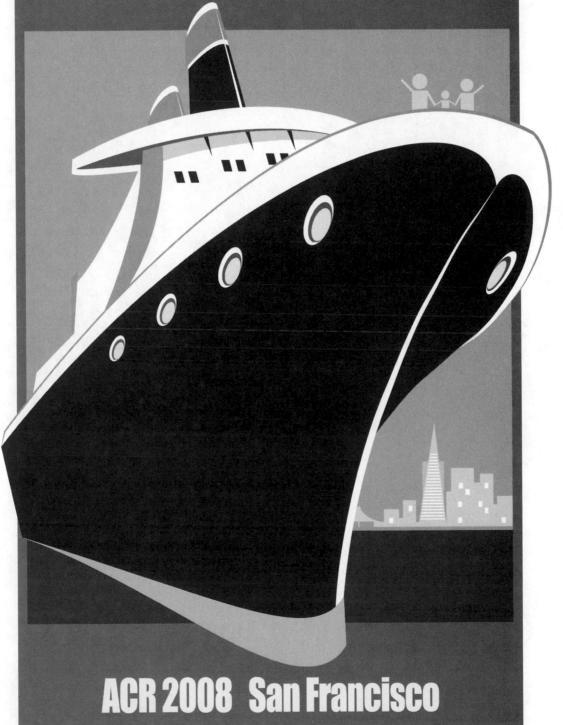

Advances In Consumer Research

Volume XXXVI   Ann L. McGill, Sharon Shavitt, Editors

ACR 2008 San Francisco

International Standard Book Number (ISBN): 0-915552-63-9

International Standard Serial Number (ISSN): 0098-9258

Ann L. McGill and Sharon Shavitt, Editors

Advances in Consumer Research, Volume 36

(Duluth, MN: Association for Consumer Research, 2009)

Preface

The 36th Annual Conference of the Association for Consumer Research was held at the Hyatt Regency Hotel in San Francisco, California, from October 23-26, 2008. These proceedings include summaries of the presentations made at the conference in symposia, competitive paper sessions, working paper sessions, roundtables, and the film festival.

ACR 2008 was the largest and most diverse ACR conference in the organization's history. The theme of the ACR2008 Conference was "Port of Call," which was intended to capture the vibrant and changing nature of our field. Researchers from thirty-three countries arrived in the commercial center of San Francisco, bringing their cargo of ideas and knowledge. Our goal was to highlight the international nature of our organization, our reliance on the conference as a marketplace of research, and the role of the conference in building intellectual and social connections. We believe the conference accomplished these objectives and highlighted new ideas, ideas that can shape the field.

ACR 2008 set records for attendance (1052 registered participants) and submissions (over 850 across all categories). We were able to accept 54% of the 104 symposium proposals submitted, 43% of the 487 competitive papers, 181 working papers, 10 films, and 7 roundtables. We wish to thank all of the authors who contributed by submitting research, reviewing papers and session proposals, serving on committees, and overseeing conference tracks. In particular, we are very grateful to Amna Kirmani and Jill Klein for chairing the working paper track, Jennifer Escalas and Lauren Block for chairing the roundtable track, Russell Belk and Marylouise Caldwell for chairing the film festival, Margaret Campbell and Robert Kozinets for chairing the doctoral symposium, and the twelve outstanding individuals who served as Associate Chairs for the competitive paper sessions: Rohini Ahluwalia, Michael Barone, Tanya Chartrand, Aimee Drolet, Ran Kivetz, Tina M. Lowrey, Rik Pieters, Linda L. Price, Aric Rindfleisch, Jaideep Sengupta, Baba Shiv, and Kathleen D. Vohs.

In addition to the usual conference sessions, one innovation this year was the organization of some paper sessions into "Embedded Conferences," which were subtracks of related work. These subtracks emerged organically from the high quality submissions we received, and were organized in sequence to highlight the connections across the sessions and allow interested conferees an opportunity to attend all of them. The Embedded Conferences covered the topics of Health and Eating, Magical Thinking, the Brand and the Self, and Quantitative Methods. The first two of these were followed by discussion sessions devoted to synthesizing the contributions across the paper sessions. We are indebted to David G. Mick and John Sherry for their valuable leadership in these sessions.

Several other people deserve our thanks for their help in running the conference, including ACR Executive Director Rajiv Vaidyanathan, ACR conference coordinator Patty Salo Downs, administrative director Jennifer Williams, Jimmy Wong for attending to a myriad details, webmaster Aleksey Cherfas for his extraordinary help with the web-based submission system, and Carol and Steve Barnett who were instrumental in preparing these proceedings. We also thank Punam Anand Keller, ACR President, for entrusting this conference to us. We will get her back someday. And we are very grateful to several previous conference chairs, particularly Angela Lee and Dilip Soman, for their support and their unfailingly helpful responses to our many random queries.

Ann L. McGill, University of Chicago
Sharon Shavitt, University of Illinois at Urbana-Champaign
2008 ACR Conference Co-Chairs and Proceedings Editors

Conference Committees and Reviewers

PRESIDENT
Punam A. Keller, Dartmouth College, USA

CONFERENCE CHAIRS
Ann L. McGill, University of Chicago, USA
Sharon Shavitt, University of Illinois at Urbana-Champaign, USA

ASSOCIATE CHAIRS
Rohini Ahluwalia, University of Minnesota, USA
Michael Barone, University of Louisville, USA
Tanya Chartrand, Duke University, USA
Aimee Drolet, University of California, Los Angeles, USA
Ran Kivetz, Columbia University, USA
Tina M. Lowrey, University of Texas at San Antonio, USA
Rik Pieters, Tilburg University, The Netherlands
Linda L. Price, University of Arizona, USA
Aric Rindfleisch, University of Wisconsin-Madison, USA
Jaideep Sengupta, Hong Kong University of Science & Technology, China
Baba Shiv, Stanford Graduate School of Business, USA
Kathleen D. Vohs, University of Minnesota, USA

PROGRAM COMMITTEE

Rashmi Adaval, Hong Kong University of Science & Technology, Hong Kong
Eduardo Andrade, University of California, Berkeley, USA
Eric J. Arnould, University of Wyoming, USA
Soren Askegaard, University of Southern Denmark, Denmark
Russell Belk, York University, USA
Lisa Bolton, Pennsylvania State University, USA
Simona Botti, London Business School, UK
Lyle Brenner, University of Florida, USA
Ziv Carmon, INSEAD, Singapore
Lan Nguyen Chaplin, University of Arizona, USA
Alexander Chernev, Northwestern University, USA
Chi-yue Chiu, University of Illinois at Urbana-Champaign, USA
Susan Dobscha, Bentley College, USA
Kent Drummond, University of Wyoming, USA
David Faro, London Business School, UK
Eileen Fischer, York University, USA
Ayelet Fishbach, University of Chicago, USA
Valerie Folkes, University of Southern California, USA
Mark Forehand, University of Washington, USA
Shane Frederick, Massachusetts Institute of Technology, USA
Guliz Ger, Bilkent University, Turkey
Markus Giesler, York University, Canada
Daniel Goldstein, London Business School, UK
Ronald Goodstein, Georgetown University, USA
Kent Grayson, Northwestern University, USA
Sonya Grier, American University, USA
Reid Hastie, University of Chicago, USA
Steve Hoeffler, Vanderbilt University, USA
Donna Hoffman, University of California, Riverside, USA
Margaret K. Hogg, Lancaster University, UK
Shailendra Jain, Indiana University, USA
Eric J. Johnson, Columbia University, USA
Annamma Jamy Joy, Hong Kong Polytechnic University, Hong Kong
Thomas Kramer, Baruch College, USA
Aparna A. Labroo, University of Chicago, USA
Ashok K. Lalwani, University of Texas at San Antonio, USA

Angela Y. Lee, Northwestern University, USA
Prashant Malaviya, INSEAD, France
A. Peter McGraw, University of Colorado at Boulder, USA
Edward McQuarrie, Santa Clara University, USA
Geeta Menon, New York University, USA
Elizabeth Moore, University of Notre Dame, USA
Chezy Ofir, Hebrew University, Israel
Cele Otnes, University of Illinois at Urbana-Champaign, USA
Hilke Plassmann, California Institute of Technology, USA
Joseph Priester, University of Southern California, USA
Suresh Ramanathan, University of Chicago, USA
Akshay Rao, University of Minnesota, USA
Julie Ruth, Rutgers University, USA
Ann Schlosser, University of Washington, USA
Sankar Sen, Baruch College, USA
Deborah Small, University of Pennsylvania, USA
Dilip Soman, University of Toronto, Canada
Jan-Benedict Steenkamp, The University of North Carolina at Chapel Hill, USA
Carlos Torelli, University of Minnesota, USA
Linda Tuncay, Loyola University Chicago, USA
Oleg Urminsky, University of Chicago, USA
Ana Valenzuela, Baruch College, USA
Leaf Van Boven, Cornell University, USA
Madhu Viswanathan, University of Illinois at Urbana-Champaign, USA
Melanie Wallendorf, University of Arizona, USA
Luk Warlop, Catholic University Leuven, Belgium
Klaus Wertenbroch, INSEAD, France
Tiffany Barnett White, University of Illinois at Urbana-Champaign, USA
Nancy Wong, University of Wisconsin-Madison, USA
Stacy Wood, University of South Carolina, USA
David Wooten, University of Michigan, USA
Carolyn Yoon, University of Michigan, USA
Marcel Zeelenberg, Tilburg University, The Netherlands
Shi (shir) Zhang, University of California, Los Angeles, USA

ACR DOCTORAL SYMPOSIUM
Margaret Campbell, University of Colorado, USA
Robert V. Kozinets, York University, Canada

FILM FESTIVAL
Russell Belk, York University, Canada
Marylouise Caldwell, The University of Sydney, Australia

LOCAL ARRANGEMENTS
Kathleen O'Donnell, San Francisco State University, USA

ROUNDTABLES
Lauren Block, Baruch College, USA
Jennifer Edson Escalas, Vanderbilt University, USA

WORKING PAPERS
Amna Kirmani, University of Maryland, USA
Jill Klein, INSEAD, Singapore

COMPETITIVE PAPER REVIEWERS

Lisa Abendroth, University of St. Thomas, USA
David Ackerman, California State University, Northridge, USA
Pankaj Aggarwal, University of Toronto, Canada
Praveen Aggarwal, University of Minnesota Duluth, USA
Nidhi Agrawal, Northwestern University, USA
Alexandra Aguirre-Rodriguez, Bryant University, USA
Aaron Ahuvia, University of Michigan-Dearborn, USA
Joseph Alba, University of Florida, USA
Paul J. Albanese, Kent State University, USA
Dolores Albarracin, University of Illinois at Urbana-Champaign, USA
Gerald Albaum, University of New Mexico, USA
On Amir, University of California, San Diego, USA
Alan Andreasen, Georgetown University, USA
J. Craig Andrews, Marquette University, USA
Charles Areni, The University of Sydney, Australia
Jennifer Argo, University of Alberta, Canada
Eric J. Arnould, University of Wyoming, USA
Zeynep Arsel, Concordia University, Canada
Laurence Ashworth, Queen's University, Canada
Sukriye Atakan, University of Michigan, USA
A. Selin Atalay, HEC Paris, France
Tamar Avnet, Yeshiva University, USA
Nilufer Aydinoglu, Koc University, Turkey
Aysen Bakir, Illinois State University, USA
Gary Bamossy, Georgetown University, USA
Syagnik Banerjee, University of Rhode Island, USA
Fleura Bardhi, Northeastern University, USA
Michael Basil, University of Lethbridge, USA
Bill Bearden, University of South Carolina, USA
Mickey Belch, San Diego State University, USA
Steven Bellman, Murdoch University, Australia
Julia Belyavsky, University of Florida, USA
Mariam Beruchashvili, California State University, Northridge, USA
Meghana Bhatt, Baylor College of Medicine, USA
Barbara Bickart, Rutgers University, USA
Baler Bilgin, University of California, Riverside, USA
Abhijit Biswas, Wayne State University, USA

Dipayan Biswas, Bentley College, USA
George Bizer, Union College, USA
Onur Bodur, Concordia University, Canada
Wendy Boland, The University of Arizona, USA
Samuel Bond, Duke University, USA
Derrick Boone, Wake Forest University, USA
Janet Borgerson, University of Exeter, UK
Stefania Borghini, Bocconi University, Italy
David Boush, University of Oregon, USA
Tonya Williams Bradford, University of Notre Dame, USA
S. Adam Brasel, Boston College, USA
C. Miguel Brendl, Northwestern University, USA
Barbara Briers, HEC Paris, France
Julie Edell Britton, Duke University, USA
Frederic Brunel, Boston University, USA
Sabrina Bruyneel, Catholic University Leuven, Belgium
James Burroughs, University of Virginia, USA
Katherine A. Burson, University of Michigan, USA
Kurt A. Carlson, Duke University, USA
Les Carlson, Clemson University, USA
Amitav Chakravarti, New York University, USA
Elise Chandon, Virginia Polytechnic Institute and State University, USA
Pierre Chandon, INSEAD, France
Sucharita Chandran, Boston University, USA
Joseph Chang, Vancouver Island University, Canada
Jennifer Chang Coupland, Pennsylvania State University, USA
Subimal Chatterjee, Binghamton University, USA
Amitava Chattopadhyay, INSEAD, Singapore
Amar Cheema, Washington University in St Louis, USA
Haipeng Chen, Texas A&M University, USA
Qimei Chen, University of Hawaii at Manoa, USA
Shirley Y. Y. Cheng, University of Illinois at Urbana-Champaign, USA
Cecile Cho, University of California, Riverside, USA
Hyejeung Cho, University of Texas at San Antonio, USA
Athinodoros Chronis, California State University, Stanislaus, USA
Catherine A. Cole, University of Iowa, USA

v

Jongwon Park, Korea University, Korea

Se-Bum Park, Korea Advanced Institute of Science and Technology, Korea

Marie-Agnes Parmentier, York University, USA

Kirsten Passyn, Salisbury University, USA

Vanessa Patrick, University of Georgia, USA

Anthony Patterson, University of Liverpool, UK

Teresa Pavia, University of Utah, USA

Cornelia Pechmann, University of California, Irvine, USA

Joann Peck, University of Wisconsin-Madison, USA

Laura Peracchio, University of Wisconsin-Milwaukee, USA

Andrew Perkins, Rice University, USA

Barbara Phillips, University of Saskatchewan, Canada

Christian Pinson, INSEAD, France

Jeffrey Podoshen, Franklin and Marshall College, USA

Cait Poynor, University of South Carolina, USA

John Pracejus, University of Alberta, Canada

Melea Press, University of Wyoming, USA

Girish Punj, University of Connecticut, USA

Stefano Puntoni, Erasmus University, The Netherlands

Priya Raghubir, University of California, Berkeley, USA

Rajagopal Raghunathan, The University of Texas at Austin, USA

Priyali Rajagopal, Southern Methodist University, USA

P. S. Raju, University of Louisville, USA

Sekar Raju, Iowa State University, USA

Brian Ratchford, University of Texas at Dallas, USA

Rebecca Ratner, University of Maryland, USA

Elena Reutskaja, Pompeu Fabra University, Spain

Marsha Richins, University of Missouri, USA

Scott Rick, University of Pennsylvania, USA

Nancy Ridgway, University of Richmond, USA

Hila Riemer, Ben-Gurion University, Israel

Jason Riis, New York University, USA

Torsten Ringberg, University of Wisconsin-Milwaukee, USA

Deborah Roedder-John, University of Minnesota, USA

Harper Roehm, The University of North Carolina at Greensboro, USA

Michelle Roehm, Wake Forest University, USA

Anne Roggeveen, Babson College, USA

Jose Antonio Rosa, University of Wyoming, USA

Gregory Rose, University of Washington, USA

Randall Rose, University of South Carolina, USA

Mark Rosenbaum, Northern Illinois University, USA

Bill Ross, Pennsylvania State University, USA

Derek Rucker, Northwestern University, USA

Salvador Ruiz, University of Murcia, Spain

Cristel Russell, Auckland University of Technology, New Zealand

Neela Saldanha, University of Pennsylvania, USA

Linda Court Salisbury, Boston College, USA

Sridhar Samu, Indian School of Business, India

Ozlem Sandikci, Bilkent University, Turkey

Shay Sayre, California State University, Fullerton, USA

Bernd Schmitt, Columbia University, USA

Jonathan Schroeder, University of Exeter, UK

Janet Schwartz, Princeton University, USA

Norbert Schwarz, University of Michigan, USA

Saskia Schwinghammer, Tilburg University, The Netherlands

Irene Scopelliti, Bocconi University, Italy

Maura L. Scott, Arizona State University, USA

Anne-Laure Sellier, New York University, USA

Edith Shalev, New York University, USA

Narendra Sharma, IIT Kanpur, India

Piyush Sharma, Hong Kong Polytechnic University, Hong Kong

Omar Shehryar, Montana State University, USA

Hao Shen, The Chinese University of Hong Kong, China

Eric Shih, Sungkyunkwan University, South Korea

L. J. Shrum, University of Texas at San Antonio, USA

Timothy Silk, University of British Columbia, Canada

David Silvera, University of Texas at San Antonio, USA

Joseph Simmons, Yale University, USA

Itamar Simonson, Stanford University, USA

Anuradha Sivaraman, University of Delaware, USA

Dirk Smeesters, Erasmus University, The Netherlands

Pamela Smith, Radboud University, The Netherlands

Jane Sojka, Ohio University, USA

Jack Soll, Duke University, USA

Michael Solomon, Saint Joseph's University, USA

Sanjay Sood, University of California, Los Angeles

Katherine Sredl, University of Illinois at Urbana-Champaign, USA

Joydeep Srivastava, University of Maryland, USA

Diederik A. Stapel, Tilburg University, The Netherlands

Douglas Stayman, Cornell University, USA

Lorna Stevens, University of Ulster, Magee Campus, Ireland

David Stewart, University of California, Riverside, USA

Michal Ann Strahilevitz, Golden Gate University, USA

Harish Sujan, Tulane University, USA

Jill Sundie, University of Houston, USA

Magne Supphellen, Norwegian School of Economics and Business Administration, Norway

Raj Suri, Drexel University, USA

Scott Swain, Boston University, USA

Siok Tambyah, National University of Singapore, Singapore

Berna Tari, Bilkent University, Turkey

Manoj Thomas, Cornell University, USA

Debora Thompson, Georgetown University, USA

Kelly Tian, New Mexico State University, USA

Zakary Tormala, Stanford University, USA

Olivier Toubia, Columbia University, USA

Marlene Towns, University of Southern California, USA

Claire Tsai, University of Toronto, Canada

Gulnur Tumbat, San Francisco State University, USA

Meltem Ture, Bilkent University, Turkey

Alice Tybout, Northwestern University, USA

Gulden Ulkumen, University of Southern California, USA

Nancy Upton, Northeastern University, USA

Rajiv Vaidyanathan, University of Minnesota Duluth, USA

Beth Vallen, Loyola College, USA

Niels van de Ven, Tilburg University, The Netherlands

Bram Van den Bergh, Catholic University Leuven, Belgium

Hester Van Herk, VU University Amsterdam, The Netherlands

Koert van Ittersum, Georgia Institute of Technology, USA

Stijn van Osselaer, Erasmus University, The Netherlands

Marijke van Putten, Tilburg University, The Netherlands

W. Fred van Raaij, Tilburg University, The Netherlands

Marc Vanhuele, HEC Paris, France

Patrick Vargas, University of Illinois at Urbana-Champaign, USA

Ann Veeck, Western Michigan University, USA

Ekant Veer, University of Bath, UK

Alladi Venkatesh, University of California, Irvine, USA

Meera Venkatraman, Suffolk University, USA

Peeter Verlegh, Erasmus University, The Netherlands

Nicole Verrochi, University of Pennsylvania, USA

Kathleen D. Vohs, University of Minnesota, USA
Joachim Vosgerau, Carnegie Mellon University, USA
Monica Wadhwa, Stanford University, USA
Echo Wen Wan, University of Hong Kong, Hong Kong
Fang Wan, University of Manitoba, Canada
Jing Wang, University of Iowa, USA
Qing Wang, University of Warwick, UK
Michaela Wanke, University of Basel, Switzerland
James Ward, Arizona State University, USA
Kimberlee Weaver, Virginia Polytechnic Institute and State University, USA
Yun-Oh Whang, Kansas State University, USA
Christian Wheeler, Stanford University, USA
Keith Wilcox, Baruch College, USA
Jerome Williams, The University of Texas at Austin, USA
Patti Williams, University of Pennsylvania, USA
Jorge A. Wise, Tecnologico de Monterrey, Mexico
Andrea Wojnicki, University of Toronto, Canada
Kachat Andrew Wong, University of Southern California, USA
Natalie Wood, Saint Joseph's University, USA
Christine Wright-Isak, Florida Gulf Coast University, USA
Lan Wu, California State University, East Bay, USA
Robert S. Wyer, Jr., Hong Kong University of Science & Technology, China
Lan Xia, Bentley College, USA
Richard Yalch, University of Washington, USA

Kenneth C. C. Yang, The University of Texas at El Paso, USA
Xiaojing Yang, University of Wisconsin-Milwaukee, USA
Baskin Yenicioglu, Henley Management College, USA
Catherine Yeung, National University of Singapore, Singapore
Sunghwan Yi, University of Guelph, Canada
Sukki Yoon, Bryant University, USA
Eric Yorkston, Texas Christian University, USA
Gal Zauberman, University of Pennsylvania, USA
Yael Zemack-Rugar, Virginia Polytechnic Institute and State University, USA
Jiao Zhang, University of Miami, USA
Jing Zhang, University of Wisconsin-Milwaukee, USA
Meng Zhang, The Chinese University of Hong Kong, China
Shuoyang Zhang, Indiana University, USA
Ying Zhang, University of Texas at Austin, USA
Yinlong Zhang, University of Texas at San Antonio, USA
Min Zhao, University of Toronto, Canada
Xin Zhao, University of Hawaii, USA
Yuhuang Zheng, Tsinghua University, USA
Rongrong Zhou, Hong Kong University of Science & Technology, China
Rui Juliet Zhu, University of British Columbia, Canada
George Zinkhan, University of Georgia, USA
Rami Zwick, Hong Kong University of Science & Technology, China

WORKING PAPER REVIEWERS

Jim Alvarez-Mourey, University of Michigan, USA
Christina I. Anthony, The University of Sydney, Australia
Sukriye Atakan, University of Michigan, USA
Rajesh Bagchi, University of Colorado at Boulder, USA
Julia Belyavsky, University of Florida, USA
Neil Bendle, University of Minnesota, USA
Christine Bennett, University of Minnesota, USA
Aaron Brough, Northwestern University, USA
Elaine Chan, Hong Kong University of Science & Technology, China
Hannah Chang, Columbia University, USA
Sunaina Chugani, University of Texas at Austin, USA
Adam Craig, University of South Carolina, USA
Olga Dorokhina, University of Maryland, USA
Ryan Elder, University of Michigan, USA
Francine Espinoza, University of Maryland, USA
Dilney Goncalves, INSEAD, France
Lauren Gurrieri, University of Melbourne, Australia
Eric Hamerman, Columbia University, USA
Haiming Hang, Lancaster University, UK
Lora Harding, Northwestern University, USA
Ashlee Humphreys, Northwestern University, USA
Mathew S. Isaac, Northwestern University, USA
Jesse Itzkowitz, University of Florida, USA
Peter Jarnebrant, Columbia University, USA
Lan Jiang, University of British Columbia, Canada
Uma Karmarkar, Stanford University, USA

Amna Kirmani, University of Maryland, USA
Jill Klein, INSEAD, Singapore
Yuliya Komarova, University of South Carolina, USA
Joseph Lajos, INSEAD, France
Juliano Laran, University of Florida, USA
Roland Leak, University of South Carolina, USA
Ab Litt, Stanford University, USA
Michael Luchs, The University of Texas at Austin, USA
Vincent Mak, Hong Kong University of Science & Technology, China
James Edward Matherly, University of Maryland, USA
Brent McFerran, University of British Columbia, Canada
Sarah G. Moore, Duke University, USA
Leonardo Nicolao, The University of Texas at Austin, USA
Nailya Ordabayeva, INSEAD, France
Ji Kyung Park, University of Minnesota, USA
Anastasiya Pocheptsova, University of Maryland, USA
Mark Ratchford, University of Colorado at Boulder, USA
Dan Rice, University of Florida, USA
Breagin Riley, Northwestern University, USA
Aner Sela, Stanford University, USA
Andrew Stephen, Columbia University, USA
Jennifer Stewart, The Ohio State University, USA
Morgan Ward, The University of Texas at Austin, USA
Eugenia C. Wu, Duke University, USA
Lifeng Yang, The Ohio State University, USA
Linyun Yang, Duke University, USA

FRANCO NICOSIA BEST COMPETITIVE PAPER AWARD COMMITTEE
Daniel Goldstein, London Business School, UK
Cele Otnes, University of Illinois at Urbana-Champaign, USA
Akshay Rao, University of Minnesota, USA

SPECIAL THANKS TO
Peggy Eppink, University of Chicago, USA
Jenny Goh, University of Illinois at Urbana-Champaign, USA
Janice Luce, University of Chicago, USA
Cassie McConkey, University of Illinois at Urbana-Champaign, USA
Jimmy Wong, University of Illinois at Urbana-Champaign, USA

ACR 2008 Conference Coordinator
Patty Salo Downs

ACR 2008 Administrative Director
Jennifer Williams, University of Chicago, USA

ACR Executive Director
Rajiv Vaidyanathan, University of Minnesota, Duluth, USA

ACR Conference Webmaster
Aleksey Cherfas

Scheduling Assistance
Aaron Brough, Northwestern University, USA
Mathew S. Isaac, Northwestern University, USA

Logo and Cover Art
Mark Otnes

SPECIAL THANKS TO OUR CONFERENCE SPONSORS FOR THEIR GENEROUS SUPPORT

Journal of Consumer Research

Dartmouth College
Tuck School of Business

Kilts Center for Marketing
University of Chicago
Booth School of Business

College of Business
University of Illinois at Urbana-Champaign

Qualtrics

SPECIAL THANKS TO OUR FILM FESTIVAL AWARDS SPONSORS

McDonough School of Business
Georgetown University

University of California, Irvine

Center for Consumer Culture

SPECIAL THANKS TO OUR EXHIBITORS FOR THEIR GENEROUS SUPPORT

Elsevier Limited

Interpretive Simulations

Noldus Information Technology

Psychology Press / Taylor & Francis Group

Qualtrics

University of Chicago Press

Table of Contents

Thursday, 23 October 2008
ACR DOCTORAL SYMPOSIUM

Friday, 24 October 2008
FILM FESTIVAL I-IV
8:00am–5:00pm

Can Buy Me Love
This Day is To Be Special: The Role of Exaggerated Contrast in an Indian Wedding
Behind Closed Doors: Gendered Home Spaces in an Arab Gulf State
Urban Archetypal Hedonistas
Bodily Experiences of Second Life Consumers
The Ties That Bind: Being Black, Buying, and Hope
Binomial Structure in Luxury: Analyzing Overseas Trip Experiences of Japanese Well-to-Dos
Everything You Always Wanted to Know About the Pre-Party
Behind Closed Doors: Opportunity Identification Through Observational Research
Consumption, Belonging, and Place

Friday, 24 October 2008
SESSION I
8:00am–9:15am

1.01   *From the Black Box to the Aquarium: How Brain Imaging Sheds 'Light' on the Underlying Mechanisms of How Marketing Actions Work*
1.02   *When the Going Gets Tough: How Metacognitive Difficulty Improves Evaluation*
1.03   *Status: Why Consumers Engage in Conspicuous Consumption and How They May Be Perceived*
1.04   *Those Troublesome Teens: Influences on Adolescent Consumption*
1.05   *Acculturation and Consumer Behavior: Building Cultural Bridges Through Consumption*
1.06   *Production and Reproduction of Consumer Culture in Virtual Communities*
1.07   *Justification and Choice*
1.08   *Materialism, Self-Esteem, and Well-Being*
1.09   *What's That I See? Visual Impact on On-line and Service Evaluation*
1.10   *Moving Beyond the Rabbit's Foot: Superstition and Magical Thinking in Consumer Behavior*
1.11   *Social Networks and Consumer Behavior*
1.12   *No Man Is an Island: Social Influences on Communications and Behavior*
1.13   ROUNDTABLE: *Understanding and Improving Consumer Personal Finances*

Friday, 24 October 2008
SESSION II
9:30am–10:45am

Friday, 24 October 2008
SESSION III
11:15am–12:30pm

Friday, 24 October 2008
SESSION IV
2:00pm–3:15pm

Friday, 24 October 2008
SESSION V
3:45pm–5:00pm

5.01 *Soft Concepts and Hard Measures: New Scales and Techniques for Understanding Brand Relationships and Affect*
5.02 *Marketing Issues in Politics*
5.03 *Brand Symbolism and Reference Groups: Perspectives on the Identity Value of Brands*
5.04 *Multifaceted Consumer Welfare: Broadening the Perspective*
5.05 *Consumer Culture: Theory, Politics, and Opportunities*
5.06 *Building an Understanding of What Makes Consumer Behavior Transformative*
5.07 *Consumer Perceptions of Value and Price*
5.08 *Food, Family, and Guns: Diverse Socialization Agents*
5.09 *Activating and Imagining the Self*
5.10 *How Can We Improve Consumers' Health?*
5.11 *Positive Emotions–Theory and Application*
5.12 *Are You Talking to Me? The Effects of Explicit and Inferred Advice in Consumer Judgment*

Friday, 24 October 2008
WORKING PAPER SESSION A
5:00pm–6:30pm

Saturday, 25 October 2008
FILM FESTIVAL V-VIII
8:00am–5:00pm

Can Buy Me Love
This Day is To Be Special: The Role of Exaggerated Contrast in an Indian Wedding
Bodily Experiences of Second Life Consumers
The Ties That Bind: Being Black, Buying, and Hope
Urban Archetypal Hedonistas
Behind Closed Doors: Gendered Home Spaces in an Arab Gulf State
Binomial Structure in Luxury: Analyzing Overseas Trip Experiences of Japanese Well-to-dos
Everything You Always Wanted to Know About the Pre-Party
Consumption, Belonging, and Place

Saturday, 25 October 2008
SESSION VI
8:00am–9:15am

6.01 *Sticker Shock: The Emotional Side of Pricing*
6.02 *Cognition and Sensory Perception: The Impact of Input from Sensory Modalities on Imagery, Memory, Information Processing, and Sensory Perception*
6.03 *Compensatory Consumption: How Threat Directs Consumers' Product Preferences*
6.04 *Objectification of the Body and the Self*
6.05 *Making Informed Product Decisions: Positioning, Customization, Co-Production, and Feature Design*
6.06 *Legitimation in the Marketplace*
6.07 *Where, When, and Why: Moderating and Mediating Effects in Judgment and Decision-Making*
6.08 *Patience, Attention to Time, and Consumer Cognition*
6.09 *Context and the Self in Memory and Emotion*
6.10 *Taking It to the Streets: Methodological Challenges of Doing Transformative Consumer Research on Health*
6.11 *Unraveling Motivation: Affective and Cognitive Processes Underlying Consumer Goals and Choices*
6.12 *Interacting with Technology: Search, Risk, and Experience*
6.13 ROUNDTABLE: *HLM: Hierarchical Linear Models*

Saturday, 25 October 2008
SESSION VII
9:30am–10:45am

7.01   *How Do You Really Feel about It? Emotional Processes and Product Evaluation*
7.02   *Context-Dependent Search*
7.03   *Symbolic Essence of a Brand: Meaning and Associations*
7.04   *Consumer Identity, Resistance, and Coping*
7.05   *Consumer Engagement in "Attention Economies"*
7.06   *Through the Looking Glass: New Ideas about the Consumption of Beauty*
7.07   *Taking the Load out of Choice Overload: Strategies for Reducing Cognitive Difficulty in Choice from Extensive Assortments*
7.08   *Time: It's a Personal Thing*
7.09   *Bottom-Up Influences on Information Integration and Decision-Making: Information Type, Format, and Intercorrelation*
7.10   *The Effect of Conflicting Information and Natural Primes on Health Related Behaviors*
7.11   *Welcome to the Jungle: Understanding How Environmental Cues Influence Consumption in "The Wild"*
7.12   *Look How Good Looks: Ideals in Product and Ad Design*
7.13   ROUNDTABLE: *Conducting Consumer Research in Emerging Markets: Challenges, Issues and New Directions.*

Saturday, 25 October 2008
SESSION VIII
11:15am–12:30pm

8.01   *Hot Like Before: Emotional Memory in Communication*
8.02   *The Psychological Consequences of Choice*
8.03   *The Role and Construction of Brand Personality*
8.04   *Come On, Get Happy*
8.05   *And Then We Came to the End: Troubled Commercial Relationships*
8.06   *'What Things Do': Examining Things That "Matter" in Consumer Research*
8.07   *How You Say it Matters: Frameworks for Understanding Message Framing*
8.08   *The Impact of Time and Temporal Orientation on Consumer Behavior*
8.09   *Inside the Eye of the Mind: Effects of Mental Imagery on Beliefs and Preferences*
8.10   *To Indulge or Not to Indulge? Self-Regulation and Overconsumption*
8.11   *Encoding, Remembering, and Using Numeric Information: Implications for Pricing*
8.12   *When Does Your Advertising Matter: New Insights from Political, Advocacy, and Sponsorship Advertising*
8.13   ROUNDTABLE: *Intro To Social Network Methods*

Saturday, 25 October 2008
SESSION IX
2:00pm–3:15pm

9.01   *Aiming Higher and Lower: Setting and Shifting Standards of Evaluation*
9.02   *Chiaroscuro: The Darker (and the Lighter) Side of Information Processing*
9.03   *Different Selves Make the World Go 'Round*
9.04   *Me, Myself, and I: The Role of Self Views in Prosocial Judgments*
9.05   *Beauty Is in the Eye (and Reaching for the Wallet) of the Beholder*
9.06   *The Consumption of Reading*
9.07   *I Want To Be Just Like Them, or Do I? Assimilation and Contrast Effects in Consumer Judgment*
9.08   *The Impact of Psychological Distance on Charitable Fundraising*
9.09   *Start Spreading the News: Personal and Impersonal Communication Effects for New and Known Options*
9.10   *Effects of Supersizing and Downsizing Packages on Consumption: Marketing and Policy Implications*
9.11   *What Makes Ideas Stick? How Characteristics and Contexts of Messages Influence Their Success*
9.12   *Bricks, Clicks, and Tricks: Influences on Consumer Shopping and Service Experiences*
9.13   ROUNDTABLE: *Consumer Neuroscience: Current State of Knowledge and Future Research Directions*

Saturday, 25 October 2008
SESSION X
3:45pm– 5:00pm

Saturday, 25 October 2008
WORKING PAPER SESSION B
5:00pm–6:30pm

Table of Contents

Competitive Papers

Competitive Papers

Film Festival

Roundtable Summaries

Chairs:
Lisa E. Bolton, The Pennsylvania State University, USA
Paul Bloom, Duke University, USA
Joel Cohen, University of Florida, USA

Participants:
David Glen Mick, University of Virginia, USA
Ron Paul Hill, Villanova University, USA
Kathleen D. Vohs, University of Minnesota, USA
Amar Cheema, Washington University, USA
John G. Lynch, Duke University, USA
Vanessa Perry, The George Washington University, USA
Gal Zauberman, University of Pennsylvania, USA
James Burroughs, University of Virginia, USA
Cynthia Cryder, Carnegie Mellon University, USA
Scott Rick, University of Pennsylvania, USA
Eldar Shafir, Princeton University, USA
Stephen Spiller, Duke University, USA

Chairs:
Henrik Hagtvedt, University of Georgia, USA
Vanessa Patrick, University of Georgia, USA

Participants:
Wesley Hutchinson, University of Pennsylvania, USA
Joan Meyers-Levy, University of Minnesota, USA
JoAndrea Hoegg, University of British Columbia, Canada
Darren Dahl, University of British Columbia, Canada
Rajagopal Raghunathan, The University of Texas at Austin, USA
Rui Juliet Zhu, University of British Columbia, Canada
Rolf Reber, University of Bergen, Norway
C. Page Moreau, University of Colorado at Boulder, USA
Frederic Brunel, Boston University, USA
Annamma Jamy Joy, University of British Columbia, Canada
Jonathan Schroeder, University of Exeter, UK
Ravi Chitturi, Lehigh University, USA
Joseph Alba, University of Florida, USA
Michael Luchs, College of William & Mary, USA
Xiaoyan Deng, University of Pennsylvania, USA
Rishtee Kumar Batra, Boston University, USA

Chair:
Julie L. Ozanne, Virginia Polytechnic Institute and State University, USA

Participants:
Dipankar Chakravarti, University of Colorado at Boulder, USA
Ron Paul Hill, Villanova University, USA
David Glen Mick, University of Virginia, USA
Benet DeBerry-Spence, University of Illinois at Chicago, USA
David Crockett, University of South Carolina, USA
Krittinee Nuttavuthisit, Chulalongkorn University, Thailand
Amitava Chattopadhyay, INSEAD, Singapore
Simone Pettigrew, University of Western Australia, Australia
Peter Wright, University of Oregon, USA
Rohit Varman, Indian Institute of Management, India
Laurel Anderson, Arizona State University, USA
Stacey Menzel Baker, University of Wyoming, USA
Lisa Bolton, Pennsylvania State University, USA
Tonya Williams Bradford, University of Notre Dame, USA
June Cotte, University of Western Ontario, Canada
Susan Dobscha, Bentley College, USA
Cornelia Pechmann, University of California, Irvine, USA
Linda L. Price, University of Arizona, USA
Jose Antonio Rosa, University of Wyoming, USA
Namika Sagara, University of Oregon, USA
Sridhar Samu, Indian School of Business, India
Andrea Scott, Pepperdine University, USA
Sonya Grier, American University, USA
Humaira Mahi, San Francisco State University, USA
Dilip Soman, University of Toronto, Canada
Ashlee Humphreys, Northwestern University, USA
John Kozup, Villanova University, USA

Chair:
Dawn Iacobucci, Vanderbilt University, USA

Participants:
Gerri Henderson, Northwestern University, USA
Adam Duhachek, Indiana University, USA
Jim Oakley, University of North Carolina, USA
Steve Hoeffler, Vanderbilt University, USA
Steve Posavac, Vanderbilt University, USA
Simona Botti, London Business School, UK
Katherine A. Burson, University of Michigan, USA
Pankaj Aggarwal, University of Toronto, Canada

Chairs:
James R. Bettman, Duke University, USA
Drazen Prelec, Massachusetts Institute of Technology, USA
Carolyn Yoon, University of Michigan, USA

Participants:
William Hedgcock, University of Iowa, USA
Mary Frances Luce, Duke University, USA
Hilke Plassmann, California Institute of Technology, USA and INSEAD, France
Baba Shiv, Stanford University, USA
Ale Smidts, Erasmus University, The Netherlands
Stacy Wood, University of South Carolina, USA
Akshay Rao, University of Minnesota, USA
Brian Knutson, Stanford University, USA
Adam Craig, University of South Carolina, USA
Vinod Venkatraman, Duke University, USA
Martin Reimann, Stanford University, USA
Scott Rick, University of Pennsylvania, USA

Working Paper Abstracts

Building Theory and Breaking Boundaries: Welcome to the Real World
Punam Anand Keller, Dartmouth College, USA

I decided on the topic for this speech on a flight home from a meeting with a group of university administrator, financial planners, and faculty. The goal of our meeting was to identify initiatives to help new university hires save more for retirement. I was so upset at everyone's impressions of consumer research that it was fitting that I wrote the outline of this speech on the only paper I could find on the plane–motion sickness bags!

I have faced similar resistance from business school colleagues, and dare I say, even marketing colleagues who are not here today. They cannot get over why we care about how consumers process simple information. They don't understand why we wash away individual differences in our random designs. They are bewildered by why we don't study the decision context since it determines the constraints that prevent consumers from achieving their goals.

It is clear to me that our crash course on the philosophy of science, starting with the premise that theories are universally generalizable, is falling on deaf ears. We can either accept that our work is going to live and die on the sheets of journal paper, or, we can enhance the impact of our work by taking it further so that others can apply it.

Today, I would like to share concrete examples of how we can use the real world to build theory–not by learning a new skill set– but simply by leveraging the wealth of knowledge in this room. My hope is that you will leave with a richer appreciation for consumer research, with fewer boundaries between different types of consumer research, and an irresistible urge to share your research in the real world!

The first part of my talk is on building theory. It contains three approaches for making both a theoretical and practical contribution. The second part of my talk describes three scholarly benefits when we break boundaries. So I begin

The first approach for building theory in the real world is based on the topics we study. At least six previous ACR presidents have urged us to undertake research that is relevant to consumers. Relevance has been defined in a number of ways, as examining consumers in natural contexts by Valerie Folkes and Terry Shimp, as macro consumer behavior by Russ Belk and Marsha Richins, and as individual and collective well-being by Alan Andreasen and David Mick. Of the thousand plus paper and film submissions for this conference, up to 25% were on transformative consumer research topics that included consumer self-control, resistance and coping, family relations and civic values, health and financial planning, the environment, and materialism and subsistence. We have growing evidence that scholars from other disciplines, applied researchers, practitioners, and even consumers themselves, are all hungry for insights on these topics. The second approach is based on the premise that theories are strengthened when they are tested in real world conditions that challenge them. The third approach suggests real world testing enables us to identify moderators and mediators for building theory. You are going to see these red boxes on all my slides for building theory.

In preparing this speech I interviewed a small, diverse group of ACR members who I refer to as the Fab Five. Some have been doing consumer research for decades, others for just a few years. These five researchers draw on a varied set of basic disciplines-such as psychology, sociology, anthropology, and economics. They use a variety of methods and live and work in different parts of the world. But all had one thing in common–they were looking for contexts that would demonstrate the value of theory while remaining open to building theory after giving it a run in the real world. They are Brian Wansink from Cornell, Jill Klein from Insead, Deborah Small from the University of Pennsylvania, Dilip Soman from the University of Toronto, and Maura Scott from the University of Kentucky. They all illustrate how real world engagement can serve both the consumer and help develop theory. I will weave their stories with my own. Let me begin first by offering some views based on my own research.

I met my co-author Annamaria Lusardi, an economist, three years ago-when she asked me to speak at a conference on retirement saving. I told her I not only did not DO research on retirement saving, but I did not know how to save! She assured me I could present my health research since health and retirement planning decisions are similar on so many dimensions. She was right and our work together began. We started by identifying barriers to savings in lab studies, focus groups, in-depth interviews and work-place observations. Some employees could be helped by opening a dialogue about how to overcome saving barriers.

However, this does not help a large percentage of employees who said they wanted to open a retirement account, but did not know where to start. Upon further prodding, we found that not knowing where to start meant not knowing how much time the decision would take, what information was needed to make the decision, and how much money was involved. It was clear to us they needed a simple how-to plan instead of a big benefits packet! We created a simple plan that contained the information they wanted.

We also made the plan concrete by breaking it up into specific tasks with time estimates because inter-temporal discounting theory indicates this method would reduce procrastination. We gave this simple, cost-effective, theory-based planning tool to Dartmouth's Human Resources department who used it with all new university employees. Compared to a control condition, this plan resulted in a 5 fold increase in enrollments-from 8% to over 42% of new Dartmouth employees. Hundreds of new employees opened a supplementary retirement account within two months. The Dartmouth study encouraged TIAA-CREF to put our research method and planning tool on their website to encourage other education institutions to use our methods.

You're probably thinking–is that all it took. That's exactly how I want you to think! Consumer research is powerful! And we gave back to the theory. There was nothing in the inter-temporal discounting literature on the role of planning to reduce procrastination? We tested this hypothesis by running experiments with undergraduates in a variety of health and wealth contexts to demonstrate that plans reduce feasibility concerns which in turn reduce procrastination. We used consumer insights and we replaced consumer insights! That is my example of how we built theory in the real world. Now on to my examples from colleagues I mentioned to you earlier.

Brian Wansink was living in Iowa in the early '80s when he was inspired by the farmland around him-to do something that would get Americans to eat a healthier diet—a very hot topic today. But when he started testing the waters two decades ago, talking with other researchers about his ideas, they were less than receptive. One person even said to him, "Why don't you do something theoretical, something important? Nobody's interested in food." That was news to Brian; he thought everybody was interested in food. Besides he knew he could build a wide array of theories in this rich context. He was right. Fast forward to today. Brian's counterintuitive findings contribute to our theoretical understanding of perceptual biases. Brian's findings on the conditions that lead to overconsumption have influenced numerous health policies. My least favorite of Brian's findings is the use of taller glasses to prevent the over pouring of alcohol.

If a topic does not grab you, there are two other ways you can use the real world for building theory. First, theories are strengthened when they are tested in conditions that challenge them. A few years ago, I was reading about a debate in the depressive realism literature. Proponents of this phenomenon believe depressed people are more realistic because they are more likely to update their risk estimates when they are given credible information, whereas people who are not depressed stick with their priors. Objectors argue that the phenomenon is not universal or "real" because it is always tested in contexts where there was an optimistic bias–thereby if one was pessimistic one was also more accurate. To support the view that depressed people would be more open to lowering their risk estimates I started looking for contexts in which people typically inflated their risks and where there was an objective measure of accurate risk.

I chose the breast cancer context for these reasons. Women overestimate their risk of breast cancer by a factor of five! The national average is about 25% as compared to what it should be– around 5%. How do I know what it should be? There is a medical algorithm that can calculate each person's risk of breast cancer based on the individual's history. Although we showed baseline risk estimates were not different for non-depressives and depressives, depressives lowered their risk estimates when they received their individual breast cancer medical risk estimate, whereas non-depressives did not update. This real context allowed me to make a theoretical contribution to the theory of depressive realism by showing depressed people were more realistic even when they had to be more optimistic to be realistic.

Not all contexts are perfect for building this theory. Earlier this year someone asked me whether the risk of terrorism attacks would be a perfect context to study the robustness of the depressive realism phenomenon. I asked the same two questions–Do we have evidence that people are inflating the risk of a terrorist attack, and is there an objective risk estimate of a terrorist attack? Along the same lines, you might ask yourself, "What are my parameters for a good context?"

Dilip Soman can tell you what he is looking for in a context to build his theories. Dilip is interested in heuristics and biases in decisions involving time, effort, and money. He is always looking for real contexts where there is an element of uncertainty–conditions that are ripe for making budgeting "mistakes"-conditions where his interventions should have the biggest impact. Picture this-Dilip gave Non Government Organization or NGO staff members from agriculture, dairy, construction, labor, artisans, and women's cooperatives a crash course in mental accounting. Dilip selected farmers for his study because their wages were seasonal and construction workers because their wages were the most unpredictable. See, he found an opportunity to build theory–are budgeting mistakes the same for unpredictability and seasonality? Dilip encouraged both farmers and construction workers to save by giving them their wages in multiple sealed envelopes instead of a single envelop. And once the microfinance institution knew the farmers were able to manage their money better, they gave them more loans to run small agriculture businesses. Dilip continues to build theory on heuristics and biases in multiple foundations.

Deborah Small selected charitable giving as the context for testing and building her theories. Can you guess some of her theories? You can play this game with your colleagues where you

reveal the context and ask others to guess the theory or vice-versa. Deborah is interested in emotional biases in judgments. She was seeking a context that connected peoples' emotions and actual behavior. Interestingly, she observed her counterintuitive idea in the field before she developed a theoretical test for it.

Contrary to the literature, the most effective charity advertisements showed pictures of happy not sad victims. The charity context also sparked her interest in sympathy biases in decision-making because it allowed her to examine why and how much people give to charity. Published in JCR and JMR, both studies have made theoretical contribution and had an impact in the arena of charitable giving. And Debra has since collaborated with different charitable organizations in various field experiments.

These examples demonstrate that synergy between lab and field studies allow us to build theory AND make a practical contribution. An observation in one context motivates testing a question in another. And it really doesn't matter where you start. I like the way Baruch Fischoff labels research as basic-applied and applied-basic to emphasize the seamlessness between the two ways to build theory.

The third theory building approach is based on finding new moderators and mediators in the real world. If you are vigilant you will observe when people around you are not behaving theoretically–according to your theory that is.

Jill Klein went to Thailand in 2005, just after that devastating tsunami, to participate in recovery efforts. She and others were handing out gifts—new possessions—to people who had lost everything. Jill discovered that contrary to the body of work that associated materialism with a host of negative outcomes, she observed the benefits of material goods, especially for teens. She and her co-author wrote an article along with a white paper for meeting the needs of teens in other similar natural disasters. She offered an examination of theoretical boundaries *and* a proposed workable solution for a real-world problem.

Maura Scott also built theory by identifying a previously unknown moderator. Maura Scott's prediction that 100 calorie packs would not result in lower calorie consumption was confirmed among a segment of the population, the restrained eater. Similar to the movie character Bridget Jones, this type of eater writes down her weight and the things she has eaten in a daily journal. Like Bridget who finds herself with two guys, the restrained eater ends up overeating. Maura's work has won awards and she published her dissertation work in JCR.

I have shared three different ways that my colleagues and I have built theories in the real world-by identifying theories that shed insights on a topic you and others care about, by selecting real contexts to test the robustness of theory, and by identifying moderators and mediators from natural settings. I see this approach as a win-win situation. We build our theories and make them more accessible to others. We may even generate the discussion and public policy changes that directly improve consumer welfare.

You, as a scholar, have even more to gain. Building theories in the real world will inspire you to reexamine your research and teaching boundaries. You will learn to appreciate new methods, get a richer, cross-disciplinary view of your theory, and you can leverage your research in the classroom. Let me give you concrete examples of each of these benefits.

First, you get to learn—really learn—again. You learn to examine your theory with new methodologies. I have found that nothing teaches you the value of different types of consumer research than when you are trying to solve a real problem. The methodological distinctions that are so important to us here in this room seem trivial to outsiders. Originally trained as an experimental information processor, Brian Wansink has worked with marketing modelers to model eating behavior such as diminishing sensitivity to meal size change. I too used to be an information processor who now devours the behavioral decision theory literature to understand how people make choices.

Like Dilip Soman, I have greater appreciation of sociology and interpretive research because it can capture the context in which consumers live and make decisions. I even took a class on ethnography in the sociology department to improve my ability to fold the context into theory.

This training was handy when a grant from The National Endowment for Financial Education enabled Anna and I to shoot videos of different employees, talking about why and how they save. In other words how they met their goals by overcoming their barriers. If you watch these videos on the Dartmouth website, you will conclude, and I concur, that I need to learn a lot from our members who participate in ACR's film festival.

Next, I learnt to develop quantitative predictive models for the Health Marketing Division of the Center for Disease Control. I was devastated when I found out CDC was uncomfortable extending consumer research lab findings without additional field tests. And if CDC cannot use our health consumer research, who can! I asked Don "Meta" Lehmann to teach me how to develop a predictive model based on a meta-analysis of all the lab research on health communications. This health communication model is based on a sample size of over 22,000 subjects, has twenty-two message factors, across several health contexts, and six individual differences. If you are interested in using the data, let me know and I will send it to you. CDC gave me the nod when I showed that the lab-based model could predict the effectiveness of their national exercise ad campaign.

Second, you will view issues from the frames of a variety of disciplines to create a more complete picture of problems and their causes, and the theories that can be used to solve them. Dilip's website states he never misses an opportunity to talk to anyone smart or famous. He regularly gets together with scholars from economics, finance, health sciences, public policy, and sociology among others. I too participate in several cross-disciplinary groups.

One group on cost effective consumerism is made up of academics from law, economics, bioethics, medicine, psychology, neuroscience, and fields I did not even know existed like neuroeconomics. I meet with another group of scholars from public health, economics, psychology, psychiatry, medicine, and public policy—all of whom share an interest in improving personal health. I also meet with marketing managers and academics at the Marketing Science Institute meetings to discuss how to increase employee participation in corporate well-being programs. And there are so many more opportunities to break boundaries at special conferences like the Transformative Consumer Research Conference in Villanova, and one on Leveraging Consumer Psychology for Effective Health Communication in Michigan.

Third, the beauty of building theory in the real world is that it is easy to leverage your research in the classroom. Who wouldn't like to break the boundaries between research and teaching? Deborah parlays her research into her Consumer Behavior class by analyzing her students' emotions in photographs. Jill Klein uses her research on consumer boycotts and crisis management in her Social Marketing elective and International Executive Programs. Brian Wansink holds his class in a food lab. Dilip's class on Foundation for Integrative Thinking has projects to challenge students to tackle critical consumer issues such as encouraging young people to save.

Like these consumer researchers, I see my career as a three-legged stool; there is a teaching leg, a research leg, and a community/public policy leg. The three are inextricably linked, which creates synergy. The more synergy I have, the more I can leverage what I do and the easier it is to take and give back to the real world.

In closing, please join me in thanking Jill, Maura, Dilip, Brian and Deborah, for sharing their stories with us. I want to acknowledge Lauren Block and Annamaria Lusardi for inspiring me to do health and wealth-related consumer research. I want to thank Brian Sternthal and Alice Tybout for teaching me how to design theoretical and applied research. A toast to Sidney Levy—You connect theory and practice with unparalleled joy and creativity. To my parents for giving me confidence that far out striped my abilities. To a true partner, my husband Kevin. And to my children, Carolyn and Allison, who insist I keep it real by asking me what I really do.

I hope you are inspired to care for your theories by giving them new meaning in a real context. For me, passion bestows meaning-so I thank you for giving me this opportunity to share my passion for consumer research.

SYMPOSIUM SUMMARY
From the Black Box to the Aquarium: How Brain Imaging Sheds 'Light' on the Underlying Mechanisms of How Marketing Actions Work
Hilke Plassmann, California Institute of Technology, USA and INSEAD, France

EXTENDED ABSTRACTS

"The Good, the Bad and the Forgotten-An fMRI-study on Ad Liking and Ad Memory"

Peter Kenning, Zeppelin University, Germany
Michael Deppe, University of Muenster, Germany
Wolfram Schwindt, University of Muenster, Germany
Harald Kugel, University of Muenster, Germany
Hilke Plassmann, California Institute of Technology, USA and INSEAD, France

Memory is a central construct in both, advertising research as well as in neuroscience. We know from research in advertising that affect-laden ads are likely to be better recalled and better recall is likely to correlate with ad effectiveness (Ray and Batra 1983; Ambler and Burne 1999). Researchers suggest that ad memory might be "the temporal link between ad input and buying occasions" (Ambler and Burne 1999, p. 27). Interestingly, based on conditioning theories most ads use positive affect-laden stimuli and only more recently marketers started also to use negative affect-laden stimuli such as for health marketing purposes (e.g. for lung cancer prevention). In neuroscience, research has shown that distinct brain areas encode positive affect-laden stimuli (e.g. parts of the Medial Prefrontal Cortex and the Striatum) and negative affect laden-stimuli (e.g. Insular, Amygdala). There is also evidence that affective (e.g. pleasant or aversive) events are better remembered than neutral events (Hamann et al. 1999). Research in neuroscience suggests that these emotional memory effects are mainly driven by attention.

In the current study we investigated whether ads that vary in ad liking elicit changes in brain activity that corresponds to areas shown to be involved in the processing of stimuli with different affective valence. In addition, we explored the existence of emotional memory effects and how these effects differ with affective valence of the ads.

We first conducted a pre-study to quasi-normalize 45 print ads by asking 160 subjects to judge their liking of the ads. Based on the results we classified 10 ads as liked, 10 as disliked and 10 as neutral. These 30 ads were then used as stimulus material in an fMRI study. We scanned brain activity of 22 healthy and right-handed subjects (12 males, aged between 24-34 years) while they judged their liking of the 30 print ads. Every 10 seconds a new ad was projected into the visual field of the subjects. The volunteers were asked to decide whether they like or dislike this ad by pressing one of the two corresponding buttons on a magnetic resonance compatible response box. The responses were recorded with the use of specific software. Immediately after scanning, we asked the subjects to fill out a questionnaire to sample their recall of the different ads.

We found that liked and disliked ads are processed in distinct neural networks. Liked ads induced increased activity changes in higher order visual areas, the fusiform face area (FFA), the ventromedial prefrontal cortex (VMPFC), the posterior cingulum (PCC) and the ventral striatum (VS), in particular the nucleus accumbens (NCC). Activity increases in higher order visual cortices may reflect increased visual attention during viewing the attractive visual material (Shimojo et al. 2003). The FFA has been characterized as an area specialized in face recognition and perception (Grill-

Spector et al. 2004). This finding is interesting because indeed most of the liked ads contained faces whereas the disliked and neutral ads did not to that extend. The VMPFC is a region that plays a fundamental role in decision-making, especially in the context of preference and value representation (Bechara et al. 1999; Bechara 2004). Finally, our data suggests that exposure to attractive ads leads to increased cerebral blood flow in areas of to the human reward system, in particular the VS/NCC (Knutson et al. 2000, O'Doherty et al. 2004). In contrast, disliked ads are accompanied with activity changes in the insular region. Activation in the insular is consistently seen in studies of pain and distress, hunger and thirst, autonomic arousal and unfairness (Sanfey et al. 2003). A recent study showed that excessive prices activated the insular prior to the purchase decision (Knutson et al. 2007). In addition, we found that disliked ads induce activity changes in areas associated with the motor cortex. The motor cortex consists of regions in the cerebral cortex involved in planning, control, and execution of voluntary motor functions. This finding might be due to the fact that our subjects responded quicker to aversive stimuli in order to make them disappear from screen.

In the next step of the data analysis, we generated recall scores and tested their correlation with different degrees of ad liking. As expected we found significant differences in ad recall between the three different ad-liking groups. We found that highly liked ads lead to the highest ad recall, followed by the disliked and, finally, the neutral ones.

Our findings offer important insights for advertising research and practice. One interesting finding is that there is a high correlation between ad liking and the use of faces in the ads. This preliminary finding calls for future research to better understand the role of faces, facial expressions and also eye gazes for ad liking, ad recall and ad memory. Then, our findings show that both, ad liking and ad disliking lead to increased ad recall as compared to neutral ads. In a next step it would be interesting to investigate how ad liking influences attitude towards the brand and brand preference. Do conditioning theories hold here that ads that trigger activation changes in areas encoding negative affect will have a negative impact on the attitude towards and preference for the advertised brand? An alternative scenario would be that positive spillover effects could be found based on contrasts effects. Taken together, this research contributes not only to a better understanding of how advertising affects consumers' perception, affective encoding and memory, but also extend knowledge referring to the role of the emotion processing for memory effects that serve as basis for every day (economic) decision-making.

"Neural Correlates of Deception Detection: A BOLD Imaging Study"

Adam Craig, University of South Carolina, USA
Yuliya Komarova, University of South Carolina, USA
Stacy Wood, University of South Carolina, USA
Jennifer Vendemia, University of South Carolina, USA

Although many definitions of deceptive or misleading advertising have been offered, most researchers agree that for an advertisement to be deceptive it must assert or imply something that is "objectively false" (e.g., Shimp and Preston 1981). However, differences in interpretation and operationalization of advertising deceptiveness have resulted in substantial theoretical dispute and consequently, research effort (e.g., Russo et al. 1981). Unsurprisingly, much research in the past has been dedicated to features and attributes of advertisements that have a potential to mislead consumers (e.g., Armstrong et al. 1979; Barone et al. 2004; Burke et al. 1988; Shimp 1978). Burke and his colleagues (1988) for instance, investigated various message forms identified in past research as having the potential to deceive consumers by implying unrealistically high levels of brand attribute performance; their results showed that certain message forms in particular increased false brand attribute beliefs, affect, and purchase intentions. More recently, Darke and Ritchie (2007) have investigated short and long-term consequences of deceptive advertising on consumer perception and subsequent behavior and found that consumers engage in defensive stereotyping and direct negative affect towards subsequent, unrelated advertisements. Consequently, there are conflicting findings pertaining to the effect of deceptive advertising on affect and subsequently, on purchase intentions which may be explained by the mechanisms that guide deception detection. However, little evidence exists for what processes underlie consumer detection of deception in advertising even though such an insight has a potential of helping resolve a number of related theoretical arguments. Hence, the objective of the present work is twofold: first, we attempt to identify the neural correlates of deception detection using fMRI methodology, and second, we investigate the differences in consumer processing of varying levels of deceptive advertisements.

Although functional MRI methodology is relatively novel in consumer research (e.g., Yoon et al. 2006; Plassman et al. 2007), it has been used in the field of psychology to study deception effort (Kozel et al. 2004; Vendemia et al. 2006) and revealed complex processes in the anterior cingulate involving attention, working memory, and executive control. In the context of deceptive advertising, fMRI may be particularly informative as the traditional cognitive expectancy disconfirmation approach has often failed to reveal consistency in what individuals perceive as misleading information (Grunert and Dedler 1987). For instance, Shimp (1978) notes that inferences made from incomplete comparisons in advertisement messages differ among people: while some consumers assess a certain advertising message as deceptive, there are others who detect no deception when exposed to the same message. Hence, idiosyncrasies in cognitive structures involved in advertisement perception have made it largely impossible to investigate the processes underlying consumer detection of advertising deception via traditional behavioral methodology. Interpersonal deception detection research shows similar inconsistency in that primed knowledge for deception likelihood does not increase observers' accuracy at detection (Toris and Depaulo 1984).

In order to explore the neural functions underlying deception detection, college students (N=25) viewed 15 advertisements for new products that varied in their level of perceived deception potential (as determined by pretesting). Each advertisement was assigned to one of three categories (based on pretesting with college students (N=180) from the same population as the subsequent imaging study): low deception potential, mildly deceptive, and highly deceptive. The advertisements consisted of a product picture and descriptive paragraphs similar to a catalog format and were viewed for 50 seconds each.

Broadly described, we observe an inverted-u effect of neural activity where greater processing resources are expended for products that seem moderately deceptive compared to products that have either low or high potential for deception. Based on results from Darke and Ritchie (2007), we predict and find that neural activity associated with comparative processes and hypothesis-testing will be greater in conditions of moderate deception than in low deception conditions as suspicion will not be active in low deception conditions. In comparing processing between moderate and high deception conditions, neural activity associated with highly deceptive advertisements shows truncated processing resulting from the discounting of invalid messages (Schul et al. 1996; Schul et al. 2004). Additionally, prior research suggests that affective processing should also be greater in conditions of higher deception (Darke and Ritchie 2007).

Neural processing evidence from this fMRI study suggests that individuals have quick attentional responses to potentially deceptive claims in accord with behavioral theories of marketplace "defensive" vigilance and biological theories of threat surveillance. Further, the pattern of neural activation suggests an early two-stage process in which heightened attention is first preferentially directed toward highly deceptive material but that this attention shifts as processing of highly deceptive material is truncated and increased attention and belief reasoning is directed toward believable and moderately deceptive material. We interpret these data as indicating a potential risk of moderately deceptive material in that such claims generate prolonged attention as well as expanded comparative processing similar to that garnered by believable claims. While our data do not speak to resulting biases, if a potentially deceptive claim is simultaneously being evaluated for credibility and relative benefit, this would provide a situation in which individual's credibility judgments may be colored by evaluations of relative benefit.

This research contributes to the existing literatures on deception by describing the brain's early processing response to potentially deceptive information and by examining this process within the domain of marketplace deception. We find neural evidence that supports recent consumer theories of "defensive surveillance" (Darke & Richie 2007) and is in accord with broader conceptualizations of persuasion knowledge in the marketplace (Friestad & Wright 1994). Like recent fMRI research on belief reasoning, we find that activation in BA 7 (Goel & Dolan 2003) and BA 40 (Sommer et al. 2007) is associated with the larger deception detection process. Our findings distinguish between claims that vary in perceived deceptiveness. Importantly we identify "stage 1" visual attention differences that suggest preferential initial processing of highly deceptive claims as well as subsequent "stage 2" processing differences that suggest preferential processing of moderately deceptive and believable claims.

"A Salesforce-Specific Theory of Mind Scale: Tests of Its Validity by Multitrait-Multimethod Matrix, Confirmatory Factor Analysis, Structural Equation Models, and Functional MRI"

Roeland C. Dietvorst, Erasmus University, The Netherlands
Willem J. M. I. Verbeke, Erasmus University, The Netherlands
Richard P. Bagozzi, University of Michigan, USA
Carolyn Yoon, University of Michigan, USA
Marion Smits, Erasmus University, The Netherlands
Aad van der Lugt, Erasmus University, The Netherlands

In order to be successful, it is imperative that salespeople immerse themselves into the nuances of the customer's organization and pay special attention to subtle cues communicated by customers. By doing so, salespeople can put themselves into the shoes of the members of the buying center and mentally simulate what customers indicate or say they want, and why they want to buy. Following recent developments in neuroscience, we term such processes, interpersonal mentalizing and define it as the activity of inferring another person's beliefs, desires, risk preferences, intentions, and other mental states or events (Frith and Frith 2003). The ability to engage in interpersonal mentalizing and read the mind of the customer has some affinity to the adaptive selling concept (e.g., Spiro and Weitz 1990); and the functioning of the drivers of adaptation in selling interactions, in turn, rests on assumptions about, and processes going on, in the mind of salespeople. Yet research to date has utilized methods based only on verbal self-reports.

Our goal is to study brain processes of salespeople who score high versus low on interpersonal mentalizing processes. The neuroscience literature suggests that interpersonal mentalizing is a hardwired brain process that occurs spontaneously and largely unconsciously in social encounters and is centralized in a distinct network of brain regions: the most consistently activated regions with mentalizing tasks are the medial prefrontal cortex (MPFC), left and right temporo-parietal junctions (TPJ), and left and right temporal poles (TP). Based on a growing body of evidence, we hypothesize that those who are high (versus low) in interpersonal mentalizing skills display greater coordinated activation of all modules implicated in this network.

We investigated the role of mentalizing in personal selling in four studies. In the first study, a paper and pencil measure that operationalized interpersonal mentalizing concepts in a selling context was designed and administered to 132 salespeople. We refer to the measure as the salesperson theory of mind (SToM) scale in order to stress the context-specific aspects of our measure and differentiate it from a generalized theory of mind (ToM) scale which we use to test criterion-related validity. The results showed that salespeople exhibit different degrees of interpersonal mentalizing which can be represented in four distinct, but related, dimensions, and further the measures of SToM achieve convergent, discriminant, and criterion-related validity. Moreover, high versus low scorers on the SToM-scale are relatively more adaptive in selling situations, are better able to take the perspective of customers, and show less fear of being evaluated negatively in selling situations. Study 2 replicated findings of Study 1 and also showed that the four dimensions of SToM relate significantly with performance. The performance measures were then validated on a new sample of high and low performers.

Study 3 examined the construct validity of measures of SToM by use of the MTMM matrix and CFA and also tested nomological validity. The measures showed high trait variance, low error variance, and very low method variance. Performance was found to be driven largely by SToM: rapport building influenced performance indirectly through social anxiety and the other three dimensions of SToM influenced performance directly.

Study 4 used functional magnetic resonance imaging (fMRI) to discover whether different functioning of brain regions provide evidence for individual differences in the ability to mentalize interpersonally, and in addition provide evidence that the four dimensions of SToM discriminate between high and low mentalizers. We tested the hypothesis that high (vs. low) interpersonal mentalizers display relatively greater activations of specific regions of the brain (i.e., the MPFC, TPJ, TP) that have been consistently reported in the literature to be associated with mentalizing tasks.

Twenty participants (10 high and 10 low scorers on the SToM-scale) were recruited for the fMRI study. The fMRI protocol consisted of three experimental conditions: Interpersonal mentalizing (IM), Process, or Unlinked sentences. Participants listened to five stories of each type presented in a counterbalanced manner while lying supine in a full-body 3.0 T GE scanner; and functional images were acquired. In the IM condition, participants listened to stories and were instructed to imagine the intentionality of the people interacting with each other in the story. In the process condition, they thought about how people operate according to well-estab-

lished scripts. The IM and process conditions were designed to be different at a subtle level; whereas the IM condition explicitly required interpersonal mentalizing, the process condition did not. Finally, in the unlinked sentences condition, participants listened to a series of sentences that did not form a coherent story. Each story was followed by a question that the participant was instructed to answer silently to oneself. The process and unlinked sentences conditions served as control conditions.

Our results were largely consistent with our hypothesis: the high (vs. low) scorers on the SToM scale showed more activity during the mentalizing task in the MPFC and TPJ regions of the brain, but this effect was much weaker in the TP regions, and was nonexistent when we compared the interpersonal mentalizing task with the unlinked sentences task. A closer inspection of the data shows that the TP regions were in fact activated highly in both the high and low mentalizing groups of salesperson participants. To the extent that such activation in the TP regions relates to the formation and use of mental scripts (e.g., Frith and Frith 2003, p. 465), we speculate that both high and low scoring salespersons equally use script-based thinking. It thus appears that only for salespersons high in interpersonal mentalizing is the entire network consisting of the MPFC, TPJ, and TP fully activated, whereas for persons low in interpersonal mentalizing, only part of the network, the TP, is activated. Hence we find evidence suggesting that salespeople differ in their utilization of the mentalizing network, and that these differences have considerable behavioral correlates. We explore possible explanations for the differences in brain activity between high and low mentalizers. Finally, implications of our findings for the selection and training of salespersons are considered.

REFERENCES

Ambler, Tim and Tom Burne (1999), "The Impact of Affect on Memory of Advertising," *Journal of Advertising Research*, Vol. 39, Number 2, 25-34.

Armstrong, Gary M., Metin N. Gurol, and Frederick A. Russ (1979), "Detecting and Correcting Deceptive Advertising," *Journal of Consumer Research*, 6 (December), 237-46.

Barone, Michael J., Kay M. Palan, and Paul W. Miniard (2004), "Brand Usage and Gender as Moderators of the Potential Deception Associated with Partial Comparative Advertising," *Journal of Advertising*, 33 (Spring), 19-28.

Bechara, Antoine (2004), "The Role of Emotion in Decision-Making: Evidence from Neurological Patients with Orbitofrontal Damage," *Brain and Cognition*, 55 (1), 30-40.

Bechara, Antoine, Hanna Damasio, Antonio. R. Damasio, and Gregory P. Lee (1999), "Different Contributions of the Human Amygdala and Ventromedial Prefrontal Cortex to Decision-Making," *Journal of Neuroscience*, Vol. 19, Issue 13, 5473-81.

Burke, Raymond R., Wayne S. DeSarbo, Richard L. Oliver, and Thomas S. Robertson (1988), "Deception by Implication: An Experimental Investigation," *Journal of Consumer Research*, 14 (March), 483-94.

Darke, Peter R., and Robin J.B. Ritchie (2007), "The Defensive Consumer: Advertising Deception, Defensive Processing, and Distrust," *Journal of Consumer Research*, 1, 114-27.

Grunert, Klaus G., and Konrad Dedler (1987), "Misleading Advertising: In Search of a Measurement Methodology," *Journal of Public Policy and Marketing*, 5, 153-59.

Frith, Uta and Chris D. Frith (2003),"Development and Neurophysiology of Mentalizing," *Philosophical Transactions of the Royal Society London: Biological Sciences,* 358 (March), 59-473.

Hamann, Stephan B., Timothy D. Ely, Scott T. Grafton, and Clinton D. Kilts (1999), "Amygdala activity related to enhanced memory for pleasant and aversive stimuli," *Nature Neuroscience*, Vol 2, 289–93.

Kozel, Frank Andrew, Padgett, Tamara M., and Mark S. George (2004), "A Replication Study of the Neural Correlates of Deception," *Behavioral Neuroscience*, 118 (August), 852-56.

Knutson, Brian, Scott Rick, G. Elliott Wimmer, Drazen Prelec, and George Loewenstein (2007), "Neural predictors of purchases," *Neuron*, Vol. 53, Issue 1, 147-56.

O'Doherty, John, Peter Dayan, Johannes Schultz, Ralf Deichmann, Karl Friston, and Raymond J. Dolan (2004), "Dissociable roles of ventral and dorsal striatum in instrumental conditioning," *Science*, Vol. 304. No. 5669, 452-54.

Plassmann, Hilke, John O'Doherty, Antonio Rangel (2007), "Orbitofrontal Cortex encodes Willingness to Pay in Everyday Economic Transactions," *Journal of Neuroscience*, 27 (37), 9984-9988.

Ray, Michael L. and Rajeev Batra (1983), "Emotion and Persuasion in advertising: What we do and don´t know about affect," *Advances in Consumer Research*, Vol. 10, 543-48.

Russo, J. Edward, Barbara L. Metcalf, and Debra Stephens (1981), "Identifying Misleading Advertising," *Journal of Consumer Research*, 8 (September), 119-31.

Sanfey, Alan G., James K. Rilling, Jessica A. Aronson, Leigh E. Nystrom, and Jonathan D. Cohen (2003), "The Neural Basis of Economic Decision-Making in the Ultimatum Game," *Science* Vol. 300, 1755-58.

Schul, Yaacov, E. Burnstein, and A. Bardi (1996), "Dealing with Deceptions that Are Difficult to Detect: Encoding and Judgment as a Function of Preparing to Receive Invalid Information," *Journal of Experimental Social Psychology*, 32, 228-53.

_____, Ruth Mayo, and Eugene Burnstein (2004), "Encoding Under Trust and Distrust: the Spontaneous Activation of Incongruent Cognitions," *Journal of Personality and Social Psychology*, 86 (5), 668-79.

Shimp, Terence A. (1978), "Do Incomplete Comparisons Mislead?" *Journal of Advertising Research*, 18 (December), 21-7.

_____, and Ivan L. Preston (1981), "Deceptive and Nondeceptive Consequences of Evaluative Advertising," *Journal of Marketing*, 45 (Winter), 22-32.

Spiro, Rosan and Barton A. Weitz (1990), "Adaptive Selling: Conceptualization Measurement and Nomological Validity," *Journal of Marketing Research*, 27 (February), 61-69.

Toris, Carol and Bella M. DePaulo (1984), "Effects of actual deception and suspiciousness of deception on interpersonal perceptions," *Journal of Personality and Social Psychology*, 47 (5), 1063-1073.

Vendemia, Jennifer M. C., Michael J. Schilliaci, and Robert F. Buzan (2006), "Credibility assessment: psychophysiology and policy in the detection of deception," *American Journal of Forensic Psychology*, 24 (4), 53-85.

Yoon, Carolyn, Angela H. Gutchess, Fred Feinberg, and Thad A. Polk (2006), "A Functional Magnetic Resonance Imaging Study of Neural Dissociations between Brand and Person Judgments," *Journal of Consumer Research*, 33 (June), 31-40.

When the Going gets Tough: How Metacognitive Difficulty Improves Evaluation

Aparna A. Labroo, University of Chicago, USA
Sara Kim, University of Chicago, USA

SESSION OVERVIEW

Ample research establishes that feelings serve as information about preferences. An important source of feelings is the subjective characteristics of a stimulus itself (Schwarz 2004). Research argues that subjective feelings of ease of processing the stimulus are beneficial and increase liking towards the stimulus (Berlyne, 1966; Bornstien, 1989; Zajonc, 1968). This is because people implicitly associate ease with familiarity and personal relevance. Consequently, subjectively easy (vs. difficult) to process stimuli are also evaluated as more familiar and self-relevant and are preferred. However, is it possible that under certain situations, feelings of metacognitive difficulty might increase evaluation? For example, looking to become a better person, might you decide to donate more to a charity simply because processing difficulty made it seem more instrumental, because usually you invest effort in what is instrumental and you unknowingly reversed this correlation in your mind? Or celebrating a special occasion, might feelings of difficulty in coming up with the name of the chosen restaurant make it seem more exclusive? After struggling through a students' hard to read assignment that employs small font might you find the next one so much more lucid but actually only its font is larger? And to what extent do these effects emerge because of feelings of familiarity or because of the misattribution of affect? For example, if after struggling to pronounce the name of a food additive you come to think it is more dangerous, is that because it feels unfamiliar or because it feels negative? These are some questions we investigate in this session.

In contrast to existing research arguing for a positive effect of ease of processing on evaluation, in this session we discuss three situations—when the target is a means to fulfill an accessible goal (paper 1), when the target is a special occasion product (paper 2), and when the target follows a difficult to process prime (paper 3)—under which subjective difficulty of processing increases liking of the target object. Finally (paper 4), we discuss how metacognitive difficulty might increase perception of effort needed to accomplish a task at hand, thus tying the session to the initial proposition (paper 1) that effort perception can sometimes be a good thing.

Paper 1 by Kim and Labroo argues that when a target product is a means to attain an accessible goal, people employ an "effort heuristic" to judge its instrumentality as a means. This is because people investing effort to pursue goals use those means that are most instrumental in accomplishing their goals. When assessing the value of the target in fulfilling an accessible goal they also reverse this correlation inferring that effort signals instrumentality. Thus, subjective difficulty increases desirability of an object that is a means to fulfill an accessible goal.

Paper 2 by Pocheptsova and Dhar adds to our understanding of the impact of metacognitive difficulty on evaluation of products in a second way. It suggests that when scarcity or infrequency is a good thing as in the case of special occasion products, a "scarcity heuristic" kicks in and subjective feelings of difficulty make products appear more rewarding by increasing perceptions of scarcity.

Paper 3 by Shen, Jiang, and Adaval next establishes a positive impact of metacognitive difficulty on subsequent evaluations. The authors suggest that subjective feelings of difficulty that arise from perceptual processing create an illusion of increased ease towards judgments that follow. Thus judgments about a target are not only affected by processing fluency of the target but also affected by processing fluency of the material preceding the target information.

Finally, Song and Schwarz discuss the situations where difficulty signals danger and where it signals required effort to pursue ones' goals. They demonstrate that when people make judgments about risk-related targets, low processing fluency signals a lack of safety increasing expected risk associated with the target. Additionally, in a situation where people make judgments about effort-related activities, low fluency signals a need to invest higher effort. They discuss the mechanism underlying these phenomena in terms of affect and familiarity.

All four papers are closely related, well grounded in theory, advancing and consolidating research on metacognition and consumer preference formation. Each paper comprises of several experiments, and presents novel findings in an area of growing interest to consumer researchers.

EXTENDED ABSTRACTS

"The 'Instrumentality' Heuristic: When Metacognitive Difficulty Signals Means Instrumentality"

Sara Kim, University of Chicago
Aparna A. Labroo, University of Chicago

Do people crave for things just because they seem subjectively difficult to get? Take a look at "Mysterious Flirting 101" on the Web, which authoritatively proclaims that "everyone's heard that you should play hard to get in order to attract the person you like." Evidence from an experiment also confirms that female rats that play hard to get are more likely to keep their male mates interested (Erskine, 2005). Even children appear to want things that simply feel difficult to get. Try holding a toy out to a young child just beyond his or her grasp, and watch the child bounce all around you. Then, hand the toy over and watch how quickly the child loses all interest in it. In the current research, we consider the following question: does a feeling of subjective difficulty (vs. ease) sometimes increase the allure of the object under consideration, and why?

Contrary to the commonplace observations just discussed, ample evidence suggests that feelings of subjective ease rather than difficulty increase preferences of objects (Berlyne, 1966; Bornstien, 1989; Schwarz, 2004; Zajonc, 1968). For example, abstract images, line drawings, and pictures are evaluated more favorably when their perceptual characteristics are subjectively easy to process (vs. blurry) or when they have been presented on a previous occasion. Because personally relevant and familiar objects come to mind easily, people implicitly associate ease with familiarity and personal relevance (Schwarz, 2004). Consequently, subjectively easy (vs. difficult) to process objects are also evaluated as more familiar, self-relevant, and desirable.

In the current research, however, we propose that when people have a highly accessible goal before evaluating a target object, subjective difficulty (vs. ease) of processing will improve its evaluation. This is because people with an accessible goal who evaluate the target object need to assess its instrumentality in fulfilling their goal. We propose that at this time an "effort heuristic" might help ascertain how instrumental the target being considered is toward fulfilling their accessible goal. In particular, we propose that because effort during goal pursuit is usually expended in whichever means is most instrumental, people implicitly associate effort with instrumentality of a means. They might reverse this correlation in their minds to also perceive effort as a signal of instrumentality of the target means in fulfilling the accessible goal. Thus, subjective difficulty (vs. ease) might improve evaluation of a target object that is a means towards fulfilling an accessible goal because, based on the belief that people generally put in effort in whichever means is most instrumental, effort signals value. When no clear goals are accessible or when the target object is not a means to fulfill an accessible goal, ease (vs. difficulty) of processing will improve evaluation, replicating the results found in previous research. We test this across three experiments.

In all three experiments, we manipulate difficulty of processing using either blurry or clear font, in line with a methodology used in previous experiments (Novemsky et al. 2007). Experiment 1 examines whether a highly accessible mood goal leads participants to prefer LeVour chocolate when information regarding the chocolate is subjectively difficult (vs. easy) to process. We find that participants primed with a mood goal evaluated LeVour chocolate more favorably and were willing-to-pay more for the collection when the ad was difficult (vs. easy) to process, but participants primed with a conflicting self-control goal preferred LeVour and were willing-to-pay more for the collection when it was easy (vs. difficult) to process, as did neutral-goal participants. In order to ensure that our results apply beyond hedonic products and to ensure that metacognitive effort is more than a justification for choosing hedonic products (Kivetz & Simonson, 2002), experiment 2 employed donation amount as the dependent variable. Charity materials, which pretested as unpleasant and negative, ensured that neither they nor the donation to the charity provided immediate pleasure. As we expected, participants primed with the goal to be a better person donated more money when they were given blurry (vs. clear) materials. In contrast, participants in the neutral-goal condition donated more money when the materials were clear (vs. blurry), replicating research on ease of processing. Finally, Experiment 3 used a chronic measure of goal to replicate this effect. It also established that instrumentality of the target object as a means to fulfilling the accessible goal mediates the effect, and the effect is attenuated when people are unable to misattribute effort to effectiveness of the target in fulfilling the accessible goal. The effects were not because of perceived scarcity of the target and people liking what is scarce. As a set these studies thus demonstrated that the effect of metacognitive ease or difficulty of processing a target object on evaluation of the target object will depend on whether metacognitive difficulty is information to the motivational system regarding effectiveness of the target object toward fulfilling an accessible goal.

"When Products Feel Special: Low Fluency leads to Enhanced Desirability"

Anastasiya Pocheptsova, University of Maryland
Aparna A. Labroo, University of Chicago
Ravi Dhar, Yale University

Existing research posits that feelings of high fluency which signal familiarity with an object improve its evaluation (e.g. Schwarz 2004, Winkielman et. al 2003). In a departure from those findings, we demonstrate that *low* fluency can sometimes enhance evaluation of a product. We argue that in the context of special occasion high-end goods, higher fluency which indicates abundance of the product makes the products feel less special, and this translates into lower value. Thus, low fluency of processing of special-occasion products will make them feel more special and positively affect judgments.

Consistent with our proposition, we find, across four studies, that consumers prefer special-occasion products more when processing fluency is low. In Study 1 we show that consumers are willing to pay more for gourmet cheese that a specialty online retailer is introducing when its description is printed in a hard-to-read vs. easy-to-read font. However, the effect of font on evaluation reverses for regular cheese, which is consistent with the existing literature. Study 2 replicates these effects in the context of a special occasion versus everyday restaurant and using a different manipulation of fluency: ease of thought generation. Study 3 provides evidence of the underlying process. Study 3 manipulates the product context by using a word jumble task to prime special vs. everyday concepts and thus making different lay theories accessible, while keeping the product constant, to show the role of lay theories in the interpretation of fluency experience. We find that ease (vs. difficulty) of processing increases evaluation of the product when participants are previously primed with "everyday," but difficulty (vs. ease) of processing increases liking of the product when participants are primed with "special." Finally, Study 4 directly measures people's lay beliefs to see if individual differences in beliefs account for the effect of fluency on preference. We find that consumers prefer chocolate truffles more when the information about them is presented in a difficult font. Interestingly, this effect of difficulty of processing holds only for people who have a belief that chocolate is for special occasions. We also show that when participants correctly attribute the difficulty of processing to the font, they correct (reduce) their evaluation.

Our findings contribute to the growing literature on fluency effects on product evaluations. We posit that the effect of fluency on judgments is context dependent and show that contrary to previous findings low processing fluency can lead to an increase in liking. Merely framing a product as special occasion or simply priming people with the construct of special occasion prior to the evaluation task can reverse the effects that have previously been observed in the ease of processing literature. Understanding the role of fluency in consumer decisions provides the marketers with the set of new tools to lure customers to buy their products. Current paper highlights the importance of consumption domains and consumers lay theories in the interpretation of fluency experiences and thus suggest more nuanced marketing tactics for creating attractive product offerings and improving sales.

"Contrast and Assimilation Effects of Processing Fluency"

Hao Shen, Chinese University of Hong Kong
Yuwei Jiang, Hong Kong University of Science and Technology
Rashmi Adaval, Hong Kong University of Science and Technology

Consumers often encounter information sequentially when browsing through magazines. For example, they might encounter articles that are perceptually easy or difficult-to-read because of the font used. These articles might be followed by ads for products. How does the subjective experience of reading an article that is easy or difficult-to-read influence readers' reactions to a product ad that is encountered subsequently?

Some streams of research suggest that the product that is encountered subsequently will be evaluated more unfavorably if it is preceded by difficult-to-read information than if it is preceded by easy-to-read information (an assimilation effect). For example, work by Winkielman and Cacioppo (2001) suggests that positive affect is elicited if there is high processing fluency and negative affect if there is low processing fluency. If this is the case, then several theories would predict that the affect elicited by the first task might transfer to the second task, leading to assimilation. Previous research by Fiske (1982) and Sujan (1985) also suggests assimilation effects. According to this work, feelings about the first stimulus could be transferred to the second stimulus if these two stimuli are perceived as belonging to the same category. However, other streams of research suggest that the second product will be evaluated more favorably if the processing of previously encountered material is difficult than if it is easy (a contrast effect). This could occur through three mechanisms. The first, a perceptual process, suggests that people adapt to the level of past stimuli and judge new stimuli in relation to an adaptation level (Helson 1964). Thus, difficult reading experiences could lead people to adapt to that low level of processing fluency and subsequently encountered ads could be contrasted with this adaptation level and might seem easier to process leading to more favorable evaluations. The second mechanism that predicts such effects (Adaval and Monroe 2002) suggests that participants might make a deliberative judgment of the ease or difficulty of processing information about the first product that is encountered (e.g., "This is so hard to read.") and then use this as a standard for judging the processing difficulty of information about the second product ("This is much easier"). Finally, contrast effects could occur because people might form unfavorable evaluations of the object described by the difficult to read information that is encountered first and use these evaluations as a basis for judging the second product.

Experiment 1 demonstrates how perceptual fluency elicited in one situation can lead to contrast effects in a second situation and whether this effect occurs without participants' awareness (as we predict) or is the result of deliberative cognitive activity. Participants were presented with a movie review (in either a difficult- or easy-to-read font) on a webpage and were told to either form an impression of the movie review or the webpage on which it was presented. Next, they were asked to evaluate a product described in an ad that used an easy-to-read font.

We assumed that participants would experience low fluency when they read the review presented in difficult font (Novemsky et al. 2007). If an easy-to-read ad is encountered later, the experienced change in fluency might be attributed to the product described in the ad and might lead participants to evaluate it more favorably than they would if the ad was preceded by an easy-to-read movie review (a contrast effect). If the above effect occurs without awareness, it should be evident only when participants focus on forming an impression of the movie review because other participants (asked to form an impression of the webpage) are more likely to evaluate aspects of its layout (such as the font, white space etc.). This process should increase sensitivity to the fonts used in the ad. The increased awareness and deliberative comparison of these fonts with those seen in the webpage earlier might reduce the effect. Results were consistent with these assumptions.

In experiment 2, participants were presented with the product ad after they had read a movie review in an easy- or difficult-to-read font. However, after they evaluated the product, they also evaluated the font of the ad and movie review. Then, they were presented with a second movie review (that was in a font similar to the first one) and a second product ad. We assumed that evaluation of the fonts in the preceding task would draw participants' attention to fonts and should lead them to attribute processing ease or difficulty to the fonts used. Consequently, they should stop using these subjective feelings to evaluate the product in the second ad. Results were consistent with this assumption and showed that the proposed contrast effect was obtained for the product in the first ad, but disappeared for the second product ad.

Experiment 3 investigated the conditions in which assimilation effects might occur by manipulating both the fluency of the first stimuli and the relatedness between the first and second stimuli. Participants were asked to read a movie review that was presented in either difficult or easy-to-read fonts. After they had read the review, they were exposed to an ad for popcorn presented in easy-to-read font. However, in one condition the relationship between the movie and the popcorn ad was made explicit. In the other condition, this relationship was not obvious. After, reading the ad, participants were asked to evaluate the popcorn. The results of experiment 3 showed that assimilation effects occur when the two experiences are categorized together. Thus, when participants read that they could enjoy popcorn while watching the movie (high related condition), they categorized the popcorn and the movie as part of the same experience. Consequently, the difficulty of processing the movie review as a result of the fonts was transferred to the popcorn leading to an assimilation effect. In contrast, when the relatedness between the popcorn and the movie was not emphasized, the evaluation of the popcorn increased (a contrast effect) because of the processes demonstrated in previous experiments.

"Safe and Easy or Risky and Burdensome? Fluency Effects on Risk Perception and Effort Prediction"

Hyunjin Song, University of Michigan
Norbert Schwarz, University of Michigan

Six experiments extend the exploration of processing fluency to risk perception and effort prediction. Familiar stimuli are often perceived as less risky than unfamiliar ones (Slovic, 1987; Zajonc, 1980). This raises the possibility that variables that affect the perceived familiarity of a product will also affect perceptions of the risks associated with the product. One such variable is the fluency with which product information can be processed. In cognitive research, the fluency-familiarity link is reflected in erroneous recognition judgments (e.g., Whittlesea, Jacoby, & Girard, 1990) and strong feelings of knowing (e.g., Koriat & Levy-Sadot, 2001) for perceptually easy-to-process stimuli. Previous research also demonstrated, however, that processing fluency is hedonically marked and that high fluency elicits a positive affective response (e.g., Winkielman & Cacioppo, 2001). Affect associated with fluency also may be involved in intuitive judgments of risk. In light of this fluency-safety link, in the first three studies, we propose and test that difficult-to-process stimuli are perceived as more hazardous than easy-to-process stimuli, using ease of pronunciation as a manipulation of fluency.

Study 1 examined people's hazard ratings of ostensible food additives that were described with easy-to-pronounce or difficult-to-pronounce names. We predicted and found that people perceived hard-to-pronounce substances as more harmful than easy-to-pronounce substances. Study 2 replicated this finding and examined the mediating roles of feeling of familiarity and affect. As a large body of research into the role of affect in evaluative judgment demonstrates, positive affect elicits more favorable evaluations than negative affect (see Schwarz & Clore, 2007, for a review), this raises the possibility that low risk perception for fluent objects in Study 1 and 2 may be based on high preference driven by positive affect. Study 3 addressed this possibility by examining the influence of processing fluency on judgments of risk in a risk-approach situation (the excitement and adventurousness of amusement park rides) as well as in a risk-avoidance situation (the sickening effects of amusement park rides). If the effect of fluency on judgments of risk is a mere preference based on affect, low processing fluency should result in negative evaluations of amusement park rides, which should be perceived as less exciting as well as more sicken ing. If risk judgment is distinct from preference associated with fluency, however, low fluency may increase risk judgments regardless of whether risks are negative (sickening effects of rides) or positive (adventurousness of rides). Study 3 supported the latter prediction: amusement park rides with difficult-to-pronounce names were rated as more exciting as well as more sickening than rides with easy-to-pronounce names. These results further indicate the distinctive effects of fluency on risk perception.

Based on the logic that people tend to misread their current feelings as about the target of judgment at hand (Schwarz, Song, & Xu, in press), the next three studies show that people mistake the fluency of reading instructions as bearing on the ease of completing the described task. In Study 4, participants read exercise instructions either in easy-to-read fonts or in difficult-to-read fonts and predicted longer completion time and low fluency of movements in an exercise when instructions were printed in difficult-to-read fonts than in easy-to-read fonts. In addition, participants were more willing to incorporate the exercise in their daily routine when they read the instructions in easy-to-read fonts than in difficult-to-read fonts. In Study 5, participants read a recipe for a Japanese roll in easy-to-read fonts or in difficult-to-read fonts. They predicted that preparing the roll would take more time, and reported less willingness to try the recipe, when the fonts were difficult rather than easy to read. Study 6 further showed that participants perceived the recipe as requiring more skill from the cook when it was presented in a difficult to read font.

SELECTED REFERENCES

Berlyne, D.E. (1966), "Curiosity and Exploration." *Science*, 153: 25-33.

Bornstein, R.F. (1989), "Exposure and Affect: Overview and Meta analysis of Research," 1968 1987. *Psychological Bulletin*, 106: 265 289.

Kivetz R. & Simonson, I. (2002), "Earning the Right to Indulge: Effort as a Determinant of Customer Preferences toward Frequency Program Rewards," *Journal of Marketing Research*, 39: 155-170.

Novemsky, N, Dhar, R., Schwarz, N., & Simonson, I. (forthcoming), "Preference Fluency in. Consumer Choice," *Journal of Marketing Research*.

Schwarz, N. (2004), "Metacognitive Experiences in Consumer Judgment and Decision Making," *Journal of Consumer Psychology*, 14(4), 332-348.

Schwarz, N., & Clore, G. L. (2007), "Feelings and phenomenal experiences," in A. Kruglanski & E. T. Higgins (eds.), *Social psychology. Handbook of basic principles* (2nd ed.; pp. 385-407). New York: Guilford.

Schwarz, N., Song, H., & Xu, J. (in press), "When thinking is difficult: Metacognitive experiences as information," in M. Wänke (Ed.), *The Social Psychology of Consumer Behavior*. New York, NY. Psychology Press.

Slovic, P. (1987), "Perception of risk," *Science, 236*, 280-285.

Winkielman, P. & .Cacioppo, J.T. (2001). "Mind at Ease Puts a Smile on the Face: Psychophysiological Evidence that Processing Facilitation Elicits Positive Affect," *Journal of Personality & Social Psychology*, 81: 989-1013.

Zajonc, R.B. (1980), "Feeling and Thinking: Preferences Need no Inferences," *American Psychologist*, 35: 151-175.

Status: Why Consumers Engage in Conspicuous Consumption and How they may be Perceived

Joseph C. Nunes, University of Southern California, USA

EXTENDED ABSTRACTS

"The Intrinsic Benefits of Status: The Effects of Evoking Rank"

Aarti S. Ivanic, University of Southern California
Joseph C. Nunes, University of Southern California

Status, defined as one's ranking in the vertical stratification of social groups, is recognized as an important motivator of human behavior. The attainability and procurement of status has evolved over time from titles bestowed by birth to those earned or achieved. Today, a consumer can obtain status by demonstrating loyalty to a firm. More and more companies have begun stratifying customers in order to award their best customers with status. Elite customers are provided perks that enhance the experience and inducements that make future purchases more appealing. Special services, whether it is preferential seating, extended store hours and special sales, differentiate classes of customers into tiers of haves and have-nots. Whether it is admission to exclusive events or waiting in a special queue at the airport, each is a signal that the consumer is one of the haves. While many benefits signal one's status to others, firms also provide consumers with benefits that are consumed in private. For example, Continental airlines provides a dedicated phone line, priority on wait lists, expanded award availability and a no middle seat guarantee to Platinum members who fly at least 100,000 miles. These are benefits that are likely to go unnoticed by other fliers and often fail to appreciably alter the travel experience. The Platinum member's wait on the help line may occasionally take longer than normal or the flier may not clear the wait list despite having been bumped to the top. Yet, we propose elite members still derive emotional benefits from these perks making the airline's decision to provide these benefits a prudent one.

Research in marketing has focused on status goods for which the primary benefit is social. Veblen (1899) suggested that individuals acquired and consumed certain goods to signal their wealth and thus place in society to others. The marketing literature has shown that consumers acquire and use status goods to convey a particular image to those around them (Bagwell and Bernheim 1996). This conspicuous consumption of ones' status generates psychological responses such as feeling unique, distinctive and different from others (Tian, Bearden and Hunter 2001; Belk 1988; Tian and McKenzie 2001; Lynn and Harris 1997). However, not all benefits of status are social. Researchers have hypothesized that the attainment of status is no different from an "intrinsic emotional goal" that generates positive, affective reactions and emotions such as happiness and pride (Berger, Wagner and Zelditch 1985; Urda and Loch 2005). Yet, the intrinsic benefits of status have largely gone unexplored. In our work, we focus on the emotional gratification that accompanies the exercise of one's position or what is commonly referred to as "pulling rank" separate from the material and social benefits. We argue that utilizing one's status is emotionally gratifying as it makes one's elevated position or status identity salient.

We propose that *achieved* status (i.e, profession, status through a loyalty programs) can be represented by *role* identities and *endowed* (i.e., gender, race) status by *social* identities. We show that this distinction differentially impacts how individuals behave when these status identities are activated. Research has suggested that by activating a particular identity, attitudes and behaviors consistent with that identity are brought to mind, which in turn cause individuals to behave in a manner consistent with these attitudes (Reed 2004; Forehand and Deshpande 2001). Identity salience has been shown to impact one's attitude towards others (Deshpande, Hoyer and Donthu 1986), performance on quantitative tests (Shih, Pittinsky and Ambady 1999) and brand loyalty as well as preferences for prestige products (Deshpande, Hoyer and Donthu 1986). Yet, individuals do not always conform to the attitudes of a particular status group. We will show that there are instances where individuals act in discordance with the group norms and activated group stereotypes. In our work we explore the crossroads of status and identity theory and show that *status* identity salience differentially impacts consumers' behavior, specifically how much they are willing to pay for a product.

In Study 1, we show that when one's *achieved* status identity is made salient, individuals engage in behaviors that match the expectations associated with that status-role. In Study 2, we demonstrate that status role-congruent behavior results in the intrinsic benefit of prestige, distinct from the social benefit of identity signaling or any material or more tangible benefit. We demonstrate that while possessing status results in an elevated sense of prestige, individuals heighten these feelings by exercising their status (choosing to wait in a special status-only queue).

We extend our result to a consumer domain in Study 3 showing how making a relatively high *achieved* status identity salient leads individuals to pay more for a product than when a low status identity is activated. In doing so, high status individuals fulfill their status-role by acting in line with the behavioral expectations (i.e., pay more than low status individuals) associated with that role. In Study 4a, we document a racial stereotype which suggests that traditionally characterized high status individuals (i.e., White Americans) will pay more for a product than low status individuals (i.e., African Americans). In study 4b, we show how making an individual's *endowed* status identity (race) *implicitly* salient results in behavior congruent with the stereotype (i.e., African Americans pay *less* than both White Americans and the baseline-control group), while making a low-status racial identity *explicitly* salient causes individuals to act in discordance with the stereotypes (i.e. African Americans voluntarily pay *more* than both White Americans and the baseline–control group).

As firms increasingly endow their most loyal customers with status, it is important to better understand how consumers respond to status rewards which are conferred by a firm. Our results underscore the importance of understanding how consumers derive intrinsic benefits, in addition to social and material benefits, from status reward consumption. Further, we provide a better understanding of how status identity salience can result in differential responses to status cues utilized by marketers.

References

Bagwell, Laurie, S., and Bernheim, D. B., (1996), "Veblen Effects in a Theory of Conspicuous Consumption", *The American Economic Review*, 86, 3, 349-373.

Belk, Russell W. (1988), "Possessions and the Extended Self", *Journal of Consumer Research*, 15, 2, 139-168.

Berger, Joseph, Wagner, D. G. and Zelditch M. Jr. (1985), "Expectation states Theory: Review and Assessment" in *Status, Rewards and Influence*, 1-72. San Francisco: Jossey Bass.

Deshpande, Rohit, Wayne D. Hoyer and Naveen Donthu (1986), "The Intensity of Ethnic Affiliation: A Study of the Sociology of Hispanic Consumption", *Journal of Consumer Research*, 13, 214-220.

Forehand, Mark R. and Rohit Deshpande (2001), "What we see makes us who we are: Priming ethnic self-awareness and advertising response, *Journal of Marketing Research*, 38, 336-348.

Forehand, Mark R., Rohit Deshpande and Americus Reed II (2002), "Identity Salience and the Influence of Differential Activation of the Social Self-Schema on Advertising Response", *Journal of Applied Psychology*, 87, 6, 1086-1099.

Lynn, Michael and Judy Harris (1997), "The Desire for Unique Products: A New Individual Differences Scale", *Psychology and Marketing*, 14, 6, 601-616.

Reed II, Americus (2004), "Activating the Self-Importance of Consumer Selves: Exploring Identity Salience Effects on Judgments", *Journal of Consumer Research*, 31, (2) 286-295.

Shih, Margaret, Todd L. Pittinsky and Nalini Ambady (1999), "Stereotype Susceptibility: Identity Salience and Shifts in Quantitative Performance", *Psychological Science*, 10, 1, 80-83.

Tian, Kelly, T., William O. Bearden and Gary L. Hunter (2001), "Consumers' Need for Uniqueness: Scale Development and Validation", *Journal of Consumer Research*, 28, 50-66.

_____ and Karyn McKenzie (2001), "The Long-Term Predictive Validity of the Consumers' Need for Uniqueness Scale", *Journal of Consumer Psychology*, 10, 3, 171-193.

Urda, J. and C. Loch (2005), "Appraisal Theory and Social Appraisals: How an Event's Social Context Triggers Emotions", *INSEAD Working Paper Series*.

Veblen, Thorstein (1899), *The Theory of the Leisure Class*, New York: MacMillan, Reprint Random House (2001).

"Effects of the Density of Status Distribution on Conspicuous and Inconspicuous Consumption by Low-Status Consumers"

Nailya Ordabayeva, INSEAD
Pierre Chandon, INSEAD

It is a well-known and well-deplored fact that less well-off people spend more on status-enhancing positional products and save less money as a proportion of their income than richer people (Bagwell and Bernheim 1996; Christen and Morgan 2005; Duesenberry 1949). Economists have argued that one solution to this problem is to increase the density of the distribution of status by redistributing wealth through income or consumption taxation (Frank 1985, 1999). Although increasing status density can reduce envy and overall positional spending, this argument overlooks that it can increase the gains in status (i.e., improvement in social rank) resulting from conspicuous consumption for people at the lower tiers of the distribution. Therefore, increasing status density may have the unintended effect of actually encouraging low-status people to choose conspicuous consumption over savings.

In this research, we examine how the distribution of status across people affects choice between spending and saving, conspicuous and inconspicuous consumption by low-status people. We hypothesize that (1) increasing status density (i.e., increasing the proportion of people with an average level of status) encourages positional spending among low-status people even though it reduces their envy, (2) this occurs because of the higher gains in status resulting from conspicuous consumption in a dense (vs. wide) distribution, and (3) this occurs only when positional utility is primed and only in a competitive social environment. We test these hypotheses in five experiments.

In Study 1, we examined the effect of status density on envy and choice between spending and saving by low-status people. We manipulated between subjects the distribution of people's endowments with a positional product—the number of rose bushes in the front garden. In the scenario, 10% of people had no rose bushes. Forty percent of people had two rose bushes in a dense distribution and only twenty percent did so in a wide distribution. Buying three bushes enabled the 10% of people with no bushes to get ahead of 40% of people in the dense distribution and only 20% in the wide distribution. We found that low-status people were less envious but spent more in the dense (vs. wide) distribution. Furthermore, we found that social comparison orientation influenced envy but not positional spending. This suggests that conspicuous consumption is driven by status gains and not by envy or social comparison orientation.

In Study 2, we tested whether our theory accurately predicts the conspicuous consumption of high-status as well as low-status individuals in the context of decisions made for themselves rather than for hypothetical others. The participants were told that they would play an ultimatum game and try to split 10 chocolates with one other participant. Prior to the game, they were randomly assigned one star (low status) or three stars (high status), and they saw a dense or a wide distribution of stars obtained by previous participants. The participants were told that the number of stars would be public during the game and could affect their final outcome in the game. Consequently, before the actual game, the participants were given a chance to buy two additional stars at their own expense. We measured the willingness to buy stars and found that, consistently with our theory, low-status individuals were more willing to buy additional stars in a dense (vs. wide) distribution, but the opposite occurred for high-status individuals.

In Study 3, we distinguished between conspicuous and inconspicuous consumption and checked whether high status density indeed enhances perceived gains in status. The participants read two scenarios (house garden and ski trip) and judged how willingly low-status people in a dense or a wide distribution would spend money on positional products (rose bushes in the front garden and branded scarves for a ski trip) or non-positional products (pine trees in the back garden and unbranded scarves for a ski trip) and to which degree each type of spending would improve their status. We found that high status density encouraged conspicuous consumption but discouraged inconspicuous consumption. We also found that perceived status gains were higher in the dense (vs. wide) distribution for both positional and non-positional products. This indicates that high status density leads low-status people to choose consumption over saving only for positional products.

In Study 4, we further tested the moderating role of positional utility, but not as an inherently given product characteristic, but as a primed mindset. We also examined whether status is inferred from rank in the distribution of income, as assumed in previous literature, as it is in the distribution possessions. First, the participants engaged in a sentence scrambling task, which primed positional or non-positional utility. Then they studied a newsletter about their rival colleagues, which featured a dense or a wide distribution of their salaries. Finally, the participants needed to choose between an expensive trendy restaurant (positional option) and an inexpensive traditional bistro (non-positional option) for dinner with these colleagues. We measured the preference for the positional option, and found that a dense distribution of income increased the preference for the positional option only when positional utility was primed.

In Study 5, we further explored boundary conditions by examining the effect of reference group competitiveness. The participants read the same newsletter with a dense or a wide distribution of income as in Study 4, except that in the competitive group condition, the scenario featured rival co-workers, and in the cooperative group condition, it featured old friends. The participants faced the same decision between a trendy restaurant and a traditional bistro. The results showed that high income density strengthened people's preference for the positional option in the "rivals" condition but not in the "friends" condition.

In summary, we show that high status density increases conspicuous consumption among people in the lowest tier of the distribution across various distributions of status, in hypothetical and real decisions, and in the distributions of product endowments and income. Our results provide insights about the drivers of conspicuous consumption and the potential effectiveness of wealth redistribution policies and thus have important implications for future research and public policy.

References

Bagwell, Laurie Simon, and B. Douglas Bernheim (1996), "Veblen Effects in a Theory of Conspicuous Consumption," *American Economic Review*, 86 (3), 349-373.

Christen, Markus and Ruskin Morgan (2005), "Keeping Up With the Joneses: Analyzing the Effect of Income Inequality on Consumer Borrowing," *Quantitative Marketing and Economics*, 3 (2), 145-173.

Duesenberry, James (1949), *Income, Saving and the Theory of Consumer Behavior*, Cambridge, MA: Harvard University Press.

Frank, Robert (1985), "The Demand for Unobservable and Other Nonpositional Goods", *American Economic Review*, 75 (1), 101-116.

Frank, Robert (1999), *Luxury Fever: Money and Happiness in an Era of Excess*, Princeton, NJ: Princeton University Press.

Veblen, Thorstein (1899), *The Theory of the Leisure Class*, New York: Sentry Press.

"Stigmatizing Materialism: On Stereotypes and Impressions of Materialistic Versus Experiential Consumers"

Leaf Van Boven, University of Colorado at Boulder
Margaret C. Campbell, University of Colorado at Boulder
Thomas Gilovich, Cornell University

Observers of consumer behavior routinely fret about modern society's materialistic pursuit of happiness and well-being. Americans are reputed to value "having" over "being," which gives rise to alienation (Fromm 1976). Childhood consumer culture (Schor 2004) is charged with stoking materialistic desires that can only be satisfied by overspending (Schor 1999) and overworking (Schor 1993)—symptoms of a "suicidal" "affluenza" (De Graaf 2001; Lasn 2000). These materialistic desires are thought to contribute to declining social engagement (Lane 2001; Putnam 2000) by "crowding out" social relations (Kasser 2002; Lane 2001).

Not just social critic hyperbole, behavioral science indicates that materialistic consumers, those who believe that material possessions can make them happy, rate their social relations less favorably (Kasser and Ryan 2001), are more likely to be from divorced families (Rindfleisch, Burroughs, and Denton 1997), and are more likely to be diagnosed with psychological disorders

reflecting poor social functioning, including separation anxiety, paranoia, and narcissism (Cohen and Cohen 1996). Most explanations of the negative correlation between materialism and social relations focus on materialistic consumers' personalities and proclivities (Burroughs and Rindfleisch 2002; McHoskey 1999; Richins and Dawson 1992).

In this paper we shift the focus from materialistic consumers themselves to the stereotypes, or mental representations, that other people have of materialistic consumers. Using consumers who purchase experiences to gain happiness and life satisfaction as a comparison, we suggest that people stigmatize materialistic behavior by applying relatively unfavorable stereotypes of materialistic versus experiential consumers. That materialistic behavior is stigmatized—regarded as "worthy of disgrace or disapproval" (dictionary.com)—leads people to form relatively unfavorable impressions of consumers who are associated with materialistic behavior.

We tested the nature of people's stereotypes of materialistic and experiential consumers in one pair of studies. Participants were asked to generate the traits associated with materialistic and experiential consumers (study 1). A separate group of participants rated the traits associated with materialistic consumers less favorably than the traits associated with experiential consumers, despite not knowing the traits' initial association. In another study, participants rated specific material purchases made by materialistic consumers as more extrinsically motivated and less intrinsically motivated than specific experiential purchases made by experiential consumers (study 2).

These stereotypes of materialistic and experiential consumers influenced people's impressions of others' consumer behavior in another study in which people from various demographic groups formed an impression of another consumer (study 3). Participants learned only that the consumer purchased a prototypically material purchase (a new shirt) or a prototypically experiential purchase (a ski pass), without explicit mention of the distinction between materialistic and experiential purchases. Participants evaluated the consumer of a prototypical material purchase less favorably than the consumer of a prototypical experiential purchase. The stereotypes of materialistic and experiential consumers were sufficiently potent to influence people's impressions of each other during face-to-face conversations about materialistic versus experiential purchases, despite the fact that the experimenter constrained the conversation topic (study 4).

In study 5, we experimentally manipulate the extrinsic versus intrinsic motives underlying consumers' acquisition of prototypical material and experiential purchases. We showed that participants formed less favorable impressions of consumers who made extrinsically motivated purchases (e.g., skiing to gain "bragging rights") than of consumers who made intrinsically motivated purchases (e.g., buying a new watch because of its enduring value), independent of whether those purchases were prototypically materialistic or experiential.

The present research indicates that because there is a stigma attached to materialistic consumers, materialistic consumer behavior may not foster successful social relationships as well as experiential consumer behavior. The results of these studies undoubtedly reflect culturally constructed and shared values, like the cultural construction of materialism more generally (Belk 1985; Burroughs and Rindfleisch 2002). Stereotypes about materialistic and experiential consumers carry cultural meaning in much the same way as do specific products (Richins 1994) and brands (Aaker, Benet-Martinez, and Garolera 2001). Our studies thus imply that consumers in a particular cultural context—predominantly members of middle socioeconomic class—attach a stigmatization to materialistic consumers that leads them to form relatively unfavorable impressions of consumers associated with materialistic purchases.

The results of these studies provide consistent evidence that materialistic consumers are stigmatized compared with experiential consumers and that people form relatively unfavorable impressions of consumers who are associated with materialistic purchases. These results have important and complementary implications both for consumer welfare and for marketing practitioners. For consumers, these results suggest that, to the degree they desire to be favorably evaluated, they might avoid being associated with materialistic consumer behavior. Or, expressed more positively, these results reiterate a useful strategy for investing their resources in pursuit of happiness—to purchase experiences rather than possessions (Van Boven and Gilovich 2003). Similarly, when making materialistic purchases, consumers should highlight their intrinsic motivations for the purchases. For marketers, these results highlight the potential benefits of emphasizing experiential products, material products' intrinsically appealing attributes, and of avoiding associations with materialistic stereotypes.

References

Aaker, Jennifer, Veronica Benet-Martinez, and Jordi Garolera (2001), "Consumption Symbols as Carriers of Culture: A Study of Japanese and Spanish Brand Personality Constructs," *Journal of Personality and Social Psychology*, 81 (3), 492–508.

Burroughs, James E. and Aric Rindfleisch (2002), "Materialism and Well-Being: A Conflicting Values Perspective," *Journal of Consumer Research*, 29 (December), 348–70.

Cohen, Patricia and Jacob Cohen (1996), *Life Values and Adolescent Mental Health*, Mahwah, NJ: Erlbaum.

De Graaf, John (2001), *Affluenza: The All-Consuming Epidemic,* New York: Berrett-Koehler

Fromm, Erich (1976), *To have or to be?*, New York: Harper and Row.

Kasser, Timothy and Richard Ryan (1993), "A Dark Side of the American Dream: Correlates of Financial Success as a Central Life Aspiration," *Journal of Personality and Social Psychology*, 65 (2), 410-22.

_____ (1996), "Further Examining the American Dream: Differential Correlates of Intrinsic and Extrinsic Goals," *Personality and Social Psychology Bulletin*, 22 (3), 280-87.

Lane, Robert E. (2001), *The Loss of Happiness in Market Democracies*, New Haven, CT: Yale University Press.

Lasn, Kalle (2000), *Culture Jam: How to Reverse America's Suicidal Consumer Binge—and Why We Must*, New York: Harper Paperbacks.

Richins, Marcia L. (1994), "Special possessions and the expression of material values", *Journal of Consumer Research,* 21, 522-533.

Richins, Marcia. L., & Dawson, S. (1992), "A consumer values orientation for materialism and its measurement: Scale development and validation", *Journal of Consumer Research*, 19, 303-316.

Rindfleisch, A., Burroughs, J. E., & Denton, F. (1997), "Family structure, materialism, and compulsive consumption," *Journal of Consumer Research*, 23, 312–325.

Schor, Juliet B. (1999), *The Overspent American: Why We Want What We Don't Need,* New York: Harper Paperbacks.

_____ (2004), *Born to Buy: The Commercialized Child and the New Consumer Culture,* New York: Scribner.

Van Boven, Leaf and Thomas Gilovich (2003), "To Do or to Have? That Is the Question," *Journal of Personality and Social Psychology*, 85 (6), 1193-202.

Acculturation and Consumer Behavior: Building Cultural Bridges Through Consumption

Lisa Peñaloza, University of Utah, USA

SESSION OVERVIEW

This Special Session focuses on one the most characteristic phenomena of the 21st century–immigration and *acculturation*. By presenting findings from four countries, it aims to advance acculturation theory and provide consumer behavior researchers with a forum to share ideas, perspectives, and theories relating acculturation to consumption. Since the acculturation-consumption link remains under-researched, scholars are likely to be interested in a cutting-edge forum on it. The session will also offer a networking opportunity for scholars pursuing acculturation research. By bringing together researchers who study the wide range of behavior of different ethnic minorities around the globe, the session can *contribute* to the consumer behavior field by advancing the theory on acculturation. The *likely audience* will include researchers interested in studying acculturation *and* cross-cultural consumer behavior.

The four papers span a wide range of consumers' acculturation aspects. The *first paper* on Indian UK immigrants argues that religion's role in acculturation is often oversimplified; it demonstrates that religion, through acculturation, should be seen as a normative political ideology. The *second paper* on US Hispanic immigrants investigates the relationships between acculturation and consumer attitudes and behaviors. Its findings suggest that individual and environmental factors affect immigrants' chosen acculturation strategy and that acculturation levels determine consumers' loyalties to brands/stores. The *third paper* extends acculturation theory by integrating a historical perspective into it. It argues that the host and the original countries' historical relationships affect immigrants' consumers' acculturation. It compares consumer identity construction of French Algerian and Turkish immigrants. The *fourth paper* on Israeli Russian immigrants argues that being immigrants involves a sense of distinctiveness from the host country's population, which may be accompanied by negative feelings of being outsiders rather than positive feelings of being unique. Consumers' need for uniqueness among immigrants was found to be associated with acculturation motivation and ethnic identification.

EXTENDED ABSTRACTS

"Acculturation, Religion and Consumption in Normative Political Ideology"

Andrew Lindridge, Open University Business School, Germany

Calls for studies into religion's influence on consumption (e.g., Douglas and Craig 1992) have not produced a significant response. We address these calls by considering how religions and related acculturation tensions affect consumption. We advance existing theories within a group of second-generation Indians living in Great Britain who have experienced, to varying degrees, segregation on the basis of their ethnicity and, more importantly, religious identity. Specifically, differing religions as acculturation agents result in consumption choices that reflect differing acculturation and political/ideological outcomes. This is illustrated by exploring these themes through the ultimate expression of Western culture; individuality expressed through materialistic consumption, a choice supported by previous research into aspects of these

themes (Crockett and Wallendorf, 2004; White and Dahl, 2007). Consumption can be identified with specific cultural-religious meanings (McCracken 1986). Religion's meaning and effect on consumption must be considered in the context of social (formal laws, informal social norms) and personal choices (individuals' religious adherence and their need to express a religious identity; Cosgel and Minkler 2004a/b). Hence, how an individuals use consumption to express their strength of and identification with religion will ultimately express their identification with their ethnic group, their acculturation level and political/ideological outcomes.

We followed Venkatesh's (1995) qualitative ethno-consumerism framework and interpretivist studies (e.g., Holt and Thompson 2004). The sample consisted of 16 British-born Indian women from a British university. All were self-identified as second generation Indian, aged 18-25, and consisted of six Hindus, six Sikhs and four Muslims. Participants were interviewed using semi-structured questions over 13 months, each on two separate occasions.

All participants' behaviours were typical of a dialogical acculturation model by switching behaviours to adapt across contexts and had similar acculturation levels on language, food and media consumption, and clothing. All had experienced difficulties over their ethnic and religious identities and acknowledged sharing similar amount of time in engaging with their religious identity and related behaviours. All noted the complexity of their religious identity within their own acculturation identity. Of particular interest was how Hindus and Sikhs religious identity reflected Cosgel and Minkler's (2004) social choice, in contrast to Muslims' personal choice.

Hindu participants viewed their religious identity only as an aspect of their life, engaged on a selective basis when needed. Religious-consumption was limited to specific festivals or family gathering. Life in Britain represented an easy transition without acculturation tension. In contrast, religion for Sikhs produced a stronger sense of religious identity, albeit one that didn't adhere closely to Sikh religious teachings. Religious orientated consumption was minimized; instead their families used conspicuous consumption to reinforce a public image of acculturation success; a public display that centred on their interactions around their local Gurdwara (a Sikh religious building). Muslims expressed a distinct distancing from Western-cultural consumption narratives. Materialistic behaviours were dismissed as un-Islamic. Their narrative reflected an acculturation paradox. Whilst they rejected aspects of their parents' Indian culture towards materialistic consumption, they attempted to forge an Islamic identity that rejected Western-cultural values of consumption whilst accepting the more liberal aspects of British society. The latter was behaviourally strongest of all participants on the basis of religious identity. Their behaviours reflected aspects of White and Dahl's consumer identity and dissociative influence (2007) and Crockett and Wallendorf's (2004) on political ideology in consumer behaviour. Why these differences emerged partly lied in participants' choices to access their religion's teachings *and* how they negotiated and understood their acculturation experiences. In sum, religion's affect on acculturation and consumption is more complex then previously thought. Normative and political ideologies need to be considered with acculturation and religion's consumption impacts.

References

Cosgel, M. M. & Minkler, L. (2004b), "Rationality, integrity, and religious behaviour", *Journal of Socio-Economics*, 33, 329-341.

Crockett, D. & Wallendorf, E. (2004) "The Role of Normative Political Ideology in Consumer Behaviour", *Journal of Consumer Research*, 31, 511–528.

Douglas, S., & Craig, S. (1997), "The changing dynamic of consumer behaviour: implications for cross-cultural research", *International Journal of Research in Marketing*, 14, 379-395.

Holt, D. B. & Thompson, C. J. (2004), "Man-of-Action Heroes: The Pursuit of Heroic Masculinity in Everyday Consumption", *Journal of Consumer Research*, 31(2), 425-440.

McCracken, G. (1986), "Culture and Consumption: A Theoretical Account of the Structure and Movement of the Cultural Meaning of Consumer Goods", *Journal of Consumer Research*, 13, 71–81.

Venkatesh, A. (1995) *"Ethno-consumerism: A New Paradigm to Study Cultural and Cross-Cultural Consumer Behaviour"*. In J. Costa and G. Bamossy, *Marketing in a multicultural world-Ethnicity, Nationalism and Cultural Identity*, Sage Publications: London, 68–104.

White, K. & Dahl, D. W. (2007), "Are All Out-groups Created Equal? Consumer Identity and Dissociative Influence", *Journal of Consumer Research*, 34, 525–536.

"A Comprehensive Model for Hispanics' Acculturation: Antecedents and Impacts on Store and Brand Loyalty"

Aviv Shoham, University of Haifa, Israel
Sigal Segev, Florida International University, USA
Ayalla Ruvio, University of Haifa, Israel

Global immigration and cultural diversification highlight the importance of acculturation. Immigrants bring cultural characteristics from their native countries, while adapting to new cultures changes attitudes and consumption behavior (Berry, 1980). Consumer behavior acculturation studies are scarce, lack integration, and tend to be theoretical rather than empirical (Ogden, Ogden & Schau, 2004). We integrate concepts from acculturation and consumer behavior literature and our empirical study identifies individual and environmental factors affecting acculturation, uses a bi-dimensional acculturation concept, and explores the impact of the chosen acculturative strategy on US Hispanics' consumption. *Acculturation* refers to social/psychological changes resulting from contacts between individuals from different cultures during which immigrants acquire attitudes, behaviors, and cultural identity of host and integrate them with their original cultures' (Herskovits, 1936). Acculturation theories address immigrants' adaptation to host cultures. A bi-dimensional model of acculturation includes original culture maintenance (OCM) and host culture adherence (HCA) (Berry, 1980), which provide a better fit to the acculturation reality, allowing individuals to maintain or neglect their original culture while participating in the host culture (Cabassa, 2003).

We include ethnic identity, adaptability to change (individual level) and intercultural peer contact (environmental level) as antecedents. *Ethnic Identity* refers to individuals' affiliation with a cultural group. While ethnic identity and acculturation are related and affect immigrants' adaptation, research on their relationship is inconsistent. Some view ethnic identity as influenced by acculturative changes in the new culture over time (Ward, 2001). Others argue that ethnic identity affects acculturation (e.g., Peñaloza, 1994). While acculturation is a process of change, ethnic identity may or may not be static (Ogden, et al., 2004). Hence, we view ethnic identity as an antecedent of integration into the host culture. *Adaptability to change* refers to individuals' ability to cope with and adapt to changes. It affects cultural adjustment and change-accepting immigrants should adapt more to the new culture (Valdes, 2002). *Intercultural Peer Contact* refers to the extent of immigrants' contact with peers from the host culture, who can inhibit or accelerate acculturation (Searle & Ward, 1990)

Notably, Hispanics may (Segal & Sosa, 1983) or may not (Saegert et al., 1985) be more brand-loyal than others. We broaden loyalty to include brands and stores, add an orientation dimension (Hispanic/General Market), and argue that assimilators will prefer General Market (GM) brands/stores and acculturating individuals will prefer ethnic ones.

Methodology, Findings, and Conclusions

A sample of 208 Hispanic-origin individuals in the Miami area provided data. English and Spanish questionnaires were used with scales for intercultural peer contact, ethnic identification, adaptability to change, acculturation, and brand and store loyalty.

Individuals with conational peers and strong ties with them used OCM acculturation strategy. As conational peers satisfy immigrants' need for a social framework in the host country, they discourage immigrants from seeking friendships with host-culture individuals. Ethnic identity was associated with OCM but not HCA acculturation strategy. Individuals' sense of pride, belongingness, and satisfaction with their original culture reduced their adoption of the host culture. Tolerance to change facilitated the utilization of HCA acculturation strategy and decreased the use of OCM strategy. The data mostly supported the proposed relationships between the two acculturation strategies and consumer behaviors. Hispanics, who adhered to the host country exhibited loyalty to Anglo stores and brands and disloyalty to Hispanic stores (but not Hispanic brand). Two possible explanations for this finding: practically, GM stores in the study's region sell a variety of Hispanic ethnic products that might satisfy the basic needs of assimilated individuals; at the image level, assimilators might deliberately refrain from being seen in ethnic stores, which might signal their differentiation and segregation and categorize them as outsiders to the dominant society. Hispanics high on OCM should be loyal to Hispanic stores and brands, and will not associate OCM with loyalty to Anglo stores and brands.

References

Berry, J. W. (1980), "Acculturation as Variation of Adaptation," in *Acculturation: Theory, Models and Some New Findings*, ed. Amado M. Padilla, Washington, DC: Boulder: American Association for the Advancement of Science, 9-26.

Cabassa, L. (2003), "Measuring Acculturation: Where We Are and Where We Need to Go," *Hispanic journal of Behavioral Sciences*, 25 (2), 127-46.

Herskovits, M. J. (1936), *Acculturation: The Study of Cultural Contact*. NY: Augustin.

Ogden, D. T., J. R. Ogden & Hope J. S. (2004), "Exploring the Impact of Culture and Acculturation on Consumer Purchase Decisions: Toward a Microcultural Perspective," *Academy of Marketing Science Review*, 8,

Peñaloza, L. (1994), "Atravesando Fronteras/Border Crossing: A critical Ethnographic Exploration of the Consumer Acculturation of Mexican Immigrants," *Journal of Consumer Research*, 21(2), 32-50.

Saegert, J., R. J. Hoover & M. T. Hilger (1985), "Characteristics of Mexican American Consumers," *Journal of Consumer Research*, 12(2), 104-9.

Searle, W. & Ward C. (1990), "The Prediction of Psychological and Socio-Cultural Adjustment during Cross-Cultural Transitions," *International Journal of Intercultural Relations*, 14(4), 449-64.

Segal, M. N. & Sosa, L. (1983), "Marketing to the Hispanic Community," *California Management Review*, 26 (Fall), 120-34.

Ward, C. (2001), "The A, B, Cs of Acculturation," in *The Handbook of Culture andPsychology*, ed. David Matsumoto, NY: Oxford University Press, 411-45.

"How Do Historical Relationships Between The Host And Home Countries Shape The Immigrants' Consumer Acculturation Processes?"

Nil Ozcaglar-Toulouse, Universite de Lille, France
Tuba Ustuner, City University London, UK

Following the deaths of two second-generation immigrants of *banlieue*, weeks of rioting in the Paris region forced the French media to pay more attention to the country's minorities. We believe that these minorities, marginalized as such, experience '*dominated consumer acculturation*' (Üstüner and Holt, 2007). Much like the rural-to-urban migrants that Üstüner and Holt studied, these minorities live in a society that undermines the building blocks of their identities: their ethnicities. In Üstüner and Holt's study the form of domination was based on social class. The rural-to-urban migrants constituted the lowest class in the city and therefore were bearing a heavy class-based social stigma. Additionally, the consumer acculturation processes they experienced were more problematic than previously argued in the literature.

Several studies have investigated the socio-historic patterning of consumption (see Arnould and Thompson 2005). In particular, there is an evolving consumer research literature which focuses on consumer acculturation and identity construction of immigrants. Peñaloza's (1994) studied the consumption experiences of Mexicans in the US and provided a dynamic approach to acculturation models. Oswald (1999) saw acculturation as a form of cultural swapping and argued that immigrants borrow cultural elements of the home *and* host country. Askegaard, Arnould, and Kjeldgaard (2005) argued that the transnational consumer culture is also an acculturative agent. While this literature contributed to our understanding of consumer acculturation it did not consider the historical, social, and cultural context within which acculturation takes place. Üstüner and Holt's study (2007) is an exception, which argued that migrants are not the sole acculturation agents: social and historical factors also matter. Coining the term 'dominated consumer acculturation' Üstüner and Holt demonstrated how class-based domination shaped rural-to-urban migrants' acculturation to their new social setting.

We extend Üstüner and Holt's critical approach to acculturation and argue that social-class is only one form of domination. Most immigration today takes place from less developed, mostly colonized countries, to more developed, mostly colonizing countries. The forms of domination these immigrants face in their host countries are not limited to social-class. There are historical tensions between the host and home countries, stigmas associated with each other's cultures. Accordingly, we are interested in uncovering the ways in which such a cultural history shapes immigrants' collective memories and consumer identities. We ask two questions: How is the colonial social memory represented in immigrants' personal identities and expressed through consumption? What are the impacts of tensions on immigrants' acculturation process?

This research considers both the generational and ethnic differences among immigrants to answer these questions. It compares consumer identity construction processes of second-generation Algerian immigrants (with a colonial past) to that of Turkish immigrants (without a colonial past, but with recent tensions with France). While Algerians' social memory carries mixed feelings and memories about France and the colonial period, Turks' does not. While Turkish immigrants do not have a similar cultural history and institutional memory, tensions have emerged between France and Turkey over Turkey's historical relationships with Armenians and Kurds and over its demand to become an EU member. The study then compares acculturation processes of second-generation immigrants. If communitarian allegiances are based on regional, village, or ethnic ties and historical narratives for first-generation immigrants, for second-generation ones, however, they often take the form of emotional /nostalgic attachments to a particular origin or to a 'second-hand memory'. This attachment is more mythic than real, and often a corresponding reinforcement of the division between 'them' and 'us'. This is particularly the case in a context of exclusion and stigmatization, like in the *banlieue*. While this study is a work-in-progress, we will present the first comparative analysis at the conference.

This research is supported by the French "Agence Nationale de la Recherche" (ANR).

References

Arnould, E. J., and Thompson, C. 2005. Consumer Culture Theory (CCT): Twenty Years of Research. *Journal of Consumer Research* 31: 868-882.

Askegaard, S., Arnould, E. J. and Kjeldgaard, D. 2005. Postassimilationist Ethnic Consumer Research: Qualifications and Extensions. *Journal of Consumer Research* 32: 160-170.

Bouchet, D. 1995. Marketing and the Redefinition of Ethnicity. *Marketing in a Multicultural World: Ethnicity, Nationalism and Cultural Identity*. Costa, J. and Bamossy, G. (Eds.). Newbury Park, Thousand Oaks: Sage, pp. 68-104

Oswald, L. R. 1999. Cultural Swapping: Consumption and the Ethnogenesis of Middle-class Haitian Immigrants. *Journal of Consumer Research* 25(March): 303-318.

Peñaloza, L. 1994. Atraversando Frontieras/Border Crossing: A Critical Ethnographic Exploration of the Consumer Acculturation of Mexican Immigrants. *Journal of Consumer Research* 21 (1): 32-54.

Üstüner, T., and Holt, D. B. 2007. Dominated Consumer Acculturation: The Social Construction of Poor Migrant Women's Consumer Identity Projects in a Turkish Squatter. *Journal of Consumer Research* 34 (1): 41-56.

"Unique or Different: The Role of Consumers' Need for Uniqueness in the Acculturation Process"

Ayalla Ruvio, University of Haifa, Israel
Walsh Gianfranco, University of Koblenz-Landau, Germany
Sigal Segev, Florida International University, USA

Uniqueness holds a positive connotation in Western societies. It involves a feeling that sets individuals apart from the crowd, but in a manner that is appreciated by others. Tian et al. (2001, p. 52) defined consumers' need for uniqueness (CNFU) as "the trait of pursuing differences relative to others through the acquisition, utilization, and disposition of consumer goods for the purpose of developing and enhancing one's self-image and social image". CNFU is a means for satisfying NFU by using possessions creatively, making unpopular consumption choices, and avoiding buying and consuming commonly used products. According to Tian et al. (2001), all individuals use these consumption behaviors to some extent to establish a unique social image. Immigrant consumers often feel different from the population in the host country on the acquisition and use of consumer goods. Such distinctiveness is often accompanied by a feeling of being outsiders rather than by being unique. Thus, consumption is culturally-bound, which requires immigrants to adapt their behavior to the host country's consumer culture (Ownbey & Horridge 1997; Peñaloza 1994). Hence, the issue of reference groups becomes more complex for immigrants. The original ethnic community has its own language, customs, and consumption behavior whilst the new host community exerts pressure on immigrants who want to build a new life and develop a sense of belonging to adopt its consumption style (e.g., Deshpande, Hoyer & Donthu 1986; Xu et al. 2004). Under these conditions, expressing uniqueness is a challenge.

Immigrants can overcome this challenge by acculturating as a means of creating a unique self-image. By adopting the consumption behaviors of the host population, immigrants can set themselves apart from their original ethnic group, but in a manner that is approved by the majority host population. In this case, a strong motivation to acculturate will be positively associated with CNFU that is benchmarked against the original ethnic group. Alternatively, immigrants can take the opposite approach for establishing a unique identity. They can express their ethnic identity in order to distinguish themselves from the majority host population. In this case, individuals will acquire, use, and display possessions that highlight their ethnic group. Choosing to express uniqueness in this manner will be appreciated by the original ethnic group but may result in social and even legal sanctions from the majority host population. We argue that immigrants' CNFU is associated with their motivation to acculturate and with consumer behavior. Consumers' susceptibility to interpersonal influence (CSII) and ethnic identity serve as predictors of CNFU, which serves as an antecedent to acculturation strategies. Innovative shopping and the desire to purchase unique products were used as consequences of acculturation strategies. All constructs were tested in relation to the host community (the general Israeli population) and to the original culture (the former Soviet Union-FSU).

Method, Findings, and Conclusions

Information was gathered using a closed-end questionnaire from a convenience sample of 177 adult immigrants from FSU. Structural equation modeling was used to test the model.

Individuals with a strong FSU identity display their uniqueness in the FSU community. No relationships were found between identification with the Israeli community and CNFU. On the other hand, susceptibility to influence from the Israeli community was associated positively with uniqueness manifestations in the FSU community and the general Israeli population. No relationships were found between susceptibility to influence from the FSU community and CNFU. The expression of CNFU in the FSU community was associated positively with the original culture maintenance strategy of acculturation and host culture adherence. CNFU's projection in the Israeli community was negatively related to the original culture maintenance strategy of acculturation and had no relationship with host culture adherence. High host-culture-adherence individuals had a strong desire for unique Russian products and a high level of shopping innovativeness for Israeli and Russian products. Immigrants who chose to preserve their original culture demonstrated a strong desire for unique products and innovative shopping for Russian products only. In sum, immigrants do fuse the formation of their unique identity with their chosen acculturation strategy, which ultimately affects their consumer behavior.

References

Deshpande, R., Hoyer, W. D., & Donthu, N. (1986). The intensity of ethnic affiliation: A study of the sociology of Hispanic consumption. *Journal of Consumer Research*, 13, 214-20.

Ownbey, S. F., & Horridge, P. E. (1997). Acculturation levels and shopping orientations of Asian-American consumers. *Psychology and Marketing*, 14(1), 1-18.

Peñaloza, L. N. (1994). Atravesando fronteras/Border crossing: A critical ethnographic exploration of the consumer acculturation of Mexican immigrants. *Journal of Consumer Research*, 21, 32-50.

Tian, K T., Bearden, W. O., & Hunter, G L. (2001). Consumers' need for uniqueness: Scale development and validation. *Journal of Consumer Research*, 28, 50-66.

Xu, J., Shim, S., Lotz, S., & Almeida, D. (2004). Ethnic identity, socialization factors and culture-specific consumption behavior. *Psychology & Marketing*, 21(2), 93-112.

Production and Reproduction of Consumer Culture in Virtual Communities

Aron Darmody, York University, Canada

Ryszard Kedzior, Swedish School of Economics and Business Administration, Finland

SESSION OVERVIEW

The emergence of consumer culture is rooted in the fact that consumption became a central facet of modern life. In order to understand consumer behavior in contemporary society it is necessary to explore the myriad consumer practices through which consumer culture is (re)produced. Such practices can be studied on the individual, societal or institutional levels, and consumer culture can also be viewed as both a material consequence and a symbolic representation of consumer actions. Many of the most recent and significant developments within consumer culture have been Internet-related phenomena such as online brand communities, social networking sites and consumer-inhabited virtual worlds. In this session we explore issues pertaining to the (re)production of a consumer culture by looking at consumer-constructed virtual identities, new interactive contexts of brand-consumer relationships and alternative regimes of materiality present in digital environments. Following is a presentation of the main themes covered in this symposium:

Online Identity Performance and Maintenance

As evidenced by previous research (e.g. Turkle 1995; Markham 1998) virtual environments represent a potent stage for identity construction and identity play. Much like in the offline world, consumers use marketplace resources such as brands and ideologies to represent their *Selves* online. Schau and Gilly (2003) for instance, demonstrate how consumers use brands and hyperlinks to create multiple non-linear cyber self-representations. However, recent developments in social networking sites (SNSs) and virtual worlds have presented consumers with myriad of other opportunities to pursue their virtual identity projects. Consumers online act as cultural bricoleurs mixing and matching different forms of digital cultural resources in order to create narratives of their identity. Consumer-generated as well as market-produced content constitutes the core of popular web platforms such as YouTube or Second Life. These examples attest to the significance of understanding consumer behavior in virtual environments, hence this track explores different practices that consumers employ to orient themselves in a new virtual reality.

Mapping Out Digital Materiality

Non-physical aspects of consumption play increasingly important roles in many facets of the economy, including production (i.e. as evident in the Post-Fordist shift from structured manufacturing to flexible, information-driven service industries), but also in the constitution of brand value (Arvidsson 2006), and of commodity value (which has become ever more dependent on non-material components such as aesthetics). The valorization of product and service experiences as means to achieving competitive advantage serves as a good illustration of this process (e.g. Pine and Gilmore 1999). In addition, the notions of the society of spectacle (Debord 1994[1967]) and hyperreality (Baudrillard 1983[1970]) demonstrate how the non-material composition of consumption is reflected in the fact that consumers frequently encounter products only in the form of mediated representations such as marketing communications (advertising), or other pop-culture outlets (TV shows, magazines). Moreover, in the information economy, even the traditionally tangible processes of production are increasingly governed by non-material functions involving knowledge, science, expertise, systems, planning and cybernetic skills. Contemporary consumption can be characterized by growing dematerialization of objects and commodities (Slater 1997). Taking as a starting point digital materiality of the virtual world (i.e. *Second Life*) we problematize new *materialities* which are beginning to dominate our contemporary culture.

Understanding the Impact of Consumer-Generated Content for Cultivating the Brand-Consumer Relationship in the Marketplace

Consumer-generated content on the Internet provides abundant and valuable resources for marketers and brands to better understand current consumer practices and to more accurately predict emergent ones. The new technology not only provides an expanding array of platforms on which consumers can share their opinions and concerns, but it also facilitates closer and more engaging ongoing relationships between consumers and brands (Cova and Pace 2006; Muniz and O'Guinn 2001). Within this relationship the consumer is more empowered and granted a more influential and active voice in the process of brand-meaning construction and (re)positioning (Muniz and Schau 2005). Moreover, in virtual communities such as *Second Life* and social networking sites (SNSs) like *Facebook*, self-organizing consumers are (re)producing consumer culture through individual and multi-level group interactions. In many instances, brands and other marketplace symbols can play important roles in developing and reinforcing individual consumer identities, and in providing substance for online consumer community formation. Current consumer practices in the virtual world create new opportunities for marketers and their brands to activate consumers and engage them in brand-consumer relationships beyond the existing website-based brand communities.

Changing Socialscapes as the result of the Intersection between Offline and Online Reality

Since the emergence of the Internet we have seen a steady extension of consumption into new digital domains as consumers are living more and more of their lives online. Tremendous amounts of time online are spent on activities such as shopping, social-networking, gaming, socializing, dating and working. Social networking sites (SNSs) such as *Facebook*, *Myspace* and *Bebo*, and virtual worlds such as *Second Life*, have in recent years grown to become some of the most important sites for consumer interactivity (largely self-organized) on the web. Many online consumer activities are now being enacted on the burgeoning range of virtual worlds and SNSs, which have become powerful vehicles for self presentation, impression management, friendship performance and relationship management (boyd and Ellison 2007). We explore how consumers use different digital cultural resources in SNSs and virtual worlds to such ends, as well as to investigate how they facilitate the continuous convergence of online and offline consumer social relationships. As these sites have become an indispensable part of our society, we seek to illustrate how the boundaries between offline and online realities merge.

References

Arvidsson, Adam (2006), *Brands. Meaning and Value in Consumer Culture*, London: Routledge.

Baudrillard, Jean (1983[1970]), *The Consumer Society*, Thousand Oaks, CA: Sage.

boyd, danah M. and Nicole B. Ellison (2007), "Social Network Sites: Definition, History, and Scholarship," *Journal of Computer-Mediated Communication*, 13(1), article 11. Retrieved March 10, 2008 at http://jcmc.indiana.edu/vol13/issue1/boyd.ellison.html.

Cova, Bernard and Stefano Pace (2006), "Brand community of convenience products: new forms of customer empowerment-the case "my Nutella The Community"", *European Journal of Marketing*. 40, 9/10, 1087-1105.

Debord, Guy (1994[1967]), *The Society of the Spectacle*, New York: Zone Books.

Markham, Annette N. (1998), *Life Online: Researching Real Experience in Virtual Space*, Walnut Creek: Altamira Press.

Muniz, Albert and Thomas C. O'Guinn (2001), "Brand Communities," *Journal of Consumer Research*, 27 (March), 412-432.

_____ and Hope Schau (2005), "Religiosity in the Abandoned Apple Newton Brand Community," *Journal of Consumer Research*, 31 (March), 737-47.

Schau, Hope Jensen and Mary C. Gilly (2003), "We Are What We Post? Self-Presentation in Personal Web Space," *Journal of Consumer Research*, 30 (December), 385-404.

Slater, Don (1997), *Consumer Culture and Modernity*, Oxford, UK: Polity Press; Cambridge, MA: Blackwell Publishers.

Turkle, Sherry (1995), *Life on the Screen: Identity in the age of the Internet*, New York: Simon and Schuster.

EXTENDED ABSTRACTS

"I Get by with a Little Help from My Friends: Consumer Creativity in Virtual Communities"

Aron Darmody, York University, Canada
Eric P. H. Li, York University, Canada

The market offers myriad opportunities for consumers' creative expression, from how they appropriate cultural and marketplace resources for their identity projects (Holt 2002; Holt and Thompson 2004), how they actively localize the global (e.g. Kjeldgaard and Askegaard 2006) to how they re-imagine consumption spaces and play within them (Kozinets et al. 2004). However, the topic of consumer creativity has not been the core focus of these studies. Instead, the majority of extant consumer creativity research has been focused on consumer creativity in problem-solving contexts (e.g. Burroughs and Mick 2004; Hirschman 1980).

In one of the first and most enduringly influential studies on the topic, Hirschman (1980) defined consumer creativity as "the problem-solving capability possessed by an individual that may be applied toward solving consumption–related problems" (p.286). Subsequent consumer creativity studies have closely adhered to that early conceptualization, wherein consumers are creative when they are required to respond to an impediment in a problem-solving context: when a problem arises, and no preexisting solution exists, the consumer must creatively construct a solution (Burroughs and Mick 2004; Dahl and Moreau 2002; Hirschman 1983; Moreau and Dahl 2005; Ridgway and Price 1994). Recent contributions in this vein include depiction of how analogical thinking by consumers facilitates originality in concept ideation and design (Dahl and Moreau 2002), and how input constraints influence the way in which consumers process information during a creative task and can lead to instances of increased creativity (Moreau and Dahl 2005). Additionally, Burroughs and Mick (2004) investigated antecedents to and consequences of creative consumption. Their findings showed that two person-based antecedents (metaphoric thinking ability and locus of control) and two situation-based antecedents (situational involvement and time constraints) influence creative consumption, and the consequence of higher levels of creativity in response to a consumption problem leads to increased positive affect, including feelings of increased accomplishment, satisfaction, pride and confidence (Burroughs and Mick 2004).

Although varied in focus and scope extant consumer creativity studies share two other interrelated features beyond the common problem-solving perspective. Firstly, the overwhelming focus in consumer creativity is on consumers' cognitive processes during the creative undertaking (Dahl, Chattopadhyay and Gorn 1999; Moreau and Dahl 2005). Secondly, the overarching focus of this research stream has been on the single consumer as a creative individual, and analyses within it concentrated on the inputs and outcomes of a consumer's particularized creative endeavors (e.g. Burroughs and Mick 2004; Moreau and Dahl 2005).

In our present study we seek to extend the notion of consumer creativity beyond that which is conventional in consumer research as we move from a predominantly individual-focused view of consumer creativity to one that more adequately accounts for dynamic and social aspects of the creative process (Berkun 2007; Csikszentmihalyi 1996, 2006; Gruber 1974; John-Steiner 1997). Indeed sociocultural approaches to examining creativity and creative lives are commonplace in other disciplines as "[researchers] became increasingly constrained by theories that limited them to an individual focus (John-Steiner 1997, p. xviii). As Csikszentmihalyi (2006) highlights, psychologists tend to see creativity exclusively as a mental process, but creativity is as much a cultural and social as it is a psychological event, and what we call creativity is not the product of atomized individuals, but of social systems making judgments about individual's products.

In a departure from individual-centric consumer creativity research, we focus on creativity as manifest in more interactive social settings to investigate how consumer creativity is expressed at a communal level in the rich social contexts of the virtual world *Second Life*. In so doing, we also demonstrate that consumer creativity transgresses reactively responding to encountered obstacles (Collins and Amabile 1999). *Second Life* is a site of immense creativity in which consumers are actively encouraged and enabled to create their own applications and experiences through the provision of user-friendly creative tools and templates. Creativity is no longer the sole purvey of those with highly developed web design skills (Ondrejka 2007), but is notionally available to all users. Users create the entirety of the world in action. Moreover, collaboration is commonplace within this virtual spaces as consumers collectively generate information and create digital artefacts (Evans 2007; Ondrejka 2007).

In this study we draw on Csikszentmihalyi's (2006) theory of creativity. In his conceptualization, creativity is a process that can be observed where individuals, domains (a cultural, or symbolic, aspect of the environment) and fields (social aspects of the environment) interact. By adopting this perspective we seek to address some of the following: what constitutes consumer creativity within interactive virtual worlds; what motivates consumer creativity within these worlds; what are the consequences of this altered conceptualization of creativity for understanding consumer behavior; and what are the implications of these creative consumer networks to companies in general (e.g. Tapscott and Williams 2006).

In pursuing the goal of this study, we employ netographic methods (Kozinets 2002) which examines consumer creative practices online. Netnography necessitates an ongoing deep engagement within the context of study (Kozinets 2002). Data used for this project comprised Blog postings on the official *Second Life Forum* and more than six months of in-world participant observation.

Through this study we hope to stimulate discussion and present a research agenda for those interested in consumer creativity and virtual communities from a sociocultural perspective, as well as to shed some insight on the adoption of SNSs and virtual worlds play in consumer creativity.

References

Berkun, Scott (2007), *The Myths of Innovation*, Sebastopol, CA: O'Reilly Media.

Burroughs, James E. and David Glen Mick (2004), "Exploring Antecedents and Consequences of Consumer Creativity in a Problem-Solving Context, *Journal of Consumer Research*, 31 (September), 402-411.

Collins, Mary Ann and Teresa M. Amabile (1999), "Motivation and Creativity," in *Handbook of Creativity*, ed. Robert J. Sternberg, Cambridge: Cambridge University Press, 297-312.

Csikszentmihalyi, Mihaly (1996), *Creativity: Flow and the Psychology of Discovery and Invention*, New York: HarperCollins.

_____ (2006), "A Systems Perspective on Creativity", in *Creative Management and Development*, ed. Jane Henry, London: Sage Publications.

Dahl, Darren W., Amitava Chattopadhyay and Gerald J, Gorn (1999), "The Use of Visual Mental Imagery in New Product Design", *Journal of Marketing Research*, 36 (February), 18-28.

_____ and Page Moreau (2002), "The Influence and Value of Analogical Thinking During New Product Ideation," *Journal of Marketing Research*, 39 (February), 47–60.

Evans, Philip (2007), "A Silicon Silicon Valley? (Virtual Innovation and Virtual Geography)", *Innovations: Technology, Governance, Globalization*, 2, 3, 55-61.

Gruber, Howard E. (1974), *Darwin on Man: A Psychological Study of Scientific Creativity*, New York: Dutton.

Hirschman, Elizabeth (1980), "Innovativeness, Novelty Seeking, and Consumer Creativity," *Journal of Consumer Research*, 1 (December), 283-95.

_____ (1983), "Consumer Intelligence, Creativity, and Consciousness: Implications for Consumer Protection and Education," *Journal of Public Policy and Marketing*, 2 (1), 153-70.

Holt, Douglas B. (2002), "Why Do Brands Cause Trouble? A Dialectical Theory of Consumer Culture and Branding," *Journal of Consumer Research*, 29 (June), 70–90.

_____ and Craig J. Thompson (2004), "Man-of-Action Heroes: The Pursuit of Heroic Masculinity in Everyday Consumption," *Journal of Consumer Research*, 31 (September), 425-40.

John-Steiner, Vera (1997), *Notebooks of the Mind: Explorations of Thinking Revised Edition*, New York: Oxford University Press.

Kjeldgaard, Dannie and Søren Askegaard (2006), "The Glocalization of Youth Culture: The Global Youth Segment as Structures of Common Difference", *Journal of Consumer Research*, 33 (September) 231-247.

Kozinets, Robert V. (2002), "The Field Behind the Screen: Using Netnography for Marketing Research in Online Communities," *Journal of Marketing Research*, 39 (February), 61-72.

_____, John F. Sherry Jr., Diana Storm, Adam Duhachek, Krittinee Nuttavuthisit, and Benet Deberry-Spence (2004), "Ludic Agency and Retail Spectacle," *Journal of Consumer Research*, 31 (December), 658–73.

Moreau, C. Page and Darren W. Dahl (2005), "Designing the Solution: The Impact of Constraints on Consumer Creativity," *Journal of Consumer Research*, 32 (June), 13–22.

Ondrejka, Cory (2007), "Collapsing Geography *Second Life*, Innovation and the Future of National Power", *Innovations: Technology, Governance, Globalization*, 2, 3, 27-54.

Ridgway, Nancy M. and Linda L. Price (1994), "Exploration in Product Usage: A Model of Use Innovativeness", *Psychology and Marketing*, 11, 1, 69-84.

Tapscott, Don and Anthony D. Williams (2006), *Wikinomics: How mass collaboration changes everything*, New York: Portfolio.

"Mapping Out Digital Materiality–Insights for Consumer Research"

Richard Kedzior, HANKEN, Finland

Theorizations of materiality are central to the cultural understanding of consumer behavior, thus much of researchers' interest has been devoted to studying subject-object relations in different contexts such as material possession attachment (Schultz Kleine and Mezel Baker 2004), extended-self (Belk 1988), or object meanings (Richins 1994). The importance of materiality for consumer research is hinging on the notion that objects take active part in a subject's identity construction, therefore consumer selves can be transformed, created, expressed, or emancipated in relation to objects and contexts in consumer culture (Borgerson 2005). In other words, the consumer 'self' emerges through consumption practices and the objects involved in them, and consumption is a process through which human beings materialize or objectify values and meanings, resolve conflicts and paradoxes (Miller 1987).

To date, however, theorizations of materiality in consumer research have predominantly assumed the physicality (tangibility) of the object of consumption neglecting growing dematerialization of consumables accompanied by the development of technology (Slater 1997). This is a considerable omission given that the advent and proliferation of the internet has resulted in digitized equivalents of books, photographs and music encroaching on the realm of everyday consumption and exposing consumers to a new regime of materiality. Many goods which were once tangible have now lost their physical referent and become accessible solely as representations. With few exceptions (e.g. Siddiqui and Turley 2006) consequences of such process for consumer research remain largely unexplored. As also noted in the previous literature, an inquiry into materiality must expand to encompass various dimensions of change brought about by technology (Sherry 2000). Therefore, this paper introduces and problematizes the notion of digital materiality as an altered regime of materiality observable in a virtual world.

In building an understanding of digital materiality this conceptualization benefits from evidence gathered during a netnographic study (Kozinets 2002) conducted in *Second Life* over the period of four months. *Second Life* is an online three-dimensional virtual world where elements of reality merge with fantasy and its residents live their virtual lives through animated representations called avatars. Being highly immersive, this environment represents a lively consumption space that is home to all possible manifestations of consumerism such as consumer activism, resistance and consumer creativity. Existence in *Second Life* can be conceived of as an exemplar of hyperreality where members of the culture realize, construct and live the simulation (Firat and Venkatesh 1995). The distinctive value of *Second Life* as a site of this inquiry stems from the fact that it epitomizes the idea of digital materiality, as not only is the object of consumption is digitized and intangible, but the consuming subject as avatar is also an intangible representation in the virtual world.

This paper delineates the concept of digital materiality in three steps. First, in order to position the concept within the context of consumer research, it reviews other consumption phenomena that entail a non-material object of consumption such as consumer fantasies (Holbrook and Hirschman, 1982; Martin 2004), consumption dreams (d'Astous and Deschênes 2005) and vicarious exploration (Stell and Paden 1999). Research, in which the tangibility of consumption objects has been transcended, has conventionally looked at symbolic aspects of consumption or aspects of consumer fantasy and imagination. In those cases, however the non-material object of consumption usually has a physical referent that can act as a locus for the meaning. Objects in digital materiality differ significantly, as even though they might have their physical referents, they do not require them in order to exist.

Second, in order to illustrate the significance of digital materiality for consumers this study adopts a symbolic interactionist view of material identity while analyzing the meaning of consumption practices and experiences in *Second Life*. In this perspective, possessions as material symbols of identity can exist in three types of social reality (Dittmar 1992). Objective social reality is conceptualized as the objective world existing outside of the individual, i.e. objects posses 'hard' quantitative and various qualitative characteristics. Next, symbolic social reality consists of any form of symbolic expression of the world in which we live in and encompasses three important symbol systems of language, non-verbal communication and material objects (which can symbolically communicate the personal qualities of individuals). When both objective and symbolic worlds are internalized a subjective social reality is created and represented as each individual's awareness and understanding. Simplifying, it can be said that symbolic social reality represents a societal level of analysis while subjective social reality corresponds to an individual level.

Finally, by bringing in evidence from other fields such as library studies (Manoff 2006) and visual arts (Sasson 2004) this investigation exposes "the tactile fallacy". This is the logical fallacy to treat objects of consumption within digital materiality as being immaterial instead of intangible. Data gathered *in situ* also support the deconstruction of false dichotomies such as virtual versus real in terms of consumption experiences in *Second Life*. One of the major findings indicates that consumers perceive their consumption in *Second Life* as real because they interpret this lived experience within the context of the virtual world. In other words, their subjectivity moved along the confines of digital materiality.

This study addresses recent concerns in conceptualizing materiality in consumer research which resulted from the proliferation of the internet and information technologies in consumers' daily lives. By introducing and delineating the notion of digital materiality as an alternative regime of materiality as experienced by consumers in a virtual world, this research aims to sensitize researchers to careful conceptualizations of different aspects of non-material consumption.

References

Belk, Russell W. (1988), "Possessions and the Extended Self", *Journal of Consumer Research*, 15 (September), 139-168.

Borgerson, Janet (2005), "Materiality, Agency, and the Constitution of Consuming Subjects: Insights for Consumer Research", *Advances in Consumer Research*, 32, 439-443.

d'Astous, Alain and Jonathan Deschênes (2005), "Consuming in One's Mind: An Exploration", *Psychology & Marketing*, 22, 1, 1-30.

Dittmar, Helga (1992), *The Social Psychology of Material Possessions: To Have is To Be*, New York: St. Martin's Press.

Firat and Venkatesh (1995), "Liberatory Postmodernism and the Reenchantment of Consumption, *Journal of Consumer Research*, 22 (December), 239-267.

Holbrook, Morris B. and Elizabeth Hirschman (1982), "The Experiential Aspects of Consumption: Consumer Fantasies, Feelings, and Fun", *Journal of Consumer Research*, 9 (September), 132-140.

Kozinets, Robert V. (2002), "The Field Behind the Screen: Using Netnography for Marketing Research in Online Communities," *Journal of Marketing Research*, 39 (February), 61-72.

Manoff, Marlene (2006), "The Materiality of Digital Collections: Theoretical and Historical Perspectives", *Libraries and the Academy*, 6, 3, 311-325.

Martin, Brett A. S. (2004), "Using the Imagination: Consumer Evoking and Thematizing of the Fantastic Imaginary", *Journal of Consumer Research*, 31 (June), 136-149.

Miller, Daniel (1987), *Material Culture and Mass Consumption*, Oxford: Basil Blackwell Ltd.

Moreau, C. Page and Darren W. Dahl (2005), "Designing the Solution: The Impact of Constraints on Consumer Creativity," *Journal of Consumer Research*, 32 (June), 13–22.

Richins, Marsha L. (1994), "Valuing things: the public and private meanings of possessions", *Journal of Consumer Research*, 21 (December), 501-521.

Sasson, Joanna (2004), "Photographic materiality in the age of digital reproduction", in Elizabeth Edwards and Janice Hart (eds.), *Photographs Objects Histories: On the Materiality of Images*, London: Routledge.

Schultz Kleine, Susan and Stacey Menzel Baker (2004), "An Integrative Review of Material Possession Attachment", *Academy of Marketing Science Review*, 1, 1-35

Sherry, John F Jr. (2000), Place, Technology, and Representation, *Journal of Consumer Research*, 27 (September), 273-278

Siddiqui, Shakeel and Darach Turley (2006), "Extending the Self in a Virtual World", *Advances in Consumer Research*, 33, 647-648.

Slater, Don (1997), *Consumer Culture and Modernity*, Oxford, UK: Polity Press; Cambridge, MA: Blackwell Publishers.

Stell, Roxanne and Nita Paden (1999), "Vicarious Exploration and Catalog Shopping: A Preliminary Investigation," *Journal of Consumer Marketing*, 16 (4), 332–346.

"Virtually Me: Youth Consumers and Their Online Identities"

Natalie Wood, Saint Joseph's University, USA
Lan Nguyen Chaplin, University of Arizona, USA
Michael Solomon, Saint Joseph's University, USA

Identity exploration is an essential developmental task for adolescents (Erikson 1963; Harter 1999; Marcia 1993). Traditionally, it was family and friends who served as a reference for identity exploration. Today, the internet affords adolescents many new and exciting opportunities to experiment with their identities (Katz and Rice 2002; Rheingold 1993; Smith and Kollock 1999; Stern 2004; Subrahmanyam, Smahel and Greenfield 2006; Turkle 1995). Online experimentation often occurs both in the presence, and with the aid of people they have never, and may never meet in the real world. Technologies like social networking sites (e.g. Facebook), chat rooms and blogs receive the majority of attention. However, much of the real action actually takes place in sophisticated virtual worlds such as MTV's The Virtual Hills, Gaia Online and Kaneva.

Individuals enter virtual worlds in the form of *avatars*–online digital personas that they create. In these worlds they socialize with each other, play games, watch videos, shop and tryout different personas. Participation rates are staggering–Habbo Hotel targets 13 -18 year olds and boasts over 100 million registered users and over 10 million unique users each month (Sulake Coproration 2008). Gaia Online attracts more than 5 million unique visitors each month with 500,000 of their members logging in for an average of *two hours per day* (Gaia Interactive Inc 2008). By 2011 an estimated 53% of children and teen internet users will be experimenting with their virtual selves in these environments ("*Kids*" 2007).

As today's youth effortlessly move back and forth between their real and virtual environments, we can only imagine the ramifications for identity formation. These virtual playgrounds allow for experimentation and self exploration at an extraordinary level of realism. Experimenting with possible selves (see Markus and Nurius 1989) can be undertaken in a short period of time, in a relatively safe environment, with minimal effort and little or no expense.

To date a small number of researchers have investigated the relationship between online identity and offline social comparison and self concept, but with mixed results (see Caplan 2005; Harman, Hansen, Cochran and Lindsey 2005; Matsuba, 2006). The most recent study by Valkenburg and Jochen (2008) examined adolescents who use the internet for chat or instant messaging. Their findings revealed that 50 percent of users are motivated to engage in internet-based identity experiments to satisfy their desire for self-exploration (to investigate how others react), social compensation (to overcome shyness) and social facilitation (to facilitate relationship formation).

The purpose of this study is to examine, motivation for in-world participation, the potential impact and influence these virtual playgrounds have on youth identity formation (real and virtual) and how the residents of these worlds function as a reference group. To explore these issues we choose to complete a netnographic (online ethnography) study (see Kozinets 1998, 2002) of popular teenage virtual worlds. Our first step involved developing a list of specific research questions and identifying appropriate virtual environments for investigation. *MTV Network* currently operates eight teenage virtual worlds. We selected two worlds that exhibit high levels of traffic and between member interactions –*Virtual Laguna Beach* and *The Virtual Hills*.

The second step was to have our researchers join and fully participate in both of these worlds on a regular basis. Three researchers engaged in over 5 hours of virtual world familiarization/orientation. They then spent over 16 hours (1 hour per day, at various times of the day and night over a 2 month period) observing in-world behavior and taking reflective/introspective field notes and photographs. Finally they completed 7 in-world interviews with in-world residents. The reported age of respondents was 15-21 and each interview lasted 45-60 minutes. Data was first analyzed independently by each researcher and then jointly to identify major

findings based on frequency of occurrence (between and within subjects).

Motivation for participation included meeting real and virtual friends, to escape real life or find a better one, and to behave in a way that they cannot, or do not feel comfortable doing in real life. We observed a significant amount of role playing with many people owning more than one avatar, sometimes with different personas. Residents verbally and behaviorally adopt the persona of their avatar. For instance, one person was dressed in "country" attire (wearing denim and boots) and started a conversation with "Hey ya'll." Five of the seven people interviewed indicated that their avatar appearance was partially based on acceptance–the need to belong. Furthermore, screen names are commonly used to express a desirable aspect of the self (e.g. Nakedsurfgod)

In terms of identity formation possessions (virtual cars, clothing etc) are used as signals and symbolic representations of real or ideal selves. Groups of similar looking avatars tend to hang out together and are generally less friendly than groups of avatars with diverse appearances. It appears that a unified appearance acts as a code signifying membership to a specific group and members of these "in-groups" are very intolerant of new people (referred to as Noobs) who are usually recognizable by their standardized appearance and wardrobe. Furthermore, they use ridicule (bullying) as a way of setting boundaries for group membership.

All of the residents interviewed alluded to the fact that they are less confident in the real world and the environment gave them the confidence to express themselves. Several commented that they see themselves as being more outgoing in-world and in some cases this virtual confidence gives them real life confidence.

In conclusion we find that in virtual environments identity and acceptance is very important and owning the right assortment of virtual possessions is essential for fitting in. Just as in the real world a social ranking system exists and virtual bullying is common. These virtual worlds give people greater freedom and confidence to act out without any serious repercussions. Future research should 1. Explore the role of brands and how products are used to form and manage impressions of the self 2. Examine how in-world relationships are developed, how they differ from, and how they impact relationships found in the real-world, 3. Examine the relationship between identity formation via virtual worlds and psychological well-being.

References

Caplan, Scott E. (2005), "A social skill account of problematic internet use," *Journal of Communication,* 55, 721-736.

Erikson, Erik (1963), *Childhood and Society.* New York: Norton.

Gaia Interactive, Inc. (2008), *About Use.* Retrieved March 19th, 2008, from Gaia: http://www.gaiaonline.com/info/about.php

Harman, Jeffrey P., Hansen, Catherine E., Cochran, Margaret E and Cynthia R. Lindsey (2005), "Liar, liar: Internet faking but not frequency of use affects social skills, self-esteem, social anxiety, and aggression," *CyberPsychology & Behavior,* 8, 1-6.

Harter, Susan (1999), *The Construction of the Self: A Developmental Perspective.* New York: Guilford Press.

Katz, James E. and Ronald E. Rice (2002), *Social Consequences of Internet Use: Access, Involvement, and Interaction.* Cambridge, MA: MIT Press.

Kids, Teens and Virtual Worlds. (2007, September 25). Retrieved October 23, 2007, from eMarketer: http://www.emarketer.com

Kozinets, Robert V. (1998), "On Netnography: Initial Reflections on Consumer Research Investigations of Cyberculture," in *Advances in Consumer Research*, 25, Joseph Alba and Wesley Hutchinson (eds.), Provo, UT: Association for Consumer Research, pp. 366-71.

_____ (2002), "The Field Behind the Screen: Using Netnography for Marketing Research in Online Communities," *Journal of Marketing Research*, 39 (February), 61-72.

Marcia, J. E. (1993), *Ego identity: A Handbook for psychosocial research*. New York: Springer.

Markus, Hazel and Paula Nurius (1986), "Possible selves," *American Psychologist*, 41 (9), 954-969.

Matsuba, M. Kyle. (2006), "Searching for Self and Relationships Online," *CyberPsychology & Behavior*, 9, 275-284.

Rheingold, Howard (1993), *The Virtual Community: Homesteading on the Electronic Frontier*. Reading, MA: Addison-Wesley.

Smith, Marc. A and Peter Kollock (1999), *Communities in Cyberspace*. London: Routledge.

Stern, Susannah R. (2004), "Expressions of Identity Online: Prominent Features and Gender Differences in Adolescent' World Wide Web Home Pages," *Journal of Broadcasting and Electronic Media*, 48, 218-243.

Subrahmanyam, Kaveri, David Smahel, and Patricia Greenfield (2006), "Connecting Developmental Constructions to the Internet: Identity Presentation and Sexual Exploration in Online Teen Chatrooms," *Developmental Psychology*, 42(3), 395-406.

Sulake Coproration. (2008, March 19th). *Habbo-Where Else?* Retrieved March 19th, 2008, from Sulake Corporate Web site: http://www.sulake.com/habbo/?navi=2

Turkle, Sherry (1995), *Life on the Screen: Identity in the Age of the Internet*. New York: Simon & Schuster.

Valkenburg, Pattie M. and Peter Jochen (2008), "Adolescents' Identity Experiments on the Internet," *Communication Research*, 35(2), 208. Retrieved March 21, 2008, from ABI/INFORM Global database. (Document ID: 1445716861).

"Pursuit of the Sacred in the Era of Infantilization: A Multisited Ethnography of Online Gaming in China"

Jeff Wang, City University of Hong Kong, China
Xin Zhao, University of Hawaii at Manoa, USA
Gary Bamossy, Georgetown University, USA

Most studies of online gaming and virtual communities have focused on identities issues and examined how the virtual world has offered unprecedented opportunities for reconstructing identities (Castronova 2005, 2007; Meadows 2008). In this paper, we take a different approach and examine how online gaming has contributed to and reflected the infantilization of society, through a netnographic inquiry of the sacred and profane in online gaming (Belk, Wallendorf, and Sherry 1989; Barber 2007). From American *kidults*, German *Nesthocker*, Italian *Mamoone*, Japanese *Freeter*, to Indian *Zippies* and French *Tanguy*, a rising infantilist ethos that encourages and legitimizes childishness is gaining momentum around the world. This market-generated infantilization induces puerility in adults and preserves a sense of childishness in children trying to grow up. An infantilist culture prefers play over work, instant gratification over long-term satisfaction, feeling over reason, picture over word, easy over hard, simple over complex, and fast over slow. The infantilization of society is tied closely to the demands of a global economy and its ethos has become the major ideology sustaining consumer capitalism (Barber 2007). However, the nature, causes, and consequences of infantilization have only been examined within Western societies. China's rise toward the most populated consumer society offers an unprecedented opportunity to examine this thesis, especially when the one-child policy has left hundreds of millions of families with their focus on the needs of little emperors (Jing 2000).

One of the most significant findings in consumer research is the sacred and profane evoked by consumption (Belk, Wallendorf, and Sherry 1989).The sacred is the opposite to what is ordinary and part of everyday life, and it refers to what is extraordinary and significant. The sacred is often beyond rationalization and can only be comprehended through devotion. It evokes momentary ecstatic experiences, in which one temporarily feels he or she stands outside his or her self. Anything could become sacred and sacredness is an investment process, in which consumers actively seek to separate ordinary objects from the world of the profane and to create sacred meanings in their lives (Belk, Wallendorf, and Sherry 1989). A material object can be sacralized through ritual, pilgrimage, quintessence, gift-giving, collecting, inheritance, and external sanction. However, these previously studied processes of sacralization focus on the transformation of existing material objects or places into the sacred. They emphasize having and being as a mode of experiencing the sacred. Although it has been noted that the investment of labor plays an important role in transforming the ordinary into the sacred, and how such experiences can become sacred is not explored. It is also unclear whether or not consumers' gaming experiences in the virtual world can be sacred and if so, whether or not the sacralization of intangible virtual possessions takes similar trajectories. We seek to address these theoretical gaps with netnographic inquiries of the online gaming in China, and within Barber's framework of an infantilized society (Barber 2007).

We conducted depth-interviews with both experienced and amateur gamers in urban China during our multisited ethnographic fieldwork from December 2006 to December 2007. We talked to gamers in Internet Cafes, their homes, game sweatshops, and cafes where they often gathered. We interviewed thirty five informants, including not only gamers, but also game developers, reporters covering the game for newspapers, and managers of Internet Cafes. Our research sites covered a wide region in both southern and northern China, and both coastal areas and inner cities, including Beijing, Changchun, Guangzhou, Nanjing, Shanghai, and Shenzhen. Our informants ranged from fifteen-year old teenagers and to adults in their late 40s. Some were affluent young consumers whereas others were poor and played the game in order to sell virtual possessions to make a living. This diversity of different gamers helps to enrich our understanding of what it means to participate in the game world. The interviews started with grand tour questions about personal background, interests, history of online gamine, life objects, and then were followed by questions about gaming experiences (McCracken 1988; Thompson 1997). The interviews lasted from forty-five minutes to three hours. All interviews were digitally recorded and supplemented by extensive field notes, photographs of gamers playing in Internet Café, and videos of on-site observation. They were then transcribed and analyzed through a systematic and iterate process (Arnould and Wallendorf 1994; Spiggle 1994). Each individual interview was taken as an idiographic illustration of a culturally shared system of meanings, similar to previous research (e.g. Holt 2002; Mick and Buhl 1992; Thompson 1997). Initial analysis has generated rich insights about the virtual world of online gaming that we will present at the symposium.

The marketplace has long been associated with a carnivalesque atmosphere, fantastic and sensuous experience, and with the possibility of magical self-transformation through purchase in a fluid and anonymous social setting (Lears 1994). In China, the popularity of online gaming has contributed to the creation of a carnivalesque culture (Twitchell 1992), in which communist creed that represses play in the name of self-sacrifice and hard work has been replaced with the new consumerist ethos that encourages playfulness and an obsession with youthful spontaneity and rebellion as also seen in Western society's theme parks, shopping malls, urban architecture, and advertising (Barber 2007). Accompanying the rise of consumerism there is often a sense of loss (Giddens 1991), and a yearning for the sacred (Ritzer 1999), for which consumption is celebrated as a form of compensation. Online games provide an ideal arena in which gamers can experience an idealized past and the sacred lost. Different games emphasize different values and offer a wide range of psychological remedies for everyday problems faced by Chinese gamers. The variety of experiences sought after in online games goes well beyond excitement, novelty, and relaxation. Although appearing profane and unimportant to others, the avatar's sacredness undoubtedly manifests itself to its creator and many gamers we interviewed. Online gaming is a play of conflicting values that offer psychological remedies for a lost sense of achievement and other desirable values in real world. Online games constitute a liminal space through which gamers seek a transcendental sacred experience and in which the rite of passage of identity cultivation takes place in the new tribal society (Maffesoli 1996).

References

Arnould, Eric J. and Melanie Wallendorf (1994), "Market-Oriented Ethnography: Interpretation Building and Market Strategy Formulation," *Journal of Marketing Research*, 31 (November), 484-504.

Barber, Benjamin R. (2007), *Consumed: How Markets Corrupt Children, Infantilize Adults, and Swallow Citizens Whole*, New York: W. W. Norton Company.

Belk, Russell W., Melanie Wallendorf, and John F. Sherry Jr. (1989), "The Sacred and the Profane in Consumer Behavior: Theodicy on the Odyssey," *Journal of Consumer Research*, 16 (June), 1-38.

Castronova, Edward (2005), *Synthetic Worlds: The Business and Culture of Online Games*, Chicago: University of Chicago Press.

_____ (2007), *Exodus to the Virtual World: How Online Fun is Changing Reality*, New York: Palgrave Macmillan.

Giddens, Anthony (1991), *Modernity and Self-Identity: Self and Society in the Late Modern Age*, Stanford, CA: Stanford University Press.

Holt, Douglas B. (2002), "Why Do Brands Cause Trouble? A Dialectical Theory of Consumer Culture and Branding," *Journal of Consumer Research*, 29 (June), 70-90.

Jing, Jun (2000), *Feeding China's Little Emperors: Food, Children, and Social Change*, Stanford, CA: Stanford University Press.

Lears, Jackson (1994), *Fables of Abundance: A Cultural History of Advertising in America*, New York: Basic Books.

Maffesoli, Michel (1996), *The Contemplation of the World: Figures of Community Style*, translated by Susan Emanuel, Minneapolis: University of Minnesota Press.

McCracken, Grant (1988), *The Long Interview*, Newbury Park, CA: Sage.

Meadows, Mark Stephen (2008), *I, Avatar: The Culture and Consequences of Having a Second Life*, Berkeley: New Riders.

Mick, David Glenn and Claus Buhl (1992), "A Meaning-based Model of Advertising Experiences," *Journal of Consumer Research*, 19 (December), 317-38.

Ritzer, George (1999), *Enchanting a Disenchanted World: Revolutionizing the Means of Consumption*, Thousand Oaks, California: Pine Forge Press.

Spiggle, Susan (1994), "Analysis and Interpretation of Qualitative Data in Consumer Research," *Journal of Consumer Research*, 21 (December), 491-503

Thompson, Craig J. (1997), "Interpreting Consumers: A Hermeneutical Framework for Deriving Marketing Insights from the Texts of Consumers' Consumption Stores," *Journal of Marketing Research*, 34 (November), 438-55.

Twitchell, James B (1992), *Carnival Culture: the Trashing of Taste in America*, New York: Columbia University Press.

SYMPOSIUM SUMMARY
Justification and Choice
Aner Sela, Stanford University, USA
Jonah Berger, University of Pennsylvania, USA

SESSION OVERVIEW

Justification, namely, the use of accessible reasons for resolving the conflict and guilt associated with choice, is important to understanding consumers' behavior and their ensuing satisfaction. However, while research has demonstrated the significance of justification-based processes in consumer choice (e.g., Simonson 1992; Kivetz and Simonson 2002; Kivetz and Zheng 2006), we still know relatively little about the factors that moderate and inform these general processes. The present session seeks to provide an in-depth look at justification-based processes by examining their situational and motivational antecedents as well as the different ways in which they shape choice and satisfaction. How do features of the choice-set, prior beliefs, and emotions both provoke and moderate justification processes? Can the same justification be used in different contexts to arrive at different choice outcomes? How much are good justifications worth to consumers? The session will address these and related questions as it works to deepen our understanding of the role of justification in choice.

Khan, Dhar, and Fishbach (paper 1) examine the motivational role of guilt in indulgent choices and justification processes. Unlike past research which has generally assumed that people who feel guilty should abstain from indulging, this research suggests that guilt can sometimes increase rather than decrease indulgence. Three studies demonstrate that priming guilt creates a motivation to feel not-guilty, leading people to interpret their mundane choices as virtuous and use these virtuous choices as justifications to relapse and indulge.

Sela, Berger, and Liu (paper 2) develop a justification-based framework to understand how assortment size influences the type of options consumers select. More options make choice more difficult which, in turn, increases reliance on available justifications for choice. Six studies illustrate that increasing the number of options often increases the choice of utilitarian options because these tend to be easier to justify. However, when situational factors provide an accessible justification to indulge, increasing the number of options can have the opposite effect, leading to increased selection of indulgences.

Botti and Burson (paper 3) examine how consumers justify successful and unsuccessful decision outcomes and propose that consumers' satisfaction can be influenced by a belief-based justification process. Three studies document instances in which participants are either more or less satisfied with expert-made choices than their own, even when the two outcomes are the same. The findings suggest that satisfaction with choice is not only due to the outcome or to who has made the choice. Beliefs about the decision-maker's ability to find the option that best matches preferences also determines consumers' ability to justify the choice's outcome.

Keinan, Kivetz, and Netzer (paper 4) examine consumers' motivated tendency to overvalue certain justifications. This research demonstrates how adding a small utilitarian feature to a luxury good can serve to justify the indulgent purchase and reduce the associated guilt. Six studies suggest that consumers tend to overvalue such minor product features that serve to justify indulgent choices. This overvaluation is found to be mediated by guilt and is more likely to occur when the purchase seems wasteful and frivolous.

Taken together, the four papers in this session extend and deepen our understanding of choice justification processes and how they interact with features of the choice set (e.g., assortment), beliefs (e.g., about choice competence), and affect (e.g., guilt). The session would be of interest to researchers and marketers interested in consumer judgment and decision making, choice theory and assortments, affect and emotions, and the effect of the choice process on preference and satisfaction.

References

Kivetz, Ran and Itamar Simonson (2002), "Earning the Right to Indulge: Effort as a Determinant of Customer Preferences Toward Frequency Program Rewards," *Journal of Marketing Research*, 39 (May), 155–70.

Kivetz, Ran and Yuhuang Zheng (2006), "Determinants of Justification and Self-Control," *Journal of Experimental Psychology: General*, 135(4), 572–87.

Simonson, Itamar (1992), "The Influence of Anticipating Regret and Responsibility on Purchase Decisions," *Journal of Consumer Research*, 19 (June), 105-18.

EXTENDED ABSTRACTS

"Guilt as Motivation: The Role of Guilt in Choice Justification"

Uzma Khan, Stanford University, USA
Ravi Dhar, Yale University, USA
Ayelet Fishbach, University of Chicago, USA

Guilt plays an important role in consumer choices and self-control (Khan et al. 2005). However, to this point, it is unclear whether guilt only influences choice through emotional experience when people *feel* guilty, or whether it can also be a motivational state whereby people strive to *avoid* experiencing guilt. Whether guilt is an emotional or a motivational state further determines what affect guilt-primes have on indulgence. Past research has generally treated guilt as an emotion that steers consumers away from indulgence. According to this research, priming guilt-related words reduces indulgence by inducing guilty experience (Giner-Sorolla 2001; Zemack-Rugar et al. 2007). The underlying assumption is that guilt-primes create an affective state through direct assimilation with the prime. That is, people actually *feel* guilty when primed with guilt-related concepts and this feeling prevents them from indulging.

An alternative view explored in current research is that guilt acts as a motivational state. We propose that guilt-primes increase the motivation to avoid guilt, which guides the interpretation of means to achieve this goal state. For example, imagine Jane, who after picking up a diet-coke and is choosing between an unhealthy pizza and a healthy salad for lunch. We argue that she will interpret her choice of a diet-coke differently depending on her level of motivation to avoid guilt. If she is primed with guilt, she is more likely to use the diet-coke as a justification to have pizza (due to heightened motivations to avoid guilty) than if she is not primed. More generally, we suggest that guilt-primes motivate consumers to interpret their decisions as virtuous in order to avoid guilt and feeling virtuous can paradoxically lead to MORE and NOT less indulgence.

Formally, we propose that 1) guilt-primes can create a motivation avoid guilt 2) higher motivation to avoid guilt promotes interpretation of mundane choices as virtuous 3) these virtuous choices then serve as guilt-reducing justifications for further indulgence. Three studies support our theory. In Study 1 we primed participants with neutral (control) or guilt-related words (guilt-prime condition) in a scrambled-sentence task. Next, they consumed chocolate as part of a taste-test. Half of them were given a diet-coke to be consumed after the taste-test. We assumed that diet-coke can serve as a guilt-reducing justification when motivation to avoid guilt is high and can justify chocolate consumption. Consistent with our theory, ANOVA of chocolate consumption yielded a 2 (Guilt-Prime: Yes vs. No) x 2 (Diet-Coke: Present vs. Absent) interaction; i.e., participants primed with guilt consumed more chocolate when they were given a diet-coke (M=51gm) as compared to when they were not (M=28gm). However, in control condition chocolate consumed was not significantly different when diet-coke was present (M=28gm) or not (M=37gm). Results support the notion that a diet-coke is interpreted as a guilt-reducing justification and allows greater indulgence when the motivation to avoid guilt is strong (i.e., when guilt is primed) but not in absence of such motivation.

Building on the motivational view of guilt, we further predict that virtuous choices in presence of a guilt-prime can directly reduce experience of guilt. Study 2 demonstrated this effect of guilt-prime on experienced guilt for a fixed amount of indulgence. We predicted that individuals primed with guilt would experience less guilt than those not primed if they are given a guilt-reducing justification (e.g., diet coke). Again we employed a 2 (Guilt-Prime: Yes vs. No) X 2 (Diet-Coke: Present vs. Absent) design. Instead of measuring consumption, all participants ate one donut and indicated their experienced guilt. ANOVA of guilt-ratings yielded the predicted *guilt-prime* X *diet-coke* interaction. Further analyses revealed that when diet-coke was offered participants primed with guilt experienced less guilt than those not primed with guilt.

Recent research has shown that initial virtuous choices serve as guilt-reducing justifications and lead to indulgence in subsequent decisions (Khan and Dhar 2006). Study 3 shows that an initial choice is more effective as a justification when guilt is primed. Specifically, participants made two choices 1) between two highbrow magazines and 2) between highbrow and lowbrow movies. Prior to the choices, half of the participants were primed with guilt. As predicted, those primed with guilt were more likely to choose a lowbrow movie (50%) than those not primed (26%). We explain that an initial virtuous choice is more likely to be viewed as a justification and lead to more indulgence when the motivation to avoid guilt is strong.

Our findings add to justification research by showing how guilt-primes can increase indulgence through a motivation to avoid guilt, which leads to interpretation of mundane decisions as virtuous justifications. Secondly, we contribute to priming research (e.g., Bargh et al. 2001) by suggesting a motivational role of guilt-primes, which is significantly different from an affect-assimilation account. This also provides a mechanism to distinguish between goal-related vs. semantic primes. We suggest that priming a motivational state can strengthen or inhibit a goal depending on the level of goal attainment experienced.

References:

Bargh, John A., Peter M. Gollwitzer, Annette Lee-Chai, Kimberly Barndollar, and Roman Trotschel (2001), "The Automated Will: Nonconscious Activation and Pursuit of Behavioral Goals," *Journal of Personality and Social Psychology*, 18 (6), 1014–27.

Giner-Sorolla, Roger (2001), "Guilty Pleasures and Grim Necessities: Afective Attitudes in Dilemmas of Self-Control," *Journal of Personality and Social Psychology*, 80 (2), 206-21.

Khan, Uzma, Ravi Dhar, and Klaus Wertenbroch (2005), "Hedonic and Utilitarian Consumption," in *Inside Consumption: Frontiers of Research on Consumer Motives, Goals, and Desires*, ed. S. Ratneshwar and David Glen Mick, Routledge, 144-65.

Khan, Uzma and Ravi Dhar (2006), "Licensing Effect in Consumer Choice," *Journal of Marketing Research*, 43 (May), 259-66.

Zemack-Rugar, Yael, James R. Bettman, and Gavan J. Fitzsimons (2007), "The Effects of Nonconsciously Priming Emotion Concepts on Behavior," *Journal of Personality and Social Psychology*, 93 (6), 927-39.

"Variety, Vice, and Virtue: How Assortment Size Influences Option Choice"

Aner Sela, Stanford University, USA
Jonah Berger, University of Pennsylvania, USA
Wendy Liu, University of California, Los Angeles, USA

Recently, there has been a resurgence of interest in how variety influences consumer choice (Iyengar and Lepper 2000) and satisfaction (Schwartz 2004). This research has offered an important corrective to the notion that more choice is always better by demonstrating that too many options can lead consumers not to choose at all, and to feel less satisfaction and more regret about the options they do choose. But while this work has provided insight into how the number of available options affects choice likelihood, could assortment size also influence the *type* of choices consumers make?

To address this question, we develop a justification-based framework that examines how assortment size influences the choice between vice and virtue. Specifically, we argue that because choosing from greater assortments is often more difficult, it may lead to greater reliance on accessible reasons and justifications. Because some options may be easier to justify than others, this in turn should affect the type of options consumers end up selecting. Prior work has demonstrated that people generally find virtues easier to justify than vices (e.g., Kivetz and Simonson 2002; Kivetz and Zheng 2006). Consequently, we propose that choosing from larger assortments should often lead people to select relatively virtuous or utilitarian options. However, when situational factors provide accessible justifications to indulge, choosing from larger assortments should lead people to select more hedonic options.

Six studies, involving both hypothetical and real choice, support these hypotheses. Compared to people choosing from a relatively small set of options, those choosing from an enlarged set were more likely to choose reduced fat ice-cream over regular ice cream (Experiment 1A), select fruit over cookies as a lunchtime snack (Experiment 1B), and use a gift-certificate to obtain a printer rather than an mp3 player (Experiment 2). The studies also provide insight into the mechanism underlying these effects. Consistent with the notion that the effect of assortment size was driven by increased effort and conflict, it was found to be mediated by experienced choice difficulty (Experiment 3). In addition, the effect depended on whether the overall number of options was increased rather than which option category saw the increase. Thus, increasing the number of just the hedonic or utilitarian options in the choice set was sufficient to increase the choice likelihood of the utilitarian options.

Moreover, consistent with the notion that variety influences choice through reliance on accessible justification, manipulations that provided accessible reasons to indulge reversed the effect (Experiments 4 and 5). People who were given false feedback that they had exerted a great deal of effort on a task, and thus had an accessible "excuse" for selecting vice, were actually more likely to select a hedonic consumer good over a utilitarian one when choosing from an enlarged choice set than when choosing from a small choice set. In contrast, people who were told they had exerted relatively little effort were more likely to choose the utilitarian consumer good when choosing from the larger choice set. Similarly, people who felt "licensed" to indulge due to a virtuous choice they had made in an unrelated task were more likely to select a hedonic product rather than a utilitarian equivalent when choosing from a larger set, but people who did not make the "licensing" choice were more likely to select the utilitarian product from the enlarged set.

Taken together, these studies illustrate that variety not only influences whether consumers make a choice, but also what they end up choosing. Furthermore, they highlight the key role of justifications in these effects. Thus, the effect of variety on option choice was contingent on what *type* of justifications was available to people at the time of choice.

References

Iyengar, Sheena S. and Mark R Lepper (2000), "When Choice is Demotivating: Can one Desire Too Much of a Good Thing," *Journal of Personality and Social Psychology*, 79(6), 995-1006.

Kivetz, Ran and Itamar Simonson (2002), "Self-Control for the Righteous: Toward a Theory of Precommitment to Indulgence," *Journal of Consumer Research*, 29 (September) 199-217.

Kivetz, Ran and Yuhuang Zheng (2006), "Determinants of Justification and Self-Control," *Journal of Experimental Psychology: General*, 135(4), 572–87.

Schwartz, Barry (2004), *The Paradox of Choice: Why More is Less*, New York: Ecco.

"Choice Satisfaction Can Be the Luck of the Draw"

Katherine A. Burson, University of Michigan, USA
Simona Botti, London Business School, UK

In this research, we explore how consumers justify both successful and unsuccessful choice outcomes depending on whether they or an expert has made the decision. We show that self-expert differences in satisfaction with choice outcomes depend on how consumers justify these outcomes. Two studies document instances in which participants' satisfaction with expert-made choices relative to their own varies even when the choice outcomes are the same. The results of these experiments show that satisfaction for the same outcome is not only due to the outcome itself or the decision maker, but on how consumers explain the outcome. When consumers justify the outcome with the decision maker's ability to make the best choice, perceived good (poor) ability generates more (less) satisfaction. However, when outcomes are justified by factors external to the decision maker's ability, there is no effect of outcome on satisfaction.

Prior research suggests that ultimate satisfaction with choice outcomes depends on the extent to which that outcome can be justified by the chooser's capability to make the best choice (Weiner 1985). Thus, factors that influence the way in which these abilities are assessed will also influence eventual outcome satisfaction. The correspondence bias (Jones & Nisbett 1972) is one of these factors. When a choice outcome can be explained entirely by context, consumers consider this fact and are likely to temper their perceptions of the role of their own ability in the outcome. However, they are likely to persist in crediting that outcome exclusively to an expert's ability. Consequently, participants will tend to be more satisfied with an expert's positive choice outcome than their own because they can justify it more readily with the expert's ability to make good choices, even when self and expert achieve identical choice outcomes. In contrast, participants will tend to be less satisfied with an expert's negative outcome than their own because they justify it more readily with the experts' *lack* of ability to make good choices.

The first study examined perceptions of abilities and subsequent choice satisfaction in the domain of medical treatment choices. Participants either chose their own treatment from a choice set or were assigned a treatment by an expert and then given feedback that the treatment had succeeded or failed. Consistent with our expectations, participants were more likely to temper their own ability assessments than an expert's when the outcome was negative. This lead to more middling satisfaction for self-chosen than expert-chosen outcomes. Mediational analyses confirmed that the self-expert difference in outcome was the result of perceived choice ability.

In the second experiment, we test these predictions in an investment domain. Participants either personally chose a mutual fund or had one assigned by an expert. Half of participants were then given feedback that the fund had either increased or decreased. They were also provided with feedback about the unchosen funds. The unchosen funds increased when the chosen fund increased and decreased when the chosen fund decreased, by the same percent as the chosen fund. When feedback was absent, self and expert ability assessment did not differ. When the feedback suggested that the market explained the choice outcome, self-ability assessments were middling while expert-evaluations were inflated for good outcomes and deflated for bad outcomes. Despite this unequivocal feedback about the market, participants were biased in their incorporation of this situational explanation for the outcome. Mediational analyses show again that the self-expert differences in outcome depends n perceived choice ability.

Taken together, these two studies show that assessments of an expert's choice ability depend mainly on the choice outcome, while self-evaluations are often tempered by contextual information if it is available. Because satisfaction depends on participants' opportunity to justify choice outcomes with choice ability, participants are frequently more satisfied with a positive choice outcome produced by an expert than by the same outcome resulting from their own choice. When the outcome is negative, participants are less satisfied with the expert-chosen outcome than the identical self-chosen outcome.

References

Jones, Edward E. and Richard E. Nisbett (1972), "The Actor and the Observer: Divergent Perceptions of the Causes of Behavior," in *Attribution: Perceiving the Causes of Behavior*, ed. E. E. Jones, D. E. Kanouse, H. H. Kelley, R. E. Nisbett, S. Valins, and B. Weiner, Morristown, NJ: General Learning Press, 79-94.

Weiner, Bernard (1985), "An Attributional Theory of Achievement Motivation and Emotion," *Psychological Review*, 92 (4), 548-73.

"Functional Alibi"

Anat Keinan, Harvard Business School, USA
Ran Kivetz, Columbia University, USA
Oded Netzer, Columbia University, USA

"Every vice has its excuse ready" (Publilius Syrus)

Marketers of luxury products face two major challenges. Marketers have to first appeal to consumers' desire and imagination, and create a demand for something which is not really needed. Accordingly, marketing scholars and practitioners have stressed the importance of appealing to consumers' fantasies and senses, connecting with their hopes, wishes and dreams, and satisfying their emotional desires (Holbrook and Hirschman 1982; Schmitt 1999; LaSalle 2003; Danziger 2005).

However, creating a desire or a craving for the luxury product is not enough; consumers may desire such products but still feel guilty spending money on non-practical luxuries and avoid purchasing them (Kivetz and Simonson 2002; Kivetz and Keinan 2006; Keinan and Kivetz 2008). Since luxuries are "by definition superfluous" and "neither beneficial nor useful" (Thomson 1987), the purchase and consumption of such products seems wasteful and even immoral, and consequently is difficult to justify.

Thus, a second important challenge that luxury marketers need to overcome is appealing to consumers' conscience and providing them with an excuse or an "alibi" that would justify their profligate purchase, and make the purchase seem "rational" and logical. Such alibis can help consumers overcome their guilt, and view their purchase decisions as influenced by product functionality rather than by non-practical considerations and desires.

In the present research, we demonstrate how righteous consumers rationalize their frivolous behavior by inflating the perceived value of minor functional features or aspects of the luxury product. We argue that small utilitarian aspects of a seemingly wasteful product or service can serve as *"functional alibis."* For example, consumers whose cars never touch a dirt road often justify the purchase of an extravagant SUV by its performance in extreme driving conditions. Similarly, consumers often mention a protective cell phone pocket to justify the purchase of the multi-hundred dollars Coach or Louis Vuitton purses.

We demonstrate that consumers tend to overvalue features (or products) that serve as a functional alibi. Such small utilitarian additions to a hedonic luxury are often valued more than their standalone value since they provide additional utility from serving as a functional alibi and justifying the purchase. Accordingly, the willingness to pay for a luxury product connected to a utilitarian product (or feature) will be higher than the WTP for each product sold separately:

WTP (Luxury + utilitarian addition)>WTP (Luxury) + WTP (utilitarian addition).

Six studies explore the effect of adding a functional alibi on consumers' willingness to pay, purchase intentions, choices, and emotions of guilt. We show that the overvaluation of the added utilitarian product (or feature) is mediated by feelings of guilt associated with purchasing the hedonic luxury. Moreover, we demonstrate that such functional alibis are valued more when the purchase seems wasteful and induces guilt. We show that consumers who view luxury purchases as wasteful will be more likely to overvalue small utilitarian features that are attached to luxury products. Additionally, we demonstrate that small utilitarian additions are valued more when they are attached to hedonic rather than utilitarian products.

We explore the effect of the functional alibi in a variety marketing contexts (and across the 4Ps of marketing planning), including product upgrades, product positioning, new products features, product bundling, pricing, cross selling, advertising, and sales promotions. Moreover, we examine the effect of connecting a variety of functional alibis to various products and services including personal luxuries (clothing and apparel, fashion accessories, watches, cosmetics and fragrances), home luxuries (consumer electronics, hi-tech gadgets, and luxury furniture) and experiential luxuries (hotels and vacations, travel, and entertainment).

References

Danziger, Pamela N. (2005), *Let Them Eat Cake: Marketing Luxury to the Masses-As Well as the Classes*, Chicago, IL: Dearborn Trade Publishers.

Holbrook Morris B. and Elizabeth C. Hirschman (1982), "The Experiential Aspects of Consumption: Consumer Fantasies, Feeling, and Fun," *Journal of Consumer Research*, 9, 132-40.

Keinan, Anat and Ran Kivetz (2006), "Remedying Hyperopia: The Effect of Self-Control Regret on Consumer Behavior," *Journal of Marketing Research*, forthcoming.

Kivetz, Ran and Anat Keinan (2006), "Repenting Hyperopia: An Analysis of Self-Control Regrets," Forthcoming in the *Journal of Consumer Research*.

Kivetz, Ran and Itamar Simonson (2002), "Self-control for the righteous: Toward a theory of precommitment to indulge," *Journal of Consumer Research*, 29, 199-217.

LaSalle, Diana and Terry A. Britton (2003), *Priceless: turning ordinary products into extraordinary experiences*, Boston, MA: Harvard Business School Press.

Schmitt, Bernd (1999), *Experiential Marketing: How to Get Customers to Sense, Feel, Think, Act, and Relate to Your Company and Brands*, New York, NY: The Free Press.

Thomson, Garret (1987), *Needs*, London: Routledge and Kegan Paul.

Moving Beyond the Rabbit's Foot: Superstition and Magical Thinking in Consumer Behavior

Eric Hamerman, Columbia University, USA

SESSION OVERVIEW

Merriam-Webster defines superstition as "an irrational belief that an object, action, or circumstance not logically related to a course of events influences its outcome". While a great deal of established consumer behavior literature has focused on violations of rational choice, superstition is unique in demonstrating that consumers may base their choices on magical thinking, *even while recognizing and acknowledging that this is irrational*.

As a phenomenon, superstition has tremendous impact in the business world. ABC News reports that people's reluctance to tempt fate results in losses of $850 million each time a Friday the 13th occurs in the calendar. More personal examples abound; almost half of all collegiate track athletes used some sort of clothing ritual such as "lucky socks" to help their performance (Bleak and Frederick, 1998). From a consumer behavior perspective, individuals who score higher in superstitious belief are more suspicious of genetically modified foods (Mowen and Carlson, 2003), and Taiwanese students were more likely to purchase a portable radio when it was priced at TW$888–8 is lucky in Asian culture–than at the lower figure of TW$777 (Kramer and Block, 2008).

Several psychological paradigms underlay the phenomenon of superstition, although there has been little investigation of these principles as they relate to marketing. First, sympathetic magic (Rozin et al, 2007) encompasses the laws of contagion and similarity. The former states that objects that have been in contact with each other will forever remain linked, even after being physically separated. The latter posits that an item which is related to another by imagery or association may take on properties of the second item. Consistent with the definition of superstition, such beliefs are acknowledged as irrational, but still manage to hold sway over behavior.

The idea of "illusory control" (Wegner and Wheatley, 1999; Wegner, 2002) identifies three principles by which individuals may be tricked into believing that they exert control over an event: priority, consistency, and exclusivity. When an action occurs prior to an outcome, when the outcome is consistent with one's intent, and when the action is the exclusively available explanation, then one is more likely to believe that he or she caused it to occur. Pronin et al (2006) demonstrated that when individuals insert needles into a voodoo doll, they are more likely to believe that this action caused a headache in an experimental confederate when the confederate previously acted rudely; the outcome (headache in a rude individual) was consistent with subjects' intent (to hurt the confederate). Again, these beliefs are often recognized as irrational by the same individuals who use these cues to direct their actions.

A culturally ingrained idea that individuals should not "tempt fate" is the third block on which the symposium rests. While there is no rational reason why discussing an uncertain event (or a string of successes) should impact its outcome (or this "hot streak"), there are many examples in which individuals believe that such discussions will bring negative consequences.

Each of the papers in this seminar addresses at least one of these psychological components of superstition in varying ways, but with the common theme that irrational beliefs about sympathetic magic, control, or tempting fate regularly influence consumer behavior, despite being acknowledged as unreasonable by their perpetrators. In Paper 1 (Kramer and Block), individual differences in intuitive processing are examined as a moderator of sympathetic

magic. The authors found that college students were more likely to purchase a used textbook from an individual with a high grade-point-average (GPA) than from someone with a low GPA, but only for highly intuitive processors. In a second study, the authors demonstrated that magical thinking can actually impact academic performance. Subjects were given a study guide to prepare for a test, and were informed that the guide had been previously used by other students. Subjects who were highly intuitive processors and who believed that their intelligence was malleable (Dweck et al, 1993) performed better when they believed that the guide had been previously used by high-GPA rather than low-GPA students.

In Paper 2, Hamerman and Johar demonstrated that when conditions were in place for individuals to perceive an ability to control outside events (based on Wegner's three principles of illusory control), they were more likely to deploy superstition as a purchase strategy. In Study 1, subjects indicated that protagonists were more likely to stay with a non-preferred brand of beer after their alma mater's performance in a basketball tournament improved, compared to when the team's performance declined. This difference only occurred when the protagonist was framed as a big fan of the basketball team. In Study 2, subjects engaged in a simulated "Trivia Night" at two hypothetical restaurants. Participants disregarded their existing preferences (based on restaurant quality) and used their trivia scores as a factor in deciding which restaurant to patronize, even though they were explicitly informed that the location of the match had no bearing on their likelihood of scoring well. Despite this result, participants still reported that their score on the trivia quiz was less important than restaurant quality in making their decision. In Study 3, subjects were given Snickers bars while watching their school perform well in an intercollegiate academic competition. When any of the principles of illusory control were violated (e.g., the broadcast was tape-delayed, individuals were not rooting intently for the school), respondents were more likely to switch their preferences away from Snickers at the close of the match.

In Paper 3, Risen and Gilovich examined the idea that "tempting fate" elevates the accessibility of negative outcomes, which in turn increases the perceived likelihood of these outcomes. In one study, a protagonist "tempted fate" by wearing a t-shirt from a university to which he applied; subjects determined that this individual was less likely to be accepted after wearing the t-shirt. In a second study, subjects who were primed with a belief in tempting fate were less optimistic and displayed a lower level of overconfidence in their abilities. A third study indicates that subjects who "tempt fate" by exchanging a lottery ticket for one with new numbers are more likely to purchase insurance against losing the drawing. The presentation also includes a hierarchical cluster analysis that identifies "hubris" and "needless risk" as behavior clusters that are associated with the concept of "tempting fate".

In Paper 4, Kruger et al extend this research with the idea that commenting on success invites failure. In two studies, they demonstrate that subjects are more likely to predict future negative outcomes for both hypothetical protagonists (Study 1) and themselves (Study 2) after a string of successes has been mentioned compared to when success has not been referenced. Study 3 shows that the mechanism for this phenomenon is a failure to recognize "regression to the mean". At the precise time when a string of successes is noticed, regression to the mean predicts that events are likely to begin evening out. As expected, participants believed that an alteration in the background screen of a video game–put in place after a string of successes–made the game more difficult.

Taken together, the four papers investigate how people apply superstitious decision-making strategies in their everyday life, even while acknowledging that these strategies are not rational. In addition to investigating several manifestations of superstition (e.g., tempting fate, inviting failure, conditioned behavior, and culturally ingrained beliefs) across a wide variety of domains, we attempt to demonstrate that superstition and magical thinking have a strong impact on actual behaviors, including consumption.

EXTENDED ABSTRACTS

"The Impact of Thinking Style on Sympathetic Magical Thinking"

Thomas Kramer, Baruch College, USA
Lauren Block, Baruch College, USA

Would you be reluctant to drink juice previously touched by a dead, sterile cockroach? How about eating a piece of chocolate fudge shaped to look like dog feces? Psychologists and anthropologists have studied these and other examples of "sympathetic magical thinking" since the turn of the 20th century (Rozin, Millman, Nemeroll 1986). As the examples illustrate, magical beliefs follow one of two laws of magical thinking. The law of contagion holds that objects that have been in contact (e.g. a cockroach in juice) remain in contact even after being physically separated. The law of similarity states that if items that are related by imagery or association, one item may take on properties of the second (e.g. chocolate dog feces).

Despite acknowledging that magical beliefs are irrational, even well-educated adults fall prey to thinking that touching an object transfers his or her qualities (or "essence") to it, which subsequently can get passed on to another person (Rozin et al. 2007). However, the effects of magical thinking do not only result in negative attitudes, such as reluctance to consume or touch, but also have positive manifestations. For example, a building at 165 University Avenue in Palo Alto has a reputation for magical qualities, having housed PayPal, Logitech, and Google (Helft 2007), on which the owners capitalize when renting out space. Likewise, objects previously owned by celebrities maintain a distinct price advantage on the secondary market. For example, Pope Benedict's 1999 Volkswagen recently sold for over $282,000.

Recent work has brought the positive effects of magical thinking into the consumer domain. Argo, Dahl and Morales (forthcoming) show that product evaluations are higher when shoppers believe they have been previously touched by an attractive other. In general, there are only a handful of published studies in marketing that explore contagion in a consumer product domain, and these are all limited to the effects of contagion on attitudes or motivation (Argo, Dahl and Morales 2006, 2008; Morales and Fitzsimons 2007). We extend this literature by demonstrating that magical thinking can have profound effects beyond attitudes and beliefs. In a series of studies, we demonstrate behavioral manifestations of magical thinking, from purchase likelihood intentions to actual increases in performance on reasoning tasks. Importantly, in doing so, we are the first to demonstrate that achievement is a property capable of being transferred through magical thinking. We also contribute to the literature by demonstrating that the impact of magical thinking depends on consumers' thinking style (Epstein et al. 1996).

Study 1 was a 2 (prior owner's academic success: high vs. low) x 2 (intuitive processing: high vs. low) design, in which 124 undergraduate subjects were told to imagine that they were majoring in music and were looking for a used textbook for a class at the beginning of the semester. Next, subjects in the high (low) academic success condition were presented with the following ad: "This text is in excellent, like new condition. Great shape, with just a little bit of writing on it. Used it just last semester. Got an A (D) in the class; kept my GPA at 3.98 (2.34). Price: $59.99." Then, subjects indicated their purchase likelihood, followed by intuitive thinking style measures (?=.83; Epstein et al. 1996). Results showed a significant main effect of prior owner's academic success [(F1, 120)=12.23, p<.001], which was qualified by the expected thinking style X prior owner's academic success interaction [F(1, 120)=4.16, p<.05]. Planned contrast showed that high intuitive processors were significantly more likely to purchase the textbook from a prior student high versus low in academic success [M=6.26 vs. 4.07; F(1, 56)=12.63, p<.001]. However, there were no differences for low intuitive processors.

The objective of Study 2 was to provide evidence that high intuitive processors believe that achievement can be transferred through magical thinking, which would be obtained if the effect depends on perceptions about the malleability of one's own intelligence. Importantly, we also sought to show the impact of magical beliefs on actual performance. One hundred and sixteen undergraduate students participated in a 2 (thinking style) x 2 (prior users' success) x 2 (intelligence perceptions) design, were told that the study tested analytical reasoning abilities of undergraduate students, and received two sets of materials. The first set, which constituted the manipulation of prior user's success, was a study guide to help subjects in term of how to solve the analytical reasoning problems. Subjects were informed that given limited budgets for graduate student research, each study guide was designed for use by multiple respondents to reduce costs. Each study guide ostensibly had been completed by six previous respondents, and that their GPA was either relatively high or relatively low. In fact, there were no previous respondents, and the GPAs had been completed by the experimenters' research assistants. Subjects wrote down their own GPA, completed ten analytical reasoning problems, followed by thinking style and intelligence perception measures (Dweck, Hong, and Chiu 1993).

Analyses on the number of problems solved correctly yielded a main effect for prior users' success [M=3.89 vs. 4.71 for the low vs. high GPA conditions; F(1, 106)=5.10, p<.05], and the hypothesized 3-way interaction between thinking style, prior user's success, and intelligence perceptions; F(1, 106)=4.35, p<.05). The interaction between prior owner's success and intuitive processing was significant for those subjects who believed intelligence to be malleable [F(1, 51)=5.75, p<.01)] but not for those who believed intelligence to be fixed (F<1). Furthermore, actual performance on the analytical reasoning tasks of high intuitive processors who believed that intelligence was malleable was significantly greater when exposed to the study guide of high versus low prior users' success [M=5.58 vs. 3.21; F(1, 26)=10.12, p<.001]; however, performance did not differ for low intuitive processors (M=4.21 vs. 4.23; F<1).

"Can Switching Brands Help Your Favorite Team Win the Big Game?"

Eric Hamerman, Columbia University, USA
Gita Johar, Columbia University, USA

A large stream of literature in psychology has demonstrated that individuals are often susceptible to the illusion that they can affect certain events through actions that–by all rational accounts–should have no impact on the event in question. This illusion of control is likely to occur when pre-requisites of priority, consis tency, and exclusivity have been fulfilled (Wegner, 2002). Priority states that an action must occur before the event. If an individual orders a beer after watching a football game, he is unlikely to believe that his beverage choice had any impact on the outcome. Consistency is fulfilled when the outcome is consistent with the individual's intent. If a fan roots hard for his team to win by wearing a "lucky shirt", he is likely to believe that his wardrobe choice impacted the game only if his team won. Exclusivity holds true when there does not appear to be an alternative explanation. If the first-place team beats a last-place team, someone who roots for the winner could easily attribute the victory to the relative strength of the two teams, rather than to the intensity of his support.

In this paper, we suggest that consumer purchases may be viewed in certain situations as instruments to control an outside event, rather than as an attempt to purchase the "best product for the money" based on an evaluation of item attributes. Therefore, consumers will be said to use "superstitious strategies" to inform their purchase behavior when their perception of control over an outside event influences their buying decisions. We demonstrate that this phenomenon occurs even when individuals are aware that this control is merely an illusion.

In our first study, we examined lay theory beliefs about the use of superstition in purchase behavior. Participants read a hypothetical scenario about an individual who is either a big fan of–or indifferent towards–a basketball team. After ordering a non-favored beer–the favorite brand is temporarily out of stock–the team begins to immediately play either better or worse.

The principle of consistency held true only when the team began to play better (vs. worse) after placing the beverage order. In all conditions, priority and exclusivity were held constant. Therefore, this was a 2x2 between-subjects design, with factors of motivation (fan/not a fan) and consistency (team plays better/worse).

Respondents predicted that avid fans of the basketball team would vary their beer orders based on whether the outcome was consistent with their intent; they were more likely to stay with their non-favored brand when the team played well (vs. poorly). When the protagonist was not a fan, the outcome of the game was not expected to impact their choice.

In a second study, individuals participated in a simulated "trivia night" event that was described as taking place at two separate restaurants that differed in quality. Respondents were explicitly instructed that they had the exact same chance of winning at either establishment. After reporting initial preferences for each restaurant, subjects participated in four rounds of trivia: two at each locale. False feedback was distributed; scores either differed between the two restaurants or were equal at both establishments. For the fifth round, half of the subjects were given the opportunity to earn an additional cash prize by scoring well on the quiz (high motivation condition); all subjects were then asked to re-rate their relative preferences for each restaurant.

The principles of priority and exclusivity were both held constant during this experiment. Those who received scores that differed between locations were considered "high" in consistency, because there was a clear restaurant choice that was consistent with their intentions (to score well on the quiz). The experiment therefore included two between-subjects factors–consistency and motivation–each manipulated at the "high" vs. "low" levels. Subjects' relative preferences for the two restaurants prior to the practice quizzes–versus after the four practice rounds–served as a within-subjects factor ("time").

A main effect was discovered for the preference ratings over time. This was qualified by a significant interaction between Time

and Consistency: Results suggest that respondents allowed the feedback regarding their performance in the first four rounds (i.e., consistency between intent and outcome) to change their preference of restaurant venue over time, regardless of their level of motivation. However, participants reported that the "score on the trivia quiz" influenced their decision significantly less than "quality of the meal", "location", and "ambience".

In a third study, participants ate Snickers bars while watching what they believed to be either live or tape-delayed updates of their school's Intercollegiate Quiz Bowl Championship match. During this session, their school performed well. After the updates, the score was either listed as tied (so the outcome was uncertain) or lopsided (the outcome was no longer in doubt). Respondents were then given an opportunity to choose another chocolate (either Snickers or KitKat); the DV was the relative preference for each brand.

Unlike in the previous experiments, the principle of priority was manipulated through live or delayed updates of the match. Consistency was measured based on intensity of rooting interest; the school's strong performance was most consistent with those who were rooting intently for this to occur. Respondents were thought to be more motivated to impact the match when the score was tied (vs. when it was lopsided). This study is a 2x2x2 experimental design, with factors of consistency (rooting intensity: high or low), priority (live or time-delayed updates), and motivation (score of the match: close or blowout). An interaction was found between consistency, motivation, and priority, suggesting that when any pre-requisite for illusory control is met, individuals believe that they can impact the outcome of an outside event through their purchase behavior.

Taken together, these studies suggest that superstition is regularly deployed as a strategy during purchase decisions in order to impact the result of outside events. This occurs even as its users admit that the idea of such control is irrational.

"Causes and Consequences for the Belief in Tempting Fate"

Jane Risen, University of Chicago, USA
Thomas Gilovich, Cornell University, USA

It is an irony of the post-Enlightenment world that so many people who don't believe in fate refuse to tempt it. Whether due to culture, age, or stress, the magical thinking literature has traditionally stressed deficits in cognitive capacities. We contend that a complete understanding of magical thinking requires that one not only understand why the absence of cognitive capacities gives rise to magical beliefs, but also why the presence of certain psychological tendencies gives rise to magical beliefs among intelligent, emotionally-stable adults, well versed in the rules of logic.

The studies presented here provide evidence for an unexplored magical belief–the belief that it is bad luck to tempt fate. First, we demonstrate that people have the intuition that tempting fate will increase the likelihood of a negative outcome. Second, we argue that actions that tempt fate elevate the perceived likelihood of misfortune because such painful possibilities are automatically called to mind and, once entertained, they gain fluency and are seen as more likely to occur. Finally, we demonstrate that when the belief in tempting fate is made salient, people avoid the types of behaviors that are thought to tempt fate.

In order to document the magical belief, Study 1 used a between-participant scenario and measured subjective likelihood. The protagonist ("Jon") either tempted fate by being overly confident and presumptuous about the future or did not. We find that people are more likely to predict a negative outcome when fate has been tempted than when it has not. Specifically, participants believed that Jon was more likely to be rejected from Stanford if he wore a Stanford t-shirt while waiting for the school' decision than if he stuffed the shirt in a drawer while waiting.

Study 2 used the same scenario to test whether negative outcomes are more accessible following behaviors that tempt fate and whether accessibility predicts likelihood judgments. Participants were asked to read stories on the computer and indicate as quickly as possible whether a one-sentence ending made sense or whether it was a non sequitur. If the ending made sense, they rated the likelihood of the ending. Replicating Study 1, we found that participants who read that "Jon" wore the t-shirt thought he was more likely to be rejected than participants who read that he did not tempt fate. In addition, the rejection ending was more accessible for those who read that he tempted fate, and accessibility mediated likelihood judgments.

Studies 3 and 4 were designed to examine the conceptual structure of this culturally-shared belief and to examine how the notion of tempting fate can influence behavior. In Study 3, we find using hierarchical cluster analysis that "hubris" and "needless risk" composed the initial behavior clusters associated with the term tempting fate. In Study 4, we find that when people are primed with the shared belief in tempting fate, they avoid those behaviors associated with the belief. For example, we find that after participants filled out a tempting fate scale, they displayed less presumptuousness and hubris compared to those not primed; they made less optimistic predictions for their future and less over-confident claims about their traits and abilities. The tendency to "restrain" displays of hubris was similar for those who indicated an explicit belief in tempting fate and those who did not.

Although the belief in tempting fate is typically considered an example of irrational, superstitious thinking, this work suggests that this "irrational" belief results from very basic cognitive processes and may promote positive, pro-social behaviors such as humility and moderation.

"Why Calling Attention to Success Seems to Invite Failure"
Justin Kruger, New York University, USA
Jane Risen, University of Chicago, USA
Thomas Gilovich, Cornell University, USA
Ken Savitsky, Williams College, USA

"Bragging about one's good fortune is to invite misfortune. To say, 'I haven't had a cold all winter' is to wake up the following day snuffling."
— *Ferm (1959/1989)*

Calling attention to an ongoing streak of success is widely believed to invite failure. Commenting on a "no-hitter" before a baseball game is over, for example, is thought to "jinx" the pitcher and undermine his success. Recalling his legendary no-hitter in the 1956 World Series against the Brooklyn Dodgers, New York Yankees pitcher Don Larson noted that "Nobody would talk to me, nobody would sit by me, like I had the plague. . . . Some of the guys didn't want to say anything, afraid they'd put a jinx on it" (Aubrecht, 2002).

The present research empirically documents and partially explains this superstition. In Study 1, participants read one of three hypothetical scenarios about two lucky individuals or groups of individuals: two gamblers who had each won six consecutive hands of blackjack, two sports car owners who had each managed to avoid hail damage to their treasured vehicles, or two rainforest expeditions that had each avoided snakebites, mudslides, and a variety of other dangers lurking in the jungle. In one version of the scenarios,

the streak of luck was pointed out by someone (the casino dealer, the car-owner's wife, or the expedition guide), and in the other it was not. As expected, participants indicated that the streak was more likely to come to an end if it was verbally mentioned than if it was not.

Study 2 examined the superstition in a non-hypothetical situation involving real behavior. Participants played a series of gambles, with the outcomes determined by drawing from three urns ostensibly made up of winning (blue) and losing (yellow) pieces. The experimenter explained that he would draw three times from the first urn, twice from the second urn, and once from the third urn, and that the number of winners and losers drawn would determine the participant's final payment.

Participants were given a form to keep track of the outcome of each draw and to estimate the composition of the urns. After making sure that participants understood the rules, the experimenter started to draw pieces from the first urn. Unbeknownst to participants, the urns contained exclusively winning (blue) pieces. After drawing 3 winning pieces from the first urn and 2 winning pieces from the second urn, he either commented on the streak by saying, "Wow, that's five in a row. You're on quite a streak. If this keeps up, you could win more money than anyone else," or he did not comment on the streak and simply said, "Blue." After making their estimates about the composition of the final urn participants were given the option of having the experimenter draw from the third urn or having the experiment end without the final draw. The experimenter explained that if participants stopped, they would leave with $4. If they continued, they would earn $6 if a blue piece were drawn and $2 if a yellow piece were drawn.

As expected, when the experimenter verbally noted participants' streak of five consecutive wins, participants expressed less confidence that they would win on the sixth trial and thought the objective odds of winning were less in their favor. As well, they were more likely to take the experimenters offer to stop playing and take a sure $4 rather than risk losing (or gaining) $2 by drawing from the third and final urn.

What causes the superstition? One possibility is a misunderstanding of regression to the mean. Because calling attention to success by definition only occurs after a run of good fortune, subsequent performance is likely to regress towards the overall mean. Commenting on a pitcher's ongoing perfect game, for instance, *is* likely to be followed by someone getting on base in the next inning—not because the pitcher has been cursed, but because teams, on average, get at least one person on base in most innings. More generally, comments about on-going success are correlated with diminished outcomes because exceptional performance at one period (which tends to elicit such comments) is followed, on average, by less exceptional performance the next. To the extent that people mistake this correlation for cause, the superstition is borne.

Study 3 was designed to test this explanation by creating a novel superstition in the lab. Participants played numerous rounds of a simple videogame. Unbeknownst to them, the outcome of each trial was random—that is, p(success)=p(failure)=.5. In addition, the background of the game changed after three hits, which, given the number of trials involved and the probability of a hit, was virtually guaranteed to occur at least once for each participant. Also virtually guaranteed was the fact that, on average, this change in background would be associated with a relative decline in performance, since a run of three hits in a row is unlikely to be followed by a similarly successful streak. We then asked participants to describe what influence, if any, the background had on the difficulty of the game (as well as a control background that occurred after three misses). Despite the fact that outcomes were unrelated to the background (i.e., the probability of a hit on a particular trial was .5 regardless of the background), we found that participants tended to view the background that appeared after a string of hits as a bad omen. Of key importance, participants not only thought that the background change tended to be followed by a decrease in performance (which it did), but that it *caused* that decrease in performance (which it did not).

Taken together, this research suggests that people believe that calling attention to success is bad luck, and traces the superstition to a misunderstanding of statistical regression (sometimes known as the regression fallacy). Discussion focuses on the scope and everyday implications of these findings.

REFERENCES

Argo, Jennifer J., Darren W. Dahl, and Andrea C. Morales (2006), "Consumer Contamination: How Consumers React to Products Touched by Others," *Journal of Marketing*, 70 (2), 81-94.

Argo, Jennifer J., Darren W. Dahl, and Andrea C. Morales (2008), "Positive Consumer Contamination: Responses to Attractive Others in a Retail Context," *Journal of Marketing Research*, forthcoming.

Bleak, Jared L. and Christina M. Frederick, (1998), "Superstitious Behavior in Sport: Levels of Effectiveness and Determinants of Use in Three College Sports", *Journal of Sport Behavior*, 21 (1), 1-15.

Dweck, Carol S., Ying-yi Hong, and Chi-yue Chiu (1993), "Implicit Theories: Individual Differences in the Likelihood and Meaning of Dispositional Inference," *Personality and Social Psychology Bulletin*, 19 (5), 644-56.

Epstein, Seymour, Rosemary Pacini, Veronik Denes-Raj, and Harriet Heier (1996), "Individual Differences in Intuitive-Experiential and Analytical-Rational Thinking Styles," *Journal of Personality and Social Psychology*, 71 (2), 390-405.

Helft, Miguel (2007), "Rental Building's Good Karma Nurtures Silicon Valley Success," *New York Times*, September 14, A1

Kramer, Thomas and Lauren Block (2008), "Conscious and Nonconscious Components of Superstitious Beliefs in Judgment and Decision Making", *Journal of Consumer Research*, 34 (6), 783-793.

Morales, Andrea C. and Gavan J. Fitzsimons (2007), "Product Contagion: Changing Consumer Evaluations through Physical Contact with 'Disgusting' Products," *Journal of Marketing Research*, 44 (2), 272-283.

Mowen, John C. and Brad Carlson (2003), "Exploring the Antecedents and Consumer Behavior Consequences of the Trait of Superstition", *Psychology and Marketing*, 20 (12), 1045-1065.

Pronin, Emily, Daniel M. Wegner, Kimberly McCarthy and Sylvia Rodriguez (2006), "Everyday Magical Powers: The Role of Apparent Mental Causation in the Overestimation of Personal Influence", *Journal of Personality and Social Psychology*, 91 (2), 218-231.

Rozin, Paul, Linda Millman, and Carol Nemeroff (1986), "Operation of the Laws of Sympathetic Magic in Disgust and Other Domains," *Journal of Personality and Social Psychology*, 50 (4), 703-12.

Rozin, Paul, Heidi Grant, Stephanie Weinberg, and Scott Parker (2007), "Head versus Heart: Effect of Monetary Frames on Expression of Sympathetic Magical Concerns," *Judgment and Decision Making*, 2 (4), 217-224.

Wegner, Daniel M., The Illusion of Conscious Will. Cambridge: MIT Press, 2002.

Wegner, Daniel M and Thalia Wheatley (1999), "Apparent Mental Causation: Sources of the Experience of Will", *American Psychologist*, 54 (7), 480-492.

Social Networks and Consumer Behavior

Andrew Stephen, Columbia University, USA
Jonah Berger, University of Pennsylvania, USA

EXTENDED ABSTRACTS

"Opinion Leadership and Social Contagion in New Product Diffusion"

Raghuram Iyengar, University of Pennsylvania, USA
Thomas Valente, University of Southern California, USA
Christophe Van den Bulte, University of Pennsylvania, USA

We investigate the role of network position and opinion leadership in social contagion. Our study combines actual network data on advice and patient referral ties among physicians in three cities, demographic data on those physicians as well as a measure of self-reported opinion leadership, individual-level prescription data for the new drug as well as two other drugs launched earlier for treatment of the same medical condition, and individual-level sales-call data for the new drug. This data set allows us to perform a modified replication of the classic study *Medical Innovation* as extended by Van den Bulte and Lilien, with the additional benefit that the marketing effort variable varies not only over time but across physicians as well. Hence, we are able to investigate the presence of contagion dynamics in real market settings in which more traditional marketing efforts are being deployed as well, a question that is of great importance to both practitioners and researchers.

Another key feature of our study is that we use both sociometric and self-reported measures of opinion leadership. Physicians who are often nominated by their peers as people they turn to for expertise and discussion about disease management are likely to be true sources of influence. Physicians, who perceive themselves to be influential, in contrast, may indeed be so but may also have an inflated sense of self-importance. As a result, not everyone who believes is an opinion leader will actually be at the cutting edge of medical practice due to above-average expertise and clinical judgment. On the other hand, early adoption may be affected more by how one perceives oneself than by one's true status. This raises the possibility that sociometric leaders and self-reported leaders do not adopt equally early, but leaves the sequence in doubt.

A final distinctive feature of our study is that we observe not only time of adoption but also the number of prescriptions (usage volume) in each subsequent month. This allows us to shed further light on who is influential when. Prior research indicates that opinion leadership is associated with product involvement, suggesting that it is also associated with usage level. Someone who is using the product extensively is likely to be more enthusiastic and credible than someone who is not. To the extent that peers' product usage affects the amount of contagion exerted on potential adopters, heavy users are more influential and hence more attractive seeding points in a viral campaign, over and above their greater "stand alone" customer value.

We address three research questions. First, is there social contagion operating over social ties such that better connected adopters exert more influence than less connected ones, over and above the effect of marketing efforts and system-wide influences that vary over time? Second, to what extent does sociometric and self-reported opinion leadership overlap, and do they have the same influence on the time of adoption? Finally, is contagion emanating from prior adopters a function of their product usage, i.e., is their social influence affected by their usage status or volume rather than simply by their having tried the product?

We find evidence of social contagion even after controlling for marketing effort and controlling non-parametrically for any other changes over time. This justifies the deployment of network-based marketing strategies with the hope of accelerating new product diffusion. It further suggests that the dyadic social influence between individuals that is often observed in the lab can aggregate into broad social phenomena such as trends. In addition, we find that the influence of prior adopters is moderated by their prescription volume of the new drug, suggesting that heavy users are attractive viral seeding points over and above their greater "stand alone" customer value. Finally, the results indicate that sociometric and self-reported leadership are different constructs. Not only are their measures only weakly correlated, but they behave differently in the theoretical or nomological network we study. Sociometric leadership has a direct, main effect on time of adoption but does not moderate the sensitivity to social contagion. Self-reported leadership, in contrast, not only has a main effect but is also associated with a lower sensitivity to social contagion.

Taken together, these results provide insight into how social networks and actual product experience influence diffusion.

"Social Hubs: Do They Exist and What is their Role?"

Jacob Goldenberg, Hebrew University, Israel
Donald Lehmann, Columbia University, USA
Sangman Han, Sungkyunkwan University, Korea

Growth processes are important to marketing in general, and new product adoption in particular, where the diffusion of an innovation is governed, among other things, by word of mouth. In social systems, growth processes are thought to be strongly influenced by individuals who have large number of ties to other people. Although recent work by Watts and Dodds (2007) suggest that this influence was overrated, a heated debate about their existence and magnitude of impact of influentials exist.

In the social network literature, such people are called influentials, opinion leaders, mavens or sometimes hubs. Somewhat surprisingly, however, until recently there has been relatively little attention paid to these individuals in the marketing literature. Further, when the marketing literature does address such individuals, the focus is typically not on how they influence the overall market, but rather on either assessing their influence on people they are in direct contact with or identifying their characteristics. Broadly speaking, influential people are thought to have three important traits: 1) they are convincing (maybe even charismatic), 2) they know a lot (i.e., are experts), and 3) they have large number of social ties, they know a lot of people.

We focus on the third trait and present empirical findings on social hubs–individuals who maintain a large number of ties to other people–and their influence on the overall process of innovation adoption. We argue, somewhat contrary to recent suggestions, that social hubs adopt sooner than other people not because they are innovative but rather because they are exposed earlier to an innovation due to their multiple social links. We examine this argument using a mapped network and data on diffusion processes. Although social hubs have a higher adoption threshold, thus making them less "innovative," they adopt sooner than less connected individuals because their exposure exceeds this threshold sooner.

We further distinguish between innovator and follower hubs. We show that the first influence mainly the speed of the adoption in a network while the latter influence mainly the number of people that eventually adopt the innovation. The reason for the difference is consistent with dual market theories: innovative hubs adopt sooner and they turn on the process. If they adopt later the entire process will be slower. However, innovators are not trusted by the majority so innovative hubs have less influence on the market size. Follower hubs however are more reliable and their adoption can influence people to consider adoption as well. Hence they have a small influence on the speed of growth but a strong influence on market size. We also show that a small sample of hubs can be used to make an early forecast of the entire diffusion process.

Finally, we examine the advice and recommendation interaction from a point of view of an advice seeker. We focus on case in which advice providers can be people with high or low technical expertise (high in technical knowledge) and/or high or low socially connection. Somewhat contrary to intuition, information sources who are high on social connectivity are hypothesized to be relatively more attractive for more innovative products in case of a low innovativeness individuals. Consistent with this, a meta-analysis indicates that the correlation between knowledge and opinion leadership is indeed lower for more innovative products. Our studies also show that innovators consistently prefer to consult with people who are high on technical expertise, while those who are less innovative prefer to consult with socially connected individuals for more radical new products. For incremental products they prefer the experts. Finally, we show that while even less innovative consumers prefer to consult with experts about technical performance attributes for radical innovations, they still prefer to talk to a socially connected person for information about attributes that require skill to use.

Overall, this research provides an array of findings about social hubs and their role in diffusion and social contagion.

"Creating Contagious: Cascades in Spatially Dispersed Social Networks"

Andrew Stephen, Columbia University, USA
Jonah Berger, University of Pennsylvania, USA

What drives social epidemics? Cultural information and practices (e.g., products, websites, songs, or ideas) often spread like viruses across social ties between people. This diffusion is a key process through which consumers learn about new products. Further, it can be responsible for a product's amazing success (or dismal failure) with relatively little, if any, investment in conventional marketing communications or promotion strategies. But what drives these situations where products spread like wildfire through a population? How does (a) the number and network position of the early adopters and (b) characteristics of the cultural item being shared influence whether the item catches on?

This paper explores these questions by studying how information spreads across a realistic social network. People belong to physical communities (e.g., geographic centers) and are socially tied to other people both within and outside their communities. We use a stochastically generated social network of 1,000 people and an agent-based simulation model to consider the diffusion of a new product across a range of conditions. In this model, information about an innovation spreads over social network ties, and consumers are "infected" on a continuous scale. Consumers who have higher infection levels can be seen as more aware or enthusiastic about the innovation, and thus more likely to influence other consumers. Every period, one of each consumer's friends is randomly chosen as a potential influencer. We then use a simple influence model where consumers' influence one another based on their own level of awareness or infection.

We examine how characteristics of the early adopters and of the innovation itself determine how widely and quickly a product catches on. Regarding early adopters, we vary the proportion of the population that is initially infected (via advertising, for example). We also vary how the early adopters are spatially distributed over the network (i.e., where they are positioned) and their connectivity characteristics (e.g., are they well-connected with many friends or less connected but within reach of many others?). The positions of the early adopters can also be thought of in terms of the "seeding strategy" that a marketer might use to try to initiate a cascade (e.g., select the well-connected people, randomly select people). Regarding the innovation itself, we vary how conducive it is to spreading. Some products or information spread easily while others are more difficult to diffuse. Specifically, some innovations are easy to try whereas others require much greater interest. Thus, we vary the trial (or adoption) threshold. Also, while products or ideas may be top of mind right after a person hears about them, their accessibility, or how enthusiastic people are about the innovation, soon declines. We therefore vary the rate at which this decline or decay occurs, with higher decay rates meaning that the innovation is harder to remember over time.

We then examine how these factors influence product adoption. In particular, how quickly and broadly the product catches on. We find that the network positions of early adopters can dramatically impact diffusion outcomes, particularly in cases that are not conducive to diffusion (e.g., information being hard to remember or adoption requiring high awareness or enthusiasm). Even when the innovation's characteristics are well suited to it catching on the network positions of the early adopters influences adoption outcomes. Interestingly, when early adopters are well-connected (the traditional definition of a social hub or an opinion leader), the innovation does not diffuse widely and does not take-off. However, when early-adopters are positioned between many other people (i.e., social intermediaries) the innovation is much more likely to achieve widespread success. In fact, even when the early adopters have few connections, but are randomly dispersed throughout the network, more people eventually adopt the product than when early adopters are well-connected. This suggests that how well-connected early adopters are is largely inconsequential; rather, where they are positioned in the network is what influences whether they trigger a successful cascade. We also find evidence of some compensatory effects between the characteristics of the innovation. In particular, the adoption-dampening effects of high adoption thresholds can be mitigated by low decay rates (although the reverse is not true: high decay rates are not offset by low adoption thresholds).

In contrast to recent findings (Watts and Dodds 2007) our results suggest that easily influenced people are not necessary for cascades to occur. Rather social epidemics depend on the positions of the early adopters. In fact, cascades can still occur "against all odds" (i.e., when conditions are not conducive to diffusion) provided that the early adopters are positioned throughout the network. Overall, these results provide insights into how different initial conditions and micro-level behaviors influence macro-level outcomes in social contagion processes. They have direct implications to research on word of mouth, social influence, and diffusion more broadly.

SYMPOSIUM SUMMARY
The IAT in Marketing

Claude Messner, University of Basel, Switzerland
Joachim Vosgerau, Carnegie Mellon University, USA

SESSION OVERVIEW

The Implicit Association Test has become a popular tool for measuring implicit attitudes, presumably because the IAT is characterized by a unique combination of impressive effect size and effortless implementation. The IAT attracted massive media attention (e.g., in "Blink" by Gladwell 2005), and was featured on TV shows (e.g. "The Oprah Winfrey Show" on 06/06/2007) as a tool to uncover implicit racism. Originally introduced to social psychology, the IAT has been extended to clinical psychology, organizational psychology, the law, and marketing. Marketing research companies have started to use the IAT as a measure of "true" preferences and brand associations.

Despite the huge interest sparked among academics and practitioners, critical examinations of the IAT's methodology and predictive validity have received only limited attention. A notable exception are Brunel, Tietje, and Greenwald (2004) who discuss some of the methodological issues surrounding the IAT in marketing. However, the two most important issues, order-effects and assumptions behind the measurement model of the IAT, have not been investigated. Because methodologies developed in clinical research settings should undergo thorough critical examination before being used in applied disciplines such as Marketing, the symposium is aimed at investigating the role and consequences of order-effects and violations of IAT assumptions.

In the first paper, Messner and Vosgerau explain the logic of the IAT design and empirically demonstrate a procedural effect (an order effect of the IAT-blocks) and its impact on correlations of the IAT with predictor criteria. Counterbalancing or keeping order constant are shown not to alleviate the problem. In the second paper, Blanton explores the underlying measurement model and assumptions for the interpretation of IAT-effects. Stuettgen and Boatwright argue in the third paper that these assumptions (as identified by Blanton) are likely to be violated in marketing contexts, and examine via simulations how violations of the IAT-assumptions impact the validity of the IAT.

Concluding, order-effects and measurement assumptions are crucial determinants for the validity of the IAT in marketing research. The three papers explore the consequences of order-effects and violations of measurement assumptions for IAT-effects, and suggest solutions to overcome these issues.

EXTENDED ABSTRACTS

"Order Effects in the IAT"

Claude Messner, University of Basel, Switzerland
Joachim Vosgerau, Carnegie Mellon University, USA

Marketing researchers are becoming increasingly interested in non-conscious influences on consumer behavior. A central concept of non-conscious influences are implicit attitudes, which are defined as "...introspectively unidentified (or inaccurately identified) traces of past experience that mediate favorable or unfavorable feeling, thought, or action toward social objects" (Greenwald and Banaji 1995, p. 8). Implicit attitudes are thought of being potentially better predictors of behavior than explicit (self-reported) attitudes, because consumers might be unwilling to reveal their attitudes when the attitude concerns stigmatized behavior (e.g., racists atti-

tudes), or because they are unable to reveal their attitudes as they might lack the ability for correct introspection (Brunel et al. 2004).

The Implicit Association Test (IAT) has become the most popular tool for measuring implicit attitudes, presumably because the IAT is characterized by a unique combination of impressive effect size and effortless implementation. The IAT was initially introduced to social psychology (Greenwald, McGhee, and Schwartz 1998), and has since been applied in clinical psychology, organizational behavior, the law, and marketing. Outside the academic realm, the IAT has attracted massive media attention as a tool to uncover implicit racism, and is used by marketing research firms as a measure of "true" preferences and brand associations.

We focus on an internal validity problem of the IAT that has not been investigated to date, so called order-effects. Consider an Coca Cola versus Pepsi IAT in which participants favor Coke over Pepsi. In the 'compatible' block participants learn to exploit the association between Coca Cola and the positive words, but in the subsequent 'incompatible' block must respond in the opposite direction, that is Coca Cola and negative words. Switching from applying one categorization rule to applying an opposite categorization rule is cognitively demanding and requires time and practice. So, ceteris paribus, cognitive inertia leads to slower responses in the second block, no matter whether it is 'compatible' or 'incompatible'. Order-effects now accrue from the interplay of cognitive inertia (slower responses in the second block) and the IAT-effect (faster responses in the 'compatible' block). When the faster 'compatible' block comes first, cognitive inertia slows down responses in the subsequent 'incompatible' block, thereby augmenting the difference in response latencies between the two blocks (i.e. enlarging the IAT-effect). In contrast, when the 'incompatible' block precedes the faster 'compatible' block, cognitive inertia slows down responses in the faster 'compatible' block (i.e., decreasing the IAT-effect).

In study 1 we conducted an Coca Cola versus Pepsi IAT and counterbalance the order of the blocks. As expected, when the 'compatible' block came first an IAT-effect in favor of Coca Cola was found (t(24)=4.41, $p<.01$), but no IAT-effect was found when the 'incompatible' block came first (t(25)=0.05, $p=.96$). Learning within blocks confirmed that the order-effect was due to cognitive inertia. Learning in the second block was always slower than learning in the first block, no matter which block came first and which second.

In study 2, we show that cognitive inertia can be so strong that it reverses the IAT-effect. We chose positive and negative stimuli such that Coca Cola was more strongly associated with either than Pepsi. The stronger association of Coca Cola with positive *and* negative words implied no IAT-effect at the aggregate level (neither in favor of Coca Cola nor Pepsi). However, an IAT-effect in favor of Coca Cola was found when the *Coca Cola & positive words* block came first (t (22)=2.91, $p<.01$), but an IAT-effect in favor of Pepsi was found when the *Coca Cola & negative words* block was administered first (t (24)=3.66, $p<.01$). And as in study 1, learning was always slower in the block that came second.

IAT-effects crucially depend on the selection of the positive and negative stimuli. Thus, the previous cognitive inertia effects might be a result of the positive and negative stimuli that were used.

We therefore conducted study 3 with the original positive and negative stimuli from Greenwald et al.'s (1998) study 1 and 2. The targets were coffee versus black tea. As in study 2, no IAT-effect was observed on the aggregate level. However, in accordance with cognitive inertia, an IAT-effect in favor of coffee was found when the *coffee & positive words* block came first (t (29)=3.34, p<.01), but an IAT-effect in favor of black tea was found when the *coffee & negative words* block was administered first (t (29)=2.68, p<.01). Again, learning was always slower in the block that was administered second.

Order-effects introduce so much noise in IAT-scores that they can wipe out (study 1) and reverse IAT-effects (study 2 and 3). Order-effects thus distort individual IAT-scores and render correlations with predictor variables almost meaningless. The common practice of counterbalancing block-order between-subjects cancels out order-effects on the aggregate level, but on the individual level IAT-scores are still contaminated with cognitive inertia effects.

We eliminate cognitive inertia-effects in study 4 by manipulating block-order repeatedly within- instead of between-subjects, using the same stimuli as in study 1. One group was administered the block-sequence CICIC where C denotes the block in which Coca Cola is paired with the pleasant stimuli, and I denotes the block where Coca Cola is paired with the unpleasant stimuli. The other group was administered the complementary block-sequence ICICI. When the first two blocks were used to compute IAT-effects, we found the same order-effect as in study 1, that is an IAT-effect in favor of Coca Cola when the compatible block came first (t (26)=5.33, p<.01), and no IAT-effect when the incompatible block came first (t (25)=0.46, p=.65). In contrast, when the last two blocks were used to compute IAT-effects, no difference in the IAT-effects was observed between the two block-sequences (F (1, 51)=0.67, p=.42).

Concluding, when block-order is manipulated between-subjects IAT-scores should only be interpreted on the group level. When individual IAT-scores are of interest, for example when IAT-scores are to be correlated with predictor variables, block-order should be manipulated repeatedly within-subjects.

"Looking Past the Claims: A Psychometric Analysis of the Implicit Association Test"
Hart Blanton, Texas A&M University, USA

The past decade has seen a dramatic increase in the use of implicit attitude measures, and the most popular measure by far has been the Implicit Association Test (IAT). Despite evidence of weak IAT-criterion relationships across many behavioral domains, strong claims have been made regarding the validity of this measure and its ability to improve our understanding and prediction of important social behaviors. Despite the excitement surrounding this new measure, closer inspection reveals a lack of psychometric justification. To date, no formal psychometric model has been published that can justify its scoring conventions. In my talk, I examine the theory, methods and analytic strategies surrounding the IAT to determine the psychometric model that a researcher embraces (knowingly or unknowingly) whenever this measure is used.

I will begin by presenting empirical data showing that the IAT has a misspecified measurement model. The equivalent in traditional questionnaire development would occur if a researcher were to incorporate a multi-dimensional scale into his or her research program and then incorrectly interpret results as though the scale were unidimensional in nature. This type of error pervades the IAT literature.

As I show, IAT scores are influenced by three latent factors. Two of these factors assess distinct and empirically uncorrelated association strengths. The third assesses a person's general processing speed. Despite the complex factor structure of the IAT, researchers commonly interpret even very small correlations between the IAT and psychological criteria as evidence of validity. Interestingly, however, the IAT's previously unexamined factor structure can help explain why (1) the IAT rarely provides strong criterion prediction and (2) IAT scores are often independent of explicit self-reports.

I next show that researchers who use the IAT impose a restricted causal model into their studies, one that typically is not germane to their research questions. The causal model built into the IAT results from its construction as a measure of *relative* implicit attitudes. Specifically, association strengths for two attitude objects are assessed simultaneously (e.g., attitude towards smoking and attitudes towards candy). Further, this assessment is done in such a way that researchers cannot justify treating one "attitude object" as the focal object being evaluated and the other as the "scale" or "metric" against which this object is evaluated. These features require a researcher to adopt strict causal assumptions that, when not met, can cause one to unwittingly model relationships that are not of theoretical interest. As I will show, failure to consider this fact has likely resulted in faulty inferences regarding the nature of implicit attitudes and the types of influences they exert on behavioral decisions (Stuettgen and Boatwright in this symposium present simulation results that quantify the consequences of embracing such faulty assumptions).

I present a study where we assess (1) attitudes towards apples and (2) attitudes towards oranges. We show that (1) the IAT measurement strategy quite literally mixes apples with oranges (along with general processing speed), (2) the IAT measurement strategy cannot be used to represent a person's true "fruit attitude structure," and (3) the IAT causal model can cause researchers to draw faulty inferences about the influence of apples and oranges in the liking of apples sauce, orange marmalade and fruit salad. Although this study was conducted somewhat tongue and cheek the implications for consumer research are quite serious.

I then review more traditional data on the IAT, including its low test-retest reliability and its responsiveness to social context and laboratory manipulations. I also explore the implications of these features for past claims that the IAT assesses stable trait constructs that influence behavioral criteria.

Finally, I turn my attention to attempts to address shortcomings by IAT researchers. IAT researchers recently have introduced a new IAT scoring algorithm, termed the "D Score" that ostensibly addresses many of the problems highlighted here. I explain how this method works and show that it not only fails to address the above but actually introduces new confounds and further undermines the measurement model.

I close by suggesting new measurement techniques that can begin to address the limitations in the IAT and that will provide marketers with a clearer guide to testing theories about consumer behavior.

"Assessing the Assumptions Behind the IAT"
Peter Stuettgen, Carnegie Mellon University, USA
Peter Boatwright, Carnegie Mellon University, USA

Imagine you go to a restaurant with your friends. One of your friends orders Coke, but the waitress tells him that they only have Pepsi. She asks him whether he would like Pepsi instead. What do you think your friend would do? Order Pepsi or order a different soft drink? What would you do in this situation?

We asked 130 undergraduate students enrolled in a marketing class these two questions ("What do you think your friend would do", and "What would you do?"). 88% expected their friend to order Pepsi instead, and 84% would also choose Pepsi themselves (both ratios are significantly different from 50%, chi-square >12.90, p<.001; we ran these scenarios also in the opposite direction, Coke being substituted for Pepsi. Results are similar).

While it is hardly surprising that most consumers are happy to substitute Coke with Pepsi or vice versa, consumer researchers have to assume exactly the opposite when using the IAT. The calculation of the IAT-effect requires the following relationship to hold: if Coke is someone's favorite choice, Pepsi should be one of her/his *least* preferred options (cf. Blanton's talk). In the IAT, averaging the within-block response latencies assumes a positive correlation between the two association strengths measured within one block, and subtracting the two blocks from each other assumes that the blocks are negatively correlated. Combined, this means that the more a consumer associates one of the target constructs (e.g., Coke) with one of the evaluative poles (e.g., positive), the more s/he should associate the other target construct (e.g., Pepsi) with the opposite evaluative pole (e.g., negative). In the example in the beginning, this assumption would imply that the consumer switched to a different soft drink altogether rather than substituting it with Pepsi.

This assumption on the relationship between the attitudes towards Coke and Pepsi is (1) never observable (since implicit attitudes are not directly observable) and (2) likely to be violated in marketing contexts where two products or brands are compared. In the case of Coke versus Pepsi, the more a consumer associates Coke with positive the more s/he also associates Pepsi with positive. The reason is that attitudes toward Coke and Pepsi are mainly driven by attitudes toward the product category "cola-drinks". The more a consumer likes cola-drinks, the more s/he will like Coke, and also Pepsi. This is illustrated in the opening scenario where, even though a consumer might prefer Coke over Pepsi (or vice versa), s/he is happy to substitute one for the other. Given these two problems with this assumption, we examine via simulations its importance for the IAT's validity.

In particular, we define 8 variables: four variables which represent the implicit association strengths to be measured in the IAT (e.g., Coke/positive, Coke/negative, Pepsi/positive, and Pepsi/negative), and another four variables that represent the IAT-measurements of these implicit attitude strengths as reaction times. We then simulate random draws from the 8x8 correlation matrix with a Gibbs sampler. By implementing constraints in the simulations of the correlation matrix we can therefore control for whether the assumption is satisfied or not. We derive a formula to calculate a measure for the IAT's validity from these correlation matrices. This measure is simply the correlation between the IAT-effect as calculated from the observed reaction times with the IAT-effect as calculated from the simulated implicit attitudes. If the IAT was a perfect measure, this correlation should be equal to 1.

The results confirm the intuition that the IAT is on average as good a measure for the relative attitude between the two target constructs as response latencies are for each individual association strength (which are measured by the correlation between the observed reaction times and the simulated implicit attitudes).

However, the IAT assumption determines crucially whether the IAT is a better instrument than the individual response latencies, or a worse instrument. In particular, when the assumption is satisfied (i.e., the correlation between the two implicit attitudes is negative), the validity of the IAT is relatively high, even if response latencies are only a crude measure of implicit attitudes. This is because in this case the calculation of the IAT-effect combines the observed measures in a way to minimize the measurement errors contained in each measure individually. In contrast, when the assumption is violated, the validity of the IAT drops to low levels even if response latencies are very good measures of implicit attitudes. Thus, in this case interpreting the IAT-effect in the standard way is questionable.

These results suggest that the question of whether the assumption behind the IAT is satisfied or not may be more important for the validity of the IAT than the currently highly debated issue of whether response latencies are an accurate measure of implicit attitudes. Concluding, we offer advice on how to use the IAT in marketing in order to ensure its validity. In particular, whether the assumption is satisfied or not is not necessarily an inherent feature of the two target constructs to be compared, but may differ with the sample taking the IAT. For instance, in Maison et al.'s (2004) study of consumer preferences between Coke and Pepsi, the IAT performed well in predicting subsequent choice for those participants who could clearly distinguish and had clear preferences between the two brands. We conclude with the demand that IAT studies in marketing should include a discussion about how likely this crucial assumption is to be satisfied for a given sample and target categories.

REFERENCES

Brunel, Frédéric F., Brian C. Tietje, and Anthony G. Greenwald (2004), "Is the Implicit Association Test a Valid and Valuable Measure of Implicit Consumer Social Cognition?," *Journal of Consumer Psychology*, 14 (4), 385-404.

Gladwell, Malcolm (2005), *Blink: The Power of Thinking without Thinking*. New York, NY: Little, Brown and Company.

Greenwald, Anthony G. and Mahzarin R. Banaji (1995), "Implicit Social Cognition: Attitudes, Self-Esteem, and Stereotypes," *Psychological Review*, 102 (1), 4-27.

Greenwald, Anthony G., Debbie E. McGhee, and Jordan L. K. Schwartz (1998), "Measuring Individual Differences in Implicit Cognition: The Implicit Association Test," *Journal of Personality and Social Psychology*, 74 (6), 1464-80.

Maison, Dominika, Anthony G. Greenwald, and Ralph H. Bruin (2004), "Predictive Validity of the Implicit Association Test in Studies of Brands, Consumer Attitudes, and Behavior," *Journal of Consumer Psychology*, 14 (4), 405-15.

New Perspectives in Global Branding
Carlos Torelli, University of Minnesota, USA

SESSION OVERVIEW

One of the most difficult choices that multinational corporations face is deciding whether to standardize their communication strategy or to customize it to the taste of consumers in different cultural settings. As new global markets emerge, and existing markets become increasingly segmented along ethnic or subcultural lines, the need to market effectively to consumers who have different cultural values has never been more important (Shavitt, Lee, and Torelli 2008). Linking a brand to the multiple, and sometimes dissimilar, valued states and identity concerns of consumers in multi-cultural environments is becoming an increasingly complex task. To succeed in this endeavor, branding professionals need to identify the types of brand associations that are more likely to appeal to consumers in global markets. What brand characteristics do consumers with different cultural orientations prefer? What brand signals are more likely to positively impact brand credibility in multi-cultural settings? Do some consumers have a more positive attitude toward global brands than others? And if so, who are these consumers? This symposium unites under a common theme of providing insights on some of the factors that impact brand preferences and the formation of brand attitudes in globalized economies.

The first paper by Torelli et al. examines the relationships that multicultural consumers establish with their brands. The authors integrate past research on the human characteristics associated with brands (Aaker 1997) with that on the universals of human values (Schwartz 1992) and on cross-cultural differences in the relative importance of values (Triandis and Gelfand 1998), to develop a measure of the values that multi-cultural consumers associate with their brands (brand values scale or BVS). Based on the notion that consumers prefer brands with characteristics congruent with those that describe them (Malhotra 1988), they further predict cross-cultural patterns of brand preferences. Results from four studies, using multi-country samples of consumers, show that the BVS is a reliable and cross-culturally general measure of brand value associations. The findings also suggest that the cultural dimensions of vertical-horizontal, individualism-collectivism predict consumers' preferences for brands associated with culturally-congruent values. This research not only provides a cross-culturally general measure of brand representations, but shows the effect of cultural factors on brand preferences.

The second paper by Erdem, Swait, and Valenzuela explores cross-cultural differences on the antecedents of brand credibility. The authors suggest that in cultures that legitimize status differentials among their members (i.e., high-power distance), brand investments may be relatively more important for creating brand credibility. This is because the commitment that is signaled by this type of branding effort can help to mitigate the general distrust of authority in these cultural environments. In contrast, in cultures that foster the subordination of individual goals to the goals of the ingroup (i.e., collectivism, Triandis & Gelfand, 1998), or in those in which their members exhibit high-levels of risk aversion (i.e., high uncertainty avoidance, Hofstede 1980), consistency in the marketing mix (e.g., price and distribution) may lead to higher levels of brand credibility. This is because brand consistency reduces ambiguity and increases the strength of brand-group connections. A survey including brands from two different product categories (juices and PCs) and administered in 5 different countries provided empirical evidence for the predicted relationships.

This stream of research provides further insight into the effects of cultural factors on the formation of brand credibility judgments.

The final paper by Zhang and Khare enhances our understanding of the effects of the self-identity concerns of global consumers on brand preferences. Arnett (2002) proposed that, in globalized economies, consumers can develop both a local identity, characterized by identification with people in one's local community, and a global identity, characterized by a view of the self as a global citizen. Building on this pioneering work, Zhang and Khare argue that the chronic or temporary accessibility of a given identity leads to preferences for identity-congruent products (e.g., local products in the case of an accessible local identity and viceversa). In three studies, the authors develop a reliable scale to measure consumers' local-global identity and provide evidence for the hypothesized patterns of brand preferences. This research reinforces the notion that consumers appropriate brand meanings for constructing their individual identities (Escalas and Bettman 2005), and that these identities can include a more homogeneous view of the world. It also helps to reconcile the debate on whether consumers prefer global or local products and whether markets should adopt a globalized or localized marketing strategy.

This session discusses very important issues in global branding and has a great potential to inform branding researchers about the factors that impact brand preferences and the formation of brand attitudes in globalized economies. We anticipate this session will attract not only those interested in global branding issues, but those interested more generally in cross-cultural consumer behavior. Debbie John, an expert in branding, will integrate the implications of the three streams of research and provide a roadmap for future research about the effect of cultural factors on branding decisions.

EXTENDED ABSTRACTS

"A Measure of Brand Values: Cross-Cultural Implications for Brand Preferences"

Carlos Torelli, University of Minnesota, USA
Aysegul Ozsomer, Koc University, Turkey
Sergio Carvalho, University of Manitoba, Canada
Hean Tat Keh, Peking University, China
Natalia Maehle, Norwegian School of Economics and Business Administration, Norway

Globalization is perhaps the most important macro trend affecting marketing (Goldsmith 2004). As new global markets emerge, and existing markets become increasingly segmented along ethnic or subcultural lines, the need to market effectively to consumers who have different cultural values and who pursue contrasting self-identity goals has never been more important (Shavitt et al. 2008). Past research suggests that one fruitful approach for identifying the types of brand representations that are more likely to appeal to consumers with different value priorities is studying the degree to which consumers' enduring human characteristics match those that describe the brand (Malhotra 1988). Within this approach, it is critical to understand the human characteristics that consumers associate with their brands.

Consumers frequently think about brands as entities associated with a set of human characteristics (e.g., personal values or traits, see Aaker 1997), and as relationship partners with whom they establish and maintain social interactions that resemble in many respects those between social partners (Fournier 1998). Understanding which consumers like which brand characteristics better is a key issue when trying to position brands in the right spot in consumers' minds. Past research has tried to identify a set of personality dimensions that can capture the different traits that consumers attach to brands (e.g., sincerity, excitement, competence, sophistication, and ruggedness, Aaker 1997) and to use these dimensions for identifying the kind of people who prefer brands associated with different traits (e.g., Aaker 1999). In this research, we extend existing work in brand personality and argue for studying the human values that people with different cultural values associate with consumer brands.

Traits and values are two distinct elements of personality and each can predict different sorts of behavior (McClelland 1951). Values are enduring goals that people wish to pursue. Extensive research has established a theory and measurement of values in over 200 samples in more than 60 countries from every inhabited continent (Schwartz 1992). Consumer values play an important role in understanding behavior in the marketplace and models linking product attributes to values are widely used by marketing practitioners (e.g., means-end chain, Gutman 1982). In the four studies reported here, we developed a reliable measure of the human values that people from different cultural settings associate with their brands, or the *brand values scale* (BVS). These studies also show the validity of this measure to predict cross-cultural patterns of brand preferences. To develop our framework, we integrate past findings in brand personality research with those from research about the universals of human values (Schwartz 1992) and about cross-cultural differences in the relative importance of values (Triandis and Gelfand 1998).

In study 1, we explored the structure and reliability of the BVS using data from a multi-country sample of consumers (from Canada, the U.S., China, and Turkey) who rated a variety of local and foreign brands in terms of the values associated with these brands. The findings, using both exploratory factor analysis and multidimensional scaling, suggested that the same 10 value dimensions identified in past research on the importance of human values can be used to describe the values associated with consumer brands (power, achievement, hedonism, stimulation, self-direction, universalism, benevolence, tradition, conformity, and security).

Study 2 was set up to further assess the psychometric properties and structure of the BVS by performing a confirmatory factor analysis on data from a second multi-country sample of consumers (from the U.S., China, Norway, Brazil, and Turkey) who rated the values associated with a variety of brands. The results suggested that a model with 10 intercorrelated factors offered the best fit to the data. Although the BVS did not show the same circular structure of relationships found using ratings of the importance of values as guiding principles in people's lives (e.g., Schwartz 1992), there was evidence that a structure of opposing individual (self-direction, stimulation, hedonism, power, and achievement) and collective values (universalism, benevolence, tradition, conformity, and security) offered a reasonable fit to the data. Congruent with past findings about the importance of personal values, brands that are perceived high in 'individual' concerns such as 'power' or 'achievement' tend to be perceived low in 'collective' concerns such as 'universalism.' However, we did not find evidence for the moderate correlation between contiguous value dimensions representative of 'individual' and 'collective' concerns that a circular structure would suggest (e.g., between universalism and self-direction, or between power and security). This may be attributed to brand images in memory that blend elements from different value domains without the rigid constraints that emerge from value priorities.

Studies 3 and 4 showed the validity of the brand values scale for predicting cross-cultural patterns of brand preferences. Using a multi-country sample of consumers (from the U.S., Canada, Norway, Brazil, Turkey, and China), we found that the cultural dimensions of vertical-horizontal, individualism-collectivism predicted consumers' preferences and attitudes toward brands associated with culturally-congruent values. For instance, horizontal collectivism predicted a higher preference for brands associated with universalism values and a more positive attitude toward brands that embody these values.

This research introduces brand values as an important construct to better understand the relationships that multicultural consumers establish with their brands. The findings here are invaluable for branding professionals interested in assessing the degree to which brand associations match intended positionings congruent with culturally-important values in a particular market. The findings here also carry important implications for brand extension research. Parent brands associated with values that may be incongruent with those needed to succeed in a different category (e.g., a benevolent brand trying to launch a hedonistic product) may be better off by avoiding the launch of a brand extension, as this could cause dilution of the associated values. These are just some illustrations of how brand values can be used to extend our understanding of global branding phenomena.

"A Cross-Cultural Study of the Antecedents of Brand Credibility"

Tülin Erdem, New York University, USA
Joffre Swait, University of Florida and Advanis Inc., USA
Ana Valenzuela, Baruch College, USA

Brand credibility is a key concept in understanding consumers' behavior towards brands, as well as the formation and management of brand equity (Erdem and Swait 1998). Erdem, Swait and Valenzuela (2004) studied the impact of brand credibility on consumer choice in a cross-cultural setting and found that although the existence of brand credibility effects is seemingly generalizable, the mechanisms through which brand credibility operates have some differences across countries with different 'macro' cultural characteristics. In this paper, we focus on the antecedents of brand credibility in such a context. More specifically, our theoretical framework suggests that there are two exogenous antecedents to brand credibility: Consistency among the marketing mix elements and absolute brand investments. Clarity, on the other hand, affects brand credibility as a mediator for both brand investments and consistency. Specifically, this research answers the empirical question of whether the relative total impact of brand investments versus consistency on brand credibility vary depending on the cultural constructs of collectivism/individualism, uncertainty avoidance, and power distance.

We conducted our analysis using survey and experimental data from two different product categories: orange juice and personal computers. We chose these product categories because they represent categories that are respectively low and high in involvement, search costs, and risk. Data on consumer brand perceptions, brand credibility judgments, and cultural dimensions were collected from subjects in Brazil, Germany, India, Japan, Spain, Turkey, and the United States. We chose these countries to vary along Hofstede's (1980) cultural dimensions of individualism/collectivism, power distance, and uncertainty avoidance, that past research has linked to cross-cultural patterns of brand perceptions and choices. We investigated the role of these cultural dimensions as potential moderators of the process that underlies the formation of brand credibility judgments. All subjects in our studies were undergraduate students in business schools (except for about half of the Brazilian sample, who were undergraduate students in engineering) who participated in exchange for course credit. The results provided strong empirical evidence for the conceptual framework proposed by Erdem and Swait (1998) across countries.

More specifically, we investigated the impact of uncertainty avoidance, collectivism-individualism, and power distance on the relative importance of consistency and brand investments on the formation of brand credibility judgments. We expected the impact of consistency on clarity and, as a result, on brand credibility to be relatively more important in collectivistic cultures that foster the subordination of individual goals to the goals of the ingroup. This is because brand consistency reduces ambiguity and increases the strength of the connection between the brand and the reference group. We also expected the impact of brand consistency on clarity to be more important in cultures whose members exhibit high uncertainty avoidance since lack of ambiguity reduces consumers' perceived risk when they use the brand to make inferences. In contrast, we expected that in cultures that legitimize the existence of status differentials among their members (i.e., high-power distance cultures), brand investments may be relatively more important for creating brand credibility. This is because the commitment that is signaled by this type of branding effort can help to mitigate the general distrust of authority in these cultural environments. On a side note, heavy brand investments may also create a signal of status or prestige (Steenkamp, Batra and Alden 2003), which is also highly valued by consumers from cultures that rate high in power distance.

Overall, empirical results supported our expected patterns. First, results were consistent across the two product categories under study (PC and juice). Second, Germany and U.S. usually formed one cluster, while Brazil, Spain, and Turkey formed a second cluster (except in the case of power distance where the second cluster included India, Brazil, and Spain). In other words, Brazil, Spain, and Turkey represented both the high collectivism and high uncertainty avoidance cluster, with a higher percentage-wise consistency effect, whereas, Germany and US represented the high individualism/low uncertainty avoidance cluster, with a lower percentage-wise consistency effect. In the case of power distance, country-clusters changed slightly: Japan, the U.S., and Turkey represented the high power distance cluster, with a higher percentage-wise investment effect, whereas India, Brazil, and Spain represented the low power distance cluster, with a lower percentage-wise investment effect (Germany being an outlier).

These findings have important managerial implications. First of all, companies have to understand what elements in their branding strategy have the higher effect on consumers' perceptions of whether the brand signal is clear or not and, as a result, credible or not. Consumers who need brands to become unambiguous signals of either group identity or just risk-less inference making would heavily base their credibility judgments on how consistent the branding strategy is. In contrast, when brands are generally not trusted, strong brand investments may be necessary to establish the commitment of the company to the brand. In this context, companies should adjust their branding strategies by country according to overall cultural differences in consumers' brand credibility formation processes. Companies could also execute communication campaigns that reinforce the consistency over the years of brand messages (e.g., using a "now and forever" type of message) or the company's commitment to support the brand with strong investments (e.g., using a "commitment to excellence" type of message) in order to match cultural beliefs and values in their markets. Finally, the consistency of brand extensions should be very carefully assessed in categories where either risk or collective identity matters.

"Consumers' Local-Global Identity: Measurement"

Yinlong Zhang, University of Texas at San Antonio, USA
Adwait Khare, Quinnipiac University, USA

With rapid globalization, local and global products are routinely pitted against each other. While global products are growing stronger (Alden, Steenkamp, & Batra 1999), local products are also successfully competing against global products (Parmar 2004; Rigby & Vishwanath 2006). Consider for instance the success of two local colas, Mecca Cola in France and Fei-Chang Cola in China, against the two global colas, Pepsi and Coke. There appear to be both local and global leanings in consumers' product judgments. Mindful of such influences, marketers have tried to devise suitable positioning strategies for their products. Take for example GM's marketing of its Buick Minivan in China as a local rather than a global product (Fairclough 2006), or P&G's marketing of its products as global in Asia and Europe stressing that consumers around the world are being offered the same products (Sexton 2004).

These market trends mirror prior research results that are divergent. While some authors (e.g., Alden et al. 1999; Batra et al. 2000) indicate that consumers like a global product more than a local product, others find just the opposite effect (e.g., De Mooij 1997; Shimp & Sharma 1987). We believe that an unexamined factor in these studies may be the degree to which consumers identify as local versus global citizens, which may help to explain the divergent findings. For instance, in the survey conducted by Batra et al. (2000), it is possible that the global identity of participants from urban regions may have been salient and led to preferences of global over local products. Similarly, in the survey conducted by Shimp and Sharma (1987) among consumers from small-to medium-sized U.S. cities, it is possible that a salient local identity led to preferences of local over global products.

Based on Arnett's (2002) research on the psychology of globalization, we reason that the accessibility of consumers' local versus global identity is a key factor for understanding their preferences for local versus global products. Throughout the discussion, we consider local products as those tailored-made for local markets, and global products as those made with the same specifications for consumers from around the world (see Steenkamp et al. 2003). We build on the notion that consumers tend to evaluate identity-consistent information favorably (e.g., Reed 2004, Wheeler, Petty, & Bizer 2005) and suggest that consumers with an accessible global identity should prefer a global (vs. a local) product more as it may reinforce their sense of being cosmopolitan. In contrast, consumers with an accessible local identity should prefer a local (vs. a global) product more as it may reinforce their sense of being connected to their local community.

In a series of three studies, we developed a reliable and valid scale to measure the construct of local-global identity, and demonstrated its ability for explaining consumers' preferences between local and global products. More specifically, our findings provide evidence for identity-consistent product preferences such that consumers high on local (global) identity scores tend to prefer a local (global) product over a global (local) one.

In study 1, using a sample of adult consumers in a Southwestern city of the U.S., we show that local-global identity is a two-dimensional construct. The corresponding sub-scales that measure local and global identity also show satisfactory reliabilities. A global identity is distinct from, and yet correlated with, attitudes toward global companies.

Study 2 further assessed the test-retest reliability and discriminant validity of the local-global identity scale. Both sub-scales show satisfactory test-retest reliabilities. Results also suggest that local identity is distinct from, and yet correlated with, consumer ethnocentrism (Shimp & Sharma 1987). Both local and global identity measures are uncorrelated with measures of chronically accessible independent and interdependent self-construals (Singelis 1994). Finally, our findings suggest that local and global identities are two independent dimensions that measure distinct, yet possibly competing, desirable identity states.

In study 3, we show the predictive validity of the local-global identity scale and show that it can be used to predict consumers' preferences for global or local products. Participants completed the local-global identity scale. In a separate session, they were primed with either a local or a global identity and subsequently indicated their favorability toward a local and a global version of a palm pilot (order of presentation was counterbalanced). The results showed that both a temporarily and a chronically accessible identity predicted favorable attitudes for identity-congruent (vs. incongruent) products (e.g., more favorable attitudes toward local over global products when a local identity was accessible).

We believe that our research offers key theoretical contributions for globalization research and important implications for branding professionals. First, we advance the emerging literature on the psychology of globalization by empirically measuring the local-global identity construct. Extending the pioneering work by Arnett (2002), we developed a reliable and valid scale to measure the temporarily or chronic accessibility of consumers' local and global identities.

Our findings also provide a theoretical explanation for the contrasting findings about the preferences for local over global products (or viceversa). We show that when a local (global) identity is more accessible consumers prefer a local (global) product to a global (local) one. Thus, our study provides a more parsimonious explanation for reconciling divergent patterns of brand preferences reported in past research. Lastly, our results have key implications for branding decisions. By understanding consumers' accessibility of local-global identities, marketers may be better able to choose between local or global positioning strategies.

SELECTED REFERENCES

Aaker, Jennifer L. (1997), "Dimensions of Brand Personality," *Journal of Marketing Research*, 34 (3), 347-56.

Arnett, Jeffrey J. (2002), "The Psychology of Globalization," *American Psychologist*, 57 (10), 774-83.

Erdem, Tulin and Joffre Swait (1998), "Brand Equity as a Signaling Phenomenon," *Journal of Consumer Psychology*, 7 (2), 131-57.

An Examination of the Complex Relationship Between the Self and Consumer Contexts

Lan Nguyen Chaplin, University of Arizona, USA

SESSION OVERVIEW

Objective, Topics, and General Orientation

The objective of the proposed symposium is to stimulate discussion and encourage research on the dynamic relationship between the self and consumer contexts. Researchers have argued that consumers evaluate and choose brands on the basis of whether they express aspects of the self to others, or fulfill some self-enhancement or self-verification goal. Although research has clearly shown that consumers evaluate and choose brands based on these self-related motivations (thereby forming self-brand connections (SBC), several research questions remain unanswered—Are there important moderators to consider that would further illuminate the relationship between the self and consumption? Additionally, research has explored the influence of brand evaluations on SBC, but to what extent might SBC affect brand evaluations? Finally, a major assumption is that consumers bring salient and relevant self concepts to the brand consumption context, however to what extent might the consumption context influence consumers' self concepts? The aim of this session is to shed some light on these research questions.

Paper #1, by Escalas and Bettman, questions the simple manner in which researchers currently view how consumers' views of the self drive consumption and present findings on how self-enhancement goals and brand symbolism moderate the influence of brand meaning on self-brand connections. Paper #2, by Cheng, White and Chaplin, challenges the unidirectional assumption that brand evaluations/attitudes determine SBC, and present results that suggest a feedback effect. Specifically, the authors suggest that when consumers make a SBC, brand-evaluation will become an important component of self-evaluation, and therefore, is likely to be affected by whether consumers make SBC. Paper #3, by Forehand, Perkins, and Reed II, add another dimension of complexity to the relationship between the self-concept and consumer contexts by questioning whether consumers always bring their identities to the context. The authors present evidence to show that social identities are automatically influenced by contextual information about others. Each paper moves away from the simple way in which researchers currently view the role of the self-concept in consumer contexts and provides empirical evidence to shed some light on the dynamic nature of this relationship (e.g., introducing moderators and challenging assumptions).

In summary, this session presents a dynamic view of the relationship between consumers' self-concepts and consumption activities. That is, while consumers' views of the self drive consumption, these views are also constantly being shaped by the consumption context itself. This perspective paves new avenues for research, such as the potential for consumption activities to transform consumers (via transformation of self-concept) and for contextual factors to determine the self-consumption relationship. The proposed session will serve as a good platform for researchers who are interested in the relationship between the self-concept and consumption as well as those interested in advertising and branding, to communicate and develop possible future research.

Theoretical Contribution

Together, these three papers provide a fresh perspective to study the relationship between the self and consumer contexts. The current view is that individuals' self-concepts shape their consumer behavior. The emerging view from these papers is that while the self certainly drives consumption, it is more complicated than we think (as paper #1 suggests). Moreover, the directional relationship between the self and consumption may also be more complicated than we think (as paper #2 suggests). Finally, the self may not always drive consumption, but rather be driven by consumption (as paper #3 suggests). Each paper makes additional contributions. First, Escalas and Bettman provide an empirical demonstration of the ideas in McCracken's (1989) theory of meaning movement by demonstrating that brands endorsed by celebrities are a source of symbolic brand meaning. In doing so, they provide additional evidence that consumers use brands to communicate their self-concept. Cheng et al., merge the brand extension/dilution and the self-concept literatures to show how SBC can have a feedback effect and influence brand evaluations. Forehand et al., contribute to the advertising literature by showing that ad exposure has a profound effect on not just changes in brand attitude or purchase intentions, but also social identities.

EXTENDED ABSTRACTS

"Celebrity Endorsement and Self-Brand Connections"

Jennifer Edson Escalas, Vanderbilt University, USA
James R. Bettman, Duke University, USA

People engage in consumption behavior in part to construct their self-concepts and to create their personal identities (Richins 1994; McCracken 1989; Belk 1988). We examine one aspect of this construction process, namely the appropriation of the symbolic meanings of brands derived from celebrity endorsement. Building on McCracken's (1989) theory of meaning movement, we propose that the symbolic properties of the celebrity become associated with the brands the celebrity endorses. These symbolic meanings can then be transferred from the celebrity to consumers as they select brands with meanings congruent with their self-concept. When the symbolic properties associated with brands via celebrities are used to construct the self or to communicate the self-concept to others, a connection is formed with the brand. Our first study provides empirical support for the notion that brands endorsed by celebrities are connected to consumers' self-concepts as they use these brands to define and create themselves. Our second study supports the hypothesis that the self-construction process is moderated by brand symbolism, that is, the degree to which the brand communicates something about its user. Our third study is designed to test the hypothesis that the self-construction process is driven by self-enhancement motivations in consumers (cf. Escalas and Bettman 2003).

Our paper provides an empirical demonstration of the ideas in McCracken's (1989) theory of meaning movement by demonstrating that brands endorsed by celebrities are a source of symbolic brand meaning. Consumers form associations between the symbolism associated with the celebrity and the brands they endorse. These meanings are in turn transferred from the brand to the consumer as consumers actively construct themselves by selecting brands with meanings relevant to an aspect of their self-concept. Consumers form connections to brands that become meaningful through this process, and self-brand connections are intended to measure the extent to which individuals have incorporated brands into their self-concept (Escalas 2004). A critical distinction in terms of such construction processes is that between brand associations derived from celebrities with whom consumers identify or feel an affinity and associations derived from celebrities that consumers do not like or do not perceive as being similar to themselves. Consumers are likely to accept meanings from brands associated or consistent with a celebrity whom they perceive as similar to themselves or whom they aspire to be and to reject meanings associated or consistent with a celebrity who does not represent either who they are or who they would like to become. We propose that when consumers appropriate or distance themselves from brand associations based on celebrity endorsement, they do so in a manner that is consistent with self-related needs, such as self-enhancement (Escalas and Bettman 2003).

Results from our first experiment show that the degree to which celebrity usage influences self-brand connections is contingent on an individual's perceived similarity with a celebrity. In this study, we measured the extent to which 52 undergraduate student participants felt that seven popular celebrities were likely to use the product they endorsed and the extent to which the participants perceived themselves to be similar to the seven celebrities (both averaged multi-item scales, with continuous variables used in the within subjects analyses). We find a significant celebrity-use by similarity-to-celebrity interaction ($F(1, 1194)=7.61$ $p<.01$), where there is a stronger positive influence of celebrity endorsement when the participants perceive themselves to be similar to the celebrity.

Results from our second study, run with 361 eLab participants, replicate the finding that the degree to which celebrity endorsement influences self-brand connections is contingent on celebrity type (here, operationalized as most vs. least favorite celebrity) and match between celebrity and brand image, with a significant celebrity-type by image-match interaction ($F(1, 318)=10.31$, $p<.01$). Furthermore, we find this effect is moderated by the degree to which the brand is symbolic, i.e., able to communicate something about the user, with more symbolic brands having stronger effects than less symbolic brands (Escalas and Bettman 2005). We find a significant three way interaction, with steeper slopes for symbolic brands ($F(1, 314)=4.76$, $p<.03$). The positive effect of celebrity endorsement on self-brand connections is stronger for brands that are perceived to communicate something symbolic about the brand's user compared to brands that do not. On the other hand, symbolic brands are more likely to be rejected when endorsed by non-similar, disliked celebrities.

Our third study, run with 311 eLab participants, examines whether self-enhancement needs moderate the influence of celebrity endorsement on self-brand connections. Research on reference groups has found that consumers with strong self-enhancement goals tend to form self-brand connections to brands used by aspiration groups, that is, groups for which the consumer wishes to become a member (Escalas and Bettman 2003). We find a similar process is at work with celebrity endorsement. In this study, we threaten self-esteem for half the participants, thus activating self-enhancement goals. This activation increases the extent to which celebrity endorsement positively influences self-brand connections for celebrities who have characteristics that the consumer aspires to possess, while lowering self-brand connections in the case of celebrities whom the consumer does not aspire to be like ($F(1, 310)=4.62$, $p<.05$). With this third experiment, we show that self-enhancement motivations drive the process by which consumers build connections to favorable celebrity images or distance themselves from unfavorable celebrity images.

References

Belk, Russell W. (1988), "Possessions and the Extended Self," *Journal of Consumer Research*, 15 (September), pp. 139-168.

Escalas, Jennifer Edson (2004), "Narrative Processing: Building Consumer Connections to Brands," *Journal of Consumer Psychology*, 14 (1 & 2), 168-179.

Escalas, Jennifer Edson and James R. Bettman (2005), "Self-Construal, Reference Groups, and Brand Meaning," *Journal of Consumer Research*, 32 (December), 378-389.

Escalas, Jennifer Edson and James R. Bettman (2003), "You Are What They Eat: The Influence of Reference Groups on Consumer Connections to Brands," *Journal of Consumer Psychology*, 13 (3), 339-348.

McCracken, Grant (1989), "Who Is the Celebrity Endorser? Cultural Foundations of the Endorsement Process," *Journal of Consumer Research*, 16 (December), 310-21.

Richins, Marsha L. (1994), "Valuing Things: The Public and Private Meanings of Possessions," *Journal of Consumer Research*, 21 (December), pp. 504-521.

"When Poor Brand Extensions Result in Favorable Brand Evaluations"

Shirley Y. Y. Cheng, University of Illinois at Urbana-Champaign, USA
Tiffany Barnett White, University of Illinois at Urbana-Champaign, USA
Lan Nguyen Chaplin, University of Arizona, USA

An impressive body of research demonstrates that individuals use products to create and communicate their self-concepts (e.g., Belk 1988; Sirgy 1982; Solomon 1986). Particularly interesting in this regard are consumer brands, which are ideally suited to this process given the wide availability of brands and the range of distinctive brand images they reflect (e.g., Fournier 1998; Muniz and O'Guinn 2001; Schouten and McAlexander 1995). Consumers can appropriate associations belonging to brands, such as user characteristics or personality traits, and incorporate them into their self-concepts, thereby forming self-brand connections (SBC; Escalas and Bettman 2003).

The prevailing view of how brands are related to the self-concept is that consumers have certain beliefs and evaluation of a brand, which affect whether consumers make SBC (i.e., Brand-evaluations $\rightarrow$ SBC). Is it possible that a feedback effect might be operative (i.e., SBC $\rightarrow$ Brand-evaluations)? In other words, once consumers have made a SBC, how resilient are their brand evaluations when, for example, the brand's favorable image becomes questionable? Are consumers likely to defend their brand-evaluations given their strong SBC? Or, are they likely to change their brand-evaluations given the obvious challenges to the brand's image? More research is needed to address questions of this nature.

This research investigates the role that self-brand connections play in brand evaluations. Of particular interest is the question of how high SBC consumers evaluate the parent brand when it launches a poor brand extension. To date, the brand extension literature has found that the effect of extension performance on parent brand evaluations depends upon the perceived typicality of the extension. Negative performance of a typical brand extension leads to brand dilution but negative performance of an atypical brand extension does not (Loken and John 1993). Our research investigates how this process could be moderated by consumers' existing SBC. We argue that when consumers make a SBC, brand evaluation becomes an important component of self-evaluation. We know from the psychology literature that individuals are predisposed to try to maintain positive self-evaluation (Tesser 2000; Brown, Collins and Schmidt 1988). Therefore, in order to maintain a positive self-evaluation and avoid a potential threat to the self, it is likely that consumers with high versus low SBC will evaluate the parent brand favorably, even when the brand extension is objectively poor on multiple dimensions.

In study 1, we test the effects of extension typicality and extension performance on brand evaluations for consumers with high versus low SBC. We successfully replicated the typicality effect on brand dilution for those with low SBC. Specifically, we found a significant typicality by performance interaction on brand evaluation. In face of negative extension performance, low-SBC participants evaluated Apple (i.e., the target brand) less favorably when the extension is a printer (i.e., typical) than when it is a watch (i.e., atypical). As predicted, however, this effect was attenuated for high-SBC participants–parent brand evaluations were equally favorable regardless of extension typicality. As previously alluded to, we suggest that two factors set the stage for this effect. First, individuals are predisposed to maintain positive self-evaluation. Second, when consumers make SBC, brand-evaluations contribute to self-evaluations. Consequently, high-SBC consumers view poor extensions as a threat to their self and therefore evaluate poor extensions favorably in order to maintain a positive self-evaluation. To further explore this account, we look to Tesser's (2000) study, which showed that when the self is threatened, people seek to self-affirm. Following this notion, we should expect the effect of SBC on brand-evaluation to be attenuated when consumers are given the opportunity to self-affirm.

In study 2 we test whether self-affirmation attenuates the effects shown in study 1 in a 2 (SBC: high versus low) x 2 (Self Affirmation Task: Present vs. Absent) factorial. Our results show that the otherwise positive influence of high SBC on parent brand evaluations was indeed eliminated when respondents were given the opportunity to self-affirm in another domain. After completing a task in which participants described the values that are most important to them, high SBC participants evaluated the parent brand less favorably than high SBC participants who do not self-affirm, and equally favorable as those low in SBC. Studies 3 and 4 further explore the proposed mechanism and rule out important alternative explanations for the SBC effect. Study 3 demonstrates that negative brand extensions more adversely affect high versus low SBC participants. High SBC participants exhibited a greater need to self-affirm than low SBC participants. In Study 4, we directly measure negative feelings generated in response to negative brand extension performance and show that high SBC participants report significantly more negative feelings than do low SBC participants. However, as expected, this difference is attenuated when high SBC participants are able to self-affirm in another domain.

Taken together, these results provide mounting evidence in support of our account of why and how SBC affect brand evaluations. In so doing, we augment existing literature on the influence of SBC as well as research in the brand extensions literature, which has not examined the influence of SBC on parent brand dilution.

Selected References

Belk, Russell W. (1988), "Possessions and the Extended Self," *Journal of Consumer Research*, 15 (September), pp. 139-168.

Escalas, Jennifer Edson (2004), "Narrative Processing: Building Consumer Connections to Brands," *Journal of Consumer Psychology*, 14 (1 & 2), 168-179.

Escalas, Jennifer Edson and James R. Bettman (2003), "You Are What They Eat: The Influence of Reference Groups on Consumer Connections to Brands," *Journal of Consumer Psychology*, 13 (3), 339-348.

Loken, Barbara and Deborah Roedder John (1993), "Diluting Brand Beliefs: When Do Brand Extensions Have a Negative Impact?", *Journal of Marketing* 57(3), 71-84.

"The Shaping of Social Identity: Assimilation/Contrast Responses to Ad Exposure"

Mark Forehand, University of Washington, USA
Andrew Perkins, Rice University, USA
Americus Reed II, University of Pennsylvania, USA

Social identity has been found to influence a wide variety of consumer behaviors and attitudes. Consumer social identity is especially powerful to the extent that the identity is salient in the immediate social or contextual environment. In these situations, the activation of a social identity motivates the consumer to actively engage in social comparison, to express identity-consistent beliefs, and to select products that reinforce the desired social identity. Although understanding the influence of social identity on consumer behavior is clearly important, the extant research within consumer behavior has largely studied the phenomenon as a unidirectional process. That is, research has started with the belief that consumers bring certain social identities to consumption contexts and that these identities influence judgment to the extent that they are salient and relevant. Although it is certainly true that consumers do bring a variety of social identities with them into consumer contexts, past research downplays the dynamic nature of social identity. Social identities do not spontaneously appear within consumers—rather, they are shaped by a lifetime of experience, social interaction, and self-expression. Research on this phenomenon has largely argued that consumers choose brands in an attempt to express aspects of the self to others, or fulfill some self-enhancement or self-verification goal. Although these motivations do drive much of consumer social identity-formation, it is also clear that social identities are automatically influenced by contextual information about others. It is this latter automatic influence on consumer social identity that we focus on in this project. Specifically, we explore the influence of advertising exposure on the association strength between depicted social identities and the consumer's sense of self, independent of any explicit attempt at self-presentation. We argue that the influence of advertising exposure on consumer social identity is greatest when the advertising makes direct use of identity-relevant cues or generally targets specific identity groups. Exposure to such advertising can activate the relevant social identity dimension in a consumer's self-concept, and this activation can lead to either assimilation toward or contrast with the depicted identity.

Following an assimilation/contrast model, we assess the extent to which ad exposure directly influences the strength of association of basic social identity dimensions in the self-concept. Moreover, we identify two factors that determined whether consumer self-concept shifted toward the presented user imagery (assimilation) or away from the presented user imagery (contrast): (1) the discrepancy between the objective age of the characters in the advertisement and the consumer's own chronological age, and (2) the relevance of this self vs. user imagery comparison. It was hypothesized that assimilation is the likely response to others that are moderately discrepant and contrast is the likely response to others that are extremely discrepant, but that these effects would only occur when the comparison was deemed relevant.

To test the effects of self-concept discrepancy and relevance on consumer assimilation/contrast responses to advertising, three experiments were conducted. In experiment 1, consumers were exposed to advertising that featured individuals who were either similar in age (college-age users), moderately older (30-something users), or extremely older (senior citizen users) than the consumers themselves. After viewing this focal age-targeted advertisement, half of the participants then evaluated the advertising and how targeted they felt while the other half evaluated the advertising but not how targeted they felt. It was hypothesized that the evaluation of targeting status would increase the relevance of the user imagery as a comparison standard. Finally, participants completed an Implicit Association Test (IAT) that measured how strongly they self-identified with youth as part of their self-concept. Consistent with this hypothesized pattern of results, an interaction of ad type and target market evaluation was observed on subsequent self-youth association: subjects assimilated their self-concepts toward the moderately discrepant targets, but contrasted away from the extremely discrepant targets. In addition, these assimilation and contrast responses only occurred when comparison relevance was high (when the consumers initially assessed their target market status).

Experiments 2 and 3 investigated the process underlying the comparison relevance moderation effect in experiment 1. Instructions to evaluate target status were expected to heighten comparison relevance by drawing attention to characteristics that might make one a member of the target market. This proposed process was tested in experiment 2 by adding a manipulation of whether participants evaluated their similarities or dissimilarities to the presented user imagery. To simplify the design, experiment 2 only included congruent user imagery (college-age users) or extremely discrepant users (senior citizens). As in experiment 1, a significant self-concept contrast effect was observed when participants evaluated their target market status or when they evaluated their similarity to the depicted users. However, when participants evaluated their dissimilarity to the user imagery and did not evaluate their target status, no contrast effect was observed. Experiment 3 extended the findings of experiment 2 by demonstrating that the elicited effects of user imagery on the self-concept carried over to the evaluation of subsequent age-targeted stimuli. Specifically, participants with heightened self-youth associations reported more favorable attitudes toward youth-targeted films than did participants with unaffected self-youth associations.

Bettering Business: When and How Consumers Value Pro-Social Marketing Efforts
Nicole Verrochi, University of Pennsylvania, USA

SESSION SUMMARY

With increasing consumer interest in pro-social causes such as environmental protection and human rights, corporations are undergoing a shift in their charitable directions. Specifically, firms are increasingly relying on pro-social actions to increase positive evaluations and product preferences. These pro-social actions can take many forms, from donating a portion of profits to a charitable cause to sponsoring fundraising races/walks to creating new products that are tailored to a particular cause (e.g. "green" products, ethically manufactured goods). In all forms, pro-social business activities are those that take into account the interests and concerns of society.

In the marketing literature, there has been growing interest in such activities, especially those classified as corporate social responsibility (CSR), which has been defined as the overall status and activities an organization undertakes with regards to its perceived societal obligations (Brown and Dacin 1997). The prevalence of these CSR efforts has been encouraged by the growing evidence that consumers prefer to patronize businesses that share their own values and ethics (Menon and Kahn 2003; Sen and Bhattacharya 2001). In addition, socially responsible corporate activity may be a source of competitive advantage, in that it can augment the overall reputation and identity of the company. As this area of corporate activities grows, there are two questions consumer researchers may ask: how do consumers perceive these pro-social activities, and, in turn, how do those perceptions impact attitudes toward the corporation?

The three papers in this proposed special topic session address these two questions, using a variety of methods and contexts. Specifically, the lens through which the issues are examined is the comparison of self-focused versus socially-focused consumer perspectives. Bennett and Chakravarti conceptualize this comparison as the signals a person can send via consumption of CSR-related goods. Specifically, these authors find that attitudes toward these CSR-associated products are strongly correlated with their ability to not only signal *to others* socially desirable traits about the consumer, but also by their ability to *self-signal* to the consumer themselves. Goldsmith and Dhar examine the self- versus social-focus comparison via mindsets which emphasize either benefits to the *self* or benefits to the *greater good*. These researchers find that the positioning of "green" products can highlight either the match between the self and concrete benefits or the greater good and abstract benefits. When there is a mismatch between the benefits and the consumers' mindset, attitudes and willingness to pay for such "green" goods are undermined. Finally, Verrochi, Reed and Tong suggest that there are individual and cultural differences in the emphasis of self- versus social-focus in moral acts. These authors capture these differences using Moral Identity, and propose that consumer perceptions of CSR activities are driven by attributions of the corporation's intrinsic motivation to do good, which are, in turn, impacted by individual differences in perceptions of the motivations for moral action.

While these three papers build upon the burgeoning literature on socially responsible business practices, they contribute to this stream in several important ways. Bennett and Chakravarti expand on the literature regarding the ability of charitable behavior to signal the benevolent identity of consumers (Glazer and Konrad 1996), to demonstrate that it is not only the social signal that consumers are concerned with, but also the ability to tell themselves (self-signal) about their socially desirable traits. Often when confronted with a charitable behavior, consumers are forced to trade off self-focused benefits (e.g. lower price) for socially-focused benefits (e.g. low emissions gasoline) (Bishop 2008). Goldsmith and Dhar demonstrate that the difference between these benefits is not only the target of the benefit, but also the mental level at which they are construed. Finally, Verrochi, Reed and Tong draw from the social identity literature (Reed 2004) to demonstrate that the reason why consumers reject or accept products that match their moral identity is determined by the attributions the consumer makes about why the company has engaged in prosocial behavior. It is this mediating process which is controlled by internal and social values of moral action (Moral Identity) that ultimately establishes the attitude toward the product.

The current consumption environment, characterized by extensive options in terms of product quality and pro-social business affiliation, increasingly puts consumers in situations where they must choose to satisfy their own needs, the needs of society, or some combination of the two. As well as consumers facing this decision, firms too must decide how to shape their offerings to meet the demands of both the socially conscious consumer and the mainstream shopper. Reflective of this trend, this proposed special topic session offers a timely and relevant examination of how to conceptualize and understand the intersection of these underlying issues. The results of these three papers not only deepen our current understanding of socially responsible actions, but also expand the viewpoints used to examine the process by which consumers ultimately evaluate each option.

EXTENDED ABSTRACTS

"The Self And Social Signaling Explanations For Consumption of CSR-Associated Products"
Aronte Bennett, New York University, USA
Amitav Chakravarti, New York University, USA

Consumers frequently encounter, and buy, products that have a corporate social responsibility (CSR) association (e.g., cell phones giving a portion of proceeds to cancer research). It is well documented that products with a CSR-association are extremely popular among consumers and consumers may even be willing to pay a premium for these products. However, the research on CSR-associated purchase decisions has focused on antecedents that influence evaluations and purchase decisions (Brown and Dacin 1997, Sen and Bhattacharya 2001); less attention has been paid to the specific motivations that drive the decision to purchase a CSR-associated product.

We address this gap in the literature through several studies in which we find that consumers like CSR-associated products for two distinct reasons. First, consumers like the fact that these products send out highly visible, *social signals* regarding their benevolence. Second, consumers also like the more private, *self-signaling* potential associated with the purchase of these products. In sum, we find that the valuation of a CSR-associated product is jointly determined by its social and self-signaling potential. Brief descriptions of the supporting theory, specific studies we conducted, and the corresponding results, are provided below.

Signaling refers to the act of conveying information about oneself in an implicit fashion, by engaging in behaviors that reveal one's traits and preferences to observers. Glazer and Konrad (1996) examined the role of social signals in the realm of charitable behavior. Their model implies that charitable donations are observable signals, and consumers are more willing to donate when there is an increased potential for signaling. We apply this theory to CSR-associated products, a specific type of charitable donation, and hypothesize that the evaluations of CSR-associated products will be positively related to the social signaling potential of the product.

Besides sending out social signals to observers, behaviors also have the capacity to *self-signal* to the individual in question. Quattrone and Tversky (1984) showed that people often engage in behaviors in order to signal to themselves that they possess a particular desirable trait, even when there are no social incentives. Thus, we posit that CSR-associated products also allow for self-signaling. These two hypotheses were investigated in the studies described below.

In the three studies that we conducted, all participants were first presented with an advertisement for a target product, and then asked several follow up questions about the target product, which served as key dependent and process measures of interest to us. We manipulated the social and self-signaling potential of the target product by altering various elements of the ad copy.

In study 1, social signaling potential is manipulated by varying the visibility of the product via color and the CSR-association was manipulated by the presence-absence of a CSR affiliation. Study 2 replicates study 1, replacing the social signaling manipulation with a more subtle manipulation of location of consumption (private vs. public). Study 3 considers the role of self-signaling; self-signaling potential is manipulated by the presence/absence of a reminder about how the purchase of the CSR-associated product would remind participants of their benevolence.

Results across these studies indicate that products with greater social signaling potential derive more benefit from CSR associations. Although evaluations in the low social signaling condition remained constant across CSR conditions, evaluations of products with high social signaling potential increased significantly when CSR-associations were added. This difference further increased when a self-signaling reminder was added. Our findings suggest that consumers generally reward CSR-associated products that have the ability to serve as social signals. Interestingly, in order for self-signaling potential to influence the evaluations of CSR-associated products, these products must also have social signaling potential.

Two more studies, which are currently in progress, are aimed at lending further credence to the fact that social and self-signaling play an important role in the purchase of CSR-associated products. In study 4, using a design that parallels Tversky and Quattrone's (1984) cold-compressor task, we investigate the potential for consumers to derive self-signaling benefits from the purchase of a CSR-associated product, even when (a) explicit reminders about its self-signaling potential are absent, and (b) a strong social signal is not plausible. In study 5, we look at individual level traits that should predispose people to differentially value the social (versus self) signaling potential of CSR-associated products.

These five studies, using disparate manipulations and dependent measures, provide convergent findings. Our findings suggest that consumers generally reward CSR-associated products for their ability to serve as social signals and are willing to punish and devalue similar CSR-associated products that do not offer the same signaling potential. Interestingly, we find this preference even when the product's social signaling potential is very subtly cued.

Furthermore, if consumers are provided with explicit self-signals, the difference between high and low social-signaling potential products is augmented. In sum, we address a gap in the literature on corporate social responsibility by showing that the valuation of a CSR-associated product is jointly determined by its social and self-signaling potential. Our findings also extend the literature on signaling by offering an addition to the relatively modest extant stream of research related to self-signaling, especially in the consumer behavior domain.

References

Brown, Tom J. and Peter A. Dacin (1997), "The company and the product: Corporate associations and consumer product responses." *Journal of Marketing* 61 (January), 68-84.

Glazer, Amihai and Kai A. Konrad (1996), "A Signaling Explanation for Charity." *The American Economic Review.* 86 (September), 1019-1028.

Quattrone, George A. and Amos Tversky (1984), "Casual Versus Diagnostic Contingencies: On Self-Deception and on the Voter's Illusion." *Journal of Personality and Social Psychology* 46(February), 237-248.

Sen, Sankar and C. B. Bhattacharya (2001), "Does doing good always lead to doing better? Consumer reactions to corporate social responsibility." *Journal of Marketing Research* 38 (May), 225-243.

"Getting Gold by Going Green: The Importance of Fitting the Message to the Mindset"

Kelly Goldsmith, Yale University, USA
Ravi Dhar, Yale University, USA

Firms today are ever-increasing the number of "green" products they offer. These products are typically positioned in terms of an associated pro-social benefit. For example, purveyors of shade grown coffee may stress how their coffee is farmed with minimal damage to the environment. Thus far, the goal of offering green products has been to cater to consumers who value these pro-social benefits; however, industry leaders have recently noted that many consumers still weigh their own personal needs above those of society when making purchase decisions. Such critics have questioned how to position green products such that mainstream consumer interest can be cultivated and product success will not remain limited to the "green ghetto" or the minority of socially conscious consumers (Bishop 2008).

As no academic research to date has explored how consumer decision processes may influence purchase considerations of green products, the current research proposes and tests how consumer mindsets and the positioning of product benefits affect interest in green goods. When positioning a green product (energy efficient light bulbs), benefits along at least two distinct dimensions can be emphasized: the product can be described in terms of the benefits to the *self* ("reduce your home energy costs") or benefits to the *greater good* ("reduce global warming"). Benefits to the self can be seen as more concrete, as they are more psychologically proximal and are associated with lower level goal attainment. Conversely, benefits to the greater good are more abstract, as they are associated with higher order, more general goals. Recent research has demonstrated that consumers' mindsets (abstract vs. concrete) can systematically influence the importance of product benefits. Consumers in a concrete mindset have been shown to prefer products offering more tangible, personal benefits (Meyvis, Goldsmith and Dhar 2008); whereas consumers in an abstract mindset prefer products whose benefits meet higher order goals (Fishbach, Zhang and Dhar 2005). As such, we argue that consumers in a concrete mindset will be persuaded by appeals for green goods promising more concrete benefits, such as benefits to the *self*. Conversely, an abstract mindset, which focuses attention on higher order goals, will cause consumers to be more persuaded by appeals for products promising benefits to the *greater good*. Thus we predict that a consumer's mindset (abstract vs. concrete) and how the product is positioned (offering benefits to the self vs. the greater good) will have an interactive effect on consumer preferences for green goods.

This proposition is tested in three studies. In Study 1, participants' read a vignette about a green product (solar panels) that they may purchase in the near future (two weeks) or distant future (six months). Temporal distance has been shown to systematically affect the level of abstraction at which consumers' process information: more distal time frames correspond to more abstract representations (Trope and Liberman 2003), thus the time frame manipulation was used as a manipulation of mindset. The green product was positioned either as offering benefits to the self ("reduce heating costs") or benefits to the greater good ("reduce global warming"). Finally, all participants indicated their willingness to pay for the product. In support of our hypothesis, the results demonstrated that consumers in an abstract mindset showed a greater willingness to pay when the product benefited the *greater good*; whereas consumers in a concrete mindset showed a greater willingness to pay for a product associated with personal benefit (interaction: p=0.028).

Study 2 was designed to extend the ecological validity of Study 1, by using a different manipulation of mindset and a different green product. The first study may have obtained the effect of mindset on willingness to pay only for a product where consumers were relatively unfamiliar with standard prices (Coupey, Irwin and Payne 1998). To address this concern, in Study 2 we used a product whose standard price was well known (a gallon of gasoline) and measured not only willingness to pay but also purchase intent. Participants first underwent a mindset manipulation then read a vignette about a green product (ethanol gasoline) that was positioned either as offering benefits to the self ("preserve the life of your engine") or benefits to the greater good ("preserve our environment"). Finally, all participants indicated the likelihood that they would consider purchasing the product on 1–9 scale (1=definitely yes, 9=definitely no), and their willingness to pay per gallon. In support of our findings from Study 1, the results demonstrated that consumers in an *abstract* mindset were more interested in purchasing the product when it offered a pro-social benefit as opposed to a personal benefit (M_{self}=4.36; $M_{pro-social}$=3.07); whereas the opposite was true for consumers in a *concrete* mindset (M_{self}=2.80; $M_{pro-social}$=3.36). This interaction replicated and was significant for willingness to pay (p's<0.04).

Finally to extend the findings of Studies 1 and 2 into the domain of choice, Study 3 tested for the moderating effect of mindsets and product positioning on choices with actual financial consequences. Participants underwent a mindset manipulation then were told that to thank them for their participation they would be entered into a lottery for a reward of their choosing. Their choices were a cash reward, described as "Ten dollars in cash that you can spend any way that you choose," or a green battery charger described as "one way for anyone to help reduce global warming and preserve the environment." In support of our hypothesis, we find that participants in an abstract mindset were significantly more likely to choose the green product over cash ($P_{abstract}$=53.8%; $P_{concrete}$=25%; p=0.038).

At present, this research achieves several goals: we demonstrate that consumer mindsets and the positioning of a green product can have an interactive effect on consumer purchases. Further we demonstrate that this effect carries over to actual choice decisions.

As many firms today feel compelled to offer green products and wish to do so successfully, we believe this research addresses an important practical question and makes a meaningful theoretical contribution.

References

Bishop, Steve (2008), "Don't Bother with the "Green" Consumer," Retrieved August 6, 2008, from http://www.hbrgreen.org/2008/01/dont_bother_with_the_green_con.html.

Coupey, Eloïse, Julie R. Irwin and John W. Payne (1998), "Product Category Familiarity and Preference Construction," *Journal of Consumer Research*, 24, 459-468.

Meyvis, Tom, Kelly Goldsmith and Ravi Dhar (2008), "Beyond Survival of the Fittest: The Influence of Consumers' Mindset on Brand Extension Evaluations," Working Paper.

Fishbach, Ayelet, Ravi Dhar and Ying Zhang (2006), "Subgoals as Substitutes or Complements: the Role of Goal Accessibility," *Journal of Personality and Social Psychology*, 91, 232-242.

Trope, Yaacov and Nira Liberman (2003), "Temporal Construal," *Psychological Review*, 119, 403-421.

"Moral Identity and Attributions of Corporate Social Responsibility"

Nicole Verrochi, University of Pennsylvania, USA
Americus Reed II, University of Pennsylvania, USA
Jennifer Tong, Singapore Management University, Singapore

Recent research has developed an instrument for measuring both the content and intensity of a person's moral identity. Moral identity has been defined as a self-conception organized around a set of collectively shared, higher-order values, principals or beliefs (Aquino and Reed 2002). While research on consumer perceptions of socially responsible corporate actions (e.g. charitable donations, foundations, etc.) have primarily focused on the either the fit between the corporation and the charity or the form of the action (e.g. Menon and Kahn 2003), we propose that individual differences in moral identity can predict consumer reactions to corporate social acts.

Two studies demonstrate that while fit and CSR form impact some types of attributions consumers make about the firm's motivations for engaging in socially responsible action, it is moral identity which predicts those attributions that ultimately determine attitudes toward the firm. In both studies, participants first filled out a "personality test" containing the Moral Identity scale (Aquino and Reed 2002) as well as other various individual difference scales. After completing these measures, participants engaged in a filler task, and then were presented with the experimental stimuli. Each participant saw one of four advertisements; either high or low on corporation-charity fit, and either a promotion format or advocacy format as per Menon and Kahn (2003).

Study 1 demonstrates that American participants' scores on the Internalization dimension of moral identity, or the degree to which moral characteristics are self-important, predicts ratings of Values-Driven attributions. This specific class of attributions, which relate to how much a firm cares about the adopted cause, predicts attitudes toward the firm. When participants' attributions are entered into the regression, we observe full mediation of the effect of Internalization on ratings of CSR. In contrast, study 2 shows that Singaporean participants' scores on the Internalization dimension of moral identity neither predict Values-Driven attributions nor ratings of CSR. Rather, Singaporean participants' scores on the Symbolization dimension of moral identity, which captures sensitivity to the moral self as a social object, predict ratings of Values-Driven attributions, which in turn predict CSR. We also observe full mediation of the effect of Symbolization on ratings of CSR when Values-Driven attributions are included in the regression.

These results are consistent with the characterization of American consumers as possessing a relatively independent self-construal; while Singaporean consumers are have a more interdependent self-construal. To this extent, independent (US) consumers follow the norm of expressing one's unique attributes (Markus and Kitayama 1991), which maps onto the Internalization dimension's conception of the *self*-importance of moral behavior. Opposing this, consumers holding an interdependent self-construal (Singapore) follow the norm of "seeing oneself as part of an encompassing social relationship" (Markus and Kitayama 1991: p. 227), evidenced by the Symbolization dimension's sensitivity to the *social* value of moral behavior.

These findings have implications beyond the realm of individual difference scales. We find that fit between the company and charity, as well as the form of the socially responsible action are less predictive of ratings of CSR than are feelings that the firm cares about the cause, regardless of cross-cultural differences. Although different dimensions of moral identity carry more or less weight in different cultures, Values-Driven attributions consistently predict CSR evaluations. With this in mind, managers should reconsider the strategies used to select between different corporate social actions. Rather than selecting those that are the best "match" with corporate identity, firms would be better served to choose activities that they are visibly passionate about, to encourage these Values-Driven attributions. Not only would attitudes toward the firm increase, but the charities themselves would be better served by engaged corporate partners.

References

Aquino, Karl and Americus Reed, II (2002), "The Self-Importance of Moral Identity," *Journal of Personality and Social Psychology*, 83 (6), 1423-1440.

Ellen, Pam Scholder, Deborah J. Webb and Lois A. Mohr (2006), "Building Corporate Associations: Consumer Attributions for Corporate Socially Responsible Programs," *Journal of the Academy of Marketing Science*, 34 (2), 147-157.

Markus, Hazel Rose and Shinobu Kitayama (1991), "Culture and the Self: Implications for Cognition, Emotion, and Motivation," *Psychological Review*, 98 (2), 224-253.

Menon, Satya and Barbara E. Kahn (2003), "Corporate Sponsorships of Philanthropic Activities: When Do They Impact Perception of Sponsor Brand?," *Journal of Consumer Psychology*, 13 (3), 316-327.

Freedom and Constraint: The Interplay of Consumer Agency, Social Relations, and the Market

Michelle Barnhart, University of Utah, USA

Lisa Penaloza, Ecole des Hautes Etudes Commerciales du Nord, France

SESSION OVERVIEW

This session on consumer agency—that is, one's ability to fully engage in all of the various aspects of consumption—is positioned as a follow up to last year's ACR epistemic panel on consumer freedom. In that session Tom O'Guinn, Rob Kozinets, and Lisa Peñaloza joined organizer David Mick in addressing the nature, extent, up/downsides, and changes in consumer freedom over time. This topic tapped a major artery running through consumer culture theory (CCT) in conveying the powerful and creative force of this social construction. As historical artifact, freedom has inspired revolutions, wars, and civil rights struggles. As modern idealization, freedom traverses a complex web of meanings interwoven in everyday and spectacular consumption practices at home and in the marketplace, with implications to larger social and government institutions. As such, the concept of freedom merits much further work.

In the spirit of such further work, this session on consumer agency is organized to contribute understanding to the micro dynamics through which consumer agency is exerted and constrained. Western ideas of agency are rooted in the tradition of philosophers such as Descartes and Hume who emphasized an autonomous, rational subject capable of individual thought. The ability to think independently and understand one's subjectivity and self interests is necessary for agency, which has been understood in terms of action and the potential for action, as in one's capacity to act in his/her own interests. When cast in the consumption domain, consumer agency is exercised in consumption practices.

In this session, we problematize consumption practices and discourses of consumer agency. In doing so, it is important to anchor our studies in relation to representations of the consumer and the social expectations held for consuming agents by significant others—family, friends, and market agents. Questions raised include: What does agency entail in the consumption domain? How do market institutions convey agency to their consumers? How does ownership of consumption artifacts enable and constrain agency? And, how is consumer agency differentially configured in the three contexts on which we focus: a family making use of their dining room table, as we get old, and when we move? These contexts allow us to bring forth various contours of personal independence and autonomy in social relations and in the market as consumers employ products and services in relation to their family and friends and with firms.

Writers such as Adam Smith and David Ricardo have positioned the market as a source of freedom from oppressive social and religious traditions, casting consumer agency as a means of liberating ourselves from social constraints. Yet previous research has shown that the market places its own constraints on individual freedom (e.g. Bernthal, Crockett, and Rose 2005; Peñaloza 1994; Peñaloza 2001), with some consumers finding the market so oppressive that they attempt to escape to an idealized, liberating social space (Kozinets 2002). In this session we examine the tension between freedom and constraint that exists in both the market and the social realms, and consider how engaging in one realm can influence the freedom/constraint balance in the other. Furthermore, this session illuminates the ways in which consumer agency is affected by significant others, the market, and one's own body.

A common thread running through each of the three papers is an emphasis on the interplay between social relations and consumer agency. In its investigation of identity construction and the use of a family's dining room table, the first paper challenges us to reconceptualize agency as something that is articulated in the practices of individual, relational and collective identity bundles rather than being manifest only by individuals. This work also uniquely contributes to this session in its emphasis on how an object, the table, may exert a constraining force over human agency. The analysis and write-up of this paper are complete. The second paper considers how consumer agency can be shared by family, paid providers, and elderly consumers when an older person is no longer able to consume independently. In this context, the focus shifts from an inanimate object to our own bodies as a source of constraint. Additionally, this research considers how the market can perpetuate an idealized concept of freedom and independence in old age. One round of data collection and analysis for this paper is complete, and the authors expect to be in the final stages of analysis by the time of the conference. Finally, in the context of house moving, the third paper analyzes the interplay and tensions between individual consumers and their social networks of family members, friends and acquaintances. Like the other papers of the session, this research questions the individualistic view of agency by focusing on how people negotiate the social expectations and relational obligations of the gift economy. More importantly, it examines how people may sometimes seek to escape the gift economy by turning to the market. As such, this paper looks at how the market helps to reconcile consumers' desire to belong to a social network and their need for freedom and autonomy. Analysis and write-up are expected to be completed by the time of the conference.

This session is expected to appeal to those interested in consumer agency and freedom, the family, identity construction, elderly consumers, materiality, and the socially embedded nature of consumption. Implications for individuals include how they can use consumption to balance personal life goals with social and market benefits and challenges. Implications for service providers such as movers and elder care services relate to how they might position themselves relative to competitors and in anticipating future market development. Finally, implications for social theory include providing insight into how consumption impacts social groups of family and friends.

EXTENDED ABSTRACTS

"Agency, Identity and Materiality: The Storied Life of a Family and their Table"

Amber M. Epp, University of Wisconsin-Madison, USA
Linda L. Price, University of Arizona, USA
Eric J. Arnould, University of Wyoming, USA

"Figured worlds, like activities, are not so much things or objects to be apprehended as processes or traditions of apprehension which gather us up and give us form as our lives intersect them," Holland, Lachicotte, Skinner and Cain 2003

Prior research in material culture studies has sought to "transcend a simple dualism in which agency is seen as a possession of persons or society, and objects merely that which is passively worked upon" promoting instead an approach based on networks of agents that "include both animate and inanimate forms" (Miller 2001, p. 119). Consistent with this evolving perspective, we view consumer agency as improvisations and potentialities that come from the interplay of individual, relational and collective identities, material objects, other cultural resources, and situations in practice (Holland et al 2003). As such, agency is socially instanced in identities produced through collective practices that are spread across the material world and located in specific times and places (Cetina 1997). Within a socio-historical or "figured world" of semiotic meanings, objects are instruments of agency, recipients of the acts of others' agency and also act as agents to transform and displace individual, relational and collective identities and practices (Miller 2005). Hence, at contrast with views of agency as individualistic, purposeful control; we emphasize how other social units (such as couples, children and families); objects; and spaces exert semiotic agency as they interplay in identity practices (Epp and Price 2008). In particular, our study illustrates "the positive blending of social and material relations" (Miller 2001, 115) that can occur at the intersection of object and personal biographies.

Our paper is based on a two-year ethnographic case study we conducted that describes linkages between the biography of the Erikson family (a pseudonym) and the biography of their kitchen table, a highly singularized object (Kopytoff 1986). Using a life-history approach (Denzin 1978), we interviewed five family members, including a mother, father, two children, and the mother's mother. We uncover how contextual shifts and constellations of objects and spaces propel and alter the uses of the table, and how the table in turn alters key family identity practices. We produce depth of understanding and triangulation across informants and events by drawing on multiple family members and collecting data at multiple time points (Yin 2003; Wallendorf and Arnould 1991). Over the two-year period one of the researchers made multiple visits to the family's home and photographed the table in various roles. Fortuitously, this case tracks a family during a transitional period (moving to a new house), making identity issues salient (Otnes, Lowrey and Shrum 1997; Schouten 1991) and allowing us to assess contextual changes that challenge the object's role in family identity.

Our research reveals that a highly singularized object can be propelled into periods of inactivity by a convergence of forces including 1) other singularized objects with complementary and/or competing biographies; 2) other complementary and/or competing individual, relational or collective identity performances; 3) shifts in contextual elements such as spaces, life events, and so on. In the case of a highly singularized object, periods of inactivity are marked by incorporation attempts and contemplation about possible futures for both object and family biographies. Objects are moved back into activity by 1) possible futures the family envisions, which create new opportunities for object-family interactions; 2) object indexicality that demands that particular identity practices require the use of THIS particular object; 3) the complementary iconicity of objects and spaces (as dining table; contamination of the object by the space and vice versa; sometimes just needs to be a big table); and 4) shifts in contextual elements.

Object movements have unprompted and unintended consequences such as displacement of identity practices, other objects, and spaces. By focusing on the consequences of movements of singularized objects in and out of activity, we are able to account for paradoxical behaviors. For example, we explain why and how individual, relational, and family identity practices are altered or abandoned in order to reincorporate singularized objects into their performances. We also show how a singularized object, as it exits and re-enters the family's social space, can precipitate a new vision of family identity. Our research provides examples of objects exerting constraining force over human agency as seen in the dramatic efforts made by two generations of family to accommodate the table, including remodeling three houses and moving the table in and out of the current house in order to provide a key prop to particular identity performances. In addition, we highlight the agency of multiple identity bundles, not just the individual, in the improvisations that unfold in the "figured world" of the Erickson family. In the Erikson family, convergent and overlapping identity practices are more prominent than divergent and competing practices. However, divergence and competition between identity bundles emerge in the family's move to a new home with new objects and spaces potent with competing identities that ultimately displace the table to the garage. In this move we see how individual, relational and collective identities collide, compete and interplay to exert agency over the next moment of activity.

"Negotiating Agency in the Elderly Consumption Ensemble"

Michelle Barnhart, University of Utah, USA
Lisa Penaloza, Ecole des Hautes Etudes Commerciales du Nord, France

While improvements in health care have greatly increased life expectancy over the last century, they have not eliminated many of the physical and mental limitations that often accompany old age. Age related changes leave many older consumers unable to consume independently. In 2005, 6.4% of Americans between the ages of 65 and 74, and 18.3% of those over the age of 75 required assistance with at least one of the following consumption activities: using the telephone, traveling outside the home, shopping, preparing meals, doing housework, taking medications, and managing money (Census 2008).

Assistance may include private, informal help from family members or friends as well as paid in-home services, and is likely to be a complex and dynamic process involving multiple people in changing configurations over time (Waldrop 2006). We refer to this group as the *elderly consumption ensemble (ECE)* and define it as an elderly consumer and one or more others who together engage in consumption activities of that elderly person. The ECE is analogous to a jazz ensemble in which members possess different competencies and are more or less engaged in activity at any particular moment.

This research investigates how consumer agency operates within ECEs that include both unpaid family or friends and paid providers. In so doing, it strives to understand how agency is constrained, enhanced, protected, contested, relinquished, and shared in consumer behavior. For example, an older person's consumer agency may be constrained by physical limitations, enhanced by adaptive devices, protected as they insist on "doing it myself," contested by family members worried about an elder's physical safety, relinquished when they ask others to do something for them, and shared when they are able to engage in a consumption activity only with assistance. For our theoretical framework, we draw eclectically from previous work on elderly consumers, family, joint consumption, and commercial friendships. Methodology includes depth interviews with members of six ECEs, each consisting of an elderly consumer, at least one family member or friend, and at least one paid care provider. Questions elicit oral histories beginning with informants' first recognition that assistance was needed, and including how levels and types of assistance and ensemble members' relationships changed over time. Additional questions explore informants' reflections on their experience as an older person, family member/friend, or caregiver; their own aging; and what it means to be old in American society. Of interest is how older consumers' agency is influenced by their own aging bodies, family members, and market providers.

While cognition has received greater attention in studies of aging consumers (Cole and Balasubramanian 1993; Yoon 1997; John and Cole 1986; Law, Hawkins, and Craik 1998), changes in the body can also make it difficult or impossible for older consumers to exercise agency. For instance, Richard (89) has macular degeneration. He is no longer able to drive and reads only with great difficulty using a special machine that he has at home. While he has experienced no marked decline in his cognitive abilities, his is unable to act independently as a consumer in a marketplace that demands a certain degree of mobility and literacy.

Family members or friends may attempt to enhance or protect the agency of an older consumer by gifting adaptive devices, such as Richard's reading machine or Jane's (82) new walker. Yet these items may also be seen as threatening markers of age that imply a gradual loss of freedom and independence. Alternatively, family/ friends may attempt to limit an older person's agency as they try to protect the older person or to advance their own self interests. When family members engage in consumption activity with an older person who previously acted alone, agency must be negotiated in consumption behavior as the elderly consumer moves into and acts from an elderly subject position.

Finally, the market both frees and constrains older consumers. Advertising images of independent, active seniors legitimize old age in ways that are gratifying but can also create unrealistic expectations of perpetual independence and autonomy. Service providers make it possible for older consumers to live independently from their families. However, this social independence is counterbalanced with increasing dependency on the market. Assisted living centers and paid caregivers are examples. At the level of the individual service provider, we conceptualize paid care providers as ECE members engaged in consumption with elderly consumers while supporting an ideal of independence. Like family members, paid care providers negotiate agency and subject position with the elderly consumer through consumption behavior. However, in this case the relationship between an older consumer's agency and the ECE member's interest is more immediately obvious. The paid provider's employment is the direct result of the older consumer's constrained agency. If the older person could act alone, the provider would not be needed. Thus, while the paid provider may out of genuine friendship or love wish to enhance the older person's agency, he/she also has a vested interest in continued or increasing constraints.

This research seeks to contribute to the consumer behavior literature by elucidating how changes in the body and changes in family and market relationships that accompany advanced age impact the nature of consumer agency. Furthermore, by asking how agency is shared by ECE members, we challenge the concept of individual consumer agency and add to previous work on the socially embedded nature of consumption. In increasing our understanding of the ECE, this work has implications for family members, marketers, and policy makers interested in maintaining and enhancing the quality of life of elderly consumers and their families.

"Moving Across the Gift Economy and the Market"
J.S. Maroux, University of Montreal, Canada

In consumer research, the gift economy has usually been considered as a sphere of exchange that is distinct from the market. The two are not only analyzed separately, however. They are also often organized into a hierarchy of values in which the gift is privileged.

Researchers like Cheal (1988), Giesler (2006) and Thompson and Arsel (2004), for instance, have analyzed the gift and the gift economy extensively. These researchers have described gift-giving as a social activity in which a humanizing logic is applied at an interpersonal level. They have also projected this idea up to the level of the gift economy (see for example Kozinets 2002; Thompson and Coskuner-Balli 2007). Few of these researchers have questioned, however, the ennobling view of the gift economy. Notwithstanding the work on the darker sides of the gift (see for example Belk 1976, 1979; Ruth, Otnes and Brunel, 1999; Sherry, McGrath and Levy, 1993), which has unveiled the emotional and relational constraints of gift-giving behavior, consumer researchers have usually failed to explore the implications of the dark side of the gift in relation to the market. In other words, they have often ignored how people may seek to escape the constraints of the gift economy, and how they may turn to the market as a result.

This presentation examines how people negotiate the social expectations of the gift economy and the relational obligations (like social indebtedness) that such a context of exchange entails. It unveils the micro-dynamics of consumption that leads people to either comply to the norm of the gift economy, subvert it, or escape it through the market. The notion of agency is useful for understanding this process. If freedom is a notion in which the choice is sometimes idealized, agency is understood for its part as a means of expressing volition and intentions within a set of norms. In this case, we can speak about the norms of reciprocity prevailing inside the gift economy. As such, turning to the market becomes a means of asserting agency.

This presentation is grounded in an ethnographic study of house moving in Montreal (Canada). In line with Arnould and Thompson (2005), moving is used here as a privileged context for acceding reciprocity relations and for revealing the tensions that may make the gift economy unattractive, and that may lead people to escape it as a result. In Montreal, using family, friends, acquaintances and social networks for the purpose of moving is the norm. Moving is a social event particularly appropriate for the emergence of reciprocity relations. During a move, members of primary support networks—and also more distantly related persons—give, swap, exchange and trade services and resources in a fringe zone of social activity that lies between the gift economy and the market. Many people who decide to move view calling upon the market as a complement to, a substitute for, or an exit from the gift economy. Thus, the analysis of moving, with this activity seen as a point of passage between the gift economy and the market, can help us to think beyond the literature on reciprocity and gift-giving.

This presentation does not only challenge expectations of specific CCT researchers. It also goes against some of the fundamental tenets of consumer research on the gift. It shows how people may subvert the hierarchy of values that underlies most of our field's research on the gift.

References available upon request.

SYMPOSIUM SUMMARY
Understanding Hedonic Misprediction: The Role of Lay Beliefs
Jane Ebert, University of Minnesota, USA

SESSION OVERVIEW

Research shows that consumers often spontaneously consider and are influenced by their anticipated feelings about consumption experiences, both in the choices they make and in how they feel about these experiences. However, people also commonly get these hedonic predictions wrong, leading them to make suboptimal or unwanted choices (e.g., see review by MacInnis, Patrick, and Park, 2005). This symposium combines 4 papers and a discussant that advance our understanding of why and how hedonic mispredictions occur, by focusing on a relatively new and unexplored explanation: the role of lay beliefs. Beyond simply providing a laundry list of lay beliefs that result in misprediction, the juxtaposition of these papers provokes thinking on when and how lay beliefs can result in misprediction,

First, misprediction can occur if consumers hold consistent, but incorrect lay beliefs. This occurs in two of the present papers, resulting in larger predicted differences in hedonic reactions than are observed in experience. In the Ebert/Meyvis paper, subjects expect the psychological distance of an experience (e.g., reading about a recent versus a distant past event) to impact both processing of the experience and its direct hedonic impact resulting in overprediction of the impact of psychological distance. In the Zhang/Hsee paper, subjects expect that differences between products that are hard to evaluate (such as the resolution of a digital camera) will affect their preferences more than they actually do. Second, consumers may hold lay beliefs that are incorrect but inconsistent across consumers or ones which lead consumers to (incorrectly) expect no impact on their hedonic reactions, resulting in no systematic effect on prediction. This is seen in the Galak/Kruger/Loewenstein paper, where subjects' enjoyment of repeated listening to songs or drinking beverages is strongly affected by the spacing of consumption, though their predictions show no effect of spacing. Third, consumers may hold accurate lay beliefs, but fail to apply them. This is the case in the Wang/Novemsky/Dhar paper, where consumers mispredict their product enjoyment over time because they fail to apply their accurate lay beliefs on adaptation—beliefs that are easily cued and moderated through subtle changes in product features.

We expect that these four papers, tightly linked around the role of lay beliefs in affective forecasting, will lead to an interesting and thought-provoking symposium. We intend that each presentation will last for 15 minutes, with an additional 15 minutes where the discussant will highlight session themes and moderate audience questions and discussion. The papers contribute to a developing research area relevant to the interests of many ACR members, notably those interested in hedonic consumption, information processing, and judgment and decision making.

EXTENDED ABSTRACTS

"Anticipating Adaptation to Products"

Jing Wang, Singapore Management University, Singapore
Nathan Novemsky, Yale University, USA
Ravi Dhar, Yale University, USA

Many consumer products deliver their value over extended periods of time. However, the level of this utility often diminishes over time due to waning novelty, shifting reference points and expectations, and various other mechanisms. Moreover, this process of *hedonic adaptation* seems to catch people by surprise (Schwartz 2004). For example, imagine that after much thought, a person chooses to spend $500 extra to buy a high-end stereo with many cutting-edge features instead of a basic model. A few months later, the initial thrill of the new stereo fades, enjoyment falls dramatically, and the person may get caught up in remorse, wondering why he chose the expensive stereo.

The purchase decision for a product with temporally extended enjoyment requires consideration of the product's utility profile integrated over its life (Kahneman and Snell 1990; Kahneman, Wakker, and Sarin 1997; Nowlis, Mandel, and McCabe 2004). In the current research, we demonstrate that when faced with such purchase decisions, consumers often fail to predict diminishing product enjoyment over time and explore the antecedents and consequences of this prediction error. We show that this failure to predict hedonic adaptation to products arises not because of erroneous beliefs about how experienced utility changes over time, but rather because of a failure to spontaneously consider adaptation and incorporate largely correct beliefs about adaptation at the moment of choice. As a consequence, consumers may over-purchase products and spend excessively on product features even when they have correct intuitions about hedonic adaptation for those products and features.

In a pilot study, we find that there is a prevalent belief in adaptation for a range of products that are consumed over time. In study 1, we show that people's predictions of future enjoyment with a product fail to reflect diminishing enjoyment observed in actual experience despite the fact that they expressed a belief in adaptation for that item in the pilot study. In study 2, we demonstrate that intuitive beliefs about adaptation can be cued by prompting people to consider enjoyment with a product at both near and distant points in time, thereby producing better hedonic forecasts. In subsequent studies we show that consideration of adaptation has important consequences for purchase intentions and choice. Specifically, study 3a shows that cuing beliefs about adaptation significantly decreases purchase intent for products whose enjoyment people believe will quickly dissipate over time. Study 3b shows that cuing beliefs about adaptation influences product feature choices, shifting preferences away from products containing features that people believe they will quickly adapt to. In studies 4 and 5 we provide evidence that salience of prospective duration of product ownership rather than direct attention to diminishing enjoyment is responsible for the effects demonstrated in our preceding studies. Specifically in study 4, we simply ask participants to imagine using a product at different points in time without asking for any hedonic predictions and obtain a similar pattern of results on choice as shown in study 3. In study 5, we show that making multiple product enjoyment predictions over a very short time period (where no adaptation is expected) is sufficient to draw attention to duration and thereby bring beliefs about adaptation to mind. And finally, study 6 examines a boundary of people's beliefs about adaptation for products. In this study, we test the idea that people may not believe in diminishing enjoyment for products that offer highly variable experiences. We show that very subtle changes in the description of a given product can influence the perceived variability of the product consumption, which in turn moderates the effect of making prospective duration salient on purchase decisions.

In summary, the present research explores how and why predictions of enjoyment with products over time may diverge from experiences even when consumers hold valid intuitive beliefs about adaptation. Moreover, we examine the consequences of this divergence for purchase decisions. Our findings offer important insights for the study of affective forecasting, overspending, and long-term satisfaction. It is important to note how our findings contrast with prior work on affective forecasting. Specifically, previous research suggests that people often hold inaccurate beliefs about affect progression, which in turn leads to prediction errors and suboptimal choices (e.g., Kahneman and Snell 1992; Nelson and Meyvis 2006; Novemsky and Ratner 2003; Wilson et al. 2000). The present research finds that even when intuitive beliefs are accurate, predictions may still diverge from actual experiences, as people frequently fail to incorporate these accurate beliefs into judgments and choices. Our findings also offer insights into issues such as consumer overspending (e.g., buyer's remorse) and Scitovsky"s "Joyless Economy."

"Too Much of a Good Thing: Insensitivity to Rate of Consumption Leads to Unintended Satiation"

Jeff Galak, New York University, USA
Justin Kruger, New York University, USA
George Loewenstein, Carnegie Mellon University, USA

Repeated consumption of hedonic experiences is ubiquitous. Consumers eat their favorite foods repeatedly, listen to their favorite songs time and time again, and socialize with the same close friends regularly. Such repetition can lead to satiation. In one study, participants listened to a 45-second sample of a favorite song 15 times in quick succession, rating their enjoyment of the experience along the way. What began as an enjoyable experience became downright unpleasant after only 6 repetitions (Ratner, Kahn & Kahneman, 1999, Expt 1). Indeed, the notion that repetition decreases enjoyment of pleasurable experiences is a central tenet both of psychological and economic theories of taste (Helson, 1947; 1964; Mas-Colell, Whinston & Green, 1995; although see Zajonc, 1968 for an important exception).

Satiation, however, is not inevitable. A delay between exposures, for instance, can attenuate (and even halt altogether) satiation. Whereas the same song might grow tiresome if repeated in quick succession, a space between exposures reduces satiation. Are consumers aware of the impact of rate on satiation? Do they maximize satisfaction by choosing a sufficient inter-consumption delay between consumption? The present research addressed these questions.

Participants in Study 1 listened to a novel but (initially) well-liked song. Some participants went on to listen to the song 6 more times (experiencers), rating their enjoyment of the song after each iteration. Other participants merely imagined listening to the song repeatedly and predicted these ratings (forecasters). Orthogonal to this manipulation, one condition had a short break between iterations, whereas in the other condition consumption was back-to-back. Rate had a considerable influence on actual satiation, but had no influence on anticipated satiation. Participants enjoyed the song considerably more if there was a delay between consumption, but showed no difference in predicted enjoyment.

One implication of the results of Study 1 is that consumers may choose inter-consumption intervals that fail to maximize their satisfaction. If consumers do not realize the extent to which an inter-consumption delay can prolong liking, then they may not optimally space consumption. The next two studies were designed to test this hypothesis.

In Study 2, participants consumed a well-liked drink (Starbucks Mocha Frappuccino) while watching a 10-minute television program. In one condition, participants drank the beverage as quickly (or slowly) as they wished. In the other condition, participants were limited to one-sixth of the beverage at six evenly spaced intervals throughout the duration of the 10-minute program (i.e., every 100 seconds). Not surprisingly, participants consumed more quickly when left to their own devices than when an inter-consumption delay was imposed upon them. Also as predicted, participants enjoyed the beverage more when consumption was spaced than when they consumed at their own (faster) rate.

Of course, one explanation for the results of Study 2 is that instead of failing to realize that they would enjoy the beverage more if they slowed their consumption, they simply lacked the self-control to do so. After all, there is no shortage of studies that attest to the occasional difficulty people have in avoiding temptation, even with full awareness that they are doing so (Loewenstein, 1996). Would participants choose a similarly sub-optimal rate of consumption if they made their choices in advance, prior to the influence of immediate temptation? Our third and final study was designed to find out.

Participants once again were offered the opportunity to repeatedly consume a well-liked stimulus while watching a television program. This time, however, participants who chose their own rate of consumption did so prior to the experiment. Specifically, participants were told they would be given 6 Hershey's Kisses during a 20-min television program and asked to choose their inter-consumption interval (from a minimum of 10 to a maximum of 200 seconds). Importantly, participants were instructed to select the interval they thought would maximize their enjoyment of the chocolates. As in Study 2, another group of participants had no such choice and consumed the Kisses at the maximum possible inter-consumption interval (200 sec). As in Study 2, participants who chose their own rate of consumption consumed the chocolates more rapidly than those who were assigned the maximum inter-consumption interval. Also as in Study 2, this resulted in decreased enjoyment.

Taken together, the results of these studies suggest consumers underestimate the impact of rate on satiation, and consume more rapidly than is optimal. In studies 2 and 3, paradoxically, participants asked to maximize their utility were less satisfied than those who had their rate of consumption decided for them. It appears that insensitivity to rate of consumption can lead to unintended satiation.

"Affective Forecasting and Psychological Distance: The Surprising Impact of Distant Events"

Jane Ebert, University of Minnesota, USA
Tom Meyvis, New York University, USA

Would you prefer to see a film based on a true story or a similar film that is entirely fictional? Does it matter if the true story occurred recently or 10 years ago? A growing literature shows that, when making experiential consumption decisions such as these, consumers are influenced by their anticipated feelings about the experience (see MacInnis, Patrick, and Park, 2005, for a recent review). Research also finds that these hedonic predictions tend to be inaccurate. In particular, consumers tend to overestimate the enduring hedonic impact of an experience. This impact bias has been demonstrated for a broad range of positive and negative hedonic experiences, such as relocations, winning prizes, receiving gifts, failing to lose weight, and electoral defeats (see reviews Kahneman and Snell, 1992, and Gilbert, Driver-Linn and Wilson, 2002). Explanations of this bias have focused on the *lack of consideration* by predictors of the internal and external context around the focal hedonic experience, such as how feelings will change or the effects of experiences that occur subsequent to the focal hedonic experience (Gilbert et al. 1998; Gilbert and Wilson 2000).

In contrast to this work, we explore a process by which people mispredict the impact of a hedonic experience by *overconsideration* of the context around the focal hedonic experience. In particular, we demonstrate that people overestimate the dulling impact of contextual factors that increase the psychological distance of a target event. As a result, people underestimate the intensity of their emotional reaction to reading fictitious or historical stories, and to winning a prize that will only be made available later.

In 4 studies, we compared people's predicted versus actual hedonic reactions to events that were either psychologically close or distant. In studies 1-3, participants read emotion-inducing newspaper stories (e.g., about a student dying from meningitis). Experiencers were first given information about the story context. Psychologically distant experiencers were told the story was "fictitious" (Studies 1 and 3) or about an event that "happened 10 years ago" (study 2), while psychologically close experiencers were told the story was "real" (studies 1 and 3) or about an event that "happened recently" (study 2). Experiencers then read the story and rated their affective reactions. Predictors read the story and then predicted their reactions if they had first been given the information about the story context. Finally, in study 4, we use a new emotional experience and psychological distance manipulation: receiving a prize in 6 weeks (psychologically distant) or immediately (close).

Across all studies, predictors predicted a greater influence of psychological distance on their emotional reactions than experiencers actually experienced. Most often, predictors accurately predicted emotional reaction to the psychologically close experience and underestimated emotional reaction to the psychologically distant experience. Furthermore, study 3 rules out a differential salience or demand explanation for this effect. Indeed, the effect persists even when participants in the experience condition are explicitly reminded of the manipulation immediately prior to the dependent measures, ruling out an account based on a greater salience of the manipulation in the predictor condition. Furthermore, when the psychological distance information was said to be presented after the story, the predictors were reliably less sensitive to this information (than when it was said to be presented before the study), showing that predictors only relied on the information when they thought it would influence the processing of the story—and were not merely reacting to experimental demand.

These results suggest that, when choosing between options that vary on attributes related to psychological distance, consumers will be influenced by these attributes more than they should, e.g., preferring films based on stories that are true and occurred recently when, in actual fact, they would be equally happy with films based on fictional or older stories. More generally, this approach connects the affective forecasting literature to work in judgment that examines unwanted or over-correction, such as work on mental contamination (Wilson and Brekke, 1994). Given the frequency of these effects in judgment, we suspect that this process may prove a common source of systematic error in hedonic prediction.

"Inconsistency Between Predicted and Actual Sensitivity of Evaluation or Liking to Attribute Values"

Jiao Zhang, University of Miami, USA
Christopher Hsee, University of Chicago, USA

Will a consumer watching TV in her home have a better experience if the TV has a 50-inch screen or a 42-inch one? More important, can she accurately predict the difference in her experience between the two alternative scenarios? Overprediction may lead the consumer to buy the 50-inch TV without having the better

experience she believes she will. Building on previous research (Hsee & Zhang, 2004), in the present research, we further examine the question of whether consumers would overpredict how sensitive their evaluation of or liking for an outcome is to the value of that outcome when they face it alone in consumption.

In Study 1, conducted in China, most participants believed that by smelling a sample of a perfume they could tell whether the perfume was from an expensive brand or a cheap brand and accordingly their liking for that perfume would be high or low. The participants were then randomly assigned to three groups, in which they smelt a piece of tissue paper scented with a drop of an expensive perfume (Chanel No. 5, 500 RMB a bottle), or one scented with a drop of a cheap perfume (a local brand, 50 RMB a bottle), or simply a piece of ordinary scented tissue paper (about 2 RMB a pack). Contrary to the participants' belief, there was no significant difference in how much they liked the perfume across the three groups. Liking for the expensive perfume was higher than that for the cheap perfume, though only slightly, for another group of participants who tried all of three samples. The results suggest that although an expensive perfume may be more pleasant to the nose than is a cheap perfume, the difference is likely to be exaggerated in consumers' belief.

In Study 2, also conducted in China, a group of "white-collar" employees in a big company were asked to indicate whether they would buy a 5-megapixel, 3000 RMB digital camera rather than a 1-megapixel, 500 RMB one, assuming that the other features were identical between the two cameras. Most of the participants chose to buy the 5-megapixel camera. The participants were also asked to indicate whether they believed that if they were presented with an 8"x10" size photo (the largest size they said they would ever use to print photos) they would be able to tell, according to the sharpness of the photo, whether it was taken by a 5-megapixel or a 1-megapixel digital camera. Most of them believed they could. Then, the participants were presented with either a photo with a 5-megapixel resolution or one with a 1-megapixel resolution and asked to rate the sharpness of the photo; the content of the two photos was identical. It turned out that the two photos received a similar rating. Considering the fact that the participants' average monthly salary was 4000 RMB, the finding is quite dramatic.

Such misprediction is less likely to happen for consumers who are knowledgeable about the attribute under evaluation and consequently have the relevant reference information to evaluate the desirability of a value on that attribute even when facing it alone. This idea was tested in Study 3, conducted in the U.S. A group of students from a large Midwestern university was randomly assigned to be predictors or experiencers. The experiencers were presented with either a 1-megapixel or 5-megapixel photo and asked to rate its sharpness; the photos had the same content and size (8" x 10"). The predictors were presented with both photos and told that each photo would be viewed by a separate student who was similar to them. The predictors were asked to predict the sharpness rating each photo would receive. All the participants were asked to report their knowledge about photography on a five-point scale ranging from 1 (*not knowledgeable at all*) to 5 (*very knowledgeable*). Participants who gave a rating of 4 or 5 were classified as experts and the rest, novices. As we expected, among novices, predictors overpredicted the impact of photo resolution on experience of photo sharpness; among experts, no overprediction occurred. Experts were sensitive to photo sharpness even when viewing a photo in isolation.

In sum, the findings of the three studies suggest that consumers tend to believe that a higher value on a positive attribute will translate into better experience. Unless they have acquired knowledge from past experience with values on that attribute or relative reference information is provided at the time of consumption, systematic overprediction often occurs.

REFERENCES

Gilbert, Daniel T., Elizabeth C. Pinel, Timothy D. Wilson, Stephen J. Blumberg, and Thalia P. Wheatley (1998), "Immune neglect: A source of durability bias in affective forecasting," *Journal of Personality and Social Psychology*, 75 (3), 617-638.

Gilbert, Daniel T., Erin Driver-Linn, and Timothy D. Wilson (2002), "The trouble with Vronsky: Impact bias in the forecasting of future affective states," in *The wisdom in feeling: Psychological processes in emotional intelligence*, eds. Lisa F. Barrett and Peter Salovey. New York: Guilford Press, 114-143.

Helson, Harry (1947), "Adaptation-Level as Frame of Reference for Prediction of Psychophysical Data," *American Journal of Psychology*, 60 (1), 1-29.

_____ (1964), *Adaptation-Level Theory: An Experimental and Systematic Approach to Behavior*, New York: Harper and Row.

Hsee, Christopher and Jiao Zhang (2004), "Distinction Bias: Misprediction and Mischoice Due to Joint Evaluation," *Journal of Personality and Social Psychology*, 86 (May), 680-695.

Kahneman, Daniel and Jackie Snell (1990), "Predicting Utility," in Insights in Decision Making: A Tribute to Hillel J. Einhorn, ed. Robin M. Hogarth, Chicago, IL: University of Chicago Press, 295–310.

Kahneman, Daniel and Jackie S. Snell (1992), "Predicting a changing taste: Do people know what they will like," *Journal of Behavioral Decision Making*, 5 (3), 187-200.

Kahneman, Daniel, Peter P. Wakker, and Rakesh Sarin (1997), "Back to Bentham? Exploration of Experienced Utility," The Quarterly Journal of Economics, 112(2), 375-405.

Loewenstein, George (1996), "Out of Control: Visceral Influences on Behavior," *Organizational Behavior and Human Decision Processes*, 65 (3), 272-292.

MacInnis, Deborah J., Vanessa M. Patrick, and C. Whan Park (2006), "Looking through the crystal ball: Affective forecasting and misforecasting in consumer behavior," in *Review of Marketing Research*, Vol. 2, ed. Naresh K. Malhotra. Armonk NY: M.E. Sharpe, 43-80.

Mas-Colell, Andreau, Michael D. Whinston, and Jerry R. Green (1995), *Microeconomic Theory*, Oxford: Oxford University Press.

Nelson, Leif D. and Tom Meyvis (2006), "Interrupted Consumption: Adaptation and the Disruption of Hedonic Experience," Manuscript under review at the Journal of Marketing Research.

Novemsky, Nathan and Rebecca K. Ratner (2003), "The Time Course and Impact of Consumer's Erroneous Beliefs about Hedonic Contrast Effects," Journal of Consumer Research, 29, 507-16.

Nowlis, Stephen, Naomi Mandel, and Deborah Brown McCabe (2004), "The Effect of a Delay Between Choice and Consumption on Consumption Enjoyment," Journal of Consumer Research, 31 (December), 502-510.

Ratner, Rebecca K., Barbara E. Kahn, and Daniel Kahneman (1999), "Choosing Less-Preferred Experiences for the Sake of Variety," *Journal of Consumer Research*, 26 (1), 1-15.

Schwartz, Barry (2004), The Paradox of Choice. New York, NY: HarperCollins.

Wilson, Timothy D. and Nancy Brekke (1994), " Mental contamination and mental correction: Unwanted influences on judgments and evaluations," *Psychological Bulletin*, 116 (1), 117-142.

Wilson, Timothy D., Thalia P. Wheatley, Jonathon M. Meyers, Daniel T. Gilbert, and Danny Axsom (2000), "Focalism: A source of durability bias in affective forecasting," *Journal of Personality and Social Psychology*, 78 (5), 821-836.

Zajonc, R. B. (1968), "Attitudinal Effects of Mere Exposure," *Journal of Personality and Social Psychology*, 9 (2) , 1-27.

"Roll Your Own" Religion: Consumer Culture and the Spiritual Vernacular

Linda Scott, University of Oxford, UK
Pauline Maclaran, Keele University, UK

SESSION OVERVIEW

Consumer researchers have long questioned the traditional separation between sacred and secular that typifies other thought in the social sciences (Belk, Wallendorf, and Sherry 1989). In this symposium, we will build on this work in several ways.

The most salient difference will derive from the focus of place: all the sites here are European, while previous study in the stream has been in America. Our three sites—Italy, Ireland, and England—not only represent a geographic departure consistent with the theme of the conference, but also represent fundamentally different circumstances for studying the approach to spiritual experience. All three countries have historically been what James Twitchell called "single-supplier" societies in his recent book, *Shopping for God* (2007), where the church is closely intertwined with, if not indistinguishable from, the state. Consequently, these countries, especially Ireland and Italy, have traditionally allowed considerably less of the religious pluralism that Twitchell argues had lead to a market-based approach to spiritual practice in America, where consumer choice and church competition are the order of the day.

Nevertheless, in all three cases, we will demonstrate a clear trend toward what Twitchell has also called "vernacular religion"—in which consumers either produce ritual objects themselves, re-purpose traditional religious props, or shop "off the shelf" from other religious traditions—to use for their own inventive, often empowering, spiritual practices. In this way, we will also be building further on the work by previous scholars in consumer behavior, who have focused primarily on the "sacralization of the secular"—where consumers imagine or treat everyday objects in a manner that echoes, but does not attempt to constitute, a religious practice (e. g., Muniz and Schau 2005).

In other work, consumer researchers have examined the commercialization of religious spaces and objects within the American experience, but framed by an existing official church (e.g., Belk and O'Guinn 1989). Again, the geographic setting makes a difference: all three of the sites examined here are places with long religious histories, reaching back hundreds of years into the pre-Christian era—yet the cultural memory of the pagan past is still manifest in practice and the places themselves are fundamentally hybridized, thus arguably more open to consumer reinvention. At the same time, these three settings are no less open to the influences of globalization than any American site; consequently, the consumers and the places both often invoke or reflect contemporary media. As a result, a layering of past knowledge and practice with presently accepted doctrine, as well as with new tropes and needs, is present at these sites in a more transparent and conscious way. Thus, our symposium will also marry the approach to religious practice with Thompson and Tian's recent work on the cultural memory of place (2008).

We will add an important methodological layer to that originally proposed by Belk, Wallendorf and Sherry (1989): we not only tack between the field and the sociological literature for insights and analysis, we also consult the sacred texts and myths invoked by the practices under study, as well as the actual religious histories of the sites—and incorporate the layering provided by contemporary texts from *Buffy the Vampire Slayer* to *Harry Potter*.

Finally, our work demonstrates poignantly that humans are still spiritual seekers, even in a consumer society that so many critics say leads to apathy and meaninglessness. Far from abandoning the thirst for meaningful existence, our subjects show an irrepressibly hopeful and creative search for the sacred.

EXTENDED ABSTRACTS

"Bidding Brigid: Objects of Petition and the Euhemerized Goddess"

Darach Turley, Dublin City University, Ireland

Often referred to as "Mary of the Gael," St. Brigid holds pre-eminent and emblematic status among Irish Catholics. Though her reputation is not confined to Ireland (there are 40 dedicated sites in Brittany, as well as 10 pre-Reformation dedications in England, the most prominent at Glastonbury), it was probably due to her popularity in this strongly Catholic country that Brigid was spared in the Vatican's recent purge of the saintly pantheon.

Brigid, like most who were thus swept away, lived in the transition period when the pre-Christian was being assimilated into Christian orthodoxy. St. Brigid is said to have died in 524AD; the Church's first life of this saint was written soon thereafter, in the 7th century. Yet even this early biography includes attributes of a Celtic, pre-Christian goddess of the same name. Indeed, there is increasing evidence that the Christian St. Brigid is in fact an euhemerization and thus an artefact of an astute and far-sighted sixth century Papal stratagem, in which pagan sites and objects were reinvested with a Christian connotation, instead of being destroyed and replaced. Attributes of the tutelary Celtic goddess appear to have been appropriated and grafted on to her saintly virginized namesake. And while the persona of the Celtic goddess has obviously been obscured in this process, there are sufficient similarities and parallels between both to posit a composite of what constitutes a Celtic goddess. Thus, an examination of surviving Brigidine festivals and lore suggests that the cult of St. Brigid represents a perfect exemplar of this pagan-Christian syncretism. For instance, the pre-Christian Brigid was a goddess of fertility and growth and the guardian of livestock; St. Brigid's feast day is celebrated on February 1st, the first day of Spring. Miracles attributed to Brigid are characterized by lavish abundance and fecundity. Her life story depicts her very much as a transitional, hybridized figure. For example, she has a noble (married) father and a slave (unmarried) mother; she is born at sunrise, a transition between night and day; on the threshold of her mother's home-in Irish folklore a symbol of the penumbra between inner and outer worlds. Later in life, Brigid becomes an abbess—thus she attains the hierarchical status of a male bishop. A superordinate female member of the Celtic pantheon, the pagan Brigid was creator of both natural land formations and the great megalithic structures of the British Isles. In keeping with the Celtic predilection for triads, she was also a poet, healer and artisan.

Today, popular devotion to the Christian St. Brigid resonates with her pre-Christian ancestry. At St. Brigid's Holy Well in County Clare, Irish consumers marshal an array of objects and possessions to both reflect and shape religious and mythological beliefs. The well itself is situated at the back of a stone grotto. Shelves along the entrance to the grotto are bedecked with a dizzying assortment of objects left by pilgrims: romantic religious artifacts such as rosaries, Italianate holy pictures and statuary together with an array of what appears to be tawdry everyday household bric a brac: pins, buttons, combs, biros, walking sticks, eyeglasses, rags, and scarves. Pilgrims leave these objects after traveling to the well to drink its waters on designated holy days— and often attach explanatory written messages to the objects they leave behind.

The aim of this paper is to examine how the pagan-Christian syncretism discussed above is refracted through this array of possessions and texts left by devotees. A key theme to emerge in this analysis is the performative roles of these goods. Unlike their counterparts in Latin Catholic countries, the objects left here do not appear to function as votive offerings, brought to a saint or Madonna in thanksgiving for favours received. Instead, pilgrims at this well, come to St. Brigid *seeking* a favour, physical or spiritual, and the good left behind appears to function more as a material metaphor enabling the supplicant to visualize in a concrete manner what they wish the saint to accomplish on their behalf. Thus, the old way of life, the illness, is 'deposited' in the rags, walking stick or eyeglasses. Obviously, this works best if the possession holds some cathectic relationship with the disease. This theme of cathexis, detachment or unfastening was further underscored by the nature of many of the possessions deposited on the shelves: buttons, pins, nails.

A second performative role was evidenced in the way many of the items–biros, combs, pins–were deliberately bent or broken. Local lore has it that this is to underscore the fact that these items are no longer intended for use in this world. For these believers, the efficacy of the material in the non-material sphere does not appear to be an issue, a fact that challenges the modernist notion of agency and embodiment as coextensive. Indeed on a wider tableau, the mindset of those who deposit possessions at the well suggests a need to re-conjugate the relationship between agency, embodiment and self. The dominance of empiricism and positivism has had ramifications for consumer behaviour that extend beyond choice of requisite methodologies; on a metaphysical level it has also perpetuated the elision of agency, empowerment and bodily incarnation. It is hoped that this paper may contribute to an exploration of alternate boundaries between embodied and disembodied agency and a metaphysic that can accommodate a world where possessions can simultaneously contribute to making a site sacred, solicit saintly intervention, and carry a semantic payload for both human and otherworldly audiences. In this regard, Brigid's euhemerized status gives the debate an added theoretical twist.

Reflexive observations will also feature, among them a discussion of the need to revisit the notion of sociality in consumer research. A fresher, more accommodating metaphysical stance might permit a more inclusive appreciation of the role of disembodied beings, saintly and not so saintly, as significant others for the consumer behaviour of their earthly, embodied, counterparts.

"'Living a Magical Life': Sacred Consumption and Spiritual Experience in the Italian Neo-Pagan Community"
Diego Rinallo, Bocconi University, Italy

Neo-paganism is "an umbrella term for various religions, or spiritual movements, whose practitioners are inspired by the indigenous, pre-Christian, traditions of Europe ... to evolve satisfying and respectful ways of celebrating human relationships with the wider, other-than-human world" (Clifton and Harvey 2004: 1). In the 1950s, early British exponents of the movement claimed to be initiates of a nature-based witchcraft religion that had secretly survived Christian prosecutions (Gardner 1954; 1959). In the US, neo-pagan traditions have been assimilated since the 1970s to the women's spirituality movement as feminist exponents (e.g.,

Budapest 1976; Starhawk 1982) popularized the emancipating idea of a Goddess immanent in nature (as opposed to a transcendent male God detached from creation), adopting at the same time the witch as a symbol of independent female power oppressed by patriarchy (Hutton 1999).

In Italy, the neo-pagan movement is still in an embryonic phase as only in the 1990s Internet enabled the constitution of the first pagan groups and associations. Most Italian neo-pagans were raised by Catholic families and adopted neo-paganism as a religion in later phases of their lives. As Italy is predominantly a Catholic country, Wiccan and other neo-pagans are often confused with devil worshippers and face considerable level of stigma, ridicule and social ostracism. My study is based on two years of ethnographic fieldwork within the neo-pagan community in the areas of Northern Italy and Sicily. Data collection consisted of formal and informal interviews and participant observation of neo-pagan gatherings, festivals, rituals, social events, workshops and online forums in 2006-2007.

Neo-pagans are avid consumers of goods such as ritual costumes; jewelry (e.g., pentacles, Goddess figurines); ritual tools like ceremonial knives, cups, incense burners, candles, incenses; Goddesses and Gods statues; CDs of neo-pagan music; and books. Many of these items are employed in the context of rituals to create a sacred space where communication between the human and Divine is made possible. To this aim, neo-pagans learn esoteric knowledge on the inherent properties of material objects for spiritual and magical purposes. The idea that objects and elements of the physical world are mystically connected to spiritual realms and entities is age-old. In the Renaissance, Cornelius Agrippa's *Philosophia Occulta* (1533) reported extended tables of correspondences between spiritual entities and herbs, metals, stones, animals and other natural phenomena. Variations of these correspondence tables are widely available through countless books and websites, and are currently employed as reference tools for magical activities. Ritual practice among the neo-pagan community is also shaped by selective readings of scientific disciplines, including history, archeology, religious studies, psychology, folklore, anthropology and even physics. As a spiritual movement, neo-paganism has been disproportionately influenced by folklore and anthropology, and works such has Sir James Frazer's *The Golden Bough* (1922), Margaret Murray's *The Witch Cult of Western Europe* (1921) and Marija Gimbutas' *The Language of the Goddess* (1989) feature prominently in the bookshelves of many neo-pagans. While the ideas reported by some of these scholars are now discredited among academic circles (see Hutton 2000), they act as "scientific" fundament for widely circulated counter-cultural mythologies that foster a sense of shared past and shape sacred consumption practices.

In this respect, another major source of influence consists of mass-mediated representations of magic, including fantasy books (e.g., Marion Zimmer Bradley's *The Mists of Avalon*, J.K. Rowling's *Harry Potter*) and popular movies or TV shows (e.g., *Harry Potter*, *Charmed*). By selectively leveraging esoteric knowledge and resonant science, history and popular culture, members of the neo-pagan community ideologically shape subcultural practices and consumption. During a ritual, incense recipes may derive from a medieval grimoire; hand-made ceremonial dresses may be inspired by the Lord of the Rings; a magic wand may be crafted after Harry Potter's, and earrings and other ceremonial jewelry may reproduce Celtic patterns found in archeology books. The same sources also shape transcendent experiences. Eclectic neo-pagans may see Divinities in popular culture characters. Buffy may thus be invoked as a Goddess of fire and passion, while the sinister pantheon of H.P. Lovecraft's *Chtulhu Mythos* may be adopted for more gothic rituals. During meditations or dreams, neo-pagans may remember past lives when they were Avalon priests, Siberian shamans or Tuscan witches. Such vivid images, at least to a certain extent, may be influenced by their readings in history, anthropology and fiction.

This paper contributes to literature on sacred consumption. While magico-religious metaphors have been widely employed in consumer behavior, most studies have been concerned with the sacralization of the secular rather than the use of consumption goods to seek transcendent experiences. In particular, this paper explores the interplay of science and fantasy in the shaping of counter-cultural mythologies and consumption practices. As they engage with alternative spirituality and magical activities, members of the pagan community expose themselves to selected body of scientific knowledge and inspiring images from popular culture that shape their experience of the spiritual otherworld. Consumer researchers have highlighted the role of mass-mediated culture and selective readings of history in shaping of consumer ideologies and fantasies (Belk and Costa 1998; Thompson 2004; Thompson and Tian 2008). These same sources may also affect spiritual experiences.

"Spiritual Tourism: Mystical Merchandise and Sacred Shopping in Glastonbury"

Pauline Maclaran, Keele University, UK
Linda Scott, University of Oxford, UK

Set in the heart of England's countryside, Glastonbury town has become the main centre in England for what Bowman (2004, 273) describes as "spiritual tourism". Dominated by Glastonbury Tor, a distorted coneshaped hill with a ruined 14th century church tower on top, the area, that is also known as the Isle of Avalon, "generates and guards a powerful magic" (Roberts 1977). The history of the area stretches far back into the mists of time with many contested stories that change according to the spiritual orientation of the teller. It is generally agreed that the ancient Isle of Avalon was a site of prehistoric worship and mystical tradition that, arguably, can be traced as far back as the Atlantean era of 10,000 BC (Mann 2004) when the Atlanteans are said to have used the Tor as a natural temple after their own temples had been destroyed by the sea.

The area's key spiritual attractions are brought together in the concept of Glastonbury Zodiac which is claimed to have been created by a race of prehistoric astronomers (Malthood 1935). They are accredited with shaping patterns of mythical and astrological significance around the natural contours of the landscape (Roberts 1971). Estimated to be 10 miles in diameter and 30 miles in circumference, the sites that make up the Zodiac harness the Isle's potent celestial and terrestial energies and are closely lined to the Arthurian legends that surround the Isle of Avalon and that have spiritual significance for both Pagans and Christians alike. King Arthur was allegedly taken there to heal after his last battle and his body is claimed by Christians to be buried in Glastonbury Abbey (Bowman 2004). The Chalice Well at Glastonbury is supposed to be where Joseph of Arimathea hid the Holy Grail after the crucifixion. The arrival of St Joseph brought Christianity to Glastonbury and is still celebrated in the Holy Thorn Ceremony that takes place there each December (Bowman 2006).

Yet, the Chalice Well's history, going back over 2000 years, predates a Christian era. It is thought to have been built by the Druids who came to the area in 600 BC and who founded a Druidic university in the area. They believed in the healing properties of the water and the well's powers as an entrance to the other world. Because the water is reddish in colour it has also been claimed by modern Neopagans as symbolizing the menstrual blood of the Goddess and a representation of the divine feminine. The story of the sorceress, Morgen Le Fay, an important icon in Goddess culture, has its origins in Arthurian legend. Known as "Lady" or "Priestess" of Avalon, she was half–human and half-faerie. Morgen attempted to bring about the downfall of Camelot and was continually thwarted by King Arthur. In recent times she has been brought to the fore through Marion Zimmer Bradley's classic novel, *The Mists of Avalon*, that was made into a film in 2001, and which retells the story of Camelot from a goddess perspective, recasting Morgen as a gifted woman demonized by patriarchal legend (Jones 2006). Her eight sister Morgens, representing the changing cycles of nature, have also become an integral part of Goddess worship.

The many contested spiritual overlays that co-exist in Glastonbury are perhaps best exemplified by Glastonbury's high street with its astonishing array of small shops that are devoted to mystical merchandise. These New Age shops–e.g. Speaking Tree Bookshop, The Celtic Thread, The Goddess and the Green Man, The Psychic Piglet, Yin Yang, Gothic Image-sell escoteric ranges of mystical symbols, jewellery, books, tarot cards, clothing, furniture, soft furnishings and arts and crafts. Together they present a veritable spiritual bricolage that is manifested through what we have termed "sacred shopping", a shopping that reflects the rich mosaic of myth and legend that surrounds the region and enables a "pic n' mix" approach to a personalised spirituality. In the heart of this shopping lies the Goddess Temple where effigies of the Nine Morgens depict the creative power of nature and the divine feminine. In a strange juxtaposition, just around the corner stands Glastonbury Abbey, built in 37 AD, and reported to be the first Christian Church in Britain. Indeed, both Christian and Goddess communities continue to stake their claims to Glastonbury's spiritual heritage in annual processions through the town (Bowman 2004).

Drawing on a vernacular religious approach that emphasizes the role of material culture, in our presentation we will argue that Glastonbury's spiritual shopping plays an important role in carving out sacred space for New Age religious beliefs, and helps legitimize their claims in the face of more traditional Christian appropriations of sites in and around Glastonbury.

REFERENCES

Agrippa, Cornelius H. ([1533] 1992), *De Occulta Philosophia Libri Tres*, ed. Vittoria Perrone Compagni, Boston: Brill.

Belk, Russell W. and Janeen Arnold Costa (1998), "The Mountain Man Myth: A Contemporary Consuming Fantasy," *Journal of Consumer Research*, 25 (December), 218-40.

Belk, Russell W. and Gulnur Tumbat (2005), "The cult of Macintosh," *Consumption, Markets & Culture*, 8 (3), 205-17.

Belk, Russell W., Melanie Wallendorf, and John F. Sherry Jr. (1989), "The Sacred and the Profane in Consumer Behavior," *Journal of Consumer Research*, 16 (June), 1–38.

Belk, Russell W., Melanie Wallendorf and John F. Sherry Jr. (1989) The sacred and the profane in consumer behavior, *Journal of Consumer Research*, 16, 1, June: 1-38

Bowman, Marion (2004), "The Holy Thorn Ceremony: Revival, Rivalry and Civil Religion in Glastonbury," *Folklore*, 115 (2), 123-140.

Bowman, Marion (2006), "Procession and Possession in Glastonbury: Continuity, Change and the Manipulation of Tradition," *Folklore*, 115 (4), 273-285.

Clifton, Chas S. and Graham Harvey (2004), *The Paganism Reader*, New York: Routledge.

Budapest, Zsuzsanna (1976), *The Feminist Book of Lights and Shadows*, Venice, CA: Luna Publications.

Carroll, Michael P. (1999) *Irish pilgrimage: Holy wells and popular Catholic devotion*, Baltimore, MD: The Johns Hopkins University Press.

Durkheim Emile (1971 [1915]) *The elementary forms of the religious life*, trans. Joseph Ward Swain, London: George Allen & Unwin.

Frazer, Sir James G. (1922), *The Golden Bough*, Abridged version, London: Macmillan.

Gardner, Gerald B. (1954), *Witchcraft Today*, London: Rider and Company.

Gardner, Gerald B. (1959), *The Meaning of Witchcraft*, London: Rider and Company.

Gimbutas, Marija (1989), *The Language of the Goddess*, Berkeley: University of California Press.

Hutton, Ronald (1999), *The Triumph of the Moon*, Oxford: Oxford University Press.

Jones, Kathy (2006), *Priestess of Avalon, Priestess of the Goddess*, Glastonbury: Ariadne Publications.

Maltwood, Katharine (1935), *Glastonbury's Temple of the Stars*, Cambridge, UK: James Clarke.

Mann, Nicholas (2004), *Energy Secrets of Glastonbury Tor*, Somerset: Green Magic.

Murray, Margaret (1921), *The Witch Cult in Western Europe*. Oxford: Oxford University Press.

O'Cathasaigh, Donal (1982) The cult of Brigid: A study of pagan-Christian syncretism in Ireland, in *Mother worship: Theme and variations*, ed. James J. Preston, Chapel Hill, The University of North Carolina Press, 75-94

O'Duinn, Sean (2005) *The Rites of Brigid, Goddess and Saint*, Dublin: The Columba Press

O'Guinn, Thomas C. and Russell W. Belk (1989) Heaven on earth: Consumption at Heritage Village, USA, *Journal of Consumer Research*, 16, 2, September: 227-238

Roberts, Anthony (1977), "Glastonbury–the Ancient Avalon", in *Glastonbury–Ancient Avalon, New Jerusalem*, ed. Anthony Roberts, UK: Rider.

Rowley, Sherry (1997) On Saint Brigit and pagan goddesses in the Kingdom of God, *Canadian Woman Studies*, 17, 3: 93-95.

Starhawk ([1979] 1989), *The Spiral Dance*, San Francisco: HarperCollins.

Thompson, Craig J. (2004), "Marketplace Mythology and Discourses of Power," *Journal of Consumer Research* 31 (June), 162-80.

Thompson, Craig J., and Kelly Tian (2008), "Reconstructing the South: How Commercial Myths Compete for Identity Vaue through the Ideological Shaping of Popular Memories and Countermemories," *Journal of Consumer Research* 34 (February), 519-613.

Twitchell, James (2007), *Shopping for God*, New York: Simon and Schuster.

Comforting Social Presence, Depleting Social Influence

Anne-Laure Sellier, New York University, USA

SESSION OVERVIEW

We know that the presence of others affects consumers' product evaluations and their purchase behavior. Past research has demonstrated that consuming with others is a different experience than consuming alone, whether social presence is real or imagined (e.g., Argo, Dahl & Manchanda 2005; Ramanathan & McGill 2007). Of particular interest, recent research showed that consuming with others favors a similar pattern of emotional experience between consumers and others (Ramanathan & McGill 2007). Our objective in this session is to examine this "togetherness" aspect of consumption. In particular, the three presentations in this symposium generally document how social presence (real or imagined) can be comforting, thereby shaping evaluations and directing choices, while social influence–in contrast-appears taxing.

Two presentations present instances of how social presence can be comforting to consumers: Loveland, Smeesters, and Mandel show that social presence motivates consumers to choose nostalgic products over recent ones. They find that this preference is mediated by consumers' desire to feel close to others. Sellier and Morwitz find that when consumers perceive time as limited, they evaluate ads picturing a supportive social cue more positively than one presenting an achievement cue or a neutral, non-social cue; a reflection of emotion-related goals (e.g., feeling close to others) taking precedence over achievement-related goals (e.g., getting a degree to bank for a future perceived to be long). Conversely, they find that when consumers perceive time as expansive, they evaluate an ad containing a social cue signaling achievement more favorably than an ad containing a social cue signaling support. Also of interest in these two presentations is the link between valuing togetherness and managing time via consumption. In Loveland et al., social presence makes consumers value options related to the past rather than the present; in Sellier and Morwitz, social presence leads to more positive evaluations when it is congruent with the social goals activated by consumers' time horizon perspective. In contrast to this first set of findings suggesting a comforting role of social presence, Sellier and Morwitz also find that social presence hurts persuasion when it is incongruent with consumers' activated social goals, observing that a non-social cue not related to either emotion goals or achievement goals leads to more persuasion than a social cue incongruent with consumers' activated social goals. Vohs, Dennis, and Janssen present an instance of the harmful impact of social influence. Their research demonstrates that when the social context involves having one individual seek compliance from another (e.g., Cialdini 1993), it is ego-depleting for the consumer who is asked to comply. Together, these findings shed further light on the importance of investigating consumer behavior in the presence of real (Loveland et al.; Vohs et al.) or represented others (Sellier & Morwitz). In particular, this symposium stresses the implications of social presence and influence on the self. Consuming with others not only feels different (Ramanathan & McGill 2007): the findings in Loveland et al. suggest it may be self-enhancing; those in Sellier and Morwitz suggest that it can be helping or harming persuasion, while those of Vohs et al. show it can be ego-depleting.

EXTENDED ABSTRACTS

"Still Preoccupied with 1985: The Effect of Imagined Interaction on Preference for Nostalgic Products"

Kathleen E. Loveland, Arizona State University, USA
Dirk Smeesters, Erasmus University, The Netherlands
Naomi Mandel, Arizona State University, USA

We sometimes have an increased interest in products that we enjoyed in the past. The successful resurrection of nostalgic brands such as Pabst Blue Ribbon, Ford Mustang, and Converse shoes suggests that many consumers are interested in products that generate favorable childhood memories. Surprisingly, little attention has been paid to the concept of nostalgia in the consumer behavior literature. This research examines potential antecedents to an increased preference for nostalgic products. We define nostalgic products as products that were popular when one was younger and are no longer in current production.

Prior research has shown that nostalgic recollections often involve interaction with close others (Wildschut et al. 2006). Additionally, Wildschut et al. (2006) found that loneliness leads to higher nostalgic tendencies and that nostalgic recollection bolsters social bonds. These findings suggest that nostalgia serves the social functions of easing loneliness and fostering social interactions. Therefore, we hypothesized (and found) that preference for nostalgic products would increase when social, as opposed to private, aspects of life were activated in consumers' memory. We also tested the underlying mechanism for this effect, and found evidence that the increased preference for nostalgic products occurred when consumers felt emotionally closer to others, as measured by the Inclusion of the Other in the Self Scale (IOS; Aron, Aron & Smollan 1992). In addition, we examined the moderating role of life transition.

We conducted three experiments that provide empirical support for our hypotheses. In Experiment 1, participants were randomly assigned to either write about activities they engage in with other people (social), or activities they do on their own (private). Next, they chose a 10-minute video clip to watch from a set of four television shows, all of which were pretested and found to be equivalent in overall liking among individuals in the participants' age group. Specifically, they chose either a television show that is currently on the air (*The Office* or *Grey's Anatomy*) or a clip from a show that is no longer in production and first aired in the early 1990s (*Saved By the Bell* or *Fresh Prince of Bel Air*). We found a significant main effect of social interaction, with 61% of participants in the social condition choosing to watch a nostalgic show and 17% of participants in the private condition choosing to watch a nostalgic show (χ^2=12.06, $p<.01$).

Experiment 2 replicated the first experiment with the addition of the IOS as a possible mediator for the relationship between social interaction and preference for nostalgic products. We found evidence that IOS mediates this relationship (z=2.58, $p<.01$), suggesting that people prefer nostalgic products when thinking about interacting with others because such thoughts lead them to feel emotionally closer to others, and the consumption of nostalgic products can prolong this feeling of emotional closeness.

In Experiment 3, we tested the moderating role of life transition on the preference for nostalgic products. Individuals may be more likely to experience nostalgia during times of transition (i.e., discontinuity hypothesis, Davis 1979). Consumer researchers have found that symbolic possessions tend to take on greater importance during times of transition as they can help ease the psychological difficulties associated with transition (Belk 1992). In support of the discontinuity hypothesis, we found that the increased preference for nostalgic products when thinking about social (as opposed to private) aspects of life was stronger when a life transition was salient. We used a 2 (social vs. private) x 2 (current vs. transition) between-participants design in which participants wrote an essay about either their *current* life, or what they think their life will be like after graduation from college (*transition*) while focusing on either the social or private aspects of that life. Participants again chose between watching either a nostalgic or a current television show. We replicated the main effect of social interaction on the preference for nostalgic products. Additionally, there was a significant interaction between life transition and social interaction, such that the preference for nostalgic products was more pronounced when the social aspects of a life transition were made salient (*Wald*=3.28, *p*=0.05). This finding is consistent with the idea that since periods of transition are marked by the adoption of new roles and relationships (Lee, Moschis, & Mathur, 2001), individuals will seek means, such as nostalgic products, to create a sense of social and identity continuity.

In Experiment 4, we replicated and extended our earlier findings by manipulating participants' self-construal (interdependent vs. independent). We found that individuals whose interdependent self was activated had a higher preference for nostalgic movies, cars, and television programs than individuals whose independent self was activated. Further analyses indicated that the effect of self-construal on the preference for nostalgic products was mediated by feelings of interconnectedness.

Importantly, our participants demonstrated an increased preference for products from the past when they wrote (in experiments 1-3) about interacting with others in the *present* and the *future*, as compared to when they wrote about solitary activities in the *present* and *future*. Therefore, it is unlikely that participants are merely matching their thoughts about friends from the past with activities associated with close others from the past. Instead, these findings support the notion of nostalgia as a socially driven phenomenon on a more general level.

This research contributes to the literature in several ways. First, while earlier research has hinted at the idea that nostalgia is social in nature, to date this issue has not been tested explicitly. We are able to add to this literature by demonstrating that individuals experience an increased preference for nostalgic products at the mere thought of interacting with others, regardless of whether those interactions are positive/negative, past/present. Second, this is the first study to examine behavioral preferences for nostalgic products as the dependent variable. Other works that have sought to investigate triggers of nostalgia have either used "attitudes towards the past" as the dependent variable (Wildschut et al. 2006), or have only considered individual differences in nostalgia proneness (Batcho 1998).

"The Impact of Social Cues on Message Persuasiveness: The Role of Time Horizon Perspective"

Anne-Laure Sellier, New York University, USA
Vicki Morwitz, New York University, USA

While the question of *whether* social presence influences consumers' evaluations and behavior has received much attention in consumer research, less research has examined (1) whether different *types* of social presence (e.g., the mere presence of another person, social presence that signals the provision of emotional support, social presence that signals what can be gained from others, etc.) have different effects on consumers' evaluations, (2) how these effects may differ across different types of consumers, for example how it would differ across consumers who hold different perceptions concerning the amount of time they have ahead of them in life, and (3) when the absence of any social cue is preferable to its presence (in contexts other than the obvious case of low social desirability). This research explores these three questions. In particular, building on socioemotional selectivity theory (SST) (Carstensen et al. 1999), we suggest that the value that consumers will place on one particular type of social presence cue, namely cues that signal emotional support from others, will vary with their perception of how much time they have ahead of them; more precisely, it will vary with whether time is perceived as limited or expansive.

SST posits that time perception determines the relative importance of two broad categories of social goals: *knowledge-related goals*, defined as goals aimed at optimizing the future, (e.g., getting a University degree), involving a focus on achievement; and *emotion-related goals*, defined as goals related to feelings, involving a focus on emotion regulation, whereby one attempts to maximize positive emotional experiences, in particular through love and caring social interaction (e.g., interacting with people in a deep rather than a superficial manner) (Carstensen et al. 1999). SST's key predictions are that when time is perceived as limited, emotion-related goals receive priority over knowledge-related goals. That is, they pay more attention to how supportive a social interaction is than to what opportunities this interaction might open up for them. In contrast, when time is perceived as expansive, knowledge-related goals are perceived to be more important than emotion-related goals.

We hypothesized that when consumers perceive time as limited [expansive], they will evaluate a message containing a social cue signaling emotional support [achievement] more positively than a message containing a social cue signaling achievement [emotional support]. We propose that goal congruence is the process generating this effect. Further, we hypothesized that when the social cue is incongruent with the activated social goal (e.g., a social cue signaling emotional support presented to a consumer with activated achievement-related goals), it is devalued compared to a neutral cue (defined as a non-social cue that is neither emotion- nor achievement-related). In other words, an incongruent social cue is disinstrumental to the activated social goals, and offers a case where social absence is preferable to social presence (disinstrumentality hypothesis).

Importantly, in our experiments, we made sure that our messages containing a support cue and those containing an achievement or a neutral cue were equally focusing participants on thoughts and on emotions, to avoid replicating prior research contributions (particularly Williams & Drolet's 2005).

Four experiments test these predictions. In Experiment 1, we found support for our hypothesis that an emotional support [achievement-related] social cue embedded in an ad for a hotel should lead to more positive evaluations of the hotel when consumers perceive time as limited [expansive]. Participants' time horizon perspective and the social cue they were exposed to were both manipulated in a storyboard.

In Experiment 2, we manipulated participants' time horizon perspective by asking them to write about events in their life for which they perceived they had limited time versus all the time in the world to achieve them. Subsequently, participants were exposed to a storyboard for a travel agency that either contained an emotional support social cue or a neutral cue, and then evaluated the storyboard. As predicted, we found that participants perceiving time as limited evaluated the storyboard containing a support social cue more positively than the storyboard containing a neutral cue. However, participants perceiving time as expansive only tended to evaluate the storyboard containing a neutral cue more favorably, failing to support our disinstrumentality hypothesis.

Experiment 3 provides a test supportive of our goal congruence explanation. We show that a limited (versus an expansive) time horizon perspective activates social goals of love and caring (versus knowledge and achievement), which in turn drives the effect observed in Experiment 2.

Experiment 4 had two purposes: to provide further support to our goal congruence account via a stronger test of our disinstrumentality hypothesis, as well as a boundary condition of our effect. Participants with a limited or an expansive time horizon perspective viewed a storyboard eliciting negative emotions. The storyboard either contained a support social cue or a neutral cue. In addition, to test for a boundary of our effect, we instructed participants to (1) let their emotions flow naturally or (2) suppress their emotions while viewing the storyboard. We reasoned that consumers with a limited time horizon, whose focus is on maximizing positive emotional experience, may choose to suppress negative emotions. When participants let their emotions flow naturally, we found a more positive evaluation of the storyboard containing a social cue compared to a neutral cue when participants perceived time as limited; we found *the reverse* when participants perceived time as expansive. This provides further support to our goal congruence account, by showing that using an incongruent social cue is not only inefficient, but disinstrumental compared to a cue unrelated to the activated social goal. In contrast, for participants who suppressed their emotions, we found a reversal of the effect in Experiment 2, thereby providing a boundary for our effect.

This research shows that social presence embedded in persuasive messages can shape evaluations, but only when consumers' focus is on congruent social goals. When the focus is on incongruent goals, social absence leads to more favorable evaluations. This work also stresses the relevance of different types of social cues depending on how much time consumers perceive they have ahead of them.

"Why Do People Fall Prey to Social Influence Techniques? A Limited-Resource Account of Compliance"

Kathleen D. Vohs, University of Minnesota, USA
Bob Fennis, University of Twente, The Netherlands
Loes Janssen, University of Twente, The Netherlands

Documenting and studying social influence techniques has fascinated scholars for over forty years. According to Cialdini (e.g., Cialdini 1993), all influence techniques aim to lure targets into a state of automaticity or "mindlessness". In these states, targets are prone to employ norms that increase compliance rates. We propose that such mindlessness comes about because the initial stage of an influence technique triggers one underlying psychological mechanism: self-regulatory resource depletion.

We present a two-stage model, in which the first step involves draining the self's finite self-control resources via consciously attending and responding to the requestors' inquiries during the initial requests of an influence technique. A meta-analysis on the most prominent influence procedure, the foot-in-the-door (FITD) technique, revealed that its effectiveness hinges on the initial request being highly involving. A closer look suggests that highly involving requests entail either (a) active self-presentation or (b) demanding cognitive operations, or both — processes that are known to elicit self-regulatory resource depletion (Schmeichel, Baumeister and Vohs 2003; Vohs, Baumeister and Ciarocco 2005).

In the second step, self-regulatory resource depletion fosters the use of norms, which increases the odds of yielding to the target request. Influence agents use norms of reciprocity, liking, and authority to compel the person to comply. These norms are more likely to be relied upon when people pay more attention to the peripheral aspects of a message and less to the message context — a pattern that is seen among people with depleted self-regulatory resources (Wheeler, Briñol, & Hermann 2007).

Hence in six studies, we examined whether influence techniques induce self-regulatory resource depletion and then whether self-regulatory resource depletion leads to a reliance on norms and hence enhances compliance. All six experiments supported our hypotheses.

In Experiments 1 and 2 we gathered evidence to test Stage 1 of our model by examining the initial request-phase of a typical foot-in-the door ploy. We show that yielding to the initial part of a foot-in-the-door technique, which involved answering a series of self-disclosing (Experiment 1) or cognitively demanding questions (Experiment 2) induces self-regulatory resource depletion. Experiment 1 mimicked traditional foot-in-the-door technique questions while also connecting with the notion that self-regulatory resources are needed to engage in high-order thought processes and intelligent responding (Schmeichel et al 2003). Experiment 2 also borrowed questions from the foot-in-the-door literature and connected this process to the notion that self-regulatory resource depletion emerges after impression management attempts (Vohs et al 2005). Moreover, both were field studies, which enhance our claims about the generalizability of the effects.

In Experiments 3a and 3b, again field experiments, we ruled out alternate explanations that the prior results were due to emotion changes, type of interaction, or norm-violation by the agent. We asked participants to not only respond (or not) to the initial requests of a compliance technique, but we asked them to complete a mood scale to rule out the potential confounding role of negative emotions; we switched experimenters (i.e., requestors) between the initial request and the dependent measure of self-regulatory resource depletion so as to rule out violations of the norm of reciprocity; and we also added a condition in which participants on the street were simply engaged in a conversation that did not resemble anything like the initial steps of an influence technique to rule out the possibility that the effects were due to the simple act of unanticipated conversation with an unacquainted person. Across all measures in both studies, we found that no indicators of these alternate explanations prevailed; instead only self-regulatory resource depletion after being a part of a scripted social influence technique emerged.

In Experiments 4 to 6, we tested Stage 2 of the model. In this series of lab and field studies, we assessed whether self-regulatory resource depletion fosters the use of heuristics in decision making, thereby increasing the chances of compliance. In Experiment 4, self-regulatory resource depletion was manipulated, as was the salience of a norm–in this case, the norm of reciprocity). Subsequently, compliance with a request was measured. We predicted and found that when participants were self-regulatory resource depleted and were presented with a norm of reciprocity, they showed a clear tendency to comply with the request. We extended the generalizability of our theorizing in Experiments 5 and 6 to include other operationalizations of self-regulatory resource depletion. These studies also demonstrated the effect in both field and lab settings involving different norms (e.g., liking and authority) and other forms of compliance. Moreover, Experiment 6 obtained converging evidence by investigating trait self-control. In this case, we found that low–but not high–trait self-control participants were induced to comply with a target request, but only when there was a norm in place.

The present findings point to a previously unexplored "theatre of operations" of principles involved in effortful self-regulation: that of dyadic social influence. Previous research has neglected instrumental dyadic interactions in which one party tries to persuade the other party into behaving in a specific manner. Our work is an exciting step forward toward understanding how, when, and why people agree to requests that perhaps even result in behaviors they did not wish to perform.

REFERENCES:

Argo, Jennifer J., Darren W. Dahl, and Rajesh V. Manchanda (2005), "The Influence of a Mere Social Presence in a Retail Context," *Journal of Consumer Research*, 32 (September), 207-12.

Aron, Arthur, Elaine N. Aron, and Danny Smollan (1992), "Inclusion of Other in the Self Scale and the Structure of Interpersonal Closeness," *Journal of Personality and Social Psychology*, 63(4), 596-612.

Batcho, Krystine I. (1998), "Personal Nostalgia, World View, Memory, and Emotionality," *Perceptual and Motor Skills*, 87, 411-432.

Belk, Russell W. (1992), "Moving Posessions: An Analusis Based on Personal Documents from the 1847-1869 Mormon Migration," *Journal of Consumer Research*, 19 (December), 339-361.

Carstensen, Laura L. (1993), "Motivation for Social Contact across the Life Span: A Theory of Socioemotional Selectivity," in *Nebraska Symposium on Motivation*, ed. J. Jacobs, Lincoln: University of Nebraska, 209-54.

Carstensen, Laura L., Derek M. Isaacowitz, and Susan T. Charles (1999), "Taking Time Seriously: A Theory of Socioemotional Selectivity," *American Psychologist*, 54 (3), 165-81.

Cialdini, Robert B. (1993), *Influence: The Psychology of Persuasion,* New York: Morrow.

Davis, Fred (1979), *Yearning for Yesterday: A Sociology of Nostalgia*, New York: Free Press.

Lee, Euehun, George P. Moschis and Anil Mathur (2001), "A Study of Life Events and Changes in Patronage Preferences," *Journal of Business Research*, 54, 25-38.

Ramanathan, Suresh and Ann L. McGill (2007), "Consuming with Others: Social Influences on Moment-to-Moment and Retrospective Evaluations of an Experience," *Journal of Consumer Research* (December), 506-24.

Schmeichel, Brandon J., Kathleen D. Vohs, & Roy F. Baumeister, (2003). Intellectual performance and ego depletion: Role of the self in logical reasoning and other information processing. *Journal of Personality and Social Psychology*, 85, 33-46.

Vohs, Kathleen D., Roy F. Baumeister, and Natalie J. Ciarocco (2005), "Self-Regulation and Self-Presentation: Regulatory Resource Depletion Impairs Impression Management and Effortful Self-Presentation Depletes Regulatory Resources," *Journal of Personality and Social Psychology*, 88 (4), 632-57.

Wheeler, S. Christian, Pablo Briñol, and Anthony D. Hermann (2007), "Resistance to Persuasion as Self-Regulation: Ego-Depletion and its Effects on Attitude Change Processes. *Journal of Experimental Social Psychology,* 43 (1), 150-56.

Wildschut, Tim, Constantine Sedikides, Jamie Arndt, and Clay Routledge (2006), "Nostalgia: Content: Trigger, Functions," *Journal of Personality and Social Psychology*, 91(5), 975-993.

Williams, Patti and Aimee Drolet (2005), "Age-Related Differences in Responses to Emotional Advertisements," *Journal of Consumer Research*, 32 (December), 343-54.

Revisiting Consumer Confidence: New Findings and Emerging Perspectives

Zakary Tormala, Stanford University, USA

SESSION OVERVIEW

Psychological confidence—that is, the general existential state of certainty or uncertainty—is a fundamental aspect of human judgment and thought. Indeed, considerable research now suggests that the confidence or certainty with which one holds one's thoughts, beliefs, and attitudes plays a crucial role in guiding the impact of those thoughts, beliefs, and attitudes on other outcomes. For instance, the more certain one is of one's attitude, the more resistant that attitude is to attack, the more stable that attitude is over time, and the more influence that attitude has over one's behavior (see Tormala and Rucker 2007). Nevertheless, despite the importance of certainty and the extensive body of research exploring its antecedents and consequences in other fields, it has been relatively understudied in the consumer domain. This symposium revisits the notion of consumer confidence by exploring new perspectives on attitude certainty and intuitive confidence. Three papers highlight the importance of these metacognitive assessments for understanding, predicting, and shaping consumer behavior.

The first paper, by Tormala and Clarkson, puts forth a new perspective on attitude certainty. These authors propose that whereas attitude certainty traditionally has been viewed as a strengthening agent, making attitudes more resistant to persuasion and more predictive of behavior, it might be more accurate to think of attitude certainty as an *amplifying* agent. In other words, rather than inevitably strengthening an attitude, certainty might accentuate the dominant effect of that attitude on thought, judgment, and behavior. In three experiments, the authors test this hypothesis by orthogonally manipulating attitude certainty and attitude ambivalence. Across experiments, they find that when ambivalence is low, becoming more certain of an attitude makes the attitude more resistant to change and more predictive of behavior. When ambivalence is high, however, becoming more certain of an attitude makes the attitude *less* resistant to change and *less* predictive of behavior. Thus, certainty has markedly different consequences depending on the structure of the underlying attitude. This research alters existing views of attitude certainty, painting a more dynamic picture of its implications for consumer thought and action.

The second paper, by Rucker and Dubois, explores a different aspect of attitude certainty. In particular, these authors examine the interpersonal transmission of certainty. Based on the logic that attitude certainty is a metacognitive assessment of an attitude and, thus, secondary to the attitude itself, they posit that certainty assessments should be less accessible than attitudes and more likely to be lost in interpersonal transmission contexts. In three experiments, participants are given favorable attitudes toward a product, with either high or low attitude certainty. When asked to write a message about the product for another individual, participants are shown to transmit their attitudes but not their attitude certainty. Consistent with the accessibility account, however, interventions that increase the accessibility of the certainty information (e.g., a certainty priming task) boost transmission. These effects have important implications for consumer behavior, particularly given the increasing prevalence of interpersonal transmission (e.g., web reviews, WOM) in real world consumer contexts.

The final paper by Nelson, Simmons, and Galak also touches upon interpersonal aspects of confidence. Specifically, these authors apply the notion of intuitive confidence to the projection, or false consensus, effect. They propose that when people form preferences, they project these preferences onto others to a greater extent when they feel confident rather than doubtful. They further hypothesize that preference confidence can be affected by the valence of the options at hand. Two experiments provide support for this hypothesis, showing that preference confidence and projection are increased when consumers choose between positive rather than negative stimuli. A third experiment reverses this effect when participants are asked to reject, rather than choose, an option. This research enhances our understanding of projection, highlighting the role of judgment confidence in guiding perceptions of other consumers.

Taken together, the papers presented in this session highlight exciting new directions in an area that has received far too little attention in consumer research. We anticipate that this session will attract researchers interested in attitudes and persuasion, metacognition, information processing, and preferences. John Lynch, an expert on consumer decision making and the roles of accessibility and diagnosticity in guiding the impact of beliefs/attitudes on other judgments/behaviors, will provide a discussion of these three lines of inquiry, addressing their implications for consumer research and identifying potential questions for future study.

EXTENDED ABSTRACTS

"An Amplification Perspective on Attitude Certainty"
Zakary Tormala, Stanford University, USA
Joshua Clarkson, Indiana University, USA

People hold their attitudes with varying degrees of certainty. For example, two consumers might report liking a new restaurant, book, movie, or pillow to the same degree, but differ in how certain they are of that evaluation. Over the years, attitude certainty has stimulated considerable research interest (for a review see Tormala and Rucker 2007). This interest stems, at least in part, from the fact that attitude certainty is thought to have a number of important consequences for attitude-relevant outcomes. In particular, the more certain one is of one's attitude, the more predictive that attitude is of behavior (e.g., Fazio and Zanna 1978) and choice (e.g., Bizer, Tormala, Rucker, and Petty 2006) and the more resistant that attitude is to persuasion (e.g., Wu & Shaffer, 1987; Tormala and Petty 2002). These findings have been interpreted as indicating that attitude certainty inherently strengthens attitudes, making them more durable and impactful. This "crystallization hypothesis" is the dominant, if not only, view of attitude certainty in classic and contemporary research.

The Amplification Hypothesis. The current research challenges the notion that attitude certainty acts only as a strengthening agent, arguing instead that it can function as an *amplifying* agent. That is, we posit that rather than invariably strengthening an attitude, attitude certainty amplifies the dominant effect of the attitude on thought, judgment, and behavior. If the dominant effect of an attitude is to be resistant to change, for instance, increasing attitude certainty should increase that attitude's resistance, as in past research. If the dominant effect of an attitude is to be susceptible to change, however, increasing attitude certainty might increase that attitude's susceptibility.

Consider the distinction between univalent attitudes (attitudes that are primarily positive or negative in valence) and ambivalent attitudes (attitudes that consist of both positive and negative reactions). It is well-documented that univalent attitudes are more resistant to persuasion than ambivalent attitudes (e.g., Armitage and Conner, 2000; Visser and Mirabile 2004). Thus, univalent and ambivalent attitudes differ in their dominant effects on attitude change. The amplification hypothesis holds that increasing attitude certainty should accentuate this difference, making univalent attitudes even more resistant to persuasion and ambivalent attitudes even less resistant to persuasion than they were to begin with. We tested this hypothesis in a series of experiments.

In our first experiment, we orthogonally manipulated ambivalence and attitude certainty by giving participants evaluatively congruent (univalent) or incongruent (ambivalent) information about a target person from a high or low credibility source. As intended, participants were more ambivalent when they received incongruent compared to congruent information, and were more certain when they received the information from a high compared to a low credibility source. Of greatest importance, later in the session we presented participants with a persuasive message about the target person and we assessed attitude change in response to this message. As predicted, there was an interaction between information congruence (univalence/ambivalence) and source credibility (high/low attitude certainty) on attitude change. When participants had univalent initial attitudes, they showed greater attitude change when the credibility manipulation gave them low rather than high attitude certainty. When participants had ambivalent initial attitudes, they showed greater attitude change when the credibility manipulation gave them high rather than low attitude certainty.

In Experiment 2, we sought to replicate these findings in a consumer setting. We presented participants with evaluatively congruent or incongruent reviews of a new department store from a high or low credibility source. Following this information, we examined the consequences of attitude certainty by presenting participants with a persuasive message about the store. As predicted by the amplification hypothesis, there was an interaction between information congruence and source credibility on attitude change in response to this second message. When participants had univalent initial attitudes (congruent information condition), they showed greater attitude change when they had low as opposed to high attitude certainty. When participants had ambivalent attitudes (incongruent information condition), this effect was significantly reversed.

In Experiment 3, we explored a different consequence of attitude certainty—the correspondence between attitudes and behavioral intentions. As noted, it is well-established that attitudes are more predictive of behavior when they are held with high compared to low certainty. The amplification hypothesis suggests that this effect might be confined to univalent attitude conditions; under ambivalent attitude conditions, attitudes might be less predictive of behavior when they are held with high compared to low certainty. To examine this issue, we presented participants with evaluatively congruent or incongruent reviews of a new department store and manipulated attitude certainty using a confidence/doubt priming task. Later in the session, participants reported their likelihood of shopping at the store. As predicted by the amplification hypothesis, greater certainty was associated with higher attitude-intention correspondence under univalent attitude conditions, but lower attitude-intention correspondence under ambivalent attitude conditions. Experiment 3 also revealed that the attitude change effect from the first two experiments was the result of thoughtful information processing.

Discussion. The current research offers support for a new conceptualization of attitude certainty. Contrary to the traditional (crystallization) view of attitude certainty as an inherently strength-

ening agent, our findings suggest that attitude certainty has dynamic effects on attitude strength that vary according to the attitude's underlying ambivalence. Specifically, increasing attitude certainty strengthens attitudes (makes them more resistant to persuasion and more influential over behavioral intentions) when those attitudes are low in ambivalence, but *weakens* attitudes (makes them less resistant to persuasion and less influential over behavioral intentions) when those attitudes are high in ambivalence. Taken together, these findings have numerous and important implications for our understanding of attitudes and attitude strength in consumer contexts.

References

Armitage, Christopher J. and Mark Conner (2000), "Attitudinal Ambivalence: A Test of Three Key Hypotheses," *Personality and Social Psychology Bulletin, 26* (November), 1421-1432.

Bizer, George Y., Zakary L. Tormala, Derek D. Rucker, and Richard E. Petty (2006), "Memory-Based Versus On-Line Processing: Implications for Attitude Strength," *Journal of Experimental Social Psychology, 42* (September), 646-653.

Fazio, Russell H. and Mark P. Zanna (1978), "Attitudinal Qualities Relating to the Strength of the Attitude-Behavior Relationship," *Journal of Experimental Social Psychology, 14* (July), 398-408.

Tormala, Zakary L. and Richard E. Petty (2002), "What Doesn't Kill Me Makes Me Stronger: The Effects of Resisting Persuasion on Attitude Certainty," *Journal of Personality and Social Psychology, 83* (December), 1298-1313.

Tormala, Zakary L. and Derek D. Rucker (2007), "Attitude Certainty: A Review of Past Findings and Emerging Perspectives," *Social and Personality Psychology Compass, 1* (November), 469-492.

Visser, Penny S. and Robert R. Mirabile (2004), "Attitudes in the Social Context: The Impact of Social Network Composition on Individual-Level Attitude Strength," *Journal of Personality and Social Psychology, 87* (December), 779-795.

Wu, Chenghuan and David R. Shaffer (1987), "Susceptibility to Persuasive Appeals as a Function of Source Credibility and Prior Experience with the Attitude Object," *Journal of Personality and Social Psychology, 52* (April), 677-688.

"The Failure to Transmit Certainty: Causes, Consequences, and Remedies"

Derek Rucker, Northwestern University, USA
David Dubois, Northwestern University, USA

Consumers often share information in face to face exchanges, over email, or by leaving feedback for products on websites, such as Amazon.com or online forums. The present research examines consumers' propensity to transmit the degree of certainty associated with their attitudes when sharing their attitudes with others. Based on prior work showing that certainty is an important catalyst in motivating consumers to act on their attitudes (e.g., Basilli, 1996; Berger and Mitchell 1989; Fazio and Zanna 1978; Rucker and Petty 2004), we submit that it is important to understand how certainty is communicated from one consumer to another. Specifically, knowing whether another consumer is certain or uncertain should have an effect on a recipient's certainty.

Although not studied empirically, we believe there is reason to postulate that information regarding one's certainty or uncertainty is less likely to be expressed and thus is often lost in transmission. Whereas attitudes are primary beliefs (e.g., I like this car), attitude certainty is a metacognition or a secondary belief (e.g., how certain am I of my attitude towards the car). Compared to attitudes, we propose that certainty, as a metacognition, is less likely to be communicated by consumers. Specifically, we suggest that because the monitoring of one's certainty requires additional effort and direction, consumers' certainty might be less accessible and thus less likely to be transmitted at the time of a communication. Indeed, work on metacognition suggests that such processes tend to operate under high levels of thinking (Tormala and Petty 2004; Rucker, Petty, and Briñol 2008). For this reason, we propose that in consumer to consumer communications, such as word of mouth, consumers' attitude certainty should be less likely to be expressed compared to their attitudes. As a result, information related to attitude certainty is likely to be lost in transmission.

That is, even when consumers hold favorable attitudes of which they are highly certain, the certainty underlying that attitude might get lost during the transmission process. Because subsequent consumers (i.e., receivers) are less likely to be aware of the certainty of the communicating consumer (i.e., sender), they might in turn be less certain of their own attitudes. More specifically, they would lack the information that the attitude is supported by a strong degree of conviction. In addition, we propose that this loss of certainty can be prevented by either alerting consumers' sending communications to their certainty or by making the senders' certainty more obvious to subsequent recipients.

Experiment 1 tested whether certainty is indeed lost in transmission more so than favorability of one's evaluation. The experiment was conducted in several phases. Participants in phase 1 read a message about a hotel. The message was positive or negative and the certainty expressed by the source of the message was either low or high. This produced initial differences in favorability and certainty among phase 1 participants. Subsequently, phase 1 participants wrote a message about the hotel that was read by another participant. This procedure was repeated until we obtained a chain of four consumers who had received a prior message and written their own message. Results indicated that although differences in expressions of favorability were stable across the chain of participants, expressions of (un)certainty decreased over time, suggesting information related to certainty was lost in transmission.

Experiment 2 tested whether the observed loss of certainty was due to its lower accessibility. A priming manipulation was used to subtly activate individuals' attention to their certainty. If the loss of certainty stems from senders not thinking about their certainty at the time of transmission, increasing consumers' awareness of their certainty before sending the message should increase its likelihood of transmission. Participants in phase 1 received an initial message from a source inducing high or low certainty about a hotel, but equally favorable attitudes. Subsequently, participants in phase 1 completed an ostensibly unrelated crossword puzzle that contained words related to certainty and uncertainty or filler words. Participants then wrote a message about the hotel that was received by participants in phase 2. Results showed that when consumers' certainty was not accessible, there was little transmission of certainty. However, when participants in phase 1 were primed with certainty/uncertainty words, they were more likely to transmit certainty. Consequently, participants in phase 2 were more certain (uncertain) when the prior participant had been certain (uncertain). Importantly, across all conditions, attitudes were positive and equivalent, suggesting an asymmetry in the transmission of attitudes and certainty. Finally, although attitudes did not differ, in both phases, participants with high certainty reported greater purchase intentions than those with low certainty.

Experiment 3 provided a further test of the asymmetrical relation between attitudes and certainty, and proposed a potential remedy to prevent the loss of certainty. Participants in phase 1 received an initial message promoting a brand of toothpaste from a source inducing high or low certainty, but equally favorable attitudes. These participants then wrote a message about the toothpaste and reported their attitudes and certainty. Subsequently, participants in phase 2 either received a message and attitude score of one prior participant, or received the message, attitudes, *and* certainty scores of one prior participant. We found that participants in phase 2 were more likely to show a difference in certainty and behavior as a function of the prior participant's certainty when that certainty was explicitly provided. Put simply, a practical response to the loss of certainty in online venues, for instance, is simply to encourage consumers to report both their attitudes and certainty to be shared with others.

Conclusion and Contributions. The present research provides a first examination of how attitude certainty is shared and transmitted. In particular, as a secondary cognition, certainty is less accessible than attitudes and is thus more susceptible to being lost in transmission. The failure of initial consumers to communicate certainty has consequences for subsequent consumers' certainty and behavior. This work explores this failure via moderation and offers remedies regarding the loss of certainty.

References

Bassili, J. N. (1996). Metajudgmental versus operative indexes of psychological attributes: The case of measures of attitude strength. *Journal of Personality and Social Psychology, 71*, 637-653.

Berger, Ida E., and Andrew A. Mitchell (1989), "The Effect of Advertising on Attitude Accessibility, Attitude Confidence, and the Attitude-Behavior Relationship." *Journal of Consumer Research*, 16 (3), 269–279.

Fazio, R. H., and Zanna, M. P. (1978). Attitudinal qualities relating to the strength of the attitude-behavior relationship. *Journal of Experimental Social Psychology, 14*, 398-408.

Rucker, Derek D., and Richard E. Petty (2004), "When Resistance Is Futile: Consequences of Failed Counterarguing for Attitude Certainty," *Journal of Personality and Social Psychology*, 86(2), 219-35.

Rucker, Derek D., Richard E. Petty, and Pablo Briñol (2008), "What's in a Frame Anyway?: A Meta-cognitive Analysis of One Versus Two Sided Message Framing on Attitude Certainty," *Journal of Consumer Psychology , 18*, 137-149.

Tormala, Zakary L., and Richard E. Petty (2004), "Source credibility and attitude certainty: A metacognitive analysis of resistance to persuasion," *Journal of Consumer Psychology, 14*(4), 427-42.

"Intuitive Confidence and the Effect of Option Valence on Preference Projection"

Leif D. Nelson, University of California, San Diego, USA
Joseph Simmons, Yale University, USA
Jeff Galak, New York University, USA

People tend to project their own preferences and choices onto others. For example, when people choose whether or not to engage in an embarrassing act, they tend to think that other people will make the same decision (Ross, Green, & House, 1977). Although this *projection effect* (which is also known as the *false consensus effect*) has received considerable research attention, much of that attention has focused on investigating the implications of projection for judgmental accuracy (Dawes 1989; Hoch 1987; Hsee, Rottenstreich, and Tang 2008) rather than on understanding the psychological processes governing the projection process.

In this research, we propose that predicting the choices of others takes the form of a dual process (cf. Hoch, Davies, and Ragsdale 1986). First, people form an *intuitive judgment* by projecting their own preference onto others. Then, they adjust this inference on the basis of *constraint information* (e.g., knowledge of base rates; knowledge that other people may be dissimilar) that suggests that others may not share their preference. Simmons and Nelson (2006) have shown that people rely more heavily on their intuitions, and less heavily on constraint information, when they are confident in their intuitions. Following from that research, we propose that a stronger projection effect will emerge for easy, high-confident choices than for difficult, low-confident choices. This effect should emerge even when the choice options themselves are held constant.

We investigated these hypotheses by manipulating the valence of the choice options. Past research suggests that although choosing between two good options feels like an easy thing to do, choosing between two bad options feels like a difficult thing to do (Higgins 2000; Miller & Nelson, 2002). Thus, people should have greater confidence when choosing between two good options than when choosing between two bad options, and a stronger projection effect should emerge when choosing between two good options than when choosing between two bad options.

Study 1 tested this hypothesis by asking people to make choices between a certain outcome and a risky outcome (e.g., a 10% chance at $200 or a certain gain of $20) that offered equivalent expected values. On half of the trials, participants chose between two outcomes with positive expected values and, on the other half of trials, participants chose between two outcomes with negative expected values. After each choice, participants were asked to estimate the percentage of other participants they thought would make the same choice. As expected, people predicted that a greater percentage of others would make the same choice when they were choosing between two potential gains than when choosing between two potential losses.

In Study 2, we sought to generalize this result to a different choice scenario, and we measured decision confidence to assess whether it in fact differed between conditions. Participants were shown pairs of attractive or unattractive faces, and they were asked to choose between them. For each pair, participants rated how confident they were in their decision and they were asked to estimate the percentage of others who agreed with them. As predicted, participants were more confident when choosing between the attractive faces than when choosing between the unattractive faces. Moreover, the projection effect was stronger for choices between attractive pairs than for choices between unattractive pairs.

Studies 1 and 2 provide strong evidence for our hypothesis, but they suffer from a potentially important confound. Specifically, the positive stimuli presented on the high confidence trials were different than the negative stimuli presented on the low confidence trials. To eliminate this confound, we manipulated choice confidence by manipulating the framing of the choice task. Although asking participants to "choose" between two options makes it harder to select between two negative options than between two positive options, asking participants to "reject" one of the options may make it easier to select between two negative options than between two positive options (Higgins 2000).

In Study 3 we once again asked participants to express a preference between two attractive faces or between two unattractive faces. However, some participants were asked to "choose" which one they preferred whereas others were asked to "reject" the option they did not prefer. When participants were given the "choose" instruction, they once again expressed greater confidence and exhibited stronger projection when choosing between attractive than unattractive faces. However, when participants were given the "reject" instruction, these results reversed: Participants were more confident rejecting between two unattractive faces, and

they exhibited a stronger projection effect when choosing between unattractive faces. These results emerged even though task instruction had no effect on which options participants actually chose.

Finally, Study 4 extended this effect by manipulating the valence *and* extremity of the choice stimuli. On each trial, participants chose (or rejected) between two extremely positive words, two moderately positive words, two moderately negative words, or two extremely negative words. In the choice condition, decision confidence, and the projection effect, increased as the positivity of the choice set increased. In the reject condition, decision confidence, and the projection effect, *decreased* as the positivity of the choice set increased.

Together, these results provide strong support for the effect of intuitive confidence on projection. People more strongly project confident choices than uncertain ones. Moreover, this effect can account for a novel finding that we have presented here–namely, the effect of option valence on projection. Because people are often more confident when choosing between two positive options, they are more likely to believe that others would have made the same choice.

References

Dawes, Robyn M. (1989), "Statistical Criteria for Establishing a Truly False Consensus Effect," *Journal of Experimental Social Psychology*, 25 (January), 1-17.

Higgins, E. Tory (2000), "Making a Good Decision: Value From Fit," *American Psychologist*, 55 (November), 1217-1230.

Hoch, Stephen J. (1987), "Perceived Consensus and Predictive Accuracy: The Pros and Cons of Projection," *Journal of Personality and Social Psychology*, 53 (August), 221-234.

Hsee, Christopher K., Yuval Rottenstreich, and Ningyu Tang (2008), "Do We Agree More About Who Is Beautiful or Who Is Ugly? A Four-Level Model of Asymmetries between Likes and Dislikes," Working Paper, University of Chicago.

Hsee, Christopher K., Yuval Rottenstreich, and J. Tang (2008), "Do People Agree More About Who Is Beautiful

Miller, Dale T. and Leif D. Nelson (2002), "Seeing Approach Motivation in the Avoidance Behavior of Others: Implications for an Understanding of Pluralistic Ignorance," *Journal of Personality and Social Psychology*, 83 (November), 1066-1075.

Ross, Lee, David Greene, and Pamela House (1977), "The 'False Consensus Effect': An Egocentric Bias in Social Perception and Attribution Processes," *Journal of Experimental Social Psychology*, 13 (May), 279-301.

Simmons, Joseph P. and Leif D. Nelson (2006), "Intuitive Confidence: Choosing Between Intuitive and Nonintuitive Alternatives," *Journal of Experimental Psychology: General*, 135 (August), 409-428.

Does Authenticity Matter? The Importance and Interplay of Authenticity and Inauthenticity

Tandy D. Chalmers, University of Arizona, USA
Linda L. Price, University of Arizona, USA

SESSION OVERVIEW

Authenticity is argued to be the new business imperative and 'buzz word' of the 21st century (Gilmore and Pine 2007) and "consumers' search for authenticity is one of the cornerstones of contemporary marketing" (Brown, Kozinets, and Sherry Jr. 2003 p. 21). Consuming and communicating authenticity are recurrent themes in academic research and consumer research approaches the topic in several ways. First, consumer research has examined the authenticity of referents such as objects, persons, and experiences (Arnould and Price 1999; Grayson and Shulman 2000; Schouten and McAlexander 1995). Second, consumer researchers have examined authentic representations of objects, persons, and experiences, such as photographs, reenactments, and ads (e.g. Belk and Costa 1998). In both cases, research examines how to create authentic referents and representations of referents (e.g. Holt 2004) and how these are viewed by observers (Rose and Wood 2005). An important underlying assumption of this work is that authenticity is an important and positive outcome.

This privileging of authenticity has resulted in the neglect of an equally important construct: inauthenticity. Trilling (1972) notes authenticity is a polemical concept, usually only thought about when called into question, with the focus on something being either authentic or inauthentic. Much of consumer life, however, is represented by situations where both authenticity and inauthenticity co-exist (Benjamin 1969; Grayson and Martinec 2004). The purpose of this symposium is to explore the interplay between authenticity and inauthenticity.

First, Markus Giesler and Marius Luedicke discuss how consumers paradoxically create an authentic self by enhancing their physical selves with market offerings, such as Botox, that are often perceived as creating an inauthentic self. Next, Tandy Chalmers and Linda Price show how consumers negotiate authenticity and inauthenticity in an advertisement context and demonstrate a complex interplay between the two, uncovering how this authentication process is linked to ad liking. Finally, Jay Handelman and Robert Kozinets present work showing how consumers' desire to create authentic identities often overrides the negative aspects of inauthentic production techniques. They also highlight how corporations actively try to restore an image of authenticity while activists work to debunk these efforts. In each of these papers, consumers negotiate between seemingly inauthentic aspects of consumption (e.g. artificial body enhancement, blatant reproductions with a persuasive purpose, and mass production) in reaching conclusions about authenticity in their consumption choices and evaluations.

The objectives of this session are three-fold: to examine (1) the paradoxes inherent in how authenticity operates in consumers' lives and marketers' practices, (2) the different manifestations of authenticity and inauthenticity in the marketplace, such as self-authenticity, advertisement authenticity, and brand and product authenticity and, (3) how these authenticity domains all benefit from an analytic perspective highlighting the interplay between authenticity and inauthenticity as a co-production of meanings between the market and consumers.

Given the broad theoretical significance of authenticity and the multi-method focus of this symposium, it should appeal to a wide range of ACR attendees. These include CCT and other researchers interested in authenticity, inauthenticity, and its rela-tion to identity, public policy oriented researchers interested in consumer resistance, and advertising and social identity scholars interested in the relationship between the self, authenticity, and advertising responses.

EXTENDED ABSTRACTS

"American Self-Enhancement Culture and the Cyborg Consumer: Consumer Identity Construction Beyond the Dominance of Authenticity"

Markus Giesler, York University, Canada
Marius K. Luedicke, University of Innsbruck, Austria

Why do Americans place so much emphasis on individual identity and self-fulfillment? Does the skyrocketing consumption of Viagra, Botox, Prozac, Propecia and countless surgical enhancements make them more true to a "real" self, or does it make them frauds? Social critics of American self-enhancement culture commonly charge that it indoctrinates individuals into a biomedical consumerism that frustrates the construction of a genuine self-identity (Elliott 2004; Kass 2004). Following this popular "lost authenticity" thesis, Americans today-members of the middle-class in particular-are replete with deep conflicts between the relentless pursuit of self-fulfillment and high performance and the insistent yearnings for authenticity and a genuine self. In one perspective, they worry that changing their bodies through biomedical intervention might make their body and their very identity inauthentic. But they also understand that they have a duty to pursue happiness and status by perfecting themselves according to the latest biomedical research and trends (Kass 2004). Sadly, Americans can look up to no authority to resolve this fundamental identity crisis. Their only escape from "anxious dislocation" is to "follow fashion" and "listen to the reigning experts" (Lawler 2005, 3).

However, reducing self-enhancement culture to pathological consumerism turns a blind eye to the potential to construct a coherent "narrative of the self" through the consumption of biomedical products and services. For example, consumer researchers have long recognized the creative role of consumption-including the use of aesthetic plastic surgery (Schouten 1991)-in people's quest for self-identity. In this perspective, Americans may partially and inconsistently transcend the entrenched dichotomy between artificial technology and the natural body to reach unprecedented levels of enhanced self, thereby challenging the modernist quest for authenticity. These heretical self-experiments and their underlying cultural incompatibility to authenticating appeals may inspire unprecedented agentic possibilities.

To give greater consideration to this alternative account, we present the concept of the cyborg consumer. Grounded in critical feminism and cultural studies (Haraway 1991; Hayles 1999; Davis 1999), the cyborg consumer illustrates how entrenched narrative dualisms–nature versus technology, authentic versus inauthentic–are partially and inconsistently transcended to construct hybrid stories of the self that challenge the modernist primacy of self-authenticity and instead aspire to an emerging ideal of unlimited agency through technological self-enhancement. From this stand-point, the social critics who are railing about consumerist inauthenticity may be expressing less of a relevant social comment than an emerging historical discontinuity between their cultural lens and an emerging experimental cyborg episteme. For Botox consumers, being inauthentic is not the driving issue. As we will demonstrate, their ideological mandate is the duty for biomedical self-enhancement by any available means.

Our analysis is threefold. After reviewing the ideological groundwork of American self-enhancement culture, we analyze the self-narratives of individual Botox users. In distinction to the classic "lost authenticity" thesis, we build the case that Botox consumption is steeped in a complex ideology of the enhanced body and that Botox consumers' routine confrontations with authenticity-inspired assessments of their bodies intensify and augment their experiences of enhanced self and its agentic possibilities. We then summarize our findings by documenting an emerging historical discontinuity between the modernist paradigm of authentic self-identity and the emerging cyborg consumer episteme and draw out implications of the cyborg consumer model for dualism-inspired theoretical debates on the body (Thompson and Hirschman 1995), and consumer identity construction (Holt and Thompson 2005; Kozinets 2002; Arnould and Price 2000). We also develop the implications of our cyborg consumer model for the critical cyborg model, as pioneered by Donna Haraway (1991).

This analysis is part of a larger ethnographic research exploring self-enhancement consumption using the Botox biomarket as an empirical context (www.doingbotox.com). We conducted depth interviews with 20 Botox consumers (6 male) in Chicago, New York, Buffalo, and Toronto. Informants hailed from a range of middle-class backgrounds and had received up to 9 cosmetic Botox shots. With the exception of two telephone and one Skype conversation, all interviews were held either at the informants' homes, in coffee shops, or during and after a Botox injection at the dermatologist's practice. To ensure that interview narratives had a broader resonance, we compared them to user entries on online Botox forums (Kozinets 2001). In addition to these netnographic procedures, one author also analyzed introspective journal notes on a Botox injection he received "in situ" during a Botox party (Gould 1991). The complete data set was analyzed using a hermeneutical process (Thompson 1997). Interpretations were formed, fed back to our informants through the research website and via email, and revised in relation to a broader network of theoretical concerns until sufficient interpretive convergence was achieved.

"Perceptions of Authenticity in Advertisements: Negotiating the Inauthentic"

Tandy D. Chalmers, University of Arizona, USA
Linda L. Price, University of Arizona, USA

Advertisements are a powerful tool through which companies can communicate authenticity to stakeholders. Successful communication of authenticity is presumed to be linked to positive downstream responses such as brand identification, loyalty, and sales (Botterill 2007), with authenticity viewed as a key mechanism for seducing consumers. Despite this rhetoric of importance, little is empirically known about how consumers respond to advertisements designed to communicate authenticity, or if authenticity even matters in an advertisement context.

The purpose of this study is to explore consumer perceptions of and reactions to ads designed to be authentic. Stern (1994) defines authentic ads as those that "convey the illusion of the reality of ordinary life in reference to a consumption situation" (388). The key premise of Stern's conceptualization of ad authenticity is a link between everyday experiences and ad content: implying a self-referencing process where consumers relate their own experiences to an ad when evaluating it (Burnkrant and Unnava 1995). The consequence of this process should, theoretically, be increased ad liking. In contrast, if an ad is deemed inauthentic, it can be presumed

that consumers will dislike the ad. The paradoxical nature of authentic ads, however, convolutes this linear relationship: an ad, a representation by definition, cannot be something authentic or real, even if it creates a convincing illusion of something that is real (Stern 1994). Thus, even 'authentic' ads contain elements of inauthenticity (Benjamin 1969; Stern 1994).

Rose and Wood (2005), for example, find that reality television viewers negotiate between authentic and inauthentic elements of shows, with viewers deciding the entertainment value of the show is worth forgoing some aspects of authenticity. In the case of reality television, consumers are motivated to enjoy the show and seek out reasons to overlook the inauthentic. In the case of ads, however, consumers may approach the representation with skepticism (Friestad and Wright 1994) and be less willing to overlook inauthentic elements. Thus, the question of how consumers negotiate between authentic and inauthentic elements of advertisements remains unclear: do consumers seek out reasons to reject the representation as inauthentic or instead look for ways they can affirm the advertisement's authenticity? And how do consumers' general attitudes toward advertising influence these authenticity judgments?

These questions are explored in a two-study, multi-method inquiry into consumer perceptions of ad authenticity and inauthenticity. The first study, consisting of stimuli based in-depth interviews with 28 distance runners, examines if and how authenticity perceptions emerge naturally in consumer assessments of ads. Running was chosen as the study's context as there are an abundance of ads in this area depicting everyday life. During the interviews, informants were shown 15 running themed ads, each of which fit Stern's 'authenticity' requirement, and were asked what they thought of the ads. The second study consisted of a survey administered to 88 undergraduate students enrolled in an upper-level marketing class. Participants responded to one of four advertisements that seemed realistic (and therefore authentic) but also contained unrealistic undertones and elements of the outrageous. For example, an Axe Body Wash ad depicts a young man standing outside a shower with a towel showing a picture of a woman's legs around his waist, creating the illusion of a real woman straddling the man. Participants assessed the authenticity and their liking of the ad. Afterwards, both authors engaged participants in a discussion about the ads to gauge their more nuanced reactions.

The findings from both studies contribute to our understanding of authenticity and inauthenticity in an advertisement context. A clear negotiation between authentic and inauthentic elements of the ads emerged. Informant discussions in study 1 show consumers naturally evaluate ads in terms of both authenticity and inauthenticity, with these evaluations linked to ad liking. In addition, discussions show an interesting interplay between authenticity and inauthenticity perceptions when ads contained elements of both. Sometimes, ads were viewed as being simultaneously authentic and inauthentic, with informants jostling between the two sets of perceptions when making final evaluations of the ads: moving between thinking the ad is authentic to thinking it is inauthentic, and vise versa. Throughout these authentication processes, consumers engage in both self- and other-referencing. A series of counterintuitive findings also emerged were consumers deemed an ad to be authentic, related to it, but did not like the ad. This occurred when consumers engaged in 'looking-glass self' referencing where they disliked how imagined others would view them based on what is depicted in the ads (Cooley 1902/1922).

Study 2 findings confirm the importance of authenticity and inauthenticity perceptions in ad liking, but also give rise to an additional authenticity structure: advertisements viewed as authentically inauthentic. In some cases, vastly exaggerated claims are viewed as having a reflective legitimacy in relationship to the advertised product that engenders ad liking without strong links to self- or other- referencing. That is, ads may be paradoxically high in both authenticity and inauthenticity. Combining the findings from the two studies, we illustrate a set of relationships between authenticity, inauthenticity, self-, other-, and looking-glass self-referencing, and ad liking. These relationships highlight the importance of ad authenticity and inauthenticity perceptions, demonstrate the complexities and nuances of the advertisement evaluation process, and illustrate how the authentic and inauthentic are negotiated by consumers.

"The Cultural Privileging of Personal Authenticity: A Critical Postmodern Perspective"
Jay M. Handelman, Queen's University, Canada
Robert V. Kozinets, York University, Canada

The quest for personal authenticity stands as an appeal to one's potentiality for self-cultivation, self-direction, creativity, identity, and individuality–a type of human re-enchantment whereby the individual is able to find meaning in life, creativity, playfulness, sensuality, and morality (Berman 1970; Firat and Venkatesh 1995). In their quest for personal authenticity, consumers are deemed to be sovereign in their creative, playful, artful employment of branded products as core ingredients in their self-identity projects (Firat and Venkatesh 1995). The consumer dissolves the illusory separation between the physical product and the imaginary as mass produced products are transformed into symbolic meaning systems, freeing the consumer from the hegemony of the marketplace (Firat and Venkatesh 1995).

However, this postmodern privileging of consumers' imaginative, creative, hedonic play conceals the fact that the physical product and its material consequences still exists. News stories about tainted products, documentaries and film clips such as *Mardis Gras Made in China* and *The Story of Stuff*, and amateur *YouTube* video footage revealing abhorrent working conditions in the factories that produce the products we consume, remind consumers that Taylorism is alive and well; that the physical resources extracted to produce consumer goods are becoming scarcer and more costly; that the environmental consequences associated with the production, use and disposal of these goods are becoming graver.

Far from a natural, inevitable evolution, our cultural privileging of consumer personal authenticity over the consequences of production occurs in the context of a socially constructed ideological framework (Berman 1970). In this paper, we examine the paradoxical essence that seems to cut to the core of our consumption-based society. In this paradox, the act of being a consumer comes to be associated with all things moral-human and economic development, re-enchantment, aesthetic experience, knowledge, skills, and even activism and social change (Heath and Potter 2004). Yet, the potential human and environmental denigration associated with the often out-sourced production feeding our consumption is downplayed or outright ignored.

We draw on Critical Postmodernism to capture a glimpse into the social construction that comes to privilege consumer personal authenticity over the material consequences associated with consumption. Critical postmodernism is the unlikely combination of critical theory and postmodernism (Alvesson and Deetz 1996), providing a potent lens through which to examine the hybridity of contemporary consumer life characterized by the interpenetration of modernist production and postmodern consumption practices (Boje 2006). By examining the interplay between marketers, activists and consumers, we present the cultural privileging of the aesthetic nature of consumption as a hotly contested and problematized social phenomenon.

Method: We draw on three empirical sites for our data collection. First, we examine a variety of tactical maneuvers deployed by consumer activists from three different activist movements (anti-advertising, anti-brand, and anti-toxin activists). Through our participation in activist organized protest events, in-person meetings, and telephone interviews with activists from across North America, we report on the depth interviews with thirteen consumer activists who stood out as highly engaged in their protest against consumer society over the decade (1996–2006) that we examined them. Second, providing insights into marketer responses, we report on in-person (five) and telephone (six) depth interviews with eleven corporate marketers. These senior marketers were drawn from eleven different North American based multinational companies that had all been the target of consumer activist campaigns. Finally, we deployed the method of netnography to study a variety of controversy-laden online consumer discussion forum (such as <alt.politics> and <misc.activism.progressive>) and corporate blogs. In total we examined over 5,000 postings that ran from April 1999 to June 2006.

Theme 1-De-Sanctifying the Consumer: Activists rework consumer brands by recoupling them with their physical, production origins. Activists associate production, and the ensuing human and environmental consequences, with the "true" source of ethics and morality. Here, activists de-sanctify, or de-privilege, the consumer's quest for personal authenticity as an immoral, self-indulgent endeavor completely decoupled from its production origins. As such, decoupling of production does not only conceal the commercial motives of the company, but it also serves to sanctify, or privilege, the consumer as removed from the product's controversial human and environmental consequences. *Theme 2-Sanctifying the Consumer Through Corporate Social Responsibility (CSR):* Faced with a threat not only to themselves, but also to the sanctity of their consumers, marketers work to re-sanctify, or re-privilege, the consumer through acts of CSR by infusing consumption with claims of morality, ethics, and community well-being. *Theme 3-Mutual De-Sanctification:* Corporate blogs foster a type of mutual de-sanctification where consumers and companies inadvertently de-sanctify, or de-privilege, each other by recoupling the brand to its production sources. This mutual de-sanctification emerges as an enactment of the critical postmodern perspective whereby symbolic meanings of brands are celebrated, but tempered by a challenge to the power relationships that have come to privilege the consumer's authenticity desires over the material consequences associated with production.

Discussion: The paper concludes with a discussion around two particular issues. First we explore the implications of branding in a critical postmodern context. Second, we discuss consumer re-enchantment not through consumption, but through *Consumer* Social Responsibility. Traditional *Corporate* Social Responsibility is critiqued as an ideological veil that works to maintain the extant power balance that privileges consumers and the companies that market to them. We reveal a type of consumer enchantment that comes through embracing the production consequences underlying the products that are consumed.

REFERENCES

Alvesson, Mats and Stanley Deetz (1996), "Critical Theory and Postmodern Approaches to Organizational Studies," in Stewart R. Clegg, Cynthia Hardy and Walter R. Nord (Eds), *Handbook of Organization Studies*, Sage: London, 191-217.

Arnould, Eric J. and Linda L. Price (1999), "Authenticating Acts and Authoritative Performances: Questing for Self and Community," in *The Why of Consumption: Contemporary Perspectives on Consumer Motives, Goals, and Desires*, ed. S. Ratneshwar and David Mick and Cynthia Huffman, New York: Routledge.

Belk, Russell W. and Janeen Arnold Costa (1998), "The Mountain Man Myth: A Contemporary Consuming Fantasy," *Journal of Consumer Research*, 25 (December), 218-40.

Benjamin, Walter (1969), "The Work of Art in the Age of Mechanical Reproduction," in *Illuminations*, ed. Hannah Arendt, New York: Schocken, 217-52.

Berman, Marshall (1970), *The Politics of Authenticity: Radical Individualism and the Emergence of Modern Society*, Atheneum: New York.

Boje, David M. (2006), "What Happened on the Way to Postmodern?" *Qualitative Research in Organizations and Management*, 1 (1), 22-40.

Botterill, Jacqueline (2007), "Cowboys, Outlaws, and Artists: The Rhetoric of Authenticity and Contemporary Jeans and Sneaker Advertisements," *Journal of Consumer Culture*, 7 (1), 105-25.

Brown, Stephen, Robert V. Kozinets, and John F. Sherry Jr. (2003), "Teaching Old Brands New Tricks: Retro Branding and the Revival of Brand Meaning," *Journal of Marketing*, 67 (July), 19-33.

Burnkrant, Robert E. and H. Rao Unnava (1995), "Effects of Self-Referencing on Persuasion," *Journal of Consumer Research*, 22 (June), 17-26.

Cooley, Charles H. (1902/1922), *Human Nature and the Social Order*, New York, NY: Scribner.

Davis. Erik (1998), *Techgnosis: Myth, Magic and Mysticism in the Age of Information*, 1st edn, Harmony Books, New York.

Elliott, Carl (2004), *Better than Well: American Medicine Meets the American Dream*, Norton & Company.

Friestad, Marian and Peter Wright (1994), "The Persuasion Knowledge Model: How People Cope with Persuasion Attempts," *Journal of Consumer Research*, 21 (June), 1-31.

Firat, A. Fuat and Alladi Venkatesh (1995), "Liberatory Postmodernism and the Reenchantment of Consumption," *Journal of Consumer Research*, 22 (December), 239-267.

Grayson, Kent and Radan Martinec (2004), "Consumer Perceptions of Iconicity and Indexicality and Their Influence on Assessments of Authentic Market Offerings," *Journal of Consumer Research*, 31 (September), 296-312.

Grayson, Kent and David Shulman (2000), "Indexicality and the Verification Function of Irreplaceable Possessions: A Semiotic Analysis," *Journal of Consumer Research*, 27 (June), 17-30.

Haraway, Donna J. (1991), *Simians, Cyborgs, and Women: The Reinvention of Nature*, Routledge, New York.

Hayles, N. K. (1999), *How we Became Posthuman : Virtual Bodies in Cybernetics, Literature, and Informatics*, University of Chicago Press, Chicago, Ill.

Heath, Joseph and Andrew Potter (2004), *The Rebel Sell: Why the Culture Can't Be Jammed*, HarperCollins Publishers Ltd.: Toronto, Canada

Holt, Douglas B. and Craig J. Thompson (2005), "Man-of-Action Heroes: The Pursuit of Heroic Masculinity in Everyday Consumption", *Journal of Consumer Research*, vol. 31, 2, 425.

Holt, Douglas B. (2004), *How Brands Become Icons: The Principles of Cultural Branding*, Cambridge, MA: Harvard.

Kass, Leon (2004), *Life, Liberty and the Defense of Dignity: The Challenge for Bioethics*, New York: AEI Press.

Kozinets, Robert V. (2002), "Can Consumers Escape the Market?: Emancipatory Illuminations From Burning Man," *Journal of Consumer Research*, 29 (June), 20-38.

Lawler, Peter A. (2005), "Enhancement Technologies," *Modern Age*, Spring.

Rose, Randall L. and Stacy L. Wood (2005), "Paradox and the Consumption of Authenticity Through Reality Television," *Journal of Consumer Research*, 32 (September), 284-96.

Schouten, John W. (1991), "Selves in Transition: Symbolic Consumption in Personal Rites of Passage and Identity Reconstruction," *Journal of Consumer Research*, 17, (March), 412-425.

Schouten, John W. and James H. McAlexander (1995), "Subcultures of Consumption: An Ethnography of the New Bikers," *Journal of Consumer Research*, 22 (June), 43-61.

Stern, Barbara (1994), "Authenticity and the Textual Persona: Postmodern Paradoxes in Advertising Narrative," *International Journal of Research in Marketing*, 11, 387-400.

Thompson, Craig J, Hirschman and Elizabeth C. (1995), "Understanding the Socialized Body: A Poststructuralist Analysis of Consumers' Self-Conceptions, Body Images, and Self-Care Practices", *Journal of Consumer Research*, vol. 22, 2, 139.

Trilling, Lionel (1972), *Sincerity and Authenticity*, Cambridge, MA: Harvard University Press.

Emotions, Social Comparison, and Deception in Interpersonal Interactions

Eduardo Andrade, University of California, Berkeley, USA

SESSION OVERVIEW

Consumers' daily activities usually rely on interpersonal interaction: a car shopper who tries to avoid the unfair offer from a car dealer, two consumers who after a quick chat realize they have gotten different deals on the same product, or a patient who exaggerates his symptoms in order to increase the chances of getting an early appointment.

In a series of three papers we address those phenomena using standard games developed in experimental economics. We hope to contribute to our understanding of the role of interpersonal interactions in consumer behavior as well as to demonstrate how incentive-based games can shed light into this realm of research.

In paper 1, Andrade & Ho address what the authors call "emotional gaming"—i.e., people's willingness to either conceal a current emotional state or display an emotional state which diverges from the true state, in a strategic attempt to optimize the chances of success in a given social interaction. Examples of such phenomenon are widespread in consumer behavior: a waiter who, in an attempt to get a bigger tip, smiles to the customer when he hands her the check; a poker player who hides his emotional expressions to avoid providing unwanted information to competitors; and an HMO patient who exaggerates his reported level of pain to the doctor as to increase the chance of getting an early appointment with a specialist. In a series of three experiments, the authors show that during a given social interaction (e.g., ultimatum games and trust games) people deliberately conceal (experiment 1) or misrepresent (experiments 2 and 3) their emotional state in an attempt to succeed in the negotiation process.

Also using a game format, the role of emotions in interpersonal interaction is also addressed in paper 2. Ho & Su argue that in many consumption-related situations, people get upset when they receive a worse deal than their peers, which limit the extent of price discrimination. For instance, Apple has recently faced this problem after their decision to significantly reduce the price of the iPhones just a few months after the launching. Angry consumers, who had bought the product previous to the price reduction, forced the company to provide "retroactive" discounts to avoid further boycotting and damage to company's brand image. Ho & Su tested such concern for peer-induced fairness in the context of two independent ultimatum games played in sequence by a leader and 2 followers. Their results show that the leader does formulate the second offer based on the second follower's expectation of what the first offer is. In addition, the second follower is more likely to reject when she believes that the first follower receives a high offer.

As already pointed out, Andrade and Ho address the extent to which people misrepresent their feelings (e.g., inflate how happy or angry they are) for purely strategic reasons. Such willingness to convey "cheap talk" in a social interaction is certainly not constrained to emotions. In paper 3, Wang, Spezio, & Camerer point out that such phenomenon is common to many companies and consumers. Companies might be tempted to inflate earning prospects, MBA students might inflate course evaluations to improve school rankings, and HMO patients might inflate whatever symptoms they might have in order to get more quickly to the specialist. To test the extent to which participants "inflate the truth," when they have an incentive to do so, the authors rely on sender-receiver games. Moreover, they use eyetracking measures to assess the potential costs of deception. Among other findings, the authors show that people indeed convey untruthful information. Moreover, deception can be tracked at the physiological level. Right before and after the message is sent, senders' pupils dilate more when their deception is larger in magnitude. This suggests that subjects feel guilty for deceiving, or that deception is cognitively difficult.

In short, all three papers attempt to understand a few of the multiple nuances consumers and companies face in any given social interaction (Do people inflate emotions [Andrade & Ho] or other types of information [Wang, Spezio, & Camerer]?, How do they physiologically react to it [Wang, Spezio, & Camerer]?, How does information about peers influence one's decision making [Ho & Su]?). Moreover, all papers adopt a similar methodology (i.e., economic games) to help us better understand how consumers and companies might interact when actual incentives are at stake.

EXTENDED ABSTRACTS

"Gaming Emotions"
Eduardo Andrade, University of California, Berkeley, USA
Teck-Hua Ho, University of California, Berkeley, USA

A car shopper pretends to feel angry in an attempt to reduce the chances of an unfair offer from a car dealer. A teacher hides his anxiety in front of students to avoid showing lack of confidence, which in turn, could reduce students' receptivity to the lectures. By wearing appropriate apparels (e.g., dark sunglasses), professional poker players hide both bad *and* good feelings from their competitors to avoid revealing any clues about their cards. Waiters smile when they hand customers the check in an attempt to get a bigger tip. Finally, parents pretend to be very angry at their kids' misbehavior just to make sure the children behave appropriately.

In short, knowing that one's expressed affective state can influence other's decisions, people are usually tempted to *game emotions*—that is, to either conceal a current emotional state or display an emotional state which diverges from the true state, in a strategic attempt to optimize the chances of success in a given social interaction.

Survey and observational-based evidence have suggested that individuals do display non-experienced emotions, especially when their jobs require them to do so. This so-called *emotional labor* literature has addressed (a) the extent to which the workplace demands specific emotional expressions and (b) how much such requirements influence employees' wellbeing. This research stream shows that employees have frequently been obliged either by implicit social norms or by explicit company policies to display, and usually fake, specific emotional states. The service industry has numerous examples. Amusement parks, airline companies, and fast food chains, to mention a few, usually suggest—or request—their employees to continuously display positive feelings when they interact with their customers.

Nevertheless, it is possible that people, when given the opportunity, may deliberately choose to game emotions on their own in an attempt to succeed in a given negotiation and, as a result, *improve* their overall wellbeing. This paper investigates this emotion gaming hypothesis experimentally. In a series of three experiments, we show that people deliberately conceal (experiment 1) or misrepresent (experiments 2 and 3) their emotional state in a negotiation setting. When given the opportunity to either hide or express their current emotions before playing an ultimatum game, receivers who have reported low (vs. high) level of anger are more likely to conceal their emotion right before the proposers decide on the division of the pie (experiment 1). When the procedure allows participants to change their previously reported emotion, receivers choose to inflate their reported level of anger prior to proposers' decision (experiment 2 & experiment 3). Moreover, gaming emotions is financially beneficial as long as the partner does not realize that the one might be msirepresenting their feelings (experiment 3).

"A Theory of Peer-induced Fairness in Games"
Teck-Hua Ho, University of California, Berkeley, USA
Xuanming Su, University of California, Berkeley, USA

A long-standing assumption in economics is that people are purely self-interested. This assumption has been challenged recently by accumulating experimental evidence based on the so-called ultimatum game. Behavioral economists propose several models of distributional fairness to relax the self-interest assumption. In this paper we introduce the concept of *peer-induced fairness* because people have a drive to make social comparison.

That is, they look to similar others as a reference in order to form their opinions and evaluate their endowments. We investigate peer-induced fairness by considering two independent ultimatum games played in sequence by a leader and two followers. In the first ultimatum game, the leader makes a take-it-or-leave-it offer to the first follower. Before the next ultimatum game is played, the second follower obtains a public signal of this offer. Then, in the second game, the leader makes an offer to the second follower. The second follower infers what the first follower receives, uses this inference to form a reference point, and is averse to accepting offers that falls short of this benchmark. This generalized model nests the standard and several existing models of fairness. This model makes two sharp predictions. First, the leader's offer to the second follower should be non-decreasing in the common belief of what the first offer is. Second, condition on an offer, the second follower's likelihood of acceptance is inversely proportional to the reference point derived from the signal. We test both predictions experimentally and find strong support for them. We structurally estimate the model and show that peer-induced fairness is 2.5 times larger than distributional fairness. We incorporate heterogeneity by allowing subjects to be either purely self-interested or fairness-minded. Our estimation results suggest that half of the subjects exhibit peer-induced fairness. We show how peer-induced fairness might influence the occurrence of labor strikes, explain low variability in CEO compensation, and limit the extent of price discrimination.

"Pinocchio's Pupil: Using Eyetracking and Pupil Dilation To Understand Truth-telling and Deception in Sender-Receiver Games"
Joseph Tao-yi Wang, National Taiwan University, Taiwan
Michael Spezio, California Institute of Technology & Scripps College, USA
Colin Camerer, California Institute of Technology, USA

During the tech-stock bubble, Wall Street security analysts were alleged to inflate recommendations about the future earnings prospects of firms, in order to win investment banking relationships with those firms. They usually gave two separate 1-5 ratings for short run (0-12 months) and long run (more than 12 months) performance. Henry Blodget, Merrill Lynch's famously optimistic analyst, "did not rate any Internet stock a

4 or 5," while privately admitting some were "POS [piece of shit]." He was later banned from the security industry for life and fined millions of dollars.

This case is an example of a sender-receiver game with divergent preferences (sometimes called a "cheap talk" or strategic information transmission game). Sender-receiver games are simple models of economic situations in which one agent has an incentive to exaggerate the truth to another agent. The central issues in these games are how well uninformed players infer the private information from the actions of players who are better-informed, and what informed players do, anticipating the inference of the uninformed players.

Incentives for strategic information transmission are common. Besides the Blodget case mentioned above, similar dramatic accounting frauds in the last few years, such as Enron, Worldcom, and Tyco, might have been caused by the incentives of managers (and perhaps their accounting firms) to inflate earnings prospects. Expert advisors in consumer markets might also be tempted to paint a rosy picture when presenting in front of their clients. In universities, grade inflation and well-polished recommendation letters help schools promote their graduates. Other examples of incentives for strategic information transmission include government-expert relationships in policy making, doctor-patient relationships in health care choices, teacher cheating on student tests and the floor-committee relationship in Congress.

This paper reports experiments on a sender-receiver game. In the game, a sender learns the true state (a number S) and sends a costless message M to a receiver who then chooses an action A. Payoffs only depend on S and A so the message M is "cheap talk." The receiver prefers to choose an action that matches the state, but the sender wants the receiver to choose an action closer to S+b, where b is a known bias parameter. The value of b is varied across rounds. When b=0 senders prefer that receivers choose S, so they almost always just announce S (i.e., M=S), and receivers believe them and choose A=M. When b>0 senders would prefer to exaggerate and announce M>S if they thought receivers would believe them.

Besides measuring choices in these games, our experiment uses "eyetracking" to measure what payoffs or game parameters sender subjects are looking at. Eyetracking software records where players are looking on a computer screen every 4 milliseconds. These data are a useful supplement to econometric analysis of choices, when decision rules which produce similar choices make distinctive predictions about what information is needed to execute these rules.

The eyetracking apparatus also measures how much subjects' pupils "dilate" (expand in width and area). Pupils dilate under stress, cognitive difficulty, arousal and pain. Pupillary responses have also been measured in the lie-detection literature for many years. These studies suggest that pupil dilation might be used to infer deceptive behavior because senders find deception stressful or cognitively difficult.

The experimental choices, eyetracking, and pupil dilation measures generate four basic findings:

1. Overcommunication in sender-receiver game is consistent with L0, L1, L2, and equilibrium (Eq) sender behavior produced by a level-k (cognitive hierarchy) model of the sender-receiver game in which L0 sender behavior is anchored at truth-telling.
2. Eyetracking data provide the following justifications for the level-k model of overcommunication:
    a. Attention to basic structure: Sender subjects pay attention to important parameters (state and bias) of the sender-receiver game.
    b. Self-centeredness: Sender subjects look at their own payoffs more than their opponents'.
    c. Incorrect beliefs: Sender subjects focus too much on the true state payoff row.

    d. Strategizing from a truth-telling anchor: Sender subjects focus on the payoffs corresponding to the action a=s, as well as actions up to a=s+b.

3. Right before and after the message is sent, senders' pupils dilate more when their deception is larger in magnitude. This suggests that subjects feel guilty for deceiving (as in Gneezy, 2005), or that deception is cognitively difficult (as the level-k model assumes).

4. Prediction: Based on the eyetracking results, we can try to predict the true state observed by the sender using lookup data, messages, and pupil dilation. This prediction exercise suggests it could be possible to increase the receiver's payoff (beyond what was earned in the experiments) by 16-21 percent. Finally, this study shows the possible relevance of psychology and neuroscience to economics. Douglas Bernheim (2008) suggests that Neuroeconomics will be successful if it can show how new non-choice data can solve a prediction or normative problem that could not be solved by standard choice data. Our data satisfy this criterion because lookups and pupil dilation enhance prediction of the true state beyond the predictions derived simply from observed messages (choice) and equilibrium theory.

This is the first study in experimental economics to use a combination of eyetracking and pupil dilation, and is, of course, exploratory and is therefore hardly conclusive. But the eyetracking and pupil dilation results by themselves suggest that the implicit assumption in theories of "cheap talk" in games with communication—namely, that deception has no cost—is not completely right. Mark Twain famously quipped, "If you tell the truth, you don't have to remember anything." The corollary principle is that if subjects want to misrepresent the state to fool receivers, they have to figure out precisely how to do so (and whether receivers will be fooled). This process is not simple and seems to leave a psychological signature in the form of looking patterns and pupil dilation. Future theories could build in an implicit cost to lying (which might also vary across subjects and with experience) and construct richer economic theories about when deception is expected to be widespread or rare.

Novel Approaches to Understanding Context Effects in Choice and Judgment

Anastasiya Pocheptsova, University of Maryland, USA

SESSION OVERVIEW

A major theme of a large body of research in psychology and consumer behavior has been that judgments and choice are influenced by temporary incidental context. The sources of these contextual effects are "as varied as the sources of information that can serve as input into evaluative judgment" (Schwarz and Clore 2007). Despite the wealth of empirical evidence on the topic, many interesting questions remain unanswered. For example, how can physical context (such as temperature) influence psychological judgments and change preferences? How does context cross modality; how do simple visual cues affect higher order processing? Finally, do context effects have a long-term influence on judgments or are they only capable of affecting immediate evaluations? Answering these questions will help consumer behavior researchers as well as marketers make better predictions about when context effects take place and provide a more integrative framework for this area of research.

By looking beyond a traditional examination of context effects, the current session provides a richer analysis of consumer behavior by proposing novel approaches to understanding context effects. In particular, the papers in the session examine the nature of context effects by looking at the role of metaphorical relationships, the interaction of perceptual fluency and attention, psychological buffers, memory effects and lay theories. Furthermore, the session expands our understanding of context effects by examining two novel context effects: psychological warmth and perceptual boundaries.

In the first paper in the session, Williams & Bargh direct our attention to a novel under researched context effect of physical warmth. They find that physical warmth that is unrelated to the stimuli being evaluated systematically affects judgment and choices. The authors hypothesize that physical warmth is capable of producing feelings of psychological warmth and thus have downstream effect on preferences. Such a metaphoric relationship between fundamental aspects of human life and psychological concepts is proposed to be a cause of this as well as other context effects.

In the next two papers, the authors examine a different context effect of perceptual boundaries. Zhang & Labroo find that perceptual boundary (a simple box) added to stimuli affects judgments of the stimuli. Further, the authors examine the mechanism underlying the effects and find that the perceptual boundary has differential influence on visual vs. verbal stimuli through it effects on perceptual fluency. Continuing this topic, Galak, Kruger & Rozin show that arbitrary perceptual boundaries can create an illusion of distance, reducing risk perceptions and one's motivation to cross those boundaries. The authors further show that observed effects are not limited to visual spatial representation, but are rather driven by the creation of the sense of isolation that serves as a psychological buffer.

Finally, Pocheptsova & Novemsky look at the mechanisms of context effects from a different angle by examining whether these effects are long-lived. The authors examine this question by looking at a well-established incidental mood effect. They find that in general the effect of context dissipates with time. However, context effects can be prolonged through the use of immediate evaluations and application of consumers' lay theories.

Taken together the research papers in this session investigate context effects in choice and judgment from multiple, yet related, theoretical perspectives with different conceptualizations of context effects. The authors of the papers span marketing and psychology offering an interdisciplinary view on the topic. As such the session will offer a novel perspective on the ways in which context affects the behavior of consumers and is expected to attract a broad audience at ACR.

EXTENDED ABSTRACTS

"Tactile Experience with Warm Objects Alters Judgments and Decisions"

Lawrence E. Williams, University of Colorado at Boulder, USA
John A. Bargh, Yale University, USA

Over the past 25 years, nonconscious priming research has demonstrated how environmental cues shape people's thoughts, feelings, and behaviors, often in a direct, literal fashion. This research examines new routes through which the external world influences people's judgments, via the metaphorical relationship between fundamental aspects of the physical environment (e.g., physical temperature), and psychological concepts (psychological warmth). A consideration of the ways in which the physical environment influences higher-order judgments and decisions increases our understanding of just how deep context effects run.

Psychological warmth is a ubiquitous feature of people's psychological realities. However, relatively little is known about the experiential basis of the concept of warmth. Based on recent treatments of concept development via metaphor, we tested the hypothesis that physical warmth is a core psychological concept capable of producing feelings of psychological warmth. To do this, we examine the effect of incidentally exposing people to warm or cold temperatures on personality impressions and social choices in two studies. In Study 1, participants who briefly and incidentally hold a hot coffee cup rate an ambiguous person as being nicer and more generous, compared to people who hold an iced coffee cup. Participants were primed with temperature by briefly holding either a cup of hot coffee, or a cup of iced coffee. To do this, a confederate blind to the study's hypotheses met participants in the lobby of the psychology building, carrying a cup of coffee, a clipboard, and two textbooks. During the elevator ride to the fourth floor laboratory, the confederate casually asked participants if they could hold the coffee cup as she recorded their name and the time of their participation. After the confederate wrote down the information, she took back the coffee cup. The temperature of the coffee cup (hot versus iced) was the only between-subjects manipulation. When participants arrived to the experimental room, they all received a packet containing a personality impression questionnaire modeled after the Solomon Asch's classic study on personality judgments. We find that this coffee cup manipulation altered people's judgments without their awareness, such that people who held the hot coffee cup judged this ambiguous person to be warmer. In Study 2, we find that people who briefly hold a hot therapeutic pad choose a gift for a friend more often than people who hold a cold therapeutic pad, extending these temperature priming effects into the realm of decision-making. Under the guise of product evaluation, participants held either a hot or cold therapeutic pad. After participants rated the effectiveness of either the hot or cold pad, they were asked to choose between a Snapple beverage and a $1 gift certificate to a local ice cream shop as a reward for participating in the study. For half of the participants, the Snapple option was framed as a personal reward for themselves, and the gift certificate option was framed as a social gift for a friend. For the remaining participants, the Snapple option was framed as a social gift for a friend, and the gift certificate option was framed as a personal reward for themselves. Consistent with our expectations, participants who held the hot pad were significantly more likely to choose reward framed as a social gift for a friend, regardless of whether it was a gift certificate or a Snapple.

These results highlight the importance of sensory experiences on higher-order psychological phenomena, improve our knowledge of how external cues can alter people's judgments, and provide marketers and managers with a new set of levers for influencing consumer behavior.

"Perceptual Boundaries: Helping You See Better but Making You Think Less"

Yan Zhang, University of Chicago, USA
Aparna A. Labroo, University of Chicago, USA

Four studies demonstrated that adding a perceptual frame (or boundary) around a stimulus improves visual processing of the object but interferes with verbal processing of the object. Building on research suggesting that visual processing relies on narrowing of attention whereas verbal processing relies on elaboration, we proposed that a perceptual boundary can help narrow attention. As a consequence, narrowed attention results in increased perceptual fluency towards a visual stimulus, making it appear more eye-catching and attractive and improving its evaluation. However, when the target object is verbal in nature, then the salience of a perceptual boundary can constrain elaboration and interfere with the ease of understanding the object, making the target appear less fluent conceptually. As a consequence, a perceptual boundary (simply adding a box) around a visual target can improve evaluation of the target but can reduce evaluation of a verbal target. A stronger positive effect of perceptual frame is observed on visual processors processing of visual objects, and a stronger negative effect of perceptual frame is observed on verbal processors processing of verbal objects.

Experiment 1 tested this basic premise. Non-Japanese speakers were informed that they would be evaluating Bank of Japan's new logo. The logo was presented either in Japanese, and was therefore not conceptually fluent to any participant, or was presented in English. In addition, for roughly half of the participants, a box was added around the logo while no box was added for the remaining participants. The data indicated the logo was evaluated more favorably when presented in Japanese and contained a frame vs. not. In contrast, when presented in English, the logo was evaluated less favorably when it contained a frame vs. not. Process measures indicated that for the Japanese logo, the improved evaluation was mediated by increased eye-catchingness of the logo. However, for the English logo, the reduced evaluation was mediated by reduced ease of understanding and elaboration. Variables such as need for cognition or need for closure do not impact the results, nor was there a reliable effect of self report measure of explicit attention to the target. A post test that manipulated perceptual salience in an alternative way by simply highlighting the Japanese and the English logo resulted in similar effects as a frame.

Experiment 2 extended these findings by showing that visual processors who presumably process a painting visually demonstrate an increased liking of an abstract painting comprised of a box vs. no box around it, presumably because the frame facilitates perceptual processing of the painting. In contrast, verbal processors who prefer to elaborate demonstrate reduced liking, presumably because the frame interferes with elaboration about the picture.

Experiment 3 replicated these findings in the context of an unfamiliar consumer product, Lanza Shampoo. It demonstrated that only among visual processors, liking was higher when the image was framed by a box (vs. not). In a final experiment, participants were asked to rate a verbal target — the description of a statement describing a psychological effect. High elaborators demonstrated reduced liking and importance rating of the theory when it contained a perceptual frame rather than not. In contrast, low elaborators demonstrated the reverse effect.

Taken together, these experiments add to our understanding of perceptual context effects. They demonstrate that a perceptual frame can serve as a context for evaluation of a target object, but its effect on evaluation diverges based on whether the target object relies on visual or verbal processing and whether people are more inclined to process information visually or verbally. Whereas perceptual frames facilitate visual processing by narrowing attention and making the visual objects appear more eye-catching, they also constrain elaboration and interfere with verbal processing when they are salient.

"Not in My Backyard: The Influence of Arbitrary Boundaries on Consumer Choice"

Jeff Galak, New York University, USA
Justin Kruger, New York University, USA
Paul Rozin, University of Pennsylvania, USA

The present research suggests that symbolic barriers such as political borders act as psychological buffers. Specifically, we show that the context that is defined by the presence or absence of a symbolic barrier affects the decisions that consumers make. Participants in Study 1 played a simple videogame in which the goal was to navigate an automobile to a virtual store as quickly as possible. Several routes were possible, some of which necessitated crossing a political boundary, some of which did not. Participants tended to choose routes that did not require crossing a town border, even though doing so did not result in a shorter (or quicker) route. This was true despite the fact the arbitrary nature of the border was clear (that is, the border was clearly unassociated with any geographical features such as lakes, rivers, etc.).

What, then, caused this reticence to cross borders? The results of Study 2 suggest that one reason is that the presence of a political border increases the perceived distance between locations. Participants were asked to image that they were in the market for a new guitar and to select which of two hypothetical music stores they would visit. The location of each store relative to the participant was depicted on a map. The map was drawn such that the two stores were in fact equidistant from the participant, but whereas one store was located in the same town as the participant, the other was not. Participants were not only more likely to choose the store that did not require crossing the border (replicating the results of Study 1), but also indicated that they were more confident in their decision when the store was "in the same town". This effect was replicated in a third study involving a non-visual border manipulation, indicating that the effect is not unique to visual spatial representations.

The results of Study 4 suggest that there is more to the buffering effect of borders than the illusion of distance, however. Participants were asked to imagine that an oil refinery was to be built a few miles from their home. A map was provided that depicted the location of both the participant's home and the proposed refinery, which in one condition included a political boundary separating the two. Participants were less bothered by the threat of toxic waste if the refinery resided on the other side of a border. Of key importance, this was true even after statistically controlling for perceptions of distance. This effect was replicated in our fifth and final study involving the proposed construction of a nuclear power plant. Here, too, participants were less concerned about the threat of contamination, despite the fact that a political border presumably offers little protection against airborne contaminants (and despite the fact that the arbitrary nature of the border was clear).

Taken together, these results suggest that arbitrary symbolic boundaries such as political borders act as a psychological buffer. Although part of this effect can be traced to the fact that borders make objects seem further away, it is also the case that borders provide a sense of isolation (from desirable objects) and protection (from undesirable ones). It appears that just as symbolic connection can convey the feeling of contamination (Morales and Fitzsimons, 2007; Rozin and Nemeroff, 2002; Rozin, Millman and Nemeroff, 1986), so too can symbolic *dis*connection serve as a psychological buffer. Discussion focuses on the relation between these findings and other findings from the judgment and decision making literature, including work on categorization (e.g., Parducci, 1965; Tajfel and Wilkes, 1963), context effects (Payne, Bettman, and Johnson 1993) and pricing (e.g., Thomas and Morwitz, 2005; Stiving and Winer, 1997).

"The Effect of Context on Memory-based Judgments"
Anastasiya Pocheptsova, University of Maryland, USA
Nathan Novemsky, Yale University, USA

Much research suggests that incidental situational factors (e.g., a transient mood) can affect immediate evaluations (Schwarz and Clore 1983, Schwarz 2004), but less is known about how such factors affect memory-based evaluations. Many (if not most) real-life consumer decisions involve memory-based judgments, where the decision is based on the evaluation of earlier experiences. For example, when consumers decide whether to come back to the restaurant they visited last week or heard about from a friend or buy a DVD based on their own or others' movie theater experience a couple of months ago, they have to rely on memories of past experiences. In the present research, we strive to expand our understanding of mood effects on memory-based judgment in two important ways. First, we investigate the effect of incidental mood present at the time of an experience on judgments made after the mood has dissipated. We propose that memory-based judgments are generally unaffected by context that is present during an experience. However, evaluations made during experience result in the "lock in" of context effects, leading to biased memory-based judgments and choices.

Consistent with these propositions, in the first two studies we found that mood had an influence on memory-based judgments when participants evaluated target stimuli in real time. This led to higher memory-based ratings for people who encountered the target in a positive mood and lower ratings for those who encountered it in a negative mood. However, the assimilating effect of mood disappeared in the absence of real-time evaluations. In the next study we extend our findings to a real choice setting. Because the choice task requires a comparison of several options, it can be argued that individuals might be motivated to recall the attributes of the experience rather than relying on the stored overall evaluation. In contrast, we show that being in a negative mood at the time of product consumption lead participants to prefer other options over the one they experienced last time, but only if they evaluated the experience at the time of consumption.

Next, we examine lay beliefs that people hold about the effect of incidental mood on memory-based judgments. In study 3 we show that people are not sensitive to time delay in their beliefs about the effect of incidental mood on memory-based judgments. Additionally, we find that real-time evaluations do not play a role in lay theories and as a result people believe that their memory-based judgments are biased by incidental mood regardless of whether real-time evaluations were made. Finally, next two studies show that when reminded about the context of an experience, participants corrected for the perceived bias in their memory-based judgments consistent with the lay theories uncovered in study 3. This led to context-dependent judgments for participants who held context-free memories of the experience.

Since a multitude of situations involve judgments based on recollections of prior experiences, this line of research sheds some light on when such judgments will be context-dependent or context-free. Our research suggests that people are more likely to make context-free memory-based judgments when 1) there is no immediate evaluation of the experience and 2) context is not brought to the individual's attention while making a memory-based judgment.

REFERENCES:
Morales, Andrea C. and Gavan J. Fitzsimons (2007), "Product Contagion: Changing Consumer Evaluations through Physical Contact with "Disgusting" Products," *Journal of Marketing Research*, 44 (May), 272-83.

Parducci, Allen1995), *Happiness, Pleasure, and Judgment: The Contextual Theory and Its Applications*, Hillsdale, NJ, England: Lawrence Erlbaum Associates, Inc.

Payne, John W., James R. Bettman, and Eric J. Johnson1993), *The Adaptive Decision Maker*, New York: Cambridge University Press.

Rozin, Paul, Linda Millman, and Carol Nemeroff (1986), "Operations of the Laws of Sympathetic Magic in Disgust and Other Domains," *Journal of Personality and Social Psychology*, 50 (4), 703-12.

Rozin, Paul and Carol Nemeroff (2002), "Sympathetic Magical Thinking: The Contagion and Similarity "Heuristics"," in *Heurstics and Biases: The Psychology of Intuitive Judgment*, ed. Thomas Gilovich and Daneil Kahneman, Cambridge, UK: Cambridge University Press, 201-16.

Schwarz, Norbert (2004), "Meta-cognitive Experiences in Consumer Judgment and Decision Making," *Journal of Consumer Psychology*, 14, 332-348.

Schwarz, Norbert and Gerald L. Clore (1983), "Mood, Misattribution and Judgments of Well-being: Informative and Directive Functions of Affective States," *Journal of Personality and Social Psychology*, 45, 513- 523

Schwarz, Norbert and Gerald L. Clore (2007), "Feelings and Phenomenal Experiences," in E. Tory Higgins and Arie Kruglanski (eds.), *Social Psychology. Handbook of Basic Principles* (2nd ed.), New York: Guilford.

Stiving, Mark and Russell S. Winer (1997), "An Empirical Analysis of Price Endings with Scanner Data," *Journal of Consumer Research*, 24 (June), 57-67.

Tajfel, Henri and A. L. Wilkes (1963), "Classification and Quantitative Judgment," *British Journal of Psychology*, 54 (2), 101-14.

Thomas, Manoj and Vicki G. Morwitz (2005), "Penny Wise and Pound Foolish: The Left Digit Effect in Price Cognition," *Journal of Consumer Research*, 22 (June), 54-64.

Beyond 2x2x2: Methodological Advances in Uncovering Consumer Decision Processes

Siegfried Dewitte, Catholic University Leuven, Belgium

SESSION OVERVIEW

This symposium presents four methodological advances for illuminating the psychological processes underlying consumer decision making. The methodologies address two main problems. First, process data are often collected via static self-reports that distort what researchers wish to unveil, as is sometimes the case in mediation studies. Second, processes are often assumed instead of inferred from process data, which is often the case in behavioral decision theory.

The converging message of the papers in this symposium is that while reality is more complex than standard measures admit, the appropriate methodologies can both capture and clarify psychological processes. Each paper presents feasible and accessible tools that promise to provide significant leaps over conventional methods used in the consumer behavior literature. The first two papers highlight the dynamic nature of decision making. Willemsen and Johnson designed the MouselabWEB methodology and illustrate how the rich information coming out of such studies may help to set apart theories about well-known phenomena (in this case context effects). Ramanathan illustrates the wealth of information that the measurement of moment-to-moment affective changes, as measured with a joy stick, may reveal about processes underlying well-known effects. Dewitte identifies criteria that a moderation-by-process design should meet before a moderation interaction can be interpreted as evidence for the hypothesized underlying process. Goldstein introduces an interactive, graphical tool for risk preference assessment that, compared to earlier techniques, allows one to more useful process information in less time.

The symposium may be of interest to experimental researchers who, because of the phenomena they tackle, struggle to find accurate process measures. Willemsen and Johnson's contribution may help decision researchers to illustrate the process underlying an emerging decision. This insight may help to put conflicting decision theories to the test. Ramanathan's contribution may help affect, goal, and social interaction researchers to illuminate the dynamics underlying affect, motivation, and decisions in a social context. Dewitte's contribution helps researchers to clearly specify and identify the process without measuring it. Goldstein's contribution will help risk researchers to model more complex risk decisions. The symposium may also inspire consumer researchers to apply the proposed methods to new domains in our field.

Eric Johnson will lead the discussion. Several methodological contributions to our field (e.g. Johnson 2001, *JCR*; Lohse and Johnson 1996, *OBHDP*) attest to his seminal role in the methodological advance of our field. He will critically weigh the contributors' suggestions against his experience as an experimentalist interested in processes. Individual presentations will take 14 minutes, which leaves 19 minutes for discussion.

References

Johnson, E.J. (2001). "Digitizing consumer research". *Journal of Consumer Research, 28,* 331-336.

Lohse, G.L., & E.G. Johnson (1996). "A comparison of two process tracing methods for choice tasks". *Organizational Behavior and Human Decision Processes, 68,* 28-43.

EXTENDED ABSTRACTS

"The Why and When of Context Effects"

Martijn Willemsen, Eindhoven University of Technology, The Netherlands

Eric J. Johnson, Columbia University, USA

Several accounts have been proposed to explain context effects like the compromise effect and the attraction effect. Though these accounts all predict choice, they differ strongly in the underlying cognitive mechanisms. To distinguish between the accounts, we look at the process predictions that can be derived from them. Process tracing tools (like MouselabWEB (Willemsen & Johnson, 2008), the tool we used in this study) allow us to gather information acquisition data that provides us with process measures on attention (acquisition frequencies and time), comparisons (transitions between information units) and dynamics (how information search changes over time). In two studies about Loss Aversion (Willemsen et al., 2008) we have applied these tools, showing that process data can help to distinguish between alternative accounts for loss aversion (reference dependence and gain-loss framing). In the current paper, we apply a similar methodology to get more insight into the cognitive processes underlying context effects.

We focus our analysis on theories that explain *both* attraction and compromise effects. In terms of process predictions, current accounts for context effects can be classified into two broad categories: biased and unbiased information search. One series of models predict a largely unbiased information acquisition process consisting of a large number of attribute-based comparisons. Some of these are based on loss aversion, such as the relative advantage model of Tversky and Simonson (1993) and the LAM model (Kivetz et al., 2004) which we extended to account for attraction effects. Recent sequential sampling models provide a computational modeling approach to explain context effects, such as Multialternative Decision Field Theory (Roe et al., 2001) and the Leaky Accumulator model (Usher & McClelland, 2004). These process models also predict an unbiased sequential sampling process, and are either based on lateral inhibition (Roe et al.) or on loss aversion (Usher and McClelland).

Another series of models predict context effects by means of a biased process. Emergent-value models explain the effects in terms of justification (Pettibone & Wedell, 2007; Simonson, 1989), an option gets extra (emergent) value by means of a qualitative argument. Recently our own work on loss aversion (Willemsen et al., 2008), suggests that decision makers show an information acquisition process that is predominantly alternative-focused, and that over time attention is directed towards the option that is preferred (i.e., sampling is biased towards the chosen alternative). Studying the phenomenon of loss aversion, we showed that a 'Decision by Distortion' account could best account for the process data (information acquisition patterns) we observed. We also observed significant presentation order effects on the choice data, which is predicted by a decision by distortion account because early preferences might affect direction of search and likewise final preference.

We tested these accounts using process data gathered online from a group of 374 ordinary US citizens, ranging from 18 to 65 years of age, and from all educational levels. Each participant made several choices for different product classes (DVD-players, cell phones, printers and small TVs), including a compromise choice, and attraction effect choice and a two option choice (control). Additional individual measures were gathered (such as importance ratings, demographics, loss aversion for money).

An important contribution of the current paper is that we present new, more advanced, methodologies to analyze and test the process data we collected. Rather than looking at global search indexes, we look in detail to attention given to each attribute/ alternative, and how this changes over time. Data was analyzed using multilevel regression to account for individual differences and repeated observations, and to include time dynamics. New representations (Icon Graphs) were used to provide a detailed qualitative view of the process measures in our data.

The choice results replicated the compromise and attraction effect. Effects of presentation order on choice proportions were observed (as predicted by a Decision by Distortion account) and some effects of individual characteristics, such as gender and age and relative importance of the attributes. Furthermore, process data was closely linked to choice, showing that process data indeed captures part of the cognitive process responsible for the construction of preference.

Secondly, the process predictions from the models were tested by contrasts within the multilevel models on attention, comparison and search dynamics. The data revealed a biased information acquisition process, showing strong shifts in attention towards the chosen option over time. This data supported an alternative-based account, and the decision by distortion account in particular. Little evidence was found for the unbiased acquisition processes such as predicted by current models like the Relative Advantage Model and current Sequential Sampling models.

The present paper demonstrates how new methodologies of analyzing process data can be used to more rigidly test processes assumptions underlying models of decision making behavior, which might help us to distinguish between models in terms of their process validity. Furthermore, insights gained from these processes might allow us to build better specified models of decision making behavior, and those insights might also inform current computational models of context effects on what assumptions underlying these accounts might be most plausible from a psychological perspective.

"Understanding Dynamic Processes in Consumer Behavior"
Suresh Ramanathan, University of Chicago, USA

Consumer behavior researchers are very familiar with the use of between-subjects cross-sectional designs wherein participants provide data on their thoughts and feelings on a single occasion. Yet, psychological processes rarely tend to be static–they are subject to substantial internal and external influences every moment. Consider a person left alone in a room with a stranger for one hour. If one were to measure the mood of the person just before entering the room and again after a few minutes, the data may reveal both an internal variability (e.g., the person may have just had an argument with a friend leading to moods becoming more negative or may have just received an A on an exam, leading to moods becoming more positive) and external variability (due to the social influence of the stranger). One common way of looking at longitudinal measures is to use repeated measures ANOVA. However, this assumes that any intrinsic dynamics within a particular variable apply in the same way to all individuals in the sample in the interval between measurements, so that intra-individual variability may be mis-represented as measurement noise (Boker and Nesselroade 2002). Put simply, each individual or class of individuals may have a unique signature pattern of psychological dynamics. In this paper,

we present two different ways of modeling intra-personal and inter-personal dynamics in two contexts–self-control and social interaction.

In the first illustration, we discuss the dynamics of ego-depletion and how depleted individuals respond to temptations on a moment-to-moment basis. Subjects were asked to suppress their emotions in response to a very sad video clip in the depletion condition (vs. no instruction in the control condition). Following this, they were presented with a tray filled with tempting desserts and instructed to move a joystick up and down (towards themselves if they felt like taking the dessert and away from themselves if they felt like pushing it away) continuously for 3 minutes. The following measures were computed from the resultant time series: a) distance from mid-point–positive if approach, negative if avoid, b) velocity computed as the first derivative of the time series and c) acceleration, computed as the second derivative of the time series. A non-linear dynamic model was fitted with acceleration being modeled as a function of distance and velocity. The interpretation of the coefficient for distance is that it represents the frequency of oscillations in emotions, with higher absolute values implying greater cyclicality in feelings towards the temptation. The coefficient for velocity is indicative of regulation or excitation–negative values suggest that the individual is dampening the feeling towards the temptation, positive values indicate that the individual is experiencing increasing desire. Results indicated that depleted individuals had both a greater frequency of oscillations and an increasing desire compared to non-depleted individuals.

In the second illustration, we discuss the dynamics of social interaction and how people's emotions change in response to the presence of others, both friends and strangers. Using a technique called cross-spectral analysis that decomposes the time series into different frequencies, we show that interacting friends who can see each other exhibit greater synchrony (as revealed by the covariation in the time series at specific frequencies) in their moment-to-moment reactions to a video clip compared to those who cannot see each other. The same is true for strangers who can see each other. However, we show that friends expect to experience this synchrony and discount it in their retrospective evaluations of the video clip while strangers misattribute the synchrony to the video clip and hence tend to use it as a heuristic to evaluate the clip.

"Good Practice in Experimental Moderation Designs"
Siegfried Dewitte, Catholic University Leuven, Belgium

The field's favorite way of gaining insight in the processes underlying an association between variables, either causal or descriptive, is by means of statistical mediation tests. Spencer, Zanna, and Fong (2005) list six concerns associated with this technique and propose two alternatives. In this paper I focus on the moderation-of-process designs, in which the process, rather than measured, is experimentally manipulated, orthogonally to the independent variable manipulation. The typical design is a two-by-two design in which the independent variable, for which a main effect has been established, further called the basic effect, is crossed with a manipulation of the process. An ordinal interaction between the two manipulations in which the main effect is either (partially) suppressed or augmented is taken as evidence for the mediating role of the process in the basic effect.

However, an ordinal interaction does not invariably indicate moderation of the process. I distinguish three ways in which a researcher could mistake an interaction as evidence for a moderated process. The moderation manipulation may not (only) affect the target process, but (also) the independent variable itself. In that case the process underlying the basic effect is not suppressed but sabotaged from the start ('the sabotage trap'). The moderation manipulation may also influence the dependent variable directly. In that case the process underlying the basic effect is not suppressed but overruled at the end ('the sledgehammer trap'). The moderation manipulation may, finally, also initiate an alternative, artificial process. In that case the process underlying the basic effect is not suppressed but replaced by another process ('the introspection trap').

I will present a set of simple checks that researchers can implement to make sure that they exclusively affect the natural process. In addition to the actual dependent variable, the researcher needs (1) a measure I that reliably reacts to the independent variable but not to the hypothesized process. The moderation manipulation should not interact with the independent variable on this variable (upstream criterion). Sabotaged processes will not pass this criterion. The researcher also needs (2) a measure P that reacts to the process but is not inherently related to the actual dependent variable. The design is safe for the sledgehammer and the introspection trap if the independent and the moderation manipulation also interact on P, provided that the partial correlation between P and the dependent variable (controlling for the experimental manipulations) is zero (= downstream criterion).

To the extent that the additional measures are sensitive to other measurements, they should be measured in separate samples. To the extent that they are intrusive, they should be measured at the end of the procedure. The rationale is generalizable to the case (1) of individual differences as moderating factors, (2) of multiple steps in the causal chain, and sheds new light on the concept 'boundary condition'.

"Measuring Consumer Risk-Return Tradeoffs"
Daniel Goldstein, London Business School, UK

Consumer choice occurs over multiple products and services, each having multiple associated risks. The numerous outcomes and probabilities facing consumers may be unknown, or as we shall explore, be known but be too numerous and interdependent for the unaided mind to process. Product and service risks cause consumers anxiety as they worry about matters such as automotive breakdown, computer failure, drug toxicity, and fund underperformance. Marketing managers have similar worries from the sell side, along with additional concerns about predicting risk attitudes in order to design promotions, loyalty programs, and sales contests.

Despite the importance of risk to marketing, the measurement of risk preferences has lagged behind the swift progress made in the measurement of riskless, attribute-level preferences. Specifically, conjoint analysis has rocketed from its humble roots in mathematical psychology to become the marketing's chief methodological export. The lack of a risk measurement method in the marketer's toolbox might limit the impact that marketing research can have on insurance, financial services, and medicine, in which risk is an inextricable component. This paper presents a new market research technique for measuring consumer preferences over complex multiple-outcome risks.

How do people think about risk and return? Since the Enlightenment, theories of risk preference have been based on choices between simple gambles. In the last century, choices among gambles have been used to show violations of Utility Theory, and motivate subsequent alternatives, such as Subjective Expected Utility Theory, Rank Dependent Utility Theory, Cumulative Prospect Theory, Reference-Dependent Subjective Expected Utility Theory, among many others. In recent years, alternative models to the alternative models have been motivated by choices between gambles as well.

With the most notable exception being the estimation of consumer utility functions, why has consumer research had so little

to say on risk preference? One possibility might be that simple prospects, while analytically tractable, are not realistic descriptions of the risks consumers regularly face. First, real product and service risks have multiple outcomes, not just two: An investment can return any percentage of its principal, and an insurance policy can be worth any percentage of its cost. Second, unlike simple prospects, consumer choice often occurs over far more than two alternatives. A consumer shopping for funds with Fidelity has over 4,500 investment products from which to choose. Each fund has a continuous distribution of outcomes, and each can be combined with other funds to create more portfolios than could be enumerated in a lifetime. As Lopes (1987) puts it, simple prospects "occur most frequently in the context of formal gambling and psychology experiments." Measuring risk in the domain of multiple-alternative, multiple-outcome prospects seems warranted.

We focus on investing for retirement, one of the largest decisions many people ever make, and certainly one of the consequential consumer decisions for which researchers have been hearing the call. Most employees in the United States, upon starting a new job, are taken down the hall to the human resources department where they are shown a list of investment products, and asked to allocate 100 percentage points of their retirement contribution between them. Many employees spend less than an hour deciding how to allocate assets for retirement, which is surprisingly little time considering that as many as 90% or more will never change their initial choice and that the decision could impact their well-being for one third of their lives or more.

We present a new market research technique for studying preferences over multiple-outcome risks. We first describe the method, present its psychological and analytical motivations, and then report the results of empirical tests of its reliability and validity both within testing sessions and across the span of one year. Empirically, we use this method to estimate the coefficient of relative risk aversion and the loss aversion parameter for a sample of working adults who have been saving for retirement for 5 to 30 years. To foreshadow our results, the method passes tests of reliability and validation and captures individual differences based on age and income. It also identifies two sub-populations, one best fit by the classical economic theory of risk preference, and the other by a behavioral model incorporating loss aversion. We conclude by discussing how the new methodology can impact research on risk and consumer decision-making.

REFERENCES

Boker, S.M. and J.R. Nesselroade (2002). "A method for modeling the intrinsic dynamics of intraindividual variability: Recovering the parameters of simulated oscillators in multi-wave panel data." *Multivariate Behavioral Research*, *37*, 127-160.

Kivetz, R., Netzer, O. & Srinivasan, V. (2004). Alternative models for capturing the compromise effect, *Journal of Marketing Research, 41*, 237-257

Lopes, LL. (1987) Procedural debiasing. *Acta Psychologica, 64*, 167-185.

Pettibone, J.C., & Wedell, D.H. (2007). Testing alternative explanations of phantom decoy effects. *Journal of Behavioral Decision Making, 20*, 323-341

Roe, R. M., Busemeyer, J. R., & Townsend, J. T. (2001). Multialternative decision field theory: A dynamic connectionist model of decision making. *Psychological Review, 108*, 370-392.Simonson, I. (1989). Choice based on reasons: The case of attraction and compromise effects, *Journal of Consumer Research, 16*, 158-174.

Spencer, S.J., M.P. Zanna, and G.T. Fong (2005). Establishing a causal chain: Why experiments are often more effective than meditational analyses in examining psychological processes. *Journal of Personality and Social Psychology, 89,* 845-851.

Tversky, A. & Simonson, I. (1993). Context-dependent preferences. *Management Science, 39,* 1179-1189

Usher, M. & McClelland, J. L. (2004). Loss aversion and inhibition in dynamical models of multi-alternative choice. *Psychological Review, 111,* 757-769.

Willemsen, M.C., Böckenholt, U. & Johnson, E.J. (2008). Value encoding, sequential sampling and decision by distortion: Three accounts of loss aversion in choice, *manuscript under review*

Willemsen, M.C. & Johnson, E.J. (2008). *MouselabWEB: Monitoring information acquisition processes on the web,* retrieved August 15, 2008, from http://www.mouselabweb.org/

Experiential and Informational Perspectives of Consumer Preference Consistency

Leonard Lee, Columbia University, USA

Marco Bertini, London Business School, UK

SESSION OVERVIEW

The notion of preference consistency lies at the roots of understanding, predicting, and influencing consumer behavior. Most marketing activities such as market segmentation, new product development, marketing communications, and customer management are based on the premise that consumers behave in somewhat consistent patterns. A substantial body of research in preference construction (see Lichtenstein & Slovic 2006 for a recent collection of work in this literature) has established that consumers do not always have stable preferences; in contrast, their preferences can be susceptible to a host of context effects such as changes in the number (Iyengar & Lepper 2000) or composition (e.g. Huber, Payne, & Puto 1982, Simonson 1989) of the choices they have.

This session brings together a series of three papers that examine how thinking about one's consumption experiences and given product information in different ways can differentially affect the consistency and stability of one's preferences. Specifically, the degree of consistency in consumers' preferences can change as a result of how consumers think about their related retrospective consumption experiences, the given attribute information of the products to be consumed, and the associations between these products and consumers' self identities.

Using a series of four experiments in three distinct domains—food, social interaction, and music—Galak, Redden, and Kruger demonstrate that making more salient related (vs. unrelated) intervening experiences since the last consumption episode can reduce the degree of product satiation and enhance the consistency of preferences over time. Simply having a wide variety of experiences might not be enough for consumers to recover from satiation since consumers tend to experience "variety amnesia;" rather, for consumers to "restore" their preferences to the products they most preferred and to maintain consistent preferences over time, *thinking* about the variety of their past related experiences might be essential.

On the other hand, Lee, Bertini, and Ariely find that how consumers think about the given product information can also influence the consistency of their preferences. In particular, they examine how the availability of price information can impact consumers' preference consistency given the inherent imprecision of mapping between monetary assessments and predicted utility. The results of a series of five experiments converge toward the same conclusion: when consumers think about prices during their purchase decisions, their choices are less consistent and transitive. Interestingly, price conscious consumers who are chronically more adept at thinking about how prices can affect their utility are less susceptible to such a negative effect of price consideration on preference consistency.

Nonetheless, the consistency of consumers' preferences over time depends not only on how consumers think about given product attributes but also the relationships between these products and their self identities. Through a series of three studies, Amir and Mazar show that consumers' preferences for products or experiences that are closely associated to consumers' self identities, when these identities are formed (e.g. during adolescence) or significantly changed (e.g. due to a life changing event such as marriage), will remain relatively stable throughout consumers' lives. Such preference consistency does not apply to products that are not associated with consumers' identities and does not depend solely on the consumers' age or the novelty of the products.

Overall, given the fundamental relevance of these papers' topics to consumers' every day lives, this special topic session should be of great interest not only to marketing researchers and psychologists, but also to anyone who is fascinated by the factors that determine how consistent our preferences are over time.

References

Huber, J., Payne, J.W..& Puto, C. (1982). Adding asymmetrically dominated alternatives: violations of regularity and the similarity hypothesis. *Journal of Consumer Research*, 9, 90-98.

Iyengar, S. S., & Lepper, M. R. (2000). When choice is demotivating. *Journal of Personality and Social Psychology*, 79, 995–1006.

Lichtenstein, S. & Slovic, P. (2006). *The Construction of Preferences*. Cambridge University Press.

Simonson, I. (1989). Choice based on reasons: the case of attraction and compromise effects. Journal *of Consumer Research,* 16, 158-174

EXTENDED ABSTRACTS

"The Construction of Satiation: Recalling Related Intervening Experiences Accelerates Recovery from Satiation"

Jeff Galak, New York University, USA

Joseph Redden, University of Minnesota, USA

Justin Kruger, New York University, USA

Consumers typically enjoy something less as they have more of it. Although such satiation is often inevitable, it does not last forever. For example, listening to a song several times in a row will get tedious, but presumably will not affect one's enjoyment of that song a year from now. We explore this temporal aspect of satiation, and show how consumers can recover from satiation more quickly.

In a process termed "spontaneous recovery" (Thompson and Spencer 1966), people seem to recover from satiation and once again enjoy their favorites with the simple passage of time. Likewise, satiation also seems to dissipate as people have other intervening experiences. For example, people salivate less from a taste of lemon after 10 trials, but a novel taste can immediately restore their salivation (Epstein et al. 1993). It seems that either the passage of time or the presence of different experiences helps people recover from satiation. We focus on how satiation depends on the salience of intervening experiences from the past.

The recall of past consumption plays an important role in determining satiation. People eat less candy if the wrappers from each piece remain visible (Polivy et al. 1986), and consume less food when they more fully account for how much they have already had (Wansink 2004). Remembering past consumption episodes seems to increase satiation for an item. We ask the complementary question of whether focusing on past episodes that were different has the inverse effect of reducing satiation for a particular item.

It is unlikely that recalling all past experiences accelerates one's recovery from satiation. We examine the distinction between the recall of related and unrelated experiences. Specifically, we predict that thoughts of unrelated experiences should have little impact on recovery. For example, thinking about music likely won't make one feel less satiated with respect to sushi, as music has little to do with food. In contrast, thinking about things related to sushi, such as other types of cuisines, should help the recovery process. More generally, thoughts of other experiences will accelerate recovery only when they fall within the same consumption context.

Finally, we distinguish between thinking about *any* episodes and thinking about *intervening* episodes. When consumers decide what to consume, thoughts of related experiences play a role in determining the amount of satiation felt. However, these thoughts can be of any experience that a consumer *has had* (intervening) or *may have* (future). We predict that that much like actual dishabituating experiences (Rolls, Rowe, and Rolls 1982), which necessarily occur since the last time a stimulus was consumed, only thoughts of intervening experiences will accelerate recovery. For example, when deciding what song to listen to, a consumer may think about songs he has recently heard or songs that he will potentially hear in the future. Thoughts of the former should decrease satiation, while thoughts of the latter should not. More formally, we predict that feelings of satiation should decrease when intervening experiences are made salient.

We find support for these predictions across four empirical studies. The first study finds that people had a greater preference for a flavor of jelly bean that they had satiated to when they were reminded of other jelly beans that they had also consumed. The second and third studies extend and replicate this effect in the domains of social interaction and music. When participants thought of "all the other music they listened to" or "all the other friends they hung out with" during the past two weeks, they wanted to hear their favorite (and presumably most satiated) song and hang out with their close friend more so than when no such thought generation task occurred. The third study also finds that this recovery from satiation appears only when listing friends they have spent time with in the past two weeks (i.e., it broke up the repetitive experience), and not for friends they expected to see in the upcoming two weeks. The fourth and final study rules out some alternative explanations in a controlled longitudinal study related to music consumption. Three weeks after being satiating to a preferred song, participants enjoyed that song again more when they thought of all the other musical artists they had heard in the intervening time, as compared to when they thought of other unrelated experiences. Importantly, this difference was only present for a satiated song, and not for another unsatiated song that they also preferred.

Many see satiation as an inevitable, but temporary, negative consequence of consumption. Although seeking out variety likely helps counter satiation, this research suggests that simply having variety is not enough. People seem to forget about this variety when they once again think about and focus on their favorite. Despite the fact that consumers work hard and pay a price to surround themselves with a great deal of variety, they seem to succumb to some sort of "variety amnesia" and forget the abundance that they live in. It seems that people construct and recover from satiation in the moment based on past episodes that easily come to mind. We find that the simple act of recalling related intervening experiences reduces satiation.

References

Epstein, Leonard H., Anthony R. Caggiula, Joshua S. Rodefer, Lucene Wisniewski, and Shari L. Mitchell (1993), "The Effects of Calories and Taste on Habituation of the Human Salivary Response," *Addictive Behaviors*, 18(2), 179-85.

Polivy, Janet, C. Peter Herman, Rick Hackett, and Irka Kuleshnyk (1986), "The Effects of Self-Attention and Public Attention on Eating in Restrained and Unrestrained Subjects," *Journal of Personality and Social Psychology*, 50(6), 1253-60.

Rolls, Barbara J., Edward A. Rowe, and Edmund T. Rolls (1982), "How Sensory Properties of Foods Affect Human Feeding Behavior," *Physiology & Behavior*, 29(3), 409-17.

Thompson, Richard F. and William Alden Spencer (1966), "Habituation: A Model Phenomenon for the Study of Neuronal Substrates of Behavior," *Psychological Review*, 73(1), 16-43.

Wansink, Brian (2004), "Environmental Factors That Unknowingly Increase Food Intake and Consumption," *Annual Review of Nutrition*, 24, 341-78.

"Money Muddles Thinking: The Effects of Price Consideration on Preference Consistency"

Leonard Lee, Columbia Business School, USA
Marco Bertini, London Business School, UK
Dan Ariely, Duke University, USA

Price is an integral part of every buying decision. Consumers not only interpret prices as signals of product/service quality (Gerstner 1985) but can also be influenced by prices in their degree of involvement with the purchase process (Wathieu and Bertini, forthcoming) and their subsequent post-purchase consumption experience (Shiv, Carmon, and Ariely, 2005).

More fundamentally, in this work, we explore consumers' *ability* to use this important attribute—price—in their decision making. Specifically, we examine the effects of prices on the reliability and consistency of consumers' preferences, or consumers' capacity to consider prices and interpret them the same way every time they make a purchase decision. Prior research has consistently demonstrated the general dissociation between monetary assessment and predicted utility and the ill-defined hedonic representation of money in the minds of consumers (Amir, Ariely, and Carmon, forthcoming). Based on the inherently imprecise mappings between price evaluations and predicted utility, we hypothesize that price considerations can deteriorate the consistency of buying decisions.

To test this hypothesis, we investigated whether the availability of price information for a set of ten differentiated products (t-shirts) affects the consistency of sequential choices in pair-wise comparisons. As a measure for preference consistency, we computed the number of transitivity violations (i.e. for any a, b, and c, $a \geq b$, $b \geq c$, $c \geq a$, where $\geq$ denotes relative preference) across experimental conditions (Kendall and Babington Smith 1940; Lee, Amir, and Ariely, forthcoming). Across five experiments, we consistently found that when consumers considered prices in their decision making, their preferences were more intransitive.

In *Experiment 1*, participants (N=103) were randomly assigned to one of two conditions: in the *price* condition, both the pictures and prices of the t-shirts were presented to participants, while in the *no-price* condition, only the pictures of the t-shirts were available. Consistent with our basic hypothesis, the results revealed that participants in the *price* condition made significantly more intransitivity errors than those in the *no-price* condition ($p=.01$).

This result was replicated in *Experiment 2* (N=43) in which we used a different preference elicitation method—a ten-point relative preference rating scale—instead of binary choice. Additionally, we modified the experimental procedure to test an alternative explanation: in Experiment 1, participants in the *no-price* condition were never given the t-shirts' prices; thus, differential learning across conditions could have contributed to the different degrees of preference consistency. To test this account, in Experiment 2, we showed all participants (in *both* conditions) the prices of all ten t-shirts before the choice task. (We used this modified design in all subsequent experiments.) Similar to Experiment 1, participants in the *price* condition made significantly more intransitivity errors than those in the *no-price* condition ($p<.05$), demonstrating that the negative impact of price on preference consistency is the result of differential availability of price information *during* choice and does not depend on how preferences are elicited.

One alternative account of the above results is that participants in the *price* condition had "more" information than those in the *no-price* condition during choice, and the salience of this additional information could have made it more difficult for participants in the *price* condition to integrate different attributes in their decision making. We rule out this alternative account in *Experiment 3* (N=174) by demonstrating that it is the *type* of information, and not the availability of *more* information, that influences the stability of consumers' preferences. Specifically, participants were randomly assigned to one of three experimental conditions: in the *price* condition, participants were asked to consider how much they thought each t-shirt would cost when making their choices, whereas in the *experience* condition, participants were asked to consider how it would feel to wear each t-shirt; in the *no-info (control)* condition, participants were simply asked to choose the t-shirt they preferred within each pair without any specific instructions to consider any particular decision factor. Thus, unlike the earlier experiments, the t-shirts' prices were *never* displayed on the screen in all three conditions. The results revealed that participants in the *price* condition made significantly more transitivity errors than participants in both the *experience* condition ($p=.03$) and the *no-info* condition ($p=.03$), indicating that, rather than the mere availability of prices during choice, it is the active consideration of such prices that deteriorates preference consistency over time.

The results of Experiment 3 were conceptually replicated in *Experiment 4* (N=194) using a 2 (Price: present, absent) x 2 (Quality Rating: present, absent) between-subjects design: participants were shown both the prices and quality ratings of the t-shirts, one of the two pieces of information, or neither during choice. A 2X2 ANOVA returned a main effect of price on preference consistency [$F(1, 190)=4.065, p=.045$]; however, neither the main effect of quality ratings [$F(1, 190)=.332, p=.57$] nor the interaction effect between price and quality ratings [$F(1, 190)=.773, p=.38$] was statistically significant, providing further evidence that the negative effect of price consideration on preference consistency cannot be adequately explained by an information complexity account.

Finally, in *Experiment 5* (N=50), we further tested our hypothesis by using an individual difference factor—price-consciousness (Lichetenstein, Ridgway, & Netemeyer 1993). We posit that price-conscious consumers chronically focused on paying low prices should find it easier to map between prices and predicted utility; thus, the availability of price information should be less likely to degrade their preference consistency, compared to consumers who are less price-conscious. Indeed, a 2 (price vs. no-price) X 2 (price-consciousness: high, low) ANOVA revealed a significant main effect of price [$F(1, 46)=4.193, p=.046$], a significant main effect of price-consciousness [$F(1, 46)=7.271, p=.009$], and a significant interaction effect between both factors [$F(1, 46)=6.152, p=.017$] on preference consistency. Planned comparisons further revealed that whereas the availability of price information led to greater preference inconsistency among relatively non-price-conscious participants [$t(23)=2.532, p=.019$], it did not affect the preference consistency of price-conscious participants [$t(23)=.482, p=.63$].

References

Amir, On, Dan Ariely, and Ziv Carmon (forthcoming), "The Dissociation between Monetary Assessments and Predicted Utility," *Marketing Science*.

Bertini, Marco and Luc Wathieu (forthcoming), "Attention Arousal through Price Partitioning," *Marketing Science*.

Gerstner, Eitan (1985), "Do Higher Prices Signal Higher Quality?" *Journal of Marketing Research*, 22 (2), 209-15.

Kendall, Maurice G. and B. Babington Smith (1940), "On the Method of Paired Comparisons," *Biometrika*, 31 (3-4), 324-45.

Lee, Leonard, On Amir, and Dan Ariely (forthcoming), "In Search of Homo Economicus: Cognitive Noise and the Role of Emotion in Preference Consistency," *Journal of Consumer Research*.

Lichtenstein, Donald, R., Nancy M. Ridgway, and Richard G. Netemeyer (1993), "Price Perceptions and Consumer Shopping Behavior: A Field Study," *Journal of Marketing Research,* 30(2), 234-245.

Shiv, Baba, Ziv Carmon, and Dan Ariely (2005), "Placebo Effects of Marketing Actions: Consumers Get What They Pay For," *Journal of Marketing Research*, 42 (4), 383-93.

"The Most Influential Age Hypothesis: Does the Self Cause Predictable Preferences?"

On Amir, University of California, San Diego, USA
Nina Mazar, University of Toronto, Canada

Preferences are formalized as the basis for behavior ranging from our everyday actions to the most significant choices in life. One of the traditional assumptions of many social sciences is that such dispositions are relatively stable throughout our lives. Life after all, demands some stability in our motivations to survive, procreate, and belong (Maslow 1943). The hallmark of this stability assumption has been the ability to predict or forecast behavior, which in turn enables the modeling of human behavior—a necessity in disciplines such as economics or public policy aiming at increasing social welfare. In this paper we attempt to shed light on the situations in which this crucial assumption is more likely to hold and its antecedents.

A growing body of research in psychology and decision making has accumulated evidence that preferences are often unstable and dependent on transient aspects of the situation. For example, preferences for risk and reward are reference dependent (Kahneman & Tversky 1979) and thus, depend on the framing of the situation (Epley et al. 2006; or McKenzie 2004; Ariely, Leowenstein, & Prelec 2003). Even preferences for high involvement decisions, such as how much to pay for real estate (Simonsohn & Loewenstein 2005) or which university to pick, may depend on recent, albeit less relevant experiences. Choosing whether to accept an offer for undergraduate studies, for example, may depend on the weather during the admissions visit (Simonsohn 2007). Moreover, even the valence of experiences may be shifted based on an initial less relevant anchor (Ariely, Loewenstein, & Prelec 2006). Termed "the Tom Sawyer Effect", Ariely and colleagues (2006) show that people categorized the experience of listening to poetry as either enjoyable or aversive depending on whether they were asked to pay for this experience or offered to be paid for it. In sum, there are many examples for which people do not seem to have well-defined predictable preferences.

Yet, at the same time, there exists evidence that some preferences are predictable. Most notably, Holbrook and Schindler (1989) contrasted people's age with their ratings of songs and find an inverted-U shape peaking at the early twenties (23.47 years old).

Their results suggest that "People seem to develop preferences for popular musical styles (typically those which prevail among their current circle of friends) during late adolescence or early adulthood, and these preferences over other styles of music tend to prevail for the rest of their lives." The mixed evidence about the stability of preferences begets questioning what mechanism might lead to their development and what may be the resulting domains in which we might expect relatively stable preferences.

In this work we investigate one theory implying the development of such stable preferences: "The most influential age hypothesis". Emerging from a vast stream of research in social and developmental psychology, this theory builds upon the idea that identity is a rather stable trait, which is formed during late adolescence (Baumeister 1998; Erikson 1968; Kroger 2000;). To the extent that some preferences are driven by one's identity, the formation of one's self may not only influence downstream attitudes (Lord, Ross, & Lepper, 1979; Visser & Krosnick, 1998) but also preferences. Based on this idea and Holbrook and Schindler's (1989) findings about the influence of the early adulthood age on preferences for popular music, we suggest that similar to moral principles, social schemas, and languages, preferences for products or experiences that are closely associated to one's identity, when it is formed or significantly changed, will remain relatively stable throughout our lives. We report three studies in support of our theory.

We begin by looking at movies and asking experts (Study 1) as well as lay people (Study 2) two simple questions: What are their favorite movies, and at what age did they see the those movies? Our data does not support a recency effect story. In contrast, we find that both, experts as well as lay people have very strong preferences for movies they have seen as early adults. We show that our results cannot be explained by age of the participant, age of the movie, nor any other movie attribute. We therefore conjecture that products or experiences that are somehow linked to one's identity-formation will be more likely to make a long lasting, predictable impression, and consequently lead to rather stable preferences. In our final study we explicitly compare the preferences for products related to one's identity (e.g., movies) versus products not related to one's identity (e.g., portable music players) to show that only preferences for the former, when linked to identity-changing events such as marriage or becoming a parent, leave a lasting impression.

References

Ariely, Dan, George Loewenstein, and Drazen Prelec (2003), "Coherent Arbitrariness: Stable Demand Curves Without Stable Preferences," *Quarterly Journal of Economics*, 118, 73-105.

Ariely, Dan, George Loewenstein, and Drazen Prelec (2006), "Tom Sawyer and the Construction of Value," *Journal of Economic Behavior and Organization*, Vol 60, 1-10.

Baumeister, Roy F. (1998), "The Self," In The Handbook of Social Psychology, Gilbert, D.T., Fiske, S.T., & Lindzey, G. (Eds), New York, NY: Oxford University Press, 680-740.

Epley, Nicholas, Dennis Mak, and Lorraine Idson (2006), "Rebate or bonus? The impact of income framing on spending and saving," *Journal of Behavioral Decision Making*, 19, 213-227.

Erikson, Erik H., (1968). Identity: Youth and Crisis. New York: Norton.

Holbrook, Morris B. and Robert M. Schindler (1989), "Some Exploratory Findings on the Development of Musical Tastes," *Journal of Consumer Research*, Vol. 16, 119-124.

Holbrook, Morris B. (1993), "Nostalgia and Consumption Preferences: Some Emerging Patterns of Consumer Tastes," *Journal of Consumer Research*, Vol. 20, 245-256.

Kahneman, Daniel, and Amos Tversky (1979), "Prospect theory: An analysis of decision under risk," *Econometrica*, 47, 263-291.

Kroger, Jane (2000). Identity development: Adolescence through adulthood. Thousand Oaks, CA: Sage Publications.

Lord, Charles G., Lee Ross, and Mark R. Lepper (1979), "Biased assimilation and attitude polarization: The effects of prior theories on subsequently considered evidence," *Journal of Personality and Social Psychology*, 37, 2098-2109.

Maslow, Abraham H. (1943), "A Theory of Human Motivation," *Psychological Review*, 50, 370-396.

McKenzie, Craig R. M. (2004), "Framing effects in inference tasks—and why they are normatively defensible," *Memory and Cognition*, 32, 874-885.

Simonsohn, Uri, and George Loewenstein (2006), "Mistake #37: The Effect of Previously Faced Prices on Current Housing Demand," *The Economic Journal*, 116(1), 175-199.

Simonsohn, Uri (2007), "Weather to Go to College (not a typo)," Working paper.

Visser, Penny S. and Jon A. Krosnick (1998), "Development of attitude strength over the life cycle: Surge and decline," *Journal of Personality and Social Psychology*, 75(6), 1389-1410.

Zajonc, Robert B. (1968), "Attitudinal effects of mere exposure," *Journal of Personality and Social Psychology*, 9, Monongraph supplement No. 2, Part 2.

Zauberman, Gal, Rebecca K. Ratner and B. Kyu Kim (2007), "Strategic Memory Protection in Choice over Time," Working paper.

Self-Expression and Brand Identity in Consumer Choice

Alexander Chernev, Northwestern University, USA

SESSION OVERVIEW

Building on the existing literature, this session contributes to a better understanding of the role of brands in consumer decision processes. Research papers presented investigate the impact of brands from multiple theoretical perspectives, offering a broader view of the role of brands in consumer choice. The findings of the individual papers are unified into a general framework which examines the role of brands as a means of self-expression.

Given the relevance of the proposed topic to central issues in consumer behavior, this symposium adds to the identity research and, in particular, the role of brands as a means of self-expression. Apart from providing theoretical insights into how brands influence choice, the proposed symposium contributes to the understanding of several context areas that are of great interest to ACR conference attendees, including attitudes, self-image, and conspicuous consumption. Specifically, the session addresses the following issues:

Research presented by Chernev and Gal explores the antecedents of the recent decline in the power of many brands. Building on the view of brands as a means of expressing one's identity, they argue that the decline in brand power could be attributed to the increase in alternative means of self-expression. They posit that the proliferation of brands, as well as other non-brand means of self-expression, has diminished the personal relevance of individual brands — a phenomenon referred to as "brand saturation". They show that the self-expressive value of a given brand is subject to diminishing returns as the number of alternative means of self-expression increases.

Research by Berger and Ward examines the role of inconspicuous brand consumption in consumer choice. Conspicuous consumption suggests that branded products help explicitly display wealth and sophistication. In contrast, they argue that inconspicuous consumption, or using subtler signals unrecognizable to most consumers, can sometimes be more effective to insiders. Eight studies demonstrate that a) certain categories show an inverted U relationship between price and explicit branding; b) mass consumers prefer high-end products with explicit branding and misidentify those that use subtle brand signals; and c) insiders or experts prefer less explicit branding and can correctly identify subtle-signal products, which implies that subtle signals can sometimes provide more effective identity signals.

Finally, research by LeBoeuf and Simmons investigates the influence of branding on attitude functions. They show that branding predictably alters the degree to which products give rise to attitudes that serve self-expressive, as opposed to utilitarian, functions. Specifically, products that support utilitarian attitudes at the category level support less utilitarian, more symbolic attitudes at the brand level, whereas products that support symbolic attitudes at the category level support more utilitarian, less symbolic brand attitudes. They further demonstrate the implications of this finding for persuasion: Whereas utilitarian appeals are best for "utilitarian" products (and symbolic appeals are best for "symbolic" products) at the category level, this advantage does not arise at the brand level, in part because attitude functions change with branding.

The individual presentations were integrated by the discussion leader Rohit Deshpande into a more general framework, facilitating a broader understanding of the role of brands as a means of self-expression.

EXTENDED ABSTRACTS

"Brand Saturation in Consumer Choice"

Alexander Chernev, Northwestern University, USA
David Gal, Northwestern University, USA

There is a growing belief among many marketers that brands are losing their power and have "run out of juice." Prior research has attributed the diminishing power of national brands to factors such as the increased degree of commoditization of the underlying products, the transparency of the product information available online, the proliferation of intelligent agents, and the deployment of new business models such as Priceline.com, which make brands invisible to consumers.

In this research, we advance a novel explanation for the recent decline in brand power. Building on the view of brands as a means of expressing one's identity, we argue that the role of brands as a means of self-expression is contingent on the availability of other means of self-expression. We posit that the proliferation of brands, as well as other means of self-identification, has diminished the personal relevance of individual brands — a phenomenon we refer to as "brand saturation."

We propose that brand saturation can be caused by a variety of available means of self-expression, including other self-expressive brands in the same category and in unrelated product categories, and by non-brand means of self-expression. For example, we argue that the relevance of the Budweiser brand is a function not only of the strength of its intrinsic associations, but also the strength of other beer brands such as Miller and Coors. Furthermore, we argue that relevance of the Budweiser brand is affected by non-beer self-expressive brands such as Apple, Swatch, and Whole Foods, as well as by non-brand means of self-expression, including involvement in online communities such as MySpace.com, Facebook.com and LinkedIn.com. In this context, we posit that the self-expressive value of a given brand is subject to diminishing returns as the number of alternative means of self-expression increases.

We examine the impact of identity saturation on consumer brand preferences in a series of four experiments. The first study aims to demonstrate that merely asking consumers to identify their favorite brands weakens their brand preferences in unrelated product categories. Consistent with our theory, respondents who were asked to articulate their most preferred brands displayed greater indifference between the available brands in subsequent choices.

Building on the findings from this study, the second experiment documents that non-brand means of self-expression–such as identifying favorite books, movies, songs, sports teams, and hobbies–are likely to decrease perceived differentiation of the target brands. We show that the brand-saturation effect holds even in the presence of non-brand means of self-expression, such that respondents who were asked to articulate personally relevant items displayed weaker brand preferences in subsequent choices.

Experiment 3 documented identity-saturation effects naturally occurring in the context of brand choice. Thus, unlike the first two experiments in which identity saturation was achieved by explicitly asking respondents to state their preferences, in this experiment identity saturation was manipulated by having respondents merely make a choice in several product categories. This manipulation was based on the notion that choice itself can serve a self-expressive function, such that making multiple selections in personally relevant categories is likely to lead to identity-saturation, which in turn will decrease consumer preferences for the subsequent brands.

Building on the first three studies, experiment 4 provides more direct evidence of the processes underlying the brand saturation effect, documenting the role of self-expression in brand saturation. In this experiment we manipulated individuals' need for self-expression by providing a feedback that was either consistent or inconsistent with their self-image, and examined its impact on subsequent brand preferences. The data lend further support to the notion that the strength of individuals' brand preferences is a function of their need for self-expression. In particular, we show that decreasing the need for self-expression (e.g., by validating individuals' unique identity) tends to weaken their brand preferences, whereas increasing their need for self-expression (e.g., by threatening their identity) has the opposite effect, strengthening their brand preferences. This experiment documented the impact of self-expression on the strength of individuals' brand preferences using three different measures: personal brand relevance, perceived brand similarity, and willingness to pay. The data show convergence across all three measures—a finding that enhances the validity of the observed effects.

From a theoretical standpoint, this research contributes to the literature of self-identity by furnishing evidence in support of the notion that individuals' need for self-expression is finite and that there are diminishing returns on increasing the variety of means of self-expression. We show that the need for self-expression is not domain-specific but rather occurs across categories and consumption occasions. In this context, we show that brands compete for a share of a consumer's identity, such that the self-expressive value of a given brand tends to decrease as the number of alternative means of self-expression (brand and non-brand) increases.

"The Subtle Signals of Inconspicuous Consumption"
Jonah Berger, University of Pennsylvania, USA
Morgan Ward, The University of Texas at Austin, USA

Branding varies across products. While some products use explicit branding (e.g., Armani Exchange emblazoned across a shirt front), others do not. The literature on conspicuous consumption suggests that price differences might drive signal explicitness. People often use products to communicate identity, and in particular to signal wealth and/or expertise to others. Consumers might want to broadcast their purchase of an expensive Lacoste polo shirt because it signals high status. They might be less interested in letting people know they purchased a generic polo shirt from Wal-Mart. Consequently, one might imagine that explicit branding might increase with price.

The data, however, display a distinctly different pattern. In Study 1, we randomly selected more than 120 pairs of sunglasses (both men's and women's) from major sunglass websites (e.g., Sunglass Hut). We then gave coders an image of each pair, and had them rate whether each pair explicitly identified the brand (i.e., the brand name or logo appeared) or not. In contrast to what would be predicted by conspicuous consumption, we found an inverted U relationship between price and brand identification. Regressing price and price squared on brand identification indicates that while brand identification increased with price, brand identification was negatively related to price squared. While only 21% of sunglasses under $50 bore brand identifiers, 84% of sunglasses between $100 and $300 identified the brand. Brand identification decreased, however, among higher priced options. Only half the sunglasses over $400 identified the brand. In Study 2, a category analysis of

handbags replicated these results. These findings provoke an interesting question. If consumers care about signaling status, why would they pay more for a product whose brand is harder to identify?

We argue that certain consumers may prefer high-end products with subtle signals because they ensure differentiation. Consider two populations: mass consumers (the general population) and insiders (those with special knowledge). If being seen as an insider carries value among the masses, then some mass consumers may attempt to "poach" or borrow insider symbols so other mass consumers will treat them like an insider. This will dilute the product's value as a marker of insider group identity, and insiders will diverge, developing new symbols to mark their group boundaries. Insiders may be able to maintain group identifiers, however, by adopting subtle signals that are only recognizable to other insiders. Because mass consumers want most others to regard them as insiders, they prefer explicit signals recognized by mass consumers. Consequently, insiders may migrate to subtle signals because they provide such differentiation.

Six additional studies support this perspective. Studies 3A-3C demonstrate that people typically misidentify products with subtle signals. Participants viewed different shirts, both low- and high-priced, which varied in their brand-signal strength from subtle (e.g., a small logo) to explicit (e.g., a large brand name). Results indicated that participants a) were more likely to misidentify the brand on shirts that used subtle brand signals; b) could not differentiate between generic and expensive shirts displaying subtle brand signals; and c) inferred no price difference between an expensive subtly marked and a generic, subtle-signal shirt. This shows that most people would misidentify someone who bought an expensive shirt with a subtle brand signal.

The data provided by Study 4 show, however, that insiders can identify products with subtler signals. For example, though members of the general college population could not differentiate between expensive and inexpensive handbags with subtle brand markings, members of a fashion school were able to identify such bags correctly.

Insider knowledge also moderated the inferences people made about others carrying subtly vs. explicitly branded bags, as well as the preferences of both groups. Study 5 showed that while members of the general population thought people with explicit bags knew more about fashion, insiders thought that people who carried more subtle (and actually, more expensive) bags, knew more. Further, Study 6 showed that given the choice between expensive bags at similar price points, members of the general population preferred explicitly branded bags while insiders preferred bags with subtler signals.

Overall, these studies indicate the utility of subtle signals. Though members of the general population prefer high-end products with explicit signals because they facilitate recognition by the general public, insiders prefer products with subtler signals that can be recognized only by their in-group of savvy insiders. Thus, while explicit signals facilitate broader recognition, subtle signals may be useful in maintaining group boundaries.

"Branding and Attitude Functions"
Robyn LeBoeuf, University of Florida, USA
Joseph Simmons, Yale University, USA

Attitudes serve different functions. Some serve a utilitarian function of maximizing rewards, whereas others serve a symbolic, value-expressive function. Prior research has shown that particular product categories are associated with particular attitude functions: Whereas some products (e.g., aspirin) typically support utilitarian attitudes, others (e.g., flags) typically support symbolic attitudes. However, such research has focused almost exclusively on product categories, and has not considered how branding might alter associations between products and attitude functions.

We propose that branding alters these associations. First, although the associations between product categories and attitude functions are often clear, brands might be less directly associated with the category's attitude function. Spreading-activation models of knowledge suggest that knowledge is often represented hierarchically, with properties associated with the entire category being stored at the highest applicable level and not necessarily re-stored for each subsidiary instance (e.g., "can fly" would be stored with "bird," but not necessarily with each bird). Thus, the links between category-level functions and subsidiary brands may be indirect, with branded products being relatively weakly associated with the category's dominant function. Second, brands may often emphasize how they differ from the generic category: brands in utilitarian categories may build symbolic associations, and brands in symbolic categories may build utilitarian associations. Because of this, consumers may expect brands in utilitarian (symbolic) categories to be more symbolic (utilitarian) than the category itself.

Thus, we predict that products that give rise to utilitarian category-level attitudes will give rise to brand attitudes that are less purely utilitarian, but that products that give rise to symbolic category-level attitudes will give rise to brand attitudes that are less purely symbolic.

We further predict that branding will alter appeal persuasiveness. Typically, "function-matching" appeals are more effective than "mismatching" appeals: for utilitarian products, appeals emphasizing tangible benefits are superior, but for symbolic products, value-laden, symbolic appeals are superior. However, because attitude functions may differ for categories and brands, appeals that match a product's category-level function may not match the product's brand-level function as clearly. As a result, an appeal that is more persuasive at the category level (because of this function-matching advantage) may not be more persuasive at the brand level. For example, for a utilitarian product, a utilitarian appeal's advantage may be smaller at the brand level, precisely because brand attitudes for the product may be less strictly utilitarian.

We first examined whether branding alters attitude functions. In Study 1, participants evaluated the attitude functions they associated with an array of utilitarian (e.g., toothpaste) and symbolic (e.g., class rings) products. Half evaluated category-level products (e.g., vitamins) and half evaluated branded products (e.g., One-a-Day vitamins). As predicted, products that supported utilitarian category-level attitudes supported somewhat more symbolic attitudes when branded, but products that supported symbolic category-level attitudes supported less symbolic attitudes after branding.

Study 2 replicated this procedure, but participants in the branded condition evaluated hypothetical, unnamed brands. Even when the brands were unnamed, branding made attitudes towards utilitarian products more symbolic but attitudes towards symbolic products more utilitarian.

Study 3 examined the implications of this effect for persuasion. Participants considered appeals for paper towels and college t-shirts, which support utilitarian and symbolic (respectively) category-level attitudes. Participants were randomly assigned to a 2 (appeal level: brand, category) x 2 (appeal type: matching or mismatching the category-level attitude) design. For paper towels, the utilitarian (matching) appeal discussed cleaning, whereas the symbolic (mismatching) appeal discussed how paper towels, made of recycled paper, symbolize conservation. For t-shirts, the utilitar-

ian (mismatching) appeal emphasized a discount associated with wearing the shirts, whereas the symbolic (matching) appeal emphasized school spirit. As predicted, matching appeals reliably outperformed mismatching appeals when delivered for the category, but this advantage disappeared—and non-significantly reversed—when the same appeals were delivered for brands. Study 4 replicated these results, using different products, appeals, and brands.

In study 5, participants evaluated an advertisement for greeting cards. Between participants, we manipulated whether the ad was symbolic or utilitarian, and whether it was a category-level or brand-level appeal. We also measured the function served by each participant's attitude towards the category of greeting cards; this allowed us to define for each participant whether the assigned appeal was a "match." Indeed, for those with utilitarian (symbolic) attitudes, the utilitarian (symbolic) appeal had an advantage at the category level, but not at the brand level. Thus, the very same appeal's success depended upon whether it matched the individual's attitude function, thereby confirming attitude functions' role in these effects. Even with appeals held constant and "matches" defined idiosyncratically, matching appeals outperformed mismatching appeals for categories, but not for brands.

Finally, in study 6, participants evaluated actual magazine advertisements, rating them on either (a) how effective each advertisement seemed, (b) the degree to which each advertisement made symbolic and utilitarian claims, or (c) the degree to which each advertised product supported utilitarian or symbolic category-level attitudes. Advertisements for branded products were more favorably evaluated to the degree that the appeals were incongruent with the attitude function associated with the product category (i.e., mismatching appeals had an advantage). This finding converges with the more controlled experimental evidence provided by the other studies, showing that the main conclusions hold even with a much broader set of appeals. Strikingly, even with these "real" stimuli, there was no evidence that the category-function-matching advantage emerged for branded products.

These results give us insight into what brands communicate about products. Branding alters attitude functions, with predictable consequences for persuasion: "Function-matching" appeals that are superior at the category level lose their superior status at the brand level, in part because appeals that are incongruent with categories are more congruent with brands. This has potentially important managerial implications, especially because most advertisements are for brands (rather than categories). It seems that the mere fact that a product has been branded can strikingly alter not only how it is perceived, but also how attitudes towards it can best be changed.

Perspectives on Shopping Involvement

Kathleen O'Donnell, San Francisco State University, USA

SESSION OVERVIEW

With the exception of Bergadaa, Faure, and Perrien (1995), previous research has framed involvement within the context of the consumer's involvement with a particular product or product class (see for example Richins, Bloch and McQuarrie 1992). While the link between product involvement and purchase behavior is clear, we propose in this session to extend Bergadaa, Faure, and Perrien's work by bringing together three different, though interrelated, perspectives on consumer involvement with shopping in general. By focusing on involvement at this level, we hope to provide additional insights into consumers' shopping motivations that will impact retailers' sales promotion, advertising, and pricing strategies.

This session considers shopping involvement within the context of a new typology that addresses the inadequacy of the traditional distinction between situational and dispositional factors in motivation. In the new typology, involvement ranges from situational excitement, through enduring enthusiasm, to obsessive fixation and beyond.

In our first paper, Schindler updates his previous work on consumers' bargain hunting games (situational involvement), and concludes with recommendations for eliciting game play, as well as a tentative framework for how games may motivate consumers.

In our second paper, O'Donnell and Strebel identify a segment of consumers–the sport shopper–whose shopping prowess goes beyond the situational context of bargain hunting games, and over time becomes an integral part of their self identities (enduring involvement). This research provides a profile of sport shoppers' unique motivations, attitudes and involvement with shopping.

Finally, Albanese, Jewell and Murtha describe a typology that distinguishes between four categories of shoppers who vary in their degrees of shopping involvement from situational to enduring to obsessive. Within the framework they provide, game players and sport shoppers would be categorized in the normal to neurotic ranges of shopping behaviors, while those exhibiting more extreme or abnormal shopping involvement would be found in the compulsive or psychotic ranges of behavior.

These papers bring together disparate lines of research to provide a richer and more comprehensive examination of shopping involvement and to extend our understanding of consumer motivation.

EXTENDED ABSTRACTS

"Games Bargain Hunters Play: An Update"
Robert Schindler, Rutgers University, USA

Considerable work on the marketplace effects of price promotions has shown that discounts and other forms of price deals have a marked ability to influence consumer choice (e.g., Blattberg and Neslin 1990; Pauwels, Hanssens, and Siddarth 2002). Past research has also suggested that "smart-shopper feelings" and other experiential variables play an important role in these effects (e.g., Schindler 1998; Chandon, Wansink, and Laurent 2000; Bardhi and Arnould 2005). To further explore how these experiential variables have a motivational impact, a sample of consumers who are highly involved in activities designed to obtain price discounts and a sample of consumers who enjoy shopping on the Internet were interviewed in depth. A total of 37 consumers were interviewed. The resulting transcripts of over 38 hours of interviews were then analyzed by interpretive methods (e.g., Thompson, Locander, and Pollio 1989).

It was apparent that the concept of the game plays a key role in how deal-prone consumers experience their bargain-hunting activities, and that the games involved can be systematically described (as in Berne 1964). There appears to be at least two types of bargain-hunting games. The first is a solitary game, against an impersonal seller. The goal is to obtain a valued item at a price lower than what you would have otherwise paid. The second is a social game, played with or against other consumers. A common goal of this second type of game is to have your bargain-hunting successes recognized by other consumers. A consumer is likely to play a complex mixture of these two types of games.

A common game of the first type could be called, "Wait." In this game, the consumer identifies a particular desired item, and then waits for its price to decrease substantially, hoping that this will occur before the item becomes unavailable. After describing successful play of this game concerning a pair of boots, one informant described the thrill of the experience: "I guess it's like bungee jumping ... scary but exhilarating."

A common game of the second type could be called, "Guess What I Paid For This." In this game, the consumer shows a second player (e.g., a friend or family member) a recent purchase and asks this second player to indicate what one would expect to pay for the item. Since responding with a low price disparages the quality of the purchase, most second players respond with a high price, to which the first player responds with delight. Play of this game can become quite involving since it invites the second player to play again later, with the tables turned.

Numerous other games were identified in these interviews. For example, in "Diamond in the Rough," the player purchases an item that is discounted because of an apparent defect, and then attempts to show the defect to be inconsequential to the benefits provided by the item. In "Radar," the player systematically scans for bargains by repeatedly carrying out a predetermined sequence of shopping activities, thus working to defeat retailers' efforts to make discount offers unpredictable. In "Tag Team," the players clips coupons or finds discount ads for friends or relatives to use, thereby enjoying the bargain vicariously and avoiding the inconveniences of actually obtaining the items. In "Santa Claus," the player purchases numerous items on deal for the purpose of giving them away, expecting to stimulate conversation about the source of this generosity.

The interviews provided some insight on how consumer game-playing behavior is elicited and maintained. At the current point in this research, it seems that there are at least three important aspects of everyday game elicitation:

1. *Actions with intrinsic appeal.* For many people, searching advertisements and/or stores for discounts are easy and pleasant activities.

2. *A goal that seems attainable.* The desired outcome of these price-search activities–to pay less for something for which you would have otherwise paid more–seems, for many people, to be easily within their reach.

3. *Clear feedback as to how well you do.* Because a retail price is so specific and objective, even a small gain or loss becomes not only readily apparent, but also publicly observable.

The descriptions of these shopping games also suggest a tentative framework of how games may act to so effectively motivate consumers. The motivational mechanisms include (1) the ability of game play to set the agenda for one's actions, (2) the ability of a game to recruit energy, both mental and physical, and (3) the ability of a game to affect one's evaluations, both by distracting attention and by bending perceptions.

"Sport Shoppers: An Important New Segment"

Kathleen O'Donnell, San Francisco State University, USA
Judi Strebel, San Francisco State University, USA

Marketers have long realized that the majority of retail shoppers are motivated by more than simply the acquisition of goods and services. In an effort to extend the previous research that has examined the dual role of economic and hedonic motives on retail shopping behaviors (Bellenger and Korgaonkar 1980, Westbrook and Black 1985, Schindler 1998, Arnold and Reynolds 2003, Bardhi and Arnold 2005, Guiry, Magi and Lutz 2006), this study explores a unique retail shopper whom we have christened the "sport shopper". For this segment, shopping is similar to sports participation in that the shoppers compete for great deals, they train to improve their performance, they experience a "high" when they perform well, and they are able to recreate that feeling both by continuing to compete and by sharing the tales of their successes with others.

This exploratory research suggests that sport shoppers are unique from other shoppers in terms of the type and nature of the competitiveness they exhibit in the shopping arena, their desire to tell others about their shopping behaviors, and the trait-like nature of the positive affect they experience from self identifying as sport shoppers. Based on our interpretation of the cognitive responses provided by 94 students at a large western university, who were asked to share their thoughts and feelings about bargain shopping (Lincoln and Guba 1985), we find that sport shoppers take great pleasure and pride in their ability to uncover exceptional bargains by carefully combing the racks of department, specialty and discount stores. Unlike recreational shoppers, sport shoppers do not enjoy all shopping, just shopping for great deals. The thrill of victory they experience with each find reinforces their motivations to shop and to boast about the bargains they've uncovered. For them shopping is an arena in which they can compete, not against other shoppers per se, but against the retail system and their own past performance. Each shopping trip brings with it the opportunity to refine and improve their bargain shopping skills, thereby motivating them to continue participating in their "sport" (Ryckman and Hamel 1995).

In order to increase the likelihood of "winning", sport shoppers develop a set of skills which includes the creation and maintenance of a vast body of knowledge about both the products (e.g. current fashion trends, brand popularity and pricing) and retail stores in the marketplace (e.g. assortment, quality and layout of each location), as well as "pre-game" strategies based on products of interest at the time, budget and time available for shopping.

Unlike their thrift-shopping counterparts, sport shoppers compete to find the best deals on new products in a wide array of retail environments including discount retail stores (e.g. T.J. Maxx, Nordstrom Rack and Marshalls), traditional department and specialty stores (e.g. Macy's, Nordstrom, Anthropologie), and online venues (e.g. eBay and Bluefly). While they may enjoy shopping in the occasional thrift or consignment store, new products are the gold standard for sport shoppers, as they allow for the most objective determination of the savings earned.

Unlike other bargain hunters, sport shoppers compete to save more, rather than to spend less. While no particular skill is necessary to buy a $20 pair of jeans at Target, the sport shopper prides herself on being able to find the coveted $300 designer jeans for $100. Though she's paying more for her jeans on a relative basis, her $200 savings and the prestige of the premium label make her feel competent, talented and happy. Sport shoppers make a game out of shopping, perceiving the great deal as a victory over the system. They obtain greater pleasure from bragging about their bargain-hunting prowess than they would from letting others believe they paid full price for the item.

Sport shoppers are motivated to share the tales of their triumphs with others because doing so allows them to prolong or relive the positive affect they experienced at the time of the purchases, but it also earns them the additional positive feelings resulting from the admiration of the people they tell. Because they are motivated by the amount of money they save, sport shoppers tend to remember with exceptional vividness, the details of the various purchases they make.

Rather than experiencing smart shopper feelings only on those occasions when they feel responsible for getting a deal (Schindler 1998), the intensity, duration and frequency with which sport shoppers experience positive affect over their shopping "careers" creates an ongoing involvement with bargain shopping that becomes more trait-like over time. The ongoing nature of their involvement with sport shopping allows them to stay motivated and to continue identifying as sport shoppers, even when they have not gotten a great deal, or shopped lately. Unlike compulsive shoppers (O'Guinn and Faber 1992), they do not need to make a purchase on each outing, and they are able to rationalize an unsuccessful trip as either an information gathering opportunity or another form of savings.

Based on our preliminary research, we believe that this previously ignored shopper segment is unique, formidable and deeply committed to its sport, and as such it is important for both academicians and retailers to better understand the motivations and behaviors they exhibit. Using the insights gained thus far, the second phase of our research will include field observation, video ethnography and in-depth interviews, with the long-term goal of developing a sport shopper scale.

"A Typology of Four Qualitatively Different Patterns of Shopping Behavior"

Paul J. Albanese, Kent State University, USA
Robert Jewell, Kent State University, USA
Katie Murtha, Corbett Accel Healthcare Group, USA

What has been missing from the rich literature on compulsive buying is a theoretical framework that differentiates between qualitatively different patterns of shopping behavior. Without a substantive theoretical foundation it has been difficult to differentiate true compulsive buying from other problematical patterns of shopping behavior that appear similar from the descriptive or observable aspects of the buying behavior when considered in isolation. This article contributes a theoretical typology of four qualitatively different patterns of shopping behavior based on the Personality Continuum (Albanese 2002, 2006). The Personality Continuum is an integrative framework for the interdisciplinary study of consumer behavior (Albanese 2002, 2006). The Personality Continuum is divided into four qualitatively different levels of personality development that are hierarchically arranged in descending order from highest to lowest level: normal, neurotic, primitive, and psychotic (Albanese 2002). With respect to shopping behavior, the qualitatively different patterns based on the Personality Continuum are the normal consumer, neurotic shopper, compulsive buyer, and psychotic spender. Normal Consumers spend less than they earn, save for future purchases they cannot afford in the present, and prudently plan consumption activities. Neurotic Shoppers spend an excessive amount of time shopping for just the right purchase, exhausting anyone who shops with them, often not buying anything, and when a purchase is made, it is sometimes returned. They typically spend money they have and do not seriously impair family and social relationships. Compulsive Buyers are driven to spend money they do not have on things they do not need in repetitive buying binges, and then hide their purchases away, often in the original packaging with the price tags left on. The shopping behavior impairs family, social and professional relationships, and results in serious financial problems. Psychotic Spenders engage in episodic spectacular spending sprees that result in serious financial and legal problems that severely impair family, social, and professional relationships, and sometimes result in hospitalization or incarceration.

The purpose of imposing the Personality Continuum onto compulsive shopping is to allow critical evaluation of shopping categories uncovered via the various existing compulsive buying scales. Without a theoretical framework as a foundation, there is no way to evaluate the output of the various scales in other than psychometric terms. The results are presented for five instruments designed to measure compulsive shopping behavior: 1. Compulsive Buying: Original Measurement Scale developed by Valence, d'Astous, and Fortier (1988) consists of thirteen items rated on a five-point Likert scale; 2. Clinical Screener for Compulsive Buying developed by Faber and O'Guinn (1992) consists of seven items rated on a five-point Likert scale; 3. Edwards (1992, 1993) Compulsive Buying Scale consists of 13 items rated on a five-point Likert scale; 4. Questionnaire about Buying Behavior developed by Lejoyeux and Ades (1994) consists of 19 dichotomous items; 5. The Yale-Brown Obsessive-Compulsive Scale—Shopping Version developed by Monahan, Black, and Gabel (1996) consists of ten items rated from 0 to 4. The five measurement instruments were administered to a convenience sample of 128 college students (68% female; 95% between the ages of 19-23) at a large Midwestern university using an online survey to explore to what extent the four qualitatively different patterns of shopping behavior would emerge in the two-stage cluster analysis. The results demonstrated that only the Questionnaire about Buying Behavior (Lejoyeux et al. 1994, 1996) yielded three different groups that represent the normal consumer (41 subjects or 33.6%), neurotic shopper (45 subjects or 36.9%), and compulsive buyer (36 subjects or 29.5%). No psychotic subjects completed the survey; therefore, we were unable to assess whether this instrument would capture the psychotic spenders. The four remaining instruments divided the subjects into two broad groups—non-compulsive and compulsive shoppers, respectively: Valence, d'Astous, and Fortier (1988) 50% and 50%; Faber and O'Guinn (1992) 44.9% and 55.1%; Edwards (1992, 1993) 30.2% and 69.8%; and Monahan, Black, and Gabel (1996) 58.7% and 41.3%.

The failure to differentiate between qualitatively different patterns of shopping behavior is problematical because the shopping behavior of neurotic shoppers and psychotic spenders are lumped together with true compulsive buyers. This makes understanding etiology and motivation for compulsive buying behavior difficult. While the prevalence of psychotic shoppers may be relatively small quantitatively, it is important to understand this level of personality development to delimit the lower boundary of true compulsive buying behavior. The challenge now is the refinement of the measurement of the four qualitatively different patterns of shopping behavior by combining items from the existing instruments, modifying existing items, and adding new items to reflect the full typology of shopping behavior.

REFERENCES

Albanese, Paul J. (2002), *The Personality Continuum and Consumer Behavior*, Westport, CT: Quorum Books.

Albanese, Paul J. (2006), "Inside Economic Man: Behavioral Economics and Consumer Behavior," in *Handbook of Contemporary Behavioral Economics: Foundations and Developments*, Morris Altman, ed., (New York: M. E. Sharpe Publishers, 2006): 3-23.

Arnold, Mark J., and Kristy E. Reynolds (2003), "Hedonic Shopping Motivations," *Journal of Retailing*, 79(2), 77-95.

Bardhi, Fleura and Eric J. Arnould (2005), "Thrift Shopping: Combining Utilitarian Thrift and Hedonic Treat Benefits," *Journal of Consumer Behaviour*, 4(4), 223-233.

Bergadaa, Michelle, Corrine Faure and Jean Perrien (1995), "Enduring Involvement With Shopping," *The Journal of Social Psychology*, 135(1), 17-25.

Belllenger, Danny N. and Pradeep K. Korgaonkar (1980), "Profiling the Retail Shopper," *Journal of Retailing*, 56(3), 77-92.

Berne, Eric (1964), *Games People Play: The Psychology of Human Relationships*. New York: Grove Press.

Blattberg, Robert C. and Scott A. Neslin (1990), *Sales Promotion: Concepts, Methods, and Strategies*, Englewood Cliffs, NJ: Prentice Hall.

Chandon, Pierre, Brian Wansink, and Gilles Laurent (2000), "A Benefit Congruency Framework of Sales Promotion Effectiveness," *Journal of Marketing*, 64 (October), 65-81.

Dawson, Scott, Peter H. Bloch and Nancy M. Ridgeway (1990), "Shopping Motives, Emotional States, and Retail Outcomes," *Journal of Retailing*, 66(4). 408-427.

Edwards, Elizabeth A. (1993). "Development of a New Scale for Measuring Compulsive Buying Behavior." *Financial Counseling and Planning*, 4, 67-85.

Faber, Ronald J., and Thomas C. O'Guinn (1992). "A Clinical Screener for Compulsive Buying." *Journal of Consumer Research*, 19, 459-469.

Guiry, Michael, Anne W. Magi and Richard J. Lutz (2006), "Defining and Measuring Recreational Shopper Identity," *Journal of the Academy of Marketing Science*, 34(1), 74-83.

Lejoyeux, Michel and Jean Ades (1994). "Les Achats Pathologiques: Une Addiction Comportementale." *Neuro-Psy*, 9, 1(January-February), pp. 25-32.

Lejoyeux, Michel, Jean Ades, Valerie Tassain, and Jacquelyn Solomon (1996). "Phenomenology and Psychopathology of Uncontrolled Buying." *American Journal of Psychiatry*, vol. 153, 12, pp. 1524-1539.

Lincoln, Yvonne and Egon G. Guba (1985), *Naturalistic Inquiry*, Newbury Park: Sage.

Monahan, Patrick, Donald W. Black, and Janelle Gabel (1996). "Reliability and Validity of a Scale to Measure Change in Persons with Compulsive Buying." *Psychiatry Research*, 64, 59-67.

Pauwels, Koen, Dominique M. Hanssens, and S. Siddarth (2002), "The Long-term Effect of Price Promotions on Category Incidence, Brand Choice, and Purchase Quantity" *Journal of Marketing Research*, 39, 421–439.

Richins, Marsha L., Peter H. Bloch and Edward F. McQuarrie (1992), "How Enduring and Situational Involvement Combine to Create Involvement Responses," *Journal of Consumer Psychology*, 1(2), 143-153.

Ryckman, Richard M. and Jane Hamel (1992), "Female Adolescents' Motives Related to Involvement with Organized Team Sports," *International Journal of Sport Psychology*, 23: 147-160.

Schindler, Robert M. (1998), "Consequences of Perceiving Oneself as Responsible for Obtaining a Discount: Evidence for Smart-Shopper Feelings," *Journal of Consumer Psychology,* 7 (4), 371.

Thompson, Craig J., William B. Locander, and Howard R. Pollio (1989), "Putting Consumer Experience Back into Consumer Research: The Philosophy and Method of Existential-Phenomenology," *Journal of Consumer Research*, 16 (September), 133-146.

Valence, Gilles, Alain d'Astous, and Louis Fortier (1988). "Compulsive Buying: Concept and Measurement," *Journal of Consumer Policy,* 11, pp. 419-433.

Westbrook, Robert A., and William C. Black (1985), "A Motivation-Based Shopper Typology," *Journal of Retailing*, 61(1), 78-96.

To Deal or Not to Deal: Exploring the Boundaries of Dynamic Inconsistency
Xianchi Dai, University of Chicago, USA, and INSEAD, France

SESSION OVERVIEW

One of the most robust findings over decades of research in intertemporal choice is that people are dynamically inconsistent; they are more patient for future trade-offs than for near trade-offs (e.g. Ainslie 1975; Strotz 1955; Thaler 1981). Previous research has provided different theoretical explanations (e.g., Hoch and Loewenstein 1991; Liberman, Trope and Stephen 2007; Loewenstein 1996; Zauberman and Lynch 2005), examined its boundary conditions, e.g., in the domain of consumer behavior (e.g., Malkoc and Zauberman 2006; Malkoc, Zauberman and Ulu 2005; Soman 1998) and investigated consumers' coping strategies (e.g., Ariely and Wertenbroch 2002; Wertenbroch 1998).

Despite the extensive research done in this field over the years, this session demonstrates that it remains a fertile area for continued research. The session presents three papers, each focusing on different aspects of the dynamic inconsistency problem. In particular, they demonstrate that (1) dynamic inconsistency might not be as serious a problem as pervious research has suggested. It might be even reversed when consumers are moving from distant to near choices. (2) Sophisticated consumers are willing to adopt commitment strategy even with the prospect of real financial losses, which is proved to be very effective in solving dynamic inconsistency problem. (3) Concern for dynamic inconsistency might lead consumers to be overly prudent, which systematically drives consumer preferences and decisions.

Dai and Fishbach demonstrate in four studies that the actual movement towards the options can increase consumers' patience, which is contrary to the prediction based on models of dynamic consistency. They show this pattern of results in hypothetical as well as real waiting and monetary consequences, with cash and consumer products. They also show that this is because consumers infer from their wait experience that they value the category more, which in turn leads to greater preference for larger later reward.

Giné, Karlan & Zinman examine consumers' precommitment strategy in a field experiment in a Philippine bank. Substantial proportion of smokers sign up to a savings account (CARES) designed to help them quit smoking. They deposit money into the account and agree to let the bank forfeit their entire balance to charity if they fail a urine test six months later. Compared with those in the control condition, those who signed up to the CARES program were about 30% more likely to pass the test. The result suggests that sophisticated consumers are willing to pay premium for such commitment products, and that these commitment products are effective in helping achieve self control.

In the third paper, Kivetz and Keinan argue that consumers often suffer from a reverse form of dynamic inconsistency problem, namely excessive farsightedness ("hyperopia") and future-biased preferences. It shows that consumers (a) require special entitlement justifications to indulge (e.g., through hard work or perceived excellence); (b) perceive themselves as suffering from insufficient indulgence, and consequently, correct this imbalance in their lives by pre-committing to future hedonic experiences; and (c) regret (in the long-run) their supposedly farsighted acts of choosing virtue over vice.

Overall, the three papers were chosen for this session because (1) they center on the same dynamic inconsistency problem, and examine new boundary conditions, which greatly enrich our understanding of intertemporal choice and self control. (2) In terms of methodology, the session represents both behavioral and economic approaches. Different approaches complement each other and can potentially inspire new insights for future research. Together, the three papers form a cohesive set of explorations into some fundamental issues of intertemporal choice.

EXTENDED ABSTRACTS

"History Matters: When Waiting Increases Patience in Intertemorporal Choice"
Xianchi Dai, University of Chicago, USA, and INSEAD, France
Ayelet Fishbach, University of Chicago, USA

An underlying assumption in the literature of intertemporal choice is that people are better able to commit to larger-later reward over a smaller-sooner reward a long time in advance compared with a short time in advance (Ainslie and Haslam 1992; Frederick, Loewenstein, and O'Donoghue 2002). It follows that people become more impatient as they get closer to making a self-control choice between a smaller-sooner reward and a larger-later reward. For example, research on the common difference effect (Frederick et al. 2002) attests that a person prefers a smaller-sooner reward (e.g., one apple today over two apples tomorrow) when the options are presented in the near future, but prefers the large-later reward when the options are presented in the distant future (e.g., two apples in 101 days over one apple in 100 days). However, whereas previous research compared distant and near futures, it is less clear how the actual movement from distant to near choices influences preference. For example, would waiting for 100 days before making a choice make one more or less likely to prefer two apples tomorrow over one apple today?

We predict that the wait experience as a person moves closer to making a choice increases patience such that people are more likely to choose the larger-later reward than before, or compared with people who face a near future choice. We propose that this happens because people learn about their preference by observing their own behavior and the wait experience signals to a person that the category of items (e.g., apple) is desirable. This heightened value inferred from wait further leads to increase in preference for larger-later reward (per magnitude effect, Frederick et al. 2002).

We tested this proposition in four studies. The first three studies compared intertemporal choice in 1) near future condition (e.g., a small reward today vs. a large reward in 20 days) 2) distant future condition (e.g., a small reward in 30 days vs. a large reward in 50 days), and 3) near future + wait condition (e.g., the above near future choice + the person has waited 30 days before making the choice). Study 1 examined the effect of waiting use monetary reward. We found that in the wait condition, the choice share of the large-later options was higher than in the distant future condition, which was higher than in the near future condition. Study 2 replicated the same effect with products (MP3 player). Furthermore, it also showed that this increased patience is associated with increase in liking for MP3 player in the wait condition than in the other two conditions. The same finding was demonstrated in study 3 with real waiting experience and real monetary reward ($50 vs. $55 lottery):

the choice share of the large-later option was the highest in the wait condition, then the distant future condition, and lowest in the near future condition. We further found that increased patience in the wait conditions was associated with an increase in the perceive importance of money.

In the final study, we tested whether perceived wait, similar to actual wait, increases patience. In addition, this study examined whether wait experience signals that the product is valuable (value inference), rather than that wait is less costly to the individual (cost inference). We manipulated waiting by asking half of the participants their waiting experience since the last time they had Godiva chocolate (for the other half we didn't ask this question, which served as control group). Similar to study 1-3, we found that for choice between smaller sooner reward (i.e., 12 pieces of Godiva chocolate in 6 days) and larger later reward (16 pieces of Godiva chocolate in 48 days), salience of wait increased patience and thus preference for the larger-later option. Whereas for choices between getting the same reward for free later (e.g., 16 pieces of Godiva chocolate in 48 days) or sooner (paying $3 premium to get the same option in 6 days), wait increased preference for expediting, which suggests a decreased patience. This later result is noteworthy because value inference would predict preference for expediting (due to increased value) whereas cost inference would predict preference for postpone (due to lower cost estimation of waiting). These results suggest further that consumers infer from wait that they value a category more, rather than that they are the type who can wait (or that waiting is not that painful).

"Put Your Money Where Your Butt is: A Commitment Savings Account for Smoking Cessation"

Xavier Gine, The World Bank, USA
Dean Karlan, Yale University, USA
Jonathan Zinman, Innovation for Poverty Action and Stickk.com, USA

The use of cash incentives, generally referred to as conditional cash transfer programs, to alter behavior in health and anti-poverty programs is becoming more common, as evidenced by the spread of PROGRESA-type anti-poverty campaigns. One less-utilized method for applying cash incentives to behavior modification is the commitment contract. A commitment contract is essentially a contract on one's own behavior, made with one's own money—if a behavior benchmark is met, the individual gets his money back; if it is not met, the individual forfeits his money.

Green Bank of Caraga in the Philippines, together with Innovations for Poverty Action and the World Bank, recently tested a commitment contract to help Filipino smokers quit. Under the contract, participants deposited money into a bank savings account and agreed to forfeit their balance if six months later they failed a urine test to detect nicotine (failure to take the test was equated with failure to quit). Bank marketers offered the product by approaching smokers in public places. The marketers administered a short survey, provided a standard pamphlet with information on smoking's harmful effects and how to quit, and then made one of three randomly assigned offers: 1) the commitment contract; 2) aversive "cues": graphic, pocket-sized pictures of the negative health effects of smoking modeled on Canada's cigarette packaging mandate; 3) nothing.

Six months after marketing the bank team returned and administered urine tests to participants from all three groups. Subjects offered the commitment contract, regardless of whether they accepted or not, were 3.1 percentage points more likely to pass the test than the control group (a 38.8 percent increase). Those offered the contract who had previously reported a desire to quit smoking at some point in their lives were 4.3 percentage points more likely to pass. The impact was even more substantial among those who signed a commitment contract. Signers overall were 29 percentage points more likely to pass the test than the control group; signers who'd stated their intention to quit at some point were 33 percentage points more likely to pass. Acceptance rates for the contract were almost double the acceptance rates reported from previous randomized controlled trials for smoking cessation aids such as the nicotine patch or gum. Success rates of those who accepted the commitment contract in this study were double reported rates of success achieved with the help of the patch or gum. (The impact of the cards was about the same as the reported impact of patches or gums.)

This product is motivated specifically from models of time inconsistency. Clearly someone with no inconsistency, no "dual-self" model of behavior, would opt in to such a contract. Hence, the mere preference for the contract is itself evidence supporting such models, and the success of the contract in changing behavior further reinforces the theoretical motivation behind the contracts.

The study also found that acceptance of the commitment contract was heavily dependent on the ease with which participants could make subsequent deposits. Some participants offered contracts were also offered a deposit collection service by the bank; all others would have been required to go to a bank branch to make deposits. Uptake of the contract without deposit collection was so low that the offer was dropped, and everyone subsequently offered the contract was also offered deposit collection. Success in quitting, unsurprisingly, was also strongly correlated with the number of deposits made.

There is still much to learn. Would a commitment contract that offers a better return be more popular, and possibly more effective, than the one designed for this study? Do those who quit using a commitment contract take up smoking again after the contract ends? Did the bank staff who came to collect weekly deposits provide a de facto reminder that was a major element in quitting success? Despite these outstanding questions, the results suggest that non-profits and policy-makers should experiment with commitment contracts in addition to conditional cash transfers in their health and anti-poverty programs.

"Hyperopia: A Theory of Reverse Self Control"

Ran Kivetz, Columbia University, USA
Anat Keinan, Harvard University, USA

Our religions, mythologies, and fables admonish us to overcome temptation, exercise self-discipline, and heed the future (see Adam and Eve, Odysseus, and the Ant and the Grasshopper). Social scientists, too, offer helpful strategies for increasing willpower and avoiding indulgence (e.g., Ainslie 1975; Trope and Fishbach 2000). The seemingly universal espousal of prudence and farsightedness as noble goals is reflected in the voluminous literature in the social sciences on self-control. This body of research is premised on the notion that people are short-sighted (myopic) and easily tempted by hedonic "sins," such as overbuying (oniomania), splurging on tasty but unhealthy food, and indulging in luxuries (e.g., Prelec & Herrnstein 1992; Thaler 1980).

The current paper advances an alternative approach. Specifically, the universality of myopia is challenged and it is proposed that people often suffer from a reverse self-control problem, namely excessive farsightedness ("hyperopia") and over-control. Such hyperopia leads people to deprive themselves of indulgence and instead overly focus on acting responsibly, delaying gratification, and doing "the right thing." The present research examines the processes underlying hyperopia (e.g., guilt, justification), the way people cope with hyperopia (e.g., by pre-committing to indulgence), and the consequences of over-control (e.g., long-term regret).

The paper begins by reviewing and integrating the empirical evidence regarding the antecedents and consequences of hyperopia, including the findings that people (a) require special entitlement justifications to indulge, relying on such justification cues as hard work or perceived excellence (Kivetz and Simonson 2002a; Kivetz and Zheng 2006); (b) perceive themselves as suffering from insufficient indulgence, and consequently, correct this imbalance in their lives by pre-committing to future hedonic experiences (Kivetz and Simonson, 2002b); and (c) regret (in the long-run) their supposedly farsighted acts of choosing virtue over vice (Kivetz and Keinan 2006; Keinan and Kivetz 2008).

The paper also reports new direct evidence for hyperopia and supports the notion that hyperopia involves time-inconsistency and preference reversals due to variations in the intensity of guilt. Specifically, a series of studies demonstrates that people select pleasurable consumption and vices when the consequences of their decisions are psychologically distal (e.g., temporally delayed, hypothetical, improbable, abstract, or self-irrelevant) but reverse their decision when the consequences are psychologically proximal (e.g., temporally imminent, real, vivid, or self-relevant). Such reversals are more pronounced among people with a chronic tendency to experience guilt. Finally, the presented paper attempts to generalize the self-control construct by reconciling myopia and hyperopia using a distinction between self-control lapses and self-control dilemmas.

REFERENCES

Ainslie, George (1975), "Specious Reward: A Behavioral Theory of Impulsiveness and Impulse Control," *Psychological Bulletin*, 82:4, pp. 463–96.

Ainslie, George and Nick Haslam(1992), "Hyperbolic Discounting," In G. Loewenstein & J. Elster (Eds.), *Choice Over Time*, (pp. 57-92), New York, NY, US: Russell Sage Foundation.

Ariely, Dan and Klaus Wertenbroch (2002), "Procrastination, Deadlines, and Performance: Self-Control by Pre-Commitment," *Psychological Science*, 13(3): 219-224.

Frederick, Shane, George F. Loewenstein, and Ted O'Donoghue (2002), "Time Discounting and Time Preference: A Critical Review," *Journal of Economic Literature*, 40, 351-74.

Hoch, Stephen J. and George F. Loewenstein (1991), "Time-inconsistent Preferences and Consumer Self-control," *Journal of Consumer Research*, 17, 492-507.

Liberman, N., Yaacov Trope, and E. Stephan (2007), "Psychological Distance," In A. W. Kruglanski & E. T. Higgins (Eds.), "*Social Psychology: Handbook of Basic Principles*" (2nd ed.). (pp. 353-381), New York, NY, US: Guilford Press.

Keinan, Anat, and Ran Kivetz (forthcoming), "Remedying Hyperopia: The Effects of Self-Control Regret on Consumer Behavior," *Journal of Marketing Research*.

Kivetz, Ran, and Yuhuang Zheng (2006), "Determinants of Justification and Self-Control," *Journal of Experimental Psychology: General*, 135 (November), 572-587.

Kivetz, Ran and Anat Keinan (2006), "Repenting Hyperopia: An Analysis of Self-Control Regrets," *Journal of Consumer Research*, 33 (September), 273–282.

Kivetz, Ran and Itamar Simonson (2002a), "Earning the Right to Indulge: Effort as a Determinant of Customer Preferences Toward Frequency Program Rewards," *Journal of Marketing Research*, 39 (May), 155-170.

Kivetz, Ran and Itamar Simonson (2002b), "Self Control for the Righteous: Toward A Theory of Pre-Commitment to Indulgence," *Journal of Consumer Research*, 29 (September), 199-217.

Malkoc, Selin A. and Gal Zauberman (2006), „Deferring Versus Expediting Consumption: The Effect of Outcome Concreteness on Sensitivity to Time Horizon," *Journal of Marketing Research*, 43(4), 618-627.

Malkoc, Selin A., Gal Zauberman, and C. Ulu (2005), „Consuming Now or Later? The Interactive Effect of Timing and Attribute Alignability," *Psychological Science*, 16(5), 411-417.

O'Donoghue, T. and M. Rabin (1999), "Doing It Now or Later," *American Economic Review* 89(1): 103-24.

Prelec, Drazen and Richard J. Herrnstein (1992), "A Theory of Addiction", in *Choice Over Time*, ed. George Loewenstein and Jon Elster, New York: Sage.

Soman, D. (1998), "The Illusion of Delayed Incentives: Evaluating Future Effort—Money Transactions," *Journal of Marketing Research*, 35(4), 427-437.

Strotz, R. H. (1955), "Myopia and Inconsistency in Dynamic Utility Maximization," *Review of Economic Studies*, 23(3): 165-80.

Thaler, Richard (1980), "Toward a Positive Theory of Consumer Choice," *Journal of Economic Behavior and Organization*, 1 (March), 39-60.

Thaler, Richard H. (1981), "Some Empirical Evidence on Dynamic Inconsistency," *Economics Letters* 8, 201–07.

Thaler, R. and S. Benartzi (2004), "Save More Tomorrow: Using Behavioral Economics to Increase Employee Saving," *Journal of Political Economy*, 112(1, Part 2 Supplement): S164-87.

Trope, Yaacov and Ayelet Fishbach (2000), "Counteractive Self-Control in Overcoming Temptation," *Journal of Personality & Social Psychology*, 79, 493-506.

Wertenbroch, K. (1998), "Consumption Self-Control by Rationing Purchase Quantities of Virtue and Vice," *Marketing Science*, 17(4), 317-337.

SYMPOSIUM SUMMARY

Attentional and Inferential Effects of Point-of-Purchase Marketing

Ana Valenzuela, Baruch College, USA
Pierre Chandon, INSEAD, France

SESSION OVERVIEW

Recent trends in marketing have demonstrated an increased focus on in-store marketing with the hope that it will generate incremental sales at the point of purchase. Despite the importance of this topic, there are still two important unresolved issues: 1) does P-O-P marketing actually work? and, if yes, 2) how exactly does it work?

Although we know that end-of-aisle displays have large effects on consumers, the evidence about the effects of less conspicuous P-O-P activities changes that keep total category shelf space constant is less conclusive. For example, while industry reports claim that the number and position of shelf facings matters, Drèze, Hoch, and Purk (1994, p. 324) concluded that "the benefits from additional facings are non existent" and that shelf position only has a limited influence on sales. There is also no consensus on what is the best location on a shelf, with prior findings supporting an extreme position advantage (Nisbett and Wilson 1977) or a middle position advantage (Christensen 1995; Shaw 2000). Even if P-O-P marketing works, we don't know how large its effects are compared to the well-known memory-based effects created by advertising and branding.

P-O-P marketing can influence consumers through an attentional and an inferential route. First, P-O-P marketing ensures that the brand is noticed, a necessary condition for purchase. Even then, it is important to determine how much of a brand's salience is due to bottom-up perceptual features (e.g., packaging color, number and position of shelf facings) and how much is due to top-down memory-based effects (e.g., consumer search goals, past brand usage). Second, the position of a brand on the shelf could affect the inferences consumers make about the product itself. This would be likely if, for example, consumers believe that retailers position brands on the shelf according to general, meaningful criteria but it could also occur outside consumers' awareness.

Despite the importance of understanding in-store marketing effectiveness and the growing theoretical interest about position effects in consumer psychology (e.g., studies showing the association between vertical position and concepts such as power and God), relatively little research work examines the effect of in-store product position and marketing support on an option's visual search, consideration and choice. The three papers in this special session are a step forward in the empirical investigation of how in-store marketing affects visual attention and inferences about products. All the three papers are interdisciplinary in the sense that the underlying theoretical questions involve both the economic and psychological aspects of consumer decision making, combine experimental interventions and verbal reports with state-of-the-art eye-tracking data and statistical models, and examine a variety of behaviors (attention, visual search, consideration, choice, and inferences about brand attributes) for existing and fictitious brands.

In the first paper, Chandon, Hutchinson and Bradlow examine the effects of important in-store factors (the number and position of shelf facings) and out-of-store factors (past brand usage, the regular and actual price of the brand, its market share, and the shopping goal of the consumer), on attention, recall of attention, consideration, and choice. They find strong effects of the number and position of facings on attention but that not all attention improvements lead to

choice. They also find that recall of attention is not a good proxy for visual attention.

In the second paper, van der Lans, Pieters and Wedel go deeper into measuring the bottom-up and top-down components of brand salience. Drawing on a framework of competitive salience and a model of the visual search process, they estimate the effects of perceptual features (color, luminance, edges) and how these are influenced by consumers' search goals using eye-movement data. They identify two key sources of brand salience: *i)* the bottom-up component is influenced by in-store activity and package design; *ii)* the top-down component is influenced by out-of-store marketing activities such as advertising.

In the third paper, Valenzuela and Raghubir propose that, people hold underlying schemas associated with the position in which options are presented that lead to inferences about the desirability of the options and formation of preferences. They find that consumers believe (inaccurately, as we show) that retailers place brands in decreasing order of price from top to bottom rows and from right to left rows, thus, showing preference for options holding center positions in both orientations as they represent a balanced price/quality tradeoff. Preferences for the middle product are moderated by shopping goals, especially for the vertical orientation, and can be temporarily attenuated through priming, but are robust in the longer term.

Xavier Drèze, the author of the seminal and award-winning paper on the effects of P-O-P marketing, and an authority on retailing, led the discussion.

EXTENDED ABSTRACTS

"Does In-Store Marketing Work? Effects of the Number and Position of Shelf Facings on Attention, Consideration, and Choice at the Point of Purchase"

Pierre Chandon, INSEAD, France
Wesley Hutchinson, University of Pennsylvania, USA
Eric Bradlow, University of Pennsylvania, USA

Marketers are diverting a growing proportion of their promotional budgets from traditional out-of-store media advertising to in-store marketing and retailers are responding by adopting increasingly sophisticated shelf layout and management tools. We already have strong evidence that end-of-aisle displays and large increases in shelf space have strong effects on brand sales (Bemmaor and Mouchoux 1991; Curhan 1974; Inman, McAlister, and Hoyer 1990; Wilkinson, Mason, and Paksoy 1982; Woodside and Waddle 1975). The evidence about the effects of less conspicuous in-store marketing changes that keep total category shelf space constant is less conclusive. While industry reports claim that the number and position of shelf facings matters, Drèze, Hoch, and Purk (1994, p. 324) concluded that "the benefits from additional facings are non existent" and that shelf position only has a limited influence on sales. A related stream of research has shown that the position of a brand in a vertical or horizontal retail display influences price and quality expectations and hence brand choice (Christenfeld 1995; Valenzuela and Raghubir 2008). However, these results have only been demonstrated for non-familiar brands or for choices among identical options. More importantly, prior research has not examined the effects of in-store marketing on visual attention and brand consideration and has not compared its effects with those of out-of-store factors such as past brand usage, shopping goals, or the market share and price of the brand.

The objective of this research was to examine the interplay between in-store and out-of-store factors on consumer attention, consideration, and choice among brands displayed on supermarket shelves. Drawing on research on shelf management effects and on eye movements in scene perception, we developed a framework of the effects of important in-store factors—the number and position of shelf facings—and out-of-store factors—past brand usage, the regular and actual price of the brand, its market share, and the shopping goal of the consumer—on attention and purchase-related behaviors. We tested the predictions derived from this framework in an eye-tracking experiment in which we manipulated or measured all these factors for established as well as for new brands of two categories. The experimental design was a between-subjects fractional design with two within-subject replications (soap bars and pain reliever tablets). We manipulated the number of a facings of each brand (4, 8, or 12), its vertical position (first, second, third, or bottom shelf), its horizontal position (far left, center left, center right, or far right of shelf), and its shelf price (regular vs. discounted). The participants were 348 adult shoppers recruited in shopping centers. They were either asked say which of the 16 brands of soap or of pain relievers they would buy (choice goal condition) or which brands they would consider buying (consideration goal condition). We tracked the movement of their eyes while they were making these decisions and measured their recall of attention and brands past usage.

We find that in-store attention is limited. One quarter of the 16 brands were never looked at and another quarter was only fixated once. Recall of visual attention was a poor indicator of actual attention, as participants forgot 58% of the brands that they had fixated at least once. Only one quarter of the brands was included in the consideration set. We also found that eye fixations increased consideration and choice for the two new brands inserted in the shelf layout. Because participants had never seen these brands before the study, this analysis showed that in-store eye fixations can cause consideration and choice, and are not just driven by memory-based out-of-store factors.

Regression analyses showed that both in store and out-of-store factors influence attention, consideration, and choice, although in-store factors primarily influence attention whereas out-of-store factors primarily influence consideration and choice. Specifically, we found that the number of facings had a strong but marginally diminishing impact on attention, that it had a positive and linear effect on purchase decisions, and that the influence on choice was particularly strong for regular users, for low market-share brands, and for consumers with a choice rather than with a consideration goal. We also found: a) that placing the brand near the center of a shelf (vs. on its extreme ends) and on the top shelves (vs. the bottom shelves) improved attention and purchase decisions, b) that being on the left or right-hand side of the shelf made no difference, and c) that a being on the middle shelves (vs. the top or bottom shelves) helped attention but neither consideration nor choice.

These findings provide insights into four of the five issues identified as important areas for future eye-tracking research in Wedel and Pieters's (2008) review: 1) studying the interplay between bottom-up salience and top-down informativeness in guiding attention, 2) examining eye movements to other marketing stimuli besides print ads, 3) testing different attention metrics, and 4) investigating the relationship between attention and downstream marketing effects such as purchases. Finally, these findings have methodological implications. Specifically, our findings that not all

attention improvements lead to choice and that recall is not a good proxy for visual attention, underscore the importance of combining eye-tracking and purchase decision data to obtain a full picture of the effects of in-store and out-of-store marketing at the point of purchase.

"Competitive Brand Salience"

Ralf van der Lans, Erasmus University, The Netherlands
Rik Pieters, Tilburg University, The Netherlands
Michel Wedel, University of Maryland, USA

Competitive clutter at the point-of-purchase is intense due to SKU proliferation, brand extensions, me-too products, private labels and copycats. As a consequence, searching brands on supermarket shelves is a daily challenge for consumers. Clutter causes consumers to accidentally pick-up the wrong brands or not to find their favorite brand at all. Therefore, manufacturers and retailers try to make the SKUs of their brands visually salient among competitors through improved package design and advertising. They seek an optimal level of differentiation of their brands and SKUs by balancing the visual salience of each SKU relative to competitors with a unique identity of the entire line of SKUs, at the same time needing to obey established codes about the visual appearance of the category. To support this management task, the visual salience of SKUs and brands needs to be assessed but how to accomplish this is far from obvious: there is no academic literature addressing this problem, but related literatures exist on variety perceptions of assortments and on the overlap within product portfolios.

We intend to fill this gap and afford a detailed analysis of visual competition between brands based on the few seconds that consumers search for them on the shelf. Using eye-movement data collected in a brand search experiment, we develop a model that allows us to assess competitive salience, establish its effects on search performance, and show improvement through marketing.

We assess brand salience using a model of eye-movement recordings, collected during a brand search experiment. During a computer-mediated brand search task for laundry detergents eye-movements were collected for a random sample of 109 regular consumers in the Netherlands (47 males and 62 females between 16 and 55 years of age). Participants were individually seated behind 21-inch LCD computer screens (1,024 x 1,280) on which a shelf with six brands of laundry detergent was shown, four brands with three SKUs each and two brands with two SKUs each (16 SKUs in total). Multiple replications (facings) of SKUs were present to mimic regular shelves at the point-of-purchase. Participants were randomly assigned to one of five conditions of a one-factorial between-subjects design, in which they searched for one out of five different brands. In all cases, the search goal was directed at a specific SKU of a brand (the "tablet" SKU). The sixth brand is the market leader and serves as a baseline. Placement of the brands in the display was rotated across conditions and consumers to eliminate possible location effects, with the same number of facings in all conditions. Participants had a maximum of 10 seconds to find the target brand, and indicated having found the target brand by touching it on the touch-sensitive LCD screen, after which the brand search task ended. Eye-movements, and latency and accuracy of search were recorded.

We propose a conceptual framework of competitive salience and a model of the visual search process, which enable diagnostic analysis of current levels of visual differentiation of brands and SKUs at the point-of-purchase. We develop a brand search model that (a) includes the effects of image features, (b) includes the effects of systematic search strategies on eye-movements, (c) assumes two unobserved states reflecting the localization of brands, respectively their identification through re-fixations. We separate top-down from bottom-up salience through a combination of experimental design and model formulation. We integrate the effects on search accuracy and latency in the model. Together, this makes it possible to comprehensively assess competitive salience and its effects on search performance.

We thus estimate brands' salience at the point-of-purchase, based on perceptual features (color, luminance, edges) and how these are influenced by consumers' search goals from the eye-movement data. We show that the salience of brands has a pervasive effect on search performance. We identify two key sources of brand salience. The bottom-up component is influenced by in-store activity and package design. The top-down component is influenced by out-of-store marketing activities such as advertising.

Our study reveals that about one-third of salience on the shelf is due to out-of-store and two-thirds due to in-store marketing. This underlines that the integration of advertising with packaging strategies should be a key concern. The relatively small top-down influences on salience that we found for some brands in our study may well be attributable to a lack of integration of packaging and advertising strategies for some brands. Although salience of brands has a pervasive effect on search performance, it appears that consumers use only one or two basic features at the same time when trying to find a brand rapidly and accurately. This has important implications for package design and for advertising that has the purpose to increase brand salience on the shelf. Such advertising would need to establish strong associations in memory with a limited number of unique features.

"Center Of Orientation: Effect of Vertical and Horizontal Shelf Space Product Position"

Ana Valenzuela, Baruch College, USA

Priya Raghubir, University of California, Berkeley, USA

Does placing a product in a central, peripheral, or extreme-end position, or a top or bottom position systematically affect consumers' attitudes toward the brand? Surprisingly, this issue has received scant attention from consumer psychologists despite the importance of shelf placement in consumers' brand choice decisions, a manufacturer's distribution decisions, and a retailer's shelf space pricing decisions. Prior research on product placement showed that the spatial positioning of products affects consumers' inferences about prices (e.g., Inman, McAlister and Hoyer 1990), their allocation of attention across brands (e.g., Chandon, Hutchington, Bradlow and Young 2007), the number and type of product choice comparisons (e.g., Breugelmans, Campo, and Gijsbrechts 2007), the level of exposure and physical interaction with a good (e.g., Folwell and Moberg 1993), as well as brand sales (e.g., Desmet and Renaudin 1998).

This paper investigates whether, how, and when consumers extract meaning from the position of products in both horizontal and vertical shelf space arrays, and how these inferences translate into their preferences. We test three basic hypotheses: consumers believe products are placed in decreasing order of price from top to bottom rows (H1: verticality) and from right to left rows (H2: horizontality), leading to preferences for center positions in both orientations as they represent a balanced price/quality tradeoff (H3: centrality). Study 1 finds evidence that consumers have shared shelf layout schemas regarding retail practice for verticality and centrality, but not for horizontality: premium brand are on top rows, cheaper brands are on the bottom rows, promoted brands are on the extremes and popular brands occupy central positions. Study 2 shows that verticality and horizontality beliefs do not universally reflect retailers' pricing practice. Study 3 shows that these schemas affect product inferences: consumers infer that products placed on the top (and on the right) have higher prices and higher quality than those placed on the bottom (or on the left). Accordingly, they prefer positions in the center of both orientations as these represent price-quality compromises.

The next two studies examine moderating conditions for the use of vertical and horizontal shelf space schemas. They test the schema interference hypothesis, which argues that the use of these schemas will be attenuated when accessible information interferes with the schema that is held (H4). They also test the schema diagnosticity hypothesis, which argues that spatial position is used as a function of its informativeness (H5). Each of these hypotheses is examined for both the vertical and horizontal orientation. Results show asymmetric effects for the horizontal and vertical schema: schema interference eliminates verticality effects and attenuates horizontality effects (Study 4), while schema diagnosticity only has an effect on verticality-based inferences (Study 5). The center effect remains robust at an overall level, because even if the specific meaning associated with order changes, the center position may still represent a compromise option. However, the preference for the center of an array is stronger in the horizontal orientation than in the vertical orientation. Finally, mediation analyses demonstrate that verticality effects are perfectly mediated by schematic inferences, while horizontal effects are not. This implies that the use of the vertical schema is contingent on its accessibility and diagnosticity, reflecting that it is a controlled and conscious process (Feldman and Lynch 1988), whereas the use of the horizontal schema may be contingent on its mere accessibility, an effect shown to reflect automatic processes in judgments (Menon and Raghubir 2003). Finally, Study 6 finds that when consumer purchase goals move towards a higher quality/higher price alternative, choice patterns move from the center to the extreme.

REFERENCES

Bemmaor, Albert C. and Dominique Mouchoux (1991), "Measuring the Short-Term Effect of In-Store Promotion and Retail Advertising on Brand Sales: A Factorial Experiment," *Journal of Marketing Research*, 28(2), 202-214.

Breugelmans, Els, Katia Campo, and Els Gijsbrechts (2007), "Shelf Sequence and Proximity Effects in Online Stores," *Marketing Letters*, 18 (1-2), 117-33.

Chandon, Pierre, J. Wesley Hutchinson, Eric T. Bradlow and Scott Young (2007), "Measuring the Value of Point-of-Purchase Marketing with Commercial Eye-Tracking-Data," in *Visual Marketing: From Attention to Action*, ed. Michel Wedel and Rik Pieters, Mahwah, New-Jersey: Lawrence Erlbaum Associates.

Christenfeld, Nicholas (1995), "Choices from Identical Options," *Psychological Science*, 6(1), 50-55.

Desmet, Pierre and Valérie Renaudin (1998), "Estimation of product category sales responsiveness to allocated shelf space," *International Journal of Research in Marketing*, 15(5), 443-457.

Drèze, Xavier, Stephen J. Hoch and Mary E. Purk (1994), "Shelf Management and Space Elasticity," *Journal of Retailing*, 70(4), 301-26.

Feldman, Jack M. and John G. Lynch Jr. (1988), "Self-Generated Validity and Other Effects of Measurement on Belief, Attitude, Intention, and Behavior," *Journal of Applied Psychology*, 73 (3), 421–35.

Folwell, Raymond J. and D. Andy Moberg (1993), "Factors in Retail Shelf Management Impacting Wine Sales," *Agribusiness*, 9(6), 595-603.

Inman, J. Jeffrey, Leigh McAlister and Wayne D. Hoyer (1990), "Promotion Signal: Proxy for a Price Cut?," *Journal of Consumer Research*, 17(2), 74-81.

Menon, Geeta, and Priya Raghubir (2003), "Ease-of-Retrieval as an Automatic Input in Judgments: A Mere Accessibility Framework?," *Journal of Consumer Research*, 30(2), September, 230-243.

Nisbett, R. E. and T.D. Wilson (1977) "Telling More than We can Know: Verbal Reports on Mental Processes," *Psychological Review*, 84(3), 231-259.

Valenzuela, Ana and Priya Raghubir (2008), "Position Based Schemas: The Center-Stage Effect," *Journal of Consumer Psychology*, forthcoming.

Wedel, Michel and Rik Pieters (2008), *Visual Marketing: From Attention to Action*, New York: Lawrence Erlbaum Associates.

Wilkinson, J.B., Mason, J. Barry and Christie H. Paksoy (1982), "Assessing the Impact of Short-Term Supermarket Strategy Variables," *Journal of Consumer Affairs*, 19(1), 72-86.

Woodside, Arch G. and Gerald .L. Waddle (1975), "Sales effects of in-store advertising", *Journal of Marketing Research*, 15(3), 29–33.

Marketing Issues in Politics

Akshay Rao, University of Minnesota, USA

EXTENDED ABSTRACTS

"Marketing of Political Candidates and Voter Choice"

Jon Krosnick, Stanford University, USA
Josh Pasek, Stanford University, USA

Voting behavior

A great deal of research has explored the determinants of citizens' vote choices in elections and the psychological processes by which citizens make those choices. In fact, voting behavior has been one of the central topics of social science research on mass political behavior. Empirical research on voter decision-making began in the late 1940's and has progressed through four stages of development, as we shall review below. During the first three phases, research focused primarily on identifying the determinants of citizens' vote choices. In the fourth stage, interest has shifted to understanding the psychological processes involved.

Social Structure

During the first phase of voting research, studies focused on the impact of social structure on vote choices. This approach was best exemplified by the classic book, *The People's Choice*, by Lazarsfeld, Berelson, and Gaudet (1948). These researchers examined data from repeated survey interviews of a panel of citizens and found that their candidate preferences were a function of their memberships in various social groups. Specifically, three demographic variables were found to be particularly strong determinants of citizens' preferences: place of residence, social class, and religion. Living in a rural area, being middle-class, and being Protestant enhanced the likelihood of voting for Republicans, whereas living in urban areas, being working-class, and being Catholic enhanced the likelihood of voting for Democrats. Citizens who belonged to social groups with conflicting tendencies (e.g., an urban, working-class Protestant) were "cross-pressured" and were found to have unstable political preferences, selected a candidate late in the election, and frequently did not vote at all.

Party Identification

During the second phase of voting research, the emphasis shifted from a sociological one to a psychological one that emphasized attitudes (See also: ATTITUDE THEORY AND RESEARCH). This new perspective was advanced by University of Michigan researchers Campbell, Converse, Miller, and Stokes (1960) in *The American Voter*. The Michigan approach acknowledged both long-term attitudinal influences on voting by party identification and political IDEOLOGY, as well as short-term influences of attitudes on specific policy issues and attitudes towards specific candidates.

The Michigan approach emphasized party identification as the key determinant of vote choice. A citizen's party identification was presumed to be a result of his or her place in the social structure as well as the interpersonal influence of family members, especially parents. Adopted early in life, party identification was hypothesized to be a highly stable orientation that directly influenced voting. Additionally, party identification was thought to function as a perceptual screen that shaped short-term influences on voting.

Although a great deal of research has consistently demonstrated that party identification is a stable and powerful predictor of vote choice, the relation between party identification and short term influences on voting has turned out to be more complex than originally thought. Specifically, in addition to influencing short term forces, party identification appears to be influenced by them as well. For example, although party identification has been found to influence citizens' perceptions of economic conditions and their preferences on policy issues, the latter seem to influence the former as well. Thus, the relation among party identification and short-term influences is reciprocal in nature. Consequently, it appears that party identification may reflect other determinants of vote choices rather than being the single, primary engine driving voters' decisions.

Additional Determinants of Voting

During the third phase of voting research, researchers maintained the psychological emphasis and have expanded the list of vote determinants. One major body of work focused on the impact of attitudes on specific policy issues. In contrast to the *American Voter*'s presumption that such attitudes play relatively peripheral roles in vote decisions, more recent work has shown that policy attitudes do indeed have significant impact when the issue is considered personally important by a voter. But when an issue is considered personally unimportant, it appears to have little or no impact on candidate preferences.

Other phase-three research has focused on retrospective judgments of the past performance of the candidates and parties in handling national problems. Judgments in domains such as the economy and foreign affairs have been shown to exert substantial influence on vote choices (e.g., Abramson, Aldrich, & Rohde, 1991).

Finally, voters' perceptions of candidates as people have been found to influence voting. Specifically, perceptions of candidates' personality traits (i.e., competence, integrity, leadership, and empathy), as well as the emotions candidates elicit (e.g., anger, pride), shape the impressions voters form of candidates and thereby determine voting in part (Kinder, 1986).

Psychological Processes

Most recently, research has moved beyond specifying the determinants of voting and has focused on the processes by which these determinants are combined. It has been suggested that this is a relatively simple process, in which voters simply add up the number of things they like and dislike about each candidate and choose the candidate with the most positive net score. However, Lodge, McGraw, and Stroh (1989) have proposed a more complex psychological process model that distinguishes between on-line and memory-based decision-making. Rather than waiting until the end of an election campaign to integrate information from memory about the candidates to formulate a vote choice (as the memory-based perspective would suggest), voters appear to form evaluations of the candidates early on and continually update these attitudes on-line as new information is encountered. This sort of on-line updating seems especially prevalent among citizens who are political experts rather than political novices.

Conclusion

This summary touches on just a very small set of the research to be reviewed in this presentation regarding the determinants of who a citizen will vote for. New work on the role of the mass media and the impact of advertising is especially interesting and has clear applications for the understanding of consumer behavior broadly.

References

Abramson, P. R., Aldrich, J. H., and Rohde, D. W. 1991. *Change and continuity in the 1988 elections*. Washington, DC: CQ Press.

Campbell, Angus, Philip E. Converse, Warren E. Miller, and Donald E. Stokes. 1960. *The American Voter*. Chicago: University of Chicago Press.

Kinder, D. R. 1986. *Presidential character revisited, Political Cognition*, L. Erlbaum Associates.

Lazarsfeld, Paul F., Berelson, Bernard, and Gaudet, Hazel. 1948. *The people's choice; how the voter makes up his mind in a presidential campaign*. 2nd ed. New York: Columbia Univ. Press.

Lodge, Milton, Kathleen M. McGraw, and Patrick Stroh. 1989. An Impression-Driven Model of Candidate Evaluation. *The American Political Science Review* 83, no. 2:399-419.

"Mere Measurement, Implementation Intentions, and Voter Turnout"

Daniel Goldstein, London Business School, UK
Kosuke Imai, Politics, Princeton University, USA
Anja Goritz, University of Erlangen-Nurnberg, Germany

Since World War II, in over 1,600 national elections in 170 independent states, voter turnout rates have averaged about 65% of the voting age population. Policy makers in 18% of these democracies have deemed electoral participation important enough to justify compulsory voting laws, under which non-voters can face fines and other punishments. Recently, the US Congress authorized 3.9 billion dollars for the Help America Vote Act, and state governments have invested in expanding early-voting methods, which accounted for roughly 20% of the votes cast in the 2004 election. Worldwide, rewards for voters have included tax breaks, job opportunities, scholarships, and even high-stakes lotteries.

What drives voter turnout? Political theory speaks of the costs and benefits of voting and the slight probability that one's vote will be decisive. In practice, these and other variables appear in policies that target two causes of weak participation: low motivation and high obstacles. Motivation-focused initiatives aim to impart the desire to vote by invoking the importance or closeness of an election, a voter's sense of duty, rewards, punishments, or social comparisons. Obstacle-focused policies aim to make voting easier, such as by introducing same-day or automatic registration, voting by mail, or early in-person voting. If voting is largely influenced by motivations and obstacles, policy makers might take inspiration from psychological research on goal attainment, which has revealed the strong effects of two simple treatments. We attempt to demonstrate that simply asking people if and how they intend to vote can increase turnout.

The technique of asking people if they intend to vote comes from research on attitude accessibility and self-fulfilling prediction. In what is called the mere measurement or question-behavior effect, people become more likely to perform certain actions if they are first asked whether they expect to perform them. That is, merely measuring intentions changes behavior. One surprising study found that asking people whether they intended to buy an automobile increased their chances of doing so.

Why does mere measurement work? One important literature suggests that people who make forecasts about the future may alter their behavior to make the predictions come true. An emerging and complementary view is that when people answer questions about intentions, their underlying attitudes become concrete and readily accessible. For this reason, questions can be polarizing. If attitudes toward electoral participation are generally positive, assessing intentions may turn voting into a goal.

Eighty years of research has looked at the effect of polls, questions, and surveys on voter turnout with some promising findings but leave an unclear picture due to mixed results and some methodological controversies. Part of the variation in results may be due to the variety of populations, instruments, and historical periods studied. Additional variation may be due to the way experiments have mixed mere measurement treatments with related political questions and even practical information on voting.

The second technique, asking people how they intend to vote, comes from research on implementation intentions, which are simple plans that help people overcome obstacles en route to goal attainment. The effects of implementation intentions have been estimated in over 100 policy-relevant studies on exercising, recycling, smoking, and beyond, however, the link to voting has not been investigated in the literature.

How do implementation intentions work? These plans are hypothesized to lead one to direct resources (such as time and attention) toward a target goal, and away from competing goals when they inevitably arise. Furthermore, implementation intentions might make one aware of goal-realization opportunities that would otherwise go unnoticed (e.g., noticing registration offices near work), and help automate responses to foreseeable obstacles (e.g., identifying a means of backup transportation to the polls).

We illustrate the application of mere measurement and implementation intentions through experiments, analyzed in order to estimate causal effects on voter turnout in two national elections: the 2006 US Midterm Election and the 2005 German Federal Election.

In the US study, 1,968 participants were invited to take part in a brief survey approximately two months before the election. In it, a mere measurement group was asked about intentions to vote, and an implementation intentions group was additionally asked to formulate simple plans to vote. The crucial difference with the German study, which involved 1,426 people, is that it took place 1 to 4 days before the election, presumably leaving treatments fresh in the minds of participants.

The experiments pose novel theoretical and applied questions. Will implementation intentions have an effect above that of mere measurement? Will the two treatments be effective on one-shot goals that can be realized only on one day (e.g., voting on Election Day) and open-ended goals that can be realized on many possible days (e.g., early and postal voting)? For both types of goals, do mere measurement and implementation intentions treatments fade over periods of days or months?

For the open-ended goal of early (e.g., postal) voting, mere measurement treatments given two months in advance (US study) had moderate positive effects on turnout, a finding consistent with studies showing that mere measurement treatments can impact the probability of undertaking an action (such as purchasing a computer) on any day within a window of several months. For early voting, estimated implementation intentions effects were similar to those of mere measurement.

For the one-shot goal of election-day voting, mere measurement was only effective when it was administered days (Germany), but not months (US) in advance. Implementation intentions treatments, in contrast, held their effectiveness for both near and distant races.

Our study contributes to a growing body of research demonstrating that policies can benefit from working in concert with psychological mechanisms. People's preference for default options, for instance, can lead to increased membership in organ donor pools, and participation in retirement savings plans. While some policies benefit from a tendency toward inaction, others must help people to act. To construct effective campaigns and messages, policy makers might consider addressing voting as a goal, one that is aided by stating intentions and making plans.

"Facial Similarity between Voters and Candidates Causes Influence"

Jeremy Bailenson, Stanford University, USA
Shanto Iyengar, Stanford University, USA
Nick Yee, Stanford University, USA

Voters identify with political candidates in many ways, from agreeing with their positions on issues, holding the same party affiliation, belonging to the same social categories such as race or gender, or even having common physical traits such as height and facial appearance. Political scientists typically focus on candidates' policy positions, performance records, and party affiliation as the fundamental determinants of voter preferences. With a few notable exceptions nonverbal cues are conspicuously absent from the list of "usual suspects". The cognitive paradigm so dominates voting studies that even when researchers detect the effects of similarity based on a candidate's physical traits (most notably, race and gender), they typically attribute the propensity to support same-gender or ethnicity candidates to voters' tendency to infer agreeable policy positions from these traits.

On the other hand, an extensive literature across the social sciences demonstrates that people are often drawn to others perceived as similar. In the current work, we examined the relative effects of different forms of similarity on candidate evaluations by using an experimental design that manipulated the degree of candidate-voter facial similarity. We were particularly interested in how facial similarity compares to other forms of similarity such as partisanship or policy agreement and with other non-verbal cues including gender and candidate familiarity.

In Experiment One, we examined the effect of facial similarity among unfamiliar political candidates and hypothesized that the effect of facial similarity would be significant due to the lack of other cues or pre-existing biases. One week before the 2006 Florida gubernatorial election we presented a national random sample of voters with photographs of unfamiliar candidates (Charlie Crist and John Davis) that had been morphed either with the voter filling out the survey or with an unfamiliar person. In other words, Experiment One allowed us to examine, as a first step, whether facial similarity could be used to sway political outcomes in the least restricted scenario.

In Experiment Two we replicated the design with familiar candidates (George W. Bush or John Kerry) one week before the 2004 Presidential election. Our hypothesis was that the effect of facial similarity among familiar candidates would be significant, but minimal, due to the presence of pre-existing biases and other information surrounding a presidential election. The effect of facial similarity would also be minimized because the study was administered so shortly before the actual election and many voters may have already made up their minds. Thus, Experiment Two tested the effect of facial similarity in the most conservative and realistic way possible.

In Experiment Three we combined different aspects of Experiment One and Experiment Two by using a set of potential candidates (some familiar, some unfamiliar) for the 2008 presidential election. In the study, we also directly pitted forms of similarity (e.g., facial similarity, gender similarity) against candidate familiarity. We also manipulated the gender of the candidate and pitted the effects of facial similarity against the effects of attitude similar-

ity on salient political issues. Thus, Experiment Three builds upon the first two studies by allowing us to understand the relative importance of facial similarity among other cues typically present in a political election.

In these three studies we demonstrated a moderate but consistent effect of facial similarity on evaluations of actual candidates. In all three studies the effect of facial similarity was heightened when other competing identity cues were less salient. In Experiment One, we examined similarity in the least restrictive situation and demonstrated that similarity increased support for unfamiliar candidates across the board. In Experiment Two, in a high information election in which voters were invested in the outcome, facial similarity increased support for familiar candidates only among weak partisans and independents. Experiment Three directly tested the relationship between familiarity and similarity and demonstrated that facial similarity proved effective only when the candidate was relatively unfamiliar. Furthermore, the effect of facial similarity was smaller than cognitive similarities such as issues and party membership.

These results convey clear implications for the study of voting behavior. While other scholars have demonstrated that candidates who look more "competent" win elections, they have not identified the characteristics of faces that make voters evaluate a candidate more favorably. Our work demonstrates that facial similarity is one such characteristic. Increasing the facial resemblance between candidates and voters can alter electoral results, especially when the candidate is unfamiliar. The effects persist on a limited basis even when the information is conveyed about familiar candidates, one week before a closely contested presidential election. Given the revolution in information technology, we have no doubt that political strategists will increasingly resort to transformed facial similarity as a form of campaign advertising.

"Reference Dependence When Tastes Differ"

Neil Bendle, University of Minnesota, USA
Mark Bergen, University of Minnesota, USA

Behavioral decision scholars have made great strides in showing that decisions can be influenced by context and references (Kahneman and Tversky 1979, Thaler 1985, Highhouse 1996). In marketing this work has developed a much deeper understanding of behavior given the decision context (Huber Payne & Puto 1982, Hedgcock, Rao & Chen 2007), and has explored areas such as reference prices (Winer 1986, Hardie, Johnson & Fader 1993) and product line strategy (Orhun 2007).

The bulk of this work typically concentrates on vertical attributes; i.e. attributes that have a clear ordering on any single dimension and a directionality which is consistent amongst people. For example all other things being equal, people prefer high to low quality, and lower prices rather than higher prices.

There are, however, many situations where attributes cannot be easily classified as vertical. For example, in political marketing voter preferences are often modeled as horizontal differentiation, such as the classic left to right continuum. This is true of many product characteristics such as color, and taste. For example, there is no commonly agreed "ideal" car color. In these situations, consumers will not all make the same choice even when they are faced with identical alternatives and all have the same information. Not only does horizontal differentiation characterize a wealth of consumer decision contexts, it allows us to consider more complex markets where tastes must be aggregated to assess the outcomes and implications of reference dependence and marketing activities.

We use the classic Hotelling model to explore "horizontal" reference dependence, introducing reference effects that are not direction specific, i.e. the references represent a consumer's attitude about the distance to the product they experience and not an attitude to the location of the reference as such. The work horse model of competition research, the Hotelling (1929) line, parsimoniously captures both a consumer's personal preference and the market outcomes incorporating other people's preferences. We develop "horizontal" reference dependence in a manner faithful to horizontal differentiation and prospect theory, using non-direction specific effects which show diminishing sensitivity to gains and losses. The reference effect is a function of both the consumer's distance to the reference and to the product being considered. We apply reference effects to utility additively (Koszegi & Rabin 2004); a parameter sets the relative power of reference effects compared to "actual" distance.

This adds discreteness which greatly complicates the Hotelling model. To maintain a manageable scope of this work we take a partial equilibrium approach. We explore the implications of reference points not the process of setting references points. To solve the model we analyze all possible permutations of gains and losses, 65 cases. We show that although references influence the relative strength of preferences, references don't change choice under horizontal differentiation in this model. However, extending the model to contexts where strength of preference matters, we show that choices can be substantially influenced by "horizontal" reference dependence. These choices move in reasonable ways given loss aversion and diminishing sensitivity which allows specific advice to be generated as to the location managers of any given product want consumers to use as a reference.

We apply this to political marketing, which is a natural market in which to consider taste differences. In politics, despite controversy about the prevalence of coherent ideology (Converse 1964, Jost 2006), many people are willing to categorize politicians and their policies on a single taste dimension (Gigerenzer 2007). The left-right continuum that is widely used in political research (Morton 1999, 2006) represents taste differences because there is no objectively agreed upon reason for the superiority of left to right or right to left. The policy position that each voter prefers depends upon where they stand on the policy continuum.

We examine primary elections. Both the primary and predicted general election choices are captured on a Hotelling line. We show that in a general election reference effects don't change the voter's choice. However we also show that when electability and uncertainty matter, references can influence voter choice in primary elections. This allows us to develop marketing advice; campaign managers shouldn't necessarily aim to anchor potential voters' references around their own candidate's position. Specifically more electable candidates, those expected to be stronger in the general election than their primary election opponents, want voters' references far from the primary contest while less electable candidates want voters to concentrate on their specific policies, they want voters concentrating on the primary election at hand.

Thus, we provide an explanation of how reference dependence can sometimes be a very powerful influence on certain political decisions and yet have no effect on others. We explore why Howard Dean's 2004 communications strategy may have helped John Kerry noting that the conventional wisdom—that the "scream" cost Dean the election is incomplete, Dean's fall in the polls and loss in Iowa preceded the scream. In 2004 Howard Dean was relentlessly attacking George Bush not his opponent in the election John Kerry. This attention to the President reinforced a focus on ousting George Bush minimizing the policy differences between John Kerry and Howard Dean. Where voters' references are focused outside the specific primary contest this is an advantage for candidates perceived as more electable like John Kerry. This work also helps explain why in 2008 republican voters confounded expert's predictions that they would choose a candidate more in tune with their core beliefs instead choosing John McCain, the candidate seen as more electable.

References

Converse, Philip. 1964. *The Nature of Belief Systems in Mass Publics. In Ideology and Discontent*, edited by David E. Apter. New York, NY: The Free Press.

Gigerenzer, Gerd. 2007. *Gut feelings : the intelligence of the unconscious*. New York: Viking.

Hardie, Bruce, Eric Johnson, and Peter Fader. 1993. Modeling Loss Aversion and Reference Dependence Effects on Brand Choice. *Marketing Science* 12, no. 4

Hedgcock, William, Akshay R. Rao, and Haipeng Chen, 2008. Could Ralph Nader's Entrance and Exit Have Helped Al Gore? The Impact of Decoy Dynamics on Consumer Choice. *Journal of Marketing Research*.

Highhouse, Scott. 1996. Context-Dependent Selection: The Effects of Decoy and Phantom Job Candidates. *Organizational Behavior and Human Decision Processes* 65, no. 1

Hotelling, Harold. 1929. Stability in Competition. *The Economic Journal* 39, no. 153

Huber, Joel, John W. Payne, and Christopher Puto. 1982. Adding Asymmetrically Dominated Alternatives: Violations of Regularity and the Similarity Hypothesis. *Journal of Consumer Research* 9, no. 1:90-98.

Jost, John. 2006. The End of the End of Ideology. *American Psychologist* 61, no. 7:651-670.

Kahneman, Daniel, and Amos Tversky. 1979. Prospect Theory: An Analysis of Decision under Risk. *Econometrica* 47, no. 2:263-263-292.

Koszegi, Botond, and Matthew Rabin, 2004. A Model of Reference-Dependent Preferences (Working Paper) Department of Economics, Institute for Business and Economic Research, UC Berkeley.

Morton, Rebecca. 2006. *Analyzing Elections: The New Institutionalism in American Politics*. W W Norton & Company.

Morton, Rebecca. 1999. *Methods and Models: a guide to the empirical analysis of formal models in political science*. Cambridge University Press.

Orhun, A. Y. 2007. Optimal Product Line Design When Consumers Exhibit Choice-Set Dependent Preferences (Working Paper) University of Chicago.

Winer, Russell S. 1986. A Reference Price Model of Brand Choice for Frequently Purchased Products. *Journal of Consumer Research* 13, no. 2:250.

Brand Symbolism and Reference Groups: Perspectives on the Identity Value of Brands
Carlos Torelli, University of Minnesota, USA

SESSION OVERVIEW

People buy products not only for what they do, but also for what the product means; thus brands can be symbols that become part of the individual identities of consumers (Levy 1959). McCracken's (1988) model of meaning transfer states that such meaning originates in the culturally constituted world and moves into brands through several instruments such as advertising, the fashion system, and reference groups. In particular, reference groups shape brand meanings via the associations consumers hold regarding the groups of individuals who use the brand (Muniz and O'Guinn 2001). These meanings can move to consumers, as consumers appropriate brand meanings for constructing their individual identities (Escalas and Bettman 2005). How do brands achieve the highest levels of symbolism and become icons of a group? How do consumers use iconic brands for signaling their identity? When do consumers feel more motivated to seek connections among fellow brand users? How do group norms impact the identity value of brands? This symposium unites under a common theme of providing insights on the dynamic processes underlying the transfer of brand meanings via reference groups and the appropriation of these meanings for constructing consumers' self-identities.

The first paper by Torelli, Chiu, Keh, and Amaral examines how brands become icons of a cultural group and how consumers use iconic brands to manage their social identity. Adopting a shared reality perspective (Hardin and Higgins 1996) to the study of the cultural significance of brands, these authors define brand iconicity as the degree to which a brand symbolizes the values, needs, and aspirations of the members of a particular cultural group. They further reason that for these brands to become culturally influential their symbolic meanings should be widely and durably distributed in the culture (Sperber 1996). Through the sharing of these meanings in an ongoing, dynamic process of social verification, they become a shared reality. In five studies, the authors develop a reliable and cross-culturally general measure of brand iconicity. They show that consumers may use preference for iconic brands over non-iconic ones as a self-symbolizing strategy. They also show that for likable brands, if their cultural significance is widely known in the community, they are more likely to become cultural icons. This research not only provides insights into the social verification process by which symbolic group meanings get transferred to iconic brands, but show how consumers use iconic brands to manage their social identity and use social information to judge the level of iconicity of brands.

The second paper by Cheng and Chiu explores how brand patronage can facilitate perceptions of group interconnectedness and homogeneity. Cheng and Chiu suggest that knowing that one's brand choice was favored only by a few people motivates individuals to seek connections among fellow brand users. They further argue that this need to seek connections motivates minority (vs. mainstream) brand users to perceive fellow brand users to be a homogenous and desirable group, and to emphasize commonalities when they talk among each other. Minority brand users would therefore be more likely to have a shared representation of who they are and what they are like. In five experiments, they found that both the need to seek connections and ingroup communication are critical for individuals to form shared representation of group members. This stream of research provides an important insight

into how brand-group associations get established and how abstract group meanings can get transferred to a brand.

The final paper by Ng and Lau-Gesk enhances our understanding of the dynamic processes underlying the appropriation of brand meanings via reference groups. Ng and Lau-Gesk suggest that the identity value of a brand can be diminished by highlighting the conflict between individual identity-signaling desires and important group values. In three experiments, the authors find that when the conflict between consumers' desire to signal status through brand usage and the group norms disapproving such behavior are made salient, consumers are less likely to choose products that feature (vs. not) brand logos prominently. This effect is particularly strong for brand choices that are made in public (vs. in private), and even extend to situations involving counterfeit products.

This session discusses a very important topic that has amazing potential to both inform consumer researchers about the antecedents of self-brand connections and help branding professionals make better decisions. We anticipate this session will attract not only those interested in branding issues, but those interested in group-processes and the cultural meanings of brands. Jennifer Escalas, an expert in the study of consumer narrative processing and brand symbolism, will integrate the implications of the three streams of research and provide a roadmap for future research about the dynamic processes underlying the transfer of brand meanings via reference groups and the appropriation of these meanings for constructing consumers' self-identities.

EXTENDED ABSTRACTS

"Brand Iconicity: A Shared Reality Perspective"
Carlos Torelli, University of Minnesota, USA
Chi-yue Chiu, University of Illinois at Urbana-Champaign, USA
Hean Tat Keh, Peking University, China
Nelson Amaral, University of Minnesota, USA

That certain brands reach an iconic status in society is a notion widely accepted by marketing practitioners and consumers alike. Although recommendations to build iconic brands are not uncommon, very little research has been devoted to basing these recommendations upon any theoretically grounded conceptualization of brand iconicity. Recently, Holt (2004) conceptualized iconic brands as consumer brands that become "consensus expressions of particular values held dear by some members of a society" (p. 4). Iconic brands carry a heavy symbolic load for consumers, who frequently rely on them to communicate to others who they are or aspire to be. For these brands to become culturally influential, their symbolic meanings should be widely and durably distributed in the culture (see Sperber 1996). Through the sharing of these meanings on an ongoing, dynamic process of social verification, or shared reality (Hardin and Higgins 1996), their symbolism becomes an objective reality. It is precisely this shared understanding of the symbolic meaning of an iconic brand that facilitates the communication of ideals and aspirations to others through brand usage or consumption.

We define brand iconicity as the degree to which a brand symbolizes the values, needs, and aspirations of the members of a particular cultural group. Brands high in iconicity have the power to connect diverse elements of cultural knowledge and can act as reminders of culturally-relevant values and beliefs. In the five studies reported here, we developed a measure of brand iconicity and provided evidence for its reliability and validity. These studies also show how consumers use iconic brands to manage their social identity and use social information to judge the level of iconicity of brands.

In study 1, we developed a scale to measure brand iconicity (BIS) and provided evidence for its reliability and cross-cultural generality using samples of American and Chinese consumers. Brand iconicity was shown to be a construct that is distinct from, and yet correlated with, involvement. Although iconic brands are very familiar ones, brand iconicity is uncorrelated with brand familiarity.

In studies 2 and 3, we demonstrated the validity of the BIS. In study 2, we asked American participants to write a story describing American culture. Participants were further instructed to use brands either high or low in iconicity as an aid in writing the story (a control condition, in which no brands were mentioned, was also included for comparison purposes). They subsequently rated the fluency in idea generation. Results showed that including iconic brands identified through the BIS when writing about their associated culture increases fluency in idea generation and the number of important cultural values mentioned in the essay. These effects remained even after controlling for participants' level of involvement with the brands. In study 3, participants were either reminded of a recent ban on a symbolic marker of their group identity (University mascot) or completed a control task. They subsequently evaluated brands with varying levels of iconicity. Results showed that consumers preferred iconic brands over non-iconic ones as a self-symbolizing strategy. They used this strategy to compensate for a tarnished group identity upon the reminder of the ban on the University mascot.

Finally, studies 4 and 5 investigated the shared reality processes that underlie judgments of brand iconicity. Participants were led to believe that a majority (vs. a minority) of fellow participants associated either a likable or a dislikable brand (in this case a celebrity name) with culturally-relevant values. They subsequently rated the brand in terms of iconicity. Results showed that for likable brands, if their cultural significance is widely known in the community, they have an increased likelihood of becoming cultural icons. However, for dislikable brands, public awareness of their cultural meanings does not increase their iconicity scores.

Findings from this research suggest a relationship between brand evaluation, public awareness of the brand's cultural significance, and brand iconicity. At least for likable brands, it is possible to increase their iconicity by strengthening its associations with important cultural values and broadening the public awareness of such associations. This idea is congruent with Holt's (2004) assertion that brands that are successful in addressing the collective desires of a cultural group are the ones raised to an iconic status. In contrast, for dislikable brands, even when the consumers know that these brands are widely known to embody important cultural values, they do not consider these brands to be iconic. This finding is consistent with theories of intergroup behavior (e.g., Tajfel 1982), which posit that people adopt a certain group identity to fulfill their need for positive distinctiveness of the self. Thus, it would be unlikely that consumers would accept a dislikable brand as an icon of their culture, as doing so may contrast with the perceived positivity of the culture.

Findings in this research carry important implications for global branding. Consumers who are aware of the symbolism of a foreign brand in its associated culture might bring to mind its attendant cultural meaning. For example, a Chinese consumer may think about the individualist values characteristic of American culture while passing in front of a Starbucks outlet in downtown Beijing. If the consumer values an independent self-identity, the activated cultural associations upon seeing the iconic American brand may increase purchase intention.

In combination, the studies in this research not only provide insights into the social verification process by which symbolic meanings associated with a group get transferred to iconic brands, but show how consumers use iconic brands to manage their social identity and use social information to judge the level of iconicity of brands. The present paper offers a framework to better understand the impact of the cultural meanings associated with consumer brands on brand perceptions and the fulfillment of identity goals.

"Emergence of Shared Representation of Brand Users"
Shirley Y. Y. Cheng, University of Illinois at Urbana-Champaign, USA
Chi-yue Chiu, University of Illinois at Urbana-Champaign, USA

One major feature of brand communities is the "consciousness of kind" (Gusfield 1978), which is the "intrinsic connection that members feel toward one another, and the collective sense of difference from others not in the community" (p. 413, Muniz and O'Guinn 2001). Intrigued by the observation that many brand communities are centered at minority brands (e.g., Apple-Mac or Harley Davidson) instead of mainstream brands, we looked into how being in a minority group may contribute to forming a shared representation of fellow brand users.

Specifically, we examined how brand users become aware of some distinctive characteristics that are shared among fellow brand users. These distinctive characteristics *define* the group, and differentiate members from non-members of the community. We proposed that the motivation to seek connections among fellow brand users and the opportunity for in-group communication contribute to the emergence of the shared group representation.

Minority brands and the motivation to seek connections. Optimal distinctiveness theory (Brewer 1991) posits that people need to see themselves as being different from others and being connected to others at the same time. For minority brand users, knowing that their brand choice is shared only by a small group satisfies the need to be different more than the need to connect, which would motivate to seek connections to others in order to restore the optimal level of distinctiveness. Motivation to seek connections would lead minority brand users to perceive commonalities among fellow brand users. For majority brand users, knowing that a majority shares their brand choice heightens the need to be different. They are motivated to perceive differences instead of commonalities among fellow brand users.

Communication as a critical mechanism. Communication is an important mechanism for forming shared representation (Latané 1996). We maintain that communication among brand users is responsible for crystallizing distinctive group characteristics. Minority brand users (because of the heightened need to connect) would be more likely to emphasize commonalities when they talk about fellow brand users. Majority brand users, however, would be more likely to emphasize the differences among fellow brand users. Therefore, we hypothesize that minority (vs. majority) brand users would be more likely to form a shared group representation.

Experiments 1 and 2–Emergence of distinctive group characteristics. In these experiments, we manipulated group membership by giving participants a choice between two brands. They were told that their choice was either popular (majority condition) or unpopular (minority condition) among previous participants, which would lead to relatively lower versus higher levels of need for connections respectively. Next, participants read information about "the most enjoyable activity of 20 other participants who made the same choice." These activities varied in the degree to which they represented openness to experience, and there was a slightly higher number of activities high (vs. low) in openness. Using this information, participants wrote an essay to communicate their impression of these participants (referred thereafter as the target group) to another participant who would also choose the same brand. Two independent coders classified each essay in terms of whether it captured a global impression of the target group or not, and in terms of whether this global impression reflected openness to experience as the main theme. As predicted, participants in the minority (vs. majority) condition were more likely to communicate a global impression of the target group and to characterize it as high in openness.

Participants also rated the target group on group homogeneity and openness. Again as predicted, participants in the minority (vs. majority) condition rated target group members as being more similar to one another and as being more open to experience, although participants in the two conditions rated openness as equally desirable. To rule out an alternative interpretation based on information representativeness, experiment 2 replicated the findings of experiment 1, but using this time a smaller target group (i.e., information about five instead of 20 participants).

Experiments 3 and 4–Testing the proposed model. These experiments were designed to show that the need to seek connections and ingroup communication are critical for forming shared group representations. In experiment 3, participants performed the same tasks but without making the initial brand choice, which presumably prevented them from associating with the target (i.e., taking an outsider's perspective). They were simply instructed to read the same 20 most enjoyable activities of participants who chose either a minority or a majority brand and wrote an essay about these participants. As expected, participants who wrote essays about such groups did not perceive a minority group to be more homogeneous or open. In fact, reversing the pattern found in previous studies, minority (vs. majority) users were perceived to be less homogeneous and less open. These results suggest that the need to connect with fellow group members may be a prerequisite for forming a shared group representation. In experiment 4, participants made the same brand choice as in experiment 1, but were prevented from communicating their impressions (i.e., they did not write an essay describing the target group) before rating the group. Congruent with the notion that ingroup communication is necessary for forming shared group representations, participants in the minority (vs. majority) condition perceived the target group to be equally homogeneous, and even perceived it as being less open.

Experiment 5–Crystallization of distinctive group characteristics. This experiment studied serial communication as an antecedent of the crystallization of brand user representations. Participants here followed the same procedure used in experiment 1, but read a sample of the essays written by the participants in experiment 1 instead of the 20 most enjoyable activities. As predicted, participants in the minority (vs. majority) condition perceived the target group as being more open, homogenous, cohesive, and trustworthy.

Results here show that minority (vs. majority) brand users perceive and talk about fellow brand users with a greater emphasis on the commonalities among them. This contributes to forming a shared representation of the distinctive group characteristics. Existing reference group research mostly focuses on how perception of a reference group affect consumers' brand choice (e.g., Escalas and Bettman 2003). Extending this stream of research, our findings show that brand choice can affect the perceptions of the reference group by group members, which might subsequently impact the meaning of being a brand user.

"One Trait, Two Images: Impact of Impression Management Goal Conflict on Brand Choice"

Sharon Ng, Nanyang Technological University, Singapore
Loraine Lau-Gesk, University of California, Irvine, USA

Consumers frequently use brands as a means to express a desired self image. Brands, indeed the more successful ones, tend to be associated with images that consumers would like to be associated with in order to help managing the impressions they make on others (Escalas and Bettman 2005). To highlight these associations, most branded products are designed such that the brand logo is prominently featured on the product (e.g., the monogram bags sold by Louis Vuitton, the logo featured on all Ralph Lauren apparels, etc). One purpose of these logos is to highlight the brand and fulfill the impression management purpose of its users.

Many brands in the marketplace, however, possess complex trait associations where more than one meaning can develop and evolve over time. A brand may possess a conflicting image through a single trait. Take prestige, for example. On the one hand, the prestige of a brand may in itself entice consumers to purchase it in view of its associated meaning of personal success and status. On the other hand, consumers may find prestige as undesirable if they think about negative group perceptions of being overly materialistic and shallow as opposed to modest and grounded. These multiple meanings associated with a single brand trait can lead consumers to experience tension balancing personal desires (e.g., showing success) with societal values (e.g., demonstrating modesty, Goffman 1959, Leary and Kowalski 1990).

Though many brands with conflicting meanings exist in the marketplace, the literature remains silent about how brand conflict could impact brand choice. To address this gap in the literature, the present research examines situations where a single brand trait arouses oppositely-valenced responses, forcing consumers to choose between satisfying personal identity-signaling desires or fulfilling important group values. We examine how this type of conflict affect consumers' choice between products that feature the brand logo prominently and those that do not feature the logo. Our findings will help firms better understand how conflicting brand image and societal norms affect consumers' choices. In addition, we extend our theory to understand consumers' purchase of counterfeit products.

Specifically, drawing from the impression management literature, we propose that saliency of the conflicting associations triggered by the purchase or use of a brand would make people more hesitant to use the brand for impression management purposes, which would ultimately impact brand choice. To test this hypothesis, study 1 manipulated the degree to which the conflict between consumers' desire to signal status through brand usage and the group norms disapproving such behavior were made salient. Those in the low conflict condition were told that signaling status through brand usage was a widely accepted behavior in their groups, whereas those in the high conflict condition were told that such behavior was in conflict with group norms. As predicted, we found that people were less likely to choose products that featured the brand logo prominently (vs. those without the brand logo) when the conflict was made salient.

We further propose that the impact of conflicting associations on one's brand choice is moderated by the extent to which the decision is made in the public or the private domain. When the decision is made in the public domain, the conflict would take on greater weight in affecting one's decision. To test this hypothesis, study 2 adopted a 2 (Evaluation Condition: Private vs. Public) X 2 (Conflict: Low vs. High) between subjects design. As expected, we found that when the decision was made in the public domain, participants were more likely to choose products that did not feature the brand logos prominently (versus those that featured the brand logos prominently). In the private domain, there was no significant difference in the choices made. Thus, findings from studies 1 and 2 supported our contention that making salient the conflict between individual identity-signaling desires and important group values do affect consumers' choices, and this effect is particularly evident when the decision is made in the public domain.

Building on studies 1 and 2, study 3 examines how conflicting associations would affect people's attitudes towards counterfeit products. Very little research has been devoted to understanding the psychological processes underlying the purchase of counterfeit products. We propose that our findings can shed light on some of these processes. Consumers may buy counterfeit products in an attempt to signal status through brand usage without having to pay a higher price. However, these consumers may also perceive that the usage of counterfeit products is a practice that is not accepted by their groups and may negatively impact how group members perceive them. This conflict between personal goals and important group values (i.e., to leverage the brand's image to impress others and societal disdain on the purchase of counterfeit products) should affect attitudes toward counterfeit products. Specifically, we argue that when such conflict is made salient to the consumers, they would exhibit a less favorable attitude towards counterfeit products. Furthermore, this effect will be stronger when the decision is made in the public (vs. the private) domain. To test this hypothesis, we conducted a 2 (Evaluation Condition: Private vs. Public) X 2 (Conflict: Low vs. High) between subjects experiment in a counterfeit product context. Results supported our prediction.

In summary, findings from three studies suggest that the use of brands for impression management purposes may be more complex than it was previously known. Brand attributes that satisfy individual identity-signaling desires may be in conflict with values that are important for the group. Making this conflict salient can impact consumers' attitudes and choices.

SELECTED REFERENCES

Brewer, Marilynn B. (1991), "The Social Self: On Being the Same and Different at the Same Time," *Personality & Social Psychology Bulletin*, 17 (5), 475-82.

Escalas, Jennifer Edson and James R. Bettman (2005), "Self-Construal, Reference Groups, and Brand Meaning," *Journal of Consumer Research*, 32 (3), 378-89.

Hardin, Curtis D. and E. Tory Higgins (1996), "Shared Reality: How Social Verification Makes the Subjective Objective," in *Handbook of Motivation and Cognition*, Richard M. Sorrentino and E. Tory Higgins, Eds. Vol. 3: The interpersonal context. NY: Guilford Press, 28-84.

Holt, Douglas B. (2004), *How Brands Become Icons: The Principles of Cultural Branding*. Cambridge, MA: Harvard Business School Press.

Muniz, Albert M. and Thomas C. O'Guinn (2001), "Brand Community," *Journal of Consumer Research*, 27 (4), 412-32.

Multifaceted Consumer Welfare: Broadening the Perspective

Behice Ece Ilhan, University of Illinois at Urbana-Champaign, USA

SESSION OVERVIEW

Current Perspectives on Consumer Welfare: In his ACR presidential address in 2006, David Glen Mick stresses that "transformative consumer research is not something new, nor has it been dormant" (page 2). Yet, the proliferation of scholarly studies and special session journals indicates consumer behavior scholars' growing interests on the topic. To date, existing consumer welfare studies have primarily examined whether a particular consumption practice enhances or impairs consumer welfare. Consumer welfare has generally been treated as a dependent variable in association with consumption practices such as eating habits (Moore 2007, Chandon and Wansink 2007), alcohol consumption (Creyer et al 2002), gambling (Wijnholds and Little 2002), and consumption of product information (Balasubramanian and Cole 2002, Wansink and Chandon 2006). Balasubramanian and Cole (2002), for example, have tested how consumers benefit from product labels that include more negative attributes (such as sodium and fat where less is better). Reiterating the product labels-consumer welfare relationship, Wansink and Chandon (2006) pointed out the negative role of 'low-fat' nutrition labels for consumers. These welfare studies in relation to consumption have largely been guided by the question 'how does consumer behavior impact consumer welfare?' The *Journal of Consumer Research*'s Call for Papers for Transformative Consumer Research Special Issue also summarizes the scope of these studies as: "consumption that has positive or negative externalities is a way to study consumer welfare".

Broadening the Construct of Consumer Welfare: Consumer behavior scholars have learned substantially from these previous consumer welfare accounts. While these prior elaborations are most relevant to our understanding of the consumer welfare concept in association with different consumption practices, they are limited in their scope and insufficient in their elaboration of what consumer welfare is and how broadly it could be studied. Consumer welfare analysis is limited to the one-step and somewhat deterministic assessment of the concept–as a dependent variable. Also, the consumer welfare concept is used interchangeably with other consumer behavior constructs such as subjective well being, consumer satisfaction, and quality of life and is also equated with higher levels of quality of life, overall happiness with life, absence of ill being, and greater social welfare (Sirgy, Lee, and Rahtz 2007). However, accepting the face-value of consumption practices for their consumer welfare implications, consumer researchers inevitably fail to notice the complex and profound layers of the consumer welfare concept.

The session *builds on* existing consumer welfare studies by exploring multiple faces of this complex and multi-layered concept. The session papers do not deem consumer welfare only as a dependent variable that is directly associated with a consumption practice but rather try to address the amorphous nature of consumer welfare that might be compromised and enriched at the same time for the same practice. The session also *extends* existing scholarship by pointing at some boundary conditions where the existing consumer welfare frameworks fall short of offering elaborate explanations and understandings. Assumptions about consumers, contexts, and units of analysis are challenged by the session papers to broaden the frameworks. Thus, the session has been designed to contribute to an attempt to theory development of consumer welfare by furthering the existing frameworks and identifying their limits.

Papers: The three papers are united in their exploratory perspective as each of them seeks to broaden the existing consumer welfare frameworks and challenge at least one assumption related to existing discussions on the topic.

Ilhan and Tumbat attempt to extend the existing studies on consumer welfare by introducing an alternative consumer choice prospect. To challenge the face value of counterfeit consumption as lessening consumer welfare, they introduce a context that offers new choice scenarios where the consumer choice is between having a counterfeit product versus not having anything. They argue that the choice dichotomy of having an 'authentic' versus a 'counterfeit (inauthentic)' product–imposed by the existing Western lenses– is an impediment to explore possible positive consumer welfare implications of counterfeit consumption. Their findings challenge the anti-counterfeit consumption discourse and propose a novel conceptualization of consumer welfare based on this alternative choice prospect.

Askegaard and Kjeldgaard, in their study of consumption of personal coaching, challenge the validity of the assumption underlying the coaching phenomenon: that it is possible to perform oneself to better consumer welfare. Starting at the self-actualization level, they formulate a framework for investigating consumption of self-improvement therapy, exemplified by personal coaching. They then, discuss both the potential, negative macro-level consequences of the self-actualization and coaching techniques for consumer welfare in spite of the positive phenomenological experience and also the legitimacy of such macro-level critiques in the face of positive consumer experiences.

Finally, adopting a different theoretical perspective, Gau and Viswanathan re-examine the concept of consumer expertise and discuss counterintuitive implications on traditional notions of consumer welfare. Using problem solving frameworks, they suggest that traditional notions of consumer welfare should be reconsidered in light of the unique cognitive tendencies observed in low-literate consumers. Challenging the assumptions about consumer expertise, they assert that a more complete understanding of the low-literate consumer experience would include a more complete incorporation affective considerations, as well as further distinctions of literacy, perhaps into individual components of literacy and numeracy. In their paper, they iterate how this greater understanding would reveal a clearer picture of what consumer welfare could be.

This special session is very up to date with the recent transformative consumer research direction that guides the consumer behavior field. As it seeks to build on, challenge, and extend prior consumer welfare frameworks and literature, this symposium appealed to a broad cross-section of ACR attendees, particularly to the ones who are interested in and in search for new and broader directions on consumer welfare. David Glen Mick, as one of the initiators of transformative consumer direction in the field and expert in the area, was the ideal discussion leader who is well positioned to comment on research that seeks to broaden the existing frameworks.

ABSTRACTS

"Counterfeit Consumption: Consumer Welfare Perspective"
Behice Ece Ilhan, University of Illinois at Urbana-Champaign
Gulnur Tumbat, San Francisco State University

Previous studies suggest that counterfeit consumption, regarded as an illegal and unethical practice, has undesirable consequences for markets, firms, and also for consumers. The focus of consumer studies on the topic is limited to the motivations for or symbolic meanings of counterfeit consumption. Yet, the potential positive consequences of counterfeit consumption on consumer's welfare haven't been explored. We argue that the Western contexts used in existing studies bring in a specific choice dichotomy–between having an 'authentic' versus a 'counterfeit (inauthentic)' product–that acts as an impediment to explore possible consumer welfare implications of counterfeit consumption. We use an alternative context where the consumer choice may be between having a counterfeit product versus none to explore consumer welfare implications of counterfeit consumption. Our findings challenge the anti-counterfeit consumption discourse and propose a novel conceptualization of consumer welfare.

"Coaching for Capacity or Incapacity? Self-Actualization and Consumer Welfare"
Søren Askegaard, University of Southern Denmark, Odense
Dannie Kjeldgaard, University of Southern Denmark, Odense

Consumption of personal coaching is growing rapidly. Based on a utopian and a dystopian vision on the contemporary culture of self-actualization, we formulate a framework for investigating consumption of self-improvement therapy, exemplified by personal coaching. Sixteen consumers were interviewed about their motivations for engaging in as well as their experiences of personal coaching and its consequences for their lives before, during and after the therapy. We analysed the results of the interviews in the light of its contribution to consumer welfare using insights from positional economy, the ideology of performance, and critical perspectives on the self-help ideology and industry.

"Consumer Welfare Considerations Across Literacy and Resource Barriers"
Roland Gau, University of Illinois at Urbana-Champaign
Madhu Viswanathan, University of Illinois at Urbana-Champaign

Our research on low-literate, low-income consumers in the U.S. and India finds a variety of behaviors indicative of concrete thinking (e.g., buying based on a single attribute, often price, buying based on immediate need), often resulting in poor marketplace decisions (e.g., buying incorrect items, buying items with higher unit prices, foregoing substitute items). However, some low-literate consumers exhibit consumer expertise, a seemingly surprising result, given extant expertise perspectives. Our experience with educational interventions also suggests some counter-intuitive results, given our understanding of literacy. Thus, aspects of consumer welfare (e.g., consumer education, communication of product information) should be reconsidered for low-literate consumers.

References available upon request

Building an Understanding of What Makes Consumer Behavior Transformative

Eric J. Arnould, University of Wyoming, USA

SESSION OVERVIEW

The purpose of this session is to create a discussion of what makes consumer behavior transformative (Mick 2006), and through presentations and discussion, to show how participatory approaches, as well as top down approaches adopted in social marketing, can be effective in accruing positive change to individual consumers and to society. More specifically, this session explores transformative consumption experiences that consumers create by appropriating marketplace resources for their own purposes. While considerable excitement has been generated by the emergence of more participatory models of market relationships, little attention has been directed to the market transformative potential of participatory consumer behavior, although evidence for these sorts of prosumptive behaviors has been reported (Craig-Lees and Hill 2002; Thompson and Coskuner-Balli 2007).

Grass roots social innovation (Young Foundation 2006) in marketing systems provides an important complement to the more top down approaches espoused by some proponents of transformative consumer research. Social marketing seeks to change behavior through marketing programs that help individuals understand and embrace prescribed positive behaviors. By contrast, participatory research approaches facilitate learning by actively engaging consumers in ways that help them define consumer-driven solutions to problems (Ozanne and Saatcioglu 2008). Both social marketing and grass roots social innovation in market systems can and should coexist within the Transformative Consumer Research vision.

Increasingly consumers are insisting on building or reformulating markets that implement, amplify and promote principles and ideals marginalized, attenuated, or neglected by mainstream commercial interests (Thompson and Coskuner-Balli 2007, 138). Consumers are interested in systemic market change; they have become active producers of their own consumption requirements. Unlike historic or classic countercultural approaches that emphasized utopian self-sufficiency or do-it-yourself models, today, consumers are becoming adept at developing marketing-informed solutions to create beneficial systems, often incorporating non-commoditized goods and/or local connectivity, as well. In other words, consumers are investing in qualitative improvements in need satisfying systems, in some cases incorporating the goal that net benefits to the society and the environment should be higher than the full systemic costs (Mont 2008, 253).

Sometimes attributed to the collective intelligence fostered by the Internet, and the democraticization of digital media technologies, a paradigm shift in consumer behavior may be occurring (Jenkins 2006; Lévy 1997). Consistent with this idea of paradigm shift, the consumers described in the current session do not passively accept the dominant marketplace conditions with which they are presented, as Melea Press shows in a paper casting Consumer Supported Agriculture as a risk management strategy. Nor do consumers in marginalized socio-economic contexts passively accept resource constraints and external policy mandates that seek to define their consumption options as Baker, Hill, and Hunt demonstrate. Nor as Rosa and Geiger-Oneto illustrate, do resource constrained consumers passively accept resource deficits that lead some to characterize them as marginalized non-consumers. In effect, this session also builds directly on a past ACR session critical of TCR and CCT (Ozanne and Dobscha 2006). Our innovative approach will show how focusing on the market transforming

capabilities of consumers may help us understand how to alter markets in the consumer interest, and concurrently destabilize inadequate theoretical binaries like mainstream vs. marginalized market actors. Moreover, the consumer strategies described here may represent a middle ground between the opt-out strategies promoted by some consumer downshifters and voluntary simplicity advocates, the legitimacy of which is contested, and the more acquiescent orientations to consumption of those in mass markets (Bekin, Carrigan and Szmigin 2005; Mont 2008; Ottman 1995; Schorr 1998).

Professor Julie Ozanne, who has long championed both participatory approaches to policy-oriented consumer research and critical approaches to consumer research generally, will provide a synthesizing discussion of the papers and lead the audience in a discussion of the implications of these papers for developing the theory and practice of transformative consumer behavior research (Murray and Ozanne 1991; Ozanne and Dobscha 2006; Ozanne and Saatcioglu 2008).

EXTENDED ABSTRACTS

"Co-Creating Alternative Markets: Consumer Efficacy in Risk Abatement"

Melea Press, University of Wyoming, USA

Many consumers are disappointed with the current food marketing system, and are concerned by the risks they feel they take and the compromises they make with preferred values by engaging with a system they do not fully trust (Rampton and Stauber 2001). In an attempt to mitigate their feelings of risk, some consumers engage in marketplace activities that lie outside of the mainstream (Beck 1992). Community Supported Agriculture (CSA) is highlighted here, as an example of how consumers are driving change in the marketplace by choosing to purchase products through non-mainstream channels.

Transformative consumer research (TCR) takes the approach that research should shed light on consumer issues, and help to improve consumers' lives (Mick 2006). In this paper, the consumer is not painted as a marginalized figure that lacks efficacy; rather, the exemplary consumers in this paper are proactive and engaged members of a community who are able to make choices that affect their own wellbeing, as well as the marketplace itself. In the case of CSA, the idea of TCR is turned on its head, as we look to consumers to show us how they engage in alternative market activities, and advocate for their own needs.

CSAs are programs through which consumers can purchase produce (and sometimes meat and dairy products) directly from a farm. Farms that offer CSAs typically meet organic growing standards, and express concern for the environment, the local food system, and the local economy (DeMuth 1993). These values and concerns are communicated through the marketing materials of the CSA, so that consumers are able to assess the level of values congruence (Posner and Schmidt 1993) between themselves and the CSA.

For many CSA members, buying food is not a low involvement purchase. Many of these consumers want to know where their food comes from, the growing practices that are used, their food production's carbon footprint, and information about how farm workers are treated, values that are shared with CSAs. These concerns are often phrased in terms of risks that consumers are taking for themselves, their families, communities, and planet earth. The desire to manage these perceived risks, coupled with the lack of trust in the industrial agricultural system, and emergent beliefs that this system imposes sub-optimal outcomes on them, have led some consumers to seek out alternative purchasing opportunities (Thompson 2005). These consumers recognize their desires as well as their efficacy in the market system and seek out, find, and/or create purchasing opportunities that suit their needs.

CSA members balance risks by trading those they feel they cannot monitor for risks that are more manageable or at least closer to home. For example, when choosing to buy produce from a CSA rather than a grocery store, they trade uncertainty about how the produce was grown, and where it really came from, for the uncertainty that the weather in their region will be good enough during the growing season so that the farmer can actually grow produce to give to them. Other CSA members may choose to pay for the "hidden costs" of their food rather than live with the lack of information about how much petroleum has been used in the growing and transport of their produce (environmental concerns). By engaging in these activities to manage and control risk, consumers take a proactive and participatory role in creating a marketplace that fits their needs. They show themselves as able to leave the dominant social paradigm for an alternative that is a better fit for their needs and their personal values, and they show that they are able to participate in transformative activities on their own, outside the mainstream marketplace. CSAs are participatory market structures insofar as they are highly responsive to consumer concerns, and in turn, use their consumers as drivers of CSA marketing materials.

The value of the product purchased from the CSA goes beyond the produce itself, to include the emotional properties ("feel good" effects), the fit with their personal values (value congruence, see (Kalliath et al. 1999)), and the linking value of the product (Cova 1997) that joins the consumers with each other, and with their broader communities. The CSA is then positioned as an organization that fulfills a variety of needs for the consumer, from minimizing risk, to reinforcing personal values, to being a connection through which the consumer can participate in the immediate community. At no point do these consumers give up their efficacy for getting what they want from the marketplace. In fact, through their experiences with the CSA community, consumers find even more opportunities to engage in alternative purchasing behavior.

Interviews with 35 CSA members illustrate how these consumers use this alternative market mechanism, and what they gain from it. These consumers do not accept that their only option for food purchasing is their local grocery store, or even that the best option is the organic selection available at the grocery store. Rather, they have joined a grass-roots subculture, built on co-creation between producers (farmers) and consumers (CSA members). CSA members have opportunities to go to the farm and see the actual place where their food comes from, which allows them to assess the "hidden costs" of their food, as well as to learn about growing practices the farm uses. These consumers also take home extremely fresh produce (often harvested less that 24 hours before they receive it), which they highly value for perceived taste differences, improved storage quality, and the belief that the food is not only good for them, but also helps keep money in their local economy and is good for the planet.

Unlike traditional views of values and value congruence, values in CSAs are not static systems (Schwartz and Bilsky 1987). CSA members demonstrate an iterative evolution in their personal values, and in the importance they place on the products they receive from the CSA and the market structure. By going outside of the mainstream market and purchasing produce from farmers who they know, from a farm they can actually visit, CSA members assuage several of the risks that come with mass-produce food (Rampton and Stauber 2001). What is perhaps most interesting, though, is the personal transformations that CSA members experience, which seem to be strongly influenced by the co-creative process of the community, coupled with the evolution of values. These changes include differences in eating habits, thinking about food and health, preparation of food, the way food is consumed (i.e. with other people vs. alone), and the role of food preparation and meals in the household.

Community Supported Agriculture (CSA) is just one example of ways in which consumers can change the marketplace by choosing not to be involved in typical options. Through this assertion of their needs, consumers drive change, and create new market opportunities that better address their concerns about the products they are buying. CSAs provide us with an opportunity to enrich our understanding of the role of the consumer in TCR.

"Rising from the Wreckage: Personal Responsibility vs. Social Welfare in Tornado Recovery"

Stacey Menzel Baker, University of Wyoming, USA
Ronald Paul Hill, Villanova University, USA
David M. Hunt, University of Wyoming, USA

This paper explores the competing consumption ideologies of personal responsibility and social welfare and shows how these constructs are not on opposite ends of a continuum, but instead are multi-faceted and domain specific. This theoretical argument extends beyond the specific empirical context we explore here, namely rural community recovery after a disaster, to show how conflict over consumption ideologies is a necessary condition for community recovery.

In August of 2005, a tornado hit a rural community (pop. ~1500) in the Mountain West. Two people died, 25 percent of the population was left homeless, and the disaster was declared a state and national emergency. Focus group and depth interview data gathered from January through November 2006 serve as the primary data for analysis, while newspaper accounts and other written materials since the time of the tornado are used to illuminate the context. Our discovery-oriented approach was guided by a desire to employ and extend theory (Wells 1993) and by a desire to improve human welfare (Ger 1997; Murray and Ozanne 1991). The theory developed here illuminates competing consumption ideologies and describes how the nature of a market mediates the disaster recovery process.

Data show that residents of this community did not just passively accept external mandates and consumption constraints; instead, they actively and constructively resisted the domination of (1) the tornado and (2) the disaster relief procedures, often referred to as the second disaster (Myers 2008). Guiding residents' grassroots recovery efforts were two competing consumption ideologies. A consumption ideology is a system of meaning reflected in attitudes and behaviors that aim to maintain the interests of dominate groups in society (Hirschman 1993). To understand the competing ideologies, we must first understand the form and content of each ideology and then see how these ideas are reflected in the actions guiding recovery efforts. In this situation, competing ideologies were evident in (1) specific consumption behaviors that helped move people toward a changed state of existence, (2) conscious decisions to deviate from the expected (e.g., breaking rules set by FEMA), and (3) in the rhetoric of the conflict between the victims and policy-setting groups in the community.

The central assumption of the ideology of personal responsibility is that individuals should take care of their own problems, or "Cowboy Up" as locals would say. This ideology was reflected in the rhetoric and actions witnessed during the recovery process: a quick clean up conducted almost entirely by resources available within the community; beliefs about whether people should have had or should now have insurance; taking storm spotting classes to empower one's self to spot tornados; and so forth.

The ideology of social welfare is to take care of your neighbor and those less fortunate, as reflected when the locals say, "we may be out here in the middle of nowhere, but we're out in the middle of nowhere together." In tornado recovery , this ideology was reflected in perceptions that those who were more victimized (less fortunate) needed more care and illustrated when community members came together to account for victims; help reunite families with their belongings; help sort valuable from valueless objects; dispose of rubbish; donate goods; volunteer time; etc.

Consumption ideologies address problems of identity construction and reconstruction and guide decisions on how to resolve conflicts (Arnould and Thompson 2005). In this community, solutions to problems about identity reconstruction at both the individual and community level and about conflict between victims and policy makers were developed at the grassroots level, which is consistent with FEMA's guiding principle that disasters are local. To understand how solutions evolved and how competing ideologies were operationalized, it is important to understand the nature of the market in Wright. Wright is a relatively isolated community with limited services including one general contractor and one grocery store. Wright residents were already in the habit of going elsewhere to have their consumption needs met. In addition, most community members are employed in mining and ranching and possess the skills and equipment common to those industries (e.g., disaster training, heavy equipment such as tractors and dump trucks). In other words, Wright has a mobile population with mobile resources. The nature of the market in Wright mediates the lifestyles of the 'hunters and gatherers' who reside there. In some ways, these market conditions facilitated recovery because people were not dependent on the market to provide their necessities. In other ways, these market conditions mandating independence detracted from recovery, as people thought they should be able to take care of themselves, which is difficult when one is in a fog and has limited resources (85% of victims were uninsured).

When one compares this community's experience to what we know about recovery in larger communities, we can understand why recovery is so difficult. For example, Hurricane Katrina hit New Orleans two weeks after this tornado struck. Though people in this community are relatively recovered, at least from a market and consumption stand point, residents in New Orleans appear to continue to struggle. People are still undecided about purchasing or leaving FEMA trailers, etc. The difference in recovery is in part explained by the nature of the market. In New Orleans, people were totally dependent on the market to provide for their needs; whereas in this community, residents were used to employing market resources as inputs to the process of fending for themselves. Thus, from a theoretical standpoint, not only does the market mediate the lifestyle, it mediates the ideologies underlying that lifestyle and the way in which individual and community identity construction and reconstruction occurs.

"Social Strain as an Antecedent of Innovativeness among Subsistence Consumers"

Stephanie Geiger-Oneto, University of Wyoming, USA
Jose Antonio Rosa, University of Wyoming, USA

Transformative consumption and innovativeness are virtually inseparable. That is to say, consumers involved in transformative consumption creatively extract meaning and benefit from products or services and transform both themselves and the product in the process. We can consequently think of transformative consumption as depending on 1) consumers recombining past knowledge and experience into novel arrays and 2) on those arrays producing valued outcomes, i.e., on consumers being innovative (e.g., Amabile 1996). Moreover, transformative consumption and innovativeness do not have to be discontinuous and occur more frequently than most people imagine. To recognize the ubiquity of transformative consumption we need look no further than the behaviors of consumers in resource constrained environments, noting how they create beneficial artifacts from what others discard, and transform their lives through the process.

Inquiry into consumer innovativeness has a long history in consumer research (e.g., Hirschman 1980, Ram and Jung 1989 and 1994, Price and Ridgway 1983, Ridgway and Price 1994, Burroughs and Mick 2004, Moreau and Dahl 1995), and has given us valuable insight into the process and its antecedents and consequences. Recurring themes are that innovativeness is draining and risky. Consumer innovativeness involves taking products and services beyond the uses for which they were engineered. In addition, consumers that engage in the innovative redefinition of artifacts work outside their domains of expertise, and learn about the possibilities and boundaries of their novel arrays through experimentation. All innovative consumers engage in such risky concerted efforts; and in the case of resource constrained consumers the risks may be more pronounced. Driven by survival needs and resources constraints, many poor consumers engage in creative endeavors daily. Moreover, they often place a higher proportion of their limited resources at risk in innovative experiments than more affluent consumers.

In order to gain a better understanding of innovativeness among subsistence consumers, we conducted exploratory ethnographic studies in several countries, in both rural and urban contexts. Participants were first asked to identify members of their communities who they felt engaged in innovative behaviors. Once identified, we interviewed those considered to be innovative and documented both their creations and their development process. We also inquired into what inspired them, what they sought to accomplish, and the general history surrounding their innovations. We learned much about the trial and error process by which they develop products to sell in the marketplace and services to augment their products, and how they persist in innovative behaviors to sustain or improve their businesses. We also learned much about their feelings, triumphs, disappointments, and aspirations.

One lens through which to view the innovativeness of subsistence consumers is Agnew's General Strain Theory (1992). The theory argues that consumers who engage in innovative behavior do so to cope with negative emotions caused by social inequality and disappointment or frustration with their own social position. Although individuals may experience many types of strain (i.e. economic, environmental, and emotional) during the course of their lives, innovative behavior is more likely to observed from individuals who believe their current undesirable state is due to circumstances beyond their control. For example, subsistence consumers who adopt specific goals (i.e. financial stability, education for children) may resort to innovative behaviors that push existing technologies in new directions because they see themselves as having no other options (Agnew 1992). They work around the system because they believe the system will not provide them with opportunities to advance their social status. In modern societies, moreover, the strain can be exacerbated if consumers are exposed to media images that suggest the consumption of certain products will lead to more idyllic lifestyle. A gap between the culturally-induced aspirations of the poor and their opportunities for achieving them forces innovative subsistence consumers to develop their own methods of obtaining or approximating (through do-it-yourself concoctions) the branded consumer goods shown in the media. Unfortunately, they often do so without awareness of the dangers of product misuse or abuse, or the toxicity of the ingredients used to create the goods.

At the level of the individual level, we find that engaging in addition to the transformations that innovativeness in consumption can entail, innovative behaviors can provide relief from negative affect such as status frustration. According to Agnew (1992), consumers experience status frustration when they recognize a gap between status expectations and actual achievement, and the frustration (negative affect) triggers pressure for corrective action as an avoidance mechanism. The pressure can in fact be a stronger motivator for consumer innovativeness than their desire for transformative outcomes. One informant, for example, compromised his successful all-purpose cleaner business by experimenting with and distributing a "new" recipe to customers who favored the old one. When asked why he experimented in this manner the response was "just in case this one works better, despite the fact that his new innovation led to a loss of customer loyalty, and ultimately impacted his family's income and well-being.." It seems plausible that the process by which his innovations were created provided him with a release from status frustration that was more valuable than the product itself. More than one of the subsistence consumers we encountered engaged in similar behavior, and we continue to distill the factors that influence whether or not innovative behavior as a coping strategy can become dysfunctional.

At a macro level we also find that not all instances of transformative consumption and innovativeness are positive, in part because the innovation process among poor consumers is inextricably social. Most poor consumers engage in innovation to benefit their families directly or to create transformative experiences they can sell to others, and the boundaries between being a producer and a consumer are fuzzy. To improve their creations, innovators rely on a continuous flow of conversation with customers. These conversations may be used to discuss existing products, possible new products, or to generate transformative problem solutions. One unfortunate consequence of this informal process is that experimentation with existing products is seldom conducted in controlled environments and therefore lacks the necessary safeguards. Suggestions arising from conversations are quickly tested but seldom documented, and the outcomes are better remembered than the process that yields them. In addition, when new product concepts prove to be ineffective or harmful, it is those closest to the innovator who may pay the price because they are often the guinea pigs used to test them. Moreover, the disposal of experiments gone awry is often done with the same abandon as the experimentation, contaminating their home environments and those of neighbors and further eroding the subsistence consumers' already fragile health.

REFERENCES

Agnew, Robert (1992), "Foundation for a General Strain Theory of Crime and Delinquency," *Criminology*, 30, 47-88.

Amabile, Theresa (1996), *Creativity in Context*, Boulder, CO: Westview.

Arnould, Eric J. and Craig J. Thompson (2005), "Consumer Culture Theory (CCT): Twenty Years of Research," *Journal of Consumer Research*, 31 (March), 868-882.

Barsalou, Lawrence W. (1999) "Perceptual Symbol Systems," *Behavioral and Brain Sciences*, 22, 577-660.

Beck, Ulrich (1992), *Risk Society*, Thousand Oaks: Sage.

Bekin, Caroline, Marylyn Carrigan and Isabelle Szmigin (2005), "Defying marketing sovereignty: voluntary simplicity at new consumption communities," *Qualitative Market Research* 8 (4), 413-429.

Burroughs, James R. and David Glen Mick (2004), "Exploring Antecedents and Consequences of Consumer Creativity in a Problem Solving Context," *Journal of Consumer Research*, 31 (2), 402-411.

Cova, Bernard (1997), "Community and Consumption: Towards a Definition of the "Linking Value" of Product or Services," *European Journal of Marketing*, 31 (3/4), 297-316.

Craig-Lees, M. and Hill, C. (2002), "Understanding Voluntary Simplifiers," *Psychology & Marketing* 19 (2), 187-210.

deMello, Gustavo E. and Deborah J. MacInnis (2005), "How and Why Consumers Hope: Motivated Reasoning and the Marketplace, " in S. Ratneshwar, and D. Mick (eds.), *Inside Consumption: Consumer Motives, Goals, and Desires*, New York: Routledge, 44-66.

DeMuth, Suzanne (1993), *Community Supported Agriculture (CSA): An Annotated Bibliography and Resource Guide*: USDA, National Agriculture Library.

Gentner, Dedre, and Arthur B. Markman (1997), "Structure Mapping in Analogy and Similarity," *American Psychologist*, 52 (1), 45-56.

Ger, Guliz (1997), "Human Development and Humane Consumption: Well-being beyond the 'good life'," *Journal of Public Policy & Marketing*, 16 (Spring), 110-125.

Hirschman, Elizabeth C. (1980), "Innovativeness, Novelty Seeking, and Consumer Creativity," *Journal of Consumer Research*, 7 (3), 283-295.

Hirschman, Elizabeth C. (1993), "Ideology in Consumer Research, 1980 and 1990: A Marxist and Feminist Critique," *Journal of Consumer Research*, 19 (March), 537-555.

Jenkins, Henry (2006), *Convergence Culture: Where Old and New Media Collide*, New York: New York University Press.

Kalliath, Thomas J., Allen C. Bluedorn, and Michael J. Strube (1999), "A Test of Values Congruence Effects," *Journal of Organizational Behavior*, 20 (7), 1175-98.

Lakoff, George (1987) *Women, Fire, and Dangerous Things*, Chicago: University of Chicago Press.

Lazarus, Richard (1999), "Hope: An Emotion and a Vital Coping Resource Against Despair," *Social Research*, 66, 653-660.

Lévy, Pierre (1997), *Collective Intelligence: Mankind's Emerging World in Cyberspace*, Cambridge: Perseus Books.

Manzini, Ezio, François Jégou and Lara Penin (2008), "Creative Communities for Sustainable Lifestyles," *Proceedings Refereed Sessions I-II, Sustainable Consumption and Production: Framework for Action, Conference of the Sustainable Consumption Research Exchange (SCORE!) Network*, 10-11 March 2008, Halles des Tanneurs, Brussels, Belgium, 259-276.

Merton, Robert K. (1938/1996), "Social Structure and Anomie," in D. H. Kelly (ed.), *Deviant Behavior*, 5th edition, New York: St. Martin's Press, 117-127.

Mick, David Glen (2006), "Presidential Address: Meaning and Mattering Through Transformative Consumer Research", in *Advances in Consumer Research*, Volume 33, eds. Cornelia Pechmann and Linda L. Price, Duluth, MN : Association for Consumer Research, 1-4

Mont, Oksana (2008), "In Search of Sustainable lifestyles: An Antithesis to Economic Growth," *Proceedings Refereed Sessions I-II, Sustainable Consumption and Production: Framework for Action, Conference of the Sustainable Consumption Research Exchange (SCORE!) Network*, 10-11 March 2008, Halles des Tanneurs, Brussels, Belgium, 245-256.

Moreau, C. Page and Darren W. Dahl (2005), "Designing the Solution: The Impact of Constraints on Consumers' Creativity," *Journal of Consumer Research*, 32 (1), 13-22.

Murray, Jeff B. and Julie L. Ozanne (1991), "The Critical Imagination: Emancipatory Interests in Consumer Research," *Journal of Consumer Research*, 18 (2), 129-144.

Myers, Diane (1994), *Disaster Response and Recovery: A Handbook for Mental Health Professionals*, U.S. Department of Health and Human Services.

Newall, Allen and Herbert A. Simon (1972), *Human Problem Solving*, Englewood Cliffs, NJ: Prentice-Hall.

Ottman, Jacquelyn (1995), "Today's consumers turning lean and green," *Marketing News*, 29 (23, Nov 6, 1995), 12; 14.

Ozanne, Julie L. and Bige Saatcioglu (2008), "Participatory Action Research," *Journal of Consumer Research*, October, in press.

Ozanne, Julie L. and Susan Dobscha (2006), "Transformative Consumer Culture Theory?" *Advances in Consumer Research*, 33 eds. Cornelia Pechmann and Linda L. Price, Association for Consumer Research, 520-522.

Posner, Barry Z. and Warren H. Schmidt (1993), "Values Congruence and Differences Between the Interplay of Personal and Organizational Value Systems," *Journal of Business Ethics*, 12, 341-47.

Price, Linda L. and Nancy M. Ridgway (1983) "Development of a Scale to Measure Use Innovativeness," in R. P. Bagozzi and A. Tybout (eds.), *Advances in Consumer Research*, 10, Provo, UT: Association for Consumer Research, 679-684.

Ram, S and Hyung-Shik Jung (1989), "The Link Between Involvement, Use Innovativeness, and Product Usage," in T. K. Srull (ed.) *Advances in Consumer Research*, 16, 160-166.

Ram, S. and Hyung-Shik Jung (1994), "Innovativeness in Product Usage: A Comparison of Early Adopters and Early Majority," *Psychology and Marketing*, 11(1), 57-67.

Rampton, Sheldon and John Stauber (2001), *Trust Us, We're Experts!: How Industry Manipulates and Gambles with Your Future*, New York: Tarcher/Putmnam.

Ridgway, Nancy M. and Linda L. Price (1994), "Exploration in Product Usage: A Model of Use Innovativeness," *Psychology & Marketing*, 11(1), 69-84.

Schor, Juliet B. (1998), *The Overspent American: Upscaling, Downshifting, And The New Consumer*, New York: Basic Books.

Schwartz, Shalom H. and Wolfgang Bilsky (1987), "Toward a Universal Psychological Structure of Human Values," *Journal of Personality and Social Psychology*, 53 (3), 550-62.

Thompson, Craig J. (2005), "Consumer Risk Perceptions in a Community of Reflexive Doubt," *Journal of Consumer Research*, 32 (September), 235-48.

Thompson, Craig and Gokcen Coskuner-Balli (2007), "Countervailing Market Responses to Corporate Co-optation and the Ideological Recruitment of Consumption Communities," *Journal of Consumer Research*, 34 (August), 135-152.

Viswanathan, Madhubalan, José Antonio Rosa, and James Harris, (2005) "Decision Making and Coping by Functionally Illiterate Consumers and Some Implications for Marketing Management," *Journal of Marketing*, 69 (1), 15-31.

Wells, William D. (1993), "Discovery-oriented Consumer Research," *Journal of Consumer Research*, 19 (4), 489-504.

Young Foundation (2006), *Social Silicon Valleys. A Manifesto for Social Innovation*, London: Young Foundation.

Consumer Perceptions of Value and Price

Leif D. Nelson, University of California, San Diego, USA

SESSION OVERVIEW

There is a (deeply hypothetical) world in which the link between price and value is simple and intuitive. In this world, marketers set prices that reflect some combination of the amount of money they need and the amount the customer is willing to pay. Customers look at a product on the shelf, decide how much they want it (in currency), and if the price is below that level, they decide to buy. Consumer research has suggested that this simple and intuitive world is a mediocre proxy for its complex and confusing reality. This symposium presents four papers investigating the relationship between value and price in an effort to further the understanding of how these factors play into the perceptions of consumers.

In a hypothetical pricing world, people first evaluate a product and then ponder that value in relation to its price. In reality, the price can influence evaluation. Numerous studies have found that increased prices increase evaluations. The first paper (Gneezy, Carmon, and Nelson) shows that even this peculiar finding is more complicated than it seems. When prices are raised to particularly high levels, they find, perceptions of quality are reduced. A cookie that was tasty at one price is spontaneously a lot less palatable at a higher price.

Intuitively, fees should reduce consumption. The second paper (Lee and Norton) challenges this assumption, by showing that fees can increase consumption. The authors consider the influence of membership fees and find a surprising result: fees increase subsequent spending. People assume that fee-requiring stores must offer low prices and so go on to buy with the belief that they are finding great deals. Paying for the privilege to shop may seem like a deterrent to customers, but the company that charges such a fee may benefit not only from revenue from membership, but also from increased sales.

If nothing else, marketers should have some mastery of consumer price sensitivity. The third paper (Hsee and Shen) suggests that this is not true either. Marketers, because they are jointly evaluating multiple price possibilities, generate fundamentally different prices than their separately evaluating customers. Joint evaluation necessarily leads to extreme price sensitivity, whereas separate evaluation (in the absence of more knowledge of price distributions) should lead to general price insensitivity. For new and unfamiliar products, marketers tend to set prices too low.

Perhaps the most well know pricing peculiarity is the *endowment effect,* in which randomly assigned ownership produces systematically higher selling prices. Classically, this has been interpreted as consistent with loss aversion and prospect theory. The fourth paper (Weaver and Frederick) offers a new account. Consumers compare trades to market prices (which typically exceed consumer value), and increase their reservation prices to a point where they think they would be getting a good deal.

These four papers take very different approach to a related problem, so we are lucky to have an expert on the dynamics of pricing and value as our discussant. Dan Ariely is an expert in experimental psychology and consumer research, and has authored numerous articles on related topics, and recently published a best-selling book about some related research.

EXTENDED ABSTRACTS

"Getting Less Than You Pay For: Very High Prices Lead to Inferences of Very Low Quality"

Ayelet Gneezy, University of California, San Diego, USA
Ziv Carmon, INSEAD, Singapore
Leif D. Nelson, University of California, San Diego, USA

Consumers often lack the time, training, or inclination to judge the actual quality of a product or service. Accordingly, to infer quality they seek simpler alternative signals (cf. Aaker 1991) like the product's country of origin, how heavily it was promoted, or its price (Huber and McCann 1982; Rao and Monroe 1989). As a result, considerable evidence demonstrates that higher priced products are judged to be higher quality (see e.g., Gerstner 1985; Riesz 1979). One step further, price and brand name, for example, can influence actual consumption experience (e.g., Allison and Uhl 1964; Levin and Gaeth 1988). Finally, prices have been shown to produce placebo effects, as products identified as price-reduced are less effective than products identified as full price (e.g., Shiv, Carmon, and Ariely 2005; Waber, Shiv, Carmon, and Ariely 2008).

Do higher prices always lead to inferences of higher quality? In this paper, we illustrate that truly high prices actually reduce perceived quality. In a pilot study, three groups of participants were given an unfamiliar cookie to taste and rate. To create a slightly negative experience for participants we served cookies that we had strategically allowed to become stale in the week prior to the experience. Participants were informed that the cookies were now being sold on the market, and were told one of three possible prices (low, medium high). Replicating past research, the moderately priced cookie was judged to be tastier than the lower priced cookie. But most notably, participants tasting the high-priced cookie judged it to be *lower* quality than participants in either of the other conditions.

In our next study (Study 1) we wanted to see if variation in actual product quality moderated this effect. We employed the same three price levels as in the pilot, but this time we presented only approximately half of the participants with a stale cookie whereas the remainder received a cookie taken from a freshly open package. Replicating the pilot results, when participants tasted a stale cookie a moderate priced cookie was judged more favorably than a low priced cookie, but the high priced cookie was judged more negatively than both. For the comparatively tasty cookies, there was a linear relationship between price and inferred quality: moderate priced cookies tasted better than low priced cookies, and high priced cookies tasted better than both. When prices are vaguely in line with actual quality we found a standard price-quality link, but when prices were more obviously out of line, the price-quality link was reversed.

Perhaps consumers are merely drawing on an unusual theory of the relationship between price and quality? If so, then people should predict the above results regardless of actual consumption. A follow up study (Study 2) then distinguished between two possible causes of the effect: (1) judgments of the quality of the high priced product as lower than that of the moderately priced product, reflect lower quality expectations; (2) an alternative cause could be that these judgments reflected contrast between expectations and the consumption experience. Our results support the latter cause—

high priced cookies were assessed as being of significantly higher quality.

Finally, we sought to investigate how higher prices influence perceived quality (Study 3). Lee and his colleagues (Lee et al. 2007) have argued that information can operate on experience only if it is presented prior to consumption. With that in mind we replicated the moderate and high priced conditions from the previous study, while manipulating whether price information was presented prior to consumption or after consumption (but before reporting a quality measure). If the earlier findings are due to an explicit rescaling effect or a recasting of quality relative to expectation, then the manipulation should have no effect. If, on the other hand, high prices fundamentally change the experienced flavor of the product as we predict, then we should only replicate our effects when the price is presented before consumption. We found strong support for the latter: if people were told the price before tasting, the expensive cookie tasted much worse than the moderately priced cookie, but when told the price afterwards this effect was entirely eliminated.

Significantly, within the same experiment, participants sampled two much more familiar product categories (water and tissue paper). We predicted that product novelty would be crucial to our effects, but though much smaller in magnitude, the effects persisted for these product categories as well. Perhaps even the consumption of well known products can be enhanced or undermined by mere price perception.

"The "Fees → Savings" Link, or Purchasing Fifty Pounds of Pasta"

Leonard Lee, Columbia University, USA
Michael I. Norton, Harvard University, USA

Discount membership clubs have a large and growing presence in retail–one recent survey reported that Costco sells to 1 in every 11 people in the United States and Canada, and warehouse clubs are estimated to be a $120 billion industry today in the United States alone. As a result, more and more people have had the experience of entering one of these popular clubs and leaving hours later with more goods than can fit in their car and enough pasta to outlast a nuclear winter; at minimum–as is the case with at least one of the authors–many are familiar with a family member who engages in this kind of behavior.

One rational reason for such behavior is that membership clubs offer lower prices (due to volume discounts and lower overhead), but we suggest that the presence of membership fees alone–independent of the actual savings on any given product–spurs this increased spending, due to perceptions of "good prices." What might account for this generalized belief in the savings offered by discount clubs? We suggest that membership fees required for the consumption of a brand or service signal dominance on the dimension most salient to the particular brand or service: for country clubs, higher fees might signal greater exclusivity; for health clubs or healthcare plans, fees may signal higher service quality; for discount stores such as Costco or Sam's Club, where the most salient dimension is cost savings, fees may signal greater price discounts. The presence of fees at membership stores thus may instantiate an implicit norm with consumers (see Grice 1975): "We wouldn't charge you this fee if we weren't making it worth your while," leading consumers to infer a "fees → savings" link.

In a series of studies, we created our own membership clubs and sold goods to participants in our stores. Some participants were allowed to purchase whatever they liked; other participants, however, were informed that the store charged a fee, which they were required to pay before making a purchase. We show that 1) the presence of fees increases spending and overall store profitability

(despite people's predictions to the contrary); 2) fees serve as a signal of price, such that stores that charge fees are perceived as offering better deals.

In addition, another study showed that the mere presence of fees may drive choice of retail outlets: when we presented participants with newspaper advertisements for stores that mentioned membership fees, such stores were preferred to stores which did not mention fees–even when both stores offered similar goods at similar prices. Finally, we explore the impact of fees on memory: several field studies show that reminding people of membership fees paid in the past (for health insurance and gym memberships) lead them to remember having used those services more. In sum, fees lead retailers to make more money both on increased sales and, ironically, on collecting the fees that cause these increased sales, and also lead customers to see themselves as more frequent users of that outlet, a potentially important precursor to customer loyalty.

Our results seem to suggest that consumers behave irrationally in response to membership fees, attributing low prices to the perceived savings offered by retailers that charge fees, and then trying to capitalize on these seeming savings by buying more than they otherwise would. At the same time, however, the feeling of getting a good deal–whether erroneous or not–likely has positive (transaction) utility for these consumers (Thaler 1985), which would only be increased the more items placed in one's shopping cart. In addition, this transaction utility gained from perceived savings is unlikely to be offset by regret upon encountering a better deal, given the difficulty of comparing prices at other retailers. Although some utility may be offset by the vocal displeasure of the shopper's loved ones when forced to lug groceries into the house for 30 minutes, consumers may on average come out ahead despite their overgeneralized perception of the link between fees and savings.

"Marketers Mispredict Price Elasticity"

Christopher Hsee, University of Chicago, USA
Luxi Shen, Fundan University, China

Price elasticity is a key concept in economics and marketing. It reflects how consumers' demand for a good varies as the price of the good varies, and thus reflects consumers' sensitivity to price variation. What determines price sensitivity? Can marketers accurately predict consumers' price sensitivity?

We propose that an important determinant of consumers' price sensitivity toward a good or service is their familiarity with the distribution information (including reference, range, etc) of the price of the given good or service. Consumers are more price sensitive when they have more price information (e.g., the price of a can of Coke) than when they have less (e.g., the price of a newly-introduced soft drink).

Marketers know much more about price distributions than do ordinary customers, and for this reason systematically overestimate consumer price sensitivity. Specifically, marketers, when pricing a product, must jointly evaluate (JE) alternative possible prices by juxtaposing those possibilities. However, consumers, when deciding whether to purchase a product, are usually confined in the single evaluation mode (SE) in which they only see the finally offered price. Consumers know much less about price ranges than do the marketers who set the price.

This mismatch in evaluation mode should lead marketers to overestimate consumers' price sensitivity with unfamiliar products, and as a result, should lead them to systematically underpricing their products or services.

Our research is important for at least four reasons: First, it addresses a fundamental issue in economics and marketing: price elasticity or price sensitivity. Second, this is the first research showing that the mismatch in evaluation mode between marketers and consumers would not only lead marketers to mispredict consumers' price sensitivity, but also leads to reduced profit. Third, we identify that product familiarity serves as a crucial moderator of this mismatch. Finally, we show that the effects we described above occur not only when marketers are 'placed' in the JE mode (that is, they are shown alternative prices), but also when marketers are naturally in the JE mode (that is, they are simply asked to set the price for the target good). We assume that to set a price, marketers would naturally consider alternative prices and naturally found themselves in the JE mode.

We tested our ideas in six studies involving different contexts (ranging from taxi ride, coffee beans, puzzles, etc.), different dependent variables (willingness to pay, and purchase intention), and involving both hypothetical scenarios and real purchasing behavior.

In one study, for example, some participants assumed the role of marketers and some assumed the role of consumers. The marketers either set the price of a taxi ride (familiar) or of a horse ride (unfamiliar). Consumers were resented with these prices and asked whether they would purchase the service at that price. As predicted, marketers overestimated consumers' price sensitivity and therefore underpriced the horse ride but not the taxi ride.

In another study, the target product was a set of psychological tests. As in the horse-ride/taxi study, we also asked some research participants to assume the role of marketers and to make a price decision on the tests, and asked other participants to assume the role of consumers and to make a purchase decision regarding the tests. For half of the marketers and consumers (the familiar condition), there was a reference price for the target product for both marketers and consumers; for the other half participants (the unfamiliar condition), there was no reference price to either marketers or consumers. Unlike the horse-ride/taxi study, this study involved real consequences to both the marketers and the consumers, that is, marketers could earn profit by selling the tests and consumers had to pay to get the tests. Again, the study confirmed our predictions: In the price-unfamiliar condition but in the price-familiar condition, marketers overestimated consumers' price sensitivity, set too low a price, and consequently made less profit than they otherwise could had if they had set a higher price.

This research has both theoretical implications for what influences price elasticity, and prescriptive implications for how to improve profitability by improving marketing prediction accuracy.

"Transaction Disutility and the Endowment Effect"

Ray Weaver, Harvard University, USA
Shane Frederick, Massachusetts Institute of Technology, USA

Buying and selling are different expressions of the value one places on a good, with money as the medium for this expression. Accordingly, the minimum amount an owner requires to relinquish an item should correspond closely to the amount a non-owner is willing to pay for it. In fact, however, this presumption is often violated: in a review of 59 studies involving market goods, Horowitz and McConnell (2002) found that minimum selling prices exceeded maximum buying prices by a factor of nearly three. This *endowment effect* is commonly attributed to loss aversion (Thaler, 1980): people are assumed to compare potential trades to the status quo, and to feel losses from their current holdings more keenly than gains. According to this model, selling prices exceed buying prices because owners charge a premium to offset the psychological pain they expect to feel when they give up possessions.

We propose an alternative explanation: the endowment effect is caused not by the anticipated pain of losing possessions, but by

a reluctance to trade on terms that are perceived to be disadvantageous or unfair — an experience Thaler (1985) calls *transaction disutility*. Stated maximum buying or minimum selling prices are based on the value consumers expect to get from ownership, but can be influenced by concerns about making "bad" deals. Consumers judge potential deals against some reference price (r), and experience transaction disutility whenever trading at their valuation would be unfavorable with respect to that price. That is, non-owners dislike stating reservation prices that are greater than r, and owners dislike stating reservation prices that are less than the r. In this way, transaction disutility tends to distort buying prices downward and selling prices upward, away from underlying values.

The degree of transaction disutility depends on the relationship between a consumer's valuation and r, and therefore may affect buyers and sellers asymmetrically. Suppose, for example, that valuations for a coffee mug vary uniformly between zero and ten dollars. If the mug's reference price is eight dollars, transaction disutility will have a large influence on potential sellers because for most people, selling at their valuations would be a bad deal. Conversely, it will have little effect on potential buyers, most of whom could pay their valuations without making a bad deal.

Reference prices are usually based on market prices, which typically exceed the value most consumers place on products: consumers turn down the opportunity to buy most goods in the marketplace. Supermarkets, for example, carry tens of thousands of items, but each shopper buys at most a few dozen on a given trip and repeatedly declines to purchase almost everything else in the store. Like the pain-of-losing account, our account of evaluation disparities implicates sellers rather than buyers. That is, we argue that buying prices closely mirror underlying valuations, whereas selling prices significantly exceed them. In contrast to the pain-of-losing explanation, however, we attribute this to the incidental fact that reference prices are generally high, rather than to a fundamentally different consideration on the part of sellers, namely an aversion to parting with possessions.

In four experiments, we test our model. Study 1 shows that reducing r from a high (typical) level to a more moderate level alleviates sellers' transaction disutility, shrinking the endowment effect. Consumers were assigned to the role of either buyer, then asked the maximum they would pay for a box of "movie theater" candy; or given a box of candy and assigned to the role of seller, then asked the minimum they would demand to sell it. The ratio of selling prices to buying prices was greater among subjects who were suggested a high r ("the Harvard Square Theater sells this candy for $4.00") than among those given a moderate r ("Target sells this candy for $1.49").

Our model predicts that very low values of r (i.e. below most consumers' underlying valuations) will induce transaction disutility in *buyers*, causing a disparity driven by a reluctance to buy, not to sell. Study 2 confirms this prediction. Consumers were randomly assigned to the role of either buyer or seller, shown a picture of a 1925 buffalo nickel, and told, "A randomly chosen person who took this survey before you would [pay at most] [sell for as little as] x," where x varied from $0 to $20. Consistent with our model, we found that the magnitude of the endowment effect was a U-shaped function of r. When r was low, the gap was large because of deflated buying prices; when r was moderate, the gap was small because neither buying nor selling prices were severely distorted; and when r was high, the gap was again large, this time because of inflated selling prices.

In Study 3, we show that internally-generated r's function similarly as externally-provided ones. We asked consumers for maximum buying or minimum selling prices for two domestic airline tickets. We then asked them to estimate the market price of those tickets. Among people who estimated a high market price, the endowment effect was substantial. But there was no endowment effect among people whose market price estimates were similar to their valuations.

The pain-of-losing account of the endowment effect suggests that owners who value a good most highly will anticipate the most psychological pain from its loss, and therefore that the gap between buyers and sellers will be largest among these "fans." Our transaction disutility model, however, predicts the opposite: given a relatively high r, selling prices will be similarly inflated among both fans and non-fans. But buying prices, which more closely reflect underlying values, will be higher for fans. Study 4 confirms our account. We categorized people as video game fans or non-fans according to how often they play and whether they own home video game systems. For a Nintendo Wii system, the endowment effect was larger for fans than for non-fans.

Our experimental evidence supports our hypothesis that an aversion to bad deals, not an aversion to losing possessions per se, causes buying and selling prices to diverge. The results also suggest that marketing efforts designed to make favorable reference prices salient will be more effective than those that try to instill a sense of ownership in potential customers.

Positive Emotions–Theory and Application

Michal Herzenstein, University of Delaware, USA

SESSION OVERVIEW

Positive emotions have been gaining more empirical attention in the last decade. The objective of this symposium is to examine the theory and application of the effects positive emotions, both specific and general, have on a range of contexts, such as motivation, choice, assessment, and risk propensity. The research presented contributes to the emotions and decision making literature by examining new effects of important specific emotions, investigating the influence of the source of the emotion on choice, and investigating applications in health care.

The first paper shows that specific positive emotions, joy and contentment, lead to different outcomes: individuals who experience joy are more likely to use approach motivation, find gain-framed messages more compelling (and change actual behavior), and be more risk seeking; individuals who experience contentment are more likely to use avoidance motivation, find loss-framed messages more compelling, and be more risk averse. The second paper focuses on attribution of one's positive mood, either to the self or to the environment. If happiness is attributed to the self, individuals are more likely to focus on internal sources of happiness (one's behavior) rather than external sources of happiness (e.g., chocolate). The reverse is true for unhappiness. The third paper shows that physicians who experience positive emotions (vs. neutral emotions) toward their patients (empathy and sympathy) tend to overestimate the risk associated with high severity diseases and offer a larger range of treatments.

EXTENDED ABSTRACTS

"All Positive Emotions Are Not Created Equal: The Case of Joy and Contentment"

Michal Herzenstein, University of Delaware, USA
Meryl Gardner, University of Delaware, USA

Positive emotions, with happiness as their representative, have been shown to promote approach behaviors because the enhanced feelings of energy and vigor increase the subjective perception that one is capable of performing these behaviors (Cacioppo et al. 1993). In this paper we investigate two distinct positive emotions, joy and contentment, and find that they have a different influence on individuals' choice of motivation and consequently their behavior. We focus on these emotions because while both are positive, they are distinct and therefore easy to manipulate and measure (Fredrickson and Branigan 2005). Building on previous literature (Fredrickson 1998) we suggest that joy is consistent with the approach system because it is a high arousal positive emotion that creates the urge to be playful, involves exploration, invention, and prompts individuals to be more willing to experience new things. We further suggest that contentment is more consistent with the avoidance system because it is a low arousal positive emotion that prompts individuals to savor their current life circumstances and recent successes, which prompt a mood regulation behavior.

We test our predictions in four experiments, in which we manipulated emotions using two short clips (c.f., Fredrickson and Branigan 2005), one elicits joy and the other contentment. A pretest and manipulation checks in all experiments show a significant difference in the levels of joy, contentment, and activation reported by participants, and no difference in pleasantness level.

In experiment 1A we wished to create a situation that encourages avoidance behavior (participants expected to be punished for sub-performance); in experiment 1B we wished to create a situation that encourages approach behavior (participants expected to be rewarded for good performance). The main dependent variables were nervousness level (in 1A) and happiness level (in 1B), because according to Carver and White (1994) these emotions are indicators of avoidance and approach behaviors respectively. As expected, in experiment 1A we found that participants in the contentment (vs. joy) condition reported a higher level of nervousness, indicating that when individuals experience contentment they are more likely to use avoidance motivation. Similarly, in experiment 1B we found that participants in the joy (vs. contentment) condition reported a higher level of happiness, indicating that when individuals experience joy they are more likely to use approach motivation. Next we explore whether joy and contentment lead to the downstream consequences prescribed by the approach and avoidance systems.

Sherman et al. (2006) show that when a health message is congruent with individuals' motivation, it is more effective in promoting health behaviors. Specifically, approach motivation was found to be congruent with gain-framed messages while avoidance motivation is congruent with loss-framed messages. Experiment 2 employed a 2 (emotion: joy vs. contentment) x 2 (framing: gains vs. losses) between subject design to test the prediction that participants who experience joy will find a gain-framed message more appealing, and participants who experience contentment will find a loss-framed message more appealing. Participants read an article about flossing, which either stressed the benefits of flossing or the negative outcomes of not flossing. Results show that there were no main effects of emotions or framing, but there was a significant interaction of emotions x framing on article effectiveness (measured during the experiment) and actual behavior (# of times participants flossed in the week following the experiment.)

The aim of experiment 3 was to test the influence of joy and contentment on risk propensity. Previous research (Friedman and Förster 2002; Dweck and Legget 1988) suggests that when individuals use approach motivation they tend to be more risk seeking because they welcome challenge and use explorative processing; when individuals use avoidance motivation they tend to be more risk-averse because they use systematic and perseverant processing to avoid negative outcomes. We hypothesize that in the gain domain joy leads to risk seeking while contentment leads to risk avoidance, and the reverse in the loss domain. We are currently collecting data to test our hypothesis. Initial results are in the direction hypothesized.

In experiment 4 we tested whether there is a differential effect of our target positive emotions on variety seeking, a behavior more congruent with the approach system. Kahn and Isen (1993) show that positive emotions, with happiness as their representative, lead to variety seeking. We suggest that this holds for joy but not for contentment, because individuals who experience joy are more likely to use approach motivation and be more risk seeking–trying different known and unknown brands, while individuals who experience contentment are more likely to use avoidance motivation and be more risk averse–confining their choices to a small set of familiar and liked brands. We tested this hypothesis by asking participants to make choices from a list of brands of crackers, some were known American brands and the other were fake brands.

Results show that compared with participants in the contentment condition, those in the joy condition chose more brands, more unfamiliar brands, and switched more.

In sum, our research shows that not all positive emotions were created equal. While we find that joy leads to consequences similar to those found in the literature for happiness (approach motivation, congruency with the gain-frame, risk seeking (in the gain domain), and variety seeking), contentment leads to a different set of consequences (avoidance motivation, congruency with the loss-frame, risk avoidance (in the gain domain), and the choice of a small number familiar brands). Our findings imply that these are two distinct, equally strong, while equally positive emotions. Implications of our results will be discussed.

"Do You "Work to Live" or "Live to Work"? The Role of Mood and Confidence in Causal Agency"

Aparna A. Labroo, University of Chicago, USA
Nidhi Agrawal, Northwestern University, USA

Take a trip to the Workaholics Anonymous website (http://www.workaholics-anonymous.org/knowing.html) and take their test on whether you are a workaholic. You will probably discover that you are a workaholic. ABC news reports that a growing number of Americans are discovering that they live to work rather than work to live. Recent research also suggests that for the most part, people are likely to over-engage in activities that presumably better them in the long term at the cost of activities that help them feel better in the moment. Are people working harder because this will provide material wellbeing that will allow them to indulge in the moment, or do they derive happiness from engaging in activities usually associated with immediate effort and negative feelings?

We investigate when and why people might demonstrate a tendency to over-engage in actions that are in their long-term interests over those that might improve their immediate feelings. Our basic proposition is that there are two modes of happiness—internal happiness which results from feelings of personal development, including things that are in our long-term interests, and external happiness which results from the consumption of material goods that immediately make us feel better—and one is the default of the other. People's choice of internal rather than external modes of happiness depends on their confidence in the self as the agency responsible for their happiness. In contrast, the choice of external rather than internal modes of happiness depends on their confidence in the environment as the agency causing their happiness.

High confidence in the self as an agent of happiness increases actions that result in personal development and investing effort in things in ones long-term interest. This is because seeing the self as responsible for happiness leads people to believe that unless they invest in their self growth and work they cannot be happy. In contrast, high confidence in the environment as an agent of happiness increases indulgent actions because happiness is seen to result only from external sources such as the consumption of hedonic or material goods. As a consequence, happy people are more likely to engage in activities that lead to long-term personal development rather than external happiness from indulgent actions when they are confident that the self (vs. environment) causes happiness. On the other hand, people feeling unhappy who are confident that the self (vs. environment) is the cause of unhappiness look externally for happiness and reduce long-term actions over indulgent ones. Additionally, confidence in the environment as agent of unhappiness would imply a need to work to resolve the problems caused by the environment. When confidence in agency is low and people doubt that the self (vs. environment) is the agency of ones happiness, their reliance on the environment as the cause of their happiness increases and they engage in increased hedonic consumption consonant with seeking external sources of happiness. The reverse is true when people doubt that the self (vs. environment) is the agency of ones unhappiness. These predictions are tested in a series of experiments.

Experiment 1 employed a 2 (mood) x 2 (high confidence in internal vs. external agency) between-subjects design to see the effects of these factors on self-control in choice. We find that that happy participants making attributions to internal (vs. external) agency are more likely to make choices that are consonant with their long-term personal development (i.e., dieters choose an apple) rather than seek external happiness (i.e., choose a chocolate). The reverse is true for unhappy participants making attributions to internal (vs. external) agency.

Experiments 2a and 2b employ a 2(mood) x 2 (low confidence in internal vs. external agency) between-subjects design to test our predictions but use different manipulation of confidence in agency. It is demonstrated that that when participants in a positive mood make attributions to internal (vs. external) agency but are low in confidence in agency, they are less likely to make choices endorsing personal development and long-term benefits (e.g., say they will get tested for herpes even though they think they are less likely to have the disease). The reverse is true for negative participants who have low confidence in an internal (vs. external) agency as responsible for feelings.

Experiment 3 employs a 2 (attribution of happiness to internal vs. external agency) x 2 (confidence in agency) between-subjects design to demonstrate that happy participants with a high confidence in an internal (vs. external) agency are more likely to endorse activities that result in long-term personal development even if they involve short-term effort. In contrast, happy participants with a low confidence in an internal (vs. external) agency are less likely to endorse activities that result in long-term benefits and more likely to endorse indulgent activities that conflict with long-term personal development.

Experiment 4 studied these effects while focusing on an external agency. In a 2 (mood) x 2 (high vs. low confidence in external agency) between-subjects design, it demonstrates that happy participants who are high (vs. low) in confidence in external agency are more likely to make material choices that reflect seeking external modes of happiness. Unhappy participants who are high (vs. low) in confidence in external agency show reversed effects. Across these experiments, confidence in agency is manipulated in a variety of ways, by instructions, by ease of attribution manipulations such as generating one versus seven instances implicating the agency and using dominant versus non dominant hand writing about agency, and by employing emotions that naturally vary in confidence (e.g., happiness vs. hope).

The literature has suggested that wanting to feel good leads to short-term oriented indulgent choices. We suggest that attributing happiness to the self moves individuals from focusing on external sources of happiness (e.g., chocolates) to internal sources of happiness (e.g., one's behavior resulting in personal development). Such liberation of the self from external sources of happiness facilitates behaviors that increase personal development and including those beneficial in the long-term. Thus, agency attributions determine whether an external or internal mode of happiness governs behavior. Implications for the literatures on emotions, self-regulation, and consumer welfare will be discussed.

"Physician, Heal Thyself: Positive Affect, Risk, and Treatment Decisions in Health Care"

Lisa A. Cavanaugh, Duke University, USA
Christine Moorman, Duke University, USA
James R. Bettman, Duke University, USA
Mary Frances Luce, Duke University, USA

Imagine you are a physician and the decisions you make each day have implications for the health and well-being of twenty to thirty patients. As a medical practitioner, your primary vehicle for improving patient health is the treatment recommendations that you make. In reviewing a course of treatment, patients often ask you about their treatment options and the risks that are involved. Clearly you want to make the best decisions possible for your patients.

Your extensive medical education (medical school, internship, and residency) has taught you a great deal about standard courses of care and the culture of medicine. You have been taught both explicitly and implicitly not to allow your emotions to cloud your clinical judgment (Landro 2005; Hafferty and Franks 1994; Smith and Kleinman 1989). Recent advances in health care have exacerbated this "affect-free" view of medical decisions by fostering increased specialization by physicians and reliance on technology, allowing doctors to provide consultations from afar without ever seeing the patient face to face.

While affective neutrality may help protect physicians from the negative affect and significant stress they face, this practice also potentially carries with it some critical costs, particularly the loss of positive affect, empathy and the benefits they offer to patient and physician. The hidden curriculum in medical culture has marginalized humanism in favor of the transmission of technical skills and ignores the most human aspects of care (Apker and Eggly 2004; Hafferty and Franks 1995) that help people heal.

We argue that some important benefits of positive affect identified in the psychology literature (Fredrickson 1998, 2001; Isen 2003) may be forgone by physicians when they employ a strategy of affective neutrality. When physicians deny feelings and fail to see their patients as people, they may be unable to fully appreciate the stakes and possible treatment risks posed to the patient, and there may indeed be costs associated with practicing affective neutrality.

The potential to experience negative affect is omnipresent in a clinical setting, where physicians deal with sick patients and communicate bad news daily. The purpose of this research is to determine if and how the introduction of positive affect (i.e., positive feelings toward patients) will influence physicians' judgments. Building on the relevant literature on positive affect, dual-process models of information processing, and risk, we identify key factors influencing physicians' judgments. We look at the interaction between mode of patient presentation (affect-rich/ affect-poor) and disease severity (low/ high) in influencing treatment considerations and perceptions of risk.

In study one, physicians were asked to either imagine that their hospital was considering using a new medical record keeping system or that the Susan B. Komen Foundation was considering the use of a new fundraising appeal (between subjects). Physicians were shown a sample photograph of a breast cancer patient and then asked to report the extent to which seeing a picture like this would influence their own judgment, other doctors' judgments, and nurses' judgments. Physicians reported that the photograph would influence their donation judgments but not necessarily their own medical judgments.

In study two, physicians were asked to evaluate a breast cancer patient. We conducted a 2 (mode of patient presentation: affect-rich/ affect-poor) x 2 (disease severity: low/ high) between subjects

experiment. Physicians were presented with identical patient information but mode of patient presentation was varied using a procedure similar to Hsee and Rottenstreich (2004). Specifically, physicians saw either a picture of the patient with her two children (affect-rich) or a picture of a female symbol with two smaller symbols representing her children (affect-poor) in conjunction with the same patient file. We manipulated disease severity to be either low (Stage 0) or high (Stage IIIB). Physicians were then asked to make a series of judgments about the treatment options they considered and the risks that the treatments posed to the patient.

We found a two-way interaction of mode of patient presentation and disease severity for both dependent measures—breadth of consideration and perceived risk. As predicted, physicians in the affect-rich condition who evaluated a patient with a high severity disease demonstrated greater breadth of consideration in treatments. Most importantly, these same physicians also showed greater willingness to recommend the use of non-traditional therapies. These results suggest that positive affect plays an important facilitative role in the breadth of treatment options that physicians consider for severe cases of disease.

In the case of risk assessments, consistent with our prediction, physicians who evaluated a patient with a high severity disease in the affect-rich condition saw more risk than the participants in the affect-poor condition. Yet, when evaluating a patient with a low severity disease, physicians in the affect-rich condition actually saw less risk than those in the affect-poor condition. Physicians' reports of sympathy and empathy offered evidence that may help in gaining additional insight into our pattern of results. In sum, the pattern of risk seems to be driven by physicians' reliance on either risk as feelings or risk as analysis.

These findings have potentially important implications for consumer health and welfare; they also raise the question—under what circumstances are these physician behaviors desirable? We are conducting additional studies to determine how these influences on consideration and risk may ultimately affect clinical practice and patient care. We hope to illuminate two key questions: 1) When will an affect-rich mode of patient presentation be helpful versus harmful to physicians' judgments and patients' outcomes? 2) When might physicians be underestimating or overestimating risk, and which estimates are most appropriate?

Our findings offer insight into the conditions under which positive affect influences judgments of consideration and risk. Equipped with additional knowledge about the interactive effects of affect and disease severity, patients may be able to receive and physicians may be able to provide improved care, as the Hippocratic Oath suggests: "promote health and healing, reduce suffering, and not act contrary to the well-being of their own patients."

REFERENCES

Apker, Julie and Susan Eggly (2004), "Communicating Professional Identity in Medical Socialization: Considering the Ideological Discourse of Morning Report," *Qualitative Health Research*, 14(March), 411-429.

Cacioppo, John T., Joseph R. Priester, and Gary G. Berntson (1993), "Rudimentary Determinants of Attitudes: II. Arm Flexion and Extension Have Differential Effects on Attitudes," *Journal of Personality and Social Psychology*, 65, 1, 5–17.

Carver, Charles S. and Teri L. White (1994), "Behavioral Inhibition, Behavioral Activation, and Affective Responses to Impending Reward and Punishment: The BIS/BAS Scales," *Journal of Personality and Social Psychology*, 67, 2, 319-333.

Dweck, Carol S. and Ellen L. Leggett (1988) "A Social-Cognitive Approach to Motivation and Personality," *Psychological Review*, 95, No. 2,256-273

Fredrickson, Barbara L. (1998), "What Good Are Positive Emotions?," *Review of General Psychology*, 2 (September), 300-319.

Fredrickson, Barbara L. (2001), "The Role of Positive Emotions in Positive Psychology: The Broaden-and-Build Theory of Positive Emotions," *American Psychologist*, 56 (March), 218-226.

Fredrickson, Barbara L. and Christine Branigan (2005), "Positive Emotions Broaden the Scope of Attention and Thought Action Repertoire," *Cognition and Emotion*, 19, 3, 313-332.

Friedman, Ronald S. and Jens Förster (2002), "The Influence of Approach and Avoidance Motor Actions on Creative Cognition", *Journal of Experimental Social Psychology*, 38, 1, 41-55.

Hafferty, Frederic W. and Ronald Franks (1994), "The Hidden Curriculum, Ethics Teaching, and the Structure of Medical Education," *Academic Medicine*, 69 (November), 861-871.

Hsee, Christopher K. and Yuval Rottenstreich, (2004), "Music, Pandas, and Muggers: On the Affective Psychology of Value," *Journal of Experimental Psychology*, 133 (March), 23-30.

Isen, Alice M. (2003), "Positive Affect as a Source of Human Strength," in *A psychology of human strengths: Fundamental questions and future directions for a positive psychology*, ed. U.M. Staudinger and L.G. Aspinwall, Washington, DC: American Psychological Association, 179-195.

Kahn Barbara E. and Alice M. Isen (1993), "The Influence of Positive Affect on Variety Seeking Among Safe, Enjoyable Products," *Journal of Consumer Research*, 20, 2, 257-270.

Landro, Laura (2005), "Teaching Doctors to Be Nicer," *The Wall Street Journal*, September 28.

Sherman, David K., Traci Mann, and John A. Updegraff (2006) "Approach/Avoidance Motivation, Message Framing, and Health Behavior: Understanding the Congruency Effect" *Motivation and Emotion*, 30, 2, 164-168.

Smith, Allen C. and Sherryl Kleinman (1989), "Managing Emotions in Medical School: Students' Contacts With the Living and the Dead," *Social Psychology Quarterly*, 52, 56-69.

Cognition and Sensory Perception: The Impact of Input from Sensory Modalities on Imagery, Memory, Information Processing, and Sensory Perception

Aradhna Krishna, University of Michigan, USA

SESSION OVERVIEW

Inputs and interactions among multiple sensory modalities affect what we imagine, what we remember, and how we process new information. The goal of this symposium is to introduce current research in the domain of cognition and sensory perception to marketing, and to inspire further exploration of this promising area. The presentations in this session will address the complex interactions of cognition and sensory perception as it applies to consumer behavior. Each of the four papers focuses on a different sensory modality, allowing for a broad, yet coherent exposition of research in the area.

The first paper by Elder and Krishna examines the impact of sensory stimulation on taste perceptions. Perceived taste is formulated from the inputs of multiple sensory modalities, including smell, touch (texture), sight, and even sound. The authors draw upon physiological and neuroscience literatures to propose that food advertisements which include multiple senses in the verbal copy can result in higher perceived taste, compared to advertisements that focus on taste alone. The effects are driven in large part by increased sensory stimulation, which is shown to mediate the process. Further, adding to the cognitive component of taste, the authors show that restricting working memory attenuates the effects.

The second paper by Peck and Barger further exhibits sensory imagery capabilities of the human mind. The endowment effect, which states that consumers value objects more highly if they own them, also arises from psychological ownership of the object. Psychological ownership, in turn, can stem from simple physical contact with the object. The authors posit that touch (haptic) imagery can act as a surrogate for actual touch, thereby increasing psychological ownership of the object and its subsequent valuation. They show that the effects of touch imagery are similar in magnitude to having consumers actually touch the object.

The third paper by Krishna, Morrin, Lwin, and Wirtz examines the impact of product-embedded scent on subsequent recall of product information. This paper presents a large body of evidence for the heightened recall effects of scented versus unscented products. In particular, across three studies the authors show that both unaided and aided recall of product information is higher for scented versus unscented products, regardless of if the scent is congruent or incongruent with the product. These effects hold even after a delay, suggesting their storage in long-term memory. In addition, the authors show that scent is more effective at enhancing memory than the visual cue of product color.

The fourth paper by Stamatogiannakis, Chattopadhyay, and Gorn examines the impact of visual processing capacity on aesthetic response. The authors show that violations of "holistic" properties of visual stimuli (e.g., symmetry, unity, simplicity, prototypicality) results in a less positive aesthetic response when ability/opportunity to visualize is low. However, when capacity to visualize is not constrained, either because the person's inherent ability to visualize is sufficiently high, or because the person has the time to fully process the stimulus, then violations do not affect aesthetic response. Additionally, the authors identify the mechanism through which these effects operate.

The underlying constructs across each of the four papers present a cohesive representation of the interaction of cognition and sensory perception. The symposium will prove beneficial not only to researchers interested in sensory perception, but also to those interested in better understanding perceptual processes and their impact on imagery, memory, and processing. The session will conclude with a discussion moderated by Priya Raghubir, seeking to increase general understanding within the area, and to encourage future research in this exciting domain.

EXTENDED ABSTRACTS

"The Effect of Advertising Copy on Sensory Stimulation and Perceived Taste"

Ryan Elder, University of Michigan, USA
Aradhna Krishna, University of Michigan, USA

Despite our seemingly constant exposure to food, we have remarkable difficulty in discerning one taste from another when other senses are inhibited. For instance, if one cannot smell or see the food, it is difficult to tell apart the taste of a potato from an apple, or red wine from coffee (Herz 2007). Part of this ineptitude stems from the limited number of distinct tastes that we can detect.

Ambiguity in taste experiences is reduced in large part by our ability to incorporate multiple sensory inputs into our ultimate taste perceptions. The primary accompanying sense for taste is olfaction (how the food smells). Taste is further affected by vision (how the product looks, including aesthetic appeal, color, shape), as well as auditory aspects (primarily the sound the item makes when bitten or chewed). The convergence of these sensory inputs occurs in the orbitofrontal cortex, labeled as a secondary taste cortex (Rolls 2005). Interestingly, sensory activation in their respective regions of the brain can occur simply by reading verbal depictions of sensory experiences. Therefore, we posit that advertising copy that address multiple-sensory inputs will result in higher taste perceptions due to increased sensory stimulation. Results across five studies, utilizing different taste stimuli add support to our hypothesis, and also delineate the underlying process of sensory stimulation on taste perceptions.

In study 1, we created multiple- and single-sense verbal ads for potato chips. Our results show that participants that read multiple-versus single-sense ads more highly evaluated the perceived taste of potato chips. This finding was replicated in study 2, where participants evaluated the perceived taste of popcorn. Study 2 also explored a potential moderator of the ad-taste effect—cognitive resource availability. Cognitive constraints that limit the availability of working memory should reduce the ad-taste effects, since construction of sensory perception depends on available working memory (Jonides, Lacey, and Nee 2005). That is, we should see an attenuation of the effects of multiple- versus single- sense ads on taste perceptions. We do obtain this attenuation of effects in Study 2; that is, participants rated the perceived taste of the popcorn higher than those exposed to the single-sense ad. Further, within the multiple-sense ad condition, participants in the no load condition rated the taste higher than participants in the high load condition.

In studies 3 and 4, we test for the processes driving the ad-taste effect. Study 3 examines the impact of "attention" to multiple-versus single-sense (taste) on perceived taste. Participants were given instructions to either focus on all five senses (multiple-sense) or on taste alone (single-sense) when eating a cookie. We found that attention to all five senses resulted in higher taste perceptions of the cookies than the focus on the sense of taste alone. Study four looks more directly at the cognitive responses from participants as a measure of sensory stimulation, using gum as the product category. In particular, we measure the number of positive sensory thoughts elicited by participants about the gum after exposure to the ad and after tasting the gum. The relationship between multiple- versus single-sense ads and taste perceptions was mediated by the number of positive sensory thoughts.

The fifth study explores a more managerially relevant consequence of our theory, showing that willingness to pay for a novel product (Incan hot chocolate) is higher in the multiple-sense ad condition than in the single-sense condition. In sum, these five experiments support our theory that multiple-sense ads will lead to more positive taste experiences than single-sense (taste) ads.

Our research makes important contributions to both the consumer behavior and sensory perception literatures. Our contribution to marketing is an explication of the effects of ads on taste perception. This extends the impact of advertising beyond variables such as awareness and purchase intentions to perceived taste. We also contribute to perception research by providing evidence for the impact of verbal stimuli on sensory evaluations. More specifically, we show that multiple-sensory stimulation can enhance single-sense perceptions. Lastly, we make an attempt to bridge the gaps between physiology, neuroscience, and consumer behavior, showing promising potential for future research.

References

Herz, Rachel (2007), The Scent of Desire: Discovering our Enigmatic Sense of Smell, New York William Morrow.

Jonides, John, Steven C. Lacey, and Derek E. Nee (2005), "Processes of Working Memory in Mind and Brain," Current Directions in Psychological Science, 14 (1), 2-5.

Rolls, Edmund T. (2005), "Taste, Olfactory, and Food Texture Processing in the Brain, and the Control of Food Intake," Physiology & Behavior, 85(1), 45-56.

"In Search of a Surrogate for Touch: The Effect of Haptic Imagery on Psychological Ownership and Object Valuation"

Joann Peck, University of Wisconsin-Madison, USA
Victor Barger, University of Wisconsin-Madison, USA

Previous research has shown that consumers value objects more highly if they own them, a finding commonly known as the endowment effect (Thaler, 1980). This effect is not limited to legal ownership; psychological ownership, characterized by the feeling that something "is mine," also produces the endowment effect. One antecedent of psychological ownership is the ability of an individual to control an object by touching it. Shu and Peck show that when individuals are given the opportunity to touch an object (versus not), they report a greater sense of psychological ownership and value the object more highly.

If touch is not available, could the act of visualizing touch act as a surrogate? According to MacInnis and Price (1987), imaging is a resource demanding process in which sensory information is represented in working memory. Bone and Ellen (1992) conjecture that imagery "may involve sight, taste, smell and tactile sensations" (p. 93). Although research on imagery and the tactile system is limited (Klatsky, Lederman & Matula, 1993), there is some evidence for the interdependence of touch and visual imagery (Katz, 1925).

Since imaging requires cognitive resources and the effects of imagery are mediated by resource availability (Bone & Ellen, 1992; Unnava, Agarwal & Haugtvedt, 1996), blocking out perceptual distractions during imaging may enhance its effects. Unnava et al. (1996) found that when imagery and perception compete for the same resources, the positive effects of imaging are reduced. Similarly, Petrova and Cialdini (2005) found that difficulty in imagery generation can reverse the positive effects of imagery appeals. In some instances, consumer behavior researchers have instructed participants to close their eyes when imaging (e.g., Bone & Ellen, 1992; Keller & McGill, 1994 (Experiment 1); Petrova & Cialdini, 2005 (Study 3)), although this was not the focus of these studies. We hypothesize that closing one's eyes while imaging touching an object leads to greater psychological ownership and valuation than imaging touching an object when one's eyes are open.

An experimental study was designed to examine the effect of touch imagery on both psychological ownership and valuation. The design was a 4 (imagery/touch: imagery eyes closed, imagery eyes open, no touch no imagery, touch with no imagery) x 2 (product: Koosh ball, blanket), with the first factor manipulated between subjects, and the second factor varied within subjects. Three hundred and twenty-six individuals participated in the study.

Our first hypothesis predicted that when participants imaged touching the product with their eyes closed, both psychological ownership and valuation would be greater than when participants imaged with their eyes open. We found a main effect of touch/imagery for both psychological and valuation. For psychological ownership, both the touch condition and the touch imagery with eyes closed condition resulted in a significantly stronger sense of ownership than the touch imagery with eyes open condition and the no touch-no imagery condition. Interestingly, there was no significant difference in either psychological ownership or valuation between the touch imagery with eyes closed condition and the condition where actual touch was possible. For valuation as the dependent measure, the results were similar.

We next conducted a second study in order to examine the process in more detail. We hypothesized that when a person closes their eyes to imagine, they are focusing their cognitive resources which results in similar effects to actual touch. In the second study, we had participants imaging touching a product (as in Study 1) but we manipulated whether haptic interference was present and also whether the interference "fit" with the imagined object. The design of this study was a 2 (vision: eyes open, eyes closed) x 3 (haptic stimulus: none, congruent, incongruent) with both factors manipulated between subjects. Three hundred and eighty seven individuals participated and we were able to replicate our first hypothesis. We also found that when a person imagines with their eyes closed, the presence or absence of a haptic stimuli does not significantly impact haptic imaging unless the stimulus is incongruent with the product being imagined.

References

Bone, Paula F. and Pam S. Ellen (1992), "The generation and consequences of communication-evoked imagery," *The Journal of Consumer Research*, 19 (1), 93-104.

Keller, Punam A. and Ann L. McGill (1994), "Differences in the relative influence of product attributes under alternative processing conditions: Attribute importance versus ease of imagability," *Journal of Consumer Psychology*, 3 (1), 29-49.

Klatzky, Roberta L., Susan J. Lederman, and Dana E. Matula (1993), "Haptic exploration in the presence of vision," *Journal of Experimental Psychology: Human Perception and Performance*, 19 (4), 726-743.

MacInnis, Deborah J. and Linda L. Price (1987), "The role of imagery in information processing: Review and extensions," *The Journal of Consumer Research*, 13 (March), 473-491.

Petrova, Petia K. And Robert B. Cialdini (2005), "Fluency of consumption imagery and the backfire effects of imagery appeals," *The Journal of Consumer Research*, 32 (December), 442-452.

Shu, Suzanne B. and Joann Peck (working paper), "To hold me is to love me: Psychological ownership, touch, and the endowment effect."

Thaler, Richard H., (1980), "Toward a positive theory of consumer choice," *Journal of Economic Behavior and Organization*, 1, 36-90.

Unnava, H. Rao, Sanjeev Agarwal, and Curtis P. Haugtvedt (1996), "Interactive effects of presentation modality and message-generated imagery on recall of advertising information," *The Journal of Consumer Research*, 13 (June), 81-88.

"Beyond the Proustian Phenomenon: The Effect of Product-Embedded Scent on Memory for Product Information"

Aradhna Krishna, University of Michigan, USA
May Lwin, Nanyang Technological University, Singapore
Maureen Morrin, Rutgers University, USA
Jochen Wirtz, National University of Singapore, Singapore

Research in psychology suggests that humans have the ability to recognize scents previously smelled, even after long periods of time. There has been relatively little research in the marketing discipline on the relationship between scent and consumer memory, particularly when the scent is embedded within the product itself, rather than coming from the surrounding environment (i.e., ambient scent). The major goal of this paper is to explore how product-based scent impacts memory for product information, and the extent to which such memory resists decay and interference. We also explore whether the effects of product-based scent are moderated by scent's perceived congruency with the product. Further, for benchmarking purposes, we compare the effectiveness of product-based scent to product-based color (i.e., a sensory modality comparison of olfaction versus vision).

We conducted two pretests to choose the stimuli and then conducted a series of three main studies designed to explore the major issues of interest. In study 1(n=151), we infuse a pencil product with either a congruent (pine) or incongruent (tea tree) scent and measure unaided and aided recall for brand attributes after different times from exposure (no delay, 24 hour delay, two week delay). A significant time delay by scent condition interaction emerged for both unaided and aided recall. Recall was higher when the pencils were scented, especially true after a time delay, and the congruent scent was sometimes better than the incongruent scent at enhancing memory.

In study 2 (n=448), we compare the effects of scent with those of color. Versus a white, unscented control moisturizer, we infuse either a congruent (rose) or incongruent (anise) scent and either a congruent (beige) or incongruent (dark red) color. We again measure unaided and aided recall after no delay, a 24 hour delay, and a two week delay. We obtained a significant time delay by scent condition interaction for both unaided and aided recall. Recall was higher when the moisturizers were scented versus unscented, this was especially true after a time delay, and the congruent scent was sometimes better than the incongruent scent at enhancing memory.

In study 3 (n=86), we test the effects of competitive interference on memory for scent-encoded product information. All participants are exposed to an orange-scented moisturizer. Later, those in the interference condition are subsequently exposed to a different brand with the same scent, whereas those in the control condition are not. Four weeks after initial product exposure, memory for brand information is tested. With no interference, recall for the scented product is better than that of the unscented product; however, when there is interference from a second product with the same scent, recall for the original product falls to the level of the unscented product. Thus, interference negated the memory-enhancing effects of product scent, suggesting a boundary condition for this phenomenon.

One of the most intriguing results of this research concerns the effect of time delay on memory for product information associated with scent-infused (versus unscented) products. For most types of information that is learned, retrieval performance declines over time as it becomes more difficult to distinguish cues that were experienced more recently versus more distantly. The greatest decline is typically observed shortly after exposure. However, in the case of scented products, we find that memory for scent-based information does not exhibit the same rapid drop off. Instead, information encoded with scent persists over time, exhibiting a much more gradual decline over time.

Nearly all of the research on scent reintroduces scent at the time of retrieval to test its effects on memory (called Proustian effects). In our research, we examine the ability of scent to produce strong associations in memory that later manifest regardless of whether or not the scent cue is re-encountered by the consumer, i.e., going beyond the Proustian phenomenon. A key focus is therefore on the ability of product-based scent to create strong memory traces at the time of encoding, as well as the extent to which these memory traces are resistant to decay over time and interference from competing information.

"Can You Fix It?: Effects of Visual Processing Capacity on Visual Aesthetic Response"

Antonios Stamatogiannakis, INSEAD, France
Amitava Chattopadhyay, INSEAD, Singapore
Gerald Gorn, Hong Kong University of Science & Technology, China

In a recent review chapter of the role of aesthetics in consumer psychology, Hoegg and Alba (2007) stress the need to understand how perceptual processing affects product design evaluation and choice. This research is a step towards such an understanding. Several properties of visual stimuli are assumed to contribute to a positive aesthetic response.(e.g. symmetry, unity, simplicity, prototypicality). We investigate one specific characteristic that is likely to influence response to violations of these properties and aesthetic response, namely visual processing capacity.

Several properties of visual stimuli, properties that emanate from Gestalt psychology principles (e.g. Katz, 1950), have been found to lead to increased liking of visual stimuli in both psychological and consumer behavior research. For example visual stimuli properties such as unity and prototypicality tend to induce a positive aesthetic response (Veryzer and Hutchinson 1998).The same for symmetric vs. asymmetric patterns, with people tending to complete unfinished ones in symmetric ways (van Lier and Wagemans, 1999). Also in general, relatively simple patterns tend to be preferred over more complex ones at sufficiently high levels of complexity, but not in low levels of complexity. (e.g. Berlyne, 1974).

Consumers do not always visually process the products they see fully. There may be too many products to process as for example in a large department store. The person may be thinking of other things, or they may be making the purchase impulsively and hence only briefly scanning the package or packages in the store. Researchers have proposed that when cognitive resources are limited (e.g. Hutchinson and Alba 1991) people tend to process information more holistically than analytically. We draw on this research and suggest that when people have a lower visual processing capacity, symmetry, unity (any aspect of visual display that connects its parts in a meaningful way, Veryzer and Hutchinson 1998), simplicity, and prototypicality will be crucial for liking. When however visual processing capacity is higher, liking will be less affected by whether or not these properties are violated.

In experiments one and two we investigate visualizing capacity in different ways. In experiment one we look at capacity using an individual difference approach, namely comparing the responses of those lower or higher in visual processing ability. In experiment two we do so by manipulating exposure time. In our first study, we used individual differences in visualization ability to capture the effect. We used a 2X2 mixed factorial design, with pattern (full or broken) as the between participants factor and shape (3 squares and 3 octagons) as the within participants factor. Participants saw each figure for 3.5 seconds, and then rated it for liking, symmetry, simplicity and prototypicality. We also had measures of visualization ability and preference for visual processing. We found a pattern X visualization ability interaction: People low in visualization ability liked full patterns much more than broken patterns, but people high in this ability preferred the two almost equally. A similar effect was found for preference for visual processing. Interestingly, visualizing preference and visual ability were not significantly correlated. The interaction effects obtained were driven by the fact that the "lows" liked the full patterns much more than the broken ones. This difference was driven by a similar difference in symmetry ratings.

In our second experiment we used a 2X2X2X2 mixed factorial design. Time (.5, 2.5 and 3.5 seconds) and pattern (full or broken) were varied between participants, while shape (circles or squares) and number of shapes (one or three) within participants. Each participant was exposed to four figures one after the other (in random order) on a computer screen: A square, a circle, three concentric squares and three concentric circles. Half the participants saw full shapes, and half saw these same figures, but broken by two gaps randomly placed on two different spots. Also, a third of the participants saw the figures for .5 seconds each, a third for 2.5, and the other third for 3.5 seconds. After each figure was presented, participants rated it on four dimensions: liking, simplicity, symmetry and unity. Liking was always first, but the other three ratings were randomized. There was a significant interaction between pattern (full vs. broken) and time short (.5 seconds) or long (2.5 or 3.5 seconds). In the short time condition full patterns were liked more than broken ones, but in long time condition there was no such difference. Overall, these results supported expectations that the more "holistic" stimulus properties examined would be crucial for a positive aesthetic response only when visual processing capacity is limited. The drop was mediated by a similar drop in the unity ratings, indicating that in this case, unity violation was the crucial one.

In our third study we use more realistic stimuli and try to manipulate orthogonally symmetry and unity and thus resolve the different results regarding the driving mechanism in the first two studies. We further manipulate visual processing ability by cognitive vs. visual load. This helps us understand whether our effects are driven by low levels of visual processing ability, or processing ability in general. In our fourth study we manipulate visual processing ability by loading the visual context to mirror a large store context where many products are simultaneously visually perceived.

References

Berlyne, Daniel E. (1974), Studies in new experimental *aesthetics,* New York: Wiley.

Hoegg, JoAndrea, and Joseph W. Alba (2007), "A role for aesthetics in consumer psychology," in *Handbook of consumer psychology,* Edited by C. Haugtvedt, F. Kardes and P. M. Herr. Sage, 733-54.

Hutchinson, J. W., and Joseph W. Alba (1991), "Ignoring irrelevant information: Situational determinants of consumer learning," *Journal of Consumer Research,* 18 (3), 325.

Katz, David (1950), *Gestalt psychology,* New York: Ronald Press.

van Lier, Rob, and Johan Wagemans (1999), "From images to objects: Global and local completions of self-occluded parts," *Journal of Experimental Psychology: Human Perception and Performance,* 25 (6), 1721-41.

Veryzer, Robert W., and J. W. Hutchinson (1998), "The influence of unity and prototypicality on aesthetic responses to new product designs," *Journal of Consumer Research,* 24 (4), 374.

Compensatory Consumption: How Threat Directs Consumers' Product Preferences

Derek Rucker, Northwestern University, USA

SESSION OVERVIEW

Classic research on consumption proposes that products are often purchased for their symbolic qualities (Belk 1988; Levy 1959; Solomon 1983). Indeed, consumer products can communicate information both to oneself (Bem 1972; Solomon 1983) and to others (Belk, Bahn, and Mayer 1982). For example, an individual who notices she enjoys artwork might conclude to herself that she values creativity; an individual who drives a Lexus might be perceived by others as wealthy and having status. Based on the idea that products have such signaling value, the present session poses the question of whether consumers' product preferences and purchases are used to cope with threat. This proposition is examined with respect to threat in three different domains: one's self-worth, one's self-views, and one's sense of power. Each paper puts forth evidence supporting the idea that threat leads consumers to prefer and select products that compensate for the dimension under threat. As a whole, the session sheds new light on the nature of consumption and the conditions under which threat produces compensatory consumption.

The first paper, by Dalton, proposes that a threat to consumers' self-worth leads to compensation by choosing products that allow for self-expression. Three experiments are presented to test the effect of threats to one's self-worth on consumption in the context of choosing whether to trade up for a higher priced item in a category. Dalton finds that a threat to one's self-worth does indeed increase consumers' propensity to trade up and choose the higher priced option in a choice between two options. Importantly, however, Dalton finds that this occurs only when the decision to trade up occurs in a highly self-relevant domain. In a less self-relevant domain, consumers showed a reduced propensity to trade up. In addition, further supporting the idea that consumers trade up on products in response to threat, Dalton finds that buffering participants prior to the threat reduces their tendency to trade up on self-relevant products.

Wheeler and colleagues examine how consumers' confidence in their self-views can be threatened via apparently innocuous tasks that stir compensatory consumption in their decision-making. In four experiments, consumers' confidence in their views of themselves is shaken either by having participants use their non-dominant (versus dominant) hand or priming doubt (versus confidence). Wheeler and colleagues find that these simple manipulations have a significant impact on consumers' choice such that they choose products that will offset the characteristic of which there is doubt. Thus, if consumers' self-views (e.g., excitingness, intelligence) are threatened by doubt, they are more likely to choose consumer products that display these characteristics. Wheeler and colleagues further demonstrate that such threats can be prevented via direct or indirect methods that bolster the self-concept.

Rucker and Galinsky present three experiments suggesting threats to consumers' power evoke compensatory consumption in an effort to regain their sense of power. Based on the notion that status provides one means of signaling one's power, Rucker and Galinsky suggest and find that experiencing a psychological state of powerlessness fosters a preference for attributes related to status, leads to an emphasis in status when developing an advertisement, and leads to more positive attitudes towards products associated

with status. Importantly, when the product attributes are described in terms of performance, the effect reverses. Compared to the powerless, the powerful evince a stronger preference for attributes related to performance, emphasize performance in developing an advertisement, and hold more positive attitudes towards products associated with performance.

As a whole, these three streams of research converge on the point that people often consume in a compensatory manner. Furthermore, each stream of research goes beyond this initial premise by demonstrating that threats do not simply provoke greater consumption. Dalton demonstrates consumers trade up when the product is relevant, but not when the product is irrelevant. Wheeler and colleagues demonstrate that consumers do not exhibit compensatory consumption if they first engage in an affirmation of the self. Finally, Rucker and Galinsky demonstrate that if a product confers performance, rather than status, threatened individuals are less favorable towards it. Thus, these findings push our thinking on several fronts.

EXTENDED ABSTRACTS

"Look on the Bright Side: Self-Expressive Consumption and Consumer Self-Worth"

Amy Dalton, Hong Kong University of Science & Technology, China

It is widely held that people who spend money to compensate for negative feelings of self-worth do so in vain; thus "retail therapy" has been relegated to the dark side of consumption. But in fact, little is empirically known about the relationship between consumption and self-worth. First, when the going gets tough, do the tough always go shopping, or might they sometimes become thriftier instead? And second, is retail therapy inevitably a hollow pursuit, or do conditions exist in which it can be an effective way to repair consumers' feelings of self-worth? In addition to addressing these two questions, the current research explores the substantive issue of trading up—what drives consumers to pay premium prices for goods and/or services in some situations and not others?

According to the current framework, events that threaten self-worth do not uniformly increase consumption, but increase a particular type of consumption: *self-expressive consumption*. *Self-expressive consumption* is consumption that is consistent with (expresses) a consumer's self-concept, his or her values and beliefs about who he or she is. Several experiments document this effect and, in doing so, highlight that retail therapy does in fact have a bright side.

First, in this framework, while self-expressive consumption can sometimes result in an increase in consumer spending (here, trading up), it can also have the opposite effect depending on consumption self-relevance. That is, material objects and consumption domains vary in the extent to which they are important to a consumer's self-concept, a dimension referred to as self-relevance. For instance, both trading up in a highly self-relevant domain and not trading up in a domain that is low on self-relevance are forms of self-expressive consumption. The basic prediction across studies was that, in response to an event that threatened their self-worth, participants would be more likely to trade up (or trade up more) in a consumption domain that was high on self-relevance and less likely to trade up (or trade up less) in a consumption domain that was low on self-relevance.

This hypothesis was tested in experiment 1 by examining how an academic failure impacted students' willingness to trade up when choosing between two t-shirts that were high on self-relevance (i.e., two Duke t-shirts) or low on self-relevance (i.e., two white t-shirts). In each choice set, the t-shirts were priced at $14 and $19. Results showed that threat did not increase trading up in both choice contexts; rather, the tendency to trade up increased only for the self-relevant choice set. For the less self-relevant choice set, threat decreased the tendency to trade up. These results are consistent with the theory that threat impacted self-expressive consumption.

Experiment 2 sought to conceptually replicate these findings. Rather than manipulating threat, this study manipulated whether the threat experience was buffered or not by having participants write about a personally important value (or a value important to others; Steele and Liu 1983) before the academic failure. Second, rather than manipulating self-relevance, it was measured as an individual difference variable. Participants completed a questionnaire that assessed their chronic perception that possessions are part of their self-concept (Sprott, Czellar, Spangenberg 2007). Finally, rather than trading up being a hypothetical choice, it was a real choice. Following the academic failure, participants were led to believe the experiment was over and were told that the lab was conducting a draw for prizes. They were asked how they would allocate $100 to two different gift cards should they win the draw. The gift cards were for the stores Nordstrom (a more expensive store) and Macy's (a less expensive store).

Results showed that compared to buffered participants, non-buffered participants engaged in higher levels of self-expressive consumption. Thus, the conceptual pattern of experiment 1's results was upheld: when self-worth was threatened (here, because a threat was not buffered against), consumption became more self-expressive, with consumers who considered material objects important to their self-concepts trading up more (allocating more money to an expensive store), and consumers who did not consider material objects important to their self-concepts trading up less (allocating less money to an expensive store).

The results of a third experiment explored how individual and choice set differences interact to predict trading up in response to threat. The findings suggest that individuals with chronically strong links to possessions responded to threat by trading up in a variety of consumption contexts, whereas individuals with weaker links to possessions responded to threat by trade up in a more restricted range of consumption contexts. Simply put, people with strong (vs. weak) links to possessions perceive more (vs. fewer) consumption contexts to be self-relevant, and therefore trade up more (vs. less) in response to threat. These findings bolster the overall argument that threat triggers self-expressive consumption.

As alluded to earlier, this research also addressed the impact of trading up on self-worth. That is, can the decision to trade up or not assuage consumers' negative feelings of self-worth? It was predicted that trading up could repair self-worth, but only in a self-relevant domain. Experiment 1 tested and supported this hypothesis and also showed that self-worth could be repaired in less self-relevant domains by *not* trading up. Thus, not only can consumer decisions repair self-worth, but consumers apparently respond to threats by consuming in a way that immediately makes them feel better about themselves.

These findings support the theory that threats to self-worth trigger self-expressive consumption: consumers trade up more (or less) when consumption domains are more (or less) relevant to who they are. Moreover, engaging in self-expressive consumption in turn repairs the self-worth of threatened consumers. These findings highlight the bright side of the relationship between consumption and self-worth: consumers respond to threats adaptively–sometimes spending more and sometimes spending less–and functionally–by making *consumption decisions that repair self-worth*.

"Products as Compensation for Self-Confidence: Subtle Actions Affect Self-View Confidence and Product Choice"

Leilei Gao, The Chinese University of Hong Kong, China
Christian Wheeler, Stanford University, USA
Baba Shiv, Stanford University, USA

It has long been postulated that consumers should choose products with brand personalities that are congruent with their own self-views (e.g. Levy 1959; Birdwell 1964). For example, Birdwell (1964) showed that automobile owners' perceptions of their cars match their self-perceptions. However, despite some promising findings such as these, extensive reviews failed to find consistent evidence that people choose products congruent with their perceived self-characteristics (Kassarjian 1971; Sirgy, 1982).

In the present research, we suggest that a key determinant of product-self congruency in choice is self-view confidence. We show that individuals' confidence in their self-views can be shaken by seemingly inconsequential actions, such as writing about their self-characteristics with the non-dominant hand, and that this lowered confidence can increase the likelihood that they will choose products congruent with the shaken self-views.

Self-view confidence refers to the certainty that one's self-view is truly characteristic of one's actual characteristics (Pelham 1991; DeMarree, Petty, and Briñol 2007). Highly confident self-views can result from consistent and coherent evidence about one's self-characteristics drawn from the environment and from one's past experiences (Campbell 1990; Pelham 1991). In this research, we suggest that self-view confidence can also be affected by very subtle situational factors, such as performing routine actions in unusual ways (e.g., writing with one's non-dominant hand) as well as by subtle priming tasks. Individuals generally desire to hold confident self-views, and evidence suggests that a lack of such confidence can be aversive, resulting in negative psychological outcomes such as low self-esteem (Baumgardner 1990; Campbell 1990), unhappiness and anxiety (Rosenberg 1979). As a result, people seek to bolster confidence in self-views that are threatened. They can do so through both direct and indirect means.

A direct bolstering strategy would involve taking actions that directly restore the shaken self-view. One direct strategy is selecting products that symbolize the dimension on which one has lowered self-confidence. Products are frequently chosen for their symbolic qualities (Belk 1988; Levy 1959; Solomon 1983), and usage of these products can indicate that one has certain self-characteristics both to oneself (Bem 1972; Solomon 1983) and to others (Belk, Bahn, and Mayer 1982). An indirect strategy, by contrast, would involve restoring overall self-views without bolstering the self-characteristic directly. For example, people can cope with self-threats by affirming unrelated self-views (Steele 1988). This affirmation process can eliminate feelings of threat without directly repairing the challenged self-view.

In the present studies, we predicted that people who experience momentarily lowered confidence in a given self-view would be more likely to select products that bolster that self-view. We also predicted that this shift in product choices would be eliminated when participants first had the opportunity to bolster their self-views through either direct or indirect means. A series of four studies provided support for these predictions.

In experiment 1, participants wrote about their excitingness before choosing between exciting products (e.g., Apple computers) or competent products (e.g., IBM computers). They were randomly assigned to write about their excitingness with either their dominant hands or their non-dominant hands. Based upon prior research (Briñol and Petty 2003), we predicted that writing about a self-view with one's non-dominant hand would lower confidence in that self-view, because doing so would be difficult and the writing would look shaky and unconfident. Participants who wrote about their excitingness with their non-dominant hands were more likely to choose exciting products than those who wrote with their dominant hands, consistent with the idea that exciting products were chosen to restore the self-views shaken by writing with the non-dominant hand.

In experiment 2, we replicated and extended these results by testing the effects in another domain (intelligence) and by testing the effect of a direct bolstering opportunity. Participants were first randomly assigned to write about their intelligence with either their dominant or non-dominant hands. They then chose among a series of products from sets containing either intelligence-related products (e.g., bookstore gift certificate) or no intelligence-related products. At the conclusion of the session, they were offered a choice between a pen (intelligence-related) and M&M's (not intelligence-related). We predicted that participants who wrote about their intelligence with their non-dominant hand would be more likely to choose the pen, but only when they did not first have the opportunity to bolster their self-view through prior choice of intelligence-related products. This is what we found.

Experiment 3 generalized these results to another domain and tested the indirect bolstering strategy. Participants were first assigned to write about their health-consciousness with either their dominant or non-dominant hands. They then engaged in a self-affirmation task, in which they wrote about an important value, or an unrelated filler task. Last, they chose between a healthy snack (apple) and an unhealthy snack (M&M's). Results indicated that those who wrote about their health-consciousness with their non-dominant hands were more likely to choose the apple, but only if they did not first have the opportunity to engage in self-affirmation.

In our final experiment, we use another means of shaking self-confidence, fully crossed our design to test for trait-specific confidence, and tested for confidence mediation. The experiment had a 2 (Prime: confidence vs. doubt) x 2 (Trait: excitingness vs. competence) design. Participants were first primed with confidence or doubt before writing about their excitingness or competence. They then chose between a series of products with exciting or competent brand personalities. Results indicated that participants chose more exciting products when primed with doubt and writing about excitingness and chose more competent products when primed with doubt and writing about competence. Moderated mediation analyses showed that these choices were mediated by participants' confidence, but that the effect of the reduced confidence depended on the trait that was activated.

"Lifestyles of the Powerless and Powerful: Compensatory and Non-compensatory Consumption"

Derek Rucker, Northwestern University, USA
Adam Galinsky, Northwestern University, USA

Power is an omnipresent force in consumers' social world. Throughout the day consumers are likely to have experiences of feeling both powerful and powerless. For example, meeting with one's boss, defending a thesis, or submitting a job application might evoke the psychological state of feeling powerless. Conversely, interviewing a potential employee, giving advice, or setting curfew for one's child may evoke the opposite state of feeling powerful.

How does power affect consumption? We propose that psychological states of low and high power have qualitatively different effects on consumers' preferences.

Powerlessness and Compensatory Consumption. On the one hand, powerlessness, or a low power state, is associated with an aversive psychological experience that consumers are motivated to reduce. One means of reducing such a state would be to consume in a manner that gives one a sense of power. In particular, past research suggests that status is one form of power (e.g., French and Raven 1959), and that consumer products serve the function of communicating information about one's status (e.g., Belk et al. 1982). Belk and colleagues note, "It may be that concern with *demonstrating* status to others comes to dominate other consumption message interests sometime after the eighth grade and that this concern then continues." Consequently, due to a motive to compensate for their lack of power, we hypothesize that low power consumers are likely to have a preference for products and product attributes associated with status. In fact, recent work by Rucker and Galinsky (2008) suggests consumers in a state of powerlessness are willing to pay more for status-related products. We suggest this increased willingness to pay should extend to consumers' general preferences.

Having Power and Internal Focus. On the other hand, being powerful, or a state of high power, is typically associated with having control. As control is often desirable, we hypothesize that such consumers should not have a compensatory motive activated. However, we believe there is reason to suspect that experiencing a state of power should be more likely to orient consumers towards performance and obtaining products associated with exceptional functionality and performance. Specifically, prior research has shown that when people are focused on their internal states they tend to focus on the quality of the product (Snyder and DeBono 1985). And, prior research suggests that feeling powerful leads to an increased focus on their own attitudes and desires (Briñol et al. 2007; Chen, Lee-Chai, and Bargh, 2001). For example, Briñol et al. (2007) found that the powerful were less likely to process information about a persuasive message because a state of power suggested their own attitude was correct and listening to others was unnecessary. Given that a focus on one's internal desires produces a focus on quality (Snyder and DeBono 1985), and power focuses people internally, we proposed that high power should intensify a focus on the quality of the products and lead to a preference for products that emphasize quality.

We tested the different preferences resulting from states of low and high power in a series of three experiments. In experiment 1, we manipulated participants' power using a role manipulation adapted from past research (Briñol et al. 2007). Specifically, participants were informed they would be participating in two separate experiments. In the first experiment participants were randomly assigned to either a high power role (Boss) or a low power role (Employee). After the role assignment, as part of a supposedly unrelated task, participants were asked to generate a slogan to accompany a picture of a BMW that they thought would be persuasive. Participants' slogans were coded with respect to whether they emphasized status or performance. Participants assigned to the low power condition generated more slogans related to status than high power participants. In contrast, participants assigned to the high power condition generated more slogans related to performance than low power participants.

Experiment 2 tested our hypothesis by measuring, rather than manipulating, participants' general sense of power and examining their preference for a product advertised as associated with status or performance. Participants were subsequently asked to report their purchasing intentions towards the product. We found that as participants' general sense of power increased they had *more* favorable purchasing intentions for the product associated with performance. Conversely, as participants' general sense of power increased they had *less* favorable attitudes towards the product emphasizing status.

Experiment 3 examined the role of power in consumers' response to ads emphasizing the status or performance aspect of a product and experimentally manipulated power. In addition, a control group was added to demonstrate that low and high power both exhibited effects relative to a control condition. Participants were assigned to control, low, or high power conditions by having them recall a past event (see Galinsky et al. 2003). Participants then read an advertisement for an executive pen and provided their attitude towards the pen. The advertisement was varied to either emphasize the status conveyed by the pen or the performance of the pen. When the pen emphasized status, low power participants held more favorable attitudes towards the pen then both high power and control participants, which did not differ from one another. In contrast, when the pen emphasized performance, high power participants held more favorable attitudes toward the pen compared to both low power and control participants.

Conclusion and Contributions. The present research provides evidence for both compensatory and non-compensatory processes in consumer behavior. Specifically, states of powerlessness foster a desire to compensate for the loss of power, which manifests itself in a proclivity to focus on, and prefer products associated with, status. In contrast, states of power invoke a preference for products associated with performance. Theoretical and practical implications of this work in understanding power in consumer behavior are discussed.

REFERENCES

Baumgardner, Ann H. (1990), "To Know Oneself Is to Like Oneself: Self-Certainty and Self-Affect," *Journal of Personality and Social Psychology*, 58 (June), 1062-72.

Belk, Russell W. (1988), "Possessions and the Extended Self," *Journal of Consumer Research*, 15 (September), 139-68.

Belk, Russell W., Kenneth D. Bahn, and Robert N. Mayer (1982), "Developmental Recognition of Consumption Symbolism," *Journal of Consumer Research*, 9 (June), 4-17.

Bem, Daryl J. (1972), *Self-perception Theory*, In L. Berkowitz (Ed.), *Advances in Experimental Social Psychology*, Vol. 6, New York: Academic Press, 1-62.

Birdwell, Al E. (1968), "A Study of Influence of Image Congruence on Consumer Choice," *Journal of Business*, 41 (January), 76-88.

Briñol, Pablo. Richard E. Petty, Carmen Valle, Derek D. Rucker, D. D. and Alberto Becerra (2007), "The Effects of Message Recipients' Power Before and After Persuasion: A Self-validation Analysis," *Journal of Personality and Social Psychology*, 93 (December), 1040-53.

Campbell, Jennifer D. (1990), "Self-Esteem and Clarity of the Self-Concept," Journal of *Personality and Social Psychology*, 59 (September), 538-49.

Chen, Serena, Annette Y. Lee-Chai, John A. Bargh, J. A. (2001), "Relationship Orientation as a Moderator of the Effects of Social Power," *Journal of Personality and Social Psychology, 80*(February), 173-187.

DeMarree, Kenneth G., Richard E. Petty and Pablo Briñol (2007), "Self-Certainty: Parallels to Attitude Certainty," *International Journal of psychology and Psychological Therapy*, 7, 141-170.

French, John R. P., Jr. and Bertram Raven (1959), "The Bases of Social Power," in *Studies in Social Power*, ed. Dorwin Cartwright, Ann Arbor: Institute for Social Research, 150–67.

Galinsky, Adam D., Deborah H. Gruenfeld, and Joe C. Magee (2003), "From Power to Action," *Journal of Personality and Social Psychology*, 85 (September), 453-66.

Kassarjian, Harold H. (1971), "Personality and Consumer Behavior: A Review," *Journal of Marketing Research*, 8 (November), 409-18.

Levy, Sidney J. (1959), "Symbols for Sale," *Harvard Business Review*, 33 (July-August), 117-24.

Pelham, Brett (1991), "On Confidence and Consequences: the Certainty and Importance of Self-Knowledge," *Journal of Personality and Social Psychology*, 60 (April), 518-30.

Rosenberg, Morris (1979), *Conceiving the Self*, New York: Basic Books.

Rucker, Derek D., and Adam D. Galinsky (2008). "Desire to acquire: Powerlessness and compensatory consumption," *Journal of Consumer Research,* 35 (August), 257-267.

Sirgy, Joseph (1982), "Self-Concept in Consumer Behavior: A Critical Review," Journal of Consumer Research, 9 (December), 287-300.

Snyder, Mark and Kenneth G. DeBono (1985), "Appeals to Image and Claims About Quality: Understanding the Psychology of Advertising," *Journal of Personality and Social Psychology*, 49(September), 586-597.

Solomon, Michael R. (1983), "The Role of Products as Social Stimuli: A Symbolic Interactionism Perspective," *Journal of Consumer Research*, 10 (December), 319-29.

Steele, Claude M. (1988), "The Psychology of Self-Affirmation: Sustaining the Integrity of the Self," in *Advances in Experimental Social Psychology*, Vol. 21, ed. Leonard Berkowitz, San Diego, CA: Academic Press, 261-302.

Legitimation in the Marketplace

Ashlee Humphreys, Northwestern University, USA

SESSION OVERVIEW

This goal of this session is to examine the role of marketplace structures (e.g. brands, products, retailers) in the creation and maintenance of legitimacy, the congruence with dominant norms, values, and institutions. Previous research on legitimacy in consumer research has studied the acceptance of brands (Fournier 1998; Holt 2002; Kates 2004), subcultures (Kozinets 2001), and business practices (Deighton and Grayson 1995), pointing to mechanisms that range from explicit manipulation of legitimacy through social cues and actions (Kates 2004; Kozinets 2001) to implicit manipulation of affective attachment through integration into daily life (Fournier 1998) and the use of cultural scripts (Holt 2002) and discourses (Thompson 2004). Although this previous work has admirably tackled a number of disparate phenomena under the rubric of legitimacy, a clearly articulated theory of the legitimation process and its relationship to market-oriented behaviors has yet to be posed and developed by consumer researchers. By bringing together several approaches to the study of legitimacy, the aim of this session is to theorize the legitimation process through both explicit and implicit cultural forms, to examine the role of larger institutions such as legal or market structures in the legitimation process, and to debate the particular role that market-oriented behaviors play in the legitimation process. Through what process does a practice or identity become stigmatized or destigmatized? How can legitimacy be constrained or enabled by the marketplace? Lastly, how can market structures be used to gain or deny legitimacy?

The session will contribute to our understanding of consumer behavior in three ways. First, the study of legitimation helps us better understand the normative structuring of consumer practice. Many consumers have stopped smoking, started gambling, or refused to buy products made with child labor, all because these practices have gained or lost legitimacy, its congruence with other values, institutions, and social norms. By understanding these normative and institutional structures, we gain insight into the ways in which consumer behavior is constrained in some domains and enabled in others. Second, because legitimation is a fundamental social process (Johnson et al. 2006), it can be used to understand a diverse set of phenomena in consumer research. Understanding legitimation as a distinct social process can shed light on the acceptance of brands, products, practices, and marketplace ideas. In turn, it can also make clear the ways in which the market is used by consumers to attain legitimacy. Finally, a study of the legitimation process can help us better understand the interactions between consumer groups, as they vie for legitimacy in the marketplace and in the social world at large.

Three papers will examine the relationship between legitimation and market structures. First, Gokcen Coskuner-Balli and Craig Thompson will provide an analysis of the creation and legitimization of a non-traditional gender identity through marketplace performances. Ashlee Humphreys will present an institutional analysis of the legitimation of casino gambling in the United States that examines the relationships between regulative, normative, and cultural legitimacy in their interaction with marketplace institutions. Next, Marius Luedicke will examine the contestation and legitimation of brand meaning through an examination of the acculturation process. Finally, John Deighton will tie together the presented empirical work and, drawing from his previous research on the topic, will offer some guidance for further research on legitimacy.

EXTENDED ABSTRACTS

"Legitimatizing an Emergent Social Identity Through Marketplace Performances"

Gokcen Coskuner-Balli, University of Wisconsin-Madison, USA
Craig Thompson, University of Wisconsin-Madison, USA

This paper explores the creation and legitimization of a non-traditional gender identity in the market place. Over the past twenty years, consumer research has explored a variety of ways consumers use market resources for identity construction and communication (Arnould and Thompson 2005). While previous research has recognized the market as a legitimating institution for consumer identities (Penaloza 1994), it has not provided an in-depth understanding of how consumers use the marketplace to legitimize new and unconventional social identities.

To explore these issues we focus on the consumption practices of Stay-at-Home Dads (SAHD from here on) and adopt multiple methods of data collection. Data from in-depth interviews, participant observation at SAHD play groups as well as annual SAHD convention, data collected through netnography (Kozinets 2002), and textual data gathered through compilation of texts/books written for SAHDs, newspaper articles all contribute to our emergent theoretical account.

Our analysis highlights key relationships between consumers' collective efforts to legitimate a new social identity and their efforts to co-create product/brand meanings that facilitate a legitimating or successful performance of this identity. These social actors undertake contextually nuanced social performances and strategically adapt these performances in response to different audience reactions. To better understand these legitimating performances, we identify the cultural scripts from which SAHDs seek to cultivate a new way of performing fatherhood (and masculinity) and the role of the market in providing social, cultural, economic resources which are employed in their legitimating project. We then present the individual and collective consumption strategies (communal, political, entrepreneurial and masculinizing domesticity) SAHDs adopt as they simultaneously seek to legitimize a new social identity while also coping with the feelings of stigma and isolation that are routinely invoked by negative social reactions to their divergence from more culturally established models of fatherhood and masculinity.

The theoretical contributions of our analysis are threefold: First, it addresses the social and cultural barriers that consumers have to negotiate in the process of legitimating new social identities through market-mediated social performances. While the previous CCT literature has repeatedly shown that consumers creatively adapt market resources to construct identities that transcend gender, age and ethnic identities (e.g. Schouten and McAlexander 1995) or to construct hybrid ethnic identities (e.g. Penaloza 1994; Oswald 1999), it has given little attention to the ways in which audience expectations, social conventions, and a paucity of marketplace resources, can impede and/or significantly complicate the performance and legitimization of a new social identity. Second, our analysis reveals that legitimization performances are often embedded in collective struggles and mobilization of market resources in these performances are done in communication with others. As the forces of globalization and postmodern detraditionalization create new spaces for identity experimentation and transformation, various consumer groups will continuously seek to rework their collective identities to better align with these dynamic socio-cultural conditions and to make new claims for social and political rights, as in the case of poor migrant women seeking to lead a middle-class consumer lifestyle (Ustuner and Holt 2007), Greenlandic consumers seeking to forge a connection with global youth culture as a means to transcend the legacy of colonial stigmas (Kjeldgaard and Askegaard (2006), or immigrant consumers seeking to create a new hybrid identity (Pe?aloza 1994). Extending this line of theorization, we highlight that a consumer group, who possesses more social and economic resources, can actively accentuate particular postmodern trends—such as the loosening of traditional gender norms—attempt to transform social perceptions and interaction rituals through their performative innovations. Third, this study further demonstrates that consumers can use market resources not only for therapeutic gain but also to create and legitimate a new social identity that diverges from dominant gender norms. SAHDs employ communal, political, entrepreneurial and masculinizing strategies to mobilize market resources towards this goal. As such this analysis suggests that the marketplace is a political forum for creating a social script that supports emergent identity project and negotiating the impediments for attaining successful performances. In sum, SAHDs' practices of product and brand meaning co-creation are embedded in a societal dialogue over the terms of an effective performance and involves legitimating new performative role and social identity; reducing or refuting social stigmas that accompany violations of conventional performative scripts; adopting market place resources and pushing market to provide more fitting resources; contesting and transforming audience expectations.

"Legitimacy and the Cultural Diffusion of Casino Gambling, 1976-2006"

Ashlee Humphreys, Northwestern University, USA

This paper will examine the legitimation of consumption practices, as it is mediated through social, cultural, and regulative institutions. In 1976, casino gambling in the United States was a marginal consumption practice, legal in one state and undertaken by only about one in ten people in United States. Today, casino gambling is a thriving industry that exists in 28 states and is a consumption practice in which one third of consumers the US participate every year. What explains the shift in gambling from marginalized practice to thriving industry? More generally, how do new industries come to be accepted in the marketplace? How does this acceptance, in turn, destigmatize certain consumer behaviors?

This article explores stigma at the macro-cultural level by evaluating the semantic shifts in discourse about casino gambling in the United States from 1980 to 2006. Previous research on consumer stigma has studied the pathology of shopping behaviors (O'Guinn and Faber 1989), the role of stigma in formations of fan community (Kozinets 2001), and the perceived pressures and consumer enactments toward normalization in response to stigma (Thompson and Hirschman 1995), all with an eye toward the consumer experience of living with stigma. While previous research has studied stigma from this lived perspective, it has not fully taken into account the larger political and social institutions in which stigmatized consumption practices change. How and why does stigmatization of consumption practices change over time and what institutional factors facilitate this change? This article will

evaluate destimatization through the theoretical lens of legitimation, as it is theorized by institutional theory (Johnson et al. 2006; Suchman 1995).

Legitimation is social process of making a practice congruent with the configuration of other values, institutions, and social norms. It occurs on three levels, regulative, normative, and cognitive (Scott 1995). Regulative legitimacy is the degree to which a practice conforms to rules and regulations set forth by a superordinate organization, usually the government. Normative legitimacy is the degree to which the practice is accepted by social actors, irrespective of legal status. Cognitive legitimacy is the degree to which the practice is "taken for granted" and can be categorized and understood according to existing cognitive schemas and cultural frameworks. All three types of legitimacy, however, draw from the same semantic repertoires. As members of a shared social world, politicians, journalists, consumers, and casino owners, work with the same basic concepts that are used to frame casino gambling. On the one hand, the meanings of casino gambling are "out there" as social facts for actors to cite (Husserl 1900/1970). On the other hand, the social meaning of gambling is actively constructed and changed by social actors, especially those with economic and political resources (Sewell 1992). Through this change in meaning, casino gambling can be legitimated or delegitimated. Evaluating this universe of shared meanings and associations, then, is crucial for understanding how legitimacy is achieved.

The data for this chapter comes primarily from a stratified random sample from the population of all newspaper articles with "casino" in the headline or lead paragraph from three periodicals, *New York Times*, *Wall Street Journal*, and *USA Today* from 1980-2006, found using the Factiva database. Several other sources of data including seven interviews and six months of participant observation provided the context with which articles were interpreted.

I find that discourse about casino gambling is structured by semantic binaries that are mobilized by journalists and their sources to frame casino gambling along the dimension of purity and filth (Douglas 1966) and the dimension of wealth and poverty. Employing the Gremsian square (Greimas 1983; Jameson 2005), I show how a number of concepts structurally align along these two semantic poles to orient the ways in which discussions about casino gambling are enacted. The concepts of purity and filth in discourse about casino gambling are evoked not only literally to describe the state of communities where gambling occurs, but are also, and perhaps more often, used figuratively to activate reader associations with crime, prostitution, rot, and decay in the case of filth or cleanliness, integrity, transparency, heroism, and integrity in the case of purity.

Wealth and poverty orient discourse about casino gambling in terms of success and failure. The image of wealth, as it's embodied in high roller clients, wealthy companies, and resort locales, implies unambiguous success. Poverty, in any form, signals failure. The concepts of wealth and poverty are complimentary to the concepts from purity and filth, but they are by no means identical with them. A broader capitalist ideology may associate wealth with purity and poverty with filth, but this view is valid only within a very particular ideological framework. From a religious ideology, for example, poverty is associated with purity and wealth with impurity. Because of the commercial nature of gambling and the American business context, however, the semantic poles of wealth and poverty take on a special role in orienting discussions of gambling and are complimentary to the poles of filth and purity.

Further, I show how these basic semantic materials evolve over time, becoming linked through narratives of contamination, disillusionment, and redemption. For example, in the case of gambling run by Native American tribes, cultural narratives of redemption can be harnessed understand and articulate the transition from poverty to wealth and thereby judge success or failure of these social-structural changes. I examine how these semantic polarities are also synthesized over time into concretizations used to describe the state of the world. Lastly, I more closely examine the ways in which these particular concepts are used to support cultural, normative, and regulatory legitimacy, and assess the degree to which these types of legitimacy are mutually reinforcing.

These findings contribute to consumer behavior in several ways. First, the findings here contribute to our knowledge of the interaction between frames, ideologies, and discourses (Ferree and Merrill 2000). Cultural binaries are the building blocks with which social actors construct frames (Gamson 1992; Gamson and Modigliani 1989). Frames, in turn, are driven by ideologies, the oppositions of which are negotiated within a discourse. Conceptually, these semantic networks are important because they unite multiple levels of analysis, from cognitive structures (i.e. individual conceptualizations of casino gambling) to social structures (i.e. norms that govern when and where one should gamble) to regulatory structures (i.e. laws that govern the enactment of casino gambling). Second, we learn more about the basic process by which consumption practices become destigmatized. Through associations with deeply resonant metaphors and meaning, proponents of casino gambling are able to normatively construct a story and identity that valorizes gambling practices to individuals and to communities. Finally, we gain greater insight into the interaction between types of legitimacy. Specifically, legitimation occurs through more than mere "talk." Rather, it is achieved through a mutually reinforcing system of explicit structural change (regulations, market growth) and more implicit normative and cultural shifts in discourse.

"Host Culture Responses to Brand-related Acculturation: Legitimation Struggles Between German and Turkish BMW Owners in Germany"

Marius K. Luedicke, University of Innsbruck, Austria
Markus Giesler, York University, Canada

Consumer acculturation is a challenge. Global migrants today must not only cope with foreign languages, diverging cultural habits, and alternative market systems (Peñaloza 1995, p. 92), but also with multiple "ascriptive identities" (Horowitz 1975) and multifaceted national discourses and practices that result from swapping between home and host cultures (Oswald 1999; Askegaard, Arnould and Kjeldgaard 2005). Particularly for consumers who lack sufficient capital to participate in the dominant cultures' desired modes of consumption, migration more often than not results in shattered identities (Üstüner and Holt 2007) and ideologically and physically segregated existences (Davis 2006).

By providing platforms for shared social experience and community, brands are commonly held to play an integrative cultural role (Kates 2004; Muñiz and O'Guinn 2001; Oswald 1999; Peñaloza 1995). As Üstüner and Holt (2007) amply illustrate, for migrating Turkish consumers the experimentation with the dominant-culture's favorite brands presents a viable option for familiarizing with the consumption patterns of their new social environment. Consumers that are capable and ideologically attuned to delve into these new consumption practices are found to enter the new culture by consuming status-relevant goods and services in ways particular to their original culture (Peñaloza 1994). In this perspective, host cultural brands are theorized as integrative resources, a unifying *lingua franca* of the marketplace that bridges cultural gaps through creative consumption. By combining their own cultural meanings and codes with the host culture's favorite

status brands, (immigrant) consumers attempt to gain social legitimacy while, at the same time, regenerating the national brand's established system of meanings.

However, when we studied the brand consumption practices of German and Turkish-immigrant BMW drivers in Germany, this optimistic protocol of brand-based acculturation revealed several theoretical incongruities. First, we found the relationship between these two ethnic consumer groups to be mostly antagonistic rather than synergistic. Second, we found that, by way of constructing competing interpretations of BMW driving, particularly German consumer groups fostered ethnic reservations and stereotyping to deny Turkish-German consumers legitimate status gains through BMW ownership rather than bridging cultural gaps. Third, we found that, through BMW consumption, tropes of innovative engineering, Christian virtue, and social achievement were generalized as German national identity traits that were either consumed (Turkish) or consumed and defended against ethnic intrusion (German). Finally, we found that these brand-based attempts to gain social legitimacy in the German culture more often than not served to intensify ethnic segregation ideologies rather than advancing cultural integration.

The goal of our paper is to document these empirical findings and discuss their theoretical, public policy, and marketing implications. We develop a dialectical theory of consumer acculturation and brand consumption that profiles the market-mediated process of acculturation as a mutually competitive legitimation struggle. Specifically, we revise the laudable, yet in parts unrealistic, goals of the brand-based acculturation model in favor of a more nuanced theory of consumer acculturation that draws from symbiotic co-optation dynamics (Thompson and Coskuner-Balli 2007; Giesler 2008) in a multi-ethnic marketplace context. We will illustrate this alternative model on microscopic practice and market-system levels. We will show that the most laudable policy goals of homogenizing national integration will inevitably collide with the ideological segregation forces of a multi-ethnic consumer culture. Yet, at the same time, we will explain that the same competitive consumption processes that hamper national homogenization foster a multi-ethnic national market of hybrid consumer segments.

Methodologically, this analysis is part of a larger ethnographic and netnographic (Kozinets 2002) investigation of German and Turkish immigrant BMW drivers in Germany. Our German BMW drivers are between 18 and 65 years of age, have German family roots of at least three generations and belong to the German middle class. These consumers drive BMW cars including new and pre-owned 3, 5 and 7 series models as well as the Z sports cars and the X sport utility types. With currently more than two million people, the Turkish immigrant community is the largest, most visible group of immigrants in Germany and has a 35+ year cultural history in Germany. Comprising of 15 Turkish-German BMW drivers, our data set consists of 20% first generation Turkish-German consumers who were born in Turkey and immigrated to Germany and 80% second generation Turkish-Germans who were born and raised in Germany but carry forth a distinct Turkish cultural and religious heritage. These consumers drive the entire range of BMW vehicles but tend to own more used and older models than the German group. To ensure trustworthiness of our findings and the representativeness of our German national sample we used data sets from Austria and Switzerland as comparison contexts with similar socio-cultural features. We solicited informants in Berlin and Frankfurt (Germany), Innsbruck (Austria) and Zürich (Switzerland) on the streets as well as through websites and analyzed our in-depth, semi-structured interviews using the established interpretive toolkit of hermeneutical analysis (Thompson 1997).

REFERENCES

Arnould, Eric J. and Craig J. Thompson (2005), "Consumer Culture Theory (CCT): Twenty Years of Research," *Journal of Consumer Research*, 31 (March), 868-882.

Askegaard, Søren, Eric J. Arnould and Dannie Kjeldgaard (2005), "Postassimilationist Ethnic Consumer Research," *Journal of Consumer Research,* 32 (1), 160-70.

Davis, Mike (2006), *Planet of the Slums*, London: Verso.

Deighton, John and Kent Grayson (1995), "Marketing and Seduction: Building Exchange Relationships by Managing Social Consensus," *Journal of Consumer Research*, 21 (4), 660.

Douglas, Mary (1966), *Purity and Danger; an Analysis of Concepts of Pollution and Taboo [by] Mary Douglas*. London,: Routledge & K. Paul.

Ferree, Myra Marx and David A. Merrill (2000), "Hot Movements, Cold Cognition: Thinking About Social Movements in Gendered Frames," *Contemporary Sociology*, 29 (3), 454.

Fournier, Susan (1998), "Consumers and Their Brands: Developing Relationship Theory in Consumer Research," *Journal of Consumer Research*, 24 (4), 343.

Gamson, William A. (1992), *Talking Politics*. Cambridge [England] ; New York, NY, USA: Cambridge University Press.

Gamson, William A. and Andre Modigliani (1989), "Media Discourse and Public Opinion on Nuclear Power: A Constructionist Approach," *American Journal of Sociology*, 95 (1), 1-37.

Giesler, Markus (2008), "Conflict and Compromise: Drama in Marketplace Evolution," *Journal of Consumer Research*, 34 (4).

Greimas, Algirdas Julien (1983), *Structural Semantics : An Attempt at a Method*. Lincoln: University of Nebraska Press.

Holt, Douglas B. (2002), "Why Do Brands Cause Trouble? A Dialectical Theory of Consumer Culture and Branding," *Journal of Consumer Research*, 29 (1), 70.

Horowitz, Donald L. (1975), "Ethnic Identity," in *Ethnicity: Theory and Experience*, eds. Nathan Glaser and Daniel P. Moynihan, Cambridge, MA: Harvard University Press, 110-40.

Husserl, Edmund (1900/1970), *Logical Investigations*. London, New York,: Routledge and K. Paul; Humanities Press.

Jameson, Fredric (2005), *Archaeologies of the Future : The Desire Called Utopia and Other Science Fictions*. New York: Verso.

Johnson, Cathryn, Timothy J. Dowd, Cecilia L. Ridgeway, Karen S. Cook, and Douglas S. Massey (2006), "Legitimacy as a Social Process," *Annual Review of Sociology*, 32 (1), 53.

Kates, Steven M. (2004), "The Dynamics of Brand Legitimacy: An Interpretive Study in the Gay Men's Community," *Journal of Consumer Research,* 31 (2), 455-465.

Kjeldgaard, Dannie and Soren Askegaard (2006), "The Glocalization of Youth Culture: The Global Youth Segment as Structures of Common Difference,"*Journal of Consumer Research*, 33 (September), 231-247.

Kozinets, Robert V. (2002), "The Field Behind the Screen: Using Netnography for Marketing Research in Online Communities," *Journal of Marketing Research*, 39 (1), 61-73.

Kozinets, Robert V. (2001), "Utopian Enterprise: Articulating the Meanings of Star Trek's Culture of Consumption," *Journal of Consumer Research*, 28 (1), 67.

Muñiz, Albert M. Jr. and Thomas O'Guinn (2001), "Brand Community," *Journal of Consumer Research*, 27 (4), 412-432.

O'Guinn, Thomas C. and Ronald J. Faber (1989), "Compulsive Buying: A Phenomenological Exploration," *Journal of Consumer Research*, 16 (2), 147.

Oswald, Laura R. (1999), "Culture Swapping: Consumption and the Ethnogenesis of Middle-Class Haitian Immigrants," *Journal of Consumer Research,* 25 (4), 303-18.

Peñaloza, Lisa (1994), "Atravesando fronteras/Border Crossings: A Critical Ethnographic Exploration of the Consumer Acculturation of Mexican Immigrants," *Journal of Consumer Research*, 21 (June), 32–54.

_____ (1995), "Immigrant Consumers: Marketing and Public Policy Consideration in the Global Economy," *Journal of Public Policy & Marketing,* 14 (1), 83-94.

Schouten, John and James H. McAlexander (1995), "Subcultures of Consumption: An

Ethnography of the New Bikers," *Journal of Consumer Research*, 22 (June), 43-61.

Scott, W. Richard (1995), *Institutions and Organizations*. Thousand Oaks: Sage.

Sewell, William H. Jr. (1992), "A Theory of Structure: Duality, Agency, and Transformation," *American Journal of Sociology*, 98 (1), 1.

Suchman, Mark C. (1995), "Managing Legitimacy: Strategic and Institutional Approaches," *Academy of Management Review*, 20 (3), 571.

Thompson, Craig J. (2004), "Marketplace Mythology and Discourses of Power," *Journal of Consumer Research*, 31 (1), 162.

_____ (1997), "Interpreting Consumers: A Hermeneutical Framework for Deriving Marketing Insights from the Texts of Consumers' Consumption Stories," *Journal of Marketing Research,* 34 (4), 438-56.

Thompson, Craig J. and Gokcen Coskuner-Balli (2007), "Countervailing Market Responses to Corporate Co-optation and the Ideological Recruitment of Consumption Communities," *Journal of Consumer Research*, 34 (2), 135-52.

Thompson, Craig J. and Elizabeth C. Hirschman (1995), "Understanding the Socialized Body: A Poststructuralist Analysis of Consumers' Self-Conceptions," *Journal of Consumer Research*, 22 (2), 139.

Üstüner, Tuba and Douglas B. Holt (2007), "Dominated Consumer Acculturation: The Social Construction of Poor Migrant Women's Consumer Identity Projects in a Turkish Squatter," *Journal of Consumer Research,* 34 (1), 41-55.

Patience, Attention to Time, and Consumer Cognition
Christopher Olivola, Princeton University, USA

SESSION OVERVIEW

Many important consumer decisions involve time. Decisions about saving money, maintaining a diet vs. splurging, or making a payment by credit card vs. with cash are just some of the numerous situations in which people must tradeoff between consumption in the present and consumption in the future. Given the importance of intertemporal choice, then, understanding how time and patience factor into the decision making process is an important goal if we are to properly understand consumer behavior. In line with this goal, the purpose of this symposium is to explore how perceptions of time and individuals' patience-levels interact to impact consumer decision making. The papers in this session explore the impact of attention to time on consumer cognition as well as some important determinants of people's discount rates (an economic measure of patience).

The first paper (Krupka) examines the relationship between patience and access to financial resources (i.e., benefits and credit) among welfare recipients and finds that discount rates increase as access to these resources decreases. The second paper (Olivola & Wang) introduces two novel incentive-compatible methods for eliciting discount rates. A comparison of these methods reveals that discount rates vary, depending on whether attention is focused on the temporal or monetary dimension of delayed rewards. The third paper (Day & Bartels) demonstrates that temporal distance impacts perceptions of similarity, with some events seeming more similar when considered in the near future (or past), while others increase in similarity as temporal distance increases. Finally, the fourth paper (Frederick) demonstrates that two intertemporal choice "anomalies" (the magnitude effect and the sign effect) are actually more pronounced when discount rates across conditions are directly compared or when respondents are encouraged to think more deeply about their pattern of responses. This last paper also considers how these results undermine the normative (rather than descriptive) validity of the discounted utility model.

The papers in this session highlight novel and important features of the interaction between patience, attention to time, and decision making. This research demonstrates that normatively irrelevant factors can impact patience and intertemporal choice (i.e., discounting). The discount rate is shown to depend, dynamically, on access to financial resources (Krupka) and varies depending on whether consumers are focused on the monetary or temporal dimension of delayed payoffs (Olivola & Wang). In fact, attempts to reduce these inconsistencies can actually aggravate them (Frederick). Additional interesting and counterintuitive results include the finding that attention to time increases patience (Olivola & Wang) and alters perceptions of similarity (Day & Bartels).

These papers also adopt creative approaches to the study of intertemporal choice, which include the use of field experiments (Krupka) and experimental auctions (Olivola & Wang). Some papers also compare two or more methodological approaches to the elicitation of discount rates, such as between-subjects vs. within-subject designs (Frederick) and hypothetical vs. real-money incentive-compatible procedures (Olivola & Wang).

In summary, the four papers in this symposium provide both original methods for studying intertemporal choice and novel findings concerning the relationship between patience, attention to time, and consumer cognition. Collectively they demonstrate interesting and surprising phenomena, as well as important theoretical

constructs to the study of intertemporal choice. This symposium should appeal to a diverse research audience for several reasons. First, research into intertemporal choice has implications for understanding the beneficial behaviors (e.g., saving for retirement), as well as the adverse choices (e.g., accumulation of credit card debt) that seriously impact the well-being of many consumers. It therefore contributes to a growing interest in transformative consumer research. In addition, a number of important areas are considered in these papers, including intertemporal choice, time perception, psychological distance, and consumer welfare.

EXTENDED ABSTRACTS

"Eliciting Subjective Discount Rates: Monthly Patterns of Impatience Among the Very Poor"
Erin Krupka, Institute for the Study of Labor (IZA), Germany

The very poor are important targets for US government policies and financial transfer programs. Broadly speaking, individual time preferences have a fundamental role to play in explaining consumption and financial decision making (eg. Angeletos et al. 2001), but some have specifically highlighted the relationship between impatience and financial decision making among the very poor (Meier and Sprenger 2007, Shapiro 2005). It has been suggested that an important source of vulnerability for the poor stems from tight financial constraints which may turn small mistakes, like over-spending at the beginning of the month, into big problems (Caskey 1994, Bertrand, Mulinathan and Shafir, 2004, Eckel et al. 2004). Several papers have found evidence for a monthly pattern in consumption and in time preferences (Shapiro 2005, Wilde and Ranney 2000). This later group of papers suggests that there is a link between rising financial desperation and changing time preferences over the course of a benefit month and the former set of papers suggests that financial constraints play a role in determining monthly patterns of behavior.

Using a sample of 975 married male welfare recipients participating in the Seattle Income Maintenance Experiment (SIME), this paper examines the relationship between rates of subjective time preference (ie discount rates elicited using hypothetical scenarios) and the timing of benefits among welfare recipients. The income maintenance experiments, from which the data for my analysis come, were conducted in the 1970's to examine the effect of negative income tax welfare programs on work behavior. In this paper I use two different and common measures of impatience to explore the relationship between elicited impatience and benefit check receipt.

This paper exploits variation in the interview date of the "Time Horizon and Planning" module, which is orthogonal to the welfare benefit disbursement date, to demonstrate a 'daily discount rate' that is increasing over the course of the benefit month while controlling for socio-economic variables and economic behaviors collected as part of the larger study. The correlation between monthly benefit receipt (or the timing of pay checks) and behavior among welfare recipients (and those with low income) has received some empirical support. In economics, Shapiro (2005) analyzes caloric intake of food stamp recipients and finds that intake declines by 10 to 15 percent over the food stamp month. Wilde and Ranney (2000) find similar patterns for food spending and energy intake after food stamp receipt. Using a sample of mostly retired US workers and a separate sample of UK households, Stephens finds that consumption expenditures are excessively sensitive to monthly receipt of social security checks and paychecks respectively (Stephens 2003, 2006). This literature has focused on the ways in which consumption varies with the timing of welfare benefits and has suggested that the 'excessive sensitivity' to monthly payments stems from credit constraints and or poor financial management. In this paper I show a similar sensitivity of subjective discount rates to the timing of benefit payments.

Using the "Attitudes to Credit" module, I can create a subjective perception of credit constraint and examine whether the increase in the daily discount rate I observe can be accounted for by controlling for perceived credit constraints. I find that those who believe themselves to be credit unconstrained have significantly lower discount rates but that the daily discount rate remains significant and increasing over the benefit month.

The design of the Seattle Income Maintenance experiment also allows me to test whether exogenous variation in the size of the monthly transfer affects the daily discount rate. In the Seattle Income Maintenance Experiments, benefit levels (and other sources of non-work related income) were replaced by the experiment at 95%, 120% or 140% of pre-experimental benefit levels for 3 and 5 years (depending on treatment status). Thus, I can examine the effect of higher benefit levels on impatience and on the monthly impatience trend. I find no significant differences between daily discount rates elicited for controls and for those receiving larger benefits, the coefficient on the daily discount rate remains significant, and is, in some cases, larger.

This paper's final contribution is an empirical one to the growing interest in the study of impatience, and its correlates, among the very poor (Lawrence 1991, Bertrand et al 2004, Eckel et al. 2004). While the data used here are from the 1970's, my main finding of an increase in the daily discount rate over the benefit month is consistent with estimates of the relationship between subjective impatience over the benefit month using more recent data. The main result of my paper resonates with a policy recommendation for distributing welfare payments in smaller installments so that households may be assisted in smoothing consumption. Further, the results would caution against simply raising benefit levels without changing how they are administered.

References

G. Angeletos, D. Laibson, A. Repetto, J. Tobacman and S. Weinberg (2001), "The Hyperbolic Consumption Model: Calibration, Simulation, and Empirical Evaluation" *The Journal of Economic Perspectives*, Vol. 15 (3): 47-68 .

M. Bertrand, S. Mullainathan and E. Shafir (2004). "A Behavioral-Economics View of Poverty." *AEA Papers and Proceedings* 94(2): 419-423

J. P. Caskey (1994). *Fringe banking: Check-cashing outlets, pawnshops, and the poor*. New York, Russell Sage Foundation.

C. C. Eckel, C. Montmarquette and C. Johnson (2004). *Saving decisions of the working poor: short-and long-term horizons*. Montréal, CIRANO.

Stephan Meier and Charles Sprenger (2007), "Impatience and Credit Behavior: Evidence from a Field Experiment", *Boston Federal Reserve Bank Working Paper* W07-3.

Jesse M. Shapiro (2005), "Is there a daily discount rate? Evidence from the food stamp nutrition cycle," *Journal of Public Economics*, vol. 89(2-3): 303-325.

Lawrance, E. C. (1991). "Poverty and the Rate of Time Preference: Evidence from Panel Data." *Journal of Political Economy* 99(1): 54-77.

M. Stephens (2003), ";3rd of tha Month': Do Social Security Recipients Smooth Consumption Between Checks?" *The American Economic Review*, vol. 93(1): 406-422.

M. Stephens (2006), "Paycheque Receipt and the Timing of Consumption", *The Economic Journal*, vol. 116(513): 680-701.

P. Wilde and C. Ranney (2000), "The Monthly Food Stamp Cycle: Shopping Frequency and Food Intake Decisions in an Endogenous Switching Regression Framework", *American Journal of Agricultural Economics*, Vol. 82(1): 200-213.

"Patience Auctions: Novel Mechanisms for Eliciting Discount Rates and the Impact of Time vs. Money Framing"

Christopher Olivola, Princeton University, USA
Stephanie Wang, California Institute of Technology, USA

How do people trade off consumption in the future with current consumption? Measuring discount rates or discount functions is crucial to answering this question, but such measurements pose many methodological challenges. The majority of current measurement methods, such as matching tasks or hypothetical choice, suffer from important weaknesses (Frederick, Loewenstein, & O'Donoghue, 2002). Either they only provide bounds on the discount parameter rather than a point estimate or they are not carried out with real payoffs, thus giving participants no incentives to provide accurate answers and possibly limiting their external validity. In contrast, auction-based approaches can overcome these limitations by providing incentive-compatible mechanisms to elicit discount rates. For example, in second-price private-value auctions, the dominant strategy is for each bidder to bid his/her true value for the good regardless of what the other bidders do (Vickrey ,1961).

We introduce, test, and compare two novel auction-based experimental methods for eliciting discount rates. In these "patience auctions", participants could either receive $10 immediately or a payoff sometime in the future, as determined by the bidding process. The two types of single-round sealed-bid "patience auctions" that we used differed with regard to the dimension that participants could bid on: money versus time. We also compare the relative merits of using first-price auctions versus second-price auctions. In each money-bid auction, the length of delay for the future payoff was pre-set and participants simultaneously bid the monetary amount for that payoff. The lowest bidder obtained the bid-determined payoff at the end of the pre-set delay period and all other bidders received $10 at the end of the session. In the first-price money-bid auction, the bid-determined payoff was the lowest bid whereas in the second-price money-bid auction, the bid-determined payoff was the second lowest bid. In each time-bid auction, the monetary amount for the future payoff was pre-set and participants simultaneously bid the length of delay for that payoff. The highest bidder obtained the pre-set payoff at the end of the bid-determined delay period and all other bidders received $10 at the end of the session. In the first-price time-bid auction, the bid-determined length of the delay was the highest bid, whereas in the second-price time-bid auction it was the second highest bid. We discuss the important advantages these auctions have over other incentive-compatible methods of elicitation, including Becker-DeGroot-Marschak (BDM) and alternative auction designs. In particular, we show that patience auctions provide a more efficient method for eliciting discount rates from large numbers of participants than previous procedures, yielding significant savings of time and money.

In each of the four experimental auction sessions, fifteen participants bid in eight money-bid auctions and eight time-bid auctions, with different pre-set parameters for the delayed payoff or the length of delay, depending on the bid type. All the auctions were first-price auctions in two of the sessions and second-price auctions in the other two sessions. Participants were given no feedback about others' bids or the outcome of each auction. They were paid based on the outcome of one of the sixteen auctions, chosen at random, after all auctions were completed, in order to avoid any incentive distortions. In addition to the auctions, we administered surveys to another group of participants. These surveys were designed to be the hypothetical matching-task equivalents of the auctions: the parameter values used and their orderings were identical to the ones used in the auctions. This allows us to compare the discount rates revealed through the incentive-compatible auctions to those obtained with the commonly used matching task method. Sixty Princeton undergraduate students participated in the experimental auction sessions and an additional thirty completed the hypothetical matching-task surveys.

Beyond their methodological advantages, these auctions allow us to examine new and important questions about the determinants of discounting. Using our within-subject bid type manipulation, we can compare how discount rates vary depending on whether the auction focuses participants' attention on the temporal or monetary dimension of delayed rewards. We find that people are more patient when they bid time than when they bid money –a difference not obtained with equivalent hypothetical matching surveys. Specifically, the estimated mean daily discount rate (DDR) was lower in the time-bid auctions than in the money-bid auctions. While this result supports a "constructed preferences" account (Lichtenstein & Slovic, 2006) of intertemporal choice, we also find a strong within-individual correlation between implied discount rates obtained under time and money bidding, suggesting that approximately half the variance is driven by stable underlying preferences for discounting. Our results are robust to varying assumptions about the curvature of the utility function (risk-aversion vs. risk neutrality), as well as the form of the discount function (exponential vs. hyperbolic). Finally, we find that, contrary to standard auction theory predictions, first-price auctions provide more coherent estimates of the discount rates than their second-price equivalents.

We discuss why standard models of discounting fail to account for the disparity we find in discount rates when people bid money versus time. We then consider how our results relate to other recent findings in psychology, regarding the way people value time versus money. We also discuss the implications of these experimental results for the design of economic mechanisms that involve intertemporal tradeoffs. One example is treasury auctions of bills and bonds that have a pre-specified payoff structure in the future. We consider the possible outcomes of alternative treasury auction designs that elicit time bids for pre-determined current prices and future payoffs rather than the existing money bid method.

References

Becker, G., M. DeGroot, and J. Marschak. (1964). "Measuring utility by a single-response sequential method." *Behavioral Science*, 9, 226–236.

Frederick, S., G. Loewenstein, and T. O'Donoghue (2002). "Time discounting and time preference: A critical review." *Journal of Economic Literature*, 40, 351-401.

Lichtenstein, S., & Slovic, P. (Eds.) (2006). *The construction of preference*. New York: Cambridge University Press.

Vickrey, W. (1961). "Counterspeculation, Auctions, and Competitive Sealed Tenders." *Journal of Finance*, 16, 8-37.

"Event Representation, Similarity, and Preference in Temporal Context"

Samuel Day, Indiana University, USA
Daniel Bartels, University of Chicago, USA

Similarity is widely believed to play a major role in determining how entities, including choice options, are grouped and considered together, and how the consideration of one entity or event brings related knowledge to mind (e.g., Shepard, 1987). In three studies, we considered a novel factor that might affect similarity: this distance in time in which the comparison is considered. Previous studies had shown that similarity can vary widely with factors such as prior knowledge (e.g., Chi, Feltovich & Glaser, 1981) and the comparison context (e.g., Medin, Goldstone & Gentner, 1993).

It is notable that several theories in intertemporal choice theorize representational change over time (e.g., that negative information is discounted at a higher rate, that "affective" information is discounted at a higher rate, or that "low-level" information is less weighty at greater temporal distance), but with few exceptions, representational change is never tested. The current studies offer one such direct test.

Construal Level Theory (CLT; Trope & Liberman, 2003; Liberman & Trope, 1998) proposes that events in the distant future are likely to be construed primarily in terms of their abstract, central, goal-related features. Conversely, representations of events that are closer to the present are likely to contain more concrete, contextual information. These are referred to as high-level and low-level construals, respectively.

The current research draws on this theory, and asks whether these differences in which information is salient may influence how similar two events are perceived to be. For instance, events that share more high-level than low-level commonalities should seem more similar in the distant future, when the abstract goal information (which is shared) is highlighted, and contextual information (which differs between the two) is less available. An example would be the two events "going to the dentist" and "joining a health club", which involve some obvious high-level similarities pertaining to long-term health goals, but are quite different in concrete and contextual details (the "low-level" features). Conversely, we should predict the opposite pattern for events that share primarily concrete features. For example, "going to the dentist" and "getting a tattoo" are surprisingly similar in terms of specific details (reclining on a chair, needles, discomfort, etc.), but seem quite dissimilar in terms of the larger goals that they reflect.

Contrary to the first pair, these sorts of events should seem more similar in the near than the distant future, since near future construals should emphasize their concrete commonalities.

In our first experiment, we asked participants to rate the similarity of event pairs such as these, which could share either high-level (abstract, goal related) commonalities, or low-level (concrete, contextual) ones. Additionally, these events were described as taking place in the near future ("this week") or the distant future ("next year"). As predicted, there was a significant interaction between commonality level (low v. high) and temporal distance (near v. distant). Pairs sharing high level commonalities were rated as more similar in the distant future, while those sharing low-level commonalities were rated as more similar in the near future.

The first experiment contained a possible confound: two events that are near to the present are also necessarily near to each other, but distant events might not be. To address this issue, we ran a second experiment that included a "distant-close" condition, in which events are described as occurring in the same week next year. We replicated our basic effect: effects appear to be based on distance from the present (not distance between events). The distant-close condition was virtually identical to the Distant condition, but significantly different from the Close condition.

In our third experiment, we replicated these findings for events described in the near and distant past. Again, we found a significant interaction, with high-level pairs rated more similar in the distant past, and low-level pairs more similar in the recent past.

A great deal of human cognition involves planning for the future, and considering and learning from the past. The current studies suggest that these temporal distances should have a significant impact on perceived similarities, and therefore have an important effect on how knowledge is organized, and which entities and events are grouped together. This, in turn, should have important consequences for people's judgments and decisions.

Similarity can impact the manner in which choice alternatives are grouped, the adoption of a reference point, and ultimately, the ranking of preferences. We plan to discuss the implications of our findings for context effects. Specifically, Dhar & Glazer (1996) found that context effects were produced by underlying changes in similarity between choice options. We will use temporal distance to induce changes in perceived similarity and make predictions about how to turn substitution effects (between alternatives that are perceived to be similar) into attraction effects (when alternatives are perceived to be less similar).

References

Chi, M. T. H., Feltovich, P. J., & Glaser, R. (1981). "Categorization and representation of physics problems by experts and novices." *Cognitive Science*, 5, 121–152.

Dhar, R. & Glazer, R. (1996). "Similarity in context: Cognitive representation and violation of preference and perceptual invariance in consumer choice." *Organizational Behavior and Human Decision Processes*, 67, 280-293

Liberman, N., & Trope, Y. (1998). "The role of feasibility and desirability considerations in near and distant future decisions: A test of temporal construal theory." *Journal of Personality and Social Psychology*, 75, 5–18.

Medin, D. L., Goldstone, R. L., & Gentner, D. (1993). "Respects for similarity." *Psychological Review*, 100, 254–278.

Shepard, R. N. (1987). "Toward a universal law of generalization for psychological science." *Science*, 237, 1317–1323.

Trope, Y., & Liberman, N. (2003). "Temporal construal." *Psychological Review*, 110, 403–421.

"Applications of the Savage Test to Intertemporal 'Anomalies'"

Shane Frederick, Yale University, USA
Daniel Read, Durham University, UK

In his classic *Foundations of Statistics* (1954), Leonard Savage discusses the criteria for judging the normative status of a decision principle. His focus was the Allais paradox, a pair of choices for which the modal responses (including Savage's) violate the sure-thing principle–an alleged tenet of rational choice. Savage decided that '*if, after thorough deliberation, anyone maintains a pair of distinct preferences that are in conflict with the sure-thing principle, he must abandon, or modify, the principle.*' In other words, if preferences are robust to deliberative reflection by intelligent individuals–if they pass "the *Savage test*"–the principle they violate ought to be discarded as a requirement of rational choice. Slovic and Tversky (1974) applied the Savage test to the Allais paradox by exposing individuals to arguments for and against the sure thing principle. After reading arguments from both sides, most continued to make the choices that jointly violate the sure-thing

principle: they preferred a 10% chance of 5 million to an 11% chance of 1 million but rejected a 99% chance of 5 million, preferring the sure million. Thus, if one grants that the participants were "intelligent individuals" and that a hearing of the evidence allowed them to achieve reflective equilibrium, the Savage test dictates that the sure thing principle be jettisoned as an axiom of rational choice.

Variants of the Savage test could be applied to many problems in judgment and decision making literature. For example, Tversky and Kahneman (1983) show that the "conjunction fallacy" is diminished when the two critical items that are normally embedded among six unrelated items are placed side by side, the juxtaposition cues the logical rule of set inclusion for some respondents; they recognize that it *can't* be more likely for Linda to be a feminist bank teller than for her to be "just" a bank teller. That is, the reflective answers of statistically sophisticated respondents shows a recognition of the validity of that logical principle.

In this paper, we use a 'minimal' Savage test to examine the status of the major "anomalies" in *intertemporal* choice. Following the aforementioned logic, we reasoned that if people are required to make two discounting judgments side by side (or in close succession), then they must consider any differentiation between them as normatively correct–because they would otherwise capitalize on the opportunity to coordinate their responses. If, for instance, people believe they *should* apply a constant discount rate to all delayed outcomes, regardless of the magnitude, valence, or timing of the delay, then the main intertemporal choice anomalies–the "magnitude effect", "sign effect", and "hyperbolic effect" should diminish if discount rates were elicited in a manner that facilitates comparisons (e.g., the magnitude effect should be less pronounced if subjects evaluate "small" and "large" amounts side by side, than if they evaluate them separately). Conversely, if people believe that differences in discount rates *are* justified, the opportunity to consider multiple judgments side by side will not eliminate the effects, and might even increase them, by drawing attention to a factor that subjects consider to be normatively relevant.

We find that the tenets of the discounted utility model (DU) have little appeal to most intelligent adults. When experimental circumstances facilitate direct comparison of discount rates across outcomes differing in valence, magnitude, and delay, respondents did not coordinate responses. Indeed, two of the so-called "anomalies" (the magnitude effect and the sign effect) were *more* pronounced under these conditions. Thus, respondents apparently believe that it is legitimate to discount different goods differently. Admittedly, if discrepant discount rates are not reconciled by additional reflection, one could always counter that respondents were not encouraged to think hard *enough*. However, we show that respondents encouraged to think more deeply about their pattern of responses diverge *further* from the dictates of the theory. On the view that normative models draw support from the reflective equilibrium of intelligent individuals, these results undermine the *normative* validity of DU as well as its *descriptive* validity.

References

Savage, L. (1954). *The Foundation of Statistics*. New York: Wiley

Slovic, P., & Tversky, A. (1974). "Who accepts savage's axiom?" *Behavioral Science*, 19, 368- 373.

Tversky, A. & Kahneman, D. (1983). "Extensional versus intuitive reasoning: The conjunction fallacy in probability judgment." *Psychological Review*, 90, 293-315.

Taking It to the Streets: Methodological Challenges of Doing Transformative Consumer Research on Health

Julie L. Ozanne, Virginia Polytechnic Institute and State University, USA

SESSION OVERVIEW

A long tradition exists of bringing the expertise of consumer researchers to pressing social problems, such as Alan Andreasen's (1975) classic work on the disadvantage consumer. Transformative consumer researchers are developing a multi-paradigmatic program of research that directly engages different stakeholders to help solve social problems and increase consumer well being. Consumer researchers stand in a unique position as informed brokers between the interests of business, consumers, and policy makers. Like other social scientists, we employ rigorous methods and theories and seek to alleviate social problems. Unlike other social scientists, our constituency is consumers, our domain is consumption, and we have a sophisticated grasp of businesses, their strategies, and techniques. Increasingly, the great social problems of our time, such as improving health, are tied to the practices of both businesses and consumers. This ability to converse intelligently with these different stakeholders gives us the potential to broker sustainable change. Nevertheless, practical challenges emerge when doing transformative research.

This special session brings together consumer researchers who are all engaged in programmatic research that examines health problems but employ different methods. Sonya Grier and Shiriki Kumanyika discuss findings from an on-going program of community-based social marketing. Their research examines marketing as a contextual factor on food practices and obesity among African-Americans (Grier and Kumanyika 2008; Grier et al. 2007). In their presentation, they discuss conceptual and methodological challenges related to assessing the marketing environments of African Americans, which occurs at a confluence of interests and generates significant media interest. Craig Andrews, Scot Burton, and Rick Netemeyer examine the effects of a statewide, anti-smoking media campaign on adolescents (Andrews et al. 2004) and adults (Netemeyer, Andrews, and Burton 2005) using telephone interviews. This study was taken to scale in this statewide effort that involved negotiations with researchers from public health and marketing and political decision makers, which had both positive and negative impacts on the research. Laurie Anderson and Julie Ozanne employ a community health approach to examine the health beliefs and cultural practices in a Mexican-American and Native-American town where diabetes rates are 23%. Engaging community members to participate in a research project required tremendous flexibility and time. A series of methods were employed as the project continued including participant observation, interviews, photography, and action methods (Anderson 2007; Ozanne & Saatcioglu 2008).

This session highlights that despite employing different methods, these field projects all examine complex social problems that invariably involve methodological ingenuity, complex trade-offs, and intricate negotiations among various stakeholders. These researchers bring insights from their field work to explore the construction of transformative knowledge that inescapably emerges within a web of social and political interests. While these researchers study health issues from different theoretical and methodological perspectives, a common set of issues and questions emerges in their field work, which offers a platform from which we can debate the challenges and opportunities of doing research aimed at improving consumer well being. This session would be relevant to researchers interested in transformative consumer research, health care, social marketing, and at-risk consumer segments.

EXTENDED ABSTRACTS

"Methodological Challenges in Assessing the Food Marketing Environment of Target Segments"

Sonya Grier, American University, USA
Shiriki Kumanyika, University of Pennsylvania, USA

The extremely high rates of obesity have led researchers, government health organizations and advocacy groups to characterize obesity as an 'epidemic' (Institute of Medicine 2005a; Institute of Medicine 2005b; World Health Organization 2003). In the United States, although obesity is population wide, it is not equally distributed among socio-demographic groups. Ethnic minority status is associated with higher than average obesity prevalence among children and adults, particularly women (Ogden et al. 2006; Ogden et al. 2002). Researchers, policymakers and health advocates debate how food marketing strategies that encourage excess consumption of food and/or discourage physical activity create "obesogenic" environments (Hawkes 2004). A review of past large-scale public health efforts with elements similar to obesity prevention indicate that changes in the marketing environment will be a critical element for success (Economos et al. 2001; Koplan et al. 2005). Research has also described contextual differences in the type and nature of marketing exposures that may limit the effectiveness of health promotion initiatives aimed at preventing obesity among ethnic minority consumers (Grier and Kumanyika 2008; Kumanyika and Grier 2006).

The parallel discussions of the excess risk in minority populations and the importance of the marketing environment underscore the importance of understanding the marketing environments of specific target segments. However, discussion of specific conceptual and methodological approaches to assess the marketing environment of specific consumer segments have not been central to academic research or public policy discussions regarding obesity. For example, although government agencies recently recommended that food companies tailor their public education programs and market more nutritious foods to specific racial/ethnic minority populations, limited mention was made of the socio-contextual barriers these efforts may encounter (The Federal Trade Commission 2006). Although knowledge about the marketing environments of specific populations is limited, it is needed to inform such discussions (Grier et al. 2007; Kumanyika and Grier 2006). A focus on understanding marketing as a contextual variable becomes especially important given the focus on social marketing and transformative consumer research as social change mechanisms underlying public health, and public policy (Esperat 2005; Andreasen 2002).

We will discuss conceptual and methodological challenges related to assessing the marketing environments of specific target segments. We will draw from several projects related to an ongoing, grant-funded research program aimed at illuminating the marketing environment of African-Americans in light of disparities in obesity. In this community-based social marketing research, we examine marketing as a contextual factor on food-related attitudes, beliefs, norms and practices from both emic and etic perspectives.

Thus, we seek to have this research driven by realities facing the community (Esperat 2008).

In one project, we conducted field observations at three health centers that varied in their ethnic composition to inform the development of protocols to assess marketing as a contextual influence on childhood obesity. The observations allowed a qualitative assessment of context-specific marketing factors that may not emerge in standard survey questions. In another project, we conducted a systematic review of the available evidence about the food marketing environments in which African Americans live. We developed an analytical framework for defining the marketing environment of a population sub-segment, created a search strategy to identify relevant articles, and developed a coding scheme to assess the quality of identified articles. The assessment of the validity and reliability of the marketing variables across diverse studies presented key challenges for understanding the quality of marketing environment data. Issues arose with regard to making appropriate comparisons between target segments who may inhibit multiple overlapping contexts. Examples will also be drawn from other research in progress.

We will integrate across several projects to propose general and specific research strategies for assessing the marketing environments of target segments. We will also discuss issues relevant to translating the conceptual frameworks for the projects into the participatory involvement of the community. Finally, we will outline the types of future research that can address deficiencies in the current evidence base regarding how differences in the "street-level' contexts of target segments, including the marketing environment, may limit the generalities that can be drawn regarding population health interventions. The presentation aims to support the development of consumer research that generates practical solutions to contribute to the positive transformation of communities.

"Insights and Challenges in Studying the Effects of Anti-Smoking Ad Campaigns and Other Transformational Consumer Research"

J. Craig Andrews, Marquette University, USA
Scot Burton, University of Arkansas, USA
Richard Netemeyer, University of Virginia, USA

The use of tobacco is the foremost preventable cause of premature death, causing approximately 5.4 million deaths and currently responsible for the death of one in ten adults worldwide (World Health Organization 2008). Sadly, half of the 650 million global smokers will die prematurely (World Health Organization 2008). In the U.S. alone, smoking results in some 438,000 premature deaths each year and $167 billion in total tobacco-related disease costs (Centers for Disease Control and Prevention (CDC) 2008). Given this level of human and financial cost, it is not surprising that advertising and marketing communication efforts aimed at reducing smoking rates are viewed as critical (Fiore et al. 2004).

In this session, we focus on a set of adolescent and adult studies based on a multi-million dollar, statewide anti-tobacco advertising campaign in Wisconsin. We examine many of the methodological difficulties and compromises involving negotiations among diverse stakeholders (i.e., ad agency creative and media professionals, public health officials, policy makers). The campaign was funded as a result of the national Master Settlement Agreement between the states and the tobacco industry. Specific ads used in the adolescent campaign were targeted at middle and high school aged youth in Wisconsin, for which smoking incidence levels were higher than national averages. These ads focused primarily on industry deception/anti-imagery, with other themes addressing addiction and harmful effects of second-hand smoke. The campaign ads had been successfully tested and run in other states and were placed in youth television and radio spots in seven major Wisconsin markets over a six month period.

In this first study, telephone interviews were conducted with over 900 adolescents aged twelve to eighteen years. (One of the presenters had some input into the design and measures for the adolescent and adult studies.) Based on prior research, we examined predicted relationships among social influence (i.e., friends, siblings, or adult smoker in the home), prior smoking trial behavior, attitudes toward specific campaign ads, anti-smoking beliefs, and adolescent smoking intent. Two primary questions were addressed: (1) Do counter ad campaign attitudes directly impact anti-smoking beliefs and intent in a manner similar to that of conventional ads? and (2) Can ad campaign attitudes have a stronger effect on beliefs and intent for adolescents with prior smoking behavior and for those exposed to social influence? Findings show that ad campaign attitudes, prior trial behavior, and social influence all directly affect anti-smoking beliefs, and that ad campaign attitudes interact with prior trial behavior to strengthen anti-smoking beliefs (Andrews, Netemeyer, and Burton 2004). Importantly, our results indicate that attitudes related to the campaign, prior trial behavior, and social influence directly influence intent, and ad campaign attitudes interact with social influence and prior trial behavior to lessen adolescent intent to smoke. Overall, our study findings point to the importance of understanding key characteristics of the target population in the evaluation of counter-marketing campaigns. Studies examining general adolescent populations, while ignoring the measurement of important factors such as prior trial behavior and social influence, may be masking significant effects of the campaign.

In addition, separate ads in the Wisconsin Anti-Tobacco Campaign were targeted at influencing adult smoker beliefs (e.g., about the harmfulness of addiction, environmental smoke, and tobacco industry deceptive practices). In this second study, our findings for 327 adult smokers show that consideration of quitting is positively influenced by the interaction between the number of children living at home and beliefs about deceptive tobacco industry practices used to induce people to smoke (Netemeyer, Andrews, and Burton 2005). In general, implications for counter-marketing communications and for the design and understanding of future anti-smoking campaigns aimed at adolescents and adult smokers are provided.

We then discuss the many methodological challenges and problems inherent to field studies that limit the control of important factors that might differ among important political stakeholders (i.e., ad agencies, public health officials, policy makers) and can lead to non-optimal research designs. Based on our set of studies, this includes dealing with multiple advertisements in a campaign (rather than a single ad), different domains of social influence, varied levels of ad exposure, different types of relevant focal antismoking beliefs, lack of true control groups, unmeasured/omitted variables, single item and more 'practitioner-based' measures, lack of causal designs and related inferences, and use of multiple media. In addition, we discuss some of the challenges regarding the political process of dealing with different constituencies with widely varying perspectives in campaigns designed to promote consumer welfare via transformative consumer research.

More generally, we draw upon additional examples from our participation in important field studies involving market-based transformative consumer research. This includes participation with the Behavioral Change Expert Panel as part of the National Youth

Anti-Drug Media Campaign, as a Consumer Research Specialist with the Federal Trade Commission, and work for the Risk Communication Advisory Committee of the Food & Drug Administration. These positions dealt with important and difficult challenges involving campaign communications, design, assessment, and advertising copy testing and tracking. Our examples also include recent involvement in the Consumer Testing Group of the Keystone Center's Food and Nutrition Roundtable, which is charged with developing a simple, easily-understood, Front-of-Pack (FOP) Icon system that aims to identify the healthier choice for consumers within each category based on pre-established nutrition criteria. Finally, based on these examples and studies, general recommendations are provided about how to best proceed in the design and implementation of projects on consumer transformational research.

References

Andrews, J. Craig, and Richard G. Netemeyer, Scot Burton, D. Paul Moberg, and Ann Christiansen (2004), "Understanding Adolescent Intentions to Smoke: An Examination of Relationships Among Social Influence, Prior Trial Behavior, and Anti-tobacco Campaign Advertising, *Journal of Marketing*, 68 (July), 110-123.

Centers for Disease Control and Prevention (2008), "Fact Sheets on Smoking and Tobacco Use," available at: [http://www.cdc.gov/tobacco/data_statistics/Factsheets/index.htm].

Fiore, Michael C., Robert T. Croyle, Susan J. Curry, et al. (2004), "Preventing 3 Million Premature Deaths and Helping 5 Million Smokers Quit: A National Action Plan for Tobacco Cessation," *American Journal of Public Health*, 94 (February), 205-210.

Netemeyer, Richard G., J. Craig Andrews, and Scot Burton (2005), "Effects of Antismoking Advertising-Based Beliefs on Adult Smokers' Consideration of Quitting," *American Journal of Public Health*, 95 (June), 1062-1066.

World Health Organization (2008), "10 Facts about Tobacco and Second-Hand Smoke," available at: [http://www.who.int/features/factfiles/tobacco/en/index.html].

"Community Action Research on Diabetes"

Laurel Anderson, Arizona State University, USA
Julie L. Ozanne, Virginia Polytechnic Institute and State University, USA

Diabetes can be envisioned as a problem involving individual consumer decision making, such as choices to eat a healthy diet and get regular exercise (Moorman et al. 2004). Alternatively, diabetes can be conceptualized as a community problem in which social and cultural forces have a significant impact on community health (Kreuter et al. 2003). For example, diabetes is at near epidemic rates in many Mexican American and Native American communities (Giachello et al. 2003). In this study, we use participatory community action methods to examine diabetes within a town where 23% of its Mexican American and Indigenous American citizens suffer from diabetes. Health care professionals in the community felt that existing preventative programs and services were ineffective in stemming the rise in diabetes. Moreover, cultural beliefs, practices, and institutions have a significant impact on individual consumer's behaviors.

Participatory action research refers to a general methodological approach that seeks to generate knowledge that is rigorous and can be used for social action (Reason and Bradbury 2001). It is widely applied in community health research because this approach is based on the assumption that those people affected by a social problem should be meaningfully included in the research process (Minkler and Wallerstein 2003). Community members are not merely polled for their opinion, but are actively involved in defining and shaping the research process (Ozanne and Saatcioglu 2008). It is assumed that when community members are involved in the research process they will gain new capacities, they will become more conscious and reflexive regarding the problem, and they will be more ready and committed to taking action that was guided by research based on the needs of their community (Lewin 1946).

We examine an ongoing research project that was first based on participatory observation within a local advocacy group and interviews with members of this community. After the initial exploratory stages of the research, the findings were presented to a group of health workers, social workers, and community members where it coincided with and sparked an interest in the development of a community-based intervention. Specifically, a program is being developed for *promotoras* who are lay health workers and educators that work and reside within the local community. Additional interviews with community members who had diabetes were then collected and the insights from these first-hand accounts were cycled back to help shape the promotoras program.

During the fieldwork a number of challenging issues had to be addressed including length of time required to conduct the research, requirements for different types of expertise (consumer, business, and medical), and the sustainability of the social interventions. For example, while traditional ethnographic work often requires time in the community to develop an understanding of local culture and build trust with potential informants, the length of time required to conduct community action research is significantly longer. This longer tenure is due to the need to forge alliances among many different stakeholders, develop high levels of trust needed to get people to participate actively in research and action, and identify the organizational and cultural capacities needed to actually implement programs of social change. The methodological challenges and empirical results will be explored in the presentation.

References

Minkler, Meredith and Nina Wallerstein (2003), "Introduction to Community Based Participatory Research," in *Community Based Participatory Research for Health,* Meredith Minkler and Nina Wallerstein, ed. San Francisco, CA: Jossey-Bass, 3-26.

Ozanne, Julie L. and Bige Saatcioglu (2008), "Participatory Action Research," *Journal of Consumer Research*, 35, (October), published online March 11, 2008.

Reason, Peter and Hilary Bradbury (2001), "Introduction: Inquiry and Participation in Search of a World Worthy of Human Aspiration," in *Handbook of Action Research*, Peter Reason and Hilary Bradbury, ed. Thousand Oaks, CA: Sage, 1-14.

Unraveling Motivation: Affective and Cognitive Processes Underlying Consumer Goals and Choices

Monica Wadhwa, Stanford University, USA

SESSION OVERVIEW

"I have come to the conclusion that my subjective account of my motivation is largely mythical on almost all occasions. I don't know why I do things." -Anonymous

Introduction. Dating back to the ancient Greeks, scholars have attempted to elucidate the motivational factors underlying human behavior. Aristotle, who proposed one of the earliest theories of motivation, suggested human behavior to be motivated by a desire to achieve an imagined or a real appetitive outcome, and avoid an aversive outcome. Similarly, Freud suggested that individuals work toward seeking pleasurable experiences and avoiding pain. The importance of understanding what motivates goals and choices has been recognized by the consumer researchers as well. Behavioral researchers have examined motivation through a variety of lenses including hedonic versus utilitarian motives (Shiv and Fedorikhin 1999; Dhar and Wertenbroch 2000; Kivetz and Simonson 2002), motivation as a drive (Hull 1951), and the goal-systems theory (Kruglanski et al. 2002). The three papers in this session integrate some of these perspectives in presenting a dynamic view of goals and motivation.

Session Objectives and Overview. The broad purpose of this session is to present work that adds significantly to the growing body of research on motivational factors that drives consumption goals and choices. The more specific objectives of this session are to 1) to explore how affective and cognitive processes underlying an activated goal drive consumption momentum, and 2) to examine the role of exogenous irrelevant sources of motivation in energizing goal striving behaviors. To meet these objectives, three papers are included in this session, all of which are in advanced stages of completion. Keeping in mind the overall theme of ACR 2008 ("Port of Call"), and the diverse audience that ACR conference attracts, the papers in this session explore the factors that impact the motivation underlying consumer behavior from different, yet related perspectives. While the first paper examines how goal related attentional biases can energize momentum toward goal satiating stimuli, the second paper extends the focus of the first paper by exploring another factor—goal-compatibility— in energizing goal related actions. Finally the third paper complements the first two papers by exploring the role of exogenous motivational sources that are irrelevant to any specific goal in energizing subsequent goal striving behaviors.

The session will begin with a focus on goal-driven attentional biases among impulsives and non-impulsives that drive indulgent behavior. Suresh Ramanathan will present his work that focuses on how two types of attentional biases, an initial visual attention bias toward temptations and a bias related to inability to avert attention from such temptations motivate indulgent behaviors. His results demonstrate that while impulsive people exhibit both forms of goal-driven biases towards tempting stimuli, it is their inability to avert attention from such temptations that drives the extent to which they show approach reactions toward such consumption stimuli and subsequently indulge themselves.

Amar Cheema will then present his work with Nidhi Agrawal that builds on the first paper by examining the role of goal-compatibility in energizing momentum toward goal relevant con-

sumption stimuli. Specifically, their results show that compatibility between goals (hedonic versus utilitarian), frames (loss versus gains) and construal levels (low versus high) motivates action aimed at acquiring the goal-compatible consumption stimuli. They find the goal-compatibility motivated consumption action toward such consumption stimuli is independent of attitudes related to such consumption stimuli that when people are energized to achieve a goal (acquire the stimulus) on the basis of compatibility, attitudes towards the stimulus do not have a significant influence on action.

Finally, Monica Wadhwa will present her work with Baba Shiv, which complements the first two papers by examining the impact of brief experiences with hedonic cue (e.g., an appetitive taste) on subsequent goal pursuit. Wadhwa and Shiv demonstrate that a brief experience with a hedonic cue can activate a general motivation drive, which, in turn, enhances pursuit for a subsequently adopted goal (e.g., performance on an intellectual goal, dieting goal etc.). Moreover, they show that given a sequence of goals, the activated motivational drive enhances the pursuit for the more salient goal, that is, the goal temporally closest to experience with the hedonic cue. Finally, their findings demonstrate that the impact of experiencing a hedonic cue on subsequent goal pursuit is attenuated if the activated motivational state is satiated prior to the goal adoption.

In an effort to increase audience participation and provide insights about the three papers, the session will have the services of Baba Shiv as a discussant. Shiv has expertise in the area of the role of emotion in decision making, the neurological bases of emotion, and nonconscious motivational processes in decision making. As a discussant, he will contribute insights about the three papers and the general session theme from not only the field of consumer behavior, but also neuroscience, which is of great interest and appeal to many consumer behavior researchers. Each presenter will limit their talk to 15-20 minutes, to allow ample time for him to speak and to engage the audience into a discussion of the research ideas.

We believe that the features of this proposal suit the evaluation criteria for ACR 2008 symposium proposals. Notably, the session includes papers that are likely to have a broad appeal, yet maintain a coherent theme. We feel that this session brings together three papers that use innovative tools to provide cutting edge counterintuitive insights into the motivational processes that drive consumer behavior and decision making. In addition to attracting researchers interested in the domains of goals and motivation, we expect further interest from those who work within the application areas represented.

EXTENDED ABSTRACTS

"Why One Can't Stop Looking at that Temptation: Dynamics of Attentional Biases in Self-Control Dilemmas"
Suresh Ramanathan, University of Chicago, USA

Why do people over-indulge? What motivates a person not just to act on impulse but to do so repeatedly in a manner counter to one's self-interest? A variety of theories have been ventured in the literature. One view, held by behavioral economists, is that such acts of excessive impulsivity may be attributed to extreme hyperbolic discounting. While this may describe the extent to which people may value the rewarding aspect of indulgence, it does not tell us much about the underlying psychological process. Two views have emerged in the literature in this regard. An affect-based explanation suggests that such indulgences may cause spontaneous activation of lower-order affective reactions that then guide behavior (e.g., Shiv and Fedorikhin 1999, 2002). On the other hand, a motivation-based explanation proposes that rewards carry high incentive value and activate hedonic goals that strengthen over time, leading to over-indulgence (e.g., Ramanathan and Menon 2006). In this paper, I provide additional support for an incentive-salience argument, showing that impulsive behavior and overindulgence are motivated by two different forms of attentional biases toward temptations—an initial visual attention bias toward temptations and bias related to an inability to avert attention from temptations. These biases emerge despite having healthier options that are rated as equally liked and are equally vivid and attractive.

In the first study, participants first completed a scrambled sentence task that was either neutral or designed to activate a hedonic goal. All participants then engaged in a visual probe task (Bradley et al. 2002), in which participants were required to respond as quickly as possible to a small dot probe which was presented immediately after the display of a pair of pictures. The pictorial stimuli used in the visual probe task consisted of 18 color photographs of tempting desserts (e.g., ice-cream, lemon meringue, chocolate cake), each paired with a photograph of a sweet but healthy option (fruit salads, cut fruits). Each picture pair was chosen on the basis of matched liking, vividness and attractiveness as well as size. Pictures were also matched as far as possible on colors. There were an additional 18 pairs of pictures of flowers and vacation spots that were rated as equally pleasant and likeable but had no immediate incentive salience. Eight pairs of neutral objects (e.g., shoes, ties) were used on practice rounds. Picture pairs were displayed side by side. Pictures were presented for either 100 ms or 1250 ms on the screen after a fixation cross that appeared for 500, 750 or 1250 ms at random. The pair of pictures was followed by the dot probe that appeared in the position of one of the two preceding pictures and remained on the screen till the respondent's response. The task consisted of 16 practice trials, followed by 64 experimental trials in two blocks of trials, presented in a new random order in every session. Each picture pair was presented four times, so that pictures and probes appeared equally often on the left and right sides. Attentional bias scores were computed for each participant by subtracting mean RTs to probes replacing the pictures of desserts from the mean RTs to probes replacing the pictures of fruits. Positive values indicate greater vigilance for temptations. Positive values at the 100 ms exposure level indicate an initial visual attention bias towards temptations, while those at the 1250 ms level indicate maintenance of attention and an inability to divert attention from desserts when the probe appeared in the position of the fruit. Next, participants completed a series of filler questions, followed by questions relating to their felt emotions and an assessment of their impulsivity on the CIS scale (Puri 1996). They were then dismissed and ushered one at a time into an adjacent room where they were left alone for 3 minutes (while waiting to complete an unrelated study) with a tray filled with chocolate cookies that the experimenter suggested were from a departmental meeting. The experimenter subsequently counted the number of cookies consumed. Results show that impulsive people showed a strong initial visual attention bias towards the desserts despite being presented with an equally vivid and attractive healthy option. There was no such bias towards either flowers or vacation spots, both of which were rated as equally liked and attractive. Interestingly, this bias did not affect the number of cookies picked up. Rather, it was the bias

related to an inability to avert attention at a more conscious level from the temptation that influenced the number of cookies taken, more so when impulsive people were primed with the hedonic goal.

In a second study, a similar visual probe task was followed by a task requiring participants to continuously move a joystick indicating whether they felt like picking up a tempting chocolate snack on a tray in front of them right at the moment or felt like pushing it away (Ramanathan and Menon 2006). Results once again indicate that impulsive people who were primed with a hedonic goal exhibited a strong attentional bias at the conscious level that prevented them from averting their attention from temptations, and that this bias resulted in more intense approach reactions towards the snack.

Together, these results provide evidence suggesting that motivational influences leading to over-indulgence is likely due to a goal-driven attentional bias that causes people to remain fixated on temptations despite having equally liked and vivid alternatives. Stated differently, these results, therefore, suggest that the motivation to indulge is likely to be based on pure incentive salience of the temptations (Berridge and Robinson 1998) rather than initial affective reactions.

"Compatibility-Driven Momentum in Redemption of Sales Promotions"

Amar Cheema, Washington University in St. Louis, USA
Nidhi Agrawal, Northwestern University, USA

In this paper, we bring together the literatures on choice between hedonic versus utilitarian options, gain and loss frames, and construal level to identify the influence of these factors on consumer decisions in response to price promotions. We identify factors related to the message (product category, frame) and the consumer (construal level) that might make the same promotion (e.g., $5 off of $25) more or less likely to be used by the consumer. In doing so, we aim to understand the process by which the compatibility of these factors affects behavior. Based on regulatory fit theory which argues that compatibility between factors generates momentum towards accomplishing the compatible goal (Higgins 2006), we propose that compatibility urges action (e.g., redemption of a coupon) towards compatible stimuli independent of product evaluations. In contrast, stimuli that are incompatible with the goal enhance the role of product evaluations in consumers' decisions to redeem the coupon for the featured product.

Theoretical Background. By examining the effects of compatibility between three factors (product category, frames, and construal level) on coupon redemption, we integrate two disparate streams of literature. First, past research in consumer choice has shown that gain framed choices are likely to favor utilitarian products over hedonic ones (Dhar and Wertenbroch 2000). In contrast, loss framed choices tend to favor hedonic rather than utilitarian options. This research suggests that hedonic items are compatible with a loss frame whereas utilitarian items are compatible with a gain frame. A second set of findings has suggested that factors that focus on losses (e.g., prevention focus) are compatible with a near time frame and factors that focus on gains (e.g., promotion focus) are compatible with a distant time frame (Förster and Higgins 2005). On the basis of these two sets of findings we propose that for products that are associated with a utilitarian goal (e.g., an energy bar), gain framed messages presented under higher levels of construal are most effective because of the enhanced compatibility. In contrast, for products associated with hedonic goals (e.g., a chocolate cake), loss framed messages presented under lower levels of construal are compatible. Compatibility, in turn, generates an enhanced momentum for action and increases redemption likelihood. Importantly, we expect the effect of compatibility on redemption to be independent of product evaluations.

Overview of Results. In four studies, participants at higher or lower levels of construals are presented with gain or loss framed coupons. These coupons either feature a product associated with a hedonic or a utilitarian goal. Redemption likelihood, evaluations of the featured product, and other process measures are collected. Study 1 shows that for a hedonic product, redemption is highest under compatibility conditions (loss frame presented to low-level construers) than for the other three conditions. Providing further support for the proposed compatibility thesis, study 2 reveals that compatibility (utilitarian product, gain frame presented to high-level construers) leads to greater redemption than the other (incompatible) conditions. Interestingly, our results show that the effect of product evaluation on redemption is not significant in the presence of compatibility, suggesting that a stronger motivation to act, rather than evaluation drives redemption under conditions of compatibility. Consistent with this expectation, study 3 reveals that participants in compatibility (vs. incompatibility) conditions make the redemption decision faster and pay less attention to the product quality. In study 4, we find that redemption of an actual coupon offered by a local restaurant varied in accord with our predictions.

Conclusion. While previous studies on compatibility have focused on elaboration or fluency as explanations for compatibility effects on attitudes, our studies show a mechanism that links compatibility directly with behavior and suggests that compatibility might affect behavior independently of attitudes. Our findings support an explanation based on the strength of engagement–in other words, a process in which compatibility creates a momentum for action–might characterize the effects of compatibility on behavior. Higgins (2006) suggested that people experience greater strength of engagement when responding to goal-compatible (vs. incompatible) stimuli, which should fuel a momentum towards performing the compatible action. Incompatibility dilutes this momentum, lowering the propensity towards action, and increases the impact of product evaluations on redemption. On a broad level, these results contribute to increasing our understanding of consumer motivation underlying goal-directed behavior.

"Kindling the Motivation System: Impact of Incident Hedonic Cues on Subsequent Goal Pursuit"
Monica Wadhwa, Stanford University, USA
Baba Shiv, Stanford University, USA

Our consumption environment is abundant in cues that are high in hedonic value (i.e., cues that are desirable). A whiff of a fragrance, a sample of a refreshing drink or an advertisement picturing romantic images are some such cues that we commonly experience in our everyday lives. While, recent research on consumption motivation suggests that experiencing such high hedonic value consumption cues can lead to generalized reward seeking behaviors (e.g., Van den Bergh, Dewitte and Warlop 2008; Wadhwa, Shiv and Nowlis 2008), relatively little is understood about whether and how experiencing such cues impact consumer's subsequent goal related behaviors. Since arguably all of consumer choices and behaviors are goal driven (Bettman, Luce and Payne 1998), investigating how such experiences with hedonic cues impact subsequent goal related behaviors is consequential both from the marketers' and consumers' perspectives. Drawing upon the synthesis of research on consumption motivation (Van Den Bergh et al.; Wadhwa et al. 2008) and the recent evidence in neuroscience (Depue and Collins 1999; Berridge 2007; Salamone 2007), in the present research, we propose that the motivational drive activated by brief experiences with hedonic cues can enhance pursuit of a subse-

quently adopted goal. To illustrate, our proposition would suggest that if a consumer adopts an environmental goal following the consumption of an appetitive beverage sample, she should now be motivated to make a larger donation for an environmental cause (than if she had not sampled the appetitive beverage).

We address the aforementioned research proposition in a series of studies across an array of consumer goals and dependent variables. In study 1, we sought to explore the basic research question—whether or not a brief experience with a hedonic cue can enhance pursuit of a subsequently adopted goal. Our findings demonstrate that participants who had experienced a hedonic cue (romantic images) set a higher health goal (i.e., number of hours they were planning to work out), but only when they were primed with a health goal. In study 2, we sought to provide further support for our core research proposition. Specifically, we argue that when the motivational drive state activated in response to experience with hedonic cues is satiated, impact of hedonic cues on subsequent goal pursuit behaviors should get attenuated. To test this logic, we carried out the motivational drive manipulation by employing a sampling paradigm. All respondents sampled either Hawaiian Punch (motivational drive-induced condition) or a neutral water drink (motivational drive-not induced condition) presented to them in the disguise of a newly launched sports drink. Subsequently, we carried out the drive state satiation manipulation, which was adopted from Wadhwa et al. (2008). Specifically, participants who had experienced the hedonic cue either received a surprise reward (candy bar) after the hedonic cue experience but before the goal adoption (motivational drive -satiated), or they received the candy bar at the end of the study (motivational drive-induced). In this study, we measure actual persistence on a subsequent goal, which in this study was an intellectual goal that involved working on anagrams. We predicted that sampling a consumption cue high in hedonic value should enhance persistence on the subsequent intellectual goal involving unscrambling anagrams. However, when the induced motivational drive state is satiated (i.e., when participants received the surprise reward in an intervening task), the impact of hedonic cues on subsequent goal pursuit behaviors (persistence on anagrams) should get attenuated. Consistent with our propositions, we show that respondents who had experienced the hedonic cue (motivational drive-induced condition) persisted longer on the anagrams than those who had not experienced the hedonic cue (motivational-drive-not induced condition). Further, our results show when the induced motivational drive was satiated by giving a surprise reward in an intervening task, the impact of experiencing hedonic cue on subsequent goal persistence was attenuated.

In study 3, we provide further support for our activated motivational drive hypothesis. Further, study 3 shows that given a sequence of goals, the induced motivational drive enhances the pursuit for the more salient goal, that is, the goal temporally proximal to the source of activated motivational drive. To elaborate, in study 3, female participants were sequentially exposed to two goals (dieting and environmental goal), the two goals being separated by a five-minute filler task. However, in one set of conditions (goal salient-dieting), motivational drive was manipulated proximal to the dieting goal—that is, respondents sampled either an appetitive drink (motivational-drive-induced) or a neutral drink (motivational-drive-not induced) as soon as the dieting goal was made salient. In the other set of conditions (goal salient-environment), respondents sampled either an appetitive drink (motivational-drive-induced) or a neutral drink (motivational-drive-not induced) proximal to when the environmental goal was made salient. Subsequently, respondents moved to another room where they made food (cookies) and drink (lemonade) choices. Finally, respondents were asked to indicate the amount of money they were willing to pay for a charity devoted to an environmental cause. They were informed that the amount they indicate will be deducted from their study compensation. Our results show that participants showed enhanced pursuit for the dieting goal when the motivational drive state was activated temporally proximal to the dieting goal. Specifically, these participants chose to consume less of cookies and sweetened lemonade. In contrast, when the motivational drive state was activated proximal to the environmental goal, participants showed enhanced pursuit for the environmental goal—these participants chose to donate more money for the environmental cause. Across these studies, I also rule out alternative accounts related to factors such as mood and arousal.

In sum, our findings suggest that a brief experience with a hedonic cue can enhance pursuit of a subsequently adopted goal that is unrelated to the experienced hedonic cue. Implications for marketers and policy makers are discussed.

REFERENCES

Bettman, James R., Mary Frances Luce and John W. Payne (1998), "Constructive Consumer Choice Processes," *Journal of Consumer Research*, 25 (December), 187-217.

Berridge, Kent (2007), "The Debate Over Dopamine's Role in Reward: The Case for Incentive Salience?" *Psychopharmacology*, 191 (April), 391-431.

Berridge Kent C. and Terry E. Robinson (1998), "What is the role of dopamine in reward: hedonic impact, reward learning, or incentive salience?," *Brain Research Reviews*, 28 (December), 309–369.

Bradley, Brendan P., Karin Mogg., Tamsin Wright and Matt Field (2003), "Attentional bias in drug dependence: vigilance for cigarette-related cues in smokers," *Psychology of Addictive Behaviors*, 17 (March), 66-72

Depue, Richard A. and Paul F. Collins (1999), "Neurobiology of the Structure of personality: Dopamine, of Incentive Motivation, and Extraversion," *Behavioral and Brain Sciences*, 22 (June), 491-569.

Dhar, Ravi, and Klaus Wertenbroch (2000), "Consumer Choice between Hedonic and Utilitarian Goods," *Journal of Marketing Research*, 37 (February), 60-71.

Förster, Jens and E. Tory Higgins (2005), "How Global vs. Local Perception Fits Regulatory Focus," *Psychological Science*, 16, 631-36.

Higgins, E. Tory (2006), "Value from Hedonic Experience and Engagement," *Psychological Review*, 113, 439-60.

Hull, Clark L. (1951). *Essentials of behavior*, New Haven: Yale University Press.

Kivetz, Ran, and Itamar Simonson (2002), "Self Control for the Righteous: Toward a Theory of Precommitment to Indulgence," *Journal of Consumer Research*, 29 (2), 199-217.

Kruglanski, Arie W, James Y. Shah, Ayelet Fishbach, Ron Friedman, Woo Young Chun and David Sleeth-Keppler (2002), "A Theory of Goal Systems," in *Advances in Experimental Social Psychology*, ed. Mark P. Zanna, San Diego: Academic Press, pp. 331-378.

Puri, Radhika, (1996), "Measuring and Modifying Consumer Impulsiveness: A Cost-Benefit Accessibility Framework," *Journal of Consumer Psychology*, 5 (2), 87–114.

Ramanathan, Suresh and Geeta Menon (2006), "Time-Varying Effects of Chronic Hedonic Goals on Impulsive Behavior," *Journal of Marketing Research*, 43 (August), 628-641.

Salamone, John D, Mercè Correa, Andrew Farrar and Susana M. Mingote (2007), "Effort Related Function of Nucleus Accumbens Dopamine and Associated Forebrain Circuits," *Psychopharmacology*, 191 (April), 461-482.

Shiv, Baba and Alexander Fedorikhin (1999), "Heart and Mind in Conflict: Interplay of Affect and Cognition in Consumer Decision Making," *Journal of Consumer Research*, 26 (December), 278- 82.

Shiv, Baba and Alexander Fedorikhin (2002), "Spontaneous versus Controlled Influences of Stimulus-Based Affect on Choice Behavior," *Organizational Behavior and Human Decision Processes*, 87 (March), 342-370.

Van den Bergh, Bram, Siegfried Dewitte, S., & Luk Warlop (2008). Bikinis instigate generalized impatience in intertemporal choice. *Journal of Consumer Research, 35*, 85-97.

Wadhwa, Monica, Baba Shiv and Stephen M. Nowlis (2008), "A Bite to Whet The Reward Appetite," *Journal of Marketing Research*, 45 (August), 403-413.

Context-Dependent Search

Kristin Diehl, University of Southern California, USA

SESSION OVERVIEW

While the notion of context-dependence has played a dominant role in the study of consumer decision-making, most research on consumer search has focused on internal or external search costs as search determinants (e.g., Urbany 1990), treating context effects mainly as determinants of consumers' search costs (e.g., Russo 1977). By focusing solely on search costs, past research fails to account for how today's complex decision environments may influence search strategies and for search in environments where search cost are inherently low (e.g., online). Addressing these gaps, this session presents novel perspectives on determinants of consumer search. The research presented investigates the role of different search contexts in the ways consumers search, ultimately linking search to the choices consumers make and the satisfaction they derive from these choices as well as the search process as a whole.

Findings presented in this session suggest that the context in which consumers search can subtly prompt different search strategies. In particular, more restricted or less expected contexts may cue greater search effort while contexts triggering withdrawal tendencies associated with task-related affect may cue truncated search. Further, this session also suggests that the extent of search consumers engage in may affect satisfaction with the process and the choice itself.

The work by Lin and Levav investigates how the structure of product configuration menus can trigger distinct mindsets and ultimately different search strategies. Encountering menus with relatively fewer options to start with, consumers find themselves in a maximizing mode, searching more exhaustively not only from the initial set but also from subsequent, larger selections. Starting off consumers with lots of options, however, triggers a satisficing mindset associated with more superficial search even among manageable sets. Ultimately deeper search leads to greater satisfaction short-term but not necessarily greater remembered satisfaction.

Relatedly, Poynor and Wood explore how different ways of structuring assortment sets affects information acquisition and choices. They compare grouping familiar products either into more conventional taxonomic sets or into less common thematic sets. Results show that for more knowledgeable consumers, thematic groupings act as newness cues that cause them to expend greater effort when deciding among options. Engaging with the decision context in a more effortful way leads to greater incidental learning among expert but not among novice consumers. Experts also seem to derive greater process satisfaction from the more effortful decision context.

Diehl, Morales, Fitzsimons and Simester investigate how the decision context, specifically purchasing a product that elicits task-related affect, can alter where and how much consumers search for and purchase other, unrelated products. Focusing on products that elicit disgust, an emotion associated with a tendency to pull away from one's surroundings, they show that in this context consumers truncate their search even for neutral products. Ultimately lack of search leads to smaller shopping baskets and is associated with lower evaluations of the overall experience.

These presentations address this area of research from diverse and novel perspectives but converge on a central theme: External search environments subtly cue different search strategies and ultimately alter product choice. Taken together, this session will provide new insights that should be interesting to a wide range of researchers, for example, those studying context effects, assortment size and structure, or the effects of retail environments.

EXTENDED ABSTRACTS

"When Choice is Motivating: Using Product Configuration Sequence to Evoke Maximization"

Claire Lin, Columbia University, USA
Jonathan Levav, Columbia University, USA

Product configuration is an increasingly common consumer experience; consumers now customize a variety of products (such as shoes, computers, cars and pre-fabricated houses). Yet little is known about one crucial variable for designing the configuration process: the sequencing of choice menus. All else equal, how does the order of choice menus affect people's choice and satisfaction?

Consistent with research on consumer mindsets, we propose that the order by which people make a sequence of decisions may determine the overall approach they take in making these decisions. A mindset refers to a cognitive process or judgmental criterion that is triggered by a task and persists in subsequent tasks (Xu and Wyer, 2007). For example, once people learn a rule for solving an initial series of problems, they persist in applying this rule to later problems (Luchins & Luchins, 1959). The effect of mindsets has also been demonstrated in consumer settings. For example, in the shopping momentum effect (Dhar, Huber and Khan, 2007), after people make a purchase decision and get into the "which to buy" mindset, they are more likely to make subsequent purchase (Xu and Wyer, 2007). Similarly, in the context of product configuration, we expect that the mindset triggered by initial choice menus may also affect people's approach to later choice menus.

We hypothesize that the sequence of choice menus may determine people's tendency to maximize vs. satisfice, which we conceptualize as a mindset either to search exhaustively through all options in order to identify the best or to stop searching as soon as a satisfactory option is encountered. To test this hypothesis, we choose the number of options of each choice menu as a variable for sequencing the choice menus. Prior research has shown that a large number of options may be demotivating (Iyengar & Lepper, 2000). As a result, we expect that when product configuration begins with a choice menu that includes a relatively large number of options, people may be more likely to resort to a simplifying heuristic like satisficing. In contrast, when product configuration begins with a choice menu that includes a relatively small number of options, people may find it relatively easy to maximize, i.e. search through the options to identify the best one for them. Based on the concept of mindset, we expect that the maximizing or satisficing heuristic/mindset that is triggered by the initial choice menu will persist throughout the product configuration process. Further, the maximizing or satisficing mindset may affect people's satisfaction in a similar pattern observed among chronic maximizers and satisficers (Iyengar, Wells and Schwartz, 2006).

We tested our hypothesis in three experiments. Participants encountered a sequence of choice menus either with an increasing number of options (the increasing-sequence condition) or a decreasing number of options (the decreasing-sequence condition). In

Experiment 1, 49 participants configured a 10-song CD, which they could take home 2 weeks after the study. The 10 songs were chosen from 10 non-overlapping music collections. In the increasing-sequence condition, the number of song options increased from one music collection to the next (5, 10, 15,…, 50), and vice versa in the decreasing-sequence condition. Our results showed that participants in the increasing-sequence condition engaged in a deeper search effort–they sampled about 50% more songs and spent 50% more time in making decision.

In Experiment 2, using a similar task, we measured the degree of self-reported "maximization tendency," and found that the maximizing measure mediated the effect of sequencing on search. In addition, we ruled out an alternative explanation that participants who encountered a small choice menu first might search more because they mistakenly expected that all subsequent choice menus would have a similarly small number of options. We found that regardless of whether participants were informed of the actual numbers of options in all choice menus in advance, they followed the same search patterns. Apparently the mindset primed by the initial choice menu exerted a strong effect that was not overcome by the information provided to participants.

In Experiment 3, we measured participants' satisfaction with their choices immediately and again two weeks after the experiment. The immediate satisfaction was measured on a scale of 1 to 7. The delayed satisfaction was operationalized as whether people were more or less likely to follow through on their earlier decisions by coming to claim their CD two weeks later. We found that participants in the increasing-sequence condition, who exhibited stronger maximizing tendencies, were more satisfied immediately yet were less likely to claim their CD gift two weeks later, reflecting lower long-term satisfaction.

Our research shows that the sequence of choice menus can determine people's mindset for maximizing vs. satisficing. Overall, people spend more effort searching through options when they encounter a sequence of decisions in which the number of options increases from one choice menu to another. Self-reported degree of goal maximization mediates the effect of menu sequence on depth of search. Finally, the maximization vs. satisficing mindset triggered by menu sequence has a downstream effect on satisfaction: temporary maximizers are more satisfied in the short-term but less satisfied in the long-term.

"Designed To Learn: How Category Design Influences Consumer Learning, Satisfaction and Choice"
Cait Poynor, University of Pittsburgh, USA
Stacy Wood, University of South Carolina, USA

Given the proliferation of product information in the marketplace, consumers should be well-equipped to acquire knowledge and make good choices. However, due to a host of individual and contextual challenges (Alba and Hutchinson 2000, Camerer and Johnson 1991), even knowledgeable consumers may not learn information they encounter. This research suggests a novel means of improving consumers' incidental learning, proposing that type of category structure used to group products in the retail environment can be adapted in ways which help consumers acquire more knowledge while shopping.

We focus on the effects of organizing an assortment in very familiar taxonomic groupings, where objects are grouped by type, or more abstract thematic groupings, a type of goal-derived structure. Two studies employing foods as our target stimulus show that category structure can impact consumers' learning of nutritional information. However, the extent of learning generated by each design depends on consumers' prior knowledge. Whereas low prior

knowledge consumers' incidental learning is low and promoted by the highly fluent context of taxonomic sets (Alba and Hutchinson 1987), for highly knowledgeable consumers thematic category designs operate as a "newness cue" (cf. Poynor and Diehl 2008, Wood and Lynch 2002). For these consumers, thematic category structures prompt more effort during shopping. Increased effort leads to superior product information encoding for experts and raises expert consumers' satisfaction with their shopping experience. In addition, we find that greater effort among experts is associated with objectively higher choice quality. For less knowledgeable consumers, however, these effects do not hold.

A pretest first identified thematic groupings which were less expected in the marketplace but equally plausible as taxonomic groupings for the same items, consistent with the nature of a "newness cue". Participants (n=38) saw a menu containing the same 16 items organized either taxonomically (soups, sandwiches, finger foods, salads) or by cuisine theme (American, Chinese, Mexican, Italian.) Participants rated the menus as equally believable, but as expected, felt that the taxonomic groupings were more expected than were the thematic groupings.

Study 1 integrated these categories into a shopping situation to see if the less-expected thematic category structure would impact consumer learning as hypothesized. Participants (n=70) first completed a test of their prior knowledge of the nutritional content in foods. During the experiment, they were asked to imagine that they were working on a class project and decided to order lunch online. They were given the general goal of choosing a "nutritious" food and shopped a website containing 16 items organized either by the taxonomic or thematic structures identified in the pretest. Participants clicked on food names to review their nutritional information. After selecting a single food, participants completed a 10-item "surprise" quiz about the nutritional content of foods on the website, which provided our main dependent measure.

Analysis suggested that the thematic structures did, in fact, operate as newness cues for expert consumers. In the taxonomic structure, higher prior knowledge consumers did not outperform novice consumers on the quiz, consistent with a complacency effect (Wood and Lynch 2002). However, higher prior knowledge consumers showed significantly better recall for nutritional information in the thematic as opposed to the taxonomic sets. Experts also demonstrated significantly better recall in the thematic sets compared to novice participants shopping in the same structure, suggesting that their complacency was overcome. Interestingly, however, the thematic organization also created marginally significant *decreases* in incidental learning among lower prior knowledge consumers relative to the taxonomic set.

For thematic structures to be aptly characterized as newness cues, it was also important to establish that their effects occur at encoding, by increasing processing effort among experts, rather than at retrieval. Therefore, in study 2, we added an external incentive to process the nutrition information prior to shopping for some participants (n=76). For the remaining participants (n=64), the incentive was given prior to recall but after exposure to the website information. We hypothesized that study 1's effects would replicate when the incentive was offered after exposure to the information, but not when the incentive occurred before encoding. In addition, we measured participants' effort, shopping satisfaction, and choice quality.

As expected, study 2 replicated study 1's findings when consumers had received external incentives after shopping. Once again, experts learned more from the thematic structures than they had in the taxonomic structures. By contrast, novices showed a significant decrease in learning in thematic as opposed to taxonomic sets. Furthermore, the effect of category design on learning was mediated by the amount of effort expert consumers reported investing during search. In addition, the increase in effort seen among expert consumers led to higher, rather than lower shopping satisfaction ratings than in taxonomic sets. Finally, results show that expert participants chose significantly more nutritious foods when selecting from thematic as opposed to taxonomic sets. By contrast, when a processing incentive was received before exposure to the choice set, only prior knowledge predicted participants' learning and choice quality.

Data from a third study will be available for discussion at ACR 2008. Thus far, we have tested taxonomic categories which are more expected than thematic structures. However, thematic categories are becoming increasingly popular in the marketplace. Thus, our third study explores the question, what happens when taxonomic structures are unexpected, or when thematic structures become expected?

Taken together, our research suggests that a relatively subtle change in the retail environment can create positive outcomes in terms of consumer well-being and retailer success. However, findings also suggest caution: what operates as a "newness cue" for experts appeared to impede novices' encoding. Thus, retailers considering thematic structures should remain cognizant of consumers' knowledge level before adopting wholesale changes in assortment layout.

"Does One Bad Apple Spoil the Barrel? Carry-over Effects of Buying Disgusting Products on Consumer Search and Shopping Basket Decisions"

Kristin Diehl, University of Southern California, USA
Andrea C. Morales, Arizona State University, USA
Gavan J. Fitzsimons, Duke University, USA
Duncan Simester, Massachusetts Institute of Technology, USA

Trash bags, diapers, dog food, and cat litter–any one of these products is likely to be on a consumer's shopping list. Now imagine two consumers in a supermarket: X needs to buy trash bags while Y needs to buy sandwich bags. Would you expect these consumers to behave differently during the *remainder* of the shopping trip? Our research suggests that a difference in the decision context as subtle as having to buy trash versus sandwich bags can alter how much time consumers spend in a store, the types of products they buy, and their evaluations of the shopping experience as a whole. What would drive such effects? We suggest that buying products such as trash bags, diapers, dog food, etc. that elicit feelings of disgust (Morales and Fitzsimons 2007) can influence search behavior and purchase decisions not just for these disgust inducing products but, more importantly, for *other* products purchased on the same occasion.

As a first step we partnered with a national chain of convenience stores to gather actual shopping basket information. The resulting sample captured items purchased in more than 27 million baskets. We combine this data with survey measures of perceived disgust for the top 45 non-food product categories. Focusing on the 11 million baskets that included at least one item from these 45 categories we used the perceived disgust measures to categorize transactions according to the "most disgusting" item in each basket. For each category we then calculated the average percentage of food items in each basket. The findings reveal a clear relationship: baskets that contain items that are more disgusting tend to contain a smaller percentage of food items.

This data documents the relationship between purchases of disgusting items and the composition of the shopping basket. However, it yields limited insight on why exactly this might happen

and how the presence of disgusting items can lead to these findings. Disgust is associated with an appraisal of being too close to an offensive object (Lazarus 1991) and triggers an implicit action tendency to pull away from the cause of disgust and one's immediate surroundings (Rozin et al. 2000). Disgust can have powerful effects on consumer actions either due to its associated appraisal tendencies (Lerner et al. 2004) or due to perceived contamination through physical contact (Argo, Dahl and Morales 2006). Results from our transactional data could indeed be explained by consumers' reluctance to add food items to their baskets so as not to "contaminate" them. However, our laboratory findings support a slightly more complex process that does not require physical contact for a disgusting purchase to influence shoppers' behavior.

Where and how much consumers search in a retail environment can alter the kind of products considered and chosen (e.g. Moorman, Diehl, Brinberg, Kidwell 2004). In contexts that elicit disgust, we expect consumer search to be truncated based on the implicit distancing reaction disgust triggers. We also expect distancing tendencies to carry over to how consumers search in other, unrelated product categories and the store as a whole. We further test these predictions in two experiments and also rule out that it is simply negative affect that leads to these results.

In study 2 participants were given a list of ten product categories typically found in a drugstore and were asked to "purchase" one product from each category at one of two computerized stores. Lists differed only with respect to the *first* category on the list. This category was either a product prone to elicit feelings of disgust (diarrhea medicine) or a neutral product (ballpoint pens). In a third condition (disgust-branded) participants saw the same shopping list as in the disgust conditions but brand names rather than more generic category labels were used (i.e. Immodium A-D instead of diarrhea medicine).

As expected, participants in the disgust condition spent less time in the target category than those in the neutral condition. Interestingly, compared to the neutral condition, those in the disgust-branded condition also spent less time searching the target category. More importantly, purchasing a disgusting or a disgust-branded product also reduced time spent searching *other, unrelated* product categories and spent less time in the store as a whole.

We find that buying a disgusting product has pronounced effects on search behavior across unrelated product categories. As such our field results may not just be driven by consumers planning separate trips for disgusting items but may actually be due to differences in search *within* the same trip. In study 3 we rule out that our findings are driven merely by negative affect in general as opposed to the avoidance tendencies specifically triggered by disgust.

Study 3 varied the target product to be either disgusting (diarrhea medicine), neutral (Vitamin C supplement) or sad (sympathy card), holding all other products on the list constant. We replicate our prior findings that search in the target category as well as *other* categories during that trip is significantly lower for those buying a disgusting product compared to those buying a neutral product. In contrast, we find that participants purchasing a sad product spent significantly *more* time in the target category than those in the neutral condition, supporting the notion that it is the specific appraisals triggered by the target purchase, and not just the valence, that leads to these effects on search. Further, replicating findings from the field, we also show that participants who purchased a disgusting product were significantly less likely to buy a food item on the same trip than participants in the sad or neutral condition. A mediation analysis shows that purchase reductions are indeed driven by decreased search, further evidence that changes in the search context can systematically alter purchase decisions across categories.

BIBLIOGRAPHY

Alba, Joseph W. and J. Wesley Hutchinson (1987), "Dimensions of Consumer Expertise," *Journal of Consumer Research,* 13 (4), 411-454.

Argo, Jennifer J., Darren W. Dahl, and Rajesh V. Manchanda (2001), "The Influence of a Mere Social Presence in a Retail Context," *Journal of Consumer Research*, 32 (2), 207-212.

Camerer, Colin F. and Eric J. Johnson (1991), "The Process Performance Paradox in Expert Judgment: How Can Experts Know So Much and Predict So Badly," in *Toward a General Theory of Expertise: Prospects and Limits,* ed. K. Anders Ericsson and Jacqui Smith, New York: Cambridge University Press, 195-217.

Dhar, R., Huber, J., & Khan, U. (2007). The Shopping Momentum Effect. Journal of Marketing Research, 44(3), 370.

Iyengar, S. S. and M. R. Lepper (2000). "When Choice is Demotivating: Can One Desire Too Much of a Good Thing." Journal of Personality and Social Psychology 79(6): 995-1006.

Iyengar, S. S., Wells, R. E., & Schwartz, B. (2006). Research Article Doing Better but Feeling Worse. Psychological Science, 17, 143.

Lazarus, Richard S. (1991), "Progress on a Cognitive-Motivational- Relational Theory of Emotion," American Psychologist, 46 (8), 819-834.

Lerner, Jennifer D. and Dacher Keltner (2000), "Beyond valence: Toward a model of emotion-specific influences on judgment and choice," *Cognition and Emotion*, 14 (4), 473-493.

Luchins, A. S., & Luchins, E. H. (1959). Rigidity of Behavior: A Variational Approach to the Effect of Einstellung: University of Oregon Books.

_____, and Gavan J. Fitzsimons (2007), "Product Contagion: Changing Consumer Evaluations Through Physical Contact with "Disgusting" Products," *Journal of Marketing Research*, 44 (2), 272-283.

Moorman, Christine, Kristin Diehl, David Brinberg, and Blair Kidwell (2004), "Subjective Knowledge, Search Locations, and Consumer Choice," *Journal of Consumer Research*, 31 (3), 673-680.

Poynor, Cait and Kristin Diehl (2008), "The Psychology of Category Design: How Product Groupings Influence Consumer Choice and Satisfaction," *working paper*, University of Pittsburgh, Pittsburgh, PA 15260.

Rozin, Paul, Jonathan Haidt, and Clark R. McCauley (2000), "Disgust," in Lewis, Michael and Jeannette M. Haviland (eds), *Handbook of emotions*, 2nd Edition, New York: Guilford Press, 637-653.

Wood, Stacy L. and John G. Lynch, Jr. (2002), "Prior Knowledge and Complacency in New Product Learning," *Journal of Consumer Research*, 29 (December), 416-426.

Xu, A. J., & Wyer Jr, R. S. The Effect of Mind-Sets on Consumer Decision Strategies. Journal of Consumer Research, 34(4), 556-566.

Through the Looking Glass: New Ideas about the Consumption of Beauty

Barbara Phillips, University of Saskatchewan, Canada

SESSION OVERVIEW

Then she began to look about, and noticed that what could be seen from the old room was quite common and uninteresting, but that all the rest was as different as possible. (Lewis Carroll, Through the Looking Glass)

Legions of consumer researchers have examined the concept of beauty from such diverse perspectives as aesthetic ideals, body image, self-concept, self-identity, and specific industries including clothing and cosmetics. Nonetheless, a review of the beauty literature reveals a certain sameness to this research endeavor. This sameness has resulted from applying a single root perspective, leading to an oversimplified view of the phenomenon of beauty consumption. We believe that it is time to step up to the looking glass. First, to mirror the conceptualizations of beauty as they are currently conceived. Second, to go through the looking glass and explore alternative ways of seeing beauty, and thus gain new perspectives for understanding the consumption of fashion advertising, body ideals, and cosmetics purchases.

The researchers participating in this symposium are not naive about previously published research in this area, nor do they seek to overturn it. Instead, they seek to build upon it to present a more complex, more elaborated, and more nuanced explanation of the consumption of beauty. The first presentation examines the idea of aspiration as the driver of fashion advertising, and finds it lacking. The authors combine interview, content analysis, and survey data to uncover what fashion ads are really like, and the diverse ways in which women actually choose to consume them. The second presentation explores women's embodied experiences of pregnancy and birth. Previous research implies that women are released from beauty ideals during pregnancy; but interviews with pregnant women suggest that body-image is much more multifaceted and mixed than a simple polarity between freedom or enslavement can explain. The third presentation investigates the common perspective that selling beauty products such as cosmetics subjugates women. A case study of the Avon lady in Africa suggests ways in which the cosmetic industry can be empowering for women, as it creates ties of economic health between them, while avoiding disastrous repercussions from the ruling powers.

All three presentations *reflect* current perspectives on beauty consumption and then go *through* the looking glass to reverse, expand, or embellish conventional wisdom and unexamined assumptions. Yet each addresses different areas of beauty consumption: fashion images, body ideals, and the cosmetics industry. In addition, each presentation relies on empirical data that have already been collected but not yet published. Consequently, these presentations form a coherent symposium containing new information of interest to a diverse audience of consumer behavior scholars.

EXTENDED ABSTRACTS

"The Aspiration Assumption: Women's Consumption of Fashion Advertising"

Barbara Phillips, University of Saskatchwan, Canada
Edward McQuarrie, Santa Clara University, USA

Fashion is a process by which the latest aesthetic styles are introduced to the public through a system that structures the reception and consumption of those styles (Entwistle 2000). The fashion process relies on continual, regular, and institutionalized changes in dress, adornment, and decorative design (Davis 1992). Ever since Richins (1991) demonstrated that women compare themselves unfavorably to the models portrayed in clothing ads, the preponderance of academic papers examining fashion advertising has focused on representations of women—both their appearance and their roles—and compared them to some standard of "reality" (for a review, see Lindner [2004]). One of the key assumptions underlying such research is that all fashion advertising is rooted in a straightforward aspirational message showing a model to be emulated. That is, fashion advertising presents an idealized image that women are taught to aspire to. Consequently, consumer response to fashion advertising is must be simple as well: a woman can accept the idealized image and strive for it, or she can reject the idealized image and define herself in opposition.

By contrast, previous research in consumer behavior has demonstrated that the reading of advertisements is a complex task nuanced by personal life themes, goals, and projects (Mick and Buhl 1992, Mick and Politi 1989, Scott 1994), and may be conducted for many non-purchase reasons (O'Donohoe 1994). We also know that clothing choices are used to build identity within a local group (Elliott and Davies 2006) using fashion discourses from the broader culture (Thompson and Haytko 1997) while attempting to avoid negative associations (Bannister and Hogg 2004). Given these perspectives, it is difficult to believe that a simple interpretive strategy, such as "accept/reject idealized image" can effectively capture the reality of consumers' readings of fashion ads.

We contend that the reading of fashion ads has been so stigmatized and denatured that the larger project of studying fashion image consumption has stalled. Women are too often forced into the narrow categories of fashion object or fashion victim, ignoring the fact that fashion is a culturally-situated practice resulting from the intersection of complex social forces and individual negotiation (Entwistle 2000). This presentation uses the perspective of consumer culture theory (Arnould and Thompson 2005) to examine how consumers' motivations and interpretations frame their consumption of mass-mediated fashion images. Under consumer culture theory, marketing scholars accept that individuals consume the symbolic meanings of products along with a product's physical characteristics. A fashion brand is just such a combination of the physical and the symbolic (Rocamora 2002). However, little research exists on how branded and heavily imaged products such as clothing come to be infused with symbolic meaning. "Lacking such knowledge, we can at best only form conclusions without quite knowing how we derived them; this is something we often have to do in everyday life, but it hardly satisfies the requirements of a science" (Davis 1992, 4). It is our hope to advance consumer science in the domain of fashion.

We will present a content analysis of three decades of fashion advertising in *Vogue* and *Vanity Fair* to demonstrate that fashion ads are not simple vessels of aspiration. We add findings from two surveys of the readers of fashion magazines to examine *how* women consume fashion magazines. Finally, the presentation reports the results of an ongoing set of interviews with "fashionista women" to develop a theory of *why* women consume fashion advertising as they do.

"Mirror, Mirror on the Wall: Consuming Ideal Images? Celebrating the Pregnant and Postpartum Body"

Margaret K. Hogg, Lancaster University, UK
Emma Banister, Lancaster University, UK
Mandy Dixon, Lancaster University, UK

In this presentation we focus on the body as the basis for the "evaluation of self in the public arena" (Turner 1994) and explore women's experiences of cultural ideals surrounding bodies, both during pregnancy and post partum. Pregnancy is often regarded as a state which frees women, at least temporarily, from their concerns with their slender ideal self, allowing them to gain weight and change shape without the risk of attracting adverse evaluation from others; or feeling inadequate in social comparisons with idealized images of women and beauty (Richins 1991, Wood 1989). Much consumer research has focused particularly on the psychological (negative) implications of cultural idealizations of beautiful and slender bodies, to the relative neglect of investigating occasions (e.g., pregnancy) when women experience positive feelings about their bodies. Pregnancy would seem to be an occasion when women can experience positive feelings about their bodies and celebrate their growing size. Our study links Duke's (2002) consideration of consumption as a social and cultural process which involves the acceptance of, and aspiration to, the ideal, with the disciplinary gaze (Foucault 1979), that recognizes the individual as "his/her own agent of surveillance conforming to normative conventions" (Thompson and Hirschman 1995, 149).

We used phenomenological interviews to understand how the embodied self is articulated during pregnancy and early motherhood; and how expectant and new mothers respond to a variety of discourses from society and the media about what constitutes an ideal body. Firstly for many women pregnancy represented a time and space for 'free play' of the embodied self, i.e., the feminist argument which describes pregnancy as "an opportunity to 'step outside' of the tyranny of slenderness… [and] enjoy a more embodied, subjective and maternal state" (Earle 2003, 250). Our data indicated that some expectant mothers experience release from the disciplinary gaze and societal expectations, which constructs the ideal feminine body in ornamental terms, and enjoy their bodies' physicality without feelings of stress or guilt. However, it could be argued that these women are not so much freed from the disciplinary gaze, but are subject to a different disciplinary gaze or a different set of 'ideals', which constructs the feminine mothering body as productive, fertile and large. This represents a development of Earle's (2003) point. She argues that because the pregnant body is temporary it offers women no reprieve from societal expectations. It is simply that the emphasis switches to an (often unspoken) interest in women's bodies as functional-producers rather than as ornamental-seducers and women are instead presented with an alternative range of conventions around pregnant bodies and consumption, promoted via public policy statements, media and maternity interest groups.

Secondly, the environment became a source of unwanted comparative ideals (Wood 1989). Expectant mothers can find themselves confronted with a different range of discourses, which are just as normative as those they experienced before pregnancy. During pregnancy, women face the challenge not so much about what they consume in order to create a sexually attractive body but rather how they discipline their appetites in order to develop and maintain their bodies as fitness machines for pregnancy and birth (e.g., eating the right foods; taking the appropriate supplements; giving up smoking and alcohol; avoiding smoky atmospheres). This theme suggests that women's bodies are just as strongly policed within the context of pregnancy as in their non pregnant states where they feel themselves subject to another range of disciplinary discourses.

A third key theme revolved around retrieval and control, and social comparison plays a vital role here as women called on their past (pre-pregnancy) self as a source of comparison as well as the idealized images that abound in media and society. New mothers faced a difficult balancing act. As new mothers they are expected to retain the functional role of their body, including the strength to care for and nurture their child; whilst also regaining their past non-pregnant self. However, our participants did not lack agency in asserting their own independent views of their bodies, illustrated by these women's construction of their bodies as a source of strength and control; and by their discussions which centered on regaining or retraining their bodies to be 'fit'. Stories revolved around various constructions of 'fitness' in relation to various selves e.g., fit enough to be effective mothering selves (e.g., breast feeding: body finely tuned for production); fit enough to climb ladders and regain competence as the DIY self (body as agile machine); fit enough to power dress within the business world to regain the professional self (body as power engine); fit enough to regain a young, svelte-like feminine self (body as female).

"Avon in Africa: Cosmetics Consumption and Women's Empowerment Through Trade"

Linda Scott, University of Oxford, UK
Catherine Dolan, University of Oxford, UK

Critics of consumer culture have often focused on cosmetics as the nadir of the wasteful, oppressive ethic of the market. Recent historical works have suggested that this view needs revision. One particularly contradictory aspect of the historical record is the way that the beauty industry has created opportunities for women with little education or capital to achieve economic autonomy. Big names like Elizabeth Arden, Estée Lauder, and Helena Rubinstein testify to the power a small investment, an entrepreneurial spirit, and a flair for style can have in a market for goods aimed at a female constituency. However, larger, less spotlighted groups have also been served by the trade between women as consumers and women as sellers. From the corner beauty salon to the local "Avon Lady," history has given us many examples of the way cosmetics consumption can be parlayed into an economic empowerment tool for women.

The premise of this study is that the historical power of the beauty industry to quietly create incomes for women could be harnessed to fight poverty in developing nations. One of the oldest female trading networks in America, the Avon Company, has already experienced significant growth in the poor nations, with more than half of their sales now coming from developing markets. Surprising as it may seem today, Avon's historical market was among factory girls and rural farmwives in the United States—so they have a long-established track record for building businesses among poor women's existing trading relationships. Since the networks are female and the products feminine, the men in such settings seldom take notice of what can be a very healthy income stream. Indeed, anecdotal evidence coming in from Brazil or Thailand suggests that not only are Avon representatives building good incomes in unlikely places, but they may be doing it without the disapproval and even violence that often comes from patriarchal cultures when women are empowered. So, this line of goods may offer a potentially safer venue for women to improve their status, which, in turn, is now seen as a central key to developing national economies.

This presentation will report the first phase results of a three year, multi-site study in South Africa, being conducted under the auspices of the Department for International Development and the Economics and Social Science Research Council (United Kingdom). We are using several methods to examine the potential for trade of these manufactured cosmetics to alleviate poverty and foster empowerment among African women. As unlikely as cosmetics may seem as a vehicle for development, direct sales of beauty products appear to offer low risk opportunities for women to become entrepreneurs, even in regions where capital, infrastructure, and institutional frameworks are weak.

First phase results suggest not only interesting findings on the practices and benefits for Avon representatives but surprising feedback from consumers of the product. Buyers of Avon are clearly imbedded in a web of trade relationships in which they not only buy cosmetics from a friend or relative, but also sell other goods to that "Avon Lady" in a reciprocal arrangement. Patterns of purchase reflect historical African aesthetics that focus on lotion and shiny skin, but also more recent and global aesthetics involving "glamour products" like lipstick and eye shadow. Further, consumers, especially in very poor areas such as the squatter's camps outside Johannesburg, show both a proclivity to reinvention and a shrewd attention to maintaining a balance between "necessities" (lotion, in this culture) and "luxuries" (mostly perfumes). Thus, the study presents some interesting learning about hybridization, global versus local culture, and consumer adaptation, in addition to contradicting most contemporary thinking about the political status of cosmetics.

REFERENCES

Arnould, Eric J. and Craig J. Thompson (2005), "Consumer Culture Theory: Twenty Years of Research," *Journal of Consumer Research*, 31 (March), 868-882.

Bannister, Emma N. and Margaret K. Hogg (2004), "Negative Symbolic Consumption and Consumers' Drive for Self-Esteem: The Case of the Fashion Industry," *European Journal of Marketing*, 38 (7), 850-868.

Bordo, Susan (1993), *Unbearable Weight*, Berkeley, CA: University of California.

Bundles, A'Lelia (2001), *On Her Own Ground*, New York, NY: Scribner.

Burke, Timothy (1996), *Lifebuoy Men, Luxe Women*, Durham, NC: Duke.

Byrd, Veronica (1994), "The Avon Lady of the Amazon," *Businessweek*, October 24, 93.

Chalfin, Brenda (2004), *Shea Butter Republic*, London, UK: Routledge.

Clark, Gracia (1994), *Onions are My Husband*, Chicago, IL: The University of Chicago Press.

Davis, Fred (1992), *Fashion, Culture, and Identity*, Chicago, IL: The University of Chicago Press.

Duke, Lisa (2002), "Get real! Cultural Relevance and Resistance to the Mediated Feminine Ideal," *Psychology & Marketing*, February 19 (2), 211-233.

Earle, Sarah (2003), "Bumps and Boobs: Fatness and Women's Experiences of Pregnancy," *Women's Studies International Forum*, 26 (3), 25-252.

Elliott, Richard and Andrea Davies (2006), "Symbolic Brands and Authenticity of Identity Performance," *Brand Culture*, Jonathan E. Schroeder and Miriam Salzer-Morling (eds.), London, UK: Routledge, 155-170.

Entwistle, Joanne (2000), *The Fashioned Body: Fashion, Dress, and Modern Social Theory*, Cambridge, UK: Polity Press.

Foucault, Michel (1979), *Discipline and Punish: The Birth of the Prison*, London, UK: Penguin.

Hansen, Karen (2000), *Salaula: The World of Secondhand Clothing and Zambia*, Chicago, IL: The University of Chicago Press.

Horn, Nancy E. (1994), *Cultivating Customers: Market Women in Harare*, Boulder, CO: Lynne Rienner.

Jordan, Miriam (2003), "Knock, Knock: In Brazil, an Army of Unemployed Goes Door-to-Door," *Wall Street Journal*, February 19, A1.

Lindner, Katharina (2004), "Images of Women in General Interest and Fashion Magazine Advertisements from 1955 to 2002," *Sex Roles*, 51 (7/8), 409-421.

Mick, David Glen and Claus Buhl (1992), "A Meaning-Based Model of Advertising Experiences," *Journal of Consumer Research*, 19 (December), 317-338.

Mick, David Glen and Laura G. Politi (1989), "Consumers' Interpretations of Advertising Imagery: A Visit to the Hell of Connotation," *Interpretive Consumer Research*, Elizabeth Hirschman, ed., Provo, UT: Association for Consumer Research, 85-96.

O'Donohoe, Stephanie (1994), "Advertising Uses and Gratifications," *European Journal of Marketing*, 28 (8/9), 52-75.

Peiss, Kathy (1998), *Hope in a Jar*, New York, NY: Henry Holt.

Richins, Marsha L. (1991), "Social Comparison and the Idealized Images of Advertising," *Journal of Consumer Research*, 18 (June), 71-83.

Rocamora, Agnes (2002), "Fields of Fashion: Critical Insights into Bourdieu's Sociology of Culture," *Journal of Consumer Culture*, 2 (3), 341-362.

Rodriguez, Deborah (2007), *The Kabul Beauty School*, London, UK: Hodder and Stoughton.

Scanlon, Jennifer (1995), *Inarticulate Longings*, London, UK: Routledge.

Scott, Linda M. (1994), "The Bridge from Text to Mind: Adapting Reader-Response Theory to Consumer Research," *Journal of Consumer Research*, 21 (December), 461-480.

Scott, Linda M. (2000), "Market Feminism: The Case for a Paradigm Shift," *Marketing and Feminism*, Miriam Catterall, Pauline MacLaran, and Lorna Stevens (eds.), London, UK: Routledge, 16-38.

Scott, Linda M. (2005), *Fresh Lipstick: Redressing Fashion and Feminism*, New York, NY: Palgrave MacMillan.

Thompson, Craig J. and Diana L. Haytko (1997), "Speaking of Fashion: Consumers' Use of Fashion Discourses and the Appropriation of Countervailing Cultural Meanings," *Journal of Consumer Research*, 24 (June), 15-42.

Thompson, Craig J. and Elizabeth C. Hirschman (1995), "Understanding the Socialized Body: A Poststructuralist Analysis of Consumers' Self-Conceptions, Body Images, and Self-Care Practices," *Journal of Consumer Research*, 22 (September), 139-153.

Turner, Bryan S. (1994), "Preface," *The Consuming Body*, Pasi Falk, London, UK: Sage, vii-xvii.

Weiss, Brad (1996), *The Making and Unmaking of the Haya Lived World: Consumption, Commoditization, and Everyday Practice*, Durham, NC: Duke.

Wheatley, Jonathan and Jenny Wiggins (2007), "Little by Little Nestle Aims to Woo Brazil's Poor," *Financial Times*, February 20, 6.

Wilson, Ara (2004), *The Intimate Economies of Bangkok*, Berkeley, CA: University of California Press.

Wolf, Naomi (1991), *The Beauty Myth*, New York, NY: Doubleday.

Wood, J.V. (1989), "Theory and Research Concerning Social Comparison of Personal Attributes," *Psychological Bulletin*, September (106), 231-248.

Taking the Load out of Choice Overload: Strategies for Reducing Cognitive Difficulty in Choice from Extensive Assortments

Gergana Spassova, Cornell University, USA

SESSION OVERVIEW

Objective of the session. Choosing from a greater number of options can increase regret and reduce satisfaction with one's choice (Iyengar and Lepper 2000). Cognitive overload, or the extra effort needed to process information about multiple options, has been proposed as one of the mechanisms underlying the choice overload phenomenon. The objective of this symposium is to outline new strategies for reducing cognitive overload and enhancing people's enjoyment and satisfaction with choice in the context of extensive assortments.

Topics and issues. The first paper, by Isen and Spassova, proposes that mild positive affect or novelty mitigate the detrimental consequences of choice overload. Studies one and two showed that people who experienced positive affect or novelty prior to choosing from an extensive assortment were just as satisfied with their choice as people choosing from a small assortment. Studies three and four extended these findings to measures of post-sampling satisfaction and shed light on the underlying mechanisms. The authors propose that positive affect and novelty have beneficial effects on choice overload by enhancing cognitive flexibility and the ability to organize and integrate information. In the second paper, by Inbar et al., time is a resource that allows people to adequately evaluate their choice options and protects them from experiencing cognitive overload. The first study showed that when people are given ample time to make a choice, those choosing from a large array are as satisfied with their selection and experience no more regret than those choosing from a small array. The second and third studies showed that it is the subjective perception of available time that generates choice overload. Even after controlling for the time available to make a choice, feeling rushed fully mediated the impact of assortment size on regret and dissatisfaction with one's choices. The third paper, by Goodman and colleagues, investigates yet another factor that influences choice difficulty-the common retailer strategy of using recommendations such as a "best seller" sign. Results from four studies show that the extent to which consumers have developed preferences is a key moderator of the effect of best seller signage on choice from large assortments. For consumers possessing more (less) developed preferences, best seller signage in large assortments increases (decreases) the size of consideration sets and exacerbates (attenuates) decision difficulty and regret.

Potential contribution and importance. Previous research has suggested that the negative consequences of choice overload on consumer satisfaction can be reversed by factors that simplify the choice process. The papers in this symposium contribute to this research by proposing strategies that enhance consumers' cognitive resources and make the choice process easier, more manageable, and ultimately more satisfying, without changing the nature or the presentation of the options in the choice set. Furthermore, by investigating new moderators, the papers in this symposium shed light on the nature of the choice overload phenomenon and on the psychological mechanisms underlying it. Cognitive flexibility and the subjective perception of time are introduced as important elements of the choice process, and factors that influence the consumer consideration set are investigated. The scope of this symposium goes beyond research on choice overload; it has impli-cations for judgment and decision making in general as it suggests mechanisms for reducing cognitive complexity and for promoting consumers' problem-solving abilities.

EXTENDED ABSTRACTS

"When Choosing is No Longer a Burden: The Mitigating Effect of Positive Affect and Novelty on Choice Overload"

Alice M. Isen, Cornell University, USA
Gergana Spassova, Cornell University, USA

Increasing the size of a choice set has been shown to have negative consequences, such as a greater tendency for consumers to defer choice (Dhar 1997; Tversky and Shafir 1992) or to feel frustrated, confused, and less satisfied with the chosen option (Huffman and Kahn 1998; Iyengar and Lepper 2000; Malhotra 1982). Researchers have argued that these negative outcomes occur because consumers experience "choice overload" (Iyengar and Lepper 2000)–they feel overwhelmed by the extra cognitive effort needed to process information about the numerous options in the choice set. Strategies suggested to decrease choice overload involve simplifying product information (Gourville and Soman 2005), presenting it in an attribute-based as opposed to alternative-based format (Huffman and Kahn 1998), or asking consumers to articulate their preferences explicitly (Chernev 2003).

This research identifies two new factors for reducing choice overload–positive affect and novelty-and explores the specific mechanisms through which they impact consumers' experience with large choice sets. We propose that positive affect may reduce the effects of choice overload because it enhances people's cognitive flexibility and their ability to process, organize, and integrate information (Isen 1993; Kahn and Isen 1993). The beneficial effects of positive affect are proposed to be mediated by increased brain levels of the neurotransmitter dopamine (Ashby, Isen, and Turken 1999). Because novelty is also related to increased levels of dopamine, we predict that novelty may also mitigate the effects of choice overload. We test our hypotheses in four studies.

Studies one and two provided initial support for the hypotheses. Participants chose from either a small (9 flavors) or a large (45 flavors) assortment of jams, all from the same brand. Black-and-white pictures of the jams, with the flavor indicated, were displayed on the computer screen. Participants indicated their choice of jam, how much they enjoyed the choice process, and how satisfied they were with the chosen jam. Prior to choosing, to induce positive affect, participants were asked to provide first associates to positive common words (study one), and participants in the novelty condition provided first associates to neutral uncommon words (study two), while controls in both studies provided first associates to neutral common words. Among controls, the effects of choice overload previously observed were confirmed. Controls choosing from the large assortment of jams reported feeling more frustrated and tired than controls choosing from the small assortment of jams and were less satisfied with their choice. Among positive affect participants, however, the effects of choice overload were not observed. People in positive affect choosing from the large assortment did not report more frustration or tiredness than people in positive affect choosing from the small assortment, and did not feel less satisfied with the choice they had made. When choosing from the small assortment, people in positive affect reported the same degree of tiredness and frustration, and the same satisfaction with their choice, as controls. When choosing from the large assortment, people in positive affect reported feeling significantly less tired and frustrated than controls. They also enjoyed the choice process more and were more satisfied with the selected option than controls.

Novelty had a similar beneficial effect on participants' satisfaction with their chosen product, but not on their frustration or tiredness. In contrast to controls, participants who had experienced novelty did not feel less satisfied with the choice they had made from a large, relative to from a small, assortment. Furthermore, when choosing from the large (but not from the small) assortment, participants in the novelty condition reported enjoying the choice process significantly more than controls. Unlike positive affect, however, novelty did not reduce the experience of frustration and tiredness with the choice process. Participants in the novelty condition reported feeling as tired and frustrated when choosing from the large assortment as controls, and significantly more so than novelty participants who chose from the small assortment.

Studies three and four were designed to test if the observed effects of positive affect and novelty extended to measures of post-sampling satisfaction with real jams, and to shed more light on the underlying psychological mechanisms. We also reduced the number of jams in the two assortments to six (small assortment) and thirty (large assortment) to be more in line with previous manipulations of choice overload. As in the first two studies, positive affect (study three) and novelty (study four) were manipulated by asking participants to provide first associates to positive common (affect condition) or neutral uncommon (novelty condition) words. Participants were run individually. After completing the word-associates task, they were asked to choose from the designated assortment of jams and to complete measures assessing their experience with the choice process. After choosing, participants were given the option to taste the chosen jam and to indicate how much they liked it, how much they regretted their choice, and how many different flavors of this brand of jam they would like to purchase if they became available in a local store. Results were in line with our predictions. Controls choosing from the large assortment experienced more regret about their choice relative to controls choosing from the small assortment and also reported that they were likely to buy fewer flavors of jam. Positive affect and novelty mitigated the negative effect of assortment size on choice regret and purchase intentions. Additional process measures provided support for our hypothesis that positive affect and novelty have their beneficial effect on choice overload by enhancing people's ability to integrate and categorize information.

Overall, these results support the hypothesis that positive affect and novelty reduce the negative consequences of large assortment size on consumer satisfaction with choice. They confirm previous findings about the beneficial effect of positive affect on cognitive flexibility and problem solving abilities and suggest intriguing possibilities for future research on the impact of novelty on cognitive processes and decision making.

"Take It Easy: Removing Time Constraints Mitigates Choice Overload"

Yoel Inbar, Cornell Univesity, USA
Karlene Hanko, University of Cologne, Germany
Simona Botti, London Business School, UK
Thomas Gilovich, Cornell University, USA

Although it has traditionally been assumed that more options can only increase satisfaction with a choice outcome, recent research has shown that choosing from large arrays of options can be

difficult, inducing choice "paralysis" and dissatisfaction with the chosen option (Iyengar and Lepper 2000). This choice overload effect has been attributed to several causes, including the cognitive difficulty involved in evaluating and comparing a large number of options and the emotional burden that this process entails, especially for consumers who are striving to make the best choice (Brenner, Rottenstreich, and Sood; Iyengar, Elwork, and Schwartz 2006; Kahn and Lehmann 1991). Prior research has identified several factors that reduce the cognitive burden created by larger choice sets and thereby mitigate the negative effects associated with too much choice. For example, clearly articulated preferences (Chernev 2003; Huffman and Kahn 1998) allow consumers to identify the best match between their preferences and the available options without engaging in extensive, and sometimes frustrating, processing of these options. On the other hand, suppliers can ease the burden on consumers by selecting options that are easy to evaluate and displaying them in a way that facilitates within- and cross-category comparisons (Broniarczyk, Hoyer, and McAlister 1998; Gourville and Soman, 2005).

In this research we focus on another factor that can reduce the cognitive effort of choosing: sufficient time and resources to consider the available options. We hypothesize that people facing large choice sets will be less satisfied than those facing smaller sets only when they do not have adequate time and resources to evaluate the available options. When time constraints are removed, we expect that people will be as satisfied when choosing from large sets as they are when choosing from smaller sets. Moreover, we argue that it is the subjective feeling of being rushed when making a choice that reduces satisfaction with the chosen options and increases regret for the forgone options. These hypotheses were tested in three studies.

Study 1 examined whether encouraging people to take their time when choosing would ameliorate the negative effects of choosing from a large set. Participants were assigned to choose and eat a Godiva chocolate from either a small (6 chocolates) or a large (30 chocolates) array, under conditions of low or high time pressure. In the *high time pressure (rushed)* condition, the experimenter remained in the room with participants and stood directly behind them while they chose. In the *low time pressure (unrushed)* condition, the experimenter encouraged participants to take as much time as they wanted and left them alone in the room while they made their choice. After choosing, participants consumed their chocolate and completed a questionnaire that measured their satisfaction, enjoyment, and regret with their choice. Consistent with prior research, participants under high time pressure were less satisfied with their choice and experienced greater regret when choosing from the large set than when choosing from the small set. However, as predicted, this difference was entirely eliminated among participants under low time pressure.

Study 2 expanded upon these findings by demonstrating that it is the subjective feeling of being rushed during the decision process that accounts for reduced satisfaction when choosing from large choice sets. Participants chose a DVD from a small (6 DVDs) or a large (30 DVDs) array, with the understanding that they had a 1 in 10 chance of winning the DVD they selected. They then completed the same choice enjoyment, satisfaction, and regret measures as in the previous study, as well as a measure of the extent to which they felt rushed during the choice process. Replicating prior research, participants experienced greater regret and lower satisfaction when choosing from a large set than when choosing from a small set. Participants also felt more rushed when choosing from a large set than when choosing from a small set. A mediational analysis revealed that the impact of set size on satisfaction with the decision outcome can be attributed to subjective feelings of time pressure, as feeling "rushed" fully mediated the impact of set size on regret and dissatisfaction with one's choices.

Study 3 bolstered the results of Study 2 by manipulating the actual amount of time participants had to make their choice. As in the previous study, participants chose a DVD from either a small (6 DVDs) or a large (30 DVDs) array. Participants in the rushed condition were given exactly 30 seconds to make their choice and were shown a timer which counted down how many seconds were still available to complete the choice task. Participants in the unrushed condition were given unlimited time and saw no timer. Supporting previous results, those who chose from a larger set under time pressure felt more rushed than other participants and subsequently felt less happy with their choice.

In conclusion, this research contributes to our prior knowledge by showing that one of the factors contributing to the greater psychological burden of making a choice from a large set, as compared to a small set, is the perception of not having enough time for making this choice. Our results suggest that it is the perceived feeling of being rushed through the decision process, rather than the objective amount of time available to consumers when making a choice, that induces lower satisfaction and greater regret when choosing from large choice sets.

"Simplify or Intensify? Best Seller Signage on Consumer Decision-Making from Large Assortments"
Joseph K. Goodman, Washington University in St. Louis, USA
Susan Broniarczyk, The University of Texas at Austin, USA
Leigh McAlister, The University of Texas at Austin, USA
Jill Griffin, Evansville University, USA

Despite the increased cognitive load required to process large assortments, consumers are attracted to such broad options (Arnold, Oum and Tigert 1981; Broniarczyk, Hoyer, and McAlister 1998); however, they experience negative consequences, such as greater decision difficulty and regret, when they ultimately must make a choice (Iyengar and Lepper 2000; Chernev 2003). In four studies we examine whether a common retailer strategy—the use of recommendations such as a "best seller" sign—attenuates or exacerbates these negative consequences in consumer choice. The studies show that the negative consequences in consumer choice in large assortments is exacerbated when signs create conflict in the decision making process.

The first study manipulated the presence of a best seller recommendation in a small assortment (6 chocolates) and a large assortment (30 chocolates). After making a choice, participants indicated their anticipated regret and difficulty with the decision across multiple measures taken from previous research. The study showed that instead of reducing the negative consequences associated with choice, best seller signs actually exacerbated decision difficulty and anticipated regret when consumers face large assortments.

The second study manipulated the location of the sign and measured participants consideration sets. The results replicated the findings from study 1 and showed that signs increased the number of signed and non-signed options in consumers' consideration sets in large assortments. This increase in consideration set size mediated the effect of signs on decision difficulty and experienced regret. The study also shows that the findings only hold when signs are on a viable, high preference option that has the potential to conflict with consumers' preferences.

The third and fourth studies provide additional evidence that the best seller signs lead to the increased difficulty and consideration set size due to conflict with consumers' preferences. Generalizing the findings to other product categories (i.e., organic juices and designer chairs), Study 3 manipulated preference development

and the presence of a sign and found that participants with more developed preferences reported experiencing greater decision difficulty when choosing from a large assortment when a sign was present versus absent. On the other hand, participants with less developed preferences exhibited the opposite pattern of results and showed that signs reduced difficulty, regret, and the size of the consideration set.

Interestingly, signs have this effect on the choice process without changing the final option that is chosen; none of the three studies showed an increase in choice share of the signed options. Study 4 manipulated the number options that participants could chose by either having participants buy one chocolate or allowing consumers to buy multiple chocolates. Study 4 also measured preference development via subjective knowledge. We again find that best seller signage led participants with more (less) developed preferences to create larger (smaller) consideration sets, primarily due to greater consideration of non-signed options. If limited to a single choice from a large assortment, the number of options considered was related to regret, with participants with more versus less developed preferences more likely to experience regret when a best seller sign was present. However, if free to act on their larger consideration sets, participants with more versus less developed preferences were more likely to buy multiple options when a best seller sign was present in a large assortment. Implications for consumers and retailers are discussed along with avenues for future research.

REFERENCES
Arnold, Stephen J., Tae H. Oum and Douglas J. Tigert (1983), "Determining Attributes in Retail Patronage: Seasonal, Temporal, Regional, and International Comparisons," *Journal of Marketing Research*, 20 (May), 149-157.
Ashby, F. Gregory, Alice M. Isen, and And U. Turken (1999), "A Neuropsychological Theory of Positive Affect and its Influence on Cognition," *Psychological Review*, 106 (July), 529-550.
Brenner, Lyle, Yuval Rottenstreich and Sanjay Sood (1999), "Comparison, Grouping, and Preference," *Psychological Science*, 10 (May), 225-229.
Broniarczyk, Susan M., Wayne D. Hoyer, and Leigh McAlister (1998), "Consumers' Perceptions of the Assortment Offered in a Grocery Category: The Impact of Item Reduction," *Journal of Marketing Research*, 35 (May), 166-176.
Chernev, Alexander (2003), "When More is Less and Less is More: The Role of Ideal Point Availability and Assortment in Consumer Choice," *Journal of Consumer Research*, 30 (September), 170-183.
Dhar, Ravi (1997), "Consumer Preference for a No-choice Option," *Journal of Consumer Research*, 24 (September), 215–231.
Gourville, John and Dilip Soman (2005), "Overchoice and Assortment Type: When and Why Variety Backfires," *Marketing Science*, 24 (Summer), 382-395.
Huffman, Cynthia and Barbara E. Kahn (1998), "Variety for Sale: Mass Customization or Mass Confusion?" *Journal of Retailing*, 74 (Winter), 491-513.
Isen, Alice M. (1993), "Positive Affect and Decision Making" In M. Lewis & J. Haivland (Eds.), Handbook of Emotions, NY: Guilford, 261-277.
Iyengar, Sheena S., and Mark R. Lepper (2000), "When Choice is Demotivating: Can One Desire Too Much of a Good Thing?" *Journal of Personality and Social Psychology*, 79 (December), 995-1006.

Iyengar, Sheena S., Rachel F. Elwork and Barry Schwartz (2006), "Doing Better but Feeling Worse: Looking for the 'Best' Job Undermines Satisfaction," *Psychological Science,* 17 (February), 143-150

Kahn, Barbara E. and Donald Lehmann (1991), "Modeling Choice Among Assortments," *Journal of Retailing*, 67 (Fall), 274-299.

Kahn, Barbara E., and Alice M. Isen (1993), "Variety seeking among safe, enjoyable products," *Journal of Consumer Research*, 20 (September), 257–270.

Malhotra, Naresh (1982), "Information load and consumer decision making," *Journal of Consumer Research*, 8 (March), 419-430.

Tversky, Amos and Eldar Shafir (1992), "Choice under conflict: The dynamics of deferred decision," *Psychological Science*, 3 (November), 358-361.

Time: It's a Personal Thing

Cassie Mogilner, Stanford University, USA

SESSION OVERVIEW

Consumer behavior is fundamentally temporally situated. For example, consumption experiences are extended in time, and consumer choice is strongly influenced by temporal distance and sequence. Despite time's ubiquity in consumer behavior, the scientific treatment of time is psychologically naïve. Consumer behavior research on time typically focuses on manipulation and measurement of objective time (minutes, days, weeks, months, and years), to the neglect of subjective time. Just as merely measuring and manipulating decibels and lumens provides an impoverished understanding of people's judgments and decisions about loudness and brightness, respectively, merely measuring and manipulating objective time provides an impoverished understanding of consumers' judgments and decisions about time. The three papers in this symposium seek a more psychologically sophisticated understanding of the role of time's subjective, personal influence on consumer behavior.

First, Mogilner and Aaker highlight the personal value of time (vs. money) for consumers. They find that because consumers' expenditure of time carries a great deal of personal meaning, merely activating the construct of time (vs. money) boosts consumers' feelings of personal connection with the product and, in turn, their attitudes toward the product.

The next two papers examine subjective temporal distance as an output—rather than an input, as is typically the case—of emotional experience, demonstrating that subjective distance is imperfectly correlated with and can vary independently of objective time. Kim and Zauberman find that emotional arousal moderates the subjective distance between now and later. They find that individuals' preference for a lesser item now over a greater item later is partly caused by immediate emotions expanding perceptions of the temporal distance between now and later, in addition to the standard explanation that immediate emotions increase the value of immediate items.

Van Boven and colleagues argue that psychological distance generally, and temporal psychological distance in particular, is emotional in nature. They demonstrate that people report less psychological distance to events about which they feel more rather than less intense emotions, holding objective distance constant. This negative correlation between emotional experience and psychological distance is significantly reduced when people are given an alternative interpretation of their immediate emotions.

Finally, John Lynch leads a discussion of these findings and their relation to the scientific understanding of time as a psychological (rather than a purely objective) construct in consumer behavior.

EXTENDED ABSTRACTS

"Life's Riches: The 'Time>Money Effect'"

Cassie Mogilner, Stanford University, USA
Jennifer Aaker, Stanford University, USA

As the most important resources consumers have at their disposal, references to time and money are pervasive in the consumer landscape. Consider, for example, the marketing campaigns of two brands of beer: Guinness's "It's worth the wait" commercials have appealed to consumers by guiding attention to time whereas Stella Artois's "Perfection has its price" campaign has appealed through focusing attention on money. Even Citibank, an institution based on monetary transactions, brings focal attention to how one chooses to spend time (not money) in their "Live Richly" campaign (e.g., "There is no preset spending limit when it comes to time with your family"). In fact, a content analysis of ads in four very different magazines (*Money, New Yorker, Cosmo,* and *Rolling Stone*) revealed that, out of the 300 advertisements, nearly half of the ads (48%) integrated the concepts of time and/or money into their messages.

Despite the preponderance of marketers' decisions to integrate these constructs into their communications, little is known about the downstream effects of directing consumers' attention to time or money. Does the mere mention of time versus money change the way consumers evaluate products? And if so, why?

To address these questions, we conducted a series of experiments both in the field and in the laboratory. The results converge to reveal a robust "time>money effect." Compared to activating money, activating time, in general, leads to more favorable product attitudes. This "time>money effect" appears to be driven by a differential focus on one's experience gained from using the product versus the value gained from merely owning the product. Whereas thinking about time fosters feelings of personal connection as consumers consider their experiences garnered with the product (Reed, Acquino, & Levy, 2007; Van Boven & Gilovich, 2003), thinking about money disconnects consumers from those same products they know and use (Vohs, Mead, & Goode, 2006). As a result, directing attention to time (rather than money) apparently helps consumers extract greater happiness from the products filling their lives.

Across four experiments, we found support for our hypothesis that activating time (vs. money) leads to more favorable product attitudes. And further, this "time>money effect" is driven by the distinct mindsets that each activates, with the temporal (vs. monetary) mindset evoking greater feelings of personal connection.

In experiment 1, student participants were first asked to report either the amount of *time* they spent on their iPod or the amount of *money* they spent on their iPod. Those who were led to think about their time spent subsequently reported more positive attitudes towards the product than those led to think about their money spent. Further, this "time>money effect" was mediated by participants' feelings of personal connection with their iPods.

Experiment 2 was conducted to examine whether the "time>money effect" is driven by increased feelings of personal connection with the product, or if a mere valence-based account could explain the results (e.g., differential attention to the monetary costs of purchasing the product versus the temporal benefits of consuming the product). Therefore, experiment 2 was conducted at an outdoor concert that was free of charge but for which some individuals spent extensive amounts of time waiting before the concert to ensure getting decent seats. Just prior to the start of the concert, participants were asked either how much time or how much money they spent in order to see the concert. The results revealed that even in instances where the expenditure of time represented a considerable cost, activating time led to more positive attitudes towards the product than activating money, and this effect was mediated by feelings of personal connection with the product.

Participants in experiment 3 were primed with either time or money using a sentence scramble task to determine whether the "time>money effect" occurs only when time and money are activated through an overt question, or whether it can also occur when the constructs are activated more subtly. Experiment 3 also offered further insight into the underlying process through a test of moderation. Specifically, if feelings of personal connection underlie the effect, we would expect it to be particularly strong for experiential purchases (those that "are made with the primary intention of acquiring a life experience") compared to material purchases (those that "are made with the primary intention of acquiring a material good"; Van Boven & Gilovich 2003, 1194). Supporting our conceptualization that the activation of time (vs. money) boosts product attitudes by leading consumers to reflect on their purchase as part of their personal life experience, we found "the time>money effect" to be stronger for experiential purchases than material purchases.

Finally, in experiment 4, individuals were primed with either time or money using the same sentence scramble task as used in experiment 3 before entering a café. Upon leaving the café, those who had been primed with time reported more positive attitudes towards the café than those who had been primed with money, revealing that the "time>money effect" is strong enough to impact how individuals actually experience the products they consume.

References

Reed, Americus II, Karl Aquino and Eric Levy (2007), "Moral Identity and Judgments of Charitable Behaviors," *Journal of Marketing,* 71 (1), 178-193.

Van Boven, Leaf and Thomas Gilovich (2003), "To Do or To Have: That is the Question," *Journal of Personality and Social Psychology*, 85 (6), 1193-1202.

Vohs, Kathleen D., Nicole L. Mead, and Miranda R. Goode (2006), "The Psychological Consequences of Money," *Science,* 314, 1154-1156.

"Deconstructing the Present Bias: Linking Visceral Factors and Mental Representation through Time Perception"

B. Kyu Kim, University of Pennsylvania, USA
Gal Zauberman, University of Pennsylvania, USA

Research on intertemporal decisions has shown individuals have a present-bias: that is, their preference for earlier outcomes over later ones gets stronger as consumption comes closer in time (O'Donoghue and Rabin 1999). This preference is often modeled using a hyperbolic discount function: the rate at which an outcome is discounted over time (delay discounting) decreases as the time horizon gets longer. Several lines of research on intertemporal choice have suggested that visceral factors (e.g., sexual desire, hunger, or alcohol; Loewenstein 1996) or concrete mental representation (Malkoc and Zauberman 2006; Zauberman and Lynch 2005) increase the degree of present-bias. While these factors are shown to drive present-biased preferences, it is not clear whether they change individuals' momentary valuation of outcomes or their sensitivity to time horizon (i.e., the duration of the delay).

Recently, in their time perception model of present bias, Zauberman, Kim, Malkoc, and Bettman (2008) showed that individuals discount the value of outcomes, as well as discount duration itself (e.g., non-linear time perception), and this combined effect results in hyperbolic discounting. In this paper, we investigate the link between affective and cognitive drivers of present bias and time perception. Specifically, we propose that some of the standard affective and cognitive drivers of the present bias operate, at least in part, through shifts in subjective time perception of the relevant time horizon such that individuals' perceived time is more contracted or non-linear when these drivers are active.

Study 1 demonstrates the impact of sexual attractiveness on sensitivity to time horizons. Participants rated the attractiveness of

15 portrait photographs of the opposite sex, which were taken from a public website (http://www.hotornot.com). About half of the participants were presented with 'hot' photos that received mean ratings of 9.5 (out of 10) or higher on the website, and the other half were presented with 'not hot' photos that were rated as 5 or lower. After viewing and rating the attractiveness of each photo, all participants indicated subjective feeling of duration between today and multiple time horizons (e.g., 3 months to 36 months). Next, they indicated how much they would have to be paid to wait to receive a gift certificate for multiple time delays (e.g., 3 months to 36 months).

Results showed that participants' subjective estimates of time horizon were less sensitive to changes in objective time horizons after viewing 'hot' photos than after viewing 'not hot' photos. Such non-sensitivity to time horizons corresponds to a greater degree of present bias according to the time perception model of hyperbolic discounting (Zauberman, Kim, Malkoc, & Bettman 2008). Supporting this, when discount rates were calculated using objective time horizons, participants in the 'hot' condition showed more deviation from exponential discounting than those in 'not hot' condition. When participants' subjective time estimates were accounted for (i.e., discount rates were calculated using subjective time estimates of objective time horizon instead of objective time horizon itself), however, discount rates in both conditions no longer decreased as a function of time delay. These results suggest that visceral factors impact perceived time horizon, and not just the valuation of the outcome itself. Moreover, these changes in time perception contribute to present-biased preferences when visceral factors are active.

Study 2 demonstrates the impact of concrete mental representation on time perception. Participants were randomly assigned to either a concrete representation or control condition. In the concrete representation condition, participants visualized the time when they would receive and spend a $75 cash prize. They were asked to imagine and describe the occasion as vividly as possible including where to go and with whom to spend the money. Participants in the control condition did not complete this task. Next, all participants indicated how long they felt the duration between today and a day in 1 month or 3 months to be. They also indicated the delay premium if they were to delay the use of the cash prize by 1 month or 3 months.

Results showed that participants' subjective perception of time horizons were less sensitive to objective time horizons in the concrete mental representation condition than in the control condition. Participants in the concrete mental representation condition showed a greater level of present bias (i.e., decrease in discount rates over time) than those in the control condition when present bias was measured using objective time horizons. When subjective time perception was used, however, discount rates in both conditions were equal over time, supporting the time perception model of hyperbolic discounting. These results imply that concrete mental representation shifted participants' sensitivity to time horizons, causing a greater level of present bias. There was also a marginally significant main effect of mental representation on discount rates calculated using subjective time estimates, implying that concrete mental representation changed participants' valuation of outcomes as well.

In sum, this paper demonstrates an important way in which emotion and mental representation affect present-biased preference. We confirmed that affective and cognitive drivers influenced present bias (measured by declining discount rates), replicating the findings in past research. Importantly, these drivers changed individuals' sensitivity to time horizons. Taken together, these results support and extend the time perception model of hyperbolic discounting (Zauberman, Kim, Malkoc, & Bettman 2008), showing that factors often assumed to operate through the valuation of outcomes, actually operate (at least in part) through changes in sensitivity to time horizons, leading to present-biased preferences.

References

Loewenstein, George F. (1996), "Out of Control: Visceral Influences on Behavior," *Organizational Behavior and Human Decision Processes,* 65, 272–292.

Malkoc, Selin A. and Gal Zauberman (2006), "Deferring versus Expediting Consumption: The Effect of Outcome Concreteness on Sensitivity to Time Horizon," *Journal of Marketing Research,* 43, 618-627.

O'Donoghue, T., and M. Rabin (1999), "Doing It Now or Later," *American Economic Review,* 89, 103-124.

Zauberman, Gal and John G. Lynch (2005), "Resource Slack and Propensity to Discount Delayed Investments of Time versus Money," *Journal of Experiment Psychology: General,* 134, 23-37.

Zauberman, Gal, Kyu B. Kim, Selin Malkoc, and James Bettman (2008), "Discounting Time and Time Discounting: Subjective Time Perception and Intertemporal Preferences," *Working Paper,* University of Pennsylvania, PA.

"Feeling Close: The Emotional Nature of Psychological Distance"

Leaf Van Boven, University of Colorado at Boulder, USA
Joanne Kane, University of Colorado at Boulder, USA
A. Peter McGraw, University of Colorado at Boulder, USA
Jeannette Dale, Denver, Colorado, USA

What can make an event psychologically close or distant? What can make high school graduation seem like "just yesterday" or "long ago?" What can make a conference presentation seem "just around the corner" or "ages away?"

Despite psychological distance's importance to everyday experience and behavior (James 1890/1950; Lewin 1951), it is not clear what psychological distance actually is. This is because psychological distance tends to be operationally equated with objective distance (e.g., Trope & Liberman 2003). This paper seeks to clarify the psychological nature of psychological distance.

We hypothesize that psychological distance is largely emotional in nature: events about which people feel stronger emotions are less psychologically distant than events about which people feel weaker emotions. Because factors unrelated to events' objective distance can influence how intensely people feel about those events, the same events can be more or less psychologically distant, independent of when they actually occur.

Psychological distance may be emotional in nature in part because emotional arousal typically signals events' importance and relevance to the self (Frijda 1988; Lazarus 1991; Neese 1990). Increases in emotional arousal are closely related to decreases in objective distance (Olson 1988; Savitsky, Medvec, Charlton, & Gilovich 1998). This naturally occurring inverse relationship between emotionality and objective distance may produce a subjective inverse association between emotionality and psychological distance that may become overgeneralized such that events of equal objective distance can be psychologically closer when people feel relatively intensely about those events.

Our analysis of the emotional nature of psychological distance yields the novel prediction that inducing people to feel more strongly about an event will reduce that event's psychological distance, holding constant the event's objective distance. We tested this prediction in four experiments

In experiment 1, people were asked to describe, either emotionally or dispassionately, positive or negative future events. People reported being psychologically closer (i.e., less distant) to emotionally (rather than dispassionately) described events. People also reported positive events to be more psychologically distant than negative events, probably because positive events are less emotionally evocative than negative events (e.g., Rozin & Royzman 2001).

In experiment 2, we sought to test whether emotional intensity would reduce psychological distance to both past and future events. Participants described either their last or next dentist visit. After estimating the number of days since or until their dentist visit, participants were asked to describe the visit, depending on random assignment, either emotionally or dispassionately. As predicted, people reported that emotionally regarded dentist visits were psychologically closer than dispassionately regarded dentist visits, independent of those events' tense (past or future) and of the number of days since or until the visit.

In experiment 3, we sought to manipulate whether people felt more or less intensely about a future event indirectly through assignment to social roles. Such an indirect manipulation helps avoid potential concern that explicit instructions to regard events more or less emotionally, as in experiments 1 and 2, elicit experimental demand or some other aspect unrelated to emotionality. People were randomly assigned either to engage in an embarrassing public performance—dancing to the Devo song, "Whip it"—or to evaluate others' performance. Dancers reported more emotional arousal than evaluators. As predicted, dancers also reported that the dancing was psychologically closer than did evaluators. In addition, the effect of being a dancer or evaluator on reported emotional intensity statistically mediated the effect of being a dancer or evaluator on psychological distance.

In experiment 4, we sought more direct evidence for the emotional nature of psychological distance, which implies that emotional intensity should reduce psychological distance to the degree that experienced emotions are attributed to emotional events, but not when experienced emotions are attributed to some other event. The negative correlation between emotional intensity and psychological distance should therefore be reduced if people are led to attribute their emotional experience to some source other than the target emotional event.

Participants were told that in 15 minutes they would dance to the Devo song "Whip It" for one minute in front of the experimenter and a video camera, and that their performance would be shown later to other students in a study of impression formation. During the wait, participants were asked to complete an unrelated "marketing" study concerning product evaluation and auditory stimuli. Participants donned a pair of headphones and listened to "New Age" whale songs while completing questionnaires. Depending on random assignment, participants were either told that the songs "did not influence cognitive performance" (control condition), or that the songs might make them feel "anxiety and fear" (misattribution condition).

Consistent with the emotional nature of psychological distance, the correlation between emotional intensity and psychological distance was more strongly negative in the control condition than in the misattribution condition. People's emotional intensity is associated with reduced psychological distance, but not when people attribute their emotions to an unrelated source. This finding indicates that emotional intensity does not reduce psychological distance of all future events, but only those events to which people attribute their emotions.

In conclusion, although psychological distance has conceptual prominence in behavioral science, the extant theoretical and empirical emphasis has been on objective temporal distance (minutes, days, weeks, months, and years) as an input to thinking, feeling, and behaving. Our studies shift focus to the subjective (rather than the objective) nature of psychological distance as an output (rather than an input) of emotion. Independent of objective distance, emotional intensity reduces events' psychological distance. Our findings highlight the importance of putting the "psychological" back in psychological distance.

References

Frijda, N. H. (1988). The laws of emotion. *American Psychologist, 43*, 349-358.

James, W. (1890/1950). *Principles of psychology.* (Vol. I). New York: Dover Publications, Inc.

Lazarus, R. S. (1991). *Emotion and adaptation.* New York: Oxford University Press.

Lewin, K. (1951). *Field theory in social science.* New York: Harper.

Neese, R. M. (1990). Evolutionary explanations of emotions. *Human Nature, 1*, 261–289.

Olson, J. M. (1988). Misattribution, preparatory information, and speech anxiety. *Journal of Personality and Social Psychology, 54*, 758–767.

Rozin, P., & Royzman, E. B. (2001). Negativity bias, negativity dominance, and contagion. *Personality & Social Psychology Review, 5*, 296-320.

Savitsky, K., Medvec, V. H., Charlton, A. E., & Gilovich, T. (1998). "What, me worry?": Arousal, misattribution, and the effect of temporal distance on confidence. *Personality and Social Psychology Bulletin, 24*, 529–536.

Trope, Y., & Liberman, N. (2003). Temporal construal. *Psychological Review, 110*, 403-421.

The Effect of Conflicting Information and Natural Primes on Health Related Behaviors

Barbara Kahn, University of Miami, USA

SESSION OVERVIEW

It is becoming increasingly common for consumers to reach for a copy of *Newsweek* or some other mainstream publication and find information pertaining to health-related behaviors. Pharmaceutical companies are spending large marketing budgets to detail physicians and to advertise their products directly to consumers. Consumers are routinely bombarded with advice as to when to get tested, how much to eat, and which disease symptoms they should be on the look out for. With all of this information and natural priming in the marketplace, there are bound to be conflicting influences. This session looks specifically on the role that conflicting information cues have on health-related behaviors.

This session should appeal to researchers who are interested in how consumers process information from conflicting sources. In the past much of the research on conflict has focused on information from the same domain, e.g., one study says one thing, another study says another. In this session, we focus on the realistic environment where the sources of conflict frequently come from non-comparable sources of information, e.g., a scientific study reports one finding and the medical industry reports something different–or behavior indicates one kind of conclusion and physical appearances indicate another. We believe this session presents research that will make important contributions both to further our understanding of consumer behavior as well as to inform policy makers about consumers' potential reactions to conflicting sources of information in the environment.

In the first paper, "The Branded Physician's Office: Effects of Exposure to Small Pharmaceutical Promotional Items on Physician Treatment Preferences," the researchers examine how the conflicting cues offered by the pharmaceutical companies in their branding strategies and recent guidelines put into place by many universities that restrict pharmaceutical company activity in University hospitals affect medical students' implicit attitudes and decisions to prescribe. In the second paper, "Super Size Me: The Social Influence of Obese Consumers on the Food Choices of Others," the researchers examine the sometimes conflicting cues between what a person looks like (fat or thin), how much s/he eats (a lot or a little), and the interaction of those effects on what others eat. Finally, in the third paper, "Change, Change, Change: Evolving Health Guidelines, Preventive Health Behaviors, and Interventions to Mitigate Harm," the researchers examine the role conflicting information sources have on the effectiveness of various medical treatments and screening tests in affecting patient decision-making. Specifically, their focus is on providing appropriate interventions to counter possible avoidance tendencies that may occur as patients try to cope with the stress of the conflict.

Each of the papers in this session has several completed studies. The discussion leader, Punam Anand Keller is a noted expert in how consumers process information in general, as well as specifically in health-related behaviors.

EXTENDED ABSTRACTS

"The Branded Physician's Office: Effects of Exposure to Small Pharmaceutical Promotional Items on Physician Treatment Preferences"

David Grande, University of Pennsylvania, USA
Dominick Frosch, Unversity of California, Los Angeles, USA
Andrew Perkins, Rice University, USA
Barbara Kahn, University of Miami, USA

The relationship between the pharmaceutical industry and physicians has received a great deal of attention in recent years. This attention is due in part to rapid growth in pharmaceutical spending in conjunction with significant increases in pharmaceutical marketing to both physicians and patients. Pharmaceutical companies focus a majority of their marketing efforts on "detailing"–visits to physicians' offices to encourage prescriptions of the company's product (IMS Health, 2006). Most of these visits include inducements in the form of branded gifts to physicians and their staff and free drug samples that can be given to patients. These relationships have raised concerns that pharmaceutical companies are inappropriately influencing physician decision-making and that these relationships represent a breach of medical professionalism and patient trust.

The concerns of the public, media and policymakers appear to be warranted based on a series of studies demonstrating that the pharmaceutical industry is effective at influencing physician prescribing through the use of financial inducements or gifts (Wazana, 2000). Much of the research is observational and focuses on gifts of relatively high value such as expensive meals or travel to conferences. This research along with a general belief that large gifts should be the focus of concern has led numerous professional societies and universities to adopt ethics guidelines that discourage gifts valued above a certain level, often in the range of $100 (Coyle et al., 2002; AMA Code of Medical Ethics). Smaller gifts such as pens, branded prescription pads, and other office supplies are typically regarded as trivial and inconsequential.

While attention has primarily focused on gifts of relatively high value reflecting a belief that influence is proportional to economic value, little is known about the influence of smaller, less valuable branded promotional items on physicians' clinical preferences. Further, few physicians believe that small branded gifts can influence medical decision-making despite social psychology theory and evidence to the contrary. The goals of the current study are twofold. First we explore any potential influence these smaller marketing trinkets might have on physician decisions. In particular we are interested in measuring the unconscious effects that branded gifts of minimal economic value may have on implicit attitudes and physician prescribing behavior. Second the study will try and assess whether in-place educational policies with regard to pharmaceutical industry activity have any effect on attitudes toward the promoted brands.

To this end, we designed a randomized control experiment to measure the impact that exposure to these brands have on attitudes and how those attitudes affect physician decisions. 180 third and fourth year medical students and internal medicine and family medicine residents at the Penn's School of Medicine participated in the study. Participants were randomly assigned to either a control condition or a treatment condition where participants were exposed to promotional items for the brand Lipitor. Following exposure, participants completed a series of vignettes requiring them to report their clinical preferences in lipid management in situations of varying cardiovascular risk and ambiguity. Participants then completed self-report measures and implicit measures of preference and attitudes. Implicit attitudes were measured using the Implicit Association Test (Greenwald, McGhee, and Schwartz 1998), a computer-based categorization task designed to uncover inaccessible or socially undesirable attitudes. The IAT assessed relative implicit attitudes between Lipitor (the promoted brand) and Zocor, a generic equivalent.

Interestingly, participants exposed to branded promotional items for Lipitor demonstrated *weaker* positive attitudes toward Lipitor compared to Zocor on the IAT (p=0.05). Further, significant differences reflecting the same paradox were found on the most ambiguous cardiovascular risk clinical vignette, with 42.1% of controls choosing to initiate Lipitor therapy compared to 26.1% of the subjects exposed to Lipitor promotional items (p=0.03). No significant effects were evident on the low and high cardiovascular risk clinical vignettes. Explicit preferences showed similar patterns among global attributes although not statistically significant (product superiority: 48% of controls and 36% of treated rated Lipitor over Zocor, p=0.13; product preference: 53% of controls and 41% of exposed rated Lipitor over Zocor, p=0.10).

These results suggest that trainees exposed to pharmaceutical branded promotional items exhibited a boomerang response with weaker preferences toward the marketed product when compared to controls. These findings were evident on implicit measures in the most ambiguous clinical decision. A similar but non-significant pattern on the explicit measures lends support to these findings. In this case, the observed boomerang effect is potentially explained by recent policies at the University of Pennsylvania that severely restrict pharmaceutical marketing on campus. This suggests that strong institutional policies may affect attitudes underlying behavioral responses to marketing. Overall, this study provides evidence that subtle branding within the environment can have significant effects on clinical decisions and treatment preferences, but not necessarily in the direction one would expect. Further studies are currently being conducted to assess responses at other institutions with less stringent policies.

"Super Size Me: The Social Influence of Obese Consumers on the Food Choices of Others"

Brent McFerran, University of British Columbia, Canada
Darren Dahl, University of British Columbia, Canada
Gavan J. Fitzsimons, Duke University, USA
Andrea C. Morales, Arizona State University, USA

Obesity and unhealthy food consumption are major public health issues, especially in North American society. Making healthy food choices is an important part of maintaining a healthy body weight. Consumers make over 200 food choices per day (Wansink 2006), and thus it is important to understand the antecedents to unhealthy food choices. However, little research in marketing has examined why consumers make the food choices they do. For instance, once inside a restaurant, what causes one to purchase the burger instead of the salad, or the large fries over the small ones? Such trivial decisions actually have large caloric consequences, as the difference between a 16 oz. McDonald's Swamp Sludge McFlurry and McDonald's Low Fat Ice Cream Cone is 560 calories (McDonald's USA 2006). Portion size has been linked to obesity (Young and Nestle 2002), as people who select larger portions tend to eat more than those given small portions, even if the food is of poor taste or consumers are not hungry (Wansink 2006).

Past research has shown that consumption decisions are influenced by those who are physically present. People are sensitive to the behavior of others in a retail context (Bearden and Etzel 1982; Dahl, Manchanda, & Argo 2001), even if such a person is only physically present but does not engage the consumer in any way (Zhou & Soman 2003; Argo, Dahl, & Manchanda 2005). In a food context, studies have found that social influence can have either a facilitating or attenuating effect on consumption, depending on the context (see Herman, Roth, & Polivy 2003 for an excellent review). They argue that food choice is influenced by a desire to convey a certain impression or adhere to social norms (Leary & Kowalski 1990; Roth et al. 2001). Although, Herman et al. (2003) argue that making a good impression usually means eating less, other research has found that people may eat more, rather than less in the presence of another person (e.g. Conger, Conger, Costanzo, Wright & Matter 1990). Indeed, the social facilitation literature has found that the presence of others can lead to increases in consumption (e.g. de Castro 1990) because the duration of the meal is longer.

Another line of research has examined the impact of obesity on consumption. Priming people with overweight images leads to an increase in quantity consumed (Campbell and Mohr 2008). Christakis and Fowler (2007) found that a person's chance of becoming obese significantly increased when a close other (e.g., friend, sibling) became obese. Moreover, the effect persisted even if they were not living in the same city; rather, social distance was a better predictor than physical distance. Effects were not seen in neighbors in the same area.

The above lines of research have focused either on how much others eat, or on the social influence of obesity, but little research has examined the influence of the two jointly. In social influence work more generally, the effects of the social "other" have been shown to be moderated by whether the person is a member of an aspirational or dissociative group (Escalas & Bettman 2005; White & Dahl 2005, 2008). Since thin models are seen as an ideal standard in North American society (Durkin & Paxton 2002) and obesity—associated with unhealthy eating and over consumption—is a stigma that most wish to avoid (Johnson 2002), the body type of others should interact with their food choice (indulgent versus moderate) in forming evaluations of them. We propose that these frameworks can be reconciled by examining the person by situation interaction. In other words, we examine how eating with (or simply ordering in the presence of) those who are thin versus obese can impact one's food intake, but that such effects are moderated by the actual food choices of the other individual.

In Study 1, we test the joint influence of others' portion selection and their body type on consumption in a 2(thin vs. obese confederate) x 2(confederate takes little vs. takes a lot) between-subjects design. We find that that if a confederate first selects a large quantity of snack food, participants chose and consumed more if the confederate was *thin* versus obese. In contrast, if the confederate selected a small portion, participants chose and consumed more if the confederate was *obese* versus thin. A sole confederate was employed across both the obese and thin conditions, and to manipulate body type a professionally-constructed obesity prosthesis was used. Identical clothes were tailored in both a size 00 and a 16 to ensure consistency.

In Study 2, a 2(thin vs. obese confederate) x 2(healthy vs. unhealthy food) between-subjects design was employed to examine whether the effect is driven by the pairing of obesity and unhealthy food, or whether it still holds for healthy food as well. We find that regardless of the perceived healthiness of the food, after seeing a confederate select a large amount of food, participants selected and consumed less when the confederate was *obese* versus thin. As such, evidence suggests that the effects generalize to foods perceived to be healthy, and thus the effects are driven by perceived over consumption, rather than by perceptions of unhealthy eating.

Study 3 used a scenario methodology where participants imagined they were ordering ice cream and overhear the person in front of them order an extra large ice cream cone. The design was a 2(other person: obese vs. thin) x 2(cognitive load: low vs. high) between subjects design that also included a continuous body image satisfaction measure. We tested whether cognitive load and body image satisfaction moderate the effects identified, and find a 3-way interaction such that the participants chose a smaller size when they were low in body image satisfaction and their processing resources were not impaired, suggesting that the process of food choice seems to have a conscious component and such social comparison effects are heightened among those less satisfied with their physical appearance.

"Change, Change, Change: Evolving Health Guidelines, Preventive Health Behaviors, and Interventions to Mitigate Harm"

Christine Moorman, Duke University, USA
Mary Frances Luce, Duke University, USA
James R. Bettman, Duke University, USA

Every day, newspapers, magazine, television, and the internet publicize new findings produced by medical researchers. As a result, consumers have become accustomed to learning which foods, dietary supplements, exercise behaviors, and work habits will affect their risk of cancer or cardiovascular disease. Studies are followed by even more studies, and consumers are left with a great deal of information, but also with doubt and confusion about what preventive behaviors are really best for them. Casual conversations reveal this confusion and consumers simply give up trying to find a health regime that fits within the conflicting stream of health guidelines delivered at their front door each morning.

Our research considers what types of changes to health guidelines cause consumers to have a negative reaction (Study 1, completed), what types of psychological processes and traits contribute to this negative reaction (Study 2, completed), and what types of interventions might attenuate these reactions (Study 3, currently in the field). All of our studies present health guidelines through mock newspaper articles to adults. Our guideline involves the cardiovascular effects of pyridoxine (Vitamin B6).

In Study 1, we observe that consumers react more negatively to a guideline that first communicates a positive effect (i.e., pyridoxine protects against cardiovascular disease) and then reverses to describe a negative effect (e.g., pyridoxine increases risk of cardiovascular disease) than to non-conflicting guidelines or guidelines moving from negative effects to positive effects. We also find three corresponding and troubling reactions to the guidelines. First, consumers reduced their intention to monitor pyridoxine, even though the guideline suggests, from either a positive or negative perspective, that monitoring would be helpful. Second, consumers reported less faith in health guidelines and health professionals. Third, consumers exhibited a negative spillover to healthy behaviors not implicated by the guideline change. Specifically, they reported reduced intentions to engage in unrelated heart-healthy behaviors (e.g., cholesterol monitoring).

Study 2 examined potential moderators and mediators of these negative reactions. In terms of moderators, we observe a guideline change x scientific literacy interaction. Scientific literacy refers to a consumer's understanding of the nature of science, its role in society, and an appreciation of what science can and can not do (Laugksch 2000). We find that consumers who score low on a scientific literacy scale exhibit the negative spillover effects described above, while consumers scoring high on the same scale actually have a positive reaction to changing guidelines. We sus-

pect this difference emerges because high scientific literacy consumers value new information because this reaffirms their faith in scientific progress. Low scientific literacy consumers overreact and exhibit the troubling spillovers. More specifically, we find that low scientific literacy consumers follow a process moving from the changing guideline to less faith in health guidelines and health professionals, which leads to less monitoring of cardiovascular threats. Tests for moderated mediation show that this pathway does not unfold for scientifically literate consumers. Similarly, consumers higher in objective health knowledge do not exhibit the negative spillover effects associated with changing guidelines. While the underlying processes for scientific literacy and objective knowledge seem similar, the two measures are not highly correlated in our sample. Finally, further additional tests show that an external (physician) health locus of control (Lau and Ware 1981) protects against the negative spillover effects. It appears that consumers who look to their doctors for medical advice show less erosion in faith in health professionals, and hence fewer spillovers following changing guidelines.

In Study 3, which is in the field at this writing, we test the effect of four interventions designed to attenuate these effects. All of these interventions are based on reasonable frames that will help consumers put the changing health guideline information into perspective, a process we believe some consumers may do naturally. The perspective may come from: (1) appreciating the larger body of scientific literature (relevant to our scientific literacy moderator in Study 2); (2) considering all of the factors that are important to cardiovascular health (relevant to our objective knowledge moderator in Study 2); (3) asking your doctor for assistance (relevant to external-physician locus of control in Study 2); and (4) understanding the goals and constraints of media. We designed these interventions not only to disrupt the negative effects of changing guidelines, but also with an eye toward their practical use in media reports of health research.

Subjects will receive one of five intervention treatments. Four groups will receive one of four "Before You Act" boxes that corresponding to one of the contexts described above. For example, box (2) notes, "Remember that your cardiovascular health is influenced by a number of factors, including genetic and lifestyle risks. Hence, you should consider how a change in behavior fits with all your heart-healthy behaviors in order to determine the best course of action. Keeping these behaviors in mind will help you put this one action in perspective." Likewise, box (4) notes, "Remember that the news can only cover medical findings at a general level and can not cover all studies on a topic. Hence, you should be aware that they will choose to selectively report on findings they consider newsworthy. Keeping their goals and constraints in mind will help you put this information in perspective." We expect each intervention, relative to the no-intervention control group, to dampen the spillover effects observed in Study 2. We also expect that the aforementioned interactions between changing guidelines and scientific literacy, objective health knowledge, and external locus of control will be weakened as a result of the interventions. If effective, these results will point to important remedies to the problem of changing health guidelines for consumers.

Welcome to the Jungle: Understanding How Environmental Cues Influence Consumption in "The Wild"

Lisa A. Cavanaugh, Duke University, USA

SESSION OVERVIEW

How do the various cues in a shopping environment affect consumer choice? Every day consumers are exposed to a myriad of sights and sounds—colorful displays, promotional stands, different store configurations, and music playing over the loudspeaker. While exposure to "primes" in the lab has reliably shown effects on consumers, considerable skepticism remains as to whether these environmental cues do much, if anything, in more complex, real world environments. The purpose of this symposium is to better understand the impact of such environmental cues on consumer behavior, though a mixture of well-controlled lab experiments and real world field studies.

While these environmental cues are recognized by consumers and marketers alike, the extent or the direction of their influence is not well understood. Do the places and people you just happen to pass on your way to the store influence the choices you make? Do crowded stores and narrow aisles influence the products you select? Does ambient music you hear influence the type of products you buy or the size of donation you make at the register? Does the sight of a prominent holiday display make you more likely to indulge yourself or more likely to indulge others? These and other questions will be examined by the papers in this symposium.

Together the three papers in this session address how a variety of sensory cues in the consumer's environment influence product evaluation, selection, and donation behavior. More importantly, they uncover the underlying mechanisms that drive these effects. To this end, the first paper shows that products are evaluated more favorably and are more likely to be purchased when the surrounding environment contains more conceptually-related cues. The second paper shows that perceptions of physical confinement affect consumers' variety-seeking behavior. The third paper shows that the imagery and sounds prevalent in store environments around popular holidays (e.g., Christmas, Valentine's Day) can trigger very different emotional reactions among consumers with counterintuitive consequences for consumption.

Tanya Chartrand will connect the three papers and serve as the symposium discussant. Tanya is well known for her research on non-conscious goal pursuit and automatic processing of social environments. Her research suggests that much of our daily life is determined by mental processes put into motion by features of the environment, which may operate above or below consumers' conscious awareness (see, e.g., Bargh and Chartrand 1999). Her comments will integrate the various papers while also encouraging discussion among the audience and suggesting interesting potential directions for future research.

EXTENDED ABSTRACTS

"Why Coastal Dwellers May Prefer Tide: The Effects of Conceptually-Related Environmental Cues on Product Evaluation"

Jonah Berger, University of Pennsylvania, USA
Grainne Fitzsimons, University of Waterloo, Canada

Every day, consumers' environments bombarded them with different stimuli. People see certain colors around particular holidays (e.g., orange on Halloween), may read a lot about Mars in the news when a NASA mission is ongoing, and may see their neighbors walking dogs as they come home from work. Might these diverse cues influence people's consumer preferences? We know that direct product exposure, through ads and point of purchase displays, should positively affect sales (e.g., Baker 1999; Zajonc 1968), but what about exposure to perceptually or conceptually linked stimuli? The more consumers see Tide advertisements, the more they should like and purchase Tide, but what about exposure to stimuli related to Tide? Might it be the case that the more consumers see stimuli like waves, the more they will like and purchase Tide?

This presentation investigates how exposure to simple cues in everyday environments can influence consumer behavior. Our hypotheses are based on psychological research regarding spreading activation. Situational cues or primes can automatically activate associated representations in memory, leading them to become more accessible (e.g., Higgins, Rholes, and Jones 1977). This accessibility cam then spread to related constructs via an associative network (Anderson 1983; Collins and Loftus 1975; Neely 1977). According to this spreading activation account, priming (or activating) a given construct in memory leads to the spontaneous activation of related constructs in memory. Building on processing fluency research (Lee and Labroo 2004; Whittlesea 1993) we argue that this activation should lead to more positive evaluations. Consequently, we argue that exposure to everyday real world stimuli can have important downstream effects on perceptually or conceptually-related products.

Four studies examined how environmental cues prevalent in real-world environments influence the accessibility and evaluation of conceptually-related products. Our first study simply sought to establish that real-world environmental cues can activate–or make more accessible–related product representations. We took advantage of a natural temporary difference in the prevalence of certain environmental cues, by using the fact that exposure to the color orange varies greatly around Halloween. Either right before Halloween, or one week later (when all the pumpkins, etc. disappear), participants were approached outside a supermarket and asked to list the first brands of candy and soda that came to mind. Results indicted that the mere increased presence of the color orange in the natural environment was enough to influence product accessibility; consumer products associated with the color orange (i.e., Reese's Pieces and orange soda) were more accessible the day before Halloween as opposed to a week later.

Field Study 2 investigated how exposure to conceptually linked environmental cues influences product evaluation. We again relied on the natural environment for stimuli exposure. Some undergraduates ate in dining halls that used trays, while others ate in dining halls that did not use trays. Consequently, participants varied in how frequently they were exposed to trays over our week long study. We also manipulated whether a digital music player (ePlay) was linked to this, versus another, environmental cue. At the onset of the study, half the participants learned a slogan that linked the music player to dining hall trays ("Dinner is carried by a tray, music is carried by ePlay") while the other half learned a control slogan that linked the music player to a cue (i.e., luggage) that did not vary across groups ("Luggage carries your gear, ePlay carries what you want to hear"). Thus in the 2 (slogan) x 2 (environment) design, only one group of participants was exposed to more frequent conceptually linked product cues. One week later, participants reported their product evaluations and indicated how frequently they had seen trays in the past week.

Results indicated that merely being exposed to conceptually linked product cues was enough to increase product evaluations. Participants who had learned a slogan linking the product to dining hall trays, and ate in dining halls which used trays, liked the digital music player more. A moderated mediation analysis further underscored our hypothesis that the effects were driven by differential exposure to conceptually-linked environmental cues. Another study (Experiment 3) found similar effects linking products to a different environmental cue (i.e., luggage). People who traveled during the study, and thus were exposed to luggage more frequently, reported higher product purchase likelihood and greater willingness to pay.

To further examine the role of conceptual fluency in producing these effects, Experiment 4 directly manipulated exposure to conceptually linked environmental cues. Participants were shown either zero, five, or ten pictures of dogs as part of a study on "brightness perception" and then, in an ostensibly unrelated experiment, reported their evaluations of various sneakers, including some from the brand Puma. The results indicated that frequent exposure to conceptually linked stimuli increased product evaluations. Participants who saw more pictures of dogs evaluated puma sneakers more favorably.

Taken together, these studies demonstrate how subtle, everyday environment cues can have an important impact on consumer behavior. Exposure to conceptually linked stimuli can increase product accessibility, which in turn can lead to increased evaluation and purchase likelihood. These findings deepen our understanding of conceptual fluency (Lee and Labroo 2004) by demonstrating the underlying role of processing ease and examining the effects of frequent (in addition to recent) exposure. They also answer calls from priming researchers (Bargh 2006) by beginning to examine how such effects play out in noisy real world contexts. Seeing dogs can increase evaluations of Puma sneakers and living near the beach (i.e., waves) might even lead people to purchase Tide…

"Physical Confinement and Variety Seeking"

Jonathan Levav, Columbia University, USA
Rui Juliet Zhu, University of British Columbia, Canada

How does physical confinement affect consumers' behavior? Imagine shopping in a grocery store with narrow aisles; will the feelings of confinement created by the narrow aisles affect your product choices? Building on reactance theory (Brehm 1966; Wicklund 1974), we argue that such physical confinement can lead to psychological reactance, and that one consequence of this reactance is variety seeking.

Reactance theory suggests that when an individual's freedom is curtailed, she will experience a state of psychological reactance, which in turn will evoke behaviors aimed at regaining her freedom. In the consumer behavior literature, reactance research has focused on the choice context that can induce reactance, such as when constraints are placed on choice sets (e.g., stock-outs, Fitzsimons 2000) or when consumers are offered unwanted advice (Fitzsimons and Lehman 2003). A commonly observed consequence of such reactance is that individuals tend to adopt or strengthen an attitude or behavior that runs counter to what was intended for or presented to them (e.g., Fitzsimons and Lehman 2004). Building on this line of research, in this paper we investigate an important yet novel source of reactance in consumer behavior: physical confinement. We propose that asking individuals to make choices in (relative) physical confinement will evoke reactance. We predict that a

unique consequence of this reactance is variety-seeking behavior because it is viewed as an expression of choice freedom (Kim and Drolet 2003). Three studies support our theorizing.

The first study tests our basic hypothesis that a relatively confining versus a relatively less-confining space will lead to more variety-seeking. We randomly assigned participants to one of the two conditions, Wide Aisle (7ft) or Narrow Aisle (3.5ft) using dividers placed in a large laboratory space. At the end of the aisle was a table with six bowls containing six different popular candy bars. Participants were instructed to proceed down the aisle and choose three candy bars of any kind, in any combination they pleased. As anticipated, participants in the Narrow Aisle condition chose a greater variety of candy bars than their Wide Aisle counterparts.

In the next study we test the implication of our finding in study 1 to the choice of lesser known brands. We reasoned that where people seek variety they would be more likely to choose brands that they are less familiar with. Another motivation of this study was to test whether aisle width affects overall category choice or only market share. We consider familiar and unfamiliar charities as our "brands" in this study. Seventy-five undergraduate students completed the study in exchange of $10. We randomly assigned participants to a narrow or a wide aisle as in study 1. We placed a table at the end of the aisle where participants were asked to complete a short questionnaire. In the target task, participants were presented with a list and short description of six charities. Three of these were familiar charities to our participants and three were obscure. Participants were asked to indicate: 1) whether they would be willing to donate any or all of their $10 to any of the charities; 2) if so, how much they would donate; and, 3) how they would allocate their donation among the six charities in the event that they elected to make a donation.

The results revealed a significant influence of aisle width on our participants' choices. We created two donation intention indices, one for the familiar charities and one for the unfamiliar charities. No treatment effect was found on donation intentions for familiar charities. However, we found a significant main effect of aisle width on intentions to donate to the less familiar charities, such that participants in the Narrow Aisle condition were more likely to donate to the less familiar charities than their Wide Aisle counterparts. Next we examined whether the amount of money people donated differed by condition. There was no treatment effect on total donation amount, which suggests that the overall category choice is not sensitive to aisle width. We did, however, find a difference in the amount of money donated to each cause. Specifically, those in the Wide Aisle condition donated slightly more to the familiar charities. In contrast—and most interestingly—Narrow Aisle participants donated significantly more money to the unfamiliar charities compared with participants in the Wide Aisle condition.

In our third study we examine whether *feelings* of physical confinement can have the same effect as *actual* physical confinement. We held constant the aisle width at approximately 5 feet, and evoked a sense of confinement (and reactance) by prompting participants think about how narrow the aisle was (confinement condition) or not (control condition). After completing a series of unrelated measures participants were presented with ten pairs of gambles, and asked to choose one gamble from each pair. Each pair included a high probability, low payoff bet ("P-bet") and a low probability, high payoff bet ('$-bet') of approximately the same expected value. We found that participants in the confinement condition were more likely to choose an equal amount of P and $ bets, representing the highest degree of variety seeking, compared with control participants, who tended to prefer $ bets.

Finally, in an in-progress study, we attempt to confirm that reactance is indeed driving our variety-seeking effect using a similar procedure to study 3 where we also measure individuals' chronic reactance tendency. We anticipate that highly reactive participants should seek more variety when they are asked to focus on the aisle's narrowness than participants who are not. However, such a difference should be reduced among those who are chronically low in reactance. Initial results seem to support this theorizing.

In sum, we demonstrate that physical confinement can evoke reactance and consequently lead to variety-seeking. Thus, we identify an important antecedent of reactance (i.e., physical confinement) and highlight a unique consequence (i.e., variety seeking). In addition, this research contributes to the study of how structural aspects of the physical environment affect behavior.

"Happy Holidays? How Sights and Sounds of the Holidays Cue Different Feelings & Consumption Behaviors"

Lisa A. Cavanaugh, Duke University, USA
Gavan J. Fitzsimons, Duke University, USA

How do emotional holiday cues affect consumer behavior in real shopping environments? Generally the holidays are expected to prime positive feelings and large scale expenditure by consumers, particularly around holidays with an emphasis on gift giving, such as Christmas and Valentine's Day. Each holiday season consumers are flooded with seasonal holiday imagery not only at the shopping malls but also at their local grocery stores. Consumers can rarely pick up a gallon of milk or loaf of bread without passing a colorful display or hearing music reminding them of the upcoming holiday at hand. How do these sights and sounds of the holidays influence consumption? We argue that seemingly small differences in how holidays are portrayed can trigger very different types of feelings and appraisals with important consequences for consumption. Our studies look at the impact on the selection of groceries, gifts, food choices, and charitable donations in a real store environment.

Holiday decorations and themed music are often thought to enhance the holiday shopping experience and make people feel happy. Building from the literature on environmental cues (Meyers-Levy and Zhu 2007) and differential response to primes (Wheeler and Berger 2007), we look at how holiday cues differentially affect consumers. We examine how personally relevant cues trigger emotional appraisals (i.e., stakes of the situation and options for coping) and hence lead to more or less indulgence. We argue that different types of cues around the same holiday will trigger different types of feelings and meanings with important consequences for consumption. Specifically we test whether different portrayals of the same holiday can shape the choices that consumers make in real store environments. For example, some environmental cues portray Christmas as a religious holiday with manger scenes and traditional music (e.g., Silent Night, Oh Come All Ye Faithful) while others portray Christmas as a non-religious holiday with emphasis on Santa Claus, reindeer, and non-religious music (e.g., Winter Wonderland, Silverbells). Moreover, Valentine's Day has traditionally been portrayed as a holiday for lovers, however, the greeting card industry and self-affirming singles have worked diligently to re-frame Valentine's Day as a holiday for loved ones more generally (e.g., cards and gifts exchanged between girlfriends and siblings). Our series of studies show that the sights and sounds associated with different portrayals of these holidays can lead to very different choices and behavior at the register.

The Christmas Study I. The Christmas studies test our hypothesis that different portrayals of the same holiday will lead to more or less indulgent behavior. We randomly assigned participants to one of two Christmas imagery conditions: Religious or Non-

Religious prior to making product selections. Under the auspices of a greeting card evaluation task, those in the Religious condition were exposed to greeting cards with religious Christmas imagery and music. Those in the Non-Religious condition were exposed to cards with non-religious imagery and music. Participants then allocated a $50 gift certificate between an indulgent and non-indulgent option. Religious affiliation (Christian/ Non-Christian) was a measured factor. We found that Christians who saw Religious portrayals were *less likely* to opt for indulgent products for themselves. Yet, Christians who saw Non-Religious portrayals of Christmas were significantly *more likely* to indulge than Non-Christians who saw the exact same portrayal.

The Christmas Study II. Participants who had been exposed to either Religious or Non-Religious Christmas imagery entered a store environment. As participants entered the store, either religious or non-religious Christmas music was playing. The key dependent measure was indulgence, specifically the number of store brands vs. national brands selected across a variety of household product categories. Those who had viewed the Religious portrayal of Christmas and heard religious music chose significantly more in-store brands (i.e., indulging the least for themselves and spending less overall). Yet, those who heard religious music were also most likely to choose more indulgent gifts for others. Notably participants did not believe that the music had impacted their choices. Our final dependent measure of interest was donation behavior. After making all their product selections, participants had an opportunity to donate to two different charities—a local charity and an international charity—at the cash register. We find that those who had seen religious imagery and heard religious music playing in store: a) donated the most money and b) donated significantly more money to the international charity than those who heard non-religious music playing in the store environment.

Valentine's Day Study I. The Valentine's Day study was designed to test the implication of Christmas study II within a different holiday context and with generation of different types of feelings. Non-partnered individuals sometimes refer to Valentine's Day as "Single Person's Awareness Day." A prevalent stereotype consists of lonely singles home alone engaging in self-indulgent behavior, but we wondered whether this stereotype would hold across contexts. We hypothesized that consumers' relationship status would affect the way consumers respond to Valentine's Day cues and indulgence opportunities. In Valentine's Day study I, female participants were randomly assigned to one of two conditions: Romantic Valentine's Day imagery or Friendly Valentine's Day imagery via a greeting card evaluation task. Relationship status (single vs. partnered) was a measured factor. We found a significant interaction of imagery and relationship status such that non-partnered individuals who had viewed the Friendly Valentine's Day cards were less likely to indulge than those who had viewed Romantic cards.

Valentine's Day Study II. Female participants were exposed to either Romantic or Friendly Valentine's Day imagery and then entered a grocery store where they encountered a large Valentine's Day display (e.g. roses, giant teddy bear, chocolates) and seasonal music playing. Participants made a series of choices in store and checked out at the register. Our key measures of interest were self-indulgence, in the form of choices of foods and money spent on personal care products, and reported feelings. We find that imagery and relationship status influence self-indulgence in distinct ways. Non-partnered females resist tempting food but indulge more with personal care products. Our results show that while Valentine's Day undoubtedly increases individuals' awareness of their own relationship status, the effects on their consumption are sometimes counterintuitive but ultimately functional.

In sum, we show that holiday cues which reaffirm important goals can dampen self-indulgence while cues that may threaten goals lead to coping through indulgence.

REFERENCES

Anderson, J. R. (1983) in *The Architecture of Cognition B2-The Architecture of Cognition*: Harvard University Press.

Baker, W. E. (1999), "When Can Affective Conditioning and Mere Exposure Directly Influence Brand Choice," in *Journal of Advertising*, Vol. 28, 31-46.

Bargh, John A. (2006), "What Have We Been Priming All These Years? On the Development, Mechanisms, and Ecology of Non-Conscious Social Behavior," in *European Journal of Social Psychology*, Vol. 36, 147-68.

Bargh, John A. and Tanya L. Chartrand (1999), "The Unbearable Automaticity of Being," *American Psychologist*, 54 (7), 462-79.

Brehm, Jack W. (1966), *A Theory of Psychological Reactance*, Academic Press, New York.

Chartrand, Tanya L. and John A. Bargh (1996), "Automatic Activation of Impression Formation and Memorization Goals: Nonconscious Goal Priming Reproduces Effects of Explicit Task Instructions," *Journal of Personality and Social Psychology*, 71 (3), 464-78.

Collins, Allan M. and F. Loftus Elizabeth (1975), "A Spreadingactivation Theory of Semantic Processing," in *Psychological Review*, Vol. 82, 407-28.

Fitzsimons, Gavan J. (2000), "Consumer Response to Stockouts," *Journal of Consumer Research,* 27(September), 249-266.

Fitzsimons, Gavan J. and Donald R. Lehmann (2004), "Reactance to Recommendations: When Unsolicited Advice Yields Contrary Responses," *Marketing Science 23*(winter), 82-94.

Higgins, Tory E., William S. Rholes, Carl R. Jones, and March (1977), "Category Accessibility and Impression Formation," in *Journal of Social Psychology*, Vol. 13, 141-54.

Kim, Heejung S. and Aimee Drolet (2003), "Choice and Self-Expression: A Cultural Analysis of Variety-Seeking," *Journal of Personality and Social Psychology*, 85 (August), 373–382.

Lee, A. Y. and A. A. Labroo (2004), "Effects of Conceptual and Perceptual Fluency on Affective Judgment," in *Journal of Marketing Research*, Vol. 41, 151-65.

Meyers-Levy, Joan and Rui Zhu (2007), "The Influence of Ceiling Height: The Effect of Priming on the Type of Processing That People Use," *Journal of Consumer Research*, 34 (2), 174-86.

Neely, J. H. (1977), "Semantic Priming and Retrieval from Lexical Memory: Roles of Inhibition Less Spreading Activation and Limited-Capacity Attention," in *Journal of Experimental Psychology: General*, Vol. 106, 226-54.

Wheeler, S. Christian and Jonah Berger (2007), "When the Same Prime Leads to Different Effects," *Journal of Consumer Research*, 34 (3), 357-68.

Whittlesea, Bruce W. A. and November (1993), ""Illusions of Familiarity," in *Journal of Experimental Psychology: Learning, Memory, and Cognition*, Vol. 19, 1235-53.

Wicklund, Robert A. (1974), *Freedom and Reactance*, Potomac, MD: Lawrence Erlbaum Associates.

Zajonc, Richard (1968), "Attitudinal Effects of Mere Exposure," in *Journal of Personality and Social Psychology Monograph Supplement*, Vol. 9, 1-28.

The Psychological Consequences of Choice
Jinhee Choi, University of Chicago, USA

SESSION OVERVIEW

Choice has been a central topic in consumer research, and in recent years, choice researchers have been mainly investigating what people choose (i.e., preference) and how they choose (i.e., choice process) (e.g., Dhar 1997; Hsee et al. 1999; Payne, Bettman, and Johnson 1992; Shafir, Simonson, and Tversky 1993). To this day, however, there is still relatively little known about the psychological consequences of choice. For example, what are the affective residual consequences of choice? How does choice affect people's mental resources? And why are some choices experienced differently than others? The objective of this symposium is to bring together a group of researchers that study these questions. They will address the consequences of choice for consumers' affective experiences and mental resources. Specifically, the symposium includes papers on consumers' experiences of depletion, replenishment, satisfaction, and regret, as a result of making choice.

The first two papers will address choosers' general psychological experience after making a choice. The first paper by Vohs et al. demonstrates that making choices depletes self-regulatory resources and further suggests why this happens by showing the various conditions of choice. Specifically, these researchers find that making choices for the self (compared to choosing for others), making unenjoyable choices (compared to enjoyable choices), and making full choices (compared to only deliberating or only implementing choices) were more depleting.

The second paper by Choi and Fishbach identifies the conditions under which the process of making choices has replenishing (vs. depleting) effects. In contrast to broad range of research showing that making choices is hard and depleting, they demonstrate that choosing can even be replenishing when it is construed as an end rather than a means to get something. Specifically, when consumers make choice for its own sake without considering getting something, it is replenishing. In contrast, when consumers make choices to get something, it is depleting. Thus, this research suggests the positive consequence of choosing based on how it is construed.

Whereas the first two papers focus on choosers' general experience after making a choice, regardless of the chosen item, the following papers focus on choosers' experience of the selected option. The third paper by Iyengar et al. investigates the implications of choice for a chooser's experience of post-choice satisfaction. They demonstrate that merely providing a categorization of the options enhances chooser's satisfaction on the chosen item. For example, choosers were more satisfied with their selection of magazine or coffee when these products were divided into more (vs. less) categories, irrespective of the information contained in the category labels. They further show that this is driven by a sense that a greater number of categories signals greater variety among the available options, which allows for a sense of self-determination from choosing.

The final paper by Ratner et al. identifies the factors that cause choosers to regret their selections and how they react to this feeling afterwards. They show that consumers switch away from a dominant option to a dominated option in subsequent choice when they experience regret after choosing the dominant option. They further demonstrate that whether consumers' regret leads them to switch depends on how they think and make attributions about the previous options. Thus, they suggest a situation leading consumers to negative affective experience (e.g., regret), which further causes switching afterwards, moderated by their cognition (e.g., attribution).

Taken together, these papers explore the psychological consequences of making choices, including depletion, replenishment, satisfaction, and regret. These different lines of research provide diverse insights on the study of choice consequences yet maintain a coherent theme.

We believe that choice is central to consumer research and therefore, this symposium will be of great interest and appeal to a large number of audiences in consumer research, including those interested in emotion, motivation, information search and processing, and consumer satisfaction. All the papers are in advanced stages of completion (two are currently in press) and at least one author from each paper has agreed to present their paper if the symposium is accepted. As this symposium includes four talks, there will not be a long discussion but Fishbach will provide a brief summarizing discussion at the end. The talks will be kept brief to allow enough time for Q&A. We believe that the presentations on the psychological consequence of choice will elicit active discussion and idea generation for future research on choice.

References

Dhar, Ravi (1997), "Consumer Preference for a Non-Choice Option," *Journal of Consumer Research*, 24, 215-31.

Hsee, Christopher K, George F. Loewenstein, Sally Blount, and Max H. Bazerman (1999), "Preference Reversals between Joint and Separate Evaluation of Options: A Review and Theoretical Analysis," *Psychological Bulletin*, 125, 576-590.

Payne, John W., James R. Bettman, and Eric J. Johnson (1992), *The Adaptive Decision Maker*, New York: Cambridge University Press.

Shafir, Eldar, Itamar Simonson, and Amos Tversky (1993), "Reason-Based Choice," *Cognition*, 49, 11-36.

EXTENDED ABSTRACTS

"Why Do Choices Tax Self-Regulatory Resources? Three Tests of Candidates to Explain Decision Fatigue"

Kathleen D. Vohs, University of Minnesota, USA
Noelle Nelson, University of Minnesota, USA
Catherine Rawn, University of British Columbia, Canada

Although many studies now detail the deleterious effects of making many choices or having many options, few have investigated why the process of choice derails the self. The current research approached this question using the limited-resource model of self-regulation, which has been a fruitful context to study the taxing nature of making choices. The current research asked about three distinctive features of choice that may underlie the effect.

It is instructive to review previous findings on self-control deficits after making choices. A series of studies by Vohs and colleagues (Vohs et al. 2008) found that making choice led people to perform worse on a subsequent act of self-control, relative to conditions in which participants previously had not made choices. This research used multiple domains of decision making, including choices about products and courses for a university degree. The dependent measures of self-regulation included enduring painfully cold water and drinking a bad-tasting but healthy liquid. In all studies, the pattern was clear: people who had made choices showed impaired self-control on a later task, relative to people who had not made choices.

Why would choice deplete the self's regulatory resources? We investigated three important aspects of the choice process in the current studies. Our model of how choice taxes the self was derived from Gollwitzer's (1996) Rubicon Model of decision making. Gollwitzer depicts choice as the move between two qualitatively different modes of thought: deliberate and implement. The first stage in a choice process is deliberation, in which options are analyzed and a rather even-handed evaluation of options occurs. The act of choosing, per se, comes when people select an option (or more than one) in a quasi-behavioral act that connects the self to the chosen option (Strack, Werth, and Deutch 2006). The second stage in the choice process is to implement the choice, which means to act upon the selected option. This stage is markedly different from the deliberate stage, insofar as it engenders a commitment to an option and a bolstering of positivity about the chosen option. Shifting from one mindset to a qualitatively different mindset ought to be taxing, given that the concept of a mindset entails a distinct orientation toward the world, manner of engaging with the world, and evaluations of incoming information due to differing standards.

The first study examined whether making choices for the self versus making choices for another differs in terms of the regulatory energy. Insofar as making choices ties the selected object to the self, making choices ought to be more taxing when it involves the self than when it is for another given that the tie between the object and selfhood is likely far weaker. Participants came to the lab and were assigned to a condition in which they made choices for the self, for a person with whom they were moderately acquainted (on a scale from 1-9, the closeness of the relationship with this person was a 5), or made no choices. Then participants completed math problems as a measure of self-control. In line with predictions about the specialness of the self in choice, participants who made choices for themselves performed worse than participants who made choices for a friend, which itself was equivalent to self-control after not making choices.

A second study tested whether making enjoyable choices was less taxing than making choices that were not enjoyable. We hypothesized that the pleasantness of the choosing process might reduce its deleterious effects. If depletion is caused by forcing oneself to do something, then a pleasant task would presumably be less depleting than an aversive one. There was also some reason to predict that choice quantity would interact with subjective enjoyment. The beneficial impact of enjoying the task will likely wane as time and exertion increases. Hence we predicted that people would be less depleted when they made only a few, enjoyable choices but that by the time they had made many choices, they would be depleted regardless of liking for the choice task. Participants who had made no choices performed the best on the subsequent act of self-control, and participants who had made many choices (12 minutes of choosing) performed the worst. In between were a group of participants who had made a moderate amount of choices (3 minutes), and in this group the effect of choices depended on enjoyability of the task. If participants enjoyed the choice task (in this case, using a gift registry), they were less depleted than if they did not enjoy the task. But again, when participants had made many choices, the effect of enjoying the task vanished.

A third experiment manipulated which part of the choice process participants completed Some participants engaged in only the deliberate aspect of choice, whereas others followed pre-selected instructions to implement an already-chosen option (this is akin to locating the right kind of peanut butter on a grocery list

someone else wrote), whereas a third group performed the full choice process of deliberating and implementing. In line with our notion of switching mindsets, the full choice process of deliberating and implementing produced the most depletion; the other two conditions of only deliberating and only implementing were better at self-control and were equivalent to each other.

In sum, three tests of three candidates for why choice is depleting found that the self is integral to when choice is depleting; making enjoyable choices helps when making moderate amounts of choices but not when many choices are made; and that the full choice process is more taxing than either simply deliberating among options or implementing pre-selected options. This research helps move the field toward a fuller understanding of the nature of choice, by detailing when, for whom, and how choice harms self-regulation.

References

Gollwitzer, P. M. (1996). The volitional benefits of planning. In P. M. Gollwitzer & J. A. Bargh (Eds.), *The psychology of action: Linking cognition and motivation to behavior* (pp. 287-312). New York: Guilford.

Strack, F., Werth, L., & Deutsch, R. (2006). Reflective and impulsive determinants of consumer behavior. Journal of Consumer Psychology, 16, 205-216.

Vohs, Kathleen D., Roy F. Baumeister, Brandon J. Schmeichel, Jean M. Twenge, Noelle M. Nelson and Dianne M. Tice (2008), "Making Choices Impairs Subsequent Self-Control: A Limited Resource Account of Decision Making, Self-Regulation, and Active Initiative," *Journal of Personality and Social Psychology*, 94 (5), 883-898.

"Choice as an End versus a Means"
Jinhee Choi, University of Chicago, USA
Ayelet Fishbach, University of Chicago, USA

Past research has distinguished the activities derived from two distinct motivators: An extrinsically motivating activity that serves other goals and hence construed as a means to achieve these goals, and an intrinsically motivating activity that does not serve other goals and hence construed as an end in itself (Shah and Kruglanski 2000). In this research, we apply this distinction to the activity of choosing and propose two different choice modes: the one that starts with an external need to which the choice is an instrumental means versus the one where the choice is its own end and it is experiential.

Based on research attesting that the same activity is experienced as effortful when it is extrinsically motivating and as enjoyable when it is intrinsically motivating (Higgins and Trope 1990), we propose that the activity of choosing is experienced differently depending on how it is framed. When choosing is construed as a means and thus instrumental, choosing is experienced as effortful and results in post-choice depletion. Conversely, when choosing is construed as an end in itself and thus experiential, it is experienced as enjoyable and results in post-choice replenishment. Thus, whereas choice research has traditionally considered the act of choosing as effortful and depleting (e.g., Baumeister et al. 2008; Dhar 1997; Luce, Bettman, and Payne 1997), choosing can also be enjoyable and replenishing if conducted for its own sake rather than conducted to get the selected item. We also propose that the subsequent interest in getting the selected item differs based on this mental framing. When choosing is instrumental and consumers experience depletion, they should express lower interest in getting their selected item than when choosing is experiential and they experience replenishment

Four studies explore these distinct consequences of choosing depending on whether it is instrumental or experiential. Study 1 ("chips choice") manipulated choosing as instrumental or experiential by directing participants to consider the next step of purchase or not. After tasting a number of chips, those who chose chips they like most (experiential choice) were more persistent in drinking healthy but bad-tasting beverage than those who chose chips they would like to buy (instrumental choice) or those who did not make any choice (control). Study 2 ("vacation choice") manipulated choosing by emphasizing the goal of choosing or not. We found that participants who chose a vacation package without a specific external reason (experiential choice) performed better in the subsequent cognitive task than those who chose a vacation package with an emphasized goal of vacationing (instrumental choice) or those who did not make any choice (control). We also found that those who made an experiential choice were more motivated to go on a selected vacation than those who made an instrumental choice. Study 3 ("book choice") framed choosing differently by leading participants to think about the goals of choosing or the means to choose. "Thinking about the goals" frames choosing as instrumental to achieve these goals, whereas "thinking about the means" frames choosing as experiential that can be achieved by these means. We found that participants who chose a fiction book under thinking about the means (experiential choice) were more motivated to engage in effortful activities after choosing than those who did not make any choice (control), whereas those who chose a book under thinking about the goals of choosing (instrumental choice) were less motivated to do effortful activities afterwards compared to those in control condition. We also found that those who made experiential choice were willing to pay more for the selected book than those who made instrumental choice. Finally, Study 4 ("flower choice") manipulated choosing by framing it as a need or want. We found that people who did flower shopping as what they want to do (experiential choice) felt more replenished than those who did not make any choice (control), whereas those who did flower shopping as what they need to do (instrumental choice) felt more depleted than those in control condition. We further found that those who made experiential choice were more motivated to purchase the selected flower than those who made instrumental choice.

Taken together, these studies provide convergent evidence that instrumental choice construed as a means makes people depleted and decreases the interest in getting the chosen option, whereas experiential choice construed as an end makes people replenished and increases the interest in the chosen option. It implies that the same choice activity has distinct consequences depending on how it is framed.

References

Shah, James Y. and Arie W. Kruglanski (2000), "The Structure and Substance of Intrinsic Motivation," in Carol Sansone and Judith M. Harackiewicz (Eds.) *Intrinsic and Extrinsic Motivation: The Search for Optimal Motivation and Performance* (pp. 106-30). San Diego: Academic Press.

Higgins, E. Tory and Yaacov Trope (1990), "Activity Engagement Theory: Implications of Multiply Identifiable Input for Intrinsic Motivation," in E. Tory Higgins and Richard M. Sorrentino (Eds.) *Handbook of Motivation and Cognition: Foundations of Social Behavior* (Vol. 2, pp. 229-64). New York: Guilford Press.

Baumeister, Roy F., Erin A. Sparks, Tyler F. Stillman, and Kathleen D. Vohs (2008), "Free Will in Consumer Behavior: Self Control, Ego Depletion, and Choice," *Journal of Consumer Psychology*, 18, 4-13

Dhar, Ravi (1997), "Consumer Preference for a Non-Choice Option," *Journal of Consumer Research*, 24, 215-31.

Luce, Mary Frances, James R. Bettman, and John W. Payne (1997), "Choice Processing in Emotionally Difficult Decisions," *Journal of Experimental Psychology: Learning, Memory, and Cognition*, 23, 384-405.

"The Mere Categorization Effect: How the Presence of Categories Increases Choosers' Perceptions of Assortment Variety and Outcome Satisfaction"

Cassie Mogilner, Stanford University, USA
Tamar Rudnick, Columbia University, USA
Sheena Iyengar, Columbia University, USA

Imagine shoppers browsing the magazine rack of a supermarket. They study rows upon rows of glossy pages, colorful pictures, and splashy headlines. They wander the aisle among hundreds of publications grouped under different category headings. Picture the magazines on the rack: Under "Fashion" there is the ultra-thick issue of Vogue. Under "Current Events" there is a copy of Newsweek. Under "Music" there is the most recent Rolling Stone. Watch the shoppers pick magazines from a set of hundreds. Did the category labels—Fashion, Current Events, Music—influence the shoppers' choices? Did the very presence of categories affect their satisfaction with their magazine selections?

We sought answers to these questions by observing customers as they shopped the magazine aisles of a Northeastern supermarket chain. The 10 branches of the chain where we conducted our observations varied in the number of magazine options (331 to 664, $M=575$) and the number of magazine categories (18 to 26, $M=23$), which were unrelated ($r(10)=-.26$, NS). Although each of the store displays identified such categories as "Fashion & Beauty," "Health & Fitness," and "Entertainment," the retailer had flexibility in deciding whether to further categorize the display to include such categories as "Women's General Interest," "Sports," and "Music." We observed 391 shoppers as they exited the magazine aisle (50% women, ranging in age from 30 to 50 years old) and asked them to participate in a short survey. Shoppers reported on a 100-point scale their perceptions of the variety offered by the magazine selection and their levels of satisfaction with their shopping experience. The results showed that while the actual number of magazine options had little impact ($?=.04$, $t=.66$, NS), the number of categories used to partition the display positively influenced perceptions of variety ($?=.18$, $t=3.44$, $p=.001$), which in turn led to greater customer satisfaction ($?=.49$, $t=11.00$, $p<.001$).

Expanding on the observations from our exploratory field study, we conducted two experiments in the choice domains of magazines and gourmet coffee to more closely examine the relationship between the presence of categories and consumers' subjective experiences of choosing. In particular, the experiments examined the effect of mere categorization, in terms of the number and content of category labels, on chooser satisfaction. The findings show that the mere presence of a greater number of categories leads to increased chooser satisfaction, irrespective of the information contained in the category labels. This "mere categorization effect" occurs by increasing choosers' perceptions of variety, which increases their feelings of self-determination.

In experiment 1, participants were presented with a display of 144 magazines from which they were instructed to choose one. Holding the magazine options constant, the display was manipulated between subjects to either offer three broad categorizes (i.e, *Men's, Women's*, and *General Interest*) or 18 more specific categories (e.g., *Cooking, Auto,* and *Sports*). Although categorization did not influence participants who were familiar with their choice set, those participants who were unfamiliar with their choice set were significantly more satisfied with their selected magazine when the display was divided into 18 categories than when the display was divided into three categories. This effect was driven by choosers' perceiving increased variety amongst the options when there were a greater number of categories.

In experiment 2, participants were presented with a menu of 50 gourmet coffee flavors from which they were instructed to choose one to taste. The coffee options were either uncategorized or divided into 10 categories with labels that were informative (e.g., "Complex," "Spicy," "Nutty,"), somewhat uninformative (e.g., "The Gathering," "Java Joe's," "Coffee Time"), or completely uninformative "Category A," "Category B," "Category C". The results showed that irrespective of the information contained in the category labels, categorization led to greater chooser satisfaction than no categorization, but only for those who were novice coffee drinkers. Mediation analyses showed that this "mere categorization effect" was driven by the sense of self-determination that choosers experience when choosing from an assortment that they perceive to offer variety.

Building on research on categorization (e.g., Schmitt and Zhang 1998), consumers' inferences from marketing communications (e.g., Carpenter, Glazer, and Nakamoto 1994), and self-determination (e.g., Ryan and Deci 2006), this research has clear implications for retailers and offers theoretical contributions to extant work on perceived variety (e.g., Broniarczyk, Hoyer, and McAlister 1998; Hoch, Bradlow, and Wansink 1999; Kahn and Wansink 2004) and assortment size (e.g., Chernev 2003; Iyengar and Lepper 2000).

References

Broniarczyk, Susan, Wayne Hoyer, and Leigh McAlister (1998), "Consumers' Perceptions of the Assortment Offered in a Grocery Category: The Impact of Item Reduction," *Journal of Marketing Research,* 35 (May), 166-76.

Carpenter, Gregory S., Rashi Glazer and Kent Nakamoto (1994), "Meaningful Brands from Meaningless Differentiation: The Dependence of Irrelevant Attributes," *Journal of Marketing Research,* 31 (August), 339-50.

Chernev, Alexander (2003), "When More is Less and Less Is More: The Role of Ideal Point Availability and Assortment in Consumer Choice," *Journal of Consumer Research,* 30 (September), 170-83.

Hoch, Stephen, Eric Bradlow, and Brian Wansink (1999), "The Variety of an Assortment," *Marketing Science,* 18 (4), 527-46.

Iyengar, Sheena S. and Mark R. Lepper (2000), "When Choice is Demotivating: Can One Desire Too Much of a Good Thing?" *Journal of Personality and Social Psychology,* 79, 995-1006.

Kahn, Barbara and Brian Wansink (2004), "The Influence of Assortment Structure on Perceived Variety and Consumption Quantities," *Journal of Consumer Research,* 30 (March), 519-33.

Ryan, Richard M. and Edward Deci (2006), "Self-Regulation and the Problem of Human Autonomy: Does Psychology Need Choice, Self-Determination, and Will?" *Journal of Personality,* 74 (December), 1557-85.

Schmitt, Bernd and Shi Zhang (1998), "Language and Structure and Categorization: A Study of Classifiers in Consumer Cognition, Judgment, and Choice," *Journal of Consumer Research,* 25 (September), 108-22.

"When Dominated Options are Chosen: The Interplay of Affect and Cognition in Repeated Risky Choice"

Rebecca Ratner, University of Maryland, USA
Kenneth Herbst, Wake Forest University, USA
Nathan Novemsky, Yale University, USA

Individuals often face repeated choices between the same risky options. For example, when choosing how to invest savings, there are classes of investments that offer different risk profiles that a single individual might choose among on many different occasions. We are interested in examining how the outcome from a previous choice influences subsequent choices in these situations. We focus on a choice where there is a dominant option in all rounds and examine when and why individuals will choose the dominated option following a disappointing outcome with the dominant option.

Previous research has examined switching behavior in this context and found that individuals experience regret following the negative resolution of uncertainty; and that this regret drives them to switch away from what they still believe is a dominant option (Ratner and Herbst 2005). Thus, emotional reactions seem to interfere with individuals' ability to make a rational choice (Shiv et al. 2005). We extend this prior research by trying to understand why individuals experience regret following the choice of a dominant option. Regret usually accompanies a sense that one should have taken a different course of action. In the present context, that means one wishes to have chosen a dominated option. Nevertheless, substantial regret does emerge in this situation. We also examine when individuals are prone to act on their feeling of regret and actually switch to a dominated option.

In all studies, we use a fixed paradigm following Ratner and Herbst (2005). In that general paradigm, all participants first choose between two risky options (e.g., stock brokers). The information given about the options is very simple and clearly points to one option as dominant over the other option: for example, participants are asked to choose between a broker with a past success rate of 54% vs. one with a past success rate of 43%. Therefore, although one option clearly dominates the other, even the dominant option includes a substantial chance of failure. Not surprisingly, almost all participants choose the dominant option on the initial choice occasion. They then receive feedback that the option they chose did not produce a positive outcome on this first occasion. Our studies focus on what participants think and feel about this outcome and how that impacts their choices on subsequent occasions.

In our first study, we find that if we do not provide information about how the foregone option fared, participants assume that it fared well. As a result, they feel regret about having chosen the dominant option despite believing that the chosen option has a better chance of success than the foregone option even after accounting for the results of the first round. This experienced regret led individuals in Study 1 to switch to the dominated option on the next occasion. In our next study, we find that although individuals feel regret whenever they believe their outcome was worse than the outcome of the foregone option, they do not always act on this regret by switching to the dominated option. That is, their affective response does not always produce a switch on the subsequent occasion. Whether their regret leads them to switch appears to depend in part on whether they expect that the unchosen option produced a qualitatively different outcome than the obtained outcome (e.g., that the foregone option would have produced an increase in the value of an investment whereas the chosen option resulted in a decrease in value).

To summarize, we examine a situation where individuals are taking substantial risks and choosing a dominant option. Nevertheless, they are experiencing regret following the negative resolution of the risk. These feelings are sufficient to cause individuals to choose what they believe is a dominated option in a subsequent choice. Our results also suggest situations in which experienced regret does not produce regret-driven switching behaviors. Together, the results suggest a complex interplay between affect (e.g., regret) and cognitions in situations in which consumers make repeated choices between options that do not guarantee successful outcomes.

References

Ratner, Rebecca K. and Kenneth C. Herbst (2005), "When Good Decisions Have Bad Outcomes: The Impact of Affect on Switching Behavior," *Organizational Behavior and Human Decision Processes*, 96, 23–37.

Shiv, Baba, George Loewenstein, Antoine Bechara, Hanna Damasio, and Antonio R. Damasio (2005), "Investment Behavior and the Negative Side of Emotion," *Psychological Science*, 16, 435-39.

"What Things Do": Examining Things That "Matter" in Consumer Research

Elizabeth Parsons, Keele University, UK

SESSION OVERVIEW

In this symposium we attempt to re-assert the role that the object has to play in our understandings of the consumption process in exploring 'what things do'. As such the symposium aims to open out recent debates surrounding materiality in consumer research (Bettany 2007, Borgerson 2005, Zwick and Dholakia 2006). While the role material objects play in meeting needs, wants and desires, and their centrality as resources for identity construction, has been discussed by consumer researchers in depth (i.e. Belk 1988), much less attention has been paid to matter and materiality. In his 2005 book 'Materiality and Society' Dant argues strongly for a closer focus on the 'material stuff of life' and observes that the mundane routine ways in which objects are taken up in everyday lives have been neglected. Of course such an approach regards the meanings of objects not as intrinsic to the objects themselves, but as socially and culturally (re)produced (see for example Miller 1998). We seek to take this one step further by exploring the agency that might be afforded the more-than-human world of objects, or in Borgerson's words objects' 'non-intentional capacity to facilitate alteration' (2005: 440).

Rather than offer a description of each of the papers here, it is perhaps more instructive to draw out key themes operating across the three papers. In seeking to explore object agency and intentionality (i.e. in thinking through 'what things do') all three papers unpack the capacity of objects to resist our attempts at meaning making. Lai and Dermody, and Brownlie both use the trope of 'hybridity' to explore the ambiguity of object intentionality. Lai and Dermody view the donor-cadaver as an ambiguous hybrid, which destabilizes the boundaries between (living) subject and (inert) object. Likewise, Brownlie observes that music is 'simultaneously abstract and concrete, physical and mental, material and social, concept and 'thing'' For Parsons a focus on the aesthetics of antique objects similarly draws out the concomitance of the substantive and communicative dimensions of things.

Through this exploration of hybridity the authors also seek to problematise prevailing understandings of subject-object relations in consumer research. This is most obviously accomplished by Lai and Dermody in their exploration of donor-cadavers, 'the living dead' which achieve a liminal quality being neither fully subject, nor fully object. Brownlie similarly persuades us to reflect on the liminal quality of music, he argues that studying music as social interaction in material context has potential to destabilize tensions between the object-subject divide. Finally, the authors in the symposium all identify the importance of understanding the embodied, performative and staged elements of the consumption experience.. As Brownlie observes, there are 'riches to be found in getting out of the object-subject divide and the production-consumption ghetto, into the area of materiality and embodied habituated social practice.'

EXTENDED ABSTRACTS

"The 'Living Dead': An Exploration of The Social Biographies of Donor-Cadavers as Intentional Objects"
Ai-Ling Lai, University of Gloucestershire, UK
Janine Dermody, University of Gloucestershire, UK

This paper seeks to advance the burgeoning interest concerning the role of the (material) object in consumer research. Bettany

(2007) observes that there has been an ontological departure within the discipline to accord greater agentic primacy to the consuming subject. This has been conceptualized most recently in Consumer Culture Theory, where consumers "*actively rework and transform symbolic meanings*' encoded within the marketplace as part of their identity-projects (Arnould and Thompson, 2005). Consequently, the object remains a passive *res-extensa* subordinated to the consuming subject (Merleau-Ponty, 1962). As such, consumer researchers are increasingly called to explicate the intentional (purposeful) orientation between the subject and object (Borgerson, 2005; Dant, 2005; Bettany, 2007; Lai *et.* al., 2008).

The aim of this paper is to 'recover' the 'agentic capability' of things, by exploring how the embedded intentionality of objects is enacted through the intersubjective network in which they are situated (Merleau-Ponty, 1945/2002; Borgerson, 2005; Bettany, 2007). This paper will answer this special session call from an embodied perspective drawing from the existential philosophy of Merleau-Ponty (1945/2002) and Heidegger (1927/1962). We will focus our analysis within the context of organ transplantation to consider the extent to which donor-cadavers can be considered as intentional objects (*what do objects do*) and how these cadavers enter into a purposeful communion with various members of the transplant community (subject). Accordingly we will present key themes emerging from the embodied narratives of 14 potential female donors, aged 21-30, who claim to be ambivalent as they explore the ideas surrounding cadaveric organ donation (Lock, 2002).

Specifically, we analyze the way in which participants trace the 'social biography' (Kopytoff, 1986) of cadaver-donors, as they consider the social significance of the body in relation to the liminality of the machine-ventilated-cadaver in organ transplantation (Hogle, 1995). This is understandable as organs are generally donated by patients who suffer from brain stem death (BSD).[1] These machine-ventilated cadavers are occasionally referred to as heart-beating cadavers or *neomorts* (Hogle, 1995). As an ambiguous hybrid, its marginal identity destabilizes the boundaries that customarily mark the donor-cadaver as (living) subject and (inert) object. In particular, the lifelike appearance of the *neomort* (Hogle, 1995; Lock, 2002) raises panhuman controversies over its agentic status as a marker of subjectivity, which is constantly being negotiated, abolished and redefined within the intersubjective network of the transplant community. In short, the *neomort* exudes an ambiguous intentionality, which problematizes the cultural meanings surrounding the status of the body as a lingering site of the donors' personhood and a biomedical production of routine cyborg (Hogle, 1995).

Our analysis of the biomedical narrative reveals that the *neomort* is stripped of its intentionality. The body is 'staged' by biomedical experts in an attempt to construct a boundary marker to reduce the ambiguity of the *neomort* (Hogle, 1995). Medical rituals and protocol are orchestrated around the body, where the 'humanness' of the donor-cadaver is eradicated. For instance, the body is

---

[1] Brain Stem Death should not be confused with Persistent Vegetative State (PVS). BSD refers to the irreversible damage of the brain stem and PVS refers to injury to the higher brain while the brain stem remains intact.

chained to a paraphernalia of technical equipment to sustain its vegetative status, which transforms the embodied patient into a docile and disembodied object (Hogle, 1995). Yet the *neomort* is firmly located within the matrix of interpersonal relationship (Hallam *et*. al, 1999), and as such continues to exhibit social intentionality, as it remains comported towards the intersubjective world. For the participants, the intervention of the life-support machine creates a tension concerning the agentic capacity of the neomort-as-subject. On the one hand, the neomort persistently displays an *ambiguous transcendence* in its lingering orientation to life (Hallam *et*. al, 1999), and thus continues to project into the potentiality-for-being (Heidegger, 1927/1962). For some participants, preserving the life of the *neomort* becomes synonymous to preserving the endurance of the embodied self. As such, the neomort-as-subject is permeated with 'social agency' (Miller, 2005) which inhibits the decision of the potential donor and their family to consider organ donation. Other participants however, consider such *ambiguous transcendence* afforded by transplant technology as limiting. Here, the *neomort* is perceived to be 'engaging' with the world in an inhibited manner (*inhibited intentionality*), and as such hampers its 'experience' for 'being-in-the-world' (Heidegger, 1927/1962). In other words, the *neomort* is 'decapitated' in its agentic capacity to meaningfully transcend the immanence of its materiality (Merleau-Ponty, 1945/2002). Consequently, the neomort emerges as an alienated presence, whose 'experience' is disjointed from the surrounding world (lost quality of life).

Our analysis therefore illustrates how the meanings and agentic properties of the donor-cadaver come to be materialized/erased through the interpersonal narratives and rituals performed through and around the body. We also uncover a number of important ethical questions surrounding the 'ownership' the neomort and the extent to which death can be defined in relations to the materiality of the body–which we will consider within our discussion. In so doing, our paper has thematized the agentic capability of objects (donor-cadaver) in enhancing/resisting the meaning-making process surrounding the consumption practice of organ donation. The donor-cadaver is therefore an intentional object that 'objects'.

"Creating 'The Look': Staging Value in the Antique Shop"
Elizabeth Parsons, Keele University, UK

This paper adds to our understanding of the way in which value is 'staged' in the consumption experience through an exploration of the antique shop. Staging and dramatic metaphors have been widely explored in the context of services marketing (i.e. Grove and Fisk 1983, Arnould et al 1998) and more recently developed through the emerging language of consumptionscapes (Ger and Belk 1996, Venkatraman and Nelson 2008). However, these accounts focus largely on the relations between consumers, employees and the consumption surroundings. Here objects often merely act as props to the business of consumption. The aim in this paper is to explore in more depth the role that objects themselves might play in the value staging process (taking centre stage as it were). Dealers typically choose, alter, repair and assemble their objects for sale to achieve a particular look. It is argued that the innate style of objects and their presentation on the shop floor to create a specific 'look' becomes a key communicator in the staging of value. The services marketing literature has identified a split between communicative and substantive modes of staging the service experience. The focus on object aesthetics in this paper (see Wagner 1999), suggests a rejoining of these two concepts. It is argued that communicative staging, in particular dealers' story telling around the histories of objects (Parsons 2008), cannot be separated from the substantive nature (physicality) of the objects themselves. In highlighting the

role of the object the paper applies a material culture perspective on consumer behaviour and markets (Gell 1992, Attfield 2000, Borgerson 2005, Dant 2005, Miller 2005, Bettany 2007). With a particular concern to further explore 'what things do' in the consumption process (Verbeek 2005).

The paper draws insights from a wider project involved with exploring the social and material dimensions of antique dealing. Discussion is based on 15 interviews with antique dealers in two UK locations: Glasgow in Lanarkshire and Leek in Staffordshire. In this paper two cases are drawn from this research population for further elaboration. In each of these cases the dealers are involved in creating and maintaining quite different and specific 'looks' in their showroom or shop floor.

The first look to be explored is '*Eccentric Englishness*'. Roger uses several freelance finders to source his unusual objects and then transforms them in his workshop for sale to dealers (mainly American). When asked if he is interested in a specific period of antiques he says 'not into a period no- more into a look, the whole look exactly'. When asked about the look he is creating he comments 'English and a bit of French'. For inspiration Roger refers to the American interior design magazine 'Veranda' which he has copies of around the showroom. The second look to be explored is '*Scandinavian Design*' Steve has a shop and workshop in the same small town as Roger but is involved in creating this very different look. He underlines that his look is 'that sort of Scandinavian Gustavian look which is really quite strong at the moment–as long as it's not too distressed'. Similar to Roger, Steve relies on interior design magazines for inspiration and to get a feel for what is popular, he cites Homes and Gardens (a British interiors magazine) as influencing his look.

In exploring these two looks it becomes clear that while the look *represents* a style or theme within the antique shop, on a deeper level this style or theme also becomes *demanding* of the dealer in choosing and/or altering the right objects to complement, and fit in with, the look. Therefore it is argued that 'looks' operate right across markets, influencing the practices and processes of producers, designers, retailers and consumers (see Entwistle's 2002 work on modelling). In this sense the look might be more usefully conceptualised as an 'aesthetic regime' around which networks of these cultural intermediaries are organised. This concept is useful in that it allows a consideration not only of the way in which aesthetics directs the purchase and consumption of goods, but also their modes of production, distribution and presentation. Geographers have explored a 'commodity chain' approach to consumption (i.e. Hughes and Reimer 2003). But further research would explore how markets are mediated by 'aesthetic regimes' and how such regimes both direct, and place demands on, those involved in networks of dealers, retailers, interior designers and consumers. For consumer researchers the focus will undoubtedly be on the last of these, however it is argued that consumer cannot be studied in isolation of these wider networks of provision.

"On the 'Hybridity' of Music"
Douglas Brownlie, University of Stirling, UK

The paper will argue that the category of 'music' as 'culture in the making'-as social interaction in material context-is worthy of further consideration within the consumer culture research cannon.

As a provocation, the claim is offered on this basis: that examination of the current status of 'music' as analytical object within consumer research reveals widely held assumptions about the relationship between subjects and objects of consumption (Wallace, 1997; Heckler & Blossom, 1997). That 'music' as it presents itself is simultaneously abstract and concrete, physical and mental, material and social, concept and 'thing'; that it simultaneously inspires ambivalence and clarity, detachment and solidarity, offers a convenient stage on which to explore distinctions between the phenomenal and the noumenal that, as Kuchler writes, "emerged from the Enlightenment to drive a theory of culture in which not things, but humankind, is at the helm" (2005: 205). She goes on to argue that "[as a result] the world as experienced and the world as ontologically framed remain in tension, despite a long line of scholarship devoted to situating thought at the heart of the individual and of culture" (2005: 206). The paper argues that such tensions are present, if apparently dormant, within the consumer culture research project too. An adequate treatment of 'music' as material culture has, we suggest, the potential to destabilise this tension, problematizing trains of thought whose architecture unwittingly draws upon essentialist ontologies and the credo of the object-subject divide they authorize.

There is something to be gained from stepping aside from the instrumental agenda that appears to have inspired previous consumer research studies-where music is often seen as way of socially engineering an atmosphere that is conducive to certain forms of behavioural outcomes. In seeking to 'reassemble' (Latour, 2007) studies of music as consumer culture, it is clear to me that the 'actant' potential of music (cf Latour, 1991, 1992; Law 1991) is not merely as another form of powerpoint adornment-i.e. playing rock anthems to lighten up the presentation and lend it fashionable capital. In its viscerality and materiality music can be experienced as a transformative agent (Sacks, 1985, 2007), a shapeshifter, having the power to transport us between worlds as a way of bringing forth altered states of consciousness (Law, 1994; Kuchler, 2005). In that sense it has things in common with witchcraft. Indeed there is a long line of musicology that investigates the important part played by music (and cuisine) in bringing forth materiality in the context of resisting colonial acculturation (oppression) and opening up spaces for alterity and emancipation. This is especially so in the history of 'code-switching', a subtle form of re-signification to be found around the rhythmic space of syncopation as a material site of identity work done on the musical and social self. This work is done on the body, constructed not only as 'other', the site of necessary distinctions and resistance to them, but in its embodied alterity, as a site of beauty, sexuality and pleasure. Social identity and musical experience are mutually constitutive and, as Negus and Velazquez argue, "the subject and collectivity are mediated through musical experience" (2002:134). In my view current discussions of music and consumers framed through the subject-object divide seem only to work through forcing upon us a rhetorical strategy which admits unnecessarily narrow views of 'music' as material sociality.

By considering the character of performance we will explore practices already inscribed on bodies (playing, dancing, clapping, participating, observing), drawing attention to the embodied and material features of social action, revealing for inspection art-world knowledge (Becker, 1974) through performing and constructing an empirical site for the observation of embodied praxiological skills. The overall idea is to explore the riches to be found in getting out of the object-subject divide and the production-consumption ghetto, into the area of materiality and embodied habituated social practice (making music as materiality). This, in my view, constitutes the contextual relevance of music as a site of materiality as embodied social action within consumer culture research. Hopefully we will also further excite interest in the materiality of social life (Appadurai 1986; Kopytoff, 1986; Latour, 1991, 1992; Dant, 2005; Miller, 2005).

REFERENCES

Appadurai. Arun (1986), *The Social Life of Things: Commodities in Cultural Perspective,* Cambridge, Cambridge University Press.

Arnould, Eric J., Linda L. Price and Patrick Tierney (1998), "Communicative Staging of the Wilderness Servicescape," *The Service Industries Journal*, 18 (3), 90-115.

Arnould, Eric J and Craig J. Thompson (2005), "Consumer Culture Theory (CCT): Twenty Years of Research," *Journal of Consumer Research*, 31(4), 868-882.

Attfield, Judy (2000), *Wild Things: The Material Culture of Everyday Life*, Oxford: Berg.

Becker, Howard (1974), "Art as Collective Action", *American Sociological Review*, 39 (6), 767-776.

Belk, Russell W. (1988), "Possessions and the Extended Self", *Journal of Consumer Research*, 15(9), 139-168.

Bettany, Shona (2007), "The Material Semiotics of Consumption or Where (And What) Are the Objects in Consumer Culture Theory?" in *Consumer Culture Theory: Research in Consumer Behaviour*, Vol. 11, eds. Russell W. Belk and John F. Sherry, Oxford: JAI Press Publications, 41-56.

Borgerson, Janet (2005), "Materiality, Agency and The Constitution of Consuming Subjects: Insights for Consumer Research," in *Advances in Consumer Research,* 32, 439-443.

Dant, Tim (2005), *Materiality and Society*, Maidenhead: Open University Press

Entwistle, Joanne (2002) "The Aesthetic Economy: The Production of Value in the Field of Fashion Modelling" *Journal of Consumer Culture*, 2 (3), 317-339

Ger, G?liz and Russell W. Belk (1996) "I'd Like to Buy the World a Coke: Consumptionscapes of the "Less Affluent World," *Journal of Consumer Policy*, 19 (3), 271-304.

Gell, Alfred (1992), "The Enchantment of Technology and the Technology of Enchantment," in *Anthropology, Art and Aesthetics* eds. Jeremy Coote and Anthony Shelton Oxford: Oxford University Press, 40–63.

Grove, Stephen, J. and Fisk, Raymond, P. (1983), "The Dramaturgy of Services Exchange: An Analytical Framework for Services Marketing", in *Emerging Perspectives on Services Marketing,* eds.Leonard, T. Berry and Lynn, G. Shostack,. Chicago, IL.: American Marketing Association, 45-49.

Hallam, Elizabeth, Jenny Hockey and Glennys Howarth (1999), *Beyond the Body: Death and Social Identity,* London: Routledge.

Heckler, Susan, E and Dudley Blossom (1997), "The Role of Music in Advertising: Does it Transform the Audience Experience?" *Advances in Consumer Research*, 24, 301.

Heidegger, Martin ([1927]1962), *Being and Time,* trans. John Macquarrie and Edward Robinson, Oxford: Blackwell.

Hogle, Linda F. (1995), "Tales from the Cryptic: Technology Meets Organism in the Living Cadaver", in *The Cyborg Handbook*, eds. Chris H. Gray, Heidi J. Figueroa-Sarrierra and Steven Mentor, New York: Routledge, 203-218.

Hughes Alex and Suzanne Reimer eds (2003) *Geographies of Commodity Chains*, London: Pearson.

Kopytoff, Igor (1986), "The Cultural Biography of Things: Commoditization as Process," in *The Social Life of Things: Commodities in Cultural Perspective,* ed. Arjun Appadurai, Cambridge, Cambridge University Press, 64-91.

Kuchler, Susanne (2005), "Materiality and Cognition: the Changing Face of Things", in *Materiality* ed Daniel Miller, London: Duke University Press, 206-30.

Lai, Ai-Ling; Dermody, Janine and Hanmer-Lloyd, Stuart (2008), "An Existential Analysis of Consumers as 'Incarnated Beings': A Merleau-Pontyian Perspective", in Stefania Borghini, Mary Ann Mcgrath and Cele Otnes (Eds.), *European Advances for Consumer Research*, Milan, Association of Consumer Research, 8: 381-389

Latour, Bruno (1991), "Technology is Society made Durable", in *A Sociology of Monsters? Essays on Power, Technology and Domination*, ed, John Law Sociological Review Monograph 38, London, Routledge, 103-31.

Latour, Bruno (1992), "Where are the Missing Masses? The Sociology of a Few Mundane Artifacts," in *Shaping Technology-Building Society: Studies in Sociotechnical Change*, eds. Wiebe Bijker, and John Law, London: MIT Press, 225-58.

Latour, Bruno (2007), "Reassembling the social: An introduction to Actor-Network-Theory", Oxford, Oxford University Press.

Law, John (1991), "Introduction: Monsters, Machines and Sociotechnical Relations", in *A Sociology of Monsters? Essays on Power, Technology and Domination*", ed. John Law, Sociological Review Monograph 38, London: Routledge, 1-23.

Law, John (1994), *Organizing Modernity*, Oxford: Blackwell.

Lock, Margaret (2002), *Twice Dead: Organ Transplants and the Reinvention of Death,* Berkeley: University of California Press.

Merleau-Ponty, Maurice ([1945] 2002), *The Phenomenology of Perception,* trans. Colin Smith, London and New York: Routledge.

Miller, Daniel (2005), *Materiality*, London: Duke University Press

Negus, Keith and Patria, R. Velazquez (2002), "Belonging and Detachment: Musical Experience and the Limits of Identity", *Poetics*, 30, 133-145.

Parsons, Elizabeth (2008) "Dealing in (Hi)stories: Durability, Authenticity and Provenance in Markets for Antiques" *European Advances in Consumer Research*, 8.112-113.

Sacks, Oliver (1985), *The Man who Mistook His Wife for a Hat*, London: Picador.

Sacks, Oliver (2007), *Musicophilia: Tales of Music and the Brain*, London: Picador.

Venkatraman, Meera and Teresa Nelson (2008) "From Servicescape to Consumptionscape: A Photo-elicitation Study of Starbucks in the New China," *Journal of International Business Studies*, advance online publication, 17 Jan 2008, 10.1057/palgrave.jibs.8400353.

Verbeek, Peter-Paul (2005), *What Things Do*, Pennsylvania: Penn State Press.

Wagner, Janet (1999), "Aesthetic Value: Beauty in Art and Fashion," in *Consumer Value: A Framework for Analysis and Research*, ed. Morris B Holbrook, London Routledge, 126-146.

Wallace, Wanda, T. (1997), "Music, Meaning and Magic: Revisiting Music Research", *Advances in Consumer Research,* 24, 301-302.

Zwick, Detlev and Nikhilesh Dholakia (2006) "The Epistenic Consumption Object and Postsocial Consumption: Expanding Consumer-Object Theory in Consumer Research", *Consumption, Markets and Culture*, 9 (1), 17-43.

To Indulge or Not to Indulge? Self-Regulation and Overconsumption

Alexander Chernev, Northwestern University, USA

SESSION OVERVIEW

Consumers often make choices among options representing conflicting goals. This session enhances understanding of various mechanisms to resolve goal conflict in consumer decision processes by investigating the impact of goal conflict and goal progress on choice from multiple theoretical perspectives, thus offering a broader view of the role of self-regulation in choice.

Apart from providing theoretical insights on how goal conflict and goal progress influence choice, this session contributes to the understanding of the domains of self-regulation, consumption, and choice. Specifically, the session examined the following issues:

Research presented by Chernev and Gal explores scenarios in which attempts by individuals to regulate their consumption is counterproductive, leading to overconsumption. In particular, they propose that when individuals face an option that represents one of two competing goals (e.g., a tasty but high-calorie steak), adding another option that favors the alternative goal (e.g., a low-calorie salad) will increase the preference for a combined option that represents both goals (steak and salad). The counterintuitive aspect of their prediction is that by choosing the combined option, individuals end up increasing their calorie intake, an outcome counter to their goal of consuming fewer calories. They theorize that individuals evaluate choice options based not only on the options' objective performance (e.g., amount of calories) but also based on their fit with the activated goal. In this context, they show that the calorie content of the combined "low-calorie" and "high-calorie" items (e.g., steak and a salad) is perceived as lower than that of the higher calorie option alone (e.g., steak only).

Research by Fishbach and Finkelstein examines how individuals infer their progress toward achieving a particular goal in the context of food consumption. They propose that healthful food labels (e.g. "low fat" or "fat free") cue people to feel hungry, which increases the consumption of unrelated food items. They assert that this effect is driven by a perception of progress towards a person's goal of being a healthy individual as a result of exposure to healthy food labels. Consequently, one feels that the competing motivation of satisfying hunger was neglected and increases food consumption. Fishbach and Finkelstein report five experiments that manipulated the exposure to healthy product labels and documented increased subjective feelings of hunger, perceived progress towards the health goal, and actual food consumption.

Finally, research by Chandon, Wansink, Werle, and Payne investigates the effect of calorie compensation after moderate changes in calorie intake or expenditures. In particular, their research seeks to answer the following question: "Even if people eat more or burn fewer calories, why aren't they restoring their calorie balance by adjusting their subsequent calorie intake and expenditures?" Homeostasis should lead people to compensate for overeating by eating less and compensate for exercising by eating more. In a series of studies involving analyses of consumption panels and laboratory and field experiments, they show surprisingly little amount of calorie compensation within and across meals. They also find that compensation is influenced by whether overeating involved healthy or tasty foods and whether people focused on the healthy or enjoyable dimensions of exercising.

At the end of the session, the discussion leader Baba Shiv integrated the individual presentations into a more general framework, facilitating a broader understanding of the role of self-regulation in choice.

EXTENDED ABSTRACTS

"When Self-Regulation Leads to Overconsumption: The Goal-Progress Illusion"

Alexander Chernev, Northwestern University, USA
David Gal, Northwestern University, USA

Consider an individual primarily concerned with calorie intake who is choosing between two meals: a steak and similar steak with a side garden salad. After some deliberation, she chooses the second meal although the combined meal contains more calories and, thus, is inconsistent with her primary goal of consuming fewer calories. This pattern of behavior is not unusual and is, in fact, consistent with anecdotal industry evidence. To illustrate, to increase sales by attracting additional traffic into its stores, McDonald's introduced to its menu healthy, low-calorie food items like salads and fruit. Yet, its sales grew not so much from increased sales of healthy, low-calorie foods but from selling more fast-food items like double cheeseburgers.

What motivates consumers to act in a way that ends up being counterproductive vis-à-vis their goals? We propose that when individuals face an option that represents one of two competing goals (e.g., a tasty but high-calorie steak), adding another option that favors the alternative goal (e.g., a low-calorie salad) will increase the preference for the combined option that represents both goals (steak and salad). This prediction is consistent with the notion that when faced with a choice among options representing two competing goals, consumers attempt to satisfy both goals by choosing outcomes that ensure progress toward both goals. The counterintuitive aspect of this prediction is that by choosing the combined option, individuals end up increasing their calorie intake, an outcome counter to their goal of consuming fewer calories.

To explain this pattern of behavior, we theorize that individuals evaluate choice options not only based on their objective performance (e.g., amount of calories) but also based on their fit with the activated goal. To illustrate, ordering a green salad is likely to be perceived as consistent with the weight-loss goal, whereas ordering a juicy steak is likely to be perceived as consistent with the goal of indulging oneself. Because the green salad in the above example fits the low-calorie-consumption goal, it is likely to be classified as a "low-calorie" item, whereas the juicy steak is classified as a "high-calorie" item. The interesting phenomenon here is that the calorie content of the combination of a "low calorie" item and a "high-calorie" one (e.g., steak and a salad) is perceived as lower than that of the higher calorie choice (e.g., steak only).

In a series of three experiments, we examine the proposition that goal-consistent evaluations of decision alternatives can lead to counterproductive decisions. Our first experiment examines how adding a low-calorie option (e.g., a green side salad) to one of two similar high-calorie meals influences consumer choice. We show that even when the primary goal is to reduce calorie intake, adding the low-calorie option increases the preference for the combined meal, although it contains more calories.

In the second experiment, we directly test the proposition that consumers' reliance on goal-consistency to evaluate choice options leads to a biased estimation of the options' objective performance (i.e., calorie content). In particular, we ask respondents to estimate the amount of calories in individual components of a meal, as well as the number of calories in the meal as a whole. The data show that when evaluated separately options satisfying competing goals are estimated to have a greater number of calories than when the same options are estimated jointly.

The third experiment examines the role of goal consistency in estimating options' performance on consumption quantity. In particular, we examine the amount of calories consumed as a function of consumers' choice from a menu. We find that when the menu includes a lower calorie item (such as a green salad or an apple) individuals end up consuming more calories (relative to those given a menu without the low-calorie option). We also show that when the menu includes a very high-calorie item (e.g., a 1000-calorie milkshake), the effect is similar to inclusion of a low-calorie item, such that individuals who selected to forgo the very high-calorie item ended up consuming more calories than those in a scenario in which the very high-calorie item was not on the menu.

Overall, our findings are consistent with the proposition that consumers evaluate choice options based on the options' fit with their active goals and that such evaluations can lead to counterproductive outcomes. In addition to its theoretical contribution, our research has important managerial and public policy implications. In particular, we show that consumers tend to underestimate the calorie content of combinations of healthy (virtues) and unhealthy (vices) products, a finding that casts a shadow on the recent attempts by many fast food restaurants to add healthy options to their menus. Thus, while providing a healthy alternative to individuals interested in a healthier lifestyle, the introduction of healthier options can paradoxically lead to overconsumption, which stems from biased estimation of the calorie content of the available options.

"When Healthy Food Makes You Hungry"
Ayelet Fishbach, University of Chicago, USA
Stacey Finkelstein, University of Chicago, USA

Research on the Dynamics of Self-Regulation (Fishbach & Dhar, 2005; Fishbach, Dhar, & Zhang, 2006) attests that in the course of pursuing multiple goals (e.g., saving and spending), whether the individual experiences commitment to or progress towards a goal influences the course of self-regulation over time. While an experience of commitment encourages goal-congruent actions because of an increased sense that the goal is valuable and attainable, an experience of progress towards one goal will result in relaxing one's effort and moving away to another, competing motivation that is presumably somewhat neglected. This second self-regulatory process, that of inferring progress, is more likely when individuals' behavior is under externally imposed control; as a consequence, they cannot infer based on their actions that the goal is important to them and that their commitment is high.

The current research documents effects of perceived progress in the domain of healthy eating. We propose that healthful food labels (e.g. "low fat" or "fat free") cue people to feel hungry, which increases the consumption of unrelated food items. This effect is driven by a perception of progress towards the goal of being a healthy individual as a result of exposure to healthy food labels. Consequently, a person feels that the competing motivation of satisfying hunger was neglected and increases food consumption.

Five studies manipulate exposure to healthy products and product labels (versus tasty products or regular product labels) and show increased subjective feelings of hunger, perceived progress towards the health goal, and actual food consumption. In study 1, participants tasted a sample of a health bar that was presented as either "health bar" or "tasty bar" and then indicated how hungry they were. Those to whom the sample was framed as "healthy" indicated that they were hungrier compared with participants who did not taste any food sample or tasted a sample that was framed as "tasty."

Study 2 extends these results by comparing participants' hunger level before and after eating a food sample. Participants who tasted a sample that was framed as healthy (tasty) showed an increase (decrease) in subjective hunger as a result of their consumption experience while participants in a third control condition that did not sample an item showed no change in hunger over time.

Study 3 investigates the link between healthy food sampling and consumption. Participants tasted a sample that was framed as healthy or tasty and were offered the opportunity to consume an unrelated snack afterwards. Participants to whom the food sample was framed as healthy consumed more of the unrelated snack – hence, they were hungrier – than participants to whom the sample was framed as tasty.

Study 4 tests the prediction that healthy food labels increase feelings of hunger when people do not experience free choice. This study manipulated the sample that people ate (healthy vs. tasty) and the nature of their consumption (free vs. imposed choice). We found that participants who were required to eat a sample framed as healthy indicated higher hunger levels than participants who were required to eat a sample framed as tasty. In contrast, participants who believed they had a free choice were similarly hungry after sampling food that was said to be healthy versus tasty.

Finally, in study 5 we tested the effect on hunger of merely being exposed to healthy labels, such as "low-fat," versus regular labels. We predicted that the association between health and hunger is basic, such that people do not need to actually consume healthy food to infer that they have made progress towards their health goal. Merely seeing these healthy food labels can increase one's perception that progress has been made and intensify feelings of hunger. Accordingly, we expected an increase in consumption of unrelated foods. To test these predictions, participants were primed with food labels for products that were either healthy (e.g. fat-free American cheese) or regular (regular American cheese) in a "product evaluation survey." We found that participants who merely viewed healthy food labels reported that they had made more progress towards their health goal compared to participants who viewed regular food labels. More important, mere exposure to healthful (vs. regular) food labels increased consumption of a neutral snack on a subsequent task.

In summary, across five studies we find that individuals who sample healthy foods or who merely see healthy food labels feel that they have made progress towards their health goals. This sense of progress, in turn, cues feeling of hunger. Thus, eating healthy food can actually whet the appetite.

"Can Healthy Eating and Fun Exercising Make Us Fat? Post-Intake and Expenditure Calorie Compensation"
Pierre Chandon, INSEAD, France
Brian Wansink, Cornell University, USA
Carolina Werle, Grenoble Ecole de Management, CERAG, France
Collin Payne, Cornell University, USA

It is clear that the simultaneous increase in calorie supply and decrease in calorie expenditures over the past decades help explain the current obesity epidemic. Still, these environmental effects leave one important question unanswered: Even if people eat more or burn fewer calories, why aren't they restoring their calorie balance by adjusting their subsequent calorie intake and expenditures?

Calorie compensation obviously occurs for very large changes in calorie intake or expenditures. Who hasn't vowed after a really big Thanksgiving dinner that "they will never eat again"? At this level, homeostatic mechanisms kick in and re-establish the nutritional balance that is necessary for our body to operate. In this research, we examine calorie compensation after moderate amounts of changes in calorie intake or expenditures. Given that a weekly 67-calorie imbalance leads to a one pound weight gain over a year (Hill, 2003), even moderate amounts of changes in calorie intake can have big impact on obesity rates if people fail to compensate for them.

Our main hypothesis is that calorie compensation after moderate changes in calorie intake or expenditures is driven by perception of goal progress and not by homeostatic physiological mechanisms. Building on research on goal balancing (Dhar, 1999), we hypothesize that two conflicting goals are salient when making food consumption decisions: the hedonic goal of maximizing pleasure and the more utilitarian goal of maintaining good health. In addition, prior research has shown that people underestimate their calorie intake but overestimate their calorie expenditures (Livingstone, 2003). We therefore expect that perception of progress toward the "healthy living" goal is higher when a food is perceived as "healthy" than when it is perceived as "pleasurable" or "tasty." Accordingly, we hypothesize that once the choice of the main course has been made consumers will choose side orders, desserts, and beverages containing more calories if the main course is positioned as healthy (and thus perceived to contain fewer calories) than if it is positioned as "tasty."

We expect the opposite pattern of results for calorie compensation following calorie expenditures. Because of the overestimation of calorie expenditures, perception of progress on the "healthy living" goal will be lower when the calorie expenditures are perceived as contributing to health than when they are perceived as contributing to pleasure. We expect that consumers will realize that they are burning fewer calories than they thought when the calorie expenditure activity is positioned as "healthy" than when it is positioned as "pleasurable." As a result, we expect lower compensation (i.e., smaller meals) after "healthy" exercising than after "pleasure" exercising. Note that by manipulating the perception of the food and the exercising while holding the actual food and the exercise constant, we isolate the effects of goal-driven compensation from those of physiological compensation.

In the first experiment, we provided participants with either a coupon for a burger perceived to be tasty (600 calories) or for a sandwich perceived to be healthy but containing, in fact, 900 calories. We then asked people to choose whether they would like to have chips, drinks, and cookies with the burger/sandwich. We found that people chose beverages, side dishes, and desserts containing up to 131% more calories when the main course was positioned as "healthy" compared to when it was positioned as "tasty," even though the "healthy" main course already contained 50% more calories than the "tasty" one. As a result, meals ordered in the "healthy" condition unknowingly contained more calories than meals ordered in the "tasty" restaurant condition.

We replicated these results in a second experiment in which we manipulated the health positioning of the food by changing the name of the restaurant and the other types of items on the menu while holding the target dish constant. We also tested whether these effects could disappear when asking participants to consider arguments contradicting the health claims. We found that participants were more likely to order chips with a Bologna sandwich served by a "healthy" restaurant than with the same sandwich served by a "tasty" restaurant unless they were asked to consider whether the health claims of the restaurant actually applied to that particular sandwich.

In the third study, we analyzed consumption diary data from a panel of 1,800 households maintained by NPD Foodworld, Inc. Drawing on previous research (Wansink, 2006) showing that people overeat "low-fat" snack food, especially when it is considered healthy (e.g., granola), we measured calorie compensation within and across meals among households eating low-fat granola and among households eating regular granola. We found that households eating low-fat granola for breakfast consumed more calories overall during that day. We also found that these extra calories came from food and not from beverages, showing that (spurious) compensation occurs only within the same type of food. Finally, consistent with prior work (Khare, 2006), we found that compensation occurred only during breakfast and lunch and had disappeared by dinner time.

The fourth study examined the effects of imagined exercising on subsequent calorie intake. We asked people intercepted in shopping centers to read a scenario describing a 30-minute walk. The scenario asked them to focus either on the music that they would be listening to during the exercising (pleasure condition) or on the amount of effort that it would require (health condition). People in the control condition did not read a scenario involving exercising. Participants were then given the opportunity to help themselves to as many snacks as they wanted. We found that people served themselves more snacks in the pleasurable-exercising condition than in either the healthy-exercising condition or in the control (no exercising) condition.

In the final fifth study, we asked people to walk for half an hour while focusing either on the amount of energy spent (health condition), on the music that they were listening to (pleasure condition), or on an unrelated task (control). We then weighed how much food they took at an all-you-can-eat buffet where they had lunch after the task. We found that people chose bigger meals in the pleasurable exercise condition than in either the health exercise or in the control conditions.

Our research seeks to make four major contributions. First, we show that exercise influences food intake differently if people just think about exercising – in which case there is compensation – or if they actually exercise – in which case the framing and the importance of staying fit will play a role. Second, we show that people focusing on having fun when exercising tend to compensate for the calories they have burned by eating more, while those focusing on exercise eat less. Third, we find that people concentrating on exercising eat less when the central objective of staying fit is very important to them. Fourth, we put forth potentially useful implications for public policymakers, health care professionals, and consumers interested in controlling their food intake.

Encoding, Remembering, and Using Numeric Information: Implications for Pricing

Manoj Thomas, Cornell University, USA

SESSION OVERVIEW

Price cognition plays a pivotal role in models of consumer behavior postulated in the economics as well as the psychology literature (Monroe 2003; Winer 2006). Both streams of literature concur on the following assumption: A buyer's subjective judgment of the magnitude of a price should be an important determinant in purchase decisions. However, the psychological processes that underlie price magnitude judgments and the strength of the association between price magnitude judgments and choice continue to be topics of debate. In this symposium, we present three new papers that offer novel perspectives on how consumers encode, process, and use price information. The first two papers draw on the numerical cognition literature and focus on how consumers encode and process price information, while the third paper examines factors that lead to a dissociation between price perceptions and choices.

The first paper by Thomas, Simon, and Kadiyali examines whether the precision or roundedness of numbers influence people's judgments of magnitude. This paper draws on the numerical cognition literature to examine how consumers encode the magnitude information from a string of digits in a multi-digit number. Specifically, drawing on previous research on the distribution of numbers and on the role of associative processes in everyday judgments, they suggest that that people nonconsciously learn to associate precise prices with smaller magnitudes, and that this association influences their price magnitude judgments and willingness to pay. They test this hypothesized precision heuristic in laboratory experiments as well as using data from real estate transactions.

The second paper by Vanhuele and Laurent examines why consumers are less adept with prices that are not rounded. They suggest that short-term memory constraints induce consumers to apply mathematical rounding, truncate price endings, or resort to approximations. Their conceptualization suggests that what typically are considered as recall errors may therefore actually be the result of adaptive simplification strategies. They analyze patterns of price recall errors to show that errors follow systematic patterns that reveal these strategies.

The third paper by Danziger, Gal, and Morwitz examines the influence of price magnitude perceptions on product and retailer choice in an environment where price discounts are sometimes offered and vary in their depth and frequency. Past research (Alba et al. 1999; Lalwani and Monroe, 2005) has studied the effects of depth and frequency of price discounts on price perceptions. In the present research, the authors challenge the implicit assumption of this past research, that price perceptions guide choices. They find that although respondents' price perceptions are lower for retailers offering deep infrequent discounts, they buy more often from retailers offering frequent shallow discounts. They discuss the implications of this finding for our understanding of how consumers encode, process, and use price information.

EXTENDED ABSTRACTS

"Do Consumers Perceive Precise Prices to be Lower than Round Prices? Evidence from Laboratory and Market Data"

Manoj Thomas, Cornell University, USA
Daniel Simon, Cornell University, USA
Vrinda Kadiyali, Cornell University, USA

Research on factors that affect consumers' magnitude judgments in general (see Krishna 2006 for a review) and price magnitude judgments in particular (Greenleaf 1995; Monroe 2003; Morwitz, Greenleaf and Johnson 1998; Wathieu and Bertini 2007; Winer 2006) has not only unveiled several new behavioral phenomena, but also has enhanced our understanding of the consumers' cognition processes. Given the centrality of perceived price magnitude in buyers' decision making, we examine a ubiquitous, yet hitherto unexplored, aspect of price magnitude judgments: Do consumers perceive round prices to be higher or lower than prices that are not rounded? Consider the following illustrative example: A seller of a house can list the house for a more round price $365,000 or $364,000 or a more precise price such as $364,578. How would the precision in the price affect buyers' evaluation of the list price?

To explore whether people use precision as a cue in magnitude judgments, and if it does, in which direction, we ran a short online survey. Sixty nine students from a university were asked to respond to the following question: "Consider two six-digit numbers X and Y. The number X is rounded to the nearest thousand. The number Y is not rounded. Which number is likely to be smaller: X or Y?" A majority of the respondents (68%) said that the number that is not rounded (Y) is likely to be smaller, and this response rate was significantly different from chance (p<.01). This result suggests that people might be using precision as a cue for smaller magnitudes in their day-to-day numerical judgments. We refer to this decision rule as the "precision heuristic" in price magnitude judgments. In this article, we examine whether this heuristic can influence on buyers' behavior in high involvement purchases such as buying a house, and try to gain some insights into the psychological basis of the precision heuristic.

Two important clarifications about our approach are due right at the outset. First, our definition and operationalization of roundness is consistent with the extant literature (Sigurd 1988, Dehaene and Mehler 1992, and Rosch 1975). We consider the number of zeroes in a number as the measure of roundness of the number. Further, our operationalization of roundness is consistent with the notion that there can be gradations in perceived roundness of numbers; that is, some round numbers might be perceived to be more round than others (Jansen and Pollmann 2001). For example, $364,500 is more round that $364,578, but less round than $364,000. Second, we note that our discussion of roundness is distinct from the well-established literature on nine-endings in pricing (e.g., Stiving and Winer 1997). A precise price can have a nine-ending (e.g., 364,999) or not (e.g., $364,578). Comparing consumers' evaluations of a nine-ending precise price with that of the corresponding round price (e.g., 364,999 vs. 365,000) is problematic, because the effect of precision will be confounded with the nine-ending effect. Therefore, in our experiments we do not use prices that end in nine, and in the analyses of the market data we find that our results are robust to controlling for the nine-ending effect.

We report four studies that test our hypotheses. We examine whether consumers systematically judge precise prices to be higher than round prices and whether this biased judgment influences their buying behavior. Our laboratory experiments provide evidence consistent with the precision heuristic and its effect on buyer behavior. Results from study 1 offer evidence for the effect of precision heuristic in price magnitude judgments. Specifically, we find that under conditions of uncertainty, buyers are more likely to judge the magnitude of a precise price (e.g., $364,578) to be lower than the magnitude of a comparable round price (e.g., $364,000 or $365,000). Study 2 was designed to demonstrate (i) that it is possible to create an association between precision and subjective magnitude judgments, and (ii) that the activation of such an association could influence participants' judgments and decisions. The results from this study show that house buyers are likely to pay more for a house with a precise list price (e.g., $364,578) than for a comparable house with a round list price (e.g., $364,000 or $365,000). Further, we show that this effect of list price precision on buyers' willingness to pay is mediated by the bias magnitude judgments. In study 3 we use responses from a nationwide sample comprising mostly homeowners and corroborate the external validity of our results. Finally, in study 4 we analyze the data from more than 27,000 residential real estate transactions to provide evidence that the precision heuristic influences buyers' behavior, even in what is likely the largest purchase that most buyers will make in their lives. We conclude with a discussion on the limitations of this research and directions for future work.

"What Recall Errors Tell Us About Price Memory"
Marc Vanhuele, HEC Paris, France
Gilles Laurent, HEC Paris, France

In order to buy at the right price many consumers verify prices, and make comparisons across products, across purchase locations, and over time. Memory plays an important role in these comparisons. When the to-be-compared prices are present at the same location, they have to be held in short-term memory. It is also often useful to call on long-term memory to retrieve prices from the past or from another purchase location.

A series of price knowledge surveys have shown that price memory is weaker than what prior research, for instance on reference price, suggested. In-the-aisle surveys (Dickson and Sawyer 1990) suggest that many consumers do not watch prices and, when they do pay attention, price information is easily erased from short-term memory. Vanhuele, Laurent, and Drèze (2006) examined the constraints of short-term memory. In experiments in which multiple prices have to be retained in short-term memory, a requirement for the price comparisons described above, they show that auditory short-term memory has a capacity constraint in terms of the time it takes to pronounce the to-be-remembered information. Two prices with decimals often surpass this capacity constraint which leads to loss of information.

We advance the thesis that consumers are somehow intuitively aware of the difficulty of retaining price information when prices become long to pronounce and adapt their price encoding by simplifying observed prices. They may apply mathematical rounding, truncate price endings, or resort to approximations. What typically are considered as recall errors may therefore actually be the result of adaptive simplification strategies. So-called recall "errors" should therefore follow systematic patterns that reveal these strategies.

The theoretical basis for our work is provided by the triple-code model of Dehaene (1992). This model is a synthesis of the key research findings in numerical cognition, a sub-domain of cognitive psychology that examines how numbers are represented and processed in the cognitive system. Dehaene (1992) proposes that numbers can be mentally represented and manipulated in three different forms, in function of the task people are executing. The visual Arabic code represents numbers on a spatial visual medium on the basis of their written form in Arabic numerals (e.g., 35). The auditory verbal code is generated through a phonological representation in which each number is represented by a sequence of phonemes (e.g., /thirty/ /five/). Finally, the analogue magnitude code represents numbers as approximate quantities on an internal dimension termed the "number line" (e.g., about 35, slightly less than 40, or somewhere between 30 and 40).

Vanhuele, Laurent, and Drèze (2006) found evidence of all three codes, but also observed the dominance of the auditory verbal code. This observation highlights the importance of the verbal capacity constraint of short-term memory. Baddeley's (1992) work examined this constraint in detail. He postulates the existence of a phonological loop, which consists of a phonological store to hold speech-based information for the duration of 1.5 to 2 seconds and an articulatory control process to hold data within the phonological store through subvocal repetition. Vanhuele, Laurent, and Drèze (2006) found three types of evidence of the impact of the phonological loop: prices that are longer to pronounce (independently of the number of digits) are less well remembered, participants who use verbal shortcuts (e.g., pronouncing 245 as two four five instead of two hundred forty-five) have better price memory, and participants who habitually speak slower have poorer price memory.

To examine our thesis that consumers use adaptive simplification strategies, we ran new price recall surveys but also examined the data used for previous publications. For these publications, the probability of a correct response, or response within a certain error range, was taken as dependent variable. Here, we examine the types of errors that are made.

We have three types of data sets: (i) Immediate memory tests in which participants make a deliberate attempt to retain price information in short-term memory for a number of seconds, (ii) Store-exit surveys where supermarket shoppers are questioned on the prices of items they just paid for, and (iii) A store-entry survey that examines long-term memory for products consumers purchased on previous shopping occasions. As first step of our analysis we made a content analysis of the errors. Each recall response was compared to the correct price and the error was then labeled. After a couple of iterations we found that the following classification covers most of the errors: interference from other prices; rounding down one or more decimals (e.g. from 3.24 to 3.20 or 3). We reserve the word "rounding" for the mathematically correct operation of rounding down decimals below 0.5 and rounding up from 0.5 onwards; rounding up (e.g. from 3.79 to 3.80 or 4); simplifying down (e.g. from 3.79 to 3.70 or 3). Simplifying refers to a mathematically incorrect operation; simplifying up (e.g. from 3.24 to 3.30 or 4); approximations.

We then examined with statistical analyses whether the occurrence of the different types of errors had systematic drivers. Our main findings are the following:

a. Price recall errors are not randomly distributed but fall instead into clear patterns because they often are the result of simplification strategies.
b. Simplification strategies are in large part determined by the structure of the price. Whether a consumer will round or simplify is determined by the first digit(s) (euro in our case) and by the price ending (the cents part). In other words, a price of 1.XY euro will be treated differently than a price of

2.XY euro, just like a price of X.85 euro will be treated differently than one of X.99 euro. This suggests that consumers scan the most notable features of a price before registering a simplified version.

c. Our initial analyses suggest that consumers with really good price recall do not use simplification strategies, but that consumers with poorer recall ability benefit from these strategies.

"Do Price Judgments Always Influence Choice? The Effects of Retailer Discount Frequency and Depth"

Shai Danziger, Ben-Gurion University, Israel
Sharon Gal, Ben-Gurion University, Israel
Vicki Morwitz, New York University, USA

According to economic and marketing theory, product price is a major determinant of consumer choice. When multiple retailers offer the same product or a single retailer offers very similar products, consumers who are aware of price differences usually purchase the cheapest product. Therefore, retailers offer various price discounts to influence consumers' perceptions of retailers' and products' prices, and ultimately their choices of which retailer to purchase from and which product to buy (Alba et al. 1999; Lalwani and Monroe, 2005). Two aspects of discounts that retailers manipulate are discount frequency (how often discounts are offered) and discount depth (the magnitude of the offered discounts). Past research has examined the effect of discount frequency and depth on consumers' perceptions of average prices, but has not examined how that in turn influences choice. In contrast our work focuses on the impact of type of discount strategy on choice and, importantly, finds a dissociation between perceptions of the average price and choice.

Alba et al. (1999) examined the effect of depth and frequency discounting on consumers' price perceptions. They presented respondents with the prices of two brands over multiple trials (simulating weekly purchases) and asked them to indicate on each trial the brand they would choose. After all trials, participants estimated the average price of each brand. The true average price was identical for both brands. They found that when each brand was priced at only two (multiple) levels, the depth (frequency) brand was perceived to have the lower average price. Lalwani and Monroe (2005) used similar procedures to test the hypothesis that relative salience determines which discount strategy yields lower perceived prices. They found that when discount frequency (depth) is more salient, a frequency (depth) effect is found. Thus, these studies demonstrate that discount frequency and depth influence perceptions of the average price and they determine conditions when one or the other strategy is more effective in lowering price perceptions. Importantly, both papers implicitly assume that perceived average price in turn influences retailer or brand choice. However, their procedures do not allow them to examine this because respondents always saw both product prices prior to choice. Under such conditions respondents can simply select the cheaper of the two prices shown. Therefore, it is likely that respondents in these studies estimated average price only when asked to do so after the choice phase and did not use it in choice. Also, their procedures only consider the case when full price information is available for both products. In many real world shopping situations, consumers must decide which retailer to visit based only on their price expectations, and not on the actual prices of retailers.

In our research, in contrast, we explicitly examine the effects of depth and frequency discounts on consumers' choice of retailer and on several price judgments. In two experiments respondents were instructed that they would be making multiple decisions (simulating weekly purchases) regarding where to purchase a product that was available at two stores. They were also told that each store offered the product at either a regular price or at a discounted price, that they would make 100 choices, and that their goal was to minimize overall spending. An incentive compatible procedure was used. Critically, as is the case in actual retailer choice situations when consumers are not exposed to price advertising, respondents were told that their decisions would be made in the absence of current retailer price information. In other words, on each purchase occasion respondents' choices likely reflect their predictions about which store they thought was offering greater savings. In the 'chosen' feedback condition that most closely mimics many real world shopping experiences, in each trial, respondents saw only the chosen retailer's price after choice. In the 'both' feedback condition, for each trial, respondents saw the prices of both retailers after choice. This condition enabled us to examine risky choice under conditions of full price information. Following the choice phase, respondents estimated each retailer's average price, discount frequency and depth, and rated each retailer's price attractiveness and price fairness.

116 respondents participated in Experiment 1. The design was 2x2x2 with independent variables price feedback (chosen retailer only vs. both retailers; between subjects), frequency of depth discount (13% vs. 25%; between subjects) and type of discount (frequent and shallow vs. infrequent and deep; within subjects). The regular price for the three distributions was 9.89 and the average price was 8.89. In the frequent discount distribution the discounted price of 7.89 was offered on 50% of the purchase trials. In the 13% (25%) discount condition the discounted price of 2.19 (5.89) was offered on 13% (25%) of the trials.

190 respondents participated in Experiment 2. The design was 2x2x2 with independent variables price feedback (chosen retailer only vs. both retailers; between subjects), EDLP (discount vs. no discount; between subjects) and type of pricing (EDLP vs. infrequent and deep; within subjects). The regular price for the EDLP no discount distribution was 8.39, for the EDLP discount distribution it was 8.89 and for the infrequent and deep distribution it was 9.89. The average price of the three distributions was 8.39. In the EDLP discount (infrequent and deep) distribution the discounted price of 7.89 (4.89) was offered on 50% (30%) of the trials.

The same pattern emerged in both experiments. The retailer offering frequent but shallow discounts (Experiment 1) or the retailer offering every day low prices (Experiment 2) was chosen more often than the retailer offering deep but infrequent discounts even though perceived average price was lower for the latter. Also, retailer choice was more associated with perceived price fairness than with perceived average price. Thus, these results suggest that when retailers' prices are unavailable, as is often the case, choice is driven by internal price perceptions other than the perceived average price.

REFERENCES

Alba, Joseph W., Carl F. Mela, Terrence A. Shimp, and Joel E. Urbany (1999), "The effect of discount frequency and depth on consumer price judgments, *Journal of Consumer Research*, 26 (September), 99–114.

Baddeley, A. D. (1992). Working memory. *Science*, 255:556–559.

Dehaene, S. (1992). Varieties of numerical abilities. *Cognition*, 44, 1-42.

Dehaene, Stanislas and Jacques Mehler (1992), "Cross-Linguistic Regularities in the Frequency of Number Words," *Cognition*, Vol. 43, No. 1, 1-29.

Greenleaf, Eric A. (1995), "The Impact of Reference Price Effects on the Profitability of Price Promotions," *Marketing Science*, 14 (Winter), 82-104.

Krishna, Aradhna (2007), "Biases in Spatial Perception: A Review and Integrative Framework", in *Visual Marketing: From Attention to Action*, Michel Wedel and Rik Pieters, Eds., New Jersey: Lawrence Erlbaum Associates.

Lalwani, Ashok K. and Kent, B. Monroe (2005), "A Reexamination of Frequency-Depth Effects on Consumer Price Judgments," *Journal of Consumer Research*, 32(December), 480.

Monroe, Kent B. (2003), Pricing: Making Profitable Decisions. New York: McGraw-Hill/Irwin.

Morwitz, Vicki G., Eric A. Greenleaf, and Eric J. Johnson (1998) "Divide and Prosper: Consumers' Reactions to Partitioned Prices," *Journal of Marketing Research*, 35 (Nov.), 453-63.

Rosch, Eleanor (1975), "Cognitive Reference Points," *Cognitive Psychology*, 7 (October), 532-47.

Sigurd, Bengt (1988), "Round Numbers", *Language in Society*, 17, 243-252.

Wathieu, Luc and Marco Bertini (2007), "Price as a Stimulus to Think: The Case for Willful Overpricing," *Marketing Science*, 26 (January-February), 118-29.

Winer, Russell S. (2006), *Pricing*, Cambridge, MA: Marketing Science Institute.

The Consumption of Reading

Cele Otnes, University of Illinois at Urbana-Champaign, USA

SESSION OVERVIEW

Surprisingly little attention has been paid in consumer research to the consumption of "everyday" hobbies and pastimes. A search for this topic in the *Journal of Consumer Research* reveals that hobbies have typically been understood as a dependent variable associated with issues such as materialism (e.g., Chaplin and Roedder-John; 2005, 2007), or have been mentioned but not really unpacked in studies of very specific consumer segments, such as people trying to be cosmopolitan (Thompson and Tambyah, 1999) or pursuing a particular masculine identity (Holt and Thompson, 2004). However, from a consumer welfare perspective, people are often encouraged to pursue hobbies and interests in order to relieve stress, engage in pleasurable activities, help them pursue self-identity and self-actualization, and escape from the mundane world. One activity that has implications not only for these outcomes, but also is linked to a more literate and skilled populace that possesses higher cultural capital, is the reading of books. Benefits of reading extend beyond merely potentially enhancing social mobility; one study finds adults who read books are likely to be more involved in cultural activities, volunteer or charity work, and sports (charityguide.org). And while U.S. sales of trade nonfiction and fiction trade publications (which excludes religious and text books) are projected to top $27 billion in 2009 (Book Industry Study Group, 2006), in fact reading books is a hobby that faces increased competition for consumers' time from other diversion (e.g., computers, in-home movies, portable music) and cultural challenges (e.g., that reading is a somewhat elitist enterprise for "eggheads."). It is explicitly because book reading is an activity that either inspires great enthusiasm (Fineberg 2007) or increasing apathy (e.g., one in four adults read no books in 2006; Fram 2007) that the presenters in this session believed it important to turn our attention to the reasons people read (or do not), and the ways the marketplace enables them to pursue reading as a pastime in contemporary consumer culture. Clearly, understanding the consumption of books is important for scholars interested in public policy and education, but it also has implications for consumers of new technology, such as Amazon's new "Kindle," which encourages consumers to eschew traditional books in favor of downloadable, electronic versions.

Springboarding off of the recent *Consuming Books* (ed. Stephen Brown), this session features new or expanded work on how consumers pursue the pastime of reading in contemporary consumer culture. In "Never Tickle a Sleeping Booklover: How Readers Devour Harry Potter," Anthony Patterson and Stephen Brown unpack the reading styles of consumers enraptured with the Harry Potter series. Pauline Maclaran and Rosalind Masterson, in "BookCrossed Lovers: Consumers and Their Relationships with Books" explore how consumers find new meanings in reading communities as they circulate books around the world through a book-sharing technology. "Reading Others' Texts: Marginalia and the Inscription of Meaning in Collectible Books" by Janet Borgerson and Jonathan Schroeder explore the benefits of marginalia (notes made by the owners/authors) in books purchased in used or vintage outlets. Finally, in "Curling Up and Reaching Out: Meanings and Motivations for Passionate Readers," Cele Otnes and Behice Ece Ilhan hone in on what passionate readers regard as the benefits and joys of reading, and unpack many active components to this "passive" hobby. All of the authors approach their topics from the interpretive research tradition, and employ a variety of methods (e.g., netnography, depth interviews, observation) to explore their topic of interest.

This symposium was designed to appeal to a broad cross-section of ACR attendees, including scholars interested in issues pertaining to 1) consumer lifestyles and consumer identity, as reading is a hobby that is intertwined with these constructs; 2) consumer entrepreneurship and co-creation, as consumers create new ways of reading and new reading communities; and 3) "consumer culture theory"–particularly those interested in everyday consumption activities. And while public policy organizations such as Reading is Fundamental (www.rif.org) no doubt have a stake in understanding what makes various forms of reading attractive and engaging to consumers, the pervasiveness and evolution of reading make it a fascinating form of consumer behavior to study in its own right.

ABSTRACTS

"Never Tickle a Sleeping Booklover: How Readers Devour Harry Potter"

Anthony Patterson, University of Liverpool, UK
Stephen Brown, University of Ulster, UK

With 400 million copies of her books in print, J.K. Rowling's Harry Potter series has turned an entire iGeneration on to the old-fashioned pleasures of reading "proper" novels. But how do her readers read the holy writ? Detailed analysis of a Harry Potter database, consisting of several hundred qualitative interviews, suggests that there are four Rowling reading styles: Gryffindor (enthusiastically competitive); Slytherin (unhealthily compulsive); Ravenclaw (forensically critical); and Hufflepuff (comfortably numb). After considering these magical reading modes, the paper compares them to G.P. Stone's classic typology of consumer behavior.

"Curling Up and Reaching Out: Meanings and Motivations for Passionate Readers"

Cele Otnes, University of Illinois at Urbana-Champaign, USA
Behice Ece Ilhan, University of Illinois at Urbana-Champaign, USA

Although reading increasingly competes and is complemented by other entertainment activities, many consumers regard reading as one of their most cherished everyday activities. Our study, based on depth interviews with 15 self-identified adult passionate readers, explores the benefits these consumers derive from their hobby, and the ways they co-create and incorporate reading activities into their lives. We find that for passionate readers, this "passive" hobby contains many more active components than the passive nature of reading implies (e.g., by fostering book clubs, reading lists, actively becoming market mavens in the area of reading).

"BookCrossed Lovers: Consumers and Their Relationships with Books"

Pauline Maclaran, Keele University, UK
Rosalind Masterson, DeMontfort University, UK

Very few studies explore how readers feel about their books and how their involvement with books affects their lives. Following Fournier's (1998) study on the relationships between consumers and brands, this paper explores the diverse relationships between readers and their books. This study draws on book lovers' experiences of BookCrossing.com; a website that encourages and facilities the circulation of secondhand books on a global basis. The research is based on a netnographic investigation which includes six months of observation and participant observation in the BookCrossing community.

"Reading Others' Texts: Marginalia and the Inscription of Meaning in Collectible Books"

Janet Borgerson, University of Exeter, UK
Jonathan Schroeder, University of Exeter, UK

The popular value of used books reveals insights into the material pleasures of reading and collecting books. Focusing on a collectible book genre, we explore how material practices such as collecting, reading, and inscribing create meaning for consumers. We analyze the materiality of these used texts, including "inscriptions" and previous owner's marginalia–written annotations, marks, and notes left in the pages. We explore the aesthetic and temporal dimensions of books via three key aspects of their appeal: 1) marginalia; 2) collectability; and 3) material pleasures.

References available upon request.

The Impact of Psychological Distance on Charitable Fundraising

Christopher Olivola, Princeton University, USA
Wendy Liu, University of California, Los Angeles, USA

SESSION OVERVIEW

The purpose of this symposium is to explore how psychological distance impacts charitable giving and philanthropic fundraising. Charitable giving has turned into a competitive business in which charities compete to advocate their causes to consumers. Of all the social causes consumers encounter each day, which one's do they give to and which ones do they pass? What are the factors that determine when and to whom people give? This session seeks to shed light on these questions by focusing on one factor that plays a significant role in consumers' decision about charity choice and level of giving, namely, the psychological distance between the individual and the cause. Four papers, each from a different angle, demonstrate how psychological distance affects giving behavior. In doing so, this session significantly contributes to the understanding of the psychology of giving, bringing the self and the cause's relation to the self into focus, and broadening the factors to be considered when studying donation behavior. Specifically, the four papers illustrate that the motivation to contribute to a prosocial cause is heavily influenced by the extent to which consumers feel *involved* in the cause, and just as important, the extent to which they feel *separated* from the costs associated with contributing. Further, they explore the factors that mediate or moderate the impact of psychological distance on charitable giving.

The first paper (Kennedy et al.) demonstrates that social distance (self vs. other) and temporal distance (now vs. later) have parallel effects on consumers' willingness to contribute to a prosocial cause, and that these effects are moderated by the relative salience of the benefits vs. costs of contributing. When cost is salient, greater social and temporal distance fostered giving. When the pro-social benefit is salient, smaller psychological distance fostered giving. The second paper (Liu & Aaker) shows that people are more generous when they are first primed with a concept that makes them feel personally engaged in a cause (donating time; volunteering) than when they are primed with a concept that distances them from the cause (donating money). The third paper (Olivola & Shafir) takes this notion of engagement even further by showing that people are willing to donate more to a prosocial cause when they have to suffer pain and effort to contribute than when the contribution process is easy and enjoyable. Finally, the fourth paper (McGraw et al.) demonstrates the effect of literal temporal separation: people respond more strongly to the most recent humanitarian crisis they happen to encounter than equivalent events that occurred earlier.

This set of projects highlight several important aspects of psychological distance in the context of giving behavior. First, distance to the self is a key construct underlying giving, and this distance can be multiply determined. In particular, it can be determined by (a) the self-other dichotomy (Kennedy et al.), (b) a temporal gap, either in looking forward (Kennedy et al.), or in retrospect (McGraw et al.), and (c) the extent to which the person's affective system is engaged—considering spending time with a cause activates emotional thoughts about giving (Liu & Aaker), and suffering a little pain in the giving process engages the person more so than an activity that incurs no pain (Olivola & Shafir).

As supporting evidence, emotionality seems to underlie the effect of psychological distance on behavior. For example, in Liu and Aaker, greater focus on happiness and emotional benefit occurred when time donation, rather than money donation is evoked, fueling donations. In McGraw et al., people rated the most recently viewed video clip about a crisis as more upsetting than a previously viewed clip, resulting in donating more to the more recent appeal.

Finally, the current set of papers highlights an insight that has received scant attention in previous charity literature. Specifically, distance relates to not only the benefit side of consideration (the focus of previous research), but also the cost side. For example, in Kennedy et al., when cost of helping is salient, large psychological distance is actually beneficial for donations. Related, in Liu and Aaker, asking people about their monetary donations intentions lead to less donations then if intentions were not first gauged, due to the distancing effect of money.

In summary, this symposium provides a novel view of the study of charitable behavior by examining the relationship between psychological distance and giving. In the process, intriguing new findings about charitable behavior is revealed. These results are worthy of discussion; moreover, they prompt important questions for future research. For example, what are the specific emotions that create greater psychological closeness (pain, guilt, upset, happiness)? Are all emotions created equal, and do negative affect create closeness or a distancing effect? Further, when feeling close to a cause, how does the act of giving to the cause impact a person's self construal and identity?

This symposium should appeal to a diverse research audience. In particular, research into the psychology of charitable giving contributes to a growing interest in transformative consumer research. In addition, a number of important areas are considered in these papers, including affect, motivation, consumption choice, and wellbeing.

EXTENDED ABSTRACTS

"Do We Give More of Our Present Selves or Our Future Selves? Psychological Distance and Prosocial Decision Making"

Kathleen Kennedy, Princeton University, USA
Christopher Olivola, Princeton University, USA
Emily Pronin, Princeton University, USA

This research investigates the types of decisions that individuals make for their present selves, their future selves, or for others. In a series of four studies, we demonstrate that individuals make uniquely different decisions for their present selves, compared to the choices they make for future selves and others, and that these differences seem to be a result of varying internal subjective experiences. Importantly, these internal experiences can affect individuals' behavior such that they are either more generous or more selfish. If the focus of the individual is on the charitable aspect of the situation, rather than the burdensome nature of the task, they may be more generous with their present selves than with their future selves or others. However, if the internal subjective experience is one of anxiety and concern over the costs, then present selves are often more selfish. Simple manipulations to remind individuals that their future self will likely resemble their present self seem effective in reducing differences in the decisions made for the two selves (present and future). Also, asking them to make a decision for another person before choosing for themselves in the present tends to move them towards that initial commitment.

In Study 1, participants were told that they were part of an experiment that required them to consume some amount of a disgusting tasting liquid. Participants made what they believed to be truly binding decisions for themselves in the present or the future, or for someone else in the present. It was emphasized that the more they drank, the more it would help the study. Participants made unique decisions for their present selves, such that they volunteered to drink less of the liquid in the present-self condition than in the future self or other conditions. In this case, the prospect of drinking the disgusting liquid was very aversive, and the salient internal subjective experience was likely one of anxiety.

In Study 2, individuals were asked how much time they would donate to help struggling freshmen study for their exams. They were either asked to volunteer time to tutor "right now" (in the middle of midterms week), to volunteer their time for next mid-terms week (the next semester), or to decide how much time other students could tutor during their next midterm week. Participants volunteered less when choosing for their present selves, compared to future selves and others. A fourth condition also asked partici-pants to make a decision for their future self, but this time they were reminded that they would likely be "the same person you are now". In this reminder condition, the time volunteered on behalf of the future self did not differ from the time volunteered for the present self. Here, reluctance, on the part of the participants, to donate their time seemed to be due to a focus on the time pressures and stresses of their midterm exams, tempering the amount of time they volun-teered.

In Study 3, individuals were approached in their dorm and asked how much money they would donate to a breast cancer charity. The decision was either on behalf of their present selves (how much money will you donate right now?), their future selves (how much money will you will pledge to donate next semester?), or someone else (how much money should the average student donate?). Participants were again less generous with their present selves than with future selves and others. In a fourth condition, participants were asked to decide how much someone else could donate, followed by a request that they themselves donate money in the present. In this present-self/other-first condition, participants offered more money than in the present-self condition where they did not make a commitment for the other person beforehand. In this case, participants' decisions about how much someone else should donate seemed to relieve some of the reluctance they had about donating in the present.

In Study 4, participants were asked to receive emails that would benefit charitable organizations and help out a fellow student who was struggling to pay for college. Students made decisions for their present selves, future selves, present others, and future others. In this experiment, the negative aspects of the task at hand (receiv-ing some annoying emails) were outweighed by the positive expe-rience of helping (helping the charities and helping the needy student who was standing right in front of them). Under these circumstances, participants actually gave more of their present self (by agreeing to receive more emails) than they gave of their future self or another person in the present or future. In addition, partici-pants reported that their primary internal subjective concern was the pro-social benefit of helping.

Altogether, these studies demonstrate that people's immediate subjective experiences play an important role in shaping how generous they will be in the present vs. the future. If the experience is one of strong pro-social goals, they may actually be more generous "in the moment" while those goals are subjectively stronger, but if the experience includes heavy costs, they may be more generous if they make a commitment for a future self instead. Finally, we found that some simple reminders (such as reminding people that they will be very much the same in the future as they are now, or that they've just committed someone else to a more generous amount) can work to make people more or less generous.

"The Happiness of Giving: The "Time-Ask" Effect"
Wendy Liu, University of California, Los Angeles, USA
Jennifer Aaker, Stanford University, USA

How to get people to give? This research proposes one source of influence on people's response to a charity request is the mindset activated by the request—people give more when under a emo-tional rather than a transactional mindset. Further, we find that two commonly asked intention questions, namely, "how interested are you to volunteer" (a time-ask), versus, "how interested are you to donate money" (a money-ask), activate distinct mindsets, due to the different mental associations of these concepts. As a result, a charity request is more successful when the donor is first approached with a time-ask, rather than a money-ask.

Specifically, because spending time is inherently a personal action, thinking about time activates thoughts of personal emotions and goals; on the other hand, because money is a major accounting unit, thinking about money activates associations of economic value and exchanges. Thus answering a question about time acti-vates an emotional mindset in which people interpret events based on their emotional meaning, whereas answering a question about money activates a transactional mindset in which people evaluate the utility of events. Consequently, because of the personal emo-tional meaning of charity, asking of time reduces psychological distance to the charity, and increases subsequent actual donations; on the other hand, a money-ask highlights the exchange nature of a donation, thereby distances the donor from the charity and thus decreases actual donations (compared to not asking about inten-tions at all).

We propose that time and money are social constructs associ-ated with distinct concepts. Following the theory of construct activation and accessibility and research on the "question-behavior effect" (e.g., Morwitz, Johnson and Schmittlein 1993; Schwarz 1999; Sherman 1980; Spangenberg 1997; Sprott et al. 2006), we propose that asking people to consider their intention to spend time versus spend money in a certain way activates discrete goals and beliefs. We argue that thinking about time activates goals of emotional well-being, whereas thinking about money suppresses such goals by activating goals of economic utility (Brendl, Markman, and Messner 2003). As a result, considering donating time leads the individual to focus on the emotional implications of helping others, thereby bring the charity closer to the self. On the other hand, considering donating money diminishes the emotional implication, creating distance. Consequently, first asking people about their volunteering intentions, compared to first asking them about mon-etary donation intentions, leads to greater amount of charitable contribution—both in time, and in money.

Evidence for the time-ask effect is found in three studies. Experiment 1 contrasts two conditions: directly asking people for a monetary donation (money-ask) to the American Lung Cancer Foundation, versus prefacing this request by first asking people for volunteering (time-ask). This time-ask significantly increased sub-sequent amount of donation (M=$36.44 vs. $24.46, p=.04).

Experiment 2 is a field study conducted with HopeLab.org. HopeLab, a remarkable non-profit organization, uses innovative technology to help improve the quality of life for children with chronic illnesses. At time 1, participants read information about HopeLab, and were asked "How interested are you to donate time?" and "How interested are you to donate money?" The key manipulation was the order of these two questions—when time-ask (money-ask) appeared first, it put people under an emotional (transactional) mindset for subsequent questions. A third group (control condition) read about HopeLab, but was not asked any intent questions. At time 2, the same participants were approached with an opportunity to donate money to HopeLab, and/or to volunteer for HopeLab. It is found when time-ask appeared first, donation was significantly higher than in the control condition ($M=\$5.85$ vs. $\$4.42$, $p=.04$); whereas when money-ask appeared first, donation was actually lower than in the control condition ($M=\$3.07$, $p=.05$). Time-ask condition also yielded more hours of volunteering.

Experiment 3 found that a stronger perception of the link between charity and personal happiness fully mediated the effect of measuring time intent on subsequent donation.

This research has significant implications for consumer research in the areas of charitable giving, the conditions for and implications of "hot" versus "cold" thinking, psychological distance, and happiness. Future research may further examine the effect of thinking about time versus money. For example, can a simple prime of time (e.g., thinking about a future time frame) have a similar effect in activating an emotional mindset? Can thinking about time versus money lead to greater subjective happiness in life in general?

References

Brendl, C. Miguel, Arthur B. Markman, and Claude Messner (2003). "The Devaluation Effect: Activating a Need Devalues Unrelated Choice Options," *Journal of Consumer Research*, 29 (March), 463-473.

Morwitz, Vicki G., Eric Johnson, and David Schmittlein (1993), "Does Measuring Intent Change Behavior?" *Journal of Consumer Research*, 20 (June), 46-61.

Schwarz, Norbert (1999), "Self-Reports: How the Questions Shape the Answers," American Psychologist, 54, 93-105.

Sherman, Steven J. (1980), "On the Self-Erasing Nature of Errors of Prediction," *Journal of Personality and Social Psychology*, 39 (August), 211-21.

Spangenberg, Eric R. (1997), "Increasing Health Club Attendance through Self-Prophecy," *Marketing Letters*, 8 (10), 23-32.

Sprott, David E., Eric R. Spangenber, Lauren Block, Gavan Fitzsimons, Vicki Morwitz and Patti Williams (2006), "The Question-Behavior Effect: What We Know and Where We Go From Here," *Social Influence*, 1 (2), 128-37.

"The 'Martyrdom Effect': When the Prospect of Pain and Effort Increases Charitable Giving"

Christopher Olivola, Princeton University, USA
Eldar Shafir, Princeton University, USA

Charitable giving is a puzzle for standard normative theories of motivation and choice for two reasons: First, the act of giving up personal wealth for the sake of others whom we may not know or ever see seems contrary to the assumption that we are primarily driven to maximize personal utility. Second, and even more puzzling, are the ways that people choose to raise money. Some of the most popular and successful fundraisers involve a good deal of pain and effort, such as charity marathons and charity fire-walks (walking over burning coals). But there is no a priori reason for this to be the case. From a rational point of view, it's hard to see what individuals could gain from suffering or watching their friends

suffer to raise money. The same holds true for the charity organizations and the recipients of charity. Given that running or biking tens of miles is both painful, effortful, and, further, that it can be done for free, why are people paying to suffer? We consider this puzzling phenomenon, wherein the prospect of pain and effort actually increases our motivation to participate in an activity; a phenomenon we call the "martyrdom effect". The name refers to the fact that people are choosing to suffer for a cause that they care about. Many theories, and lay intuitions alike, assume that making a task more painful and effortful should decrease its appeal. The implication, then, is that to maximize participation and contributions, fundraisers ought to be easy and enjoyable for donors. In contrast, we provide evidence that the prospect of pain and effort can promote charitable giving. Across a series of experiments, participants reported that they would contribute more to a cause when the contribution process was painful and effortful than when it was neutral or even enjoyable. Additional studies showed that this "martyrdom effect" could not be explained by a taste for painful-effortful donation activities, cognitive dissonance, social norms, or a cognitive attribute substitution heuristic.

Experiment 1 tests the hypothesis that making the donation process more difficult and painful will increase the amount that people are willing to donate relative to a pleasant control, while ruling out the simple possibility that people have a preference (whatever the reasons) for the painful-effortful fundraising event. Participants considered a hypothetical scenario in which they had to decide whether to donate some of their own money in order to participate in a charity fundraiser. The nature of the fundraiser was manipulated between participants. Participants who considered a fundraiser in which donating was contingent on performing a painful or effortful activity (running 5 miles) reported that they would donate more than participants who considered an enjoyable fundraising event (attending a picnic), suggesting that they valued painful-effortful fundraisers more. However, a third group of participants who jointly considered and compared the two fundraisers indicated (by a large majority) that they would prefer attending the pleasant fundraiser to the painful-effortful one, thereby ruling out a standard economic explanation based on a 'taste for painful fundraising'.

Experiment 2 extended these findings by using real payoffs and actual pain. Participants played a Public Goods Game, in which they decided how to allocate a budget between themselves and the public pool (where money was doubled and redistributed evenly between the players). We found that players allocated more of their budget to the public pool when doing so would require enduring pain (a cold-pressor task) than did players in the painless control condition. We also found that this contribution increase was not related to beliefs about others' allocation decisions.

Experiment 3 examined whether the 'martyrdom effect' could be attributed to beliefs about the relative popularity of painful-effortful vs. enjoyable fundraisers. Participants read about a hypothetical charity that was transitioning from using one kind of fundraiser to another (from a painful-effortful one to a pleasant one or vice-versa) and were asked to predict how this transition would affect attendance and donations. Results show that participants believed the pleasant fundraiser would be more popular, ruling out the possibility that the 'martyrdom effect' is the product of social norm beliefs (e.g., Prentice & Miller, 1993).

Experiment 4 tested whether the 'martyrdom effect' occurs because people rely on a simple cognitive attribute substitution heuristic (Kahneman & Frederick, 2002) that uses amount of pain-effort as a cue when deciding how much to donate. We show that, although participants are sensitive to the amount of effort and pain involved in running various distances, they do not use this cue to determine how much they should donate to participate in a charity fundraiser.

In all of our experiments, participants decided how much to donate BEFORE experiencing any pain or effort, thereby ruling out standard dissonance theory (Festinger, 1957) as a possible explanation for our results. We discuss how the prospect of suffering for a cause may lead people to ascribe more value to their future contributions, thus motivating them to donate more and providing them with greater satisfaction.

References

Festinger, Leon (1957), *A Theory of Cognitive Dissonance*, Stanford, CA: Stanford University Press.

Kahneman, Daniel and Shane Frederick (2002), "Representativeness Revisited: Attribute Substitution in Intuitive Judgment," in T. Gilovich, D. Griffin, & D. Kahneman (Eds.), *Heuristics and Biases: The Psychology of Intuitive Judgment* (pp. 49-81). Cambridge: Cambridge University Press.

Prentice, Deborah A. and Dale T. Miller (1993), "Pluralistic Ignorance and Alcohol Use on Campus: Some Consequences of Misperceiving the Social Norm," *Journal of Personality and Social Psychology*, 64, 243-256.

"Whom to Help? Immediacy Bias in Humanitarian Aid Allocation"

A. Peter McGraw, University of Colorado at Boulder, USA
Leaf Van Boven, University of Colorado at Boulder USA
Michaela Huber, University of Colorado at Boulder, USA
Laura Johnson-Graham, University of Colorado at Boulder, USA

Deciding how to allocate charitable resources toward minimizing human suffering is among the most important and most difficult decisions consumer face. Donation decisions are difficult largely because people are exposed to information about different sources of human suffering over time, in sequences that may reflect the whims of popular media (CNN) and pop icons (Bono and Angelina) more than genuine differences in the severity of human suffering. The question we examine is how consumers perceive different, emotionally arousing sources of human suffering presented over time, and how these perceptions influence consumers' decisions about humanitarian aid allocation.

Previous research indicates that people exhibit an immediacy bias in emotion perception such that immediate emotions seem more intense than previous emotions, all else equal (Van Boven, White, & Huber, 2008). This immediacy bias occurs for at least two reasons. First, immediate emotions attract and hold attention. Second, information about immediate emotions is more available in memory than information about previous emotions. Immediate emotions may therefore seem more intense than distant emotions to the degree that people use attention and availability to judge emotional intensity.

Judgment and decision making research indicates that affect strongly influences economic preferences, including preferences about allocating humanitarian aid (Kahneman, Ritov, and Sckade 1999; Slovic et al. 2002). People donate more money to victims who arouse more intense affect than to victims who arouse less intense affect, independent of, and sometimes in spite of, information about the mortality magnitude of human crises. For instance, people sometimes donate more money to single victims than to large numbers of victims because the large numbers of undermine affective reactions (Small, Loewenstein, and Slovic 2007).

Integrating research on the immediacy bias and on the affective basis of economic preferences, we hypothesize that consumers perceive human suffering that happens to arouse immediate emotional arousal as more severe compared with human suffering that happened to have aroused previous emotional arousal. We also test whether this immediacy bias is associated with neglect of information about the crises' deadliness, and whether the immediacy bias decays over time as emotions decay.

In Study 1 participants watched two short films provided by Doctors Without Borders (DWB) regarding humanitarian crises in Sudan and Niger. Participants viewed the videos in random order, separated by 20 min. Directly after learning about the second crisis, participants were asked to allocate charitable money to DWB's activities in the two locations. Consistent with the immediacy bias, most participants (67%) allocated significantly more charitable funds to the crisis they happened to learn about second than to the crisis they happened to learn about first.

In Study 2 we sought to conceptually replicate the immediacy bias demonstrated in Study 1 with two extensions. First, we explicitly provided participants with (fictional) information about the deadliness of the two crises; this allowed us to test whether people would exhibit an immediacy bias in spite of information about the crises' deadliness. Second, we measured perceptions of human suffering and charitable actions both immediately after learning about the crises and after one day's delay, which allowed us to test whether the immediacy bias declined over time as emotions presumably subsided.

Participants watched two short DWB videos, in random order and separated by a 20 min delay, about malnutrition in Angola and Niger. Participants also read summaries of the circumstances of the two crises, which made clear that 60,000 more people were dying in one randomly determined crisis. Consistent with the immediacy bias, participants reported that they were significantly more upset while watching the second rather than the first video, and that the crisis they happened to learn about second was more deserving of humanitarian aid than the crisis they learned about first. When participants were asked to write a letter to their Senator calling attention to the suffering in one of the crises, 65% chose to write about the country they happened to learn about second. Importantly, people exhibited this immediacy bias even when it was clear that more people were dying in the first rather than the second crisis participants learned about. Finally, there was no hint of an immediacy bias when participants returned the following day, when their emotions had presumably subsided.

In our final study, we sought to replicate the immediacy bias, but with an extended sequence of four (rather than two) DWB videos of crises separated by minimal delay of 2 min (rather than 20 min). Doing so would minimize concerns that the immediacy bias is due primarily to memory decay. We also sought to reconcile an apparent inconsistency between our results and previous research suggesting that people allocate more funds to charitable causes that occur earlier rather than later in a sequence (Payne et al. 2000). We hypothesize that both patterns reflect an immediacy bias, rather than some other difference between our research (e.g., our focus on humanitarian suffering and the previous research's focus on environmental programs). Regardless of the type of pattern (immediacy or primacy) people respond to their immediate emotions, and these emotions are influential late in the sequence when allocations are made after viewing all the videos (i.e., post hoc) but emotions are influential early in the sequence when allocations after made after watching each video (i.e., sequentially).

Participants watched four randomly ordered videos about African humanitarian crises. When participants allocated funds after viewing all four videos, as in our previous studies, they allocated a disproportionately higher amount to the final crisis. In contrast, when participants allocated funds sequentially, as in previous research on sequence effects, they tended to allocate more money to the first (rather than the last) crisis.

These studies document an important bias in people's judgments and decisions about allocating charitable resources toward mitigating humanitarian suffering. Integrating research on emotion perception and the affective basis of economic preferences, these studies demonstrate that people exhibit an immediacy bias in judgments and decisions about humanitarian suffering.

References

Kahneman, Daniel, Ilana Ritov, and David Schkade (1999), "Economic Preference or Attitude Expressions? An Analysis of Dollar Response to Public Issues," *Journal of Risk and Uncertainty*, 19, 203-35.

Payne, John W, David Schkade, Willliam Desvouges, and Chris Aultman (2000), "Valuation of Multiple Environmental Programs," *Journal of Risk and Uncertainty*, 21 (1), 95–115.

Slovic, Paul, M. Finucane, E. Peters, and D. MacGregor (2002), "The Affect Heuristic," in *Heuristics and Biases: The Psychology of Intuitive Judgment*, ed. T Gilovich, D. Griffin and D Kahneman, New York, NY: Cambridge University Press, 397-420.

Small, Deborah A, George Loewenstein, and Paul Slovic (2007), "Sympathy and Callousness: The Impact of Deliberative Thought on Donations to Identifiable and Statistical Victims," *Organizational Behavior and Human Decision Processes*, 102 (2), 143–53.

Van Boven, Leaf, Kate White, and Michaela Huber (2008). "Immediacy bias in perceptions of the intensity of different emotions over time." Manuscript under review.

Effects of Supersizing and Downsizing Packages on Consumption: Marketing and Policy Implications

Pierre Chandon, INSEAD, France

EXTENDED ABSTRACTS

"Downsize in 3D, Supersize in 1D: Effects of the Dimensionality of Package and Portion Size Changes on Size Estimations, Consumption, and Quantity Discount Expectations"

Pierre Chandon, INSEAD, France
Nailya Ordabayeva, INSEAD, France

Marketers have significantly supersized package and portion sizes because it can increase consumer expenditures. However, supersizing has been under attack by regulators and consumer advocacy groups because it can lead to over-consumption. On the other hand, downsizing can help marketers hide unit price increases but is not liked by consumers. In addition, retailers are pushing manufacturers to change the shape of their packages (e.g., to switch to rounder bottles) to reduce the environmental cost of package waste. In these circumstances, the issue of how consumers respond to changes in both the size and shape of portions and packages has become important for marketers who seek to increase the purchase and consumption of their products, as well as for consumers and regulators who are concerned about improving size estimations and reducing overconsumption.

In this research, we examine how the dimensionality of changes in portion and package sizes influences consumers' estimations of product volume, size of resized doses that they produce for consumption, their preference for buying supersized or downsized packages and portions, and price discounts expected and offered for buying larger sizes.

Research in psychophysics (Stevens 1986) has shown that the subjective experience of physical intensities (e.g., weight, volume) follows an inelastic power function of their actual magnitude, which means that people underestimate the magnitude of size changes. Research has also shown that size estimations are even less elastic when estimating changes in volume (3D change) than when estimating changes in areas (2D change) or lengths (1D change) (Frayman and Dawson 1981). Drawing on these findings, we make the following hypotheses. First, size estimations are more elastic when packages change in one dimension (e.g., height) than when they change in two or more dimensions (e.g., height and diameter). Second, consumers' willingness to pay for larger package sizes—and hence their quantity discount expectations—are influenced by their biased size estimations and follow an inelastic function of actual size. Third, providing size information reduces but does not eliminate the effects of package dimensionality. Finally, this effect of dimensionality leads consumers to pour more product into and out of product containers when supersizing and downsizing a dose in 3D (vs. 1D) and to prefer packages supersized in one dimension and those downsized in multiple dimensions. Five studies provide support for our hypotheses.

Study 1 examined consumers' perceptions of package size when it changes in 1D vs. 3D. The study involved 2 between-subjects size change dimensionality conditions (1D vs. 3D) and 6 within-subjects package sizes (a candle of 50, 100, 200, 400, 800, 1600 grams). Participants saw the pictures of 6 sizes of a candle increasing either in 1D (height) or in 3D (height and diameter). Participants knew the size of the smallest candle (50 g) and had to estimate the remaining 5 sizes. We found that size estimations followed an inelastic power function (with a power exponent b smaller than 1) and that estimations were even less elastic when size changed in 3D (b=.63) than when it changed in 1D (b=.87).

Study 2 examined the effect of size change dimensionality on willingness to pay for size increases and the effect of providing size information. The study involved 6 within-subject sizes, 2 between-subject dimensionality conditions (1D vs. 3D), 2 between-subject size information availability conditions (size info available vs. unavailable) and a control condition. The participants saw 6 sizes of two actual products (vs. pictures as in Study 1), wool and dishwashing detergent, which increased either in 1D or in 3D. Participants in the unavailable-information condition saw the products and provided both size estimations and WTP for each size of each product. Participants in the available-information condition knew the actual product sizes and only provided their WTP for each size. Participants in the control condition knew the actual sizes of the products but did not see them and only provided their WTP for each size. We found that, as in Study 1, size estimations were inelastic, especially when size increased in 3D (b=.68) vs. 1D (b=.93). Partly due to size estimations, WTP also followed an inelastic power function, with lower elasticity in 3D (b=.56) than in 1D (b=.72), and dimensionality influenced WTP even when the actual package sizes were available (b=.69 in 3D vs. b=.83 in 1D).

Study 3 examined the effect of resizing dimensionality on consumption dosage. The participants increased or decreased the doses of three products provided in three containers (a vodka glass, a cocktail glass, and an infant syrup cup). In the 1D condition, the participants used cylindrical containers, in which product volume changed only in height (1D). In the 3D condition, the participants used conical containers, in which product volume changed in height and diameter (3D). Because the participants were less sensitive to size changes in 3D than to size changes in 1D, they poured more of each product into and out of conical (vs. cylindrical) containers.

Study 4 consisted of two field experiments examining how the dimensionality of size change in real product packages affects people's supersizing (Study 3a) and downsizing (Study 3b) decisions. In Study 3a, participants made a choice between a control beer or cider in a 22 Cl mug and a target brand which was either in a similar 22 Cl mug (control condition) or in a 33 Cl mug, supersized in 1D (height) or in 3D (height and diameter). The choice share of the target brand was significantly higher in the 1D condition (100%) than in the 3D (68%) or the control (55%) condition. In Study 3b, consumers chose between regular-size packages of regular Coke (50 Cl) and popcorn (94 Cl) and smaller packages of diet Coke (33 Cl) and popcorn (63 Cl) downsized in 1D or in 3D. We found that participants were more likely to choose the downsized option in the 3D condition (69%) than in the 1D condition (48%).

The final study was a field survey of the prices of regular and large product packages supersized in 1D or in 3D. Across 70 pairs of regular and supersized packages in 4 product categories (cosmetics, sandwiches, beverages and snacks), we found that the elasticity of price to size change was lower for packages supersized in 3D (.55) than for packages supersized in 1D (.88).

In sum, we found that people underestimate the magnitude of package and portion size changes, especially when they occur in

3D. Providing size information helps consumers improve their price expectations and make better resizing decisions, even if it doesn't eliminate dimensionality effects. Finally, we showed that these effects explain why supersizing is more effective in 1D and downsizing is more effective in 3D.

References

Frayman, Bruce J. and William E. Dawson (1981), "The Effect of Object Shape and Mode of Presentation on Judgments of Apparent Volume," *Perception and Psychophysics*, 29 (1), 56-62.

Stevens, Stanley Smith (1986), *Psychophysics: Introduction to Its Perceptual, Neural, and Social Prospects*. Oxford: Transaction Books.

"Packaging Cues that Frame Portion Size: The Case of the Red Potato Chip"

Brian Wansink, Cornell University, USA
Andrew B. Geier, University of Pennsylvania, USA
Paul Rozin, University of Pennsylvania, USA

What leads people to continue eating past the point of satiety (Rozin et al. 1998)? First, they might ineffectively monitor how much they have eaten (Chandon and Wansink 2007); second, they may simply eat what they believe is an appropriate amount for that situation (Geier, Rozin, and Doros 2006; Wansink 2004); third, they may be engaged in a semi-automated habitual activity, which simply continues until interrupted. A solution to all three of these problems could take the form of various types of markers which would call attention to food intake.

An increasing amount of research suggests that people use visual indications to tell them when to stop eating (Wansink 2006). A serving portion creates a consumption norm, which indicates to people when they should stop eating (Geier, Rozin, and Doros 2006). To some extent, this is what small-size portions (e.g., 100-calorie packages) do. When people reach the end of a small package they need to decide whether to continue eating by opening another package. This interrupts their hand-to-mouth behavior and forces them to consider whether they want more. Such interrupts reduce consumption of food and improve estimations of the food intake (Wansink, Painter, and Lee 2006). Less "intrusive" segmentation cues may not interrupt consumption, but simply call attention to norms and the amount consumed.

This research examines whether inserting "segmentation cues" within a package can reduce total intake of a snack within a single sitting. We propose that the use of consumption markers decrease intake of a food because: 1) they call attention to eating, 2) they provide consumption norm cues, and 3) they break the eating script by introducing a pause. Our study investigates whether visually segmenting snack food in a package will decrease how much a person eats in a single occasion.

The study involved a 3-level between-subject design where fifty-nine undergraduate respondents were randomly given one of 3 different tubes of 82 potato chips (of 11 grams each, 10 calorie/chip) while watching a documentary video. The consumption interrupt or segmentation-framing cue was a red-colored potato chip of the same size and composition as the ordinary yellow ones. Two pilot studies showed that the red chip was treated as a "regular" potato chip, except subconsciously with regard to its effect as a segmentation marker. The chips were emptied from the tube and then replaced. In one group, red-colored chips were used to mark every group of seven chips (i.e., every seventh chip was colored red) (7-marker group). In the second group, red-colored chips marked every group of fourteen chips (14-marker group). The control group had no red chips in the tube. Following the program, the respon-

dents estimated how many chips they ate, how many calories they consumed, and how many chips they usually ate when watching a one-hour show. Finally, they were asked to provide their gender, height, weight, and the number of hours since their last meal.

As anticipated, the inclusion of a divider had a dramatic influence on how many chips were consumed. Participants in the control condition on average ate 45 chips, those with 14-chip segments ate 24 chips, and those with 7-chip segments ate 20 chips. The simple use of any segmenting divider significantly reduced intake by about half, regardless of whether the dividers were present at intervals of 7 or 14 chips. There was no significant difference between the 7 and 14 dividers. The control group overestimated their actual intake significantly more than 7- and 14-marker groups, in which the participants were reasonably accurate in estimating their intake (33 vs. 19 vs. 24 chips, respectively, $p<.001$).

These results present evidence that segmentation cues and/or consumption interrupts may help reduce intake and improve estimates of calories consumed. The effects are substantial in size (around 50%). Further research is needed to determine what types of segmentation cues are most effective and in what contexts. Our results have important policy implications. Small reductions in food intake, maintained over months, can lead to substantial weight losses over years. If using consumption interrupt strategies cuts 200 calories out of a person's daily intake, it translates into the cut of 20 pounds in one year. Thus small interruptions to mindless eating can provide large aggregate results. Helping consumers understand and develop their own segmentation cues could be an effective way to reduce mindless eating.

References

Chandon, Pierre and Brian Wansink (2007), "Obesity and the Calorie Underestimation Bias: A Psychophysical Model of Fast-Food Meal Size Estimation", *Journal of Marketing Research*, 44 (February), 84-99.

Geier, Andrew B., Paul Rozin and Gheorghe Doros (2006), "Unit Bias: A New Heuristic that Helps Explain the Effect of Portion Size on Food Intake", *Psychological Science*, 17, 521-525.

Rozin, Paul, Sara Dow, Morris Moscovitch and Suparna Rajaram (1998), "What Causes Humans to Begin and End a Meal? A Role for Memory for What Has Been Eaten, as Evidenced by a Study of Multiple Meal Eating in Amnesic Patients", *Psychological Science*, 9, 392-396.

Wansink, Brian (2004), "Environmental Factors that Increase the Food Intake and Consumption Volume of Unknowing Consumers", *Annual Review of Nutrition*, 24, 455-479.

Wansink, Brian (2006), *Mindless Eating: Why We Eat More Than We Think*, New York: Bantam.

Wansink, Brian, James E. Painter and Yeon-Kyung Lee (2006), "The Office Candy Dish: Proximity's Influence on Estimated and Actual Candy Consumption", *International Journal of Obesity*, 30 (5), 871-875.

"Consumer Usage of Ultra-Concentrated Products"

Maura L. Scott, University of Kentucky, USA
Stephen M. Nowlis, Arizona State University, USA
Naomi Mandel, Arizona State University, USA

Ultra-concentrated products, often offered in smaller packages with greater potency, are available in various categories including medications, detergents, and beverages. We explore when consumers overuse ultra-concentrated products, and which cues communicate potency.

Three factors influence consumption of ultra-concentrated products: prior usage behavior, package size, and product potency.

Consumers anchor on their prior usage and fail to adjust appropriately, leading to over-consumption (Tversky and Kahneman 1974). Consumers use more of a product when dispensing from larger packages than smaller ones (Wansink 1996). We propose that product potency changes exert a unique force that causes consumers to overuse ultra-concentrated products. We explore which cues signal potency changes, and examine how these cues translate to consumption.

Study 1 examined whether consumers overuse higher potency products, and which cues assist consumers in using the prescribed quantity. It was a 2 (bottle size: large, small) × 2 (recommended regular-strength quantity: yes, no) × 2 (ultra-concentrated defined: yes, no) between-subjects experiment, $N=338$. The dependent variable was the amount of ultra-concentrated detergent used, relative to regular-strength detergent usage.

Participants viewed a 200 oz. regular-strength detergent bottle, an ultra-concentrated detergent bottle, and a list of items in one laundry load. Bottle size was operationalized with the ultra-concentrated bottle as either large (200 oz.) or small (100 oz.); the regular-strength bottle was always 200 oz., and the regular and ultra-concentrated bottle caps were identical. Recommended regular-strength quantity reflected whether or not a recommended use amount was given for the regular-strength detergent. For example, in conditions providing a recommended regular-strength amount, an entire capful was identified as the amount required for the laundry load, and participants indicated how much ultra-concentrated detergent they would use for this load; otherwise, participants indicated regular-strength quantity and the corresponding ultra-concentrated quantity they would use to wash this load. Ultra-concentration was operationalized by either indicating that the "ultra-concentrated detergent is two-times as strong as regular-strength detergent", or the packages were labeled as ultra-concentrated with no definition. The dependent variable was the percentage of over-/under-usage of ultra-concentrated product, relative to usage of the regular-strength product. For example, if a participant used one cup of regular-strength detergent and three-fourths of a cup of ultra-concentrated detergent for the same load, the over-consumption rate would be reflected as 25%; if a participant used exactly half the amount of the regular-strength when using the ultra-concentrated detergent, the over-usage rate would be 0%. Under-usage is reflected in a negative percentage.

In the result, we found that participants over-consume the ultra-concentrated product relative to the regular-strength version ($M=12.24\%$). Participants over-consume by more from a large ultra-concentrated package ($M=16.70\%$) than a small one ($M=7.94\%$); however, participants significantly overuse both the large bottle size *and* the small bottle size. Hence, a bottle size reduction slows consumption, but does not eliminate the effect.

When the regular-strength recommended usage quantity is one full cup, participants use 8.25% more than one-half cup using the ultra-concentrated version. When participants indicate *both* the amount they would use of the regular-strength and ultra-concentrated detergent, they overuse the ultra-concentrated detergent by 15.99%. That is, when given freedom to demonstrate their usage behavior of both regular and ultra-concentrated strengths, participants overuse by significantly more. Verbally defining ultra-concentrated as '2× as strong as regular-strength' should help consumers use one-half as much ultra-concentrated detergent, relative to regular-strength. However, there was no consumption difference when ultra-concentrated was defined versus not defined, although both over-usage rates were significantly greater than zero ($M=10.97\%$ and 13.45%, respectively).

Study 2 examined how trust influences consumption. It was a between-subjects experiment with 2 trust conditions (high trust, low trust), $N=386$. The trust factor manipulated the information source communicating "ultra-concentrated strength is two times as strong as regular-strength," *Consumer Reports* in the high trust condition and an advertisement in the low trust condition. The dependent variables were identical to study 1, plus measures of perceptions of regular and ultra-concentrated products.

In the result, participants significantly over-consumed the ultra-concentrated detergent in both the high ($M=9.7\%$) and low trust ($M=26.8\%$) conditions; and the directional difference in consumption rates ($p=.092$) indicates that consumers' trust in potency cues may influence their consumption. Participants trusted and believed *Consumer Reports* more than advertisements. Interestingly, even though participants perceived that potency levels of ultra-concentrated products are higher than regular-strength products; and that greater adverse effects are possible from using too much ultra-concentrated product relative to using too much regular product; consumers were not convinced that differences in effectiveness exist between ultra-concentrated and regular-strength products.

In these studies consumers persistently overused the more potent product. Understanding what factors drive wasteful consumption rates and what cues help consumers more accurately use products has marketing theory, practice, and public policy implications.

References

Tversky, Amos and Daniel Kahneman (1974), "Judgment under Uncertainty: Heuristics and Biases," *Science*, 185 (4157), 1124-31.

Wansink, Brian (1996), "Can Package Size Accelerate Usage Volume?" *Journal of Marketing*, 60 (3), 1–14.

What Makes Ideas Stick? How Characteristics and Contexts of Messages Influence Their Success

Rebecca Ratner, University of Maryland, USA
Jonah Berger, University of Pennsylvania, USA
Jason Riis, Harvard University, USA

SESSION OVERVIEW

Most approaches to persuasive communication focus on aspects of people. Certain individuals are more credible (e.g., experts; Petty et al. 1983) or influential (e.g., opinion leaders; Rogers 1995) and consequently are important to increase persuasion or help messages diffuse. Rather than focusing on people, however, a new stream of research has begun to examine how characteristics of ideas or messages themselves influence their staying power.

This session showcases some of this emerging research and illustrates how focusing on characteristics of ideas or messages themselves provides insight into what sticks and succeeds. For example, when consumers are initially exposed to an idea, what characteristics lead the idea to be perceived as compelling? Over time, which ideas are more memorable, and how do message and environmental characteristics determine people's ability to recall the messages? And what additional factors might one incorporate to revisit the question of source credibility, such as to examine how the timing of source information impacts stickiness of information? Four papers and a discussant address these ideas.

Alter and Oppenheimer (Paper #1) investigate which ideas seem most compelling on initial exposure. How does the fluency of stock names and ticker codes influence their performance? Results of several lab and archival studies demonstrate the surprising impact of fluent stock names and ticker codes.

Ratner and Riis (Paper #2) investigate how message characteristics impact stickiness after a delay. They show that the relatively simple USDA MyPyramid guideline is not simple enough, and that an even simpler guideline is much easier to remember, is more motivating, and leads to better food choices a full month after a brief exposure. Such a sticky guideline could improve many of the myriad poor choices that contribute to an individual's obesity.

When are certain urban legends more prevalent and how can we use these findings to get people to eat more fruits and vegetables? Berger (Paper #3) examines how the prevalence of related stimuli in the environment influences stickiness and success. Four studies demonstrate that products are more likely to be chosen and messages are more likely to be successful when their habitats, or set of related environmental triggers, are more prevalent and lead the messages to be remembered.

Finally, Birk, Johar, and Sengupta (Paper #4) consider how the timing of source credibility information influences stickiness. They find that the impact of source credibility is particularly pronounced when source information is provided after the message. Bad news attributed to a low-credibility source is less sticky when provided after the message. Results suggest that the stickiness therefore can depend critically on the timing of source information.

Chip Heath (Stanford University), the discussant, will integrate the talks, provide his own insights, and suggest directions for future research. Taken together, this symposium addresses how message characteristics influence staying power, and how the environment can enhance or undermine the success of the message. The papers contribute to a research area that is relevant to the diverse interests of many ACR members, including those interested in what makes ideas catch on, attitudes, persuasion, decision making, memory, health behavior, and attitude-behavior consistency.

EXTENDED ABSTRACTS

"Easy on the Mind, Easy on the Wallet: Fluency Predicts Stock and Currency Valuation"

Adam Alter, Princeton University, USA
Daniel Oppenheimer, Princeton University, USA

Why do some items seem more valuable than others? Although people routinely assess the value of stimuli in the environment, the processes that underlie valuation estimates are not well understood. Across six studies, we found that processing fluency—the subjective experience of ease with which people process information—influenced valuation estimates for monetary currency and financial stocks.

We first examined the effects of fluency on currency valuation. In three studies, participants estimated how many of each of ten inexpensive items (e.g., thumbtacks, gumballs) they could purchase with one of two monetary instruments that shared the same nominal value, but differed according to their familiarity (and, therefore, the ease with which they were processed).

In Study 1, participants either estimated the purchasing power of a common (and therefore fluently processed) $1 bill or a rare (and therefore disfluently processed) $1 Susan B. Anthony coin, one of which was depicted at the top of the questionnaire. Participants presented with the $1 bill believed they could purchase significantly more of the ten items than those who were presented with the rare $1 coin. Supporting our proposed mechanism, participants' familiarity with the rare coin was positively correlated with their estimates of its purchasing power.

We were concerned that participants may have perceived less value in coins than bills, so participants in Study 2 estimated the purchasing power of two common (fluently processed) $1 bills or a rare (disfluently processed) $2 bill. As in Study 1, participants believed the two $1 bills had significantly greater purchasing power than the rare $2 bill. Again, participants who were more familiar with the $2 bill assumed that it had greater purchasing power.

One concern with Study 2 was that participants may have overvalued the two $1 notes merely because there were two notes compared with the single note in the disfluent condition. Accordingly, in Study 3 participants estimated the purchasing power of a common $1 bill or a subtly altered $1 bill that differed from the original in several barely noticeable respects. We were also concerned that disfluency might generally attenuate valuation estimates, so we included a third condition with a real $1 bill in which the 10 items were printed in a difficult-to-read (disfluent) font. We expected participants to perceive the items as less valuable, thereby assuming the $1 bill had greater purchasing power relative to participants in the other conditions. As in Studies 1 and 2, participants believed the real $1 bill had greater purchasing power than the fake $1 bill, despite failing to recognize that it was in fact fabricated. Furthermore, participants believed the real $1 bill had greater purchasing power when the items were printed in a disfluent font. This result suggests that stimuli are valued according to how fluent they are specifically, and that disfluency does not generally depress the tendency to consume or perceive value in the environment at large.

Having shown that fluency influenced perceptions of purchasing power, we sought to show that fluently perceived purchasable commodities—in this case, financial stocks—seem more valuable than their disfluently perceived counterparts. In Study 4, undergraduates predicted how stocks with fluent (e.g., Barnings) and disfluent (e.g., Xagibdan) names would perform over six months. Participants anticipated appreciation in the stocks with simple names, and depreciation in the stocks with complex names.

Although Study 4 demonstrated a causal link between fluency and valuation, we were concerned that investors might ignore fluency when faced with many other cues. Accordingly, in Studies 5 and 6 we investigated the performance of real stocks shortly after they entered the New York Stock Exchange (NYSE) and American Exchange (AMEX).

In Study 5, undergraduates rated how easily they could pronounce the names of 89 companies that entered the NYSE between 1990 and 2004. We then compared these ratings to each stock's performance, and found that more fluently named stocks performed more strongly during their first week in the market.

The fluent names in Study 5 may have conveyed different semantic information from the disfluent names, so in Study 6, we examined whether 660 stocks with pronounceable ticker codes (e.g., LAM) outperformed stocks with unpronounceable ticker codes (e.g., HLY) in the NYSE and AMEX. Again, stocks with pronounceable ticker codes outperformed those with unpronounceable ticker codes over the first day of trading.

In sum, students and investors valued fluently processed currency and financial stocks more highly than their disfluently processed counterparts. These findings suggest that marketers benefit from creating simple, straightforward, and "sticky" products and advertising campaigns.

"What Good is A Guideline That People Can't Remember?: The Benefits of Extreme Simplicity"

Rebecca Ratner, University of Maryland, USA
Jason Riis, Harvard University, USA

Marketers provide consumer guidelines for many purposes, including product care and consumer well-being. Many such guidelines do not require stickiness, because written documents can be consulted when needed. Some guidelines, however, are needed so frequently that stickiness should be a high priority. Dietary guidelines are one example, as people make numerous food choices each day. The Department of Agriculture's (2005) customized MyPyramid nutrition guideline was designed to be simple enough to change consumer behavior. Its colorful display provides a visualization of the recommended daily consumption from each of 5 food groups. However, even this relative simplicity may be insufficient to make MyPyramid stick. With obesity levels rising, there is little evidence that consumers are following the guideline. Given the urgency of the obesity epidemic, the stickiness of nutritional guidelines needs to be better understood. We report several studies suggesting that only extremely simple guidelines have much chance of motivating consumers to adopt a more healthful diet.

Previous research has linked complex information and complex choice sets (Iyengar and Lepper 2000) with inferior decision making. Here, we suggest that even modest complexity in a guideline hampers both a consumer's ability to remember it and motivation to follow it. In one study, participants were presented either with a simple guideline (to eat fruits and vegetables as half of their food intake) or the more complex guideline from the USDA's interactive MyPyramid website. Immediately after the self-paced exposure to one of the guidelines, participants rated their interest in adhering to the guideline, the ease of remembering the guideline,

and the scientific rigor of the guideline. One month later, participants completed a food selection task and then were tested for recall of the guideline.

At Time 1, respondents reported greater motivation to adhere to the simpler guideline than to MyPyramid. Motivation to adhere to the guideline was predicted significantly by how accurately they thought they would be able to remember it (and only marginally by their perceptions of the guideline's scientific rigor). Most importantly, these same participants showed significant behavioral effects of the guideline manipulation after a delay of one month: participants in the simpler guideline condition selected significantly more fruits and vegetables than did the MyPyramid participants. Recall measures indicated that a majority who had been in the simpler guideline condition correctly recalled their guideline after one month, whereas less than one percent in the MyPyramid condition was able to recall all five recommended numbers after one month. These results are particularly noteworthy given that the MyPyramid participants spent an average of almost 30 seconds studying the guideline, compared to under 10 seconds for participants in the simpler guideline condition.

The results suggest that the compliance benefits of very simple consumer guidelines can be substantial. Consumers are more motivated to follow such guidelines, and they find them much easier to remember, although they believe these are based less on scientific research. We show that even a brief exposure to such a guideline has positive effects on dietary choices after a month-long delay. Future studies should include more extensive tests of diet change, and additional manipulations of guideline exposure. But given that obesity results from thousands of poor food choices over many years, it is encouraging that substantial improvements in the stickiness of dietary guidelines may eliminate some of those poor choices.

"Cultural Habitats: How Fit with the Environment Influences the Stickiness of Products and the Success of Ideas"

Jonah Berger, University of Pennsylvania, USA

Why do some products and ideas succeed and spread contagiously while others fail? Though researchers have often focused on how aspects of individuals (e.g., how "influential" they are, Katz and Lazarsfeld 1955), or social network structure (e.g., Watts and Dodds 2007) influences whether cultural items spread, much less research has looked at how aspects of these cultural items themselves (e.g., characteristics of products and ideas) influence their success.

We argue that fit with, or frequency of cueing by, the surrounding environment has an important influence on success. Product recall is important to purchase (Nedungadi 1990), but for something to be recalled it must first be cued by the environment, and little work has examined how the *distribution* of cues in the environment might influence success. We suggest that products or ideas have a habitat, or set of environmental triggers that encourage people to recall, transmit, and act on them. Just as certain regions or areas contain the food and conditions particular plants and animals need to survive, products and ideas have triggers that prime people to be more likely to think about and act on them. These triggers can be self-generated, or encountered in the environment, and can be any sort of stimuli (e.g., newspaper articles, conversation topics, or stimuli encountered while walking down the street) that activate or prime the related product or idea (Anderson 1995).

Importantly, cue prevalence varies across different environmental contexts. People encounter the color green more around St. Patrick's Day and more articles about politics in election years. We argue that the success of products and ideas will vary with the prevalence of such related cues. Specifically, we suggest that products and ideas will be more likely to stick in memory and succeed more broadly if they are cued more frequently by the environment.

Study 1 examined whether people would eat more fruits and vegetables if a slogan reminding them to do so was linked to a prevalent environmental cue. Participants recorded what they ate every day over two weeks. Half-way through the period, as part of an ostensibly unrelated study, they were repeatedly exposed to a slogan about fruit and vegetable consumption. Importantly, students' real-world environments varied: some ate in dining halls that used trays while others did not. Building on this difference, some students received a slogan which linked fruit and vegetable consumption to this cue. Others received a control slogan which was liked more in a pre-test but not cued by the environment. Results indicated that increased cueing by the environment led to greater fruit and vegetable consumption. Compared to the control conditions (same environment, different slogan and different environment, same slogan) participants whose environments cued them to think of the slogan ate 25% more fruits and vegetables.

Study 2 investigated how habitat prevalence influences the success of catchphrases. Participants had dyadic conversations regarding pre-selected topics. They were also given a long list of catchphrases and asked to use some of them in their conversations. Pretesting generated topics that provided more frequent cues for certain catchphrases (e.g., fuzzy math) as opposed to others (e.g., lockbox). Results indicated that particular catchphrases were more likely to be used in conversations which provided more frequent cues.

The next two studies examined whether habitat prevalence would predict success in the broader cultural environment. In the late 1990s, an email circulated suggesting that Microsoft needed people to forward a particular message to test their new email tracing program. If the message reached 1000 people, everyone who forwarded it would get $1000. We tracked the prevalence of this rumor over time using a searchable newsgroup database (Study 3). To proxy for habitat prevalence, we recorded the number of Top 50 newspaper articles that mentioned Bill Gates over that same period. An OLS regression found that habitat prevalence predicted rumor success; the rumor appeared more frequently in times when there was greater public attention to related cues (i.e, Bill Gates). Study 4 found similar results examining the success of a political factoid (about the school problems of the 1940s vs. the 1980s). The factoid appeared more frequently in times when there were more frequent cues to related issues in the public discourse.

This research demonstrates that the prevalence of related cues influences stickiness and success. While people often focus on making messages read more persuasively, these findings illustrate the importance of linking public health campaigns and other initiatives to prevalent environmental cue. Attending to the structure of the environment can increase success.

"When Bad News Sticks: The Effect of Valence and the Timing of Source Credibility on Attitude Strength"

Matthias Birk, Humboldt-University of Berlin, Germany
Gita Johar, Columbia University, USA
Jaideep Sengupta, Hong Kong University of Science & Technology, China

What makes bad news stick? When will they hurt consumers' brand attitudes and shake their confidence in their evaluations? Consumers are frequently confronted with negative brand information without a clear understanding of how trustworthy the information really is. With the rise of consumer self reports on the Internet, source credibility often remains ambiguous or it becomes clear only after reading the information. In our context, "stickiness" refers to how the negative information affects the strength of the attitude, so that it can continue to have an impact in the future (e.g., the link to behavioral intentions). We propose that negative information can have either a strengthening or weakening effect on brand attitudes depending on two critical factors: a) the credibility of the source providing the information; and b) whether the recipient is made aware of source credibility before or after processing the negative information.

Prior research has shown that early knowledge that a message source is highly credible lowers message elaboration, as recipients accept the new information without much processing (Priester et al. 1999). Based on Grice's work on conversational maxims (see Grice, 1975) we predict that when relevant (i.e. either credible or non-credible) source information is provided *after* negative brand information, this will alert consumers to feel that they should have paid greater heed to the brand information. This will cause them to carefully re-think the information that they have just processed. In contrast, when irrelevant or ambiguous source information is given *after*, this should not lead to heightened elaboration. When the source is credible, such heightened elaboration should lead to increased attitude ambivalence, thus producing an overall weakening effect (cf. Sengupta and Johar 2002). A different prediction obtains, when the source of information is viewed as non-credible. In this case, once again, being made aware of the source's lack of credibility *after* exposure to the negative brand information should cause consumers to carefully rethink this information–however, the low source credibility should cause the elaboration to primarily take the form of counter-argumentation. Such counterarguing should lead to the strengthening of the original attitude, in line with recent findings in the arena of attitude resistance (see Tormala and Petty 2002). When source information is ambiguous neither a weakening nor a strengthening effect should be obtained.

Experiment 1 tested these hypotheses by first providing participants with initial positive brand information about a DVD-Player, followed by negative brand information under four conditions: negative information from a credible source vs. an ambiguous source and whether the source was known prior to or after processing the negative information. The two critical dependent variables were: a) the extent to which the negative information was elaborated; and b) the accessibility of the final brand attitude. In line with our prediction, given a credible source, elaboration was heightened when the credibility of the source was revealed after exposure to the negative information (vs. before); further, this heightened elaboration led to the hypothesized lowering of attitude accessibility. For the ambiguous source, however, no differences in elaboration or accessibility were obtained for the source-before vs. source-after conditions.

Experiment 2 provided participants with a credible source vs. a non-credible source, varying time of source information as in experiment 1. Additional strength-related dependent variables were included. Results from this study supported both the predicted strengthening and weakening effects. Replicating Experiment 1, results for the credible source conditions revealed a weakening effect: making participants aware of source credibility after (vs. before) exposure to the negative brand information led to increased elaboration, increased attitude ambivalence, lowered accessibility and a lowered correspondence between attitudes and behavior. On the other hand, results for the non-credible source supported a strengthening effect: the source-after (vs. source-before) condition led to heightened elaboration, no difference in ambivalence, higher attitude accessibility and a stronger attitude-intention link.

Our results suggest that consumers re-access and elaborate on information when they are subsequently told that the source of the information was either extremely credible or extremely non-credible, not however when subsequent source information is ambiguous. As a result, bad news is most sticky when presented by a high-credibility source *after* the information is initially processed, and by a low-credibility source *before* the information is processed. A third experiment, now in progress, tests the elaboration mechanism presumed to underlie the findings by manipulating the ability to process information. The results have interesting implications on how and when bad news should be presented for maximal impact.

REFERENCES

Anderson, John R. (1995). *Cognitive Psychology and its Implications* , W.H. Freeman, New York .

Katz, Elihu, and Paul F. Lazarsfeld (1955), *Personal influence: The part played by people in the flow of mass communication* . Glencoe , IL : Free Press.

Grice, Herbert P. (1975), "Logic and conversation," in *Syntax and Semantics,* ed. Peter Cole and Jerry L. Morgan, New York: Academic Press. 41-58.

Iyengar, Sheena S., & Mark R. Lepper (2000), When choice is demotivating: Can one desire too much of a good thing? *Journal of Personality and Social Psychology, 79,* 995-1006.

Nedungadi, Prakash (1990), "Recall and Consumer Consideration Sets: Influencing Choice Without Altering Brand Evaluations," Journal of Consumer Research, 17 (December), 263–76.

Priester,Joseph, Duane Wegner, Richard Petty, Leandre Fabrigar (1999), "Examining the Psychological Process Underlying the Sleeper Effect: The Elaboration Likelihood Explanation," *Media Psychology*, 1, 27 48.

Sengupta, Jaideep, and Gita V. Johar (2002), "Effects of Inconsistent Attribute Information on the Predictive Value of Product Attitudes: Toward a Resolution of Opposing Perspectives," Journal of Consumer Research, 29(June), 39-56.

Tormala, Z.L., and Richard E. Petty (2002), What doesn't kill me makes me stronger: The effects of resisting persuasion on attitude certainty. *Journal of Personality and Social Psychology*, 83(6), 1298-1313.

Watts , Duncan J. and Peter S. Dodds (2007), "Influentials, Networks, and Public Opinion Formation," *Journal of Consumer Research*, 34, 441-458.

Goals Shared with Others: How to Increase Motivation Toward Social Goals

Minjung Koo, University of Chicago, USA

SESSION OVERVIEW

The majority of goal research has focused on consumers' personal goals, such as losing weights or saving money. However, consumers often strive toward group or social goals, defined as goals that are achieved by a group of individuals working together toward a common cause. For example, consumers in a focus group meeting work together to generate opinions on a product, people make pledges to a charity organization to meet the campaign goal, and family members join forces to complete a common task. Classic research finds that whenever a group of individuals work on a collective rather than individual task, they often exhibit less effort, typically labeled social loafing or free riding (Karau and Williams 1993; Kidwell and Bennett 1993; Ringelmann 1913). Accordingly, the focus of this symposium is on understanding the motivation to contribute to a social goal and how to reduce social loafing. Across several lines of research, we further wish to identify how marketers, managers, and other social agents can motivate people to contribute to their social goals.

Three papers explore the motivation to pursue goals shared with others. The first two papers examine what motivates individuals to contribute to a shared social goal. The third paper explores how people respond to goal conflicts between social goals and their own personal goals.

In the first paper, Koo et al. examine what factors best motivate individuals to work toward group goals. These authors find that individuals who are not highly identified with members of a group are most affected by information on other group members' contribution to date, because this information suggests that a group's goal is valuable. In contrast, individuals who are already highly identified with members of a group are most affected by information on required contributions to complete the goal, because this information emphasizes the need to progress to complete the goal. For example, the information on accumulated donations to date (vs. remaining donations to go) increased participants' contributions, when the victims were presented as out-group ("they"; low identification) versus in-group ("we"; high identification).

In a second paper, Ratner et al. investigate how to motivate individuals toward a social goal in the context of charitable giving. They find that advocates for a cause (e.g., individuals making a fundraising request on behalf of an organization such as American Cancer Society) are more effective if they have a personal connection to a victim of that cause (e.g., they lost a family member to cancer) than if they do not have a personal connection. That is, having a relationship with a victim renders one a more effective advocate for the cause thus increases contributions, because such an advocate exerts powerful social influence on potential donors.

The third paper, by Fitzsimons, addresses the problem of goal conflict. With limited time and energy, people are often faced with a conflict between personal goals (e.g., career pursuit, academics) and social goals (e.g., relationship with family members). This paper investigates how people respond to conflicts between social and personal goals when making choices about their future actions. It finds that perceived goal conflict increases both commitment and ambivalence towards the more chronically important goal. For example, participants who chronically valued relationships more than academics reinforced their commitment to relationship goals in the face of conflict; however, they also showed increased negative affect and frustration about their relationship goals. The pattern was mirrored for participants who chronically valued academics more than relationships.

Taken together, the three papers provide an overview of how people pursue goals shared with others, which have important theoretical as well as practical implications for goal research. Data collection in all papers is complete and the session includes a total of 9 studies. All participants have agreed to present should the session be accepted. Each presentation will be for 20 minutes, which will allow 15 minutes for discussion by Dilip Soman (the discussion leader) and Q&A at the end of the session.

We expect that this session will be of interest to a broad audience of consumer researchers but of special interest to those researchers interested in issues regarding goals, motivation and social influences. The area of goals is one that has generated considerable interest over the past several years, and we hope that our presentation of recent findings on how people pursue group goals will result in active debate and generate ideas for future research.

EXTENDED ABSTRACTS

"Group Goals and Sources of Motivation: When Others Don't Get the Job Done, I (Might) Pick Up the Slack"

Minjung Koo, University of Chicago, USA
Ayelet Fishbach, University of Chicago, USA
Marlone Henderson, University of Chicago, USA

Many goals that people strive to attain qualify as group goals, which are defined as goals that a collection of individuals works together to achieve (Zander 1980). Examples include goals such as engaging in social movements, pledging to charity, volunteering for community outreach programs, generating ideas in team meetings, and accomplishing chores with housemates. Interestingly, despite the benefits group goals produce, individuals do not always work efficiently or effectively in collective settings. While much inefficiency of groups can be explained by incongruence in values and demographic differences amongst members (Jehn, Chadwick and Thatcher 1997), group productivity or performance also tends to suffer because of motivational deficits that occur when a goal is shared with others (e.g., social loafing, Ringelmann 1913, and free riding, Kerr and Bruun 1983). Acknowledging this general tendency to underperform, the present work addresses the different sources of motivation to contribute to group goal striving.

The theory and research on the dynamics of self-regulation (Fishbach and Dhar 2005; Koo and Fishbach 2008) attest that people ask themselves one out of two questions when deciding to invest in a personal goal: is the goal valuable? Or, is the pace of pursuing the (already valuable) goal adequate? For example, students can decide to study for an exam because they believe it is important to master that topic of knowledge or, alternatively, because they think they have not made enough progress. We propose that the sources of motivation described above not only apply to personal goals but to group goals as well. Group members may wish to assess whether a group goal is valuable, in which case they seek social proof for goal value in others' contributions (Cialdini 1993). Under such circumstances, prior contributions by others would increase one's own contribution through a dynamic of highlighting other group members' actions. Group members may also wish to assess whether a goal has progressed to a sufficient level, in which case they infer need for progress on the basis of others' inadequate efforts. In such situations, people would compensate for or balance out the actions of others with their own contributions.

What, then, determines people's concern with whether others are pursuing a valuable goal versus pursuing a goal sufficiently? We propose that the level of identification with other group members determines whether one's source of motivation is the perceived value of the goal versus need for progress by group members. Individuals identify highly with others that they categorize as part of themselves, but identify less so with others that they deem as separate from themselves (Tajfel and Turner 1986; Turner 1987). In turn, high group identifiers feel more committed to their group and experience the positive and negative outcomes of their group as their own, whereas low group identifiers wish to evaluate the importance of the group to their identity (Ellemers, Spears and Doosje 1997; McCauley 2001).

We predict low group identifiers are posited to ask whether a group's goal is valuable. Therefore, an emphasis on prior effort expenditures by other group members that signal high goal value should increase their own efforts. High group identifiers, on the other hand, are already committed to their group's goal, and, consequently, are posited to focus on need for progress. Therefore, emphasizing lack of effort by others rather than prior effort expenditures should increase their own efforts more.

Three studies tested these predictions. Study 1 examined the contribution of ideas to a focus group. To assess each individual's contribution, participants work individually but assume their input will be collapsed with other group members (Jackson and Williams 1985). The group goal was to generate ten promotion ideas for a new cellular phone (iPhone). We manipulated identification by describing other team members as affiliated with an out-group (rival universities; low identification) or salient in-group (same university; high identification). We manipulated the framing of progress information (presumably, 50%) by informing participants that other group members had contributed about half of the ideas to date, or that half the ideas were missing to meet the goal. As expected, we found that the focus on to-date (vs. to-go) contributions increased idea generation for low identifiers but decreased idea generation for high identifiers.

Study 2 and 3 extended these findings in the context of a charitable fundraising. We predict that the level of identification with a victimized group influences the source of motivation for people's actions toward the group, particularly their responses to solicitations when information about to-date versus to-go contributions is made salient. Specifically, Study 2 assessed Americans' willingness to help the victims of Southern California wildfires after fall 2007. We manipulated identification with the victimized group by describing them as members of an out-group ("they, the residents of Southern California") or in-group ("we, Americans"). We further provided information on money raised to date or money still required to achieve the campaign goal. As predicted, we found that emphasizing donations to date (vs. to go) increased willingness to donate for out-group members, but decreased willingness to donate for in-group members. Study 3 was a large-scale field experiment (with Compassion International), which assessed actual contributions. Following Kenya riots in December 2007, we created a campaign that established a special crisis fund to support affected children. In the solicitation letter, we manipulated identification with the victims (they vs. we) and the focus on accumulated versus remaining donations. Consistent with

Study 2, we found that group identification determined the relative impact of focus on accumulated versus remaining contributions.

Taken together, the current article provides important lessons with respect to how to increase contributions to a group goal. First, it suggests that situational factors such as background of group members or semantic framing (they vs. we) can push people to increase or decrease their group identification. Second, it suggests that boosting group identification does not necessarily guarantee greater contribution to a group goal but one should employ appropriate strategies that correspond to the sources of motivation (value vs. need for progress) as determined by the group identification. Such strategies will be successful at increasing contributions and can reduce the robust social loafing and free riding.

"How Can You Say "No"? Deference Granted to Advocates Who Are Victims"

Rebecca Ratner, University of Maryland, USA
Min Zhao, University of Toronto, Canada
Dale Miller, Stanford University, USA

What factors impact whether consumers will donate their money and time to others? Organizations like the American Cancer Society rely on individual donations, and understanding the factors that impact individual donation behavior is of interest to a growing number of consumer researchers. Recent findings suggest several factors that impact the degree to which individuals feel sympathetic toward victims of causes and their likelihood to engage in actions to support the cause. For example, an identifiable victim produces greater sympathy and donation compared with an unidentifiable victim (Small and Loewenstein 2003), and friendship with a victim leads to greater sympathy towards other victims of the same misfortune (Small and Simonsohn 2008). Related work indicates that people feel more sympathy toward a single victim than toward many victims who suffer the same fate (Slovic 2007).

In the present research, we explore the role that social influence can play in impacting people's willingness to engage in donation behaviors. Specifically, we test the hypothesis that being a victim gives one psychological standing to have one's requests honored, even when a victim is not more effective at changing people's attitudes toward the cause for which they are advocating. In these studies, we look both at those who were directly impacted by a cause (e.g., the person suffered physical harm) or indirectly via a close relationship to the immediate victim (e.g., the parent of a child who died due to an unsafe product).

Our first study tests people's lay theory and demonstrates that people expect an advocate who is a victim to be more knowledgeable, persuasive and sympathetic than a non-victim. Further, we find that people have a lay belief that victims are more effective spokespeople than non-victims because of the greater persuasion that the former engender about the importance of the cause.

Our subsequent studies investigate whether the social influence produced by the victims comes about because they are more persuasive, or whether they simply elicit more compliance. One study employed a 2 (illness that caused suffering for the advocate: heart attack vs. cancer) X 2 (organization: American Heart Association vs. American Cancer Society) between-subjects design. Results indicated that people find it harder to say no to another person who asks them to attend a meeting when the cause of the meeting is the same as the cause of the advocate's suffering. Respondents felt significantly more disrespectful saying no when the advocate's parent had cancer and the organization was the American Cancer Society than the American Heart Association and significantly more disrespectful saying no when the parent had a heart attack and the organization was the American Heart Association than the American Cancer Society. Information about the advocate did not change people's perception of the importance of the cause.

Another study provides further evidence that people find it hard to say no to a victim because of perceived standing, rather than because of attitude change. In this study, people find it harder to say "no" to help a victim who provides weak arguments in support of the cause than a non-victim who provides strong arguments in support of the cause.

A final study provides additional evidence that the greater deference provided to appeals made by those who have suffered personally is due to compliance rather than persuasion. This study presented the respondents with a question of how much they will donate (i.e., WTP) to a Cancer Society after learning of a charitable appeal by someone who identified their status as a victim (i.e., that their parent had cancer) versus non-victim of the target disease (i.e., the had a heart attack). Half of the respondents were asked to indicate an amount between $0 and $10 whereas the other half of the respondents were asked to indicate a donation amount that is either $0 or $10 to the Cancer Society. We found that when respondents could choose any amount between $0 and $10, the number of people donating $10 did not differ significantly as a function of whether the advocate had suffered because of cancer. However, when asked whether they would donate $0 vs. $10 to the cause, significantly more participants who read about the appeal from the individual whose parent died of cancer (rather than heart disease) opted to make the $10 donation. Therefore, when the advocate indicated a connection to the cause as a victim, it increased donors' willingness to give something rather than nothing. People did not want to refuse to help the person who identified their victimhood because they otherwise felt guilty.

Together, these results suggest that being a direct or an indirect victim not only makes a person more sympathetic to a cause (Small & Simonsohn in press) but also makes the person him or herself a more effective advocate for the cause because others find it hard to reject their requests. Although we find that people endorse a lay belief that the effectiveness of a victim is driven by attitude change, our results suggest that the effectiveness is driven by their psychological standing to make requests. An advocate's status as a victim makes it hard to say no them, as long as the request relates to the issue about which the victim suffered. As a result, a consumer's own willingness and motivation to engage in donation behavior can be strongly influenced by the social context in which the donation request unfolds.

References

Slovic, Paul. (2007) "If I Look at the Mass, I Will Not Act: Psychic Numbing and Genocide," *Judgment and Decision Making*, 2, 79-95.

Small, Deborah A., & George Loewenstein. (2003). "Helping *a* Victim or Helping *the* Victim: Altruism and Identifiability," *Journal of Risk and Uncertainty*, 26, 5–16.

Small, Deborah A., & Uri Simonsohn. (in press). "Friends of Victims: Personal Experience and Prosocial Behavior," *Journal of Consumer Research*.

"Effects of Personal vs. Interpersonal Goal Conflicts on Goal Commitment and Goal-based Choice"

Grainne Fitzsimons, University of Waterloo, Canada

With limited time and energy, people are often faced with conflicts between important goals. For many people, a primary goal conflict is between personal goals (goals to improve one's health or to advance one's career) and interpersonal goals (goals to maintain or improve the quality of relationships with friends, family members, and romantic partners.) For example, an individual may feel torn about whether to work late (advancing career goals) or return home early to spend time with her family (advancing social goals.) In a series of experiments, we investigated how people respond to goal conflicts when making choices about their future actions and preferences, testing the hypothesis that perceived goal conflict would increase commitment to the more chronically important goal, but would also cause increased ambivalence and negativity about the chosen goal.

In the first study, we set out to test the basic hypothesis. Participants completed pre-measures of the importance of their academic achievement and romantic relationship goals. In the experimental session, participants read an article apparently from a popular magazine reviewing research that either (a) showed that relationships and academics were a zero-sum game in that most people struggled to successfully pursue goals in both domains, or (b) showed that relationships and academics were not a zero-sum game in that most people could easily successfully pursue goals in both domains. Participants then evaluated their commitment and affect towards their relationship and academic goals. As predicted, participants who chronically valued relationships more than academics reinforced their commitment to relationship goals in the face of conflict; however, as predicted, they also showed increased negative affect and frustration about their relationship goals. The pattern was mirrored for participants who chronically valued academics more than relationships.

In the second study, we set out to manipulate the importance of the goal, and to examine the consequences of personal-interpersonal goal conflicts for choice. Participants (all undergraduate females) completed pre-measures of the importance of their dieting/fitness goals and their friendship/social life goals. In the experimental session, the importance of the fitness goal was temporarily manipulated via a goal salience manipulation, in which participants were led to feel they were doing well or poorly on this goal. The manipulation was taken from Fishbach & Dhar (2005): Participants are asked to mark the divergence of their ideal from current weight on a scale. In the low goal salience condition, the scale ranged only a small amount, leading participants to perceive a large discrepancy between their current and ideal weights. In the high goal salience condition, the scale ranged a large amount, leading participants to perceive a smaller discrepancy between their current and ideal weights. Participants then read an article modified from a recent popular fitness magazine reviewing research that either (a) suggested that friendships often interfere with achieving dieting goals, or that (b) friendships do not interfere with dieting goals. Participants evaluated their commitment and affect towards their social and dieting goals, evaluated dieting-consistent (e.g., organic energy bars and fruit) and inconsistent products (e.g., candy and chocolate bars) that served as rewards for experimental participation, filled out ballots to enter in a draw for dieting-consistent gift baskets (i.e., filled with healthy foods, gift certificates for local gyms and fitness clothing stores, and subscriptions for fitness magazines) and neutral gift baskets (i.e., filled with gift certificates for local clothing stores and movie theaters, and subscriptions for entertainment magazines), and chose a reward (fruit or candy). As predicted, participants in the high dieting goal salience condition, for whom the dieting goal was temporarily of increased importance, responded to perceived goal conflict by enhancing their commitment to the dieting goal as shown in their self-reported ratings and their choices. They were likelier to fill out ballots to win dieting-consistent gift baskets and to choose a dieting-consistent reward. However, as predicted, the increase in commitment was again accompanied by an increase in negative affect towards the dieting goal in self-report ratings of the goal and goal-consistent products. Participants in the high dieting goal salience condition responded to perceptions of conflict by choosing goal-consistent products, but by providing more ambivalent ratings of the goal-consistent products.

In these two studies, participants responded to perceptions of goal conflict by increasing commitment to the focal or chronically important goal, as evidenced in their self-reports and their goal-consistent product choices. However, the perceived goal conflict produced an additional cost: Participants also felt more negatively and ambivalently towards the goals and the goal-consistent products. Thus, in everyday life, when people face these common personal vs. interpersonal goal conflicts, there are important consequences for goal commitment and goal-based choice.

Going Green and Seeing Green: Social Routes to Conservation and Monetary Roadblocks to Consideration

Eugene M. Caruso, University of Chicago, USA

SYMPOSIA OVERVIEW

In consumer contexts, purchase decisions that benefit the individual (e.g., buying a sports car) can often impose costs on others (e.g., damaging pollution of the environment). In this session, four papers explore the factors that facilitate or inhibit consumers' motivation to consider others in their beliefs and behaviors—including behaviors that have a direct impact on the welfare of society as a whole. The first two papers offer novel strategies for promoting environmentally friendly ("green") consumption, and the final two papers pinpoint a pervasive roadblock to such prosocial behavior. By providing both theoretical and practical contributions, this symposium raises new questions about the effects of status, social norms, and money on consumer behavior specifically and social interaction more generally.

In the first paper, Griskevicius, Tybur, and Van den Bergh investigate the role of status-attainment goals in consumption. Drawing on evolutionary theories of altruism and status, this research shows that activating status motives can actually increase the tendency of people to choose green products over superior non-green products. Goldstein, Griskevicius, and Cialdini examine the role that certain reference groups play in motivating hotel guests to conserve environmental resources, showing how such consumers give greater consideration to the normative behaviors of reference groups whose immediate surroundings most closely match their own.

In contrast to such prosocial behavior, the remaining two papers examine how a factor inherent to consumption activities–money–can serve as a barrier to the consideration of others' needs and perspectives. Because money can remind people how they can achieve their own goals without the input or influence of others, it can reduce their dependency on others and their desire for social connectedness. Mead and Baumeister show that individuals who are primed with money are less driven by self-presentation concerns and are less well liked by an interaction partner. Unlike priming status goals, priming money seems to reduce the motivation to make a good impression on others in the service of forging interpersonal bonds. Caruso, Mead, and Vohs examine the underlying mechanism for the asocial effects of money. This research finds that the mere presence of money leads people to behave in a more self-centered (egocentric) manner, which makes them less likely to take the perspective of others and less likely to help a stranger (unless they were financially dependent on that stranger). As such, money may hinder people's ability to understand social norms, anticipate others' reactions to their behavior, or be sensitive to the needs of other people–all of which may prevent them from pursuing behaviors that benefit not only the welfare of others but of society as a whole.

Taken together, the papers in this symposium offer some specific strategies for promoting prosocial behavior and some important barriers that can prevent it. Considering that the bulk of the consumer literature has tended to focus on the factors that incline consumers toward self-focused consumption rather than other-oriented consumption and conservation (Mick 2006), we think that this symposium will be part of the movement to address this imbalance. We feel that a deeper understanding of the goals that are active in various consumer contexts can further our efforts to increase the motivation and execution of actions that embrace, rather than eschew, the concerns of others.

This symposium should be of interest to researchers in the areas of persuasion, motivation, social influence, prosocial behavior, decision-making, and consumer cognition. Because the papers in this symposium utilize multiple and diverse methodologies, it should also appeal to those who value the combination of field and laboratory experiments. The speakers will integrate the presentations by highlighting their contribution to the consumer behavior literature and their implications for marketing research and practice. Each speaker has agreed to serve if the proposal is accepted, and all papers have data from several experiments and are in advanced stages of completion.

EXTENDED ABSTRACTS

"Conspicuous Conservation: Promoting Green Consumption through Status Competition"

Vladas Griskevicius, University of Minnesota, USA
Joshua M. Tybur, University of New Mexico, USA
Bram Van den Bergh, Catholic University Leuven, Belgium

How can we motivate consumers to go green? Traditional approaches suggest providing people with information (about the plight of the environment) or with incentives (to switch to green products). Although both techniques can certainly spur conservation, such approaches largely ignore the social nature of—and the social motivation behind—conservation.

Consider what a person communicates about himself by going green. By purchasing a hybrid car rather than a gas-guzzler, for example, a person can signal to others that he is a relatively altruistic, rather than a selfish, individual. That is, instead of purchasing an environmentally wasteful product that will benefit only him, he chose a product that will benefit others by helping the environment, even though choosing the green product often means foregoing the luxury of having a more powerful engine and ample trunk space.

Engaging in prosocial behaviors such as green consumption can earn people a prosocial reputation (Semmann, Krambeck, and Milinski 2005). Individuals with such reputations are seen as more trustworthy (Barclay 2004) and more desirable as friends, allies, and leaders (Cottrell, Neuberg, and Li 2007). Considering that prosocial individuals are highly valued, prosocial actions are directly associated with status. Indeed, self-sacrifice for the benefit of the group has been shown to increase a person's status in the group (Hardy and Van Vugt 2006).

An altruistic reputation can be so valuable that individuals across modern and traditional societies (and even across species) are known to compete for status by trying to be seen as more altruistic—an evolutionary theory called *competitive altruism* (Van Vugt et al. 2007). Given the relationship between prosocial behavior and status, the theory of competitive altruism suggests that people should engage in prosocial actions particularly when they are motivated to compete for status. Thus, because green products enable a person to signal that he is cooperative and prosocial, activating a motive for status should lead people to prefer green over non-green products.

The current research examined how activating a status motive influenced product choice. Consider one choice facing a person in a bustling car show room: Should he buy the relatively luxurious, higher-performance, but energy-wasteful car, or the less luxurious, lower-performance, but energy-efficient Hybrid car. If he is motivated to gain status at the time of the decision, a traditional perspective suggests that he should choose the more luxurious option (e.g., Godoy et al. 2007). After all, this car has better performance, comfort, and indulgence. But the theory of competitive altruism suggests that status should lead him to choose the green product because there is an important public cost to choosing the more luxurious non-Hybrid car: Such a choice may signal to others that the owner is selfish and doesn't care about the welfare of others.

The first experiment examined how status motives influenced product choices between three types of green products (e.g., Toyota Camry HYBRID) and a more luxurious non-green counterpart product (e.g., Toyota Camry XL V-6). Findings showed that although the more luxurious products were generally more preferred (in the control condition), activating status motives significantly increased people's tendency to choose the green product.

According to competitive altruism theory, a key factor in how status motives should influence product choices is whether the act of purchasing can publicly signal the buyer's prosocial or selfish nature. The second experiment thus examined how status motives influenced choices when purchases were made in public versus in private (e.g., shopping alone at home on the Internet). Consistent with traditional perspectives, when shopping in private, status motives led people to prefer the more luxurious products. However, in line with competitive altruism, when shopping in public, status motives led people to choose the green (rather than luxurious) products. The third experiment examined how the relative price of the green vs. non-green products influenced their desirability. Results showed that status motives led green products to be particularly desirable when such products cost more than their non-green counterparts.

In summary, although status has been traditionally associated with luxury and "status goods," this research shows that activating status motives can lead people to forego such products. Instead, consistent with the theory of competitive altruism, status motives can lead people to choose non-luxurious and poorer-performing green products because such products can signal a prosocial rather than the selfish nature of the person. This research has both theoretical contributions and practical implications for consumer behavior.

"Limitations of Global Norms on Global Conservation: Using Provincial Norms to Motivate Pro-Environmental Behavior"

Noah J. Goldstein, University of California, Los Angeles, USA
Vladas Griskevicius, University of Minnesota, USA
Robert B. Cialdini, Arizona State University, USA

Recently, many consumer researchers have noted that very little research has been conducted on the factors that influence consumers' prosocial behaviors, and even less on pro-environmental behaviors (Menon and Menon 1997; Mick 2006; Robin and Reidenbach 1987; see also Bendapudi, Singh, and Bendapudi 1996). We sought to better understand such actions in several domains, including the domain of hotel towel reuse. With the adoption of environmental programs by hotels, more and more travelers are finding themselves urged via signs to reuse their towels to help conserve environmental resources by saving energy and reducing the amount of detergent-related pollutants released into

the environment. Guests are almost invariably informed that reusing one's towels will conserve natural resources and help save the environment from further depletion, disruption, and corruption. Notable in its complete absence from these surveyed persuasive appeals was one based on a potentially powerful motivator of prosocial behavior: descriptive social norms.

When consumers learn that seven out of ten people choose one brand of automobile over another or that teeth-whitening toothpaste has become more popular than its less functional counterpart, they are getting information about descriptive social norms, which refer to how most people behave in a given situation. Descriptive norms motivate both private and public action by informing individuals of what is likely to be effective or adaptive behavior in that situation (Cialdini, Kallgren, and Reno 1991).

The complete absence of a descriptive normative approach to hotel conservation programs is especially remarkable considering that studies conducted by the largest manufacturer of hotel towel reuse signs indicate that approximately 75% of guests who have the opportunity to participate in such programs do reuse their towels at least once during their stay. From a practical perspective, then, one purpose of this research was to investigate whether utilizing an appeal that conveys the descriptive norm for participation in such programs would be more effective at encouraging towel reuse than the current industry standard appeal. We tested this hypothesis in Experiment 1 by creating our own towel reuse cards and recording the extent to which each of the two appeals spurred guests to participate in a hotel's conservation program. Consistent with predictions, we found that the sign employing the descriptive norm approach produced significantly greater towel reuse than one employing the standard environmental approach.

A second purpose of the present investigation was to examine how hotel guests' conformity to a descriptive norm varies as a function of the type of reference group tied to that norm. In Experiment 2, we examined whether the norm of hotel guests' immediate surroundings, which we refer to as the *provincial norm*, motivates conformity to the norm to a greater extent than the norm of guests' less immediate surroundings, which we refer to as the *global norm*. Specifically, we investigated whether guests who learn the descriptive norm for their particular room (provincial norm) are more likely to participate in the program than guests who learn the same descriptive norm for the whole hotel (global norm), even though the provincial norm in this context is rationally no better an indicator of correct or proper behavior than the global norm. Consistent with predictions, the sign employing the provincial norm led to the greatest amount of towel reuse, even though individuals considered this group to be comparatively much less meaningful to their personal identities than to other reference groups used for other descriptive normative appeals in Experiment 2.

The more powerful influence of provincial norms was conceptually replicated in Experiment 3. In that experiment, participants went to a large on-campus computer center, where they learned the (pro-environmental) norms for either the entire computer center (global norm) or simply for the people who had previously sat at their particular computer (provincial norm). Consistent with the field data, those who learned the provincial norm were more likely to engage in pro-environmental behavior than were those who learned the global norm. Several other experiments in the computer center setting help reveal potential mechanisms for the effect. Theoretical and pragmatic implications of this work are discussed.

"Money Reduces Self-Presentation and Interpersonal Likability in Novel Social Situations"

Nicole L. Mead, Florida State University, USA
Roy F. Baumeister, Florida State University, USA

Because humans have a fundamental need to belong, they often try to put their best face forward when meeting new people in an attempt to be perceived as likable (Baumeister 1998). In fact, self-presentation is vital for success in life. Many desirable outcomes, such as making friends, success in one's occupation, and maintaining healthy relationships, are influenced by the ability to manage one's impression according to situational demands (e.g., Schlenker 1980).

However, people are not always successful at getting their desired impression across to others. Because self-presentation is a conscious and effortful process, people are not always willing or capable of exerting the resources that self-presentation requires (Vohs, Baumeister, and Ciarocco 2005). The current research examined how money influences self-presentation and interpersonal likability. It was expected that, because money reduces people's desire for social connectedness (Vohs, Mead, and Goode 2006), nonconscious reminders of money would reduce self-presentation strategies and interpersonal likability.

Experiment 1 tested the hypothesis that reminders of money would reduce concern with creating a desirable impression on a new interaction partner. After completing filler questionnaires in front of a money or a fish screensaver, participants were told they would engage in a 5 min conversation with another participant. The experimenter explained that, because it can be difficult for people to have a conversation with a stranger, both participants would record an introductory video that would be viewed by the partner before the interaction. Self-presentation was measured by having a group of independent raters code how hard participants were trying to create a good impression in their video. Consistent with our hypotheses, results indicated that money-primed participants tried less hard than neutral-primed participants to create a good impression on their partner.

In Experiment 2, we tested the hypothesis that money would reduce interpersonal likability by having two previously unacquainted participants engage in a semi-structured conversation for 5 min. In each pair, one participant was assigned to be the target of the interaction (the person who rated for interpersonal likability) and the other the rater. Participants, naïve to experimental condition, were put in separate rooms and completed a jumbled phrase task. Half of the targets descrambled phrases containing money-related words whereas the other half of targets descrambled sentences containing only neutral words. Raters always performed the neutral version of the descramble task. After a 5 min interaction, raters were asked to indicate how likable, competent, and friendly the target was during the interaction. Both the target and the rater were asked to indicate how much they cared about the impression they made on their partner during the interaction. Results indicated that, compared to participants who descrambled neutral-phrases, participants who unscrambled money phrases were rated as less likable. Moreover, money-primed participants were seen as less friendly during the interaction, which mediated the effect of the money-prime on reduced likability. Money-primed participants also cared less than about the impression they made on their partner than neutral-primed participants. Additional analyses indicated that results were not attributable to mood or differences in perceived competency.

Results of two experiments suggest that money reduces the likelihood that people will self-present to a new acquaintance. Although this could have positive implications for the self, such as ability to stand up for one's rights, it may have negative implications for others, such as reduced prosocial behavior.

"There's No "You" in Money: Thinking of Money Increases Egocentrism"

Eugene M. Caruso, University of Chicago, USA
Nicole L. Mead, Florida State University, USA
Kathleen D. Vohs, University of Minnesota, USA

The psychological effects of money long have been suspected, and now are beginning to be revealed in experimental research. Particularly in consumer contexts, money is a potent incentive because it enables consumers to obtain the goods and services necessary to achieve their personal needs (Lea and Webley 2006). Because money tends to engender a self-sufficient state of heighten personal goal pursuit and reduced dependency on others (Vohs, Mead, and Goode 2008), reminders of money may harm interpersonal sensitivity by increasing attention to the self and away from others.

Theoretically, money's ability to reduce social sensitivity can be understood as resulting from the exchanged-based rules that govern the use of money in consumer contexts–rules that are diametrically opposed to the forces that promote communal behaviors (Fiske 1991). Empirically, participants reminded of money tend to offer less help to others, request less help from others, and put more physical distance between themselves and others relative to those not reminded of money (Vohs, Mead, and Goode 2006). In the current research, we explored whether money has the effect on basic human cognition of increasing egocentrism–the fundamental tendency to interpret the world in terms of the self.

Because money heightens personal goal pursuit (Vohs et al. 2006), and because active goals direct cognitive resources (Bargh et al. 2001), reminders of money may focus the mind on the self. Given finite cognitive resources, increased focus on the self means reduced focus on other aspects of social life, including other people. In addition, egocentric correction is a costly controlled process that is less likely to be activated when people are insufficiently motivated (Epley et al. 2004). Because money stimulates self-sufficient behavior, it may well reduce attempts to understand others' perspectives. In four studies, we tested the hypothesis that reminders of money may reduce people's willingness to correct their own egocentric perspective.

In Study 1, we asked participants to draw a symbol on their foreheads (Hass 1984). We manipulated the salience of money by having some participants draw a dollar sign ($) and others draw the letter *S*. A greater percentage of participants drew the symbol egocentrically (as though the writer would read it herself) when drawing the symbol $ than when drawing the symbol *S*, suggesting that they were less likely to spontaneously adopt another's visual perspective.

In Study 2, we activated the concept of money for some participants but not others before they read some social information (facts about another student) and some nonsocial information (a list of nonsense words). On a subsequent surprise memory test, those reminded of money made more errors when recalling information about the other student but not the nonsense words, suggesting that money's effects on information processing may be specific to social information.

To test whether money reduces the tendency to adjust one's egocentric beliefs, Study 3 asked participants to rate both how much they personally, and how much other people, agree with various statements about abortion (Ross, Greene, and House 1977). Participants who were subtly reminded of money through a faint background image on the computer showed greater egocentric projection of their own beliefs and their predictions of another's beliefs.

Finally, Study 4 tested whether a financial incentive for accuracy would overcome the effects of money primes on egocentric behavior. Because a financial incentive provides direct benefits to the self and may allow consumers to fulfill their own goals and needs more effectively, we predicted that money-primed participants would be more inclined to work for a financial incentive than a social one. In a maze task that required participants to give directions to help a blindfolded participant navigate a series of paths, the financial incentive (but not the social one) reduced the number of egocentric errors made by participants primed with money.

Money has become an integral part of consumer societies, as people desire to accumulate the goods, services, and (presumed) happiness that it affords. When a consumer has enough resources to be self-sufficient and meet her own goals, she has little need to interact, trade, or negotiate with other consumers or sellers in a marketplace. Furthermore, moving beyond one's egocentric perspective may be a necessary step in promoting prosocial behavior, such as empathizing with those in need or donating to charitable causes (e.g., Batson 1994). We feel that a deeper understanding of the effects of money on human cognition and behavior in general–and on the egocentric tendencies it appears to engender in particular–should help both consumers and marketers develop strategies that enable the perspective taking necessary to facilitate efficient exchanges and promote choices that benefit both the individual decision makers and the societies to which they belong.

REFERENCES

Barclay, Pat (2004), "Trustworthiness and Competitive Altruism Can Also Solve the 'Tragedy of the Commons,'" *Evolution and Human Behavior*, 25, 209–20.

Bargh, John A., Peter M. Gollwitzer, Annette Lee-Chai, Kimberly Barndollar, and Roman Troetschel (2001), "The Automated Will: Nonconscious Activation and Pursuit of Behavioral Goals," *Journal of Personality and Social Psychology*, 81, 1014-27.

Batson, C. Daniel (1994), "Prosocial Motivation: Why Do We Help Others?" In *Advanced Social Psychology*, ed. A. Tesser, Boston: McGraw-Hill, 333-81.

Baumeister, Roy F. (1998), "The Interface Between Intrapsychic and Interpersonal Processes: Cognition, Emotion, and Self as Adaptations to Other People," in *Attribution and Social Interaction: The Legacy of Edward E. Jones*, ed. John M. Darley and Joel Cooper, Washington, DC: American Psychological Association, 201–23.

Bendapudi, Neeli, Surendra N. Singh, and Venkat Bendapudi (1996). "Enhancing Helping Behavior: An Integrative Framework for Promotion Planning," *Journal of Marketing*, 60, 33-49.

Cialdini, Robert B., Carl A. Kallgren, and Raymond R. Reno (1991), "A Focus Theory of Normative Conduct: A Theoretical Refinement and Reevaluation of the Role of Norms in Human Behavior," in *Advances in Experimental Social Psychology*, Vol. 24, ed. Leonard Berkowitz, San Diego, CA: Academic Press, 201-34.

Cottrell, Catherine A., Steven L. Neuberg, and Norman P. Li (2007), "What Do People Desire in Others? A Sociofunctional Perspective on the Importance of Different Valued Characteristics," *Journal of Personality and Social Psychology*, 92, 208-31.

Hardy, Charlie L. and Mark Van Vugt (2006), "Nice Guys Finish First: The Competitive Altruism Hypothesis," *Personality and Social Psychology Bulletin*, 32, 1402-13.

Epley, Nicholas, Boaz Keysar, Leaf Van Boven, and Thomas Gilovich (2004), "Perspective Taking as Egocentric Anchoring and Adjustment," *Journal of Personality and Social Psychology*, 87, 327-39.

Fiske, Alan P. (1991), *Structures of Social Life: The Four Elementary Forms of Human Relations*, New York: Free Press.

Godoy, Ricardo A., Victoria Reyes-García, William R. Leonard, Tomas Huanca, Thomas McDade, Vincent Vadez, and Susan Tanner (2007), "Signaling By Consumption in a Native Amazonian Society," *Evolution and Human Behavior*, 28, 124-34.

Hass, R. Glen (1984), "Perspective Taking and Self-Awareness: Drawing an E on Your Forehead," *Journal of Personality and Social Psychology*, 46, 788–98.

Lea, Stephen E. G. and Paul Webley (2006), "Money as Tool, Money as Drug: The Biological Psychology of a Strong Incentive," *Behavioral and Brain Sciences*, 29, 161-209.

Menon, Ajay and Anil Menon (1997), "Enviropreneurial Marketing Strategy: The Emergence of Corporate Environmentalism as Market Strategy," *Journal of Marketing*, 61, 51-67.

Mick, David G. (2006), "Meaning and Mattering Through Transformative Consumer Research," in *Advances in Consumer Research*, Vol. 33, ed. Cornelia Pechmann and Linda L. Price, Provo, UT: Association for Consumer Research, 297-300.

Robin, Donald P. and Eric Reidenbach (1987), "Social Responsibility, Ethics, and Marketing Strategy: Closing the Gap between Concept and Application," *Journal of Marketing*, 51, 44-58.

Ross, Lee, David Greene, and Pamela House (1977), "The 'False Consensus Effect': An Egocentric Bias in Social Perception and Attribution Processes," *Journal of Experimental Social Psychology*, 13, 279-301.

Schlenker, Barry R. (1980), *Impression Management: The Self-Concept, Social Identity, and Interpersonal Relations*. Monterey, CA: Brooks/Cole.

Semmann, Dirk, Hans-Jurgen Krambeck, and Manfred Milinski (2005), "Reputation is Valuable Within and Outside One's Social Group," *Behavioral Ecology and Sociobiology*, 57, 611–16.

Van Vugt, Mark, Gilbert Roberts, and Charlie Hardy (2007), "Competitive Altruism: Development of Reputation-Based Cooperation in Groups," In The Oxford Handbook of Evolutionary Psychology, *ed.* Robin Dunbar and Louise Barrett, Oxford: Oxford University Press, 531-40.

Vohs, Kathleen D., Roy F. Baumeister, and Natalie J. Ciarocco (2005), "Self-Regulation and Self-Presentation: Regulatory Resource Depletion Impairs Impression Management and Effortful Self-Presentation Depletes Regulatory Resources," *Journal of Personality and Social Psychology*, 88, 632-57.

Vohs, Kathleen D., Nicole L. Mead, and Miranda R. Goode (2006), "The Psychological Consequences of Money," *Science*, 314, 1154-56.

Vohs, Kathleen D., Nicole L. Mead, and Miranda R. Goode (2008), "Merely Activating the Concept of Money Changes Personal and Interpersonal Behavior," *Current Directions in Psychological Science*, 17, 208-12.

When Consumer Behavior Meets Islam

Elizabeth Hirschman, Rutgers University, USA

SESSION OVERVIEW

This special session will offer an initial look at consumption behavior in one of the most under-studied cultural domains–the Islamic world. As the process of globalization intensifies, the need for knowledge about the consumption behavior of other cultures has become imperative. However, though the cross-cultural literature generally recognizes the importance of studies in this area, in most cases it focuses on Western and Asian countries. The research on consumer behavior in the Islamic culture in general and, in Islamic countries in particular, is scarce.

Thus, this special session will attempt to provide consumer behavior scholars with the opportunity to acquire a unique insight into various aspects of consumption in the Islamic world. Hopefully, this session will stimulate an exchange of ideas and promote collaboration among researchers revolving around the issue of consumption behavior in different cultures, which ultimately will contribute to the development of the consumer behavior field.

The *likely audience* will include researchers interested in studying cross-cultural aspects of consumer behavior.

The three papers in this special session revolve around the concept of consumers' acculturation, spanning a wide range of issues. The *first paper* explores the meaning of home, space and personal possessions for women and men in Qatar. Using an ethnographic approach, the study finds that, as in Western culture, homes and possessions are expressions of self and family. However, the meaning of home spaces and possessions differs from their interpretation in the West. Middle Eastern cultures generally have a more restricted sense of what is totally private, making a sharper distinction between men's and women's spaces and between public and private spaces. The study also examines favorite possessions within Arab Muslim households in Qatar, seeking those characteristics that are unique and common to Middle Eastern and Western cultures.

The *second paper* examines the meaning of Christmas from the minority point of view of Tunisian Christians. Relying on in-depth interviews, its findings suggest considerable differences between the manner in which Christmas is constructed by Christians living in a Muslim setting vs. those who celebrate it in North America. Expatriates often import holiday food and decorations from their homelands and overstuff their homes with external representations of Christmas in an attempt to create a Christian haven for themselves that resembles the celebration of the holiday in a mythologized childhood in their countries of origin. While they may integrate certain iconic and sensory elements of Islamic traditions into their celebration of Christmas, the holiday creates a cross-cultural bond among Christians that, temporarily at least, distances them from their Muslim friends.

The *third paper* reports on a four-year ethnographic study in Turkey about the discourse between Islam and consumption. Its results contradict the common Western perception that Islam is opposed to capitalism and consumerism. On the contrary, Islam is deeply embedded in a consumerist and capitalist ethos. As in Western culture, Islamic consumers take pleasure in the consumption experience and adopt global brands. Islamist companies compete in the international market and utilize modern tools of marketing. This paper concludes that the logic and ideology of capitalism and consumerism coexist with the logic and ideology of Islam, and

that Islamic consumers exhibit behaviors that are similar to those observed in the Western world.

Each of the following presenters has agreed to serve if the proposal will be accepted: Rana Sobh, Mourad Touzani and Özlem Sandıkcı.

Finally, our discussant will be Prof. Elizabeth Hirschman, a leading, internationally recognized scholar on cultural aspects of consumer behavior.

EXTENDED ABSTRACTS

"Consuming Gendered Space in Islam"
Rana Sobh, University of Qatar, Qatar
Russell Belk, York University, Canada

The idea of personal versus shared spaces within homes is relatively new. Tuan (1982) shows that it is only within the last few hundred years that notions of privacy and separate public and private spaces within the home have emerged. Notions of private space are also encoded architecturally (Sommer 1969). Intimacy within the nuclear family is a concept that has grown as extended families have diminished (Rybczynski 1986). There are also differences in the use and sense of ownership of various spaces within the home by individual family members. Different family members think of areas of the home as being their territories (Altman 1975). Even when a particular area like the bathroom must be shared it is common to temporarily claim private space for hygienic, purifying, and beautification rituals (Kira 1970). When these spaces are encroached upon by others, there is a sense of contagion or violation (Belk 1988). We formally or informally designate boundaries defining personal space, spaces for close kin, and spaces where friends, neighbors, and strangers can meet within the home (Allan 1989). Such concepts have been extensively studied in the West (e.g., Gallagher 2006; Marcus 1995; Munro and Madigan 1999), but little comparable work has been done in non-Western homes.

Compared to the West, Middle Eastern standards of privacy involve a more restricted sense of what is totally private (e.g., Kadivar 2003), due largely to the moral concerns of Islam. This results in a sharper distinction between public and private space, often with high exterior perimeter walls and inward facing courtyards (Waly 1992). Public and private spheres within Muslim cultures also differ from Western Paradigms (Tarvis, 1992). Within the home, women's public sphere for instance includes being in the company of non-mahrems (family members/those permanently ineligible for marriage to her). But outside the home women may paradoxically have a more private sphere restricted to Mahrems (Boulanouar, 2006). Furthermore, there is a sense of private space that a Muslim woman carries with her as she goes from home to marketplace (e.g., Asad 2003), facilitated by various forms of veiling.

Within Arab Muslim homes, there is also a sharper distinction between men's and women's spaces as well as transitional spaces in moving from one to another, as Farah and Klarqvist (2001) found in Sudan. The basis for such spatial gendering are cultural and do not seem to arise from prescriptions within Islam (Farah and Klarqvist, 2001), although there is some disagreement on this point (Nageeb 2004). While some contend that having a space of their own is extremely important to women's identities as well as their sense of social and economic status (Cooper 2001), others call such a space a "neo-harem" and find that it reduces women's sense of space and of control over their lives (Nageeb 2004).We discuss these contending perspectives based on our findings regarding gendered areas within and boundaries within Qatari homes.

Favorite possessions within the home are a part of our extended self (Belk 1988) and thus serve a key function in our self-definition and expression of cultural values. These possessions and the meanings ascribed to them vary with culture and gender. For instance, Wallendorf and Arnould (1988) found that Americans' favorite objects were more likely to be linked to personal memories, while those from Niger were more likely to mention objects linked to social status. They also found gender differences, with men in Niger more likely to cite the Quran and women more likely to cite silver jewelry as well as objects given to them by others. While some research in this vein has been conducted in other, largely non-Islamic parts of the world, we examine favorite possessions within Arab Muslim households in Qatar and attempt to identify local and regional specifics as well as what is unique and common in Middle Eastern and Western cultures relating to homes and meanings of possessions.

References

Allan, Graham (1989), "Insiders and Outsiders: Boundaries Around the Home," in Graham Allan and Graham Crow, eds., *Home and Family: Creating the Domestic Sphere*, Houndsmills, UK: Macmillan, 141-158.

Altman, Irwin (1975), *The Environment and Social Behavior: Privacy, Personal Space, Territory, Crowding*, Monterey, CA: Brooks/Cole.

Asad, Talad (2003), "Boundaries and Rights in Islamic Law: Introduction," *Social Research*, 70 (3), 683-386.

Belk, Russell W. (1988), "Possessions and the Extended Self," *Journal of Consumer Research*, 14 (September), 139-168.

Boulanour, Aisha W. (2006), " Dressing for Success: A background to Muslim women's clothing," *New Zealand Journal of Asian Studies*, 2 (December), 135-157.

Campo, J. E. (1991), *The Other Side of Paradise: Explorations into the Religious Meanings of Domestic Space in Islam*, Columbia, SC: University of South Carolina Press.

Cooper, Barbara M. (1997), "Gender, Movement, and History: Social and Spiritual Transformations in 20th Century Maradi, Niger," *Environment and Planning D: Society and Space*, 15 (April), 195-221.

Farah, Eman Abelrahman and Bjorn Klarqvest (2001), "Gender Zones in the Arab Muslin House," *Proceedings, 3rd International Space Syntax Symposium*, Atlanta, GA, 42.1-42.15.

Gallagher, Winifred (2006), *House Thinking: A Room-by-Room Look at How We Live*, New York: Harper Collins.

Kadivar, Mohsen (2003), "An Introduction to the Public and Private Debate in Islam," *Social Research*, 70 (Fall), 689-680.

Kira, Alexander (1970), "Privacy and the Bathroom," in Proshansky, et al., 269-275.

Marcus, Claire Cooper (1995), *The House as a Mirror of Self: Exploring the Deeper Meaning of Home*, Berkeley, CA: Conari.

Munro, Moira and Ruth Madigan (1999), "Negotiating Space in the Family Home," in Irene Cieraad, ed., *At Home: An Anthropology of Domestic Space*, Syracuse, NY: Syracuse University Press,107-117.

Nageeb, Salma Ahmed (2004), *New Spaces and Old Frontiers: Women, Social Space, and Islamization in Sudan*, Lanham, MD: Lexington Books.

Rybczynski, Witold (1986), *Home: A Short History of an Idea*, New York: Penguin.

Sommer, Robert (1969), *Personal Space: The Behavioral Basis of Design*, Englewood Cliffs, NJ: Prentice-Hall.

Tuan, Yi-Fu (1982), *Segmented Worlds and Self: Group Life and Individual Consciousness*, Minneapolis, MN: University of Minnesota Press.

Wallendorf, Melanie and Eric J. Arnould (1988), "'My Favorite Things': A Cross-Cultural Inquiry into Object Attachment, Possessiveness, and Social Linkage," *Journal of Consumer Research*, 14 (March), 531-547.

"Looking for Christmas in a Muslim Country"
Mourad Touzani, University of Tunis, Tunisia
Elizabeth Hirschman, Rutgers University, USA
Ayalla Ruvio, University of Haifa, Israel

Despite the fact that Christmas is celebrated by Christians around the world (e.g., Liebeson 2001; Wernecke 1979),virtually all the research on Christmas familiar to consumer researchers has been conducted in North America (e.g., Barnett 1954; Caplow 1984; Laroche, Saad, Kim and Browne 2000; Time-Life Books 1998; Schauffler 1907; Guttman 2007). Within this body of inquiry, themes of hedonism (Hirschman and LaBarbera 1989), materialism (Belk 1987), communalism (Caplow 1982), generosity (Pollay 1986), selfishness (Moschetti 1979), joy (Hirschman and LaBarbera 1989), and anxiety/resentment (Hirschman and LaBarbera 1989) have been identified. Further, the familiar secular Christmas iconography of snowy winter sleigh rides, strings of glittering green and red lights, Santa's reindeer and elves, Christmas trees, mistletoe and holly (despite their Celtic, pagan origins) have been examined from multiple vantage points. As have, of course, the sacred symbols including Mary and Joseph standing near Baby Jesus lying in a manger, while the shepherds, angels and wise men look on (e.g., Belk 1987; Kasser and Sheldon 2004). One reason for the distinctive pattern (and perhaps the narrowness, as well) of these findings is that they emanate from studies set in Christian-dominant cultures. In both the United States and Canada, Muslims, Jews, Hindus, Buddhists and Jains, Sikhs and Wiccans are but small minorities operating within a dominant Christian society.

Our purpose in the present study is to learn what happens when the tables are turned, that is, when Christians must celebrate their primary holiday within a non-Christian culture, especially one which is far removed topographically from the Currier and Ives settings associated with the North American Christmas. What happens when Christmas is re-located to North Africa, where Muslims are the majority religion and snow-covered ponds, horse-drawn sleighs and even chimneys are absent?

Tunisia, the site of our study, is positioned on the Mediterranean coast between Libya, Egypt and Algeria. It is hot, arid and sandy, features more palm, date and olive trees than evergreens, and contains a Christian community comprising less than 2% of the population, most of whom are European expatriates drawn from Italy, France, Spain and North America.

In-depth interviews conducted with these Tunisian Christians revealed a dramatically different meaning structure vis a vis that found in North America. Among the most notable differences are:

The necessity of importing holiday-appropriate foodstuffs and decorations from ethnic Christian homelands in Europe and North America, which are viewed as more authentic and nostalgia-inducing than those purchasable locally.

Casting oneself back to a mythologized childhood or ancestral setting in which Christmas is celebrated openly and widely.

A feeling of Christmas scarcity, sparseness and frugality within the surrounding society, contrary to the desired sense of abundance, grandiosity and frivolity found in Christian-dominant cultures. This external sparseness is compensated for by over-stuffing the interior of the home with food, decorations, music and other signifiers of the holiday, creating a Christian/Christmas refuge/haven.

A willingness to embrace iconic and sensory syncretism in which Islamic traditions, foods, songs and décor are blended with the traditional Christmas rituals.

The development of a sense of cross-Christian communality that binds together these minority religious affiliates, despite their disparate national origins in Africa, Arabia, Italy, France and North America. The result is a submerging of the racial, ethnic, and national boundaries that usually separate these Christian celebrants.

Concurrently, there is a tendency to temporarily distance oneself from Muslim friends and associates, in order to maintain a sense of sacred and social boundaries.

References

Barnett, James H. (1954), *The American Christmas: A Study in National Culture*, Salem, New Hampshire, Ayer Company

Belk, Russell W. (1987), A Child's Christmas in America: Santa Claus as Deity, Consumption as Religion", *Journal of American Culture*, Spring.

Caplow, Theodore,, (1982), "Christmas Gifts and Kin Networks", *American Sociological Review*, 47, June, 383–392.

Caplow, Theodore, (1984), "Rule Enforcement without Visible Means: Christmas Gift-Giving in Middletown", *American Journal of Sociology*, 1306–1323.

Gurman, Peter, (2007), *Christmas in America*, Denver, CO: Skyhorse

Hirschman, Elizabeth C. and Priscilla LaBarbera, (1989), "The Meaning of Christmas" in Elizabeth C. Hirschman (editor), *Interpretive Consumer Research*, Association for Consumer Research, Provo, Utah, 136–147.

Liebeson, Maureen, (2001), *Christmas in Greece*, Chicago, Ill, World Book.

Moschetti, Gregory J., (1979), "The Christmas Potlatch: A Refinement on the Sociological Interpretation of Gift Exchange", *Sociological Focus*, 12, 1, January, 1–7.

Pollay, Richard W. (1986), "It's the Thought that counts: A Case Study in Xmas Excess", in *Advances in Consumer Research*, Vol. 14, editors Melanie Wallendorf and Paul Anderson, Provo, Utah, Association for Consumer Research, 140 -143

Schauffler, Robert H. (1907), *Christmas: Its Origin, Celebration and Significance as Related in Prose and Verse*, New York: Dodd Mead & Comp.

Time-Life Books, (1998) *An Old Fashioned Country Christmas*, New York

Wernecke, Herbert H. (1979), *Christmas Around the World*, New York, W. L. Jenkins

"Islam and Consumption: Beyond Essentialism"

Ozlem Sandikci, Bilkent University, Turkey
Guliz Ger, Bilkent University, Turkey

The rise of Islam is generally seen as an opposition to capitalism and Western consumerism (Barber 1996; Bocock 1993; Ray 1993; Witkowski 1999). For instance, Turner argues that "consumerism offers or promises a range of possible lifestyles which compete with, and in many cases, contradict the uniform lifestyle demanded by Islamic fundamentalism" (1994, p.90). According to Turner the cultural, aesthetic and stylistic pluralism fostered by postmodernism and the spread of global system of consumption contradict with the fundamentalist commitment to a unified world organized around incontrovertibly true values and beliefs. While "the consumer market threatens to break out into a new stage of fragmented postmodernity in late capitalism," fundamentalism "acts as a brake on the historical development of world capitalism" (Turner 1994, p.80).

We argue that such essentialist readings mystify the relationship between Islam and consumption and willingly or unwillingly contribute to the discourse of the "clash of civilizations". Drawing upon a four-year long ethnographic project we have undertaken in Turkey we argue that Islam, at least in the context of urban Turkey, does not oppose consumption or offer an alternative to consumerism. Rather, Islamism is deeply embedded in a consumerist and capitalist ethos.

We find that the more ascetic and orthodox Islamists may restrict their consumption and refrain from purchasing products or brands that are perceived to be associated with the West: e.g., Coca Cola or McDonalds. However, most of the Islamists do not oppose consumption–they actively engage in consumption albeit in an Islamic way: for example, hanging a picture of Kaba rather than a figurative painting on the wall, or drinking juice rather than beer. The urban Turkish case demonstrates that consumption patterns can be and are appropriated into religiously acceptable styles without undermining consumption itself. This is perhaps even easier in the case of Islam for which hedonism is an accepted way to life and is less of a sin than Christianity. Islam permits the pursuit of desires as long as they are integrated with moral principles such as generosity, sharing, giving to the poor, and fairness, and one is not enslaved by passionate attachment (Belk, Ger and Askegaard 2000). Islam accepts that material things are important in life. However, it requires that acquisitiveness and competition are balanced by fair play and compassion. That is, material goods are to be distributed and wealth is to be shared among all in a just manner. Being honest, fulfilling commitments, seeking virtue, providing for dependents generously, and being socially conscious legitimize consumption.

We also find that Islamism is in alliance with capitalism. Since the 1980s, companies which identify themselves as Islamist businesses have emerged in Turkey. However, far from opposing capitalism, these companies utilize capitalist tools and compete with national and global brands both in Turkey and in foreign markets. The development of the Islamist companies coincided with the economic restructuring of the Turkish economy beginning in the mid 1980s. As the economy was privatized, liberalized, and globalized, both the manufacturingscape and the consumptionscape changed. In order to boost export revenues, the governments encouraged both the big, established companies as well as the entrepreneurs of conservative smaller towns to develop their businesses and form transnational connections. Backed with government incentives as well as international funding coming mainly from the Islamist organizations in Germany and Saudi Arabia, the small- to mid-size companies grew rapidly, creating an Islamist business sector that came to compete head on with the secular sector in almost every field. A wide variety of products and services positioned as "Islamic," ranging over summer resorts, financial institutions, clothing, food, newspapers, decorative objects, and shopping centers targeted the newly-emerging Islamist middle/upper classes.

In 1990, an association called MUSIAD (the Independent Industrialist and Businessmen Association) was founded to represent the interests of Islamist companies. MUSIAD supports market capitalism with an accentuated Islamic business ethics. It has close ties to the Islamist parties and strong transnational connections, including a very prominent presence in Germany. MUSIAD emphasizes the compatibility of Islam with capitalism and uses Islam as a basis for cooperation and solidarity among both local and international producers, and advocates a model of development sensitive to the cultural identities (Bugra 1998). Given that the prophet Mohammed himself was a merchant and Islam had always been wedded to commerce, the development of globally-oriented Islamist businesses suggest a "natural" course of economic progress.

We observe greater differences between social classes than between Islamists and Westernized seculars. Religious convictions seem to blend with cultural capital, taste, and related discourses of aesthetics all of which construct different lifestyles and consumption patterns along class lines. Religion provides yet another discourse, one among many others that shape and legitimize consumption practices. Religious or not, so long as consumers invent justifications for their consumption, they consume what they deem desirable and affordable.

Overall, we find that Islamism, as it is experienced in urban Turkey, does not oppose capitalism and the consumerist ethos. Islamist companies adopt and utilize the tools of modern marketing and forge international business connections. Similarly, consumers who identify with Islamism do not generally oppose consumption or global brands. On the contrary, they enjoy the fleeting pleasures of consumption. The logic of capitalist markets and the ideology of consumerism coexist with the logic and ideology of Islam, constructing consumption practices that negotiate daily tensions, just like in any other context.

References

Barber, Benjamin R. (1995) *Jihad vs. McWorld*, New York: Random House.

Belk, Russell W., Güliz Ger, and Søren Askegaard (2000) "The Missing Streetcar Named Desire," in: S. Ratneshwar, David Glen Mick, and Cynthia Huffman (eds.), *The Why of Consumption*, London: Routledge, 98-119.

Bocock, Robert (1993) *Consumption*, London: Routledge.

Buğra, Ayşe (1998), "Class, Culture, and State: An Analysis of Interest Representation by Two Turkish Business Associations," *International Journal of Middle East Studies*, 30, 521-539.

Ray, Larry (1993), *Rethinking Critical Theory*, London: Sage.

Turner, Brian (1994) *Orientalism, Postmodernism and Globalism*, London and New York: Routledge.

Witkowski, Terrence H. (1999) "Religiosity and Social Meaning in Wearing Islamic Dress," paper presented at the *7th Cross Cultural Research Conference*, Cancun, Mexico, 12-15.

Exclude or Include? Consideration Set Strategies and the Choice Process

Joseph K. Goodman, Washington University in St. Louis, USA

SESSION OVERVIEW

Decision making research shows that there are two ways to narrow down a set of options—an include and an exclude strategy—and that they can have systematic consequences on consideration set construction and choice (Heller, Levin, and Goransson 2002). Related research has also used the terms *accept, select, choose,* or *retain* versus *reject* or *eliminate* to refer to a choice between two (or three) options (e.g., Meloy and Russo 2004; Ordóñez et al. 1999; Shafir 1993). This session will bring these two research streams—which have predominately been investigated separately—together to find common ground and promising avenues for future research. Across the three papers we investigate a) what factors affect the use of include and exclude strategies (paper 2), b) how these strategies affect the weighting of attributes and the composition of consideration sets (papers 1 and 2), and c) how these strategies affect final choice and consumer satisfaction (papers 2 and 3).

The first paper, by Irwin and Naylor, investigates the influence of include and exclude strategies on attribute weighting, demonstrating that forming a consideration set by excluding (vs. including) alternatives results in greater weighting of ethical attributes. Interestingly, they also show that consumers judge others' behavior more negatively if they exclude ethical product alternatives. The second paper, by Goodman and Broniarczyk, proposes that, contrary to the findings of prior research, an exclude strategy may not be the default strategy when forming a consideration set. They provide evidence that consumers are more likely to use an include strategy as the assortment size increases and that this strategy choice can have subsequent effects on consideration set formation. They also provide evidence that the use of an include strategy can increase decision difficulty and regret in the final choice phase. The third paper, by Machin, focuses on including and excluding in the choice phase (termed *selecting* and *rejecting*) and finds that rejection can lead to greater satisfaction than selection. Five studies, using actual and imagined consumption experiences, identify two mediating processes and two moderators, and show that a rejection-(versus selection-) based decision strategy increases negative thoughts about foregone options.

This symposium provided a unique opportunity for researchers to broaden the traditional focus of the include/exclude and reject/select domains. The symposium format allowed researchers to explore alternative ways of understanding differences in decision strategies and how these strategies can affect consumer consideration set construction and choice and to discuss how to blend these two streams of research. In addition, the symposium was especially important because it addressed other current consumer issues: how consumers use and weight ethical attributes in choice, how consumers choose decision strategies, and consumer satisfaction. Researchers interested not only in judgment and decision making, but also in ethical attributes and choice, consideration set satisfaction, and satisfaction, were particularly attracted to this session. The papers presented and the insightful discussion provided by Lisa Bolton went beyond an exploration of the include/exclude phenomenon to create a lively discussion for fruitful avenues of future research.

EXTENDED ABSTRACTS

"Ethical Decisions and Response Mode Compatibility: Weighting of Ethical Attributes in Consideration Sets Formed by Excluding versus Including Product Alternatives"

Julie Irwin, The University of Texas at Austin, USA
Rebecca Naylor, University of South Carolina, USA

One of the most pervasive and puzzling inconsistencies in human behavior is the discrepancy between stated values and actual behavior. Psychologists have studied this attitude-behavior link across many contexts and have paid special attention to instances when people appear to be practicing "moral hypocrisy" (Batson et al. 1999) by not reflecting their supposed moral beliefs in their observed actions. For marketers, this puzzle takes a concrete form; it is surprising that products embodying commonly-held values do not perform better in the marketplace. Why, for instance, does furniture made from rainforest (vs. tree farm) wood continue to sell? Why have market forces not eliminated animal testing in the cosmetics industry? Why are corporations able to continue to mistreat workers, often with no obvious market reaction? Ehrich and Irwin (2005) showed that part of the problem is that consumers will not ask for ethical product information even though they would use it if it were available.

For some product categories, however, ethical attribute information is readily available. In those cases, why might there be a discrepancy between values and behavior? Along with the myriad of other possibilities, such as hypocrisy (Batson et al. 1999), there may be contextual elements of the decision that guide consumers toward (or away from) considering the ethical possibilities. In this set of four studies, we establish that "exclusion" versus "inclusion" (Heller et al. 2002) results in greater weighting of ethical attributes in consideration set formation, even though normatively which task is used should not have any systematic influence.

In our first two studies, we demonstrate that ethical attributes are weighted more in consideration sets formed using exclusion versus inclusion because the exclusion and inclusion tasks are differentially compatible (Fischer et al. 1999; Tversky, Sattath, and Slovic 1988) with ethical attributes. We argue that ethical attributes are weighted more in exclusion than in inclusion because the goal of exclusion tasks is to indicate which alternatives one does not want to further consider. Although, normatively, both modes make a statement about one's values, we argue that the expression of moral values feels more natural in exclusion than in inclusion: ethical issues are compatible with the goal of indicating what you do not want. Explicitly rejecting the "bad" items (the items unattractive on the ethical attribute) allows for an indication of adherence to the ethical principle. This explicit rejection seems to match the reaction people have to values that are protected (or at least strongly held); the typical response to a particularly egregious ethical violation is to reject everything about it (Lichtenstein, Gregory, and Irwin 2007). In our first two studies, we also test another proposition based on our compatibility argument; namely that there should be no difference in weighting for attributes without direct ethical implications. As predicted, we find no differences in the weighting of nonethical attributes such as price and performance across response mode.

Although we theorize that compatibility is driving our expected result, there are two alternate explanations for this finding, which we rule out in our studies. First, attribute framing could induce our results, making them redundant with past research (e.g., Shafir 1993). Ethical attributes often are expressed negatively (i.e., in terms of the number of exploited children, the amount of wasted environmental resources, etc.). To establish that it is the ethicality of these attributes, not their frame, driving our results, in Study 2 we demonstrate that manipulating the framing of the ethical attribute to be positive or negative does not affect the weighting of the ethical attribute across response modes. Second, differential weighting across the two modes might also be influenced by increased emotion in the exclusion mode that leads to avoidance of the ethical attribute. Loss modes, which may include exclusion contexts, induce negative emotion and concomitant coping strategies, such as avoidance (Luce et al. 2000). It is possible that the increased emotion of exclusion and/or adding an ethical attribute to the decision process causes participants to avoid making tradeoffs and to simply not act on the ethically attractive options, resulting in their being left in the consideration set. This possibility would be interesting, but not particularly new given the literature on loss and coping. The explanation we propose is not driven by how emotionally involved participants are with a given ethical issue but rather by differential compatibility between ethical attributes and response modes. To address this possible affect-based explanation, in our first two studies we provide statistical evidence that affect does not drive our effects.

In our third study, we provide direct evidence that consumers use the principle of compatibility when evaluating an ethical decision by demonstrating that consumers judge others' behavior more negatively if they exclude ethical products (as opposed to not including ethical products). Finally, in our fourth study, we demonstrate that ethical attributes are given greater weight in exclusion than in inclusion in a laboratory study involving real (vs. hypothetical) consideration set formation and an actual monetary decision.

Together, the results of these four studies suggest that consumer consideration of ethical products is driven not only by motivational issues such as hypocrisy and guilt, but also by simple cognitive issues such as how context guides the decision in one direction versus another. Our results therefore have important implications for the marketing of ethical products, both specifically (e.g., it is important to encourage exclusion modes) and generally (e.g., the failure to consider ethical products may reflect seemingly minor contextual issues guiding the decision process and not consumer disinterest in ethical issues).

"Screening from Large Assortments: The Use of Include and Exclude Strategies in Consideration Set Construction"

Joseph K. Goodman, Washington University in St. Louis, USA
Susan Broniarczyk, The University of Texas at Austin, USA

Decision making research shows that there are two ways to narrow down a set of options an include and an exclude strategy—and that they can have systematic consequences on consideration set construction and choice. The research has argued that an exclude strategy is the default strategy and is more likely to be used in consideration set construction (Ordóñez et al. 1999; Heller et al. 2002). Consideration set construction strategies, or screening strategies, are particularly important as assortment size and choice difficulty increase because a consideration set is more likely to be formed as the choice set size increases (Lussier and Olshavsky 1979). Thus, an important question is whether assortment size can lead consumers to use a different strategy to narrow down the set of options given that they use a consideration set. Could this influence what attributes and options are considered, and ultimately influence

decision difficulty and regret? If consumers faced with a large assortments are more likely to use an include strategy, then an include strategy may be the more common strategy overall.

Though little attention has been given to how assortment size may affect the decision strategy, there is evidence that strategy choice may affect the consideration set. Prior research shows that compared to an exclude strategy, an include strategy can decrease the size of the consideration set (Heller et al. 2002). There is evidence from the binary choice literature (Meloy and Russo 2004; Shafir 1993) that the use of include strategy will lead consumers to weight positive attributes more and negative attributes less (see also Irwin and Naylor in this symposium). Thus, we propose that consumers faced with larger assortment will be more likely to use an include strategy and that this strategy choice will lead consumers to have more positive thoughts and fewer negative thoughts when constructing consideration sets.

Across three studies we show how assortment affects the use of an include versus exclude strategy in consideration set construction and its consequences on consideration sets and final choice. In the first study we manipulate the size of the assortment by presenting participants with either a small assortment (6) or large assortment (30) of gourmet chocolates. Participants are instructed to either select an include strategy or an exclude strategy and narrow down the set of options to those that they "would actually consider buying" (adapted from Heller et al. 2002). They then respond to questions measuring decision difficulty and anticipated regret. The results show that contrary to previous research, an exclude strategy is not always the "default" strategy, and that participants are more likely to use an include (vs. exclude) consideration set strategy in large (65%) compared to small assortments (31%). The results also indicate that consideration sets are significantly smaller when participants choose an include compared to an exclude strategy, and this is especially true as the assortment size increases. Lastly, the study shows that consumer's experience heightened decision difficulty and anticipated regret when they use an include strategy in large assortments compared to an exclude strategy.

In the second study we test whether the use of an include strategy changes the thought process of consumers during consideration set formation. We collect written protocols during the consideration set formation process and have two independent judges code their thoughts. In addition, we use two product replicates to extend our results to a new category, backpacks, and we investigate an important moderator to strategy selection, maximization. Maximizers tend to seek out the best options in choice whereas satisficers simply seek acceptable options (Schwartz 2004); likewise, maximizers will likely seek the best strategy (i.e., switch to an include strategy) depending on the assortment. The results show that compared to satisficers, maximizers are especially likely to show a difference in strategy in large versus small assortments. In addition, we demonstrate that an include (vs. exclude) strategy leads consumers to focus more (less) on positive (negative) attributes, express more (fewer) positive (negative) thoughts in the consideration set construction process, compose smaller consideration sets, and focus more (less) of their thoughts on options (not) in the consideration set.

Since studies 1 and 2 allow participants to choose which strategy to use when forming their consideration set, it is possible that the results are due to self selection. Study 3 manipulates which strategy consumers use and finds consistent results with the previous studies.

This research suggest that an exclude strategy may be the "default" strategy in small assortments, but when consumers are faced with large assortments they are more likely to use an include strategy to form their consideration set. Marketers and consumers should be aware that not only will their strategy change as the size of the choice set increases, but that it can systematically influence the composition of final consideration set and final choice.

"Choosing by Selecting or Rejecting: How Decision Strategy Influences Consumer Satisfaction"

Jane Machin, Virginia Polytechnic Institute and State University, USA

Two moviegoers face a choice between caramel and buttered popcorn. One selects an alternative ("Mmm, caramel popcorn") while the other rejects an alternative ("Yuck, buttered popcorn"). Both eat the same popcorn. But who is more satisfied? Prior research suggests that selection and rejection are not complementary strategies and can have different and non-trivial effects on which options are chosen (e.g. Shafir 1993). There are occasions, however, when there will be no systematic difference in choice between selectors and rejecters — for example, choices among functionally equivalent options (Levin, Jasper, and Forbes 1998) or choices with a clearly superior option (Shafir 1993). This begs the question of whether decision strategy matters when there are no systematic differences in choice. There is currently little understanding of the down-stream, post-choice consequences of decision strategy. The present research addresses this gap focusing specifically on consumption satisfaction. Over four studies I provide evidence for the novel proposition that using a rejection-based decision strategy ("Yuck, buttered popcorn") can lead to greater consumption satisfaction compared to a selection-based decision strategy ("Mmm caramel popcorn").

Study 1 demonstrates that rejecters experience greater satisfaction compared to selectors when they have a relatively negative experience, such as eating stale popcorn. Differences in counterfactual thought direction (Roese 1993) mediate the relationship between decision strategy and satisfaction. Compared to selectors I find that rejecters generate more *downward focused* counterfactuals ("things could have been worse") when the experience is negative. I demonstrate in study 3 that this difference in counterfactual thought direction occurs because of a divergence in information focus during the decision process. A rejection-based decision strategy not only focuses attention on more negative information in general, but focuses attention specifically on negative aspects of the foregone alternative. When a rejecter later reflects upon what might have been, thoughts about how the outcome could have been worse are more easily generated because the initial decision focused on the negative aspects of that alternative outcome. Consistent with the principal of affective contrast (Markman et al. 1993) rejecters then recruit these thoughts to mitigate dissatisfaction with the negative experience. Satisfaction does not differ when the consumption experience is positive, since positive experiences do not prompt counterfactual thinking (Landman and Petty 2000). Evidence for mediated moderation is presented.

Using a multi-alternative (rather than binary) choice set and a new choice context, study 2 provides additional evidence that using a rejection-based decision strategy increases satisfaction after a negative consumption experience. Study 2 also introduces a second moderator: salience of the foregone alternative. In study 1, the foregone alternative was visible to all participants when they consumed the chosen item. Since salience of the foregone alternative is important in the ability to generate any counterfactual thoughts (van Dijk and Zeelenberg 2005), decision strategy should only influence satisfaction if the foregone alternative is salient at the time of consumption. As predicted, study 2 finds that, compared to a selection-based decision strategy, a rejection-based decision strategy generates more downward focused counterfactual thoughts, which mitigate satisfaction, only when participants are reminded of

the foregone alternative and the consumption experience is sufficiently negative.

Study 3 provides more direct evidence of the psychological processes that lead to the difference in counterfactual thought direction. Participants' thoughts while making their decision were coded for the number of positive, negative, and neutral thoughts about the chosen and foregone alternatives. Analysis reveals that rejecters have more negative thoughts about the foregone alternative compared to selectors (both in absolute terms and when compared to the number of positive thoughts). A multi-step mediated moderation process demonstrates that (1) thoughts during the decision process mediate the relationship between decision strategy and counterfactual direction and that (2) counterfactual direction mediates the relationship between decision thoughts and satisfaction. Combined, decision thoughts and counterfactual thought direction fully mediate the relationship between decision strategy and satisfaction.

Study 4 replicates the basic finding using participants' self-generated decision strategy, thus providing some real world validity. Participants who spontaneously use a rejection-based decision strategy to make their choice are more satisfied with their consumption experience compared to participants who spontaneously use a selection-based decision strategy, when the consumption experience is negative and the foregone alternative is salient. Counterfactual thought direction again mediates the relationship between decision strategy and satisfaction.

Together, these studies demonstrate that *how* a decision is reached has implications beyond the actual choice. Compared to a selection-based decision strategy, a rejection-based decision strategy leads to greater satisfaction when the consumption experience is negative and the foregone alternatives are salient. Thoughts at the time of the decision and counterfactual direction after the consumption process play mediating roles. The studies find either no difference in expectations and/or supportive results for a relative satisfaction measure that controls for initial expectations helping to rule this out as an alternative explanation. There are also no differences in perceived ease of strategy or perceived amount of choice.

Inasmuch as consumers may not be perfectly satisfied once a product is consumed, my research suggests that marketing managers may wish to encourage consumers to adopt a rejection-based decision strategy. Subsequent reminders of the foregone options would mitigate dissatisfaction and could prevent further downstream consequences, such as brand switching. From the consumer's perspective, my research suggests it would be better to use a rejection-based decision strategy whenever a negative consumption experience is possible.

REFERENCES

Batson, D.C., Thompson, E.R., Seuferling, G., Whitney, H., and Strongman, J.A. (1999), "Moral Hypocrisy: Appearing Moral to Oneself without Being So," *Journal of Personality and Social Psychology*, 77, 525-37.

Ehrich, K.R. and Irwin, J.R. (2005), "Willful Ignorance in the Request of Product Attribute Information," *Journal of Marketing Research*, 42, 266-77.

Fisher, G.W., Carmon, Z., Ariely, D., Zauberman, G. (1999), "Goal-based Construction of Preferences: Task Goals and the Prominence Effect," *Management Science*, 45, 1057-75.

Heller, D., Levin, I.P., and Goransson, M. (2002), "Selection of Strategies for Narrowing Choice Options: Antecedents and Consequences," *Organizational Behavior and Human Decision Processes*, 89, 1194-1213.

Landman, J. and Petty, R. (2000), ""It Could Have Been You": How States Exploit Counterfactual Thought to Market Lotteries," *Psychology & Marketing*, 17 (4), 299-321.

Levin, I.P., Jasper, J.D., and Forbes, W.S. (1998), "Choosing versus rejecting options at different stages of decision making," *Journal of Behavioral Decision Making*, 11 (3), 193-210.

Lichtenstein, S., Gregory, R. and Irwin, J.R. (2007), "What's Bad is Easy: Taboo Values, Affect, and Cognition," *Judgment and Decision Making*, 2, 169-188.

Luce, M.F., Payne, J.W., and Bettman, J.R. (2000), "Coping with Unfavorable Attribute Values in Choice," *Organizational Behavior and Human Decision Processes*, 81, 274-99.

Markman, K. D., Gavanski, I., Sherman, S. J., and McMullen, M. N. (1993), "The Mental Simulation of Better and Worse Possible Worlds," *Journal of Experimental Social Psychology*, 29 (1), 87-109.

Ordóñez, Lisa D. Lehman Benson, III, and Lee Roy Beach (1999), "Testing the Compatibility Test: How Instructions, Accountability, and Anticipated Regret Affect Prechoice Screening of Options," *Organizational Behavior and Human Decision Processes*, 78 (April), 63-80.

Roese, N. J. (1993), "The Structure of Counterfactual Thought," *Personality and Social Psychology Bulletin*, 19 (3), 312-19.

Schwartz, Barry (2004), *The Paradox of Choice*, New York: Harper Collins.

Shafir, E. (1993), "Choosing versus Rejecting: Why Some Options are Both Better and Worse Than Others," *Memory and Cognition*, 21 (July), 546-56.

Tversky, A., Sattath, S., and Slovic, P. (1988), "Contingent Weighting in Judgment and Choice," *Psychological Review*, 95, 371-84.

van Dijk, E. and Zeelenberg, M. (2005), "On the Psychology of 'If Only': Regret and the Comparison Between Factual and Counterfactual Outcomes," *Organizational Behavior And Human Decision Processes*, 97 (2), 152-60.

Exploring the Concept of Brand Embarrassment: The Experiences of Older Adolescents

Ian Grant, University of Strathlyde, UK

Gianfranco Walsh, University of Koblenz-Landau, Germany

ABSTRACT

Although consumer behavior researchers pay continuing attention to brands and their importance to consumers, not much is known about the negative emotional effects of brands. The authors extend prior research by introducing a new construct called 'brand embarrassment'. Brand embarrassment refers to anxiety and negative emotions evoked by brands in certain consumption contexts. A qualitative study with older adolescents in the United Kingdom finds that embarrassment is experienced in the private and public domains. Brand embarrassment is explained in terms of issues of the *personal-self* and *relationships with brands*. Overwhelmingly, the participants claim that they try to avoid possible brand embarrassment.

INTRODUCTION

Branding research is largely premised on the belief that consumers want brands as they form a shortcut in the minds of consumers when making a purchase decision, make a quality promise, package meaning, and define the consumer's sense of self (e.g., Aaker and Biel 1993; Chan et al. 2003). However, a perspective that is largely absent from the literature is that brands can evoke negative feelings in consumers. The position advanced in this research suggests that in certain consumption contexts, brands can cause embarrassment to consumers. Growing attention has been dedicated in recent years to deepening our understanding of the emotion of embarrassment in consumption contexts. It has been recognized as a "familiar and widely occurring emotion that affects many facets of our social behavior" (Dahl et al. 2001: 473) and hence deserving of scholarly attention. It remains an under-researched subject however in comparison to the dominant moral emotions of shame, anger, empathy and guilt (Haidt 2003: 853). And yet as Miller (1995) highlights, embarrassment is an emotion that all humans experience at some point, as it is unlikely that an individual will never be affected by what others think of him or her.

In a consumption context, a growing body of researchers have focused on identifying incidents of embarrassment through different stages of the consumer purchasing cycle, from initial purchase through usage until disposal (Dahl et al. 2001; Verbeke and Bagozzi 2002; Iacobucci et al. 2003; Grace 2007). Researchers to date have detailed instances of product and service-related embarrassment irrespective of the existence and importance of brand meaning in that experience. This ignores the symbiotic relationship between consumer's emotional feelings, both positive and negative, and the influence of brand associations, image and meaning (Edel and Burke 1987; Aylesworth et al. 1999). The paper will examine links between the negative emotion of embarrassment and theories of branding before detailing a qualitative study exploring the conceptualization of brand embarrassment.

EMBARRASSMENT IN A CONSUMPTION CONTEXT

Embarrassment is an emotion almost all humans feel at some point, given the importance of how individuals are influenced by what others think of them (Miller 1995). It can be defined as a commonly occurring, short-lived, negative emotional response arising from a perceived threat to the presented or public-self, in the presence of real or imagined audiences (Miller and Leary 1992). Unlike other self-conscious emotions such as guilt and shame, embarrassment involves social interaction. If embarrassment is experienced in private, it is thought to be because individuals are imagining what others might think of them (Sabini et al. 2001). Protecting the public-self from unflattering and unwanted evaluation is a powerful motive that underlies such behavior. In this way, embarrassment can be viewed as an important regulator of social behavior (Goffman 1956).

Miller (1996) reminds us that negative relationships occur between embarrassment and previous events and so researchers have focused on the importance of familiarity as an influence on embarrassing experiences (Dahl et al. 2001). Uncertainty following an unwanted event can produce feelings of embarrassment for either party (Parrott et al. 1988). Baumeister et al. (1995) remind us however of the importance of social context in any evaluation of self-conscious emotions, defined by individual's socialization experiences. This might include issues of social environment and place (Verbeke and Bagozzi 2002), social composition and social status.

LINKING BRAND ASSOCIATIONS TO EMBARRASSMENT

Negative emotions have a significant influence on consumers' purchase and consumption patterns (Kapoor 2008). Mizerski and White (1986) argue that brand-related cues seek to overcome such negative affective reactions. It has long been recognized that branded products are capable of influencing, even shaping consumer emotions and feelings. Dobni and Zinkhan's (1990) definition of brand image specifically highlights the emotional, as well as reasoned perceptions consumers attach to brands. As Levy (1959) argues, products are often purchased (or avoided) not for their functional qualities, but because of how, as symbols, they impact on the user's status and self-esteem. According to Aaker (1997), brands have distinct personalities (defined along the dimensions of sincerity, excitement, competence, sophistication, and ruggedness) and consumers are generally expected to seek brands that are consistent with their personality. The concept of brand image is therefore a shared mental concept, steeped in emotional as well as rational interaction. It therefore suggests a relationship between emotional states (both positive and negative) and consumer brand image. Banister and Hogg (2003: 850) discovered in the UK fashion context that "consumers often decide whether to accept or reject products and brands on the basis of their symbolic (as opposed to functional) attributes".

Researchers have detailed relationships between advertising (the dominant driver of brand image) and such positive and negative feelings (Batra and Ray 1986; Aylesworth et al. 1999). This covers both conscious and more involuntary consumption conditions. Edel and Burke (1987) extended this work to include the impact of emotions toward branded associations but remind us that negative feelings will not always predict advertising and hence brand attitudes. One rare study linking embarrassment with brand advertising (Ray 2001) focused on embarrassment communicated by advertising acknowledging that over time, a process of image transfer occurs with repeated exposure to negative stimuli.

An important link between the emotional state of embarrassment and brands is the involvement of reference or peer groups (Stafford 1966). Sirgy (1982) suggests that consumers attach varying degrees of importance to how they believe others view their preferred brand. Given the prerequisite for self-conscious evaluation before experiencing embarrassment, it is likely that negative feelings such as embarrassment may emerge if the values and attributes collectively held amongst peers are deemed socially unacceptable. A consumer's need for social approval often leads consumers to evaluate the perceived risks attached when purchasing a specific brand. Certain brands inevitably carry negative consequences, either physical or social. Consumers are therefore more susceptible to group influence and perceived risk when a brand decision involves social interaction. There are also instances of consumer avoidance of social encounters where negative feelings toward brands might occur. Leith and Baumeister (1996) referred to this as the dark side of embarrassing situations. Consumers may disown their favored brands if they foresee the potential for embarrassment as was recently evidenced by the problems for the Burberry brand in the United Kingdom.

In summary therefore, we hypothesize the existence of what we have termed 'brand embarrassment', a form of social anxiety that occurs when a person's public identity in a particular situation is threatened. This form of embarrassability refers to an individual's general susceptibility to feelings of awkwardness and uncomfortableness in connection with a branded encounter. The embarrassment might be experienced by either party in anticipation, during or shortly after the event.

AN EXPERIENTIAL UNDERSTANDING OF BRAND EMBARRASSMENT

In this study, we seek to explore stories of embarrassment as they relate to past, present and anticipated branded experiences. Our focus on the negative emotional experiences of late adolescence (aged from 18 to 22), reflects their transition from highly brand conscious years as adolescents through to a growing sense of maturity in adulthood (see Wooten 2006). In this sense, we hoped to tap into their experiences of brand embarrassment, reflecting adolescents' status as media and marketing literate (Buckingham 2002) yet highly self-conscious consumers. This age group merits special attention because theirs is a time of experimentation and risk-taking (Larson 2001), embroiled in issues of peer-influenced identity formation and the projection the 'self' identity (Moschis and Churchill 1979). According to Chaplin and John (2005: 121) "adolescence brings an even greater appreciation of brand images along with an increased understanding of the role that brands play in defining the self" suggesting a time in which negative branded experiences could be highly influential.

Thompson et al. (1989) argued that an approach based on the principles of existential phenomenology allows for analysis of context-dependent, 'lived-in' experiences; researchers ask participants to articulate their own "personalized understandings of consumption phenomena" (Thompson and Haytko 1997: 19). This implies that any meanings derived from an experience are always situated in their current experiential context. In this study, we treat embarrassment as intrinsically embedded rather than distinct from the phenomenological surrounding (Tangney 1995). Experiences of brand embarrassment were recounted in the context of older adolescents' everyday lives thereby providing thematic descriptions of the consumption phenomena in question.

Research Method

In keeping with phenomenological principles, this study used a series of in-depth discussion sessions, conducted amongst friendship pairs. According to Hunt and Miller (1997 cited in Banister and Hogg 2003: 857), 'friendship pairs' provide a naturalistic, intimate setting encouraging participants to more openly discuss issues of identity and consumption. Six initial sessions comprising of twelve

participants were conducted in the summer of 2007, providing opportunities to explore different lines of questioning and to pilot naturally-forming 'friendship pairs'. A further thirteen sessions were then held from autumn 2007 till early 2008, allowing for the emergence and exploration of core themes. Although there emerged a balance of gender across the study, 'pairs' were as often mixed as single sex, reflecting participants' ease in the company of mixed gender. All respondents were United Kingdom undergraduates, or friends of undergraduates. A £15 incentive linked to a local record store was used as incentive to encourage participation.

Participants were encouraged to provide visual representation of potential embarrassing brands to discuss, including newspaper and online images, and even digital photographs. These were used in a projective manner to help alleviate any issues of inhibitions before recalling embarrassing incidents, and to enrichen discussions surrounding those events. Discussions were unstructured, but covered initial experiences, differences across product categories, the nature of embarrassment and resultant behaviors and linked emotions. Once transcribed, the data was analyzed using phenomenological interpretation (Thompson et al. 1989). Salient themes, recurring ideas and patterns of beliefs linking people and cultural setting together were identified. A second stage then involved relating patterns of commonality between different transcripts and seeking different interpretations of similar phenomena.

FINDINGS

This paper will focus on the range of influences that combine to create and perpetuate brand embarrassment. Influences are artificially separated into those relating to the *personal-self* and then *relationships with brands* although such distinctions are difficult to separate given the interlinked, symbiotic nature when discussing experiences of brand embarrassment.

Influences of the Personal-Self
Issues of social class and status

Given the nature of embarrassment with its signaling of a perceived or actual threat to the presented or public-self, many of the initial and more obvious experiences related to participants' perceived social status with class distinctions apparent. Such examples were most marked when discussing secondary school experiences where issues of class distinction are marked and on view. As Andy explains when discussing his embarrassing memories of drinking branded vodka when seventeen:

It wholly depends on the class thing, when I look at what Glen's (vodka) … it completely reminds me of people that I knew in school and the phrase "drinking Glen's by Inverness Castle".

In this example, the cheaper brand of vodka serves to remind Andy of unpleasant memories of school amongst fellow classmates he did not want to be associated with. The brand of vodka plays a central associative link, providing a strong emotional tie between the social status of its users, the matching downmarket associations of the brand and his implicit reaction. Experiences of such ties between brand and social status extended across many different product categories, from retail stores visited, to cars driven, to mobile phones owned. Most prolific were stories relating to fashion clothing brands as Iain explains:

I would never go and buy another pair of trainers or a Kappa tracksuit—it's the connotation, you can just hear the screech of 'neds' in the back. That is not something you want to be associated with. .. that's the thing, because Kappa do produce some really good clothes and it is generally reasonably priced and I am sure I have got a t-short that I use for training now and again–I do my best to sort of hide it.

In his case, it was not the product quality of the clothing that was in question but the user-associations that caused the embarrassment. 'Neds' is a euphemism for socially undesirable adolescents, often from underprivileged backgrounds who hang around in gangs, clearly distinguishable by prominent branded clothes they display. In certain cases (such as the commonly reported Burberry brand), high quality expensive fashion brands were requisitioned by such groups resulting in a transferal of negative user imagery to the clothing brand. Other examples in this study included Berghaus (outdoor wear), Lacoste and Firetrap. Branded clothing was recognized as a form of tribal uniform causing embarrassment for companies and others who came into close proximity.

In school environments, especially those with restricted uniform policies, adolescents use brands as a means of establishing social standing. As Tracey explains, branded clothing creates social status and inevitably feelings of awkwardness and a very visual sense of social inferiority:

It was always like when you were doing PE in school and stuff you always had brand names and without like, say the two stripes down your trousers instead of three like the adidas ones and it would be "why are you wearing them kind of things?". It was always like "oh, you don't have any money?" and we were always paranoid about what kinds of tops you wore…. not realizing you were judging people.

Social judgments, through the clothes displayed, extended to more functional items such as the make of white shirt or the choice of black shoe, with the brand recognizable just by the style:

Fraser: At my state school, the only freedom you had was the type of shirt, it has to be white but you could buy an expensive or a cheap white Asda shirt and the shoes, they were the most obvious because they had to be black but the type of shoes … these were the only two items you really had any freedom of choice over; it became whether you had a Calvin Klein shirt or a George shirt from Asda, or whatever cool shoes were in. If you did not have the best in these, it defined your social standing.

Feelings of embarrassment were not however linked exclusively to concerns over downmarket stigma. There were also a few examples of embarrassment when faced by brands that signified more upmarket associations according to Jamie:

Where I was brought up, and where my dad was brought up, it was a sort of rougher area. I notice it when I go back, my dad has got quite a nice brand of car and you are parking it and heads are turning. It is not an outrageous one, it is an Audi. You are almost embarrassed to have such a good car when you are driving about and stuff–it stands out a mile.

Both however indicate that brands play an important part in creating feelings of discomfort and social stigma and highlight how the brand imagery and related user associations create both personal embarrassment (in defense against the ridicule of the accusers) or projected toward others who might be the focal point for the brand in question.

Transitions in adolescence

For adolescents in particular, the rapidly changing public and private worlds, with its associated issues of experimentation and social risk, provided fertile ground for stories of branded embarrassment. In one particularly vivid episode, Grant tells us how his lack of social knowledge in a new school setting provided the impetus for an acute case of brand embarrassment:

This is really peculiar because I went to a private school for high school but still lived with a lot of friends that I had gone to primary (state) school with so it was obviously two completely different worlds. Especially at that age and it was sort of like my 1st year at high school, first school disco. I turned up with a Helly Hansen jacket which would have been really cool (at my primary school), but it meant different things at the private school. It gets worse because underneath I had a Kappa tracksuit. The tracksuit was really acrylic shiny fabric …there was a complete scene at the disco. In retrospect, I am really embarrassed about it but at the time, I wasn't so much because I had this kind of feeling that I was right and they were wrong. But as time progressed and they educated me in the ways of fashion, I was mortified … meeting lots of new people and trying to create my own identity.

This case demonstrates a temporal aspect to brand embarrassment. Embarrassment can emerge unexpectedly with changing circumstances and although not always overtly obvious to the recipient, the effects in terms of reduced social standing and a feeling of inadequacy are evident. Identification with brands can change very quickly during the formative identification years of adolescence with both the changing cycles of fickle fashion and the constant movement between social circles. It is likely that brand embarrassment may also occur in other situations of transition, such as the move to a new job or a geographical re-location as consumers move between social expectations and social norms. This was however beyond the scope of this research study.

Generational and age distance

There were numerous examples of how brand embarrassment might emerge when faced with an age-related generational gap. Such embarrassment typically emerged between adolescents and their parents, even grandparents. Examples such as highlighted by Jamie below, illustrate how powerful user associations from one generation compare with ignorance or ambivalence from an older one:

My dad used to climb when he was younger but he is quite a savvy shopper, like he usually gets the cheap stuff normally, but decent stuff–he comes into the house one day with a big grin on his face, he has bought the most expensive jacket of his life, and I was like, "…all right, let's see it", and he tells me it was £320, puts it on and we just start laughing. It was a Berghaus Europeak jacket–he works down in Parkhead (east Glasgow), that's where all his patients are, lots of 'neds', so he does not wear it there any more!

The experiences of Jamie's father illustrate the complex mix of generational differences, social status and negative brand associations. Stories of adolescents being embarrassed to be associated with the brands displayed by their parents included dissociation with downmarket supermarket brands purchased by their parents, expensive designer clothes worn by image-conscious mothers and even the brands of cars driven by parents on the school run.

Embarrassment, sometimes never revealed, led to examples of masking the brand, parental avoidance and even lying to their friends. For many, their parents either lacked the same brand-driven values or were ignorant of the depth of meaning implicit.

Socialization: Distance, tribes and environments

Brand embarrassment was also a function of the nature of the socialized relationship between parties growing up in a peer driven culture. For many of those spoken to, brand embarrassment occurred not between the very best of friends but between those they knew less well or not at all. Tracey highlights how a feeling of embarrassment relates to a past friend:

When we were younger, even still now, I would say that say you are in Asda and you buy Smart Price (Asda Own Label) and you go to the check out, and then your pal who you were at school with, is serving you, it is an embarrassing thing. We kind of recognize that it should not be an embarrassing thing because it is, because of the cheap associations.

This type of avoidance behavior is consistent with Goffman's (1956) description of efforts to avoid the gaze of others as visible signs of embarrassment. Indeed, the highly tribalized nature of adolescent lives leads to stories of embarrassment between the brand conscious cliques and social circles. Adolescents are known to join such groups for the purposes of ego enhancement, achievement of status superiority and identity formation (Danesi 1994). In the formative secondary school years, brands were used to define social acceptance and for those not able to, or unwilling to display those brands, a sense of embarrassment was felt as a result of ridicule and social exclusion:

Amanda: In high school, it was always because you were in such tightly packed social environment, where everyone was sort of competing to be popular, so if you did not wear Kickers shoes, you were excluded.

Fraser: When I was back in school, it was just my mates, and I had a pair of shoes and I just wore them with jeans one day and just got a ripping because of the pressure to wear branded trainers like, sort of more skate brands like Vans or Ethies, and all that sort of thing, and I was wearing, I think they were from Clarks or somewhere, just black normal shoes.

Such stories bear a close resemblance to Leary's (1995) understanding of embarrassment as an aversive stimulus that encourages circumspection of public image and importantly, discourages behaviors that might threaten that desired peer-driven image. Furthermore, such cases of embarrassment were often shared amongst observers around, in which teasing and social degradation was a shared social norm (Miller 1987). Wooten (2006) argues that embarrassment in such circumstances is a consequence of the peer ridicule that has arisen and such individuals will become conditioned over time to recognize and takes steps to avoid grounds for potential embarrassment.

Participants also emphasized the importance of social context and place. Environments such as the sports changing room in which the wrong choice of brand of deodorant or make-up displayed could lead to feelings of embarrassment through teasing, ridicule or even fears of bullying. In such circles, the need to establish and maintain social approval became dominant. Haidt (2003) locates this within individuals' powerful desire to 'belong' in group situations. This need to belong extends toward the consumption of branded products and the desire to keep up with group fashions. In fast moving markets such as mobile phones, brand embarrassment was perceived to occur when individuals in the group were left behind by the latest technological fashion as Colin comments on:

In 2nd year, the first phone I got was really top of the range at the time, a Nokia 3310 which is now a brick, but at the time, it was fantastic but within a couple of months, all my mates had them and I was "ok, you had a perfectly good phone anyway", and they do the same thing, but maybe they felt they needed to get them because they felt embarrassed about their against mine.

Feelings of brand embarrassment were also contingent upon the occasion as much as the brand in question. Alcoholic drinks were perceived to be potent territory for brand embarrassment given the image-conscious nature of drinks marketing and changing brand loyalties between differing social groups and drinking occasions. In the example below, Martin talks about an experience in which embarrassment was caused as much by a change in social environment, from one which was acceptable to one that was clearly not:

About three months ago, I was with this person who was the only person I knew. All his friends were drinking Bacardi Breezers and I was like "this is not the way we do it in my group of friends", we always bought a few pints .. I think in that sort of environment, you're a bit embarrassed and everyone else is drinking this so…you feel pressured because you don't want to stand out … whereas if I was with my mates, I would feel embarrassed to drink that.

Issues of self perception and identity

Finally, participants believed that embarrassment with brands was also a function of issues of self-perception, a lack of self-confidence and individuals' personality and character. Negative images and associations linked to brands worn or consumed produced feelings of undesirability, similar to what Banister and Hogg (2001: 244) described as the "undesired self". This was often based on experiences resulting in teasing, ridicule and isolated cases of bullying. In one such example, a fifteen-year-old boy was so embarrassed to be wearing the wrong choice of school bag that he still remembers the hurtful taunts that followed. Some six years on, he feels that this and several other branded incidents led to a draining of confidence and arguably a deep rooted negative self-portrayal.

Relationships with Brands

In her study, Fournier (1998), drawing on interpersonal relationship theory, suggests that consumers form different types of relationships with their brands. A deeper understanding the phenomenon of brand embarrassment relates not just to issues of the self and socialized environment but also the types of branded relationships consumers establish, maintain or disown.

Brand familiarity and knowledge

Consistent with theories of embarrassment which recognize that a lack of familiarity can encourage the formation of embarrassment (Miller 1992) and also studies of product and purchase embarrassment (Dahl et al. 2001), participants in this study such as Scott below recounted examples in which a lack of knowledge about either a brand's attributes or a lack of confidence in the brand image might result in possible future embarrassment:

It would be different if you did have a really good brand, say you bought a big Sony, I am not saying you would be like "check out my Sony television" but you would maybe slide it in there. At the other end, I would be embarrassed if I had a television like say a Matsui

In the same vein, stories of embarrassment, either actual or anticipated, occurred in situations in which the participant risked perceptual ridicule if they revealed their lack of branded knowledge in keeping with Gilovich et al.'s (2000) concept of the 'spotlight effect'. In one such example, the choice of a brand of malt whisky to present to a twenty-one year's father as a gift was fraught because he was concerned that the brand of whisky he chose, Glenfiddich, might reveal his lack of knowledge about the sophistication in choice of Scottish malt whisky brands.

The scrutiny of brand attributes and brand knowledge also worked in reverse with examples of feelings of embarrassment because of a lack of knowledge amongst others consuming the brand in question. As Kai explains, he anticipates embarrassment as he does not want to be associated with a brand of wrist bands because of the ignorance of its users:

The *Make Poverty History* (wrist bands)–I found really difficult–everybody just jumped on the bandwagon and obviously became a fashion statement around that summer … never mind the whole politics behind the whole actual event, I just thought it would be really embarrassing to be walking round because I would be seen to be like somebody who just like, you know, they may not even know the ins and outs of the campaign and stuff. They just wanted a wrist band to prove a fashion point.

Therefore, the lack of brand knowledge can create both experienced embarrassment and projected embarrassment, amongst known individuals and in the case of Kai, unknown passer-bys.

Associations and meaning

As Levy (1959) argues, the symbolism of brands plays an important part in the creation of meaning influencing positive and negative associations with brands. In this research, there were different forms of symbolism creating feelings of embarrassment toward the brand in question. Perhaps the most frequently cited example was the Burberry 'check' design, the most visible emblem of the 'ned' culture so prevalent in the United Kingdom from the late nineties onwards. But other examples included the design patches on jeans pockets, the archway 'M' for McDonalds and even the crocodile label for Lacoste. In Judith's case, it relates to Diesel jeans:

Some folk were going out to spend more money on buying, say, a £150 pair of Diesel jeans or something. And I think folk did, well I certainly did, feel kind of pressured as such, but you would buy say like jeans that had like the brand name plastered across the back pocket so that you would be seen to be wearing them.

In such examples, the brand through its most visible association becomes synonymous with those who visit, purchase and consume it. The embarrassment becomes more vivid with a single symbolic focal point for negative feelings. In a similar vein, embarrassment was also evident toward those who sought to identify with a faked or imitation brand. In such situations, the embarrassment was more akin to sympathy, even antipathy toward the recipient. One participant described occasions in which she would always look down to check whether a passer-by was indeed wearing original 'ugg' boots, identified by their minimal label on the back heel. When noticing individuals wearing the fake version without the original label, she felt embarrassed that such individu-

als should be seeking a shared identity with genuine 'ugg' owners. The concept of a shared mental image (Dobni and Zinkhan 1990) was therefore compromised and negative emotions are fostered.

Participants described how brand names and logos were sometimes covered over to avoid potential embarrassment including the removal of labels from bottles of own-label water, the covering up of laptop logos, the scratching of a brand name off a skateboard with childish associations and the customization of a fashion brand label to disguise its true provenance. In the example below, the increased importance of ethical credentials for branded foods is evident in the actions of a mother seeking to avoid embarrassment when serving coffee. The mere sight of the wrong label was sufficient to provoke a negative reaction as Judith tells us:

Take my mother–she would be embarrassed to buy a brand that was not ethical. She would be embarrassed to say to her friends that it was not ethical so she would be embarrassed to buy Nestle. I remember when we were growing up and my brother Stephen really wanted something from Nestle and she would buy it and hide it in the cupboard or put it in a different package so that when her friends came round, they would not see she had bought Nestle.

In common with theories of symbolic consumption and image transfer, there were many examples of anticipated embarrassment because of the negative associations these might infer:

Mediums of branded embarrassment

Studies have shown that advertising socially sensitive products can cause embarrassment through the awkward nature of how the product is promoted, classically through its advertising, causing feelings of awkwardness and discomfort (Ray 2001). This research suggests that embarrassment can also be caused through the branded communication, creating a sense of embarrassment in a product category not normally associated with embarrassment. Examples centered around either the style of the advertising or the characteristics of the source celebrity used to communicate the branded message. Carlenes explain why she would be embarrassed to be associated with a perfume promoted by an infamous UK celebrity:

I would really have to push myself before I would buy it. Because I just think that it is the tackiest concept in the world and that I would just feel really embarrassed if someone said "oh what are you wearing" and I would have to say "oh, it's Jade perfume"–I would just feel that would be really embarrassing.

In other commonly cited examples, several participants claimed to no longer shop at a well known frozen foods retailer because of a recent association with a fallen pop celebrity, Kerry Katona. Once an ideal role model for families with young children, the celebrity suffered a downward slide in popularity with several high profile incidents eroding her family-friendly image. For Gary, who took pride in the quality of his cooking, the negative brand associations caused by the fallen celebrity were enough to cause acute embarrassment avoidance.

Beyond the negative associations of celebrity promotion, sometimes the style and tone of the advertising was sufficient to cause mild forms of embarrassment causing the viewer to 'cringe' and feel negatively disposed toward the advertiser. Although such examples were often 'enjoyed' for their awfulness, any thoughts of association with the advertiser would undoubtedly have lead to personal ridicule and social stigma. Examples discussed included past advertising for Ferrero Rocher, current campaigns for Esure online insurance and finally a well known DIY chain.

DISCUSSION AND CONCLUSIONS

A review of the literature highlights how previous studies focusing on the consuming aspects of embarrassment take little or no account of anticipated or experienced embarrassment centered on the 'branded encounter'. Our findings confirm that this is rich territory to explore; the embedded nature of brand associations, image and meanings in adolescents' everyday lives making experiences of embarrassment almost inevitable. Brand embarrassment was found to be influenced by the symbiotic relationships between the *personal-self* and individuals' *branded relationships*. The findings enhance our understanding of the processes of advanced socialization, identifying how issues of status and class, age and generational differences, interaction within and between groups, social transitions and finally the development of self-identity contribute toward feelings of embarrassment when faced by negative branded encounters. Given the brand-saturated society through which adolescents now navigate, such feelings are widespread. This research gave rise to a range of behavioral consequences, from playful teasing and awkwardness through to possible long-term harm from social stigma and even bullying.

The research also provides a bridge between our understanding of embarrassment and the symbolic consumption of branded products and services. It recognizes the symbolic importance of consumption during adolescent years (Belk et al. 1992) but refines our understanding of how branded associations, images and meaning contribute toward negative as well as positive emotional feelings amongst adolescents (Chaplin and John 2005) through the conceptual lens of embarrassment.

We recognize that this is a small scale study with an emphasis at this stage on exploration but believe it provides fertile ground for continued extensive research which seeks to examine the conceptual links between causes, nature and consequences of brand embarrassment.

REFERENCES

Aaker, Jennifer (1997), "Dimensions of Brand Personality," *Journal of Marketing Research*, 34 (3), 347-356.

Aaker, David A and Alexander L Biel (1993), "Brand Equity and Advertising: Advertising's Role in Building Strong Brands," Hillsdale, NJ, Lawrence Erlbaum Associates, Inc., 83-96.

Fournier, Susan (1998), "Consumers and Their Brands: Developing Relationship Theory in Consumer Research," *Journal of Consumer Research*, 24 (4), 343-373.

Aylesworth, Andrew B., Ronald C. Goodstein and Ajay Kalra (1999), "Effect of Archetypal Embeds on Feelings: An Indirect Route to Affecting Attitudes?" *Journal of Advertising*, 28 (3), 73-82.

Baumeister, Roy F., Stillwell, Arlene M. and Todd F. Heatherton (1994), "Personal Narratives about Guilt: Role in Action Control and Interpersonal Relationships," *Basic and Applied Social Psychology*, 17 (1/2), 173-198.

Banister, Emma N. and Margaret K. Hogg (2003), "Negative Symbolic Consumption and Consumers' Drive for Self Esteem: The Case of the Fashion Industry," *European Journal of Marketing*, 38 (7), 850-868.

Batra, Rajeev and Michael L. Ray (1986), "Affective Responses Mediating Acceptance of Advertising," *Journal of Consumer Research*, 13 (2), 234-249.

Belk, Russell W., Bahn, Kenneth D. and Robert N. Mayer (1982), "Developmental Recognition of Consumption Symbolism," *Journal of Consumer Research*, 9 (June), 4-17.

Buckingham, David. (2002), "The Electronic Generation? Children and New Media," in *Handbook of New Media: Social Shaping and Social Consequences,* eds. L. Lievrouw & Sonia. Livingstone, Sage Publications: London, 77-89

Chan, Priscilla Y. L., John Saunders, Gail Taylor, and Anne Souchon (2003), "Brand Personality Perception: Regional or Country Specific?" *European Advances in Consumer Research*, Vol. 6, eds. Darach Turley and Stephen Brown, Provo, UT: Association for Consumer Research, pp. 300-307.

Chaplin, Lan N. and Deborah R. John (2005), "The Development of Self-Brand Connections in Children and Adolescents," *Journal of Consumer Research*, 32 (1), 119-129

Dahl, Darren W., Rajesh V. Manchanda and Jennifer J. Argo (2001), "Embarrassment in Consumer Purchase: The Roles of Social Presence and Purchase Familiarity," *Journal of Consumer Research*, 28 (3), 473- 481.

Dobhi, Dawn and George M. Zinkhan (1990), "In Search of Brand Image: A Foundation Analysis," *Advances in Consumer Research*, 17, 110-119.

Danesi, Marcel (1994), *Cool: The Signs and Meanings of Adolescence,* Toronto: University of Toronto Press.

Edell, Julie A. and Marian Burke (1987), "The Power of Feelings in Understanding Advertising Effects," *Journal of Consumer Research*, 14 (3), 412-434.

Goffman. Erving (1956), "Embarrassment and Social Organization," *American Journal of Sociology*, 62, 264-271.

Grace, Debra (2007), "How Embarrassing! An Exploratory Study of Critical Incidents including Affective Reactions," *Journal of Service Research*, 9 (3), 271-285.

Haidt, Jonathan (2003), "The Moral Emotions," *Handbook of Effective Sciences*, eds. R. Davidson and H. Goldsmith, Oxford University Press: Oxford, 852-870.

Iacobucci, Dawn, Bobby J. Calder, Edward C. Malthouse and Adam Duhachek (2003), "Psychological, Marketing, Physical, and Sociological Factors Affecting Attitudes and Behavioral Intentions for Customers Resisting the Purchase of an Embarrassing Product," *Advances in Consumer Research*, 30, 236-240.

Larson, R. W. (2001), "How US Children and Adolescents Spend Their Time: What it Does (and Doesn't) Tell Us About Their Development," *Current Directions in Psychological Science*, 10 (5), 160-164.

Leith, Karen Pezza and Roy. F. Baumeister (1996), "Why Do Bad Moods Increase Self-Defeating Behavior? Emotion, Risk Taking, and Self-Regulating Behavior," *Journal of Personality and Social Psychology*, 71, 1250-1267.

Levi, Sidney (1959), "Symbols for Sale," *Harvard Business Review*, 37 (July-August).

Kapoor, Harish (2008), "Negative Emotions as Motivators of Consumption," *Advances in Consumer Research*, 35, forthcoming.

Miller, R. S. (1995), "On the Nature of Embarrassability: Shyness, Social Evaluation, and Social Skills," *Journal of Personality*, 63 (June), 315-339.

Miller, Rowland S. and Mark R. Leary (1992), "Social Sources and Interactive Functions of Emotion: The Case of Embarrassment," *Emotion and Social Behavior*, ed. M. S. Clark, Newbury Park, CA: Sage, 202-221.

Mizerski, Richard, W. and Dennis J. White (1986), "Understanding and Using Emotions in Advertising," *Journal of Consumer Marketing*, 3 (4), 57-70.

Moschis, George P. and Roy L. Moore (1979), "Decision Making Among the Young: A Socialization Perspective," *Journal of Consumer Research*, 6 (September), 101-112.

Parrott, W. Gerrod, John Sabini and Maury Silver (1988), "The Roles of Self-Esteem and Social Interaction in Embarrassment," *Personality and Social Psychology Bulletin*, 14 (March), 191-202.

Sabini, John, Garvey, Brian and Amanda. L. Hall (2001), "Shame and Embarrassment Revisited," *Personality & Social Psychology Bulletin*, 27 (1), 104-117.

Sirgy, M. Joseph (1982), "Self-Concept in Consumer Behavior: A Critical Review," *Journal of Consumer Research*, 9 (3), 287-300.

Stafford, J. (1966), "Effects of Group Influence on Consumer Brand Preferences," *Journal of Market Research*, 3 (1), 68-76.

Tangney, June P. (1995), "Shame and Guilt in Interpersonal Relationships," *Self Conscious Emotions*, eds. J. P. Tangney and K.W. Fischer, New York: Guildford Press.

Thompson, Craig J. and Diane L. Haytko (1997), "Speaking of Fashion: Consumers' Uses of Fashion Discourses and the Appropriation of Countervailing Cultural Meanings," *Journal of Consumer Research*, 24 (June), 15-42.

Thompson, Craig J., William B. Locander and Howard R. Pollio (1989), "Putting Consumer Experience Back into Consumer Research: The Philosophy and Method of Existential Phenomenology," *Journal of Consumer Research*, 16, 133-146.

Verbeke, Willem and Richard P. Bagozzi (2003), "Exploring the Role of Self- and Customer-Provoked Embarrassment in Personal Selling," *International Journal of Research in Marketing*, 20, 233-258.

Wooten, David B. (2006), "From Labeling Possessions to Possessing Labels: Ridicule and Socialization Amongst Adolescents," *Journal of Consumer Research*, 33 (September), 188-198.

Extending the Research in Relation to Materialism and Life Satisfaction

Eda Gurel Atay, University of Oregon, USA
M. Joseph Sirgy, Virginia Polytechnic Institute and State University, USA
Muris Cicic, University of Sarajevo, Bosnia and Herzegovina
Melika Husic, University of Sarajevo, Bosnia and Herzegovina

ABSTRACT

This paper builds on Sirgy's (1998) theory of materialism by integrating exposure to materialistic advertising and social influence into a more comprehensive model. The data collected in Bosnia/Herzegovina showed that exposure to materialistic advertising and social influence contribute to materialism. Materialism, in turn, leads to the use of all types of standard of comparisons (affective- and cognitive-based expectations) to make judgments about standard of living. As the use of these standards of comparisons increases, people start to evaluate their standard of living more negatively, and this negative evaluations of standard of living leads to dissatisfaction with life.

INTRODUCTION

Materialism, defined as "the importance ascribed to the ownership and acquisition of material goods in achieving major life goals or desired states" (Richins 2004, pg. 210), has been studied extensively in the past 20 years. Several studies demonstrated that the more materialistic people are less satisfied with their lives than their less materialistic counterparts because the more materialistic people believe that any given level of possessions is inadequate to meet their living standards. (La Barbera and Gurhan 1997). For instance, Belk (1984) found that aspects of materialism (i.e. possessiveness, nongenerosity, and envy) were negatively related to happiness and life satisfaction. Similarly, Richins and Dawson (1992) found a negative correlation between life satisfaction and three subdimensions of materialism (centrality, success, and happiness). Sirgy, Lee, Larsen, and Wright (1998) also were able to demonstrate that materialistic people are less satisfied with their material possessions and less satisfied with life than non-materialistic people. However, these findings did not explain the negative relationship between materialism and life satisfaction. To address this issue, Sirgy (1998) advanced an explanation to account for this negative relationship. The gist of the explanation is that materialistic people have inflated expectations of their standard of living, whereas non-materialistic people have realistic expectations. These inflated expectations cause materialistic people to evaluate their standard of living negatively. This negative affect spills over to judgments of life overall, making materialistic people feel dissatisfied with life. Thus, one goal of this paper is to test this explanation in a formal way.

Our second goal is to further develop the research tying TV viewership to materialism (e.g., Goldberg and Gorn 1978; Greenberg and Brand 1993; Rahtz, Sirgy, and Meadow, 1989). For instance, Sirgy et al. (1998) were able to empirically demonstrate that TV viewership contributes to materialism, which in turn plays an important role in negative evaluations of standard of living and life dissatisfaction. How? We designed our study to help answer this question. Specifically, we believe that TV viewership affects materialism through exposure to materialistic advertising. That is, exposure to ads that links consumer goods and services with status and prestige is hypothesized to be a key factor influencing the development of materialism (cf. Moschis and Moore 1982; Buijzen and Valkenburg 2003; Pine and Nash 2002).

HOW DOES MATERIALISM LEAD TO LIFE DISSATISFACTION?

Sirgy (1998) developed a theory explaining how materialism leads to life dissatisfaction. He reasoned that in evaluating standard of living, materialistic people tend to employ affective-based expectations (e.g., ideal, deserved, and need-based expectations) rather than cognitive-based expectations (e.g., past, predictive, and ability-based expectations). Affective-based expectations are value-laden and they lead to experiencing intense emotions. These emotions can be positive feelings of elation, joy, and pride as well as negative feelings of anger, envy, and possessiveness. In contrast, cognitive-based expectations generate cognitive elaboration in evaluations of one's standard of living.

There are at least three types of affective-based expectations. The first type is *ideal expectations*. Ideal expectations are standards of comparisons based on remote referents rather than situational ones. For example, an ideal expectation of becoming "filthy rich" is remote in the sense that is cultivated by adopting standards and goals of people that are imaginary, distant, and based on vicarious experiences not grounded by the reality of one's situation. Materialistic people are more likely to compare their own standard of living with people who are "filthy rich" making them feel dissatisfied with their own standard of living. That ideal image of being "filthy rich" may be an image cultivated from watching too much television and seeing the lives of the rich and famous—remote referents. The second type of affective-based expectations is *deserved expectations*. This type of expectations reflects the tendency to make equity-based comparisons involving income and work. Materialistic people, compared to their non-materialistic counterparts, tend to think that they work harder than others but earn less. These equity-based comparisons generate feelings of injustice, anger, or envy. Lastly, *minimum-need expectations* of a standard of living reflect spending money to meet minimum (basic) needs. Materialistic people believe that they need more money to make ends meet. That is, their basic needs tend to be much more inflated than non-materialistic people.

In contrast to materialistic people, people who are not materialistic are more likely to use cognitive-based expectations in evaluating their standard of living. For instance, they may compare their standard of living with their *past* (their past material possessions). That is, nonmaterialistic people evaluate their income by assessing how far they have come along—compared to last year, a couple of years ago, or further back in time. Alternatively, nonmaterialistic people tend to evaluate their standard of living using *predictive expectations* (expected future wealth). Another type of cognitive-based expectations reflects the perceptions of *ability* to achieve in life a certain standard of living. That is, non-materialistic people use their perception of their ability to achieve a certain amount of wealth based on their education and occupational skills in evaluating their standard of living.

Overall, affective-based expectations can be viewed as unrealistic and inflated goals that result in dissatisfaction with standard of living, whereas cognitive-based expectations are more realistic and non-inflated goals. Evaluations of standard of living based on cognitive-based expectations are not likely to lead to feelings of dissatisfaction with one's standard of living.

Based on the preceding discussion, our study will test the following hypotheses with respect to the relationships between materialism and the use of specific types of expectations in evaluating one's standard of living:

H1a: Materialistic people are more likely to use ideal expectations in evaluating their standard of living than non-materialistic people.

H1b: Materialistic people are more likely to use deserved expectations in evaluating their standard of living than non-materialistic people.

H1c: Materialistic people are more likely to use minimum need expectations in evaluating their standard of living than non-materialistic people.

H1d: Non-materialistic people are more likely to use past expectations in evaluating their standard of living than materialistic people.

H1e: Non-materialistic people are more likely to use predictive expectations in evaluating their standard of living than materialistic people.

H1f: Non-materialistic people are more likely to use ability expectations in evaluating their standard of living than materialistic people.

Furthermore, our study will test the following hypotheses with respect to the relationships between the frequency of using certain types of expectations of standard of living and satisfaction with standard of living:

H2a: The greater the frequency of evaluation of standard of living based on ideal expectations, the lower the satisfaction with standard of living.

H2b: The greater the frequency of evaluation of standard of living based on deserved expectations, the lower the satisfaction with standard of living.

H2c: The greater the frequency of evaluation of standard of living based on minimum-need expectations, the lower the satisfaction with standard of living.

H2d: The greater the frequency of evaluation of standard of living based on past expectations, the higher the satisfaction with standard of living.

H2e: The greater the frequency of evaluation of standard of living based on predictive expectations, the higher the satisfaction with standard of living.

H2f: The greater the frequency of evaluation of standard of living based on ability expectations, the higher the satisfaction with standard of living.

Feelings of satisfaction or dissatisfaction with standard of living plays an important role in the evaluation of life overall. There is a huge literature and much empirical evidence in the quality-of-life literature that suggests that life satisfaction is a judgment made by evaluating a variety of life domains such as leisure life, social life, work life, family life, spiritual life, and material life. The latter (material life) reflects one's overall feelings related to one's standard of living. Thus, life satisfaction is determined mostly by evaluations of important life domains, including material life (see Diener 1984, and Diener et al 1999 for a review of that literature). Based on the preceding discussion, our study will test the following hypothesis:

H3:   The higher the satisfaction with standard of living the higher the satisfaction with life.

HOW DOES TV VIEWERSHIP AFFECT MATERIALISM?

One of the most examined antecedents of materialism is *TV viewership* (e.g., Goldberg and Gorn 1978; Greenberg and Brand 1993; Rahtz, Sirgy, and Meadow, 1989). For instance, Sirgy et al. (1998) were able to empirically demonstrate that TV viewership contributes to materialism, which in turn plays an important role in negative evaluations of standard of living and life dissatisfaction. However, *exposure to materialistic advertising* might mediate the relationship between TV viewership and materialism. In other words, TV viewing might lead to exposure to materialistic advertising, which in turn, augments materialism. Therefore, exposure to ads that links consumer goods and services with status and prestige is hypothesized to be a key factor influencing materialism (Moschis and Moore 1982; Buijzen and Valkenburg 2003; Pine and Nash 2002). Therefore, our study will test the following hypothesis:

H4a: The higher the exposure to materialistic advertising the greater the materialism.

H4b: The greater the TV viewership the higher the exposure to materialistic advertising.

Social influence has also been found as an antecedent of materialism (e.g., Churchill and Moschis 1979; Clark, Martin, and Bush 2001). Social influence, in this context, can be defined as the impact of family and peers on consumer behavior. Moschis and Moore (1979), for instance, found that family communication structures influences adolescents' materialism levels. Similarly, Churchill and Moschis (1979) found that materialism levels of children tended to increase as the frequency of communication with peers increased. Therefore, based on previous studies, it can be said that there is a positive relationship between materialism and social influence. Formally stated:

H5:   The greater the social influence the higher the materialism.

THE OVERALL HYPOTHESIZED MODEL

Our overall hypothesized model builds on Sirgy's (1998) theory of materialism by integrating TV viewership, exposure to materialistic advertising, and social influence into a more comprehensive model. Specifically, it is hypothesized that TV viewership contributes significantly to exposure to materialistic advertising. Exposure to materialistic advertising, in addition to social influence in buying behavior, contributes significantly to materialism. Materialism, in turn, contributes to setting affective-based (inflated and unrealistic) expectations of standard of living. Materialism and inflated, unrealistic expectations are negatively related to the satisfaction with standard of living (SOL). Satisfaction with SOL, on the other hand, contributes to life satisfaction. The conceptual model depicting these hypothesized relationships is shown in Figure 1.

METHOD

To test the conceptual model depicted in Figure 1, a consumer survey was conducted in a major city in Bosnia and Herzegovina. First, consistent with the Anderson and Gerbing's (1988) 2-step method, the measurement model was estimated in the first step. Then, in the second step, the structural model was estimated and

FIGURE 1

The Conceptual Model Linking TV Viewership with Life Satisfaction

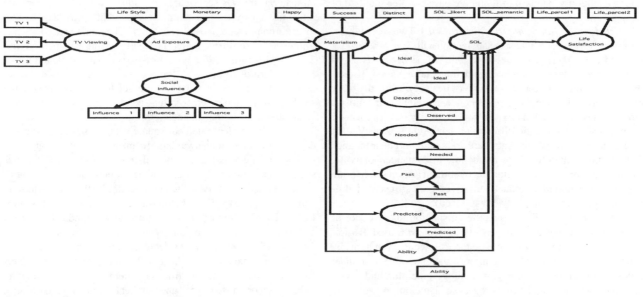

modified. LISREL 8.80 (Joreskog and Sorbom 2006) was used to analyze the covariance matrices in all analyses.

Sample

The data were collected from 301 adults in Bosnia and Herzegovina in 2007. Cluster sampling technique was used to collect the data. Specifically, the city was divided into neighborhoods and these neighborhoods were categorized as high, medium, and low income. After selecting two sample neighborhoods from each category, the researcher used the systematic random sampling to collect survey data. Once a potential respondent agreed to complete the questionnaire, the researcher made arrangements to pick up the questionnaires 4-7 days later. One hundred and one, 100, and 100 questionnaires were collected from low, medium, and high-income neighborhoods, respectively. Of 301 respondents, 120 (39.9%) were men, 180 (59.8%) were women, and gender was missing for one participant. The age of respondents ranged from 18 to 84 with a mean of 36.36. The percentage of missing data was less than 5% for each variable and those missing data were randomly distributed. Therefore, they were handled by using maximum likelihood estimation.

Measures

TV viewership. To measure TV viewership, three questions were adapted from Churchill and Moschis (1979). Two questions assessed how many hours they spent watching television in a day during the weekdays and weekend. The response sets included 17 responses ranged from 0 to 16+ hours. The third question assessed how many hours they watched television in total per week and the response set included seven categories.

Exposure to materialistic advertising. Participants were instructed to think about their image of most of the ads they had noticed about consumer goods and services in the last few weeks. Then, they were asked to describe their images of these ads along the following attributes on 7-point scale: high status/low status; affluent/non-affluent; high prestige/low prestige; high class/low

class; extraordinary/ordinary; glamorous/non-glamorous; luxurious/non-luxurious; expensive/not-expensive; for the rich/for the poor; and snobbish/non-snobbish. The first five of these attributes reflect lifestyles while the second half reflects the monetary values of goods/services. Therefore, this construct was considered a two-factor correlated construct. Indeed, an exploratory factor analysis and a confirmatory factor analysis verified this 2-factor structure (Satorra-Bentler scaled $\chi2$ (34, N=301)=67.17, p<.001; CFI=.99; SRMR=.044; and RMSEA=.057).

Social influence. Social influence was conceptualized as the impacts of friends and family on buying behaviors. It was measured by three questions adapted from Churchill and Moschis (1979) on five-point scales (1=all of the time, 5=never). These items assessed whether participants talked with their friends and family about buying things and whether they learned from them what to look for in buying things.

Materialism. Materialism was measured by using nine items (Gurel-Atay and Sirgy 2007) with 5-point scales (1=strongly agree, 5=strongly disagree). Materialism was conceptualized as a 3-factor construct: happiness (the belief that material possessions bring happiness to life; e.g., "Having luxury items is important to a happy life."), success (the belief that possessions symbolize achievement and success; e.g., "I feel good when I buy expensive things. People think of me as a success."), and distinctiveness (the belief that possessions make people feel distinctive from others; e.g., "I usually buy expensive things that make me look distinctive").

Standards of comparison (affective and cognitive-based expectations of standard of living). We developed the measure of standards of comparison for this study. Respondents were provided with the following prompt: "Most people have strong feelings about their standard of living because they compare their family's current financial situation with different types of standards of comparisons. The questions below are designed to capture the *standard of comparison* you use in evaluating your family's standard of living." Single items were used to measure each of the six standards of comparison in evaluating standard of living on ten-point scales where 1 means "no, my feelings about my standard of living are not based on this standard of comparison" and 10 means "yes, my feelings about my standard of living are based on this standard of comparison."

Satisfaction with standard of living (SOL). Two sets of questions were developed to measure satisfaction with SOL. The first set included two Likert-type questions. One of the questions asked respondents to describe their current financial situation of their immediate family (1=very poor; 5=very healthy), while the other question probed the feelings of respondents about their family's current financial situation (1=very bad; 5=very good). The second set included five semantic differential items (Ogden and Venkat 2001). Specifically, participants were asked to report their feelings about the things their family owns, their family's standard of living, and their family's financial situation overall on a seven-point scale (happy/angry; good/bad; elated/tense; contended/frustrated; fulfilled/disappointed; and pleased/displeased).

Life satisfaction. To measure life satisfaction, short version of Campbell, Converse, and Rodgers (1976) scale was used. Participants were asked to rate their life on the following seven items by using seven-point scales: boring/interesting; enjoyable/miserable; useless/worthwhile; full/empty; discouraging/helpful; and disappointing/rewarding; and brings the best in me/doesn't give me much chance.

Item Parceling: Before conducting the analyses, parceling was used on four sets of measures: exposure to materialistic advertising, materialism, satisfaction with SOL, and life satisfaction. Based on Bagozzi and Heatherton's (1994) advice, at least two parcels were created for each construct to account for measurement error. Because exposure to materialistic advertising is considered as a two-factor construct, the indicators of each factor were summed to develop two parcels. Similarly, each dimension of materialism constituted a parcel. That is, materialism was represented by three parcels. Satisfaction with SOL, on the other hand, was represented by two parcels. One parcel included the Likert-type items while the other parcel included six semantic differential items. To develop the item parcels for life satisfaction, this measure was subjected to one-factor model. Then, the items were rank ordered based on their loadings on this factor and assigned one of two groups to provide the item-to-construct balance (Little, Cunningham, Shahar, and Widaman 2002; Russell, Kahn, Spoth, and Altmaier 1998). That is, the average loadings of each item parcel on the factor were approximately equal. These item parcels were used in subsequent analyses.

RESULTS

Measurement Model Results

Prior to conducting the CFA, normality of the observed variables was inspected. Some of the variables had high skewness and kurtosis values. Even though maximum likelihood (ML) estimation method is considered to be very robust even with highly skewed/kurtosis data, West, Finch, and Curran (1995) argue that ML produces too high chi-square statistic and leads rejecting too many true models when the variables are highly nonnormal. To deal with this problem, Satorra-Bentler correction was reported in all analyses.

To estimate the measurement model, the constructs were modeled as freely correlated first-order factors with their respective indicators. The Anderson and Gerbing (1988) convention was followed to fix the loadings and measurement errors of item parcels. First, composite reliabilities for each item parcel were computed. Then, the highest composite reliability for a given construct was chosen. For instance, materialism had three parcels (i.e. happiness, success, and distinctiveness) and composite reliabilities for each of

these parcels were .899, .924, and .929, respectively. Because distinctiveness had the highest value, the loading of distinctiveness on materialism was set equal to the square root of its composite reliability. Lastly, the measurement error of distinctiveness was set to one minus its composite reliability. The same procedure was followed for exposure to materialistic advertising, satisfaction with SOL, and life satisfaction. For the constructs with single indicators (i.e. standard of comparison constructs), the loadings were set to unity and measurement errors were set to .25, which was the smallest measurement error value found for the other, estimated error variances (Anderson and Gerbing, 1988).

Satorra-Bentler scaled chi-square value was 306.83 with 163 degrees of freedom and it was significant at .001. Even though chi-square statistic was significant, other goodness of fit statistics suggested a close fit to the data with the root mean square error of approximation (RMSEA; Steiger and Lind 1980; Browne and Cudeck, 1993)=.054 (confidence interval=.045-.063, PCLOSE=.22), Bentler's (1990) comparative fit index (CFI)=.96, and standardized root mean square residual (SRMR; Bentler 1995)=.051. Therefore, it was decided that fit was adequate.

The summary of tests related to the convergent validity (internal consistency) of the constructs and item parcels is included in Table 1. According to Fornell and Larcker (1981), average variance extracted (AVE) by each construct should be greater than .50 and the composite reliability of a factor should be equal to or greater than .60 to verify convergent validity. As Table 1 shows, the only construct that had AVE less than .50 was social influence and its AVE was .49. All other AVE values ranged from .55 to .87. Composite reliabilities were greater than .60 with a range of .74 to .94. Similarly, coefficient alphas were high and ranged from .73 to .93 with a mean of .83. Furthermore, all factor loadings were significant at .05 level. All these results imply that convergent validity (internal consistency) was satisfactory for the constructs.

To test for discriminant validity, the squares of correlations between any two constructs were compared with the AVE estimates of those two constructs (Fornell and Larcker 1981). Because the AVE for each construct was greater than its squared correlation with any other construct, discriminant validity was supported.

Structural Model Results

Table 2 presents the results for the original model as shown in Figure 1. As can be seen from the table, the fit of the model to the data was not adequate. The Satorra-Bentler scaled chi-square value was significant and other fit indices were not in acceptable ranges. The results showed that the path from TV viewership to exposure to materialistic advertising was nonsignificant. Indeed, only 1% of the variance in exposure to materialistic advertising was explained. Therefore, this path was dropped from the analysis by removing the TV viewership construct from the model. As stated in the methods section, standards of comparison constructs were represented by single indicators. Inspection of modification indices revealed that these indicators were interrelated. Moreover, the standardized residuals between these single indicators were large (greater than 2.58), meaning that those residuals were correlated. Further, modification indices for the *psi* matrix (the matrix that includes structural residuals) showed that the residuals of the standard of comparison constructs are correlated. All these findings implied that these constructs have something in common. Indeed, they are all types, or standards, of comparison people can use to evaluate their standard of living. Theoretically, one can propose that materialistic people use all kinds of comparisons more often than nonmaterialistic people do. Actually, the signs of the path coefficients from materialism to each of these standards of comparison were positive. Therefore, it was decided to include a single construct called

TABLE 1
INTERNAL CONSISTENCY RESULTS (N=301)

	Coefficient Alpha	Composite Reliability	AVE
TV Viewership	0.792	0.839	0.643
Social Influence	0.732	0.737	0.490
Materialistic Ad Exposure		0.843	0.735
Parcel 1: Lifestyles	0.888	0.902	0.650
Parcel 2: Monetary Values	0.868	0.874	0.580
Materialism		0.863	0.683
Parcel 1: Happiness	0.866	0.899	0.750
Parcel 2: Success	0.891	0.924	0.803
Parcel 3: Distinctiveness	0.892	0.929	0.813
Satisfaction with SOL		0.827	0.715
Parcel 1: Likert type questions	.642*	0.900	0.810
Parcel 2: Semantic differential	0.932	0.940	0.730
Life Satisfaction		0.898	0.815
Parcel 1	0.745	0.794	0.563
Parcel 2	0.800	0.826	0.545

Notes. AVE=Average variance explained.

Composite reliability and AVE values for parcels were calculated from separately conducted confirmatory factor analyses; composite reliability and AVE values for latent constructs were calculated from the final confirmatory factor analysis that included all constructs.

* Pearson correlation for two items

TABLE 2
STRUCTURAL MODEL RESULTS

Model Tested	χ^2	df	p	CFI	SRMR	RMSEA (C.I.)
Original Model	867.56	183	.001	.820	.110	.112 (.110-.112)
Modified Model	355.02	134	.001	.920	.097	.074 (.065-.084)

Notes. χ^2= Satorra-Bentler Scaled Chi-Square; CFI=Comparative Fit Index; SRMR=Standardized Root Mean Square Residual; RMSEA (C.I.)=Root Mean Square Error of Approximation (Confidence Interval); N=301

standard of comparison in the model and use six types of comparison as indicators of this construct. This model is shown in Figure 2.

The modified model fit the data better with Satorra-Bentler scaled χ^2 (134, N=301)=355.02. Even though the chi-square was significant, it can be expected given the relatively large sample size. Other goodness of fit statistics were in acceptable ranges: CFI=.92, SRMR=.097, and RMSEA=.074.

Table 3 shows unstandardized parameters with standard deviations, the standardized parameters, critical ratios that were calculated by dividing unstandardized parameters by the estimates of corresponding standard errors, and the level of significance (*p* values) for parameters. As expected, materialism was affected significantly by both exposure to materialistic advertising and social influence. Approximately, 11% of the variance in materialism was explained by these two variables. Materialism, in turn, explained 10% of the variance in standard of comparison. The positive path coefficient between these two constructs suggests that

as materialism increases, the use of standards of comparison increases. Standard of comparison, on the other hand, influenced satisfaction with SOL negatively. That is, as people use standards of comparison to evaluate their SOL more often, they become more dissatisfied with their SOL. Eleven percent of the variance in satisfaction with SOL was explained by standard of comparison. As predicted, satisfaction with SOL contributed to life satisfaction positively. Twenty six percent of the variance in life satisfaction was explained by satisfaction with SOL. Overall, general support was found for the modified model.

DISCUSSION

Two goals guided the current study. The first goal was to test the theoretical explanation of the negative relationship between materialism and life satisfaction as provided by Sirgy (1998). After modifying the original model, the results provided a moderately good fit to the data. As expected, all relationships between variables

FIGURE 2
The Modified Model

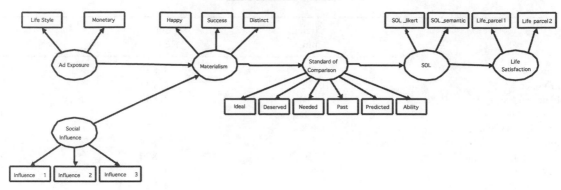

TABLE 3
PARAMETER ESTIMATES

Path	ML Estimates (Std. Dev.)	Std. ML Estimates	C. R.	p values
Materialistic Ad Exposure → Materialism	0.06 (0.02)	.15	3.00	0.003
Social Influence → Materialism	1.23 (0.29)	.30	4.24	0.001
Materialism → Standard of Comparison	0.26 (0.06)	.31	4.33	0.001
Standard of Comparison → Satisfaction with SOL	-0.53 (0.24)	-.16	-2.21	0.027
Satisfaction with SOL → Life Satisfaction	0.34 (0.05)	.51	6.80	0.001

Notes. ML=Maximum likelihood; Std. Dev.=standard deviation; C.R.=critical ratio

were significant. The study findings did not support Sirgy's explanation but the same findings shed new light on a possible different explanation: the more materialistic people are, the more they seem to use all types of standard of comparisons (affective- and cognitive-based expectations) to make judgments about their standard of living. And the more they use these standards of comparison (irrespective of whether these expectations are affective or cognitive) the more they judge their standard of living negatively. The more negative their evaluations of their standard of living the more they feel dissatisfied with their lives. Of course we expected that the more-materialistic people use affective-based standards of comparison (ideal-, deserved-, and minimum-need expectations) the more likely they are to evaluate their standard of living negatively. But we didn't expect the fact that the more they use cognitive-based expectations the more likely they are to make negative evaluations about their standard of living. We expected the opposite. Perhaps the reality is that the more people are materialistic the more they preoccupy themselves with all kinds of thoughts related to standard of living. These thoughts are likely to conjure up all kinds of expectations, cognitive and affective-based expectations. And the more they think about their standard of living, the more their expectations become inflated and unrealistic. This may be one

explanation for our study findings. Another explanation may be that our standard-of-comparison measures were not sensitive enough to force respondents to make distinctions among cognitive versus affective-based expectations. Yet another methodological explanation may be a response bias effect. Respondents were biased by the way these measures captured their expectations and responded in the same manner across all six items designed to capture these expectations. Future research should explore this issue further and conduct studies with more sensitive expectation measures. The expectation measures should be captured with multiple indicators and the placement of these measures should be varied in the survey questionnaire to minimize response bias.

The second goal of this study was to test the explanation that materialism is not directly affected by TV viewership but through exposure to materialistic advertising (controlling for the effects of social influence). The study findings showed that materialism can indeed be predicted significantly by exposure to materialistic advertising and social influence. However, the same data failed to show that TV viewership has any predictive effects on exposure to materialistic advertising. Why did our study fail to replicate previous studies linking TV viewership with materialism? Is it possible that this finding is idiosyncratic (i.e., an outlier)? That is, could it be that television advertising in Bosnia/Herzegovina is significantly different from advertising in other countries (e.g., USA) that the frequency of television watching may not influence consumers' recall of recent advertising as being status-oriented? Future research should explore this issue by collecting data across different countries (including Bosnia/Herzegovina) and conduct cross-cultural analysis.

There are additional study limitations that should be aired. First, all variables were measured concurrently. Therefore, the statistical relationships among the constructs may not reflect causation. Future research should conduct longitudinal studies and perhaps experimental studies too. Another limitation may be related to the sample. The percentage of females participated in this study was higher than that of males. The study should be replicated with equal percentages of males and females. In addition, all analyses were conducted on a single sample. The findings should be replicated with a new sample. Lastly, the data were collected in Bosnia/Herzegovina, a collectivist country. Cross-validation of results is needed across different cultures, to include both individualistic and collectivistic cultures.

REFERENCES

Anderson, James J., and David W. Gerbing (1988), "Structural Equation Modeling in Practice: A Review and Recommended Two-Step Approach," *Psychological Bulletin*, 103 (3), 411-423.

Belk, Russell W. (1984), "Three Scales to Measure Constructs Related to Materialism: Reliability, Validity, and Relationships to Measure of Happiness," in *Advances in Consumer Research*, Vol.11, ed. Thomas F. Kinnear, Ann Arbor MI: Association of Consumer Research, 291-297.

Bagozzi, Richard P., and Todd F. Heatherton (1994), "A general Approach to Representing Multifaceted Personality Constructs: Application to State Self-Esteem," *Structural Equation Modeling*, 1(1), 35-67.

Bentler, Peter M. (1990), "Comparative Fit Indexes in Structural Models," Psychological Bulletin, 107, 238–246.

Bentler, Peter M. (1995), EQS Structural Equations Program Manual, *Encino, CA: Multivariate Software.*

Browne, Michael W., and Robert Cudeck (1989), "Single Sample Cross-Validation Indices for Covariance Structures," Multivariate Behavioral Research, 24, 445–455.

Buijzen, Moniek, and Patti M. Valkenburg (2003), "The Effects of Television Advertising on Materialism, Parent–Child Conflict, and Unhappiness: A Review of Research," *Journal of Applied Developmental Psychology*, 24 (4), 437-456.

Campbell, A., P. E. Converse, and W. L. Rodgers (1976), *The Quality of America Life*, New York: McGraw-Hill Book Company.

Churchill, Gilbert A. Jr., and George P. Moschis (1979), "Television and Interpersonal Influences on Adolescent Consumer Learning," *Journal of Consumer Research*, 6 (1), 23-35.

Clark, Paul W., Craig A. Martin, and Alan J. Bush (2001), "The Effect of Role Model Influence on Adolescents' Materialism and Marketplace Knowledge," *Journal of Marketing Theory and Practice*, 9 (4), 27-36.

Diener, Ed (1984), "Subjective Well-Being," *Psychological Bulletin*, 75(3), 542-575.

Diener, Ed, E. Suh, R. Lucas, and H. Smith (1999), "Subjective Well-Being: Three Decades of Research," *Psychological Bulletin*, 125, 276-302.

Fornell, Claes, and David F. Larcker (1981), "Evaluating Structural Equation Models with Unobservable Variables and Measurement Errors," *Journal of Marketing Research*, 18, 39-50.

Greenberg, Bradley S., and Jeffrey E. Brand (1993), "Television News and Advertising in Schools: The "Channel One" Controversy," *Journal of Communication,* 43 (1), 143-151.

Goldberg, Marvin E., and Gerald J. Gorn (1978), "Some Unintended Consequences of TV Advertising to Children," *Journal of Consumer Research*, 5 (1), 22-29.

Gurel-Atay, Eda, and M. Joseph Sirgy (2007, October), "Developing a New Measure of Materialism," Poster session presented at the annual meeting of the *North American Conference of the Association for Consumer Research*, Memphis, TN.

Joreskog, Karl, and Sorbom, D. (2006), *Lisrel 8.80 User's Guide*, Lincolnwood, IL: Scientific Software International.

La Barbera, Priscilla A., and Zeynep Gurhan (1997), "The role of Materialism, Religiosity, and demographics in Subjective Well-Being," *Psychology & Marketing*, 14 (1), 71-97.

Little, Todd D., William A. Cunningham, Golan Shahar, and Keith F. Widaman (2002), "To Parcel or Not to Parcel: Exploring the Question, Weighing the Merits," *Structural Equation Modeling*, 9 (2), 151-173.

Moschis, George P., and Roy L. Moore (1979), "Decision Making among the Young: A Socialization Perspective," *Journal of Consumer Research*, 6 (2), 101-112.

Moschis, George P., and Roy L. Moore (1982), "A Longitudinal Study of Television Advertising Effects," *Journal of Consumer Research*, 9 (3), 279-286.

Ogden, Harold J., and Ramesh Venkat (2001), "Social Comparison and Possessions: Japan vs. Canada," *Asia Pacific Journal of Marketing and Logistics*, 13 (2), 72-84.

Pine Karen J., and Avril Nash (2002), "Dear Santa: The Effects of Television Advertising on Young Children," *International Journal of Behavioral Development*, 26 (6), 529-539.

Rahtz, Don, M. Joseph Sirgy, and Meadow, H. L. (1989), "Correlates of Television Orientation Among the Elderly," *Journal of Advertising*, 18(3), 9-20.

Richins, Martha L., and Scott Dawson (1992), "A Consumer Values Orientation for Materialism and its Measurement: Scale Development and Validation," *Journal of Consumer Research*, 19 (3), 303-316.

Richins, Martha L. (2004), "The material Values Scale: Measurement Properties and Development of a Short Form," *Journal of Consumer Research*, 31 (1), 209-219.

Russell, Daniel W., Jeffrey H. Kahn, Richard Spoth, and Elizabeth M. Altmaier (1998), "Analyzing Data from Experimental Studies: A Latent Variable Structural Equation Modeling Approach," *Journal of Counseling Psychology*, 45 (1), 18-29.

Satorra, Albert, and Peter M. Bentler (1988), "Scaling Corrections for Chi-Square Statistics in Covariance Structure Analysis," *Proceedings of the Business and Economic Statistics*, Section (308-313), Alexandria, VA: American Statistical Association.

Sirgy, M. Joseph (1998), "Materialism and Quality of Life," *Social Indicators Research*, 43, 227-260.

Sirgy, M. Joseph, Dong-Jin Lee, Van Larsen, and Newell D. Wright (1998), "Satisfaction with Material Possessions and General Well-Being: The Role of Materialism," *Journal of Consumer Satisfaction/Dissatisfaction and Complaining Behavior*, 11, 103-118.

Sirgy, M. Joseph, Dong-Jin Lee, Rustan Kosenko, H. Lee
    Meadow, Don Rahtz, Muris Cicic, Guang X. Jin, Duygun
    Yarsuvat, David Blenkhorn, and Newell D. Wright (1998),
    "Does Television Viewership Play a Role in the Perception
    of Quality of Life?" *Journal of Advertising*, 27 (1), 125-142.
Steiger, James H., and Lind, J. C. (1980, May), "Statistically
    Based Tests for the Number of Factors," Annual spring
    meeting of the *Psychometric Society*, Iowa City, IA.
West, Stephen G., John F. Finch, and Patrick J. Curran (1995),
    "Structural Equation Models with Nonnormal Variables:
    Problems and Remedies," in *Structural Equation Modeling:
    Concepts, Issues, and Applications*, ed. Rick H. Hoyle,
    Thousand Oaks, CA: Sage, 56-75.

At Face Value: Visual Antecedents of Impression Formation in Servicescapes

Joost W. M. Verhoeven, University of Twente, The Netherlands
Thomas Van Rompay, University of Twente, The Netherlands
Ad Pruyn, University of Twente, The Netherlands

ABSTRACT

Consumers may base employee impressions on physical appearance and displayed personal objects. In a scenario experiment, using photos of a physician and a 360-degree panorama of his consultation room, we examined the effects of appearance and tangibles on impression formation. Study 1 shows that observers employ various strategies of combining information from different sources when forming an impression of the employee's friendliness and competence. Whereas previous research has shown that impression formation based on personal appearances proceeds in an automatic fashion, the findings of study 2 indicate that impression formation grounded in the perception of tangibles requires more elaborate processing.

INTRODUCTION

In the MTV Dating Show "Room Raiders", a young woman examines the bedrooms of three men to decide who she would like to go out with. Through a careful investigation of the rooms she tries to find out as much as possible about the tastes, hobbies, and personalities of the three candidates. For instance, upon finding a comic book, she may draw the conclusion that the guy is immature, a snowboard may signal that he is adventurous and sporty, while a messy room may suggest that he is too lazy to clean up. Without meeting even one of them, she has formed a detailed impression of the three men and she has made her decision. When she is to announce the winner, she meets the three candidates for the very first time. Even before any interaction has taken place, she is confronted with a new wealth of information: she sees what the three guys look like. However, it's too late to change her mind.

This example illustrates how people find out more about others by studying their personal living environments. By altering and customizing personal working- and living environments people express and confirm their (desired) identities (Belk 1988; Schlenker 1985). Consequently, the environments that people live in are rich with information about the personality, values and lifestyle of the occupant (Gosling et al. 2002). Observers, in turn, use those elements of the tangible environment as a 'lens' through which they view underlying constructs such as the personality, preferences, and lifestyle of the occupant (Brunswik 1956). In addition, personality impressions are affected by personal appearance. For instance, people use others' facial features to infer the personality (Berry and Wero 1993). In all, the example shows how people use different sources of information to assemble personality impressions.

The role of visual cues in social perception is not only interesting from the viewpoint of interpersonal communication; it is particularly prevalent in customer judgments of services. Since in services the 'product' consists of actions or performances rather than goods, the impressions consumers hold of service employees are central in the quality perception and satisfaction (Zeithaml, Bitner and Gremler 2006). As customers largely lack the information and skills to reliably assess the service providers' capacities, they search for alternative indicators (Hoffman and Bateson 2006; Zeithaml 1988). Visual cues may be used as such alternative indicators. In the present studies we will focus on the ways in which a consumer bases an impression of a service provider on the tangible service environment and personal appearance.

PERSONAL APPEARANCE AND IMPRESSION FORMATION

Personal appearance may be the most direct source of information about other people (Shevlin et al. 2003). Zero-acquaintance studies have found that personality ratings of strangers that are solely based on personal appearance are significantly correlated with self-ratings (Borkenau and Liebler 1992) and personality ratings of acquaintances (Berry 1990; Borkenau and Liebler 1993). This does not only imply that others use personal appearance as a source of information in impression formation, but that this information, at least with respect to some personality traits, is often fairly accurate (Shevlin et al. 2003).

In many services, competence appears to be among the most important traits that consumers use when they evaluate employees (Czepiel, Solomon and Surprenant 1985; Gronroos 2000). Even though service encounters usually comprise rather short interactions with service employees who are usually unknown to the customer, customers are generally quite capable of forming a first impression based on brief exposures to employee appearance (Czepiel et al. 1985; Grandey et al. 2005). In the political domain, Todorov (2005) illustrated the far-reaching consequences of competence judgments at zero acquaintance: Competence judgments based solely on minimal exposure to photographs of politicians significantly predicted the outcomes of elections for the U.S. Congress. Impressions following from zero-acquaintance seem to be primarily based on faces (Berry and Wero 1993). However, besides faces, a number of other appearance attributes cues may be at play, such as clothing (Mangum et al. 1997), posture, and locomotion. In this article, we will argue that personal attributes may also be incorporated into impressions of service employees.

TANGIBLE ENVIRONMENTS AND IMPRESSION FORMATION

Individuals design and alter their environments in such a way that they reinforce and express their personal identities (Belk 1988). Observers are confronted with this information, which they process and use in impression formation processes (Gosling et al. 2002). Several studies have examined the effects of tangibles on perceived traits of occupants (e.g., Burroughs, Drews and Hallman 1991; Gosling et al. 2002; Tedeschi and Melburg 1984). Occupants of high-status offices, for instance, are judged as more neat, critical, sincere, intelligent and less noisy than occupants of low-status offices (Cherulnik and Sounders 1984). Likewise, friendliness perceptions may be based on furniture arrangement: In an 'open' office setup (desk against the wall), occupants are perceived as more friendly than in a closed setup (Morrow and McElroy 1981). In a physician's consultation room, an impressive set of medical handbooks and a diploma on the wall signal competence, whereas personal objects reinforce the image of a friendly and involved person (Verhoeven, van Rompay and Pruyn 2007). These studies all illustrate how, in the eyes of observers, certain characteristics of the environment 'transfer' to the occupant.

Gosling and colleagues (2002) proposed two mechanisms through which these inference may be made. First, inferences may be the result of stereotype activation. Some object or symbol in the environment may trigger a stereotype (Kay et al. 2004), which is typically associated with a set of traits. Observers, in turn, may more or less automatically infer that these stereotypical traits apply to the occupant of the place. For instance, a poster with a peace symbol may activate the hippie stereotype, which may lead observers to believe that the occupant is laid back and is sympathetic towards certain social and political movements. Second, inferences may be the result of a two-step inference mechanism. Because behaviors that take place in an environment naturally leave residuals, observers may infer the behaviors that have taken place in an environment from the residues. Subsequently, observers infer the dispositions that underlie these behaviors (Buss and Craik 1983). Upon finding a full ashtray, one may infer that the occupant has been smoking, which may lead the observer to believe that the occupant has certain dispositions that are typical for smokers. In conclusion, tangible possessions on display may affect a wide variety of inferences about the 'displayer'.

HOLISTIC IMPRESSIONS

Personal appearances and tangible environments are seldom perceived in isolation, but observers are usually confronted with these sources of information simultaneously. Their combined effects give rise to a holistic image that shapes consumers experiences (Grove and Fisk 1989). Apart from the importance of congruence among various elements in the servicescape (Mattila and Wirtz 2001), different elements may also complement each other in terms of the meanings that are portrayed. For instance, in a healthcare setting, consumers' needs are typically twofold (Arneill and Devlin 2002; Laine *et al.* 1996). First, one needs to be assured that the care providers have the technical competence needed for successful outcomes (Czepiel *et al.* 1985). Second, patients have a desire for a service provider that shows empathy. In line with Driver and Johnston (2001), we expect that physicians will make the best impression when they express both professional and empathic qualities, through either their appearance or personal environment. In other words, we expect that information from different cues will complement each other. This prediction was tested in study 1. We used a healthcare setting to explore the role of personal appearance and tangibles in impression formation.

STUDY 1

Pretest

To make an informed decision regarding the selection of stimulus material, a pretest was conducted among 41 student (13 men, 28 women; mean age = 20.0, SD = 1.40). They were instructed to carefully watch 10 photos of physicians. The physicians were photographed in white coats, from the waist up without any environmental features visible. They varied in age and appearance. Patients rated the physician's friendliness (6 items, α = .74) and competence (13 items, α = .93). For study 1, we used photos of the physician (physician 1) that was rated friendly (M = 7.33, SD = .67), but relatively incompetent (M = 5.86, SD = 1.18) and the physician (physician 2) that was rated as competent (M = 7.28, SD = .84), but relatively unfriendly (M = 6.11, SD = .88). The physicians differed significantly in terms of friendliness as well as anticipated competence: t(19) = 5.36, p<.001 and t(19) = -5.21, p<.001 respectively.

Method

In the main study 77 students participated (32 men, 45 women; mean age = 21.0, SD = 2.37). Participants were randomly assigned to one of the four cells in a 2 (friendly vs. competent appearance) x 2 (professional vs. personal objects) between-subjects experimental design. They were asked to imagine having an appointment with a lung specialist in a general hospital because of respiration com-

plaints. The patient was asked to take a seat in the consultation room and to wait for the specialist to get ready. Next, participants used a 360 degree panorama photo to look around in the room. Using the mouse, they were able to control the speed and angle of the presentation of the room. This room contained either professional objects (such as a diploma, medical handbooks and scale models of organs) or personal objects (such as decorative sculptures, a miniature sailboat and a shawl of a sports team). After 60 seconds, participants were told the physician came in and his photo appeared on the screen. This was the physician that was rated in the pretest as either friendly but relatively incompetent, or as competent but relatively unfriendly. After exposure to the scenario, the 360 degree panorama, and the photo of the physician, participants were asked to indicate to what extent they thought the physician was competent (13 items, α = .95), friendly (6 items, α = .84) and to what extent they would be satisfied with this physician (2 items, r = .70). All items were scored on 7-point scales.

Results

In an analysis of variance, we found replication of the pretest results: participants rated physician 1 as more friendly (M = 6.98, SD = .75) than physician 2 (M = 6.50, SD = 1.12, F(1,73) = 4.71, p = .03). The environmental manipulation did not exert and effect on perceived friendliness and neither did the interaction between both factors (F>1).

Analysis of variance showed no significant main effects of our manipulations on perceived competence (F<1.4). However, the interaction between both factors was significant: F(1, 73) = 4.19, p = .04. Analysis of the simple main effects showed that the physician with a friendly appearance was perceived as more competent when he displayed professional (M = 6.21, SD = 1.00) rather than personal objects (M = 5.41, SD = 1.68): F(1,37) = 3.31, p = .08. The physician that looks competent, on the other hand, is judged as competent regardless of the objects he is surrounded with (professional objects: M = 5.95, SD = 1.32, personal objects: M = 6.35, SD = 1.07, F<1.1).

Furthermore, results showed a 2 x 2 interaction on anticipated satisfaction (see Figure 1). Examination of the simple effects shows that patients are more satisfied with a physician that looks friendly in a professional consultation room than they are with the same physician in a room with personal possessions: F(1,37) = 6.05, p = .02. For a physician that looks competent, this effect reverses: F(1,37) = 3.26, p = .08. The main-effects of both factors are non-significant: F<1.

Discussion

In line with studies in patient satisfaction (Arneill and Devlin 2002; Laine *et al.* 1996), study 1 shows that patients are only satisfied with physicians when they express both their technical and their empathetic qualities. However, the way patients infer competence seems to differ from the way they infer friendliness. Friendliness judgments in our study are based on personal appearance, but not on our manipulation of displayed possessions. On the other hand, when assessing the physician's level of technical competence, patients seem to combine information from different sources (appearance and the tangible environment). Patients infer that a physician is competent when either his appearance or his consultation room signals competence (or both).

The present study is an investigation into the cues that patients use to assess the physician. Many factors may be involved in impression formation. It is very likely that patients use all their senses and cues may include visual, auditory, and even olfactory stimuli (Grove and Fisk 1989). Although our study only examines two visual factors, it does provide us with insights as to how

FIGURE 1

Effects of appearance and tangible objects on anticipated satisfaction.

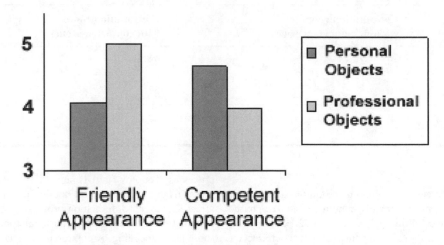

observers combine information from various sources into one meaningful impression.

First, the effects of our manipulations on perceived friendliness indicate that one cue in the environment may be so dominant that the influences of other sources become negligible. Observers will try to attend to those cues that they believe are most accurate for a specific trait, while ignoring inaccurate cues (Brunswik 1956). For instance, observers may believe that faces are most accurate in conveying information about personalities (Cloonan 2005), whereas physical spaces may be believed to hold cues as to characteristics such as a person's tidiness, values and recreational pursuits (Gosling *et al*. 2002). Hence, when judging information derived from various sources, personal appearance may be thought of as a far more direct and reliable indicator of friendliness than the tangible environment is.

Second, and more interestingly, observers may find ways to combine information from various sources in interesting ways (Grove and Fisk 1989). When inferring the level of competence from indirect cues, the default assumption may be that a physician is competent. This default belief may be so strong that a single (visual) source of information is insufficient to overrule this standard belief. Yet when a number of factors simultaneously reinforce an image that deviates from the default, an observer may discard this default belief.

Finally, when it comes to patient satisfaction, the cues seem to complement each other: patients are only satisfied when personal appearance and possessions have signaled both technical and empathetic qualities (Czepiel *et al*. 1985). It should be noted that patient satisfaction may not only be based on cues that are informative about the primary care provider (in this case the lung specialist), but also on cues that are telling about other care providers (nurses, administrative personnel etc.). Such information was not included in the study.

When consumers are confronted with an employee, they will direct their attention toward the cues they believe most accurately describe this person. As study 1 illustrates, an impression may very well result from a synthesis of different sources of information. However, not all information is processed simultaneously. As an observer's processing capacity is limited, there is a restricted amount of information that can be processed in the immediate stages after perception (Ambady and Rosenthal 1992; Peracchio and Luna 2006). In their two-stage model, Raghubir and Krishna

(1996) suggest that consumer judgments are formed and framed in an initial automatic stage, which is followed by conscious deliberate processing.

Previous research indicates that upon perceiving a target person, people usually incorporate information abstracted from his or her appearance in this initial snap-shot processing stage (Todorov *et al*. 2005). However, it remains unclear in what stage of processing environmental information is attended to. The tangible environment seems to be a rather indirect indicator, requiring more interpretation and hence more elaborate, thoughtfull processing. Therefore, we predict that information derived from tangible environments is typically attended to in later stages of information processing. This prediction was tested in study two.

STUDY 2

Method

A total of 126 undergraduate students participated in a single-factor between subjects design. They were invited into the research lab and guided to separate rooms with a computer. Instructions were provided on-screen. Participants were confronted with two photos of physicians in their working environments (at the left and right side of the screen). Next, they were instructed to click on the photo of the physician that they thought was the more competent of the two. The two physicians were selected from the pretest of study one. Their appearance was rated as approximately equally competent (M = 6.83, SD = 1.11 vs. M = 6.49, SD = .95; t (20) = 1.08, p>.10). In every set, one of the physicians was displayed in a room with competence cues (medical handbooks and mock-ups), the other one was displayed with personal objects (decorative sculptures and a set of luxurious toy cars). The position on the screen (left and right) and the appearance of the physician were counterbalanced, so that we can be sure that these factors did not affect the results in any way. Half of the participants were instructed to choose between the photos as fast as possible. The other half of the sample looked at the photos for at least 30 seconds and was subsequently asked to make their decision. This procedure was adopted from Todorov and colleagues (Todorov *et al*. 2005) to measure participants' impressions in the early stages of information processing. We omitted 11 participants from the rapid response condition whose response time was above 3 seconds.

TABLE 1

Choices between rooms as a function of length of exposure

	Consultation room without competence cues	Consultation room with competence cues	Total
t<3 sec	28	25	53
t>30 sec	10	52	62
Total	38	77	115

Results

In line with the pretest, we found that both physicians were chosen as the more competent equally in both the rapid response- and the long exposure condition: $\chi^2(1, 115) = .002$; $p>.10$.

Competence cues in the environment did not exert an effect on the chosen photo when participants responded within 3 seconds, while the vast majority of participants in the long-exposure condition did choose the physician with competence cues over the one without them (see table 1): $\chi^2(1, 115) = 17.40$; $p<.001$. These results confirm the prediction that impression formation based on tangibles requires more elaborate processing: only when participants are given the time for elaborate processing do tangible cues affect their choices.

GENERAL DISCUSSION

"During a consultation there are two people at work. While the doctor is searching for a diagnosis, the patient is quietly summing up the doctor. And it is often the patient who reaches his conclusion first" (Short 1993).

In a healthcare setting, patients may feel like their faith is in the hands of strangers. In such a situation, one naturally feels the need to assess the service provider's competence level (Czepiel *et al.* 1985). As the results of our studies show, empathic qualities are also required. Customers may turn to both personal appearances and tangible elements in the service environment to assess these characteristics but, in this study, only those cues related to personal appearance are processed in a quick, rapid fashion. Whereas rapid judgments are made without deliberate effort on the part of the consumer, conscious processes, on the other hand, are intentional, controllable and consume cognitive resources (Dijksterhuis *et al.* 2005). The findings reported suggest that this deliberate effort is needed for tangibles to affect impressions. The results from the present studies seem to suggest that in impression formation, tangibles can only be effective when they are consciously being processed. This does not mean that individuals cannot be affected by tangibles at an unconscious level. A considerable and growing body of literature stresses otherwise (Meyers-Levy and Zhu 2007). For instance, Kay et.al. (2004) showed that, at a subconscious level, objects can prime certain constructs and steer behaviors. However, our results suggest that, when competing, more direct cues are available (such as personal appearance), consumers appear to attend to those cues first. Only later, they direct their attention to tangible cues.

Models of social cognition and decision making are of special interest to our findings. These models posit a distinction between unreflective effortless "system 1" processes and slow, deliberate effortful "system 2" processes (Chaiken and Trope 1999; Kahneman 2003). Many inferences about other people, such as those based on facial expressions, can be characterized as effortless system 1 processes (Todorov and Uleman 2003). Interestingly, person impressions that are formed on-line in the very first encounter can affect subsequent information processing. Arguably, immediate system 1 judgments based on personal appearance can steer the subsequent encoding of environmental cues that are subject to multiple interpretations. This means that tangible competence symbols are likely to be interpreted as sincere and authentic when they are displayed by a person that looks competent, but may be regarded phony when displayed by someone who does not have a competent appearance. Likewise, system 1 processing of facial personality cues can affect the encoding of verbally expressed information.

Apart from the availability of cognitive resources, the extent and elaboration of processing of environmental cues is also likely to vary with customer involvement. Arguably, high-involved customers are more likely to engage in deliberate processing of various sources of information embedded in the servicescape, incorporating effects of tangible elements, whereas low involved customers are less likely to attend to these more 'subtle' or indirect sources of information. In addition, elaboration of processing may vary as a function of dispositional differences such as need for cognition (Cacioppo and Petty 1982).

In addition, future research should explore whether other types of environmental factors, such as atmospherics (e.g., scent, color or music) and layout, also affect impression formation processes in the same or different ways as the visual stimuli that were under investigation in the present studies. Arguably, such influences are more pervasive and therefore may be more likely to receive attention in an earlier stage of the impression formation process than the tangible objects discussed in this paper. Furthermore, in future research, ecological validity of scenario methods should be increased by studying consumer responses to (transcripts of) actual interactions that are open to multiple interpretations. This would provide additional proof for the relevance of the findings in actual service encounters. In the meantime, the findings reported confirm the importance of the tangible servicescape in consumer decision-making and hint at the importance of exploring and establishing the ways in which environmental cues are processed.

REFERENCES

Ambady, Nalini and Robert Rosenthal (1992), "Thin slices of expressive behavior as predictors of interpersonal consequences: A meta-analysis," *Psychological Bulletin,* 111(2), 256-274.

Arneill, Allison B. and Ann Sloan Devlin (2002), "Perceived quality of care: The influence of the waiting room environment," *Journal of Environmental Psychology,* 22(4), 345-360.

Belk, Russell W. (1988), "Possessions and the extended self," *Journal of Consumer Research,* 15(2), 139-168.

Berry, Diane S. (1990), "Taking people at face value: Evidence for the kernal of truth hypothesis," *Social Cognition,* 8, 343-361.

Berry, Diane S. and Julia L. Finch Wero (1993), "Accuracy in face perception: A view from ecological psychology," *Journal of Personality,* 61(4), 497-520.

Borkenau, Peter and Anette Liebler (1992), "Trait inferences: Sources of validity at zero acquaintance," *Journal of Personality and Social Psychology,* 62(4), 645-657.

_____ (1993), "Convergence of stranger ratings of personality and intelligence with self-ratings, partner ratings, and measured intelligence," *Journal of Personality and Social Psychology,* 65(3), 546-553.

Brunswik, Egon (1956). *Perception and the representative design of psychological experiments.* Berkeley: University of California press.

Burroughs, W. Jeffrey, David R. Drews and William K. Hallman (1991), "Predicting personality from personal possessions: A self-presentational analysis.," *Journal of Social Behavior and Personality,* 6, 147-163.

Buss, David M. and Kenneth H. Craik (1983), "The act frequency approach to personality," *Psychological Review,* 90(2), 105-126.

Cacioppo, John T. and Richard E. Petty (1982), "The need for cognition," *Journal of Personality and Social Psychology,* 42(1), 116-131.

Chaiken, Shelly and Yaacov Trope (Eds.). (1999). *Dual process theories in social psychology.* New York: Guilford.

Cherulnik, Paul.D. and Susan. B. Sounders (1984), "The social contents of place schemata: People are judged by the places where they live and work," *Population and Environment,* 7, 211-233.

Cloonan, Thomas F. (2005), "Face value: The phenomenology of physiognomy face value: The phenomenology of physiognomy," *Journal of Phenomenological Psychology,* 36(2), 219-246.

Czepiel, John A. , Michael R. Solomon and Carol F. Surprenant (1985). *The service encounter.* Lexington: Lexington.

Dijksterhuis, Ap, Pamela K. Smith, van Rick B. Baaren and Daniel H.J. Wigboldus (2005), "The unconscious consumer: Effects of environment on consumer behavior," *Journal of Consumer Psychology,* 15(3), 193-202.

Driver, Carole and Robert Johnston (2001), "Understanding service customers: The value of hard and soft attributes," *Journal of Service Research,* 4(2), 130-139.

Gosling, Samuel D., Sei Jin Ko, Thomas Mannarelli and Margaret E. Morris (2002), "A room with a cue : Personality judgments based on offices and bedrooms," *Journal of Personality and Social Psychology,* 82(3), 379-398.

Grandey, Alicia A., Glenda M. Fisk, Anna S. Mattila, Karen J. Jansen and Lori A. Sideman (2005), "Is "Service with a smile" Enough? Authenticity of positive displays during service encounters," *Organizational Behavior and Human Decision Processes,* 96(1), 38-55.

Gronroos, Christian (2000). *Service management and marketing : A customer relationship management approach.* Chichester, NY: Wiley.

Grove, Stephen J. and Raymond P. Fisk. (1989). Impression management in services marketing: A dramaturgical perspective. In Robert A. Giacalone and Paul Rosenfeld (Eds.), *Impression management in the organization* (pp. 427-438). Hillsdale, NJ: Erlbaum.

Hoffman, K. Douglas and John E. G. Bateson (2006). *Services marketing: Concepts, strategies & cases.* Mason: Thomson.

Kahneman, Daniel (2003), "A perspective on judgment and choice: Mapping bounded rationality," *American Psychologist,* 58(9), 697-720.

Kay, Aaron C., Christian Wheeler, John A. Bargh and Lee Ross (2004), "Material priming: The influence of mundane physical objects on situational construal and competitive behavioral choice.," *Organizational Behavior and Human Decision Processes,* 95, 83-96.

Laine, Christine, Frank Davidoff, Charles E. Lewis, Eugene C. Nelson, Elizabeth Nelson, Ronald C. Kessler, *et al.* (1996), "Important elements of outpatient care: A comparison of patients' and physicians' opinions," *Ann Intern Med,* 125(8), 640-645.

Mangum, Sandra, C. Garrison, C. Lind and H. Gill Hilton (1997), "First impressions of the nurse and nursing care," *Journal of Nursing Care Quality,* 11(5), 39-47.

Mattila, Anna S. and Jochen Wirtz (2001), "Congruency of scent and music as a driver of in-store evaluations and behavior," *Journal of Retailing,* 77(2), 273-289.

Meyers-Levy, Joan and Rui Zhu (2007), "The influence of ceiling height: The effect of priming on the type of processing that people use," *Journal of Consumer Research,* 34(2), 174-186.

Morrow, Paula C. and James C. McElroy (1981), "Interior office design and visitor response: A constructive replication," *Journal of Applied Psychology,* 66(5), 646-650.

Peracchio, Laura A. and David Luna (2006), "The role of thin-slice judgments in consumer psychology," *Journal of Consumer Psychology,* 16(1), 25-32.

Raghubir, Priya and Aradhna Krishna (1996), "As the crow flies: Bias in consumers' map-based distance judgments," *Journal of Consumer Research,* 23(1), 26-39.

Schlenker, Barry K. (1985). *The self and social life.* New York: McGraw-Hill.

Shevlin, Mark, Stephanie Walker, Mark N. O. Davies, Philip Banyard and Christopher Alan Lewis (2003), "Can you judge a book by its cover? Evidence of self-stranger agreement on personality at zero acquaintance," *Personality and Individual Differences,* 35(6), 1373-1383.

Short, David (1993), "First impressions," *British Journal of Hospital Medicine,* 50(5), 270.

Tedeschi, James T. and Valerie Melburg (1984), "Impression management and influence in the organization," *Research in the sociology of organizations,* 3, 31-58.

Todorov, Alexander, Anesu N. Mandisodza, Amir Goren and Crystal C. Hall (2005), "Inferences of competence from faces predict election outcomes," *Science,* 308(5728), 1623-1626.

Todorov, Alexander and James S. Uleman (2003), "The efficiency of binding spontaneous trait inferences to actors' faces," *Journal of Experimental Social Psychology,* 39(6), 549.

Verhoeven, Joost W.M., Thomas J.L. van Rompay and Ad Th.H. Pruyn. (2007). Let your workspace speak for itself: The impact of material objects on impression formation and service quality perception. In Gavan J. Fitzsimons and Vicki G. Morwitz (Eds.), *Advances in consumer research* (Vol. 34, pp. 669-674). Duluth, MN: Association for Consumer Research.

Zeithaml, Valarie A. (1988), "Consumer perceptions of price, quality, and value: A means-end model and synthesis of evidence," *Journal of Marketing,* 52(3), 2-22.

Zeithaml, Valarie A., Mary Jo Bitner and Dwayne D. Gremler (2006). *Services marketing: Integrated customer focus across the firm.* (4th ed.). Boston: McGraw-Hill/Irwin.

Disentangling the Effect of Culture and Language on Imagery Generation

Beichen Liang, East Tennessee State University, USA

ABSTRACT

This study attempts to isolate the effect of culture and language on imagery generation. By asking subjects from China, Singapore, and the U.S. to read Chinese and English messages, my findings show that it is not language, but culture, that drives the higher imagery generation capability of the Chinese people. The Chinese generate more mental images than do both Singapore Chinese and Americans, even when all groups are tested in English because Chinese have a predominantly concrete way of thinking. Singapore Chinese generate the same number of images when exposed to both languages because they have a balanced mental representation.

Past research has maintained that certain words have higher imagery value and were more likely to facilitate imagery generation than other words (Paivio and Foth 1970; Paivio 1971; Paivio and Csapo 1973; Paivio, Yuille, and Madigan 1968; Richardson 1980). For example, concrete words, such as apple, watch, or table, are more likely to create an image in one's mind than abstract words, such as love, freedom, or justice.

However, recent studies have shown that these finding on imagery generation may not hold for more distinctive cultures. When exposed to low imagery words, Chinese subjects tend to generate more images than do their American counterparts. However these studies do not differentiate the effect of culture from the effect of language. The high imagery generation capability of the Chinese may be due to a higher imagery value of ideographic language or the Chinese concrete way of thinking. This paper tries to disentangle the effect of culture versus language on imagery generation and examines in more detail which influence, language or culture, will contribute more to the high imagery generation capability of Chinese people.

LANGUAGE AND IMAGERY GENERATION

Language plays an essential role in an individual's cognitive development (Vygotsky 1962) from childhood onwards. First developed as a way of communication, language later becomes an important tool in shaping the cognitive process (Ji, Zhang, and Nisbett 2004). Recent studies in marketing have shown that linguistic differences between the Chinese and English-speaking people can influence their way of thinking (Logan 1986; Nisbett et al. 2001), categorization (Ji, Zhang, and Nisbett 2004), a consumer's verbal information memory (Schmitt, Pan, and Tavassoli 1994), judgment and choice (Schmitt and Zhang 1998), and even verbal processing (Tavassoli, 1999). It is well known that Chinese is an ideographic language while English is an alphabetic language. Such language differences may influence consumers' ability to generate imagery.

The earliest Chinese characters were formed by drawing pictographs. These characters were originally pictures of people, animals, or other objects. For example, the sun was written as ⊙ , the moon as 𝌆, water as 𝌆, and so on. Second, Chinese created indicatives by adding a kind of sign to a character to indicate a certain meaning. For example, by adding a point to "刀" (knife), a new word "刃"(blade) is formed. Third, in order to express abstract ideas or concepts, the ancient Chinese created "associated compounds" by combining two or more elements or characters. For example, pictographs of the sun and moon were written together to form a new character, 明, to express the meaning of "bright or brightness". Over the centuries, Chinese characters have evolved from irregular drawings to stylized forms, from picture-based hieroglyphics to ideographic "square characters," but they do continue to have a similar structure and grammar. So, the inference is that the processing of Chinese is more likely to generate pictures in people's minds than other language will.

Moreover, the structure of Chinese characters has nothing to do with their pronunciation. The pronunciation is based on "rote associative learning" (Tavassoli 1999, p.171). So, the learning, reading, and memory of Chinese characters rely heavily on visuospatial information or on how to discern subtle structural differences between characters.

The Chinese language widely uses classifiers to categorize words into different groups (Schmitt and Zhang 1998). Words are classified based on their physical properties, such as shape, size, thickness, and length, and also their conceptual properties, such as bendable, elastic, and graspable. For example, "zhang" is used as a classifier for objects (such as tables, desks, photos, and paper) that have properties of flatness and extendedness. The processing of such classifiers also relies heavily on visual code. On the other hand, English, French, German, and Spanish never use such classifiers.

In contrast, the entire English alphabet consists of 26 meaningless letters whose orthography represents the pronunciation of words (Tavassoli 1999). English speakers subvocalize (phonologically recode) written words (McCusker, Hillinger, and Bias 1981) and rehearse words in a phonological loop of short-term (Baddeley 1986). Moreover, English speakers tend to phonologically recode visual information as well (McCusker, Hillinger, and Bias 1981). So, the process of English is dominated by phonological representation (Schmitt, Pan, and Tavassoli 1994; Tavassoli 1999) and thus the ability to generate imagery may be inhibited by allocating mental resources to such subvocalizing of words.

In summary, the processing of Chinese words may rely heavily on visual code and ignore, at least partly, phonemic recoding (Rozin, Poritsky, and Sotsky 1971; Sasanuma 1975; Schmitt, Pan, and Tavassoli 1994; Tavassoli 1999). In contrast, the processing of English words may rely mainly on phonological code. So, the unique structures of Chinese characters may facilitate the imagery generation of Chinese subjects while English letters have no such effect.

CULTURE AND IMAGERY GENERATION

Scholars have found that the Chinese have an interdependent view of self. They view the self as part of a surrounding social context and believe one's behaviors are primarily organized, controlled, or contingent upon the thoughts, feelings, and actions of others (Markus and Kitayama 1991). Thus they attach more importance to others and emphasize their relationship and harmony with others.

The appreciation of the relationship between self and others makes Chinese people, including self and others, an integral part of the context in which they are imbedded (Markus and Kitayama 1991). The behavior of a person is strongly based on the nature of context, especially when others are present (Markus and Kitayama 1991). One learns about the self in reference to others in a particular situation; conversely, one learns about others in reference to the self in a specific context. As a result, persons are only parts of the context and cannot be fully understood when separated from the surrounding social context (Phillips 1976; Shweder 1984). So, for Chinese, specific social contexts are more likely to serve as the unit of representation than one's unique internal attributes (Markus and Kitayama 1991). Therefore, Chinese develop a concrete way of thinking (Cousins 1989; Kühnen, Hannover, and Schubert 2001) and tend to direct their attention to a specific daily context (Cousins 1989; Nisbett et al. 2001). This way of thinking is defined as "a boundedness to perceptual stimuli, a tendency to perceive things as part of the real-life settings from which they normally take their meaning, rather than to mentally isolate objects or their attributes and generalize across contexts on the basis of conceptual similarity" (Cousins 1989, p. 124).

In contrast, Westerners view the self as a bounded, unitary, and stable entity that is separated from social context. They emphasize attending to self, the appreciation of one's uniqueness from others, and the importance of asserting the self. Therefore, their attitudes, feelings, and behaviors should be determined by themselves without being controlled by any external factors (Markus, Mullally, and Kitayama 1997). They learn about the self without considering others and the context (Nisbett et al. 2001). They organize knowledge about self into a hierarchical structure, with the person's distinctive internal attributes as the superordinate nodes, resulting in a greater cognitive elaboration of attributes of the self across contexts (Markus and Kitayama 1991). So, for Westerners, the specific internal attributes will serve as the unit of representation. They develop an abstract way of thinking whose definition is to "mentally isolate objects or their attributes and generalize across contexts on the basis of conceptual similarity" (Cousins 1989, 124).

In sum, even when facing abstract words, Chinese tend to think concretely because abstract stimuli are unnatural for them and must be supplemented with contexts (Cousins 1989). So, Chinese are more likely to generate imagery when exposed to abstract words because they tend to retrieve scenes from specific daily life to fill in the missing context (Markus and Kitayama 1991), whereas Americans are less likely to do so because they tend to think in an abstract manner.

OVERVIEW OF EXPERIMENT 1

According to the above discussion, both language and concrete thinking may result in the high imagery generation ability of Chinese. But it is not easy to separate these two factors because culture influences people's thinking through language (Whorf 1956). Based on drawings, the Chinese writing system reflects the concrete way of thinking of Chinese (Logan 1986). Therefore, language is a medium that the Chinese use to transmit and internalize their culture (Ji, Zhang, and Nisbett 2004). As a result, culture and language are embedded in each other. However, these two factors can be separated by using bilinguals as research subjects (Ervin and Osgood 1954; Ji, Zhang, and Nisbett 2004).

Ervin and Osgood (1954) indicate that there are two types of bilinguals: Compound and coordinate. Compound bilinguals are individuals who learned two languages as a child, whereas coordinate bilinguals learned a second language later or even in adulthood. In other words, compound bilinguals generally learn native and second languages simultaneously, whereas coordinate bilinguals generally learn two languages consecutively (Ji, Zhang, and Nisbett 2004). An individual's age and the context of learning a second language are often closely related (Ji, Zhang, and Nisbett 2004). For example, learning a second language at a very early age often takes places in the same family context, whereas learning the second language later often involves a school context that is quite different from a family context. Therefore, compound bilinguals who learned

two languages during childhood are more likely to have a single cognitive representation. In comparison, coordinate bilinguals may have two distinctive representations, one for each language (Ervin and Osgood 1954), because learning different languages in different contexts results in more functional separation between the bilinguals' two codes (Lambert, Havelka, and Crosby 1958). Compared with compound bilinguals who have a higher degree of interdependence in the organization of a word and its translation equivalent, coordinate bilinguals have two relatively independent association networks for translation equivalents and tend to make more semantic distinctions between these two codes (Lambert, Havelka, and Crosby 1958).

Moreover, since coordinate bilinguals learned a second language later, they should be more proficient in their native language, and their ways of thinking would tend to be dominated by native culture because their cognition had been shaped significantly by their native culture before they learned the second language. Even in the process of learning the second language, their ways of thinking were also enhanced by their native culture because they were exposed to their native culture significantly more than they were exposed to the foreign culture. As a result, bilingualism for coordinate bilinguals is not balanced (Ji, Zhang, and Nisbett 2004).

The findings of Ji, Zhang, and Nisbett's (2004) study provide evidence for these arguments. In their study, which examined the effect of language or culture on categorization, Ji, Zhang, and Nisbett (2004) found that language had no effect on categorization preference of Hong Kong and Singapore Chinese (compound bilinguals). Their finding shows that compound bilinguals tend to have a single representation, while mainland Chinese tend to have an unbalanced one.

The distinction between compound and coordinate bilinguals is also supported by evidence from neurology. Kim et al. (1997) examined the spatial relationship between native and second languages in the cortex by using functional magnetic resonance imaging (fMRI). They found that for coordinate bilinguals who learned their second language in adulthood, the second language was spatially separated from the native language. In contrast, the native and second language of compound bilinguals who learned their second language at an early age are represented in common frontal cortical areas. Chee et al. (1999) found a similar result after using fMRI to examine Singapore Chinese bilinguals. They found that Singapore Chinese bilinguals use the same neuroanatomical regions during the conceptual and syntactic processing of a written sentence, regardless of testing the language, because they were exposed to Chinese and English in early childhood.

In this experiment, I examine whether culture and language have relatively independent effects on imagery generation by testing bilingual subjects in two languages (Chinese vs. English). Although it is very hard, if not impossible, to completely separate culture from language, testing bilinguals allows me to examine the effect of one, while controlling the effect of another one.

If culture is the primary driving factor behind imagery generation, then bilinguals, especially coordinate bilinguals, should generate a similar number of images when exposed to different languages. Since coordinate bilinguals have an unbalanced representation (the native language dominates the second one), and compound bilinguals have a shared representation (equal representation from both languages), I expect that coordinate bilinguals will generate more images than compound bilinguals, regardless of languages used in the test, if culture is the key driver of imagery generation. However, if language plays a key role in imagery generation, I should observe a language effect among bilinguals, especially among compound bilinguals. In other words, bilinguals should generate more images when exposed to Chinese than when

TABLE 1
ABSTRACT MESSAGES

Abstract Messages
A Classa digital camcorder has ultra compact size and weighs less than one pound.
A Classa digital camcorder performs very well under low light conditions. With its new filters and lenses, a light as dim as a candle is enough.
The Classa allows you to capture a scene clearly from a long distance with its 12X optical and 480X digital zoom. Because of the high zoom, you can get clear pictures even from a mile away.
The Classa can help you in several sports, too. It records all your movements with great accuracy. You play them back in the minutest detail, using slow motion and freeze-frame to analyze and correct your mistakes

exposed to English. Moreover, there will not be a significant difference among coordinate bilinguals, compound bilinguals, and Americans when tested in English if languages matter.

EXPERIMENT 1

The purpose of this experiment is to examine the effect of culture when controlling the effect of language and the effect of language when controlling the effect of culture.

Method

Participants. Fifty-two Chinese students from a southwestern university in mainland China, 48 Singapore Chinese students from a university in Singapore, and 26 American students from a southeastern university in the U.S. were selected. All Mainland Chinese subjects were majors in English to ensure that their English skills were strong enough. Both mainland and Singapore Chinese read stimuli in Chinese and English. Americans only read English stimuli.

Singapore Chinese were selected because Singapore has been a British colony for more than 100 years and is more westernized than Mainland China. Second, since English is one of the official languages in Singapore it is learned from kindergarten and used frequently in daily communication. Third, both Singapore and mainland China use simplified Chinese, so the effect of language is comparable. In contrast, for the majority of mainland Chinese, English is generally learned after elementary school and is rarely used in daily communication outside English classes. Hong Kong Chinese will not be used, because Hong Kong uses traditional Chinese, which differs significantly from simplified Chinese in terms of structural variations. So the effect of language is not comparable.

Stimuli. Stimuli were adapted from those used by Unnava and Burnkrant (1991) to ensure that there was no significant difference on such dimensions as believability, understandability, meaningfulness, distinctiveness, self-referencing, informativeness, or the perceived strength of arguments. A digital camcorder was used as the target product because the product category was of enough interest for the participants to be able to process the ads meaningfully. I chose a digital camcorder because participants were probably quite familiar with it even if they did not have one. So, the ability to generate images may not be inhibited here as might occur in situations where little or no schematic knowledge exists (Wright and Rip 1980). A completely fictitious name (Classa) was used to

eliminate the effect of prior experience with established brands. The ad described four attributes of the digital camcorder (size, low-light performance, zoom, and the ability to capture sports action).

Message. Only abstract word messages were adapted from those used by Unnava and Burnkrant (1991) because both literature and studies suggest that culture difference occurs only when people are exposed to abstract words. The messages are shown in Table 1.

Procedure. Participants were first asked to read a cover story and advertisement messages. Participants were also told they were taking part in an important survey and were in a small group of students whose opinions would be valued greatly, which is a typical mechanism to increase involvement. After reading the ad, the participants were asked to do a two-minute math quiz to clear their short-term memory. Then the participants were asked to write down the imagery generated in their minds when they read the ad. Next, participants completed a series of ancillary measures and a "Ten Statement Test" (TST) in which they were asked to respond ten times to the question, "Who am I?" Finally, the participants were thanked and dismissed.

Cousins (1989) used a Twenty Statement Test. However, I used a Ten Statement Test (TST) because in a pretest students found it very difficult to complete twenty statements. The coding schema used by Cousins (1989) was adapted to code the statements into two categories, concrete or abstract thought. Physical (e.g., I am 23 years old), social (e.g., I am a marketing major student), concrete preference (e.g., I like swimming; I like cats), concrete wish (e.g., I hope to be an accountant), activity (I am doing a project for my marketing class), and qualified attribute (I am nice to my friends) were coded as concrete statements. Global preference (e.g., I like music/sports/animals), global wish (e.g., I wish the world to be better), pure attribute (e.g., I am friendly), or other global statements were coded as abstract statements.

Result

Manipulation Check. Two bilingual judges who were blind to the purpose of the study coded the responses to TST into two groups: concrete or abstract thought. The reliability was 92%. A 3 (country) x 2 (language) ANOVA with the number of concrete thoughts as the dependent variable was conducted. A main effect of country emerged (M_{China}=5.61, $M_{Singapore}$=4.58, $M_{U.S.}$=3.19; $F(2, 120)$=11.957, $p<.01$). The Tukey Test showed that mainland Chinese generated more concrete thoughts than both Singapore Chinese and Americans ($ps<.01$). Singapore Chinese also generated

TABLE 2
STUDY 1 RESULTS: MEANS AND STANDARD DEVIDTIONS

Country	Language	Image	SD	n
ChinaChinese	2.44	1.67	27	
	English	2.00	1.10	24
Singapore	Chinese	1.64	1.11	25
	English	1.65	1.30	23
U.S.English	0.92	0.84	26	

FIGURE 1
IMAGES GENERATED BY SUBJECTS FROM CHINA, SINGAPORE, AND U.S.

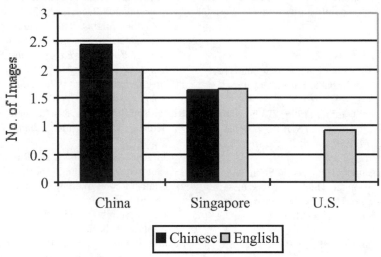

more concrete thoughts than Americans ($p<.01$). When exposed to English, the Tukey Test showed that there was no significant difference between mainland and Singapore Chinese ($M_{China}=5.13$, $M_{Singapore}=4.48$; $p>.1$). But both mainland and Singapore Chinese generated more concrete thoughts than Americans ($M_{China}=5.13$, $M_{U.S.}=3.19$, $p<.01$; $M_{Singapore}=4.48$, $M_{U.S.}=3.19$, $p<.05$) when exposed to English. When exposed to Chinese stimuli, mainland Chinese generated more concrete thoughts than Singapore Chinese ($M_{China}=6.04$, $M_{Singapore}=4.68$; $F(1, 50)=8.393$, $p<.01$).

Generated Images. A 3 (country: China, Singapore, and U.S.) x 2 (language: Chinese vs. English) ANOVA with a number of images as a dependent variable was conducted (please see Table 2 for means and standard deviations). Only a main effect of culture emerged ($M_{U.S.}=0.92$, $M_{China}=2.24$, $M_{Singapore}=1.65$; $F(2, 120)=7.126$, $p<.01$; see Figure 1). Mainland Chinese generated more images than Singapore Chinese ($p<.08$); both mainland and Singapore Chinese generated more images than Americans (China vs. U.S., $p<.01$; Singapore vs. U.S., $p<.05$).

When exposed to English, the Games-Howell Test (Levene's Test, $p<.1$) showed that both mainland and Singapore Chinese generated more images than Americans ($M_{China}=2.00$, vs. $M_{American}=0.92$, $p<.01$; $M_{Singapore}=1.65$, $M_{American}=0.92$, $p<.07$). However, there was no significant difference between mainland and Singapore Chinese subjects ($p>.1$), although mainland Chinese subjects generated a few more images. When exposed to Chinese stimuli, Chinese participants generated more images than Singapore

Chinese ($M_{China}=2.44$, $M_{Singapore}=1.64$; $F(1, 50)=4,101$, $p<.05$). For mainland Chinese subjects, there was no significant difference between Chinese and English stimuli ($M_{Chinese}=2.44$, $M_{English}=2.00$; $F(1,49)=1.222$, $p>.1$). Singapore Chinese subjects generated almost the same number of images when exposed to Chinese and English stimuli ($M_{Chinese}=1.64$, $M_{English}=1.65$; $F(1, 46)=0.001$, $p<.01$).

Discussion. My findings show that it is not language but culture that drives the higher imagery generation capability of Chinese. Imagery generation capability ranks high for mainland Chinese subjects, medium for Singapore Chinese, and low for Americans because mainland Chinese are on the concrete side and Americans are on the abstract side, while Singapore Chinese are in the middle. Singapore Chinese subjects have a balanced cognitive representation, so they generated almost the same number of images when exposed to both Chinese and English stimuli. Since mainland Chinese have a predominantly concrete mode of thinking, they generated more images than both Singapore Chinese and American subjects, even when tested in English.

GENERAL DISCUSSION

This paper attempts to differentiate the effect of culture from that of language on imagery generation. My findings show that culture is the main factor driving imagery generation. Mainland Chinese have higher imagery generation capability than both Singapore Chinese and Americans because they are more likely to think concretely. Singapore Chinese generate the same number of images when exposed to both Chinese and English stimuli because they have a balanced mental representation. Moreover, since their representation is a mix of Eastern and Western cultures, Singapore Chinese are in the middle in terms of imagery generation. Although my study did not find that language affected imagery generation significantly, its effect should not be ignored because mainland Chinese generated fewer images when exposed to English stimuli than when exposed to Chinese stimuli. Moreover, culture shapes individuals' cognition through language.

This study did not examine the possible effect of location on imagery generation. Studies have shown that the cognitive process could be modified after living in another culture for even a short period of time (Brewer and Gardner 1996; Ji, Zhang, and Nisbett 2004). Future studies should examine whether mainland Chinese have a lower imagery generation capability after living in Western cultures for some time.

REFERENCES

Baddeley, Alan (1981), "The Concept of Working Memory: A View of Its Current State and Probable Future Development," *Cognition*, 10 (1-3), 17-23.

Brewer, Marilynn B. and Wendi Gardner (1996), "Who Is This 'We'? Levels of Collective Identity and Self Representations," *Journal of Personality and Social Psychology*, 71 (1), 83-93.

Chee, Michael W. L., David Caplan, Chun Siong Soon, N. Sriram, Edsel W. L. Tan, Thorsten Thiel and Brendan Weekes (1999), "Processing of Visually Presented Sentences in Mandarin and English Studied with fMRI," *Neuron*, 23 (1), 127-37.

Cousins, Steven D. (1989), "Culture and Self-Perception in Japan and the United States," *Journal of Personality and Social Psychology*, 56 (1), 124-31.

Ervin, S. M. and C. E. Osgood (1954), "Second Language Learning and Bilingualism," *Journal of Abnormal and Social Psychology*, 49, 139-46.

Ji, Li-Jun, Zhiyong Zhang, and Richard E. Nisbett (2004), "Is It Culture or Is It Language? Examination of Language Effects in Cross-Cultural Research on Categorization," *Journal of Personality and Social Psychology*, 87 (1), 57-65.

Kim, Karl H. S., Norman R. Relkin, Kyoung-Min Lee, and Joy Hirsch (1997), "Distinct Cortical Areas Associated with Native and Second Languages, *Nature*, 388 (July 10), 171-74.

Kühen, Ulrich, Bettina Hannover, and Benjamin Schubert (2001), "The Semantic-Procedural Interface Model of the Self: The Role of Self-Knowledge for Context-Dependent versus Context-Independent Modes of Thinking," *Journal of Personality and Social Psychology*, 80 (3), 398-409.

Lambert, W. E., J. Havelka, and C. Crosby (1958), "The Influence of Language-Acquisition Contexts on Bilingualism," *Journal of Abnormal and Social Psychology*, 56, 239-44.

Logan, Robert K. (1986). *The Alphabet Effect*. New York, NY: Morrow.

Markus, Hazel Rose and Shinobu Kitayama (1991), "Culture and the Self: Implications for Cognition, Emotion, and Motivation," *Psychological Review*, 98 (2), 224-53.

Markus, Hazel Rose, Patricia R. Mullally, and Shinobu Kitayama (1997), "Selfways: Diversity in Modes of Cultural Participation," in *The Conceptual Self in Context: Culture, Experience, Self-Understanding*, ed. Ulric Neisser and David A. Jopling, Cambridge, England: Cambridge University Press, 13-61.

McCusker, Leo X., Michael L. Hillinger, and Randolph G. Bias (1981), "Phonological Recoding and Reading," *Psychological Bulletin*, 89 (2), 217-45.

Nisbett, Richard E., Kaiping Peng, Incheol Choi, and Ara Norenzayan (2001), "Culture and systems of thought: Holistic vs. analytic cognition," *Psychological Review*, 108 (2), 291-310.

Paivio, Allan (1971), *Imagery and Verbal Process*, New York: Holt, Rinehart, and Winston.

Paivio, Allan and Kalman Csapo (1973), "Picture Superiority in Free Recall: Imagery or Dual Coding," *Cognitive Psychology*, 5 (2), 176-206.

Paivio, Allan and Dennis Foth (1970), "Imaginal and Verbal Mediators and Noun Concreteness in Paired Associate Learning: The Elusive Interaction," *Journal of Verbal Learning and Behavior*, 9, 384-90.

Paivio, Allan, John C. Yuille, and Stephen A. Madigan (1968), "Concreteness, Imagery and Meaningfulness Values for 925 Nouns," *Journal of Experimental Psychology Monograph Supplement*, 76 (1), 1-25.

Phillips, Denis Charles (1976), *Holistic Thought in Social Science*, Stanford, CA: Stanford University Press.

Richardson, John T. (1980), "Concreteness, Imagery, and Semantic Categorization," *Journal of Mental Imagery*, 4, 51-58.

Rozin, Paul, Suan Poritsky, and Raina Sotsky (1971), "American Children with Reading Problems Can Easily Learn to Read English Represented by Chinese Characters," *Science*, 171 (3976), 1264-67.

Sasanuma, Sumiko (1975), "Kana and Kanji Processing in Japanese Aphasics," *Brain and Language*, 2 (3), 369-83.

Schmitt, Bernd H., Yigang Pan, and Nader T. Tavassoli (1994), "Language and consumer memory: The Impact of Linguistic Differences between Chinese and English," *Journal of Consumer Research*, 21 (December), 419-31.

Schmitt, Bernd H. and Shi Zhang (1998), "Language Structure and Categorization: A Study of Classifiers in Consumer Cognition, Judgment, and Choice," *Journal of Consumer Research*, 25 (September), 108-22.

Shweder, Richard A. (1984), "Preview: A Colloquy of Culture Theorists," in *Culture Theory: Essays on Mind, Self, and Emotion*, ed. Richard A. Shweder and Robert A. LeVine, Cambridge, England: Cambridge University Press, 1-24.

Solso, Robert L. (2001), *Cognitive Psychology* (6th ed), Needham Heights, MA: Allyn & Bacon.

Tavassoli, Nader T. (1999), "Temporal and Associative Memory in Chinese and English," *Journal of Consumer Research*, 26 (September), 170-81.

Unnava, Rao H. and Robert E. Burnkrant (1991), "An Imagery-Processing View of the Role of Pictures in Print Advertisement," *Journal of Marketing Research*, 28 (May), 226-31.

Vygotsky, Lev S. (1962), *Thought and Language*, Cambridge, MA: MIT Press.

Whorf, Benjamin Lee (1956). *Language, Thought, and Reality*, Cambridge, MA: Technology Press of MIT.

Wright, Peter and Peter Rip (1980), "Product Class Advertising Effects on First-Time Buyers' Decision Strategies," *Journal of Consumer Research*, 7 (September), 176-88.

Successful Brand Alliance and Its Negative Spillover Effect on a Host Brand: Test of Cognitive Responses

Ji-Yeon Suh, Korea Advanced Institute of Science and Technology, Korea
Se-Bum Park, Korea Advanced Institute of Science and Technology, Korea

ABSTRACT

The current research demonstrates that a high-favorability host brand can benefit from co-branding with a moderate-favorability partner brand due to greater (fewer) positive (negative) cognitive responses. By contrast, a moderate-favorability host brand can enhance the evaluation of its co-branded product by partnering a high-favorability partner because the partner brand can facilitate more positive cognitive responses while blocking cognitive responses. We also found that a high-favorability partner brand may do more harm than good to a moderate-favorability host brand's new product because the partner brand does not block the activation of counter-arguments after co-branding is terminated.

INTRODUCTION

Brand alliance, defined as the situation in which two or more brands are joined together in some fashion (Rao, Qu, and Ruekert 1999; Rao and Ruekert 1994; Simonin and Ruth 1998), provides means to examine the effects of brand equity on consumer reaction to brand combinations. Several empirical studies on brand alliance have documented mostly positive effects of brand alliance on consumer brand evaluations. Rao and Ruekert (1994), for example, have claimed that brand alliance allows consumers to assume that high-quality products will only partner with other high-quality products. Brand alliance triggers the transfer of positive affect from the high-quality brands to the low-quality brands (Levin, Davis, and Levin 1996), improves the image of one or the other partners and signals greater product quality (Park, Jun, and Shocker 1996), and conveys information about the quality of a product even when its quality has not or cannot be observed (Rao et al. 1999). Relatedly, Simonin and Ruth (1998) demonstrate that an attitude toward a co-branded product influences subsequent impressions of each partner's brand such that positive spillover effects emerge.

The current research, however, maintains that partnering with high-quality brands may do more harm than good to host brands. Sternthal, Phillips, and Dholakia (1978), for example, have demonstrated that individuals who are favorably predisposed to message appeal are more persuaded by a moderate-credibility than a high-credibility message source because individuals are not highly motivated to retrieve thoughts that are presumably positive or the high-credibility source may engender a feeling that the position is adequately represented and thus no more support argumentation is necessary when the high-credibility message source advocates a view that individuals initially favor. In contrast, individuals freely generate and rehearse their own repertoire of thoughts as well as those included in the message when a moderate-credibility source endorses the message. However, a high-credibility message source exerts a greater persuasive impact on attitudes of message recipients with a negative initial opinion toward an advocated issue because the high credibility blocks the retrieval and rehearsal of counterarguments (Sternthal, Dholakia, and Leavitt 1978; Sternthal et al. 1978). For example, Voss and Tansuhaj (1999) find that consumer evaluation of an unknown brand from another country becomes more positive when it partners with a well-known domestic brand. Drawing on the cognitive response theory, we thus hypothesize that consumer evaluation of a co-branded product will be moderated by the degree of a partner brand's favorability in the brand alliance context.

Regarding the spillover effect of brand alliance, Keller and Aaker (1992) maintain that a prior, successful extension increases consumer evaluation of not only a proposed brand extension but also of a core brand itself. By contrast, a poor brand extension dilutes consumer evaluation of a core brand (Loken and Roedder John 1993; Sullivan 1990). Considering a brand alliance between a moderate-favorability host brand and a high-favorability partner brand, one would expect a positive spillover of the brand alliance on a host brand to emerge because consumer evaluation of a co-branded product between these two brands becomes positive based on the cognitive response account. We hypothesize, however, that negative cognitive responses will be activated once the host-brand does not carry the high-favorability partner brand any more, resulting in a contrast effect, a negative spillover effect of the brand alliance. To test these hypotheses, we conduct an experiment in which the favorability of a host and that of a partner brand are varied to examine their impact on consumer evaluation of the brand alliance and its spillover effect on the host brand's new product.

BURBERRY AND LOUIS VUITTON STUDY

Overview of the Study

The objectives of the current research were twofold. First, we intended to investigate how a host brand's favorability and a partner brand's favorability would influence the evaluation of their co-branded product. Second, we aimed to examine whether or not the favorability of the co-brand evaluation would help or hurt the evaluation of the host brand's new product launched after their brand alliance is terminated. Toshiba and Sony were chosen as representing a moderate- and a high-favorability host brand respectively, and Burberry and Louis Vuitton were selected as representing a moderate- and a high-favorability partner brand respectively.

Method

Participants and Design. Two-hundred and ten adults participated in this experiment for a cyber-money gift certificate. Of 210 participants, females were 102 (51.9%), and their mean age was 32.3 years old. Their occupation were undergraduates (27.6%), graduates (6.2%), businessmen (58.6%), and self-employed and housewives (7.6%).

The current research employed a 2 (host brand's favorability: Toshiba or Sony) x 2 (partner brand's favorability: Burberry or Louis Vuitton) between-subjects design in which Toshiba (Sony) represents a moderate (high) favorability host brand, and Burberry (Louis Vuitton) represents moderate (high) favorability partner brand.

Procedure and Measures. At the beginning of the experiment, participants were asked to read a product description about either a Toshiba's or a Sony's new laptop partnered with either Burberry or Louis Vuitton. As shown in the appendix, participants were shown the color pictures of the co-branded laptop including one standard interior cut and one exterior cut embroidered with the partner brand's prototypical patterns and colors. In addition, identical hardware specifications such as CPU, memory, hard disk, and LCD size were provided across all treatment conditions. Next, participants were asked to evaluate the co-branded laptop on the following

Advances in Consumer Research
Volume 36, © 2009

FIGURE 1
CO-BRANDED LAPTOP: TOSHIBA VERSUS SONY

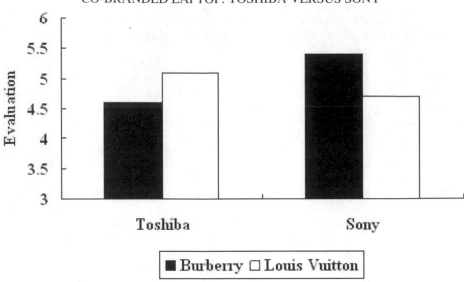

six seven-point bi-polar items: dissatisfied-satisfied, unfavorable-favorable, dislike-like, unreliable-reliable, unappealing-appealing, and unattractive-attractive. These six items were loaded on a single factor and were averaged to form a reliable co-brand's evaluation index (α=.92). Right after the evaluation of the co-branded laptop, participants were asked to list their thoughts about the co-branded laptop, which were coded and categorized into positive, neutral, and negative thoughts by three independent judges.

Next, participants were told that either Toshiba or Sony would launch this new laptop of its own, and were shown its pictures that did not vary across the treatment conditions except for brand logos. Participants were then asked to evaluate the host brand's new laptop on the identical bi-polar items to the co-branded laptop. Again, the six evaluative items were averaged to form a reliable host brand evaluation index (α=.92). After participants evaluated the host brand's new laptop, they were asked to list their thoughts about the laptop. Participants were then asked to evaluate the partner brand on the following eight seven-point scale items (1=not at all, 7=very much): interested, attention-getting, familiar, preferred, aspiring, luxurious, unique, and valuable. These eight evaluative items were also averaged to form a reliable evaluation index for the partner brand (α=.95). Last, participants' prior attitude toward the host brand was evaluated on the same bi-polar items used for the co-branded and the host brand laptop. Again, these six evaluative items were averaged to form a reliable prior attitude index toward the host brand (α=.93). Participants were then debriefed and thanked.

Results and Discussion

Manipulation Checks. A 2 (host brand's favorability) x 2 (partner brand's favorability) ANOVA was conducted to check participants' prior attitude toward the host brand and their evaluation of the partner brand. Our analysis first yielded a significant main effect of the host brand on the prior attitude toward the host brand, indicating that participants preferred Sony (M=5.0) to Toshiba (M=4.5, $F(1, 185)$=10.02, p<.01). Our analysis also found that participants evaluated Louis Vuitton (M=4.7) more favorably than Burberry (M=3.4, $F(1,183)$=62.95, p<.001).

Co-Brand and Host Brand Evaluation Indices. First, the analysis conducted a 2 (host brand's favorability) x 2 (partner brand's favorability) ANOVA on the evaluation index for the co-brand. As shown in figure 1, the analysis only yielded a significant host-partner brand interaction ($F(1,206)$=18.05, p<.001), suggesting that participants evaluated the Toshiba-Louis Vuitton laptop (M=5.1) more favorably than the Toshiba-Burberry laptop (M=4.6, $t(104)$=2.67, p<.01). By contrast, participants preferred the Sony-Burberry laptop (M=5.4) to the Sony-Louis Vuitton laptop (M=4.7, $t(102)$=3.33, p<.01).

Second, a 2 (host brand's favorability) x 2 (partner brand's favorability) ANOVA on the evaluation index for the host brand's new laptop was conducted. As figure 2 indicates, the analysis yielded a significant main effect of the host brand, suggesting that participants liked the Sony's laptop (M=4.9) more than the Toshiba's (M=4.6, $F(1, 206)$=5.1, p<.05). The analysis also revealed a significant host-partner brand interaction ($F(1, 206)$=6.2, p<.05), demonstrating that participants evaluated the Sony's new laptop more favorably after exposure to the Sony-Burberry's laptop (M=5.2) than the Sony-Louis Vuitton's laptop (M=4.8, $t(102)$=2.65, p<.01), whereas no significant difference was found for the Toshiba's own laptops.

Spillover Effect of Co-Branding on the Host Brand Evaluation. Consistent with Simonin and Ruth (1998), the analysis offered strong support for the spillover effects of co-branding on the host-brand evaluation except for the Toshiba-Louis Vuitton condition. As shown in figures 1 and 2, participants' evaluations of the Toshiba's and the Sony's new laptops were assimilated to their prior evaluations of the Toshiba-Burberry, the Sony-Burberry, and the Sony-Louis Vuitton co-branded laptops. However, the analysis found a contrast between the Toshiba's own laptop (M=4.7) and the Toshiba-Louis Vuitton's laptop (M=5.1, $t(52)$=2.45, p<.05). To further examine the underlying cognitive mechanism of the spillover effects, we analyzed participants' cognitive responses next.

Test of the Cognitive Response Hypothesis. First, our analysis demonstrated significant host-partner brand interactions for positive thoughts ($F(1, 204)$=23.64, p<.001) and negative thoughts ($F(1,$

FIGURE 2
HOST BRAND'S LAPTOP: TOSHIBA VERSUS SONY

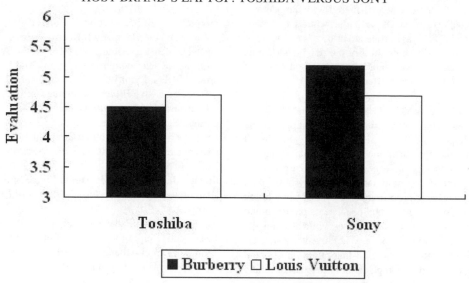

TABLE 1
COGNITIVE RESPONSES: MEANS (AND STANDARD DEVIATIONS)

Host brand		Partner brand			
		Louis Vuitton		Burberry	
		Co-brand's	Host brand's	Co-brand's	Host brand's
Toshiba					
	Positive	1.47 (.14)	1.00 (.12)	.89 (.11)	1.06 (.11)
	Neutral	.16 (.06)	.13 (.05)	.09 (.04)	.13 (.05)
	Negative	.18 (.05)	.46 (.11)	.74 (.16)	.31 (.07)
Sony					
	Positive	.91 (.12)	.96 (.11)	1.60 (.16)	1.24 (.12)
	Neutral	.19 (.07)	.30 (.08)	.12 (.06)	.18 (.05)
	Negative	.67 (.11)	.54 (.10)	.14 (.05)	.24 (.07)

204)=27.48, $p<.001$) for the co-brand evaluation. As table 1 shows, the findings suggested that participants generated more positive ($M_{POSITIVE}$=1.47) and fewer negative thoughts ($M_{NEGATIVE}$=.18) for the Toshiba-Louis Vuitton laptop than for the Toshiba-Burberry laptop ($M_{POSITIVE}$=.89, $t(102)$=3.28, $p<.01$; $M_{NEGATIVE}$=.74, $t(102)$=-3.36, $p<.01$, respectively). By contrast, participants generated more positive ($M_{POSITIVE}$=1.60) and fewer negative thoughts ($M_{NEGATIVE}$=.14) for the Sony-Burberry laptop than for the Sony-Louis Vuitton laptop ($M_{POSITIVE}$=.91, $t(102)$=3.59, $p<.01$; $M_{NEGATIVE}$=.67, $t(102)$=-4.28, $p<.01$, respectively).

On the other hand, only a significant main effect of the partner brand on negative thoughts emerged for the evaluation of the host brand's new laptop ($F(1, 204)$=5.77, $p<.05$), suggesting that participants generated more negative thoughts when two host brands, Toshiba and Sony, did not carry the Louis Vuitton (M=.50) name than when they did not carry the Burberry brand name (M=.28). These findings were considered providing empirical support for the cognitive response hypothesis such that a moderate-favorability partner brand (Burberry) prompted greater elaboration of positive thoughts when partnered with a high-favorability host brand (Sony), whereas a high-credibility partner brand (Louis Vuitton) generated greater positive thoughts and blocked the activation of negative thoughts when partnered with a moderate-favorability host brand (Toshiba). Of particular, when a moderate-favorability host brand (Toshiba) introduced its own brand after the co-branded product with a high-credibility partner brand (Louis Vuitton), the deactivated negative thoughts were released, resulting in a negative spillover, the contrast effect.

SUMMARY AND CONCLUSION

The current research has successfully tested and supported the cognitive response hypothesis that the high-favorability host brand can benefit from co-branding with the moderate-favorability partner brand because greater (fewer) positive (negative) cognitive responses are generated. By contrast, the moderate-favorability host brand can enhance the evaluation of its co-branded product by partnering with the high-favorability partner brand because its partner brand can facilitate more positive cognitive responses while blocking the activation of negative cognitive responses. The current research has also shown that the evaluation of the high-favorability host brand may backfire when co-branding a high-favorability partner brand because individuals generate more counter-arguments than supporting arguments. From the managerial standpoint, these findings suggest that marketers for moderate-favorability host brands should keep in mind that high-credibility partner brands both help and hurt their brand. In addition, marketers for high-favorability host brands should be reminded that teaming-up with equally high-favorability partner brands may do more harm than good in certain conditions. From the theoretical standpoint, the current research contributes to brand alliance research in that the underlying cognitive mechanisms of consumer evaluation of co-branding and its spillover effects are identified. Also, the current research has provided further empirical support for the cognitive response such that the favorability of a partner brand either enhance or undermine consumer evaluation of brand alliances. However, the current research is limited in that the role of cognitive resources is not taken into consideration. Individuals with lack of cognitive resources, for example, low-involvement individuals may prefer a high-favorability host and partner's co-branded product because their thought generations are restricted and thus use a brand-name heuristic.

REFERENCES

Keller, Kevin L. and David A. Aaker (1992), "The Effects of Sequential Introduction of Brand Extensions," *Journal of Marketing Research*, 29 (February), 35-50.

Levin, Aron M., James C. Davis, and Irwin P. Levin (1996), "Theoretical and Empirical Linkages between Consumers' Responses to Different Branding Strategies," in *Advances in Consumer Research*, Vol. 23, ed. Kim P. Corfman and John G. Lynch, Jr., Provo, UT : Association for Consumer Research, 296-300.

Loken, Barbara and Deborah Roedder John (1993), "Diluting Brand Beliefs: When Do Brand Extensions Have a Negative Impact?" *Journal of Marketing*, 57 (3), 71-84.

Park, C. Whan, Sung Youl Jun, and Allan D. Shocker (1996), "Composite Brand Alliances: An Investigation of Extension and Feedback Effects," *Journal of Marketing Research*, 33, 453-66.

Rao, Akshay R., Lu Qu, and Robert W. Ruekert (1999), "Signaling Unobservable Product Quality through a Brand Ally," *Journal of Marketing Research*, 36, 258-68.

Rao, Akshay R. and Robert W. Ruekert (1994), "Brand Alliances as Signals of product Quality," *Sloan Management Review*, 36 (Fall), 87-97.

Simonin, Bernard L. and Julie A. Ruth (1998), "Is a Company Known by the Company It Keeps? Assessing the Spillover Effects of Brand Alliances on Consumer Brand Attitudes," *Journal of Marketing Research*, 35, 30-42.

Sternthal, Brian, Lynn W. Phillips, and Ruby Dholakia (1978), "The Persuasive Effects of Source Credibility: A Situational Analysis," *Public Opinion Quarterly*, 42 (3), 285-314.

Sternthal, Brian, Ruby Dholakia, and Clark Leavitt (1978), "The Persuasive Effect of Source Credibility: Tests of Cognitive Response," *Journal of Consumer Research*, 4 (March), 252-60.

Sullivan, Mary (1990), "Measuring Image Spillovers in Umbrella-Branded Products," *Journal of Business*, 63 (3), 309-29.

Voss, Kevin E. and Patriya Tansuhaj (1999), "A Consumer Perspective on Foreign Market Entry: Building Brands through Brand Alliances," *Journal of International Consumer Marketing*, 11(2), 39-58.

APPENDIX
EXPERIMENTAL STIMULI

(a) Toshiba-Burberry Co-Branded Laptop

TOSHIBA-BB-1

EXTERIOR

INTERIOR

CPU	Intel Core2 Duo Santarosa T7700 (2.4GHz)
RAM	2GB DDR2 667 SDRAM
L2 CACHE	4MB
LCD	14.1" TFT
RESOLUTION	SXGA+ (1,440 x 1,050)
VGA	Intel GMA X3100
VRAM	128MB
HDD	120GB (S-ATA, 5,400rpm)
OPTICAL DRIVE	DVD±RW
WIRELESS LAN	802.11a/b/g/n
WEIGHT	5.9 (lbs)
PRICE	2,150,000 (Won)

(b) Sony-Louis Vuitton Co-Branded Laptop

SONY-LV-1

EXTERIOR

INTERIOR

CPU	Intel Core2 Duo Santarosa T7700 (2.4GHz)
RAM	2GB DDR2 667 SDRAM
L2 CACHE	4MB
LCD	14.1" TFT
RESOLUTION	SXGA+ (1,440 x 1,050)
VGA	Intel GMA X3100
VRAM	128MB
HDD	120GB (S-ATA, 5,400rpm)
OPTICAL DRIVE	DVD±RW
WIRELESS LAN	802.11a/b/g/n
WEIGHT	5.9 (lbs)
PRICE	2,150,000 (Won)

(c) Toshiba's Own Laptop

TOSHIBA Satellite S40

EXTERIOR

INTERIOR

CPU	Intel Core2 Duo Santarosa T7700 (2.4GHz)
RAM	2GB DDR2 667 SDRAM
L2 CACHE	4MB
LCD	14.1" TFT
RESOLUTION	WSXGA+ (1,680 x 1,050)
VGA	nVIDIA Quadro NVS 140M
VRAM	224MB
HDD	160GB (S-ATA, 5,400rpm)
OPTICAL DRIVE	DVD±RW
WIRELESS LAN	802.11a/b/g/n
WEIGHT	5.6 (lbs)
PRICE	2,100,000 (Won)

(d) Sony's Own Laptop

SONY VAIO S40

EXTERIOR

INTERIOR

CPU	Intel Core2 Duo Santarosa T7700 (2.4GHz)
RAM	2GB DDR2 667 SDRAM
L2 CACHE	4MB
LCD	14.1" TFT
RESOLUTION	WSXGA+ (1,680 x 1,050)
VGA	nVIDIA Quadro NVS 140M
VRAM	224MB
HDD	160GB (S-ATA, 5,400rpm)
OPTICAL DRIVE	DVD±RW
WIRELESS LAN	802.11a/b/g/n
WEIGHT	5.6 (lbs)
PRICE	2,100,000 (Won)

"…Do I need it, do I, do I really need this?": Exploring the Role of Rationalization in Impulse Buying Episodes

Andreas Chatzidakis, Royal Holloway University of London, UK
Andrew P. Smith, Nottingham University, UK
Sally Hibbert, Nottingham University, UK[1]

ABSTRACT

The paper complements existing research regarding the interplay between impulsive and deliberative processes in consumer decision making, by examining how cognition (in the form of rationalizations or motivated judgements) enables people to proceed with (rather than control) their impulses. It applies the concept of neutralization (Sykes and Matza, 1957), in the manner of a theory of motivated cognition and as a taxonomy of pre- and post-behavioral rationalizations; and presents findings from a preliminary study which suggests that neutralization theory can be applied to accounts of impulse buying episodes.

INTRODUCTION

The negative externalities of consumption are often rehearsed (e.g. environmental impact); whereas the personal negative consequences of consumption are often neglected in the policy domain (with the possible exception of debt). Likewise impulse buying is often represented as a benign activity in many forums. However, it can have negative consequences for the participant, particularly if the consumer succumbs to impulses on a regular basis or has limited financial means. Consumer debt in developed economies is excessive (e.g. Brown et al. 2005) and causes concern for policy makers, debt related charities and consumer interest groups. Household bankruptcy rates are increasing, and this appears to be attributable to excessive spending on consumer durables and services rather than more run of the mill household expenses. Indeed, there is an established empirical link between indebtedness, bankruptcy and the propensity to succumb to *Akratic* repeated 'excessive' impulse purchase (Wood 1998). Research has also shown that impulse purchases can have negative psychological consequences for the participants (Wood 1998; Green and Smith 2002) as well as lead to domestic conflict and other negative social consequences (Green and Smith 2002). Repeat impulse purchase can be a problematic form of buying behavior whatever the financial resources of the consumer. Even those who can afford it may experience the negative familial and psychological consequences (the research reported here does not explore impulse buying which is attributable to an impulse disorder-Lejoyeux et al. 1996).

Research into impulse buying has provided many insights, which are explored below, however there is still some ambiguity about a] the exact role of cognition on impulse restraint and enactment and b] how consumers deal with impulses that carry negative consequences both in post-behavioral (i.e. as a result of an impulsive purchase) and pre-behavioral stages (i.e. at the time of purchase) of the impulse formation and enactment process (Dholakia 2000). Indeed, the consumers' cognitive ability to cope with any doubts or internal conflicts should be a key facilitatory factor of repeated impulsive behavior. In an attempt to redress this issue, the current paper advances the concept of neutralization (Sykes and Matza 1957) and explores its applicability in twenty consumer accounts of impulse buying episodes.

CONCEPTUAL CONTEXT

Impulsiveness in any context is a difficult construct, and one that can be defined in many ways (Coscina 1997, Webster and Jackson 1997a, 1997b), nonetheless the basic elements of these generic psychological definitions are evident in most existing definitions of impulse buying, such as that offered by Rook and Hoch (1985): 1. Sudden and spontaneous desire to act; 2. Temporary loss of control; 3. Psychological conflict and struggle; 4. Reduction of cognitive evaluation; 5. Disregard for consequences. This perspective is reflected in Rook's (1987) definition of impulse purchasing as "a sudden, often powerful and persistent urge to buy something immediately" (Rook 1987, 191). Vohns and Faber (2007) note that recent research continues to reflect this viewpoint, by for example, distinguishing between people that are impulsive and those that are not. They caution, however, that this distinction overlooks the fact that nearly everyone occasionally engages in impulse purchases and even the most impulsive people sometimes do manage to control their impulses.

Impulse buying has been consistently linked with mood states (e.g. Hill and Ward 1989, Rook and Gardner 1993). Interestingly Rook and Gardner (1993) found that positive mood states are more favorable to impulse buying than negative ones, but also suggested that consumers may use impulse purchasing to extend or alter mood states, for example people might buy on impulse in negative moods, that is, as a "therapeutic mood alteration tactic" (Rook and Gardner 1993, 19). Luomala (1998) provides support for this in a study of self-gift behavior, arguing that the self-regulation of negative moods through consumption related activities was a "common and integral part of consumers' lives" (Luomala 1998, 109). Other studies of self-gift behavior and compensatory consumption have also shown that consumption can be used as a device for mood repair (Mick, DeMoss and Faber 1992, Woodruffe 1997a, Woodruffe-Burton 1998a). The link between these forms of consumption and impulse buying remains largely unexplored however. Moreover as Rook and Gardner (1993) postulate it is a not only negative mood that may encourage impulse buying. Youn and Faber (2000) investigated cues that might trigger impulse buying and found that both negative and positive moods or feeling states might prompt impulse buying. It should also be remembered that mood is both an 'input' and an 'output' to impulse buying.

Several studies have emphasized the influence of external situational and environmental factors on impulse buying; including atmospherics, exciting shopping environments, in-store promotions, point of purchase stimuli, physical proximity, layout and space allocation of products within the store (Bellenger and Korgaonkar 1980; Desmet and Renaudin 1998; Faber and Vohs 2004; Hoch and Loewenstein 1991; Kollat and Willett 1967; Peck and Childers, 2006). However their exact effect on the process of impulse buying is still under-investigated. There is also a dearth of research into the effect of companion shoppers and other social effects (for exceptions see Green and Smith 2002; Luo 2005).

Studies into impulse buying have been criticized for focusing mostly on the emotional and situational elements of the phenomenon, as opposed to adequately considering the potential of the cognitive perspective (Burroughs 1996; Piron 1991). Burroughs

---

[1] The authors would like to acknowledge Sarah Green for collecting the data.

(1996) argued that the cognitive processes of impulse buying were particularly important when one considers how consumers map the symbolic meaning of objects onto conceptions of the self. Moreover, Rook and Hoch (1985) suggest that even at the height of impulse buying episodes, customers often engage in 'inner dialogue'. Additionally some studies have examined how consumers may reject the impulse to buy something and exert self-control when negative normative evaluations reach some critical level (Rook and Fisher 1995). Other consumers may actively employ strategies to prevent impulse buying. For example, people may attempt to regulate their own behavior through willpower, not going shopping or leaving credit cards at home (Hoch and Loewenstein 1991, Lehtonen 2000).

Related to the above, the perceived and actual consequences of impulse buying and their exact role on impulse restriction or enactment remain a neglected area of study. Although many definitions of impulse buying suggest that it occurs with a disregard for consequences (Rook 1985), impulse is typically perceived as having negative psychological consequences that trigger internal conflict (Emmons et al.. 1993). For example, impulsive persons often exhibit a sense of guilt (Wishnie 1977) and regret (Spears 2006). Research on compulsive buying and addictive consumption has explored negative consequences of consumer behavior that might be relevant to impulse buying. For example addictive consumption is viewed as having long-term and serious negative consequences, not least guilt, self-loathing and debt (Elliot, Eccles and Gournay 1996; Friese 1999; Green and Smith 2002; O'Guinn and Faber 1989).

Recent research into impulse buying (and consumer behavior more broadly) has re-emphasized the interplay of impulsive (affective) and cognitive (deliberative) processes (Shiv and Fedorikhin 1999; Strack, Werth, and Deutsch 2006). In the context of consuming candies, Hofmann, Rauch, and Gawronski (2007) found that under conditions of high cognitive capacity, dietary restraint standards were more influential on behavior than implicit attitudes, however, this trend was reversed under conditions of low cognitive capacity. Similarly, in a series of experiments Vohs and Faber (2007) showed that depletion of self-regulatory (primarily cognitive) resources in preceding tasks leads to increased willingness to behave impulsively in subsequent tasks. From this perspective, consumer decisions can be viewed as ongoing conflicts between desires, triggered for example by mood states and environmental stimuli, and willpower; or more reflective, cognitive attempts to exercise control over these impulses (Hoch and Lowenstein 1991). Nonetheless, desires can affect cognitive processes in more perplexing ways (e.g. Eagly and Chaiken, 1993). For example, under a "motivated reasoning" perspective, (Baumeister 1996; Ditto et al. 1998; Kunda 1990), urges, desires and similar motivational states "may affect reasoning through reliance on a biased set of cognitive processes: strategies for accessing, constructing and evaluating beliefs" (Kunda 1990, 480). Cognition, in the form of biased judgments or rationalizations, may therefore facilitate rather than inhibit impulse enactment. In this respect, the exact role of "inner dialogue" (Rook and Hoch, 1985) on impulse buying episodes remains unexplored.

THE ROLE OF NEUTRALIZATION

In an attempt to understand the Consumption Impulse Formation and Enactment process (CIFE) holistically, Dholakia (2000) distinguishes between consonant (harmonious) and dissonant (conflicting) impulses. Consistent with the above, he notes that while cases of consonant impulses (no perceived constraints from impulse formation to enactment) are theoretically possible, most often, consumers experience psychological conflict or dissonance,

arising from incongruence between their emotional (desires) and cognitive preferences (Emmons et al. 1993; Rook 1987). Importantly, this results in a more thought-based evaluation of the consequences of impulse enactment. If they are evaluated negatively, the consumer's cognitive system is activated, to employ a variety of resistance strategies, such as self-control, selective attention to information and control of emotions (Dholakia 2000). Cognition, however, in the form of rationalizations or motivated judgments may also play a facilitatory role on impulse enactment. Whereas the impulse buying literature have so far considered only the post-behavioral role of rationalizations (Rook 1987; Sparks 2006), they represent generic mechanisms of adding consonant cognitions, (versus changing existing cognitions or behavior; Beauvois and Joule 1996), that should be equally applicable when the purpose is to alleviate feelings of anticipated (pre-behavioral) as opposed to post-behavioral dissonance (Baumeister and Newman 1994; Tsang 2002) Indeed, the importance of rationalization has been highlighted in recent social psychological research concluding that most claims of irresistible impulses are a matter of rationalization rather than of genuinely being helpless against strong desires (Baumeister 2002; Baumeister et al.. 1994). Nonetheless, even the broader cognitive dissonance/social psychological literature has largely focused on the post-behavioral role of rationalizations (see e.g. Beauvois and Joule 1993, 1996). Inevitably, this stream of research has lacked a comprehensive theory of pre- and post-behavioral rationalizing strategies: "although many different examples of self-justification have been documented in the psychological literature, this has not produced a comprehensive taxonomy of self-justification strategies" (Holland et al. 2002, 1714). Originally applied in the context of norm violating behaviors, neutralization is both a theory of motivated cognition and a taxonomy of pre- and post-behavioral rationalizations that has been widely applied as a way to advance understanding of these processes (Bersoff 1999; Fritsche 2005; Hazani 1991).

In 1957, Sykes and Matza published their seminal article on juvenile delinquency criticising the predominant theoretical viewpoint that delinquency is a form of behavior based on the values and norms of a deviant sub-culture in the same way as law-abiding behavior is based on the norms and values of the larger society. These authors suggested that rather than learning moral imperatives, values or attitudes standing in a complete opposition to those of his/her society, the delinquent learns a set of justifications or rationalizations, that is the techniques of neutralization, which can insulate him/her from self-blame and the blame of others. Furthermore, while these patterns of thought can be viewed as following delinquent behavior, ultimately they can precede it, and make dissonant behavior possible. That is, once successfully internalized, they can truly become neutralizing devices as opposed to post behavioral rationalizations (Grove et al. 1989). Existing longitudinal (Agnew 1994; Minor 1981, 1993; Shields and Whitehall 1994) and experimental studies (Bersoff 1999; Bohner et al. 1998; Fritsche, 2003) have generally found support for this etiological assumption.

Sykes and Matza (1957) originally identified five major categories-labelled 'neutralization techniques'-that describe the rationalizations that people apply to their problematic behaviors. Later applications have identified additional ones which are arguably more applicable in specific contexts (Fritsche 2005; Maruna and Copes 2005). The original five techniques, are listed below (as adapted in a consumer context by Strutton et al. 2004, 254) along with illustrative examples in the context of impulse purchasing:

1) Denial of responsibility: A circumstance in which one argues that one is not personally accountable for the behavior because factors beyond one's control are operating; e.g. "Was such a one-off bargain and my friends insisted that I buy it".

2) Denial of Injury: A circumstance in which one contends that the consequences of the behavior are not really serious e.g. "What's the big deal, it was such a small purchase anyway".

3) Denial of Victim: A circumstance in which one counters the blame for personal actions by arguing that somebody else is the victimizer; e.g. "It's the retailer's fault; the way they promote these things, it's like you buy them before you realize it".

4) Condemning the condemners: A circumstance in which one deflects fault by pointing out that those who would condemn engage in similar activities; e.g. "Nowadays, everybody indulges him/herself by buying something absolutely unnecessary once in a while".

5) Appeal to higher loyalties: A circumstance in which one argues that behavior is the result of an attempt to actualize some higher order ideal or value; e.g. 'I was so tired and frustrated, and I really needed something to lift my mood so I just had to do it'.

Since its formulation by Sykes and Matza, neutralization theory has been one of the most widely known and frequently cited theories in the sociology of deviance and beyond (for recent reviews see Fritsche 2005; Manura and Copes 2005). Furthermore, neutralization theory has been the subject of more intuitive applications, both within and beyond the boundaries of what is typically labelled as deviant behavior. Examples include bingo playing (King 1990), organizational rule enforcing (Fershing 2003), religious dissonance (Dunford and Kunz, 1973), mothers entering preteen daughters into beauty contests (Heltsley and Calhoun 2003) and eating unhealthily during pregnancy (Copelton 2007).

Neutralization theory has been successfully applied in consumer contexts but research in this domain remains limited (Chatzidakis et al. 2004, 2006; Mitchell and Chan 2002; Rosenbaum and Kuntze 2003; Strutton et al. 1994, 1997). It has not been applied to impulse purchasing, although the importance of social norms underlying this context has often been highlighted in the literature (e.g. Cobb and Hoyer 1986; Bayley and Nancarrow 1998; Peck and Childers 2006; Rook and Fisher 1995). For example, Rook and Fisher (1995) mention how impulsive behavior has traditionally been associated with immaturity, weakness or lack of intelligence and therefore classified as "bad". Accordingly, impulse purchasing is often cited as an example of the so-called "dark side of consumer behavior" (Hirschman 1991). Consumers who violate these norms may need to neutralize in order to alleviate any feelings of guilt or dissonance they could otherwise experience when acting on their impulses.

Nonetheless, it is not only the existence of social norms against impulse purchasing that suggests applicability of the concept of neutralization in this domain. As mentioned earlier, within the consumer impulse formation and enactment process, dissonance might arise after the consideration of various negative consequences, which may relate to societal but also more personal concerns (e.g. monetary waste, weight gain, domestic conflict, anticipatory emotions of guilt and regret; Dholakia 2000; Green and Smith 2002). Within a cognitive dissonance framework, once a specific behavior is perceived as problematic, neutralization, as a generic strategy of adding consonant cognitions, should be more widely applicable to impulsive episodes. Lastly, it is important to note that neutralizing processes neither assume nor require extensive cognitive processing prior to impulse enactment. On the contrary, the techniques represent readily available patterns of thought or "cognitive heuristics" (Chatzidakis et al. 2006) that are compatible with both reflective and impulsive modes of decision-making (Strack et al. 2006); such as peripheral versus central (Petty

and Cacioppo 1986) or heuristic as opposed to systematic (Chaiken, Liberman and Eagly 1989) modes of processing. Accordingly, the aim of the preliminary study reported below, was to identify the types of neutralizations that may be employed in impulse buying contexts and to gain an indication of their cognitive accessibility both at pre- and post-behavioral stages of impulse formation and enactment.

METHODOLOGY

A qualitative method of data capture was deemed appropriate in order to gain preliminary insights on the applicability of neutralization to the impulse buying domain. The study was in the main deductive because the codes were predetermined, that is the 'neutralization techniques'. Nonetheless, additional techniques, sub-themes and issues relating to the process of neutralization emerged in the interviews. The twenty participants were female, aged 18-51, and had varied backgrounds. They were recruited through targeted publicity at community resource centres. All had got into debt at some point directly as a result of their impulse purchasing. The study focussed specifically on women, as previous research has shown that overall women buy proportionately more on impulse than men (Dittmar, Beattie and Friese 1995). Clothes were the primary focus of the study, because women often impulsively buy goods that are symbolic and express their self-image (Dittmar et al. 1995; Rook and Hoch 1985; Criak 1994). Nonetheless, some participants moved on to mention additional impulse buying experiences.

The interviews were humanistic in nature (see Chamaz 1997), and were designed to give respondents the opportunity to tell their own story and fully discuss their own feelings and behaviors (Elliott, Eccles and Gournay 1996; O'Guinn and Faber 1989). A general structure and interview schedule was established before the interviews but the guide was designed to be flexible (Kvale 1983; O'Guinn and Faber 1989; Willis 1990). This inductive element of the study helped illuminate the accessibility of neutralization-type of arguments in the consumers' minds (and therefore their compatibility with both reflective and impulsive modes of processing), and is a key characteristic for successful neutralization (Fritsche 2003). Accordingly, the interplay of deductive and inductive principles has been widely adopted for exploratory inquiries into other applications of neutralization theory (e.g. Byers et al. 1999; Chatzidakis et al. 2004; Ferraro and Johnson 1983; Gauthier 2000; Hazani 1991). The interviews began by asking respondents to describe their most recent impulse buying episode, similar to the strategies adopted by Gardner and Rook (1988) and O'Guinn and Faber (1989). Further questions and the direction of the conversation were based on respondents' comments, in order to explore their experiences (Ritson, Elliott and Eccles 1996). All respondents were fully de-briefed and offered counselling services and the annotated transcripts were cross-referenced.

"Theoretical thematic analysis" was used in order to systematically code and analyse the data with the aim of identifying common patterns, salient themes and sub-themes, which were then contrasted with the pre-existing theoretical framework (Braun and Clarke 2006; Fereday and Muir-Cohrane 2006). Initially, data were coded separately by each of the authors of this paper and then findings were compared to ensure inter-coder agreement and validity (Braun and Clarke 2006). During the coding process it was evident that different neutralization techniques were often used in combination to justify impulsive behavior, which reflects what researchers have remarked in other contexts (e.g. Forsyth and Evans 1998; Hazani 1991). In such instances, data were allocated multiple category codes to indicate the interrelationships between themes. Coding also highlighted that the semantic borders between single techniques were on few occasions fuzzier (Fritsche 2002). In these cases, the broader context and framing of the statement was an important determinant of how the data were coded. The findings reported below include verbatim extracts and some commentary to give a flavor of the overall nature and recurrent themes from the interviews.

FINDINGS

There was ample evidence to suggest that respondents were readily employing neutralizing techniques to alleviate feelings of dissonant impulses. Indeed, none of the participants was challenged to rationalize their impulses, but all of them did so at various stages in the interviews. In many instances, respondents moved on to explicitly acknowledge the importance of rationalization on the impulse formation and enactment process:

"You've always got to justify yourself and think well yeah I really needed that cardie, and I really needed that pair of pants even though I've got ten others, and I will use them, and I will wear it and if I'm going wear it and they feel comfortable, that's all that matters, it was a bargain so think how much I've saved." s

However, in line with previous consumer applications (Grove *et al.* 1989) not all five techniques were equally represented in the impulse buying context. The most popular techniques proved to be denial of responsibility, denial of injury and appealing to higher loyalties whilst there was only tenuous reference to denial of victim and condemnation of the condemners. Furthermore, two additional techniques were identified, and seemed to resemble what has been identified in previous research as "metaphor of the ledger" (Klockars 1974) and "defence of necessity" (Minor 1981).

Denial of responsibility centers on notions of control or the extent to which the consumers view themselves as "acted upon" rather than "acting" (Sykes and Matza 1957). This theme of attribution was evident in several consumer accounts and was perhaps not surprising given the documented evidence on the importance of "self-control" in the impulse formation and enactment process (Dholakia 2000; Vohns and Faber 2007). For example, some participants suggested that it was their friends or partners who were in effect responsible for their impulsive behavior:

"We went into, erm, a shop once to buy a fridge freezer and I came out with a television and a video as well (laughs) but that's really...that's more my husband than me...he's quite bad at things like that, he's like just get it, he sort of encourages me, I try and...not to, he is sort of quite a big influence on me, makes me do things like that, spend extra, six hundred quid on something when it was only going to be three or something."

Other participants denied responsibility on the grounds that they were influenced by atmospherics or other environmental and situational characteristics, somewhat implying their function at levels beyond their conscious control:

"Well if, its nice discreet lighting, subtle and the mirror makes you look good, yes it will certainly encourage you..."
"Alright, because sometimes when you're on holiday you buy things and because you're in a hot country, it's all flowery or whatever, brighter colours, because you're in, I don't know what the heat does to you..."

Denial of injury was primarily based on financial considerations, especially for products that were considered to be within a very affordable range and hence unproblematic purchases:

"I thought, they're cheap, I'll buy them."

A different version was based not on the absolute monetary value of the product, but relative to longer term considerations, such as frequency and occasions of usage:

"...this was fifty quid, and I was with my friend when I bought it and I went but I really like it, and she went yeah but you know its fifty pounds, and I said I know but I could wear it to work and I would wear it outside of work and she went oh well if you're going to wear it for both then perhaps you will get your moneys worth out of it."

Interestingly, few participants felt the need to justify potential injuries to their household as opposed to personal finances (e.g. the fact that the family might have to forgo other consumption events such as vacations because of any spending was hardly ever alluded to). Likewise, broader negative consequences for the environment (e.g. waste of resources) or society (e.g. fair trade clothing), were rarely mentioned, but this could be because ethical clothes shopping is still a trend in its infancy (Shaw et al. 2006).

Appeal to higher loyalties can be perceived as the technique which comes closer to a situation of a behavioral dilemma, whereby the "negative (unintended) consequences of one action are logically implied in positive (intended) consequences of the other action and vice versa" (Villenave-Cremer and Eckensberger 1986 in Marks and Mayo 1991, 720). In line with the existing impulse buying literature, the higher loyalties served by the (impulsive) behavior mostly related to personal desires and self-gratification:

"...erm I just thought it'll really cheer me up if I get something new for the weekend, you know if I go out at the weekend I've got something new to wear and er, I just kind of felt a bit better about myself."
"...well, sometimes I try things on but sometimes I'm just so happy that I've found something I like I just take them to the till there and then and buy it."

Other frequently mentioned higher-ordered values, related to notions of deservedness or the existence of an opportunity:

"Erm, cos you think well, I've worked for this money, I've worked to buy this..."
"Sometimes you think oh well I'll get it before somebody else gets it, yet everybody else is seen in it, or you think well maybe if I come back and its really popular, there'll be none left, you know what I mean, like your size and none'll be left and they won't be able to order you another one, and its frustrating then. (AtHL)

Additional Techniques: Some additional themes were also identified in the interviews, which seemed to relate to techniques that have been previously identified in neutralization research as "metaphor of the ledger" (Klockars 1974) and "defence of necessity" (Minor 1981). The metaphor of the ledger refers to circumstances in which individuals justify their behavior in question based on other activities which have led to credits they can somewhat "cash in" (Hollinger 1991; Minor 1981). In the context of impulse buying this was often translated into excuses for self-giving, such as having accomplished certain ends or having done more than what is required for one's friends or family:

> *"...the children have far more clothes than I do really, they get far more presents and I think as they get older you realize that you can't spend your whole life spending all your pay on them, you've got to have a life yourself, so maybe as they get older it gets far easier to spend money on me (laughs)"*.

Lastly, defences of necessity were based on reasons such as special occasions and circumstances, urgency of satisfying specific emotional or functional needs and which somewhat rendered the impulsive purchase prudent, if not necessary:

> *"...we'd got all the kids presents which were quite a lot, and then this computer came up at a good price, so I bought it. And I justified it by saying that my daughter, being in the new school now needed a computer, would help her and also her brother with their schoolwork."*
> *"Yeah, I usually try and justify them as a necessity. Cos I don't usually, if it's Christmas or birthdays and things I don't tend to ask for clothes cos, they're a necessity."*

DISCUSSION AND CONCLUSIONS

Given that most consumers engage in inner dialogue even at the peak of impulse buying episodes (Rook and Hoch 1985), it is imperative that theories of impulse buying evolve to explain the multiplicity of roles that cognition may play on the impulse formation and enactment process (Dholakia 2000). Accordingly, this paper advances the concept of neutralization in an attempt to illustrate how (motivated) cognition, in the form of pre- and post-behavioral rationalizations may also facilitate rather than inhibit impulse enactment; and ultimately sustain repeated impulsive behavior. An exploratory study probed the applicability of the concept and identified the types of neutralizing arguments that consumers may use in relation to impulsive purchases.

The findings from the present study are mostly illustrative however, because the sample was restricted in terms of size, demographic and psychographic profile and, of course, it could not demonstrate causation and therefore confirm that the arguments are used as neutralizing devices. However, the study did shed some light on the chronological ordering question because the need to justify even at the point of purchase was very commonly cited by almost all the respondents (as was the experience of guilt in the post-purchase phase). Furthermore, it provided strong indication that consumers have a sufficient range of accessible neutralization techniques to alleviate feelings of dissonant impulses. This is particularly important in the context of impulse formation and enactment, as it implies that neutralizing processes should not necessarily require extensive cognitive effort. As such, they are also compatible with impulsive modes of processing (Strack et al. 2006). Future research could benefit from studies that probe the applicability of the concept in more diverse contexts of impulse buying, with different sample profiles and methods that may help better understand contemporaneous cognitive processes such as "shopping with consumers" (Lowrey et al. 2005; Otnes et al. 2005). At a second stage of research, experimental approaches would be needed, in order to directly address the causal ordering issue as well as specify conditions and moderating variables that affect the influence of neutralization on enactment and persistence of consumer impulses. For example, intervening variables could relate to anticipated or post-purchase guilt, mood state and adjustment, and deprivation of a need (see e.g. Strack et al. 2006).

Such a research endeavor could have important implications for marketing communications and public policy initiatives against impulsive behaviors that carry negative personal, broader societal and environmental consequences. For example, marketing campaigns could challenge specific neutralizing arguments by pointing to their logical fallacy or dangerously prevailing nature. Furthermore, creative attempts to counter the employment of neutralization techniques can even be found in cognitive-behavioral treatments and therapeutic communities such as narcotic and alcoholic anonymous (Maruna and Copes 2005). This is of increasing relevance given the emergence of specialist anti-impulse buying programmes.[2]

REFERENCES [3]

Baumeister, Roy F. (2002), "Yielding to temptation: Self-control failure, impulsive purchasing, and consumer behavior," *Journal of Consumer Research*, 28, 670-676.

Baumeister, Roy F. and Newman, Leonard S. (1994), "Self Regulation of Cognitive Inference and Decision Processes," *Personality and Social Psychology Bulletin, 20*, 3–19.

Beauvois, Jean-Leon and Joule, Robert-Vincent (1996), *A Radical Dissonance Theory*, London: Taylor and Francis.

Bersoff, David M. (1999), "Why Good People Sometimes Do Bad Things: Motivated Reasoning and Unethical Behavior," *Personality and Social Psychology Bulletin*, 25(1), 28-39.

Braun, Virginia and Clarke, Victoria (2006), "Using Thematic Analysis in Psychology," *Qualitative Research in Psychology, 3*, 77-101.

Burroughs, James E. (1996), "Product Symbolism, Self-Meaning, and Holistic Matching: The Role of Information Processing in Impulsive Buying," *Advances in Consumer Research, 23:* 463-469.

Chatzidakis, Andreas, Sally Hibbert, and Andrew P. Smith (2006), "Ethically Concerned, yet Unethically Behaved": Towards an Updated Understanding of Consumer's (Un)ethical Decision Making, *Advances in Consumer Research, 33*, 693-698

Chatzidakis, Andreas, Sally Hibbert, Darryn Mitussis, and Andrew P. Smith (2004), "Virtue in Consumption?" *Journal of Marketing Management*, 20(5/6), 527-544.

Dholakia, Utpal M. (2000), "Temptation and Resistance: An Integrated Model of Consumption Impulse Formation and Enactment," *Psychology and Marketing*, 17 (11), 955-982.

Dittmar, Helga, Jane Beattie, and Susanne Friese (1995), "Gender Identity and Material Symbols: Objects and Decision Considerations in Impulse Purchases," *Journal of Economic Psychology, 16*, 491-511.

Ditto, Peter H., James A. Scepansky, Geoffrey D. Munro, Anne-Marie Apanovitch, and Lisa K. Lockhart (1998), "Motivated Sensitivity to Preference-Inconsistent Information," *Journal of Personality and Social Psychology*, 75(1), 53-69.

Elliott, Richard, Sue Eccles, and Kevin Gournay (1996) "Man Management? Women and the Use of Debt to Control Personal Relationships," *Journal of Marketing Management*, 12, 657-669.

---

[2]See e.g. http://www.stoppingovershopping.com/
[3]Due to space constraints, the full list of references is available from the first author upon request.

Emmons, Robert A., Laura A. King, and Ken Sheldon (1993), "Goal Conflict and the Self Regulation of Action," in Wegner Daniel M. and James W. Pennebaker (Eds.), *Handbook of Mental Control* (528–551). Englewood Cliffs, NJ: Prentice Hall.

Fritsche, Immo (2005), "Predicting Deviant Behavior by Neutralisation: Myths and Findings," *Deviant Behavior,* 26(5), 483-510.

Grove, Stephen J., Scott J. Vitell, and David Strutton (1989), "Non-Normative Consumer Behavior and the Techniques of Neutralization," *Proceedings of the 1989 AMA Winter Educators Conference*, 131-135.

Hazani, Moshe (1991), "Aligning Vocabulary, Symbols Banks and Sociocultural Structure," *Journal of Contemporary Ethnography*, 20, 179-202.

Hoch, Stephen J. and George F. Loewenstein (1991), 'Time-inconsistent Preferences and Consumer Self-Control," *Journal of Consumer Research*, 17, 492-507.

Hofmann, Wilhelm, Wolfgang Rauch, and Bertram Gawronski (2007), "And Deplete us not into Temptation: Automatic Attitudes, Dietary Restraint, and Self-Regulatory Resources as Determinants of Eating Behavior," *Journal of Experimental Social Psychology,* 43(3), 497-504.

Holland, Rob W., Ree M. Meertens, and Mark van Vugt (2002), "Dissonance on the Road: Self-Esteem as a Moderator of Internal and External Justification Strategies," *Personality and Social Psychology Bulletin*, 28(12), 1713-1724.

Kunda, Ziva (1990), "The Case for Motivated Reasoning," *Psychological Bulletin,* 108(3), 480-498.

Lejoyeux, Michel, Jean Ades, Valerie Tassain, and Jacquelyn Solomon (1996), "Phenomenology and Psychopathology of Uncontrolled Buying," *American Journal of Psychiatry*, 153(12), 1524-1529.

Luomala, Harri T. (1998), "A Mood-Alleviate Perspective on Self-Gift Behaviors: Stimulating Consumer Behavior Development," *Journal of Marketing Management,* 14(1-3), 109-132.

Marks, Lawrence J. and Michael A. Mayo (1991), "An Empirical Test of a Model of Consumer Ethical Dilemmas," *Advances in Consumer Research,* 18, 720-728.

Maruna, Shadd and Heith Copes (2005), "Excuses, Excuses: What Have We Learned from Five Decades of Neutralisation Research?" *Crime and Justice: A Review of Research*, 32, 221-320.

Piron, Francis (1991), "Defining Impulse Purchasing," *Advances in Consumer Research,* 18, 509-514.

Rook, Dennis W and Stephen J. Hoch (1985), "Consuming Impulses," *Advances in Consumer Research,* 12, 23-27.

Rook, Dennis W. (1987) 'The Buying Impulse', *Journal of Consumer Research,* 14(Sept): 189-199.

Rook, Dennis W. and Robert J. Fisher (1995), "Normative Influences on Impulsive Buying Behavior," *Journal of Consumer Research,* 22(3), 305-312.

Rook, Dennis W. and Meryl P. Gardner (1993), "In the Mood: Impulse Buying's Affective Antecedents," in Belk, Russell W. and Janeen A. Costa (eds), *Research in Consumer Behavior*, 6, 1-28, London: JAI Press Ltd.

Spears, Nancy (2006), "Just Moseying Around and Happening Upon it versus a Master Plan: Minimizing Regret in Impulse versus Planned Sales Promotion Purchases," *Psychology and Marketing*, 23(1), 57-73.

Strack, Fritz, Lioba Werth, and Deutsch Roland (2006), "Reflective and Impulsive Determinants of Consumer Behavior," *Journal of Consumer Psychology,* 16(3), 205-216.

Strutton, David, Scott J. Vitell, and Lou E. Pelton (1994), "How Consumers May Justify Inappropriate Behavior in Market Settings: An Application on the Techniques of Neutralization," *Journal of Business Research,* 30, 253-260.

Sykes, Gresham M. and David Matza (1957), "Techniques of Neutralization: A Theory of Delinquency," *American Sociological Review*, 22(6), 664-670.

Vohs, Kathleen D. and Ronald J. Faber (2007), "Spent Resources: Self-regulatory Resource Availability Affects Impulse Buying," *Journal of Consumer Research,* 33, 537-547.

Wood, Michael (1998), "Socio-Economic Status, Delay of Gratification, and Impulse Buying," *Journal of Economic Psychology,* 19(3), 295-320.

Youn, Seounmi and Ronald J. Faber (2000), "Impulse Buying: Its Relation to Personality Trasits and Cues," *Advances in Consumer Research,* 27,179-185.

The Involved Ostrich: Mothers' Perceptions of Fathers' Participation in the Transition to Parenthood

The VOICE Group[1]
VOicing International Consumption Experiences

ABSTRACT

This study focuses on mothers' perceptions of fathers' attitudes toward consumption decisions related to the introduction of the first child in the family. Two interviews were conducted with each respondent, pre- and post-natal, using the long interview method; in this paper we focus on pre-natal data. Data revealed that men, according to their partner's perceptions, used consumption as a virtual umbilical cord, although levels of consumption involvement varied from co-involvement for most purchases, to limited involvement, and/or involvement for 'large' items, particularly travel systems and technical items. This research also revealed that men partook in highly masculinized forms of "nesting," and in general shunned pregnancy book reading; although some did engage in "research" activities such as searching the internet for product safety information. We conclude from this study that the transition into parenthood can be difficult for men due to their lack of a physical connection to the pregnancy, a perception that the baby industry is not designed for them, the continuance of male stereotypes in the media, and also the time available to men to become involved in consumption activities immediately prior to a baby's birth.

INTRODUCTION

Parenting is one of the most studied and discussed facets of the human experience. There are thousands of popular press books on the subject as well as journals, dissertations, and monographs with topics ranging from sleep strategies, disciplining models, educational excellence, and sibling rivalry.

Within consumer behavior, the topic of the family took center stage as traditional marketers found the household a useful unit of analysis for promoting goods and services (Commuri and Gentry 2000). The family quickly emerged in the marketing literature as a "unit of analysis" that made decisions as a group. Beyond this cursory analysis, the complexities of family life have remained largely unstudied. While recently new mothers have begun to garner attention from consumer researchers (e.g. Prothero 2002; Hogg, Curasi, and Maclaran 2004), there continues to be a dearth of research on fathers, fatherhood, and fathering styles within the field of consumer behavior (see Harrison and Gentry 2007 (a) and (b) for notable exceptions). Although fathers were classified as a 'consumer group' as early as 1990 (Barbour 1990), we know very little about the extent to which fathers participate in consumption decisions, especially when related to children.

This study serves to shed some initial light on the processes that men use in the transition into parenthood. And while the light is being shed through the perspectives of their female partners, it is an important place to begin as it allows researchers to formulate some initial ideas that can be then supported or refuted once studies with men commence. Using pre-natal interviews of twenty women from four countries, this study looks at the perceptions of their partners' participation in the consumption decisions related to getting ready for a new baby. While previous research has focused on the role of others on mothers' preparations for the baby and the impact of the marketplace on new mothers' confidence in their new role (Davies et al 2007), no work in the consumer behavior field has been conducted to consider how mothers perceive fathers' level of interest, amount of effort, or perceived role in this transitional stage to parenthood.

MOTHERHOOD, FATHERHOOD, AND CO-PARENTING

Who is the modern day father? This is perhaps a more complicated question than appears on the surface. Each decade seems to capture through television or movies the stereotypical father of the times, for example Father Knows Best in the 1950s and the Cosby Show of the 1980s. Media today paints a fragmented picture of fathers; oftentimes, either showing (disproportionately) the single dad struggling to raise children on his own (Two and a Half Men) or the well-balanced co-parent who willingly contributes equally to all activities domestic (Medium). In advertising, fathers are often shown as inept buffoons or disinterested and useless appendages (Harrison and Gentry 2007a).

In certain circles, fathers are attempting to take a more active role than in previous generations. There appears to be a shift in how fathers are participating in family activities, including childrearing, housework, household maintenance, and kinship work. This shift is less voluntary and more of a requirement when the family is headed by a single father (Harrison and Gentry 2007a). The father must learn to manage a household, including grocery shopping, school clothes shopping, and homework preparation, in the absence of the mother who previously took care of those things. The current generation of fathers is the first to truly embody the fourth and ultimate level of parenting as outlined by Pleck and Pleck (1997). The movement away from the "genial dad and breadwinner" to "equal co-parent" has emerged without explicit expectations and guidelines, without scripts or role models. This more egalitarian approach has left many heterosexual couples grappling with issues of femininity and masculinity and a need to improve upon the parenting styles of their own parents. Both mothers and fathers in a co-parenting household seem to be following a "making it up as we go" mentality that transcends social class, racial, and ethnic boundaries (Summers et al 1999).

Recently, Harrison and Gentry (2007) studied the effects of single fatherhood on family consumption decisions. This groundbreaking work further strengthened the pre-existing belief that women are the primary arbiters of the marketplace when it comes to family purchases such as school clothes and groceries and that, in their absence through either divorce or death, when men enter the marketplace they are often strangers in a strange land (de Certeau 1984), lacking the skills or knowledge of what or how to buy. Imagine a single father having to help his daughter choose tampons, for example.

Researchers also point out that advertising often depicts fathers as helpless, inept, or ignorant when it comes to household processes and purchases. Research in the 1970s and 1980s portrayed both men and women in highly stereotypical roles (Harrison and Gentry 2007). Images began to shift in the 1990s with women being shown more favorably (Coltrane and Allan 1994). Yet, men continue to be portrayed in stereotypical ways. The image of the

[1]This paper is the result of collective, collaborative research undertaken by members of The VOICE Group. The members of this group, in alphabetical order, are Andrea Davies, Susan Dobscha, Susi Geiger, Stephanie O'Donohoe, Lisa O'Malley, Andrea Prothero, Elin Brandi Sørenson, and Thyra Uth Thomsen.

family man is still extremely rare in ad campaigns. Kaufman (1999) stated that ads are socializing agents for all parents but particularly fathers because they have chosen not to use their own fathers for this purpose.

Recent ad images are showing fathers in a different light. In some cases the father exerts superhuman powers to complete a task (for instance washing the dishes) that the mother was unable to accomplish using her merely human powers. Also, images of fathers holding or otherwise engaging young children have begun to emerge in parenting magazines and on certain TV ads but they are still the exception rather than the norm (Harrison and Gentry 2008.

While consumer research has ignored this facet of family consumption decision making, the parenting research is abounding with models of positive father involvement and the measurement of mothers' perceptions of fathers' participation in parenting.

RESEARCH FROM THE FAMILY AND PARENTING LITERATURE

The role of the father has been well studied in the family and parenting research. The seminal article by Lamb, Pleck, Charnov, and Levine (1987) created three constructs that measure fathers' involvement: "accessibility, engagement, and responsibility" (p. 259). Summers et al (1999) use this same model to measure mothers' perceptions of fathers' engagement by measuring "interaction or direct engagement between father and child; accessibility or availability to the child, and taking responsibility for the child (p. 293)." Summers et al (1999) go on to say that "this framework appears to be emerging as a generally accepted view of the critical dimensions of positive fathering (p. 293)."

Also, much of the family literature on fathering has used as a central measurement mothers' perceptions (Fagan and Barnett 2003; Futris and Schoppe-Sullivan 2007; Krishnakumar and Black 2003). This use of mothers' perceptions stems from the fact that while co-parenting appears to be the aspirational parenting model of the moment, mothers "continue to assume the primary role in child rearing (Simmerman, Blacher, and Baker 2001; p. 325)." At the same time, while men are playing a greater role in the family and especially inside the home, one study showed that they were largely unable to report on specific details of their children's lives, such as teachers' names and outside activities (Lareau 2000). The mothers' level of knowledge of the children's day to day activities was much higher and much more specific than the fathers'. Douglas and Michaels (2004) point this out as well: "after all, a dad who knows the name of his kid's pediatrician and reads them stories at night is still regarded as a saint; a mother who doesn't is a sinner (p. 8)." Therefore, while it is extremely important that fathers' voices be recorded and studied, this study focuses on mothers' perceptions of fathers' participation in the period prior to the arrival of their first child in order to learn more about fathers' role in this period of transition. It also gives the opportunity to test McMahon's findings that "men and women may both be parents, I was told, but they act, think, and feel differently as parents (1995, p. 234)."

METHOD

The data for this paper was collected as part of a larger project on the role consumption plays in the management of a woman's transition into first time motherhood. The project includes two interviews each with twenty mothers across four countries (Denmark, Ireland, the UK, and the USA). The interviews were conducted prior to and after the birth of the first child by one of eight researchers who comprise the research group. Other forms of data were also collected, including consumption diaries and photographs of certain goods that were either purchased or received in

other means, such as gifts or on loan. The interviews were driven by the long interview method (McCracken 1988), the photographs were reviewed using autoelicitation techniques (Heisley and Levy 1991) and a snowballing technique was used to garner the participants (Miles and Huberman 1994).

For this paper we are focusing on the pre-birth interviews with mothers, conducted between 32-39 weeks gestation, and are looking specifically at the women's perceptions of the involvement of their male partners in the buying of items needed for the imminent arrival of their baby. It should be stressed at this point that all of our participants were heterosexual, and from middle-class backgrounds.

FINDINGS

The path to parenthood is lined with fear, excitement, intrepidation, and preparation. And while women have many guideposts along this path, men have relatively few. During pregnancy, women are privy to hundreds of book options, constant updating from doctors, and a willingness to dip into their social network's shared wealth of knowledge. Men, on the other hand, are less targeted by the pregnancy book market, are sometimes absent from doctor's visits, and are not used to discussing such intimate issues with their social networks. So, how does a father manage this transition? Murphy (2004) states that "it takes a very long time to negotiate the shift from partners to parents" and that the mother and father's paths will never be "parallel," especially during the initial postpartum phase.

Between 1970 and 2000 Douglas and Michaels (2004) pointed out that over eight hundred books were published on the topic of motherhood, while in recent years only a small number of 'how to' manuals have been published for fathers (Parsons 1997; Smith 2004; Berkmann 2005; Brott 2005). While the literature suggests that many women feel the need to read books and research products men do not necessarily feel the same need. So how then are men transitioning from fathers-to-be to fathers? Does consumption play a role during this period of liminality? There were a number of different areas in which the consumption related activities of fathers were highlighted and below we discuss three prominent areas—namely the use of consumption as a virtual umbilical cord; the 'nesting' activities of fathers; and the ways in which father's both desire and seek out information in relation to pregnancy and fatherhood.

Consumption as a virtual umbilical cord

Because men are unable to physiologically perform the act of pregnancy, a number of our participants talked of how their partners felt disconnected from the pregnancy or that the pregnancy did not 'seem real' to them:

Sarah: He's only really realizing it's happening now. He can see the bump getting bigger now, but he kind of feels outside it…So in certain kinds of respects he's really prepared and geared towards it, but in others then he's still a bit of an ostrich on it as well, I think.
Int: And why do you think that is?
Sarah: I think it's just because it's not quite real yet. …..We've talked about this kind of bonding thing before; like I can feel it moving around, trashing around, but he'll talk to it like, he's really into it that way, but at the same time he can walk away from that where for me there's no walking away now (laughs). (Ireland)
"But also—of course it's different for a man, because he cannot feel the baby and all of these things the same way that I can. He doesn't feel it with his own body. (Heidi, Denmark,)

One of our Danish participants also talked of how she felt marketing activities were also geared towards women, because men were somehow 'on the sideline':

It's like it's always directed at women. And I know what they say about hormones and all that; and that we are easier to manipulate into buying all kinds of things. But my husband cares about this at least just as much as I do. But he is not the kind who is falling for the pink clothes. But I believe it has a lot to do with women and their pregnancy and the husband is out here on the sideline. And that's not how I experience it. (Nina, Denmark)

Thus, in the same way that the mothers saw consumption as a way of helping them to 'prepare' for the arrival of their baby, our participants also suggested that fathers used consumption to remain connected and engaged, but the amount of involvement varied both within and across cultures. A number of our mothers-to-be talked of how their partners were very involved for most of the purchases made and indeed became emotional at times:

Lise: He is probably just as excited as I am, and he has participated in everything. Right from the beginning he has been with me at the doctor and the scannings and the midwife and he is very involved. It is not just my project. It is the two of us all the way through. He would be very unhappy if bought anything and he was not part of the decision. He likes to be part of the decisions-down to almost the smallest details. It is a big thing for him too. (Denmark)

Int: What was it like to go shopping for a pram–how did you go about doing that?
Karen: I was touched, but in fact it was only because Kasper is so sensitive. When he tried to push the pram he started crying. His sister accompanied us. It was in [a town in Jutland]. And when he was to push it, he started crying, and then I just got so touched, and it really was an extremely nice experience, (Denmark)

Similarly some participants talked about the fun they had shopping for baby items. Here Megan talks about her husband's involvement, even though he normally dislikes shopping:

Even Terry, poor guy, doesn't have a choice of what he wears, he hates shopping; so I just literally go in and go boom, boom, boom and come home and go there you are love, and he's delighted, usually [laughs], most of the time anyway. But, I must say I've liked some of the things we've gone shopping for together. In the States now when we were shopping Terry is a real Irish guy and there were two real beautiful looking girls inside the baby shop we were in buying and Terry was telling them about the U2 concert that we went to the night before and that we were from Ireland, and it was our first baby. I was over looking at the shelves of clothes while he was up at the counter chatting the two women up [laughs], and I could hardly get a word in edge ways as to what colours etc, but he's that type of person. He's very outgoing, he's very chatty, and he loved the shopping with an element of doing his own thing in the middle of it [laughs]. But we've had a good laugh actually through the whole lot of it. (Megan, Ireland)

In contrast to those fathers who were very much co-partners in consumption preparations, some of our participants talked about their partners finding "large purchases" to be important in terms of shopping time and effort, yet, had very little interest in, and left the smaller purchases to the women:

Int: So Duncan's come along on a couple of trips but…
Caroline: Yeah, but not, I think the final decision is still mine, as in because it's knowing a bit more and reading a little bit more about things, and then he was quite happy to go along with it. The bigger things, probably like the cot and the pushchair, and that, the more practical things, yeah, he did have more on an input, but like cotton wool and lotion and all that sort of thing, it goes over his head, oh, do we need that, yeah, oh, we do, yes, we do. (UK)

Indeed, sometimes the mother's did not want the father's to be involved in buying some of the smaller items:

Nina: Well, mostly they were joint decisions–buying a car seat or buying a sleeping bag. Also the bigger things, really. We talked about those and agreed on what it should be. I think I was the one pushing it but then my husband also said that we should go ahead and then we did. And now we go get it done in order to be able to leave it alone.
I: And so you did that together?
Nina: But then, these last clothes, I was definitely the one. I didn't let him in on that. (Denmark)

When asked about the level of joint decision making, Claire underscored her leadership role: "he's been very good" taking her places, he defers to her, yet she sees things as "joint decisions, with me leading!" (UK)

Some participants, again in contrast, talked of their partners feeling very happy to leave most, if not all, consumption decisions up to them:

Int: And does Tony feel it will be nice for the baby to sleep in it?
Sarah: I think he does yeah; in some respects he's like 'oh you decide, it's your kind of area' if you like. (Ireland)

There were also cases where some of our participants talked about how their partners would like to be more involved in all sorts of activities, related to the baby, including buying things, but circumstances did not allow this. Ella, for instance talks of how her husband Fintan was not as involved because he was working incredibly hard within his own small business:

I really feel having talked to you that Fintan has really been kind of left out. But to be fair it's probably more circumstances than anything that he hasn't been as involved in stuff. Even from the point of view of reading and everything; if he actually had two minutes he'd probably read some of the books with me. And he did particularly in the beginning when we had that book with all the pictures, every week. He was thrilled with that, it was so amazing to read that, you know after so many weeks this organ was developed. I suppose I feel a bit sorry for him because he hasn't been able to be as involved, but he's a very hands-on kind of person, and he will be. And he's come to the hospital with me a lot. I really feel like I'm defending him, its not that, I just feel it's a bit unfair that he hasn't been able to be as involved. (Ireland)

There has been much talk in the literature of the involvement of men in the bringing up of their children, and also recently discussions as to how difficult this can sometimes be, due to limited paternity leave, for instance. Warner (2005) points out that at the turn of the century American men were working on average more than fifty hours per week. Such long hours coupled with both limited paternity and maternity leave created an environment where some fathers were not as involved as they would like to have been. This is also true in our study where the men were all working full-time in the weeks prior to their babies' arrival, and as such would have had limited time to become involved with purchasing, particularly when their partners had began their own maternity leave from work.

Even those partners who had very little involvement in purchasing most items did play a role in the purchasing of bigger and/or technical items for the baby. Indeed, one area where most of our participants talked of their partner's involvement, either in purchasing, or in afterwards assembling, was the buying of the baby 'travel system'. As Megan laughingly told us:

> Basically it was very light-weight, very easy to manoeuvre, and my husband thought it was the best thing since his brand new car that he bought a couple of years ago [laughs]. So that's why we bought that. (Ireland)

Ella, also from Ireland, who had highlighted how her husband Fintan had little involvement in most purchases talked of how he was 'adamant' that they purchase a particular type of travel system. Abigail, from the USA, also talks of her husband's enthusiasm over technical items:

> Int: Oh, okay. So, has he, how involved has he been?
> Abigail: He's been surprisingly involved. More, much more than I expected him. He's an engineer and like he loves all the, like when we went to register, he's looking at all the stuff, you know, yeah looking at gadgets to see how things go together and you know, we had a shower and I came home and he had every box opened already and I'm like, wait, we might need to return it. I want to see, this is cool. Did you see the car seat? I'm like this time it won't work. Show me what to do. (USA)

Thus in the same way that the mothers in our study used consumption to help them prepare for their babies arrival, fathers, who often felt that the pregnancy was 'not real' to them also used consumption to help them prepare. The level and types of involvement however, varied both within and between countries and ranged from co-decision making for most purchases, to limited and little involvement in other instances. The only area in which there appeared to be consistency was in the purchase of a travel system for a baby, where all fathers had some involvement in the decision making and/or assembly of the product purchased.

Father's Nesting

Many of our participants talked of their partners engaging in a highly masculine form of "nesting," an activity typically attributed to pregnant women. Nesting has been described as a hormonally triggered desire to make the home as clean, orderly, and ready as possible prior to the baby's arrival and tends to 'kick-in' around the fifth/sixth month of pregnancy (Johnston 2004). While there has been limited research about the physiological and behavioral changes of expectant fathers (Storey et al 2000) the authors note hormonal changes in men just before and after their babies' birth have been identified. At the same time, other studies have shown, that men also suffer from post-partum depression (Ballard and Davies 1996; Leathers, Kelley, and Richman 1997), although other research suggests these levels are much higher for women (Douglas and Michaels 2004). Consequently if men's hormones and physiology

also change during this time period do such changes also lead to a male form of 'nesting'? From our interviews, we found many examples of men undertaking 'projects' that could be considered nesting. Activities took the form of large home improvement projects and also putting together complicated baby equipment. Even the men who had been less involved in purchasing items were very involved in various 'projects', with examples including, converting an attic; converting a spare bedroom into a nursery for the baby; and putting together 'complicated' items such as cribs, travel cots, etc. Here, Sarah talks of how her husband has been involved very little in the purchase of things and is also unsure about what will happen when the baby actually arrives, yet is still involved in 'big' projects and is also planning to work less hours following their babies birth:

> Int: Does he want to switch off and wait until the baby arrives for everything?
> Sarah: No, he's funny, he's quite prepared, in like the attic is underway, you know what I mean, and he's doing all of that like, and from a furniture point of view, what chair will we use, what will we use as a changing table, and he's got involved with the Moses basket. He got a bit of a shock yesterday when I said "we might leave the Moses basket here" [in the bedroom], and he was like, "is it going to sleep here", and I was like "yes". I just assumed he knew (laughs) so there might be a bit of a debate about that one, but I mean even for the first few weeks it will have to be in with us you know. (Ireland)

Karen explains how her partner, Kasper, builds a new chest for the baby: "I am sort of picky. So we ended up making one ourselves. That was fine. It was Kasper who decided, that he would like to do that. And I don't have to interfere. It is his project. That's nice (Denmark, pre-interview)." Karen also remarks that Kasper restored another piece of furniture:

> Yes, the cupboard. I think that is because there is such a funny story behind my purchase of it, and then Kasper restored it. He really has done a lot, I reckon. It was a total ramshackle. He really has restored it from scratch. And that has also been a project for him. [...] It means a lot. He also told me, that I do not have to paint it. He wants to do it all himself. That's his project. It has really been great. He has also sewn a curtain for the nursery station. He has made the nursery station and the cupboard. All himself. Sewn and measured and everything. Yes. (Denmark)

There is much said about a woman's nesting instinct kicking in toward the end of the pregnancy but nothing appears to be mentioned about a man's desire to "get his house in order" for the baby. From our data, it appears that for some men, the desire to construct new things or put together complicated baby apparatuses may be a way of making the impending changes seem more real or provide a physical connection in lieu of the physical changes happening to their pregnant partners. Thus, while some father's such as Fintan and Tony had little involvement in buying items for the baby they had engaged in very significant 'projects' in their houses, even though their partners had stressed how busy they were with their jobs and thus unable to engage with other preparations, such as buying products. 'Nesting' for fathers therefore can be an important way of managing role uncertainty and the 'projects' they engaged with can be seen as a way of staging the self (Goffman 1959) and also helping fathers cope with the role disruption they are facing (Solomon 1983).

Fathers Desiring and Seeking Out of Information

The amount and type of information sought out in relation to the pregnancy varied between partners . While a few of our mothers-to-be read very little, most were highly engaged and saw reading about their pregnancy and birth as playing a big role in helping them prepare for their babies' arrivals. The women talked of how their partners did very little or no reading, or who read in a different way:

The only other one (books consulted) was one that I think Duncan's friend bought him, but it was to do with a chap, you're pregnant, too, mate. I did flick through it, but it's written for a guy. It's not something that I would say go and read, because it's written like they're down the pub and they're chatting, and you know the way lads will have a few pints. They're ... and they're fantastic, because it explained everything that would happen or that was happening in boy talk, I think. That's the only way to describe it. I think there must be quite a few of those types of books for chaps. It was completely different to what I would have. I was surprised, initially, that he enjoyed it. You know lads laugh at you, I'm thinking, and then I look at the bit he's just read and think, OK. It's not the most polite about us girls, but, yeah. (Caroline, UK)

So, while women's pregnancy books and publications are often quite graphic, technical, and medically thorough, this particular publication geared toward a man was tongue-in-cheek and almost poking fun of the entire pregnancy process. Indeed, the front cover of one of the few books for men on pregnancy The Bloke's Guide to Pregnancy (Smith 2004) has a picture of a football on the front cover, in stark contrast to the often idyllic mother and baby photographs sporting the front cover of most mothering manuals.

The next example is particularly compelling because Karen repeatedly describes Kasper as heavily involved with all aspects of her pregnancy:

Karen: It has been much like 'Kasper, I would really like you to read some of all those books'–but he doesn't bother.
Int: No, he prefers the Internet?
Karen: Yes, he does that too. But he is more like looking things up. He is more like, well, he says 'It is not necessary to read this book from one end to another–you don't get any wiser of that.' You know, that is one thing I have been a bit disappointed about him not participating. (Denmark)

Kasper goes so far as to make Karen question the degree to which she is studying up on pregnancy and parenting:

But Kasper thinks I am exaggerating, he tells me to use them as reference books, not read them as such. I do have a tendency to read them and to find out that oh we have to remember. (Karen, Denmark)

Sarah's partner is so disgusted by the pictures in the pregnancy books and he refuses to look at them:

Int: And what about any of the books, has he looked at any of them?
Sarah: He won't even look at any of the pictures.
Int: Why?
Sarah: What I do is, the book will be on the bed or something, and he'll find it and it will fall open on what he would call really horrendous pictures and he'll go 'agh'. (Ireland)

Sadie's partner also did not look at the pregnancy books but for different reasons:
Int: Did Ed look at it (book on pregnancy)as well?
Sadie: Never, well he doesn't, he's not into reading anyway, and he certainly wouldn't be reading that. He's kind of an old fashioned, macho guy. 'That's women's stuff.' (Ireland)

There were exceptions; here Abigail talks of her husband's involvement at pre-natal doctor's visit as a result of being 'up to speed' from reading baby manuals:

Abigail: We were lucky because he was in school too and it was flexible. Then he's, you know, all freaked out because the last two appointments or whatever, now he starts work and he's like, I can't come, your mom's going to have to go. He's so bummed out that he can't but he's been (inaudible) and he'll ask more questions than I do. I kind of, whatever the doctor tells me, that's fine. And he's like, what about and like, I heard. You know 'cause we have the What to Expect When You're Expecting book and yet in this chapter it's and he's all up to speed. (USA)

A clear picture of how fathers prepare for the role of fatherhood does not emerge from these findings. The mothers' perceptions of their partners' involvement shows both similarities and differences; involvement in buying items for instance varies from co-involvement and joint-decision making, for most, if not all purchases, to limited involement at the other end of the spectrum. Further research to assess what mediates these relationships is therefore warranted. For example, existing research in the parenting literature suggests these differences are not related to class, ethnicity or race. Our study serves to confirm this viewpoint as well as there. were difference and similarities both within and across cultures.

DISCUSSION

This study serves to uncover men's consumption activities in the biologically female and culturally feminine experience of pregnancy and childbirth. As the zeitgeist of parenting has shifted to the notion of co-contribution, the implementation of this philosophy has proved problematic during this particular transitional period. During pregnancy especially and to a certain extent after a child is born, nature necessarily forces a different experience on men and women and it is only now that researchers and parents alike are beginning to figure out what equal parenting really means. Murphy (2004) states "whatever you do, keep in mind that it takes a very long time to negotiate the shift from partners to parents…The overwhelming majority of moms I spoke to found that the birth of their baby transformed even the most egalitarian marriage into a kind of Leave it to Beaver time warp… (p. 53)." And while women want their partner to be an equal contributor, as one participant (Claire) said, the reality may be that they want joint decision making with the woman in the lead. In her extremely successful book The Girlfriend's Guide to Pregnancy, Vicky Iovine described it this way: "perhaps we new mums are secretly terrified that Daddy is going to be at least as skillful at childcare as we are. Where does that leave us?…So many of us secretly suspect that we are really amateurish at this mothering business and if a man…can do the job proficiently, then our self-esteem and identity lie in shattered little pieces on the bedroom floor (p. 52)."

The complex set of emotions and physiological changes that both men and women experience when transitioning into parenthood is sometimes softened by consumption experiences, such as when Danish consumers buy their first prams, a product laden with social and cultural capital (Thomsen and Sørensen 2006). Yet, it also appears from related research that the baby marketplace actually exacerbates the fears and concerns of new parents, creating feelings of inadequacy and resistance. How women perceive their partners to be coping with the transition appears to be an important piece in the larger study of how becoming a parent is informed by identity, gender roles and norms, socialization, marketplace ideologies, and sociocultural beliefs. This paper has focused on women's perceptions of their partner's involvement in consumption prior to the birth of their baby; future research is therefore warranted, for perceptions following the birth of the baby on the one-hand, with a need for also investigating the perceptions and opinions of fathers themselves. As stated in the literature review, mother's perceptions of fathers have been utilized as a central measurement in the parenting and family literatures and this study also follows this practice; in the future it is also important to consider father's opinions on their roles and also father's perceptions of mother's involvement, to broaden our understanding and help build on the new ideas, from the differing countries, brought together and highlighted in this paper.

REFERENCES

Ballard C. and Davies R. (1996), "Post Natal Depression in Fathers", *International Journal of Psychiatry*, 8(1), 65-71.

Barbour R. (1990) "Fathers: The Emergence of A New Consumer Group", in Garcia J., Kilpatrick R. and Richards M. (eds), *The Politics of Maternity Care*, Oxford: Clarendon Press.

Berkmann M. (2005) *Fatherhood: The Truth*. Vermilion.

Brott A. (2005), *The New Father: A Dad's Guide to the First Year* New York: Abbeville Press.

Coltrane, S. and K. Allan (1994), "New Fathers and Old Stereotypes," *Masculinities*, 2(4), 43-66.

Commuri and Gentry. (2000), "Opportunities for Family Research in Marketing", *Academy of Marketing Science Review*. Vancouver: 1.

Davies Andrea, Dobscha Susan, Geiger Susi, O'Donohoe Stephanie, O'Malley Lisa, Prothero Andrea, Sørensen Elin Brandi, Thomsen Thyra Uth, (2007), "Guiding, Chiding Providing: Consumption and the Social Networks of Expectant Mothers," in *European Advances in Consumer Research*, Milan, IT.

Douglas, S.J., and M.W. Michaels. (2004), *The Mommy Myth: The Idealization of Motherhood and How It Has Undermined All Women*. New York: The Free Press.

Fagan J. and Barnett M. (2003), "The Relationship Between Maternal Gatekeeping, Paternal Competence, and Mothers' Attitudes about the Father's Role and Father's Involvement", *Journal of Family Issues*, 24, 1020-1043

Futris T.G.and Schoppe-Sullivan S.J (2007), "Mother's Perceptions of Barriers, Parenting Alliance, and Adolescent Father's Engagement with their Children", *Family Relations*, 56(July), 258-269.

Goffman, E. (1959), *The presentation of self in everyday life*, New York, Anchor Books.

Harrison R.and Gentry J. (2007a), "Single Fathers and Household Production and Consumption: Their Story and Their Children's" in *European Advances in Consumer Research*, volume 8.

Harrison and Gentry (2007b), "The Vulnerability Of Single Fathers Adjusting To Their New Parental Role," in *European Advances in Consumer Research*, volume 8.

Harrison, Robert and James W. Gentry (2008), "Marketing Forces Slowing Male Movement Toward Gender Neutral," in *9th ACR Conference on Gender, Marketing, and Consumer Behavior*, Bettany, Dobscha, O'Malley, Prothero, eds.; Boston, MA: 530-567.

Hogg, M., C. F. Curasi , and P. Maclaran. (2004), "The (Re-) Configuration of Production and Consumption in Empty Nest Households/Families", *Consumption, Markets and Culture*, 7 (3), 329-350.

Heisley, D. and Levy, S. (1991), "Autodriving: a photoelicitation technique", *Journal of Consumer Research*, 18, 257-272

Iovine V. (1997), *The Best Friends Guide to Surviving the First Year of Motherhood*, London: Bloomsbury.

Johnston, J. (2004), "The Nesting Instinct," *Midwifery Today/ International Midwife*, Autumn (71), 36-7.

Kaufman, G. (1999), "The Portrayal of Men's Family Roles in Television Commercials," *Sex Roles*, 41 (Nos. 5/6), 439-458.

Krishnakumar A. and Black M.M. (2003), "Family Processes within Three Generation Households and Adolescent Mothers' Satisfaction with Father Involvement", *Journal of Family Psychology*, 17(488-498).

Lamb, M.E., Pleck J.H., Charnov E.L., and J.A.Levine (1987), "A Bio-social Perspective on Paternal Behavior and Involvement", in J. Lancaster, J Altmann, A. Rossi and L. Sherrod, *Parenting Across the Lifespan: Bio-Social Dimensions*, 111-142, New York: Aldine de Gruyter.

Lareau, Annette (2000), "My Wife Can Tell Me Who I Know: Methodological and Conceptual Problems in Studying Fathers," *Qualitative Sociology*, 23(4), 407-433.

Leathers, S.J., Kelley, M.A., and Richman, J.A. (1997), "Postpartum Depressive Symptomatology in New Mothers and Fathers: Parenting, Work and Support", *Journal of Nervous and Mental Disease*, 185(3), 129-139.

McCracken, G. (1988), *The Long Interview*. Newbury Park, California: Sage.

McMahon, M. 1995. *Engendering Motherhood; Identity and Self Transformation in Women's Lives*. New York: The Guilford Press.

Miles, M. B. and Huberman A.M. (1994) *Qualitative data analysis-Second edition*, London: Sage.

Murphy A.P. (2004), *The Seven Stages of Motherhood: Making the Most of Your Life as a Mum*. New York: Random House.

Parsons R. (1997), *The Sixty Minute Father*. London: Trafalgar Square Publishing.

Pleck E.H.and Pleck J.H. (1997), "Fatherhood Ideals in the United States: Historical Dimensions, in Lamb M.E. (ed.), *The Role of the Father in Child Development* (3rd Ed.), New York: Wiley.

Prothero, A. (2002), Consuming Motherhood: an Introspective Journey on Consuming to be A Good Mother. *Gender and Consumption*: ACR Gender Conference, Dublin, June.

Storey A.E., Walsh L.J., Quinton R.L. and Wynn-Edwards K.E. (2000), "Hormonal Correlates of Paternal Responsiveness in New and Expectant Fathers" *Evolution and Human Behavior*, 21(2): 79-95.

Solomon, M. R. (1983), "The Role of Products as Social Stimuli: A Symbolic Interactionism Perspective", *Journal of Consumer Research*, 10(December), 319-329.

Simmerman S., J. Blacher, and B.L. Baker (2001), "Father's and Mother's Perceptions of Father Involvement in Families with Young Children With A Disability", *Journal of Intellectual and Developmental Disability*, 26(4), 325-338.

Smith J. (2004). *The Bloke's Guide to Pregnancy*. London: Hay House Inc.

Summers J.A., H. Raikes, J. Butler, P. Spicer, B. Pan, S. Shaw, M. Langager, C. Mcallister, M.K. Johnson (1999), "Low-Income Fathers' and Mothers' Perceptions of the Father Role: A Qualitative Study in Four Early Head Start Communities", *Infant Mental Health Journal*, 20(3), 291-304.

Thomsen, T. U., and E.B. Sørensen E. B. (2006), "The First Four-wheeled Status Symbol: Pram Consumption as a Vehicle for the Construction of Motherhood Identity", *Journal of Marketing Management* 22 (Nov): 907-927.

Warner, J. 2005. *Perfect Madness: Motherhood in the Age of Anxiety*. New York: Riverhead Books.

The Appeal of Our New Stuff: How Newness Creates Value

Aimee Dinnin, The University of Western Ontario, Canada

ABSTRACT

This conceptual paper accounts for the thrill associated with a brand new possession. I propose that the perception of newness is an important part of the consumption experience because it creates short-term value. Three factors create the perception of newness: situational product involvement, a sense that the product is pristine, and physical possession. Value is then derived from the hedonic experience of ownership and the motivational force of attraction to be the first user of a pristine, virgin product. The sense of newness fades over time, through product usage, and as the consumer hedonically adapts to possession.

INTRODUCTION

Consider the following hypothetical example of two individuals at a local police station. Both have had their bicycles stolen, and are distressed about their losses. The first person, who has owned his bike about six months, reports that his bike has been stolen. The second person reports "my *brand new* bike has been stolen". Presumably, the second person uses the term brand new to imply that the loss was greater than the first person's. She uses the term to indicate that her bike was, somehow, more valuable and more special because it was brand new.

Next, consider a consumer who has purchased a new car. Initially, he takes great pride in his brand new car; he diligently washes and waxes it, does his best to protect it from scratches, and prohibits his friends from eating inside it. Eventually, despite his best efforts to keep the car in its brand new state, the odometer creeps upward and a coffee is spilled on the front seat. After a finite amount of time and regular use, it is no longer his *brand new* car.

A brand new product is more appealing, and, at some point, the newness fades from new purchases. But why is a brand new bike more appealing than a somewhat new bike? What is different about the brand new bike? In this paper, I offer a description of the factors necessary to create a sense of brand new, and I suggest that the appeal of new possessions creates additional short-term value for the consumer, beyond mere ownership and endowment effects. I also offer an answer to the question: Why and how does my *new* car turn into my car? I argue that our perceptions of the product, and the product itself, change, and I will explain why the newness, and its attendant value, fades.

I believe that newness can be considered a perceived aspect of a product. Sensing that a possession has newness creates value for the consumer by fostering a positive hedonic experience and sense of attraction toward the new possession. Perceiving that a product has newness generates a thrill for the consumer, and this thrill lasts until the person perceives that new newness has faded. Coupland alludes to this, noting that attention to the product fades as newness fades (2005). This suggests that newness creates some sort of value or special appeal for the consumer.

To my knowledge, the concept of newness–as I introduced it– has received limited attention in consumer research. Richins and Bloch discuss newness in their account of why the "new wears off" of new possessions (1986, 280), but they account for the fading sense of newness by linking it to situational product involvement. Product involvement comprises interest and arousal, but it does not explain the pleasure or enjoyment that seem to accompany a perception of newness. Accordingly, I would argue that involvement does not adequately account for newness. Further investigation of how the authors consider newness reveals that they may be

describing a form of novelty, which is conceptually different from newness; any stimulus is considered novel when it is first introduced, but not every new stimulus has a sense of *newness* about it. For example, there may be nothing novel about the tenth pair of Nike running shoes a runner/consumer purchases, but the new pair may seem *brand new* for a short time. Other researchers have discussed the idea of newness in a similar manner, considering new as new-to-market (Wasson 1960), different (Oropesa 1995), or innovative (Hirschman 1980). I suggest that newness is a bona fide concept, distinct from novelty, and worthy of theoretical attention.

This paper will consider the special appeal and value associated with brand new products, with the understanding that the product has not had a previous owner. Additionally, I will only consider newness in the context of a purchase in a product category from which the consumer has previously purchased, and I will not consider novel products in the sense of consumer innovation and early adoption of new product categories. The model does not specifically account for newness in relation to products received as gifts, although there is opportunity for gift literature to inform future model development. Further, because I contend that physical perfection is an essential determinant for newness, this phenomenon will not be considered in relation to services or intangible products.

The purpose of this paper is to explain why and how new possessions create short-term value for consumers. In the first section of this paper, I argue that newness is developed in response to three determining factors: situational product involvement, perception of the product's pristine physical qualities, and possession of the product. In the second section of the paper, I define and discuss the notion of newness, and how it is defined by increased short-term value and loss aversion. In the third section of the paper, I suggest that newness declines as a result of time passage, product usage, and hedonic adaptation. The final section of the paper discusses the propositions put forth in the preceding sections, and identifies some research questions inspired by the model. First, to the question: what makes a product seem new?

DETERMINANTS OF NEWNESS

Situational Product Involvement

Involvement with a new product is necessary but not sufficient to foster a sense of newness. Product involvement can be defined as the consumer's level of interest, arousal, enthusiasm, or excitement toward a product, although it is important to note that involvement is determined by the consumer's interpretation of the product, not the product itself (Antil 1984). Consumer research has demonstrated that this psychological state can be understood as either enduring involvement or situational involvement, and that the principal distinction between them is temporal duration (Richins and Bloch 1986).

Consumers temporarily exhibit situational product involvement when their interest, arousal, and excitement toward a product peak. This peak generally occurs when a purchase decision is made (Richins and Bloch 1986). Situational involvement is experienced during pre-purchase search activities, during the purchase itself, and while the consumer still feels the excitement of having a new product. By definition, it declines over time (Antil 1984).

Situational involvement motivates pre-purchase search activities independently of the level of enduring involvement, which is the consumer's ongoing or baseline level of interest in a particular product (Richins, Bloch, and McQuarrie 1992). For example, a consumer who has minimal enduring involvement with a car will experience temporary situational involvement when she is in the process of choosing and buying a new car. Consumers can be involved in the purchase but not in the product; as purchase needs are identified and options are analyzed, the consumer becomes involved in the purchase in order to make a satisfactory decision but she does not require a high level of interest in the product in order to become engaged in the purchase (Bloch, Sherrell, and Ridgway 1986). This suggests that only situational product involvement is required to create a sense of newness, because a consumer can sense newness for a product with which she has either a great deal or very little enduring involvement.

Pristine Product

The second necessary determinant of newness is that the consumer must believe that the product is pristine in order to sense that the product is truly new. *Pristine* is a subjective notion, and for the purposes of this paper, it will refer to a product that the consumer perceives to be in its perfect, unblemished, ideal form.

The consumer's evaluation of a product's physical appearance is the first form of connection with the product (Bloch, Brunel, and Arnold 2003), and consumers desire to purchase products that are as physically perfect as possible. When people purchase an apple, for example, they are drawn to choose apples with brilliant color, symmetrical shape, and clean, shiny skin. Blemishes, dirt, and physical damage deter us, just as they do for manufactured consumer products; we are likely to infer that quality and product performance will be compromised when we perceive the product as physically imperfect (Kotler and Mantrala 1985). However, we are also deterred by imperfections that do not explicitly indicate damage to the product or inferior quality. Although consumers differ in their individual levels of focus on product appearance (Bloch et al. 2003), product appearance is considered a universal signal of product quality (Dawar and Parker 1994).

Packaging plays an important role in maintaining a sense of pristine because consumers are less likely to question quality or performance when the original packaging is still intact. Underhill uses, as an example to demonstrate that consumers are deterred by damaged packaging, the following dialogue about shopping for bed linens:

How does it feel? The problem is that most sheets are sold in plastic bags, which allow you to look but not touch. So you tear open the bag with your nail and furtively rub the fabric. Now if you decide to buy, you'll choose another package, because who wants one that's been damaged (even if you did the damaging)? (Underhill 1999, 170)

A product can be considered imperfect if it is physically damaged or otherwise altered from its intended or ideal form. However, a product can also be considered imperfect if the consumer perceives it to be contaminated in some respect. Argo, Dahl and Morales (2006) found that consumers can consider a product to be contaminated if they believe that another consumer has simply touched the product. That is, a consumer can develop a sense of contamination in spite of an unblemished physical appearance. Argo et al. found that that perceived contamination of a product resulted in lower product evaluations, which were driven by the consumers' feelings of disgust. This is interesting because disgust is one of the strongest human emotions (Zaltman 2003), and consumer perceptions of a product can significantly worsen if other consumers are perceived as contaminating a product through touch

(Argo et al. 2006). This reveals that perceiving a product as pristine is more complex than an objective evaluation of its undamaged appearance.

Possession

I propose that physical possession is the third necessary determinant to the experience of newness. In order to sense that the product is brand new, the consumer must actually possess the product and be able to call it mine. Economic theory says the rational consumer takes possession of a particular product to derive utility from its functional benefits. We know, however, that consumers behave in ways that are both consistent and inconsistent with economic theories of choice (Okada 2001). Consumers can be simultaneously rational and emotional, reflective and impulsive, when they choose to take possession of a new product (Strack and Werth 2006). Indeed, "…much, if not all, consumption has been quite wrongfully characterized as involving distanced processes of need fulfillment, utility maximization, and reasoned choice." (Belk, Ger, and Askegaard 2003, 326).

Recently, researchers have espoused a middle ground position, positing that consumers engage in consumption activities to gain utilitarian benefits, which are derived from the functional benefits of the product, and to gain hedonic benefits, which are derived from the sensations of experiencing the product (Voss, Spangenberg, and Grohmann 2003). Thus, actual possession of a product gives the consumer access to the product's usefulness, and allows the consumer to sense the pleasure associated with the possession experience. Additionally, possession entitles the consumer to be the first to use the new product, which is an important stage in the consumption experience.

VALUE FROM NEWNESS

When the consumer senses that a new possession is truly brand new, there is a distinct level of additional value associated with the product. The consumer's sense of newness is generated by his situational involvement in the product, a sense of the product's pristine physical qualities, and possession of the product. These three factors work together to create the additional value associated with newness and the heightened loss aversion associated with the value assessment.

The concept of value is psychologically complex, and involves more than the monetary amount that one ascribes to something. Value can be derived from hedonic experience and from a force of attraction (Higgins 2006). That is, the value of newness can be considered both as the pleasurable experience of owning a pristine, new product, and the strong motivational force to be the first to use the product. Higgins notes that "although the hedonic experience and the motivational force experience often are experienced holistically, conceptually they are distinct from each other" (2006, 441).

I believe that value of newness is partially derived from the pleasure associated with ownership of a new possession. Situational involvement creates a short-term state of arousal for the consumer in relation to his very recent acquisition of a new possession. If the product is physically pristine and "untouched", the consumer should derive a distinct sense of pleasure in relation to his new possession immediately following its acquisition. In fact, many consumers are able to derive some value from the pleasure experienced by merely seeing a physically appealing product (Creusen and Schoormans 2005). It is this source of value that generates the "thrill" associated with a brand new possession, and most consumers should be able to acknowledge and describe the pleasurable excitement that comes from a new product.

I propose that the value from newness is also gained from being the first user of the product. This value is derived from the motivational force experience associated with the consumer's desire to be the first to use a pristine, previously "untouched" product. Higgins describes this source of value as "the experience of the motivational force to make something happen (experienced as a force of attraction)" (2006, 441). Instinctively, most consumers likely have a sense of the product owner's entitlement to be the first user of a pristine, virgin product. The privilege of being the first to wear, drive or operate a product whose newness is salient should be familiar to most of us. In some cases the consumer may be able to derive this value over a long period of time (e.g., a new car) because the product itself seems to hold its newness over several usage experiences. In other cases, however, the value associated with first use may be derived from simply opening the packaging (e.g., a new calculator). Few of us would consider driving a friend's brand new car before she had driven it, because we recognize that the product's owner is entitled to the privilege of first use. Conversely, there can be a distinct sense of disappointment associated with someone else being the first to use your own new possession.

LOSS AVERSION

When a person possesses something, he is motivated to avoid losing it. This motivation to avoid loss is termed loss aversion, which is a general preference to avoid a loss over experiencing a gain (Kahneman and Tversky 1984). In other words, the pain associated with a loss is more pronounced than the pleasure associated with an acquisition (Zhang and Fishbach 2005). Loss aversion reveals itself in a price discrepancy between an individual's willingness to pay to obtain a product, and his willingness to accept to part with the same product (Kahneman, Knetsch, and Thaler 1990). This discrepancy is known as the endowment effect (Thaler 1980), and it explains why owners demand higher prices than potential buyers. The endowment effect occurs immediately: willingness to accept increases substantially as soon as the individual acquires the item. Thus, an object's value increases as soon as the individual takes possession of it (Kahneman et al. 1990).

I propose that newness will create an amplified endowment effect. As previous research has demonstrated, a product's value will increase after the consumer takes possession of it. However, part of this increase in value should be attributed to the value derived from newness; the product's value and the associated loss aversion will decrease as the newness fades.

Owners of hedonic possessions attributed more value to their possessions and were more sensitive to possession loss than owners of utilitarian possessions (Dhar and Wertenbroch 2000). This suggests that possessions that evoke a strong hedonic reaction, such as products for which the newness is highly salient, are valued more highly and instill a higher degree of loss aversion in their owners. The endowment effect can therefore account for the increased hedonic impact of a potential loss (Nayakankuppam and Mishra 2005). In support of this, Belk (1988) reported that people are more likely to invest emotional energy in their possessions when the possessions are newer.

WHY NEWNESS FADES

I propose that the sense of newness fades as the additional value associated with newness dissipates; the appeal of the new product wanes as the hedonic experience and motivational force experience cease to provide value. Richins and Bloch allude to this, noting that "once the purchase has been made, consumer arousal and time spent thinking about the product decline as purchase needs and product novelty subside" (1986, 280). The temporal boundary of newness can be defined as the point at which *my new car* has become *my car*. Until this point, the value of newness declines over time, through product usage, and as the consumer hedonically adapts to possession.

Product usage and the passage of time since purchase affect newness in three ways. First, situational involvement naturally fades over time, resulting in diminishing value and a declining sense of newness. Second, product usage usually results in the product losing its original pristine characteristics, which will also have a negative impact on newness. Third, the value associated with being the first to use a possession is fully derived through direct experience with the possession.

Hedonic Adaptation

As the consumer becomes familiar with his new possession, he becomes psychologically accustomed to level of stimulation it provides and to the nature of his affect associated with the possession (Strahilevitz and Loewenstein 1998). As time passes, the intensity of his affect decreases, and this process is known as hedonic adaptation (Frederick and Loewenstein 1999). In their investigation of new car buyers, Richins and Bloch (1986) found evidence of hedonic adaptation: as the owners became accustomed to their new cars, their levels of product involvement diminished to pre-purchase levels. Thus, hedonic adaptation takes places as newness fades. The consequences of this adaptation are two-fold: the consumer experiences a reduced hedonic response to his new state of being, and he experiences an exaggerated sensitivity to reverting back to his original state of being (Strahilevitz and Loewenstein 1998). Additionally, hedonic adaptation can explain why a consumer does not experience increased happiness from acquiring more material goods; as the consumer acquires more his aspirations and actual gains are raised equally (Easterlin 2003).

DISCUSSION

The endowment effect explains the consumer's tendency to increase product valuation after taking it into possession; valuation increases when possession occurs. However, the literature on hedonic adaptation suggests that value declines over time, if value is considered in terms of hedonic experience and force of attraction. Thus, it appears that possession valuation may involve a pattern different from–but not contradictory to–the endowment effect; valuation may be amplified for the period of time immediately following endowment. Figure 1 depicts valuation over time according to this model. The solid line demonstrates valuation according to the endowment effect, where value increases after possession occurs and, presumably, stays constant. The dotted line depicts the pattern in valuation according to my theory; valuation increases after possession occurs, but declines over time. Strahilevitz and Loewenstein (1998) allude to this pattern, noting that although the endowment effect occurs immediately after possession occurs, more time is needed for the consumer to completely adapt to ownership. This suggests the possibility that the consumer may value her new possession somewhat less after she hedonically adapts to ownership than she did when first endowed with it.

Conceptualizing newness in this way inspires some research questions that may permit empirical tests of the theory or allow for the future development of the model. A simple experiment could determine if monetary valuation peaks immediately after possession endowment and subsequently declines after time or usage. Further manipulations could identify the extent to which a peak in valuation is dependent on temporary enthusiasm toward the product, the perception of the product as being pristine, or belief that the product has not been previously used. It would also be necessary to assess how usage of a new possession influences valuation.

FIGURE 1
Possession Valuation Over Time

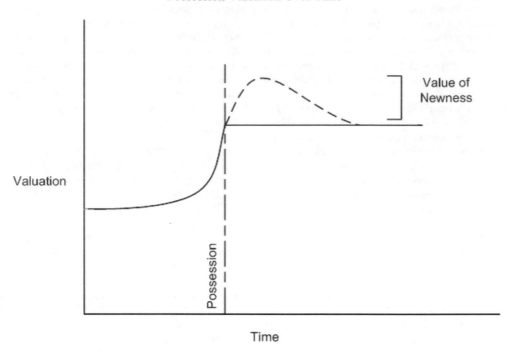

Determining the boundary conditions of the model will be useful in improving our understanding of possession newness. Subsequent testing might address the ways in which product categories influence newness. Do different product categories prompt the consumer to have a heightened sense of newness? What are the characteristics of these categories, and to they involve higher levels of enduring involvement? Is newness enhanced by monetary outlay for purchase, rarity of the product, or the amount of time and emotional energy invested in the pre-purchase search? The influences of individual consumer characteristics should also be addressed. Is newness influenced by personality characteristics, such that some consumers sense newness more strongly than others? Are more materialistic individuals more inclined to sense newness because they place more value on the acquisition of material objects than other people (Burroughs and Rindfleisch 2002)? Does consumer optimism influence newness because people who are more optimistic about the future experience more pleasure in buying new things (Oropesa 1995)? Further, since possessions not only become part of the self, but also help to construct identity (Belk 1988), are consumers more likely to be stimulated by possessions in which they have invested emotional energy? Is newness more salient for possessions that contribute more to identity or sense of self?

Experimental design could also incorporate differences in the nature of the endowment situation. Although this model does not consider products given as gifts, newness may be affected by perceptions of a gifted possession. For example, how is newness influenced by pleasure associated with receiving the perfect gift, by disappointment associated with receiving a bad gift, or by suspicion that the giver has "re-gifted" the item? Further, can newness be perceived in relation to a previously owned product, such as a used car or an antique item?

In addition to empirical testing, it will be important to understand how newness is actually experienced by consumers. This could involve a phenomenological approach, focusing on individual consumer experiences with new possessions. From this perspective, we might gain insights into the emotions and behaviors involved in perceiving newness. If consumers know that the newness will eventually fade, are they sometimes motivated to maximize the intensity and duration of newness because they enjoy the associated hedonic experience? How do consumers try to maximize or maintain a sense of newness? Addressing these questions may help us to understand why consumers are not willing to pay the same price for a physically flawed product, even if the flaw will not affect product performance. Further, it will be important to understand how newness is "used up". What are the behaviors associated with consumption of newness? Are consumers less willing to share possessions for which the newness is still salient? Are consumers conscious of a privilege associated with the first use of a possession or with using up the newness? Attention to these research questions will allow for a better appreciation of how consumers experience value from their new possessions.

CONCLUSION

In this paper, I described the factors necessary to create a sense of possession newness: situational product involvement, perception of the product's pristine physical state, and actual possession of the product. When these factors are present, the consumer is able to derive short-term value from the new possession in the form of a distinct, pleasurable response to the product and the privilege of being the first to use the product. The value of newness fades over time, with use of the product, and as the consumer hedonically adapts to ownership.

Considering the concept of newness within this framework can allow for an understanding of how and why consumers perceive some new possessions to hold special appeal. The notion that newness creates a distinct form of short-term hedonic value and a compulsion to be a new product's first user can help to explain behavior toward these possessions and the pattern of valuation. Further, this concept of value from newness integrates literature concerning the endowment effect and hedonic adaptation, thereby deepening our understanding of possession valuation.

REFERENCES

Antil, John H. (1984), "Conceptualization and Operationalization of Involvement," in *Association for Consumer Research*, Vol. 11, ed. Thomas C. Kinnear, Provo, UT, 203-09.

Argo, Jennifer J., Darren W. Dahl, and Andrea C. Morales (2006), "Consumer Contamination: How Consumers React to Products Touched by Others," *Journal of Marketing*, 70, 81-94.

Belk, Russell W. (1988), "Possessions and the Extended Self," *Journal of Consumer Research*, 15, 139-68.

Belk, Russell W., Guliz Ger, and Soren Askegaard (2003), "The Fire of Desire: A Multisited Inquiry into Consumer Passion," *Journal of Consumer Research*, 30, 326-51.

Bloch, Peter H., Frederic F. Brunel, and Todd J. Arnold (2003), "Individual Differences in the Centrality of Visual Product Aesthetics: Concept and Measurement," *Journal of Consumer Research*, 29, 551-65.

Bloch, Peter H., Daniel L. Sherrell, and Nancy M. Ridgway (1986), "Consumer Search: An Extended Framework," *Journal of Consumer Research*, 13, 119-26.

Burroughs, James E. and Aric Rindfleisch (2002), "Materialism and Well-Being: A Conflicting Values Perspective," *Journal of Consumer Research*, 29 (348-370).

Coupland, Jennifer Chang (2005), "Invisible Brands: An Ethnography of Households and the Brands in Their Kitchen Pantries," *Journal of Consumer Research*, 32 (June), 106-18.

Creusen, Marielle E. H. and Jan P. L. Schoormans (2005), "The Different Roles of Product Appearance in Consumer Choice," *The Journal of Product Innovation Management*, 22, 63-81.

Dawar, Niraj and Philip Parker (1994), "Marketing Universals: Consumers' Use of Brand Name, Price, Physical Appearance, and Retailer Reputation as Signals of Product Quality," *Journal of Marketing*, 58, 81-95.

Dhar, Ravi and Klaus Wertenbroch (2000), "Consumer Choice between Hedonic and Utilitarian Goods," *Journal of Marketing Research*, 37 (1), 60-71.

Easterlin, Richard A. (2003), "Explaining Happiness," in *National Academy of Sciences of the United States of America*, Vol. 100, 11176-83.

Frederick, Shane and George Loewenstein (1999), "Hedonic Adaptation," in *Well-Being: The Foundations of Hedonic Psychology*: Russel Sage Foundation Press.

Higgins, E. Tory (2006), "Value from Hedonic Experience and Engagement," *Psychological Review*, 113 (3).

Hirschman, Elizabeth C. (1980), "Innovativeness, Novelty Seeking, and Consumer Creativity," *Journal of Consumer Research*, 7 (December), 283-95.

Kahneman, Daniel, Jack L. Knetsch, and Richard H. Thaler (1990), "Experimental Tests of the Endowment Effect and the Coase Theorem," *Journal of Political Economy*, 98 (6), 1325-48.

Kahneman, Daniel and Amos Tversky (1984), "Choices, Values and Frames," *American Psychologist*, 39, 341-50.

Kotler, Philip and Murali K. Mantrala (1985), "Flawed Products: Consumer Responses and Marketer Strategies," *The Journal of Consumer Marketing*, 2 (3), 27-37.

Nayakankuppam, Dhananjay and Himanshu Mishra (2005), "The Endowment Effect: Rose-Tinted and Dark-Tinted Glasses," *Journal of Consumer Research*, 32, 390-95.

Okada, Erica Mina (2001), "Trade-Ins, Mental Accounting, and Product Replacement Decisions," *Journal of Consumer Research*, 27, 433-46.

Oropesa, R. S. (1995), "Consumer Possessions, Consumer Passions, and Subjective Well-Being," *Sociological Forum*, 10 (215-244).

Richins, Marsha L. and Peter H. Bloch (1986), "After the New Wears Off: The Temporal Context of Product Involvement," *Journal of Consumer Research*, 13 (September), 280-85.

Richins, Marsha L., Peter H. Bloch, and Edward F. McQuarrie (1992), "How Enduring and Situational Involvement Combine to Create Involvement Responses," *Journal of Consumer Psychology*, 1 (3), 143-54.

Strack, Fritz and Lioba Werth (2006), "Reflective and Impulsive Determinants of Consumer Behavior," *Journal of Consumer Psychology*, 16 (3), 205-16.

Strahilevitz, Michal A. and George Loewenstein (1998), "The Effect of Ownership History on the Valuation of Objects," *Journal of Consumer Research*, 25 (December).

Thaler, Richard (1980), "Toward a Positive Theory of Consumer Choice," *Journal of Economic Behavior and Organization*, 1 (1), 39-60.

Underhill, Paco (1999), *Why We Buy: The Science of Shopping*, New York: Simon & Schuster Paperbacks.

Voss, Kevin E., Eric R. Spangenberg, and Bianca Grohmann (2003), "Measuring the Hedonic and Utilitarian Dimensions of Consumer Attitude," *Journal of Marketing Research*, 40 (3), 310-20.

Wasson, Chester R. (1960), "What Is "New" About a New Product?," *Journal of Marketing*, 25 (1), 52-56.

Zaltman, Gerald (2003), *How Customers Think: Essential Insights into the Mind of the Market*, Boston, MA: Harvard Business School Press.

Zhang, Ying and Ayelet Fishbach (2005), "The Role of Anticipated Regret in the Endowment Effect," in *Advances in Consumer Research*, Vol. 32, ed. Geeta Menon and Akshay R. Rao, Duluth, MN: Association for Consumer Research, 66.

Consuming the Black Gospel Culture: An Interpretive Study of Symbolic Exchanges

Yuko Minowa, Long Island University–Brooklyn Campus, USA
David S. Glover, Long Island University–Brooklyn Campus, USA

ABSTRACT

This paper investigates the meanings of Black gospel music and symbolic exchanges of gospel culture within and across gospel and non-gospel communities. Based on an ethnographic account, we analyze our informants' lived experiences with consuming gospel music and culture. Based on the consumption orientation and based on the nature of experience, we find that gospel music consumption is characterized as indulgent, contemplative, communicative, and transcendent. We discuss how gospel music mediates to define and redefine the meanings of the culture within and across gospel communities and Others. While being commodified as a cultural product, gospel music spawns new consumer identities.

INTRODUCTION

Music evolves, metamorphoses, and its meanings and consumer experiences are intricately interwoven, begetting a mandala of symbols while letting the consumer immerse in the vast sea of emotional undulation. Black gospel music is a genre par excellence. Originating in the Negro spirituals, one definition of gospel music may be "a religious music of African Americans that emerged in urban centers during the early decades of twentieth century" (Burnim and Maultsby 2006, 51). It is an expression of the aesthetics, values, and experiences of their community (Jackson 1995). Today, however, gospel music is consumed by both descendants of Africa and those who do not share at all the African American heritage and tradition. It is appreciated through an MP3 player by a lonesome jogger as well as in church as part of liturgical ceremony. The music is sung by religious African Americans in a choir as well as by groups of Japanese Buddhists or Australian atheists. Gospel music is not only sung, but the choir is an object of spectation by tourists. Then, what does it mean to different individuals to consume such supposedly religious and ethnocentric gospel music? How do people consume their experience with the music and culture? The multivocal character of gospel music seems to expand unbounded and continues to augment its multiplicity.

On a Wednesday morning, for instance, a deluge of foreign tourists fills up the sightseeing bus at Times Square and cruises New York City. They head toward Harlem to explore and experience what they believe to be authentic African American urban culture including gospel music. In one of the churches, a few locals walk down the aisle with Chinese takeout in a plastic bag and start rocking their bodies as they approach an open pew, while a group of young Japanese female tourists indifferently listens to the tour guide's explanation about where the donation would go. All of a sudden, a pencil-thin woman staggers up to the stage and speaks to the audience about her personal problems. Then, a man in a red and yellow robe recites the bible while the gospel choir, made up of members of the local addiction rehabilitation center, sings frantically, and some locals, in trance, sing together and shout intermittently "thank you," "hallelujah," and "amen." Chaos and madness permeate this newly renovated church; the site is an apt simulacrum of an "authentic" Black church in Harlem appropriated for a commercial purpose in the global age.

Another way to apprehend gospel music and culture is to critically examine its meanings in relation to consumer culture theory (Arnould and Thompson 2005). Gospel music is a subject of study in various disciplines. Its history and the history of performance are topics in music history as well as cultural studies (Darden 2004; Smith Pollard 2008). As the music of a subculture, in ethnomusicology, its musical tradition in its cultural context is examined (Burnim 1985; Jackson 1995). In sociology, the function of gospel music in symbolic interaction and its power in social influence are explored (Semmes 1974). In anthropology, the hybridization of indigenous and gospel music by locals in the age of globalization has been explored (Magowan 2007).

On the other hand, in consumer research, experiential consumption of music is profoundly related to the subculture represented by age group (Holbrook and Schindler 1989; Blair and Hatala 1992), ethnicity (Schroeder and Borgerson 1999), and religion (Davis and Yip 2004), or any combination of these variables (Gooch 1996). Previous studies on religion or spirituality in conjunction with consumption (O'Guinn and Belk 1989; Kozinets 2001) did not integrate the role of music in cultivating and enhancing religiosity or consumption. On the other hand, there seems to be little research efforts made to investigate consumer behavior of African Americans with few exceptions (Edson Escalas 1994; Stamps and Arnould 1998; Hirschman and Hill 1999).While the postmodern social phenomenon unveils "cocooning" lifestyle and fragmented social identities in urban landscape (Thompson and Holt 1996), previous inquiries about minority communities (Üstüner and Holt 2007) neglected the significance and role of aesthetic consumption in the sustenance of consumer identity. In this regard, gospel music is an integral part of consumer identity, and it is driven by outer-directed forces.

Therefore, the present study investigates the experiential consumption of gospel music by incorporating multidisciplinary perspectives. In particular, the objectives of the current study are: 1) to examine the meanings and structure of the experiential consumption of gospel music, and 2) to explore symbolic exchanges of the gospel culture within and across the communities defined by gospel music consumption. There is a dearth of research on consumer behavior related to African Americans and their cultures in general. There is no prior study on the experiential consumption of Black gospel music in consumer research. While the shortage alone does not rationalize our motivation for the study, we justify the significance of our study because of the tacit impact of the music making and symbolic exchanges on consumer well-being and welfare aside from its contribution to consumer culture theory.

METHODS

We conducted an interpretive study to empirically explore how consumers of Black gospel music inside and outside the gospel communities consume the musical experience and the entire gospel culture. Following methodological approaches stemming from contemporary social sciences that have been applied to consumer research (Arnould and Wallendorf 1994; Charmaz 2000), we employed participant observation and a variety of interviewing techniques, such as ethnographic interviewing, focus group interviews, and in-depth personal interviews. Ethnographic interviewing is a particularly valuable method to apprehend consumer experiences because the interview setting *in situ* evokes the consumption experiences in the past and the present (Holt 1997). Specifically, interviews took place in the lounge of churches, the dining room of the local addiction rehabilitation center, in the living room of the informant's home, and inside the sightseeing bus. People were more likely to talk about their experiences with gospel music and culture in these sites than in the conference room that was also used for formal interviews.

The study was conducted in several sections of New York City between April 2007 and March 2008. The selection of interview sites was crucial because gospel culture was objectified, consumed, and marketed in divergent ways depending on the geographical location within the city. Harlem, predominantly the home of the African American community, in particular, is considered a focal point for our study since it is socio-historically the center of the development of gospel culture in the North East along with Philadelphia. Also, Harlem is the strategic site for the gospel industry as it became the tourism destination for Others to view and appreciate supposedly authentic black community and gospel culture.

In sum, 27 people were interviewed, which consisted of 12 males and 15 females. All of them but three were descendents of Africans and, to a varying extent, part of gospel communities. When they were asked to identify their cultural background, most of them preferred to call themselves simply New Yorkers. Seven people identified themselves as something else, such as Caribbean or Southerner. Three people from non-gospel communities consisted of two tourists from Japan and one Jewish female from New York. The ages of informants ranged from 14 to 83, with the median age of 40 years. These people were selected on the basis of their self-claimed, highly involved consumption experience with gospel music and culture. The duration of the interviews ranged between 20 and 60 minutes. The informants included students, administrative staff, office clerks, the music director of gospel choirs, the executive director of an addiction rehabilitation center, recovering addicts, and retired school teachers. In other words, the sample included both white- and blue-collar, lower to middle class, and urban gospel consumers. We began interviews with less structured questions and modified them as we felt needed, adjusting to emergent research questions and to informants' responses. All the interviews were either video or audio recorded, and they were subsequently transcribed for analysis and interpretation.

Along with the interviews, we conducted participant observations. We studied participants of concerts, special events during Black history month at the local historical society, which was targeted to a general audience, and at the large concert hall which was targeted to descendants of Africa, supposedly heavy gospel music consumers. We joined an organized commercial sightseeing tour and traveled to Harlem with tourists by chartered bus and saw a gospel concert performed by members of the local addiction rehabilitation center. We took notes manually where digital recording was not allowed. We talked informally with participants of concerts and sightseeing tours about their experience with consuming gospel music and culture.

In analyzing the data, we tried letting the data speak first rather than approaching them with a theoretical frame postulated ex ante. Before coding the data, we explicated, explained, and explored the narratives in the transcription following the hermeneutic triad (Czarniawska 2004). Then, we examined data instances, compared conceptual similarities and differences, and sorted emergent themes. During the core analysis when we discussed emerging concepts, we went back to the narratives and examined data iteratively. We repeated the cycles of inquiry until it had reached saturation. All the names that appear in this paper are pseudonyms, followed by the informant's age in parentheses.

SYMBOLIC CONSUMPTION OF GOSPEL MUSIC

Black gospel music is symbolic of the Christian, African American subculture. Various meanings are embedded in the consumer's experiential consumption of the music within the fuzzy perimeter of subculture. For some, the subculture is well defined with the reinforcement of a strong religious boundary. For example, Tamara (31), whose father was a pastor, says "the whole being raised in church is a part of it. So, it in a way is a culture because the people in church, you know, we all have our own way." Inspirational, encouraging, uplifting, and strengthening are the words most frequently used by our informants to characterize the meanings of the gospel music.

Lyrics of gospel music are the good news, the Devine message. For Daria (58), it is her extended self, symbolic at different levels simultaneously, as it connects her with her ancestry, faith, and culture and music. Spreading activation, shifting the meaning back and forth, she states: "To have the Gospel come from the Book and the Book is old and it was my mother's, it was my father's and now it's mine, so my children, it's just old stuff hereditary. It carries the message in music." The message reminds the faithful that they should continue to stand up and not to give up. Ronald (31) claims that it not only evokes emotion but also invokes a motion; gospel music helps him to take the extra step.

Gospel music is perceived to possess remedial and analgesic properties. Jim (83) says it is a remedy for both physical and psychological pains, and quoted Mahalia Jackson out of his memory: "Blues tells the world your troubles, but, Gospel tells the world your troubles *and* what the solution is." Troubles may be specifically related to consumer behavior: dilemmas and frustrations caused by acquisitions and possessions. Brenda (40) claims: "gospel music allows me to look beyond the material things and see what the real quality, the substance of life is." Gospel music in the religious context helps people tolerate personal difficulties in quotidian circumstances as Imogene (61) says:

I take Him into the doctor's office, my Lord and Savior Jesus Christ and anyone else who would go with me—that's John, Paul, Peter—they all go into the waiting area to get it together cause most times our best bet is to take notes before going into the doctor's office that includes prayer and anything else you got going on.

Clinical and therapeutic uses of music have been studied, and their effectiveness in medical, psychoanalytic, and behavioral fields has been attested to (Bunt 1997). However, gospel music can be beyond therapeutic; it comes to the mind of the faithful as a form of prayer, which is invocatory, and aids consumer decision making as discussed by Imogene above.

Nature of Experience versus Consumption Orientation

Analyzing the narratives of the informants, we found the texts can be categorized in terms of the nature of experience and the orientation of consumption. The nature may be either purely musical with a void of religious context or liturgical within ceremonial context. On the other hand, the consumption orientation may be autonomous or syncratic. The music alone can be consumed by individuals, while gospel music, as part of cultural experience, can be shared with other members of the community, or Others who do not share the heritage yet desire to have the cultural experience.

Some of our informants said that gospel music is both a form of worship and a kind of entertainment. As a means of entertainment, Johnson (2005, 59) points out that "we live out the contradictions of our lives, and an aversion to religion does not exclude persons from making personally meaningful connections to gospel music…" But such purely musical experience may be regarded as sacrilegious by the faithful. For example, when listening to gospel music in a concert hall, both the choir and the audience get "lost"

FIGURE 1
Symbolic Consumption of Gospel Music

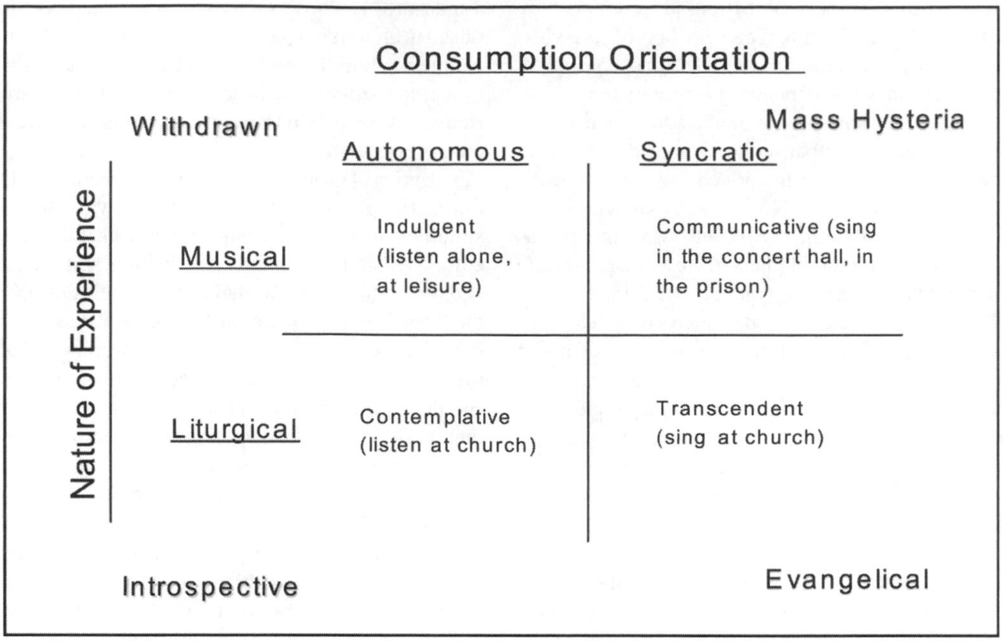

while entertaining each other in antiphonal reverberations. Tamara (31), an informant from the gospel culture, says: "it's a lack of sincerity."

The Symbolic Consumption of Gospel Music

Based on the nature of experience and the consumption orientation, we consider that music as a conduit for indulgence, a means to induce personal reflection, a device for communication with others, and a channel for transcendent experience. These are diagrammatically summarized in Figure 1. The following narratives of informants provide us with insights.

Music as Indulgence. Excessive consumption of gospel music may signal the individual's proclivity towards withdrawal. The moderate state may be considered as indulgent behavior. Some informants discussed the relaxing efficacy of indulging in gospel music. Linda (52), for instance, is likely to spend her Sunday morning with a cup of coffee listening to gospel music. It enlightens her day. She is Catholic but does not go to church regularly. Nevertheless, starting a day with gospel music is the right course of behavior.

Gospel music, like popular music, can evoke a nostalgic past while indulging with it. For example, Linda (52) recollects her difficult youth and how she dealt with problems by listening to *What a Friend I Have in Jesus.* Similarly, Jim (83) recollects how his aunts on the farm used to always sing as they worked: "They picked cotton, and they chopped cotton ... and when the season was over, they would sing songs like: 'So glad, I done got over, I'm so glad.'"

With its hypnotic quality, some gospel music help induce the consumer to withdraw from the outside world temporarily to recollect things from the past, to relieve from present pains, and to avoid confronting future difficulties. For instance, it induces Jim (83) to recollect his hard days:

I was addicted to heroin for many, many years... And during one of my drying out periods, I heard this guy singing and playing the guitar, ah, a gospel song, and his voice was so beautiful and clear that it got me back into gospel ... And it's always had a deep spiritual meaning and something so spiritual. It was so different from other music that you can hardly explain it.

When the music is felt sublime, it brings the consumer a spiritual cleansing. More recently, Jim's indulgence with the music led him to acquire an iPod so that he can play gospel songs and sing along with them while he is cooking in the kitchen. The technology has aided enhancing consumer's indulgent behavior while it united sublime and mundane, or sacred and secular, in consumers' daily lives.

Music as Personal Reflection. Storr (1993, 95), in criticizing Freud, discusses true sources of religious sentiments, which originated from "a sensation of eternity, a feeling as of something limitless, unbounded-as it were, 'oceanic.'" Such sentiments may be provoked by introspection, keenly conscious observation of the self. Linda (52) says that gospel music helps her feel closer to her spiritual "ultimate" relationship with God. For Tamara (31), it is a way to put her beliefs to music, a form of expression for her, as she could identify herself with the messages.

Not only personal nostalgia, but gospel music also evokes collective historical experience. Malcom (35) associates it with slavery and the repugnant ordeals that African Americans underwent. Roy (29) links the historical experience and personal sentiments through gospel music. He explains:

I like the earthliness of the Negro spirituals that remind me of the Black experience. In Orangeburg, South Carolina, where

I went to high school, … they used to do a lot of breeding of slaves. And they sold them in the slave market in Charleston… so when you hear those Negro spirituals … it speaks to an experience that I'm basically a product of the breeding.

Roy is a southerner who was born after Jim Crow. Although he did not experience segregation, he learned about the hardships of black people at church while growing up. As an indigenous South Carolinian, he believes that he is a descendant of slaves. Thus the collective history is felt immediate as his personal history. Gospel music is not only juxtaposed to his memory of the history, but also it has served to condition him to reflect on his identity.

Music as Communication. When the music is sung in a group, the shared music-making experience is a powerful source of communication. Gospel music is important to Malcom (35) because "it's [his] connection to the community." When Leticia moved from New York to Cleveland, the first thing she did was to look for the right church to join. She had three evaluative criteria: the preacher, church members, and the gospel choir. Our other informants similarly narrate the significance of gospel music as a galvanizing and solidifying force in the community.

The music, however, does not have to be communicated in a large group. The musician and an individual audience can have deep philosophical communication. For Krista (28), listening to the Yolanda Adams song *Open My Heart* gave an answer to her personal problem, because of the perceived similarity between her circumstances and those of the singer: "you know, [the singer] is in a room and she's talking to God and … she's questioning I guess the situation and she just has to make her decision…" Religion, spirituality, and consumer decision making are united through Krista's subjective feeling and thoughts in communicating with the Divine, which is mediated by her musical experience.

Furthermore, the communication is aimed to salvage the doomed. Steve (52) who traveled with the gospel choir to a prison in Louisiana describes his recollection from "the Underground Railroad Tour":

We were at a prison in Louisiana called the Louisiana State Penitentiary. We were on death row singing for young men, 16 and 17 years old, and no one had ever done a concert on death row before at this Angola State Penitentiary. And I recall … these were young men who were maybe never going to see outside or maybe they were going to die there. And, I can remember singing for these young men and just hoping that they can get some kind of idea of freedom, even inside of death row….

Having grown up in a dysfunctional family, Steve became a problem child, and then, a drug addict. Then he was taken to a gospel choir, and the music-making experience changed his life. In penitentiaries he visited, he and the choir members were self-designated missionaries. While communicating the good news with inmates, Steve thought he could have been there if he had not been exposed to gospel music. Thus the communication through music can also function to reflect the self and enhance the self respect.

Music as Transcendent Experience. Daniel (49), the director of the gospel choir at one of the African Episcopal Methodist churches, differentiates gospel music from other types of Western music by pointing out that it is an oral tradition rather than being written down. As such, he believes, "it's kind of in a different way and it comes more, you know, initially from within and it just keeps

coming from within." Malcom (35), a musician, plays both gospel and jazz. When he plays jazz, he caters to the crowd's mood. On the contrary, when he plays gospel music, he concentrates on the spirituality and his feelings for appreciating Creator for life, health, strength. He says: "the connection [with the Creator] is so important. I shy away from what the audience vibes or what the congregation would get me to do. But, I communicate with the Creator first."

For Catherine (60), a singer and a devotee in the choir, the performance is a dedication to the Divine:

When I first sang in the choir, you said to me, 'good job my sister.' And I said, 'to God be the glory.' It's not about me, it's about Him. It's not a performance to us, it's a ministry. We don't sing these songs because we want the congregation to say, 'Good job Catherine,' 'Good job Imogene.' No. We want God to get the glory. We want those persons who hear us to feel God is within us when we project these songs.

Her zealous and affirmative pronouncement in a heroic tone suggests that she experiences a kind of psychic syncope while feeling a divine purpose in music. Similarly, during music making, singers and audience in call-and-response often appear not to be fully in conscious control of their behavior; they are out of quotidian time and space, or experiencing "cerebral eclipse" (Becker 2004). These trancers experience positive musical emotions, often accompanied by physiological arousal. The "forestructure of understandings" about musical experience is, however, conditioned by the community (Gergen 1991 cited in Becker 2004, 69) as musical emotion is culturally constructed (Geertz 1983). Transcendent and evangelical experiences can be elicited strategically by the religious community (Becker 2004, 98).

SYMBOLIC EXCHANGES OF GOSPEL COMMUNITIES AND OTHERS

Gospel music functions more than a source of entertainment or a liturgical accompaniment. As a social and cultural agent, it intermediates symbolic exchanges of gospel communities and other communities. In that process, authenticity of blackness was appropriated and re-appropriated reflecting the efforts to adjust to the perceived authenticity of each other. As Johnson argues (2005, 80) "'blackness' may exist as a floating signifier in various cultures, but the consequences of its signification vary" and manifest in various ways, such as music, depending on the cultural environment. The opinions toward the consequences vary: the expropriation of black culture; the co-optation of the cultural products by Others. Such amalgamation is viewed as the problem of cultural hegemony (Semmes 1994). In Figure 2, we illustrate the exchange process among and between gospel and non-gospel communities.

Consuming the Gospel Culture as Others

Consumers from non-gospel communities market, diffuse, assimilate, participate, and spectate the gospel culture. Some consumers approach gospel music with intrinsic motives to experience humanistic-oriented spirituality (Emmons and Paloutzian 2005) which is characterized as a universal human phenomenon, and its manifestation phenomenological. Granpsie (65), a Jewish New Yorker, occasionally goes to church in her neighborhood, to listen to gospel music. Her experience exemplifies such spirituality induced by experiential consumption of gospel music:

At joint Passover and Easter celebration, the rabbi and the pastor talk about the similarity. About two years ago, at the end

FIGURE 2
Symbolic Exchanges of Gospel Culture

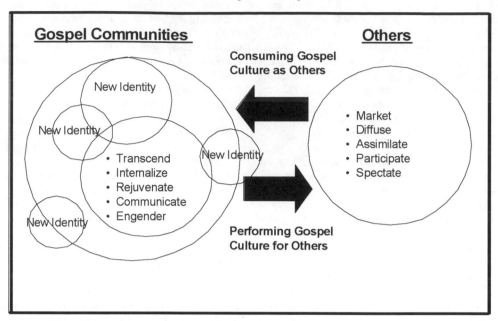

of the service, everybody got up and sang *We Shall Overcome* together holding hands. And, that made me cry because it brought me back to the 60s, the whole Civil Rights Movement, and all the things that had not happened. So, it was a very emotional experience. I started teaching in 1964, and that was the height of the Movement, and I was teaching in the Black communities in Brooklyn... It was a difficult time because those of us were idealistic.

The propinquity of Jews and Christians she heard and experienced in her personal history and the collective history of her cohorts created a collage of memories, which were synthesized by her musical experience. By participating in the liturgical service as Others, the consumer seems to experience the music as an agent to personal reflection and nostalgic feelings.

Performing the Gospel Culture for Others

Gospel music is a creative agent of the Black community. It expresses and disperses their cultural ethos and aspirations (Semmes 1994). On the other hand, music, in general, influences the behavior of society. Summarizing the prior studies, Crozier (1995) contends that multiple factors–affect, arousal, emotion, and mood–induced by music contribute to social influence. Comparing the influence of rock and rap music and that of gospel music on young people, Jim (83) observes: "their behavioral patterns followed the pattern of the music."

On the other hand, Jim (83) is a cathartic agent as the director of a choir and addict rehabilitation center: "I probably would not be so strong in the Lord if it wasn't for gospel; but, it gives me a chance to express, really, to get people's attention." He does not do it as a show, though. Once Jim met a young man from Japan, a sound technician, who blatantly stated, "I don't believe in God." But when the recording project was completed, the young Japanese said, "You know, I'm going to try that Bible you were talking about," and for Jim, it was the ultimate gratification of singing; introducing to

somebody who does not believe in God, so that he may say "Hey look, maybe there's something to it, the God thing."

Performing and consuming music is a form of social identity. It provides the security of identification, assuring its own group identity while distinguishing the self from the others (Larson 1995). Our informants' narratives further suggest that singing gospel music and performing gospel culture for Others function to engender new identities for those in the gospel communities. For example, at one church, singers are dressed in Africanized costumes at the concert. These costumes are not authentic but help the singers enhance their perceived African heritage. Each singer has two flags in their hands to wave at the audience. These flags, seemingly real, are only props to enhance their image of being descendents of Africa.

When performing and consuming the culture of Other, the music, as a creative agent, plays an intermediary role. In the process, music and other cultural products are accommodated to spawn and shape a new identity and new culture. Daniel (49) says, "Gospel will always be contemporary... [and] influenced by things that are happening outside of the church." Leticia (33) who worked with Jay Moss, a prominent gospel singer, for a Black Heritage Celebration in Cleveland, Ohio, by inviting the Latino community, had this experience:

... I've never been in a particularly Latino church. But, they rocked it. You know, when they performed, they rocked it. A lot of people were into it. And it was something different. Now I was amazed. I was just like wow, okay. I need to visit your church too. Maybe I'll learn some Spanish, but, I need to visit your church, too, you know.... I think contemporary music, gospel music has helped that grow... at a very fast pace.

The new identity engendered as a result of the heterogeneity of the audience has necessitated a new music to grow to address the differences. Gospel music with the tint of rap has spawned the new gospel culture (Gooch 1996; Smith Pollard 2008). Referring to the controversial holy hip-hop, Daria (58) tells us, "I think if it reaches the people, it's all good, 'cause you need a variety to reach different people. So it's all good as long as the message is being put out there." As part of the new generation of the gospel culture, Kelly (14) is insightful: "Young kids that don't believe in God do not listen to gospel unless it's hip-hop." She says nobody should be offended, however, "because God is giving them that gift."

CONCLUSIONS

In this paper, we investigated the meanings of gospel music and symbolic exchanges of gospel culture within and across gospel and non-gospel communities. Based on an ethnographic account, we analyzed the narratives of the informants and interpreted their lived experiences with consuming gospel music and culture. Based on the consumption orientation (i.e., whether the consumption is autonomous or syncratic) and based on the nature of experience (i.e., whether the gospel consumption is musical or liturgical), we found that gospel consumption was characterized as indulgent, reflexive, communicative, and transcendent. We discussed how gospel music mediates to define and redefine the meanings of gospel culture within and across gospel communities and Others.

Consumer culture theory is inclusive of "blurred genres," reflecting the nature of social sciences (Geertz 1983). It does not seem, however, to raise a question whether experiential consumption of music gives us a good life or a happy one. The current study shows Black gospel music does not necessarily lead to either end. Poverty and the resultant social problems continue to exist despite the personal and cultural significance and the edifying properties of gospel music. Then why do we continue consuming the musical experience? Kivy (1993, 31) contends, "the best that we can hope from music … is that it help to *humanize*." Neither does the humanizing influence of gospel music alone contribute to improving consumer welfare. "The mind strives to imagine only those things which posit its power of acting" (Spinoza 1677 quoted in Curley 1994, 182). The results of the present study are best hoped to bring about more inquiry in to transformative consumer research.

REFERENCES

Arnould, Eric J. and Melanie Wallendorf (1994), "Market-oriented Ethnography: Interpretation Building and Marketing Strategy Formulation," *Journal of Marketing Research*, 31 (November), 484-504.

Arnould, Eric J. and Craig J. Thompson (2005), "Consumer Culture Theory (CCT): Twenty Years of Research," *Journal of Consumer Research*, 31 (March), 868-82.

Becker, Judith (2004), *Deep Listeners: Music, Emotion, and Trancing*, Bloomington, IN: Indiana University Press.

Blair, M. Elizabeth, and Mark N. Hatala (1992), "The Use of Rap Music in Children's Advertising," in *Advances in Consumer Research*, Vol.19, ed. John F. Sherry, Jr. and Brian Sternthal, Provo, UT : Association for Consumer Research, 719-24.

Burnim, Mellonee V. (1985), "Culture Bearer, Tradition Bearer: An Ethnomusicologist's Research on Gospel Music," *Ethnomusicology*, 29 (3), 432-47.

_____ and Portia K. Maultsby (2006), *African American Music: An Introduction*, New York: Routledge.

Bunt, Leslie (1997), "Clinical and Therapeutic Uses of Music," in *The Social Psychology of Music*, ed. David. J. Hargreaves and Adrian C. North, New York: Oxford University Press, 249-67.

Charmaz, Kathy (2000), "Grounded Theory: Objectivist and Constructivist Methods," in *Handbook of Qualitative Research*, ed. Norman K. Denzin and Yvonna S. Lincoln, Thousand Oaks, CA: Sage Publications, Inc., 509-35.

Crozier, W. Ray (1995), "Music and Social Influence," *The Social Psychology of Music*, ed. David. J. Hargreaves and Adrian C. North, New York: Oxford University Press, 68-83.

Curley, Edwin (1994), *A Spinoza Reader: The Ethics and Other Works*, Princeton: NJ, Princeton University Press.

Czarniawska, Barbara (2004), *Narratives in Social Science Research*, Thousand Oaks, CA: Sage Publications.

Darden, Robert (2004), *People Get Ready! A New History of Black Gospel Music*, New York: The Continuum International Publishing Group, Inc.

Davis, Teresa, and Jeaney Yip (2004), "Reconciling Christianity and Modernity: Australian Youth and Religion," in *Advances in Consumer Research*, Vol. 31, ed. Barbara E. Kahn and Mary Frances Luce, Valdosta, GA: Association for Consumer Research, Pages: 113-17.

Edson Escalas, Jennifer (1994), "African American Vernacular English in Advertising: A Sociolinguistic Study," in *Advances in Consumer Research*, Vol. 21, ed. Chris T. Allen and Deborah Roedder John, Provo, UT: Association for Consumer Research, 304-9.

Emmons, Robert A. and Raymond F. Paloutzian (2003), "The Psychology of Religion," *Annual Review of Psychology*, 54, 377-402.

Geertz, Clifford (1983), *Local Knowledge: Further Essays in Interpretive Anthropology*, New York: Basic Books.

Gooch, Cheryl Renée (1996), "Rappin' for the Lord: The Uses of Gospel Rap and Contemporary Music in Black Religious Communities," in *Religion and Mass Media: Audiences and Adaptations*, ed. Daniel A. Stout and Judith M. Buddenbaum, Thousand Oaks, CA: Sage Publications, 228-42.

Hirschman, Elizabeth C. and Ronald P. Hill (1999), "On Human Commoditization: A Model Based Upon African-American Slavery," in *Advances in Consumer Research*, Vol. 26, ed. Eric J. Arnould and Linda M. Scott, Provo, UT: Association for Consumer Research, 394-98.

Holbrook, Morris B. and Robert M. Schindler (1989), "Some Exploratory Findings on the Development of Musical Tastes," *Journal of Consumer Research*, 16 (June), 119-24.

Holt, Douglas B. (1997), "Poststructuralist Lifestyle Analysis: Conceptualizing the Social Patterning of Consumption in Postmodernity," *Journal of Consumer Research*, 23 (March), 326-50.

Jackson, Joyce Marie (1995), "The Changing Nature of Gospel Music: A Southern Case Study," *African American Review*, 29 (2), 185-201.

Johnson, E. Patrick (2005), "Performing Blackness Down Under: Gospel Music in Australia," in *Black Cultural Traffic: Crossroads in Global Performance and Popular Culture*, ed. Harry J. Elam, Jr. and Kennel Jackson, Ann Arbor: The University of Michigan Press, 59-82.

Kivy, Peter (1993), *The Fine Art of Repetition: Essays in the Philosophy of Music*, New York: Cambridge University Press.

Kozinets, Robert V. (2001), "Utopian Enterprise: Articulating the Meanings of *Star Trek*'s Culture of Consumption," *Journal of Consumer Research*, 28 (June), 67-88.

Magowan, Fiona (2007), "Globalisation and Indigenous Christianity: Translocal Sentiments in Australian Aboriginal Christian Songs," *Identities: Global Studies in Power and Culture*, 14, 459-83.

Nelson, Angela M. S. (2001), "Why We Sing: The Role and Meaning of Gospel in African American Popular Culture," in *The Triumph of the Soul: Cultural and Psychological Aspects of African American Music*, ed. Ferdinand Jones and Arthur C. Jones, Westport, CT: Praeger Publishers, 97-126.

O'Guinn, Thomas C. and Russell W. Belk (1989), "Heaven on Earth: Consumption at Heritage Village, USA," *Journal of Consumer Research*, 16 (September), 227-38.

Schroeder, Jonathan E., Janet L. Borgerson (1999), "Packaging Paradise: Consuming Hawaiian Music," in *Advances in Consumer Research*, Vol. 26, ed. Eric J. Arnould and Linda M. Scott, Provo, UT: Association for Consumer Research, 46-50.

Semmes, Clovis E. (1974), "The Dialectics of Cultural Survival and the Community Artist: Phil Cohran and the Affro-Arts Theater," *Journal of Black Studies*, 24 (4), 447-61.

Smith Pollard, Deborah (2008), *When the Church Becomes Your Party: Contemporary Gospel Music*, Detroit, MI: Wayne State University Press.

Stamps, Miriam B., and Eric J. Arnould (1998), "The Florida Classic: Performing African-American Community," in *Advances in Consumer Research* Vol. 25, ed. Joseph W. Alba and J. Wesley Hutchinson, Provo, UT: Association for Consumer Research, 578-84.

Storr, Anthony (1992), *Music and the Mind*, New York: Ballantine Books.

Thompson, Craig J. and Douglas B. Holt (1996), "Communities and Consumption: Research on Consumer Strategies for Constructing Communal Relationships in a Postmodern World," in *Advances in Consumer Research*, Vol. 23, ed. Kim P. Corfman and John G. Lynch Jr., Provo, UT: Association for Consumer Research, 204-5.

Üstüner, Tuba and Douglas B. Holt (2007), "Dominated Consumer Acculturation: The Social Construction of Poor Migrant Women's Consumer Identity Projects in a Turkish Squatter," *Journal of Consumer Research*, 34 (June), 41-56.

Changes in Self and Interpersonal Relationships Over Time: A Study of Important Gifts from Gift-Recipients' Perspectives

Phoebe Wong, Lancaster University, UK
Margaret K. Hogg, Lancaster University, UK

ABSTRACT

This paper examines the impact of gift-recipients' self and identity changes on the meanings of the important gifts that they received a long time ago; and the strategies they employ when dealing with these changes in the context of their "existing on-going" and "disconnected" relationships. This paper addresses the research gap in our understanding of how changes in interpersonal relationships with the gift-givers are incorporated into the changing meanings associated with the gifts over time. Our findings expand upon the existing gift-giving research by examining how old gifts signify different aspects of changes to the self in life transitions within consumers' identity projects.

INTRODUCTION

This paper examines the impact of changes in gift-recipients' self and identity on the meanings associated with their important gifts that were often received a long time ago; and the strategies they employ when dealing with these changes in the context of their "existing on-going" and "disconnected" relationships. We aim to address the research gap in our understanding of the impact which changes in self and interpersonal relationships with the gift-givers has on the meanings associated with the original gifts over time.

How people interpret, and often give new meanings to, their gifts as their possessions gain in importance over time has not been explored in earlier consumer research. Most gift-giving research focuses on the actual gift-giving process from the perspectives of the givers, recipients, or even of a third person in the decision making process of buying a gift. Earlier research has concentrated on the process of searching for a gift, purchasing a gift, choosing the right place or the right time to give a gift, the reaction of recipients when receiving a gift; and how a third person often influences the decision of a giver in purchasing a gift (Joy, 2001, Curasi, 1999, Belk and Coon, 1993, Otnes, Lowrey and Kim, 1993, Sherry, McGrath and Levy, 1992, Lowrey, Otnes and Ruth, 2004, Sherry 1983).

However, Josselson, Lieblich and McAdam (2007) commented that "relationships are central, from the very beginning of and throughout life, to the constitution and expression of the self" (p. 3). Through their narratives about the important gifts that they have received, informants reveal how their selves are maintained, modified or changed in two contrasting relationships, i.e. the "existing on-going" and "disconnected" relationships, with the gift-givers. Four informants' narratives about their important gifts are used to explore how the sense of self, and the associated interpretation and meanings of important gifts, change and co-evolve over time.

Earlier research used six relational meanings of gifts to examine the creation and maintenance of relationships from the perspective of gift-recipients (Ruth, Otnes and Brunel 1999). However, how gift-recipients' identities, and the meanings of their important gifts, change over time has not been explored. Building upon Ruth et al's (1999) study of "how relational meanings are created through gifts" (p. 385), this paper focuses firstly, on the interpersonal relationships between gift-givers and gift-recipients; and secondly on the gifts that recipients received a long time ago and whose meanings have evolved over time. The emotionally and symbolically-laden meanings of gifts may change over the life course (Belk,

1988, Solomon, 1983) so that gift recipients reinterpret the meanings of these gifts. These gifts often become special possessions for recipients, bearing witness to their different relationship life stages such as dating, getting married, divorced, or losing their loved ones. Each relationship transition offers an opportunity for recipients to redefine and renegotiate their identities (McAlexander, 1991). Throughout these trajectories of different transitions, some recipients maintained and strengthened their relationships with the gift-givers, whereas some recipients struggled or even ended their relationships with the gift-givers due to relationship breakdowns, personal disputes or death. These relationship changes lead to self-modification and self-change.

In this exploratory study of self-change and self-continuity, we collected and analysed consumers' narratives so that we could access discourses around the self in different settings. Selves and identities are embedded in discourse in the format and construction of stories (Georgakopoulou, 2002). We begin by reviewing the literature on gift-giving, possessions and the use of narratives; before outlining the research design and the method of narrative analysis; then we present the stories from four informants about how they modified their self and identity, and re-interpreted their relationships with their important gifts. We conclude by discussing the different strategies informants employ when dealing with these changes.

GIFT-GIVING

Gift-giving has been studied for decades in anthropology (i.e. the economic reciprocity exchange), sociology (i.e. the social exchange) and psychology (i.e. the motivation of reciprocity exchange) (Mauss 1954, Homans 1961, Schwartz 1967). In marketing, Sherry (1983) proposed a three-stage framework of the gift-giving process involving the gestation stage (i.e. searching for, choosing and buying a gift), then the presentation stage (i.e. the time and place of the actual exchange) to the final stage of reformulation (i.e. realignment and reformulation of the relationships between the gift-giver and gift-recipient). Building upon the economic and social reciprocity exchange of gift-giving, Belk and Coon (1993) identified gift-giving among dating couples as agapic love gift-giving and suggested that the reciprocal exchange is not a requisite feature of gift-giving between lovers. Similar findings were found in studies of romantic couples in Minowa and Gould (1999) and Joy (2001).

Most gift-giving research focuses on the actual gift-giving process and activities (1) from the perspectives of the gift-givers (Joy, 2001, Minowa and Gould, 1999, Curasi, 1999, Belk and Coon, 1993, Otnes et al., 1993) in terms of the decision making process involved in buying a gift (i.e. searching for a gift, purchasing a gift, choosing the right place or a right time to give the gift); (2) from the perspectives of the gift-recipients (Minowa and Gould, 1999, Ruth et al., 1999, Fischer and Arnold, 1990, McGrath, 1989) (i.e. the reaction of recipients when receiving a gift and how they evaluate their relationships after the gift-receiving experiences); (3) the disposition of the gift (Sherry et al., 1992); or (4) how a third person influences people's Christmas gift purchasing (Lowrey et al., 2004). Furthermore, gifts carry many emotional and symbolic meanings including love (Belk and Coon 1993, Fischer and Arnould 1990) and sadness (Mick and Demoss, 1990).

273

Consistent with the nature of possessions, meanings of gifts will change and evolve according to the recipients' life experiences and social contexts. Andersen (1993) suggested that a relationship trajectory exists between the giver and recipient and consists of the interpretation of the relationship in the past, the current state of the relationship, and the possible relationship in the future. For our study, we are interested in how the relationship trajectory is reflected in and embodied by the different meanings which are invested in the gifts that have become important possessions, over time.

POSSESSIONS AND THE SELF

Belk (1988) argued that people extend the concept of self through their possessions, i.e. products, places, other people and pets. "Our possessions are a major contributor to and reflection of our identities" (p. 139). There are five stages of role-identity development throughout the identity project life cycle, i.e. pre-socialization, discovery, construction, maintenance and disposition (Kleine and Kleine, 2000). People reveal different aspects of their self and identity by retelling stories of possessions. Although aspects of the self are viewed and emphasized in various ways in different cultures, "the fact that these conceptions of self are expressed to some degree through objects seems to be universal" (Wallendorf and Arnould, 1988: 532). Furthermore, Csikszentmihalyi and Rochberg-Halton (1981) commented that "things tell us who we are, not in words but by embodying our intentions. In our everyday traffic of existence, we can also learn about ourselves from objects, almost as much as from people" (p. 91).

In terms of temporality and possessions, items that people acquired in the past carry meanings in the present time and may anticipate meanings in the future (Kleine and Baker, 2004). The temporal features of attachments are consistent with narratives. In narratives, people retell and reorganise their past events and provide evaluations and add new meanings to them in the present time and sometimes also predict possible futures. Therefore, people's selves are revealed through stories about their attachments. As Kleine et al. stated (1995: 327), "a special possession could facilitate self-continuity by connecting a person with a desirable past self (e.g. memories), a present self (me now), or a future self (who I am becoming)".

NARRATIVES

"People live storied lives" (Creswell, 2005: 87). People are natural storytellers who share their stories with friends or colleagues, on a daily basis. "Relationships require narrative to evoke the empathy and multilayered attention necessary for one person to have some sense of the nature of someone else's relational experience" (Josselson et al., 2007: 4). One of the advantages of narratives is that "they organise life, i.e. social relations, interpretations of the past, present and future" (Daiute and Lightfoot, 2004: xi). From their past experience, narrators learn and make who they are at present and who they might want to be in the future. It is clear that narratives provide a sense of self as continuous through time. Furthermore, possessions and narratives are closely linked together. Possessions have a function in helping people to narrate their stories as Kleine et al. (1995) emphasize "possessions to which there is attachment help narrate a person's life story; they reflect "my life" (p. 327).

RESEARCH METHOD: NARRATIVE RESEARCH DESIGN

In the present study, informants were asked to share stories about their gifts as possessions that were special, meaningful and important to them. Their selves and identities are embedded in their stories as Georgakopoulou (2002) says that "if selves and identities are constituted in discourse, they are necessarily constructed in stories" (p. 428). The snowball technique[1] was used to identify twenty informants (ten males, ten females).

The informants were young professionals aged between 29 and 37; either single or married. Semi-structured narrative interviews were conducted in Hong Kong and lasted on average one hour. Some guided questions were used in order to stimulate a discussion. However, interviews were not strictly constructed and this was in line with Wagner and Wodak's (2006) method of narrative interview. Rather, the flow of topics varied depending on their stories. All the interviews were digitally recorded and transcribed.

The transcripts were read a number of times in order to achieve familiarity with the material. Then, a three-dimensional narrative structural analysis (Clandinin and Connelly, 2000) was applied in order to examine how narrators told their stories under the dimension of interaction (i.e. their belief and values on the personal level and interactions with other people on the social level), the dimension of temporality (i.e. how the past event or experience leads to the present self and will possibly influence informants' future decisions), and the dimension of situations (i.e. time and context). Finally, the story fragments from each narrator were linked up in order to compose a coherent "story line" for each person (Fournier and Mick, 1999, Tagg, 1985).

In this study of gift-recipients' interpretation of the meanings of their important gifts, informants narrated stories about the gifts that had become important possessions. They described gifts that they had owned between 5 and 25 years. We analysed and examined how these narrators told their stories about different aspects of their selves in terms of their relationships with their gift-givers. We chose four informants' narratives for this paper which illustrate the central emergent themes of the "existing on-going" and "disconnected" relationships.

FINDINGS

Data analysis yielded a number of themes that revealed gift-recipients' interpretation of their selves and interpersonal relationships with the gift-givers, and changes in the meanings of their important gifts. Themes will be examined under two dimensions, i.e. "the disconnected relationships" and "the on-going relationships" between the gift-givers and the gift-recipients. Strategies of how informants maintain, modify or negotiate their self and the relationships with their gift-givers will be covered in the discussion section.

DIMENSION: DISCONNECTED RELATIONSHIPS

Ada: Her disconnected relationships with her ex-husband and her deceased father

Ada told five stories about gifts which represented important possessions for her. Four stories related to her ex-husband and one story was about her father who had died 6 years before. Ada is a 39-year old fashion boutique owner who has always wanted to improve her quality of life by challenging herself at different stages of her life. She first narrated her love story in a temporal sequence starting from how Ada and John, her ex-husband, had met in high school and how she had received her first gift from him when dating.

---

[1]The purpose of the snowballing technique is to identify and accumulate informants as each located informant recommends other people to researchers (Babbie 1996, Creswell 1998).

Ada: "We were dating at that time… It (the watch) was so popular at that time to have vintage style watches. He noticed that I like one of the watches there. He secretly bought it and gave it to me at Christmas. He was very fond of me at that time."

After they completed their GCSEs (a high school public exam), John, her ex-husband, was sent to study at university in the US. That was the first time they were apart. Before he left Hong Kong, he bought a Titus watch from their special love series and had it engraved with the words "Everlasting Love" on the back of the watch for Ada as a reassurance of his love for her. Ada narrated how they were apart and how happy and sweet she felt when she received it. However, all of the sudden, she came back to the reality from her narrative and realized that the relationship was over. *"Forget it. It's over. It was the past!"*

Ada: "The second watch is from him. When he studied aboard, he bought me a Titus. It was the first time we were separated. I didn't wanna let him go. Therefore, he bought me that watch. It was that special love series with the slogan of "It doesn't matter whether we cannot be together forever, the important thing is we have each other at this moment…(pause) Forget it. It's over. It was the past!"

Ignoring her family's objections, Ada went to the U.S. in order to be with John. They had a happy time together in the US. Both of them were students and enjoyed their lives without their parents. John always wanted to surprise Ada by buying or getting something special for her. He secretly asked his friend to buy a "Big Mouth Boy" Japanese cartoon watch, i.e. Ada's favourite cartoon character, for her. The watch was not available in Hong Kong. Therefore, John asked his friend to buy it from Japan.

Ada: ""Little Big Mouth" watch. We were in the US at that moment. He knew that I loved that cartoon character. He asked somebody who was on the way to Hong Kong… bought it… via Japan… came back to the US."

They got married in Canada and then John returned to Hong Kong where he worked as an architect. Ada stayed in San Francisco and tried to complete her studies. Separation was not easy. Ada decided to quit her studies and went back to Hong Kong. Once again, John wanted to show his affection by using his first salary to buy her an expensive watch, i.e. Rolex.

Ada: "We were separated for four months (after the wedding). He saved it for four months. When we met again at the airport, he gave it to me. It was a surprise again. This is my first luxury watch and still the only luxury watch. I think the current price of that model is about HKD 30,000 something."

Sadly the marriage ended after 8 years. It was John who made the decision to end the relationship. Ada was in shock and could not believe that John was going to leave her. Looking back, Ada realized that she had not shown enough appreciation and had taken John for granted. She had not cherished the times that she had had with him. When looking at all the gifts she received from him, she is more touched than before.

Ada: "Currently, I am more touched. I didn't cherish them at that time. When I looked back, I realized nobody would treat me that nice. Not any more… Forget it. Don't talk about it. (Note: She started to cry)"

Ada is still struggling to redefine her sense of self and identity after her divorce. She could not correct the mistakes she had made in the past and that had destroyed her marriage. However, she wanted to move on from this disconnected relationship. During her narration Ada, from time to time, re-emphasized how the interviewer and herself should address John as "her EX-HUSBAND". She consciously kept trying to remind herself of her current status of being "divorced".

The other important possession that she described was a gift from her father who had died 6 years before. She received a watch from her father when she was 15 years old. It was a ritual in her family that all the children received a watch from their father when they reached 15 years old. When Ada received the watch, she felt like she had reached the stage of adulthood. While narrating the story about the watch that she received from her father, she came to a realization that she shared some similarity with her father, being an authoritative figure in her own marriage. She believed that was the reason why her marriage had broken down.

Ada: "I got this watch from my dad when I was 15 years old. The brand was popular at that time… even advertising on TV. It was the first watch I wore at school. Dad gave us a watch when we reached 15. It's like when you are an adult, you got a watch coz at that time watches were quite precious. …We had some good times and bad times. He was very authoritative and my mum is always gentle and listens to him. I guess I picked my dad's role and became "my dad" in my own marriage. I destroyed my own marriage. Anyway, the feeling not having my dad around is now different. I could console myself that it's gone. But when it comes to details, say see some elderly… that reminds me of my dad. Then I realized I still miss him."

Ada received those gifts more than 20 years ago. The original feelings of receiving those gifts were sweet, touching, full of surprises and feeling like a grown-up. As time went by, Ada faced different life transitions, from dating, getting married, experiencing a divorce and the death of her father. The attachments represented by those gifts intensified and increased as Ada offered new interpretations and meanings for her important gifts.

Ping: his disconnected relationship with his mother, the lost loved one

Ping's mother was his role model. Mrs Wong was hard working and full of love and care. In Ping's eyes, his mother was "invincible". Mrs Wong could cook delicious Chinese food, knit and mend old clothes in order to save money as well as taking care of the church where she worked as a janitor at the same time. Although his mother had died 9 years ago, he still missed her a lot. He wanted to hold on to the gifts that she had given to him so that he could feel her presence. As time has gone by, he has gradually tried to let go of some of the gifts as a sign of learning how to live without his mother's presence.

Ping's mother was good at knitting. She had knitted a lot of sweaters for him when he was young. He did not cherish them at that time. Once his mother passed away, he realized how important it was to keep these sweaters in order to feel her presence. He only has one sweater left now, and it is so precious that he does not dare to wear it as he said *"you will never have a second one"*.

Ping: "A sweater that my mother knitted for me. I have only one left. I cherish it so much that I do not dare to wear it. I used to have quite many sweaters knitted by her. I didn't cherish

them at that time. I have one left and I don't want to wear it…
I might take it out and have a look… coz no more… you will
never have a second one. I quite cherish it."

His family was not that well-off. His mother always tried to
mend clothes and blankets instead of buying new ones for him in
order to save money. Ping viewed these as part of the gifts that he
had received from his mother. It is a good image of her virtue that
he always remembered. In his opinion, Mrs Wong sacrificed herself
for the family, especially for her children. He used to have a blanket
that Mrs Wong had mended, darning the edges in order to repair it.
Ping kept it for several years. As time went by, he started to find the
courage to look at some of the gifts that reminded him of his mother.
It has been 9 years and he is still learning how to let go of some of
the emotion by disposing of some of his precious items.

*Ping: "I think I can let go. For example, I just threw a worn out
blanket away today. The reason I kept it for a while is that my
mum mended the edges of the blanket. I didn't want to throw
it away. But I realized I have to let go something.*

DIMENSION: EXISTING ON-GOING
RELATIONSHIPS

Stephanie: Her on-going relationships with her sister and husband

Stephanie narrated 6 stories about her important possessions,
half of which she had received as gifts from her sister and her
husband. Stephanie is very close to her sister, Jenny. The age gap
between them is so small that they played, cried and fought for toys
or clothes when they were young. Jenny sometimes can be quite
competitive. For example, Stephanie wanted to be a flight attendant. Immediately, Jenny applied for the same position in a different
airline company. Stephanie received a watch from her sister as a
birthday gift almost 10 years ago. It was the first time that Jenny had
left Hong Kong and lived in another place for a long time. When she
was not around, Stephanie missed her greatly. Jenny sent a funny
watch to Stephanie as her birthday present during the time she was
in the US. Stephanie appreciated the watch because of her relationship with her sister. She has worn the watch for almost ten years.

*"Another one (watch)…my sister sent it to me from the US. She
and I are very close… sometimes quite competitive… like I
decided to become a flight attendant and she immediately did
the same. Anyway, I missed her when she was not around. My
sister was there with her husband for more than a year. She
sent the watch to me as my birthday present. I like it VERY
much and have been wearing it for many years… almost ten
years."*

Stephanie and Alex got engaged in 2001. Alex proposed in a
traditional way with a bunch of flowers, a diamond ring and a
surprise dinner. Stephanie personally does not particularly like
diamond rings. She had bought one for herself in the past. But she
emphasized that the ring from Alex is different from any other ring.
It is her engagement ring with a heart-shape diamond on it. It is a
sign of Alex's promise and love for her. Although the diamond is
not that big, it has a significant meaning for her that makes her
happy. She cherishes it so much that she does not wear it every day.
She only wears it when attending *"somebody's wedding"* to signify
her marital status.

*"I am not a big fan of diamond rings. The size of the diamond
is not important to me coz I don't like it too big. The big*

diamonds don't suit my image. The way I dress…don't match.
I like the one I got from Alex… small and a heart shape…
because it is meaningful and I like the heart shape diamond. I
bought a diamond ring for myself before. But when I go out, I
wear Alex's diamond ring not mine. I like that one. But I don't
wear it every day. Only when I attend to somebody's weddings.
…I like it (the ring). It makes me happy. It is meaningful and
beautiful."*

Stephanie also received a diamond pendant cross from Alex on
her baptism before they were married. It has a symbolic meaning
because now she is a Christian with a cross around her neck. In
addition to the symbolic meaning of the necklace, there were
additional lived experiences associated with the pendant because
she accidentally dropped the pendant down the sink. The experience taught her that it is always better to solve problems together
rather than alone and she appreciated Alex's support and help. The
pendant cross carries not only the original meaning of celebrating
her baptism, but also an additional experientially-derived meaning
that they will always share.

*"Alex gave it to me on my baptism… the day to celebrate that
I became Christian. I dropped in the sink and took me the
whole night to fetch it… Now when I think about it, it is still
quite sad coz it took me the whole night and I felt really down.
…I did not want to wake up Alex. I thought he could not help
me. I thought men are careless. How wrong and silly I was?!
At the end, we had to solve the problem together and got the
pendant out of the tube of drain of the sink. Alex did it with
some "Blue tap"… I wouldn't get it out by myself. It was him
who did it for me. That was an experience that we learned…
to try to solve problems together"*

Peter: His existing on-going relationships with his father and wife

Peter was born into a complex family. His father had two
wives, or rather an official wife and an unofficial wife (a mistress),
more typical of pre-war China. His father owned factories in Hong
Kong and China which exported electronic parts to the US. His
family was very well-off. Peter is the mistress' son, meaning that he
was not recognised by the family. Although Peter has a complicated
background, he had a happy childhood with his mother and sister.
His father came to visit them as often as he could in order to provide
a fatherly figure to him. Peter and his sister went to live with his
father's family, consisting of a elder half brother and half sister,
when he was about 12 years old.

Peter has a close relationship with his father although his father
did not live with him when he was child. He respects his father as
an entrepreneur setting up factories on his own. Peter believes his
father had a reason to do what he did in the past and does not feel
any resentment towards him. Peter received a watch from his father
as a sign of reaching adulthood. The watch is important and
memorable for Peter because his father gave it to him.

*Peter: "Another one I got is from my dad… can't remember
the brand… it got a vintage feel of it. My dad likes watches as
well… He just gave it to me to wear. He thought I had grown
up as an adult and it was time to give me one. Therefore, he
passed the watch to me. For me, this is a memorable item. My
dad gave it to me.*

His father used to own a lot of cars when the businesses were
doing very well. However all the companies were closed down,
following a financial crisis. Peter's father sold almost everything he

owned in order to pay off his debt. The only thing his father kept for himself, and later passed it on to Peter, was the licence plate BD 2822. His father bought this licence plate when he started his business. The number "2822" has a meaning in Chinese that "2" sounds like the word "easy" in Chinese and "8" sounds like "rich" in Chinese. The licence plate has two symbolic meanings for Peter. First of all, it is a precious item marking his father's success in the past. His father passed this precious item onto him. Peter wants to continue the spirit of the family legacy to the next generation. The second symbolic meaning of the licence plate is a special link between Peter and his father. Peter admires his father who is a very traditional Chinese father who does not show much of his emotion through words but through objects that he passed on to his son. His father did not give the licence plate to any of his other children, not even to Peter's older half-brother who is traditionally the heir in the family. The recognition and love from his father meant a great deal to Peter.

Peter: An item… hmm… a licence no. of BD 2822. Dad passed it on to me. He used to have this licence no. to his car. The number is very special. For me, first the Chinese pronunciation of 2822. Also, he gave it to me. If I could pass it on to the next generation, that would be great. This gives me… a family… it doesn't worth any money… but it is like a family legacy you pass it on to the next generation. It is not the jewel of the family. But it has a special link between me and my dad… keeping it. I hope I could pass it on to the next generation some day.

Bonnic, his then-girlfriend and now wife, bought a lover watch set of Agnes B for Peter during the time they were dating because she wanted to have some proper watches for both of them to wear when attending formal occasions, e.g. Chinese banquets. Peter likes the watch because it is different from the watch he wears at work as a PE teacher. As he said, "*it is a proper watch*". Also, it is a lover set of watches that they can use to show their commitment to each other as a couple by wearing them together.

Peter: "Bonnie bought me a watch, Agnes B lover watches. No…no… no… it was a lover set. It was the first love set watches we had but were stolen last year. We always have sporty watches because of our work (PE teachers)… like that kind of digital… Casio… Bonnie wanted to buy watches that we can wear them together in different formal occasions like Chinese banquets. I like it… she had the same watch and I had the same… quite nice… as a couple."

From dating to getting married, Bonnie and Peter have built up their dreams together through different transitions. Their love has grown strong so that the this gift has acquired additional meanings. Peter had a calling/ vision that he wanted to study theology and to dedicate himself to his church. After serious discussions with Bonnie and attending different retreat camps, he made up his mind to give up his job as a PE teacher and to enrol himself in the Christian ministry and study theology for three years. Although the financial burden fell on Bonnie's shoulders, she did not complain about helping Peter fulfil his dream. In fact, she was very proud of her husband's decision. As Peter said, "*I really have to thank Bonnie for her unconditional support and patience. The family… that is the most important thing.*"

DISCUSSION

Our findings expand upon the existing gift-giving research to illustrate how old and established gifts can signify the evolution of

interpersonal relationships over time, and these meanings co-evolve with self-change and self-continuity. Different strategies are adopted in order to manage the changes within the "disconnected" and "existing on-going" relationships.

In the disconnected relationships our story-tellers often found themselves facing a dialectic tension in their narratives. They were often caught between the stages of identity disposition, identity discovery and identity construction within role identity development (Kleine and Kleine, 2000). The negotiation process of letting go of some things whilst keeping hold of other things amongst their meaningful possessions often helped them cope with loss and to adjust to change in this liminal phase of life transitions. "Possessions bring past meanings into the present and maintain present meanings. Possessions also help them project themselves in to the future, even beyond death" (Kleine and Baker, 2004: p. 9). Due to the fact that they will not or cannot have any further contact with the gift givers, they are in the process of self-reconstruction, moving from disposing of their past identity (e.g. Ada as a married person) to acquiring a new identity (e.g. Ada becoming a divorcee), giving new emotional and symbolic meanings to their gifts that they had received from their gift-givers. In Ada's case, she did not want a divorce. In general, people who did not take the initiative in the divorce proceedings tend to hold on to possessions or gifts that are related to their partners as if they are still holding on to the relationships (McAlexander, 1991). The strategy of holding on to her gifts implies that she is still in the liminal phase; that she is in "a limbo between the past state (i.e. a married woman) to the current one (i.e. a divorcee)" (Schouten, 1991: 421). Ada is in the process of identity reconstruction, and her narrative captures the dialectic tension experienced as a divorcee within her identity role project. "Attachment itself, and the meanings of attachment possessions, tend to be dynamic in order to manage the relentless conflict between desiring self-continuity and needing self-change" (Kleine and Baker, 2004: p. 5).

In the disconnected relationships with the gift-giver caused by death, Ada and Ping used a strategy of "re-membering"[2] their lost loved ones on a different level (Myerhoff, 1982). "The parent may be dead, but the relationship did not die" (Silverman and Nickman, 1993: 315). Over time, people accept the reality of the loss and learn how to find a way to include the lost loved ones in their life (Nasim, 2007). Ada had both good and bad times with her father in the past. But she focused on the good times, e.g. a gift that she received from him as a sign of reaching adulthood embodied the best image of their relationship and meant that "*I could console myself that it's gone.*" Similar to Ada, Ping tried to find a strategy to balance the dialectic tension in his narrative between "holding on" and "letting go". The sacredness that Ping invests in his sweater reflects the importance of his mother's status in his heart (Belk et al., 1989). His disposition of the blanket is a step that he takes in order to try and redefine his relationship with his mother. Both Ada and Ping have kept their relationships with their deceased parent alive at another level in order to help their own self-change within their life transitions (Nasim, 2007).

The strategy for Stephanie and Peter in their "existing on-going" relationships with the gift-givers was to maintain and cultivate a promising future together. In the case of existing on-going relationships with the gift-givers, the symbolic and emotional meanings and values of the possessions were enhanced through interactions (i.e. wearing or using the important gifts on different occasions) (Richins, 1994). In contrast to the role-identity develop-

---

[2]Myerhoff (1982) suggested the term re-membering to describe how people redefine their relationships with the deceased and include them in their lives.

ment in the "disconnected" relationships, informants in the "existing on-going" relationships sought identity maintenance in their role-identity development (Kleine et al 2005). Stephanie and Peter focus not only on the past and the present but also look forward to strengthening and cultivating a promising future together.

Peter was a mistress' son and was not recognised in the family when he was a child. Having moved in to live with his father's family when he was a teenager, he was eager to be accepted as part of the family. Receiving a watch from his father when he reached adulthood, and a family licence plate as a sign of carrying on the "family legacy", signified his recognition by his father and the family. These gifts represented the family's inalienable wealth and carried significant symbolic meanings for Peter (Curasi et al., 2004). Stephanie, in her turn, had been wearing the watch that her sister had given her, for more than 10 years. The watch "evokes richly textured webs of her personal memories" and her relationship with her sister (Belk 1991).

In an interpersonal romantic relationship, a person's self tends to overlap with his/ her partners (Aron et al., 1992). Peter received a watch from Bonnie when they were dating. The watches are symbols of their love. They wear them in public as a signal to other people that they are united, illustrating continuity, affiliation and love. Similar to Peter, Stephanie wore her engagement ring to indicate that she had been engaged in the past and was now married, and working on building a solid foundation for her relationship with her husband (Kleine and Baker, 2004). In terms of her story about her pendant diamond cross, the pendant carries not only the original meaning of celebrating her baptism, but also an additional layer of new meaning that was created by the shared memories of Stephanie and Alex of losing and then regaining the cross.

Collecting and analyzing consumer narratives allowed a deeper understanding in terms of how informants view themselves and their relationships with their loved ones through their important gifts, i.e. the possession value of objects. This captures temporal notions of the self-change/ continuity as possessions provide "symbolic benefits delivering self-change/ continuity value" (Kleine and Baker, 2004: 25). These informants shared their inner most feelings about their possessions and revealed who they were, how they became who they are, and sometimes also who they want to be in the future, which meant that different views of the self started to emerge around the axes of continuity and change, and different views of the strategies used to manage ongoing relationships with gift-givers also emerged, whether the giftgivers were living or dead.

REFERENCES

Andersen, P. A. (1993) "Cognitive Schemata in Personal Relationships," in Duck, S. and N. Park (Eds.) *Individuals in Relationships*. CA, Sage.

Aron, A., E. N. Aron, and D. Smollan (1992) "Inclusion of Other in the Self Scale and the Structure of Interpersonal Closeness," *Journal of Personality and Social Psychology*, 63, 596-612.

Belk, R. W. (1988) "Possessions and the Extended Self," *Journal of Consumer Research*, 15, 139-168.

Belk, R. W. and G.S. Coon (1993) "Gift Giving as Agapic Love: An Alternative to the Exchange Paradigm Based on Dating Experiences," *Journal of Consumer Research*, 20, 393-417.

Belk, R. W., M. Wallendorf and J. F. J. Sherry (1989) "The Sacred and the Profane in Consumer Behavior: Theodicy on the Odyssey," *Journal of Consumer Research*, 16, 1-38.

Clandinin, D. J. and R. M. Connelly (2000) *Narrative Inquiry: Experience and Story in Qualitative Research*, San Francisco, Jossey-Bass.

Creswell, J. W. (2005) *Educational Reseach: Planning, Conducting and Evaluating Quantitative and Qualitative Research*, New Jersey, Person.

Csikszentmihalyi, M. and E. Rochberg-Halton (1981) *The Meaning of Things: Domestic Symbols and the Self*, Cambridge, Cambridge University Press.

Curasi, C. F. (1999) "In Hope of an Enduring Gift: the Intergenerational Transfer of Cherished Possessions; a Special Case of Gift Giving," in *Advances in Consumer Research*, 26, eds. Eric J. Arnould and Linda M. Scott, Provo: UT: Association for Consumer Research, 125-132.

Curasi, C. F., L. L. Price and E. J. Arnould (2004) "How Individuals' Cherished Possessions Become Families' Inalienable Wealth," *Journal of Consumer Research*, 31, 609-622.

Daiute, C. and C. Lightfoot (Eds.) (2004) *Narrative Analysis: Studying the Development of Individuals in Society*, London, Sage.

Fischer, E. and S. J. Arnold (1990) "More than a Labor of Love: Gender Roles and Christmas Gift Shopping," *Journal of Consumer Research*, 17, 239-267.

Fournier, S. and D. G. Mick (1999) "Rediscovering Satisfaction," *Journal of Marketing*, 63, 5-23.

Georgakopoulou, A. (2002) "Narrative and Identity management: Discourse and Social identities in a Tale of Tomorrow," *Research on Language and Social Interaction*, 35, 427-451.

Homans, G. C. (1961) *Social Behavior: Its Elementary Forms*, New York, Harcourt, Brace and World.

Josselson, R., A. Lieblich A. and D. P. McAdam (2007) "Introduction," in Josselson, R., A. Lieblich and D. P. McAdam (Eds.) *The Meaning of Others: Narrative Studies of Relationships*, Washington D.C., American Psychological Association.

Joy, A. (2001) "Gift Giving in Hong Kong and the Continuum of Social Ties," *Journal of Consumer Research*, 28, 239-256.

Kleine III, R. E. and S. S. Kleine (2000) "Consumption and Self-Schema Changes Throughout the Identity Project Life Cycle," in *Advances in Consumer Research*, Volume 27, eds. Stephen J. Hoch and Robert J. Meyer, Provo, UT: Association for Consumer Research, 279-285.

Kleine, S. S. and S. M. Baker (2004) "An Integrative Review of Material Possession Attachment," *Academy of Marketing Science Review*.

Kleine, S. S., R. E. Kleine III and C. T. Allen (1995) "How is a Possession "Me" or "Not Me"? Characterizing Types and an Antecedent of Material Possession Attachment," *Journal of Consumer Research*, 22, 327-343.

Lowrey, T. M., C. C. Otnes and J. A. Ruth (2004) "Social Influences on Dyadia Giving Over Time: A Taxonomy from teh Giver's Perspective," *Journal of Consumer Research*, 30, 547-558.

Mauss (1954) *The Gift*, London, Cohen and West.

McAlexander, J. H. (1991) "Divorce, the Disposition of the Relationship, and Everything," in *Advances in Consumer Research*, Volume 18, eds. Rebecca H. Holman and Michael R. Solomon, Provo, UT: Association for Consumer Research, 43-48.

McGrath, M. A. (1989) "An Ethnography of a Gift Store: Wrappings, Trappings, and Rapture," *Journal of Retailing*, 65, 421-441.

Mick, D. G. and M. DeMoss (1990) "Self Gifts: Phenomenological Insights from Four Contexts," *Journal of Consumer Research*, 17, 322-332.

Minowa, Y. and S. J. Gould (1999) "Love My Gift, Love Me or Is It Love Me, Love My Gift: a Study of the Cultural Construction of Romantic Gift Giving among Japanese Couples," in *Advances in Consumer Research,* Volume 26, eds. Eric J. Arnould and Linda M. Scott, Provo, UT: Association for Consumer Research, 119-124.

Myerhoff, B. (1982) "Life History among the Elderly: Performance, Visibility and Re-membering," in Ruby, J. (Ed.) *A Crack in the Mirror: Reflexive Perspectives in Anthropology.* Philadelphia, University of Pennsylvania Press.

Nasim, R. (2007) "Ongoing Relationships: Recounting a Lost Parent's Life as a Means to Re-member," in Josselson, R., A. Lieblich and D. P. McAdam, D. P. (Eds.) *The Meaning of Others: Narrative Studies of Relationships.* Washington D.C., American Psychological Association.

Otnes, C. C., T. M. Lowrey and Y.C. Kim (1993) "Gift Selection for Easy and Difficult Recipients: a Social Roles Interpretation," *Journal of Consumer Research,* 20, 229-244.

Richins, M. L. (1994) "Valuing Things: The Public and Private Meanings of Possessions," *Journal of Consumer Research,* 21, 504-521.

Ruth, J. A., C. C. Otnes and F. F. Brunel (1999) "Gift Receipt and the Reformulation of interpersonal Relationships," *Journal of Consumer Research,* 25, 385-402.

Schouten, J. W. (1991) "Selves in Transition: Symbolic Consumption in Personal Rites of Passage and Identity Reconstruction," *Journal of Consumer Research,* 17, 412-425.

Schwartz, B. (1967) "The Social Psychology of the Gift," *the American Journal of Sociology,* 73, 1 - 11.

Sherry, J. F. J. (1983) "Gift-giving in Anthropological Perspective," *Journal of Consumer Research,* 10, 157 - 168.

Sherry, J. F. J., A. McGrath and S. J. Levy (1992) "The Disposition of the Gift and Many Unhappy Returns," *Journal of Retailing,* 68, 40-65.

Silverman, P. and S. Nickman (1993) "Children's reaction to the Death of a Parent," in Stroebe, M and R. O. Hansson (Eds.) *Handbook of Bereavement: Theory, Research, adn Intervention,* New York, Cambridge University Press.

Solomon, M. R. (1983) "The Role of Products as Social Stimuli: A Symbolic Interactionism Perspective," *Journal of Consumer Research,* 10, 219-329.

Tagg, S. K. (1985) "Life Story Interviews and Their Interpretation," in Brenner, M., J. Brown and D. Canter (Eds.) *The Research Interview: Uses and Approaches,* London, Academic Press.

Wagner, I. and R. Wodak (2006) "Performing Success: Identifying Strategies of Self-presentation in Women's Biographical Narratives," *Discourse and Society,* 17, 385-411.

Wallendorf, M. and E. J. Arnould (1988) ""My Favorite Things": A Cross-Cultural Inquiry into Object Attachment, Possessiveness, and Social Linkage," *Journal of Consumer Research,* 14, 531-547.

Buy Genuine Luxury Fashion Products or Counterfeits?

Boonghee Yoo, Hofstra University, USA
Seung-Hee Lee, Kent State University, USA[1]

ABSTRACT

The research examined the effect of three groups of variables on purchase intention of luxury fashion designer brands and their corresponding counterfeits: past behavior (past purchases of counterfeits and originals), attitudes toward buying counterfeits (by economic and hedonic benefits), and individual characteristics (materialism, perception of future social status, and self-image). Data of 324 Korean female students confirmed that the variables were determinants of purchase intention of counterfeits and originals and that purchase intention of counterfeits was positively related to purchase intention of originals whereas purchase intention of originals was negatively related to purchase intention of counterfeits.

INTRODUCTION

Counterfeiting prevails throughout the world, accounting for about ten percent of the world trade or worth of about 500 billion dollars, and the U.S. loses a quarter of a trillion dollars due to global piracy and counterfeiting (Heffes 2008). The most popular counterfeit market is clothing, followed by shoes, watches, leather goods, and jewelry. Louis Vuitton, Gucci, Burberry, Tiffany, Prada, Hermes, Chanel, Dior, Yves St Laurent, and Cartier are frequently pirated. Knockoffs of fashion brands are usually manufactured in China, South Korea, Taiwan, and South America (Ritson 2007). While most studies have focused on how to control the supply side of counterfeits, few studies have investigated the demand side, in particular, what factors explain purchase decision-making between counterfeits and originals (see Penz and Stöttinger 2005). The last statement is very true for luxury fashion designer products, whose counterfeits are popular among individual consumers across countries, poor or wealthy. Therefore, the purpose of this research was to examine the impact of three groups of antecedents on intent to buy luxury fashion designer brands versus their corresponding counterfeits. The three groups of interest refer to past behavior (represented by past purchases of counterfeits and originals), attitudes toward buying counterfeits (by economic and hedonic benefits), and individual characteristics (materialism, perception of future social status, and self-image). Figure 1 summarizes the research framework of the study.

RESEARCH HYPOTHESES

Past Behavior

Past behavior is found to be a more significant predictor of later behavior than the effects of intentions and perceptions of behavioral control (Bagozzi 1981; Ouellette and Wood 1998). As long as circumstances remain stable, past behavior forms a habit with repeated performance and later behavior relies more on past behavior than cognitive consideration (Bamberg, Ajzen, and Schmidt 2003). Therefore, past purchases of counterfeits are supposed to result in purchase intention of counterfeits whereas past purchases of originals are supposed to result in purchase intention of originals. In particular, the strong brand equity of luxury fashion brands that has been established over years provides stable image and prestige, which would consequently make consumers rely heavily on their habit of purchasing luxury fashion brands. Therefore, we hypothesize:

H1: Past purchases of counterfeits positively affect purchase intention of counterfeits.

H2: Past purchases of originals positively affect purchase intention of originals.

Attitudes toward Buying Counterfeits

As the theory of planned behavior predicts, attitudes toward an act positively affect behavioral intentions (Ajzen 1991; Ajzen and Fishbein 1980). Attitudes refer to the degree to which a person has a favorable appraisal of the behavior in question and are an immediate indicator by which her/his intention of conducting the specific behavior can be predicted. Therefore, positive attitudes toward buying counterfeits are expected to affect purchase intention of counterfeits positively whereas they are expected to affect the opposite act (purchase intention of originals) negatively.

We recognize economic benefits and hedonic benefits of counterfeits as two major reasons that make consumers develop positive attitudes toward buying counterfeits. First, because counterfeits' prices are a mere fraction of genuine items' prices, consumers enjoy economic benefits and feel values (Albers-Miller 1999). A counterfeit is a lower-quality, lower-price choice whereas a genuine item is a higher-quality, higher-price choice (Gentry et al. 2006; Prendergast et al. 2002). However, counterfeit consumers do not mind low quality and poor materials because they do not see counterfeits as inferior choices when they experience budget constraints and appreciate economic benefits of counterfeits (Dodge et al. 1996; Nia and Zaichkowsky 2000). They perceive purchase of counterfeits to be worthier and enhance societal welfare (Ang et al. 2001; Van Kempen 2003). On the other hand, as consumers are likely to buy originals when they can afford, economic benefits of counterfeits would not necessarily affect their intention to buy originals.

Second, consumers view that the brand name, the label, and identifying design characteristics such as logo, color, pattern, and accessories are themselves valuable. Such hedonic benefits value a product for its own sake (Babin, Darden, and Griffin 1994). When consumers pursue hedonic rather than utilitarian needs, they will easily accept counterfeits. Furthermore, they are not much concerned about low quality. Even in case others notice they consume counterfeits, consumers who do so for a pure hedonic reason will not feel embarrassed. They do not consider a consumer image built on fake products an issue of fragility. Therefore, hedonic benefits of counterfeits are expected to be linked positively to purchase intention of counterfeits and negatively to purchase intention of originals. Therefore, we hypothesize:

H3: Attitudes toward buying counterfeits by economic benefits positively affect purchase intention of counterfeits.

H4: Attitudes toward buying counterfeits by hedonic benefits positively affect purchase intention of counterfeits.

H5: Attitudes toward buying counterfeits by hedonic benefits negatively affect purchase intention of originals.

Individual Characteristics

Among many other individual characteristics, we examined the impact of materialism, perception of future social status, and

[1]The authors acknowledge that this research was supported by a summer research grant from the Frank G. Zarb School of Business, Hofstra University.

FIGURE 1
Antecedents of Purchase Intention of Counterfeits versus Genuine Luxury Fashion Brands

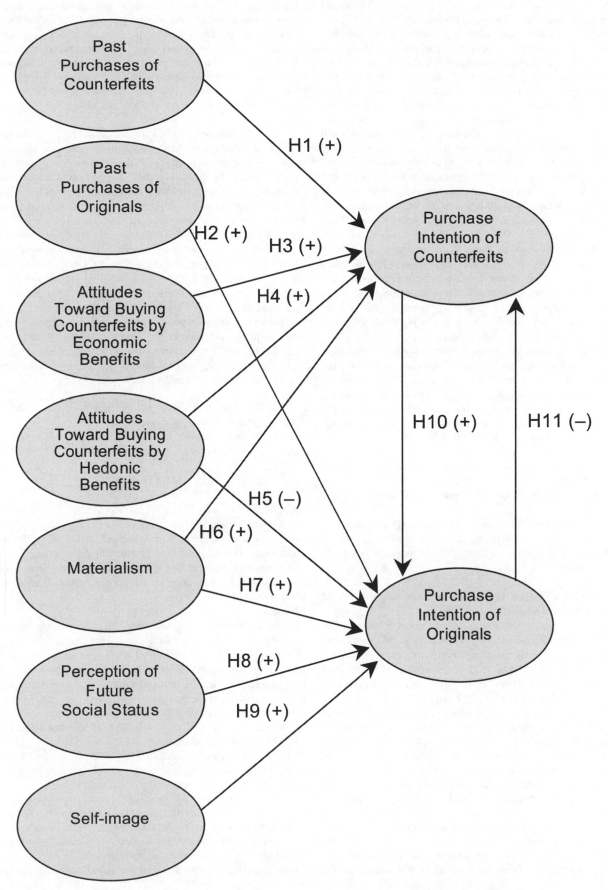

self-image on purchase intention of counterfeits and originals. Materialists place "possessions and their acquisition at the center of their lives" and view them "as essential to their satisfaction and well-being in life." (Richins and Dawson 1992, p. 304). Their primary goal of material possessions is to impress others rather than themselves. From that perspective, both counterfeits and originals fit the purpose of consumers' external physical vanity because they provide the image of prestige through the display effect despite significant quality differences. External physical vanity refers to "an excessive concern for, and/or a positive (and perhaps inflated) view of, one's physical appearance" (Netemeyer, Burton, and Lichtenstein 1995, p. 612). Consumers will have the identical appearance whether they wear a counterfeit or an original. The only difference is that consumers for originals purchase originals for what luxury brands mean, whereas consumers for counterfeits, who need only verisimilitude, purchase just the prestige of the originals without paying for it (Penz and Stöttinger 2005). Nevertheless, both products provide identical appearances, satisfying the materialistic mind.

One major element of social status is personal economic power (Sorokin 1959). When a consumer evaluates her or his future social status to be high, she or he will become less price-sensitive and select genuine fashion products whose prices are, for instance, ten times more expensive than those of corresponding counterfeits. That way, perceived future social status is positively linked to intention of buying the genuine products.

Consumers purchase products whose image matches their self-image to impress others. Self-image concerns itself with issues like "how I am seen by others" (Sirgy and Danes 1982). Therefore, status consciousness and high self-image positively affect purchase intention of originals because genuine products convey the image of affluence, wealth, and social class that match high self-image (Wee, Tan, and Cheok 1995). Therefore, we hypothesize:

H6: Materialism positively affects purchase intention of counterfeits.

H7: Materialism positively affects purchase intention of originals.

H8: Perception of future social class positively affects purchase intention of originals.

H9: Self-image positively affects purchase intention of originals.

Reciprocal Causation between Purchase Intentions of Counterfeits and Originals

In this section, we examine the reciprocal relationship or feedback-loop between the two types of intention: the intent to buy the counterfeits and the intent to buy the originals. First, counterfeit experiences are expected to cause consumers to develop more preference of genuine luxury fashion products through perceived risks involved with counterfeits. For instance, consumers would realize a high social risk as a result of the discomfort that they would feel if others might notice their use of counterfeits. That risk is derived from the poor physical quality, materials, and delicate design differences of counterfeits. According to Nia and Zaichkowsky (2000), the dominant majority of consumers disagrees that the value, satisfaction, and status of originals are devalued by the counterfeits available in the market. Counterfeits do not decrease the sense of ownership of originals because consumers strongly believe in the inferiority of counterfeits, and, therefore, counterfeits do not affect the demand for originals, which provide the exclusivity, durability, better quality, after-sales service, status, ethicality, and legality (Cheung and Prendergast 2006). Contradictory to the

concerns of luxury brand name manufacturers, consumers are well aware of key attributes and quality of genuine luxury brand names. This is even more true when consumers purchase counterfeits as a trial before committing to the originals (Gentry, Putrevu, and Shultz 2006). Therefore, consumers desire genuine luxury even when buying counterfeits. In a report, a third of consumers for counterfeits wanted to buy the original in the future as a result of negative counterfeit experiences (Ritson 2007). Consumers believe that being counterfeited attests to the fact that the counterfeited brands are well recognized, valued, and desired (Bian and Veloutsou 2007).

Second, consumers who buy originals do not desire counterfeits. Nia and Zaichkowsky (2000) found that owners of originals, perceiving counterfeits as inferior, believe the ownership of genuine luxury brands bring them admiration, recognition, and acceptance by others; thus these consumers demand counterfeits less. Once consumers earn an income high enough to afford genuine luxury fashion items, they are less likely to purchase counterfeits (Wee, Tan, and Cheok 1995). When consumers are highly involved with the product category, care about brands, and are brand-loyal, they are also less likely to purchase counterfeits (d'Astous and Gargouri 2001). Consumers who prefer legitimate originals do not desire counterfeits because they are more satisfied with the originals than the counterfeits in every aspect, except price (Tom et al. 1998). Experiences of originals provide more satisfaction through better physical quality and interpersonal approvals of the products, and, accordingly, make consumers lose interest in counterfeits. Originals serve social and psychological motives better in improving social standing and prestige. Therefore, we hypothesize:

H10: Purchase intention of counterfeits positively affects purchase intention of originals.

H11: Purchase intention of originals negatively affects purchase intention of counterfeits.

METHODS

Sample

Female college students in South Korea voluntarily participated. We selected South Korea because it is a major fashion counterfeit manufacturing and consuming country and female college students because they are active buyers and consumers of both counterfeits and originals of luxury fashion brands. We obtained 324 eligible responses.

Measures

Table 1 shows the measure items. All measures, except those for past purchases and future social class, were measured in a seven-point scale format. We developed a six-item scale of positive attitudes toward buying counterfeits by economic benefits and a five-item scale of positive attitudes toward buying counterfeits by hedonic benefits. These two scales measured how positively the consumer considers buying the counterfeits thanks to economic and hedonic benefits, respectively. Reliability of the scales was 0.84 and 0.71. As for materialism, we used Richins and Dawson's (1992) 18-item scale of materialism. Reliability of the scale was 0.81. We used Ahn et al's (2001) 19-item scale of self-image to measure a consumer's self-image. Reliability of the scale was 0.84.

We examined five different luxury fashion products: handbags, designer shoes, apparel, sunglasses, and jewelry. The purchase intention of counterfeits was measured by the mean score of the participant's responses to the questions worded, "How much would you like to purchase x counterfeits in the future?" in which x represented the most popularly counterfeited brands from each of

TABLE 1
Constructs Measured

Purchase Intention of Counterfeits (Reliability=0.88)
How much would you like to purchase x counterfeits in the future? (Five-item scale)
Where x=a group of selected brands for each of handbags, designer shoes, apparel, sunglasses, and jewelry.

Purchase Intention of Originals (Reliability=0.91)
How much would you like to purchase x originals in the future? (Five-item scale)
Where x=a group of selected brands for each of handbags, designer shoes, apparel, sunglasses, and jewelry.

Positive Attitudes toward Buying Counterfeits by Economic Benefits (Reliability=0.84)
1. I buy counterfeit products if I think genuine designer products are too expensive.
2. I buy counterfeit products if I cannot afford to buy designer products.
3. I buy counterfeit products without hesitation if I have a chance to buy the counterfeits.
4. I buy counterfeit products, instead of the designer products, if I prefer specific brands.
5. I boast about counterfeit products as if they are the genuine brand products.
6. I usually purchase counterfeits when it is difficult to distinguish between the counterfeits and the genuine products.

Positive Attitudes toward Buying Counterfeits by Hedonic Benefits (Reliability=0.71)
1. I like counterfeit goods because they demonstrate imitative abilities and ingenuity on the part of the counterfeiters.
2. I buy counterfeit products because counterfeiters are "little guys" who fight big business.
3. Buying counterfeit products demonstrates that I am a wise shopper.
4. I like buying counterfeit products because it is like playing a practical joke on the manufacturer of the non-counterfeit products.
5. I would buy counterfeit products even if I could easily afford to buy non-counterfeit products.

Materialism (Reliability=0.81)
1. I admire people who own expensive homes, cars, and clothes.
2. Some of the most important achievements in life include acquiring material possessions.
3. I do not place much emphasis on the amount of material objects people own as a sign of success.*
4. The things I own say a lot about how well I am doing in life.
5. I like to own things that impress people.
6. I do not pay much attention to the material objects other people own.*
7. I usually buy only the things I need.*
8. I try to keep my life simple, as far as possessions are concerned.*
9. The things I own are not all that important to me.*
10. I enjoy spending money on things that are not practical.
11. Buying things gives me a lot of pleasure.
12. I like a lot of luxury in my life.
13. I put less emphasis on material thing than most people I know.*
14. I have all the things I really need to enjoy life.*
15. My life would be better if I owned certain things I do not have.
16. I would not be any happier if I owned nicer things.*
17. I would be happier if I could afford to buy more things.
18. It sometimes bothers me quite a bit that I cannot afford to buy all the things I would like.

Perception of Future Social Class (9-point single-item measure)
How would you rank your future socio-economic class? Upper-Upper (= 9), Upper-Middle, Upper-Low, Middle-Upper, Middle-Middle, Middle-Low, Low-Upper, Low-Middle, Low-Low (= 1)

Self-Image (Reliability=0.84)
1. Modesty / not modesty
2. Intelligent / not intelligent
3. Mature / not mature
4. Sophisticated / not sophisticated
5. Neat / not neat
6. Sexy / not sexy
7. Feminine / not feminine
8. Classic / not classic
9. Intense / not intense
10. Bold / not bold
11. Gorgeous / not gorgeous
12. Simple / not simple*
13. Fashionable / not fashionable
14. Comfortable / not comfortable
15. Individuality / not individuality
16. Active / not active
17. Cute / not cute
18. Sporty / not sporty
19. Young / not young

* Reverse-coded.

TABLE 2

Construct Intercorrelations and Reliability

	1	2	3	4	5	6	7	8.	9
1. Purchase Intention of Counterfeits	1								
2. Purchase Intention of Originals	0.11	1							
3. Past Purchases of Counterfeits	0.57	0.20	1						
4. Past Purchases of Originals	-0.03	0.44	0.22	1					
5. Positive Attitudes toward Buying Counterfeits By Economic Benefits	0.33	0.05	0.27	-0.09	1				
6. Positive Attitudes toward Buying Counterfeits By Hedonic Benefits	0.43	-0.20	0.28	-0.17	0.40	1			
7. Materialism	0.20	0.45	0.22	0.28	0.13	0.02	1		
8. Perception of Future Social Status	-0.01	0.32	0.08	0.22	0.13	-0.03	0.25	1	
9. Self-image	0.07	0.25	0.09	0.23	0.07	-0.00	0.12	0.21	1
Reliability alpha	0.88	0.91	n.a.	n.a.	0.84	0.71	0.81	n.a.	0.84
Number of items	5	5	1	1	6	5	18	1	19
Mean	2.89	4.47	1.35	1.46	3.85	2.35	3.97	7.34	4.30
Standard deviation	1.48	1.68	1.26	1.50	1.33	0.90	0.71	1.15	0.72
Minimum value	1.00	1.00	0.00	0.00	1.00	1.00	1.85	4.00	2.36
Maximum value	7.00	7.00	5.00	5.00	6.50	5.20	6.55	9.00	6.68

$p < .01$ for correlation of 0.14 or greater.

the five luxury fashion product categories. Likewise, the purchase intention of originals was measured by the mean score of the responses to the five purchase-intention questions worded for originals. Reliability of the purchase-intention scale was 0.88 for counterfeits and 0.91 for originals. Perceived future social status was measured by a nine-point single item: one (low-low status) to nine (high-high status). Participants were also asked to answer yes or no as to whether they had ever purchased counterfeits or originals of the selected brands for each of the five product categories. The count of yes answers, ranging from zero to five, was the measure of past purchases of counterfeits and originals. Participants' counterfeit and genuine item purchase experiences were 54% and 20% for the selected handbag brands respectively; 17% and 13% for the designer shoes brands; 25% and 50% for the apparel brands; 7% and 26% for the sunglasses brands; and 34% and 38% for the jewelry brands. Table 2 shows the intercorrelations of the scales and summary information.

RESULTS

We ran a path analysis to test the research hypotheses simultaneously. A completely standardized solution, produced by the maximum likelihood method of LISREL 8.8 (Jöreskog and Sörbom 1993), showed adequate overall goodness-of-fit statistics of the path model. Specifically, chi-square was 6.01 (d.f.=13, p=0.95). AGFI was 0.99. CFI and NFI were 1.00 and 0.99, respectively. Both of RMSEA and SRMR were 0.01. Table 3 summarizes the results of hypothesis testing, which find all hypotheses supported at the significance level of lower than 0.05.

The results showed that purchase intention of luxury fashion counterfeits was positively predicted by past purchase experiences of counterfeits (H1: Estimate=0.49, p<0.0001), positive attitudes toward buying counterfeits by economic benefits (H3: Estimate=0.10, p<0.05), positive attitudes toward buying

counterfeits by hedonic benefits (H4: Estimate=0.21, p<0.0001), and materialism (H6: Estimate=0.17, p<0.01). Purchase intention of genuine luxury fashion products was positively predicted by past purchase experiences of originals (H2: Estimate=0.26, p<0.0001), materialism (H7: Estimate=0.27, p<0.0001), perceived future social status (H8: 0.17, p<0.001), and self-image (H9: Estimate=0.10, p<0.05) and negatively predicted by positive attitudes toward buying counterfeits (H5: Estimate=-0.2, p<0.0001). In addition, the reciprocal paths were supported as hypothesized: purchase intention of counterfeits was positively related to purchase intention of originals (H10: Estimate=0.30, p<0.0001), whereas purchase intention of originals was negatively related to purchase intention of counterfeits (H11: Estimate=-0.21, p<0.01).

GENERAL DISCUSSION

This study provides insights into what factors make consumers purchase luxury fashion product counterfeits (versus originals) and how successfully managers can handle the counterfeiting troubles and market the genuine brands more successfully. First, past purchase behavior is the strongest antecedent of purchase intention of counterfeits. Manufacturers have focused on developing technologies making counterfeiting difficult and policing counterfeit manufacturers, distributors, and sellers, but these measures are relevant mainly to businesses but irrelevant to individual consumers. A new, effective measure should focus on consumers and discourage them to buy counterfeits and consequently form a habit of buying counterfeits. In other words, luxury brand-name manufacturers need to promote buying or consuming of counterfeits as something similar to a crime. Note that the same logic has been applied to consumption of illegal drugs, weapons, and music downloading. Counterfeit buying behavior is indeed anti-social, illegal, and unethical in a sense. For instance, terrorist organizations and regimes are often involved with counterfeiting as a means of

TABLE 3
Path Model Estimates: Completely Standardized Solution

Hypothesized Relationship and Sign	Estimate	t-value	Conclusion
H1: Past Purchases of Counterfeits →			
Purchase Intention of Counterfeits (+)	0.49	9.79	Supported****
H2: Past Purchases of Originals →			
Purchase Intention of Originals (+)	0.26	5.62	Supported****
H3: Positive Attitudes toward Buying Counterfeits by Economic Benefits →			
Purchase Intention of Counterfeits (+)	0.10	2.16	Supported*
H4: Positive Attitudes toward Buying Counterfeits by Hedonic Benefits →			
Purchase Intention of Counterfeits (+)	0.21	3.88	Supported****
H5: Positive Attitudes toward Buying Counterfeits by Hedonic Benefits →			
Purchase Intention of Originals (−)	-0.28	-5.09	Supported****
H6: Materialism → Purchase Intention of Counterfeits (+)	0.17	2.98	Supported**
H7: Materialism → Purchase Intention of Originals (+)	0.27	5.50	Supported****
H8: Perception of Future Social Status →			
Purchase Intention of Originals (+)	0.17	3.67	Supported***
H9: Self-image → Purchase Intention of Originals (+)	0.10	2.22	Supported*
H10: Purchase Intention of Counterfeits →			
Purchase Intention of Originals (+)	0.30	3.77	Supported****
H11: Purchase Intention of Originals →			
Purchase Intention of Counterfeits (−)	-0.21	-2.42	Supported**

* $p < 0.05$; ** $p < 0.01$; *** $p < 0.001$; and **** $p < 0.0001$.

fundraising. Counterfeiters also damage tax revenues by not reporting their production and transactions. The new legal measures targeting buyers and consumers would certainly create strong negative social norms toward buying counterfeits once a society develops a consensus on the seriousness of the social damage due to counterfeits. Manufacturers should pursue this measure to create fear among consumers for a possible legal penalty. This measure, when implemented, will also help consumers to develop negative attitudes toward buying counterfeits.

Second, luxury fashion product manufactures should investigate the possibility that they might benefit from counterfeits. As H10 and H11 were supported, purchase intention of luxury fashion counterfeits positively affects purchase intention of originals while purchase intention of originals negatively affects purchase intention of counterfeits. This finding clearly implies that counterfeit consumers are very likely to become ultimate consumers for originals over time and do not return to counterfeits, a likelihood that is consistently found in pirated software or illegal music file downloading research, where counterfeits aid a full and fast market penetration of the originals (Haruvy, Mahajan, and Prasad 2004). Likewise, fashion counterfeits might function as a risk-free trial version, generate interest among consumers, and make them spread positive word-of-mouth to other consumers. This could be an immature conclusion, but it is one that is worth investigating.

Third, for luxury fashion brands, social status and self-image must be better promotional themes than materialism because social status and self-image are linked to purchase intention of originals whereas materialism is linked to purchase intention of both originals and counterfeits. This strategy would make consumers buy originals over counterfeits because originals better serve and match their social status and self-image. However, when fashionability or physical appearance is emphasized as the promotional theme,

consumers will choose either counterfeits or originals depending, for instance, on their income, shopping convenience, and hedonic purposes because both provide a good look despite a significant difference in product and service quality.

Limitations and Future Research

Some limitations to this study should be noted, and efforts to resolve them would serve as avenues for future counterfeiting research. First, the findings of the study may have limited generalizability. The sample, which seemed appropriate for a fashion brand counterfeit study, was South Korean female college students. However, it would be more meaningful if the same findings hold consistent in different types of consumers (professional females, high-income females, or older females), in different regions (far more or far less developed countries than South Korea), in different cultures (East versus West; collectivist versus individualist societies), and in functional product categories (cameras, golf clubs, or cell phones). Second, the factors investigated were limited to behaviors and characteristics of individual consumers. Future research needs to examine other factors to explain counterfeit behaviors. Examples include marketing activities (advertising, pricing, store image, warranty, and after-purchase services), brand characteristics (brand quality, brand image, and market leadership), and environmental factors (regulations related to counterfeiting activity, market availability of counterfeits, and national-level animosity against the manufacturing country of the luxury brand). Third, the study used cross-sectional survey data to test the hypotheses whose nature was causal. However, survey data provide correlational, not causal, data at best. Therefore, to overcome this limitation, future research needs to adopt experiments to test the hypotheses properly. Such an approach would bring confident answers to luxury-brand manufacturers and researchers. For instance, it is yet to be examined whether luxury fashion counterfeit experiences indeed increase the sales of the originals. Not survey data, but experimentation, would answer the question without raising unnecessary controversy or doubt.

CONCLUSION

Responding to the call for investigation of consumer-side explanations of buying behavior of fashion counterfeits, this study found that past purchase experiences, attitudes toward buying counterfeits by economic and hedonic benefits, and individual characteristics (that is, materialism, perception of future social status, and self-image) are major determinants of the purchase intention of counterfeits and originals. In addition, the study confirmed that purchase intention of originals decreases purchase intention of counterfeits, whereas purchase intention of counterfeits increases purchase intention of originals.

REFERENCES

Ahn, Chun-Soon, Seung-Hee Lee, Sookja Lim, Yoon Yang, and Shannon J. Lennon (2001), "A Comparative Analysis between the Kawabata Instrumental Evaluation and the Subjective Evaluation of Korean and American Consumers," *Journal of the Korean Society of Clothing and Textiles*, 25 (2), 217–227.

Ajzen, Icek (1991), "The theory of Planned Behavior," *Organizational Behavior and Human Decision Processes*," 50, 179-211.

Ajzen, Icek and Martin Fishbein (1980). *Understanding Attitudes and Predicting Social Behavior*. Englewood Cliffs, NJ: Prentice-Hall.

Albers-Miller, Nancy D. (1999), "Consumer Misbehavior: Why People Buy Illicit Goods," *Journal of Consumer Marketing*, 16 (3), 273-287.

Ang, Swee Hoon, Peng Sim Cheng, Elison A.C. Lim, and Siok Kuan Tambyah (2001), "Spot the Difference: Consumer Responses towards Counterfeits," *Journal of Consumer Marketing*, 18 (3), 219-235.

Babin, Barry J., William R. Darden, and Mitch Griffin (1994). "Work and/or Fun: Measuring Hedonic and Utilitarian Shopping Value," *Journal of Consumer Research*, 20 (March), 644-656.

Bagozzi, Richard P. (1981), "Attitudes, Intentions, and Behavior: A Test of Some Key Hypotheses," *Journal of Personality and Social Psychology*, 41 (4), 607-627.

Bamberg, Sebastian, Icek Ajzen, and Peter Schmidt (2003), "Choice of Travel Mode in the Theory of Planned Behavior: The Roles of Past Behavior, Habit, and Reasoned Action," *Basic and Applied Social Psychology*, 25 (3), 175–187.

Bian, Xumemei and Cleopatra Veloutsou (2007). "Consumers' attitudes regarding non-deceptive counterfeit brands in the UK and China," *Journal of Brand Management*, 14 (February), 211-222.

Cheung, Wah-Leung and Gerard Prendergast (2006), "Buyers' Perceptions of Pirated Products in China," *Marketing Intelligence & Planning*, 24 (5), 446-62.

d'Astous, Alain and Ezzedine Gargouri (2001), "Consumer Evaluations of Brand Imitations," *European Journal of Marketing*, 35 (1/2), 153-167.

Dodge, H. Robert, Elizabeth A. Edwards, and Sam Fullerton (1996), "Consumer Transgressions in the Marketplace: Consumers' Perspectives," *Psychology and Marketing*, 13 (8), 821-835.

Gentry, James W., Sanjay Putrevu, and Clifford Shultz, II (2006), "The Effects of Counterfeiting on Consumer Search," *Journal of Consumer Behaviour*, 5 (September), 1-12.

Haruvy, Ernan, Vijay Mahajan, and Ashutosh Prasad (2004), "The Effect of Piracy on the Market Penetration of Subscription Software," *Journal of Business*, 77 (April), S81-S107.

Heffes, Ellen M. (2008), "Fending Off Pirates," *Financial Executive*, 24 (March), 40-42.

Jöreskog, Karl G. and Dag Sörbom (1993), *LISREL 8.02*. Chicago: Scientific Software International, Inc.

Netemeyer, Richard G., Scot Burton, and Donald R. Lichtenstein (1995), "Trait aspects of Vanity: Measurement and Relevance to Consumer Behavior," *Journal of Consumer Research*, 21 (March), 612-626.

Nia, Arghavan, and Judith Lynne Zaichkowsky (2000), "Do Counterfeits Devalue the Ownership of Luxury Brands?" *Journal of Product and Brand Management*, 9 (7), 485-497.

Ouellette, Judith A. and Wendy Wood (1998), "Habit and Intention in Everyday Life: The Multiple Processes by which Past Behavior Predicts Future Behavior," *Psychological Bulletin*, 124, 54–74.

Penz, Elfriede and Barbara Stöttinger (2005), "Forget the 'Real' Thing-Take the Copy! An Explanatory Model for the Volitional Purchase of Counterfeit Products," *Advances in Consumer Research*, 32, 568-575.

Prendergast, Gerald, Leung Hing Chuen, and Ian Phau (2002), "Understanding Consumer Demand for Non-Deceptive Pirated Brands," *Marketing Intelligence and Planning*, 20 (7), 405-416.

Richins, Marsha L. and Scott Dawson (1992), "A Consumer Values Orientation for Materialism and its Measurement: Scale Development and Validation," *Journal of Consumer Research*, 19 (December), 303-316.

Ritson, Mark (2007), "Fakes Can Genuinely Aid Luxury Brands," *Marketing*, July 25, 21-21.

Sirgy, M. Joseph and Jeffrey E. Danes (1982), "Self-Image/Product-Image Congruence Models: Testing Selected Models," *Advances in Consumer Research*, 9, 556-561.

Sorokin, Pitirim (1959), *Social and Cultural Mobility*. New York: The Free Press.

Tom, Gail, Barbara Garibaldi, Yvette Zeng, and Julie Pilcher (1998), "Consumer Demand for Counterfeit Goods." *Psychology & Marketing*, 15 (5): 405-21.

Van Kempen, Luuk (2003), "Fooling The Eye of the Beholder: Deceptive Status Signaling Among the Poor in Developing Countries," *Journal of International Development*, 15 (March), 157-177.

Wee, Chow-Hou, Soo-Jiuan Tan, and Kim-Hong Cheok (1995), "Non-Price Determinants of Intention to Purchase Counterfeits Goods," *International Marketing Review*, 12 (6), 19-46.

Impression Formation in a World Full of Fake Products

Sezayi Tunca, University of Innsbruck, Austria
Johann Fueller, University of Innsbruck, Austria

ABSTRACT

This study extends existing theories on impression formation taking the fact of product piracy into consideration. The conducted qualitative study on Rolex watches confirms the suggested process of impression formation and brand appraisal consisting of four components. Our findings contribute to the theory of impression formation and lead to a better understanding of how people wearing fake products are perceived. The results of this study also have major practical implications, suggesting that under certain circumstances product piracy may entail an overall positive brand reputation which in part contradicts the predominant negative view of brand piracy.

INTRODUCTION

"Counterfeit and pirated goods are a big problem for global business, costing hundreds of billions of dollars, according to manufacturers and trade groups" (The Wall Street Journal 2007, p.B1). Trade in counterfeited and pirated products has been spreading at alarming rates and has reached incredible high proportions. According to McDonald and Roberts (1994) "piracy has developed a momentum all of its own" (p.56). They argue that counterfeiting and product piracy have spread from areas such as music and video recording, garments, watches, leather goods, cosmetics and software to products such as aircraft and automobile parts, prescription drugs, baby pacifiers, mannequins, alcoholic drinks, foodstuffs, contraceptives et cetera. Therefore, it can be argued that nearly no product categories are left unscathed. OECD (2007) suggests based on analysis of international trade data that up to USD 200 billion of internationally traded products could have been counterfeit or pirated in 2005. Additionally, OECD (2007) points out that "the figure does not, however, include counterfeit and pirated products that are produced and consumed domestically, nor does it include non-tangible pirated digital products being distributed via the Internet. If these items were added, the total magnitude of counterfeiting and piracy worldwide could well be several hundred billion dollars more" (p.6).

As counterfeiting and product piracy have evolved into a global problem, research on counterfeiting and piracy has been extensive, and many marketing researchers have addressed different aspects of counterfeiting and piracy. Although, these researchers have not delivered a unanimous definition of counterfeiting and piracy, the most common definitions of these terms indicate, that counterfeit brands refer to a 100 per cent copy of the authentic brand, with the objective of deceiving the consumer into believing that it is the genuine brand (cf. McDonald and Roberts, 1994; Prendergast et al., 2002; Papadopoulos, 2004). In contrast to counterfeit brands the term pirated brand also involves the unauthorised reproduction of patented brands, but without the intention of deceiving the consumer that it is the authentic brand (cf. McDonald and Roberts, 1994; Prendergast et al., 2002; Papadopoulos, 2004). Brand piracy is a supply and a demand side phenomenon as consumers consciously buy the fake brands.

As already indicated counterfeiting and brand piracy have been investigated from supply and demand side, and due to the global impact of counterfeiting or product piracy researchers have given some implications of how this phenomenon could be battled (e.g. Jacobs et al., 2001; Tom et al., 1998; Wee et al., 1995). Therefore, it is well accepted among researchers that this phenomenon might lead to direct sales losses for the brand holder and

consequently it also might result in job losses, and further entails tax revenue losses for the economy of a country. Further, it is also agreed on that product piracy leads to a deterioration of the brand image (c.f. Jacobs et al., 2001; McDonald and Roberts, 1994; Wee et al., 1995; Prendergast et al., 2002; Nia and Zaichkowsky, 2000; Tom et al., 1998).

This study tries to demonstrate that product piracy needs not always be negative. Bamossy and Scammon (1985) hint that if imitation is indeed the highest form of flattery, then companies whose brands are faked have much to be flattered about. In other words, a brand that is not copied is neither desirable nor valued. This study especially argues that the brand reputation of genuine products needs not necessarily be effected negatively by the fakes if looked at the matter in a differentiated way. Therefore, in this study a further interesting approach to this phenomenon, which has been neglected so far, might be to investigate, how people buying pirated products are perceived by others, and based on this perception the argument is that the reputation of pirated products might be evaluated differently. Consequently, this work is based on the assumption that depending on the overall impression formed of a person, a brand is perceived as a fake or a genuine product, and therefore it is argued that product piracy might have positive implications for the overall brand reputation under certain conditions. Thus, it is all about differentiating easily between authentic and fake owners in reference to their overall impression and also deducing positive implications for the overall brand reputation from the usage of fake products by people who can easily be recognized as owning a fake.

THEORY

"Clothes make the man" or "Fine feathers make fine birds"

Those sayings were formed in times when product piracy or counterfeits did not exist, at least to this extent. Also, when scholars introduced their theories how clothes and other material possessions contribute to the formation of an impression about a person, they did not consider that one has to check if the person's belongings are real or fake products when forming an overall impression about the person. This study extends existing theories on impression formation taking the fact of product piracy into consideration.

This section delivers a sound overview of existing theories contributing to an understanding of impression formation, role of fake and real products, distinction of it and consequences on the perception of fake bearers. Based on the theoretical foundations, it introduces an impression formation and brand appraisal process consisting of four components. The first component comprises the first impression theories and Veblen's conspicuous consumption (Veblen, 1945 [1899]) and demonstrates the formation of an overall impression of a person and the inferences made from this overall impression. The second component contains Goffman's dramaturgic perspective (Goffman, 1951, 1959) and illustrates the detection of misrepresentations and the resulting judgement of possessions as fake or authentic. The third component embraces Bourdieu's social space (Bourdieu, 1989a, 1989b) and describes the differentiation aspects from people belonging to other social classes. Finally, the fourth component incorporates the implications on overall brand reputation in accordance to the other three components.

Impression Formation: We meet a variety of people in every day life and tend to form first impression of others even in short time encounters. According to Bierhoff (1989) "first impressions do not emerge slowly over a long period of time but are formed almost immediately during the first encounter with the target person"(p.2). He further concludes that "impression formation is best considered as a process by which an organized overall impression emerges in which single traits receive specific meanings" (p.2). Jones (1990) argues that the importance of appearance cues cannot be overestimated in a first impression formation situation, and notes that such appearance cues include the attributions of commonly recognized physical attraction, clothes and grooming, facial expression, and posture. Further, research has shown that in a society where brief social contacts are numerous, clothing has become an important aspect in impression formation (cf. Douty, 1963; Holman, 1980; Judd et al., 1975; Lennon, 1986; Rosencranz, 1962). These studies further indicate that clothes worn are a major element in appearance, and therefore play a significant role in impression formation and in accrediting socioeconomic class. Research has also placed emphasis on the importance of material possessions in impression formation (cf. Hunt et al., 1996; Belk, 1978; Belk, 1980; Belk, 1981; Belk et al., 1982a; Belk et al., 1982b;). These studies imply that people first use possessions when they present themselves to others and second, also resort to similar possessions when they gather information about others. In other words, people use products to encode information about themselves, and as they develop a knowledge which products can be used to provide certain information, they also refer to these experiences when they decode information about others. Therefore, it can be argued that all these attributes are used to make inferences about others. Consistent with the presented research, this study argues that people refer to attributes like physical attractiveness, posture, facial expressions, material possessions, speech patterns etc. to make inferences about others. Further, it is argued that these single attributes receive specific meanings, and that an overall impression of others emerges according to these assigned single attributes.

Veblen's Conspicuous Consumption: Veblen (1945 [1899]) introduced in his treatise "The Theory of the Leisure Class" the widespread term conspicuous consumption. He states that with growing industrial development the distinction between classes shifted more towards the acquisition of property. He points, "it is even more to the point that property now becomes the most easily recognized evidence of reputable degree of success as distinguished from heroic or signal achievement. It therefore becomes the conventional basis of esteem. Its possession in some amount becomes necessary in order to any reputable standing in the community. It becomes indispensable to accumulate, to acquire property, in order to retain one's good name" (pp.28-29). Therefore, people are exerted to differentiate themselves from others and try to achieve this in acquiring goods, which are out of reach for people in lower social classes. Accordingly, Schulz (2006) outlines that in Veblen's theory a simple and direct relationship between the owners' status and their possessions of expensive goods exists. He implies that Veblen's elite distinguishes herself from the others in consuming goods, which are out of reach for others, and this enables the holders of elite status to enhance their privileged status. Bagwell and Bernheim (1996) suggest that the signaling of wealth is best achieved with "expensive durable goods, including one's automobiles, jewelry, and clothing", which "are all observed regularly by numerous other individuals during the normal course of social interaction, and provide durable emblems of substantial resource dissipation" (p.367). So far with first impression formation and Veblen's theory of conspicuous consumption we have a theoretical foundation for the first component of the suggested impression formation and brand appraisal process. As soon as people meet each other, they are inclined to form an overall first impression of each other in reference to their clothing, possessions (especially luxury products), facial hair, posture et cetera, and they are also inclined to make inferences regarding socioeconomic status and characteristic of the encountered person.

Goffman's Dramaturgic Perspective: Goffman (1959) suggests that "when an individual enters the presence of others, they commonly seek to acquire information about him or to bring into play information about him already possessed", and that "they will be interested in his general socio-economic status, his conception of self, his attitude toward them, his competence, his trustworthiness, etc. If unacquainted with the individual, observers can glean clues from his conduct and appearance which allow them to apply their previous experience with individuals roughly to the one before them or, more important, to apply untested stereotypes to him" (p.1). He argues that the individual plays a role and requests his observers to take seriously the impression fostered. He further indicates that the role is presented in a front (a setting), and this setting involves furniture, décor, physical layout, and other background items. Further, as part of personal front he includes insignia of office or rank; clothing, sex, age, and racial characteristics; size and looks; posture; speech patterns; facial expressions; bodily gestures; and the like. He suggests that once the proper sign-equipment has been obtained and familiarity gained in the usage of it, this equipment can be used for the performance of a favourable social style. Further he claims that "perhaps the most important piece of sign-equipment associated with social class consists of status symbols through which material wealth is expressed" (p.32). But Goffman (1951) also alerts that it is possible "that symbols may come to be employed in a "fraudulent" way, i.e. to signify a status which the claimant does not in fact possess" (p.296). Consequently, Goffman (1959) indicates that it is natural for the audience to judge if the impression the performer seeks to foster may be true or false. As he constitutes: "So common is this doubt that, as suggested, we often give special attention to features of the performance that can not be readily manipulated, thus enabling ourselves to judge the reliability of the more misrepresentable cues in the performance. And if we grudgingly allow certain symbols of status to establish a performer's right to a given treatment, we are always ready to pounce on chinks in his symbolic armour in order to discredit his pretensions" (p.51). The presented research demonstrates that as soon as people encounter others, they are apprehensive to detect if the fostered image of others is reliable or if a misrepresentation is current. They fulfil this task by applying to restrictive devices of misrepresentation. For example, in connection with pirated brands the overall impression of the owner may contradict the personalities conveyed by the brand. Hence, the person observed may be perceived as owning a fake product. This comprises the second component of the impression formation and brand appraisal process, in which it is decided if a product is fake or genuine.

Bourdieu's Social Space: Vogt (2000) argues that Bourdieu has changed the traditional Marxist approach of the economic capital concept in adding cultural, social and symbolic capital to the concept.[1] Bourdiue (1989b) states that people position themselves according to their distributions of these resources in the social space. In *Distinction* Bourdiue (1989a) describes how these various capitals, in particular economic and cultural capital, work in the social field of consumption. Income, financial- and material assets compose economic capital. Thus, economic capital can be equated with wealth (cf. Vogt 2000, Holt 1998, Veenstra 2005). Cultural and factual knowledge, attitudes, preferences, behaviours, educa-

---

[1]For detailed elaboration see Bourdieu 1983, 1989a, 1995

tional attainment, skills, experiences, worldviews, vocabulary, modes of speech etc. compose cultural capital (cf. Lamont and Lareau, 1998; Allen and Anderson, 1994). Further, Bourdieu (1989a) predicates in *Distinction* that cultural capital is an indicator of class position, and that cultural capital is accumulated by family upbringing and social background; formal education and personal educational experiences; and occupational culture (see also Holt, 1998; Veenstra, 2005). Accordingly, for people who hold both types of capital in high and low quantities different lifestyles can be classified. For example, people such as lawyers and doctors not only have high amounts of money to consume luxuries goods, but they also have the necessary cultural capital to position themselves in higher social classes. Further, Bourdieu (1989b) argues that "the representations of agents vary with their position (and with the interest associated with it) and with their habitus, as a system of schemes of perception and appreciation of practices, cognitive and evaluative structures which are acquired through the lasting experience of a social position. Habitus is both a system of schemes of production of practices and a system of perception and appreciation of practices" (p.19). Correspondingly, he concludes that habitus leads to the classification of oneself by choosing clothes, sports, friends etc. that suit ones position, and it also makes one "capable of perceiving the relation between practices or representations and positions in social space (as when we guess a person's social position from her accent)" (p.19). Consequently, the habitus enables people to distance or differentiate themselves of people who vary in some kind of resource endowment. This can be exemplified in regards to new money people or people who own small businesses. These people may as well possess financial assets to position themselves in a high social status class, but this may be inhibited because they lack the cultural knowledge, which is accumulated via socialization during the family and social upbringing. This displays the third component of the impression formation and brand appraisal process, in which the habitus, which is predominantly shaped by cultural capital, enables to sense one's and others place in the social space.

The perception of a person as owning a fake or a genuine product might have negative or positive effects on the overall brand reputation depending on the context of the situation. As above explained the bearers of genuine products form an overall impression of others (first component) and judge the same products on others based on their first impressions and distinguish between owners of fake or genuine products (second component). As the users of the authentic products might be prone to think that everybody can easily distinguish between fake and legal product due to first impression formation, they might regard the users of the pirated brands as not intruding in their social status sphere (third component). Quite the contrary, they might regard the users of the pirated brands as individuals who admire their social status and affluence and therefore, regard their social self as affirmed, and this might help them to enhance their self-esteem and might lead to an overall positive brand evaluation (fourth component). To determine if the suggested theory of an impression formation and brand appraisal process consisting of four components can be hold, a qualitative research is conducted.

RESEARCH FIELD

Of concern in this study are luxury brand products. Nia and Zaichkowsky (2000) point out the special characteristics of luxury brands being prestige and rarity, and assume that "the counterfeits may negatively affect the image of the original and hence the desire to own the original" (p.486). "What we have here are uninvited guests to the market party and, like any other party, there are those who will object to the gatecrashers" (McDonald and Roberts,

1994). This implies that the loss of rarity leads to a decline of the prestige aspect, and further the existence of pirated brands produces an area of conflict, which can have a negative effect on the overall perception of the authentic brands, as brand image incongruity might be the consequence of this market practice. A further reason, why luxury brands are chosen is that appearance and visibility are critical for these brands but not salient for functional products such as music CDs and software programs (cf. Tom et al., 1998). Following these arguments, the brand Rolex is used for the qualitative research section. Rolex enjoys a high reputation among all interest groups of the brand, whether they can afford the brand or not. A brand such as Rolex with an excellent reputation is consequently committed to product piracy. This follows the argumentation that a brand that is neither desirable nor valued will not be copied (cf. Bamossy and Scammon, 1985). Further, the argumentations offered in this section are also effective for the brand Rolex, as the loss of rarity might lead to a decline in prestige, and appearance and visibility seem to be critical for this brand as well.

METHODOLOGY

To detect if the presented research and especially the process of impression formation and brand appraisal consisting of four components can be hold, twelve authentic Rolex owners were interviewed. The interview method is used as it enables to "understand themes of the lived daily world from the subjects' own perspective" (Kvale 1998, p.27). The interview also enables to "reach areas of reality that would otherwise remain inaccessible such as people's subjective experiences and attitudes" (Peräkylä 2005, p.869). Consequently, as in this qualitative research the perceptions and experiences of the participants are of primary concern, the qualitative in-depth interview research is applied. Twelve interviews with authentic brand holders were conducted, and the interviews lasted from 30 to 50 minutes and were audio recorded. All interviews were transcribed to text for analysis. During the interviews visual aids in form of pictures were used. Five pairs of Rolex pictures representing an authentic and a fake product were used to detect if the interviewees could distinguish between the fake and the authentic product. This is of importance as this study claims that people do not distinguish between fake or real in reference to the appearance of the product, but make inferences from the overall image of the bearer to decide if the product is fake or genuine. Therefore, it is important that people are aware of the fact that some products cannot be distinguished only in reference to the appearance of the product and that they might rely on other facts to distinguish between fake and real. Further, five pictures of different people were shown during the interview, and it was claimed that all of these people had a Rolex. The intention was to detect if the interviewees decided in reference to the perceived overall image of the people if the Rolex was authentic or pirated, and if they identified or compared themselves with them. This exploratory study should help to clarify if the suggested process of impression formation and product piracy can be hold and what implications can be derived for the overall brand reputation of pirated brands.

RESULTS

The participants refer to many attributes when they form an impression of an encountered person. The most mentioned ones are clothes, shoes, watches, brands carried, personal appearance or public manner, jewelry or accessories, trimness and speech of the person encountered. Other attributes some interviewees rely on when forming an impression of others are trimness of face, hair or hairstyle, facial expression, posture, movement, physical appearance, occupation, age and even how spruce the finger nails are. Some interviewees indicate that they first rely on attributes like clothes and shoes or public appearance to form an impression of the encountered person, and that these attributes compose the most important ones and are used more intensively than other attributes, as interviewee#6 remarks: "Clothes make up most for me. The first impression for me is, how somebody is dressed, particularly the shoes. And then the next impression is the talk. Thus, how he acts, how he answers, how the language is. And then a first impression is formed. The first impression is appearance and clothes." This aspect also emerges when encountered people are described in a context. As soon as a context is included to the impression formation process, some attributes are more chosen to describe the impression they have of the person. In the most cases when the pictures are shown, immediately the occupation of the person is mentioned and the resulting implications for the overall impression formed are noted. Almost all participants mention attributes without objection, which indicates that they are aware of the process of attribute seeking in impression formation, and that they do it consciously. Therefore, it can be concluded that the interviewees rely on several attributes like clothes, speech, occupation, accessories, brands carried etc. to form an overall impression of the encountered person.

Further, the interviews evidence that the impression formation process also comprises categorization of the encountered people. The response of interviewee#5 illuminates this aspect: "It is looked at the overall picture. How the occurrence is, and of course it is looked at the clothes, at the movement and then in this context the person is positioned in a group, which is classified by oneself." The categorization results from deduction of several characteristics from the overall impression formed. This means that first an overall image with reference to attributes like clothes, appearance etc. is formed, and that next from this overall image other characteristics are deduced. The mentioned characteristics, which the interviewees derive from the overall impression are financial resources or income, education level, and class membership. In respect to class membership, they distinguish between middle class and upper class or between blue-collar worker and white-collar employee or just wealthy people. Some interviewees notice that their inferences are based on prejudice, but remark that they are aware that they do it and assume that others behave in the same manner. The interviews reveal that the interviewees infer consciously or unconsciously from the overall image formed especially attributes such as financial success, education and class membership.

The next step was to identify if the interviewees classify, based on the overall image formed of others and the inferences they make from this overall image, the bearers of the Rolex as owning a real or a fake product. For the detection if the interviewees refer to other attributes than only the product observed when they distinguish between fake and real, it might be important to elaborate what the brand Rolex meant for these people. As in the theoretical part of this work already exemplified, the detection of misrepresentations might depend on mismatches between brand reputation and the overall impression formed of the person. Therefore, it is intended to detect what Rolex represents for the interviewees in order to be able to determine if their decisions are based on these representations of the brand in their minds. When asked what Rolex represents for them, some interviewees mention both which attributes the person should have who owns it and brand specific attributes. Other interviewees only mention brand specific attributes without considering traits of the people who own it. Among the attributes which the person should have are that the person should be self-confident,

should be stylish, should be well dressed, should have a sense for quality, should be spruce, should be educated, should have a smart occurrence and should have a good income. Further, these people are regarded as not showing off, as people who consciously spend money on luxury and as people who indulge oneself in buying such things. When they refer to the specific attributes of Rolex, they mention the high quality of the product, the durability of the product, the timelessness and the constancy of the product, luxury, the stable value of the product, the product being an asset, status symbol, perfection and as being the crown of the watches, as its brand label indicates it. Next, it was of interest to detect if the interviewees having specific brand representations refer also to other attributes than product appearance when they evaluate the bearers as owning a fake or an authentic Rolex. People who are perceived as having an overall elegant appearance or as being stylish dressed, as having a good job or working at higher levels, as being wealthy or as having higher income and as being well educated are assigned as owning an authentic brand. In the most cases the interviewees use these descriptions in some combination to reason their decisions. In contrast, people who are perceived as working at low qualification jobs, as being not so wealthy or as having less income, as being young and as not being well dressed were assigned as owning a fake brand. Again in the most cases the interviewees use these descriptions in some combination to reason their judgments. Therefore, the interviews highlight the aspect that people do not only differentiate between fake and real in reference to the observed brand or product, but they also refer to the overall impression formed of a person or to the deductions made from this overall impression to distinguish between fake and real bearer. The response of interviewee#11 evidences this argument: "You recognize it immediately from the quality. But it should not be forgotten that really good imitations exist. Thus, it exists A and B, average, normal and one to one very excellent imitations, with which even the expert has difficulties to recognize. But you recognize it from the person who has it. Certainly, you look at that person and ask yourself, can such a person afford for example such a watch or a product like that."

The next step is to assess if the interviewees compared or identified themselves with the people who are identified as fake or real owners and what implications this has on brand reputation. When the pictures of the people, who are judged as owning a real Rolex, are presented to the interviewees and asked if they identify themselves with these people, the responses are manifold. First, some interviewees respond that they identify themselves with the person presented in reference to his or her style; appearance; occurrence; clothes; and with the context in which the person is, like being in a convention. Second, others respond that they identify themselves with the person presented only in some attributes like style, and that they differ in regards to other characteristics like the person is more conservative or classical. Third, some interviewees tell that they could not identify themselves with the person presented, but give positive descriptions of the person like being nobler, more elegant and more career-minded. Although the responses are differing no one mentions any negative associations in reference to these people. When asked what it meant for the brand or for their perception of the brand if such a person owns an authentic Rolex, the responses are predominantly positive. Such positive responses are that they have a good feeling; that Rolex is worn by people, who are esteemed; that it has a positive smack; that it is a good promotion, which strengthens Rolex; that they have a positive attitude towards these people, and therefore as well a positive attitude toward the brand; that it strengthens their relation to the brand; and that they are confirmed in their product choice. As no negative perceptions are mentioned and with reliance to these references it can be concluded that these people in the main enhance the perception of the brand reputation.

When the pictures of the people, who are judged as owning a fake, are shown and asked if they identify with these people, most of the interviewees respond that they could not identify themselves with these people. Whereas some of the interviewees only reply that they simply cannot identify or compare themselves with these people, some also reason why they do not compare or identify themselves with them. The reasons mentioned are how they dressed; the milieu they are in; the age of the person; these people did not amount to much, if they are satisfied with a fake; the job of the people; and that they are in a different income class. Therefore, it can be concluded that in general the interviewees do not identify themselves with these people. In the next step the interviewees are asked what they think why these people buy a fake Rolex. The most common responses are that these people esteem or admire the brand, as otherwise they would not buy the fake product; that the brand is in demand, but they cannot afford it; that they buy it just for fun; that they want to cheat; that they want to show off; that they want to keep up; and that they want to enhance their prestige. When asked what it meant for the brand or for their perception of the brand when such people own a fake brand. The responses again are predominantly positive, although beforehand as above indicated some negative responses such as they want to cheat or show off were stated, most of the interviewees argue that it proves that the brand is esteemed, admired and wanted, and they add that only valued products are copied. Ten interviewees state these descriptions and always conclude that therefore the owning of fake products by these people should not have negative implications for the brand. The interviews demonstrate that most of the interviewees do not regard the usage of fake products by these people as a problem, but quite the contrary, it is thought to enhance brand reputation.

Finally, the interviewees are asked if they believe that others perceive them as owning a real Rolex and how they deal with this situation. Nine interviewees state that they believe that others perceive them as owning a real Rolex. Three interviewees tell that they pay attention to their appearance, and that others surely regard them as owning a real Rolex because of the overall impression they display. The other six interviewees assert that they surely are regarded as having a real Rolex because of the profession they perform. One interviewee who is an army officer mentions that it depends on if he wears plain clothes or if he is in uniform. If he wears plain clothes, he is sure that people refer to him because of his appearance as owning a real Rolex, but if he is in uniform, he supposes that he is considered as having a fake product, as people think that such people do not earn enough money. But he tells that this does not bother him, as he values the brand in any case. Two other interviewees tell that they are probably not regarded as having a Rolex because of their overall impression displayed. One of them tells that he has a young appearance and due to that people might consider him as having a fake product. The other tells that she performs lots of free time activities like sports and because of her appearance at that time people might refer to her as having a fake product. But again both tell that their relation to the product is very intense, and therefore they do not care what others think of them.

DISCUSSION

This study extends existing theories on impression formation taking the fact of product piracy into consideration. It frames an impression formation and brand appraisal process consisting of four components. The first component comprises the impression formation theory and Veblen's conspicuous consumption (Veblen,

1945 [1899]) and indicates the formation of an overall impression of an encountered person and the inference of attributes such as wealth or social status. The findings of the qualitative research confirm the reliance on several attributes to form an overall impression and the inference of further characteristics, such as class membership, education and income or wealth. The second component demonstrates the detection of misrepresentations. This study confirms Goffman's (1951, 1959) detection of misrepresentations in regards to social status and extends it by including the detection of the authenticity of brands and products. The third component embraces Bourdieu's social space (Bourdieu, 1989a, 1989b) and describes the differentiation aspects from people belonging to other social classes. The interviews reveal that people compare or identify themselves with others who have similar economic and cultural capital and distance themselves from people with different economic and cultural capital endowment. Finally, the fourth component incorporates the implications on overall brand reputation in accordance to the other three components. The results of the interviews indicate that people clearly distinguish between real and fake owners with reference to their formed overall image and the detected misrepresentations (component one and two). As people who own fakes can easily be identified, they do not get the opportunity to cheat and position themselves in a higher position (component three). In reliance to the specification of these three components the authentic users conclude that fake owners in most cases use a fake brand because they admire or esteem it, and not for deceiving others. Further, the admiration of the brand by these people proves according to the authentic owners that the product is really wanted and this again enhances brand reputation. Further, they also indicate that the existence of the fakes is positive for the brand, as only brands are copied which are valued, and that this again confirms their product choice (these arguments comprise component four indicating an overall positive brand reputation). Our findings contribute to the theory of impression formation and add a better understanding of how people wearing fake products are perceived. Due to the found clear distinction of fake and real bearers of products, the results of this study also have major practical implications, suggesting that under certain circumstances product piracy may serve as counter-intuitive marketing instrument which in part contradicts the predominant negative view of product piracy for brands.

However, the presented results comprise first findings. In this research we concentrated on one product category (watches), one brand (Rolex) and one interest group (owners of the authentic brand). Further research could demonstrate if the findings can be generalized or extended to other product categories or interest groups such as potential customers.

REFERENCES

Allen, Douglas E. and Paul F. Anderson (1994), "Consumption and Social Stratification: Bourdieu's Distinction," *Advances in Consumer Research*, Volume 21, 70-74.

Bagwell, Laurie S. and B. Douglas Bernheim (1996), "Veblen Effects in a Theory of Conspicuous Consumption," *The American Economic Review*, Vol. 86, No. 3, Jun., 349-373.

Bamossy, Gary and Debra L. Scammon (1985), "Product Counterfeiting: Consumers and Manufacturers Beware," *Advances in Consumer Research*, Vol. 12, 334-339.

Belk, Russell W. (1978), "Assessing the Affects of Visible Consumption on Impression Formation," *Advances in Consumer Research*, Vol. 5, Issue 1, 39-47.

_____ (1980), "Effects of Consistency of Visable Consumption Patterns on Impression Formation," *Advances in Consumer Research*, Vol. 7, Issue 1, 365-371.

_____ (1981),"Determinants of Consumption Cue Utilization in Impression Formation: an Association Derivation and Experimental Verification," *Advances in Consumer Research*, Vol. 8, Issue 1, 170-175.

_____, Kenneth D. Bahn and Robert N. Mayer (1982a), „Developmental Recognition of Consumption Symbolism," *Journal of Consumer Research*, Vol. 9, June 1982, 4-17.

_____ Russell, Robert Mayer and Kenneth Bahn (1982b), „The Eye of the Beholder: Individual Differences in Perception of Consumption Symbolism," *Advances in Consumer Research*, Vol. 9, Issue 1, 523-530.

Bierhoff, Hans-Werner (1989), *Person Perception and Attribution*, Berlin, Heidelberg, New York, London, Paris, Tokyo, Hong Kong: Springer Verlag.

Bourdieu, Pierre (1983), Ökonomisches Kapital, kulturelles Kapital, soziales Kapital. In Reinhard Kreckel (ed.), *Soziale Ungleichheiten (Soziale Welt, Sonderband 2)*, Göttingen, 183-198.

_____ (1989a), *Die feinen Unterschiede: Kritik der gesellschaftlichen Urteilskraft*, 3.Aufl., Frankfurt am Main: Suhrkamp.

_____ (1989b), "Social Space and Symbolic Power," *Sociological Theory*, Vol.7, No.1, Spring, 14-25.

_____ (1995), *Sozialer Raum und >>Klassen<<*, 3.Aufl., Frankfurt am Main: Suhrkamp.

Douty, Helen I. (1963), "influence of clothing on perception of persons," *Journal of Home Economics*, Vol. 55, No.3, 197-202.

Goffman, Erving (1951), "Symbols of Class Status," *The British Journal of Sociology*, Vol.2, No.4, Dec., 294-304.

_____ (1959), *The Presentation of Self in everyday Life*, London: The Pinguin Press.

Holman, Rebecca H. (1980), "Clothing as Communication: An Empirical Investigation," *Advances in Consumer Research*, Vol. 7, Issue 1, 372-377.

Holt, Douglas B. (1998), "Does Cultural Capital Structure American Consumption," *Journal of Consumer Research*, Vol. 25, June, 1-25.

Hunt, James M., Jerome B. Kernan and Deborah J. Mitchell (1996), "Materialism as Social Cognition: People, Possessions, and Perception," *Journal of Consumer Psychology*, 5(1), 65-83.

Jacobs, Laurence, A. Coskun Samli and Tom Jedlik (2001), „The Nightmare of International Product Piracy: Exploring Defensive Strategies," *Industrial Marketing Management*, 30, 499-509.

Jones, Edward E. (1990), *Interpersonal Perception*, New York: W. H. Freeman and Company.

Judd, N., Bull, R.H.C., Gahagan, D. (1975), "The Effects of Clothing Style Upon the Reactions of a Stranger," *Social Behavior and Personality*, 3 (2), 225-227.

Kvale, Steinar (1998), *Interviews: An Introduction to Qualitative Research Interviewing*, Thousand Oaks, London, New Delhi: Sage Publications.

Lamont, Michele and Annette Lareau (1988), "Cultural Capital: Allusions, Gaps and Glissandos in Recent Theoretical Developments," *Sociological Theory*, Vol.6, No.2, Autumn, 153-168.

Lennon, Sharron J. (1986), "Additivity of Clothing Cues in First Impressions," *Social Behavior and Personality*, 14 (1), 15-21.

McDonald, Gael and Christopher Roberts (1994), "Product Piracy: The Problem that Will not Go Away," *Journal of Product & Brand Management*, Vol. 3 No.4, 55-65.

Nia, Arghavan and Judith L. Zaichkowsky (2000), "Do counterfeits devalue the ownership of luxury brands?," *Journal of Product & Brand Management*, Vol.9 No.7, 485-497.

OECD (2007), The Economic Impact of Counterfeiting and Piracy: Executive Summary, viewed 10 June, 2007,<http://www.oecd.org/dataoecd/13/12/38707619.pdf

Papdopoulos, Theo (2004), "Pricing and pirate product market formation," *Journal of Product & Brand Management*, Vol. 13 No.1, 56-63.

Peräkylä, A. (2005), "Analyzing Talk and Text". In: Denzin, N.K. and Lincoln, Y.S. (eds.): *The Sage Handbook of Qualitative Research*, third edition, Thousand Oaks, London, New Delhi: Sage Publications, 869-886.

Prendergast, Gerard, Leung H. Chuen and Ian Phau (2002), „Understanding consumer demand for non-deceptive pirated brands," *Marketing Intelligence & Planning*, 20/7, 405-416.

Rosencranz, Mary L. (1962), "clothing symbolism," *Journal of Home Economics*, Volume 54, Number 1, 18-22.

Schulz, Jeremy (2006), "Vehicle of the Self: The social and cultural work of the H2 Hummer," *Journal of Consumer Culture*, 6(1), 57-81.

The Wall Street Journal (2007), "Efforts to Quantify Sales of Pirated Goods Lead to Fuzzy Figures", viewed 19 October 2007, <http://online.wsj.com/public/article/SB119274946863264117.html

Tom, Gail, Barbara Garibaldi, Yvette Zeng and Julie Pilcher (1998), „Consumer Demand for Counterfeit Goods," *Psychology and Marketing*, Vol.15(5), 405-421.

Veblen, Thorstein (1945 [1899]), *The Theory of the Leisure Class, An Economic Study of Institutions*, New York: The Viking Press.

Veenstra, Gerry (2005), „Can Taste Illumine Class? Cultural Knowledge and Forms of Inequality," *Canadian Journal of Sociology / Cashiers canadiens de sociologie*, Vol.30, No.3, Summer, 247-279.

Vogt, Ludgera (2000), „Identität und Kapital. Über den Zusammenhang von Identitätsoptionen und sozialer Ungleichheit". In: Hettlage, R. and Vogt, L. (eds.): *Identitäten in der modernen Welt*, Wiesbaden: Westdeutscher Verlag, 77-100.

Wee, Chow-Hou, Soo-Jiuan Tan and Kim-Hong Cheok (1995), "Non-price determinants of intention to purchase counterfeit goods: An exploratory study," *International Marketing Review*, Vol. 12 No.6, 19-46.

The Present Location of Temporal Embeddedness: The Case of Time Linked Consumption Practices in Dual Career Families

Shona Bettany, Bradford University, UK
Caroline Gatrell, Lancaster University, UK

ABSTRACT

This paper examines the time linked consumption practices of professional dual career families, examining the kind of consumption practices these families use to manage their lives. The study found that rather than being slaves to time scarcity, professional dual career parents actively 'speed up' and 'slow down' time through particular consumption practices to take more control of their family lives and times. This paper utilises these empirical accounts to develop theory on time and the family in consumer research which not only enriches understanding of families and familial consumption but also provides a theoretical development of the concept of time within consumer research

INTRODUCTION: PROFESSIONAL DUAL CAREER FAMILIES AND TIME

In previous work on this subject matter (Bettany and Gatrell 2007), we presented an empirical interpretive analysis of time linked consumption practices in professional dual career families. Our argument for this work was that, to date, consumer research on the family, being focused primarily on decision making, life cycle and roles had presented a narrow conceptualisation of 'the family' as a construct (Ekstrom 2005, Price and Epp 2005). Moreover, that this narrow conceptualisation was also highly gendered and gender/role normative around the notion of the "normal" nuclear family with father as breadwinner and mother as carer, housewife and nurturer (Commuri et al 2005). Conversely to this picture, as Ekstrom (2005) has argued a plurality of families exists today leading us to the conclusion that the family itself may not be the most appropriate construct with which to theorise what we might call 'kin'. As Price and Epp (2005) have argued examining how families are enacted might be more worthwhile than taking the family as an already self evident construct. Examining these alternative family enacting constructions led us, as well as others (Gentry and McGinnis 2003) to a concern with the most quickly growing family construction (Macran et al 1996), the "peer marriage" of professional dual career parents with small children. "Peer marriages" are defined as those marriages where *'partners are social equals, have careers, share equal responsibility for finances and other decision making, and where the husband assumes far greater responsibility for child-rearing'* (Gentry and McGinnis 2003). As a family form, peer couples with children, defined here as "professional dual career families" have risen exponentially. Professional dual-career couples, have *'jobs which require a high degree of commitment and which have a continuous developmental character'* (Rapoport and Rapoport 1969) with a lifestyle career pattern including high levels of career responsibility and personal investment of time and energy (Johnson, Kaplan, and Tusel 1979, Bird and Schnurman-Crook 2005). However, and perhaps not surprisingly, when we examined the concept of the peer marriage within consumer research the primary focus of consumer research on the family is still upon decision making and family roles in these decision making processes. This often reduces these monumental changes in family form, structure and activities to 'families with working wives' becoming a variable in family decision making research (see for example Mangleburg 1999). Traditional decision making research and research on family roles does not, and can not,

begin to understand the complex entanglement of family 'making' processes and consumption activities in contemporary families, especially professional dual career families that have highly complex lives.

'Time' is a central theme in studies of the family in consumer research, particularly those that focus on the "working" mother. The working mother emerges in these studies as the key figure in terms of time pressure, time management and time scarcity (Gross 1987). Thompson's (1996) study of "the juggling lifestyle" of professional working mothers, for example, as well as others (Joag, Gentry, and Ekstrom 1991, Joag 1985, Joag, Gentry, Gentry et al 1996, Commuri and Gentry, 2005 among others) predominantly focus on mothers only and by doing so, these studies implicitly position women *only* as functioning and managing in both the work and domestic spheres and thus subtly act to reinscribe the domestic sphere as the feminine domain. The ability of women to balance home and work through time management is studied (or put under question), while the father is not considered. This therefore doesn't consider the specificity of professional dual career families. It has been documented in the consumer behaviour field that there is little evidence in the consumer research literature that husbands have taken on more household roles. However, as Rudd (1987) points out, if the research has asked the woman about shared roles (e.g. Foxman and Burns 1987), this may have skewed the findings somewhat. In other fields it has been documented that fathers undertake an increased level of childcare and other roles (Gatrell 2005, Hochschild 1997) and interdependence of roles is common (Bird and Schnurman-Crook 2005). Research on the dual career family and the division of domestic labour is a contested field and in professional dual career households, management of, and juggling between, the domestic sphere and the work sphere has been reported as highly complex (Sullivan 2000, Windebank 2001). As well as this focus on the mother as primary time manager, many of the studies in marketing emphasise the negativity of working women's lives with a focus on concessions, compromises and guilt. Thompson's paper opens with a quote from a respondent which begins 'sometimes I go through guilt trips…'. The article goes on to assert that *'women…must find ways to cobble together a compromise between the competing cultural ideals of traditional motherhood and career oriented professionalism'* (1996:388-our emphasis). This may be correct, but the message is that families with professional working mothers are highly problematic and that living in these families is likely to be a negative experience.

In trying to develop an understanding of this negativity in the literature and in the public and political commentaries given above we kept returning to the issue of time and how time was being conceptualised. We concluded that this negativity was predominantly linked to the idea of "time scarcity" in these families as the root of their "problem". From our own experience as professional working mothers we could endorse the idea that time was scarce from our own households, but we both felt that the understanding of the phenomenon of time needed a more nuanced analysis and that the idea of "time scarcity" as a central factor may be a little simplistic. Supporting this, Southerton (2003) argues in his study of suburban households that although his respondents all presented narratives of "time harriedness", in depth examination of their experiences of this phenomenon led him to assess that this did not automatically equate to "time scarcity" and that their consumption, management and experience of time was highly complex.

The combination of a scarcity of research on "alternative" family constructions and the rather outdated and one might say naïve conceptualisations of both 'the family' and 'time' in consumer research led us to our interpretive study of professional dual career families and time. In the initial paper from this study we presented a rich interpretive study of peer families actively managing and subverting time through complex consumption patterns. In this presentation, we utilise a portion of that empirical evidence to make a further contribution concerning the conceptualisation of time within consumer research.

TIME AND CONSUMER RESEARCH

Future consumer research should emphasize analyses of the socio-temporal contexts of consumer behavior. This means that consumer behavior should not only be related to clocks and calendars. It should also be temporally related to other activities, and to specific patterns of interaction and location. The social temporality of consumer behavior should be identified by specifying the particular preceding, succeeding or coinciding events, and by examining the consumer's own perceptions and reflections regarding these temporal relations between the consumer behavior and other events...[Consumer researchers need] to develop more insight into how consumers themselves perceive and reflect on this temporal coordination of consumer behavior in relation to other events, including action, actors and arenas, within particular contexts.
(Gronmo 1989:341)

The quote above was taken from the groundbreaking article by Sigmund Gronmo (1989) where he effectively exploded the myth of a one-dimensional concept of time with which consumer researchers had previously been theorising their research concerning time and the consumer (see also Hirschman 1987). Research on time in consumer research, until then had been dependent upon a concept of time borrowed from economics (Jacoby, Szybillo and Berning 1976). This concept of time, where time is seen as an external, objective fact, as a mechanical, clock based, linear and standardised resource led to consumer research on time that focused on time allocation (Robinson 1975, Wilson 1984), time as a resource to be spent and/or saved (Hendrix 1984), time scarcity (Gross 1987) and time expenditure choices (Chapin 1974, Holman and Wilson 1982). In general, all time conceptualising consumer research concerned the 'use of time' as a finite, objective and limited resource (see also Anderson, Karns and Venkatesan, 1988; Arndt and Gronmo, 1977; Golden, Umesh, Weeks and Anderson, 1988; Hawes, 1977; Hendrix, Kinnear and Taylor, 1978). In his article, Gronmo argued that there were at least three different conceptualisations of time, and that this mechanical, economics based view was only one of these. The most important conceptualisation of time for consumer research, he argued, is social time, that is the concept of time as defined through the subjective perception and experience of time as embedded within specific socio-cultural contexts, this he called 'social temporality'.

Given our concerns as researchers regarding what we considered as the rather simplistic conceptualisation of time within peer families as related to "time scarcity", and given that "time scarcity" fits within the mechanical economics based concept of time, we looked for research in the consumer behaviour discipline that developed Gronmo's call for a broader and more multi dimensional theorisation of time. More specifically we looked for work that developed Gronmo's call for attention to social temporality. The two major pieces of work that have used the concept of social temporality are Szmigin and Carrigan's (2001) study of elderly consumers and Thompson's (1996) study cited above, of the juggling lifestyle of working mothers. Szmigin and Carrigan (2001) argue that very little research indeed has been done in consumer behaviour discipline regarding time as a social concept embedded within particular social and cultural groups, citing only their own and Thompson's study.

Both the Szmigin and Carrigan (2001) and Thompson (1996) articles utilize Dapkus' (1985) phenomenological framework of time experiences to organize their analyses. However, both use this framework only as a methodological and analysis organizing tool, neither develop any further time and consumption based theory. Moreover, both articles, as they rely on Dapkus phenomenological approach, cannot extend the theory of time beyond the mechanical model. Phenomenology, because of its focus on pure experience takes linearity (as a key element of participant narratives) for granted. As a result, although the work is "social" in its approach, the concept of time per se, remains as a mechanical, economic, linear and fundamentally objective concept.

Given the lack of theoretical development of this area and order to develop the theoretical contribution of this work, there is a requirement to go outside the discipline of consumer research and examine how time is being conceptualized in sociology and cultural theory, particularly how time is being used to theorize family life and the case of peer families. Although, as posited by Weik (2004) "many authors in the field of sociology and social theory have integrated temporal features into their theories, there is still a lack of theories based on time" and Torres (2007) complains of the "theoretical shortfall" with regard to time in the social sciences, one theory has emerged concerning the highly complex experience of time and the management of work and home by professional couples. This is the theory of "the extended present" (Brennan 2002, 2005). Time as the extended present, is not a linear and measurable construct, but rather a subjective experience. Analysing the extended present means focusing upon the nature and intensity of the time experienced, and how time itself is constructed through activities, practices and experiences. In the extended present, there is a heightened sense of the present, and the past and future are backgrounded and often distorted (Brown 1998). In the extended present the focus is on the here and now, activities are viewed in relation to the present, not the long term future, work/home times and practices become fragmented, entwined, complex and multiple and not easily explained in terms of simple "time scarcity". "The extended present" has three characteristics, outlined by Brennan and Nilsen (1994) *time simultaneity, time compression* and *time autonomy*. *Time simultaneity* is the experience and management of "multiple times". This might be expressed in terms of the practice of multi-tasking, but is more akin to simultaneously managing different worlds with highly different time bases and expectations. *Time compression* is the feeling that more and more tasks have to be concentrated into a shorter time period, but also that there is a requirement to be ultimately flexible to any unexpected occurrence in the present time. In time compression, people are constantly switched on and available for action demanded from many different (and often incommensurate) sources. *Time autonomy* is the state of being self managing in terms of time, but that this self management extends into a timetabling of every waking moment, there is a sense with time autonomy that one can manage ones own time, but that the tasks are potentially never ending, and there is no "off-time" without awareness of things that need to be done.

The extended present as a theory provided an interesting way to organise our initial analysis, and certainly went beyond the previous analyses of time in consumer research. In terms of the negativity presented in research on peer families it provides an alternative viewpoint. Living in the extended present is not simply dystopian or utopian but shows multiple heterotopias of temporality that peer families have to manage, and live within. However, although this is undoubtedly useful, it still adheres to a basic ontology of time as an objective 'thing' to be managed, and relies heavily on the typical economic metaphors of the mechanical conceptualisation of time. We felt that the behaviour of our respondents required more dimensionality of analysis, respondents were not slaves to time, just 'coping with' time and 'managing' time, they were far more active in their negotiations. Parents were 'enacting' time, engaging in consumption practices to actively slow down and speed up time in the present. This points to not only the different conditions that structure time, but to a different ontology of time. The challenge here, then, is how to theorise time in a way that avoids the traps of the mechanical conceptualisation that positions peer families in this simplistic way.

Beginning with the extended present as a starting point begins to address the ontological traps of prior analyses in that its focus is on "the present" rather than presenting some kind of temporal progress narrative. In studies of time and discourse, Cooren *et al* (2005:265) also begin with this starting point but add the ontological progression of enactment to their analysis arguing that, "the structuration of time occurs through the articulation of different agents *doings*" (emphasis ours). In other words, they analyse time not as something external, to be managed, spent and saved, but as a discursive achievement or enactment within specific social settings. The authors argue that in these discursive analyses of time, the past, present and future are simultaneously embedded within the discursive event of the research situation, and their analytical focus is on the processes of engagement and disengagement that indicates enactment of these different time "zones", not as things in themselves, but as produced in the present. This analytical focus and ontological approach can be applied to this analysis concerning enactment not of past present and future in the present, but as enactment of different concepts of time itself. This analytical focus of the present oriented enactment of different concepts of time within very specific research settings and research moments we have called "a present location of temporal embeddedness".

EMPIRICAL EXAMPLE

From Coping with Time to Enacting Time: A Present Location of Temporal Embeddedness in Peer Families

Speeding up time: consuming surrogates, 'not doing' and the Taylorisation of the home

Theorists have discussed how the management of home and work for dual career parents has led to a 'Taylorisation' (Hochschild 1997, Lyon and Woodward 2004) of the home and there was some evidence for this in our interpretations. Taylorisation (Taylor 1911) is associated with mass production methods in manufacturing and is better known as scientific management. The basic premise is to discover the most efficient way to do particular work tasks to improve productivity . This sort of task-oriented optimization is found in manufacturing (E.g. production lines) and in services (E.g.fast food resaurants). Taylorisation is based upon a highly masculinised conceptualisation of time (Odih 1999), as it is measurable, linear, commodifible and instrumental, and thus, this Taylorisation of the home has been seen as running counter to trandtional feminine time conceptualisations of family life

(Hochschild 1997, Tietze and Musson 2002). There was some evidence to support the idea that some aspects of home life were being 'Taylorised' as a way to speed up time and increase efficiency through specific consumption related practices.

One of the ways that this was being managed was by a compartmentalising of certain 'drudge' tasks that required little thought, as Angela explains

Domestic mamagement, the real boring repetitive stuff, the ironing, the washing etc. is a real bone of contention. I hate the chores, I hate laundry and the the endless repetitive trips upstairs, empty the airing cupboard, put stuff away, fill it with new things, put another wash on…and then you look around and the linen basket is full…(Angela Academic)

Parents used various strategies to speed up the time these tasks took. Sharing of tasks was one route that respondents took to increase efficiency. It was clear from the data that although some sharing of some tasks was being used as a way to speed up time, management of this still usually fell to the woman, for example in organising slots of time for the man to contribute and in the case of men's data, discourses of helping the wife were common, which did not go unnoticed…

(my wife) will prompt me by saying the bath hasn't been cleaned for ages which usually means Charles go and clean the bath and ill do it… (Charles Scientist)

I feel like I'm dragging my husband like a donkey, and he has said on occasion "I'll help you out, I'll help you out by cleaning the bath" and I always make a big fuss about it because there is no 'helping me out' to it! We live here its two adults , you and me…(Lianne A Level Teacher)

Some women in the sample resented this bitterly, and it was obviously a cause for contention for both parties. As a result, they had to find other ways of offloading routine chores, and one of the ways they did this was through the consumption of 'domestic surrogates' in the form of paid help, or outsourcing. Consumption of surrogates was an important time linked consumption practice for these parents. Largely, it was the mother that organised these surrogates.

I manage it…its amazes me how much time that takes. So I organise that the washing is done, to leave out in the basket so that (the cleaner) can take it out and iron it, and I tidy up so that it isn't too bad when she is trying to clean (Eleanor, Senior Education Manager)

This phenomenon of doing domestic tasks for the surrogate was very common, especially cleaning before the cleaner arrives. Further to this, the mother often paid for the surrogates out of her own salary.

A further strategy deployed by respondents to speed up time was 'not doing'. Many reported having 'dropped their standards' by simply not engaging in particular activities.

The house gets cleaned only when people are coming, because something has to give. I know that I can't do everything… (Sonia, nurse manager)

It became clear through the analysis of the data that there was evidence to suggest that the home had become 'Taylorised', although it was much more complex than it might first appear. Clearly, the women in the study felt under more pressure than the men to be more efficient in the home and reported that they used skills developed in the workplace to speed time up significantly. Tasks *were* more shared, but the traditional model of the family seemed to impinge upon the women more strongly. The discourses emerging from the men in the study (and quite a few of the women) of *helping* and responsibility indicated that in the main, however equitable the task allocation was, the implication was that in 2004, a was found in the 1980s by Coltrane (1989), management of the home was still largely the woman's domain.

Slowing down the extended present: slow parenting and the subversion of speed

What became clear in terms of the Taylorisation of the home thesis is that it applied to very specific tasks and activities. In relation to other activities it did not hold. The respondents appeared to have selected certain practices which were subject to a *slowing down* of time linked to heightened and meaningful experiences. The slowing of time has been described as *'conscious negotiation of the different temporalities which make up our everyday lives deriving from a commitment to occupy time more attentively…a deliberate subversion of the dominance of speed'* (Parkins 2004). We felt that this described other practices the parents were doing in contrast to the 'speeding up' of time. This could not be conceptualised as simply 'saving time' to get 'free time' but in terms of spending time differently, slowly and meaningfully. Urry (2000) has argued that choosing slowness over speed equals a heightened sensory or aesthetic experience. In terms of time linked consumption practices, this became another important area for our analysis.

Parents were slowing time using very specific time linked consumption practices that were often described in terms of *'real parenting'*. Often these activities were highly time consuming, for example, Angela, an academic recalled how she made some sugar mice for her daughter's birthday:

She had seen the picture of these mice in a children's magazine about a mouse who is a ballet dancer, and she wanted them for her birthday party. I had never done anything like that and I had no idea how difficult it would be. Fortunately, we had a 'dry run' in advance of the day, because it took me several goes to get it right. The first couple of tries just produced a sticky mess; you certainly couldn't shape a mouse out of it. Anyway I looked through some old cookery books and I found a recipe for peppermint creams which were similar. And it turned out that the magazine had got the quantities wrong, so no wonder it didn't work. So I tried again and this time I got it right and I was able to make these little mice, and I put icing roses for ears, and pink liquorice tails and little silver balls for the eyes. And when the actual birthday came, I knew I could do it and they were perfect, and my daughter was so pleased, and that made it all worthwhile (Angela Academic)

Sometimes these time linked consumption practices were linked to special purchases. However, we must make it clear here that in all cases this did not extend to the consumption of expensive toys or over consumption. Sophie, a solicitor, preferred her son to involve himself in creative play, rather then relying on expensive presents to keep him entertained.

I've never thought that as far as my son is concerned he must have x, y and z just because I didn't have it as a child. It is quite the reverse, I don't want him to be spoilt…(Sophie Solicitor)

Special purchases seemed to be not hugely expensive or extravagant, but imbued with particular meaning and usually this was meaning that could be linked to 'slow' parenting practices.

I was really busy, away on business and I wanted to buy her these special pyjamas, ones you could get in New York but no where else I had seen them the last time I was away and told her about them…well I hunted all day and finally I found these b**** things I couldn't remember… Anyway it was all worth it when I saw her little face. My job is putting her to bed in the evening and we get the pyjamas and make sure the fairy on them is smiling…we get so much fun out of them in the evening, the fairy reads the book and whispers to me… (Peter Accountant)

Peter emphasised here that his purchase was not to compensate for him being away, but to enjoy his parenting on his return. His explanation of this was that compensation, for him meant the father perfunctorily buying toys and sending the child away to play with them. For Peter, the pleasure of these consumption activities were in facilitating a special 'slow' parenting time that had a high cost in terms of time he could spend doing other activities..

This slowing of time for parenting included aspects of parenting and consumption which were quite surprising given the degree of disposable income that this group often had access to. For example, going to the library seemed to be considered a much more rewarding parenting practice than buying books for many of the parents even though this was much more time consuming for them. This indicated for us an important aspect of these activities which was not that the respondents were slowing time to do less, but slowing time to do *more*, often highly labour intensive practices. An example of this concerned food consumption as part of parenting.

Although most parents used 'convenience' foods there seemed to be a commitment to eat better and to feed children in a more natural way at least some of the time. Organic foods were often mentioned as well as home made baby food and 'proper' family meals. This was an aspect of consumption activity that fathers seemed happier to be involved with and enjoyed the preparation of some meals which became complex time linked consumption practices. This father explains…

What I do enjoy is at the weekend there is a market in the town, often a French market and we go down and choose nice veg and go to the butchers for meat and the deli for nice bits then I cook a lovely meal for the family on Saturday evening. It is a special time now that they are getting a little bit older. They learn about things…what kind of things err well…we were looking at celeriac, it is so ugly why would you want to eat it but it tastes lovely so you have to get them over the ugliness of it…they did eat it (laughter) its important that they understand how…how to eat actually (James Senior Manager)

One of the important aspects of this 'slow parenting' was that the fathers, like James above, actively sought these time linked consumption practices as a way to significantly develop the parent-child relationship. All of the fathers in the study exhibited high levels of commitment to developing this key relationship, often over and above the commitment to the relationship with their wives/partners. Parents might experience conflict over who is responsible for the rationalised, 'Taylorised', mundane tasks, but where these special 'relationship forming' times were concerned both parents wanted to engage in them. Parents were prepared to expend signifi-

FIGURE 1
Gronmo's Model of relationships between time concepts
(From Gronmo 1989)

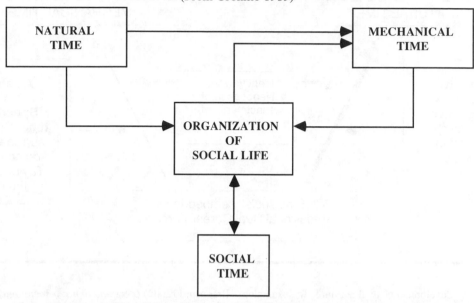

cant amounts of time and energy, often mediated through specific consumption practices as has been illustrated above.

MODELLING THE PRESENT LOCATION OF TEMPORAL EMBEDDEDNESS: A RETURN TO GRONMO

As Knights (2006) has argued, one of the common problems shared by mechanical models of time, and research which takes an oppositional stance to that conceptualisation of time and instead utilise the theory of social time is that both still adhere to a concept of time that is basically essentialist, external, objective and linear. Neither approach appreciates the social processes through which alternative conceptions of time are enacted. It is certainly the case, as argued above, that the scant literature using the concept of social time in consumer research does not consider these issues. In the analysis above, we have gone beyond the idea of both social time as it is conceptualised in consumer research and the extended present, demonstrating instead how parents are actively enacting different time concepts to create a 'present location of temporal embeddedness' where time is enacted or discursively constituted in particular ways. This conceptualisation does not rest ontologically upon the concept of time as essential, objective and linear but as enacted, subjective, socially and discursively embedded and 'in the present'.

Developing Gronmo's model (Figure 1) we will develop a model of the "present location of temporal embeddedness" in peer families that represents the research above. Gronmo's initial model is a very useful model to begin with, as it already admits the existence of multiple time concepts and that these are interconnected and impact upon one another.

For Gronmo, the organisation of social life is based upon a negotiation between what he calls 'natural time' and 'mechanical time'. Mechanical time has already been defined, natural time is dictated by changes and rhythms in nature, social or familial processes and is cyclical. This negotiation results in social time/ social temporality which is the focus of analysis he calls for in consumer research. It is quite easy to make the connections between our analysis of slowing down and speeding up time with these categories. Natural time is most often associated with the home, motherhood and nurturing and mechanical time is most often associated with work. Where we depart from Gronmo is that rather than social time being the outcome of a negotiation between natural and mechanical time, in our model (Figure 2) social time, or rather the social embeddedness of time (in this case within the context of peer marriage) enacts natural and mechanical time concepts in specific ways.

In our research, thinking about our data in terms of the present location of temporal embeddedness allowed us to develop our analysis into the realms of asking what is being achieved in these social settings, what is being enacted, achieved and mobilised through these enactments of time. In the model we show how the embeddedness of enactments of time focus around complex enacted negotiations between natural and mechanical time where natural time is privileged through slowing down and mechanical time is de-emphasised by speeding it up. We concluded that these discursive strategies reflect a social setting in which the actual parameters of parenting itself is being redefined. Parents are actively securing their identity as 'good parents' through their enactment of time and furthermore 'being a good parent' is being achieved in the research setting through these complex time enactments. There is a clear speeding up and de emphasis of tasks not directly connected with active parenting experiences and a slowing down of heightened parenting engagements with children.

Further to this, within this shared discursive achievement of being a good parent there are quite clear battlegrounds associated with the enactment of each time concept. Power and gender roles are quite clearly evident and being played out across the enactment of these times. One of the most important findings of the research concerns the changing roles of fathers within peer families. Our research found that fathers emphasised relationship forming times with their children (as reported above) This was an important finding for this research, fathers as well as mothers wanted to invest a significant amount of time and emotional capital to develop close relationships with their children, and these were often mediated through consumption practices. As well as being a source of pleasure for the fathers, they often discussed this in terms having

FIGURE 2

The present location of temporal embeddedness in professional dual career families

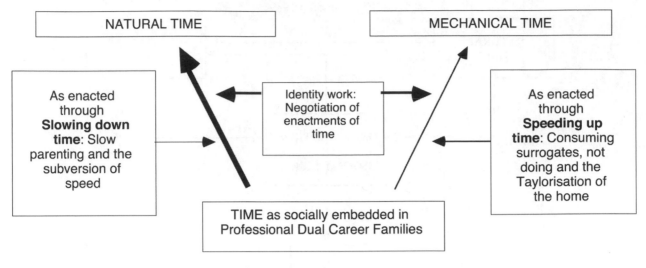

choices removed by developments in the future, for example, redundancy or divorce. Fathers seemed to want significant parenting time at least partly as a response to uncertainty over their roles in the future of their children's lives.

Mothers in our study focused on the other time concept, which as can be seen from the empirical example became a battleground not only over who was doing these mundane everyday tasks, but over the actual conceptualisation of what is 'is to be a mother' in peer families. There are clear battle lines being drawn over tasks such as cleaning the bath, which the father quite proudly admits that he does "to help his wife", and the mother then has to remind him that his language assumes the task is owned by her and she has to strongly resist that. This shows production and reproduction of gender within the peer family. This illustrates the importance of looking at this phenomenon through this particular ontological lens, and demonstrating how whereas experience based research might report that tasks are shared and gender discrimination in peer families is being eroded, discursive analysis instead shows that the task is still discursively constituted as a female one, and presumably then, one that is still ultimately the mother's responsibility!

In conclusion, our model of the present location of temporal embeddedness in professional dual career families shows these families actively using time enactment of different time concepts and actively slowing and speeding up the time/s associated with each concept. Time enactments are used as a discursive resource to cope with a highly complex life situation, as parents try to make their identities 'as parents' coherent but also use these time enactments to help negotiate and renegotiate power charged gender and parenting roles.

REFERENCES

Adam, B (1995) *Time watch: the social analysis of time.* Cambridge Polity Press

Bergadaa, M (1990) "The role of time in the action of the consumer," *Journal of Consumer Research* 17 (December) pp 33-42.

Bernandes, J. (1997) *Family Studies, An Introduction*, London, Routledge.

Bird, Gloria W. & Schnurman-Crook, Abrina (2005) "Professional Identity and Coping Behaviors in Dual-Career couples." *Family Relations* 54 (1), 145-160.

Brannen, J (2002) *Lives and times: a sociological journey*, London Institute of Education.

Brannen, J (2005) "Time and the negotiation of work/family boundaries: autonomy illusion?" *Time and Society* 14/1 pp 113-131.

Brown, A (1998) "'Doing Time': The Extended Present of the Long-Term Prisoner," *Time & Society*, Vol. 7, No. 1, 93-103.

Carrigan, M and Szmigin, I (2004) "Time uncertainty and the expectancy experience: an interpretive exploration of consumption and impending motherhood," *Journal of Marketing Management* 20 p771.

Commuri, Suraj and James W. Gentry (2000), "Opportunities for family research in marketing," *Academy of Marketing Science Review*, http://www.amsreview.org.

Commuri, S and Gentry, J (2005) "Resource Allocation in Households with Women as Chief Wage Earner," *Journal of Consumer Research*. Gainesville: Sep 2005.Vol.32, Iss. 2; pp185, 11 pgs.

Daly, K (1996) *Families and time: keeping pace with a hurried culture*. London Sage.

Dapkus, M. A. (1985). "A thematic analysis of the experience of time." *Journal of Personality and Social Psychology*, 49(2), 408–419.

Darier, E (1998) "Time to be lazy: work, the environment and subjectivities," *Time and Society* 7/2 pp 193-208.

Karin M. Ekstrom (2005), "Roundtable: Rethinking Family Consumption By Tracking new Research Perspectives," in *Advances in Consumer Research* Volume 32, eds. Geeta Menon and Akshay R. Rao, Duluth, MN: Association for Consumer Research, Pages: 493.

Felstead, A and Jewson, N (2000) *In work at home: towards an understanding of home working*. London Routledge

Foster, I.R. and Olshavsky, R.W. (1989), "An Exploratory Study of Family Decision Making Using a New Taxonomy of Family Role Structure," in *Advances in Consumer Research* Volume 16, eds. Thomas K. Srull, Provo, UT: Association for Consumer Research, Pages: 665-670.

Foxman,E and Burns AC (1987), "Role Load in the Household," in *Advances in Consumer Research* Volume 14, eds. Melanie Wallendorf and Paul Anderson, Provo, UT: Association for Consumer Research, Pages: 458-462.

Gatrell, C (2005) *Hard labour, The Sociology of Parenthood*, Maidenhead, Open University Press.

James W. Gentry, Lee Phillip McGinnis (2003), "Doing Gender in the Family Household Production Issues," in *Advances in Consumer Research* Volume 30, eds. Punam Anand Keller and Dennis W. Rook, Valdosta, GA: Association for Consumer Research, Pages: 309-313.

Gentry, J, Joag, S anf Ekstrom, K. "The Role of Goals in Family decision making," *Asia Pacific Advances in Consumer Research* Volume 2, Pp 93-99.

Gross, B (1987) "Time scarcity, interdisciplinary perspectives and implications for consumer behaviour," In Sheth and Hirschman (Ed) *Research in Consumer Behaviour* 2 pp 1-54.

Hassard, J (2002) "Essai: Organisational time: modern symbolic and postmodern reflections," *Organisation Studies* 23/6 pp885-892.

Hochschild, A (1997) *The time bind: when home becomes work and work becomes home*. Henry Holt CA.

Hogg, M, Curasi, C and Maclaran, P (2004) "The (re-)configuration of production and consumption in empty nest households/families," *Consumption, Markets and Culture* 7/3 pp 239-259.

Holt, D (1995) "How consumers consume: a typology of consumption practices," *Journal of Consumer Research* 22/1 pp 1-16.

Johnston, D and Swanson, D (2003) "Invisible mothers: a content analysis of motherhood ideologies and myths in magazines," *Sex Roles: a journal of research* 49/1-2 pp 21-33.

F. A. Johnson, E. A. Kaplan, and E. J. Tusel, "Sexual Dysfunction in the 'Two-Career' Family," *Medical Aspects of Human Sexuality*, XIII(January, 1979), 7-17.

Kahne, H (1981), "Women in Paid Work: Some Consequences and Questions for Family Income and Expenditures," in *Advances in Consumer Research* Volume 08, eds. Kent B. Monroe, Ann Abor: Association for Consumer Research, Pages: 585-589.

Kohen, JA (1981), "Housewives, Breadwinners, Mothers, and Family Heads: The Changing Family Roles of Women," in *Advances in Consumer Research* Volume 08, eds. Kent B. Monroe, Ann Abor: Association for Consumer Research, Pages: 576-579.

Lyon, D and Woodward, A (2004) "Gender and Time at the top," *European Journal of Women's studies* 11/2 pp205-221

Mangleburg, T.F. Grewal, Bristol, D.T. (1999), Family Type, Family Authority Relations, and Adolescents' Purchase Influence," in *Advances in Consumer Research* Volume 26, eds. Eric J. Arnould and Linda M. Scott, Provo, UT: Association for Consumer Research, Pages: 379-384.

Miller, D (1998), *A Theory of Shopping*, Ithaca, New York: Cornell University Press.

Nowotny, H (1994) *Time: the modern and postmodern experience*. Cambridge Polity Press.

Macran, S., Joshi, H. and Dex, S. (1996) "Employment after childbearing: a survival analysis," *Work, Employment and Society*, 10: 273–296.

Odih, P (1999) "Gender time in the age of deconstruction," *Time and Society* 8/1 pp9-38.

Parkin, W (2004) "Out of time: fast subjects and slow living," *Time and Society* 13/2-3 pp 363-382.

Price, L. L. and Epp, A.M. (2005), "Special Session Summary: Finding Families: Family Identity in Consumption Venues," in *Advances in Consumer Research* Volume 32, eds. Geeta Menon and Akshay R. Rao, Duluth, MN: Association for Consumer Research, Pages: 9-13.

Pullinger, J. and Summerfield, C. (1998) *Social Focus on Women and Men, Office for National Statistics*, London: The Stationery Office.

Qualls, WJ (1982), "Changing Sex Roles: Its Impact Upon Family Decision Making," in *Advances in Consumer Research* Volume 09, eds. Andrew Mitchell, Ann Abor: Association for Consumer Research, Pages: 267-270.

R. Rapoport and R. N. Rapoport, "The Dual-Career Family," *Human Relations*, XXI I (No. 1, 1969), 3-30.

Rindfleisch, A, Burroughs, J and Denton, F. (1997) "Family structure, materialism, and compulsive consumption," *Journal of Consumer Research* 23 (4): 312-325.

Rudd, J (1987), "The Household as a Consuming Unit," in *Advances in Consumer Research* Volume 14, eds. Melanie Wallendorf and Paul Anderson, Provo, UT: Association for Consumer Research, Pages: 451-452.

Runte, M and Mills A (2004) "Paying the toll: a feminist post structuralist critique of the discourse bridging home and family," *Culture and Organisation* 10/3 pp237-249

Schaninger, Charles M. and William D. Danko (1993), "A Conceptual and Empirical Comparison of Alternative Household Life Cycle Models," *Journal of Consumer Research*, 19 (March), 580-594.

Southerton, D. and Tomlinson, M. (2005) "'Pressed for time'-the differential impacts of a 'time squeeze'," *Sociological Review* 53 (2): 215-239.

Southerton, D (2003) "Squeezing time: allocating practices, coordinating networks and scheduling society," *Time and Society* 12/1 pp 9-25.

Stephens, D, Hill, R.P., Commuri, S., and Gentry, J.W. (2001) "Issues of control in two extreme household types," *Asia Pacific Advances in Consumer Research* Volume 4 pp. 355-361.

Sullivan, O (2000) "The division of domestic labour: 20 years of change?" *Sociology* 34, 537-546.

Taylor, F (1911) *The principles of scientific management*, New York, Harper.

Thair, T. and Risdon, A. (1999) "Women in the Labour Market," Results from the Spring 1998 *Labour Force Survey, Labour Market Trends, Office for National Statistics* 107:103–128.

Tietze, S and Musson, G (2002) "When work meets home: temporal flexibility as lived experience," *Time and Society* 11/2-3 pp315-334.

Thompson, C.J. (1996) "Caring consumers: gendered consumption meanings and the juggling lifestyle," *Journal of Consumer Research* (22) March.

The Feeling of Love Toward a Brand: Concept and Measurement

Noel Albert, CERAG and WESFORD, France
Dwight Merunka, University Paul Cezanne Aix-Marseille (IAE-CERGAM) and Euromed Marseille, France
Pierre Valette-Florence, IAE and CERAG, France

Since the 90's, research concerning brands has strongly developed and notably the brand-consumer relationship or consumer connections to brands thematics through constructs such as brand trust, brand commitment or brand loyalty (Chaudhuri and Holbrook, 2001; Fournier, 1998; Fournier and Yao, 1997; Samuelsen and Sandvik, 1998). Among these different constructs, the feeling of love toward a brand appears to be recent and researchers (Ahuvia, Bagozzi and Batra, 2007; Caroll and Ahuvia, 2006; Whang and al., 2004) and pratitioners (Roberts, 2006) manifest their interest for this novel construct when applied to objects or brands.

First investigations concerning the brand love construct dealt with the definition and conceptualization of the construct (Shimp and Madden, 1988; Ahuvia, 1993). More recent research aims at measuring the feeling of love a consumer might hold for a brand (Caroll and Ahuvia, 2006). This research current leads to a better understanding of the non-interpersonal love feeling and to more managerial relevance. Uncovering and measuring dimensions of love and consequences of love for a brand may help managers in the definition of their brand strategies.

This research focuses on the measurement of the love construct. It points to conceptual limitations in love scales available in marketing and develops, tests and validates a new scale to apprehend the feeling of love toward a brand. This scale leads to a better understanding of consumer brand relationships. This article is composed of two parts. In the first section, we discuss the state of the art in consumer love literature pertaining to three main domains: (a) conceptualizations of the love construct in a marketing context, (b) limitations in the studies of love in marketing, and (c) measurement issues linked to the two brand love scale currently available in a marketing context. In the second part we present the construction of the proposed new love scale, from exploratory studies to the dimensionality of the brand love scale and the presentation of its reliability and validity assessments.

CONCEPTUALIZATIONS AND MEASUREMENTS OF THE FEELING OF LOVE TOWARDS A BRAND

Main conceptualizations of love in marketing

The first authors introducing the feeling of love in marketing are Shimp and Madden (1988). They adapt in a marketing context the interpersonal love theory of Stenberg (1986) named the Triangular theory of love. The three dimensions of love (passion, intimacy and decision/commitment) are slightly transformed in a consumption context and become: yearning, liking and decision/commitment. The presence, or not, of these components in a brand-consumer context lead to 8 different relationships (Nonliking, Liking, Infatuation, Functionalism, Inhibited Desire, Utilitarianism, Succumbed Desire, Loyalty). Ahuvia (1993, 2005a, 2005b) also thoroughly study the concept of love applied to various object categories (places, ideas, pets, consumption objects, etc.). According to him, the feeling of love toward an object is composed of 12 characteristics (excellence, irreplaceability, sense of meaning, etc.). This early work enables better understanding the meaning of the love feeling toward an object. However, it also contains some conceptual problems and limitations. For example, Ahuvia (1993) considers satisfaction or well-being as dimensions of the love feeling whereas these constructs are usually considered as outputs or consequences of interpersonal love (see for example Hendrick, Hendrick and Adler (1988) for satisfaction and Kim and Hatfield (2004) for well being).

Ahuvia (1993) proposes a conditional integration theory to explain the feeling of love toward an object. The starting point of Ahuvia's thesis is the Aron and al. (1986) theory who claim that love is the inclusion of others in the self. He distinguishes two kinds of variables linked to the self: the actual level of integration into the self and the desired level of integration into the self. Ahuvia (1993, p. 87) explains that : « *Love then, can be defined as the situation in which both the desired and the actual level of integration are high*". Later, Ahuvia (2005b) compares interpersonal love and the feeling of love toward an object. Results of this comparison indicate that they have more common points (the lover finds the object attractive, the object provides something the lover wants or needs, a sense of natural fit, love is enduring, etc.) than differences (non-presence of negative emotions in love for objects, self sacrifice). Whang and al. (2004) measure the feeling of love of bikers toward their motorcycles using an interpersonal love scale that they apply without adaptation (that of Hendrick and Hendrick, 1986). Results indicate that bikers love for their machines is made of passion (Eros), possessiveness (Mania) and altruism (Agape). Caroll and Ahuvia (2006, p.5) define brand love as: "*the degree of passionate emotional attachment a satisfied consumer has for a particular trade name*". According to those authors, five caracteritics describe brand love: (1) passion for the brand, (2) attachment for the brand, (3) positive evaluation of the brand, (4) positive emotions in response to the brand and (5) declaration of love for the brand. This helps us understand what the feeling of love is in a consumption context. Nevertheless those studies have some important limitations.

Limits of the study of love in a marketing context

We identify three main limitations in the studies of love in marketing: theoritical, methodological and managerial.

Theoretical limitations: two main frameworks are currently used to approach the brand love feeling. Some studies specifically rely on one interpersonal love theory and apply it in the marketing context (Ahuvia, 1993; Shimp and Madden, 1988; Whang and al., 2004). Love is a complex feeling and phenomenon and it seems difficult to claim that an interpersonal theory will capture all of this particular feeling when applied to objects or brands. Moreover, selecting one of the available interpersonal theories and adapting it to marketing also means not taking into account the findings from other studies in the search of the understanding of love. Another approach is characterized by the fact that authors do not refer to any interpersonal theories on love (Fournier, 1998). These studies may be deemed a-theoritical and may lead to some problematic interpretations. For example, why are intimacy, commitment and integration to the brand proposed by Fournier (1998) not linked to the passion/love dimension as it is in interpersonal theories (e.g.: Sternberg, 1986; Aron et al., 1986)?

Methodological limitations: Some authors explicitly use the term "love" during their qualitative interviews and indicate it may help understanding the prototype of love (Ahuvia, 1993, 2005b).

Advances in Consumer Research
Volume 36, © 2009

However, the explicit use of the word "love" may well introduce an important bias. The responses of the respondents may well be made with reference to their conceptualization of interpersonal love, since the concept of love in memory is more strongly linked to interpersonal concepts than to brand or object concepts (Fehr and Russel, 1991). Moreover, this method probably falls short of enabling to uncover specific brand love dimensions since the dominant pattern in memory is undoubtedly that of interpersonal love.

Managerial limitations: Many authors have worked on the feeling of love applied to objects (Ahuvia, 1993, 2005b; Shimp and Madden, 1998; Whang et al., 2004). From a brand management standpoint, these studies may be limited since objects can be diverse from pets to homes and places. We believe more interesting to propose a love scale applied to brands with a clear concept of a brand such as defined by many authors (Keller, 2007). New developments in the field of love towards brands should try to circumvent these limitations.

1.2. Brand love measurement scales.

We present the two brand love scales currently available in marketing and point to some limitations.

Caroll and Ahuvia's Brand Love Scale (2006)

Caroll and Ahuvia (2006) propose a brand love scale composed of ten items composing a unique dimension. The items are: (1) this is a wonderful brand; (2) this brand makes me feel good; (3) this brand is totally awesome; (4) I have neutral feelings about this brand (reverse-coded item); (5) this brand makes me very happy; (6) I love this brand; (7) I have no particular feelings about this brand (reverse-coded item); (8) this brand is a pure delight; (9) I am passionate about this brand; (10) I am very attached to this brand. The important question concerning this scale is its claimed unidimensionality. Firstly, in the interpersonal love literature, love is generally presented as a multidimensional construct (Hatfield, 1988; Sternberg, 1986). Secondly, examining the items of the scale questions its possible unidimensionality. Items composing the scale carry different meanings (passion, happiness, attachment, well being, etc.) and probably favor multidimensionality. Also, passion and attachment which here belong to the scale and therefore to the same dimension are considered as two different dimensions or steps in interpersonal love theories (Hatfield, 1988; Sternberg, 1986).

The Thomson, MacInnis and Whan Park Brand Love Scale (2005)

The second scale in marketing which may be used to measure a love feeling towards brands is that of Thomson et al. (2005). This scale is remarkably constructed and tested from a methodological standpoint. However, while the authors label the construct to be measured as '*Emotional Attachment*', we contend that the proposed scale deals more with the love construct than the attachment construct. In particular, the conceptualisation of '*attachment*' integrates here the dimension of "*passion*". Beyond rare exceptions, the attachment component of a love relationship does not include the passion dimension (Hatfield, 1988; Baumeister et al., 1999; Fisher, 2006). With the inclusion in the scale of the "*Passion*" dimension (one dimension out of three, the two others being Affection and Connection), and the use of the item "*Loved*" which belongs to the Affection dimension, we believe that the construct studied and measured is similar to that of Love. Dimensions and measurement items of the Thomson et al. scale are given in Figure 1.

From a conceptual standpoint, the two dimensions, Affection and Connexion are considered as a unique dimension in the interpersonal love literature. Affection is also called intimacy (Hatfield, 1988) or attachment (Fisher, 2006). Connection is generally con-

sidered as an element defining affection or intimacy. For example Sternberg (1997, p.315) defines intimacy as "(...) *feelings of closeness, connectedness, and bondedness in loving relationships*". According to Baumeister and Bratslavsky (1999, p.50): "*intimacy refers to the way the two people feel that they are close to the other*". Also, Hendrick and Hendrick (1983, p.18 cited by Baumeister and al., 1999) explain that: "*Intimacy means the degree of closeness two people achieve*". Recent findings on interpersonal love from neurosciences (Fisher, 2006) and social psychology (Hatfield, 1988) demonstrate that the feeling of love is composed of two dimensions: affection and passion. There is no mention of a connection dimension. Of course, the scale may be different because applied to brands. However these conceptual difference at least call for more research on the theme. Finally, there are important correlations between the three dimensions of the Thomson et al. (2005) scale. In study 4 of the research, the three dimensions have correlations superior to 0.72 (connection–passion: r=0.79; connection–affection: r=0.72; passion–affection: r=0.75) which we believe to be high and may question the dimensionality of the construct.

METHODOLOGY AND RESULTS

The scale construction is first detailed following procedures recommended by Churchill (1979). We then present the structure of the scale and its reliability and validity tests. Finally, we focus on the nomological validity of the love scale and its predictive validity of three common constructs: brand loyalty, brand trust and positive word of mouth.

2.1 Scale construction

We first present the procedures used to generate the items of the love scale. We show how the steps followed here attempt to overcome precedent limitations mentioned. We then present data collection procedures and data collected for the scale development.

Item generation

Two exploratory studies are conducted in order to understand the brand love construct and generate the items for the scale. These two studies (interviews and an internet survey) are designed to overcome limitations uncovered in previous research.

Seventeen structured interviews are conducted with 7 women and 10 men aged 19 to 59. During these interviews the word love is explicitly mentionned in order to help understanding the brand love prototype (Ahuvia, 1993, 2005b). However, this procedure may also impose a pre-established model of interpersonal love on the respondents. Therefore, we conduct an internet survey using projective methods and not mentioning the word "love". Nineteen pictures are chosen to represent brand consumer relationships and among the 19 images, three symbolize the feeling of love. We use different open-ended questions to understand brand consumer relationships without using the word love (e.g.: "*Why did you choose this image to represent your relationship with the brand?*", "*Is the brand special for you? If yes, please explain why?*").

In opposition to previous research (Ahuvia, 1993, 2005b; Whang et al., 2004) which applied one specific interpersonal theory to a marketing context, both studies conducted here are truly exploratory and no underlying theory was referred to. The exploratory dimensions obtained are confronted to the intersponal literature in order to retain only true dimensions of love and avoid selecting antecedents or consequences. This should enable to avoid conceptual limitations previously mentionned.

Data collection for scale development

For scale construction purposes, we integrate two categories of items: (1) items identified in our two exploratory studies and (2) items used in three interpersonal love scales. We select items from

FIGURE 1
Items and dimensions of brand love feeling (Thomson and al., 2005)

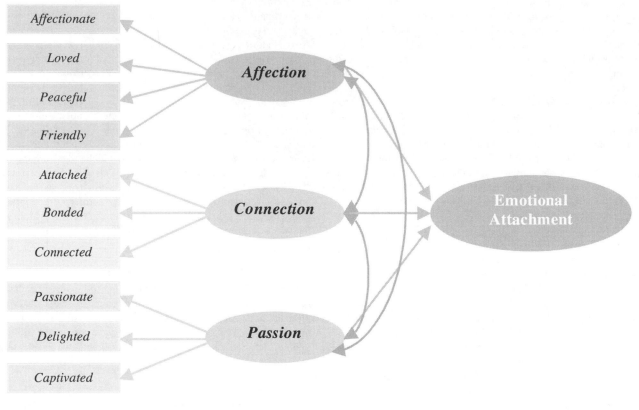

the Passionate Love Scale (Hatfield and Sprecher, 1986), the Triangular Theory Love Scale (Sternberg, 1986), and the Romantic Love Scale (Rubin, 1970) which are largely referred to in the love literature. A total of 248 items are used to construct the instrument. All those items are linked to the love feeling and include its dimensions, its antecedents and its consequences. Among those 248 items, 107 of them measured love dimensions. Respondents used a 10 points Likert scale, ranging from 1 (does not apply at all) to 10 (totally applies), to describe the extent to which the items could apply to the brand they chose for the survey.

The Internet survey offered 4 versions of the questionnaire in which the order of the items was randomized. We also developed a peper and pencil questionnaire. All in all, 825 fully completed questionaires were used for analysis. The final sample of respondents consists of 35.8% of men (64.2% women) with a majority of younger persons (66.3% less than 30 years of age). 43% are students, 23% executives, 17.8% employees. 65.6% of respondents are single and 25.6% are married. Table 1 presents the product categories and the 10 brands most mentioned by the participants.

Model

Exploratory and confirmatory analyses

We first conducted an exploratory Factor Analysis on the 107 items (corresponding to real love dimensions) and for the 825 observations. Items that refer to antecedents or consequences of the love feeling were not taking into account for scale construction. A

bootstrap analysis, based on 300 new samples, was used. Two kinds of items were eliminated at this step of the analysis. First, the items with a small loading or with cross loading on two or more factors. Items that correspond to constructs only related to love (i.e. its antecedents or consequences) were also eliminated from the analysis. The final set of items retained (22 items) reflected a seven-factor solution (see Table 3).

The structure uncovered for the brand love feeling is easy to understand and seems to offer a good description of the concept. In ordrer to check the validity of this solution, a set of CFA using structural equations modeling (SEM) was conducted. Table 2 presents the goodness of fit of the model which is satisfactory.

We now detail the 7 dimensions of the brand scale. The first factor indicates that the consumer considers the brand as unique and/or special ('*Uniqueness*'). The second factor highlights the pleasure given by the brand to the consumer ('*Pleasure*'). Items from interpersonal love compose the third factor which underlines the proximity between the consumer and its brand ('*Intimacy*'). The fourth factor ('*Idealization*') is also composed of interpersonal items. The long relationship between the consumer and the brand constitutes the fifth factor ('*Duration*'). The sixth factor represents important persons or events for the consumer and symbolized by the brand ('*Memories*'). Finally, the seventh factor translates the fact that the brand is present in the consumer's mind ('*Dream*'). The correlations between the factors are positive and significant. Beacause of the presence of interpersonal items in the scale ob-

TABLE 1
Brand and Product Categories

Brands	Nb	% cit.
Sony	24	14,1%
Apple	21	12,4%
Adidas	19	11,2%
L'Oreal	18	10,6%
Chanel	17	10,0%
Zara	17	10,0%
Esprit	15	8,8%
Nutella	14	8,2%
Audi	13	7,6%
BMW	12	7,1%

Product Categories	Nb	% obs.
Clothes	272	33,0%
Perfume	69	8,4%
Grocery	78	9,5%
Car	90	10,9%
Cosmetics	61	7,4%
Hi-fi/Audio/Vidéo	46	5,6%
Shoes	43	5,2%
Music	16	1,9%
Computers	36	4,4%
Lingerie	25	3,0%
Hygiene	17	2,1%
Various	49	5,9%

TABLE 2
Results of the AFC

Index	Results
RMSEA	0.08
GFI	0.91
AGFI	0.89

tained, the feeling of love towards a brand is identical or highly similar to an interpersonal love feeling as Whang and al. (2004) have already demonstrated.

Results also indicate the presence of two second order dimensions. The first second order dimension is linked with five first order factors (duration, dream, memories, intimacy and uniqueness). This factor is named '*Affection*'. The second factor is linked with the two last first order dimensions: idealization and pleasure. This second order factor is named '*Passion*'. Affection for the brand highlights a long relationship with the brand and the proximity between the consumer and the brand. The brand is perceived as unique by the consumer and the consumer often thinks about it. Passion for the brand is due to the idealization and pleasure provided to the consumer by the usage or possession of the brand. This second order solution is notably interesting with respect to the interpersonal love literature. Affection and Passion are present in numerous theories on the subject (Hatfield, 1988; Sternberg, 1986; Rubin, 1970). Moreover, neuroscience research (Fischer, 2006) also demonstrate that the love feeling is composed of the same two dimensions, passion and affection. Loadings between the factors of the first and second order are given in Figure 2.

Reliability

Scale's reliability is good as shown through the Joreskog coefficients. Six of the seven factors have a reliability coefficient superior to 0.7 and one factor has a reliability coefficient of 0.672 which can be judged satisfactory.

Convergent validity

We followed the The Fornell and Larcker (1981) recommendations for the estimation of convergent validity. Bootstraps analysis are used to compute the variance shared between each factor and its indicators. Results from Table 3 indicate good convergent validity for 5 of the 7 factors. Factors 4 and 5 exhibit a lower convergent validities (respectively 0.447 and 0.446) but it is still satisfactory, mainly due to the fact that the respective loadings are greater or equal to 0.63. All t tests are superior to 2, which confirms the good convergent validity of the scale.

Discriminant validity

The discriminant validity is tested by comparing the chi-square from a constrained model (factors' correlations constrained to one) to the chi-square from a free model (correlations between factors are free) (Bagozzi and Yi, 1991). The chi-square difference between the constrained model and the free model is always

FIGURE 2
Second order conceptualization of the brand love scale

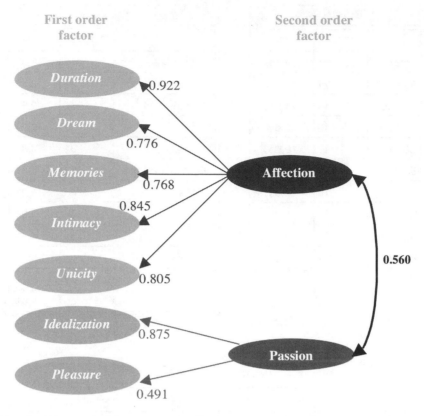

superior to the theoretical chi-square which confirms discriminant validity.

Nomological Validity

The love feeling is linked to a lot of different behaviors, emotions or feeling in the interpersonal relationship literature. In a consumption context, Caroll and Ahuvia (2006) demonstrate a positive direct effect of brand love on both loyalty and word of mouth. Thomson et al.'s (2005) emotional attachment construct is linked to four attachment behaviors (proximity maintenance, emotional security, safe haven, separation distress) and predicts brand loyalty and the willingness to pay a premium price. Our survey contains love items but also items which measure other constructs usually considered as outputs of love. We test the relation between the brand love scale uncovered and the constructs of brand trust, brand loyalty and positive word of mouth. The measurement of these constructs are ad hoc measurements since we did not use scales already tested in the literature but items about brand trust, brand loyalty and word of mouth that were identified in our exploraroty studies.

Several characteristics of passion could explain its link with positive word of mouth. According to Sternberg (1986) or Shimp and Madden (1988), the passion component of a romantic relationship leads to infatuation. Passion is also considered as the motivational dimension of love. Morever, Hatfield (1988) indicates that passion is characterized by excitation. Infatuation, motivation and excitation are supposed to be linked to positive word of mouth about

the brand. In a marketing context, Caroll and Ahuvia (2006) have demonstrated a positive link between brand love and positive word of mouth. Bauer and al. (2007) also demonstrate that brand passion influences word of mouth.

Loyalty has been defined as an element present in the description of affection love (Fehr, 1988) but loyalty is also not the same construct than love. Caroll and Ahuvia (2006) have demonstrated that brand love has a positif effect on brand loyalty. Consumers who feel affection for the brand are expected to be loyal to this brand.

Finally, we think that brand affection could explain brand trust. Trust has been often considered has an antecedent of attachment/affection (Palmentier and al., 2006). However, as Belaid and Bekhi (2008, p.8) explain: *"Trust is not necessarily a perequisite to brand attachment but it plays a main role in enhancing this affective bond. Moreover, brand attachment could reinforce brand trust."*. Love is a complex phenomenom and its relations with other constructs are usually hard to define. Hendrick, Hendrick and Adler (1988, p.981) indicate for the relation between love and satisfaction (one of love's consequence): *"However, process and outcome in a close personal relationship are part of the same feedback loop, with satisfaction in turn affecting the levels of love or investment that initially predicted satisfaction"*. The same phenomenon applies to the others antecedents and consequences of love. Consumers who feel affection for the brand are expected to trust the brand.

Results support our hypothesis. Passion is linked to positive word of mouth while affection is linked to brand trust and brand loyalty. In Table 4 are shown the loadings of the items measuring

TABLE 3

Loadings, Reliability and Convergent validity of the brand love scale

Factor	Items	Loadings (*t test>2*)	Reliability *Rho of Järeskog*	Convergent validity (*% of shared variance*)
Uniqueness	This brand is special	0.703	0.672	0.506
	This brand is unique	0.720		
Pleasure	By buying this brand, I take pleasure	0.845	0.822	0.538
	Discovering new products from this brand is a pure pleasure	0.718		
	I take a real pleasure in using this brand	0.612		
	I am always happy to use this brand	0.741		
Intimacy	I have a warm and comfortable relationship with this brand	0.752	0.771	0.530
	I feel emotionally close to this brand	0.694		
	I value this brand greatly in my life	0.736		
Idealization	There is something almost ' magical' about my relationship with this brand.	0.675	0.707	0.447
	There is nothing more important to me than my relationship with this brand	0.631		
	I idealize this brand	0.697		
Duration	(I feel that) this brand has accompanied me for many years	0.694	0.707	0.446
	I have been using this brand for a long time	0.670		
	I have not changed brand since long	0.638		
Memories	This brand reminds me someone important to me	0.825	0.856	0.666
	This brand reminds me memories, moments of my past (childhood, adolescence, a meeting, ...)	0.723		
	I associate this brand with some important events of my life	0.891		
Dream	This brand corresponds to an ideal for me	0.682	0.812	0.521
	I dream about that brand since long	0.682		
	This brand is a childhood dream	0.721		
	I dream (or have dreamt) to possess this brand	0.796		

each of the three constructs (word of mouth, brand trust and brand loyalty). Relationships between the two second order factors (Passion and Affection) and the three outcome variables are given in Figure 3.

DISCUSSION

Consumers may experiment a real feeling of love toward some brands as demonstrated in numerous research findings. Concerning the measurement of the love construct, two brand love scales have been developed but they are subject to conceptual limitations according the definition of love. The main objective of this research

is to propose a valid scale enabling measurement of the feeling of love towards a brand. The solution obtained is composed of 22 items and 7 first order dimensions: Uniqueness, Pleasure, Intimacy, Idealization, Duration, Dream and Memories. The seven factors offer a second order solution with two factors labelled Passion and Affection, which is consistent with the most recent findings on interpersonal love in social psychology and neuroscience. This validates the proposed scale from a conceptual standpoint. Our findings confirm that love towards a brand is highly similar to interpersonal love. Statistical analysis confirms the reliability, validity and the quality of the structure of the porposed model.

TABLE 4
Results from the CFA of the outcomes of the brand love feeling

	Items	Loadings (*t test>2*)	Reliability *Rho de Jöreskog*
Trust	This brand does not disappoint	0.411	0.576
	In the event of failure from the brand, I think I will forgive. Everyone can make mistakes	0.636	
	I have never been disappointed by this brand	0.619	
Word of Mouth	I defend this brand at any cost	0.712	0.801
	Sometimes I talk a lot about this brand	0.758	
	I think it is a good brand, I will recommend it to friends and family	0.658	
	I often speak about this brand	0.576	
Loyalty	I am loyal to this brand and I think I will be for a long time	0.740	0.764
	I am very loyal to the brand	0.709	
	I do not intend to switch to another brand	0.548	

FIGURE 3
Test of the nomological validity (path coefficient)

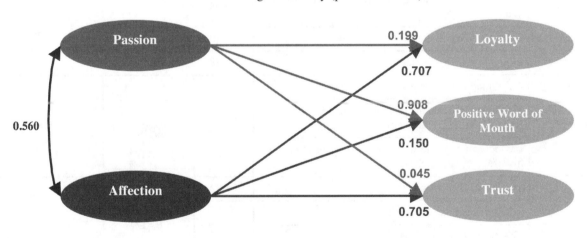

Finally, the brand love scale predicts three positive behaviors, namely Trust, positive word of mouth and loyalty. The use of the brand love scale may now help managers to detect consumers who feel love toward their brand, measure the importance and the dynamics of the phenomenon and help them propose adapted communications, loyalty programs or novel consumer segmentation schemes.

These interesting results must be tempered by some limitations. First, although the brand love scale predicts brand loyalty, brand trust and positive word of mouth, we did not use scales developed and tested in the literature. Although we believe that the items used do a good job in measuring the constructs, a more formal test is required in further research.

Given current limitations with this research and the very limited number of studies on the subject of brand love, we encourage future research in the area. Both antecedents and consequences of brand love need further exploration. What creates brand love? Are brand image, brand differentiation, brand uniqueness an issue? Is the type of brand both in terms of its category or its positioning an issue? Are some consumers more love prone than others? May the love feeling be linked to history or nostalgia? The nomological validity tests indicate that the dimensions of passion and affection do not have the same outputs. Could it be the same about brand love antecedents? Are there specific antecedents and consequences for brand affection and brand passion? What mixture of antecedents is then required to generate both passion and affection? Another interesting issue is the level of analysis to which the brand love concept may apply. Can a consumer be in love with a brand independent of the products that carry the brand? Or is the consumer in love with a branded product? Does love transfer with brand extensions? We believe that this concept is in its preliminary phases of development. Cultural variations may also affect the concept and measurement of love towards a brand. Much research is yet needed to better understand, measure and assess the importance of the brand love construct.

REFERENCES

Ahuvia, Aaron. C. (1993), *I love it! Towards an unifying theory of love across divers love objects*, Ph. Dissertation, Northwestern University.

Ahuvia, Aaron C. (2005a), "Beyond the extended self: Love objects and consumer's identity narratives," *Journal of Consumer Research*, 32 (June), 171-184.

Ahuvia, Aaron C. (2005b), "*The love prototype revisited: A qualitative exploration of contemporary folk psychology*," Working Paper. University of Michigan-Dearborn.

Ahuvia, Aaron C., Bagozzi Richard P. and Batra Rajeev (2007), "*Brand love*": the "*what*" and "*so what*", Marketing Science Institute Conference, Mineapolis.

Aron, Arthur A. and Aron Elaine N. (1986), *Love as expansion of the self: understanding attraction and satisfaction*, New York: Hemisphere.

Bagozzi, Richard P. and Yi Y. (1991), "*Multitrait-multimethod matrices in consumer research*," *Journal of Consumer Research*, 17, August, 426-439.

Baumeister, Roy F. and Bratslavsky Ellen (1999), "Passion, intimacy and time: passionate love as a function of change in intimacy", *Personality and Social Psychology Review*, vol.3, n°1, 47-67.

Bauer, Hans H., Heinrich Daniel and Martin Isabel (2007), *How to create high emotional consumer brand relationships? The causalities of brand passion*, ANZMAC Annual Conference, Dunedin.

Belaid Samy and Behi Azza T. (2008) *The outcomes of brand attachment: An empirical investigation of the role of attachment on building brand consumer's relationships for utilitarian products*, International Congres "Marketing Trends" Venice.

Caroll, Barbara. A. and Ahuvia Aaron C. (2006), "Some antecedents and outcomes of brand love," *Marketing Letters*, 17 (2), 79-89.

Chaudhuri, Arjun and Holbrook Morris B. (2001), "*The chain of effects from brand trust and brand affect to brand performance: The role of brand loyalty*," *Journal of Marketing*, 2, 91-93.

Churchill, Gilbert A. (1979), "*A paradigm for developing better measures of marketing construct*," Journal of Marketing Research, 16, February, 64-73.

Fehr, Beverley (1988), "Prototype analysis of the concepts of love and commitment," *Journal of Personality and Social Psychology*, 55, 4, 557-570.

Fehr, Beverley and Russel James A. (1991), "The concept of love viewed from a prototype perspective," *Journal of Personality and Social Psychology*, 60, 3, 425-438.

Fornell, Claes and Larcker, David F. (1981), "Evaluating structural equations models with unobservable variables and measurement error," *Journal of Marketing Research*, 18, February, 39-50.

Fournier, Susan (1998), "Consumers and their brands: Developing relationship theory in consumer research," *Journal of Consumer Research*, 24 (March), 343-373.

Fournier, Susan and Yao Julie. (1997), "Reviving brand loyalty: a reconceptualization within the framework of consumer–brand relationships," *International Journal Research in Marketing*, 14, 5, 451-472.

Fisher, Helen (2006), *Pourquoi nous aimons*, Ed. Robert Laffont, Paris.

Hatfield, Elaine (1988). Passionate and companionate love. In R. J. Sternberg & M. L. Barnes (ed.), *The psychology of love* (pp. 191-217), New Haven, CT: Yale University Press.

Hatfield, Elaine and Sprecher Susan (1986), "Measuring passionnate love in intimate relationships," *Journal of Adolescence*, 9, 383-410.

Hendrick, Clyde and Hendrick Susan S. (1983), *Liking, loving, and relating*, Monterey, CA: Brooks/Cole.

Hendrick, Clyde and Hendrick Susan S. (1986), "A theory and method of love," *Journal of Personality and Social Psychology*, 50, 392-402.

Hendrick, Susan S., Hendrick Clyde and Adler Nancy L. (1988), "Romantic Relationship: Love, Satisfaction and Staying Together," *Journal of Personality and Social Psychology*, 54, 6, 980-988.

Keller, Kevin L. (2007), *Best Practices Cases in Brandind*, Prentice Hall, 3rd edition.

Kim, Jungsik and Haftield Elaine (2004), "Love-types and Subjective Well Being : a cross cultural study," *Social Behavior and Personality*, 32 (2), 173-182.

Palmatier, Robert W., Dant Ravij P., Grewal Dhruv and Evans Kenneth R. (2006), "Factors influencing the effectiveness of a relationship marketing: a meta analysis," *Journal of Marketing*, 70, 136-153.

Roberts, Kevin (2006), *The lovemarks Effect: Winning in the Consumer Revolution*, PowerHouse Books.

Rubin, Zick (1970), "Measurement of romantic love," *Journal of Personality and Social Psychology*, 16, 2, 265-273.

Samuelsen, Bendik and Sandvik Kare (1998) "*Effects of customer state of commitment to service provider*," In Proceedings of the 27th EMAC Conference, vol. 1. p. 345–50.

Shimp, Terence A. and Thomas J. Madden (1988), "Consumer-object relations: A conceptual framework based analogously on Sternberg's triangular theory of love," *Advances in Consumer Research*, 15, 163-168.

Sternberg, Robert J. (1986), "A triangular theory of love," *Psychological Review*, 93 (2), 119-135.

Sternberg, Robert J. (1997), "Construct validation of a triangular love scale," *European Journal of Social Psychology*, 27 (3), 313-335.

Thomson, Matthew, MacInnis, Deborah J. and Whan Park C. (2005), "The ties that bind: Measuring the strength of consumers' emotional attachment to brands," *Journal of Consumer Psychology*, 15 (1), 77-91.

Whang, Yun-O., Allen, Jeff, Sahoury, Niquelle and Zhang, Haitao (2004), "Falling in love with a product: The structure of a romantic consumer–product relationship," *Advances in Consumer Research*, 31, 320-327.

Can Brands Make Us Happy? A Research Framework for the Study of Brands and Their Effects on Happiness

Jean-Francois Bettingen, University of Innsbruck, Austria
Marius K. Luedicke, University of Innsbruck, Austria

ABSTRACT

Brands permeate consumer culture. Yet, despite their ubiquitous presence, one of the societally most relevant and fundamental questions of brand existence remains among the most difficult to capture: Can brands make us happy? Academics have identified emotional and cognitive influences of brands on loyalty and studied the broader well-being effects of income and consumption. This paper adds to this discourse by analyzing the roads and barriers of researching correlations between brands and happiness. We first evaluate methods to reliably assess general influences on happiness. Then, we differentiate three levels of the consumer-brand experience and discuss if and how their respective correlations with happiness can meaningfully be measured. As a result, we offer a roadmap for brand-related happiness research that directs and inspires further inquiry.

INTRODUCTION

When Apple's first cellular phone, the "iphone," hit the U.S. Market in June 2007, the most devoted fans went to such lengths as to spend several nights in front of the Apple stores to get a hand on the device. Once acquired, they petted the product, showed it around, cheered the brand, and thus rejuvenated the brand-based market system. Has the owners' happiness been driven by the device itself? Was it the brand? Or was it the entire system of brands that molded the iphone in to being such a powerful identity resource?

Brands have been important since about 1885. Since these early days, brands have become means not only for making better-informed purchasing decisions, but also for advancing individual identity projects (Elliott and Wattanasuwan 1998); as symbols of taste, wealth, and belonging (Levy 1959), as objects of desire (Belk, Ger and Askegaard 2003, Ahuvia 2005), as motives for social community building (McAlexander, Schouten and Koenig 2002), and as relationship partners (Fournier 1998). Whereas these functions have been perceived as implicitly positive for consumer well-being, brands have also long been criticized (Fisk 1967). Over the last decade, a rising number of authors have investigated the darker side of corporate branding, the brand's potential backlash (Handelman 1999; Holt 2002; Klein 1999; Kozinets and Handelman 2004; Lasn 2000). The key point of these studies is that the "branding of cultures" by corporations advances a superficial culture of over-consumption, resulting ultimately in the destruction of human and environmental resources, a reduced quality of human relationships and diminished overall well-being (Csikszentmihalyi 1999).

The above findings evoke the fundamental question of whether brands can make us happy. Existing research has illuminated various influences of consumption on happiness, such as car possession, smoking, or leisure activity levels, and scrutinized demographic influences such as income, employment, or race on happiness, but remains silent on the level(s) at which brands might influence consumers' and society's psychological well-being. This paper offers an important next step towards closing this gap in knowledge by reflecting on the roads and barriers of brand-related happiness research. We first discuss the concept of happiness, its various influences, and its most reliable measures. Then, we de-scribe three distinct levels of brand experience from which consumers might derive happiness; brand clues, brand systems, and the overall system of brands. Lastly, we combine the suitable happiness measures with these three realms of experience to present a research framework for future brand-related happiness research.

THE LEVELS OF BRAND EXPERIENCE

A brand is a "name, term, sign, symbol, or design, or a combination of them, intended to identify the goods or services of one seller or group of sellers and to differentiate them from those of competitors" (Chernatony and Dall'Olmo Riley 1998, 419). This and various other more cultural and multi-faceted concepts of brands underlie an extensive body of literature that has illuminated the individual-psychological (Aaker, Fournier and Brasel 2004; Tybout and Carpenter 2001), communal-sociological (Arnould and Thompson 2005; Hellmann 2003; McAlexander, Schouten and Koenig 2002), and economic-managerial (Aaker 1995) merits of branding. However, for our purpose, we need a definition of the brand that differentiates the tangible, observable elements of a brand (e.g. a specific thing) from the meanings of them (e.g. its community associations) and again from the meanings of the entirety of brands in society (i.e. attitude towards bands in general). We next describe these three levels of brand experience as brand clues, brand systems and the system of brands.

Brand Clues

A "brand clue" is a set of distinctions that consumers experience with their physical senses-sight, hearing, smell, touch and taste. As manifestations of brands, brand clues include logos, products, price tags, stores, sounds, smells and other clues through which consumers identify the derivation, quality, or function of a particular good or service. For an observer, that is an owner or non-owner, a brand clue in itself is experiential and meaningless. However, brand clues are also links to the brand system.

Brand Systems

Brand systems are systems of communication that organize the meanings of brand clues for an observer (Giesler 2003). Such meanings may include the particular identity connotations of a brand (e.g. the innovative spirit of Apple products), the connotations of group belonging (e.g. the community of Harley Davidson owners), and the (largely imagined) social responses that consumers derive from interpreting brand meanings (e.g. responses to wearing fashion brands).

Brand systems are characterized by three markers (Luedicke 2005). First, brand systems are established through social communication about brand clues. They proliferate with every reference made to the brand, but are as oblivious as human minds. Second, distinctive clues with high social relevance influence the brand systems' communicative "noise." That social noise is independent of whether consumers accept, alter, or oppose the suggested meanings of the brand clues. Third, being intelligent in their social reproduction, brand systems negotiate and perpetuate specific programs and structures that guide, constrain, and inspire communication. Programs and structures allow consumers, marketers and other observers to communicate in accordance with–or against–the

FIGURE 1

Three ontological levels of brand experience

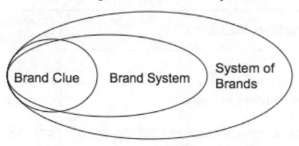

---

predominant meanings of a brand system and use these meanings for their marketing or identity goals.

The System of Brands

The system of brands is a theoretical concept for studying the entire presence and role of brands for an observer. Brands and their social utilization by organizations and consumers are understood as a functional subsystem of consumer societies, and operate with particular programs and codes. In distinction to the brand system, which embraces communications around a specific brand, the system of brands refers to the general logic of brands that enables consumers to recognize brands as parts of a larger system. The shared knowledge about the system allows consumers to employ brands both as a means for social distinction as well as for better making purchasing decisions.

In concert, these three notions allow us to meaningfully define the notion of brands, and to correlate brand experiences with consumer happiness (see Figure 1). Observers (e.g. consumers, marketers, journalists) perceive brand clues independent of brand knowledge (e.g. a Ferrari is a loud red car). When they learn about the brand's social attributes and how they are perceived in a particular cultural context (e.g. a Ferrari is a high status vehicle, or a "pimp ride"), they experience the brand system. Observers that, for instance, have their first experiences with consumer cultures will get an understanding of the system of brands in this particular context. They will learn that particular brands have an effect on social responses or that some social realms demand the usage of brands whereas others rather despise it. Differentiating these three levels of brand experience enables us to distinguish suitable measures for their assessment.

WHAT IS HAPPINESS?

Ancient Greek philosophy understood happiness as the absence of pain (e.g. Epicure), and was focused largely on the body or the result of intelligent reflection (e.g. Cicero). The hedonist philosophy of Aristippus of Cyrene, however, theorized that happiness was the sum of material pleasures, and the meaning of life was the maximization of delight (Layard 2005, Fromm [1976] 2007). This hedonistic concept of happiness was particularly influential for the Italian metropolitan elite of the Renaissance, and the British and French bourgeoisie of the 18th and 19th centuries. Hedonism continues to be expressed in contemporary consumer culture with the creed of "having more" is "being more" (see Fromm 2007 for a critique). Whether happiness is–or should be–the ultimate goal in life remains an unresolved philosophical question. However, it is evident that American consumers accept the "pursuit of happiness"

since the Declaration of Independence in 1776 as a salient life goal and consumption as a central means for leveraging it.

The definition of happiness is largely author dependant. In the literature, a person's "happiness" is determined in at least four different ways. Psychologists tend to use the construct of "subjective well-being" (Diener et al. 1999). This term reflects the idea of happiness as a non-physical state that cannot be objectively measured (as opposed to body temperature or blood pressure). In this view, subjective well-being is "the degree to which an individual judges the overall quality of his/her own life-as-a-whole favorably" (Veenhoven 2001, p. 4). Economists, in contrast, understand well-being as a function of a person's income and the utility derived from consumption (Sunanyi-Unger 1981). Another stream of literature theorizes happiness as one of many human affects. For these researchers, happiness levels can be derived from the observation- and averaging-of a person's affects over a period of time. Lastly, researchers in the field of neurobiology perceive happiness as an activation state within a particular region of the brain.

What Influences Happiness?

Generic influences on happiness (using measures of satisfaction) were found to include income, personal characteristics, socially-developed characteristics, how respondents spend their time, attitudes and beliefs towards self/others/life, relationships, and the wider economic, social and political environment (Dolan, Peasgood and White 2008, p. 97). Such research has found, for instance, significant differences in the evaluation of subjective well-being depending on people being employed versus unemployed and single versus living with a partner (ibid.). People with high self-esteem, a sense of personal control, optimism, and extraversion were found to be generally happier (Myers and Diener 1995). Research has also tested for happiness correlations with gender, age, education, and ethnicity, but results vary among the various studies (Andrews and Withey 1976; Diener 1984). It seems that money can buy happiness, but only temporarily (Myers and Diener 1995).

The question underpinning all these analyses is whether happiness can be influenced. Some authors argue that about 50% of one's satisfaction is predefined in the human genetic program and that life circumstances only marginally affect human happiness (Lykken and Tellegen 1996). Others believe that a change in behavior, such as an eventual grateful gesture to a friend, can change overall happiness levels (Wallis et al 2005, Seligman 2002). Self-evaluation has been variously used in studies correlating consumption with happiness (see Table 1)(Diener and Suh 1999, Frey and Stutzer 2002, Layard 2005). It has been reported, for

TABLE 1

Correlates of Consumption Measures and Happiness (Source: The World Database of Happiness)

Consumption Measure	Correlation with Happiness
Car Ownership	r=+.17
Active involvement in sports	r=+.19
Possession of micro-wave and dish-washer	r=+.15
Leisure activity level	r=+.14
Smoking	r=-.10

instance, that among 3,500 Dutch consumers above 18 years of age car ownership correlates moderately positive with happiness (r= + .17, p<.05 in 1997 and r= + .12, p<.05 in 1993).

Whereas these above studies provide some evidence of consumption influences on happiness, they tell little about brands and remain vague on both the various levels of brand experiences and on the direction of causality. Consequentially, the ultimate question of whether-and how-brands influence consumer happiness has yet to be answered.

HOW IS HAPPINESS MEASURED?

Approaches to measuring happiness are many fold. As stated above, scholars understand happiness in at least four different ways. However, the economists' reductionism approach of objective well-being does not add to our quest as this stream abstracts from subjective and individual evaluations. In the sections that follow, we describe the key approaches of subjective well-being, hedonic affect, and physiological activation in more detail.

Measuring Happiness as Subjective Well-Being

A broad variety of scales have been used to quantify peoples' quality or satisfaction with life. Among the former, the "Satisfaction with Life Scale" of Pavot and Diener (1993) ranks as the most reputed. It evaluates overall happiness with five questions rated on a scale from 1 (strongly disagree) to 7 (strongly agree). Other examples of multi-item scales include the "Oxford Happiness Inventory" (Argyle et al. 1989) with 29 items and the "Depression-Happiness Scale" (McGreal and Joseph 1993) with 40 items.

For some authors, single-item scales are, on average, as valid as multi-item scales (Burisch 1984). Such scales typically use a question such as "On the whole, are you very satisfied, fairly satisfied, not very satisfied, or not at all satisfied with the life you lead?" (European Commission 2008), or "Taken all together, how would you say things are these days? Would you say that you are…?" Answers on a 7 point Likert type scale range from "completely unhappy" to "completely happy" (Andrews and Whitney 1976). For these single-item scales it was found to make no empirical difference in results if the word "satisfied" or "happy" was used (Hirata 2006). This makes the single-item scale applicable for large-scale surveys.

The subjective well-being approach and its underlying beliefs have two important implications for our study. First, happiness is not understood as a peak of life evaluation, but being happy means that a person judges his or her life favorably rather than unfavorably at a particular point in time. Typically, such measures are repeated over months and years to measure changes in correlations and to abstract from punctual emotions. Second, happiness is understood as a subjective appreciation of one's life without any objective standard. Hence, if consumers judge themselves to be happy, then, as far as the researcher is concerned, they are happy. Difficulties with studying satisfaction with life arise from whether it is a stable personal trait or an evaluation that depends on life circumstances (Veenhoven 1994), and whether happiness is perceived as absolute or relative (Veenhoven 1991). As it currently stands, most researchers in the satisfaction of life paradigm agree that happiness depends on both personal traits and life circumstances. It is further found to depend on both the respondents' social environments and as absolute in the sense that happiness cannot occur unless basic human needs–such as security, health, and food–are satisfied.

Measuring Happiness as Hedonic Affect

Happiness correlates not only with the subjective evaluation of the degree to which personal expectations have been met (see Bentham 1789, Veenhoven 1984, Myers and Diener 1995), but also with the relative presence of positive and negative affects. These include the pleasantness of emotions (e.g. love), sensory feelings (e.g. taste), and mood (a mixture of affects). The World Database of Happiness lists more than 200 different scales for measuring hedonic affects. Affect scales explicitly ask for affective states, in contrast to subjective well-being scales that avoid words referring to feelings or moods, but ask for achievements, wants, and goals. Furthermore, researchers applying affective measures are not restricted to self-reports, but can also draw on external observations such as those of family members or the researchers themselves (Noelle-Neumann 1977).

Affective experiences can be evaluated simultaneously good and bad, and should therefore be described as bivalent rather than bipolar (Kahneman 1999). The Positive and Negative Affect Schedule (PANAS) measure of affect rates among the most frequently used affect scales (Watson, Clark, and Tellegen 1988). Participants are asked to rate ten positive affects (interested, excited, strong, enthusiastic, proud, alert, inspired, determined, attentive, and active) and ten negative affects (distressed, upset, guilty, scared, hostile, irritable, ashamed, nervous, jittery, and afraid) according to their emotional strength at various points in time. Answers range from 1="very slightly or not at all," to 5="extremely" (ibid.). As affects change in situ, they must be measured repetitively to inform about a participant's overall happiness. The "Experience Sampling Method" (ESM, Csikszentmihalyi, Lason and Prescott 1977) acknowledges this dynamic by asking respondents several times per day to report the situation they are engaged in at that moment and to evaluate the presence or absence of various feelings. Although this method reveals valuable insights on the intensity of current feelings in a specific situation, it remains difficult to be implemented for larger scale surveys. Therefore, Kahneman et al (2004) developed the "Day Reconstruction Method" (DRM) that combines elements of time diaries and experience sampling. Respondents are asked to reconstruct the previous day by dividing it into various episodes and to indicate the time dedicated to that episode. In a second step, respondents are asked to report the intensity of feelings along nine affect dimensions on a scale ranging from 0 (not at all) to 6 (very much). The assessed net affect of an experience is defined as the average of the 3 positive affect dimensions (happy, warm, enjoying myself) less the average of the 6 negative affect dimensions (frustrated, depressed, hassled, angry, worried, criticized) (Kahneman and Krueger 2006). These dimensions are nevertheless not fixed and the list can vary depending on the research goals.

The measure of happiness via affect is not without its disputes. Kahneman and colleagues, for instance, argue that remembering effects disturb the correct assessment of happiness. Therefore, their approach inquires into the lived experiences of people in situ. They found, for instance, that the five most positive activities for Texas housewives are (in descending order) sex, socializing, relaxing, praying or meditating, and eating, rather than taking care of children (Wallis et al 2005). Seligman (2002) and others argue against this position because they find memories and stories telling more about authentic happiness than the actual experiences. Seligman concludes that engagement and meaning are more influential to happiness than the pursuit of pleasure.

Measuring Happiness via Physiological Responses

Since neurobiologist have found reliable correlations between self-reported happiness and the activation of particular brain regions, happiness is considered to some extend measurable objectively. Methods for deriving results are electrophysiological (EEG, EKG) and imaging (e.g. fMRI, PET) response techniques. Subjects respond to various stimuli, such as haptic experiences or social stimuli (e.g. family pictures or a movie), with changes in their skin conductivity, heart rate, or activation of brain areas. These findings largely abstract from cultural influences on happiness evaluations and from individual interpretation of emotions. However, researchers must define the levels of activation that translate reliably into self-reported happiness. Hence, as they entail the opposite strength and weaknesses of the self-report techniques, these measures are useful as complementary methods. Realistically, however, most researchers will be unable to cover the financial expenses of an fMRI study with a representative sample of consumers.

ROADS AND BARRIERS FOR MEASURING BRAND-RELATED HAPPINESS

Consumption inspires human senses as much as it evokes their thoughts (Holbrook and Hirschman 1982). With their refined qualities, brands are likely to do so in specific ways at the above three experiential levels. Consumer researchers have inquired at various occasions into the short and long term hedonic responses of consumers to brand or product stimuli (cf. Chaudhuri and Holbrook 2001; Ruth 2001; Sundie et al 2006). Some studies have also

considered how the evaluation of these affects or responses may be mediated by the cognitive appraisal of emotions (Edell and Burke 1987), personality (Matzler, Bidmon and Grabner-Kräuter 2006), and experience and background knowledge (Ruth 2001; Washburn, Till and Priluck 2004). Most of these studies, however, focus too narrowly on selected emotions (e.g. Di Monaco et al 2004) or character traits (e.g. Matzler, Bidmon and Grabner-Kräuter 2006) and ignore well-being outcomes. They also use the brand notion rarely distinct from the products or companies they represent, so that the particular effect of brand clues and systems remains unappreciated. In their attentive study of the influence of brand trust and affect on market performance, Chaudhuri and Holbrook (2001, p. 87) come closest to an explicit study of brand-related happiness. They measure correlations of brand affect and loyalty by asking three direct questions: "I feel good when I use this brand", "This brand makes me happy", and "This brand gives me pleasure." While these authors provide insightful information, we find such unconcealed, intrusive questions not only likely to provoke biased answers, but also unsuitable for capturing consumer experiences with brands comprehensively (see Kahneman and Krueger above). Hence, we next evaluate potential methods for understanding the role of brands for happiness based on the above distinct levels of brand experience and the most reliable measures. Figure 2 provides an illustrative overview of the various options and limitations that we discuss next.

Brand Clues and Happiness

A brand clue was defined as a visual, audible, haptic, olfactory, or gustational experience that can be evaluated via physiological response tests and affect measures. The experiencing of brand clues, such as driving a Porsche, will have little (if any) direct influence on cognitive appraisals of well-being, but probably a mediated one. Brand clues can be evaluated by participants that have no previous experience with, or knowledge of the social meaning of the branded good or service. Hence, discrimination of hedonic or physiological responses can be attributed to experiences with goods of different sensual qualities. Researchers may consider various sorts of high and low end branded products for comparison.

From the above methodical and conceptual findings we derive three suitable ways for measuring potential brand clue effects on happiness. First, we suggest conducting laboratory or field experiments at which consumers are confronted with high and low quality, status, price, etc. brand clues. Subjects' physiological responses can be measured via electrophysiological (EEG, EKG) and imaging (e.g. fMRI, PET) techniques and related to subjective well-being measures.

Second, the day reconstruction method appears useful for evaluating emotional responses to brand clues over a period of several days, weeks, or even months. These brand-specific in situ self-evaluations can be flanked with external observations of these consumers' emotional responses to brand clues over this period of time. For such external data, the researcher or the friends and family observe and note facial expressions, posture, voice, and other physical behaviors.

Websites and mobile computer applications allow for more timely evaluations of brand-related affects then previously. The "hedonimeter.net" art project of Christine Wong Yap foreshadows such an empirical approach where respondents record and comment their emotions throughout their day (see e.g. http://www.hedonimeter.net/results/index.php?op=view&id=2 [03/18/2008]). Results can be averaged and deviations can be calculated to reveal the respondent's amplitude and frequency of positive and negative brand-related feelings. An ascription of "happy" or "unhappy" requires the setting of threshold values.

FIGURE 2

A research roadmap for brand-related happiness research

Happiness Measure ⟍ Brand Experience Level	Physiological Responses	Emotional Responses / Affects	Subjective Well-being Evaluations
Brand Clues Sensory consumption experiences	Electrophysiological (EEG, EKG) and imaging (e.g. fMRI, PET) comparative experiments with brand clues	Brand-specific in situ self-evaluations (via DRM, ESM) and external evaluations of emotional responses to brand clues	Correlates of self and external SWB evaluations with physiological and emotional responses; potential new measure to correlate brand clue and system influences with satisfaction.
Brand Systems Ideological and social consumption experiences	Electrophysiological (EEG, EKG) and imaging (e.g. fMRI, PET) comparative experiments with social brand perceptions	Brand-specific in situ self-evaluations (via DRM, ESM) and external evaluations of emotional responses to social brand perception	
System of Brands Societal systemic brand experiences	-	-	

Third, for understanding influences of brand clues on satisfaction, we suggest (if applicable) calculating correlates of self and external measures of well-being with the physiological and emotional responses noted above. In addition, we suggest to develop a new scale that allows for measuring indirect brand clue influences on happiness, such as the number of high and low end brands owned, the amount of pleasure derived from consuming the brand in public, the number and type of responses to brand consumption, or the enjoyment with acquiring new products. Such a scale development process would require a qualitative study to evoke relevant brand clue effects. It seems though unlikely that a single temporally limited affect may influence significantly and permanently a consumer's overall subjective well-being. Causality between a favorable appreciation of a brand clue and a high level of subjective well-being may also be difficult to define.

Brand Systems and Happiness

Brand systems capture the social meanings of a brand that evolve through communication about brand clues (Giesler 2003, Luedicke 2005). Understanding the meaning of these communications within a particular culture requires cognitive processing of brand-related messages, such as corporate advertisements, the brand tales of friends, or the symbolic references that brand clues (e.g. shape, material, or style) make in a popular culture. Ownership of a branded good that is perceived as signaling high status-such as a Rolex watch-might influence owners' self-evaluations of their well-being because wearing a brand clue with high status recognition-rather than a socially less relevant product-might be perceived as an indicator for success and social achievement. In consumer cultural research, the symbolic value of brands has often been studied but seldom refined for a subsequent study of happiness. Among others, Fournier (1998) and Ahuvia (2005), for instance, report on consumers experiencing brand-related emotions from love to hate and Pichler and Hemetsberger (2007) argue that consumers develop extreme devotional relationships with brands. However, these authors remain ambiguous on specific happiness influences. Further examples of emotional responses to brand systems resides in the consumer resistance literature (e.g. Kozinets and Handelman 2004). This body of literature offers accounts of

strong responses to brands and organizations that, again, unfold their cultural and marketing relevance both on the level of affect and of cognitive evaluation.

Two ways of measuring brand systems' influences on happiness appear viable on the above methodical and theoretical grounds. As a first approach, we suggest inquiring into the affects that brand-related communications provoke (cf. Ruth 2001 for partial findings). This exercise largely overlaps with evaluating the role of brand clues for happiness. However, while using the same empirical approaches-e.g. ESM or DRM-the researcher focuses on in situ reports of social relationships that a brand inspires and on reports of symbolic use and consumer responses. The measure can be flanked by subjective well-being evaluations for consistency tests.

Alternatively or additionally, researchers may seek to reveal potential correlations between a person's general brand appreciation, brand ownership, and subjective well-being by means of multi-item scales. This approach operates on the level of a specific brand system (probably around a high profile brand) symbolizing the achievement of life goals. For instance, the possession of a Porsche may serve as mediator for the life goal "successful career." To understand this relationship, the researcher measures in a first set of items the respondents' general sensitivity towards brand meanings that is expressed, for instance, in brand knowledge, brand experience levels, brand name recall for product categories and the across-respondents overlap of brand associations. These questions need to be developed and tested carefully and should be less intrusive and obvious than existing ones. The second set of questions captures the effective use and meanings of brands that matter to respondents in particular social ways. The scale would allow for self-evaluations of brands that evoke high to low social responses and for indicating the type of responses that these brands evoke, such as surprise, rejection, or respectful recognition from others. Further it is of interest, what kind of relationships the respondents form with those meaningful brands, including positive and negative, short-lived and traditional relationships (see Fournier 1998). These data would provide an idea of the respondents' usage frequency and direction of brand meanings and allow for revealing potential correlations among the various appreciations of brand systems and happiness.

We hypothesize that the influence of brands systems on subjective well-being is existent but limited whereas the physiological and attitude measures may evoke more vivid responses. However, most likely, it will be difficult to separate the brand clue from the brand system level responses.

The System of Brands and Happiness

On the system of brands level, we expect brands to influence individuals in their entirety as a social mechanism that not only facilitates purchase choices and (partially) quality evaluations, but also provides a cultural structure for symbolic uses of goods and services. Consumer culture theorists have used notions such as the "world of consumer products" (Fournier 1998) and "the web of brands" (Klein 1999) for describing brands on this systemic level. The major critique against brands also operates on this level of experience. The guiding question on this ontological level is, if the overall existence and influence of brands on consumers' lives has an impact on happiness evaluations, and if so, in which direction(s)? A broad range of answers is possible. Respondents might feel that the symbolic communication that brands reinforce changes their social life to the worse (argued e.g. by Klein 1999), because they have to actively consider what their products are telling others about themselves to avoid trouble. Yet, they might also and even simultaneously be positive towards the system of brands as it allows them to facilitate other aspects of social life, including even symbolic rebellion (Holt 2002). As an example, not having an Apple ipod has almost become a social stigma in some European schools. Parents that pay for their children not to be plagued at school experience this system in a particularly direct way.

Similar abstract constructs have been tested elsewhere for their influence on happiness. Frey, Leuchinger and Stutzer (2004) have, for instance, measured the influence of terrorism on overall happiness using the number of attacks and the number of people killed to define the periods with more or less terrorist activity. Later, they compared these data to longitudinal national happiness surveys. We might consider data such as national advertising expenses, density of billboards in downtown, or the number of brands in a country as comparable indicators, but they abstract from actual perceptions. We suggest conducting an explorative study for developing an appropriate measure of individual brand perceptions. Such a measure of the respondents' appreciation of the system of brand must allow for multi-faceted responses. Respondents must be able to appreciate and disapprove of aspects of the system at the same time, rather than rating the system in its entire social effect. Again, these responses would later be correlated with the same respondents' ranking on a subjective well-being scale. Such correlations are likely to occur for some groups of consumers (e.g. less affluent parents) and less for others (e.g. young urban professionals), depending on life circumstances, social comparison groups and particularly on income levels.

Combining Measures

Depending on scale length and complexity, it appears useful to combine the evaluations of brand clues, brand systems, and the system of brands for testing the measures for further correlations. It seems logical to combine the system of brands evaluation with the affect reports evaluated using the day reconstruction method.

CONCLUSIONS

This study offers an important step towards answering the question of whether brands can make us happy. We have argued that happiness (or frustration) may result from consumers' experiences with sensory brand clues, social brand systems and the overall system of brands in a particular society. We have shown that three distinct paths can lead to a reliable evaluation of happiness: physiological responses, emotional responses (affect measures), and subjective well-being evaluations. On these conceptual and methodical grounds, we have developed a research framework; a guide to the most viable directions and approaches for further research into brand-related happiness. The limitations of this study coincide with its purpose; to invite fellow researchers to work on measures for hedonic responses to brand clues, on scales for the cognitive appreciation of brand systems, on evaluations of the system of brands, or on refining the directional guide with further options.

This ongoing research contributes to consumer behavior research, marketing theory, and public policy in three important ways. First, we seek to provide empirical evidence of consumers' multifaceted evaluations of brands and how they relate to each other in everyday consumption contexts. Second, we expect to learn more about the sources of happiness in brands for deriving marketing implications. And lastly, we hope to respond to social activists' critiques of the system of brands with reliable empirical data. This lack of empirical research has led to an abundance of populist critiques and affronts against corporations and brands, and cries out for independent scientific scrutiny.

REFERENCES

Aaker, David A. (1995), "Building Strong Brands," *Brandweek*, 36 (Oct), 28-34.

Aaker, Jennifer, Susan Fournier and S. Adam Brasel (2004), "When Good Brands Do Bad," *Journal of Consumer Research*, 31 (1), 1-17.

Ahuvia, Aaron C. (2005), "Beyond the Extended Self: Loved Objects and Consumers' Identity Narratives," *Journal of Consumer Research*, 32 (1), 171-84.

Andrews, Frank M. and Stephan B. Withey (1976), *Social indicators of well-being: American's perceptions of life quality*, New York: Plenum Press.

Argyle, Michael, Maryanne Martin and Jill Crossland (1989), "Happiness as a function of personality and social encounters," in *Recent advances in social psychology: An international perspective*, ed. Joseph P. Forgas and Michael Innes, Amsterdam: Elsevier Science Publishers.

Arnould, Eric J. and Craig J. Thompson (2005), "Consumer Culture Theory (CCT): Twenty Years of Research," *Journal of Consumer Research*, 32 (4), 868-83.

Babin, Barry J., William R. Darten and Mitch Griffin (1994), "Work and/or Fun: Measuring Hedonic and Utilitarian Shopping Value," *Journal of Consumer Research*, 20 (4), 644-56.

Belk, Russell W., Guliz Ger and Soren Askegaard (2003), "The Fire of Desire: A Multisited Inquiry into Consumer Passion," *Journal of Consumer Research*, 30 (3), 326-52.

Bentham, Jeremy (1789), *An introduction into the principles of morals and legislation*, Dover: Dover Publications.

Burisch, Matthias (1984), "You don't always get what you pay for: Measuring depression with short and simple versus long and sophisticated scales," *Journal of Research in Personality*, 18 (1), 81-98.

Chaudhuri, Arjun and Mooris B. Holbrook (2001), "The Chain of Effects from Brand Trust and Brand Affect to Brand Performance: The Role of Brand Loyalty," *Journal of Marketing*, 65 (2), 81-94.

Csikszentmihalyi, Mihaly (1999), "If we are so rich, why aren't we happy?" *American Psychologist*, 54 (10), 821-7.

Csikszentmihalyi, Mihaly, Reed Larson and Suzanne Prescott (1977), "The ecology of adolescent activity and experience," *Journal of Youth and Adolescence*, 6 (3), 281-294.

de Chernatony, Leslie and Francesca Dall'Olmo Riley (1998), "Defining A "Brand": Beyond The Literature With Experts' Interpretations," *Journal of Marketing Management*, 14 417-443.

Di Monaco, R., S. Cavella, S. Di Marzo and P. Masi (2004), "The effect of expectations generated by brand name on the acceptability of dried semolina pasta," *Food Quality & Preference*, 15 (4), 429-37.

Diener, Ed (1984), "Subjective Well-Being," *Psychological Bulletin*, 95 (3), 542-575.

Diener, Ed and Eunkook Suh (1999), "National Differences in Subjective Well-Being," in *Well-Being: the Foundation of Hedonic Psychology*, ed. Daniel Kahneman, Ed Diener and Nobert Schwarz, New York: Russell Sage Foundation.

Diener, Ed, Eunkook M. Suh, Richard E. Lucas and Heidi L. Smith (1999), "Subjective Well-Being: Three Decades of Progress," *Psychological Bulletin*, 125 (2), 276-302.

Dolan, Paul, Tessa Peasgood and Mathew White (2008), "Do we really know what makes us happy? A review of the economic literature on the factors associated with subjective well-being," *Journal of Economic Psychology*, 29 (1), 94-122.

Edell, Julie A. and Marian Chapman Burke (1987), "The Power of Feelings in Understanding Advertising Effects," *Journal of Consumer Research*, 14 (3), 421-34.

European Commission (2008), "Europabarometer Survey," http://ec.europa.eu/public_opinion/, [03/01/2008]

Elliott, Richard and Kritsadarat Wattanasuwan (1998), "Brand as symbolic resources for the construction of identity," *International Journal of Advertising*, 17 (2), 131-145.

Fisk, George (1967), *Marketing Systems: An Introductory Analysis*, New York et al: Harper and Row.

Fournier, Susan (1998), "Consumers and Their Brands: Developing Relationship Theory in Consumer Research," *Journal of Consumer Research*, 24 (4), 343-373.

Frey, Bruno S. and Alois Stutzer (2002): *Happiness and Economics*, Princeton: University Press.

Frey, Bruno S., Simon Leuchinger and Alois Stutzer (2004), "Valuing Public Goods: The Life Satisfaction Approach," CESifo Working Paper.

Fromm, Erich ([1976] 2007), *Haben oder Sein*, München: dtv.

Giesler, Markus (2003), "Social Systems in Marketing," in *European Advances in Consumer Research*, Vol. 6, ed. Darach Turley and Stephen W. Brown, Valdosta, GA: Association for Consumer Research, 249-256.

Handelman, Jay M. (1999), "Culture Jamming: Expanding the Application of the Critical Research Project," in *Advances in Consumer Research*, Vol. 26, ed. Eric J. Arnould and Linda L. Price, Provo, UT: Association of Consumer Research, 399-404.

Hellmann, Kai-Uwe (2003), *Soziologie der Marke*, Frankfurt am Main: Suhrkamp.

Hirata, Johannes (2006), Happiness, Ethics and Economics (unpublished doctoral thesis), St. Gallen: University of St. Gallen.

Holbrook, Morris B. and Elizabeth C. Hirschman (1982), "The Experiential Aspects of Consumption: Consumer Fantasies, Feelings, and Fun," *Journal of Consumer Research*, 9 (2), 132-140.

Holt, Douglas B. (2002), "Why Do Brands Cause Trouble? A Dialectical Theory of Consumer Culture and Branding," *Journal of Consumer Research*, 29 (1), 70-90.

Kahneman, Daniel and Alan B. Krueger (2006), "Developments in the Measurement of Subjective Well-Being," *Journal of Economic Perspectives*, 20 (1), 3-24.

Kahneman, Daniel, Alan B. Krueger, David A. Schkade, Norbert Schwarz and Arthur A. Stone (2004), "A Survey Method for Characterizing Daily Life Experience: The Day Reconstruction Method," *Science*, 306 (5702), 1776-1780.

Klein, Naomi (1999), *No Logo-Taking Aim at the Brand Bullies*, New York: Picador.

Kozinets, Robert V. and Jay M. Handelman (2004), "Adversaries of Consumption: Consumer Movements, Activism, and Ideology," *Journal of Consumer Research*, 31 (3), 691-704.

Lasn, Kalle (2000), *Culture Jam: The Uncooling of America TM*, New York: Quill.

Layard, Richard (2005), *Happiness: Lessons from a New Science*, London: Penguin Books.

Levy, Sidney J. (1959), "Symbols for sale," *Harvard Business Review*, 37 (4), 117-125.

Luedicke, Marius K. (2005), "Brand Systems: A Conceptual Framework for the Sociological Analysis of Brand Phenomena," in *European Advances in Consumer Research*, Vol. 7, ed. Karin M. Ekström and Helene Brembeck, Valdosta, GA: Association for Consumer Research.

Lykken, David and Auke Tellegen (1996), "Happiness is a stochastic phenomenon," *Psychological Science*, 7 (3), 186-9.

Matzler, Kurt, Sonja Bidmon and Sonja Grabner-Kräuter (2006), "Individual determinants of brand affect: the role of the personality traits of extraversion and openness to experience," *Journal of Product & Brand Management*, 15 (7), 427-34.

McAlexander, James H., John W. Schouten and Harold F. Koenig (2002), "Building Brand Community," *Journal of Marketing*, 66 (1), 38-54.

McGreal, Rita and Stephen Joseph (1993), "The Depression-Happiness Scale," *Psychological Reports*, 73 (3), 1279-1282.

Myers, David G. and Ed Diener (1995), "Who is Happy?," *Psychological Science*, 6 (1), 10-9.

Noelle-Neumann, Elisabeth (1977), "Politik und Glück," in *Freiheit und Sachzwang*, ed. Horst Baier and Helmut Schelsky, Opladen: Westdeutscher Verlag.

Pavot, William and Ed Diener (1993), "The Affective and Cognitive Context of Self-Reported Measures of Subjective Well-Being," *Social Indicators Research*, 28, 1-20.

Pichler, Elisabeth A. and Andrea Hemetsberger (2007), "Hopelessly Devoted to You-Towards an Extended Conceptualization of Consumer Devotion," *Advances in Consumer Research*, 34.

Ruth, Julie A. (2001), "Promoting a Brand's Emotion Benefits: The Influence of Emotion Categorization Processes on Consumer Evaluations," *Journal of Consumer Psychology*, 11 (2), 99-113.

Seligman, Martin E.P. (2002), *Authentic Happiness: Using the New Positive Psychology to Realize Your Potential for Lasting Fulfillment*, New York: Free Press/Simon and Schuster.

Sundie, Jill M., James Ward, Wynne W.; Chin and Stephanie Geiger-Oneto (2006), "Schadenfreude as a Consumption-Related Emotion: Feeling Happiness about the Downfall of Another's Product," *Advances in Consumer Research*, 33 (1), 96-7.

Tybout, Alice M. and Gregory S. Carpenter (2001), "Creating and Managing Brands," in *Kellogg on Marketing*, ed. Dawn Iacobucci, New York: Wiley, 74-102.

Veenhoven, Ruut, World Database of Happiness, Erasmus University Rotterdam., Available at: http://worlddatabaseofhappiness.eur.nl

_____ (1984), "Conditions of Happiness," Dorbrecht/Boston: Kluwer Academic.

_____ (1991), "Is Happiness Relative?," *Social Indicators Research*, 24, 1-34.

_____ (1994), "Is Happiness a Trait?," *Social Indicators Research*, 31, 101-160.

_____ (2001), World Database of Happiness, Item Bank, Introductory Text, Available at: http://worlddatabaseofhappiness.eur.nl [01/20/2008].

Washburn, Judith H., Brian D. Till and Randi Priluck (2004), "Brand Alliance and Customer-Based Brand-Equity Effects," *Psychology & Marketing*, 21 (7), 487-508.

Wallis, Claudia, Elizabeth Coady, Dan Cray, Alice Park and Jeffrey Ressner (2005), "The New Science of HAPPINESS," *Time*, 1/17/2005, pA2-A9.

Watson, David, Lee Anna Clark and Auke Tellegen (1988), "Development and Validation of Brief Measures of Positive and Negative Affect: The PANAS Scales," *Journal of Personality and Social Psychology*, 54 (6), 1063-70.

Shopping for Civic Values: Exploring the Emergence of Civic Consumer Culture in Contemporary Western Society

Janine Dermody, University of Gloucestershire, UK
Stuart Hanmer-Lloyd, University of Gloucestershire, UK
Richard Scullion, Bournemouth University, UK

ABSTRACT

In this paper we critique how consumerism is considered an antithesis of citizenship, how acting as a consumer and acting in a civic manner are often viewed as detached parts of our lives. We seek to do this by exploring the blurring of consumerism and citizenship, which is culminating in an emerging area of politicised consumption based on citizenly rights, obligations and social inclusion together with competition and autonomous choice. We illustrate this emergence with specific reference to 'green' citizen-consumers to demonstrate the changing face of civic society in the west, where shopping can act as a vector for civic values and hence facilitates the emergence of civic consumer culture in contemporary western society.

INTRODUCTION–A CRISIS IN CIVIC SOCIETY?

With consumerism dominating the ideology and behaviour of western society, the halcyon days of civic engagement, where individuals act as 'good citizens', are purported to be in decline. This concern exists because of the negative consequences associated with consumerism, in particular the charge of self-indulgence with little consideration for others. This has been compounded by the increasingly visible connections between consumerism and climate change, which is resulting in some profound implications for human, social and environmental capital. All western governments are undoubtedly concerned about the degradation of our society and planet, and have been for some time. In this paper, we are advocating that some of the underlying causes that threaten our planet can be linked to a breakdown in western civic society, and that, what might initially seem paradoxical, we believe combining civic and consumerist values may hold the key to reinvigorating the health of our planet and our society.

Concern about the breakdown in the traditions of civic society is echoed in academic work on social capital and active citizenship. For example David Putnam (2000), in 'Bowling Alone', portrays the unparalleled collapse, since the 1960s, of social capital in America. The research of Hoskins et al (2006) indicates a mixed pattern of active citizenship in Europe. While David Halpern (2004) concurs that the strength of social capital in some western societies is cause for disquiet, he is much more concerned with the transformation of social capital per se. Halpern argues that what is more important is recognition that traditional types of social capital are in decline globally and are being replaced with more issue-specific and less time-demanding forms, with the most explicit manifestation residing within a universal increase in individualistic social capital. We argue that this mirrors many of the influences of consumerism in individuals' life-worlds and underlines the challenges associated with consumerism and climate change.

The British government is so concerned by this 'shift' in society, they have implemented educational policy to ensure citizenship now features highly on the educational curriculum in British schools, and are currently considering citizenship ceremonies for British school children to convey what it means to be a citizen of Britain-a sense of shared belonging, higher social cohesion, and for children to understand their rights and responsibilities as British citizens (BBC News24 2008). This concern is also reflected in wider educational networks, for example the CiCe thematic framework (see cice.londonmet.ac.uk).

Are we then facing a crisis in western society while we wait for an enlightened new generation to brandish the torch of citizenship as adults? Of course this depends on what is meant by citizenship and civicness. Professor Bernard Crick, who was asked to advise the British Government on introducing classes in citizenship into schools, makes a distinction between being a good citizen -obeying laws-and being an active citizen-getting involved in prescribed types of activity that are deemed of civic worth (for example voluntary work). However, this offers a somewhat narrow view of what it means to be a modern citizen living in the west, particularly if we accept that being civic and having a sense of community are perceived experiences, (Couldry et al 2007). Hence, it becomes necessary to look beyond the obvious places to better understand the state of 'civicness' in contemporary western society. At the same time it is also necessary to understand consumerism and its implications for civic society. In this paper we seek to do this by exploring the blurring of what has been viewed by traditionalists as two contrasting concepts, namely that of consumerism and citizenship, which is culminating in an emerging area of politicised consumption based on citizenly rights, obligations and social inclusion, together with competition and autonomous choice. We illustrate this emergence with specific reference to 'green' citizen-consumers to demonstrate the changing face of civic society in the west, where shopping can act as a vector for civic values. We begin our exploration by considering the underlying premises of civic culture, citizenship and consumerism.

THE UNDERLYING PREMISES OF CIVIC SOCIETY, CULTURE AND CITIZENSHIP

The attributes of a civic society and culture are considered essential for a healthy public sphere and thus for legitimate democracy to survive and flourish. Civic society is generally considered to be the terrain in our lives between those spaces occupied by the economy and the State. It is within this terrain that citizens reside. Taking its cue from Habermasian theories of the public sphere, civic society has to be situated in accessible spaces where the flow of information and ideas are largely unfettered so that a communicative interaction between citizens is encouraged. Thus, *"norms of equality and symmetry"* prevail (Dahlgren 2006, 277), allowing all an opportunity to participate. Discussion of a civic nature, about issues that affect society generally, is considered vital for democracy to survive. Without such activity the hollow institutions of democracy may remain but without moral authority (Dahlgren 2006). These somewhat abstract notions have to be rooted in the everyday, the personal and the subjective lives of individuals and it is from this assumption that the idea of civic culture becomes crucial.

Dahlgren (2000, 2003) argues that civic culture requires social agents to act as citizens because it is through and by such acts that road markers are set out shaping future patterns of civic thought and behaviour. Traditionally this civic space has been located between that occupied by state and private life spheres, where consumption would have been placed firmly within the private sphere. He

TABLE ONE

Dahlgren's Civic Culture model

Values	Must include positive disposition towards democracy as the best way of organising political life.
Identity	People must see themselves as a political entity, as a citizen among the many identities they hold.
Affinity	Minimal sense of commonality must exist based on recognition of mutual needs.
Knowledge	A degree of understanding about democracy and the literacy skills to participate.
Experience	There must be some recurring practices that concretise democracy from an abstract to an actual occasion/ event for people.
Discussion	Forms of civic interaction and discussion must take place in accessible locations.

Source: synopsis of the ideas of Dahlgren (2003), Reconfiguring Civic Culture in the New Media Milieu.

outlines six variables making up civic culture-table one. At any given point the specific mix of these variables shapes the civic environment that might then be characterised and positioned on a continuum of empowering–disempowering for those living within such a culture.

Within this civic environment, citizens are afforded a trio of rights: personal freedom, participation in political processes and a sharing of the benefits from societal wealth (Marshall 1964). Marshall's notion of citizenship places it beyond individual self-determination despite being centred on entitlement, because the benefits of citizenship result largely through the collective development of a civil society (Turner 2001). Citizens are concerned with solving public problems (Boyte and Skelton 1998), through possessing a sense of belonging to a wider community (Abala-Bertrand 1996). Citizenship is thus about rights balanced with responsibilities, where agency is manifest through voice, where decision-making involves giving due consideration to justice, equality and the widest possible consequences, a space that ultimately affords superiority to broad societal wishes. Crick (2000) makes it clear that citizenship involves more than passive adherence to law *and* it also entails a willingness to take part in the public domain, which in itself, presupposes a belief in some sense of the 'common good'. Thus citizenship offers a notion of freedom that includes duty, which, in effect, imposes a certain direction and purpose on that freedom. In this way being a citizen involves the checking of some individual rights because the collective rights supersede them. Citizenship is then, to varying degrees, about equity, participation, delayed gratification and some form of representation.

The liberal model of citizenship-premised on individual rights (Isin and Turner 2002)-is well entrenched in many Western societies. Accordingly liberty is promoted through allowing individuals to pursue their own interests, and, because a certain form of rational choice is assumed, the actions of one such individual is thus considered unlikely to limit the liberty of others. This form of citizenship is the political equivalent of a lassiez-faire market. Alternative theories of citizenship challenge the dominance of this liberal perspective, arguing that communitarianism affords a much greater role for community cohesion, (Etzioni 1993), where the emphasis is on our socio-cultural obligations to one another. This is the political equivalent of social economy models that call for vigorous State intervention. In his polemic, Dahlgren (2006, 269) argues that a republican model of citizenship acknowledges elements of both liberal and communitarian thinking, it is *"citizenship as a mode of social agency within the context of pluralistic interests"*. This articulation of citizenship thus offers a vision of society that creates space for us to move between individual and collective states of liberty. All three views of citizenship offer a view on the appropriate relationship between individual agency and community or social cohesion, between liberty and responsibility, between a freedom to and a freedom from. Parallels are evident in market spaces where the equivalent key relationship might be between consumer sovereignty and producer power. Nonetheless it is evident, from this brief account, how notions of the citizen and civic culture appear distant from a more consumerist-orientated culture.

THE CORE NOTIONS OF CONSUMERISM AND CONSUMERS

Consumerism is typically associated with hedonism, narcissism, nihilisism, decadence, instant gratification and social control (Cohen 2003; Desmond 2003; Durning 1991; Ewen 1976; Firat and Dholakia 1998; O'Shaughnessy and O'Shaughnessy 2002; Thompson 1996; Thompson and Tambyah 1999). It is therefore not surprising that, as Kass and Kass (2000) observe, the more people grow to love their freedom and to view it as a distinct element of their lifestyle, the more they will view themselves as having no obligation but to self-indulge. O'Shaunnessy and O'Shaunessy (2002) argue that it is this sovereignty and liberty of choice that is complicit in the negative reputation of consumerism. Consumerism is thus often perceived as a negative influence on the morals of society–encouraging 'false values', materialism, unrestrained choice and indulgence and the isolation of individuals from their traditional communities as they seek 'never-to-be fulfilled' promises from their consumption choices. This, in turn, feeds consumers anxiety and self-doubt, undermining their sense of subjective wellbeing, and so reducing their levels of happiness with their lives (Chaplin and John 2007; Borgmann 2000; Csikszentmihalyi 1990, 2000).

It is thus interesting to note that for an increasing number of people, the influence of consumption on their lives is growing, and with it, an increase in individualism. Consequently, around the world, mass consumer society has emerged as the major source of economic and social influence (Bauman 1998; Borgmann 2000; Desmond 2003; Schor 1998). As a result, a modernist perspective has emerged from this evolution (civilising) of society that emphasises the modern, self-disciplined, individual self (Elias 1994), where consumers, in accordance with the pursuit of scientific enlightenment and Cartesian control, are perceived as rational, self-maximising economic individuals in control of their emotions. This, at least initially, seems to strengthen a belief in the *distinction* between notions of civic and consumer culture.

However this modernist account of consumerism and its consequences for consumers fails to appreciate more contemporary understanding of consumers and their expanded consumption choices and meanings they ascribed to them. That is, the varied traditions, dialogue and practices that constitute their *'cultures of consumption'* (Arnould and Thompson 2005; Belk 1988; Bevir and Trentmann 2007; Holt 2002; McCraken 1986; Mick and Buhl 1992), as advocated by scholars exploring consumer culture theoretics. Within this more culturally-focused perspective, consumerism is regarded as a process of shared, social learning, laden with emotion, symbolic meaning and identity, and consumers less as culture bearers and more as culture-producers (Arnould and Thompson 2005; Belk 1988; Dermody and Scullion 2001; Maffesoli 1996; McCraken 1986, 1990; Mick and Buhl 1992). Consequently the marketplace, where the balance of power has, in some ways, shifted in favour of consumers, provides consumers with an assorted repertoire of mythic and symbolic resources enabling them to create their individual and collective identities–through their (expanded) consumption choices (Arnould and Thompson 2005; Baudrillard 1993; Belk 1988; Belk et al 2003; Elliott 1997, 1999; Holt 2002; Mick and Buhl 1992; Schau and Gilly 2003; Taylor and Saarinen 1994). What then emerges about contemporary consumers and their consumption is that they are interpretative agents who, in creating meaning from their consumption, play, individually and collectively, within a spectrum ranging from acceptance to (pseudo)rejection of the dominant identity and lifestyle images conveyed by advertising and mass media (Holt 2002; Kozinets 2002; Kozinets and Handelman 2004; Murray 2002; Thompson 2004). From this account, we see how consumerism has become a powerful influence on both individual and collective behaviour. Consequently can the empowering dimension of consumerism also be used to nurture additional civic threads within modern British society? We will now move our discussion on to consider the idea of the citizen-consumer.

EVALUATING THE IDEA OF THE CITIZEN-CONSUMER

Critics of consumerism typically perceive citizenship and consumerism to reside at opposite ends of the spectrum, a contrast between outward-looking, public interest versus private, inward-looking self-interest, where citizens are 'worthy' and consumers are 'unworthy'. Certainly the traditional version of civic culture and citizenship has been seen in stark contrast with what being a consumer entails; with, as we have previously discussed, the two positions residing within different cultural values and norms (Lasch 1978). Sharply contrasting world visions have been developed; one based on involvement in society as citizens of a nation, the other with involvement in a corporate world as consumer units (Elliott 1982). Sennett (cited in Bull 2000) argues that our immersion in consumerism leads to apathy about others, for him, being a consumer is instead of being a citizen. A dichotomy is thus exposed between a fundamental principle of the market, namely segmentation, which places emphasis on difference and a first order principle of citizenship-the idea of a common good (Cohen 2003). Consumerism is rooted in self-interest, whilst citizenship takes its inspiration from a regard for others. Citizenship is rooted in trust of others, consumerism in self-reliance (Sennett 1998). The dominance of a consumer culture has thus been articulated as a withdrawing from citizenship, with this void being filled by a small, anti-political group of activists, devoid of claims for legitimacy beyond their own pet projects and pet hates (Bauman 2001). Lash's (2002) notion of the 'loss of the common', related to common good, common experience and common troubles, has negative consequences for civic culture. He argues that this has resulted in an offloading of once public functions into private spaces (Lash 2003). Beck and Beck-Gernsheim (2002, 26) talk of how individualisation has

become culturally embedded, thus public space is now characterised by *"conflictual coexistence"*. Couldry (2006) maintain that our predominant orientation is away from anything considered public, many of us choose to place 'the other', the more distant, and the things we are less sure of in a public space. All of these are signs that we use 'public' to denote remoteness from our own responsibility and agency. Couldry's study concludes that any vague sense of a 'public connectedness' that their respondents felt did not generate civic deliberation or action. Accordingly they talk of a disarticulation between awareness of public issues and the place such issues are afforded in individuals' life-worlds. One discourse sees the rise of consumerism at the expense of citizenship contributing to a decline of the public over the private sphere (Marquand 2004). Consumer culture is thus distinctly different from the articulation of civic culture expressed by Dahlgren (2003) in table one. For example, with respect to values, there is more individuality and materialistic values, whilst for identity, choice becomes the arbiter of truth–table two.

Overall, then, for many, the impact of contemporary consumer society on traditional citizenship and civic culture has been regarded as negative because this distinct consumer culture has become so dominant.

Historically, however, these divergent positions are untrue (Cohen 2003). As Cohen observes, citizens and consumers have at times been in conflict and sometimes in harmony as the political and economic landscape changes. For example during 1890-1920, activist citizen consumers used their power in the marketplace, through boycotts and buycotts, to achieve progressive political reform in American society (Cohen 2003). The consumer boom then dominated the British and American political landscape, and in particular, according to Hilton (2001) and Bauman (2008), undermined the majestic collective ideals of citizenship by crushing the critical faculties of individuals as citizens in favour of individuals as shoppers. While this might have been true for rational, self-maximising, economic consumers, as our preceding discussion of contemporary consumers indicates, while consumers are embedded in capitalism, they are not passive, complacent nor non-evaluative in their consumption choices, which they weave into their complex, fluid identity projects–for their individual and collective purposes. Consequently they are *"not the unwitting dupe of legend, who responds rat like to environmental stimuli of Skinnerian caprice. Nor…transfixed, rabbit-like, in the headlights of multinational capital"* (Foxall et al 1998, 244). For some consumers, then, particularly those who are better educated, with high levels of political interest (Scammel 2003), and who have a particular personal values orientation, they are using their analytical talents and their economic power to achieve political reform in twenty-first century consumerist society. Widespread and often localised boycotts are illustrative of this. As a result what emerges is the distinction between materialistic and more citizenly-orientated types of consumers, as motivated by their personal values system rather than a broad distinction between citizens and consumers. Mapping this orientation to the values research of Schwartz (1992), materialistic consumers will reside within the domain of self-enhancement, based on the values of power, achievement and hedonism, while citizen-consumers reside within the domain of self-transcendence based on the values of benevolence and universalism. We see, for example, the growth in concern for the welfare of animals in the supermarkets and a growing interest being taken in the production processes of our favourite brands (Klein 2001). Therefore polarised classifications that see the concepts of citizenship and consumerism as only and always in opposition are under increased scrutiny (Bevir and Trentmann 2008; Chambers and

TABLE TWO
Adaptation of Dahlgren's Civic Culture model-Consumer Dominant *over* Citizen

Values	Individuality dominates in our constant quest for self-expression, understanding and high self-esteem. Immediacy is privileged over transience. Personal values are promoted at the expense of others and those identified as civic i.e. equality, justice and reciprocity are superseded. (Bauman 1998, 2001; Giddens 1991, 1998).
Identity	As self-enterprising individuals our sense of agency is realised most readily through consumer choice where personal taste and preference becomes the arbiter of truth and where our high self-efficacy is encouraged. (Rose 1996; Campbell 2001).
Affinity	Weak relationships are formed with brands and retailers based on an extended form of exchange e.g. loyalty schemes. Rights are seen to be actualised through individual not common actions-through notions of consumer sovereignty-thus located in the marketplace. (Gabriel and Lang 1995).
Knowledge	Little sociological imagination is required to operate successfully in the consumer sphere where knowing your own desires is considered to be most important. The linguistic capability/dominant discourse of marketing is, if not alien to civic speak, not supportive of it. (Belk et al 2003; Couldry 2004)
Experience	Experiences as a consumer dominate establishing our sense of expertise and everyday routines and practices. These tend to be framed in a way that eschews collective or public considerations. Our memory bank is characterised as fragmented rather than collective and is dominated by our experiences as consumers. (Warde 2005, Scullion 2006).
Discussion	Efforts are made to avoid talking politics with shopping and its associated interests acting as a key deflector. Little direct connection is made between our daily consumer lives and political action. Acceptable forms of public discourse are limited and increasingly personalised and local. Marketing tends to offer a single non critical type of discourse/form of discussion (about best deals not questioning the very ethics of deals). Closed loop so anti-pluralist. (Couldry 2005; Eliasoph 1998).

Kymlickc 2002; Dahlgren 2006; Edwards 2004; Soper and Trentmann 2008), particularly with the acknowledgement that consumption is now a key political site (Miller 1997; Michellette et al 2004; Nava 1991; Schudson 2007; Stevenson 2002). Thus, an alternative view to this idea that consumer culture *has replaced* civic culture is one that suggests they coalesce and this has brought about a change in the character of citizenship. Consequently the boundaries between private market and political spheres have broken down. This blurring of public and private, of what it signifies to be a consumer and a citizen, means actions once considered part of civic life are increasingly part of what we do as contemporary consumers. For example, in Britain in the last few years we have witnessed a consumer revolt over 'excessive' bank charges, a campaign against the practices of 'ticket touts' making huge profit margins on resold concert tickets and collective pressure being exerted on business and government alike over fuel prices. Of course original motives for involvement may have been about self-interest, but all have also resulted in a greater sensitivity to fairness and reasonableness. This is reflected in our second reiteration of Dahlgren's model of civic culture, where we illustrate how this synthesis reinvents interactions in a fusing of a civic and consumerist society–table three.

Accordingly we argue that this *changes* rather than simply *challenges* the nature of civic culture. Dahlgren (2003, 161) acknowledges that placing any notion of civic culture into a contemporary setting *"we find consumerism as an ideological vector in political discourse."* And this is particularly apparent within more ethically-orientated consumption, for example increasing consumption of fair-trade brands, and among consumers who 'force' commercial organisations to adopt more responsible business practices, for example the pressures placed on the British food industry and retailers, by parents, to make children's' food more healthy.

Furthermore, while civic-consumers tend to take a lead on creating a 'better society', they are also more likely to revise their own already civic-consumption choices to strengthen their 'civic cause', for example cycling rather than using public transport or getting involved in car share schemes to help save fuel and the environment. It is also interesting to observe that, similar to the persona typically portrayed of citizens (Collins and Butler 2003), the citizen-consumer takes an enduring rather than episodic approach to their market engagements; for example willingly entering into relationships with ethical investment organisations who emphasise a long term and more holistic perspective (Zwick et al 2008). We have developed a clearer sense of links between the various life-spheres we occupy, *"the notion of public has been sequestrated by 'electorate' consequently increasing the areas of life open to general scrutiny"* (Giddens 1991, 152). This has led to a heightened awareness and salience that our personal lives are wrapped up with global perils.

However, Bauman (2008) and Stevenson (2002) make important caveats to this merging of citizen and consumer. Bauman (2008) argues that consumer activism, including politicised consumption, is dangerous because it undermines the traditions of democracy; since it is the unelected select few acting for what *they* perceive as the good of others. While we acknowledge an undemocratic element within politicised consumption, this does not mean that it is inherently bad, particularly when considered within the context of climate change, discussed later in our paper. Furthermore, it must also be recognised that traditional avenues for democratic expression in western society are weakened by declining voter turnout and a low sense of efficacy, caused in part by public cynicism towards the tarnished reputation of politicians and parties (Dermody et al 2010), reinforcing doubt in the traditions of democracy to further causes that augment human, social and

TABLE THREE
Adaptation of Dahlgren's Civic Culture model–The Merging Citizen-Consumer

Values	Personal versions of humanist values are held where self-reliance and self-responsibility are fused with understanding the need for reciprocity and a desire for fairness. (Bauman 1998, Beck and Beck – Gurnsheim 2002).
Identity	This involves an increased reference to global and cosmopolitan identity with community and tribal alliances formed through shared consumer practices (Rose 1996, Warde 2005).
Affinity	Growth of single issue personalised political participation results in episodic collective action often through the marketplace. Through environmental concerns, there is a growing sense, in the west, of sharing responsibility for the fate of worlds future. (Stevenson 2002, Micheletti et al 2006, Zwick et al 2008).
Knowledge	A growing awareness emerges of the links between consumer actions and their impact on the broader world. There is a greater desire for transparency from both commercial and governmental organisations. (Klein 2001, Couldry 2004).
Experience	The ability to influence commercial and political organisations-often through marketplace actions– has increased. The mass media give widespread coverage of consumerist political campaigns. (Stevenson 2002, Scullion 2006).
Discussion	There is almost universal access to marketplace discussions that take on a political quality (for example the origins and fairness of food production). A choice agenda discourse emerges related to increased expectations of both private and public service delivery. (Collins and Butler 2003; Marquand 2004).

environmental capital. Stevenson (2002, 310) warns *"while consumption may raise 'ethical questions', it does so only by being connected to more formal citizenship criteria of rights, obligations and social exclusion."* Thus, not all consumers will act in a civic way–the distinction between the personal values orientations of materialists vs. citizen-consumers discussed above; and in addition, the cognitive capability and sense of personal efficacy to believe that their behaviour can make a difference. As Castells (1997, 359) remarks, the *"sites of this power are people's minds."* Hence the notion of a citizen-consumer appears to be reflective of consumers who, as interpretative agents, are immersed within the capitalist cultural production system, but who can choose to become politicised through their consumption, which they use collectively and individually to interact with their lived world, and in so doing aim to enhance civic society. A vital outcome of this blurring of consumer and citizen, as illustrated in table 3, is a greater sense of transparency and reflexivity. Hence we increasingly see and experience the connections-the politics of being a consumer-and so they shape what it means to live in contemporary society. Accordingly, we now illustrate and explore this within the context of sustainable consumption, which offers a pertinent illustration of this blurring of consumer and citizen.

THE GREEN CITIZEN-CONSUMER

Ecological destruction, for example current predictions of climate change and finite resources, means that we are *"currently living in the shadow of our own annihilation"*, (Stevenson 2002, 312). The latest United Nations Intergovernmental Panel on Climate Change states that evidence of global warming is incontrovertible, with catastrophic consequences, (IPCC 2007). Set within this shadow, environmentally responsible-'green' citizen-consumers-will be pursuing issues surrounding rights, obligations and social exclusion–as part of their economic power of consumption choices. Typically this will involve boycotts and buycotts (Friedman 1999, 2006; Micheletti et al 2006; Shaw et al 2006); where consumers pursue sustainability issues pertinent to human, social

and environmental capital, for example goods that are fairly traded, organic, cruelty-free, resource-efficient, recyclable, and/or local. As Friedman (1999) observes, boycotts–as expressions of *"economic democracy"* (198) that fuel media interest-are a highly attractive tactic that enable ordinary people to fight for a more sustainable future. Indeed, the involvement of more civic-orientated consumers in the development of more sustainable consumption patterns has been advocated for some time, (see for example Rio, 1992). Accordingly, political consumerism is becoming a core part of civic life as consumption becomes increasingly *"suffused with citizenship characteristics"* (Scammell 2000, 351). Consequently it is reflective of the start of a shift in political power in the UK that allows politicised consumers, albeit still a minority with limited influence (Kennedy 2006), to take immediate action to preserve our planet; and as Follesdal (2006, 8) observes, *"political consumerism can…be a stopgap measure until global structures are in place with sufficient enforcement power."* Clearly given the latest findings from the IPCC, political consumerism constitutes an important interim and ongoing response to help combat climate change.

Evidence has shown that the intensity of consumers' commitment towards environmentally responsible -'green'-consumption can vary (Dermody and Hanmer-Lloyd 1999 Kilbourne 1995). In turn this reflects the different roles that political consumerism can have per se. The work of Follesdal (2006) is pertinent here. He proposes five different notions of the role of political consumerism, which are not mutually exclusive. We have located these within the realms of sustainability and added indicators of the status (strength) of each role–table four.

As can be seen the more activist green political consumers adopt a role of 'reforming business practices'–which includes reforming government policy, while the more passive role is one of 'mutual respect' where repugnance is expressed but no action is taken.

It is also important to reflect on these roles in relation to engendering a more green civic society. Hence we will now

TABLE FOUR
Roles of Green Civic-Consumers

Role	Summary	Status
1. Agency	Green civic-consumers use their own agency to distance themselves from ' evil acts' , for example environmental pollution and corporate exploitation of child labour. Through boycotting these offending brands and companies they avoid complicity in evil behaviour that they believe is damaging to human, social and environmental capital. Thus they are attempting to break the causal chain between their own acts and immoral, non-sustainable outcomes.	Active
2. Expression of Self (Identity)	Green civic-consumers, through their ' green' consumption choices are actively expressing their post-materialist values. Their consumption choices fall within the realms of ethical and responsible, for example actively choosing organic fair-trade brands to strengthen human, social and environmental capital.	Active
3. Expression of Mutual Respect (Identity)	Behaviour is based on the belief that certain companies are violating fundamental normative constraints, e.g. a coffee company abusing the rights of coffee growers (human capital). These green civic-consumers, as individuals, will express repulsion at these violations by refusing to buy the offending brands, but they will not attempt to change the behaviour of others. Protecting economic capital will be important.	Moderately active
4. Instruments for Reforming Wrong-doers	Green civic-consumers will pressurise individuals to change their ' wrong' behaviour, e.g. driving SUVs in cities, non- recycling, by attempting to re-socialise them using, for example, the principles of punishment (shunning, rejection, etc). There is an orientation towards strengthening social capital– to reform the values of society for communal benefit.	Active
5. Instruments for Reforming Business Practices	Green civic-consumers– mainly through protests and boycotts– will drive/punish companies and governments to change their values and thus their behaviour/policies to secure better human rights and human security and so build human, social and environmental capital.	Very active

Source: adapted from the ideas of Follesdal, (2006), Political Consumerism as Chance and Challenge, pp 8-10.

elaborate on the merging citizen-consumer we presented in table three, contrasting this with the original ideas of Dahlgren (2003) in table one. Potentially the most distinctive difference occurs within *values*, where Dahlgren maintains that a positive disposition towards democracy must exist as the best way of organising political life. Yet for the citizen-consumer, they possess a sense of self-reliance and self-responsibility, which go beyond the traditional vessels of democracy to include the 'power' of the marketplace. Accordingly these individuals will possess the self-belief that they can make a contribution to democracy through their values-orientation of benevolence and universalism that directs their behaviour. This combination will be very potent in achieving the behaviour and policy changes needed to engender a more sustainability-orientated, civic-consumer culture. All of the roles identified by Follesdal (2006) will be influential here, but mutual respect may be the weakest. Consequently a picture begins to emerge of individuals actively pursuing the cause of human, social and environmental capital through the actions they take on behalf of others within the marketplace as 'agent' and as 'reformer'. In so doing, they express the fundamentals of their self-identity as green civic-consumers. Illustrations of these behaviours can be found in table four. Secondly, with respect to *identity*, people seeing themselves as a green citizen-consumer will regard themselves as politicised consumers with a global and cosmopolitan identity who, with reference to their community and tribal alliances, operate politically within the marketplace to further the cause of sustainability as a whole. With reference to Follesdal's roles, we can envisage strong connections

with 'self identity'–principally post-materialist values that engender the pursuit of ethical and responsible consumption–namely fairly-traded, organic, local, energy-efficient, etc. There is also likely to be a strong relationship with 'agency'. Thirdly, with Dahlgren's notion of *affinity,* where a growing sense of commonality is needed based on recognition of mutual needs, 'mutual respect' could be influential here and certainly the pursuit of social and environmental capital would be pertinent in working towards a civic culture that embraces sustainability. Fourthly, regarding *knowledge,* while individuals will need to understand democracy and possess the literacy skills to participate, equally important will be their cognisance of the market and how they can influence corporate, government and consumer behaviour to further the cause of sustainability by enhancing human, social, environmental and economic capital. 'Agency' and 'reform' will be important in achieving this. Dahlgren maintains in his fifth element of civic culture, namely *experience,* that there must be some recurring practices that concretise democracy from an abstract to an actual occasion and/or event for people. Consequently while elections will be important events, the positive outcomes of environmental and societal boycotts and protests will also concretise a broader sense of civicness through democracy-using the marketplace to further the cause of sustainability. 'Agency' and 'business/government reform' will be integral here. Finally, with respect to *discussion,* civic interaction and discussion must include integration of marketplace issues, both in terms of a critique of materialism as well as activism through political consumption that enables change to be achieved and thus furthers the sustainability agenda. The diversity of communication resources this engenders must be accessible to all. 'Agency' and 'business/government reform' will be important in facilitating this. Accordingly some interesting relationships begin to emerge between the persona of the green citizen-consumer and the roles they can play in enhancing the health of civic society. Clearly, though, further research is needed to empirically explore these relationships.

Becoming a 'green' citizen-consumer, however, is not easy since sustainability is, in itself, a complex issue (Giddens 1994; Goodland 2002). The pursuit of sustainability requires us to evolve to a higher plane of consciousness, for our orientation to become one of self-transcendence (Schwartz 1992), as we become more civic in our orientation (Berglund and Matti 2006; Doherty and de Geus 1996), which enables us to make more responsible and equitable choices as we interact within our capitalist system. It requires us to envision the world differently to enable us to re-engage with it. In many ways, it reflects Dahlgren's (2003) vision of civic society embedded with rights, obligations and social inclusion, but coupled with consumer power within the market system. This, in turn, mirrors the words of Kofi Annan, UN Secretary-General, (2000) when he stated: *"We have to choose between a global market driven only by calculations of short-term profit, and one which has a human face....Between a selfish free-for-all in which we ignore the fate of the losers, and a future in which the strong and the successful accept their responsibilities, showing global vision and leadership. Let us choose to unite the powers of the markets with the authority of universal ideals."*

CONCLUSION: THE EMERGENCE OF CIVIC CONSUMER CULTURE

In conclusion, our preceding discussion demonstrates that consumerism and citizenship can reside together, and in so doing, they can change each other. Hence contemporary citizenship is alive and active through politicised consumption–where shopping acts as a vector for nurturing civic values. Consequently this expression of citizenship operates through a 'cultures of consumption' paradigm–where individuals have a voice through their consumption choices, which they use to pursue social, human and environmental capital, which, in turn reflects a self-transcendence orientation, in accordance with the tenets of civic culture. Consumerism, then, can be empowering, and it has triggered a new expression of personal politics–through shopping–for increasingly powerful, compassionate, reflexive and self-consciously politicised consumer groups. Accordingly we are witnessing the emergence of a civic consumer culture, rooted in consumerism merged with citizenship, which has the potential to enhance the future health of our planet and civic society in the west.

REFERENCES

Albala-Bertrand, L (1996), *Open File: Citizenship and Education: Towards Meaningful Practice*, Unesco International Bureau of Education.

Arnould, E.J. and C.J. Thompson (2005), "Consumer Culture Theory (CCT): Twenty Years of Research," *Journal of Consumer Research*, Vol. 31 (March), 868-882.

Baudrillard, J. (1993), *Symbolic Exchange and Death*, London: Sage.

Bauman, Z. (1998), *Work, Consumerism and the New Poor*, Milton Keynes: Open University Press.

Bauman, Z. (2001), *The Individualized Society*, Oxford: Blackwell Publishing.

Bauman, Z. (2008), "Exit Homo Politicus, Enter Homo Consumens," in Soper, K. and Trentmann, F. (Eds.), *Citizenship and Consumption*, Palgrave Macmillan, Chapter 9 (139-153).

BBC News 24 (2008), "Pupils to Take Allegiance Oath," 11th March. http://www.bbc.co.uk

BBC News website (2007), Monday, 23 April. http://news.bbc.co.uk/1/hi/uk_politics/6582423.stm

Beck and Beck–Gurnsheim (2002), *Individualization. Institutionalized Individualism and its Social and Political Consequences*, London: Sage.

Belk, R. (1988), "Possessions and the Extended Self," *Journal of Consumer Research*, Vol. 15. (September), 139-168.

Belk, R.W., G. Guliz and S. Askegaard (2003), "The Fire of Desire: A Multisited Inquiry into Consumer Passion," *Journal of Consumer Research*, Vol. 30 (December), 326-352.

Berglund, C. and S. Matti (2006), "Citizen and Consumer: the Dual Role of Individuals in Environmental Policy," *Environmental Politics*, Vol. 15, No. 4, (August), 550-571.

Bevir, M. and F. Trentmann (2008), "Civic Choices: Retrieving Perspectives on Rationality, Consumption, and Citizenship," in K. Soper and F. Trentmann (Eds.), *Citizenship and Consumption*, Palgrave Macmillan, Chapter 2 (19-33).

Bevir, M. and F. Trentmann (2007), *Governance, Consumers and Citizens. Agency and Resistance in Contemporary Politics*, Basingstoke, UK: Palgrave.

Borgmann, A. (2000), "The Moral Complexion of Consumption," *Journal of Consumer Research*, Vol. 26 (March), 418-422.

Boyte and Skelton (1998), Available online at: http://www.publicwork.org/pdf/workingpapers/Reinventing%20Citizenship.pdf

Bull, M. (2000), *Sounding out the city. Personal stereos and the management of everyday life*, Oxford: Berg.

Castells, M. (1997), *The Power of Identity*, Oxford: Blackwell.

Chambers, S. and W. Kymickc (Eds.) (2002), *A Critical Theory of Civic Society*, NJ:Princeton University Press.

Chaplin, L.N. and D.R. John (2007), "Growing up in a Material World: Age differences in Materialism and Adolescents," *Journal of Consumer Research*, Vol. 34, No. 4 (December), 480-493.

Cohen, L. (2003), *A consumers' republic: The politics of mass consumption in postwar America*, New York: Knopf.

Collins, N. and P. Butler (2003), "When Marketing Models Clash with Democracy," *Journal of Public Affairs*, Vol. 3, 52-62.

Couldry, N. (2004), "The Productive 'Consumer' and the Dispersed 'Citizen'," International *Journal of Cultural Studies*, Vol 7 (March), 21-32.

Couldry, N. (2006), "Culture and Citizenship: The Missing Link?", *European Journal of Cultural Studies*, Vol 9. No.3, 321-340.

Couldry, N., S. Livingstone, and T. Markham (2007), *Media Consumption and Public Engagement: Beyond the Presumption of Attention*, Palgrave, New York, USA

Crick, B. (2000), *Essays on Citizenship*, London: Continuum.

Csikszentmihalyi, M. (1990), *Flow: The Psychology of Optimal Experience*, New York: Harper & Row.

Csikszentmihalyi, M. (2000), "The Cost and Benefits of Consuming," *Journal of Consumer Research*, Vol. 27 (September), 267-272.

Dahlgren, P. (2000), "Media, Citizenship and Civic Culture," in J. Curran and M. Gurevitch (Eds.), *Mass Media and Society* (3rd Edn.), London: Edward Arnold, 310-328.

Dahlgren, P. (2000), "The Internet and the Democratization of Civic Culture," *Political Communication*, Volume 17 No.4 (October), 335-340.

Dahlgren, P. (2003), "Reconfiguring Civic Culture in the New Media Milieu," in J. Corner and D. Pels (Eds.), *Media and the Restyling of Politics*, London: Sage. (Chapter 9).

Dahlgren, P. (2006), "Doing Citizenship The Cultural Origins of Civic Agency in the Public Sphere," *European Journal of Cultural Studies*, Vol. 9 No. 3, 267-286.

Dermody, J. and S. Hanmer-Lloyd (1999), *From Dolphin-Friendly Cornflakes to Ecological Revolution: Reflections on the Meanings of Greening*, Proceedings of Academy of Marketing Annual Conference, University of Stirling, 7-9 July.

Dermody, J. and R. Scullion (2001), "Delusions of Grandeur? Marketing's Contribution to "Meaningful" Western Political Consumption," *European Journal of Marketing*, Vol.35 No.9/10, 1085-1098.

Dermody, J., S. Hanmer-Lloyd and R. Scullion (2010), "Young People and Voting Behaviour: Alienated Youth and (or) an Interested and Critical Citizenry?," *European Journal of Marketing* (special edition on political marketing), Forthcoming.

Desmond, J. (2003), *Consuming Behaviour*, Basingstoke, UK: Palgrave.

Doherty, B. and M. de Geus (1996), *Democracy and Green Political Thought. Sustainability, Rights and Citizenship*, London: Routledge.

Durning, A. (1991), "Asking How Much is Enough," in L. Brown et al (Eds.), *State of the World, 1991*, New York: Norton.

Edwards, M. (2004), *Civic Society*, Cambridge: Polity Press.

Elias, N. (1994) (original 1939), *The Civilising Process: The History of Manners and State Formation and Civilization*, (Trans. Edmund Jephcott), Oxford: Basil Blackwell.

Eliasoph, N. (1998), *Avoiding Politics: How Americans Produce Apathy in Everyday Life*, Cambridge University Press.

Elliott, P. (1982), "Intellectuals, the 'Information Society' and the Disappearance of the Public Sphere," *Media Culture and Society*, Volume 4 No 3 (July), 243-253.

Elliott, R. (1997), "Existential Consumption and Irrational Desire,"*European Journal of Marketing*. Volume 31. Issue 3. 285-296.

Elliott, R. (1999), "Symbolic Meaning and Postmodern Consumer Culture," in D. Brownlie, M. Saren, R. Wensley and R. Whittington (Eds.) (1999), *Rethinking Marketing. Towards Critical Marketing Accountings*, London: Sage.

Etzioni, A. (1993), *The Spirit of Community: Rights, Responsibilities, and the Communitarian Agenda*, New York: Crown Publishers.

Ewen, S. (1976), *Captains of Consciousness: Advertising and the Social Roots of the Consumer Culture*, New York: McGraw-Hill.

Firat, A.F. and N. Dholakia (1998), *Consuming People: From Political Economy to Theatres of Consumption*, New York: Routledge.

Follesdal , A. (2006), "Political Consumerism as Chance and Challenge," in M. Micheletti, A. Follesdal and D. Stolle (Eds.), *Politics, Products and Markets. Exploring Political Consumerism Past and Present*, London: Transaction Publishers, Chapter 1.

Foxall, G.R., R.E. Goldsmith, and S. Brown (1998), *Consumer Psychology for Marketing* (second edn.), Thomson.

Friedman, M. (2006), "Using Consumer Boycotts to Stimulate Corporate Policy Changes: Marketplace, Media and Moral Considerations," in M. Micheletti, A. Follesdal and D. Stolle (Eds.), *Politics, Products and Markets. Exploring Political Consumerism Past and Present*, London: Transaction Publishers, 45-62.

Giddens, A. (1991), Modernity *and Self-Identity: Self and Society in the Late Modern Age*, Cambridge: Polity Press.

Giddens, A. (1994), *Beyond Left and Right: The Future of Radical Politics*, Cambridge: Polity Press.

Giddens, A. (1998), *The Third Way: The Renewal of Social Democracy*, Cambridge: Polity Press.

Goodland, R. (2002), "Sustainability: Human, Social, Economic and Environmental," in *Encyclopaedia of Global Change*, John Wiley.

Halpern, D. (2004), *Social Capital*, John Wiley.

Hilton, M. (2001), "Consumer politics in post-war Britain," in M. Daunton and M. Hilton, *The Politics of Consumption: Material Culture and Citizenship in Europe and America*, Oxford: Berg.

Holt, D.B. (2002), "Why do Brands Cause Trouble? A Dialectical Theory of Consumer Culture and Branding," *Journal of Consumer Research*, Vol. 29 (June), 70-90.

Hoskins, B., J. Jesinghaus, M. Mascherini, G. Munda, M. Nardo, M. Saisana, D. Van Nijlen, D. Vidoni and E. Villalba (2006), "Measuring Active Citizenship in Europe," Institute for the Protection and Security of the Citizen. *CRELL Research Paper 4*. EUR 22530 EN. http://farmweb.jrc.cec.eu.int/ CRELL/ http://www.jrc.cec.eu.int

IPCC (2007), UN's Intergovernmental Panel on Climate Change, *Summary for Policymakers of the Synthesis Report of the IPCC Fourth Assessment Report*, 17 November. Downloaded from http://www.ipcc.ch/# (accessed 23 November 2007).

Isin, E. and B. Turner (2002), *Handbook of Citizenship Studies*, London: Sage Publications.

Jones, G. (2005), "Labour worries in marginals may just be a ploy," *The Telegraph*, 4 May.

Kass, A. and L.R. Kass (2000), *Wing to Wing, Oar to Oar*, University of Notre Dame Press, Notre Dame, IN.

Kennedy, P. (2006), "Selling Virtue: Political and Economic Contradictions of Green/Ethical Marketing in the UK," in M. Micheletti, A. Follesdal and D. Stolle (Eds.), *Politics, Products and Markets. Exploring Political Consumerism Past and Present*, London: Transaction Publishers, Chapter 2.

Kilbourne, W.E. (1995), "Green Advertising: Salvation or Oxymoron?," *Journal of Advertising*, Vol. XXIV, No. 2 (summer), 7-19.

Klein, N. (2001), *No Logo*, Harper Collins, London.

Kozinets, R.V. (2002), "Can Consumers Escape the Market? Emancipatory Illuminations from Burning Man," *Journal of Consumer Research*. Vol. 29. (June). 20-38.

Kozinets, R.V. and J.M. Handelman (2004), "Adversaries of Consumption: Consumer Movements, Activism, and Ideology," *Journal of Consumer Research*, Vol. 31 (December), 691-704.

Lasch, C. (1978), *The Culture of Narcissism: American life in an Age of Diminishing Expectations*, New York: Norton.

Lash, S. (2002), Foreword in Beck and Beck–Gurnsheim, *Individualization. Institutionalized Individualism and its Social and Political Consequences*, London: Sage.

Lash, S. (2003), "Reflexivity as Non-linearity," *Theory, Culture and Society*, Vol. 20 No. 2 (April), 49-57.

Maffesoli, M. (1996), *The Time of Tribes*, Thousand Oaks, CA: Sage.

Marquand, D. (2004), *Decline of the Public. The Hollowing out of Citizenship*, Cambridge: Polity Press.

Marshall, T. (1964), *Citizenship and Social Class and Other Essays*, Cambridge: Cambridge University Press.

McCraken, G. (1986), "Culture and Consumption: A Theoretical Account of the Structure and Movement of the Cultural Meaning of Consumer Goods," *Journal of Consumer Research*, Vol. 13 (June), 71-84.

McCraken, G. (1990), *Culture and Consumption*, Bloomington and Indianapolis: Indiana University Press.

Micheletti, M A. Follesdal and D. Stolle (Eds.) (2006), *Politics, Products and Markets. Exploring Political Consumerism Past and Present*, London: Transaction Publishers.

Mick, D.G. and C. Buhl (1992) "A Meaning-Based Model of Advertising Experiences," *Journal of Consumer Research*, Vol. 19 (December), 317-338.

Miller, D. (1997a), "Consumption and its Consequences", in H. Mackay (Ed.), *Consumption and Everyday Life*, London: Sage. 14-50.

Miller, D. (1997b), "Could Shopping Ever Really Matter?," in E. Pasi and C. Campbell (Eds.), *The Shopping Experience*, London: Sage, 31-55.

Murray, J.B. (2002), "The Politics of Consumption: A Re-Inquiry on Thompson and Haytko's (1997) 'Speaking of Fashion," *Journal of Consumer Research*, Vol. 29 (December), 427-440.

Nava, M. (1991), "Consumerism Reconsidered: Buying and Power," *Cultural Studies*, Vol. 5. No. 2, 157-173.

O'Shaughnessy, J. and N.J. O'Shaughnessy (2002), "Marketing, the Consumer Society and Hedonism," *European Journal of Marketing*, Vol. 36 No. 5/6, 524-547.

Putnam, R. D. (2000), *Bowling Alone. The Collapse and Revival of American Community*, NY:Simon & Schuster.

Rio. (1992), *The United Nations Conference on Environment and Development*, Rio de Janeiro, 3-l4 June.

Rose, N. (1996), "The Death of the Social? Re-figuring the Territory of Government," *Economy and Society*, Vol 25, No.3, 327-356.

Scammell, M. (2000), "The Internet and Civic Engagement: The Age of the Citizen-Consumer." *Political Communication*, Vol.17, 351-5.

Scammell, M. (2003), "Citizen-Consumers: Towards a New Marketing of Politics," in J. Corner and D. Pels (Eds.), *Media and the Restyling of Politics*, London: Sage, (Chapter 7).

Schau, H.J. and M.C. Gilly (2003) "We Are What We Post? Self-Presentation in Personal Web Space," *Journal of Consumer Research*, Vol. 30 (December), 385-404.

Schor, J.B. (1998), *The Overspent American*, New York: Basic Books.

Schudson, M. (2007), "Citizens, Consumers and the Good Society," *The Annals of the American Academy of Political and Social Science*, Vol. 611 (May), 236-249.

Schwartz, SH. (1992), "Universals in the Content and Structure of Values: Theoretical Advances and Empirical Tests in 20 countries," *Advances in Experimental Social Psychology*, Vol.25, 1-65.

Scullion, R. (2006), "Investigating Electoral Choice through a Consumer as Choice-Maker Lens," in D. Lilleker, N. Jackson and R. Scullion (Eds.), *The Marketing of Political Parties. Political Marketing at the 2005 British General Election*, Manchester University Press, (Chapter 8).

Sennett, R. (1998), *The Corrosion of Character*, New York: Norton.

Shaw, D., T. Newholm, and R. Dickinson (2006), "Consumption as Voting: an Exploration of Consumer Empowerment," *European Journal of Marketing*, Vol. 40. No. 9/10, 1049-1067.

Soper, K. and F. Trentmann (2008), "Introduction", in Soper, K. and F. Trentmann (Eds.), *Citizenship and Consumption*, Palgrave Macmillan. Chapter 1 (1-16).

Stevenson, N. (2002), "Consumer Culture, Ecology and the Possibility of Cosmopolitan Citizenship," *Consumption, Markets and Culture*, Vol. 5. No. 4, 305-319.

Taylor, M. and E. Saarinen (1994), *Imagologies: Media Philosophy*, London: Routledge.

Thompson, C.J. (1996), "Caring Consumers: Gendered Consumption Meanings and the Juggling Lifestyle," *Journal of Consumer Research*, Vol. 22. (March), 388-407.

Thompson, C.J. (2004), "Marketplace Mythologies and Discourses of Power," *Journal of Consumer Research*, Vol. 31. (June), 162-180.

Thompson, C.J. and S.K. Tambyah (1999), "Trying to be Cosmopolitan," *Journal of Consumer Research*, Vol. 26. (December), 214-241.

Turner, B. (2001), "The Erosion of Citizenship," *British Journal of Sociology*, Volume 52. No 2. (June), 198-209.

Warde, A. (2005), "Consumption and Theories of Practice," *Journal of Consumer Culture*, Vol 5. No 2., 131-153.

Zwick, D., J. Denegri-Knott, and J. Schroeder (2008), "Unintended Political Investing: The Social Pedagogy of Wall Street," in D. Lilleker and R. Scullion (Eds.), *Voters or Consumers. Imagining the Contemporary Electorate*, (2008), Cambridge Scholars Publishing, UK.

Exploring How Perceived Store Price-Level and Customer Characteristics Influence Price-Related Emotions

Stephan Zielke, University of Göttingen, Germany

ABSTRACT

This paper demonstrates how the perceived price-level of a retail store and individual differences between customers impact on several price-related emotions as parts of a retailer's price image. The findings support the hypothesis that the perceived store price-level influences price-related emotions such as enjoyment, distress, anger, fear, interest, contempt, shame and guilt. Price consciousness and price-quality inferences moderate these relations and they also have direct effects on some of the emotions. The findings extend the limited knowledge regarding price-related emotions and illustrate the importance of customer characteristics in understanding emotional reactions to prices.

INTRODUCTION

Emotions receive attention in marketing research (Bagozzi, Gopinath, and Nyer 1999; Erevelles 1998). However, only a few studies mention the role of emotions in price perception and processing. They discuss smart shopper feelings (Schindler 1989) and price-related emotions theoretically (Raghubir 2006), analyze the role of emotions in explaining price fairness (Campbell 2007) and price acceptance (O'Neill and Lambert 2001), or treat emotions as a part of a retailer's price image (Zielke 2006). The limited number of studies about price and emotion is surprising as many people know from their own experience that cheap or expensive prices cause feelings of enjoyment, distress, anger, fear or interest. In addition, shopping in cheap stores may also trigger emotions like contempt, shame or guilt.

Knowledge of these effects is very important from a practical point of view as emotions may have a substantial behavioral relevance. Several studies prove that emotions mediate the relation between cognitions and response variables, such as attitudes, spending and customer migration (Chebat and Michon 2003; Chebat and Slusarczyk 2005; Holbrook and Batra 1987), and that they improve the prediction of such variables (Agarwal and Malhotra 2005; Allen, Machleit, and Schultz Kleine 1992; Allen et al. 2005). In a retail context, price-related emotions should accordingly have an important impact on attitudinal and behavioral store loyalty. Therefore, retailers have to understand the emotional consequences of their pricing activities, and should be aware of individual differences in the process of emotion formation, which are an important basis for segmentation approaches.

This study contributes to the understanding of price-related emotions by analyzing their antecedents. Building on price-image research (Zielke 2006), the paper focuses on the impact of price-level perception (as a belief) on different price-related emotions that are part of the retailer's price image. Thus, this paper concentrates on associating or anticipatory emotions rather than emotions in concrete shopping situations. The emotions analyzed as dependent variables are enjoyment, distress, anger, fear, interest, contempt, shame and guilt. This selection is based on Izard's (1977) catalogue of emotions and prior research (O'Neill and Lambert 2001).

In addition, this paper analyzes individual differences in the relationship between price-level perception and the different emotions. Previous studies identified the customers' price consciousness and price-quality inferences as antecedents of price acceptance (Lichtenstein, Bloch, and Black 1988; O'Neill and Lambert 2001). Building on the appraisal theory (Bagozzi et al. 1999), these characteristics can influence the relevance of different goals, which

play a role in emotion formation. They should therefore have effects on price-related emotions and moderate the emotional impact of price-level perception.

In summary, the central research questions of this paper are the following:

- What is the impact of price-level perception on different price-related emotions like enjoyment, distress, anger, fear, interest, contempt, shame and guilt?
- What is the impact of price consciousness and price-quality inferences on price-related emotions?
- How do price consciousness and price-quality inferences moderate the emotional impact of price-level perception?

Answering these research questions extends the existing literature on price-image research and exploratory studies on the role of emotions in price perception and processing.

DEFINING PRICE-RELATED EMOTIONS

In the psychological literature, many definitions of emotions emphasize different aspects of this construct (Kleinginna and Kleinginna 1981). Building on cognitive theories of emotion, Bagozzi et al. (1999) define emotion as "a mental state of readiness that arises from cognitive appraisals of events or thoughts". They illustrate further that appraisal is "an evaluative judgment and interpretation thereof" and that "emotions arise in response to appraisals one makes for something of relevance". Thus, in the context of this paper, evaluative judgments (e.g. price-level perceptions) and the relevance of these judgments (that depends e.g. on the customers' price consciousness) can cause different price-related emotions. Hence, price-related emotions are defined as emotions that result from evaluating a firm's pricing activities.

LITERATURE REVIEW ON PRICE-RELATED EMOTIONS

Only a few studies in the literature mention the impact of price perception and processing on price-related emotions. Schindler (1989) argues that cheap prices result in ego-expressive feelings, which he describes as smart-shopper feelings. However, he does not analyze these feelings empirically. Raghubir (2006) also discusses several emotions related to pricing, spending and saving in a theoretical paper. Campbell (2007) found that general affective reactions to price situations have an impact on price fairness judgments. O'Neill and Lambert (2001) investigate the role of emotions on the relationship between price consciousness, price-quality inferences, product involvement, internal reference price and the latitude of price acceptance for a pair of sports shoes. In their study, they measure six of Izard's (1977) basic emotions. However, their model only includes enjoyment of prices and surprise, while the iterative process of model fitting excluded distress, anger, disgust and contempt. Emotions also play a role in price image research. Zielke (2006) argues that remembered emotions are an integral part of a retailers' price image. He empirically identified an emotional image dimension, which correlates strongly with price-level perception. However, the study does not analyze the relationship between price-level perception and specific emotions.

To sum up, the literature analysis indicates that the perceived store price-level is related to emotions and that price consciousness and price-quality inferences may have an impact on this relation.

However, no study in the literature analyzes these relations empirically.

CONCEPTUAL FRAMEWORK

The present paper builds on existing research, analyzing the impact of perceived store price-level, price consciousness and price-quality inferences on different price-related emotions. Perceived store price-level is defined as the perception of a store's prices without taking differences in product quality or services into account. In the literature, many studies interpret price-level perception as the price image of the store (e.g. Büyükkurt 1986; Desai and Talukdar 2003; Nyström 1970; Zeithaml 1984). Therefore, the term price-level image is used in the following. High scores for the price-level image mean that perceived prices are low, while low scores mean that perceived prices are high.

Price consciousness and price-quality inferences are conceptualized according to definitions by Lichtenstein and his colleagues. Price consciousness refers to "the degree to which the consumer focuses exclusively on paying low prices" and the price-quality schema is the "generalized belief across product categories that the level of the price cue is related positively to the quality level of the product" (Lichtenstein, Ridgway, and Netemeyer 1993).

Two approaches are available to conceptualize price-related emotions. The first develops catalogues of basic emotions, which are building blocks for other higher order emotions (Ortony and Turner 1990). Izard (1977) differentiates between ten fundamental emotions, namely interest, enjoyment, anger, disgust, contempt, distress, fear, shame, guilt and surprise. A lot of empirical studies in the marketing field build on these catalogues (e.g. Allen et al. 1992; Oliver 1993; Westbrook 1987; Westbrook and Oliver 1991). The second describes and measures emotional experiences according to the dimensions pleasure, arousal and dominance (Mehrabian and Russell 1974). This approach is mostly applied to the analysis of store atmosphere (Baker, Grewal, and Levy 1992; Donovan and Rossiter 1982; Donovan et al. 1994).

According to Machleit and Eroglu (2000), discrete emotions contain more information and are better predictors of shopping satisfaction than general emotional dimensions. Hence, Izard's catalogue of basic emotions is an appropriate basis to conceptualize price-related emotions. For the present paper, eight out of the ten basic emotions suggested by Izard were selected. Disgust is left out, because of the difficulty to relate this emotion to prices. Surprise is also excluded because the relationship between price-level perception and surprise is probably non-linear and thus requires special treatment in the analysis. Interest is included, although interest might be more of a cognitive state than an emotion (Richins, 1997) or a mode of action readiness (Frijda, Kuipers, and ter Schure 1989). To sum up, eight emotions, namely enjoyment, distress, anger, fear, interest, contempt, shame and guilt, are included in the following analysis.

HYPOTHESES

In the first stage, hypotheses regarding the impact of price-level image on the different price-related emotions were developed. The theoretical basis for the following hypotheses is the appraisal theory, according to which *goal relevance* and *goal congruence* play an important role in emotion formation (Bagozzi et al. 1999; Lazarus 1991; Smith and Lazarus 1993). In the context of price-level perception, different goals are potentially affected:

- Firstly, low prices support the goal of saving money while expensive prices violate this goal.
- Secondly, buying in cheap stores has an impact on the goal of social status (Ashworth, Dark, and Schaller 2005).

- Thirdly, low prices can affect the goal of social responsibility because buying budget-priced groceries may have negative consequences for small local shops, farmers and the environment (Lavorata and Pontier 2005).

Thus, low prices are congruent to the goal of saving money, but at the same time incongruent to other goals.

Furthermore, the specific goals can produce different emotions (Lazarus 1991). The congruence or incongruence to the saving goal should be related to enjoyment, distress, anger, fear and interest. According to appraisal theorists (e.g. Roseman, Spindel, and Jose 1990), these emotions occur in situations, for which the retailer (his pricing policy) or other circumstances (e.g. cost structures) are responsible. Assuming that congruence or incongruence to the saving goal are attributed to the retailer or circumstances, lower prices should lead to increased enjoyment and decreased distress, anger and fear. In addition, lower prices should also decrease interest. Interest should be stronger in expensive stores, where the incongruence to the saving goal makes customers more attentive, focused and alert regarding prices.

Incongruence to the goals of social status and social responsibility might be perceived as more self-induced, as customers can sacrifice these goals in favor of making a good deal. Emotions resulting from the incongruence of self-induced goals are shame and guilt (Roseman et al. 1990). Thus, low prices might lead to the incongruence of social goals, resulting in higher levels of shame and guilt. The same effect should hold for contempt because contempt can be interpreted as a projection of shame. The individual's own blameworthy behavior that induces shame should induce contempt if it is performed by others (Ortony, Clore, and Collins 1988).

In summary, low prices lead to the congruence of the saving goal and thus have a positive impact on enjoyment but a negative one on distress, anger, fear and interest. However, they also lead to the incongruence of social goals, resulting in stronger feelings of contempt, shame and guilt.

H1: The lower a customer perceives a retailer's price-level, the stronger the price-related enjoyment, contempt, shame and guilt and the weaker price-related distress, anger, fear and interest is.

The next hypotheses refer to the impact of price consciousness. By definition, price consciousness has a positive impact on the relevance of saving money. An increased relevance of the saving goal has two effects: firstly, respondents might experience enjoyment, distress, anger, fear and interest on a higher level, irrespective of the prices in a store. Secondly, price-conscious customers will react more emotionally to differences in price levels.

H2: The stronger the price consciousness, the bigger the enjoyment, distress, anger, fear and interest.

H3: For high price-conscious customers, the impact of price-level perception on enjoyment, distress, anger, fear and interest is stronger (compared to customers who are less price-conscious).

Similarly, price-quality inferences also affect the relevance of the saving goal. However, the effect is in the opposite direction. Customers with strong price-quality inferences might evaluate the saving goal as less relevant because it conflicts with quality goals. Consequently, the levels of enjoyment, distress, anger, fear and interest should be smaller, and customers with strong price-quality inferences should react less emotionally to changes or differences

TABLE 1
Item-scale (extract)

Price-level image	The prices are generally very low here.
Price consciousness	I mostly buy very cheap products when shopping for groceries.
Price-quality inferences	If I pay more for groceries, they are generally better quality.
Enjoyment	I am often delighted by the prices in this shop.
Distress	The prices in this shop make me sad.
Anger	I become angry when I think about the prices in this shop.
Fear	I am scared of paying too much in this shop.
Interest	I am very attentive when it comes to prices in this shop.
Contempt	I find that more strange people shop here than elsewhere.
Shame	I feel a bit embarrassed when I have to shop here.
Guilt	I have a bad conscience when I buy groceries here.

in price levels, regarding these emotions. However, for the level of fear and interest, cue utilization and uncertainty can mask this effect. This is explained in more detail in the discussion section.

Price-quality inferences also affect the goals of social status and social responsibility. If low prices signal poor quality, buying in cheap stores may become more embarrassing and thus the incongruence of low prices with the goal of social status increases. As a consequence, customers experience higher levels of contempt and shame, and they react more emotionally to differences in price levels. In addition, price-quality inferences should have an impact on guilt, especially if credence qualities like the environmental compatibility of the production process or animal welfare are affected. Thus, the level of guilt increases and customers react more emotionally with regard to this emotion.

H4: The stronger the price-quality inferences, the smaller the enjoyment, distress, anger, fear and interest and the stronger are contempt, shame and guilt.

H5: For customers with strong price-quality inferences, the impact of price-level perception on enjoyment, distress, anger, fear and interest is weaker while the impact on contempt, shame and guilt is stronger (compared to customers with weak price quality inferences).

MEASURES

Testing the hypotheses empirically requires measures for the different constructs. The price-level image was measured with five items, price consciousness and price-quality inferences with four. The item scales for these constructs were used by the author in various earlier studies (e.g. Zielke 2007). Three to four items measured each price-related emotion. Most items were generated based on the Differential Emotions Scale from Izard (1977). However, the original items were adapted to relate the emotions to prices. Table 1 presents an extract of the item scale (the complete scale is available from the author upon request). Following the recommendation of Bagozzi et al. (1999), unipolar seven-point scales were used. The scales ranged from totally disagree (1) to totally agree (7).

RESEARCH DESIGN AND SAMPLE

The different measures were embedded into a questionnaire. The questionnaire included questions on the respondents' buying behavior, a scale measuring price perception and price-related emotions, scales for price consciousness, price-quality inferences and questions regarding the socio-demographic and socio-economic status of the respondents.

Each respondent rated the price-level image and price-related emotions for two stores, which are different in their price positioning. They selected the two stores from a list of several grocery retailers, including discounters, supermarkets, hypermarkets and small grocery businesses. No particular criteria were given for store selection, except that the stores differ in their price positioning. This procedure should guarantee a sufficient amount of variance in the data. Furthermore, the procedure has the advantage that respondents rate the stores relatively to each other, which should be closer to real world shopping situations.

University students collected the data. They were advised to distribute the questionnaires to respondents of different ages, gender, household size and income. The generated sample comprises 291 respondents or 582 cases (because each respondent evaluated two stores). The mean age of the respondents is 37 years, 64% are female and 74% live in a household with two or more persons. The median income is between 1,500-2,000 Euros. In 39.9% of all cases the respondents rated their preferred store, and in 39.5% they rated stores where their grocery expenditures do not exceed 25 percent. Hence, the results are not biased towards preferred stores.

RESULTS

For all constructs, the alpha coefficients are similar to those reported by Izard (1977), and they exceed the value of .70. The discriminant validity is also sufficient according to Fornell and Larcker's (1981) criterion. One exception is fear, which correlates strongly with the price-level image. Therefore, the results for fear should be interpreted with some caution.

The hypotheses are tested with covariance structure analyses, using the MLR estimator in Mplus (Muthén and Muthén 2007). The

TABLE 2

The emotional impact of price-level image, price consciousness and price-quality inferences

Independent Variables	Dependent variables							
	Enjoyment	Distress	Anger	Fear	Interest	Contempt	Shame	Guilt
Price-level image	.67*	-.46*	-.51*	-.86*	-.52*	.10*	.13*	-.08
Price consciousness	.06	.26*	.25*	.22*	.54*	.01	.05	.17*
Price-quality inferences	-.09	.07	.10	.11*	.25*	.21*	.35*	.36*
R^2	.48	.23	.27	.73	.43	.06	.13	.11
CFI	.92	.92	.92	.93	.94	.94	.94	.93
SRMR	.05	.05	.06	.05	.05	.05	.04	.05

* significant effect for p<.05

results for H1, H2 and H4 are presented in table 2. All fit-indexes are acceptable, but not outstanding. R-square values are large for fear, but small for contempt, shame and guilt.

H1 stated that the lower a customer perceives a retailer's price-level (indicated by high scores for the price-level image), the stronger the price-related enjoyment, contempt, shame and guilt and the weaker the price-related distress, anger, fear and interest is. This hypothesis is supported by significant positive coefficients for enjoyment (.67), contempt (.10) and shame (.13) and negative coefficients for distress (-.46), anger (-.51), fear (-.86) and interest (-.52). Only the coefficient for guilt is contrary to H1 negative but not significant.

H2 assumed that price consciousness influences the levels of emotions, which are related to the saving goal. Supporting H2, price consciousness significantly increases the level of distress (.26), anger (.25), fear (.22) and interest (.54). The effect on enjoyment is also positive but small and not significant. In addition, price consciousness has a positive impact on the level of guilt (.17). This effect was not hypothesized.

According to H4, price-quality inferences should decrease the level of enjoyment, distress, anger, fear and interest, while they increase the levels of contempt, shame and guilt. The hypothesis is only supported for emotions that are related to social goals. Price-quality inferences have a positive impact on contempt (.21), shame (.35) and guilt (.36). The results do not support the hypothesis for emotions that are related to the saving goal. The coefficients for enjoyment, distress and anger are not significant. The effects for fear (.11) and interest (.25) are significant but contrary to the hypothesis positive.

H3 and H5 assumed that price consciousness and price-quality inferences have an impact on how emotionally customers react to changes or differences in the perceived store price-level. According to H3, the impact of the price-level image on enjoyment, distress, anger, fear and interest should be stronger for high price-conscious customers. Using a scale split, the respondents were separated in two groups with high and low price consciousness. Differences

between both groups were tested with multiple group covariance structure analyses in Mplus. Table 3 presents the results.

Supporting H3, high price-conscious customers react more emotionally to differences in the perceived store price-level for enjoyment, distress and anger. For fear and interest, the coefficient is also larger in the high price-conscious group. However, the multiple group model does not differ significantly from a restricted model, where the effects are identical in both groups. In addition to the hypothesized effects, more differences between both groups were found. The price-level image influences shame only for low price-conscious customers (.25). The results for guilt are most interesting. If customers are not price conscious, lower prices increase guilt (.18), but for high price-conscious customers, lower prices reduce guilt significantly (-.32).

H5 was also analyzed using a multiple group covariance structure analysis. Table 4 presents the results. According to H5, for customers with high price-quality inferences, the impact of the price-level image on enjoyment, distress, anger, fear and interest is weaker while the impact on contempt, shame and guilt is stronger (compared to customers with weak price-quality inferences). The results support H5 for enjoyment, distress, interest and shame. For anger and contempt, the size of the effects is as hypothesized, however the effects or differences are not significant. Contrary to H5, the coefficients for fear are identical. Again, the effect for guilt is most interesting. If price quality-inferences are strong, lower prices increase guilt (.26). However, if these inferences are weak, lower prices have negative impact on guilt (-.34).

DISCUSSION

After presenting the results, some unexpected findings should be discussed in more detail. Firstly, without considering moderating effects, the price-level image has no impact on guilt. Interestingly, whether low prices increase or reduce guilt depends on customer characteristics. If the price consciousness is small or the price-quality inferences are large, low prices increase guilt. Otherwise, low prices reduce this emotion. However, there is an explana-

TABLE 3
How price consciousness (pc) moderates the emotional impact of the price-level image

	Dependent variables							
	Enjoyment	Distress	Anger	Fear	Interest	Contempt	Shame	Guilt
Beta (pc low)	.61*	-.31*	-.35*	-.76*	-.36*	.16	.25*	.18*
Beta (pc high)	.76*#	-.58*#	-.64*#	-.91*	-.51*	.08	.21#	-.32*#
CFI	.93	.95	.92	.95	.95	.95	.92	.95
SRMR	.06	.05	.08	.05	.06	.06	.07	.06

* significant effect for p<.05; # effects between both groups differ significantly for p<.05 (chi-square difference test according to Satorra and Bentler (2001))

TABLE 4
How price-quality inferences (pqi) moderate the emotional impact of the price-level image

	Dependent variables							
	Enjoyment	Distress	Anger	Fear	Interest	Contempt	Shame	Guilt
Beta (pqi low)	.75*	-.52*	-.56*	-.81*	-.50*	.08	.06	-.34*
Beta (pqi high)	.59*#	-.17#	-.27*	-.81*	-.23*#	.15	.27*#	.26*#
CFI	.94	.95	.93	.95	.97	.96	.94	.95
SRMR	.06	.05	.07	.05	.05	.06	.07	.07

* significant effect for p<.05; # effects between both groups differ significantly for p<.05 (chi-square difference test according to Satorra and Bentler (2001))

tion for these effects. A violation of the social responsibility goal is not the only thing that might result in guilt; price conscious customers and those with small price-quality inferences might feel guilty if they buy in expensive stores, resulting in a negative relation between low prices and guilt.

Secondly, price-quality inferences do not have a direct effect on enjoyment, distress and anger. Contrary to the hypotheses, the impact on fear and interest is positive and significant. As indicated in the hypotheses section, it is possible to explain the results for interest and fear. If price-quality inferences are strong, customers might use prices as cues for product quality. Hence, they are more interested in prices. The impact on fear might be positive, because price-quality inferences can cause uncertainty in the price evaluation process, resulting in stronger fear.

Finally, price consciousness influences the impact of low prices on shame. This impact only exists for low price-conscious respondents. An explanation for this finding might lie in social desirability and consistence effects. High price-conscious customers who usually buy in cheap stores might not admit to or suppress feelings of contempt and shame.

IMPLICATIONS, LIMITATIONS, AND FUTURE RESEARCH

The results have important implications because they widen the understanding of the antecedents of price-related emotions. The perceived store price-level is an important predictor of several emotions. Price consciousness and price-quality inferences moderate this impact and they have direct effects on some of the emotions. The findings extend the prior research on retail price images (Zielke 2006), individual differences in price perception and processing (Lichtenstein et al. 1988) and exploratory studies on price-related emotions (O'Neill and Lambert 2001).

Besides these theoretical implications, the results are also important from a management perspective as they underline the fact that emotional reactions to prices depend on customer segments with different levels of price consciousness and price-quality inferences. Therefore, retailers should consider these variables in their segmentation approaches. The results also show that retailers can influence price-related emotions without changing their price levels, for example by influencing price consciousness or price-quality inferences.

The study also has certain limitations. Firstly, the measurement of emotions is based on Izard's Differential Emotions Scale. Richins (1997) argues that this scale does not capture the full range of consumption-related emotions, and this argument might also hold for price-related emotions. Secondly, the independent variables explain the emotions to a limited extent. Some R-square values are small, especially for contempt, shame and guilt. Furthermore, the fit-indexes of the models are improvable. Thirdly, in the hypotheses section, most arguments are based on goal relevance and goal congruence. However, these constructs were not measured explicitly.

Hence, future studies should analyze additional emotions, for example surprise or pride. They should also introduce more antecedents of price-related emotions, for example value for money, and they should measure goal relevance and goal congruence explicitly. It might be also interesting to investigate the moderating effects of other customer characteristics, for example prestige consciousness or ethics orientation. Future studies might also consider alternative methods, for example experimental approaches. Finally, future research should analyze the consequences of the different price-related emotions. Consequently, this paper is hopefully a starting point for subsequent studies on price-related emotions.

REFERENCES

Agarwal, James and Naresh K. Malhotra (2005), "An Integrated Model of Attitude and Affect: Theoretical Foundation and Empirical Investigation," *Journal of Business Research*, 58 (4), 483-493.

Allen, Chris T., Karen A. Machleit, and Susan Schultz Kleine (1992), "A Comparison of Attitudes and Emotions as Predictors of Behavior at Diverse Levels of Behavioral Experience," *Journal of Consumer Research*, 18 (3), 493-504.

Allen, Chris T., Karen A. Machleit, Susan Schultz Kleine, and Arti Sahni Notani (2005), "A Place for Emotion in Attitude Models," *Journal of Business Research*, 58 (4), 494-499.

Ashworth, Laurence, Peter R. Darke and Mark Schaller (2005), "No One Wants to Look Cheap: Trade-Offs Between Social Distinctiveness and the Economic and Psychological Incentives to Redeem Coupons," *Journal of Consumer Psychology*, 15 (4), 295-306.

Bagozzi, Richard P., Mahesh Gopinath, and Prashanth U. Nyer (1999), "The Role of Emotions in Marketing," *Journal of the Academy of Marketing Science*, 27 (2), 184-206.

Baker, Julie, Dhruv Grewal, and Michael Levy (1992), "An Experimental Approach to Making Retail Store Environmental Decisions," *Journal of Retailing*, 68 (4), 445-460.

Büyükkurt, B. Kemal (1986), "Integration of Serially Sampled Price Information: Modeling and Some Findings," *Journal of Consumer Research*, 13 (3), 357-373.

Campbell, Margaret C. (2007), "Says Who?! How the Source of Price Information and Affect Influence Perceived Price (Un)fairness," *Journal of Marketing Research*, 44 (2), 261-271.

Chebat, Jean-Charles and Richard Michon (2003), "Impact of Ambient Odors on Mall Shoppers' Emotions, Cognition, and Spending. A Test of Competitive Causal Theories," *Journal of Business Research*, 56 (7), 529-539.

Chebat, Jean-Charles and Witold Slusarczyk (2005), "How Emotions Mediate the Effects of Perceived Justice on Loyalty in Service Recovery Situations: An Empirical Study," *Journal of Business Research*, 58 (5), 664-673.

Desai, Kalpesh K. and Debabrata Talukdar (2003), "Relationship between a Product Groups' Price Perceptions, Shopper's Basket Size, and Grocery Store's Overall Store Price Image," *Psychology & Marketing*, 20 (10), 903-933.

Donovan, Robert J. and John R. Rossiter (1982), "Store Atmosphere: An Environmental Psychology Approach," *Journal of Retailing*, 58 (1), 34-57

Donovan, Robert J., John R. Rossiter, Gilian Marcoolyn, and Andrew Nesdale (1994), "Store Atmosphere and Purchasing Behavior," *Journal of Retailing*, 70 (3), 283-294.

Erevelles, Sunil (1998), "The Role of Affect in Marketing," *Journal of Business Research*, 42 (3), 199-215.

Fornell, Claes and David F. Larcker (1981), "Evaluating Structural Equation Models with Unobservable Variables and Measurement Error," *Journal of Marketing Research*, 18 (1), 39-50.

Frijda, Nico H., Peter Kuipers, and Elisabeth ter Schure (1989), "Relations Among Emotions, Appraisal, and Emotional Action Readiness," *Journal of Personality and Social Psychology*, 57 (2), 212-228.

Holbrook, Morris B. and Rajeev Batra (1987), "Assessing the Role of Emotions as Mediators of Consumer Responses to Advertising," *Journal of Consumer Research*, 14 (3), 404-420.

Izard, Caroll E. (1977), *Human Emotions*, New York, NY: Plenum Press.

Kleinginna, Paul R. Jr. and A. M. Kleinginna (1981), "A Categorized List of Emotion Definitions, with Suggestions for a Consensual Definition," *Motivation and Emotion*, 5 (4), 345-379.

Lavorata Laure and Suzanne Pontier (2005), "The Success of a Retailer's Ethical Policy: Focusing on Local Actions," *Academy of Marketing Science Review*, 5 (12), 1-9.

Lazarus, Richard S. (1991), *Emotion and Adaptation*, New York: Oxford University Press.

Lichtenstein, Donald R., Peter H. Bloch, and William C. Black (1988), "Correlates of Price Acceptability," *Journal of Consumer Research*, 15 (2), 243-252.

Lichtenstein, Donald R., Nancy M. Ridgway, and Richard G. Netemeyer (1993), "Price Perceptions and Consumer Shopping Behavior: A Field Study," *Journal of Marketing Research*, 30 (2), 234-245.

Machleit, Karen A. and Sevgin A. Eroglu (2000), "Describing and Measuring Emotional Response to Shopping Experience," *Journal of Business Research*, 49 (2), 101-111.

Muthén, Linda K. and Bengt O. Muthén (2007), *Mplus User's Guide* (4th ed.), Los Angeles, CA: Muthén & Muthén.

Mehrabian, Albert and James A. Russell 1974), *An Approach to Environmental Psychology*, Cambridge, MA: MIT Press.

Nyström, Harry (1970), *Retail Pricing: An Integrated Economic and Psychological Approach*, Stockholm, Sweden: EFI.

O'Neill, Regina M. and David R. Lambert (2001), "The Emotional Side of Price," *Psychology & Marketing*, 18 (3), 217-237.

Oliver, Richard L. (1993), "Cognitive, Affective, and Attribute Bases of the Satisfaction Response," *Journal of Consumer Research*, 20 (3), 418-430.

Ortony, Andrew, Gerald L. Clore, and Allan Collins (1988), *The Cognitive Structure of Emotions*, Cambridge, UK: Cambridge University Press.

Ortony, Andrew and Terence J. Turner (1990), "What's Basic about Basic Emotions?," *Psychological Review*, 97 (3), 315-331.

Raghubir, Priya (2006), "An Information Processing Review of the Subjective Value of Money and Prices," *Journal of Business Research*, 59 (10/11), 1053-1062.

Richins, Marsha L (1997), "Measuring Emotions in the Consumption Experience," *Journal of Consumer Research*, 24 (2), 127-146.

Roseman, Ira J., Martin S. Spindel, and Paul E. Jose (1990), "Appraisals of Emotion-Eliciting Events: Testing a Theory of Discrete Emotions," *Journal of Personality and Social Psychology*, 59 (5), 899-915.

Satorra, Albert and Peter M. Bentler (2001), "A Scaled Difference Chi-Square Test Statistic for Moment Structure Analysis, " *Psychometrika*, 66 (4), 507-514.

Schindler, Robert M. (1989), "The Excitement of Getting a Bargain: Some Hypotheses Concerning the Origins and Effects of Smart-Shopper Feelings," *Advances in Consumer Research*, 16, 447-453.

Smith, Craig A. and Richard S. Lazarus (1993), "Appraisal Components, Core Relational Themes, and the Emotions," *Cognition and Emotion*, 7 (3/4), 233-269.

Westbrook, Robert A. (1987), "Product/Consumption-Based Affective Responses and Postpurchase Processes," *Journal of Marketing Research*, 24 (3), 258-270.

Westbrook, Robert A. and Richard L. Oliver (1991), "The Dimensionality of Consumption Emotion Patterns and Consumer Satisfaction," *Journal of Consumer Research*, 18 (1), 84-91.

Zeithaml, Valarie A. (1984), "Issues in Conceptualizing and Measuring Consumer Response to Price," *Advances in Consumer Research*, 11, 612-616.

Zielke, Stephan (2006), "Measurement of Retailers' Price Images with a Multiple-item Scale," *The International Review of Retail, Distribution and Consumer Research*, 16 (3), 297-316.

Zielke, Stephan (2007), "Why are Discount Stores so Cheap? An Analysis of Customer Attributions," in *Proceedings of the 34th International La Londe Research Conference in Marketing*, ed. Søren Askegaard, Dwight Merunka, and Joseph M. Sirgy, La Londe, France.

Moderating Effects of Emotion on the Perceived Fairness of Price Increases

Tobias Heussler, University of Muenster, Germany
Frank Huber, University of Mainz, Germany
Frederik Meyer, University of Mainz, Germany
Kai Vollhardt, University of Mainz, Germany
Dieter Ahlert, University of Muenster, Germany

ABSTRACT

Previous research on price changes has focused on the analysis of price increases on the basis of rational processes. This paper focuses on the examination of the moderating role of emotions on the relationship between the magnitude of price increases and perceived price fairness. In addition, we analyze the effect of perceived price fairness and willingness to pay in consideration of the moderating influence of emotions. The empirical results demonstrate that emotions have the potential to compensate for the negative impact of price increases on perceived price fairness and the willingness to pay.

INTRODUCTION

A great many companies today are acting on markets that are suffering from saturation of consumption. Overcapacities lead to price wars. Although most managers are aware of the negative influence of price decreases on financial performance, such price decreases are common practice (see Diller 2008). According to Marn and Rosielle, "Improvements in price typically have three to four times the effect on profitability as proportionate increases in volume" (Marn and Rosielle 1992, 82). Further empirical evidence is provided by Simon and Dolan (1996). Their empirical study demonstrates that a price increase of 20% leads to a quintuple gain in company profit in the chemical industry. To set effective prices, marketers need to predict how consumers are likely to respond to price changes (Campbell 1999).

The acceptance of price increases has been identified as one critical factor of profit gains. Therefore, the knowledge about customers reaction to price increases is indispensable in order to realize effective prices. However, knowledge about customers' reaction to price increases is rarely addressed in marketing literature (Homburg, Hoyer and Koschate 2005). Critical determinants of the evaluation process are presumably the quality (Monroe 1973) and the perceived fairness (Hermann, Wricke and Huber 2000) of an offer. Xia, Monroe, and Cox (2004) state that the consumer will be more sensitive to the price of a product or service if the price leaves a corridor in which the price is perceived as fair and appropriate.

Most articles in behavioral pricing literature focus on cognitive aspects of unfairness perceptions (Homburg and Koschate 2005). While marketing research confirms the role of emotions (Westbrook and Oliver 1991; Bagozzi, Gopinath and Nyer 1999) in information processing and behavior, the influence of emotion[1] on price fairness judgments has been neglected so far (Cohen and Areni 1991). O'Neill and Lambert (2001) and Babin, Hardesty and Suter (2003) suggest that there is likely to be a relationship between price and emotion. We propose that emotion is an important element that accompanies the cognition of perceived price fairness.

The neglected integration of emotional factors into the information processing is surprising. Churchill and Surprenant (1982) maintain that in some situations cognitive aspects as moderator variables are of less importance than are emotional aspects. Empirical support is given by Westbrook and Oliver (1987). Their research examined the hypothesis that emotional components may even dominate cognitive components. In this context, an academic discussion of the emotional aspects of the customer within the behavioral pricing literature is valuable.

Therefore, this article enhances the understanding of situations in which consumers evaluate price increases as fair. Thus, in study 1 we assess price increases in the context of positive and negative emotions, and identify conditions in which a price increase may be considered as unfair. The phrasing of our hypotheses is based on equity theory (Adams 1965; Walster, Walster and Berscheid 1978).

In a second study we intend to confirm the positive relationship between perceived price fairness and the willingness to pay, as did an earlier study by Bolton, Warlop, and Alba (1999). However, our study considers interaction effects due to emotions as well.

The article is divided as follows: (1) Hypotheses are derived from the theoretical background of how price increases affect perceived price fairness, and for this we review literature on equity theory and dual entitlement principle. (2) We conduct two experiments to confirm the stated hypotheses. (3) The results of the ANOVA provide implications to realize "successful" price increases and combine price actions with corporate communications.

THEORETICAL BACKGROUND AND HYPOTHESES DEVELOPMENT

Relationship between the magnitude of price increases and perceived price fairness

Price fairness research is based on the idea that consumers evaluate prices as fair or not fair, rather than evaluating prices rationally. Fairness is achieved if there is a balance between the contributions individuals make and the outcomes (rewards) they receive. Relative to those of other persons (Adams 1965), individuals seek distributive equity. Over the last ten years, several authors have focused on price fairness issues (Campbell 1999; Bolton, Warlop and Alba 2003; Xia, Monroe and Cox 2004). Kahnemann, Knetsch and Thaler (1986a) explain that judgments on fairness neither refer to cost-plus considerations nor to ask-and-bid relations. Rather, the profit could be identified as a critical influencing factor of perceived price fairness. Consequently, price fairness is determined by economic and psychosocial components (Maxwell 1995; Campbell 1999).

In marketing literature the explanation of fairness judgments is usually based on equity theory (Huppertz, Arenson and Evans 1978; Dickson and Kalapurakal 1994; Maxwell 1995). According to equity theory, fairness results from the means of decisions and allocations (Adams 1965; Walster, Walster and Berscheid 1978). The basic question, answered by equity theory, addresses what individuals perceive as fair and how they react to unfair relations. Judgments are based on a precise concept of exchange proportion-

---

[1] There are divergent views about the emotion construct and its terminology. For purposes of this study, we focus on emotion as a state of affect. The term "affect" is typically defined as a valenced feeling state. Emotion is one example of this feeling state. While mood is lower in intensity, emotion is higher in intensity and is object-specific (Cohen and Areni 1991).

ality, the equity function (Adams 1965), which opposes outcomes to inputs of exchange partners. Walster, Berscheid and Walster (1973) extend the theory by explaining that inputs can be allocated by positive inputs (assets) and negative inputs (liabilities). While positive inputs enable the exchange partner to achieve positive outcome, negative input enables to achieve negative outcome (Walster, Berscheid and Walster 1973). If input-outcome-relations do not differ significantly, the individual perceives equity or fairness. The perception of inequity results from an imbalance of the equity function. Adams (1965) claims that outcomes and inputs are subjective perceived values. Therefore, individuals evaluate input and outcome differently.

In the context of reactions to price increases, two equations play a major role: (1) a comparison of input-outcome relations before and (2) a comparison of input-outcome relations after the price increase (Homburg, Hoyer and Koschate 2005).

The higher the increase in price (price as input variable), the stronger the imbalances of the equity equation will be. We assume that the equity equation is balanced before the increase in price. Consequently, the stronger the imbalance of the equations after the increase in price is, the stronger the decrease in perceived price fairness. Extreme price increases result in perceived inequity (Maxwell 1995). On the basis of this discussion we propose the following basic hypothesis:

H1: The higher the magnitude of price increase, the lower the perceived price fairness.

Moderating effects of emotions on the relationship between price increases and perceived price fairness

Marketing literature on price fairness has, to date, concentrated on the cognitive influencing factors (Xia, Monroe and Cox 2004). In their comprehensive study, Bolton, Warlop and Alba (2003) explore a variety of factors that contribute to consumer perception of price fairness.

The authors investigated the role of three reference points—past prices, competitor prices, and costs—on price fairness judgments (Bolton, Warlop and Alba 2003). Using two studies, Campbell (1999) confirms the influence of the inferred motive for a firm's price increase in perceptions of price fairness. The data analysis indicates a positive impact on price fairness (Campbell 1999). However, the role of emotions within the cognitive information processing has been neglected by the literature so far. Also, the study of Kalapurakal, Dickson and Urbany (1991), which identifies a positive relationship between the reputation of a company and the perceived price fairness, did not control for emotions. Considering Izard's (1981) basic emotions, O'Neill and Lambert (2001) explore the influence of emotions on several price perceptions constructs and define the expression "price affect." The authors analyze the relationships between price quality, internal reference prices, price consciousness, and willingness to pay, and integrate the emotions "surprise" and "happiness" in their model.

This neglect of attention to emotion is surprising since, for decades, literature on emotion has confirmed that individuals tend to adapt perceptions according to their needs, wishes, and goals (Izard 1981; Frijda 1988). Izard (1981) has revised the relationship between emotion and cognition. Several authors agree on this interaction, and even more importantly, the interaction's impact on consumers' perceptions (Forgas 2001; Adolphs and Damasio 2001; Harmon-Jones 2001; LeDoux 1998; Zajonc 1980).

Emotions are also associated with equity theory. As a powerful social-psychological theory, equity theory can shed light onto the subjective view of fairness. Equity theory claims that the

comparison processes among buyers lead to the idea that their rewards should be proportional to their investments (Homans 1961). Emotions may lead to the revaluation of equity. Provided that there are constant outcomes, a price increase leads to cognitive dissonance (Festinger 1962). This is caused by the difference of the input-outcome relations before and after the price increase. Based on the argument of Zajonc (1980) and LeDoux (1998), which states that emotion and cognition are interrelated, it can be concluded that the cognitive inconsistency of inputs and outcomes has to interact with emotions. Emotions may influence the perceptions of the inputs and the outcomes, as well as the proportion of both inputs and outcomes to the other.

Understanding inputs and outcomes as subjective elements (Homburg, Hoyer and Koschate 2005), an acceptance of a price increase may be higher in the context of positive emotions. Emotions will influence perceived price fairness such that individuals confronted with positive emotions will adapt their inequity to a greater degree than individuals confronted with negative emotions. From an equity theory perspective, that means that a price increase leads to a raised input for the consumer, and to a reduced input-outcome relation. In this case positive emotions initiate a reinterpretation of the input- and outcome-variables, which in turn balance the input-outcome equation. In contrast to positive emotions, negative emotions cannot equalize the equity equation.

In summary, research based on the equity theory indicates that people make inferences about emotions, and that whether the emotion is positive or negative influences the perceptions of input-outcome relation before and after the price increase. We extend this research and suggest that the factor of emotion is likely to provide insights as to when a price increase is likely to be perceived as fair or unfair. The perception of the price increase will depend on the magnitude to which the consumer evaluates the new input-outcome relation in the context of emotion. Especially in buying decisions of high-involvement and branded products, Zeitlin and Westwood (1986) demonstrate that emotions, prices, and their individual perception play major roles.

Based on the consideration of emotions as influencing factor of the equity theory, we add to the literature by proposing that positive and negative emotions are another factor that influences perception of price fairness.

H2: Emotions moderate the relationship between the magnitude of a price increase and the perception of price fairness. Positive emotions increase the perception of price fairness more than negative do emotions.

Price fairness and willingness to pay

To quantify willingness to pay Thaler (1985) states that fairness is the "most important factor in determining p" (Thaler 1985, 205). Willingness to pay is defined as the maximum amount of money a customer is willing to pay for a product or a service (Winer 1985). Therefore, the construct provides a good measure of the value in monetary units (Goldman, Leland and Sibley 1984). To theoretically justify the nature of the relationship between price fairness and willingness to pay, we turn to Maxwell (2002), whose study determined that fairness of price practices influences attitude towards both a seller and willingness to pay. In general, it is feasible to maintain that customers who perceive a price increase as fair are more willing to accept a higher price (Maxwell 2002).

An unexpected price increase is likely to lead consumer considerations about why the firm raised the price. Consistent with Kahnemann, Knetsch and Thaler (1986b), price increases will be perceived as fair if the company's profit stays constant. To evaluate

TABLE 1

Picture	IAPS-No.	Name	Pleasure rating		Arousal rating	
			Mean	Standard deviation	Mean	Standard deviation
Positive Emotion						
1	7230	Banquet	7.38	1.65	5.52	2.32
2	5830	Sunset	8.00	1.48	4.92	2.65
3	2160	Father and baby	7.58	1.69	5.16	2.18
4	4220	Surfer	6.60	1.72	5.18	2.33
5	8030	Ski jumping	7.33	1.76	7.35	2.02
6	4533	Beach Volleyball	6.22	2.24	5.01	2.47
7	4660	Kiss	7.40	1.36	6.58	1.88
8	8080	Sailing	7.73	1.34	6.65	2.20
9	1710	Puppies	8.34	1.12	5.41	2.34
10	2540	Mother and baby	7.63	1.51	3.97	2.33
11	2530	Married couple	7.80	1.55	3.99	2.11
12	1750	Rabbit	8.28	1.07	4.10	2.31
Negative Emotion						
1	9180	Seal	2.99	1.61	5.02	2.09
2	9160	Soldier	3.23	1.64	5.87	1.93
3	1300	Pit Bull	3.55	1.78	6.79	1.84
4	9040	Famished dog	1.67	1.07	5.82	2.15
5	3160	Swollen eyes	2.63	1.23	5.35	1.79
6	9050	Plane crash	2.43	1.61	6.36	1.97
7	6230	Revolver	2.37	1.57	7.35	2.01
8	3170	Baby with tumor	1.46	1.01	7.21	1.99
9	9140	Dead cow	2.19	1.37	5.38	2.19
10	9250	War victim	2.57	1.39	6.60	1.87
11	9000	Cemetery	2.55	1.55	4.06	2.25
12	3230	AIDS patient	2.02	1.30	5.41	2.21

an inferred motive of pricing acts, cost transparency has to be given. Consequently, increasing prices, which function as input variable can be compensated by an increase in outcome. A balanced equity equation means, in turn, perceived price fairness (Walster, Berscheid and Walster 1973). It is fair for a firm to raise prices when faced with increasing costs. Hence, we hypothesize

H3: The higher the perceived fairness of price practice, the higher the willingness to pay.

Moderating effects of emotions on the relationship between perceived price fairness and willingness to pay

Loomes and Sudgen (1986) developed the disappointment theory, which integrates the expected utility model with emotions. The disappointment theory states that the perceived product value depends on the difference between the real value and the expected value. Loomes and Sudgen (1986) refer to the specific emotion function $D(u(x)-u(\overline{x}))$, with $u(x)$ as the perceived value and $u(\overline{x})$ as the expected value, based on experience. Consistent with the expected value theory, we assume that consumers intend to maximize their utility. Because the intensity of emotions increases the higher the intercept, the authors conclude that the function is convex for positive values of $u(x)-u(\overline{x})$ and concave for negative values of $u(x)-u(\overline{x})$. Consequently, the intensity of emotions rises for extreme differences between the expected value and the per-

ceived value (LoomesSudgen 1986). Referring to the emotion function of Loomes and Sugden (1986), positive emotions may increase the willingness to pay, while negative emotions disproportionally decrease the willingness to pay.

H4: Emotions moderate the relationship between the perception of price fairness and the willingness to pay. Positive emotions increase the willingness to pay, whereas negative emotions decrease the willingness to pay.

METHODOLOGY
Sample design and experimental procedure

Two studies were conducted to test these hypotheses. The sample was comprised of 210 students from a German university. The average age of the participants was 26. 7 years, and the sample included 134 men and 76 women. The stimuli consisted of written scenarios describing a sports shoe retailer that realized to increase prices. Laurent and Kapferer (1985) and Zaichkowsky (1985) identified athletic shoes as a high-involvement product and tested them within several experimental designs (Laurent and Kapferer 1985; Zaichkowsky 1985). The basic scenario described a situation of buying athletic shoes.

We did not pay incentives to participants. While it is common practice in experimental economics to employ financial incentives to increase performance, we doubt that such a practice is worth the effort in our context (Hertwig and Ortmann 2001). Decision within our experiments cannot be evaluated in terms of right or wrong and thus, give no basis for performance-oriented payments.

In all studies we used a 3x2 between subjects designs (Hair et al. 2007). In order to control confounding variables, we assigned subjects to the experimental groups in a randomized way (Homburg, Hoyer and Koschate 2005).

STUDY 1

Study 1 uses a 3x2 between subject design, crossing the magnitude of a price increase and emotions (positive, negative). The dependent measure was the perceived price fairness.

The pricing literature offers little guidance when it comes to manipulating price levels. The price increase was changed at three levels. Thus, to pretest the level of price increases we conducted a Vickrey auction (Vickrey 1961). Based on a starting price of 80¤, the three proper levels of price increase were 5 ¤ (6.25%), 15 ¤ (18.75%) and 20 ¤ (25%).

The experimental factors of emotion were manipulated before describing the scenarios and collecting the data. There are several methods to manipulate emotions (Gerrards-Hesse, Spies and Hesse 1994; Lang, Bradley and Cuthbert 1997). We used the International Affective Picture System (IAPS) by Lang et al. (1988). The success of IAPS was confirmed in several studies (Bradley and Lang 1994; Lang, Bradley and Cuthbert 1997). Positive and negative emotions were manipulated by 12 pictures each. The pictures used are presented in Table 1.

Participants completed manipulation checks. To measure emotions, we used the PAD (Pleasure-arousal-dominance) scale developed by Mehrabian and Russel (1974), which has been used by marketing scholars to assess emotional response to interpersonal aspects of shopping (Izard 1981; Plutchik 1989; Mehrabian and Russel 1984). The scale contains 18 semantic differential items, six each of pleasure, arousal, and dominance.

The manipulation in experimental groups perceiving positive and negative emotions was confirmed by the PAD-scale. Subjects confronted with positive pictures reported more positive emotions (Mean $_{pos.\ Emotion}$=4.35) than did subjects to whom we presented negative pictures (Mean $_{neg.\ Emotion}$=3.69). A pairwise t test on the locus of emotion measure between the two scenarios was large in the intended direction (t=8.23; p<.001). The pretest to measure the level of price increases served as a manipulation check. The use of a pretest study is adopted when it is difficult to obtain a manipulation check within the main study (Perdue and Summer 1986).

After reading through one scenario, subjects provided fairness evaluations. Consistent with Kahneman, Knetsch, and Thaler (1986) and Maxwell (1995), we measured price fairness by using a four-item scale from 1 ("fully agree") to 7 ("fully disagree"). The midpoint of the scales are described as neither. Scales were: "The price is fair," "The price increase of the shoe is appropriate." "All consumers were treated fairly," and "Price calculation of the athletic shoe is understandable." The scale had an acceptable Cronbach reliability (Cronbach's Alpha=.84). Also, exploratory factor analysis of the scale returned a single factor solution.

It was hypothesized that participants will perceive price increases as more fair in a scenario with positive emotions. Results strongly support this hypothesis. In order to test the significance of the differences a 3x2 ANOVA using the fairness as dependent measure revealed the desired main effect of the price increase (F=91.64; p<.001). Also, the interaction effect, which means that emotions moderate the main effect, can be confirmed (F=7.137; p<.012). Results indicate that the higher the price increase; the less important are emotions as influencing factors.

As well, the second main effect is tested significantly (F=18.993; p<.000). This means that subjects find the price increase in the positive emotion scenario to be more fair than in the negative emotion scenario. However, in the context of low price increases, emotions are even more relevant. This effect is presented in Figure 1. Surprisingly, results indicate that positive emotions have a greater impact in price fairness than do negative emotions.

STUDY 2

Study 2 examined different levels of price fairness as the independent variable. Experiment 2 assessed the impact on the willingness to pay (Hypothesis H3). Additionally, we test hypothesis H4, which maintains that emotions mediate the relationships between the magnitude of price fairness and the willingness to pay (Hypothesis H4). Study 2 involved a 3x2-between subject design. Before measuring the willingness to pay, subjects were confronted with a similar scenario in the shoe store, as used in study 1. The experimental groups with different emotions (Mean$_{positive\ Emotion}$>Mean$_{negative\ Emotion}$) were manipulated in terms of three different levels of price fairness.

The levels of price fairness are positive inequity, negative inequity, and perceived equity. Thus, the scenarios read as follows: "To buy a athletic shoe, you visit a store shop. A friend has recommended a certain shoe. But the price of the shoe has increased. The salesperson, who is a friend of yours, explains that the company raised the prices of their shoes due to increased R&D and production costs"(equity). Because the marketing literature does not provide an appropriate manipulation procedure, we manipulated the scenario using Campbell's (1999) inferred motive for price increases for a firm's price increase. When participants inferred that the company had a negative motive for the price increase, the increase was perceived as less fair than the same increase when consumers inferred that the company has a positive motive (e.g., rising production costs) (Campbell 1999). Therefore, the reason for the price increase varied between three different groups: In one group the price increase was justified by rising production costs. Consequently, participants should perceive the price increase as fair (equity). When the price stays the same despite rising production costs, we expected the perception of fair prices (positive inequity). When the salesperson does not explain the price increase, the price increase shifts the input-outcome relation of the equity function to the disadvantage of the producer. Negative inequity would be the consequence (Campbell 1999). We used the same measurement of price fairness as in the first experiment. Positive and negative emotions were manipulated using IAPS-pictures. Subjects were confronted with the same type of emotions as in the first experiment. These pictures guaranteed a well-founded manipulation. The results of the PAD –Measurement of Mehrabian and Russel (1984) supported this approach.

Willingness to pay was measured using the card method (Hoevennagel 1996). The subjects were given a certain number of cards with prices printed on them. Subjects are instructed to choose the card of the highest price they were willing to pay (MitchellCarson 1989). Even if the presentation of cards restricts the choices, the procedure eliminates anchoring-effects (Hoevennagel 1996). At the same time, the presentation of prices is easily implemented. Participants can chose between different cards on a scale from 25 ¤ to 150¤. Results of the measurements indicated that prices range from 45 ¤ to 145 ¤. Ignoring the manipulations, the mean price of the athletic shoe was about 87 ? (Mean$_{WTP}$=86.59).

The same items used in the first interviews were used to measure the price fairness (Cronbach's Alpha=.93). The item-to-total correlation gives no reason to skip an item. The measurement

FIGURE 1
Means of price fairness by experimental condition

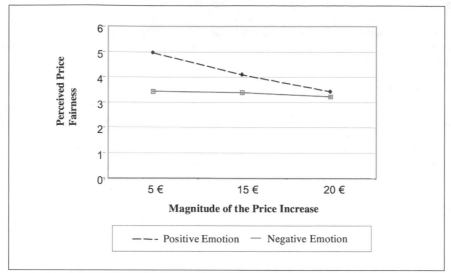

of emotions reveals a high difference between positive and negative emotions (t=7.63; p<.001).

The manipulation checks do not justify the differentiation in equity, positive inequity, and negative inequity. Positive inequity and equity do not provide a significantly different mean value (t Positive InequityEquity =1.53). Therefore, we use a 2x2-between subject design and limit the experiment to negative inequity and positive inequity. Subjects of the "negative inequity" scenario (Mean Negative Inequity=3.753) perceive the price increase as more unfair than do the subjects of the "positive inequity"-scenario (Mean Positive Equity=5.18).

Hypotheses H3 and H4 were tested by means of a 2x2-ANOVA with willingness to pay as dependent variable. Both main effects were significant. In terms of the results for willingness to pay, there was a main effect for emotion (F=7.387; p<.007). Participants in the positive emotion condition were willing to pay a higher price than participants in a negative emotion condition. The positive relationship between price fairness and willingness to pay was also tested significantly, meaning that participants who perceive price increases as fair are willing to pay more (F=12,264; p<.001). However, the interaction effect cannot be confirmed.

IMPLICATIONS AND FUTURE RESEARCH

This is an exploratory study. Thus, there are few strong conclusions, and many limitations. Our study extends previous research in the area of price fairness research by investigating how emotions moderate the relationship between perceived price fairness and consumer's willingness to pay. The implementation of price increases is easier if price increases are perceived as fair. Our paper indicates the impact of emotions on the relationship between the magnitude of price increases and the perception of price fairness. We add emotion as an important element of price fairness perceptions that accompany the cognition considerations of equity theory. It is logical, therefore, to speculate about the nature of the relationship between emotions and price fairness. However, our study focused on positive and negative emotions. Further research should extend the spectrum of emotions and investigate whether positive and negative emotions compensate each other or negative

emotions dominate positive emotions, as stated by Izard (1981). In addition, we did not measure the negative emotions caused by the price increase itself.

As with any methodology, there are limitations associated with experimental research. The results refer to a limited data set. Additionally, the use of the athletic shoe scenarios is not complex enough to generalize the findings. Consequently, future research should explore the relationship between emotion and price for other consumer groups and buying situations.

Our results provide explanations for irrational behavior of consumers. Cognitive behavioral theories have to consider emotional aspects. This article supports the rising attention of marketing literature towards emotions because cognitive theories are revealed to be limited in explaining consumer behavior. Price judgments are complex and intrapersonal procedures. Emotions and emotion-induced actions cannot, therefore, be neglected. The integration of emotions revalues the prognosis of pricing actions and consumer behavior.

With regard to the moderating effect of emotions in the impact of price increases on the consumer's willingness to pay, our study indicates that a 20% increase in price can be absorbed by positive emotions. The impact of positive emotions declines for higher price increases. Hence, firms should consider emotional and cognitive aspects within their price measures. Advertising needs to pay more attention to the role of emotions in all aspects of marketing (O'Neill and Lambert 2001). Advertising currently relies on repetitions, while strong emotions are avoided. Feelings of delight, joy, sympathy, and happiness should be reflected in the store appearance. Especially pictures have an impact in this concern.

REFERENCES

Adams, Stacy J. (1965), "Inequity in Social Exchange," *Advances in Experimental Social Psychology*, Berkowitz, Leonard (ed.), New York, 267-299.

Adolphs, Ralph and Antonio R. Damasio (2001), "The Interaction of Affect and Cognition: A Neurobiological View", *Handbook of Affect and Social Cognition*, Forgas, J. P. (ed.), New Jersey, 27-50.

Babin, Barry J., David M. Hardesty and Tracy Suter A. (2003), "Color and shopping intentions: The intervening effect of price fairness and perceived affect," *Journal of Business Research*, 56 (7), 541-551.

Bagozzi, Richard P., Mahesh Gopinath, and Prashanth U. Nyer (1999), "The Role of Emotion in Marketing," *Journal of Academy of Marketing Science*, 27 (2), 184-206.

Bolton, Lisa E., Luk Warlop and Joseph W. Alba (2003), "Consumer Perceptions of Price Fairness," *Journal of Consumer Research*, 29 (4), 474-491.

Bradley, Margaret, M. and Peter J. Lang (1994), "Measuring emotion: The self-assessment manikin and the semantic differential," *Journal of Behavior Therapy and Experimental Psychiatry*, 25 (1), 49-59.

Campbell, Margaret C. (1999), "Perceptions of Price Unfairness: Antecedents and Consequences," *Journal of Marketing Research*, 36 (2), 187-199.

Churchill, Gilbert A. and Carol Surprenant (1982), "An Investigation into the Determinants of Customer Satisfaction," *Journal of Marketing Research*, 19 (4), 64-73.

Cohen, Joel B. and Charles S. Areni (1991), "Affect and Consumer Behavior," *Handbook of Consumer Behavior*, Robertson, Thomas S. and Harold H. Kassarjian (eds.), Englewood Cliffs, 183-240.

Dickson, Peter D. and Rosemary Kalapurakal (1994), "The Use and Perceived Price Fairness of Price-Setting Rules in the Bulk Electricity Market," *Journal of Economic Psychology*, 15, 427-448.

Diller, Hermann (2008), *Preispolitik*, 4th. Edn, Stuttgart.

Forgas, Joseph P. (2001), "Affect and Social Cognition", *Handbook of Affect and Social Cognition*, Forgas, Joseph P. (ed.), New Jersey, 1-27.

Frijda, Nico H. (1988), "The Law of Emotions," *American Psychologist*, 43 (5), 349-358.

Gerrards-Hesse, Astrid, Kordelia Spies and Friedrich W. Hesse (1994), "Experimental Inductions of Emotional States and their Effectiveness: A Review," *British Journal of Psychology*, 87 (1), 55-78.

Goldman, Berry M., Hayne E. Leland and David S. Sibley (1984), "Optimal Nonuniform Prices," *Review of Economic Studies*, 51 (165), 305-316.

Hair, Joseph F., Ronald T. Tatham, Rolph E. Anderson and William Black, *Multivariate Data Analysis*, 5th Edn, Englewood Cliffs.

Harmon-Jones, Eddie (2001), "The Role of Affect in Cognitive-Dissonance Processes," *Handbook of Affect and Social Cognition*, Forgas, Joseph P. (ed.), New Jersey, 237-256.

Herrmann, Andreas, Martin Wricke and Frank Huber (2000), "Kundenzufriedenheit durch Preisfairness," *Marketing ZFP*, 22, 131-143.

Hertwig, Ralph and Andreas Ortmann (2001), "Experimental practices in economics: A methodological challenge for psychologists," *Behavioral and Brain Science*, 24, 383-451.

Hoevennagel, R. (1996), "An Assessment of the Contingent Valuation Method" *Valuing the Environment: Methodological and Measurement Issues*, Pething, R. (ed.), Dordrecht 1996, 195-227.

Homburg, Christian, Wayne D. Hoyer and Nicole Koschate (2005), "Customer Reactions to Price Increases: Do Customer Satisfaction and the Perceived Motive Fairness matter?," *Journal of the Academy of Marketing Science*, 33 (1), 36-49.

Homburg, Christian and Nicole Koschate (2005), "Behavioral Pricing-Forschung im Überblick-Erkenntnisstand and zukünftige Forschungsrichtungen," *Zeitschrift für Betriebswirtschaft*, 75, 383-423.

Homburg, Christian and Harley Krohmer (2003), *Marketingmanagement-Strategien-Instrumente-Umsetzung-Unternehmensführung*, Wiesbaden: Gabler.

Huppertz, John W., Sidney J. Arenson and Richard H. Evans, (1978), "An Application of Equity Theory to Buyer-Seller Exchange Situations," *Journal of Marketing Research*, 15 (2), 250-260.

Izard, Carroll E. (1981), *Die Emotionen des Menschen–Eine Einführung in die Grundlagen der Emotionspsychologie*, Weinheim.

Kahneman, Daniel, Jack L. Knetsch and Richard H. Thaler, (1986a), "Fairness and the Assumptions of Economics," *The Journal of Business*, 59 (4), 285-300.

Kahneman, Daniel, Jack L. Knetsch and Richard H. Thaler, (1986b), "Fairness as a constraint on Profit Seeking: Entitlements in Markets," *The American Economic Review*, 76 (4), 728-741.

Kahneman, Daniel and Amos Tversky (1979), "Prospect Theory: An Analysis of Decision Under Risk," *Econometrica*, 47, 263-291.

Kalapurakal, Rosemary, Peter P. Dickson and Joel Urbany (1991), "Perceived Price Fairness and Dual Entitlement," *Advances in Consumer Research*, (18) 1, 788-793.

Lang, Peter J., Margaret M. Bradley and Bruce N. Cuthbert (1997), "International Affective Picture System (IAPS): Technical Manual and Affective Ratings, Gainesville NIMH Centre for the Study of Emotion and Attention", *Working Paper*, University of Florida.

Laurent, Gilles and Jean-Noel Kapferer (1985), "Measuring Consumer Involvement Profiles," *Journal of Marketing Research*, 22 (1), 41-53.

LeDoux, Joseph E. (1998), *Das Netz der Gefühle -Wie Emotionen entstehen*, Munich.

Loomes, Graham and Robert Sugden (1986), "Disappointment and Dynamic Consistency in Choice under Uncertainty", *Review of Economic Studies*, 53 (173), 271-282.

Marn, Michael V. and Robert L. Rosiello (1992), "Managing price gaining profit," *Harvard Business Review*, September-October, Boston.

Maxwell, Sarah (1995), "What makes Price Increase seems fair?," *Strategy & Practice*, 21 (3), 21-27.

Maxwell, Sarah (2002), "Rule-based price fairness and its effect on Willingness to purchase," *Journal of Economic Psychology*, 23, 191-212.

McConnel, J. Douglas (1968), "An Experimental Examination of the Price-Quality Relationship," *Journal of Business*, 41 (4), 439-444.

Mehrabian, Albert and James A. Russel (1974), *An Approach to Environmental Psychology*, Cambridge.

Mitchell, Robert C. and Richard T. Carson (1989), *Using surveys to value public goods: The contingent valuation method*, Washington D.C.

Monroe, Kent B. (1973), "Buyers´ subjective perception of price," *Journal of Marketing Research*, 10, 70-80.

O'Neill, Regina M. and David R. Lambert (2001), "The Emotional Side of Price," *Psychology & Marketing*, 18 (3), 217-237.

Plutchik, Robert (1989), "Measuring Emotions and Their Derivatives", in Emotion -Theory, Research, and Experience: The Measurement of Emotions, Plutchik, Robert and Henry Kellermann, (eds.), New York, 1-37.

Simon, Hermann and Robert J. Dolan (1996), *Profit durch Power Pricing*, New York.

Thaler, Richard H. (1985), "Mental Accounting and Consumer Choice," *Marketing Science*, 4 (3), 199-214.

Vaidyanathan, Rajiv and Praveen Aggarwal (2003), "Who is the fairest of them all? An attributional approach to price fairness perceptions," *Journal of Business Research*, 56, 453-463.

Vickrey, William (1961), "Counter speculation, Auctions, and Competitive Sealed Tenders," *Journal of Finance*, 16, 8-17.

Walster, Elaine, Ellen Berscheid and William G. Walster (1973), "New Directions in Equity Research," *Journal of Personality and Social Psychology*, 25, 151-176.

Walster, Elaine, William G. Walster and Ellen Berscheid (1978), *Equity: Theory and Research*, Boston.

Westbrook, Robert A. and Richard L. Oliver, (1991), "The Dimensionality of Consumption, Emotion Patterns, and Customer Satisfaction," *Journal of Consumer Research*, 18 (1), 84-91.

Winer, Russel S. (1985), "A Price Vector Model of Demand for Consumer Durables: Preliminary Developments," *Marketing Science*, 4 (1), 74-90.

Xia, Lan, Kent B. Monroe and Jennifer L. Cox (2004), "The Price is unfair! A Conceptual Framework of Price Fairness Perceptions," *Journal of Marketing*, 68 (4), 1-15.

Zaichkowsky, Judith L. (1985), "Measuring the Involvement Construct," Journal of Consumer Research, 12 (3), 341-52.

Zajonc, Robert B. (1980), "Feeling and Thinking Preferences need no Inferences," *American Psychologist*, 35 (2), 151-75.

Zeitlin, David M. and Richard A. Westwood (1986), "Measuring Emotional Response," *Journal of Advertising Research*, 26 (5), 34-44.

Cannibal or Commodity Fetish: Body as Material Interaction

Ai-Ling Lai, University of Gloucestershire, UK
Janine Dermody, University of Gloucestershire, UK

ABSTRACT

This paper seeks to address the call to bridge the dichotomous divide between subject and object within consumer research. Adopting an embodied perspective and drawing on our empirical research, we highlight the paradoxical meanings surrounding the fetishization of the body as a commoditized object as well as a kernel of personal history. We explore the extent to which participants are willing to overcome the depersonalizing transformation to their embodied self, as they negotiate the meanings surrounding the progressive objectification of the body, inherent in the practice of organ transplantation. Our analysis suggests the difficulty in delineating where the embodied subject ends (donor as self) and the commoditized object (donor as cadaver) begins. As such, the boundaries that mark the agentic capability of the embodied donor as commodity/intentional subject are mutable, indeterminate and intersubjectively emergent. We therefore seek to create a dialogue among consumer scholars to reconsider the body as the 'material interaction' between consuming subjects and material objects. Only in so doing, can we begin to advance the discipline beyond its essentialist roots.

'Transplanted organs become one of many examples of objects rendered culturally significant by new medical technology. Their cultural value lies in their economic and their social worth; they are rare commodities in part because they are personalized objects'

- Sharp, 1995: pp. 378

INTRODUCTION

This paper seeks to address the need to transcend the subject-object dualistic legacy of Cartesianism within consumer research. Increasingly, consumer researchers are called to reflexively elucidate the relationships between subjects (consumers) and objects (commodities) and how the ensuing cultural meanings are mediated within marketplace cultures (Borgerson, 2005; Arnould and Thompson, 2005; Elliot and Wattanasuwan, 1998; Wallendolf and Arnould, 1988). Accordingly we are responding to recent calls for consumer researchers to bridge the dichotomous divide between the consuming subject and commodity object, by reflecting on:

"...the radical indeterminacy of both 'subject' and 'object'....which begin from the assumption of an emergent ontology with bodies, objects and meaning entangled, co-constituted, fragile and often ambivalent." (Bettany, 2007; 45)

This call is reflective of a shift in consumer research, away from the *'essential characteristics of consumption objects'* (Bettany, 2007: 42) towards the agentic primacy of the consuming subject, as exemplified recently by CCT (Arnould and Thompson, 2005). By privileging either the subject *or* the object, consumer researchers have yet to appreciate the purposive (intentional) communion between the consumer and the material world (Merleau-Ponty, 1945/2002; Dant, 2006; Joy and Venkatesh, 1994; Heidegger, 1927/1962; Borgerson, 2005; Miller, 1987; Latour, 1987), and have therefore reinforced the legacy of Cartesian philosophy (Thompson *et.* al. 1989; Arnold and Fischer, 1994). In other words, by endorsing the binary opposition between subject/object, consumer researchers have overlooked the concept of *intentionality*[1]–which is

considered to be at the root of agency (Borgerson, 2005). This paper will therefore adopt an embodied perspective, drawing from the phenomenology of Merleau-Ponty (1945/2002) and Heidegger (1927/1962) to address the intentional comportment (Merleau-Ponty, 1945/2002), which connects consumers to material culture. As Dant (2006) suggests, it is through embodiment that the embedded material capital of objects emerges. In the light of this, Dant (2006) defines 'material interaction' as:

"...the meeting of the materiality of peoples' bodies, including the mind and imagination that are part of those bodies, with the materiality of objects, including the qualities and capacities that has been designed and built in by the combined and collective actions of a series of other people." (Dant, 2006: 300)

This is important because it helps us to realize the dialectical connection between subject and object (Merleau-Ponty, 1945/2002; Borgerson, 2005)-which is mutable and indeterminate (Bettany, 2007). As such, we can begin to appreciate that *agency* is necessarily co-determined through the intersubjective network of embodied beings. We propose to situate our analysis within the context of cadaveric organ donation, by establishing the body (cadaver) as the point of 'material interaction' (Dant, 2006) between different stakeholders within the transplant community,[2] who contest what the body is, the extent to which the body can be considered a constituent of selfhood and how its boundaries should be defined (Seale *et.* al., 2006). The decision to become an organ donor is therefore embedded within a nexus of competing narratives, through which the body is thematized as a battleground where the battle concerning its agentic capability (*i.e.* are bodies intentional or inert) is fought. The body therefore occupies an ambiguous position within the discourse of organ transplantation, as it is at once a commoditized object and a biographical marker of the self (Sharp, 2005). Through empirical research, this paper presents accounts of the negotiated meanings of potential donors, as they attempt to relate their embodied experience to the progressive objectification of the body, inherent in the medical practice of organ transplantation. We begin our analysis by considering pertinent themes within the literature, namely: (1) the body as enfleshment of the world, (2) the body in plenum and (3) the objectification of the body.

THEMES FROM THE LITERATURE

The Body as Enfleshment of the World: Towards the Dissolution of the Subject-Object Dualism

Within consumer research, the body has often been conceptualized as an inert object. Its status as a kernel of existence and locus of knowledge is subordinated to the superiority of the mind (Burkitt, 1999; Joy and Venkatesh, 1994). The body has therefore assumed

---

[1]Intentionality is a concept first introduced by Franz Brentano (1837-1917) to explicate the relationship between the subject and the object. To say that the subject is intentional is to say that it is always directed towards or refers to some objects.

[2]The intersubjective connection between donors, recipients, donor/recipient families, medical professionals and marketers

a liminal presence in the discipline, where it has long been eclipsed by the hegemonic legacy of Cartesianism (Joy and Venkatesh, 1994; Thompson *et. al*, 1989) and rendered docile under the panoptic gaze of the 'inscriptive perspective' (e.g. Thompson and Hirschman, 1995; Grosz, 1994). More recently, consumer researchers have begun to acknowledge the 'lived experience' of consumers as essentially 'incarnated' (Patterson and Elliot, 2002; Lai *et. al*, 2008; Joy and Sherry, 2003). In order to fully embrace the consumers as 'incarnated beings', researchers are called to reinstate the body as the conduit of intentionality by *'re-establishing the roots of the mind in its body, and its world'* (Merleau-Ponty, 1963:3 in Grosz, 1994). As Merleau-Ponty (1945/2002) suggests, human beings cannot simply be reduced to 'purely mind' (subject) or merely bodies (object) for our mind is always incarnated and vice versa (Grosz, 1994; Howson and Inglis, 2001). By introducing the notion of 'body-subject', Merleau-Ponty demonstrated that the body is not merely a *possession* of the subject (having a body); rather it reveals the primordial intertwining of our subjectivity and corporeality (being a body), which is purposefully orientated towards the world it inhabits. Consequently we both *have* and *are* bodies (Turner, 1996). From a Merleau-Pontyian perspective, objects (materiality) are constructed (designed) as the enfleshment of consumer culture, which are then embodied by the consuming subjects who, in so doing, consecutively shape the process of material civilization (Merleau-Ponty, 1968; Lai *et. al*, 2008; Dant, 2006). We will now move on to consider the body as the conduit of intentionality, with reference to Merleau-Ponty's and Heidegger's ideas on embodiment.

The Body in Plenum: The Existential Conceptualization of the Body as a Conduit of Intentionality

While Heidegger has very little to say about the body, on closer reading it becomes apparent that his hermeneutic account of *Dasein* is essentially embodied (Heidegger, 1927/1962). In the German language *Dasein* literally means Being-*there* (Macquarrie, 1972). As the body is our anchorage of being-in-the-world, Being-*there* necessarily implies that Dasein is an embodied being (Macquarrie, 1968). In *Being and Time,* Heidegger (1927/1962) criticized the prevailing Western thinking that tends to regard Being in terms of thinghood (Macquarrie, 1972). The Cartesian dualistic substance of Mind/Body is one such example. Similarly, Merleau-Ponty (1945/2002) is vehemently opposed to the reduction of the embodied subject to a passive *res extensa* (1945/2002: 381), in which it is rendered as a thing-in-itself (Sartre, 1943/1956). To regard embodied beings as passive objects is to engage in an 'act of depersonalization' (Heidegger, 1927/1962: 73) that withdraws from the person, his right to dignity, mystery and humanity (Marcel, 1949 in Macquarrie, 1972: 176). For Heidegger, Dasein is embodied through and through–where man comports himself towards his *Being* as a 'holistic fusion of body, soul and spirit' (1927/1962: 73). By taking up the issue of *Being*, Dasein is responsible for who he is and what he may become. Here, the parallels between Heidegger's concept of *Dasein* and Merleau-Ponty's '*body-subject*' begin to emerge.

As a body-subject, Dasein *projects* into future possibilities as *ahead-of-itself* (Heidegger, 1927/1962: 279). Such *projection* into future trajectory is what Heidegger called *transcendence* (Dreyfus and Rubin, 1999: 300). Thus, as a transcendental being, *Dasein-as-embodied* has an *intentional* comportment towards the world (space) and his project (time), through which he plays an active part in the meaning-making process. Accordingly, through our embodied experience, we creatively infuse our life-narratives with meanings, drawing from the *possibilities* open to us in our purposeful communion with the world.

Our embodied existence is therefore a dynamic process, which suggests 'being in a plenum' (Merleau-Ponty, 1945/2002: 525)–i.e. to exist is to always be in action. The precursor to existence, then, is our embodied transcendence. To exist is to 'perform' life-*I do therefore I am*. It is in '*doing*' that we attain concreteness and fullness of existence (Macquarrie, 1972). Inverting the *cogito*, it is because '*I can that I am*' (Merleau-Ponty, 1945/2002: 446), and thus '*I am therefore I think*' (Macquarrie, 1972; Craib, 1998). Merleau-Ponty and Heidegger have therefore reversed Descartes' claim to the certainty of existence by relocating it's locus from the dispassionate '*I think*' to the embodied '*I can*'.

Death therefore represents the transformation from '*I can*' into '*I no longer can*' (Leder, 1990). The silent sphinx of the cadaver heralds the annulment of intentionality (Bauman, 1992). Thus, the omnipresence of death reveals to Dasein his underlying nullity, where he can no longer 'perform' life (I can't therefore I'm not). For Heidegger (1927/1962) then, nonbeing is in the fibre of our very being. As Merleau-Ponty argues, we as intentional beings are betrothed to the world through which we are held *responsible* for our '*commitment*' to exist.

"I can no longer pretend to be a nihilation (néant), and choose myself continually out of nothing at all. If it is through subjectivity that nothingness appears in the world, it can equally be said that it is through the world that nothingness comes into being. ... We are always in a plenum, in being, just as a face, even in repose, even in death, is always doomed to express something." (Merleau-Ponty, 1945/2002: 525)

In short, our dialogical engagement with the world means that we, as embodied beings are not simply inert entities lying around, indifferent to our surrounding. In Heideggerian terms, we are never simply *present-at-hand* (1927/1962: 67). A synthesis between the ideas of Merleau-Ponty and Heidegger thus portray Dasein as *chiasmatically* conjoint to his world as *one flesh*–i.e. the *flesh of the body* is also the *flesh of the world* (Merleau-Ponty, 1968; Lai *et. al*, 2008; Dant, 2006)–thereby rendering the traditional subject-object dualism obsolete. If the body-as-subject defies objectification, to what extent can body parts be commoditized as social gifts within the discourse of cadaveric organ donation? To what extent does the tension between the subject-object status of the body (cadaver) mediate the material interactions between different members of the transplant community?

The Objectification of the Body within the Discourse of Cadaveric Organ Donation

As organ transplantation becomes increasingly routinized, concerns have been raised with regards to the slippery slope of body commodification (Scheper-Hughes, 2001; Hogle, 1995; Lock, 2002; Belk, 1990). This is not surprising as organ donation inevitably entails the fragmentation of the embodied self. As the body is isolated into interchangeable components, it can then be commoditized as a form of merchandise (Helman, 1988; Seale et. al., 2006). Thus, by objectifying the body, organ donation becomes conceivable as it is stripped of its emotive and social value, i.e. an object devoid of personhood. This reflects the Cartesian conception of the mind/body dualism, which reinforces the inert quality of the body.

Within the medical context, the body is further reified through the clinical gaze (Foucault, 1973) and various medical rites (e.g. pathological examination). Medical professionals are required to engage in what William Hunter called 'necessary inhumanity' or clinical detachment (Armstrong, 1987; Lock, 2002; Richardson,

1987; Lynch, 1990) in order to achieve medical objectivity. This clinical gaze transforms the cadaveric donor into a 'thing-in-itself'— an assemblage of body parts (Lynch, 1990; Helman, 1988). Thus organ transplant procedures have been described as a form of late modern cannibalism (Scheper-Hughes, 2001), where organs are 'extracted', 'salvaged' and 'replaced' (Robbins, 1996), mirroring the taking of functioning parts from a machine (e.g. cannibalizing car parts) to repair another that is broken (Youngner, 1996; Richardson, 1996; Fox and Swazey, 1992). As Heidegger (1927/ 1962) feared, such medical construction has reduced the body into an undignified object of biology-a corporeal thing. As the integrity of the embodied self is violated, the status of body parts as the locus of the self becomes a matter of social dispute (Seale *et. al*, 2006). In breaching bodily boundaries, transplantation has given birth to hybrids that threaten to undermine the western conception of the coherent self (Helman, 1988; Hallam *et. al*, 1999). In other words, the leaky bodies of organ transplantation violate the 'taken-for-granted' modernist western assumptions about the 'bounded body', where *'being whole'* is defined in terms of corporeal solidity, immutability and impermeability by otherness (Hallam *et. al*, 1999; Douglas, 1902/1966). Furthermore, upon receiving an organ, transplant recipients often undergo transformative experience that alter their sense of self (Sharp, 1995)—which they *fetishize* with lingering animism (Lock, 2002; de Brosses, 1760/1970). Such anthromorphism of the body thus reflects broader societal concerns over the reconfiguration of body boundaries (Douglas, 1902/1966; Hallam *et. al*, 1999).

Belk (1990) contends that body parts and organs can retain their sacredness by being given and received as gifts (see also Titmuss, 1972). Hogle (1995) and Lock (2002), however, are perturbed by the gift exchange of organs, arguing that such ritualistic practice of gift-giving merely conceals the progressive objectification of the body and obscure the darker side of organ transplantation (Youngner, 1996; Richardson, 1996). By normalizing the 'gift-of-life' discourse, potential donors are promised a *ressurective appeal* to become technologically "immortalized". Thus, donors can "live on" literally in the body of organ recipients (Sharp, 1995) and symbolically in the collective memory of society (Lock, 2002); while remaining oblivious of the cultural production that transforms donor cadavers into routine cyborgs (Hogle, 1995). Marx (1867/1976) called this the *fetishization* of commodity, where consumers are removed from the production process through the medium of commodity. Hence, through the promotional rhetoric of the 'gift-of-life', the body becomes commoditized as social object (Helman, 1988; Seale *et. al*., 2006; Kopytoff, 1986). Such objectification of the body violates the integrity of the embodied self, *'causing tension between the status of body parts as 'self' (subject) or not self (object)'* (Seale *et. al*, 2006: 26).

For the potential donors, the body continues to carry a personalized imprint of the self (Sharp, 1995). Biographical narratives are told *through* and *with* the bodies. As such, the *'biographical body'* is also a historical body-engraved with the epiphany of life, where personal triumphs and tragedy are chronicled. It is through their 'historical body' that potential donors are able to experience a sense of continuity, which unites the past, the present and the future (Thompson, 1997; Giddens, 1991; Mick and Buhl, 1992) as their ongoing existential project (Thompson and Hirschman, 1998; Merleau-Ponty, 1945/2002). Hence, the body is a conduit of intentionality that perpetually comports towards its *potentiality-for-being* (Heidegger, 1927/1962) and cannot be easily depersonalized.

Having reviewed the premises and paradoxical meanings underlying the *fetishization* of the body as a commoditized *object-in-itself* as well as an animistic site of lingering subjectivity, we now present the methodology of this empirical study.

METHODOLOGY

In recognition of the need to transcend the Cartesian legacy of subject-object dualism, we have adopted the philosophical perspective of hermeneutic-phenomenology (Arnold and Fischer, 1994; Thompson *et.* al, 1994) to inform our interpretive inquiry of cadaveric organ donation. Hermeneutic philosophy emphasizes the ontological status of Being (Heidegger, 1927/1962), in which the interpreter (researcher as subject) enters into a dialogical relationship with the interpreting-object (participants as co-author) to arrive at a mutual understanding of new possibilities of what it means to be human (embodied subjects). Hence both the researcher and the participants are embodied beings, who are intersubjectively comported towards each other (Merleau-Ponty, 1945/2002) in a *'continuous state of coming into understanding'* (Arnold and Fischer, 1994: 59). Through the collaborative approach of active interviewing (Holstein and Gubrium, 1995), the researcher (first author) engaged the participants in a shared narratological dialogue (Thompson, 1997). Multiple active interviews, of approximately 4 hours each, were conducted with 14 British female potential organ donors, aged 21-30, who harbour ambivalent perceptions towards organ donation–generating extremely 'rich' and complex data.

Hermeneutic-phenomenology also insists that researchers must first understand the pre-objective 'lived experience' of the participants (*emic perspective)* prior to the construction of knowledge (Merleau-Ponty, 1945/2002; Thompson *et.* al, 1994). Hence the construction of knowledge necessarily emerges as a *fusion of horizon* (Gadamer, 1989) between the participants and the researcher (Holstein and Gubrium, 1995; Thompson, 1997). Thus, in this study, this *fusion of horizon* occurred when the participants' perspectives slipped into the perspectives of the researcher (first author) and vice versa (Merleau-Ponty, 1945/2002; Langer, 1989), mutually enriching and expanding horizons of understanding of all involved. The interpretation of data presented in this paper is therefore the concretized form of understanding (Gadamer, 1989) derived from this *fusion*. In this way, the subject-object dichotomy is bridged (Arnold and Fischer, 1994)

THEMATIC ANALYSIS AND DISCUSSION

Our findings reveal that participants have predominantly depicted organ donation as involving the disintegration of the body. The 'fragmented' and 'leaky' body emerge as overriding representations in participants' narratives, which collide with their embodied experience for *'being whole'* (Lock, 2002). The 'fragmented body' also implies the transgression of body boundaries, where participants fear the *'cannibalistic'* repercussions of merging with the bodies of anonymous others (Kopytoff, 1986; Sharp, 1995; Dant, 2006). In our thematic analysis, we explore various perspectival standpoints from which participants negotiate the situated meanings surrounding the mortal body. In doing so, we can begin to illustrate how they attempt to make sense of the depersonalizing transformation of their embodied self and thus, reconcile the competing narratives surrounding the transgression of corporeal boundaries that underlie the practice of cadaveric organ transplantation.

Being Whole/Being Fragmented: Negotiating the Progressive Objectification of the Disintegrated Body

In their pre-objective description (emic perspective), participants have predominantly depicted cadaveric organ donation as involving the fragmentation of the body. For example, the body is portrayed as being *'scattered about'*, *'cut up in little pieces'*, *'hacked up'*, *'butchered'*, and *'chopped up'*. It is therefore not surprising that transplant surgeons and/or doctors are often depicted as *'psychotic'*, *'crude'*, *'monstrous'* and *'horrendous'*. Meanwhile, organ transplantation, as a practice, is deemed '*barbaric*', '*crude*', '*gruesome*' and '*intrusive*'. Estelle's description below is an archetypal portrayal of organ donation:

"*I see it in a crude sense. I am just like 'oh they just take an organ out of someone and plonked it in someone else's.' It is just in a horrible, disrespectful way that is just pictured in my head. And they just make it sound like really nice but unpersonal type thing......Like if someone's had their like organs donated they'll be all hacked up.... it'll be taken out of them and that's just horrible because they'll be cut up for no reason. They don't have...like time to pass away peacefully or time for the family to say goodbye. It is more like, they are just the donor. They are not a person that's kindly giving you something. It is just like, "right, another one." Seems quite horrible.....it's not a person any more, we'll just get out the organs because we need them and they (the donors) don't matter.*" (Estelle, Age 21, Interview 1)

Like all the participants, Estelle sketched a somewhat '*crude*' representation of organ transplantation, which she perceives to be a *de-humanizing* procedure that routinizes body mutilation. Here, the transplant professionals are demonized through the 'othering process', as the '*they*'–who '*just take organs*' from an anonymous pool of donors and '*plonked*' them into the collective bodies of transplant recipients (*someone else*). Donor-cadavers are '*hacked up*' or '*cut up for no reason*' in order to fulfill 'greater' social needs. Therefore, emphasis is placed on the utilitarian concern of organ shortages, while the potential donor as a person pales into insignificance. As a result, donor-cadavers are transformed into routine cyborgs (Hogle, 1995), that can be replaced like interchangeable spare-parts that are merely present-at-hand (*they are not a person that's kindly giving you something. It is just like, "right, another one*'). No longer able to project into the *potentiality-of-being*, the cadaver donors thus lose their intentionality as embodied beings (*they are just donors*). Drawing from her embodied standpoint, Estelle argues that the practice of transplantation has crudely neglected the social significance of the donor, whose body continues to express an orientation to the '*Being who has just lost his life*' (Heidegger, 1927/1962: 282). For her, the body continues to be the locus of personhood, whose 'subjectivity' is co-defined through the interpersonal network in which it is located. As a point of intersubjective interaction, the body must therefore be left in peace to allow the bereaved to say their final goodbye. While the appeal for organ donation has been 'gift-wrapped' to make it '*sounds nice*', such an intuitive appeal stands in contradiction to Estelle's pre-objective understanding of organ transplantation, which she considers to be '*disrespectful*' and '*horrible*'. Similarly, in her narrative below, Kierra provides a macabre depiction of cadaveric organ donation as involving the practice of clinical detachment, which she deems as the ultimate sign of disrespect to the donors and their families.

"*I know one of my friends is studying to be a doctor. And he just tells me about cadavers, is that the right word?...Anyway, he tells me about the story about cutting people up and....they don't seem to....it is not really a personal thing to them. It's like the body is a piece of meat and they fix it and sew it up, you know. It is like, the body is on the cutting board you know, (they) open you up gradually, sew it up and fix it and change it and do what you need to do. And that's how I think of it. But for me, I think of body in terms of people and I think life is very important. Well, the medical students see them as...although they know they are people...the doctors would have to detach*

themselves, haven't they, I think..."there are some people here who donated themselves for our benefit and aren't we lucky and we must respect these people and appreciate it". I don't think I can walk into a room with a dead person and laugh and take pictures and drink coffee really. And I think of that and I think of people laughing around cadavers and not thinking about them as people. It is kind of.....it is a natural.....it is somebody....they may be dead but still you know....very significant....that person is dead." (Kierra, Age 24, Interview 1)

Kierra is cognizant of the term *cadaver* being a discursive construction specific to medicine (Youngner, 1996). For her, the medical concept of the disembodied *cadaver* clashes with her *pre-objective understanding* of the deceased person in her lifeworld. As a medical construction, the *cadaver* is a pathological specimen of objective science (Foucault, 1973; Williams and Calnan, 1996). Sequestrated to the private realm of the operating theatre (Walter, 1996), the *cadaver* undergoes the rite of *dehumanization*, where it lies submissively on the '*cutting board*' (operating table) like a '*piece of meat*', ready to be '*sewn*', '*fixed*', '*opened up*' and '*changed*' by the clinically detached professional. As Heidegger (1927/1962) has forewarned, such acts of depersonalization (*it is not really a personal thing to them*) have denied embodied subjects their last shreds of dignity (Lynch, 1990). Despite acknowledging that such 'necessary inhumanity' (William Hunter circa 1780 in Richardson, 1987) is essential to achieve medical objectivity, (*doctors would have to detach themselves*), Kierra insists that the body continues to be a significant embodiment of the deceased donor whose life is '*very important*'. As such, the fragmentation of the body into medical objects is unthinkable for the majority of the participants. Not only does it disrupt the intersubjective bond between the deceased and the bereaved, it also signifies the disintegration of the embodied self, as Carmen explains below:

"*Because of just how important I am to me and my body. The body is to me how I was made up here, so it's almost like you are shattered (laugh) when you are scattered about. Erm...so that's why....cause you can't keep a hold of it. You can't keep track of everything.*" (Carmen, Age 23, Interview 2)

For Carmen, the integrity of the body represents '*how she is made up*'. Transplantation involves the breakup of the intact body, as it is '*shattered*' to pieces before being dispersed (*scattered about*) into the bodies of anonymous others. As such, she fears the 'loss of control' over the management of her body. For Carmen, this powerlessness to exercise control over the '*scattered body*' will '*shatter*' the concreteness of her Being, and thus herald the collapse of her identity project. Carmen then reflects on what it means for her to '*be whole*':

"*You want to be whole; everything is working in conjunction to each other. You as a person, you know, you have got nothing missing, you have got nothing wanting. ....You know I want to feel at home where I am...and whole where I am. My own perceptions of being whole in everything, being yours in its right place even if it is not working, you know, you are not needing it....because without it (the body) we wouldn't be <u>here</u>.*" (Carmen, Age 23, Interview 2, our emphasis)

In this narrative, Carmen suggests that *being whole* affords her a permanent sense of corporeal familiarity (*everything is in its right place*)–which she can then weave around her as a protective cocoon (Giddens, 1991) to help her '*feel at home*' in the world (Heidegger,

1927/1962). Such a refuge furnishes her *ontological security* (Giddens, 1991) and facilitates her ongoing project of the self. It is therefore important for Carmen to maintain the integrity of the body despite the cessation of its biological life. In existential terms, it is through the body that she is able to 'be-in-the-world' (Heidegger, 1927/1962). As Carmen insists, *"without the body, we wouldn't be here"*. This implies that 'being-a-body' is to be '*somewhere* in the world' (Heidegger, 1927/1962; Macquarrie, 1972)–that is to be in the continuity in terms of time and space. As such, a *disembodied* existence is inconceivable for participants; as the body represents the concreteness that anchors their lived experience and thereby supports the fullness of their existence (Macquarrie, 1972; Bauman, 1992). As a kernel of existence, the body is in perpetual transcendence and must continue to *"emerge or stand out from nothing"* (Macquarrie, 1972: 62). This is expressed below by Willa:

"Nothingness is frightening, you know, it's a void. It's…erm….it's out of….it's beyond my perception and therefore because I…because it's beyond my imagination I suppose that makes me afraid of it. Like some general sort of existence I suppose. Some general being part of time and space…..Erm….because we are…we're sort of Earth-bound aren't we? We are physically rooted to the ground in a sense…erm…Sort of constrained (by the) body. Gravity keeps us…keeps us down on the Earth and…erm….we're as rooted really as… almost as a tree is rooted into the earth. I mean we're rooted on Earth because of….erm…because of gravity and so on. I'm…I'm…I'm scared of (cosmic) space …that's… beyond my imagination…Because…because to me the idea of being unearthed, sort of ungrounded….it takes me out of life as I…as I know it, and it moves too far towards concepts I don't understand …… so the thought of…the thought of being in a spaceship or some rocket thing and looking down on Earth, I think my sanity would go immediately" (Willa, Age 31, Interview 2, our emphasis).

For Willa, to exist is to be part of the space-time continuum, anchored by her body. Drawing from her embodied experience of '*being earth-bound*', Willa describes her incarnated *existence* as analogous to a tree taking roots in the soil of the earth. In contrast, Willa equates *nothingness* to being in the void of cosmic *space*, which she claims to be '*beyond her imagination*'. As perception is intentional (i.e. the perceiving subject is comported towards an object in the world), nothingness is imperceptible to her as her (and our) imagination cannot stretch beyond what she has no experience of (Merleau-Ponty, 1945/2002; Bauman, 1992). Being adrift in the abyss of the cosmos creates in her an empty vacuousness, akin to Sartre's 'Nausea' (1938). Her perception cannot entertain the '*idea of being ungrounded*', as it defies the familiarity of her embodied senses that '*takes her out of life as she knows it*'. For Willa, nothingness is therefore a boundless void that offers no refuge to her perceptual need for groundedness (Bauman, 1992). As she loses the concreteness for being-in-the-world (Macquarrie, 1972), she also loses the 'wholeness' for Being (*my sanity would go immediately*) and thus the 'liquidation' of her (and our) self (Heidegger, 1927/1962). For the participants then, 'Being-in-the-world' entails *having* and *being* a 'bounded' body, through which they are able to project *ahead-of-themselves* towards the *possibilities-for-Being* (Heidegger, 1927/1962). The body is therefore permeated with intentionality as it is always in a plenum, incessantly 'performing' the act of living (Merleau-Ponty, 1945/2002). From an embodied standpoint, then, we can begin to appreciate our female participants' apprehension concerning the objectification of the body through cadaveric organ donation, as this implies being in a *stasis*

where they are no longer capable of meaningful transcendence. We will now move on to consider this.

Cannibalistic/Transcendental Potential of Organ Donation: On Merging With Anonymous Other

As participants contemplate the intercorporeal exchange of organs, their narratives take on a sinister undertone as they problematize the 'ressurective' promise to 'live on' in the body of anonymous transplant recipients. The merging and breaching of body boundaries evokes considerable anxiety among the participants as it violates the 'taken-for-granted' assumptions about the 'bounded body'. In other words, organ transplantation thematizes the 'leaky body'-a marginal construct, permeated with dangerous intent, as Carmen describes below:

"I think that's WRONG. It's eerie and not right …"No, I don't want to do that."….Erm…You know, I don't actually want to live on forever more and erm….I want me to be me, special as I am. Erm…And it….just it sounds like almost like something out of a horror film if you feel that parts of you is going to live on in other people. I think that's a bad way to go. It doesn't sit easy with me. Cause it's adulterated. It is like you are not pure anymore because it would be somebody else as well. So I think you are truly you when you are you, not bits of you and bits of somebody else". (Carmen, Age 22, Interview 2).

For Carmen, the idea of being technologically immortalized is met with a strong sense of repulsion. By situating her interpretive position within the genre of horror films, Carmen implies that the '*ressurective*' potential of organ transplantation is verging on the realms of the 'supernatural'. Her narrative can therefore be read as a cautionary tale (Thompson, 2004) that forewarns of the 'menacing' ramifications ingrained in the promise of technological transcendence. For Carmen, the breaching of bodily boundaries is 'adulterating' (Douglas, 1902/1966), as it threatens to defile the 'purity' of the embodied self. The practice of transplantation has therefore created a new class of hybrids, whose ambiguous coupling throws us into 'radical doubt' as to what the body is (Shilling, 1993; Hogle, 1995; Ohnuki-Tierney, 1994) and what constitutes our selfhood (Shilling, 1993, Seale et. al, 2006). To consolidate her sense of individuality (*I want me to be me, special as I am*), Carmen expresses a strong resistance to such hybridity, arguing that '*you are truly you when you are you, not bits of you and bits of somebody else*'. Such violations to the 'bounded body' have therefore provoked a sense of unease among our participants, insinuating that organ donation is saturated with cannibalistic potential (Scheper-Hughes, 2001).

For the participants, transplanted organs are *fetishized* objects, enlivened with animistic qualities (Sharp, 1995; Lock, 2002). This has created room for participants to 'give voice' to the 'knowing body' (Merleau-Ponty, 1945/2002), thereby substantiating it as an agentic field of resistance. Such anthromorphism of the body is pervasive among the participants, best captured in the narrative constructed by Chloe below:

"I don't know….probably something just like a mental image more than anything else. With everything the doctors seem to be able to do now, you would be able to survive rejection. But there's …the organ itself would always be…you can…almost see the heart itself going, "No, I don't belong in here", and sort of …erm…you having to take drugs to stop rejection, it's almost like the organ going, 'No, I don't belong in here. Let me out'. erm…..which is why they, you know, they sort of give drugs to sort of…I don't know, calm the organ, to pacify it, to

make it sleepy, so it isn't permanently sort of going "Let me out! Let me out! I don't belong in here!" Probably like a joke, saying, you know, that ….in obviously donating an organ, you know, you'll know that you're helping somebody else walk around with your heart. This is in my imagination just….you just know it was that person down there has got what was once yours. There's probably a selfish element …. like me, you know, it's like, "That's mine! You shouldn't have it. Put it back, it's only borrowed". Despite the facts that you don't…you're not going to need it again." (Chloe, Age 24, Interview 2)

In her narrative, Chloe forewarns of the peril that may befall the transplant recipient when the barricade of the bounded body is breached (Sharp, 1995; Hallam *et. al*, 1999). Specifically, she portrays the heart as bewildered and rebellious, seemingly taking on a life of its own, as it struggles to liberate itself from the fleshy casing of a foreign body. Like Chloe, most participants in this study depict the heart as the strongest site of defiance, as it is culturally considered to be the seat of personhood and emotion (Manning-Steven, 1997; Haddow, 2000; Belk, 1988). The 'imagined biography' (Kopytoff, 1986) constructed around the heart is therefore richly elaborated (Sharp, 1995).

By constructing a social biography of the transplanted heart, Chloe envisages the alienation of the self, which is manifested through the biological (natural) rejection of foreign body parts (in this case the heart). In order to avoid being discounted as 'irrational', Chloe draws on the scientific discourse of immunosuppressive rejection to 'legitimize' her embodied standpoint. As Chloe observes, it is on the corporeal frontiers that the battle of power and control commence between biomedicine (a cultural invention) and the biological body. Immunosuppressant drugs such as cyclosporine are weapons wielded by medical professionals to pacify the wilful organs to subordinate them to the power of science. And in so doing, fulfilling the modernist project that upholds the superiority of culture (science) to overcome the limitations of the 'natural' body (Bauman, 1992; Hirschman, 1990; Shilling, 1993). Chloe indicates that such medical infringement of the body has also blurred the boundaries that have culturally marked the ownership of our body (Sharp, 1995). Disputes therefore arise as to who (i.e. donor or recipient) should be accorded the rightful control over the transplanted organs. In her narrative, Chloe vehemently maintains that selfhood is an incarnated phenomenon, emphasising the body's 'natural' defences to protect its borders from the invasion of alien objects. In other words, the 'knowing body' has 'declared' its 'natural' allegiance to its owner (donor), who should therefore retain their rightful dominion over their organs. Not surprisingly then, organ donation is imbued with vampirish tendencies where the transfer of personalized organs is tantamount to the transference of the donor's agentic life-force. Further illustrating this, Cyd states:

"I've heard stories about people that say they have flashbacks that aren't their memories or that they feel things or that they like certain foods now because they have someone else's body parts and things, and it just doesn't seem right that we should take on somebody's else's that's not ours. It's…yeah..(laugh) Yeah, I don't know really… I don't know, because I've seen things on telly before where people have never met and they don't know anything about the other person's life but yet they've got a memory of their wife or something….I don't know, I think perhaps your body and your body parts take on more than we really think and so then to transfer it, maybe you

do take a little piece of that soul with you….If that really is true, then for that person that might not be a great experience either to have like parts of you in…because they might not always be good bits, maybe there would be bad bits too…. Yeah. They could pass on your demons or something. (laugh)" (Cyd, Age 22, Interview 2)

Cyd suggests that the body is saturated with the donor's personal history, which becomes embodied as 'memories'. Such 'embodied memories' are sedimented within their corporeal schema (Merleau-Ponty, 1945/2002). Thus, by donating their organs, they may also transfer their 'embodied memories' onto recipients', and hence modify their corporeal schema. This transference of 'embodied memories' is euphemized as *'passing on her demons'*. As Cyd implies, her 'embodied demons' may transform the recipients' experience of being-in-the-world (*say they have flashbacks that aren't their memories or that they feel things or that they like certain foods*) and thus alter their personal history. For Cyd, the transplanted organs are more than just inert biological objects. Rather, they are intentional objects that have the potential to inhibit the social agency of the organ recipient.

In their narratives, participants often make intertextual reference to the genre of thriller and horror films. Posed as a counter-narrative, these films provide cultural commentaries, warning the dangers of violating body boundaries. Participants tend to sensationalize various urban myths represented in these films, such as the horror of identity swap (*Face/Off, All About My Mother*), seeing ghosts (*The Eye*), the tyranny of gifts (Fox and Swazey, 1992), where the donor family stalks transplant recipients to seek reciprocation to their grief (*21 Grams*). This is exemplified below by Estelle:

"Carrie (friend) told me this film she watched (The Eye) and I am just picturing that. It is really scary. She had a… I think it is a retina transplant ….. And she looked into the mirror, and she sees the donor's ghost reflected in the mirror. Like she sees her eyes…that other person's reflection. That's why it was freaking me out there. It's just the whole idea of….someone else's identity mixed up with yours because…Oh! Have you seen Face/Off the film? It's like really unrealistic, because it's just like the different actors playing the different characters but…this guy has…erm…got this criminal arrested, but he has been given or he's been knocked out and his face has been stolen, so the criminal lives the life of him and he the cop. And….that'd be awful. Just…just the idea that you're assumed to be someone else." (Estelle, Age 21, Interview 1)

CONCLUSION

In their narratives, participants imply that the decision to become an organ donor relies on individuals being willing to overcome the depersonalized transformation of the body to embrace the redemptive spirit of the 'gift'. Hence, participants are actively engaged in a reflexive negotiation, to establish the parameters to which their embodied self can be objectified, fragmented and reincorporated as medicalized objects (Hogle, 1995; Youngner, 1996). Thus, while the idea of breaking up the body seems abhorrent to our participants, this does not mean they reject cadaveric organ donation outright. Instead, as it thematizes competing narratives surrounding the mortal body, it feeds their confusion, and thus their ambivalence surrounding becoming an organ donor.

Specifically, our participants perceive body parts as permeated with 'imagined social agency' (Miller, 2002 in Borgerson, 2005), which have the potential to (1) hinder the agency of the organ recipient whose embodied self becomes cannibalized, and/or (2) annul the embodied intentionality of the donors whose embodied self becomes 'literally' devoured by the recipient. The 'ressurective' appeal of the 'gift-of-life' is therefore rife with ideological contradictions (Sharp, 1995); as participants are presented with the *transcendental promise* to 'extend their biographies' while simultaneously being confronted with its *cannibalistic potential*. As Lock (2002) argues, the fetishism of the body is doubly at work. On the one hand, the promotional discourse of organ donation has concealed the progressive objectification of the body through the fetishization of the 'gift' (Richardson, 1996; Youngner, 1996). For the potential donors, however, the body is infused with animistic quality that mystifies it as a fetishized object akin to religious relics (Sharp, 1995, Lock, 2002; de Brosses, 1760/1970).

Embedded within this nexus of competing narratives, the body therefore occupies an ambiguous position within the discourse of organ transplantation, as it is at once a commoditized cadaver and the vessel of personal history (Sharp, 1995). It is therefore difficult to establish where the embodied subject ends and the commoditized object begins. Consequently, the boundary that distinguishes the embodied/disembodied constituent of selfhood is indeterminate, mutable and emergent (Dant, 2006; Bettany, 2007), as its locality is co-defined through the intersubjective network that makes up the transplant community. As such, the 'agentic capability' attributed to the body is negotiated through the 'material interaction' between members of the transplant community. In summary, organ donation has thrown into confusion what the body is, how it should be treated and to what extent the body can be considered as the kernel of existence. The corpse, though lifeless, continues to express an orientation to life and is imbued with social and personal significance.

Accordingly this paper therefore seeks to create a dialogue among consumer scholars to reconsider the relationships between consuming subjects and material objects. Only in so doing, can we begin to advance the discipline beyond its essentialist roots. We propose mortal embodiment as a promising area of study that enables us to recognize that material civilization is cultivated through the bodily utilization of cultural objects-molded in the enfleshment of consumers' experience of being-in-the-world. We leave you with the thoughts of Merleau-Ponty -

"The body is our general medium for having a world. Sometimes, it is restricted to the action necessary for the conservation of life, and accordingly posits around us a biological world...Sometimes, finally, the meaning aimed at cannot be achieved by the body's natural means; it must then build itself an instrument, and it projects thereby around itself a cultural world" (Merleau-Ponty, 1945/2002: 169).

REFERENCES

Armstrong, David (1987), "Silence and Truth in Death and Dying", *Social Science and Medicine,* Vol. 24(8): 651-658.

Arnold, Stephen J., and Fischer, Eileen (1994), "Hermeneutics and Consumer Research", *Journal of Consumer Research,* Vol. 21: 55-70.

Arnould, Eric J., and Thompson, Craig J. (2005), "Consumer Culture Theory (CCT): Twenty Years of Research", *Journal of Consumer Research,* 31(4): 868-882.

Bauman, Zygmunt (1992), *Mortality, Immortality and Other Life Strategies,* Stanford: Stanford University Press.

Belk, Russell W. (1988), "Possessions and the Extended Self", *Journal of Consumer Research,* Vol. 15(9): 139-168.

Belk, Russell W. (1990), "Me and Thee Versus Mine and Thine: How Perceptions of the Body Influence Organ Donation and Transplantation", in James Shanteau, Richard Jackson and Richard Harris (Eds.), *Organ Donation and Transplantation: Psychological and Behavioral Factors*, Washington, DC: American Psychological Association, 139-149.

Bettany, Shona (2007), "The Material Semiotics of Consumption or Where (And What) Are The Objects In Consumer Culture Theory?" in Russell W. Belk and John F. Sherry (Eds.), *Consumer Culture Theory: Research in Consumer Behaviour*, Oxford: JAI Press Publications, Vol. 11: 41-56.

Borgerson, Janet (2005), "Materiality, Agency and The Constitution of Consuming Subjects: Insights for Consumer Research", in Geeta Menon and Akshay R. R. Rao (Eds.), *Advances in Consumer Research*, Duluth, MN, Association for Consumer Research, Vol. 32: 439-443.

Burkitt, Ian (1999), *Bodies of Thought: Embodiment, Identity and Modernity,* London: Sage Publications.

Craib, Ian (1998), *Experiencing Identity,* London: Sage.

Dant, Tim (2006), "Material Civilization: Things and Society", *The British Journal of Sociology,* 57(2): 289-308.

de Brosses, Charles ([1970]1760), *Du culte des dieux fetiches, ou Parallele de Vancienne religion de I'Egypte avec la religion actuelle de Nigritie,* Westmead: Farnborough, Hants.

Douglas, Mary ([1902]1966), *Purity and Danger: An Analysis of Concepts of Polution and Taboo,* London: Routledge and Keegan Paul.

Dreyfus, Hubert L. (1999), *Being-In-The-World: A Commentary on Heidegger's Being and Time, Division I,* Cambridge and London: The MIT Press.

Dreyfus, Hubert L. and Rubin, Jane (1999), "Kierkegaard, Division II, and Later Heidegger", in Hubert L. Dreyfus (Ed.), *Being-in-the-world: A Commentary on Heidegger's Being and Time, Division I*, Cambridge and London: The MIT Press, 283-340.

Elliot, Richard and Wattanasuwan, Kritsadarat (1998), "Brands As Symbolic Resources for the Construction of Identity", *International Journal of Advertising,* Vol. 17 (2): 131-144.

Foucault, Michel (1973), *The Birth of the Clinic,* trans. A. M. Sheridan Smith, London: Tavistock.

Fox, Rene C. and Swazey, Judith P. (1992), *Spare Parts: Organ Replacement in American Society,* New York and Oxford: Oxford University Press.

Gadamer, Hans-Georg (1989), *Truth and Method,* New York: Crossroad.

Giddens, Anthony (1991), *Modernity and Self-Identity: Self and Society in the Late Modern Age,* Cambridge: Polity Press.

Grosz, Elizabeth (1994), *Volatile Bodies: Toward a Corporeal Feminism,* Bloominton and Indianapolis: Indiana University Press.

Haddow, Gillian (2000), "Organ Transplantation and (Dis)Embodiment", *Edinburgh Working Papers in Sociology,* Edinburgh: University of Edinburgh.

Hallam, Elizabeth; Jenny Hockey and Glennys Howarth (1999), *Beyond the Body: Death and Social Identity,* London: Routledge.

Heidegger, Martin ([1927]1962), *Being and Time,* trans. John Macquarrie and Edward Robinson, Oxford: Blackwell.

Helman, Cecil (1988), "Dr. Frankenstein and The Industrial Body", *Anthropology Today,* Vol. 4(3): 14-16.

Hirschman, Elizabeth C. (1990), "Secular Immortality and the American Ideology of Affluence", *Journal of Consumer Research,* Vol. 17(June): pp. 31-42.

Hogle, Linda F. (1995), "Tales from the Cryptic: Technology Meets Organism in the Living Cadaver", in *The Cyborg Handbook*, eds. Chris H. Gray, Heidi J. Figueroa-Sarrierra and Steven Mentor, New York: Routledge, 203-218.

Holstein, James A. and Gubrium, Jaber F. (1995), *The Active Interview*, Thousand Oaks, CA: Sage.

Howson, Alexandra and Inglis, David (2001), "The Body in Sociology: Tension Inside and Outside Sociological Thought", *The Editorial Board of The Sociological Review*: 297-317.

Joy, Annamma and Sherry, John F. (2003), "Speaking of Art as Embodied Imagination: A Multisensory Approach to Understanding Aesthetic Experience", *Journal of Consumer Research*, Vol. 30(September): 259-282.

Joy, Annamma and Venkatesh, Alladi (1994), "Postmodernism, Feminism and the Body: The Visible and the Invisible in Consumer Research" *International Journal of Research in Marketing*, Vol. 11(September): 333-357.

Kopytoff, Igor (1986), "The Cultural Biography of Things: Commoditization as Process", in Arjun Appadurai (Ed.), *The Social Life of Things: Commodities in Cultural Perspective*, Cambridge: Cambridge University Press.

Lai, Ai-Ling; Dermody, Janine and Hanmer-Lloyd, Stuart (2008), "An Existential Analysis of Consumers as 'Incarnated Beings': A Merleau-Pontyian Perspective", in Stefania Borghini, Mary Ann Mcgrath and Cele Otnes (Eds.), *European Advances for Consumer Research*, Milan, Association of Consumer Research, 8: 381-389

Langer, Monika (1989), *Merleau-Ponty's Phenomenology of Perception*, Basingstoke and London: The MacMillan Press.

Latour, Bruno (1987), *Science in Action: How to Follow Scientists and Engineers Through Society*, Milton Keynes: Open University Press.

Leder, Drew (1990), *The Absent Body*, Chicago and London: The University of Chicago Press.

Lock, Margaret (2002), *Twice Dead: Organ Transplants and the Reinvention of Death*, Berkeley: University of California Press.

Lynch, Abbyann (1990), "Respect for The Dead Human Body: A Question of Body, Mind, Spirit, Pscyhe", *Transplantation Proceedings*, Vol. 22 (June): 1016-1018.

Macquarrie, John (1968), *Martin Heidegger*, London: Lutterworth Press.

Macquarrie, John (1972), *Existentialism: An Introduction, Guide and Assessment*, New York: Penguin Book.

Manning-Stevens, Scott (1997), "Sacred Heart and Secular Brain", in Carla Mazzio and David Hillman (Eds.), *The Body In Parts: Fantasies of Corporeality in Early Modern Europe*, London and New York: Routledge.

Marx, Karl ([1867]1976), *Capital*, Volume One, London: Penguin Books.

Merleau-Ponty, Maurice ([1945] 2002), *The Phenomenology of Perception*, trans. C. Smith, London and New York: Routledge.

Merleau-Ponty, Maurice (1968), *The Visible and the Invisible and The Working Notes*, Evanston: Northwestern University Press.

Mick, David G. and Buhl, Claus (1992), "A Meaning-based Model of Advertising Experiences", *Journal of Consumer Research*, Vol. 19 (December): 317-338.

Miller, Daniel (1987), *Material Culture and Mass Consumption*, Oxford: Basil Blackwell.

Ohnuki-Tierney, Emiko (1994), "Brain Death and Organ Transplantation: Cultural Bases of Medical Technology", *Current Anthropology*, Vol. 35(3): 233-254.

Patterson, Maurice and Elliot, Richard (2002), "Negotiating Masculinities: Advertising and the Inversion of the Male Gaze", *Consumption, Markets and Culture*, Vol. 5(3): 231-246.

Richardson, Ruth (1987), *Death, Dissection and the Destitute*, London: Routledge.

Richardson, Ruth (1996), "Fearful Symmetry: Corpses for Anatomy, Organs for Transplantation?", in Renee C. Fox, Laurence J. O'Connell and Stuart J. Youngner (Eds.), *Organ Transplantation: Meanings and Realities*, Madison: The University of Wisconsin Press, 66-100.

Robbins, Margaret (1996), "The Donation of Organs for Transplantation: the Donor Families", in Glennys Howarth and Peter C. Jupp (Eds.), *Contemporary Issues in the Sociology of Death, Dying and Disposal*, Basingstoke: MacMillan, 179-192.

Sartre, Jean-Paul (1938), *Nausea*, trans. Robert Baldick, London: Penguin

Sartre, Jean-Paul ([1943]1956), *Being and Nothingness: An Essay on Phenomenological Ontology*, trans. Hazel E. Barnes, New York: Washington Square Press.

Scheper-Hughes, Nancy (2001), "Commodity Fetishism in Organs Trafficking", *Body and Society*, 7(2-3): 31-62.

Seale, Clive; Cavers, Debbie and Dixon-Woods, Mary (2006), "Commodification of Body Parts: By Medicine or by Media?", *Body and Society*, 12(1): 25-42.

Sharp, Lesley A. (1995), "Organ Transplantation as a Transformative Experience: Anthropological Insights into the Restructuring of the Self", *Medical Anthropology Quarterly*, Vol. 9(3): 357-389.

Shilling, Chris (1993), *The Body and Social Theory*, London: Sage.

Thompson, Craig J. (1997), "Interpreting Consumers: A Hermeneutical Framework for Deriving Marketing Insights From The Text of Consumers' Consumption Stories", *Journal of Marketing Research*, Vol. XXXIV: 438-455.

Thompson, Craig J. (2004), "Marketplace Mythology and Discourses of Power", *Journal of Consumer Research*, 31(6): 162-180.

Thompson, Craig J. and Hirschman, Elizabeth C. (1995), "Understanding the Socialized Body: A Poststructuralist Analysis of Consumers' Self Conceptions, Body Images and Self-Care Practices", *Journal of Consumer Research*, Vol. 22 (9): 139-153.

Thompson, Craig J. and Hirschman, Elizabeth C. (1998), "An Existential Analysis of the Embodied Self in Postmodern Consumer Culture" *Consumption, Markets and Culture*, Vol. 2(4): 337-465.

Thompson, Craig J.; Locander, William B. and Pollio, Howard R. (1989), "Putting Consumer Experience Back into Consumer Research: the Philosophy and Method of Existential-Phenomenology", *Journal of Consumer Research*, Vol. 19(2): 133-147.

Thompson, Craig J.; Pollio, Howard R. and Locander, William B. (1994), "The Spoken and the Unspoken: A Hermeneutic Approach to Understanding the Cultural Viewpoints That Underlie Consumers' Expressed Meanings", *Journal of Consumer Research*, Vol. 21(3): 432-452.

Thompson, Craig J. and Haytko, Diana L. (1997), "Speaking of Fashion: Consumers' Uses of Fashion Discourses and the Appropriation of Countervailing Cultural Meanings", *Journal of Consumer Research,* Vol. 24(June): 15-42.

Titmuss, Richard M. (1972), *The Gift Relationship: From Human Blood to Social Policy,* New York: Vintage Book.

Turner, Bryan S. (1996), *The Body and Society,* London: Sage Publications.

Wallendorf, Melanie and Arnould, Eric J. (1988), "My Favorite Things: A Cross-Cultural Inquiry into Object Attachment, Possessiveness and Social Linkage", *Journal of Consumer Research,* 14(3): 531-547.

Walter, Tony (1996), "Facing Death Without Tradition", in Glennys Howarth and Peter Jupp (Eds.), *Contemporary Issues in the Sociology of Death, Dying and Disposal,* London: Macmillan, 193-204.

Williams, Simon J. and Calnan, Michael (1996), "The 'Limits' of Medicalization? Modern Medicine and the Lay Populace in Late Modernity'", *Social Science and Medicine,* Vol. 42(12): 1609-1620.

Youngner, Stuart J. (1996), "Some Must Die", in Renee C. Fox, Laurence J. O'Connell and Stuart J. Youngner (Eds.), *Organ Transplantation: Meanings and Realities,* Madison: The University of Wisconsin Press, 32-55.

Living with the Obesity Stigma: Perceptions of Being Obese from Three Cultures

Ekant Veer, University of Bath, UK

ABSTRACT

One defining antecedent of marginalized consumer groups is their status as being stigmatized. Although much research has investigated the perceptions of onlookers of a stigmatized person or group, little research has been conducted regarding the stigmatized person themselves and what impact the stigma has on his or her behavior. Using qualitative methods, this paper investigates the way in which an understanding of the obesity stigma develops within the individual, the impact that the obesity stigma has on consumers' perceptions of themselves and finally, their ability to internalize and act upon social marketing interventions.

INTRODUCTION

The increasing interest in marginalized consumer research has led to a recent increase in exploratory work in the area. One defining antecedent of a marginal consumer is his or her status as being stigmatized or separated from society in some way (Burden 1998). Many studies have elucidated the range of effects expressed by onlookers of stigmatized consumers; however, little research has focussed on the effect a stigma can have on afflicted consumers themselves. This paper uses the visible stigma of obesity as the context for understanding how consumer perceptions and actions may change as the stigma attachment is internalized in the obese individual's life. As such, the questions are asked: how does the sense of stigmatization develop in an obese person, and secondly, how do obese people cope with this feeling of stigmatization? Qualitative research methods were employed to understand how informants' lives have been affected by their stigmatized status as being obese, and subsequently offer avenues of investigation for social marketers in order to more effectively target marginalized groups with their campaigns.

After exploring the extant literature surrounding stigmas and prejudices a brief discussion of the methodology is presented. This is followed by a summary of findings, a discussion of main themes from the research and some implications for social marketers, public policy makers and academicians.

WHAT IS A STIGMA?

A stigma, in its simplest form, is any distinguishing mark or characteristic that distinguishes a consumer as being different (Allport 1954). Although stigmas do not necessarily need to be negatively valanced, stigmas are often reported as being negative marks or characterisations. For example, Link and Phelan (2001) note that stigmatisation is the combination of distinguishing a person or group based on known differences; associating these differences with negative attributions; separating these individuals or groups based on these negative differences and assigning a loss of status to this stigmatized individual or group. This definition, based on the earlier research of Goffman (1963), outlines both the distinguishing quality of stigmas but also the dynamic, processual nature of stigmas.

In the case of obesity, known differences between an obese person and a non-obese person can result in the obese person being stigmatized and therefore, thought of as being lesser by the non-obese person. For example, obese persons are excluded from certain social groups (Crocker and Luhtanen 1990), thought of as having lowered self control (Brown, et al. 2003) and academically less superior than non-obese persons (Tiggeman and Anesbury 2000).

One of the precursors to modern stigma research stems from Gordon W. Allport's work in the 1950's and Henri Tajfel and John Turner's work on Social Identity Theory (SIT), beginning in the mid 1970's. SIT is grounded in the premise that consumers, as social beings, categorize themselves into separate groups and protect their 'in-group' from the distinct 'out-groups' (Tajfel 1979, Turner 1991). In-groups are characterized as being groups that one currently belongs to or wishes to belong to, while an out-group is any group that one does not belong or does not wish to belong to. Stigmas form the basis for forming in-groups and out-groups. For example, a male consumer may walk into a women's clothing store with his partner. Generally speaking, the male consumer in outside of his normal domain and surrounded by persons he represents as being part of his out-group. In an attempt to feel some form of belonging and comfort in his surroundings he may instinctively approach another male in the store who appears equally uncomfortable. Even though the two persons may never associated with one another in a 'normal' setting, when surrounded by a distinct out-group a male in-group is formed. The two consumers may never have met however, if the stigma of discomfort was not perceived by both members. That is, the discomfort of the two men drew them together to form an in-group. If one of the consumers expressed extreme ease and comfort with the situation the other male may not have been able to associate himself with the comfortable consumer and no contact would have been made.

A prejudice, in its mildest form, can be thought of as the relative preference of one's in-group over the out-group, expressed in evaluation, liking, or allocation of resources (Struch and Schwartz 1989). The strength and explicitness of an individual's prejudicial tendencies was dichotomized by Allport (1954) from the bigoted individual to the compunctious individual. The actual strength of prejudice seems to vary from individual to individual from a mild annoyance to a true hatred of a stigmatized group. Although a compunctious individual may feel a sense of guilt once his or her prejudicial behavior has been brought to light, the fact remains that subconscious favoritism towards one's in-group and the relative discrimination of an out-group is endemic of natural human behavior.

The two-factor Justification-Suppression Model (JSM) of prejudice by Crandall and Eshleman (2003) operationalizes prejudicial expression as a function of both suppressive factors (the internally or externally motivated attempt to control or reduce the expression or awareness of prejudice) and justifying factors (the internal or external process that can serve to express genuine prejudice without the threat of sanctions). The JSM model determines that an individual's prejudicial behavior and thoughts are expressed in such a way based on their ability to control or justify innate prejudicial desires (genuine prejudice).

Although genuine, an innate prejudice may exist within an individual but it may or may not be expressed overtly based on his or her ability to justify or suppress the prejudice respectively. Allport's (1954) notion of the bigot would have relatively high justification factors in play compared with his or her suppression factors; whilst a compunctious individual would have the reverse. That is, the prejudice exists innately within the compunctious individual, but is repressed rather than expressed.

Renfrew's (1997) study into the causes of aggression showed that certain 'noxious stimuli' can elicit escape, avoid or punishment strategies. In a similar way, stigmas can elicit prejudicial or aggressive tendencies toward a stigmatized individual or group. A stigma can be seen as an activator or initiator for prejudicial expression; that is, the stigma is used as the distinguishing mark that leads to favoritism towards unstigmatized persons or groups and aggression, avoidance or animosity towards stigmatized persons.

Explicit stigmas include sex, age, ethnicity or weight and are easily identified by onlookers. A person may have an innate or genuine prejudice towards persons of Asian descent but this would only be expressed either when in the physical presence of an Asian person or the subject of Asian ancestry is highly salient in the minds of the racist, such as when persons of Asian descent are discussed amongst others. As the name suggests, latent stigmas are more concealed than the above examples, which may result in prejudicial behavior not being expressed until the stigma is unveiled. For example, an environmentalist may have a strong attachment with a commercial whaler until realising their ideologies clash (latent stigma), at which point it is likely that varying levels of prejudicial expression would surface depending on the strength of the participant's use of available justification and suppression factors. Obesity falls into the first of the two stigma categories. Obesity is often easily identifiable, allowing those with prejudicial beliefs about the obese to make quick assumptions (Ferraro and Holland 2002). Some overt consequences of prejudicial behavior often include, but is not restricted to, physical detachment; social segregation, fear, reduced family cohesion, secrecy and lowered social status (Phelan, et al. 1997).

Hebl and Mannix (2003) extend the stigma literature to show that it is not only the stigmatized individual that is subject to prejudicial expression, but also persons that associate with the stigmatized individual. In their study, Hebl and Mannix (2003) found that an unstigmatized person standing with their obese partner was seen as less favorable than an unstigmatized person standing with their nonobese partner.

WHY OBESITY?

The clinical definition of obesity is an excess of fatty tissue to the point that the person is in significant medical risk (Aronne and Segal 2002). However, it is not the presence of fatty tissue that is of concern in the present study, but rather the perceptions that are associated with the excess fat that an individual carries. One may be slightly overweight and feel far more stigmatized than one who is extremely overweight.

Obesity not only defines a person as being different, but is still considered by many to be a point of negative differentiation (Crandall 1994, Ferraro and Holland 2002). Weiner, Perry, and Magnusson (1988) empirically showed that the stigma associated with obesity is one of the most damaging of the 10 they studied. Obese persons were seen as being highly responsible and to blame for their current size, one of the least liked groups in society and worthy of little pity or financial assistance. Respondents identified obesity as one of the least likely stigmas to deserve social welfare. Other than drug abusers and child abusers, obese persons are ranked as being the stigmatized group most undeserving of affection.

Aside from the extreme effects obese consumers may experience by being stigmatized are the increasing rates of obesity across much of the Asia Pacific region. The New Zealand Ministry of Health rated research designed to curb the rise of obesity rates as being its most important goal in the near future (Minister of Health 2003, New Zealand Ministry of Health 2001). The Australian Department of Health and Ageing has ranked Australia as being one of the fattest developed nations in the world and has instigated a number of initiatives to control the onset of obesity in Australian society (Australian Department of Health and Ageing 2004). Further research into all aspects associated with obesity has been called for

from a number of academic sources, including the Journal of Consumer Research (Mick 2003).

The greater understanding there is surrounding obese consumers' perceptions towards themselves and the obesity stigma, the greater likelihood that more effective social marketing campaigns can be developed that meet their needs as well as promote healthy weight goals. Qualitative research methods were employed so as to provide richness of data regarding the obesity stigma. The following section discusses the methodology drawn on and the respondents that participated in the investigation.

METHODOLOGY

Qualitative methods were employed in order to gain a greater understanding of the perceptions, motivations and feelings behind the informants' actions. As with much interpretivist work the research was undertaken with the aim to inform and develop theory, rather than to generalize or predict actions and behavior to populations (Walsham 1995). Two main qualitative methods were undertaken. Firstly, focus groups were used to help individuals open up and discuss the topic of obesity amongst peers who were in a similar situation. It was reasoned that a group forum would allow greater flow of conversation and interaction with the sensitive topic of obesity stigma (Onkvisit and Shaw 1987). Following the focus groups depth interviews were conducted to gain further insight based on individual cases. Depth interviews provided a more private setting where an informant was able to express themselves without the fear of social judgement (Thornton and Moore 1993). With obesity becoming increasingly prevalent in the South Pacific region the countries of Fiji and New Zealand were used as a source of data for the current research.

Four focus groups were conducted in three distinct populations. Two focus groups were conducted in an indigenous Fijian community based outside of Suva, Fiji. One group was made up entirely of male informants, and the other comprised solely of female informants. One focus group was conducted with Indo-Fijian women living outside of Suva, Fiji. The final group was taken from high school students studying in the south Auckland suburb of Mangere, which is recognized as having a high proportion of Pacific Island and Maori students. All respondents felt they were overweight or obese. Actual weights and body fat measures were not completed so as to not further emphasize the obesity stigma in the minds of the respondents.

Although each group may be distinct from one another in many ways all groups were well represented by high levels of obesity, generally low levels of education and income in their communities and very little understanding regarding the consequences of obesity and its related illnesses. For the Fijian and Indo-Fijian groups a local interviewer was used to conduct the focus group and translate the transcripts into English for analysis. Local interviewers were chosen so that informants can communicate in their native language, providing greater expression and more effective communication. Each interviewer was provided with a standard set of questions, but also encouraged to ask questions along a line they felt may be useful. Interviewers were hired from a local medical college and were both experienced in qualitative interviewing techniques as well as obesity related issues.

During each focus group a second researcher was present to take fieldnotes of general observations made during the focus groups. Even though the second researcher may not understand the language being spoken, the observations made provided valuable insight into the setting in which the focus was conducted as well as the overall tone and atmosphere of the focus group; qualities that the moderator may not have had time to note. Table 1 outlines the make up of each focus group.

TABLE 1
DESCRIPTION OF FOCUS GROUP INFORMANTS

Group	Number of Informants	Language Spoken	Length	Researchers present
Fijian males	7– ranging in ages from 25 to 50 years old.	Fijian	90 minutes	1 Fijian speaking moderator, 2 non Fijian speaking observers. All male.
Fijian females	9– ranging in ages from 30 to 52 years old.	Fijian	65 minutes	2 Fijian speaking moderators, 1 non Fijian speaking observer. All female.
Indo-Fijian females	7– ranging in ages from 18 to 55 years old.	Fijian Hindi	80 minutes	1 Hindi speaking moderator (female), 2 non Hindi speaking observers (male).
Mangere High School students	8– ranging in ages from 15 to 18 years old.	English (all informants fluent in English as a first language)	55 minutes	1 English speaking interviewer (male), 1 English speaking observer (Female).

One on one depth interviews were then conducted with selected focus group participants. Snowballing data sampling was used to acquire further informants. Depth interviews were conducted in order to obtain greater clarification about issues the researcher felt were important to discuss but not appropriate for a group forum. That is, issues that may be deemed shameful to the social group, such as binge eating, depressive feelings or suicide, could be more readily discussed with an interviewer in a private setting. Eight depth interviews were completed in total. Table 2 provides a brief description of informants who participated in depth interviews.

Each transcript was analysed by two researchers, one using the native language and one using the English translation. Open ended and Axial coding methods were used in order to obtain a number of coherent emergent themes within each transcript and then across all transcripts (Spiggle 1994).

Final inter-coder reliability was ascertained by comparing themes and major quotes from transcripts pertaining to each theme. Conflicts were discussed between the coders and resolutions made. When no resolution was possible a third coder, independent from the research collection process, was called to examine the discrepancies and offer a final opinion. Final agreed upon themes were then independently scrutinized by two judges in order to determine their value in aiding the understanding of stigmatized consumer groups.

FINDINGS

Three major themes emerged as being both salient and valuable in informing extant theory. These themes have been labelled *Hopelessness*, *Blindness*, and *Variable Salience*. Each theme will be discussed in greater detail with relevant implications for theory.

Hopelessness

Although the notion that the obese can suffer from depressive disorders is not novel, the consistent theme of hopelessness indicated a strong sense of a deeper, more enduring feeling of despair.

Interestingly it was not exacted at other aspects of the individual's life. Divya recounts her previous experiences with dieting and her weight as being a never ending cycle.

"It's not…It's not as if my life, my size is not a problem. I know it is…I know the pain I suffer from the diabetes and the puffing [breathlessness]…but it [weight loss] can't be done…I have done it before and I…I just can't do it…it's too hard and too difficult…if it was easy and I could do it, it would still be too hard I think…I just have no more power or fight left…" Divya, 55 year old Indo-Fijian female

Lei narrates how his father and mother continue to talk to him about his size and what it means to them.

"I don't understand it sometimes…I know I can do it but my Mum keeps saying "it's too late…it's too late for me to, to be healthy-but you, you have [a] chance…" I guess they've given up and accepted it…" Lei, 18 year old Asian male.

The sense of hopelessness in the older informants and the desire for the younger ones not to lose hope or stop trying is also evident in the way the parents purchase and cook foods for themselves and for their children.

"it's not right I know…but the children need to run and the children need to play and they need to have good food…we give them a little bread and some butter and some milk and they play…while we buy for ourselves the bad [fatty] foods and the drink…I don't want my son to be me this way…I want him to be big and strong…but not big…like me…" Joeli, 38 year old Fijian male.

There is also a sense of fear espoused by the older informants. However, rather than dispossess the feared self as suggested by self

TABLE 2
DESCRIPTION OF DEPTH INTERVIEW INFORMANTS

Name[1]	Relationship to other groups	Language Spoken	Length	Age	Researchers present
Sitiveni	Male, part of Fijian community	Fijian	70 minutes	26	1 Fijian speaking interviewer (male)
Joeli	Male, part of Fijian community	Fijian	65 minutes	38	1 Fijian speaking interviewer (male)
Adi	Female, part of Fijian community	Fijian	45 minutes	45	1 Fijian speaking interviewer (female)
Rangi	Male, high school student in Mangere	English	45 minutes	16	1 English speaking interviewer (male)
Lei	Male, high school student in Mangere	English	65 minutes	18	I English speaking interviewer (male)
Hine	Female, high school student in Mangere	English	45 minutes	17	1 English speaking interviewer (male)
Asha	Female, part of Indo-Fijian community. Daughter of Divya	Indo-Fijian	60 minutes	18	1 Hindi speaking interviewer (female)
Divya	Female, part of Indo-Fijian community. Mother of Asha	Indo-Fijian	80 minutes	55	1 Hindi speaking interviewer (female)

[1]Note that names have been replaced with synonyms to retain the anonymity of informants.

regulation theory (Carver and Scheier 1981) Joeli has chosen to accept his status but attempts to protect his dependents from the consequences of his actions.

Blindness

The theme name was chosen as it highlights the lack of understanding, especially amongst the younger informants, about the risks of obesity and the reality of being stigmatized until they were confronted with a situation in which prejudice was expressed.

"I really didn't understand it aye…you know, they are all the same…well…they are all us…but it was like they didn't want to have anything to do with me and wanted to look at me as the fat guy that people like to laugh at you know…I was like only 12 then and I didn't think about it until then…it's like I just [expletive deleted] woke up for the first time…I had to look at myself for a while…you know…think about it and wonder what happened to me…" Rangi, 16 year old Maori male.

Lei continues with his narrative of his parent's history with obesity

"My dad tells me that he gets looked at you know…by the family and the other people at work…I didn't even think of it that way…he's just my dad…it's like some people look at him…at his weight…and then others look at *him* (emphasis present) at himself…not what he looks like, but who he is…I only thought of it afterwards when some people look at me differently…like at the dairy [local shop] there's always bad food there and people watch me as I buy it…it's not like I noticed before…but now I do…" Lei 18 year old Asian male

Not only is there a sense of distress, as with those informants who expressed hopelessness, but also a 'loss of innocence' regarding their perceived self. There is a turning point where suddenly the stigma becomes apparent to the obese informant, and it is from this awareness that his or her perceptions and actions change. Lei's father seems to have been subject to ongoing situations that significantly impact his life, which in his mind, continue to reinforce the stigma attachment. These situations or *negative interventions* are now being seen by Lei himself, which also heightens his awareness about his size and the stigma associated with it.

FIGURE 1
PROCESS OF STIGMA REINFORCEMENT

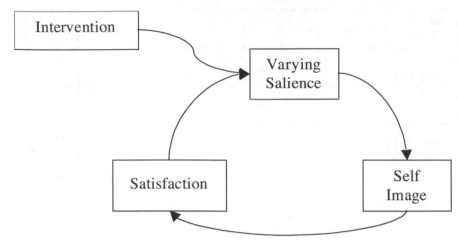

Variable Salience

The final theme discussed here is that of variable salience regarding the obesity stigma. It was seen from the data that at various times the felt importance of informant's obese stigma was more or less pronounced. That is, situations arose where informants would think more about their physical size in a negative sense. As with Rangi's account these interventions could lead to a time of personal reflection and introspection. That is, after an intervention is a time of reflection about the prior occurrence and a time of self examination. Sitiveni recounts occasions such as this in his time at school.

"yeah...there were times when I knew I was bigger...I mean...we'd play rugby against people...small people and everyone would laugh at me as I would be bigger than two people and they said we just need four Sitiveni's and we'd win...I mean...It was good that I am thought of as strong...but not then...but at other times...like with my family...I don't think of my size...I like fit in with the group and I'm just normal...but then I remember where I have just been and I think again about myself...it's different for us you know..." Sitiveni, 26 year old Fijian male.

Reed (2004) discusses how varying levels of heightened awareness about a personal characteristic may lead to altered perceptions and behavior; however, with the nature of a prejudicial stigma being a negatively valanced characteristic the effects are far more pronounced.

"I hate it when I feel ugly...when it's my bigness that makes me ugly...it's when the younger girls I know are laughing...but with my husband I know I am not ugly...it's a way of think[ing] I know...it's my way of thinking more and more about what my belly is doing...and more and more about my looks...it's not right..." Adi, 45 year old Fijian female.

This quote by Adi reinforces the sentiment that there are occasions or interventions when the negative connotations associated with her obese size can lead to feelings of negative self worth and subsequent levels of dissatisfaction about her size. However, the relatively short lifespan of such feelings is also evident. That is, as quickly as negative feelings may appear in her life they also disappear when she is with her husband. The cumulative effect on her overall body satisfaction may be of no consequence; however, with ongoing interventions that continue to make her feel negatively about her self it is anticipated that a more enduring feeling of being stigmatized and 'ugly' could occur.

DISCUSSION

The findings indicate a definite change from a state of blindness about the obesity stigma and its effects on obese individuals to a state of hopelessness about ever changing state. Understandably there are a multitude of intermediary stages, for example acceptance, apathy, motivation or narcissism. However, it is at the extreme poles of the scale that the most explicit findings can be discussed. The relationship between salience and self image is key to understanding exactly how the iterative process operates. As shown in Figure 1, it is theorized that an intervention at some point has led to an increased sense of salience about the obesity stigma. This starts a period of personal self reflection and personal dissatisfaction, as Rangi discussed, which then comes back to a sense of varied salience. Depending on the valance and the frequency of the interventions the process continues to reinforce the stigma attachment in the mind of the victim to the point, over many years possibly, whereby the individual feels a sense of hopelessness about his or her situation.

The process of moving from a state of blindness to that of hopelessness does appear to be an iterative one, developed over time over a number of intervening situations. For example, Lei's account of his father being stared at by colleagues or family members can lead to increased salience about his size, and depending on the messages being internalized the outcome could be a positive or negative self image. Figure 2 shows how the process of stigma reinforcement can continue in a vicious cycle manner from a point of blindness to a state of hopelessness.

Figure 2 represents a deterioration in self efficacy regarding an individual's perceived ability to lose weight (Wilson, Wallston and King 1990). This is in contrast to a notion of external locus of

FIGURE 2
ITERATIVE PROCESS FROM BLINDNESS TO HOPELESSNESS

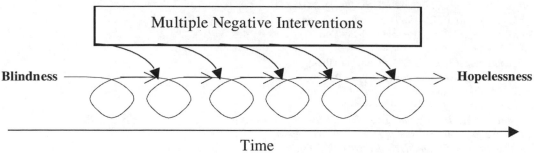

control whereby the blame may be directed elsewhere (Weiner, Perry and Magnusson 1988). Here we see that these informants know that they had control, however, have since lost the ability to enact any significant change in themselves.

Hopelessness is theorized here as being a state of zero self efficacy that is a result of longitudinal deterioration. The methods needed to alter an individual who exhibits signs of no personal self worth or no perceived ability to change would need to be both rigorous and ongoing. Early positive interventions are critical.

CONCLUSION

The role of the intervention as a method for social change has been discussed in length by many leading social marketing academicians (Andreasen 1995, Donovan and Henley 2003, Kotler and Roberto 1989). However, understanding how the everyday interventions, such as family meetings and social interactions may lead to a feeling of negative self worth has not been investigated. From this study there exists a gap in the extant literature regarding the importance of stigma salience as a driving force for understanding how consumers can go from total unawareness about the need to lose weight to a state of hopelessness regarding their ability to lose weight.

The premise therefore exists that one off ad hoc campaigns are unlikely to provide any significant impact on the consumer's sense of personal efficacy. That is, when ongoing negative interventions surround the consumer there needs to be adequate positive interventions to ensure that the consumer does not continue to spiral into a deeper feeling of hopelessness. This is not to say that obese consumers are praised for their size, rather that they are encouraged and motivated by their in-group to maximize their feelings of personal self efficacy. Ideally any intervention would be targeted early on when the consumer has been fraught with only a few negative interventions and he or she still feels the ability to make significant changes to his or her weight. The evidence presented here directs greater attention towards the need for more social marketing interventions to be targeted at younger populations before hopelessness takes hold and self efficacy deteriorates. Further research is needed to identify specific motivating antecedents that may increase self efficacy, motivation to lose weight and locus of control so that more effective social marketing campaigns can be developed and implemented.

REFERENCES

Allport, Gordon Willard (1954), *The Nature of Prejudice*, Cambridge, M.A.: Addison-Wesley.

Andreasen, Alan R. (1995), *Marketing Social Change: Changing Behavior to Promote Health, Social Development, and the Environment*, San Francisco: Jossey-Bass Publishers.

Aronne, Louis J. and Segal, Karen R. (2002), "Adiposity and fat distribution outcome measures: Assessment and clinical implications," *Obesity Research*, 10 (November (Suppl)), 14S-21S.

Australian Department of Health and Ageing (2004), "About Overweight & Obese." http://www.health.gov.au.

Brown, Lucy Scott, Waller, Glen, Meyer, Caroline, Bamford, Bryony, Morrison, Tamara and Burditt, Emily (2003), "Socially Driven Eating and Restriction in the Eating Disorders," *Eating Behaviors*, 4 (3), 221-228.

Burden, Ramil (1998). *"Vulnerable Consumer Groups: Quantification and Analysis,"* Office of Fair Trading, Hayes, UK.

Carver, Charles S. and Scheier, Michael (1981), *Attention and Self-Regulation: A Control-Theory Approach to Human Behavior*, New York: Springer-Verlag.

Crandall, Christian S. (1994), "Prejudice Against Fat People: Ideology and Self-Interest," *Journal of Personality and Social Psychology*, 66 (5), 882-894.

Crandall, Christian S. and Eshleman, Amy (2003), "A Justification-Suppression Model of the Expression and Experience of Prejudice," *Psychological Bulletin*, 129 (3), 414-446.

Crocker, Jennifer and Luhtanen, Riia (1990), "Collective Self-Esteem and Ingroup Bias," *Journal of Personality and Social Psychology*, 58 (1), 60-67.

Donovan, Robert J. and Henley, Nadine (2003), *Social Marketing: Principles & Practice*, East Hawthorn: IP Communications.

Ferraro, Kenneth F. and Holland, Kimerlee B. (2002), "Physician Evaluation of Obesity in Health Surveys: "Who are you Calling Fat?"" *Social Science and Medicine*, 55 1401-1413.

Goffman, Erving (1963), *Stigma: Notes on the Management of Spoiled Identity*, Englewood Cliffs, NJ: Prentice Hall.

Hebl, Michelle R. and Mannix, Laura M. (2003), "The Weight of Obesity in Evaluating Others: A Mere Proximity Effect," *Personality and Social Psychology Bulletin*, 29 (1), 28-38.

Kotler, Phillip and Roberto, E. L. (1989), *Social Marketing: Strategies for Changing Public Behavior*, New York: The Free Press.

Link, Bruce G. and Phelan, Jo C. (2001), "Conceptualizing Stigma," *Annual Review of Sociology*, 27 363-385.

Mick, David Glen (2003), "Editorial," *Journal of Consumer Research*, 29 (March), 1-9.

Minister of Health (2003). *"Implementing the New Zealand Health Strategy 2003: The Minister of Health's Third Report on Progress on the New Zealand Health Strategy,"* Ministry of Health, Wellington.

New Zealand Ministry of Health (2001). *"DHB Toolkit: Obesity-To Reduce the Rate of Obesity,"*

Onkvisit, Sak and Shaw, John (1987), "Self Concept & Image Congruence: Some Research and Managerial Implications," *Journal of Consumer Marketing*, 4 (Winter), 13-24.

Phelan, Jo C., Link, Bruce G., Moore, Robert E. and Stueve, Ann (1997), "The Stigma of Homelessness: The Impact of the Label "Homeless" on Attitudes Toward Poor Persons," *Social Psychology Quarterly*, 60 (4), 323-337.

Reed, Americus (2004), "Activating the Self-Importance of Consumer Selves: Exploring Identity Salience Effects on Judgements," *Journal of Consumer Research*, 31 (September), 286-295.

Renfrew, John W. (1997), *Aggression and its Causes: A Biopsychosocial Approach*, New York: Oxford University Press.

Spiggle, Susan (1994), "Analysis and Interpretation of Qualitative Data in Consumer Research," *Journal of Consumer Research*, 21 (December), 491-503.

Struch, Naomi and Schwartz, Shalom B. (1989), "Intergroup Aggression: Its Predictors and Distinctness From In-Group Bias," *Journal of Personality and Social Psychology*, 56 (3), 364-373.

Tajfel, Henri (1979), "Individual and Groups in Social Psychology," *British Journal of Social and Clinical Psychology*, 18 183-190.

Thornton, Bill and Moore, Scott (1993), "Physical Attractiveness Contrast Effect: Implications for Self-Esteem and Evaluations of the Social Self," *Personality and Social Psychology Bulletin*, 19 (4), 474-480.

Tiggeman, Marika and Anesbury, Tracy (2000), "Negative Stereotyping of Obesity in Children: The Role of Controllability Beliefs," *Journal of Applied Social Psychology*, 30 (9), 1977-1993.

Turner, John C. (1991), *Social Influence*, Milton Keynes: Open University Press.

Walsham, Geoff (1995), "Interpretive Case Studies in Information Systems Research: Nature and Method," *European Journal of Information Systems*, 4 (2), 74-81.

Weiner, Bernard, Perry, Raymond P. and Magnusson, Jamie (1988), "An Attributional Analysis of Reactions to Stigmas," *Journal of Personality and Social Psychology*, 55 (5), 738-748.

Wilson, Dawn K., Wallston, Kenneth A. and King, Joan E. (1990), "Effects of Contract Framing, Motivation to Quit and Self-Efficacy on Smoking Reduction," *Journal of Applied Social Psychology*, 20 (7), 531-547.

Commodify Thyself: Neither MySpace® nor Your Space but a Space for Mass-Objectification of Subjects

Soonkwan Hong, The University of Texas-Pan American, USA

ABSTRACT

The blogosphere that promotes objectified and commodified identities is contested by individual bloggers and the blogger body as a whole. In the blogosphere, the discourse of power haunts not only between a blogger and the blogger body, but also between the blogger and the blogosphere as a market system providing identity project services. Netnographical data reveal a triadic power relationship in the online market system that facilitates the traffic of identity resources. Notwithstanding the ever more complex power structure, the market still serves its function as expected. The unparalleled magnetism of the viral marketing tranquilizes the observed tension among the three parties and lubricates the market system.

INTRODUCTION

Online self-portrayal has drawn much attention from consumer research because its theoretical importance as to identity projects of consumers today and the ubiquitous interests in personal websites represented mostly by blogs (e.g., Arnould and Thompson 2005; Schau and Gilly 2003). A number of websites in U.S., such as *MySpace, Facebook*, and *Blogger* successfully attract more subscribers. Blogging in China has also been widespread and reported as disseminators of consumer culture, including but not limited to fashion, food, and travel (Zhao and Belk 2007). A particular Korean blog (*Cyworld®*) has accomplished a tremendous success as more than 20 million people, out of 48 million total population, have subscribed to the blog (e.g., Jung, Youn, and McClung 2007). European countries are no exception. This exponential growth of the blogosphere can be attributed to the identity-laden nature of contemporary consumer culture (e.g., Giddens 1991) and the commodification-facilitating nature of online consumption activities. A blogger may act as an iconic celebrity as s/he "sells" the identity through his/her blog, or spontaneously become popular when many others wish to appropriate his/her identity and the relevant images.

The blogosphere, as such, invites a substantial portion of consumers and provides commodified and commodifying self-expressive contrivances. It should be, nevertheless, noted that the identity projects of consumers executed on the blogosphere are distinct from those conducted in off-line contexts in that consumers choose to become objects as they disclose their identities online. The subject/object dichotomy (see Firat and Venkatesh 1995) is overtly defied as consumers objectify themselves in their blogs and make their identities transparent. Despite this theoretical significance of blog as a new agent for identity projects, studies on online consumer self-presentation are centered only on the consumptions of signs, symbols, cultures, experiences, and materials (e.g., Peñaloza 2000, 2001). Those consumption activities and experiences as elements of one's identity become widely available, as they are posted online, and exchangeable for the same kinds of consumptions with different cultural substances created and distributed by other online consumers. The blogosphere has become another type of market in which embodied, audio-visualized, and embellished cultural materials-different types of consumptive actions-are put up for sale. Commodification of the cultural materials is evident because consumers seek more and varied materials in the market at the expense of their own materials available for other consumers (c.f., Benjamin 1973).

The commodification of the objects that belong to a subject will, however, erode the subjectivity. Celebrities are neither subjects nor objects. They become objects on the day they make their debut on TV. Correspondingly, the demarcation between subjects and objects blurs in online settings. Subjectivity can be maintained intact only until the blogger posts his/her identity-relevant cultural products and/or artifacts. The blogosphere is not only a completely commodified, commercialized, and marketized agent for identity projects, but also a commodifying and objectifying agent.

Given the theoretically intricate yet particularly significant online consumer culture, a few questions need to be addressed. What theoretical lenses can be utilized to explicate the selective commodification of identity? Do all bloggers want to commodify their identity? If not, why and how do they protect their identities from an over or unnecessary commodification? Hence, this study first seeks to provide theories that address voluntary commodification of identity and potential withdrawal of the commodified identity. Second, the present study identifies the preventive measures that bloggers employ to shield their identities from excessive or reprehensible commodifications. Third, the study also provides a discussion on the opposition of bloggers to the mass-culture on the blogosphere necessitating the commodification of subjectivity.

The second and third objectives are especially important because they evince that the discourse of power must be embedded in online consumption activities. Insightfully, the discourse of power (see Foucault 1977, 1980) in an online context envisages a novel structure of power. Dissimilar to the dyadic discourse of power as to identity projects in the conventional market system (e.g., Thompson 2004; Thompson and Tian 2008), the power may possibly circulate in a triadic relationship among the market, a blogger, and other bloggers. The nature of the relationship is seen neither as a conflict between blogging consumers and the market, nor a friction between "me" and "others." The relationship rather appears to compel each blogger to manage his or her appropriate power level in order to culturally benefit from each other, and the market may also be required to control the level of its influence and intervene between two or more bloggers.

The complex mechanism of identity protection in the blogosphere is a peculiar phenomenon of interest for two reasons. First, it seems a self-contradiction of bloggers because they are in opposition to the objectification of subjectivity even though they have chosen to objectify themselves online as they subscribe to the websites. Second, bloggers have to wrestle with two different entities: the market (blogosphere as a mainstream cultural arena that obliges identity disclosure) and other bloggers (they require a constant and unlimited identity disclosure). In order to unearth the tangled power relationship in the blogosphere, a particular blogging website called *Cyworld* in Korea is selected as the site for the theorization. A literature review as to "commodified identity" will be followed by a netnography-aided grounded theory (Glaser and Strauss 1967; Kozinets 2002) that should stimulate a more profound discussion on the triadic power relationship in the blogosphere.

THEORETICAL BACKGROUND OF COMMODIFIED IDENTITY

Reciprocity of Identity Disclosure in the Blogosphere

"Give and take" must be emphasized and necessitated in the blogosphere. The reciprocity seems the most prominent catalyst of commodified identity. The function of reciprocity of intimate disclosure of self is described as "[d]isclosure seems to beget disclosure, such that people who receive intimate disclosure feel obligated to respond with a personal disclosure of equal intimacy" (Moon 2000, p. 324). Whether or not identity is seen as a purely private or public concept, the description applies to the blogosphere quite fitly. If a blogger deems identity more public than private, disclosure does not require but assumes reciprocity. On the contrary, reciprocity will be imposed strictly on the blogging activity as an identity project when identity is conceived totally private. The quintessence of identity is, however, neither private nor public; rather, it is always balanced (e.g., Brewer 2003; Grubb and Grathwohl 1967). Therefore, reciprocity of identity-disclosure confuses bloggers with respect to the selection between "exhibition and concealment" of identity.

Bloggers have to determine the appropriate level of identity-disclosure as they understand both requirements for identity. Nevertheless, there are two forces that bloggers should confront when they determine the level. First, the disclosure of identity will only be greatened and deepened. Simply, everything and anything about a blogger's identity is asked to be revealed as the disclosure interacts with other identities disclosed (Derlega, Metts, Petronio, and Marguilis 1993). Second, the online context does promote face-to-face human-interaction-like social activities (e.g., Moon and Nass 1996). Bloggers might be unconsciously involved too much with identity-disclosure albeit the potential pitfall of identity-replication by other bloggers. The unconscious or unrealized involvement with "online identity showcase" is either due to the numbing nature of online environment (e.g., Hoffman and Novak 1996) or because of the bloggers' daydream of a perfect reciprocity in the blogosphere.

Disclosure generally means a chance to be commodified and objectified just as we have seen in many cases of artistic products. The two aforementioned reasons for disclosure-required by others and stimulated by the market (blogging websites)-also concretize the newly proposed notion of the triadic relationship of power in the blogosphere. A management of only one relationship with either entity will not ameliorate the convolution of the extended discourse of power.

Appropriated Identity

Commodification of identity in the blogosphere operates as a process that enables bloggers to assimilate to other bloggers' identity projects as constituents of the mass-culture of blogging. Bloggers, however, "deassimilate" themselves from the others so as to maintain unique identities in the blogosphere as an ultimate reservoir of identity. Baudriallard (1998) marks a noteworthy characteristic of commodification that idealizes a double-barreled praxis of commodified identity projects in blogs. Simultaneous homogenization and the differentiation of bloggers' identity-presentation, which is possibly analogous to each other's, beget a self-contradictory tension among bloggers. Echoing this notion of dual-meaning commodification, Rindfleish (2005) postulates, "once a self-identity is formed it is immediately appropriated, eventually consumed, and a different form of self-identity must be reconstructed" (358). Identity reconstruction has long been inculcated since postmodern thinkers and researchers defied identity

as a consistent and uncontested concept (e.g., Featherstone 1995; Gergen 1991; Schouten 1991). Technology-enhanced identity projects accelerate the dissemination of popular identities, and thus the necessity to revise bloggers' identities is intensified and detected earlier than before. Consequently, bloggers-intimidated by the speed and scale of identity simulation and emulation in the blogosphere-are required to protect their own identities and further culturally rebel against the "identity-theft" promoted by the market.

METHODOLOGY

A pool of narratives, excerpts, and notes is developed through a netnographical field study (see Kozinets 1998, 2002). The data collection method employed is to justify the interpretation procedure in a naturalistic setting. The textual discourses automatically transcribed online are culturally enriched "thick descriptions" (Clifford 1990). The descriptions are also expected to be identity-laden as the bloggers narrate their deep-hearted emotions, ideologies, and internal struggles. The data collection ceases when there seem no more insightful categories of interest and importance found. The methodology can be judged as a grounded-theory (see Glaser and Strauss 1967) because an induction will derive a theory explaining the individual bloggers' power management strategies.

A keyword searching method is used due to the immense (over 20 million bloggers) resources of data in *Cyworld*, a blogging website in Korea. The choice of the research site is rationalized through three reasons. First, liberatory expressions of self in online settings are more prevalent in Korea across different age groups because the country has not fully adapted to modernism. A place where modernity did not prevail or at least sufficiently permeate tends to be more open to postmodern ideas (e.g., Firat and Dholakia 1998). Second, ironically, the fast acceptance of postmodern lifestyles and cultures in those places also appears to be contested more easily and earlier than elsewhere because of the "root-absent" nature of the culture. Lastly, the collectivistic cultural orientation of Korea may evidently entail the power relationship with other bloggers, which may not be manifest elsewhere yet.

The narratives and excerpts, translated from Korean to English, as well as the researcher's observational fieldnotes compose the data set to be interpreted (Note that the names for direct quotes that appear in later sections are all initials). Disjunct and less meaningful textual data are sorted and bundled together for a codified schema of identity protection from external power sources (e.g., Arnould and Wallendorf 1994). Following Thompson (1997) and Spiggle (1994), a creative, playful, subjective, and yet substantially translative hermeneutics is expected to yield a meaningfully concentrated and culturally fertile model of the triadic power relationship in the blogosphere.

FINDINGS: A TRIADIC POWER RELATIONSHIP

Postings on the personal online diary (or repository) type of blogs in *Cyworld*, field observations, and the researcher's personal (also familial) direct interactions with other blogger friends reveal the immanent and yet conspicuous management of the tensions with the market and other participants in the market (blogosphere). The ideological commotions of bloggers as consumers of identity project service in the blogosphere emanate the fever from the cycle of acceptance, commensalism, and repudiation. The relations of bloggers with two different power sources, wielding isomorphic influences over individual blogging service consumers, entail unique management strategies respective to each influence. Moreover, there accrues a schema of the triangulate power relationship in the blogosphere (see Figure 1), in which each entity operates to contribute to the sustainability and transformation of the marketplace.

FIGURE 1
Triadic Power Relationship in the Blogosphere

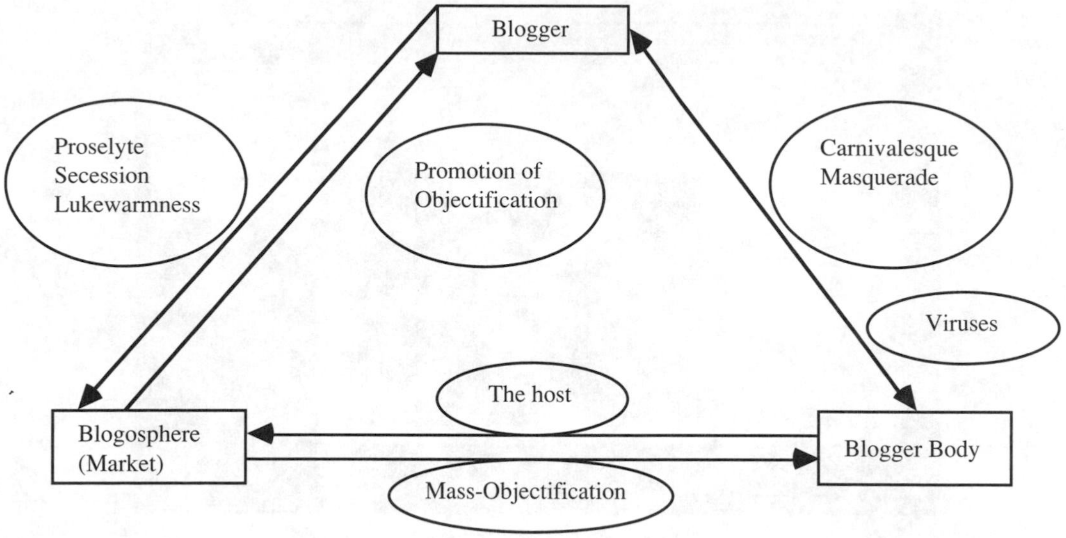

Carnivalesque in the Blogosphere

Bloggers obtain various entertainments from the blogosphere that frees bloggers to enunciate conventionally unexposed aspects of their identities. The blogosphere seems an extremely enjoyable milieu (c.f., Kozinets et al. 2004) because of the widely accessible repertories for identity projects, and owing to the learning experience as to different craftsmanship of identity projects by the blogger body. A blogger KY notes:

I know I have to present my own color in my blog, but it is very hard to find one that fits me. Too much fun, too much to learn… For the time being, I'd rather get so much fun around without thinking anything serious. Having a fun identity in my blog is just great because I have been thinking that it should always be something serious. I think blogging will make me able to have some kind of orgy and an identity at the same time.

Enjoyment, craze, fetishisization, and bizarreness in the blogosphere attract more users to the identity project service, and the degree to which the users reflexively indulge in the fiesta intensifies. This escalation of reflexivity, however, only produces bloggers' anxiety for over-exposure and misuse of their identities, and the anxiety appears to exceed the perceived benefit and fun from blogging (c.f., Hong 2008). In association with the contradictory apprehension of bloggers, HS concedes:

I hate somebody taking my postings and using them as if they are his own creations. I think it should be banned somehow, but I can blame only myself because I love to put my stuff up online. Once we started doing so, we can never stop but just confuse other bloggers with too much going on in our blogs. Then, they get bombarded or intimidated by the extreme presentations of our identities. You know what? I had a visitor to my blog that left a message, saying "you're really something disgusting, pervert, and never acceptable." That's exactly what I wanted, so I got happy because they wouldn't want to fake my stuff but just let them go. No worries anymore. ☺

Difficult to replicate but extremely ludic expressions of one's identity are repeatedly witnessed guards from the overuse and exploitation of identity expression. Bloggers strive to be superordinate to others with regard to their identities' cultural meaningfulness and profoundness while accentuating playfulness. The carnivalesque in the blogosphere increases the difficulty level to appropriate the identities available in blogs but constantly require better quality creativeness from the defensive bloggers. The "overly enriched" cultural manifestations, however, still serve as an apparatus for a blogger to retain a superior power over the other identity (re)creators.

Masquerade in the Blogosphere

Another way to handle the ever complex task of identity show-off and the subsequent shrink of the presenter to maintain a preferable power level in the blogosphere is to bewilder other presenters with a multitude of camouflages. It seems impossible to pinpoint the salient identity of a blogger because s/he introduces as many personas as possible; therefore, the mission of protection of the blogger's focal identity among multiple identities is more likely to be accomplished (see Laverie, Kleine, and Kleine 2002 for identity salience). HM posts:

I know who I am, but nobody seems to. Maybe, I have too many characters to show, but it doesn't matter as long as I do not lose, nor am confused, with myself. I hope everybody feels the same…

Bloggers do not appear to want to explore a new and/or inimitable type of identity and declare a preoccupancy of the newly created identity; rather, they provide unnecessarily central identity artifacts. Perhaps, bloggers conceive that this is the only plausible way to commodify and exchange identity and the relevant resources with others. Accordingly, the maintenance of power level is continuously achieved, provided a blogger's central identity is not "degraded" for others' identities. The harder to figure one's real façade, the less worry about unwanted objectification of identity.

FIGURE 2
A Bizarre Presentation of Identity in Cyworld ®

The blogger narrated that she failed to communicate with the heater shown in the picture. Interestingly, the subtitle of the photo section is "managing boredom."

The wishfully authentic identity, which the blogger distances from the objectification and the following commodification is still misinterpreted and misapplied in the worst case because of the other "cluttering" identities. In her monologue, SM confesses her identity presentations have unconsciously and unintentionally become a multiple-personality type of self-disclosure:

> Today, my friends told me I must be crazy or something and said I had to stop this thing. They said I was not supposed to claim myself to be a Christian if I'm regularly drinking and trashed in clubs so often. But I don't care whatever they say because, as everyone knows, people have so many different phases of life that may or may not represent them. If others think all the things are my identities, that's their choice. I just want to keep updating things about me whether or not they make me look really crazy. I want to let you judge…

The masked or possibly distorted identities offered in the blogosphere are different from the carnivalesque of identities in that the former intoxicate and obfuscate other bloggers with irresistible but unrealistic amusement, and that the latter reduces the odds of losing the pivotal identity, not to be copied, by showing ostensibly unrelated and disjointed identities. An individual blogger and the blogger body as a whole enforce and defend the identity-commodification as they concurrently exchange their identity supplies and try to "demarketize" their identities. As a result, the power flow between the two entities is always egocentric, which thus can never be contributing to the market system unless the market commercially intermediates (e.g., viral marketing) between the two.

Proselyte

Bloggers' management of power in relation to the market (blogosphere) is surprisingly simple and prompt. They simply explore and connect their identities to a new form of marketplace, such as the UCC (user created contents) in *YouTube®* that enables more in-depth and culture-rich expression of identity. DR feels a compulsion when he posts in his blog:

> I started it (blogging) as a hobby, but now it's become a burden in my life. So sometimes I stretch myself all the way, but it doesn't work at all. To convey myself only through writings and some pictures certainly has a limitation. I feel I am going to collapse pretty soon, which oppresses me harder.

The converts explain that they need a better "distribution system" of identities. The market (blogosphere) only promotes and implicitly obliges bloggers to supply the merchandises (identity and the relevant creativeness) without intermediaries for a better system. Consequently, they seek a more effective system that prevents the identities from being "sublimated" due to systematic incompleteness. These bloggers do not resist the idea of commodified identity but seem to contest the market system, which promotes the traffic of abstracted commodification of identities. The market may never suggest the sublimation of one's identity presentation. Intriguingly, the proselytes, however, do not always move to a more liberal place. SE utters:

> There is much emotion, culture, information, and other things to learn and help me better express myself in traditional media, like papers, news, and books. Newspapers are 50 cents a day and ten dollars per month. My blog doesn't deliver anything but some funny things about me so it is supposed to be about one cent. It should just be a hobby because it doesn't help me nor others either.

Bloggers may choose traditional media through which they find the necessary "raw materials" for identity (re)construction and discontinue blogging because of the less meaningful contents found in the blogosphere. The bloggers admit the fact that they may not meet the quality standard of the identity presentation in the market because of the "tacky" nature of the postings and that they also find fun but possibly low-class identities drifting in the blogosphere. This resistance to the commodification of identity denotes a self-critical withdrawal of self from the market. In sum, bloggers retire from the market if they detect the system to be inefficient for their fully descriptive expression of identity, and when they become self-reflective due to the inability to aid others in collecting quality resources for identity. In either case, bloggers abandon the commodifying proposal by the market as a counterproposal for the market system.

Secession

The other type of bloggers who vie with the market hegemony, requiring commodification of identity, abscond or leave the market temporarily or permanently. The temporary escape of bloggers from the market corroborates Kozinets's (2002) account that indoctrinates the unfeasibility of complete aloofness from the market. They "submerge and surface (a direct translation of a Korean slang)" as they perceive the commodification of identity differently in terms of the level of exploitation, distortedness, sublimation, and showiness of the commodified identities in the blogosphere. The bloggers who leave the market temporarily are lukewarm identity creators and suppliers; they return to the system as they find it necessary. They may once again need some ingredients for their identity renovation, or want to be a popular identity supplier. TK writes:

I'm going to submerge for the time being or maybe forever. Please don't ask me why because I know you feel like doing the same thing sometimes for some reasons. Doing this thing is just sick and tired and exhausts me. People talk whatever way they want…talk too much about my stuff, and the problem is that I keep doing this even though I hate them. Actually, I don't hate the people, but I hate this thing existing for us. For us??? Well, for somebody else, not me…

Whether the submergence is an escape or just an impermanent lukewarmness depends on whether the blogger opts to come back to the commodifying space or vanishes from the market for identity projects service. Bloggers, however, tend to make a second or further launch of their identity showcases after an optimal length of cessation of work. A back-to-work blogger JW advertises in his blog:

Folks, I'm back here. I hope you haven't missed me too much. I will post so enthusiastically from now on. I think I have found more things to amuse you guys. Well, I think I was wrong to think this is a totally crappy thing to do. I am happy to realize that I need this thing because it makes me alive. Unexposed existences are all dead.

Bloggers who actually disappear from the blogosphere are also observed. Nevertheless, it is also detected that many of them still opportunistically peep into the market as they visit blogs. They are still consumers of commodified identities but not producers of them. Their effort to manage the relationship in the blogosphere is partially successful, which, in turn, signifies that consumers may imperfectly escape the market by discarding one of the roles (consuming and producing) in the market. The discourse of power in the marketplace becomes nihilistic if both roles are disposed.

Viruses

Although the discussion of viral marketing may not be thorough in this study, the significance of the phenomenal marketing activity is exceptional because of its potential to be a new promotional device for voluntary commodification of identity. The market sustains its efficiency and dominion over consumers in the blogosphere through the incorporation of more explicit marketization of identity symbols. Branding itself and the following instillation of brand images and meanings can be more effective and widespread as intended (c.f., Leskovec, Adamic, and Huberman 2007). The blogger body serves as a host of the viruses, even though they oppose the mass-objectification of subjectivity, insomuch as the market provides novel, acceptable, and utilizable identity materials: brands and the brand spirit. Figure 3 illustrates the use of a brand by the market in order to coordinate the power flow in the blogosphere. Moreover, the paradoxical tension between a blogger and the blogger body is diminished as they agree to transmit and share mutually beneficial brand images and cultures as identity resources. Consequently, the market always functions as an unavoidable power source that nullifies the superfluous struggle for power and encourages sustainable symbiosis (e.g., Schouten and McAlexander 1995) in the online identity project service market.

DISCUSSION

The marketplace conflict stabilized and digested through the transmittance of viral branding strategies reorganizes the market system (e.g., Giesler 2008). Therefore, the commensal relationship between the market and consumers is again substantiated. The historically and theoretically irrefutable concept of co-optation in a close relation to the discourse of power is also to appear in the online marketplace (see Thompson and Coskuner-Balli 2007 for co-optation). That is, the theoretical twist found in this study is that the triadic power relationship possibly renders a new type of co-optation. In the power structure, the market appears to co-opt the ability of consumers to efficiently and immediately distribute the brands and the relevant ideas, instead of appropriating the consumers' cultural competency that may well be marketized. This co-optation may generate less negative repercussions in the marketplace than the co-optation in the traditional viewpoint does because the consumers in search of identity resources can collaborate in obtaining and delivering brands as identity resources.

The viral brands can, nonetheless, regress to the historical model of branding that Holt (2002) presents. The pursuit of sovereignty of consumers again contradicts the viruses (brands) that may be transmitted too fast and too widely. After a certain point, the brands do not serve as the identity project service due to the possibility that consumers' identities can no longer be individuated but manufactured. The marketplace turmoil may be just around the corner once again.

In response to this dialectical discussion on the evolutionary market, consumer culture research should embark upon two agendas. First, the discourse of power in the triadic power structure found in the study must be followed by a closer investigation of the "modest" power management of the market. The nature of the power management realized by the concept of viral marketing should differentiate it from the historical market hegemony, which may be more explicit, coercive, and homogenizing. It is certainly of interest and significance because the bloggers voluntarily participate in the "totalizing logic" (c.f., Firat and Venkatesh 1995). Second, the concept of co-optation also needs to be theoretically dissected due to the newly explored type of co-optation in the study. Consumers' cultural creativeness and the capability of disseminating brand cultures may not be the all to be co-opted.

FIGURE 3
Viral Brand in the Blogosphere

EXR is an apparel brand in Korea that cooperates with Cyworld to promote their brand and infuse their brand culture into the blogger body. A large number of bloggers visit the blog to obtain resources for their identity.

REFERENCES

Arnould, Eric J. and Melanie Wallendorf (1994), "Market-Oriented Ethnography: Interpretatioin Building and Marketing Strategy Formulation," *Journal of Marketing Research*, 31 (November), 484-504.

_____ and Craig J. Thompson (2005), "Consumer Culture Theory (CCT): Twenty Years of Research," *Journal of Consumer Research*, 31 (March), 868-882.

Baudriallar, Jean (1998), *The Consumer Society*, London: Sage.

Benjamin, Walter (1973 [1936]), "The Work of Art in the Age of Mechanical Repoduction," in *Illuminations*, trans. Harry Zohn, London: Fontana, 211-244.

Brewer, Marilynn B. (2003), "Optimal Distinctiveness, Social Identity, and the Self," in *Handbook of Self and Identity*, ed. Mark R. Leary and June Price Tangney, New York: The Guilford Press.

Clifford, James (1990), "Notes on (Field)notes," in *Fieldnotes*, Roger Sanjek, ed. Ithaca, NY: Cornell University Press, 47-70.

Derlega, Valerian J. Sandra Metts, Sandra Petronio, and Stephen T. Marguilis (1993), *Self-Disclosure*, Newbury Park, CA: Sage.

Featherstone, Mike (1995), *Undoing Culture: Globalization, Postmodernism, and Identity*, Thousand Oaks, CA: Sage Publications.

Firat, A. Fuat and Alladi Venkatesh (1995), "Liberatory Postmodernism and the Reenchantment of Consumption," *Journal of Consumer Research*, 22 (December), 239-267.

_____ and Nikhilesh Dholakia (1998), *Consuming People: From Political Economy to Theaters of Consumption*, London and New York: Routledge.

Foucault, Michel (1977), *Discipline and Punish: The Birth of the Prison*, trans. Alan Sheridan, New York: Vintage.

_____ (1980), *Power/Knowledge: Selected Interviews and Other Writings 1972-77*, ed. Colin Gordon, New York: Pantheon.

Gergen, Kenneth J. (1991), *The Saturated Self*, New York, NY: Basic Books.

Giddens, Anthony (1991), *Modernity and Self-Identity*, Stanford, CA: Stanford University Press.

Giesler, Markus (2008), "Conflict and Compromise: Drama in Marketplace Evolution," *Journal of Consumer Research*, 34 (April), 739-753.

Glaser, Barney G. and Anselm L. Strauss (1967), *The Discovery of Grounded Theory*, Chicago: Aldine.

Grubb, Edward L. and Harrison L. Grathwohl (1967), "Consumer Self-Concept, Symbolism, and Market Behavior: A Theoretical Approach," *Journal of Marketing*, 31 (October), 22-27.

Hoffman, Donna L, and Thomas P. Novak (1996), "Marketing in Hypermedia Computer-Mediated Environments: Conceptual Foundations," *Journal of Marketing*, 60 (July), 50-68.

Holt, Douglas B. (2002), "Why Do Brands Cause Trouble? A Dialectical Theory of Consumer Culture and Branding," *Journal of Consumer Research*, 29 (June), 70-90.

Hong, Soonkwan (2008), "The Entropy of Symbolic Consumption: Demand Side Market Failure and the Counterproposals," *Advances in Consumer Research*, 35, forthcoming.

Jung, Taejin, Hyunsook Youn, and Steven McClung (2007), " Motivations and Self-Presentation Strategies on Korean-Based "Cyworld" Weblog Format Personal Homepages," *CyberPsychology and Behavior*, 10 (February), 24-31.

Kozinets, Robert V. (2002), "The Field Behind the Screen: Using Netnography for Marketing Research in Online Communities," *Journal of Marketing Research*, 34 (February), 61-72.

_____ (2002), "Can Consumers Escape the Market? Emancipatory Illuminations from Burning Man," *Journal of Consumer Research*, 29 (June), 20-38.

_____, Johan F. Sherry, Jr., Diana Storm, Adam Duhachek, Krittinee Nuttavuthisit, and Benet Deberry-Spence (2004), "Ludic Agency and Retail Spectacle," *Journal of Consumer Research* 31 (December), 658-672.

Laverie, Debra A., Robert E. Kleine III, and Susan Schultz Kleine (2002), "Re-examination and Extension of Kleine, Kleine. and Kernan's Social Identity Model of Mundane Consumption: The Mediating Role of the Appraisal Process," *Journal of ConsumerResearch,* 28 (4), 659-69.

Leskovec, Jurij, Lada A. Adamic, and Bernado A. Huberman (2007), "The Dynamics of Viral Marketing," *ACM Transactionson the Web*, 1 (1).

Moon, Youngme and Clifford I. Nass (1996), "How Real' Are the Computer Personalities? Psychological Responses to Personality Types in Human-Computer Interaction," *Communication Research*, 23, 651-674.

_____ (2000), "Intimate Exchanges: Using Computers to Elicit Self-Disclosure form Consumers," *Journal of Consumer Research*, 26 (March), 323-339.

Peñaloza, Lisa (2000), "The Commodification of the American West: Marketers' Production of Cultural Meanings at a Trade Show," *Journal of Marketing,* 64 (October). 82-109.

_____ (2001), "Consuming the American West: Animating Cultural Meaning at a Stock Show and Rodeo," *Journal of Consumer Research,* 28 (December), 369-98.

Rindfleish, Jennifer (2005), "Consuming the Self: New Age Spirituality as 'Social Product' in Consumer Society," *Consumption, Markets, and Culture*, 8 (December), 343-360.

Schau, Hope Jensen and Mary C. Gilly (2003), "We Are What We Post? Self-Presentation in Personal Web Space," *Journal of Consumer Research*, 30 (December), 385-404.

Schouten, John W. (1991), "Selves in Transition: Symbolic Consumption in Personal Rites of Passage and Identity Reconstruction," *Journal of Consumer Research*, 17 (March), 412-425.

_____ and James H. McAlexander (1995), "Subcultures of Consumption: An Ethnography of the New Bikers," *Journal of Consumer Research*, 22 (June), 43-61.

Spiggle, Susan (1994), "Analysis and Interpretation of Qualitative Data in Consumer Research," *Journal of Consumer Research*, 21 (December), 491-503.

Thompson, Craig J. (1997), "Interpreting Consumers: A Hermeneutical Framework for Deriving Marketing Insights from the Texts of Consumers' Consumption Stories," *Journal of Marketing Research*, 34 (November), 438-455.

_____ (2004), "Marketplace Mythology and Discourses of Power," *Journal of Consumer Research*, 31 (June), 162-180.

_____ and Gokcen Coskuner-Balli (2007), "Countervailing Market Responses to Corporate Co-optation and the Ideological Recruitment of Consumption Communities," *Journal of Consumer Research*, 34 (August), 135-152.

_____ (2008), "Reconstructing the South: How Commercial Myths Compete for Identity Value through the Ideological Shaping of Popular Memories and Coutermemories," *Journal of Consumer Research*, 34 (February), 595-613.

Zhao, Xin and Russell W. Belk (2007), "Live From Shopping Malls: Blogs and Chinese Consumer Desire," *Advances in Consumer Research*, 34, 131-137.

The Effect of Gender and Product Categories on Consumer Online Information Search

Jooyoung Park, Korea Advanced Institute of Science and Technology, Korea
Yeosun Yoon, Korea Advanced Institute of Science and Technology, Korea
Byungtae Lee, Korea Advanced Institute of Science and Technology, Korea

ABSTRACT

This article analyzes clickstream data collected from a popular online retailer to observe actual consumers' information search behavior in terms of both gender and product categories. The results show that, compared to males, females tend to be comprehensive processors, searching for more product information including customer reviews and using an assistant agent more while shopping online. Also, unlike males, females use both customer reviews and the assistant agent significantly more when shopping for experience goods than when shopping for search goods. These results will help academics and practitioners to have a deeper understanding in consumer behavior in the online context.

INTRODUCTION AND BACKGROUND

With the advance of Internet accessibility and the reduction in service delivery costs, online shopping has continued to grow over the past years. In 2005, the volume of consumption through online retailing in the United States rose by more than 20% compared to 2004 (Mulpuru, Johnson, and Tesch 2006), and reached $100 billion in 2006, indicating that the Internet has emerged as a significant marketplace today (Cassis 2007).

As more and more consumers visit the Internet to shop, researchers have explored various characteristics of the Internet to observe their influences on consumer behavior in the online shopping environment. Many studies have addressed that the most commonly cited reason that consumers purchase online is the widespread availability of information on the Internet (Wolfinbarger and Gilly 2001). In addition to the voluminous information, online retailers also enable consumers to have interactive experience by providing shopping aids, such as customer reviews or assistant agents. The abundant information and the interactive experience seem to enable the Internet to realize the expectation that it would become an important retailing channel.

Even though the growth of the online marketplaces appears to be evident, both academics and marketing managers argue that consumers are still reluctant to shop on the Internet. Researchers said that, contrary to the traditional shopping environment, consumers perceive greater risks toward online shopping due to limited physical contact with products or services (Korgaonkar and Wolin 2006). According to Korgaonkar et al. (2006), consumers are especially less willing to purchase experiential products online, because they are unable to determine the product quality prior to the actual purchase (Nelson 1974). In addition, several researchers suggest that the perceived risks are significantly affected by personal factors such as gender (Kehoe, Pitkow, and Morton 1997). Kehoe et al. (1997) said that since females have higher levels of computer anxiety and are more emotionally vulnerable to lack of interaction with other people, they tend to perceive greater risks toward online shopping than men and become reluctant to shop and purchase online.

Past studies imply that both product characteristics and gender are important factors that influence online shopping and purchasing. However, there has been little research into the influence of gender and product characteristics on consumer behavior in the online shopping context. As a result, despite prior research efforts, less is known about how males and females differ in their information search behavior in the online shopping process. Since understanding consumers' information search behavior is critical to provide consumers with better shopping experience, the primary objective of this research is to examine gender differences in information search behavior in the online channel and to show how gender differences are manifested in shopping for different types of product categories.

LITERATURE REVIEW AND HYPOTHESES

Gender Differences in the Variety of Information Search

A commonly cited theory related to gender differences, the selectivity model (Meyers-Levy 1989; Meyers-Levy and Maheswaran 1991; Meyers-Levy and Sternthal 1991) describes gender differences in the information process. According to this model, males are regarded as 'selective processors', while females are considered 'comprehensive processors' in terms of information processing, That is, males acquire information in a heuristic fashion, therefore missing subtle cues, whereas females tend to engage in an effortful, comprehensive and itemized analysis of all possible information.

Several studies have observed gender differences in the consumer shopping context as well. Campbell (2000) proposed the principal ideological differences between males and females in the context of shopping. He said that males generally view shopping as something that is 'needs-driven', so they tend to form negative attitudes toward it. Additionally, they see it as a work to be accomplished with minimum input of time and effort. On the other hand, females consider it enjoyable and associate it with a leisure frame and form highly positive attitudes. Corresponding to previous research on the information search process, several studies centered on the shopping context found that, unlike females, males simplify the shopping process by attending to a smaller number of information sources, with the intention of obtaining the actual goods with the least "fuss" (Laroche, Saad, Cleveland, and Browne 2000). Following the previous research on gender differences in the information search process, we expect that females would search for more information by visiting a greater number of product pages than males would in the online shopping process. Therefore, the first hypothesis follows:

> *H1*: Compared to males, females are likely to search for more information by visiting more product pages in the online shopping process.

Gender Differences in Social Interaction

According to Carlson (1971), males are more likely to be guided by agentic goals, whereas females may be guided by communal goals. Specifically, studies on gender differences in motivational orientation found that males are motivated by achievement needs and directed towards individualistic tasks (Venkatesh and Morris 2000). Males are also more likely to be independent or assertive (Venkatesh et al. 2000), while females are more sympathetic and prefer harmony (Briton and Hall 1995). Also, Meyers-Levy (1989) further suggested that these gender differences in the goal orientation have a significant effect on information processing.

Especially, females are generally more willing to share personal information and change their behaviors through interactions with others compared to males (Brannon 1999).

Unlike the direct face-to-face relationships between sellers and buyers in the traditional shopping context, the relationship in the online context is between buyers and the mediated environment, resulting in lack of social interaction. Instead of physical contact with products and face-to-face interactions with a salesperson in the brick-and-mortar retailers, online retailers try to offer similar experiences through interactive decision aids such as customer reviews and an assistant agent. Customer reviews are defined as a type of product information created by users based on their own experiences, working as sales assistants to help consumers identify the products that best match their expected usage conditions (Chen and Xie 2004). Acknowledging the interactive characteristics of customer reviews, Chen et al. (2004) stated that customer reviews are a new element of marketing communications.

Abundant research has stated that salespersons play an important role in the market place. Specifically, Meyer (1990) suggested two distinct benefits of consumers' interaction with salespersons. Firstly, the functional benefit is defined as a consumer's desire to get help from a salesperson to fulfill his or her needs. Also, researchers argue that the social aspects of a customer-salesperson relationship are critical as much as the functional benefit (Czepiel 1990) since customer's emotional reactions to a personal interaction with a salesperson may influence the customer's overall satisfaction with the purchase experience (Westbrook 1981) and future purchase intentions (Babin 1995). In the online context, a salesperson is not physically present, even though a help from salespersons is indeed necessary. In order to resolve consumers' frustrating experience caused by the lack of salesperson's assistance, online retailers provide an assistant agent to enhance consumers' shopping experience by responding consumers' inquiries and requests. Importantly, this agent also provides online consumers with a kind of social interaction with salespersons, allowing the consumers to ask for information about their orders, products or services on the website.

Given that distinct goal orientations generate the gender differences in the information processing, we assume that females will be more likely to interact with other consumers through customer reviews and an assistant agent.

H2a: Compared to males, females are likely to read customer reviews on products or services more in the online shopping process.

H2b: Compared to males, females are likely to use an assistant agent more in the online shopping process.

Gender Differences in the Perceived Risks

One stream of research on gender differences has addressed that specifically females perceive greater risks in a wide variety of domains (Garbarino and Strahilevitz 2004). In the online context, researchers have also found that females tend to perceive greater risks toward online purchasing (Garbarino, et al. 2004). As consumers are less willing to purchase when they perceive more risks (Shimp and Bearden 1982), results from previous studies indicate that women are less willing to purchase online and spend less money than men (Allen 2001), while men perceive the characteristics of online shopping more favorably than women (Slyke, Comunale, and Belanger 2002).

With the purpose of exploring the influence of the characteristics of products or services on the consumer information search process, researchers have categorized products in terms of whether the quality of goods or services can be verified prior to purchase.

Most commonly cited, Nelson's (1974) theory suggests two product categories: search goods and experience goods. Search goods refer to products or services for which the most critical attributes can be evaluated before purchase. On the other hand, experience goods are products or services for which the cost to evaluate the most essential attributes is so high that direct experience is often the evaluation method with the lowest costs in terms of time, money, cognitive effort, or other resources (Nelson 1974).

Although the Internet enables consumers to search for enormous information, the Internet interrupts consumers' experiences involving the sense of touch or feel (Burke 1997). According to Korgaonkar, Silverblatt, and Girard (2006), the perceived risks are greater for experience goods than for search goods because of this limited experience like directly touching or feeling products in the online environment.

Since female customers tend to perceive greater risks than males, and the risks are even enhanced when shopping for experience goods than when shopping for search goods, we believe that females would read more customer reviews and use an assistant agent more frequently when shopping for experience goods than when shopping for search goods. We propose the following:

H3a: Compared to males, females are likely to read customer reviews more when shopping for experience goods than when shopping for search goods in the online shopping process.

H3b: Compared to males, females are likely to use an assistant agent more when shopping for experience goods than when shopping for search goods in the online shopping process.

METHOD

Data Collection

When a consumer visits several pages of an online retailer, the separate records of those pages construct a "path", sometimes called "clickstream" in the form of a log file. This clickstream data includes information about each customer's ID, requested pages, visited time, software connected through, and personal information such as the email address and name. Based on the information involved in the clickstream data, we can directly observe what kinds of pages consumers visit while shopping online. For this reason, researchers commonly analyze the clickstream data to examine consumer behavior on the Internet (Bucklin, Bell, and Sismeiro 2000).

Online retailers collect records of visits by all customers on visits in their database. The information provided by this data is quite realistic, companies are often reluctant to provide data due to customer privacy. Fortunately, however, seeing the significance of our research, the online retailer that we contacted provided us with their data, given the condition that consumer privacy is protected. The online retailer providing the data opened the online website in August 2001, and became one of the biggest online retailers in Korea, earning more than $108 million in 2006. Similar to one of most popular online retailers in the US, Amazon.com, the online retailer places various products and services ranging from electronics to groceries.

We asked for all records of pages that customers have viewed during a month from July 1 through July 31 in 2006. In order to make the data usable for our research, we went through several steps of dividing the data into analyzable forms. Since we focus on the information search behavior during each visit to the online retailer, we divided the whole data into individual visits by each consumer, which are called "sessions." Practitioners often define a session when a consumer is inactive for a certain amount of time. The online retailer that provided the data also defined each session by 60 minutes of inactivity. In this basis, we first separated the data into a set of sessions of each visitor, and then kept only one visit for each consumer to make the data more representative. We also deleted data containing less than five pages, because it is meaningless to examine those data including little information. Finally, after preprocessing the data, we matched them with the customer demographic file to identify consumer information.

Measurement

Independent Variables

Gender. To compare the information search behavior in the online shopping context between males and females, we included gender information in the preprocessed data, denoting gender by 0 or 1 (0=female, 1=male).

Product Category. In order to observe the effect of product characteristics in the online retailers, we chose two product categories: clothing and electronic appliances including personal computers. These two product categories are most frequently purchased in the online retailer. Also, Girard, Silverblatt, and Korgaonkar (2002) categorized personal computers as search products and clothing as experience goods. Consistent with this categorization, we selected clothing for experience goods and electronic appliances including personal computers for search goods. We denoted the electronic appliances category by 1 and the clothing category by 2.

Dependent Variables

Pageviews. Studies that analyzed clickstream data commonly measure pageviews, the number of pages viewed, to observe consumer information search behavior. Similarly, we measured the number of product pages that the consumers visited to measure the variety of information search.

Customer Reviews. To identify how males and females rely differently on customer reviews, we counted the number of customer reviews that a consumer read during a session. Therefore, a greater number of customer reviews implies a higher tendency to rely on customer reviews.

Assistant Agent. For the purpose of observing gender differences in the use of an assistant agent, we counted the number of clicks on an assistant agent to request information about the products or services. The result implies that the greater the number of clicks on an assistant agent is, the more consumers request for assistants.

RESULTS

Sample Description

Over a period of a month, 377,797 visits were recorded in the database of the online retailer, but only 890 data items, consisting of 618 females and 272 males who visited clothing and electronic appliances categories, satisfied our criteria and were included in the data analysis. According to the statistics of total visitors to the retailer, 59.4% of the visitors were females and the average age of the visitors was 39. Because females are generally more interested in the clothing category (Zhou, Dai, and Zhang 2007), the final data includes a higher percentage of females than the average of total visitors. Specifically, 151 females and 155 males were examined in the electronic appliances category, whereas 467 females and 117 males were considered for clothing category.

Hypothesis Testing

To investigate gender differences in the variety of searching for information in the online context, we first compared the numbers of product pages visited between males and females. As expected, the number of product pages visited by females differed significantly from that of males (Mmales=5.73, Mfemales=8.36). An ANOVA showed that the mean of the number of products that viewed for females was greater than that of males ($F(1,888)=9.707$, $p<.003$).

Secondly, we observed gender differences in the use of decision aids. Hypothesis 2a suggests gender differences in the utilization of customer reviews in the online shopping process: females will read more customer reviews than males. The result shows that females actually used customer reviews significantly more than males (Mmales=.91, Mfemales=3.83, $F(1, 888)=26.247$, $p<.001$). Additionally, females were also more likely to read customer reviews than males. While 21.7% of males read customer reviews, 46.3% of females did so ($\chi^2=48.100$, $p<.001$). Hypothesis 2b addresses gender differences in the use of an assistant agent in the online shopping process. The results show that females asked for help more often than males do (Mmales=0.67, Mfemales=1.17, $F(1, 888)=7.174$, $p<.009$). Furthermore, females were more likely to use an assistant agent than males (Mmales=19%, Mfemales=29%, $\chi^2=9.244$, $p<.004$). As we have hypothesized, females used customer reviews as well as an assistant agent more frequently than males.

Finally, we observed the interaction effect of gender and product categories on consumer information search behavior. According to the results of an ANOVA analysis, females read more customer reviews when shopping for experience goods than when shopping for search goods (Mexperience=4.42, Msearch=2.01). On the other hand, there was no difference in the use of customer reviews for males across product categories (Mexperience=.91, Msearch=.91). This interaction effect ($F(3, 886)=12.488$, $p<.001$) implies that only females were sensitive to product categories when shopping online (figure 1). By comparing the percentage of online shoppers' use of customer reviews across two product categories, we also found that females were more likely to read customer reviews when shopping for experience goods than when shopping for search goods (Mexperience=49.9%, Msearch=35.1%, $\chi^2=10.044$, $p<.003$). Again, unlike females, males did not show significant difference in the willingness to rely on customer reviews across product categories (Mexperience=24.8%, Msearch=19.4%; $\chi^2=1.158$, $p>.301$). Lastly, we observed gender differences in the use of an assistant agent when shopping for different product categories. An ANOVA reveals that only females showed significant differences in the use of an assistant agent depending on product categories ($F(3, 886)=3.917$, $p<.01$) (figure 2). Females used an assistant agent to a greater degree when shopping for experience goods than when shopping for search goods (Mexperience=1.29, Msearch=0.81). The additional analysis demonstrates that females were more willing to use an assistant agent when shopping for experience goods than when shopping for search goods (Mexperience=32%, Msearch=19%, $\chi^2=8.975$, $p<.004$). Again, males did not show any significant differences in the use of an assistant agent across two product categories (Mexperience=21%, Msearch=17%, $\chi^2=.672$, $p>.439$).

DISCUSSION

The purpose of this research is to understand how gender and product categories influence the consumer information search behavior in the online context. Our results show that, compared to males, females tend to search for various information including both product and customer reviews and to use an assistant agent more frequently in the online shopping process. Consistent with the selectivity model (Meyers-Levy 1989; Meyers-Levy et al. 1991; Meyers-Levy et al. 1991), the results imply that females are more likely to be comprehensive processors than males in the online

FIGURE 1

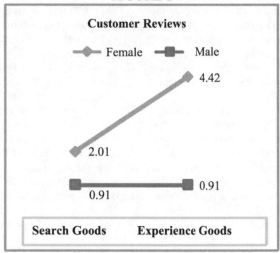

Customer Reviews

◆ Female ■ Male

4.42

2.01

0.91 — 0.91

Search Goods Experience Goods

FIGURE 2

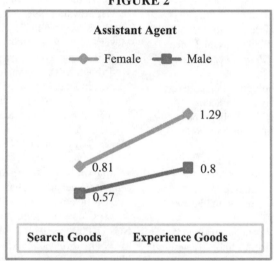

Assistant Agent

◆ Female ■ Male

1.29

0.81

0.57 — 0.8

Search Goods Experience Goods

environment. According to previous studies on perceived risks in the online context, we suggest the interaction effect of gender and product categories on the consumer information search behavior with the online retailers where the physical contact with products or services is limited. Specifically, females consulted customer reviews and used an assistant agent more often when shopping for experience goods than when shopping for search goods. On the other hands, males showed no significant differences in information search across product categories. This implies that the influence of product characteristics on consumers' information search differs between males and females.

The findings of the present study have significant theoretical implications. Foremost, unlike most behavioral studies that examined perception or attitudes of consumers, this article observed actual behaviors by analyzing data derived from a popular online retailer. Therefore, by keeping track of the actual consumer behaviors in the shopping process, the present research would contribute to making more accurate predictions on the consumer behaviors in the online context. The present research also expands theorists' current understanding of online consumers in terms of both personal factors and product characteristics.

Our findings from the real world data could help practitioners apply the results directly to their online retailers. Considering the evidence that females perceive greater risks toward online shopping, managers should try to decrease the perceived risks felt by females by providing various information sources, such as customer reviews. Our research also suggests that degrees of consumers' desire for interactive experiences differ depending on gender and product categories in the online context. We recommend online retailers to furnish various interactive website features, such as real-time interaction with salespersons, to make the online shopping experience more comparable to the traditional shopping experience especially for females who are shopping for experience goods.

LIMITATIONS AND FUTURE RESEARCH

Despite several contributions, this research should have some limitations. First of all, the data included in this research is collected from one single online shopping retailer. Therefore, further data collection from globally dominant online retailers will help to generalize the results.

Second, the present research involves only two types of product categories, clothing and electronic appliances. However, researchers have categorized products or services in various ways. For instance, Copeland (1923) classified goods according to the degree of effort consumers are likely to expend and the degree of preference formation at the beginning of the shopping process: convenience, shopping, and specialty goods. Therefore, future research can examine the influence of product characteristics on consumer information search behaviors based on different classifications of product types.

Previous studies have suggested that computer experience (Slyke et al. 2002), the amount of computer training (Liao and Cheung 2001), and the knowledge of online shopping are positively related to consumers' adoption of online shopping. Since consumers' knowledge and experience of shopping increase as their use of the Internet grows, consumer information search behavior will also change accordingly. Therefore, further research is needed to observe how consumer online shopping behavior, especially information search behavior, evolves over time with more experience.

REFERENCES

Allen, Darren. (2001), "EMarketer: Women on the Web," http://www.ebusinessforum.com/analysis/ecommerce_b2c.20010028_b2c.html.

Babin, Barry J., Boles, James S., and Darden, William R. (1995), "Salesperson Stereotypes, Customer Emotions, and Their Impact on Information Processing, " *Journal of Academy of Marketing Science*, 23(1), 94-105.

Brannon, Linda. (1999). "Gender Psychological Perspectives," 2nd ed. Needham Heights (MA): Allyn and Bacon.

Briton, Nancy J. and Hall, Judith A. (1995), "Beliefs about female and male nonverbal communication," *Sex Roles*, 32, 79–90.

Bucklin, Randolph E., Bell, David R., and Sismeiro, Catarina (2000), "Consumer Shopping Behaviors and In-Store Expenditure Decisions," aagsm.ucla.edu, http://www.anderson.ucla.edu/documents/areas/fac/marketing/bbs.pdf.

Campbell, Colin (2000), "Shopaholics, Spendaholics, and the Question of Gender," In A. Benson(Ed.), I Shop, Therefore I Am: Compulsive Buying and the Search for Self, New York: Aronson, 57-75.

Cassis, Christine (2007), "College Students Help Fuel Ever-Growing Internet Sales, " http://media.www.dailyfreepress.com/media/storage/paper87/news/2007/01/22/News .

Carlson, Rae (1971), "Sex Differences in Ego Functioning: Exploratory Studies of Agency and Communication, " *Journal of Consulting and Clinical Psychology,* 37, 267-277.

Chen, Yubo and Xie, Jinhong (2004), "Online Consumer Reviews: A New Element of Marketing Communications Mix," University of Arizona Working Paper, http://papers.ssrn.com/sol3/papers.cfm?abstract_id=618782.

Copeland, Melvin T. (1923), "The Relation of Customers' Buying Habits to Marketing Methods," *Harvard Business Review*, April, 282-289.

Czepiel, John A. (1990), "Service Encounters and Service Relationsihps Implications for Research, " *Journal of Business Research*, 20(1), 13-21.

Garbarino, Ellen and Strahilevitz, Michal (2004), "Gender Differences in the Perceived Risk of Buying Online and the Effects of Receiving a Site Recommendation," *Journal of Business Reseach*, 57, 768-775.

Girard, Tulay, Silverblatt, Ronnie, and Korgaonkar, Pradeep (2002), "The Influence of Product Class on Preference for Shopping on the Internet, " *Journal of Computer-Mediated Communication*, 8(2), http://jcmc.indiana.edu/vol8/issue1/girard.html.

Korgaonkar, Pradeep, Silverblatt, Ronnie and Girard Tulay (2006), "Online Retailing, Product Classifications, and Consumer Preferences," *Internet Research,* 16(3), 267–288.

Kehoe, Colleen, Pitkow, James, and Morton, Kimberly (1997), "*Eighth WWW user survey* [On-line]," http://www.gvu.gatech.edu/user_surveys/survey-1997-10/.

Korgaonkar, Pradeep and Wolin, Lori D. (1999), "A Multivariate Analysis of Web Usage," *Journal of Advertising Research,* 39(2), 53-88.

Laroche, Michel, Saad, Gad, Cleveland, Mark, and Browne, Elizabeth (2000), "Gender Differences in Information Search Strategies for a Christmas Gift," *Journal of Consumer Marketing*, 17(6), 500-522.

Liao, Ziqi and Cheung Michael Tow (2001), "Internet-based e-shopping and consumer attitudes: an empirical study," *Information and Management* 38(5), 299–306.

Meyer, Edward (1990), "Retail on the Rebound," *Directing Marketing*, 53(1), 7.

Meyers-Levy, Joan (1989), "Gender Differences in Information Processing: a Selectivity Interpretation," in Cafferata and Tybout (Eds), Cognitive and Affective Responses to Advertising, Lexington Press, Lexington, MA.

Meyers-Levy Joan and Maheswaran, Durairaj (1991), "Exploring Differences in Males' and Females' Processing Strategies," *Journal of Consumer Research*, 18, 63-70.

Meyers-Levy Joan and Sternthal, Brian (1991), "Gender Differences in the Use of Message Cues and Judgments," *Journal of Marketing Research*, 28, Feb. 84-96.

Mulpuru, Sucharita, Johnson, Carrie, and Tesch, Brian (2006), "US ECommerce: The Year in Review." Forrest Research, www.forrester.com.

Nelson, Phillip (1974), "Advertising as Information," *Journal of Political Economy*, 81(4), 729-754.

Shimp, Terence A. and Bearden, William O. (1982), "Warranty and Other Extrinsic Cue Effects on Consumers' Risk Perceptions," *Journal of Consumer Research*, 9, 38-46.

Slyke, Craig V., Comunale, Christie, L., and Belanger, France (2002), "Gender differences in perceptions of web-based shopping," *Communications of the ACM*, 47(7), pp. 82–86.

Venkatesh, Viswanath and Morris, Michael G (2000), "Why Don't Men Ever Stop to Ask for Directions? Gender, Social Influence, and Their Role in Technology Acceptance and Usage Behavior," *MIS Quarterly*, 24(1), 115-139.

Westbrook, Robert (1981), "Sources of Consumer Satisfaction with Retail Outlets," *Journal of Retailing*, 57(3), 68-85.

Wolfinbarger, Mary and Gilly, Mary C. (2001), "Shopping Online for Freedom, Control and Fun," *California Management Review*, 43(Winter), 73-93.

Zhou, Lina, Dai, Liwei, and Zhang, Dongsong (2007), "Online Shopping Acceptance Model: A Critical Survey of Consumer Factors in Online Shopping," *Journal of Electronic Commerce Research,* 8(1), 41-62.

The Body and Technology: Discourses Shaping Consumer Experience and Marketing Communications of Technological Products and Services

Margo Buchanan-Oliver, The University of Auckland, New Zealand
Angela Cruz, The University of Auckland, New Zealand

ABSTRACT

Frontiers of thought in other disciplines, popular culture, and marketing communications are continually 're-visioning' technology and influencing how consumers think about and experience technology-based products and services. Providing a glimpse into these frontiers, this paper re-introduces the body into theorisations of consumer-technology interaction and reviews interdisciplinary discourses shaping views of the body and technology. The key theoretical discourses of body-machine liminality, control and freedom, embodied interaction, and identity are discussed. These discourses expand conceptualisations of technology beyond a limiting focus on functional benefits, offering new frames and foundations for investigating consumer experience and marketing communications of technology-based offerings.

INTRODUCTION

How do consumers understand and experience technology? How do marketers and advertisers communicate these experiences in a compelling way? In addressing these issues, present theorisations of consumer-technology interaction in marketing literature offer a narrow perspective, with a lack of attention to the body restricting the focus of marketing theory to the functional benefits of technology.

Underlying this pervasive disembodiment of the consumer is an assumed Cartesian dualism which not only separates the mind from the body but also privileges the former over the latter. Such dualism is evident, for instance, in the assumption of a simple dichotomy between the online self and the physical self in explaining consumers' construction of online identities (Schau and Gilly 2003). However, this Cartesian dualism underlying dominant conceptions of the self in consumer research is profoundly unsettled by consumers' interaction with increasingly ubiquitous technologies. Today, there is a proliferation of mechanical, digital, and biomedical technologies which not only allow consumers to transform and communicate their bodies across time and space (e.g. avatars in immersive virtual environments such as Second Life), transport themselves beyond their immediate physical location (e.g. cell phones), but also increasingly merge with and enter consumers' bodies in a more literal sense (e.g. pacemakers). Thus, such interactions are destabilising the traditional mapping of the individual self onto a single biological body.

In addition, rather than a natural, pre-determined, and discretely-bounded entity, the body is increasingly revealed as a malleable and porous construction. Not only does the body function as a site for multiple, shifting layers of cultural meaning (Schroeder and Dobers 2006), but its actual materiality is similarly elastic. Featherstone (2000), for instance, sees body modification ranging from simple prosthetic devices to enhance body motor and sensory functions (e.g. spectacles), to the building of technological environments around the body, to the incorporation of technology into the body. These interactions reveal a complex negotiation occurring in the boundary between the body and technology than is initially apparent through a Cartesian-framed first glance. In essence, the ubiquity of machines and the diversity of consumers' interactions with them are dramatically dissolving the boundaries between the body and technology and raising fundamental questions about what it means to be and to have a body, and what it means to be human, in an environment saturated with technology.

Conversations around these issues have circulated in other academic disciplines, popular imagination, and in marketing communications viz. Apple's classic '1984' advertisement (Scott 1991). Ericsson's 'Designer Technology' print campaign (Schroeder and Dobers 2006), Sony's print campaign for the Memory Stick™ (Venkatesh, Karababa, and Ger 2002), and Nike Lab's 'Les Jumelles' and 'Eye(D)' (Campbell, O'Driscoll, and Saren 2006) television commercials (TVC) have recently been analysed as exemplifying the merger of the body with technology.

These explorations have emerged from a visual cultural approach in marketing communications research. Schroeder and Dobers (2006), for instance, illustrate how visual rhetoric is used in a range of print advertisements to represent information technologies in increasingly corporeal ways, using the body as a means of anthropomorphising abstract technologies and rendering them familiar and accessible. Campbell et al. (2006) have presented a brief typology of visual tropes used to represent the posthuman technologised body, as exemplified in Nike's TVC 'Les Jumelles'.

However, understanding visual rhetoric per se, while insightful, requires contextualisation within existing discourses which inform the construction and interpretation of specific tropes. As Arnould and Thompson (2005, p. 869) note, these "manifestations of consumer culture are constituted, sustained, transformed, and shaped by broader historical forces (such as cultural narratives, myths, and ideologies)." These discourses therefore provide a discursive context to ideologies articulated in consumer narratives around technology (Kozinets 2008). Conversely, as these discourses are largely implicated in the social construction of shared cultural meanings, understanding these discourses also enhances understanding of the wider psychological and socio-cultural implications of such representations in marketing communications. These can be linked to emerging works (Venkatesh et al. 2002; Giesler 2004; Giesler and Venkatesh 2005) exploring the notion of 'posthuman consumer culture' as a theoretical lens for consumer research. Thus, an awareness and understanding of these conversations about the body and technology frames not only visual rhetoric in marketing communications involving the body and technology, but also consumers' phenomenological experience of technology. Clearly, these are fundamental discourses which marketing theory cannot afford to ignore.

METHODOLOGY

To uncover and clarify these discourses, key conceptual and philosophical texts were selected based on their salience for lensing consumers' embodied experience of technology. These were sourced through keyword searches in online ACR proceedings and the ABI/Inform database, and informed by the authors' backgrounds in semiotics, literary theory, postmodern theory, and film, television, and media studies, with further scans conducted through reference lists and Google Scholar. These key works encompassed a range of disciplines including cybernetics, cognitive neuropsychology, media studies, cultural studies and critical theory.

A theoretical discourse analysis methodology guided the induction of discursive categories and related sub-themes from these sources. From each text, main concepts and key themes were identified, which were then categorised into broader themes based on perceived commonalities and linkages. A process of iteration between the emerging discursive categories and the source texts permitted the development of provisional categories, constructs, and conceptual connections for subsequent exploration, thereby aiding the induction of broader, underlying themes from these sources (Spiggle 1994). Triangulation was further ensured through regular discussions of emerging interpretations between the authors.

DISCOURSES OF THE BODY AND TECHNOLOGY

The key discourses which emerged from this analysis were: body-machine liminality, a dialectic between control and freedom, consumers' embodied interaction with technology, and the body as a site for the (re)production of identity.

Body-Machine Liminality

Liminality refers to "a state of transition between two or more boundaries" (Campbell et al. 2006, p. 3). In the context of consumers' interactions with technology, being liminal describes a condition of hybridity, that is, being simultaneously human and machine, and neither human nor machine. Here the boundaries between the human and machine are confounded and revealed as porous and permeable. As Hayles (1999, p. 2-3) writes, "In the posthuman, there are no essential differences or absolute demarcations between bodily existence and computer simulation, cybernetic mechanism and biological organism, robot teleology and human goals."

This discourse of body-machine liminality is fleshed out in various conceptions of posthumanism and cyborgs. Some writings on posthumanism envisage a dramatic discontinuity between the 'human' and 'posthuman'. For instance, when body performance artist Orlan (1996, p. 91) declares that "the body is obsolete," she makes a distinction between the 'natural' body as defined by evolution and the body that is defined by technology. Such conceptions privilege the idea of a 'natural' body which has only been recently surpassed through technology.

This dichotomy between the pre-technological and post-technological body is challenged by Zylinska (2002) who perceives human identity as "inherently prosthetic" (2002, p.3) and by Clark (2003) who conceives of humans as 'natural-born cyborgs' who utilise technology in such a way that it becomes transparent in use and inseparable from our bodies to "extend our sense of presence and our potential for action" (Clark 2003, p. 125). As Clark notes, the plasticity of the brain permits human subjectivity to range over an interactive network of biological and non-biological components, unconstrained by the "biological skin-bag" (Clark 2003, p. 27).

This posthuman dissolution of boundaries is embodied conceptually, figuratively, and metaphorically in the figure of the cyborg which speaks to the inseparability of the body and machine and as a visual representation of this contradictory union (Haraway 1991). The cyborg not only exemplifies the posthuman era (Clarke 2002, Orlan 1996), it is also a manifest representation that technology is an integral aspect of human identity (Clark 2003; Zylinska 2002a).

Specific aspects of body-machine liminality are outlined below.

Liminality of Substance. There is an increasing difficulty in distinguishing as separate entities the human body from the machines with which it interacts, such that the emergent entities are always human-machine symbionts (Clark 2003). Furthermore, in the more literal sense of cyborgism, non-biological material is already embedded within the body (e.g. pacemakers, hearing aids, contact lenses).

Liminality of Form. Liminality of form occurs when the body and the machine are perceived to resemble one another through repeated metaphorical associations in visual rhetoric (Schroeder and Dobers 2006) and in behavioural repertoires. Developments in

cybernetics and artificial life also illustrate the increasing divestment of human agency onto machines.

Liminality of form is also referenced in the increased plasticity of a biological body in its interaction with technologies such as cosmetic surgery.

Liminality of Location. Human-machine interactions are characterised by an indeterminate mapping of the subject with respect to the corporeal body such as occurs in the immersive virtual environment of *Second Life* where users create real-time three-dimensional online bodies which interact with others. In such spaces location of the self proves problematic. Is the self located in the physical body or the online body, in both, or in neither? Steuer's (1992) concept of 'telepresence', in which the consumer simultaneously perceives both their immediate physical environment and the hypermedia computer-mediated environment (Hoffman and Novak 1996), is apposite here.

Control and Freedom

The body can be seen as both master of and slave to technology. This dialectical master-slave relationship is linked to the indeterminate location of agency within individual and communal bodies.

Agency. In its interaction with technology, the body is no longer privileged as the true site of agency, as the self and its associated capacities for independent action extend beyond the boundaries of the skin and are invested in non-biological artefacts. The notion that humans are not the only ones that have an ability to act is explored in Actor-Network Theory (Latour 1993), in which the distinction between human and non-human agents is seen to be an artificial construction of modernity. What emerges in this discourse is a conception of agency which is not unique to the biological body, but rather distributed over a network of hybrid actors.

Enabled and Dependent Body. While new technologies have the ability to extend or enhance human capability and introduce new functionality in human life, this is accompanied by an increased dependency on these same technologies. Shilling (2005), suggests that prosthetic technologies can be perceived as dependent 'corporeal replacement' (e.g. crutches), or 'cyborgian enhancement', enabling new functionality (e.g. running shoes).

Emancipated and Disciplined Body. Technology can be deployed as an apparatus for the production and control of 'docile bodies' (Foucault 1977) by institutional processes, including marketing (Venkatesh, Meamber, and Firat 1997). Since the industrial era, a drive towards increased control and efficiency have led to the body being seen as an appendage to machines inasmuch as machines are seen to extend the body.

Conversely, interactions with technology may not be reduced to the totalising effects of powerful institutions (de Certeau 1984), as new technologies and cyberspace can promise an emancipatory potential where these computer-mediated environments create an idealised 'public sphere' removed from institutional interest (Habermas 1989; Poster 1997, cited in Lister, Dovey, Giddings, Grant, and Kelly 2003). Clark's (2003) promotion of a 'global informational free lunch' in cyberspace, and Rheingold's (1993) conceptualisation of the virtual community as an 'electronic agora' free from the constraints of the 'electronic panopticon' provide such promise.

Creative and Emulative Body. The question of agency encompasses not only interaction between individual consumers and technology, but also communal interaction between consumers where the social 'linking value' of technology products and services takes precedence over their 'use value' (Cova and Cova

2002), and enables intercorporeality, a sense of being connected to and in communication with other embodied beings.

A similar dialectic to that of emancipation and discipline is theorised with regards to communal bodies, with bodies either mirroring or emulating the meanings available in the surrounding consumer culture (Frank 1990) or creatively subverting these meanings and creating alternatives to mainstream consumer culture (Firat and Venkatesh 1995; Giesler and Venkatesh 2005).

Embodied Interaction

Another central informing discourse concerns embodied interaction at the interface, within which the following themes are articulated.

Sensory Body. Consumers' interface with technology involves the senses and engenders embodied experiences of pleasure or pain. The pleasure of interacting with technology has been explored in concepts such as 'flow' and 'telepresence' in computer-mediated environments (Hoffman and Novak 1996), as instantiated by experiences of 'vicarious kinaesthesia' in the immersive video game experience (Darley 2000). In relation to this, Mirzoeff (1999, p. 92) conceptualises virtuality as the transformation of space away from three-dimensional reality to the "polydimensional interior world of the self," asserting that this is not unique to digital technology. In addition, using the example of putting one's avatar on display in public online platforms, Mirzoeff (1999) describes the pleasure of a highly visualised and sensual experience of being both consumer and commodity.

Conversely, the notion of pain at the interface with the machine is highlighted by considering the violence entailed in body modification and prostheticism. As Zylinska (2002b, p. 214) writes, "Physical violence is a manifestation [...] of power exerted on weak but unsubmissive bodies which are then prosthesized (extended, adjusted, bent, etc.) in an attempt to deprive them of their integrity and inviolability." Consider, for instance, the pain experienced in cosmetic surgery, or the strain of sitting at a computer terminal for extended periods.

Erotic Body. Technology facilitates the reproduction of sexual desire, constructing a body which is either/both desired and desiring. Visual culture is particularly implicated in the production of erotic bodies, with relations of desire constructed between gazing subjects (usually male) and gazed objects (usually female), in which the gazing subject is placed in a position of power and domination over the gazed object. Such relations are evident in the use of pornographic codes, particularly the fetish, in the marketing of digital cameras (Schroeder and McDonagh 2006) to signify liminal zones of danger and excitement. In relation to this, Campbell et al. (2006) explore the liminal characteristics of the 'technological gaze' deployed in Nike's 'Les Jumelles', producing a paradoxically sexualised yet empowered female body.

Identity

Identity is another central informing discourse of the body and technology. In this discourse, the body is viewed as a site of difference between subjects, with technology as an apparatus for the (re)production of such difference. Such 'investments of difference' (Grosz 1994) are crucial to the constitution of identity–a sense of who one is as distinct from some other. From a critical perspective, such investments of difference are also seen to produce differential power relations in society, with hierarchical structures of class, gender, and race persisting in new media in different forms, contrary to utopian notions (Mirzoeff 1999). Discourses of identity centre on the following 'modern' categories of difference.

Gendered Body. Bodies are differentiated in terms of gender and sexuality, producing a binary opposition between male and female bodies, as well as between 'straight' (heterosexual) and 'queer' (non-heterosexual) bodies. Implicated in the construction of gendered identities are particular technologies and modes of visual representation such as 'faceism' (Schroeder and Borgerson 2007) which reinforce these dichotomies. With respect to the body and technology, the figure of the cyborg is contradictory in that it can be seen to offer both liberatory identifications for women while simultaneously confirming gendered stereotypes (Gonzalez 1999).

Ethnic Body. Bodies are also differentiated in terms of race and ethnicity, producing a binary opposition between Western bodies and 'Oriental' (non-Western) bodies, as framed by a Eurocentric view which privileges the former over the latter (Said 1978). In this view, bodies are conceptualised as semiotically charged carriers of meaning, such that the potential for action in racialised bodies is delimited by their history of meaning (Klesse 2000). In this vein, Gordon (1995, cited in Schroeder 2003) posits the concept of an 'epidermal schema' which suggests a variance in cultural associations attached to different skin colours. Moreover, with regards to the technological reproduction of ethnicity, Hammonds (1999) shows how visual technologies have always been, and still are, implicated in the attempts to establish categories of race.

Political Body. In addition, bodies are differentiated in terms of access to technological resources, producing a hierarchical relation in which the privileged upper class comes to dominate the excluded lower class. An increasing inequality between the technological 'haves' and 'have-nots' led Castells (1996) to coin the term 'digital divide', describing a situation in which access to advanced technology and the ability to realise its full potential is concentrated in the developed world. Inequitable class relations are sustained through this concentration of economic and educational capital in the hands of a privileged few (Bourdieu 1984).

Mutable Body. Bodies are also differentiated in terms of age, with discourses of the cyborg implicitly privileging youth over old age. On one hand, authors such as Farquhar (1999) champion the liberatory potential of the cyborg concept, citing the example of reproductive technologies which enable previously excluded women to become mothers. On the other hand, Woodward (1999) writes of normalising discourses in which 'bad' or monstrous mothers are constructed in relation to 'good' or 'natural' mothers, effectively preventing older women from accessing reproductive technologies. This underlines the differential access to technology for people of different ages, as well as the differential meanings ascribed to different kinds of cyborgs. As Woodward (1994) writes, "most of us fear the future prospect of frailty as a cyborg, "hooked up" [...] to a machine."

IMPLICATIONS AND FURTHER RESEARCH

Communicating Technology

These discourses, which pervade consumer culture predominantly through popular texts and marketing communications, reflect an expanding, if not shifting, cultural zeitgeist with regards to how technology is viewed: technology is not merely all around us; it is (inside) us. Marketing communications needs to reflect these concerns in order to pierce the heart of what technology means to consumers.

With regards to visual rhetoric in marketing communications, therefore, one might ask what discourses predominate and what discourses are missing in the communication of technology, how these might differ across product categories and brands, and how these might relate to advertising resonance. Such an inquiry will not only enable a description of dominant practices in marketing communications, but also highlight under-utilised opportunities for creating more compelling appeals and increasing the cut-through of marketing messages. It is notable, for instance, that the print advertisements analysed in Schroeder and Dobers (2006) predominantly deploy discourses of functionality or enablement. However, it is conceivable that a message based on the sensory aspects of interaction, or on the 'negative' aspects of interaction such as dependency or addiction, can be equally, if not more, compelling (e.g. video game advertisements).

Thus, for brand managers, marketing communications managers, and advertisers, these discourses provide a compass for navigating the turbulent and mysterious waters of socio-cultural meaning. For a marketer of technology-based products and services in a cluttered communications environment, such a compass is essential for illuminating creative blind spots and finding ways to break out of existing formulations. The ability to create unique and resonant messages, based on knowledge of these discourses and the ways in which these are being deployed in one's industry, would certainly endow one's communications with a competitive edge.

Discourses in Consumer Culture

Moreover, this analysis raises questions around the wider socio-cultural repercussions of deploying these discourses in advertising. With regards to gender identity, for instance, one might consider how the visual trope of representing technology using the female body might reflect and perpetuate differential power relations between men and women. On this note, Clarke (2002, p. 35) observes that "Liminal beings are […] perceived as polluting […] and are more often than not characterized as monstrous, diseased, queer, marginal, black, insane or female." In a similar vein, advertisements which deploy 'Oriental' (i.e. non-European) bodies as a more potent symbol of liminality may be seen to reinforce binary narratives of ethnicity.

However, it is interesting to consider not only the ways in which traditional dichotomies are articulated, iterated, and reinforced, but also the ways in which these are disrupted. While technology can be seen as an apparatus for the reproduction of such dichotomies, the multiplicity of ways in which consumers interact with machines underlines the artificial and constructed nature of these oppositions and allows for the emergence of ambiguous 'thirdspaces of knowledge' which unsettle traditional binary categories (Campbell et al. 2006). As Campbell et al. (2006, p. 7) write, "Posthuman images produce paradoxical social meaning," in that they blur "the lines that separate the masculine from the feminine, the mechanical and the visceral, and even the divide between nature and culture." Fundamental questions can therefore be raised about the ontological implications of body-machine liminality, and how this might raise questions about what it means to be human or posthuman (Giesler 2004; Giesler and Venkatesh 2005).

Understanding Consumer Experience

Since images of posthumanism already proliferate in the realm of marketing communications (Schroeder and Dobers 2006; Venkatesh et al. 2002), we need to explore how such images might impact consumer experiences with technology. Consumer ambivalence towards technology as examined by Mick and Fournier (1998) might be impacted by the destabilising effect of posthumanism on 'essential' human nature. It might also be shaped by the socio-culturally contested figure of the cyborg (Clarke 2002).

CONCLUSION

In summary, this paper presented and discussed key discourses shaping consumers' views of the body and technology. Through a discourse analysis methodology, theoretical perspectives on the body and technology from key works across a range of disciplines were summarised. The central discourses found were: body-machine liminality, a dialectic between control and freedom, consumer experience at the interface, and the (re)production of identity.

These discourses of the body and technology represent the frontier in theorisations of technology and provide a promising platform for further research. In order to create compelling communications resonant with consumers' experiences of technology, a deep understanding of the meanings surrounding the body-technology interface and how these are being read by consumers is required. This can provide an insight not only into the ways in which these representations influence how consumers think about and interact with technology, but also how consumers think about themselves and construct their own identities, thereby opening up and framing much-needed discussion around the wider phenomenological, ideological, and ethical implications of marketing communications practice.

REFERENCES

Arnould, Eric J. and Craig J. Thompson (2005), "Consumer Culture Theory (CCT): Twenty Years of Research," *Journal of Consumer Research*, 31 (March), 868-82.

Bourdieu, Pierre (1984), *Distinction: A Social Critique of the Judgement of Taste*, London: Routledge and Kegan Paul.

Campbell, Norah, Aidan O'Driscoll, and Michael Saren (2006), "Cyborg Consciousness: A Visual Culture Approach to the Technologised Body," in *European Advances in Consumer Research*, 7, in press.

Castells, Manuel (1996), *The Rise of the Network Society*, Oxford: Blackwell.

Clark, Andy (2003), *Natural-Born Cyborgs: Minds, Technologies, and the Future of Human Intelligence*, New York: Oxford University Press.

Clarke, Julie (2002), "The Human/Not Human in the Work of Orlan and Stelarc," in *The Cyborg Experiments: The Extensions of the Body in the Media Age*, ed. Joanna Zylinska, New York: Continuum, 33-55.

Cova, Bernard and Veronique Cova (2002), "Tribal Marketing: The Tribalisation of Society and Its Impact on the Conduct of Marketing," *European Journal of Marketing*, 36 (5/6), 595-620.

Darley, Andrew (2000), *Visual Digital Culture: Surface Play and Spectacle in New Media Genres*, London and New York: Routledge.

de Certeau, Michel (1984), *The Practice of Everyday Life*, Berkeley: University of California Press.

Farquhar, Dion (1999), "(M)Other Discourses," in *The Gendered Cyborg: A Reader*, ed. Gill Kirkup, Linda Janes, Kathryn Woodward, and Fiona Hovenden, New York: Routledge, 209-20.

Featherstone, Mike (2000), "Body Modification: An Introduction," in *Body Modification*, ed. Mike Featherstone, London: Sage, 1-14.

Firat, A. Fuat and Alladi Venkatesh (1995), "Liberatory Postmodernism and the Reenchantment of Consumption," *Journal of Consumer Research*, 22 (December), 239-67.

Foucault, Michel (1977), *Discipline and Punish: The Birth of the Prison*, New York: Pantheon Books.

Frank, Arthur W. (1990), "For a Sociology of the Body: An Analytical Review," in *The Body: Social Process and Cultural Theory*, ed. Mike Featherstone, Mike Hepworth, and Bryan S. Turner, London: Sage, 36-102.

Giesler, Markus (2004), "Consuming Cyborgs: Posthuman Consumer Culture and Its Impact on the Conduct of Marketing," in *Advances in Consumer Research, Vol. 31*, ed. Barbara E. Kahn and Mary Frances Luce, Valdosta, GA: Association for Consumer Research, 400-02.

Giesler, Markus and Alladi Venkatesh (2005), "Reframing the Embodied Consumer as Cyborg: A Posthumanist Epistemology of Consumption," in *Advances in Consumer Research, Vol. 32*, ed. Geeta Menon and Akshay R. Rao, Duluth, MN: Association for Consumer Research, 661-69.

Gonzalez, Jennifer (1999), "Envisioning Cyborg Bodies: Notes from Current Research," in *The Gendered Cyborg: A Reader*, ed. Gill Kirkup, Linda Janes, Kathryn Woodward, and Fiona Hovenden, New York: Routledge, 58-73.

Grosz, Elizabeth A. (1994), *Volatile Bodies: Toward a Corporeal Feminism*, Bloomington: Indiana University Press.

Hammonds, Evelynn M. (1999), "New Technologies of Race," in *The Gendered Cyborg: A Reader*, ed. Gill Kirkup, Linda Janes, Kathryn Woodward, and Fiona Hovenden, New York: Routledge, 305-14.

Haraway, Donna Jeanne (1991), *Simians, Cyborgs, and Women: The Reinvention of Nature*, New York: Routledge.

Hayles, N. Katherine (1999), *How We Became Posthuman: Virtual Bodies in Cybernetics, Literature, and Informatics*, Chicago: University of Chicago Press.

Hoffman, Donna L. and Thomas P. Novak (1996), "Marketing in Hypermedia Computer-Mediated Environments: Conceptual Foundations," *Journal of Marketing*, 60 (3), 50-68.

Klesse, Christian (2000), "'Modern Primitivism': Non-Mainstream Body Modification and Racialized Representation," in *Body Modification*, ed. Mike Featherstone, London: Sage, 15-38.

Kozinets, Robert V. (2008), "Technology/Ideology: How Ideological Fields Influence Consumers' Technology Narratives," *Journal of Consumer Research*, 34 (April), 865-81.

Latour, Bruno (1993), *We Have Never Been Modern*, Cambridge, MA: Harvard University Press.

Lister, Martin, Jon Dovey, Seth Giddings, Iain Grant, and Kieran Kelly (2003), *New Media: A Critical Introduction*, London: Routledge.

Mick, David Glen and Susan Fournier (1998), "Paradoxes of Technology: Consumer Cognizance, Emotions, and Coping Strategies," *Journal of Consumer Research*, 25 (September), 123-43.

Mirzoeff, Nicholas (1999), *An Introduction to Visual Culture*, London and New York: Routledge.

Orlan (1996), *This Is My Body, This Is My Software*, London: Black Dog Publishing.

Rheingold, Howard (1993), *The Virtual Community: Homesteading on the Electronic Frontier*, Reading, MA: Addison-Wesley.

Said, Edward (1978), *Orientalism*, New York: Pantheon Books.

Schau, Hope Jensen and Mary C. Gilly (2003), "We Are What We Post? Self-Presentation in Personal Web Space," *Journal of Consumer Research*, 30 (3), 385-404.

Schroeder, Jonathan (2003), "Special Session Summary on Branding the Body: Skin and Consumer Communication," in *European Advances in Consumer Research, Vol. 6*, ed. Darach Turley and Stephen Brown, Provo, UT: Association for Consumer Research, 23-28.

Schroeder, Jonathan E. and Janet L. Borgerson (2007), "Identity and Iteration: Images and the Constitution of Consuming Subjects," working paper, School of Business and Economics, University of Exeter, Exeter, EX4 4PU.

Schroeder, Jonathan E. and Peter Dobers (2006), "Imagining Identity: Technology and the Body in Marketing Communications," in *Advances in Consumer Research, Vol. 34*, ed. Gavan Fitzsimons and Vicki Morwitz, Orlando, FL: Association for Consumer Research, in press.

Schroeder, Jonathan E. and Pierre McDonagh (2006), "The Logic of Pornography in Digital Camera Production," in *Sex in Consumer Culture: The Erotic Content of Media and Marketing*, ed. Tom Reichert and Jacqueline Lambiase, Mahwah, NJ: Lawrence Erlbaum Associates, 219-42.

Scott, Linda M (1991), "For the rest of us: a reader-oriented interpretation of Apple's '1984' commercial", *Journal of Popular Culture*, 25(1), 67-82.

Shilling, Chris (2005), *The Body in Culture, Technology and Society*, London: Sage.

Spiggle, Susan (1994), "Analysis and Interpretation of Qualitative Data in Consumer Research," *Journal of Consumer Research*, 21 (December), 491-503.

Venkatesh, Alladi, Laurie A. Meamber and Fuat A. Firat (1997) "Cyberspace as the next marketing frontier(?)", ed. Stephen Brown and Darach Turley, *Consumer Research: Postcards from the Edge*, Routledge, London/New York, 300-21.

Venkatesh, Alladi, Eminegul Karababa, and Guliz Ger (2002), "The Emergence of the Posthuman Consumer and the Fusion of the Virtual and the Real: A Critical Analysis of Sony's Ad for Memory Stick," in *Advances in Consumer Research, Vol. 29*, ed. Susan M. Broniarczyk and Kent Nakamoto, Valdosta, GA: Association for Consumer Research, 446-52.

Woodward, Kathryn (1994), "From Virtual Cyborgs to Biological Time Bombs: Technocriticism and the Material Body," in *Culture on the Brink: Ideologies of Technology*, ed. Gretchen Bender and Timothy Druckery, Seattle: Bay Press, 47-64.

_____ (1999), "Introduction to Part Three (Representing Reproduction: Reproducing Representation)," in *The Gendered Cyborg: A Reader*, ed. Gill Kirkup, Linda Janes, Kathryn Woodward, and Fiona Hovenden, New York: Routledge, 161-70.

Zylinska, Joanna (2002a), "Extending Mcluhan into the New Media Age: An Introduction," in *The Cyborg Experiments: The Extensions of the Body in the Media Age*, ed. Joanna Zylinska, New York: Continuum, 1-12.

_____ (2002b), "'the Future... Is Monstrous': Prosthetics as Ethics," in *The Cyborg Experiments: The Extensions of the Body in the Media Age*, ed. Joanna Zylinska, New York: Continuum, 214-36.

Getting Lost "Into the Wild": Understanding Consumers' Movie Enjoyment Through a Narrative Transportation Approach

Wided Batat, University of Poitiers, France
Markus Wohlfeil, University College Cork, Ireland

ABSTRACT

As consumers enjoy watching movies for many reasons, this paper takes an existential-phenomenological perspective to discuss movie consumption as holistic private lived experiences. By using interactive introspection, the two researchers examined their own individual private consumption experiences with the recently released movie *Into the Wild* (US 2007) as a complex tapestry of interrelated factors. The introspective data indicates that a consumer's personal engagement with the movie narrative, its characters and underlying philosophy is of particular importance for one's enjoyment of the movie. This allows for and even enhances the consumer's temporary feeling of complete immersion into the movie's imaginary world.

INTRODUCTION

For more than a century, consumers all over the world have enjoyed watching movies for many reasons that can range from mere short-term entertainment to the personal experience of complete immersion into the movie narrative (Green, Brock and Kaufman 2004) and identification with its characters (Cohen 2001). Yet, a closer review of the literature on movie consumption indicates that we still lack a full understanding of how an ordinary consumer experiences the consumption of movies and what subjective contribution it makes to one's quality of life. This scant attention may have resulted from marketing's primary interest in the economic dimensions of movie consumption, where the focus is often limited to box office performances or the sales and rentals of DVDs in specified markets (De Vany and Walls 2002; Hennig-Thurau, Walsh and Bode 2004; Ravid 1999). In doing so, movie consumption is usually reduced to the mere purchase of individual tangible media formats (Basil 2001; Krugman and Gopal 1991) rather than investigated as the actual consumption of movies as intangible brands in themselves (Wohlfeil and Whelan 2008). In film studies, on the other hand, researchers seek to explain the effects of movies on their audiences by means of audience-response theory (Mulvey 1975; Phillips 2003). This involves trained expert viewers discussing in theory how an imaginary, idealised viewer would respond to movie texts and the cinematic experience by assuming probable motives, expectations and prior knowledge (Hirschman 1999). However, a synthesis of ideas from psychoanalysis, linguistics, semiotics, Marxism and feminism has hereby created the image of a passive viewer, who is vulnerable to the manipulative qualities of the cinematic experience (Phillips 2003). Moreover, expert viewers have often discussed suspected audience responses as a means to advance their own political-ideological agenda (see Mulvey (1975) as an excellent example).

A very different approach was recently taken by Wohlfeil and Whelan (2008), in which one of the authors observed introspectively his own experiential consumption of the movie *Pride & Prejudice* (UK 2005). While they identified a complex tapestry of interconnected factors contributing to a consumer's movie enjoyment, they found a consumer's personal engagement with the film narrative and its characters to be of particular importance and provided thereby evidence for the applicability of narrative transportation theory (Gerrig 1993; Green and Brock 2000) to movie consumption. Though primarily applied to reading, this theory suggests that enjoyment can benefit from the experience of being immersed in a narrative world through cognitive, emotional and imaginary involvement as well as from the consequences of that immersion, which include emotional connections with characters and self-transformations (Green et al. 2004: 311). Transportation is hereby seen as a process by which the consumer actively seeks to be taken away from one's everyday life into different narrative worlds, where one could experience a different self and engage empathetically with media characters like real friends (Gerrig 1993). This private engagement is further enhanced through out-of-text intertextuality by which the consumer connects the movie to one's own personal life experiences (Hirschman 2000a; Wohlfeil and Whelan 2008). In a recent study, Argo, Zhui and Dahl (2008) found that consumers' immersion into melodramatic narratives may be dependent on the level of fictionality, whereby females tend to empathise more readily with narratives that feature factual contents, while males prefer to loose themselves in narratives with highly fictional contents.

But similar to previous studies (i.e. Green and Brock 2000; Rapp and Gerrig 2006), their hypotheses were only tested within laboratory experiments, where the staged and artificial setup had little resemblance to consumers' real-life experiences. The findings also contradict Wohlfeil and Whelan's (2008) introspective data, which provide clear evidence that the male researcher empathised and even identified strongly with the rather factual narrative and characters in *Pride & Prejudice* (UK 2005). Hence, the question remains whether there is any evidence that those findings on transportation theory would reflect consumers' real-lived movie consumption experiences. Taking an existential-phenomenological perspective (Thompson 1997; Thompson, Locander and Pollio 1989), this study therefore aims to provide alternative insights into consumers' holistic movie consumption experiences. As both authors happen to be of different gender, come from different cultural backgrounds and live in different countries, we will compare, examine and discuss our own individual private lived consumption experiences with the recently released movie *Into the Wild* (Dir.: Sean Penn, US 2007) and how we connected the movie to our personal life experiences by using interactive introspection (Ellis 1991; Wallendorf and Brucks 1993).

METHODOLOGY

In order to truly understand movie consumption as a holistic phenomenological experience from an insider perspective, the focus has to be on the consumer experience in the way it presents itself to consciousness (Merleau-Ponty 1962; Thompson et al. 1989). Subsequently, we used a research method known as subjective personal introspection (SPI), which is an experiential, private self-reflection on joys and sorrows related to consumption and found in one's own everyday participation in the human condition (Holbrook 1995: 201). This method has an advantage of allowing the researcher for an easy, unlimited 24-hour access to an insider's lived experiences with the investigated phenomenon without having to wrestle with ethical concerns regarding the informants' privacy (Brown 1998; Gould 2006). However, this also means that we now have to disappoint all those readers who were expecting to find hard, scientific data obtained through hypothetical-deductive methods. Instead, we followed for this study an approach that could be broadly described as interactive introspection and involves gaining illuminative subjective insights through comparing, contrasting and interpreting introspective essays (Ellis 1991; Patterson et al. 1998; Wallendorf and Brucks 1993).

As it happens, both authors are of different gender and live in different countries. The first author is female, in her 20s, Algerian, lives in Southern France and is for the purpose of this paper referred to as the female viewer (FV). The second author is male, in his 30s, German, lives in the South of Ireland and is now referred to as the male viewer (MV). Both researchers wrote independently from each other an extensive introspective essay on their personal experiential consumption of the movie *Into the Wild* (Dir.: Sean Penn, US 2007), which, by coincidence, they have both watched recently. Based on Jon Kracauer's bestselling book, the movie retells the true story of Christopher McCandless, a young college graduate who decided to abandon his worldly possessions and leave his perfectly planned out life behind in order to escape the trappings of a society he despised by experiencing natural life in all its immediacy in the Alaskan wilderness. While his journey and view on life touched a number of people along the way, his romantic idealism ultimately leads to his doom at the unforgiving hands of Mother Nature. We then exchanged the two essays and each researcher compared and analysed them for both common emic themes and individual differences (Thompson 1997). Finally, we compared our two personal interpretations of the introspective essays for similarities and/or differences and summarised them accordingly (Gould 2006; Patterson et al. 1998).

MAJOR FINDINGS AND DISCUSSION OF THE DATA

The thorough analysis of the introspective data obtained from our personal holistic lived experiences of consuming *Into the Wild* (US 2007) has revealed some very interesting findings. For both viewers, the essence of our private movie enjoyment was the arousal, pleasure and emotional stimulation obtained from the cinematic consumption experience (Holbrook and Hirschman 1982) rather than from maximising some ominous economic benefits (Basil 2001; Eliashberg and Shugan 1997). However, while a tapestry of interrelated factors contributed to the overall movie consumption experience, both viewers experienced the strong personal emotional engagement with the movie narrative and our subsequent ability to loose ourselves mentally *Into the Wild* (US 2007) as essential to our enjoyment of the movie. This confirmed Wohlfeil and Whelan's (2008) earlier findings, as evidenced in the following extracts:

In terms of the lead character Chris, my relationship with him changed several times over the film. At the beginning, I disliked him because he appears to be another spoiled, rebellious and stupid rich kid that feels himself to be totally misunderstood. Then, when the family history was revealed I started to understand his motivations and even empathised with him in his search for a better, more harmonic life based on love and mutual respect. I even understood when he failed to grab his first opportunity. After all, I have failed to notice a few times as well that everything I was looking for was directly in front of my eyes and I just had to take it, but I was too scared or too stupid to see it. However, after he obviously knew that he has found what he was looking for in the flesh right in front of his eyes and feet and still left to fulfil a naïve, romanticised fantasy, then I thought again "what an idiot!" (MV)

"Into the Wild" left me sobbing like a baby; I would go as far as to say uncontrollably–Thank God, I saw this alone and in the darkness. Regarding the character, one scene that stands out in particular is McCandless killing a moose. It both vividly illustrates an intimate aspect of living in the wild and provides an almost existential moment-to-moment take on the newly discovered aspects of the character. (FV)

The story itself is an incredibly important one. Ever had that feeling of wanting to abandon your existing life and living one step closer to nature? I can't deny being touched by the relationships that Alexander (Emile Hirsch) makes on his travels and I was haunted by images of Alexander desperately trying to get food in the Alaskan wilds, in particular his efforts with a moose. This was storytelling so good it could bring you to tears. I was convinced as to touching the nature of Christopher/Alexander. (FV)

It was a captivating movie experience and I believe that it is one of those movies that you can watch over and over again and each time you will discover something new and different. It's also kind of going on a journey of self-discovery yourself each time you watch the film. My relation to the characters differed. I didn't really identify with anyone of them, but empathised strongly with the hippie couple (Catherine Keener and Brian Dierker), Ron Franz (Hal Holbrook) and even Carine–but the latter could be influenced by my admiration for Jena Malone as the actress who portrayed her. (MV)

Both viewers also experienced an equally intensive level of immersion and empathy with the factual movie narrative. Thus, the introspective data would contradict Argo et al.'s (2008) prediction that a consumer's ability to empathise with melodramatic narratives–whether factual or fictional–would be determined by one's gender. In fact, the data would contradict the suggestion that a consumer's ability to immerse in and empathise with a melodramatic movie narrative would be determined by any of the common socio-demographic variables such as age, ethnicity, nationality or cultural background. But while its intensity may appear to be similar, we discovered nonetheless some interesting differences in each viewer's account of our private lived movie consumption experiences, which influenced the nature of the personal transportation experience and, hence, warrant a closer examination. Although both viewers agreed that each of our private *Into the Wild* (US 2007) consumer experiences started with a search for relevant information across similar media (i.e. magazines, IMDb, websites, TV or YouTube) long before actually watching the movie in the cinema, the type of information we sought and our underlying motivations to do so differed significantly:

Once a couple of years, there comes a movie that is both unapologetically soulful and offers a gentle philosophical take on one of the timeless myths and human tendencies. ...The first time I heard about the film was in January 2008 in a French TV talk show. I decided to learn more about the movie by looking for information on the Internet. ... I ensured myself of the quality of the movie by gathering much information on the story, the character, the moviemaker Sean Penn, magazine criticisms; comments comparison between French and English websites. In addition, I checked for the box office of the English media on Yahoo UK. (FV)

My interest and experiential consumption of this movie actually started already as early as October 2006, when I read in an interview with Jena Malone in Mean magazine that it was just being filmed…As it so happened, in this article she talked not only about her then recent film release "*The Go-Getter*" and her increasing interest in expressing herself in self-produced music and short films, but also that she would soon starting to film "*Into the Wild*" with Sean Penn. Jena Malone then vividly recalls how she had accidentally hung up on Sean Penn when he phoned her at home near Lake Tahoe to cast her, because due to a defective connection she couldn't hear him and thought it was an obscene call. I really loved the way she told the story during the interview…In September 2007, the movie trailer of "*Into the Wild*" appeared on YouTube. Without hesitation I used YouTube Catcher to download the trailer. Not that the trailer was giving much away, but it definitely stimulated an appetite for more in me….Jena Malone being in the movie was enough reason for me to must see it anyway!!! (MV)

As it turned out, the male viewer is the self-confessed fan of a movie actress and much of his interest in the movie, subsequently, stems from her involvement in the movie production. In fact, he became only aware of the movie as a result of reading an interesting interview with her. Furthermore, much of his information search was directly associated with the actress, such as catching glimpses of her in the movie trailer, downloading video clips of her interviews or photos of her at the movie premiere. The female viewer, on the other hand, had no fan-related interests and learnt only by chance about the film in a TV show. Her search for information about the movie was driven by her awakened interest in its mythological narrative (Hirschman 2000b), the true background story and the lead character's philosophical ideals, which have touched her emotionally. The movie, nevertheless, has also awakened in her an admiration for the leading actor Emile Hirsch–though her perception of him blurred increasingly by merging his off-screen persona with his on-screen character.

Emile Hirsch gave the best performance of his career and he literally carried the whole movie on his shoulders….I shared the same values as Emile Hirsch who goes on to display a person, who is selfless and whose goal is simply to go somewhere where he can live peacefully… Throughout, it was Emile's smiles and caring advice that seem to be constant reminders to me to have hope, to believe that there's more out there than the rat race we're so wrapped up in. (FV)

As a result of those different individual motivations for watching this movie, both viewers also differed in our personal engagement with the movie's melodramatic narrative and the characters as well as in the way we actually lost ourselves in the movie experience. As is already evident in the earlier extracts and confirming Wohlfeil and Whelan's (2008) earlier findings, the male viewer engaged very closely and emotionally with the individual characters in the movie–a response that most previous literature only ascribed to female audiences. Oatley (1999) and Cohen (2001) argued that personal engagement with literary characters and their stories in novels can take with increasing level of immersion broadly three different forms. On the weakest level, a consumer merely sympathises with the characters (= feels with them) as a side-participant who likes them. On the next level, the consumer feels empathy for the character (= shares the character's emotions) because of perceived similarities to one's own private experiences. Finally, the consumer identifies with the character (= feels the character's emotions as one's own) for the moment similar to an actor playing a role.

While sympathising with the parents in their desperate, but fruitless search for their son, the male viewer empathised during his movie consumption experience strongly with the hippie couple, Ron Franz and Chris's sister Carine. However, much of his empathy for her may result from his admiration for the actress Jena Malone, who portrayed her. On the other hand, though he didn't directly admit to it, there is also evidence that his ambivalent emotional engagement with the lead character Christopher McCandless is more than positive and negative empathy, but in fact a form of identification (Cohen 2001). Indeed, the use of out-of-text intertextuality (Wohlfeil and Whelan 2008), by which the male viewer connected Christopher's experiences on screen with his personal life experiences, suggests that the character's naivety, idealism, motives and even foolishness served as a mirror through which the male viewer relived his own experiences.

While Chris moves on and meets a kind couple of hippies (Catherine Keener and Brian Dierker) with their own sad background story of a lost son, we can see in flashbacks behind the façade of the McCandless family life. His father is a career-minded individual for whom his family is more or less a necessary status symbol… Chris and Carine are consistently caught up in the middle of [their parents regular] fights or even recipients to the fighting. More and more I was beginning to understand the motivation behind Chris's actions. His journey wasn't really the expressed statement of an over-ideological kid, but a desperate attempt of escaping from the white suburban middle-class society that his family represented. (MV)

And I could fully empathise with him now, as I also sought myself to escape desperately from a (lower working-class) living environment I was growing up in and deeply despised… Most of the time, I was told what I couldn't do and any dream, creativity or ambition for experiencing and doing something different, something that matters, was cruelly slaughtered [by parents, teachers, career counsellors] right from the start… Instead, I ended up working in retailing for years. In all those years, movies provided me with the only source of escape and the only source of inspiration–like Jack London novels did for Chris McCandless. I needed to get out… (MV)

Interestingly, the female viewer did not really sympathise, empathise or even identify with any of the characters as such. In taking a macro-perspective, her transportation experiences were instead based on her personal engagement with the lead character's (and, thus, the story's) philosophical view on looking for the human condition and the meaning of life in modern Western societies rather than with his person. Thus, the female viewer seemed to empathise or even identify herself essentially with the presented ideals by connecting them through out-of-text intertextuality with her own personal ideals and philosophical views–an aspect that the literature on narrative transportation theory has overlooked so far, but would warrant further, more detailed investigation at a different occasion.

The mission of Christopher seemed to be showing that at some point a long time ago, we got so far from what it's really all supposed to be about. He lived by example in showing that the best way to try to figure out, where we went wrong, would be to go back to when man lived in the wild, surviving only on his wits and his instincts. At the end, he made the ultimate sacrifice trying to figure out the answer for us–and he did–that we are social beings, who need companionship and society to be really happy. (FV)

I think that *Into the Wild* is a gentle mediation on the poetry of the road and the extent to which personal philosophy is coloured by our own bruised sensibilities (some people don't feel they deserve to be loved, says McCandless to the ageing hippie at one point) and drive to be free, primarily free of emotional attachment to people. It explores the thin line between idealism and escapism, freedom from and responsibility to others, and the degree to which our tendency to sleepwalk through our choices can sneak up on the ideal of living in the wild far from the modern society. (FV)

However, despite our different motivations for watching the movie and, subsequently, the different nature of our personal transportation experiences with *Into the Wild*, for both viewers watching a film is like being in a dream where we can enjoy the peaceful moment of loosing ourselves into the melodramatic narrative for awhile. Hence, both reviewers engaged in a certain routine of additional consumer behaviour to enhance their movie consumption experiences in advance. The female viewer, for example, discovered that the film was not shown in her local cinema, so that she had to carefully plan for a 1 hour train journey to the nearby city on the weekend, where the movie was actually screened. In order to make the trip worthwhile, she decided to meet up with friends and to go shopping, which she arranged around her main event–the cinematic movie experience.

I learnt that "*Into the Wild*" had only been released in Poitiers, which is an hour journey away from the town I live in. I decided to go there on the next weekend to watch the movie and to spend some time with my friends there. Before booking my train tickets, I first phoned the cinema to enquire about their time schedules for showing *Into the Wild*… The next weekend, I arrived on the morning to have lunch with my friends and do some shopping in the area before going to the cinema. But I did not ask them to go with me to the cinema, because I preferred to be on my own and not to share the movie experience with them for the simple reason that I didn't want to listen to other people's troubles, but to loose myself in the movie's story. (FV)

The male viewer also faced the difficulty that the film wasn't screened in a cinema nearby and had to consider a 50 minutes bus trip towards to a multiplex further away or to wait for the DVD release. Fortunately for him, the local arthouse cinema was showing *Into the Wild* (US 2007) four weeks later and he chose this option at the end. But this also turned out to be an advantage, as he prefers the more personal and intellectual atmosphere of arthouse cinemas in comparison to that of modern multiplexes, which he perceives to be noisy, commoditised and disrespectful to film as an art form with their blockbuster & popcorn diet. Interestingly, both viewers had in common that we prefer to watch movies on our own and not to share the experience with others. While this doesn't necessarily mean that we won't sometimes (but not always) discuss the movie with friends afterwards (!), both of us simply feel that the presence of friends during actually watching the film may only invite continuous comments or chats about private matters that disrupt or even prevent us from enjoying our transportation experiences. In fact, we experience all disruptive influences on our movie enjoyment, which also include late-comers, talking audience members, chatty teenagers and noisy families with kids running wild around, simply as quite annoying and frustrating.

I know only to well that many people decide to go to the cinema on a rather short notice and then often choose the respective movie on the spot–a regrettable habit that has probably emerged from the rise (and partial monopolisation) of the multiplexes and their brainless blockbuster & popcorn diet–but I'm not one of them. … The good thing about Kino [an arthouse cinema] is that it is visited by an older and more intellectual clientele, which means that the chance of being surrounded by consistently chatting teenagers, running kids and permanently interrupting insensible families, which has become such a common and annoying feature experience with the multiplexes, is close to zero. The diet of independent movies is anyway beyond their interest and intellectual horizon. Thus, the chance to genuinely and truly loose myself in the movie was quite good. (MV)

However, the movie consumption experience didn't stop for both viewers with watching the movie in the cinema. Instead, both of us engaged in efforts to transform our temporary, intangible movie experiences into tangible objects to prolong our enjoyment of the movie, its melodramatic narrative and its atmospheric audiovisual impression on our minds. Therefore, each of us enhanced our movie consumption experience by purchasing movie-related items and merchandising such as a CD of the soundtrack, an original cast-signed movie poster, movie stills and, maybe most important of them all, the movie itself on DVD. The overall aim of this kind of consumer behaviour enabled both viewers to experience the movie enjoyment either once again and/or to provide clues for remembering one's feelings from watching the movie for the first time.

The film went around in my head for days. I purchased on eBay this autographed movie poster, which was personally signed by the entire cast, to decorate the wall of my office directly over my desk. It still hangs there. In the meantime, I also bought on eBay the official press booklet for $2.99. And I placed already a pre-order on Amazon.com for the region 1 double-disc DVD pack of the film, which will be released on 4th March 2008. The region 2 DVD will be released in the UK one week later and I hope it will also be available in Ireland, because I intend to buy it for my collection as well. (MV)

I was interested in the awesome movie soundtrack of "*Into the Wild*" as well, which was so beautiful and so touching. Eddie Vedder of Pearl Jam was simply brilliant and deserves an Oscar for this effort. All the songs are just so powerful and bring back the deep emotion from the movie. It's simply amazing how Eddie Vedder wrote songs that fit perfectly with Christopher McCandless's story. However, I did not know the singer, but I knew how to deal with this problem. Indeed, I've gone through the same research process in relation to "*Blood Diamond*" in order to identify the singer's name on the Internet. Of course, my primary interest was to check for a free video on YouTube and, then, to buy the soundtrack on CD, because it remembers me of the movie–even if it was a little bit expensive. (FV)

As can be seen from the last extract, the soundtrack of the movie served to enhance the nature of the female viewer's experienced immersion into the movie melodramatic narrative based on her identification with the presented underlying philosophy on the human condition. Yet, not only had the musical soundtrack provided her with this kind of stimulation, but also the impressive and captivating cinematography of the Alaskan wilderness, which fascinated and drew her literally into the narrative. Urry (1990) proposed that, as an individual chooses to gaze upon a specific place, anticipation is sustained through a variety of distant non-tourist practices, such as films that construct and reinforce the gaze. In recent years, the *Lord of the Rings*-Trilogy and *Whale Rider* are known to have increased public awareness and demand among international tourists for travelling to New Zealand. Hence, by watching *Into the Wild* (US 2007), the female viewer experienced in her the growing desire to visit the shown landscape of Alaska in its natural beauty and purity herself as a tourist one day soon, which also stimulated an interested search on information about Alaska.

After watching Into the Wild, my interest in visiting Alaska has intensified. I was inspired to visit some of the locales and landscapes featured in the film. I learned about Alaska through the movie and I was positively influenced by the beautiful areas in the US displayed in "*Into the Wild*". (FV)

CONCLUSIONS

The study's findings clearly prove that movie enjoyment should be understood as a private lived consumption experience that depends on a holistic tapestry of interrelated factors and, subsequently, should be studied in its entire complexity. Subjective personal introspection offers hereby the potential for gaining interesting insights into the private domain of movie consumption that is less accessible to the traditional methods, which focus mainly on the collective domain. In line with previous studies, we found that an individual's personal emotional engagement with the narrative, its characters and underlying philosophy, which allow for the temporary immersion into the movie's world, is of particular importance for one's movie enjoyment. The level and nature of a consumer's experienced immersion into the movie narrative is determined less by age or gender, but by one's very private motives and interests.

The managerial implication of these findings is for film producers to stop heeding the calls of consultants (i.e. De Vany and Walls 2002; Eliashberg and Shugan 1997) for mass-produced, family-friendly, made-by-standard-formula movie packages that serve the smallest common denominator. As consumers want to enjoy the feeling of loosing themselves in the movie consumption experience for diverse personal and intimate motives, the narrative has to be challenging and stimulate personal engagement from a variety of different angles. This would require each movie to be created again as an artistic product rather than as an interchangeable commodity. The point seems to be supported in particular by the recent global success and the growing popularity of both independent films and world cinema movies that tend to provide audiences with unique, interesting, involving, challenging and much more demanding narratives than Hollywood's current standardised and family-friendly blockbuster-diet. Moreover, after loosing their former elitist image, arthouse cinemas and film-clubs in Europe are becoming increasingly popular alternatives to the multiplex cinema chains, which are often the vertically-integrated exhibition division of the major Hollywood studios (Kerrigan and Özbilgin 2002, 2004). Maybe, rather following the advice of accountants and consultants, it is time for film producers to listen again to real consumers as to how and why they enjoy watching movies in order to understand what movie consumption is really all about…

REFERENCES

Argo, Jennifer, Zhui Rui and Darren W. Dahl (2008), "Fact or Fiction: An Investigation of Empathy Differences in Response to Emotional Melodramatic Entertainment", *Journal of Consumer Research*, 34 (3), 614-23.

Basil, Michael D. (2001), "The Film Audience: Theater versus Video Consumers", *Advances in Consumer Research*, 28, 349-52.

Brown, Stephen (1998), "The Wind in the Wallows: Literary Theory, Autobiographical Criticism and Subjective Personal Introspection", *Advances in Consumer Research*, 25, 25-30.

Cohen, Jonathan (2001), "Defining Identification: A Theoretical Look at the Identification of Audiences with Media Characters", *Mass Communication & Society*, 4 (3), 245-64.

De Vany, Arthur and W. David Walls (2002), "Does Hollywood Make Too Many R-Rated Movies? Risk, Stochastic Dominance and the Illusion of Expectation", *Journal of Business*, 75 (3), 425-51.

Eliashberg, Jehoshua and Steven M. Shugan (1997), "Film Critics: Influencers or Predictors?", *Journal of Marketing*, 61 (1), 68-78.

Ellis, Carolyn (1991), "Sociological Introspection and Emotional Experience", *Symbolic Interaction*, 14 (1), 23-50.

Gerrig, Richard J. (1993), *Experiencing Narrative Worlds: On the Psychological Activities of Reading*, New Haven: Yale University Press.

Gould, Stephen J. (2006), "Comparing, Not Confirming Personal Introspection: A Comment on Woodside (2004)", *Psychology & Marketing*, 23 (3), 253-56.

Green, Melanie C. and Timothy C. Brock (2000), "The Role of Transportation in the Persuasiveness of Public Narratives", *Journal of Personality and Social Psychology*, 79 (5), 701-21.

Green, Melanie C., Timothy C. Brock and Geoff F. Kaufman (2004), "Understanding Media Enjoyment: The Role of Transportation into Narrative Worlds", *Communication Theory*, 14 (4), 311-27.

Hennig-Thurau, Thorsten, Gianfranco Walsh and Mathias Bode (2004), "Exporting Media Products: Understanding the Success and Failure of Hollywood Movies in Germany", *Advances in Consumer Research*, 31, 633-38.

Hirschman, Elizabeth C. (1999), "Applying Reader-Response Theory to a Television Program", *Advances in Consumer Research*, 26, 549-54.

Hirschman, Elizabeth C. (2000a), "Consumers' Use of Intertextuality and Archetypes", *Advances in Consumer Research*, 27, 57-63.

Hirschman, Elizabeth C. (2000b), *Heroes, Monsters & Messiahs: Movies and Television Shows as the Mythology of American Culture*, Kansas City: Andrews McMeel.

Holbrook, Morris B. (1995), *Consumer Research: Introspective Essays on the Study of Consumption*, London: Sage.

Holbrook, Morris B. and Elizabeth C. Hirschman (1982), "The Experiential Aspects of Consumption: Consumer Fantasies, Feelings and Fun", *Journal of Consumer Research*, 9 (2), 132-40.

Kerrigan, Finola and Mustafa F. Özbilgin (2002), "Art for the Masses or Art for the Few? Ethical Issues in Film Marketing in the UK", *International Journal of Non-Profit and Voluntary Sector Marketing*, 7 (2), 195-203.

Kerrigan, Finola and Mustafa F. Özbilgin (2004), "Film Marketing in Europe: Bridging the Gap Between Policy and Practice", *International Journal of Non-Profit and Voluntary Sector Marketing*, 9 (3), 229-237.

Krugman, Dean M. and Yasmin Gopal (1991), "In-Home Observations of Television and VCR Movie Rental Viewing", *Advances in Consumer Research*, 18, 143-49.

Merleau-Ponty, Maurice (1962/2002), *Phenomenology of Perception*, New York: Routledge.

Mulvey, Laura (1975), "Visual Pleasure and Narrative Cinema", *Screen*, 16 (3), 6-18.

Oatley, Keith (1999), "Meeting of Minds: Dialogue, Sympathy and Identification in Reading Fiction", *Poetics*, 26 (5-6), 439-54.

Patterson, Anthony, Stephen Brown, Lorna Stevens and Pauline Maclaran (1998), "Casting a Critical "I" Over Caffrey's Irish Ale: Soft Words, Strongly Spoken", *Journal of Marketing Management*, 14 (7-8), 733-48.

Phillips, Patrick (2003), "Spectator, Audience and Response", In: *An Introduction to Film Studies*, 3rd Edition, (Ed.) Nelmes, Jill, London: Routledge, 91-128.

Rapp, David N. and Richard J. Gerrig (2006), "Predilections for Narrative Outcomes: The Impact of Story Contexts and Reader Preferences", *Journal of Memory and Language*, 54 (1), 54-67.

Ravid, S. Abraham (1999), "Information, Blockbusters and Stars: A Study of the Film Industry", *Journal of Business*, 72 (4), 463-92.

Thompson, Craig J. (1997), "Interpreting Consumers: A Hermeneutical Framework for Deriving Marketing Insights from the Text of Consumers' Consumption Stories", *Journal of Marketing Research*, 34 (6), 438-55.

Thompson, Craig J., William B. Locander, and Howard R. Pollio (1989), "Putting Consumer Experiences Back into Consumer Research: The Philosophy and Method of Existential Phenomenology", *Journal of Consumer Research*, 16 (2), 133-46.

Urry, John (1990), *The Tourist Gaze: Leisure and Travel in Contemporary Societies*, London: Sage.

Wallendorf, Melanie and Brucks, Merrie (1993), "Introspection in Consumer Research: Implementation and Implications", *Journal of Consumer Research*, 20 (3), 339-59.

Wohlfeil, Markus and Whelan, Susan (2008), "Confessions of a Movie-Fan: Introspection into a Consumer's Experiential Consumption of 'Pride & Prejudice'", *European Advances in Consumer Research*, 8, 137-143.

Adults' Consumption of Videogames as Imaginative Escape From Routine

Mike Molesworth, Bournemouth University, UK

ABSTRACT

This paper considers the adult consumption of videogames as a form of escape from routine and often unsatisfactory aspects of consumers' everyday lives. Drawing from a phenomenological study of 24 adult players, I illustrate aspects of escapism through play, specifically: nostalgia; 'everyday' daydreams; media-derived fantasies, and; virtual tourism. I consider these themes in light of the sociology of consumption and of play to highlight adult videogame consumption as a significant trajectory of experiential economies where the market provides commodities that allow for the actualisation of the imagination.

A GROWN-UP VIDEOGAME MARKET

According to Mintel (2006a) UK videogame sales were £2,626m in 2006 and growing at 17%, significantly more than other leisure activities such as pre-recorded music, cinema, live entertainment, or visiting museums and galleries. Globally a similar picture is presented. Kolodny (2006) cites PricewaterhouseCoopers data that predicts that the 2010 global market for videogames may be worth $46.5billon. The message from this data and its reporting is that we should 'take videogames seriously' on the basis of their considerable economic contribution.

This market expansion also defies the popular view of videogames as the preoccupation of male teenagers, obsessively playing alone (see Poole, 2001). For example, the Entertainment Software Association's (2007) claims that the average age of players is now 33 and that less than a third are under 18. In the UK over half of adults between 20 and 55 play videogames at least occasionally (Mintel, 2006a) and 17% of adults (over 18) play video games in any one week Mintel (2006b). To reinforce the 'importance' of adult digital play, Mintel's (2006b) analysis of UK leisure highlights the very limited amount of time adults have for such activities. Leisure time is precious and more adults than in the past are choosing videogames to fill it. In this paper I therefore provide one account of what adults do with videogames. In doing so I note consumers' use of the imagination-aided by the consumption of technology-to 'escape' the limitations of everyday life.

THE CONSUMPTION OF THE IMAGINATION

It is easy to dismiss escapism as idle daydreaming. Yet there is an established body of work in consumer culture that places the imaginary at the heart of our consumer society. First let's consider imaginative play. The imagination is implicit in the most significant play theories of the 20th century. For example, it is seen in the non-materiality of the 'magic circle' articulated by Huizinga (1938) who goes on to argue for play as a foundation of culture, and in Caillois's (1958) *paidia*, the chaotic, 'free-play' that is the opposite of rule-bound *ludus*. Other theorists such as Turner (1982) and Schechner (1984) are more explicit about the role of imaginative play as an outlet for fantasies that cannot be actualised in everyday social life. Here, aesthetic endeavours are a way to 'deal with' societal issues in a way that is separate from everyday life.

This recognition of the significance of play of the imagination, according to Sutton-Smith (1997), has its roots in the Romantic period as a reaction against the growth of industrialisation and urban lifestyles. As thought and behaviour was increasingly ordered through work practices, a movement grew to free individuals from these constraints. And such a need to escape routine is a central focus of Cohen and Taylor's *Escape Attempts*, (1992). Their account of resistance to everyday life suggests that as individuals become aware of limitations in the apparently scripted life-plans that society gives them to follow, they seek various strategies to escape them.

What consumer researchers add to this is the detail of how the market now provides both the source material for this imagination, and activities that aid emancipation from routine. The call to consider the fantasy in consumption was first made 25 years ago by Holbrook and Hirschman (1982) and there is now a significant 'playful turn' in consumer research. For example, McCracken (1988) argues that goods may act as bridges to desired, but 'displaced' meanings. Individuals create idealised states of being in their imagination-a golden past, a utopian future, or a promised other land-that are then deliberately removed from the everyday context to avoid possibly that they are revealed as less than what is imagined. Commodities are then used to access these desirable daydreams. This suggests a speculative, 'wishing' mind, discontented with everyday arrangements, and seeking to actualise fantasy through consumption. The implication is that 'daydreaming' about commodities is more than simple distraction, but rather an activity for meaning making and personal transformation.

Campbell's (1987) sociology of consumption is also consistent with this discourse. He describes a 'modern hedonism' that has developed from a Protestant ethic that suppressed overt desires, and that flourished as indulgent imagination as a result of a Romantic influence. Consumers have therefore become dream-artists who: "*employ their creative, imaginative powers to construct mental images, which they consume for the intrinsic pleasure they provide*" (1987:77). This resonates with characteristics of play, especially Sutton-Smith's (1997) 'play of the imagination' that is based on the same Romantic foundations. For Campbell pleasure is derived from emotional experiences created by the imagination rather than physical ones, but 'modern hedonism' is not, as Boden & Williams (2002) suggest, only a disembodied-mentalist experience, but one where daydreaming *may* result in actualisation in the form of consumption. Consumer goods allow for daydreams to come true and therefore anchor abstract thoughts to the material world. In other words, daydreams are bolted onto material objects or experiences.

Although fantasy *may* feed from an unlimited use of the imagination–i.e. may have no grounding in material existence–such extremes are a problematic way of escaping mundane reality because they cannot transform that reality. As Belk Ger & Askegaard (2003) explain, desire requires there to be hope that the object of desire can be obtained. They also argue that desire is not attached to an object because of its intrinsic qualities, "*but on the consumers' own hopes for an altered state of being*" (Belk et al, 2003:348). Cohen and Taylor express it like this: "*Our sense of the specialness of our inner life, coupled with our fears about allowing it to 'run away with us' may lead us to attempt transformations of reality by bringing our fantasies into the real world. In other words, instead of allowing fantasies to be mere adjuncts to existing scripts, we actually set out to script our fantasies, to give some concrete expression to our imaginings.*" (1992:109)

For example I may happily desire a new car (and subsequent transformed life), but to desire to be a wizard or Jedi would 'normally' be 'futile'. Society therefore has established imagination 'norms', especially related to commodities. Yet Campbell also recognises the potential for novels, films and TV to provide individuals with the raw material for daydreams. We might now want to add videogames to Campbell's list of media and note that through these technologies, even the desire to do magic may be actualised. This is relatively new. The result, as has been previously argued (Molesworth & Denegri-Knott, 2007), is that there may be a continuum of imaginative labour from daydream to fantasy with varying degrees of potential for actualisation through both material and digital virtual consumption.

So play is at the heart of culture and now of our consumer society and videogames represent a trajectory towards the consumption of fantasy, aided by technology.

RESEARCH METHODS

To understand the lived experience of adult videogame consumption I draw on part of a larger phenomenological study of adult videogame consumption.

There has been growth in the acceptance of interpretive research methods in consumer behaviour over the last 20 years (Arnould & Thompson, 2005; Goulding 1999) with Thompson in particular becoming associated with phenomenology (Thompson, Locander & Pollio, 1989; Thompson 1990; Thompson, Pollio & Locander, 1994; Thompson, 1997) and other consumer researchers also drawing from the lived experiences of consumers. For example Belk and Costas' (1998) investigation of mountain man retreats; Kozinets's (2001) study of Star Trek culture; Kozinets's (2002) study of the Burning Man Festival; Holt's (2002) investigations into consumer resistance to brands; Belk, et al's (2003) investigation into consumer desire; Martin's (2004) study of *Magic the Gathering*, and; Stevens and Maclaren's (2005) study of the use of women's magazines to evoke the imagination. Such studies also provide example of the market's ability to either aids the 'escape', or re-imposes itself after a temporary, 'carnivalesque' period. The result is recognition in consumer research of a desire for escape from societal norms, and a range of interpretive approaches that might be used in such studies. I have drawn on such methods here.

Thompson et al (1989) explain that phenomenological interviews focus on actual experiences of the phenomena under investigation. A phenomenology then seeks to reveal patterns of experience or 'global themes' that are supported by direct references the reported experiences, and as a result the analysis remains closely tied to the specific data generated, and in the 'emic' world of the participant (Thompson et al, 1989). Hence the idea is to generate nuanced narratives of consumers' experiences rather than generalisable theory. The value of such accounts lies in the insight they provide into consumer experiences rather than predictive models.

For a phenomenology sampling is based on participants' ability to relate in detail their experiences of the phenomena under investigation. A small number of participants may be sufficient to arrive at global themes. For example, Thompson (1990) considers the lives of working women with reference to just four interviews; Woodruffe-Burton (1998) considers male shopping using case studies of three men, and; and Holt (2002) considers consumer resistance to brands using 12 participants. Ideally a researcher simply continues to talk with different participants until no new experiences are revealed so that 'exhausting' the range of experience is more important than large samples. For this study I interviewed a total of 24 adult videogame players from a range of social backgrounds, professions, and domestic arrangements in order to understand experiences of consuming videogames. Fieldwork took place in the South of England, over a 5 month period in 2006. Here I draw on the experiences of six participants as illustrative of the themes specifically relating to 'escapism'.

VIDEOGAME CONSUMPTION AND THE IMAGINATION

Four themes emerged from discussions with adult players in the context of escapism: a form of nostalgia; the enactment of 'daydreams' (aspects of people's lives that they would like to be true, or that they once desired, but now cannot hope to achieve in the material world); the exploration of fantasies that are beyond what they might ever experience in the material world, (but which may have been stimulated by books or films), and; the experience of novelty, through 'visiting another world'. I will now illustrate each.

Nostalgia (being as you were)

Most of players I spoke to re-played old games from time to time. For example Matthew is a 26 year-old Soldier who lives with his fiancé in a small house a few miles from the army base where he works. He has recently been posted in Bosnia and in the Middle East and has now decided to get married and leave the army. He explains that most of his friends live either some distance away, or on the base and therefore he seldom socialises with them. Throughout the interviews Matthew recalls playing videogames as a child and teenager. He also explains that he still plays some of these childhood games.

"I asked for the Amiga because what I wanted it for was the Football Manager game you see. And to this day I'm still a massive football manager fan…. And I actually got it for my laptop. I got Championship Manager 94, 95, you know. And it's not so much, it's not a great management game, well it was then, but you know compared to what you've got now, but it's just more the retro thing about going back and doing it. I sit and play; it's good fun. It kind of takes you back to be honest, to whenever you where that age, kind of thing."

Later Matthew tells me more about playing retro games:

"Nothing was better than Championship Manager you know. And that was me, my cousin and my mate, used to sit up for days on end….. And that's why it's on my computer. I guess it's trying to go back to that, but it doesn't feel the same. It's good and it's fun and it's enjoyable, but you know, it's more of a novelty. Whereas before it was…. Because you're not 17 any more. And because the games have progressed I would say. I mean, you're going back, I'm going back, say to Doom, after playing Halo, which is not necessarily the same game but is a game later on and they've evolved so much you know. But when you go back to it, it's not as good as now, At the time that was the best game on the market and it was the best game in the genre that you had and for me there was nothing that could compare at the time, but now there's an absolute host of games that are better, you know, but what they don't have is my cousin and my mate sat there, you know, at whatever age and drinking coke and eating sweets, and eating crisps, playing it, you know…. For me, I had an enjoyable childhood, you know, and even in my teenage years it was enjoyable you see, And I enjoyed it and I enjoyed doing that stuff, you know and ten years, twelve years on and it's responsibility."

Matthew explains a dissatisfaction with the re-experience of playing old games. He is drawn to play them to recapture an experience he remembers as pleasurable, but the experience doesn't live up to the memory that it allows him to access. This is a recurring theme amongst those players that re-played old games. Players have fond memories of games that may have taken up a significant amount of their younger years. They seek these out, often using emulators, but sometimes re-buying old consoles and games. But the reported experience of re-playing such games is ultimately of disappointment. The warm feeling of nostalgia that accompanies familiar graphics and controls soon fades. The 'problem' with nostalgic play is that players soon realise that 'things have moved on'. At the time players had never seen or experienced anything like it, but in subsequent years technology has developed and the things that make the game originally special, are now 'routine'. Perhaps more significantly, those that they played with are absent. Recognition of this prompts reflection on their own life that has continued along a plan they cannot now change.

Actualising daydreams (being a better you)

Players may look to games for experiences based on things they feel they should have done, but never actually achieved. So Matthew also tells me about playing military combat videogames, explaining why he enjoys such games, and comparing them to actual combat that he has not experienced despite his recent tours of duty.

"You never get to go what you do in the game. Apart from the select few that have been to war and actually done it, you never get to shoot back and this, that and the other, and be involved in real sort of dangerous situations. And I always sort of tell people when they ask, 'would you want to go to war, or would you want to, you know' and soldiers say 'yes'. And why would you want to do that, you say well you know 'would you want to train as a bricklayer and never build a wall', you know, it's what you've been trained for all this time. And you want to see what you are made of when it comes down to it."

Janice is a 39 year-old forklift and delivery driver who lives with her partner in the suburbs of a large city, a long and slow commute from her work. She explains her enduring interest in motor sport. Again she plays games, for example *Grand Turismo*, based on these activities as a substitute for driving in the material world, even though she seems clear that the games are in many ways an inferior experience:

"I enjoy driving and I've done single-seater racing car driving and I enjoy motorcycling, I enjoy going at speed. But you can't do that out on the highways and byways. But you can-it's escapism isn't it-like all of the games and stuff? It doesn't compare to the real thing really, because it's not you know, it's not the real thing is it, but it's as near as damn it and it's probably more than you are ever going to do. You are never going to be able to get into a top class car and drive round the streets of Paris or London or whatever, but it's just escapism isn't it and it's a matter of going at some speed...."

Later in the interview Janice returns to this idea:

"You can't do on the roads, or in my job, what I can do in the game. I can't get into a top class sports car and go hurtling down the road in a race and winning the pot of four grand. I can't do that at work. I take a box of black things over to someone so they can fill them and then bring them back again. At work I behave myself because I don't want to loose my licence and I don't want to loose my job."

Here Janice actualises her interest in racing through a videogame, recognising and overcoming what she perceives as impossibilities in her work and financial limitations of a low paid job. She cannot afford the exotic cars that she enjoys driving in games, or afford to risk losing her driving licence. Luke, a 29 year-old single web designer provides another account. Here at least part of his actions in videogames are about consumer daydreams that he may still hope to materially actualise. He talks a lot about sports and hobbies, and in particular about his interest in customising cars. He uses games to explore these interests:

"Need for Speed, I would say, has taught me a lot about cars. It's taught me what bits do what to some extent, what you can do to a car to change its performance, that kind of thing. It gives you an incentive to learn things in a way. You are virtually experiencing doing that thing. If they have got it anyway near right, then you will learn. You are not going to learn the handling obviously because there is no feel, but you do learn stuff about travelling on the road.... It's one of the reasons I buy them. It's what I'm interested in. It's a way to learn about things I'm interested in, so it's different to buying books on the subject [laughs] or actually doing them. I've got a Honda CRX, but I haven't done anything to it. I was going to change the air filter on it, maybe the exhaust, and take it from there.... But I would do it in Need for Speed, but I probably wouldn't go out and waste my money in reality [laughs]. That was the reason I bought it, was because I wanted a racing game.... And just this whole modifying thing.... It's crossed my mind to go out and modify the car, but I'm too sensible now, I've had a lot of debts in my time and I hate them so I won't put anything huge on my credit card even though I'd like to.... Because it's easier and cheaper in the game than trying to do it properly [laughs].... To some extent if you want to be at the top of the NBA, or whatever you can do it in a game, probably in a weekend, whereas in life all you are going to hit is rejection and well you might succeed, but the chances are small. So in the game you can achieve it, you know it's achievable, it's not just a pipe dream, sort of thing."

Everyday life seems to produce desires to do things that are not possible because of physical, legal, financial or time constraints. Some of these may be fleeting (a sudden urge to drive fast as a result of a frustrating traffic jam, tempered by threat of speed camera); some may be more enduring such as the desire to be good at sports. These may accumulate over years, yet never be acted on, leaving individuals with a sense of something that might have been and that may be re-visited through game-play. With other daydreams there may still be a hope of some achievement (when finances allow, for example). In various ways games seem to be a way for players to access these daydreams and in doing so keep them alive and/or compensate in some way for their inability to made them happen. This is a role for games that allows specific and managed access to the imagination.

Actualising fantasy (being someone else)

Although the interest of some gamers remains in the order of daydreams, for others games are pleasurable because they address more fantastic imaginings. For example Elaine is an 18 year-old student who lives in a cramped apartment with her divorced mother who often works long hours. They are under considerable financial hardship. Elaine explains that she has few friends and little money to go out socialising. She provides an account of playing *The Sims* that suggests that an individual may use the same game for both daydreaming about their future and to engage with a fiction-derived fantasy. She starts by explains how she creates the 'perfect' life:

"In The Sims I make my own life and it's like me but it's perfect. It's just the way you want your whole life to go, you can just make it happen. Ok, this is where I use the cheat codes, because you can give them lots of money [laughs].... A good house, they don't have to have a job, so they can spend all their time at home [laughs]..., the cheats I use mean that they don't have to cook meals, they don't have to sleep. And I spend the whole time I guess making friends with all of the ones already in the game, so it's just you can see what it would be like if your life was perfect."

Elaine then goes on to tell me about her other 'neighbourhoods' in *The Sims:*

"Well I've got two, I've got one called the Wizarding World, which has all Harry Potter characters in, as well as myself. And then I've got one called Sphera, out of Final Fantasy V. And I've got all of the characters from that in there.... I downloaded all sorts of things, so I can make them fly on broomsticks and things, which you couldn't normally do in the game. And I guess it's just unique and it's kind of like creating your own game. Or your own film. And you can have things go just the way you want them with characters from other things. I mean I've written–sorry about the Harry Potter fixation–fan fiction which is like 400 pages long at the moment, but I can just put that into The Sims and just make that happen. It just feels really good when you see it all done."

Max provides a similar story. He is a 31 year-old overseas PhD student who lives in student accommodation, isolated from friends and family. He explains an enduring interest in the *Star Wars* films and how games have allowed him to inhabit this 'universe'. Like Elaine, Max explains that he has his own version of the films 'in his head'. He has built and maintained his own fantasy space from the raw materials of Lucas's films. Max tells me in detail about many of the *Star Wars* games that he plays but there is a recurring theme:

Jedi Outcast is a game that I play. I've been playing it since it came out. I haven't finished it yet because it has some frustrating bits and then I just put the game away for months and don't touch it.... And Rebel Strike is just a game that I play for the quick fix, you know, flying around, shooting, destroying stuff. I don't like the tactical element in it. I think it's just that I can finally sit in an X-Wing or in a TIE-fighter and shoot stuff, because that's always been one of my dreams.

People gain access to other worlds and experiences through films and books. They come to know of these places and people (or creatures), but only in third person. However games may give them more direct access to these fantasies. They allow players to become the heroes of fictions, or to experience these worlds 'firsthand'. This seems to be a slightly different strategy for dealing with the mundane familiarity of everyday life. Rather than change aspects of that life and live out those changes in a game, players opt to negate the material world altogether in favour of some other type of 'ideal' existence, first imagined, then actualised through a videogame.

Virtual tourism (being somewhere different)

The final way in which these players articulated escapism was in terms of simply wanting to 'be somewhere else' or 'experience something new, beautiful, or exciting'. For example Carl is 40 year-old IT manager. He is married (for the second time) and has 3 children (2 from his first marriage). Carl explains that for him

games are a space away from demanding work and from his complicated family arrangements:

"If I am just having a stroll about in the game then I will play something like Breed where I can go anywhere and I'll just avoid the bad guys, I know where they are so I'll just avoid them and I might have a pop with my snipers rifle occasionally, but really while I'm in there I'm just seeing what is over the next hill. It's quite a clever game Breed is..., it's a bit more free form, which allows you then to take a stroll."

Later Carl returns to explaining the pleasure from simply taking in the beauty of a game.

"I mean sometimes the effects are just so beautifully done and so detailed in the way that they have been produced; how the sprites on the screen are actually detailed and there is a whole area of that that actually draws you into playing the game, you know. Yeh, the aesthetics of it is also something that's important. I suppose that's part of the 'what if'. I mean if I wander about in Breed it is partly the aesthetics, you know, the way that they have designed the building and some of the complexes, it's fascinating, you know. It's actually quite a beautiful game, in quite a raw way.... There is almost a beauty to it, you know the drop ship is like the drop ship out of Aliens with quite a square body and there is a practical feel to it that actually appeals to me and I think that's actually quite real you know."

Towards the end of one interview Carl explains a specific time in his life when he had a need to escape into another world; to 'get away!'

"I think for me personally it was about leaving the world behind. You can do that.... when I went through the divorce I would be at work at seven o'clock sometimes, doing legitimate stuff, but that was also one of my strategies for losing myself. But when I was at home then, especially when the children had gone to bed, I would play games, because I could turn the lights off and my whole world then would be what's on that screen and I could get very, very involved and it didn't involve the pain I was going through. I'm very sure there wasn't transference there. I didn't want to play violent games, so it wasn't me transferring my anger at my ex-wife into a game. I just wanted to get away from it. I wanted to be somewhere else. And in a non-physical way, that was a way of doing that."

Players report taking pleasure in exploring game worlds. Rather than acting out a daydream or fantasy, here the pleasure is in the unknown; the excitement of not knowing what comes next and of having no clear script to act out. So rather than actualising the imagination players are asking for their imagination to be stimulated. Again this may be taken as an attempt to somehow 'deal with' every day life. The same furnishings in the same house, the same desk in the same office, or same shop floor, the same routine tasks re-experienced every day may feed a desire to escape. And in Carl's case, the routine 'pain' of a failing marriage creates an especially strong desire to 'be somewhere else' and videogames facilitate this.

PLAY, THE IMAGINATION AND 'ESCAPE' FROM ROUTINE

I now want to consider the implications for such imagination-based consumption. I start by reviewing the consistency of these observations with existing 'Romantic' consumption theories and more broadly with theories of play. Here I argue that there is a need for more theoretical consideration of the interactive between consumption, the imagination *and technology*. I also want to consider possible critiques of such consumption activity, noting the tension between the libratory discourse of 'escape' and the market structuring of the imagination.

Players imagine times past, 'lost' and ideal futures, and fantastic worlds, both familiar and novel. In doing so they may temporally and spatially extend their existence in a series of digital virtual activities that seem to confirm McCracken's (1988) strategies for displaced meaning. We might also see such behaviour as contemporary examples of the 'escape attempts' articulated by Cohen and Taylor (1992). As they put it: "*At any moment it is as though we can throw a switch inside our heads and effect some bizarre adjustment to the concrete world which faces us–make horses fly, strip the women, assassinate the boss–or else conjure up an alternative reality...*" (1992:90). Only now the switch is on the console and not just in our head. Videogames provide various ways for the player to remove themselves from their everyday lives. As an ideal commodity form of our time (see Kline Dyer-Witheford & De Peuter, 2003) games therefore represent a significant point in consumer culture; not just a move from Fordism to experiential consumption, but perhaps to consumption as the actualisation of the imagination, aided by technology. In consuming videogames we are literally buying into our fantasies and this seems a solution to economic and material limitations in markets and in consumers themselves. There is almost no limit to what may be produced and consumed in the digital virtual spaces of videogames. This is also an expanded view of the consumer imagination that doesn't just desire novelty, or desire itself, but also craves the past, fantasy, or just to 'get away' from material reality. Videogames are therefore not trivial, but for there users are significant resources for the management of everyday life.

In terms of Caillois's (1958) broader sociology derived from play videogames and the experiences they create are a reflection of society's rules and freedoms. This idea is also articulated in iterative relationship between the aesthetic and the social that Turner (1982) and Schechner (1984) articulate. The popularity of videogames tells us something about the society we live in. We see adults dealing with a life-world that promises so much more than they might ever materially achieve. This is perhaps less a Romantic society (see Campbell, 1987) than one where consumers' imaginations are over-stimulated, (there is so much to want) in contrast to the reality of a rather mundane adult existence. They then look to marketised technology to bridge this gap.

For example Players find and re-play old games as a conscious way to access memories of pleasurable times in their lives that are now lost to them. However this is seldom a satisfactory approach as such memories provoke a realisation that the past may never be recreated; that they are stuck in their adult world. This is also McCracken's (1998) complaint against nostalgia as a suitable location for displaced meaning.

Other locations may be more suitable for successful actualisation. Games allow for the maintenance of a long-held interest in sport, driving or other 'possible' activity, allowing a player to maintain an interest, but at a distance. Players hold an ideal scenario in which, for example, they are a professional basketball player, or a skilled race driver. Games become a way to access many such desires. When they play, players may experience a temporary and partial actualisation of their daydreams without risk of 'breaking them' by subjecting them the harsh reality of material attempts at such activity with their legal, physical, or financial implications.

For others the media (books and films in particular) form the basis of an imaginary world that exists in their mind in some detail and which may then be enacted in a game. For this group of adults existing media narratives were articulated clearly (*Star Wars* and *Harry Potter)*. These 'public' fantasies are sufficiently detailed to allow them to be evoked in the imagination. Players may spend considerable time playing these games, diverting their attention from the circumstances of their daily lives. This is also like the form of distancing described by Cohen and Talyor. By being able to tell themselves that their everyday life isn't 'all they are', players may better manage the scripts of daily routine. And material commodities no longer limit such imaginative acts, as Campbell (1987) and others suggest in theories of imagination-based consumption. Now fantasy becomes that which may be consumed and the limit is the imaginations of writers and filmmakers who may produce fantastic adventures for us to fill our minds with, and then the skills of videogame producers who may create these worlds in a form that we may inhabit. The player is therefore involved in the sort of mental management of scripts that Cohen and Taylor (1992) articulate, balancing a 'mundane' and/or unsatisfactory existence with fantastic escapes.

Cohen and Taylor also see the holiday-that other favourite of the experiential economy-as a potential source of escape from routine and here videogames provide the opportunity for 'virtual tourism', (although perhaps tripism, the term Lehtonen and Maenpaa (1997) give to short recreation shopping excursions, is a better description). Players may take these trips for just an hour or so in the evening. The desire is to simply lose oneself in the spectacle of a previously unseen landscape. As Featherstone (1991) suggests of other contemporary consumer practice, it is controlled decontrolling; a measured and managed sense of other-worldliness, now enabled by technology. We might question the nature of authenticity in such activity. For example both Urry (1990) and Cohen and Taylor (1992) highlight that tourism for many has become the futile search for an authentic experience against the recognition of a manufactured lifestyle. But in games, authenticity is abandoned in favour of endless, novel manufactured worlds. The result is a space where players are free to enjoy an aesthetic experience, and to forget their paramount reality for a while (especially where this reality is depressing or unsatisfactory).

This may all sound liberating, but a critical analysis of such 'escapes' might present videogames as complex leisure 'pacifiers' like those described by Huxley in *Brave New World* (1932). Videogames combine aspects of *Soma, Centrifugal Bumble-puppy* and the *Feelies*; they may calm those frustrated with life, involve them in complex and expensive leisure consumption, and/or distract with interactive spectacle. They are a technological cure for the consumer ennui Shankar, Whittaker & Fitchett (2006) describe, leaving players to carry on with the rest of their life-script as planned. Yet we might note that much of their angst for a better life *results* from market and media derived desire. As consumer culture, games may therefore serve a conservative role, channeling resistance into activities that deflect criticism away from broader market ideology. Like other studies about emancipation from the routines of our *consumer society*, the conclusion is that such escape is ultimately 'futile'.

Yet when Cohen and Taylor re-evaluated their first edition of *Escape Attempts* they noted that they should have: "*shown rather more appreciation of the comic/heroic diversity of people's search for something outside paramount reality..., more sensitivity to the idea that the very activity of 'attempting' to escape is an imaginative way to understand more about the limitations of our world.*" (1992:28). Perhaps the same might be true of these players. In negotiating a mapped-out life with largely predictable scripts these players find ways of using videogames to 'cope' with the frustrations of life and their occasional recognition of its futility, to feed, experience and to actualize their imagination. To reduce players to a predictable 'alienated consumer' script would be a denial of their complex and nuanced life-worlds. Emancipation from the market may be an impossibly for these consumers, as might the material actualization of an 'ideal' life, but their skill and success in 'making the best of it' might still be acknowledged.

REFERENCES

Arnould, E. J. & Thompson, C. J. (2005). "Consumer culture Theory (CCT): Twenty Years of Research," *Journal of Consumer Research*, Vol. 31. (March). 868-882.

Belk R. W, Ger G. & Askeergard S. (2003). "The Fire of Desire: A multisided inquiry into consumer passion," *Journal of Consumer Research* Vol. 30. (December). 326-351.

Belk, R.W. & Costa, J.A. (1998). "The mountain man myth: a contemporary consuming fantasy," *Journal of Consumer Research*. Vol. 25. (December). 218-40.

Boden S. & Williams, S. (2002). "Consumption and Emotion: The Romantic Ethic Revisited." *Sociology*. Vol. 36. No. 3. 493-512.

Caillois, R. (1958). *Man Play and Games*. Urbana and Chicago: UIP.

Campbell, C. (1987). *The Romantic Ethic and the Spirit of Modern Consumerism*. London: Blackwell-IDEAS.

Cohen, S. & Taylor, L. (1992), *Escape Attempts: the Theory and Practice of Resistance to Everyday Life*. London: Routledge.

Entertainment Software Association. (2007). Downloaded from www.theesa.com/facts/gamer_data.php , accessed July 26th.

Featherstone, M. (1991). *Consumer Culture & Postmodernism*, UK: Sage Publications.

Goulding, C. (1999). Consumer research, interpretive paradigms and methodological ambiguities. European Journal of Marketing, Vol. 33. Issue 9/10. 859-881

Holbrook, M. B. & Hirschman, E.C (1982). "The Experiential Aspects of Consumption: Consumer Fantasies, Feelings, and Fun," *Journal of Consumer Research*, Vol 9 (September).132-140.

Holt, D.B. (2002) "Why do brands cause trouble? A dialectical theory of consumer culture and branding," *Journal of Consumer Research*. Vol. 31. (June). 1-26

Huizinga, J. (1955). *Homo Ludens: a study of the play element in culture*, Boston: The Beacon Press.

Huxley, A. (1932). *Brave New World*. London: Harper.

Kline, S., Dyer-Witheford, N. & de Peuter, G. (2003). *Digital Play, The Interaction of Technology, Culture, and Marketing*, Montreal: McGill-Queen's University Press

Kolodny, L. (2006). "Global Video Game Market Set to Explode." *Business Week*. June 23rd.

Kozinets, R. (2001). "Utopian Enterprise: articulating the meanings of Star Treks Culture of Consumption." *Journal of Consumer Research*. Vol. 28. (June). 67-89.

Kozinets, R (2002). "Can Consumers Escape the Market? Emancipatory Illuminations from Burning Man." *Journal of Consumer Research*. Vol. 29. (June). 20-38.

Lehtonen, T-K. & Maenpaa, P. (1997). "Shopping in the east centre mall." In. Falk, P. & Campbell, C. (eds) *The Shopping Experience*. London: Sage.

Martin, B. A. (2004). "Using the Imagination: consumer evoking and thematizing of the fantastic imaginary." *Journal of Consumer Research*. Vol. 31. (June). 136-149.

McCracken, G. (1988) *Culture & Consumption*, Bloomington: University of Indiana Press.

Mintel. (2006a). *Video and Computer Games*. September.

Mintel. (2006b). *Leisure Time–UK*. February.

Molesworth, M. & Denegri-Knott, J. (2007). "Digital Play and the Actualisation of the Consumer Imagination." *Games and Culture*. Vol. 2. No. 1. 114-133.

Poole, S. (2001). *Trigger Happy*. London: Fourth Estate.

Schechner, R. (1988) *Performance Theory*. London and New York: Routledge.

Shankar, A., Whittaker, J. & Fitchett, J.A. (2006). "Heaven knows I'm miserable now." *Marketing Theory*. Vol. 6. No. 4. 485-505.

Stevens, L, & Maclaran, P, (2005), "Exploring the 'Shopping Imaginary': the dream world of women's magazines." *Journal of Consumer Behaviour*. Vol. 4. No. 4. 282-292.

Sutton-Smith, B. (1997). *The Ambiguity of Play*. USA: Harvard.

Thompson, C. J., Locander, W. B. & Pollio, H. R. (1989). "Putting Consumer Experiences Back into Consumer Research: the philosophy and method of existential-phenomenology." *Journal of Consumer Research*. Vol. 16. (September). 133-146

Thompson, C. J. (1997). "Interpreting Consumers: a hermeneutical framework for deriving marketing insights from the texts of consumers' consumption stories." *Journal of Marketing Research*. Vol. 34. No. 4. 438-455.

Thompson, C. J. (1990). "The Lived Meaning of Free Choice: an existential-phenomenological description of everyday consumer experiences of contemporary married women." *Journal of Consumer Research*. Vol. 17. (December). 346-361.

Thompson, C. J., Pollio, H. R. & Locander, W. B. (1994). "The Spoken and the Unspoken: a hermeneutic approach to understanding the cultural viewpoints and underlie consumers' expressed meanings." *Journal of Consumer Research*. Vol. 21. (December). 432-452.

Turner, V. (1982). *From Ritual to Theatre: The human seriousness of play*. New York: PAJ Publications.

Urry, J. (1990). *The Tourist Gaze*. London: Sage.

Woodruffe-Burton, H. (1998). "Private desires, public display: Consumption, postmodernism and fashion's 'new man'." *International Journal of Retail Distribution Management*. Vol. 26. Iss. 6. 301-.

Baby-blue "Bullet-proof" Satin Bras: The Excursion Into The Soviet Consumer Realities

Natasha Tolstikova, University of Gloucestershire, UK

INTRODUCTION

Researchers debate if consumer culture in the Soviet Union was a valid phenomenon. Traditional Western view on consumption in the Soviet Union is captured in the statement by Karpova et al (2007). The authors argue that in the Soviet planned economy neither marketplace nor consumers existed in the Western understanding of the terms, mainly because the freedom of choice did not exist (106). However, several researchers demonstrated that Soviet consumer culture, albeit different from that of the Western one, was valid and existed throughout, citing a number of manifestations and elements (e.g. Reid (2002); Kelly and Volkov (1998); Cox (2003)). At the start, it was characterized by shortages and later by the black market; consumer culture has manifested itself through such powerful consumer drives and desires that in post-Soviet times it resulted in the explosion of the market economy. To satisfy purists, we shall call this phenomenon "para-consumer culture," where the state encouraged the population "to consume in *particular* ways" (Reid 2002, 216) and consumers were skillful in obtaining and interacting with the goods.

To study particulars of Soviet consumer realities has an additional allure because it becomes an arena of the struggle between an ordinary citizen and the state, thus destroying the myth of totality in the totalitarian state. "It was . . . in the everyday that the grand master narrative of the Soviet Union moved in a Bakhtinian sense from the monologic to the polylogic as Soviet citizens proceeded to reformulate or subvert it–not with the intent of bringing down the system, but simply to buy a decent pair of shoes" (Baker 1999, 22). Some researchers argue that it was shortages of goods and faulty distribution that eroded Socialist economies and led to the collapse of the whole system (i.e. Reid 2002).

For the most part of the Soviet history everyday mundane objects such as underwear and undergarments have been ignored or neglected by the economy. The state also instilled certain policies toward underwear not only through its limited production but also though non-action: by ignoring the issue. Yet, the people's attitudes toward underwear demonstrate a complex web of ingenuity, creativity, and desires. Understandably, there was no need to advertise for the item produced in limited quantities. However, a few images were uncovered. This paper analyses the history, representation, and meaning of Soviet women's underwear as a manifestation of consumer attitudes and resistance.

This article claims that the gradual strengthening of the Soviet consumer culture was evident in changing social beliefs and attitudes evident in advertising. These changes were reflected in the visual and verbal gestalt of the advertisements. The paper analyzes four advertising posters corresponding to the leadership periods of Lenin, Stalin, Khrushchev, and Brezhnev. Using historical analysis and textual reading, it provides a contextual background to the images that act as "bearers of meaning, reflecting broad societal, cultural and ideological codes" (Schroeder 2006, 9). My method rests upon the iconographic approach envisioned by Panofsky and interpreted by Leeuwen (2001).

Unlike most semiotic analyses that are concerned with signs and their relationships, iconography additionally is preoccupied with the context and "how and why cultural meanings of their visual expressions come about historically" (92). There are three levels of pictorial meaning: representational (similar to "decoding" or description of the images), iconographical symbolism (or relation between objects and signs that concentrates on the concepts attached to images), and iconological symbolism (that identifies ideological meaning of the image) (ibid, 100-101). My analysis will be employed along these three dimensions.

BRIEF HISTORY OF WESTERN WOMEN'S UNDERWEAR

There are two prevalent positions explaining the reason for undergarments to come about: symbolic and practical. Saint-Laurent argued that "the birth of [under]clothing must be placed between that of religion and art, it cannot be compared with weapons, hunting implements or agricultural tools" (1974, 7). As such, social classes signified their status through different wears; different sexes who sported same type of outer clothing (such as togas in Ancient Greece) wore underclothes that were strictly feminine and masculine (36). The other theory holds that early underwear appeared for the reason of protecting the bodies from scratchy and stiff fabric of outerwear and also of protecting expensive costumes "from the dirt of the bodies they adorned" (Wilson 2003, 102). The early underwear did not even resemble contemporary lingerie; in ancient times women wore slips that progressed to Victorian bifurcated undergarments (not, however, connected at the crotch) (Entwistle 2000). Women's panties in a contemporary form appeared only in the 20th century (Wilson 2003, 102). Whatever the start was, fairly quickly it gained one more function: women's underwear became a tool of seduction, turning into the kind of clothing that is "more naked than nudity" (Carter 1982, 97). Already in the late Victorian era the appearance and meaning of women's underwear changed, making it "more elaborate and sexually codified" (Entwistle 2000, 203). Its mere proximity to the skin and its intricate construction with lace, frills, and see-though fabrics made it erotically charged. Particularly, stockings has been a common sex fetish (ibid, 204).

Historically, underwear has been a personal item, visible only to the wearer and to intimate partners. The wide universe of lingerie: panties and brasseries, stockings and garter belts, corsets and girdles long have been mechanisms of transforming the woman's body into a fashionable shape. With its enhancements, such as pads and whale bones, undergarments have been deceptive by nature; "their function is to make artificial shape seem real" (Saint-Laurent 1974, 68). Jantsen et al. argued that undergarments have been instruments of containment and control of women's bodies that made them fit the "aesthetic ideals and political concerns of a male-dominated society" (2007: 178). At the same time, their article demonstrates that lingerie empowers women even when she is not in public (ibid).

Curiously, lingerie becomes a meeting point for the public and the private, where outerwear signifies the public and underwear stands for the private. Historically, the first undergarments were originally outer garments (Saint-Laurent 1974, 12). While the underwear grew in numbers and complexity, it was intermittently worn either under the clothes or over the clothes (i.e., according to Renaissance fashion, the bustier was worn over the dress). The distinction is fluid. In the Western culture of the 20th century the deliberate visibility of underwear parallels "ambiguity surrounding privacy, intimacy and sexuality" (Wilson 2003, 107).

Generally, advertising is designed to stir emotions and desires in its target. At first, advertising for underwear was rather modest, praising functionality of the product. At the end of the 19th century, American advertising for corsets emphasized their ability to enhance one's figure as well as the comfort and ease of wear (Reichert 2003, 56-60). But soon the practicality was replaced by sensuality and seductive abilities of underwear. By the 1900s, advertisements for stockings commonly displayed women lifting their hems to show off the product (ibid, 83). With the increase in variety of underwear brands, their promotion became more explicit and suggestive, relying on sexual images that activate biological instincts. In his study of sexual images in advertising, Reichert suggested that women in undergarments have been often used as an allure for selling everything—including products that have nothing to do with neither women, nor underwear (ibid).

SOVIET UNDERWEAR

The Bolsheviks had an aspiration to build a new society where the personal would be eliminated and equal citizens would enjoy collective property. Reportedly in the early Soviet communes people shared not only pots and pans but personal clothing, including underwear (see Tolstikova 2001). The ideology of eradicating distinctions between sexes was reflected in the style of the New Soviet body and the style of clothing. The cult of muscular bodies and asceticism was manifested in mass sports parades and unisex clothing, particularly underwear. There were two main unisex items of Soviet underwear, knitted cotton undershirts and boxers which meant to signify comfort, ease of movement, simplicity, and hygiene. Practical Soviet women underwear was designed to better serve the new roles of women's physical activities in the factory and the kitchen (Abrahams, 2006). In the process of creating a New Soviet person, Soviet sexes were merging; a woman meant to be attractive not because of her sexual attributes (highlighted by sexualized underwear), but through her class dignity (Bulgakova 2002).

A woman could easily become an ideological suspect for wearing a dress adorned with frills or silk stockings (Starshinina 2007). In the 1930s, when the country began to militarize, the garment industries worked overtime, producing military uniforms in massive quantities with men's underwear as a part of it. Although, women's underwear was produced as well, the outputs were very limited and it was difficult to buy. As in pre-Industrialization period, women continued to sew their undergarments themselves or to seek services of private seamstresses (ibid). In the planned economy, standards for women underwear were limited. In the 1940, it assumed a single prototype of a brasserie with three sizes (Sevriukova 2006). In the West, since 1920s artificial silk became the fabric of choice for producing intricate underwear and stockings, making them affordable for the masses (Ewing 1974, 88). Similar Soviet items were made of natural fibers such as cotton and wool making them practical but unappealing and even uncomfortable.

In the 1950s, Stalin wanted to project an image of imminent abundance in the desolated war-torn country. Artificial fibers began to be used by consumer industries introducing a Soviet equivalent of nylon—kapron (Fillipov 2007). For the first time, Soviet women could experience an affordable luxury, see-through, sleek, leg-shaping kapron stockings. Nevertheless, women exposed to foreign lingerie in the Second World War became weary of the unseemliness of their underwear. In public perception, undergarments were almost obscene; semantics reflected this attitude—people referred to the specific types by their folk nicknames, such as "the anthracite" for the men's cotton black boxers or "the bullet-proof" for reinforced blue satin bras (Anon 2004-2005). According to the Soviet oral mythology, in the late 1950s, a French movie actor, either Yves Montand or Gérard Philipe or Alain Delon (the mythological details vary depending on the speaker) was so shocked by Soviet underwear that he bought it in large quantities and created a

sensation by displaying his private collection in Paris (Sevriukova 2006).

Soviet attitude towards underclothing was ambiguous. Women were ashamed of its plainness, and while wearing it they exercised rules of modesty. Nevertheless, bras and panties, sometimes, very unsightly, worn and mended, without a shame were hanged outdoors or in communal hallways to dry up after the wash. There was a paradox of chastity bordering on sanctimony when people ignored or even pretended not to notice each other underpants openly displayed in the communal spaces. Because specialized clothing such as swimming or sports suits was difficult to come by, both women and men often wore underwear as outerwear when working on their garden plots, swam or sunbathed (Starshinina 2007), creating ambiguity between private and public.

Living in the system where apparel industries produced uniform-style clothing, and perhaps, because they were forced to have public existence, Soviet women wanted to make their underwear different and distinct. There were few choices available to express their individuality through the underwear. Those, lucky to have a slender built preferred to shop in children's departments: made from multi colored fabrics, the panties for girls was more appealing that adult underwear. In home economics classes, schoolgirls learned how to sew panties; they often made them from colorful calico and adorned with ribbons and lace (Denisova 2002). When a Soviet person was going abroad, usually on business, his female relatives supplied him with a list of everybody's measurements of waists, chests, and the lower bodies so women were able to establish their uniqueness and if not to express their identity, at least to differentiate themselves from others (Culloudon 2004).

The Soviet state tried to control all aspects of human existence, including the underwear. The system supplied the utilitarian bare necessities, depriving women of the symbolic and the sensual. However, after Stalin's death Khrushchev came to power and lifted the symbolic Iron Curtain, exposing the country to foreign fashions, images, and culture. As a by-product, during the 1960s period nicknamed A Thaw, the culture of romanticism with its symbolism and anti-materialism took hold (see Tolstikova 2001). However Brezhnev's times brought individualism, erasing the altruistic revolutionary spirit. The long neglect of consumer desires made some authors to suggest that underwear was never advertised (Culloudon 2004). Using recently published collections of Soviet advertising posters, I was able to uncover a few examples. Soviet underwear advertising reflected the trend shift from the functional to the symbolic. Advertising examples from different eras will provide the visual proof of this transformation.

ANALYSIS

The first example is an agitation poster from 1934 by A. Kokorekin (Snopkov et al. 2004, 158) (Figure 1). The country was in the midst of industrialization with large population migrating to urban centers (Filtzer, 1999). Women had important roles as able-bodied workers and procreators of future generations. The poster propagates physical culture among women. On a representational level, there is a woman in her black underwear in a household setting doing an exercise routine. There is a window behind her and a Vienna back chair with a kitchen towel hanging from it. What looks like a domestic striped rug lies underneath her white sports slippers. The vertical panel on the right shows different exercises for the routine with the words underneath "Daily physical exercise routine–necessary for passing the physical state norms." The slogan underneath the image states "Be ready for labor and defense!"

Iconographic symbolism that reflects relations between objects signifies the importance of the woman; her stocky and muscular figure with spread arms occupies the center of the poster.

FIGURE 1

FIGURE 2

Traditional fascination with pale refined beauties gave way to respect for the red cheek healthy ideals. The strength of the woman's body symbolizes the changed roles of women in a proletarian state and the importance of being physically fit and ready to land her hand to the cause of building the new world order. She, nevertheless, exhibits traditional female traits: she retained long hair gathered in the back of her head, her home is tidy and clean, the kitchen towel is pristine white. The picture is also connected with the future: a traditional peasant physique of a woman is exposed to urban industrial landscapes in her background.

Because it is an example of political agitation, iconological symbolism or ideological meaning of the image, reflects in straightforward verbal propaganda of the text. With particular interest to our central concern, the underwear, there is an affirmation of the naturalness of the women's body minus its carnal attributes. The woman is primary a worker and a mother, an equal social participant approaching a man in physicality. She wears black underwear that

in Western societies is synonymous with naughtiness (Carter 1974, 96) but was used as sports wear in Soviet Russia on the 1930s. The woman is comfortable in her body and wants to improve it for physical labor. The underwear here is a functional utilitarian item.

The second image is the advertising poster from 1952 by V. Pimenov (Snopkov et al. 2007, 224) (Figure 2). Stalin was still in power, the country was recovering from devastations of the war. Propagating "the myth of abundance," Stalin forged an ideological consensus with the party elite by improving their everyday life with consumer goods (Fitzler 1999). Developments in chemistry secured new consumer products; one example was women's stockings. At the first, representational level of the image, we see an upper body of a woman in a frontal position wearing a short-sleeved dress and showing a sheer stocking to the viewer. She occupies the center of the poster, done in a lavender-pink palette. She looks directly at the viewer; her lips are slightly parted into a tentative smile. The headline states, "Kapron stockings. Beautiful, durable, hygienic." The word "kapron" is in large red cursive serif whereas

FIGURE 3

the rest is in white blocky sans serif on a pink background. The text on top identifies the distributor, "The Ministry of the Light Industry of U.S.S.R. Moscow Distributor of Sewing Goods." Typical of Soviet merchandize world, there is no brand name or trade mark; we cannot even be sure that the stockings were Soviet made.

Iconographic symbolism of colors tied stockings to delight and calmness; curved lines and the delicacy with which the woman's hands hold the stocking probably elicited association with femininity and exquisiteness of the product. The oversized lettering of the product name and a half-smile of the model hinted at the reserved excitement about the product. Her style of dress suggests casual environment thus she is probably not a sales clerk but a perspective user. However, rather than showing the product in use, the poster demonstrates a mere existence of the product somewhere in the Soviet universe.

The artistic style and colors inform ideological symbolism. Through the realistic style the woman depicted in this advertisement communicates qualities of an exemplary Soviet woman; she is modest, her dress is not revealing or seductive yet she is fit; she does not wear any cosmetics or jewelry yet her eyebrows suggest that they have been tweezed; her casual interaction with the stocking demonstrates her sedated joy. Her eyes look directly communicating equality with the viewer thus expressing the principals of collectivity. Even in Soviet fashion one is expected to be modest and simple: the ideology of collectivism prohibited anybody to stand out from the masses (Vainshtein 1996, 71). This woman is rather a display prop for the Soviet stockings. The heart palpitations are non-detectable in this image of a woman who came into a physical contact with the product that is known to have magical transformation capabilities for the female consumer. The stocking can be replaced by any other Soviet product without compromising its general message, "Life is becoming ever better and more joyous!" (the often cited Stalin 1936 quote). This advertising poster possesses "grandeur of purpose" and "somber dignity."

The third image is an advertising poster from 1966 by S. Lapaev (Snopkov et al. 2007, 238) (Figure 3). Technically, Khrushchev was already ousted but the initiatives that he had started had long lasting effects. Khrushchev wanted to restore the Communist ideals through changing ideological discourse and by spreading state authority into consumption, taste and fashion, areas of life considered private in other societies (Reid 2002: 216). Youth's cultural values of romanticism and enthusiasm manifested in developing new virgin territories but also were signified by the "softer" artistic styles (see Tolstikova 2001). On a representational level the advertising image is a drawing of female legs below the knee from the back angle. The rest of the woman is invisible to the viewer. She wears white heels and a sheer skirt/dress/slip. The white background has an abstract spot in grey with a thistle "catching" a stocking which the woman tries to untangle with her hand. The headline reads, "Seamless kapron stockings fashionable and inexpensive." The advertiser, "The Russian Clothing Distributor of the Ministry of the Trade or R.S.F.S.R," is identified with a barely readable text in a vertical side line in the lower right corner. There are five different typefaces used in this advertisement: two of them are serifs and three are sans serifs.

Body cropping/symbolic dismemberment has been a persistent topic in the analysis of Western advertising images (e.g. Kilbourne 1999). The theory holds that when a woman is represented by just a body part, this symbolically signifies that her body is separated from her mind and she ceased to be a whole person and therefore she looses her individuality (Cortese 2005, 38). The iconographic symbolism of this image rests on the assumption that S. Lapaev had chosen to concentrate on female legs for the purpose of calling attention to the product in use—it calls to the viewer to witness how beautiful it makes women's legs, but also how delicate the product is (but inexpensive too, even if it is damaged by a thistle there will be no trouble to replace it!). Traditionally in art, "the special sexual emphasis was given to women's legs" (Berger 1972, 138). However, in this case rather than evoking sexual feelings, the visual details celebrate sensuality and romanticism—the angle, the sheerness of the hem, and even the thistle.

The iconological symbolism of this image is a mix of contradictory signs. On the one hand it speaks of modernity (typography, abstractedness of the thistle), elegance and femininity (elongated limbs, dainty gesture of releasing the stocking), sensuality (forces a viewer to concentrate on female legs), and dynamism (the movement rather than stationary position of the 1952 woman). In short the image signifies a new reality by challenging the suffocating

FIGURE 4

artistic Socialist Realist canons. On the other hand, rather than being abstractedly indifferent as in the 1952 advertisement, the depiction is more realistic through a narrative (a thistle).

The final image is a 1965 advertising poster by E. Filimonov (Snopkov et al. 2007, 239) (Figure 4). Brezhnev was already in power and the image reflects the values propagated. Already by the 1960s the state had realized the impossibility of the speedy achievement of Communism; both ideologically and economically the country was in stagnation. The acquisitiveness of material goods intensified. For the first time in the history of the Soviet ideology, material possessions lost its negative connotations. Collectivist socialist ideas had gradually been replaced by individualism (Millar 1985: 703). The poster depicts a female silhouette wearing a fitted pink see-through flowing camisole on a black background. The heading underneath the image states, "Rayon lingerie, elegant and practical." The producer is identified as The Ministry of the Trade of the Russian Federation. The "female" curves to the back in a coquettish pose, her eyes are turned downward; her arms are stretched to the front and rolled toward her body. She has a full figure with small waist. There are no legs depicted below the hem. The "female" has long hair that falls below the shoulders. Her underwear is visible through the transparent rayon of the camisole.

On the iconographic level, there is a stark contrast between the pink of camisole and the black of background which makes the product to stand out. The pose of the figure is artificial, allowing for demonstration of the details of the camisole, such as its transparency, lace details of the bodice and hem. The "female" is depicted alone in her intimate moment. Unlike women in the 1952 advertisement, she is not only the user of the product but she is emotionally involved with the product, apparently enjoying herself. E. Filimonov chose to represent this user in a "dream-like" image, allowing the imagination of the viewer to do additional work. This depiction of a curvaceous female figure in her undergarments is an open advertising text suggesting sensuality, sex appeal, and fantasy on the part of the viewer, thus opening the dialogic space.

The iconological symbolism of the image suggests the "softening" of the official ideology toward women by recognizing their feminine appeal and even the right to being sex objects. The contrasting colors attest to the courage to deal with the issue. Factors such as the soft curves of the "female," manner of representation, chosen point of view (suggesting to the viewer this intimate image as if by accident)—all speak of increasing importance of femininity and recognition of privacy in the society. The clear enjoyment of the product by the subject of the advertisement signifies the growing significance of consumer goods and more favorable attitude toward personal possessions.

IDEOLOGICAL ROLE OF ADVERTISING IN THE SOVIET SYSTEM

In the immediate post-revolutionary years, advertising techniques were used to create ideological agitation and propaganda. For only a few years in the 1920s, the private trade enjoyed a temporary comeback with explosion of street advertisements. After much debates about the role of the advertising under Soviet conditions, whether this capitalist tool should be adopted for different realities (e.g. Tolstikova 2007), the purposes of the socialist advertising were officially defined in 1957 by a Conference of Advertising Workers of Socialist Countries; they were to inform the rational norms of consumption, to assist trade, and, lastly, to educate consumers' taste (Crowley and Reid 2000, 10-11). Everything that was published in the Soviet Union, be it an article, a book or an advertisement, was authorized by the state—the state was the advertiser and the advertising agency. There were no disagreements between the client and the executor, since they were the same.

Rather than create excitement and desire for the product, the post-war Soviet advertising transmitted the rationality of a material world of Soviet goods. It was important for Soviet advertising to communicate the idea that there were enough material goods for every Soviet consumer. Under these conditions, material goods symbolized the stability of a peaceful Soviet existence. It was often enough to show that the product was simply available (Sal'nikova 2001, 174-175).

Not surprisingly, food was the top priority for the long deprived population. In 1948 Food Advertising Organization, started to dress "the shop window of socialism" perpetuating the "myth of abundance" (Shkliaruk 2007, 6). Print advertisements depicted oversized tins of crabs and champagne floating in the air and sometimes smiling citizens next to the products. The depiction of an idealized product was intended to create delight and admiration in the customer used to asceticism of the war period.

Khrushchev's increased output of consumer industries which often resulted in surpluses urged the improvement of product distribution. He considered advertising to be an important tool of the newly developing Soviet marketing that helped to move the goods (c.f. Goldman 1963). Advertising of the 1960s operated under a slogan "Soviet means excellent!" and carried a symbolic meaning of priorities of socialism over capitalism.

The Soviet character prohibited a person from demonstrating extreme desires for material goods therefore Soviet advertising exhibited restraint. The purpose of socialist advertising was not to generate consumer desires but to promote "rational consumption" (Reid 2002, 218). In Stalin's time, advertising did not surprise or entertain but attracted the consumer's attention to mostly food items, such as vitamins, fish oil, or toothpaste that would be nutritious for restoring or maintaining health. Advertising photographs were rare; illustrations drawn in the style of Socialist Realism were more likely to promote the idea of abundance. Khrushchev's regime had a goal of modernizing the country not only through industrialization but through daily life. The realistic representational style of the earlier advertising became inappropriate for the Khrushchev's Communism project. It required artistic laconism and allowed empty spaces (Shkliaruk 2007, 7).

The advertisements analyzed are advertising posters. Posters were large, colorful and were displayed near the point of purchase, inside the shops. Unlike in the West where in-store advertising would serve as a reminder and an encouragement for a purchase, Soviet advertisements often served as a visual replacement for the physical merchandize (Shkliaruk 2007, 6). Advertising posters were consumed in the public space of a store; depending on its specific location customers either glanced at it briefly or looked it at intently if they happened to have it in their view when they stood in line. During Stalin's era they demonstrated the promised abundance, during Khrushchev's they were the window into Communism where citizens were to have everything and during Brezhnev's they were empty signs or meaningless decorations.

DISCUSSION

Comparison of the four advertisements demonstrates the changes that, on one level, can be explained with the internal historical trends, namely with changing Soviet values and attitudes. Ideological perception of women's social roles evolved from an equal partner to the proletarian man to the traditional view where a woman was perceived as a vessel for a new life to modern patriarchal where external values such as good looks and fashion started to be important. The analysis also reveals the changes in Soviet advertising from ideological propaganda to a neutral store window to a communication vehicle for symbolism. But, on another level, the changes can also be attributed to macro historical developments. Martens and Casey (2007) argue that after the World War II, the winning countries encountered affluence which was more pronounced in the West where consumption shifted away from the practical/functional to luxury/symbolic (220). Apparently, similar processes manifested itself in the Soviet Union. The attitudes toward individual consumption were changing; contemporary Soviet advertising reflected the changes and confirmed the trend.

REFERENCES

Abrahams, Marc (2006), "Red stars and bras," *Education Guardian Weekly*, 21 February, http://education.guardian.co.uk/egweekly/story/0,,1713784,00.html, last assessed on 8 February 2008.

Anon (2004-2005), "Stories about the underwear: beauty", *Beauty, Health, Fitness*, December-January, http://www.kzfspb.ru/material92.html, last assessed on 2 March 2008.

Berger, John (1972), *Ways of Seeing* (New York: Penguin books).

Bulgakova, Oksana (2002), "Soviet beauty in Stalinist cinema," in Marina Balina, Evgeny Dobrenko and Yurii Murashov, eds., *Soviet Heritage On culture, literature and cinema*, 391-411 (Saint-Petersburg: Academic Project).

Barker, Adelie Marie (1999), "The Culture Factory: Theorizing the Popular in the Old and New Russia," in Adelie Marie Barker, ed., *Consuming Russia: Popular Culture, Sex, and Society Since Gorbachev*, 12-48 (Durham and London: Duke University Press).

Carter, Angela (1982), *Nothing Sacred: Selected Writings* (London: Virago).

Cortese, Anthony J. (2005), *Provocateur: Images of Women and Minorities in Advertising*. Lanham (Maryland: Rowman & Littlefield Publisher).

Crowley, David and Susan E. Reid (2000), "Style and Socialism: Modernity and material culture in post-war Eastern Europe," in Susan E. Reid and David Crowley, eds., *Style and Socialism: Modernity and Material Culture in Post-War Eastern Europe*, 1-24 (Oxford, New York: Berg).

Culloudon, Virginia (2004), "Discovering Russia. History of underwear: closer to the body," *Radio Liberty*, Moscow, transcript, 1 April, http://www.svoboda.org/programs/or/2001/or.040101.asp, last assesed on 8 February 2008.

Cox, Randi (2003), "All this can be yours!: Soviet commercial advertising and the social construction of space, 1928-1956," in Evgeny Dobrenko and Eric Naiman, eds., *The Landscape of Stalinism: The Art and Ideology of Soviet Space*, 126-162 (Seattle and London: University of Washington Press).

Denisova, Sasha (2002), "Underwear. What? Where? When?," No. 9, http://www.ogoniok.com/archive/2002/4768/40-58-61/, last assesed on 2 March 2008.

Entwistle, Joanne (2000), *The Fashioned Body: Fashion, Dress and Modern Social Theory* (Cambridge: Polity Press).

Filippov, A. V. (2007), *A Contemporary History of Russia. 1945-2006*, http://www.prosv.ru/umk/istoriya/2.html, last assessed 25 Nov. 2007.

Filtzer, Donald (1999), "The standard of living of Soviet industrial workers in the immediate postwar period, 1945-1948," *Europe-Asia Studies*, 51 (6), 1013-1038.

Goldman, Marshall (1963), *Soviet Marketing: Distribution in a Controlled Economy* (London: Collier-McMillan).

Jantzen, Carl, Per Østergaard and Carla M. Sicena Vieira (2007), "Becoming 'a woman to the backbone:' Lingerie consumption and the experience of feminine identity," *Journal of Consumer Culture*, 6, 177-202.

Karpova, Elena, Nancy Nelson-Hodges and William Trevor (2007), "Making sense of the market: An exploration of apparel consumption practices of the Russian consumer," *Journal of Fashion Marketing and Management*, 11 (1), 106-121.

Kelly, Catriona and Vadim Volkov (1998), "Directed desires: kul'turnost' and consumption," in Catriona Kelly and David Shepherd, eds., *Constructing Russian Culture in the Age of Revolution: 1881-1949*, 291-313 (Oxford: Oxford University Press).

Kilbourne, Jean (1999), *Deadly persuasion: why women and girls must fight the addictive power of advertising* (New York: Free Press).

Leeuwen, Theo Van (2001), "Semoitics and iconography," in Theo van Leeuwen and Carey Jewitt, eds., *Handbook of Visual Analysis*, 92-118 (London, Thousand Oaks, New Delhi: SAGE).

Martens, Lydia and Emma Casey (2007), "Afterward: Gender, consumer culture and promises of betterment in late modernity," in Emma Casey and Lydia Martens, eds., *Gender and Consumption: Domestic Cultures and the Commercialisation of Everyday Life,* 219-242 (England: Ashgate).

Millar J. (1985), "The little deal: Brezhnev contribution to acquisition socialism," *Slavic Review*, 44, 694-706

Reichert, Tom (2003), *The Erotic History of Advertising* (Amherst, NY: Prometheus Books).

Reid, Susan E. (2002), "Cold War in the kitchen: Gender and the de-Stalinization of consumer taste in the Soviet Union under Khrushchev," *Slavic Review* 61, 2 (Summer), 211-252.

Saint-Laurent, Cecil (1974), *The History of Ladies Underwear* (London: Michael Joseph).

Sal'nikova, E. V. (2001), *Aesthetics of advertising. Cultural roots and leitmotifs* (Moscow: State University of Art Studies, Ministry of Culture of Russian Federation).

Schroeder, Jonathan E. (2006), "Editorial: Introduction to the special issue on aesthetics, images, and vision," *Marketing Theory*, 6 (5), 5-10.

Sevriukova, Vita (2006), "Soviet underwear: An attempt to interfere, *History of fashion*, 2 November, http://www.modnoe.ru/interes/detail.php?ID=1524, last assessed on 8 February 2008.

Shkliaruk, Aleksandr (2007), "An essay on the history of Russian trade poster," in Aleksandr Snopkov, Pavel Snopkov and Aleksandr Shkliaruk, eds., *Advertising Art in Russia* (Moscow: Kontakt-Kul'tura).

Snopkov, Alexander, Pavel Snopkov and Alexander Shkliaruk, eds. (2007), *Advertising Art in Russia* (Moscow: Kontakt-Kul'tura).

Snopkov, Alexander, Pavel Snopkov and Alexander Shkliaruk, eds. (2004), *600 Posters* (Moscow: Kontakt-Kul'tura).

Starshinina, Elizaveta (2007), "Closer to the body: History of women's underwear in memory of Soviet contemporaries," *Friday*, 2, http://pressa.irk.ru/friday/2007/08/021001.html, last assessed on 8 February 2008.

Tolstikova, Natalia (2001), "Reading *Rabotnitsa*: Ideals, Aspirations, and Consumption Choices for Soviet Women, 1914-1964" (PhD Diss., University of Illinois at Urbana-Champaign).

Vainshtein, Ol'ga (1996), "Female fashion, Soviet style: Bodies of ideology," in Helena Goscilo and Beth Holmgren, eds., *Russia—Women—Culture*, 64-93 (Bloomington, Indiana: Indiana University Press).

Wilson, Elizabeth (2003), *Adorned in Dreams: Fashion and Modernity* (New York, London: I.B. Taurus).

Effects of Nostalgic Advertising through Emotions and the Intensity of the Evoked Mental Images

Silke Bambauer-Sachse, University of Fribourg, Switzerland
Heribert Gierl, University of Augsburg, Germany

ABSTRACT

In this paper we analyze effects of nostalgic versus non-nostalgic advertising through elicited emotions and the intensity of evoked mental images on consumers' attitudes and purchase intentions. In addition, we examine if imagery instructions are helpful in the context of nostalgic advertising. We conducted two empirical studies to examine these processes. Our results show that nostalgic advertisements evoke more positive emotions and more intensive mental images than non-nostalgic advertisements which in turn affect consumers' attitudes toward the ad and toward the product and their purchase intentions.

INTRODUCTION

People are often not only influenced by immediate circumstances, but also by their pasts and their anticipated futures (Belk 1990). Consumers cannot return to the past, but they can try to preserve it through nostalgic consumption activities (Rindfleisch and Sprott 2000; Sierra and McQuitty 2007; Stern 1992). Nostalgia is a part of people's consumption experience and, therefore, a part of preference or choice (Goulding 2001). Furthermore, nostalgia is an important marketing topic (Gabriel 1993; Havlena and Holak 1991; Reisenwitz, Iyer, and Cutler 2004) that influences trends in designing, decorating, entertaining, collecting, retailing, media, arts, and advertising (Holbrook 1994). Nostalgic advertising is used in different product categories such as food, beverages (Muehling and Sprott 2004; Rindfleisch, Freeman, and Burroughs 2000), music, movies (Holak and Havlena 1992; Baker and Kennedy 1994; Sierra and McQuitty 2007), toy, clothing, candy, chocolate, furniture, vehicle, outdoor equipment, perfume (Belk 1990; Reisenwitz, Iyer, and Cutler 2004; Rindfleisch and Sprott 2000), financial planning (Rindfleisch and Sprott 2000), coffee, watches, cigarettes, medicine (Reisenwitz, Iyer, and Cutler 2004). Marketing practitioners increasingly use nostalgic cues such as themes, images, jingles, and old slogans in advertising and nostalgic products (Havlena and Holak 1991; Baker and Kennedy 1994) to offer consumption experiences which are characterized by a taste of youth (Stern 1992), to evoke memories of consumers' past personal experiences (Sujan, Bettman, and Baumgartner 1993), and to elicit emotions (Braun, Ellis, and Loftus 2002). Nostalgic cues are used with regard to different aspects of life such as buildings, organizational leaders, colleagues (Gabriel 1993), family members, special events (Holak and Havlena 1992; Muehling and Sprott 2004), entertainment (Havlena and Holak 1991), literature, artwork, technology, home (Sierra and McQuitty 2007), odors (Hirsch 1992), vacations, weddings (Baker and Kennedy 1994), restaurants (Reisenwitz, Iyer, and Cutler 2004), and religion (Holak and Havlena 1992).

The effectiveness of nostalgia in an advertising context with regard to effects such as increasing the level of brand awareness and brand attitude has not been broadly analyzed in the literature (Muehling and Sprott 2004; Reisenwitz, Iyer, and Cutler 2004). Moreover, many former studies on nostalgia are rather exploratory than driven by a theory that could explain and predict consumer behavior in nostalgic contexts (Braun, Ellis, and Loftus 2002; Rindfleisch and Sprott 2000; Sierra and McQuitty 2007).

There are only a few studies that deal with emotions in the context of nostalgic advertising. Early studies in this field of research rather exploratively examine emotional components of nostalgia on the basis of descriptions of nostalgic experiences (Holak and Havlena 1992, 1998). A more recent study focused on effects of nostalgic advertisements through evoked emotions on advertisement and brand attitudes and on purchase intentions, and provided the finding that nostalgic advertising evokes positive emotions which have direct positive effects on the attitude toward the ad and rather indirect effects on the attitude toward the brand and on purchase intention (Pascal, Muehling, and Sprott 2002). However, the authors of this study only tested nostalgic advertisements and did not consider control advertisements which are helpful as a reference. Thus, it is necessary to examine effects of nostalgic advertising versus non-nostalgic advertising through emotions on attitudes toward the ad and the product and on purchase intentions in a new empirical study.

Studies on mental images that are evoked in the context of nostalgic advertising are scarce as well. For example, Holak and Havlena (1996) examined nostalgia imagery exploratively by asking consumers to create collages. In a more recent study, Muehling and Sprott (2004) found that nostalgic advertisements generate nostalgia-related thoughts in consumers which are not always positively valenced. This finding provides a first insight in mental processes that can be triggered by nostalgic advertising. However, measuring mental images seems to capture the mental processes evoked by nostalgic advertising more comprehensively than just recording thoughts.

Consequently, the purpose of this paper is to analyze effects of nostalgic versus non-nostalgic advertising through elicited emotions and mental images on consumers' attitudes toward the ad and toward the advertised product as well as on their purchase intention. The focus here is on shedding light on possible processes that are triggered by nostalgic advertising in consumers.

This paper contributes to the existing body of research by providing a new theoretical approach to predict effects of nostalgic advertising and by presenting the results of two empirical studies which aim at analyzing effects of nostalgic advertising through emotions and mental imagery on consumers' attitudes toward the ad and toward the product, and on their purchase intention. The findings of the studies presented here enable marketers to understand the processes triggered by nostalgic advertising in consumers in more detail and to consequently use nostalgic cues more target-oriented.

THEORETICAL AND EMPIRICAL BACKGROUND

The Concept of Nostalgia

Nostalgia is not a theory in itself. It is rather a concept that can provide an explanation of a given situation (Goulding 2001). Nostalgia is a feeling or a mood that causes a preference for things that tend to evoke nostalgic responses (Holak and Havlena 1998). In addition, nostalgia is distinct from autobiographical memory (Muehling and Sprott 2004). Nostalgia is often described as a longing for past times. Thus, people try to recreate aspects of the past in their present life by reproducing past activities and focusing on possessions that remind them of the past (Davis 1979; Holbrook 1993; Holbrook and Schindler 1991; Nawas and Platt 1965; Sierra and McQuitty 2007; Stern 1992). Furthermore, nostalgia is described as a coping mechanism (Best and Nelson 1985; Davis 1979; Goulding 2001) which is characterized by a mythologization or symbolization of the past (Brown and Humphreys 2002; Rindfleisch, Freeman, and Burroughs 2000) as well as by an imaginary character (Belk 1990) and which helps people to come to terms with their present life circumstances (Gabriel 1993) or with concerns over the future (Nawas and Platt 1965). Belk (1990) and Holak and Havlena (1992) see nostalgia as an emotion consisting of both pleasant and unpleasant components. One the one hand, people reminiscing in memories of the past are happy, but on the other hand, people are sad because they would like to relive the past times and because they realize that this is impossible at the same time (Baker and Kennedy 1994).

Effects of Nostalgic Advertising through Emotions on the Attitude toward the Ad

Evoking nostalgic feelings through advertising generates predominantly positive emotions (Baumgartner, Sujan, and Bettman 1992; Holak and Havlena 1998; Pascal, Sprott, and Muehling 2002) because, due to a positivity bias of the memory, people tend to remember rather positive episodes from their lives and because advertisements often aim at retrieving pleasant rather than unpleasant memories (Sujan, Bettman, and Baumgartner 1993). This argument leads to our first hypothesis:

H1: Ceteris paribus, nostalgic advertising evokes more positive emotions than non-nostalgic, modern advertising.

Consistent with affect transfer models of persuasion (MacKenzie, Lutz, and Belch 1986; Zajonc 1980), experiencing nostalgic feelings due to nostalgic appeals in advertisements can influence consumers' judgment processes (Sujan, Bettman, and Baumgartner 1993) and lead to the formation of positive attitudes (Muehling and Sprott 2004). Consequently, emotional responses to nostalgic advertisements are believed to have positive effects on consumers' attitudes toward the ad (Batra and Ray 1986; Baumgartner, Sujan, and Bettman 1992; Machleit and Wilson 1988; Muehling and Sprott 2004; Reisenwitz, Iyer, and Cutler 2004). These considerations lead to:

H2: The more positive the emotions that are evoked by a nostalgic versus a non-nostalgic, modern ad, the more positive is consumers' attitude toward the ad.

Effects of Nostalgic Advertising through Mental Images on the Attitude toward the Advertised Product

Nostalgic advertising messages arouse attention and are entertaining (Reisenwitz, Iyer, and Cutler 2004). Furthermore, they can evoke nostalgic reflections in consumers (Muehling and Sprott 2004) and stimulate an imaginative recreation of a past which can be associated with the advertised product (Stern 1992). Consequently, imagery theory can serve as an explanation for effects of nostalgic advertising on consumers' attitude toward the advertised product. Imagery is a sensory representation of a memory that enables people to relive past experiences (Lutz and Lutz 1978) that they ascribe a special meaning (Baker and Kennedy 1994). A mental image is an imagination of a certain event (Sherman et al. 1985). Imagery processing can either consist in retrieving information from memory or in having fantasies (Hoyer and MacInnis 2004; MacInnis and Price 1987; Sherman et al. 1985) that are elicited by pictures, concrete verbal stimuli, or imagery instructions. Imagery instructions are statements that direct the recipients to form a mental picture of a certain concept (Lutz and Lutz 1978).

According to Burns, Biswas, and Babin (1993) mental images work as a mediator in the relation between predictor variables such as cues or instructions to imagine and the target variable attitude.

Transferred to the context of nostalgic advertising, consumers are believed to have mental images of former consumption situations and experiences (Baumgartner, Sujan, and Bettman 1992). Imagery processing can be evoked by nostalgic advertisements or advertisements with a nostalgia-related imagery instruction. Thus, the contact with a nostalgic advertisement for a certain product or a nostalgia-related imagery instruction evokes nostalgic mental images in consumers that are related to the advertised product. These mental images can contain autobiographical memories and are predominantly positive (Sujan, Bettman, and Baumgartner 1993). These considerations lead to:

H3: Ceteris paribus, nostalgic advertising evokes a more intensive mental image associated with the advertised product than non-nostalgic, modern advertising.

As comparatively concrete cues evoke more comprehensive and clearer mental images than comparatively abstract cues (Unnava, Agarwal, and Haugtvedt 1996), we assume that a nostalgic advertisement with a concrete imagery instruction elicits a more intensive nostalgic image than a nostalgic advertisement without such a concrete cue. Thus:

H4: A nostalgic advertisement with an imagery instruction evokes an even more intensive mental image than a nostalgic advertisement without such an instruction.

Having nostalgic thoughts evokes a higher identification with the communicated information (Braun, Ellis, and Loftus 2002). Consequently, the information processed in this way is comparatively persuasive (Baumgartner, Sujan, and Bettman 1992). Thus, a mental image evoked by nostalgic advertising is believed to have predominantly positive effects on consumers' attitude toward the product (Babin and Burns 1997; Bone and Ellen 1992; MacInnis and Price 1987; Sujan, Bettman, and Baumgartner 1993) because the advertisement recipients tend to not consider negative aspects of the advertised product when processing the evoked mental images (MacInnis and Price 1987).

H5: The higher the intensity of the evoked mental image the more positive is consumers' attitude toward the advertised product.

Effects of Nostalgic Advertising through the Attitude toward the Ad on Product Evaluation and Purchase Behavior

Consumers who are exposed to a nostalgic advertisement, are supposed to transfer evoked memories of former times to products (Hirsch 1992). Thus, having nostalgic feelings as well as having mental images of former times in mind may positively influence consumers' judgment processes (Sierra and McQuitty 2007; Sujan, Bettman, and Baumgartner 1993), which results in more favorable product evaluations (Braun, Ellis, and Loftus 2002; Pascal, Sprott, and Muehling 2002; Reisenwitz, Iyer, and Cutler 2004; Sujan, Bettman, and Baumgartner 1993). Furthermore, nostalgic feelings and thoughts drive the behavior of people (Hirsch 1992). When experiencing nostalgia in a consumption context, consumers are supposed to show higher purchase likelihood with regard to the advertised products (Reisenwitz, Iyer, and Cutler 2004) and to purchase especially nostalgia-related products (Goulding 2001; Sierra and McQuitty 2007).

FIGURE 1
RESEARCH MODEL

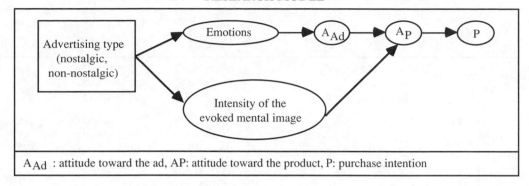

A_{Ad} : attitude toward the ad, AP: attitude toward the product, P: purchase intention

TABLE 1
OVERVIEW OF THE TWO EMPIRICAL STUDIES

Aspect	Study	
	1	2
Analyzed Variables	attitude toward the ad attitude toward the product purchase intention emotions	attitude toward the ad attitude toward the product purchase intention intensity of the evoked mental images
Sample size	480 participants	465 participants
Respondents	students, employees, retirees	students
Mean age	45.12 years	24.26 years
Gender distribution	242 women, 238 men	231 women, 234 men
Tested products	detergent, pudding, band-aids, cookies	chocolate, soft drinks, fast food, facial cream

Research Model

The theoretical considerations presented above are summarized in the research model shown in figure 1. This research model is tested in an empirical study, which is presented in the next section.

EMPIRICAL STUDIES ON NOSTALGIA EFFECTS IN ADVERTISING

Overview of the Empirical Studies

In order to examine the processes triggered by nostalgic advertising in consumers as comprehensive as possible, we conducted two empirical studies to be able to clearly separate the assumed effects. The two studies differ in one variable: in the first study we measured the emotions, in the second study we measured the intensity of the mental images evoked by nostalgic advertisements. With regard to all other variables the studies are comparable so that the existence of the relations between these variables can be validated by comparing the results of the two empirical studies. Table 1 gives an overview of the two studies.

The study descriptions show that both studies are largely comparable. As nostalgic cues such as nostalgic pictures are believed to be comparatively effective in low involvement advertising situations (Reisenwitz, Iyer, and Cutler 2004), we chose every day low involvement products as examples. We used different product examples in each study to cover a wide range of product categories. We chose brands that had already existed during the childhood of the respondents because early childhood brand relationships are the emotional basis for later adult brand relationships (Braun, Ellis, and Loftus 2002).

Moreover, we intentionally used a sample consisting of people of different age groups in one study and a student sample in the other study to prove that the results hold across age groups.

Nostalgia Manipulation and Measures

In both studies nostalgia was manipulated in the respective advertisements by including nostalgic pictures from former advertisements. The nostalgic advertisements were tested against non-nostalgic modern advertisements from current advertising campaigns for the respective products. In addition to testing nostalgic

TABLE 2
MEASURES APPLIED IN THE TWO EMPIRICAL STUDIES

Model variable	Statement	Factor loadings		Alpha/ correlation
		Study 1	Study 2	
Attitude toward the ad (AAd)	The ad is appealing.	.89 (t=26.50)	.95 (t=43.06)	.86
	I like this ad.	.87 (t=30.05)	.92 (t=25.05)	.92
	This ad is interesting.	.88 (t=32.55)	.91 (t=29.14)	
Attitude toward the product (AP)	This product is attractive.	.85 (t=21.26)	.92 (t=42.52)	.71
	This product is interesting.	.86 (t=23.92)	.90 (t=46.06)	.87
	This product is appealing.	.76 (t=7.92)	.86 (t=21.23)	
Emotions (E)	I am fine	.90 (t=31.74)	-	.60
	I feel happy.	.90 (t=32.73)		
Purchase intention (I)	I would like to buy this product.	1.00	1.00	-

Scale: 1 = totally disagree, ..., 7 = totally agree

versus non-nostalgic advertisements in both studies, we had nostalgic advertisements with imagery instructions in the second study. As this study aimed at analyzing the intensity of evoked mental images we intended to additionally examine whether including imagery instructions in advertisements positively influences this intensity. The imagery instruction consisted in the question: "Do you remember the good old days?"

The measures used in the empirical studies are summarized in table 2. Emotions had been operationalized by measuring subjective feelings because those represent the conscious awareness of the emotional state a person is experiencing (Desmet 2004). As the study was conducted in Germany, the items had been translated into German. Each model variable that was used in both studies is ascribed two alpha values (one value for each study). Table 2 additionally contains the factor loadings of the respective items. The significantly positive factor loadings as well as the high alpha values and correlations show that the applied items are appropriate for measuring the respective model variables.

In addition to the variables listed in table 2 we needed to measure the intensity of the nostalgic mental images elicited by the contact with the advertisements in the second study. As the quantity and the vividness of evoked images are the most important dimensions of the intensity of mental images (Ellen and Bone 1991) we measured these two aspects as follows. The respondents were asked to document the mental images that had come to their mind as follows: "Please describe the images that came to your mind when regarding the ad." Instead of asking the respondents to indicate the vividness of these mental images, we coded the images reported by the respondents according to the detailedness with which the respondents described the images (1=low, 2=moderate, and 3=high vividness). The two dimensions of the intensity of the mental images were combined by weighting the number of mental images by the respective vividness.

Procedure

In both studies, each participant saw only one print advertisement for a brand of one of the chosen product categories (either a nostalgic or a non-nostalgic, modern advertisement) because we wanted to avoid that the respondents would be primed for the relevant measures (emotions, intensity of evoked mental images) when evaluating further advertisements. The procedure, which was the same for both studies, was as follows. The participants saw one advertisement and were subsequently asked to fill in a questionnaire with measures for their emotions/for the intensity of the evoked mental images, and with statements concerning their attitudes toward the ad and toward the brand, and their purchase intention. Finally the respondents had to answer demographic questions which were used to prove that the different experimental groups were structurally equal with regard to age and gender.

Effects of Nostalgic versus Non-Nostalgic Advertisements

For all of the data analyses presented below, we pooled the data across products. In a first step we basically analyze possible effects of nostalgic versus non-nostalgic advertisements on emotions and the intensity of mental images. The results of a t test and an ANOVA show that the advertising type (nostalgic versus non-nostalgic, modern advertising) has significantly positive effects on emotions (E_{Ad_nos}=3.10, E_{Ad_mod}=2.85, t=2.71, p<.01) and on the intensity of the evoked mental images (MI_{Ad_nosII}=1.10, MI_{Ad_nos}=1.09, MI_{Ad_mod}=.65, F=4.79, p<.01). Thus nostalgic advertisements elicit significantly more positive emotions and significantly more intensive mental images than non-nostalgic, modern advertisements. However, the data show that the difference between a nostalgic advertisement with and a nostalgic advertisement without an imagery instruction is not significant. Thus, H4 is not supported. Based on these findings, a more detailed analysis of the effects of nostalgic versus non-nostalgic advertising through emotions and the intensity of the evoked mental images on the response variables attitude toward the ad, attitude toward the product and purchase intention is presented in the following section of the paper.

Methods of Data Analysis and Model Fit in Both Studies

In order to test our research model, we applied two structural equation models. The most common procedures to estimate structural equation models are LISREL and PLS. As our independent variable is nominal (nostalgic versus non-nostalgic advertisement) we had to choose the most appropriate procedure. A review of research in high reputation journals has shown that PLS models are preferred over LISREL models if categorical data are used as exogenous variables because PLS models do not require metric input data (e.g., Fichman and Kemerer 1997; Kahai, Avolio, and

TABLE 3
MODEL FIT, RELIABILITY, AND VALIDITY MEASURES IN BOTH STUDIES

	R^2		Composite reliability		Average variance extracted		Correlations between endogenous variables (squared correlations)					
							A_{Ad}		A_P		I	
Study	1	2	1	2	1	2	1	2	1	2	1	2
AAd	.34	.01	.91	.95	.78	.86						
AP	.26	.18	.84	.92	.63	.79	.49 (.24)	.26 (.07)				
Purchase intention (I)	.17	.56	1.00	1.00	1.00	1.00	.24 (.06)	.18 (.03)	.41 (.17)	.75 (.56)		
Emotions (E)	.15	-	.89	-	.81	-	.57 (.32)	-	.39 (.15)	-	.18 (.03)	-
Intensity of the evoked mental images (MI)	-	.12	-	-	-	-	-	.05 (.00)	-	.11 (.01)	-	.05 (.00)

A_{Ad}: attitude toward the ad, A_P: attitude toward the product

TABLE 4
PATH COEFFICIENTS OF THE PLS MODEL IN STUDY 1

Effect of... on	E	A_{Ad}	A_P	I
Nostalgic versus non-nostalgic ad	.22 (t=1.79**)	n.s.	n.s.	n.s.
E	-	.56 (t=7.23****)	.15 (t=1.39*)	n.s.
A_{Ad}	-	-	.41 (t=3.96****)	n.s.
A_P	-	-	-	.42 (t=4.41****)

E: emotions, A_{Ad}: attitude toward the ad, A_P: attitude toward the product, I: purchase intention
****: p<.001, ***: p<.01, **: p<.05, *: p<.10, n.s.: not significant

Sosik 1998). Therefore, we used two PLS models to test the effects assumed in our hypotheses. Both PLS models differ with regard to one variable: the first model contains emotions whereas the second model contains the intensity of the evoked mental images. Emotions are included in the first PLS model as a metric variable measured by reflective indicators. The intensity of the evoked mental images is included as a metric variable with one formative indicator in the second PLS model. Besides this difference, both models contain the same variables. Consumers' purchase intention is the target variable. The attitude toward the product and the attitude toward the ad are integrated as mediator variables. Thus, both models have three endogenous variables in common that are measured by reflective indicators. In the first model the exogenous model variable (advertising type: nostalgic ad versus non-nostalgic, modern ad) is included through one formative indicator which is a common procedure for binary exogenous variables (e.g., Crilley and Sharp 2006; Kahai, Sosik, and Avolio 2004; Li et al. 2006). In the second model the advertising type (nostalgic ad, nostalgic ad with imagery instruction, and non-nostalgic, modern ad) is included through two formative binary indicators (reference: non-nostalgic, modern ad). The model fit, reliability and validity measures for both models are shown in table 3.

The R^2 values of the partial models are acceptable. Furthermore, the composite reliability values are sufficiently high (Bagozzi and Yi 1991). Moreover, the average variance extracted values exceed the squared correlations between the model variables proving discriminant validity (Fornell and Larcker 1981).

Results of Study 1: Effects of Nostalgic Advertising through Emotions

The purpose of the first study is to analyze the effects of nostalgic versus non-nostalgic advertising through emotions that are triggered by nostalgic appeals on consumers' attitudes toward the ad and toward the product, and on their purchase intention. The estimated path coefficients of the first PLS model are summarized in table 4.

The results show that the advertising type (nostalgic versus non-nostalgic advertising) has a significantly positive effect on the extent to which consumers experience emotions. Thus, H1 is supported and the data indicate that nostalgic advertisements arouse

TABLE 5
PATH COEFFICIENTS OF THE PLS MODEL IN STUDY 2

Effect of... on	MI	A_{Ad}	A_P	I
Nostalgic versus non-nostalgic ad	.24 (t=2.37**)	n.s.	n.s.	n.s.
Nostalgic ad with imagery instruction versus non-nostalgic ad	.26 (t=2.59**)	n.s.	n.s.	n.s.
MI	-	n.s.	.34 (t=3.45****)	n.s.
A_{Ad}	-	-	.27 (t=2.68***)	n.s.
A_P	-	-	-	.75 (t=15.17****)

MI: intensity of the evoked mental images, A_{Ad}: attitude toward the ad, A_P: attitude toward the product
I: purchase intention; ****: $p<.001$, ***: $p<.01$, **: $p<.05$, *: $p<.10$, n.s.: not significant

more positive emotions in the ad recipients than non-nostalgic, modern advertisements. The results also mirror the fact that the advertising type does not have any direct effects on the attitude toward the ad, the attitude toward product, or on purchase intention.

Moreover, the data show that the emotions aroused by the respective advertisement have a significantly positive effect on consumers' attitude toward the ad supporting H2. Thus, the more positive the emotions that are triggered by an advertisement, the more positive is the recipients' evaluation of the ad. The additional effect of emotions on the attitude toward the product is only significant at the 10 percent level. Furthermore, emotions do not influence consumers' purchase intention. Thus, the results show that emotions evoked by an advertisement predominantly influence consumers formation of an attitude toward the ad. In addition, the results indicate that the attitude toward the ad has a significantly positive effect on the attitude toward the product which in turn has a significantly positive influence on purchase intention. The findings of our first study are in line with previous findings of Pascal, Sprott, and Muehling (2002).

Results of Study 2: Effects of Nostalgic Advertising through the Intensity of Evoked Mental Images

The purposes of the second study were to gain additional insights in effects of nostalgic versus non-nostalgic advertising through the intensity of mental images that are activated in consumers on their attitudes toward the ad and toward the product as well as to validate the findings of the first study. The estimated path coefficients of the second PLS model are shown in table 5.

The results indicate that nostalgic advertising evokes a significantly more intensive mental image than non-nostalgic advertising. Thus, H3 is supported. Again, the advertising type does not have any direct effects on consumers' attitudes toward the ad and toward the product and on their purchase intention. Moreover, the results show that the intensity of the evoked mental images neither has effects on consumers' attitude toward the product nor on their purchase intention, but it does have a significantly positive effect on the attitude toward the product. Thus, H5 is supported. Analogous to the results of study 1, the path coefficients of the second PLS model show that consumers' attitude toward the ad has a significantly positive effect on their attitude toward the product, but no effect on consumers' purchase intention. Finally, the attitude to-

ward the product has a significantly positive effect on purchase intention.

CONCLUSION

The purpose of this paper has been to analyze effects of nostalgic versus non-nostalgic advertising through emotions and the intensity of evoked mental images on consumers' attitudes toward the ad and toward the product, and on their purchase intention. The results of two empirical studies show that, ceteris paribus, nostalgic advertisements evoke more positive emotions and more intensive mental images than non-nostalgic, modern advertisements. Furthermore, the results indicate that the evoked emotions are rather ad-related, whereas the elicited mental images are rather product-related.

Positive emotions evoked by nostalgic advertisements positively influence consumers' attitude toward the ad and have positive indirect effects through the attitude toward the ad on the attitude toward the product and on purchase intention. Consequently, marketers can profit from using nostalgic advertisements best when advertising emotional products that are advertised by emotional advertisements because nostalgic instead of modern advertisements evoke additional positive emotions and thus enhance the effect of other positive emotions in this context.

Nostalgic instead of non-nostalgic modern advertisements additionally evoke a more intensive mental image which has direct positive effects on consumers' attitude toward the product. Thus, nostalgic advertising is especially appropriate when advertising products that are likely to be subject to mental images. Moreover, as the effect of nostalgic advertising on the intensity of the evoked mental images can only be slightly enhanced by using an additional imagery instruction, marketers can omit such an instruction when it would cause an information overload in an advertisement.

Moreover, the fact that the positive effects of nostalgic versus non-nostalgic, modern advertising have been shown for a student sample as well as for a sample consisting of younger and older people shows that positive effects of nostalgic advertising do not necessarily depend on the age of the advertising recipients.

In further research, it might be interesting to analyze emotion and mental imagery paths in a comprehensive study because there might be interesting interaction effects. Moreover, further research might focus on controlling for personality variables such as nostalgia proneness, visual-verbal style of processing, and need for cognition.

REFERENCES

Babin, Laurie A. and Alvin C. Burns (1997), "Effects of Print Ad Pictures and Copy Containing Instructions to Imagine on Mental Imagery that Mediates Attitudes," *Journal of Advertising*, 26(3), 33-44.

Bagozzi, Richard P. and Youjae Yi (1991), "Multitrait-Multimethod Matrices in Consumer Research," *Journal of Consumer Research*, 17(4), 426-439.

Baker, Stacey M. and Patricia F. Kennedy (1994), "Death by Nostalgia: A Diagnosis of Context-Specific Cases," in: *Advances in Consumer Research*, eds. Chris T. Allen and Deborah Roedder John, Provo: Association for Consumer Research, 169-174.

Batra, Rajeev and Michael L. Ray (1986), "Affective Responses Mediating Acceptance of Advertising," Journal of Consumer Research, 13(2), 234-249.

Baumgartner, Hans, Mita Sujan, and James R. Bettman (1992), "Autobiographical Memories, Affect, and Consumer Information Processing," *Journal of Consumer Psychology*, 1, 53-82.

Belk, Russel W. (1990), "The Role of Possessions in Constructing and Maintaining a Sense of Past," in: *Advances in Consumer Research*, ed. Marvin E. Goldberg, Provo, UT: Association for Consumer Research, 669-676.

Best, Joel and Edward E. Nelson (1985), "Nostalgia and Discontinuity: A Test of the Davis Hypothesis," *Sociology and Social Research*, 69, 221-233.

Bone, Paula F. and Pam S. Ellen (1992), "The Effect of Imagery Processing and Imagery Content On Behavioral Intentions," in *Advances in Consumer Research*, ed. Marvin E. Goldberg, Gerald Gorn, and Richard W. Pollay, Provo: Association for Consumer Research, 449-454.

Braun, Kathryn A., Rhiannon Ellis, and Elizabeth F. Loftus (2002), "Make My Memory: How Advertising Can Change Our Memories of the Past," *Psychology and Marketing*, 19(1), 1-23.

Brown, Andrew D. and Michael Humphreys (2002), "Nostalgia and the Narrativization of Identity: A Turkish Case Study," *British Journal of Management*, 13, 141-159.

Burns, Alvin C., Abhijit Biswas, and Laurie A. Babin (1993), "The Operation of Visual Imagery as a Mediator of Advertising Effects," *Journal of Advertising*, 22(2), 71-85.

Crilley, Garry and Colin Sharp (2006), "Managerial Qualities and Operational Performance: A Proposed Model," *Measuring Business Excellence*, 10(2), 4-18.

Davis, Fred (1979), *Yearning for Yesterday: A Sociology of Nostalgia*, New York: Free Press.

Desmet, Pieter M.A. (2004), "Measuring Emotions," in: *Funology: From Usability to Enjoyment*, ed. Mark A. Blythe, Kees Overbeeke, Andrew F. Monk, and Peter C. Wright, Dordrecht: Kluwer Academic Publishers, 111-123.

Fichman, Robert G. and Chris F. Kemerer (1997), "The Assimilation of Software Process Innovations: An Organizational Learning Perspective," *Management Science*, 43(10), 1345-1363.

Fornell, Claes and David F. Larcker (1981), "Evaluating Structural Equation Models with Unobservable Variables and Measurement Error," *Journal of Marketing Research*, 18(1), 39-50.

Gabriel, Yiannis (1993), "Organizational Nostalgia–Reflections on "The Golden Age"," in: *Emotion in Organizations*, ed. Stephen Fineman, London: Sage Publications, 118-141.

Goulding, Christina (2001), "Romancing the Past: Heritage Visiting and the Nostalgic Consumer," *Psychology and Marketing*, 18(6), 565-592.

Havlena, William J. and Susan L. Holak (1991), "The Good Old Days: Observations on Nostalgia and its Role in Consumer Behavior," in: *Advances in Consumer Research*, eds. Rebecca H. Holman and Michael R. Solomon, Provo, UT: Association for Consumer Research, 323-329.

Hirsch, Alan R. (1992), "Nostalgia: A Neuropsychiatric Understanding," in: *Advances in Consumer Research*, eds. John F. Sherry and Brian Sternthal, Provo, UT: Association for Consumer Research, 390-395.

Holak, Susan L. and William J. Havlena (1992), "Nostalgia: An Exploratory Study of Themes and Emotions in the Nostalgic Experience," in: *Advances in Consumer Research*, eds. John F. Sherry and Brian Sternthal, Provo, UT: Association for Consumer Research, 380-387.

Holak, Susan L. and William L. Havlena (1998), "Feelings, Fantasies, and Memories: an Examination of the Emotional Components of Nostalgia," *Journal of Business Research*, 42, 217-226.

Holbrook, Morris B. (1993), "Nostalgia and Consumption Preferences: Some Emerging Patterns of Consumer Tastes," *Journal of Consumer Research*, 20(2), 245-256.

Holbrook, Morris B. (1994), "Nostalgia Proneness and Consumer Tastes," in: *Buyer Behavior in Marketing Strategy*, 2nd edition, ed. John A. Howard, Englewood Cliffs, NJ: Prentice-Hall, 348-364.

Holbrook, Morris B. and Robert M. Schindler (1991), "Echoes of the Dear Departed Past: Some Work in Progress on Nostalgia," in: *Advances in Consumer Research*, eds. Rebecca H. Holman and Michael R. Solomon, Provo, UT: Association for Consumer Research, 303-333.

Hoyer, Wayne D. and Deborah J. MacInnis (2004), *Consumer Behavior*, 3rd edition, Boston: Houghton Mifflin.

Kahai, Surinder S., Bruce J. Avolio, and John J. Sosik (1998), "Effects of Source and Participant Anonymity and Difference in Initial Opinions in an EMS Context," *Decision Sciences*, 29(2), 427-460.

Kahai, Surinder S., John J. Sosik, and Bruce J. Avolio (2004), "Effects of Participants and Directive Leadership in Electronic Groups," *Group & Organizational Management*, 29(1), 67-105.

Li, Ji, Kevin Lam, Gongming Qian, and Yongqing Fang (2006), "The Effects of Institutional Ownership on Corporate Governance and Performance: An Empirical Assessment in Hong Kong," *Management International Review*, 46(3), 259-276.

Lutz, Kathy A. and Richard J. Lutz (1978), "Imagery Eliciting Strategies: Review and Implications of Research," in: *Advances in Consumer Research*, ed. H K Hunt, Provo: Association for Consumer Research, 611-620.

Machleit, Karen A. and R. Dale Wilson (1988), "Emotional Feelings and Attitude toward the Advertisement: The Roles of Brand Familiarity and Repetition," *Journal of Advertising*, 17(3), 27-35.

MacInnis, Deborah J. and Linda L. Price (1987), "The Role of Imagery in Information Processing: Review and extensions," *Journal of Consumer Research*, 13, 473-491.

MacKenzie, Scott B., Richard J. Lutz, and George E. Belch (1986), "The Role of Attitude Toward the Ad as a Mediator of Advertising Effectiveness: A Test of Competing Explanations," *Journal of Marketing Research*, 23, 130-143.

Muehling, Darrel D. and David E. Sprott (2004), "The Power of Reflection–An Empirical Examination of Nostalgia Advertising Effects," *Journal of Advertising*, 33(3), 25-35.

Nawas, M. Mike and Jerome J. Platt (1965), "A Future- Oriented Theory of Nostalgia," *Journal of Individual Psychology*, 21, 51-57.

Pascal, Vincent J., David E. Sprott, and Darrel D. Muehling (2002), "The Influence of Evoked Nostalgia on Consumers' Responses to Advertising: An Exploratory Study," *Journal of Current Issues and Research in Advertising*, 24(1), 39-49.

Reisenwitz, Timothy H., Rajesh Iyer, and Bob Cutler (2004), "Nostalgia Advertising and the Influence of Nostalgia Proneness," *Marketing Management Journal*, 14(2), 55-66.

Rindfleisch, Aric, Dan Freeman and James E. Burroughs (2000), "Nostalgia, Materialism, and Product Preferences: An Initial Inquiry," in: *Advances in Consumer Research*, eds. Stephen J. Hoch and Robert J. Meyer, Provo, UT: Association for Consumer Research, 36-41.

Rindfleisch, Aric and David E. Sprott (2000), "Moving Forward on Looking Backward: Advancing Theory and Practice in Nostalgia," in: *Advances in Consumer Research*, eds. Stephen J. Hoch and Robert J. Meyer, Provo, UT: Association for Consumer Research, 34-35.

Sherman, Steven, Robert B. Cialdini, Donna F. Schwartzman, and Kim D. Reynolds (1985), "Imagining Can Heighten or Lower the Perceived Likelihood of Contracting a Disease: The Mediating Effects of Ease of Imagery," *Personality & Social Psychology Bulletin*, 11, 118-127.

Sierra, Jeremy J. and Shaun McQuitty (2007), "Attitudes and Emotions as Determinants of Nostalgia Purchases: An Application of Social Identity Theory," *Journal of Marketing Theory and Practice*, 15(2), 99-112.

Stern, Barbara (1992), "Historical and Personal Nostalgia in Advertising Text: The Fin de Siècle Effect," *Journal of Advertising*, 21, 11-22.

Sujan, Mita, James R. Bettman, and Hans Baumgartner (1993), "Influencing Consumer Judgments Using Autobiographical Memories: A Self-Referencing Perspective," *Journal of Marketing Research*, 30, 422-436.

Unnava, H. Rao, Sanjeev Agarwal, and Curtis P. Haugtvedt (1996), "Interactive Effects of Presentation Modality and Message-Generated Imagery on Recall of Advertising Information," *Journal of Consumer Research*, 23(1), 81-88.

Zajonc, Robert B. (1980), „Feeling and Thinking: Preferences Need no Inferences," *American Psychologist,* 35, 151–175.

The Effects of Humor on the Processing of Word-of-Mouth

Dave Bussiere, University of Windsor, Canada

ABSTRACT

Exploratory qualitative analysis of 127 actual on-line conversations revealed the presence of humor in word-of-mouth (WOM). This use of humor seemed to weaken the impact of the WOM advice. While there is a rich history of research on the impact of humor on advertising, there is no equivalent research in the WOM literature. Using a 2x2 experimental design, the impact of humorous WOM on behavioral intentions, WOM intentions, evaluations of source credibility and evaluations of message persuasiveness are analyzed. Humor was found to decrease the impact of positive and negative WOM messages.

"At its most basic level humor is an intended or unintended message interpreted as funny. Yet curiously, the communication field has only skimmed the surface of the world of humor." (Lynch 2002, p. 423)

For almost 35 years, marketing research has acknowledged the impact of humor on message processing. This research has focused primarily on the role of humor in advertising and its impact on message persuasiveness, source credibility and behavioral intentions. In contrast, research on word-of-mouth (WOM) has focused on neutral, positive or negative WOM comments. This paper will provide a literature base for future humor research in WOM.

Humor in Advertising

Since Sternthal and Craig's pivotal article (1973), there have been numerous articles that have analyzed various implications of humor in advertising. As Duncan (1979) notes, learning theory suggests that humor should positively impact advertising results through increased distraction, higher arousal, positive conditions and increased source credibility:

"Advocates of humor in advertising argue that light-hearted copy secures audience attention, increases advertisement memorability, overcomes sales resistance, and enhances message persuasiveness." (Duncan 1979, p. 286).

While some studies have found a positive relationship between the use of humor and ad results (c.f. Madden & Weinberger 1984), there are mixed results overall. In fact, the impact of a humorous message seems to be contingent on who receives the message:

"If humor is used in a persuasive communication, its function may also vary depending on how humor is processed by the message recipient." (Zhang & Zinkhan 2006, p. 114).

Message Persuasiveness

While there has been a substantial amount of research on the impact of humor on message persuasiveness, the understood direction of the effect is mixed (Weinberger and Gulas 1992). Duncan and Nelson (1985), for example, found that humor in radio ads had positive impact on lower-order processes like attention, but weakened persuasion. Other studies found that humor increased message persuasion because it reduced resistance to the message (Lammer et al 1983, Zhang 1996).

More common, however, were studies that support Sternthal and Craig's (1973) proposition that humor may, in theory, increase persuasiveness, but that it does not appear to influence actual persuasion when compared to serious appeals because of the moderating impact of other variables (Booker 1981, Madden and Weinberger 1984). In fact, much of the past research has found indirect effects that moderated the impact of humor such as the need for humor (Cline, Altsech and Kellaris 2003), liking of the ad (Gelb and Pickett 1983), the need for cognition (Zhang 1996) and the attitude towards the ad (Zhang and Zinkhan 2006).

Source Credibility

The impact of humor on source credibility is far less studied and yet the same mix of results exists (Weinberger and Gulas 1992). While Sternthal and Craig (1973) found that "Humor tends to enhance source credibility," (p.17), the only other study found that advertising executives, both researchers and creative directors generally did not agree (Madden and Weinberger 1984).

Behavioral Intentions

There is also mixed support for using humor to increase the likelihood of message recipients intending to follow the advice in the message. One study found that humor did, in fact, increase intentions to purchase the product (Perry et al 1997). In contrast, Gelb and Pickett (1983) and Duncan and Nelson (1985) found an opposite effect. Madden and Weinberger (1984) found mixed support for the impact of humor on purchase intention amongst advertising executives. In a study of humor in promotion for events, Scott, Klein and Bryant (1990) found that humor increased attendance at social events, but had no impact on business event attendance.

Word-of-Mouth Intentions

Only one study analyzed the impact of humor in advertising on word-of-mouth intentions. Perry et al (1997) found that humor increased the likelihood that the message recipient would pass on the massage to other consumers.

As the preceding highlights, despite 35 years of research, the impact of humor in advertising remains unsettled. As Weinberger and Gulas (1992) note:

"Though the broad question of humor's effectiveness in advertising is unanswerable, we can compile the accounts of humor research in the proper constraints to gain insights about its effects." (Weinberger and Gulas 1992, p. 35)

Following this line of reasoning, this article will acknowledge imperfect understanding of humor, and expand research to humor in word-of-mouth messages.

Word-of-Mouth

For over 50 years, WOM has been actively researched (Brooks 1957) and yet there is general agreement that the research is incomplete (c.f. Bowman & Narayandas 2001, Wangenheim 2005).

In general, WOM has been found to provide an easy, credible source of information and more effective than ads (c.f. Goldenberg, Libai & Muller 2001). Research has also found that individuals turn to strong-tie, rather than weaker social connections (Brown & Reingen 1987, Gilly, Graham, Wolfinbarger & Yale 1998, Goldenberg, Libai & Muller 2001, Yale & Gilly 1995).

Research indicates that there are many reasons for consumers to participate in WOM discussions. Some participate post-consumption, and want to discuss their experience. Others participate pre-purchase and want to better their purchase decision.

Post Consumption Word-Of-Mouth

Post consumption research has focused on within the consumer complaint literature. This research has examined how service failure increases the likelihood of complaining to the service provider and to other consumers. One of the prime drivers of WOM is the desire to complain about a service failure (Bone 1995, Halstead 2002, Maxham & Netemeyer 2003, Maxham & Netemeyer 2002, Maxham 2001, Nyer & Gopinath 2005, Richins 1983).

The desire to participate in negative word-of-mouth/complaining behavior is lessened by a company's reaction to complaints. Company reaction to complaints influences the degree to which people participate in negative WOM (Brown, Barry, Dacin & Gunst 2005, Halstead 2002, Maxham 2001, Nyer & Gopinath 2005, Richins 1983, Wangenheim 2003, Voorhees, Brady & Horowitz 2006).

Pre-Consumption Word-Of-Mouth

Consumers cannot know everything and so must turn to others for advice and information. In general, this research has found that positive and negative WOM massages have different impacts on consumers–with negative being more effective (DeCarlo et al 2007, Wangenheim 2005).

This negative WOM has been shown to negatively influence consumers' brand perceptions (Bone 1995, Gruen, Osmonbekov & Czaplewski 2006), intentions to buy (Bone 1995, Gruen, Osmonbekov & Czaplewski 2006, Keiningham, Money 2004, Lee, Lee and Feick 2006, Maxham 2001, Mayzlin 2006, Perkins-Munn & Evans 2003, Woodside & Delozier 1976,) and intentions to pass of further WOM (Brown, Barry, Dacin & Gunst 2005, Maxham 2001).

Interestingly, negative WOM has been found to result in stronger perceptions of source credibility (Godes & Mayzlin 2004).

Humor in Word-of Mouth

It is not surprising that humor would exist within WOM messages. As Lynch (2002) notes: "Jokes and humor, in general, play an important part in determining who we are and how we think of ourselves, and as a result how we interact with others." (Lynch 2002, p. 425)

EXPLORATORY RESEARCH

Given the importance of humor within the communication process, it can be expected that it will impact the message exchange within WOM conversations. As such, exploratory qualitative research was undertaken to understand the role of emotions and humor in WOM.

Internet based WOM has become increasingly used in consumer research (Chevalier & Mayzlin 2006, Dellarocas 2003, Godes & Mayzlin 2004, Goldenberg, Libai & Muller 2001, Gruen, Osmonbekov & Czaplewski 2006, Mayzlin 2006, Phelps et al 2004,). In keeping with this line of research, electronic WOM was used in the exploratory research. Prior qualitative research indicated that online home improvement forums contained ample electronic WOM conversations (Bussiere 2000), so 127 naturally-occurring online conversations from the internet newsgroup *alt.home.repair* were analyzed. The conversations varied in length from two comments to over 40 comments. Some conversations included over 20 individuals. All conversations dealt with home improvement issues.

The conversations were analyzed for evidence of any emotion or mood that moved the word-of-mouth message away from a neutral statement. The impact on the flow of conversation was then analyzed. The primary focus of the analysis was the tone of the WOM advice rather than the advice seeker. Samples of the complete text were also coded by two additional researchers to assess reliability.

Findings

Approximately a quarter of messages included elements of humor. This not only altered the tone of the conversation, but also resulted in further use of humor or, at times, angry responses to the humor. In the following conversation, the humorous comment seems to be intentional and seems to seek to make the other participants smile or comment.

After a 264 word question about his furnace, Edge concludes (Conversation 3):

Have I got a faulty thermostat or is there something wrong down at the furnace?
Thanks a million-Edge

The conversation maintains a focus on the question, and yet the humor also becomes an integral part of the conversation. Participants even began using emoticons (e.g. :-) the sideways smile) to make sure that the comment was being understood as humor.

ANSWER 1: You should have 24 volts ac. (measure again with the meter in the ac mode). If the voltage is still low, check the wiring for a bad connection. this can cause an intermittent problem)
> Thanks a million -
No problem, just send a half a million, please!!! :-)(want the address to send it??)Better yet, I'll pick it up personally. :-)(wouldn't want it to get lost in the mail) :-)
RESPONSE TO ANSWER: Thanks for the tip! It was a loose wire, where the thermostat connects to the gas valve. Hmmm. Half a million? Maybe I can talk you down?
COMMENT FROM OBSERVER: Do what everyone else does—just don't pay.
Christopher

Similarly, a request for help in hanging wallpaper resulted in the following comment (Conversation 29):

Use longer nails?

Alternatively, the humor is essentially tangential to the conversation. The participants likely see it, but it does not actually influence the flow of conversation. Consider, for example, the following conversation. At the end of a conversation that actually addresses the issue, a new participant enters the conversation and takes advantage of the wording of the question to add some adult humor. The question asks about mounting a toilet flange. The final answer is less than useful (Conversation 123).

for good sex i alwayze mount it.

This tangential humor, however, can actually influence the flow of conversation. Consider, for example, the following conversation. The questioner, Stormin Mormon, begins with mild humor in describing his vehicle. More importantly, Stormin Mormon signs his question with additional references to his religion. Because some participants have multiple postings, it is worthwhile noting the commentor's name (Conversation 76).

QUESTION: Stormin Mormon
My land tank is a 87 Dodge, with the 8 engine, and has about 150K miles. Running about 8 or 9 MPG. Recently had the tune up parts. Cap, rotor, sparks, air filter, fuel filter. What else might help improve mileage?
Christopher
Learn more about Jesus www.lds.org www.mormons.org
ANSWER 1: Tony
Hi, You mean V8? Advancing timing as much as you can will help. Changing
advance curve by trying different springs in the distributor can help changing the thermostat with hotter one (if that old engine can take it without leaking coolant) can help Trying to get lower idle RPM can help. Tranny shift kit may help. Changing the jet in the carb, etc., etc. No new ignition wires?
ANSWER 2: Randd01
Jack it up and put a GMC under it!
ANSWER 3: Loose Cannon
Don't think putting a GMC under it would help get better mileage. I have an
older GMC 'Gaucho' van with a 350. What a pig on gas! Don't know which Chrysler V8 the Stormin Mormon has in his Dodge van, but if it is the 318, the gas mileage should be better than he is getting. Had a few big old Chrysler cars with the 318 engine and got pretty good mileage out of them. Seldom, if ever had any engine problems either.
ANSWER 4: Randd01
My new GMC with 5.3 V8 averages 20 mpg got up to 23 on highway with automatic overdrive tranny. Way better then my 1995 GMC with 350 got.
ANSWER 5: Swampy
get a few of your wives to push it
RESPONSE TO ANSWER 5: Stormin Mormon
Oddly enough, I'm a bachelor. But thanks for the idea.

Note that the humor moved the conversation into a GM versus Chrysler debate. In addition, Stormin Mormon's Mormon status elicited the multiple wife joke. In each case, the actual issue became a side issue.

Yet, at times, humor is used to add strength to the message. The cutting aspect of the humor actually speaks to the seriousness of the issue. In the following conversation, the questioner asks about soldering a natural gas control valve. The response is humorous and serious (Conversation 118):

Increase your life insurance twofold. Have your next of kin two counties away with copies of all important papers when you do this.

This exploratory research indicates that the presence of humor in WOM messages can alter the flow of a conversation. Specifically, the presence of humor seems to weaken the impact of the WOM message on behavioral intentions–the likelihood that an individual who receives the WOM message will be more likely to follow the advice in a purchase decision—and on the likelihood of passing on the advice to others through future WOM.

RESEARCH QUESTIONS

Based on the literature review and the exploratory research, the following behavioral intention, WOM intention, source credibility and message persuasiveness hypotheses were developed.

Behavioral Intentions
H1a: Positive humorous WOM messages will evoke weaker behavioral intentions than positive neutrally-toned WOM messages
H1b: Negative humorous WOM messages will evoke weaker behavioral intentions than negative neutrally-toned WOM messages

Word-of-Mouth Intentions
H2a: Positive humorous WOM messages will evoke weaker WOM intentions than positive neutrally-toned WOM messages.
H2b: Negative humorous WOM messages will evoke weaker WOM intentions than negative neutrally-toned WOM messages.

Source Credibility
H3a: Positive humorous WOM messages will evoke weaker perceptions of source credibility than positive neutrally-toned WOM messages.
H3b: Negative humorous WOM messages will evoke weaker perceptions of source credibility than negative neutrally-toned WOM messages.

Message Persuasiveness
H4a: Positive humorous WOM messages will evoke weaker perceptions of message persuasiveness than positive neutrally-toned WOM messages.
H4b: Negative humorous WOM messages will evoke weaker perceptions of message persuasiveness than negative neutrally-toned WOM messages.

METHOD

Participants and Design

Participants were 492 American adults who participated in the survey as part of a paid survey panel. The design was a two (positive/negative WOM message) by two (neutral and humorous WOM) experimental design. Each participant was presented with two WOM scenarios.

Stimuli and Procedure

Four WOM messages were created for the experiment (a positive and negative version of the neutral and humorous messages). All stimuli were based closely on actual messages found in the 127 conversations from the exploratory research. All WOM messages were changed to a fictional brand name (Granger). In keeping with the home improvement focus of the exploratory research, all WOM messages dealt with garage door openers. Five business professors and three adult non-academics rated a total of 16 potential scenarios to ensure internal validity. Additional WOM descriptors were provided to avoid leading the responses (e.g. impatient, confused, shy, curious, etc.). The four scenarios that were used had agreement from all raters.

Participants completed the experiment online. After viewing each WOM message, participants were asked to evaluate the credibility of the source, persuasiveness of the message, behavioral intention and WOM intentions. Using existing scales ensured high reliability of the scales as is demonstrated in Table 1.

Source credibility measured the trustworthiness of the WOM message provider using a 5 item scale that focused on trustworthiness. Persuasiveness of the Message uses a 4 item scale to measure the strength of the WOM message. Behavioral Intentions measures the inclination of the message recipient to follow the advice given

TABLE 1
SCALE RELIABILITY

Scale	Source	
Source Credibility	Mackenzie and Lutz 1989	0.90
Persuasiveness of the Message	Gurhan-Canli and Maheswarn 2000	0.89
Behavioral Intention	Mackenzie, Lutz and Belch 1986	0.92
WOM Intention	Price and Arnould 1999	0.93

in the WOM message using a 3 item scale. The WOM Intention scale measured the willingness to recommend the brand discussed in the WOM message using a 3 item scale.

RESULTS

Behavioral Intentions

The behavioral intentions scale was used to determine the inclination of the respondent to purchase the Granger garage door opener if they needed a garage door opener based on the WOM message that they read.

There was strong support for H1a. Behavioral intentions for positive neutral WOM messages (M=0.80) were reduced for positive humorous comments (M=0.26; T(261)=15.25, p<0.01). Similarly, H1b was supported—behavioral intentions for negative neutral WOM messages (M=0.70) were reduced for negative humorous messages (M=0.21; T(231)=12.48, p<0.01).

Overall, there was strong support for the hypotheses that neutral WOM messages have a larger impact on behavioral intentions than do humorous WOM messages.

Word-of-Mouth Intentions

The WOM intentions scale was used to determine the inclination of the respondent to pass on the WOM comment about Granger garage door openers to others through future WOM conversations.

There was strong support for H2a. WOM intentions for positive neutral WOM messages (M=0.76) were reduced for positive humorous comments (M=-0.92; T(261)=12.55, p<0.01). Similarly, WOM intentions for negative neutral WOM messages (M=0.35) were reduced for negative impatient messages (M=-1.11; T(231)=11.28, p<0.01), thereby supporting H2b.

Overall, there was general support for the hypotheses that neutral WOM messages have a larger impact on WOM intentions than do humorous WOM messages.

Dissecting The Results

In order to understand why behavioral intentions and WOM intentions decreased with the presence of humor, the role of positive versus negative messages was analyzed.

Positive versus Negative Messages

While the flow of the WOM conversations altered when humor was present, there was some indication that negative and positive comments impacted the flow differently. It was, however, difficult to forecast a directional effect for each of the message types.

Behavioral Intentions

Positive and negative messages influenced behavioral intentions differently, based on the message tone. Neutrally-toned com-

ments that were positive (i.e. supported the Granger brand), exhibited slightly stronger behavioral intentions (M=0.80) than negative messages (M=0.70; T(261)=2.82, p<0.01). This was consistent with previous research.

Humorous WOM demonstrated no significant difference on behavioral intentions between positive and negative comments.

Word-of-Mouth Intentions

In general, positive comments had a weaker impact on WOM intentions than negative comments. WOM intentions for positive neutral comments (M=0.76) were greater than WOM intentions for neutral negative messages (M=0.35; T(261)=3.22, p<0.01). This was not consistent with previous research.

Humorous WOM demonstrated no significant difference on WOM intentions between positive and negative comments.

Source Credibility and Message Persuasiveness

In addition to answering questions about behavioral and WOM intentions following each WOM, participants also asked to evaluate the credibility of the message giver and the persuasiveness of the message.

Hypothesis 3a was supported. Positive neutral WOM resulted in higher ratings of source credibility (M= 0.84) than humorous WOM (M=0.50; T(261)= 10.33, p<0.01).

Similarly, hypothesis 3b was supported. Negative neutral WOM resulted in higher ratings of source credibility (M= 0.77) than humorous WOM (M=0.47; T(231)= 8.47, p<0.01). This is consistent with Godes & Mayzlin (2004).

In judging message persuasiveness, hypotheses 4a and 4b were both supported. Positive neutral WOM also resulted in higher ratings of message persuasiveness (M=0.67) than humorous WOM (M=0.28; T(261)= 10.40, p<0.01). Negative neutral WOM resulted in higher ratings of message persuasiveness (M=0.63) than humorous WOM (M=0.23; T(231)= 10.77, p<0.01).

DISCUSSION

The complete analysis of hypotheses found significant differences between neutrally-toned and humorous WOM comments. These differences are partially explained by the degree of positivity or negativity in the messages. The WOM message tone and degree of negativity have significant influences on perceived source credibility and persuasiveness of the message.

These findings have important implications for our understanding of WOM dynamics and consumer behavior. First, the findings in general indicate that word-of-mouth is a more complicated construct than previously believed. Second, it indicates that the tone of the message may be as important as the actual message. Humor generally detracts from the impact of the message.

Managers will benefit from understanding that WOM is more complicated that previously understood. This means that companies may want to spark neutral WOM comments rather than using humorous appeals to spark WOM. This is increasingly important given recent interest in viral marketing campaigns.

Future research could evaluate the ways in which these changes interact. Specifically, research that attempts to model the interactions between message positivity/negativity and message tone would provide important insight into consumer analysis of WOM messages.

Given Zhang and Zinkhan's (2006) finding that the impact of a humorous message seems to be contingent on who receives the message, research that further investigates the recipients of humorous messages would be beneficial. As such, demographic analysis may also provide insight into the differing views of males versus females, experienced consumers versus inexperienced, and individuals with varying personal traits. Similarly, an analysis of how market mavens–those most likely to pass on marketplace advice– react to humorous WOM would be beneficial.

This research is limited by its data collection method. Online word-of-mouth messages may not be representative of off-line WOM behavior. Also, the fact that message givers were unknown to the participants may impact results. Again, this may speak to the differences between electronic WOM and traditional WOM. Also, any research based on humor is subject to differing views of the humor. While statistical differences were found, studies that replicate the findings would be useful.

REFERENCES

Alden, Dana, Ashesh Mukherjee, and Wayne Hoyer (1993), "An Examination of Cognitive Factors Related To Humorousness," *Journal of Advertising,* 22(2), 29-38.

Alden, Dana, Ashesh Mukherjee, and Wayne D Hoyer (2000), "The Effects of Incongruity, Surprise And Positive Moderators On Perceived Humor," *Journal of Advertising,* 29(2), 1-15.

Arndt, Johan (1967), "Role of Product-related Conversations in the Diffusion of a New Product," *Journal of Marketing Research,* 4 (3), 291.

Athanassopoulos, Antreas, Spiros Gounaris, and Vlassis Stathakopoulos (2001), "Behavioral Responses to Customer Satisfaction: An empirical study," *European Journal of Marketing,* 35 (5/6), 687.

Bone Paula F. (1995), "Word-of-Mouth Effects On Short-Term and Long-Term Product Judgments," *Journal of Business Research,* 32, 213–23.

Bowman, Douglas and Das Narayandas (2001), "Managing Customer-Initiated Contacts With Manufacturers: The Impact on Share of Category Requirements and Word-Of-Mouth Behavior," *Journal of Marketing Research,* 38 (3), 281.

Brooker, George (1981), "A Comparison of The Persuasive Effects of Mild Humor And Mild Fear Appeals," *Journal of Advertising,* 10(4), 29-40.

Brooks, Robert (1957), "'Word-of-Mouth' Advertising In Selling New Products," *Journal of Marketing,* 22(1), 154-161.

Brown Jacqueline and Peter Reingen (1987), "Social Ties And Word-of-Mouth Referral Behavior," *Journal of Consumer Research,* 14(4), 350–362.

Brown, Tom, Thomas Barry, Peter Dacin, and Richard F Gunst (2005), "Spreading The Word: Investigating Antecedents of Consumers' Positive Word-of-Mouth," *Academy of Marketing Science. Journal,* 33(2), 123-138.

Bussiere, Dave (2000), "Evidence and Implications of Electronic Word-of-Mouth," Proceedings of the Academy of Marketing Science Conference.

Chevalier, Judith A., and Dina Mayzlin (2006), "The Effect of Word of Mouth On Sales: Online Book Reviews," *Journal of Marketing Research,* 43 (August), 345–354.

Cline, Thomas, Moses Altsech, and James Kellaris (2003), "When Does Humor Enhance Or Inhibit Ad Responses?: The Moderating Role of the Need for Humor," *Journal of Advertising,* 32(3), 31-45.

Decarlo Thomas, Russell Laczniak, Carol Motley, and Sridhar Ramaswami (2007), "Influence of Image and Familiarity on Consumer Response to Negative Word-of-Mouth," *Journal of Marketing Theory And Practice,* 15(1) 41–51.

Dellarocas, Chrysanthos (2003), "The Digitization of Word of Mouth: Promise and Challenges of Online Feedback," *Management Science,* 49(10), 1407- 1424.

Duhan, Dale F, Scott D Johnson, James B Wilcox, and Gilbert D Harrell (1997), "Influences on Consumer Use of Word-of-Mouth Recommendation Sources," *Academy of Marketing Science. Journal,* 25 (4), 283.

Duncan, Calvin (1979), "Humor In Advertising: A Behavioral Perspective," *Academy of Marketing Science. Journal,* 7(4), 285–306.

Duncan, Calvin, and James Nelson (1985), "Effects of Humor In A Radio Advertising Experiment," *Journal of Advertising,* 14(2), 33-40.

Engel, James, Roger Blackwell, and Robert Kegerreis (1969), "How Information Is Used To Adopt An Innovation," *Journal of Advertising Research,* 9, 3– 8.

Gelb, Betsy, and Charles M Pickett (1983), "Attitude-Toward-The-Ad: Links To Humor And To Advertising Effectiveness," *Journal of Advertising,* 12(2), 34-42.

Gilly, Mary C, John L Graham, Mary Finley Wolfinbarger, and Laura J Yale (1998), "A Dyadic Study of Interpersonal Information Search," *Academy of Marketing Science. Journal,* 26 (2), 83.

Godes, David, and Dina Mayzlin (2004) "Using Online Conversations To Study Word-of-Mouth Communication," *Marketing Science,* 23(4), 545–560.

Goldenberg Jacob, Barak Libai and Eitan Muller (2001), "Talk of The Network: A Complex Systems Look At The Underlying Process of Word-of-Mouth," *Marketing Letters,* 12(3), 211-223.

Gruen, Thomas, Talai Osmonbekov, and Andrew Czaplewski (2006), "Ewom: The Impact of Customer-To-Customer Online Know-How Exchange On Customer Value And Loyalty," *Journal of Business Research,* 59, 449–456.

Gurhan-Canli, Zeynep and Durairaj Maheswaran (2000), "Determinants of Country-of-Origin Evaluations," *Journal of Consumer Research,* 27(1), 96-108.

Halstead, Diane (2002), "Negative Word of Mouth: Substitute For Or Supplement To Consumer Complaints?" *Journal of Consumer Satisfaction, Dissatisfaction And Complaining Behavior,* 15, 1-12.

Keiningham, Timothy, Tiffany Perkins-Munn, and Heather Evans (2003), "The Impact of Customer Satisfaction on Share-of-Wallet in a Business-To-Business Environment," *Journal of Service Research,* 6(1) 37-50.

Lammers, Bruce, Laura Leibowitz, George Seymour, and Judith Hennessey (1983), "Humor and Cognitive Responses to Advertising Stimuli: a Trace Consolidation Approach," *Journal of Business Research* 11(17), 173-185.

Lee, Jonathan, Janghyuk Lee, and Lawrence Feick (2006), "Incorporating Word-of-Mouth Effects in Estimating Customer Lifetime Value," *Database Marketing & Customer Strategy Management*, 14(1), 29–39

Lynch, Owen (2002), "Humorous Communication: Finding a Place for Humor in Communication Research," *Communication Theory*, 12(4), 423–445.

Madden, Thomas and Marc Weinberger (1984), "Humor in Advertising: A Practitioner View," *Journal of Advertising Research*, 24(4), 23-29.

Maxham James G. III (2001), "Service Recovery's Influence on Consumer Satisfaction, Positive Word-of-Mouth, and Purchase Intentions," *Journal of Business Research*, 54, 11–24.

Maxham, James G and Richard G Netemeyer (2003), "A Longitudinal Study of Complaining Customers' Evaluations of Multiple Service Failures and Recovery Efforts," *Journal of Marketing*, 66 (4), 57.

_____ (2002), "Modeling Customer Perceptions of Complaint Handling Over Time: The Effects of Perceived Justice on Satisfaction and Intent," *Journal of Retailing*, 78 (4), 239.

Mayzlin, Dina (2006), "Promotional Chat on The Internet," *Marketing Science,* 25(2), 155–163.

MacKenzie, Scott and Richard Lutz (1989), "An Empirical Examination of the Structural Antecedents of Attitude Toward the Ad in an Advertising Pretesting Context," Journal of Marketing, 53(April), 48-65.

MacKenzie, Scott, Richard Lutz and George Belch (1986), "The Role of Attitude Toward the Ad as a Moderator of Advertising Effectiveness: A Test of Competing Explanations," *Journal of Marketing Research*, 23(May), 130-143.

Money, Bruce (2004), "Word-of-Mouth Promotion and Switching Behavior in Japanese and American Business-To-Business Service Clients," *Journal of Business Research*, 57, 297– 305.

Nyer, Prashanth, and Mahesh Gopinath (2005), "Effects of Complaining Versus Negative Word of Mouth on Subsequent Changes in Satisfaction: The Role of Public Commitment," *Psychology & Marketing*, 22(12): 937–953.

Perry, Stephen, Stefan Jenzowsky, Cynthia King, Huiuk Yi, Joe Bob Hester and Jeanne Gartenschlaeger (1997), "Using Humorous Programs as a Vehicle for Humorous Commercials," *Journal of Communication,* 47(1), 20-39.

Phelps, Joseph, Regina Lewis, Lynne Mobilio, and David Perry (2004), "Viral Marketing Or Electronic Word-of-Mouth Advertising: Examining Consumer Responses and Motivations to Pass Along Email," *Journal of Advertising Research*, 333-348.

Price, Linda and Eric Arnould (1999), "Commercial Friendships: Service Provider-Client Relationships in Context," *Journal or Marketing*, 63(October), 38-56.

Richins, Marsha L. (1983), "Negative Word-of-Mouth by Dissatisfied Consumers: A Pilot Study," *Journal of Marketing*, 47(68).

Scott, Cliff, David Klein, and Jennings Bryant (1990), "Consumer Response to Humor in Advertising: A Series of Field Studies Using Behavioral Observations," *Journal of Consumer Research,* 16(4), 498-501.

Spotts, Harlan, Marc Weinberger, and Amy L Parsons (1997), "Assessing the Use and Impact of Humor on Advertising Effectiveness: A Contingency Approach," *Journal of Advertising,* Fall 1997; 26(3), 17-33.

Stern, Barbara (1996), "Advertising Comedy in Electronic Drama: The Construct, Theory and Taxonomy," *European Journal of Marketing,* 30(9), 37-59.

Sternthal, Brian and Samuel Craig (1973), "Humor in Advertising," *Journal of Marketing*, 37(4), 12-18.

Voorhees Clay, Michael Brady and David Horowitz (2006), "A Voice from The Silent Masses: An Exploratory and Comparative Analysis of Noncomplainers," *Journal of The Academy of Marketing Science*, 34(4), 514-527.

Wangenheim, Florian, and Tomas Bayon (2004), "The Effect of Word of Mouth on Services Switching: Measurement And Moderating Variables," *European Journal of Marketing,* 38(9/10), 1173-1185.

Wangenheim, Florian (2005), "Postswitching Negative Word of Mouth," *Journal of Service Research,* 8(1), 67- 78.

Weinberger, Marc, and Charles Gulas (1992), "The Impact of Humor in Advertising: A Review," *Journal of Advertising,* 21(4), 35-59.

Woodside, Arch and Wayne Delozier (1976), "Effects of Word of Mouth Advertising On Consumer Risk Taking," *Journal of Advertising,* 5(4), 12-19.

Zhang, Yong, and George M Zinkhan (2006), "Responses to Humorous Ads," *Journal of Advertising,* 35(4), 113- 127.

Emotional Network in Control of Cognitive Processes in Advertisement

Andrzej Falkowski, Warsaw School of Social Psychology, Poland
Alicja Grochowska, Warsaw School of Social Psychology, Poland

ABSTRACT

The theoretical background for the presented research are network models of memory and emotion, and the prospect theory. The research examines cause-effect relationships between emotions elicited by the advertisement and the processes of evaluation and memory for ads appealing to positive or negative emotions. Structural equation modeling has been applied as a method of statistical analysis. The two studies show the significance of emotions and the specificity of autobiographical ads and PSA's (non-commercial advertisements), with reference to a consumer's personal gains and losses in the light of the prospect theory.

INTRODUCTION

One of the crucial factors determining the way consumers process information of advertisement are emotional reactions elicited by ads. Ad-triggered emotions, transferred to the ad, can influence the evaluation and memory of both an ad and the advertised brand (Burke, Edell, 1989; Holbrook, Batra, 1987; Morris et al., 2002; Escalas et al., 2004). Recent studies suggest that positive and negative emotions have an asymmetrical effect on reactions to ads (Moore, Hutchinson, 1983; Brown et al., 1998). However, different roles of positive and negative emotions in evaluation and memory of ads have not been explained yet (Cotte, Ritchie, 2005; Faseur, Geuens, 2006; Tanner, 2006). This problem can be solved in the light of network models in which relationships between emotion and cognition are considered. The role of positive and negative emotions in evaluation and memory of advertisement can be modified by the context of ad perception and by instrumental or prosocial motivational factors. Friestad and Thomson (1993) showed that memory of ads was dependent on the context in which they were perceived (ad-directed processing vs. brand-directed processing). Emotional advertisements were better remembered when perceived in the ad-directed context. Furthermore, Sujan, Bettman and Baumgartner (1993) and Baumgartner, Sujan and Bettman (1992) found that consumers' autobiographical memories involving products and product usage experiences were affectively charged and retrieval of autobiographical memories influenced evaluation and memory of advertisement. The stronger the emotions (net-affect) elicited by the ad were, the better the ad and brand were evaluated. The better the brand evaluations, the better memory for brand claims was, but only in strong argument conditions. Relationships between positive vs. negative emotions and evaluation and memory of ads can be analyzed in the light of gains and losses which the consumer incurs by purchasing or not purchasing the product. Such an approach to research matches the prospect theory by Kahneman and Tversky (1979).

The goal of our research is to investigate cause-effect relationships between emotions elicited by the advertisement and the processes of evaluation and memory for ads appealing to positive or negative emotions. Our purpose also is to show the significance of emotions and the specificity of autobiographical ads and PSA's (non-commercial advertisements), with reference to a consumer's personal gains and losses in the light of the prospect theory.

THEORETICAL BACKGROUND

Network organization of emotions

Relationships between emotion and cognition can be well explained by network models of the mind. In the PDP model, McCllelland (1995) explains information processing of objects and events, but not emotions. Parallel and cooperative processing of emotional information were emphasized by Suarez Araujo and colleagues (2005). Bower (1992) took emotions into consideration as well as events and objects in his network model of memory. A constructivist and contextual approach to emotion and memory was presented by Parrot and Spackman (2000). Panksepp's (2000) studies indicated the cooperation of emotional and cognitive processes. The emotional system can be considered as a network structure as well as in other perspectives. There are neurobiological, psychophysiological and psychological arguments that systems responsible for processing positive and negative emotions are independent (Cacioppo, Berntson, 1994; Cacioppo, Gardner, 1999). Research into influences of positive and negative emotions on cognitive processes showed that positive affect improved creative problem solving: it led to cognitive elaboration and flexibility, giving rise to more thoughts, more nontypical thoughts, and innovative solutions to problems. Therefore, it can be claimed that positive affect activates a wide area of a cognitive network. On the other hand, research on negative affect showed that the negative affect is not simply the opposite of positive affect in either its behavioral or cognitive effects. Negative affect increases vigilance more than positive affect, while activating a narrower area of the cognitive network (Ashby, Isen, Turken, 1999).

Positive and negative ads and gains and losses

According to the prospect theory by Kahneman and Tversky (1979), 'losses loom larger than gains'. Kahneman and Tversky's research has been concerned mainly with monetary outcomes. However, the authors suggest that the theory is applicable to choices involving other attributes. Positive and negative emotions in advertisement can be significant not only in evaluation and memory of ads but also in experiencing satisfaction of purchase (gains) or dissatisfaction with not having purchased the product (losses). Therefore, one can expect that ads can elicit strong negative emotions and high sensitivity by suggesting what consumers can lose by not purchasing the product, whereas ads implying gains by purchasing the product elicit moderate positive emotions and low sensitivity to the ad. The effect of gains and losses in advertisement can be modified by different motivational factors elicited by both commercial and non-commercial ads. The effect is stronger if gains and losses concern the consumer directly, which is related to instrumental motivation.

Theoretical model

On the basis of the assumptions presented above we propose a theoretical model for print advertisement (Figure 1). Our model is based on Burke and Edell's (1989) research which examined relationships between emotions elicited by advertisement and evaluation of the ad and brand. In Burke and Edell's analyses the fit of structural models to the empirical data was excellent.

In our model, advertisement, as an emotional stimulus, activates nodes in the emotional network. Emotions elicited by the advertisement influence ad and product evaluation, and memory. Furthermore, according to the effect of familiarity, familiar stimuli are more attractive (Zajonc, 1980). Therefore, one can expect that the more familiar the advertisement, the more positive the evaluation of the product. Since we tested memory for brand claims, we did not expect the effect of ad evaluation on memory: Even in

Advances in Consumer Research
Volume 36, © 2009

FIGURE 1
Theoretical model: emotions in evaluation and memory of advertisement

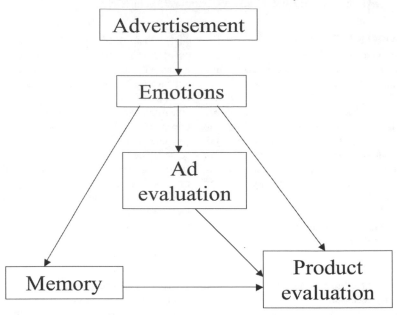

positively evaluated ads, brand claims can be processed peripherally. Our model can be interpreted as the emotional-cognitive network, sensitive to the context and emotions elicited by the ad.

STUDY 1

Emotions in evaluation and memory of the autobiographical ad

Personal experiences stored in autobiographical memory have specific properties which are important for research into autobiographical advertisement. First, autobiographical knowledge can be considered a constructive process. Therefore, autobiographical memories are sensitive to the context in which they are retrieved. Second, accessing autobiographical memories is likely to enhance the involvement in communicated information. In autobiographical advertisement emotions are elicited by autobiographical text, referring to personal experiences. Krugman (1965, 1967) emphasized the importance of accounting for the personal experiences that individuals accessed during exposure to an advertisement and assumed that autobiographical memories have an important influence on the process of product evaluation. According to Baumgartner, Sujan and Bettman (1992), encouraging autobiographical memories with an advertisement influences evaluation and memory of the ad. Personal involvement encouraged by the advertisement can also be significant for perceiving gains or avoidance of losses while in possession of the product. This perception depends on whether the advertisement refers to positive or negative autobiographical memories.

In Study 1 we examine cause-effect relationships between emotions elicited by the advertisement and the processes of evaluation and memory for ads appealing to positive or negative emotions. We also investigate the significance of the context in which the ad was perceived (ad-directed processing vs. brand-directed processing) and the significance of positive vs. negative emotions elicited by the ad in its evaluation and recall. Finally, we analyze the results obtained with reference to the consumer's personal gains and losses in the light of prospect theory.

Participants, Materials, and Procedure

One hundred and eighty-eight undergraduate students, age 19–25, took part in Study 1. Participants were volunteers, from universities and colleges in Warsaw.

Two *print advertisements* were designed for the purpose of the experiment. Both ads presented a DVD case. Brand claims of fictitious brand General Master were located at the bottom of each ad. The two ads included different autobiographical texts, one referring to positive and the other to negative autobiographical memories.

The Emotional Network Scale was used to measure emotions elicited by the advertisement. The construction of our scale was inspired by Burke and Edell's (1989) *The Feelings Scale* and Sujan, Bettman and Baumgartner's (1993) *Net Affect Scale*. The categorical and network structure of emotions constituted the theoretical background for the Emotional Network Scale. Multidimensional scaling methods were applied to establish the network structure of emotions. Psychometric properties of the 21-item scale were described by Grochowska and Falkowski (in print). Three indices of emotions were analyzed: positive emotions, negative emotions and the difference between positive and negative emotions (net-affect). There were 13 and 8 items for positive and negative emotions, respectively. Participants marked their answers on the 7-point Likert scale.

The *Ad Evaluation Scale* was used to measure the subjects' assessment of the ads. In constructing the scale a principal components analysis yielded two factors: positive and negative evaluation. In preliminary studies three ads (positive, negative, and neutral) were investigated and adjectives loaded more than .60, shared by the three ads, were selected. Thus, the scale consisted of 32 adjectives, 16 for positive and 16 for negative evaluation. The index of ad evaluation was the difference between sums of positive and negative items, according to the methodology described by Burke and Edell (1989).

Product evaluation was assessed on four 100-millimeter-long scales, in which 0 was low and 100 was high: satisfaction with, and

FIGURE 2

Structural equation models for the ad referring to positive autobiographical memories

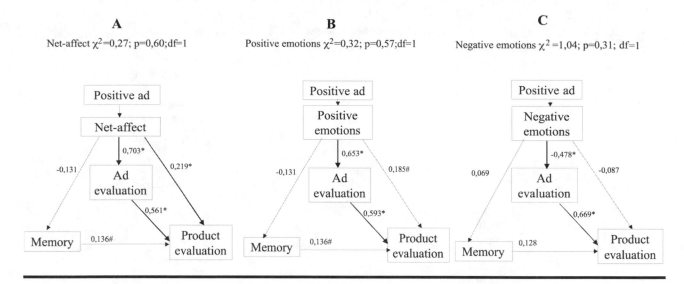

quality, durability, and utility of the product advertised. The four measures were totaled to form an overall measure of product evaluation. Cronbach-alpha was .94.

Brand claim recall. Subjects were asked to list all the brand claims that they could recall from the ad. The number of brand claims correctly recalled was counted. The recall score could vary between 0 and 10.

Procedure and methods of statistical analysis

The study was conducted individually, in laboratory conditions. Subjects were asked to either evaluate the merits of the advertised brand (brand-directed processing) or to judge the merits of the actual advertisement for the brand (ad-directed processing). At first, a buffer ad was implemented. Then, forty seconds were given to view an experimental advertisement. Two groups viewed the ad referring to positive autobiographical memories and the other two viewed the ad referring to negative. Then the subjects were asked to list all the brand claims they could recall from the advertisement, in the order that first came to mind. They were then asked to fill The Emotional Network Scale, The Ad Evaluation Scale and product evaluation scales. Assumptions on the network structure of cause-effect relationships between analyzed variables allowed the testing of the theoretical model applying structural equation modeling as a method of statistical analysis.

Results

Emotions in memory and evaluation of autobiographical ads

The proposed model of effects of emotion on evaluation of ads and products and on memory for brand claims, similar to Burke and Edell's (1989) models, was tested in structural equations modeling. The system was tested by translating the variables presented in Figure 1 into a system of structural equations expanded to include the positive and negative emotions as well as the difference between them (net-affect) elicited by the ad, for the two ads referring to positive or negative autobiographical memories. In this way, the six empirical models were tested. Structural equation models for the ad referring to positive autobiographical memories are presented in Figure 2.

As we can see in Figure 2A, net-affect elicited by the ad referring to positive autobiographical memories had a direct effect on the ad and product evaluation. Although emotions elicited by the ad had no direct influence on the memory of brand claims, the fit of the model to empirical data was worse after removing the path between emotions and the memory of brand claims.[1] This means that cause-effect relationships presented in the model are significant for the entire model. Furthermore, there was an effect of brand claims on product evaluation (at the level of statistical tendency, p=0,08). Familiar stimuli were evaluated more positively. Thus, there were three determinants in product evaluations in the analyzed model: memory of brand claims, ad evaluation and emotions elicited by the ad. Similar regularity could be observed in the ad referring to positive autobiographical memories, in the case of eliciting positive emotions (Figure 2B). But this effect did not occur in the case of eliciting negative emotions (Figure 2C) nor in the ad referring to negative autobiographical memories (Figure 3). Thus, positive emotions activated a wide area of the cognitive network. On the other hand, negative affect was not simply the opposite of positive affect in its cognitive effects.

Negative emotions elicited by the ad (Figure 2C and 3C) had a direct effect on one variable only: evaluation of the ad. Negative emotions had an effect on the negative ad evaluations but not on the evaluations of the product itself. In product evaluation subjects relied upon ad evaluation. Relationships between negative emotions and the memory of brand claims and the evaluations of the product were not significant in this model. However, after remov-

---

[1] Akaike's Information Criterion (AIC), (Akaike 1987), has been used for selecting the best model among a number of candidate models. We compared AICs for six models respecting the path between emotions and the memory (-1.729; -1.9; -1.68; -1.62; -0.96; -1.991) to AICs for six models after removing this path (-2.369; -3.739; 39.75; 54.05; 17.23; 34.01, respectively). The model that yields the smallest value of AIC is considered the best. Models respecting the path between emotions and the memory had lower AICs than the models after removing this path.

FIGURE 3
Structural equation models for the ad referring to negative autobiographical memories

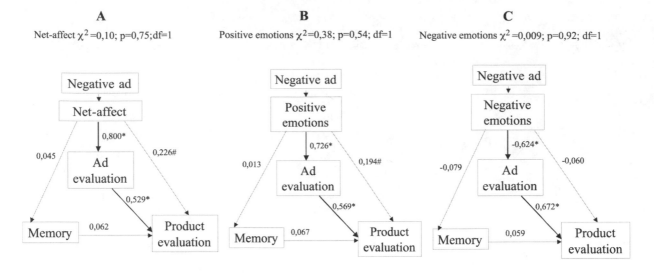

A

Net-affect χ^2=0,10; p=0,75;df=1

B

Positive emotions χ^2=0,38; p=0,54; df=1

C

Negative emotions χ^2=0,009; p=0,92; df=1

FIGURE 4
Values of fits (χ^2) for models of advertisements referring to positive vs. negative autobiographical memories, in two contexts of ad perception

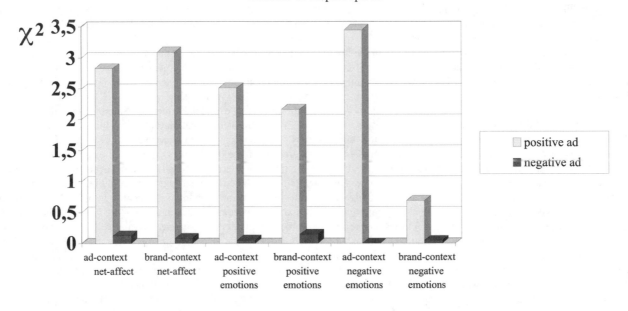

ing the path between negative emotions and the memory of brand claims, the fit of the model to empirical data was worse. This means that relationships between emotions elicited by the ad and brand claims recall were significant for the entire model, as in models for net-affect or for positive emotions. Furthermore, it can be observed that negative emotions activated a narrow part of the cognitive network compared to positive emotions.

Emotions in evaluation and memory of autobiographical ads, in the two contexts of ad perception

It was expected that the structure of relationships between emotions elicited by the ad, evaluations of the ad and brand, and brand claims recall were modified by the context of ad perception.

In the following analyses the theoretical model was tested for the data obtained in two contexts of ad perception: ad-directed and brand-directed processing. In subsequent analyses, emotions elicited by the ad (positive emotions, negative emotions and net-affect), in two contexts of ad perception, for ads referring to positive vs. negative autobiographical memories, were taken into consideration. Thus, the χ^2 tests were used to estimate the fit of empirical data to twelve theoretical models (Figure 4).

An interesting regularity may be seen in Figure 4: in models for ads referring to positive autobiographical memories the fit of the model to empirical data was much worse than in models for ads referring to negative autobiographical memories. This means that

FIGURE 5
Structural equation models for the PSA referring to positive emotions

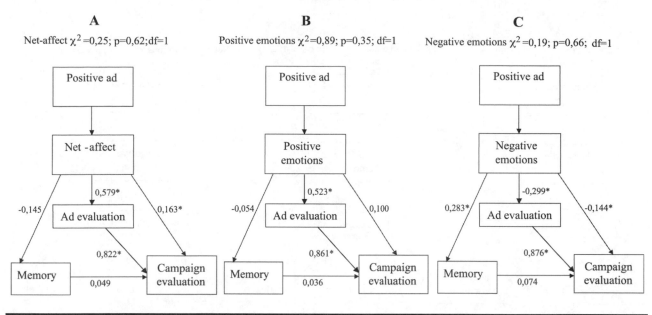

subjects were more sensitive to losses (negative, threat message) than to gains (positive message). This result is in accordance with prospect theory by Kahneman and Tversky (1979)–'losses loom larger than gains'. The same product presented in the perspective of gains vs. losses was remembered and evaluated differently. Moreover, in ads referring to positive autobiographical memories, there was an effect of brand claims memory on product evaluation in the ad-directed context, while in the brand-directed context this relationship was not significant. This means that relationships between memory of brand claims and product evaluation in the ad-directed context had an emotional nature-familiar stimuli were more attractive. In the perspective of marketing application one can say that through positive emotions the ad is better remembered, whereas negative emotions cause deeper, more thorough information processing.

STUDY 2

Emotions in evaluation and memory of PSA,'s (non-commercial ads)

The particular feature of Public Service Advertisements is that they usually elicit negative emotions. PSA messages often refer to anxiety or compassion. Appeals to anxiety encouraging the viewer to take action for his own good (for example, to give up smoking) are often used in PSA's. Appeals to compassion are efficient in PSA's encouraging viewers to help others (e.g. to support starving children). According to Bagozzi and Moore (1994) negative emotions elicited by the PSA lead to empathic reactions and facilitate making decisions to help others.

The aim of Study 2 was to investigate cause-effect relationships between emotions elicited by the PSA and the processes of evaluation and memory for such ads. The significance of positive and negative emotions in evaluation and memory of PSA's was also examined. Unlike Study 1, the persuasive message did not refer to personal gains or losses.

Participants, Materials, and Procedure

Ninety-eight undergraduates and postgraduates participated in Study 2. Participants were volunteers, from Warsaw and Lodz universities.

Two *print public service advertisements* were designed for the purpose of experiment. Both ads presented the logo of the fictitious foundation "Loving Bears", its slogan and information about the campaign. The two ads presented different photographs: one referring to positive emotions (showing a healthy and cheerful child) and the other to negative emotions (showing a sad and scruffy child).

Emotions elicited by the ads were measured with *The Emotional Network Scale*.

Advertisement and the campaign (advertised idea) evaluations were measured on five 7-point adjective scales adapted for PSA's.

An index of *memory for the ad and the campaign* was a sum of scores on questions on the feeling of familiarity of the ad and campaign.

Procedure and methods of statistical analysis. The study was conducted individually. Each participant was presented one advertisement. One group viewed the ad referring to positive emotions and the other to negative emotions. Then the subjects were asked to fill The Emotional Network Scale, scales for ad and campaign evaluation, and answer the questions on familiarity of the ad and campaign. Structural equation modeling was used as a method of statistical analysis.

Results

The theoretical model was tested by translating the variables presented in Figure 1 into a system of structural equations expanded to include the positive and negative emotions as well as the difference between them (net-affect) elicited by the ad, for the two PSA's referring to positive or negative emotions. That way, all six empirical models were tested. Structural equation models for the ad referring to positive emotions are presented in Figure 5, and to negative emotions, in Figure 6.

FIGURE 6
Structural equation models for the PSA referring to negative emotions

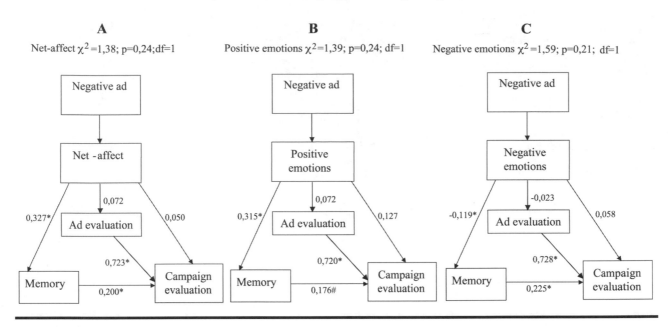

As we can see in Figures 5 and 6, there was only an effect of emotions on the evaluation of the ad and the campaign when the ad referred to positive emotions, but not to negative. Whereas in the case of the ad referring to negative emotions, an effect of emotions was observed on the feeling of familiarity with the ad and the campaign. The more positive the emotions elicited by the ad presenting a sad and scruffy child, the more familiar the ad and the campaign were reported to be. However, the foundation was fictitious and the ad was constructed for the purpose of the experiment. In the case of the ad presenting a healthy and cheerful child, the evaluations of the ad and the campaign were based on emotions. Whereas in the ad presenting a sad and scruffy child evaluations of the ad and the campaign were based on cognition–i.e. the feeling of familiarity of the ad and the campaign.

Figure 7 presents the fits of the model to empirical data (χ^2) for PSA's referring to positive and negative emotions.

When the ad was not coherent with the problem advertised (presenting a healthy and cheerful child), the fit of the theoretical model to the empirical data was better than in the case of the ad coherent to the problem advertised (i.e. presenting sad and scruffy child). This means that people are more sensitive to dissonant stimuli. The ad presenting a cheerful child could elicit a dissonance, and cause astonishment and more careful attention to the ad.

FINAL REMARKS

The research showed that positive emotions activated a wide area of the cognitive network. Therefore, one could expect that more cues of ad recall are available. On the other hand, negative emotions activated a smaller area of the cognitive network and elicited high sensitivity to the perceived ad, so messages in the advertisement are processed more thoroughly. Therefore, one can say that *cooperation* of positive and negative emotions enables better memory of the ad. It is worth noting that only positive emotions are transferred to product evaluation; negative emotions are not significant here.

Public service advertisements which elicited dissonance and high sensitivity, caused astonishment and more careful attention to the ad. This way the persuasive message in the ad could be remembered better.

Commercial ad referring to losses was processed more sensitively than the ad referring to gains. This result is congruent with prospect theory by Kahneman and Tversky (1979). This effect appeared only in the case of persuasive messages referring to personal gains and losses. The results of our research suggest that advertisers can control the form of persuasive messages to influence the perceived satisfaction of purchase (gains) or dissatisfaction with not having purchased the product advertised (losses).

REFERENCES

Akaike, Hirotugu (1987), "Factor analysis and AIC," *Psychometrika*, 52, 317-332.

Ashby, F.Gregory, Alice M. Isen and And U. Turken (1999), "A neuropsychological theory of positive affect and its influence on cognition," *Psychological Review*, 106 (3), 529-550.

Bagozzi, Richard P. and David J. Moore (1994), "Public service advertisements: emotions and empathy guide prosocial behavior," *Journal of Marketing*, 58 (1), 56-70.

Baumgartner, Hans, Mita Sujan and James Bettman (1992), "Autobiographical memories, affect, and consumer information processing," *Journal of Consumer Psychology*, 1 (1), 53-82.

Bower, Gordon H. (1992), "How might emotions affect learning," In: S.A. Christianson (ed.), *The handbook of emotion and memory: Research and theory* (p. 3-31). Hillsdale, NJ: Erlbaum.

Brown, Steven P., Pamela Homer and Jeffrey J. Inman (1998), "A meta-analysis of relationships between ad-evoked feelings and advertising responses," *Journal of Marketing Research*, 35, 114-126.

FIGURE 7
Values of fits (χ^2) for models of PSA's referring to positive and negative emotions

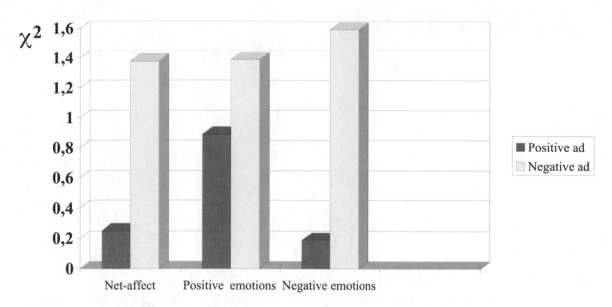

Burke, Marian C. and Julie E. Edell (1989), "The impact of feelings on ad-based affect and cognition," *Journal of Marketing Research*, 26, 69-83.

Cacioppo, John T. and Gary G. Berntson (1994), "Relationship between attitudes and evaluative space: a critical review, with emphasis on the separability of positive and negative substrates," *Psychological Bulletin*, 115, 401-423.

Cacioppo, John T. and Wendi L. Gardner (1999), "Emotion," *Annual Review of Psychology*, 50 (1), 191-214.

Cotte, June and Robin Ritchie (2005), "Advertiser's theories of consumers: why use negative emotions to sell?," *Advances in Consumer Research*, 32 (1), 24-31.

Escalas, Edson J., Chapman M. Moore and Edell J. Britton (2004) , "Fishing For Feelings? Hooking Viewers Helps", *Journal of Consumer Psychology*, 14 (1-2), 105-114.

Faseur, Tine and Maggie Geuens (2006), „Different positive feelings to different ad evaluations," *Journal of Advertising*, 35 (4), 129-142.

Friestad, Marian and Esther Thorson (1993), "Remembering ads: The effects of encoding strategies, retrieval cues, and emotional response," *Journal of Consumer Psychology*, 2 (1), 1-23.

Grochowska, Alicja and Andrzej Falkowski (in print), „Sieciowa struktura emocji: podstawy teoretyczne i wlasciwosci psychometryczne skali do badania reakcji emocjonalnych na reklam?" [Network structure of emotions: Theoretical background and psychometric properties of the scale measuring emotions elicited by advertisement], *Studia Psychologiczne*.

Holbrook, Morris B. and Rajeev Batra (1987), "Assessing the role of emotions as mediators of consumer response to advertising," *Journal of Consumer Research*, 14 (3), 404-420.

Kahneman, Daniel and Amos Tversky (1979), „Prospect theory: an analysis of decision under risk," *Econometrica*, 47 (2), 263-291.

Krugman, Herbert E. (1965), "The impact of television advertising: learning without involvement," *Public Opinion Quarterly*, 29 (3), 349-356.

Krugman, Herbert E. (1967), "The measurement of advertising involvement," *Public Opinion Quarterly*, 30 (4), 583-596.

McClelland, James L. (1995), "Constructive memory and memory distortions: a parallel distributed processing approach" In: D. Schacter (ed.), *Memory distortion* (p. 69-90). Cambridge, MA: Harvard University Press.

Moore, Danny. L. and Wesley Hutchinson (1983), "The effects of ad affect on advertising effectiveness," *Advances in Consumer Research*, 10 (1), 526-531.

Morris, Jon D., ChongMoo Woo C., James A. Geason and Jooyoung Kim (2002), "The power of affect: predicting intention", *Journal of Advertising Research*, 42 (3), 7-17.

Panksepp, Jaak (2000), "Emotions as natural kinds within the mammalian brain," In: M. Lewis, J.M. Haviland-Jones, *Handbook of emotions* (p. 137-156). New York-London: The Guilford Press.

Parrot, Gerrod W. and Matthew Spackman (2000), "Emotion and memory," In: M. Lewis, J.M. Haviland-Jones, *Handbook of emotions* (p. 476-490). New York-London: The Guilford Press.

Suárez Araujo Carmen Paz, Isabel Barahona da Fonseca, José Barahona da Fonseca and José Simões da Fonseca (2004), "Beyond reason: Emotion," *AIP Conference Proceedings*, 718 (1), 465-473.

Sujan, Mita, James R. Bettman and Hans Baumgartner (1993), "Influencing consumer judgments using autobiographical memories: a self-referencing perspective," *Journal of Marketing Research*, 30, 422-436.

Tanner, Jeff F. (2006), "Read this or die: a cognitive approach to an appeal to emotions," *International Journal of Advertising*, 25 (3), 414-416.

Zajonc, Robert B. (1980), "Feeling and thinking: preferences need not inferences," *American Psychologist*, 35, 151-175.

Pushing the Envelope of Brand and Personality: Antecedents and Moderators of Anthropomorphized Brands

Marina Puzakova, Drexel University, USA
Hyokjin Kwak, Drexel University, USA
Joseph F. Rocereto, Monmouth University, USA

ABSTRACT

The tendency for consumers to perceive brands as actual human beings has significant implications in the area of branding. However, there is a large gap in the marketing literature regarding the process and conditions that may influence the degree to which consumers perceive brands as complete human beings. The present research introduces the concept of anthropomorphized brands and discusses the psychological mechanisms that underlie the process of brand anthropomorphization. Our study builds on the three-factor theory of anthropomorphism to explain how self-concept/brand image congruity may influence the inference process of brand anthropomorphization. Furthermore, we suggest that sociality and effectance motivation variables may moderate the relationship between self-concept/brand image congruity and anthropomorphized brands. Theoretical and managerial implications are also discussed.

INTRODUCTION

The concept of Anthropomorphization has been explored in various academic disciplines: a religious context (Gilmore 1919), application to pets (Cheney and Seyfarth 1990), and even to gadgets (Epley et al. 2008). Among philosophers, the concept of anthropomorphism has been discoursed for more than two thousand years. Anthropomorphization theory has also significant implications in marketing research. For example, Fournier (1998) claims that individuals experience little difficulty in assigning personality features to brands; Levy (1985) and Plummer (1985) provide evidence that consumers easily view brands as possessing human characteristics . It is a widely accepted notion that consumers form different types of relationships with brands (Fournier 1998). However, for a brand to become an actual partner in the relationship, it must be perceived as a complete, literal human.

As marketing practitioners direct their promotional campaigns to attempt to persuade consumers to view brands as fully human, no reasonable explanation has been provided in regards to potential key variables that may impact consumers' ability and motivation to perceive brands as humans. Furthermore, a considerable number of psychological theories have been employed in order to better understand consumer-brand relationships (e.g., theories of love (Shimp and Madden 1988) or trust (Hess 1995)) without exploring the phenomenon of brand anthropomorphization, its antecedents, and underlying psychological mechanisms.

The anthropomorphization phenomenon has been extensively noted in varying streams of literature, but it has not received meaningful psychological account within the consumer behavior literature. Moreover, researchers in various fields of social science have been considering anthropomorphization as an invariant psychological process. Following this tradition, marketing researchers who have utilized the notion of somehow personalized or humanized brands have considered the process of consumers prescribing human characteristics to nonhuman objects as a chronically occurring consumer judgment. However, the three-factor anthropomorphization theory introduced by Epley et al. (2007) posits that different people are more or less likely to anthropomorphize objects, and that the anthropomorphization process is greatly determined by the accessibility of human knowledge, by the presence of specific situational cues, and by individuals' motivation at the time of judgment.

In summary, the purpose of the present study is threefold: 1) to advance the theory of anthropomorphization by introducing the notion of anthropomorphized brands in marketing research and explaining how anthropomorphized brands are different from other existing marketing brand concepts (e.g., brand personality); 2) to examine the antecedents of anthropomorphized brands; 3) to investigate the moderating roles of sociality motivation and effectance motivation on the relationship between self-concept/brand image congruity and anthropomorphized brands. The overall conceptual model is presented in Figure 1.

CONCEPTUAL BACKGROUND AND PROPOSITIONS

Anthropomorphization and Anthropomorphized Brands (AB)

Marketing communication efforts have encouraged consumers to view brands in human terms (Aggarwal and McGill 2007; Yoon et al. 2006). There is evidence in the marketing literature that consumers may perceive humanlike features in products and brands (Aggarwal and McGill 2007; Tremoulet and Feldman 2000). The psychological process of imbuing brands with personalities is referred by Aaker (1997) as *animism*. In marketing research, animism and anthropomorphism are frequently used interchangeably to demonstrate the process of product or brand animation. For instance, Fournier (Fournier 1998) refers to theories of animism when discussing the anthropomorphization process. However, social psychologists explicitly differentiate between the two psychological processes. For example, Guthrie (1993) describes animism as a person's wishful thinking of instilling life into objects when some motion or noise from the object is discerned. More importantly, the author defines anthropomorphism as the perception and recognition of humans in objects in the surrounding environment. Additionally, Epley et al. (2007, p. 865) argue that, "anthropomorphism involves more than simply attributing life to the nonliving (i.e., animism)". Consequently, prescribing selective human characteristics to nonhuman objects or merely simply enlivening nonhuman objects (animism) is not synonymous with viewing these objects as complete humans (anthropomorphism).

Furthermore, results of a qualitative study regarding consumer-brand relationship formation conducted by Fournier (1998) show some evidence that consumers may form relationships with brands. Extensive research in consumer behavior supports the notion of the existence of strong consumer-brand relationships (Aaker, Fournier, and Brasel 2004; Aggarwal and McGill 2007; Kim, Lee, and Ulgado 2005). However, Fournier (1998) argues that, in order for a brand to serve as a viable relationship partner and become a legitimate member of a consumer-brand bond, a brand should possess multiple qualities of a human being, embracing emotionality, thoughtful behavior, soul, and feelings. The fact that consumers form strong relationships with brands suggests that individuals perceive these brands as complete humans. Therefore, in the present paper, we apply the notion of anthropomorphization to brands and define anthropomorphized brands as *brands perceived by consumers as actual human beings with various emo-*

FIGURE 1
Conceptual Model

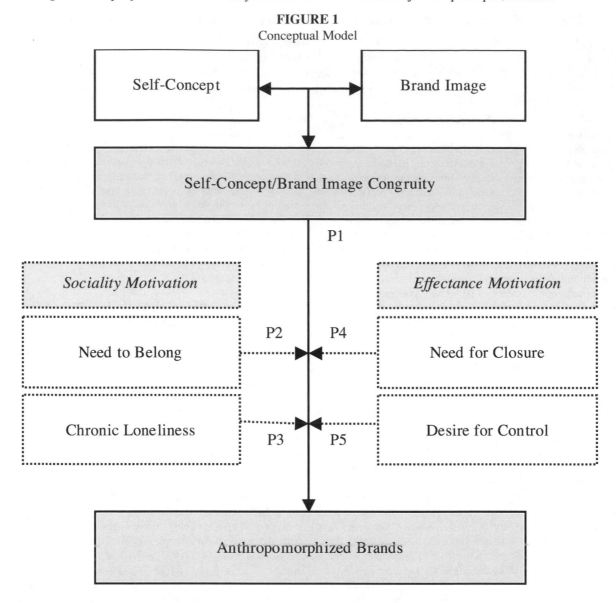

tional states, mind, soul, and conscious behaviors that can act as prominent members of social ties.

More than a decade ago, marketing scholars explored the concept of brand personality (BP) (Aaker 1997). Consumers' perceptions of brand personality became an extensively utilized phenomenon in the practitioners' world. Multiple examples can be identified in the brand world, such as sincere brands (e.g. Hallmark and Ford) (Smith 2001) or exciting brands (e.g. Mountain Dew and BMW) (Aaker et al. 2004). For example, Aaker (1997) states that Dr. Pepper is considered to possess a nonconforming, unique, and fun personality.

In the psychology and marketing literature, personality is commonly defined as the consistency of an individual's behaviors and reactions to surrounding stimuli (Kassarjian 1971). "Anthropomorphism involves going beyond behavioral descriptions of imagined or observable actions" (Epley et al. 2007, p. 865). More specifically, the anthropomorphization of nonhuman objects means perceiving them as absolute humans (Epley et al. 2007). This

involves attributing mind (intentions, effortful thinking, and consciousness) (Gray, Gray, and Wegner 2007), soul (Gilmore 1919), emotional states (Leyens et al. 2003), and behavioral features (Epley et al. 2007). Additionally, anthropomorphism entails the inference process of unobservable human features. Many characteristics of human nature are not readily recognizable, and personality, though being an essential observable part of humans, does not exhaust the transcended concept of humanness (Haslam et al. 2005). Furthermore, Haslam et al. (2005) argue that uniquely human characteristics involve human-nonhuman comparisons, while personality, being the differentiator of humans, is relevant to only person-to-person comparisons. Also, personality develops within the course of life. However, humanness is inherent to humans from the moment of birth. Thus, BP represents only one facet of the multiple components of AB. Additionally, in the marketing literature, BP has been defined as the set of human features that are associated with a brand and strictly applicable to brands (Azoulay and Kapferer 2003). This definition of BP substantially limits the range of personality characteristics that can be attributable to humans. Therefore, this fact provides additional evidence that the AB concept transcends the construct of BP.

Self-Concept/Brand Image Congruity

Self-concept theory, being the subject of psychological and sociological academic interest for many decades, has multiple implications in marketing research (Aaker 1999; Grubb and Grathwohl 1967; Hong and Zinkhan 1995; Kleine, Kleine, and Kernan 1993; Rocereto, Kwak, and Puzakova 2008; Sirgy 1982). There are many conceptualizations of self-concept in the consumer behavior literature. One such definition is that, "the self is what one is aware of, one's attitudes, feelings, perceptions, and evaluations of one's self as an object" (Grubb and Grathwohl 1967, p.24). Another definition of the self comes from the nineteenth century when James (1890, p.291) conceptualized the self as, "...a sum of all that he (man) can call his, not only his body and psychic powers, but his clothes and his house...". It is obvious from James' definition that the self goes beyond one's personal perception of their own inner state, but includes external elements that a human owns. The self is extremely important and valuable to individuals, and they are expected to behave in ways that protect and enhance their self-concept (Kleine et al. 1993; Sirgy 1982; Underwood 2003; Wallendorf and Arnould 1988). One way to extend and bolster a consumer's self-concept is through the symbolic meanings of brands that consumers possess (Belk 1988; Kassarjian 1971). That is, consumers are able to strengthen their own self-concept by owning brands whose symbolic images are congruent with important aspects of one's own self-concept. Therefore, the present study elaborates on the notion of self-concept/brand image congruity that is defined as the level of congruity between key elements of one's own self-concept and brand image.

The tendency for consumers to utilize brands as symbols in expressing one's self-concept arises from the fact that consumers imbue brands with human personality traits (Aaker 1997). Consumers make evaluations of brands based upon the perceived similarity between their own self-concept and perceived human personalities that they view in brands. If the result of such self-concept/brand image evaluations is positive, that is, in cases wherein consumers perceive the images of brands as being similar to their own self-concept, then they may develop higher levels of brand preferences and brand loyalty and will seek to own and surround themselves with brands that are congruent with their own self-concepts (Grubb and Grathwohl 1967; Hong and Zinkhan 1995; Kassarjian 1971). In the present study, we argue that self-concept/brand image congruity may be positively associated with consumers' perception of AB. We provide the psychological account for the relationship between self-concept/brand image congruity and AB further.

Self-Concept/Brand Image Congruity as an Antecedent to AB

According to Epley et al. (2007), the primary determinant of nonhuman object anthropomorphization is the activation of individuals' self-knowledge or human category knowledge, that is, the accessibility of the human cue at the point of judgment. The elicitation of human knowledge, in general, or self-knowledge, in particular, is based to a great extent upon the physical disability of humans to imagine how to be an object, and individuals' natural tendency to merely experience what it is to be a human due to their sensory limitations (Epley et al. 2007). Guthrie (1993) argues that individuals are extremely sensitive to the availability of any human cue and are very proficient in detecting its presence. Additional reasoning that Epley et al. (2007) provide is that egocentric knowledge is automatically accessible in making judgments for both humans and nonhumans. Psychology literature provides evidence

that supports the notion that self-knowledge operates naturally in the inference processes. For example, Tremoulet and Feldman (2000) show that similarity in motion may stimulate the anthropomorphic processes, and Dennett (1982) demonstrates that facial features or voices may increase the anthropomorphic induction processes. There is a support for the claim that human schema is primed by human cue in marketing literature, as well. For example, in Aggarwal and McGill's (2007) study, the process of product anthropomorphization occurs when human self-schema is activated by the physical appearance of the front of a car that closely resembles the human feature of a smile or of the shape of a bottle that emulates the human physical shape. Furthermore, as the three-factor theory of anthropomorphism postulates, human category or self knowledge application and anthropomorphic inference are likely to be corrected by giving further thought to the object of induction. Thus, when nonhuman information about brands is present, consumers may exhibit the tendency to cognitively process that information and to overcome the anthropomorphic representations of brands in their minds.

Building on the three-factor theory of anthropomorphism (Epley et al. 2007), we argue that when individuals identify that a brand possess aspects of their own unique human personality, the availability of the human cue activates human category knowledge. Sequentially, specific human personality dimension of a brand elicits consumer's self-schema that entails the same personality characteristics (Sirgy 1982). Similarly, previous research has shown that, based on the self-consistency motivation theory (Epstein 1980), consumers approach brands by making comparisons between their own self-concept and the images of these brands (Sirgy 1982). Successively, when making these comparisons, consumers are applying their self-knowledge to brands. When accessible at the point of judgment, human knowledge or self-knowledge may give a consumer a hint to make anthropomorphic inferences about brands. However, at this point, consumers may consider the other non-anthropomorphic brand features that allow for the overcoming and correcting of the initial inference pursuant to AB. For example, consumers may notice some non-anthropomorphic representation in an advertisement, such as the unrealistically fast movements of the image representing the brand in an advertisement that do not resemble the human motion, or a brand message using, instead of the words "family of products" (contains human cue), the words "line of products" (does not contain anthropomorphic cue) (Aggarwal and McGill 2007).

A consumer's consequential psychological process results in making decisions about the level of perceived similarity or dissimilarity between one's own self-concept and the image of a brand that has been defined above as self-concept/brand image congruity. Self-concept/brand image congruity is based on the notion of values that consumers project to brands (Grubb and Grathwohl 1967; Sirgy 1982). Furthermore, voluminous research has shown that brand value is derived from the symbolic meaning of a brand and is embedded in consumers' affective components of their attitudes (Belk 1988; Richins 1994; Wallendorf and Arnould 1988). Thus, when consumers are making comparisons between their own self-concepts and images of brands, they are comparing their own values with those of the values that a particular brand image carries.

On the other hand, marketing researchers have given sparse consideration to the dehumanization theory that has received the vast attention of scholars in psychology and sociology (Haslam et al. 2007). This theory has been primarily applied to explain racial and ethnical intergroup antagonism, conflict, and violence. Haslam et al. (2007) suggest that the dehumanization theory may be applied, not only to the realm of ethnocentric intergroup problems, but also to the interpersonal context, that is, the dehumanization phenomena can be present in subtle and everyday forms. The central position of dehumanization theory is that if individuals perceive the values of the outgroup as being dissimilar to the values of their ingroup, then they are likely to deprive the outgroup of humanness (Schwartz and Struch 1989). Schwartz and Struch (1989) discuss that values reflect the group humanness and convey the group's humanity. Translated into the interpersonal context, dehumanization theory postulates that when the values of other individuals significantly differ from the values of one's self, then the dehumanization process is likely to occur (Haslam et al. 2007). In the present study, we argue that when consumers' human category knowledge or self-knowledge is primed, they are likely to make anthropomorphic inferences about brands and to perceive these brands as being completely human. Consequently, we posit that dehumanization theory may explain consumer-brand relationships as well. In the light of dehumanization theory, we claim that when brand values are incongruent with consumers' values, consumers are likely to overcome and correct their anthropomorphic inferences of AB. On the contrary, when self-concept/brand image congruity is established, that is, in cases wherein consumers perceive their own values and the values of the images of brands as being congruent, consumers exhibit the tendency to perceive AB without further correction.

Additionally, voluminous research has shown that self-concept/brand image congruity results in affective responses towards brands (Belk 1988; Klein, Kleine, and Allen 1995; Wallendorf and Arnould 1988). Similar streams of research support the notion that consumers experience high levels of attachment toward brands that are most congruent with their own self-concept (Kleine et al. 1993; Richins 1994). In addition, consumers are expected to be more loyal to brands that are more congruent with their own self-concept (Bhattacharya, Rao, and Glynn 1995; Underwood 2003). As ample marketing literature suggests, attitudinal loyalty provides a strong barrier against competitor attempts to persuade consumer switching behavior that is based upon superior functional features of brands or any situational influences (Oliver 1999). Consequently, in the present paper, we propose that consumers' positive affective states "protects" consumers' perception of AB from correction to the perception of non-AB through subsequent possible cognitive non-anthropomorphic considerations. In the absence of congruity, consumers may observe nonhuman features of brands and access some alternate nonhuman representations that may switch their perception of AB to non-AB (Epley et al. 2007).

P1: Self-concept/brand image congruity is positively associated with anthropomorphized brands.

The Moderating Role of Sociality Motivation

Sense of social connection or belonging is one of the most important human values (Kahle, Beatty, and Pamela 1986) and significantly influences one's success and mental health (Adler and Brett 1998). Prior research has shown that individuals satisfy their need for social connections with evident ease, for example, by establishing close connections with religious objects or pets (Epley et al. 2007). Here, we argue that individuals may satisfy their need for social connections through forming affective bonds with AB. First, the state of sociality motivation may increase consumers' social cues accessibility involving humanlike features in brands, influencing the inference process of brand anthropomorphization. Second, sociality motivation stimulates individuals to energetically search for any clues of social connections. Previous marketing research literature suggests that brands may satisfy the need for social connections. For instance, consumers experience the feeling of intrinsic connection through membership in brand communities

(Muniz and O'Guinn 2001). Moreover, individuals whose need for social connection is not satisfied experience the same pain as physical pain (MacDonald and Leary 2005). To recover from this social pain, individuals may tend to anthropomorphize nonhuman objects, and they are more likely to perceive AB. Thus, we propose that consumers who exhibit a high level of the individual need for belonging, and those with higher level of chronic loneliness may have the tendency to anthropomorphize brands.

Need to Belong Generally, the need to belong can be defined as the desire to establish interpersonal attachments (Pickett, Gardner, and Megan 2004). Although the need to belong is an important individual difference variable inherent to consumer behavior literature, it has been neglected in recent marketing studies. However, it has received vast consideration in social psychology. Social psychology researchers have established the fact that individuals' need to belong is the fundamental motivating principle that results in the crucial consequences related to social performance (Smith and Mackie 2000). In support, Leary (1990) argues that the lack of belonging may result in negative outcomes, such as depression, anxiety, or low self-esteem. Prior social psychology research demonstrates that when individuals' needs to belong are unmet, then the social monitoring system assists individuals in adjusting to social information and stimulates the behavior that may lead to social connections (Pickett et al. 2004). Thus, individuals become very attentive and accurate in detecting social cues in the environment. More specifically, Gardner, Pickett, and Brewer (2000) experimentally find that when individuals' need to belong are not satisfied, they exhibit increasing attention toward social vs. nonsocial information. This increased attention to social cues in social psychology literature has been termed as the interpersonal sensitivity that is defined as, "the ability to sense, perceive accurately, and respond appropriately to one's personal, interpersonal, and social environment" (Bernieri 2001, p.3). According to Epley et al.'s (2007) theory, increased sensitivity to social cues may lead to higher degrees of anthropomorphization. That is, consumers who are high in the need to belong may tend to observe humanlike features and human cues more frequently and, therefore, anthropomorphize brands more actively than those who are low in the need to belong.

P2: The relationship between self-concept/brand image congruity and AB is moderated by the need to belong. That is, for consumers who are high in the need to belong, self-concept/brand image congruity will have higher positive association with AB than for their counterparts.

Chronic Loneliness The fact that individuals differ in the extent to which they feel chronically lonely, that is, the degree to which they experience a persistent lack of social inclusion (Pickett et al. 2004), has been well established in the social psychology literature (Cacioppo et al. 2006). Similar to research relating to the need to belong, prior research regarding loneliness provides evidence that when individuals are chronically lonely, they prefer social information within their immediate environment as opposed to nonsocial information (Gardner et al. 2005). Chronically lonely individuals exhibit a tendency to be very creative in instilling humanlike agents within nonhuman objects (Epley et al. 2008). There is support for this notion in the social psychology literature. For example, in their study, Epley et al. (2008) show that after exposure to a loneliness stimuli, individuals tend to perceive gadgets with humanlike features, including the possession intentions, free will, consciousness, and experienced emotion.

Hollywood provides a particularly poignant scenario of the impact that chronic loneliness can have on the likelihood of the occurrence of AB. In the popular movie, Castaway, the character played by Tom Hanks finds himself completely alone on a deserted tropical island following a plane crash. Completely void of any human contact for weeks, he inexplicably befriends a Wilson branded volleyball, whom he affectionately names "Wilson". Throughout his extended solitude and increasing level of chronic loneliness, the character, more and more, views this inanimate object as slowly, yet clearly, evolving into a complete human being. The relationship between the character and the brand becomes so intense that the character is left utterly distraught at the "loss" of "Wilson" at sea.

Therefore, in the present study, we argue that for chronically lonely consumers, anthropomorphic cues are more readily accessible, more easily activated, and are utilized as a path to recover from the social pain caused by social disconnection. That is, chronically lonely consumers are more prone to fulfill the social connection gap with AB and form various types of social relationship with AB. In sum, chronically lonely consumers may tend to be more likely to perceive brands as complete humans, as members of their social ties, and are less likely to overcome or correct their anthropomorphic representations, because such correction of initial anthropomorphic inferences will result in the severance of the pre-established social connection with these brands and cause a recurrence of social pain.

P3: The relationship between self-concept/brand image congruity and AB is moderated by chronic loneliness. That is, for consumers who are high in chronic loneliness, self-concept/brand image congruity will have higher positive association with AB than for their counterparts.

The Moderating Role of Effectance Motivation

The perception of AB by consumers is substantially influenced by effectance motivation-motivation of individuals to act and cooperate effectively in the surrounding environment (Epley et al. 2007). A growing body within psychological research suggests that individuals differ in their motivation to feel efficaciously in their immediate environment (White 1959). Effectance motivation has emerged from the desire of consumers to comprehend and predict their environment, along with an inherent need to reduce its uncertainty. We propose that anthropomorphism satisfies consumers' desire to efficaciously understand the symbolic meanings of brands. Efficaciously motivated individuals, while observing millions of marketing messages in their environment, will tend to seek meaning through the anthropomorphization process. More specifically, Dawes and Mulford (1996) argue that individuals are inclined to anthropomorphize to increase both the comprehensibility and the predictability of nonhuman objects' behaviors in the same way as egocentric knowledge serves as a reference point in making judgments regarding the behavior of another individual. Self knowledge in the anthropomorphic processes increases the individual's controllability of the environment (Burger and Copper 1979) and assists in finding better explanations regarding ambiguous elements within their current environment. Therefore, the extent to which consumers demonstrate their desire to master their environment (Harter 1978) will influence the anthropomorphic tendencies of persons to see humans in brands. In the present study, consumers' effectance motivation is represented by such individual differences traits as the need for closure and the desire for control that may both affect the likelihood of anthropomorphization.

Need for Closure The need for closure is an individual difference trait that explains the extent to which a person desires the precise answer to one's inquiry vs. ambiguity and disorder (Kruglanski and Mayseless 1988). Individuals who are high in the need for closure display the tendency to instantaneously acquire

primarily available cues in their environment and to make judgments based on these cues without engaging in an effortful search for additional and more meaningful information in their environment (Kruglanski and Webster 1996). Thus, individuals who are high in the need for closure are highly motivated to comprehend existing situations and stimuli, immediately abandoning any further cognitive incentives. Considering the apparent ease of self-knowledge accessibility, as has been discussed a forehead, and the ease of seizing upon first available cues, we argue that consumers high in the need for closure tend to perceive brands as humans to a greater extent than those consumers who are low in the need for closure. That is, marketing communication efforts entailing any human cue are utilized by consumers in the formation of impressions and in anthropomorphic judgments about brands. Individuals experience negative affect if their need for closure is undermined or threatened and, therefore, we argue that consumers with a high need for closure exhibit higher sensitivity to any anthropomorphic representations of brands and even facilitate the anthropomorphic representations in their minds. According to Kruglanski and Webster (1996), consumers will be prone to "freeze" their initial anthropomorphic inductions about brands. Thus, those consumers with a high need for closure will not tend to overcome and correct their first anthropomorphic inferences regarding the humanness of brands, because they will rather be motivated to seek a quick, primarily available resolution and, consequently, preserve this resolution from any extant interferences (Kruglanski and Webster 1996).

P4: The relationship between self-concept/brand image congruity and AB is moderated by the need for closure. That is, for consumers who are high in the need for closure, self-concept/brand image congruity will have higher positive association with AB than for their counterparts.

Desire for Control The desire for control construct has received scarce attention in the consumer behavior literature. On the opposite, the construct has been examined by many psychological theorists. For example, Adler (1930) and Burger (1992) propose a striving or motivation of individuals to demonstrate their ability to control the events in their lives. More generally, the concept of control is a commonly accepted driving force of humans that is defined as the psychological need to display the superiority and competence over situations (White 1959). Psychological research has provided evidence that individuals are not identical in terms of the desire for control, and they will exhibit different levels in their general desire to gain control over situations and objects (Burger and Copper 1979). Satisfaction of the desire for predictability of situations and mastery of the environment evokes positive emotions in individuals. For example, previous studies have investigated the role of perceived control in relationship to service quality (Hui and Bateson 1991) where it has been shown that the opportunity to cognitively reinterpret situations and display competence positively affects consumers. Therefore, desire for control motivates consumers to create order regarding the elements of their surroundings, which also allows for the predictability of consequent interactions with brands in the future. In other words, individuals high in the desire for control will tend to predict and comprehend nonhuman objects through the process of anthropomorphization. Consumers with a high degree of the desire for control will possess stronger proclivity to explain brands' behaviors through anthropomorphic representations of brands and, particularly, through attributions of intentions and desires to brands (Burger and Hemans 1988). The result of such attributional activity will facilitate individuals' perception of acting efficaciously in their environment (Epley et al. 2007). Moreover, the existence of humans in brands for consumers who are high in the desire for control will serve favorably in increasing individuals' desire for efficacious functioning due to the clear understanding of brand behavior at the current stage and in the future. Taken jointly, these results suggest the following proposition:

P5: The relationship between self-concept/brand image congruity and AB is moderated by the desire for control. That is, for consumers who are high in the desire for control, self-concept/brand image congruity will have higher positive association with AB than for their counterparts.

DISCUSSION

Although marketing practitioners frequently persuade consumers to view brands as if they are real humans, in the present study, we argue that the marketing literature has been lacking the concept of consumers' perception of brands as complete humans. We theoretically introduce the concept of anthropomorphized brands in the consumer behavior literature. We further theorize the important antecedents (i.e., self-concept/brand image congruity) and moderators (i.e., effectance motivation and sociality motivation) of AB. Establishing the notion of consumers' perception of AB discloses new avenues for research pursuant to the creation of consumer-brand relationships and provides new perspectives for understanding these relationships in light of psychological theories of social interaction between consumers and brands. Prior research has shown that the process of brand anthropomorphization occurs in an automatic manner. However, research in social psychology has provided evidence supporting the variability of anthropomorphism. Thus, the major contribution of the present paper is to provide a psychological account for the mechanism of brand anthropomorphization.

Future empirical testing of the propositions defined in this paper should provide significant insights for both academic researchers and practitioners regarding what factors may influence consumers' perceptions of brands as fully, literally humans. The theoretical underpinning of the present paper may shed light into the manner in which self-concept/brand image congruity influences the perception of brands as humans. Furthermore, the theoretical findings of the present paper illustrate a more clear understanding of the manner in which the relationship between self-concept/brand image congruity and AB can be moderated by individual differences of personality traits.

Future directions for marketing researchers might be to delve deeper into the understanding of the drivers of AB. For example, one potential line of research may investigate the manner in which the physical appearance of products or the increasing number of interpersonal contacts may influence the development of AB. Moreover, there are additional avenues for future examination regarding how advertising variables and marketing communication efforts may impact the inferences about AB. Furthermore, future research may better clarify under what conditions consumers may have formed strong bonds with their brands and even have become to identify themselves with these brands, however, still may have not yet transcended their perceptions of these brands as complete humans.

Although, in the present paper, we argue that self-concept/ brand image congruity is the driver of AB, future research may be directed towards the investigation of whether similarities between one's own self-concept and the images of brands may not only strengthen the self, but also create 'the other' that is the important part of actualization, maintenance and construction of the self. Specifically, a fruitful line of future inquiry is the examination of the underlying psychological processes that make the anthropo-

morphized brand lead consumer-brand relationships and contribute to consumers' identity transformations under the conditions of the increasing individualization of society.

Additionally, while we argue in the present paper that effectance motivation may moderate the relationship between self-concept/ brand image congruity and brand anthropomorphization due to the better prediction and control over brands' unexpected behaviors and contingencies, future research should explore in greater detail a wider range of factors and more specific mental processes occurring in consumers' minds that lead to the intensification of the anthropomorphization processes and perceptions of brands as actual humans with various subject-to-change goals, evolving needs, and relationship effort requirements versus mere perceptions of brands as commercial entities with the dominant goal of delivering market value to their owners. As brands and their products are converting into more sophisticated and intricate entities, consumers may suffer more from being baffled with the escalating brands' complexities. Consequently, during the rapid diffusion of innovation and technologically advanced brands, individuals' effectance motivation may play an especially important role as consumers' need for closure and control is triggered further. Therefore, additional research should address these important questions regarding under what particular conditions do consumers' perceptions of brand as real humans become more difficult than the perceptions of brands as a profit-making unit.

In conclusion, the present paper advances the marketing literature regarding the development of strong consumer-brand relationships. We believe that this study is a first step in gaining a better understanding of the mechanisms that underlie the process of brand anthropomorphization, a process that is a crucial element in establishing legitimate relationships between consumers and brands. The practical implications of these findings show that, in an attempt to create anthropomorphized brands, marketing practitioners may follow the laws and principles of consumers' interpersonal/social relationships with brands in order to eventually push the envelope of brands and human personality.

REFERENCES

Aaker, Jennifer L. (1997), "Dimensions of Brand Personality," *Journal of Marketing Research*, 24, 347-356.

_____ (1999), "The Malleable Self: The Role of Self-Expression in Persuasion," *Journal of Marketing Research*, 36 (1), 45-57.

Aaker, Jennifer L., Susan Fournier, and S. Adam Brasel (2004), "When Good Brands Do Bad," *Journal of Consumer Research*, 31 (June), 1-16.

Adler, A. (1930), "Individual psychology," in *Psychologies of 1930*, ed. C. Murchinson. Worcester, Massachusetts: Clark University Press, 1930,

Adler, A. and C. Brett (1998), *Social Interest: Adler's Key to the Meaning of Life*, Oxford, United Kingdom: Oneworld Publications.

Aggarwal, Pankaj and Ann L. McGill (2007), "Is This Car Smiling at Me? Schema Congruity as Basis for Evaluating Anthropomorphized Products," *Journal of Consumer Research*, 34 (December), 468-479.

Azoulay, Audrey and Jean-Noel Kapferer (2003), "Do Brand Personality Scales Really Measure Brand Personality," *Journal of Brand Management* 11 (2), 143-155.

Belk, Russell W. (1988), "Possessions and the Extended Self," *Journal of Consumer Research*, 15 (September), 139-168.

Bernieri, F.J. (2001), "Interpersonal Sensitivity: Theory and Measurement," in *Toward a Taxonomy of Interpersonal Sensitivity*, Mahwah, NJ: Lawrence Erlbaum, 3-20.

Bhattacharya, C. B., Hayagreeva Rao, and Mary Ann Glynn (1995), "Understanding the Bond of Identification: An Investigation of its Correlates among Art Museum Members," *Journal of Marketing*, 59 (4), 46-57.

Burger, J.M. and H.M. Copper (1979), "The Desirability of Control," *Motivation and Emotion*, 3, 381-393.

Burger, J.M. and L.T. Hemans (1988), "Desire for Control and the Use of Attribution Processes," *Journal of Personality*, 56 (531-546).

Burger, J.M. (1992), *Desire for Control: Personality, Social and Clinical Perspective*, New York: Plenum.

Cacioppo, J. T., M.E. Hughes, Waite L.J., L.C. Hawkley, and R.A. Thisted (2006), "Loneliness As a Specific Risk Factor For Depressive Symptoms: Cross Sectional and Longitudinal Analyses," *Psychology and Aging*, 21, 140-151.

Cheney, D. and R. Seyfarth (1990), *How monkeys see the world*, Chicago: University of Chicago Press.

Dawes, R. and M. Mulford (1996), "The False Consensus Effect and Overconfidence: Flaws in Judgment or Flaws in How We Study Judgment?," *Organizational Behavior and Human Decision Processes*, 65, 201-211.

Dennett, Daniel C. (1982), *Kinds of Minds: Towards an Understanding of Consciousness*, New York: Basic.

Epley, Nicholas, Scott Akalis, Adam Waytz, and John T. Cacioppo (2008), "Creating Social Connection through Inferential Reproduction: Loneliness and Perceived Agency in Gadgets, Gods, and Greyhounds," *Psychological Science*, 19 (2), 114-120.

Epley, Nicholas, Adam Waytz, and John T. Cacioppo (2007), "On Seeing Human: A Three-Factor Theory of Anthropomorphism," *Psychological Review*, 114 (4), 864-886.

Epstein, Seymour (1980), "The Self-Concept: A Review and the Proposal of an Integrated Theory of Personality," in *Personality: Basic Issues and Current Research*, eds. Ervin Staub and Englewood Cliffs.

Fournier, Susan (1998), "Consumers and Their Brands: Developing Relationship Theory in Consumer Research," *Journal of Consumer Research*, 24, 343-373.

Gardner, W. L., C.L. Pickett, and M.B. Brewer (2000), "Social Exclusion and Selective Memory: How the Need to Belong Influences Memory for Social Events," *Personality & Social Psychology Bulletin*, 26, 486-496.

Gardner, W. L., V. Jefferis, M.L. Knowles, and C.L. Pickett (2005), "On the Outside Looking In: Loneliness and Social Monitoring," *Personality & Social Psychology Bulletin*, 31, 1549-1560.

Gilmore, George W. (1919), *Animism or Thought Currents of Primitive Peoples*, Boston: Marshall Jones Company.

Gray, H. M., K. Gray, and D.M. Wegner (2007), "Dimensions of mind perception," *Science*, 315, 619.

Grubb, Edward L. and Harrison L. Grathwohl (1967), "Consumer Self-Concept, Symbolism and Market Behavior: Theoretical Approach," *Journal of Marketing*, 31, 22-27.

Guthrie, Stewart (1993), *Faces in the Clouds: A New Theory of Religion*, New York: Oxford University Press.

Harter, S. (1978), "Effectance Motivation Reconsidered: Towards a Developmental Model," *Human Development*, 21, 34-64.

Haslam, Nick, Paul Bain, Lauren Douge, Max Lee, and Brock Bastian (2005), "More Human Than You: Attributing Humanness to Self and Others," *Journal of Personality and Social Psychology*, 89 (6), 937-950.

Haslam, Nick, Stephen Loughnan, Catherine Reynolds, and Samuel Wilson (2007), "Dehumanization: A New Perspective," *Social and Personality Compass*, 1 (1), 409-422.

Hess, Jeffrey S. (1995), "Construction and Assessment of a Scale to Measure Consumer Trust," *American Marketing Association Educators' Conference*, Vol. 6, eds. B. Stern and G. Zinkhan. Chicago: American Marketing Association

Hong, Jae W and George M Zinkhan (1995), "Self-Concept and Advertising Effectiveness: The Influence of Congruency, Conspicuousness, and Response Mode," *Psychology and Marketing*, 12 (1), 53-77.

Hui, Michael K. and John E.G. Bateson (1991), "Perceived Control and the Effects of Crowding and Consumer Choice on the Service Experience," *Journal of Consumer Research*, 18 (September), 174-184.

James, William (1890), *The Principles of Psychology*, New York: Henry Holt.

Kahle, Lynn R., Sharon E. Beatty, and Homer Pamela (1986), "Alternative Measurement Approaches to Consumer Values: The List of Values (LOV) and Values and Life Style (VALS)," *Journal of Consumer Research*, 13 (December), 405-409.

Kassarjian, Harold H. (1971), "Personality and Consumer Behavior: A Review," *Journal of Marketing Research*, VIII (November), 409-418.

Kim, Hae Ryong, Moonkyu Lee, and M. Francis Ulgado (2005), "Brand Personality, Self-Congruity and The Consumer-Brand Relationship," *Asia Pacific Advances in Consumer Research*, Vol. 6, eds. Yong-Uon Ha and Youjae Yi. Association for Consumer Research.

Klein, Susan Schultz, Robert E. Kleine, III, and Chris T. Allen (1995), "How is a Possession "Me" or "Not Me"? Characterizing Types and an Antecedent of Material Possession Attachment," *Journal of Consumer Research*, 22 (December), 327-343.

Kleine, Robert E., Susan Schultz Kleine, and Jerome B. Kernan (1993), "Mundane Consumption and the Self: A Social-Identity Perspective," *Journal of Consumer Psychology*, 2 (3), 209-235.

Kruglanski, A.W. and O. Mayseless (1988), "Contextual Effects in Hypothesis Testing: The Role of Competing Alternatives and Epistemic Motivations," *Social Cognition*, 6, 1-21.

Kruglanski, A.W. and D.M. Webster (1996), "Motivated Closing of the Mind: "Seizing" and "Freezing"," *Psychological Review*, 103, 263-283.

Leary, M. R. (1990), "Responses to Social Exclusion: Social Anxiety, Jelousy, Loneliness, Depression, and Low Self-Esteem," *Journal of Social and Clinical Psychology*, 9, 221-229.

Levy, Sidney J. (1985), "Dreams, Fairy Tales, Animals, and Cars," *Psychology &Marketing*, 2 (Summer), 67-81.

Leyens, J.P., B.P. Cortes, S. Demoulin, J. Dovidio, S.T. Fiske, R. Gaunt, and et al. (2003), "Emotional prejudice, essentialism, and nationalism," *European Journal of Social Psychology*, 33, 703-717.

MacDonald, G. and M.R. Leary (2005), "Why Does Social Exclusion Hurt? The Relationship between Social and Physical Pain," *Psychological Bulletin*, 131, 202-223.

Muniz, Albert M., Jr. and Thomas C. O'Guinn (2001), "Brand Community," *Journal of Consumer Research*, 27 (March), 412-432.

Oliver, Richard L. (1999), "Whence Consumer Loyalty?," *Journal of Marketing*, 63 (Special), 33-44.

Pickett, Cynthia, Wendi. L. Gardner, and Knowles Megan (2004), "Getting a Cue: The Need to Belong and Enhanced Sensitivity to Social Cues," *Personality & Social Psychology Bulletin*, 30 (September), 1095-1107.

Plummer, Joseph (1985), "How Personality Makes a Difference," *Journal of Advertising Research*, 24 (December/January), 27-31.

Richins, Marsha L. (1994), "Valuing Things: The Public and Private Meanings of Possessions," *Journal of Consumer Research*, 21 (December), 504-521.

Rocereto, Joseph F., Hyokjin Kwak, and Marina Puzakova (2008), "The Role of Self-Concept Congruency on Product-Brand Image and Store-Brand Image: Antecedents and Consequences," *Unleashing the Power of Marketing to Transform Consumers, Organizations, Markets, and Society*, Vol. 19, eds. James R. Brown and Rajiv Dant. IL, Chicago: American Marketing Association.

Schwartz, S.H. and N. Struch (1989), " Values, Stereotypes, and Intergroup Antagonism," in *Stereotypes and Prejudice: Changing Conceptions*, eds. D. Bar-Tal and A.W. Grauman and A.W. Kruglanski and W. Stroebe. New-York: Springer-Verlag, 151-167.

Shimp, Terence A. and Thomas Madden (1988), "Consumer-object relations: A Conceptual Framework Based Analogously on Sternberg's Triangular Theory of Love," *Advances in Consumer Research* Vol. 15, ed. M. Houston. Provo, UT: Association for Consumer Research

Sirgy, Joseph (1982), "Self-concept in Consumer Behavior: A Critical Review," *Journal of Consumer Research*, 9 (December), 287-300.

Smith, E. and D. Mackie (2000), *Social Psychology*, New York, USA: Psychology Press.

Smith, Stephen (2001), *America's Greatest Brands*, New York: America's Greatest Brands.

Tremoulet, Patrice D. and Jacob Feldman (2000), "Perception of Animacy from the Motion of a Single Object," *Perception*, 29 (8), 943-951.

Underwood, Robert L. (2003), "The Communicative Power of Product Packaging: Creating Brand Identity via Lived and Mediated Experience," *Journal of Marketing Theory and Practice*, 11 (1), 62-76.

Wallendorf, Melanie and Eric J. Arnould (1988), "My Favorite Things: A Cross-Cultural Inquiry into Object Attachment, Possessiveness, and Social Linkage," *Journal of Consumer Research*, 14 (March), 531-547.

White, R. (1959), "Motivation Reconsidered: The Concept of Competence," *Psychological Review*, 66, 297-330.

Yoon, Carolyn, Angela Gutchess, Fred Feinberg, and Thad A. Polk (2006), "A Functional Magnetic Resonance Imaging Study of Neural Dissociations between Brand and Person Judgments," *Journal of Consumer Research*, 33 (June), 31-40.

Brand Avoidance: A Negative Promises Perspective

Michael Shyue Wai Lee, The University of Auckland Business School, New Zealand
Denise Conroy, The University of Auckland Business School, New Zealand
Judith Motion, University of Wollongong, Australia[1]

ABSTRACT

Previous research lacks a unifying construct that is both parsimonious enough to account for the multiple reasons that motivate brand avoidance, and flexible enough to remain workable. We address this gap by providing a core construct that may aid in the understanding of brand avoidance. Specifically, we use grounded theory to analyse qualitative data from 23 in-depth interviews, and we introduce the negative brand promises idea as a powerful yet practical metaphor for understanding brand avoidance.

"The creation of meaning via consumption involves both positive and negative choices." Professor Margaret Hogg (1998 p.133)

"Your most unhappy customers are your greatest source of learning." Bill Gates (Microsoft)

"Oh my God! Starbucks!!! I hate Starbucks… Oh there are many reasons; they make sh*t coffee. It's horrible! It's really bad tasting coffee, and you can never get a decent size, you can't just get your average normal cup of coffee you have to get a bucket, which then costs twice as much and tastes bad… and the whole multi-national thing… they're really slow… and they're wasteful! They have individual plastic spoons and there's extra packaging and stuff. So Starbucks I avoid, I'd rather not have a coffee than drink a Starbuck's coffee." CI (First sensitization interview)

INTRODUCTION

The broad domain of anti-consumption, and the specific topic of brand avoidance, is becoming more interesting and important to scholars, managers, and consumers. The quotations above are evidence of this growing interest, as are the increasing number of academic and managerial articles, journal special issues, popular books, magazines, and websites dedicated to the subject area of anti-consumption (Banister and Hogg 2004; Englis and Soloman 1997; Gabriel and Lang 1995; Hogg and Banister 2001; Holt 2002; Klein 2000; Kozinets 2002; Kozinets and Handelman 2004; Lee, Fernandez, and Hyman 2008a; Rumbo 2002; Thompson and Arsel 2004; Thompson et al. 2006; Zavestoski 2002a). Yet, despite this growing interest, the extant literature still lacks a comprehensive, and parsimonious, understanding of anti-consumption and its related topics. Therefore, the purpose of this paper is to explore, in depth, a specific type of anti-consumption, brand avoidance, and in doing so contribute a more complete, integrative, and elegant understanding of the area.

To date, the majority of marketing scholars and practitioners have espoused the many positive aspects of branding and brand equity, and have focused primarily on brands as market-based assets (Srivastava et al. 2001; Srivastava et al. 1998). Consequently, this perspective of brands has resulted in an emphasis on exploring the reasons behind why consumers select brands and how firms can increase brand loyalty. In consumer research, the notion that people express themselves and construct their identities/self-concepts through the brands and products they use has been well documented (Aaker 1999; Dolich 1969; Grubb and Grathwohl 1967; Heath and Scott 1998; Hogg, Cox, and Keeling 2000; Levy 1959; McCracken 1989; Sirgy 1982; Solomon 1983).

However, equally valid is the idea that some people avoid certain products and brands because of negative associations/meanings (Banister and Hogg 2004; Englis and Soloman 1997; Levy 1959; Thompson and Arsel 2004). Yet, until recently (Banister and Hogg 2004; Kozinets and Handelman 2004; Lee et al. 2008b; Thompson and Arsel 2004; Thompson et al. 2006), the notion of consumers rejecting specific *brands* to avoid adding undesired meaning to their lives has received little attention. As a consequence, the negative characteristics of brands, and their potential to become market-based liabilities for their firm, have not really been explored by marketing academia and practice. This paper directly addresses the issue of negative brand meaning by specifically exploring why consumers avoid certain brands.

When we look closely at the extant literature, it becomes apparent that most studies in the area of anti-consumption actually focus on dissatisfaction with products and services, or counter-cultural phenomenon such as voluntary simplification and consumer resistance (Banister and Hogg 2004; Craig-Lees and Hill 2002; Halstead 1989; Hogg 1998; Kozinets 2002; Oliver 1980; Penaloza and Price 1993; Zavestoski 2002b). Therefore, with the exception of a few researchers (Holt 2002; Lee et al. 2008b; Thompson and Arsel 2004; Thompson et al. 2006), the main unit of analysis in most anti-consumption studies has been general product or service categories, rather than specific brands. Since this research looks at the anti-consumption of *brands*, it is necessary to clarify this concept.

The notion of the brand as a multi-dimensional value constellation is a convincing idea that underlies most conceptualisations of brand (de Chernatony and Dall'Olmo Riley 1998 p. 436-437); and is the notion of brand that we use for this research. This holistic view of the brand is distinct from the traditional product-centric view of the brand (Ambler and Styles 1996) and posits that a brand's value constellation could mean many different things to a consumer, for example: a legal instrument, a logo, a promise/covenant, a risk reducer, an identity, a value system, an evolving entity, or a corporation (Ambler and Styles 1996; Balmer and Gray 2003; Berry 2000; Brodie, Glynn, and Little 2006; Dall'Olmo Riley and de Chernatony 2000; de Chernatony and Dall'Olmo Riley 1998; de Chernatony and Dall'Olmo Riley 1997; Erdem and Swait 2004; Erdem, Swait, and Valenzuela 2006).

A brand is considered a market-based asset, or has positive equity, when it adds value to the company by helping to enhance and sustain cash flow for the company and its shareholders (Srivastava, Shervani and Fahey 1998). However, Keller (1993) states that a brand has customer-based equity when consumers act more, or *less*, favourably to the brand than an identical product or service that is un-named or fictitiously named. Berry (2000), also suggests that brand equity may be positive or *negative*. In considering the importance of brands within marketing, two points become evident. First, it is clear that brands are important to marketers and positive brand equity is a valuable component of a company's brand asset.

[1] Acknowledgements: The authors would like to thank Professor Rod Brodie for his comments and the Foundation of Research Science and Technology, project number UOWX0227 for funding for this study.

Second, there is a negative component to brand equity, although this idea has not been sufficiently considered. In exploring the incidents where the association with a brand name actually reduces the worth of, and preference for, an object, this paper contributes to the notion of negative brand equity.

Brand avoidance is defined as a phenomenon whereby consumers deliberately choose to keep away from or reject a brand (Lee et al. 2008b). Two key concepts lie close to the study of brand avoidance. The first is the anti-constellation, which comprise products that are rejected by consumers (Hogg and Michell 1997). Unlike this study, there is less emphasis on brands in the study of anti-constellations. The second concept which closely resembles brand avoidance is the inept set (Narayana and Markin 1975), where the main reasons for negative evaluation have been attributed to a dislike of the advertisement and poor product performance. Another study using two surveys of 100 and 180 consumers concluded that 'extrinsic' factors such as price, availability, and salesperson's recommendations were most likely to influence rejection of a brand (Abougomaah, Schlater, and Gaidis 1987).

We argue that the previous classifications of brand anti-consumption are too simplistic, especially since the rejection of a brand owing to issues of price and availability may not constitute a deliberate act of brand avoidance. This paper demonstrates that there are a myriad of reasons contributing to brand avoidance, and offers a parsimonious, yet flexible, metaphor for understanding brand avoidance.

METHOD

As part of an ongoing project exploring brand avoidance, we used an existing data set gathered by Lee et al (2008). Details of the recruitment method are discussed in their article; therefore we provide more detail regarding our coding process. The lead author applied the grounded theory method of constant comparison to 23 in-depth interview transcripts, in an attempt to abstract from the raw data to a theory of brand avoidance. This technique is similar to other iterative and hermeneutical approaches used in previous studies of anti-consumption (Kozinets and Handelman 2004; Thompson and Arsel 2004; Thompson et al. 2006).

The coding and analysis of the qualitative data first involved the breaking down of the data into smaller units or open coding (Strauss and Corbin 1990; Strauss and Corbin 1998). Practically, this means that for every interview, the lead author read each line of transcription and highlighted all points of interest. At this early stage of analysis, the lead author created codes as frequently as necessary to capture all the possible reasons for avoidance.

The abundant number of codes generated at the end of open coding meant the next logical step in constant comparison was to compare the categories for similarities and differences. Axial coding was used (Strauss and Corbin 1990; Strauss and Corbin 1998), thus, categories that were very similar were collapsed into higher-order categories.

Analysis then progressed to a higher level of abstraction as theoretical coding, or Strauss and Corbin's 'selective' coding (1990), continued. The main emphasis of grounded theory is on how these relationships increase understanding of a particular phenomenon. Figure 1 displays the hierarchical relationships between the four main types of brand avoidance and their sub-themes. It also proposes some relationships between the central themes, revealed in this study, and other pertinent concepts in brand avoidance.

In hermeneutics, 'dialectical tacking' refers to the development of understanding by comparing and contrasting the findings of the present research with existing knowledge (Thompson 1997).

Thus, one of this paper's main contributions is that it integrates the emergent themes into an original theoretical model. This comprehensive approach to understanding brand avoidance directly addresses the limits of previous knowledge, which has been based on studies focusing only on singular reasons for brand avoidance. These new insights into brand avoidance and the study's core category are discussed next.

FINDINGS AND DISCUSSION

Negative brand promises and the four types of brand avoidance.

Our analysis of the data reveal four types of brand avoidance: experiential, deficit-value, identity, and moral avoidance. Figure 1 displays the main reasons motivating each type of brand avoidance, in addition to their sub-themes. For example, unmet expectations motivates most instances of experiential avoidance; but it was poor performance, the extra hassle and inconvenience associated with failed consumption experiences, and an unpleasant store environment that comprised the emic incidents from which the category of experiential avoidance emerged (Lee et al. 2008b).

Experiential Avoidance: Undelivered Brand Promises

Whilst previous literature from the areas of: disconfirmation and dissatisfaction, (Halstead 1989; Hirschman 1970; Oliva, Oliver, and MacMillan 1992; Oliver 1980; Swan and Combs 1976); negative shopping experiences (Arnold, Reynolds, Ponder, and Lueg 2004; Keaveney 1995); and unpleasant store environments (d'Astous 2000; Turley and Milliman 2000) were used to inform the emergent themes, by further abstracting from the data we are able to provide a new metaphor for understanding these instances of experiential avoidance. We suggest that it is the participant's construction of the brand as an *undelivered brand promise*, which motivates him or her to avoid the brand.

Brands are a multifaceted construct (de Chernatony and Dall'Olmo Riley 1998) and, the brand promise is one important aspect of a brand's constellation of values. The promises framework suggests that the act of branding involves making promises to consumers (Balmer and Gray 2003; Berry 2000; Bitner 1995; Brodie et al. 2006; Dall'Olmo Riley and de Chernatony 2000; Vallaster and De Chernatony 2005). A promise creates a reason to expect something; therefore it is undeniable that brand promises lead to expectations (Gronroos 2006). Indeed, within a consumer's mind, the meaning of a brand is partially made up of a set of expectations about what is supposed to happen when the consumer purchases a brand (Dall'Olmo Riley and de Chernatony 2000). Promises may be explicit or implicit (Gronroos 2006), and when brand promises are delivered in a way that is consistent with consumer expectations, it encourages repurchase (Dall'Olmo Riley and de Chernatony 2000). However, with regards to brand avoidance, if consumers' actual experiences do not match what they have been led to expect by the brand promise, dissatisfaction may result (Halstead 1989; Oliver 1980; Swan and Combs 1976), and brand avoidance may occur (Lee and Conroy 2005; Lee et al. 2008b; Oliva et al. 1992; Thompson et al. 2006).

Thus, one potential disadvantage of branding is that if the company is unable to deliver its promise, it risks disappointing the consumer. Therefore, by heightening consumer expectations, sometimes a brand may be a liability. The following participant clearly illustrates this potential:

I purchased a Sony walkman... maybe after a year, it started rolling [jamming] the tape... So I decided to discard the Sony

FIGURE 1
EMERGENT THEORETICAL MODEL OF BRAND AVOIDANCE

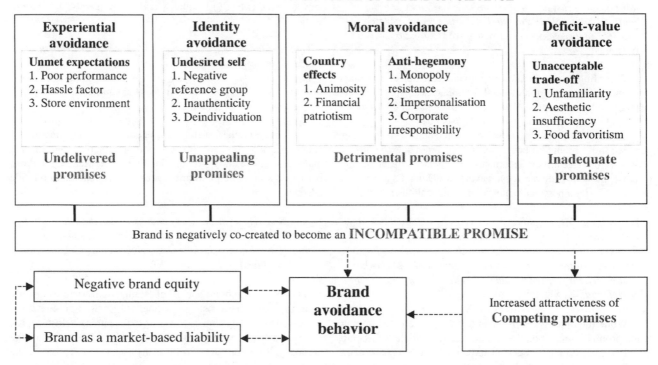

and I didn't get a replacement... sometimes the brand name does not equate to the quality that you'd expect from the brand. RH Int 12 (Male, 26)

The expectations that RH had of his walkman were created by his interpretation of the Sony brand promise. However, it is clear that the implicit brand promise was not delivered, thereby resulting in future brand avoidance.

Identity Avoidance: Symbolically Unappealing Promises

Identity avoidance occurs when consumers perceive certain brands to be inauthentic, or associate certain brands with a negative reference group. Some consumers may also avoid mainstream brands, believing that the use of such brands detract from their own unique sense of individuality (Lee et al. 2008b). Literature in the area of undesired self (Hogg and Banister 2001; Ogilvie 1987; Sirgy 1982), self-image congruency (Dolich 1969; Graeff 1997; Grubb and Grathwohl 1967; Heath and Scott 1998; Hogg et al. 2000; Sirgy 1982), and disidentification (Bhattacharya and Elsbach 2002; Elsbach and Bhattacharya 2001) helped to inform our understanding of this type of brand avoidance. However, we contribute to the literature by offering the notion of a *symbolically unappealing promise* as a new, and more managerially meaningful, way of understanding identity avoidance. Specifically, we suggest that it is possible for some consumers to perceive certain brand promises as symbolically unappealing, and that such brands have the potential to move them closer towards their undesired selves. Consequently, the consumer disidentifies with the brand's symbolically unappealing promises, and through the process of brand avoidance, the individual is able to manage his or her self-concept, as the following participant illustrates:

It's just not my style... [Amazon-surf/beach wear]... they don't suit what I wear, my image, cause it's not like I'm going

to go walking around in little tank top... I don't have the body for it anymore... you know what I mean?... I'm married now I don't need to attract anyone anymore. VL Int 14 (Female, 28)

VL chooses to avoid this brand because its implicit promise, to provide a young and flirty style, is symbolically unappealing to the self concept she is currently attempting to maintain.

Moral Avoidance: Socially Detrimental Promises

The third type of brand avoidance is moral avoidance. Our analysis of the data suggests that moral avoidance consists of two main reasons for brand avoidance: country effects and anti-hegemony. In terms of country effects, some well known brands (such as Coke and McDonald's) are iconic representatives of the countries from which they originate. When consumers feel animosity towards a country, sometimes their dislike also transfers to the iconic brand of those countries. In other cases, participants who are financially patriotic may avoid brands that they believe will not contribute to the economic development and well being of their country.

Avoidance owing to anti-hegemony, or against domination, is informed by previous work in the area of consumer resistance (Fischer 2001; Holt 2002; Klein 2000; Kozinets and Handelman 2004; Penaloza and Price 1993; Thompson and Arsel 2004). The data reveal that some consumers avoid dominant brands in order to prevent the development of monopolies, large companies who are suspected of corporate irresponsibility. Typically, only hegemonic and large multi-national companies are held accountable for their actions. The bias against multi-national organisations may be due to their higher visibility, which means they are often under higher scrutiny:

I think that when things are operating on a really big scale like that that they are often doing more damage to the environ-

ment… I'm not saying that all the little guys added up aren't doing damage as well, because probably every little coffee store is doing just as much damage as Starbucks in terms of pollution but I don't know, so that doesn't really make sense does it? But it seems worse when it's like McDonald's. KB Int 10 (Female, 27)

These findings are in line with previous research on consumer resistance, where large and successful companies are more likely to be targets of consumer criticism (Holt 2002; Klein 2000; Kozinets and Handelman 2004; Thompson and Arsel 2004).

Other participants also avoid hegemonic brands because they perceive those brands as being impersonal and disagree with the way in which large brands dehumanize the agents of the brand. For instance, the following participant avoids McDonald's because he prefers to foster a personal connection with local businesses:

You walk into McDonald's…what's the chance that they know who you are…I can send my children down to the fish and chip shop knowing that the fish and chip shop guy knows who my kids are, so if they're not back in half an hour, I can ring him up and say did you see my kids down there? I cannot do that at McDonald's. MT Int 16 (Male, 42)

While the other types of brand avoidance are based on how brand promises impact on the individual's immediate well-being, moral avoidance, on the other hand, is based on the perception of the brand at an ideological level and how it negatively impacts on the wider society.

A further distinction of moral avoidance is the existence of a dominating or oppressive force that the participant resists; for our participants, that oppressive force was normally a hegemonic corporation/brand or another country. This characteristic of moral avoidance is supported by previous literature in the area of consumer resistance and other similar domains (Dobscha 1998; Gramsci 1971; Holt 2002; Klein 2000; Kozinets and Handelman 2004; Moisio and Askegaard 2002; Penaloza and Price 1993; Rumbo 2002). It is this power imbalance, between the multi-national brand and the consumer that makes moral avoidance distinct from other types of brand avoidance.

The final distinguishing criterion of moral avoidance is that it is motivated by the participants' beliefs that they are doing the right thing. In other words, because certain brands are perceived to be oppressive and overly dominant, some participants believe that it is their moral duty to avoid such brands. This ethical component is another integral characteristic of moral avoidance that is not present in the other types of brand avoidance.

Although our findings are in line with previous literature, we suggest that it is the consumer's perception of a brand as a *socially detrimental promise* that drives moral avoidance of certain brands. The promise of fast and convenient food, cheaper prices on mass merchandise, and standardized consumption experiences are not appreciated by all consumers. In fact these brand promises are actually incompatible with some consumers' moral values, and as a consequence, some participants choose to avoid brands for ethical reasons.

Deficit-Value Avoidance: Functionally Inadequate Promises

We expand existing work on brand avoidance (Lee et al. 2008b) by introducing the concept deficit-value avoidance, which occurs when consumers perceive brands as representing an unacceptable cost to benefit trade-off. Previous literature on value and quality help to inform this type of brand avoidance (Dodds, Monroe, and Grewal 1991; Grewal, Monroe, and Krishnan 1998;

Parasuraman and Grewal 2000; Parasuraman, Zeithaml, and Berry 1985; Zeithaml 1988). Some participants avoid budget brands that they construe to be of low quality and, consequently, deficient in value:

I don't go for the real cheap stuff, so I suppose I do avoid them, like No Frills and Basics [budget brands]… if it's real cheap then I don't place much value on it because if it's real cheap then it means that it doesn't cost much to make and it's usually inferior. SP Int 18 (Male, 26)

In contrast, other participants feel that obtaining a product of adequate quality for low cost is a more acceptable trade-off than gaining a high quality product for high cost. Hence, for those participants, it is the premium brands that are unable to provide adequate value:

Sometimes I feel you pay that much just to get the status… 'Oh it's a Sony'… the quality will most likely be the same, but the money we've added doesn't really give you anything, it's just extra profit. KL Int 11 (Male, 20)

Since the symbolic benefit of 'status' appears to be of little value to KL, the extra cost he associates with a Sony product is not perceived to add any tangible benefits to the purchase. Instead, KL believes that the price premium only adds 'extra profit' to the company. Therefore, KL avoids Sony because he perceives the brand as being deficient in value.

From an emic perspective, some participants avoided unfamiliar brands, evaluating such brands to be lower in quality and higher in risk (Richardson, Jain, and Dick 1996), and therefore providing less value when compared to brands with which they were more familiar.

Another sub theme within deficit-value avoidance is aesthetic insufficiency. Some consumers use the appearance of a brand as an indicator of functional value and avoid aesthetically insufficient brands because ugly packaging or a lack of colours signify an inability to satisfy the individual's utilitarian requirements. Socio-culturally, much value is placed on aesthetic beauty in society and the halo-effect of attractiveness is well known. Marketers use attractive packaging and models in their promotional campaigns hoping the positive connotations that people have of beauty will be associated with the product (Belch and Belch 2004; Chitty et al. 2005; Soloman 2002). Simply put, from a functional perspective, beauty inspires confidence, while aesthetic insufficiency does the opposite.

However, the data also reveal that some participants will seek aesthetic value as an end in itself, rather than as an indicator of performance:

It's [Budget brands] something that's cheap and nasty it's not nice, I mean the packaging it's just not nice…I know it sounds hopeless, but it's because I know it just looks nicer, so I want it to look nice. SR Int 2 (Female, 40)

Throughout her transcript, SR was dubious that the appearance of a brand could be directly related to its quality; nonetheless she still prefers her things 'to look nice'.

The final sub-theme in deficit-value avoidance concerns a phenomenon whereby consumers avoid food associated with certain value-deficient brands, but are comfortable with purchasing other products bearing the same brand name. We term this phenomenon food favoritism, and research on perceptions of food and safety suggest that when it comes to decisions regarding food choice, people are more likely to be cautious and use 'better safe than sorry' cues, avoiding the unfamiliar, contaminated, cheap, or harmful (Green, Draper, and Dowler 2003; Occhipinti and Siegal 1994).

> *Low budget brands...I would buy like pet food and toilet rolls, but when it came to food I wouldn't buy cheap, I'd go for maybe the slightly higher price... probably down to health.*
> AR Int 4 (Male, 29)

In AR's mind, the No Frills brand promise (lower quality for a cheap price) is adequate for certain products, but inadequate for food.

Overall, the common defining property of the sub-themes in deficit-value avoidance is that they all involve an unfavourable perception of the brand's utility. Thus, from an etic perspective, at the core of deficit-value avoidance is the rejection of a brand because of the unacceptable trade-off that it represents to the participant. In keeping with the negative promises framework, we believe the concept of a *functionally inadequate promise* is a suitable metaphor for understanding deficit-value brand avoidance.

The incompatible brand promise.

As figure 1 indicates, the four negative brand promises that participants are motivated to avoid may be further abstracted into a core category termed an *incompatible promise*. This study employs a holistic definition of brand, whereby brands are considered bundles of meaning, or multi dimensional value systems (Dall'Olmo Riley and de Chernatony 2000; de Chernatony and Dall'Olmo Riley 1998). In line with this perspective, a number of marketing scholars have argued that one important aspect of brand meaning, and marketing in general, is the notion of a brand as a 'promise' or 'covenant' (Balmer and Gray 2003; Berry 2000; Bitner 1995; Brodie et al. 2006; Calonius 2006; Dall'Olmo Riley and de Chernatony 2000; de Chernatony and Segal-Horn 2003; Gronroos 2006; Levitt 1981; Vallaster and De Chernatony 2005; Ward, Light, and Goldstine 1999). As the previous sections have indicated, this idea of the brand as a promise is also particularly useful for helping to understand brand avoidance.

A promise is an assurance or declaration that something will or will not happen and, as a result, promises create a reason to expect something (Gronroos 2006; Merriam-Webster 1998). However, an interesting aspect of promises is that they may be based on real or imaginary resources, and can be either implicit or explicit. Furthermore, like any other form of social communication, promises involve an element of subjective interpretation/evaluation by the parties involved, both before and after a transaction (Calonius 2006; Gronroos 2006). Thus, in the consumer's mind, a brand promise is an assurance that by purchasing a specific brand, certain events should follow.

Since many consumers cannot fully experience nor assess a product or service in advance, many purchase decisions are essentially based on implicit or explicit promises or 'metaphorical reassurances' (Levitt 1981), and, therefore, promises are a crucial component of marketing. This study suggests that not all brand promises are positively interpreted. Instead, some brand associations may be re-constructed in the mind of the consumer to represent a promise of an undesirable outcome; one that is incompatible with the individual's requirements.

We argue that brand avoidance may arise from incidents where brand promises have been undelivered/broken, or when brand promises have been negatively re-constructed in the mind of the consumer to represent an assurance of something symbolically unappealing, socially detrimental, or functionally inadequate. In all cases of brand avoidance, the brand and what it is interpreted to deliver, is perceived to be incompatible with the consumer's needs or wants. A consequence of this negative re-construction of the brand promise is that the consumer is motivated to avoid the brand.

Increased Attractiveness of Competing Promises.

Most consumer purchase decisions are influenced by both approach and avoidance. So, individuals are pushed away from undesired end states, just as much as they are pulled towards achieving desired end states, and in most cases the two forms of motivation operate simultaneously (Bourdieu 1984; Elliot 1999; Markus and Nurius 1986; Ogilvie 1987; Soloman 2002; Wilk 1997). When a consumer re-constructs a brand's value constellation to represent an incompatible promise, not only may that act lead to avoidance of the brand, but the promises of competitors may also become more attractive to the consumer. As a result, the consumer approaches competing brands to satisfy his or her consumption needs and wants. This preference for competing promises may indirectly exacerbate the avoidance of the offending brand. This proposition is displayed in figure 1 by the arrow leading from competing promises to brand avoidance. The way in which an incompatible promise may motivate consumers to approach competing brands holds an interesting insight for the concept of brand loyalty.

Brand loyalty is a well researched area (Baldinger and Rubinson 1996; Chaudhuri and Holbrook 2001; Jacoby and Kyner 1973; Oliver 1999; Roselius 1971); however, as early as the 1970's, brand loyalty was suggested to consist of both acceptance *and* rejection. Therefore, "not only does [brand loyalty] 'select in' certain brands; it also 'selects out' certain others" (Jacoby and Kyner 1973 p. 2). Similarly, we contend that brand avoidance not only results in the active rejection of certain brands, but at a broader level, it is also a phenomenon that impacts on the attractiveness of competing brands.

Some participants' narratives of brand avoidance were mentioned alongside notions of brand loyalty, which provides an interesting juxtaposition that contributes to the understanding of both brand loyalty and brand avoidance. For instance SR's avoidance of McDonald's does not operate in isolation within the consumption system. What becomes apparent is the inextricable link between the incompatible promises of McDonald's and the increased attractiveness of competing brands:

> *I like Wendy's because I like their chicken burgers, and just cause they make them fresh they haven't been sitting their for ages. You know at McDonald's they could have been sitting there for a while. At Wendy's they make them fresh and they have fresh salads in them and stuff. I think the quality at Wendy's is better, probably paying more but I think its better quality and they use real chicken.* SR Int 2 (Female, 45)

SR's avoidance of McDonald's is mentioned alongside her loyalty for Wendy's. Therefore, is SR's hatred of McDonald's pushing her towards the competing promises of Wendy's? Or is her love of Wendy's pulling her away from the offending brand? The most sensible answer is probably both, since approach and avoidance are able to operate concurrently within each person (Elliot 1999).

Negative Brand Equity.

Another interesting proposition that has emerged from our interpretation of the qualitative data, relates to the resource-based view of the firm (Barney 1991; Barney, Wright, and Ketchen Jr. 2001; Hooley, Broderick, and Moller 1998; Hooley, Greenley, Cadogan, and Fahy 2003; Srivastava et al. 2001; Srivastava et al.

1998), and is illustrated on the bottom left corner of figure 1.

Brand equity was originally defined as a set of assets or liabilities linked to the brand's name that adds value to, or subtracts from, the firm or its customers. Thus, positive brand equity is the added value that the brand provides to the company through the extra money a consumer is willing to pay for the branded service or product (Aaker 1996; Keller 1993). The concept of brand equity as a balance of both negative and positive components has still been relatively ignored in most branding research, with most studies focussing only on the positive components of brand equity.

With regards to the resource-based view of the firm, Srivastava, Fahey, and Christensen (2001) have elucidated the multitude of ways in which a brand is able to enhance shareholder value. Although there is little dispute that a well-managed brand is a market-based asset, there has been scarce discussion over the idea of the brand as a market-based liability. Thus, there still exists a gap in this area, despite the recommended importance of exploring the reasons why a market-based asset might "deprecate, decay, or decline" (Srivastava et al. 2001).

We develop the notion of the brand as a market-based liability by drawing upon Barney's (1991) conceptualisation of a firm's resources, where an asset is described as one of a number of resources that "improve a firm's efficiency and effectiveness" (Barney 1991p. 101). We consider a liability to be the opposite of an asset; and therefore define a market-based liability as anything that decreases a firm's efficiency and effectiveness in the marketplace. This research uses qualitative data in the form of participant quotations to demonstrate that, within the marketing and consumption system, certain incidents may result in a brand promise becoming negatively re-constructed, thereby leading to brand avoidance attitudes and behaviors. A brand that suffers from sustained periods of brand avoidance or failing consumer relationships may develop negative brand equity, since customers consistently react unfavourably to the brand (Aaker 1996; Keller 1993). The brand could then develop negative network equity, as the perceptions and behaviors of additional distributors, retailers, and the market place in general, co-mingle to form an unfavourable impression of the brand. Since the avoided brand decreases a firm's efficiency and effectiveness in the marketplace, the brand might be considered a market-based liability, because it is actually a disadvantage for the company to possess such a brand.

From the firm's perspective, the simplest method of dealing with a market-based liability may be to discard the brand as soon as negative promises begin to develop. However, we argue that the reality of the situation is not black and white. Since negative brand promises are constructed within a complex marketing and societal environment, it is likely that a state of flux exists between the positive brand building efforts of the firm and the negative brand associations that exist within any market. Brand managers should acknowledge that both aspects contribute to the co-constructed meaning of most brands.

MANAGERIAL IMPLICATIONS, LIMITATIONS, FUTURE RESEARCH, AND CONCLUSION

Traditionally, marketing managers have concentrated on strategies that aim to persuade customers to select their brands, but some consumers actively avoid certain brands. Lack of research and knowledge relating to this area means that "conventional brand management literature offers little concrete advice on how brand strategists can proactively diagnose the cultural vulnerabilities that could eventually erode their customer-based equity" (Thompson et al. 2006 p. 61). To this end, we offer the negative promises framework as a tool which managers may use to diagnose any brand avoidance issues that they encounter.

One caveat that accompanies any research using a relatively small number of informants is that the findings must be considered alongside the context in which the study has taken place. In this study, the reasons for brand avoidance emerged from a relatively small group of informants; thus, the findings should only be interpreted as being representative of the participants' attitudes and behaviors. For instance, although several participants expressed an avoidance of McDonald's, this is a successful brand that is clearly satisfying its target market. Therefore, any implications that have emerged from the participants of this study must be interpreted within the context of this research. Thus, we offer a theoretical contribution of why some brands are avoided by some consumers, rather than representative account of brand avoidance in the wider consumer population.

Another limitation of this study, lies in the question: how important is it for managers to deal with brand avoidance? If the majority of target consumers are satisfied with a brand, then there is no need for a company to risk its strategic positioning by addressing people's perception of a brand's incompatible promise. Thus, the brand manager must decide whether the net gain of new customers, as a result of addressing an incompatible brand promise, is greater than the net loss of the original target market. However, it would still be prudent for companies, particularly controversial ones like McDonald's, to monitor the opinion of brand avoiders, if only to be aware of the anti-consumption attitudes directed at their brand. The ability to understand and possibly change brand avoidance attitudes and behaviors in consumers should be considered an important long-term goal of any organisation, even if the number of complaining consumers is relatively small.

Even more managerially useful, would be for future research to interview people who avoid the very brands that have been designed to target them. Many companies use brand guidelines that describe, exactly, the type of person to whom each brand is designed to appeal, such information may be requested from a brand's parent company. Future studies could then recruit participants based on two criteria: (1) they fit a certain brand's target consumer profile and, (2) they actively avoid that brand. Results of such studies, focusing on actual target markets, should help to bridge the gap between the theoretical contributions of this paper and the practical requirements of brand managers.

A final limitation of our study may be that the core concept of an incompatible promise could have been abstracted further to arrive at an even more parsimonious explanation of brand avoidance. For instance, it could be argued that *negative brand meaning* may be the most parsimonious explanation for brand avoidance. Thus, the reason for brand avoidance is because the brand represents negative meaning to the consumer; the implication follows that all a brand manager needs to do is to ensure that their brand meaning does not become negative. Obviously, not only would this be an overly simplistic, and somewhat naive, view of the marketing world, but it is also does not provide a practical way of understanding brand avoidance. Such an abstracted view is too parsimonious and becomes unworkable, particular if it does not elaborate on the elements that constitute negative brand meaning. Although it is important for grounded theory research to abstract from the qualitative data to provide a higher order construct/theory, it is equally important (especially in marketing) that the theory is not too abstract or unworkable. The negative promises framework is a perspective that provides an elevated understanding of brand avoidance but remains practical.

In conclusion, the challenge of balancing between parsimony and complexity has not been successfully negotiated previously in brand avoidance research. The majority of prior studies have been too narrow, failing to account for the myriad of reasons motivating brand avoidance. Further, the area has lacked a unifying construct that is both abstract enough to account for the many reasons for brand avoidance, yet concrete enough so that managers may find it useful. We address this challenge by offering the notion of an incompatible brand promise as a unifying concept that accounts for the majority of brand avoidance behaviors and attitudes. We suggest that this metaphor provides an elevated, yet workable, understanding of brand avoidance.

REFERENCES

Aaker, David (1996), *Building Strong Brands*. New York: Free press.

Aaker, Jennifer L. (1999), "The malleable self: The role of self-expression in persuasion," *Journal of Marketing Research*, 36 (1), 45-57.

Abougomaah, Naeim H., John L. Schlater, and William Gaidis (1987), "Elimination and choice phases in evoked set formation," *The Journal of Consumer Marketing*, 4 (4), 67-73.

Ambler, Tim and Chris Styles (1996), "Brand development versus new product development: Towards a process model of extension decisions," *Marketing Intelligence & Planning*, 14 (7), 10-19.

Arnold, M. J. , K. E. Reynolds, N. Ponder, and J. E. Lueg (2004), "Customer delight in a retail context: Investigating delightful and terrible shopping experiences," *Journal of Business Research*, Forthcoming.

Baldinger, Allan L. and Joel Rubinson (1996), "Brand loyalty: the link between attitude and behavior," *Journal of Advertising Research*, 36 (6), 22-34.

Balmer, John M T and Edmund R Gray (2003), "Corporate brands: What are they? What of them?," *European Journal of Marketing*, 37 (7/8), 972-97.

Banister, Emma N. and Margaret K. Hogg (2004), "Negative symbolic consumption and consumers' drive for self-esteem," *European Journal of Marketing*, 38 (7), 850-68.

Barney, Jay (1991), "Firm resources and sustained competitive advantage," *Journal of Management*, 17 (1), 99-120.

Barney, Jay, Mike Wright, and David J. Ketchen Jr. (2001), "The resource-based view of the firm: Ten years after 1991," *Journal of Management*, 27 (6), 625-41.

Berry, Leonard L. (2000), "Cultivating services brand equity," *Journal of the Academy of Marketing Science*, 28 (1), 128-37.

Bhattacharya, C. B. and Kimberly D. Elsbach (2002), "Us versus them: The role of organizational and disidentification in social marketing initiatives," *Journal of Public Policy & Marketing*, 21 (1), 26-36.

Bitner, Mary Jo (1995), "Building service relationships: It's all about promises," *Journal of Academy of Marketing Science*, 23 (4), 246-51.

Bourdieu, Pierre (1984), "Distinction: A Social Critique of the Judgement of Taste. Translated by Richard Nice," in. London: Routledge & Keagan Paul plc.

Brodie, Roderick J, Mark S Glynn, and Victoria Little (2006), "The service brand and the service-dominant logic: Missing fundamental premise or the need for stronger theory?," *Marketing Theory*, 6 (3), 363-79.

Calonius, Henrik (2006), "Contemporary research in marketing: A market behavior framework," *Marketing Theory*, 6 (4), 419-28.

Charmaz, Kathy (2000), "Grounded theory: Objectivist and constructivist methods.," in Handbook of Qualitative Research, Norman K Denzin and Yvonne S Lincoln, Eds. Thousand Oaks: Sage.

Chaudhuri, Arjun and Morris B. Holbrook (2001), "The chain of effects from brand trust and brand affect to brand performance: The role of brand loyalty," *Journal of Marketing*, 65 (2), 81-93.

Craig-Lees, Margaret and Constance Hill (2002), "Understanding voluntary simplifiers," *Psychology & Marketing*, 19 (2), 187-210.

Dall'Olmo Riley, Francesca and Leslie de Chernatony (2000), "The service brand as relationship builder," *British Journal of Management*, 11, 137-50.

d'Astous, Alain (2000), "Irritating Aspects of the Shopping Environment," *Journal of Business Research*, 49 (2), 149-56.

de Chernatony, Leslie and Francesca Dall'Olmo Riley (1998), "Defining a "brand": Beyond the literature with experts' interpretations," *Journal of Marketing Management*, 14, 417-43.

_____ (1997), "Modelling the components of the brand," *European Journal of Marketing*, 32 (11/12), 1074-90.

de Chernatony, Leslie and Susan Segal-Horn (2003), "The criteria for sucessful service brands," *European Journal of Marketing*, 37 (7/8), 1095-118.

Dobscha, Susan (1998), "The lived experience of consumer rebellion against marketing," *Advances in Consumer Research*, 25, 91-97.

Dodds, Williams B, Kent B. Monroe, and Dhruv Grewal (1991), "Effects of price, brand, and store information on buyers' product evaluations," *Journal of Marketing Research*, 28 (August), 307-19.

Dolich, Ira J. (1969), "Congruence relationships between self images and product brands," *Journal of Marketing Research*, 6 (February), 80-84.

Elliot, Andrew J. (1999), "Approach and avoidance motivation and achievement goals," *Educational Psychologist*, 34 (3), 169-89.

Elsbach, Kimberly D. and C. B. Bhattacharya (2001), "Defining who you are by what you're not: Organizational disidentification and the National Rifle Association," *Organization Science*, 12 (4), 393-413.

Englis, Basil G. and Michael R. Soloman (1997), "Special session summary: I am not therefore, I am: The role of avoidance products in shaping consumer behavior," *Advances in Consumer Research*, 24, 61-63.

Erdem, Tulin and Joffre Swait (2004), "Brand credibility, brand consideration, and choice," *Journal of Consumer Research*, 31 (1), 191-98.

Erdem, Tulin, Joffre Swait, and Ana Valenzuela (2006), "Brands as signals: A cross-country validation study," *Journal of Marketing*, 70 (1), 34-49.

Fischer, Eileen (2001), "Special session summary: Rhetorics of resistance, Discourses of discontent," *Advances in Consumer Research*, 28, 123-24.

Gabriel, Yiannis and Tim Lang (1995), *The Unmanageable Consumer*. London: Sage publications Ltd.

Goulding, Christina (2001), "Grounded Theory: A Magical Formula or a Potential Nightmare," *The Marketing Review*, 2, 21-34.

Graeff, Timothy, R. (1997), "Consumption situations and the effects of brand image on consumers' brand evaluations," *Psychology & Marketing*, 14 (1), 49-70.

Gramsci, A (1971), *Selections from the Prison Notebooks*. London: Lawrence & Wishart; edited and translated by Quintin Hoare and Geoffrey Nowell Smith.

Green, Judith M., Alizon K. Draper, and Elizabeth A. Dowler (2003), "Short cuts to safety: risk and 'rules of thumb' in accounts of food choice," *Health, Risk & Society*, 5 (1), 33.

Grewal, Dhruv, Kent B. Monroe, and R Krishnan (1998), "The effects of price-comparison advertising on buyers' perceptions of acquisition value, transaction value, and behavioral intentions," *Journal of Marketing*, 62 (April), 46-59.

Gronroos, Christian (2006), "On defining marketing: Finding a new roadmap for marketing," *Marketing Theory*, 6 (4), 395-417.

Grubb, Edward L. and Harrison L. Grathwohl (1967), "Consumer self-concept, symbolism and market behavior: A theoretical approach," *Journal of Marketing*, 31 (October), 22-27.

Halstead, Diane (1989), "Expectations and disconfirmation beliefs as predictors of consumer satisfaction, repurchase intention, and complaining behavior: An empirical study," *Journal of Consumer Satisfaction, Dissatisfaction and Complaining Behavior*, 2, 17-21.

Heath, Adam P. and Don Scott (1998), "The Self-concept and Image Congruence Hypothesis," *European Journal of Marketing*, 32 (11/12), 1110-24.

Hirschman, Albert O. (1970), *Exit, Voice and Loyalty: Responses to declines in Firms, Organizations, and States*. Cambridge, MA: Harvard University Press.

Hogg, Margaret K. (1998), "Anti-constellations: Exploring the impact of negation on consumption," *Journal of Marketing Management*, 14 (April), 133-58.

Hogg, Margaret K. and Emma N. Banister (2001), "Dislikes, distastes and the undesired self: Conceptualising and exploring the role of the undesired end state in consumer experience," *Journal of Marketing Management*, 17, 73-104.

Hogg, Margaret K., Alastair J. Cox, and Kathy Keeling (2000), "The impact of self monitoring on image congruence and product/brand evaluation," *European Journal of Marketing*, 34 (5/6), 641-66.

Hogg, Margaret K. and Paul C. N. Michell (1997), "Special session summary: Exploring anti-constellations: Content and consensus," *Advances in Consumer Research*, 24, 61-63.

Holt, Douglas, B. (2002), "Why do brands cause trouble? A dialectical theory of consumer culture and branding," *Journal of Consumer Research*, 29 (June), 70-90.

Hooley, Graham, Amanda Broderick, and Kristian Moller (1998), "Competitive positioning and the resource-based view of the firm," *Journal of Strategic Marketing*, 6 (2), 97-115.

Hooley, Graham J., Gordon E. Greenley, John W. Cadogan, and John Fahy (2003), "The performance impact of marketing resources," *Journal of Business Research*, Forthcoming, 10.

Jacoby, Jacob and David B. Kyner (1973), "Brand loyalty vs. repeat purchasing behavior," *Journal of Marketing Research*, 10 (1), 1-9.

Keaveney, Susan M. (1995), "Customer switching behavior in service industries: An exploratory study," *Journal of Marketing*, 59 (2), 71-82.

Keller, K. L. (1993), "Conceptualising, measuring and managing customer-based brand equity," *Journal of Marketing*, 57 (January), 1-22.

Klein, Naomi (2000), *No Logo: Taking Aim at Brand Bullies*. London: Flamingo.

Kozinets, Robert V. (2002), "Can consumers escape the market? Emancipatory illuminations from burning man," *Journal of Consumer Research*, 29 (June), 20-38.

Kozinets, Robert V. and Jay M. Handelman (2004), "Adversaries of consumption: Consumer movements, activism, and ideology," *Journal of Consumer Research*, 31 (3), 691-704.

Lee, Michael S W, Karen Fernandez, and Mike R Hyman (2008a), "Anti-consumption: An Overview and Research Agenda," *Journal of Business Research* (Special issue on Anti-consumption), 1-3.

Lee, Michael S W, Judith Motion, and Denise Conroy (2008b), "Anti-consumption and brand avoidance," *Journal of Business Research* (Special Issue on Anti-consumption), 12.

Lee, Michael S. W. and Denise Conroy (2005), "Brand Avoidance: The brand as a market-based liability," in EMAC: Rejuvenating Marketing. Milan.

Levitt, Theodore (1981), "Marketing intangible products and product intangibles," *Harvard Business Review*, 59 (3), 94-102.

Levy, Sidney J. (1959), "Symbols for sales," *Harvard Business Review*, 37 (4), 117-24.

Markus, Hazel and Paula Nurius (1986), "Possible selves," *American Psychologist*, 41 (9), 954-69.

McCracken, Grant (1989), "Who is the celebrity endorser? Cultural foundations of the endorsement Process," *Journal of Consumer Research*, 16, 310-21.

Merriam-Webster (1998), "Merriam-Webster's Online Dictionary." 10th ed. Springfield MA: Merriam-Webster Incorporated.

Moisio, Risto J and Soren Askegaard (2002), "Fighting Culture: Mobile phone consumption practices as means of consumer resistance," *Asia Pacific Advances in Consumer Research*, 5, 24-29.

Narayana, Chem L. and Rom J. Markin (1975), "Consumer behavior and product performance: An alternative conceptualization," *Journal of Marketing*, 39 (October), 1-6.

Occhipinti, Stefano and Michael Siegal (1994), "Reasoning and food and contamination," *Journal of Personality and Social Psychology*, 66 (2), 243-53.

Ogilvie, Daniel M. (1987), "The undesired self: A neglected variable in personality research," *Journal of Personality and Social Psychology*, 52 (2), 379-85.

Oliva, Terence A., Richard L. Oliver, and Ian C. MacMillan (1992), "A catastrophe model for developing service satisfaction strategies," *Journal of Marketing*, 56 (3), 83-95.

Oliver, Richard L (1980), "A cognitive model of the antecedents and consequences of satisfaction decisions," *Journal of Marketing Research*, 17 (November), 460-69.

_____ (1999), "Whence consumer loyalty?," *Journal of Marketing*, 63, 33-44.

Parasuraman, A. and Dhruv Grewal (2000), "The impact of technology on the quality-value-loyalty chain: A research agenda," *Journal of Academy of Marketing Science*, 28 (1), 168-74.

Parasuraman, A., Valarie A. Zeithaml, and Leonard L. Berry (1985), "A conceptual model of service quality and its implications for future research," *Journal of Marketing*, 49 (4), 41-50.

Penaloza, Lisa and Linda L. Price (1993), "Consumer resistance: A conceptual overview," *Advances in Consumer Research*, 20, 123-28.

Richardson, Paul, S., Arun Jain, K., and Alan Dick (1996), "Household store brand proneness: A framework," *Journal of Retailing*, 72 (2), 159-85.

Roselius, Red (1971), "Consumer rankings of risk reduction methods," *Journal of Marketing*, 35 (1), 56-61.

Rumbo, Joseph D. (2002), "Consumer resistance in a world of advertising clutter: The case of adbusters," *Psychology & Marketing*, 19 (2), 127-48.

Ryan, Gery W and H Russell Bernard (2000), "Data management and analysis methods," in Handbook of Qualitative Research, Norman K Denzin and Yvonne S Lincoln, Eds. Thousand Oaks: Sage.

Sirgy, Joseph M. (1982), "Self-concept in consumer behavior: A critical review," *Journal of Consumer Research*, 9 (December), 287-300.

Sivakumar, K and S P Raj (1997), "Quality tier competition: How price change influences brand choice and category choice," *Journal of Marketing*, 61 (3), 71-84.

Soloman, Michael R. (2002), *Consumer Behavior: Buying, Having, and Being* (Fifth ed.). Upper Saddle River: Prentice Hall.

Solomon, Michael R. (1983), "The role of products as social stimuli: A symbolic interactionism perspective," *Journal of Consumer Research*, 10 (3), 319-29.

Spiggle, Susan (1994), "Analysis and interpretation of qualitative data in consumer research," *Journal of Consumer Research*, 21 (December), 491-503.

Srivastava, Rajendra K., Liam Fahey, and H. Kurt Christensen (2001), "The resource-based view and marketing: The role of market-based assets in gaining competitive advantage," *Journal of Management*, 27 (6), 777-802.

Srivastava, Rajendra K., Tassadduq A. Shervani, and Liam Fahey (1998), "Market-based asscts and sharcholder value: A framework for analysis," *Journal of Marketing*, 62 (January), 2-18.

Stern, Barbara B (2006), "What Does Brand Mean? Historical-Analysis Method and Construct Definition," *Journal of the Academy of Marketing Science*, 34 (2), 216-23.

Strauss, Anselm L and Juliet Corbin (1990), *Basics of Qualitative Research: Grounded Theory Procedures and Techniques*. Newbury Park: Sage Publications.

_____ (1998), *Basics of Qualitative Research: Techniques and Procedures for Developing Grounded Theory*. Thousand Oaks: Sage.

Swan, John E. and Linda Jones Combs (1976), "Product performance and consumer satisfaction: A new concept," *Journal of Marketing*, 40 (2), 25-33.

Thompson, Craig J. (1997), "Interpreting consumers: A hermeneutical framework for deriving marketing insights from the texts of consumers' consumption stories," *Journal of Marketing Research*, 34 (4), 438-55.

Thompson, Craig J. and Zeynep Arsel (2004), "The Starbucks brandscape and consumers' (anticorporate) experiences of glocalization," *Journal of Consumer Research*, 31 (3), 631-42.

Thompson, Craig J., Aric Rindfleisch, and Zeynep Arsel (2006), "Emotional branding and the strategic value of the doppelganger brand image," *Journal of Marketing*, 70 (1), 50-64.

Turley, L. W. and Ronald E. Milliman (2000), "Atmospheric effects on shopping behavior: A review of the experimental evidence," *Journal of Business Research*, 49 (2), 193-211.

Vallaster, Christine and Leslie De Chernatony (2005), "Internationalisation of services brands: The role of leadership during the internal brand building process," *Journal of Marketing Management*, 21 (1/2), 181-203.

Ward, Scott, Larry Light, and Jonathan Goldstine (1999), "What High-Tech Managers Need to Know About Brands," *Harvard Business Review*, 77 (4), 85-95.

Weitzman, Eben A. (2000), "Software and qualitative research," in Handbook of Qualitative Research, Norman K Denzin and Yvonne S Lincoln, Eds. Thousand Oaks: Sage.

Wilk, Richard (1997), "A critique of desire: Distaste and dislike in consumer behavior," *Consumption, Markets and Culture*, 1 (2), 175-96.

Zavestoski, Stephen (2002a), "Guest editorial: Anticonsumption attitudes," *Psychology and Marketing*, 19 (2), 121-26.

_____ (2002b), "The social-psychological bases of anticonsumption attitudes," *Psychology & Marketing*, 19 (2), 149-65.

Zeithaml, Valarie A. (1988), "Consumer perceptions of price, quality, and value: A means-end model and synthesis of evidence," *Journal of Marketing*, 52 (July), 2-22.

"Bye Bye Love"-Why Devoted Consumers Break Up With Their Brands

Andrea Hemetsberger, Innsbruck University, Austria
Christine M. T. Kittinger-Rosanelli, Innsbruck University, Austria
Sandra Friedmann, Innsbruck University, Austria

ABSTRACT

Consumer devotion and brand love have recently attracted rising interest in consumer research. Due to their high emotional attachment, brand devotees love and adore their brands and even fervently defend them against all odds. Yet, some of these relationships break down. This article addresses the question why strong emotional bonds with brands are weakened, and how consumers experience the process of emotional detachment and relationship termination. Phenomenological interviews with brand devotees revealed that–similar to personal relationships–personal transformation and physical and psychological injuries are two main categories of reasons for brand love to vanish.

INTRODUCTION

Apple, the iconic cult brand (Belk and Tumbat, 2005) is undoubtedly one of the brands which is said to be loved by its users and fans. Apple fans are devoted brand evangelists and defend the brand fervently, if necessary. However, even the most convinced Apple devotees were at least irritated by Steve Jobs' pricing policy of the recently introduced Apple iPhone in the US. People were eagerly awaiting the new iconic iPhone. They were spending their nights in front of the stores in order to pay 599 Dollars and get one of the first iPhones. When Apple reduced prices to 399 $ after two months, some were furious and ended their relationship with the brand, although they still loved Apple. Sounds like personal relationship problems? Probably very much so.

The Apple story is just one out of many examples of brand relationship termination with a loved brand. Literature on brand switching behavior and relationship termination in general is rich (Andreasen, 1984; Schouten, 1991; McAlexander, 1991; Fajer and Schouten, 1995; van Trijp et al., 1996; Fournier, 1998; Mathur, Moschis and Lee, 2003 Perrin-Martinenq, 2004). However, we have only limited evidence of dissolutions of consumer-brand relationships that were once highly emotional and committed partnerships (see: Fournier, 1998; Aaker, Fournier and Brasel, 2004; and Price, Arnould and Folkam Curasi, 2000 about older consumers' disposition of possessions). Firstly, consumers who are highly committed are brand loyal by definition. Secondly, enthusiast consumers and brand devotees are usually much more forgiving and tolerant in case of transgressions from the side of the brand (Fournier, 1998). But when, and under what circumstances do they decide to cut these strong emotional bonds? How do they experience this break up?

This article aims to research and theorize about the termination of strong consumer-brand relationships and contribute to a more thorough understanding of brand love dissolution. To this end we will briefly review the literature on brand relationships and strong emotional bonds with brands in general. We will further summarize literature on possible reasons for brand relationship dissolution, and provide empirical insights into consumer stories of breaking up with a brand they love. In the discussion section we draw a parallel to marital relationship dissolution, and add some thoughts for future research.

STRONG EMOTIONAL BONDS BETWEEN CONSUMERS AND THEIR BRANDS

Susan Fournier's (1998) expanded relationship perspective entailed a wealth of empirical and theoretical insights into emotional bonds between consumers and their brands, which was fuelled from mainly two streams of research. While one of them is rooted in a quantitative view on consumer-brand relationships, and called (product) attachment (Ball and Tasaki, 1992), attachment to brands (Thomson, MacInnis and Park, 2005), or brand love (Ahuvia, 2005), the other stream of research is more qualitative and interpretive in nature and comprises work on brand relationships (Fournier, 1998; Aaker, Fournier and Brasel, 2004), and devotion (Pimentel and Reynolds, 2004; Pichler and Hemetsberger, 2007, 2008). In general, the importance of such relationships for consumers' identity projects, personal style, social categorization, and self-definition is unquestioned.

Brand attachment is a construct which has been introduced in consumer research in order to explain high degrees of emotional attachments to brands (Thomson, MacInnis and Park, 2005). Individuals form attachment to a myriad of objects (Belk, 1988; Wallendorf and Arnould, 1988; Richins, 1994), brands (Schouten and McAlexander, 1995), film series (Kozinets, 2001), places (Maclaren and Brown, 2005), or activities (Hemetsberger, 1999), which evoke feelings of connection, affection, love, and passion. Attachment theory in psychology predicts that individuals who are attached to a person are more likely to be committed to, invest in, and make sacrifices for that person. Emotional attachment to brands is expected to lead to similar results with regard to beloved objects, which has major implications for brand loyalty and emotional commitment, in particular.

Ahuvia (2005) introduced a similar construct, termed brand love. He contends that love objects have a strong influence on our sense of who we are. Hence, they determine our self-concept, contribute to our self definition, and also demarcate the boundaries between ourselves and the identities that we reject. Viewed from this perspective, brand love may actually be highly relevant for times of change, and personal transformation. As a matter of fact, research on brand detachment has found particular life events, and phases of transition to be major causes for brand detachment or brand switching (Andreasen, 1984; Mathur, Moschis and Lee, 2003). It is thus unclear when, and under what circumstances, times of transition foster band love or rather constitute a peril to the consumer-brand relationship.

Devotion is defined as a somewhat distinct concept in that it concentrates on the private side of consumer-brand relationships on the one hand, and on the behavioral patterns and acts of devotion as a proof for a balanced self- *and* other-related concerns, on the other hand (Pichler and Hemetsberger, 2008). Devotion is said to be similar to mature love relationships which are defined by passion, intimacy, and dedication. Researchers (Pimentel and Reynolds, 2004; Belk and Tumbat, 2005; Pichler and Hemetsberger, 2007) also emphasize that devotion implies feelings of spiritual and religious excitement, fervor, zeal, and adoration. Similar to love relationships, brand devotees' adoration is not very likely to vanish out of the blue.

Although Pichler and Hemetsberger (2007), for instance, criticize the view that brand love and consumer devotion may be seen as an ideal state of 'endless love' and highest consumer-brand relationship quality, they leave the question untouched when and why consumers would terminate strong brand relationships, and how consumers emotionally detach themselves from their brands.

TERMINATING BRAND LOVE

Consumers terminate brand relationships and change their brand preferences several times in their lifetime. From research into brand-switching behavior we learn that some consumers tend to get bored more easily with brands and products, are variety seekers (van Trijp, Hoyer and Inman, 1996). Other reasons include marketing strategies employed by marketers, or situational influences. Drawing on literature on interpersonal relationships, Fajer and Schouten (1995) identified three typical patterns of termination: (1) physical separation, (2) new brands replace old ones, or (3) a partner in the dyad reveals or does something to alienate the other. In the case of highly committed partnerships we propose that these patterns are likely to be accompanied by strong triggers, as for instance severe transgressions on the side of the brand, or important transitory stages on the side of the consumer that cause the relationship to deteriorate.

Fournier (1998) suggests two general models of relationship deterioration. The entropy model is based on the assumption that relationships fall apart if they are not actively maintained. As brand devotees are active maintainers by definition, the entropy model as a single cause for relationship termination seems implausible. The stress model (Andreasen, 1984; Fournier, 1998) refers to forceful destructions of brand relationships through brand dyadic, personal, or environmental stress factors which are not relationship specific. Consumers may move to another place where they cannot buy the brand, or other alternatives are found to be even more tempting.

Brand dyadic stress is caused by someone breaking the rules of a relationship, a breakdown of trust, or failure to keep a promise. Other failures refer to poor conduct in the relationship, such as poor brand performance, or a failure to reinforce consumer commitment. Similar failures might also occur in consumer-brand love relationships yet such failures are likely to be forgiven and/or downgraded by real brand devotees (Fournier, 1998). Some relationships even show signs of reinvigoration after such transgressions, primarily with exciting as opposed to sincere brands, and in response to recovery efforts (Aaker, Fournier and Brasel, 2004). Although transgressions vary in severity and cause, all are significant in their potential to affect consumer-brand relationships. 'Sudden death' refers to utterly devastating transgressions which lead to immediate termination of the relationship.

Personal stress factors occur with life disturbances, role changes, or changes in personality, caused by important life events (Andreasen, 1984, Schouten, 1991, Mathur, Moschis and Lee, 2003). Life events and role transitions are associated with significant changes in consumer behavior in general. New brands can help to cope with distress associated with the adoption of new roles and relinquishing old ones. However, loved brands may also serve as a refuge in turbulent times. It is therefore unclear whether, and which life events do actually have an impact on strong consumer-brand relationships.

Termination of brand love is certainly not a spontaneous decision but rather an ongoing process of dissolution (Duck, 1982). Drawing on Duck's work, Fajer and Schouten (1995) describe ending processes of brand relationships as a sequence of break-down, decline, disengagement, and dissolution. The time needed to end a relationship most certainly depends on whether termination had been triggered by a disruptive event, or had been rather a series of experiences or developments which contribute to a continuous 'fade-out'. It is important to distinguish between relationship termination and brand detachment. Brand relationships may be terminated although consumers are still emotionally attached to the brand; on the other hand, consumers may still stick to a brand but affectively detach from the brand (Perrin-Martinenq, 2004). We argue that it is important to look at the process of relationship deterioration, the idiosyncratic sequence of disturbances and related reactions, in order to understand why love relationships fall apart. We aim to elicit stories of relationship termination; the triggers, reactions, and subsequent processes of dissolution that, in combination, mark the end of a brand love story.

METHOD

Our empirical work followed a 2-step process. First we identified brand proponents who have had strong emotional bonds with brands that for some reason were terminated. Participants were asked to briefly outline their 'love story' with a favorite brand of theirs. To determine whether brand commitment was really strong and emotional we used the brand-relationship-quality dimensions and respective descriptions suggested by Fournier (1998), and additional scale items (Kressmann et al., 2003) and indicators (Aaker, Fournier and Brasel, 2004) for strong brand relationships. Content analysis of the stories, guided and categorized by these dimensions enabled us to decide, if the participants qualified. The final sample consisted of 4 female and 6 male respondents from age 20 to 62, and comprised 10 stories of 10 different passed brand-relationships, including diverse products like cars, clothing, cosmetics, drinks, electronics, and skis. Participants were informed about the goal of the study and ensured confidentiality.

In the second step we conducted phenomenological interviews (Thompson, Locander and Pollio, 1989) to attain first person experiences on the relationships with their beloved brand, and their end. We chose this form of interview to attain deep insights into this very personal, not always easy to verbalize, and in some cases even painful process. To stimulate the expression of emotions undergone during the process we applied the photo-elicitation technique (Zaltman, 1997). Respondents were asked to bring 3 photos or pictures illustrating or symbolizing their brand relationship and their feelings during the termination process. The pictures were used either at the beginning to stimulate stories about the brand relationship, or in the course of the interview. Some respondents used the pictures to express their feelings. If the pictures were not mentioned by the respondent, the interviewer asked for their deeper symbolic meaning, in order to stimulate additional narratives. At the end of the interview the researchers also asked for a picture which is most representative for the ending of the relationship, again with the intention to eventually evoke additional memories or feelings of the detachment process (Zaltman, 1997).

We tape-recorded the interviews and transcribed them verbatim. Analysis followed a two step process (Thompson, 1989). An idiographic analysis documented the single termination experiences including motives, triggers, emotions and processes. Integrative analysis revealed similarities and differences and allowed us to formulate themes, and relate them to processes of brand detachment.

FINDINGS

Consumers' stories of breaking up with the brands they loved revealed how important those brands are for real brand devotees, and thus how central relationship termination and emotional detachment are for consumers' selves and identities. Some stories sound quite familiar, some are extreme in a way, some seem to belong to the category of 'never-ending stories', and some are even heartbreaking. We found two main categories of relationship termination of brand devotees, which are related to self healing on the one hand and personal transformation on the other hand. In the following we will describe *how* relationship termination develops, and how behavioral (re)actions of both partners and brand detachment are related to relationship ending.

Personal transformation

My ™ just couldn't keep up with me and my new life

Sebastian, 29 years old and self-employed with a creative agency told us about his detachment from the Sony brand and his Sony notebook in particular. He had admired Sony since he was a child and all electronic equipment he owned was Sony. His love for Sony culminated in his notebook which he even took along to parties and evenings with friends.

"… at that time I was really crazy. I even took my notebook when going out. I took photos with the first digital cameras and there just was my notebook to transmit them right on spot (to the notebook)…. Everybody could have a look and we emailed them immediately. At that time you were really important and cool if you did that. Looking backward I have to say that I had bats in my belfry, but at that time it was important." (…) (My Sony-Laptop) was something like my best friend who I could share with everything and who I took everywhere. (…) Who never lets you down, my Sony Notebook never crashed. Like your very best friend, who you can rely on and who is always with you."

Sebastian's passion for Sony started to lag when he quit his job in an advertising agency (which he had started right after college) and started his own business.

"When starting my own business, I also went through a strong personal transformation. I started to refuse run-of-the-mill products, which somehow everybody seemed to have. … Now I am self-employed, experienced in my job, I am successful and in this situation I wanted new things, not these ordinary ones. (…) I frequently looked at Apple–ads. After all, their claim is "think different". This seemed like the right motto for me and my life."

During this transition he actually buys an Apple Notebook + iPod and after a while gives away his Sony Vaio as a gift to a friend who needed a computer for college. He describes his feelings when he passed on his Sony to his friend.

"It was quite ok. I already had my Powerbook and was super happy with it. I had my new profession, my self-employment and was full of pleasant anticipation, expecting what future might bring for me. So it was not bad to let loose my Sony. And of course I was happy that my friend would still use it. After all I had been really proud of "the Thing" and I was happy that it is in good hands and that it will be treated with diligence. If I had given it to a stranger it would definitely have been different."

Actually Sebastian never completely detached from his Sony brand but rather decided to let it 'fade-out'. It was quite okay for him; a new (love) brand replaced the old one (Fajer and Schouten, 1995) but he could not bear throwing it away; it was so much part of him and part of his former life that he wanted his old brand to find a good place, a refuge. Sebastian actually still shows much respect for his former love brand but feels unable to treat it with the same passion as before. Hence, he passes it on in an attempt to help the brand have the life it deserves; a behavior common for brand devotees (Pichler and Hemetsberger, 2008). Price, Arnould and Folkman Curasi (2000) reported similar findings with older consumers who pass on symbolic-laden special possessions to their heirs. Brands may actually want to help with these rituals in order to preserve the object from becoming secularized.

Falling in love with another ™

Susanne, 26 works as an office clerk in a medium sized company in a small town in upper Bavaria. Before she was an active athlete within the German Skiing Union and participated in World Series ski-races. She drove "Völkl ski" as a child and also during her career as a ski-racer where she was happy and proud to be selected by Völkl to be sponsored.

"The skis were really great and it fitted so well with my driving style. That simply was mine. They were my one and only. In the evening I brought them along to my room, because I did not want anything to happen to them. (…) They were my sanctuary." (…) we were a team.

When she finished her active racing career she continued to buy Völkl for her private use until she got to know Hermann Maier [Austrian top skiing athlete] who drove Atomic skis.

"I simply adored him. (…)…the way he skied, with all his power. And also this bundle of muscles, that was impressing. … and he drove Atomic."

She started looking for and test-driving Atomic-skis and Völkl just was not so important any more. For about two years she drove Völkl *and* Atomic skis and then changed completely to Atomic.

"Now I am a confident driver of Atomic skis. I could not say that I dislike Völkl or so, but that just occurred because I admired Hermann Maier so much. Ok, now I also need Atomic skis. They are, of course, really good skis, nothing can be said against that. It's simply different from driving Völkl. That's how it was."

Susanne actually exhibits typical adolescent behavior where falling in love with someone and adoring him is part of this transitory phase. At first sight Susanne's case looks like a typical brand switching behavior in light of perceived superior alternatives. Yet leaving someone whom she used to love is difficult for her, even if another option seems much more tempting. That is why Susanne actually needs two years of parallel relationship. What is interesting though is that actually the brand testimonial infatuated her which seems decisive for her brand switching behavior. Her admiration for his skiing skills, and the prospect of getting closer to her 'ideal skier self' exceeded the fascination with the new brand. Personified brands are strong attractors. Particularly when they enjoy iconic status, they are seductive and predestined objects for adoration.

De-Glorification

Simone, a student of the social sciences in her early twenties was a Benetton fan from the age of 5. At that age she "inherited" most of her clothes from older friends. When she occasionally got new outfits, she traveled with her Mum to the next small city to go to a Benetton store. She remained a devoted Benetton customer for many more years, being particularly fond of the quality, the cosmopolitanism, the cultural diversity.

"It was a little bit like a part of me in a certain way, also their advertising campaigns. The cheerful children from the diverse nations, and all dressed up with the bright colors of Benetton. So everywhere on the world children wear these garments and I got to do so as well. I am among them. That's what impressed me when I was a girl."

Towards her high school graduation she started being less satisfied. She has some bad experiences with the quality of the materials and also senses a drawback in style; too dysfunctional for her changing lifestyle (more travel). She starts buying other brands but keeps buying Benetton. After about 2 years she completely turns to other brands without finding any particular favorite. Simone's story elicits a quality of brand love that we may actually call 'glorification' at a rather young age. In the course of the years, and when naivety changes into informed and emancipated consumer decision-making, the brand cannot keep up. Similar to what Belk, Wallendorf and Sherry (1989) have called desacralization, deglorification is a process of brand deterioration, here caused by an eye-opening personal transition into adulthood.

We slowly drifted apart

The following case demonstrates that it may actually be the brand that changes personality in the eye of the relationship partner, which led to a slow but destructive alienation (Fajer and Schouten, 1995). Hans, 62 years old, worked as an engineer and retired last year. For almost his whole life he had a strong emotional bond to Volkswagen (VW), especially the old beetle. He owned beetles, sometimes more than one at a time, and enjoyed almost anything with them like driving, traveling, fixing and tuning it, trading second hand spare parts, Volkswagen ads, and the company behind. VW, especially the beetles were for him exactly what the literal translation of Volkswagen means: a car for all people-solid, sound technology, good value, and suitable for young and old alike. His passion for the brand faded very, very slowly and after 15 years of increasingly ambivalent feelings towards the brand he finally turned his back on VW. He still liked the Golf 1 and 2 model, although he was unhappy that the warranty expired as soon as one fixed anything himself.

"But the (Golf) 3 was not so neat. Actually the time had come then. The (Golf) 2, by the way, I drove it for quite some time; I was quite thrilled. But the 3, it was so bad then, there were complaints all the time so that I had already refused to buy one. Starting with the 4, it was completely over; they got more and more expensive. That had nothing to do anymore with a "Folkeswagen", not to talk about "Folkesprices". No, that's not for me no more. And with these new models, there was nothing you could do yourself, you always hat to go to a garage, and that was costly again. Also the others (models), Phaeton or whatever it is called. In my eyes that does not fit VW. Why would VW need a luxury limousine? That sure is not a car for the people, but the others aren't either. So what!"

He still had an old beetle until a year ago but he sold it because he needed the space in the garage and had problems getting spare parts anyway. That was the end of the story. The process of detachment actually started after many years of love and faithfulness. Hans and his VW had a symbiotic relationship of two very stable and dependable personalities. Nostalgia proneness is one of the person-

ality characteristics of Hans thus the relationship ended when the brand became too fierce in its rejuvenation efforts. Furthermore, when the brand refused to let him engage in 'labors of love', he decided to let go. This is actually a commonly observed reaction of brand devotees, who want their brand to develop continuously but who refuse to accept radical changes. This particular process of relationship ending takes years or even decades of slowly drifting apart.

From the Hurt to the Healing Self
The torn self

Maria is 37 and works and lives in her own Living-Design Studio in Munich. Her first true love with an Italian guy entailed her love for "Prosecco Valdobbiadene" (light sparkling wine). This Prosecco "Valdo" saw the two of them through all special occasions of their relationship and was also part of her boyfriend's family life back in Italy. The Valdo actually became the embodiment of this love affair and had a very special significance in her life. The end of this love affair was very painful and disappointing, and also determined the end of her relationship with the Valdo.

"I wanted to ban everything that I related to him (former boyfriend) from my life. Yes, also the Valdo. Once during that time I bought one more bottle together with a girlfriend, because I liked it so much-maybe to drown my grief a little bit. The next morning I had a terrible headache. Maybe it was simply too much (laughs). Anyway, I decided to buy Valdo never again. … to protect myself a little. … so that it does not hurt when I see it. Especially at the beginning of the first year (after the break up) it was fairly bad."

During that year of grief she occasionally checks in the stores if the Valdo is still available, but does not buy again.

"I had to separate irrevocably from the Valdo to cope with the whole disappointment and to let bygones be bygones. The memories kept being too strong. Even if I had adored the Valdo; it would not work any more. I would have destroyed myself."

Even today, 7 years after the breaking, memories of this tremendous disappointment come up when by chance she sees a Valdo. As we know from research on special possessions (Belk, 1988), when brands become imbued with strong meanings and memories, they become symbols and manifestations of our experiences. They become part of the extended self thus are hard to let go. The torn self engages in a healing process of emancipation from persons/things that hurt.

A 'healing hand'

Andreas has had a strong emotional relationship with Audi. He is hotelier and this year he is going to celebrate his 50th birthday. He brought the picture of a red heart which symbolized his feelings for Audi, *"this strong feeling that I felt for Audi, almost love"*. He switched from Audi to Ferrari recently, a pretty radical move. Andreas' left leg was severely injured in a ski accident last year which partly explains his dramatic break up with Audi. He underwent a hard process of physical rehabilitation and cannot do his favorite sports like skiing or golfing any more.

"I simply have to avoid sports. (…) I cannot live like I used to live before. I had to realign my life and in the course of it I replaced my Audi and bought a Ferrari. (…) I just hoped that my parting from Audi would ease the farewell from my

PICTURE 1
Manfred sitting on his father's DKW

previous life. That it would be easier for me to recognize the facts. That I would not permanently think of old memories and experiences; simply get more involved with new things."

He also finished the relationship with his wife and experienced hard times. A picture showing a teardrop is what he considers most representative for the whole change process, including the change from Audi to Ferrari. He still holds Audi in high respects and still uses Audis for his hotels, but "it's not my life to that extent any more"; for his new, private life it's definitely Ferrrari now. From a psychological perspective, Andreas faced a similar challenge of physical and psychological 'healing'. As described by Schouten (1991), consumption activities, including disposition and acquisition, play vital roles in the restoration of harmony to an ambiguous and, in Andreas' case, physically hurt self. He gave up his wife and his Audi—symbols of his old life. Ferrari, a much stronger brand, serves as a support in times of re-orientation, because it could compensate at least his bodily disabilities, and act as a symbol of regaining strength. With Andreas, too, the personifications of the two brands were decisive for his move. In times of troubles you need a helping hand, in times of recovery, Andreas needed a healing Hero.

Breach of faith
Stefan, a passionate biker was sure to own the best road bike of the world. After having desperately longed for an "Eddy Merckx -Bike" (named after the legendary German bike racer Eddy Merckx) he finally bought (credit financed) the "Ferrari among bikes" for 10.000 German Marks. He was very proud and enjoyed the admiration from his fellows and other bikers.

"It was the most exquisite (bike) one could think of. It was the dream of every biker" (…) It meant incredibly much to me. It symbolized success and a great technical standard. It gave me the feeling to be better, more successful and unbeatable against my fellows. Actually it was sheer lunacy to have myself decorated with this device (…) but I was possessed by it."

The "dream" did not last long. Despite being "death sure to have the very best material" the frame broke without any premonition on a downhill passage of a dolomite mountains pass and Stefan had a horrible accident. He was catapulted off the road and by great chance survived with minor injuries.

"It was like awakening from a dream. Due to the overturn and the material defect they (my strong feelings) simply vanished.

The great feeling, the dream of being invincible was replaced by sheer fear of this bike."

The reactions from the company were more then disappointing and hardly went beyond the attitude that "shit happens. There is no 100% safety." Stefan never again touched this or any other Eddie Merckx bike not to speak about driving one. "So from blind enthusiasm for the bike I hit the zero point or was even below that." If the company had reacted differently, he thinks, he might have overcome his fear related to the product. But after this reaction he set seals on this chapter and bought a conventional and simple bike without a "big name" and did not have any problems ever since. Stefan's detachment from the brand could actually have been prevented if the brand had reacted differently. But the brand turned his back on him and Stefan lost his faith in it. From a psychological standpoint Stefan–similar to Andreas–had to cope with substantial fears, which he managed by making a clear cut. However, although Stefan was deeply hurt by the brand in a physical and in a psychological sense, he refrained from buying another "big name". Similar to other cases where the brand spoiled the relationship, consumers' feelings are so deeply hurt that they never again engage in another love relationship within the same product category.

Humiliation and contempt
Manfred, Head of Logistics of a big Bavarian company located in Munich was enthused by the car brand Audi and DKW (the former name of the brand who at that time also manufactured motor bikes). Being a child he already adored his fathers DKW bike (see Picture 1). Right after getting his drivers license he kept owning and loving different Audi models for decades. He was always very proud of his cars and convinced to get good value for money until several problems and unpleasant experiences with his last A6 provoked a revaluation of the brand and finally a break of the relationship.

The problem started on the 3rd day with his last A6. Heading for a meeting he parked in front of his head office and locked the car with the remote key. The car not only locked but opened all 4 windows at the same time. … Once, twice, three times he tried with the same results and an increasing crowd of spectators was giving him advices. Running late for his meeting he called the hotline that kept being busy. Finally he reached somebody who told him that this was not a new problem and that he should just keep trying.

"I was pissed off. I was the mock of the people. My meeting had long begun and my windows kept opening. I called the hotline again and was told by a friendly voice to disconnect the battery *and boot up the electronic system. Anyhow, the laughs were on the other side and I was humiliated and embarrassed with my new car. That stank!"*

Three weeks later he went to the Audi- garage because his back door would not close, or reopened when he closed the drivers-door. The serviceman closed it almost forcibly without checking the mechanism and accused him of not being able to shut doors himself and making up complaints. Manfred ran mad again, and had his problem solved by another mechanic.

"First the window story, then the garage, where they proofed to be extremely arrogant and treated me like I was no Audi-customer at all, though this was my 6ᵗʰ Audi. I was nobody for Audi. Well, so other cars started to attract me; according to the motto there are plenty more fish in the sea."

He also started to look at car statistics and tests in magazines and realized that other cars might be better value. When the period of mounting unpleasant events added up to about 2–3 years he broke up with Audi, and ended up choosing a Skoda as his next car.

"I would never have put aside Audi overnight. No, no, I was far too attached to them. But as things go, there is one straw that breaks the camels back."

Manfred's story is the typical story of several severe transgressions from the side of the brand, which eventually leads to relationship termination. What is stunning though is the fact that it took him years to terminate the relationship and detach from the brand. Detachment itself was an active process of looking for a car with purely functional value. No love involved here at all.

Marion, a housewife, 54 years old, told us about her story with the cosmetics mail-order (internet) supplier Yves Rocher (YR) with limited direct distribution in YR-stores in some cities. More than 20 years she loved and used her YR products and convinced many friends of her beloved products.

"I simply could trust the brand and I knew I was right when I used the brand and that they were just the thing for me. These cosmetics very soon became a part of me. It was a ritual to go to the bathroom and use my cosmetics which almost seemed to have waited for me well arranged in the mirror cabinet. (…) It was my one and only. (…) Using the cosmetics in the morning was like the sun rising in the morning, simply fantastic."

When she moved to Skopje, Mazedonia with her husband, the relationship came to a sudden end. After having settled in Skopje she wanted to restock her inventory of personal care items. Her new address was fairly long and did not fit into the online-form provided. So she called an operator for help. After a few unpleasant calls and emails she was informed that there was no solution for this problem and that she could not order to this address.

"I had to abandon the products I needed. That really annoyed me. The whole bureaucracy, I was really frustrated and disappointed. I was angry at YR. I could not order and I will not order because I was so furious. I had ordered for decades and spent a lot of money (…). I was an absolutely loyal customer and this makes me just sad. You do not expect such things. (…) It still offends me, when I talk about it. The whole anger comes back up in me. ….I even asked her, if she could

eventually write the address by hand on the parcel, but even that was too much for them. They told me it's not possible because everything is automatized. Bullshit, nobody can believe that, right?"

On her occasional visits back home in Germany she could actually buy YS products in one of the stores, but now she refuses to buy them.

"I could not even imagine a life without YR products. Now I realized that it does go without. Nobody can take me back to one of the stores… it hurts being disappointed so deeply. I still think a lot of my YR creams and such. For some I still haven't found alternatives … They are the ones I miss particularly. Nonetheless I will not buy from them again. Who do they think I am!"

At this point of enragement, forgiveness is not possible any more. As Gottman (1993) contends, at this stage of hypervigilance, attribution bias would cause even negative interpretation of positive behavior. Humiliation and contempt are the worst that could happen in a relationship, because they communicate disgust (Gottman, 1993). Inevitably contempt leads to greater conflict and negativity, the remaining wounds are hard to heal, if ever. What is interesting though is that Manfred made a clear cut, whereas Marion is still emotionally attached to the brand. One possible interpretation could be a gender effect. Another interpretation Marion's highly emotional decision to take revenge and not to buy any more. As she immediately terminated the relationship she was lacking time to emotionally detach from the brand. Hence, she reported that she is still suffering from the painful break up.

DISCUSSION

Consumers and brands divorce. Whereas it is not new that consumers are more or less brand loyal, terminating relationships with brands they love is no impulse reaction, goes much deeper in its emotional quality, and–as indicated above–has a deep impact on consumers' lives. Although our research is exploratory in nature, and many more stories might exist, we could carve out two main factors that contribute to the termination of a love relationship with brands: personal transformation and coping with physical and psychological injuries. When consumers break up with their brands, it is always connected to a major life event and/or phase of personal development and emancipation, or with a changing brand personality, which contributes to a growing incompatibility of the consumer and his brand. Hence, our findings support current knowledge, particularly regarding times of transition and changes in consumption patterns (Andreasen, 1984, Schouten, 1991, Fajer and Schouten, 1995), but also clearly transcend what is currently known in literature in at least two ways.

First, the findings indicate that the termination of a love relationship with a brand has to be clearly distinguished from the process of emotional detachment. Consumers may break up but still love their old brands, as is the case with Andreas' Audis, or Marion's story with Yves Rocher. Even in cases where the company has caused relationship termination, it seems hard for consumers to let their love brand go. Vice versa, consumers may need years of detachment from a brand before they actually terminate the brand relationship. As our study shows, emotional detachment is a long (see also Coulter and Ligas, 2000) and active process. The findings indicate that consumers need to actively detach themselves from their love brands, either through cognitive degradation or behavioral engagement in retaliation, searching for alternatives, passing it on, or similar. These processes of detachment are accompanied by ambiguous feelings and behavior, as exemplified in several cases.

Secondly, we found that breaking up with a love brands exhibits parallels to breaking up with a strong personal relationship. In some cases people fall in love with another brand, which is qualitatively different from a typical 'fling' (Fournier, 1998) where relationship termination is foreseeable; in other cases, proactive sustaining behavior and communication is missing for a long time; other stories reveal that consumers are not willing to accept the personality development of the brand in the course of the years. In cases of relationship endings that are 'caused' by the love brand, transgressions are either severe, causing highly affective reactions, or relationship ending is an extremely long process of steadily growing misfits between the person and the brand. Emotions that were triggered by brand transgressions range from anger and enragement, to grieve, feeling betrayed, or even fear, and eventually lead to relationship termination or even retaliation (Grégoire and Fisher, 2008). Accordingly, triggers that cause such strong emotions are much more severe and usually occur not only once.

Drawing on research about marital divorce, we can distinguish several deteriorating factors, which contribute to the termination of a love relationship. Gottman, in an interview (2007), contended that the best predictors of breakup are 'criticism', 'defensiveness', 'stonewalling', and 'contempt'. Interestingly, all four of these "Horsemen of the Apocalypse" (Gottman, 1993) have been reported by our informants as behaviors enacted by the brands they loved and broke up with, probably the most devastating being stonewalling and contempt as exemplified by the Yves Rocher story. Defensiveness is a rather common 'brand behavior', portrayed by Stefan's Eddie Merckx story, and brought to perfection by Audi's reaction to Manfred's quest for help, which was additionally spiced with criticism.

Viewed from a positive perspective, brands that are loved can do a lot to support a positive, life-long love relationship by treating consumers with respect and showing affection. Several of our cases indicate that, even after severe transgressions, consumers are reluctant to give up their emotional relationships. Similarly, times of transition could open up new opportunities for consumer-brand relationships and deepen the emotional bonds. Ahuvia (2005) has pointed out the importance of love brands for supporting personal identity that combines potentially conflicting aspects of selves, enable personal growth, and renewal of the self. Future research into consumer-brand relationships that successfully mastered turbulent times could elicit possible courses of action. Future research is also needed to highlight whether gender differences, or other personality characteristics, influence processes of emotional detachment. Love stories and strong emotional relationships might be highly idiosyncratic in their particular development and thus need emphatic brands that are familiar with 'The Art of Loving' (Fromm, 1956).

REFERENCES

Aaker, Jennifer, Fournier, Susan and S. Adam Brasel (2004), "When Good Brands do Bad," *Journal of Consumer Research*, 31 (June), 1-16.

Ahuvia, Aaron C. (2005), "Beyond the Extended self: Loved Objects and Consumers' Identity Narratives," *Journal of Consumer Research*, 32 (June), 171-184.

Andreasen, Alan (1984), "Life Status Change and Changes in Consumer Preferences and Satisfaction," *Journal of Consumer Research*, 11 (December), 784-794.

Ball, A. Dwayne and Lori H. Tasaki (1992), "The Role and Measurement of Attachment in Consumer Behavior," *Journal of Consumer Psychology*, 1 (2), 155-172.

Belk, Russell (1988), "Possessions and the Extended Self," *Journal of Consumer Research*, 15 (September), 139-168.

_____, Wallendorf, Melanie and John F. Sherry Jr. (1989), "The Sacred and the Profane in Consumer Behavior: Theodicy on the Odyssey," *Journal of Consumer Research*, 16 (June), 1-38.

_____, and Gülnur Tumbat (2005), "The Cult of Macintosh," *Consumption, Markets and Culture*, Vol. 8, 3 (September), 205-217.

Benson, Gary (2007), "Making Relationships Work: A Conversation with Psychologist John M. Gottman," *Harvard Business Review*, December 2007, 45-50.

Coulter, Robin A. and Mark Ligas (2000), "The Long Good-Bye: The Dissolution of Customer-Service Provider Relationships," *Psychology & Marketing*, 17 (8), 669-695.

Duck, Steve (1982), "A Topography of Relationship Disengagement and Dissolution," in: Duck, Steve ed., *Personal Relationships 4: Dissolving Personal Relationships*, Academic Press: London, 1-30.

Fajer, Mary T. and John W. Schouten (1995), "Breakdown and Dissolution of Person-Brand Relationships," *Advances in Consumer Research*, 22, 663-667.

Fournier, Susan (1998), "Consumers and Their Brands: Developing Relationship Theory in Consumer Research," *Journal of Consumer Research*, 24 (March), 343-373.

Fromm, Erich (1956), *The Art of Loving*, New York: Harper & Row.

Gottman, John M. (1993), "A Theory of Marital Dissolution and Stability," *Journal of Family Psychology*, 7 (19), 57-75.

Grégoire, Yany and Robert J. Fisher (2008), "Customer betrayal and Retaliation: When your Best Customers become your Worst Enemies," *Journal of the Academy of Marketing Science*, 36 (2), 247-261.

Hemetsberger, Andrea (1999), "Explaining the Social Basis for the Emergence of Extreme Activity Attachment–a Social Representations Perspective," *Proceedings of the 28th annual conference of the EMAC* 1999 in Berlin: CD-ROM.

Kressmann, Frank, Herrmann, Andreas, Huber Frank and Stephanie Magin (2003), "Dimensionen der Markeneinstellung und ihre Wirkung auf die Kaufabsicht," *Die Betriebswirtschaft*, 63 (4), 401-418.

Kozinets, Robert V. (2001), "Utopian Enterprise: Articulating the Meanings of Star Trek's Culture of Consumption," *Journal of Consumer Research*, 28 (June), 67-88.

Maclaran, P. and S. Brown (2005), "The Center Cannot Hold: Consuming the Utopian Marketplace, *Journal of Consumer Research*, 32 (September), 311-323.

Mathur, Anil, Moschis, George P. and Euehun Lee (2003), "Life events and Brand Preference Changes," *Journal of Consumer Behaviour*, 3 (2), 129-141.

Perrin-Martinenq, Delphine (2004), "The Role of Brand Detachment on the Dissolution of the Relationship Between the Consumer and the Brand," *Journal of Marketing Management*, 20, 1001-1023.

Pichler, Elisabeth A. and Andrea Hemetsberger (2007), ""Hopelessly Devoted to You"-Towards an Extended Conceptualization of Consumer Devotion," in G. Fitzsimons and V. Morwitz (eds.), *Advances in Consumer Research*, Vol.34, 194-199.

Pichler, Elisabeth A. and Andrea Hemetsberger (2008), "Driven by Devotion–How Consumer Interact with their Objects of Devotion," in (eds.), *Advances in Consumer Research*, Vol. 35, forthcoming.

Pimentel, Ronald W. and Reynolds, Kristy E. (2004), "A Model for Consumer Devotion: Affective Commitment with Proactive Sustaining Behaviors," *Academy of Marketing Science Review*, 5, 1-45.

Price, Linda L., Arnould, Eric J. and Carolyn Folkman Curasi (2000), "Older Consumers' Disposition of Special Possessions," *Journal of Consumer Research*, 27 (September), 179-201.

Richins, Marsha L. (1994), Valuing Things: The Public and Private Meanings of Possessions," *Journal of Consumer Research*, 21 (December), 504-521.

Schouten, John W. (1991), "Personal Rites of Passage and the Reconstruction of Self," *Advances in Consumer Research*, 18, 49-51.

Schouten, John W. and James H. McAlexander (1995), "Subcultures of Consumption: An Ethnography of the New Bikers," *Journal of Consumer Research*, 22 (June), 43-61.

Thompson, Craig J., Locander, William B. and Howard R. Pollio (1989), "Putting Consumer Experience Back into Consumer Research: The Philosophy and Method of Existential-Phenomenology," *Journal of Consumer Research*, 16 (2), 133-146.

Thomson, Matthew, MacInnis, Deborah J. and C. Whan Park (2005), "The Ties That Bind: Measuring the Strength of Consumers' Emotional Attachment to Brands," *Journal of Consumer Psychology*, 15 (1), 77-91.

Van Trijp, Hans C.M., Hoyer, Wayne D. and Jeffrey J. Inman (1996), "Why Switch? Product-Category-Level Explanations for True Variety-Seeking Behavior," *Journal of Marketing Research*, 33 (3), 281-292.

Wallendorf, Melanie & Arnould, Eric J. (1988), ""My Favorite Things": A Cross-Cultural Inquiry into Object Attachment, Possessiveness, and Social Linkage," *Journal of Consumer Research*, 14 (March), 531-547.

Zaltman, Gerald (1997), "Rethinking Market Research: Putting People Back In," *Journal of Marketing Research*, 34 (4), 424-437.

Exploring Consumers' Conflict Styles: Grudges and Forgiveness Following Marketer Failure

Michael B. Beverland, Royal Melbourne Institute of Technology, Australia
Emily Chung, Royal Melbourne Institute of Technology, Australia
Steven M. Kates, Simon Fraser University, Canada

ABSTRACT

To date, research has not extensively examined consumer conflict styles following a transgression of commercial relationship norms by firms. We examine instances of service failure between consumers and long-time service providers using critical incident interviews with 30 informants. The findings indicate that the decision to perpetuate grudges or forgive service providers following a transgression is moderated by consumers' self- vs. other-orientation, emotional intelligence, and attachment style. The findings provide a new perspective on grudge holding and highlight the dark side associated with strong emotional bonds between consumers and service providers.

INTRODUCTION

One downside to close dedication-based relationships (relationships based on trust and voluntary membership; Bendapundi and Berry 1997) between firms and consumers is that customers in these relationships may react more negatively to severe service failures—"a violation of the implicit or explicit rules guiding relationship performance and evaluation" (Aaker, Fournier, and Brasel 2004, p.2). Bendapundi and Berry (1997, p. 33) propose that such violations lead to "ill-will and consequent negative repercussions." Repercussions may include negative twist behaviors ("unwanted behaviors of resistance against the company"; Arnould, Price, and Zinkhan 2004, p. 784) including long-term grudgeholding, theft, vandalism, negative word-of-mouth, anti-brand websites, and in rare cases physical abuse of service personnel (Andreassen 2001). These outcomes often occur even when seemingly reasonable efforts at service-recovery have been undertaken. Since many service organizations position themselves as sincere relationship partners that espouse consumer centricity (Bolton, Smith, and Wagner 2003) the betrayal of relationship norms potentially represents a significant moment in the consumer-brand relationship (Aggarwal 2004) because consumers place greater emphasis on negative events than on positive performances, and an "updating of expectations may take hold when disconfirmation exceeds a certain threshold" (Rust, Inman, Jia, and Zahorik 1999, p. 90). Such transgressions may result in counter factual thinking about the service provider resulting in a negative reassessment of the brands' motives (McColl-Kennedy and Sparks 2003). Moreover, the literature suggests that relationships *are* renegotiated (for the worse) following a transgression regardless of whether service recovery efforts were successfully undertaken (Maxham and Netemeyer 2002.

We examine why some consumers continue to perpetuate grudges against service providers and why and how consumers come to forgive transgressing firms. This paper examines these questions by drawing on the relational conflict literature. Although service provider transgressions have been examined from the perspective of dissatisfaction and justice (Smith and Bolton 2002), research on interpersonal conflict reveals a broader range of conflict responses or styles, and a range of moderators that go beyond concerns of justice to include a complex range of post-betrayal outcomes and moderators. For example, research on the nature of betrayal by romantic partners covers a broad range of possible cognitive, emotional and behavioral outcomes (McCullough et al. 1998). In particular, this research focuses on explaining how and why betrayed partners may engage in acts that seek to repair or end relationships. Such research on helps to explain why some consumers perpetuate grudges following a transgression.

METHODS

Long in-home interviews were performed with consumers, focusing on service brand choice, usage, and instances of serious failure. Service brand consumption is a rich context in which to investigate topics of relationship realignment, dissatisfaction, and forgiveness because consumers establish ongoing relationships with brands or marketing organizations (Fournier 1998). Further, transgressions sometimes occur in marketers' relationships with consumers (Aaker et al. 2004), and consumers adjust their meanings of, and relationships with them, accordingly. Our dataset consisted of thirty interviews with consumers (16 women and 14 men aged between 17 and 61) that had experienced failures in commercial relationships—thus theoretical sampling was employed. To probe into and elaborate on motivations for switching, types of transgressions, and eventual outcomes of transgressions, we employed some projective techniques by providing informants a range of images to help them elaborate on their reactions (Zaltman 2004). In each case we asked informants to discuss the nature of the relationship prior to the transgression, the nature of the transgression and the outcomes. Where relevant, we asked informants to compare the transgressing brand with any new brands that the informant switched to. As well, further probes into informants' emotional responses to transgression addressed personal life themes.

Interviews lasted approximately sixty to ninety minutes and were subsequently transcribed. These interviews were then analyzed by classifying the types of transgressions, processes of dealing with transgressions, and the outcomes that occurred using coding methods described by Strauss and Corbin (1998). Data was read over and analyzed independently by the authors, and then jointly discussed during face-to-face meetings and ongoing email correspondence. Overall, interpretive analysis was performed on the data in order to understand the rich details surrounding types of transgressions and their outcomes, and connecting data derived circumstances to constructs of interest such as relationship change and forgiveness. Finally, categories derived from the data were connected to and enriched by prior research, furthering our understanding of realignment in consumers' relationships service providers. For building theory, attention was paid to those consumption stories that appeared to challenge and extend extant findings (due to space limitations we focus on four informants).

FINDINGS

Consumer Forgiveness

Forgiveness relates to the release of negative feelings associated with a transgression and overcoming such resentments for restoring the relationship to its original state (Sells and Hargrave 1998). In a comprehensive review of the literature Sells and Hargrave (1998, p. 28) identified six necessary conditions of forgiveness: a violation occurs that causes one partner emotional or physical pain; the violation results in a broken relationship between the parties; perpetuation of the injury is halted; a cognitive process is pursued where the painful event or action is understood or reframed within a fuller context; there is a release or letting go of justifiable emotion and retaliation related to the event; and, there is a renegotiation of the relationship. Of the sampled informants, 16 forgave the transgressor, with nine remaining in the relationship and seven exiting.

In describing examples of forgiveness, informants recounted incidences in a calm manner and although engaging in negative word-of-mouth, they only did so when people asked them about certain service classes. In cases where negative word-of-mouth occurred, the focus was on poor service standards—a functional assessment of the partner's performance. As well, these informants' transgressions involved a pattern of constant failures and in some cases illegal behavior before the consumers decided that the relationship should be terminated. And, these informants often engaged in intense efforts to repair the relationship and reconcile with the transgressor during incidences of failure, often stating how they "followed the rules," or "played their part"—characteristics absent in instances of grudgeholding. Thus, even when exit resulted, these informants met the six conditions of forgiveness identified by Sells and Hargrave (1998).

For example, Peter (WM30) recounted his experience with the National Bank, identifying multiple small failures including sending credit cards to the wrong address, failing to send personal security codes for the card, and poor service-recovery efforts from the bank's credit card center. Such failures had practical repercussions for Peter and his wife because all their credit cards and bank accounts were interlinked—therefore failures often made accessing money difficult, or in cases where new cards had to be sent out, account and internet banking details had to be constantly changed. However, despite these incidences of failure, Peter and his wife kept their anger under control, engaged in efforts at repairing the relationship, and were prepared to extend forgiveness. For example:

"Well their service was terrible! They were rude, unhelpful. Again, we tolerate mistakes, but if the service is good and they try and rectify it, you can be very forgiving, but if they continually, and they did, continually do the same thing and treated us very poorly and we sent them letters about granting my wife access to the accounts and they had it on system, but they always said she couldn't deal with the account. So this went on and on and on, we had really, really had enough."

Peter's passage above was reflective of the stance of many of our informants experiencing small service slippages or failures (anger was followed by a reframing of the event, calming down, attempts to repair the relationship, and eventual exit when it dawned upon the informant that these efforts would not be reciprocated). Peter only sought to exit the relationship after it was clear that his generosity and benevolence within the relationship would not be reciprocated. Peter's unwillingness to exit the relationship immediately was also moderated by his empathy with staff (he described many service personnel as "victims of the system" rather than being intrinsically rude individuals). As such, Peter ultimately attributed fault to the brand *per se*.

"Yes, the bank as an entity, because you can forgive one or two service failures, you know, you can have bad days, you can cop a bad one but generally you don't have them all bad, but it was very consistent and we had enough and it was their system, whatever they did, it was their information system, they always got it wrong. And obviously they didn't have the power to deal with it."

Peter's ability to explain one-off failures as poor timing or bad luck is evidence of his desire to empathize with service staff. However, ongoing failures led Peter to reconsider his stance. Peter's instances of anger and frustration were therefore used to generate counter-factual thinking about the brand (McColl-Kennedy and Sparks 2003), and the likely future experiences—a reexamination of the likely future value of a continued relationship with the offending partner. As such, what were perceived as "one-off" service failures were seen as part of a wider systemic failure that undermined the ability of bank representatives to authentically deliver on their promises. Peter, who defined his expectations of the service provider in terms of "fast, prompt and friendly professional service," realized that these expectations would never be met given the firm's wider problems. However, during this period of time, Peter was still reluctant to leave the bank, describing himself as "too forgiving" and "very patient" and also identifying that although alternatives exist, switching costs in terms of changing account information with employers, suppliers of regular services, and the hassles involved with setting up new phone and internet banking were also involved. For example:

"No, no, we try and get it right. Too much hassle to keep changing banks. As long as they respond and they communicate the problem, or their explanation, and they are up front about it and you know what's going on. Even when it's a human error, you can live with it, as long as they fix it properly."

The final act of betrayal involved a serious violation of customer confidentiality, when a friend working at the bank accessed their account and gave details of their finances to other friends (an illegal act under Australian law). However, even here, Peter's concern that informing the bank would result in the staff member losing their job ("we wouldn't them to lose their job") led him to quietly exit the relationship. Peter forgave because he saw that the outcomes of complaining would impact negatively on the service staff—a result he did not desire because of his empathy with staff. Peter's post-transgression experience was typical of several consumers that emotionally moved on from a negative relationship, rather than ruminating on past events and bearing a grudge. Although Peter will not return to the National Bank in the future, the transgression effectively no longer plays any role in his life.

Peter chose his service providers on the basis of functional performance. In contrast the next example involves a stronger emotional bond between the informant (Tom) and the service provider. Tom (WM18) formed an emotional bond with his chosen service provider, a local retailer of surf equipment because one of his goals was to become a proficient surfer. When he used his new high performance wetsuits it failed dramatically. For example:

"Unfortunately it stretched while I was in the freezing cold water… and let everything in, the water, everything and I froze…came out shaking…and I was numb…I didn't think it would stretch like that but it stretched quite considerably, which they are meant to do, but at the time, I think it was one of my first wet suits, and I didn't think it would because my Rip Curl [wetsuit] hadn't…it did something that was unexpected to me."

Because of this failure, Tom returned to the Billabong retail store and was told most wetsuits stretch and it was necessary for him to buy a new suit. Tom could have reacted angrily (and switched back to Rip Curl or demanded compensation) at this point given that this retailer prides itself on surfing expertise and could have been expected to advise him to buy a smaller suit first time (wetsuits are an expensive purchase and usually require customers to interact closely with retail staff in order to get the right fit). Instead, Tom reframed the experience and apportioned the blame to himself: "that was just my error that I didn't know. I hadn't researched it well enough and didn't look." He subsequently bought another Billabong wetsuit and vest. Tom has many choices of wetsuit providers and there is a wide range of high quality retail outlets that will ensure he gets a suit suited to his needs. As well, Tom had previously experienced an alternative as a child with his Rip Curl suit. So why did Tom forgive the brand and remain within the relationship?

First, Tom views this experience as part of a learning curve to become a proficient surfer and thus gains value from the experience because he is now better paced to make informed purchase decisions in the future and has actually gained a better wetsuit as a result. Second, although Tom experienced the Rip Curl brand, he did so as a youngster and thus views it as a "kid's brand" rather than a high performance one. Third, retail stores are located close to beaches and therefore employ people who can provide equipment to deal with local wave and weather conditions (whereas stores away from beaches often focus on selling surf-inspired fashion accessories). Thus, by continuing to frequent the retailer he can improve his chances of achieving his goal. Fourth, because of his brand beliefs (partly formed due to his relative novice status as a surfer) he prefers to choose tried and tested brands like Billabong over others. Therefore, despite the seeming available of alternatives, for all intents and purposes, Tom perceives he has little choice of service provider. Research identifies that aggrieved partners extend forgiveness when they believe that there are benefits in doing so, the partner will reciprocate, and there are no alternatives (McCollough et al. 1997). In these cases, aggrieved partners may reframe the transgression and even accept some of the blame for its occurrence (Finkel et al. 2002). This helps explain Tom's conflict style in this case.

Consumer Grudge Holding

According to the literature, there are various forms of forgiveness and alternatives to forgiving a transgression (McCullough, Worthington, and Rachal 1997). For example, an individual may experience unforgiving responses such as harboring a grudge, rehearsing the hurt, perpetuating on negative emotions, seeking revenge, or maintaining estrangement from the transgressor. Unforgiveness and grudge holding following a transgression generally leads to vindictive behavior because transgressions create a "debt" that motivates a person to "get even" with the transgressor through seeking vengeance (Finkel et al. 2002). Unforgiveness could be reduced without explicitly promoting forgiveness, such as by accepting the hurt, reframing the events and circumstances around the offence, seeking justice, managing the stress related to the event, and controlling the anger resulting from the offence (Wade and Worthington 2003).

As noted, 14 informants maintained grudges against the service provider, with eight exiting the relationship and six staying. For example, Jack (WM20s) discussed two poignant examples of exit that remained emotionally charged (these had occurred some time earlier), and in one case, engaged actively in negative twist behaviors. Thus, although the relationships were ended from a commercial standpoint, they still played a prominent role in his life. Jack's examples are more emotionally charged, and he attributes moral failure to the brand and in the case of banks, the product class as a whole. For example:

"Basically what cemented my opinion of the Commonwealth Bank and what convinced me to leave it was the service I got from the staff member in the bank. I was waiting for quite a long time and the staff member was busy with another customer helping them with some new account, but she would dawdle and she wasn't hurrying up at all and I was in the bank for over half an hour, just waiting for her. I was waiting and there was another woman there who was serving someone else as well and that customer actually walked out the door, leaving the one woman free and instead of that woman saying I will be with you in a moment or something like that, she just walked out the back and she didn't come back. And, meanwhile the other person who was serving the one who's dawdling with the new customer, wouldn't look up at me, wouldn't look up at me at all and finally the customer leaves and I walk over there and she didn't apologize for the wait or anything and it's like, well, okay, this is the service you should expect in banks anyway. That was more or less the attitude I got from her and I wasn't impressed with that, so basically if her attitude had have been different, then I guess I wouldn't have been so harsh with the bank. But, basically it cemented my attitude and contributed to my decision to leave it."

Jack's response sits in stark contrast to Peter's more tolerant attitude regarding episodes like this. Jack describes this event as "the straw that broke this camel's back" and then described a long line of seemingly small service failures that were characterized by a lack of customer centricity including poor service in branches, lack of friendliness, and bureaucratic service rules. However, Jack also recognized that he may have been harsh with the bank by judging it based on his encounter with two staff members. Rather than reflect on this seeming rash act he generalizes from this incident first to the bank, and then to all banks as a class.

"I felt angry that the Commonwealth Bank as a corporation had allowed it to get to a stage where they purposely want you to wait in the bank with the aim of not going back to the branch, with you getting fed up with it, so you have to go and use your phone banking or your internet banking and I believe that that's what it's all about, that they are trying to deter you from going in the bank, that's why they keep you waiting and that's why they don't provide the service and people in the finish just give up and don't go into the branches anymore. [*I. Can you explain a bit more about giving up?*] People think, okay, this is the service that we can expect from banks, so we are not going to put up with it, so we will just, won't go into the branch. [*I. Do you think you just had her on a bad day, or do you think she is always like that?*] No, no I think it is in regards to banks, yes. Yes, definitely. I think it's, over the years because they have been closing branches and putting off staff, I think that the attitude of the staff and the banks has gotten worse, because they are putting up with so much abuse from the public and I did actually say something to the girl about waiting, about the length of time that I had to wait in the bank and I said, you know, it's nothing against you, but I think it's ridiculous that I had to wait so long and so on. And, she said well, yes I know, but the Commonwealth Bank has actually put off staff and this is the way they like things to be done now and we do apologize for the wait, but they are actually trying to get people to use the phone banking, instead of coming into the branches. And I said, well it's just not good enough, I understand that, but it's just not good enough. I said, you have lost me as a customer and she, basically, yeah, okay, there goes another one. *[I. How did she react, was she angry that you were leaving, or didn't care?]* No, she didn't care. It was like okay, yeah, this is number 567 for today...."

Jack's anger generated during the service encounter triggered a cognitive reappraisal of the brand, and then of banks *per se*. Like Peter, Jack engages in counterfactual thinking where he compared his experiences to his expectations of service (McColl-Kennedy and Sparks 2003), the result of which was a realization that there was little value congruence between him and the brand (value congruence is believed to moderate responses to transgressions; Aggarwal 2004; Macintosh and Stevens 2006). Jack considers the failures to be part of a wider systemic problem at the bank, but rather than simply attribute it to poor functional processes, Jack judges the bank's (and product class') motives—by blaming the failure on the greed of the banks and belief that the owners are conspiring to deliberately create a negative experience so they can increase profits by shutting down branches and laying off staff.

"Basically they have just become more money hungry over the years. Their profits are just out of hand, and the media keeps reporting on that obviously, saying that they are in the tens and millions of dollars and so on. And account keeping fees keep going up, they are closing branches all the time and they are trying to force people out of the branches and onto the phone network and the Internet network."

To understand Jack's viewpoint one also needs to consider his attachment to bank. Jack had stronger emotional ties to the Commonwealth Bank. As a schoolboy he had banked his weekly pocket money with this bank as part of a national scheme to encourage savings. As such, the relationship is full of rich self-relevant meanings and memories (cf. Thomson et al. 2005). As a result, Jack built up an expectation that the bank would care for him because of his long loyalty.

"I have always actually banked with them from primary school, that's when my first account started and I was sort of disappointed that with the service I received, they were just prepared to allow me to close my accounts, without any queries with, nothing. I guess because I had been with them for so long that I sort of had a trust that the Commonwealth Bank would be there for me, when I say be there for me, that they wouldn't be as harsh as what I thought they could be, as what I had learnt to believe banks were."

Jack's belief in the benevolence of the Commonwealth Bank as a brand partner was challenged when despite a long period of loyalty, he realized that the bank simply did not care about him either way—reinforced by the service worker's lack of surprise or emotional concern at his request to close his accounts. Such an experience was described by Jack as a "wake up call" to the true nature of banks as commercial entities (despite their espoused rhetoric of partnership). Jack realized that he was not truly in a genuine relationship, and had little influence on the bank, or value to it.

Veronica (WF20s), who describes herself as "not very forgiving" discussed a number of instances of "instant exit"—cases where a small infraction led to immediate exit, at much emotional and practical cost to her. For example, despite knowing that requests for large sums needed to be made 24 hours in advance, Veronica wanted the bank to wave this requirement. Following an initial rebuff from a service provider and Veronica's anger, a manager relented and waved the wait period as part of a service recovery effort. Yet, Veronica exited.

"I said, "I give you my money and I really don't want to be treated like this." It wasn't about money, it was more about the attitude...It's like they're a bank, but "please don't bank with us, just give us your money." Anyway, I spoke to the manager and I explained that I needed this money urgently, and she said, "that's no problem, you can come back in about an hour and a half and you will have the cash." I was shocked and surprised, because I could not understand on what basis she actually made this decision because all of a sudden I could have anything and in that afternoon I came back, I got my cash and I said, "can I please close the account?" "Oh, why are you doing this?" And I said because I was not treated the way I wanted to be treated."

This seemingly rash decision to exit following one-off "failures" characterized all of Veronica's examples, including product and service providers. For example, she dropped L'Oreal as a brand partner despite many years of preference due to one small failure and a recognition that alternatives are difficult to find in cosmetics given the intimate nature of the product (after two years of searching for a satisfactory alternative to no avail Veronica returned to L'Oreal). Veronica recognizes that she has a lost a sense of perspective in her responses yet nevertheless constantly exits relationships following seemingly small slights.

"She was really sorry and she apologized and I was kind of sorry. She was the nice person and I didn't want to be nasty or anything to her. I just said this has happened once and I just– you know, I don't want to deal with you guys, that's it, so she was really upset that I closed the account and afterwards I got a letter from her, where she actually tried to win me back as a customer and I said it's too late, because you could have prevented this from happening that day and now it's just too late, I'm not interested."

Even allowing for the lack of procedural justice, Veronica did not view what was a one-off encounter as the result of a bad experience, or perhaps a trainee staff member's inexperience. Veronica's experience and reaction is also highly emotive. For example:

[I. What was it about that particular situation that prompted the all or nothing decision?] As a customer, you should actually have access to your funds all the time. I knew about the 24 hours notification, but after I asked for a cheque and she said no, then I thought something was wrong, because this is not right and then five minutes later, I speak to her manager and all of a sudden, I get a completely different service and that's what I didn't like. *[I. What did you attribute this to?]* Maybe lack of knowledge by this person. She should have actually told me I'm not sure or can you come back later and I'll find out, but not just, no, you can't. I just said if I actually have to put in requests 24 hours in advance, then I just don't bank with you, it's that simple... although she kind of didn't deserve that response, they kind of provided this overall image and that's what I associate with the St George Bank. Again, sometimes just individuals standing behind a counter or a person are having a bad day, but I'm a customer and this is a bank and that's all I know. I don't really want to deal with their individual problems or their bad days...."

Veronica's choice of the St George bank is not coincidental. This particular bank positions itself as the "non-bank, bank" (banks within Australia are regularly placed last in consumer satisfaction surveys). In contrast, St George has adopted an emotional branding strategy, positioning themselves around authentic service, customer centricity, friendliness, and at a time when many banks are closing branches, this bank is expanding their branch network. For Veronica, the choice of banking partner was driven by the emphasis they placed on her value as an individual, the strong sense of service and customer centricity and their flexibility in responding to customer needs. Therefore, Veronica's action (identified by her as "unreasonable") can be explained partly by her high sense of entitlement (Exline et al. 2004) and her belief that she has a number of other alternatives in the product class. Thus she reacts to conflict by seeking to dominate the offending partner (Macintosh and Stevens 2006). By exiting, Veronica reaffirms herself as a powerful consumer, even though later on (as with her car repair agency and L'Oreal) she returns to the relationship after failing to find an alternative (in the projective techniques, Veronica referred to a picture of a boxer in a fighting pose to characterize her attitudes to brands). Veronica's use of a fighting metaphor suggests she will be perpetually disappointed in commercial relationships, thus increasing her search and trial costs.

DISCUSSION

Based on the informant passages above we suggest three moderators of consumers' post-transgression conflict style: self- vs. other-orientation, emotional intelligence, and attachment style. First, research on conflict styles suggests aggrieved individuals may respond to transgressions in one of four ways: integration (cooperative behavior with transgressor), dominating (aggressive behavior towards transgressor), obliging (acquiescence to transgressor) or avoiding. These outcomes are moderated by concern for self and others (Macintosh and Stevens 2006; Rahim 1983; Twomey 1978). For example, both Jack and Veronica have a high degree of self-orientation and as such seek to dominate the offending partner, whereas Peter exhibits a high degree of other-orientation and seeks integration and obligation.

Peter's actions may be explained by their over emphasis on other-orientation at the expense of self-orientation. Rahim (1983) proposed that individuals exhibiting a high concern for self and other were likely to engage in genuine efforts at repairing the relationship in order to maximize the benefits to both parties. In cases where other orientation dominates, the aggrieved party may be more forgiving of the aggressor and seek to understand and rationalize the aggressor's actions so they can move forward. This suggests that self- vs. other-orientation may moderate forgiveness outcomes. For example, Sells and Hargrave (1998) suggest that cessation of injury is necessary for forgiveness to occur, yet Peter engages in many actions consistent with a forgiving stance even though he continued to suffer ongoing hurt. By way of contrast, Tom exhibits greater balance in self- vs. other-orientation. In these cases, consumers are predicted to engage in genuine efforts at repairing the relationship in order to maximize the benefits to both parties (Macintosh and Stevens 2006; Rahim 1983; Twomey 1978), just as Tom does.

Second, Peter and Tom's attempts at reconciliation and the ability to put the transgression in perspective and ultimately move beyond it, can also be attributed to a high degree of emotional intelligence, or "the ability to manage one's own emotions and deal with others' emotions in problem solving and decision making" (Yang and Mossholder 2004, p. 594). Yang and Mossholder suggest that emotional intelligence involves four interrelated abilities: accurately appraising and expressing emotions, generating emo-

tions to facilitate thought processes, understanding emotions and emotional knowledge, and regulating emotions in the self and in others to promote emotional and intellectual growth. Such abilities are believed critical to strong relationships because they ensure that task related conflicts do not get blown out of proportion nor become personal. Individuals with strong emotional intelligence are proposed to engage in more cooperative approaches to conflict, whereas highly emotional and coercive responses to conflict are the result of limited levels of emotional processing. Against these criteria, Peter and Tom exhibit high levels of emotional processing and seek to repair the relationship. Thus service failures ultimately do not result in ongoing grudges among these informants. In contrast, Veronica openly acknowledges that she is quick to anger and is "not very forgiving." She also identifies that her reactions may have been unfair given the attempts made at service recovery. These reactions reflect lower levels of emotional processing than Peter or Tom.

Third, we believe that different attachment styles influence forgiveness outcomes. Attachment is defined as "an emotion-laden target-specific bond between a person and a specific object" (Thomson, MacInnis, and Park 2005, p. 77-78). Attachments vary in strength and form part of consumer relationships with brands or service providers (Fournier 1998). In Peter's case, although he had remained in the relationship for some time and valued the bank as a relationship partner, his attachment was defined primarily in functional terms ("fast, prompt and friendly professional service"). Thus, despite ongoing interaction with the service provider, Peter did not form a strong attachment with them (defined by "a rich set of schemas and affectively laden meanings that link the object to the self" Thomson et al. 2005, p. 79), and did not suffer separation distress. By way of contrast, Jack's relationship with the bank was richer in meaning and based on a deeply felt sense of trust—therefore Jack's reaction to the partner's betrayal was ultimately more painful and severe than Peter's. In contrast, Tom's close attachment to the brand and retailer, coupled with his balanced self- vs. other-orientation and strong emotional processing results in forgiveness. Veronica's relationships were also characterized by less rich (in comparison with Tom and Jack) emotional attachments (e.g., her response to strong emotional campaigns such as St George's friendly customer centric bank advertisements and L'Oreal "Because You're Worth It") although unlike Tom and initially Jack, she believes that such brands are easily replaced (Twomey 1978).

Such findings enrich our understanding of consumer grudgeholding and contribute to emerging debates on consumer conflict styles (Macintosh and Stevens 2006). In regards to self- vs. other-orientation we identify that for consumers at either extreme, reconciliation is likely to be difficult. In cases where self-orientation dominates relationships are terminated quickly following a transgression, with the aggrieved party unlikely to seek reconciliation or respond to service recovery efforts. This is particularly so for high self-oriented consumers with low levels of emotional intelligence. In contrast, high self-oriented consumers with stronger emotional intelligence are likely to remain within relationships because they engage in some level of emotional processing that result in them placing the transgression within a wider context of benefits. Consumers high on other-orientation are more likely to tolerate constant errors, forgive small failure, and in cases of severe transgressions (such as Peter) simply exit relationships without holding a grudge (and engaging in costly negative behaviors for the brand).

Research is necessary to confirm the findings herein by using attachment scales (Thomson et al. 2005), conflict orientations (Rahim 1983), and emotional intelligence (Yang and Mossholder 2004). Experimental scenarios of transgressions could be developed to examine the relationship between personality type and propensity to forgive could be developed. These scenarios could also take into account perceived switching costs (choice of alternatives). Research could also examine barriers to forgiveness such as narcissism. As consumer culture can be characterized by an entitlement mentality (Boyd and Helms 2005), research could draw on narcissism scales to assess consumers' proneness to forgive (Exline et al. 2004).

REFERENCES

Aaker, Jennifer, Susan Fournier, and Adam S. Brasel (2004), "When Good Brands Do Bad," *Journal of Consumer Research*, 31 (1), 1-16.

Aggarwal, Pankaj (2004), "The Effects of Brand Relationship Norms on Consumer Attitudes and Behavior," *Journal of Consumer Research*, 31 (June), 87-101.

Andreassen, Tor W. (2001), "From Disgust to Delight: Do Customers hold a Grudge?" *Journal of Service Research*, 4 (1), 39-49.

Arnould, Eric, Linda Price and George Zinkhan (2004), *Consumers*. Boston, MA: McGraw-Hill.

Bendapundi, Neeli and Leonard Berry (1997), "Customers' Motivations for Maintaining Relationships with Service Providers," *Journal of Retailing*, 73 (1), 15-37.

Bolton, Ruth N, Amy K. Smith and Janet Wagner (2003), "Striking the Right Balance: Designing Service to Enhance Business-to-Business Relationships," *Journal of Service Research*, 5 (4), 271-293.

Exline, Julie J., Roy F. Baumiester, Brad J. Bushman, W. Keith Campbell, and Eli J. Finkel (2004), "Too Proud to Let Go: Narcissistic Entitlement as a Barrier to Forgiveness," *Journal of Personality and Social Psychology*, 87 (6), 894-912.

Finkel, Eli J, Caryl E. Rusbult, Madoka Kumashiro and Peggy A. Hannon (2002), "Dealing With Betrayal in Close Relationships: Does Commitment Promote Forgiveness," *Journal of Personality and Social Psychology*, 82 (6), 956-974.

Fournier, Susan (1998), "Consumers and Their Brands: Developing Relationship Theory in Consumer Research," *Journal of Consumer Research*, 24 (March), 343-373.

Grayson, Kent and Tim Ambler (1999), "The Dark Side of Long-Term Relationships in Marketing Services," *Journal of Marketing Research*, 36 (1), 132-141.

McColl-Kennedy, Janet R. and Beverly A. Sparks (2003), "Application of Fairness Theory to Service Failures and Service Recovery," *Journal of Service Research*, 5 (3), 251-266.

McCullough, Michael E., Steven J. Sandage, Susan Wade Brown, Chris K. Rachal, Everett L. Worthington Jr and Terry L. High (1998), "Interpersonal Forgiving in Close Relationships: II Theoretical Elaboration and Measurement," *Journal of Personality and Social Psychology*, 75 (Dec), 1586-1603.

McCullough, Michael E, Everett L. Worthington Jr and Kenneth C. Rachal (1997), "Interpersonal Forgiving in Close Relationships," *Journal of Personality and Social Psychology*, 73 (2), 321-336.

Macintosh, Gerard and Charles Stevens (2006), "Consumer Conflict Management Strategies in Everyday Service Encounters," *Advances in Consumer Research*, 33, 279-280.

Maxham III, James G. and Richard G. Netemeyer (2002), "Longitudinal Study of Complaining Customers' Evaluations of Multiple Service Failures and Recovery Effort," *Journal of Marketing*, 66 (Oct), 57-71.

Rahim, M. Afzalur (1983), "A Measure of Styles of Handling Conflict," *Academy of Management Journal*, 26 (2), 368-376.

Rust, Roland T, J. Jeffrey Inman, Jianmin Jia and Anthony Zahorik (1999), "What You *Don't* Know About Customer-Perceived Quality: The Role of Customer Expectation Distributions," *Marketing Science*, 18 (1), 77-92.

Sells, James N. and Terry D. Hargrave (1998), "Forgiveness: A Review of the Theoretical and Empirical Literature," *Journal of Family Therapy*, 20, 21-36.

Smith, Amy K. and Ruth N. Bolton (2002), "The Effect of Customers' Emotional Responses to Service Failures on their Recovery Effort Evaluations and Satisfaction Judgments," *Journal of the Academy of Marketing Science*, 30 (1), 5-24.

Strauss, Anselm M. and Juliet Corbin (1998), *Basics of Qualitative Research*. Newbury Park, CA: Sage.

Thomson, Matthew, Deborah J. MacInnis and C. Whan Park (2005), "The Ties That Bind: Measuring the Strength of Consumers' Emotional Attachments to Brands," *Journal of Consumer Psychology*, 15 (1), 77-91.

Twomey, Daniel F. (1978), "The Effects of Power Properties on Conflict Resolution," *Academy of Management Review*, Jan, 144-150.

Wade, Nathaniel G. and Everett L. Worthington, (2003), "Overcoming Interpersonal Offenses: Is Forgiveness the Only way to Deal with Unforgiveness?" *Journal of Counseling & Development*, 81 (Summer), 343-353.

Yang, Jixia and Kevin W. Mossholder (2004), "Decoupling Task and Relationship Conflict: The Role of Intragroup Emotional Processing," *Journal of Organizational Behavior*, 25, 589-605.

Zaltman, Gerald (2004), *How Customers Think*. Cambridge, MA: Harvard Business School Press.

Salvation of the Second Shift: Are Wives Immune to Monday Blues?

Charles Areni, The University of Sydney, Australia

ABSTRACT

In an internet survey, 702 Australians reported momentary and typical moods for each day of the week (DOW). Both mood measures indicated a gender x marital status x DOW interaction, wherein wives were relatively immune to Monday blues compared to husbands and single adults. Due to traditional gender stereotypes and roles within the household, wives may not associate Mondays with the loss of discretionary leisure and the onset of paid work. Consistent with this explanation, wives reported doing housework on the weekend more frequently than single women and men. They also experienced weekend leisure less frequently and performed substantially fewer hours of paid labor during the week compared to men, although there was no difference between single and married women on either variable. However, none of these variables mediated the gender x marital status x DOW effect on reported moods, suggesting that additional factors underlie wives' immunity to Monday blues.

INTRODUCTION

Stereotypes found in aphorisms (e.g., Monday blues, Wednesday hump day, and T.G.I.F.–Thank God It's Friday), song titles (e.g., I Don't Like Mondays–the Boomtown Rats, Friday on My Mind–the Easybeats, Saturday Morning in the City–Brian Wilson, Gloomy Sunday–Billie Holiday), and literary works (e.g., "something unromantic as Monday morning"–Charlotte Bronte (Shirley), "as lonesome as a Sunday"–Mark Twain (A Connecticut Yankee in King Arthur's Court), "He that laughs on Friday may cry on Sunday"–Proverbs (The Bible)) suggest that some days of the week are consistently better than others. These aspects of popular culture imply that moods vary over the course of a typical week according to a sinusoidal pattern, with a positive gradient between the nadir on Monday and the peak on Friday or Saturday, a transition from the negative to the positive portion of the week on Wednesday (i.e., the hump day), and a steep decline in mood late on Sunday. Day of the week (DOW) stereotypes stem from an assumption that people are generally happier when they are free to choose their activities compared to when they are engaged in paid work (Beatty & Torbert, 2003; Dupre & Gagnier, 1996). The sinusoidal pattern emerges because weekdays (weekends) are associated with paid work (free time) (Zerubavel, 1985), and because people anticipate the number of days before the transition from one to the other (Larsen & Kasimatis, 1990). Hence, Monday morning is the worst part of the week because it is the first work day after two days of free time, and because four work days follow before the next period of free time. Likewise, Friday evening is the best part of the week because it marks the beginning of an extended period of free time (i.e., T.G.I.F.) (Areni, 2008).

Given this explanation for DOW stereotypes, factors affecting the amount of free time experienced on the weekend, and the amount of paid work experienced during the week, should also affect the extent to which Mondays are associated with negative moods. Along these lines, previous studies have shown that men are more prone to the stereotypical weekly mood pattern than women (Rossi & Rossi, 1977; Almagor & Ehrlich, 1990). In short, men have distinct, compartmentalized portions of the week for paid work (i.e., Mon-Fri, 9 to 5) and leisure (i.e., evenings and weekends), whereas these boundaries are blurred for women (Almagor & Ehrlich, 1990; Deem, 1996), who often fulfill multiple social and professional roles simultaneously (Thompson, 1996). Additional research suggests that role conflict is magnified for wives compared

to single women (Stevens, Kiger & Riley, 2001; Roxburgh, 2006). The research reported below uses survey data obtained from a cross-section of the Australian population to test the hypotheses that wives will report less negative moods on Mondays compared to husbands and single adults. The following section expands on this prediction, explaining why wives may be immune to Monday blues compared to single women and men.

WORK TIME, LEISURE TIME AND GENDER INEQUALITY

Perhaps the most fundamental defining aspect of leisure is the freedom or discretion to pursue pleasurable activities (Unger & Kernan, 1983). By this simple definition, contemporary gender roles rob wives of this most basic of human pursuits because of their greater involvement in household production (Hunt & Kiker, 1981), their adoption of multiple, often conflicting, social and professional roles (Thompson, 1996), a perceived lack of freedom to act on their personal wishes (Thompson, Locander & Pollio, 1990), and a tendency to put the needs of others ahead of their own (Meyers-Levy, 1988; Thompson et al., 1990). All of this suggests that wives experience less leisure compared to husbands and single adults (Bittman & Wajcman, 2000; Mattingly & Bianchi, 2003).

Hochschild (1989) coined the phrase "second shift" to describe the fate of working wives who, after a full day of work at the office, come home to a disproportionate amount of household work due to husbands who do not pull their own weight. Despite the social impetus for husbands to increase their share of domestic labor to accommodate the careers of their wives (Thornton, 1989; Mattingly & Bianchi, 2003), husbands often define themselves in terms of their abilities as "breadwinners" for the household (MacMillan & Gartner, 1999; Rogers & DeBoer, 2001; Commuri & Gentry, 2005). Perhaps because of this narrow criterion, husbands do less household work than wives (Hochschild, 1989; Bittman & Pixley, 1997; Roxburgh, 2006), even after correcting for hours of paid labor per week. Some studies have found that wives do more than twice as much household work as their husbands (Bittman et al., 2003), so as wives increase the amount of time spent in paid work, their available leisure time evaporates (Cantwell & Sanik, 1993).

Although wives experience a relative loss of leisure and a higher proportion of housework throughout the week, these gender inequities are more pronounced on weekends, where husbands and children enjoy pure leisure experiences that are often produced by wives' household labor activities (Graham, 1984; Deem, 1996). A husband's experience of drinking a cold beer while watching football on television is produced by a wife who shops for the household (i.e., puts the beer in the refrigerator), pays the utility bills (i.e., supplies the television programming), does the laundry (i.e., provides the clean clothes the husband is presumably wearing), and keeps the children entertained (i.e., stops them from interrupting the viewing experience), among other things. Wives experience free time during different parts of the week compared to husbands and single adults; since they have less free time during the weekend, they squeeze it into weekday evenings, after the kitchen has been cleaned and the children have been put to bed (Hewitt, 1993; Le Feuvre, 1994). Hence, for wives, weekends are less likely to be experienced as two days of free time for leisure activities (Larson & Richards, 1994; Deem, 1996).

Moreover, despite changing gender roles and attitudes toward women pursuing careers, women still work fewer hours per week than men (Coleman & Pencavel, 1993; Roxburgh, 2006), and wives work fewer hours per week than unmarried women, although the gap is narrowing (Coleman & Pencavel, 1993; Pencavel, 1998). Wives are also less likely to work in traditional "9 to 5, Monday through Friday" positions, instead occupying part time jobs that better accommodate their childcare activities (Presser & Cox, 1997). Wives often choose to participate in paid labor because of financial or marital distress. Indeed, research suggests that wives who increase their participation in paid labor often do so because of unhappiness in their marriage, which is why increases in wives' paid labor hours is correlated with subsequent divorces initiated by wives but not those initiated by husbands (Schoen, Rogers & Amato, 2006). So wives are less likely to experience Mondays as the beginning of a period of paid work. Many will not begin a full week of work on Monday, and for others, paid work may be a welcome respite from more stressful domestic labor (Larson & Richards, 1994; Deem, 1996).

These gender differences in work and leisure time have been explained in terms of rational allocations of economic resources (Becker, 1981). That is, men spend more hours in paid work because they have greater opportunities to earn money. But this argument seems rather tautological, and even when wives work as many hours and earn as much money as their husbands, they still do more household work, suggesting that gender stereotypes have more to do with this uneven division of domestic labor (Hochschild, 1989; Bittman et al, 2003; Commuri & Gentry, 2005). Wives earning more than 50% of household income may actually do more housework as a consequence (Bittman et al., 2003), because their husbands contribute even less to domestic labor (Brines, 1994; Greenstein, 2000). In other words, a wife who earns more than her husband is "compensated" by having to do even more housework, suggesting a possible ego defense explanation for husbands' failure to contribute equally to household work. Having children magnifies these differences between husbands and wives (Mattingly & Bianchi, 2003). Research has even shown that married mothers do more household work than single mothers, suggesting that "husbands create more household work than they perform" (Mauldin & Meeks, 1990, p. 67).

In a more general sense, compared to men, and to a lesser extent, single women, wives are less likely to experience the transition from the weekend to the week as a loss of free time to paid work. Instead, household responsibilities permeate every day regardless of how many hours of paid work they perform (Larson & Richards, 1994; Deem, 1996). Since the perceived loss of free time is a critical aspect of Monday blues (Areni, 2008), this suggests that wives should be relatively immune to actual and perceived downward swings in mood from Sunday to Monday compared to husbands and single adults. The research reported below tests this basic hypothesis, and also predicts that wives will report (a) fewer hours of paid labor during the workweek, (b) lower frequencies of leisure experiences during the weekend, and (c) higher frequencies of household production activities during the weekend compared to husbands and single adults. These variables are also tested as mediators of the gender x marital status interaction effect on perceived and actual Monday blues.

METHOD

Design and Procedure

An internet survey was conducted in order to collect data on momentary moods over the course of a week and the typical moods people experience on each DOW. The data were collected from the 5th to the 12th of October in 2005 to avoid public holidays and major sporting events. Husbands, wives, and single men and women reported their momentary moods once per day at their discretion over one week. On the eighth day, they reported how they typically feel on each DOW. Hence, *mood measure* (momentary, typical) and *DOW* were within-subjects factors, and *gender* and *marital status* were between-subjects factors.

Sample

Seven hundred and two subjects were selected from the panel of an Australian market research company, which included 369 males (52.6%) and ages ranging from 16 to 65. The distribution of ages was approximately normal, with a mean of 38.0 years and a standard deviation of 10.2. There was no significant difference in the mean ages of males and females, and distribution by metropolitan area was uniform when weighted by population. Sixty-nine percent of the subjects were employed in some capacity, 42.5% in full-time work. The remaining 31% who did not report being employed were split between those having home duties (17.5%), retirees (4.3%), and those who were unemployed (9.7%).

Independent Variables

Momentary versus Typical Moods: For the momentary mood measures, subjects were asked "What is your mood like right now?" on seven successive days. On the eighth and final day of the survey, subjects were asked "On a typical (DOW), what is your mood like over the course of the whole day?" This question was repeated seven times for each DOW. The momentary and typical mood measures used the same response format, which is described below.

Marital Status and Gender: Subjects were asked "Which of the following best describes you?" using the response categories "single", "in a relationship, separate residences", "in a relationship, living together", and "married couple". Given research suggesting that married couples differ from cohabitating couples, who are more comparable to other singles (Stack & Eshleman, 1998), only subjects selecting the last option were classified as married. All other responses were coded as single. Subjects were then prompted with "Are you…" using the response categories "male" and "female".

Mediating Variables

Hours of Paid Work: Subjects were asked "How many hours per week do you normally work?" using an open-ended response format.

Frequency of Weekend Housework and Leisure: After each of the 7 momentary mood reports, subjects were asked "In what activity are you presently involved?" using an open-ended response format. The responses were coded into 49 categories by two experienced researchers using the Daily Life Experiences (DLE) taxonomy (Stone & Neale, 1982; Stone, 1987). The DLE classifies daily activities into five broad categories (paid work, leisure, family and friends, financial matters, and other), with 14 sub-categories and 49 final classifications. For purposes of this analysis, family and friends was separated into two sub-categories: household work and social leisure. Social leisure, involving discretionary time spent with friends or family members, was grouped with other leisure activities, whereas childcare and other activities involving the care of family members were classified as household work. This resulted in four main categories: paid work, leisure, household work, and other, which was an aggregation of the financial matters and other categories in the original taxonomy.

Two judges independently coded the open-ended responses into the 49 classifications. Inter-coder reliability was assessed for each DOW. Cohen's K values ranged from .80 on Thursday to .88 on Sunday and Monday. When the data were aggregated up into the four main activity categories, Cohen's K values increased, ranging from .87 on Wednesday and Saturday to .92 on Monday. These results reflect "substantial" to "almost perfect" inter-coder reliability (Landis & Koch 1977, p. 165); differences were resolved via discussions between the author and the two coders. So, subjects reporting momentary moods on a given day also indicated whether they were experiencing leisure or household work at that time. Hence, it was possible to count the number of experiences in each category on the weekend. Since Fridays are experienced as part of the weekend rather than the workweek (Rossi & Rossi, 1977), this research adopted a 3-day definition of the weekend. Subjects could report between 0 and 3 leisure activities and household work activities on the weekend.

Dependent Variable

The two mood measures involved a single, bi-polar response scale in order to reduce subject fatigue given that eight successive daily surveys were required (see Kahneman et al., 2005). Although single, bi-polar measures fail to capture qualitative differences between positive (e.g., pride vs. relief) and negative (e.g., loneliness vs. anger) affective states, previous research suggests "that most moments of experience can be adequately characterized by a single summary value on the GB (good-bad) dimension" (Kahneman, 1999, p. 8). Nine horizontally arrayed circles one quarter inch in diameter were anchored on the left side by "very bad" and on the right side by "very good". Subjects used a mouse to indicate their mood. For purposes of data analysis, the scale was treated as ranging from -4 (very bad) to +4 (very good), with the middle circle taking on the value 0.

RESULTS

In order to test the hypothesis that wives would be relatively immune to Monday blues, a 4-way mixed-factor ANOVA was run with gender and marital status as between-subjects factors and DOW and mood measure as within-subjects factors. Results indicated that the main effects of gender ($F_{1,698}$=4.5, p<.05), marital status ($F_{1,698}$=7.0, p<.01), DOW ($F_{1,698}$=110.5, p<.0001), and mood measure ($F_{1,698}$=8.3, p<.01) were all significant. Women (M=1.60) reported more positive moods than men (M=1.37); married subjects (M=1.63) reported more positive moods than single subjects (M=1.36); and overall, subjects reported more positive typical moods (M=1.54) than momentary moods (M=1.42). The DOW effect was more or less consistent with the stereotypical sinusoidal pattern, with moods on Monday (M=1.10) significantly lower than moods on Tuesday (M=1.31), Wednesday (M=1.26), Thursday (M=1.40), Friday (M=1.53), Saturday (M=1.60) and Sunday (M=1.61); and moods on Tuesday–Thursday lower than moods on Friday–Sunday, all at a=.05.

However, these main effects must be qualified by significant measure x DOW ($F_{6,4188}$=71.8, p<.0001), gender x DOW ($F_{6,4188}$=2.7, p<.01), and gender x DOW x marital status ($F_{6,4188}$=3.6, p<.001) interaction effects. The mood measure x DOW interaction effect revealed that the stereotypical pattern was more obvious for typical moods compared to momentary moods. Specific mean contrasts on each day revealed that typical moods were less positive than momentary moods on Monday (0.57 vs. 1.24) and Tuesday (0.89 vs. 1.47), but more positive than momentary moods on Wednesday (1.29 vs. 1.16), Thursday (1.46 vs. 1.33), Friday (2.05 vs. 1.54), Saturday (2.36 vs. 1.53), and Sunday (2.19 vs. 1.65), all at the a=.05 level of significance, except for Thursday, which was significant at a=.10. So while there was some evidence for Monday blues in momentary moods, it was more pronounced in typical moods.

Perhaps more importantly, given the focus of the research, the gender x DOW interaction revealed that most of the gender main effect reported above occurred on Monday ($F_{1,698}$=6.4, p<.01), where women (M=1.30) reported more positive moods than men (M=0.92). No other gender differences for the remainder of the week were significant at α=.10. This suggests that men are more prone to Monday blues than women, but the gender x DOW x marital status interaction revealed that this conclusion depends on marital status. Paired comparisons revealed that moods declined from Sunday to Monday for single men (1.34 vs. 0.79, $t_{1,224}$=4.7, p<.0001), married men (1.81 vs. 1.13, $t_{1,143}$=5.9, p<.0001), and single women (1.74 vs. 1.00, $t_{1,160}$=5.6, p<.0001), but not for married women (1.66 vs. 1.57, $t_{1,171}$<1). As hypothesized, wives were immune to Monday blues.

The underlying explanation for wives' relative immunity to Monday blues stems from differences in gender roles within the household. Because they do more housework on weekends, experience less leisure on weekends, and work fewer hours of paid labor during the week, wives are less likely to experience Mondays as a loss of free time and the onset of paid work. If this explanation is correct, then hours of paid labor during the week and the frequency of leisure and housework during the weekend may mediate the effects of gender and marital status on Monday moods. In order to explore the first possibility, hours worked per week was included as the dependent variable in a 2-way, between-subjects ANOVA with gender and marital status as the independent variables. Results indicated only a main effect of gender ($F_{1,698}$=52.7, p<.0001). Men (M=33.13) worked more hours per week than women (M=16.52), regardless of marital status. Moreover, when hours worked was included as the covariate in an ANCOVA with DOW and mood measure as within-subjects factors and gender and marital status as between-subjects factors, it was not predictive of moods on Monday ($F_{1,697}$<1) or any other day of the week. So the relative immunity to Monday blues does not apparently stem from wives working fewer hours of paid labor during the week.

To examine whether the amount of weekend housework is related the gender x DOW x marital status interaction effect on reported moods, frequency of housework was included as the dependent variable in a 2-way, between-subjects ANOVA with gender and marital status as independent variables. Results indicated main effects of gender ($F_{1,697}$=36.7, p<.0001) and marital status ($F_{1,697}$=23.5, p<.0001). Women (M=0.87) were more frequently engaged in weekend housework than were men (M=0.48), and married subjects (M=0.85) reported housework activities more frequently than single subjects (M=0.52). The gender x marital status interaction was marginally significant ($F_{1,697}$=3.6, p<.06). Consistent with traditional gender stereotypes, wives (M=1.06) reported doing housework on the weekends more frequently than single women (M=0.66), husbands (M=0.59), or single men (M=0.41) at the α=.10 level of significance. Frequency of weekend housework was then included as a covariate in a 4-way, mixed-factor ANCOVA with gender and marital status as between-subjects factors and DOW and mood measure as within-subjects factors. However, results indicated that the frequency of weekend housework was not predictive of moods reported on Monday ($F_{1,696}$<1) or any other day. So wives immunity to Monday blues is not explained by the amount of housework done on the weekend.

Frequency of weekend leisure was also included as a dependent variable in a 2-way, between-subjects ANOVA with gender and marital status as independent variables. Results indicated main effects for gender ($F_{1,697}$=3.3, p<.10) and marital status ($F_{1,697}$=4.7, p<.05). Men (M=2.02) experienced weekend leisure more frequently than did women (M=1.87) and single subjects (M=2.02) reported weekend leisure more frequently than married subjects (M=1.86). However, when frequency of weekend leisure was included as a covariate in a 4-way ANCOVA with gender and marital status as between-subjects factors and DOW and mood measure as within-subjects factors, it was not predictive of the moods reported on Monday ($F_{1,696}<1$) or any other day of the week. So, the frequency of weekend leisure activities also fails to account for the gender x day x marital status effect on reported moods.

DISCUSSION

The results reported above support the hypothesis that wives are immune to Monday blues compared to single women and men, who experienced a marked decline in mood from Sunday to Monday. The explanation given for this immunity stemmed from wives not experiencing Monday as the onset of negatively valued paid work following a weekend of positively valued leisure. Instead, wives were thought to experience all days as complex mixes of leisure and domestic and paid labor, with Mondays even experienced as a relief from the domestic labor of the weekend. However, subsequent analyses did not support this explanation. Hours of paid work during the week, frequency of weekend leisure, and frequency of weekend housework did not mediate the effect of gender and marital status on moods by DOW, suggesting that other factors may mitigate Monday blues.

Despite research indicating changes in attitudes toward more egalitarian gender roles, these results suggest that actual behavior within the household seems to have changed substantially less (Cantwell & Sanik, 1993). Women continue to do more household work than men, and this difference is magnified among married couples. As a result, wives experience less leisure time during the weekend than their husbands do. There is some indication in the literature that the failure of husbands to bring their behavior in line with their supposed attitudes is ego defensive. Contributing more household labor may unconsciously be interpreted as an indication that husbands are inadequate in the traditional role of "bringing home the bacon" (Stevens, Kiger & Riley, 2001). Career-oriented women may feel guilty about being inadequate in their traditional roles as wives and mothers, and domestically-oriented men may feel ashamed about being inadequate in their traditional role as breadwinners.

Along these lines, attitudes toward traditional and progressive gender roles may play a more important role in determining whether Monday mornings are experienced as a loss of freedom or an escape from domestic labor. For a woman adopting a more traditional gender role, domestic labor on the weekend might not be viewed as onerous and paid work during the week may be minimal. On the other hand, a woman with more progressive values may well resent weekend housework, and look forward to resuming her career-oriented work on Monday (Hochschild, 1997). In addition to looking at the allocation of time to household and work-related behaviors, future research might examine attitudes toward gender roles and related issues as potential mediators of Monday blues.

The DOW x mood measure interaction effect reported above indicates that Monday blues and other DOW stereotypes may be more in the mind rather than in the reality of moment by moment affective states. There is some evidence of a weekly mood cycle in the momentary mood reports, but it is at odds with the stereotypical pattern in some respects. Although subjects reported relatively low momentary moods on Monday, which increased substantially on Tuesday, momentary moods were lowest on Wednesday; and though they rose steadily from Thursday to Saturday, momentary moods continued to improve on Sunday, which runs counter to the stereotypical pattern. By contrast, the typical mood reports followed the stereotypical pattern perfectly, with more pronounced differences between the "good" and "bad" parts of the week. Asking people how they typically feel, on a "Monday" for example, explicitly mentions the DOW, which may activate schemas and stereotypes related to that day. It also encourages people to consider a wide span of previous experiences, and to consider common rather than unique aspects of those experiences. One of the most accessible common aspects of Mondays is the return to paid work after a period of weekend leisure, which should trigger the stereotype, and lead to an exaggeration of how bad Mondays are. By contrast, the momentary mood measure makes no mention of the specific DOW. When asked how they feel at the moment, people are more likely to be influenced by their local surroundings and recently passed and immediately anticipated events, rather than DOW stereotypes. Hence, the stereotypical pattern is relatively muted (Areni, 2008).

It is also intriguing that reported typical moods were more favorable than the actual momentary moods people experienced. Based on momentary mood reports from a number of cultures, Biswas-Diener, Vitterso & Diener (2005) have concluded that "most people are pretty happy" (p. 2005). The caveat suggested here is that people may not be quite as happy as they think. Perhaps this also reflects an ego defensive mechanism. Is may be acceptable to admit that things are not going well at the moment, but to admit that things typically do not go well may be threatening to the self. People are motivated to feel good about themselves and others, and typical moods may be more diagnostic than momentary moods as indications of how things are going, so they are biased in a positive direction.

REFERENCES

Almagor, M. & Ehlich, S. (1990). Personality correlates and cyclicity in positive and negative affect. *Psychological Reports*, 66, 1159-1169.

Areni, C.S. (2008). (Tell me why) I don't like Mondays: Does an overvaluation of discretionary time underlie reported weekly mood cycles? *Cognition and Emotion*, 22, 1228-1252.

Beatty, J.E. & Torbert, W.R. (2003). The false duality of work and leisure, *Journal of Management Inquiry*, 12, 239-252.

Becker, G.S. (1981). *A Treatise on the Family*. Cambridge, MA: Harvard University Press.

Biswas-Diener, R., Vitterso, J. & Diener, E. (2005). Most people are pretty happy, but there is cultural variation: The Inughuit, the Amish, and the Maasai, *Journal of Happiness Studies*, 6, 205-226.

Bittman, M. & Pixley, J. (1997). *The Double Life of the Family: Myth, Hope, and Experience*. Sydney: Allen & Unwin.

Bittman, M. & Wajcman, J. (2000). The rush hour: The character and leisure time and gender equity. Social Forces, 79, 165-189.

Bittman, M., England, P., Sayer, L., Folbre, N. & Matheson, G. (2003). When does gender trump money? Bargaining and time in household work. *American Journal of Sociology*, 109, 186-214.

Brines, J. (1994). Economics dependency, gender, and the division of labor at home. *American Journal of Sociology*, 100, 652-688.

Cantwell, M.L. & Sanik, M.M. (1993). Leisure before and after parenthood. *Social Indicators Research*, 30, 139-147.

Coleman, M.T. & Pencavel, J. (1993). Trends in market work behavior of women since 1940. *Industrial and Labor Relations Review*, 46, 653-676.

Commuri, S. & Gentry, J.W. (2005). Resource allocation in households with women as chief wage earners. *Journal of Consumer Research*, 185-195.

Deem, R. (1996). No time for a rest? An exploration of women's work, engendered leisure and holidays. *Time & Society*, 5, 5-25.

Dupre, J. & Gagnier, R. (1996). A brief history of work. *Journal of Economic Issues*, 30, 553-559.

Graham, H. (1984). *Women, Health and the Family*. London: Harvester.

Hewitt, P. (1993). *About Time: The Revolution in Work and Family Life*. London: Rivers Oram Press.

Hochschild, A.R. (1989). *The Second Shift: Working Parents and the Revolution at Home*. New York: Viking.

Hochschild, A.R. (1997). *The Time Bind: When Work Becomes Home and Home Becomes Work*. New York: Henry Holt.

Hunt, J.C. & Kiker, B.F. (1981). The effect of fertility on the time use of working wives. *Journal of Consumer Research*, 7, 380-387.

Kahneman, D. (1999). Objective happiness. In Kahneman, D., Diener, E. & Schwartz, N. (Eds.), *Well-Being: The Foundations of Hedonic Psychology*, New York: Russell Sage Foundation, 3-25.

Kahneman, D., Krueger, A. B., Schkade, D.A., Schwartz N. & Stone A.A. (2005) A survey method for characterizing daily life experience: the day reconstruction method. *Science*, 306, 1776-1780.

Landis, J.R. & Koch, G.G. (1977). The measurement of observer agreement for categorical data, *Biometrics*, 33, 159-174.

Larsen, R. J. & Kasimatis, M. (1990). Individual differences in entrainment of mood to the weekly calendar. *Journal of Personality & Social Psychology*, 58(1), 164-171.

Larson, R.W. & Richards, M.H. (1994). *Divergent Realities: The Emotional Lives of Mothers, Fathers and Adolescents*. New York: Basic Books.

Le Feuvre, N. (1994). Leisure, work and gender: A sociological study of women's time in France. *Time and Society*, 3, 151-178.

MacMillan, R. & Gartner, R. (1994). When she brings home the bacon: Labor-force participation and the risk of spousal violence against women. *Journal of Marriage and the Family*, 61, 947-958.

Mattingly, M.J. & Bianchi, S.M. (2003). Gender differences in the quantity and quality of free time: the U.S. experience. *Social Forces*, 81, 999-1030.

Mauldin, T. & Meeks, C.B. (1990). Time allocation of one- and two-parent mothers. *Lifestyles: Family and Economic Issues*, 11, 53-69.

Meyers-Levy, J. (1988). The influence of sex roles on judgment. *Journal of Consumer Research*, 14, 522-530.

Pencavel, J. (1998). The market work behavior and wages of women: 1975-1994. *Journal of Human Resources*, 33, 771-804.

Presser, H.B. & Cox, A.G. (1997). The work schedules of low-educated American women and welfare reform. *Monthly Labor Review*, April, 25-34.

Rogers, S.J. & DeBoer, D.D. (2001). Changes in wives' income: Effects on marital happiness, psychological well-being, and the risk of divorce. *Journal of Marriage and the Family*, 63, 458-472.

Rossi, A.S. & Rossi, P.E. (1977). Body time and social time: Mood patterns by menstrual cycle phase and day of the week. *Social Science Research,* 6, 273-308.

Roxburgh, S. (2006). "I wish we had more time to spend together…" the distribution of perceived family time pressures among married men and women in the paid labor force. *Journal of Family Issues*, 27, 529-553.

Schoen, R., Rogers, S.J. & Amato, P.R. (2006). Wives' employment and spouses' marital happiness. *Journal of Family Issues*, 27, 506-528.

Stack, S. & Eshleman, J.R. (1998). Marital status and happiness: A 17-nation study. *Journal of Marriage and the Family*, 60, 527-536.

Stevens, D., Kiger, G. & Riley, P.J. (2001). Working hard and hardly working: Domestic labor and marital satisfaction among dual-earner couples. *Journal of Marriage and Family*, 63, 514-526.

Stone, A. A. (1987). Event content in a daily survey is differentially associated with concurrent mood. *Journal of Personality and Social Psychology*, 52, 56-58.

Stone, A.A. & Neale, J.M. (1982). Development of a methodology for assessing daily experience. In A. Baum & J. Singer (Eds.), *Environment and Health* (Vol 4, pp. 49-83). Hillsdale, NJ: Erlbaum.

Thompson, C.J. (1996). Caring consumers: Gendered consumption meanings and the juggling lifestyle. *Journal of Consumer Research*, 22, 388-407.

Thompson, C.J., Locander, W.B. & Pollio, H.R. (1990). The lived meaning of free choice: An existential-phenomenological description of everyday consumer experiences of contemporary married women. *Journal of Consumer Research*, 17, 346-361.

Thornton, A. (1989). Changing attitudes toward family issues in the United States. *Journal of Marriage and the Family*, 51, 873-893.

Unger, L.S. & Kernan, J.B. (1983). On the meaning of leisure: An investigation of some determinants of the subjective experience. *Journal of Consumer Research*, 9, 381-392.

Zerubavel, E. (1985). *The seven day circle: The history and meaning of the week*, New York, The Free Press.

(Waiting) Time Flies When the Tune Flows: Music Influences Affective Responses to Waiting by Changing the Subjective Experience of Passing Time

Charles Areni, The University of Sydney, Australia
Nicole Grantham, Information Tools Pty Ltd, Australia

ABSTRACT

Researchers often focus on perceived (i.e. estimated) duration or deviations from expected duration when examining the effects of atmospheric music on waiting and customer satisfaction. Comparatively little attention has been given to whether an interval feels as though it has "dragged" on versus "flown" by compared to the normal pace of time passage. In a laboratory experiment, subjects waiting for an important event to begin reported more negative affective states when disliked rather than liked music was played during the interval. This effect was completely mediated by their subjective experience of the interval as having passed more slowly or quickly than usual when disliked versus liked music was played, respectively, whereas neither deviations from their expected waiting time nor estimates of actual duration were related to reported affective states.

INTRODUCTION

Previous research has found that perceived waiting time is negatively correlated with overall satisfaction in customer settings as diverse as restaurants (Jones and Peppiatt 1996; Davis and Heineke 1998), supermarkets (Tom and Lucey 1997), video rental stores (Evangelist et al. 2002), banks (Houston, Bettencourt and Wenger 1998), emergency healthcare (Dansky and Miles 1997), general healthcare (Pruyn and Smidts 1998), and airlines (Taylor 1994). Presumably, consumers get annoyed when they have to wait for an extended period (Houston et al. 1998), so longer waits are associated with lower levels of satisfaction (Cameron et al. 2003). The marketing literature has made the distinction between perceived duration and actual duration, and researchers have explored how commercial environments influence the perceived duration of a given interval apart from its duration as measured by a clock or watch (Bailey and Areni 2006; Hornik 1984; Haynes 1990; Taylor 1994; Hui and Tse 1996).

However, most conceptualizations of perceived duration have either involved estimates of the interval in standard time units (Jones and Peppiatt 1996; Dansky and Miles 1997; Evangelist et al. 2002), measures of duration relative to some context-specific expectation (Hedges, Trout and Magnusson 2002; Boudreaux, Mandry and Wood 2003), and/or some combination of the two (Taylor 1994; Tom and Lucy 1997; Davis and Heinke 1998; Houston, Bettencourt and Wenger 1998; Pruyn and Smidts 1998; Roper and Manela 2000; Hedges et al. 2002). These kinds of measures have produced mixed results, sometimes resulting in a direct negative relationship between perceived duration and satisfaction as noted above, sometimes an indirect negative relationship (Pruyn and Smidts 1998; Evangelist et al. 2002), and other times no relationship at all (Boudreaux et al. 2003).

The research reported here posits that an interval may seem long not because it is long or because it is longer than expected given the context, but because time seems to pass more slowly than usual even though the actual duration may be known. Although the first two possibilities have been examined in detail, no research has examined the relationship between whether a given waiting period *feels* as though it has passed more quickly or slowly than usual and resulting affective states. Based on attentional models of time perception, the research presented below argues that, of these three

measures, the subjective experience of the pace of passing time is the most important determinant of affective state in waiting contexts. Consistent with this explanation, a laboratory experiment demonstrates that the effect of atmospheric music on the affective states of respondents waiting for an upcoming event was mediated by their subjective experience of time as passing more quickly or slowly than usual, whereas neither perceived duration nor deviations from expected duration were related to affective state.

SUBJECTIVE EXPERIENCES OF PASSING TIME: ATTENTIONAL MODELS

Attentional models hold that attention is divided between processing temporally-relevant versus temporally irrelevant information. An increase in attention devoted to temporally relevant information results in more information recorded regarding the passage of time (Block 1990). As more and more attention is devoted to the passage of time, perceived duration increases (Zakay 2000). Attentional models are particularly relevant to waiting contexts because people who are waiting for an upcoming event pay closer attention to the passage of time than they would in other situations (Zakay 1990). Attentional models are best captured by the familiar cliché "Time flies when you're having fun", and also suggest that time drags when you are not having fun (i.e., waiting). However, in a waiting context, the relationship also operates in reverse; a wait that feels as if it is passing quickly is far less annoying than one which seems to drag on. In other words, attentional models suggest that the effect of waiting on affective states is mediated by the subjective experience of the rate at which time seems to pass. Any stimulus that distracts customers from thinking about the passage of time should speed up the subjective experience of passing time, making the wait seem more bearable. One of the most frequently studied stimuli in this regard is atmospheric music (Baker et al. 2002).

For example, MacNay (1996), North and Hargreaves (1999), Roper and Manela (2000), and Guegen and Jacob (2002) found that respondents reported shorter duration estimates when atmospheric music was present versus absent in a medical exercise facility, an experimental laboratory, a psychiatric care waiting room, and a telephone on-hold setting, respectively. Assuming that music diverts attention away from monitoring time, less temporal information is encoded and elapsed time seems shorter. Yalch and Spangenberg (1990) reported that shoppers under the age of 25 gave shorter estimates of shopping time when they heard Top 40 as opposed to Muzak, whereas the reverse was true for shoppers 25 years of age or older. It is possible that younger shoppers liked and listened to the Top 40 music more, hence diverting attention from the passage of time and reducing perceived duration, whereas the reverse may have been true for older shoppers (Yalch and Spangenberg 1993). Also consistent with attentional models, Lopez and Malhotra (1993) and Cameron et al. (2003) found that respondents' time estimates were negatively correlated with their reported liking of atmospheric music. Collectively, these results suggest that people exposed to atmospheric music that they like will devote less attention to the passage of time, thus making time seem to pass quickly and the wait seem more bearable (Cameron et al. 2003). This suggests the following two hypotheses:

H_{1a}: People exposed to music they like during a waiting period will report feeling that time has passed more quickly than usual compared to people exposed to disliked music.

H_{1b}: The effect of music likeability on affective states will be mediated by the subjective experience of time as passing more slowly or quickly than usual.

Much of the research examining customer satisfaction has adopted a disconfirmation of expectations paradigm, wherein satisfaction judgments are driven by differences between perceptions of the actual service experience and prior expectations of the service (Parasuraman, Zeithhaml and Berry 1985). Not surprisingly, previous research on customer waiting has largely relied on measures of perceived duration and/or deviations from expected duration as indicators of the negative effects of waiting on satisfaction (see Houston, Bettencourt and Wenger 1998; Pruyn and Smidts 1998). Many of these studies have found that perceived waiting time is negatively correlated with overall satisfaction in settings as diverse as restaurants (Jones and Peppiatt 1996; Davis and Heineke 1998; Luo et al. 2004), supermarkets (Tom and Lucey 1997), video rental stores (Evangelist et al. 2002), banks (Houston et al. 1998), emergency healthcare (Dansky and Miles 1997), general healthcare (Pruyn and Smidts 1998), and airlines (Taylor 1994). In other words, these studies found that the longer customers think they have waited, the less satisfied they are with their service experience.

Research has also found that various aspects of atmospheric music reduce perceived duration in contexts as diverse as healthcare (MacNay 1996), psychiatric care (Roper and Manela 2000), telephone on-hold (Gueguen and Jacob 2002), university registrations (Oakes 2003), department stores (Yalch and Spangenberg 1990, 1993), supermarkets (Gulas and Schewe 1994), and among students participating in laboratory experiments (Kellaris and Altsech 1992; Kellaris and Kent 1992; Lopez and Malhotra 1992; Kellaris and Mantel 1996; Kellaris, Mantel and Altsech 1996; Hui, Dube and Chebat 1997; North and Hargreaves 1999; Yalch and Spangenberg 2000; Bueno, Firmino and Engelman 2002; Cameron et al. 2003; Mantel and Kellaris 2003).

However, other researchers have reported little or no direct relationship between atmospheric music and perceived duration in contexts such as telephone on-hold (North, Hargreaves and McKendrick 1999), banks (Chebat, Gelinas-Chebat and Filiatrault 1993), gymnasiums (North, Hargreaves and Heath 1998), restaurants (Caldwell and Hibbert 1999), and among students participating in laboratory experiments (Boltz 1998; Brown and Boltz 2002). Moreover, many of the effects reported above are in opposition to the predictions of attentional models (Kellaris and Kent 1992; Hui et al. 1997; Gulas and Schewe 1994; Yalch and Spangenberg 2000), and some involve direct contradictions. For example, Lopez and Malhotra (1992) reported that, compared to disliked music, liked music reduced perceived duration among students participating in a laboratory study, whereas Hui et al. (1997) reported that liked music actually increased perceived duration compared to disliked music. This may reflect the finding that attentional models hold mainly when people focus on the passage of time during the target interval (Block and Zakay 1997), which would be expected of customers waiting for an upcoming event (Zakay 1990; North and Hargreaves 1999), but not necessarily in all retailing contexts (Bailey and Areni 2006).

Moreover, when attentional models do operate, as is the case in waiting contexts, the subjective experience of time passage has a more direct effect on resulting affective states than does perceived duration (Friedman 1990; Flaherty 1999). For example, given certain environmental conditions (e.g., waiting while listening to disliked atmospheric music), time may feel like it is dragging on even though a customer has a rough idea of how long he has been waiting (e.g., due to periodically checking his watch). In these kinds of situations, subjective experience and not perceived duration would capture the effect of prolonged thinking about the passage of time on resulting affective state. Hence, the following hypothesis is advanced.

H_2: The perceived duration of the wait period will not mediate the effect of music likeability on reported affective states.

With respect to differences between perceptions and expectations, some researchers have found that waits perceived as exceeding expectations are associated with lower levels of satisfaction in hospitals (Pruyn and Smidts 1998; Boudreax, Mandry, and Wood 2003), emergency healthcare facilities (Hedges, Trout and Magnusson 2002), airline travellers (Taylor 1994), fast food restaurants (Davis and Heineke 1998), and among students participating in laboratory studies (Kumar, Kalwani and Dada 1997; Hui, Thakor and Gill 1998; Cameron et al. 2003). However, results regarding deviations from expected duration are also equivocal. Other studies have found that negative gaps between perceived and expected wait times did not result in lower levels of satisfaction in hospitals (Boudreaux, Mandry and Wood 2003), banks (Houston et al. 1998), restaurants (Luo et al. 2004), and among students participating in laboratory studies (Hui and Tse 1996). Moreover, research has not examined the effects of atmospheric music on deviations from expected duration because expected duration judgments are, by definition, formed prior to exposure to the wait setting. This limits the effects of any atmospheric variable, and results in deviation judgments being strongly correlated with perceived duration measures. Hence, the following hypothesis is advanced.

H_3: Deviations from the expected duration of the wait period will not mediate the effect of music likeability on reported affective states.

METHOD

Eighty-six undergraduate students studying business at a major Australian university were recruited for participation in the experiment. Course credit (2%) was offered as an incentive to participate. In addition, respondents who successfully completed the experiment were entered into a draw for 4 prizes of $500 each. They were told that the study involved knowledge of brand names in various product categories and that they would be required to perform a recall task followed by the completion of a questionnaire. On arrival, they were greeted by a laboratory assistant, asked to sign a consent form, and asked to wait until the study began. When all the respondents for a given session had arrived, the researcher led them in groups of 6–8 into a room set up to appear like a waiting room, with little or no visual stimuli, and no clocks. They were instructed to place all hand bags, backpacks, etc. on a table, to turn off their mobile phones, and to refrain from talking to one another so as not to bias the outcome of the study. The researcher then explained that "the sessions are being run in multiple rooms to save time and things are running a bit behind schedule", and that he would "return shortly to begin the study when the previous session ends". The actual time spent in the waiting area was 17.5 minutes. This prevented respondents from guessing correctly simply by rounding up (i.e., 20 minutes) or down (i.e., 15 minutes) to a "standard" time interval. The experimenter began the target period when the last respondent entered the room. He returned to the room after 17 minutes, and distributed the questionnaire containing the dependent measures. Respondents were instructed to complete the questionnaire 17.5 minutes after the last person entered the room.

Independent Variable: Music Likeability

Several selections of music were selected from two categories, recent number one hits versus uncharted songs from the 1950s. Despite the face validity of the manipulation (i.e., university students would presumably prefer recent number one songs to music created long before they were born), a manipulation check measure prompted respondents with the open-ended statement: "To what extent did you find the music…" and asked them to circle the number corresponding to their perception of the music on five 7-point scales anchored by "unpleasant (1)–(7) pleasant", "unappealing (1)–(7) appealing", "unlikable (1)–(7) likable", "boring (1)–(7) interesting", and "unexciting (1)–(7) exciting". The results of an exploratory factor analysis indicated a single factor solution with an eigenvalue of 3.1 and with all factor loadings exceeding 0.7. Using a mean weighted by factor scores as the dependent variable, a one-way ANOVA revealed a significant effect of music likeability ($F_{1,73}$=27.1, p<.0001, w^2=.27), wherein the recent number one songs were rated as more likable (M=4.7) than the 1950s songs (M=3.3).

Mediating Variables

Perceived Duration: Similar to the approaches used by Hui and Tse (1996) and Mantel and Kellaris (2003), the first item on the questionnaire asked respondents: "Without looking at your watch, please estimate how long you have been in this room. _____ minutes _____ seconds." This open-ended approach is common in time perception research because it tends to eliminate any rounding off to the nearest minute (Block (1990).

Subjective Experience of Time Passage: The next two items in the questionnaire measured respondents' subjective experience of time passage using 7-point semantic differential response scales. Both items were based on work by Friedman (1990) and Flaherty (1999). Respondents were prompted with: "During the period I've been in this room:" using a response scale anchored by "time has flown by" (1)–(7) "time has dragged on", and "Since I've entered this room: "time has passed quickly" (1)–(7) "time has passed slowly". The subjective experience measure was the mean of the two items.

Deviation from Expected Duration: The next item measured deviations from prior expectations of duration. Adapted from earlier research by Houston, Bettencourt and Wenger (1998) and Boudreaux, Mandry and Wood (2003), the item prompted respondents with the statement: "The amount of time I've been in this room has been" and used a response scale anchored by "shorter than expected" (1)–(7) "longer than expected". Respondents were instructed to circle the number that best corresponded to their perception of the wait period.

Dependent Variable: Affective state

The affective state measure involved the five items used to measure the pleasure-displeasure dimension of Mehrabian and Russell's (1974) PAD model of affect. This measure has been used in several studies examining retail atmospherics (Donovan and Rossiter 1982; Hui and Tse 1996), and more specifically, the impact of music likeability on time perception and affective states (Cameron et al. 2003). Respondents were prompted with the statements "This question is about how you feel now. For each scale, circle the number that corresponds with your current mood." Five 7-point scales followed, with the anchors: "depressed (1)–(7) contented", "unhappy (1)–(7) happy", "unsatisfied (1)–(7) satisfied", "annoyed (1)–(7) pleased", and "bored (1)–(7) relaxed".

Given the importance of distinguishing among perceived duration, deviation from expected duration, and the subjective experience of passing time, an exploratory factor analysis of the items comprising the mediating and dependent variables was conducted. As shown in Table 1, the results indicated a four factor solution. The five pleasure-displeasure items loaded on the first factor, which produced an eigenvalue of 3.62. Factor loadings ranged from .79 to .87, and communalities ranged from .65 to .79. The two subjective experience items loaded on the second factor, which produced an eigenvalue of 1.82. The factor loadings were .83 and .93 and the communalities were .87 and .91, for the first and second item, respectively. The third factor, which produced an eigenvalue of 1.05, directly corresponded to the deviation from expected duration measure, which had a loading and communality of .97 and .99, respectively; and the final factor, with an eigenvalue of 1.04, corresponded to the perceived duration measure, which produced a loading of .99 and a communality of .98. These results suggest that perceived duration, deviation from expected duration, and the subjective experience of a time interval are distinct constructs with the potential to differentially mediate the effect of music likeability on affective state. Hence, the measures for subjective experience and affective state were the mean scores of the corresponding items, weighted by factor loadings, and the measures for perceived duration and deviation from expected duration were simply the responses to the corresponding single items.

RESULTS

Hypotheses 1–3 were tested via four 1-way ANOVAs with music likeability as the independent variable and affective state, subjective experience, perceived duration and expected duration as the dependent variables; and 3 ANCOVAs with likeability as the independent variable, affective state as the dependent variable and subjective experience, perceived duration, and expected duration as the three covariates. All hypotheses essentially required that respondents exposed to the liked atmospheric music would report more favourable affective states than respondents exposed to disliked music. The results of the first ANOVA supported this expectation. The effect of music likeability on reported affective states was significant ($F_{1,81}$=7.2, p<.01, w^2=.07), with respondents reporting more positive affective states in the liked condition (M=4.3) compared to the disliked condition (M=3.7).

Hypothesis 1a predicted that respondents hearing liked music would report that the waiting interval passed more quickly than usual compared to respondents hearing disliked music, and hypothesis 1b predicted that the effect of music likeability on affective state would be mediated by the subjective pace of time passage. A second ANOVA with likeability as the independent variable and subjective experience as the dependent variable revealed a significant result ($F_{1,83}$=11.9, p<.001, w^2=.11), with respondents in the disliked condition reporting that time passed more slowly (M=5.0) than did respondents in the liked condition (M=3.9), hence supporting hypothesis 1a. As shown in Table 2, when subjective experience was included as a covariate in an ANCOVA with music likeability as the independent variable and affective state as the dependent variable, it was a significant predictor ($F_{1,80}$=19.6, p<.0001), and the effect of music likeability on affective state was all but eliminated ($F_{1,80}$=1.4, p<.25). Hence, the effect of music on affective state was mediated by the subjective experience of time passing more slowly or quickly than usual; hypothesis 1b was supported.

Hypothesis 2 predicted that perceived duration would not mediate the effect of music likeability on reported affective states. A third ANOVA revealed that music likeability had little or no effect on perceived duration ($F_{1,84}$<1). Moreover, when perceived duration was included as a covariate in an ANCOVA with music

TABLE 1
Factor Analysis Results for the Measures of Affective States, Subjective Experience, Perceived Duration, and Expected Duration

	Factor1	Factor2	Factor3	Factor4
pleas1	*0.82957*	-0.24452	0.02014	0.07644
pleas2	*0.87467*	-0.06717	-0.12940	0.03805
pleas3	*0.84804*	-0.24671	-0.06956	-0.08752
pleas4	*0.80566*	-0.26879	-0.14824	-0.21156
pleas5	*0.78962*	-0.14382	-0.06431	-0.07276
subjtime1	-0.33378	*0.83376*	0.24504	-0.06184
subjtime2	-0.19916	*0.93182*	0.06061	-0.02741
deviation1	-0.12659	0.19185	*0.96717*	0.00097
pertime1	-0.08153	-0.06438	-0.00158	*0.98595*

Variance Explained by Each Factor

Factor1	Factor2	Factor3	Factor4
3.61874	1.82250	1.04723	1.04167

TABLE 2
Mediation Results for Subjective Experience, Perceived Duration, and Deviation from Expected Duration

Model	F stat	p value	Effect	Result
Pleasure = Liking	$F_{1,81} = 7.2$	p < .01	$\omega^2 = .07$	H_1 supported
Pleasure = Subjective Experience	$F_{1,80} = 19.6$	p < .0001		H_2 supported
Liking	$F_{1,80} = 1.4$	p < .25	$\omega^2 < .01$	
Pleasure = Perceived Duration	$F_{1,80} = 1.9$	p < .19		H_3 supported
Liking	$F_{1,80} = 7.7$	p < .01	$\omega^2 = .07$	
Pleasure = Deviation from Expectations	$F_{1,80} = 3.6$	p < .10		H_4 supported
Liking	$F_{1,80} = 5.1$	p < .03	$\omega^2 = .04$	

likeability as the independent variable, it was not predictive of affective state ($F_{1,80}=1.9$, p<.18). Hence, although failing to reject the null hypothesis cannot be construed as supporting a prediction, these results are at least consistent with hypothesis 2. Hypothesis 3 predicted that deviation from expected duration would not mediate the effect of music likeability on reported affective states. A fourth ANOVA revealed that music likeability had a significant effect on expected duration ($F_{1,83}=4.8$, p<.04, $w^2=.04$). Respondents reported that the wait period was longer than expected when they heard disliked (M=5.6) compared to liked (M=4.8) music. Moreover, when expected duration was included as a covariate in an ANCOVA it was marginally significant as a predictor of affective state ($F_{1,80}=3.6$, p<.06); however, the effect of music likeability remained significant ($F_{1,80}=5.1$, p<.03, $w^2=.04$). Hence, these results are consistent with hypothesis 3.

DISCUSSION

The research reported above assumed that the ultimate impact of atmospheric music is on affective state, with the subjective experience of time passage as the mediating variable. However, previous research has examined the mediating role of affective state in accounting for the effect of music on time perception (Wansink 1992; Hui, Dube and Chebat 1997). In order to examine whether this alternative view applies to the results reported above, affective state was examined as a possible mediator of the effect of atmospheric music on deviation from expected duration and the subjective experience of time passage (it has already been established that music had little or no effect on perceived duration). Two ANCOVAs were conducted with atmospheric music as the independent variable, affective state as the covariate, and deviation from expected duration and the subjective experience of time passage as the two dependent variables.

For the ANCOVA with the deviation measure as the dependent variable, the effect of affective state as a covariate was marginally significant ($F_{1,80}=3.6$, p<.06), and the effect of music was no longer significant ($F_{1,80}=2.0$, p<.17). Moreover, the size of the effect of music declined noticeably when affective state was included as a covariate (from $w^2=.04$ to $w^2=.01$). Hence, consistent with Wansink (1992) and Hui et al. (1997), affective state does mediate the effect of atmospheric music on expected duration. In the ANCOVA with subjective experience as the dependent variable, the effect of affective state as a covariate was highly significant ($F_{1,80}=19.6$, p<.0001). However, the effect of music on subjective experience remained significant ($F_{1,80}=6.0$, p<.02), though the effect size was reduced (from $w^2=.11$ to $w^2=.04$). On the basis of these results one could conclude that the effect of atmospheric music on the subjective experience of time passage is partially mediated by affective state. However, given the conceptual foundation underlying hypotheses 1 and 2, and the result that subjective experience completely accounted for the effect of music on affective state, the more parsimonious conclusion is that former mediates the effect of music on the latter. Hence, attentional models appear to be more useful than other conceptual models for explaining the effects of atmospheric music on affective states in waiting contexts.

A number of other factors have been shown to reduce perceived waiting time in addition to atmospheric music, including giving estimates of the duration of a delay (Hui and Tse 1996; Roper and Manela 2000), involving customers in the provision of the service (Chebat and Filiatrault 1993), giving people tasks to complete during a wait (Dansky and Miles 1997), providing entertainment (Jones and Pepiatt 1996), asking about customers' well-being (Roper and Manela 2000), and avoiding interruptions (Chebat and Filiatrault 1993). The assumption underlying much of this research is that reducing perceived duration will make the wait more bearable and result in higher levels of satisfaction (Jones and Pepiatt 1996; Dansky and Miles 1997).

However, the results reported above question whether this assumption holds. For example, giving repeated updates on the estimated duration of a delay may reduce perceived duration by giving customers a basis for making more accurate estimates, but this may have little or no influence on how much attention is devoted to monitoring the passing time or whether time seems to drag on during the wait. By contrast, engaging customers in conversation will almost certainly divert attention away from monitoring time; this would result in time seeming to pass more quickly than usual, and hence, a more favourable affective state. In short, perceived duration is related to affective state and/or customer satisfaction mainly when attentional models operate.

The research reported above has a number of limitations which should be disclosed and further discussed. Given the goals of this research, the most directly relevant shortcoming is the measure of the subjective experience of passing time. Although perceived duration and expected duration are often measured using single items, the subjective experience of passing time is, on the face of it, a more complex construct, potentially having multiple dimensions. The two items reported here reflect the conceptualization of Friedman (1990) and Flaherty (1999), but a more comprehensive approach would involve the development of numerous potential items, the elimination of items that are not highly correlated with the majority of the items, assessing the dimensionality and reliability of the remaining items, and an examination of the resulting scale on a new sample (Churchill 1979). Future research should proceed along these lines, as better measures of cognitive processes will be needed if research examining the effects of waiting on affective state is to progress further.

The artificial laboratory setting is another potential limitation of this research. Much of the literature in this area involves actual customers waiting in actual retail settings. Although field studies do not necessarily provide higher levels of external validity, they are useful for establishing the relevance of the theory to an actual consumer behavior setting. Finally, the dependent variable in this research was general affective state rather than satisfaction with the waiting experience, as is often used in this area of research. It could be the case that listening to music influenced respondents' affective states directly, quite apart from any influence on the perceived passage of time. Future research should use a more direct measure of whether respondents were satisfied with the wait experience to better test the proposed mediating processes.

REFERENCES

Bailey, Nicole and Charles S. Areni (2006). "When a Few Minutes Sound Like a Lifetime: Does Atmospheric Music Expend or Contract Perceived Time?" *Journal of Retailing*, 82 (3), 189-202.

Baker, Julie, A. Parasuraman, Dhruv Grewal and Glenn B. Voss (2002), "The Influence of Multiple Store Environment Cues on Perceived Merchandise Value and Patronage Intentions." *Journal of Marketing*, 66 (2), 120-141.

Block, Richard A. (1990), "Models of Psychological Time," in *Cognitive Models of Psychological Time*, Richard A. Block (Ed.), Hillsdale, NJ: Lawrence Erlbaum, pp. 1-35.

_____ and Dan Zakay (1997). "Prospective and Retrospective Duration Judgments: A Meta-Analytic Review," *Psychonomic Bulletin and Review*, 4 (2), 184-197.

Boltz, Marilyn (1998), "The Processing of Temporal and Nontemporal Information in the Remembering of Event Durations and Musical Structures," *Journal of Experimental Psychology: Human Perception and Performance*, 24 (4), 1087-1104.

Boudreaux, Edwin D., Cris V. Mandry and Karen Wood (2003), "Patient Satisfaction Data as a Quality Indicator: A Tale of Two Emergency Departments," *Academic Emergency Medicine*, 10 (3), 261-268.

Brown, Scott W. and Marilyn G. Boltz (2002), "Attentional Processes in Time Perception: Effects of Mental Workload and Event Structure," *Journal of Experimental Psychology: Human Perception and Performance*, 28 (3), 600-615.

Bueno, Jose Lino Oliveira, Erico Artioli Firmino and Arno Engelman (2002), "Influence of Generalized Complexity of a Musical Event on Subjective Time Estimation," *Perceptual & Motor Skills*, 94 (2), 541-547.

Caldwell, Clare and Sally A. Hibbert (1999), "Play That One Again: The Effect of Music Tempo on Consumer Behaviour in a Restaurant," in *European Advances in Consumer Research*, Vol. 4, Bernard Dubois et al. (Eds.), Provo, UT: Association for Consumer Research, pp. 58-62.

Cameron, Michaelle Ann, Julie Baker, Mark Peterson and Karin Braunsberger (2003), "The Effects of Music, Wait-Length Evaluation, and Affective state on a Low-Cost Wait Experience," *Journal of Business Research*, 56 (6), 421-430.

Chebat, Jean-Charles and Pierre Filiatrault (1993), "The Impact of Waiting in Line on Consumers," *The International Journal of Bank Marketing*, 11 (2), 35-40.

_____, Claire Gelinas-Chebat and Pierre Filiatrault (1993), "Interactive Effects of Musical and Visual Cues on Time Perception: An Application to Waiting Lines in Banks," *Perceptual & Motor Skills*, 77 (3), 995-1020.

Churchill, Gilbert A. Jr. (1979), "A Paradigm for Developing Better Measures of Marketing Constructs," *Journal of Marketing Research*, 16 (February), 64-73.

Dansky, Kathryn H. and Jeffrey Miles (1997), "Patient Satisfaction with Ambulatory Healthcare Services: Waiting Time and Filling Time," *Hospital & Health Services Administration*, 42 (2), 165-177.

Davis, Mark M. and Janelle Heineke (1998), "How Disconfirmation, Perception and Actual Waiting Times Impact Customer Satisfaction," *International Journal of Service Industry Management*, 9 (1), 64-72.

Donovan, Robert J. and John R. Rossiter (1982), "Store Atmosphere: An Environmental Psychology Approach," *Journal of Retailing*, 58 (1), 34-57.

Dube-Rioux, Laurette, Bernd H. Schmitt, and France Leclerc (1989), "Consumers' Reactions to Waiting: When Delays Affect the Perception of Service Quality," in *Advances in Consumer Research*, Vol. 16, Thomas. K. Srull (Ed.), Provo, UT: Association for Consumer Research, pp. 59-63.

Evangelist, Shane, Badger Godwin, Joey Johnson, Vincent Conzola, Robert Kizer, Stephanie Young-Helou and Richard Metters. (2002), "Linking Marketing and Operations: An Application at Blockbuster, Inc.," *Journal of Service Research*, 5 (2), 91-100.

Flaherty, Michael G. (1999), *A Watched Pot*. New York: New York University Press.

Friedman, William (1990), *About Time: Inventing the Fourth Dimension*. Cambridge, MA: The MIT Press.

Guegen, Nicolas and Celine Jacob (2002), "The Influence of Music on Temporal Perceptions in an On-hold Waiting Situation," *Psychology of Music*, 30 (2), 210-214.

Gulas, Charles and Charles Schewe (1994), "Atmospheric Segmentation: Managing Store Image with Background Music," in *Enhancing Knowledge Development in Marketing*, Ravi Acrol and Andrew Mitchell (Eds.), Chicago, IL: American Marketing Association, pp. 325-330.

Haynes, Paula J. (1990), "Hating to Wait: Managing the Final Service Encounter," *Journal of Services Marketing*, 4 (4), 2-26.

Hedges, Jerris R., Andrew Trout and A. Roy Magnusson (2002), "Satisfied Patients Exiting the Emergency Department (SPEED) Study," *Academic Emergency Medicine*, 9 (1), 15-21.

Hornik, Jacob (1984), "Subjective and Objective Time Measures: A Note on Perception of Time in Consumer Behavior," *Journal of Consumer Research*, 11 (1), 615-618.

Houston, Mark B., Lance A. Bettencourt and Sutha Wenger (1998), "The Relationship Between Waiting in a Service Queue and Evaluations of Service Quality: A Field Theory Perspective," *Psychology & Marketing*, 15 (8), 735-753.

Hui, Michael K. and David K. Tse (1996), "What to Tell Consumers in Waits of Different Lengths: An Integrative Model of Service Evaluation," *Journal of Marketing*, 60 (2), 81-90.

_____, Laurette Dube and Jean-Charles Chebat (1997), "The Impact of Music on Consumers' Reactions to Waiting for Services," *Journal of Retailing*, 73 (1), 87-104.

_____, Mrugank V. Thakor and Ravi Gill (1998), "The Effect of Delay Type and Service Stage on Consumers' Reactions to Waiting," *Journal of Consumer Research*, 24 (4), 469-479.

Jones, Peter and Emma Peppiatt (1996), "Managing Perceptions of Waiting Times in Service Queues," *International Journal of Service Industry Management*, 7 (5), 47-61.

Kellaris, James J. and Moses B. Altsech (1992), "The Experience of Time as a Function of Musical Loudness and Gender of the Listener," in *Advances in Consumer Research*, Vol. 19, John Sherry and Brian Sternthal (Eds.), Provo, UT: Association for Consumer Research, pp. 725-729.

_____ and Robert J. Kent (1992), "The Influence of Music on Consumers' Temporal Perceptions: Does Time Fly When You're having Fun?" *Journal of Consumer Psychology*, 1 (4), 365-376.

_____, and Susan Powell Mantel (1996), "Shaping Time Perceptions with Background Music: The Effect of Congruity and Arousal on Estimates of Ad Durations," *Psychology & Marketing*, 13 (5), 501-515.

_____, Susan Powell Mantel and Moses B. Altsech (1996), "Decibels, Disposition, and Duration: The Impact of Musical Loudness and Internal States on Time Perceptions," in *Advances in Consumer Research*, Vol. 23, Kim Corfman and John Lynch (Eds.), Provo, UT: Association for Consumer Research, pp. 498-503.

Lopez, Linda and R. Malhotra (1991), "Estimation of Time Intervals with Most Preferred and Least Preferred Music," *Psychological Studies*, 36 (3), 203-209.

Luo, Wenhong, Matthew J. Liberatore, Robert L. Nydick, Q. B. Chung and Elliot Sloane (2004), "Impact of Process Change on Customer Perception of Waiting Time: A Field Study," *Omega*, 32, 77-83.

MacNay, Sterling K. (1996), "The Influence of Preferred Music on the Perceived Exertion, Affective state, and Time Estimation Scores of Patients Participating in a Cardiac Rehabilitation Exercise Program," *Therapy Perspectives*, 13 (2), 91-96.

Mantel, Susan Powell and James J. Kellaris (2003), "Cognitive Determinants of Consumers' Time Perceptions: The Impact of Resources Required and Available," *Journal of Consumer Research*, 29 (4), 531-538.

North, Adrian C. and David J. Hargreaves (1999), "Can Music Move People?: The Effects of Musical Complexity and Silence on Waiting Time," *Environment and Behavior*, 31 (1), 136-149.

_____, _____ and Sarah J. Heath (1998), "Music Tempo and Time Perception in a Gymnasium," *Psychology of Music*, 26 (1), 78-88.

_____, _____ and Jennifer McKendrick (1999), "Music and On-Hold Waiting Time," *British Journal of Psychology*, 90 (1), 161-164.

Oakes, Steve (2003), "Music Tempo and Waiting Perceptions," *Psychology & Marketing*, 20 (8), 685-706.

Parasuraman, A., Valarie A. Zeithaml, and Leonard L. Berry (1985), "A Conceptual Model of Service Quality and Its Implications for Future Research," *Journal of Marketing*, 49 (Fall), 41-50.

Pruyn, Ad and Ale Smidts (1998), "Effects of Waiting on the Satisfaction with the Service: Beyond Objective Time Measures," *International Journal of Research in Marketing*, 15 (4), 321-334.

Roper, Janice M. and Julita Manela (2000), "Psychiatric Patients' Perceptions of Waiting Time in the Psychiatric Emergency Service," *Journal of Psychosocial Nursing*, 38 (5), 19-27.

Taylor, Shirley (1994), "Waiting for Service: The Relationship between Delays and Evaluations of Service," *Journal of Marketing*, 58 (2), 56-69.

Tom, Gail and Scott Lucey (1997), "A Field Study Investigating the Effect of Waiting Time on Customer Satisfaction," *Journal of Psychology*, 131 (6), 655-660.

Wansink, Brian (1992), "Listen to the Music: Its Impact on Affect, Perceived Time Passage, and Applause," in *Advances in Consumer Research*, Vol. 19, John Sherry and Brian Sternthal Eds.), Provo, UT: Association for Consumer Research, pp. 715-718.

Yalch, Richard F. and Eric R. Spangenberg (1990), "Effects of Store Music on Shopping Behavior," *Journal of Services Marketing*, 4 (1), 31-39.

_____ and _____ (1993), "Using Store Music for Retail Zoning: A Field Experiment," in *Advances in Consumer Research*, Vol. 20, Leigh McAlister and Michael L. Rothschild Eds.), Provo, UT: Association for Consumer Research, pp. 632-636.

_____ and _____ (2000), "The Effects of Music in a Retail Setting on Real and Perceived Shopping Times," *Journal of Business Research*, 49 (2), 139-147.

Zakay, Dan (1990), "The Evasive Art of Subjective Time Measurement: Some Methodological Dilemmas," in *Cognitive Models of Psychological Time*, Richard A. Block (Ed.), Hillsdale, NJ: Lawrence Erlbaum, pp. 59-81.

_____ (2000), "Gating or Switching? Gating Is a Better Model of Prospective Timing (A Response to 'Switching or Gating' by Lejeune)," *Behavioral Processes*, 52 (2/3), 63-69.

Post-Purchase Consumer Regret: Conceptualization and Development of the PPCR Scale

Seung Hwan Lee, University of Western Ontario, Canada
June Cotte, University of Western Ontario, Canada

ABSTRACT

We conceptualize and operationalize a new definition of post-purchase consumer regret. Consumers can regret both the *outcome* and the *process* of their purchase. While previous researchers have identified the existence of these two components, there has been a lack of exploration of how outcome regret and process regret are experienced in a consumer context. In terms of outcome regret, we posit two dimensions: regret due to foregone alternatives and regret due to a change in significance; we believe these influence consumers. In terms of process regret, we expect regret due to both under- and over-consideration during decision-making. We propose and conceptualize these multiple dimensions of post-purchase consumer regret, and report three studies that, taken together, validate a scale for measuring this construct (PPCR). We conclude by identifying possible new research opportunities in this area, outlining why more consumer behavior research can, and should, be devoted to the topic of consumer regret.

INTRODUCTION

When consumers experience regret after a certain purchase, are they regretting what they bought (the outcome), how they bought it (the process), or both? The purpose of our paper is to propose and validate a multidimensional framework for each of these two components of regret. While previous researchers have identified the existence of these two components (e.g. Zeelenberg and Pieters 2006), there has been a lack of exploration of the components of outcome regret and process regret, and how each of these components are experienced in a consumption context. Therefore, we propose a new theoretical definition of post-purchase consumer regret. First, we describe regret in greater detail and also differentiate it from a potentially related construct (disappointment). Second, we conceptually redefine the current definitions of outcome regret and process regret. Third, we present the results of three studies that create a PPCR scale. Fourth, we conclude by identifying implications and questions to stimulate additional research.

CONSUMER REGRET

Regret is an aversive cognitive emotion that people are motivated to avoid, suppress, deny, and regulate should they experience it (Zeelenberg and Pieters 2006). Traditionally, regret has been known to be a painful sensation that arises as a result of comparing 'what is' with 'what might have been' (Sugden 1985). In other words, regret transpires when an obtained outcome compares unfavourably with an outcome that could have been better had the individual chosen differently (Bell 1982; Tsiros and Mittal 2000). This is known as outcome regret (Zeelenberg and Pieters 2006). That is, post-purchase *outcome* regret is a comparison of individual's assessment of the outcomes between what has been bought and what could have been bought.

But recently, scholars have also hypothesized that, independent of outcomes, the quality of the decision *process* can also be regretted (Connolly and Zeelenberg 2002; Zeelenberg and Pieters 2006). Process regret is evoked when an individual compares their inferior decision process to a better alternative decision process. When individuals regret due to process, instead of comparing the outcomes, they compare the decision processes (e.g., I should have checked more stores before buying). These two components of regret can occur independently of one another, which suggest that

it is possible for someone to regret the process, even if the purchase experience resulted in a good outcome. Using Decision Justification Theory (DJT), Connolly and Zeelenberg (2002) argue that individuals regret due to the evaluation of outcomes, and also because of a decision made in an unjustifiable way. DJT postulates that the total amount of regret experienced is a sum of regret experienced as a result of an outcome that is inferior to another outcome that has been rejected, plus the feeling of self-blame for the poor decision process. Below, we go into more depth by closely examining what regret is, and what regret clearly is not.

What is Regret?

Responsibility. Regret arises from individuals expending cognitive efforts to consider the chosen option against the rejected options (Inman, Dyer, and Jia 1997). Individuals must think in order to feel regret. For individuals to experience regret, they have to cognitively process and cross-compare one option (chosen) to another option (foregone). If the result of the comparison is perceived to be unfavorable (i.e. the foregone option is perceived to be better than the present option), then individuals are prone to feeling regret over their actions.

Self-blame is a major component of regret. When individuals perceive that their decision was unreasonable or inexplicable, they tend to feel responsible for making the poor decision (van Dijk, van der Pligt, and Zeelenberg 1999). Sugden (1985) contends that the intensity of regret is often influenced by the level of individual responsibility taken, as well as self-blame. One consistent finding is that regret tends to be greater when individuals had more control over their decisions than when individuals have had little control over their decisions (Gilovich and Medvec 1994).

Counterfactual Thinking. In addition to feeling responsible, in order to experience regret, individuals must also be able to construct alternative scenarios other than the current state (Zeelenberg and Pieters 2006). Counterfactual thinking (CFT) is the process of comparing reality with alternative possibilities by constructing hypothetical scenarios to assess the attractiveness of alternative possibilities (Kahneman and Miller 1986). In essence, CFT is not an evaluation of the outcome, but rather the thought-process of how an outcome could have been prevented or altered to yield a more positive or a negative outcome.

There are two forms, or directions, of counterfactual thinking: upward CFT and downward CFT (Kahneman and Miller 1986). When individuals think about how circumstances could have been worse, it is referred to as downward CFT. Conversely, upward CFT is when individuals think about how circumstances could have been better. Because people engage in greater CFT after a negative outcome than after a positive outcome (Kahneman and Miller 1986), it is likely that people engage in upward CFT more often than downward CFT. And subsequently, when individuals generate upward CFT, it is likely that they will experience regret (Kahneman and Miller 1986).

In the context of consumer behavior, individuals tend to engage in upward CFT after a negative purchase outcome, and CFT helps them analyze what went wrong, to assess why they potentially made a poor choice, and to discover what better opportunities they may have missed. When a negative outcome occurs, people use CFT which can subsequently intensify the feeling of regret (Kahneman and Miller 1986). Indeed, the greater the CFT that

FIGURE 1
CONCEPTUAL MODEL

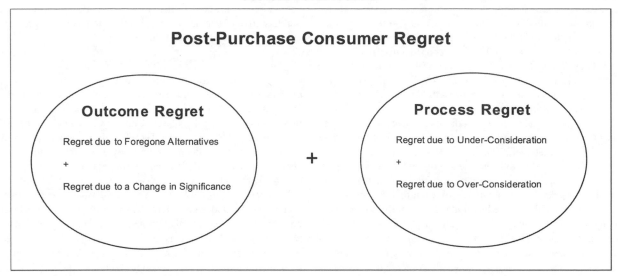

FIGURE 1
CONCEPTUAL MODEL

occurs, the greater the potential for regret to be experienced by the individual (Landman 1993). Therefore, CFT is not only a necessary condition of regret, but also has the potential to influence the magnitude of regret experienced by the individual.

What Regret is Not

Disappointment. Disappointment is an unpleasant feeling induced by the discrepancy between the desired expected outcome versus the actual outcome (Bell 1985). Regret is sometimes used inappropriately as a synonym for other negative emotions, including disappointment. This is because, like regret, disappointment is also a function of post-purchase valuation (Inman et al. 1997). Both are negative-based emotions that are induced by outcomes and risky decision-making. While the two may appear similar, they can be clearly distinguished from one another in three main ways: phenomenology, appraisal patterns and attributions, as well as the varying behavioral consequences of regret and disappointment.

First, building on the idea that specific emotions have distinctive goals, action tendencies, thoughts, and feelings associated with each emotion, Zeelenberg et al. (1998b) compared the phenomenological differences between regret and disappointment (for a review, see Zeelenberg et al. 1998b). Overall, those who experienced regret tended to rethink about past events, while those who experienced disappointment tended to dismiss their negative experience.

Second, in terms of appraisal and attribution, disappointment is appraised as something that caused by events beyond the individual's control, while regret is appraised as something that caused by oneself (van Dijk and Zeelenberg 2002). Zeelenberg and Pieters (2004) posited that one of the major differences between regret and disappointment lies in control. Regret typically arises as a result of having made the wrong decision and is associated with self-blame. On the other hand, disappointment arises as a result of unfulfilled expectations and is associated with blaming others or circumstances beyond individual's control (Zeelenberg et al. 1998a).

Finally, research in emotion theory has shown that discrete emotions have different idiosyncratic behaviors, and behavioral tendencies, associated with them. For example, Zeelenberg and Pieters (1999) conducted multiple studies to assess the differences in consequences between regret and disappointment after a failed service encounter. They found that regret was more associated with

switching behavior than disappointment, while disappointment was more associated with word-of-mouth than regret.

POST-PURCHASE CONSUMER REGRET

As we have argued, Decision Justification Theory suggests individuals can regret due to a) evaluation of the outcomes and b) evaluation of the process (Connolly and Zeelenberg 2002). We believe these two dimensions are themselves multidimensional, and that the total regret experienced by a consumer is a sum of four components. Within outcome regret, we propose that there are two components: regret due to foregone alternatives and regret due to a change in significance. Within process regret, we also propose two components: regret due to under-consideration and regret due to over-consideration (Fig. 1).

OUTCOME REGRET

Regret due to Foregone Alternatives. When individuals regret due to foregone alternatives, they regret that they have chosen an alternative in favour of another alternative. This is perhaps the most classic understanding of post-purchase regret. When the chosen alternative is believed to be inferior to the foregone alternatives that could have been purchased, people are open to experiencing "regret due to foregone alternatives". A key note concerning this dimension is that individuals can compare their chosen alternative to the *known* foregone alternative and/or *unknown* foregone alternative.

People evaluate outcomes by comparing what they have received to what they could have received (Sugden 1985). They feel regret if the foregone outcome is, or is perceived to be, better than the current outcome. Regret is related to choice and the very nature of choice implies that there were other possibilities that could have been chosen over the selected alternative (Zeelenberg and Pieters 2006). These possibilities can be explicitly known to the buyer or unknown to the buyer in which case the person would have to hypothetically construct these possibilities. Traditionally, researchers assumed that outcomes of the rejected alternative must be known to the buyer in order for regret to occur (Bell 1982). Known foregone alternatives are choices that were available to the buyer at the time of the purchase. (e.g., buying A, when one knew about options B and C).

However, studies have suggested that individuals can experience regret even in the absence of known foregone alternatives.

Ritov and Baron (1995) posit that foregone alternatives can be imagined or hypothetically imagined. Regret is not restricted to circumstances in which the outcomes of the rejected alternatives are always known to the buyer (Tsiros and Mittal 2000).

Tsiros and Mittal (2000) developed a model of post-purchase regret by outlining the antecedents and consequences of consumer regret. They demonstrated that regret can still be experienced even when the rejected alternatives are not known to the consumer. These authors argued that when the rejected alternatives are unknown to the buyer, the individual will trigger their upward CFT to construct hypothetical scenarios. Individuals have the tendency to think of outcome scenarios that are often better than the current scenario (Kahneman and Miller 1986). If a person deploys CFT to imagine a better product than the one that they have already chosen, then this person is likely to regret having chosen the current alternative. Therefore, unknown foregone alternatives are choices that were not available to the buyer at the time of the purchase but were hypothetically imagined following the purchase. In this case, individuals wonder whether or not there could have been better options than the one they purchased. (e.g., buying the only option noticed at the time, later wondering whether other options existed). In short, regret due to foregone alternatives is triggered by choice. This phenomenon exists because individuals may make wrong choices and experience regret afterwards, even if the decision at the time seemed to be the right one.

Regret due to a Change in Significance. Researchers have used means-end theory to explain the goal-directed nature of a particular purchase (Zeithaml 1988). In the context of consumer behaviour, the theory suggests consumers tend to judge products based on the ability of the product to fulfill a desired consequence. The level in which the product has fulfilled its desired consequence will act as a cue to determine if the product was a worthwhile purchase.

Regret due to a change in significance is caused by the individual's perception of diminished product utility from the time of the purchase to a certain point in time after the purchase. When an individual buys a product, there is a certain expected use for it. However, if something happens to make the product less appropriate for that use, or the entire usage situation disappears, then the individual is open to feeling regret due to change in significance. If a product was bought for a specific purpose, but the product was unable to fulfill that purpose, then the individual's perception of the product's utility value has changed from time 1 (the time of purchase) to time 2 (time after purchase). That is, in T1, the product carried a purpose, but in T2, the product's purpose has been diminished. Basically, the focus here is whether or not the product has fulfilled the needs of the consumers, when the need has changed.

One of the main distinctions between regret due to change in significance and regret due to foregone alternatives is that the former does not require the comparing of chosen versus the rejected alternatives. In this dimension, the chosen alternative is being compared to itself, but at a different time dimension (T1 vs. T2). Essentially, the product is being compared to what it was at the time of the purchase (T1) to a time when the buyer's perceived utility value of the product has diminished (T2). (e.g., buying a bottle of wine to take to a party that was cancelled).

This dimension has been never explored in previous regret-related literatures. While some may argue that this is a case of disappointment, the distinction needs to be made between the events that have occurred and the purchase that has been made. The buyer may have been disappointed at the series of events that have occurred, but regrets the actual purchase that was made. This dimension highlights that foregone purchase alternatives are not required for individuals to feel regret after a purchase. Regret due to change in significance is the diminishing change in the individual's perception of product utility value from T1 (the time it was purchased) to T2 (a point in time after the purchase). The greater the utility difference, the greater the regret.

PROCESS REGRET

The two dimensions mentioned above strictly focus on the *outcomes* of a purchase. However, researchers have pointed out that, independent of outcomes, the quality of the decision *process* itself can also engender regret (Connolly and Zeelenberg 2002; Zeelenberg and Pieters 2006). Therefore, it is important to discuss the results of the outcomes separately from the quality of the decision process, and delineate how each of the components separately influences post-purchase consumer regret.

Regret Due to Under-Consideration. When individuals feel regret due to under-consideration, regardless of the purchase outcome, they are sceptical of the heuristic processing that led them to the purchase. Individuals assess the quality of their decision process by examining both implementation/execution and the amount of information they gathered (Janis and Mann 1977). Thus, there are two ways in which individuals can regret due to under-consideration. First, individuals can regret if they feel that they have failed to implement the decision process as they intended it, an intention-behavior inconsistency (Pieters and Zeelenberg 2005). Second, individuals can feel regret if they believe, in hindsight, that they lacked the desired quality and/or quantity of information needed to make a good decision.

People are inherently motivated to do what they set out to do. However, even when behavioral intentions are formed and goals are clearly determined, not all plans go according to plan. Intention-behavior inconsistency is the failure to implement one's behavioral intention in the decision process (Pieters and Zeelenberg 2005). Regret occurs when individuals compare their factual decision process (inconsistent with their behavioral intention) to the counterfactual decision process (consistent with their behavioral intention). When individuals realize that the action that they have taken is not what they intended, they deploy upward CFT to imagine what it would have been like had they executed their desired behavioral intentions. Hence, regret is induced when there is a perceived discrepancy between the intended course of action (how they planned to make a decision) and the actual course of action taken (how they actually made their decision).

Intention-behavioral inconsistency can be due to internally or externally attributed causes. When cause is externally attributed, individuals are likely to be disappointed rather than regretful. When cause is internally attributed, individuals believe they put insufficient effort into the decision, or they deviated from their original intentions through irrational decisions. (e.g., buying the first car that one test drove). Individuals can also feel regret due to under-consideration if they believe, in hindsight, that they lacked the desired quality and/or quantity of information needed in their decision-making process. This differs from behavioral intention inconsistency because even if the decision-making process does go as intended, individuals can still feel regret if, in the post-purchase stage, they feel that they have not done enough to make the best decision. Decisions that were well-justified can sometimes appear to be unjustified at a later point in time (Crawford et al. 2002). This means there are likely situations where individuals feel that they could have done more to change the results, even though at the time of the purchase it seemed to be justified.

A critical distinction needs to be made between regret due to unknown foregone alternatives versus regret due to under-consideration. While the two may appear similar in nature, they are indeed distinct from one another. Thinking about an unknown foregone alternative requires the individual to construct hypothetical products to be compared against the chosen product. Thinking about how one under-considered his/her purchase requires rethinking the buying process. While re-thinking the buying process may lead to the construction of hypothetical products, the two are different from one another because one focuses on comparing the chosen product to a hypothetical product (regret due to foregone alternatives) while the other focuses on comparing the actual decision process to an decision heuristic process (regret due to under-consideration).

In short, regret due to under-consideration is regretting the process of how one arrives at a decision. The consumer can feel regret because what they intended to do was not executed properly and/or the consumer can regret because they feel they should have done more (e.g. more thought, acquire more information, expend more effort, etc.) during decision-making.

Regret Due to Over-Consideration. When individuals regret due to over-consideration, regardless of the outcome, they are regretting that they have put too much time and effort into the buying process. Similar to regret due to under-consideration, this dimension also centers on heuristic processing. However, the critical distinction between the two is that regret due to under-consideration focuses on how one could have done more to *alter* the decision for a better outcome, whereas, regret due to over-consideration focuses on how one could have done less and still achieve the *same* result. Individuals often base their judgment of the quality of their decision process on the amount of information gathered (Janis and Mann 1977). When individuals over-consider their decision process, they are regretting that they have gathered unnecessary information which may or may not have factored into the final result.

In general, more thinking leads to better decisions (Pieters and Verplanken 1995; Pieters and Zeelenberg 2005). Thinking helps individuals search, and weigh the pros and cons of options, which has been known to increase the intention-behavior consistency (Pieters and Verplanken 1995). Thinking also helps individuals achieve a fuller range of objectives, gather more information, and make better arguments in their decision-making process (Pieters and Zeelenberg 2005). Individuals are generally motivated to put extra effort in order to avoid or minimize post-decision regret (Janis and Mann 1977). Therefore, because people behave in a way to reduce future regret, it is common for individuals to avoid or delay their final decision by putting more effort into gathering more information.

However, there comes a threshold where acquiring more information, and expending more effort, does not change or influence the final decision. This means any information that is acquired thereafter can be considered unnecessary and wasteful. Any effort perceived by the consumer as unnecessary effort potentially could be regretted, because the same decision could have been reached with less information and effort. Furthermore, excess information and effort are not the only things that can be regretted when individuals over-consider. Individuals can regret the emotional burden, the cognitive overload, and the stress that was experienced during the decision-making process. (e.g., spending a lot of time looking at alternatives, when the first option was the best choice).

In summary, similar to regret due to under-consideration, regret due to over-consideration is also regretting the process of how one arrives at a decision. Individuals regret having expended too much effort on the decision process, when they could have arrived at the same decision in a shorter amount of time, with less information, or with less effort.

POST-PURCHASE CONSUMER REGRET (PPCR) SCALE DEVELOPMENT

We developed a scale which measures the four components of post-purchase consumer regret as we conceptually defined it above. Previous measures have not sufficed in measuring the multidimensional components of regret, or carried the necessary rigor and the proper validation technique required for developing scales, as proposed by Churchill (1979). Arguably, the closest existing scale that measures experienced regret is the regret experience measure (REM) developed by Creyer and Ross (1999). The REM scale is an 8-item scale that measures level of regret experienced and self-recrimination. However, this measure of regret is uni-dimensional, and it focuses on measuring the level of regret experienced had one chosen differently, and the self-recrimination for selecting the wrong alternative. Other regret scales available were deemed psychometrically insufficient, or were not directly relevant to the consumer behavior context. In this section, we briefly present our scale development process and then discuss the results of our empirical work.

Study 1–Item Generation

A preliminary study involved a focus group of consumers to gain insights in their recent purchasing experience where they regretted a certain purchase. A content analysis of the discussion along with a literature review, brainstorming, and consulting with academics helped generate a total pool of 223 items designed to measure the four facets of post-purchase consumer regret. Following this step, ambiguous items were eliminated as well as those items which were worded with formal academic language, resulting in a revised pool of 174 items.

Study 2–Face Validity

Face validity of the items was assessed in two stages (Bearden, Netemeyer, and Teel 1989). In the first analysis, a marketing faculty was exposed to short descriptions of each of the dimensions and was asked whether or not the item should be retained or removed from the list. Items that received "not applicable" were subsequently removed from the list, leaving us with 153 remaining items. Next, these remaining items were submitted to 10 additional judges (a panel consisting of marketing academics across North America). This panel of judges was also given definitions of each dimension, and were asked to rate each item as "clearly representative", "somewhat representative", or "not representative". For each of the dimensions, items that were deemed to be clearly representative by at least six of the judges were retained. We retained 45 items and the resulting items were arranged in an arbitrary order and interspersed in all subsequent questionnaires to avoid explicit categorization of the dimensions. Each item was formatted into a five-point Likert scale ranging from 1 (strongly disagree) to 5 (strongly agree).

Study 3–Item Refinement

Separate item analysis was performed for the remaining 45 items using the responses obtained from a convenience sample of 174 undergraduate students from several northeastern universities. The students were recruited via an opportunity to win a raffle for a movie gift certificate. The purpose of purification study was to verify the existence of the dimensions and to further reduce the number of items to a manageable number.

The correlation of each item with the total score for each of the four susceptibility dimensions was computed. Items that did not have item-to-total subscale correlations above .50 were deleted. In addition, items that did not have statistically higher correlations with the dimension to which they were hypothesized to belong, in

TABLE 1

FINAL POST-PURCHASE CONSUMER REGRET SCALE

PPCR Scale	EFA	CFA
Regret due to Foregone Alternatives *(Composite Reliability=0.929, AVE=0.765)*		
1. I should have chosen something else than the one I bought.	.782	.862
2. I regret the product choice that I made.	.793	.911
3. I now realize how much better my other choices were.	.714	.824
4. If I were to go back in time, I would choose something different to buy.	.775	.900
Regret due to a Change in Significance *(Composite Reliability=0.885, AVE=0.659)*		
1. I regret getting the product because it was not as important to me as I thought it would be.	.817	.842
2. I wish I hadn't bought the product because it is now useless to me.	.758	.894
3. I regret my purchase because the product never served its purpose.	.707	.786
4. I regret my purchase because I did not need the product.	.804	.714
Regret due to Under-Consideration *(Composite Reliability=0.925, AVE=0.754)*		
1. With more information, I feel that I could have made a better decision.	.758	.862
2. I feel that I did not put enough consideration into buying the product.	.754	.871
3. With more effort, I feel that I could have made a better decision.	.745	.879
4. I regret not putting enough thought into my decision.	.708	.861
Regret due to Over-Consideration *(Composite Reliability=0.928, AVE=0.764)*		
1. I expended too much effort in making my decision.	.856	.815
2. I wasted too much time in making my decision.	.869	.820
3. I think I put too much thought in the buying process.	.894	.933
4. I feel that too much time was invested in getting this product.	.903	.921

comparison with item correlations with the remaining dimension total scores, were also deleted (Ruekert and Churchill 1984). Principal components analysis with varimax rotation was also performed, resulting in a five factor solution. Based on the resulting relative eigenvalues, we retained the first four factors, consisting of items with loadings exceeding .70. These analyses resulted in a reduction of 9 items, leaving 36 items for reliability and confirmatory factor analysis.

The remaining items were examined via confirmatory factor analysis using AMOS version 7.0. First, a confirmatory factor analysis (i.e. a four-factor correlated structure) revealed items with low item reliabilities. In addition, we removed items that potentially cross-loaded onto other dimensions, and we further reduced the items for parsimony. After this refinement, a second confirmatory factor analysis was performed on the remaining 16 items (four items per factor). The four-factor correlated structure fits the data relatively well (*CMIN/DF=1.965, NNFI=.922, CFI=.96, RMSEA=.075*), thereby indicating unidimensionality (Steenkamp and van Trijp 1991). Composite reliability, average variance extracted, and individual item loadings of the 16 retained items (four items per dimension) are listed in Table 1.

DISCUSSION

We have used the foundation provided by Decision Justification Theory to introduce a new theoretical definition of post-purchase consumer regret. Consumers can regret both the outcome and the process of their purchase (Zeelenberg and Pieters 2006). We proposed that subsumed within *outcome* regret, individuals can feel regret due to foregone alternatives and/or feel regret due to a change in significance. Subsumed within *process* regret, individuals can feel regret due to under-consideration and/or feel regret due to over-consideration.

With the PPCR scale we have established a concise measure that makes it easy to capture one's level of post-purchase consumer regret. The three studies operationalized PPCR and validated the scale items. Our results are consistent with our conceptual definition, demonstrating a multidimensional factor structure, as well as adequate reliability.

It is important to note that individuals can experience all dimensions of post-purchase consumer regret, or might just experience one (or none) of the dimensions at a certain given time. Furthermore, individuals can experience a particular dimension of regret at a certain point in time and another dimension of regret a different point in time after purchase. Individuals can also feel different magnitudes of regret arising from each of the dimensions. Therefore, in order to better understand post-purchase consumer regret, it is important to consider each of the dimensions and the magnitude of regret experienced. It is the sum of regret experienced, through each of the four dimensions, that determines how much the individual regrets a purchase.

Future research in this area should focus on continued empirical work with the four dimensions of the PPCR and studying how each of the dimensions functions within a larger nomological network of antecedents and consequences. Additional studies would test convergent and discriminant validity of the dimensions, and also provide evidence of strong nomological and predictive validity. In particular, we encourage researchers to look at post-consumption behaviors such as repeat purchase intentions, change in attitudes toward brands, and complaint behavior. We believe that different dimensions of regret will have unique influences on these post-consumption behavior variables. Also, future research in this area should try to address the following questions. In what circumstances do individuals regret one dimension more than another dimension? Why do individuals feel regret in some ways and not in others? How does time play a role in the magnitude of regret experienced by the individual?

Understanding why consumers regret after a purchase is critical to marketers, as they are constantly looking for ways to minimize the negative experiences experienced by their customers. By having a greater awareness of the different forms of post-purchase regret, businesses can focus on helping individuals attain a better consumption experience. For instance, if marketers know that their customers are experiencing regret primarily due to foregone alternatives, then they can direct their attention to improving their own product and making it more appealing to the customer over other alternatives (e.g. better features, cheaper prices). If they know that their customers are experiencing regret due to a change in significance, then they can direct their attention to devising ways to add more significance to the product (e.g. market multiple uses of the product, add more value to the product, more liberal return policies). If marketers know that their customers are experiencing regret due to process (under-consideration and over-consideration), then they can direct their attention to assisting customers in their decision-making process through helpful customer service, and providing easy accessibility to information to guide them along the way. In sum, if marketers have a better understanding of what is causing consumer to regret over their purchase, then they can place greater emphasis in reducing that particular dimension of regret.

REFERENCES

Bearden, William O., Richard G. Netemeyer, Jesse E. Teel (1989), "Measurement of Consumer Susceptibility to Interpersonal Influence," *Journal of Consumer Research*, 15 (March), 473-81.

Bell, David E. (1982), "Regret in Decision-making under Uncertainty," *Operations Research*, 30 (September-October), 961-81.

_____ (1985), "Disappointment in Decision-making Under Uncertainty," *Operations Research*, 33, 1-27.

Churchill, Gilbert A. Jr. (1979), "A Paradigm for Developing Better Measures of Marketing Constructs," *Journal of Marketing Research*, 16 (February), 64-73.

Connolly, Terry, and Marcel Zeelenberg (2002), "Regret in Decision-making," *Current Directions in Psychological Science*, 11, 212-16.

Crawford, Matthew T., Allen R. McConnell, Amy C. Lewis, and Steven J. Sherman (2002), "Reactance, Compliance, and Anticipated Regret," *Journal of Experimental Social Psychology*, 38, 56-63.

Creyer, H. Elizabeth and William T. Ross Jr. (1999), "The Development and Use of a Regret Experience Measure to Examine the Effects of Outcome Feedback on Regret and Subsequent Choice," *Marketing Letters*, 10 (4), 373-86.

Gilovich, Thomas and Victoria H. Medvec (1994), "The Temporal Pattern to the Experience of Regret," *Journal of Personality and Social Psychology*, 67 (3), 357-65.

Inman, J. Jeffrey, James S. Dyer, and Jianmin Jia (1997), "A Generalized Utility Model of Disappointment and Regret Effects on Post-Choice Valuation," *Marketing Science*, 16 (2), 97-111.

Janis, Irving L. and Leon Mann (1977), *Decision-making: A Psychological Analysis of Conflict, Choice, and Commitment*, New York, NY: The Free Press.

Kahneman, Daniel, and Dale T. Miller (1986), "Norm Theory: Comparing Reality to Its Alternatives," *Psychological Review*, 92 (April), 136-53.

Landman, Janet (1993), *Regret: The Persistence of the Possible*, New York, NY: Oxford University Press.

Pieters, Rik and Bas Verplanken (1995), "Intention-Behavior Consistency: Effects of Consideration Set Size, Involvement and Need for Cognition," *European Journal of Social Psychology*, 25, 531-43.

Pieters, Rik and Marcel Zeelenberg (2005), "On Bad Decisions and Deciding Badly: When Intention Behavior Inconsistency is Regrettable," *Organizational Behavior and Human Decision Processes*, 97 (March), 18-30.

Ritov, Ilana and Jonathan Baron (1995), "Outcome Knowledge, Regret, and Omission Bias," *Organizational Behavior and Human Decision Processes*, 64 (November), 119-27.

Ruekert, Robert W. and Gilbert A. Churchill, Jr. (1984), "Reliability and Validity of Alternative Measures of Channel Member Satisfaction," *Journal of Marketing Research*, 21 (May), 226-33.

Steenkamp, Jan-Benedict E.M. and Hans C.M. van Trijp (1991), "The Use of Lisrel in Validating Marketing Constructs," *International Journal of Research in Marketing*, 8 (4), 283-99.

Sugden, Robert (1985), "Regret, Recrimination, and Rationality," *Theory and Decision*, 19, 77-99.

Tsiros, Michael and Vikas Mittal (2000), "Regret: A Model of Its Antecedents and Consequences in Consumer Decision-making," *Journal of Consumer Research*, 26 (March), 401-17.

Van Dijk, Wilco W. and Marcel Zeelenberg (2002), "Investigating the Appraisal Patterns of Regret and Disappointment," *Motivation and Emotion*, 26 (December), 321-31.

Zeelenberg, Marcel, and Rik Pieters (1999), "Comparing Service Delivery to What Might Have Been: Behavioral Responses to Regret and Disappointment," *Journal of Service Research*, 2 (August), 86-97.

_____ (2004), "Beyond Valence in Customer Dissatisfaction: A Review and New Findings on Behavioral Responses to Regret and Disappointment in Failed Services," *Journal of Business Research*, 57, 445-55.

_____ (2006), "Looking Backward With an Eye on the Future: Propositions toward a Theory of Regret Regulation," in *Judgments over Time: The Interplay of Thoughts, Feelings, and Behaviors*, eds. L.J. Sanna and E.C. Chang, New York, NY: Oxford University Press, 210-29.

Zeelenberg, Marcel, Wilco W. van Dijk, and Antony S.R. Manstead (1998a), "Reconsidering the Relation between Regret and Responsibility," *Organizational Behavior and Human Decision Processes*, 3 (June), 254-72.

Zeelenberg, Marcel, Wilco W. van Dijk, Antony S.R. Manstead, Joop van der Pligt (1998b), "The Experience of Regret and Disappointment," *Cognition and Emotion,* 12 (2), 221-30.

Zeithaml, Valarie (1988), "Consumer Perceptions of Price, Quality and Value: A Means-End Model and Synthesis of Evidence", *Journal of Marketing*, 52 (July), 2-22.

Influencing Willingness to Pay by Supraliminally Priming the Concept of Honesty

Robert Schorn, University of Innsbruck, Austria
Barbara Maurhart, University of Innsbruck, Austria[1]

ABSTRACT

Previous research has shown that priming can be used to influence peoples' perception, evaluations, motivations, and even behavior. Most of these studies have been conducted using laboratory experiments. We examined whether supraliminal priming can be effectively applied to affect peoples' behavior in a real consumption situation. In an experiment to test if supraliminally priming the concept of honesty via "mirrored words" influences peoples' behavior, we found that users of a toilet contributed significantly more money for using the bathroom when being primed with the concept of honesty than when that concept had not been primed. Implications and ethical considerations are discussed.

INTRODUCTION

When James Vicary, in 1957, claimed to have increased Coke sales by 18% and popcorn sales by over 50% by secretly flashing the words "EAT POPCORN" and "DRINK COKE" onto the movie screen at a local theatre, people were outraged and alarmed (Weir 1984). Today, we know that it was just a hoax. Nevertheless, numerous studies have been conducted over the last few decades, especially in social cognition research, to demonstrate that priming can be used to influence peoples' perception, evaluations, motivations, and even behavior (see Bargh 2006; Dijksterhuis, Aarts, and Smith 2005 for an overview). For example, Bargh and Pietromonaco (1982) showed that people previously subliminally primed with words semantically related to hostility rated a stimulus person according to the priming words: the more hostile the words presented earlier, the more negative the impression of the stimulus person became. Maxwell, Nye, and Maxwell (1999) demonstrated that, by priming a consideration for fairness, a seller can increase a buyer's satisfaction without sacrificing profit. In simulated negotiations, participants primed to consider fairness demonstrated more cooperative behavior, making greater concessions that led to faster agreement. Fairness-primed buyers consequently had a more positive attitude toward the seller and expressed significantly greater positive subjective disconfirmation of their expectations. Bargh, Chen, and Burrows (1996) found that participants primed with the concept of rudeness, interrupted the experimenter more quickly and frequently than did participants primed with politeness-related stimuli. Furthermore, participants for whom an elderly stereotype was primed walked slower down the hallway when leaving the experiment than did control participants, consistent with the content of that stereotype. Recently, much attention has been focused on the affect of non-conscious influences on consumer behavior and choice, but the field of consumer research is still largely dominated by the rationale of deliberate and cognitive decision-making processes (Bargh 2002). In terms of the latter, a consumer acting as a result of non-conscious stimuli would be succumbing to "hedonic impulses" (Alba 2000; Baumeister 2002). This study evaluates whether supraliminal priming can be used to influence consumer behavior (non-consciously) in a real consumption situation.

"Priming refers to the presentation of a stimulus that either facilitates or inhibits the processing of a subsequent stimulus. The prime precedes the target and has consequences for how well the target is processed." (Kellogg 1997, 83) Several different types of priming can be distinguished. One basic separation is between direct priming and indirect priming. Direct–or repetition–priming is the facilitation of the processing of a stimulus as a function of a recent encounter with the same stimulus (Cofer 1967; Schacter 1987). In studies in which subjects are free to generate any response they wish to the test stimulus, prior study of items increases the likelihood that those items will be generated as responses. Indirect priming is any change in performance resulting from the presentation of information related in some way (associatively, semantically, graphically, phonemically, or morphologically) to test stimuli (Richardson-Klavehn and Bjork 1988). Here, changes in test results can be observed when information that is related to test stimuli is presented prior to the test. The typical example is the decrease in lexical decision latency as a consequence of presenting associatively or semantically related words prior to the test stimulus; a phenomenon known as associative or semantic priming (Fischler 1977; Meyer and Schvaneveldt 1971). Bargh and Chartrand (2000) refer to three priming techniques: conceptual priming, mindset priming, and sequential priming. In conceptual priming, the activation of mental representations in one context is used to exert a passive, unintended, and nonaware influence in subsequent, unrelated contexts. In mindset priming manipulations, the participant is actively engaged in a goal-directed type of thought in one context, to show that this mindset is more likely to operate later in an unrelated context. Sequential priming techniques test for chronic connections between two representations, across which activation automatically spreads. It is used to study the associative structure of the mind rather than to examine the residual effects of recent experience.

Priming stimuli (or primes) can be delivered in two ways: subliminally or supraliminally. In social cognition research, both forms have been shown to be successful in influencing judgments, motivations, and behaviors (Bargh 1992, 1999). Delivered subliminally, the primes themselves are not accessible to the person's awareness. For instance, they can be presented so weakly or briefly that subjects do not recognize them consciously. If primes are delivered supraliminally, the persons are aware of the primes but not of their potential influence. The "scrambled sentence test" is a very frequently used supraliminal priming technique (Bargh et al. 1996; Srull and Wyer 1979). In an ostensible test to measure language ability, participants are instructed to make coherent, grammatical sentences out of each string of words. The test contains some words related to the concept intended to be primed. Another established supraliminal priming technique is a word-search puzzle where priming words are embedded in a matrix of letters (Bargh et al. 2001). Crossword puzzles are also used to place priming words. While these priming techniques have been used successfully in various laboratory experiments, they seem not to be applicable in most real consumer behavior situations. Our aim was to find and evaluate a priming technique that can be used in real consumption situations, outside the laboratory. A supraliminal priming technique–used in laboratory experiments–but applicable in real consumption situations is where words are mirrored vertically on the baseline. We refer to these words as "mirrored words". Perrig, Wippich, and Perrig-Chiello (1993) used mirrored words in a perceptual priming task. In the learning phase, participants were shown 20 mirrored words for 1.5 seconds each. They were asked

[1]This research was supported by OENB-Jubilaeumsfonds 12012

Advances in Consumer Research
Volume 36, © 2009

FIGURE 1
Priming stimuli: honest, dishonest, and control stimulus

about how many enclosed areas they were able to find in each mirrored word. In a second–seemingly independent–task, they had to identify words in a perceptual identification task. Words that had been presented as mirrored words before were identified more quickly than those not previously presented.

In our study, we examine whether supraliminal priming can be effectively applied to affect peoples' behavior in a real consumption situation. In a field experiment we test whether priming the concept of honesty would cause users of a toilet at a motorway service area to pay the requested contribution (30 cents) by putting the money voluntarily into a box without being obviously observed. Even though we expect people primed with the concept of honesty to contribute more money, we conservatively formulate a two-tailed hypothesis.

H1: There is a significant difference in money contributed for using a toilet between people whose concept of honesty was primed and people whose concept of honesty was not primed.

Guidebooks about affirmation techniques and autosuggestion recommend that affirmations be formulated positively, without negations or a prefix that negates a word because the unconscious does not consider such a prefix. Irrespective of the scientific credibility of these sources, we examine whether using the word "dishonest" as a prime would influence people when paying the requested contribution. This leads to hypotheses two and three:

H2: There is a significant difference in money contributed for using a toilet between people primed with the word "dishonest" and people not primed.
H3: There is a significant difference in money contributed for using a toilet between people primed with the word "dishonest" and people primed with the word "honest".

Finally, we investigate whether there is a difference in money contributed between men and women, leading to our fourth hypothesis:

H4: Men and women differ significantly in money contributed for using the toilet.

METHOD

Participants
Participants were all people (1033 male, 896 female) who visited a toilet in a motorway service area over six consecutive days between 10 am and 1 pm or between 1 pm and 4 pm.

Materials
The priming manipulation took the form of words mirrored vertically over the baseline. Three different priming stimuli were used, constructed using the words "honest," "dishonest", or a meaningless control word (see figure 1).

Before carrying out the experiment, the stimuli were pre-tested in order to find out whether people could detect a stimulus word. None of the 30 pre-test participants recognized a word. Each of the stimuli was printed in black color on a light brown sheet of paper (297 x 210 mm), compatible with the color of the doors of the toilet cubicles. Each stimulus covered about two thirds of the sheet. The stimuli could be seen as posters, picturing some form of art. They were fixed on the inside of each door of the 22 toilets (14 for women, 8 for men) at the motorway service area. Additionally, a sticker (100 x 70 mm) of black print on white background, compatible with the background surface, was fixed above each of the 11 urinals in the men's bathroom. Each stimulus was placed at eye level. At the exit of each bathroom was a box with a sign requesting people to pay 30 cents for using the toilet. People directly encountered the box before leaving the bathroom.

Procedure and design
Our experiment was carried out at the (only) bathroom of a relatively modern and very clean motorway service area, downstairs from the restaurant. People did not recognize that they participated in an experiment. Our independent variable was the kind of priming condition: honest, dishonest, or control condition. Data were collected separately for men and women. One collection box was located at the women's bathroom exit and another at the exit of the men's bathroom. The amount of money people contributed was our dependent variable. Participants were not directly observed, in order to avoid unintended experimenter effects. When people left the bathroom, they came directly to a corridor leading back to the restaurant. Here, the experimenter (disguised as a staff member obviously working on something) counted the people leaving the two bathrooms. After one hour, the money received was counted and the priming condition was changed. Priming conditions were counterbalanced by time of day and day of the week. In total, 160 people (81 male, 79 female) were randomly selected after leaving the bathroom and were questioned about their satisfaction with the bathroom (cleanliness, etc.). They were also asked, whether they noted something strange. If their answer was yes, they were asked to specify it. None of the 160 people asked appear to have recognized a word in the priming stimuli.

RESULTS
Each of the three priming conditions (honest, dishonest, and control) was observed for a total of 12 hours. As we knew the total

TABLE 1
Descriptive statistics for the three priming conditions

Prime	People	Money received in €	€ per person x 1000	Units of observation
Honest	763	27.96	36.64	12
Dishonest	653	21.72	33.26	12
Control stimulus	513	13.82	26.94	10
Total	1929	63.50	32.92	34

amount of money received and the amount of people visiting the bathrooms each hour, we could calculate an average amount (money/person) for each of the 36 hours of observation (dependent variable). During the experiment, a cleaning lady–obviously uninformed about the experiment–removed the collection boxes from both the men's and the women's bathrooms, leaving us with a total of 34 units of observation. For each unit (= hour) of observation we generated a value "€ per person" by dividing the amount of money received within that unit by the amount of people studied within that unit. We call this value "average amount per unit." These values were then used to statistically compare the different priming conditions.

A total of €63.50 was collected from the 1929 people studied (Table 1). The highest average per person donation was when the "honest" stimulus was used (€36.64 per 1000 people).

To test our first hypothesis, we compared the average donation per sampling unit in the "honesty" primed condition with those of the control condition. Since the distribution of the variable "average amount per unit" was determined to be non-normal and the number of values low, we used non-parametric tests. A Mann-Whitney U test revealed a significant difference (z=-2.110, p=.035, 2-tailed) between these two conditions. Participants in the "honesty"-primed condition contributed more money (mean rank=14.17) than did participants in the control condition (mean rank=8.30). This result supports our first hypothesis that there is a difference in contributing requested money for using a toilet between people whose concept of honesty was primed and people whose concept of honesty was not primed. People whose concept of honesty was primed by a supraliminal prime contributed significantly more money for using the bathroom.

The average donation per sampling unit in the "dishonesty"-primed condition was compared with that of the "honesty"-primed condition to test hypothesis two. A Mann-Whitney U test did not reveal a significant difference between these two conditions (z=-1.328, p=.184, 2-tailed). There was no significant difference in contributing money for using a toilet between people primed by the concept of dishonesty and people primed by the concept of honesty.

In order to test our third hypothesis we compared the average donation per sampling unit under the "dishonesty"-primed condition with those of the control condition. The Mann-Whitney U test did not reveal a significant difference between these two conditions (z=-.198, p=.843, 2-tailed). People whose concept of dishonesty was primed did not differ significantly from people whose concept of dishonesty was not primed (control stimulus).

In testing our fourth hypothesis, we found no significant gender difference for the total experiment (two tailed Mann-Whitney U test z=-.034, p=.973), the "honesty"-primed situation (z=-.160, p=.873), the "dishonesty"-primed situation (z=-.241, p=.810), or the control (z=-.313, p=.754).

DISCUSSION

In our experiment to test if supraliminally priming the concept of honesty influences peoples' behavior, we found out that users of a toilet at a motorway service area contributed significantly more money (p=.035) for using the bathroom when being primed with the concept of honesty than when that concept had not been primed. Whereas most priming experiments have been carried out in laboratory situations, we have been able to show that priming can also be applied to real consumption situations.

As many of the established supraliminal priming techniques–like scrambled sentence tests or word search puzzles–seem not to be applicable in most real consumption situations, we have been able to show that mirrored words are both applicable and useful as a priming stimulus. As far as we know, mirrored words have thus far only been employed as priming stimuli in perceptual priming tasks (Hofer 1992; Perrig et al. 1993). We have shown that mirrored words can also be effectively used for conceptual priming tasks. This finding suggests important consequences for the use of supraliminal priming in a variety of consumption environments, including shops, restaurants, and insurance companies, but also in fields such as health care and road safety. Priming for honesty in bathrooms can also be adapted to related situations such as self-service newspaper racks and supermarket checkouts, as well as other situations that seek to maximize honesty; most especially in courts, legal institutions, financial services and tax collection.

Our study only found a significant difference in money contributed between people primed with the concept of honesty and the control group. People primed with the concept of dishonesty did not differ significantly from people primed with the concept of honesty or the control group. One reason for this result could be that the word dishonesty could have been processed non-consciously in an ambivalent manner. It could be that the prefix "dis" was considered differently than the rest of the word, which could have led to the result that some people processed the prime dishonest similar to that of the prime honest. Further research would be necessary to confirm/negate this explanation. A variety of antonyms could be tested: some that differ only by a prefix, as well as others that are completely different, like "crooked" (vs. "honest"). As the amount of money people contributed for using the toilet was quite low in the control group (on average 2.69 cents per person, Table 1), the floor effect could make it difficult to undercut this amount. Another reason for the lack of significant differences could be that people did not face the stimuli very intensively as they were not instructed to do so, as in many other priming experiments. In almost all experiments using visual supraliminal primes, participants were required to deal with the priming stimuli in some way–like writing the words to make sentences in a scrambled sentence test (Bargh et al. 1996) or counting the closed areas of mirrored words (Perrig et al. 1993)–but in our experiment, people were not actively engaged in dealing with the primes. Some people might only have gone to the bathroom to wash their hands or to freshen up and so may not have encountered the priming stimuli (located above the urinals and on toilet doors). Future experiments should attempt to further minimize the number of participants that do not encounter the priming conditions.

This study shows that the behavior of people can be influenced by supraliminal stimuli whose message can not be detected. The effectiveness of our priming experiment also highlights some important ethical considerations. Because stimuli are not consciously detected, the source of the influence is unknown to the individuals that are manipulated. It is impossible to deliberately avoid being exposed to stimuli that are genuinely undetectable. As the stimuli circumvent certain conscious processes–like critical analysis or evaluation of the context of the stimulus–the possibility of conscious counter-control over subliminal effects is minimal. Because non-conscious influences induce attitude and behavior changes without providing information regarding the source of the influence, people are forced to create post-hoc explanations for their attitudes and behaviors, justifying and rationalizing these attitudes and behaviors to themselves and others (Bornstein 1989).

The aim of this article, and of research in priming generally, should not be to identify techniques that allow companies or other organizations to influence people without their consent or awareness, but to show what kinds of influencing techniques work under what conditions and how misuse can be prevented. For instance, to successfully prime it is critical that people are not aware of how the primes might affect them (Bargh 2002). If people are informed about the function of priming techniques, they can have some control over unwanted influences and so allowing impure manipulations to be thwarted. The results of studies concerning the non-conscious manipulation of people should provide the basis for company policies, as well as political decision making, to avoid the misuse of influencing techniques.

REFERENCES

Alba, Joseph W. (2000), "Presidential Address Dimensions of Consumer Expertise or Lack Thereof," in *Advances in Consumer Research*, Vol. 27, ed. Stephen J. Hoch and Robert J. Meyer, Provo, UT: Association for Consumer Research, 1–9.

Bargh, John A. (1992), "Why Subliminality Does Not Matter to Social Psychology: Awareness of the Stimulus versus Awareness of Its Influence," in *Perception without Awareness*, ed. Robert F. Bornstein and Thane S. Pittman, New York: Guilford, 236–255.

_____ (1999), "The Most Powerful Manipulative Messages are Hiding in Plain Sight," *Chronicle of Higher Education*, (January 29), B6.

_____ (2002), "Losing Consciousness: Automatic Influences on Consumer Judgment, Behavior, and Motivation," *Journal of Consumer Research*, 29 (September), 280–5.

_____ (2006), "What have we been priming all these years? On the development, mechanisms, and ecology of nonconscious social behavior," *European Journal of Social Psychology*, Vol. 36, 147–68.

Bargh, John A., and Tanya L. Chartrand (2000), "The Mind in the Middle: A Practical Guide to Priming and Automaticity Research," in *Handbook of Research Methods in Social and Personality Psychology*, ed. Harry T. Reis and Charles M. Judd, Cambridge: Cambridge University Press, 253–85.

Bargh, John A., Mark Chen, and Lara Burrows (1996), "Automaticity of Social Behavior: Direct Effects of Trait Construct and Stereotype Activation," *Journal of Personality and Social Psychology*, Vol. 71, No 2, 230–44.

Bargh, John A., Peter M. Gollwitzer, Annette Lee-Chai, Kim Barndollar, and Roman Troetschel (2001), "The Automated Will: Nonconscious Activation and Pursuit of Behavioral Goals," *Journal of Personality and Social Psychology*, 81 (December), 1014–27.

Bargh, John A. and Paula Pietromonaco, (1982) "Automatic Information Processing and Social Perception: The Influence of Trait Information Presented Outside of Conscious Awareness on Impression Formation," *Journal of Personality and Social Psychology*, Vol. 43, No 3, 437–49.

Baumeister, Roy F. (2002), "Yielding to Temptation: Self-Control Failure, Impulsive Purchasing, and Consumer Behavior," *Journal of Consumer Research*, 28 (March), 670–6.

Bornstein, Robert F. (1989), "Subliminal Techniques as Propaganda Tools: Review and Critique," *Journal of Mind and Behavior*, 10 (Summer), 231–62.

Cofer, Charles N. (1967), "Conditions for the Use of Verbal Associations," *Psychological Bulletin*, 68, 1–12.

Dijksterhuis, Ap, Henk Aarts, and Pamela K. Smith (2005), "The Power of the Subliminal: On Subliminal Persuasion and Other Potential Applications," in *The New Unconscious*, ed. Ran R. Hassin, James S. Uleman, and John A. Bargh, Oxford, NY: Oxford University Press, 77–106.

Fischler, Ira S. (1977), "Semantic Facilitation Without Association in a Lexical Decision Task," *Memory & Cognition*, Vol. 5 (3), 335–9.

Hofer, Daniel (1992), *Unbewusste Verhaltenssteuerung: Funktionsprinzipien perzeptueller Repraesentationen im Lernen*, Regensburg: Roderer.

Kellogg, Ronald T. (1997), *Cognitive Psychology*, London: Sage Publications.

Maxwell, Sarah, Pete Nye, and Nicholas Maxwell (1999), "Less Pain, Same Gain: The Effects of Priming Fairness in Price Negotiations," *Psychology & Marketing*, 16 (October), 545–62.

Meyer, David E. and Roger W. Schvaneveldt (1971), "Facilitation in Recognizing Pairs of Words: Evidence of a Dependence in Retrieval Operations," *Journal of Experimental Psychology*, 90, 227–34.

Perrig, Walter, Werner Wippich, and Pasqualina Perrig-Chiello (1993), *Unbewusste Informationsverarbeitung*, Bern: Huber.

Richardson-Klavehn, Alan and Robert A. Bjork (1988), "Measures of Memory," *Annual Review of Psychology*, Vol. 39, 475–543.

Schacter, Daniel L. (1987), "Implicit Memory: History and Current Status," *Journal of Experimental Psychology: Learning, Memory, and Cognition*, Vol. 13, No. 3, 501–18.

Srull, Thomas K. and Robert S. Wyer, Jr. (1979), "The Role of Category Accessibility in the Interpretation of Information about Persons: Some Determinants and Implications," *Journal of Personality and Social Psychology*, Vol. 37, 1660–72.

Weir, Walter (1984), "Another Look at Subliminal 'Facts'," *Advertising Age*, October 15, 46.

Less is More When Learning By Analogy: The Disruptive Impact of Attribute Information on Consumers' Benefit Comprehension of Really New Products

Amina Ait El Houssi, University of Wollongong, Australia
Kaj Morel, Delft University of Technology, The Netherlands
Erik Jan Hultink, Delft University of Technology, The Netherlands

ABSTRACT

The presented study had two purposes. First, it pursued to demonstrate that it is more effective to use analogies in advertisements for really new products to increase consumers' comprehension of the new product's benefits than not to use analogies. Second, it aimed to test the (counterintuitive) assumption that inclusion of product attribute information in the advertisement in addition to the analogy would actually frustrate benefit comprehension. The results of the experiment showed that advertisements with an analogy lead to greater benefit comprehension than advertisements without an analogy. Further, it is more effective in print advertising in managing consumer learning of the benefits of really new products to use an analogy without than with additional product attribute information. We discuss these findings and outline directions for future research.

INTRODUCTION

New product marketers are constantly seeking ways to ensure that their advertisements not only attract consumers' attention and generate interest, but educates them about their new products' benefits as well (cf. Aaker, Batra, and Myers 1992). Educating consumers is especially relevant in the case of really new products, because such products are relatively complex and often combine several functionalities. As a result, advertisements for really new products typically contain a lot of information. Moreover, this information is likely to consist of technical features and language that consumers are unable or unwilling to understand (Bradley and Meeds 2004; Meeds 2004). In interviews with prospective consumers of several really new products, Veryzer (1998) found that "quite often customers had no experience with the technologies underlying these products and thus they had little or no frame of reference for understanding them" (p.143). Therefore, the communication objective for such really new products should not be on emphasizing the product's new technologies and innovative features. Rather, a more effective communication objective would be to persuade consumers of the new benefits that the new product provides to them (Lee and O'Connor 2003). The question is how marketers should do this?

Recent research in marketing and consumer behaviour has suggested that analogies may be useful to enhance consumer learning of really new products (Ait El Houssi, Morel, and Hultink 2005; Gregan-Paxton, Hibbard, Brunel, and Azar 2002; Moreau, Lehmann, and Markman 2001a; Roehm and Sternthal 2001). Analogies are believed to be effective learning aids because they provide consumers with a familiar frame of reference that helps them to comprehend the unfamiliar new product (Gregan-Paxton and Roedder John 1997). These studies, however, have provided interesting but inconclusive results. Roehm and Sternthal (2001) compared the use of analogy with literal similarity in advertising and demonstrated that messages containing an analogy are better comprehended and are more persuasive, but only when the recipient has expertise with regard to the base. They further found that the effectiveness of an analogy is not only moderated by consumers' ability to map structural relations, but also by the availability of cognitive resources to perform the comparison task. In another

study, Gregan-Paxton et al. (2002) showed that the use of analogy directs consumers' attention to the corresponding relations between target and base. Although it is suggested that the structural relation between the base and the target is more informative about what benefits a product offers (Gregan-Paxton and Roeder John 1997), this assumption has not been empirically tested by Gregan-Paxton et al. (2002). Hence the important question remains whether a focus on corresponding attributes actually enhances consumer's comprehension of the key benefits of a really new product. Answering this question constitutes the first objective of the present study.

Gregan-Paxton et al. (2002) have also shown that analogy triggers selective processing of new product information. They have suggested that analogy can effectively direct consumer's attention to some attributes and away from others. Having said this, we believe that one reason why the use of analogies in previous research (see e.g., Ait El Houssi et al. 2005; Hoeffler 2003; Gregan-Paxton et al. 2002) has not worked as well as expected, may be that the investigated advertisements used attribute information in addition to the analogy. It is proposed here that the inclusion of technical attribute information in an ad copy is likely to prevent consumers from paying sufficient attention to the analogy and thus from forming a concrete representation of the new product and the benefits it offers (Bradley and Meeds 2004). The second objective of the present study is to investigate the plausibility of this proposition by means of an experiment in which consumers' comprehension of a new product's benefits advertised through both an analogy and attribute information is compared with consumers' comprehension of a new product's benefits advertised through an analogy only.

COMPREHENDING NEW PRODUCT BENEFITS THROUGH LEARNING BY ANALOGY

How do analogies assist consumers in comprehending a really new product and in particular its distinctive benefits? In order to answer this question, we first explain how analogical learning is understood to take place.

Analogical Learning

Analogical learning takes advantage of the structural similarities that exist between something that a consumer already knows (i.e., the base domain) and something new to the consumer (i.e., the target domain). It is essential for analogical learning to take place that the knowledge that is transferred from the base to the target domain is predominantly related to a common relational structure (i.e., how the base and target relate to each other) and not to physical resemblance (i.e., how many surface properties the base and target share). Comparing a PDA (target) to a secretary (base), for instance, helps consumers to understand what a PDA does (i.e., performing routine tasks for the individual) in spite of the fact that there are no physical similarities between a PDA and a secretary.

Learning by analogy occurs through a series of three stages: access, mapping and transfer (Gentner 1989; Keane, Ledgeway, and Duff 1994). In the access stage, a relevant base domain becomes active in a person's memory and serves as a source of information about the target. Access is likely to occur spontaneously when the target shares a number of surface properties with the base (Gentner, Ratterman, and Forbus 1993). It is characteristic of analogies that the base and target do not share (many) surface properties. This lack of common surface properties makes spontaneous activation of a relevant base less likely (see, e.g., Gick and Holyoak 1980; Reed, Ernst, and Banerji 1974). Therefore, the base is usually prompted by an external source such as a print ad in a marketing communications setting (Gregan-Paxton et al. 2002; Moreau et al. 2001a/b). Once the base has been activated, its content and structure are compared with the target domain in the mapping stage. Unlike access, mapping is characterised by a preference for relation-based rather than attribute-based comparisons between domains (Clement and Gentner 1991; Gentner et al. 1993). Finally, in the transfer stage, the base and target domains are aligned based on the relational commonalities between the two. It is in this stage that learning occurs when knowledge is moved from the base to the target along the paths that have been created during the mapping stage.

Beneficial Effects of Analogies

The basic premise of our study is that using analogies in appeals for really new products may be the most effective tool to direct consumers' attention to and increase their comprehension of the benefits of a really new product. When processing an analogy, cognitive effort is likely to be allocated to the structural relations between the base and the really new product rather than to attribute similarities between them. Hence, an ad containing an analogy will generate greater attention to structural relations than an ad containing merely attributes. Recent research in marketing confirmed that the use of analogies in product descriptions causes consumers to focus on corresponding relationships between the target and the base and to disregard feature similarity (Gregan-Paxton et al. 2002). The focus on structural relationships enhances comprehension of the distinctive benefits of the really new product because structural relations are thought to be more informative than attributes about the benefits that a new product offers (Gregan-Paxton and Roeder John 1997). Support for this hypothesis is found in studies showing that analogies, rather than literal similarity or mere-appearance comparisons, are generally perceived to be more sound (Gentner et al. 1993) and more goal-relevant (Read 1984). An analogy permits the consumer to focus on the shared data structure (between the base and the target) that is sparse enough to allow the learner to isolate the key principles (Gentner 1989). Continuing with our example, a secretary is known for performing many routine tasks and a comparison with a PDA highlights the shared commonalities implying that like a secretary the PDA also performs many routine tasks. Thus, it is reasonable to assume that an analogy increases the salience of the distinctive benefits of a really new product via corresponding relationships with the base domain thereby simplifying the new product. Separate attributes, on the contrary, may complicate encoding relevant information about a really new product in a coherent way. A really new product described by merely attributes will be difficult to understand since it involves complex relationships between largely unfamiliar attributes, technologies and benefits (Menon and Soman 1999). In sum, the use of analogies is likely to promote understanding of the main benefits of a really new product due to an increased focus on and an enhanced elaboration of the key benefits. We therefore hypothesise:

H1: Consumers will better comprehend the distinctive benefits of a really new product from ads featuring an analogy than from ads not featuring an analogy.

Attribute Information as a Disruptive Factor

In practice, companies often communicate attributes when introducing new products (Hoeffler 2003). Since really new products are relatively complex, advertising of these products is especially prone to technical features and language (Bradley and Meeds 2004; Meeds 2004). Including attribute information to an ad containing an analogy may be very demanding for consumers, because most consumers do not have the knowledge to evaluate such technical information. Previous research has demonstrated that even consumers with expertise in the domain of a really new product experience difficulties with comprehending and appreciating the benefits of this type of products (Moreau et al. 2001). The inclusion of technical characteristics of a really new product may induce consumers to focus on what is not known (Lee and O'Connor 2003) and thus impose significant learning requirements upon the consumer (Lehmann 1997).

Roehm and Sternthal (2001) offered evidence that the processing of an analogy is a resource-demanding task. This is because analogies rely on the mapping of structural relations that can be difficult to detect and resource demanding to map. When technical attribute information is presented in an ad that also contains an analogy, consumers´ cognitive resources are used to search memory for representations that are capable of making sense of the highly unfamiliar product attributes. Simultaneously, however, substantial resources must be allocated to the processing of the analogy if the analogy is to be successful (Roehm and Sternthal 2001). In other words, consumers' cognitive resources must be divided over the task of comprehending the technical characteristics of the really new product on the one hand, and the task of comprehending the analogy on the other. When the former task demands a great percentage of the available resources, comprehension of the analogy may be compromised. If this happens, the merits of using an analogy are likely to be reduced or even nullified. In support of this account, Gregan-Paxton et al. (2003) found that consumers who processed advertisements containing an analogy recalled significantly fewer new product features than those who processed advertisements without an analogy. In short, we hypothesize that the positive effects of the use of analogies on benefit comprehension will be weakened by the inclusion of attribute information in the advertisement. Hence, hypothesis 2 reads:

H2: Consumers will better comprehend the distinctive benefits of a really new product when it is advertised through an analogy only than through an analogy plus attribute information.

METHOD

Participants

Participants were 122 students from a Dutch high school who participated voluntarily. Sixty-one percent was female and the average age was 16.6 years. They were recruited at the school during breaks and free periods. High school students were selected as they were likely to be interested in the new products examined and they are less likely to have a special interest or expertise in advertising.

Design and Stimuli

The study employed a single-factor (message type: attributes only, analogy only, analogy plus attributes) between-subject design. The design was applied to two really new products. The experimental treatment consisted of exposure to one of the message types for one of the two products. The PH 530 is a mobile phone

TABLE 1
LIST OF THE PRODUCT CHARACTERISTICS OF THE PH 530 AND RP 530

	The PH 530...	The RP 530...
1.	is made of synthetic material[f].	is made of synthetic material[f].
2.	has a talk time of 6 hrs max[a].	has a microcomputer[a].
3.	makes it possible to create your own music[b].	translates words[b].
4.	has a melody editor[am].	has a scanner[am].
5.	has an audio recorder[am].	has a speech function[am].
6.	makes it possible to create your own ring tones[b].	spells words[b].
7.	has exchangeable covers[a].	has a dictionary Dutch-English / English-Dutch[am].
8.	has a standby time 300 hrs max[a].	has a summary function[a].
9.	makes it possible to mix music[b].	gives the correct pronunciation of words[b].
10.	has FM radio[am].	comes with a headset[a].
11.	is for sale online[f].	is for sale online[f].

[a] Attribute of the product not mentioned in the body copy text.
[am] Attribute of the product mentioned in the body copy text.
[b] Benefit of the product.
[f] Filler.

with music functionality to mix and create music and ring tones. The RP 530 is a portable pen-like reading device that provides definitions, spelling and pronunciation of words. These two products were selected because they were unfamiliar to participants and because sound analogies were available.

Six different print ads were developed corresponding to the experimental conditions for the two really new products (see Appendix). All versions of the ad were constructed to be as similar as possible to eliminate the lay-out of the ad as a possible confound. No brand names were provided because we did not want participants' judgments to be based on such peripheral cues (Ozanne, Brucks, and Grewal 1992). The original product names (i.e., ReadingPen and Philips 530) were changed to fictitious names (i.e., RP 530 and PH 530, respectively) in order to minimise associations regarding the brand or product name. The ad for the attribute condition and the analogy plus attributes condition consisted of a headline at the top of the page, a coloured picture of the new product at the centre of the page, and a body copy text at the bottom of the page. The analogy was manipulated in the headline (i.e., PH 530: "Be your own DJ"; RP 530: "With the RP 530 you always have your language teacher close at hand"). The body copy text described general features of the new product. The ad version for the analogy only condition lacked the body copy text containing the product attributes.

Procedure

Each participant received a booklet containing the instructions, stimulus and measures. To stimulate realistic viewing conditions, participants were asked to view the ad as they would normally do when reading a magazine. They were allowed to examine the ad at their own pace and they could freely turn back to the ad while filling out the questionnaire. After participants completed the questionnaire, the purpose of the experiment was explained. The whole procedure took less than 10 minutes.

Measures

Benefit comprehension. Inspired by the measure of Roehm and Sternthal (2001), participants were given a list of 11 character-

istics of the advertised products presented in random order (see table 1). This list resulted from a literature search into the attributes and benefits of both new products. Participants were asked to tick the three main characteristics *that were clarified by the ad for the new product* from the list. To reduce possible primacy and recency effects, the first and last characteristic on the list were fillers. Apart from the fillers, the list included three distinct benefits of the new product, three attributes that were presented in the body of the text, and three attributes that the advertised product possessed but that were not mentioned in the ad. The number of benefits from the list marked by participants, ranging from zero to three, determined the degree of participants' comprehension of the new product benefits.

Product familiarity. The use of an analogy is thought to be more effective when consumers have limited or no prior knowledge of the target product. Therefore, participants rated their familiarity with the really new product on a two-item scale ($r=.64$, $p<.001$) as an additional check that product familiarity was indeed low, as was observed in the pretest: "How familiar are you with the [product]?" (1="not familiar at all"; 7="highly familiar"), and "Have you ever read, seen or heard anything about the [product]?" (1="never"; 7="very often").

Product interest. To ensure the relevance to the sample group participants were asked to rate the extent to which they were interested in the new product presented in the ad on three items ($\alpha=.84$): 1="not interesting at all"/7="very interesting", 1="dislike it very much"/7="like it very much", and 1="does not interest me at all"/7="interests me very much".

Results

To ensure the selected products were relevant to high school students interest in the advertised product was measured. Results show that participants were equally interested in both products (PH 530: 4.5, RP 530: 4.5; $F(1,121)=.04$ $p=.85$). Product familiarity was measured to control for the degree of participants' familiarity with the new product and an insignificant relationship with benefit comprehension was found (PH 530: $F(1,62)=2.26$, $p=.14$; RP 530: $F(1,58)=.75$, $p=.39$). Product familiarity was therefore not included as a covariate in testing the hypotheses. In order to test whether ads

TABLE 2
MEANS OF DEPENDENT VARIABLE IN EACH OF THE EXPERIMENTAL CONDITIONS

	PH 530 (n= 63)			RP 530 (n=59)		
	Attributes only	Analogy plus attributes	Analogy only	Attributes only	Analogy plus attributes	Analogy only
Benefit comprehension[1]	.24[a]	1.05[b]	1.76[c]	.56[a]	.73[a,b]	1.32[b]

[1] Ratings on benefit comprehension ranged in score from 0 to 3. Higher means indicate higher scores on the variable.
[a, b, c] Different superscripts indicate which means differ significantly from each other.

containing an analogy generated higher understanding of the benefits of the really new products than ads not containing an analogy (H1), an ANOVA was run separately for both products with message type as the independent variable and benefit comprehension as the dependent variable. Table 2 presents the means of the dependent variable for the experimental conditions for both the PH 530 and RP 530. The analysis yielded a significant main effect for message type for the PH 530 (Attributes: M=.24; Analogy plus attributes: M=1.05; Analogy: M=1.76; $F(2,62)$=25.63 p< .01) and for the RP 530 (Attributes: M=.56; Analogy plus attributes: M=.73; Analogy: M=1.32; $F(2,58)$=4.55, p< .05). For the PH 530, a Tukey post-hoc comparison test showed that all differences were significant (Analogy plus attributes vs. Attributes: *mean difference*=.81, p< .01; Analogy vs. Attributes: *mean difference*=1.52, p< .01; Analogy vs. Analogy plus attributes: *mean difference*=.71, p< .01). For the RP 530, the Tukey post-hoc comparison test revealed a significant difference between the analogy only condition and the attributes only condition (*mean difference*=.76, p< .05). The difference between the analogy only and analogy plus attributes conditions was marginally significant (*mean difference*=.59, p=.06). In short, for both really new products, ads featuring an analogy increased benefit comprehension significantly more than ads not featuring an analogy, confirming hypothesis 1. In addition, for the mobile phone, the ad featuring only an analogy boosted benefit comprehension significantly more than the ad featuring an analogy plus attributes. A similar, but not-significant difference was observed for the ReadingPen. Hypothesis 2, therefore, needs to be rejected for the RP 530, but not for the PH 530.

GENERAL DISCUSSION

The presented study had two purposes. First, it pursued to demonstrate that it is more effective to use analogies in advertisements for really new products to increase consumer comprehension of the distinctive benefits of the new product than not to use analogies. Second, it aimed to test the (counterintuitive) assumption that inclusion of product attribute information in the advertisement in addition to the analogy would actually frustrate benefit comprehension. The rationale for this assumption is that inclusion of relatively complex technical attribute information in an advertisement requires consumers to spend a disproportional part of their available processing resources to it in order to comprehend it. As a result, limited attention is dedicated to comprehension of the analogy, decreasing its potential beneficial effects on product benefit comprehension.

With respect to the first purpose, the results showed that advertisements with an analogy lead to greater benefit comprehen-

sion than advertisements without an analogy. These findings provide support for our argument that consumers who process an analogy focus on the relational structures that exist between a base and a target, and that these relational structures are more informative about what benefits a really new product offers than attribute information. Regarding the second purpose, the results showed that ads featuring only an analogy had a stronger positive effect on benefit comprehension than ads featuring an analogy plus attribute information, especially for the mobile phone.[1] This effect may be explained by the availability of cognitive resources theory (Roehm and Sternthal 2001). These authors argue that combining attribute information with an analogy distracts attention away from an analogy, thereby leaving less cognitive resources available for elaborating on the analogy. Indeed, in their study, Roehm and Sternthal found that experts only showed greater comprehension of an analogy and were more persuaded by it when they were able to devote substantial cognitive resources to it. When insufficient cognitive resources were made available for processing the analogy, its beneficial effects were absent.

Although the cognitive resources theory seems a likely candidate to explain our findings, we cannot be too sure about it as participants in our experiment could spend as much time as they liked on processing the ads. Under these conditions, participants had ample opportunity to pay attention to the analogy in spite of the presence of attribute information. Of course, the question remains whether participants will spend as much attention to an analogy when presented with attribute information as they would in the alternative situation where there is only the analogy to process. In the latter situation, participants confronted with the line "Be your own DJ" in the ad for the PH 530 mobile telephone, for instance, would be forced to come up with their own inferences regarding the meaning of this claim. Given the nature of this claim, such inferences would most probably constitute common relations between the base (i.e., a DJ) and the target (i.e., the PH 530) rather than specific attribute information. The fact that participants have to come up with these inferences themselves without any additional help, in contrast to the situation in which attribute information is available, may cause them to experience greater comprehension of the distinctive benefits. Future research is necessary to establish which explanation is most appropriate for our findings.

---

[1] In a pilot study similar to this experiment with a different sample (n=123), we also found significantly higher benefit comprehension for the ads featuring only an analogy than ads featuring an analogy plus attributes. This finding thus appears to be rather robust.

An interesting finding that has not been reported earlier, but that should be mentioned here is that although the ads containing an analogy only scored higher on consumer benefit comprehension, consumers found this ad less informative than the ad containing an analogy plus attributes. This finding is surprising because it suggests that while consumers perceive attribute information to be informative, inclusion of such information in an ad with an analogy actually leads to lower product benefit comprehension. This finding may be the result of a kind of 'more is better' heuristic that consumers apply and that, as is the case with most heuristics, is generally effective. In case of the particular circumstances that were investigated in this study more information appears to be worse.

IMPLICATIONS FOR MARKETING AND NEW PRODUCT DEVELOPMENT

This research contributes to a better understanding of consumer comprehension of new product benefits in the context of really new products. Specifically, the results suggest that the use of analogies in ads for these products improves consumer comprehension of really new product benefits, and that adding attribute information to an ad containing an analogy lowers rather than improves consumer comprehension. These results have important implications for marketers responsible for the launch process (or the marketing communications) of really new products. As really new products tend to be complex and consist of several technical features that consumers often do not understand, managers should resist the temptation to communicate the product's new technologies and innovative features to consumers as this communication strategy will only confuse consumers and makes them less likely to adopt. A more appropriate launch strategy would focus on the really new product's distinctive benefits. Our study shows that analogies can be helpful in conveying these benefits to consumers. In order for such a strategy to be successful, companies should spend sufficient time on identifying an analogy that is sound; i.e., a comparison that is strong enough so that the consumer can infer relevant benefits from the base to the really new product. The choice of such an appropriate analogy is not easy. The soundness-rating task of Gentner et al. (1993) and the task that we employed may help companies to identify such strong analogies.

When companies have identified a sound analogy it may be better to only include this analogy in the ad for the really new product without adding attribute information as the results in our experiment show. Although it may seem intuitively more logical that analogies will serve as the "the explanatory context" for the complex attributes (Bradly and Meeds 2004), our findings tell another story. Consumers usually spend little time on processing an ad. According to Chisolm (1995) newspaper ads are looked at for an average of 0.84 seconds. It may therefore be more useful when consumers spend this limited time and their available cognitive resources on processing the analogy, rather than be distracted by the often long list of technical features.

Overall, our research provides valuable information for marketers on how consumers react to really new products. The results reinforce a broader strategic lesson that marketers should prepare the customer cognitively for really new products (Hoeffler 2003; Moreau et al. 2001b). This cognitive preparation can, for example, be achieved by visualisation exercises (Dahl and Hoeffler 2004) but also by the use of sound analogies as our results show. Although the last word has surely not been written on the use of analogies in communicating really new product benefits, our results showed that a DJ and a language teacher were helpful in comprehending the distinctive benefits of a mobile phone with music functionality and a portable pen-like reading device that provides definitions, spell-

ing and pronunciation, respectively. We are looking forward to new research that will investigate if and when other analogies such as, for example, a guardian angel or a sheep are helpful in explaining the distinctive benefits of a car safety protection system or an autonomous lawn mower to consumers, thereby hopefully improving the market success of such innovative products.

REFERENCES

Aaker, David. A., Rajeev Batra, and John G. Myers (1992), *Advertising Management* (4th ed.). Englewood Cliffs: Prentice Hall.

Ait El Houssi, Amina, Kaj P.N. Morel, and Erik J. Hultink (2005), "Effectively communicating new product benefits to consumers: The use of analogy versus literal similarity," In *Advances in Consumer Research*, Vol. 32, ed. Geeta Menon and Akshay R. Rao, Duluth, MN: Association for Consumer Research, 554-559.

Bradley, Samuel D. I. and Robert Meeds (2004), "The effects of sentence-level context, prior word knowledge, and Need for Cognition on information processing of technical language in print ads," *Journal of Consumer Psychology*, 14 (3), 291-302.

Chisolm, Jim (1995), "Does color make a difference?," *Admap*, December, 17-21.

Clement, Catherine A. and Derdre Gentner (1991), "Systematicity as a Selection Constraint in Analogical Mapping," *Cognitive Science*, 15 (January), 89-132.

Dahl, Darren W. and Steve Hoeffler (2004), "Visualizing the self: Exploring the potential benefits and drawbacks for new product evaluation," *Journal of Product Innovation Management*, 21 (July), 259-267.

Gentner, Dedre (1989), "The mechanisms of analogical transfer," In *Similarity and Analogical Reasoning* ed. Stella Vosniadou and Andrew Ortony. Cambridge: Cambridge University Press,199-242.

Gentner, Dedre, Mary Jo Ratterman, and Kenneth D. Forbus (1993), "The roles of similarity in transfer: Separating retrievability from inferential soundness," *Cognitive Psychology*, 25 (October), 524-575.

Gick, Mary L. and Keith J. Holyoak (1980), "Analogical problem solving," Cognitive Psychology, 12 (July), 306-355.

Gregan-Paxton, Jennifer, Jonathan D. Hibbard, Frédéric F. Brunel, and Pablo Azar (2002), "So That's What That is: Examining the Impact of Analogy on Consumers' Knowledge Development for Really New Products," *Psychology & Marketing*, 19 (June), 533-550.

_____ and Deborah Roedder John, (1997), "Consumer learning by analogy: A model of internal knowledge transfer," *Journal of Consumer Research*, 24 (December), 266-284.

Hoeffler, Steve (2003), "Measuring preferences for really new products," *Journal of Marketing Research*, 40 (November), 406-420.

Keane, Mark T., Tim Ledgeway, and Stuart Duff (1994), "Constraints on Analogical Mapping: A Comparison of Three Models," *Cognitive Science*, 18 (July), 387-438.

Lee, Yikuan and Gina C. O'Connor (2003), "The impact of communication strategy on launching new products: The moderating role of product innovativeness," *Journal of Product Innovation Management*, 20 (January), 4-21.

Lehmann, Donald (1997), "A different game: Setting the stage" in: *A different game: Really new products, evolving markets, and responsive organizations*, ed. Page Moreau, Boston: Marketing Science Institute report No. 97-118

APPENDIX A

Example of the ad for the PH 530

Attributes only condition

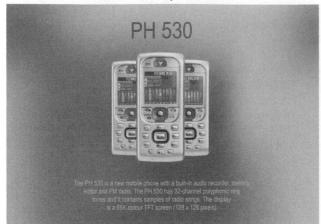

Analogy plus attributes condition

Analogy only condition

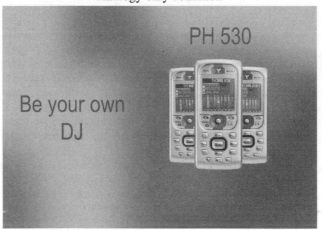

Meeds, Robert (2004), "Cognitive and attitudinal effects of technical advertising copy: the roles of gender, self-assessed and objective consumer knowledge," *International Journal of Advertising*, 23 (3), 309-335.

Menon, Satya and Dilip Soman (1999), "Managing consumer motivation and learning: Harnessing the power of curiosity for effective advertising strategies," Working paper of the Marketing Science Institute report No. 99-100.

Moreau. Page., Donald R. Lehmann, and Arthur B. Markman, (2001a), "Entrenched Knowledge Structures and Consumer Responses to New Products," *Journal of Marketing Research*, 38 (February), 14-29.

_____ Arthur B., Markman, Donald R. Lehmann, (2001b), "'What is it?' Categorization Flexibility and Consumers' Response to Really New Products," *Journal of Consumer Research*, 27 (March), 489-498.

Ozanne, Julie L., Merrie Brucks and Dhruv Grewal (1992), "A study of information search behavior during the categorization of new products," *Journal of Consumer Research*, 18 (March), 452-463.

Read, Stephen (1984), "Analogical reasoning in social judgment," *Journal of Personality and Social Psychology*, 46 (January), 14-25.

Reed, S.K., Ernst, G.W., & Banerji, R. (1974). The role of analogy in transfer between similar problem states. *Cognitive Psychology*, 6 (July), 436-450.

Roehm, Michelle L. and Brian Sternthal, (2001), "The Moderating Effect of Knowledge and Resources on the Persuasive Impact of Analogies", *Journal of Consumer Research*, 28 (September), 257-272.

Veryzer, Robert W., Jr. (1998), "Key factors affecting customer evaluation of discontinuous new products," *Journal of Product and Innovation Management*, 15 (March), 136-150.

The Role of Exploration in Creating Online Shopping Value

Catherine Demangeot, University of Strathclyde Business School, UK
Amanda J. Broderick, Coventry University Business School, UK

ABSTRACT

This study draws attention to the integrating role of exploration in online shopping. Online, the shopping experience, product search and product information search all happen through the exploration of different pages of a website. A survey among 301 respondents who first navigated an online bookstore for eight minutes was analyzed using structural equation modeling. Results show that exploratory potential (the perceived ability of a retail website to provide scope for further exploration) plays a central role in creating utilitarian and hedonic value, which in turn contribute to site commitment. Further, sense-making potential only produces utilitarian value if mediated by exploratory potential, thus further reinforcing the notion that exploratory potential is the real 'killer attribute' of a retail website.

INTRODUCTION

This paper demonstrates the importance of exploratory potential for online research by examining its explanatory power on shopping behavior. Environmental psychologists Kaplan and Kaplan (1982) suggest that exploration is, alongside sense-making, a major human need in an environment. Thus, if one considers the screen on which the successive pages of a retail website are displayed as an environment, consumers perceive the succession of pages in terms of their exploratory potential and their sense-making potential (Demangeot and Broderick, forthcoming). Exploratory potential is defined as the perceived ability of the site to provide scope for further exploration over and beyond what is visible to consumers on the page they are viewing, and sense-making potential is defined as the perceived ability of a retail website to facilitate the consumer's orientation, navigation and task accomplishment.

Exploration can apply to the retail environment, the shopping experience, the product range available on the website, or the information available about a particular product. It can happen at the level of an individual page, whose different components and overall design can be inviting, and at the level of the whole site, when the depth of content prompts the discovery of more material and the overall 'feel' of the site enriches the navigation experience. Thus, this paper contends that exploration is an important concept in studying online consumer behavior, because it reflects the manner in which, fundamentally, the shopping experience and product information search take place in the online context, as a result of the internet medium's characteristics.

Most studies of online consumer behavior have echoed discrete streams of the consumer behavior literature, focusing on separate elements of the overall shopping experience. In particular, Hoffman and Novak (1996) discuss the distinction between surfers and goal-directed online users, echoing the distinction made by Bloch, Ridgway, and Sherrell (1989) between browsing and pre-purchase information search. Klein (1998) and Li, Daugherty, and Biocca (2001) have considered the manner in which products may be experienced differently online and offline, adding to the literature concerned with different types of product experiences (Hoch, 2002; Singh, Balasubramanian, and Chakraborty, 2000; Wright and Lynch, 1995). Several authors have also considered the atmospheric qualities of online shopping environments (e.g. Eroglu, Machleit, and Davis, 2003; Richard, 2005), leaning on the extensive body of literature on the use of the 'silent language' of environmental cues to produce desirable consumer responses (Kotler,

1973; Mehrabian and Russell, 1974; Turley and Milliman, 2000). However, none of these studies takes account of the fact that in an online context, the processes of shopping, assessing product range and gathering product information are one and the same, consisting of clicks and searches.

In this paper, the concept of exploration is used to integrate these different streams, reflecting the reality that when shopping online, information search, product experience and store navigation are performed in the same manner. The paper investigates the behavioral consequences of the exploratory potential of a retail website. It first outlines the study's conceptual framework, before presenting the method and measures chosen. The main results are reported and implications are drawn. Finally, limitations are acknowledged and directions for further research suggested.

CONCEPTUAL FRAMEWORK

Online exploration

The rationale for studying the concept of online exploration stems from the common manner in which online, consumers shop, navigate the virtual environment, find products and gather product information.

Online, the process of acquiring product information and shopping generally is fundamentally different from offline. Because it is not possible to survey a whole website at once, consumers have to find their way, form impressions and gather information by progressing through consecutive clicks and searches. Besides, electronic data is stored and can be retrieved in a manner which gives shoppers access to quasi-unlimited amounts of information from a variety of sources (the marketer, other users, experts, opinion leaders etc.). The data can be accessed immediately (via competently-executed searches) or can facilitate, through a series of hyperlinks, in-depth information gathering, to browse or make a purchase decision. Thus, the scrolling up or down of long pages or the clicking of successive hyperlinks are different forms of exploration, of the virtual shop, of the product range or of a particular product's information. Offline, the gathering of information from different sources is carried out as a series of discrete activities (reading a review, visiting a shop to ask questions to the sales assistant, consulting a colleague or friend); it involves different people and takes place in different locations. Shopping online can encompass, in the same locus, the simultaneous performance of activities which, offline, are separate in time and place. The ability to do this is likely valued by consumers, since it greatly reduces the effort and costs of searching for information (Nelson, 1974).

Information can be accessed at very little cost and in any sequence, because searches can return both the expected product or information, and a series of alternatives, and because individual product pages often provide links to other products. Thus, the distinction between browsing and pre-purchase information search is less pronounced online than offline. Consequently, the distinction in the literature between browsing and pre-purchase information search (Bloch et al., 1989), may be less relevant online. In fact, consumers likely switch from one mode to the other during the course of one shopping navigation, committing some information to memory (or, for instance, to the website's 'wish list') while concurrently deciding to make a particular purchase. The concept of exploration encompasses both motives.

The activity of shopping and the products for sale are experienced differently online and offline in two major ways. First, the online retail environment itself is less intuitive than a real shop; it is only revealed to the consumer one page at a time, and navigated virtually, with the help of informational cues. Hence, a sense of the 'depth' of the website and its product range is acquired not through a visual assessment of the volume of the store or a walk around the aisles, but by calling up a succession of two-dimensional pages. To move on from the scene and information on the screen, it is necessary to click on a hyperlink or perform a search. The concept of exploration is appropriate because it accounts for the fact that online, retail environment, products and product information do not appear to consumers all at once, but they are explored in the same manner, by calling up a succession of pages or scrolling up and down the same page.

Second, the products are not physically present, and experiencing them consists in clicking on different parts of a screen, to look at different images, perhaps simulate their manipulation (as, in the case of cameras, clicking on a hotspot to zoom in or take a photograph), watching a video or obtaining more textual information. Klein (1998) shows how goods which offline cannot be experienced before they are purchased, may, online, have more attributes which can be searched and assessed. Similarly, online user reviews enable consumers to obtain a vicarious experience of goods such as experiential goods, which can be difficult to assess offline (Varlander, 2007). Further, Senecal, Kalczynski, and Nantel (2005) found that consumers who consult product recommendations display a more complex shopping behaviour (in terms of number of pages visited, the linearity of the navigation pattern, and the number of product pages visited) than those who did not consult recommendations, suggesting that they use product recommendations as just one of several factors contributing to their decisions. This behavior is different from offline, where recommendations are often used to reduce decision-making effort and time (Solomon 1986).

Demangeot and Broderick (forthcoming) have conceptualized exploratory potential to reflect four dimensions: (1) *visual impact*, defined as the attention-grabbing, aesthetic visual diversity of individual pages; (2) *experiential intensity*, defined as the ability of the website to produce an involving shopping experience; (3) *marketer informativeness*, defined as the extensiveness of marketer information available on the site; and (4) *non-marketer informativeness*, defined as the extensiveness of product information available on the site, which originates from non-marketer sources, and is used differently than marketing information by consumers (Solomon, 2004). In essence, visual impact and experiential intensity describe the shopping and environmental exploration, while marketer informativeness and non-marketer informativeness concern the informational exploration. Further, the distinction between visual impact and experiential intensity reflects the distinction between perceptions at the level of an individual page and at the level of the entire navigation, experienced as a succession of pages. Other studies have considered the entertaining (e.g. Kim and Stoel, 2004), aesthetic (e.g. Yoo and Donthu, 2001) or informational (e.g. Loiacono, Watson, and Goodhue, 2007) qualities of retail websites. However, the construct of exploratory potential, while encompassing these three dimensions, has the advantage of integrating them since they are all apprehended by consumers through the same process of exploration. Therefore, they are expected to have a common core, motivated by people's fundamental need to explore environments (Kaplan and Kaplan, 1982). Demangeot and Broderick's (forthcoming) study found empirical support to the conceptualization of exploratory and sense-making potential as higher-order constructs.

They conceptualized sense-making potential as reflecting two dimensions: (1) *page clarity*, defined as "the ease with which one can grasp the organization of the scene" (Kaplan, 1992); and (2) *site architecture*, defined as the shopper's perception of the organization of the different pages of the website as a coherent, understandable whole. The distinction between the two dimensions again reflects the distinction between the level of an individual web page and the succession of pages visited during a shopping navigation.

There is an obvious tension between the needs to make sense and to explore, since attempts to facilitate sense-making can reduce an environment's exploratory potential and vice versa. However, both needs have to co-exist: while familiarity is sought after, it also breeds contempt (Kaplan and Kaplan 1982), and exploration satisfies the need for stimulation (Berlyne, 1960).

Several studies using the Technology Acceptance Model (Davis, Bagozzi, and Warshaw, 1989) have found an antecedent-consequence relationship between the model's two main constructs: perceived ease of use and perceived usefulness (Henderson and Divertt, 2003; Karahanna and Straub, 1999). Ease of use is similar, conceptually, to sense-making potential, and usefulness is similar to exploratory potential. It is possible that, as is the case between ease of use and usefulness, sense-making potential is an antecedent of exploratory potential, because the online environment needs to make sense first, before its exploratory qualities can be apprehended fully. Thus:

H1: A retail website's sense-making potential is a predictor of its exploratory potential.

Online exploration and shopping value

Value is considered as a main outcome of shopping experiences (Babin, Darden, and Griffin, 1994; Holbrook, 1986). Since people shop to satisfy a variety of needs, some of which are independent of the acquisition of products (Bloch et al., 1989; Tauber, 1972), shopping value encompasses an appreciation of the whole experience rather than just the success of the shopping trip or navigation with regard to product acquisition (Babin et al., 1994; Diep and Sweeney, 2008). The outcome of a shopping trip or navigation may result in both utilitarian and hedonic shopping value (Babin et al., 1994). Utilitarian value is defined as "an overall assessment of functional benefits and sacrifices" (Overby and Lee, 2006, p. 1161) and hedonic value as "an overall assessment of experiential benefits and sacrifices, such as entertainment and escapism" (Overby and Lee, 2006, p. 1161). Thus, consumers shopping online can potentially draw utilitarian value, if they have gained more from the navigation than the costs expended (financial, time, cognitive), as well as hedonic value, if the experience was rewarding in its own right.

The exploration of landscapes is involving (Kaplan and Kaplan, 1982) and similarly, shopping navigations can be involving due to the medium's potential for interactivity and vividness (Fortin and Dholakia, 2005). More complex information displays (Gammack and Hodkinson, 2003) and image interactivity (Kim, Fiore, and Lee, 2007) increase attention and involvement. The mere presence of involvement suggests that the experience is hedonically rewarding (Bloch and Richins, 1983). Consumers may be able to enjoy a lively interaction with the website or with the product without proceeding with a purchase, and this in itself can produce hedonic value (MacInnis and Price, 1987). Exploratory potential can provide further product knowledge for its own sake, and be perceived as an intrinsically rewarding experience. Thus:

H2: A retail website's exploratory potential provides consumers with hedonic value.

FIGURE 1
CONCEPTUAL MODEL

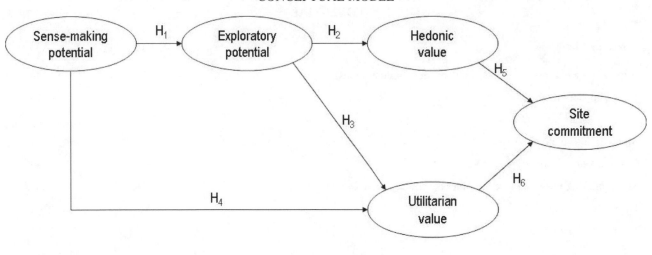

Furthermore, the involvement elicited by the exploratory potential of a website makes consumers pay more attention (Celsi and Olson, 1988), which facilitates instrumental tasks (Hoffman and Novak, 1996). Cognitively involved consumers are known to increase information processing abilities and search for more information (Beatty and Smith, 1987). Further exploration of the site and interest in looking at more products and more information can lead consumers to find more suitable products, thus making the shopping trip also more successful in utilitarian terms (Kroeber-Riel, 1979). Thus:

H3: A retail website's exploratory potential provides consumers with utilitarian value.

Further, when consumers perceive the website to be easy to make sense of, they are likely to find products or product information more easily. As they accomplish what they set out to do, the navigation will likely produce some utilitarian value (Babin et al., 1994). Hence:

H4: A retail website's sense-making potential provides consumers with utilitarian value.

Value and site commitment

Each online shopping navigation is a 'moment of truth', which will influence the consumer's future intentions and behavior. Obtaining consumer commitment as a result of any site navigation is important (Christopher, Payne, and Ballantyne, 2002), since it explains future behavioral intentions (Park and Kim, 2003). Whether consumers purchase or not during a particular navigation, the ongoing relationship between consumer and retail website–or absence thereof–is subject to the consumer's site commitment. In this study, site commitment is defined as the degree to which the consumer is willing to remain associated with the retail website. It indicates a future-focused assessment of a consumer's recent navigation, linking past and future behavior (Park and Kim, 2003). Because shopping value, whether hedonic or utilitarian, is a positive outcome and increases shopper satisfaction (Babin et al., 1994), it is likely to produce approach behaviors (Jones, Reynolds,

and Arnold, 2006). Therefore the following hypotheses are formulated:

H5: Hedonic value drawn from navigating a retail website is positively related to site commitment.
H6: Utilitarian value drawn from navigating a retail website is positively related to site commitment.

The conceptual model shown in Figure 1 summarizes the six hypotheses derived.

METHOD AND MEASURES

To test the conceptual model, data were collected from a sample of 301 respondents recruited on a voluntary basis among the students and staff of a British university. Respondents were asked to shop at an online bookstore (www2.uk.bol.com) for eight minutes, then answer a questionnaire about that particular navigation experience. The duration was established based on the need for respondents to get to know the site well enough to answer specific questions about its attributes, while keeping the overall duration under 25 minutes.

A relatively unknown site was chosen (only 7.3% of the sample reported having visited it once or occasionally; no-one was a regular user) to capture instant, 'fresh' perceptions, thus overcoming validity concerns expressed about the likely halo effects of studies which call on consumers' memory to describe past experiences (Chen, Wigand, and Nilan, 1999; Lowrey, Otnes, and McGrath, 2005). To maximize the 'naturalness' of the shopping exercise, the site was chosen in a product category which students and university staff typically purchase; the setting for the navigation (computer lab, desk or home) is typical of the setting the respondents use when they shop online; and the instructions themselves asked the respondents to shop "as [they] would normally shop online if [they] were at home, in an internet café or at [their] desk", thus they clearly aimed to induce the sense of shopping, rather than just aimless or experimental browsing.

Exploratory potential and sense-making potential were conceptualized as higher-order constructs. They were operationalized as such, and to measure their respective dimensions, the scales

TABLE 1
PSYCHOMETRIC PROPERTIES OF THE MEASURES OF EXPLORATORY POTENTIAL AND SENSE-MAKING POTENTIAL

Construct/dimension	CR	AVE
Exploratory potential (second-order construct, 4 dimensions)	.76	.46
Visual impact (4 items)	.87	.63
Experiential intensity (4 items)	.79	.48
Marketer informativeness (5 items)	.82	.49
Non-marketer informativeness (3 items)	.81	.59
Sense-making potential (second-order construct, 2 dimensions)	.79	.67
Page clarity (3 items)	.86	.68
Site architecture (6 items)	.86	.51

CR: composite reliability; **AVE**: average variance extracted

FIGURE 2
FINAL MODEL RESULTS

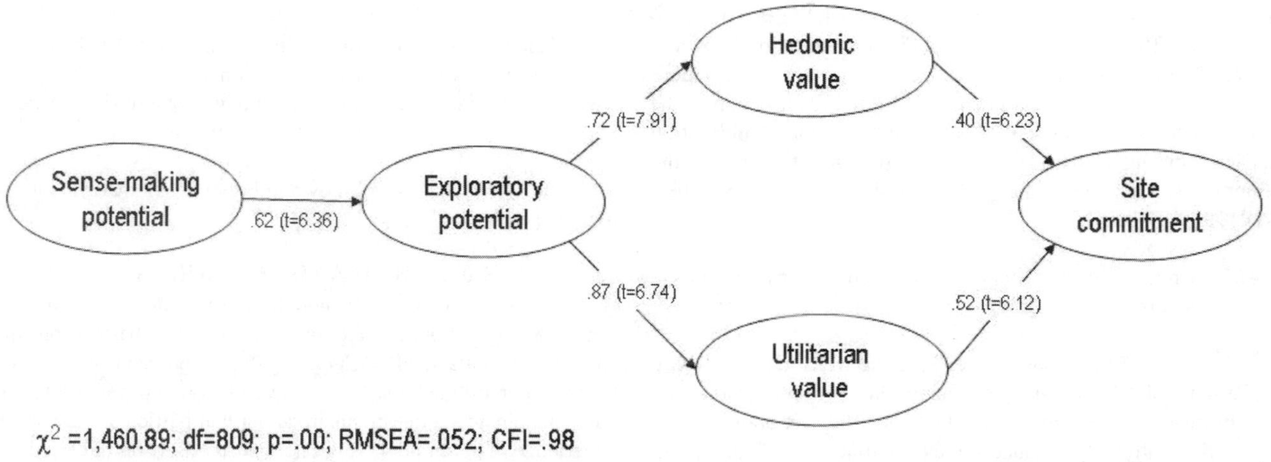

χ^2 =1,460.89; df=809; p=.00; RMSEA=.052; CFI=.98

developed and validated in Demangeot and Broderick (forthcoming) were used. The psychometric properties of the two higher-order constructs and their respective dimensions are summarized in Table 1.

To measure hedonic and utilitarian value, Babin, Darden, and Griffin's (1994) scales of 11 and 4 items respectively were used. To meet the unidimensionality requirement (Gerbing and Anderson, 1988), the hedonic value scale was reduced to 6 items, consistent with other studies (e.g. Babin, Chebat, and Michon, 2004). To measure site commitment, items from existing scales (Agarwal and Karahanna, 2000; Coyle and Thorson, 2001) were combined with items developed during a previous, qualitative exploration stage. As recommended by Baumgartner and Steenkamp (2001) to reduce the possibility of response bias, items were ordered randomly and all scales contained both positively- and negatively-worded items.

The Appendix, which details the items retained to tap each measure, shows that all measures display strong psychometric properties. Discriminant validities between all measures of the model were assessed and supported by, first, ensuring that a confidence interval of two standard errors on either side of the correlation coefficients did not include 1, and second, through the testing of nested models to confirm that correlation coefficients between each set of factors were significantly different from 1 (Anderson and Gerbing, 1988).

FINDINGS
The path model was tested using structural equation modeling, and produced strong goodness-of-fit indices (χ^2=1,459.65; df=808; p=.00; RMSEA=.052; CFI=.98). Of the path coefficients freely estimated, all except one have strong values, significant at the .001 level. However, the path from sense-making potential to utilitarian value is not significant. Its coefficient (-.04) has a t-value of -.59. As a result, the model was re-specified to exclude that path. The results of this final model are shown in Figure 2.

Hypothesis 1, which posits a positive relationship between sense-making potential and exploratory potential, is supported, with a path estimate of .62 (t=6.36; p<.001). When a website makes sense, it is more likely perceived to be worth exploring too. Hypothesis 2 posits a positive relationship between exploratory potential and hedonic value, and it is supported by a path estimate of .72 (t=7.91, p<.001). When consumers are on a shopping website which has exploratory potential, they draw hedonic value from it. Hypothesis 3, which posited a positive relationship between exploratory potential and utilitarian value, is supported by a path estimate of .87 (t=6.74, p<.001). This supports the argument that when consumers navigate a site which has potential for exploration, they gain utilitarian value, possibly because the site's exploratory attributes enable them to achieve such shopping objectives as purchasing the most suitable item, being able to compare between several products, or being able to inspect products by clicking on them, etc.

Hypothesis 4 which suggested that sense-making potential is an antecedent of utilitarian value, was rejected. This was an unexpected, yet most interesting finding. The entirety of the effect of sense-making potential on utilitarian value is mediated by exploratory potential. Consumers therefore do not appear to draw *any* value from sense-making attributes if they cannot use them to explore the site. Sense-making potential may be a necessary condition for consumers to be able to explore a site, but it is not sufficient for them to draw value from their visit or form a commitment. This is consistent with Kaplan and Kaplan's (1982) argument that people are not satisfied with just making sense of an environment. They quickly become bored and seek exploration as a way to expand the boundaries of their world.

Hypothesis 5, which posited a positive relationship between hedonic value and site commitment, is supported by a path estimate of .40 (t=6.23; p<.001). Similarly, Hypothesis 6, which posited a positive relationship between utilitarian value and site commitment, is supported, with a path estimate of .52 (t=6.12; p<.001). These results suggest that consumers form a commitment to a site based on both kinds of value.

DISCUSSION AND CONCLUSION

Several implications arise from this study. First, the results confirm and further reinforce the notion that exploration plays a central role in providing consumers with shopping value. The strength of the relationship between exploratory potential and both kinds of value, and the absence of a direct relationship between sense-making potential and utilitarian value suggest that exploratory attributes are essential for consumers to draw value from their navigation. Exploratory potential, then, plays a significant role in producing shopping value, and may be thought of as the 'killer attribute' of retail websites. Thus, exploratory potential is the most strategic attribute of retail websites, because by producing shopping value, it creates commitment to the site.

Exploratory potential was found to reflect both spatial exploration and informational exploration attributes. Exploration applies to both the virtual environment and to product-related information. The internet, with its unique characteristics, presents marketers with different opportunities to create a shopping environment and manage product communication, which are equally worth exploring. Online, products can come to life through telepresence (Steuer, 1992); for the first time in consumers' lives, all sources of information they value most (personal, marketer, opinion formers, other users) are available at once; the quantity of information is potentially quasi-unlimited, and it can be searched effectively. The potential for the exploration of online shopping environments can

only grow, as technology and increasing bandwidth provide more ways to bring environments and products to life.

Second, the study found that hedonic value and utilitarian value contribute to site commitment in similar proportions. This is an important finding because although the utilitarian benefits of online shopping are well known (e.g. convenience, absence of crowding, access to more information and access to a wider product range), and the limitations of virtual experiences compared to direct ones have been considered (Grewal, Iyer, and Levy, 2004), online shoppers nevertheless appear to place a high value on hedonic factors when considering their future relationship with a retail website. Online also, the ability to stage intrinsically rewarding experiences is likely to be a source of competitive advantage (Pine and Gilmore, 1998). Marketers' ability to provide, on each visit, a shopping experience which produces high levels of both hedonic and utilitarian value is especially important online where, unless they form the intention of returning to a site during a navigation, shoppers are unlikely to 'stumble into it' again with the ease one stumbles into a store in the high street or a mall.

Managerially, the model developed and tested implies that a major concern of online marketers should be to create and design retail websites which facilitate exploration. The model also suggests ways in which they can manipulate the design of their websites to produce stronger customer commitment. In particular, exploratory potential, which is central to gaining consumer commitment to the site, was found to concern both the shopping environment itself, and the product information. Consequently, as they work closely with IT and design professionals, marketers can use these concepts to ensure that the results of site development or re-designs do indeed result in higher perceptions of exploratory potential. As technology evolves, they will have to keep finding new ways to facilitate the exploration of their online environments and of their products and information.

The study's results need to be considered in the context of its limitations. First, the use of a convenience sample of university students and staff limits the generalizability of its findings. Students have been exposed to virtual environment for a higher proportion of their lives, and are more computer literate and avid online shoppers than average consumers (Marsh, Case, and Burns, 2000). In this respect though, they are perhaps more representative of tomorrow's consumers, and should be a prime concern to marketers, as they consider the future of online retailing.

Second, due to their age and lighter time pressures, students may also have more exploratory behavior tendencies. This could have raised the observed levels of hedonic value. Further research could consider the possible moderating effect of exploratory behavior tendencies. Baumgartner and Steenkamp (1996) have found that both exploratory information seeking tendencies and exploratory acquisition of product tendencies affect actual exploratory consumer behaviors. This begs the question of whether these two constructs moderate the relationship between sense-making and exploratory potential (consumers with high levels of exploratory behavior tendencies may seek and therefore be able to identify exploratory cues more proficiently than others), or between perceived exploratory potential and hedonic value.

A third source of vulnerability lies in the single context (online bookstores) in which the measures and overall model have been developed and tested. Replication applied to a different product category might return different strengths in relationships. In particular, exploratory attributes may have less importance on websites selling less gratifying product categories such as groceries or computer accessories. However, because all online shopping necessitates exploration to move from one webpage to another, exploratory potential is expected to remain a crucial attribute of all retail websites.

A further avenue for future research would be to establish whether, when consumers are in a hurry to make a decision, exploration may be a hindrance. Offline, Chernev (2006) found that, while consumers relish the flexibility offered by large assortments, they are more confident–when the time comes to make a choice–when choosing among smaller assortments. However, it is possible that the manner in which information is stored, searched, sorted and categorized online, can assist consumers in making sounder decisions among larger assortments, by reducing the amount of cognitive processing required to compare between items of a similar nature. There may also be circumstances when the relationship between sense-making potential and exploratory potential does not exist or, even, is reversed. For instance, in the case of highly technical or really new products, one could conceive that making sense of the site and its information is the result of exploring it more.

Fourth, while the use of an ex post facto design precludes any claim of causality, a number of measures were taken to limit the influence (confound) of extraneous elements–the respondents navigated the same site, at the same download speed, with the same browser display and for the same duration. Nevertheless, a true experimental design would be useful to study the impact of cue manipulations on consumer responses.

Importantly, in view of the central role played by exploration in online shopping behavior, the concept requires further theoretical development. A qualitative approach would be useful in further understanding and distinguishing between different exploration situations during the course of an online shopping navigation. Observational methods, for example by tracking the different pages visited during a single shopping navigation, could help researchers understand consumers' trajectories during a shopping navigation, and perhaps associate different types of trajectories with distinct behavioral outcomes. Further research is also needed, to extricate the possible role of such phenomena as learning, internal information search, information overload, on the relationship between exploratory potential and site commitment.

By highlighting the central role of exploratory potential in committing consumers to a site, a major contribution of this study is to draw attention to the integrating role of exploration in online shopping, and re-focus the main challenge of online retailing as the design of virtual retail environments and the communication of product information in a manner which invites exploration. The consumer behavior literature, which so far has focused mostly on goal-directed search (Janiszewski, 1998), will need to turn its attention towards the exploratory manner in which online, goal-directed shoppers and browsers alike shop and search for products and information. This will become especially important if consumers keep using the internet as part of a cross-channel strategy (Muse, 2006).

In conclusion, this study has revealed, and its findings further emphasized, the central role played by exploratory potential as it increases commitment to a retail website by producing both hedonic and utilitarian value. Further research on the exploratory potential of retail websites holds a great deal of promise, since one can only assume that the constantly evolving technology will provide ever more opportunities and novel ways for retailers to increase the potential for exploration on their website. Furthermore, as internet speeds increase and internet use becomes more widespread and more second-nature to consumers (as the young 'generation internet' comes of age and becomes the consuming majority), the relative importance of sense-making and exploratory potential is likely to irrevocably and permanently tilt towards exploratory attributes.

REFERENCES

Agarwal, Ritu and Elena Karahanna (2000), "Time flies when you're having fun: Cognitive absorption and beliefs about information technology usage", *MIS Quarterly,* 24(4), 665-94.

Anderson, James C. and David W. Gerbing (1988), "Structural Equation Modeling in Practice: A Review and Recommended two-step Approach", *Psychological Bulletin,* 103, 411-23.

Babin, Barry J., Jean-Charles Chebat, and Richard Michon (2004), "Perceived appropriateness and its effect on quality, affect and behavior", *Journal of Retailing and Consumer Services,* 11(5), 287-98.

Babin, Barry J., William R. Darden, and Mitch Griffin (1994), "Work and or Fun-Measuring Hedonic and Utilitarian Shopping Value", *Journal of Consumer Research,* 20(4), 644-56.

Baumgartner, Hans and Jan-Benedikt B. Steenkamp (2001), "Response Styles in Marketing Research: A Cross-National Investigation", *Journal of Marketing Research,* 38, 143-56.

Baumgartner, Hans and Jan-Benedikt Steenkamp (1996), "Exploratory consumer buying behavior: Conceptualization and Measurement", *International Journal of Research in Marketing,* 13, 121-37.

Beatty, Sharon E. and Scott M. Smith (1987), "External Search Effort: An Investigation Across Several Product Categories", *Journal of Consumer Research,* 14, 83-95.

Berlyne, Daniel E. (1960), *Conflict, Arousal and Curiosity*, New York, NY: McGraw Hill.

Bloch, Peter H., and Marsha Richins (1983), "A Theoretical Model for the Study of Product Importance Perceptions:, *Journal of Marketing,* 47, 69-81.

Bloch, Peter H., Nancy M. Ridgway, and Daniel L. Sherrell (1989), "Extending the Concept of Shopping: An Investigation of Browsing Activity", *Journal of the Academy of Marketing Science,* 17(1), 13-21.

Celsi, Richard L. and Jerry C. Olson (1988), "The Role of Involvement in Attention and Comprehension Process", *Journal of Consumer Research,* 15(2), 210-24.

Chen, Hsiang, Rolf T. Wigand, and Michael S. Nilan (1999), "Optimal experience of Web activities", *Computers in Human Behavior,* 15(5), 585-608.

Chernev, Alexander (2006), "Decision Focus and Consumer Choice among Assortments", *Journal of Consumer Research,* 33(1), 50-9.

Christopher, Martin, Adrian Payne, and David Ballantyne (2002), *Relationship Marketing-Creating Stakeholder Value*, Oxford: Butterworth Heinemann.

Coyle, James R. and Esther Thorson (2001), "The effects of progressive levels of interactivity and vividness in web marketing sites", *Journal of Advertising,* 30(3), 65-77.

Davis, Fred D., Richard P. Bagozzi, and Paul R. Warshaw (1989), "User Acceptance of Computer Technology: a Comparison of Two Theoretical Models", *Management Science,* 5(8), 982-1003.

Demangeot, Catherine and Amanda J. Broderick (forthcoming), "Consumer Perceptions of Online Shopping Environments: A Gestalt Approach", *Psychology & Marketing.*

Diep, Vien C. S. and Jillian C. Sweeney (2008), "Shopping trip value: Do stores and products matter?", *Journal of Retailing and Consumer Services,* 15(5), 399-409.

Eroglu, Sevgin A., Karen A. Machleit, and Lenita M. Davis (2003), "Empirical testing of a model of online store atmospherics and shopper responses", *Psychology & Marketing, 20*(2), 139-50.

Fortin, David R. and Ruby R. Dholakia (2005), "Interactivity and vividness effects on social presence and involvement with a web-based advertisement", *Journal of Business Research, 58*(3), 387-96.

Gammack, John and Christopher Hodkinson (2003), "Virtual Reality, Involvement and the Consumer Interface", *Journal of End User Computing, 15*(4), 78-96.

Gerbing, David W. and James C. Anderson (1988), "An Updated Paradigm for Scale Development Incorporating Unidimensionality and its assessment", *Journal of Marketing Research, 25*(2), 186-92.

Grewal, Dhruv, Gopalkrishnan R. Iyer, and Michael Levy (2004), "Internet retailing: enablers, limiters and market consequences", *Journal of Business Research, 57*(7), 703-13.

Henderson, Ron and Megan Divett (2003), "Perceived Usefulness, Ease of Use and Electronic Supermarket Use", *International Journal of Human-Computer Studies, 59*(3), 383-95.

Hoch, Stephen J. (2002), "Product experience is seductive", *Journal of Consumer Research, 29*(3), 448-54.

Hoffman, Donna L. and Thomas P. Novak (1996), "Marketing in hypermedia computer-mediated environments: Conceptual foundations", *Journal of Marketing, 60*(3), 50-68.

Holbrook, Morris B. (1986), "Emotion in the Consumer Experience: Toward a new Model of the Human Consumer", In W. R. Wilson (Ed.), *The Role of Affect and Consumer Behavior: Emerging Theories and Applications* (pp. 17-52), Lexington MA: Heath.

Janiszewski, Chris (1998), "The influence of display characteristics on visual exploratory search behavior", *Journal of Consumer Research, 25*(3), 290-301.

Jones, Michael A., Kristy E. Reynolds, and Mark J. Arnold (2006), "Hedonic and utilitarian shopping value: Investigating differential effects on retail outcomes". *Journal of Business Research, 59*(9), 974-81.

Kaplan, Stephen (1992), "Environmental Preference in a Knowledge-Seeking, Knowledge-Using Organism", In J. Tooby (Ed.), *The Adapted Mind: Evolutionary Psychology and the Generation of Culture* (pp. 581-98), New York: Oxford University Press.

Kaplan, Stephen and Rachel Kaplan (1982), *Cognition and Environment*, New York, NY: Praeger Publishers.

Karahanna, Elena and Detmar W. Straub (1999), "The psychological origins of perceived usefulness and ease-of-use", *Information & Management, 35*(4), 237-50.

Kim, Jihyun, Ann Marie Fiore, and Hyun Hwa Lee (2007), "Influences of online store perception, shopping enjoyment, and shopping involvement on consumer patronage behavior towards an online retailer", *Journal of Retailing and Consumer Services, 14*(2), 95-107.

Kim, Soyoung and Leslie Stoel (2004), "Dimensional hierarchy of retail website quality", *Information & Management, 41*(5), 619-33.

Klein, Lisa R. (1998), "Evaluating the Potential of Interactive Media through a New Lens: Search versus Experience Goods", *Journal of Business Research, 41*(3), 195-203.

Kotler, Philip (1973), "Atmospherics as a Marketing Tool", *Journal of Retailing, 49*(4), 48-64.

Kroeber-Riel, Werner (1979), "Activation Research: Psychobiological Approaches in Consumer Research", *Journal of Consumer Research, 5*(March), 240-50.

Li, Hairong, Terry Daugherty, and Frank Biocca (2001), "Characteristics of Virtual Experience in Electronic Commerce: A Protocol Analysis", *Journal of Interactive Marketing, 15*(3), 13-30.

Loiacono, Eleanor T., Richard T. Watson, and Dale L. Goodhue (2007), "webQual: An Instrument for Consumer Evaluation of Web Sites", *International Journal of Electronic Commerce, 11*(3), 51-87.

Lowrey, Tina M., Cele C. Otnes, and Mary Ann McGrath (2005), "Shopping with Consumers: Reflections and"Innovations", *Qualitative Market Research, 8*(2), 176-88.

MacInnis, Deborah J. and Linda L. Price (1987), "The Role of Imagery in Information Processing: Review and Extensions", *Journal of Consumer Research, 13*(March), 473-91.

Marsh, Robert, Thomas Case, and O.Maxie Burns (2000), "Demographic Variables Related to On-Line Purchasing by University Students", paper presented at the 3rd Annual Conference of Southern Association for Information Systems, Atlanta, GA.

Mehrabian, Albert and James A. Russell (1974), *An Approach to Environmental Psychology*, Cambridge (MA): The MIT Press.

Muse, Dan (2006), "Online Shopping to Grow-Are you Ready?", www.ecommerce-guide.com/news/reearch/article.php/3583651.

Nelson, Philip J. (1974), "Advertising as Information", *Journal of Political Economy, 82*(4), 729-54.

Overby, Jeffrey W. and Eun-Ju Lee (2006), "The Effects of Utilitarian and Hedonic Online Shopping Value on Consumer Preference and Intentions", *Journal of Business Research, 59* (10-11), 1160-66.

Park, Chung-H., and Young-G. Kim (2003), "Identifying key factors affecting behavior in an online shopping context", *International Journal of Retail & Distribution Management, 31*(1), 16-29.

Pine, B. Joseph I., and James H. Gilmore (1998), "Welcome to the Experience Economy" *Harvard Business Review, 76*(4), 97-105.

Richard, Marie-Odile (2005), "Modeling the impact of internet atmospherics on surfer behavior", *Journal of Business Research, 58*(12), 1632-42.

Senecal, Sylvain, Pawel J. Kalczynski, and Jacques Nantel (2005), "Consumers' decision-making process and their online shopping behavior: a clickstream analysis", *Journal of Business Research, 58*(11), 1599-608.

Singh, Mandeep, Siva K. Balasubramanian, and Goutam Chakraborty (2000), "A comparative analysis of three communication formats: Advertising, infomercial, and direct experience", *Journal of Advertising, 29*(4), 59-75.

Solomon, Michael R. (1986), "The Missing Link: Surrogate Consumers in the Marketing Chain", *Journal of Marketing Research, 50*(4), 208-218.

Solomon, Michael R. (2004), Consumer behavior, New Jersey: Prentice Hall.

Steuer, Jonathan (1992), "Defining Virtual Reality: Dimensions Determining Telepresence", *Journal of Communication, 42*(4), 73-93.

Tauber, Edward M. (1972), "Why Do People Shop?", *Journal of Marketing, 36*(October), 46-59.

APPENDIX
MEASURES USED IN THE MODEL AND THEIR PSYCHOMETRIC PROPERTIES

Construct/item wording	CR	AVE	Completely stand. loading (t-value)
Visual impact–4 items	.87	.63	
The website had a visually pleasing design			.86 (t=12.70)
This website was dull visually (R)			.82 (t=12.11)
The website was aesthetically appealing			.82 (t=12.25)
This site had no visual impact (R)			.67 (*)
Experiential intensity–4 items	.79	.48	
This website replicated the kind of experience I have when I shop			.69 (t=9.31)
The experience of shopping was not there when I navigated on this site (R)			.75 (t=9.89)
When I navigated this website I felt I was shopping for real			.71 (t=9.50)
This website was incapable of reproducing the experience of shopping (R)			.62 (*)
Marketer informativeness–5 items	.82	.49	
There was enough information on this website to assess the products			.57 (t=9.89)
I could learn a lot about the products			.64 (t=11.42)
The information on this website was helpful			.73 (t=13.39)
The information on this website was useful			.71 (t=12.89)
This website adequately met my information needs			.81 (*)
Non-marketer informativeness–3 items	.81	.59	
This site had customer reviews of products			.82 (t=12.14)
From this site it was impossible to see what other users thought of the products (R)			.70 (t=11.25)
This website only gave me its own product information, and not other users' impressions (R)			.79 (*)
Page clarity–3 items	.86	.68	
There was too much text on the screen (R)			.86 (t=16.53)
There was an awful lot of things on every page (R)			.75 (t=14.18)
The pages on this website were too crowded (R)			.85 (*)
Site architecture–6 items	.86	.51	
During the navigation, I felt confused (R)			.70 (t=11.16)
I felt lost on this website (R)			.67 (t=10.81)
My interaction with this website was clear and understandable			.73 (t=11.59)
The web pages were easy to read			.69 (t=11.01)
The content on this site was clear			.77 (t=12.20)
The organization of the information presented on the screen was confusing (R)			.71 (*)
Utilitarian value–4 items	.79	.49	
I accomplished just what I wanted to on this navigation			.76 (t=8.23)
I couldn't find what I really needed on this website			.79 (t=8.36)
While shopping I found just the item(s) I was looking for			.71 (t=7.99)
I was disappointed because I would have to go to another site to complete my shopping (R)			.49 (*)
Hedonic value–6 items	.88	.55	
The navigation on this website was truly a joy			.78 (t=13.88)
Shopping on this website truly felt like an escape			.77 (t=13.71)
I enjoyed this navigation for its own sake, not just for the items I may have purchased			.66 (t=11.43)
I had a good time on this site because I was able to act on "the spur of the moment"			.74 (t=13.12)
During the navigation I felt the excitement of the hunt			.74 (t=13.15)
While shopping on this site I felt a sense of adventure			.77 (*)

APPENDIX (CONTINUED)
MEASURES USED IN THE MODEL AND THEIR PSYCHOMETRIC PROPERTIES

Construct/item wording	CR	AVE	Completely stand. loading (t-value)
Site commitment–7 items	**.94**	**.70**	
I will visit this site first when I want to buy books			.79 (t=12.97)
I plan to use this website in the future			.91 (t=14.71)
I intend to continue using this website in the future			.94 (t=15.22)
I expect my use of this website to continue in the future			.91 (t=14.79)
I am unlikely to use this website again (R)			.78 (t=12.75)
I will recommend this site to other people			.82 (t=13.37)
I would have only good things to say about this website			.69 (*)

$\chi^2=1,259.50$, df=783 (p=.000); RMSEA=.045 ; CFI=.98; n=301
(R): reverse-scored item. *: the metric for each scale was established by fixing one of the construct indicators to 1.
CR: Composite reliability; **AVE**: Average variance extracted

Turley, Lou W. and Ronald E. Milliman (2000), "Atmospheric Effects on Shopping Behavior: A Review of the Experimental Evidence", *Journal of Business Research,* 49(2), 193-211.

Varlander, Sara (2007), "Online information quality in experiential consumption: An exploratory study", *Journal of Retailing and Consumer Services,* 14(5), 328-38.

Wright, Alice A. and John G.J. Lynch (1995), "Communication effects of advertising versus direct experience", *Journal of Consumer Research,* 21(4), 708-18.

Yoo, Boonghee and Naveen Donthu (2001), "Developing a scale to measure the perceived quality of an Internet shopping site (SITEQUAL)", *Quarterly Journal of Electronic Commerce,* 2(1), 31-46.

Culinary Culture, Gastrobrands and Identity Myths: 'Nigella', An Iconic Brand in the Baking

Paul Hewer, University of Strathclyde, UK
Douglas Brownlie, University of Stirling, UK

INTRODUCTION

"They say that stars give you something to dream about...[the] screen idols are immanent in the unfolding of life as a series of images. They are a system of luxury prefabrication, brilliant syntheses of the stereotypes of life and love. They embody one single passion only: the passion for images, and the immanence of desire in the image. They are not something to dream about; they are the dream. And they have all the characteristics of dreams" (Baudrillard 1988, 56).

In his perceptive and persuasive rendering of the nature of consumer society and its obsession with fame and celebrity, McCracken (2005) states that "the celebrity world is one of the most potent sources of cultural meaning at the disposal of the marketing system and the individual consumer"(ibid, 113). Indeed, as Pringle (2004) so bluntly puts it, 'celebrity sells'. While both authors transport us back to the 1960s and McLuhan's powerful analysis of the "transforming power of media" (1964, 20), Pringle offers a managerial take on the growing complexity of the media environment, where media fragmentation, global reach and the explosion of celebrity culture go hand in hand. Olsen (1999) trenchantly observes that by virtue of the global distribution of its manufactured media product, the US Film and TV media industry is effectively assembling a "Hollywood Planet". Pringle takes the view that "the celebrity phenomenon has largely been created by [US] movies and television [although] there is no doubt that other media have play[ed] a significant part" (ibid, 10).

To consumer researchers it will come as no surprise that, while generating enormous growth in the demand for media content, rapidly circulating flows of mass media product have bombarded us with stories and images of many manufactured celebrity figures. But, by adding to the growing media clutter, this has made it increasingly difficult for brands to gain and hold consumer attention. In what he terms the '*era of consent*', where brands increasingly need consumers' permission to communicate with them, Pringle (2004) concludes that commodity celebrities "who themselves have a high standing in the public eye, [provide] one of the more powerful tools for brand [building]" (ibid, 50). Hence, equally unsurprisingly, building brand visibility through harnessing the 'cut through' of celebrity iconography continues to make sound commercial sense.

Paradoxically, while celebrity 'product' feeds off fame, it is also embedded within the constitutive logic of promotional culture, for which exposure to the glare of media attention is a mode of economic production (Wernick, 1991). It recursively organises the conditions of possibility of celebrity, not merely as media product and content, but as a medium of communication. And if the message or meaning content is celebrity, while the medium is also celebrity, we then have an example of McLuhan's pronouncement that "the medium is the message" (1964, 13). This is also an instance of what Baudrillard refers to as '*the implosion of meaning*', where message and "all the contents of meaning are absorbed in the dominant form of the medium. The medium alone makes the [communications] event-and does this whatever the contents" (1983, 100). In more prosaic words, commodified celebrities, whose fame derives from carefully calculated media activity and self-presentation, must also manipulate media attention to develop and sustain the visibility and viability of their own marketplace visibility and viability. Celebrity may be commonly understood as a highly prized, if fleeting, condition that attaches itself to an object of media attention, but as Cashmore and Parker (2003) advise, "...it is [the] commodification of the human form [...] the process by which people are turned into "things", things to be adored, respected, worshipped, idolized, but perhaps more importantly, things which are themselves produced and consumed" (ibid, 215). The celebrity of celebrity and its product, celebrity, function in fiercely contested cultural domains where competing celebrity brands nurture the visibility of their visibility, while levering it to penetrate the ambient noise of competing media products. Thus are the thematic features of the celebrity and the *celebritized*[1] brand not only the product of careful composition and premeditation, but of recursively organized modes of production built around everyday conventions that articulate celebrity, so giving a media object meaning within specific social relations. So, as the opening extract suggests, celebrity is not simply something to dream about; it is the dream.

Pringle (2004), like Rein, Kotler and Stoller (1987) before him, situates managerial interest in branding technology in the device of personalization by means of which commodities come to acquire extraordinary, figurative meanings. Brand identity is made intelligible through the symbolizing capacity of consumers. This feeds into and off iconic media content that promotes chains of associations between face, figure and personality. McCracken (1989) describes as 'meaning transfer' the personification by means of which product properites become associated with desirable qualities of the commodified celebrity character. A process of appropriation takes place. McCracken's argues that celebrities are "key players in the meaning transfer process" (2005, 112) and that "celebrity endorsement and the marketing system are cultural undertakings in which meaning is constantly in circulation" (ibid, 113). He sets out a three-stage process through which "culture and consumption interact to create a system of meaning movement [whereby] some of the meanings of the celebrity [become] the meanings of the product" (1989, 314). Sternberg (1998) describes this transfer as 'iconographic work', where, through a combination of facial expression, costume, bearing, gesture, voice and word,

---

[1] We use the terms *celebritized* and *celebritization* in this sense: that if we understand the brand as 'media object'-the object or thing that is itself the product of media attention paid to it-an example of what Lury refers to as "*the broadcast distribution of commodities*" (2004,6); and the media object feeds off and into circulating cultural codes, unstable subject positions circulating around, eg, gender roles and identity, or in our case 'domesticity'; and those subject positions are temporarily stabilized through the deliberate media manipulations of branding and personification; and where, as a media brand a subject position itself is framed and narrativised through the lens of celebrity iconography; then, the cultural logic of celebrity (including the celebrity of celebrity), organized recursively as a mode of production, works through discursive practices of *celebritization*. So, *celebritization* describes what happens when the logic of celebrity is exploited as a mode of production in the service of marketing ends. In this sense the cultural logic of celebrity (and of the celebrity of celebrity) is at the core of consumer society, for, as Warhol famously remarked in 1968, 'in the future everyone will be world-famous for fifteen minutes'.

celebrities personify sought-after brand features or attributes. In another article, he observes that "everywhere we look, goods and services are suffused with images [and] capitalism is burgeoning from the calculated production of meanings" (1999, 3). Marketplace activity that draws upon cultural resources to 'thematize a commodity' so to heighten its meaning is understood by Sternberg as "iconic production" (ibid, 3). He argues that the activity of loading everyday consumer products with evocative meaning, with what Jameson (1991, 91) refers to as a 'sign flow' or 'inner logic', generates the brand content that animates desire. We suggest that if the commodified celebrity can be understood as a medium of translation, then the brand itself can be seen as a media object, an essential interface in the cultural logic of consumption.

The purpose of this paper is to explore ways in which celebrity functions as a mode of economic production whereby cultural resources, especially differentiating subject positions currently in circulation, are *celebritized* in pursuit of rhetorical appeal. We explore these issues through developing case material from an investigative site that consists of the branding of a celebrity chef through a collection of superior photographic print images situated within a contemporary 'lifestyle' cookery book. We take the photographic content of the cookbook, the representations of the commodified celebrity, as constructed spaces or environments with *celebritizing* characteristics.

Within the built environments of the photographic images we argue that representations perform iconographic work as spatialized forms of discursive practice, allowing us to explore the work of celebrity as the content of those images. In other words, the images make available for inspection models of *celebritized* social relations, in this case framed by the narratives into which particular representations of <u>domesticity</u> have been inserted. As in a previous study (Brownie and Hewer 2008) we investigate the mediating role played by the cookbook as cultural artefact, seeing it as a way of further circulating powerful cultural codes of masculinity in pursuit of commercial success. In the context of this study we focus on domesticity as an unstable symbolic form which is put to cultural work, appropriated towards the production of meaning and the amelioration of cultural anxieties within the landscaped environments of the images.

CCCT*[2]

Within discussions around CCT (Arnould and Thompson 2005) we note that the notion of celebrity seems curiously absent, with exception possibly of O'Guinn (1991) and Schroeder (2006). This strikes the authors as strange, given the fact that contemporary consumer culture is literally awash with commodified celebrity product (Wicks et al. 2007) labouring to help us fashion consumer selves with their wiles, charms and managed identities. To the list of celebrity feminine 'cooks'-the term 'chef' reserved for their hypermasculine male counterparts-Martha Stewart, Elizabeth David, Fanny Craddock and Delia Smith, must surely be added that of *Nigella*, (to not italicize it would surely be a sin!). Nigella joins that long list of celebrity actresses: Marilyn Monroe, Rita Hayworth, Audrey Hepburn to name but three; and celebrity divas, Madonna and Kylie-all of whom exist in the hallowed territory of fame, celebrity stardom and fandom. Residing in a mythic land in which one's surname becomes entirely unnecessary, redundant to communicate the appeal, magnetism and sway held and wielded by such iconic celebrity characters.

We argue in this paper that the iconicity of the *Nigella Brand* has as much to do with the *recipes* (Brownlie and Hewer 2008; Holt 2004) which it offers for rethinking feminine identities, domesticity and womanhood within contemporary consumer culture. Hence to explain the attraction, the constructedness of the *Nigella Brand* and

its marketplace appeal, we consider the cultural logic of celebrity, unpacking the role that celebrities play in assuaging doubts and managing cultural anxieties, what Holt (2004) refers to as "meaningful stories, myths that work as salves for contradictions in the nations's culture" (ibid: xi). While we pay tribute to the insighful work of Holt (2004), especially his concepts of cultural branding and identity myths, in exploring the cultural meanings that celebrity brands circulate, we also recognise the significance of thinking of them as constituting a particular form of *Myth Today* (Barthes, 1985). In this regard, we also draw upon the inspirational work of McCracken who suggests that since "all of us labor to fashion manageable selves, it is inevitable that we should cultivate a knowledge of this [celebrity] world." (1989, 318).

THERE'S SOMETHING ABOUT NIGELLA

"This is a book about baking, but not a Baking Book. The trouble with much modern cooking is not that the food it produces is not good, but that the mood it induces in the cook is one of skin-of-the-teeth efficiency, all briskness and little pleasure. Sometimes that's the best we can manage, but at other times we don't want to feel stressed and overstretched, but like a domestic goddess, trailing nutmeggy fumes of baking pie in her languorous wake..." (Lawson 2000, inset page to front cover)

The *Nigella* brand includes all manner of cookware items, from swanky red measuring cups to nifty serving hands, from cookie cutters to an all-purpose pot (well who needs lots of pots cluttering up the kitchen when you can have one), and a wipe-clean laminated shopping bag adorned with cocktails and delectable deli goodies, or as she explains on Nigella.com "I have a terrible habit of walking around town with tatty plastic bags and this is my attempt to rehabilitate in style. I can get a spare pair of shoes, books, magazines, emergency rations and the usual rubbish in here, and it actually looks good on the arm too: no more bag lady." (Nigella.com, accessed 28/11/07).

This *Living Kitchen* cookware range is available globally from selected retail outlets. It generates annually more than seven million pounds. The product range is enlivened by a number of glossy-stylized cookbooks (Lawson 2000, 2001, 2007), which can be likened to the 'How To' manuals of yesteryear, presenting ready-made solutions or 'salves' to our cultural doubts and anxieties–like those of *How to Eat, How to be a Domestic Goddess*. This also includes a variety of TV programmes and accompanying books which are exported overseas, from those of the *Nigella Bites* (2000) era, to the most recent offering, *Nigella Express* (2007). Herein, viewers and readers are transported to that fantasyland where the impossible is made possible[3]–a land in which it is possible to not only *have your cake and eat it*–but a land in which we are drawn into a particular version of feminine identity, a branded subject position around which it is possible to do the cooking whilst caring for others, to give others pleasure, if that choice works for you. However, it is not necessary to be chained to the kitchen sink catering for the needs of others to feel loved, loving and needed. It is also possible to choose to care for yourself, say through taking trouble to feed yourself and choosing food you like rather than deferring to the choices of significant others. In constructing her version of the celebrity chef, pleasures of cooking, eating and caring

---

[2]CCCT, ie Consumer Culture Celebrity Theory!!
[3]For copyright reasons we are unable to reproduce the images from the book here. To view the images seek out Lawson (2007) or Nigella.com.

are linked in representations of domestic life which admit the importance of caring and hedonism to dealing with the conflicts and anxieties experienced by working women.

In Nigellaland we are transported to a magical place of plenty, a consumer culture where supermarkets reign supreme; a land in which you can literally *express* it all (but at a cost). This narrativization seeks to assuage any doubts or anxieties experienced by her cash-rich, time-poor, viagra-induced cosmopolitan constituency. This is a hegemonic land of taste and distinction (Bourdieu, 1984), where everybody has that most desired and cherished of kitchen adornments the salt pig (and it has to be full size measuring 16cm x 18cm), to those not in the know a pot for holding salt, but for Nigella aficionados this commonplace object is magically transformed through the story-telling capabilities of our 'brand author':

> "I am a complete *Maldon* salt addict, and like to be able to keep my salt out at grabbable distance near the stove at all times. Again, the salt pig I own is functional, but no more, and I wanted one as a part of the range, one I really wanted to live with and take pleasure from just seeing it on the kitchen top."

Woodside et al. (2008) argue that storytelling plays a central role in how people relate to one another and that brands are important actors in the myths that inform such stories and move people to action. Building on this line of thought, we suggest that GastroBrands are thus constructed around their story-telling potential; stories which inevitably do a seamless job of promoting particular 'brand authors' in their pursuit of difference.

ALL ABOARD THE NIGELLA EXPRESS

All aboard the *Nigella Express* then, a homey spectacular realm in which the kitchen becomes a magical familial and social place. A site not simply for domestic toil and drudgery; but a space for self-fulfilment, emancipation, calculated hedonism and premeditated fun. Here we are being sold a particular version of commodified pleasure and liberation: where the gals all look great, even in the morning, and even when making the meals for her imaginary cosmo gastronista guests, for (yummy) dad and for the (yummy) kids. This is a magical liminal realm where the washing-up never needs doing; a land where the inevitable messiness of everyday living and cooking is banished never to be seen; a land where the clamouring pressures of kids and the daily grind of employment are remarkably and effortlessly erased. A glamourous and all too seductive version of femininity and homeyness then, where the mundane and ordinary are never allowed to set foot. Within this gastroporn vista the character of Nigella rules, as a celebrity we all love to hate. And perhaps it is this collectivized hatred that propels the brand and its all too seductive and sex-suggestive myths. In a contemporary consumerland where size zero's rule the celebrity zeitgeist, Nigella stands out in her all too retro-voluptuousness. For her 2000 cookbook offering *How to be a Domestic Goddess*, the inset pages contain golden-hued (sepia would be just too old-looking) images of what can only be likened to 1950's *Stepford Wives* revelling in the delights of taking the Sunday roast from the oven, exuding poise, grace and what can only be described as ecstatic delight at the marvels of deftly wielding a rolling pin and measuring milk from a *milk bottle* (and look what happened to those objects). The blurb for the book offering reads:

> "This is a book about baking, but not a Baking Book. The trouble with much modern cooking is not that the food it produces is not good, but that the mood it induces in the cook is one of skin-of-the-teeth effiency, all briskness and little pleasure. Sometimes that's the best we can manage, but at

other times we don't want to feel stressed and overstretched, but like a domestic goddess, trailing nutmeggy fumes of baking pie in her languorous wake..." (Lawson 2000, inset page to front cover)

So what the Nigella brand offers we might argue is a particular version of 'doing domesticity'; her currency and widespread appeal the result of the Nigella brands' ability to navigate, negotiate and even side-step tricky cultural and feminist contradictions, especially that of drudgery of the domestic sphere. Or as Nigella exhorts in the introduction for *How to be a Domestic Goddess*:

> "I neither want to confine you to kitchen quarters nor even suggests that it might be desirable. But I do think that many of us have become alienated from the domestic sphere, and that it can actually make us feel better to claim back some of that space, make it comforting rather than frightening. In a way, baking stands both as a useful metaphor for the familial warmth of the kitchen we fondly imagine used to exist, and as a way of reclaiming our lost Eden." (Lawson 2000: vii).

Here the brand liturgy (in its earliest form) considers the salve (Holt, 2004) for the anxieties of domesticity as female identity to flow from the mythical craft and comforts to be had from baking and enjoying the fulfillment that comes from caring for others and giving them pleasure. In this manner, the success of *Nigella* the celebrity brand cannot simply be explained by recourse to her perceived credibility, or her trustworthiness, expertise, attractiveness, or even her beauty, as the Brand Management literature (Keller 2004: 376) would have us believe.

Rather the *Nigella* brand exploits multiple competing subject positions in circulation around the identity myth of domesticity. Representations assembled from those subject positions suggest a new narrative of domesticity for the time-starved, body-conscious, self-indulgent contemporary woman. Thus constructs a version for our post-feminist, post-gender, postmodern times that, while sounding overwrought and precious, also strikes an alluring and comforting note. That is to say, the *Nigella* brand does not simply reiterate such brand propositions and values. Rather it performs and enacts such propositions of culinary sexyness and culinary homeyness to thereby rolling-pin out any of the inherent contradictions of our mundane, firefighting, reality tv, work-obsessed everyday lives. The brand, especially in its later form, responds to such collective existential and ontological dilemmas over experiences of time scarcity and stress generated by juggling the roles of worker, wife, parents and yummy mummy (O'Donohoe 2007), to name but a few. Moreover, Nigella's celebritized brand of domesticity generates compensatory resources–Holt's salve (2004)-to help readers respond creatively to erasing the existential tensions and anxieties commonly experienced in their everyday lives. Suggestive perhaps of Baudrillard's (1988) notions of the constraint of pleasure and the view of consumption as a form of production (1988). The introductory blurb of the latest extension of the brand, the *Nigella Express* (2007) cookbook thus reveals:

> "The Domestic Goddess is back but this time it's instant. Nigella and her style of cookery have earned a special place in our lives, symbolising all that is best, most pleasurable, most hands-on and least fussy about good food. But that doesn't mean she wants us to spend hours in the kitchen, slaving over a hot stove.
>
> Featuring fabulous fast foods, ingenious short cuts, terrific time-saving ideas, effortless entertaining and simple, scrump-

tious meals, Nigella Express is her solution to eating well when time is short.

Here are mouthwatering recipes, quick to prepare, easy to follow, that you can conjure up after a long day in the office or on a busy weekend, for family or unexpected guests. This is food you can make as you hit the kitchen running, with vital tips on how to keep your store cupboard stocked, freezer and fridge stacked. When time is precious, you can't spend hours shopping, so you need to make life easier by being prepared. Not that the recipes are basic-though they are always simple-but it's important to make every ingredient earn its place in a recipe. Minimise effort by maximising taste. And here too is great food that can be prepared quickly but cooked slowly in the oven, leaving you time to have a bath, a drink, talk to friends, or do the children's homework. Minimum stress for maximum enjoyment..." (www.nigella.com/books/detail.asp?area=5&article=3510)

As a slogan for the brand 'Minimise effort by maximising taste' ain't a bad one. And seeking clarity through recourse to Bourdieu on habitus and social class, especially in his discussion over the role of the new petite bourgeoisie, we might suggest that an ethics of consumption is being enacted:

"Seeking its occupational and personal salvation in the imposition of new doctrines of ethical salvation, the new petite bourgeoisie is predisposed to play a vanguard role in the struggles over everything concerned with the art of living, in particular, domestic life and consumption, relations between the sexes and the generations, the reproduction of the family and its values...the new ethical avant-garde urges a morality of pleasure as duty. This doctrine makes it a failure, a threat to self-esteem, not to 'have fun'...The fear of not getting enough pleasure, the logical outcome of the effort to overcome the fear of pleasure, is combined with a search for self-expression and 'bodily expression and for communication with others ('relating'–echange), even immersion in others (considered not as a group but as subjectivities in search of their identity)." (1984, 366-367).

This is perhaps why the naturalistic *denouement* for every TV programme always has to be the ritualistic display of food as a means for, what Maffesoli (1996) might refer to as, our *being-togetherness*-a culinary gift which makes material the ineluctable and ephemerality of the everyday as a form of *immersion in others*. Communicating and conveying those all-important ethical brand qualities of taste and distinction, but achieved with minimum effort and toil, justified and legitimised visually as doing one's bit for the greater good of others, especially the voracious gastronistas of dinner-partyland.

As a brand then, the Nigella Brand ain't that shy about coming forward; ain't that shy about maximising it's brand assets (as they say in the Brand Management textbooks, cf. Keller 2004); ain't that shy about responding to any lingering doubts over the earlier *Domestic Goddess* message, with it's all-encompassing, all-too-labour-intensive, back-to-the-kitchen mentality. But most importantly, the Nigella Brand works hard to enjoin us against the choices and dispositions of the *necessary*, an all too terrifying place signalled as Bourdieu suggests by a "resignation to the inevitable." (1984, 372). Instead, through living the *Nigella* way, we might say that the everyday becomes a site for the re-chantment of the labour of identity, pleasure and fun around an ethics of consumption and the all too consuming delights of the spectacular.

CELEBRITIES, FEMININITIES AND THE DRAMATISATION OF THE SPECTACULAR

Within the cultural studies literature on celebrities, Chaney (2002) argues that "celebrities work at the dramatisation of mundaneity" (2002, 113). In this way such manufactured characters are said to embody that thin line between communicating and displaying, for all to see, the ordinariness of the everyday and the flight to the spectacular and extra-ordinary. In being able to blur this distinction then rests their appeal. Likewise, Bell and Hollows (2005) explore how celebrities (or 'lifestyle experts') take upon the role of "advising us on consumer choice–*interpreting* the lifestyle landscape for us rather than dictating how to live" (2005, 15, italics in original). They continue by suggesting: "Voice and manner are important here, too, in making expertise ordinary, which also means making it accessible and inclusive." (2005, 15). Perhaps this is why *Brand Delia*[4] was doomed to fail for the late nineties and early noughties, as all too schoolmarmish, and all too hectoring Nanny Mummy. *Brand Nigella* also treads a tricky line here as a cultural intermediary. But it is clearly the case that her TV gastro-makeover programmes (as do the images within the book) work hard at the dramatisation of mundane spaces, such as the kitchen, garden and dining room table, coupling this with her own silky dulcet tones, cover-girl looks, friendly and flirtatious affectations which work hard to convey the possibilities of the spectacularity of the domestic sphere. In this light, it's useful to turn to Cashmore and Parker's (2003) assessment of the appeal of *Brand Beckham* as a bringing together of seemingly contradictory representations of masculinity "that contradicts, confuses and conflates all in one. He is 'new man' (nurturer, romantic, compassionate partner) and 'new land'/ 'dad-lad' (soccer hero, fashionable father, conspicuous consumer–some would argue, all round, cosmetically conscientious 'metrosexual') while demonstrating vestiges of 'old industrial man' (loyal, dedicated, stoic, breadwinning)." (2003, 225). Perhaps we can say that the *Nigella* brand works in a similar way, syncretically blurring the distinctions, the apparent inconsistencies of traditional-stay-at-home-mummy (caring, pinny bedecked-homemaker), with professional-entrepreneurial mummy (smooth operator, woman-on-top, out-competing men), but also managing to conflate such modes of femininity with that of yummy-mummy (sexy, desirable, clad in designer-clothes).

Nigella also has the perfect credentials for that of a Celebrity Gastronista–a colourful and tragic past. Prior to publishing her swathe of cookery books (2000, 2001, 2007), as Nigella Lawson she was not only the daughter of the UK Chancellor of the Exchequer during the Thatcher years, Nigel Lawson, she was also the food writer for that ultimate fashionista publication *Vogue*. The death of her first husband, journalist John Diamond, and subsequent second marriage to Charles Saattchi is further evidence of her strong media appeal. Her continuing appeal is also assured in blogland, as the range of Nigella's books remain popular in those all-important Amazon reviews with *How to be a Domestic Goddess* scoring a cool 44 out of 51 reviews at the all-important Five Star level. *Nigella Express* appears less popular, but still 21 out of 38 reviews rated it at Five Star. One such review on Amazon.com is typical of most and suggests on the theme of Nigellahood:

"We all adore (or want to be) Nigella in our house! We love time spent fiddling around with a zillion ingredients, gallons of cream and a dozen eggs BUT this is fabulous too!!

---

[4]Delia Smith is a well-known UK cookbook writer, whose most famous book *Delia Smith's Complete Cookery Course*, published originally in 1978, but since reprinted over 20 times stands not so proud on many a budding cooks' top shelf.

I have two children who love tasty food (who doesn't?) and I needed some new ideas for quick meals! You will find plenty of them in this book and your kids will love trying out some new flavours!! Popular with my two are the white bean mash, chicken schnitzel with bacon and green eggs and ham (frequently accompanied by the Dr Seuss story of the same name!).

Don't be put off by the "Express" element of the title! This is a great book with just enough Nigella chat to also make it a good read when you're not cooking." (http://www.amazon.co.uk/Nigella-Express-Lawson).

A review which 104 out of 118 fellow readers found 'useful'. Another reviewer was less popular and suggested a counter side to her appeal:

"Nigella herself is possibly the most irritating person on TV today-her simpering, her over-the-top adjectives and her ridiculous outings with her 'friends' who have obviously never set eyes on her before make me reach for the off button. BUT I have to admit that her recipes in this new book are terrific." (http://www.amazon.co.uk/Nigella-Express-Lawson)

For us, such vitriol and loathing serves to merely add more vitality and dynamism to the relationships (Fournier, 1996) and connections, consumers generate around the *Nigella brand.*

CONCLUSIONS

By way of a contribution we argue that what makes the *Nigella* brand phenomenon of interest to consumer researchers is not only that it employs circulating subject positions of domesticity and feminisms, but that it is playful with them. It self-consciously nudges away at their assumed limits, subtly disrupting uncontested norms, bending them ever so gently to the imperatives of wider contemporary debates about domestic lifestyles. And in offering resources to help undo, or at least resist embedded assumptions about socially acceptable forms of domesticity, we argue that the 'Nigella Express' cookbook also offers material that is suggestive of strategies for the transformative performance of domesticity. We find that the content of those strategies is generated by means of images informed by ideas that turn on the blurring of boundaries between the pursuit of pleasure through caring for others, and the pursuit of pleasure through caring for the self (which in some cases is achieved through caring for others); between the leisured self and the employed self; between the public world of the workplace and the intimate, private world of domesticity; between the stressed, time-short self and the self-indulgent self; between the controlled self and the decontrolled, calculated hedonist self; between self of deferred pleasures and the self of immediate gratifications; between the cooking as pleasure self and the cooking as additional hassle self. It is then possible to understand those images as sites for rethinking, not only how domesticity is performed, but also how we seek to fashion seductive representations of such conduct. Deeply rooted anxieties can surround the disruption of even apparently minor details defining social differentiation, especially fears over the balance achieved between restraint and self-indulgence, between giving and taking pleasure and what that might say about your ability to conduct yourself in a recognizably acceptable way within contemporary consumer culture.

REFERENCES

Arnould, Eric J. and Thompson, Craig J. (2005), "Consumer Culture Theory (CCT): Twenty Years of Research", *Journal of Consumer Research* 31, (March): 868-882.

Barthes, Roland (1985, orig. 1957) *Mythologies*, translated by Annette Lavers. Palidin: London.

Baudrillard, Jean (1983), *In the shadow of the silent majorities. Or the end of the social*, New York, semiotext(e).

Baudrillard, Jean (1986), *America*. London. Verso.

Baudrillard, Jean (1988), *Selected Writings*. Polity Press: Oxford.

Bourdieu, Pierre (1984), *Distinction: A Social Critique of the Judgement of Taste*. London: Routledge.

Bell, David and Hollows, Joanne (2005), "Making Sense of Ordinary Lives". In *Ordinary Lifestyles: Popular Media, Consumption and Taste*, 1-18. Open University Press: Maidenhead.

Brownlie, Douglas and Hewer, Paul (2007), "Prime Beef Cuts: Culinary Images for Thinking Men", *Consumption, Markets and Culture*, vol.10, (3): 229-250.

Cashmore, Ellis and Parker, Andrew (2003), "One David Beckham? Celebrity, Masculinity, and the Soccerati", *Sociology of Sport* 20, (3): 214-231.

Chaney, David (2002), *Cultural Change and Everyday Life*. Palgrave: Basingstoke.

Fournier, Susan (1998), "Consumers and their Brands: Developing Relationship Theory in Consumer Research", *Journal of Consumer Research*, Vol.24, (March), 343-353.

Holt, Douglas (2004), *How Brands Become Icons: The Principles of Cultural Branding*. Harvard Business School Press: Harvard.

Jameson, Fredric (1991), *Postmodernism or the Cultual Logic of Late Capitalism*. London. Verso

Keller, Kevin Lane (2004), *Strategic Brand Management: Building, Measuring, and Managing Brand Equity*. Prentice Hall: New Jersey.

Lawson, Nigella (2000), *How to be a Domestic Goddess*. Chatto and Windus: London.

_____ (2001), *Nigella Bites*. Chatto and Windus: London.

_____ (2007), *Nigella Express*. Chatto and Windus: London.

Lury, Celia (2004), *Brands: The Logos of the Global Economy*. London. Routledge.

Maffesoli, Michel (1996), *The time of the tribes: The decline of individualism in mass society*. Sage: London.

McCracken, Grant (1989), "Who is the Celebrity Endorser? Cultural Foundations of the Endorsement Process", *Journal of Consumer Research* 16, (3): 310-321.

McCracken, Grant (2005), *Culture and Consumption II: Markets, meaning and brand management*, Bloomington, Indiana University Press.

McLuhan, Marshall (1964), *Understanding Media: the extensions of man*. London. Routledge.

O'Donohoe, Stephanie (2007), "Yummy Mummies: The Clamour of Glamour in Advertising to Mothers", *Advertising and Society Review* 7, (3): 1-17.

O'Guinn, Thomas (1991), "Touching Greatness: The Central Midwest Barry Manilow Fan Club," in *Highways and Buyways: Naturalistic Research from the Consumer Behavior Odyssey*, Russell W. Belk, ed. Provo, UT: Association for Consumer Research, 102–11.

Olsen, S (1999), *Hollywood Planet: Global media and the competitive advantage of narrative transparency*. Mahwah, NJ. Lawrence Erlbaum Associates.

Pringle, H (2004), *Celebrity Sells*. London. Wiley.

Rein, I., Kotler, P and M Stoller (1987), *High Visibility*. London. Heinemann.

Schroeder, Jonathan (2006), "The Artist and the Brand", *European Journal of Marketing*, vol.39, (11): 1291-1305.

Sternberg, E (1998), "Phantasmagoric Labour: The new economics of self-presentation." *Futures,* 30, 1, 3-21.

Sternberg, E (1999), *The economy of Icons: how business manufactures meaning*, Westport, Ct. Praeger.

Wernick, Andrew (1991), *Promotional Culture: Advertising, ideology and symbolic expression*. London. Sage.

Wicks, Patricia; Nairn, Agnes and Griffin, Christine (2007), "The Role of Commodified Celebrities in Children's Moral Development: The Case of David Beckham", *Consumption, Markets and Culture*, vol.10, (4): 401-424.

Woodside, Arch G, Sood, Suresh and Miller, Kenneth E. (2008), "When Consumers and Brands talk: Storytelling theory and research in psychology and marketing", *Psychology and Marketing*, vol.25, (2): 97-145.

Defining the Brand Hero: Explorations of the Impact of Brand Hero Credibility on a Brand Community

Toni Eagar, Australian National University, Australia

ABSTRACT

This article presents a definition of brand hero based on the literature surrounding celebrity endorsement with particular emphasis on source credibility and attractiveness. Three brand communities and their brand hero(es) were analyzed using an ethnographic–grounded theory approach. Findings indicate that brand hero credibility does not solely include expertness, trustworthiness and attractiveness but is complicated by the inter-relationship between the brand, community and hero to include the attributes of integrity and affinity. These are key constructs in the effectiveness of the brand hero in motivating the brand community to act for the benefit of the brand.

INTRODUCTION

While the nature of celebrity is often lamented in modern society (Caughey 1987) marketers have held a positive view of celebrities as potential tools for gaining and holding the attention of potential customers through a focus on celebrities as endorsers of a product or brand (McCracken 1989). However, there is a gap in the research in understanding the nature of brand community celebrities, which are people who are recognized by the brand community for their role within the brand's creation. This article seeks to offer an alternative perspective to that outlined by celebrity endorsement. Through the application of the source credibility framework a more comprehensive understanding of brand hero effectiveness is achieved. The difference in source and audience effects has a profound impact on the application of brand hero credibility. This article will define the concept of brand hero in order to understand the issues surrounding credibility.

THE LITERATURE

A feature of modern society is the rise of fan culture within popular media, which has led to an increasing interest in consumption related social networks, such as brand communities. A brand community is "a specialized, non-geographically bound community, based on a structured set of social relations among admirers of a brand" (Muniz and O'Guinn 2001, p.412). Brand community research has focused on how brand communities positively influence marketing outcomes in terms of brand commitment and meaning, and also for the consumer in the development of self and social identity (McAlexander, Schouten and Koenig 2002, Muniz and Hamer 2001, Muniz and O'Guinn 2001, Muniz and Schau 2005). However, while there has been acknowledgement that there are celebrity influences within a brand community (Belk and Tumbat 2005, Muniz and Schau 2005) there has been little research into the relationship between brand community members and these celebrity figures.

In contrast, there has been extensive research into the area of using celebrities to endorse a brand or product in marketing communications, specifically in advertising. McCracken (1989, p.310) defines a celebrity endorser as "any individual who enjoys public recognition and uses this recognition on behalf of a consumer good appearing with it in an advertisement". A basic assumption of this definition is that a celebrity's public recognition is developed separately from the brand and this recognition is then used to endorse a brand. From this assumption of externally developed recognition, celebrity endorsement research has focused on finding appropriate celebrities and presenting them in persuasive and symbolically representative communications with the brand (McCracken 1989). This has overshadowed study of internally generated celebrities whose public recognition is tied to their role with the brand, thus issues of appropriateness and symbolic congruence are not relevant.

A number of endorsement roles that the celebrity can fulfill have been identified; (1) the celebrity is an expert; (2) is associated with the manufacturer in some long-term capacity; or (3) has no special knowledge, or association with, the product in question (Friedman, Termini and Washington 1976, McCracken 1989). The first role of celebrity endorser as expert can be applied to the brand hero. The brand hero derives their perceived expertise from their involvement in the creation or production of the brand. However, the literature in celebrity endorsement tends to use examples of experts external to the brand, such as a racing car driver endorsing motor oil (McCracken 1989), where their perceived expertise is a consequence of their profession and would impart knowledge about motor products. The second role of the celebrity endorser in association with the manufacturer in a long-term capacity also can be applied to the brand hero concept. For example, singer Kylie Minogue has a long-term relationship with lingerie maker Holeproof in a capacity of designing a range of co-branded lingerie; she doesn't just endorse the product but is involved in its creation. In terms of brand heroes where the brand is the sole creation of that celebrity the association between the celebrity and the manufacturer is indelibly linked. However, not all brand heroes require a long-term relationship, for example, a director may have only worked on one Star Trek movie to be considered a brand hero for the Star Trek brand community. The third role includes only celebrities well-known from external sources, which does not fit within the brand hero concept (McCracken 1989), examples of this include Christina Aguilera and LL Cool J, both singers, appearing in television commercials for Virgin Mobile. Neither celebrity has a special association with the brand through expertness or through a long-term association, as these were one-off appearances. This final role has no equivalent to the concept of brand hero, where the core assumption is some special association to the brand in a capacity internal to the creation or production of the brand.

There have been three main approaches to celebrity endorsement developed. The first two approaches are similar in their application and rely on the target market viewing the celebrity as either a credible source of information or as an attractive source. The third is referred to as the 'meaning movement' approach, where a celebrity is an appropriate endorser when there is congruence in the symbolic images evoked by both the celebrity and the brand. The 'meaning movement' approach may be of importance in understanding the effectiveness of a brand hero, but it is beyond the scope of this article. Source credibility states that the celebrity will be viewed as a credible source when it is perceived that celebrity has the ability to make valid assertions (expertness), and a willingness to make valid assertions (trustworthiness) (McCracken 1989). Source attractiveness has been considered as a separate factor in explaining source effectiveness (Kahle and Homer 1985) or as an additional component of credibility (Kamins 1990). Attractiveness as an indicator of credibility is considered the most appropriate conceptualization, as the focus for brand heroes is not physical attractiveness, but rather their attractiveness is a function of their contribution to the brand's success. However, the nature of brand

FIGURE 1
CASE SELECTION CRITERIA AND CASE SITES SELECTED

	Single Brand Hero	**Multiple Brand Heroes**
Single Role	Discworld	The Brumbies
Multiple Roles		Star Trek

hero credibility is somewhat different which will be explored further in the findings section.

The definition of celebrity does not fully encompass the brand hero concept, as the special association the brand hero has with the brand means that other factors beyond mere recognition are present. The definition that is most widely used is "celebrity is a person who is known for his well-knowness" (Boorstin 1964, p.57). In particular, the key-determining factor of a brand hero being influential in a brand community is their perceived credibility with the brand and the community. However rather than being limited to expertness, trustworthiness, and attractiveness, for the brand hero, credibility takes on additional dimensions as the relationship between the brand, brand community and the brand hero create a more complex relationship of perceptions than the simple brand-endorser memory matrix proposed by McCracken (1989). The findings presented will discuss how current definitions of endorser credibility apply to the brand hero context. Also, credibility will be extended to include the added complexity of the brand community situation and the effect this has on brand community outcomes.

METHOD

The objective of this article is to define the concept of the brand hero and the outcome of credibility on brand hero effectiveness. A qualitative approach was applied as the nature of understanding brand hero credibility is exploratory. Both the grounded theory approach, particularly the principles of building theory from data through constant comparison and theoretical sampling (Glaser and Strauss 1967), and ethnography, and its concern for culturally based patterns of behavior (Goulding 2005) were applied in this research. Theoretical sampling of cases was conducted for analysis (Glaser and Strauss 1967), where sampling was based on a single/multiple role by single/multiple brand hero matrix, with three sites selected that are discussed below, see Figure 1. The analysis method applied was derived from grounded theory, with data being open-coded, then built into categories that through systematic comparison were developed into theoretical constructs and relationships.

Site 1: Discworld

The principal site of investigation was the Discworld brand community. Terry Pratchett as the author of Discworld books represents a single brand hero with a single role. Discworld is a fantasy-comedy series that has sold over 40 million books worldwide. There are 38 books, aimed at adults, in the series. Data collection was ethnographically based with the researcher forming an embedded role in online and real-world Discworld communities. This involved participant observation in online forums and real-world conventions, and in-depth interviews with brand community members and Terry Pratchett

Site 2: The Brumbies

The Brumbies are a rugby union team that competes in the Super14 competition comprising teams from Australia, New Zealand and South Africa. The Brumbies have multiple brand heroes that perform a single role as players. Data collection involved participant observation of fans at games held in Canberra, Australia over a three-year period.

Site 3: Star Trek

Star Trek has multiple brand heroes who have multiple roles from actors, directors, authors and creators of the television series, books and movies. Star Trek is one of the most successful television science fiction series ever, with continuous production of Star Trek related entertainment since the sixties. Data collection was non-participant in nature and involved analyzing the question and answer sessions that were held online at the official Star Trek website (www.startrek.com) between community members and various Star Trek celebrities.

WHO IS THE BRAND HERO?

The different sites of investigation underlined the differences that exist between the traditional conceptualization of the celebrity endorser credibility and how credibility is applied to brand heroes. Figure 2 shows the attributes of the brand, the brand hero and the

FIGURE 2
THE ATTRIBUTES OF BRAND HERO CREDIBILITY

---

brand community that combine to create brand hero credibility. The findings suggest that while the brand hero needs to be seen as an expert and trustworthy, these concepts take on different dimensions in the brand hero context as the brand hero is placed within the milieu of the brand community. As the relationship is more complex there are also additional dimensions to brand hero credibility that will be presented. The findings from the analysis of the different brand community sites indicate that credibility is extended through brand hero integrity and affiliation.

Brand Hero Integrity

The research revealed that for the brand community one of the key brand hero attributes was integrity. The celebrity endorsement literature refers to source credibility in terms of expertness and trustworthiness. Expertness is defined as the perceived ability of the celebrity to make assertions about a product, and trustworthiness is the perceived willingness of the celebrity to make valid assertions (McCracken 1989). These definitions have an underlying assumption that the celebrity's credibility is based on their activities external to the brand, which is then matched-up to the brand and the message (McCracken 1989). Such an assumption does not take into account the credibility that a celebrity might attain through their association with the brand. For instance, Terry Pratchett the brand hero to the Discworld brand community hardly needs to establish his expertness in the Discworld brand or in the fantasy literature product category as his creation of the brand itself has established his legitimacy. When respondents were asked whether they believed Terry Pratchett was a celebrity the responses were mixed but respondents referred to his credibility as an author and his integrity as a representative of the Discworld brand.

"Yes essentially Terry Pratchett is a giant of literature, he's a god. There's nothing else you need to say about Terry Pratchett in my mind he's a giant of literature he's something out there, I don't need him in my life, he's there. His books are in my life and occasionally I go to his lectures and go 'oh wow this is fascinating' it really is." (Chris, Personal Interview)

The statement by Chris indicates that Terry Pratchett's credibility is enhanced because of his perceived status in the product category. One of the core aspects of brand hero credibility is the belief that they represent the top of their field. This status in the field is often expressed in comparative terms between competing brands and brand heroes.

"I completely agree with what Terry Pratchett says. Sorry, but JK is not the only author in the world, and she's a long way short of the best authors around. I am a big Harry Potter fan, but she in no way compares to the Discworld series. She has only wrote one series of books about one main group of characters, and it will be interesting to see where her writing goes after here. Will she be able to take the world that she has invented for HP and write about different people, or will we be stuck with the same people & personalities. Pratchett's discworld series has many different characters with different storys that all somehow complement each other. You very rarely meet a character that you feel you have already encountered in a different person. Lets just look back in twenty years, and see whether there is still such a great demand for the discworld series, & discworld memorabilia, and compare it to how JK is doing.
Mind you, the Harry Potter books are so similar to the star wars series, that maybe we'll be up to the prequels by then!!" (Harry Potter Forum post in TP vs JKR Thread)

For the Discworld community, as a smaller brand in the market, most of the comparisons are made with the largest brand, Harry Potter (Muniz and Hamer 2001, Muniz and O'Guinn 2001). When comparing Terry Pratchett's status to J.K. Rowling the consensus of the community was that he was the better author and deserved more success but that J.K. Rowling was an adequate author who had won the 'lottery', as one online member described it. So for the brand hero the issue of expertness not only depends on their ability to make assertions but also on their perceived status within the product category based on their contribution to the brand's success. This linking of expertness to the brand's success is also present in understanding the notion of trust in source credibility.

> "He doesn't strike me as a kind of arrogant celebrity and I think he would be interesting. I think he writes books because he genuinely wants people to read them not because he's cashing in. I don't get that impression, I don't think he could write the books as well as he does if he was just going: 'Right, I could do with another half mil so you know I'll churn another one out'. I think he genuinely wants you to read them. If you're intelligent you realize that if you're going to make money out of people they're going to have some demand on you." (Tegan, Personal Interview)

For Tegan, Terry Pratchett represents someone who is credible because his motivation for producing Discworld is a love of the brand and the fans. This perception imbues a great deal of trust in Terry Pratchett's management of the brand. Other respondents referred to the notion of 'selling out' and that Pratchett never would, an example of this is in the denial that any Discworld figurines would ever be sold at McDonald's as Happy Meal toys. There was vehement denial that Pratchett would ever allow his brand to be used in such a way, one respondent said that he would have to be 'dead and buried, very dead and very buried before Discworld would be sold out' (David, Personal Interview) and even then another respondent believed that Pratchett's wife and daughter would not 'sell-out' the brand in this way as 'they love it too much' (Sandra, Discworld Convention). The belief that the brand hero creates and manages the brand for the benefit of the brand and its values underpins perceptions of brand hero credibility. So for the brand hero, credibility is defined as the perceived integrity of the brand hero in maintaining the brand's values.

Brand Hero Affiliation

Besides the integrity of the brand hero in maintaining the brand's values another aspect of brand hero credibility related to their attractiveness to the brand community. Source attractiveness as a component of credibility refers to the celebrity's perceived familiarity, likeability and similarity (McGuire 1985). In terms of the brand hero the most salient attractiveness dimension was similarity, where the brand hero had to demonstrate a similar sense of being affiliated to the brand and the community as that felt by the brand community. Familiarity and likeability were not useful constructs in the brand hero context, as familiarity was a part of the brand community experience and likeability was based on a sense of affinity, so they are not covered further. Similarity of perceived affinity was achieved in two ways, (1) the demonstration of a long-held affinity to the brand, and (2) the appearance that the brand hero was just another fan. In order for the brand hero to be accepted by the community the brand hero needed to show that on some level they were 'just like the community members'.

In the first instance when a potential brand hero was presented to the community the brand hero was required to demonstrate that they held the similar affinity with the brand as that of the brand community. This was prevalent in the Star trek brand community where there are a number of brand heroes who perform different roles within the brand. A case that demonstrates this was the Question and Answer (Q&A) session held between the online Star Trek community and the director Robert Wise. This brand hero only had one instance of contributing to the Star Trek brand through his direction of the first Star Trek movie. Many of the questions asked of this brand hero revolved around Robert Wise establishing his credentials as a Star Trek fan.

> "Had you ever seen any "Star Trek" show before Paramount asked you to direct the Motion Picture?" (Romain NIGITA, Robert Wise Q&A, 02.05.2004)

> "Mr. Wise, did you have anything to do with the 1983 TV version, aka the Special Longer Version? Did you re-edit the film specifically for television and video? What prompted the 1983 longer version? Thanks," (James B., Robert Wise Q&A, 02.05.2004)

As Robert Wise had only a brief association with the Star Trek brand the questions that the brand community asked him revolved around his work in the brand and his history with the Star Trek brand. In this Q&A session only one question was asked about Robert Wise's career outside of Star Trek, this in contrast with Leonard Nemoy (Dr. Spock, a long running character from the original television series and movies) where half the questions asked concerned his life outside of Star Trek, with questions such as:

> "Your voice talent is excellent. Will we be seeing more voice work from you?: (designationlocutus, Leonard Nemoy Q&A, 03.04.2003)

> "As a writer and advanced amateur photographer myself for many years now, there are many questions I would like to ask you about your passion for still photography, culminating in your latest, and remarkable, "Shekhina" project. For example, how did your interest in photography evolve, and did you begin with 35mm?" (gundar Leonard Nemoy Q&A, 03.04.2003)

This was interpreted to indicate what Leonard Nemoy had already established his affiliation with the Star Trek brand and as such the community did not need to ascertain his commitment to the brand. The less the brand hero is viewed as having a similar affiliation to the brand the more likely the brand community is to attempt to establish this credibility. So for Robert Wise, who had little long-term affiliation with the brand there was a need to establish the perception of him being committed to the Star Trek brand. Whereas, a brand hero like Leonard Nemoy with a long history of Star Trek involvement did not need to establish his brand affiliation.

The second aspect of brand hero affiliation is the appearance the brand hero is just another fan. This goes beyond merely establishing an affiliation for the brand as discussed previously, but includes those aspects of brand community involvement that define membership activities. For example, Terry Pratchett was considered a credible Discworld community member because he would behave just like any other fan at community events.

> "Now, the question is, why does he do it? Why give up three days of precious free time to spend them in a field with people who would buy your books anyway? Even if it did increase sales, the amount would be a drop in the ocean compared to what he's selling already. So I'm left with the notion that he enjoys it. He walks around, chatting to fans, occasionally being photographed but not, I hope, being hassled too much. He doesn't appear to have an entourage (we saw him walking down from the top barn to his car on Sunday morning, presumably to pick up something) or to have any security worries (if he had any 'minders', they were very well hidden) and because he acts like a 'regular person', that's how he gets treated. It might be that he feels he 'owes' it to the fans to turn

up at events like this. In the Q&A, he was asked whether he was going to be at the Australian Convention, and after saying that the date had been changed a couple of times already, he said that whatever date it finally ended up on, he'd be there, because "they've gone to so much trouble" (and that he never misses a chance to go to Australia). I don't know of any author with a comparable level of sales who gives so much time to keeping fans happy.'" (Diane L, alt.fan.Pratchett, 05.08.2005)

For this Discworld brand community member they perceive that Terry Pratchett is motivated by enjoyment of fan contact rather than by commercial concerns. In her mind this gives added credibility and appeal to Pratchett as a brand hero. The 'regular person' aspect of his credibility presents a persona that the brand community is able to identify as someone similarly committed to the community and the brand. This was also evident in the Brumbies case where the captain, Stirling Mortlock was sidelined due to injury. He demonstrated his commitment to the brand by acting as the waterboy for half the team's season. He also demonstrated an affinity for the community while being the waterboy by interacting with the crowd. For example after an apparently incorrect line call the following exchange occurred:

"Ref are you blind?!" Male 20s
"Ref you can borrow my glasses if you like!" Male 40s
"This guy is useless, isn't he?" Stirling Mortlock to the men yelling
"You should get out there, Waterboy! We need you!" Male 20s

Such exchanges create a sense of the brand hero being on the same side as the brand community, that they are all working together for the benefit of the brand. A similar affinity was found in the Star Trek community:

"What can the fans do to help get more publicity for *Star Trek: Enterprise*?" (Pam, Scott Bakula Q&A, 19.11.2003)

This apparent sense of affinity of the brand hero for the brand community and the resultant expectation from the brand community that they are working with the brand hero for the benefit of the brand is a crucial function of a brand hero. While the celebrity endorser is attempting to persuade the audience (McCracken 1989) the brand hero is attempting to motivate a communal effort between themselves and the brand community for the benefit of the brand. The broader scope of brand hero credibility, that extends to encompass aspects such as integrity and affinity are important considerations in developing effective marketing strategies using a brand hero to communicate to a brand community. The implication of these findings will be discussed in the following section.

IMPLICATIONS AND FURTHER RESEARCH

The results of this research indicate that while the celebrity endorsement literature offers a key foundation in the consideration of the brand hero concept it does not fully encompass the phenomenon. While brand heroes display some similarity to celebrities in their attributes to celebrities these are influenced by the more complex nature of the interaction between the brand, the brand community and the brand hero. This apparent feedback in effects offers an alternative perspective for the study of celebrity endorser effectiveness, which would be a valuable addition to the increasing amount of research in the 'meaning movement' approach (McCracken 1989). McCracken (1989) proposed transference of

meaning between the celebrity and the brand, however, the current research suggests that the transference may be two-way and include social or group meanings. Further research is needed to analyze reciprocity in meaning transference and the effect that social/group meaning has on this relationship.

The definition of the brand hero is distinct from celebrities, as brand heroes are well known by the brand community for their role in the creation, production or consumption experience of a brand. This is in contrast with the common approach to celebrity as something that happens separately to a brand. The findings show that the brand hero has a great deal of influence in providing the motivation for the brand community to engage in behaviors for the benefit of the brand. This sense that the brand hero and the brand community are working together for the continued success of their brand is something that has been alluded to in previous research (Belk and Tumbat 2005, Muniz and Schau 2005), however, it is something that requires further research. This communal effort goes beyond simple persuasion or communicating with the brand community but may form a fundamental core of social identity, where a brand hero may be the most effective tool a marketer could use in developing and maintaining a group of highly committed customers.

The concepts of expertness, trustworthiness and attractiveness as indicators of source credibility are adapted and extended to include brand hero integrity and affinity in the brand hero context. The additional concepts of integrity and affinity are important considerations. The brand hero needs to represent themselves as a symbolic agent of the brand and community's values. Further research is needed on how marketers can build this brand community celebrity, in particular how do you build celebrity for a brand hero while emphasizing the brand hero's credibility? The notion of 'selling out' is inherently anti-corporate or anti-marketing, marketers need to understand how they can create integrity and affinity without creating the perception of 'selling out'. A starting point for this research would be in defining the term 'selling out' and under what conditions the perception of 'selling out' occurs.

Additional research is also required into the effect that brand heroes have on brand community outcomes. This research indicates that being perceived as credible leads to the perception of a communal effort to advance the brand. Important areas of study would be in the nature of the relationships formed between the brand hero and the brand community and an investigation into the effects on community identity and involvement. This additional research would assist marketer's in understanding the nature of the brand hero as a brand community communication source and also the limits that marketers have in controlling the brand hero and in turn the brand community.

The research is limited by the three cases chosen, which represent certain types of brand communities and brand heroes. Further research is needed to ascertain whether the influence of a brand hero is community or hero determined, and a wider selection of brand community sites is required to achieve this. This study is further limited by not including the 'meaning movement' hypothesis in defining brand hero effectiveness. While the current study focused on brand hero credibility, further research into the symbolic transfer of meaning between the brand and the brand hero would be a valuable and interesting extension of the current study. However, understanding the nature of brand hero credibility, in terms of integrity and affinity, is important to our knowledge of the brand community phenomenon. Brand heroes are influential tools in the creation and management of social networks around consumption objects.

REFERENCES

Belk, Russell W., and Gulnur Tumbat (2005), "The Cult of Macintosh," *Consumption, Markets and Culture*, 8(3), 205-217.

Boorstin, Daniel J. (1964), *The Image: A Guide to Pseudo-Events in America*, New York: Harper & Row

Caughey, John L. (1987), "Mind Games: Imaginary Social Relationships in American Sport," in *Meaningful Play, Playful Meaning*, ed. Fine, Gary, Champaign, IL: Association for the Anthropological Study of Play, 19-33

Friedman, Hershey H., Salvatore Termini, and Robert Washington (1976), "The Effectiveness of Advertising Utilizing Four Types of Endorsers," *Journal of Advertising*, 5(Summer), 22-24.

Glaser, Barney G., and Anselm L. Strauss (1967), *The Discovery of Grounded Theory*, Chicago: Aldine

Goulding, C. (2005), "Grounded theory, ethnography and phenomenology: A comparative analysis of three qualitative strategies for marketing research," *European Journal of Marketing*, 39(3/4), 294-308.

Kahle, Lynn R., and Pamela M. Homer (1985), "Physical Attractiveness of the Celebrity Endorser: A Social Adaption Perspective," *Journal of Consumer Research*, 11(March), 954-961.

Kamins, Michael A. (1990), "An Investigation in the "Match-up" Hypothesis in Celebrity Advertising: When Beauty May be Only Skin Deep," *Journal of Advertising*, 19(1), 4-13.

McAlexander, James H., John W. Schouten, and Harold F. Koenig (2002), "Building Brand Community," *Journal of Marketing*, 66(January), 38-54.

McCracken, Grant (1989), "Who is the Celebrity Endorser? Cultural Foundations of the Endorsement Process," *Journal of Consumer Research*, 16(December), 310-321.

McGuire, William J. (1985), "Attitudes and Attitude Change," in *Handbook in Social Psychology*, ed. Gardner, Lindzey, and Elliot Aronson, New York: Random House, 233-346

Muniz, Albert M. Jr., and Lawrence O. Hamer (2001), "Us Versus Them: Oppositional Brand Loyalty and the Cola Wars," *Advances in Consumer Research*, 28, 355-361.

Muniz, Albert M. Jr., and Thomas C. O'Guinn (2001), "Brand Community," *Journal of Consumer Research*, 27(March), 412-432.

Muniz, Albert M. Jr., and Hope Jensen Schau (2005), "Religiosity in the Abandoned Apple Newton Brand Community," *Journal of Consumer Research*, 31(4), 737-747.

When the Brand is Bad, I'm Mad! An Exploration of Negative Emotions to Brands

Simona Romani, DEIR, University of Sassari, Italy
Hamdi Sadeh, Al Quds Open University, Palestine
Daniele Dalli, DEA, University of Pisa, Italy

ABSTRACT

This paper attempts to identify the nature and characteristics of individual negative emotions to brands and the antecedent conditions which affect them. Using introspective essays with consumers in two very diverse cultural contexts (Italy and Palestine), our findings reveal that the negative emotions of dislike and anger are experienced to a much greater extent than others, such as sadness, fear, disappointment. At the same time, we observed the presence of three conditions which consumers focus on and react to in the context of brand, noting that these systematically relate to specific negative emotions.

Lastly, we examined the consistencies and differences between our qualitative results and those of previous quantitative research conducted on negative emotions in general.

INTRODUCTION

The website called "Hatebook", a parody of the famous "Facebook", can be seen to presently be enjoying much success on the internet. Identical to its reputable cousin, but red in color, this site presents itself by way of an elucidatory phrase: "Hatebook is an anti-social utility that disconnects you from the things YOU HATE".

Its users, who are called haters, do not spare anyone and free rein is given to gossip and backbiting. It is possible to hate anything and everything and to do it in company is considered to be much more rewarding. Not by chance, upon entrance, pops up the message: "welcome to the site of bad".

Examination of whether these "hate clans", created "to get rid of all annoying things around you", include some specifically dedicated to brands, revealed that there were indeed 45 with those most targeted featuring a number of classic cases such as Starbucks, Microsoft, Pepsi, and McDonalds, but notably also Burberry, D&G and Vuitton, etc.

For example, in the description of the "I hate Starbucks" clan, the founder, *bartbrains*, writes: "Do you think that Starbucks are not really selling coffee but something like water with syrup, cream and sugar? Do you miss the taste of real coffee? Do you think that people go to Starbucks just to be in fashion? Then this clan is for you".

Similarly, on the hate-board of the "I hate Microsoft" clan Rocker wrote 2007-11-25 at 01:05:55 h. "Linux Rules. Fuck Windows"; coolzone wrote 2007-11-13 at 14:28:49 h. "I HATE BUGS, I HATE microsoft's BSOTD!!" and josefstalin wrote 2007-11-03 at 12:36:18 h "All capitalist pigs should suffer for their lack of equality".

These cases demonstrate that, while it is possible for consumers to like or even love some brands, have an emotional attachment to or in any case generally positive feelings toward them, at the same time it is also true that consumers can express negative feelings, such as hate, dislike, anger, etc.

Yet most prior examination of consumer-brand relationships has given little consideration to these negative aspects.

This is not to say that negative feelings have not featured in certain brand research; some studies touch upon phenomena closely related to negative emotions and feelings (e.g. Holt 2002; Hollenbeck and Zinkham 2006), but an explicit development of the topic is still notably lacking in the literature.

Above all, the research available on negative emotional reactions to brands is significantly limited, especially in comparison with that conducted on those positive. In terms of negative emotions regarding brands, the almost exclusive focus on brand dissatisfaction is far outweighed by the wide range of positive responses explored-e.g., brand love (Shimp and Madden 1988; Whang, Allen, Sahoury, and Zhang 2004; Carroll and Ahuvia 2006; Keh, Pang and Peng 2007), brand attachment (Thomson, McInnis, and Park 2005; Thomson 2006; Park, MacInnis and Priester 2007), brand passion (Fournier 1998), brand satisfaction (Oliver 1997; Fournier and Mick 1999; Giese and Cote 2000) and brand delight (Oliver, Rust and Varki1997; Durgee 1999; Swan and Trawick 1999; Kumar, Olshavsky and King 2001).

In addition, there is limited marketing research addressing the situational conditions, or antecedents, associated with specific consumption emotions (as exceptions, see Folkes 1984; Folkes, Koletsky and Graham 1987; Nyer 1997; Ruth, Bruner and Otnes 2002; Soscia 2007).

This paper aims to address these research gaps in an attempt to identify the nature of individual negative emotions to brands and the antecedent conditions that cause them.

This investigation would provide considerable insights, on a theoretical level, in order to better understand and explain consumer-brand relationships; what's more, this type of knowledge could be of great benefit to brand managers who need to enhance their understanding of the situational conditions associated with negative emotions in the selected targets and to verify the possibility of devising specific countermeasures.[1]

In comparison with the prevailing research on emotions and appraisals this study employs a non traditional approach based on unstructured introspective essays involving consumers in two extremely diverse socio-cultural contexts: Italy and Palestine.

This approach allows for stepping back from the dominant paradigms to investigate and describe negative emotions to brands from the firsthand viewpoints of those directly involved (analogous logics are present in, among others, Fournier and Mick 1999 and Kwortnik and Ross 2007). Our goal can therefore be seen to be threefold: 1. develop a realistic account of negative emotions to brands as they arise in everyday life, 2. identify relevant antecedent conditions capable of generating varying negative emotions to brands, and 3. compare this knowledge with prevailing paradigms on emotions in order to reveal possible similarities and differences.

EMOTIONAL RESPONSES AND CONSUMPTION

Emotions can be said to have a specific referent (e.g. consumer is angered by poor shop service).

More explicitly, emotions arise in response to an appraisal of something of relevance to one's well-being. As specified by Bagozzi, Gopinath and Nyer (1999) "appraisal" means an evaluative judg-

---

[1]In some situations, negative emotions toward a brand could actually be the result of a particular brand positioning strategy that necessarily implies a negative reaction from some specific targets considered not interesting by the company.

ment and interpretation thereof, while "something of relevance" implies a personally experienced incident or episode, an action performed or result produced by oneself, or changes in an object person of thought with personal meaning.

It is important to consider that although types of events or physical circumstances are frequently associated with particular emotional responses, there is not a direct, causal relationship between the two but rather the latter is the result of each individual's unique psychological appraisal, evaluation and interpretation of the former.

It is possible for the same stimulus to be interpreted in a number of ways, thus giving rise to various emotions: a parent's forbiddance of his/her child buying a desired product could be interpreted by the child as an unforeseen and intolerable obstacle, perhaps producing anger; or it could well be construed as a way of limiting personal independence, possibly generating sadness. Thus, the resulting emotion is essentially an experience of the emotion producing situation and its potential positive or negative significance for the individual person, and so, varying emotions can be said to be characterized by different situational meaning structures (Frijda 1986).

This central role of appraisal in the formation of emotions has led to the definition of what are aptly called appraisal theories in psychology (e.g., Frijda 1986; Lazarus 1991; Ortony, Clore, and Collins 1988; Roseman 1991; Roseman, Antoniou and Jose 1996; Smith and Ellsworth 1985).

Appraisal theorists maintain that cognitive elements are: a) an integral part of the emotion, in that each emotion corresponds to a specific meaning structure or cognitive examination of the situation; and b) the direct cause of the emotional experience and behavior.

A distinctive feature of appraisal theories is the number and type of cognitive elements that give rise to discrete emotional responses. The literature is extremely rich, but there is also a strong degree of convergence between the different approaches (Scherer 1988; Watson and Spence 2007).

While the confines of this paper do not allow us to present a full review of these theories, we do focus on their use for studying negative consumption emotions, their cognitive appraisal and possible effects.

Folkes (1984) and Folkes, Koletsky and Graham (1987) manipulate the three principal dimensions of causality (locus, stability and controllability) in order to examine their relation to anger. It is clear that respondents in situations where product failure is due to a firm's controllable actions report higher levels of anger than when it is consumer-related or beyond the firm's control. Also, anger stemming from failure on the part of the service provider can be seen to be associated with increased negative post-purchase consumer behavior (refund, demanding apology, complaining, etc.).

Likewise, Nyer (1997) manipulates certain appraisals (goal relevance and congruence, attribution and coping potential) ascertaining that various combinations can influence respondents' anger and sadness in the evaluation of computer products. These emotions are also shown as determinants of post-consumption behavior such as negative word of mouth.

More recently, Soscia (2007) demonstrates the correlation between two different appraisals (goal congruence and agency), guilt and also certain post-consumption behavior such as negative word of mouth and customer complaint.

Ruth et al. (2002), further demonstrate the systematic relationship between nine cognitive appraisals from Ellsworth and Smith (1988) and six specific negative emotions (fear, anger, sadness,

guilt, uneasiness and embarrassment) in a consumption context, making use of variance and multiple discriminant analysis.

However, these studies focus on emotions generated by general consumption situations–subjective states that occur when considering, buying or using a product-and not on those specifically elicited by brands; it is possible, therefore, that additional research is required to identify a specific set of negative emotions in relation to brands.

In fact, in the case of a specific focus on emotions in relation to brands we can expect much more emphasis on emotions brought about by reactions to the object and its possible meanings rather than on emotions determined by decision making processes and subjective experiences that characterize consumption situations considered in a broader and more generic sense.

Additionally, it is worth noting that previous research has been experiment-focused or correlational in nature, providing evidence regarding the possible systematic relationship between appraisals and certain negative consumption emotions, based on existing psychological theories; however, a thorough examination of negative emotions as experienced and expressed through the consumer is lacking. Those concerned with marketing have yet to accurately and comprehensively assess these types of emotions in the context of normal everyday life and with regards to brands.

Consequently, this study attempts to address the following research questions:

1. What kind of negative emotions do consumers experience in relation to a specific brand?
2. What are the relevant antecedent conditions capable of generating various negative emotions to brands?
3. And finally, is it possible to relate this set of conditions to salient cognitive appraisals, or an interpretation of situations according to the likely impact on one's well-being (Bagozzi et al. 1999) as documented in various emotion appraisal theories put forward by a number of authors?

METHODOLOGY

In order to address these research questions and further our knowledge of the nature and characteristics of consumer negative emotions to brands, this study employs a projective method. This technique has proven useful in a variety of contexts where more traditional quantitative and qualitative methods fail to achieve an adequate understanding of consumer behavior processes and consumption symbolism (among others, Belk, Ger and Askegaard 2005; Havlena and Holak 1996; Zaltman and Coulter 1995).

Our informants consisted of consumers in both Italy and Palestine. The Italian consumers totaled one hundred and fifteen male and females (equally distributed) aged between 18 and 51 and the Palestinian consumers numbered fifty six (equally distributed) aged between 20 and 25.

Our main intent in selecting these two cultural contexts was to avoid the narrow confines of an individual, typically western country, with an interest in broadening the scope of our data rather than necessarily creating the basis for a cross-cultural, comparative investigation.

We made use of introspective essays as a qualitative, projective method. These essays allowed us to evoke consumers' feelings and emotions without their being directly guided by an interviewer (Lupton 1996). They were requested to write down the name of a brand capable of generating negative emotional responses, specify these feelings, and provide an open and detailed account of the reasons for their reactions.

Questions and responses were in Italian or Arabic, where appropriate. The essays were analyzed independently by two of the native tongued authors, and additionally we collectively re-evaluated our interpretations a number of times.

Not surprisingly, we found both similarities and differences between the two locations, and naturally, our findings are particular to the culture and people studied. However, we found that some differences had more to do with emphasis and specifics than essential content. Indeed, an initially extensive list of areas of difference was progressively reduced during our collective meetings.

From this iterative process, we are able to present our findings by way of topic, noting cultural differences in the presence of systematic evidence.

FINDINGS

Our findings are divided into two parts, beginning with a description of the nature of negative emotions to brands as experienced by our informants and then turning to the antecedent conditions of their occurrence. The latter gives place to most of the discussion about possible cultural effects on emotions toward brands. Following these two sections, we then discuss the possibility of relating this set of conditions to the salient appraisals well documented in emotion appraisal theories by certain authors and consider the potential implications for brand theory.

Dislike and anger as main negative emotions to brands

Firstly, it is worth noting that, with rare exception, respondents were able to effectively describe the emotions they felt toward the brand and differentiate not only between the different basic positive and negative emotional states, but also those more analogous such as sadness, anger, dislike, etc.

Indeed, after focalizing on their chosen brand, respondents' accounts often concentrate on one particular emotion, describing it in detail and generally keeping it separate from others that can be considered similar in terms of valence, yet distinct in terms of nature and content.

We witness in both research contexts that respondents are by and large spontaneously drawn toward one specific negative emotional state and much less frequently inclined to describe a combination of such emotions.

It appears, therefore, that each emotional state is distinct and characterized by something peculiar to it; a set of psychological sensations capable of making it possible to distinguish one from another.

The two fundamental groups of negative emotions consumers experience to brands can be seen to be centered around dislike and anger.

Dislike emotions[2] are typical, affective and aesthetic reactions to brands based on evaluations of unappealingness, which are, in turn, dependent on personal attitudes and tastes.

These emotions are characterized by different levels of intensity, covering a continuum of feelings from simple dislike and to the extreme and global, negative emotion of hate. The typical emotion terms within this range chosen by consumers to express their negative feelings toward brands are aversion, distaste, disgust and revulsion.

So, I felt dislike and distaste toward this brand (P-M, 18)
I don't trust this brand and I honestly, really hate it (P-M, 20)

Consumers also report feeling cross, irritated, spiteful, indignant toward a brand, expressing prototypical features of the emotion anger.

I feel very cross, irritated and spiteful toward all the Tuna Marina brand products (P-M, 21)
I feel indignant and hostility toward the Coca Cola brand, for many reasons (P-F, 21)

The role assigned to other negative emotions such as sadness,[3] fear and disappointment[4] is extremely marginal.

Our findings corroborate the suggestion by Bagozzi et al. (1999) that the dominance of the dissatisfaction construct in marketing is possibly due more to its being the primary emotion to receive attention rather than constituting a unique, fundamental construct in and of itself, and that, therefore other negative emotions could be of equal or even greater importance in consumption contexts.

Antecedent conditions of negative emotions to brands

The three main brand-related antecedent conditions which consumers can focus on, evaluate and react to, are the:

* physical object
* symbolic cultural object
* agent

Physical object

Whilst acknowledging the central role of a product's symbolism in consumption culture, it is also essential to recognize that its physical attributes and functions continue to play an important role. In fact, consumers' negative feelings can result from an attenuation of their relationship with a brand due to an intentional or inadvertent disruption in its conduct (Fajer and Schouten 1995; Fournier 1998). Such a breakdown can have a multitude of causes, including the undoubtedly important role played by unmet promises by marketers in terms of brand performance, as reported below:

I literally hate Clinique products. They're really expensive, and claim to be hypo-allergenic, but I still got an allergic reaction. I felt totally cheated. I mean, I'd practically thrown my money away for nothing (I-F, 20)

Additional factors also capable of generating consumers' negative feelings toward brands are changing consumer needs, criteria of liking or even the appearance of potentially superior alternatives:

I really don't like Onyx. It's okay for a young adolescent target, but it doesn't go with my way of dressing. When I was younger, I liked the brand a lot, but then I grew up and their stuff just stayed the same. I think it's a brand that needs updating (I-F, 25).
I really don't like Lotto products! They've hardly changed in years, and have never known how to reinvent themselves in any way (I-M, 19)

---

[2]This concept of dislike differs from that put forward by Dalli, Romani and Gistri (2006). In that case dislike was a global, negative consumer response to a brand and not a group of emotions, as in this paper.

[3]Sadness is often associated with anger; this mix of emotions will be discussed subsequently.

[4]The absence of this emotion, usually present in consumption situations (Zeelenberg and Pieters 1999), could be explained by the fact that disappointment is specifically related to decision making whereas here consumers' accounts that focus on decision processes related to brands are decidedly marginal.

In the above cases the brand is considered as a physical object with material characteristics and functionalities with the negative consumer reaction resulting from its relative unattractiveness.

In addition to this type of negative consumer responses to brands that is common to both Italian and Palestinian respondents, we see an interesting phenomenon emerging solely for the latter. It appears that Palestinians' resentment toward the state of Israel leads to their denigrating the quality of Israeli products and services, perceiving them as personal and culture specific, and consequently disliking these particular brands.

This can be seen to be especially true for products such as food and services, which are particularly culturally imbedded and difficult to disconnect from those who produce them; Palestinian consumers' animosity can be seen to have a significant negative impact on their perception and assessment of the quality of Israeli products.

I hate all of this Israeli brand's products and I don't like seeing any of them on the Palestinian market. I view this brand as an enemy of Palestinian, and so I advise everyone I know not to buy any of its products. I don't trust them either because they could contain toxic substances, especially given Israeli policy (P-F, 19).

This kind of milk is produced in Israel for children. One day, I bought it for my little brother from an Israeli market and it was wonderful. When my mother asked me to buy another carton, and I bought it in a Palestinian area, it gave him many health problems. This must be due to Israel's mean and devious policy of allocating toxic containers to Palestinian markets and harmless ones to their own. I hate this brand because of its differentiation policy and the fact that it isn't concerned about children's health. (…) I won't trust any Israeli brands in the future (P-F, 23)

This type of negative response to brands, due to the presence of animosity toward an ethnic group, resulting in negative product-quality judgments is also documented by Shoham et al (2006) in a comparable cultural context. This study examines Jewish Israeli reactions to Arab Israelis regarding the purchase and consumption of products and services produced or marketed by the latter.

Here, this result is extremely noteworthy given that previous research (Klein 2002; Klein, Etterson and Morris 1998) concludes that such animosity has no effect on product/brand judgments and emotions.

The symbolic cultural object

It appears that people buy brands for something other than their mere physical attributes and functions (Levy 1999).

Consumers attach positive and negative meanings to their consumption choices in order to create and maintain social and cultural identities (McCracken 1986); they also use these meanings to establish similarity and difference and in doing so, call for inclusion within or exclusion from particular social settings.

Wilks (1997) provides an example of this, demonstrating that distaste and refusal are often given greater importance than taste and choice in their being more effective as social indicators, despite the fact that likes tend to be much easier to communicate than dislikes.

Hogg's research can also be considered from the viewpoint that consumers' anti-choices are aimed at creating distance from the undesired self they want to be disassociated from (Banister and Hogg 2004; Hogg and Banister 2001). According to Hogg's findings, consumers are able to define themselves by means of the formation of distaste and associated negative stereotypes.

In their written reports, a number of consumers can be seen to express negative feelings toward brands that, due to their symbolic associations, are not self-expressive or are connected to one or more specific stereotypes or social groups from which they want to distance themselves.

The sense of dislike expressed below by Rossana is based on the fact that she cannot identify with the brand's image and, furthermore, that the brand actually appears to her to be associated with a profile she finds objectionable: showgirls. It is clear that this brand does not contribute to her identity construction and, in addition, is capable of shifting her identity toward an undesired self.

I really don't like Monella Vagabonda! I consider it to be a brand that doesn't represent me at all; a brand for showgirl types! (I-F, 21)

On the other hand, the negative feelings expressed below by Angela toward Paciotti depend on an association between the brand and particular stereotypical characteristics of the typical user. Angela believes that those who possess Paciotti products have character traits she dislikes. In terms of emotion, the effect is stronger, resulting in "disgust".

The brand Paciotti really disgusts me! In my experience, people who wear these shoes are usually loutish and pay a lot of attention to appearances (I-F, 27)

Generally speaking, at times brands represent actual or ideal human profiles from which consumers want to distance themselves since they dislike them as such or because of their specific traits and characteristics. In this sense, by association, brands are capable of conveying negative or positive symbolic meanings, and are used as a means for communicating one's idiosyncrasies to others.

As a matter of fact, our informants from Italy and Palestine can be seen to significantly differ with regards to this dimension. While many Italian subjects make reference to brands as carriers of negative symbolic meanings, no Palestinian expresses such attitudes.

This asymmetry can be explained in a number of ways. Firstly, the situation in the Palestinian territories (the Israeli occupation and acute social and economic recession) can be said to be devastating, with harsh and continual threats to social, cultural and even physical conditions. Understandably, the vast majority of Palestinians concentrate on their primary needs for survival and not on desires (Annajjar 2007; Abdelhameed 2004). Consequently, they attach little or no importance to differentiation, inclusion or exclusion as a matter of cultural and/or symbolic identity construction mediated by consumer goods and brands.

From the situation above it follows that Palestinians live according to a commonly shared subsistence or survival existence that is not a matter of choice as in affluent Italy, but of providence: these consumers are condemned to considering solely the functional aspects of consumption and not those symbolic. In this sense there is little differentiation between these "consumers" and–even for religious or moral beliefs–they give no importance to material goods as a means for social and cultural distinction.

In addition, the Palestinian community can be said to be a sort of tribal community in which everyone is strictly embedded in a complex network of clans and sects. They have no additional "need" for inclusion/distinction as occurs in western societies where individuals have lost their sense of belonging and ask for "linking value" (Cova 1997). They do not "need" goods or services to feel closer to other consumers, since their self is already well-rooted in a specific tribal structure (Abdelhameed 2004; Alsorany 2006; Annajjar 2007; Helal 2005; Helles 2003).

Moreover, this tribal configuration has the effect of reducing the individual dimension of living: personal expression undergoes "communal" processes such as discipline, obedience and self-sacrifice for group benefit. Individual identity depends on integration within the group structure and–almost by definition–one's clan or tribe affiliation ensures no need for further "distinction".

In other words, if properly integrated within the social structure, one's culture becomes an integral part of belonging to a group, removing the need for "individual" expression.

The agent

According to that presented above, it is evident that consumers attach functional or symbolic properties to the brand as an inanimate object. However, recent studies have developed a richer and more variegated picture of the consumer-brand relationship: the brand's role appears to be more complex than it used to be. Researchers have put forward the idea of the brand as an active partner in a dyadic relationship (Fournier 1998), a real agent. Consumers actively infer and construct brand meaning, generating emotions toward them, but it can also be argued that brands have their own attitudes to their target markets, which iteratively affects consumers' evaluations (Dall'Olmo Riley and de Chernatony 2000; McEnally and de Chernatony 1999). This premise is based on the fact that brands act by way of their "parent" company's actions, such as the everyday execution of marketing strategies and overall (in)activity related to social, ethical and/or political issues.

Following this line of reasoning, brands are considered not only for what they represent, symbolize and communicate, but also for what they actually do with this active role being played mainly through their company's actions. Consumers make little or no distinction between the brand and its manufacturer and the brand becomes a sort of synonym for the company: the company is perceived as the brand and the brand as the company (Aggarwal 2004). When something occurs that is perceived as incorrect, consumers say "brand x did this, brand y did that", explicitly referring to the brand when speaking about company behavior.

As a result, consumers commit themselves to brands that behave in ways that give the appearance of their sharing common views and values, whilst they are troubled by those seen to have an incorrect conduct, evading the civic responsibilities expected of a community pillar (Holt 2002).

The following excerpts are clear examples of this aspect: consumers explicitly associate regrettable behavior and even forethought and hypocrisy to brands. Brands are capable of doing bad things and it appears they can do it purposefully and with satisfaction.

I feel indignant toward Nestlé. I can't stand its opportunistic and unethical behavior and the fact that it tries to conceal this by using a false and misleading exterior appearance (I-F, 22) Sometimes they like making people angry with them. I am angry and indignant because of their shameful advertisements. They should respect the regional culture and religion of where they are broadcast (P-M, 20)

In the Palestinian reports the brand's country of origin can be seen to be of great relevance in this perspective. Respondents express strong negative emotions toward brands manufactured in "enemy" countries for political (e.g. Israel or the USA) as well as religious reasons (e.g. Denmark for its publication of cartoons perceived as offensive to Muslims). These consumers recount

feeling negative emotions to brands that come from these countries because of their very origin. In these cases, it is not company behavior, but that of certain individuals from the country in question that is extended to the population as a collective subject (the Americans/Danish do this or that) and even to the country itself as an agent (the U.S./Denmark did something).

I feel really cross, irritated, and spiteful toward all products with the brand-name Tuna Marina; simply because it's Israeli (P-M, 21) I feel indignant and hostile toward Coca Cola, for many reasons; firstly, it is an American company (P-M, 21) I feel angry and annoyed with this brand because of its country's disrespect for Muslim feelings and Islam.(P-M, 19).

In short, brands can be conceived as agents: they are given the "personality" to do things, put ways of behaving into practice. They can also be considered as representative of collective agents (people, countries). This occurs when consumers associate specific events and individual conduct with "collective" properties of the community/country of origin on an ideological, ethical and/or religious level and when their normative implications are perceived as different from those of the consumer.

In these circumstances, the brand acts as an agent and, as such, is able to elicit emotions that can differ from those elicited by the brand as an object, as is apparent in the discussion below.

Relating brand negative emotions and appraisal theories

Analysis of our data reveals that the brand-related conditions on which consumers focus, or an individual's interpretation of brand were often related to particular emotional responses. More specifically, in both research contexts, we see the majority of dislike emotions being associated with the brand perceived as a physical object and those of anger with its interpretation as an agent.

This product is a replacement of an Israeli one called "Tapozena". Marawi is not a good choice.

The bottle shape is unattractive, the taste is bad, and bearing these qualities in mind, the price is high. Therefore, I dislike and feel distaste toward this brand's product (P-M, 18). I feel indignant toward Nestlé. Of all the multinationals it is the symbol of exploitation, abuse of power and a total lack of ethics. Also, it produces so many products that at times it becomes impossible to avoid buying one of them (I-F, 27)

In the Italian context, dislike emotions can also be seen to be related to the brand interpreted as a symbolic cultural object.

These systematic relationships between negative emotions and an individual's brand interpretation strongly relate to salient appraisals documented by various emotion theories.

As observed primarily by Ortony et al (1988), but also, with slight differences, by a number of authors (among others, Ben-Ze'ev 2000; Roseman et al. 1996), the group of dislike emotions result primarily from reactions to objects qua objects whose intensity tends to be influenced by the "unappealingness" of the item of interest.

We found this salient appraisal to be consistent with our data since the majority of dislike emotions are related to an interpretation of a brand as an inanimate object with utilitarian and functional and/or symbolic values. In addition, respondents' reports on disliked brands can be seen to closely relate to the characteristic feelings, thoughts, action tendencies and goals of dislike identified by Roseman, Wiest and Swartz (1994). A number of respondents describe sentiments like wanting to reject and distance themselves from the brand, as illustrated below:

I hate Datch! I would never wear it. It's a rough and vulgar brand...in fact it's represented by a big-head like Costantino. I wouldn't ever want anyone to think that I identify with that style, I'd feel terrible. (I-M, 28)

On the other hand, anger emotions differ from those of dislike since they derive from disapproval of someone else's questionable actions (and their consequences) rather than a global and detailed evaluation of an object's appealingness (Ortony et al. 1988). Anger is the classic example of emotions that are "other oriented" (Smith and Ellsworth 1985; Roseman et al. 1996), that is, generated from others' responsibility. As with dislike, this involves a negative evaluation, but it is the appraisal of particular actions performed by others rather than of an object.

Once again, we found this salient theoretical appraisal of anger emotions to be consistent with our data, since consumers' interpretations consider the brand as an active agent (Fournier, 1998) by way of its administering managers' activities or country of origin's policies. Consumers can be seen to feel anger when these actions are considered unfair and/or questionable.

Respondents' reports on brands capable of generating anger can also be seen to correlate closely with hypotheses upheld by Roseman et al. (1994) that considers it to be an emotion that involves the desire to attack in order to injure someone else.

Indeed, we see that respondents can feel extremely negative towards brands whose behavior they consider unfair, and wish to seriously damage them, as illustrated below:

Buck is just one of the Danish brands about which I couldn't care less about quality. I feel hate and aggression toward all Danish products because of the great insult to the Prophet Mohammed in a Danish newspaper. This offends over one billion Muslims. Indeed, this was condemned and denounced by the Muslim world by way of an economic boycott of Danish brands. So, let this be a lesson to those who attempt to insult Islam in the future. I boycott Danish brands, and I urge all my friends and relatives to do likewise until the government of Denmark apologizes to the Muslim world. I despise all Muslims who buy any Danish brands, considering them to be disloyal to Islam (P-M, 23).

Whereas in the presence of dislike emotions individuals are inclined to avoid confronting the brand, in the case of anger they often wish to correct the brand's behavior, at times through extreme action or forms of punishment, in order to be able to (re)create a possible relationship with it.

Lastly, some consideration can be given to sadness; this particular emotion is marginally present in consumers' descriptions, but when it is, it is rarely alone, and often associated with anger. Consumers that disapprove of a brand's culpable actions are often contemporarily unhappy about the related undesirable events that could derive from them.

I feel anger and indignation toward Adidas, but also sadness. I saw a documentary in Germany, about how Pakistani children of three years and up make Adidas shoes and other items that I could never buy (I-F, 26)

The emergence of this emotional mix in respondents' descriptions is somewhat unaligned with the theoretical models presented by various appraisal theorists, which tend to emphasize the underlying differences that exist between these two emotions. Ortony et al. (1988) are the only authors that consider a possible association between these two emotional states. Nevertheless, this evidence is somewhat weak and additional research is required to investigate this issue further.

CONCLUSION

Using a qualitative projective method, we found that similar consumer negative emotions to brands occur in two diverse cultural contexts. Our findings demonstrate that the negative emotions of dislike and anger are experienced to a greater extent than others, such as sadness, fear and disappointment. At the same time, we observed the presence of three conditions on which consumers focus and react to in the context of brand, noting that these systematically relate to specific negative emotions.

Lastly, we examined the consistencies with and differences between our qualitative results and those of previous quantitative research conducted on negative emotions in general.

This study complements research on specific negative emotions in the context of consumption. Our findings also prove to be consistent with past causal research on individual consumption emotions such as anger, where we observed the salience of other-oriented responsibility and control, as does Folkes (1984), Nyer (1997) and Ruth et al. (2002).

In addition, we are contributing to that line of research by providing a foundation for studying under-considered consumption emotions, such as dislike.

However, this paper's main contribution is on the subject of brand, by providing preliminary and relatively new evidence for the vastly under-researched phenomenon of negative emotions to brands. A particular aspect of our findings can also be said to be intriguing from a theoretical standpoint. The fact that anger and dislike are the negative emotions most commonly experienced by consumers, both in isolation and combination with others, offers ample space for reflection on the possibility of enriching the analysis of negative emotional paths in the consumer brand relationship, given the, until now, sole consideration of dissatisfaction as the typical negative emotional response to brands.

The expansion of this investigation could have important theoretical, but also managerial implications given the importance of limiting, or even better, avoiding the diffusion of negative emotions toward brands for their managers.

This study's use of a projective method allows for advantages in collecting data about actual rather than prompted or manipulated emotions. However, this needs to be further complemented by alternative projective as well as qualitative methods, in order to evaluate the strength and validity of our results and the possibility to enrich them. Additional research is in progress to address these issues.

REFERENCES

Abdelhameed, Mazen (2004), *The Social Aspects of the Palestinian Culture*, Amman: The Jordanian for Printing and Publication, 1st Ed.

Aggarwal, Pankaj (2004), "The effects of brand relationship norms on consumer attitudes and behaviour," *Journal of Consumer Research*, 31 (June), 87-101.

Alsorany, George (2006), "The Palestinian Cultural Reality," a brochure of the Palestinian Ministry of Culture, The Palestinian Ministry of Culture.

Annajjar, Salem (2007), "Reading the Palestinian Cultural Scene," *Periodical of the Civilized Dialogue*, Vol. 1299.

Bagozzi, Richard P., Mahesh Gopinath, and Prashanth U. Nyer (1999), "The role of emotions in marketing," *Journal of the Academy of Marketing Science*, 27 (2), 184-206.

Banister, Emma N. and Margaret K. Hogg (2004), "The role of the negative self in Consumption," Paper presented at the EMAC Conference, Murcia, Spain.

Belk, Russel W., Guliz Ger, and Soren Askegaard (2003), "The fire of desire: a multisided inquiry into consumer passion," *Journal of Consumer Research*, 30 (December), 326-351.

Ben-Ze'ev, Aaron (2000), *The subtlety of emotions*, Cambridge, MA: MIT Press.

Carroll, Barbara A. and Aaron C. Ahuvia (2006), "Some antecedents and outcomes of brand love," *Marketing Letters*, 17 (2), 79-89.

Cova, Bernard (1997), "Community and consumption: toward a definition of the 'linking value' of products or services", *European Journal of Marketing*, 31 (3/4), 297-316.

Dalli, Daniele, Simona Romani, and Giacomo Gistri (2006), "Brand Dislike: Representing The Negative Side of Consumer Preferences," in *Advances in Consumer Research*, Vol. 33, eds. Cornelia Pechmann and Linda L. Price, Duluth, MN : Association for Consumer Research, 87-95.

Dall'Olmo Reilly, Francesca and Leslie de Chernatony (2000), "The service brand as relationships builder", *British Journal of Management*, 11, 137-150.

Durgee, Jeffrey F (1999), "Deep soulful satisfaction," *Journal of Consumer Satisfaction, Dissatisfaction and Complaining Behavior*, 12, 53–63.

Ellsworth, Phoebe C. and Craig A. Smith (1988), "From appraisal to emotion: differences among unpleasant feelings," *Motivation and Emotion*, 12 (3), 271-302.

Fajer, Mary T. and John W. Schouten (1995), "Breakdown and dissolution of person-brand relationships," in *Advances in Consumer Research*, 22, 663-667.

Folkes, Valerie S. (1984), "Consumer reactions to product failure: an attributional approach", *Journal of Consumer Research*, 10 (March), 398-409.

Folkes, Valerie S., Susan Koletsky and John L. Graham (1987), "A field study of causal inferences consumer reaction: the view from the airport", *Journal of Consumer Research*, 13 (March), 534-539.

Fournier, Susan (1998), "Consumers and their brands: Developing relationship theory in consumer research," *Journal of Consumer Research*, 24 (March), 343-373.

Fournier, Susan and David G. Mick (1999), "Rediscovering satisfaction," *Journal of Marketing*, 63 (October), 5-23.

Frijda, Nico H. (1986), *The emotions*, Cambridge: Cambridge University Press.

Giese, Joan L. and Joseph A. Cote (2000), "Defining consumer satisfaction," *Academy of Marketing Science Review*, 1, 1-24.

Havlena, William J. and Susan L. Holak (1996), "Exploring nostalgia imagery through the use of consumer collages," in *Advances in Consumer Research*, Vol. 23, ed. Frank R. Kardes, Provo, UT: Association for Consumer Research, 35-43.

Helal, Jamal (2005), *Secularism in the Palestinian Political Culture*, Amman: Zahran House for Publication, 1st Ed.

Helles, Mahmoud (2003), "Culture in the Palestinian Education," *Humanities Studies Periodical Journal*, 27 (1), 67–95.

Hogg, Margaret K. and Emma N. Banister (2001), "Dislikes, distastes and the undesired self: conceptualising and exploring the role of the undesired end state in consumer experience," *Journal of Marketing Management*, 17, 73-104.

Hollenbeck, Candice R. and George M. Zinkhan (2006), "Consumer Activism on the Internet: The Role of Anti-brand Communities," in *Advances in Consumer Research*, Vol. 33, eds. Cornelia Pechmann and Linda L. Price, Duluth, MN: Association for Consumer Research, 479-485.

Holt, Douglas B. (2004), "Why do brands cause trouble? A dialectical theory of consumer culture and branding", *Journal of Consumer Research*, 29 (June), 70-90.

Keh, Hean Tat, Jun Pang and Siqing Peng (2007), "Understanding and measuring brand love", Paper presented for the 2007 *Advertising and Consumer Psychology: New Frontiers in Branding: Attitudes, Attachments, and Relationships*. Santa Monica, CA, June 7th to 9th.

Klein, Jill P. (2002), "Us versus them, or us versus everyone? Delineating consumer aversion to foreign goods," *Journal of International Business Studies*, 33 (2), 345–63.

Klein, Jill P., Richard Ettenson and Marlene D. Morris (1998), "The animosity model of foreign product purchase: an empirical test in the people's Republic of China," *Journal of Marketing*, 62 (January), 89–100.

Kumar, Anand, Richard W. Olshavsky, and Maryon F. King (2001), "Exploring alternative antecedents of customer delight," *Journal of Consumer Satisfaction, Dissatisfaction and Complaining Behavior*, 14, 14–26.

Kwortnik, Robert J. and William T. Ross (2007), "The role of positive emotions in experiential decisions," *International Journal of Research in Marketing*, 24 (December), 324-335.

Lazarus, Richard S. (1991), *Emotions and adaptation*, New York: Oxford University Press.

Levy, Sidney J. and Dennis W. Rook (1999), *Brands, consumers, symbols, and research. Sidney J Levy on marketing*, Thousand Oaks: Sage Publications, Inc.

Lupton, Deborah (1996), *Food: the body and the self*, London: Sage Publications.

McCracken, Grant. (1986), "Culture and Consumption: a Theoretical Account of the Structure and Movement of the Cultural Meaning of Consumer Goods," *Journal of Consumer Research*, 13 (1), 71-84.

McEnally, Martha R. and Leslie de Chernatony (1999), "The evolving nature of branding: consumer and managerial considerations," *Academy of Marketing Science Review*, 2, 1-38.

Nyer, Prashamth U. (1997), "A study of the relationships between cognitive appraisals and consumption emotions", *Journal of the Academy of Marketing Science*, 25 (4), 296-304.

Oliver, Richard L. (1997), *Satisfaction: A behavioral perspective on the consumer*, New York: McGraw Hill Companies, Inc.

Oliver, Richard L., Roland T. Rust, and Sajeev Varki (1997), "Customer delight: foundations, findings, and managerial insight," *Journal of Retailing*, 73 (3), 311-336.

Ortony, Andrew, Gerard L. Clore, and Allan Collins (1988), *The cognitive structure of emotions*, Cambridge: Cambridge University Press.

Park, Whan C, Deborah J. MacInnis, Joseph R. Priester (2007), "Beyond attitudes: attachment and consumer behavior," *Seoul National Journal*, 12 (2), 3-36.

Roseman, Ira J. (1991), "Appraisal determinants of discrete emotions," *Cognition and Emotion*, 5 (3), 161-200.

Roseman, Ira J., Ann Aliki Antoniou and Paul E. Jose (1996), "Appraisal determinants of emotions: constructing a more accurate and comprehensive theory," *Cognition and Emotion*, 10 (3), 241-277.

Roseman, Ira J., Cynthia Wiest, and Tamara S. Swartz (1994), "Phenomenology, behaviours, and goals differentiate discrete emotions", *Journal of Personality and Social Psychology*, 67 (2), 206-221.

Ruth, Julie A., Frédéric F. Brunel and Cele C. Otnes (2002), "Linking thoughts to feelings: investigating cognitive appraisals and consumption emotions in a mixed-emotions context", *Journal of the Academy of Marketing Science*, 30 (1), 44-58.

Scherer, Klaus R. (1988), "Criteria for emotion-antecedent appraisal: a review", in *Cognitive perspectives on emotion and motivation*, Eds. Vernon Hamilton, Gordon H. Bower, and Nico H. Frijda, Dordrecht, Netherlands: Kluwer, 89-126.

Shimp, Terence A. and Thomas J. Madden (1988), "Consumer-object relations: a conceptual framework based analogously on Sternberg's triangular theory of love," in *Advances in Consumer Research*, Vol. 15, ed. Michael J. Houston, Provo, UT: Association for Consumer Research, 163-168.

Shoham, Aviv, Moshe Davidow, Jill G. Klein and Ayalla Ruvio (2006), "Animosity on the home front: the Intifada in Israel and its impact on consumer behavior," *Journal of International Marketing*, 14 (3), 92-114.

Smith, Craig A. and Phoebe C. Ellesworth (1985), "Patterns of cognitive appraisals in emotion," *Journal of Personality and Social Psychology*, 48 (4), 813-838.

Soscia, Isabella (2007), "Gratitude, delight, or guilt: the role of consumers' emotions in predicting post consumption behaviors," *Psychology & Marketing*, 24 (October), 871-894.

Swan, John E. and Fredrick I. Trawick, Jr (1999), "Delight on the nile: an ethnography of experiences that produce delight," *Journal of Consumer Satisfaction, Dissatisfaction and Complaining Behavior*, 12, 64–70.

Thomson, Matthew (2006), "Human brands: investigating antecedents to consumers' strong attachments to celebrities," *Journal of Marketing*, 70 (July), 104-119.

Thomson, Matthew, Deborah J. MacInnis, and C. Whan Park (2005), "The ties that bind: measuring the strength of consumers' emotional attachments to brands," *Journal of Consumer Psychology*, 15 (1), 77-91.

Watson, Lisa and Mark T. Spence (2007), "Causes and consequences of emotions on consumer behaviour. A review and integrative cognitive appraisal theory", *European Journal of Marketing*, 41 (5/6), 487-511.

Whang, Yun-Oh, Jeff Allen, Niquelle Sahoury, and Haitao Zhang (2004), "Failing in love with a product: the structure of a romantic consumer-product relationship," in *Advances in Consumer Research*, Vol. 31, eds. Barbara Kahn and Mary Frances Luce, Valdosta, GA: Association for Consumer Research, 320-327.

Wilk, Richard (1997), "A critique of desire: distaste and dislike in consumer behavior," *Consumption, Markets & Culture*, 1(2), 175-196.

Zaltman, Gerard and Robin A. Coulter (1995), "Seeing the voice of the customer: metaphor-based advertising research," *Journal of Advertising Research*, 35 (July-August), 35-51.

Zeelenberg, Marcel and Rik Pieters (1999), "Comparing service delivery to what might have been, Behavioral responses to regret and disappointment", *Journal of Service Research*, 2 (August), 86-97.

Salsa Magic: An Exploratory Netnographic Analysis of the Salsa Experience

Kathy Hamilton, University of Strathclyde, UK
Paul Hewer, University of Strathclyde, UK

"The anticipation of the night, Your skin prickling with electricity thinking about going dancing... The feeling in your stomach as you enter the dancehall and look around. The first beat of the drum reverberating around your soul. The automatic smile when you see people enjoying themselves. The wonder and amazement at all the bodies moving so well and so naturally. Being kissed by the magic in the air from all the chemistry, charisma and the good energy flowing all around. The nervousness of my first dance, yet the beautiful realisation that my body and soul remembers what to do and shall guide me through it. The 'thank God' feeling that my body and mind can take me to that beautiful place of euphoria again that comes from dancing" (Male, Salsa Dancer, Australia).

INTRODUCTION

This is a paper about the promise of dance as unfolding social drama. Such promise has clearly been recognised in attempts to represent dance cinematically: from Powell and Pressburger's *The Red Shoes*, to the classic *Singin in the Rain*; from Fred Astaire in *Shall We Dance* (or even Richard Gere in the 2005 remake) to the disco inferno of Tony Manero swinging his butt to recognition in *Saturday Night Fever*. Representations of dance as re-enchanting and reinvigorating have always remained to the fore within cinematic discourses. This rich potential has also been recognised in TV advertisements, with the Apple Ipod 'Silhouettes' campaign clearly feeding off such liberatory experiences. In this paper we foreground one such dance technique, that of Salsa, to reveal and explore the appeal of the experiences provided by this dance form. We suggest that the scene has grown significantly over the last ten years from its roots in the Caribbean (mainly Puerto Rico and Cuba) and initial transfer to New York and Los Angeles to a phenomenon sweeping the world. As a global export (Madrid 2006) the appeal of Salsa appears much more than this culturally, especially when we turn to the significant rise in popularity achieved by this dance form. Here we can draw attention to the continuing emergence of a gamut of Salsa Congresses, Latin Dance clubs and classes springing up across the globe in countries as diverse as the UK (Evening Chronicle 1998; Sunday Times 1999), Singapore (Singapore Times 2004), Ghana (Africa News 2006), the US (Miami New Times 2000; New York Times 2007) and Canada (Montreal Gazette 2006; Vancouver Sun 2005); to even the success of the Broadway musical *In the Heights* and Jennifer Lopez starring in *El Cantante*, which depicts the life of 1970s Salsa songster Hector Lavoe. Or even *Dirty Dancing 2* subtitled *Havana Nights*, where formal ballroom dancing in the form of Katey meets the steamy passionate embrace of Javier in the Cuban dance halls of the 1950s.

DANCE WITHIN CONSUMER RESEARCH

Within consumer research what strikes the authors as somewhat surprising is the lack of studies which have taken dance seriously, the absence of studies made more explicit by the value of those exceptions (Wort and Pettigrew 2003; Goulding et al 2002; Goulding and Shankar 2004). For us this absence is troubling, as we explore how as a research context a turn to dance forms, cultures and representations would appear to offer us much potential to reinvigorate our own understanding of consumer cultures (see Featherstone 1991) and ways of theorizing consumer culture. A dance turn within consumer research necessites we take seriously

notions of (tribal) aesthetics (Maffesoli 2007) and ephemeral communities (Hamera 2007), but also notions of embodiment (Featherstone 1991; Frank 1991; Goulding et al 2002; Joy and Sherry 2003). Dance then promises transformation and transcendence, but also as Frank reveals is communal, bringing forth particular "forms of dyadic associatedness which transcend the individual body to that of the other" (Frank 1991, 80). The experience of embodiment offered through a turn to dance becomes all important for a rethinking of consumers, especially as what we glimpse through attention to dance and the performative realm is a reconsideration of the "human body as a moving agent in time and space" (Thomas 2003, 78). A moving body which questions notions of fixed structures, where agency becomes the ability to "negotiate movements within those structures" (McDonald 2004, 200). The moving body in other words becomes pivotal in exploring consumer culture afresh, suggestive of rethinking our relationship with this world, and the imagined limits cast upon that relationship. For as Meamber and Venkatesh indicate: "the body is a site of exploration and experimentation...a way to understand, explain, refashion our notion of our world." (1999, 194).

Both Turner (1991) and Featherstone (1991) draw upon the work of Foucault to explore notions of the regimentation and disciplining of the body, as he suggests "Bodily domination is never imposed by some abstract societal Other; only bodies can do things to other bodies. Most often, what is done depends on what bodies do to themselves" (1991, 58). For Featherstone, we might suggest that *bodies matter* (to take a line from Judith Butler 1993) within consumer culture, especially evinced through notions of the performing self where management of one's appearance and look become paramount. Or as Bourdieu expresses: "The body, a social product which is the only tangible manifestation of the "person" is commonly perceived as the most natural expression of innermost nature...The legitimate use of the body is spontaneously perceived as an index of moral uprightness, so that its opposite, a 'natural' body, is seen as an index of *laisser-aller* ('letting oneself go')" (1992, 193). For Foucault (1990, 152) then a turn to bodies and their histories becomes a turn to the body as the site for the deployment of power/knowledge relations, but also to reimagine the body as simply unfinished business that is unstable and therefore constitutive in constructing potential resistances.

It is here that the significance of dance as a cultural form and sensibility reveals itself, not simply individual leisure time but a form of letting oneself go, a space for constructing resistance, offering transcendence and transformative potential through becoming "other", for as Carter (1996) suggests: "The spatial aspects of movement and the situation of the action in the performing space can also be considered for their significance in forming or replicating notions of gender" (1996, 50-51). Dance then as a performative act reveals its significance, the ability to blur and overcome (if only symbolically) contradictions, its ability to provide as Turner reveals a "liminal period...betwixt and between one context of meaning and action and another" (1982, 113). For as Hamera suggests "They [Dance techniques] offer vocabularies for writing, reading, speaking and reproducing bodies. In doing this, they do much more: organize communities around common idioms, rewrite space and time in their own images, provide alibis, escape clauses, sometimes traps, sometimes provisional utopias" (Hamera 2007, 208).

Wort and Pettigrew (2003) explore such symbolic and material refashionings through a group of Australian womens' experiences of belly dancing to challenge the assumptions around this dance form. They argue that participation is performed by women to "fulfil their own needs for femininity and sensuality, rather than being an activity designed for the male gaze" (2003, 190). Belly dancing thus becomes a way of "dabbling in the exotic" (ibid, 190), but also for the women a way "to come to terms with the shapes of their bodies" (ibid, 190). In this way, Wort and Pettigrew draw attention to the transformative potential of dance, as illustrated through the importance of adorning their bodies with accoutrements such as costumes but also the application of henna and their associated beauty rituals for making material this transformation from their everyday to dance selves. But perhaps more importantly, as a form of transcendence achieved through a "connection" with other women (ibid, 191). Or as McRobbie proposed: "Dance is where girls were always found in subcultures. It was their only entitlement" (1993, 25). On this entitlement, she continues by writing about the rave experience for women: "This gives girls new-found confidence and a prominence. Bra tops, leggings and trainers provide a basic (aerobic) wardrobe. In rave (and in the club culture with which it often overlaps) girls are highly sexual in their dress and appearance...The tension in rave for girls comes, it seems, from remaining in control, and at the same time losing themselves in dance and music" (1993, 25).

The work of Maffesoli (2007) explores a similar theme but from another conceptual position; he explores the nature and "advent" of the tribal aesthetic itself where he seeks to explain the emergence of this logic, that is to say, aesthetics are defined in terms of their etymological meaning as "people feeling emotions together" (Maffesoli 2007, 27). More so, he argues that the tribal aesthetics speak of an ecological dialectic versus that of simply economic means-ends activities–a spirit which captures the sense of aesthetics as expressing a "passion for life" (ibid, 27), where "situations are the only things of any import" (ibid, 29), since within such contexts (Maffesoli uses the example of the "orgy") lies the possibility for the "loss of oneself in another" (ibid, 30), or better, of a "re-enchantment of the world" acheived essentially through the collapse of the individual and the foregrounding of "shared passion and social empathy" (ibid, 30). The approach of Maffesoli then takes seriously the social sphere as the starting point for any investigation of tribal aesthetics, or as he explains:

> "Big meetings, large gatherings of all kinds, group trances, sporting events, musical excitement and religious or cultural effervescence–all raise the individual to a form of plenitude that s/he cannot find in the grayness of economic or political functionality. In each of these phenomena, there is a sort of magic participation in strange things and strangeness..." (ibid, 32).

Salsa dancing then can be understood as one such instance of *social effervescence* where the consumer moves beyond their position of isolated individual through involvement and participation with the emergent social. Parallels can be drawn with the work of Goulding et al. (2002) and Goulding and Shankar (2004) which employs notions of Maffesoli's (1996) neotribalism to explore the emergent rave scene–"the music, the laser light shows, and in some cases the ingestion of drugs like ecstasy and cocaine, and the nature of the dance itself" (Goulding and Shankar 2004, 649)-for producing new dramas and communities constructed around a particular dance form. Or as Sash, one of the respondents better articulates: "You have enough hassle all week at work. What you want to do at the weekend is break free of all that, go a bit mad, get it all out of your system, dancing is like a release, you can lose yourself...On Friday the fun starts early" (Goulding et al 2002, 275). Dance in other words becomes a useful context to explore the intimacies and embodiments brought into being through such new communities, or as Hamera reveals: "It is a testament to the power of performance as a social force, as cultural poesis, as communication infrastructure that makes identity, solidarity and memory sharable. Communities are danced into being in daily, routine labor, time and talk...emerg[ing] at dance's busy intersections of discipline and dreams, repetition and innovation, competition and care" (Hamera 2007, 1).

METHODOLOGY

In this section we reveal the methodology adopted to obtain the "deep contextualization of meaning" (Cova, Kozinets and Shankar 2007, 9) necessary for a fuller and richer understanding of Salsa. The material presented in this paper was collected through a netnographic analysis of an online salsa forum (http://www.salsaforums.com). Drawing on the excellent work of Kozinets (1997, 1998, 2001, 2002) we argue that a netnographic analysis is able to transcend the 'limits of asking' through observation of people's talk. Salsaforum is an international forum that attracts people from all over the world. The forum began in February 2004 and a testament to its growing popularity is the fact that there are now 3382 registered users, who have made a total of 74638 postings since its outset. Members vary dramatically in the usage of the forum; some have not made any postings and the most active user has made a total of 7265 posts, averaging 4.92 posts per day (figures correct on 14 March 2008). The forum provides an arena for members to discuss salsa music, share salsa video clips, announce events and offer reviews of salsa clubs, DVDs etc. For our analysis, we focused on the "Just Dance" section of the forum. There are a total of 1750 discussion threads in this section of the forum covering a wide range of salsa dance issues. Some threads only receive a few replies while others have received almost 1000 replies. Interpretation was constructed around moving between individual postings, chunks of postings, entire discussion threads and the emergent understanding of the complete data set (de Valck 2007). In addition, our interpretation of the Salsa experience is also aided by knowledge gained through participant observation and interviews. The posting presented at the beginning of the paper highlights a number of issues that will now be explored. Specifically the findings are organised into three key experiential themes: the first exploring the salsa experience; followed by understanding the "magic" of the salsa dance floor; finally, we explore the apparent interaction between the music, the self and the body engendered by the salsa experience.

'JUST DANCE': THE SALSA EXPERIENCE

From our analysis of the internet forums, a key experiential theme is that Salsa appears as a shared experience that links individuals together resulting in a relaxed, friendly and comfortable atmosphere on the salsa forum. The forum is viewed as a place where salseros (salsa dancers) can seek advice, support and encouragement from other salsa lovers in all corners of the world. As one participant suggests:

> *I love this forum* 😄 *. This place can even out the wildest of emotional roller coasters and hopefully has kept some people going when they might otherwise have given up.* (UK, male)

Others concur that the forum provides a helpful support network and analysis reveals that members use the forum as a venue to share positive (e.g. the perfect dance) and negative (e.g. embarrassment at being abandoned mid-song on the dance floor) salsa stories. There is evidence of a sense of camaraderie amongst forum members, as demonstrated through the incessant use of compliments, both written (such as "well said") and symbolic (smiling or bowing emoticons) during discussions as members praise each other for what are perceived to be beautiful or inspiring words. For example, as one of the participants suggests:

You can tell from all your posts here that you would be GREAT to dance with. You have a passion for dancing and music plus you appreciate and understand your partner. A winning combination 😀😀 (male, Australia)

This camaraderie is extended to newcomers who often receive words of welcome after their initial postings. As a result of the powerful and often poetic communication between members, the forum serves, we argue, as a rich repository of cultural meanings seeking to embody the social dramas (Turner 1982) of contemporary consumer culture.

"BEING KISSED BY THE MAGIC IN THE AIR": CONSTRUCTING MAGICAL EXPERIENCES ON THE DANCE FLOOR

The passion felt for salsa shines through in both observation in salsa classes and clubs and analysis of the forum postings. In addition to well-being and health benefits created by physical movement, Salsa is also seen as an activity that has "the power to generate so much happiness." One member defines a salsa "fix" as "THAT euphoric, satisfying feeling" while another suggests that salsa "gives me all the energy in the world. It makes me feel alive!" One of the reasons for this feel-good factor is because salsa dancing results in a sense of escape from the mundane realities of everyday life and provides relief from feelings of stress or tension (similar to Goulding et al 2002). More so, in terms of the way in which space appears as a social construct, the dance floor is viewed as somewhere that can be separated from the rest of the world akin we would suggest to Turner's anti-structure "wherein human beings stripped of their roles, statuses, memberships, and moralities, are in communion as human selves–against the demands of organization and structure" (1982, 113). Or, the signature of one of our forum members more succinctly conveys this idea: "Mild-mannered corporate guy by day...raging Salsero by night." The salsa dance floor offers dancers the possibility of being transported to a liminal space: "another world—where there's no pain, suffering, worries that life abundantly confronts you with." In this world salseros experience a sense of peace, it is a world where "everything is effortless, no performance anxiety, no feelings of superiority or inferiority." The following two postings provide effective illustrations of this otherworldness associated with the salsa dance floor:

Participant 1: I love it when everything around me seems to disappear, when there's just me, my dance partner and music. In those moments I feel so much passion, so much energy... I truly feel life in my veins. That's better than...well…anything! (Male, Slovenia)

Participant 2: It offers an environment where you can walk in feeling like a nobody, or maybe just down after a hard day, and walk out feeling completely special and very much appreciated. The best thing is that it comes with no strings attached and there seems to be an understanding and respect for the bound-

aries that separate the dance floor from the rest of the world. For five minutes you can loose yourself and focus all your attention on another human being! (Male, UK).

A vital space of emergence and possibility, for example, a number of salseros compare the emotions generated through salsa with the experience of falling in love suggesting that the "spirit of salsa" makes "time stand still" as people lose themselves in the moment. One forum member commented that: "Looking back on some of the best dances; they now seem like dreams. Maybe they happened maybe they didn't." In this way, the dance floor becomes a sacred place (Belk 1989) to be imagined and eulogized.

Some salseros extend their love of salsa from the dance floor to other aspects of their lives. Some suggest that salsa "starts to become a part of you" while others go further and suggest that it becomes a lifestyle and an overarching guiding philosophy:

Participant 3: "Salsa isn't about girls, it isn't about who is looking at you, it isn't about patterns/moves, it isn't about partying, it isn't stepping. It is about LOVE, it is a lifestyle where salsa is your world and your mate the subject of all interactions within that world and its love…. It is a lifestyle, a lifestyle, it is nothing less..."

For some, devotion to salsa dancing not only encroaches on lifestyle but can actually become a way of life in its own right (de Burgh-Woodman and Brace-Govan 2007).

The previous postings place especial emphasis on the relationship between the dancing couple which is described by the forum members as a "mysterious union," "gratifying connection" and "magical moment." In an ideal partnership "you cease being two people dancing with each other, and become a couple dancing together." This highlights the central role of the social in the salsa experience, defined by one forum member as follows: "Social-in dance terms?-The ability to participate, engage in, and collaborate, with someone-known or unknown- who is of a like disposition". The reference to "like disposition" in this definition does not refer to demographic or socio-economic characteristics, rather, salsa appears to attract people from all walks of life who are connected through their love of the dance. The internet forum makes possible a sharing of this interest, but also a global connection where talk of people's salsa experiences is central. As one member suggested, salsa provides an opportunity for "Meeting and dancing with a wide variety of people that I normally would never meet in my nerdy, high-tech world." It is precisely this tendency that caused Gilroy (1991) to comment that the dance floor could be viewed as a cultural space marked by an absence of the usual hierarchies of society. It could be suggested that salsa provides an opportunity to break down barriers as it creates an automatic link and point of communion between dancers:

Participant 4: "It's always funny, when I'm hanging out with my salsa friends, to see the puzzled looks on people's faces. They're like…what are all of these black, white, latino (you name it) folks doing hanging out together. In fact, we were asked what group we were from or the reasons we were hanging out! LOL It's all about the dance and the music, baby!"

Salsa congresses are a popular venue for meeting other salsa aficionados and appear to provide a chance for people from many different countries to congregate. It is commonly suggested that even language differences do not inhibit union through salsa; the dancing is the central element. Thus the dance floor offers a space that is beyond the barriers that may typically prevent meaningful interaction in everyday life. As one member suggested, salsa is "the global language of dance." Indeed communication through dance is sometimes deemed superior to oral communication offering a way to "perfectly capture and convey something you could never express with words."

The above definition of social also suggests that even complete strangers can be united through salsa. Observation at salsa clubs indicates that partner switching is the norm as participants rarely dance with the same partner for two songs in a row. As one forum member suggests, "the more you dance with people you don't know, the better." Stories of dancing with strangers then appears to offer the potential to generate deep emotions, as articulated in the comment below:

> Participant 5: That surprise dance. Someone you've never met before, maybe never even seen dancing, asks you to dance, or you ask them, and from the first step, you're in tune with each other. It just feels so "right" it makes me wanna laugh (and cry) my way across the dance floor. (UK)

As such, the dance floor becomes a space where norms of touch are challenged and where the relationship between private and public space is blurred (Bringinshaw 2001). The presence of "chemistry" between a couple, even those who are strangers off the dance floor, leads to a particularly intense emotion. This was defined by one Salsero as follows: "Chemistry is when both partners are listening, and both are hearing. Chemistry is nuance, appreciated and acknowledged." The difficulty of putting this chemistry into words motivated participants to use various metaphors to express and understand such extraordinary experiences: "When that spark ignites it's great; it's like a story being read for the first time" and "We're painting a story together and the dancefloor is our canvas." Thus in Maffesoli's (2007) words, in order for the "loss of oneself in another," there needs to a connection between two people through the sharing of emotions and particular dance experiences. Salsa draws our attention to the boundaries of the body, and the extent to which such boundaries are fluid and can be blurred and merged (Bringinshaw 2001). Whereas Douglas (1973) maintains that physical bodily experiences are modified by the social body through adherence to social norms, we suggest that the salsa dance floor may be viewed as one space where this modification is less evident. Whereas bodily behaviour in public spaces is often rule-governed as individuals maintain "territories of the self" (Goffman 1966), in salsa dancing, that personal space can expand to include the extended body, that is, the body of the other.

"MY BODY AND SOUL REMEMBERS WHAT TO DO AND SHALL GUIDE ME THROUGH"

The interaction between the music, the self and the body is of central importance in salsa dancing. The previous section highlighted the strong emotional bonds that exist on the dance floor. It appears that connections between the couple are accentuated through the music. As one forum member suggests: "The two of you have become *one* WITH the music." Music is seen as powerful and energising and as a force that vitalizes the body:

> Participant 6: To me, as soon as "the right music" comes on (has to have that certain groove), it touches me deeply, it pulses through me, like electricity, and I want to become one with it. The pleasure I get from the music alone is intense, very much like....you know what I mean ;-)... and if I can dance and click with someone it becomes perfect. I go straight to heaven.

> Participant 7: my ultimate goal is to be a true representation of the music that is being played.... on the moment, creative, imaginative, response to the music, that is what I strive for every time I walk in a dance floor ...... someday someday (male).

While mastery of the steps undoubtedly makes participants feel good, especially when learning a new move for the first time, this is not deemed to produce the best style of dance. Rather many believe that truly good dancers are those who not only listen but "feel" the music in their "heart and soul" and are capable of translating such emotion into movements of the body. Even those who do not understand the Spanish lyrics, can be guided by the emotion in the singer's voice. As another Salsero remarked:

> "In fact, when a person is deeply in touch with feelings and the music, changes in a song never heard before are felt way before they happen, they all have nothing to do with technique nor musical knowledge of salsa, rather ability to feel..."

In salsa dancing, the accounts suggest that people's bodies can be one step ahead of levels of consciousness as people become caught up in the vitality and spontaneity of the "materiality of being-together" (de Certeau 1996, 75). It is this process that leads to self-expression as salseros interpret the music in different ways. As one member suggests, "we aren't robots, we are all different, so shouldn't we all display the true US on the dancefloor?" An important goal for many salseros is to achieve flair or "sabor," that is "an innate response to self expression that can not be taught through a set of physical rules" as participants attempt to "find yourself in the dancefloor" and contact with "inner dancers." Indeed, one member comments that "Even though this is a partner dance, I would say the most important thing I have learned is to dance for myself." The dance floor appears as a space characterised by a freedom of expression and freedom of movement and the release of aspects of the self that are often hidden to others:

> Participant 3: I like the fact that people get to enjoy you and vise versa. Sometimes the you on the floor can be more 'you' than the person off the floor just like an artist might express the deepest part of themselves through their paintings but nowhere else. (Female, UK)

Thus "the way people treat their bodies reveals the deepest dispositions of the habitus" (Bourdieu 1992, 190). Similarly, Fraleigh (1995, 19) suggests, "We dance to enact the bodily lived basis of our freedom in an aesthetic form.....We move for the moving, but more, we dance for the dancing." In other words, salsa appears to provide a form of freedom from everyday constraints where movement is not directed at instrumental or practical goals but rather is channeled into forms of self-expression and action centered upon pleasure and enjoyment. Salsa is a way to allow self-expression and emotion to escape or "burst" as a "radiating essence." In this sense, Salsa can be seen as a medium of expression through the communicative body, that is, a body in process of creating itself (Frank 1991).

As social drama, salsa dancing appears to demand that participants are in touch with their inner emotions. One forum member provides a particularly rich description of the way in which this may conflict with societal expectations and norms:

> "society at large does not teach us how to become in tune with our feelings but rather, how to look to the outside and be lost

in exoteric ideals; a material world that is only to be happy with external possessions. Hence, we go on following what society tells us and forget about the innerself and feelings..." (male)

This member suggests that those who focus on technique rather than letting the music move them are driven by "instant gratification," a central driver of consumer society (O'Shaughnessy and O'Shaughnessy 2002). They are driven to dance in such a way that fits with others' expectations rather than attempting to dance in tune with their inner selves which would enable "real achievement" in the future. The issue of rationality versus emotion is central to this discussion and Salsa appears as a way to fulfil the "emotional hunger" (Cushman 1990, 600) generated by consumer culture. Or as our participant continues:

> "while the mind is busy thinking the body can't feel. The mind is blocking the body from feeling.....Listen to your soul not what step the brain thinks you should do....
> Dancing comes from the soul, not the mind, but to a thinking society such a belief doesn't come easy to stress.....So, while we are taught the do this and do that, our soul has been waiting to be let loose. Our mind (ego) needs something to feel good about, that something happens to be patterns and the thought of achievement through more and more complicated patterns. While the ego rules there isn't telling someone that true fulfillment comes from the soul."

These posts generated a great deal of enthusiasm with forum members suggesting that "his inspirational words are like diamonds" and "jewels". Others agreed that the best dances are those when the moves "just happen". Dancers who are driven by the head are bound by "limits, correctness, and rationale" and therefore fail to realise that "true greatness [comes] from that something inside of you." Creativity is therefore not as constrained as one might imagine (cf. Madrid 2006). As Frank (1991) suggests, for the communicative body, discourses enable more than they constrain. Thus once primary steps have been learnt, salseros can allow their bodies to "play with the music" and thereby overcome the cultural contradictions that they experience in their everyday lives through the medium of dance.

CONCLUSIONS

"The presumption of bodies already in motion, what dance takes as its normative condition, could bridge the various splits between mind and body, subject and object, and process and structure that have been so difficult for understandings of social life to navigate." (Martin 1998).

From the ecstatic bodily gestures of the shaman to the magic of ritual within archaic cultures dance has always been central for the construction, production and reconstruction of our notions of society. From the hypnotic beats of Salsa music and its associated global marketing industries, to its continued representation and commodification within films and advertising, to the multitude of global clubs, congresses and dance classes; Salsa culture has always offered a rich and fertile ground for the transcendence of cultural forms. Our exploratory study foregrounds the lack of attention with the CCT tradition (Arnould and Thompson 2005) to notions of the body and embodiment (Joy and Sherry 2003); Goulding et al (2002) make a similar point on the importance of the body. On the basis of our exploratory netnographic study of the salsa experience we reveal in this study how dance forms such as salsa are rooted in a renegotiation of the relationship with our own bodies and those of others. That is how dance responds to and may

compensate for a need for movement within our everyday lives; moving bodies are always then about a release and transcendence, even when such movement is underscored with a dance technique which is itself disciplining. The desire to dance then responds to a reclaimation and renegotiation within the confines of existing structures; navigating and traversing within the confines of those structures whilst offering a partial imaginative release through resolving cultural contradictions on the dance floor. Through touch, sustained eye contact and a "magical" connection with others; through the creation of art with one's body; and through the tendency to forget what one looks like in order to follow one's "inner dancer" to the beat of a style of music which is "infectious". We start to see how dance, but also through the discourses constructed around it, promises a kind of transcendence, an attempt to rethink the rules of association with not only others, but also ourselves within consumer society. Whereas conventional thinking dictates that the body mediates the relationship betwee self identity and social identity (Goffman 1966), it appears that salsa dancing offers the opportunity for a union between the outer representational body and the subjective experiential body (Thomas 2003). Using Csikszentmihalyi's (1990) terminology, we can suggest that's salsa dancing offers a "flow experience," that is a state of total involvement where one moment flows holistically into the next without conscious intervention (cited in Celsi et al. 1993). More so, we might concur with Turner when he suggests that: "The group or community does not merely 'flow' in unison at these performances, but, more actively, tries to understand itself in order to change itself" (Turner 1982, 101). Herein lies the promise of salsa, as for some, the experiential consumption of salsa provides meaning in life and offers enjoyment and ecstasy through connection (Belk 1989) and "rare imaginative transcendences" (Turner 1982, 101). More so, the online interactions makes possible a continued dialogue around such experiences, where we witness the group generating new forms of understanding and knowledge.

Dance then comes to be seen as a reflexive form of knowledge enacted in and through our bodies, where the settled and fixed is disturbed and placed in motion. Here the importance of dance for an understanding of consumer culture reveals itself. While others may rule out the possibility of escape from consumer culture (Arnould 2007); a turn to dance brings in its gyratory wake a reimagining of consumer action embedded within not only economic and market forces. Rather we see how dance embodies an unquenchable thirst to escape beyond the mundane, a desire for "freedom", especially if understood as the continual and never-ending "attempt at self-disengagement and self-invention" (Rajachman cited by Sawicki 1991, 101). In our minds this speaks of how dance makes possible shared passions, exhilarations and desires lacking from people's everyday lives, compensating and granting them a space for articulation and expression. Whereas previous research has suggested that high octane white knuckle experiences such as skydiving (Celsi, Rose and Leigh 1993) and white water rafting (Arnould and Price 1993) may offer such an opportunity to transcend mundane experience; here we suggest that salsa dancing can result in total absorption as the dance floor becomes a "beautiful place of euphoria." While at the same time we acknowledge and appreciate the role of consumer culture itself in this economy of passions and desire, since it is the character of contemporary consumer culture which furnishes and makes possible the emphatic and constant rejoinder to seek out desire, producing the will to desire desire and passion itself. But to end, we argue that what dance ultimately makes possible, is what de Certeau refers to as a "materiality of being-together" (1996, 75). That is, through its emergent qualities, and brought into being by the sensual and exotic qualities of the music, but also most importantly through the synchronic movements of the dancers themselves to produce a community space for rethinking the social and notions of shared emotions through a dance form which is itself affiliative and sharable. By way of closure, the promise of dance then can be understood as a social drama which through its performances serves to, as Turner suggests: "keep us alive, give us problems to solve, postpone ennui, guarantee at least the flow of our adrenalin, and provoke us into new, ingenious cultural formations of our human condition and occassionally into attempts to ameliorate, even beautify it" (1982, 110-111).

REFERENCES:

Arnould Eric J. and Thompson, Craig J. (2005), "Consumer Culture Theory (CCT): Twenty Years of Research", *Journal of Consumer Research* 31, (March), 868-882.

Arnould Eric (2007), "Can consumers escape the market?" In *Critical Marketing: Defining the Field,* eds. Michael Saren, Pauline Maclaran, Christina Goulding, Richard Elliott, Avi Shankar and Miriam Catterall, 140-155. Butterworth-Heinemann: Oxford.

Arnould, Eric J. and Price, Linda L. (1993), "River Magic: Extraordinary Experience and the Extended Service Encounter", *Journal of Consumer Research*, Vol.20, June, (1), 24-44.

Belk, Russell W.; Wallendorf, Melanie and Sherry, John F. (1989), "The Sacred and the Profane in Consumer Behavior: Theodicy on the Odyssey", *Journal of Consumer Research*, Vol.16, June, (1), 1-38.

Bringinshaw, Valerie A. (2001), *Dance, Space and Subjectivity,* Palgrave: New York.

Brownlie, Douglas; Hewer, Paul and Treanor, Steven (2007), Sociality in motion: exploring logics of tribal consumption among cruisers. In *Consumer Tribes,* eds. Bernard Cova, Robert V. Kozinets and Avi Shankar, 107-128. Butterworth-Heinemann: Oxford.

Bourdieu, Pierre (1992), *Distinction: A social critique of the judgement of taste.* Routledge: London.

Butler, Judith (1993), *Bodies that matter: on the discursive limits of 'sex'.* Routledge: London.

Canniford, Robin and Shankar, Avi (2007), "Marketing the savage: appropriating tribal tropes." In *Consumer Tribes,* eds. Bernard Cova, Robert V. Kozinets and Avi Shankar, 35-48. Butterworth-Heinemann: Oxford.

Carter, Alexandra (1996), "Bodies of knowledge: dance and feminist analysis". In *Analysing Performance: A Critical Reader* ed. Patrick Campbell, 43-69. Manchester University Press: Manchester.

Celsi, Richard L.; Rose, Randall L. and Leigh, Thomas W. (1993), "An Exploration of High-Risk Leisure Consumption through Skydiving", *Journal of Consumer Research*, Vol.20, June, (1): 1-23.

Cova, Bernard and Cova, Veronique (2002), "Tribal Marketing: the tribalisation of society and its impact on the conduct of marketing", *European Journal of Marketing* 36, no.5/6: 595-620.

_____, Kozinets, Robert V. and Shankar, Avi (2007), "Tribes, Inc: the new world of tribalism." In *Consumer Tribes* eds. Bernard Cova; Robert V. Kozinets and Avi Shankar, 3-26. Butterworth-Heinemann: Oxford.

Csikszentmihalyi, Mihaly (1990), Flow: The Psychology of Optimal Experience. Harper and Row: New York.

Cushman, Phillip (1990), "Why the Self is Empty: Towards a Historically Situated Psychology", American Psychologist, Vol.45, (May), 599-611.

De-Burgh-Woodman, Helen and Brace-Govan, Jan (2007), "We do not live to buy: Why subcultures are different from brand communities and the meaning for marketing discourse", *International Journal of Sociology and Social Policy*, Vol.27, (5/6), 193-207.

De Certeau, Michel (1984), *The Practice of Everyday Life,* University of California Press: London

De Vlack, Kristine (2007), "The War of the eTribes: Online Conflicts and Communal Consumption," In *Consumer Tribes* eds. Bernard Cova; Robert V. Kozinets and Avi Shankar, 260-274. Butterworth-Heinemann: Oxford.

Dempster, Elizabeth (1994), "Women writing the body: Let's watch a little how she dances". In *Bodies of the Text: Dance as Theory, Literature as Dance* eds. Ellen W. Goellner and Jacqueline Shea Murphy, 21-38. Rutgers: New Jersey.

Douglas, Mary (1973), *Natural Symbols: Explorations in Cosmology*, Routledge: London.

Featherstone, Mike (1991), "The body in consumer culture". In *The Body: Social Process and Cultural Theory* eds. Mike Featherstone, Mike Hepworth and Bryan S. Turner, 170-196. Sage: London.

Foucault, Michel (1990), *The History of Sexuality Volume 1: An introduction.* Penguin Books: London.

Fraleigh, Sondra Horton (1995), *Dance and the lived body: A descriptive aesthetics*, Univ. of Pittsburgh Press: Pittsburgh.

Frank, Arthur W. (1991), "For a sociology of the body: An analytical review." In *The Body: Social Process and Cultural Theory* eds. Mike Featherstone, Mike Hepworth and Bryan S., 36-102. Sage: London.

Gilroy, Paul (1991), *'There ain't no black in the union jack': The cultural politics of race and nation.* Univ. of Chicago Press: Chicago.

Goffman, Erving (1966), *Relations in Public,* Harper & Row: London.

Goulding, Christina and Shankar, Avi (2004), "Age is just a number: Rave culture and the cognitively young 'thirty something'". *European Journal of Marketing* 38, no.5/6: 641-658.

Goulding, Christina; Shankar, Avi and Elliott, Richard (2002), "Working weeks, rave weekends: identity fragmentation and the emergence of new communities", *Consumption, Markets and Culture* 5, no.4: 261-284.

Hamera, Judith (2007). *Dancing communities: performance, difference and connection in the Global City.* Palgrave: Basingstoke, Hampshire.

Joy, Annamma and Sherry, John F. Jr. (2003), 'Speaking of Art as Embodied Imagination: A Multisensory Approach to Understanding Aesthetic Experience', *Journal of Consumer Research*, Vol.30, no.2, 259-282.

Kozinets, Robert V. (1998), 'On Netnography: Initial Reflections on Consumer Research Investigations of Cyberculture', *Advances in Consumer Research*, Vol.25, 366-371.

_____ (1997), '"I Want To Believe": A Netnography of The X-Philes' Subculture of Consumption', *Advances in Consumer Research,* Vol.24, 470-475.

_____ (2001), 'Utopian Enterprise: Articulating the Meanings of Star Trek's Culture of Consumption', *Journal of Consumer Research*, Vol.28, (June), 67-88.

_____ (2002), 'The Field Behind the Screen: Using Netnography for Marketing Research in Online Communities', *Journal of Marketing Research*, Vol.39, no.1 (February), 61-72.

LaPointe-Crump, Janice (2003), "Of Dainty Gorillas and Macho Sylphs: Dance and Gender." In: *The dance experience: insights into History, Culture and Creativity* eds. Myron Howard Nadel and Marc Raymond Strauss, 159-172. Princeton: Canada.

McDonald, Paul (1998), "Reconceptualising Stardom". In *Stars* ed. Richard Dyer, New Edition, with supplementary chapter, 175-212. British Film Institute Publishing: London.

McRobbie, Angela (1993), "Shut up and dance: youth culture and changing modes of femininity", *Young* 1, 13-31.

Madrid, Alejandro L. (2006), Dancing with desire: culture embodiment in Tijuana's Nor-tec music and dance. *Popular Music* 25, no.3, 383-399.

Maffesoli, Michel (2007), "Tribal Aesthetic". In *Consumer Tribes* eds. Bernard Cova, Robert V. Kozinets and Avi Shankar, 27-34. Butterworth-Heinemann: Oxford.

Maffesoli, Michel (1996), *The time of the tribes: The decline of individualism in mass society*. Sage: London.

Martin Randy (1998), *Critical moves: dance studies in theory and practice*. Duke Univ. Press: Durham, NC.

Meamber, Laurie A. and Venkatesh, Alladi (1999), "The flesh is made symbol: an interpretive account of contemporary bodily performance art". In: *Advances in Consumer Research* eds. Eric J. Arnould and Linda M. Scott, 190-194. Association for Consumer Research: Provo, UT.

Nadel, Myron Howard (2003), "Social dance: A portrait of people at play". In *The Dance Experience: Insights into History, Culture and Creativity* eds. Myron Howard Nadel and Marc Raymond Strauss, 55-80. Princeton: Canada.

O'Shaughnessy, J. and O'Shaughnessy, N. (2002), "Marketing, the consumer society and hedonism", *European Journal of Marketing*, Vol.36, (5/6), 524-547.

Sawicki, Jana (1991), *Disciplining Foucault: Feminism, Power and the Body*. Routledge: London.

Schouten, John W.; Martin, Diane M. and McAlexander, James H. (2007), "The evolution of a subculture of consumption". In: *Consumer Tribes* eds. Bernard Cova, Robert V. Kozinets and Avi Shankar, 67-75. Butterworth-Heinemann: Oxford.

Spiggle, Susan (1994), "Analysis and interpretation of qualitative data in consumer research." *Journal of Consumer Research* 21, (December), 491-503.

Thomas, Helen (2003), *The body, dance and cultural theory*. Palgrave: London.

Turner, Bryan (1991), "Recent developments in the theory of the body". In: *The Body: Social Process and Cultural Theory* eds. Mike Featherstone, Mike Hepworth and Bryan Turner, 1-35. Sage: London.

Turner, Victor (1982), *From Ritual to Theatre: The Human Seriousness of Play*. PAJ: New York.

Wort, Fiona and Pettigrew, Simone (2003), "Consuming the belly dance". In *European Advances in Consumer Research* eds. Darach Turley and Stephen Brown, 187-192. Association for Consumer Research: Provo, UT.

Just a sampling of some of the Newspaper Articles on Salsa

Africa News 2006. Strictly Salsa 2006 (First National Salsa Championship). *Africa News*, December 22nd 2006.

Miami New Times 2000. Salsa and Be Counted, *Miami New Times*, May 25th 2000.

Newcastle Evening Chronicle 1998. Salsa night is all a bit of a wiggle. *Newcastle Evening Chronicle*, July 22nd 1998.

New York Times 2007. Salsa Spins Beyond Its Roots. *New York Times*, July 29th 2007.

Sunday Mirror 1999. Salsa: The Sexiest Hobby Ever?. *Sunday Mirror* January 3rd 1999.

The Singapore Straits Times 2004. Salsa Seduction. *The Straits Times*, October 10th 2004.

Vancouver Sun 2005. Salsa! For many, salsa, a sensual fusion of Afro-Cuban-Latino street music with early American jazz, isn't just a dance, it's a way of life. *Vancouver Sun* October 3rd 2005.

Exposing the 'Credogenic' Environment: Where does Responsibility Lie?

Isabelle Szmigin, The University of Birmingham, UK
Deirdre O'Loughlin, University of Limerick, Ireland

ABSTRACT

This paper explores the nature of the consumption environment of credit, termed the 'credogenic' environment and identifies its key players including financial services providers, regulators and consumers. Perspectives from both students and key informants from a range of consumer and debt advice agencies, regulatory bodies and banks in the UK and Ireland are presented. The pervasive culture of credit and the issue of responsibility emerge as key themes. While there is recognition of marketing's role in creating and sustaining the credogenic environment, there are differing views regarding lender and borrower responsibility and accountability. The adequacy and effectiveness of current legislation is questioned.

INTRODUCTION: THE MARKETING ENVIRONMENT

While the marketing environment is recognised as a critical factor for both management and customers, it is a relatively underexplored and underdeveloped concept. The ideological power of neo-liberalization has resulted in the 'exaltation of the individual' (Evans, 2002:56) in marketing discourse, while the influence of marketing to shape and control the consumption environment has been largely ignored. A case in point has been what we term the credogenic environment, where the continued availability of credit for many of those already in debt inevitably affects the choices they make and their perception of their financial situation. The term 'credogenic' is purposely derived from another term describing a particular environment in which marketing could be seen as complicit. This is the obesogenic environment (Swinburn et. al. 1999) whereby a surfeit of fat, sugar and salt and a lack of physical exercise have led to an increase in obesity. In particular, Swinburn et al., (1999) highlight the importance of the physical, economic, social and cultural environments of most industrialised countries and we suggest that a similar argument could be made regarding the proliferation of credit and the acceptance of high levels of debt in western societies today. This paper begins by acknowledging the nature and importance of this credit environment in terms of how it is constructed and examines how much real freedom and choice consumers have in their behaviour within it. We consider research which identifies the individual's cognitive limitations faced with a complex purchase such as credit before presenting a more detailed analysis of the current credogenic environment with a particular emphasis on the growth of consumerism and the pervasiveness of the culture of credit across all strata of society. Empirical research with regulators, representatives of financial institutions and advisory agencies and one potentially vulnerable group (students) is presented to identify roles and responsibilities.

THE ENVIRONMENT AND CONSUMER CHOICE

The dominant neo-liberal view coming from standard welfare economics is that of rational, well informed consumers. Consumers are, however, still constrained by their own cognitive limitations and product complexity. Complexity is an important issue in terms of how much real control consumers have. It has been suggested that consumers cannot rationally process all the information neces-sary to optimize their behavior (Hanson and Kysar, 1999). This argument could be made for the consumption of credit where increasing product complexity and limited financial literacy result-ing in poor financial decision-making is a growing cause for concern (Atkinson and Kempson, 2004). Thus, any argument for consumer empowerment has to be framed within the complexity of the context.

Furthermore, we also have to consider how people frame choices in relation to their needs now and in the future. If we use too much credit today it is unlikely that we do it while considering the implications for our future needs. This reflects Pigou's (1920) defective telescopic faculty whereby most people prefer present pleasures to future satisfaction. Increased choice today has little regard for the future; we must instead consider how the individual's imperfect faculty operates in the sophisticated marketing environment alongside a rampant consumer culture where pursuit and possession of goods is all important (Roberts and Jones, 2001). The evaluation of a product's potential harmfulness is not always clear-cut as the marketing of seemingly beneficial products can some-times become damaging because of the particular characteristics of the consumer (Rittenburg and Parthasarathy, 1997) who through their lack of knowledge, experience or maturity may abuse or misuse the product (Cui and Choudhury, 2003). For example, university students accept bank loans to enable them to study and support themselves at university but in doing so they are required to assess their financial capabilities in terms of budgeting for this commitment and forecast their ability to pay in the future once employed. While the use of credit cards to finance consumer purchases has become 'a way of life' (Hayhoe et al. 2000), it has been suggested that the dramatic growth in credit card usage among college students in the US is placing them at greater risk for high debt levels and misuse and mismanagement of credit after gradua-tion (Lyons, 2004). If young people enter the market place unable and ill-equipped to manage the further demands and attractions offered by the credit industry their future may already be blighted. Thus, the ethical evaluation of many products depends on their interaction with consumer characteristics and marketing practices (Cui and Choudhury, 2003).

THE CREDOGENIC ENVIRONMENT

Higher levels of credit consumption and debt accumulation have led to an economic and, importantly, psychological transfor-mation in society from a saving to a spending culture (Griffiths, 2000; Berwick, 2004). This in turn, appears to be accompanied by a change in consumer behaviour and attitude where debt has become perceived as part of normal modern life (Lea et. al., 1993). Recent statistics show that Ireland is ranked first in terms of personal indebtedness compared to euro area countries using per-sonal-sector credit to GDP and GNP ratios (ECB, 2007). Similarly, secured and unsecured debt figures in the UK have reached £1.2 trillion (Datamonitor, 2006) with UK consumers accounting for two thirds of all outstanding credit card debt in the EU (Fleet Street Letter, 2007). Alongside changing behaviour there has been an increasing level of aggressive unethical and undesirable marketing practices (Burton, 2008), a rise in 'predatory lending' to vulnerable groups (Hill and Kozup, 2007) and promises of 'easy money'

TABLE 1
Profile of Agency/Supply-side Participants

Position	Institution
Director of Consumer Information	Financial Regulator, Ireland
Director	Office of Director of Consumer Affairs, Ireland
Head of Policy and Research	Money Advice & Budgeting Service (MABS) Ireland
Head of Student Banking	Irish Retail Bank, Ireland
President, Students' Union	University of Limerick, Ireland
Financial Advisor and Media Presenter	Personal Finance Consultancy, Ireland
Consumer Sector Team Manager	Financial Services Authority, UK
Senior Social Policy Officer	Citizens Advice, UK
Training and Information Officer	National Debtline UK
Director	British Bankers Association, UK
President, Students' Guild	University of Birmingham, UK

(Griffiths, 2000) by traditional and non-traditional financial institutions. In this credogenic environment the decision to take on credit is strongly shaped by a desire to attain a lifestyle (Chien and Devaney, 2001) in order to satisfy a range of hedonistic and utilitarian desires in turn shaped marketing practice.

Coupled with the increased range and access to credit, there is also a high level of asymmetric information between borrower and lender (Oxera, 2004) which is particularly relevant for people who may be classed in the "vulnerable" category, such as students and low-income groups. A recent Irish study found that debt among low-income consumers includes a greater element of "middle-class, lifestyle–related" consumption and debt including credit card debt and luxury goods debt, which is often driven by aggressive marketing tactics and increased access to credit, coupled with pressures from a consumption-driven society (O'Loughlin, and O'Brien, 2006). While the life-cycle hypothesis of saving (Modigliani, 1986) suggests that people in the early stages of their career may have more favourable attitudes towards spending and borrowing, assuming future strong earnings (Chien and Devaney, 2001), more recent research suggests that indebtedness may move across lifecycle stages (Soman and Cheema, 2002), signalling that young people will continue to carry debt throughout their lifecycle. Taking a student perspective, O'Loughlin and Szmigin (2006) found that changing expectations and intense promotion of unsolicited and unsecured credit by financial providers signals a pattern of attitude tolerance and debt-accumulating behaviour among students that will ensue throughout their adult lives. The empirical part of this paper presents findings from in-depth discussions with students in the UK and Ireland, considered to be a particularly susceptible consumer group, in addition to key informants who are directly engaged with the credogenic environment from a policy, practice and advisory capacity. The research illustrates the nature and pervasiveness of the culture of credit and outlines a range of views with regard to where and how the ultimate responsibility for managing the current credogenic environment should lie.

METHODOLOGY
The study focused on exploring the level and division of responsibility held by key players including consumers, government agencies and financial providers in the credogenic environment and the power relations therein through an inductive exploratory approach (Miles and Huberman, 1994; Zaltman, 1997; Silverman, 2000).

A purposive sample of 5 UK and 6 Irish agency and supply-side key informants were selected across a range of key Irish and UK banking representative bodies, government support bodies, debt advice bureaus, consumer agencies and student representatives.

In addition, a range of consumer interviews were conducted with a purposive sample of 3rd level students based at the University of Limerick, Ireland and Universities of Bath and Birmingham, UK across a range of demographics, (age, gender, geographic and economic background). A purposeful sampling method was used to recruit 20 UK and Irish students in total, 10 from each country. As one of the key areas of interest was range and use of credit, including attitudes and behaviour in relation to credit cards, each student in the sample was recruited on the basis of credit card ownership.

Personal interviews were chosen as the most appropriate means of data collection for sensitive financial issues due to their superior ability to build depth and intimacy (Denzin and Lincoln, 1994) and optimally reveal participant in-depth insights and interpretations (Carson et al. 2001) in relation to credit and debt consumption. Following Miles and Huberman (1994), the transcripts were independently coded by both researchers and the themes were subsequently discussed and agreement was reached in terms of any differences in interpretation.

DISCUSSION OF FINDINGS

Ease of Access to Credit

Most of the students in this study found it easy to access both loans and credit cards from their banks. Importantly, many students are opening a back account for the first time and it gives banks the opportunity to market further products to them:

'It wasn't me going out and saying I need a credit card, it was more, there's an option of getting a credit card, why not?' (UK, Male)

'It was very easy for me to obtain a credit card, I wasn't going to have it but they said to me I might as well have it because it's there' (UK, Female)

Neither student has intended to obtain a credit card but accepted them when offered. They readily, and perhaps with little thought, accepted them. The possible consequences of getting into the credit card 'way of life' (Hayhoe *et al.*, 2000) are highlighted by the representative from the National Debtline who expressed her concern that people as young as 18 were calling on their service:

'It's so easy to get and people are starting off a lot younger and they're just acquiring more credit and then inevitably, they reach a point where they can't pay it and it might not be because their income drops but it just can't sustain it' (Training Information Officer, National Debt Line)

She continued by saying that young people do not necessarily have the 'training' to know how to deal with the credit offered them and then they accept more credit until they are no longer able to cope, thus echoing the issue of financial capability and literacy highlighted in the literature (e.g. Atkinson and Kempson, 2004).

The director from the British Bankers Association also pointed to a supply side issue in relation to the ease of credit for young people by pointing out that credit could be acquired from many sources so no one provider really knew how indebted a customer was. In addition he recognised that students were a particularly attractive marketing proposition:

"If they're promising in terms of university calibre then of course they have a future potential, and it's that future potential that makes them such an attractive marketing proposition" (Director, British Bankers Association).

That students require money to support their education at a time when they will be limited in terms of how much they can earn makes them an easy target for marketing and in particular for point of sale offers. None of the student participants had been rejected for loans or credit cards. But while the financial providers' telescopic abilities forecast that students are likely to be earning reasonably within a relatively short period of time, they do not accommodate the potential financial difficulties such students may face during their studies or already be in. Although previous studies (Mendoza and Pracejus, 1997) have recognised that students may display a future temporal orientation associated with holding more credit cards, debt still requires careful management in the period before future earnings are realised.

Marketing and Responsibility

Students were aware of and critical about the marketing they encountered. They suggested that marketing messages often only gave them one side of the agreement:

"You know, it's like we are giving you the freedom to do all this but actually on the sly we are keeping you hostage for the next few years until you pay us back" (Irish, Female).

Another student suggested that providers present a picture of 'free' money to students:

"For me, they make it out as if this is free money, you don't really need to worry about it, spend it on what you want we'll sort you out a good deal, have a good time, that's probably the way they market, and I don't think it's a good way because it comes across as free money, not you've got to think about the consequences" (UK, Female).

That the marketing of credit may play on a consumer's desire to engage fully with a culture of materialism (Calder, 1999) was recognised by all of the agency and supply participants. The policy officer from Consumers Advice described a recent piece of research they had conducted which had identified what she refereed to as the 'seven deadly sins of credit marketing':

'It's all about how easy it is and it's all appealing to people's aspirations and also particularly in the loans, they say; 'why don't you take out a little bit more? Go on, spoil yourself!' (Senior Policy Advisor Citizens Advice)

The British regulator was more circumspect in his comments, recognising the importance of education for individuals but also acknowledging that the decision as to whether or not to take credit is theirs:

'Our job is to make sure that people understand the decisions that they need to take in relation to taking on debt and the consequences of it and make sure they've got enough information and the tools available to make those decisions, not to tell them what their decisions are' (Consumer Sector Team Manager, Financial Services Authority).

The idea that there is a responsibility to ensure people understand what they are getting themselves into was echoed by the director of the British Bankers Association, who suggested that some kind of interrogation was needed to assess whether the finance was needed and the nature of repayment fully understood at the time of purchase:

'(We should) provide them with more understanding....how could I best help you in any future credit you might want to take, and I'd say, do you need it, do you understand it and can you afford it?' (Director, British Bankers Association).

In conclusion the supply side participants echoed the students' comments in relation to the freedom extended to them in terms of being able to engage with a product for which they did not necessarily have enough information and understanding to recognise their future obligations. This supports the notion that the effective evaluation of complex products such as credit is dependent on both the vulnerability of the consumer, marketing practice (Cui and Choudhury, 2003) but also meaningful consumer information and advice.

Individual Responsibility

Despite the fact that many financial providers aggressively promoted credit offerings to consumers and were perceived to be "putting an idea in a student's head", many students acknowledged their responsibility. This individual level responsibility related to assessing the level of credit each person required and ensuring that he/she did not incur unmanageable debt. Several students emphasised the importance of the individual assuming the responsibility for taking on credit, over-spending and paying back the debt:

"[It's a] nightmare...I think people take too much credit out–they go beyond their means and it can be a downward spiral into debt and you shouldn't really take it up unless you need to... that's my thoughts really" (UK, Female)
"Yeah, I don't believe in any of this crap when people sue for spending too much and being in debt and get it written off. No, you spend, it's your own fault you pay it back" (UK, Female)

Both comments suggest a high level of awareness and maturity regarding their role and responsibility in relation to credit and debt which they clearly feel should not be passed on to others to manage. Some students recounted bad experiences from which they had learned to manage their finances better. For example one student recalled her immature behaviour:

'I should have just paid off the minimum payment but I thought if I don't think about it it's not there' (Irish, Female)

Since this time, however, she has set up a minimum payment to leave her account each month. Conversely, other participants recounted stories of how they or their peers assumed little or no responsibility for their spending and instead relied on parents to support them and pay off any debts they incurred:

"No, some of my friends...they will just go into a shop and spend all around them. Some of them have their parents...they just pay it back for them" (Irish, Female)

Similarly, others spoke of their "nice parents" and that they were "spoiled" as their parents not only paid off their loans and debts but also provided them with an allowance.

While some students freely used their parents as a source of non-repayable income to finance their lifestyle, others recognised the extensive support provided by their parents and were very mindful of taking responsibility for their own debt.

"My family do so much for me already. The student debt that I will pick up is my own responsibility I mean I can't ask them to go off paying other parts after they do everything, all the other financial things for me" (UK, Male)

While previous research has shown that parental attitudes to finance offer a context to their children's behaviour (Hesketh, 1999), this can also contain mixed messages with regard to the use of credit (Atkinson and Kempson, 2004). The role of parents in this study was complex with some being very active, even cutting up their children's' credit cards following excessive use, while others regularly paid off debts of hundreds of pounds.

The concept of responsibility varied across participants with some acknowledging and exercising individual responsibility while others focused more on the instant gratification of spending and supporting their lifestyle (Webley and Nyhus, 2001), without reflecting on the long-term consequences of debt, instead relying on their family to "bail them out" if they incurred unmanageable debt. There were clearly major economic differences amongst students that reflected how they were able to behave with regard to debt as

is reflected by this comment from the President of the Students' Guild:

'The amount of people I know who take all their student loan out and put it in a high interest bank and Mum and Dad give them money every month and have a copy of their parent's credit card so that they can just go and spend.' (President, Students' Guild, University of Birmingham)

From a supplier perspective, the notion of individual responsibility was also met with mixed responses with some emphasising that "responsibility works both ways" (Financial Advisor, Ireland). Another suggested that "there has to be responsible lending and there has to be responsible borrowing" (Director of Consumer Information, Financial Regulator, Ireland). Individual level responsibility was also contingent on the consumer being fully informed and equipped to make the best financial decision and there was acknowledgement by some that not only were financial products complex but that financial capability varied, signalling the "need for better financial literacy from school age" (Director, Office of Director of Consumer Affairs, Ireland). Others believed, however, that there was sufficient consumer information and public awareness in addition to legislation in regard to credit and debt and that it was the responsibility of the individual to exploit resources available to them:

"We give them information and leaflets–we don't tell them what to do... regulation should be minimised" (Consumer Sector Team Manager, Financial Services Authority, UK).

While the notion of individual responsibility unveiled disparate thoughts from both consumers and supply-side participants, it did not detract from the shared view that increased access and consumption of credit was pervasive. Those involved directly with indebted individuals recognised a change in culture regarding the acceptance of credit with young people becoming socialized into the normalization of debt (O'Loughlin and Szmigin, 2006), such that they 'carry this philosophy with them' (Financial Advisor, Ireland). However, successfully or not students manage their current situation their attitudes and behavior are likely to continue to develop in a pattern which may be difficult to change and adjust leading to a life-long relationship with debt (Soman and Cheema, 2002).

CONCLUSIONS AND IMPLICATIONS

This paper has argued for the importance of understanding the environment in the modern consumption context. The case study of the credogenic environment effectively illustrates the nature of the power relationships which support the continued dominance of marketing's role in a neo-liberal context. Despite the exaltation of the individual as rational and well informed, the challenges facing consumers to exercise true choice and freedom within this arguably marketing-governed environment are clear. Reflecting many western societies, the consumer and supplier research highlights the pervasiveness of the culture of credit in Ireland and the UK which is predominantly fueled by increased access to and intensive marketing and promotion of "easy credit" and "free money". This is particularly concerning given the individual cognitive limitations associated with a complex purchase such as credit which may be particularly acute for susceptible groups such as students, where their ability to evaluate and act responsibly may be unfairly tested. The consumer and supplier research clearly highlights that students are perceived as an attractive marketing proposition and targeted at the point of sale with unsolicited seemingly harmless credit offerings, often without clear explanation of the long term implications. The direct consequence is a "buy now pay later" culture and the normalization of debt, some of which becomes unsustainable for consumers such as students who may not have the present ability, if perhaps the future potential to repay their debts. That consumer agencies report increased usage of their services by consumers as young as 18 is testimony to the power of the credogenic environment, within which a sophisticated financial marketing force continues to offer attractive credit options while failing to include the consequential dark side to credit which is unmanageable debt.

The issue of where responsibility should lie for creating and sustaining this credogenic environment unveiled much debate and diverse perspectives among both consumer and supply-side participants. On one hand, there was clear consensus among both groups of participants regarding marketing's dominant role in creating a consumerist society in actively promoting a lifestyle to consumers which in turn was facilitated by a range of credit options offered by financial providers. On the other hand, there were mixed views regarding the extent to which responsibility should be assigned at the individual consumer level, particularly as the issue of varying levels of financial capability and literacy was a key factor. Regarding the issue of lender responsibility, recent Irish legislation has been introduced through the Consumer Protection Codes (2006) which have outlawed many unethical lender practices such as unsolicited limit increases and pre-approved loans. Reflecting similar initiatives in other counties, this may go some way towards providing augmented regulation of the credit-led environment which is focused on protecting the consumer rather than on crippling the supplier. As for individual responsibility, while the notion of financial education from an early age and ongoing "training" of consumers as suggested by participants is part of the solution, there does not appear to be sufficiently meaningful or accessible information in the public domain. Indeed, considering many of the students were offered credit at the point of sale, it is perhaps here that attractively packaged and promoted credit offerings should be accompanied by simple but hard-hitting guidelines and warnings regarding the total cost of repayment and penalties.

REFERENCES

Atkinson, Adele and Kempson, Elaine (2004), Young People, Money Management, Borrowing and Saving, *A Report to the Banking Code Standard*.

Berwick, Isabel (2004) "The Heavy Burden of 'Have Now Pay Later'", *Financial Times*, [London] June 5.

Burton, Dawn (2008) *Credit and Consumer Society*, Routledge, UK.

Calder, Lendol (1999) *Financing the American Dream: A Cultural History of Consumer Credit*, Princeton University Press, Princeton University.

Carson, David, Audrey Gilmore, Chris Perry, and Kjell Gronhaug. (2001) *Qualitative Market Research*, London: Sage Publications.

Chien, Yi-Wen and Sharon A Devaney. (2001) "The Effects of Credit Attitude and Socioeconomic Factors on Credit Card and Instalment Debt", *The Journal of Consumer Affairs*, 35 (1), 162-179.

Cui, Geng and Pravat Choudhury. (2003) "Consumer Interests and the Ethical Implications of Marketing: A Contingency Framework", *Journal of Consumer Affairs*, 37 (2), 364-378.

Datamonitor (2006) "Credit Risk and Bad Debt Management in the UK Retail Lending Market", *Datamonitor*, July.

Denzin, Norman K. and Lincoln, Yvonne S. (1994) *Handbook of Qualitative Research*, Thousand Oaks: Sage.

Evans, Peter 2002. "Collective Capabilities, Culture, and Amaartya Sen's Development as Freedom", *Studies in Comparative International Development*, 37(2), 54-60.

Fleet Street Letter (2007) "Debt, The UK's Epidemic", *Fleet Street Letter*, 27th November, (www.fspinvest.co.uk).

Griffiths, Margaret (2000) "The Sustainability of Consumer Credit Growth in Late Twentieth Century Australia", *Journal of Consumer Studies & Home Economics*, 24(1), 23-33.

Hanson, Jon D. and Douglas A Kysar. (1999) *Taking Behaviourlism Seriously: The Problem of Market Manipulation*, 74, NYUL rev. 632.

Hayhoe, Celia., Leach, L., Pamela Turner, Marilyn Bruin and Frances Lawrence. (2000) "Differences in Spending Habits and Credit Use Among College Students", *Journal of Consumer Affairs*, 34(1), 113-133.

Hesketh, Anthony J. (1999), "Towards an economic sociology of the student financial experience of higher education", *Journal of Education Policy*, Vol. 14 No. 4, 385-410.

Hill, Ronald, P. and John C. Kozup (2007) "Consumer Experiences with Predatory Lending Practices", *Journal of Consumer Affairs*, 41(1), 29-46.

Lea, Stephen E. G. Paul Webley and Mark R. Levine, (1993) "The Economic Psychology of Consumer Debt", *Journal of Economic Psychology*, 14(1), 85-119.

Lyons, Angela (2004) "A Profile of Financially At-Risk College Students", *Journal of Consumer Affairs*, 38 (1), 56-80.

Miles, Mathew. B. and Huberman, A. Michael, (1994) *An Expanded Sourcebook Qualitative Data Analysis*, 2nd Ed, Thousand Oaks, CA: Sage.

Mendoz, Noram, A. and Pracejus, John W. (1997) Buy Now, Pay Later: Does a future Temporal Orientation affect credit overuse? In *Advances in Consumer Research*, (24) eds. Merrie Brucks and Deborah J. MacInnis, Provo, UT: Association for Consumer Research, 499-503.

Modigliani, Franco (1986) Life Cycle, Individual Thrift and the Wealth of Nations, *American Economic Review*, 76 (3), 297-314.

O'Loughin, Deirdre and Ronan O'Brien (2007), "Emerging Perspectives On Credit And Debt Among Low Income Consumers", *Irish Business Journal*, 3, (1), 4-15.

_____ Deirdre and Isabelle Szmigin (2006), "'I'll Always Be in Debt': Irish and UK Student Behaviour in a Credit-Led Environment'", *Journal of Consumer Marketing*, 23 (6), 335-353.

Oxera (2004), "Are UK Households over-indebted?" Oxera Consulting Ltd., UK

Pigou, Arthur C. (1920), *The Economics of Welfare,* London: MacMillan.

Rittenburg, Terri L. and Madhaven Parthasarathy (1997), "Ethical Implications of Target Market Selection", *Journal of Macromarketing*, 17, (2), 49-64.

Roberts, James, A. and Eli Jones (2001), "Money Attitudes, Credit Card Use, and Compulsive Buying among American College students", *Journal of Consumer Affairs,* 35, (2), 213-240.

Silverman, David (2000), *Doing Qualitative Research: A Practical Handbook*, London: Sage.

Soman, Dilip and Amar Cheema (2002), "The Effect of Credit on Spending Decisions: The Role of the Credit Limit and Credibility", *Marketing Science*, 21, (1), 32-53

Swinburn, Boyd, Gary Egger and Fazeela Raza, (1999), "Dissecting Obesogenic Environments: the Development and Application of a Framework for Identifying and

Prioritizing Environmental Interventions for Obesity", *Preventive Medicine,* 29, 6, 563-570

Webley, Paul and Ellen K. Nyhus, (2001), "Life-cycle and Dispositional routes into Problem Debt", *British Journal of Psychology*, 92, (3), 423-446.

Zaltman, Gerald (1997), "Rethinking Market Research, Putting People Back", *Journal of Marketing Research*, 34, (4), 424-437.

Classifying Customers with Multidimensional Customer Contact Sequences

Sascha Steinmann, University of Goettingen, Germany
Guenter Silberer, University of Goettingen, Germany

ABSTRACT

We used a multidimensional sequence alignment method to cluster customers (N=151) of a German tour operator according to the multidimensional sequences of their customer contacts (dimension 1), their functions (dimension 2) and importance of the customer contact (dimension 3). In doing so, we obtained four clusters. Results reveal differences in the customers' behavior concerning the customer contacts and their functions in the whole purchase process, as well as between the customer segments identified. Customer segmentation based upon demographic or psychographic variables would not have been able to enrich the knowledge of the customers in this manner.

INTRODUCTION

Knowledge of one's customers is a strategic success factor for any supplier. The fundamental element for the attainment of customer knowledge is the contact between the retailer or service provider and her/his customers in the different channels of the marketing and distribution system. Not only are the kind and number of the customer contacts in a specific process phase relevant to this, but also their functions and importance to the customer, not to mention the sequence of these three dimensions during the purchase process. Such multidimensional sequences have practically been ignored in previous marketing research, especially the problem of collecting, connecting and analyzing the relevant data from the different marketing and distribution channels in all phases of the purchase process to present a single, unified view of the customers (Payne and Frow 2004).

However, it can be assumed that multidimensional customer contact sequences (MCCS) are of great relevance to marketing: for example, it can be expected that different contact sequences are accompanied by different product purchases or e.g. in the tourism industry through the booking of different journeys and that different customers have different sequences according to their individual behavior. Knowledge of these connections facilitates the purposeful control of the customers throughout the purchase process by the retailer or service provider and thus extends his/her commercial possibilities to interact with customers within the bounds of marketing. Furthermore, such sequences can provide important insights into potential existing cross-channel synergies (Verhoef, Neslin, and Vroomen. 2007). Hence, an analysis of the multidimensional sequence of the customer contacts (dimension 1), their functions (dimension 2) and their importance (dimension 3) could provide crucial insights into customer behavior, as well as the needs and preferences of the customers over time, as it has become routine for the consumer to use different channels in the purchase process to approach a retailer or a service provider (Rangaswamy and van Bruggen 2005). Therefore, this study contributes to the marketing literature by addressing how the MCCS can be measured and form the basis for multidimensional customer segmentation. Besides this we are also interested in evaluating possible determinants and effects of the customer contacts, their functions and importance.

CONCEPTUAL BACKGROUND

Customer Touch Points and Customer Contacts

It is increasingly common for firms to employ online distribution channels alongside its offline distribution channels and further marketing channels to rely on these complex combinations as a source of competitive advantage and better serve their customers needs and preferences (Geykens, Gielens, and Dekimpe 2002). In such environments, many customers have become multi channel users. They realized contacts between the firm and themselves at different contact points (e.g. store, agency, homepage) in the different phases of the purchase process. Therefore, there are many opportunities to establish contacts between a supplier and customers in the different process stages.

In retailing, we can differentiate the pre-purchase, purchase and post-purchase phases, but in other branches or when we are interested in specific problems or research questions it is more meaningful to use a more detailed modeling of the process. For example, with regard to tourism industry differentiation into five successive process phases (the pre-booking, booking, pre-journey, journey and post-journey phase) including all customer contacts is reasonable. Furthermore, we can distinguish the variability of the contact points (personal, semi-personal and impersonal contacts) (Silberer, Steinmann, and Mau 2006). Payne and Frow (2004) define these categories of customer contacts as a continuum of forms ranging from the physical to the virtual contact.

Functions and Importance of Customer Contacts

Every customer contact fulfills different functions in the various process phases. Consequently, speech, sale and service functions can be distinguished (Simons and Bouwman 2004). Therefore, the functions of the customer contacts in the different channels range from general and selective information regarding the desired product or service, price comparisons and purchasing up to using different kinds of customer services as well as advisory and complaining. Hence, in the contact, not only is purchasing a product of relevance to the customer, but also information and communication prior to, during and following the purchase (Wallace, Giese, and Johnson 2004). According to the media-richness theory (Daft and Lengel 1984), during the process customers will subsequently find it easier to establish contact with a supplier in a way that best fits their needs. This requires that the respective channels and their combination to be capable of fulfilling customer needs and preferences concerning the desired functionality in the different process phases.

According to Payne, Bettman, and Johnson's (1993) concept of adaptive decision-making, a customer shifts between the pre-purchase to the purchase phase from an attribute-based search to an alternatives-based search as she/he progresses in the decision-making process. Thus, the customers will be less focused on information gathering but more focused on comparing the alternatives they have decided to consider. In the case of complex products or services such as vacations, these alternatives are complex bundles of attributes and benefits that need to be processed. In cases where many relevant aspects of the decision cannot be controlled, customers seek some kind of help in the decision-making, and hence the customer is more likely to use the desired benefit as the basis to evaluate the characteristics of the different contacts points and the importance of the specific contact in the purchase process (Frambach, Roest, and Krishnan 2007). However, there are channel related differences in fulfilling customer's needs and preferences across the purchase process, including richness of information presented (Daft and Engel 1984) and accessibility or convenience (Ward

2001). For example, on the internet products cannot be physically examined, which leads to less product information than in the case of brick-and-mortar stores (Venkatesan, Kumar, and Ravishankar. 2007). Therefore, the internet is often considered to be risky for purchasing (Alba et al. 1997). Conversely, the offline channels are amongst other things characterized by richer information on the product (Venkatesan et al. 2007). Verhoef et al. (2007) used an extended version of the theory of reasoned action (Fishbein and Ajzen 1975) in their model for explaining the interdependencies of customers' channel choice across different process phases. Their results show that customers can benefit from the channel related differences within the purchase process by using the channels according to their individual channel behavior (see also Silberer et al. 2006) because channels do not differ in their functionality but also in their ability to fulfill individual customer needs to the same extent across the different process phases (Balasubramanian, Raghunathan, and Mahajan 2005). Research also shows that benefits and therefore the importance of the several contacts sought change across the process phases (Mittal, Kumar, and Tsiros 1999).

Concerning the booking of a vacation, we can expect personal contacts in offline channels to be more likely and more important to the customer than semi- or impersonal contacts because personal advisors are in the best position to help the customers identify and explain the important aspects in the pre-purchase and purchase phase. Because of the limited functionality of the mostly impersonal contacts in online channels compared to face-to-face contacts in offline channels, many customers commonly use the internet as an information source in the purchase process. Especially in the case of complex products or services, customers have to come to categorize it in their minds as an important information source, not as a shopping revenue (Balasubramanian et al. 2005; Verhoef et al. 2007). The previous comments show that not only does the usage of the different contact points by the customers differ during the purchase process, but it also supports the assumption that the functions, as well as the importance of the customer contacts, also change during the purchase process. We assume that this is reflected in the multidimensional customer contact sequences (MCCS).

Customer Segmentation

For our study, research regarding different approaches for customer segmentation is of particular interest. Ruiz, Chebat, and Hansen (2004) and Ganesh, Reynolds, and Luckett (2007) provide an overview of a large number of empirical studies on this topic. The procedure for the formation of customer segments can thus be divided into two different approaches. Demographic variables (e.g. age and gender) on the one hand and on the other psychographic variables (e.g. motives or attitudes) are drawn upon for the segmentation. By doing so, the constituted customer groups reveal *who* is buying in the investigated stores and *why*. The customer's actual buying behavior during and after the purchase, however, is hardly taken into account, i.e. *how* the customers inform themselves prior to purchase, *how* the purchase in the store goes and *how* the relationship between retailer and customer is organized after the purchase. Kim and Park (1997) classified the customers of food stores by the frequency of their visits. Ruiz et al. (2004) use the behavior during a shopping trip, and that only related to a visit in one store or shopping mall, as a basis for customer segmentation. Although they had partially different results in the end, the mentioned studies show the usefulness of customer segmentation based on their customer's behavior. However, different essential aspects are not taken into account: the specified studies only examine the behavior in a specific channel of a supplier *in* the purchase phase. It should be expected that different behavior during the purchase is reflected in different behavior *prior* to and *after* the purchase.

Another aspect deals with the variables used in the segmentation analysis: to consider only the behavior leads to the neglect of other contacts between customers and suppliers. However, as shown by studies mentioned first, such contacts are important influential factors for customer behavior.

According to Hägerstrand (1970) customer behavior can be viewed as a sequence of interdependent actions over time. However, customer behavior in the studies mentioned is mostly treated as a chain of independent activities. Thus, the sequential order and obvious relations of the activities are often neglected. Therefore, Abbott's (1995, p. 94) statement "We assume intercase independence even while our theories focus on interaction" regarding social science is also largely true for marketing research concerning the segmentation of the customers with regard to their individual behavior through the phases of the purchase process. Therefore, in the aforementioned approaches important aspects reflecting the customers' behavior are not addressed.

The sequential behavior of the customers throughout the purchase process also in different channels has barely been taken into account in the formation of segments. For marketing purposes, Larson, Bradlow, and Fader (2005) for example used a sequence-analytical clustering approach to evaluate the shopping behavior in a supermarket for the foundation of customer segments. Silberer et al. (2006) used the sequence of the customer contacts in retailing to evaluate differences in the customer's behavior with regard to the whole purchase process. Segmentation of this kind can give a retailer or service provider important insights into the requirements, preferences and behavior of the customers over a period of time. By tracking the multidimensional customer behavior across channels, firms can improve their understanding of their customers' decision-making and develop a basis for creating strong relationships and improving retention (Dholakia, Zhao, and Dholakia 2005).

The previous discussion shows that not only do the customer contacts (dimension 1) differ across the successive phases of the purchase process, they also support the assumption that the functions (dimension 2), as well as the importance (dimension 3) of the customer contacts, also change during the purchase process. The actual behavior of the customers over a period of time is taken into account for the customer segmentation through the use of the multidimensional customer contact sequences. This facilitates a differentiation of customers that is not possible on the basis of demographic or psychographic variables. Such insights are an important confirmation as to the usefulness of customer segmentation regarding the multidimensional customer contact sequence.

METHOD: MULTIDIMENSIONAL CUSTOMER CONTACT SEQUENCES

Measures and Procedure

The aim of this segmentation is to identify powerful customer clusters which are very similar with regard to their individual behavior reflected in their multidimensional customer contact sequence in the purchase process. We investigated multidimensional customer contact sequences regarding the five different phases of the purchase process in the tourism industry-pre-booking, booking, pre-journey, journey and post-journey phase-with a German tour operator based upon a structured questionnaire (comparable to Silberer et al. 2006). To support the recollection of events dated far away back a proceeding was chosen that took pattern from cognitive psychology (Ericsson and Simon, 1980; Anderson, 1995). Therefore, the questionnaire leads the customer through her/his memories step by step-starting with events that are most accessible to him because they are closest to the interview (post-journey phase)-up to those situations that are initially difficult to remember without any support because they date a long way back (booking and pre-booking phase).

The surveyed multidimensional sequences included the different customer contacts (dimension 1: e.g. advertising, travel agency staff, tour guide), their functions (dimension 2: general and selective information, price comparison, booking, advisory and complaining) as well as the importance (dimension 3) of the different customer contacts across the purchase process. The importance of the customer contacts was inquired on a six-step rating scale ranging from 1=*entirely unimportant* to 6=*very important*. To ensure the recording of the multidimensional customer contact sequence over the whole purchase process, only those customers were recruited who had actually finished a journey booked with the tour operator. Furthermore, we only surveyed customers who booked a journey in the last 6 months prior to the study to ensure that they could still remember it well.

In the final questionnaire, not only the multidimensional contact sequences actually realized were examined but also possible determinants (previous bookings, price category, journey category, internet affinity, and demographic variables) as well as final variables (customer satisfaction, intention of recommendation, intention of repeat booking, trust).

A total of N=151 customers of the tour operator took part in the survey. Every participant in the survey was entered in a lottery, where two wellness weekends and tickets to a German leisure park were drawn. Women represented 44.2% of the sample. The average age=51.12 (SD=13.52) years.

Multidimensional Sequence Alignment and Sequence Clustering

The Sequence Alignment Method (SAM) was originally developed in molecular biology to compare DNA or protein sequences (Sankoff and Kruskal 1983). The idea of the SAM is to equalize two different sequences with regard to the operations insertion, deletion and substitution. Mostly the weight of one is assigned to the operations insertion and deletion, for substitutions the sum of the consecutive operations deletion and insertion (Joh et al. 2002). Usually there are different ways to transfer one sequence to another in the aforementioned operations, therefore the minimal sum of the weighted operations, the Levenshtein distance (Levenshtein 1966), is commonly used as similarity measure for the considered sequences.

In this study, the customer behavior is not represented as the customer contacts by a single attribute. To gain deeper insights in the differences of customer behavior and powerful clusters, the multidimensional customer contact sequences were characterized by three dimensions: the customer contact sequence (dimension 1), the sequence of the functions related to the customer contacts (dimension 2), and the sequence of the importance (dimension 3) of the contacts to the customers. The easy way to compare such sequences is to calculate the Levenshtein distance for each dimension separately and then add up the measured distances of all the dimensions. This approach is based on the assumption that all attributes are independent. In our case, this clearly is not true because there are obviously dependencies between the customer contacts, their functions and their importance. Therefore the calculation of measured attributes for each dimension would distort the result. To avoid such distortions with regard to the different measurement scales of the dimensions, we used a multidimensional approach proposed by Joh et al. (2002) which identifies elements that can be aligned simultaneously without calculating the costs twice, called "optimal trajectory multidimensional SAM" (OTMSAM). Joh et al. (2002) proposed to treat the operations that are applied to the elements of a dimension belonging to the same

event to be treated as a single operation. This integrated operation combines a set of elements that can be aligned simultaneously as if it were one element. Such sets of elements are called a segment. In the case of no interdependencies, the resulting alignment cost equals the simple sum of uni-dimensional optimum alignment costs. Any costs-savings are indicative of interdependencies across the dimensions underlying the activity-travel patterns. In general, the alignment of two multidimensional activity patterns will involve varying degrees of cost reductions. The stronger the interdependencies between attributes, the higher the cost reduction. For a more detailed description see Joh et al. (2002). The distances were calculated with the Software DANA as a basis for our cluster analysis using the Ward Method. The results of our cluster analysis show that the differentiation into four clusters proved to be the optimal cluster solution.

RESULTS: MULTIDIMENSIONAL SEQUENCE CLUSTERS

Description of the Clusters using Constituent Variables

In order to describe the clusters, the active variables that have entered the cluster analysis are cited. The clusters identified are therefore described using the customer contact sequences (centroids) typical for them (see table 1).

The typical representative of the first cluster has two contacts with the travel agency staff in the booking phase. These contacts were used for "selective information" and for the "booking" of the desired journey. In virtue of the minimal customer contacts in this cluster, it is not surprising that they were rated as "very important" contacts. The centroid of cluster 2 shows that these customers realized contacts in all different phases of the purchase process. They sought contact with the travel agency staff in the pre-booking phase for "selective information". During the booking phase they used the catalog to obtain "general information" combined with the travel agency staff for "selective information" and the "booking" of the desired journey. Prior to their journey they used the tour operators catalog and the travel vouchers to get "general" and "selective information" about their travel destination and for recreational activities. All contacts in this phases were "very important" to the customers. During their vacation these customers contacted the tour guide for a "price comparison" of different recreational activities. In the post-journey phase they realized a contact with the travel agency staff to obtain "advice" on different problems. The contacts in the journey and post-journey phase are of significantly lower importance to these customers. The customers in the third cluster sought their first contacts in the booking phase. They used the tour operators catalog combined with the travel agency staff for obtaining "general and selective information" about the travel destination and different hotels as well as the "booking" of the considered journey. It is noticeable that the catalog is of much lower importance to these customers compared to cluster 2. As in cluster 2, the customers from cluster 3 also used the tour operators catalog and the travel vouchers for "general and selective information" about the travel destination and for information about recreational activities, but evaluated these contacts as less important. During the journey and in the post-journey phase, these customers display a similar behavior regarding their realized contacts than the customers in cluster 2. Customers in cluster 4 used the tour operators catalog for obtaining "general information" and a "price comparison" of the tour operator's different offers and only contacted the travel agent only for the "booking" of the desired vacation. During their vacation they sought contact with the tour guide for "general and selective information" and the "booking" of recreational activities. In the post-journey phase they used their travel vouchers and

TABLE 1
Description of the clusters by centroid sequences

Cluster 1	Contacts		*Travel agent*		*Travel agent*								
	Functions[a]		*SI*	→	*B*								
	Importance[b]		6		6								
Cluster 2	Contacts	*Travel agent Agent*		*Catalog*		*Travel Agent*		*Catalog*		*Travel vouchers*		*Tour guide*	*Travel Agent*
	Functions	*SI*	→	*GI*	→	*SI & B*	→	*GI & SI*	→	*GI*	→	*P*	→	*A*
	Importance	6		6		6		6		6		3	3
Cluster 3	Contacts	*Catalog*		*Travel Agent*		*Catalog*		*Travel vouchers*		*Tour guide*		*Travel Agent*	
	Functions	*GI*	→	*SI & B*	→	*GI & SI*	→	*GI & SI*	→	*GI & SI*	→	*A*	
	Importance	4		6		5		5		4		3	
Cluster 4	Contacts	*Catalog*		*Travel Agent*		*Tour guide*		*Travel vouchers*		*Catalog*			
	Functions	*GI & P*	→	*B*	→	*GI, SI & B*	→	*A*	→	*A*			
	Importance	5		5		5		2		2			

Note: [a] GI="general information", SI="selective information", P="price comparison", B="booking", A="advisory";
[b] inquired on a six-step rating scale, 1 corresponds to *entirely unlikely*; 6 corresponds to *very likely*

the catalog for "advisory" functions or, maybe, finding a telephone number to contact the tour operator, but such contacts were only of low importance.

Description of the Clusters using Contact-related Variables

For the description of the cluster solutions within the four clusters, selected differences regarding the three dimensions of the MCCS are referred to here in the different phases of the purchase process which differentiate the clusters (see table 2). The results in describe the clusters by way of different customer contacts in the purchase process. Overall, the customers in the first cluster realized the fewest number of contacts with regard to the whole purchase process as well as concerning the proportion of contacts in different process phases, except the booking phase, compared to the other clusters. In the pre-booking phase the high proportion of contacts with the tour operators-advertising in the travel agency is remarkable for the customers in cluster 3. The customers of the other clusters realized such contacts significantly less. We obtained similar results for catalog contacts in the booking phase.

The customers in all clusters mostly booked the desired journeys in the travel agency having personal contacts with the travel agency staff. Prior to the journey the customers in the second cluster had the highest proportion of contacts concerning the stated contacts. We obtained similar results in the journey phase. In the post journey phase, only the customers in cluster 2 only had considerably more contacts with the travel agency staff compared to cluster 1 and cluster 3. Customers in cluster 1 hardly had any contact with the stated contact points. The customers in cluster 4 used the catalog and the travel vouchers most often, the proportions distributed equally across the stated contact points here. All these results are reflected in the first dimension of the centroid-sequences of clusters.

The differences in the functions of the customer contacts provide important findings regarding the intention of the contacts during the overall purchase process (see table 3). In the pre-booking phase we obtain highly significant differences regarding the function "general information" of the tour operator's catalog. Customers in cluster 1 and cluster 4 used the catalog least for this function, but the customers of cluster 1 used the catalog for more differentiated functions than the customers in cluster 4. They also used the catalog for "selective information" and "price comparison".

The same behavior was obtained for the customers in cluster 2. Concerning the catalog functions we obtained a similar result in the booking phase. There are no significant differences between the clusters regarding the functions of the travel agency staff in this phase, but it is remarkable that these contacts had to fulfil most different functions. The customers of all clusters used them for "general and selective information" regarding the tour operator's offers, the travel destination, and recreational activities, as well as for "price comparison", "advice", and, of course, for the "booking" of the desired journey. We did not obtain any significant differences in the functions of all contact points during the journey. In this phase the customer contacts, especially contacts with the tour guide, were mostly used for "selective information" and the "price comparison" of recreational activities as well as for "advice" and "complaining". After the journey, our results show significant differences in the functions of the contacts with the travel agency staff. The customers of cluster 2 and cluster 4 mostly used this contact point for "advisory" functions, while the customers in cluster 1 and cluster 3 mostly had contact for "complaints" in this phase.

Overall, the customers of cluster 2 evaluated the contacts as most important compared to the other clusters (see table 4). Interestingly, this is the only cluster that evaluated the contacts in the pre-

TABLE 2
Cluster description using selected contact points

	Cluster 1	Cluster 2	Cluster 3	Cluster 4	
Number of Contacts	*M*=5.1 (2.4)	*M*=12.7 (4.6)	*M*=10.2 (4.5)	*M*=9.9 (3.3)	*p*<.001
Pre-booking phase	*64.4%*[a]	*93.8%*	*93.3%*	*93.1%*	*p*<.001
Advertising in the travel agency	2.2%	3.1%	22.2%	6.9%	*p*<.05
Tour operator's catalog	33.3%	68.8%	62.2%	48.3%	*p*<.01
Booking phase	100%	100%	100%	100%	n.s.
Tour operator's catalog	28.9%	78.1%	45.5%	55.2%	*p*<.001
Other websites	8.9%	34.4%	15.6%	13.8%	*p*<.05
Bookingchannel					
Travel agency	*86.7%*	*75%*	*73.3%*	*72.4%*	n.s.
Internet	*11.1%*	*21.9%*	*15.6%*	*20.6%*	
Other	*2.2%*	*3.1%*	*11.1%*	*7%*	
Pre-journey phase	51.1%	98.9%	91.1%	86.2%	*p*<.001
Tour operator's catalog	8.9%	68.8%	42.2%	20.7%	*p*< .001
Travel documents/vouchers	31.1%	68.8%	57.8%	32.5%	*p*<.01
Travel agency staff	17.8%	53.1%	24.4%	48.3%	*p*<.01
Journey phase	48.9%	98.9%	82.2%	89.7%	*p*<.001
Tour operator's catalog	11.1%	40.6%	8.9%	10.3%	*p*<.05
Tour guide	37.8%	81.3%	71.1%	65.5%	*p*<.001
Post-Journey phase	51.1%	75.0%	62.2%	82.8%	*p*<.05
Tour operator's catalog	13.6%	31.3%	22.2%	51.7%	*p*<.001
Travel documents/vouchers	9.1%	28.1%	24.4%	51.7%	*p*<.001
Travel agency staff	25%	56.3%	28.9%	48.3%	*p*<.05

Note: [a]100 % correspond to the customers in cluster 1; SD in brackets; all significant differences between the four clusters were calculated with a χ^2-adaptation test or *F*-Test; n.s.=not significant.

TABLE 3
Cluster description by functions of selected contact points

	Cluster 1	Cluster 2	Cluster 3	Cluster 4	
Number of different functions	*M*=2.4 (1.1)	*M*=4.1 (0.8)	*M*=3.3 (0.7)	*M*=2.9 (1.0)	*p*<.001
Pre-booking phase					
Tour operator's catalog					
General information	*35.7%*[a]	*86.4%*	*78.6%*	*35.7%*	*p*<.001
Booking phase					
Tour operator's catalog					
General information	*58.3%*	*88%*	*73.7%*	*46.7%*	*p*<.01
Pre-journey phase					
Travel vouchers					
Selective information	*16.7%*	*21.1%*	*47.8%*	*22.2%*	*P*<.01
Advisory	*2.2%*	*21.1%*	*21.7%*	*66.7%*	*p*<.01
Post-Journey phase					
Travel agency staff					
Advisory	*2.1%*	*50%*	*20%*	*77.8%*	*p*<.01
Complaining	*16.7%*	*11.1%*	*40%*	*22.2%*	*p*<.01

Note: [a]100 % correspond to the customers in cluster 1 who realized a catalog contact; SD in brackets; all significant differences between the four clusters were calculated with a χ^2-adaptation test or *F*-Test.

TABLE 4
Cluster description by importance of the customer contacts

	Cluster 1	Cluster 2	Cluster 3	Cluster 4	
Average importance of contacts	*M*=5.1 (0.8)[a]	*M*=5.4 (0.4)	*M*=5.0 (0.5)	*M*=5.0 (0.7)	*p*<.05
		Pre-booking phase			
Other websites	*M*=5.0 (1.4)	*M*=5.6 (0.8)	*M*=4.4 (1.2)	*M*=4.0 (1.4)	*p*<.05
		Booking phase			
All contacts	*M*=5.7 (0.6)	*M*=5.4 (0.4)	*M*=5.3 (0.7)	*M*=5.2 (0.7)	*p*<.05
		Pre-journey phase			
Tour operator's homepage	*M*=4.2 (0.6)	*M*=5.3 (0.5)	*M*=4.4 (0.6)	*M*=5.0 (1.0)	*p*<.01
		Journey phase			
All contact points	*M*=4.6 (1.3)	*M*=5.4 (0.7)	*M*=5.1 (0.7)	*M*=4.8 (1.2)	*p*<.05
Tour guide	*M*=4.8 (1.2)	*M*=5.5 (0.7)	*M*=5.1 (0.9)	*M*=4.6 (1.5)	*p*<.05
		Post-Journey phase			
Tour operator's catalog	*M*=5.2 (1.3)	*M*=5.0 (0.9)	*M*=4.2 (1.3)	*M*=3.7 (0.9)	*p*<.05
Tour operator's homepage	*M*=4.9 (0.8)	*M*=4.9 (0.7)	*M*=4.2 (0.9)	*M*=5.2 (0.7)	*p*<.01

Note: [a] inquired on a six-step rating scale: 1 corresponds to *entirely unimportant*, 6 corresponds to *very important*

booking phase as the most important, while for the customers in the other clusters the contacts in the booking phase were of the highest importance.

Prior to the journey, we obtained significant differences with regard to the importance of the tour operator's homepage. Regarding the customers in cluster 1, this contact point was of considerably lesser importance compared to the other clusters. During the journey the tour guide was the most important to cluster 2. After the journey our results show significant differences in the importance of contacts with the tour operator's catalog and homepage. In this phase the contacts with the travel agency staff were of great importance to all customers, probably due to the fact that this contact point was mostly used for "advice" and especially for "complaining". Finally, table 5 characterizes the clusters of the different segments by its size and essential demographic reference numbers.

We also analyzed the behavior of the customers in our cluster solution regarding the customer contacts, their functions and importance over time. As expected, we obtained significant differences in the customer behavior in each cluster across the successive phases of the purchase process. For the customers in cluster 1, we found highly significant differences concerning the number of contacts across the different phases ($Hotelling's\ Trace\ F_{(4, 41)}$_26.152; $p<.001$) but no significant differences with regard to the functions and importance of the customer contacts. Only 64.4% of these customers realized contacts in the pre-booking phase and after the booking of the vacation, they also have a significantly lower proportion compared to the other clusters ($p<.001$). In cluster 2, we detected significant differences in the customer contacts ($Hotelling's\ Trace\ F_{(4, 28)}$_3.182; $p<.05$) and highly significant differences for the functions ($Hotelling's\ Trace\ F_{(4, 12)}$_16.001; $p<.001$). Compared to the others, these customers had the highest proportion of contacts in the pre-booking phase (93.8%), the pre-journey phase (98.9%) and also during the journey (94.6%). For cluster 3, we obtained a similar pattern concerning the customer contacts ($Hotelling's\ Trace\ F_{(4, 41)}$_10.797; $p<.001$) and the functions ($Hotelling's\ Trace\ F_{(4, 14)}$_22.589; $p<.001$). We also

found such characteristics for the customers in cluster 4 (customer contacts: $Hotelling's\ Trace\ F_{(4, 26)}$_4.308; $p<.01$; functions: $Hotelling's\ Trace\ F_{(4, 11)}$_11.971; $p<.01$). According to cluster 1, there are no significant differences in the importance of the contacts across the purchase process phases.

Determinants of the Multidimensional Customer Contact Sequence Clusters

As we have already illustrated, different factors can determine contact sequences. In this context, the duration of the purchase consideration, the price of the journey and the journey category are conceivable. Furthermore, the time of day and the day of the week can be regarded as determinants for customer contacts. However, only the most important differences between the cluster solutions of both segments are considered more closely here (see table 6).

Effects of the Multidimensional Customer Contact Sequence Clusters

Besides the determinants, the effects of the MCCS on final variables such as customer satisfaction with the tour operator's prices, the journey, and the tour operator's service across the successive phases of the purchase process are also of great interest. We were also interested in the satisfaction with the reachability of the tour operator, as well as the satisfaction with of the tour operator compared to other tour operators. Furthermore, we examined the effects of the customer contacts on the intent to recommend, willingness for repeated bookings, perceived risk and trust (see table 7).

DISCUSSION AND CONCLUSIONS

The results of our study demonstrate that the customers can be classified with regard to their multidimensional contact sequences. These indicate differences in the purchasing process, as for example our results on differences in the customers' behavior concerning the usage and functions of the different contact points across the purchase process suggest between the customer clusters identified. Customer segmentation based upon demographic or

TABLE 5

Cluster description by essential reference variables

	Cluster 1	Cluster 2	Cluster 3	Cluster 4	
Cluster size	n_1=45	n_2=32	n_3=45	n_4=29	
Age	M=53.7 (12.4)	M=45.9 (13.2)	M=50.9 (14.2)	M=52.5 (13.3)	n.s.
Women's quota	51.1%	50%	42.2%	31%	n.s.

Note: n.s.=not significant

TABLE 6

Description of the clusters by possible determinants

	Cluster 1	Cluster 2	Cluster 3	Cluster 4	
Selected determinants for MCCS					
Previous bookings	93.9%[a]	65.6%	77.8%	89.7%	p<.01
Duration of booking consideration (in days)	M=32.6 (28.4)	M=48.9 (38.9)	M=79.2 (86.7)	M=53.5 (32.2)	p<.05
Journey category					n.s.
Long-haul journey	*8.9%*	*34.4%*	*20.0%*	*20.7%*	
Beach holiday/Last-Minute	*46.7%*	*46.9%*	*55.6%*	*34.5%*	
City tour	*6.7%*	*9.4%*	*4.4%*	*17.2%*	
Club vacation	*13.3%*	*0%*	*0%*	*10.3%*	
Wellness/Spa vacation	*6.7%*	*0%*	*6.7%*	*10.3%*	
Other	*17.7%*	*9.3%*	*13.3%*	*7.0%*	
Price category					n.s.
< 1000 ?	*15.9%*	*29.1%*	*28.6%*	*24.1%*	
1001–1500 ?	*13.6%*	*16.1%*	*21.4%*	*24.1%*	
1501–2000 ?	*27.3%*	*19.4%*	*14.3%*	*20.7%*	
2001–2500 ?	*15.9%*	*16.1%*	*9.5%*	*3.4%*	
2501–3000 ?	*4.5%*	*6.5%*	*4.8%*	*10.3%*	
> 3000 ?	*22.7%*	*12.9%*	*21.4%*	*17.1%*	
Internet usage (in general)					
Several times a week	59.2%	74.2%	74.7%	64.3%	*n.s.*

Note: [a]100 % correspond to the customers in cluster 1; SD in brackets; all significant differences between the four clusters were calculated with a χ^2-adaptation test or F-Test; n.s.=not significant.

TABLE 7

Cluster description with possible effects

	Cluster 1	Cluster 2	Cluster 3	Cluster 4	
Satisfaction[a]					
with journey and prices	M=5.3 (0.9)	M=5.0 (0.8)	M=4.6 (1.2)	M=5.0 (0.6)	p<.05
Tour operator	M=4.9 (1.1)	M=4.7 (0.9)	M=4.2 (1.1)	M=5.0 (0.8)	p<.05
Meet customer's expectations[b]	M =5.3 (0.8)	M=5.0 (1.2)	M=4.5 (1.3)	M=4.9 (0.9)	p<.01
Intent to recommend[c]	M=5.1 (0.9)	M=5.0 (0.8)	M=4.6 (1.2)	M=5.0 (0.6)	p<.05
Willingness for repeat bookings[d]	M=5.3 (1.3)	M=4.6 (1.3)	M=4.6 (1.4)	M=5.4 (1.1)	p<.01

Note: [a] inquired on a six-step rating scale: 1 corresponds to *entirely dissatisfied*, 6 corresponds to *very satisfied;* [b] inquired on a six-step rating scale, 1 corresponds to *not at all,* 6 corresponds to *completely;* [c] & [d] inquired on a six-step rating scale, 1 corresponds to *entirely unlikely*; 6 corresponds to *very likely*; *SD* in brackets all significant differences between the four clusters were calculated with a F-Test psychographic variables would not have been able to enrich the knowledge of the customers in this manner.

In observing the differences between all of the results, we can classify each cluster with a name–even if simplified: customers in the first cluster could be characterized as "satisfied repeat bookers" in view of their very high proportion of previous bookings with the tour operator, low number of contacts, and the results concerning the final variables. The second cluster can be categorized as "information seekers", as the customers in this cluster already had the highest proportion of contacts, especially with the tour operator's catalog, in nearly all phases of the purchase process bar the post-journey phase. In the pre-booking and booking phase, they mostly used the different contact points for "general and selective informa-tion" on the tour operator's offers and the travel destination. Prior to their journey and in the journey phase, they sought information regarding recreational activities. In view of the proportion of contacts with offers through the tour operator's advertising in the pre-booking phase, and with regard to the results concerning the final variables, the customers in the third cluster can be referred to as "unsatisfied offer bookers". Finally, customers from the fourth cluster could be classified as "complicated travelers". They have the highest proportion of contacts in the post-journey phase, not to mention a high proportion of contacts with the tour guide during their vacation. The contacts in these phases mostly served "advi-sory" or "complaining" purposes.

This new kind of information puts a supplier in a position to adapt the establishment of individual customer contact points to the different customer segments and guide customers via contacts in the purchase process. Knowing these segments and their sequences enables the retailer to anticipate further contacts and offer suitable measures. If the supplier pursues a particular strategy with regard to the sequence of the contacts, these results provide information on the proportion of the customers who behave accordingly. There-fore, the balance between the aspired and actual sequence of the customer contacts could be used to monitor the marketing commu-nication, as well as the whole marketing strategy. The multidimen-sional contact sequences could also provide crucial insights into potential existing cross-channel synergies. Such insights will con-tribute to an approach towards optimal multi channel integration as well as an optimal multi channel mix and also a successful CRM. This will increase customer satisfaction as well as gaining profit-able and long-term customer relationships.

There are also important implications for marketing science as individual customer contacts or parts of the purchasing process have primarily been explained through partial theories in previous research (Kumar and Venkatesan, 2005). However, the differences identified in the multidimensional customer contacts sequences cannot be explained with such approaches. A comprehensive theory is necessary which, ideally, would integrate all the individual phenomena from the purchasing phases and can explain the differ-ences of the customers in their contact sequences. Besides this, our results also imply the application of other sequence analytical methods, such as Markov-Models, for predicting customer behav-ior as well as the cluster membership based on the multidimensional sequences. Furthermore, we only analyzed customer contacts and contact sequences in one branch with one tour operator, so a lot of research in other branches is necessary to generalize our findings.

REFERENCES

Anderson, John R. (1995), "Cognitive psychology and its implications," New York: Freeman.

Abbott, Andrew (1995), "Sequence Analysis: New methods for old ideas," *Annual Review of Sociology*, 21 (2), 93-113.

Alba, Joseph, John Lynch, Barto Weitz, Chris Janiszewski, Richard Lutz, Alan Sawyer, and Stacy Woods (1997), "Interactive Home Shopping: Consumer, Retailer, and Manufacturer Incentives to Participate in Electronic Marketplaces," *Journal of Marketing*, 51 (3), 38-53

Balasubramanian, Sridar, Rajagopal Raghunathan, and Vijay Mahajan (2005), "Consumers in a multichannel environment: Product utility, process utility, and channel choice," *Journal of Interactive Marketing*, 19 (2), 12-30.

Daft, Richard L. and Richard H. Lengel (1984), "Information richness: a new approach to managerial behavior and organizational design", in: Cummings, L.L. & Staw, B.M. (Eds.), Research in organizational behavior 6, Homewood, IL: JAI Press, 191-233.

Dholakia, Ruby R., Miao Zhao, and Nikhilesh Dholakia (2005), "Multichannel Retailing: A Case Study of Early Experi-ences," *Journal of Interactive Marketing*, 19 (2), 63-74.

Ericsson, Anders K. and Herbert A. Simon (1980), "Verbal reports as data," *Psychological Review*, 87, 215-251.

Fishbein, Martin and Icek Ajzen (1975), "Belief, attitude, intention, and behavior: An introduction to theory and research", Reading, MA: Addison-Wesley.

Frambach Ruud T., Henk C.A. Roest, and Trichy V. Krishnan (2007), "The Impact of Consumer Internet Experience on Channel Preference and Usage Intentions across the different stages of the buying process," *Journal of Interactive Marketing*, 21 (2), 26-41.

Ganesh, Jaishankar, Kristy E. Reynolds, and Michael G. Luckett (2007), "Retail patronage behavior and shopper typologies: a replication and extension using a multi-format, multi-method approach," *Journal of the Academy of Marketing Science*, 35 (3), 369-381.

Geyskens, Inge, Katrijn Gielens, and Dekimpe, Marnik G. (2002), "The Market Valuation of Internet Channel Audi-tions," *Journal of Marketing*, 66 (2), 102-119.

Hägerstrand, Torsten (1970), "What about people in regional science?," *Papers of the Regional Science Association*, 24 (1), 7-21.

Joh, Chang-Hyeon, Theo A. Arentze, Frank Hofman, and Harry J.P. Timmermans (2002), "Activity pattern similarity: A multidimensional sequence alignment method," *Transporta-tion Research B*, 36 (5), 385-483.

Kim, Byung-Do and Kyundo Park (1997), "Studying Patterns of Consumer's Grocery Shopping Trip," *Journal of Retailing*, 73 (4), 501-517.

Kumar, Vipin and Rajkumar Venkatesan (2005), "Who are the multichannel shoppers and how do they perform? Correlates of multichannel shoppinmg behavior," *Journal of Interactive Marketing*, 19 (2), 44-62.

Larson, Jeffrey S., Eric T. Bradlow, and Peter S. Fader (2005), "An exploratory look at supermarket shopping paths," *International Journal of research in Marketing*, 22 (4), 395-414.

Levenshtein, Vladimir I. (1966), "Binary codes capable of correcting deletions, insertions, and reversals," *Soviet Physics Doklady*, 10 (8), 707-710.

Mittal, Vikas, Pankaj Kumar, and Michael Tsiros (1999), "Attribute-Level Performance, Satisfaction, and Behavioral Intentions over Time: A Computation-System Approach," *Journal of Marketing*, 63 (2), 88-101.

Payne, John W., James R. Bettman, and Eric J. Johnson (1993), "The Adaptive Decision Maker," Cambridge, UK: Cam-bridge Press.

Payne, Adrian and Pennie Frow (2004), "The role of multichannel Integration in customer relationship management." *Industrial Marketing Management,* 33 (2004), 527-538.

Rangaswamy, Arvind and Gerrit H. van Bruggen (2005), "Opportunities and challenges in multichannel marketing: an introduction to the special issue," *Journal of Interactive Marketing*, 19 (2), 5-11.

Ruiz, Jean-Paul, Jean-Charles Chebat, and Pierre Hansen (2004), "Another trip to the mall: a segmentation study of customers based on their activities," *Journal of Retailing and Consumer Services*, 11, 333-350.

Sankoff, David and John B. Kruskal (1983), "Time Warps, String Edits, and Macromolecules: The Theory and Practice of Sequence Comparison," Addison-Wesley Reading: Mass.

Silberer, Günter, Sascha Steinmann, and Gunnar Mau (2006), "Customer Contact Sequences as a Basis for Customer Segmentation," *RETAILING 2006: Strategic Challenges in the New Millennium*, Special Conference Series Volume XI 2006. Ed. by J. R. Evans, Hempstead/NY: AMS, 232-237.

Simons, Luuk P.A. and Harry Bouwman (2004), "Designing a channel mix," *International Journal of Internet Marketing and Advertising*, 1 (3), 229–250

Verhoef, Peter C., Scott A. Neslin, and BjörnVroomen (2007), "Multichannel Customer Management: Understanding the research-shopper phenomenon," *International Journal of Research in Marketing*, 24 (2007), 129-148.

Venkatesan, Rajkumar, Vipin Kumar, and Nalini Ravishankar (2007), "Multichannel Shopping: Causes and Consequences," *Journal of Marketing*, 71 (2), 114-132.

Wallace, David W., Joan L. Giese, and Jean L. Johnson (2004), "Customer retailer loyality in the context of multiple channel strategies," *Journal of Retailing*, 80 (4), 249-263.

Ward, Michael R. (2001), "Will Online Shopping Compete More with Traditional Retailing or Online Shopping?," *Netnomics: Electronic Research and Electronic Networking*, 3 (2), 103-117.

Towards an Understanding of Media Usage and Acculturation

Manel Hadj Hmida, Universite de Lille, France
Nil Ozcaglar-Toulouse, Universite de Lille, France
Marie-Helene Fosse-Gomez, Universite de Lille, France

ABSTRACT

This investigation focuses on the role of the media in the acculturation processes of Maghrebins in France. It seeks to assess the extent to which the media are an agent for acculturation in this specific immigrant population. We carried out thirteen in-depth interviews with a varied sample group, using an interpretative approach. We considered three types of media in this research: the 'French' media, the 'Arab' media, and the 'ethnic' media produced in France but directed at the Maghrebins. Results are then presented and discussed. The limits of this research are underlined, and some future openings for research are proposed.

INTRODUCTION

Immigration is a study topic for human and social sciences. Demographers thus take an interest in population movements; historians are interested in the spread of cultures and in colonisations; anthropologists see immigrants as 'the others'; and sociologists investigate the social transformations brought about by the arrival of immigrants. More recently, marketing researchers have become interested in immigration, initially because immigrants represent a market and because understanding the acculturation process is key to penetrating that market, but also from a point of view of transformative research, since this understanding makes it possible to improve immigrants' well-being.

Most studies of consumer acculturation have studied immigrants in the US, while relatively less attention has been paid to immigrants living in Europe (e.g. Askegaard et al. 2005; Lindridge et al. 2004; Jamal 2003). France has the highest rate of immigration in Europe (INSEE, 2006). Immigration in France, which originally was chiefly motivated by economic considerations, is now motivated more by family reunification. According to INSEE,[2] mainland France had 4.9 million immigrants in mid-2004, representing 8.1% of the population. In light of France's republican and egalitarian tradition and its chosen position as a strong and centralising nation state, immigration is currently a hot topic for debate (Hetzel 2003). The recent creation of the 'Ministry of Immigration, Integration, National Identity and Co-development' has been seen by some as going against the founding principles the French Republic, intended to be universalist and egalitarian. The debate is heating up even further with the increasing emergence of 'communitarian' behaviours or the protest movements in the suburbs of major cities that have large immigrant populations.

The media is playing a part in this change. Thus, France has seen the recent appearance of newspapers and magazines (such as Amina, Jeune Afrique, Salama, Arabies Magasine and Yasmina) and radio or television stations are specifically targeted at ethnic populations. This rapid growth in the number of media making use of the ethnic variable as a criterion for defining their target market raises numerous questions. In particular: which role will these media play in the acculturation process for immigrants? Marketing literature presents the media as an essential agent for acculturation, but this significance is supported by little empirical work. This article is intended to assess the extent to which the media constitute an agent for acculturation in a specific immigrant population: that of Maghrebins in France. According to INSEE (2006), maghrebin immigrants are the largest immigrant population in France (with the exception of intra-EU immigration). They represent a growing market for marketers, since in 2005 the number of immigrants originating from the Maghreb was 1.5 million, 220,000 more than in 1999 (+17%). The fact that the Maghreb is composed of three countries (Algeria, Morocco and Tunisia) means that it represents certain homogeneity of cultural identity. This shared culture is first and foremost based on the Berber origin of most of the region's inhabitants–even if many of them do not speak Berber. In addition, all the inhabitants speak Arabic (a language that has been spoken in the region for thirteen centuries) in classical and/or dialect form. Classical Arabic is essentially a vehicle for Islam, the religion shared by Maghrebins and for official institutions such as schools and the public administration. However, dialectal Arabic is the mother tongue and language used in everyday life by the majority of Maghrebins.[3] Finally, these three countries share a common history with France, linked initially with colonisation (19th and beginning of the 20th Century) and then to immigration (essentially since 1960). The majority of French people tend to react to this strong shared identity by stigmatising these three countries on account of their 'Arab-Muslim' identity, and this stigmatisation in turn reinforces the 'homogeneity' of Maghrebin identity in France.

In order to study the role of the media in the acculturation process of Maghrebins in France, we will first adress to the theories of acculturation and the role that the media play in this regard. We will then present the methodology and the main results of our qualitative study. Finally, we will end this article with a discussion, including the main limits of this research and the avenues of research.

Immigration and research into consumer behaviour

Most research into consumer behaviour studies the process by which individuals adapt to a culture different from their own, by concentrating on two phenomena: assimilation and acculturation. Research employing the assimilationist approach studies how individuals adjust to a new culture by how quickly they appropriate elements of that new culture, at the expense of their own culture of origin (Deshpande et al. 1986; Hirschman 1981; Kim et al. 1990; Wallendorf and Reilly 1983). Since the 1990s, research has concentrated on the acculturation approach. According to this doctrine, different individuals adapt to different extents and borrow elements from their own culture of origin as well as from their host culture (Berry 1980; Jun et al. 1993; Mendoza 1989; Peñaloza 1994). More recent work has focused on the 'swapping' between the culture of origin and the host culture, and this movement has given rise to

---

[1] This research is supported by the French "Agence Nationale de la Recherche" (ANR). *Financé par* ANR.

[2] INSEE is the French National Institute for Statistics and Economic Studies.

[3] The significance of its proximity to classical Arabic depends on the sociocultural position of the speaker.

different acculturation models (Askegaard et al. 2005; Lindridge et al. 2004; Oswald 1999; Üstüner and Holt 2007).

However, all this research takes the work of Berry (1980) as its source, which assigns different degrees of acculturation to individuals based on the extent to which they associate themselves with their culture of origin and their host culture. There are therefore four modes of acculturation: assimilation, integration, separation and marginalisation (Berry 1980). Integration is the situation in which immigrants partially maintain the cultural integrity of their ethnic group and partially demonstrate an increasingly marked participation in their new society. In this situation, immigrants retain their identity and certain other of their own cultural characteristics (languages, dietary customs, religious festivals, etc.) whilst simultaneously taking part in economic, political and legal structures with the other ethic groups in the new society. On the other hand, immigrants are considered to be assimilated if they abandon their cultural identity in favour of that of the host society. They do not wish to retain their cultural identity and actively seek contact with the host culture. Separation describes the situation of individuals who do not seek to establish relations with the dominant community and who wish to keep their cultural identity. They preserve their culture of origin and their practices and keep themselves apart from the dominant group. Marginalisation is where immigrants lose their identity (often as a result of assimilationist policies practised by the dominant group) but yet do not have the right to participate in the running of institutions and the life of the dominant group.

For some researchers, acculturation manifests chiefly at a behavioural level. The authors first addressed linguistic preferences (Hui et al. 1992; Valencia 1985), particularly at work, at school, within the familiar or in situations where there is confrontation with the media, together with shopping behaviour. Other works (Gentry et al. 1995; Jun et al. 1993; Laroche et al. 1991; Valencia 1985) have studied the choice of neighbourhood (ethnic/non-ethnic) and friends, the celebration of religious festivals and the choice of holidays and social activities, together with the issue of mixed marriages. Peñaloza (1994) stresses however the limits of an approach that measures the degree of adherence or integration of a minority to a dominant culture without examining the nature of this process, and omits to take account of the influence of marketing strategies on the process of adaptation amongst the populations studied. That author states that in a globalised world with porous frontiers, the presence of transnational consumers and products has an effect on local consumer cultures. In the host society, some immigrants tend to consume products attached to their culture of origin, thereby displaying ethnic consumption, whereas others appropriate or do not hesitate to opt for products representing the dominant culture; they thus demonstrate a considerable degree of cultural change and are progressively becoming more and more acculturated, at the expense of their culture of origin. The individual characteristics of immigrants (demographic, geographic, linguistic and the date of their arrival) are determining factors in the process of consumer acculturation, as are the various agents of acculturation: family, friends, religious institutions, the media and the institutions of the culture of origin and the host society (see Ogden, Ogden and Schau 2004). Within this context of acculturation, this paper will concentrate on the specific agent of the media.

THE MEDIA: AN AGENT OF ACCULTURATION?

Since the inaugural work of Nagata (1969 *in* Lee 1989), many researchers (Hui et al. 1998; Lee 1989; O'Guinn and Faber 1985; O'Guinn et al. 1986; Kim, Laroche et al. 1990; Peñaloza 1994, etc.) have presented the media as a crucial element in the acculturation process. However, relatively little research (Kara and Kara 1996)

has been devoted to studying the impact of the media on acculturation.

The media can have an effect on two levels. On the one hand, they enable immigrants to become symbolically familiar with their host society (Lee 1989). This is however not a question of intense, concrete contact with the new society. By making use of the radio, the television, magazines, newspapers, cinema, theatre, museums or lectures, immigrants can acquire certain closeness to the host society (Tzu 1984). They learn which products they 'must use and own' in order to be properly looked on as a member of the dominant society (O'Guinn et al. 1985; O'Guinn et al. 1986). This is especially important where the immigrants do not have a comfortable command of the language of the host country. Television can be a solution to this problem, since images enable a relative understanding to be gleaned (Lee 1989). Garcia (1982) has shown the preference of Mexican-Americans for the media over and above other agents as a source of information and advice. Similarly, Lee (1989) shows that television is perceived by Chinese immigrants in the USA as a reliable source of information and an easily accessible agent of acculturation when learning the lifestyle and values of the host country. Indeed, Lee and Tse (1994, 68) write that: "exposure to mass media, [...] contributed to attitudinal and/or behavioral change. It appears that acculturating individuals' adoption of the majority norms may be related to their exposure to mass media".

Moreover, immigrants seek to remain in contact with their country of origin via forms of media that are relevant to their ethnic cultural community. This research can be interpreted as the need to return to the well-known and the familiar, and as being linked to the pleasure of hearing one's language of origin or of coming back into contact with familiar cultural elements. It may also be a question of the need to stay informed of what is going on in the country of origin. This research into contact via the media is not limited to the initial phase of arrival in the host country. In their consumption of ethnic media, immigrants can seek out this contact even several years after their immigration. In their work on immigrants from Hong Kong to Canada, Lee and Tse (1994, 68) report that: "even after living in Canada for at least seven years, the long-time immigrants spent 41% of their media time on ethnic media".

Over the course of immigrants' settlement in the host society, they are bathed in an intensive consumption of dominant media, at the expense of ethnic media. Immigrants are therefore simultaneously in contact with the media from the host country and the media from their country of origin. The media should thus be distinguished more precisely according to their target language and their relationship with Maghrebin immigrants. As part of this research, we will consider three types of media.[4]

- the 'French' media: French-language television channels, radio stations, newspapers and magazines targeted at the French population living within the country;
- the 'Arab' media from the countries of origin: Algerian, Moroccan and Tunisian national newspapers from the countries of the Maghreb that are sold in France and channels; and radio stations broadcast from Arab countries such as Al-Jazeera. These media are essentially targeted at the populations living in the Maghreb or in Arab countries.
- 'Ethnic' media produced in France but for the Maghrebin minority in France. These media cover subjects of interest to the Maghrebin community living in France.

---

[4]Only television, radio and the press will be considered here, since cinema and posters are of very secondary importance as media.

How do Maghrebin immigrants living in France consume these different media, and to what extent do these media contribute to their acculturation process? This was the key question addressed by this research.

METHODOLOGY

In order to answer these questions, it would have been limited for us to restrict ourselves to a quantitative study of the consumer behaviour of Maghrebin immigrants in France. It is not sufficient to know whether these immigrants are aware of the different media and whether they consume them; the method of that consumption and the relationship these immigrants have with the media–the way they integrate them into their life and their identity–must also be known. A qualitative approach was therefore required. We decided to carry out in-depth interviews with a varied sample group of Maghrebin immigrants in France, using an interpretative approach.

We carried out 13 in-depth interviews of an approximate length of 90-120 minutes with Maghrebin immigrants aged between 19 and 54; 12 of these immigrants are from the middle class backgrounds, and one is from lower class. In total, thirteen people were approached for a total of 21 hours and 26 minutes' interview time. We favoured variety of information over choosing a representative sample of the population. For this reason we opted for a theoretical sampling process by trying to vary the gender, age and generation of the people involved. The theoretical sampling was achieved after the 13th interview, since the accounts received displayed a considerable degree of diversity and the last interviews contributed relatively little new information (Glazer and Strauss 1967). This figure is higher than the minimum recommended by McCracken (1988) and is within the range of 3-20 interviews for interpretativist research (Fournier 1998; Thompson and Haytko 1997).

Our interviews were carried out in the north of France, a region marked by an initial economic Maghrebin immigration for the purpose of working in the textile or mining industry; these immigrants were subsequently joined by the immigration of their families. The Maghrebin immigration is in fact the result of multiples waves of migration motivated by economic, political or family considerations. According to INSEE data (1999), Algerians form the majority of Maghrebin immigrants in France (44%, or 574,208 immigrants), followed by Moroccans (40%, or 522,504 immigrants) and then Tunisians (16%, or 201,561 immigrants). Over the course of their settlement in France, Maghrebins have spread throughout the whole of France. Of the thirteen people, nine are Algerian, two are Moroccan and two are Tunisian. The sample is composed of seven women and six men. Seven arrived in France at various ages and have been living in France for between 5 and 44 years; they form the first generation. The others, born in France, are deemed to be the second generation. We took into account their place of residence in France and their background (rural/urban) in their country of origin.

The interviews were recorded and transcribed in their entirety. The interviews touched on several aspects pertaining to the dominant culture and the culture of origin (their arrival in France, the story of their immigration, and their current life in France). In terms of life in France, the interviews sought to understand the immigrants' sociability, their cultural practices in the host country, their consumption of media and how they perceive, identify and define themselves in French society.

The relationship with the media was studied via different themes. The respondents were asked to speak about programmes they watched, stations to which they listened and newspapers and magazines that they read. The discussion on the media led the respondents to voice the reasons that drive their choices of the French or Arabic media.

Some of them are of an identity concern:

"I watch French TV because I'm French, because it's my life, because France is my country." (Faiçal, 23 years old, 2nd).

Others are related to nostalgia to the language:

"It's nice to watch Tunisian TV from time to time, to hear people speaking with Tunisian accents, but that's the only reason." (Kamel, 23 years old, 2nd).

Whereas for some immigrants, the media choice is a sign of their acculturation in the host society:

"I'll never switch on an Arab channel, ever. To start with, I don't understand literary Arabic, and also because I prefer to watch French TV, because I'm French and that's all there is to it." (Faiçal, 23 years old, 2nd)

We analysed the comments of our thirteen respondents using an interpretative approach. By alternating between the specific case of each interview and the interviews taken as a whole, and by making use of literature, we sought to understand the role of the media in acculturation, and whether this role appears as major as the literature stemming from research done in non-French-speaking contexts suggests (Jamal 2003; Kim and Kang 2001; Lee and Tse 1994; Peñaloza 1994; Samad 1998).

MAIN RESULTS

The profile of media consumption shown by the interviews as a whole does not seem to depart significantly from that of the French population as a whole. Television is a very widespread medium and was appreciated to varying degrees in the interviews, with some people criticising the choice of programmes available, but everyone watched it (with the exception of students who did not have a television set in their student accommodation, but who nevertheless had the opportunity to watch it whenever they returned home to their family). In the minds of the respondents, it is thus the most significant medium in the minds of the respondents. Radio is seen as a medium to be used as an accompaniment, to be listened to in the car, or in the background at home, but also a medium that enables people to stay informed (the news station France Info). More people are familiar with the press than actually read it: the respondents cited titles of daily newspapers and magazines, but then said that they read newspapers only very occasionally, with the exception of the free ones given out in the metro. People seem to be more regular readers of magazines, since magazines address the interests of their readers (Femme Actuelle, France Football, Sciences et Vie, etc.). Finally, the younger respondents referred to the internet: some visit newspaper sites to read the news, and others use it to find Arab music.

We will focus on three types of media as defined above: French media, Arab media and ethnic media, by following the comments made by our respondents more closely than we will follow their consumer behaviour itself.

With regard to French media, which are the media consumed most heavily by all the respondents, comments on television showed two opposing viewpoints. For some people, the choice of a programme or a French channel was simply a matter of personal taste, and bore no connotations of integration or involvement in French society.

TABLE 1
Informants Characteristics

Names	Sex	Age	Arrival date	Generation	Origin	Occupation	Language ability	Education level
Dorsaf	F	35	1992	1st	Tunisian	Benevolent (NGO fields)	French, Tunisian dialect, Classical Arabic	University
Louiza	F	26	Born in France	2nd	Algerian	Cashier	French	High school
Faiçal	M	23	Born in France	2nd	Moroccan	Student	French, Moroccan dialect	University
Farid	M	19	Born in France	3rd	Algerian	Student	French	University
Kamel	M	23	Born in France	2nd	Tunisian	Student	French, Tunisian dialect	University
Warda	F	21	Born in France	2nd	Algerian	Student	French	University
Samir	M	35	2002	1st	Algerian	Waiter	French, Algerian dialect	University
Mohamed	M	53	1963	1st	Algerian	Professor/researcher in Physics	French	University
Zora	F	54	1978	1st	Algerian	Maintenance staff	French, Algerian dialect	Graduate school
Rachida	F	52	1955	1st	Algerian	Nurse	French	Second grade
Lynda	F	23	1989	2nd	Algerian	Student	French	University
Chérif	M	34	2001	1st	Algerian	Security gard	French, Algerian dialect Classical Arabic	University
Nourah	F	20	Born in France	2nd	Moroccan	Student	French, Moroccan dialect	University

"Sometimes there are good programmes on, with good guests, so I watch them. It depends on the programme. When there is something I like on one of the channels, I'll watch it. I like M6 on Sunday nights when there is something good on like 'Zone Interdite' or something like that; it depends on the programme. If there's a film on that I like, I'll watch that too." (Louiza, 26 years old, 2nd)

"I put on any channel at all, really, and I fall asleep in front of it after half an hour." (Rachida, 52 years old, 1st)

"Actually I channel-hop; I don't have a favourite channel either but I guess I watch M6 the most because I think it's the channel that shows the most entertainment programmes." (Nourah, 20 years old, 2nd)

Others have a more all-encompassing view of the consumption of French television channels and associate it with a strategy of integration. Television characterises the society that is accepting them and they find it perfectly understandable to incorporate it into their media habits, since they feel themselves to be members of French society. It is via this form of communication that the respondents are in contact and in step with their surroundings and what makes up their daily lives. This is what Peñaloza (1994) calls an agent for acculturation.

"French channels are about my life after all, since they mean something to me and they talk about what is happening in France. I feel more affected by what is happening in France, and France is important to me because it's my country, and I spend more time following events in France." (Dorsaf, 35 years old, 1st)

These media represent their present-day and everyday life in a country that most of them think of as their own.

"Things about the French system, because I do live in this country, after all, I feel it important to follow the French media in order to be aware of things even if only from a political and administrative point of view, in society." (Lynda, 23 years old, 2nd).

Some people go further and appear aware of the role played by the French media in general, and television in particular, in their acculturation process.

"It depends how you think of yourself and which attitude you adopt. If you think of yourself as once an immigrant, always an immigrant, you're obviously going to be interested by everything to do with your home country, so as long as it's about your home country, you're happy, which is not at all the case for me. Or you might think to yourself that you're here but you're different; for example, I'm here but I'm different, but first and foremost I'm here, so obviously whatever goes on in France is of interest to me." (Dorsaf, 35 years old, 1st).

The newspapers and magazines that are read cater more for the interests of their readers: older people read daily regional newspapers, students read the economic press, and football fans read sports journals. With regard to the radio, some people listen to it very occasionally, whereas others mentioned a list of stations to which they listened, but comments on the radio were very limited, and the immigrants did not seem to attach any particular importance to it.

With regard to Arab media, the role discovered was different. These constitute an invaluable source of information on political events and on troubles and unrest, both in the world at large and more specifically in Arab countries in particular. This preoccupation with politics was shared by all the respondents, although their comments were particularly alarmist with relation to Algeria. All respondents relied mainly on the Arab channels in order to avoid being cut off from the Arab-Muslim world.

"Al-Jazeera is an information channel, so they take the time to go into things in detail, and to examine issues from different angles and discuss them at length, so you don't take what they tell you at face value: it does more than just present the information; there are analyses and everything; so it's very important, when you think that on the other hand it's not a channel...I mean it doesn't do all that because it's an Arab channel, or because it's a famous channel; it also presents analyses about the Israelis and the Americans and everything. It does nonetheless handle information in a way that seems objective to me; in any case they give everyone the right to express themselves." (Dorsaf, 35 years old, 1st)

"I watch Tunisian television, and a bit of Al-Jazeera to find out what's going on in the Middle East." (Kamel, 23 years old, 2nd)

Arab television also has another function entirely: as an integrator within the family itself. For the second generation, who do not always have a good command of Arabic, watching television with those from the first generation is an essential form of sharing. The process of acculturation is different between the 1st generation and the 2nd generation, which creates a distance between parents and children. French and Maghrebin societies keep these groups apart by virtue of the specific experiences that each of them has had: children have not experienced what their parents have in their country of origin, and parents do not experience what their children are going through on a daily basis. Young people are aware of this distance and try to diminish it by watching Maghrebin television with their parents from time to time, particularly during religious festivals (Ramadan). They use Algerian or Moroccan television as a means of bridging the gap between themselves and the first generation, even though some admit that they do not understand everything or that the content is of no interest to them. For the respondents from the second generation, it is a question of 'respect' for their elders: they symbolically try to be close to their parents, to share some aspects of their parents' original culture to which these young people are not accustomed in their daily lives. Thus, the country, which can sometimes be a source of differences between the two generations, can sometimes be a means of reuniting them.

"I only watch it when my father watches it; I wouldn't switch on something like that myself." (Faiçal, 23 years old, 2nd),

"When my parents are around and I feel like spending some time with them. There are programmes in Arabic on the Algerian channel, and there are sketches, that I sometimes watch with them, or alternatively when something major is happening in Algeria or whatever, or when my parents tell me that such-and-such is happening." (Louiza, 26 years old, 2nd)

Arab television is also a cultural echo for people who live in France but are very attuned to their culture of origin. It is also a means of heightening the sensitivity of children to certain cultural aspects, such as their language of origin, that they only rarely get the opportunity to hear in the home. Religious festivals are particularly appropriate occasions:

"We all end up watching during Ramadan because the whole family comes together for dinner. There are some nice things on in Ramadan, so we watch as a family, and it's enjoyable." (Louiza, 26 years old, 2nd)

Finally, the media mirror immigrants' shifting identities. Some respondents clearly state that they use their choice of channels or programmes as a way of asserting their own identity:

"Arab channels are an insight. I'm more interested in what's going in in France, and of course what's going on in the world, although now the world has become a village, but it's really a matter of choice. France is important to me because it's my country, so events in France are the ones I follow the most regularly. Arab channels are an insight as well as an entertainment; they are an insight into a world that is no longer my world but that still has something to offer me, as well as meeting my cultural expectations and expectations in terms of information, and they mean I can stay in touch with the pace of life going on over there, of which I'm still a part in a way." (Dorsaf, 35ans, 1st)

However, this attitude was not shared by all the respondents; some made less consistent use of the Arab media because they had got accustomed to their life in France in terms of culture, specifically their consumer culture.

The situation is basically the same with regard to newspapers, with the added issue that a command of written Arabic is required. Immigrants who read newspapers written in the Maghreb or in Arab countries and 'imported' to France do so because these newspapers present information in a different way from French newspapers. Comments from these immigrants share the same underlying search for a connection with their identity is present in their comments. Finally, with regard to radio, no respondent mentioned any stations broadcast from the Maghreb or from any Arab country as forming part of their listening habits.

With regard to ethnic media, the situation is different, because television is absent from the choice of media available. There is no channel targeted specifically at Maghrebins in France. The analysis covered solely newspapers, magazines and radio stations. These media appear to be relatively poorly known, especially the press. No respondent mentioned any ethnic magazines without being prompted. Most of them were completely unaware of their existence. However, the media targeted at a Maghrebin public in France are both numerous and (above all) varied. Some are information magazines, others are women's magazines and yet others discuss culture. They are targeted at Maghrebins from France, not just Maghrebins who live in France. These magazines represent the Maghrebin community in France and cover current affairs topics such as mixed marriages, relationships between 'Maghrebin' women and 'French' men and discrimination, as well as cultural activities including music, cinema or shows intended for Maghrebin audiences from France, not to mention articles on beauty products sold in France and made from plants that come from the Maghreb. Their content therefore differs radically from that of the Arab media, which discuss the life of Maghrebins living in the Maghreb. When respondents learned of the existence of these newspapers and magazines, they immediately showed an interest.

"I could identify with the feelings they talked about, and with their way of thinking, because I've got a side to me like that." (Lynda, 23 years old, 2nd),

"Ah, now that's interesting; that way we can stay informed about other things than the regular news about all the troubles

and everything going on back at home. Like here, for example–look, they're talking about cookery, and since I like cooking and everything, it's very interesting to watch the recipes and things, all the things you can watch." (Zora, 54ans, 1st)

With regard to ethnic radio, only the radio station 'Pastel FM' was mentioned by the respondents in their comments. 'Pastel FM' is a formal communication medium for France's Maghrebin community. This station addresses some aspects of Maghrebin culture, chiefly cinema and music. Information on the release dates for films at the cinema (such as for the film Indigène,[5] which was mentioned by several respondents) or concerts by Maghrebin groups is given out via this radio station. However, the majority of ethnic information is transmitted via informal networks, which use word of mouth and social connections. These informal networks are used almost exclusively to transmit information about religious events (demonstrations of solidarity, social debates on religious themes, etc.) and the celebration of religious festivals. For most Maghrebins in France, the ethnic cultural activities in which they are involved are connected with religion and the practice thereof.

DISCUSSION AND CONCLUSION

This research worked from literature on ethnicity in marketing and focused on the potential role of the media in the acculturation process of Maghrebin immigrants in France. The results obtained largely corroborate the earlier work done in this field. The media have a strong presence in the life of this immigrant population, and above all are very varied: alongside traditional French media, this population consumes Arab media (chiefly television programmes, more rarely newspapers, and hardly ever the radio) and marginally consumes ethnic media, despite the fact that these media are theoretically targeted at them. The media definitely play a role in acculturation, which takes two complementary forms: the French media enable Maghrebin immigrants to gain a better understanding of the society in which they live, whereas the Arab media give them the opportunity to remain in contact with their country and culture of origin. Encouraging as these results are, they do however raise numerous questions, which we will discuss in this last section. First of all, however, the unique aspects of our research need to be set out, since this is the first study of its kind on Maghrebins in France in marketing literature; previous research has dealt with Mexican (e.g. Garcia 1982) or Chinese (e.g. Lee 1989) immigrants in a North American context.

The first unique aspect is the Arabic language, which lends itself very poorly to the written press. It is not uncommon for a spoken language to differ from its written equivalent, but with Arabic, a Moroccan, a Tunisian and an Algerian will all speak a very different dialect from the language they will find printed in a newspaper or a magazine. There is therefore a considerable problem in terms of making newspapers accessible, since a certain degree of education is required. Classical Arabic thus makes it more difficult to maintain links with the culture of origin. On the other hand, the use of classical Arabic promotes communication across national frontiers, and enables Maghrebins to follow programmes broadcast by an Egyptian or Saudi channel. Moreover, classical Arabic is strongly linked to Islam. The second-generation immigrants who participated learned Arabic either within the French school system (as a foreign language) or, more frequently, in schools dedicated to Islam, since a fluent command of Arabic is

essential in order to read the Qur'an. This situation is by no means exceptional; for example, Hebrew is linked with reading the Bible in the Jewish faith, but it also has repercussions on relationships with culture. Thus, one of the female respondents who rejected Islam as a religion ended up rejecting Arabic as a language as well, and as a result found herself cut off from the culture entirely. Finally, the last unique aspect of this research pertains to the historic relations between France and the Maghreb in a colonial context. French was the language of the elite in these three countries, and a large number of people in the Maghreb still speak the language, including the current political and economic elite. Needless to say, this makes French extremely important as a language, and enables second-generation immigrants who do not speak the relevant national dialect to enter into contact with their family or with certain media published in French (e.g. the Le Matin newspaper in Morocco). It goes without saying that the combined effect of these elements makes it difficult to extend this research to other immigrant populations in other countries without taking the necessary precautions.

The first question raised by our results pertains to the actual content of the media that are intended to transmit a vision and the behavioural codes of the host society. Thus, a number of our respondents mentioned that they chiefly watched American series on television (Columbo, Desperate Housewives, One Tree Hill, etc.). As Hirschman (1988) showed in her work on the competing series of 'Dallas' and 'Dynasty', series such as these do illustrates codes and methods of consumption, but these codes are completely different from French codes. In addition, the respondents highlighted, totally consistently, the difference between the Egyptian series broadcast on Maghrebin television and the methods of behaviour–not to mention the expressions–observed in those societies. First-generation immigrants however appear relatively enthusiastic consumers of this type of programme, certainly more so than their descendants. Although we reasonably can state with regard to information and news that the medias of each of the countries–the country of origin and the host country–participate in a process of acculturation between the two cultures, numerous television programmes tend more to broadcast a 'universal' or generic culture, using American society and culture as its reference.

The second question relates to the similarities and differences observed between the consumption of media within the French population and that within the Maghrebin immigrant population. Of course, since an interpretative approach is being used, this does not involve making a quantitative comparison; rather, the determining factors for the consumption of media must be established. Cultural capital, and thus to a certain extent social class (Bourdieu 1984), appear to be essential elements in terms of determining the consumption of media amongst both French people and immigrants. Although television reaches all populations, the number of media consulted increases in proportion to the level of education, and the media become more diverse: newspapers and the internet play an increasing role, and the type of channels watched changes. Age is another dividing factor: older people (generally first-generation immigrants) say that they read the regional press (La Voix du Nord in our study), whereas younger people use the internet to look for information.

The third question relates to the issue of ethnic media. These seem to be largely unfamiliar to respondents, particularly with regard to magazines and newspapers. Two reasons can be put forward to explain this unfamiliarity: either these ethnic media have not benefited from sufficient publicity and distribution, or they genuinely do not respond to a latent need in the Maghrebin immigrant population. The second scenario obviously raises questions of its own: does it indicate that being a Maghrebin immigrant in France

---

[5]A French film about North African soldiers sent to liberate France from Nazi occupation during World War II. The five actors are all descendants of Maghrebin immigrants.

today does not confer any particular status and does not give rise to any requirements sufficiently specific to create an independent need for media? This question needs to be examined in more detail.

Finally, the central question raised by this research is that of the relationship between acculturation and media. Should the media be considered as an agent of acculturation or rather as an indicator of it? The literature insists that the former role is correct; our research indicates that the latter concept is also worth consideration. However, it is not so much the quantity of media consumed as the type and variety of these media that counts when assessing the degree of acculturation. The quantity of media consumed is in fact linked to the cultural capital of the individual concerned and it increases in proportion to the level of education. Variety here must be defined as a recourse to media that fall within the different categories we identified during this research: French, Arab and ethnic. Separated immigrants are more likely to consume Arab media, whereas assimilated immigrants will restrict themselves to French media. Consumption of the broadest variety of media will most likely be observed amongst integrated immigrants, who will simultaneously consume French media (because they feel affected by what goes on in France), Arab media (in order to stay in contact with the Arab-Muslim culture) and ethnic media (because they have to face problems specific to them). Furthermore, the generation effect must be taken into account: for people who arrived in France as adults (1st generation) and whose mother tongue is Arabic, the acculturation of these individuals seems to be indicated by their consumption of French media. For young people born of immigrant parents (2nd generation), on the other hand, who can speak and read French more spontaneously, it is more their consumption of Arab or ethnic media that acts as a gauge of acculturation. The development of a gauge for assessing the degree of acculturation via the variety of media consumed thus appears to be a promising topic for future research work.

REFERENCES

Askegaard, Soren, Eric J. Arnould, and Dannie Kjeldgaard (2005), "Postassimilationist Ethnic consumer Research: Qualifications and Extensions," *Journal of Consumer Research*, 32, (June), 160-70.

Berry, John (1980), "Acculturation as Varieties of Adaptation," in *Acculturation: Theory, Models and Some New Findings*, ed. Amado M. Padilla, Boulder, CO: Westview, 9-26.

Bourdieu, Pierre (1984), *Distinction: A Social Critique of the Judgment of Taste*, Cambridge, MA: Harvard University Press.

Deshpande, Rohit, Wayne Hoyer, and Nareen Donthu (1986), "The Intensity of Ethnic Affiliation: A Study of The Sociology of Hispanic Consumption," *Journal of Consumer Research*, 13 (September), 214-20.

Fournier, Susan (1998), "Consumer and their Brands: Developing Relationship Theory in Consumer Research," *Journal of Consumer Research*, 24, (March), 343-73.

Garcia, John A. (1982), "Ethnicity and Chicanos: Mesurement of Ethnic Identification, Identity and Consciousness," *Hispanic Journal of Behavioral Sciences*, 4 (March), 295-314.

Gentry, James W., Sunkyu Jun and Patriya Tansuhaj (1995), "Consumer Acculturation Process and Cultural Conflict: How Generalizable is a North American model for Marketing Globally?," *Journal of Business Research*, 32, 2 (February), 129-39.

Glaser, Barney and Anselm Strauss (1967), *The Discovery of Grounded Theory*, Chicago: Aldine.

Hetzel, Patrick (2003), "Pratiques et Tabous du Marketing: Segmenter par les Critères Ethniques et Communautaires," *Décisions Marketing*, 32, Octobre-Décembre, 97-103.

Hirschman, Elizabeth C. (1988), The Ideology of Consumption: A Structural-Syntactical Analysis of 'Dallas' and 'Dynasty'," *Journal of Consumer Research*, 15 (December), 344-59.

Hirschmann, Elizabeth C. (1981), "American Jewish Ethnicity: Its relationship to Some Selected Aspects of Consumer Behavior," *Journal of Marketing*, 45 (Summer), 102-10.

Hui, Michael K., Annamma Joy, Chankon Kim, and Michel Laroche (1992), "Acculturation as a determinant of consumer behaviour: Conceptual and methodological issues", in AMA Winter Educator's conference, 3, Chris T. Allen, et al., ed. Chicago, IL. *American Marketing Association*, 466-73.

Insee (2006), "Enquêtes annuelles de recensement 2004 et 2005: Près de 5 millions d'immigrés à la mi-2004," *Insee Première*, 1098 (Août)

Jamal, Ahmad (2003), "Retailing in a multicultural world: the interplay of retailing, ethnic identity and consumption," *Journal of Retailing and Consumer Services* 10, 1 (January), 1-11.

Jun, Sunkyu, A. Dwayne Ball, and James W. Gentry (1993), "Modes of consumer acculturation," in *Advances in Consumer Research*, Vol. 20, ed. Leigh McAlister and Michael L. Rothschild, Provo, UT : Association for Consumer Research, 76-82.

Kara, Ali and Natasha R. Kara (1996), "Ethnicity and Consumer Choice: A study of Hispanic Decision Processes Across Different Acculturation Levels," *Journal of Applied Business Research*, 12(2), 22-34.

Kim, Chankon, Michel Laroche, and Annamma Joy (1990), "An empirical Study of Ethnicity on Consumption Patterns in a Bi-Cultural Environement," in *Advances in Consumer Research*, Vol.17, ed. Marvin E. Goldberg, Gerald Gorn, and Richard Pollay, Ann Arbor, MI: Association for Consumer Research, 839-46.

Kim, Youn-Kyung and Jikyeong K. Kang (2001), "The effects of ethnicity and product on purchase decision making," *Journal of Advertising Research*, 41(2), 39-48.

Laroche, Michel, Annamma Joy, Michael Hui and Chankon Kim (1991), "An Examination of Ethnicity Measures: Convergent Validity and Cross-Cultural Equivalence," in *Advances in Consumer Research*, Vol.18, ed. Rebecca H. Holman ad Michael R. Solomon, Provo, UT: Association for Consumer Research, 150-57.

Lee, Wei Na (1989), "The Mass-Mediated Consumption realities of Three Cultural Groups," in *Advances in Consumer Research*, Vol. 16, ed. Thomas K. Srull, Provo, UT: Association for Consumer Research, 771-78.

Lee, Wei Na and David K. Tse (1994), "Changing Media Consumption Strategies: Acculturation patterns among Hong Kong immigrants to Canada," *Journal of Advertising*, Vol. 23, 1 (March), 57-70.

Lindridge, Andrew M., Margaret K. Hogg, and Mita Shah (2004), "Imagined Multiple Worlds: How South Asian Woman in Britain Use Family and Friends to Navigate the 'Border Crossings' Between Household and Societal Contexts," *Consumption, Markets and Culture*, Vol. 7, 3 (September), 211-38.

McCracken, Grant (1988), *Culture and consumption : New approches to the symbolic character of consumer goods and activities*, Bloomington and Indiapolis, Indiana University Press

Mendoza, Richard H. (1989), "An empirical Scale to Measure Type and Degree of Acculturation in Mexican-American Adolescents and Adults," *Journal of Cross-Cultural Psychology*, Vol. 20, 4, 372-85.

Ogden, Denise T., James R. Ogden and Hope Jensen Schau (2004), "Exploring the Impact of Culture and Acculturation on Consumer Purchase Decisions: Toward a Microcultural Perspective," *Academy of Marketing Science Review*, 03: Available: http://www.amsreview.org/articles/ogden03-2004.pdf

O'Guinn, Thomas, Ronald Faber, and M. D. Rice (1985), "Popular Film and Television and Consumer Acculturation Agents: America 1900 to Present," in *Historical Perspectives in Consumer Research: National and International Perspectives*, J. Sheth and C. T. Tan, eds. Singapore : National University of Singapore , 297-301.

O'Guinn, Thomas and Ronald Faber (1985), "New Perspectives on acculturation: The Relationship of General and Role Specific Acculturation with Hispanics' Consumer Attitudes," *Advances in Consumer Research*, Vol. 12, ed. Elizabeth C. Hirschman and Morris B. Holbrook, Provo, UT: Association for Consumer Research, 113-17.

O'Guinn, Thomas, Wei-Na Lee, and Ronald Faber (1986), "Acculturation: The Impact of Divergent Paths on Buyer Behavior," in *Advances in Consumer Research,* Vol. 13, ed. Richard Lutz, Provo, UT: Association for Consumer Research, 579-83.

Oswald, Laura R. (1999), "Culture Swapping: Consumption and the Ethnogenesis of Middle-Class Haitian Immigrants," *Journal of Consumer Research*, 25 (March), 303-18.

Peñaloza, Lisa N. (1994), "Atravesando Fronteras / Border Crossing: A critical Ethnographic Exploration of the Consumer Acculturation of Mexican Immigrants," *Journal of Consumer Research*, 21 (June), 32-54.

Samad, Yunas (1998), "Media and Muslim Identity: Intersections of Generation and Gender," *Innovation*, 11(4), 425-38.

Thompson, Craig and Diane L. Haytko (1997), "Speaking of Fashion: Consumer's Uses of Fashion Discourses and the appropriation of Countervailing Cultural Meanings," *Journal of Consumer Research*, 24 (June), 15-42.

Tzu, Lao (1984), "Strangers' Adaptation to New Cultures," in *Communicating with Strangers: An Approach to Intercultural Communication,* Gudykunst, William B. and Young Y. Kim, Addison-Wesley Publishing Company, Inc., 205- 22.

Üstüner, Tuba and Douglas B. Holt (2007), "Dominated Consumer Acculturation: The Social Construction of Poor Migrant Women's Consumer Identity Projects in a Turkish Squatter," *Journal of Consumer Research*, 34 (June), 41-56.

Valencia, Humberto (1985), "Developing an Index to Measure "Hispanicness," in *Advances in Consumer Research*, Vol. 12, ed. Elizabeth C. Hirschman and Morris B. Holbrook, Provo, UT: Association for Consumer Research, 118-21.

Wallendorf, Melanie and Michael Reilly (1983), "Ethnic migration, assimilation and consumption," *Journal of Consumer Research*, 10 (December), 293-302.

Adolescents Yet Again Speak of Fashion: An Account of Participation and Resistance

Cagri Yalkin, King's College, UK
Richard Elliott, University of Bath, UK

EXTENDED ABSTRACT

This paper aims to examine the female adolescent friendship groups' consumption of fashion from a perspective of participation and resistance in the marketplace, and intends to build a case for analyzing the consumption of fashion and 'peer pressure' outside of the traditional belonging vs. independence dichotomy; both in order to bring a new perspective to the adolescents' relationship with the market and one another, and to fill the gap arising from the absence of the female adolescents' voice from the resistance literature.

Resistance to marketing efforts (Dobscha 1998) and to the domination of corporations (Holt 2002), and the emancipatory efforts to avoid the market (Kozinets 2002) have been studied and given way to new conceptualizations regarding the general issues of resistance and emancipation. Although Thompson and Haytko (1997) have studied the interpretive acts of naturalizing, problematizing, juxtaposing, resisting, and transforming in the case of fashion, their analysis is based on adult informants' narratives. Understanding how fashion and related marketing communications fit into adolescents' daily lives and how they are employed in the process of participating in and/or resisting fashion will fulfill some of the gaps in the literatures of both adolescents' consumption practices and marketplace resistance. Taking into account the above-mentioned gaps, we explored the resistive/participative practices of adolescent consumers by making use of adolescents' narrations of fashion and its communications. The extended case method (Burawoy 1991) was used, based on three friendship groups (popular, unpopular, normal), and two 12.5-13 year-old adolescents from each friendship group were interviewed; the data was analyzed using a hermeneutic approach (Thompson 1997). The name and nature of the groups emerged from the preliminary conversations with the adolescents, and were later used to define cases; the three groups' understanding of the social spaces they occupied at school matched one another.

The key results of data analysis are twofold: the first is that the adolescents narrate readings/acts of both resistance and participation in fashion; they use several tactics to resist the hegemonic practices and images of fashion. The second, and unexpected, key result is that the patterns of reading and the resistive/participative acts described seem to be consistent within friendship groups; small friendship groups act as micro-interpretive communities (Fish, 1980; Kates 2002; Yannopoulou and Elliott 2008).

The data analysis revealed three resistive tactics used by the adolescents: the trivialization of fashion, ascribing tyrannical qualities to fashion, and surrealizing the images in fashion and beauty communications. Trivializing fashion or projecting it as a not-so-important part of one's life and consumption practices has as its main building block the claims of *not*-following fashion seasonally, if at all, and *'just wearing what I wanna wear'*. Similar to the way Dobscha's (1998) informants who defined themselves as "I'm not a consumer", the adolescents defined themselves as "I'm not into fashion". However, these claims do not exclude them from consuming fashion. Secondly, seeing fashion and its related beauty imagery as one of the root causes of the 'size zero' buzz, the adolescents ascribed tyrannical qualities to fashion, blaming it for the eating disorders they see both around themselves and in distal references such as Kiera Knightley: *'It is a dangerous industry because fashion is super skinny people, which is forcing people just to feel bad about themselves if they are slightly over weight or something'*. Finally, regardless of the 'interpretive position' (Thompson and Haytko 1997), the adolescents surrealize the images in fashion and beauty communications as a form of passive resistance. However, this derealization emerges not as a suppressive force in that its' way of existence (surreal imagery) is the very tool used by adolescents in order to resist fashion communications, evident in such quotes as *'They [models] are just impossibly thin, impossibly happy... They just don't seem like real people to me'*; echoing deCerteau's (1984) viewpoint that subversion can be found in people's daily practices, tactics that are grounded in the signification system foreign to the system they have no choice but to accept.

Penaloza and Price (1993) argued that the range of actions viewed as resistance was narrow and that altering the meaning of consumption and consumption objects were neglected. Trivializing the meaning of consuming fashion and treating fashion imagery as surreal classify as attempts at altering the meaning of consumption (e.g. Wallendorf and Arnould 1991). As the accounts of resistance seem to be embedded in the grander act of participation, as "the effective strategies and tactics of consumer resistance are limited to those stemming from outside the market" (Penaloza and Price 1993), and as the adolescents are still taking part in the fashion 'system', their resistive interpretations/acts are not likely to have large-scale effects on the way they are treated by fashion communication and marketing; although this does not exclude the presence of 'agency' in the adolescents' narratives.

Adolescents continuously took up of different interpretive positions from which to ascribe meanings to their fashion behaviors and to describe the motivations for others' fashion behaviors (Thompson and Haytko 1997). There seem to be different meanings attached to some of the resistive acts at the micro-group level: how the 'popular' girls view resistive actions versus how the 'unpopular' group views resistive actions differ. There is a difference between how friendship groups read the resistive/participative practices of the other friendship groups, giving way to sanctions that further induces differentiation of friendship groups, which resonates with the viewpoint that it is the form of resistance that is sanctioned, not resistance itself. The adolescent identities seem to be located within micro-communities of interpretation and practice (friendship groups); the self has been integrated with the social and the material (Elliott 2004). Finally, the female adolescents view fashion as dominant because it is what is available; given that the informants are very young, they have still not experimented with alternative shops or ways of getting dressed, and to them, fashion is dominant not because it is capitalism's tool, as consumption is seen by the respondents in Dobscha (1988) and Holt (2002), but because it is what makes clothes *available*.

Overall, Thompson and Haytko's (1997) study on the interpretation of fashion and Murray's (2002) re-interpretation are contrasted by the adolescents' interpretations in that the interpretive positions need not be individualistic, they can rest on a common point of reading. While this study does not argue that a friendship group 'causes' a particular interpretive strategy and the accompanying resistive/participative practices to emerge, it suggests that the friendship groups as micro-interpretive communities should be explored. Understanding close-friendship groups as the context within which the complex background of established cultural meanings and belief systems are formed and as a part of cultural background (Thompson 1997) leads the way to conceptualizing close-friendship groups as interpretive communities (Yannopoulou and Elliott 2008), which follow-up research will explore.

REFERENCES

de Certeau, Michel (1984), *The Practice of Everyday Life*, London University of California Press.

Dobscha, Susan (1998), "The Lived Experience of Consumer Rebellion Against Marketing," in *Advances in Consumer Research*, Vol. 25, ed. Joseph W. Alba and Wesley J. Hutchison: Provo, UT: Association for Consumer Research, 91-97.

Elliott, Richard (2004), "Making Up People: Consumption as a Symoblic Vocabulary for the Construction of Identity," in *Elusive Consumption*, ed. Karen M. Ekstrom and Helene Brembeck, Oxford: Berg, 129-43.

Fish, Stanley (1980), *Is There A Text In This Class? The Authority of Interpretive Communities*, London, England: Harvard University Press.

Holt, Douglas B. (2002), "Why Do Brands Cause Trouble? A Dialectical Theory of Consumer Culture and Branding," *Journal of Consumer Research*, 29 (June), 70-90.

Kates, Steven M. (2002), "Doing Brand and Subcultural Ethnographies: Developing the Interpretive Community Concept in Consumer Research," in *Advances in Consumer Research*, Vol. 29, ed. Susan Broniarczyk and Kent Nakamoto, Valdosta, GA: Association for Consumer Research, 43.

Kozinets, Robert V. (2002), "Can Consumers Escapt the Market? Emancipatory Illuminations from Burning Man," *Journal of Consumer Research*, 29 (June), 20-38.

Murray, Jeff B. (2002), "The Politics of Consumption: A Re-inquiry on Thompson and Haytko's (1997) "Speaking of Fashion"," *Journal of Consumer Research*, 29 (December), 427-40.

Thompson, Craig J. (1997), "Interpreting Consumers: A Hermeneutical Framework for Deriving Markcting Insights from the Texts of Consumers' Consumption Stories," *Journal of Marketing Research*, 34 (November), 438-55.

Thompson, Craig J. and Diana L. Haytko (1997), "Speaking of Fashion: Consumers' Uses of Fashion Discourses and The Appropriation of Countervailing Cultural Meanings," *Journal of Consumer Research*, 24 (June), 15-42.

Wallendorf, Melanie and Eric J. Arnould (1991), "'We Gather Together': The Consumption Rituals of Thanksgiving Day," *Journal of Consumer Research*, 18 (June), 13-31.

Yannopoulou, Natalia and Richard Elliott (2008), "Open versus closed advertising texts and interpretive communities," *International Journal of Advertising*, 27 (1), 1-28.

The Effect of Parenting on Adolescent Susceptibility to Peer Influence: Mediating Role of Self-Esteem

Zhiyong Yang, University of Texas at Arlington, USA
Michel Laroche, Concordia University, Canada
Ashesh Mukherjee, McGill University, Canada

EXTENDED ABSTRACT

Individuals are often influenced by the opinions of peers, such as their friends, activity partners, and colleagues at work (Price and Feick 1984). This is especially true during adolescent years, a time when individuals are particularly sensitive to ideas and trends popular among their peers (Bachmann, John, and Rao 1993). Peer influence on adolescents has significant marketing and public policy implications, since many adolescent decisions ranging from brand choice to substance abuse are affected by the opinions of peers (Kandel 1996; Rose, Boush, and Friestad 1998; Wooten and Reed 2004). In fact, peers influence not just adolescents' choices at the brand level, but also their attitudes towards retailers, amount of money spent shopping, and attitudes towards consumption in general (Batra, Homer, and Khale 2001; Mangleburg, Doney, and Bristol 2004). Peer influence is also viewed as one of the most important factors, if not the most important one, to affect adolescent smoking or other forms of consumer misbehaviors (Akers and Jensen 2006).

Acknowledging the important role peers play in individuals' consumption-related decisions, previous research in marketing has validated the fundamental role of susceptibility to peer influence (SPI) and its powerful impact on consumer behavior, where SPI is defined as the tendency for individuals to look to standards from peers to develop their own motivations, attitudes, and behaviors (Bearden, Netemeyer, and Teel 1989). Despite the vital role SPI plays in understanding consumer behavior, little research has been conducted to investigate the driving forces of susceptibility. This issue is important because knowing about the key antecedents of SPI allows researchers and practitioners can develop effective intervening strategies to alter individuals' vulnerability to peer influence.

In the present research, we fill this gap through examining the effects of parenting strategies on SPI among adolescents. Specifically, we develop an integrative model of adolescent susceptibility to peer influence that includes parenting strategies (parental responsiveness and parental psychological control) as driver, adolescents' self-esteem as mediator, and stage at adolescence as moderator of susceptibility to peer influence. The overarching finding in our studies is that responsive parenting decreases susceptibility by bolstering adolescents' self-esteem, while psychologically controlling parenting increases susceptibility without influencing adolescents' self-esteem. This is especially true for children at their mid- and late-adolescence stages. Notably, these results were observed in both cross-sectional (Studies 1 and 2) and longitudinal data (Study 3), as well as data from both adolescents and their parents. Implications of the results for improving the effectiveness of parent-oriented anti-smoking campaigns are discussed.

REFERENCES

Akers, Ronald L., and Gary F. Jensen (2006), "The Empirical Status of Social Learning Theory of Crime and Deviance: The Past, Present, and Future," In *Taking Stock: The Status of Criminological Theory* (pp. 37-76), F. Cullen, J. Wright and K. Blevins (eds.). New Brunswick, NJ: Transaction Publishers.

Bachmann, Gwen, Deborah Roedder John and Akshay R Rao (1993), "Children's Susceptibility to Peer Group Purchase Influence: An Exploratory Investigation," *Advances in Consumer Research*, 20, 463-468.

Batra, Rajeev, Pamela M. Homer, and Lynn R. Khale (2001), "Values, Susceptibility to Normative Influence, and Attribute Importance Weights: A Nomological Analysis," *Journal of Consumer Psychology*, 11(2), 115-128.

Bearden, William O., Richard G. Netemeyer, and Jesse E. Teel (1989), "Measurement of Consumer Susceptibility to Interpersonal Influence," *Journal of Consumer Research*, 15(March), 473-481.

Kandel, Denise B. (1996), "The Parental and Peer Context of Adolescent Deviance: An Algebra of Interpersonal Influences," *Journal of Drug Issues*, 26 (Summer), 298-315.

Mangleburg, Tamara F., Patricia M. Doney, and Terry Bristol (2004), "Shopping with Friends, and Teen's Susceptibility to Peer Influence," *Journal of Retailing*, 80 (2), 101-116.

Price, Linda L. and Lawrence Feick (1984), "The Role of Interpersonal Sources in External Research: An Informational Perspective," In Thomas Kinnear (Ed.), *Advances in Consumer Research, 11* (pp. 250-255), Chicago, IL: Association for Consumer Research.

Rose, Gregory M., David M. Boush, and Marian Friestad (1998), "Self-Esteem, Susceptibility to Interpersonal Influence, and Fashion Attribute Preference in Early Adolescents," *European Advances in Consumer Research*, 3, 197-203.

Wooten, David B. and Americus Reed II (2004), "Playing It Safe: Susceptibility to Normative Influence and Protective Self-Presentation," *Journal of Consumer Research*, 31(December), 551-556.

Advances in Consumer Research
Volume 36, © 2009

Building Consumption Skills through Teenage Empowerment: A Powerful and Invisible Determinant of Customer Relationships

Wided Batat, University of Poitiers, France

EXTENDED ABSTRACT

Social networking and Web 2.0 enable young people to connect and collaborate easily and productively, online tools and spaces allow them to create collective knowledge about any consumption subject. The Internet and the mobile phone have become a central force that fuels the rhythm of teenage daily life. Among other things, there has been significant growth over the past five years in the number of teens who play games on the Internet, get news, check-in and shop online. In addition, the changing media landscape has become a battleground for the adolescents' share of voice. The 'YouTube' generation uses many forms of media simultaneously and average over six hours a day using the various forms (Hempel and Lehman 2005). Consequently, authors argue that today's teenagers are more competent than their parents in dealing with media and digital products (McDonnell 1994; Tapscott 1998) as their consumption learning is mostly made by practising social and entertainment activities *via* digital equipments and media which enable them to develop consumption skills. However, modern-day adolescents are competent or vulnerable consumers, depending on their age, gender, family, social background, consumption experience and other influences on their daily lives (Tufte 2003). In order to develop a better understanding of young consumers' empowerment, who represent the most highly sought for researchers and marketing practitioners, it is important to explore teens' competencies as consumers of media and new technologies. By examining how teens aged 11-15 define a competent consumer and how they perceive themselves as competent consumers within their own normative framework of new technologies' usages, we should be better able to understand the consumption behaviours they exhibit, the purchase decision they make and the limitations they feel they must overcome to become fully competent consumers. In order to examine these issues, the exploratory research was the best means for getting at these unspoken cultural and social patterns that shape consumer behaviour. The main thrust of this research involved 20 French schoolchildren aged 11-15 both boys and girls for 6 months (from January to June). This study was delimited to the schoolchildren population enrolled at Sainte Marthe Chavagnes elementary school in the city of Angoulême (south west of France).

The key findings for this study illustrated the behaviours associated with competent consumers and areas for improvement as competent consumers. Moreover, the study showed that teenagers are not mere followers of marketing strategies and they develop consumption skills in relationship to their experience, their peers and media which are more often associated with their consumption learning. We believe that nowadays teenagers are active participants and producers of their cultural consumption processes and that state of things can also be seen in the consumption of entertainment electronic technologies. In answering the question of competencies and savvy teens, our investigation gives evidence about the process of skills' construction within the consumption of digital product by the schoolchildren aged 11-15. Hence, teenagers' perception of the competence that they must have to be able to consume lies first and foremost on skills associated with preventive behaviours.

Being responsible consumer also means having the ability to resist to marketers influences. In order to do so, getting information, evaluating and comparing the options, looking for the best price-quality ratio and the awareness about the environment' protection are one of the characteristics of a competent and responsible consumer. The present exploratory research seems to confirm that the mother and specifically the father remain the most influential consumer learning agent, in addition of peers, media, Internet, learning through trial and error, observation and the virtual peers *via* blogs. Therefore, the consumption skills emerge within the teens' experience of the purchase and the use of new technologies within their entertainment activities (playing video games) as well as their social activities (chatting on the Internet). Therefore, for companies understanding individuals' experiences remains the foundation for innovation and empowering young customers to communicate the message will become a vital part of both brand value and customer relationships management (CRM).

REFERENCES

Ahava, Maija A. and Palojoki, Päivi (2004), "Adolescent Consumers: Reaching Them, Border Crossings and Pedagogical Challenges", *International Journal of Consumer Studies*, 28 (4), 371-379.

Alba, Joseph W. and Wesley J. Hutchinson (1987), "Dimensions of Consumer Expertise", *Journal of Consumer Research*, 13, 411-454.

Bandura, Albert. (1977), "Self-Efficacy: Toward a Unifying Theory of Behaviour Change", *Psychological Review*, 84 (2), 191-215.

Batat, Wided. (2006), "L'usage du Téléphone Mobile par les Adolescents. In: *Innovations Technologiques*", (Ed.). Chatal Ammi, Paris: Hermès Lavoisier, 300-313

Benn, Jette. (2004), "Consumer Education Between 'Consumership' and 'Citizenship': Experiences from Studies of Young People", *International Journal of Consumer Studies*, 28, 108-116.

Buckingham, David. (2005), "Constructing the Media Competent Child: Media Literacy and Regulatory Policy in the UK. [WWW document]. URL http://www.medienpaed.com/05-1/buckingham05-1.pdf

Ekström, Karin M. (2005), "Rethinking Family Consumption-Tracking New Research Perspectives", *Advances in Consumer Research*, 32, 493-497.

Hall, Stuart. (1996), "Introduction: Who Needs Identity? ", In: *Questions of Cultural Identity* (Ed. by Hall, S.) Sage, London.

Hempel, Jessi. and Lehman, Paula. (2005), "The MySpace Generation", *Business Week*, 3963, 86-96.

Hoffman, Donna L. and Novak, Thomas P. (1996), "Marketing in Hypermedia Computer-Mediated Environments: Conceptual Foundations", *Journal of Marketing*, 60, 50-68.

Lee, Christina K. and Conroy, Denise M. (2005), "Socialisation Through Consumption: Teenagers and the Internet", *Australasian Marketing Journal*, 13 (1), 8-19.

McDonell, Katheleen. (1994), "*Kid Culture: Children as Adults and Popular Culture*", Second Story Press, Toronto.

Mick, David G. and Fournier, Susan. (1998), "Paradoxes of Technology: Consumer Cognizance, Emotions and Coping Strategies", *Journal of Consumer Research*, 25, 123-143.

Moschis, George P. and Churchill, Gilbert A. (1978), "Consumer Socialization: A Theoretical and Empirical Analysis", *Journal of Marketing Research*, 15 (4), 599-609.

Newell, Frederick (2002), " Why CRM Doesn't Work: How to Win by Letting Customers Manage the Relationship", CRM Magazine www.destinationcrm.com/articles/default.asp?ArticleID=3107

Ritchie, Jane. and Spencer, Liz. (1994), "Qualitative Data Analysis for Applied Policy Research", In: *Analysing Qualitative Data* (ed. by A. Bryman and R.G. Burgess). London: Routledge.

Roedder-John, Deborah. (1999), "Consumer Socialization of Children: A Retrospective Look at Twenty-five Years of Research", *Journal of Consumer research,* 26, 183-213.

Rogers, Everett M. (1995), *"Diffusion of Innovations"*, New York: Free Press.

Ross, Christine. (2005), "Saving For Your Children", [WWW document]. URL *http://news.bbc.co.uk/2/hi/business/3112942.stm*

Shih, Chen F. (1998), "Conceptualising Consumer Experiences in Cyberspace", *European Journal of Marketing*, 32(7), 655-663.

Tapscott, Don. (1998), *"Growing up Digital: The Rise of the Net Generation"*, New York: McGraw-Hill.

Tufte, Birgitte. (2003), "Children, Media and Consumption", *Advertising & Marketing to Children,* 5 (1), 69-75.

Ward, Scott. (1974), "Consumer Socialization", *Journal of Consumer Research*, 1 (2), 1-17.

Winner, Landon. (1994), "Three Paradoxes of the Information Age", In: *Culture on the brink: Ideologies of technology* (ed. by B. Gretchen and D. Timothy).

Strauss, Judy. and Frost, Raymond. (2001), *"E-Marketing, Prentice-Hall"*, New Jersey

More Than Meets the Eye: The Influence of Implicit Self-Esteem on Materialism

Ji Kyung Park, University of Minnesota, USA
Deborah Roedder John, University of Minnesota, USA

EXTENDED ABSTRACT

One of the most consistent findings reported in the materialism literature is the link between self-esteem and materialism, with lower feelings of self-worth related to higher levels of materialism (Chaplin and John 2007; Richins and Dawson 1992). Material goods are viewed as a way for individuals with low self-esteem to cope with or compensate for doubts about their self-worth.

However, recent self-esteem research suggests that the relationship between self-esteem and materialism may be more complicated than current findings suggest. Two forms of self-esteem have been identified: explicit versus implicit self-esteem (Greenwald and Banaji 1995). *Explicit self-esteem* is defined as conscious evaluations of the self, whereas *implicit self-esteem* is defined as unconscious evaluations of the self. Consistent with Wilson, Linsey and Schooler (2000)'s dual attitude model, people can have two different attitudes toward the self, such as implicit versus explicit self-esteem. In fact, explicit self-esteem is only weakly correlated with implicit self-esteem, which is considered a distinct dimension of self-esteem (Bosson, Brown, and Zeigler-Hill 2003).

In this article, we propose that explicit self-esteem alone is not sufficient to capture the relationship between self-esteem and materialism, and that implicit self-esteem is an important determinant in the adoption of materialism. We report three studies that demonstrate the usefulness of this construct for understanding materialism. Each of the studies and findings are described below.

Study 1: The Joint Effect of Implicit and Explicit Self-Esteem on Materialism

Prior research has found that individuals with high (explicit) self-esteem exhibit lower levels of materialism. However, individuals with high (explicit) self-esteem are not a homogeneous group. In fact, this group includes two distinct subgroups of individuals: those with *congruent high self-esteem* (high explicit/high implicit self-esteem) and those with *discrepant high self-esteem* (high explicit/low implicit self-esteem).

Not surprisingly, these two groups exhibit different behavioral patterns. Individuals with discrepant high self-esteem have underlying negative self-feelings associated with low implicit self-esteem. To conceal such nagging self-doubts, these individuals use various forms of self-enhancing strategies. Relative to individuals with congruent high self-esteem, they tend to exhibit overt grandiosity, higher levels of narcissism, and indirect forms of self-enhancement, such as out-group derogation and in-group biases (Bosson et al. 2003; Jordan et al. 2003; Kernis et al. 2005). In sum, individuals with discrepant high self-esteem possess some of the same characteristics usually attributed to individuals with low (explicit) self-esteem, with both groups engaging in self-enhancing strategies to compensate for negative self-feelings.

Thus, we predict that individuals with discrepant high self-esteem will exhibit higher levels of materialism than individuals with congruent high self-esteem. We measured intact levels of implicit and explicit self-esteem, comparing how combinations of these types of self-esteem relate to materialism. Explicit self-esteem was measured using the Rosenberg Self-Esteem Scale (Rosenberg 1965); implicit self-esteem was measured using the self-esteem Implicit Association Test (IAT: Greenwald and Farnham 2000). As a measure of materialism, we used a qualitative task in which levels of materialism were revealed by asking participants to construct a collage to answer the question: "What makes me happy?" (see Chaplin and John 2007).

The results support the idea that materialism depends not only on the levels of explicit self-esteem, but also on implicit self-esteem. Contrary to prior materialism research, individuals with high (explicit) self-esteem are not always immune to the appeals of materialism. Indeed, individuals with discrepant high self-esteem (high explicit/low implicit self-esteem) are more materialistic than individuals with congruent high self-esteem (high explicit/high implicit self-esteem).

Study 2: The Causal Impact of Implicit Self-Esteem on Materialism

Next, we proceed with our examination of implicit self-esteem by examining the causal relationship between implicit self-esteem and materialism. In Study 1, intact levels of implicit and explicit self-esteem were measured rather than manipulated, leaving open the possibility that materialism affects implicit self-esteem rather than the reverse. In Study 2, while measuring the intact levels of explicit self-esteem, we primed high implicit self-esteem through subliminal evaluative conditioning (Dijksterhuis 2004).

The results replicated those of Study 1. High implicit self-esteem priming reduced materialism; indeed, among participants with high explicit self-esteem, those in the control group who did not receive a prime were more materialistic than those primed with high implicit self-esteem.

Study 3: Why Does Discrepant High Self-Esteem Cause Materialism?

Individuals with discrepant high self-esteem, who tend to have relatively strong materialistic tendencies, present the most interesting case when compared to prior materialism research. In Study 3, we explore why discrepant high self-esteem can lead to materialism in more detail. They tend to use self-protective and self-enhancing strategies, not only to compensate for underlying negative self-feelings, but also to deal with threats to the self (McGregor et al. 2005). Because these individuals are concerned about protecting their exaggerated self-images, they overly react to self-threats.

We thus predict that individuals with discrepant high self-esteem will respond to a situation where a self-threat is present by focusing on material possessions as a self-enhancing behavior. Further, we expect their response to self-threats to be unique, in that not all individuals with low implicit self-esteem will react this way. We manipulated the level of self-threat in performing a memory task. As in Study 1, we measured the intact levels of explicit and implicit self-esteem, and used Richins and Dawson (1992)'s materialism scale as a measure of materialism.

We found that individuals with discrepant high self-esteem exhibit defensive responses to threats to their self-image. When a self-threat was present, individuals with discrepant high self-esteem exhibited heightened materialistic tendencies, which was not the case for individuals with low explicit and low implicit self-esteem.

Summary

Prior research has found that individuals with high self-esteem are less materialistic than those with low self-esteem. We add to these findings by distinguishing two types of self-esteem—explicit and implicit self-esteem—and demonstrating that they have a joint influence on materialism. Specifically, we find that individuals with high explicit self-esteem vary in their tendency to self-enhance through material things as a function of their levels of implicit self-esteem. Thus, contrary to prior research, individuals with high explicit self-esteem can be susceptible to materialism.

REFERENCES

Bosson, Jennifer K., Ryan, P. Brown, Virgil Zeigler-Hill, and William B. Swann, Jr. (2003), "Self-Enhancement Tendencies among People with High Explicit Self-Esteem: The Moderating Role of Implicit Self-Esteem," *Self and Identity*, 2, 169-187.

Chaplin, Lan Nguyen and Deborah Roedder John (2007), "Growing Up in a Material World: Age Differences in Materialism in Child and Adolescents," *Journal of Consumer Research*, 34 (4), 480-93.

Dijksterhuis, Ap (2004), "I Like Myself but I Don't Know Why: Enhancing Implicit Self-Esteem by Subliminal Evaluative Conditioning," *Journal of Personality and Social Psychology*, 86 (2), 345-355.

Greenwald, Anthony G. and Mahzarin R. Banaji (1995), "Implicit Social Cognition: Attitudes, Self-Esteem, and Stereotypes," *Psychological Review*, 102 (1), 4-27.

_____ and Shelly D. Farham (2000), "Using the Implicit Association Test to Measure Self-Esteem and Self-Concept," *Journal of Personality and Social Psychology*, 79 (6), 1022-1038.

Jordan, Christian H., Steven J. Spender, Mark P. Zanna, Etsuko Hoshino-Browne, and Joshua Correll (2003), "Secure and Defensive High Self-Esteem," *Journal of Personality and Social Psychology*, 85 (5), 969-978.

Kernis, Michael H., Teresa A. Abend, Brian M. Goldman, Ilan Shrira, Andrew N. Paradise, and Christian Hampton (2005), "Self-Serving Responses Arising from Discrepancies between Explicit and Implicit Self-Esteem," *Self and Identity*, 4, 311-330.

McGregor, Ian, Paul R. Nail, Denise C. Marigold, and So-Jin Kang (2005), "Defensive Pride and Consensus: Strength in Imaginary Numbers," *Journal of Personality and Social Psychology*, 89 (6), 978-96.

Richins, Marsha L. and Scott Dawson (1992), "A Consumer Values Orientation for Materialism and Its Measurement: Scale Development and Validation," *Journal of Consumer Research*, 19 (December), 303-16.

Wilson, Timothy D., Samuel Lindsey, and Tonya Y. Schooler (2000), "A Model of Dual Attitudes," *Psychological Review*, 107 (1), 101-126.

The Bi-directional Effects of Consumption and Well-being; An Empirical Examination

Vincent-Wayne Mitchell, City University London, UK
Jing Yang Zhong, City University London, UK

EXTENDED ABSTRACT

The present study seeks to investigate how much people have to spend in order to achieve happiness; and how much happy people are more likely to spend. The concept of life satisfaction occupies a central place in marketing theory, and the model has been successfully applied to Quality-of-Life (QOL) issues (Day 1987; Lee, et al. 2002; Leelakulthanit, Day, and Walters 1991). However, individuals' actual consumption has not been linked to well-being issues and fully investigated in consumer behavior.

The theoretical foundation of the present study is the integration of subjective well-being (SWB) bottom-up and top-down theories. Bottom-up theories propose that "SWB is caused by the (summation of) pleasurable and unpleasurable moments and experiences, and a happy individual is happy simply because he or she experiences many happy moments" (Brief et al. 1993:646). This suggests that an individual's level of overall happiness is primarily predicted by his or her objective life circumstances such as the consumption behavior in this context (Feist et al. 1995). Top-down theories, by contrast, assume "there is a global propensity to experience things in a positive way, and this propensity influences the momentary interactions an individual has with the world. In other words, a person enjoys pleasures because he or she is happy" (Diener 1984:565). From this perspective, a person's overall well-being is the cause rather than consequence of his or her experience of specific phenomena such as specific consumption experiences (Feist et al. 1995; Headey, Veenhoven, and Wearing 1991). That is, we argue there is a bi-directional causality between SWB and consumption on hedonic products. In the present study, we look at two consumption categories, that of leisure consumption and durables consumption. This is because the increases of the consumption on these two categories are the highest for the past 4 decades in the UK (Porritt 2003), and they are important to consumers in modern life.

Data for this study are from the British Household Panel Survey wave 10-15 which were collected in late 2001-early 2002 for wave 10, in late 2002-early 2003 for wave 11, and so on. The observations for these 6 waves are over 50,000. Methodologically, panel data is the way of establishing the directional causality, which is the key aspect of the present study (Graham, Eggers, and Sukhtankar 2004). In the present study, subjective well-being is measured with the inverse of the 'caseness score' form of the multi-item scale GHQ12, ranging from 0 to 12. It is widely recognized to be a reliable measure of psychological well-being (Argyle 1987). Leisure consumption includes a) consumption on leisure activities, entertainment and hobbies; b) consumption on eating out. Variables a) and b) are ordinal in nature and ranging from 0, 1 (under £10) until 12 (over £160). Consumption on hedonic durables is measured with consumers' annual expenditure on each and aggregate of the 7 household hedonic electronics in the past year. Control variables include gender, age, age2, marital status, household size, number of children and pre school children, education, vocational qualification, job status and the partner's job status, property ownership, health status, household net wealth, household annual income, and region in accordance with existing literature on consumption (Ameriks, Caplin and Leahy 2002; Oropesa 1995). Random-effects ordered probit estimations and panel fixed effects estimations are employed to test the directional causations. Stata 10 is used for the data analysis in this study.

Our ordered probit estimations reveal that compared to spend nothing on leisure per month, leisure consumption at all other categories significantly affect a consumer's well-being. For example, the increase of leisure consumption from under £10 to over £160 per month weakly decreases the probability of being less happy, but strongly increases the probability of being in the highest well-being level (by 7.25% on average). However, consumption on hedonic durables does not affect well-being. These results seem to indicate that rather than deriving satisfaction from consumption activities as suggested in existing theories, only spending on experiential hedonic products correlate with being active and social contribute to well-being.

For the other causal direction, our ordered probit estimations suggest compared to well-being at reference level 0, well-being at levels over 3 all report highly significant effects on leisure consumption. For example, when well-being increases from level 1 to 12, people are 5.63% less likely to spend nothing per month on leisure, while they are 1.53% more likely to spend £50-£59 per month. The estimates for the effects of SWB on eating out and aggregate leisure consumption reveal qualitatively similar results. Additionally, we also find that when an individual's SWB increases from 0 to 12, the weighted average leisure consumption increased by approximately 20%. Our findings indicate compared to unhappy consumers, happy consumers enjoy more and are more likely to spend on hedonic products, but they do not tend to spend too much or buy very expensive ones. The findings seem to indicate that happy consumers spend on hedonic products primarily for meeting intrinsic goals such as intrinsic fun, regulating emotions (consumption on hedonic durables), social connectedness, and physical health (leisure consumption) which can be at no-cost or low-cost, rather than for extrinsic goals such as social comparison, material symbols, and identity seeking which are much more expensive, and they do not prefer expensive indulgent hedonic products.

Theoretically, this research extends well-being research into the consumer behavior area, and supplements the consumer literature that short-lived emotions influence consumers' temporal buying intention such as self-gifting, impulse buying, and compulsive buying and reaction to marketing stimuli. We suggest chronic well-being has potential impacts on consumers' general consumption behavior, especially on hedonic products, and the consumption it leads to is primarily goal pursuit and oriented. One implication for marketers of hedonic products is that happy consumers could be their target audience. Consumers can also use the results to guide their consumption behavior to improve their long-term happiness and quality of life.

REFERENCES:

Ameriks, John, Andrew Caplin, and John Leahy (2002), "Retirement consumption; insights from a survey," National Bureau of Economic Research (NBER) Working Paper Series, Working Paper 8735.

Argyle, Michael (1987), *The Psychology of Happiness*, Routledge, London.

Brief, Authur P., Ann H. Butcher, Jennifer M. George, and Karen E. Link (1993), "Integrating bottom-up and top-down theories of subjective well-being: the case of health," *Journal of Personality and Social Psychology*, 64 (4), 646-53.

Day, Ralph L. (1987), "Relationship between life satisfaction and consumer satisfaction," In *Marketing and Quality-of-Life Interface*, ed. by A. Coskun Samli, Westport, CT: Greenwood, 289-311.

Diener, Ed. (1984), "Subjective well-being," *Psychological Bulletin*, 95, 542-75.

Graham, Carol, Andrew Eggers, and Sandip Sukhtankar (2004), "Does happiness pay? An exploration based on panel data from Russia," *Journal of Economic Behavior and Organization*, 55(3), 319-42.

Feist, Gregory J., Todd E. Bodner, John F. Jacobs, Marilyn Miles, and Vickie Tan (1995), "Integrating top-down and bottom-up structural models of subjective well-being: a longitudinal investigation," *Journal of Personality and Social Psychology*, 68 (1), 138-50.

Headey, Bruce, Ruut Veenhoven, and Alex Wearing (1991), "Top-down versus bottom-up theories of subjective well-being," *Social Indicators Research*, 24, 81-100.

Lee, Dong-Jin, M. Joseph Sirgy, Val Larsen, and Newell D. Wright (2002), "Developing a subjective measure of consumer well-being," *Journal of Macromarketing*, 22 (2), 158-69.

Leelakulthanit, Orose, Ralph Day, and Rockney Walters (1991), "Investigating the relationship between marketing and overall satisfaction with life in a developing country," *Journal of Macromarketing*, 11, 3-23.

Porritt, Jonathon (2003) *Redefining Prosperity: Resource Productivity, Economic Growth and Sustainable Development*, London: Sustainable Development Commission.

Oropesa, R. Sal (1995), "Consumer possession, Consumer passions, and subjective well-being," *Sociological Forum*, 10 (2), 215-44.

Imagery-Text Congruence in Online Commerce and its Influence on Attitude Formation: A Processing Fluency Account

Thomas J. L. van Rompay, Twente University, The Netherlands
Peter W. de Vries, Twente University, The Netherlands
Ad T. H. Pruyn, Twente University, The Netherlands

EXTENDED ABSTRACT

Recent research indicates that design features of products and (online) environments may influence consumer choice and attitude formation (e.g., Griffith 2005; Mandel and Johnson 2002). Part of this influence relates to whether, and the extent to which, meanings connoted across different design elements match or mismatch (e.g., Van Rompay and Pruyn *in press*). For instance, online environments comprise many different elements (e.g., color, layout, textual information, and visuals) whose connotations require integration in order for a consumer to form an opinion or make a (purchase) decision. The authors propose that meaning (in)congruence impacts the relative ease with which informational elements are integrated. Ease of information integration, in turn, is expected to shape consumer response. To test these predictions, an experimental study is reported in which meanings connoted throughout product visualization and product description on a hotel booking site were manipulated.

In motivating these predictions, of particular interest is recent theorizing on processing fluency (e.g., Lee and Labroo 2004; Reber, Schwarz, and Winkielman 2004). The kernel of this proposal holds that people evaluate stimuli more positively the more fluently they can be processed. Arguably, meaning congruence also impacts processing fluency. For instance, when confronted with online vendor sites connoting various meanings through text (e.g., product description) and visuals (e.g., thumbnails of products), consumers face the task of integrating these various meanings into an overall impression in order to assess product quality and relevance, and to decide on purchase. Compared to highly incongruent information, matching or congruent information connoted by different website elements requires less integration, and, thus, makes the target product's meaning easier to grasp (cf. Lee and Labroo 2004).

Based on the above, it was predicted that online vendor sites in which product description and product visualization connote congruent meanings pose less information integration requirements, i.e., are more easily processed, compared to websites connoting incongruent meanings through product description and visualization. In line with the proposed relation between processing fluency and product evaluations, fluent processing was, in turn, expected to positively affect consumers' attitude towards the product presented. Since meaning integration requires, at least to some extent, elaborate processing, it was predicted that congruence effects would be particularly pronounced for participants high in need for cognition, as opposed to participants low in need for cognition.

To test these hypotheses, an experimental study was conducted in which participants were asked to evaluate a hotel booking site in which meaning congruence was manipulated. Based on pretesting, three hotel images were selected; a hotel image connoting coziness, a hotel image connoting modernity and a hotel image neutral with respect to these constructs. Similarly, two hotel descriptions were selected either stressing the hotel's cozy atmosphere or its modern atmosphere. By cross pairing the product visualizations and product descriptions, six versions of the website were created, crystallizing in a 3 (Product appearance: cozy versus neutral versus modern) * 2 (Product description: cozy versus modern) * 2 (Need for Cognition: low versus high) between-participants design. Dependent measures comprised measures of processing fluency and attitude formation.

Results indicated that meaning congruence, as opposed to meaning incongruence, indeed facilitated processing and positively affected attitude formation. Hence, processing fluency and attitude ratings were highest when a modern hotel appearance was accompanied by a hotel description stressing the hotel's modern atmosphere, and when a cozy hotel appearance was accompanied by a description stressing its cozy atmosphere. In contrast, websites connoting incongruent meanings through text and visuals received lower ratings on the fluency and attitude measures. In line with predictions, congruence effects were particularly apparent for participants high in need for cognition. Furthermore, using moderated mediation analyses (Muller, Judd, and Yzerbyt 2005), it was shown that meaning congruence indeed impacts attitude formation via processing fluency, confirming that meaning congruence is an important antecedent of processing fluency and via this route affects consumer attitude formation.

The findings reported are of practical relevance, not in the least because product descriptions and product visualizations are the two most important sources of product information on online vendor sites. Considering that this particular type of service (i.e., a hotel booking site) is also high in experience characteristics (i.e., the service can only be evaluated after consumption; Klein 1998), the importance of information congruence is all the more apparent. Under these conditions in particular, information gathering to reduce uncertainty and perceived risk associated with the wrong choice (e.g., booking a modern hotel high in formalized procedures when looking for a warm and personal atmosphere) benefits from information congruence.

Taking note of these considerations, the findings reported can be integrated with, seemingly contradictory, findings from research addressing congruence effects in advertising (e.g., Heckler and Childers 1992; Lee and Mason 1999). Findings from these studies indicate that text-image incongruence in ads may attract attention and positively affect consumer response in low involvement situations. The results reported here indicate that, when consumer involvement and perceived risks are high, information incongruence should be avoided. Nonetheless, incongruence may yield positive effects when applied to peripheral or stylistic website elements (e.g., color, layout or typeface) that are not central to information processing (cf. Eroglu, Machleit, and Davis 2001). In addition, future research should explore to what extent moderators such as browsing intentions and online experience qualify congruence effects.

Awaiting further studies addressing these and related issues, in the meantime the findings presented testify to the importance of careful consideration of textual and visual elements comprising the online environment, and stress the importance of website design in general.

REFERENCES

Eroglu, Sevgin A., Karen A. Machleit, and Lenita M. Davis (2001), "Atmospheric Qualities of Online Retailing: A Conceptual Model and Implications," *Journal of Business Research*, 54 (2), 177-84.

Griffith, David A. (2005), "An Examination of the Influences of Store Layout in Online Retailing," *Journal of Business Research*, 58 (10), 1391-96.

Heckler, Susan E. and Terry L. Childers (1992), "The Role of Expectancy and Relevancy in Memory for Verbal and Visual Information: What is Incongruency?," *Journal of Consumer Research*, 18 (4), 475-92.

Klein, Lisa R. (1998), "Evaluating the Potential of Interactive Media through a New Lens: Search versus Experience Goods," *Journal of Business Research*, 41 (3), 195-203.

Lee, Angela Y. and Aparna A. Labroo (2004), "The Effect of Conceptual and Perceptual Fluency on Brand Evaluation," *Journal of Marketing Research*, 41 (2), 151-65.

Lee, Yih H. and Charlotte Mason (1999), "Responses to Information Incongruence in Advertising: The Role of Expectancy, Relevancy, and Humor," *Journal of Consumer Research*, 26 (2), 156-69.

Mandel, Naomi and Eric J. Johnson (2002), "When Web Pages Influence Choice: Effects of Visual Primes on Experts and Novices," *Journal of Consumer Research*, 29 (2), 235-45.

Muller, Dominique, Charles M. Judd, and Vincent Y. Yzerbyt (2005), "When Moderation is Mediated and Mediation is Moderated," *Journal of Personality and Social Psychology*, 89 (6), 852-63.

Reber, Rolf, Norbert Schwarz, and Piotr Winkielman (2004), "Processing Fluency and Aesthetic Pleasure: Is Beauty in the Perceiver's Processing Experience?," *Personality and Social Psychology Review*, 8 (4), 364-82.

Van Rompay, Thomas J. L. and Ad T. H. Pruyn (in press), "Effects of Product Shape-Typeface Congruence on Brand Perception," *Advances in Consumer Research*.

How a Consumption Failure Influences an Observing Customer's Attribution and Perceived Service Quality: The Role of Regulatory Focus

Elisa K. Y. Chan, The Chinese University of Hong Kong, China
Lei Su, The Chinese University of Hong Kong, China
Lisa C. Wan, The Chinese University of Hong Kong, China

EXTENDED ABSTRACT

Past literature has largely focused on how a failure in consumption influences customer satisfaction and behavioral reactions to the company (e.g., Folkes and Graham 1987; Smith, Bolton, and Wagner 1999), but very little attention has been paid to examine how a failure influences other customers (or potential customers) who are not directly involved in a consumption failure. Interestingly, existing marketing literature regarding the role of other customers has investigated how the presence of other customers influence decision making of customers involved in a consumption context (e.g., Argo, Dahl, and Manchanda 2005); however, the reciprocal influence that the customer involved has on other customers has remained untapped. This research attempts to fill this gap by examining how customers react to an observed consumption failure. It also highlights the moderating influences of regulatory focus on observing customer's attribution behavior and perceived service quality. It reports a study that tested several hypotheses.

Research Hypotheses

According to defensive attribution theory (Walster 1966), when observers witness a negative event in a context that is relevant to them, feeling of threat would arise. This feeling would then lead to attribution driven by self-protective motives. These defensive attributions may also be subjected to the influence of perceived personal similarity with the target person involved in an incident (Shaver 1970). Drawing on the defensive attribution theory, we argue that an observing customer will attribute more (vs. less) responsibility to the service provider if the customer involved in the failure incident is similar (vs. not similar) to him/her. These attributions, in turn, will influence an observing customer's perceived service quality of the company. In addition, an individual's regulatory focus may moderate this pattern of attribution due to their differences in sensitivity to loss (prevention-focused) versus gain (promotion-focused). Since prevention-focused (vs. promotion-focused) customers are more sensitive to loss, they are vigilant against harmful consequences of a similar service failure that might befall them. It follows that in a similarity condition, prevention-focused (vs. promotion-focused) customers may attribute more responsibility to the company, and therefore possess a poorer perceived service quality.

The research hypotheses are summarized as follows:

H1: When there is perceived personal similarity with the customer involved, an observing customer will attribute more responsibility to the service provider

H2: The effect of perceived personal similarity on responsibility attribution will be moderated by regulatory focus. *(a)* When there is perceived personal similarity, prevention-focused (vs. promotion-focused) observing customer will attribute more responsibility to the service provider, and *(b)* When there is no perceived personal similarity, regulatory focus of an observing customer will have no effect on responsibility attribution.

H3: The effect of perceived personal similarity on perceived service quality will be moderated by regulatory focus. *(a)* When there is perceived personal similarity, prevention-focused (vs. promotion-focused) observing customer will have a poorer perception of service quality, *(b)* when there is no perceived personal similarity, regulatory focus of an observing customer will have no effect on perceived service quality, and **(c)** this effect is mediated by attribution.

Method and Results

A total of 100 undergraduate students (61% females) of a University in Hong Kong participated in the study. Participants were randomly assigned to either a similarity or non-similarity condition, and their regulatory orientation scores were measured. Median split was used to classified participants into prevention-focused and promotion-focused orientation. Finally, a total of 92 undergraduate students were used to test the hypotheses.

The results from an experiment provide general support for the hypotheses. In general, participants attributed more responsibility to the service provider in the similarity condition (vs. non-similarity condition). As predicted, prevention-focused participants attributed more responsibility in the similarity condition than did promotion-focused participants. No significant difference between the two groups was found in the non-similarity condition. Moreover, participants perceived poorer service quality in the similarity condition (vs. non-similarity condition). In particular, prevention-focused (vs. promotion-focused) participants perceived service quality to be poorer in the similarity condition, and no significant difference between the two groups was found in the non-similarity condition. More importantly, results indicated that attribution partially mediated the effect of regulatory focus on perceived service quality in the similarity condition.

REFERENCES

Argo, Jennifer J., Darren W. Dahl, and Rajesh V. Manchanda (2005), "The Influence of a Mere Social Presence in a Retail Context," *Journal of Consumer Research*, 32(September), 207-12.

Folkes, Susan Koletsky, and John L. Graham (1987), "A Field Study of Causal Inferences and Consumer Reaction: The View from the Airport," *Journal of Consumer Research*, 13 (March), 534-539.

Shaver, Kelly G. (1970), "Defensive Attribution: Effects on Severity and Relevance on the Responsibility Assigned for an Accident," *Journal of Personality and Social Psychology*, 18, 380-383.

Smith, Amy K., Ruth N. Bolton, and Janet Wagner (1999), "A Model of Customer Satisfaction with Service Encounters Involving Failure and Recovery," *Journal of Marketing Research*, 36(August), 356-372.

Walster, Elaine (1966), "Importance of Physical Attractiveness in Dating Behavior," *Journal of Personality and Social Psychology*, 4, 508-516.

Two Types of Language Bias in Word of Mouth

Gaby A. C. Schellekens, Erasmus University, The Netherlands
Peeter W. J. Verlegh, Erasmus University, The Netherlands
Ale Smidts, Erasmus University, The Netherlands

EXTENDED ABSTRACT

Product-related conversations, or word of mouth, form an important part of consumers' responses to products and services. While the role of language in other areas of consumer behavior has received considerable attention (Luna and Peracchio 2005; Tavassoli 1999), there has been no research on the role of language in word of mouth. Language is fundamental to word of mouth and the study of language use could uncover fundamental psychological processes and gain insight in the context of word-of-mouth communication (Fiedler 2008).

To study the role of language in word of mouth, we made use of the framework provided by the Linguistic Category Model (Semin and Fiedler 1988). The linguistic category model has been used to study a variety of aspects of language use in interpersonal behavior. It distinguishes four categories of interpersonal terms based on the sentence verbs and predicates from the most concrete level (*descriptive-action verbs*) to the intermediate (*interpretive-action verbs* and *state verbs*) to the most abstract level *Adjectives*). The use of more abstract language increases the extent to which a description is informative about the subject, as well as increased temporal stability and perceived likelihood of repetition of the behavior that is being described (Semin and Fiedler 1988). In general, people are unaware of the level of abstraction they apply, and cannot access their reasons for chosing a certain level of abstraction (Franco and Maass 1996).

Research in social psychology has demonstrated a linguistic expectancy bias (Wigboldus, Semin and Spears 2000). That is, behavior is described more abstractly when it is congruent (rather than incongruent) with one's expectations of the actor. Up till now, this bias has only been demonstrated with interpersonal behavior and has never been examined for communication about inanimate objects. Even though many of peoples daily conversations are about objects, such as product related conversations. This paper intends to fill this gap and examines the *linguistic expectancy bias* in word of mouth. In addition, and perhaps even more importantly, we will focus on the role of the receiver. In social psychology, language abstraction has mostly been studied in settings were participants are asked to describe the behavior of an actor (often depicted in a cartoon). In word-of-mouth communication, however, product experiences are communicated to another consumer. Research has frequently shown that receivers have a strong impact on the nature of word of mouth (e.g., Brown and Reingen 1987). We therefore extend the concept of linguistic expectancy bias to include the perceived or inferred expectations of the receiver. We will show that a *receiver's* attitude toward a product or brand will influence the abstraction level that is chosen by the sender of a word-of-mouth message. We label this phenomenon the *"receiver linguistic expectancy bias"*.

Experiment 1 demonstrates the linguistic expectancy bias in word of mouth. In the experiment the product attitudes about fictitious brands (positive vs. negative) and product experiences (positive vs. negative) were manipulated and the participants were asked how they would communicate the product experience to another person by choosing from several predetermined product descriptions according to the levels of the linguistic category model (Semin & Fiedler, 1988). Consistent with our hypotheses, study 1 revealed the linguistic expectancy bias in word of mouth: product experiences congruent to ones product opinion were communicated more abstractly, compared to expectancy incongruent experiences. More specifically, favorable product experiences were communicated more abstractly by participants with a positive product attitude compared to a negative attitude, and unfavorable experiences were communicated more concretely by participants with a positive compared to a negative product attitude. The findings of experiment 1 were replicated in two additional studies. The first one demonstrated the linguistic expectancy bias with existing brand attitudes (using actual brand names, such as Nike and Apple Ipod) and the second replication showed the linguistic bias with an open-ended response format as dependent variable, in which participants' responses were coded according a schema developed by Semin and Fiedler (1988).

Experiment 2 demonstrates the *receiver linguistic expectancy bias*. It was expected that characteristics of receivers affect the language that senders use to describe their product experiences. We anticipate that people will use more abstract or more concrete language to accommodate the receiver's expectations about a product.

In the experiment, the participants were asked to communicate a product experience to a receiver of whom they knew the product attitude. We found that positive experiences were communicated more abstractly when the receiver held a more favorable (vs. unfavorable) attitude of the product under consideration. Likewise, negative experiences were communicated more abstractly when receivers held a less favorable (vs. favorable) attitude of the product. This bias parallels the "classical" linguistic expectancy bias, but has its cause in a different source, namely the attitude of the receiving party.

Our research sheds new light on the oft-studied topic of word of mouth, by providing insights into the subtleties of product-related conversations. We provide a first application of the linguistic category model outside the context of (inter)personal behavior, and demonstrate a linguistic expectancy bias for inanimate objects. Secondly, we propose and demonstrate a receiver linguistic expectancy bias. Our studies show that language abstraction is responsive to the influence of the communication context: a communicator's use of language abstraction is biased to fit the expectations of the receiver. Opportunities for future research are identified in the paper.

REFERENCES

Brown, Jacqueline Johnson and Peter H. Reingen (1987), "Social Ties and Word-of-Mouth Referral Behavior," *Journal of Consumer Research*, 14 (3), 350-362.

Fiedler, Klaus (2008), "Language: A Toolbox for Sharing and Influencing Social Reality," *Perspectives on Psychological Science*, 3 (1), 38-47.

Franco, Francesca M. and Anne Maass (1996), "Implicit Versus Explicit Strategies of Out-Group Discrimination-The Role of Intentional Control in Biased Language Use and Reward Allocation," *Journal of Language and Social Psychology*, 15 (3), 335-359.

Luna, David and Laura A. Peracchio (2005), "Advertising to bilingual consumers: The impact of code-switching on persuasion," *Journal of Consumer Research*, 31 (4), 760-765.

Semin, Gün R. and Klaus Fiedler (1988), "The Cognitive Functions of Linguistic Categories in Describing Persons-Social Cognition and Language," *Journal of Personality and Social Psychology*, 54 (4), 558-568.

Tavassoli, Nadar T. (1999), "Temporal and Associative Memory in Chinese and English," *Journal of Consumer Research*, 26 (2), 170-181.

Wigboldus, Daniel H. J., Gün R. Semin, and Russell Spears (2000), "How do we Communicate Stereotypes? Linguistic Bases and Inferential Consequences," *Journal of Personality and Social Psychology*, 78 (1), 5-18.

Selective Consumer WOM Communication and Its Consequences

Yu Hu, Salem State College, USA

EXTENDED ABSTRACT

Consumers' interpersonal, word-of-mouth (WOM) communications have long been recognized as an effective channel to disseminate market information (Frenzen and Nakamoto 1993) and, perhaps more importantly, to influence consumers' product judgments and choices (Herr, Kardes and Kim 1991). Accordingly, much of the research attention has been focused on the recipient of the WOM message (i.e., the *audience*). However, for an interpersonal social interaction like WOM, surprisingly very little is known about the effect of WOM on the communicator of the message (i.e., the *speaker*). Specifically, two issues are largely overlooked: First, the speaker's retelling of past experience to an audience is not a verbatim recall of what has happened (Marsh 2007); instead, the speaker's message construction is a selective process, a process that is under the influence of many individual and situational forces. Second, this selective communication process itself might drive important cognitive changes in the minds of the speaker. In other words, communicating consumption experience with others might affect the speaker's subsequent judgments of the experience itself.

For the WOM speaker, communications of consumption information with others can serve many different interpersonal or situational goals, such as self-presentation, impression management, or entertainment, and more importantly, accuracy is often not the main objective; thus, the communicated message should not be a simple relay of the stored knowledge. In fact, message modifications, such as interpretation, evaluation, exaggeration, omission, or even falsification (e.g., Argo, White, and Dahl 2006; Sengupta et al. 2002) are ubiquitous in consumers' daily conversations. "This means, in effect, that one has to lie. We must leave out the details that don't fit, and invent some that make things work better (Schank and Abelson 1995, p. 34)."

Borrowing a term from social psychology (e.g., Higgins 1992), I use *audience-tuning* to refer to the WOM speaker's adaptive message construction behavior, in which the speaker tailor his/her message to suit the audience's characteristics or meet situational demands. I posit that the speaker's audience-tuning behavior not only affects the quantity and quality of the WOM messages transmitted to the audience but also has a significant cognitive impact on the speaker's subsequent memory and judgments of the communication topic. As Schank and Abelson (1995, p. 58) put it, "We lose the original and keep the copy". That is to say, as a consequence of the communication, the speaker's recollections or evaluations of the consumption knowledge might be realigned with the contents of the communicated messages.

Many researchers have reasoned that memory differences after communications could be attributed to the fact that communicators selectively rehearsed certain aspects of the past events during communications and the rehearsals enhanced the subsequent retrievals of those details. In addition to the rehearsal mechanism, McGregor and Holmes (1999) proposed a heuristic explanation that people develop a heuristic version or interpretation of the past events to effective retelling of past story and this interpretation heuristics directly biased later judgments and remembering of those events. Regardless, either due to enhanced rehearsal or heuristic interpretation, selectively modifying past experiences to serve communication purposes is bound to have a cognitive impact on the speaker.

In an effort to provide empirical evidence of WOM speakers' message modification behavior and its consequent cognitive changes, this research developed a memory-based, two-step experiment approach. Subjects first learned some evaluatively complex (positive, negative and ambiguous) product information and formed initial judgments. After a brief delay, they were supraliminal primed with different social relations: best friend vs. stranger (i.e., communal vs. exchange relation; see Clark and Mills 1979, 1993). Immediately afterwards, in an ostensibly unrelated task, they were asked to freely communicate the product information to a relation-ambiguous audience. Subjects' responses revealed the following patterns: Those primed with a best-friend audience communicated more negative product information than those primed with a stranger; they were also more likely to negatively interpret ambiguous information.

Twenty-four hours later, product attitude was reassessed via an online questionnaire. Results showed a significant attitude change. More importantly, subjects in the best friend condition presented significantly decreased evaluations of the product, which could be attributed to the fact that these participants recounted significantly more negative product information during the communication stage and this selective rehearsal affected their subsequent judgments. Interestingly, audience-tuning behavior did not seem to have an evaluative impact on subjects in the stranger group: Although they rehearsed more positive product information than those in the best friend condition, they seemed to have a mechanism in place to filer out or not register the audience effect during either the message production process or the later reevaluation of the product. This unexpected finding pointed to a promising direction for future research. For example, if it is reasonable to expect that the speaker needs to monitor the retelling-induced cognitive change, then what factors would contribute to the enhancing or discounting of this ability? What are the roles of the audience in this monitoring process?

The intended contribution of this research is twofold. First, by priming a common relationship variable to demonstrate the WOM speaker's selective message construction and the resultant cognitive changes (and non-change), this paper attempts to raise researchers' attention to the social co-construction nature of consumer WOM behaviors. It is necessary for researchers to adopt a broader, interpersonal, co-constructive view of the WOM behaviors and to identify the antecedents and consequences of this complex process (see Pasupathi 2001 for a review). Second, as a meaningful addition to the WOM research methodology, this research introduces a new memory-based experimental approach that could be used to systematically investigate the process of WOM communications and its consequences.

REFERENCES

Argo, Jennifer J., Katherine White, and Darren W. Dahl (2006), "Social Comparison Theory and Deception," *Journal of Consumer Research*, 33 (June), 99-108.

Clark, Margaret S. and Judson Mills (1979), "Interpersonal Attraction in Exchange and Communal Relationships," *Journal of Personality and Social Psychology*, 37 (January), 12-24.

Clark, Margaret S. and Judson Mills (1993), "The Difference between Communal and Exchange Relationships: What It Is and Is Not," *Personality and Social Psychology Bulletin*, 19 (December), 684-91.

Frenzen, Jonathan, and Kent Nakamoto (1993), "Structure, Cooperation and the Flow of Market Information," *Journal of Consumer Research*, 20 (December), 360-75.

Herr, Paul M., Frank R. Kardes, and John Kim (1991), "Effects of Word-of-Mouth and Product-Attribute Information on Persuasion: An Accessibility-Diagnosticity Perspective," *Journal of Consumer Research*, 17 (March), 454-62.

Higgins, E. Tory (1992), "Achieving 'Shared Reality' in the Communication Game: A Social Action That Creates Meaning," *Journal of Language and Social Psychology*, 11 (September), 107-31.

Marsh, Elizabeth J. (2007), "Retelling Is Not the Same as Recalling: Implications for Memory," *Current Directions in Psychological Science*, 16, (February), 16-20.

McGregor, Ian and John G. Holmes (1999), "How Storytelling Shapes Memory and Impressions of Relationship Events Over Time," *Journal of Personality and Social Psychology*, 76 (March), 403-19.

Pasupathi, Monisha (2001), "The Social Construction of the Personal Past and its Implications for Adult Development," *Psychological Bulletin*, 127 (September), 651-72.

Sengupta, Jaideep, Darren W. Dahl, and Gerald G. Gorn (2002), "Misrepresentation in the Consumer Context," *Journal of Consumer Psychology*, 12 (2), 69-79.

Schank, Roger C. and Robert P. Abelson (1995), "Knowledge and Memory: The Real Story," in *Knowledge and Memory: The Real Story*, ed. Robert S. Wyer, Jr., Hillsdale, NJ: Erlbaum, 1-85.

The Interpersonal Determinants of Sniping in Internet Auctions

Michael A. Kamins, Stony Brook University, USA
Avraham Noy, University of Haifa, Israel
Yael Steinhart, University of Haifa, Israel
David Mazursky, Hebrew University of Jerusalem, Israel

EXTENDED ABSTRACT

The current research explores the intrapersonal and social factors of the sniping phenomenon. Sniping occurs in on-line auctions when the auction closes at a specified pre-determined time (a "hard close"). Sniping is placing a bid on an item in the very ending stages of the auction in an attempt to win the auction, while leaving other bidders a short period of time or no time to respond.

Four studies were conducted to examine the social factors affecting the sniping strategy. The first study was based on on-line survey among 144 eBay bidders. Its findings pointed out that consumers perceive sniping to be an effective auction strategy by which the bidders can achieve a higher probability of winning the auction at a lower price. The second study was based on an on-line auction simulation setting among 62 participants. Its results revealed that participants were more likely to snipe when there was a higher number of other bidders showing an interest in the auction than when the number was low. The last two studies were conducted in actual eBay auctions. The third study was conducted among 141 eBay bidders in the presence of high or low counter. eBay counter is a visual representation of the number of viewers who inspected the specific item. The results demonstrated that the tendency to snipe was higher in case of high counter (many other potential bidders) than in case of low counter. The fourth study was conducted among 286 eBay bidders. The findings indicated that when the auction displayed the counter, sniping took place more often in public auction (i.e. when knowing the bidders' identity) compared to private auctions (i.e. when the bidder's identity is concealed). However, when the counter was hidden, there was not a significant difference in the percentage of sniping.

The findings of this research shed new light on the determinants affecting bidding behavior, specifically–sniping in internet auctions. The research also uncovers extant beliefs that bidders have about sniping effectiveness. It would be interesting to further explore the boundaries of the social impact on sniping. It can be implemented through controlling for other factors which earlier studies observed that they have an effect on sniping. The closing rule of the auction and the experience of the bidders are such factors which come to mind. These studies will enable the researchers to evaluate boundary conditions regarding the effect of the other bidders on sniping behavior as well as the interaction among the factors.

Consumer Emotional Intelligence: A Comparison between the U.S. and China

Robert Jewell, Kent State University, USA
Annie Peng Cui, West Virginia University, USA
Blair Kidwell, University of Kentucky, USA
Desheng Wang, Shandong University, China

EXTENDED ABSTRACT

Consumption decisions often satisfy consumers' various psychological needs and serve a social purpose by reflecting ties to one's family, community, and cultural groups. These distinct orientations may provide important insights into how consumers process emotional information and how they use that information to make brand decisions. In this research, we explore the antecedent role of consumer emotional intelligence on decision making differences between collectivist and individualistic orientations; specifically Chinese and American consumers. Further, we compare the consumer emotional intelligence scale across these two distinct cultures to better understand its validity and dimensionality.

In the present paper, we first highlight the importance of cross-cultural instrument testing, followed by a brief discussion of CEI and its measurement. Then, we compare differences in the CEI instrument across a US and Chinese sample, followed by an examination of the influence of CEI on brand selection.

Emotional intelligence is defined as one's ability to recognize, perceive, and effectively use emotional information, such as the meaning of emotions, emotional patterns, and emotional relationships (Caruso, Mayer, and Salovey 2002, Mayer and Salovey 1997). Emotional intelligence operates in a complementary fashion with the more traditional, cognitively-based knowledge in decision making. That is, emotional intelligence is conceptualized to supplement rather than supplant cognitive intelligence in decision-making contexts (Mayer, Salovey, and Caruso 2004). Research has consistently indicated that emotional intelligence predicts performance beyond the effects of cognitive intelligence (Mayer et al. 2004).

Recently, a scale has been developed that evaluates emotional intelligence specifically as it relates to consumer domain-specific issues such as product choice (Kidwell, Hardesty, and Childers 2008). The Consumer Emotional Intelligence Scale (CEIS; www.ceis-research.com) was developed to measure the domain of consumer decision making. The CEIS is comprised of four specific branches; *perceiving*, *facilitating*, *understanding*, and *managing* emotion.

Research on culture has shown that differences exist on a number of dimensions. For example Hofstede has found that cultures tend to differentiate along five dimensions: power distance, individualism versus collectivism, masculinity versus femininity, uncertainty avoidance, and long- versus short-term orientation (Hofstede 2001). With respect to the difference between the U.S. and China, the dimension that is most-often invoked is the individualism versus collectivism dimension. Individualist societies are believed to be characterized by low identification and loose integration into social groups. The implication is that people in individualist societies are largely on their own in terms of dealing with issues and problems. Conversely, those in collectivist societies are characterized by strong identification and a high degree of cohesiveness with social groups. The implication is that that people in collectivist societies perceive individual issues and problems as problems for the group to solve (Hofstede 2001).

With respect to emotional intelligence, such a taxonomy of cultural differences may suggests, on the one hand, difference between U.S. and Chinese consumers. China, representing a more collectivist society, may reward emotional intelligence to a higher degree than an individualist society such as the U.S. Thus, one expectation related to emotional intelligence may be that consumers in China have higher levels of emotional intelligence. Moreover, the emotional skills necessary to function in a collectivist society may be qualitatively different than the skills necessary to function in a collectivist society. Thus, with respect to emotional intelligence, the expectation may be that rather than the amount of emotional intelligence, the structure of emotional intelligence would be different between China and the U.S.

On the other hand, there is reason to believe that cognitive representation and cognitive processing characteristics, such as intelligence, are invariant with respect to culture (Sternberg 2004). That is, perhaps the ability to perceive, use, understand, and manage emotions is a fundamental characteristic of the human condition. With respect to emotional intelligence, such a perspective would lead one to predict structural invariance for CEI as it pertains to a comparison between U.S. and Chinese consumers. Given these two distinct yet equally viable possibilities, we view this study as exploratory. As a result, we make no specific hypotheses or predictions as to the nature of the similarities or differences between China and the U.S. with respect to emotional intelligence; we will allow the question to be addressed empirically.

To examine the construct of CEI and its structure in two countries that are culturally distinct, we conducted two studies in China, representing a collectivistic culture, and the United States, representing an individualistic culture. The results of our studies suggest that the basic structure for the Chinese data indicated a good model fit with the CEIS model proposed by Kidwell, Hardesty and Childers (2008). This supports the notion that CEI is a general construct that appropriately applies to consumers in a country that is culturally distinct from the U.S., where the scale was developed. Thus, we can conclude that the construct itself and its four-factor structure are robust and have a high external validity. This finding is further supported in a choice task that indicates that consumers high in emotional intelligence evaluate attribute information more objectively than consumers with lower levels of emotional intelligence.

Our second important finding indicates that although the basic structure for the Chinese data showed a good model fit, there is a clear indication of structural difference between the two samples. In particular, the dimension of *Understanding* determines the difference between the Chinese and the U.S. samples. One possible explanation might be that Chinese consumers, coming from a collectivist culture, may pay more attention to the contextual cues when giving the task to understand and process the information presented than American consumers. This may lead to a different perception of the same scenario between Chinese and American consumers, which eventually presented via their answers.

The present study suggests that consumer emotional intelligence provides a unique lens for researchers and marketers to study consumers from different cultures. Future research should explore this construct in other cultures, group dynamics, and other marketing applications.

REFERENCES

Adaval, Rashmi (2001), "Sometimes It Just Feel Right: The Differential Weighting of Affect-Inconsistent Product Information," *Journal of Consumer Research*, 28 (June), 1-17.

Barone, Michael J., Paul W. Miniard, and Jean B. Romeo (2000), "The Influence of Positive Mood on Brand Extension Evaluations," *Journal of Consumer Research*, 26 (March), 386-400.

Belk, Russell W. (1988), "Possessions and the Extended Self," *Journal of Consumer Research*, 15 (September), 139-168.

Byrnes, Babara M. (2001), *Structural Equation Modeling with AMOS*, Mahwah, New Jersey: Lawrence Erlbaum Associaates, Inc.

Campbell, Donald T., and Julian C. Stanley (1963), *Experimental and Quasi-Experimental Designs for Research*, Chicago, Rand McNally.

Cook, T. D., and D. T. Campbell (1979), *Quasi-Experimentation: Design and Analysis Issues for Field Settings*, Boston, MA: Houghton Mifflin.

Cousins, Steven D. (1989), "Culture and Self-Perception in Japan and the United States," *Journal of Personality and Social Psychology*, 56 (January), 124-131.

Escalas, Jennifer Edson and James R Bettman (2005), "Self-Construal, Reference Groups, and Brand Meaning," *Journal of Consumer Research*, 32 (December), 378-89.

Hofstede, Geert (2001), *Culture's Consequences: Comparing Values, Behaviors, Institutions and Organizations Across Nations*, Sage, Thousand Oaks, CA.

Kidwell, Blair, David M. Hardesty, and Terry L. Childers (2008), "Consumer Emotional Intelligence: Conceptualization, Measurement, and the Prediction of Consumer Decision Making," *Journal of Consumer Research*, 35 (June).

Kleine, Susan S., Robert E. Kleine, and Chris Allen (1995), "How is a possession 'me' or 'not me'? Characterizing types and an antecedent of material possession attachment," *Journal of Consumer Research*, 22 (December), 327-343.

Markus, Hazel Rose and Kitayama, Shinobu (1991), "Culture and the Self: Implications for Cognition, Emotion, and Motivation," *Psychological Review*, 98 (April), 224-253.

Mayer, John D., Peter Salovey, and David R. Caruso? (2004), "Emotional Intelligence: Theory, Findings, and Implications," *Psychological Inquiry,* 15 (3), 197-215.

Mayer, John D., David R. Caruso and Peter Salovey (1999), "Emotional Intelligence Meets Traditional Standards for an Intelligence," *Intelligence,* 27 (1), 267-98.

Mayer, John D., and Peter Salovey (1997), "What is Emotional Intelligence?," in *Emotional Development and Emotional Intelligence: Implications for Educators*, ed. Peter Salovey and David Slusher, New York, NY: Basic Books, 3-31.

Mayer, John D., Peter Salovey and David Caruso (2000), "Models of Emotional Intelligence," In *The Handbook of Intelligence,* ed. Robert J. Sternberg, New York, NY: Cambridge University Press, 396-420.

_____ (2002), *Mayer-Salovey-Caruso Emotional Intelligence Test (MSCEIT) Item Booklet*. Toronto, Canada: MHS Publishers.

Mayer, John D., Peter Salovey and David Caruso, and Gill Sitarenios (2004), "Measuring Emotional Intelligence with the MSCEIT V2.0," *Emotion*, 3 (1), 97-105.

Robert J. Sternberg (2000), *The Handbook of Intelligence,* ed., New York, NY: Cambridge University Press

Roberts, Richard D., Moshe Zeidner, and Gerald Matthews (2001), "Does Emotional Intelligence Meet Traditional Standards for an Intelligence? Some New Data and Conclusions," *Emotion,* 1 (3), 196-231.

The Effect of Culture on Sequential Choice in Group Settings

Song-Oh Yoon, Korea University, Korea
Kwanho Suk, Korea University, Korea
Seon Min Lee, Korea University, Korea
Eunyoung Park, Korea University, Korea

EXTENDED ABSTRACT

Past research has indicated that people tend to seek variety in their choices. This effect has been demonstrated in both intrapersonal and interpersonal choices, although variety-seeking has been shown to result in lower overall satisfaction with their choices (Ariely and Levav 2000). Many of these findings are explained by people's desire to portray a positive self-image by appearing unique (Ariely and Levav 2000; Ratner and Kahn 2002). However, the findings of some cross-cultural studies have challenged the generalization of such assessments (Kim and Markus 1999). According to these studies, variety-seeking is less pronounced in Eastern cultural members, as they share different assumptions regarding uniqueness and individuality. Specifically, in contrast to the more individualistic Western culture, where uniqueness and being different from others are considered positive traits, negative associations are attached to uniqueness and individuality in the more collectivistic Eastern culture.

While past research has provided insights into cultural influences on variety-seeking behavior and the underlying motivations, its implications with regard to consumer's interpersonal decision have yet to be clearly understood. This is mainly because past cross-cultural studies in this area have focused on individual choice situations (Kim and Markus 1999). In particular, it is still ambiguous as to whether the negative meanings associated with uniqueness in Eastern culture will result in a mere lack of conscious attempts to vary their choice from those of others (i.e., lack of variety-seeking) or it will result in greater efforts to conform to others' choices in interpersonal decision situations. One line of research (e.g., Markus and Kitayama 1991) suggests that individuals from collectivistic cultures are expected to follow others' choices when the choice is made in a group setting, since being similar to others and conformity to group is an important cultural value in this context. However, another research finding (e.g., Kim and Drolet 2002) suggests that other's choices would exert minimal effects on the individual's choice, because choice is not an act of self-expression for collectivistic cultural members. Accordingly, members of collectivist cultures will not necessarily make similar choices with those of others, while the amount of variety-seeking behavior is less, compared to individualistic cultural members.

Therefore, the primary purpose of current research is to test these two competing predictions. In particular, we focus on the impact of others' choices on conformity-seeking tendency among individuals from collectivist cultures. We also attempt to examine the conditions under which such cultural orientations have particularly profound impacts on individual's choice. In line with previous research highlighting that culture is not a constant meaning but often dissipates or activates depending on situational demands (Briely and Aaker 2006), we show that culture has greater implications for choice only when individual's choice is made based on cultural, rather than personal, knowledge. Finally, we investigate the potential differences between Eastern and Western cultural members in the emotional consequences of aligning one's behavior (e.g., choice) with cultural norms. Unlike the members of Western culture, whose emotional well-being has been shown to be lowered after complying with cultural norms (e.g., variety-seeking), individuals in Eastern culture are not expected to experience such reductions in emotional well-being, as aligning oneself with cultural norms (e.g., conformity) is more consistent with their definition of personal happiness.

We test our predictions in two studies, involving real restaurant order data and a field study. In the first study, the analysis of 517 meal order slips, representing 1,475 diners from two local restaurants in Korea, showed that real tables dining in a group tended to choose less varied dishes as compared to what would be expected from a random sampling of population of all individual choices across tables (i.e., simulated data representing menu selections in the absence of any group influence). Similar findings are observed in restaurants that differ in terms of cuisine, average dish price, and familiarity to participants. Next, we replicate our findings in a setting that allows more experimental control. In our field experiment, we manipulate the conditions in which individuals choose their options, such that in one condition they select their options under group influence (i.e., sequential choice condition) and in the other condition, group is dissolved and thus the choice becomes a strictly individual one (i.e., individual choice condition). We found that Koreans tended to select options identical to those of their group members when they make selections collectively as opposed to individually. We further show that, unlike previous findings based on individuals from Western cultures, adherence to the cultural norm (i.e., conformity) did not result in lower overall satisfaction with their chosen options for Koreans. Lastly, we show support for the hypothesized mechanism underlying the above effects, by demonstrating that the tendency to seek variety or conformity is associated significantly with decision maker's individualistic-collectivistic dispositions.

REFERENCES

Ariely, Dan and Jonathan Levav (2000), "Sequential Choice in Group Settings: Taking the Road Less Traveled and Less Enjoyed," *Journal of Consumer Research*, 27 (December), 279-290.

Briley, Donnel A. and Jennifer L. Aaker (2006), "When Does Culture Matter? Effects of Personal Knowledge on the Correction of Culture-Based Judgments," *Journal of Marketing Research*, 43 (August), 395-408.

Kim, Heejung and Aimee Drolet (2003), "Choice and Self-Expression: A Cultural Analysis of Variety-Seeking," *Journal of Personality and Social Psychology*, 85 (2), 373-382.

Kim, Heejung and Hazel Rose Markus (1999), "Deviance or Uniqueness, Harmony or Conformity? A Cultural Analysis," *Journal of Personality and Social Psychology*, 77 (4), 785-800.

Markus, Hazel Rose and Shinobu Kitayama (1991), "Culture and the Self: Implications for Cognitions, Emotion, and Motivation," *Psychological Review*, 98 (2), 224-253.

Ratner, Rebecca K. and Barbara E. Kahn (2002), "The Impact of Private versus Public Consumption on Variety-Seeking Behavior," *Journal of Consumer Research*, 29 (September), 246-257.

Do Ethnic Marketing Efforts Pay Off?: Interaction Effects of Accomodated Brand and Price on Product Evaluation and Purchase Intention

Manuel Michaelis, University of Muenster, Germany
Hai Van Duong Dinh, University of Muenster, Germany
Tobias Heussler, University of Muenster, Germany
Mareike Meyer, University of Muenster, Germany
Dieter Ahlert, University of Muenster, Germany

EXTENDED ABSTRACT

In the course of history, especially through globalization and the coalescence of many different countries to confederations (e.g., the European Union), migration has become a common phenomenon all over the world–resulting in large ethnic groups in many domestic markets. As a result of this changing ethnic landscape, marketers increasingly target ethnic groups with culturally accommodated marketing. Consequently, consumer researchers are engaged with the questions of whether ethnicity is a viable variable to segment markets, and whether targeting ethnic groups with culturally oriented marketing pays off. In spite of this growing interest in ethnic marketing, research in this field is still fairly limited, even in the U.S. where ethnic marketing has evoked most attention (Burton 2000). Furthermore, the range of issues addressed in the studies is narrow. First, due to the dominance of U.S. research papers, studies focus on ethnic groups in the U.S. Second, most of these studies focus on ethnic advertising and neglect accommodation options of other marketing tools, such as culturally oriented brands (Burton 2000). Last, in large part the studies are limited to efforts to determine behavioral differences between consumers of various cultural groups, and trying to account for these to cultural factors (Holland and Gentry 1999; Hirschman 1981).

Extending our knowledge about consumer responses to ethnic marketing, our contribution to the literature is threefold. First using an accommodated brand we analyze a marketing tool other than advertising. Second, we differentiate between consumer affective, cognitive, and conative responses to ethnic marketing measures. Third, we investigate the specific impact of an accommodated brand on price premium options for a German ethnic group.

Drawing on accommodation theory (Holland and Gentry 1999) and existing findings of research on ethnic marketing, brand, and price, we derived our hypotheses. We propose that culturally accommodated brands improve cognitive and affective product evaluation as well as purchase intention. Moreover, we propose that accommodated brands moderate the relationships between price and cognitive product evaluation, affective product evaluation, and purchase intention.

We tested our hypotheses in collaboration with a German mobile telephone service provider, gathering data from 100 Turkish respondents, and using a scenario-based experimental fixed-factor 2 x 2 between-subjects research design. Our stimuli were four different fictitious products which were presented randomly to the participants. Price (high vs. low single surcharge per call to Turkey) and brand (neutral vs. Turkish brand name with Turkish national symbols) were selected as independent variables, whereas the phone rates were reduced to four fixed connections for the ease of presentation to the test subjects (calls on German landline and all German mobile networks, calls on Turkish landline, calls on all Turkish mobile networks, single surcharge per call to Turkey).

The effects of accommodated brand and price on the dependent constructs were tested by conducting a MANOVA. The results indicate significant main effects and a significant interaction effect. In order to determine the effect of the stimuli on each dependent construct we conducted Follow-Up-ANOVAS, which revealed that the affective product evaluation and the purchase intention were both influenced by an interaction effect (brand x price). In contrast to our proposition, we did not find a significant interaction effect on the cognitive product evaluation. Moreover, we found no significant direct effect of brand on cognitive product evaluation. Last, we conducted post-hoc tests to determine whether the hypothesized effects work in the proposed direction. In the case of a high price, the accommodated brand has a positive impact on the affective product evaluation as well as on purchase intention, whereas, in the case of a low price, mean values do not differ significantly from those when no accommodation takes place. Thus, ethnical accommodation at lower prices does not have a significant impact on affective product evaluation or on purchase intention.

Our results have implications for marketing management. In the case of low prices ethnic marketing efforts increase neither affective product evaluation nor purchase intention because the price dominates other cues (here: brand) which affect consumer response. In the case of high prices, purchase intention is higher with accommodated brands than with brands that have not been accommodated. Consequently, cultural adaptations allow higher prices, justifying expenditure on ethnic marketing efforts. As a result, accommodated branding tends to pay off, particularly in situations of larger targeted ethnic groups and those with higher purchasing power.

The effect of price level and branding on cognitive product evaluation is less clear. In contrast to our hypothesis, we found no effect of price and brand on cognitive product evaluation. Holland and Gentry (1999) give a reasonable explanation of this result. Due to the mere exposure effect, accommodation may have an affective response even if consumers do not consciously recognize the targeted marketing efforts (here: accommodated brand). In contrast, recognition is a prerequisite for consumers to evaluate products cognitively. Therefore, more research is needed to understand the underlying process of product evaluation in an ethnic context. Further research could also draw on Oliver's loyalty model, which differentiates between four stages of loyalty—cognitive, affective, conative, and action loyalty (Oliver 1997; Evanschitzky, and Wunderlich 2006)—to extend our knowledge of consumer response to ethnic marketing.

As with all empirical studies, this study has limitations. The key limitation here is the design as a laboratory experiment. In order to extend an examination of the results, the experiments can be replicated with heterogeneous samples (field experiments). Moreover, replications with different ethnic groups and in different service industries are needed in order to confirm our findings.

REFERENCES

Burton, Dawn (2000), "Ethnicity, Identity and Marketing: A Critical Review," *Journal of Marketing Management*, 16 (8), 853-77.

Evanschitzky, Heiner and Maren Wunderlich (2006), "An Examination of Moderator Effects in the Four-Stage Loyalty Model," *Journal of Service Research*, 8 (4), 330-45.

Hirschman, Elizabeth C. (1981), "American Jewish Ethnicity: Its Relationship to some Selected Aspects of Consumer Behavior," *Journal of Marketing*, 45 (3), 102-10.

Holland, Jonna and James W. Gentry (1999), "Ethnic Consumer Reaction to Targeted Marketing: A Theory of Intercultural Accommodation," *Journal of Advertising*, 28 (1), 65-77.

Oliver, Richard L. (1997), *Satisfaction: A Behavioral Perspective on the Consumer*, New York: McGraw-Hill.

Seize The Day! Encouraging Indulgence for the Hyperopic Consumer

Kelly L. Haws, Texas A&M University, USA
Cait Poynor, University of Pittsburgh, USA

EXTENDED ABSTRACT

The luxury market in the United States alone generated over $445 billion in 2005 (Mintel 2005). Though some luxury items are associated with frivolity, there also appear to be short and long-term benefits associated with indulgence, beginning with the enjoyment of everyday pleasures and extending to profound effects on life satisfaction (Kivetz and Keinan 2006). However, recent research suggests that consumers may display what has been called "hyperopic" behavior, exhibiting aversion to luxury-related products and actions. Some degree of hyperopia may exist in a broad segment of the population. Therefore, both in order to enhance consumer well-being and provide guidance for luxury marketers, understanding ways in which consumers and marketers can alter such hyperopic tendencies, within reason, is important (Kivetz and Simonson 2002). In the present research, we measure hyperopia as an individual difference, identify mechanisms which drive hyperopic behavior and validate prior assumptions about its nature. We then examine how the level at which goals or purchases are construed can impact the behavior of hyperopic consumers, helping those with high levels of hyperopia to overcome their aversion to indulgence and learn to "Seize the day."

In the present research, we use a 6-item measure of hyperopia based on the work of Kivetz and Simonson (2002) and examined further by Kivetz and Keinan (2006). This scale captures hyperopia's main characteristics: First, hyperopia lowers a consumer's present likelihood of pursuing and consuming indulgences. Second, hyperopic individuals acknowledge their own difficulty with indulgence, and therefore should be capable of reporting these tendencies. Third, the hyperopic tendency to consistently forego indulgence can lead to retrospective regret and a sense of missing out on life (Kivetz and Keinan 2006).

In our first study, we measure individual level hyperopia and examine its relationship to basic outcomes. We propose that consumers high in hyperopia will generally consider a given set of products as more luxurious than will consumers low in hyperopia. Furthermore, we demonstrate that even when controlling for differences in perceived level of luxury, high hyperopia consumers have lower purchase intentions for luxuries than consumers low in hyperopia. Study 1 also provides evidence that high hyperopia is different from excessive self-control, suggesting that hyperopia is distinct from excessive levels of self-control.

Studies 2 and 3 seek to demonstrate a construal based level remedy for hyperopic consumers. In Study 2, we asked participants to adopt and elaborate on an indulgence goal:

Imagine that you have decided that although your financial future is important, you really should enjoy life more by worrying less about how you are spending your money or sticking to a particular budget, and instead focus more on the overall enjoyment of your life.

Immediately following these instructions, the level of construal at which participants were to consider the indulgence goal was manipulated using a laddering technique based on Fujita et al. (2006). For the low-level construal condition, participants were asked to consider *how* they might pursue the goal. For the high-level construal condition, participants were asked to consider *why* they might pursue the goal.

We then assessed perceived ease of achieving the indulgence goal. Results showed a significant interaction of hyperopia level and the level at which the goal was construed. Closer examination of this interaction reveals that the effects of construal were primarily among high hyperopia participants. When high hyperopia participants construed the indulgence goal at a higher level, they exhibited a significantly higher sense that they could pursue the goal in question than did those construing at a lower level.

In study 3, we manipulate the construal of an indulgence product through marketing communications. Specifically, participants read about a BMW, either in terms of specific, concrete attributes or higher-level benefits. Then, embedded among a series of distracter questions, we measured their sense that the car constituted a good investment (i.e., that it was consistent with long-term gains) and their purchase likelihood for the car. As in study 2, the ad containing the higher-level construal significantly increased perception of the vehicle as a good investment among high hyperopia consumers. This perception, in turn, mediated an increase in purchase likelihood among that group.

Overall, we reveal that hyperopia operates at a fundamental, perceptual level, creating an upward tendency in the degree to which a given item is seen as luxurious. Furthermore, hyperopic consumers express lower purchase intentions for luxury products, even when controlling for their own luxury perceptions. Studies 2 and 3 reveal that construal level moderates the effect of trait hyperopia. Importantly, we demonstrate that this occurs by altering the extent to which the luxury is seen as a long-term investment or gain, and is, therefore, consistent with the hyperopic consumer's tendencies. Thus, the present research provides insight into means of overcoming hyperopic tendencies (Kivetz and Simonson 2002). These theoretical contributions suggest that marketing communications can externally influence construal levels in ways that make luxury products less unappealing to the high hyperopia consumer. Practically, the present research suggests that retailers and consumers can create situations which are conducive to the hyperopic individual's ability to occasionally "Seize the day!" and make the most out of the opportunities life has to offer.

REFERENCES

Fujita, Kentaro, Yaacov Trope, Nira Liberman, and Maya Levin-Sagi (2006), "Construal Levels and Self-Control," *Journal of Personality and Social Psychology*, 90 (3), 351-67.

Kivetz, Ran and Itamar Simonson (2002), "Self-Control for the Righteous: Toward a Theory of Precommitment to Indulgence," *Journal of Consumer Research,* 29 (September), 199-217.

Kivetz, Ran and Anat Keinan (2006), "Repenting Hyperopia: An Analysis of Self-Control Regrets," *Journal of Consumer Research,* 33 (September), 273-82.

Liberman, Nira and Yaacov Trope (1998), "The Role of Feasibility and Desirability Considerations in Near and Distant Future Decisions: A Test of Temporal Construal Theory," *Journal of Personality and Social Psychology*, 75 (July), 5-18.

Mintel (2005), "Luxury Goods Retailing–US," accessed online at http://academic.mintel.com.

Schedules of Reinforcement, Learning, and Frequency Reward Programs

Adam Craig, University of South Carolina, USA
Timothy Silk, University of British Columbia, Canada

EXTENDED ABSTRACT

Recent studies have applied principles of operant conditioning to provide insight into consumer behavior in response to frequency reward programs (FRP's). Operant conditioning describes how both animals and humans acquire (learn) behavior through punishments and reinforcements experienced while behaving successively in the environment. With FRP's, consumers are rewarded each time they shop at a particular company, repeatedly purchase a product, or fly with a specific airline. They also avoid the loss of potential rewards by being loyal to the program. In all cases, effort (usually measured in time or dollars spent) is rewarded in the hope that consumers will exhibit loyalty and continue their purchasing efforts.

Consumer research on FRP's has focused primarily on fixed ratio (FR) reinforcement schedules. For example, Kivetz et al. (2006) employed a FR10 schedule that rewarded consumers after every 10 purchases and found that operant effort (i.e., the rate of purchase) increases as perceived distance to the goal decreases. While consumer research has reliably demonstrated that FR schedules can accelerate purchases, it has yet to examine other types of schedules found to generate higher response rates in other research domains. Research in operant conditioning and neuroscience has shown that variable ratio (VR) schedules generate faster rates of response than fixed ratio (FR) schedules using the same number of reinforcements (Ferster and Skinner, 1957). This implies that VR schedules have the potential to generate higher revenues with no increase in the cost of rewards. The current research examines the impact of variable ratio schedules in an FRP context.

The different response rates for FR and VR schedules is attributed to differences in the rate of learning each schedule. Fixed schedules are learned relatively easily since the reward recurs consistently after every nth purchase. Once the schedule is learned, subjects accelerate their behavior as they approach the next reward (i.e., as the psychological distance to the next reward decreases). However, participants in FR schedules tend to exhibit periods of inactivity immediately following a reward when the perceived distance to the next reward is at its greatest.

In contrast, VR schedules are learned less easily because the timing of each reinforcement varies over successive trials. The impeding affect of variability on learning is supported by research on multiple-cue learning (e.g., Mellers 1980), which shows that people have difficulty learning patterns that contain small amounts of error or randomness. The number of rewards administered by a VR schedule is the same as with an FR schedule, but the exact timing of the rewards in the behavioral sequence varies randomly. Because the reward occurs randomly and can be acquired (potentially) after any single operant response, perceived distance to the reward decreases, motivation to respond increases, and participants respond without cessation. This eliminates the post-reward pause observed with FR schedules, resulting in higher response rates. Variability also influences preference for reinforcement schedules. Wilson et al. (2005) find that people forecast that they will be happier when the timing of reinforcements is predictable. Yet, paradoxically, positive moods (Wilson et al. 2005) and neural responses (Berns et al. 2001) tend to last longer when the timing of reinforcements is uncertain.

Consistent with Wilson et al. (2005), we predict that consumers will prefer FRPs that administer rewards on a more certain or predictable schedule when given a choice among reward schedules. Consistent with Ferster and Skinner (1957), we predict FRPs that employ VR schedules will produce faster rates of purchase. The results of two experiments demonstrate the predicted response paradox: consumers predict they will purchase more and be more satisfied with predictable fixed ratio schedules, yet response rates are fastest when rewards are administered using unpredictable variable ratio schedules.

Experiment 1 examined consumer's self-predicted behaviors in response to three reinforcement schedules under consideration at their favorite coffee shop. The study employed a within-subjects design involving 33 undergraduates. Subjects were presented with descriptions of three reinforcement schedules: (1) FR5, (2) VR5 with high variability, (3) VR5 with low variability. As expected, consumers' predicted satisfaction and predicted purchase frequency were inversely related to the variability of the schedule.

Experiment 2 examined whether VR schedules generate faster, more frequent responses than FR schedules. Experiment 2 also examined whether increasing the variability of reward timing results in slower rates of learning and faster response times. One hundred and forty-four subjects were randomly assigned to one of four reinforcement schedules: (1) FR5 in which participants were rewarded after every 5th trial, (2) VR5 with low variability in which participants were rewarded after every four to six trials, (3) VR5 with high variability in which participants were rewarded after every two to eight trials, and (4) a no-reward control condition. The VR5 schedule with high variability generated the fastest rate of response, followed by the VR5 schedule with low variability, the FR5 schedule, and the no-reward control condition. Differences in response rates were attributable to differences in the rate at which consumers learned the schedules and anticipated rewards. Further, the rate of learning was inversely related to the variability of reward timing. In summary, the findings suggest that variable ratio schedules may be more profitable despite consumers' preferences for predictable rewards.

The Anticipation of Chosen Pleasures: Temporal Variations in the Valuation of Delayed Consumption

Elaine Chan, Hong Kong University of Science and Technology, Hong Kong, China
Anirban Mukhopadhyay, University of Michigan, USA

EXTENDED ABSTRACT

Consumers often make purchase decisions now for products and services to be consumed in the future. Research on the valuation of delayed consumption has mixed findings. Discounted utility theory (Ainslie 1975) demonstrates that delayed consumption is valued less than immediate consumption ("discounting"). However, other research (Loewenstein 1987) indicates that individuals may savor the pleasantness of future consumption, implying that delayed consumption is instead valued more ("anticipation"). This research investigates the conditions under which individuals discount versus anticipate future consumption, and proposes that the extent of intrinsic motivation towards the consumption is an important moderating factor. Specifically, we predict that two variables—autonomy, as manifested by choosing agent, and perceived control, as manifested by length of delay—which we predict influence intrinsic motivation and hence the temporal valuation of delayed consumption.

Extant research has demonstrated that choosing one's option provides autonomy and increases motivation to persist at the chosen activity (Deci and Ryan 1985). We therefore hypothesize that when individuals choose their own consumption, the associated autonomy provides intrinsic motivation to engage in the consumption, and a goal of consumption is activated. If this goal is not satiated over time, its intensity may increase (Bargh et al. 2001), leading to anticipation. In contrast, if the consumption is chosen by someone else, the lower autonomy and correspondingly intrinsic motivation will lead not to anticipation, but rather discounting of the delayed consumption—causing evaluations to decrease with time.

However, two factors may be at play here. When the delay extends beyond a certain point, individuals may perceive other uncontrollable external factors decreasing their perceived control over the consumption thereby reducing the intrinsic motivation. Hence as the length of delay increases, the positive effect of autonomy on intrinsic motivation may get swamped by the increasingly negative effect of decrease in perceived control. As a result, beyond a certain point there should be a net negative effect on intrinsic motivation. Therefore, we hypothesize that when individuals make their own choices, the valuation of delayed consumption will first increase and then decrease as the temporal separation between choice and consumption increases.

We tested these hypotheses in three experiments. In experiment 1, participants were told that a drama festival was due to start either the same day or one week later. They then read descriptions of three dramas, of which one had been pretested to be significantly more interesting. Next, half the participants chose which drama they would like to watch, while the other half were told which drama their friend had chosen for them (the "more interesting" option). Subsequently, they were asked to imagine that the drama was to start in a few hours but there was a thunderstorm outside (as in Gourville and Soman 1998). Given this scenario, participants were asked how likely they would go to watch the drama. As predicted, results revealed that intention increased with delay in the self-choice condition, but decreased in the other-choice condition.

Experiment 2 used real delays between choice and consumption, and included an additional longer delay condition. We also directly manipulated inherent interest to test whether the anticipation effect is driven by intrinsic motivation. We expected that the inverted u-shaped relationship between evaluation and time would occur only for consumption that is of high (vs. low) inherent interest. In contrast, evaluations should decline with time when someone else chooses the option, regardless of the level of inherent interest. The fourth aim of this experiment was to test the proposed mediating effect of intrinsic motivation. Similar to experiment 1, participants were told that a music festival was to be held either the same day, one week later, or two weeks later. Inherent interest was manipulated using genre: participants in the high [low] interest condition read about two pop [classical] music concerts. The procedure was the same as before: participants either chose the concert for themselves or were told which concert their closest friend had chosen. Subsequently (vs. after a week / two weeks), participants reported their evaluations and intrinsic motivation towards the concert. Consistent with our prediction, when they chose their own concert, there was a significant quadratic trend (i.e. more positive evaluations in the short-delay than in no-delay and long-delay conditions) but only in the high interest condition. When the concert was chosen by someone else, there was a linear trend such that participants in the no-delay condition reported more positive evaluations than in the delay conditions. Further, as hypothesized, this effect was fully mediated by intrinsic motivation.

Experiment 3 aimed to further increase confidence in the inverted u-shaped relationship in the self-choice condition by using real decisions as well as delays. We also wanted to investigate the effect on post-consumption evaluations. Participants were first asked to choose between two variants of chocolate. Then, either immediately, one week, two weeks, or one month later, they provided their pre-consumption evaluations. Finally, after tasting their chosen chocolate, they reported post-consumption evaluations. Replicating the previous pattern, pre-consumption evaluations showed a significant quadratic trend such that evaluations were more positive in the one-week condition than in the same day, two-week and one-month conditions. As before, this effect was mediated by intrinsic motivation. In contrast, post-consumption evaluation measures revealed an ironic negative effect—participants evaluated the chocolate more *negatively* in the one-week condition than in the other three conditions. Evidently, those who anticipated more prior to consumption reported lower post-consumption evaluations.

Taken together, our results demonstrate that when consumers make their own choices, there is an inverted u-shaped relationship between pre-consumption evaluation and delay. We also show that the anticipation effect is driven by consumers' intrinsic motivation towards the consumption, and thus only occurs for consumption that is of high inherent interest. When somebody else makes the choice for them, evaluations decline as consumption is delayed. The moderating effect of choice on the discounting and anticipation effects; the fact that that this is due to differences in intrinsic motivation; and the inverted u-shape of the anticipation effect; the three are key contributions of this paper.

REFERENCES

Ainslie, George (1975), "Specious Reward: A Behavioral Theory of Impulsiveness and Impulse Control," *Psychological Bulletin*, 82 (July), 463-96.

Bargh, John A., Peter M. Gollwitzer, Annette Lee-Chai, Kimberby Barndollar, and Roman Trotschel (2001), "The Automated Will: Nonconscious Activation and Pursuit of Behavioral Goals," *Journal of Personality and Social Psychology,* 81 (6), 1014-27.

Deci, Edward L. and Richard M. Ryan (1985), *Intrinsic Motivation and Self-Determination in Human Behavior*, New York, Plenum Press.

Gourville, John T. and Dilip Soman (1998), "Payment Depreciation: The Behavioral Effects of Temporally Separating Payments from Consumption," *Journal of Consumer Research*, 25 (September), 160-74.

Loewenstein, George (1987), "Anticipation and the Valuation of Delayed Consumption," *The Economic Journal*, 97 (September), 666-84.

The Role of Goals in the Relationship Between Counterfactual Thinking and Behavioral Intentions

Anu Sivaraman, University of Delaware, USA
Parthasarathy Krishnamurthy, University of Houston, USA

ABSTRACT

This paper focuses on why and how counterfactual thinking (CFT) affects information processing and behavioral intentions. Earlier research has indicated that CFT influences the ability to discriminate between superior and inferior arguments, but did not directly examine the underlying process. Also, even when CFT affects future behavioral intentions, it is not clear how it does so. Across three studies we find that the underlying process is more akin to elaboration than priming. Also, we find that, when CFT influences behavioral intentions, it does so by increasing goal strength.

Counterfactual Thinking as a Post-hoc Consumption Expectation

Jessica Y. Y. Kwong, The Chinese University of Hong Kong, China
Candy K. Y. Ho, The Chinese University of Hong Kong, China

EXTENDED ABSTRACT

Consumer expectation of a consumption experience is seen as pivotal in determining consumer responses to the consumption experience because it serves as a comparison standard against which the consumption is evaluated (e.g., Oliver 1980; Oliver and DeSarbo 1988). Research to date has conceptualized consumer expectations as a set of prior beliefs about a product or service (Olson and Dover 1979), indicating that they are formed before consumption. While these prior expectations are useful as generic and relatively stable standards for evaluating any consumption experience, they might be too general for assessing one particular incident. We argue that after receiving an outcome, consumers may also retrospectively generate case-to-case "customized standards" to evaluate that particular consumption incident. These instantaneous standards are highly contextualized that they may be relevant to the current situation only, and may even be contradictory to general preexisting expectations. In the present research, we investigate consumers' retrospective construction of a "customized standard" for a particular consumption instance and examine its effects on consumer responses to the consumption.

It is proposed that in instances of negative consumption experience, consumers' counterfactual thoughts of "what the company *could* have done" serve as a retrospectively constructed expectation of "what the company *should* have done" and determine consumers' postpurchase responses. Counterfactual thinking is the imagination of alternatives to a factual event in which the factual outcome is undone by altering an antecedent event. For instance, a customer who finds that a fast food shop has stopped selling food just a few minutes before he/she arrives may generate a counterfactual thought that he/she would have made the purchase had the counter extended the service hours just a little bit longer. At that instance, the customer may take that hypothetical action that the company could have done, that is, close later, as what the company should have done. By underscoring what the company should have done and yet failed to do, company-related counterfactuals signal the company is at fault. This will lead to negative reactions toward the company.

We further propose that the extent of negative reactions toward the company depends on the ease of generating those counterfactual actions. The easier it is for the consumers to imagine a company could have done something differently, the stronger is the belief that the company should have acted accordingly. Hence, we hypothesize that consumers would react more unfavorably towards the company in situations where it would be easier to generate company-related counterfactual thoughts.

In addition, we also hypothesize that consumers' negative reactions will be tempered in the presence of self-related counterfactual thoughts. For example, consumers may react less negatively to the fast food shop when they dropped by somewhere (e.g., grocery store) on their way to the fast food shop than when they did not. The counterfactual of not visiting another place suggests the self as another antecedent that could have turned the situation around. People in general have a tendency to discount the weight of one antecedent given another (Kelley 1972). Thus, the impact of the company-related counterfactual thoughts on consumers' reactions may depend on the availability of other company-unrelated counterfactual thoughts, such that this effect

may be attenuated when it is easy to generate company-unrelated counterfactual thoughts, such as those related to oneself.

We assessed our ideas using scenario experiments, in which undergraduate students participated for course credits. Study 1 tested the effect of company-related counterfactuals on consumers' postpurchase responses. In the scenario, the ease of generating company-related counterfactuals was altered by temporal closeness. It was easier to generate such thoughts when the temporal closeness for the counterfactual actions was high than when it was low.

Consistent with our contention that temporal closeness should facilitate the construction of company-related counterfactuals, participants in the temporally-close condition (vs. the temporally-far condition) elicited a significantly higher proportion of company-related thoughts. Parallel to our predictions, participants in the temporally-close condition reported significantly higher dissatisfaction toward the company and also higher negative postpurchase intentions than did those in the temporally-far condition. More important, these findings could not be explained by the idea that consumers' reactions are driven by their prior beliefs about the consumption experience. In fact, the findings were in a direction opposite to those predicted by consumers' preexisting beliefs.

Study 2 was conducted to show that the impact of company-related counterfactuals was attenuated by the presence of self-related counterfactuals. The study independently manipulated the ease of generating company-related counterfactuals and that of generating self-related counterfactuals.

Consistent with study 1, participants who generated more company-related counterfactuals reported greater dissatisfaction and negative postpurchase intentions towards the company. However, as our discounting argument predicted, this pattern was attenuated among those who generated a higher proportion of self-related counterfactuals. The thought protocols yielded further support that the participants relied on the post-hoc-generated company-related counterfactuals as the standard for evaluations. Again, the results were opposite to the predictions derived on the basis of consumers' preexisting general beliefs.

To conclude, this research highlights the role of post-hoc-constructed expectations in influencing consumers' responses from a counterfactual thinking perspective. Results from two studies provide converging evidence that counterfactual thoughts of what the company could have done to bring a better outcome set as post-hoc standards for evaluations. The easier is this process, the more dissatisfied are the consumers. This tendency, nevertheless, is attenuated when company-unrelated counterfactual thoughts, such as those related to the consumers themselves, are generated simultaneously. Findings in the current studies could not be readily explained by consumers' prior expectations. This highlights the uniqueness of post-hoc expectation as standards for evaluations.

REFERENCES

Kelley, H. H. (1972), "Causal Schemata and the Attribution Process," in *Attribution: Perceiving the Causes of Behavior*, eds. Edward E. Jones, D. E. Kanouse, H. H. Kelley, R. E. Nisbett, S. Valins, and B. Weiner, Morristown, NJ: General Learning Press, 151–74.

Oliver, Richard L. (1980), "A Cognitive Model of the Antecedents and Consequences of Satisfaction Decisions," *Journal of
Marketing Research*, 17 (November), 460–9.

_____ and Wayne S. DeSarbo (1988), "Response Determinants
in Satisfaction Judgments," *Journal of Consumer Research*,
14 (March), 495–507.

Olson, Jerry C. and Philip Dover (1979), "Disconfirmation of
Consumer Expectations Through Product Trial," *Journal of
Applied Psychology*, 64 (April), 179–89.

The Role of Alternative Causes and Disabling Conditions on Consumers' Acceptance of Product Claims

Elise Chandon, Virginia Tech, USA
Chris Janiszewski, University of Florida, USA

EXTENDED ABSTRACT

Causal conditional reasoning involves making inferences on the basis of an "if p then q" statement (i.e., a conditional premise), where p is the antecedent (i.e., cause) and q is the consequent (i.e., effect). In the field of marketing, product claims often take the form of a conditional premise. The goal of advertisers is to convince consumers that brands are a "true" cause of beneficial effects. For instance, Crest toothpaste uses the slogan *Crest fights cavities* in an attempt to persuade potential customers that if they use Crest toothpaste, then they will not develop cavities.

Product claims can be formulated in many different ways. First, product claims can either focus on the presence (i.e., usage) or absence (i.e., non-usage) of the brand and the resulting impact on the effect. Second, ad claims can lead with the cause (e.g., *Pantene Pro-V: For hair so healthy it shines*) or the effect (e.g., *How do you spell relief: R-O-L-A-I-D-S*). Manipulating these two variables (usage or non-usage of the brand and presentation order) offers four possible ways to express a product claim. Examples of product claims that fit into each of these classifications (see Table).

Prior research investigating a person's willingness to accept a causal claim has focused on two types of counterarguments (Cummins 1995; Cummins et al. 1991; Dieussaert, Schaeken, and D'Ydewalle 2002): the availability of alternatives causes and the availability of disabling conditions. An alternative cause is a possible cause that can generate the effect and a disabling condition is a situation which prevents the effect from happening despite the presence of the cause. A person's ability to think of *disabling conditions* can make a claim less believable. For example, knowing that people with high sugar diets are more likely to have cavities may decrease a person's willingness to believe that Crest prevents cavities. The presence of disabling conditions cast doubt on the sufficiency of the cause (e.g., using Crest). Second, the person's ability to think of *alternative causes* can make a claim less believable. For example, knowing that good oral hygiene also prevents cavities may reduce a person's willingness to believe that Crest prevents cavities. The presence of alternative causes casts doubt on the necessity of the cause.

We contend that the persuasiveness of a product claim will depend on the accessibility and diagnosticity (e.g., Feldman and Lynch 1988; Wyer and Hartwick 1980) of disabling conditions and alternative causes. Experiment 1 investigates the diagnosticity of disabling conditions or alternative causes for assessing the believability of a conditional premise. We ask participants to read a conditional premise, to list disabling conditions or alternative causes, and to make a conditional inference. We show that listing disabling conditions influences the acceptance of a modus ponens (MP) and a modus tollens (MT) conditional premise, but not an affirmation of the consequent (AC) and a denial of the antecedent (DA) conditional premise. Similarly, we show that listing alternative causes influences the acceptance of an AC and a DA conditional premise, but not a MP and a MT conditional premise.

Experiment 1 focused on documenting the types of counterarguments (i.e., reasons) that influence the acceptability of a conditional premise. In effect, it investigated the diagnosticity of specific type of counterarguments. Yet, when a person assesses the validity of an advertising claim, counterarguments are self-generated. Are there factors that influence the type of counterarguments that are accessible (Rholes and Pryor 1982; Roese, Sanna, and Galinsky 2005)? The conditional reasoning literature is silent on that issue but there is suggestive evidence in the counterfactual literature that the accessibility of different types of counterarguments will depend on the framing of the causal claim (Roese, Hur, and Pennington 1999).

In experiment 2, we investigate the joint influence of the accessibility and diagnosticity of disabling conditions or alternative causes on the believability of a causal claim. We show that a claim framed as achieving a gain is more believable in a MP argument format (e.g., "If you use a deodorant soap, then you will remove body odor.") than a DA argument format (e.g., "If you do not use a deodorant soap, then you will not remove body odor."). In contrast, a claim framed as preventing a loss is more believable in a DA argument format (e.g., "If you do not use a deodorant soap, then you will not prevent body odor.") than a MP argument format (e.g., "If you use a deodorant soap, then you will prevent body odor.").

The results show a complex, but predictable, pattern of acceptance of product claims depending on the claim frame and the argument format. Most importantly, the results show that one argument format (i.e., MT) is not universally the best argument type. It is also interesting to note that a number of existing product claims are being stated in a manner that limits their acceptance.

REFERENCES

Cummins, Denise D. (1995), "Naive Theories and Causal Deduction," *Memory & Cognition*, 25 (September), 646-658

Cummins, Denise D., Todd Lubart, Olaf Alksnis, and Robert Rist (1991), "Conditional Reasoning and Causation," *Memory & Cognition*, 19 (May), 274-82.

Dieussaert, Kristien, Walter Schaeken, and Gery D'Ydewalle (2002), "The Relative Contribution of Content and Context Factors on the Interpretation of Conditionals," *Experimental Psychology*, 49 (July), 181-95.

Feldman, Jack M. and John G. Lynch (1988), "Self-generated Validity and Other Effects of Measurement on Belief, Attitude, Intention, and Behavior," *Journal of Applied Psychology*, 73 (August), 421-435.

Rholes, William S. and John B. Pryor (1982), "Cognitive Accessibility and Causal Attributions," *Personality and Social Psychology Bulletin*, 8 (December), 719-727.

Roese, Neal J., Taekyun Hur, and Ginger L. Pennington (1999), "Counterfactual Thinking and Regulatory Focus: Implications for Action versus Inaction and Sufficiency versus Necessity," *Journal of Personality and Social Psychology*, 77 (December), 1109-1120.

Roese, Neal J., Lawrence J. Sanna, and Adam D. Galinsky (2005), "The Mechanics of Imagination: Automaticity and Control in Counterfactual Thinking," in *The New Unconscious*, eds. Ran R. Hassin, James S. Uleman, and John A. Bargh, New York, NY, US: Oxford University Press, 138-170.

TABLE

Conditional Premise	Product Claim	Argument Format
Cause, therefore effect	*Pantene Pro-V: For Hair So Healthy It Shines*	Modus Ponens (MP)
Not effect, therefore not cause	*If it is not trail rated, it is not a Jeep 4x4*	Modus Tollens (MT)
Effect, therefore cause	*How do you spell relief: R-O-L-A-I-D-S*	Affirmation of the Consequent (AC)
Not cause, therefore not effect	*If you haven' t relaxed on a French Quarter balcony, you haven' t lived yet*	Denial of the Antecedent (DA)

Wyer, Robert S. and Jon Hartwick (1980), "The Role of Information Retrieval and Conditional Inference Processes in Belief Change," in *Advances in Experimental Social Psychology; Volume 13*, ed. L. Berkowitz, New York: Academic Press, 243-284.

Is that Bargain Worth My Time?

Ritesh Saini, George Mason University, USA
Raghunath Singh Rao, University of Texas at Austin, USA
Ashwani Monga, University of South Carolina, USA

EXTENDED ABSTRACT

Consumers love bargains. The possibility of cheaper products urges people to drive to far-flung outlet malls; the prospect of getting a discount makes them clip and save coupons; and the promise of instant savings at the time of purchase is reason enough to sign up for the store-specific credit card. But how far are consumers willing to go in order to get such bargains? Consider an example of two stores: Store A sells a shirt for $20 but Store B sells the same shirt for $10. Would a consumer, who is already in Store A, be willing to take a five-minute drive to Store B in order to save $10? Furthermore, would the consumer be willing to drive to save $10 if the price at Store A were $60?

Traditional economic theories suggest that consumers should base this decision simply on how much they value the benefit of $10 versus the cost of a five-minute drive (Stigler 1987). However, research on relative thinking suggests that a discount of $10 seems *less* appealing if the price is $60 rather than $20. In other words, people demonstrate relative thinking (Azar 2007; Thaler 1980; Tversky and Kahneman 1981). This notion is significant for marketers because it implies that, given a fixed sales-promotion budget aimed at increasing store traffic, a manager ought to make discounts more attractive by applying them on products that are priced low rather than high. We delineate the conditions under which this strategy would make sense, but also other conditions in which managers ought to do the opposite. We show that a $10 discount can sometimes seem *more* appealing on a price of $60 rather than $20.

Relying on the strength of multidisciplinary research, we rely on a mathematical model to derive new predictions that we then test in behavioral studies. Our theorizing involves a consideration of referent thinking, which involves the reference price that one expects to pay (Kalyanaram and Winer 1995; Winer 1986). We employ an analytical model to study how two behavioral tendencies—relative and referent thinking—interact when they are jointly incorporated into the prospect theory value function. This leads to three novel predictions: (1) A relative-thinking effect will emerge when the actual price turns out to be the same as expected. That is, consumers will be more willing to seek a bargain on a product that is priced low rather than high. (2) A referent-thinking effect, which is opposite to the relative-thinking effect, will emerge when the actual price deviates from the expected price. That is, consumers will be more willing to seek a bargain on a product that is priced high rather than low. (3) A relative-thinking effect will emerge yet again when actual prices become extremely discrepant from the reference price.

The above predictions are supported in three laboratory experiments that employ an infrequently-purchased product category (blankets) and a frequently-purchased product category (gasoline). An additional study attests to the counter-intuitiveness of our results and provides evidence that these effects might be occurring without people being aware of them. Specifically, when a group of participants were given details about one of our experiments and asked to predict what the results would have been, they suggested a pattern that was consistent with relative thinking, but opposite to the referent-thinking results that we actually found.

From a theoretical standpoint, we help better understand the factors that determine the effectiveness of bargains such as price promotions. We also help provide a more nuanced view of prior research on relative thinking (Tversky and Kahneman 1981). To research on internal reference prices (Kalyanaram and Winer 1995), we add the notion that the influence of reference prices stretches beyond perceptions of actual prices; they also change perceptions of promotions that are offered on those prices. Finally, we present a framework that affords wide applicability. For instance, our framework can be extended to incorporate time-money differences (Okada and Hoch 2004; Saini and Monga 2008) in order to examine how bargain-seeking behavior varies with whether the cost of seeking a bargain is in terms of time or money. Similarly, it can help understand the effect of other consumer benefits, beyond the monetary promotions that we studied.

From a managerial standpoint, our results offer direct suggestions regarding enhancing the effectiveness of a fixed sales promotion budget by considering not only product prices, but also the deviations of those prices from expected prices. Depending on the situation, a fixed sales-promotion budget should sometimes be allocated to cheap products (loss leaders) but to more expensive products (big-ticket items) at other times. Finally, recommendations arise in terms of when promotions ought to be framed in absolute terms ($X off), and when in relative terms (Y% off).

REFERENCES

Azar, Ofer H. (2007), "Relative Thinking Theory," *Journal of Socio-Economics*, 36 (1), 1-14.

Darke, Peter R. and Jonathan L. Freedman (1993), "Deciding Whether to Seek a Bargain: Effects of Both Amount and Percentage Off," *Journal of Applied Psychology*, 78 (6), 960-65.

Ho, Teck H., Noah Lim, and Colin F. Camerer (2006), "Modeling the Psychology of Consumer and Firm Behavior with Behavioral Economics," *Journal of Marketing Research*, 43 (August), 307-31.

Kahneman, Daniel and Amos Tversky (1979), "Prospect Theory: An Analysis of Decision Under Risk," *Econometrica*, 47 (March), 263-92.

Kalwani, Manohar U., Chi Kin Yim, Heikki J. Rinne, and Yoshi Sugita (1990), "A Price Expectations Model of Customer Brand Choice," *Journal of Marketing Research*, 27 (August), 251-62.

Kalyanaram, Gurumurthy and Russell S. Winer (1995), "Empirical Generalizations From Reference Price Research," *Marketing Science*, 14 (3), G161-69.

Koszegi, Botond and Matthew Rabin (2006), "A Model of Reference-Dependent Preferences," *Quarterly Journal of Economics*, 121 (November), 1133-65.

Miller, Richard L. (1962), "Dr. Weber and the Consumer," *Journal of Marketing*, 26 (January), 57-61.

Monroe, Kent B. (2003), *Pricing: Making Profitable Decisions*, New York: McGraw-Hill/ Irwin.

Moon, Philip, Kevin Keasey, and Darren Duxbury (1999), Mental Accounting and Decision Making: The Relationship Between Relative and Absolute Savings," *Journal of Economic Behavior and Organization*, 38 (February), 145-53.

Mowen, Maryanne M. and John C. Mowen (1986), "An Empirical Examination of the Biasing Effects of Framing on Business Decisions," *Decision Sciences*, 17 (October), 596-602.

Nunes, Joseph C. and C. Whan Park (2003), "Incommensurate Resources: Not Just More of the Same," *Journal of Marketing Research*, 40 (February), 26-38.

Okada, Erica M. and Stephen J. Hoch (2004), "Spending Time versus Spending Money," *Journal of Consumer Research*, 31 (September), 313-23.

Ranyard, Rob and D. Abdel-Nabi (1993), "Mental Accounting and the Process of Multiattribute Choice," *Acta Psychologica*, 84 (2), 161-77.

Saini, Ritesh and Ashwani Monga (2008), "How I Decide Depends on What I Spend: Use of Heuristics is Greater for Time than for Money," *Journal of Consumer Research*, 34, 6 (April), 914-922.

Stigler, George J. (1987), *The Theory of Price*, New York: Macmillan.

Thaler, Richard H. (1980), "Toward a Positive Theory of Consumer Choice," *Journal of Economic Behavior and Organization*, 1 (1), 39-60.

Thaler, Richard H. (1985), "Mental Accounting and Consumer Choice," *Marketing Science*, 4 (Summer), 199-214.

Tversky, Amos and Daniel Kahneman (1981), "The Framing of Decisions and the Psychology of Choice," *Science*, 211 (4481), 453-8.

Tversky, Amos and Daniel Kahneman (1991), "Loss Aversion in Riskless Choice: A Reference-Dependent Model," *Quarterly Journal of Economics*, 106 (November), 1039-61.

Tversky, Amos and Daniel Kahneman (1992), "Advances in Prospect Theory: Cumulative Representation of Uncertainty," *Journal of Risk and Uncertainty*, 5 (October), 297-323.

Winer, Russell S. (1986), "A Reference Price Model of Brand Choice for Frequently Purchase Products," *Journal of Consumer Research*, 13 (September), 250-6.

The Differential Promotion Effectiveness on Hedonic versus Utilitarian Products

Yuhuang Zheng, Tsinghua University, China
Ran Kivetz, Columbia University, USA

EXTENDED ABSTRACT

Prior research in social sciences (e.g., Kivetz and Simonson 2002; Kivetz and Zheng 2006; Maslow 1970; Prelec and Loewenstein 1998; Weber 1998) suggests that consumers feel more difficult to justify spending money on hedonic than utilitarian products because of the inherent disadvantages of hedonic luxuries compared with utilitarian necessities. Consequently, we propose that consumers have a stronger need for justification and are more likely to rely on external justifications such as promotions to help them make a purchase decision when buying hedonic products than buying utilitarian ones. Therefore, it is predicted that promotions have a stronger effect on the purchase likelihood of hedonic rather than utilitarian products. This and other related propositions are tested in a series of studies using a variety of promotion programs and product categories in different price ranges.

Study 1 tests the proposition that promotions have a stronger effect on the purchase likelihood of hedonic products than utilitarian ones in three separate tests using different types of products. In each test, respondents were randomly assigned to one of the four conditions in a 2 (product type: hedonic vs. utilitarian) X 2 (promotion availability: available vs. unavailable) between-subjects design. Consistent with our hypothesis, in all three tests, promotions had a stronger positive effect on the purchase likelihood of the hedonic products than utilitarian products (all p's<.05). Specifically, in the first test (DVD movie vs. ink cartridge), for the hedonic product (DVD movie), promotion had a significant positive effect on the purchase likelihood (13% vs. 47%, $p<.001$). In contrast, for the utilitarian product (ink cartridge), promotion did not have a significant positive effect on the purchase likelihood (77% vs. 87%, $p>.1$). The difference in the observed promotion effects between hedonic product and utilitarian product conditions is statistically significant ($p<.05$). Similarly, in the second test (LCD TV vs. desktop PC), for the hedonic product (LCD TV), promotion had a significant positive effect on the purchase likelihood (46% vs. 81%, $p<.001$). In contrast, for the utilitarian product (desktop PC), promotion did not have any effect on the purchase likelihood (78% vs. 78%, $p>.1$). The difference in the observed promotion effects between hedonic product and utilitarian product conditions is statistically significant ($p<.01$). Finally, in the third test (Time Out New York magazine vs. Time magazine), for the hedonic product (Time Out New York magazine), promotion had a significant positive effect on the purchase likelihood (12% to 42%, $p<.01$). In contrast, for the utilitarian product (Time magazine), promotion did not have a significant positive effect on the purchase likelihood (54% vs. 37%, $p>.1$). The difference in the observed promotion effects between hedonic product and utilitarian product conditions is statistically significant ($p<.01$).

Study 2 further tests the proposed conceptualization by holding constant the product in all conditions while manipulating consumption goals (hedonic vs. utilitarian) across conditions. Specifically, Study 2 employed a 2 (consumption goal: hedonic vs. utilitarian) X 2 (promotion availability: available vs. unavailable) between-subjects design. The results show that while promotions had a significant positive effect on the purchase likelihood of a digital camcorder when the consumption goal was hedonic (for vacation) (32% vs. 68%, $p<.001$), the same promotion did not have a significant effect on the purchase likelihood of the same camcorder when the consumption goal was utilitarian (for study) (63 vs. 74%,

$p>.1$). The interaction effect between promotion availability and consumption goal was significant ($p<.05$).

Study 3 was designed to test the conceptualization by investigating the differential effects of promotions when a product is purchased for self compared to when a product is purchased as a gift for others. Specifically, Study 3 employed a 2 (hedonic product vs. utilitarian product) X 2 (promotion available vs. promotion unavailable) X 2 (for the self vs. for others as a gift) between-subjects design. Consistent with the proposed conceptualization, the results demonstrate that for hedonic products, promotions had differential effects on the purchase likelihood of the hedonic product when it was purchased for the self (25% vs. 73%, $p<.001$) compared to when it was purchased as a gift for others (71% vs. 86%, $p<.1$) (interaction effect $p<.05$). In contrast, for utilitarian products, there was no significant differential effects of promotion on the purchase likelihood of the utilitarian product when it was purchased for self (20% vs. 40%, $p<.05$) compared to when it was purchased as a gift for others (46% vs. 61%, $p<.1$) (interaction effect $p>.1$). The 3-way interaction effect between product type, promotion availability and whether the product is purchased for the self or for others as a gift was marginally significant in the predicted direction ($p<.1$),

Study 4 investigates the underlying psychological processes of the differential promotion effectiveness by examining the moderating role of justifications in the positive effect of promotions on purchasing or choosing hedonic products. Specifically, Study 4 employed a 2 (justification availability: available vs. unavailable) X 2 (promotion availability: available vs. unavailable) between-subjects design. The results show that while promotions have a strong positive effect on the purchase likelihood of hedonic products (28% vs. 75%, $p<.001$), such effect is eliminated when consumers are asked to carefully think of reasons before they make their decisions (50% vs. 56%, $p>.1$). The interaction effect was significant in the predicted direction ($p<.01$), supporting the moderating role of justifications in the positive effect of promotions on the purchase likelihood of hedonic products.

In sum, the findings of Studies 1-4 are consistent with our proposed conceptualization that consumers find it more difficult to justify spending money on hedonic luxuries for themselves and therefore they have a stronger need for and are more sensitive to external justifications such as promotions. In the final section, we discuss the implications of the findings for marketing managers and for the literature of sales promotion.

REFERENCES

Kivetz, Ran and Itamar Simonson (2002), "Self-Control for the Righteous: Towards a Theory of Pre-commitment to Indulgence," *Journal of Consumer Research*, 29 (September), 199-217.

Kivetz, Ran and Yuhuang Zheng (2006), "Determinants of Justification and Self-Control," *Journal of Experimental Psychology: General*, 135 (4), November, 572-587.

Maslow, Abraham H. (1970), *Motivation and Personality*, 2nd ed. New York: Harper and Row.

Prelec, Drazen and Richard J. Herrnstein (1991), "Preferences or Principles: Alternative Guidelines for Choice," in *Strategy and Choice*, ed. R. J. Zechenhauser, Cambridge, MA: MIT, 319-340.

Weber, Max (1998), *The Protestant Ethic and the Spirit of Capitalism*, 2nd ed. Los Angeles: Roxbury.

Gambling for a Discount: Preferring Discount Per Item to Discount Per Purchase?

Bernadette Kamleitner, University of London, UK
Mandeep K. Dhami, University of Cambridge, UK
David R. Mandel, DRDG Toronto, Canada

EXTENDED ABSTRACT

Price discounts are a well-studied promotional method (e.g., Hardesty and Bearden 2003). How discounts are offered has an influence on consumers' deal perception (e.g., DelVecchio, Krishnan, and Smith 2007). Although various discount frames have been investigated, there remains a paucity of research on risky discounts. These are discounts that are determined by a chance procedure (e.g., 'scratch & save" cards). Research on risky discounts is needed because they are actually offered and because they differ from other discount formats in at least one important respect: even after choosing a product, consumers do not know how much discount they will receive. Consumers receiving risky discounts are playing a gamble with an unknown outcome.

To enhance our understanding of risky discounts we assess in three studies whether consumers prefer to get risky discounts per purchase or per item and why they prefer one discount format over the other. In fact, these options differ with regard to several respects (e.g., saving distribution) but they do not differ with regard to expected values.

Study 1 was conducted in an environment where risky discounts are offered, in Canada. 150 participants completed a questionnaire on a 'scratch & save' card discount policy. According to this policy customers pick a card and scratch it to reveal their particular discount rate. Each card informs about possible discount rates (e.g., 10%, 25%, 50%) and their associated probabilities. Participants were asked to choose between getting such a discount per item (i.e., separate cards for each item) or per purchase (i.e. one card overall). Options do not differ with regard to expected value. After choosing a discount format, participants were asked to report their main reason for their choice.

A significant majority of participants (82%) chose the item-specific discount. The main reason given was that participants thought that this option would be more likely to provide them with a higher discount. Some thought they would get a higher discount overall, others thought that they would get a higher discount at least once, but most did not further clarify their claim. Some of those choosing the purchase-specific discount also did so because they believed that purchase-specific discounts would be superior with regard to expected discount. However, most choosing the purchase-specific discount did so because they preferred to keep things simple.

Participants of Study 1 were familiar with risky discounts in general but they were not familiar with item-specific discounts. To ensure that results were not due to a familiarity bias Study 2 replicated Study 1 in a country where purchase-specific and item-specific risky discounts are equally novel to consumers, the UK. 67 participants participated in an exact replication of Study 1. Again, a significant majority of participants (67%) preferred the item-specific discount. The differences in reasons mentioned across options largely corresponded to those established in Study 1. Most participants preferred one discount per item because the probability of receiving a higher discount was perceived as being higher, i.e. participants appeared to be more hopeful.

Study 3 aimed to corroborate these findings using a different design. 54 participants read a scenario that was based on the discount policy used in the previous studies. Participants were told that one shopper, Susan is offered one 'scratch & save' card for her purchase of four items whereas another shopper, Molly, is offered four cards for the same items. Participants answered four questions designed to shed light on their underlying preferences: They had to indicate whether Susan, Molly or both equally would (a) be more hopeful when starting to scratch, (b) have better chances to get an overall discount of more than 25% off, (c) and of at least 50% off, and (d) spread more positive word-of-mouth communication about the shop. Separate analyses for each of these questions show that item-specific discounts are perceived as inspiring more hope, as more likely to lead to a higher discount and as more likely to lead to positive word-of-mouth communication.

Across studies we found that consumers prefer risky item-specific discounts to risky purchase-specific discounts, mainly because they seem to inspire more hope. Interestingly, this hope does not seem to relate to actual characteristics of savings distributions. In study 3, consumers were not able to realize actual changes in overall outcome probabilities that result from splitting a purchase-specific discount into multiple discounts per item. Rather, across studies many consumers seemed to be hopeful either because of a biased perception of probabilities or because the item-specific discount option led to a shift in mindset: many consumers choosing the item-specific discount seemed to aim to at least once "hit the jackpot" rather than making a good deal overall. From a retailer's perspective, offering item-specific risky discounts is rational as long as discount administration is feasible. In particular the observed shift in mindsets may lead to more satisfied consumers: In the case of purchase-specific discounts, only those getting an overall high rare discount will be especially satisfied. In the case of item-specific discounts, all those getting a high discount on one single item will be satisfied.

Considering that not everyone preferred item-specific discounts and that there is still much to learn (e.g., verifying the observed preference across product categories and different amounts of items) we recommend offering a choice between purchase-specific and product-specific risky discounts rather then forcing consumers into one discount format. Risky discounts make it possible to offer consumers such a choice.

REFERENCES

Chakraborty, Goutam and Catherine Cole (1991), "Coupon Characteristics and Brand Choice," *Psychology and Marketing*, 8 (3), 145-59.

Chandrashekaran, Rajesh and Dhruv Grewal (2003), "Assimilation of Advertised Reference Prices: The Moderating Role of Involvement," *Journal of Retailing*, 79 (1), 53-62.

Chen, Shih-Fen S., Kent B. Monroe, and Yung-Chien Lou (1998), "The Effects of Framing Price Promotion Messages on Consumers' Perceptions and Purchase Intentions," *Journal of Retailing*, 74 (3), 353-72.

DeKay, Michael L. and Tai Guy Kim (2005), "When Things Don't Add Up," *Psychological Science*, 16 (9), 667-72.

DelVecchio, Devon, H. Shanker Krishnan, and Daniel C. Smith (2007), "Cents or Percent? The Effects of Promotion Framing on Price Expectations and Choice," *Journal of Marketing*, 71 (3), 158-70.

Dhar, Sanjay K., Claudia Gonzalez-Vallejo, and Dilip Soman (1999), "Modeling the Effects of Advertised Price Claims: Tensile Versus Precise Claims?," *Marketing Science*, 18 (2), 154.

Estelami, Hooman (2003), "The Effect of Price Presentation Tactics on Consumer Evaluation Effort of Multi-Dimensional Prices," *Journal of Marketing Theory & Practice*, 11 (2), 1.

Green, Leonard, Joel Myerson, and Pawel Ostaszewski (1999), "Amount of Reward Has Opposite Effects on the Discounting of Delayed and Probabilistic Outcomes," *Journal of Experimental Psychology-Learning Memory and Cognition*, 25 (2), 418-27.

Ha, Hwan Ho, Jung Suk Hyun, and Jae H. Pae (2006), "Consumers' "Mental Accounting" In Response to Unexpected Price Savings at the Point of Sale," *Marketing Intelligence & Planning*, 24 (4), 406-16.

Hardesty, David M. and William O. Bearden (2003), "Consumer Evaluations of Different Promotion Types and Price Presentations: The Moderating Role of Promotional Benefit Level," *Journal of Retailing*, 79 (1), 17-25.

Kamleitner, Bernadette and Erik Hölzl (in press), "Cost-Benefit-Associations and Financial Behavior," *Applied Psychology: An International Review*.

Kim, Hyeong and Thomas Kramer (2006), ""Pay 80%" Versus "Get 20% Off": The Effect of Novel Discount Presentation on Consumers' Deal Perceptions," *Marketing Letters*, 17 (4), 311-21.

Klos, Alexander (2005), "Investment Decisions and Time Horizon: Risk Perception and Risk Behavior in Repeated Gambles," *Management Science*, 51 (12), 1777-90.

Krishna, Aradhna, Richard Briesch, Donald R. Lehmann, and Hong Yuan (2002), "A Meta-Analysis of the Impact of Price Presentation on Perceived Savings," *Journal of Retailing*, 78 (2), 101-18.

Kruger, Justin and Patrick Vargas (2008), "Consumer Confusion of Percent Differences," *Journal of Consumer Psychology*, 18 (1), 49-61.

Munger, Jeanne Lauren and Dhruv Grewal (2001), "The Effects of Alternative Price Promotional Methods on Consumers' Product Evaluations and Purchase Intentions," *Journal of Product & Brand Management*, 10 (3), 185 -97.

Prelec, Drazen and George Loewenstein (1991), "Decision-Making over Time and under Uncertainty-a Common Approach," *Management Science*, 37 (7), 770-86.

Rachlin, Howard, Jay Brown, and David Cross (2000), "Discounting in Judgments of Delay and Probability," *Journal of Behavioral Decision Making*, 13 (2), 145-59.

Raghubir, Priya, Jeffrey J. Inman, and Hans Grande (2004), "The Three Faces of Consumer Promotions," *California Management Review*, 46 (4), 23-+.

Samuelson, Paul A. (1963), "Risk and Uncertainty: A Fallacy of Large Numbers," *Scientia*, 98, 108-13.

Sinha, Indrajit and Michael F. Smith (2000), "Consumers' Perceptions of Promotional Framing of Price," *Psychology & Marketing*, 17 (3), 257-75.

Stafford, Marla Royne and Thomas F. Stafford (2000), "The Effectiveness of Tensile Pricing Tactics in the Advertising of Services," *Journal of Advertising*, 29 (2), 45-58.

Tan, Soo-Jian and Seow Hwang Chua (2004), ""While Stocks Last!" Impact of Framing on Consumers' Perception of Sales Promotion," *Journal of Consumer Marketing*, 21 (5), 343-55.

Thaler, Richard H. (1980), "Toward a Positive Theory of Consumer Choice," *Journal of Economic Behavior & Organization*, 1 (1), 39-60.

Thaler, Richard H. and Eric Johnson (1990), "Gambling with the House Money and Trying to Break Even: The Effects of Prior Outcomes on Risky Choice," *Management Science*, 36 (6), 643-60.

Tversky, Amos and Daniel Kahneman (1974), "Judgment under Uncertainty-Heuristics and Biases," *Science*, 185 (4157), 1124-31.

Weber, Bethany J. and Gretchen B. Chapman (2005), "Playing for Peanuts: Why Is Risk Seeking More Common for Low-Stakes Gambles?," *Organizational Behavior and Human Decision Processes*, 97 (1), 31-46.

Wirtz, Jochen and Patricia Chew (2002), "The Effects of Incentives, Deal Proneness, Satisfaction and Tie Strength on Word-of-Mouth Behaviour," *International Journal of Service Industry Management*, 13 (2), 141-62.

Neuroscience in Marketing and Consumer Research: Using Functional Magnetic Resonance Imaging

Martin Reimann, Stanford University, USA
Andreas Aholt, University of Hamburg, Germany
Carolin Neuhaus, University of Bonn, Germany
Oliver Schilke, Stanford University, USA
Thorsten Teichert, University of Hamburg, Germany
Bernd Weber, University of Bonn, Germany

EXTENDED ABSTRACT

Advances in brain imaging have made it possible for researchers to enhance their knowledge about how the brain functions. Recently developed forms of neuroimaging, such as functional magnetic resonance imaging (fMRI), allow for a direct measurement and localization of brain activations. In some respect, fMRI may be considered superior to more traditional measurement approaches, such as questionnaire surveys, in that it promises: (1) the ability to provide confirmatory evidence about the existence of an intrapersonal phenomenon; (2) the generation of a more fundamental conceptualization and understanding of underlying processes; and (3) the refinement of existing conceptualizations of various phenomena.

Although the use of neuroscientific methods has a long history within the social sciences, e.g. in the discipline of neuropsychology, applications in the field of consumer neuroscience are still relatively scarce. While consumer neuroscience–also referred to as neuromarketing–has excited growing interest in recent times, both in the business practice and as a focal point of academic research, its use is still far from being wide-spread among marketing and consumer behavior scholars. A possible diffusion barrier may be that familiarity with neuroscientific methods in the consumer behavior area is low, making it difficult for most researchers to properly evaluate its use. Exacerbating this problem of limited familiarity, existing applications of neuroimaging in the consumer behavior area have used the technique inconsistently and, at times, inappropriately.

The purpose of our research is to provide insights into the field of fMRI, which is the most frequently-used neuroscientific methodology in marketing and consumer research in past years. We will focus on the advantages it provides and the problems it faces. Moreover, we will suggest guidelines for how to implement fMRI in marketing and consumer research.

References can be obtained from the first author upon request.

An Innovative Approach Examining the Asymmetrical and Nonlinear Relationship between Attribute-Level Performance and Service Outcomes

Xiaomeng Fan, Purdue University, USA
Sandra Liu, Purdue University, USA
Michael Zhu, Purdue University, USA

EXTENDED ABSTRACT

Studies in customer satisfaction suggest that the relationship between the attribute-level performance and overall satisfaction/behavioral intentions may be nonlinear; attributes with differing characteristics can affect customer satisfaction differently. This study employs an innovative approach for a step-by-step evaluation of said relationships within a hospital service context.

Conceptualization

The prospect theory predicts that people follow an S-shaped value function when making decisions under risk. This curve changes from a reference point, steeper for losses than for gains, indicating a negative asymmetrical effect. In addition, the curve suggests a diminishing sensitivity of service outcomes to attribute-level performances, with changes at higher levels of positive/negative performance failing to influence service outcomes as dramatically as changes at the intermediate range.

However, empirical studies have revealed that both directions of asymmetrical effects (positive/negative asymmetry) and types of nonlinear relationships (increasing/diminishing sensitivity) vary depending on the nature of service attributes. For example, Anderson and Mittal (2000) posited that attributes with satisfaction maintaining qualities often exhibited negative asymmetrical effects, because these could be viewed as core attributes and were taken for granted by consumers. Moreover, higher order constructs were likely to have a decreasing sensitivity towards extreme levels of performance on these attributes. Meanwhile, for attributes with satisfaction enhancing qualities, positive performance was rarely expected by the consumer. Thus, changes in the positive domains of these attributes would bring about greater impacts than would changes in the negative domains and might create increasing rates of improvement on service outcomes.

In our study regarding the relationship between attribute-level performance and patient behavioral intention in terms of the likelihood to recommend the hospital (LTR), attributes are established through four aspects: Physiological Care, Psychological Care, Physical Environment, and Spiritual Care, and these specific attributes each has a particular nature. For instance, "competence" under Physiological Care may have satisfaction maintaining qualities, given the essential importance of this attribute to hospital services. LTR is expected to drop significantly if staff "competence" is viewed negatively. Meanwhile, attributes reflecting Spiritual Care may have a satisfaction enhancing nature, since these have been less addressed in hospitals previously and patients may be surprisingly delighted by positive experiences on these attributes. Therefore, we hypothesize that these attributes can be classified into three types according to the direction of asymmetrical effects: for Type I attributes, LTR can only be influenced if negative performances are encountered; for Type II attributes, LTR can only be influenced if positive performances are encountered; for Type III attributes, both positive and negative performances can significantly influence LTR. We then hypothesize that Type I and Type III attributes will display diminishing marginal returns on LTR, given the satisfaction maintaining qualities of these attributes; Type II attributes will be perceived as "delights" for customers, providing an increasing marginal return of LTR.

Method

Telephone-survey data was gathered from 2000 inpatients hospitalized in 2006. Patients were asked to indicate their experiences with 24 descriptors of hospital services on a seven-point likert-like scale and were also asked to rate, on an eleven-point scale, how likely they would recommend the hospital.

Five hidden aspects of hospital services were extracted through an exploratory factor analysis: "Compassionate Care", "Mutual Communication", "Procedure Efficiency", "Reputation", and "Spiritual Care". A score for each factor was generated by taking the weighted average of ratings on items under the corresponding factor and ranged from 1 to 7. The authors then centered these scores, creating five new variables representing performances on each factor.

Next, a three-step approach was utilized to examine the asymmetrical and nonlinear relationships existent between performance on each aspect of hospital services and LTR. First, the original scale measuring attribute performance was divided into four parts: "extreme-positive", "low-positive", "low-negative", and "extreme-negative". Second, on each of these parts, LTR was regressed along the perceived performance on the individual aspect of hospital services. If either low-negative or extreme-negative performance was significant in predicting LTR, while neither part of the positive domains could influence LTR, said aspect of hospital service belonged to Type I attributes. If either part of the positive domains was significant in predicting LTR, while neither part of the negative domains could influence LTR, said attribute belonged to Type II. It was also possible to find some attributes on which both positive and negative performances could influence LTR. These attributes belonged to Type III. To assess nonlinearity (increasing/diminishing sensitivity), the regression coefficients on low versus extreme levels of perceived performance were compared by using Z-Test. Finally, for each attribute, the curves representing the relationship between LTR and attribute-level performance were delineated in both the positive and negative domains.

Major Findings

Spiritual Care was established as a Type II attribute; negative performance did not have a significant impact on LTR, but positive performance could significantly enhance LTR. Z-test also indicated an increasing rate of improvements of LTR as the Spiritual Care performance approaches "perfect". The other four aspects of hospital care are regarded as Type III attributes, since both the positive and negative domains of perceived performances on these attributes could have a significant impact on LTR. However, Type III attributes did not relate with LTR in an S-shaped value function. For "Mutual Communication" and "Compassionate Care", LTR was particularly sensitive to extremely negative performance and exhibited decreasing sensitivity towards the extreme upper end of positive domains. For "Procedure Efficiency", LTR also demonstrated particular sensitivity towards extremely negative performance, while maintaining a linear relationship with perceived performance on its positive domain. For "Reputation", LTR indicated decreasing sensitivity towards extreme values within the negative domain, but had a linear relationship with attribute-level performance on the positive domain. Finally, no care aspect was identified as a Type I attribute.

Based on these research findings, we advocate that for hospitals that wish to advance from "good" to "great", the priorities of service improvement programs should target levels of "Spiritual Care", since continuous improvements on this attribute will bring increasing marginal returns of LTR.

REFERENCES

Anderson, Eugene W. and Vikas Mittal (2000), "Strengthening the Satisfaction-Profit Chain," *Journal of Service Research,* 3(2), 107-20.

_____ and Marry W. Sullivan (1993), "The Antecedents and Consequences of Customer Satisfaction for Firms," *Marketing Science,* 12(2), 125-43.

Balmer, Sylvia and Tom Baum (1993), "Applying Herzberg's Hygiene Factors to the Changing Accommodation Environment," *International Journal of Contemporary Hospitality Management,* 5(2), 32-35.

Blizzard, Rick (2004), "Praying For Patient Satisfaction," *Gallup Poll Tuesday Briefing,* 3/30/2004, 1-3.

Ganzach, Yoav and Benjamin Czaczkes (1995), "On Detecting Nonlinear Noncompensatory Regression Models," *Organizational Behavior and Human Decision Processes,* 61(2), 168-76.

Kahn, Barbara E., and Robert J. Meyer (1991), "Consumer Multiattribute Judgments under Attribute-Weight Uncertainty," *Journal of Consumer Research* 17 (4), 508-22.

Kano, Noriaki, Nobuhiko Seraku, Fumio Takahashi, and Shinichi Tsuji (1984), "Attractive Quality and Must-Be Quality," *The Journal of the Japanese Society for Quality Control,* 14 (2), 39-48.

Koenig, Harold G. (2003), "Meeting the Spiritual Needs of Patients" (accessed May 31, 2007), [available at http://www.pressganey.com/products_services/readings_findings/satmon/article.php?article_id=94].

Liu, Sandra S., Eklou Amendah, En-Chung Chang, and Lai Kwan Pei (2006), "Satisfaction and Value: A Meta-Analysis in the Healthcare Context," *Health Marketing Quarterly.* 23 (4), 49-73.

Macrae, Janet (1995), "Nightingale's Spiritual Philosophy and Its Significance for Modern Nursing," *Image: The Journal of Nursing Scholarship,* 27(1), 8-10.

MacStravic, Scott (2006), "Take a Complement," *Marketing Health Services,* 26(2), 24-27

Mittal, Vikas and Patrick M. Baldasare (1996), "Eliminate the Negative," *Journal of Health Care Marketing,* 16(3), 24-31.

_____, William T. Ross, and Patrick M. Baldasare (1998), "The Asymmetric Impact of Negative and Positive Attribute-level Performance on Overall Satisfaction and Repurchase Intentions," *Journal of Marketing,* 62(Jan), 33-47.

Moschis, George P., Danny N. Bellenger, and Carolyn F. Curasi (2003), "What Influences the Mature Consumers?," *Marketing Health Services,* 23(4), 16-21.

Oliva, Terence A., Richard L. Oliver, and William O. Bearden (1995), "The Relationship Among Consumer Satisfaction, Involvement, and Product Performance: A Catastrophe Theory Application," *Behavioral Science,* 40 (2), 104-32.

Otani, Koichiro, Richard S. Kurz, Thomas E. Burroughs, and Brian Waterman (2003), "Reconsidering Models of Patient Satisfaction and Behavioral Intentions," *Health Care Management Review,* 28(1), 7-20.

Rust, Roland T. and Richard L. Oliver (2000), "Should We Delight the Customer," *Journal of the Academy of Marketing Science,* 28(1), 86-94.

Sheldon, Joanne E. (2000), "Spirituality as a Part of Nursing," *Journal of Hospice and Palliative Nursing,* 2(3), 101-8.

Streukens, Sandra and Ko D. Ruyter (2004), "Reconsidering Nonlinearity and Asymmetry in Customer Satisfaction and Loyalty Models: An Empirical Study in Three Retail Service Settings," *Marketing Letters,* 15(2-3), 99-111.

Taylor, Shelley E. (1991), "Asymmetrical Effects of Positive and Negative Events: The Mobilization –Minimization Hypothesis," *Psychological Bulletin,* 110 (1), 67-85.

Ting, Shueh-Chin, and Cheng-Nan Chen (2002), "The Asymmetrical and Non-linear Effects of Store Quality Attributes on Customer Satisfaction," *Total Quality Management,* 13(4), 547-69.

Yoon, Sung-Joon and Joo-Ho Kim (2000), "An Empirical Validation of a Loyalty Model Based on Expectation Disconfirmation," *Journal of Consumer Marketing,* 17(2), 120-36.

The "Right" Consumers for the Best Concepts: A Methodology for Identifying Emergent Consumers for New Product Development

Donna Hoffman, University of California, Riverside, USA
Praveen Kopalle, Dartmouth College, USA
Thomas Novak, University of California, Riverside, USA[1]

EXTENDED ABSTRACT

Consumer firms are generally interested in learning which consumers might be the "right" ones they might use to further develop product concepts and improve their chances for success in the marketplace. Which consumers are the most appropriate to engage in the product development process is important because while new product development is a major activity of firms (Chandy and Tellis 1998), most of the 25,000 products introduced in the United States each year fail (Goldenberg, Lehmann, and Mazursky 2001). While much research has emphasized improving current new product concept techniques (e.g. Dahan and Hauser 2002; Dahl and Moreau 2002; Green, Krieger, and Vavra 1997), except for the lead user approach (von Hippel 1986), little work has focused on *which* consumers to use in the new product development process, particularly in the consumer goods industry.

We propose such a methodology to identify these "right" consumers. We argue that the right consumers possess what we call an "emergent nature," i.e., the ability to process information in a synergistically experiential and rational thinking style, and exhibit a unique set of personality traits such that interactions among them in a new product development context will produce a product that mainstream consumers would find more appealing and useful relative to one that is developed by mainstream or even innovative consumers. We draw on information processing theory to develop the emergent nature construct and test our hypotheses in four studies.

A considerable body of research in dual-processing theory has differentiated among two types of information processing styles: experiential thinking style and rational thinking style (e.g. Epstein 1994; Pacini & Epstein 1999; Sloman 1996; Smith and DeCoster 2000) and substantiated the existence of individual differences in these two thinking styles (Epstein, Pancini, Denes-Raj, and Heier 1996; Pancini and Epstein 1999; Norris and Epstein 2003a, 2003b). Rational thinking style involves goal-directed, active, logical processing, and permits consumers to make optimal judgments about the utility of adopting a particular product innovation. Experiential thinking style, on the other hand, involves holistic, emotional, associative processing. Immediate experience is critical for experiential thinking, while logic and evidence are critical for rational thinking. The two thinking styles are not mutually exclusive processing styles; empirically they tend to have a very small positive correlation. Epstein and his colleagues have shown that these two processing styles reliably relate to a variety of psychological constructs (e.g. Pacini & Epstein 1999), with rational thinking style appearing to be adaptive for good judgment in specific decision-making situations, and an experiential style adaptive for interactions and creative pursuits.

Novak and Hoffman (2007) suggest that some tasks "might demonstrate *synergistic* effects" in which *both* experiential and rational situation-specific thinking style might correlate positively with performance. We propose that consumers with an emergent nature are high in both experiential and rational thinking style and are able to use the two thinking styles in a synergistic manner. That is, we argue that *emergent nature is defined largely by the complementary interaction between the experiential and rational thinking styles.*

We propose that emergent consumers, owing to the synergies among their thinking styles, are able to engage successfully in both idea generation to enhance the original concept and logical analysis to refine and develop the concept further. In other words, emergent consumers are able to synergistically apply intuition and judgment to improve product concepts. Consumers with a high emergent nature develop an intuitive, almost "instinctive" understanding, i.e., visualizing the latent uses of a new product, through a sequence of small scale, affective, and associative perceptions. They are able to generate these ideas focused on the future because they possess a high degree of experiential processing ability. The experiential system generates the "gut feelings" underlying the intuitive understanding of the potential usefulness of a new product concept. Following this automatic, associative stage, emergent consumers, owing to their high degree of rational processing ability, then employ a rational thinking style in a conscious, logical and analytic effort to evaluate and refine the concept. In our conceptualization, the thinking styles work together in a complementary and iterative fashion, where a rational effort to analyze a product concept may activate further implicit, experiential associations about that concept, followed by another round of rational analysis, and so on. The essence of emergent nature is that consumers so possessed are able to inform their experiential impressions and associations with rational evaluation and judgment and vice versa.

The results from Study 1, a comprehensive calibration and validation phase involving scale development and construct measurement, provide strong support for the idea that emergent nature is a useful construct in the product development context. We have developed a highly reliable and valid scale to measure emergent nature in consumers and showed that the emergent nature construct is empirically distinct from other product development constructs such as lead user status, as well as dispositional innovativeness (Steenkamp and Gielens 2003).

In study 2, five mutually exclusive groups of consumers, including those high on emergent nature, lead user status, and dispositional innovativeness, develop a new product concept using an online bulletin board methodology, and in studies 3 and 4, those concepts are market tested demonstrating that consumers high on emergent nature can develop product concepts that are perceived by typical consumers as significantly better than concepts developed by groups high on domain-specific lead user status or dispositional innovativeness.

The strong showing of the concept developed by the high lead user group reinforces research that argues that lead users represent a good segment for developing radical new product concepts (von Hippel 1986). It also provides strong face validity to our results. We also note that we have developed a highly reliable and valid scale to measure domain-specific lead user status in a consumer context and marketing researchers may also find value in this scale.

Although work remains to be done, the idea of identifying and using emergent consumers in the development of consumer prod-

[1]The authors thank David Porter, an entrepreneur and the inventor of SmartBox, a patented storage device for the delivery and pickup of goods (U.S. Pat. #5,774,053), for permission to use the SmartBox descriptions in this research.

ucts that mainstream consumers will find appealing seems viable and worthy of the effort required to understanding it more fully.

REFERENCES

Chandy, R., G. J. Tellis. 1998. Organizing for Radical Innovation: The Overlooked Role of Willingness to Cannibalize. *Journal of Marketing Research* 35 (November) 474–487.

Dahan, Ely and John R. Hauser (2002), "The Virtual Customer," *Journal of Product Innovation Management*, 19 (5), 332-353.

Dahl, Darren W. and Page Moreau (2002), "The Influence and Value of Analogical Thinking During New Product Ideation," *Journal of Marketing Research*, 39 (February), 47-60.

Epstein, S. (1994), "Integration of the Cognitive and the Psychodynamic Unconscious," *American Psychologist*, 49, 709-724.

Epstein, S., Pacini, R., Denes-Raj, V., & Heier, H. (1996). Individual differences in intuitive-experiential and analytical-rational thinking styles, *Journal of Personality and Social Psychology*, 71, 390-405.

Goldenberg, J. Lehmann, R. D., and Mazursky, D. (2001), "The Idea Itself and the Circumstances of its Emergence as Predictors of New Product Success," *Management Science*, 47 (1), 69-84.

Green, Paul E., Abba M. Krieger, and Terry G. Vavra (1997), "Evaluating New Products," *Marketing Research*, Winter, 12-21.

Novak, Thomas P. and Donna L. Hoffman (2007), "The Fit of Thinking Style and Situation: New Measures of Situation-Specific Experiential and Rational Cognition," UCR Sloan Center for Internet Retailing Working Paper, August 27.

Norris, P. and S. Epstein (2003a), "The Investigation of Some Fundamental Issues Concerning Rational-Analytical and Intuitive-Experiential Thinking Styles with a Short Form of the Rational-Experiential Inventory," working paper.

Norris, P. and S. Epstein (2003b), "Objective Correlates of Experiential Processing." Working paper.

Pacini, R., & Epstein, S. (1999). The relation of rational and experiential information processing styles to personality, basic beliefs, and the ratio-bias phenomenon. *Journal of Personality and Social Psychology, 76*, 972-987.

Sloman, Steven A. (1996), "The Empirical Case for Two Systems of Reasoning," *Psychological Bulletin*, 119(1), 3-22.

Smith, Eliot R. and Jamie DeCoster (2000), "Dual-Process Models in Social and Cognitive Psychology: Conceptual Integration and Links to Underlying Memory Systems," *Personality and Social Psychology Review*, 4(2), 108-131.

Steenkamp, Jan-Benedict E.M. and Katrijn Gielens (2003), "Consumer and Market Drivers of the Trial Rate of New Consumer Products," *Journal of Consumer Research*, 30 (December), 368-384.

Von Hippel, E. (1986), "Lead Users: A Source of Novel Product Concepts," *Management Science* 32(7), 791–805.

Effects of Lower and Higher Quality Brand Versions on Brand Evaluation: An Opponent-Process Model Plus Differential Brand-Version Weighting

Timothy B. Heath, Miami University, USA
Devon DelVecchio, Miami University, USA
Michael S. McCarthy, Miami University, USA
Subimal Chatterjee, Binghamton University, USA

EXTENDED ABSTRACT

Despite threats of image dilution, sellers commonly extend brand names to lower quality (*Charmin Basic, Levi Strauss Signature, BMW 1-Series,* etc.). To assess potential outcomes of such strategies as well as underlying processes, this study tests the effects on overall brand evaluation of middle-quality brands also offering versions of either lower or higher quality.

Experiments 1 and 2

An exploratory choice experiment comparing control conditions within two product classes (target brands offering a single middle-quality product) with experimental conditions (target brands also offering a lower-quality or higher-quality version) found no effect of offering lower-quality versions. However, offering a higher-quality version bolstered choice of the middle-quality offering in one of the two product classes tested. A small follow-up experiment extended this by having participants rate the brands on various perceptual dimensions. Consistent with the choice results, offering higher quality improved perceptions of brand knowledge and perceived marketplace respect, whereas lower-quality versions failed to have an effect.

These opening experiments implicate opponent processes in the context of lower-quality versions. Whereas quality-association effects should be negative due to brand associations with lower quality, variety effects should be positive because additional offerings signal greater knowledge of production processes (expertise), increased ability to produce and market a range of products, greater sensitivity to diverse consumer tastes, etc. These potential positive effects may then temper the negative effects of brands offering lower-quality versions (although both effects should be positive in the case of higher-quality versions). Experiment 3 was then conducted to replicate the brand-quality asymmetry with better measures of underlying processes.

Experiment 3

Methodological Overview. Two-hundred-forty-eight upperclassman at a large U.S. university were randomly assigned to conditions. A 7 (brand-quality levels: control plus six experimental conditions) by 2 (product-class: pasta sauce, portable CD players) by 2 (name: *Formaggio's* or *Giovanni's* pasta sauce, *Acoustix* or *Earshot* CD players) between-subjects design was used. In addition to the control condition that included only the flagship product (e.g., *Giovanni's* pasta sauce), the six experimental conditions added (1) a brand version one level up in quality (*Giovanni's Tuscano*), (2) one two levels up in quality, (3) versions at both one and two levels up in quality, (4) a brand version one level down in quality (*Giovanni's Basiqué*), (5) one two levels down in quality, and (6) versions at both one and two levels down in quality.

Participants imagined living abroad where they were venturing into an early shopping experience there. They viewed a table of brands listed by brand name, price, and average quality rating ostensibly from a survey of the retailer's customers, and then rated the target brand on three items per each of the following: brand attitude, prestige, innovativeness, and ability.

Results and Discussion. Experiment 3 replicated the brand-quality asymmetry. Whereas higher-quality versions significantly improved brand attitudes as well as perceived brand prestige, innovativeness, and ability, lower-quality versions had (1) null effects on brand attitude, (2) smaller negative effects on perceived brand prestige, (3) smaller positive effects on perceived brand innovativeness, and (4) null effects on perceived brand ability.

Consistent with the opponent-process model, lower-quality versions reduced perceived brand prestige but increased perceived brand innovativeness. The opponent-process model was also supported by the fact that statistically controlling for perceived innovativeness eliminated the asymmetric effects of higher-quality and lower-quality versions on brand attitude

Experiment 4

Although the prior experiments implicate a robust brand-quality asymmetry, Experiment 4 proposes and tests a process in addition to opponent processes: Consumers may "discount" or under-weight lower-quality versions when judging brands. Even if a flagship brand adds lower-quality versions, the brand continues to offer the same quality offerings as before, thereby suggesting no change in the brand's ability to design, produce, and market quality products, and no change in the brand's commitment to offering quality products. However, when brands offer higher-quality versions, these versions signal the greater skill necessary to produce and market such products, as well as an organizational commitment to offering higher-quality products.

Method. Experiment 4 replicated Experiment 3's procedures using only a single additional higher-quality or lower-quality version to simplify. To enhance generalizability, Experiment 4 used different product classes (restaurants and beers) plus both real and fictitious brands (*Metro* was the new (fictitious) target brand in both product categories, and real target brands were *Ruby Tuesday* in restaurants and *Fosters* in beers). Experiment 4 supplemented Experiment 3's measures with questions assessing how much weight participants in experimental conditions accorded the flagship brand version when evaluating brand liking, prestige, expertise, and innovativeness (constant-sum to 100).

Results and Discussion. The brand-quality asymmetry again arose across multiple measures as well as within both real and fictitious brands (although effects were weaker within real brands, they remained statistically significant). Unlike Experiment 3, however, none of the perceptual measures could statistically account for the asymmetry in brand attitudes. Nonetheless, consistent with an opponent-process account, lower-quality versions reduced perceived brand prestige significantly. Whereas higher-quality versions consistently improved brand perception and evaluation, lower-quality versions failed to change brand attitudes, perceived brand innovativeness, or perceived brand expertise.

Regardless of the dimension being judged, consumers reported giving grater weight to higher-quality versions than to lower-quality versions. Higher-quality versions were also weighted as much or more than flagship versions, whereas lower-quality versions were consistently rated less than flagship versions. It appears that consumers do, in fact, consider lower-quality versions less relevant to brand evaluation than flagship and higher-quality versions.

Discussion

Four experiments find that higher-quality brand versions boost brand image and evaluation more than lower-quality brand versions damage them. This brand-quality asymmetry emerges in part from lower-quality versions stimulating both negative and positive effects that then partially cancel out one another, and in part from consumers seeing lower-quality versions as less relevant to brand evaluation than higher-quality brand versions. It appears that offering higher-quality versions has multiple positive effects, whereas offering lower-quality versions has a mix of positive, negative, and null effects that fail to threaten brand image as much as negative quality-associations alone might otherwise suggest.

Are Well-Known Brands Held to a Higher Standard of Performance: The Moderating Influence of Pre vs. Post Purchase of the Product

M. Deniz Dalman, Binghamton University, USA
Kalpesh K. Desai, Binghamton University, USA
Manoj K. Agarwal, Binghamton University, USA

EXTENDED ABSTRACT

Prior research in branding has clearly demonstrated the multitude of benefits (e.g., inclusion in consideration sets, greater advertising efficiency) that well-known brands (or WKB) enjoy over less known brands (or LKB) (Feinberg et. al. 1992; Johnson et. al. 2006; Park and Srinivasan 1994). With some exceptions, most such research focus either on the pre- or post-purchase stage and that too for either WKB or LKB. In the current research, we fill this important gap in the literature by comparing the relative evaluations of WKB and LKB in both pre- vs. post-purchase stages. Similarly, the current research fills an important gap in the satisfaction literature (Caruana, Money, and Berthon 2000; Oliver and Swan 1989) by highlighting the moderating impact of brand equity on the influence of deviation of objective performance of a brand relative to its claimed performance on consumer satisfaction.

Consider a consumer choosing between a laptop manufactured by SONY, a WKB, and AVERATEC, a LKB. SONY is likely to be priced higher compared to AVERATEC due to its strong brand equity. Each brand makes specific claims about the battery life that its product will provide. Brands often claim a specific level of performance on an objective attribute (e.g., battery life and laptops). However, because of manufacturing and usage variability, consumers will experience uncertainty about the actual performance relative to the claimed level. Thus, the actual performance delivered by a brand could be higher or lower than the claimed level. We argue that at the pre-purchase stage, consumers will entertain lower level of uncertainty about the WKB's (vs. LKB's) performance relative to the claim because of its strong brand equity. This will result in WKB having a competitive advantage in the pre-purchase stage in terms of preference and buying likelihood even if both LKB and WKB claimed the same level of performance on an objective attribute. However, based on the literature in standards of judgment and stereotyping (Biernat, Manis, and Nelson 1991; Linville and Jones 1980) we posit that the LKB will have an advantage in the post-purchase stage (i.e., after using the product) because WKB will be held to a higher standard of performance. More specifically, if both brands exceed their claims, LKB will be rewarded more than WKB. If both brands fail to meet their claims, WKB will be punished more than LKB.

Results of the first study employing two category replicates of tires and online web service confirm our hypotheses in the pre-purchase and post-purchase stages and confirm the uncertainty of performance underlying the evaluations in the pre-purchase stage. In Study 2, we establish the robustness of the effects by replicating the Study 1 results for both categories. The regression analyses confirmed our posited process underlying the evaluations in post-purchase stage. Specifically, it showed that it is the deviation from claim that influences the satisfaction and not the deviation from participant's expectation formed during the pre-purchase stage. The results show that WKB is held to a higher standard than LKB for the same deviated level of performance—if both brands exceed their claims, LKB is evaluated more favorably than WKB. However, when both brands fail to meet their claims, WKB is punished more than LKB.

Along with important managerial implications, this research has important theoretical implications for both the satisfaction and brand equity literature. Regarding the former, we show that, contrary to the satisfaction literature, it is not the deviation from the expectation (which we controlled for in this study) that influences the levels of satisfaction for a given performance but it is the different evaluations of the same deviated performance of brands varying in their brand equities. As for brand equity literature, we show that while WKB have advantages over LKB in the pre-purchase stage, WKB are held to a higher standard and thus they have less room for error in the post-purchase stage. Managers of such brands should carefully manage the expectations of consumers in the post-purchase stage. LKB should take full advantage of being held to a lower standard of performance in the post-purchase stage. However, managers of such brands need to be more conservative when they are deciding the claimed level of performance to communicate to consumers and should work to reduce the perceived uncertainty in performance of such claimed performance in the pre-purchase stage.

REFERENCES

Biernat, M., Manis M., and Nelson T. E. (1991). "Stereotypes and Standards of Judgment." *Journal of Personality and Social Psychology* 60(4): 485-499.

Caruana, A. Money, A. H., and Berthon, P. R. (2000). "Service quality and satisfaction-the moderating role of value". *European Journal of Marketing*, 34(11/12), 1338.

Feinberg, F. M., Kahn, B. E. and McAlister, L. (1992) "Market share response when consumers seek variety." *Journal of Marketing Research* 29(2): 227–237.

Johnson, M. S., E. Garbarino, et al. (2006). "Influences of customer differences of loyalty, perceived risk and category experience on customer satisfaction ratings." *International Journal of Market Research* 48(5): 601-622.

Linville, P. W. and E. E. Jones (1980). "Polarized Appraisals of Out-Group Members." *Journal of Personality and Social Psychology* 38(5):689-703.

Oliver, Richard L. and John E. Swan (1989). "Consumer Perceptions of Interpersonal Equity and Satisfaction in Transactions: A Field Survey Approach," *Journal of Marketing*, 53 (April), 21-35.

Park, C. S. and V. Srinivasan (1994). "A survey-based method for measuring and understanding brand equity and its extendibility." *Journal of Marketing Research* (JMR) 31(2): 271.

Self-Regulation and Consumer Ethnicity: Resisting Undesirable Eating Temptations

David J. Moore, University of Michigan, USA

ABSTRACT

Intense emotional distress is capable of depleting one's capacity for self-control, thus increasing one's vulnerability to yielding to an undesirable eating temptation (Baumeister and Heatherton 1996). This study found that Caucasian women, compared to their African American counterparts, engage in more weight reduction activities, but nevertheless, experience greater emotional concern about gaining weight, and this elevated level of emotion helped to undermine self-regulation. Furthermore, African American women displayed greater transcendence-a more positive attitude toward disappointment in achieving immediate weight reduction goals, and this, in turn, boosted self-regulation. Implications for marketing and public policy are also discussed.

Pledges and Competitions as Health Interventions

Sekar Raju, Iowa State University, USA
Priyali Rajagopal, Southern Methodist University, USA

EXTENDED ABSTRACT

Public policy makers have attempted to influence the development and prevalence of healthy eating habits through various recommendations with respect to food content. While these efforts have contributed to increased awareness and knowledge of what constitutes healthy eating, research has documented that just this increased knowledge may be insufficient to motivate people to eat in healthier ways (e.g. CDC 1996). Further, little is known about how children of different age groups react to such interventions. Children and young adults are important groups to address in the context of healthy eating because past research has shown that these groups fail to meet the recommended daily consumption levels of fruit and vegetables in the United States and because eating patterns that are established in childhood tend to persist throughout life, indicating the importance of starting healthy eating habits early (Lien, Lytle, and Klepp 2001). Our research aims at understanding two different public policy interventions (pledges and competitions) that can be used by marketers and public policy makers to increase healthy eating attitudes and behaviors amongst school and college age students. We report the results of two empirical studies conducted amongst school children and college students.

Study 1

Objective: To compare the relative effects of pledges, and competitions on healthy eating choices amongst school children and understand how the age of the child plays a role in the effectiveness of the intervention.

Study background and design: A total of approximately 31,000 public school students in grades one to eight participated in this longitudinal field study conducted over a six month period. Schools participating in this study were provided an enhanced lunch menu consisting of an additional serving of a fruit and a vegetable during the study period.

Method: Schools were randomly assigned to one of three study conditions-control, pledge, or competition condition. The second independent variable was age, a measured variable. Grades 1 through 3 were coded to represent younger children and grades 4 to 8 were coded to represent older children. Incentives were offered to all the students in the study and were small in nature (e.g. pencils). The baseline condition participants received only the incentive instructions. The pledge condition participants were told about the incentives and asked to make a personal pledge to eat healthier by signing their name on a special poster prepared for the occasion and placed in the classroom for the duration of the study. The competition condition participants were told about the incentives and were also told that they were in a friendly healthy eating competition with students from other participating schools.

Procedure

Six weeks prior to the start of the main study, baseline consumption of fruits and vegetables were recorded. For a one week period, the same enhanced menu that was used during the main study was provided to students in the participating schools (BE). The following week, the enhanced menu was withdrawn but student's fruits and vegetable consumption with the regular menu was recorded (BR). These two baseline measures allowed us to account for any variation in novelty and availability effects. The main study was conducted over six consecutive weeks and the consumption of fruits and vegetables was recorded for each day of the week for each student in each school. At the end of the sixth week, all students were told that the healthy eating program had ended. In the week immediately following the main study, the enhanced menu was again provided and consumption recorded to track immediate follow-up behavior (IF). Finally, ten weeks after the completion of the main study, long-term follow-up behavior (DF) was tracked by offering the enhanced fruit and vegetables menu for a week and recording the consumption. Therefore, the study was designed as a 3 (study condition: control, pledge, or competition) x 2 (age: younger or older children) x 8 (study week: W1–W6) mixed design. Study condition and age were between-subject variables and study week was a within-subject variable.

The data was collected at the individual level, but due to privacy concerns, aggregated to the homeroom level.

Results

A repeated measures ANOVA conducted on the two baseline measures BE and BR revealed no significant differences between the measures (M_{BE}=.45, M_{BR}=.45, F (1, 673)=.46, p>.10).

The data was subjected to a two-way ANCOVA with experimental condition and grade as the between-subject variables, study week as the within-subject variable, change in consumption of fruits and vegetables over the baseline period as the dependent variable, and enrollment size as the covariate. The results revealed a significant three-way interaction between study condition, age, and study week (F (11.7., 3902)=2.83, p<.001; χ^2=.01). To understand the nature of the three-way interaction better, the data were analyzed separately for the younger and older children.

Younger children

The results of a one-way ANOVA revealed that the increase in the proportion of competition condition participants taking fruits and vegetables was greater than pledge condition participants for younger children. The data relating to the follow-up period revealed that the increase in the proportion of students taking fruits and vegetables continued to be significantly greater for the competition condition participants compared to the pledge or control conditions. However, the difference between the pledge and control conditions became non-significant. These results suggest that in the follow-up period (both immediate and delayed), the competition condition participants maintained their consumption of fruits and vegetables, but the pledge condition participants dropped to a level not different from the control condition participants.

Older children

For the duration of the six study weeks, there was a significantly larger increase in the proportion of pledge condition participants taking fruits and vegetables compared to the competition condition participants, except in weeks three and four where the results were not significant. Similarly, the difference between the pledge and control condition participants was also significantly different for all the study weeks. Taken together, these results suggest that the increase in the proportion of pledge condition participants taking fruits and vegetables was greater than competition condition participants for older children. In the immediate and delayed follow-up period, the difference between the pledge and competition conditions became insignificant indicating that the effects of the intervention did not extend beyond the intervention period.

Our results hold important implications for health educators, marketers and public policy makers since they suggest that different interventions may be appropriate for children of different ages.

REFERENCES

Center for Disease Control (1996), "Guidelines for School Health Programs to Promote Lifelong Healthy Eating," *Mortality and Morbidity Weekly Report*, 45 (RR-9).

Lien, Nanna, Leslie Lytle and Knut-Inge Klepp (2001), "Stability in consumption of fruit, vegetables, and sugary foods in a cohort from age 14 to age 21," *Preventive Medicine*, 33 (September), 217-26.

The Effect of Past Usage Pattern on Preference for Current Tariff: Can I Control Myself?

Young-Soo Kim, KAIST Business School, South Korea
Do-Hyung Park, LG Electronics Inc., South Korea

EXTENDED ABSTRACT

In spite of the importance of past usage patterns on tariff choice, in our knowledge, there are few studies investigating the effect of past usage patterns on tariff choice. The purpose of this article is to examine the relationship between past usage patterns and current tariff choice by using self-control theory.

Past usage patterns of consumers may range from being stable to fluctuating. Depending on the past usage pattern which tariff, pay-peruse or flat-rate tariff, will be preferred? We try to explain consumers' tariff choice by using self-control and perceived risk of tariff choice failure. Basically, when the pattern is stable a person tends to choose pay-per-use tariff if their usage is less than the minimum beneficial rate for flat-rate tariff or choose flat-rate tariff if their usage is excessive in order to maximize economic utility. However, a person can not be sure of next usage of certain content if variance of the past usage pattern is high, which results in that he/she is concerned about self-control for future usage as well.

Our study focuses on the case in that the past usage pattern is fluctuating. This research proposes the two different mechanisms depending on the self-controllability when the past pattern is fluctuating. Specifically, if consumers think themselves to have the high level of self-controllability, they choose the tariff that fits the norms of each content usage. Otherwise, they choose the tariff based on the risk related to the failure of tariff choice.

According to prior research on self-control, hedonic contents make people feel guiltier as the usage volume increases (e.g., Kivetz and Simonson 2002; Prelec and Herrnstein 1991; Thaler 1980). Therefore, in general, people strive to decrease the usage volume of hedonic contents as possible and increase the usage volume of utilitarian contents (e.g., Ainslie 1975; Hoch and Loewenstein 1991; Trope and Fishbach 2000; Wertenbroch 1998). Thus, if people perceive that they can control their future usage, utilitarian contents users are more likely to choose flat-rate tariff to increase the usage volume. On the other hand, hedonic contents users are more likely to choose pay-per-use tariff in order to decrease the usage of hedonic contents.

The decrease in the self-controllability of future usage leads him/her to focus on a future tariff choice failure which is either the case of that he/she chose pay-per-use tariff but used more than their estimated usage rate or the case that he/she chose flat-rate tariff but used less than their estimated usage rate. In the case of the hedonic content, if consumers who chose pay-per-use tariff are unsuccessful in the choice, they can not justify the added costs easily. In contrast, if consumers who chose flat-rate tariff experience the tariff choice failure, they can justify the unused usage more easily. Finally, it is predicted that consumers exposed to the fluctuated usage of hedonic contents are more likely to prefer flat-rate tariff to pay-per-use tariff. In the case of the utilitarian content, if consumers who chose flat-rate tariff are unsuccessful in the choice, they can not justify the unused usage easily. In contrast, if consumers who chose pay-per-use tariff experience the tariff choice failure, they can justify the added costs more easily.

Study 1 examined the effect of past usage patterns on preference for two tariff options and the moderating role of a content type. Participants were given the scenario in which they have been using an online web site providing online contents. Depending on the manipulation of content type, they were involved in the online site offering either hedonic or utilitarian contents. After, the table showing the past pattern of each content usage was provided. The data of the table had twelve month usage in terms of time. After exposed to the stimuli, participants were asked to evaluate preference for the two different tariffs. Study 1 showed that when the past usage pattern had high variance, preference for tariffs is different depending on the content type. Specifically, hedonic content users preferred flat-rate tariff, while utilitarian content users preferred pay-per-use tariff.

Study 2 was initiated in order to support our theory more strongly by conducting the experiment to manipulate the level of self controllability. We hypothesize that utilitarian contents users are more likely to prefer flat-rate tariff than the hedonic contents users do when they have the high level of self-controllability. On the other hand, hedonic contents users are more likely to prefer flat-rate tariff than the utilitarian content users do when they have low level of self-controllability. In study 2, the same pattern of past usage with the target usage of 30 hours was provided across all conditions, but the average usage was different from 25 hours per month to 35 hours per month. We intended for participants in the utilitarian content condition to experience failure in self-control given the past usage pattern with 25 average hours per month whereas success in self-control given the past usage pattern with 35 average hours per month. As hypothesized, in the case of the high level of self-controllability condition, participants exposed to the utilitarian content reported a higher score of preference for flat-rate tariff than those exposed to the hedonic contents. As for the case of the low level of self-controllability condition, participants exposed to the hedonic contents reported a higher score of preference for flat-rate tariff than those exposed to the utilitarian contents

Contributions made by the present research are twofold. First, we examined how consumers' preference between the two tariffs changes when the overall past usage pattern has high variance. Second, we proposed the underlying mechanism to explain consumers' tariff choice by using perceived risk and self-control. In study2, we showed that if people perceive that they have control over their future usage, they choose the tariff that fits the norms of each content usage even when the past usage pattern is highly fluctuating. On the other hand, if people perceive that they have less control over their future usage, they choose the tariff based on the risk related to the failure of tariff choice.

REFERENCES

Ainslie, G. (1975). Specious reward: A behavioral theory of impulsiveness and impulse control. *Psychological Bulletin, 82,* 463-509

Hoch, S. J., and Loewenstein, G. (1991), "Time-inconsistent preferences and consumer self-control," *Journal of Consumer Research.* 17, 492-507.

Kivetz, Ran and Itamar Simonson (2002), "Earning the Right to Indulge: Effort as a Determinant of Customer Preferences towards Frequency Program Rewards," *Journal of Marketing Research*, 39 (May), 155–170.

Kling, John P. and Stephen S. van der Ploeg (1990), "Estimating Local Elasticities with a Model of Stochastic Class of Service and Usage Choice," *Telecommunications Demand Modelling: An Integrated View, A. de Fontenay, M.H. Shugard, and D.S. Sibley, eds. Amsterdam: North Holland, 119–36.*

Kridel, Donald J., Dale E. Lehman, and Dennis L. Weisman (1993), "Option Value, Telecommunication Demand, and Policy," *Information Economics and Policy*, 5 (2), 125–44.

Lambrecht, Aanja and Bernd Skiera (2006), "Paying too much and being happy about it: Existence, Causes, and Consequences of Tariff-Choice Biases," *Journal of Marketing Research*, 43, 212-223.

Miravete, Eugenio J. (2002), "Choosing the Wrong Calling Plan? Ignorance and Learning," *American Economic Review*, 93 (1), 297–310.

Nunes, J. (2000), "A Cognitive Model of People's Usage Estimations," *Journal of Marketing Research*, 37 (November), 397–409.

Prelec, Drazen and George Loewenstein (1998), "The Red and the Black: Mental Accounting of Savings and Debt," *Marketing Science*, 17 (1), 4–28.

Thaler, R. H. (1980), "Toward a Positive Theory of Consumer Choice," *Journal of Economic Behavior and Organization*, 1, 39–60.

_____ (1985), "Mental Accounting and Consumer Choice," *Marketing Science*, 4 (Summer), 199–214.

Train, Kenneth E. (1991), "Optimal Regulation: The Economic Theory of natural Monopoly," Cambridge, MA: MIT Press.

_____, Daniel L. McFadden, and Mosche Ben-Akiva (1987), "The Demand for Local Telephone Service: A Fully Discrete Model of Residential Calling Patterns and Service Choices," *Rand Journal of Economics*, 18 (1), 109–123.

Trope, Yaacov and Ayelet Fishbach (2000), "Counteractive Self-Control in Overcoming Temptation," *Journal of Personality and Social Psychology*, 79 (4), 493–506.

Wertenbroch, Klaus (1998), "Consumption Self-Control by Rationing Purchase Quantities of Virtue and Vice," *Marketing Science*, 17, 317-337.

The Social Construction of Consumer Needs: A Case Analysis of the "Healing Boom" in Japan

Takeshi Matsui, Hitotsubashi University, Japan and Princeton University, USA

EXTENDED ABSTRACT

This paper examines the development process of the healing boom, the largest consumer culture in Japan at the turn of the century, which developed consumers' collective sense of consumption environments and oriented their experience and lives (Kozinets 2001). Since the late 1990s, many firms in different industries launched a large number of "healing" products and services; such a category had not existed until this boom. The more the boom developed, the wider the category of healing products and services expanded. Finally, hair dryers that generate negative ions, talking stuffed dolls, tourist resorts, spa, and compilation CDs of easy listening were advertised as "healing" products or services.

Due to the massive launch of "healing" products and services, the meaning of healing was drastically changed. According to K?jien 5th edition (1998), the most authoritative Japanese dictionary, Iyasu (heal) means to cure somebody's disease or injury, satisfy hunger, or mitigate emotional pain. Gendai Y?go no Kiso Chishiki (Encyclopedia of Contemporary Words) 2003 Edition explains that Iyashi Sij? (healing market) is a market of goods and services that are useful for creating psychological security, and nowadays, various kinds of consumer goods such as books, music, paintings, movies, massage, drink, food, and clothing, which help us relax, fall under this rubric.

This study argues that this linguistic change is evidence of the cognitive institutionalization of healing, which means that healing is accepted as an objective reality among the members of society (Berger and Luckmann 1966). Neo-institutional sociology has been interested in this cognitive process (DiMaggio 1997; DiMaggio and Powell 1983; Meyer and Rowan 1977; Powell and DiMaggio 1991; Zucker 1983). Agents such as firms and consumers take some actions not because of rules or obligations forced by their society but because such an action is taken for granted as the way we do these things (Scott 2008).

To analyze the interplay among corporate behavior, media discourse, and consumer needs, this study adopts two concepts from neo-institutional sociology: firms' mimetic isomorphism and the media's theorization. Mimetic isomorphism is the mechanism that forces organizations to imitate other organizations' behavior that they perceive as successful when the relationship between means and ends is uncertain (DiMaggio and Powell 1983). Successful products or services are now easily imitated by their competitors because marketers' ceaseless effort to offer hit products or services always faces uncertainty about the relationship between means (the 4Ps) and ends (sales and/or profit). The imitative process in the healing boom can be considered as a typical instance of mimetic isomorphism. Theorization is the self-conscious development and specification of abstract categories and the formulation of patterned relationships such as chains of cause and effect (Strang and Meyer 1993). Nikkei newspapers, the counterpart of Wall Street Journal, theorized that people bought healing products because they hoped to eliminate their stress. This causal explanation triggered imitative behavior by firms.

This study includes three content analyses. First, in order to understand firms' mimetic isomorphism, all healing products and services launched were listed by investigating 5,371 articles of Nikkei newspapers published from 1982 to 2007. Second, in order to understand the media's theorization, a qualitative content analysis on the contents of Nikkei articles was conducted. Third, to understand the views of ordinary people on healing (cognitive institutionalization), the study analyzed the environment of ideas to which ordinary magazine readers were exposed. A content analysis on 8,038 article titles from 466 types of magazines published from 1984 to 2007 was carried out. Content analysis was adopted because it is a useful research tool to understand consumption value through time (Tse, Belk, and Zhou 1989).

Three cognitive institutionalization processes are found. First, it is now taken for granted that healthy people have the need to be healed. Second, it is also considered natural that these needs can be satisfied by purchasing and using healing products or services. Third, the new expression Iyashi-kei (healing kind) began to be used frequently for describing certain kinds of laypersons who just help us relax and are not religious persons or healers. Most celebrities considered as Iyashi-kei are young actresses, which endorses the implicit shared views on the gendered division of labor: women heal men. In summary, consumers' needs for healing are socially constructed by media discourse and the imitative behavior of firms.

REFERENCES

Berger, Peter L. and Thomas Luckmann (1966), *The Social Construction of Reality: A Treatise in the Sociology of Knowledge*, Garden City, N.Y.: Doubleday.

DiMaggio, Paul (1997), "Culture and Cognition," *Annual Review of Sociology*, 23, 263-87.

DiMaggio, Paul J. and Walter W. Powell (1983), "The Iron Cage Revisited: Institutional Isomorphism and Collective Rationality in Organizational Fields," *American Sociological Review*, 48 (2, April), 147-60.

Kozinets, Robert V. (2001), "Utopian Enterprise: Articulating the Meaning of Star Trek's Culture of Consumption," *Journal of Consumer Research*, 28 (June), 67–89.

Meyer, John W. and Brian Rowan (1977), "Institutionalized Organizations: Formal Structure as Myth and Ceremony," *American Journal of Sociology*, 83 (2), 340-63.

Powell, Walter W. and Paul J. DiMaggio (1991), "Introduction," in *The New Institutionalism in Organizational Analysis*, ed. Walter W. Powell and Paul J. DiMaggio, Chicago: University of Chicago Press, 1-38.

Scott, W. Richard (2008), *Institutions and Organizations: Ideas and Interests*, Los Angeles: Sage Publications.

Strang, David and John W. Meyer (1993), "Institutional Conditions for Diffusion," *Theory and Society*, 22 (4), 487-511.

Tse, David K., Russell W. Belk, and Nan Zhou (1989), "Becoming a Consumer Society: A Longitudinal and Cross-Cultural Content Analysis of Print Ads from Hong Kong, the People's Republic of China, and Taiwan," *Journal of Consumer Research*, 15 (4), 457-72.

Zucker, Lynne G. (1983), "Organizations as Institutions," in *Research in the Sociology of Organizations*, Vol. 2, ed. S. B. Bacharach, Greenwich, CT: JAI Press, 1-47.

Why Do People Shop Second-Hand? A Second-Hand Shoppers' Motivation Scale in a French Context

Dominique Roux, Universite Paris 12- IRG, France
Denis Guiot, Universite Paris Dauphine (DRM-DMSP), France

EXTENDED ABSTRACT

Despite the marked interest in second-hand markets and thrift shopping (Bardhi and Arnould 2005; Belk, Sherry, and Wallendorf 1988; Sherry 1990; Soiffer and Hermann 1987), no measurement tool has been developed to capture the range of motivations that drive consumers to buy second-hand. In particular, little can be predicted either in term of behavior related to second-hand buying, or of the consequences that stem from it. This study thus offers a measure of second-hand shoppers' motivations, the types of products they bought and of channels they frequent as well as with other economic or ludic practices such as recycling and browsing.

We first show that second-hand commerce has ancient roots in France and is experiencing comparable growth to Anglo-Saxon contexts: proliferation of garage sales, expansion of specialized second-hand stores, and growing use of the Internet. Then, in line with previous research (Bauhain-Roux and Guiot 2001), we assume that purchasing second-hand consists both of not buying new and of resorting to forms of supply that have their own distinctive characteristics. As Westbrook and Black' (1985) contribution on shopping, we assume that motivations toward second-hand buying conform to this combination of reasons that encourage consumers to look for original and less expensive products and to prefer the informal and recreational world of certain places of exchange. The concept of motivation thus appears to be a wide-ranging tool for studying second-hand buying, both in regard to products and distribution channels.

Following Churchill's (1979) paradigm revised by Rossiter (2002), we develop a measure of motivations toward second-hand buying within a French socio-cultural context. We define motivations for second-hand buying as the psychological and material impulses that orient individuals toward second-hand products and/ or channels. As previous research was carried out in Anglo-Saxon contexts and only within specific channels, a preliminary qualitative study was deemed necessary to explore the motivations of French purchasers. We identified six main areas of motivation, broken down into 15 sub-dimensions and 77 items: an economic dimension (I) is reflected by four factors: the search for a fair price (1), bargain hunting (2), the wish to pay less (3), and the allocative aspect of price (4); a recreational dimension appears to be linked both to the second-hand product offering (II)—the originality of the products (5), nostalgia for items from the past (6), self-expression (7), and congruence sought with the items purchased (8)—and also to the characteristics of certain shopping outlets (III) such as social contact (9), stimulation (10), and treasure hunting (11); a power motive (IV) is also revealed by the way purchasers control the power of sellers by means of bargaining (12), and through a wish to escape from conventional channels (13); ethical and ecological motives (V) show concerns of certain purchasers in regard to recycling and avoidance of waste (14); and finally, "anti-ostentation" motives (VI) for some respondents reveal the conscious and voluntary rejection of everything associated with fashion and mass consumption (15).

Two data collections gathered from 708 second-hand buyers enabled us successively to calibrate and replicate the scale. Scale purification was achieved through an initial data collection (224 Parisians), and exploratory and confirmatory factor analysis. We examined the hierarchical structure of the scale, its reliability, and its convergent and discriminant validity. The findings reveal a hierarchical structure characterized by two second-order factors, one corresponding to economic motives—with 3 subfactors: "fair price", "ethics and ecology" and "distance from the system"—and the other to recreational motives—with 4 subfactors: "treasure hunting", "originality", "social contact" and "nostalgia". An alternative first-order model comprising 7 correlated sub-factors was tested and rejected in favor of the hierarchical structure hypothesis.

We successfully replicated the hierarchical model on a validation sample of 484 Parisians with the same survey conditions. A measurement model using the 7 dimensions and 21 items remaining after the purification stage provides a satisfactory goodness-of-fit to the data. Reliability was estimated through Jöreskog's (1971) indices (>.70). Observation of factor contributions (all significant and >.669), application of the Fornell and Larcker (1981) procedure, and comparison of nested structural models indicate that the convergent and discriminant validity conditions are satisfactorily met. The nomological and predictive validities were assessed by testing the relations between second-hand shoppers' motivations and the types of products bought and channels frequented, as well as behaviors related to economic and recreational motives such as recycling (Leonard-Barton 1981) and browsing (Lombart 2004). Three types of effect corresponding to the different dimensions of the construct were assumed:

H1: Economic motives for second-hand buying are positively linked to recycling behaviors, measured by items included in the voluntary simplicity scale (Leonard-Barton 1981)

H2: Recreational motives for second-hand buying are positively linked to browsing behaviors, (defined as wandering around for pleasure and without any specific intention of buying, Lombart 2004).

H3: Motivations for buying second-hand are positively linked to the frequency of buying second-hand products and to the number of second-hand product channels visited.

The results confirm the stability of the causal model with significant structural coefficients enabling all the hypotheses to be validated. Additionally, the capacity of the scale to explain the choice of products bought and the second-hand channels frequented was tested by logistic regression, while controlling the effects of age, income and educational level. 10 of the 32 product categories and half the 11 channels proposed show correct classification percentages by logistic regression. Finally, the scale successfully captures a variety of motives that give rise to a specific form of purchasing. It incorporates motivations toward products and channels and no longer relies on contextualized approaches. It also lends itself to different uses involving a total score corresponding to all dimensions of the aggregated construct, as well as disaggregated scores. It can further be used to explain variables linked either to the economic or recreational dimensions such as preferences toward private labels, sensitivity to brands or perceived market authenticity. New avenues of research are also envisaged on possible links between the second-hand shopping motivations and emerging phenomena such as sustainable or socially responsible consumption, dissatisfaction with the market system, and consumer resistance.

REFERENCES

Bardhi, Fleura and Eric J. Arnould (2005), "Thrift Shopping: Combining Utilitarian Thrift and Hedonic Treat Benefits," *Journal of Consumer Behavior*, 4 (4), 223–33.

Bauhain-Roux, Dominique and Denis Guiot (2001), "Le développement du marché de l'occasion. Caractéristiques et enjeux pour le marché du neuf, " *Décisions Marketing*, 24, sept-dec, 25–35.

Belk, Russell W., John F. Sherry Jr., and Melanie Wallendorf (1988), "A Naturalistic Inquiry into Buyer and Seller Behavior at a Swap Meet," *Journal of Consumer Research*, 14 (March), 449–69.

Churchill, Gilbert A., Jr. (1979), "A paradigm for developing better measures of marketing constructs," *Journal of Marketing Research*, 16, 1, 64–73.

Fornell, Claes and David F. Larcker (1981), "Evaluating structural equation models with unobservable variables and measurement error," *Journal of Marketing Research*, 18 (February), 39–50.

Jöreskog, Karl G. (1971), "Statistical Analysis of Set Congeneric Tests," *Psychometrika*, 36, 109–33.

Leonard-Barton, Dorothy (1981), "Voluntary Simplicity Lifestyles and Energy Conservation," *Journal of Consumer Research*, 8 (December), 243–52.

Lombart, Cindy (2004), "Le butinage : proposition d'une échelle de mesure," *Recherche et Applications en marketing*, 19, 2, 1–30.

Rossiter, John R. (2002), "The COARSE procedure for scale development in marketing," *International Journal of Research in Marketing*, 19, 4, 305–35.

Sherry, John F. Jr. (1990), "A Sociocultural Analysis of a Midwestern American Flea Market," *Journal of Consumer Research*, 17 (June), 13–30.

Soiffer, Stephen S. and Gretchen M. Herrmann (1987), "Visions of Power: Ideology and Practise in the American Garage Sale," *Sociological Review*, 35, 1, 48–83.

Westbrook, Robert A and William C. Black (1985), "A Motivation-Based Shopper Typology," *Journal of Retailing*, 61, 1, 78–103.

The Meanings of 'Kod-sa-na-faeng'- Young Adults' Experiences of Television Product Placement in the UK and Thailand

Amy Rungpaka Tiwsakul, University of Surrey, UK
Chris Hackley, University of London, UK

EXTENDED ABSTRACT

"… when I see they use it in *Sex and the City*, I feel like if I use it I can be like Jessica Parker … Jessica guarantees it." (Female, Thai, 24)

Young adults around the world have a commonality in their experience of brands and marketing practices. Product placement has no direct translation in Thai, it is known as 'kod-sa-na-faeng' or 'implicit advertising'. This is partly because product placement and sponsorship are not separate categories on Thai television but aspects of the same practice. Nevertheless, consumers in Thailand, as well as those in the UK, are well aware of the various promotional techniques deployed in their television viewing. Television offers a powerful medium for the promotion of brands. Consumers often have an intimate engagement with their favourite television shows. Television is a medium conducted in a localised vernacular. In Thailand and the UK even where syndicated foreign shows or advertisements are broadcast they are framed by localised announcements and locally produced shows. TV is often engaged with on a daily basis in domestic environments. It has the dual quality of both normalising and glamorising consumption practices. Brands are ubiquitous in television as they are in everyday life: studio directors need brands in order to populate storylines with familiar objects which connect with the viewers' own reality. Television is consequently an ideal vehicle for product placement, yet its role as a vehicle for consumer cultural meaning transfer (McCracken, 1988) and a resource for personal identity projects in an international context is still relatively under-researched.

Previous studies have begun to conceptualise some of the dynamic characteristics of product placement in, for example, explorations of the influence on consumer attitudes towards the brand of the connection between plot and brand (Russell, 2002), character-product associations (Chang and Roth, 2000) and the alignment of consumer attitudes towards the placed brand with those of a character with whom viewers identify (Russell and Stern, 2006). However, most previous studies have been attitudinal and individual in orientation (e.g. Karrh 1994, 1995, 1998; Balasubramanian, 1991; Vollmers and Mizerski, 1994; Nelson, 2002; Gupta et al., 2000; Nebenzahl and Secunda, 1993). So far, more studies have focused on movies as a television as a product placement medium than television (exceptions include LaFerle and Edwards, 2006; Russell, and Puto, 1999; Russell et al, 2004; Tiwsakul et al., 2005) but thus far phenomenological approaches have been rare and non-US national contexts have seldom been explored in their consumer cultural context.

Attempts to define and categorise product placement practices suffer from the limitation that they do not take account of differences in regulation and practice in different countries. For example, Balasubramanian (1994), Gupta and Gould (1997), Ford (1993) and Baker and Crawford (1995) suggest that product placement is 'paid for' with cash or other considerations going to the studio, usually in the person of the producer or broadcaster. This ignores two issues: one is the fact that many brands appear in entertainment as content simply directors need them. Placements give a brand much-needed visibility and credibility regardless of whether payment was made and public relations agencies go to great lengths to bring about 'coincidental' placements. The second issue is that, in the UK, product placement is common but brand owners are forbidden by current regulations from paying programme makers. Instead, they pay product placement agencies who use their contacts with studios to push heir clients' brands into programmes as freely supplied scene props.

This paper describes research among consumers in two differing cultural contexts, the UK and Thailand. In each country the media infrastructure is mature with many domestic television shows being made. Each country has a vital consumer culture and lively interest in brands both domestic and non-domestic (although in Thailand consumer culture is concentrated in the major urban centers where buying power is highest). One important difference between them is that in Thailand television product placement is well-established and although there is media censorship there are relatively lax regulations governing placement practices. In contrast, in the UK under current regulations television programme makers are forbidden from receiving payment from brand owners for featuring their brands as scene props or in storylines. Nevertheless, this does happen legally under the 'free prop supply' system. It is widely assumed that UK regulations will soon change to allow paid-for placements. The UK thus has an immature and highly regulated television product placement environment while Thailand has a mature and relatively under-regulated one.

This paper draws on interviews and written narratives from a selective sample of UK-based and Thai-based television-viewing young adult consumers supplemented by interviews with leading practitioners. Taking an interpretive theoretical stance, the findings suggest that young adult consumers in both countries are similarly attuned to television product placement incidents: they seek them out, describe them vividly, and clearly enjoy their sophistication in discerning not only brands, both global and local, but also the marketing techniques by which brands are inserted into their entertainment. Consumers displayed a high degree of reflexive self-awareness in being aware of their subjective responses to brands placed in television shows and articulating the underling motivations for their affective response. Specifically, they deployed their knowledge and awareness of brands in identity strategies. The paper develops these themes using direct quotes and then draws on the findings to develop and integrated discussion around international consumers' experience of television of product placement, identity, brand symbolism and the movement of consumer cultural meaning.

REFERENCES

Babin, Laurie A. and Carder, Thompson S. (1996), "Viewers' recognition of brands placed within a film", *International Journal of Advertising*, 15:2, 140-151.

Baker, Michael J., and Crawford, Hazel A., (1995), "*Product placement*", working paper, Department of Marketing, University of Strathclyde, Glasgow, Scotland, unpublished.

Balasubramanian, Siva K. (1994), "Beyond advertising and publicity: hybrid messages and public policy issues", *Journal of Advertising*, 23:4, 29-47.

Balasubramanian, Siva K. (1991), *Beyond advertising and publicity: the domain of hybrid messages*, Cambridge, MA: Marketing Science Institute.

Advances in Consumer Research
Volume 36, © 2009

Baudrillard, Jean (1998), *The consumer society: Myths and structures, trans. Turner, C.*, London: Sage.

Chang, Jennifer E. and Roth, Edward W. (2000), "When is cranberry sauce shaped like a can? An investigation of cultural capital, gender and consumption in television programming", Schroeder, J. E., and Otnes, C. (eds.), *Association of Consumer Research on Gender, Marketing, and Consumer Behavior*, Urbana, University of Illinois, 107-123.

d'Astous, Alain and Seguin, Nathalie (1999), "Consumer reactions to product placement strategies in television sponsorship", *European Journal of Marketing*, Vol. 33:9/10, 896-910.

Danesi, Marcel (2006), *Brands*, New York: Routledge.

Elliott, Richard and Ritson, Mark (1999), "The social uses of advertising: an ethnographic study of adolescent advertising audiences", *Journal of Consumer Research*, 26:3, 260-277.

Fiske, John (1987), *Television culture*, London: Routledge.

Ford, Bianca, and Ford, James (1993), *Television and sponsorship*, Oxford: Butterworth-Heinemann.

Gould, Stephen J. and Gupta, Pola B (2006), ""Come on down" How consumers view game shows and the products placed in them", *Journal of Advertising*, 35:1, 65-81.

Gupta, Pola B., Balasubramanian, Silva K., and Klassen, Michael (2000), "Viewers' evaluations of product placements in movies, public policy issues and managerial implications", *Journal of Current Issues and Research in Advertising*, 22:2, 41-52.

Gupta, Pola B. and Gould, Stephen J. (1997), "Consumers' perceptions of the ethics and acceptability of product placements in movies: Product category and individual differences", *Journal of Current Issues and Research in Advertising*, 19:1, 37-50.

Hackley, Christopher and Tiwsakul, Rungpaka (2006a), "Entertainment marketing and experiential consumption", *Journal of Marketing Communications*, 12:1, 63-75.

Hirschman, Elizabeth C. (1986), "Humanistic inquiry in marketing research, philosophy, method and criteria", *Journal of Marketing Research*, 23, 237–249.

Hirschman, Elizabeth C. (1988), "The ideology of consumption: A structural-syntactical analysis of 'Dallas' and 'Dynasty'", *Journal of Consumer Research*, 15, 344-359

Hirschman, Elizabeth C., and Holbrook, Morris B. (1992), *Postmodern consumer research: The study of consumption as text*, Newbury Park, CA: Sage.

Hirschman, Elizabeth C. and Thompson, Craig (1997), "Why media matter–toward a richer understanding of consumers relationships with advertising and mass media", *Journal of Advertising*, Vol. 16:1, 43–60.

Holt, Douglas (2004), *How do brands become icons: the principles of cultural branding*, Boston: Harvard Business School Publishing Corporation.

Jansson, Andre (2002), "The mediatisation of consumption: towards an analytical framework of image culture", *Journal of Consumer Culture*, 2:1, 5-31.

Karrh, James A. (1995), "Brand placements in feature films: the practitioners' view", Madden, C. S., *The American Academy of Advertising, Waco, TX, Hankamer School of Business, Baylor University*, 182-188.

Karrh, James A. (1998), "Brand placement: A review", *Journal of Current Issues and Research in Advertising*, 20:2, 31-49.

La Ferle, Carrie, and Edwards, Steven M. (2006), "Product placement: how brands appear on television", *Journal of Advertising*, 35:4, 65-86.

Lincoln, Yvonna S., and Guba, Egon G. (1985), *Naturalistic inquiry*, Beverly Hills, CA: Sage.

McCracken, Grant (2005), *Culture and consumption II: markets, meaning, and brand management*, Bloomington: Indiana University Press.

McCracken, Grant (1988), *Culture and consumption: New approaches to the symbolic character of consumer goods and activities*, USA: Indianna University Press: Bloomington and Indianapolis.

Miles, Matthew B., and Huberman, Michael A. (1994), *An Expanded sourcebook: qualitative data analysis*, London: Sage.

Mortan, Cynthia, and Friedman, Meredith (2002), ""I saw it in the movies": Exploring the link between product placement beliefs and reported usage behaviour", *Journal of Current Issues and Research in Advertising*, 24:2, 33-40.

Nebenzahl, Israel D., and Secunda, Eugene (1993), "Consumers' attitudes towards product placement in movies", *International Journal of Advertising*, Vol. 12, Iss. p. 1-11.

Nelson, Michelle R. (2000), "Recall of brand placements in computer/video games", *Journal of Advertising Research,*, Vol. 42:2, 80-93

O'Donohoe, Stephanie (1997), "Raiding the postmodern pantry-advertising intertextuality and the young adult audience", *European Journal of Marketing*, 31:3/4, 234-253.

Peñaloza, Lisa (2001), "Consuming the American West: animating cultural meaning and memory at a Stock Show and Rodeo", *Journal of Consumer Research*, 28, December, 369-398.

Potter, Jonathan and Wetherell, Margaret (1987), *Discourse and social psychology*, London: Sage.

Russell, Cristel A. and Puto, Christopher P. (1999), "Rethinking television audience measures: An exploration into the construct of audience connectedness", *Marketing Letters*, 10:4, 387-401.

Russell, Cristel A. (2002), "Investigating the effectiveness of product placements in television shows: the role of modality and plot connection congruence on brand memory and attitude", *Journal of Consumer Research*, 29:3, 306-319.

Russell, Cristel A., Norman, Andrew T., and Heckler, Susan E. (2004), "*People and their television shows: An overview of television connectedness"*, In: Shrum, L. J., *The psychology of entertainment media*, Mahwah, NJ: LEA, p. 275-290.

Russell, Cristel A. and Stern, Barbara B. (2006), "Consumers, characters and products: A balance model of sitcom product placement effects", *Journal of Advertising*, 35:1, 7-21.

Russell, Cristel A. (1998), "Towards a framework of product placement: Theoretical propositions", *Advances in Consumer Research*, 25, 357-362.

Schroeder, Jonathan E. and Salzer-Mörling, Miriam (2006), *Brand culture*, New York: Routledge.

Shermach, Kelly (1995), "Casting Catt Goes Out", *Marketing News*, 29, 11.

Spiggle, Susan (1994), "Analysis and interpretation of qualitative data in consumer research", *Journal of Consumer Research*, 21, 491-503.

Storey, John (2003), *Cultural studies and the study of popular culture*, 2nd ed., Edinburgh: Edinburgh University Press.

Thompson, Craig J., Pollio, Howard R., and Locander, William B. (1994), "The spoken and the unspoken: a hermeneutic approach to understanding the cultural viewpoints that underlie consumers' expressed meanings", *Journal of Consumer Research*, 21, December, 431-453.

Thompson, Craig, Locander, William, and Pollio, Howard (1989), "Putting consumer experience back into consumer research: the philosophy and method of existential phenomenology", *Journal of Consumer Research*, 17, 133-147.

Tiwsakul, Rungpaka, Hackley, Christopher, and Szmigin, Isabelle (2005), "Explicit, non-integrated product placement in British television programmes", *International Journal of Advertising*, 24:1, 95-111.

Vollmer, Stacy M. and Mizerski, Richard W. (1994), "A review and investigation into the effectiveness of product placements in films", *In Conference Proceedings of the 1994 Conference of the American Academy of Advertising*, Athens, 97-102.

A Multivariate Model of Partitioned Country-of-Origin on Consumer Quality Perceptions

Md. Humayun Kabir Chowdhury, East West University, Bangladesh

EXTENDED ABSTRACT

A substantial body of literature has accumulated showing that consumers adjust their attitudes toward a product according to its country-of-origin (Chao 1993; Cordell 1992; Han 1989; Han and Terpstra 1988). This bias may be categorized as either "home country bias" or "foreign country bias". With "home country bias" consumers prefer products made in their own country to identical products made in foreign countries. "Foreign country bias" exists when differential differences are expressed for products made in different foreign countries (Schooler 1965; Wang and Lamb 1983).

Understanding consumers' opinion toward products from various countries can be useful in developing multinational strategic marketing policies. If country-of-origin is to be used as a competitive tool, managers must also understand the mechanism of country-of-origin on consumer quality perceptions. Research on evaluation of foreign products infers that the producing country affects consumers' judgments of product quality (Bilkey and Nes 1982; Hong and Wyer 1989). For example, a country's image regarding workmanship and technological advancement logically will be projected onto the features of products produced by that country. Product quality evaluation is conceptualized as the attitudes consumers hold towards their targeted products.

The main objective of this research was to examine the cognitive processes by which country-of-origin information influences consumer's evaluation of a product. In doing so, structural equation modeling approach has been used to test a hypothetical model containing relationships among psychological constructs including country associations, the evaluation of the product's functional characteristics and appearance and the quality perceptions with regard to the product. The second objective was to develop a better understanding of the country-of-origin effect by separately examining the effects of the country-of-design (COD), the country-of-assembly (COA), the country-of-parts (COP), and consumer brand mage (CBI) of a product.

To study the psychological process by which the country-of-origin associations are integrated in the formation of related behavioral deliberation, a hypothetical structural model was developed. The model contained eight theoretical constructs. These constructs were considered to be latent psychological variables that cannot be measured directly and without error. Instead, each of them has to be measured indirectly through multiple indicators. The eight constructs of the hypothetical model may be grouped into the following three categories:

- Evaluation of the country-of-Origin associations;
- Evaluation of the product; and,
- Evaluation of the quality.

Therefore, current study dealt with eight constructs and their observed measures. The questionnaire contained multiple measures of all seven latent variables of the model. The selection of these indicators was based on an extensive literature review. All measures used in the present study had already been used and found to be valid and reliable indicators in one or more previous studies. The main sources used in this selection process were: Insch and McBride (1998), Parameswaran and Yaprak (1987), Bandyopadhyay and Banerjee (2002), Ahmed and d'Astous (1999), Han and Terpstra (1988). For all these directly observed variables, ratings were obtained on a seven-point scale ranging from 7="Strongly Agree" to 1="Strongly Disagree".

Since COD, COA, COP and CBI deal with overall country and brand image, description and scales for each construct thus contained the same contents except the specific country name. For example, a description for COD such as "Japan has designed a television ——" has been changed into–"China/Bangladesh has designed a television —". Similarly, the description for COA is– "China assembled the final product——" has been changed into- "Japan/Bangladesh assembled the final product——". Finally, the description for COP is–"Major parts have been produced in Bangladesh" has been changed into–"Major parts have been produced in Japan/China".

The data were first tested for reliability using Cronbach's alpha to assess reliability. Internal consistency (reliability) values of the measurement items were assessed before entering into the structural analysis. Data were analyzed via structural equation models using Amos (Analysis of MOment Structures) 5.0.

The Maximum-Likelihood Method was selected as the method of model estimation. The fit of the structural model was estimated by various indices, and the results demonstrated good fit. For models with good fit, most empirical analyses suggest that the ratio of chi-square normalized to degree of freedom (χ^2/df) should not exceed 3.0 (Carmines and McIver 1981). In addition, the obtained goodness-of-fit (GFI) measure was 0.92 and the adjusted goodness-of-fit (AGFI) measure was 0.89, respectively, which are both higher than the suggested values. The other two indices of good fit– the normalized fit index (NFI) and the comparative fit index (CFI) are recommended to exceed 0.90. The results also meet these requirements. Finally, the discrepancies between the proposed model and population covariance matrix, as measured by the root mean square error of approximation (RMSEA), are in line with the suggested cutoff value of 0.08 for good fit (Byrne 1998).

The results of this study provide evidence that country associations can influence product responses. Moreover, when COD, COA, COP and CBI associations are available to consumers, these associations appear to affect product responses in different manners. The results raise the possibility that countries that already have positioned themselves around a reputation for technological innovation or other skills and abilities related to product development and manufacturing may expect consumers to transfer those associations to new products from the country.

REFERENCES

Ahmed, Sadrudin A. and Alain d'Astous (1999), "Product-Country images in Canada and in the People's Republic of China," *Journal of International Consumer Marketing*, 11(1), 5-22

Bandyopadhyay, Subir and Banerjee, Bibek (2002), "A Country-of-Origin Analysis of Foreign Products by Indian Consumers," *Journal of International Consumer Marketing*, 15 (2), 85-109

Bilkey, Warren. J., and Erik Nes (1982), "Country-of-Origin Effects on Product Evaluations," *Journal of International Business Studies*, 13 (Spring/Summer), 89-99

Han, C. M. (1989), "Country Image: Halo or Summary Construct?" *Journal of Marketing Research*, 26 (May): 222-229

Han, C. M. and Terpstra V. (1988), "Country-of-origin: Effects for Uni-national and Bi-national Products," *Journal of International Business Studies*, 16 (Summer), 235-256

Hong, S. T. and Wyer R. S. Jr. (1989), "Effects of Country of Origin and Product Attribute Information on Product Evaluation: An Information Processing Perspective," *Journal of Consumer Research*, 16 (September), 175-187

Insch, Gary S. and McBride, J. Brad (1998), "Decomposing the Country-of-Origin Construct: An Empirical Test of Country of Design, Country of Parts and Country of Assembly," Journal of International Consumer Marketing, 10 (4), 69-91

Chao, P. (1993), "Partitioning Country of Origin Effects: Consumer Evaluations of a Hybrid Product," *Journal of International Business Studies*, 24 (2), 291-306

Cordell, V. V. (1992), "Effects of Consumers Preferences for Foreign Source Products," *Journal of International Business Studies*, 23 (2), 251-269

Parameswaran, R. and Yaprak, A. (1987), "A Cross-National Comparison of Consumer Research Measures," Journal of International Business Studies, (Spring), 35-49

Schooler, R. (1965), "Product Bias in the Central American Common Market," Journal of Marketing Research, 2 (November), 394-397

Changing Mealtime Rituals: The Mediating Influence of the Television on Family Dynamics

David P. Chitakunye, Keele University, UK
Pauline Maclaran, Keele University, UK

EXTENDED ABSTRACT

Eating at home has always been regarded as a time when all family members come together from their diverse and separate activities to affirm their relatedness and love (Levy 1996). Yet traditional mealtimes have become more fragmented with members of a family often eating at different times to suit their own personal schedules (Warde 1997). Although food meanings, and the rituals and practices in which these are embedded, contribute to family identity and domestic life (Charles and Kerr 1988), our knowledge is still limited as to how these are changing, and how material objects, such as the television or computer games, are influencing these changes.

Whilst the family serves as a consuming, producing, distribution and socialising unit interacting with other elements of society (Price and Epp 2005), consumer researchers have devoted relatively little attention in understanding them. Extant research has investigated food consumption behaviour with particular focus on specific consumption events such as Thanksgiving Day (Wallendorf and Arnould 1991); Christmas (Hirschman and LaBarbera 1989); public eating venues (Fischer and Wayne 1999); food culture of particular societies or ethnic groups (Hetzel 1999); and consumer micro-cultures (Thompson and Troester 2002).Yet, apart from Hirschman et al. (2004), there has been a paucity of consumer research that examines the differing contexts of eating, and how these affect the meanings attached to food consumption. Importantly, in relation to this study, there is silence about the actual practices in regard to eating together as families (Murcott 1997).

Given this background, our present purpose is to explore how the television is mediating family mealtime relationships, and their concomitant rituals. In particular, we are interested in naturalistic everyday food consumption practices in the domestic context of consumption, rather than specific consumption events or food consumption in public places.

This study uses an interpretive research strategy. Stage 1 of the research was school-based and gathered data from school children aged between 13 and 17 through observation, semi-structured and in-depth interviews as well as visual diaries. Stage 2 was an observation during family mealtimes; we talked informally with family members. The research followed a theoretical sampling approach for recruiting informants, i.e. a sample that typifies the population, the theoretical category or the phenomenon to be studied and was chosen purposefully with consideration to representativeness (Mason, 2002; Silverman, 2000). In addition, online research was used to sensitise the researchers to the culturally resonant categories (Hirschman et al. 2004). In total the dataset so far consists of 13 personal interviews, 9 online interviews, 23 visual diaries, and mealtime observations with 3 families.The data analysis is following the principles for the analysis and interpretation of qualitative data as recommended by Spiggle (1994) and others (Strauss and Corbin, 1998; Arnould and Wallendorf, 1994), and continuing in an iterative fashion across offline and online environments.

Two overarching conceptual categories are used to organise our interpretation of the meanings of mealtime rituals, and how these are mediated by the television: (1) the formal environment for food consumptions; and, (2) the informal environment for food consumption. Our findings show that when eating in a formal environment, such as the dining room, the table is usually set in a specific way, making it easier to maintain a routinised seating order, which may also be hierarchical, for example, with a father or mother at the head of the table. This formal configuration facilitates interactions between family members which take place on a face-to-face basis, with few external distractions. Appropriate eating and serving utensils (e.g. knives, forks, plates, dishes etc) will also be used. By contrast, the informal environment (usually a lounge or 'den') tends to be dominated by the television, with seating arrangements organised accordingly in order to ensure good viewing. In this environment it is not always convenient to use traditional eating or serving utensils and it thus encourages a more relaxed style of consumption. The seating of family members often follows a random pattern, depending on who comes first into the room, and an available seat's proximity to the television. Because everyone faces the television rather than each other, conventional mealtime interactions may prove difficult, not least because family members will usually be absorbed in what is happening on the television.

Drawing from these findings, we argue that, family identity may be enacted through everyday mealtime interactions and the various communication processes therein that include parents, children, television, the Internet and so forth. Of particular importance in our findings, is the link between food, family identity and domestic life, and how this is mediated by the television in several ways. Our study demonstrates how the mealtime reality of everyday life is frequently shared with the television. We argue that the television is becoming part of the nucleus family. Just as people share not only food, but also conversation and a social life, so too, does the television become part of that social life when informants' conversations are centred on television programmes, rather than on other family members.

REFERENCES

Arnould, E.J. and Wallendorf, M. (1994), "Marketing-oriented ethnography: Interpretation building and marketing strategy formulation", *Journal of Marketing Research*, 31(4), 484-504.

Charles, N. and Kerr, M. (1988), *Women Food and Families*, Manchester: Manchester University Press.

Fischer, E. (1999), "Special Session Summary: Tales of Food and Eating ", in Eric J. Arnould and Linda M. Scott, eds., *Advances in Consumer Research Volume 26*, Provo, UT: Association for Consumer Research, p. 483.

Hetzel, P. (1999), "Consumption, food and taste", Special session summary, *Advances in Consumer Research,* Vol. 26, Provo, UT: Association for Consumer Research, 330.

Hirschman, E. C. and LaBarbera, P. A. (1989), "The Meaning of Christmas", in E. C. Hirschman, ed., *Interpretive Consumer Research,* Provo, UT: Association for Consumer Research, pp. 136-147.

Hirschman, E.C., Carscadden, N., Fleischauer, L., Hasak, M. and Mitchell, M. (2004), "Exploring the architecture of contemporary American foodways", in E.C. Hirschman, ed., *Advances in Consumer Research,* Vol. 31, Provo, UT: Association for Consumer Research, 548-553.

Levy, S.J. (1996), "Stalking the Amphisbaena," *Journal of Consumer Research*, 23 (December), 163-176.

Mason, J. (2002), 'Qualitative interviewing: Asking, listening and interpreting', in T. May, ed., *Qualitative Research in Action*, London: Sage Publications.

Murcott, A. (1997), "Family meals–a thing of the past?", in P. Caplan, ed., *Food, Health and Identity*, Routledge, London, pp.32-49.

Price, L.L. and Epp A.M.(2005), "Special Session Summary Finding Families: Family Identity in Consumption Venues", in Geeta Menon and Akshay R. Rao, eds., *Advances in Consumer Research* Volume 32, Duluth, MN : Association of Consumer Research, pp. 9-13.

Silverman, D. (2000), *Doing Qualitative Research: A Practical Handbook*, London: Sage.

Spiggle, S. (1994), "Analysis and Interpretation of Qualitative Data in Consumer Research", *Journal of Consumer Research*, 21(December), 491-503.

Strauss, A. and Corbin, J. (1998), *Basics of Qualitative Research*, Thousand Oaks, CA: Sage.

Thompson, C.J. and Troester M. (2002), "Consumer Value Systems in the Age of Postmodern Fragmentation", *Journal of Consumer Research,* 28(4), 550-571.

Wallendorf, M. and E. J. Arnould (1991), "We Gather Together: Consumption Rituals of Thanksgiving Day," *Journal of Consumer Research,* (18) 1, 13-32.

Warde, A. (1997), *Consumption, Food and Taste: Culinary Antinomies and Commodity Culture*, London: Sage.

Ties that Bind and Blind: The Negative Consequences of Using Social Capital to Facilitate Purchases

Bryan R. Johnson, Pennsylvania State University, USA
William T. Ross, Jr., Pennsylvania State University, USA

EXTENDED ABSTRACT

Conceptualization

As the fabric of civilization, social relationships play an important, yet often subtle, role in society. Relationships bind individuals together by facilitating correspondence and collaboration among them. Because of their intrinsic function in social interactions, relationships have the capacity to impact numerous aspects of human behavior, including those related to consumption. Consequently, given the influence of these ties, many consumers draw upon social connections as they purchase everyday products and services (Beaty et al. 1996; DiMaggio and Louch 1998; Frenzen and Davis 1990). Accordingly, the purpose of this paper is to examine the impact of using these social relationships to make purchases. While scholars have recently begun to address the basic questions of whether and why consumers leverage personal relationships in the marketplace, very little has been done to determine the implications of such actions for consumers.

To highlight the consequences of incorporating social relationships into consumption experiences, we draw upon social capital theory, which posits that individuals obtain benefits or returns as a result of their social relationships with others (Lin 2001; Portes 1998). Generally speaking, social capital theory focuses on how the resources embedded in social relationships provide benefits to individuals. These resources, such as advice, information, and ideas, are considered social because they can only be accessed through direct and indirect ties with others. Hence, to possess social capital, one must possess relationships with others; it is only through social interactions that the benefits of social capital can be realized (Lin 2001; Portes 1998).

Like most social capital research conducted in the social sciences, research on social capital in the consumer domain has focused primarily on the positive benefits of this behavior, while largely ignoring the hidden liabilities that may be associated with leveraging social relationships for personal gains. Consequently, our main objective is to identify the negative outcomes of social capital mobilization for consumers drawing upon their relationships to make purchases in the marketplace. Ultimately, uncovering and explaining these negative outcomes is important if scholars are to understand this meaningful social dimension of consumer behavior.

Method

To understand the consequences of leveraging social relationships in the marketplace and to expand and refine social capital theory in the consumer domain, we utilize the grounded theory approach (Glaser and Strauss 1967; Strauss and Corbin 1998). We conducted semi-structured depth interviews with 19 U.S. consumers, who were purposively selected using established theoretical sampling techniques. Our analysis employed *open coding* to identify important concepts in the data and *axial coding* to identify how emerging codes related to larger categories of interest (Strauss and Corbin 1998). We followed the "constant comparative approach" (Glaser and Strauss 1967) to ensure that the emerging theory was well-grounded in the data. This method of data analysis led to rich conceptual density among our categories and allowed us to refine our code list, yielding a core set of categories regarding the consequences of social capital mobilization. In order to ensure trustworthiness of the data, we conducted member checks with study participants, as advocated in previous research (Belk, Sherry, and Wallendorf 1988; Lincoln and Guba 1985).

Findings

The fundamental premise of social capital theory is that individuals obtain returns from leveraging their social relationships. However, we have suggested that these returns may, at times, be negative. As expected, during the course of our interviews, we uncovered experiences in which negative outcomes unexpectedly occurred as a result of social capital mobilization.

Our analysis identified three categories of these negative outcomes: *recourse bridling*, *trust decay*, and *relationship atrophy*. These outcomes are important because they have not previously been connected to individual social capital theory. Identifying such experiences extends and refines social capital theory, both within marketing and in the larger social science arena.

Recourse bridling occurs when consumers face challenges during the consumption experience, yet they feel constrained from addressing them, given the relationships involved. This bridling effect likely occurs due to the perceived discomfort associated with confronting friends, as well as the perceived awkwardness that may result in future social interactions. *Trust decay* also results as a consequence of problems that arise when using personal relationships to facilitate purchases. When things do not work out as anticipated, many consumers lose trust in their friends' judgments and subsequently discount their recommendations and opinions in future interactions. Finally, *relationship atrophy* occurs when problems associated with the transaction permanently tarnish the relationships involved. When problems arise and expected benefits fail to materialize, individuals are often put in the unfortunate position of making a choice between the anticipated benefits and the relationship. When anticipated benefits win out, relationships degenerate.

Surprisingly, we find that many consumers underestimate the risks involved with leveraging their relationships for personal gains. Nearly all participants failed to contemplate the possible impact of negative experiences on the relationships involved. Instead, they tended to fixate completely upon the potential benefits available to them. Our data suggest that consumers' ability to foresee these negative consequences is a function of their experience using social capital. Consequently, those with more experience may be more adept at calculating the true cost of using their social connections, as they are more likely to have experienced negative consequences in the past.

Ultimately, this study makes several important contributions. It highlights the notion that social capital may not be the panacea it was once believed to be. Although social capital mobilization frequently results in positive outcomes for individuals, there are situations in which it has negative consequences. In addition, this study identifies the different categories of negative outcomes typically experienced by consumers when employing social capital in the marketplace.

Interestingly, these consequences are typically unanticipated and frequently take consumers by complete surprise. Ironically, the same social forces that facilitate access to resources can also constrain and impair those who seek them. Collectively, these findings add depth to our understanding of social capital theory, both within marketing and in the larger social science arena.

REFERENCES

Adler, Paul S. and Seok-Woo Kwon (2002), "Social capital: Prospects for a new concept," *Academy of Management Review*, 27 (1), 17-40.

Beaty, Sharon E., Morris Mayer, James E. Coleman, Kristy Ellis Reynolds, and Jungki Lee (1996), "Customer-Sales Associate Relationships," *Journal of Retailing*, 72 (3), 223-47.

Belk, Russell W., John F. Sherry, and Melanie Wallendorf (1988), "A Naturalistic Inquiry Into Buyer And Seller Behavior At A Swap Meet," *Journal of Consumer Research*, 14 (4), 449-70.

Belk, Russell W., Melanie Wallendorf, and John F. Sherry (1989), "The Sacred And The Profane In Consumer-Behavior-Theodicy on The Odyssey," *Journal of Consumer Research*, 16 (1), 1-38.

Bergadaa, Michelle M. (1990), "The Role of Time In The Action of The Consumer," *Journal of Consumer Research*, 17 (3), 289-302.

Bourdieu, Pierre (1986), "The Forms of Capital" in *Handbook of Theory and Research for the Sociology of Education*, J.G Richardson, Ed. Westport, CT: Greenwood Press.

_____ (2002), "The Sociological Theory of Pierre Bourdieu" in *Contemporary Sociological Theory*, Craig Calhoun, Joseph Gerteis, James Moody, Steven Pfaff, and Indermohan Virk, Eds. Malden, MA: Blackwell Publishing.

Boxman, Ed, Paul M. De Graaf, and Hendrik D. Flap (1991), "The Impact of Social and Human Capital on the Income Attainment of Dutch Managers," *Social Networks*, 13 (1), 51-73.

Burt, Ronald. S. (2000), "The Network Structure of Social Capital," *Research in Organizational Behavior*, 22, 345-423.

_____ (2004), "Structural Holes and Good Ideas," *The American Journal of Sociology*, 110 (2), 349-99.

Charmaz, Kathy (2006), *Constructing Grounded Theory*. Thousand Oaks, CA: Sage.

Cohen, Sheldon, William J. Doyle, David P. Skoner, Bruce S. Rabin, and Jack M. Gwaltney, Jr. (1997), "Social ties and susceptibility to the common cold," *JAMA*, 277 (24), 1940-44.

Coleman, James S. (1988), "Social Capital in the Creation of Human Capital," *The American Journal of Sociology*, 94, 95-120.

DiMaggio, Paul and Hugh Louch (1998), "Socially Embedded Consumer Transactions: For What Kinds of Purchases Do People Most Often Use Networks?" *American Sociological Review*, 63, 619-637.

Dominguez, Silvia and Celeste Watkins (2003), "Creating networks for survival and mobility: Social capital among African-American and Latin-American low-income mothers," *Social Problems*, 50 (1), 111.

Frenzen, Jonathan and Harry L. Davis (1990), "Purchasing Behavior In Embedded Markets," *Journal of Consumer Research*, 17 (1), 1-12.

Gabbay, Shaul M. and Ezra W. Zuckerman (1998), "The Contingent Effect of Contact Density on Mobility Expectations," *Social Science Research*, 27, 189-217.

Glaser, Barney G. and Anselm Strauss (1967), "The Constant Comparative Method of Qualitative Analysis," in *The Discovery of Grounded Theory: Strategies for Qualitative Research*. Chicago, IL: Aldine.

Granovetter, Mark (1985), "Economic Action and Social Structure: The Problem of Embeddedness," *American Journal of Sociology*, 91 (3), 481-510.

_____ (1983), "The Strength of Weak Ties: A Network Theory Revisited," *Sociological Theory*, 1, 201-33.

_____ (1973), "The Strength of Weak Ties," *American Journal of Sociology*, 78 (6), 1360-80.

House, James S., Karl R. Landis, and Debra Umberson (1988), "Social relationships and health," *Science*, 241 (4865), 540-45.

Kawachi, Ichiro, Bruce P. Kennedy, Kimberly Lochner, and Deborah Prothrow-Stith (1997), "Social capital, income inequality, and mortality," *American Journal of Public Health*, 87 (9), 1491-500.

Lin, Nan (2001), *Social Capital: A Theory of Social Structure and Action* (1 ed.). Cambridge: Cambridge University Press.

_____ (1999), "Social networks and status attainment," *Annual Review of Sociology*, 25, 467-88.

Lin, Shu-Chi and Yin-Mei Huang (2005), "The role of social capital in the relationship between human capital and career mobility: Moderator or mediator?" *Journal of Intellectual Capital*, 6 (2), 191-216.

Lincoln, Yvonna S. and Egon G. Guba (1985), "Designing a Naturalistic Inquiry," in *Naturalistic Inquiry*, Yvonna S. Lincoln and Egon G. Guba, Eds. Beverly Hills, CA: Sage.

Marx, Karl (1933), *Wage-Labour and Capital*. New York, NY: International Publishers.

Mouw, Ted (2003), "Social Capital and Finding a Job: Do Contacts Matter?" *American Sociological Review*, 68 (6), 868-98.

Neuman, W. Lawrence (2000), *Social Research Methods* (4th ed.). Boston, MA: Allyn & Bacon.

Patton, Michael Q. (1990), *Qualitative Evaluation and Research Methods* (2nd ed.). Newbury Park, CA: Sage Publications.

Portes, Alejandro (1998), "Social capital: Its origins and applications in modern sociology," *Annual Review of Sociology*, 24, 1-24.

_____ (2000), "The Two Meanings of Social Capital," *Sociological Forum*, 15 (1), 1-12.

Portes, Alejandro and Patricia Landolt (1996), "The Downside of Social Capital," *The American Prospect*, 26, 18-22.

Portes, Alejandro and Julia Sensenbrenner (1993), "Embeddedness and immigration: Notes on the social determinants of economic action," *The American Journal of Sociology*, 98 (6), 1320-50.

Price, Linda L. and Eric J. Arnould (1999), "Commerical friendships: Service provider—client relationships in context," *Journal of Marketing*, 63 (4), 38-56.

Putnam, Robert D. (1993), "The Prosperous Community: Social Capital and Public Life," The American Prospect, 24, 34-48.

_____ (1995), "Bowling Alone: America's Declining Social Capital," *Journal of Democracy*, 6, 65-78.

Ream, Robert K. (2005), "Toward Understanding How Social Capital Mediates the Impact of Mobility on Mexican American Achievement," *Social Forces*, 84 (1), 201-24.

Seidel, Marc-David L., Jeffrey T. Polzer, and Katherine J. Stewart (2000), "Friends in high places: The effects of social networks on discrimination in salary negotiations," *Administrative Science Quarterly*, 45 (1), 1-24.

Smith, Adam (1937), *The Wealth of Nations*. New York, NY: Modern Library.

Smoldt, Robert K. (1998), "Turn word of mouth into a marketing advantage," *The Healthcare Forum Journal*, 41 (5), 47-49.

Spiggle, Susan (1994), "Analysis and Interpretation of Qualitative Data In Consumer Research," *Journal of Consumer Research*, 21 (3), 491-503.

Strauss, Anselm and Juliet Corbin (1998), *Basics of Qualitative Research: Techniques and Procedures for Developing Grounded Theory* (2nd ed.). Thousand Oaks, CA: Sage.

Teachman, Jay D., Kathleen Paasch, and Karen Carver (1997), "Social capital and the generation of human capital," *Social Forces*, 75 (4), 1343-1359.

Temkin, Kenneth and William M. Rohe (1998), "Social Capital and Neighborhood Stability: An Empirical Investigation," *Housing Policy Debate*, 9 (1), 61-89.

Thompson, Craig J., William B. Locander, and Howard R. Pollio (1990), "The Lived Meaning of Free Choice: An Existential-Phenomenological Description of Everyday Consumer Experiences of Contemporary Married Women," *The Journal of Consumer Research*, 17 (3), 346-361.

The Comparative Mindset: From Animal Comparisons to Increased Purchase Intentions

Alison Jing Xu, University of Illinois at Urbana-Champaign, USA
Robert S. Wyer, Jr., Hong Kong University of Science & Technology, China

EXTENDED ABSTRACT

Xu and Wyer (2007) found that when consumers consider their preference for one of a set of products without having decided whether they want to buy anything at all, they develop a "which-to-buy" mind-set that increases their likelihood of ultimately making a purchase both in the present situation and in other, unrelated situations. In one study, for example, more participants reported a willingness to purchase a vacation package if they had previously reported a preference for one of two computers than if they had not. In another experiment, participants who stated preference for five pairs of products or services were significantly more likely to purchase candies that were on sale after the experiment than were participants who had not made preference judgments before. Thus, merely stating a preference for choice alternatives in one product domain not only can increase the willingness to make a purchase in other hypothetical situations but also can have an impact on actual purchase behavior.

Preference judgments are only one type of comparative judgments, however. In the present research, we proposed that a which-to-buy mind-set may be a manifestation of a more general, comparative mind-set that, once activated, persists to influence decisions and behavior in other situations in which comparison processes come into play. Furthermore, this mind-set may be activated by making different kinds of comparative judgments in non-product domains.

Four experiments examined these possibilities. Participants in the first experiment received information about two vacation packages, A and B. One group of participants indicated which vacation they preferred. A second group of participants, however, indicated which vacation they disliked more. Then, both these participants and control participants (who had not been exposed to the vacation packages) received information about two computers and indicated whether they would want to purchase A, to purchase B, or to defer making a choice. Compared with control participants who had not made judgments of vacation packages, participants who either made preference or dislike judgment of vacation packages were more likely to choose one of the computers rather than defer choice.

In experiment 2, some participants were exposed to pairs of animals (e.g., elephants, hippos, etc.) and asked to indicate which animals in each pair they preferred. Other participants were asked to compare the animals with respect to a specific attribute (heaviness, jumping ability, eye sight, etc.). Then, both these participants and control participants who did not make judgments of animals performed the same computer-decision task we employed in Experiment 1 Both groups of participants who made comparative judgments of animals expressed a greater willingness to buy one of the computers than control participants.

Furthermore, a third experiment showed that participants who had made comparative judgments of animals were actually more likely than control participants to purchase one of several products (candy, potato chips, etc.) that were on sale after the experiment.

Experiment 4 manipulated the comparative mind-set by asking participants to make a series of similarity judgments on countries, educational institutions, etc. Making these similarity judgments reflected the nature of making directional comparisons suggested by Tversky (1977). These participants also expressed greater willingness to purchase a computer in the subsequent choice task than were control participants.

REFERENCES

Xu, A. J. & Wyer, R. S. (2007). The effect of mind-sets on consumer decision strategies. *Journal of Consumer Research*, *34*, 556-566.

Tversky, A. (1977). Features of similarity. *Psychological Review*. *84, 327-352*.

The Illusion of the Illusion of Control

Francesca Gino, University of North Carolina, USA
Zachariah Sharek, Carnegie Mellon University, USA
Don A. Moore, University of California, Berkeley, USA

EXTENDED ABSTRACT

In the 1970s, New York City installed buttons at intersections with traffic lights. Helpful signs instructed pedestrians: "To cross street, push button. Wait for walk signal." Pedestrians in New York routinely assume that pushing the button speeds the arrival of the walk signal. As it happens, their faith is misplaced. Since the late 1980s, traffic signals in New York have been controlled by a computer system that determines when the walk signal is illuminated (Luo, 2004). Pushing the button has no effect. But the city has not paid to remove the signs or the buttons, and pedestrians push the buttons anyway. Are they suffering from the illusion of control?

According to Langer (1975), people are suffering from the illusion of control when they behave as if they have control when in fact they do not. Many studies have shown how easy it is to get people to behave as if they think they have control over purely chance outcomes (see Thompson, Armstrong, & Thomas (1998) for a thorough review). These experimental paradigms set up situations like New York City intersections, and then point the finger of bias at people who press the "walk" button when given the chance to do so. But is it any surprise that when people have zero control, they are more likely to overestimate than underestimate their control?

A simpler alternative explanation is that people have an imperfect sense of how much they control probabilistic events—when they have very little control, they tend to overestimate it. This alternative explanation implies the need for an experimental condition that is missing from most research on the illusion of control: A high control condition. If people with no control systematically overestimate their control when they have little because they are unsure about how much control they have, then they should systematically underestimate their control when they have objectively high control. This is the hypothesis we test in our experiments.

In two studies, we manipulated whether control was objectively high or objectively low and asked participants to estimate their control. Our main goal was a critical test of the claim that people generally overestimate their control. As predicted, people overestimated their level of control in the low control condition and underestimated it in the high control condition. These results are consistent with our hypothesis and suggest that people systematically overestimate their control when it is objectively low and systematically underestimate it when it is objectively high.

The first study used a novel paradigm that allowed us to manipulate the actual amount of control participants had over a feature of a task in which they were engaging. The results show that when participants had low control (15%) they tended to overestimate it, but that when they had high control (85%) they tended to underestimate it. The second study replicates this result using the classic button-light paradigm in which participants are given a button that may or may not influence the chances that a light comes on subsequent to them pressing the button. Again, when the button provided them with high control (80%) over the light's onset, they tended to underestimate that control. When the button provided them with low control (20%) over the light, they tended to overestimate that control.

Our studies offer little evidence of systematic overestimation of control. Indeed, the only circumstance in which we found that our participants overestimated their control was when they had very little and our measure made it difficult or impossible for them to underestimate their control. We offer an alternative account for findings that people overestimate their control when control is low: It is common for people to be uncertain about how much control they have. Consequently, when control is objectively low people tend to overestimate it. By focusing on domains in which people have little control, prior research has created the illusory impression that overestimation of control is more frequent than it actually is.

REFERENCES

Langer, E. J. (1975). The illusion of control. *Journal of Personality and Social Psychology,* 32(2), 311-328.

Luo, M. (2004, February 27). For exercise in New York futility, push button. *New York Times.*

Thompson, S. C., Armstrong, W., & Thomas, C. (1998). Illusions of control, underestimations, and accuracy: A control heuristic explanation. *Psychological Bulletin,* 123(2), 143-161.

The Impact of Social Categorization on Persuasion Attempts

Mirjam A. Tuk, University of Groningen, The Netherlands
Peeter W. J. Verlegh, Erasmus University Rotterdam, The Netherlands
Ale Smidts, Erasmus University Rotterdam, The Netherlands
Daniel H.J. Wigboldus, Radboud University Nijmegen, The Netherlands

EXTENDED ABSTRACT

Research examining social categorization effects on persuasiveness, has mainly focused on understanding the precise impact of persuasion attempts from in-group members on attitudes. It has been argued that in-group membership can serve as a cue for systematic processing (Mackie Worth and Asuncion 1990; Van Knippenberg 1999), because in-group members are more similar and usually share the same opinions. This causes people to process information from in-group members in a more systematic way than information from out-group members. As a consequence, people are relatively more persuaded by strong arguments from in-group members than by weak arguments from in-group members, whereas they are relatively unpersuaded by both strong and weak arguments from out-group members. This implies that persuasion attempts from out-group members are relatively less influential than persuasion attempts from in-group members, and do not (or to a lesser extent) influence attitudes.

However, research examining the impact of out-group members within other domains, suggests that people do show strong reactions towards out-group members. People have a strong tendency to differentiate themselves from out-group members in terms of resource allocation (less points or credits for the out-group), and evaluations of group members (evaluate in-group and out-group members as even more different than they already are; Jetten, Spears and Postmes 2004). Furthermore, recent research examining the impact of group membership in relation to product evaluations (Berger and Heath 2007; Escalas and Bettman 2003, 2005; White and Dahl 2006, 2008), shows that people tend to avoid products that are associated with dissociative out-groups.

The above described research shows that people tend to differentiate themselves from out-groups in terms of resource allocation and product preferences, but remains silent about the precise impact of persuasion attempts from out-groups. In the current research, we examine whether out-group members are either less persuasive (i.e., have relatively less influence on attitudes, as is suggested by the research showing stronger persuasion effects of in-group members) or whether people differentiate their attitudes after persuasion attempts from out-group members (as is suggested by the research showing differentiation tendencies in other domains). A crucial test to gain more insight in the exact impact of persuasion attempts from out-group members, is to examine the impact of persuasion attempts that differ in opinion valence. A differentiation effect does not predict differences in responses to weak versus strong arguments from out-group members, and this previously found result is thus in line with both a differentiation effect and a difference in persuasiveness effect. However, a differentiation effect predicts that people will report attitudes that are clearly different from the one stated by the out-group member. This implies reporting a positive (product) attitude after a negative recommendation, and a negative attitude after a positive (product) recommendation. If the out-group member is less persuasive than the in-group member, this does not predict a flip of attitudes in a direction that is clearly different from the out-group member, but rather a relatively neutral opinion.

We tested these predictions with four experiments. In the first three experiments, we manipulated recommendation valence (positive versus negative) and group membership (in-group versus out-group). Across these three experiments, we used different manipulations of group membership. This had two purposes, first of all, this increases the reliability and generalizability of the results. And second, the type of group manipulation is quite easily open to alternative explanations (unknown to the researchers, a particular group might for example be a dissociative out-group for the participants). Showing the hypothesized effects with different types of group manipulations (one of which was a minimal group paradigm; Billig and Taifel 1973) rules out such group specific alternative explanations. In these three experiments, respondents read the (positive or negative) opinion of either an in-group or an out-group member about a specific painting. After seeing a picture of the painting themselves, respondents were asked to indicate their opinion about this painting (seven-point scale, 1=ugly, 7=beautiful). Results of the three individual studies showed that people were more positive about the painting after a positive in-group recommendation than after a positive out-group recommendation (in line with previous research). These studies also showed that people were more positive about the painting after a negative out-group recommendation than after a positive out-group recommendation, which is in line with a differentiation effect. Furthermore, a pooled analysis over these three studies also showed that respondents were more positive about the painting after a negative out-group recommendation than after a negative in-group recommendation. Together, these studies and the pooled analysis over these three studies provide convincing evidence that people react to persuasion attempts from out-group members by differentiating their own attitude away from the out-group member, and that this effect is caused by pure social categorization.

Remarkably, none of the studies showed any difference in attitude after the positive versus the negative in-group recommendation. In the final experiment, we examined whether this was caused by a lack of salience of shared (in)group membership (Wilder 1984). We argued that a recommendation from an in-group member can be perceived on a more interpersonal level as a recommendation from a stranger rather than on an intergroup level (as a recommendation from a fellow in-group member). Confronting people with the existence of the out-group should make the intergroup context relatively more salient and subsequently also highlight the fact that someone belongs to the in-group. In this study, we confronted half of the respondents with out-group members, and we found the expected effect of recommendation valence (more positive after a positive than after a negative in-group recommendation), which was again absent in the condition where respondents were not confronted with the out-group.

These set of studies showed that out-group members have an important impact on attitudes in an unexpected manner. This is important to take into account with regard to persuasion attempts (such as word of mouth) and advertisement campaigns, just like the finding that in-group membership only has an impact on attitudes when an intergroup context has been made salient.

REFERENCES

Berger, Jonah and Chip Heath (2007), "Where consumers diverge from others: Identity signaling and product domains," *Journal of Consumer Research,* 34(August), 121-134.

Billig, Michael and Henri Tajfel (1973), "Social categorization and similarity in intergroup behavior," *European Journal of Social psychology,* 3(February), 27-51.

Escalas, Jennifer E. and James R. Bettman (2003), "You are what they eat: The influence of reference groups on consumers' connections to brands," *Journal of Consumer Psychology,* 13(), 339-348.

Escalas, Jennifer E. and James R. Bettman (2005), "Self-construal, reference groups, and brand meaning," *Journal of Consumer Research,* 32(December), 378-389.

Jetten, Jolanda, Russel Spears and Tom Postmes (2004), "Intergroup distinctiveness and differentiation: A meta-analytic integration," *Journal of Personality and Social Psychology,* 86(June), 862-879.

Mackie, Diane M., Leila T. Worth and Arlene G. Asuncion (1990), "Processing of persuasive in-group messages," *Journal of Personality and Social Psychology,* 58(May), 812-822.

Van Knippenberg, Daan (1999), "Social Identity and Persuasion: Reconsidering the Role of Group Membership," In D. Abrams and M. A. Hogg (Eds.), *Social Identity and Social Cognition* (pp. 315-331). Malden, Massachusetts: Blackwell Publishers Inc.

White, Katherine and Darren W. Dahl (2006), "To be or not be? The influence of dissociative reference groups on consumer preferences," *Journal of Consumer Psychology,* 16(4), 404-414.

White, Katherine and Darren W. Dahl (2008), "Are all out-groups created equal? Consumer identity and dissociative influence," *Journal of Consumer Research,* 34(February), 525-538.

Wilder, David A. and Peter N. Shapiro (1984), "Role of Out-Group Cues in Determining Social Identity," *Journal of Personality and Social Psychology,* 47(February), 342-348.

The Persuasive Role of Incidental Similarity on Attitudes and Purchase Intentions in a Sales Context

Lan Jiang, University of British Columbia, Canada
Darren Dahl, University of British Columbia, Canada
Amitava Chattopadhyay, INSEAD, Singapore
JoAndrea Hoegg, University of British Columbia, Canada

EXTENDED ABSTRACT

The study of similarity in persuasion has a long history. The majority of research in this area has been conducted to examine the role of attitude similarity between individuals, but this research has recently been extended to examine the role of incidental similarity, i.e., chance similarities between individuals that provide little relevant information and few implications in a specific context (Burger et al. 2004). For example, a shared birthday with another individual provides no diagnostic information regarding compatibility as business partners.

In most instances, logic would indicate that incidental similarities should not play a significant role in social environments. However, existing research has shown that incidental similarity can play a role in social situations and can increase liking, persuasion, and cooperative behavior between individuals (e.g., Burger et al. 2004). In this paper we extend these initial findings for incidental similarity to an interpersonal context. Specifically, we examine the effects of incidental similarity shared between a salesperson and a potential consumer in an actual face-to-face sales situation. Further, we provide an explanation for how and why incidental similarity can have a persuasive influence, in this instance. To do this, we draw on the theoretical framework of a need for belongingness (Baumeister and Leary 1995), where people strive to achieve social connectedness with those around them. This framework is particularly relevant in an interpersonal situation, which is the context of our investigation.

Four experiments show our contributions: 1) we establish social connectedness as an important underlying mechanism for the effect of incidental similarity. While previous research (e.g., Brendl et al. 2005) has shown that self-esteem enhancement can underlie incidental similarity effects, we show that in the interpersonal context social connectedness drives the effects of incidental similarity and that our results cannot be explained on the basis of self-esteem, 2) we identify two boundary conditions that qualify our findings: the valence of sales person's behavior towards an unknown other and the length of the interpersonal relationship as being critical moderators to the process we outline. We show that when the need for social connectedness is mitigated, i.e., when the salesperson is disliked or when the relationship is not expected to continue, the positive effects of incidental similarity are lost.

We propose that discovering an incidental similarity with a negative or disliked other will decrease the need for connectedness and cause individuals to distance themselves from the similar other. Since connectedness can underlie the relationship between incidental similarity and attitudes/purchase intentions, we expect that distancing in the sales context investigated will mean negative implications for attitude formation and the resulting purchase intentions. We also expect the negative outcome caused by an incidental similarity during an unpleasant social interaction to be mitigated when the social interaction is brief and unlikely to continue.

Using an actual sales situation, Study 1 tests for the effects of incidental similarity in a service context and identifies the role of connectedness in the process. We manipulated incidental similarity through shared birthday. After a sales promotion for a personal training program, consumers who accidentally found out that they share the birthday with the trainer reported a more favorable attitude towards the program as well as a higher intention to enroll in the program. The direct measure on the sense of connectedness and the mediation analysis corroborated our hypothesis that social connectedness could be the underlying mechanism for the incidental similarity effect.

Study 2 further validates the role of connectedness by comparing the effects of incidental similarity for individuals differing in their chronic tendency to connect with others. We found that people who have a low social connectedness orientation are least influenced by the shared birthday and on the other hand, people with a high social connectedness orientation are influenced most strongly.

Study 3 tests the potential boundary condition for the observed effect of incidental similarity by identifying the importance of the valenced behavior of the referent other in achieving both a social connection and an effect for incidental similarity. We showed a reversed effect of the shared birthday when the salesperson displays some negative traits during the promotion. When participants discover that they share the same birthday with a person who is rude, the similarity no longer helps establish connection and instead it makes them feel more disconnected. The decreased feeling of connectedness leads to a more negative attitude towards the program and lowers their intention to purchase.

Our final study tests another possible boundary condition of the incidental similarity effect–the anticipated length of the interpersonal relationship with the salesperson. We show that this negative effect that was realized was mitigated when the social interaction was just a brief encounter with no future interactions expected. In non-aversive conditions, an incidental similarity increased attitude favorability and purchase intentions even when the interaction with the similar other was a brief encounter.

To our knowledge, this research is the first empirical test of social connectedness as a theoretical explanation for when and why individuals will be affected by an incidental similarity. Drawing from the theory of belongingness (Baumeister and Leary 1995), we tested two features of the need for belongingness, the valence of the interaction and the length of the relationship, as moderators for incidental similarity effects. Our results not only confirmed the impact of these two situational factors, but also extended Baumeister and Leary's (1995) proposition by demonstrating a negative effect of incidental similarity in an aversive condition.

From a managerial perspective, our research provides insight into the power of cultivating similarity between consumers and sales agents in the retail context. Matching sales people with consumers to enhance shared similarity is an obvious recommendation for marketing practice. Our research suggests that even matching based on incidental similarities may have an influence on consumer decision making. It is important to note however, that salespeople that share a similarity also have the capacity to alienate consumers if their behavior is perceived to be negative.

REFERENCES

Baumeister, Roy F. and Mark R. Leary (1995), "The Need to Belong: Desire for Interpersonal Attachments as a Fundamental Human Motivation," *Psychological Bulletin*, 117 (May), 497-529.

Brendl, C. Miguel, Amitava Chattopadhyay, Brett W. Pelham, and Mauricio Carvallo (2005), "Name Letter Branding: Valence Transfers when Product Specific Needs are Active," *Journal of Consumer Research*, 32 (December), 405-415

Burger, Jerry M., Nicole Messian, Shebani Patel, Alicia del Prado, and Carmen Anderson (2004), "What a Coincidence: The Effects of Incidental Similarity on Compliance," *Personality and Social Psychology Bulletin*, 30 (January), 35-43

Contagious Likes and Dislikes–Neighborhood Effects in Attitudes and Preferences

Jayati Sinha, University of Iowa, USA
Dhananjay Nayakankuppam, University of Iowa, USA

EXTENDED ABSTRACT

We examine the influence of neighborhood effects on attitudes and preferences. Specifically, does exposure to the attitudes of others in a group influence one's own attitudes and preferences? The primary goal of the present research was to explore how individual attitudes are shaped by neighborhood effects-that is, people living in close proximity could influence each others attitudes and preferences. By neighborhood effects, we refer to interdependencies between individual attitudes and the attitudes of others in a group. Said differently, exposure to others' attitudes and preferences influences one's own attitudes and preferences. Specifically, we suggest that there are (a) *direct influences* (e.g., a neighbor provides information and/or opinions about some issue or product) as well as (b) *indirect influences* (where no direct information needs to be exchanged).

The notion of direct influences is suggested by the effects such as the *group polarization* phenomenon (Moscovici and Zavalloni, 1969) and the *chameleon effect* (Chartrand and Bargh, 1999). A sizeable body of social psychology literature has demonstrated that an individual's attitude toward a given issue tends to polarize during a group discussion with other people who hold a similar opinion on that issue (Myers, 1978; Myers and Lamm, 1976). We base the hypothesis regarding the indirect influence from recent work in social psychology (Ambady and Rosenthal, 1992; Ambady et al., 1999) which suggests that there are domains where people are remarkably accurate at gleaning information from very little information.

We show that neighborhood effects do emerge for issues where one is exposed to group attitudes. More intriguingly, neighborhood effects also emerge for issues where one was never exposed to group attitudes. We suggest that this is due to the fact that exposure to some group attitudes allows individuals to make shrewd guesses about group attitudes on other issues that were never discussed. Further, these guesses bias one's own attitudes.

We present evidence for one mechanism through which neighborhood effects emerge, namely that exposure to the preferences of others (which is more likely when individuals are in close contact) influences one's own preferences. Thus, Bill telling Bob about his attitude towards Scott's lawn feed changes Bob's attitude towards Scott's. More startlingly, we show that it does not require exposure to the attitude towards the target object. Neighborhood effects emerge even for non-discussed target objects. Exposure to attitudes towards some objects appears sufficient to allow individuals to make fairly shrewd guesses about attitudes towards other objects, which in turn influence their own attitudes. That is, Bill telling Bob about his attitude towards Scott's lawn feed changes not only Bob's attitude towards Scott's lawn feed, but also Bob's attitudes towards other issues such that Bob's and Bill's attitudes converge even on non-discussed issues (such as Scott's lawn mowers).

Strong Attitudes Versus Strong Situations: Social Pressure on Recycling

Iris Vermeir, University College Ghent & Ghent University, Belgium

EXTENDED ABSTRACT

Previous researches show contradictory results concerning attitude strength, social pressure and attitude-behavioural consistency. Either strong situations (Wallace et al. 2005) or strong attitudes (Pomerantz et al. 1995) predict attitude-behavior consistency. We argue that these contradictory results could be explained when personal factors like perceived control and self-monitoring are taken into account. The purpose of this study is to investigate the relation between attitudinal (attitude strength), contextual (social pressure) and personal (self-monitoring and perceived control) variables in influencing attitude-behavior consistency. More specifically, we investigate if the level of self-monitoring and perceived control could influence the predicitive value of attitude extremity (as a measure of attitude strength; Krosnick et al. 1993) and social pressure on the attitude-behavior consistency.

Openess to social pressure is not at the least influenced by personal characteristics like self-monitoring. High self-monitors are particularly sensitive to others in social situations and use the expressions of others as guidelines for their own behavior (Gangestad and Snyder 2000). Hence, in strong social pressure situations, attitudes of high-self monitoring respondents shouldn't necessarily determine behavior (H1a). While, for low-self monitoring respondents, strong attitudes could overcome social pressure (H1b). Low-self monitors perform behavior according to their own beliefs, instead of paying attention to beliefs or behaviors of others (Gangestad and Snyder 2000).

Previous research already demonstrated a decreased attitude-behavior consistency due to a lack of perceived control (Vermeir and Verbeke 2006). Individuals have to feel they are able to act environmentally conscious in order to intend environmental behavior (Knussen et al. 2004) or actually perform this behavior (Tanner 1999). Hence, we can expect that strong attitudes would not be followed if perception of perceived control is low, regardless of social pressure (H2a). When perceived control is high, attitude strength can be a determinant of behavior, especially in low pressure situations (H2b).

In order to test our hypotheses, an experiment was set up concerning recycling of soda cans. To manipulate social pressure, participants studied research results –ostensibly the results of a recent study on student opinion- that indicated that an in-group (defined by connectedness to the group) strongly or weakly engaged in recycling behavior. Manipulation checks confirmed that our respondents experienced high (versus low) social pressure when recycling behavior described in the text was high (versus low).

In total, 284 students participated in our experiment in exchange of a reward. When entering into the room, respondents were offered a soda. First, participants were asked attitudinal questions on recycling. Attitudes toward recycling were measured using a four-item semantic differential on a 7-point scale. Attitude extremity was used as a measure of attitude strength. Extremity scores were created by computing the absolute value of the deviation of each attitude score from its conceptual midpoint (cfr. Fabrigar, Petty, Smith and Crites 2006). Next, participants were asked to carefully read a text on recycling behavior of 18-25 year old adults. After completing some filler items, respondents indicated their perceived level of control to engage in recycling behavior and completed the self-monitoring scale (Snyder and Gangestad 1986). A median split was performed to identify low/high self-monitors and low/high perceptions of control. Next, respondents were asked

to go to another room to collect their reward. On their way to the other room, respondents could dispose of their cans on their own, without any peers around. They could drop their soda can in either an ordinary bin or a recycling bin (meant for cans). Both bins were equally visible. About 45% of our respondents (N=119) used the ordinary bin, while 141 respondents (55%) used the recycling bin. The soda cans were marked so we could link each soda can to a corresponding number on the questionnaire.

Results showed that attitude strength and social pressure do indeed influence attitude-behavior consistency. In general, respondents who experienced high (versus low) social pressure, did act more on their positive recycling attitudes. However, strong attitudes were not always associated with high consistent behaviors. High self-monitoring respondents who experience high social pressure do not differ in their attitude extremity according to their behavioral pattern, confirming our first hypothesis (H1a). Furthermore, we found that attitude extremity did not differ for consistent and inconsistent respondents who did not experience high social pressure. High self-monitoring respondents who act consistently with their attitudes do not have stronger attitudes compared to inconsistent respondents regardless of social pressure. Possibly, high self-monitoring respondents have a natural tendency to act on their expressed attitudes, regardless of their strength and regardless of contextual factors. We found that low self-monitors, who are more prone to follow their own ideas, follow their attitudes when they are strong (versus weak), especially when there is no social pressure. However, social pressure does seem to influence low-self monitors on some occasions: low-self monitors who experience social pressure to act on their positive attitudes, do engage in recycling regardless of the strength of their attitude (rejecting H1b). These results show the vast influence of social pressure in determining behavior, even for low-self monitoring respondents.

Furthermore, respondents who feel they can decide for themselves if they engage in recycling, engage in recycling behavior when their attitudes are stronger (versus weaker), especially when they do not experience social pressure (confirming H2b). Respondents who feel they have less control over their recycling behavior, do act on their recycling attitudes when they experience high social pressure and when their attitudes are stronger (versus weaker) (partly rejecting H2a). Moreover, under conditions of social pressure, respondents with high perceived control, act consistently on their positive attitudes, if their attitudes are strong (versus weak). Although the latter result was only marginally significant, these results show that strong attitudes can predict attitude-behavioral consistency regardless of the perception of control when they experience high social pressure. When less social pressure exists, low (versus high) control makes attitude strength less a determinant of behavioral consistency (partly confirming H2a). Possibly, these respondents do not engage in recycling behavior because they have no control over their behavior on one hand and because there is no social pressure to act on their attitudes.

REFERENCES

Bagozzi, Richard, P., Wong, Nancy, Abe Shuzo and Bergami Massimo (2000), "Cultural and Situational Contingencies and the Theory of Reasoned Action: Application of Fast Food Restaurant Consumption", *Journal of Consumer Psychology*, 9(2), 97-106.

Bright Alan D. and Michael J. Manfredo (1995), "The quality of attitudinal information regarding national resource issues: the role of attitude strength, importance and information", *Society and Natural Resources*, 8, 399-414.

Chaiken, Shelly, Eva M. Pomerantz and Roger Giner-Sorolla (1995), "Structural consistency and attitude strength", In R.E. Petty, J.A. Kronsick (eds.), *Attitude Strength: Antecedents and Consequences,* (pp 387-412). Mahwah, NJ: Lawrence Erlbaum Associates, Publishers.

Eagly, Alice H. and Shelly Chaiken (1993), *"The psychology of attitudes"*, Fort Worth: Harcourt Brace Jovanovich College Publishers.

Fabrigar, Leandre R., Richard E. Petty, Steven E. Smith and Stephen L. Jr. Crites (2006), "Understanding Knowledge Effects on Attitude-Behaviour Consisteny: The Role of Relevance, Complexity, and Amount of Knowledge", J*ournal of Personality & Social Psychology*, 90(4), 556-577.

Fazio, Russell H. (1990), "Multiple processes by which attitude guide behaviour: the mode model as an integrative framework", *Advances in Experimental Social Psychology*, 23, 75-109.

Fazio, Russell H. and Zanna, Mark P. (1978a), "On the predictive validity of attitudes. The role of direct experience and confidence", *Journal of Personality*, 46, 228-243.

Fazio, Russel H., and Zanna, Mark P. (1978b), "Attitudinal qualities relating to the strength of attitude-behavior relationship", Journal of Experimental Social Psychology, 14, 398-408.

Follows, Scott B. and David Jobber (2000), "Environmentally Responsible Purchase Behavior: A Test of a Consumer", *European Journal of Marketing*, 34 (5/6), 723-746.

Gangestad, Steven, W. and Mark Snyder, (2000) "Self-monitoring: Appraisal and Reappraisal", *Psychological Bulletin*, 126(4), 530-555.

Gardner, Gerald T. and Paul C. Stern (1996), *"Environmental Problems and Human Behavior"*. Boston: Allyn and Bacon.

Glasman, Laura R. and Dolores Albarracín, (2006), "Forming Attitudes That Predict Future behaviour: A Meta-Analysis of the Attitude-Behaviour Relation", *Psychological Bulletin*, 132(5), 778-822.

Haugtvedt, Curtis P. , Schumann, David W., Schneier, Wendy L. and Wendy L. Warren (1994), "Advertising Repetition and Variation Strategies–Implications for understanding Attitude Strength", *Journal of Consumer Research*, 21(1), 176-189.

Hume, Scott (1991), "Consumer Doubletalk Makes Companies Wary", *Advertising Age*, 62 (October 28), GR4.

Jackson, Anita L., Janeen E. Olsen, Granzin, Kent L., and Alvin C. Burns (1993), "An Investigation of Determinants of Recycling Consumer Behavior," *Advances in Consumer Research*, 20, 481-487.

Knussen, Cristina, Yule, Fred, MacKenzie, Julie and Wells, Mark (2004), "An analysis of intentions to recycle household waste: The roles of past behaviour, perceived habit and perceived lack of facilities", *Journal of Environmental Psychology*, 24, 237-246.

Kraus, Stephen J., (1995), "Attitudes and the Prediction of Behaviour: A Meta-Analysis of the Empirical Literature", *Personality and Social Psychology Bulletin*, 21(1), 58-75.

Krosnick, Jon A. and Richard, E. Petty (1995), "Attitude strength: an overview", In R.E. Petty, J.A. Kronsick (eds.), *Attitude Strength: Antecedents and Consequences,* (pp 387-412). Mahwah, NJ: Lawrence Erlbaum Associates, Publishers.

Krosnick, Jon A., Boninger, David S., Chuang, Yao C., Berent, Matthew K. and Catherine G.Carnot (1993), "Attitude strength: One Construct or Many Related Constructs", *Journal of Personality and Social Psychology*, 65(6), 1132-1151.

Lee, Julie Anne and Stephen J. S. Holden (1999), "Understanding the Determinants of Environmentally Conscious Behavior," Psychology & Marketing, 16 (August), 373-392.

Mischel, Walter (1977), "The Interaction of Person and Situation", In D. Magnusson and N.S. Endler (Eds.), *Personality at the crossroads: Current Issues in interactional psychology,*(pp.333-352). Hillsdale, NJ: Erlbaum.

Osgood, Charles E. and Percy H. Tannenbaum (1955), "The Principle of congruity in the prediction of attitude change", *Psychological Review*, 62, 42-55.

Peterson, Karen K. and Jeffrey E. Dutton (1975), "Centrality, Extremity, intensity: Neglected variables in research on attitude-behavior consistency", *Social Forces*, 54, 393-414.

Pomerantz, Eva M., Chaiken, Shelly and Rosalind Torsedillas (1995), "Attitude strength and resistance process" *Journal of Personality and Social Psychology*, 69, 408-419.

Roozen, Irene T.M. and Patrick De Pelsmacker (2000), "Polish and Belgian consumers' perception of environmentally friendly behavior" *Journal consumer studies and home economics*, 24, 9-21.

Shook, N.J., Fazio, R.H., Eiser, J.R. (2007), "Attitude generalization: similarity, valence & extremity", *Journal of experimental social psychology*, 43, 641-647.

Smith, Joanne, R. and Deborah, J. Terry (2003), "Attitude-behaviour consistency: the role of group norms, attitude accessibility and mode of behavioural decision-making", *European Journal of Social Psychology*, 33, 591-608.

Snyder, Mark (1974), Self-monitoring of expressive behaviour, *Journal of Personality and Social Psychology*, 30, 526-537.

Snyder, Mark and Steven W. Gangestad (1986), "On the nature of self-monitoring: matters of assessment, matters of validity", *Journal of Personality and Social Psychology*, 51, 125-139.

Snyder, Mark and William B. Swann (1976), "When actions reflect attitudes: The politics of impression management", *Journal of Personality and Social Psychology*, 34, 165-183.

Spira, Joan, S. (2002), "Attitude Strength and Resistance to Persuasion", *Advances in Consumer Research*, 29, 180-185?

Stern, PaulC. and Thomas Dietz (1994), "The value basis of environmental concern", *Journal of Social Issues*, 50(65-84).

Tanner, Carmen (1999), "Constraints on environmental behavior", *Journal of Environmental Psychology*, 19, 145-157.

Tonglet, Michelle, Phillips, Paul S. and Margaret P. Bates (2004), "Determining the drivers for householder pro-environmental behaviour: waste minimisation compared to recycling", *Resources, Conservation and Recycling, 42,* 27-48.

Vermeir, Iris and Wim Verbeke (2006), "Sustainable food consumption: exploring the consumer "attitude-behavioural intention" gap", *Journal of Agricultural and environmental Ethics*, 19(1), 1-18.

Vermeir, Iris and Wim Verbeke (2008), "Sustainable food consumption among young adults in Belgium: Theory of planned behaviour and the role of confidence and values", *Ecological Economics*, 64, 542-553.

Wallace, David S., Paulson, René M., Lord, Charles G., and
  Charles, F. Bond (2005), "Which behaviors do attitudes
  predict? Meta-analyzing the effects of social pressure and
  Perceived difficulty", *Review of General Psychology, 9(3)*,
  214-227.

The Emotional Information Processing System is Risk Averse: Ego-depletion and Investment Behavior

Bart De Langhe, RSM Erasmus University, The Netherlands
Steven Sweldens, RSM Erasmus University, The Netherlands
Stijn Van Osselaer, RSM Erasmus University, The Netherlands
Mirjam Tuk, University of Groningen, The Netherlands

EXTENDED ABSTRACT

Previous research has shown that self-regulatory strength is crucial to exert willpower. It has been found that a depletion of self-regulatory resources very often leads to detrimental behavior such as overeating and impulsive buying (Vohs and Faber 2007; Vohs and Heatherton 2000). However, not much is known about how the availability of these resources is related to risky decision making. The current research shows that a state of ego-depletion leads to higher levels of risk aversion in mixed gambles (involving mixtures of gains and losses).

Risk aversion for mixed gambles refers to the tendency of people to reject a gamble with an equal chance to win or to lose, even when the expected value of gambling is higher than the expected value of not gambling (Tversky and Kahneman 1992). Recent developments in the field of neuroscience and psychology indicate that anticipatory emotional reactions that are elicited by features of the risky decision alternatives are crucial in understanding risk taking and risk seeking (Damasio 1994; LeDoux 1996; Loewenstein et al. 2001).

In the current research, we adopt a dual-process framework that distinguishes between a rational (cognitive) and an experiential (emotional) information processing system (Epstein and Pacini 1999), in order to explain greater risk avoidance in a state of ego-depletion. In a situation where one has to make a choice between a risky and a less risky alternative, both the rational and the experiential system generate an "advice" concerning the most desirable behavior. The outcome of the rational system is determined by a cognitive assessment of probabilities of decision outcomes and outcome severity, whereas the outcome of the experiential system is determined by an automatic retrieval of accumulated knowledge from previous experiences. Since the experiential system attaches greater weight to previously experienced negative contingencies than to previously experienced positive contingencies of the choice options (De Houwer, Thomas, and Baeyens 2001), it guides the decision maker away from risky alternatives.

Given that the rational system is the slower, analytical system it is in an ideal position to monitor and inhibit the output of the faster, associative experiential system. However, building on previous research that puts forward self-regulatory resources as the necessary fuel for the rational system (Vohs 2006), we hypothesize that a depletion of self-regulatory resources impairs the inhibiting capacity of the rational system. As a consequence, the output of the experiential system is weighted more heavily in the final decision, resulting in more risk aversive behavior among ego-depleted individuals.

Two experiments provide support for this reasoning. In both experiments, the availability of self-regulatory resources was manipulated by a modified version of the Stroop task (Stroop 1935). Inhibiting first responses (which is the general purpose of this task) has been shown to consume self-regulatory resources (e.g., Inzlicht and Gutsell 2007; Muraven, Tice, and Baumeister 1998; Wallace and Baumeister 2002), and is therefore an effective way of inducing a state of ego-depletion.

In Study 1, the Stroop task was followed by an investment task which has previously been used to compare decision making of patients with lesions to the brain's emotional circuitry and patients with substance dependence to decisions made by a normal control group (Shiv et al. 2005a; Shiv et al. 2005b). The task consists of 20 decision rounds in which one can choose between investing $1 or not investing $1. An investment decision is followed by a coin toss; heads results in losing the $1, tails results in gaining $2.50. If a participant decides not to invest, the game advances to the next round. Since the expected value of risk seeking behavior (invest) is higher than the expected value of risk aversive behavior (not invest), a rational decision maker should always decide to invest. Participant's predisposition to rely on experiential processing was measured with the experientiality subscale of the Rational-Experiential Inventory (Pacini and Epstein 1999).

As the experiential system is an associative information processing system that generates emotional responses based on previous outcomes, we only expected it to influence investment decisions of depleted participants after some experience with the task at hand (i.e. in the second block of 10 trials). Additionally, we expected a moderation of the effect by experientiality. Indeed, if the weighting of the outcomes of the experiential system is dispositionally low, the rational monitoring system should still be able to override the responses generated by the experiential processing system.

As predicted, the three-way interaction between state of self-regulation (control; depleted), experientiality (high; low) and decision block (first block of 10 decisions; second block of 10 decisions) was significant. After having gained some experience with the investment task, ego-depleted participants with a tendency to rely on their experiential "hunches" clearly showed higher levels of risk aversion.

The goal of the second study was to demonstrate that a lower availability of self-regulatory resources can be beneficial for decision making in a situation where the expected value of risk avoidant behavior is higher than the expected value of risk seeking behavior. After completing the modified Stroop task, participants continued with the Iowa Gambling Task (see Bechara et al. 1994, for exact procedures and pay-off structure). Participants had to choose 100 times between cards from four different decks. Two decks are low-risky decks with a high expected value, and two decks are high-risky decks with a lower expected value. Results showed that ego-depleted participants selected significantly more cards from the low-risky decks with a higher expected value.

In sum, in two experiments we showed that a lower availability of self-regulatory resources increases risk aversion in mixed gambles (study 1 & study 2). This finding can be explained by an increased weighting of experiential processing in decision making (study 1) and implies that ego-depletion is not always detrimental for decision making, but can also guide people towards more beneficial choice options (study 2).

REFERENCES

Bechara, Antoine, Antonio R. Damasio, Hanna Damasio, and Steven W. Anderson (1994), "Insensitivity to future consequences following damage to human prefrontal cortex," *Cognition*, 50, 7-15.

Damasio, Antonio R. (1994), *Descartes' error: emotion, reason, and the human brain*, New York: Grosset/Putnam.

De Houwer, Jan, Sarah Thomas, and Frank Baeyens (2001), "Associative learning of likes and dislikes: A review of 25 years of research on human evaluative conditioning," *Psychological Bulletin*, 127 (6), 853-869.

Epstein, Seymour and Rosemary Pacini (1999), "Some basic issues regarding dual-process theories from the perspective of cognitive-experiential self-theory," in *Dual-process theories in social psychology*, eds. S. Chaiken and Y. Trope. New York: The Guilford Press,

Inzlicht, Michael and Jennifer N. Gutsell (2007), "Running on empty-Neural signals for self-control failure," *Psychological Science*, 18 (11), 933-937.

LeDoux, Joseph E. (1996), *The Emotional Brain*, New York: Simon & Schuster.

Loewenstein, George F., Elke U. Weber, Christopher K. Hsee, and Ned Welch (2001), "Risk as feelings," *Psychological Bulletin*, 127 (2), 267-286.

Muraven, Mark, Dianne M. Tice, and Roy F. Baumeister (1998), "Self-control as limited resource: Regulatory depletion patterns," *Journal of Personality and Social Psychology*, 74 (3), 774-789.

Pacini, Rosemary and Seymour Epstein (1999), "The relation of rational and experiential information processing styles to personality, basic beliefs, and the ratio-bias phenomenon," *Journal of Personality and Social Psychology*, 76 (6), 972-987.

Shiv, Baba, George Loewenstein, and Antoine Bechara (2005a), "The dark side of emotion in decision-making: When individuals with decreased emotional reactions make more advantageous decisions," *Cognitive Brain Research*, 23 (1), 85-92.

Shiv, Baba, George Loewenstein, Antoine Bechara, Hanna Damasio, and Antonio R. Damasio (2005b), "Investment behavior and the negative side of emotion," *Psychological Science*, 16 (6), 435-439.

Stroop, John R. (1935), "Studies of interference in serial verbal reactions," *Journal of Experimental Psychology*, 18, 643-662.

Tversky, Amos and Daniel Kahneman (1992), "Advances in prospect theory: Cumulative representation of uncertainty," *Journal of Risk and Uncertainty*, 5, 297-323.

Vohs, Kathleen D. (2006), "Self-regulatory resources power the reflective system: Evidence from five domains," *Journal of Consumer Psychology*, 16 (3), 217-223.

Vohs, Kathleen D. and Ronald J. Faber (2007), "Spent resources: Self-regulatory resource availability affects impulse buying," *Journal of Consumer Research*, 33 (4), 537-547.

Vohs, Kathleen D. and Todd F. Heatherton (2000), "Self-regulatory failure: A resource-depletion approach," *Psychological Science*, 11 (3), 249-254.

Wallace, Harry W. and Roy F. Baumeister (2002), "The effects of success versus failure feedback on further self-control," *Self and Identity*, 1, 35-42.

A Model of Investment Decision-Making: How Adaptation to Losses Affects Future Selling Decisions

Carmen K.M. Lee, VU University Amsterdam, The Netherlands
Roman Kräussl, VU University Amsterdam, The Netherlands
André Lucas, VU University Amsterdam, The Netherlands
Leonard J. Paas, VU University Amsterdam, The Netherlands

EXTENDED ABSTRACT

The well-known disposition effect postulates that investors tend to sell their winners (appreciated investments) too soon and hold their losers (depreciated investments) for too long (Shefrin & Statman, 1985). The prominent explanation for this disposition effect is based on prospect theory (Kahneman & Tversky, 1979), which posits that investors are more risk-averse in the domain of gains and more risk-seeking in the domain of losses. Thus, when facing paper gains, investors tend to be risk-averse implying the tendency to sell their winners. By contrast, when facing paper losses, investors tend to choose the risky option and hold on to their losers. However, it is not clear why and when investors eventually do sell at a loss. The aim of the present study is to address this gap in the current literature by integrating a theory of adaptation, adaptation level theory (Helson, 1964), a theory of reference point dependence, prospect theory (Kahneman & Tversky, 1979), and a theory of dual process decision-making, cognitive-experiential self-theory (Epstein, 1994) to propose a model of investment decision-making.

Our model disentangles the effects of time in losing position and size of loss on reference point adaptation. The adaptation of the reference point (from prospect theory) can be modeled as changes in adaptation level (from adaptation level theory), which are determined by time and size of each stimulus. These are linked to the investor's decision-making process using the framework of cognitive-experiential self-theory, which suggests there are two systems in decision making: experiential and rational (Epstein, 1994). The experiential system can automatically and effortlessly process information. Also, it interacts with the rational system as a source of intuitive wisdom and creativity. On the other hand, the rational system is a deliberative and effortful system, processing at high levels of abstraction and handling long term delay of gratification.

In the integration of prospect theory, adaptation level theory and experiential self-theory, we develop on the results of a recent study by Arkes, Hirshleifer, Jiang and Lim (2008). They find investors adapt to financial gains and losses as their reference point shifts after the value of the investment increased or decreased. However, the link between reference point adaptation and decision-making is still lacking. Therefore, we conduct an experimental study to examine how the adapted reference point influences one's emotions and expectation about an investment's future performance, and eventually leads to the decision to hold or to capitulate a losing investment.

We hypothesize that (H1) the size of total loss and the time in losing position are negatively related to an individual investor's adapted reference point; (H2a) the adapted reference point is positively related to one's optimistic expectations towards the losing investment; (H2b) in turn, more optimistic expectation leads to a smaller probability of an investor's capitulation of the losing investment; (H3a) the size of previous loss is negatively related to one's positive emotion towards the losing investment; (H3b) in turn, more positive emotion leads to a smaller probability of capitulation. We ran an experiment, in which 111 participants incurred various sizes of stock losses over a course of maximum 10 investment periods. At the end of each period, participants received information of the stock's performance. Before making the decision to hold or to capitulate on the stock, participants answered several questions concerning their emotions, expectations and adaptation to losses.

We applied the partial least squares (PLS) approach to estimate the proposed model. Significant effects were observed from both time in losing position and size of total loss on reference point adaptation. We show that the investors' adapted reference point significantly shifts downwards when total loss and time in losing position increase. These experimental results give support to hypothesis 1. Moreover, a higher adapted reference point predicts more optimistic expectations about the stock's future performance, while a larger previous loss predicts more negative emotions. These results give support to hypotheses 2a and 3a. To test hypothesis 2b and 3b, we examine the relation among emotion, expectation and the decision to hold or capitulate on a losing investment. More optimistic expectations about the stock's future performance are positively and significantly related to the tendency to keep the losing investment, although a more positive emotion does not significantly predict a stronger tendency to hold. Thus, hypothesis 2b is supported, but hypothesis 3b is not.

Our results are consistent with Arkes et al. (2008) that investors do adapt to losses, but we contribute to the existing literature by demonstrating that a lower adapted reference point is predicted by a larger size of total losses and/or a longer time in losing position. Moreover, our results add more insight into the separate effects of time in a losing position and the size of investment losses as we have disentangled the unique effect of past stimuli and time. We also show that adaptation of the reference point indirectly affect an investor's decision to hold or to capitulate on a losing investment, thus, we have demonstrated the link between reference point adaptation and decision-making.

REFERENCES

Arkes, Hal R., David Hirshleifer, Danling Jiang, & Sonya Lim (2008), "Reference Point Adaptation: Tests in the Domain of Security Trading," *Organizational Behavior and Human Decision Processes,* 105, 67-81.

Epstein, Seymour (1994), "Integration of the Cognitive and the Psychodynamic Unconscious," *American Psychologist,* 49, 709-724.

Helson, Harry (1964), *Adaptation Level Theory,* New York: Harper and Row.

Kahneman, Daniel & Amos Tversky (1979), "Prospect Theory: An Analysis of Decision Under Risk," *Econometrica,* 47, 263-292.

Shefrin, Hersh & Meir Statman (1985), "The Disposition to Sell Winners Too Early and Ride Losers Too Long," *Journal of Finance,* 40, 777-790.

Cost-Benefit Associations and Their Influence on Loan Experience

Bernadette Kamleitner, University of London, UK
Erik Hoelzl, Universitaet Wien, Austria
Erich Kirchler, Universitaet Wien, Austria

EXTENDED ABSTRACT

Most decisions are determined by costs and benefits. We investigate whether it matters to which degree consumers mentally associate costs and benefits of a transaction. In 1998 Prelec and Loewenstein suggested that the pleasure of consumption decreases, if thoughts related to consumption strongly evoke thoughts of payment. Also, they suggested that the pain of paying decreases, if thoughts related to payment strongly evoke thoughts of consumption. Or to put it differently: if the benefits of a transaction make people think of the cost, the benefits themselves become devaluated. If the cost of a transaction make people think of the benefits, the cost become less onerous. To ascertain whether cost-benefit associations (CBAs) really have these suggested consequences it seems necessary to assess and manipulate the actual degree of cost-benefit associations. Even though some studies have drawn on Prelec and Lowenstein's concept of coupling (Gourville and Soman 1998; Heath and Fennema 1996; Kivetz 1999; Soman and Gourville 2001) they did not directly measure cost-benefit associations. Rather, it has been assumed that certain differences in transaction characteristics lead to differences in cost-benefit associations (e.g., assuming weak CBAs due to price bundling Soman and Gourville 2001) which in turn contribute to differences in consumer evaluations and behaviour (for an exception, see an interview study by Kamleitner and Kirchler 2006). We aim to fill this gap.

In three studies, we assessed the consequences of cost-benefit-associations on consumer evaluations of a personal loan. Personal loans were chosen as a context because buying a good on a loan entails several consumption and payment episodes over a long time period. Consequently, costs and benefits are likely to be salient and in turn loan users are likely to be able to report on CBAs.

Study 1 was a field study among 143 personal loan users. CBAs were assessed by two straightforward items asking for the strength of each direction of association (e.g., 'When I think of the loan I always also think of the goods I bought with it'). Subjective evaluations of the loan and the good were assessed as dependent variables. Separate regressions were run to predict both dependents. The subjective burden of the loan significantly regressed on the degree to which the benefits evoked thoughts of the cost (B2C-association) whereas it did not regress on the degree to which the cost evoked thoughts of the benefits (C2B-association). This result holds even if possible income effects are controlled for. Contrary to that, the subjective evaluation of the loan financed good does not relate to the degree of CBAs. Hence neither of the assumed consequences was observed. Strong B2Cs did not reduce the utility of consumption and strong C2Bs did not reduce the burden of the loan. Rather, strong C2Bs seemed to relate to the burden of the loan. The more the benefit (i.e. loan financed good) made people think of the cost (i.e., loan), the more burdensome the loan was experienced.

To make sure that CBAs have a causal impact on subjective evaluations, Study 2 manipulated CBAs in a paper pencil experiment. 128 Participants were asked to immerse into a short scenario about a person who took up a loan for a car. In particular, the scenario contained two short episodes and thoughts the person had during that episode. Wording of the thoughts was varied so that both directions of CBAs were manipulated independently. After immersing into the scenario, participants were asked to provide subjective evaluations of loan and car. A manipulation check indicated that the manipulation was successful. A 2x2 MANOVA tested for an effect of B2C- and C2B-associations on evaluations. As in Study 1, there only was a main effect of the B2C-association. If benefits strongly led to thoughts of cost, the loan was experienced more burdensome and the car was experienced less positive than if this association was weak. In sum, Study 2 reconfirms and adds to findings of Study 1. As in Study 1 B2C-associations had an effect on loan burden. In addition, the hypothesized effect of B2C-associations on the utility of the good was observed.

Study 3 was designed to assure generalizability across designs and samples. 235 people participated in an online experiment: Participants were asked to imagine that they had among other goods a loan-financed car. They then had to work through several slice-of-life episodes, some of them featuring the car or the loan. Slight changes in wording and in accompanying pictures were successfully used to prime B2C- and C2B-associations. Subjective evaluations were again assessed. Results of a 2x2 MANOVA are in line with the previous studies. There was only a main effect of B2C-associations. The subjective loan burden was higher if the car strongly evoked thoughts of the loan. No effect on the subjective utility of the car was observed.

To conclude it seems that—at least with loan-holders—CBAs do not have the consequences often assumed. This finding is of practical importance and it is worthwhile to investigate why we did not observe the theorized relations, e.g., strong B2Cs had a consistent effect on cost rather than benefit perception. One possibility is that associations are influential because of a meta-cognitive impact. Strong associations can increase the cognitive accessibility of the associated concept. Accessibility in turn may act as cue to the affective quality of the concept (e.g., Wanke, Bohner, and Jurkowitsch 1997). For example, if a good strongly evokes thoughts of payment, consumers may focus on their intense thoughts of payment and interpret them as indicative of a massive pain of paying. The current studies allow for this possibility. Future research is needed to show to which degree our findings can be generalized across transaction contexts, measurements and manipulations.

REFERENCES

Gourville, John T. and Dilip Soman (1998), "Payment Depreciation: The Behavioral Effects of Temporally Separating Payments from Consumption," *Journal of Consumer Research*, 25 (2), 160-74.

Heath, Chip and M. G. Fennema (1996), "Mental Depreciation and Marginal Decision Making," *Organizational Behavior and Human Decision Processes*, 68 (2), 95-108.

Kahneman, Daniel and Amos Tversky (1984), "Choices, Values and Frames," *American Psychologist*, 37 (4), 341-50.

Kamleitner, Bernadette and Erik Hölzl (in press), "Cost-Benefit-Associations and Financial Behavior," *Applied Psychology: An International Review*.

Kamleitner, Bernadette and Erich Kirchler (2006), "Personal Loan Users' Mental Integration of Payment and Consumption," *Marketing Letters*, 17 (4), 281-94.

Kivetz, Ran (1999), "Advances in Research on Mental Accounting and Reason-Based Choice," *Marketing Letters*, 10 (3), 249-66.

Kounios, John, Roderick W. Smith, Wei Yang, Peter Bachman, and Mark D'Esposito (2001), "Cognitive Association Formation in Human Memory Revealed by Spatiotemporal Brain Imaging," *Neuron*, 29 (1), 297-306.

Novemsky, Nathan, Ravi Dhar, Norbert Schwarz, and Itamar Simonson (2007), "Preference Fluency in Choice," *Journal of Marketing Research*, 44 (3), 347-56.

Prelec, Drazen and George Loewenstein (1998), "The Red and the Black: Mental Accounting of Savings and Debt," *Marketing Science*, 17 (1), 4-28.

Schwarz, Norbert (2004), "Metacognitive Experiences in Consumer Judgment and Decision Making," *Journal of Consumer Psychology*, 14 (4), 332-48.

Schwarz, Norbert, Lawrence J. Sanna, Skurnik Ian, and Carolyn Yoon (2007), "Metacognitive Experiences and the Intricacies of Setting People Straight: Implications for Debiasing and Public Information Campaigns," *Advances in Experimental Social Psychology*, 39, 127-61.

Soman, Dilip and John T. Gourville (2001), "Transaction Decoupling: How Price Bundling Affects the Decision to Consume," *Journal of Marketing Research*, 38 (1), 30-44.

Thaler, Richard H. (1985), "Mental Accounting and Consumer Choice," *Marketing Science*, 4 (3), 199-214.

_____ (1990), "Saving, Fungibility, and Mental Accounts," *Journal of Economic Perspectives*, 4 (1), 193-205.

Tversky, Amos and Daniel Kahneman (1981), "The Framing of Decisions and the Psychology of Choice," *Science*, 211, 453-58.

Wanke, M., G. Bohner, and A. Jurkowitsch (1997), "There Are Many Reasons to Drive a BMW: Does Imagined Ease of Argument Generation Influence Attitudes?," *Journal of Consumer Research*, 24 (2), 170-77.

Effects of Belief in Global Citizenship on Branding Discourse in the U.S. and Russia

Yuliya Strizhakova, Michigan Technological University, USA
Robin Coulter, University of Connecticut, USA
Linda Price, University of Arizona, USA

EXTENDED ABSTRACT

Global brands appeal to managers because of their ability to provide economies of scale and secure high brand equity. Their appeal for consumers is more widely debated, especially in emerging markets where global brands are frequently blamed for disruptions of local value systems. Past research (Appadurai 1990) suggests that the potential of global brands to transform cultural meanings depends on whether consumers believe that global brands can provide them with the means of participation in the global consumer culture and expression of their identity. Holt, Quelch, and Taylor (2004) posit: *global brands create an imagined global identity that [the consumer] shares with like-minded people* (p. 71); they report that approximately 12% of consumers across 12 countries prefer global brands for this reason.

Drawing on research on branded products, globalization, and consumer culture as related to developed and emerging markets, we attempt to further explicate the concept of belief in global brands as a passport to global citizenship. Specifically, we posit and test relationships between several concepts, including: belief in global citizenship, the symbolic use of branded products as a means of identity, and the importance of branded products. We further consider the effects of cultural openness and consumer ethnocentrism on belief in global citizenship. The overarching goal of our research is to move beyond preference prediction for global brands and to assess effects of belief in global citizenship on a symbolic system of meanings consumers associate with branded products in developing and developed cultures. We consider belief in global citizenship as an antecedent to the symbolic meaning of personal identity that branded products project and to importance that consumers assign to branded products. Effects of consumer ethnocentrism and cultural openness on belief in global citizenship are also examined.

Our research takes an adapted etic approach (Douglas and Craig 2006) and focuses on the global youth segment in one developed (U.S., n=218) and one developing (Russia; n=292) market. College students in the two countries were asked to complete a questionnaire that presented them with shortened measures of consumer ethnocentrism (Shimp and Sharma 1987) and cultural openness (Sharma et al. 1995). Based on past research (Alden, Steenkamp, and Batra 1999; Holt et al. 2004; Steenkamp, Batra, and Alden 2003), we developed three items to measure belief in global citizenship. We also developed fifteen items to measure the meaning of personal identity of branded products (five items each to reflect the meanings of self-identity, group-identity, and status). Because of past challenges with self-reported general measures of consumer involvement with branded products in emerging markets (e.g., Coulter, Price and Feick 2003), we developed an index measure of branded product importance for each individual based upon his/her expressed importance for branded products in ten product categories (i.e., mineral water, soda, beer, coffee, cigarettes, chocolates, personal care/cosmetics, clothing, automobiles, and televisions).

We used structural equation modeling (AMOS, 7.0) to address our goals and hypotheses. The models exhibited configural and metric invariance (Steenkamp and Baumgartner 1998), which allowed us to make model comparisons between the two countries. Both pan- and intra-country analyses were performed. As pre-dicted, belief in global citizenship was a strong positive predictor of the brand meaning of personal identity, and this effect was stronger in Russia. The meaning of identity increased importance of branded products to an equal degree across countries. Both cultural openness and consumer ethnocentrism had positive effects on belief in global citizenship, but, contrary to our prediction, the effect of cultural openness was stronger in the U.S. and the effects of ethnocentrism were not different across the two countries. Consistent with past research, there was a moderate negative correlation between consumer ethnocentrism and cultural openness in the U.S. (Sharma et al. 1995; Shimp and Sharma 1987), but we found no relationship between these two concepts in Russia.

Our work draws attention to belief in global citizenship and importance of branded products, and examines relationships between these concepts, as well as their relationship to symbolic meanings associated with antecedents of ethnocentrism and cultural openness. Our research identifies several important opportunities for future research. First, we show that young consumers in the U.S. and Russia vary in the extent to which they believe in belongingness to the global world and view global brands as symbols of identity meanings. Global brands empower branded product discourse by enriching meanings of brands and facilitating consumer involvement with branded products. Second, we find that individuals in the U.S. and Russia who are culturally open and those who are patriotic about their locally-made products are likely to believe in global citizenship. The latter finding speaks to the notion of emerging "glocal" identities of young consumers, especially in developing markets where global brands signal a path for national empowerment and value sharing. Future research should examine potentially different, possibly curvilinear relationships between ethnocentrism and belief in global citizenship in samples of more ethnocentric consumers and over time. Finally, the relative novelty of brands and branding in Russia makes the constructs of culture and consumer culture rather distinct. Multinational corporations and local firms need to be aware of consumer's limited understanding of branding and determine appropriate local mechanisms to further develop consumer culture.

The Demand for Counterfeits-An Extended TPB Approach with Empirical Evidence from Seven Countries

Elfriede Penz, Wirtschaftsuniversitaet Wien, Austria

Barbara Stoettinger, Wirtschaftsuniversitaet Wien, Austria

EXTENDED ABSTRACT

This paper aims to broaden the knowledge on why consumers buy counterfeit products, a global concern to manufacturers of original products. Extended through the concept of self-identity, the Theory of Planned Behavior is used as theoretical underpinning in a seven-country study. Overall, findings support the usefulness of the extended TBP to explain the demand for fakes in a multi-country setting. A more in-depth look into individual linkages reveals national idiosyncrasies and provides interesting avenues for future research.

Introduction

The trade with counterfeit products has been growing dramatically across the globe, and manufacturers of the original products find themselves in a constant battle against this malpractice. In order to curb the demand for counterfeits, the knowledge on what drives customers to buy the copy rather than the original is crucial. As pointed out in the literature (Eisend & Schuchert-Güler, 2006), the knowledge base in the field is still fragmented and lacks theoretical substantiation. Thus, with our contribution, we aimed at extending existing research in various ways: (1) responding to the frequent call for more theoretical underpinning by using the Theory of Planned Behavior (Ajzen, 1991) as a framework, (2) extending it with the concept of self-identity and (3) applying the model to a multi-country sample to meet frequent calls for more cross-national research in this area (Fullerton & Punj, 1997; Husted, 2000).

Conceptual Background

In consumer misbehavior research, which uses the purchase of counterfeits as one of its classic examples (Fullerton & Punj, 2004; Green & Smith, 2002), the TPB was used previously (d'Astous, Colbert, & Montpetit, 2005); yet only in the context of software and music piracy, i.e., product categories with highly functional benefits (e.g., Kwong & Lee, 2002). For the product categories that we selected for our research; counterfeits of widely used branded products (such as textiles, handbags, accessories), the TPB was not used so far as a theoretical framework.

Branded products are used to improve the self-concept through the transfer of attributed meanings and thus the enrichment of self-value. People who are buying branded products are especially concerned about the impression they make and more sensitive to interpersonal rejections (Ang, Cheng, Lim, & Tambyah, 2001; Nia & Zaichkowsky, 2000). For this process to work, interaction with others is necessary. Others deliver meaning to brands, as brands are interpreted differently by different consumer groups (Hogg, Cox, & Keeling, 2000).

Through the concept of subjective norm, the TPB takes the role of social influences on the purchasing behavior into account (Terry, Hogg, & White, 2000). Theoretically, the purchase of counterfeits is based on similar contentions: buying fake products means getting the prestige of branded products without paying for it (Cordell, Wongtada, & Kieschnick, 1996), thus indicating suitability of TPB also in our research context. Recently, concerns were raised that subjective norm exhaustively covers external influences on purchasing decisions (Thorbjörnsen, Pedersen, & Nysveen, 2007). Research strongly points towards self-identity as a meaningful extension of the TPB (Armitage & Conner, 2001; Mannetti, Pierro, & Livi, 2002; Thorbjörnsen et al., 2007). In that respect, self-identity has been used in purchasing settings, where ethical considerations are an important influence (Shaw & Shiu, 2003; Sparks, 2000). While buying counterfeits represents unethical consumer behavior, the underlying arguments related to self-identity may apply similarly in our research context.

Methodology

Based on existing literature and the contentions outlined above, a model was developed. Attitudes towards counterfeits/counterfeiting, the subjective norm (operationalized in three ways: as direct social influence through immediate peers, interpersonal influence susceptibility, consumer motivation), perceived behavioral control, perceived access to counterfeits and price consciousness were outlined as drivers of intention. Ethical disposition, self identity and fashion consciousness were modeled as antecedents. The model was tested at two different price levels (counterfeit is significantly/slightly cheaper than the original).

We tested our theoretical model in seven countries, namely Mexico, Thailand, Ukraine, Slovakia, the U.S., Austria and Sweden. Country selection is based on Husted's (2000) work who identified three factors as important drivers of the demand for counterfeits (GNP per capita, distribution of income, individualism). Data were gathered by means of a questionnaire survey. After pre-testing and checking for content validity of the measures, the final questionnaire was made available in the languages pertinent in the countries chosen. Linguistic equivalence between the different versions was established through back-translation (Brislin, 1970).

Findings and Discussion

As results show, the general model structure we proposed appears to be universal with an acceptable fit across the seven countries and the two different price levels. So, with our research goals in mind, the extended Theory of Planned Behavior on an overall level serves well as a theoretical framework to predict the demand for counterfeits across countries.

A more in-depth look into individual linkages revealed a multi-faceted picture. While attitudes do have an effect on intentions to purchase, linkages differ in strength on a country basis. This holds even truer, when it comes to the antecedents to attitudes. Influences other than attitudes turned out to be more stable across countries when predicting purchase intention. Perceived behavioural control was a particularly important influence on the intention to buy. Similarly important and consistently, price consciousness does NOT influence the intention to buy. This contradicts the conventional notion and arguments put forward in the literature. The access to counterfeits turned out to be influential in explaining intentions to buy, yet less strongly and consistently than the other two factors.

The importance of social norm as proposed in TPB holds true to a large extent. Particularly, the immediate social environment plays an important role, while on a more general level (interpersonal influence susceptibility, consumer motivation) the impact of social norm is fading. Self-identity does not impact intention directly, but very much indirectly via the subjective norm.

In terms of future research, given the national idiosyncrasies, it appears called for to investigate in more depth how attitudes are formed on a national level and in what way the antecedents proposed influence this formation. Moreover, deepening the insights into how and on what level self-identity and subjective norm are related and influence other constructs would contribute to the theoretical advancement of TPB. Finally, while the general model structure appears to be universal, the specific variable values at national levels point to cultural influences. Exploring and explaining these national/cultural idiosyncrasies will be helpful to deepen the understanding of why consumers buy fakes.

REFERENCES

Ajzen, I. (1991). The theory of planned behavior. *Organizational Behavior and Human Decision Processes*, 50, 179-211.

Ang, S. H., Cheng, P. S., Lim, E. A. C., & Tambyah, S. K. (2001). Spot the difference: Consumer responses towards counterfeits. *Journal of Consumer Marketing*, 18(3), 219-235.

Armitage, C. J., & Conner, M. (2001). Efficacy of the Thoery of Planned Behaviour: A Meta-Analytic Review. *British Journal of Social Psychology*, 40, 471-501

Brislin, R. W. (1970). Back translation for cross-cultural research. *Journal of Cross-Cultural Psychology*, 1(3), 185-216.

Cordell, V. V., Wongtada, N., & Kieschnick, R. L. J. (1996). Counterfeit purchase intentions: Role of lawfulness, attitudes and product traits as determinants. *Journal of Business Research*, 35, 41-53.

d'Astous, A., Colbert, F., & Montpetit, D. (2005). Music Piracy on the Web-" How Effective are Anti-Piracy Arguments? Evidence from the Theory of Planned Behaviour. *Journal of Consumer Policy*, 28(3), 289-310.

Eisend, M., & Schuchert-Güler, P. (2006). Explaining counterfeit purchases: A review and preview. *Academy of Marketing Science Review*, 2006, 1.

Fullerton, R. A., & Punj, G. (1997). What is consumer misbehavior? *Advances in Consumer Research*, 24, 336-339.

Fullerton, R. A., & Punj, G. (2004). Repercussions of promoting an ideology of consumption: consumer misbehavior. *Journal of Business Research*, 57, 1239-1249.

Green, R. T., & Smith, T. (2002). Countering brand counterfeiters. *Journal of International Marketing*, 10(4), 89-106.

Hogg, M. K., Cox, A. J., & Keeling, K. (2000). The impact of self-monitoring on image congruence and product/brand evaluation. *European Journal of Marketing*, 34(5/6), 641-666.

Husted, B. W. (2000). The impact of national culture on software piracy. *Journal of Business Ethics*, 26(3), 197.

Kwong, T. C. H., & Lee, M. K. O. (2002). Behavioral intention model for the exchange mode Internet music piracy. Paper presented at the 35th Annual Hawaii International Conference on System Sciences.

Mannetti, L., Pierro, A., & Livi, S. (2002). Explaining Consumer Conduct: From Planned to Self-Expressive Behavior. *Journal of Applied Social Psychology*, 32(7), 1431-1451.

Nia, A., & Zaichkowsky, J. L. (2000). Do counterfeits devalue the ownership of luxury brands? *Journal of Product & Brand Management*, 9(7), 485-497.

Shaw, D., & Shiu, E. (2003). Ethics in consumer choice: A multivariate modelling approach. *European Journal of Marketing*, 37(10).

Sparks, P. (2000). Subjective expected utility-based attitude-behavior models: The utility of self-identity. In D. J. Terry & M. A. Hogg (Eds.), *Attitudes, behavior, and social context. The role of norms and group membership* (pp. 31-46). Mahwah, New Jersey: Lawrence Erlbaum.

Terry, D. J., Hogg, M. A., & White, K. M. (2000). Attitude-behavior relations: social identity and group membership. In D. J. Terry & M. A. Hogg (Eds.), *Attitudes, behavior, and social context. The role of norms and group membership* (pp. 67-93). Mahwah, New Jersey: Lawrence Erlbaum.

Thorbjörnsen, H., Pedersen, P. E., & Nysveen, H. (2007). "This is who I am": Identity expressiveness and the theory of planned behavior. *Psychology & Marketing*, 24(9), 763-785.

An Exploratory Study of Media Multitasking Practices and Experiences among Young Consumers

Andrew Rohm, Northeastern University, USA
Fleura Bardhi, Northeastern University, USA
Fareena Sultan, Northeastern University, USA

EXTENDED ABSTRACT

An increasingly important line of inquiry in consumer behavior is the study of the ways consumers multitask across multiple forms of media in a simultaneous fashion (Pilotta and Schultz 2005). Simultaneous media consumption, which we call media multitasking, is a phenomenon born from the plethora of media and communications platforms available and easily accessible to consumers, especially among young consumers. The media landscape and delivery system itself has changed dramatically in recent times. Contemporary media employs multitasking formats, such as television newscasts displaying multiple messages on one screen, enabling viewers to access several different news items simultaneously. Further, consumers are no longer passive media spectators, but interact with media in co-production settings, such as seen with consumer-generated advertisements or text-message voting for a favorite singer in television shows such as *American Idol*. However, marketing research continues to examine media consumption and treat marketing communication issues under a sequential, traditional marketing communication model where the consumer is a passive receiver of one type of media at one time. This study represents a first attempt to examine the phenomenon of media multitasking and its implications for marketing communication concepts and strategy.

Media multitasking, the simultaneous consumption of multiple media platforms seems to be the norm, especially among young Gen Y consumers who have grown up amidst today's vast media landscape. According to a nation-wide survey study reported by *Time* magazine, Americans aged 8 to 18 not only consume the greatest amount of media, but through electronic media they can compress 8.5 hours worth of media time a day into a 6.5 hour time-period through simultaneous consumption (Wallis 2006). This study attempts to a) examine media multitasking behavior among young consumers and b) provide an understanding of their motivations, experiences, and coping with media multitasking.

The study of multitasking has primarily been the domain of cognitive psychology, concluding that multitasking threatens consumers' task effectiveness, learning and well being. However, the cognitive perspective ignores the socialization aspect of behavior. Mick and Fournier (1998) illustrate the ways individuals attempt to cope with the ubiquity of technology. Consumers may also develop specific skills with which to manage and even automate performance involving multiple tasks (Kanfer and Ackerman 1996). In some instances, consumers may be more effective while multitasking when they are able use technology to complement or supplement other media (Sinan, Brynjolfsson, and Alstyne 2007; Jenkins 2006). For example, consumers may seek to complement and add depth to their media experience by searching for results of a sporting event online while they are simultaneously watching the event on television. Therefore, consumers may adopt multitasking strategies in order to increase comprehension and effectiveness in the consumption of online and offline media. Highly practiced skills, such as sequential or simultaneous multitasking across sources of media, may be developed as strategies to deal or cope with vast amounts of media communications sources or outlets (Sinan, Brynjolfsson, and Alstyne 2007). In what he refers to as the participatory culture,

Jenkins (2006) also suggests that because of the rise in access to digital media, particularly among the youth market, multitasking and attention should not be viewed as an "either, or" proposition, given that the nature of attention to media among young consumers has changed to that of continuous partial attention. In other words, consumers born and raised during the Internet era are perhaps becoming more skilled at navigating between and effectively managing multiple sources of information and media content.

The goal of the study is to examine the experience of media multitasking from the perspective of the young Gen Y consumer. Therefore, we selected as a purposeful sample for the study 64 undergraduate students at a university in the northeastern U.S. The students were also screened on their media consumption to insure that they continuously participate in media multitasking. As this is an exploratory study, a qualitative approach was taken. Data were collected through semi-structured interviews and collages developed to portray their media consumption.

We found that media multitasking is a normal activity in students' lives driven by a) the ease of accessibility and the interactive nature of contemporary media; and b) the participatory culture in which they live. For Gen Y, work, leisure, socialization, and personal self-development are closely related with exposure to various media and communications technologies. We found that most media multitasking evolved around the offline (television) and the online (computers). Consistent with past research, our findings suggest that television is typically consumed as a background media, whereas online sources (e.g., the Internet) act as foreground media characterized by discrete burst of engagement and attention. Two types of media multitasking behaviors emerged that differ in terms of the role of the consumer as either *active participant* or *passive victim*, as well as in terms of the individual's level of attention and engagement. The first type of media multitasking behavior involves *strategic switching* between various media platforms. The second type of multitasking is a passive mode of behavior, characterized by the individual constantly tuning in and out various media with the goal of simply being "always on".

Media multitasking is considered by our informants as paradoxical. Our data suggests that the multitasking experience parallels a subset of consumer paradoxes of technology developed by Mick and Fournier (1998): efficient/inefficient, connectivity/isolation, and freedom/enslavement. To cope with these paradoxes consumers develop various coping strategies (Mick and Fournier 1999) from restriction of media usage to the refinement of personal media consumption practices. The majority of our informants claimed that, while they were aware of personal issues and challenges associated with their media consumption, they have become effective multitaskers as a result of their active participation as consumers of contemporary media and the associated role of media as a socialization agent within the youth participatory culture. Based on these findings the paper provides implication for theory and practice.

The Role of Symbolic Consumption in Identity Projects: The Case of Fostered Children

Margaret K. Hogg, Lancaster University, UK
Maria G. Piacentini, Lancaster University, UK
Sally Hibbert, Nottingham University Business School, UK[1]

EXTENDED ABSTRACT

Consumption impacts identity projects especially when it facilitates, accelerates, ameliorates or impedes identities in transition. Earlier studies have largely examined identity transitions within the context of privileged groups of consumers, to the relative neglect of less privileged consumer groups. Negative experiences such as stigmatization can impede identity transitions by interrupting the acquisition not just of an adult identity, but also of some of the essential consumer skills for operating in the marketplace, thus threatening self-esteem. The empirical context represented by less privileged groups such as fostered children, for instance, could offer significant additional theoretical insights into the impact of consumption experiences on identity projects. The literatures on transition and emerging adulthood informed our examination of the lived experiences of young fostered people.

Young people in the transition to adulthood in post-industrial societies have the opportunity to explore a wider range of potential identities because the current cultural environment is less normatively structured (Bauman 2001; Cote 2002). While this brings opportunities for self development, the task of configuring a coherent identity that will provide the basis for adult roles in work, family and home life, often creates a psychological burden (Schwartz et al. 2005). Evidence suggests that a sense of agency and the ability to exercise free choice are crucial to successfully undertaking future adult roles such as parenthood, employment and marriage (Schwartz 2004); and yet the ability to exercise agency and free choice are not necessarily enjoyed by all sections of society, often reflecting structural inequalities in the marketplace. During their transitions to young adulthood, fostered children often face the additional burden of managing social stigma and stereotyping in their identity projects because "at its core, the experience of stigma is fundamentally a threat to the self" (Crocker and Garcia 2006: 289).

We used a range of contacts (e.g. charities that support fostered young people; a lobbying organisation run by care-experienced young people; and support workers) to recruit sixteen young adults for group and individual interviews over an eight month period. All participants were aged between 16 and 21; and had either left care to live independently or were preparing to do so. A token incentive was paid to each participant. Focus group discussions with nine participants lasted between sixty and ninety minutes; and were held in single-sex groups (four men and five women). Nine individual interviews were held (7 women and 2 men). Each interview lasted between one and two hours. Open-ended questions were used to elicit the experiences of young fostered adults, and about how the fostered children had coped with those experiences in the transition to adulthood. Intratextual and intertextual interpretive analyses (Adkins and Ozanne 2005) were used, moving between deductive and inductive approaches. The interview framework was used for deductive analysis around themes such as experiences of leaving care. Inductive analysis was used to identify emergent themes (e.g. different views of the self; vulnerability; and coping strategies).

These fostered children's experiences showed how consumption was used to achieve selfhood and personal identity (Hirschman and Hill 2000); the role of the material in identity formation processes; and particularly the creation of meaning via consumption including symbolic consumption and the extended self (Belk 1988). For the purposes of this paper, we follow Thompson (2005) and focus on three participants' stories (Veronica, Theresa, Krista) to illustrate the major themes which emerged from our overall data set about symbolic consumption in relation to transitional objects; precious possessions and relationships; and identity threats from stereotyping (that is, the fear that one's behavior will confirm an existing stereotype of a group with which one identifies).

At times of transition, possessions play an important role, symbolising relationships and helping to enhance feelings of psychological well-being during liminality (Noble and Walker, 1997). Our informants tended to have few material goods but these were very important to their psychological well-being, reinforcing the importance of transitional objects as identity markers. Krista's desk was a transitional, almost epiphanic (Woodward 2001) object, that had moved with Krista from her care home into her new flat, marking also her transition to adult status by living independently, and managing her household expenses via careful budgeting (e.g. the desk demonstrated her ability to save and to allocate resources carefully). This suggests scope for seeing the extended self (Belk 1988) in a much more nuanced way within the context of individuals' earlier consumption and attachment histories. In the context of the vulnerable youth coming out of foster care, the role of possessions is particularly important, confirming the role of symbolic consumption in transitions (Gentry et al. 1995; McAlexander 1991; Price et al. 2000; Roster 2001; Schouten 1991; Young 1991). Our research also builds on Hirschman and Hill's (2000) work on the role of possessions and the impact of restricted consumption on identity; and resonates too with recent work on refugees (Parkin 1999) who share characteristics in terms of the uncertainty of life, the transitoriness of possessions, and the brittleness of relationships.

Their children were sacred possessions, representing very important attachment objects for the fostered young women who themselves had experienced very poor histories of attachment in their own young lives. Veronica's story about the birthday party she had held for her daughter Megan illustrated how symbolic consumption was used to mark her precious daughter's birthday, and inscribe familial relationships. Veronica could thereby demonstrate that she had the means to be an indulgent, as well as caring, mother, and thus pass one of the key tests of adult identity (i.e. parenthood, George 1993).

Symbolic consumption emerged as a response when an identity threat was perceived from stereotyping, even when a young person's foster care status was concealed. For Theresa it was very important to be able to 'pass as normal' and to be accepted as a mother. She felt her physical appearance was instrumental in allowing her to disconnect from an earlier negative identity that might be attributed to her; and her physical appearance was closely tied to her self-esteem. Theresa fought hard to conceal aspects of her past that directly related to her being fostered (particularly the

[1] Acknowledgements: The authors would like to thank all the young people who participated in this study as well as the U.K. national children's charity, Barnados and the local government Morecambe Leaving Care Team (U.K.) for their generous assistance. We would also like to thank Russell Belk and Pauline Maclaran for their comments on earlier drafts of this paper.

people who had constituted her social network when she was fostered). Her appearance served to 'disguise' her from past social ties; she had changed her hair colour and had facial piercings to avoid being recognized by former friends. She was particularly anxious to protect her child and her partner from her past. This earlier youthful (negative) identity was in tension with the adult (positive) identity that she was trying so hard to move towards, particularly that of a caring mother who could be a good role model for her child.

Stories from fostered children show how they employ symbolic consumption in their strategies to resist and counteract the threats from their earlier negative identities as 'fostered children' as they forge new identities as young emergent adults and consumers. From their stories we see how they employ contingencies of self-worth in order firstly, to enhance their self-esteem in the key transitions to establishing an adult identity (becoming parents and establishing family life); and secondly to counter feelings of low self-esteem which contribute significantly to consumer marginality, vulnerability and disadvantage.

REFERENCES

Adkins, Neve Ross and Julie L. Ozanne (2005), "The Low Literate Consumer," *Journal of Consumer Research*, 32 (June), 93-105.

Arnett, Jeffrey J. (2000), "Emerging Adulthood," *American Psychologist*, 55 (5), 469-481.

Arnould, E. and C.J. Thompson (2005) "Consumer Culture Theory (CCT): Twenty Years of Research" Journal of Consumer Research 31 (March) 868-882.

Barn, Ravinder, Linda Andrew and Nadia Mantovani (2005), *Life After Care: The Experiences of Young People from Different Ethnic Backgrounds*, York, UK: York Publishing Service for Joseph Rowntree Foundation.

Bauman, Zygmunt. (2001), *The Individualised Society,* Cambridge: Polity

Belk, Russell W. (1988), "Possessions and the Extended Self," *Journal of Consumer Research*, 15, 139-168.

Belk, Russell W, Melanie Wallendorf and John F. Sherry (1989), "The Sacred and the Profane in Consumer Behavior: Theodicy on the Odyssey," *Journal of Consumer Research*, 16 (June), 1-38.

Bertrand, Marianne, Sendhil Mullainathan and Eldar Shafir (2006), "Behavioral Economics and Marketing in Aid of Decision Making Among the Poor," *Journal of Public Policy and Marketing*, 25 (1), 8-23.

Caplovitz, Kevin (1963), *The Poor Pay More*, New York: The Free Press.

Cornwell, T. Bettina and Terrance G. Gabel (1996), "Out of Sight, Out of Mind: An Exploratory Examination of Institutionalization and Consumption," *Journal of Public Policy and Marketing*, 15 (2), 278-95.

Cote, James E. (2000), *Arrested adulthood: The changing nature of maturity and identity in the late modern world*, New York: New York University Press.

Cote, James, E. and C. Levine (2002), *Identity formation, agency, and culture: a social psychological synthesis.* Mahwah, NJ: Lawrence Erlbaum Associates.

Crocker, Jennifer and Connie T. Wolfe (2001), "Contingencies of self-worth," *Psychological Review*, 108, 593-623.

Crocker, Jennifer and Julie A. Garcia (2006), "Stigma and the Social Basis of the Self: A Synthesis," in *Stigma and Group Inequality: Social Psychological Perspectives*, ed. Shana Levin and Colette van Laar, New York: Lawrence Erlbaum Associates, 287-308.

Crocker, Jennifer and Park, Lora E. (2004), "The costly pursuit of self-esteem," *Psychological Bulletin*, 130, 392-414.

Crocker, Jennifer, Andrew Karpinski, Diane M. Quinn, and Sara K. Chase (2003), "When Grades Determine Self-Worth: Consequences of Contingent Self-Worth for Male and Female Engineering and Psychology Majors," *Journal of Personality and Social Psychology*, 85 (3), 507-16.

Crocker, Jennifer, Brenda Major, and Claude M. Steele (1998), "Social Stigma," in *The Handbook of Social Psychology*, Vol. 2, ed. Daniel T. Gilbert, Susan T. Fiske, and Gardner Lindzey, New York: McGraw-Hill, 504–53.

Crockett, David, Sonya A. Grier and Jacqueline A. Williams (2003), "Coping with Marketplace Discrimination: An Exploration of the Experiences of Black Men", Academy of Marketing Science Review, [Online] 2003 (4)

Gentry, James, Patricia F. Kennedy, Catherine Paul, and Ronald Paul Hill (1995), "Family Transitions During Grief: Discontinuities in Household Consumption Patterns," *Journal of Business Research*, 34, 67-79.

George, Linda K. (1993), "Sociological Perspectives on Life Transitions," *Annual Review of Sociology*, 19, 353-73.

Goffman, Erving (1963), *Stigma: Notes on the Management of Spoiled Identity*, Englewood Cliffs, NJ: Prentice Hall.

Hagan, John and Holly Foster (2003), "S/He's a Rebel: Toward a Sequential Stress Theory of Delinquency and Gendered Pathways to Disadvantage in Emerging Adulthood," *Social Forces*, 82 (1), 53-86.

Hill, Ronald Paul (1991), "Homeless Women, Special Possessions, and the Meaning of "Home": An Ethnographic Case Study," *Journal of Consumer Research*, 18 (December), 298-310.

Hill, Ronald Paul (2002), "Stalking the Poverty Consumer: A Retrospective Examination of Modern Ethical Dilemmas," *Journal of Business Ethics*, 37 (2), 209-19.

Hirschman, Elizabeth C. and Ronald P. Hill (2000), "On Human Commoditization and Resistance: A Model Based upon Buchenwald Concentration Camp," *Psychology & Marketing*, Vol. 17 Issue 6, 469-491

Kaufman-Scarborough, Carol (2001), "Sharing The Experience of Mobility Disabled Consumers: Building Understanding Through the Use of Ethnographic Research Methods," *Journal of Contemporary Ethnography*, 30 (August), 430-64.

McAlexander, James H. (1991), "Divorce, the Disposition of the Relationship, and Everything," *Advances in Consumer Research*, Vol. 18 Issue 1, p43-48.

Noble, Charles H. & Beth A. Walker (1997), "Exploring the relationships among liminal transitions, symbolic consumption and the extended self," *Psychology & Marketing*, 14 (1), 29-47.

Office of the Deputy Prime Minister, Social Exclusion Unit (2005), *Improving Service, Improving Lives* Report to UK Government.

Ozanne, Julie L., Ronald Paul Hill, and Newell D. Wright (1998), "Juvenile Delinquents' Use of Consumption as Cultural Resistance: Implications for Juvenile Reform Programs and Public Policy," *Journal of Public Policy and Marketing*, 17 (2), 185-96.

Parkin, Kevin J. (1999) "Mementoes as Transitional Objects in Human Displacement," *Journal of Material Culture*, 4 (3), 303-21.

Price, Linda L., Eric J. Arnould and Carolyn Folkman Curasi (2000), "Older Consumers' Disposition of Special Possessions," *Journal of Consumer Research*, 27, (September), 179-201.

Propp, Jane, Debora M. Ortega and Forest NewHeart (2003), "Independence or Interdependence: Rethinking the Transition from "Ward of the Court" to Adulthood," *Families in Society*, 84 (2), 259-66.

Quinn, Diane M. (2006), "Concealable Versus Conspicuous Stigmatized Identities" in *Stigma and Group Inequality: Social Psychological Perspectives*, ed. Shana Levin and Colette van Laar, New York: Lawrence Erlbaum Associates, 83-104.

Ridge, Tess and Jane Millar (2000), "Excluding Children: Autonomy, Friendship and the Experience of the Care System," *Social Policy and Administration*, 34 (2), 160-175.

Schouten, J. W. (1991) "Selves in Transition: Symbolic Consumption in Personal Rites of Passage and Identity Reconstruction" *Journal of Consumer Research* 17 (March) 412-425

Schwartz, B. (2004), *The paradox of choice: why more is less,* New York: Ecco.

Schwartz, Seth J., James E. Cote and Jeffrey Jensen Arnett (2005), "Identity and Agency in Emerging Adulthood: Two Developmental Routs in the Individualization Process," *Youth & Society*, 37 (2), 201-229.

Thompson, Craig J. (1996), "Caring Consumers: Gendered Consumption Meanings and the Juggling Lifestyle," *Journal of Consumer Research,* 22 (March), 388-407.

Thompson, C. J. (2005) Consumer Risk Perceptions in a Community of Reflexive Doubt. *Journal of Consumer Research.* Vol. 32, pp 235-248.

Woodward, Ian (2001), "Domestic Objects and the Taste Epiphany: A Resource for Consumption Methodology," *Journal of Material Culture* 6 (2)115-136.

The Roles of Affective and Cognitive Components of Attitudes in the Context of High-Stakes Healthcare Decisions

Tracey King, American University, USA

EXTENDED ABSTRACT

This study is an attempt to shed light on the interplay of affective responses and cognitive beliefs in determining consumer attitudes towards high-stakes healthcare decision behaviors. High-stakes consumer decisions are defined as those involving subjectively important and risky outcomes (Kahn and Baron 1995; White 2005). The primary goal is to test the hypothesis that affective responses, compared to cognitive beliefs, are more important in determining attitudes towards hormone replacement therapy (HRT) use. Using structural equations modeling, attitudes and intentions towards HRT use are predicted within a network of relationships based on the theory of planned behavior framework (Ajzen 1991). The basic theory of planned behavior model was expanded to include the separation of affective and cognitive predictors of attitude towards HRT use (Edwards 1990).

One particular high-stakes decision context in which consumers are actively determining their choice of treatment is the decision of whether or not to use HRT. This treatment involves both risks and benefits, remains controversial among healthcare professionals, and is a decision almost every female consumer makes as she reaches menopausal age. In the literature on high-stakes decision making, it is argued that individuals may have a tendency to make these types of decisions using heuristics or general rules of thumb, including an overall affective reaction (Kunreuther et al. 2002; Loewenstein et al. 2001). Although there have been a number of studies that examine the cognitive influences on attitudes and intentions towards HRT use (Spatz et al. 2003), there is only limited research that considers the importance of affective responses in determining attitudes towards HRT use.

A sample of women (N=369; median age=51) provided the data to test the above hypothesis and the relationships in a model predicting intentions to use HRT. The respondents were administered a questionnaire containing self-report measures for constructs including (1) cognitive beliefs (e.g., "I think that using HRT is safe (vs. unsafe)"; α=.81) (2) affective responses (e.g., "Using HRT makes or would make me feel anxious (vs. not worried)"; α=.83), (3) subjective norms (e.g., "People who are important to me would encourage me to use HRT"; α=.93), (4) perceived behavioral control (e.g., "I am confident that I could use HRT if I wanted to"; α=.86), (5) attitude towards HRT use (e.g., "My overall attitude towards HRT use is favorable (vs. unfavorable)"; α=.96), and (6) intentions towards HRT use (e.g., "I expect to use or continue to use HRT in the future"; α=.99). All items were measured using 7-point semantic differential or Likert scales.

The first step in the analysis of the conceptual model and hypotheses tests was to assess the properties of each measurement instrument by performing a confirmatory factor analysis (CFA) using LISREL (Jöreskog and Sörbom 1996). The fit indices of the measurement model showed good fit ($\chi 2$=279.46, df=120, p<.01, CFI=.98, RMSEA=.60) and the validity and reliability of the measures were confirmed. The next step was to examine the structural relationships in the model and assess model fit. The fit indices showed that the model had an acceptable fit ($\chi 2$=194.36, df=124, p<.01, CFI=.98, RMSEA=.61) based on the criteria published by Jaccard and Wan (1996).

The structural results indicate that attitude (β=.49, t=11.78, p<.01) and subjective norms (γ=0.40, t=9.57, p<.01) both had positive and significant effects on intentions to use or continue to use HRT. However, perceived behavioral control (γ=.07, NS) had a nonsignificant effect on intentions to use or continue to use HRT. The path between affective responses and attitude towards HRT use was also positive and significant (γ=.82, t=14.17, p<.01). However, the path from cognitive beliefs to attitudes towards HRT use was positive but nonsignificant (γ=.09, NS).

The results provide support for the hypothesis that affective responses are a stronger predictor of attitudes compared to cognitive beliefs. Although the nonsignificant relationship between cognitive beliefs and attitudes towards HRT use was surprising, it is consistent with research on high-stakes decision making that shows that ambiguity as to what would constitute a 'right' answer can lead individuals to make choices by focusing on affective cues instead of cognitive beliefs (Kunreuther et al. 2002). To formally test this assertion, feelings of attitudinal ambivalence were measured using a four-item scale (α=.76) regarding how 'torn' one feels about the behavior. When entered into a linear regression, cognitive beliefs are shown to be a significant predictor of attitudinal ambivalence (β=.13, t=2.12, p<.05) whereas affective responses are nonsignificant (β=.04, t=.65, NS).

REFERENCES

Ajzen, Icek (1991), "The Theory of Planned Behavior," *Organizational Behavior and Human Decision Processes,* 50 (2), 179-211.

Edwards, Kari (1990), "The Interplay of Affect and Cognition in Attitude Formation and Change," *Journal of Personality and Social Psychology,* 59 (2), 202-16.

Jaccard, James and Choi K. Wan (1996), *LISREL Approaches to Interaction Effects in Multiple Regression,* Thousand Oaks, CA: Sage.

Jöreskog, Karl and Dag Sörbom (1996), *LISREL8: User's Reference Guide,* Chicago, IL: Scientific Software International.

Kahn, Barbara and Jonathan Baron (1995), "An Exploratory Study of Choice Rules Favored for High Stakes Decisions," *Journal of Consumer Psychology,* 4 (4), 305-28.

Kunreuther, Howard, Robert Meeyr, Richard Zeckhauser, Paul Slovic, Barry Schwartz, Christian Schade, Mary Frances Luce, Steven Lippman, David Krantz, Barbara Kahn, and Robin Hogarth (2002), "High Stakes Decision Making: Normative, Descriptive, and Prescriptive Considerations," *Marketing Letters,* 13 (3), 259-68.

Loewenstein, George F., Elke U. Weber, Christopher K. Hsee, and Ned Welch (2001), "Risk as Feelings," *Psychological Bulletin,* 127 (2), 167-286.

Spatz, Barbara A., Dennis L. Thombs, T. Jean Byrne, and Betsy J. Page (2003), "Use of the Theory of Planned Behavior to Explain HRT Decisions," *American Journal of Health Behavior,* 27 (4), 445-55.

White, Tiffany Barnett (2005), "Consumer Trust and Advice Acceptance: The Moderating Roles of Benevolence, Expertise, and Negative Emotions," *Journal of Consumer Psychology,* 15 (2), 141-8.

The Role of Cultural Identity and Personal Relevance on Risk Perception and Avoidance

Sergio W. Carvalho, University of Manitoba, Canada
Lauren G. Block, Baruch College, USA
Subramanian Sivaramakrishnan, University of Manitoba, Canada
Rajesh Manchanda, University of Manitoba, Canada
Chrissy Mitakakis, Baruch College, USA

EXTENDED ABSTRACT

In the globalized world that we now live, the media keeps warning us about health threats such as the avian flu, mad cow disease, E.coli, etc. from different countries. It is generally assumed that perception of risk among citizens depends largely on the perceived likelihood of occurrence of the threat (Luce and Kahn 1999; Menon, Block, and Ramanathan 2002). However, little is known on whether risk perception depends on how culturally similar the origin of the threat is to one's own? For instance, would Californians feel more at risk if the health threat originated in England versus in Japan, although both countries are advanced and at almost the same distance? This paper attempts to answer these important questions.

Scholars investigating the psychological closeness phenomenon suggest that people are more likely to assimilate self-evaluation to the standard if they feel psychologically closer to him or her (Brown et al. 1992). Along similar lines, Teigen's (2005) proximity heuristic theory in judgment of risk suggests that perceptions of proximity influence people's perceptions of their own and other people's risk. He exemplifies this proximity phenomenon by saying that the death of a close relative is more threatening than the death of a distant one, even when genetics is not the cause of death. A somewhat opposing view to the heuristic proximity theory is the one on defensive processing of threatening messages. Liberman and Chaiken (1992) suggest that threatening messages that are personally relevant may lead people to engage in defensive and biased processing in an attempt to reduce the threat. In this case, we can expect that health risky situations that are perceived to be highly personally relevant may lead to message avoidance or denial of susceptibility and hence reduce the perception of risk.

It is common knowledge that people feel psychologically closer to culturally similar groups. We propose that this feeling of closeness with the origin of a threat increases one's perception of risk and behavioral intentions. However, when personal relevance is increased, it can lead to a rejection of the risk.

In this research, using a context of people being affected by contaminated beef and dairy products, we conducted three studies to examine consumers' perception of risk from potentially consuming the contaminated food and their consequent willingness to engage in behaviors to avoid the risk. We demonstrate that when the risk is highly likely to occur, perceived risk and behavioral intentions are high only when the threat originates in a culturally similar country. However, when risk is less likely to happen, perceived risk and behavioral intentions are unaffected by the cultural similarity with the originating country. Furthermore, we show that even in the case of a culturally-dissimilar country, perceived risk and behavioral intentions can be high when the threat is high, provided that personal relevance is also high. In the case of the culturally-similar country, when personal relevance is high, it lowers their perception of risk and behavioral intentions.

Participants in studies 1 and 2 were given a fictitious news article that reported a food contamination in a foreign country and some citizens in that country being affected as a result. Likelihood of threat occurrence was communicated by manipulating the strength of the warning issued by local (Canadian) health officials about the possibility of food imported from that country being contaminated. In study 1, our data show that when the contaminated food was said to be imported from a culturally similar country (UK), consumers perceive a greater risk and behavioral intentions when the likelihood of threat occurrence is high and a lower risk when the likelihood of threat occurrence is low. However, when the contaminated food was said to be imported from a culturally dissimilar country (France), risk perception and behavioral intentions were low regardless of the likelihood of occurrence of the threat. These results indicate that the likelihood of threat occurrence impacts risk perceptions and behavioral intentions only when the threat originates in a culturally similar context. When the origin of the threat is seen as culturally distant, consumers underestimate the risk and are less willing to engage in behaviors to avoid the risk even when the risk is highly likely to occur.

In study 2, we manipulated personal relevance by the news article specifying that the persons affected by the contaminated food were students (high personal relevance) or not specifying (low personal relevance). We demonstrate that when the origin of the threat is a culturally-dissimilar country, perceived risk and behavioral intentions are high when the likelihood of threat occurrence is high only in the highly personally relevant condition. Interestingly, in the case of the culturally-similar country (UK), when the victims were reported to be students, perception of risk and behavioral intentions drop in the case of high likelihood of threat occurrence. We argue that this happens because consumers activate a defensive mechanism (Liberman and Chaiken 1992) that makes them reject the threat as not being credible. The results of study 2 mirror study 1 when the victims were said to be just people.

In study 3, using Germany as our culturally similar condition and Spain as our culturally dissimilar condition, we were able to replicate the findings from studies 1 and 2. This was done to eliminate any potential dissociative biases arising from English Canadians' perceptions of France.

This paper makes two important contributions. First, it demonstrates the moderating role of cultural similarity in perception of risk and behavioral intentions to avoid the risk in the face of an external threat. Second, it shows that when the message concerns a possible negative outcome, increasing the personal relevance of the threat results in rejecting the risk, counter to common knowledge that communications need to help the consumer relate to them in order to be effective.

REFERENCES

Brown, J. D., Novick, N. J., Lord, K. A., & Richards, J. M. (1992). When Gulliver travels: Social context, psychological closeness, and self-appraisals. *Journal of Personality and Social Psychology*, 62(May), 717–727.

Liberman, A., & Chaiken, S. (1992). Defensive processing of personally relevant health messages. *Personality and Social Psychology Bulletin*, 18(6), 669-679.

Luce, M. F., & Kahn, B. E. (1999). Avoidance or vigilance? The psychology of false positive test results. *Journal of Consumer Research*, 26(December), 242-259.

Menon, G., Block, L. G., & Ramanathan, S. (2002). We're at as much risk as we are led to believe: Effects of message cues on judgments of health risk. *Journal of Consumer Research,* 28(March), 533-549.

Teigen, K. H. (2005). The proximity heuristic in judgments of accident probabilities. *British Journal of Psychology*, 96, 423-440.

Certainty Appraisal and Health Communications

Canan Corus, St. John's University, USA

EXTENDED ABSTRACT

Introduction

Individuals employ defensive mechanisms when faced with health information that might perturb their sense of security. Efficacy of health communications are undermined as high risk individuals who are the target of most campaigns are also those who are most likely to reject or ignore them (Block and Williams 2000). Recent research suggests that aversion towards relevant health information is diminished under positive emotions. If the benefits of negative information are essential, as in the case of self relevant messages, then positive affect acts as a resource for buffering the mood hurting influence of threatening information, while under negative affect, one lacks the confidence to deal with the adverse emotional effects of threatening health information (Raghunathan and Trope 2002).

Conceptual Framework

This research examines the role of discrete incidental emotions on the effectiveness of health communications. Certainty appraisal (Smith and Ellsworth 1985) differentiates emotions on the basis of predictability that they convey about the environment. For example, when people feel angry, they report thinking that the situation is unpleasant but that they are certain and confident about what is happening. In contrast, when one feels anxious, the situation is unpleasant but also less predictable.

It is proposed that emotions high on certainty appraisal can provide the confidence to cope with the insecurity instigated by relevant but threatening health messages. Previous research shows that high certainty (e.g., anger, pride) makes one feel more resilient to risk (Lerner and Keltner 2001) or assess the situation as manageable (Johnson and Stewart 2005). It is proposed that those feeling certain might conclude that they need not refrain from processing an aversive but useful message. On the other hand, individuals feeling uncertainty associated emotions (e.g., anxiety, hope) are motivated to decrease their uncertainty (Raghunathan and Pham 1999). We suggest that the threatening nature of highly relevant health information is likely to be in conflict with uncertainty reduction goals, leading to decreased processing of this information. Thus, we suggest that when a health message is highly self-relevant, uncertainty related emotions will impede processing whereas certainty related emotions will facilitate processing of relevant health messages.

A different mechanism is likely to be at work when the health risk is *not* self relevant and therefore *not* as threatening. We predict that when relevance is low, the projected effect of the message for one's affective state will be less influential (Andrade 2005). Therefore, the message's implications for one's uncertainty related goals will be less relevant. In this case, emotions low (high) on certainty appraisal signal insufficient (sufficient) confidence about the surroundings, leading to increased (decreased) processing. These predictions would be in agreement with Tiedens and Linton (2001) findings that certainty related emotions lead to heuristic processing.

Studies 1-3

When individuals are at low (high) risk, those who are induced with uncertainty (certainty) related emotions will process a health related message to a higher extent compared to participants who are induced with certainty (uncertainty) related emotions. The first 2 studies directly test this hypothesis.

In study 1 participants were induced to feel anger (negative-certain emotion), pride (positive certain emotion), worry (negative-uncertain emotion) or surprise (positive -uncertain emotion). They then read an article about Chlamydia, a prevalent STD. Individuals were categorized as high versus low risk according to their past sexual behavior. The dependent measures were: message related thoughts, correct answers to a quiz about the article and a message persuasion intention measure. As expected, High risk individuals showed higher message recall and were more persuaded under certainty related emotions while the opposite was true for low risk individuals.

Study 2 replicates the results of study 1. In this study, perceived vulnerability was manipulated by conveying either high or low prevalence of the health threat. Further, emotions different from those in study 1 were used (i.e., hope and happiness). The procedure and dependent variables were similar to those of study 1 but this study focused on a different health issue, Hepatitis C. The results of study 1 were replicated. Further, in study 2, we wanted to rule out alternative explanations which may involve other relevant appraisals (i.e., pleasantness, situational control and intensity). Hence, we regressed vulnerability and a composite appraisal measure on the dependent variables. Results show that certainty was the *only* emotional dimension that interacts with vulnerability in the predicted direction. The regression results confirm that in the high risk condition, the more certain participants felt about the situation (i.e., higher certainty appraisal) the more they processed the message. Thus, it provides further support for the proposed effect that high certainty provides encouragement for processing useful but intimidating health information.

Study 3 not only extends the findings to a different health context (i.e., caffeine consumption) but also provides evidence that the demonstrated effects are indeed a function of the threatening nature of health related information. In this study, participants are presented with negative as well as positive information on caffeine consumption. Inducing four negative emotions that range in their certainty appraisals (i.e., fear, sadness, anger, disgust) we show that emotions that are associated with higher certainty increase individuals recall of negative information as compared to positive information and this effect is reversed for uncertainty related emotions.

Conclusion

In sum, the findings support the proposition that certainty-related emotions provide confidence to attend relevant but threatening information. Whereas, when feeling uncertain emotions, reading threatening health information clashes with uncertainty reduction goals, decreasing message processing and persuasion. These findings are in agreement with affect regulation theories and extend them to involve emotional uncertainty as an emotional state to be "repaired", by avoiding further uncertainty or striving for reassurance. The implications of this research concern the context (e.g., emotion laden program) in which a health message should be placed as well as its tone (e.g., high vs. low threat) that should be used in that context.

The Effects of Retrieval Ease on Health Issue Judgments: Implications for Campaign Strategies

Chingching Chang, National Chengchi University, Taiwan

EXTENDED ABSTRACT

A common opinion among psychologists studying metacognition is that "there is more to thinking than thought content" (Schwarz, 2004, p. 332). The literature on metacognition suggests that recall tasks render two types of information accessible: the retrieved content and the subjective experience of retrieving the content (see Schwarz, 1998, 2004, for reviews). Both types of information can influence judgments. Content-based thinking models (e.g., Wyer & Srull, 1989) hold that the more instances of an event that individuals are asked to recall, the more instances they will retrieve, and the higher they will thus estimate the frequency of the event to be. In contrast, metacognition models suggest that the more instances individuals are asked to recall, the more difficulty they will experience with retrieval (Schwarz, 1998, 2004). This subjectively experienced retrieval difficulty is then taken as an indicator that such events do not happen frequently.

Accordingly, thinking about the severity of a disease can render two types of information available: the retrieved consequences of the disease and the ease or difficulty with which they were brought to mind. Rothman and Schwarz (1998) found that, when asked to list many as opposed to a few factors leading to a disease, participants experienced more difficulty with the retrieval task, decreasing their perceived vulnerability to the disease. By extension, when people are asked to list possible outcomes or symptoms regarding an ailment, the difficulty with which such information comes to mind should affect their judgments of the ailment's severity. This question was tested in the first experiment of the present study.

In order to maximize willingness to seek treatment, it is also crucial to increase perceived self-efficacy in dealing with an ailment. Thus it is relevant to ask whether the difficulty of retrieving prevention or treatment options influences perceived self-efficacy. This issue was addressed in the second experiment.

When thinking about health issues, people often consider the severity of the issue. If it is difficult to retrieve many instances of serious consequences, the issue should be seen as less serious. Therefore, it is important for health campaigners to work to reduce ease of retrieval effects by reminding people about the severity of health issues. Experiment three addressed the prediction that when public service announcements (PSAs) render more information accessible, subjective experiences will not be used as judgment inputs and the retrieval ease effect will be weaker.

Experiment four focused on the idea that, for issues of higher general concern, people will tend to engage in content-based processing. This mode of processing should also be more prevalent among individuals who are particularly concerned about the specific target health issue. When individuals who are thus motivated to engage in content-based processing attempt to list many disease consequences, they should perceive the disease as more severe and their vulnerability to it as higher, and find the health message to be more effective.

In sum, the present study had four objectives: first, to test for ease of retrieval effects on issue severity when the retrieval task involves listing disease consequences; second, to examine ease of retrieval effects on self-efficacy when the retrieval task involves listing prevention or treatment options; third, to test whether making more relevant information accessible attenuates the effects of retrieval ease; and finally, to examine the effects of retrieval ease when PSAs encourage content-based processing.

Findings supported the predictions. In the first experiment, ease of retrieval was manipulated by asking participants to list either a high or low number of consequences of an ailment. As expected, retrieval difficulty resulted in lower perceived disease severity. In the second experiment, ease of retrieval was manipulated by varying the number of disease prevention or treatment measures participants attempted to list. As predicted, retrieval difficulty resulted in lower self-efficacy regarding prevention and treatment. In two additional experiments, participants viewed a public service announcement (PSA) highlighting the consequences of contracting a particular disease. Ease of retrieval effects were observed only when the manipulation involved irrelevant information (number of prevention/treatment options) and not relevant information (number of consequences). Furthermore, when the health issues were of greater concern, content-based rather than experience-based judgment appeared to be stimulated, and attempting to list more disease consequences resulted in higher ratings of disease severity.

Toward a More Comprehensive Theory of Attitude Change: The Effects of Inter-Attitudinal Concept Structure on Attitude Dynamics

Leslie D. Dinauer, University of Maryland University College, USA

EXTENDED ABSTRACT

Theories of inter-attitude relationships and attitude change have failed to identify the architecture of inter-attitudinal structures and then clarify its relationship to attitude and belief change. Such a failure is critical to consumer researchers for whom understanding attitudes is a primary pursuit. This theoretical study examined two competing models of inter-attitudinal structure that explicitly address the influence of inter-attitudinal structure on attitude change dynamics: a hierarchical model (Hunter, Levine, Sayers, 1976, 1984; Poole and Hunter, 1979) and the Galileo spatial-linkage model (Woelfel and Saltiel, 1988; see also Kaplowitz & Fink, 1988; Woelfel & Fink, 1980). The results should inform consumer attitude research and lead to more accurate measurement of consumer attitudes, as well as to the production of more effective persuasive messages.

Each of the models in the study posits an inter-attitudinal structure that makes a number of predictions regarding how attitude change occurs between and among associated concepts. In a hierarchical model, a change in attitude toward a concept in a hierarchy is hypothesized to be constrained by the structural relationships of the hierarchy (i.e., one's attitude towards animals in general is not affected by a change in one's attitude towards dogs). In the Galileo spatial-linkage model such constraints are loosened and it is hypothesized that attitude change toward any concept in a group of linked concepts will result in absolute change across all linked concepts.

The between-subjects experiment in this study presented participants with pictures of either an *explicit* hierarchy (i.e., one that consists of concepts that are super- and subordinate to each other as a result of their denotative meanings) or an *implicit* hierarchy (i.e., one that consists of concepts that are not obviously super- and subordinate to each other as a result of their denotative meanings; however, when people are asked to organize a set of concepts that form such a hierarchy, the super- and subordinate relationships emerge) and then measured participants' attitudes after they processed a persuasive message. To accomplish this, three hundred ninety-one students enrolled at a large eastern university were randomly assigned to one of 26 questionnaire conditions: 2 (Hierarchy: explicit vs. implicit) x 2 (Priming: primed vs. unprimed) x 3 (Persuasive Message Target: Superordinate concept vs. Subordinate Concept 1 vs. Subordinate Concept 2) x 2 (Question Order: ascending vs. descending) plus two control groups. They were exposed to the randomly assigned hierarchy exposure and priming conditions and consequenltly administered the questionnaire. Additionally, prior to the study, ten pilot studies (N=271) had been conducted that determined the content of the explicit and implicit hierarchies and the measurement instrument used in the study.

Adjusted geometric mean distances among nine experimental concepts as measured in the questionnaire were input into the Galileo computer program V56 (Woelfel, 1993). This generated 14 multidimensional spaces, one for each of 2 x 3 x 2 experimental conditions plus two controls. The program rotated each space to the same orientation and transformed it to a least-squares best fit so that the spaces could be similarly aligned and visually compared. The first two dimensions in each space accounted for at least 79% of the variance of the real space involved as per Miller's (1988) procedures to check the reliability of the paired-comparison judgments.

Thus, the true spaces were very close to two-dimensional and the generated spaces were relatively accurate representations of the arrangements of their respective concepts. This "true" two dimensionality increased the validity of conclusions drawn from examinations of the graphs, however, supplemental analyses of variance and structural equation modeling offered additional support.

Analyses of the multidimensional cognitive spaces show that linguistic organizational structures influence attitude change. However, it is the Galileo spatial-linkage model that provides a theoretical structure which makes the more correct set of predictions about how concepts affect one another. The results also support the spatial-linkage model's suggestion that such inter-attitudinal change is constrained less by a concept's relative position in the structure and more by the strength of the concept's association with other concepts in that structure. Furthermore, within these inter-attitudinal structures, concepts directly targeted by a persuasive message often exhibit less attitude change than related concepts.

The results hold several important implications for consumer researchers, and should lead to more accurate measurement of consumer attitudes, as well as to the production of more effective persuasive messages across consumer influence areas. First, the results support the Galileo model's operationalization of a process of inter-attitudinal influence that has been previously described but for which no consistent cognitive mechanism has been suggested. For example, Converse's (1964) renown and popular discussion of belief systems in mass publics proposes that people's attitudes and beliefs are enmeshed in a greater network of peculiar, often irrelevant, ideas that exert influence over the network. The Galileo spatial-linkage model provides a model of cognitive processing that explains why such influence occurs. Moreover, because the model suggests that this influence is not uncommon, support for the Galileo model as demonstrated in this study also suggests that consumer attitude researchers should pay more attention to the seemingly irrelevant attitudes that might provide access to a difficult to reach attitude of interest.

Because the results suggest that it is possible to affect attitudes indirectly, there are tremendous implications for those in the applied consumer research field who design persuasive messages about sensitive topics (e.g., obesity, debt). For example, the results of the study suggest that talking to individuals about specific purchases, as opposed to talking about shopping in general, may be more effective as a debt counseling strategy. Moreover, simply the act of making accessible an individual's specific shopping-related cognitive space, and revealing the implicit associations to him or her, may increase the effectiveness of debt counseling by creating a new awareness of the previously unknown links and influences between attitudes and behaviors.

Portions of the conference paper presented have previously appeared in Dinauer L.D., & Fink E. L. (2005). Inter-attitude structure and attitude dynamics: A comparison of the hierarchical and Galileo spatial-linkage models. *Human Communication Research, 31*, 1-32.

REFERENCES

Converse, P. E. (1964). The nature of belief systems in mass publics. In D. E. Apter (Ed.), *Ideology and Discontent* (pp. 206-261). New York: The Free Press.

Hunter, J. E., Levine, R. L., & Sayers, S. E. (1976). Attitude change in hierarchical belief systems and its relationship to persuasibility, dogmatism, and rigidity. *Human Communication Research, 3,* 1-29.

Hunter, J. E., Levine, R. L., & Sayers, S. E. (1984). Attitude change in concept hierarchies. In J. E. Hunter, J. E. Danes, & S. H. Cohen (Eds.), *Mathematical models of attitude change: Vol. 1. Change in single attitudes and cognitive structure* (pp. 231-259). Orlando, FL: Academic.

Kaplowitz, S. A., & Fink, E. L. (1988). A spatial-linkage model of cognitive dynamics. In G. A. Barnett & J. Woelfel (Eds.), *Readings in the Galileo system: Theory, methods and applications (pp. 117-146). Dubuque, IA: Kendall/Hunt.*

Miller, M. M. (1988). Using generalizability theory to assess the dependability of direct magnitude separation estimates (Galileo data). In G. A. Barnett & J. Woelfel (Eds.), *Readings in the Galileo system: Theory, methods and applications* (pp. 203-217). Dubuque, IA: Kendall/Hunt.

Poole, M. S., & Hunter, J. E. (1979). Change in hierarchically organized attitudes. In D. Nimmo (Ed.), *Communication yearbook* 3 (pp. 157-176). New Brunswick, NJ: Transaction.

Woelfel, J. (1993). GALILEO (Version 5.6) [Computer software]. Amherst, NY: The Galileo Company.

Woelfel, J., & Fink, E. L. (1980). *The measurement of communication processes: Galileo theory and method.* New York: Academic Press.

Woelfel, J., & Saltiel, J. (1988). Cognitive processes as motions in a multidimensional space. In G. A. Barnett & J. Woelfel (Eds.), *Readings in the Galileo system: Theory, methods and applications* (pp. 35-53). Dubuque, IA: Kendall/Hunt.

The Illusion of Avoiding Bias: How Correcting for Perceived Bias Can Make a Recommendation More Effective

Francine Espinoza, University of Maryland, USA
Rebecca Hamilton, University of Maryland, USA

EXTENDED ABSTRACT

Based on previous research, we expect that consumers would be more influenced by a recommendation coming from a trusted source (e.g., a friend) than by a recommendation coming from a distrusted source (e.g., a salesperson; Wilson and Sherrell 1993). However, we demonstrate that this is not always the case. Research on bias correction shows that individuals correct for perceived bias in their judgments by making adjustments in the direction opposite to which they believe the context is influencing their judgments (Wegener and Petty 1995). Because consumers may naturally resist a recommendation from a distrusted source, attempting to remove bias from their judgments may, ironically, increase rather than decrease the effectiveness of a recommendation from a distrusted source. As a result, a recommendation from a distrusted source can become not only more effective, but just as effective as a recommendation from a trusted source.

We examine three potential explanations for the moderating effect of correction on source trustworthiness effects: Changes in perceptions of ulterior motives of the recommender; changes in overall attitudes towards the recommended product; and changes in judgment (attitude) certainty. Building on previous research (Tormala and Petty 2002, 2004, Tormala, Clarkson, and Petty 2006) we propose that judgment certainty is mediating the effect.

We focus on the role of certainty because research suggests that attitude certainty can change as a result of consumers' observing their reactions to a persuasive attempt (Tormala and Petty 2002, 2004). Assuming that correction instructions motivate individuals to observe their reactions and to resist the influence of a recommendation (Briñol et al. 2004), we predict that asking consumers to correct their judgments will change the certainty with which participants hold their judgments. Therefore, we propose that certainty, rather than perceived ulterior motives of the recommender or overall attitudes toward the products, will mediate the effect of source trustworthiness and correction on willingness to buy.

Study 1 (N=71) employed a 2 source trustworthiness (friend vs. salesperson) x 2 correction (no-correction vs. correction) between-subjects design and a jacket purchase scenario adapted from Campbell and Kirmani (2000). A 2x2 ANOVA reveals an interaction ($F(1, 67)$=4.53, p<.05) suggesting that correction eliminated the effect of source trustworthiness. Participants were more willing to buy a product when the trusted source (friend) recommended it, than when the distrusted source (salesperson) recommended it ($F(1, 30)$=8.61, p<.01). However, when participants were instructed to correct their judgments (based on instructions adapted from Wegener and Petty 1995), the effect of trustworthiness was no longer significant ($F(1, 37)$=.01, p>.90). Notably, no significant effects emerged for the overall attitude measure (all p>.12), and although the salesperson was perceived to have more ulterior motives than the friend ($F(1, 67)$=48.86, p<.001), the effect of correction was not significant (p>.33).

Study 2 (N=267) employed a 3 source trustworthiness (federal agency vs. control) x 2 correction (no-correction vs. correction) design. Participants read a pamphlet describing the benefits of phosphate detergents and learned that the pamphlet was either produced by a federal agency or by the manufacturer (Briñol, Petty, and Tormala 2004). The correction manipulation was adapted from study 1.

As predicted, an interaction between source and correction in a 3x2 ANOVA ($F(1, 259)$=4.13, p<.02) indicates that, in the no correction condition, participants were more willing to buy the product when the trusted source recommended it than when the distrusted source recommended it (M_{agency}=5.15, $M_{manufacturer}$=4.35, $M_{control}$=5.02), $F(1, 130)$=5.43, p<.26). Correction eliminated this difference (M_{agency}=4.58, $M_{manufacturer}$=4.89, $M_{control}$=5.17), ($F(1, 129)$=1.36, p>.26). A 3x2 ANOVA with certainty as dependent variable reveals a similar interaction ($F(1, 259)$=5.43, p<.01).

We conducted regressions to test mediation by certainty. In the first regression, the interaction between source and correction (t=2.83, p<.005) affected the dependent variable willingness to buy. In the second regression, the interaction between source and correction (t=2.47, p<.02) affected the mediator variable attitude certainty. In the third regression, attitude certainty (t=3.27, p<.001) affected willingness to buy, and the interaction between source and correction was no longer significant (t=1.79, p=.08, Sobel z=2.41, p<.01). These results support the mediating role of certainty.

Study 3 (N=163) provides further support for the process mechanism by manipulating certainty subliminally and holding the source of the recommendation constant. Using a 2 certainty (uncertainty vs. certainty) x 2 correction (no-correction vs. correction) design, we first subliminally exposed participants to certainty and uncertainty-related words. Then, participants indicated their willingness to rent an apartment recommended by a realtor. If certainty affects behavioral intentions, we should detect a difference in willingness to rent the recommended apartment in the no correction condition. If, as proposed, correction changes certainty, after correction the change in certainty should be reflected in the behavioral intentions measure.

As predicted, a significant interaction between certainty and correction on behavioral intentions in a 2x2 ANOVA ($F(1, 159)$=5.41, p<.02) suggests that, in the no correction condition, participants primed with certainty had more favorable behavioral intentions towards the recommended apartment than participants primed with uncertainty ($M_{certainty}$=5.02, $M_{uncertainty}$=4.16), ($F(1, 86)$=5.26, p<.02). When participants were instructed to correct, this difference was eliminated ($M_{certainty}$=4.18, $M_{uncertainty}$=4.54), ($F(1, 73)$=.99, p>.3).

Across three studies, we show the basic effect and support mediation by judgment certainty. The results contribute to the bias correction literature by suggesting a new process mechanism through which correction operates to influence judgments, and to persuasion research by showing one condition in which behavioral intentions can change directly as a function of certainty, while attitude favorability remains unchanged.

REFERENCES

Briñol, Pablo, Derek D. Rucker, Zachary Tormala, and Richard E. Petty (2004), "Individual Differences in Resistance to Persuasion: The role of Beliefs and Meta-Beliefs," in *Resistance and Persuasion*, ed. Eric S. Knowles and Jay A. Linn., Mahwah, NJ: Lawrence Erlbaum, 83-104.

Briñol, Pablo, Richard E. Petty, and Zakary L. Tormala (2004), "Self-Validation of Cognitive Responses to Advertisements," *Journal of Consumer Research*, 30 (4), 559-573.

Campbell, Margaret C. and Amna Kirmani (2000), "Consumers' Use of Persuasion Knowledge: The Effects of Accessibility and Cognitive Capacity on Perceptions of an Influence Agent," *Journal of Consumer Research*, 27 (June), 69-83.

Tormala, Zakary L. and Richard E. Petty (2002), "What Doesn't Kill me Makes me Stronger: The Effects of Resisting Persuasion on Attitude Certainty," *Journal of Personality and Social Psychology*, 83 (6), 1298-313.

_____ (2004), "Source Credibility and Attitude Certainty: A Metacognitive Analysis of Resistance to Persuasion," *Journal of Consumer Psychology*, 14 (4), 427-42.

Tormala, Zakary L., Joshua J. Clarkson, and Richard E. Petty (2006), "Resisting Persuasion by the Skin of One's Teeth: The Hidden Success of Resisted Persuasive Messages," *Journal of Personality and Social Psychology*, 91 (3), 423-35.

Wegener, Duane T. and Richard E. Petty (1995), "Flexible Correction Processes in Social Judgment: The Role of Naïve Theories in Corrections for Perceived Bias," *Journal of Personality and Social Psychology*, 68 (1), 36-51.

Wilson, Elizabeth J. and Daniel L. Sherrell (1993), "Source Effects in Communication and Persuasion Research: A Meta-Analysis of Effect Size," *Journal of the Academy of Marketing Science*, 21 (2), 101-13.

Feeling Fatigued Leads to Feeling Certain: Regulatory Resource Depletion and Attitude Certainty

Echo Wen Wan, University of Hong Kong, China
Derek D. Rucker, Northwestern University, USA
Zakary L. Tormala, Stanford University, USA
Joshua J. Clarkson, Indiana University, USA

EXTENDED ABSTRACT

This research examines the impact of regulatory resource depletion on attitude certainty. Regulatory resources have been conceptualized as a pool of resources that people use to override urges or exert controlled behavior (Baumeister et al. 1998). Attitude certainty is the subjective feeling of conviction one has about one's attitude, or the extent to which one believes one's attitude is correct (Gross, Holtz and Miller 1995). We focus on studying how regulatory resource depletion affects attitude certainty in the absence of differences in attitudes. We also uncover the mechanism using measured and manipulated approaches and demonstrate that differences in certainty have a meaningful effect on behavior.

Previous research has established attitude certainty as an independent construct from attitudes (Bassili 1996; Rucker and Petty 2004). Attitude certainty is particularly interesting for consumer research because *behavior* is influenced not solely by one's attitude but also the certainty placed in that attitude. In particular, attitudes held with high certainty serve as stronger guides for judgment and behavior.

Past research has shown that depletion significantly impacts consumer behavior such as impulse purchases (Vohs and Faber 2007). Recently Wheeler, Briñol, and Hermann (2007) found that depletion leads to poorer resistance against the counterattitudinal message when individuals were allowed to vary the effort exerted to counterargue. Our research focuses on the situation where depleted individuals are sufficiently motivated to exert equal effort on the subsequent task as non-depleted individuals and thus generate similar thought profiles (Muraven and Slessareva 2003). In such situations depleted and non-depleted individuals should have processed the same information to the same degree, which would produce similar attitudes. However, under such circumstances we asked whether depletion might affect attitude certainty.

Intuitively, one might expect that depleted (vs. non-depleted) individuals would perceive processing messages as more difficult. Based on prior findings that processing ease is associated with attitude certainty (Haddock et al. 1999), depletion might undermine attitude certainty. However, we propose that depletion might actually lead to greater attitude certainty. Research has shown that depleted (vs. non-depleted) individuals perceive themselves as exerting greater effort overestimating the amount of time they spend (Vohs and Schmeichel 2003; Wan and Sternthal 2008) on the same task. Previous studies suggest that people might use the amount of time or effort spent as indicators of the thoroughness of information processing (Vonk and van Knippenberg 1995). And the perception of thoroughness of thinking is associated with attitude certainty. For example, Berger and Mitchell (1989) suggest that repeated ad exposures enhanced individuals' product-related processing and thus their attitude certainty. Furthermore, recent research suggests that *perceived elaboration* (one's subjective assessment of how carefully one has processed information) affects attitude certainty even when there are no differences in actual elaboration (Barden and Petty forthcoming).

Drawing on the work linking depletion to perceived elaboration and the work linking perceived elaboration to attitude certainty, we predict that in situations where depleted individuals are motivated and able to process messages extensively, depletion will increase attitude certainty, and this effect is accounted by an enhanced perceived elaboration among depleted individuals.

Three experiments tested and supported these propositions. In all experiments, participants first completed a depletion manipulation, followed by reading an ad message about a consumer product. We strived to hold the actual amount and type of thinking constant across conditions in multiple ways: First, we induced high motivation to process by emphasizing the importance of the task. Second, we held actual ad exposure time constant. Finally, to test the success of our efforts we included measures that prior research has shown to be sensitive to differences in actual information processing.

In experiment 1, participants completed either a depletion manipulation, read an ad about one brand of answering machine, reported their attitude and attitude certainty, and reported their perceived elaboration and processing ease. The results show that depleted and non-depleted participants did not differ in their attitudes or processing ease. However, depleted participants were more certain of their attitudes and perceived their information processing as more thorough than non-depleted ones. Perceived elaboration mediated the effect of depletion on attitude certainty.

Experiment 2 used a different depletion manipulation in a different product category and with a different ad exposure time. In addition, we added two independent variables. One manipulated the naïve theories about the relationship between depletion and perceived elaboration. This tested whether varying the relationship between depletion and perceived elaboration affected certainty, and thus provided a moderation approach to testing the role of perceived elaboration. The other varied the argument strength in the message to test whether actual processing between depleted and non-depleted was constant. As another means of testing individuals' actual processing, we included a thought listing measure. The results showed that attitudes only differed between strong and weak arguments conditions, but depletion had no effect. The naïve theory results showed that manipulating the relationship between depletion and perceived elaboration affected attitude certainty, supporting the perceived elaboration mechanism. Moreover, both depleted and non-depleted participants had more favorable thoughts in the strong than weak argument conditions.

Experiment 3 tested the behavioral consequence of our effects following the same procedure as used in the strong argument condition in experiment 2 except that no naïve theory was manipulated. At the end participants made a real purchase decision. The results showed that 1) the attitude-purchase correlation was significantly stronger among depleted (vs. non-depleted) participants; 2) among participants holding positive attitudes, depleted (vs. non-depleted) individuals chose to purchase the snack more frequently; and 3) these effects were mediated by difference in attitude certainty. Depletion led participants to be more certain, and thus they became more likely to act based on attitudes.

Our research contributes to literature on regulatory depletion and persuasion by revealing a hidden effect of depletion on attitude certainty. We also enrich the understanding of attitude certainty by showing that a subjective perception of elaboration (vs. objective differences) impacts attitude certainty. Finally, this research finds evidence that consumer behavior (e.g., actual purchase) can be affected by depletion due to the variation in attitude certainty.

REFERENCES

Barden, Jamie. and Richard E. Petty (2008), "The Mere Perception of Elaboration Creates Attitude Certainty: Exploring the Thoughtfulness Heuristic," *Journal of Personality and Social Psychology*, 95 (3), 489-509.

Bassili, John. N. (1996), "Meta-judgmental versus operative indexes of psychological attributes: The case of measures of attitude strength," *Journal of Personality and Social Psychology*, 71(4), 637-53.

Baumeister, Roy F., Ellen Bratslavsky, Mark Muraven, and Dianne M. Tice (1998), "Ego Depletion: Is the Active Self a Limited Resource?" *Journal of Personality and Social Psychology,* 74(5), 1252-265.

Berger, Ida E., and Andrew A. Mitchell (1989), "The Effect of Advertising on Attitude Accessibility, Attitude Confidence, and the Attitude-Behavior Relationship," *Journal of Consumer Research*, 16(3), 269–79.

Gross, Sharon R., Rolf Holtz, and Norman Miller (1995), "Attitude Certainty," In *Attitude Strength: Antecedents and Consequences*, ed. Richard E. Petty and Jon A. Krosnick, Mahwah, NJ: Erlbaum.

Haddock, Geoffrey, Alexander J. Rothman, Rolf Reber, and Norbert Schwarz (1999), "Forming judgments of attitude certainty, intensity, and importance: The role of subjective experience," *Personality and Social Psychology Bulletin,* 25(7), 771–82.

Muraven, Mark and Elisaveta Slessareva (2003), "Mechanisms of Self-Control Failure: Motivation and Limited Resources," *Personality and Social Psychology Bulletin*, 29(July), 894-906.

Rucker, Derek. D, and Richard E. Petty (2004), "When Resistance Is Futile: Consequences of Failed Counterarguing for Attitude Certainty," *Journal of Personality and Social Psychology,* 86(2), 219-35.

Vohs, Kathleen D. and Ronald J. Faber (2007), "Spent Resources: Self-Regulatory Resource Availability Affects Impulse Buying," *Journal of Consumer Research*, 33(March), 537-47.

Vohs, Kathleen D. and Brandon Schmeichel (2003), "Self-Regulation and the Extended Now: Controlling the Self Alters the Subjective Experience of Time," *Journal of Personality and Social Psychology*, 85(August), 217-30.

Vonk, Roos and Ad, van Knippenberg (1995), "Processing attitude statements from in-group and out-group members: Effects of within-group and within-person inconsistencies on reading times," *Journal of Personality and Social Psychology,* 68(2), 215-27.

Wan, Echo W. and Brian Sternthal (2008), "Regulating the Effects of Depletion through Monitoring," *Personality and Social Psychology Bulletin*, 34(1), 32-46.

Wheeler, S. Christian., Pablo Briñol, and Anthony Hermann (2007), "Resistance to persuasion as self-regulation: Ego-depletion and its consequences for attitude change processes," *Journal of Experimental Social Psychology, 43(1),* 150-56.

This Brand is Me: A Social Identity Based Measure of Brand Identification

Amy E. Tildesley, University of Queensland, Australia
Leonard V. Coote, University of Queensland, Australia

EXTENDED ABSTRACT

Of particular importance to practitioners and academics in the marketing field is the ability to recognize, analyze and utilize information regarding the voluntary relationships that consumers engage in with the brands they purchase. Fournier (1998) and Aaker (1999) make an explicit plea to researchers regarding the need for research in marketing to examine the deep, enduring brand relationships that lead to beneficial outcomes for firms. Accordingly, recent consumer behavior research has investigated the psychological connections individuals build with brands, brand communities and the brand relationships that surpass loyalty (Carroll and Ahuvia 2006; Fennis and Pruyn 2007; Fournier 1998; McAlexander, Shouten, and Koenig 2002). One commonly accepted perspective stemming from the consumer behavior literature is that products and brands are able to fulfill the self-definitional needs of consumers (Belk 1988; Dolich 1969). This notion has proliferated a variety of academic fields of study including possessions as extensions of self (Belk, Bahn, and Mayer 1982; Kliene, Kleine, and Allen 1995), brand personality (Aaker 1997; Kassarjian 1971), relationship marketing (Fournier 1998), the congruence or fit literature (Birdwell 1968; Dolich 1969; Gardner and Levy 1955) and more recently, consumer-company and brand identification (Bagozzi and Dholakia 2006; Bhattacharya, Glynn, and Rao 1995; Bhattacharya and Sen 2003). Thus, the self-concept related benefit of brands is well accepted in the literature; however, the numerous and varied manifestations of the construct have perpetuated a fragmented and inarticulate area of study.

This paper purports that strong consumer-brand relationships may be attributed to theories of social psychology, namely, social identity and self-categorization theory. The basic premise of these theories is that individuals group within society to achieve meaningful self-definition through intergroup homogenization and intragroup difference (Tajfel 1978, 1982). Social psychologists have historically applied these theories to an organizational context (Brown et al. 1986; Hogg and Abrams 1988) and concurrently, organizational behaviorists adopted theories of social psychology to explain desirable employee behavior such as employee citizenship and conscientiousness (Ashforth and Mael 1989; Bergami and Bagozzi 2000; Cheney 1983). Thus, organizational identification has received much academic attention in recent years (Dutton, Dukerich, and Harquail 1994; Pratt 1998; Riketta 2005; Van Dick 2001). Following this and entering the realm of marketing, Bhattacharya and Sen (2003) introduced the concept of consumer-company identification and posit that individuals, regardless of formal membership ties, are able to identify with companies.

Unfortunately, identification theory in marketing remains in its infancy. This may be partly attributed to the theoretical foundation of consumer-company identification being somewhat detached from the marketing literature and companies being the incorrect focus in marketing. Brand identification is the focus of few studies, and has never been conceptualized as a construct truly separate from that of organizational identification. Equally as problematic, the operationalization of the construct is inconsistent, underdeveloped, and always adapted from the organizational literature. The aim of the present research was threefold: (1) to conceptually develop brand identification by firmly grounding the construct in the social psychology literature, and hence to establish it as distinct from organizational and consumer-company identification, (2) to establish a valid and reliable measure of brand identification, and one appropriate for a branding context and, (3) to compare the new measure to existing measures of identification used in the marketing literature.

Drawing on domain sampling theory, three components of brand identification were developed that were thought to capture the entire domain of the construct. Specifically, brand identification was hypothesized to consist of a self-brand connection component, to reflect the process of social classification and affiliation, a brand salience component, to capture of the importance of the brand to one's self-identity and finally, a brand signaling component, to reflect the utility of the brand in signaling one's self-identity to others. Studies using data from twelve samples and over 2,000 subjects were conducted to refine and validate the final 11-item measure of brand identification.

In the initial scale purification studies, the scale was refined using factor analyses on multiple samples. Subsequently, antecedents and outcomes of brand identification were proposed and the scale was shown to have nomological validity. The developed scale was found to have the same antecedents as established identification scales; however, the outcomes differed substantially. In particular, one component of the developed scale, self-brand connection, was shown to consistently outperform the other two components of the developed scale as well as the established scales. Specifically, the self-brand connection component explained more variance in a set of outcome variables including loyalty, willingness to pay a price premium, and brand advocacy and defense. In a test of known-group validity, it was shown that the new scale was able to distinguish between those who should score highly on the scale and the general population. The brand identification scale was then subject to two quasi-experimental studies to test its predictive ability. The first study demonstrated that consumers with high levels of brand identification were more resilient to negative information about the brand. In the second study, a choice task demonstrated that brand identification was positively related to brand preference.

Overall, the evidence obtained from the studies in this paper for the validity and reliability of the brand identification scale is encouraging. Marketers intuitively understand the importance of brands and the possibility of consumer identification with brands and as such, the identification concept is quickly becoming a recurrent theme within much of the consumer behavior and marketing literatures. Despite this, more work needs to be done in testing our conceptions of brand identification and the role it plays in shaping consumer behaviors. The brand identification measure reported in this paper is offered to the field as an impetus to further empirical work and theory testing, with the ultimate aim of truly understanding brand identification and its importance.

REFERENCES

Aaker, Jennifer L. (1997), "Dimensions of Brand Personality," *Journal of Marketing Research*, 14, 347-56.

_____ (1999), "The Malleable Self: The Roles of Self-Expression in Persuasion," *Journal of Marketing Research*, 36, 45-57.

Ashforth, Blake E. and Fred A. Mael. (1989). "Social Identity Theory and the Organization," *Academy of Management Review*, 14, 20-39.

Bagozzi, Richard. P. and Utpal M. Dholakia. (2006), "Antecedents and Purchase Consequences of Customer Participation in Small Group Brand Communities," *International Journal of Research in Marketing*, 23, 45-61.

Belk, Russell W. (1988), "Possessions and the Extended Self," *Journal of Consumer Research*, 15, 139-68.

Belk, Russell W., Kenneth D. Bahn, and Robert N. Mayer. (1982), "Developmental Recognition of Consumption Symbolism," *Journal of Consumer Research*, 9, 4-17.

Bergami, Massimo and Richard P. Bagozzi. (2000), "Self-Categorization, Affective Commitment and Group Self-Esteem as Distinct Aspects of Social Identity in the Organization," *British Journal of Social Psychology*, 39, 555-77.

Bhattacharya, C. B., MaryAnn Glynn, and Hayagreeva Rao. (1995), "Understanding the Bond of Identification: An Investigation of its Correlates Among Art Museum Members," *Journal of Marketing*, 59(4), 46-57.

Bhattacharya, C. B. and Sankar Sen. (2003), "Consumer-Company Identification: A Framework for Understanding Consumers' Relationships with Companies," *Journal of Marketing*, 67(2), 76-88.

Birdwell, Al E. (1968), "A Study of the Influence of Image Congruence on Consumer Choices," *Journal of Business*, 41, 76-88.

Brown, Rupert, Susan Condor, Audrey Mathews, Gillian Wade, and Jennifer A. Williams. (1986), "Explaining Intergroup Differentiation in an Industrial Organization," *Journal of Occupational Psychology*, 59(4), 237-68.

Carroll, Barbara A. and Aaron C. Ahuvia. (2006), "Some Antecedents and Outcomes of Brand Love." *Marketing Letters*, 17, 79-89.

Cheney, George. (1983), "On the Various and Changing Meanings of Organizational Membership: A Field Study of Organizational Identification." *Communication Monographs*, 50, 342-62.

Dolich, Ira J. (1969), "Congruence Relationships Between Self Images and Product Brands," *Journal of Marketing Research*, 6, 80-4.

Dutton, Jane E., Janet M. Dukerich, and Celia V. Harquail. (1994), "Organisational Images and Member Identification," *Administrative Science Quarterly*, 39, 239-63.

Fennis, Bob M. and Ad Th. H. Pruyn. (2007), "You Are What You Wear: Brand Personality Influences on Consumer Impression Formation," *Journal of Business Research*, 18, 39-50.

Fournier, Susan. (1998), "Consumers and Their Brands: Developing Relationship Theory in Consumer Research," *Journal of Consumer Research*, 24(4), 343-74.

Gardner, Burleigh B. and Sidney J. Levy (1955), "The Product and the Brand," *Harvard Business Review*, 33, 33-9.

Hogg, Michael A. and Dominic Abrams. (1988), *Social Identifications: A Social Psychology of Intergroup Relations and Group Processes*. London: Routledge.

Kassarjian, Harold H. (1971), "Personality and Consumer Behavior: A Review," *Journal of Marketing Research*, 8, 409-18.

Kleine, Susan S., Robert E. Kleine, and Chris T Allen. (1995), "How is a Possession 'Me' or 'Not Me'? Characterizing Types and an Antecedent of Material Possession Attachment," *Journal of Consumer Research*, 22(3), 327-43.

McAlexander, James H., John W. Schouten, and Harold F. Koenig. (2002), "Building Brand Community." *Journal of Marketing*, 66(1), 38-54.

Pratt, Michael G. (1998), "To Be or Not to Be? Central Questions in Organizational Identification," In D. A. Whetten, & P. C. Godfrey (Ed.), *Identity in organizations: Building theory through conversations*, 171-207, London: Sage.

Riketta, Michael. (2005), "Organizational Identification: A Meta-Analysis," *Journal of Vocational Behavior* 66, 358-84.

Tajfel, Henri. (1978), *Differentiation Between Social Groups: Studies in the Social Psychology of Intergroup Relations*. London: Academic Press.

_____ (1982), "Social Psychology of Intergroup Relations," *Annual Review of Psychology*, 33:1-39.

Van Dick, Rolf. (2001), "Identification in Organizational Contexts: Linking Theory and Research from Social and Organization Psychology," International *Journal of Management Reviews*, 3(4), 265-83.

Is Consumer Culture Theory Research or Realpolitik? A Sociology of Knowledge Analysis of a Scientific Culture

Matthias Bode, University of Southern Denmark, Denmark
Per Østergaard, University of Southern Denmark, Denmark

EXTENDED ABSTRACT

When Consumer Culture Theory (CCT) was introduced by Arnould and Thompson (2005) it was part of a branding strategy to create legitimacy for interpretive research. The general direction of these branding procedures is a necessary step towards a more developed discussion of academic research as they explicitly take into account the "realpolitik complexities" of science (Arnould and Thompson 2007, 6). Unfortunately, the discussion rests upon unreflected assumptions about the relationships between theory/knowledge and the status and social reproduction of academic cultures. The goal of this paper is twofold. First, the CCT discussion is embedded in a wider theoretical and empirical frame of academic cultures. As the higher education landscape is confronted with severe challenges of globalization, underfinanced mass universities and a managerial spirit with a drive for efficiency and productivity (Henkel 1997; Becher and Trowler 2001), a thorough research stream is exactly focussing on the link between science and the real world context. Second, it is intended to make the inherent logic of thought procedures in the CCT construction explicit by a deconstructive reading (Atkins 1983; Harland 1987). It is revealed how CCT represents a different perception of knowledge compared to the way knowledge was perceived among research taking part in The Interpretive Turn (Sherry 1991). The latter was focused on groundbreaking research and less interested in the realpolitik consequences, which is opposed to the CCT focus on realpolitik in its strive for legitimacy. It is shown how there have been an ongoing discussion in the sociology of scientific knowledge (e.g., Becher and Trowler 2001; Henkel 2000; Pickering 1992) about the consequences in scientific cultures when they are confronted with the requirements of the real world. This is a debate that is not reflected in CCT and there is a lot to be learned from that stream of research.

The basic insights are based on a multi layered conception of dynamic scientific cultures that emerge form the informal, scientific community as a network, incorporating direct and indirect interaction with other colleagues outside of the local academic institution. If we want to deliberately change and manage these cultures, it is not enough to focus on individual academics in their assumed loyal commitment to the community. Rather, the individual academic is an actor, embedded in a system of internal and external variables. Primarily, there are micro layers of individuals, meso layers of institutions and discipline, and macro layers of national and international relationships. Instead of presupposing a homogeneity of interest and orientations, the heterogeneity of the specific constellations of institutional, disciplinary and national cultural layers and the individual researcher's negotiation of value tensions has to be taken into account.

The deconstructive analysis of CCT is done on the basis of Greimas' (e.g., 1987; 1990) semiotic square. It is shown how CCT reveals the classical dichotomy between knowledge and power. It is a dialectical contradiction, which are the constituting elements for the university as an institution. The Interpretive Turn can be seen as a scientific culture where there was no interest in being pragmatic and thereby a strive for recognition from the mainstream. Instead there was a tendency to stay outside the mainstream in an isolated position with no power. Arnould and Thompson (2005; 2007) want to change that by introducing CCT. Where the former stream of research had an idealistic attitude towards doing research, CCT is instead focused on the pragmatic aspects in order to get legitimacy from the mainstream and thereby being a part of the power game in the discipline. To do this the CCT researchers must leave their idealistic and isolated position and instead participate actively in realpolitik. There are logically some inherent dangers in these different movements. The Interpretive Turn has been characterized by groundbreaking research and it can be difficult to continue this kind of research if the researchers become a part of the mainstream and the power position, which is characterized by a "suppose to know" attitude. There is no easy solution to the dilemma of whether to choose the power position or to stay isolated in the knowledge position. One answer to the dilemma is a new way of dealing with this kind of research. Instead of being in one of the camps we think there is a third position in between the two camps, which we define as reflexive research. It is the pragmatic position striving for an idealistic mentality among the researchers. It is a position with a focus on pragmatic aspects of research, but at the same time leaving room for the anarchistic nature of groundbreaking research. Reflexive research is characterized by a meta-level where the scientific culture openly can reflect upon the how-to dealing with the conflicting reality of today's research landscape.

REFERENCES

Altbach, Philip G. (2001), "Academic Freedom: International Realities and Challenges," *Higher Education*, 41 (1-2), 205-19.

Anderson, Paul F. (1983), "Marketing, Scientific Progress, and Scientific Method," *Journal of Marketing*, 47 (Fall), 18-31.

Anderson, Paul F. (1989), "On Relativism and Interpretivism-With a Prolegomenon to the „Why Question," in *Interpretive Consumer Research*, ed. Elizabeth Hirschman, Provo: ACR, 10-23.

Arnould, Eric J. and Craig J. Thompson (2005), "Consumer Culture Theory (CCT): Twenty Years of Research" *Journal of Consumer Research*, 31 (March), 868-882.

Arnould, Eric J. and Craig J. Thompson (2007), "Consumer Culture Theory (and We Really Mean Theoretics): Dilemmas and Opportunities Posed by an Academic Branding Strategy," *Research in Consumer Behavior*, 11, 3-22.

Arnould, Eric J. and Craig J. Thompson (2008), The story is verified by email correspondence with Arnould and Thompson, March 2008.

Atkins, Douglas G. (1983), *Reading Deconstruction/Deconstructive Reading*, Lexington: The University Press of Kentucky.

Austin, Ann E. (1990), "Faculty Cultures, Faculty Values," in *Assessing Academic Climates and Cultures*, ed. William G. Tierney, San Francisco, 61-74

Bagozzi, Richard P. (1976), "Science, Politics, and the Social Construction of Marketing', in *Marketing 1776–1976 and Beyond*, ed. Kenneth L. Bernhardt, Chicago, IL: AMA, 586–592.

Becher, Tony (1989), *Academic Tribes and Territories. Intellectual Enquiry and the Culture of Disciplines*, Milton Keynes: Open Univ. Press.

Becher, Tony and Paul R. Trowler (2001), *Academic Tribes and Territories. Intellectual Enquiry and the Culture of Disciplines*, 2nd ed., Buckingham: Open Univ. Press.

Belk, Russell W. (1976), "What Should ACR Want to Be When It Grows Up?" in *Advances in Consumer Research*, Vol. 13, ed. Richard J. Lutz, Provo, UT: ACR, 423–24

Brown, Stephen (1995), *Postmodern Marketing*, London: Routledge.

Brown, Stephen (2002), "The Spectre of Kotlerism: A Literary Appreciation," *European Management Journal*, 20 (2), 129-146.

Brown, Stephen and Hope Jensen Schau (2007), "Writing Consumer Research: The World According to Belk," *Journal of Consumer Behaviour*, 6 (6), 349-368.

Bush, Ronald and Shelby D. Hunt (1982), *Marketing Theory: Philosophy of Science Perspectives*, Chicago: AMA.

Deshpande, Rohit (1983): „Paradigms Lost": On Theory and Method in Research in Marketing, *Journal of Marketing*, 47 (Fall), 101-110.

Enders, Jürgen (1999), "Crisis? What Crisis? The Academic Professions in the ‚Knowledge' Society," *Higher Education*, 38 (1), 71-81.

Fine, Seymour (1981), *The Marketing of Ideas and Social Issues*, New York: Praeger.

Greimas, Algirda J. (1987), *On Meaning: Selected Writings*, Minneapolis: University of Minnesota Press.

Greimas, Algirda J. (1990), *The Social Sciences: A Semiotic View*, University of Minnesota Press: Minneapolis.

Hackett, Edward J. (1990), "Science as a Vocation in the 1990s: The Changing Organizational Culture of Academic Science," *The Journal of Higher Education*, 61 (3), 241-279.

Harland, Richard (1987), *Superstructuralism. The Philosophy of Structuralism and Post-structuralism*, London, New York: Methuen.

Henkel, Mary (2000), *Academic Identities and Policy Change in Higher Education*, London: Jessica Kingsley.

Hirschman, Elizabeth C. (1985), "Scientific Style and the Conduct of Consumer Research," *Journal of Consumer Research*, 12 (September), 225-239.

Hirschman, Elizabeth C. ed. (1989), *Interpretive Consumer Research*, Provo: ACR 1989.

Hirschman, Elizabeth C. and Morris B. Holbrook (1992), *Postmodern Consumer Research. The Study of Consumption as Text*, Newbury Park: Sage.

Hirschman, Elizabeth C. and Morris B. Holbrook eds. 1981, *Symbolic Consumer Behavior*, Ann Arbor: ACR

Holbrook, Morris B. (1985), "Why Business is Bad for Consumer Research: The Three Bears Revisited," in *Advances in Consumer Research*, Vol. 12, eds. Elizabeth C. Hirschman and Morris B. Holbrook, Provo, UT: ACR, 145-156.

Holbrook, Morris B. (1986), "Whither ACR? Some Pastoral Reflections on Bears, Baltimore, Baseball, and Resurrecting Consumer Research," in *Advances in Consumer Research*, Vol. 13, Richard J. Lutz, Provo, UT: ACR, 436-441

Holbrook, Morris B. and John O'Shaughnessy (1988), "On the Scientific Status of Consumer Research and the Need for an Interpretive Approach to Studying Consumption Behavior, " *Journal of Consumer Research*, 15 (December), 398-402.

Hudson, Laurel Anderson and Julie L. Ozanne (1988), "Alternative Ways of Seeking Knowledge in Consumer Research," *Journal of Consumer Research*, 14 (March), 508-521.

Hunt, Shelby D. (1983): *Marketing Theory. The Philosophy of Marketing Science*, Homewood: Richard D. Irwin.

Kogan, Maurice (1999): "The Culture of Academe," *Minerva*, 37 (1), 63-74.

Kogan, Maurice, Ingrid Moses and Elaine El-Khawas (1994), *Staffing Higher Education–Meeting New Challenges*, London: J. Kingsley.

Leong, Siew Meng, Jagdish Sheth and Chin Tiong Tan (1994), "An Empirical Study of the Scientific Styles of Marketing Academics," *European Journal of Marketing*, 28 (8/9), 12-26.

Malcolm, Tight (2004), "The Organisation of Academic Knowledge: A Comparative Perspective," *Higher Education*, 46 (4), 389-410.

Meja, Volker and Nico Stehr eds. (1999), *The Sociology of Knowledge*, Cheltenham, Northampton

Merton, Robert K. (1942/1973), "The Normative Structure of Science," in *The Sociology of Science*, ed. Norman W. Storer, Chicago, 267-278.

Peter, J. Paul (1992), "Realism or Relativism for Marketing Theory and Research: A. Comment on Hunt's 'Scientific Realism'," *Journal of Marketing,* 56 (April), 72-79.

Peter, J. Paul and Jerry C. Olson (1983), "Is Science Marketing?" *Journal of Marketing*, 47 (4),), 111-125.

Pickering, Andrew (1992), "From Science as Knowledge to Science as Practice," in *Science as Practice and Culture*, ed. Andrew Pickering, Chicago: UC Press, 1-26.

Scott, Linda M. (1994): "The Bridge from Text to Mind: Adapting Reader-Response Theory to Consumer Research," *Journal of Consumer Research*, 21 (December), 461–80.

Snow, Charles P. (1959), *The Two Cultures and the Scientific Revolution*, New York: Univ. Press.

Stiles, David R. (2004), "Narcissus Revisited: The Values of Management Academics and their Role in Business School Strategies in the UK and Canada," *British Journal of Management*, 15 (2), 157-175.

Tadajewski, Mark (2006), "The Ordering of Marketing Theory: The Influence of McCarthyism and the Cold War," *Marketing Theory,* 6 (2), 163-199.

Thompson, Craig J. (1997), "Buy Brown's Book! A Fully Impartial Commentary on Postmodern Marketing," *European Journal of Marketing*, 31 (3/4), 254-263.

Thompson, Craig J. (1997), "Interpreting Consumers: A Hermeneutical Framework for Deriving Marketing Insights from the Texts of Consumers' Consumption Stories," *Journal of Marketing Research*, 34 (November), 438-455.

Thompson, Craig J. (2004), "Marketplace Mythology and Discourses of Power," *Journal of Consumer Research*, 31 (June), 162-180.

Tuire, Palonen and Lehtinen Erno (2001), "Exploring Invisible Scientific Communities: Studying Networking Relations within an Educational Research Community. A Finnish case," *Higher Education*, 42 (4), 493-513.

Välimaa, Jussi (1998), "Culture and Identity in Higher Education Research," *Higher Education*, 36 (2), 119-138

Weber, Max (1919/1973), "Wissenschaft als Beruf," in *Gesammelte Aufsätze zur Wissenschaftslehre von Max Weber,* ed. Johannes Winckelmann, Tübingen: Mohr, 582-613.

Whitley, Richard (1984), *The Intellectual and Social Organization of the Sciences*, Oxford: Clarendon.

Ylijoki, Oili-Helena (2000), "Disciplinary Cultures and the Moral Order of Studying. A Case-Study of Four Finnish University Departments," *Higher Education*, 39 (3), 339-362.

Potential Contributions from Contemporary Social Science Literature: Expanding Cultural Understanding in Consumer Research

Kivilcim Dogerlioglu-Demir, Washington State University, USA
Jeffrey Radighieri, Washington State University, USA
Patriya Tansuhaj, Washington State University, USA

EXTENDED ABSTRACT

Prior research has examined the state of culture based consumer research (Sojka and Tansuhaj (1995), yet to our knowledge there are no published works that study the issue from a cross-disciplinary and non-marketing/consumer perspective. The purpose of this paper is to review and integrate recent cultural research in social science disciplines in order to gain insights into theories and related concepts that will help further our understanding of consumers in diverse cultures.

Two independent judges reviewed 323 articles from the top ten cited journals in five social science disciplines: anthropology, psychology, communication, philosophy and sociology. We aim at exploring and assessing the breadth, not depth, of knowledge in contemporary social science research. Therefore, articles published in the past two years (2006 and 2007) were included in order to identify contemporary research. Our analysis includes studies between cultures and nations as well as investigations within one culture or nation. The articles were coded on additional criteria, including cultural dimension, format (conceptual vs. empirical), and method (qualitative vs. quantitative).

Our findings reveal some prominent cultural themes in each discipline. While contemporary sociology papers tend to focus on transnational migration and role of religion, communication research centers on race and racial bias. Recent anthropology articles tend to emphasize macro issues of imperialism and capitalism. Philosophy papers focus on the meaning of globalization, diversity and sympathy. Psychology research examines acculturation, discrimination, and ingroup/outgroup issues. The main recent theme that seems to cut across all disciplines is globalization and its differential effects on various peoples across the globe.

Identified articles were content analyzed by the judges and classified into six dimensions: 1) language and communication, which includes studies that explore the cultural functions of communication; 2) religion and beliefs, covering studies that have theological and ethical perspective on cultural issues; 3) ethnicity, race and nationality, which comprises research that emphasizes race, ethnicity, acculturation, and nationality; 4) family and gender, examining marriage, sexual identity, and family issues; 5) government and law including works that focus on legal structures as they affect everyday life; and 6) regionalization and globalization, reflecting studies that examine the origins and consequences of integration of economies and political systems and their repercussions on individuals.

Relevant theories and concepts were identified and discussed for each dimension. In the language and communication dimension, we discuss two particular theories: cultural sensitivity/centered approaches and pictorial realism. Moral cosmology theory was chosen as a significant contribution in the religion and values dimension. The ethnicity, race, and nationality dimension provides the largest quantity of relevant theories, including dramaturgical theory, "I-know-you-but-you-don't-know-me," cultural frame switching, social unity, and material cultural evolution concepts. Applicable theories in the family and gender dimension include the demand/withdraw pattern of communication and transformative processes. In the government and law dimension, resistance and affect control theory seem to have a high potential for providing a significant contribution to consumer research. Finally, in the regionalization and globalization dimension, the theory of globalization of law and authenticity were identified and discussed as applicable and useful for introducing to the consumer research in marketing.

Our research suggests the presence of a bias toward the United States and its respective cultural groups. Future research should entail more work in South America, Africa, and Eastern Europe. In addition, more research on religion and beliefs could provide significant contributions to the field. While the family has been researched in the social sciences, it has not received much attention in consumer behavior. In addition, more work is needed in sexual identity issues. Finally, consumer research has also not addressed regionalization and globalization in any serious manner. We cannot ignore such a global phenomenon and how it affects consumers at the macro and micro levels (i.e., collective consumer trends such as hypermodernism in China, versus changes in individual consumer attitudes, values and behavior changes).

With this study, we hope to provide consumer researchers with new and exciting research directions that might help us better understand consumer behavior in diverse settings. Despite repeated calls, cross-cultural consumer research continues to use nationality as a proxy for culture. We wish to reemphasize the need to move away from treating culture and nationality as equivalent. Amid globalization, we can also learn from the same weakness shown in social science research, the need to reduce our bias toward focusing mostly on studying America or the American culture. Finally, scholars have stressed the need for consumer research to become more interdisciplinary (Deighton 2005; Mick 2006; Shimp 1994; Wells 1993), yet these calls have gone unheeded. The ultimate goal of this work is for the reported results and suggestions to serve as a starting point for researchers to begin to move the field toward a multidisciplinary emphasis.

REFERENCES

Deighton, John (2005), "From the Editor-Elect," *Journal of Consumer Research*, 32 (1), 1-5.

Mick, David Glen (2006), "Meaning and Mattering through Transformative Consumer Research," in *Advances in Consumer Research*, Vol. 33, ed. Cornelia Pechmann and Linda L. Price, San Antonio, TX: Association for Consumer Research, 1-4.

Shimp, Terence A. (1994), "Academic Appalachia and the Discipline of Consumer Research," in *Advances in Consumer Research*, Vol. 21, ed. Chris Allen and Deborah Roedder John, Provo, UT: Association for Consumer Research, 1-7.

Sojka, Jane Z. and Patriya S. Tansuhaj (1995), "Cross-Cultural Consumer Research: A Twenty-Year Review," *Advances in Consumer Research*, 22 (1), 461-74.

Wells, William (1993), "Discovery-Oriented Consumer Research," *Journal of Consumer Research*, 19 (March), 489-503.

The Impact of Family Micro-Environments on Children's Consumer Socialization

Ben Kerrane, Bradford University, UK
Margaret K. Hogg, Lancaster University, UK

EXTENDED ABSTRACT

The purpose of this paper is to explore the family environment in which children learn to become consumers. It aims to contribute towards filling the significant gaps which exist in our current understanding of the role that the family environment plays in the socialization of children (Roedder John, 1999). This paper also offers support for Cotte and Wood's (2004) assertion that parents can create different family environments for their children, and explores the possible implications of such environments in terms of consumer socialization.

With the family described as *the* socialisation unit (Commuri and Gentry, 2000), it is perhaps surprising that relatively little is known abut how such a social environment impacts on the consumer socialization process. Moschis and Churchill (1978), too, point towards the importance of the family in the consumer socialization process, and Moschis and Churchill (1978) offer their classic conceptualization of consumer socialization.

Theories such as *parental socialisation style* (Carlson and Grossbart, 1988) and *family communication pattern* (Carlson et al., 1994) have been presented which aim to shed greater light on the family socialization environment. However, such theories have failed to adopt an internal focus. Instead, families are often compared to one another, and consumer research has ignored the possible differences which may exist within the same family.

Research in the fields of genetics and behavioural psychology suggest that multiple environments, or *familial micro-environments* (Harris, 1995), exist within the same family. This study, therefore, seeks to explore the family environment in greater detail in relation to the consumer socialization of children. A wide variety of family forms were chosen as the sites of consumption due to marketing's preoccupation with nuclear family types (Commuri and Gentry, 2000), and the voices of children alongside adults are actively sought.

Six families were recruited to participate; one lesbian headed family with both adopted and biological children; one blended family; a family headed by a cohabiting couple; a family headed by a single mother; and two nuclear families. Each family member was invited to take part in the research process in a move away from the early family studies which recruited only a limited number of respondents. Generally every family member who was living in the family home chose to participate, although there were a few exceptions (most notably with very young children, adolescent children and certain fathers who chose not to be involved).

Consent was sought from both parents and children alike to participate in phenomenological interviews and family observation. The families were seen between three and five times over a period ranging from four to twelve months. The interviews were conducted in the family home, where a parent or guardian was always present, and interviews were conducted with individuals and family groups depending on which family members were available.

The interviews were recorded and transcribed. The data was analysed following Spiggle's (1994) data analysis steps in which marginal notes were made on each transcript. This allowed similar topics to be grouped under broader emergent themes. Each family was analysed initially on an idiographic basis and then across-family analysis occurred which allowed for global themes to emerge. The interpretation of the interview texts used a hermeneutical approach (Thompson, 1991; Thompson, Locander and Pollio, 1990) which involved an iterative process of moving back and forth within and across interview texts and between transcripts and the literature.

Across all six family cases significant differences were found to exist *within* the families studied. Family members, parents and children alike, treated various family members in different ways, creating very unique familial micro-environments for the family members. Two family cases, in a similar vein to Thompson (2005), are presented; the Baldwin family story to illustrate the differences in the family environment that are created by parents; and the Jones family story to illustrate how children themselves can treat their fellow siblings in different ways.

The familial micro-environments which exist within each family story suggest that one universal family environment does not exist. Empirical support is not found to support the universal parental socialization style and family communication pattern that Carlson and Grossbart (1988) and Carlson et al. (1994) respectively present. Rather, different socialization tendencies exist within the same family, with parents and children acting as important socialization agents within the family for other children.

The unique familial environments fostered by parents (*paternal micro-environments*) and children (*fraternal micro-environments*) impact the consumer socialization environment in families, and the *antecedent variables* and *socialization process variables* which Moschis and Churchill (1978) identify, and thus the learning outcomes for children within families. A child's familial micro-environment affects the opportunities which are made available to the child to discuss consumption related issues, and thus the ability to acquire consumer skills.

REFERENCES

Carlson, L., and Grossbart, S. (1988) Parent Style and Consumer Socialisation of Children. *Journal of Consumer Research*. Vol. 15 pp. 77–94.

Carlson, L., Walsh, A., Laczniak, R. N. and Grossbart, S. (1994) Family Communication Patterns and Marketplace Motivations, Attitudes, and Behaviours of Children and Mothers. *The Journal of Consumer Affairs*. Vol. 28 (1) pp. 25-53.

Commuri, S., and Gentry, J. W. (2000) Opportunities for Family Research in Marketing. *Academy of Marketing Science Review*. Vol. 2000 (8) pp. 1–34.

Cotte, J. and Wood, S. L. (2004) Families and Innovative Consumer Behaviour: A Triadic Analysis of Sibling and Parental Influence. *Journal of Consumer Research*. Vol. 31, pp. 78–86.

Harris, J. R. (1995) Where Is the Child's Environment? A Group Socialisation Theory of Development. *Psychological Review*. Vol. 102 (3) pp. 458-489.

Moschis, G. P. and Churchill, G. A. (1978) Consumer Socialization: A Theoretical and Empirical Analysis. *Journal of Marketing Research*. Vol. 15, pp. 599–609.

Roedder John, D. (1999) Consumer Socialisation of Children: A Retrospective Look at Twenty-Five Years of Research. *Journal of Consumer Research*. Vol. 26 pp. 183–213.

Spiggle, S. (1994) Analysis and Interpretation of Qualitative Data in Consumer Research. *Journal of Consumer Research*. Vol. 21, pp. 491-503.

Thompson, C. J. (1991) May the Circle Be Unbroken: A Hermeneutic Consideration of How Interpretive Approaches to Consumer Research Are Understood by Consumer Researchers. *Advances in Consumer Research.* Vol. 18, pp. 63-69.

Thompson, C. J. (2005) Consumer Risk Perceptions in a Community of Reflexive Doubt. *Journal of Consumer Research.* Vol. 32, pp. 235-248.

Thompson, C. J., Locander, W. B. and Pollio, H. R. (1990) The Lived Meaning of Free Choice: An Existential-Phenomenological Description of Everyday Consumer Experiences of Contemporary Married Women. *Journal of Consumer Research.* Vol. 17, pp. 346-361.

Consumer Socialization: The Role of Hunting and Gun Rituals in Becoming a Man

Jon Littlefield, Berry College, USA
Julie L. Ozanne, Virginia Polytechnic Institute and State University, USA

EXTENDED ABSTRACT

The modern practice of recreational hunting is a domain that has been understudied in the sociological and anthropological literature and completely neglected in the consumer research literature. Anthropology has largely focused on the history of hunting as interpreted via modern day hunter-gatherer societies as a means of studying human development, while sociology has focused on the extremities of the hunting culture such as poaching or on the ethics of hunting or eating meat. The neglect in consumer research is particularly surprising for two reasons. First, hunting in pre-historic times represents the earliest representation of key consumption and acquisition activities. While today we shop, previously we hunted. And activities such as sharing meat that continue to exist today, both among modern hunters and among still-existing hunter-gatherer societies, suggest remnants of one of the earliest forms of exchange. Second, hunting is an area in which study of the extended consumer socialization process in families—typically between fathers and their sons—can be examined. New hunters, along with their male mentors, undergo a years- or decades-long process of socialization into the skills, social norms, and values of the hunting culture. This socialization process, along with the ensuing expression of masculinity by hunters, is the focus of this study.

Children develop through both cognitive and social means and both have been suggested as important foci for the study of consumer socialization (Moschis and Moore 1979; Roedder John 1999). In consumer research, however, the cognitive development of socialization has attracted the most attention. In this stream of literature, socialization is envisioned as progressing through a series of three stages that are related to the child's age (Roedder John 1999): a perceptual stage focused toward "immediate and readily observable perceptual features of the marketplace" (186), an abstract analytic stage where the child shifts to more symbolic thought where s/he can see multiple perspectives, and a reflective stage in which the child is able to grasp not only functional meanings of the consumption experience but also its more subtle social meanings. This approach sees the child attaining specific skills at universal stages with this progression depending on the complexity of the child's existing cognitive structures and is based on theory developed originally by Jean Piaget (1963). In contrast to this Piagetian perspective, we find that an explanation that explicitly includes the influence of family members and other mentors more richly explains the socialization process into hunting.

The primary method of data collection was semi-structured, in-depth interviews of approximately two hours with twenty-seven adult male hunters and a wildlife manager, including interviewing separately 5 fathers and sons who hunt. The secondary method was participant observation of the hunting community, including hunter safety classes, hunting and gun shows, informal interviews with hunting-related retailers, and participation in hunting trips. A hermeneutical analysis of the text was conducted, based on the assumption that consumers' personal histories are embedded within a context of personal meanings expressed by "culturally shared narrative forms" (Thompson 1997, 439-40), involving an *intra*-textual analysis resulting in a written interpretation of each informant and an *inter*-textual analysis comparing themes across informants.

Our findings suggest that consumer socialization can be conceptually expanded to include the dynamics by which social influences such as family impact the process through which young men learn to hunt, making use of Lev Vygotsky's theory of development (Vygotsky 1978; Tudge and Scrimsher 2003) that stresses the importance of interpersonal interaction in the socialization process. Hunters progress through four distinct stages that are characterized by support, challenge, and encouragement by their mentors. *Pre-hunters* accompany their mentors hunting, participating in scouting and retrieving activities, while *neophytes* have proven they are responsible enough to carry a loaded gun. *Apprentice* hunters hunt independently without their mentors, exhibiting camaraderie and challenge with their peers, and *competent* hunters have moved past the need to prove themselves and have achieved actualization of their masculinity in ways discussed in the following section.

Competent hunters negotiate masculinity in ways that relate both to the mediating role that equipment plays in constructions of the "extended self" (Belk 1988) and to the primary motivation achieved from participating in the activity of hunting. Their equipment meanings vary on a continuum between meanings that are intrinsic to the equipment (e.g., accuracy, technical aspects) and meanings that are extrinsic to the equipment (e.g., personal history, nostalgia). The second factor relates to the approach to the hunt, which varies from a focus on the experience of the hunt (a process orientation) to a focus on the final kill (an ends orientation).

Thus, four subgroups of hunters emerged: traditionalists, gearheads, experientialists, and transcendentals, and we found that masculinity is both expressed and understood differently by the four types of hunters. For *traditionalists,* hunting is deeply intertwined with rural family traditions and results in easily achieved close male social bonds. Technology mediates the hunting experience for the *gearhead* through mastery of equipment in both skill development and customization, he expresses his masculinity through his desire for control, order, precision, and accuracy, and is unique among hunters in his focus on a hierarchy based on technical expertise. Masculinity for the *experiential* hunter harkens back to finding his particular place in both the natural and the social worlds. Rather than dominating nature, the experiential is interconnected with nature. *Transcendental* hunters represent a category of masculinity that affirms emotional bonds to both family and nature by using their family socialization and life long hunting experience to achieve a balance between stereotypically feminine characteristics of empathy and caring and a stereotypically masculine activity of hunting and killing in competition with other men.

REFERENCES

Arnould, Eric J., and Linda L. Price (2003), "Authenticating Acts and Authoritative Performances: Questing for Self and Community," in *The Why of Consumption: Contemporary Perspectives on Consumer Motives, Goals, and Desires*, ed. S. Ratneshwar, David Glen Mick, and Cynthia Huffman, London: Routledge, 138-61.

Belk, Russell W. (1988), "Possessions and the Extended Self," *Journal of Consumer Research*, 15 (September), 139-68.

Belk, Russell W. and Janeen A. Costa (1998), "The Mountain Man Myth: A Contemporary Consuming Fantasy," *Journal of Consumer Research*, 25 (December), 218-40.

Bye, Linda Marie (2003), "Masculinity and Rurality at Play in Stories about Hunting," *Norwegian Journal of Geography,* vol. 57, 145-53.

Fine, Lisa M. (2000), "Rights of Men, Rites of Passage: Hunting and Masculinity at Reo Motors of Lansing Michigan, 1945-1975," *Journal of Social History,* 33 (4), 805-23.

Holland, Dorothy, William Lachicotte, Jr., Debra Skinner, and Carol Cain, ed. (1998), *Identity and Agency in Cultural Worlds,* Cambridge: Harvard University Press.

Holt, Douglas B. and Craig J. Thompson (2004), "Man-of-Action Heroes: The Pursuit of Heroic Masculinity in Everyday Consumption," *Journal of Consumer Research,* 31 (September), 425-40.

Kiesling, Scott Fabius (2005), "Homosocial Desire in Men's Talk: Balancing and Re-creating Cultural Discourses of Masculinity," *Language in Society,* 34, 695-726.

Martin, Diane, John W. Schouten, and James H. McAlexander (2006), "Claiming the Throttle: Multiple Femininities in a Hyper-Masculine Subculture," *Consumption, Markets and Culture,* 9 (3), 171-205.

McKenzie, Callum (2005), "Sadly Neglected—Hunting and Gendered Identities: A Study in Gender Construction," *The International Journal of the History of Sport,* 22, 4 (July), 545-62.

Moschis, George P. and Roy L. Moore (1979), "Decision Making Among the Young: A Socialization Perspective," *Journal of Consumer Research,* 6 (September), 101-12.

Muñiz Jr., Albert M. and Thomas C. O'Guinn (2001), "Brand Community," *Journal of Consumer Research,* 27 (March), 412-32.

Piaget, Jean (1963), "The Attainment of Invariants and Reversible Operations in the Development of Thinking," *Social Research,* 30 (3), 283-99.

Roedder John, Deborah (1999), "Consumer Socialization of Children: A Retrospective Look at Twenty-Five Years of Research," *Journal of Consumer Research,* 26 (December), 183-213.

Rook, Dennis W. (1985), "The Ritual Dimension of Consumer Behavior," *Journal of Consumer Research,* 12 (December), 251-64.

Schouten, John W. and James H. McAlexander (1995), "Subcultures of Consumption: An Ethnography of the New Bikers," *Journal of Consumer Research,* 22 (June), 43-61.

Schroeder, Jonathon E., and Detlev Zwick (2004), "Mirrors of Masculinity: Representation and Identity in Advertising Images," *Consumption Markets and Culture,* 7, 21-52.

Smalley, Andrea (2005), "'I Just Like to Kill Things': Women, Men, and the Gender of Sport Hunting in the United States, 1940-1973," *Gender and History,* 17 (1), 183-209.

Thompson, Craig J. (1997), "Interpreting Consumers: A Hermeneutical Framework for Deriving Marketing Insights from the Texts of Consumers' Consumption Stories," *Journal of Marketing Research,* XXXIV (November), 438-55.

Tudge, Jonathan R.H., and Sheryl Scrimsher (2003), "Lev S. Vygotsky on Education: A Cultural-historical, Interpersonal, and Individual Approach to Development," in *Educational Psychology: A Century of Contributions,* *ed.* Barry J. Zimmerman and Dale H. Schunk, Mahwah, NJ: Lawrence Erlbaum, 207-28.

Turner, Victor W. (1967), *The Forest of Symbols: Aspects of Ndembu Ritual,* Ithaca: Cornell University Press.

Van Gennep, Arnold (1960/1909), *The Rites of Passage,* Chicago: University of Chicago Press.

Vygotsky, Lev S. (1978), *Mind in Society: The Development of Higher Psychological Processes,* Cambridge, MA: Harvard University Press.

Ward, Scott (1974), "Consumer Socialization," *Journal of Consumer Research,* 1 (September), 1-14.

Wink, Joan, and LeAnn G. Putney (2002), *A Vision of Vygotsky,* Boston: Allyn and Bacon.

The "Proper Meal" and Social Capital in Urban China

Ann Veeck, Western Michigan University, USA
Hongyan Yu, Jilin University, China
Alvin C. Burns, Louisiana State University, USA

EXTENDED ABSTRACT

The concept of a "proper meal" has been studied as a symbol of the family and as a means to identify the roles and the power structure of family members as they negotiate the divisions between the public and private spheres for decades (e.g. Murcott 1982; Charles and Kerr 1988; DeVault 1991). Building on the "proper meal" literature, this study investigates conceptualizations of the "proper meal" in urban China. Via interviews with twenty Chinese families, we examine how activities related to domestic meals serve to generate and transmit social capital (Bourdieu 1984, Coleman 1988, Putnam 2000) during this era of dramatic economic and social change.

Descriptions of what constitutes a proper meal in western studies generally start with the dishes necessary for a nutritious meal. For example, British studies in the 1980's found that a proper meal had to be home cooked and consisted of meat, potatoes, vegetables, and gravy (Charles and Kerr 1986; Murcott 1982). In the U.S. DeVault (1991) also found strict definitions related to the appropriate constitution of meals, although the particular choice of dishes could vary according to the families' ethnicities. Earlier studies also emphasized that for a meal to be proper it was expected that a woman had cooked the meal at home and that all family was in attendance (Charles and Kerr 1988; DeVault 1991; Murcott 1982). More recent conceptualizations on meal norms have found more forgiving standards on the composition of the meal, as well as more sharing of meal tasks by younger couples (Bugge and Almas 2006; Makela 2000; Marshall and Anderson 2002).

Representations of the "proper meal" are useful for studying how family routines facilitate the transmission of social capital. Social capital is defined as a set of resources that accrue to individuals as a result of their membership in particular social groups, with the most fundamental group in most societies being the family (Bourdieu 1984, Coleman 1988, Putnam 2000). The form of social capital transmitted among family members would be what Putnam (2000) would call 'bonding,' or exclusive, social capital that would reinforce the solidarity and mutual benefit of being a member of the family. Social capital has been seen as a conceptual tool for understanding the nature of family life and the communities in which they are imbedded (e.g. Edwards 2004; Putnam 1998).

This research is part of a larger study of family meals, conducted in Changchun, Jilin Province, P.R. China, that has included focus groups, family interviews, food shopping trip observations, and a household survey over a multiple year period. For this research, we conducted interviews with twenty families who had at least one child living at home in their home. The interviews included numerous questions about family meals, including the participation of family members in activities surrounding breakfast, lunch, and dinner and perceptions and attitudes towards food-related tasks and meals. We analyzed the interviews to identify definitions of the "proper meal," and to pinpoint how family meals served to transmit social capital.

An analysis of data related to definitions of the proper meal found the following components to be most salient: 1) food, 2) atmosphere, 3) mood, 4) conversation, and 5) participants. As in other studies of "proper meals" (e.g. Murcott 1982; Lupton 2000), family members defined a proper meal as having food that is tasty and nutritious as a fundamental requirement. A pleasant, or perhaps special, atmosphere was also cited as being important, with family members retaining a relaxed and happy mood. Quite a few participants noted the need for good conversation that was about light and happy topics, with an avoidance of stressful topics, particularly related to work. Finally, and most importantly according to many of the respondents, all of the family members had to be present for the meal to be "proper."

Via the definitions of "proper meals" provided by the families we interviewed, along with elaborations on how domestic meals actually functioned in their lives, we were able to identify how social capital might be generated and transmitted via these food-related activities. In the end, we coined and categorized three distinctive forms of social capital that were propagated via family meals, and, by extension, family life: identity capital, moral capital, and emotional capital. The first form of social capital that we identified as being enhanced through shared meals is identity capital, which functions to provide feelings of belonging and purpose to family members. The second form of social is moral capital, which serves to transmit proper mode of conduct and values to family members. A final form of social capital is emotional capital, which allows the transmission of feelings of love and emotional support to family members

With a sample consisting of twenty intact families, this study omits the viewpoint of individuals who live outside these strict boundaries. The conceptualization of a "proper meal" might be seen quite differently by residents of Chinese cities who are, for example, very rich, or single, or migrant workers, or any number of characterizations that were not represented in our sample. The study of the formation of social capital using other family forms and household types would provide wider understandings of the place of family in society.

REFERENCES

Bourdieu, Pierre (1984), *Distinction: A Social Critique of the Judgement of Taste*, London: Routledge and Kegan Paul.

Bugge, Annechen Bahr and Reidar Almas (2006), "Domestic Dinner: Representations and Practices of a Proper Meal among Young Suburban Mothers," *Journal of Consumer Culture*, 6 (2), 203-228.

Charles, Nickie and Marion Kerr, (1988), *Women, Food, and Families*, Manchester: Manchester

Coleman, James S. (1988), Social Capital in the Creation of Human Capital," *American Journal of Sociology*, 94, pp. S95-S120.

DeVault, Margaret L. (1991), *Feeding the Family: The Social Organization of Caring as Gendered Work*, Chicago: University of Chicago Press.

Edwards, Rosalind (2004), "Present and Absent in Troubling Ways: Families and Social Capital Debates," *Sociological Review*, 1-21.

Lupton, Deborah (2000), "'Where's Me Dinner?': Food Preparation Arrangements in Rural Australian Families," *Journal of Sociology*, 36 (2), 172-188.

Makela, Johanna (2000), "Cultural Definitions of the Meal," in *Dimensions of the Meal: The Science, Culture, Business, and Art of Eating*, ed. Herbert L. Meiselman. Gaithersburg, MD: Aspen Publishers.

Marshall, D. W. and A. S. Anderson (2002), "Proper Meals in Transition: Young Married Couples on the Nature of Eating Together," *Appetite*, 39, 192-206.

Murcott, Anne (1982), "On the Social Significance of 'Cooked Dinner' in South Wales, *Social Science Information*, 21 (4/5), 677-696.

Putnam, Robert D. (1998), "Foreword," *Housing Policy Debate*, 9 (1), 1-4.

Putnam, Robert D. (2000), *Bowling Alone: The Collapse and Revival of American Community*, New York: Simon and Schuster.

The Self-Activation Effect of Advertisements: Ads Can Affect Whether and How Consumers Think About the Self

Debra Trampe, University of Groningen, The Netherlands
Diederik A. Stapel, Tilburg University , The Netherlands
Frans W. Siero, University of Groningen, The Netherlands

EXTENDED ABSTRACT

One of the signature strengths of the advertising industry lies in its ability to transfer seemingly mundane objects into highly desirable products. Products can transform into different entities once they are placed in advertisements. In their everyday appearance, products are relatively distant, self-defining stimuli: Shoes are for walking and cars are for driving. However, the meaning that is conveyed by such products can change dramatically once they are placed in an advertisement. Then, these products can become consumer products, things that can be bought and owned. Then, shoes and cars are for buying. To give an example, the meaning signaled by a high-heeled shoe in an advertisement is radically different from the meaning that is conveyed when one encounters the exact same shoe outside of its advertisement context. In the latter situation, the shoe is a relatively distant, neutral product. However, in the former advertisement context, the shoe is a desirable, potentially self-relevant product that one can buy and that suggests a possible self-image of beauty and attractiveness.

The present paper looks at important but understudied consequences of the different meaning that advertised versus non-advertised products can convey. In three experiments, we test the proposed self-activation effect of advertisements, which suggests that the different meaning products convey once they are placed in an advertisement can trigger important self-processes. By postulating the self-activation effect of ads, we suggest that when placed in an advertisement context, products become potentially desirable consumer products that address people in their capacity as consumers—people who buy and own things, and thus make specific consumer choices and decisions. Moreover, we expect this effect to be especially true for hedonic products, but not for more utilitarian products. Specifically, we suggest that advertised hedonic products, as opposed to non-advertised hedonic products, can affect both *the extent* to which individuals think about the self, and *how* they think about the self.

Interestingly, the relevant literature has not yet explicitly acknowledged the idea that the meaning that is conveyed by advertised products may be very different from the meaning that is conveyed by non-advertised products. However, previous studies have focused on how advertisements can employ all sorts of techniques to convey their message in an implicit fashion, such as implicatures (Phillips 1997) and stylistic properties (Peracchio and Meyers-Levy 2005). Contemporary consumer research acknowledges that advertisements can possess symbolic features and that advertisements are often highly stylized representations that compel consumers to engage ads as symbolic systems (Aaker 1999; Philips and McQuarrie 2004; Scott 1994; Solomon 1983). That is, rhetorical theory posits that advertisements can convey meaning that goes beyond their physical characteristics and as a consequence, consumers must draw upon associations and cultural knowledge to grasp the implicit meaning the ad conveys. However, past studies have commonly focused on how the content of ads can affect product perceptions, evaluations, and processing style. In other words, most consumer research has studied variations within consumer situations, rather than variations between consumer and non-consumer situations. Or, using Folkes' (2002) words "… little consumer research directly compares consumption with non-consumption or customer with non-customer behavior". The present paper attempts to fill a void in the current literature by making comparisons between consumer and non-consumer situations.

Taken together, the results of three experiments indicate that very subtle manipulations (merely adding a brand name and a relatively simple background) can interact with the hedonic level of the products to transform products into advertised consumer products. The consequences of this change in meaning were found to be substantial. First, Study 1 found that a hedonic product that was placed in an ad activated the self (as exemplified by an increase in the salience of first-person pronouns), as compared to the same hedonic product when it was not advertised. That is, when research participants had been exposed to an ad featuring eye shadow (a product previously rated as relatively hedonic), they were more likely to translate fictitious words as first-person pronouns than when they had viewed the eye shadow without the ad context.

Study 2 was designed to address the self-evaluative consequences of Study 1's finding that ads can interact with the hedonic level of products to activate the self. Study 2 revealed that ads for hedonic products (as opposed to a more utilitarian product) were used as a standard against which consumers evaluated the self. Specifically, individuals were found to evaluate their self-image more negatively when they had viewed, for example, a high-heeled shoe (a product previously rated as relatively hedonic) in an ad than when they were exposed to the exact same shoe when it was cut out from its advertisement context.

Further support for the notion that the activation of the self is an important underlying mechanism was provided by Study 3's finding that experimentally activating the self interacted with the hedonic level of products to produce similar effects on self-evaluation as did exposure to advertised products. That is, when the self was directly activated, exposure to the hedonic products in ads resulted in more negative self-evaluations than when the self was not activated.

To sum up, the three experiments provide evidence for the self-activation effect of ads: placing products in an advertisement context can interact with the hedonic level of products to activate the self, and as a consequence, ads can exert self-evaluative effects on consumers. By demonstrating this, the current studies contribute to the literature on visual imagery in ads. This literature has revealed important knowledge about how consumers draw meaning from ads. The current studies add to this research body by demonstrating that an advertisement context itself can also serve as a "figure of thought" that should not be processed literally, but rather by using implicit associations and knowledge. Stated differently, the current research adds to the existing literature on rhetorical theory by examining how people interpret themselves on the basis of advertisements, rather than looking at how people interpret the advertisement on the basis of themselves (i.e., their knowledge structures).

REFERENCES

Aaker, Jennifer L. (1999), "The Malleable Self: The Role of Self-Expression in Persuasion," *Journal of Marketing Research*, 36 (1), 45-57.

Folkes, Valerie (2002), "Presidential Address: Is Consumer Behavior Different?" Susan Broniarczyk, ed. *Advances in Consumer Research*, 14, 1-4.

Peracchio, Laura A., and Joan Meyers-Levy (2005), "Using Stylistic Properties of Ad Pictures to Communicate with Consumers," *Journal of Consumer Research*, 32, 29-40.

Phillips, Barbara J. (1997), "Thinking into it: Consumer Interpretation of Complex Advertising Images," *Journal of Advertising*, 16 (2), 77-87.

— and Edward F. McQuarrie (2004), "Beyond Visual Metaphore: A New Typology of Visual Rhetoric in Advertising," *Marketing Theory, 4* (1/2), 113-136.

Scott, Linda M. (1994), "Images in Advertising: The Need for a Theory of Visual Rhetoric," *Journal of Consumer Research*, 21, 252-273.

Solomon, Michael (1983), "The Role of Products as Social Stimuli: A Symbolic Interactionist Perspective," *Journal of Consumer Research*, 10, 319-329.

My Brand and I: The Impact of Self-Construal on Self-Brand Closeness

Jia Liu, Monash University, Australia
Dirk Smeesters, Erasmus University, The Netherlands
Els Gijsbrechts, Tilburg University, The Netherlands

ABSTRACT

Three studies demonstrate that consumers with independent self-construals are more inclined to incorporate brands into the self and hence maintain close connections with them than consumers with interdependent self-construals. We demonstrate the underlying role of self-expression in explaining this effect. Unlike interdependent consumers, independent consumers have a high need for self-expression, and are inclined to use brands to communicate the self, which should further strengthen their self-brand connections.

Imagining the Self: The Effect of Self-Focus and Visual Perspective on Persuasion

Massimiliano Ostinelli, McGill University, Canada
Ulf Böckenholt, McGill University, Canada

EXTENDED ABSTRACT

When evaluating products, consumers often imagine future consumption-related behaviors (e.g., MacInnis & Price, 1987; Shiv & Huber, 2000). Drawing on James's (1982) classical distinction between the "Me" and the "I", we suggest that when projecting themselves into the future, consumers can focus either on their *future being-self*, by reflecting on what consumption can make them become (e.g., a better student, an expert, a caring parent), or their *future experiencing-self*, by anticipating the thoughts, feelings, and emotions they will experience in a consumption episode (e.g., the excitement of a snowboard downhill, the relaxation of a spa).

To persuade people to engage in the imagined behavior, images of future being-selves have to successfully convey how the scene pictured enhances one' sense of self, whereas images of future experiencing-selves have to transmit the feelings and emotions that could be experienced in a particular situation. We propose and provide evidence that the persuasiveness of being-selves and experiencing-selves is moderated by visual perspective in imagination.

Future selves can be imagined through a *first-person* perspective, when people visualize the scene through their own eyes, or a *third-person* perspective, when people visualize the scene through the point of view of an external observer (e.g., Nigro & Neisser, 1983). Empirical findings indicate that the adoption of a specific vantage point can determine the inferences people make about their future selves. In particular, the third-person perspective leads to more dispositional attributions (e.g., Frank & Gilovich, 1989) and highlights the broader meaning of an imagined situation (Libby & Eibach, 2004 cited in Libby et al. 2005; Vasquez & Buehler, 2007). On the other hand, the first-person discloses more information about future states of mind (i.e., affective reactions and psychological states) experienced by a person (McIsaac & Eich, 2002).

We propose that the third-person perspective, by highlighting the broader meaning of a behavior and its dispositional consequences, is more suitable to imagine future being-selves, whereas the first-person-perspective, by disclosing more information about one's state of consciousness, is more suitable to imagine future experiencing-selves.

Moreover, although people can deliberately decide to adopt a specific visual perspective (Nigro & Neisser, 1983), we suggest that unfamiliar scenarios, being imagined through a constructive process that focuses attention on the spatial relation between the self and its surrounding environment, tend to be visualized through a third-person perspective. This, in turn, increases the persuasiveness of future being-selves over experiencing-selves.

Three studies were conducted to test our hypotheses. Study 1 had a 2 (visual perspective: first vs. third) x 2 (self-focus: being vs. experiencing) between-subjects factorial design. Participants were presented with a short description of a new book that provided techniques to improve performance at school and imagined either themselves having a better way of studying, mastering course material, and becoming an expert in a subject domain (being-self) or the feelings of getting a good grade on a difficult exam (experiencing-self). The visualization task was performed either through a first- or a third-person perspective. As expected, future being-selves led to to significantly more favorable attitudes toward the book when imagined through a third- as opposed to a first-person perspective, whereas the experiencing-self-focus led to directionally (although not significantly) more favorable attitudes when the scene was visualized through a first-person as opposed to a third-person perspective. Further analysis suggested that vividness of imagination, but not ease of imagination, mediated the interaction effect between self-focus and visual perspective on attitude.

Drawing on empirical evidence suggesting that near-future events are more likely imagined through a first-person perspective than distant-future events (Pronin & Ross, 2006), Study 2 replicated findings from Study 1 through a naturalistic manipulation of visual perspective. Participants imagined enjoying an exotic vacation (experiencing-self) either in the near-future (a week later) or in the distant-future (three years later). As expected, the vacation was more likely imagined through a third-person perspective in the distant-future than in the near-future condition. Moreover, participants who adopted a third-person perspective liked significantly less the vacation destination than those who adopted a first-person perspective. A distribution of products test (MacKinnon, Lockwood, Hoffman, West, & Sheets, 2002) showed that temporal distance had a significant indirect effect on attitude via visual perspective, although its direct effect on attitude was not significant.

Study 3 analyzed the impact of scenario familiarity on visual perspective and future selves' persuasiveness. The experiment had one between-subjects factor (scenario: familiar vs. unfamiliar) and one within-subject factor (self-focus: being vs. experiencing) design. Participants were asked to imagine either incorporating the product into their daily routine (familiar scenario) or an original use of the product (unfamiliar scenario) and evaluated the product by focusing either on their being- or experiencing-selves (within-subject factor). In the being-self-focus, respondents were first asked to consider the extent to which the e-book reader made them more efficient/effective and then rate the product attractiveness by focusing on that particular aspect of their imagination. In the experiencing-self-focus, respondents were asked to consider the extent to which they experienced positive emotions and feelings while using the product, and rate the product attractiveness by focusing on that particular aspect of their imagination. As expected, the unfamiliar scenarios were more likely imagined through a third-person perspective than familiar ones. Moreover, the e-book reader was evaluated significantly more positively in the being-self-focus than in the experiencing–self–focus when the scene was visualized through a third-person perspective but no significant differences was found when the scene was visualized through a first-person perspective. This finding suggests that the attractiveness of future being-selves over experiencing-selves was enhanced by the adoption of a third-person perspective. Although the direct effect was not significant, a distribution of products test (MacKinnon et al., 2002) showed that familiarity had a significant indirect effect on attitude via visual perspective.

This work has two main implications for product positioning and advertising. First, marketers can manipulate visual perspective to match future self-focus; situations that draw attention on one's being-self (e.g., future achievements, symbolic consumption) are more attractive when visualized through a third- rather than a first-person perspective, whereas the opposite is true for future experiencing-selves (e.g., the excitement of a snowboard downhill). Second, marketers can draw attention on either being- or experiencing-self to match the visual perspective in imagination. As shown in Study 3, unfamiliar consumption imaginations, such as the use of a radical new product, are more effectively promoted by drawing consumers' attention on their being-selves (e.g., becoming more efficient) rather than on their experiencing-selves (e.g., experiencing positive feelings).

REFERENCES

Frank, M. G., & Gilovich, T. (1989). Effect of Memory Perspective on Retrospective Causal Attributions. *Journal of Personality and Social Psychology, 57*(3), 399-403.

Libby, L. K., & Eibach, R. P. (2004). *Seeing Meaning: Visual Perspective and Action Identification in Mental Imagery.* Paper presented at the Society for Personality and Social Psychology.

MacInnis, D. J., & Price, L. L. (1987). The Role of Imagery in Information Processing: Review and Extensions. *Journal of Consumer Research, 13*(4), 473-491.

MacKinnon, D. P., Lockwood, C. M., Hoffman, J. M., West, S. G., & Sheets, V. (2002). A Comparison of Methods to test Mediation and other Intervening Variable Effects. *Psychol Methods, 7*(1), 83-104.

McIsaac, H. K., & Eich, E. (2002). Vantage Point in Episodic Memory. *Psychonomic Bulletin & Review, 9*(1), 146-150.

Nigro, G., & Neisser, U. (1983). Point of View in Personal Memories. *Cognitive Psychology, 15*(4), 467-482.

Pronin, E., & Ross, L. (2006). Temporal Differences in Trait Self-Ascription: When the Self Is Seen as an Other. *Journal of Personality and Social Psychology, 90*(2), 197.

Shiv, B., & Huber, J. (2000). The Impact of Anticipating Satisfaction on Consumer Choice. *Journal of Consumer Research, 27*(2), 202-216.

Vasquez, N. A., & Buehler, R. (2007). Seeing Future Success: Does Imagery Perspective Influence Achievement Motivation? *Personality and Social Psychology Bulletin, 33*(10), 1392.

Public Commitment Leads to Weight Loss

Stephanie Dellande, University of New Orleans, USA
Prashanth U. Nyer, Chapman University, USA

EXTENDED ABSTRACT

In compliance dependent services (CDS), e.g., weight loss programs, the client is expected to continue to perform for himself or herself once away from the service provider in order to ensure positive outcomes and customer satisfaction (Dellande and Gilly 1998). Given that the customer of CDS must provide the inputs as well as create a major portion of the service, it is important to understand the underlying motivation-compliance process. Motivating the customer to comply with his or her service roles becomes all-the-more difficult/important when the customer must carry out his or her roles for extended periods of time. The research objective of this investigation is to explore aspects of motivation in long-term customer compliance behavior. We examine public commitment and its influence on motivation, and the effect of these on customer compliance behavior in a weight loss program. Further, we investigate the role of susceptibility to normative influence (SNI), to understand the underlying relationship between public commitment and customer compliance behavior.

Conceptualization

This paper investigates the role of public commitment in influencing motivation and compliance behavior in weight loss. In addition, susceptibility to normative influence (SNI) is also examined. The theoretical model suggests that public commitment to weight loss leads to long-term weight loss compliance behavior; further, weight loss motivation partly mediates the effect of public commitment on weight loss and SNI moderates the effect of public commitment on weight loss. As such, we offer the following hypotheses:

H1: Higher levels of public commitment to a target behavior will result in higher levels of compliance with that behavior.

H2: The effect of public commitment on long-term customer compliance behavior will be, in part, mediated by weight loss motivation.

H3: Susceptibility to normative influence (SNI) will moderate the relationship between public commitment and compliance such that, at high levels of susceptibility to normative influence (SNI), the positive influence of public commitment on compliance will be strengthened.

Method

Design

The study uses a 3 x 2 full factorial design manipulating three levels of public commitment (no public commitment, short-term public commitment, and long-term public commitment), and a median split to generate two levels (low and high) of Susceptibility to Normative Influence (SNI).

Subjects

The subjects in this study were 211 women between the ages of 20 and 45 enrolled in a women's weight loss program at a center in southern India. The subjects were selected from clients who signed up for a 16 week weight loss program designed to help clients lose modest amounts of excess weight (typically 15 to 20 pounds). Weight loss goals were set for the 8th week and the 16th week of the 16 week program. The weight loss goal for the follow-up visit held during the 24th week was the same as the week 16 goal, i.e., participants were expected to maintain their weight loss during the eight week period following the program.

Subjects completed a survey that included measures of susceptibility to normative influence (SNI), and weight loss motivation using modified versions of the sub-scales from Snell and Johnson's (1997) Multidimensional Health Questionnaire. Versions of this survey were also administered during the 4th week and during the 12th week of the 16 week program. During the second and third administrations of this questionnaire an additional question was included to assess the manipulation of public commitment. Subjects were randomly assigned to one of three manipulated experimental conditions in a 3x2 full-factorial experimental design.

In this study we investigated the effect of long-term versus short-term public commitment, and consequently public commitment was manipulated as follows. Each subject in the long-term public commitment condition had their weight loss goal, and their name printed on an index card and displayed in a locked glass-faced bulletin board for the duration of the 16 week program. Subjects in the short-term public commitment condition had their weight loss goal and their name displayed in the bulletin board for the first three weeks of the program. Subjects in the no public commitment condition did not have their information posted in the bulletin board. After eliminating participants who did not complete the entire 16 week program, 211 subjects remained.

Subjects were weighed at the start of the program, eight weeks into the program, at the end of the 16 week program, and once more during the follow-up visit during the 24th week. The percentage of weight loss goal achieved (WL) was computed for each of these weigh-ins and these form the major dependent variables in this study. Thus a subject with weight loss goals of 10, 20 and 20 pounds (for weeks 8, 16 and 24) who achieved weight loss of 9, 16 and 14 pounds respectively, would have WL scores of 90%, 80% and 70% for the three weigh-ins.

Major Findings

In this study, we investigated the effect of making public "the commitment" to lose weight. Subjects who made a long-term public commitment to a weight loss goal were found to have achieved greater results compared to subjects who made a short-term public commitment, and compared to those who made no commitment at all. Further it was found that weight loss motivation partly mediated the effect of public commitment on weight loss. Higher levels of public commitment resulted in increased weight loss motivation which in turn resulted in increased levels of weight loss. In addition, the personality trait *susceptibility to normative influence* (SNI) was found to be a moderator of the effect of public commitment on weight loss. Subjects high in SNI were more likely to be affected by public commitment, compared to those lower in SNI. Finding significant differences in compliance behavior lends greater support to our hypothesis that the "public-ness" with which a commitment is made will have a significant and favorable impact on long-term compliance behavior.

REFERENCES

Dellande, Stephanie and Mary C. Gilly (1998), "Gaining Customer Compliance in Services," *Advances in Services Marketing and Management*, 7, 265-292.

Snell, William E. and Georgette Johnson (1997), "The Multidimensional Health Questionnaire," *American Journal of Health Behavior*, 21, 33-42.

Does Precipitation Affect Consumers' Smoking Tendency?

Yinlong Zhang, University of Texas at San Antonio, USA

EXTENDED ABSTRACT

Smoking consumption perhaps is the most striking example of a harmful pattern of consumer behavior. Yet, smoking consumption is still very common in developed markets, nearly 25% of the U.S. population smokes tobacco despite the well-known negative consequences (Centers for Disease Control and Prevention, 1997), and its usage seems to be getting increasingly higher in emerging markets (World Health Organization 2004).

Due to the health and social significance of smoking consumption, over the years academic attention has been paid to understand the determinants for smoking consumption tendency. Different literatures seem to emphasize the relative importance of different factors. For example, the economic literature has mostly stressed that economic factors such as prices as the most critical driver for smoking consumption. While the social psychology literature tends to recognize that psychological, and interpersonal social determinants are important in understanding the smoking consumption, the role of social environmental factors such as family or peer group has been demonstrated as extremely important determinants. But, the role of natural environment factors such as temperature or precipitation has not been systematically investigated. These factors arguably are the very important factor in explaining consumers' consumption activities (Parker 1997), so the current research aims to offer an initial step to understand the impact of these factors in smoking consumption.

Starting with two secondary data sources, we show that measure of precipitation correlates significantly with percentage of adult smokers at both country and state levels, even after controlling for many plausible alternatives. This relationship was further confirmed with a survey on smokers' belief and their smoking tendency. Next, we present data from two experiments in which we manipulated perceived precipitation to determine its effect on smoking consumption. From the two experiments, we show that manipulations of imagined rainy weather influence intention to engage in smoking consumption in predictable ways, and this influence is mediated by negative mood, moderated by smoking status and whether smokers are in hedonic or utilitarian processing objectives.

REFERENCES

Aaker, J.L., & Lee, A.Y. (2001). "I" seek pleasures and "we" avoid pains: the role of self-regulatory goals in information processing and persuasion. *Journal of Consumer Research*, 28, 33-49.

Baron, R. M., & Kenny, D.A. (1986). The moderator-mediator variable distinction in social psychological research: conceptual, strategic, and statistical considerations. *Journal of Personality and Social Psychology*, 51, 1173-82.

Bushman, Brad J., Morgan C. Wang and Craig A. Anderson (2005), "Is the Curve Relating Temperature to Aggression Linear or Curvilinear? Assuaults and Temperature in Minneapolis Re-examined," *Journal of Personality and Social Psychology*, 89 (1), 62-66.

CDC (2004), National center for chronic disease prevention & health promotion. Apps.nccd.cdc.gov.

Cunningham. Michael R. (1978), "Weather, Mood, Helping Behaviour: Quasi Experiments with Sunshine Samaritan," *Journal of Personality and Social Psychology*, 37 (11), 1947-1956.

Duarte, Rosa, Jose Julian Escario, and Jose Alberto Molina (2006), "The Psychological Behaviour of Young Spanish Smokers," *Journal of Consumer Policy*, 29, 176-189.

Hughes, J.R., Higgins, S.T., and Hatsukami, D., (1990), Effects of Abstinence from Tobacco: A Critical Review," in L.T. Kozlowski, H.M. Annis, H.D. Cappell, F.B. Glaser, and M.S. Goodstadt (Eds), *Research Advances in Alcohol and Drug Problems*, 10, 317-398, New York: Plenum Press.

Kassel, Jon D., Laura R. Stroud, and Carol A. Paronis (2006), "Smoking, Stress and Negative Affect: Correlation, Causation, and Context Across Stages of Smoking," *Psychological Bulletin*, 129 (2), 270-304.

Kenny, D.A. (2001). *Mediation: Issues and questions*. Retrieved from http: // nw3.nai.net / ~dakenny / mediate.htm

McMorrow, Martin J., and R.M. Foxx (1983), "Nicotine's Role in Smoking: An Analysis of Nicotine Regulation," *Psychological Bulletin*, 93 (2), 302-327.

Ornstein, S., & Hanssens, D. (1985). Alcohol control laws and the consumption of distilled spirits and beer. *Journal of Consumer Research*, 12 (2), 200-13.

Oyserman, D., Coon, H.M., & Kemmelmeier, M. (2002). Rethinking individualism and collectivism: evaluation of theoretical assumptions and meta-analyses. *Psychological Bulletin*, 128, 3-72.

Parker, Philip M. (1997), *National Cultures of the World: A Statistical Reference*, Westport, CT: Greenwood Press.

Schwarz, Norbet and Gerald Clore (1983), "Mood, Misattribution, and Judgments of Well-Being: Informative and Directive Functions of Affective States," *Journal of Personality and Social Psychology*, 45 (3), 513-523.

Sobel, M. E. (1982). Asymptotic intervals for indirect effects in structural equations models. In S. Leinhart (Ed.), *Sociological methodology 1982* (pp.290-312). San Francisco: Jossey-Bass.

Trafimow, D., Triandis, H.C., & Goto, S.G. (1991). Some tests of the distinction between the private self and the collective self. *Journal of Personality and Social Psychology*, 60, 649-655.

When is a Salad Not a Salad? The Impact of Product Category on Perceived Nutritional Value

Caglar Irmak, University of South Carolina, USA
Beth Vallen, Loyola College, USA

EXTENDED ABSTRACT

The American marketplace has been inundated with "healthy" alternatives to "unhealthy" foods. For instance, smoothies are positioned as healthy alternatives to milkshakes and salads are suggested as replacements for burgers. While salads and smoothies sound like healthy options, objective nutritional information, such as caloric content and number of fat grams, might indicate that they are not really healthier choices. Yet when we do not have complete access to this information, it is hard to decipher the nutritional difference between a healthy option and its unhealthy counterpart. Instead, we may rely on cues to infer an item's nutritional value. Under certain conditions, however, using cues to infer the healthiness of food items may lead to increased consumption of unhealthy foods. For example, recent research demonstrated that when a fast-food restaurant claims to serve healthy food (e.g., Subway), consumers are more likely to underestimate the caloric content of main dishes and to choose higher-calorie side dishes, drinks, or desserts compared to when no such claims are made (e.g., McDonald's; Chandon and Wansink 2007). Essentially, the healthy claim associated with the restaurant creates a "health halo," such that all restaurant items are perceived as healthy, irrespective of their objective nutritional content.

In the present research, we demonstrate that the product category associated with a food item provides another cue that consumers use to infer the healthiness of the item. For instance, imagine that you are ordering dinner from a restaurant menu that presents the items under different category titles (e.g., pastas and salads). Our results suggest that you will perceive a food item that is presented in a relatively healthier food category (e.g., salad) to be healthier than a food item with identical ingredients that is presented in a relatively less healthy food category (e.g., pasta). Moreover, we show that these effects are more likely to be demonstrated by those who are more knowledgeable about nutrition (i.e., experts) because they are more likely to rely on category-based heuristics to form inferences about products (Sujan 1985; Sujan and Dekleva 1987). In four studies, we demonstrate that product category information may bias experts' perceptions of the nutritional value of food items, such that food items that belong to relatively healthy categories are perceived to be more nutritious than those that belong to less healthy categories. These perceptions of nutritional value, in turn, impact consumption behavior.

In the first two studies, participants were presented with a dish containing identical ingredients, but with different product category assignment as communicated by the item name (i.e., salad vs. pasta or veggie links vs. sausage links). They then evaluated the item's healthiness and nutritional value and responded to items assessing nutrition expertise. As expected, the results showed that while novices showed no difference in their nutrition perceptions of the items, experts perceived the items assigned to healthier categories (i.e., salad and veggie links) to be significantly healthier than the items assigned to less healthy categories (i.e., pasta and sausage links).

In the third study we sought to investigate the proposed categorization process underlying the effects observed in the prior studies. To do so, we manipulated the processing approach of study participants. After providing participants with the same pasta-salad pair used in study 1, half of the participants engaged in an effortful, piecemeal process by estimating the healthiness of each ingredient of the food item before evaluating its overall healthiness. The remaining participants engaged in a holistic, categorization process by estimating the healthiness of each ingredient after they evaluated the overall healthiness of the food item. In line with the categorization explanation, the results show that when individuals first estimated healthiness of each ingredient (i.e., piecemeal process), neither novices nor experts perceived any significant difference between the healthiness of the two items. On the other hand, experts–but not novices–considered the salad to be healthier than pasta when they evaluated perceived healthiness of the item before its ingredients (i.e., categorization process).

In our final study, we explored the impact of food category assignment on various product inferences as well as consumption quantity. We provided participants of this study with a sample of an actual confectionary product identified as either "Candy Chews" or "Fruit Chews" and measured perceptions of nutritional value, attitude towards, and purchase likelihood of the item, as well as the amount of the product consumed. As in prior studies, when the category name was associated with healthfulness (i.e., Fruit Chews), experts perceived the item to be healthier. They also expressed more positive attitudes towards and showed stronger intentions to purchase the item. Importantly, these inferences translated into behavior; nutrition experts consumed greater quantities of the item when it was positioned as a member of a relatively healthy category. Novices, on the other hand, did not demonstrate these category-based inferences nor was their consumption influenced by the category manipulation.

Together, these findings demonstrate that perceptions of the nutritional value of food items with identical ingredients can differ depending on the food category in which they are presented. For experts, food items that belong to relatively healthy categories are assumed to be more nutritious, are liked more, and are more likely to be purchased than items with identical ingredients that belong to less healthy categories. In turn, these items are likely to be consumed in greater quantities. Novices, on the other hand, are far less likely to rely on category-based heuristics. Ironically, this suggests that the knowledge that was acquired to make informed decisions may accentuate the impact of health halos created by food categories. These findings contribute to the emerging body of literature that examines cues that consumers utilize to infer unknown information about food items (e.g., Chandon and Wansink 2007) by showing that product category information–which might simply be provided by the item's name– can drive health perceptions of food items and resulting consumption behavior.

REFERENCES

Chandon, Pierre and Brian Wansink (2007), "The Biasing Health Halos of Fast-Food Restaurant Health Claims: Lower Calorie Estimates and Higher Side-Dish Consumption Intentions," *Journal of Consumer Research*, 34(3), 301-314.

Sujan, Mita (1985), "Consumer Knowledge: Effects on Evaluation Strategies Mediating Consumer Judgments," *Journal of Consumer Research*, 12, June, 31-46.

Sujan, Mita and Christine Dekleva (1987), "Product Categorization and Inference Making: Some Implications for Comparative Advertising," *Journal of Consumer Research*, 14(3), December, 372-378.

Inferred Informational Cascades and Their Effects on Choice: The Relative Stocking Level Effect

Jeffrey R. Parker, Columbia University, USA
Donald R. Lehmann, Columbia University, USA

EXTENDED ABSTRACT

Consumers use multiple heuristics in making (sometimes non-optimal) choices. Here we introduce another heuristic, the *relative-stocking-level* effect, which consumers use to choose among similar alternatives. Specifically, we present evidence that consumers use the relative stocking level of available alternatives to infer the popularity of those alternatives and then use the inferred popularity as an input in making choices, leading them to select the less stocked alternative. We suggest that even though consumers do not directly observe the behavior(s) of their predecessors, they use stocking levels to infer it, ignoring other information (e.g., brand and quality) and potential extremeness aversion; a process we call an *inferred informational cascade*. In other words, this paper investigates whether informational cascades manifest themselves in the absence of direct observation.

Participants in four studies made choices between intra-category products, each of which was stocked at a different level. A separate study (not reported here) also examined the effect of different stocking levels when options were presented individually and found no evidence of a stocking level effect, demonstrating that it is a relative effect and, hence, not the same as a scarcity effect.

In study 1, participants chose items from three product categories (white wine, red wine and cheese) where two similar alternatives were available. Across categories, 79% of respondents chose the lesser-stocked alternative. Importantly, of those choosing the lesser-stocked alternative, 52% reported perceived popularity of that alternative as the main reason for their choice, supporting the inferred informational cascade explanation. Interestingly, participants choosing the more-stocked alternative often gave product appearance (the label) as an explanation which, since items here (and in the other studies) were rotated (balanced) in the treatments, seems to have been a convenient, and possibly post hoc, rationalization.

Study 2 extended study 1 by increasing the number of alternatives per category. Participants were asked to choose one white wine and one red wine with each category offering three alternatives stocked at three distinct levels. Replicating the results of study 1, participants preferred products that were relatively less stocked. Across categories, 53% of participants chose the least-stocked alternative, 32% chose the mid-stocked alternative and 15% chose the most-stocked alternative. A binary logistic regression revealed that stocking level was a significant predictor of preference. As in study 1, participants choosing the lesser-stocked alternatives largely indicated they had done so based on perceived popularity. Importantly, participants in this study most frequently chose the extreme option, counter to what extremeness aversion would predict.

Neither of the first two studies provided participants with information about the products other than their stocking levels and a small picture of the items. Such information could potentially reduce or eliminate the relative-stocking-level effect. Therefore, in study 3, brand information was introduced. Participants were asked to choose from six different product categories (paper towels, toilet paper, air freshener, shampoo, deodorant and spray cleaner). To simplify administration, the brands were combined into two equally appealing groups of products. One brand from each category was placed in Group A, and one in Group B. For example, the two brands of paper towels were Scott (which was placed in Group A) and Bounty (which was placed in group B). Pretests indicated that the brands in each group were equally recognizable. As in study 1, all choices were binary. Participants made their choices either from sets where both products were equally stocked (these choices were used to determine baseline preferences in each category) or where one product was less stocked. Across brands, 53% of participants preferred Group B products when both products were equally stocked, which is not significantly different from chance. However, when the brands in Group A were less stocked, they were preferred by 60% of the participants. Similarly, when the brands from Group B were less stocked, they were preferred by 63% of the participants. Overall, lesser-stocked brands were preferred by 62% of the participants. Therefore, the relative-stocking-level effect still exists in the presence of well-known brands.

Finally, in study 4 we directly tested whether participants were making quality inferences based on perceived popularity. If participants make a quality inference, and use this information to make a selection, this would suggest our explanation of inferred informational cascades is at best an indirect effect (with stocking leading to a popularity inference which, in turn, leads to a quality inference). Thus, each participant was provided a quality rating for each of the alternatives. If a quality inference is driving the relative-stocking-level effect, then participants' choices should be random when the products are of equal quality. However, even when both alternatives were of equal quality, 78% to 85% chose the lesser-stocked product, replicating the findings of study 1. When the lesser-stocked alternative was of higher quality, 93% of participants preferred it. Most interestingly, when the lesser-stocked alternative was of lower quality, 27% of participants still preferred the lesser-stocked alternative. Thus, the relative-stocking-level effect is not dependent on quality inferences.

Taken together, the four studies present evidence that a relative-stocking-level effect exists and that it is robust in the face of extremeness aversion and brand and quality information. That participants choose the alternative they believe to be most popular, and do so despite information suggesting this might be suboptimal, supports our contention of the presence of an inferred informational cascade.

This type of consumer behavior may have significant practical implications for managers such as optimal stocking quantity and restocking timing. Further, retailers could potentially use this information to direct customers to more profitable private labels. It also suggests consumer welfare may be decreased when consumers utilize the "relative-stocking-level" heuristic. Finally, our findings suggest that consumers do not have automatic negative reactions towards either the brand (e.g., "This brand must not be good if they don't keep it in stock.") or the store (e.g., "This store is disorganized.") when a product is not fully stocked. Instead, it seems that consumers find imperfect stocking levels to be positive information.

CAM: A Spreading Activation Network Model of Subcategory Positioning when Categorization Uncertainty is High

Joseph Lajos, INSEAD, France
Zsolt Katona, INSEAD, France
Amitava Chattopadhyay, INSEAD, France
Miklos Sarvary, INSEAD, France

EXTENDED ABSTRACT

In this era of digital convergence, consumers often encounter new, hybrid products that do not fit unambiguously into their existing mental categories. For example, when consumers encountered the Motorola Envoy, which would later be acknowledged as the first personal digital assistant (PDA), they had difficulty categorizing it, since it shared features with portable computers and organizers, yet was distinctly different from products in both categories (Keller, Sternthal, and Tybout 2002).

When consumers encounter a new product, such as the Envoy, which has features that differ significantly from existing categories, they respond by creating a new subcategory (e.g., the PDA subcategory) within their existing category structure for products (Sujan and Bettman 1989). If the new product could conceivably be placed into more than one category due to similarities (e.g., shared features) with several categories (i.e., categorization uncertainty is high; Gregan-Paxton et al. 2005), consumers must determine where to position the new subcategory. For example, upon encountering the Envoy, which shared features with both portable computers and personal organizers, consumers had to decide under which of these two categories to position the new PDA subcategory.

Understanding how consumers determine where to position a new subcategory is important, since new products, including really new products, are often derived from existing product categories (Goldenberg, Mazursky, and Solomon 1999). A recent example is Sony-Ericsson's Walkman phone, which also functions as an mp3 player, camera, pedometer, and organizer.

Furthermore, consumers' categorization decisions can have striking implications for firms. Research has shown that consumers use information contained in product categories to make inferences about the features, functions, and performance of new products, and to predict the retail store departments in which they will be stocked (Gregan-Paxton and Moreau 2003). Furthermore, the manner in which consumers categorize products affects their thoughts about, attitudes toward, and overall evaluations of these products (Moreau et al. 2001b; Sujan 1985; Sujan and Bettman 1989), their memory for product features (Gregan-Paxton and Moreau 2003; Sujan and Bettman 1989), and their likelihood of recalling and subsequently choosing the products in memory-based choice (Nedungadi 1990).

In this paper, we address the question of how consumers position subcategories for new products when categorization uncertainty is high by developing and testing an analytical process model. The Category Activation Model (CAM) differs from extant models of categorization in two important ways. First, whereas extant models primarily seek to describe how category knowledge is represented and to predict into which categories objects will be placed, the goal of the CAM is to predict where entire new subcategories will be positioned. Second, whereas extant models are largely based on the notion of selective attention, the CAM relies on category accessibility.

We build on previous research that shows that priming a category increases its accessibility and subsequent use (Herr 1986, 1989). We assume that when a category is accessed (e.g., by thinking about a product in the category), some of the resulting activation remains with the category and the rest spreads through the entire network. Furthermore, we assume that the increase in activation that results when a category is accessed increases the probability that a new subcategory will be positioned under it. Combining these assumptions, it follows that if we accurately describe the process by which activation spreads through the network, we should be able to predict the probability that a new subcategory will be positioned at any relevant location within the category structure. We show that these probabilities depend on the existing link structure, since these links determine how activation spreads through the network. Our model leads to the following hypothesis:

H: The probability that an individual will position a new category subordinate to a particular category i is proportional to the relative number of categories that are already subordinate to i.

We find support for this hypothesis in three studies. First, in a pilot study, we performed a preliminary test of our hypothesis by asking participants to build category structures for 100 products and then examining some properties of the structures that they formed. The results indicated that these structures were congruent with the CAM, and that those participants who spent less time on the task were more likely to rely on the heuristic represented by the CAM.

In study 1, we formally tested our hypothesis in the context of a new, hybrid product, and also tested our proposition that accessibility underlies the effect. In the experiment, we varied the relative number of subcategories that were subordinate to two parent categories. The results indicated that, following a neutral prime, participants were more likely to position a new subcategory for a new, hybrid product under the parent category to which more subcategories were connected. Furthermore, we found that first priming the parent category to which fewer subcategories were connected using a proofreading task eliminated this effect, providing evidence in favor of accessibility.

However, one could argue that the results of study 1 were driven by differences in perceived category breadth or abstraction, rather than accessibility, across the subcategory numerosity conditions. In study 2, we ruled out perceived breadth as an alternative explanation by manipulating subcategory numerosity and the breadth of each category independently. The results indicate that subcategory numerosity influenced participants' positioning of a new subcategory, above and beyond any effect attributable to differences in category breadth.

The CAM provides a means for firms to assess how consumers are likely to position a subcategory for a new product. A firm could then use this prediction to estimate the level of marketing effort that would be needed to alter or support the manner in which consumers position the subcategory, to the firm's advantage. Furthermore, the CAM suggests one means by which such influence might be exerted. Since, based on our findings, consumers will be more likely to position a new subcategory within a category that already has many subcategories, it follows that advertising that prompts consumers to think about several subcategories within a particular domain should increase the likelihood that they will position the new subcategory within that domain.

REFERENCES

Alba, Joseph W. and Amitava Chattopadhyay (1985), "Reducing the Size of the Retrieval Set: The Effects of Context and Part-Category Cues on the Recall of Competing Brands," *Journal of Marketing Research*, 22 (August), 340-349.

Alba, Joseph W. and J. Wesley Hutchinson (1987), "Dimensions of Consumer Expertise," *Journal of Consumer Research*, 13 (March), 411-454.

Barabasi, Albert-Laszlo and Reka Zsuzsanna Albert (1999), "Emergence of Scaling in Random Networks," *Science*, 286, 509-512.

_____ (2002), "Statistical Mechanics of Complex Networks," *Reviews of Modern Physics*, 74 (1) 47-96.

Barsalou, Lawrence W. (1983), "Ad Hoc Categories," *Memory and Cognition*, 11, 211-227.

_____ (1985), "Ideals, Central Tendency, and Frequency of Instantiation as Determinants of Graded Structure in Categories," *Journal of Experimental Psychology: Learning, Memory, and Cognition*, 11, 629-649.

_____ (1987), "The Instability of Graded Structure in Concepts," in *Concepts and Conceptual Development: Ecological and Intellectual Factors in Categorization*, ed. Ulric Neisser, New York, NY: Cambridge University Press, 101-140.

_____ (1991), "Deriving Categories to Achieve Goals" in *The Psychology of Learning and Motivation: Advances in Research and Theory*, Vol. 27, ed. G. H. Bower, New York, NY: Academic Press, 1-64.

_____ (1992), *Cognitive Psychology: An Overview for Cognitive Scientists*. Hillsdale, NJ: Erlbaum.

Cohen, Jacob (1988), *Statistical Power Analysis for the Behavioral Sciences*, 2nd ed., New York: Academic Press.

Cohen, Joel B. (1982), "The Role of Affect in Categorization: Towards a Reconsideration of the Concept of Attitude," in *Advances in Consumer Research*, Vol. 9, ed. Andrew A. Mitchell, Ann Arbor, MI: Association for Consumer Research, 94-100.

Cohen, Joel B. and Kunal Basu (1987), "Alternative Models of Categorization," *Journal of Consumer Research*, 13 (March), 455-472.

Coley, John D., Douglas L. Medin, and Scott Atran (1997), "Does Rank have its Privilege? Inductive Inference within Folkbiological Taxonomies," *Cognition*, 64, 73-112.

Fiske, Susan T. (1982), "Schema-Triggered Affect: Applications to Social Perception," in *Affect and Cognition: The 17th Annual Carnegie Symposium on Cognition*, ed. Margaret S. Clark and Susan T. Fiske, Hillsdale, NJ: Erlbaum, 55-78.

Fiske, Susan T. and Mark A. Pavelchak (1986), "Category-Based Versus Piecemeal-Based Affective Responses: Developments in Schema-Triggered Affect," in *The Handbook of Motivation and Cognition: Foundations of Social Behavior*, ed. Richard M. Sorrentiono and E. Tory Higgins, New York: Guilford Press.

Goldenberg, Jacob, David Mazursky, and Sorin Solomon (1999), "Toward Identifying the Inventive Templates of New Products: A Channeled Ideation Approach," *Journal of Marketing Research*, 36 (May), 200-210.

Gregan-Paxton, Jennifer, Steve Hoeffler, and Min Zhao (2005), "When Categorization is Ambiguous: Factors that Facilitate the Use of a Multiple Category Inference Strategy," *Journal of Consumer Psychology*, 15 (2), 127-140.

Gregan-Paxton, Jennifer and Deborah Roedder John (1997), "Consumer Learning by Analogy: A Model of Internal Knowledge Transfer," *Journal of Consumer Research*, 24 (3), 266-284.

Gregan-Paxton, Jennifer and C. Page Moreau (2003), "How Do Consumers Transfer Existing Knowledge? A Comparison of Analogy and Categorization Effects," *Journal of Consumer Psychology*, 13 (4), 422-430.

Hamilton, David L. and Steven J. Sherman (1996), "Perceiving Persons and Groups," *Psychological Review*, 103 (2), 336-355.

Herr, Paul M. (1986), "Consequences of Priming: Judgment and Behavior," *Journal of Personality and Social Psychology*, 51 (6), 1106-1115.

_____ (1989), "Priming Price: Prior Knowledge and Context Effects," *Journal of Consumer Research*, 16 (June), 67-75.

Higgins, E. Tory, John A. Bargh, and Wendy Lombardi (1985), "Nature of Priming Effects on Categorization," *Journal of Experimental Psychology: Learning, Memory, and Cognition*, 11 (1), 59-69.

Higgins, E. Tory and Gillian A. King (1981), "Accessibility of Social Constructs: Information-Processing Consequences of Individual and Contextual Variability," in *Personality, Cognition, and Social Interaction*, ed. Nancy Cantor and John F. Kihlstrom, Hillsdale, NJ: Earlbaum, 69-121.

Higgins, E. Tory, William S. Rholes, and Carl R. Jones (1977), "Category Accessibility and Impression Formation," *Journal of Experimental Social Psychology*, 13 (March), 141-154.

Keller, Kevin Lane, Brian Sternthal, and Alice Tybout (2002), "Three Questions You Need to Ask About Your Brand," *Harvard Business Review*, 80 (9), 80-6.

Kruschke, John K. (1992), "ALCOVE: An Exemplar-Based Connectionist Model of Category Learning," *Psychological Review*, 99 (1), 22-44.

Langville, Amy N. and Carl D. Meyer (2004), "Deeper inside Page Rank", *Internet Mathematics*, 1 (3), 335-400.

Malt, Barbara C., Brian Ross, and George Murphy (1995), "Predicting Features for Members if Natural Categories when Categorization is Uncertain," *Journal of Experimental Psychology: Learning, Memory, and Cognition*, 21 (3), 646-661.

Markman, Ellen M. (1989), *Categorization and Naming in Children: Problems of Induction*. Cambridge, MA: MIT Press.

Medin, Douglas L. and Stephen M. Edelson (1988), "Problem Structure and the Use of Base-Rate Information from Experience," *Journal of Experimental Psychology: General*, 117, 68-85.

Medin, Douglas L., Elizabeth B. Lynch, John D. Coley, and Scott Atran (1997), "Categorization and Reasoning Among Tree Experts: Do All Roads Lead to Rome?" *Cognitive Psychology*, 32, 49-96.

Medin, Douglas L. and Marguerite M. Schaffer (1978), "Context Theory of Classification," *Psychological Review*, 85 (May), 207-238.

Medin, Douglas L. and Edward E. Smith (1984), "Concepts and Concept Formation," *Annual Review of Psychology*, 35, 113-138.

Mervis, Carolyn B. and Eleanor Rosch (1981), "Categorization of Natural Objects," *Annual Review of Psychology*, 32, 89-115.

Meyers-Levy, Joan and Alice M. Tybout (1989), "Schema Congruity as a Basis for Product Evaluation," *Journal of Consumer Research*, 16 (June), 9-54.

Minda, John Paul and J. David Smith (2000), "Prototypes in Category Learning: The Effects of Category Size, Category Structure, and Stimulus Complexity," *Journal of Experimental Psychology: Learning, Memory, and Cognition*, 27, 775-799.

Moreau, C. Page, Donald R. Lehmann, and Arthur B. Markman (2001a), "Entrenched Knowledge Structures and Consumer Response to New Products," *Journal of Marketing Research*, 38 (February), 14-29.

Moreau, C. Page, Arthur B. Markman, and Donald R. Lehmann (2001b), "What Is It?' Categorization Flexibility and Consumers' Responses to Really New Products," *Journal of Consumer Research*, 27 (March), 489-498.

Mori, Tamas F. (2002), "On Random Trees," *Studia Scientiarum Mathematicarum Hungarica*, 39, 143-155.

Murphy, George and Brian Ross (1994), "Predictions from Uncertain Categorizations," *Cognitive Psychology*, 27 (October), 148-193.

_____ (1999), "Induction with Cross-Classified Categories," *Memory and Cognition*, 27, 1024-1041.

Murphy, Gregory L. and Douglas L. Medin (1985), "The Role of Theories in Conceptual Coherence," *Psychological Review*, 92, 289-316.

Nedungadi, Prakash (1990), "Recall and Consumer Consideration Sets: Influencing Choice without Altering Brand Evaluations," *Journal of Consumer Research*, 17 (December), 263-76.

Nedungadi, Prakash, Amitava Chattopadhyay, and A. V. Muthukrishnan (2001), "Category Structure, Brand Recall, and Choice," *International Journal of Research in Marketing*, 18 (September), 191-202.

Nosofsky, Robert M. (1986), "Attention, Similarity, and the Identification-Categorization Relationship," *Journal of Experimental Psychology: General*, 115, 39-57.

Nosofsky, Robert M. and Thomas J. Palmeri (1997), "An Exemplar-Based Random Walk Model of Speeded Classification," *Psychological Review*, 104 (2), 266-300.

Nosofsky, Robert M., Thomas J. Palmeri, and Stephen C. McKinley (1994), "Rule-Plus-Exception Model of Classification Learning," *Psychological Review*, 101 (1), 53-79.

O'Sullivan, Chris S. and Francis T. Durso (1984), "Effect of Schema-Incongruent Information on Memory for Stereotypical Attitudes" *Journal of Personality and Social Psychology*, 47 (July), 55-70.

Rehder, Bob and Aaron B. Hoffman (2005), "Eye Tracking and Selective Attention in Category Learning," *Cognitive Psychology*, 51, 1-41.

Rosch, Eleanor (1978), "Principles of Categorization," in *Cognition and Categorization*, ed. Eleanor Rosch and Barbara B. Lloyd, Hillsdale, NJ: Erlbaum.

Rosch, Eleanor and Carolyn B. Mervis (1975), "Family Resemblances: Studies in the Internal Structure of Categories," *Cognitive Psychology*, 7, 573-605.

Rosch, Eleanor, Carolyn B. Mervis, Wayne D. Gray, David M. Johnson, and Penny Boyes-Braem (1976), "Basic Objects in Natural Categories," *Cognitive Psychology*, 8, 382-439.

Ross, Brian H. (1997), "The Use of Categories Affects Classification," *Journal of Memory and Language*, 37 (August), 240-267.

Ross, Brian H. and Gregory L. Murphy (1996), "Category-Based Predictions: Influence of Uncertainty and Feature Associations," *Journal of Experimental Psychology: Learning, Memory, and Cognition*, 22 (3), 736-753.

_____ (1999), "Food for Thought: Cross-Classification and Category Organization in a Complex Real-World Domain," *Cognitive Psychology*, 38, 495-553.

Shepard, Roger N. (1964), "Attention and the Metric Structure of the Stimulus Space," *Journal of Mathematical Psychology*, 1, 54-87.

Shepard, Roger N. and Jih-Jie Chang (1963), "Stimulus Generalization in the Learning of Classifications," *Journal of Experimental Psychology*, 65 (1), 94-102.

Shepard, Roger N., Carl I. Hovland, and Herbert M. Jenkins (1964), "Learning and Memorization of Classifications," *Psychological Monographs: General and Applied*, 75 (13), 1-41.

Smith, Edward E. and Douglas L. Medin (1981), *Categories and Concepts*. Cambridge, MA: Harvard University Press.

Smith, Edward.E., Andrea L. Patalano, and John Jonides (1998), "Alternative Strategies of Categorization," *Cognition*, 65, 167-196.

Smith, J. David and John Paul Minda (1998), "Prototypes in the Mist: The Early Epochs of Category Learning," *Journal of Experimental Psychology: Learning, Memory, and Cognition*, 24, 1411-1436.

Smythe, Robert T. and Hosam M. Mahmoud (1995), "A Survey of Recursive Trees," *Theoretical Probability and Mathematical Statistics*, 51, 1-27.

Srull, Thomas K. and Robert S. Wyer Jr. (1979), "The Role of Category Accessibility in the Interpretation of Information About Persons: Some Determinants and Implications," *Journal of Personality and Social Psychology*, 37 (10), 1660-1672.

Sujan, Mita (1985), "Consumer Knowledge: Effects on Evaluation Strategies Mediating Consumer Judgments," *Journal of Consumer Research*, 12 (June), 31-46.

Sujan, Mita and James R. Bettman (1989), "The Effects of Brand Positioning Strategies on Consumers' Brand and Category Perceptions: Some Insights from Schema Research," *Journal of Marketing Research*, 26 (November), 454-67.

Sujan, Mita and Christine Dekleva (1987), "Product Categorization and Inference Making: Some Implications for Comparative Advertising," *Journal of Consumer Research*, 14 (December), 372-378.

Taylor, Shelley E. (1981), "A Categorization Approach to Stereotyping," in *Cognitive Processes in Stereotyping and Intergroup Behavior*, ed. David L. Hamilton, Hillsdale, NJ: Erlbaum, 88-114.

Taylor, Shelley E. and Jennifer Crocker (1981), "Schematic Bases of Social Information Processing," in *Social Cognition: The Ontario Symposium*, Vol. 1, ed. E. Tory Higgins, C. Peter Herman, and Mark P. Zanna, Hillsdale, NJ: Erlbaum, 89-134.

Ward, Thomas B. (1995), "What's Old about New Ideas?" in *The Creative Cognition Approach*, ed. Steven M. Smith, Thomas B. Ward, and Ronald A. Fiske, Cambridge, MA: MIT Press, 157-78.

Weber, Renee and Jennifer Crocker (1983), "Cognitive Processes in the Revision of Stereotypic Beliefs," *Journal of Personality and Social Psychology*, 45 (November), 961-977.

Wyer, Robert S. Jr. (2007), "The Role of Knowledge Accessibility in Cognition and Behavior: Implications for Consumer Information Processing," in *Handbook of Consumer Psychology*, ed. Curtis Haugvedt, Frank R. Kardes, and Paul M. Herr, Mahwah, NJ: Erlbaum.

Wyer, Robert S. Jr. and Gabriel A. Radvansky (1999), "The Comprehension and Validation of Social Information," *Psychological Review*, 106 (1), 89-118.

Wyer, Robert S. Jr. and Thomas K. Srull (1981), "Category Accessibility: Some Theoretical and Empirical Issues Concerning the Processing of Social Stimulus Information," in *Social Cognition: The Ontario Symposium*, Vol. 1, ed. E. Tory Higgins, C. Peter Herman, and Mark P. Zanna, Hillsdale, NJ: Erlbaum,

_____ (1989), *Memory and Cognition in its Social Context*, Hillsdale, NJ: Erlbaum.

Yamauchi, Takashi and Arthur B. Markman (2000), "Inference Using Categories," *Journal of Experimental Psychology: Learning, Memory, and Cognition*, 26 (May), 776-795.

The Effect of Adding Features on Product Attractiveness: The Role of Product Perceived Congruity

Matteo De Angelis, Luiss Business School, Italy
Gregory S. Carpenter, Northwestern University, USA

EXTENDED ABSTRACT

Manufacturers offer consumers an ever-increasing number of features to differentiate products. Even simple devices often add a relatively broad range of features. Research shows positive (e.g., Carpenter et al. 1994) and negative effects of adding features (e.g., Mick and Fournier 1998). However, all studies assume that buyers make calculations based on perceived benefits and costs associated with additional features. Using the cost-benefit framework, scholars (Thompson et al. 2005; Gill 2008) show that the outcome of the calculation depends on the context of evaluation.

We propose that calculation buyers make, weighing benefits and costs, depends on more than simply the benefits, the costs, and the context; it depends on the cognitive resources applied. We argue that the resources consumers apply to the evaluation of the added features depend on the number of features, the similarity between the features and the brand, and the time frame over which consumers anticipate making their choice. Contrary to many scholars, we specifically examine the case of one versus more additional features, and explore the role of time frame in buyers' evaluation, examining how varying the future time horizon affects buyers' valuation of added features.

When valuing novel features, consumers may rely on their existing knowledge about the brand. Consumers confronting a brand with a small or large number of new features may react depending on their ability to resolve the apparent incongruities between new features and brand. The value they attach to the features may depend both on the number and their perceived brand congruence. When exposed to congruent features, consumers need not expend great cognitive effort to resolve incongruity. As a result, as the number of congruent features increases consumers should perceive an overall benefit from such an increase, increasing valuation. When exposed to moderately incongruent features, consumers face a dilemma, because resolving such incongruities requires effort, but this resolution leads to enhanced evaluation (Mandler 1982). However, this effect should exist for any small to modest number of features. Finally, resolution of highly incongruent features would require making undesired structural changes to the schema: the resources required exceed those available, leading to consumers not positively valuing the newly added features. This should be true for one or more extremely incongruent features.

Next we focus on the case in which new features' number is high. Previous analysis suggests that consumers avoid spending the resources necessary to resolve the incongruity when the number of incongruent features is high. But evidence suggests that consumers apply more resources in some instances. Then, what is the impact of added resources on the valuation of a large number of added features? When the features and the brand are highly congruent, applying additional resources should produce no difference, because features do not need extensive elaboration. The same is predicted when features are highly incongruent, because of the undesired, structural changes to the schema required. When features are moderately incongruent, things change. Encouraging people to think carefully about new stimuli results in resolution of moderate incongruity and greater preference (Meyers-Levy et al. 1994; Maoz and Tybout 2002). The nature of that effect will, however, vary with the resources applied to the task. With greater resources, buyers will more easily be able to reduce the incongruity,

leading to more detailed information processing and more positive evaluation.

Further, are the cases where a larger number of moderately incongruent features is preferred to a smaller number? One possible answer is provided by temporal construal theory, according to which the outcomes of increasing the number of moderately incongruent features may differ depending on the temporal frame of consumers' evaluation. Liberman and Trope (1998) argue that distant future events are more abstract, whereas near future events are more concrete. Hence, when focused on near future, consumers will develop a concrete construal of the product: as the number of incongruent features increases, perceived difficulty to reconcile more features with the current configuration of the product increases, and product evaluation should not increase. However, when considering a number of moderately incongruent features in a distant time frame, consumers will develop a more abstract construal of the product, focusing on higher-level considerations, related to the desirability to have more features. Consequently, product evaluation increases as the number of features increases.

We tested these predictions in three experiments. The first one focused on the interaction between number and congruity of features. Pre-tests identified the brand (Apple), the product (Ipod Nano), and three features for each of three congruity conditions (high, moderate, low). A 2x3 was employed, in which the number of new features (one, three) and their product congruity were manipulated. Subjects were asked to rate the attractiveness of the Ipod Nano compared to $200 cash. Results showed that product attractiveness increased as the number of congruent features increased, whereas it did not increase as the number of moderately or extremely incongruent features increased.

The second study was a 2x3 in which level of resources (high, low) and congruity were manipulated, whereas the number of features was set at three. We found a significant difference in evaluation between high and low resources only when features were moderately incongruent.

The third study was a 2 x 2 design, in which temporal construal (near, distant future) and number of new moderately incongruent features (one, three) were manipulated. An increase in product evaluation as the number of features increased was observed only in the distant future.

This contribution of this paper consists in suggesting that the perceived costs and benefits associated with adding multiple product features depend on the resources consumers are willing to devote to the evaluation and on the level of abstraction at which costs and benefits are considered. All else equal, greater number of features and greater perceived incongruence between features and brand increase the perceived cost of the features. But those same features are perceived to be less costly or more valuable when consumers devote more resources to considering them or when they do so at a higher level of abstraction.

REFERENCES

Anderson, Lynn R. and Martin Fishbein (1965), "Prediction of Attitude from the Number, Strength, and Evaluative Aspect of Beliefs about the Attitude Object: A Comparison of Summation and Congruity Theories", *Journal of Personality and Social Psychology*, 3 (September), 437-43.

Broniarczyk, Susan M. and Andrew D. Gershoff (1997), "Meaningless Differentiation Revisited", *Advances in Consumer Research*, 24, 223-228.

_____ and _____ (2003), "The Reciprocal Effects of Brand Equity and Trivial Attributes" *Journal of Marketing Research*, 40 (May), 161-175.

Brown, Christina L. and Gregory S. Carpenter (2000), "Why Is the Trivial Important? A Reasons-Based Account for the Effects of Trivial Attributes on Choice", *Journal of Consumer Research*, 26 (March), 372-385.

Burnkrant, R.E. (1976), "A Motivational Model of Information Processing Intensity" Journal of Consumer Research, 3 (1), 21-30.

Campbell, Margaret C. and Ronald C. Goodstein (2001), "The Moderating Effect of Perceived Risk on Consumers' Evaluations of Product Incongruity: Preference for the Norm", *Journal of Consumer Research*, 28, 439-449.

Carpenter, Gregory S., Rashi Glazer, and Kent Nakamoto (1994), "Meaningful Brands from Meaningless Differentiation: The Dependance on Irrelevant Attributes", *Journal of Marketing Research*, 31 (August), 339-350.

Eagly, Alice H. and Shelley Chaiken (1993), *The Psychology of Attitudes*, Orlando, FL: Harcourt Brace.

Farquhar, Peter H. (1994), "Strategic Challenges for Branding", *Marketing Management*, 3 (2), 8-15.

Fishbein, Martin (1963), "An Investigation of the Relationship between Beliefs about an Object and the Attitude toward that Object" *Human Relations*, 16 (August), 233-240.

Fiske, Susan T. and Shelley E. Taylor (1984), *Social Cognition*, New York: Random House.

Gill, Tripat (2008), "Convergent Products: What Functionalities Add More Value to the Base?", *Journal of Marketing*, 72, 46-62.

Gilovich, Thomas, Margaret Kerr, and Victoria Husted Medvec (1993), "Effect of Temporal Perspective on Subjective Confidence", *Journal of Personality and Social Psychology*, 64, 552-560.

Kraus, Paul and Gregory S. Carpenter (2005), "Brand Differentiation: The Role of the Context in Creating Valuable Differences" Working paper, Northwestern University.

Lancaster, Kevin J. (1971), *Consumer Demand: A New Approach*, New York: Columbia Univerisity Press.

Liberman, Nira and Yaacov Trope (1998), "The Role of Feasibility and Desirability Considerations in Near and Distant Future Decision: A Test of Temporal Construal Theory", *Journal of Personality and Social Psychology*, 75 (1), 5-18.

Maheswaran, Durairaj and Brian Sternthal (1990), "The Effect of Knowledge, Motivation, and Type of Message on Ad Processing and Product Judgments", *Journal of Consumer Research*, 17, 66-73.

Mandler, George (1982), "The Structure of Value: Accounting for Taste" in *Affect and Cognition: The 17th Annual Carnegie Symposium*, eds. Margaret S. Clark and Susan T. Fiske. Hillsdale, NJ: Lawrence Erlbaum Associates, 3-36.

Maoz, Eyal and Alice M. Tybout (2002), "The Moderating Role of the Involvement and Differentiation in the Evaluation of Brand Extensions", *Journal of Consumer Psychology*. 12, 119-31.

McGuire, William J. (1969), *The Nature of Attitudes and Attitude Change*, The Handbook of Social Psychology, Addison-Wesley Publishing Company.

Meyers-Levy, Joan and Alice M. Tybout (1989), "Schema Congruity as a Basis for Product Evaluation", *Journal of Consumer Research*, 16, 39-54.

_____, Therese A. Louie, and Mary T. Curren (1994), "How Does the Congruity of Brand Names Affect Evaluations of Brand Name Extensions?" *Journal of Applied Psychology*, 79, 46-53.

Mukherjee, Ashesh and Wayne D. Hoyer (2001), "The Effect of Novel Attributes on Product Evaluation", *Journal of Consumer Research*, 28 (December), 462-472.

Nisan, Mordecai (1972), "Dimension of Time in Relation to Choice Behavior and Achievement Orientation". *Journal of Personality and Social Psychology*, 21 (2), 175-82.

Nowlis, Stephen M. and Itamar Simonson (1996), "The Effect of New Product Features on Brand Choice", *Journal of Marketing Research*, 33 (February), 36-46.

Payne, John W. (1982), "Contingent Decision Behavior", *Psychological Bulletin*, 92 (September), 382-402.

Peracchio, Laura A. and Alice M. Tybout (1996), "The Moderating Role of Prior Knowledge in Schema-Based Product Evaluation", *Journal of Consumer Research*, 23, 177-192.

Petty, Richard E. and John T. Cacioppo (1981), *Attitude and Persuasion: Classic and Contemporary Approaches*, Dubuque, IA: Wm.C. Brown.

_____, and _____ (1984), "The effects of Involvement on Responses to Argument Quantity and Quality: Central and Peripheral Route to Persuasion", *Journal of Personality and Social Pshycology*, 46, 69-81.

_____, and _____ (1986), "The Elaboration Likelihood Model of Persuasion", in *Advances in Experimental Social Psychology*, 19, 123-205, ed. Berkowitz. Orlando, FL: Academic.

_____, _____ and David W. Schumann (1983), "Central and Peripheral Routes to Advertising Effectiveness: The Moderating Role of Involvement", *Journal of Consumer Research*, 10, 135-46.

Russo J. Edward, and Barbara A. Dosher (1983), "Strategies for Multiattribute Binary Choice", *Journal of Experimental Psychology: Learning, Memory and Cognition*, 9, 676-96.

Shafir, Eldar (1993), "Choosing versus Rejecting: Why Some Options are both Better and Worse than Others", *Memory and Cognition*, 21 (July), 546-556.

Stayman, Douglas M., Dana L. Alden, and Karen H. Smith (1992), "Some Effects of Schematic Processing on Consumer Expectations and Disconfirmation Judgments", *Journal of Consumer Research*, 19, 240-255.

Thompson, Debora V., Rebecca W. Hamilton, and Roland T. Rust (2005), "Feature Fatigue: When Product Capabilities Become Too Much of a Good Thing", *Journal of Marketing Research*, 42 (November), 431-442.

Trope, Yaacov (1986), "Identification and Inferential Processes in Dispositional Attribution", *Psychological Review*, 93, 239-257.

_____ (1989), "Levels of Inference in Dispositional Judgment", *Social Cognition*, 7, 296-314.

Vallacher, Robin R. Daniel M. and Wegner (1987), "What Do People Think They're Doing? Action Identification and Human Behavior", *Psychological Review*, 94, 3-15.

Wiklund, Michael E. (1994), *Usability in Practice: How Companies Develop User-Friendly Products*, San Diego: Academic Press.

Wilkie, William L. and Edgar A. Pessemier (1973), "Issues in Marketing's Use of Multi-Attribute Attitude Models", *Journal of Marketing Research*, 10 (November), 428-41.

Preference Fluency in Sequential Customization: The Unexpected Ease or Difficulty of Product Feature Decisions

Keith Wilcox, Baruch College, The City University of New York, USA
Sangyoung Song, Baruch College, The City University of New York, USA

EXTENDED ABSTRACT

Product customization has become so ubiquitous that companies in thousands of different categories tailor some aspect of their product designs to meet individual customer needs. To date, a significant amount of academic research on customization has focused on finding ways to develop better customization recommendations in order to create a stronger fit between firms' product offerings and customer preferences. Inherent in much of this research is the assumption that consumers have stable preferences that, once revealed, will allow managers to better anticipate customer needs and achieve a strong competitive advantage. However, other research on the construction of preferences suggests that customer preferences are not well-defined and that factors, which seem unrelated to consumer preferences, may influence product customization decisions. For example, individuals will retain more optional features while customizing a car when they are endowed with a fully-loaded model and asked to reject features from the car compared to when they begin with a base model car that requires them to add features (Park, Jun, and MacInnis 2000).

Building on recent research in sequential decision-making and processing fluency, this current research identifies preference fluency—the subjective feeling of ease or difficulty experienced while making a decision—as another factor that affects customer preference during product customization. Previous research on preference fluency (Novemsky et al. 2007) has found that increasing the difficulty of a decision, without changing the content of decision-makers' thoughts, can have a substantial impact on preference. However, the effect of fluency on judgment may have less to do with the level of difficulty, and more to do with whether there is a discrepancy between the experienced difficulty and an expected baseline value (Whittlesea and Williams 2000). Thus, increasing the difficulty of a decision may not lead to preference fluency if individuals expect the decision to be more difficult. Interestingly, this also suggests that altering individuals' expectations may lead to preference fluency without changing the actual difficulty of a decision.

We conceptualize product customization as a sequential decision-making process where individuals use their experiences from earlier decisions to form their expectations for subsequent decisions. We find that when the difficulty of subsequent customization decisions deviates from that of initial decisions, it creates a discrepancy between consumers' actual and expected decision difficulty. This, in turn, results in preference fluency and leads individuals to select more premium features during customization compared to when they perform a similar task where the level of difficulty is expected. Thus, we demonstrate that the sequential nature of customization processes can lead to preference fluency without changing the actual difficulty of consumers' decisions.

In study 1, we compare consumer preference for laptop computer features when there is low versus high discrepancy, which we manipulated via option framing. Respondents were presented with one of four configurations of a laptop computer (two high discrepancy and two low discrepancy configurations). In one high discrepancy configuration, respondents were endowed with an initial set of features that they were asked to reject before adding a subsequent feature set. In the other high discrepancy configuration, respondents were asked to add the initial feature set before rejecting the subsequent feature set. We then compared preferences in these configurations to those in two low discrepancy configurations where the framing of features remained constant (i.e., respondents only added or rejected the two feature sets). We found that participants' choices in the high discrepancy customization processes were consistent with enhanced or reduced preference fluency.

In study 2, we directly link discrepancy to preference by holding the framing of alternatives constant and manipulating expectations. To manipulate expectations, we provided respondents with consensus information about whether other people found the subsequent feature set to be easier than the initial feature set. The results provided additional support for our discrepancy theory. When people expected a decision to be more difficult than it actually was, the unexpected ease of the decision led to choices that were consistent with enhanced fluency. Similarly, when individuals expected a decision to be easier that it was, the unexpected difficulty of the decision resulted in choices that were consistent with reduced fluency.

This paper contributes to our understanding of preference fluency in decision-making. While previous research has shown that preference fluency will arise when the difficulty of a decision increases, we demonstrated that preference fluency is not only determined by the difficulty of the decision, but by the extent to which it deviates from individuals' expectations. We believe these findings have important managerial implications as well. Previous research has suggested that endowing consumers with a premium version of a product may be the managerially optimal solution because they will retain more higher-priced, higher-performance features compared to the basic model (Park et al. 2000). However, it may be difficult to implement this idea in practice since the higher initial price of the premium model is likely to decrease the likelihood that consumers will consider that model. This paper demonstrates that individuals will select as many (and in some cases more) higher-priced, higher-performance features as the premium version when they are initially endowed with a mid-priced, standard version, which may be a more attractive option for customization.

REFERENCES

Novemsky, Nathan, Ravi Dhar, Norbert Schwarz and Itamar Simonson (2007), "Preference Fluency in Choice," *Journal of Marketing Research*, 44 (3), 347-356.

Park, C. Whan, Sung Youl Jun and Deborah J. MacInnis (2000), "Choosing What I Want Versus Rejecting What I Do Not Want: An Application of Decision Framing to Product Option Choice Decisions," *Journal of Marketing Research*, 37 (2), 187-202.

Whittlesea, Bruce W. A. and Lisa D. Williams (2000), "The Source of Feelings of Familiarity: The Discrepancy-Attribution Hypothesis," *Journal of Experimental Psychology: Learning, Memory, and Cognition*, 26 (3), 547-565.

Effects of Consumer Co-Production on Perceived Authenticity of Consumption Experience and Input Product

Magne Supphellen, Norwegian School of Economics and Business Administration, Norway
Sigurd V. Troye, Norwegian School of Economics and Business Administration, Norway

EXTENDED ABSTRACT

In two studies we examine the effects of *prosumption* (Toffler 1980; Xie, Bagozzi, and Troye 2008) on the perceived authenticity of a food product (taste and input product). Prosumption (*production* + con*sumption*) is "value creation activities undertaken by the consumer that result in the production of products they eventually consume and that become their consumption experiences" (Xie et al. 2008, p. 110). We suggest that subjective feelings of authenticity are stimulated when consumers actively participate in the value-creation process (prepare food) and that this sense of authenticity transfers to the outcome (the taste of food) and the input product (a dinner toolkit). It is further suggested that stronger perceptions of authenticity are obtained when consumers are highly involved with the prosumption domain (cooking). Specifically, we tested the following hypotheses:

H1: Consumer prosumption has a positive effect on outcome authenticity, i.e. self-produced outcomes will be perceived as more authentic than ready-made solutions of comparable quality

H2: Consumer prosumption has a positive effect on perceived authenticity of the input product

H3: The positive effects of consumer prosumption on perceived authenticity of outcomes (H1) and input product (H2) will be more pronounced for consumers who are highly involved in the prosumption domain compared to those who are less involved.

Study 1: Effects of Real Prosumption

Participants and Design

A professional research agency recruited subjects randomly from a Scandinavian city (n=98; 52.4 percent females, mean age: 33). All participants were users of the focal product category (Asian food). The study used a 2 (Low prosumption/High prosumption) by 2(Low involvement/High involvement) between-subjects design. The product was a Tikka Masala dinner toolkit.

Stimuli, procedure and measures. The experiment took place in a laboratory kitchen with 8 pairs of ovens. In the Low Prosumption condition (n=47), the food was ready-made and subjects only heated and stirred the food. In the High-Prosumption condition (n=51), subjects were asked to fry meat and prepare the meal as prescribed on the product package (the package contained coco milk and dehydrated sauce and rice).

Before tasting the food, subjects filled in a small booklet of measures on perceived prosumption level (manipulation check) and demographic questions in an adjacent room. While subjects filled in this questionnaire, their casseroles were secretly swapped with food prepared by our chef. Subjects were let to believe that they were going to taste the food they had prepared themselves. Next, subjects were instructed to taste the food.

After the taste session, subjects responded to a questionnaire with measures of outcome and input authenticity and prosumption domain involvement. Outcome- and input authenticity were measured on two seven-point semantic differential scales (not at all authentic–very authentic; not really Indian–really Indian). Product domain involvement was measured by three items on seven-point scales.

Results of study 1

Manipulation checks. The manipulation of prosumption was successful ($F(1,82)=5.679$, $M_{\text{high prosumption}}=3.492$ vs $M_{\text{low prosumption}}=2.881$, p<.05).

Test of hypotheses. In line with H1, we find that subjects who prepared the dish themselves, rate the taste as more authentic than subjects who tasted ready-made food ($M_{\text{HighPros}}=4.66$ vs $M_{\text{LowPros}}=4.37$, $F(1, 81)=3.93$, $p=.051$). A similar, but even stronger effect is observed for authenticity of the input product (the Tikka Masala toolkit), lending support to H2 ($M_{\text{HighPros}}=4.76$ vs $M_{\text{LowPros}}=4.14$, $F(1, 81)=4.86$, $p=.00$). Also, the Prosumption level x Domain involvement interaction is significant for both taste authenticity ($F(1, 81)=11.83$, $p=.00$) and product authenticity ($F(1, 81)=4.43$, $p=.04$). The patterns of means and the results of contrast analyses are consistent with H3 for both variables.

Study 2

Participation involves three aspects that may partly determine perceived authenticity of the outcome. First, the prosumer gains insight into how the dish is made. Second, it allows an association between the self and the outcome. Third, what is self-made is also hand-made. In study two we used a scenario manipulation to assess whether "self-made" had an effect over and beyond the effect of the outcome being "hand made".

Participants and Design

Subjects were 240 bachelor students in an introductory marketing course. Two subjects did not use Asian food and were removed from the analyses. In line with previous research (Bendapudi and Leone 2003), prosumption was manipulated by means of scenarios. All scenarios focused on the same product as in study 1 and described a situation in which friends were expected to visit in 90 minutes. Three scenarios described three different prosumption conditions: 1) food purchased from a firm specializing in delivery of fast food (low prosumption), 2) food prepared by a friend (handmade, low prosumption), or 3) food prepared by the subject (high prosumption). After reading a scenario, subjects tasted the food (prepared in the same way as in study 1) and responded to a questionnaire with the same measures as in study 1.

Results Study 2 and conclusion

Manipulation checks. The prosumption manipulation was successful ($F(2,236)=7,631$, p<.05; $M_{\text{self-made}}=2.753$; $M_{\text{made by friend}}=2.259$, $M_{\text{purchased}}=2.162$, p <. 05 for both contrasts).

Test of hypotheses. The main effect of prosumption on outcome authenticity (taste authenticity) was not significant (F= 1,980, p=.139). Thus, H1 was not supported ($M_{\text{self-made}}=3.97$; $M_{\text{made by friend}}=3.65$, $M_{\text{purchased}}=3.80$). ANOVAs for the effects of prosumption on input product authenticity (H2) and the interaction between prosumption and domain involvement on outcome- and input authenticity (H3) revealed no significant findings (all p-values>.30).

To our knowledge, this research presents the first experimental evidence of positive effects of consumer co-production on authenticity perceptions. A methodological contribution is also offered to research on consumer prosumption. The scenario manipulation in study 2 was too weak to produce any of the effects observed in study 1. This finding suggests that real participation is needed in future experiments on the effects of prosumption.

REFERENCES

Bendapudi, Neeli and Robert P. Leone (2003), "Psychological Implications of Customer participation in Co-Production", *Journal of Marketing*, 67 (January), 14-28.

Toffler, Alvin (1980), *The Third Wave*, NY: William Collins Sons & Co. Ltd.

Xie, Chunyan, Richard P. Bagozzi and Sigurd V. Troye (2008), "Trying to Prosume: Toward a Theory of Consumers as Co-Creators of Value", *Journal of the Academy of Marketing Science*, 36, 109-122.

The Role of Attribute Importance in the Effect of Defaults on Choice: The Moderating Effect of Budget Range and Justification

Sehoon Park, Sogang University, Korea
Moon-Yong Kim, Korea Advanced Institute of Science and Technology, Korea

EXTENDED ABSTRACT

There are several product/service categories in which consumers have some control over the number, type, and configuration of options they select (Park, Jun, and MacInnis 2000). For instance, consumers are allowed to create their own consumable products by either starting with a basic product and adding desired components or starting with a fully loaded product and deleting undesired components (Levin, Schreiber, Lauriola, and Gaeth 2002; Park et al. 2000). That is, there are many everyday examples of additive (or upgrading) or subtractive (or downgrading) default designations for relatively less expensive nondurable products (e.g., pizzas) or more expensive products (e.g., PCs, automobiles): the default is the choice alternative a consumer automatically receives if he/she does not explicitly request otherwise (Brown and Krishna 2004, p. 530).

Much prior research concerning default effects has demonstrated that defaults can change the likelihood that a particular item is chosen (Brown and Krishna 2004; Johnson, Bellman, and Lohse 2002; Levin et al. 2002; Park et al. 2000). Especially loss aversion or an endowment-based account (cf. Kahneman, Knetch, and Thaler 1991) offers a clear explanation for why the strength of the default may vary according to which alternative receives the default designation, and thus it predicts that high (i.e., more expensive) defaults will have a stronger effect on choice than will low (i.e., less expensive) defaults (see Brown and Krishna 2004).

Tversky and Kahneman's reference-dependent model (1991) suggests that loss aversion may vary systematically across attributes. Among some of the determinants of the differences in loss aversion, it was demonstrated that attribute importance is a strong predictor of loss aversion (Johnson, Gächter, and Herrmann 2006). Given that default effects are typically described as a manifestation of loss aversion, thus, we proposed that the effect of the ordinal position of defaults (low vs. high) on choice differs depending on the importance of attributes that constitute the defaults.

In addition, recent research has identified critical moderators that help define the boundaries of loss aversion (Ariely, Huber, and Wertenbroch 2005; Camerer 2005; Novemsky and Kahneman 2005a, 2005b). Although there may be several pathways through mechanisms that underlie loss aversion, we proposed that consumers' budget range and justification for choice differentially affect the dual mechanisms that vary the degree of loss aversion (i.e., changes in cognitive perspective and emotional attachment) as suggested by Ariely et al. (2005), and thus they serve to moderate the effect of defaults on choice. Finally, we suggested the role of attribute importance in the low- or high-default condition that varies the differential effect of two extrinsic, contextual factors (i.e., budget range and justification) on the dual mechanisms that underlie loss aversion, which would, in turn, influence the effect of defaults on choice.

We tested our hypotheses in a series of three studies. We selected automobiles as the product category for these studies. A set of 10 product attributes was selected, five of which were rated as important or less important. Eighty-eight undergraduate students at a large university participated in study 1. Under both no financial constraint (i.e., wide budget range) and no justification (i.e., participants not instructed to provide reasons for their choice) conditions, one factor (i.e., the ordinal position of defaults: low vs. high) was manipulated across two experimental cells. To manipulate the

ordinal position of defaults, we followed the same manipulation established by Park et al. (2000). In the context of product attributes choice decisions, the participants were asked to either add desired product attributes to a base model (i.e., low-default condition) or delete undesired product attributes from a fully loaded model (i.e., high-default condition). The participants for study 2 consisted of 89 undergraduate students at a large university. Under both financial constraint (i.e., narrow budget range) and no justification condition, the ordinal position of defaults (low vs. high) was manipulated across two experimental cells as in study 1. The control group was the 88 respondents in two experimental cells from study 1. In study 3, a 2 x 2 between subjects design was used in the justification condition: the ordinal position of defaults (low vs. high) and budget range (narrow vs. wide). A total of 173 undergraduate students at a large university were randomly assigned to one of the four experimental conditions. The control group was the 177 respondents in four experimental cells from studies 1 and 2.

In study 1, it was demonstrated that under no financial (budgetary) constraint, there arises a positive effect of default designation (low vs. high) on choice. And, the positive effect of default designation on choice was shown to increase in proportion to the importance of attributes that constitute the defaults. That is, the difference in consumer choice outcomes between low- and high-default conditions was observed to be larger when important (vs. less important) attributes are added to (deleted from) a low (high) default.

Study 2 demonstrated the moderating role of budget range in the effect of defaults on choice: As the range of budget narrows, it was shown that choice outcomes decrease more greatly among consumers in the high-default condition than among consumers in the low-default condition. Also, it was found that the moderating role of budget range in the effect of defaults on choice arises when important attributes are added to (deleted from) a low (high) default, whereas it does not have a significant moderating role in the effect of defaults on choice when less important attributes are added to (deleted from) a low (high) default.

In study 3, we examined the moderating role of justification in the effect of defaults on choice. It was shown that justification increases the difference in consumer choice outcomes between low- and high-default conditions under no financial constraints (i.e., under the wide budget range), unlike under the narrow budget range. Also, it was revealed that when less important (vs. important) attributes are added to (deleted from) a low (high) default, justification plays a moderating role in the effect of defaults on choice under the wide budget range, unlike under the narrow budget range.

REFERENCES

Ariely, Dan, Joel Huber, and Klaus Wertenbroch (2005), "When Do Losses Loom Larger Than Gains?" *Journal of Marketing Research*, 42(2), 134-38.

Brown, Christina L. and Aradhna Krishna (2004), "The Skeptical Shopper: A Metacognitive Account for the Effects of Default Options on Choice," *Journal of Consumer Research*, 31(3), 529-39.

Camerer, Colin (2005), "Three Cheers-Psychological, Theoretical, Empirical-for-Loss Aversion," *Journal of Marketing Research*, 42(May), 129-33.

Johnson, Eric J., Steven Bellman, and Gerald L. Lohse (2002), "Defaults, Framing, and Privacy: Why Opting In≠Opting Out," *Marketing Letters*, 13(1), 5-15.

Johnson, Eric J., Simon Gächter, and Andreas Herrmann (2006), "Exploring the Nature of Loss Aversion," IZA Discussion Paper No. 2015, [available at http://ssrn.com/abstract =892336].

Kahneman, D., Jack Knetch, and Richard Thaler (1991), "The Endowment Effect, Loss Aversion, and Status Quo Bias," *Journal of Economic Perspectives*, 5, 193-206.

Levin, I. P., Schreiber, J., Lauriola, M., and Gäeth, G. J. (2002), "A Tale of Two Pizzas: Building Up from a Basic Product versus Scaling Down from a Fully Loaded Product," *Marketing Letters*, 13, 335-44.

Novemsky, Nathan and Daniel Kahneman (2005a), "The Boundaries of Loss Aversion," *Journal of Marketing Research*, 42(May), 119-28.

Novemsky, Nathan and Daniel Kahneman (2005b), "How Do Intentions Affect Loss Aversion?" *Journal of Marketing Research*, 139-40.

Park, C. Whan, Sung Youl Jun, and Deborah J. MacInnis (2000), "Choosing What I Want Versus Rejecting What I Do Not Want: An Application of Decision Framing to Product Option Choice Decisions," *Journal of Marketing Research*, 37(May), 187-202.

Tversky, Amos and Kahneman, Daniel (1991), "Loss Aversion in Riskless Choice: A Reference-Dependent Model," *The Quarterly Journal of Economics*, 106(4), 1039-61.

Understanding the Role of Materialism in the Endowment Effect

Inge Lens, Katholieke Universiteit Leuven, Belgium
Mario Pandelaere, Katholieke Universiteit Leuven, Belgium

EXTENDED ABSTRACT

People generally demand more money to give up an object in their possession, than they are willing to pay to obtain this object (Thaler 1980). This asymmetry between willingness to pay and willingness to accept is referred to as the 'endowment effect' (Kahneman, Knetsch, and Thaler 1990; Thaler 1980). It is widely assumed that the reluctance to exchange possessions observed in the endowment effect, can be explained in terms of loss aversion (Kahneman et al. 1990). The theory of loss aversion suggests that the positive experience of gaining an object cannot compensate for the pain of giving up a possession. As a result people are inclined to value possessions more than (monetary) alternatives of similar objective value (Kahneman and Tversky 1979; Tversky and Kahneman 1991). However, the same loss appears not to be as aversive for everyone at any time. Previous research revealed a number of moderators of the endowment effect (e.g., Liberman et al. 1999; Lin et al. 2006; Loewenstein and Issacharoff 1994; Strahilevitz and Loewenstein 1998). This paper aims to extend this line of research by proposing materialism as an additional moderator.

People who strongly endorse material values consider the acquisition of possessions as a central life-occupation, bringing forth happiness and success (Richins and Dawson 1992). Given the attachment of materialists to their possessions, we propose that materialistic 'sellers' are more reluctant to exchange endowments for money than less materialistic sellers, resulting in higher minimum selling prices (hypothesis 1). Next, we assume that materialistic 'buyers' are more willing to spend money on an object they don't possess, relative to buyers low on materialism (hypothesis 2). Finally, we assume that the influence of materialism is more pronounced for sellers than for buyers, suggesting that the endowment effect increases with increasing materialism (hypothesis 3).

To test the hypothesis that materialism moderates the endowment effect, one hundred eighty-seven students participated in a first study. Half of them were endowed with a coffee mug (sellers), the other half were not (buyers). Buyers stated a maximum buying price for the mug, whereas sellers reported their minimum selling price. Materialistic values were assessed with the Material Values Scale (Richins and Dawson 1992). The results suggest that materialistic sellers demand higher minimum prices than less materialistic sellers. No relationship between buying prices and materialism is found. Hypotheses 1 and 3 are thus supported, hypothesis 2 is not. A second experiment with 68 male students replicates these findings with more valuable endowments (six technologically innovative gadgets, e.g., an optical, wireless computer mouse). Additionally, two alternative explanations are ruled out. The impact of materialistic values on selling prices cannot be attributed to a higher desirability of the gadgets for materialistic relative to less materialistic sellers or to differences in affect between more and less materialistic participants. In line with Terror Management Theory (e.g. Solomon, Greenberg and Pyszczynski 2004) and empirical evidence that reminding consumers of their own mortality induces or reinforces materialistic behavior (e.g. Mandel and Heine 1999; Kasser and Sheldon 2000), we predict in a third experiment that an increased endowment effect will be observed after a mortality salience induction and we assume that this increase will be stronger for materialistic consumers than for less materialistic consumers. In this experiment we first measured levels of materialism of two

hundred eighty-two participants. Subsequently, we instructed half of the participants to write a short essay about their own death (experimental condition with death-related thoughts). Participants in the control condition wrote about a more neutral topic: their favorite music or a visit to the dentist. After a number of unrelated tasks, half of the participants in each condition stated their maximum buying price for a small gadget, the other half of the participants indicated their minimum selling price. The data again support the assumption that chronic levels of materialism moderate the endowment effect. Furthermore, evidence is found for the predicted three-way interaction between endowment condition (buyer-seller), mortality salience condition (death-related thoughts-neutral thoughts) and materialism. It appears that reminding participants of their own mortality results in an increased endowment effect, at least to the extent they endorsed material values prior to the mortality salience induction. These findings again support hypotheses 1 and 3. Similar to the previous studies, no influence of materialism on stated buying prices is found.

In sum, in two correlational studies and one experimental study we found that materialists demand higher prices for their endowments, relative to less materialistic individuals. Materialism, however, has no predictable impact on buying prices. These implications of materialism in the occurrence of the endowment effect enhance our insight in this extensively documented phenomenon, and, in doing so, advance our understanding of the (economic) consequences and the nature of materialism. Materialism has previously been associated with a near-sighted consumption pattern (Dittmar 2005; Watson 2003) and high aspirations for possessions and wealth (Kasser and Ryan 1996; Kasser and Sheldon 2000). However, our data suggest that materialists don't necessarily want to have everything at any cost. On the other hand, the endorsement of material values seems to motivate people to demand higher prices for their goods, even when cheap or rather unattractive commodities are traded. So far, research on the effect of materialism on consumer behavior has mainly focused on spending tendencies and intentions of prospective buyers, whereas this paper shows that materialism might as well have important implications for the supply-side of market relations (e.g., in second-hand markets like eBay).

The current paper has demonstrated a robust relationship between materialism and the endowment effect. Although the current paper did not focus on any underlying mechanism, it is likely that materialistic consumers experience more loss aversion, resulting in higher selling prices and an increased endowment effect. Future research may assess the validity of this hypothesis

REFERENCES

Dittmar, Helga (2005), "A New Look at "Compulsive Buying": Self Discrepancies and Materialistic Values as Predictors of Compulsive Buying Tendency," *Journal of Social and Clinical Psychology,* 24 (6), 832-59.

Kahneman, Daniel, Jack L. Knetsch, and Richard H. Thaler (1990), "Experimental Tests of the Endowment Effect and the Coase Theorem," *Journal of Political Economy,* 98 (6), 1325-48.

Kahneman, Daniel and Amos Tversky (1979), "Prospect Theory: An Analysis of Decision Under Risk," *Econometrica,* 47 (March), 263-91.

Kasser, Tim and Richard M. Ryan (1996), "Further Examining the American Dream: Differential Correlates of Intrinsic and Extrinsic Goals," *Personality and Social Psychology Bulletin*, 22 (March), 280-87.

Kasser, Tim and Kennon M. Sheldon (2000), "Of Wealth and Death: Materialism, Mortality Salience, and Consumption Behavior," *Psychological Science*, 11 (July), 348-51.

Liberman, Nira, Lorraine Chen Idson, Christopher J. Camacho, and E. Tory Higgins (1999), "Promotion and Prevention Choices Between Stability and Change," *Journal of Personality and Social Psychology*, 77 (6), 1135-45.

Lin, Chien-Huang, Shih-Chieh Chuang, Danny T. Koa, and Chaang-Yung Kung (2006), "The Role of Emotions in the Endowment Effect," *Journal of Economic Psychology*, 27 (4), 589-97.

Loewenstein, George and Samuel Issacharoff (1994), "Source Dependence in the Valuation of Objects," *Journal of Behavioral Decision Making*, 7 (3), 157-68.

Mandel, Naomi and Steven J. Heine (1999), "Terror Management and Marketing: He Who Dies With the Most Toys Wins," *Advances in Consumer Research*, 26, 527–32.

Richins, Marsha L. and Scott Dawson (1992), "A Consumer Values Orientation for Materialism and Its Measurement: Scale Development and Validation," *Journal of Consumer Research*, 19 (December), 303-16.

Solomon, Sheldon, Jeff Greenberg, and Thomas A. Pyszczynski (2004), "Lethal Consumption:

Death-denying Materialism," in *Psychology and Consumer Culture: The Struggle for a Good Life in a Materialistic World*, ed. Tim Kasser and Allen D. Kanner, Washington, DC: American Psychological Association, 127-46.

Strahilevitz, Michael A. and George Loewenstein (1998), "The Effect of Ownership History on the Valuation of Objects," *Journal of Consumer Research*, 25 (3), 276-89.

Thaler, Richard H. (1980), "Toward a Positive Theory of Consumer Choice," *Journal of Economic Behavior and Organization*, 1 (1), 39-60.

Tversky, Amos and Daniel Kahneman (1991), "Loss Aversion in Riskless Choice: A Reference-Dependent Model," *The Quarterly Journal of Economics*, 106 (4), 1039-61.

Watson, John J. (2003), "The Relationship of Materialism to Spending Tendencies, Saving, and Debt," *Journal of Economic Psychology*, 24 (6), 723-39.

Inclusion versus Exclusion: The Effect of Perceived Uncertainty on Screening Strategies

Rajani Ganesh Pillai, North Dakota State University, USA
Xin He, University of Central Florida, USA
Raj Echambadi, University of Central Florida, USA

EXTENDED ABSTRACT

Screening refers to the process that governs the admission of options into the choice set (Beach 1990; 1993). Extant literature notes that screening strategies play an important role in consumer decision making (Beach 1990, 1993; Payne, Bettman, and Johnson 1993). For example, research shows that the type of screening strategy employed influences the composition of the consideration set (Levin, Huneke, and Jasper 2000; Yaniv and Schul 1997, 2000), and impacts the final choice and purchase likelihood as well (Chakravarti, Janiszewski, and Ulkumen 2006; Levin et al. 2002; Park, Jun, and MacInnis 2000).

Consumers typically use two types of strategies in screening: an exclusion strategy wherein alternatives not worthy of further consideration are eliminated, and an inclusion strategy wherein attractive alternatives are selected for additional evaluation (Yaniv and Schul 1997; 2000). While prior literature has predominantly focused on the consequences of the two screening strategies, such as the characteristics of the consideration set (Yaniv and Schul 1997, 2000) or final choice (Park, Jun, and MacInnis 2000; Shafir 1993), little attention has been devoted to the antecedents of screening strategies. We do so here. Specifically, we argue that perceived uncertainty has a systematic influence on the preference of screening strategies, such that consumers with high perceived uncertainty are more likely to adopt an exclusion strategy whereas those with low perceived uncertainty are more likely to employ an inclusion strategy.

Prior research shows that consumers frequently experience uncertainty in decision making, and such uncertainties arise from multiple sources: from not knowing the potential outcomes of the options, the individual's intrinsic preferences, or the attributes and decision rules that are relevant to the task at hand (Simonson 1989; Urbany, Dickson, and Wilkie 1989). The theoretical underpinnings of the proposed relationship between perceived uncertainty and screening strategy are drawn from the literatures on consumer learning (c.f. Alba and Hutchinson 1987; Johnson and Russo 1984) as well as probabilistic reasoning (c.f. Tversky and Kahneman 1974). Drawing from and building upon these two streams of literature, we suggest that consumers high in uncertainty are more likely to use exclusion screening strategies because exclusion is more likely to increase the perceived accuracy in decision making.

Empirical Studies

We test our theoretical hypotheses in two separate studies. In Experiment 1 (n=126), we demonstrate the effect of perceived uncertainty on screening strategies using a 2(uncertainty) x 2 (task complexity) between-subjects design. We manipulated task complexity in order to rule out an alternate explanation. Uncertainty was manipulated by varying the clarity of preferences and familiarity with the product category (Urbany, Dickson, and Wilkie 1989) while task complexity was manipulated by varying the number of alternatives available to choose from (Payne, Bettman and Johnson 1993). Results indicated that participants who were highly uncertain were more likely to prefer exclusion screening strategy. We also examined the underlying psychological process through the mediation analysis of perceived accuracy. Results of the mediation analysis (Baron and Kenny 1986) indicate strong support for the mediating role of perceived accuracy of the screening strategy as opposed to effort savings. Finally, in Study 2, we seek to demonstrate the external validity of our findings (Winer 1999) by analyzing the verbal protocols from the popular TV game show "*Who Wants to be a Millionaire?*" Verbal protocols from twenty-four shows were coded following Ericsson and Simon (1993) and analyzed using various (OLS, fixed effects regression, Logit, and mixed-Logit) models. Results corroborates our experimental findings—contestants high in uncertainty were more likely to adopt exclusion screening strategies whereas those contestants low in uncertainty were more inclined to employ inclusion strategies.

Discussion

This paper highlights the important role of perceived uncertainty in consumer decision making. It not only influences final choice but also the specific screening strategy used in prechoice screening. The consistent pattern of results using different methodologies (experiment and verbal protocol analysis), samples (students and adult contestants), decision contexts (apartment rental and TV game show), and models for analysis (OLS, fixed effects regression models, Logit, and mixed-Logit models) lend robustness to our findings. Further, we show that the preference of screening strategy is mainly driven by accuracy considerations rather than effort savings, a finding consistent with the idea that screening improves quality of decisions by preventing bad options from being considered for choice (Beach 1990, 1993). These findings have important implications in a wide variety of decision contexts like choosing among investment alternatives or medical procedures, where uncertainty is an inherent component of the decision process, and where the final choice carries not only lasting but often irrevocable consequences. We hope that future research will continue to examine inclusion and exclusion strategies and help consumers make informed decisions through a better understanding of the underlying screening process.

REFERENCES

Alba, Joseph W. and J. Wesley Hutchinson (1987), "Dimensions of Consumer Expertise," *Journal of Consumer Research*, 13 (March), 411-54.

Baron, Reuben M. and David Kenny (1986), "The Moderator-Mediator Variable Distinction in Social Psychological Research: Conceptual, Strategic, and Statistical Considerations," *Journal of Personality and Social Psychology*, 51 (December), 1173-82.

Beach, Lee R. (1990), *Image Theory: Decision Making in Personal and Organizational Contexts*. Chichester: Wiley.

Beach, Lee R. (1993), "Broadening the Definition of Decision Making: The Role of Prechoice Screening of Options," *Psychological Science*, 4 (July), 215-20.

Chakravarti, Amitav, Chris Janiszewski, and Gulden Ulkumen (2006), "The Neglect of Prescreening Information," *Journal of Marketing Research*, 43 (November), 642-53.

Ericsson, Anders A. and Herbert A. Simon (1993), *Protocol Analysis: Verbal Reports as Data*. Cambridge, MA: MIT Press.

Johnson, Eric J. and Edward J. Russo (1984), "Product Learning and Learning New Information," *Journal of Consumer Research*, 11 (June), 542-50.

Levin, Irwin P., Judy Schreiber, Marco Lauriola, and Gary J. Gaeth (2002), "A Tale of Two Pizzas: Building Up from a Basic Product Versus Scaling Down from a Fully-Loaded Product," *Marketing Letters*, 13 (November), 335-44.

Levin, Irwin P., Mary E. Huneke, and J.D. Jasper (2000), "Information Processing at Successive Stages of Decision Making: Need for Cognition and Inclusion-Exclusion Effects," *Organizational Behavior and Human Decision Processes*, 82 (July), 171-93.

Park, Whan C., Sung Youl Jun, and Deborah J. MacInnis (2000), "Choosing What I Want Versus Rejecting What I Do Not Want: An Application of Decision Framing to Product Option Choice Decisions," *Journal of Marketing Research*, 37 (May), 187-202.

Payne, John. W., James R. Bettman, and Eric J. Johnson (1993), *The Adaptive Decision Maker*. Cambridge, UK, Cambridge University Press.

Shafir, Eldar (1993), "Choosing Versus Rejecting: Why Some Options are Both Better and Worse Than Others," *Memory and Cognition*, 21 (July), 546-56.

Simonson Itamar (1989), "Choice Based on Reasons: The Case of Attraction and Compromise Effects," *Journal of Consumer Research*, 16 (September), 159-74.

Tversky, Amos and Daniel Kahneman (1974), "Judgment under Uncertainty: Heuristics and Biases," *Science*, 185 (July–September), 1124-30.

Urbany, Joel E., Peter R. Dickson, and William L. Wilkie (1989), "Buyer Uncertainty and Information Search," *Journal of Consumer Research*, 16 (September), 208-15.

Winer, Russel S. (1999), "Experimentation in the 21st Century: The Importance of External Validity," *Academy of Marketing Science Journal*, 27 (Summer), 349-58.

Yaniv, Ilan and Yaacov Schul (1997), "Elimination and Inclusion Procedures in Judgment," *Journal of Behavioral Decision Making*, 10 (September), 211-20.

Yaniv, Ilan and Yaacov Schul (2000), "Acceptance and Elimination Procedures in Choice: Non Complementarity and the Role of Implied Status Quo," *Organizational Behavior and Human Decision Processes*, 82 (July), 293-313.

The Glass Is Both Half Full And Half Empty: The Strategic Use Of Mixed Counterfactual Thoughts

Christina I. Anthony, The University of Sydney, Australia
Elizabeth Cowley, The University of Sydney, Australia

EXTENDED ABSTRACT

Why is it that after experiencing inevitable losses, heavy gamblers continue to spend money on gambling? Consumers often engage in a variety of consumption behaviors that are not necessarily in their best interest, apparently paying little attention to previous experiences that yielded questionable outcomes. The decision to gamble again, for example, should be influenced at least in part by one's success on previous occasions. And evaluations of these experiences should, on average, discourage repeat behavior. The purpose of this research is to examine how mixed counterfactuals may contribute to our understanding of potentially dysfunctional consumer behaviors. More specifically, we investigate frequent gamblers dysfunctional use of mixed counterfactuals in order to justify a loss, and devalue a win.

Relevant Literature and Hyposteses

Counterfactual thinking is the process of imagining alternative outcomes that could have, but did not occur (Roese 1997). Theorists have categorized counterfactuals in terms of their directionality. Upward counterfactual thoughts (UCTs) involve the generation of better alternative outcome(s). Downward counterfactuals thoughts (DCTs) involve the generation of worse alternative outcome(s) to reality. UCTs increase negative affect with our actual outcome, via a comparison to the better imagined alternative. DCTs increase positive affect with our actual outcome, via a comparison to the worse imagined alternative. An important determinant of the directionality of counterfactual thoughts is outcome valence. Research shows that people are more likely to spontaneously generate UCTs following failure, and DCTs following success (Gleicher et al. 1995; Grieve et al. 1999; Markman et al. 1993; Sanna, Chang, and Meier 2001). This can be explained in terms of the functional value of counterfactual thoughts.

Functional accounts assume that counterfactuals can beneficially serve people's goal states and motivations (Roese 1994; Roese and Olson 1995). UCTs generally serve a preparatory function, and DCTs generally serve an affective function (McMullen 1997; McMullen and Markman 2000; Roese and Hur 1997). Therefore, using UCTs following failure may be functional as the resulting negative affect helps one to learn from the past and avoid similar failures. On the other hand, generating DCTs following success may be functional as the resulting positive affect allows one to appreciate their success. Thus, we hypothesize that infrequent gamblers should show a significant difference in the direction of their counterfactual thoughts for a loss compared to a win (more UCTs for loss, more DCTs for win), further they should feel more disappointed with a loss relative to a win.

Whereas functional accounts are concerned with the beneficial role of counterfactual thinking in people's understanding of events, the dysfunctional perspective implicates the potentially adverse use of counterfactuals (Sherman and McConnell 1995). We propose that mixed counterfactuals (both UCT and DCT) may be generated in response to an outcome to justify continuing an activity. Frequent gamblers may use DCTs dysfunctionally to discount a loss and gloss over any problems signaled by their UCTs. Frequent gamblers may use UCTs dysfunctionally to devalue a win and dismiss their appreciation for an outcome which could have been worse as was signaled by their DCTs. In effect, we hypoth-

esize that mixed counterfactuals are strategically generated to counteract more spontaneous functional responses in order to justify replaying the game. Thus, we predict that frequent gamblers unlike infrequent gamblers, should generate mixed counterfactuals, and should not reveal any differences in their affective reaction to a loss relative to a win.

Method

One hundred and forty two gamblers played 300 games on a computer displaying a simulated poker machine game called Maid Marion. The design included one manipulated independent factor and one measured factor. The patterns of wins and losses in the games were pre-determined to manipulate the outcome of the experience (win, loss). A series of questions were asked to determine whether the participant was a frequent gambler. After the game ended, gamblers counterfactual thoughts and affective reactions were collected.

Results

We demonstrate that infrequent gamblers generated significantly more upward relative to downward counterfactuals for a loss, and more downward relative to upward counterfactuals for a win. Further, they were more disappointed (less pleased) with a loss, and more pleased (less disappointed) with a win. These results supported our predictions regarding a functional use of counterfactual thoughts which enable the infrequent gambler to learn from a loss and appreciate a win.

In contrast, we demonstrate that frequent gamblers generated mixed counterfactuals. Further, unlike infrequent gamblers, they did not reveal any significant differences in their disappointment with a loss relative to a win. These results supported our predictions regarding a potentially dysfunctional use of counterfactual thoughts which enable the frequent gambler to gloss over a loss and devalue a win, in order to justify replaying. Interestingly, our results suggest that mixed counterfactuals may have been generated sequentially, as evidenced by the additive/subtractive changes in frequent gamblers affective response. Further, our results suggest that frequent gamblers dysfunctional response may be mediated via their negative affect rather than their positive affect.

Discussion

This paper examined the potentially dysfunctional use of mixed counterfactuals in the context of gamblers evaluations of poker machine outcomes. Evidence of mixed counterfactuals and their dysfunctional influence on affect was demonstrated for frequent gamblers. In this paper, 'mixedness' was defined in terms of the direction of counterfactual thoughts; generating both UCT and DCT in response to an outcome. Interestingly, our results support the idea that mixedness stems from the direction of counterfactuals bearing an additive/subtractive influence on affect, rather than from dual modes of affective processing. However, future research should examine and compare the multiplicity of forms through which duality, or mixed counterfactuals may manifest.

Further, in this research we were not able to directly measure the sequential nature of dysfunctional counterfactuals, rather this was inferred from the pattern of affective response. However, this effect and other mixed counterfactual process mechanisms should be empirically tested. While the context of investigation in this paper is limited to gambling, our findings provide a platform for research into the effects of mixed counterfactuals and their potentially dysfunctional effects. We conclude by acknowledging the possibility that in other situations, mixed counterfactuals may serve a functional purpose, this remains to be examined.

REFERENCES

Gleicher, Faith, David S. Boninger, Alan Strathman, David Armor, John Hetts, and Mina Ahn (1995), "With an Eye toward the Future: The Impact of Counterfactual Thinking on Affect, Attitudes, and Behavior. ," in *What Might Have Been: The Social Psychology of Counterfactual Thinking*, ed. Neal J. Roese and James M. Olson, Hillsdale, NJ, England: Lawrence Erlbaum Associates, Inc. , 283-304.

Grieve, Frederick G, David A Houston, Susan E Dupuis, and Deborah Eddy (1999), "Counterfactual Production and Achievement Orientation in Competitive Athletic Settings," *Journal of Applied Social Psychology*, 29 (10), 2177-202.

Markman, Keith D., Igor Gavanski, Steven J. Sherman, and Matthew N. McMullen (1993), "The Mental Simulation of Better and Worse Possible Worlds," *Journal of Experimental Social Psychology*, 29 (1), 87-109.

McMullen, Matthew N (1997), "Affective Contrast and Assimilation in Counterfactual Thinking," *Journal of Experimental Social Psychology*, 33 (1), 77-100.

McMullen, Matthew N. and Keith D. Markman (2000), "Downward Counterfactuals and Motivation: The Wake-up Call and the Pangloss Effect," *Personality and Social Psychology Bulletin*, 26 (5), 575-84.

Roese, Neal J and Taekyun Hur (1997), "Affective Determinants of Counterfactual Thinking," *Social Cognition*, 15 (4), 274-90.

Roese, Neal J. (1994), "The Functional Basis of Counterfactual Thinking," *Journal of Personality and Social Psychology*, 66 (5), 805-18.

Roese, Neal J. (1997), "Counterfactual Thinking," *Psychological Bulletin*, 121 (1), 133-48.

Roese, Neal J. and James M. Olson (1995), "Functions of Counterfactual Thinking," in *What Might Have Been : The Social Psychology of Counterfactual Thinking*, ed. Neal J. Roese and James M. Olson, Mahwah, N.J.: Erlbaum Associates.

Sanna, Lawrence J., Edward C. Chang, and Susanne Meier (2001), "Counterfactual Thinking and Self-Motives," *Personality and Social Psychology Bulletin*, 27 (8), 1023-34.

Sherman, Steven. J. and Allen. R. McConnell (1995), "Dysfunctional Implications of Counterfactual Thinking: When Alternatives to Reality Fail Us," in *What Might Have Been: The Social Psychology of Counterfactual Thinking*, ed. N. J. Roese and J. M. Olson, Mahwah, NJ: Erlbaum, 199-231.

Self-positivity in Risk Judgments: The Role of Processing, Encoding, and Recall Biases

Parthasarathy Krishnamurthy, University of Houston, USA
Magdalena Cismaru, University of Regina, Canada

EXTENDED ABSTRACT

Self-positivity bias refers to the tendency of people to consider themselves as more fortunate than others. In the context of health judgments, this illusion of invulnerability can lead to poor choices and unfortunate consequences such as not getting medical attention in a timely manner or becoming obese. Therefore, examining the process may open up ways to manage such biases with important implications for designers of public policy campaigns advocating changes in behavior such as preventing obesity.

Although literature demonstrates self-positivity in a variety of contexts, including health, there are no empirically tested accounts of how self-positivity occurs. According to Chambers and Windschitl (2004), self-positivity might arise from biased retrieval of risk information. In the present research, we (a) present a first empirical test of biased retrieval of risk information, and (b) argue that self-positivity begins with biased encoding and biased processing of information. We report three studies examining self-positivity in encoding, processing and recall of risk information in the context of health estimates.

The principal goal of Study 1 was to assess biased retrieval of risk information. Students participated in 2 (target person) x 2 (order of elicitation) mixed design, with the target person manipulated within-subjects and the order of elicitation manipulated between-subjects. The design, measures, and procedure were based on Menon, Block, and Ramanathan (2002); Menon, Raghubir, and Schwarz (1995); and Raghubir and Menon (1998). Participants were exposed to a series of slides about Chronic Fatigue Syndrome (CFS) that described the condition, the symptoms, the severity, the difficulty of being diagnosed, and the people at risk. Participants then judged their own risk of developing CFS, the risk of an undergraduate student of developing CFS, and the risk-increasing and risk-decreasing factors that they used in providing the risk estimate for each target person (self and the average student). Results show that participants retrieved relatively more risk-increasing factors when the target person was the average person than when it was the self. Mediation analyses indicate that self–other differences in retrieval associated with risk-increasing and risk-decreasing factors mediate the effect of target person on risk estimates, consistent with Chambers and Windschitl's proposed model (2004) and our expectations.

The goal of Study 2 was to assess whether self-positivity is observed even in the processing of risk-behaviors, and whether such biases lead to positivity in risk-judgments. The online study involved two target persons, self versus average student, administered in two phases separated by a 10-minute distraction task. In phase 1, all participants were exposed to a condensed version of the CFS presentation and then presented with a list of eight behaviors— four risk-increasing (i.e., "consuming a lot of sugar") and four risk-decreasing (i.e., "eating plenty of fruits, vegetables, whole grains, and beans") — in regard to one's chance of developing CFS. Participants in the self-target person condition were instructed to think of these behaviors and to describe themselves performing them, one behavior at a time. Those in the other-target person condition were asked to think of the same behaviors and to describe an average student performing them. Following this, participants were asked to indicate how clearly they were able to visualize the target person (self or average student) engaging in each of those behaviors (imagery). A difference in the clarity of imagery was employed as an indication of information processing. After about 10 minutes or so, in phase 2 of the study, participants generated risk estimates for their assigned phase 1 target. The results from Study 2 suggest that self-positivity is not limited to retrieval, as noted in the three-stage model of Chambers and Windschitl (2004), but extends to processing of information. The same risk-behavior when processed with respect to one's self is visualized more readily if the behavior is risk-decreasing and less readily if the behavior is risk-increasing. Furthermore, the relative readiness to visualize risk-increasing behaviors (relative to risk-decreasing behaviors) significantly mediates the impact of the target person on risk-judgments.

The goal of Study 3 was to assess whether there are systematic biases in the encoding of risk information. Students participated in an online study with two target persons, self versus average student. They were exposed to a scenario that described oneself or an average student buying a lunch. They were then asked to evaluate the meal's content of fiber, sugar, whole grains etc., and indicate the extent to which the lunch was healthful, likable, etc. The effect of target on encoding was examined by looking at whether the target person influenced the evaluation of the meal. Results indicate that the target person affects encoding of ingredients, therefore suggesting that self-positivity is not limited to retrieval and processing of information, but extends to encoding of information. In general, participants considered their meal to be lower in undesirable ingredients such as sugar, fat, or calories, and higher in desirable ingredients such as grains and beans in contrast to evaluating the same meal for an average student. These results help extend the Chambers and Windschitl' model (2004) to include encoding biases as well as retrieval and processing biases documented in Study 1 and Study 2.

Although our findings extend our understanding of the mechanism behind self-positivity bias, identifying ways to manage self-positivity with important practical implications for designers of public policy campaigns remains to be investigated by future work. Specific research questions concern framing the information provided in a way to minimize encoding biases as well as processing biases and further retrieval biases when warranted.

REFERENCES

Chambers, John R. and Paul D. Windschitl (2004). "Biases in Social Comparative Judgments: The Role of Nonmotivated Factors in Above-Average and Comparative-Optimism Effects". *Psychological Bulletin*, 5 (September), 813-838.

Menon, Geeta, Lauren G. Block and Suresh Ramanathan (2002). "We're at as Much Risk as We are Led to Believe: Effects of Message Cues on Judgments of Health Risk". *Journal of Consumer Research*, 28 (March), 533-550.

Menon, Geeta, Priya Raghubir and Norbert Schwarz (1995). "Behavioral Frequency Judgments: an Accessibility-diagnosticity Framework". *Journal of Consumer Research*, 22 (September), 212–228.

Raghubir, Priya and Geeta Menon (1998). "AIDS and Me, Never the Twain Shall Meet: The Effects of Information Accessibility on Judgments of Risk and Advertising Effectiveness". *Journal of Consumer Research*, 25 (June), 52-64.

Gender Identity Salience and Perceived Vulnerability to Breast Cancer

Steven Sweldens, RSM Erasmus University, The Netherlands
Stefano Puntoni, RSM Erasmus University, The Netherlands
Nader T. Tavassoli, London Business School, UK

EXTENDED ABSTRACT

Breast cancer is one of the world's leading causes of death and breast cancer awareness campaigns aim to increase women's risk awareness and promote early screening behavior. Health campaigns aimed at increasing women's breast cancer awareness often stress women's vulnerability to breast cancer using images and appeals related to the female sex and to femininity. Estimates of personal risk are constructed by individuals based on environmental cues and personal experience. In particular, personal risk perceptions are closely tied to individuals' sense of self due to the link between aspects of one's self-concept (e.g., lifestyle, age or gender) and actual risk. Despite the large body of literature devoted to understanding the psychological processes involved in the estimation of perceived vulnerability, the relationship between risk estimates and self-identity is still unclear.

This paper explored how inherent characteristics of a risk interact with self-identity salience to influence estimates of perceived vulnerability. In particular, we investigated how and under which conditions the salience of a certain identity trait (e.g., gender) can influence one's perceived susceptibility to risks associated with this trait (e.g., breast cancer). Two alternative theoretical accounts—cognitive accessibility and defense mechanisms—provide opposing predictions with regard to the direction of the influence of identity salience in perceived risk.

Cognitive accessibility predicts an increase in gender-related risk perception following an increase in gender salience. Contextual factors that increase the salience of a dimension of self-identity should increase the accessibility of knowledge structures associated with this dimension and result in higher likelihood estimates for risks that are associated to this activated dimension through the operation of judgmental heuristics. For example, increased (decreased) accessibility of AIDS-related information had a positive (negative) effect on associated risk perceptions (Raghubir and Menon 1998). The cognitive accessibility account therefore predicts that increased gender salience should increase estimates of gender-specific risks.

A different line of reasoning, based on defense mechanisms, leads to the opposite prediction for identity aspects that are central to the self. The sexual self is a central aspect of women's multifaceted self and a disease such as breast cancer is inextricably bound to women's perception of their gender identity. Under conditions of heightened gender identity salience, the thought of contracting breast cancer may be perceived as especially threatening. Consequently, defensive mechanisms—which are intimately related to ego threat—may occur in these conditions, leading to a minimization of subjective risk estimates. For example, participants who were made to believe they suffered from a fictitious enzyme deficiency evaluated this deficiency as less serious than controls (Jemmott, Ditto, and Croyle 1986) and personal relevance increases the likelihood that threatening health messages are defensively processed (Liberman and Chaiken 1992).

To summarize, two distinct accounts make opposing predictions regarding the effect of identity salience on identity-specific risk perception. Cognitive accessibility predicts that heightening women's gender identity increases perceived vulnerability to risks such as breast cancer. A motivational defense mechanism account predicts instead that when a central aspect of the self (e.g., women's gender) is made more salient, threats (e.g., breast cancer) to this aspect are likely to trigger defensive mechanisms (e.g., risk minimization). Neither account predicts an effect of increased gender salience on gender-neutral risks.

We conducted a series of experiments with female participants to test these theories. Significant interactions and simple effects provide evidence for the defensive mechanism account and explored boundary conditions for the effect of identity salience on perceived risk. In experiment 1, 2, and 4 identity salience was manipulated using an essay writing task. Relative to a control condition, in the gender prime condition we observed a decrease in women's perceived risk of contracting breast cancer (experiments 1 and 4) whereas no effect was evident on risks without a link to gender identity. Behavioral implications were apparent in experiment 2, in which we found that gender priming leads to a decrease in donations to research on ovarian cancer treatment. Confirming the role of nonconscious defensive mechanisms, fear appraisal prior to the risk rating task muted the effect of gender identity salience on risk perceptions (experiment 4). In experiment 3 we used a more subtle gender priming task in which participants determined the gender of Dutch words. Establishing the importance of self-identity, perceived breast cancer vulnerability was lower when women were primed with their own gender, but not with the general category of gender.

These experiments contribute to literature on subjective risk estimates, defensive mechanisms and cognitive priming. Moreover, the results have implications for the design of health campaigns. Breast cancer awareness campaigns almost inevitably stress womanhood or women's sense of gender identity and along with it the relative importance of this identity aspect for their self-concept. Our findings indicate that an increase in gender identity salience can trigger defensive mechanisms of risk minimization, thus potentially attenuating or even reversing a campaign's intended consequences. The results of the experiments provide a number of suggestions on how to reduce the likelihood of defensive mechanisms interfering with the intended aim of health campaigns.

REFERENCES

Jemmott, John B., Peter H. Ditto, and Robert T. Croyle (1986), "Judging Health Status: Effects of Perceived Prevalence and Personal Relevance," *Journal of Personality and Social Psychology*, 50 (5), 899-905.

Liberman, Akiva and Shelly Chaiken (1992), "Defensive Processing of Personally Relevant Health Messages," *Personality and Social Psychology Bulletin*, 18 (December), 669-679.

Raghubir, Priya and Geeta Menon (1998), "AIDS and Me, Never the Twain Shall Meet: The Effects of Information Accessibility on Judgments of Risk and Advertising Effectiveness," *Journal of Consumer Research*, 25 (June), 52-63.

Measuring Internet Product Purchase Risk

Brent L S Coker, University of Melbourne, Australia

EXTENDED ABSTRACT

Despite general agreement amongst researchers that risk is an important phenomenon influencing online consumer decision making, there has been little consistency in the way risk has been defined and measured. Although the nature of online risk has been well defined, a psychometrically robust scale to measure this risk has yet been developed.

Internet Product Purchase Risk (IPPR) is defined as "the degree of uncertainty an individual perceives towards purchasing a product on the Internet". Perceptions of risk are activated during product evaluation and transaction stages of purchase decision making (Howard, 1973).

Evaluation Judgment Risk (EJR) is activated from an assessment of how easy or difficult a product is to evaluate online. It is defined as the degree of uncertainty aroused from an individual's belief in their ability to make an accurate judgment of product quality on the Internet. Given that some products are comprised of more experiential type attributes than others, EJR is influenced to a large extent by the physical characteristics of a product (Swaminathan, 2003). However, because consumers differ in which attributes are considered important when evaluating a product, EJR also differs between people for the same product (Alba et al., 1997; Klein, 1998).

Internet Security Risk (ISP) is an evaluation of how insecure the Internet is for shopping, and is defined as the degree of uncertainty and mistrust aroused from thoughts about providing personal and financial information over the Internet. An individual with low ISP is likely to have more confidence in their ability to shop on the Internet than an individual with high ISP. Low ISP consumers are characterized by a positive self-evaluation of their Internet shopping ability, displaying more robustness against contradictory cues and perceived inhibiting factors in their Internet shopping behavior than those who are risk averse (Eagly & Chaiken, 1993).

The Internet product purchase risk (IPPR) scale was developed and tested in four studies. In the first study (n=100) a preliminary pool of items was generated with evidence of content validity. In the second study (n=600) the IPPR scale was purified using principal axis factor analysis. In the third study (n=600) evidence of criterion-related, known-group, nomological, and discriminant validity was demonstrated. In the fourth study (n=184), the moderating effect of IPPR on trust-purchase intentions was empirically examined.

The IPPR scale was found to be internally consistent, exhibiting high criterion-related, known-group, and discriminant validity. Evidence of content validity was shown during initial selection of the items, and when open-ended questions of risk were matched to IPPR scores by expert judges (Zaichkowsky, 1985). The comparison of IPPR scores to open ended questions by expert judges also tested the criterion-related validity of the scale. The IPPR scale was also shown to have known-groups validity by demonstrating how those who were frequent online shoppers had higher IPPR then infrequent shoppers. Evidence of nomological validity was demonstrated by showing how IPPR was affected by perceived behavioral control, and correlated to intentions to purchase online. The metric invariance between item scores when measuring four products differing in experiential attributes suggested the items were robust in terms of interpretation.

Two main findings were found in the development. First, IPPR was found to have a quadratic relationship with experience purchasing from the product category. The results showed that although the frequency of purchase initially reduced IPPR, levels of IPPR actually increased for those who had purchased more than 6 times from the product category in the past 12 months. The second main finding was that IPPR was found to moderate a trust-purchase incompatibility tendency, with risk averse participants trusting a different seller than the one they preferred to purchase from. The results from the fourth study suggest that negative framing may be used to enhance trust for those with high perceptions of Internet purchase risk.

We conclude that IPPR plays an important role in influencing consumers' decisions to adopt the Internet for purchase, and suggest the scale is likely to be useful for academics seeking to further our understanding of online consumer related phenomena.

REFERENCES

Alba, J. W., Lynch, J., Weitz, B., Janiszewski, C., Lutz, R., Sawyer, A., et al. (1997). Interactive home shopping: Consumer, retailer, and manufacturer incentives to participate in electronic marketplaces. *Journal of Marketing, 61*(3), 38-53.

Bandura, A. (1998). *Self-efficacy: The exercise of control* (2nd ed.). New York: NY: W. H. Freeman and Company.

Bhatnagar, A., & Ghose, S. (2004). Segmenting consumers based on the benefits and risks of Internet shopping. *Journal of Business Research, 57*(12), 1352-1360.

Dinev, T., & Hart, P. (2005). Internet privacy concerns and social awareness as determinants of intention to transact. *International Journal of Electronic Commerce 10*(2), 7-29.

Eagly, A. H., & Chaiken, S. (1993). *Psychology of Attitudes* (1st ed.). Fort Worth, TX: Harcourt Brace Jovanovich.

Howard, J. A. (1973). Confidence as a validated construct. In J. A. Howard & L. E. Ostlund (Eds.), *Buyer behavior: Theoretical and empirical foundations* (1st ed., pp. 426-433). New York: Alfred A Knopf.

Klein, L. R. (1998). Evaluating the potential of interactive media through a new lens: Search versus experience goods. *Journal of Business Research, 41*(3), 195-203.

Miyazaki, A. D., & Fernandez, A. (2001). Consumer perceptions of privacy and security risks for online shopping. *The Journal of Consumer Affairs, 35*(1), 27.

Park, J., Lennon, S. J., & Stoel, L. (2005). On-line product presentation: Effects on mood, perceived risk, and purchase intention. *Psychology & Marketing, 22*(9), 695.

Swaminathan, V. (2003). The impact of recommendation agents on consumer evaluation and choice: The moderating role of category risk, product complexity, and consumer knowledge. *Journal of Consumer Psychology, 13*(1&2), 93-101.

Zaichkowsky, J. L. (1985). Measuring the involvement construct. *Journal of Consumer Research, 12*(3), 341-353.

Advances in Consumer Research
Volume 36, © 2009

APPENDIX 1
The Internet Product Purchase Risk Scale

Internet Product Purchase Risk (IPPR) Scale
—*for measuring the degree of uncertainty*
towards purchasing a product on the Internet

Buying a _____ **on the Internet is...**
(Insert name of product)

Unpredictable	Predictable
Safe	Risky*
Uninformative	Informative
Reliable	Unreliable*
Untrustworthy	Trustworthy
Secure	Not Secure*
Not Credible	Credible
Clear	Unclear*
Uncertain	Certain
Responsible	Irresponsible*

Instructions:
1. Write the name of the product to judged at the top
2. Write a cross (x) in one of the intervals for each word pair
3. Work quickly, but carefully, through the list. Do not pause

Examples:

Neutral   Slightly

Quite   Extremely

Scoring:
1. Reverse score items marked with an asterisk (*)
2. Total the scores from each word pair (from 1 on the left to 7 on the right)
3. Scores range from 11 (extremely low perceived risk) to 70 (extremely high perceived risk)

© Brent Coker

Flow in Consumer Research: A Novel Approach

Jan Drengner, Chemnitz University of Technology, Germany
Manuela Sachse, Chemnitz University of Technology, Germany
Pia Furchheim, Chemnitz University of Technology, Germany

EXTENDED ABSTRACT

Since the seminal article by Hoffman and Novak (1996) flow has gained more attention in consumer research. Reviewing the literature, there have been several attempts to develop a conceptualization of flow, whereby the following characteristics seem to make up the core of the construct: action-awareness merging (1), loss of self-consciousness (2), transformation of time (3), sense of control (4), clear goals (5), unambiguous and seamless feedback (6), challenge-skill balance (7), concentration on task at hand (8), and autotelic experience (9).

However, our examination shows disparity between the different conceptualizations. First, there is no overall agreement on the use of the flow characteristics. Some researchers (Chen, Wigand, and Nilan 2000; Jackson and Eklund 2002; Stavrou et al. 2007) take all of the above mentioned characteristics into consideration. Alternatively, others confine themselves to selected characteristics and/or use additional ones (Huang 2006; Novak, Hoffman, and Yung 2000; Shin 2006). Second, there is often no discussion whether these characteristics are formative or reflective dimensions, or even if they might be seen as antecedents or consequences of flow. Only a few researchers (Drengner, Gaus, and Jahn 2008; Sánchez-Franco 2006; Sánchez-Franco and Roldán 2005; Shin 2006; Siekpe 2005) discuss the nature of the dimensions (reflective vs. formative) intentionally.

Generally, both problems seem to be based on the fact that flow has often been defined with special focus on the respective subject of investigation. Therefore, we develop a new and universal conceptualization and test it empirically.

With the help of some decision rules by Jarvis, MacKenzie, and Podsakoff (2003), we classified the characteristics 1 to 4 and 8 as reflective dimensions and the characteristics 5 to 7 as antecedents. Since it is neither an antecedent nor a formative dimension or a manifestation of flow, we see characteristic 9 rather as a consequence of the flow experience. Hence, we excluded this characteristic from our 3 empirical studies.

In study 1, subjects were 618 online-game players (81 female, 537 male; 23.0 mean age). Study 2 contained 1,556 soccer World Cup viewers (742 female, 854 male; 25.7 mean age). The sample of study 3 consisted of 120 attendees of soccer World Cup public viewing points (48 female, 72 male; 23.6 mean age). We assessed the antecedents and dimensions, each with 3 items following the Flow Scales by Jackson and Eklund (2002).

In all three studies, there was no differentiation between respondents who experienced flow and those who did not with respect to their perceived control. These findings can be corroborated by the theory of planned behavior (Ajzen 1991), stating that perceived control is a precondition for behavioral intention and behavior. Following this idea, control would lead to the behavior, which might result in a flow experience. Hence, we exclude characteristic 4 from further analyses.

The remaining characteristics were evaluated by two different second-order models in study 1 with the help of CFA. Model 1, which draws upon the mostly used perspective (e.g., Chen et al. 2000; Csikszentmihalyi 1975; Jackson and Eklund 2002; Stavrou et al. 2007), incorporates all characteristics (1 to 3, 5 to 8) as dimensions. Model 2 distinguishes the characteristics between dimensions (1 to 3, 8) and antecedents (5 to 7) of flow according to our suggested conceptualization. The fit values (χ^2, RMSEA, SRMR, NNFI, CFI, PNFI, CVI), the loadings of the characteristics as well as their explained variance attest superiority to model 2.

Given the need for generalizability we retested model 2 in study 2 and 3 with different subjects of investigation. Again, the empirical findings support our conceptualization with 4 reflective dimensions (1 to 3, 8). Therefore, we suggest the following flow definition: Flow is a holistic experience, explaining the state in which the acting individual experiences a loss of self-consciousness, loses all sense of time while being highly concentrated and having the impression of his or her consciousness and action merging. This definition provides first directions towards a universal conceptualization of flow, which is applicable in various fields of consumer research.

REFERENCES

Ajzen, Icek (1991), "The Theory of Planned Behavior," *Organizational Behavior and Human Decision Processes*, 50 (2), 179–211.

Chen, Hsiang, Rolf T. Wigand, and Michael S. Nilan (2000), "Exploring Web Users' Optimal Flow Experiences," *Information Technology & People*, 13 (4), 263–81.

Csikszentmihalyi, Mihaly (1975), *Beyond Boredom and Anxiety*. San Francisco: Jossey-Bass.

Drengner, Jan, Hansjoerg Gaus, and Steffen Jahn (2008), "Does Flow Influence the Brand Image in Event Marketing?," *Journal of Advertising Research*, 48 (1), 138–47.

Hoffman, Donna L. and Thomas P. Novak (1996), "Marketing in Hypermedia Computer-Mediated Environments: Conceptual Foundations," *Journal of Marketing*, 60 (3), 50–68.

Huang, Ming-Hui (2006), "Flow, Enduring, and Situational Involvement in the Web Environment: A Tripartite Second-Order Examination," *Psychology & Marketing*, 23 (5), 383–411.

Jarvis, Cheryl B., Scott B. MacKenzie, and Philip M. Podsakoff (2003), "A Critical Review of Construct Indicators and Measurement Model Misspecification in Marketing and Consumer Research," *Journal of Consumer Research*, 30 (September), 199–218.

Jackson, Susan and Robert C. Eklund (2002), "Assessing Flow in Physical Activity: The Flow State Scale-2 and Dispositional Flow Scale-2," *Journal of Sport & Exercise Psychology*, 24 (2), 133–50.

Novak, Thomas P., Donna L. Hoffman, and Yiu-Fai Yung (2000), "Measuring the Customer Experience in Online Methodological Environments: A Structural Modeling Approach," *Marketing Science*, 19 (1), 22–42.

Sánchez-Franco, Manuel J. (2006), "Exploring the Influence of Gender on the Web Usage via Partial Least Squares," *Behaviour & Information Technology*, 25 (1), 19–36.

_____ and José L. Roldán (2005), "Web Acceptance and Usage Model–A Comparison between Goal-directed and Experiential Web Users," *Internet Research*, 15 (1), 21–48.

Shin, Namin (2006), "Online Learner's 'Flow' Experience: An Empirical Study," *British Journal of Educational Technology*, 37 (5), 705–20.

Siekpe, Jeffrey S. (2005), "An Examination of the Multidimensionality of Flow Construct in a Computer-Mediated Environment," *Journal of Electronic Commerce Research*, 6 (1), 31–43.

Stavrou, Nektarios A., Susan A. Jackson, Yannis Zervas, and Konstantinos Karteroliotis (2007), "Flow Experience and Athletes' Performance with Reference to the Orthogonal Model of Flow," *The Sport Psychologist*, 21 (4), 438–57.

The Impact of Matching Between Emotion Types and Product Offerings on Evaluations

Kiwan Park, Seoul National University, Korea
Hakkyun Kim, Concordia University, Canada
Norbert Schwarz, University of Michigan, USA

EXTENDED ABSTRACT

In conceptualizing how affect plays an informational role, the valence of affect, such as positive or negative, has been of focal interest. Although the differential role of positive versus negative affect has been well documented as a mechanism accounting for people's different behaviors or decisions (depending on the valence of the affect), and has been proven useful for our understanding as to how human cognition and affect interplay, many questions are still unanswered. Will sad people behave in the same manner as angry people, assuming both are equally negative? Or, will excited consumers prefer a trip to an amusement park as much as consumers experiencing a peaceful mood, given the same degree of positivity? Actually, the significance of the specificity of emotions has been a bit neglected, in favor of the parsimony of research programs.

Inasmuch as the same positive or negative affect serving as an informative cue is context-dependent, distinct emotions within positive or negative mood can carry different informational values, depending on how well the context can be understood with the prevailing mood state. Since discrete emotions (of the same valence) are associated with their unique meanings respectively and are followed by different types of appraisal, or the accessibility of semantically congruent information that matches those emotional states (Lazarus 1991), it appears to be plausible that incidental emotions (beyond positive or negative valence) can influence how people incorporate discrete emotions in generating evaluative judgments. In fact, an exploration into the premise that discrete emotions have distinct effects on people's judgments has only begun recently.

For example, by adopting appraisal theories of emotion, Lerner and Keltner (2001) show that angry people express optimistic risk estimates and make risk-seeking choices while anxious people express pessimistic risk estimates and make risk-averse choices. Similarly, DeSteno et al. (2000) show that sad individuals believe that sad events are more likely to occur than angering events, whereas angry individuals believe that angering events are more likely to occur than sad events. These findings reflect the notion that sadness being experienced in the moment is used as input for coloring one's environment as a sad place and influences the likelihood of sad events occurring. In the same vein, momentary feelings of anger are used as a cue indicating one's environment as a place full of angering events, which then affects the likelihood of angering events occurring.

Following that it is the match with the current domain of concern, rather than the emotional valence or congruence in a general sense, that determines the information that is given processing priority, we reason that a match between felt emotion and the emotional appeal of a product will generate more favorable evaluations toward a product. This prediction is based on theorizing that consumers will better empathize with product claims when they are in the same emotional vein (e.g., feelings of excitement), which will lead them to believe that the product will surely give them the claimed benefits (e.g., adventure). Consequently, people are expected to find certain messages or product claims as more convincing or appealing in the matching versus the mismatching condition.

Two experiments were conducted to test the above hypotheses. Study 1 aimed to assess whether a match versus a mismatch between emotional state and product appeals yields differences in evaluation by participants whose ambient emotions differ. To accomplish this goal, we employed a 2 (Emotion: excited vs. peaceful) × 2 (Product: adventurous vs. serene) between-subjects design and measured participants' evaluations of a target object when the overtones associated with distinct emotions varied. The results from study 1 provided support for our hypothesis. More specifically, we found that people's evaluations toward travel products in the form of advertisements depend on a match versus a mismatch between an individual's emotional state and emotional appeals of a product. When the travel destination was described as a place full of adventurous offerings, people showed more favorable attitudes toward the destination under excitement than under serenity. Conversely, when the same destination was depicted as a place full of serene offerings, people showed more favorable attitudes toward the destination when people felt peaceful than when they felt excited.

In a follow-up study, we further investigated the mechanism underlying the emotion congruency bias observed in study 1. In evaluating a product built on emotional benefits, people may (implicitly) ask themselves "how would I feel if..." and can get a direct answer from their current emotional state. Specifically, when there exists a match, people may increase their likelihood estimates of a matching emotional benefit, as people tend to infer how they would feel from how they are feeling in the moment. On the other hand, when there exists a mismatch, what people infer from their current emotion can actually play a disturbing role, in that their current emotion blocks people's imagery regarding the proposed product's emotional benefits. Thus, it is predicted that the positive impact of a match (vs. a mismatch) will influence people's evaluations via enhanced estimates of the occurrence of product benefits. The results from study 2 confirmed this premise. Specifically, by using structural equation models, we showed that individuals experiencing a specific emotion are more likely to believe events associated with their emotions prevail in their environment: as a consequence, they make more positive evaluations of products whose nature is more consistent with their emotional states, as those products are expected to reflect corresponding emotions that are promised from their consumption. Thus, study 2 replicates the results of study 1 and further determines the underlying process that explains the emotion congruency bias for positive discrete emotions.

Taken together, these findings add to the emergence of emotion specificity and fluency effects as factors affecting consumer judgments. In addition, the managerial implications from the current research can be important, in that that firms have an opportunity to make use of mood to their advantage by employing tactics in advertisements and interpersonal sales designed to enhance consumers' emotional states, in combination with positioning decisions.

REFERENCES

Aaker, Jennifer L. and Angela Y. Lee (2001), "I Seek Pleasures, We Avoid Pains: The Role of Self Regulatory Goals in Information Processing of Persuasion," *Journal of Consumer Research*, 28 (June), 33-49.

Albarracin, Dolores and G. Tarcan Kumkale (2003), "Affect as Information in Persuasion: A Model of Affect Identification and Discounting," *Journal of Personality and Social Psychology*, 84 (3), 453-69.

Bless, Herbert, Gerald L. Clore, Norbert Schwarz, Verena Golisano, Christina Rabe, and Marcus Wölk (1996), "Mood and the Use of Scripts: Does a Happy Mood Really Lead to Mindlessness?," *Journal of Personality and Social Psychology*, 71 (4), 665-79.

Bodenhausen, Galen V., Lori A. Sheppard, and Geoffrey P. Kramer (1994), "Negative Affect and Social Judgment: The Differential Impact of Anger and Sadness," *European Journal of Social Psychology*, 24, 45-62.

Clore, Gerald L. and Stanley Colcombe (2003), "The Parallel Worlds of Affective Concepts and Feelings," in *The Psychology of Evaluation: Affective Processes in Cognition and Emotion*, Jochen Musch and Karl Christoph Klauer, Eds. Mahwah, NJ: Lawrence Earlbaum.

DeSteno, David , Richard E. Petty, Derek D. Rucker, Duane T. Wegener, and Julia Braverman (2004), "Discrete Emotions and Persuasion: The Role of Emotion-Induced Expectancies," *Journal of Personality and Social Psychology*, 86 (1), 43-56.

DeSteno, David, Richard E. Petty, Duane T. Wegener, and Derek D. Rucker (2000), "Beyond Valence in the Perception of Likelihood: The Role of Emotion Specificity," *Journal of Personality and Social Psychology*, 78 (3), 397-416.

Forgas, Joseph P. (1995), "Mood and Judgment: The Affect Infusion Model (AIM)," *Psychological Bulletin*, 117 (1), 39-66.

Gorn, Gerald, Marvin E. Goldberg, and Kunal Basu (1993), "Mood, Awareness, and Product Evaluation," *Journal of Consumer Psychology*, 2 (3), 237-56.

Gorn, Gerald, Michel Tuan Pham, and Leo Yatming Sin (2001), "When Arousal Influences Ad Evaluation and Valence Does Not (and Vice Versa)," *Journal of Consumer Psychology*, 11 (1), 43-55.

Johnson, Eric J. and Amos Tversky (1983), "Affect, Generalization, and the Perception of Risk," *Journal of Personality and Social Psychology*, 45 (1), 20-31.

Lavine, Howard and Mark Snyder (1996), "Cognitive Processing and the Functional Matching Effect in Persuasion: The Mediating Role of Subjective Perceptions of Message Quality," *Journal of Experimental Social Psychology*, 32 (6), 580-604.

Lazarus, Richard S. (1991), *Emotion and Adaptation*. New York: Oxford University Press.

Lerner, Jennifer S. and Dacher Keltner (2001), "Fear, Anger, and Risk," *Journal of Personality and Social Psychology*, 81 (1), 146-59.

Loken, Barbara (2006), "Consumer Psychology: Categorization, Inferences, Affect, and Persuasion," *Annual Review of Psychology*, 57, 453-85.

Martin, Leonard L., Teresa Abend, Constantine Sedikides, and Jeffrey D. Green (1997), "How Would I Feel If...? Mood as Input to a Role Fulfillment Evaluation Process," *Journal of Personality and Social Psychology*, 73 (2), 242-53.

Martin, Leonard L., David W. Ward, John W. Achee, and Robert S. Wyer, Jr. (1993), "Mood as Input: People Have to Interpret the Motivational Implications of Their Moods," *Journal of Personality and Social Psychology*, 64 (3), 317-26.

Mathews, A. and C. MacLeod (1994), "Cognitive Approaches to Emotion and Emotional Disorders," *Annual Review of Psychology*, 45, 25-50.

Mayer, John D., Yvonne N. Gaschke, Debra L. Braverman, and Temperance W. Evans (1992), "Mood-Congruent Judgment Is a General Effect," *Journal of Personality and Social Psychology*, 61 (July), 119-32.

Pham, Michel Tuan (2004), "The Logic of Feeling," *Journal of Consumer Psychology*, 14 (4), 360-74.

_____ (1998), "Representativeness, Relevance, and the Use of Feelings in Decision Making," *Journal of Consumer Research*, 25 (September), 144-59.

Raghunathan, Rajagopal and Michel Tuan Pham (1999), "All Negative Moods Are Not Equal: Motivational Influences of Anxiety and Sadness on Decision Making," *Organizational Behavior and Human Decision Processes*, 79 (1), 56-77.

Raghunathan, Rajagopal, Michel Tuan Pham, and Kim P. Corfman (2006), "Informational Properties of Anxiety and Sadness, and Displaced Coping," *Journal of Consumer Research*, 32 (March), 596-601.

Schwarz, Norbert (1990), "Feelings as Information: Informational and Motivational Functions of Affective States," in *Handbook of Motivation and Cognition: Foundations of Social Behavior*, Richard M. Sorrentino and E. Tory Higgins, Eds. Vol. 2. New York: Guilford Press.

_____ (2004), "Metacognitive Experiences in Consumer Judgment and Decision Making," *Journal of Consumer Psychology*, 14 (4), 332-48.

Schwarz, Norbert, Herbert Bless, and Gerd Bohner (1991), "Mood and Persuasion: Affective States Influences the Processing of Persuasive Communications," in *Advances in Experimental Social Psychology*, M. P. Zanna, Ed. San Diego, CA: Academic Press.

Schwarz, Norbert and Gerald L. Clore (2007), "Feelings and Phenomenal Experiences," in *Social Psychology: Handbook of Basic Principles*, Arie W. Kruglanski and E. Tory Higgins, Eds. 2nd ed. New York: Guilford.

_____ (1983), "Mood, Misattribution, and Judgments of Well-Being: Informative and Directive Functions of Affective States," *Journal of Personality and Social Psychology*, 45 (3), 513-23.

_____ (2007), "Feelings and Phenomenal Experiences," in *Social Psychology: Handbook of Basic Principles*, ed. A. W. Kruglanski and E. T. Higgins, New York: Guilford, 385-407.

Skurnik, Ian, Carolyn Yoon, Denise C. Park, and Norbert Schwarz (2005), "How Warnings About False Claims Become Recommendations," *Journal of Consumer Research*, 31 (March), 713-24.

Wegener, Duane T., Richard E. Petty, and Stephen M. Smith (1995), "Positive Mood Can Increase or Decrease Message Scrutiny: The Hedonic Contingency View of Mood and Message Processing," *Journal of Personality and Social Psychology*, 69 (1), 5-15.

The Effect of Experiential Analogies on Consumer Perceptions and Attitudes

Miranda R. Goode, University of Western Ontario, Canada
Darren W. Dahl, University of British Columbia, Canada
C. Page Moreau, University of Colorado, USA

EXTENDED ABSTRACT

Microsoft has compared playing the Xbox 360 to participating in a city-wide water balloon fight and Alfa Romeo has compared driving a sports car to a first kiss. These are prime examples of experiential analogies. By comparing a product to a familiar but disparate experience, these analogical comparisons have the power to shift consumer focus from objective information, such as functionality and performance, to the evaluative, emotional and multi-sensory information associated with the product experience. This shift in focus highlights the importance of base preference (i.e., a consumer's liking for the comparison experience) as an important influence on analogical persuasiveness. This shift in focus also highlights the power of an analogy to tap into the emotional knowledge that individuals have gained from their own experiences. Surprisingly, previous research has focused almost exclusively on analogies designed to transfer objective knowledge in the context of strategic and functional oriented comparisons (Gregan-Paxton 2001; Gregan-Paxton and Moreau 2003; Hoeffler 2003; Roehm and Sternthal 2001). In doing so, not only has the consumer's ability to transfer unique, personally-experienced emotional information been ignored, but the effect of prior preferences on an analogy's persuasiveness has not been investigated. Addressing these gaps and building on previous speculation on the role of emotions in analogical thinking (Thagard and Shelley 2001), our research defines and isolates the effects of base preference, emotional knowledge, and experienced emotion on consumer attitudes.

When processing an experiential analogy, it is anticipated that consumers will access their knowledge of the base experience and any knowledge they might have of the target product experience. With the Alfa Romeo Spider ad, individuals would think about what happened and the emotions experienced during a first kiss. Any similarities between what takes place during a first kiss and what an individual knows or thinks driving the sports car might entail would be cognitively identified. Finally, based on these identified similarities, emotional inferences (i.e., predictions about the emotions that would be experienced during target product use) would be generated. We predict that whether or not the generation of emotional inferences will have a positive or negative effect on target attitudes will depend on the favorability of the base preference (i.e., how much the base experience is liked). This moderating hypothesis implies that target attitudes will be more positive when preference for the base experience is favorable and a high number of emotional inferences are generated. When preference for the base experience is less favorable and a high number of emotional inferences are generated, we would expect target attitudes to be more negative. Note that the current investigation focuses on the more common use of experiential analogies to positively influence consumer attitudes.

Three studies were designed to test our theorizing. This was done using three different analogies across several base and target categories, thus contributing to the generalizability of our effects. Across all three studies, we also compared the persuasiveness of an experiential analogy to more general emotion-oriented appeals. This provided us with additional insight on the contributors to analogical persuasiveness and the ability to make substantive recommendations for whom experiential analogies may be more persuasive.

Study 1 involved direct measures of base preference and emotional inferences to test the main moderating prediction. Participants were randomly assigned to view either an experiential analogy ad or an emotional appeal control ad. The findings were consistent with expectations and suggest that experiential analogies cue the transfer of emotional knowledge from the base experience to the target product. The effect of emotional inferences on target attitudes was moderated by base preference. The more participants liked the base experience and the more emotional inferences they generated then the more favourable were consumer attitudes. The analogy ad was also liked significantly more than the emotional appeal ad.

Study 2 was designed to provide additional evidence for the main moderating prediction and for the cognitive nature of the emotional knowledge transfer process. This was done by manipulating participants' ability to generate emotional inferences through cognitive load. Measures of experienced emotion were included in this study and in study 3 to further show that emotional knowledge transfer is cognitive and has an effect on product attitudes independent from experienced emotion. In study 3, the soundness construct (which captures the extent to which the base and target share deeper underlying similarities) was introduced to further demonstrate that base preference moderates the effect of emotional knowledge transfer on target attitudes. Across studies 2 and 3, we found evidence that the processing of experiential analogies results in the generation of emotional reactions which also predict consumer attitudes. Importantly, accounting for experienced emotion did not reduce the significant effect of base preference and emotional inferences on consumer attitudes. This suggests that experienced emotion and emotional knowledge transfer, a more cognitive process, may be viewed as having complementary effects on the persuasiveness of an experiential analogy.

The contribution of this research is three-fold. First, analogy researchers have highlighted the need to move beyond the identification of factors that affect analogy comprehension to identify the factors that affect an analogy's persuasiveness (Perrott, Gentner, and Bodenhausen 2005). Addressing this, we establish base preference as an important influence on an analogy's persuasiveness. This research is the first to examine how preference for a disparate base is integrated into a target product evaluation. Second, we demonstrate that product attitudes can be significantly influenced by directing people to consider their own subjective experience as a basis for understanding the emotions that may be experienced when using a new product. We find evidence that this involves the cognitive consideration of emotions, which we have labeled emotional knowledge transfer. This is perhaps surprising and of central interest to marketing practitioners, since we show that the persuasiveness of an experiential analogy is not limited to emotional reactions. Finally, on a broader level, our research provides the first known empirical investigation of analogies involving experiential comparisons, thus establishing their value in persuasion.

REFERENCES

Gregan-Paxton, Jennifer (2001), "The Role of Abstract and Specific Knowledge in the Formation of Product Judgments: An Analogical Learning Perspective," *Journal of Consumer Psychology*, 11 (3), 141-58.

Gregan-Paxton, Jennifer and Page Moreau (2003), "How Do Consumers Transfer Existing Knowledge? A Comparison of Analogy and Categorization Effects," *Journal of Consumer Psychology*, 13 (4), 422-30.

Hoeffler, Steve (2003), "Measuring Preferences for Really New Products," *Journal of Marketing Research*, 40 (4), 406-20.

Perrott, David A., Dedre Gentner, and Galen V. Bodenhausen (2005), "Resistance is futile: The unwitting insertion of analogical inferences in memory," *Psychonomic Bulletin & Review*, 12 (4), 696-702.

Roehm, Michelle L. and Brian Sternthal (2001), "The Moderating Effect of Knowledge and Resources on the Persuasive Impact of Analogies," *Journal of Consumer Research*, 28 (September), 257-72.

Thagard, Paul and Cameron Shelley (2001), "Emotional Analogies and Analogical Inference," in *The Analogical Mind*, ed. Dedre Gentner, Keith J. Holyoak and Boicho N. Kokinov, Cambridge, MA: The MIT Press, 335-62.

Evaluative Conditioning 2.0: Direct and Indirect Attachment of Affect to Brands

Steven Sweldens, RSM Erasmus University, The Netherlands
Stijn van Osselaer, RSM Erasmus University, The Netherlands
Chris Janiszewski, University of Florida, USA[1]

EXTENDED ABSTRACT

When initially neutral stimuli such as new brands co-occur repeatedly with positively valenced stimuli (such as beautiful pictures, nice music, celebrity-endorsers etc..), we observe that as a result the brand becomes more positively evaluated itself. This repeated-pairings procedure is referred to as "evaluative conditioning" in the literature (for a review, see De Houwer et al. 2001). According to the established theory by De Houwer et al., positive affect only becomes *indirectly* attached to the brand. The brand becomes more positively evaluated through mediating memory links to the affective stimuli it co-occurred with in the past. Thus, after a sufficient number of co-occurences, the brand starts to evoke (un)conscious memories to the affective stimulus it co-occurred with in the past. Positive affect experienced towards the brand is caused by the triggering of such memories. In this article, we introduce a new theory, in which we show that–only in specific circumstances–affect can also become *directly* attached to the brand. In this case, it is the brand itself that acquires the positive affect, without the necessity for further intermediating memories to the affective stimuli.

We show when direct versus indirect affect transfer occurs, which is critically dependent on the way the brands and affective stimuli are presented together. We also show that direct transfer of affect (compared to indirect affect transfer) results in much more stable brand attitudes which are uniquely resistant to retroactive interference from new learning (e.g., advertising clutter) and uniquely resistant to post-conditioning devaluations of the affective stimuli (e.g., celebrity endorsers falling from grace).

We identified two properties of conditioning procedures that determine whether affect becomes directly or indirectly attached to the brand. First, the time gap between the presentations of brand and affective stimulus should be zero for direct affect transfer to be possible. This matches on the distinction between a *sequential conditioning* procedure and a *simultaneous conditioning* procedure.

Second, we manipulated whether the brand was repeatedly paired with the same affective stimulus (*same pairings* condition) versus always with different affective stimuli (*different pairings* condition). In a *same pairings* conditioning procedure, it becomes more likely that the brand will evoke (un)conscious memories to the affective stimulus in the future, hence indirect affect transfer is promoted. However, in a *different pairings* conditioning procedure, there's no such establishment of a strong link between a brand and a certain affective stimulus, making it unlikely that one will be recalled upon future presentation of the brand. Therefore, different pairings inhibit the indirect transfer of affect.

Combining these deductions, we conclude that in a sequential same pairings conditioning procedure, only indirect affect transfer will occur. In a simultaneous different pairings conditioning procedure, only direct affect transfer will occur. In a simultaneous same

pairings conditioning procedure, both types of evaluative learning can occur. In a sequential different pairings conditioning procedure however, evaluative learning should be inhibited because it is not conducive of indirect (due to the different pairings), nor direct (due to the sequential presentation) affect transfer.

We set up a first experiment to test the hypothesis that a sequential different pairings conditioning procedure should lead to less transfer of affect than other procedures.

Experiment 1

Fifty-seven students at a large Southeastern university participated in this experiment in exchange for course credits. We employed a 2 (simultaneous vs. sequential conditioning) x 2 (same vs. different pairings) x 2 (attitudes towards positively vs. neutrally conditioned brands) mixed design with the first two factors manipulated between subjects and the latter manipulated within subjects. We used pictures of unknown Belgian beers as brands and positive and neutral pictures from the International Affective Pictures System as the affective stimuli.

Confirming our prediction, evaluative conditioning was strongly significant in all conditioning procedures, except in a sequential different pairings condition.

Experiment 2

We directly tested the indirect versus direct nature of the attitude changes caused by evaluative conditioning by investigating what happens when the valence of an affective stimulus suddenly changes after the conditioning phase. On the one hand, when affect transfer is indirect, a brand derives its valence by (un)consciously retrieving the associated affective stimuli. Therefore, the brand's valence will be tied to the affective stimuli's valence and a devaluation of the affective stimuli will cause a devaluation of the brand. On the other hand, when affect becomes directly attached to the brand, it is of no further consequence what happens to the affective stimuli that were previously paired with the brand.

Ninety-seven students at a large Southeastern university participated. The design of the study was a mixed 2 (sequential vs. simultaneous conditioning) x 2 (same vs. different pairings) x 3 (attitudes towards normally positively conditioned, positively conditioned with a posteriori devaluated affective stimuli, and neutrally conditioned brands). The first two factors were manipulated between subjects, the latter one within subjects.

In accordance with our theory, we found that a devaluation of the affective stimuli negatively impacts the affect towards the brand in a sequential same pairings condition, in a simultaneous same pairings condition, but not in the simultaneous different pairings condition. As in experiment 1, no affect transfer occurred with a sequential different pairings condition.

Discussion

In an unreported third experiment we also found that attitudes generated by a simultaneous different pairings procedure (leading to direct affect transfer) are much more stable and hence not sensitive to forgetting induced by other learning tasks after conditioning, whereas attitudes generated by a sequential same pairings procedure (leading to indirect affect transfer) are very vulnerable to forgetting of the associations induced by new learning tasks.

[1]Support from the Department of Marketing Management at the Rotterdam School of Management, the Marketing Department at the Warrington College of Business Administration, the Erasmus Research Institute of Management and the Trust Fund Erasmus University Rotterdam is gratefully acknowledged. This paper is based on the first author's dissertation.

It can be concluded that achieving direct transfer of affect carries distinctive advantages for the brand. First, it shields the brand from devaluation of associated affective stimuli (such as celebrity endorsers falling from grace). Second, it's much more stable with regard to interference by subsequent learning as in advertising clutter situations.

REFERENCE

De Houwer, Jan, Sarah Thomas, and Frank Baeyens (2001), "Associative learning of likes and dislikes: A review of 25 years of research on human evaluative conditioning," *Psychological Bulletin*, 127 (November), 853-69.

How and When Alpha-Numeric Brand Names Affect Consumer Preferences

Kunter Gunasti, Pennsylvania State University, USA
William T. Ross, Jr., Pennsylvania State University, USA

EXTENDED ABSTRACT

"…An alpha-numeric brand name is defined as a name that contains one or more numbers either in digit form (e.g., "5") or in written form (e.g., "five"). This means that alpha-numeric brand names include referential or non-sense mixtures of letters and digits (e.g., WD-40), mixtures of words and digits (e.g., Formula 409), or any of the preceding where the figure is written out in word form…" (Pavia and Costa, 1993, 85).

There are millions of registered and unregistered alpha-numeric trademarks in use (US Patent and Trademark Office 2006). The increase in the market segmentation; spread of technology; difficulty of finding and implementing new brand names; decrease in product life cycles; and the tendency to stretch a favorable brand name to new products have led marketers to use alpha-numeric brands (see Boyd 1985 for a review). Even highly successful non-alpha-numeric brands like Lincoln and Acura have recently switched to alpha-numeric brands that dominate the automotive industry.

Some alpha-numeric brands make it fairly simple to draw inferences about the product. For instance, the BMW 3.20 refers to a 2 liter engine volume for the 3 series cars, and you can easily tell that the 3.28 is a relatively better product due to its larger engine (2.8 liters). Correspondingly, Audi A8 and A6 indicate larger size and higher luxury levels than A4 and A3. However, it is not always so easy to understand alpha-numeric brand names. Mercedes has over ten letter classes resulting in a rather complicated set of some forty alpha-numeric brand names and not many people know the difference between an S550 and an E550 car. Sometimes alpha-numeric brands are not consistent with the consumers' intuitions. For example, contrary to intuition, Nokia 6110 is inferior to Nokia 6102 and average consumer has no idea what 6110 really refers to.

Most past studies on alpha-numeric brands have focused on the perception of the brands and how consumers associate them with different product categories. In their benchmark study, Pavia and Costa (1993) investigated how consumers react to the magnitude of the numbers and the symbolisms of the letter combinations used in alpha-numeric brands. Authors found that the numeric portions of the brands play a vital role in the perception of the product generation, whereas the letters usually help consumers identify the product type. In parallel, Ang (1997) investigated the effects of phonetics, lucky numbers and letters on consumers' processing of alpha-numeric brand names and showed that various linguistic properties of the brands affect consumers' general opinions of the products.

While past research has provided us with important insights about the perception of the alpha-numeric brands, the effects of these brands on consumers' choices have not been explored. It is well-known that the brand name is the foundation of a brand's image and it has a vital role on customers' purchase decisions in the marketplace (Kohli and LaBahn 1997). On the other hand, despite their widespread use in numerous industries, we know very little about how alpha-numeric brands actually affect the choice outcomes. Our research contributes to literature by extending on past studies and identifying the systematic effects of alpha-numeric brand names on consumers' preferences under different circumstances. Building on previous findings, we demonstrate how and when alpha-numeric brand names can improve or reduce the accuracy of consumer choices. We consider situations, when there is complete or incomplete attribute information and explore the different cognitive processes through which alpha-numeric brands have an effect on consumers who have different levels of need for cognition.

This research reveals that alpha-numeric brands have a systematic effect on product choices. We show that given an identical choice set, labeling a product option with a higher or lower alpha-numeric brand (X-100 vs. X-200) increases or decreases its choice share. We also consider the situations when choice options are missing important attributes and reveal that under missing information, alpha-numeric brands can still affect (potentially mislead) consumer choices. We further examine the different cognitive processes through which alpha-numeric brands affect consumers with low and high need for cognition (Cacciopo and Petty 1982). Our findings indicate that consumers with low need for cognition use a simple brand name heuristics and make their decisions based on the assumption that alpha-numeric brands with higher numeric portions correspond to more advanced products. On the other hand, those with high need for cognition process alpha-numeric brands more deeply trying to infer brand-attribute correlations and understand the relations among the brand names and attribute values.

Besides its contribution to different streams of literatures such as branding, missing information and inference making, our research has important managerial and practical implications. The fact that product familiarity did not prevent the effects of alpha-numeric brands on choices highlights the serious implications of our research for marketers and consumers. Our results further show that consumers' choices can be fairly easily manipulated by marketers in real life purchases. If sales people strategically expose their customers to various product options with alphanumeric brands they may maximize the possibility that consumers will make a choice based on alphanumeric brand names.

REFERENCES

Ang, Swee Hoon (1997), "Chinese Consumers' Perception of Alpha-numeric Brand Names," *Asia Pacific Journal of Marketing and Logistics*, 8(1), 31-48

Boyd, Colin W. (1985), "Point of View: Alpha-Numeric Brand Names," *Journal of Advertising Research*, 25 (5), 48-52.

Cacciopo, John T. and Richard E. Petty (1982), "The Need For Cognition," *Journal of Personality and Social Psychology*, 42 (1), 116-31.

Kohli, Chiranjeev and Douglas W. LaBahn (1997), "Observations: Creating Effective Brand Names: A Study of the Naming Process," *Journal of Advertising Research*, 9(1), 18-37

Pavia, Teresa A., and Janeen Arnold Costa (1993), "The Winning Number: Consumer Perceptions of Alpha-Numeric Brand "Names," *Journal of Marketing*, 57 (July), 85-98

United States patent and trademark office official website, www.uspto.gov, Feb, 12th, 2006

Broadening Perceptions of Familiar Brands

Robert Jewell, Kent State University, USA
Christina Saenger, Kent State University, USA

EXTENDED ABSTRACT

When changes in the market reveal the need for a well-defined brand to broaden its consumer perceptions, such attempts are often met with resistance. Perceptions of well-defined brands are typically strongly held, inhibiting the ability of a brand to broaden perceptions when faced with changes in the market, such as shifts in consumer preferences or flat revenues. This research examines how a well-defined brand can encourage the assimilation of discrepant information into the brand meaning via comparative advertising. We propose that the comparison brand acts as a referent, facilitating the development of associations between the advertised brand and new attribute information. Further, we argue that the characteristics associated with the comparison brand will moderate the ability of a brand to expand its meaning via comparative advertising.

It is generally accepted that brands are stored as concept nodes and are defined based on linkages to category-relevant attributes (Nedungadi 1990). To broaden perceptions of a brand, links to new attributes must be established. One way to establish these links is to make salient relevant context cues (Meyers-Levy and Tybout 1997); when context cues become accessible, the evaluation of an item is not only derived from the characteristics of the item, but also from the interaction of the characteristics of the item and the context in which the item is evaluated (Meyer and Johnson 1995). Thus, employing a context cue or referent should facilitate consumers' interpretation of the extent to which a brand is associated with new attributes; however, a brand-attribute link will be rejected for a brand attempting to associate with a product-class category that is inconsistent with existing brand linkages. Well-defined brands are constrained by strong associations to existing product-type attributes; the association of new information is likely to be resisted due to the high level of discrepancy between the new information and the existing associations. Combining new information with a contextual cue that dissociates the brand from, but still ties to membership in, its existing product type, should result in relative acceptance of the new attribute information.

Comparative advertising is often used in marketing to make a context cue salient. The comparison brand serves as a reference point by which the new claim of the advertised brand is, in part, judged. When selecting a comparison brand, a competitor may be chosen from either the brand's current product-type category, or from the product-type category of the new attribute information. When comparing a brand to a competitor in its existing product class category, the advertisement communicates points of distinction of the brand from that competitive group (i.e., a dissociative strategy). When comparing a brand to a competitor in the product-type category of the new attribute information, points of similarity between the brands are emphasized (i.e., an associative strategy).

When communicating the link between a brand and a new attribute from a different product-type category with a noncomparative advertisement, we expect the highly discrepant attribute information to be rejected due to its inconsistency with current perceptions of the brand (cf. Meyers-Levy and Sternthal 1993); the development of the link would be met with resistance. In a dissociative comparative advertisement, however, we expect that the reference point increases the likelihood that the link will be developed between the brand and the new attribute information because the comparison brand has links to the current product-type category, providing a schema-consistent reference point that makes the link between the advertised brand and new attribute seem less discrepant. In an associative comparative advertisement, this tempering of the new claim is not expected. The associative reference point should amplify the discrepancy between the advertised brand and the new attribute information because the advertised brand would be compared to two referents from a different product-type category: both the attribute and the competitor from the new product-type category.

We hypothesized that a dissociative comparative advertising strategy would be more effective in broadening perceptions of a well-defined brand than both an associative strategy and a noncomparative strategy, and that there would be no difference between the associative and noncomparative strategies. Further, we hypothesized that an associative strategy would result in evaluations that are more consistent with the current product-type category than would a dissociative or noncomparative strategy. Results of our first study confirmed that the use of a reference point facilitates the broadening of the meaning of a brand, and that the nature of the reference point (dissociative or associative) matters. Further, results of the associative strategy showed that associative comparative advertising strengthens the association to the existing product-type category.

While the dissociative comparative advertising strategy proved successful in our first study, it may have a significant weakness. Repeated encoding of dissociative information may strengthen the linkages of the advertised brand to the existing product-type category due to repeated activation of the schema-consistent reference point as the comparison brand. Thus, we proposed that a comparative advertising approach combining both dissociative and associative strategies will be successful, over time, in pushing the brand away from the existing product-type category and pulling the brand toward the new product-type category. We hypothesized that this combination approach would be more effective than a purely-dissociative approach, and that the dissociative approach would be perceived as more consistent with current product-type category attributes than the combination strategy. Results confirmed that context cues from multiple product-type categories were more effective in broadening perceptions, and that multiple exposures to context cues from the current product-type category reinforce the existing meaning of a brand.

The present paper contributes to the comparative advertising literature by demonstrating how comparative advertising can be used to broaden perceptions of a well-defined, existing brand. Previous research on comparative advertising has focused on the effects of a comparison brand on perceptions of new or unfamiliar brands, where the process of assimilation is fairly straightforward. This paper examines the impact of existing linkages on the acceptance of new information and provides a framework through which a well-defined brand may broaden the way it is defined in the marketplace.

REFERENCES

Aaker, David A. and J. Gary Shansby (1982), "Consumer Evaluations of Brand Extensions," *Journal of Marketing*, 54 (January), 56-62.

Churchill, Gilbert A. Jr. (1976), *Marketing Research: Methodological Foundations*, Hinsdale IL: Dryden Press.

Droge, Cornelia and Rene Y. Darmon (1987), "Associative Positioning Strategies Through Comparative Advertising: Attribute Versus Overall Similarity Approaches," *Journal of Marketing Research*, 24 (November), 377-88.

Gorn, Gerald J. and Charles B. Weinberg (1984), "The Impact of Comparative Advertising on Perception and Attitude: Some Positive Findings," *Journal of Consumer Research*, 11 (September), 719-27.

Grewal, Dhruv, Sukumar Kavanoor, Edward F. Fern, Carolyn Costly and James Barnes (1987), "Comparative Versus Noncomparative Advertising: A Meta-Analysis," *Journal of Marketing*, 61 (October), 1-15.

Herr, Paul M. (1989), "Priming Price: Prior Knowledge and Context Effects," *Journal of Consumer Research*, 16 (June), 67-75.

Herr, Paul M., Steven J. Sherman, and Russell H. Fazio (1983), "On the Consequences of Priming: Assimilation and Contrast Effects," *Journal of Experimental Social Psychology*, 19 (July), 323-40.

Meyer, Robert and Eric J. Johnson (1995), "The Building Blocks of a Unified Mathematical Theory of Consumer Perception, Judgment, and Choice," *Marketing Science*, 14 (3), G180-189.

Myers-Levy, Joan and Brian Sternthal (1993), "A Two-Factor Explanation of Assimilation and Contrast Effects," *Journal of Marketing Research*, 30 (August), 359-68.

Myers-Levy, Joan and Alice M. Tybout (1997), "Context Effects at Encoding and Judgment in Consumption Settings: The Role of Cognitive Resources," *Journal of Consumer Research*, 24 (June), 1-14.

Narayana, Chem L. (1977), "Graphic Positioning Scale: An Economical Instrument for Surveys," *Journal of Marketing Research*, 16 (February), 118-22.

Nedungadi, Prakash (1990), "Recall and Consumer Consideration Sets: Influencing Choice without Altering Brand Evaluations," *Journal of Consumer Research*, 17 (December), 263-76.

Pechmann, Cornelia and S. Ratneshwar (1991), "The Use of Comparative Advertising for Brand Positioning: Association versus Differentiation," *Journal of Consumer Research*, 18 (September), 145-60.

Sujan, Mita and James R. Bettman (1989), "The Effects of Brand Positioning Strategies on Consumer's Brand and Category Perceptions: Some Insights From Schema Research," *Journal of Marketing Research*, 26 (November), 454-67.

Whence Brand Evaluations? Investigating the Relevance of Personal and Extrapersonal Associations in Brand Attitudes

Sandor Czellar, HEC Paris, France
Benjamin Voyer, HEC Paris, France
Alexandre Schwob, HEC Paris, France
David Luna, Baruch College, USA

EXTENDED ABSTRACT

A recent conceptualization of attitude structure in social psychology proposes that individuals may have in their memories different types of salient associations about an object, each type with a different role in personal attitude formation (Olson and Fazio 2004). According to this conceptualization, some of these salient associations, called *personal associations*, contribute directly to the formation of personal attitudes about the object. However, other associations, called *extrapersonal associations*, may be accessible in memory, but because individuals may not necessarily endorse them, these associations do not contribute directly to the formation of personal attitudes about the object. Those extrapersonal associations may be based on a variety of sources, including cultural knowledge, social influence or media information (Karpinski and Hilton 2001).

As this new typology bears potentially important implications for attitude conceptualization and measurement, it has promptly generated considerable research interest. Thus, experiments across several attitude domains highlight the importance of the personal-extrapersonal distinction for a better understanding of the associations affecting the outcomes of different attitude measures (De Houwer, Custers, and De Clercq 2006; Han, Olson, and Fazio 2006; Olson and Fazio 2004). The purpose of the present research is to investigate the validity and boundary conditions of Olson and Fazio's (2004) framework in a consumer attitude domain—brand evaluations. We present three studies on different car brands that are globally supportive of the new typology.

Study 1 suggests the presence of extrapersonal associations for all brands investigated, by showing that some highly accessible brand associations indeed do contribute to global attitudes about those brands, but others do not. In particular, we found that, for each of the car brands used in the study, at least one of the thoughts among the first five reported by the respondents did not correlate significantly with the overall attitude toward the brand.

Study 2 shows that an individual difference, consumer expertise with the category, impacts the accessibility of personal associations in a brand evaluation context. An important difference with respect to Study 1 is that, instead of using thought protocols, Study 2 assessed the personal-extrapersonal nature of associations with an implicit procedure by implementing the Implicit Association Test. We administered two different versions of the Implicit Association Test (IAT): the traditional IAT (Greenwald, McGhee, and Schwartz 1998) and the personalized IAT (Olson and Fazio 2004). The traditional IAT, according to Olson and Fazio (2004), is potentially affected by extrapersonal associations that are accessible at the time of categorizing the target object. Olson and Fazio (2004) devised a "personalized" version of the IAT that should be affected by personal associations to a greater extent than the traditional IAT. Our study found that increasing levels of category expertise lead to a greater correspondence of IAT measures with explicit attitude measures in the personalized (but not in the traditional) IAT.

Study 3 further highlights the value of the new typology for consumer research by showing that it can meaningfully explain changes in brand knowledge structures in a persuasion context. As in Study 2, we find that individuals with different levels of expertise use knowledge in different ways when they report their brand evaluations. Further, this study finds that personal associations (those used in the construction of brand evaluations) are made accessible by either strong or weak messages, depending on whether individuals are experts or novices, respectively.

Taken together, our three studies provide strong support for the value of Olson and Fazio's (2004) framework and provide a better understanding of the nature of the brand associations that form consumer brand attitudes. We conclude the paper with a discussion of the theoretical implications of our results with respect to recent research on the personal-extrapersonal distinction between associations. For instance, our results contribute to our knowledge on attitude structure and provide valuable results for current conceptualizations of attitude processes (Fabrigar, MacDonald, and Wegener 2005). Recently, Gawronski and Bodenhausen (2006, 2007) advanced a distinction between two kinds of evaluative processes: associative and propositional. Associative processes are claimed to provide the basis for primitive affective reactions in evaluative judgments, while propositional processes involve thoughtful assessments of the validity of evaluative statements. Gawronski and Bodenhausen (2006) argue that the personal-extrapersonal distinction is likely to operate at the propositional level but less so at an associative level. Indeed, the explicit attitude measures used in our three studies likely implied some level of propositional reasoning and thus support this view. However, our second study using different variants of the Implicit Association Test corroborates recent findings in other research (Olson and Fazio 2004; Han et al. 2006) suggesting that the distinction between personal and extrapersonal information may, in some domains at least, also operate at a low-thought, associational level. Our findings suggest that attitudes for long-standing, established brands are likely to be part of such domains. However, the new typology may not apply to, for example, freshly formed attitudes toward new brands. Further research is certainly warranted to investigate which consumption domains are more or less likely to entail the relevance of the personal-extrapersonal distinction at both associative and propositional levels.

REFERENCES

De Houwer, Jan, Roel Custers, and Armand De Clercq (2006), "Do Smokers Have a Negative Implicit Attitude Toward Smoking?," *Cognition and Emotion*, 20 (8), 1274-84.

Fabrigar, Leandre R., Tara K. MacDonald, and Duane T. Wegener (2005), "The Structure of Attitudes," in *The Handbook of Attitudes*, Dolorès Albarracín and Blair T. Johnson and Mark P. Zanna, Eds. Mahwah NJ: Lawrence Erlbaum.

Gawronski, Bertram and Galen V. Bodenhausen (2006), "Associative and Propositional Processes in Evaluation: An Integrative Review of Implicit and Explicit Attitude Change," *Psychological Bulletin*, 132 (5), 692-731.

Gawronski, Bertram and Galen V. Bodenhausen (2007), "Unraveling the Processes Underlying Evaluation: Attitudes from the Perspective of the APE Model," *Social Cognition*, 25 (5), 687-717.

Greenwald, Anthony G., Debbie McGhee and Jordan L. K Schwartz (1998). "Measuring Individual Differences in Implicit Cognition: The Implicit Association Test," *Journal of Personality and Social Psychology,* 74 (6), 1464-80.

Han, Anna H., Michael A. Olson, and Russell H. Fazio (2006), "The Influence of Experimentally Created Extrapersonal Associations on the Implicit Association Test," *Journal of Experimental Social Psychology,* 42 (3), 259-72.

Karpinski, Andrew and James L. Hilton (2001), "Attitudes and the Implicit Association Test," *Journal of Personality and Social Psychology,* 81 (5), 774-88.

Olson, Michael A. and Russell H. Fazio (2004), "Reducing the Influence of Extrapersonal Associations on the Implicit Association Test: Personalizing the IAT," *Journal of Personality and Social Psychology,* 86 (5), 653-67.

Encounters of Accidental Tourists: Maintaining Boundaries through Food Consumption

Fleura Bardhi, Northeastern University, UK
Anders Bengtsson, Suffolk University, USA
Jacob Ostberg, Stockholm University, Sweden

EXTENDED ABSTRACT

The study attempts to provide an understanding of the ways that tourists relate to local and home food and the role that these relationships play in personal management of tourist experiences. Tourism involve boundary crossing and may generate a sense of fragmentation and discontinuity. Tourist traveling may even threaten our familiar sense of who we are. Thus, tourists do not only engage in adventurous explorations, but also in boundary maintenance practices (Belk 1997). Acculturation studies have pointed at several such practices and have emphasized the role of possessions and rituals in boundary maintenance practices during long term mobility. However, research that examines the ways that tourists manage their experiences abroad is lacking. Further, mobile consumers behave conservatively when it comes to food consumption and foods tastes are among the most resistant practices during acculturation. Considering the relationship between food, identity, and home, we intend to provide an explanation and perspective on such tourist food experiences. Food consumption is fundamental for human life and we take the perspective that food is never just about eating and eating is never just a biological process (Rozin 1999; Watson and Caldwell 2005). In this paper, we examine how food becomes a cultural resource for consumers that are temporarily away from their everyday life contexts.

One of the reasons that tourists feel distressed when being faced with the local food at the tourist destinations is that "food consumption simultaneously asserts the oneness of the ones eating the same and the otherness of whoever eats differently" (Fischler 1988: 275; Mintz and Du Bois 2002). Food consumption is not only about defining oneself towards or from various groups, it is also about being unique, which is a fundamental aspect of our sense of self-identity (Giddens 1991). On this more individual level food consumption is central since any human is constructed, biologically, psychologically and socially by the food he or she chooses to incorporate. When the self is threatened by the abundance of unfamiliar cultural cues at the tourist destination, food becomes an anchor that reminds the tourist of who they really are.

Food plays a salient role during boundary crossing and maintenance also because it is an essential and portable part of the materiality of home (Miller 2001), and as such can be used to recreate an experience of home and a sense of stability when away (Petridou 2001). Additionally, food tastes reflect socialization processes that work directly on the body and these embodied tastes tend to be enduring and difficult to transform (Allen 2004). Prior research has shown that mobile consumers resist changes in such embodied food preferences and long for the cultural environments similar to their home country (Thompson and Tambyah 1999). Thus, we expect that tourists may cope with cultural and existential alienation through maintenance of these embodied food preferences to recreate a sense of home in the body and abroad.

The empirical data for this study consists of accounts of 29 middle-class American consumers' experiences of food consumption during a trip to China that lasted for 10 days. This particular context (i.e. first time tourists to a culture that is distinctly different from their native culture) was deemed appropriate for understanding the a) consumer alienation experiences as tourists; and b) the existential role of food as a coping mechanism. Data collection took place during and after the trip. Informants were instructed to keep a personal journal of their food encounters during their trip. When they returned to United States, we used their personal journals as the backbone for one-to-one in-depth interviews that lasted from 30 to 90 minutes with each of them. The interviews evolved around their overall tourist experience in China, their experiences with Chinese foods and other types of foods they selected to consume. An interpretative and semiotic perspective was followed in analyzing and interpreting the data.

Informants make sense of their tourist experiences and consumption of food through continuous categorization and interpretation of the host and home food cultures illustrated in the paper by a model inspired by Greimas' semiotic square. We find that the category Chinese Food creates considerable discomfort whereas the remaining three categories of the semiotic square (Domestic, Non-Chinese, and Non-Domestic food) represent positive food encounters because these enable informants to cope with experiences of alienation. Consistent with prior work, we find that the mass tourist typically lacks the local cultural capital to make sense of the experience abroad and makes little effort do so (Hannerz 1990). Thus, food encounters with the Other challenge tourist as competent consumers, decision makers, and alienate them from the local Other. Tourists attempt to grapple with these negative experiences by creating a symbolic distance towards the Other through food categorizations and judgments. Further, we find that negative judgments that informants made about the local Chinese food were extended to the judgments about the social Other.

Another important finding in the study is the fact that cultural and food regimes continue to play a salient role in making sense of daily consumption experiences. We find that they become even more salient during boundary crossing situations (such as tourism) when the home culture is symbolically threatened (Swidler 1986). Our informants resisted local foods and practices and strived to sustain the home-based cultural interpretation framework and practices. Consumers may not be as open to food experimentation as it is often suggested in the food consumption literature. This research shows that the familiar ways of eating food are still strongly connected to the consumers' sense of self as embodied practices (Allen 2004). This leads us to wonder whether the suggested condition of gastronomy is exaggerated (Warde 1997) and traditional food-ways continue to structure our eating in the same way as before.

Additionally, globalization processes and food transnationals have created in some way a reassuring standardized servicescape for tourists that enable them to experience "home" abroad through patronization of these predicable, safe, and familiar spaces and tastes. We find that while informants reject transnational fast foods at home, they embrace it with longing and satisfaction abroad. For many informants search and consumption of non-Chinese food became a symbolic project of finding and experiencing a sense of home and normality. They expressed greater satisfaction with non-Chinese food that was also transferred to quality and customer satisfaction evaluations with the overall servicescape. Further, we find that iconic authenticity (Grayson and Martinec 2004) with the 'home food' was sufficient for tourists to reduce cultural and personal anxieties and feel comfortable, at home abroad.

Living with Uncertainty: The Impact of Terrorism

Krittinee Nuttavuthisit, Chulalongkorn University, Thailand

EXTENDED ABSTRACT

Terrorism has become a global event that creates a continuous effect on not only killing and destruction but also on significant changes in people's behavior. Nevertheless, in consumer research there have been few studies on the impact of terrorism on consumer behaviors. Possibly this is because of limited access to the victims of terrorism and affected locations. Literatures in related areas include studies of uncertainty, coping strategies, and terror management. The major findings are that when people feel uncertain about what will happen, they try to regain a sense of control which helps to reduce the stress of uncertainty. However, prior research mainly specified control over situation while the circumstance of terrorism is inexplicable and out of control.

This research explores the effects of the ongoing terrorist violence in the southern provinces of Thailand. It aims to address the theoretical gap in studying how people cope with their experiencing uncertainty when they feel victimized and powerless under the uncontrollable situation. Moreover, this study reflects recent terror management research which has emphasized cultural-specific responses (Rindfleisch and Burroughs 2004).

Thailand is considered a peaceful country with Buddhism as the dominant religion. Thai Muslims are mostly concentrated in the southern provinces of Thailand, particularly in Narathiwat, Yala and Pattani. With their different lifestyle, some Thai Muslims feel estranged from the rest of the country and, together with the chronic concerns of poverty, underdevelopment and discrimination by some abusive officials, these problems led to the insurgency led by Muslim separatists. In the beginning the targets of the terrorist attacks were government officials but now include all kinds of people, ranging from Buddhist monks to school teachers, Muslim farmers and innocent children. The reason for these attacks is unclear and no group has claimed responsibility for these events. The daily random attacks have resulted in sustained uncertainty and dramatic changes to the lifestyles of residents and their families.

Uncertainty is a dynamic state of discomfort, a situation that exists when people feel that they cannot predict what will happen. Uncertainty has long been recognized as a critical issue and different means of managing uncertainty have been identified in various fields of studies. Pavia and Mason (2004) emphasized the experience of uncertainty and coping strategies as a rich field for consumer research. Generally, the specified coping strategies can be categorized into two basic concepts, avoiding suspected causes of uncertainty and seeking what brings stability and a sense of future. The two major coping strategies may appear antithetical but they are linked by the common goal of regaining a sense of control.

This research study began early in 2005 with respondents including residents of the three southern provinces, soldiers stationed in the region and their families. Eight long interviews and two focus group interviews, one with soldiers and another with their wives, were conducted. Due to the upsurge in violence field visits were not possible, and interviews with residents in the troubled areas were carried out when they visited Bangkok. Verbatim transcripts were interpreted by means of a hermeneutical process (Thompson, Locander, and Pollio 1989).

The research data illustrates that, in accordance with the previous theory of uncertainty management, people try to avoid suspected causes of uncertainty and seek what provides a sense of stability. The means to address their fear, worry and tension are reflected in their consumptions of time, place, faith and social affiliations which also suggest the unique responses to managing uncertainty depending on the context and cultural values. In this case, rather than avoiding the suspected causes of uncertainty (i.e., dangerous areas, or 'ghostly terrorists' which are impossible to identify), local residents instead attempt to adjust their own routines or lifestyles. Although theories of uncertainty management emphasize increased flexibility in creating alternatives (Lazarus and Folkman 1984; Courtney, Kirkland and Viguerie 1999), this study found that people prefer the familiar even when this is unsafe to encounter the odds of daily attacks at anytime. In seeking what brings stability or sense of future, they relied on faith or miracles rather than performing concrete preventive acts within the community or with the authorities. They trust that fate will bring a natural end to these events over which they feel they have little or no control.

To some people, these coping behaviors may appear gullible, insubstantial or short-sighted, but they serve the purpose, as specified in previous theory, of enabling people to regain a sense of control which helps to reduce the stress of uncertainty. However, a difference must be noted here as the sense of control in this study is rather control over self rather than the situation. Based on the notion that uncertain events cause the sense of uncertainty, prior research suggested that constructing a new normalcy can enable individuals to restore order and envision a sense of future (Becker 1997; Pavia and Mason 2004). Creating a new normalcy in which individuals can *explain the situation*, i.e., what has happened and what will happen, enables them to choose the way to live their lives (Weitz 1989). However, the findings of this research illustrate that people rather try *to recognize the situation* and adjust the self (e.g., lifestyle and beliefs) to handle the experience of uncertainty. Instead of constructing a new normalcy they familiarize themselves with the uncertain events and, in this way, they can also gain the sense of control, but over self rather than the situation. The focus is on dealing with the present rather than unveiling the past or the future. Uncertainty is rooted in the individual's perception of the outcome or meaning of a situation (Penrod 2007). Hence, whether it is managing the situation or managing the self should also induce changes in an individual's perceptions of the circumstances. This study proposes extension of the theory regarding management of uncertainty to incorporate coping mechanisms from the perspective of self. It also endorses the view that cultural differences (i.e. belief in fate occurring by law of karma in Buddhism or by god's will in Islam) significantly influence how individuals respond to uncertainty.

REFERENCES

Becker, Gay (1997), *Disrupted Lives: How People Create Meaning in a Chaotic World*, Berkeley: University of California Press.

Courtney, Hugh, Jane Kirkland, and Patrick Viguerie (1999), "Strategy Under Uncertainty," in *Harvard Business Review on Managing Uncertainty*, Boston, MA: Harvard Business School Press.

Lazarus, Richard S. and Susan Folkman (1984), *Stress, Appraisal, and Coping*, New York: Springer.

Pavia, Teresa M. and Marlys J. Mason (2004), "The Reflexive Relationship between Consumer Behavior and Adaptive Coping," *Journal of Consumer Research*, Vol. 31 (September), 441-54.

Penrod, Janice (2007), "Living with Uncertainty: Concept Advancement," *Journal of Advanced Nursing*, Vol. 57 (March), 658-67.

Rindfleisch, Aric and James E. Burroughs (2004), "Terrifying Thoughts, Terrible Materialism? Contemplations on a Terror Management Account of Materialism and Consumer Behavior," *Journal of Consumer Psychology*, 14 (3), 219-224.

Thompson, Craig J., William B. Locander, and Howard R. Pollio (1989), "Putting Consumer Experience Back into Consumer Research: The Philosophy and Method of Existential-Phenomenology," *Journal of Consumer Research*, 16 (September), 133-146.

Weitz, Rose (1989), "Uncertainty and the Lives of Persons with AIDS," *Journal of Health and Social Behavior*, Vol. 30 (September), 270-81.

Cultures of Unruly Bricolage: 'Debadging' and the Cultural Logic of Resistance

Douglas Brownlie, University of Stirling, Scotland
Paul Hewer, University of Strathclyde, Scotland

EXTENDED ABSTRACT

Abstract

Arnould and Thompson note that the "marketplace has become a pre-eminent source of mythic and symbolic resources through which [people] construct narratives of identity" (2005: 871). Not only do consumers "actively rework and transform symbolic meanings" (ibid: 871), but in everyday practices they use "marketplace cultures [to] define their symbolic boundaries through an ongoing opposition to dominant lifestyle norms and mainstream consumer sensibilities (ibid: 874). The paper examines identity work done with cherished possessions, in this case cars. By means of a netnography we focus on everyday practices where consumers rework brand identity towards their local identity projects.

Introduction

A rich stream of research has explored consumers' resistance to commodity culture and brands (Arnould & Thompson, 2004; Holt, 2001, 2002; Dobscha, 1998; Fournier, 1998; Schor, 1998). Research has thus focused upon the anti-brand movement (Fischer, 2001), lovers of the natural world (Dobscha, 1998), downshifters (Schor, 1998), to the voluntary simplicity movement (Murray, 2002) or the burning man movement (Kozinets, 2002b). Murray (2002) draws our attention to how such consumers, who are often cynical of commodity culture, seek to construct their sense of who they are, through what he terms their 'salient negations' to commodity culture. We reveal how consumer subcultures are engaged in forms of guerrilla warfare to affirm, maintain and consolidate their group identity through their appropriations of marketing brands.

Conceptualisation

In their recent synthesising overview of consumer culture theory, Arnould and Thomson discuss the constitutive and productive aspects of consumption, noting that the "marketplace has become a pre-eminent source of mythic and symbolic resources through which [people] construct narratives of identity" (2005: 871). They remind us that not only do "consumers actively rework and transform symbolic meanings" (ibid: 871), but that through a variety of everyday practices they also use "marketplace cultures [to] define their symbolic boundaries through an ongoing opposition to dominant lifestyle norms and mainstream consumer sensibilities (ibid: 874). In this paper we construct a line of argument based on those thematic observations, exploring in particular the identity work that is done by consumers through modifying cherished possessions, in this case cars. We focus, paradoxically perhaps, on the site of everyday practices by means of which consumers de-badge, or perhaps, re-badge their vehicles, or otherwise rework its brand identity, in pursuit of local identity projects.

Methodology

In our quest to understand the consumer practices and tactics of 'debadging' we drew inspiration from the netnographic work of Kozinets (2001, 2002a). We started by 'lurking' at a number of web forums devoted to car cultures. These included amongst others: MBWorld Discussion forum, otherwise known as the forum for Mercedes-Benz enthusiasts; VWvortex forum, otherwise know as the Volkswagon enthusiast website; Mini2.com, otherwise known as 'fuel for your mini obsession'; Hondacivicforum.com; and 7thGenCivic.Com. Most of the forums advertise themselves in much the same way that the Honda Civic forum does: "as a discussion forum & one stop resource for all Honda Civic related discussions, with forum topics including Honda Civic vehicle maintenance, tech help with car repairs, and performance upgrades."

Findings

The findings are organised under three key themes: first to unravel what we mean by the practice of debadging; second to theorize the consumer as a designer; and third, to explore the forms of exchange, and affiliation exhibited by car enthusiasts. For instance, we find that design at the everyday level is about finding solutions to identity tasks and overcoming contradictions through bricolage. For many the changes made through de-badging their vehicles focus upon the achievement of a particular look, where the reclamation of de-signing is intended to achieve a degree of anonymity, but also a form of cultural capital in itself in which such practices were engineered to speak to those who understand, and exclude others for their lack of aesthetic and technical knowledge and appreciation. The informants display a sophisticated understanding and appreciation of the state of things and are restless in their pursuit to change the things that matter in their lives.

Conclusions

The analytical focus of the paper is directed towards a virtual community of car enthusiasts and a series of online reports of consumer bricolage in the empirical setting of car modification. This opens a window on a variety of everyday practices that characterize how consumers actively use cars and other resources of popular culture in creative ways as symbolic resources for constructing and sustaining social identity. Also illuminated are ways in which arenas of anti-consumption are invested with particular meanings that are grounded within practices of daily life. Through analysing forms of reportage naturally occurring in those online sites, textual data is generated about consumption practices that can be read as constitutive of forms of consumer resistance. Theorising resistance through de Certeau's (1984) lens of everyday practice brings analysis to 'grounded aesthetics' (Willis, 1990) as a potential arena in which practices of consumer resistance are played out. Over an eight-month period an internet-based methodology generated observations of online posting activity on five different internet newsgroups attracting those with an interest in the highly particular pursuit of car modification. Participants used those web-forums not only to share information and insights, but to give individual and collective voice to enthusiasms towards car modification and customization as a way of improving vehicle aesthetic appeal. The term 'grounded aesthetics' (Willis, 1990) is used to describe 'articulations' (Kozinets, 2001, p. 70) between practices of everyday life and the creativity that consumers bring to their 're-appropriation of the product-system' (de Certeau 1984, p xxiv). For some informants the practice of debadging is a tactic to improve the look of the vehicle; for others it expresses a more radical practice that feeds-off desires to be free of what is seen as the thinly concealed calculation and manipulation of visible brand livery. Findings show that, as Denzin (2001) observes, "grounded aesthetics function both as vehicles and sites of resistance" (ibid, p.

328). The paper concludes that the discussion threads of the studied web-forums offer access to the interplay of discursive resources in circulation among interest-based collectives; and that they can usefully be understood as arenas for following how the discursive resource-base is nurtured, sustained and transformed through various interpellations, including the rehearsal of anti-consumption rhetoric and sentiment. But rather than being anxious or defensive about such forms of unruly re-appropriation, we advise that businesses, especially designers and consumer researchers, would benefit from following the discussion occurring on such sites–for this speaks of fragments of cultural change that, should it gather impetus, will circulate more widely within contexts of consumption.

REFERENCES

Arnould, Eric J. and Thompson, Craig J. (2005), "Consumer Culture Theory (CCT): Twenty Years of Research". *Journal of Consumer Research*, vol.31:868-882 [March].

De Certeau, Michel. (1984), *The Practice of Everyday Life*. Berkeley: University of California Press; 1984.

Denzin, Norman K. (2001), "The Seventh Moment: Qualitative Inquiry and the Practices of a More Radical Consumer Research", *Journal of Consumer Research*, vol.28:324-330 [September].

Dobscha, Susan. (1998), "The Lived Experience of Consumer Rebellion against Marketing" (1998), *Advances in Consumer Research*, vol.25:91-97.

Fournier, Susan. (1998), "Consumers and their brands: developing relationship theory in consumer research", *Journal of Consumer Research*, vol.24:343-373 [March].

Holt, Douglas B. Why do Brands Cause Trouble? A Dialectical Theory of Consumer Culture and Branding (2002), *Journal of Consumer Research*, vol.29:70-90 [June].

_____ (2001), Deconstructing Consumer Resistance: How the Reification of Commodified Cultural Sovereignty is entailed in the Parasitic Postmodern Market, *Advances in Consumer Research*, vol.28:123.

Kozinets, Robert V. (2002a), "The Field Behind the Screen: Using Netnography for Marketing Research in Online Communities", *Journal of Marketing Research*, Vol.XXXIX:61-72 [February].

_____ (2002b), "Can Consumers Escape Market? Emancipatory Illuminations from Burning Man", *Journal of Consumer Research*, vol.29: 20-38 [June].

_____ (2001) "Utopian Enterprise: Articulating the Meanings of Star Trek's Culture of Consumption", *Journal of Consumer Research*, vol.28, June, 67-88.

_____ (1997), "I Want To Believe": A Netnography of The X-Philes' Subculture of Consumption. *Advances in Consumer Research,* vol.24, 470-475.

Lury, Celia. (2004), *Brands: The Logos of the Global Economy*. London: Routledge.

Schor, Juliet *The Overspent American: Upscaling, Downshifting and the New Consumer*. Harper Collins: New York; 1999.

Willis, Paul; Jones, Simon; Canaan, Joyce; and Hurd, Geoff *Common Culture: Symbolic Work at Play in the everyday cultures of the young*. Milton Keynes: Open University Press; 1990.

Consumer Mourning and Coping with the Loss of Strategic Rituals: The Case of Marshall Field & Co.

Cele C. Otnes, The University of Illinois at Urbana-Champaign, USA
Behice Ece Ilhan, The University of Illinois at Urbana-Champaign, USA
Jenny Yang, The University of Illinois at Urbana-Champaign, USA
Nicole Tami, The University of Illinois at Urbana-Champaign, USA

EXTENDED ABSTRACT

It is a well-supported assertion in the social sciences and in consumer behavior that rituals provide structure and meaning to people's lives (e.g., Driver, 1991; Rook 1985). Furthermore, through commitments of time, energy and money, consumers demonstrate their attachment not only to consumer-generated rituals such as family holidays, but also to "strategic rituals"–repeated, dramatic events engineered by retailers and marketers in order to achieve key customer and profit objectives. Although current research on consumer/retailer relationships examines the importance of retail aesthetics and the ways retailers enhance brand meaning (e.g., Sherry 1998; Sherry, et al, 2004; Thompson and Arsel, 2004), our understanding of the benefits consumers accrue from such relationships remains underdeveloped. In this paper, we focus on the how consumers mourn and cope with the loss of strategic rituals offered by a retailer. By focusing on the loss of these strategic rituals, we illuminate the specific benefits consumers glean from them, and the ways consumers cope with aspects of ritual loss.

Our interest in the topic was spurred by the outpouring of negative emotions accompanying the announcement that the landmark Chicago-based department store chain Marshall Field & Co. (hereafter, "Field's") would be rebranded as Macy's as of September, 2006. The significance of Field's as a venue for its own strategic rituals was well-documented in media accounts and on web blogs. In addition, Field's was highly significant as a pioneering retailer in the United States, and offered many "firsts"–such as the first restaurant in a retail store, the first delivery, the first return/exchange policies, and one of the first stores to recognize the importance of the aesthetic experience of shopping (as evidenced by its Tiffany windows, fountain and large staff devoted to store display). We employed an interpretive approach, beginning with a few preliminary depth interviews with friends and acquaintances who confirmed that they were mourning the loss of Field's. We then placed an ad on a Midwest university bulletin board, asking for volunteers to discuss their thoughts and feelings on the renaming of the store. Informants include key players involved in maintaining websites dedicated to the memory and/or resurrection of Field's, such as fieldsfanchicago.com and darrid.com. Our fifteen informants (one was interviewed twice) were all middle- or upper-middle class in their 20s-50s, and were primarily white females. However, three were African-American females and two were men. Three of the four research team members, all women between their 20s and 40s, conducted the interviews. We conducted the first few in pairs to facilitate discussion among the research team of emergent issues, with the last half being conducted by single researchers. Transcripts of these interviews yielded over 125 pages of single-spaced text.

Three of the four team members participated in the analysis, reading and re-reading the data and focusing our research questions to those we believed could best help us understand the ritual mourning and coping we observed. These questions are: 1) What cherished rituals did Field's create or co-create with consumers? 2) What benefits of these rituals do consumers miss the most? 3) How do consumers cope with the loss of these strategic rituals? The authors negotiated the interpretation of these questions and discussed the most salient issues to include in this paper, as well as other issues to pursue as our interviews continue. Our findings reveal that Field's created or co-created at least six strategic rituals for consumers: selection of focal ritual artifacts (such as the first pair of high heels, prom dresses, and wedding gowns), enhancement of the Christmas ritual, customized shopping experiences, sources of iconic brands/gifts, inclusion on a tour of Chicago, and bargain shopping. Furthermore, consumers elicited five key benefits from these strategic rituals at Field's. Specifically, the source provided a venue for aspirational but democratic consumption, a source of aesthetic pleasure, a source of civic pride given the importance of Field's and the Fields family to Chicago, a locus for family traditions, and the quintessential shopping experience through the offering of unique, high-quality merchandise, unparalleled customer service and even a highly desirable work environment complete with rituals designed to enhance employees' work experiences. Further, in coping with the loss of Field's, consumers exhibit both avoidant and accepting behavioral coping strategies. Avoidant strategies include venting their unhappiness over the loss of Field's, rejecting Macy's and other alternatives to the strategic rituals Field's had created, and distancing themselves physically and cognitively from the memories of Field's. Active coping strategies include accepting the loss, but also engaging in more active civic-oriented strategies such as staging protests outside the store and boycotting Macy's. Our paper reveals that consumers do find strategic rituals supported or co-created by retailers as meaningful experiences in their lives, and when the opportunities for these rituals disappear, must mourn and cope with these losses.

References available upon request.

The Construction of Value in Attention Economies

Ashlee Humphreys, Northwestern University, USA
Robert V. Kozinets, York University, Canada

EXTENDED ABSTRACT

In this paper, we view YouTube through the lens of the "attention economy" and use it as a site to further develop our understanding of the hierarchical processes of attention consumption and the construction of value within attention economies. Originally developed by Herbert Simon, the concept of an attention economy comes from considering the many effects implied by an abundance of information. As Simon (1971) says, "[w]hat information consumes is rather obvious: it consumes the attention of its recipients. Hence a wealth of information creates a poverty of attention and a need to allocate that attention efficiently among the overabundance of information sources that might consume it" (p. 41). Although Simon perceptively notes that attention becomes a resource and therefore comes to have value, he does not elaborate the process by which attention becomes transformed into something valuable. More recently, popular management writers have built off of Pine and Gilmore's (1999) idea of an "experience economy" to argue that this experience economy is underlain by an interest-driven "attention economy" (Davenport and Beck 2001). A number of authors take the attention economy principle to speculative lengths, predicting that, one day, "attention transactions" will replace financial transactions (Franck 1999; Goldhaber 1997). We take this speculation to pose several specific research questions. How do attention transactions occur on and through YouTube? How do the partners to an attention exchange form an idea of their role in this system of exchange? What roles are normatively available to them and how do they find a place within these roles? Further, how do these roles change over time?

Previous research has suggested that that people in an exchange network can vary in their roles as giver and receiver. However, when we consider attention economies we do not yet have a theory for how people assume an exchange role, how they conceive of these roles, or how these roles change over time, as the system evolves. Research on fan communities and fandom explores affective exchange both amongst fans and between fans and celebrities (Jenkins 1992; Kozinets 2001; O'Guinn 2000). On the one hand, fans actively interact with the objects of their admiration, contributing texts made from cultural materials (Lanier, Muñiz, and Schau 2006; Schau and Russell 2004) and forming social groups based on affiliation (Kozinets 2001). These characteristics of activity and involvement are particularly relevant to forming conceptions of an attention-based economy in an environment where interaction drives value and exchange. On the other hand, celebrities come to have value as a result of many of these fan activities and attentions. The precise nature of the relationship between fan feedback and celebrity value in attention economies, and particularly the fluidity of these concepts within electronically media, present a unique opportunity to develop a theory of the ways in which value is constructed through consumer/producer/fan/celebrity interaction, activity, and exchange.

To understand how people view themselves within attention exchange systems, we interviewed users of the YouTube network, an internet community where people exchange videos, post comments, and maintain personal profiles. Sixteen interviews were conducted in situ over the internet via private messages (Giesler 2006; Kozinets 2002). A netnography of site content, including analysis of videos produced by informants and those 'favored' by informants, was also conducted (Kozinets 2002). In addition to self-reports from interviews, several observations—the number of videos watched represented the level of consumption, and the number of videos posted to the site represented the level of production—were used to indicate the users' status as a consumer, producer, fan, and/or celebrity.

From this data, we find that in the attention exchange system, several ideal typical roles emerge from the ways in which people talk about their place in YouTube network, consumer, producer, fan, and celebrity. Although these ideal-typical roles—consumer, producer, fan, or celebrity—are not often fully-realized empirically, they orient consumer's conception of their place within the system. These dialectically-formed roles are often mutually exclusive within one exchange. That is, if one person discursively takes the producer role as the provider of value, the other person in the exchange takes the consumer role as the user of value.

We can then model the process of value creation through attention exchange as a four stage movement between these identities along two dimensions, the affective dimension and the market dimension. On the affective dimension, people exchange affect—words of encouragement, notes on the video's content, related thoughts or jokes. In general, the affective dimension represents attention being given to the producer of a video. Most often, the receivers of these comments are heralded as 'celebrities,' and the givers of the comments think of themselves 'fans.' Celebrities also give affect in return by sending messages to their fans or responding to posted comments. The market dimension represents the dimension on which content is exchanged. The ideal-typical producer actually makes the substantive components of the video and the ideal-typical consumer actually receives the content. In the case of YouTube, the material exchange is either the video itself or the verbal statements that make up the comments. As a result of this exchange process, four market identities with specific orientations arise: the productive celebrity, the fan-as-consumer, the fan-as-producer, and the produced celebrity. Each identity in the system is dialectically constructed through the process of exchange, the interaction between two parties in a given stage.

From the study of YouTube as an attention exchange system, we learn several things about identities within an exchange system. First, people construct their role in relation to the other people in the exchange in systematic ways. These identities change systematically both temporally within the exchange itself and between exchanges in the system. Second, value is created through the interaction of affect and material exchange. When videos are produced, they do not immediately have value. Value is bestowed by fan response, not only toward the producer, but by the interaction of fans. Affect alone, however, does not produce value; this affect must be directed toward some product or some person that comes to represent value itself. Vital to this celebrity value are two elements—commonness and uniqueness—that fans work to collectively monitor and maintain these. Third, by studying this 'sharing' system, we gain insight into the factors that motivate people to share and to reciprocate. The exchange of comments, as "currency" repays sharers for their work and motivates them to produce again. User comments form a more reified indicator of value when they are used as metrics for measuring celebrity/producer value. In this sense, they truly are the capital on which this non-monetary exchange system functions.

REFERENCES

Davenport, Thomas H. and John C. Beck (2001), *The Attention Economy : Understanding the New Currency of Business*. Boston: Harvard Business School Press.

Franck, Georg (1999), "The Economy of Attention," *Telepolis*, http://www.heise.de/tp/r4/artikel/5/5567/5561.html,

Giesler, Markus (2006), "Consumer Gift Systems," *Journal of Consumer Research* (September 2006), forthcoming.

Goldhaber, Michael H. (1997), "The Attention Economy and the Net," *First Monday*, 2 (4), http://www.firstmonday.org/issues/issue2_4/goldhaber/.

Jenkins, Henry (1992), *Textual Poachers : Television Fans & Participatory Culture*. New York: Routledge.

Kozinets, Robert V. (2001), "Utopian Enterprise: Articulating the Meanings of Star Trek's Culture of Consumption," *Journal of Consumer Research*, 28 (1), 67.

_____ (2002), "The Field Behind the Screen: Using Netnography for Marketing Research in Online Communities," *Journal of Marketing Research (JMR)*, 39 (1), 61.

Lanier, Clinton , Jr. Albert Muñiz, and Hope Jensen Schau (2006), "Write and Wrong: Ownership, Access and Meaning in Consumer Co-Created Online Fan Fiction," *Advances in Consumer Research*, 33.

O'Guinn, Thomas (2000), "Touching Greatness: The Central Midwest Barry Manilow Fan Club," *The Consumer Society Reader*, Juliet Schor and Douglas Holt, Ed. New York: The New Press.

Pine, B. Joseph and James H. Gilmore (1999), *The Experience Economy: Work Is Theatre & Every Business a Stage*. Boston: Harvard Business School Press.

Schau, Hope Jensen and Cristel A. Russell (2004), "Consuming Television: Connectedness and Community in Broadcast Media," *Advances in Consumer Research*, 31 (1), 544.

Simon, Hebert (1971), "Designing Organizations for an Information-Rich World," *Computers, Communications, and the Public Interest*.

Are Consumers Intuitively Bayesian? The Role of Consumer Metacognition

Dipayan (Dip) Biswas, Bentley College, USA
Guangzhi (Terry) Zhao, University of Kansas, USA
Donald Lehmann, Columbia University, USA
Dhruv Grewal, Babson College, USA

EXTENDED ABSTRACT

To reduce the uncertainty of product purchase decisions, consumers frequently resort to product rating information provided by third-party rating agents. Such rating agents and rating information are ubiquitous in the marketplace, ranging from stock rating by financial institutions, movie rating by film critics, product rating by consumer reports, product safety rating by government agencies to product ratings posted online in blogs by individual consumers (Jadad and Gagliardi 1998).

This paper attempts to examine how consumers might process such information about product rating and source accuracy, how their judgment updating might be influenced by the data format, and whether their updated judgments would be consistent with a normative Bayesian framework. Prior research reports contradictory results regarding how consumers will update their judgments when processing sequential numerical data. While the Bayesian belief updating theory is perhaps the most widely used theoretical framework to examine how people are likely to update their beliefs based on sequential information (Diaconis and Zabell 1982), researchers have reported mixed empirical findings regarding the extent to which human judgments are consistent with Bayesian predictions. Some studies (e.g., Kahneman and Tversky 1972) came to the conclusion that people are not at all Bayesian. In contrast, another line of research (e.g., Gigerenzer and Hoffrage 1995), using an evolutionary psychology perspective found that under certain conditions (e.g., frequency data), people can be intuitively Bayesian. Yet a third line of research approached a middle-ground, and suggested that people do update their beliefs in a fashion that are directionally consistent with Bayesian predictions, but the extent to which people update their beliefs are conservative in comparison to the predictions by Bayes' theorem (see e.g., Edwards 1968; Rust et al. 1999). We attempt to resolve this apparent inconsistency in prior findings by examining the role of difficulty of computation of the numerical data in consumer belief updating. We ask the question: Would consumers update their beliefs with each piece of sequential numerical information, and will the final updated judgments/ beliefs be consistent with a normative Bayesian model, or follow a different pattern of updating? More specifically, using a model based on consumer metacognition (e.g., Gollweitzer and Schaal 1998), we identify conditions under which participants will update their beliefs to an extent that is consistent with Bayesian theory, as well as conditions under which they will update their beliefs in a way deviating from Bayes' theorem. We propose that when the numerical information is easy to compute mathematically (e.g., for percentage format), consumer judgments are likely to be conservative than the Bayesian predictions, since an averaging rule will be applied. For difficult-to-compute frequency data (e.g., *Consumer Reports* has been correct 121 out of 173 times in its ratings), consumer judgments are likely to be in line with the Bayesian prediction. Our proposition might seem to be somewhat counterintuitive because Bayes' theorem is a normative model, while we are proposing that consumers are likely to have judgments consistent with Bayesian predictions when the numbers are difficult to compute mathematically and require extra cognitive capability. We provide the underlying theoretical causes for this counterintuitive pattern of results, and in the process, hope to resolve some of the inconsistency in prior findings.

As mentioned earlier, we use a consumer metacognition framework to examine processing of difficult-to-compute data (e.g., frequency data) versus easy-to-compute data (e.g., percentage data). "Metacognition" refers to a person's knowledge about their own cognitive processes and/or abilities, and the consequent regulation of the cognitive processes (Garafalo and Lester 1985; Gollweitzer and Schaal 1998). Metacognition theory would predict that a consumer would utilize the optimal amount of cognitive resources to process any mathematical information (Garafalo and Lester 1985). This implies that a consumer would regulate their cognitive processing in the most efficient manner.

Therefore, applying the averaging algorithm for the processing of numerical data would depend on the processing fluency involved in the task (Schwarz 2004). One key distinction between easy-to-compute percentage versus difficult-to-compute frequency data is that sequential data presented in the former format is relatively easier to compute mathematically (Dehaene 1992, 2001; Waters et al. 2006; Sloman 1996). In other words, it is relatively easier to apply the averaging algorithm in the case of percentage data than it is for frequency data.

Hence, when evaluating a sequence of percentage data, consumers are likely to average out the information. In contrast, with the computational difficulty of applying the averaging algorithm in the case of frequency data, consumers are likely to apply a different type of algorithm. Specifically, we propose that for frequency data, with the difficulty of applying the averaging algorithm, consumers would have very little incentive to allocate cognitive resources to such an algorithmic task. Instead, consumers are likely to form an overall impression or hypothesis of the given information (e.g., Product B is better than Product A), and use subsequent sequential information to test that hypothesis.

In Study 1, we found support for our hypothesis that consumers would have greater degree of belief updating and judgments consistent with Bayesian predictions for difficult-to-compute frequency data than for easy-to-compute frequency or percentage data. Study 2 showed that highlighting data distinctiveness enhances belief updating for percentage data, but does not make a difference in the case of frequency data. Finally, Study 3 showed that the results of Study 1 hold when the data are presented in consistent frames, but not in alternate frames. That is, when the data are presented in consistent frames, participants have updated judgments consistent with Bayesian predictions. However, for data presented in alternate frames, updated judgments for frequency data get conservative than the Bayesian predictions, while for percentage data, judgments are conservative than Bayesian predictions irrespective of data presentation frame.

REFERENCES

Dehaene, Stanislas (1992), "Varieties of numerical abilities," *Cognition*, 44, 1-42.

Dehaene, Stanislas (2001), "Précis of the number sense," *Mind & Language*, 16, 16-36.

Diaconis, Persi and Sandy L. Zabell (1982), "Updating Subjective Probability," *Journal of the American Statistical Association*, 77(380), 822-30.

Edwards, W. (1968), "Conservatism in Human Information Processing," in B. Leinmuntz (ed.), *Formal Representation of Human Judgment*, New York: Wiley.

Garafalo, J. and F. K. Lester (1985), "Metacognition, cognitive monitoring, and math performance," *Journal for Research in Mathematics Education*, 16, 163-176.

Gigerenzer, G. and U. Hoffrage (1995), "How to improve Bayesian Reasoning without Instruction: Frequency Formats," *Psychological Review*, 102, 684-704.

Gollwitzer, P. M. and B. Schaal (1998), "Metacognition in action: The importance of implementation intentions," *Personality & Social Psychology Review*, 2, 124-136.

Jadad, Alejandro R. and Anna Gagliardi (1998), "Rating Health Information on the Internet," *Journal of the American Medical Association*, 279, 611-614.

Kahneman, Daniel and Amos Tversky (1972), "Subjective Probability: A Judgment of Representativeness," *Cognitive Psychology*, 3, 430-54.

Rust, Roland T., J. Jeffrey Inman, Jianmin Jia, and Anthony Zahorik (1999), "What You Don't Know About Customer Perceived Quality: The Role of Customer Expectation Distributions," *Marketing Science*, 18(1), 77-92.

Schwarz, Norbert (2004), "Metacognitive experiences in consumer judgment and decision making," *Journal of Consumer Psychology*, 14(4), 332-348.

Sloman, Steven A. (1996), "The empirical case for two systems of reasoning," *Psychological Bulletin*, 119, 3-22.

Waters, Erika A., Neil D. Weinstein, Graham A. Colditz, and Karen Emmons (2006), "Formats for improving risk communication in medical tradeoff decisions," *Journal of Health Communication*, 11, 167-182.

Translation Errors in the Aggregation of Consumer Recommendations

Boris Maciejovsky Massachusetts Institute of Technology, USA
David V. Budescu, University of Illinois at Urbana-Champaign, USA

EXTENDED ABSTRACT:

An increasing number of consumers uses the internet rather than brick and mortar stores for their purchase decisions. One important difference between traditional stores and virtual marketplaces is that the latter do not allow consumers to inspect directly the physical properties of goods and commodities. This lack of immediate experience triggers uncertainty about the specific properties and the overall quality of the products. One way to reduce this uncertainty is to allow consumers to share their experiences in the form of reviews and recommendations. Indeed, many of the leading internet marketplaces (e.g., Amazon.com, EPionions.com) offer consumers the opportunity to publicize their experiences in the form of verbal statements and numerical ratings. Verbal statements usually are free-format short essays, whereas numerical ratings provide a complementary summary in the form of quantitative ratings.

These two different information formats, verbal and numerical, need to be integrated by consumers to adequately aggregate the available information. Prior research on the internal consistency of preferences suggests that such integration might often be less than optimal. One explanation for such preference reversals is based on the compatibility between stimulus and response. According to the compatibility hypothesis (Fitts and Seeger, 1953), "the weight of any input component is enhanced by its compatibility with the output" (Tversky, Sattath and Slovic, 1988, p. 376). We extend this line of research by studying compatibility effects in information aggregation across different information formats (verbal and numerical). We predict higher rates of preference reversals when the stimulus format (verbal or numerical) does not match the response format (verbal or numerical).

We used a two-stage design to test this conjecture. On stage 1, participants rated the attractiveness of 12 fictitious products. This allowed us to derive an individual ranking of the products. For each product, participants saw 10 recommendations that were presented either as brief verbal statements (e.g., "this product was excellent" or "this product was average"), or as numerical ratings on a 5-point scale (1 to 5 stars). The verbal statements were pre-tested, and rated by independent raters, to match the 5-point numerical scale. We also varied the variance (low or high) and the mean (low, intermediate, or high) of the recommendations. Each of the 12 products was described by a unique combination of the presentation mode, the variance, and the mean of the recommendations.

After a 10-minute filler task, subjects entered stage 2 of the experiment. They were shown pairs of the products as used on stage 1. For each product subjects saw the corresponding 10 recommendations. Subjects were asked to provide a summary evaluation of each of the two products. The evaluation was either in a matching or a non-matching format. For instance, if the products were accompanied by verbal recommendations, subjects in the matching-format condition were asked to provide a summary evaluation of the products in the form of verbal statements (they were shown 5 pre-tested verbal statements) and asked to summarize the product. The options ranged from "this product was very bad" to "this product was excellent." In the non-matching condition, subjects were asked to click on a 5-point rating scale (1 to 5 stars). After summarizing each of the two products, subjects had to pick their preferred one. Comparing the evaluations of the rankings derived from stage 1 and the choices of stage 2 allowed us to study the internal consistency of preferences for each individual.

In study 1 we employed a 2 (stimulus mode: verbal or numerical format) x 2 (response mode: matching or non-matching format) between-subjects design to study how preferences are affected by the compatibility of the provided information. Our results confirmed that preference reversals are significantly higher for non-matching formats as compared to matching formats. Preference reversals were particularly pronounced for high variance products. In study 2 we allowed participants to select the response mode, verbal or numerical, by themselves. The majority of subjects preferred the numerical response mode, even in cases in which the products were presented verbally. This led to in an increase in preference reversals. This finding suggests that subjects did not anticipate the importance of compatibility between stimulus and response format on preference consistency. In all studies DMs showed the highest levels of preference inconsistencies for products with identical means but different standard deviations, suggesting that DMs have more trouble exhibiting consistent preferences for high variability options (and considerably less difficulty for options with mean differences).

REFERENCES

Fitts, P. M. and Seeger, C. M. (1953). S-R compatibility: Spatial characteristics of stimulus and response codes. *Journal of Experimental Psychology*, 46, 199-210.

Tversky, A., Sattath, S. and Slovic, P. (1988). Contingent weighting in judgment and choice. *Psychological Review*, 95, 371-384.

Interactive Restructuring: Implications for Decision Processes and Outcomes

Nicholas Lurie, Georgia Institute of Technology, USA
Na Wen, Georgia Institute of Technology, USA
Doe Hyun Song, Georgia Institute of Technology, USA

EXTENDED ABSTRACT

Many online environments offer tools that allow consumers to interactively restructure decision environments. Examples include the ability to sort alternatives on different attributes and to eliminate alternatives from consideration. For example, when planning a trip on Expedia, a consumer can sort hotels by price if her goal is to find a low-priced hotel. Alternatively, when comparing hotels, Travelocity allows the consumer to eliminate those she does not like. In theory, such tools should help online consumers avoid information overload and make better decisions. However whether, and the conditions under which, such tools lead to better decisions is not well understood.

Although prior research in offline environments has shown that consumers sometimes restructure decision environments to facilitate the comparison of alternatives, it also suggests that restructuring is contingent on the effort involved (Coupey 1994). Given that the effort involved in restructuring offline environments is high, such restructuring should only occur when consumers are highly motivated. Relatedly, a large body of research has found support for Slovic's (1972) "concreteness principle," which proposes that consumer rarely restructure decision environments and instead make decisions consistent with the way in which information is presented (Bettman and Kakkar 1977; Bettman and Zins 1979; Jarvenpaa 1989; Kleinmuntz and Schkade 1993). Moreover, other research has shown that the extent to which consumers adapt their decision strategies depends on the effort and accuracy associated with using these alternative decision strategies within a given information environment (Payne, Bettman, and Johnson 1988, 1993).

By dramatically lowering the costs to consumers of restructuring information environments, interactive restructuring tools have important implications for decision processes and outcomes. The extent and conditions under which they enhance decision-making quality, however, is unclear. On the one hand, tools such as sorting and elimination may create a better match between the task and the decision environment, which should reduce information overload, improve decision quality and/or reduce decision effort (Hoch and Schkade 1996; Lurie 2004). In addition, previous research suggests that restructuring leads to more compensatory decision making by freeing up cognitive resources (Coupey 1994); this suggests that the availability of tools that lower the cost of restructuring information should lead to more compensatory processing. In particular, consumers using restructuring tools may be more likely to consider multiple factors than those without access to such tools. At the same time, there is a reason to believe that the availability of interactive restructuring tools may actually be detrimental to decision quality in some information environments. For example, to the extent that sorting leads to heuristic decision processes, such tools may lead to lower quality choices in environments in which attributes are negatively correlated (Bettman et al. 1993).

We propose that the availability of restructuring tools is likely to lead to two types of adaptive behavior (Payne et al. 1993). First, to the extent that interactive restructuring tools serve as substitutes for cognitive effort, decision makers will be adaptive in their use of these tools. For example, decision makers should be more likely to use such tools in difficult choice environments—such as those in which attributes are negatively correlated. Second, decision makers

should adapt to the environments created by using such tools. For example, they should be more likely to process by attribute after using sorting tools that order alternatives by a given attribute.

To address these issues, two experiments were conducted that manipulated the availability of interactive restructuring tools as well as the correlation among product attributes. Study 1 compared decision quality in the presence versus absence of sorting tools for choice sets characterized by positively or negatively correlated attributes. Study 2 extended Study 1 by examining the impact of providing elimination as well as sorting tools to consumers. In addition, Study 2 used process-tracing techniques to examine how the availability of interactive restructuring tools affects decision processes as well as outcomes.

Results from both studies show that the availability of sorting tools increases choice accuracy in positively correlated environments but not in negatively correlated environments. In support of the idea that consumers are adaptive in their use of such tools, consumers sort more when product attributes are negatively correlated than when attributes are positively correlated. However, they are no more likely to use elimination tools. In support of the idea that consumers adapt to the restructured environments that they themselves create, the availability of sorting tools increases time per acquisition and selectivity in negatively correlated environments. Moreover, a significant 3-way interaction was found between attribute correlation, sorting tools, and elimination tools. When product attributes are negatively correlated, the availability of sorting tools lowers choice quality when elimination tools are not available but increases choice quality when elimination tools are available. When attributes are positively correlated, the ability to sort improves decision quality regardless of the availability of elimination tools.

REFERENCES

Bettman, James R., Eric J. Johnson, Mary Frances Luce, and John W. Payne (1993), "Correlation, Conflict and Choice," *Journal of Experimental Psychology: Learning, Memory, and Cognition*, 19 (July), 931-51.

Bettman, James R. and Pradeep Kakkar (1977), "Effects of Information Presentation Format on Consumer Information Acquisition Strategies," *Journal of Consumer Research*, 3 (March), 233-40.

Bettman, James R. and Michel A. Zins (1979), "Information Format and Choice Task Effects in Decision Making," *Journal of Consumer Research*, 6 (September), 141-53.

Coupey, Eloise (1994), "Restructuring: Constructive Processing of Information Displays in Consumer Choice," *Journal of Consumer Research*, 21 (June), 83-99.

Hoch, Stephen J. and David A. Schkade (1996), "A Psychological Approach to Decision Support Systems," *Management Science*, 42 (1), 51-64.

Jarvenpaa, Sirkka L. (1989), "The Effect of Task Demands and Graphical Format on Information Processing Strategies," *Management Science*, 35 (March), 285-303.

Kleinmuntz, Don N. and David A. Schkade (1993), "Information Displays and Decision Processes," *Psychological Science*, 4 (July), 221-27.

Lurie, Nicholas H. (2004), "Decision Making in Information-Rich Environments: The Role of Information Structure," *Journal of Consumer Research*, 30 (March), 473-86.

Payne, John W., James R. Bettman, and Eric J. Johnson (1988), "Adaptive Strategy Selection in Decision Making," *Journal of Experimental Psychology: Learning, Memory & Cognition*, 14 (July), 534-52.

_____ (1993), *The Adaptive Decision Maker*, New York, NY: Cambridge.

Slovic, Paul (1972), "From Shakespeare to Simon: Speculation—And Some Evidence—About Man's Ability to Process Information," *Oregon Research Institute Bulletin*, 12 (3), 1-29.

Good from Far but Far from Good: The Effects of Visual Fluency on Impressions of Package Design

Ulrich R. Orth, Christian-Albrechts-Universität Kiel, Germany
Keven Malkewitz, Oregon State University, USA

EXTENDED ABSTRACT

Consumers often make initial judgments about brands based solely on the brand's packages, and the accuracy of these impressions influences brand selection and evaluation. This paper examines the accuracy of meaning (brand personality and quality impressions) derived from package design (Bloch 1995). More specifically, we examine three areas where there are gaps in our knowledge concerning the effect of package design on impressions, the areas of consensual accuracy, spatial accuracy, and individual differences in spatial accuracy.

The first area concerns the consensual accuracy of brand impressions which are derived from the design of packages. Brand managers, designers, consumers and other stakeholders have a vested interest in having consumers form similar impressions from their packaging. This provides a consistency in impressions, allowing managers to more accurately convey information, and allowing consumers to receive more accurate knowledge. The second area concerns spatial accuracy. Many situations exist where consumers see marketing stimuli from more than one distance. For example, a billboard viewed from a distance may result in different impressions than the same billboard viewed from up close, and a wine bottle in a retail store might evoke one set of brand impressions from a distance, and yet another set of impressions when held in the hand. A third area where we have little knowledge is the influence of interpersonal differences on impressions formed from packages, specifically brand and quality impressions. Individuals who are highly involved in a product category, or those whom have a great deal of acumen in the design of packages, may process package information differently than those who are less involved or those who have less design acumen.

We designed and conducted two studies to examine these three gaps in our knowledge, specifically 1) consensual accuracy, 2) spatial accuracy, and 3) the affect of individual differences in involvement and design acumen on spatial accuracy. In our first study, we examine fifty examples from five different types of holistic package designs identified in prior research (massive, contrasting, natural, delicate, and non-descript packages, Orth and Malkewitz 2008), and we examine the influence of the five package designs on brand personality (Aaker 1997) and quality impressions. We find that the five designs significantly differ in their ability to generate the consistent impressions needed for consensual accuracy. Natural and delicate designs had more consensual accuracy, and massive, contrasting, and delicate designs had less. These differences are thought to be due to difference in the perceptual fluency of the stimuli (Janiszewski 1993; Reber, Winkielman, and Schwarz 1998)

Study 2 was conducted to examine the spatial accuracy of the five types of package designs, the situation where a package is viewed from more than one distance, as if approaching a package on a shelf in a retail environment. Subjects were shown smaller and larger package images, and the difference in brand and quality impressions was examined. Consumer also provided additional information on their level of involvement with their level of involvement in the category (Zaichkowsky 1985) and their design acumen (Bloch, Brunel, and Arnold 2003). Changes in brand personality (independent of design) were found for "exciting" brand personality impressions (packages rated more exciting for the smaller "seen at a distance" packages), while ruggedness, competence, and sophistication brand impressions were stronger for the larger "seen up close" packages. Quality ratings were also higher for larger "seen up close" packages.

The influence of the five holistic package designs was also significant, Massive and contrasting designs had significantly greater changes in personality and quality impressions, while changes in the natural and delicate designs were not as great. There was little change in non-descript designs. Additionally, there were several situations where there were differential impressions of brand personality due to package design. For example, massive designs gave the impression of being more sophisticated when viewed from a distance, while delicate designs gave the impression of being more sophisticated when viewed up close.

We also found that being more involved in the product category, or having more design acumen, resulted in a decreased spatial accuracy of these individuals. The addition of more information to the process of evaluating packages results in significant differences in the brand personality evaluations.

The implications of this research are of interest for all brand and package stakeholders. We provide evidence that package design has an influence on the consensual accuracy of the brand and quality impressions formed by consumers, that certain package designs are more (or less) consistent in the impressions that they generate when viewed at different distances, and we show that consumers high in involvement and design acumen form package impressions that are different from those with less involvement or less acumen. This evidence suggests that brand managers should more closely examine their packages to insure consumers form consistent impressions from their packages (consensual accuracy), to insure consumers form consistent impressions regardless of viewing distance (spatial accuracy), and to insure that their packages are appropriate for consumers differing in levels of acumen and involvement.

REFERENCES

Aaker, Jennifer L. (1997), "Dimensions of Brand Personality," Journal of Marketing Research, 34(August), 347-356.

Bloch, Peter H. (1995). "Seeking the Ideal Form: Product Design and Consumer Response," *Journal of Marketing*, 59(July), 16-29.

Bloch, Peter H., Frederic F. Brunel, and Todd J. Arnold (2003). "Individual Differences in the Centrality of Visual Product Aesthetics: Concept and Measurement," *Journal of Consumer Research*, 29(March), 551-565.

Childers, Terry L., Michael J. Houston, and Susan E. Heckler (1985). "Measurement of Individual Differences in Visual versus Verbal Information Processing," *Journal of Consumer Research*, 12(September), 125-134.

Fang, Xiang, Surendra Singh, and Rohini Ahluwalia (2007). "An Examination of Different Explanations for the Mere Exposure Effect," *Journal of Consumer Research*, 34(June), 97-103.

Grill-Spector, K., and N. Kanwisher (2005). "Visual Recognition: As Soon as You Know it is There, You Know What it is," *Psychological Science*, 16, 152-160.

Hassin, R., and Y. Trope (2000). Facing Faces: Studies on the Cognitive Aspects of Physiognomy," *Journal of Personality and Social Psychology*, 78, 837-852.

Henderson, P. W., and Cote, J. A. (1998). Guidelines for Selecting or Modifying Logos. *Journal of Marketing*, 62(April), 14-30.

Henderson, P. W., Giese, J. L., and Cote, J. A. (2004). Impression Management Using Typeface Design, *Journal of Marketing*, 68(October), 60-72.

Janiszewski, Chris (1993). "Preattentive Mere Exposure Effects," *Journal of Consumer Research*, 20(December), 376-392.

Janiszewski, Chris, and Stijn M.J. Van Osselaer (2000). "A Connectionist Model of Brand- Quality Associations," *Journal of Marketing Research*, 37(August), 331-350.

Kenny, David A. (1991). "A General Model of Consensus and Accuracy in Interpersonal Perception, *Psychological Review*, 98, 155-163.

Kruglanski, A.W. (1989). "The Psychology of Being "Right": The Problem of Accuracy in Social Perception and Cognition," *Psychological Bulletin*, 106, 395-409.

Little, Anthony C., and David I. Perrett (2007). "Using Composite Images to Assess Accuracy in Personality Attribution to Faces," *British Journal of Psychology*, 98, 111-126.

Malloy, Thomas E., Linda Albright, David A. Kenny, Fredric Agatstein, and Lynn Winquist (1997), "Interpersonal Perception and Metaperception in Nonoverlapping Social Groups," *Journal of Personality and Social Psychology*, 72(2), 390-398.

Novemsky, Nathan, Ravi Dhar, Norbert Schwarz, and Itamar Simonson (2007). "Preference Fluency in Choice," *Journal of Marketing Research*, 45(August), 347-356.

Olson, Ingrid R., Jiang Yuhong, and Katherine Sledge Moore (2005). "Associative Learning Improves Visual Working Memory Performance," *Journal of Experimental Psychology*, 31(5), 889-900.

Orth, U. R., and Malkewitz, K. (2008). "Holistic Package Design and Consumer Brand Impressions," *Journal of Marketing, 72* (May).

Petty, R. E., and Cacioppo, J. T. (1986). *Communication and Persuasion: Central and Peripheral Routes to Attitude Change,* New York, Springer.

Reber, Rolf, Norbert Schwarz, and Piotr Winkielman (2004). "Processing Fluency and Aesthetic Pleasure: Is Beauty in the Perceiver's Processing Experience?" *Personality and Social Psychology Review*, 8(4), 364-382.

Reber, Rolf, P. Winkielman, and Norbert Schwarz (1998). "Effects of Perceptual Fluency on Affective Judgments," *Psychological Science*, 9, 45-48.

Underwood, Robert L. (2003). "The Communicative Power of Product Packaging: Creating Brand Identity via Lived and Mediated Experience," *Journal of Marketing Theory and Practice*, 9 (Winter), 62-76.

Van Osselaer, Stijn M.J., and Chris Janiszewski (2001). "Two Ways of Learning Brand Associations," *Journal of Consumer Research*, 28(September), 202-223.

Vernon, David, and Toby J. Lloyd-Jones (2007). "Effects of Delay on Color Priming for Natural Objects," *Psychological Reports*, 100(1), 275-293.

Veryzer, R. W. (1999). "A Nonconscious Processing Explanation of Consumer Response to Product Design," *Psychology and Marketing*, 16(6), 497-522.

Zaichkowsky, Judith L. (1985). "Measuring the Involvement Construct." *Journal of Consumer Research, 12* (December), 341-352.

Zhao, Shenghui, and Robert J. Meyer (2007). Biases in Predicting Preferences for the Whole Visual Patterns from Product Fragments," *Journal of Consumer Psychology*, 17(4), 292-304.

When Good Looks Kill: An Examination of Consumer Response to Visually Attractive Product Design

Rishtee Kumar Batra, Boston University, USA
Frederic Brunel, Boston University, USA
Sucharita Chandran, Boston University, USA

EXTENDED ABSTRACT

In a time when companies are able to match each other on dimensions of quality and price, superior design is seen as a key to winning customers. In the past several years the issue of design and its role as a strategic tool for marketplace success has been pursues by manufacturers of consumer goods from small appliances to automobiles. But while design has been an area of growing concern, it remains unclear whether superior design should be a goal sought after by all. The present paper examines the effect of visually attractive design upon consumers' perceptions of quality and argues that under certain circumstances, firms benefit from investing in superior visual design while in other circumstances companies might be adversely impacted in pursuit of highly attractive visual design. We develop and empirically test a model of visual information processing based on theories assimilation-contrast and implicit personality. It is shown that a under normal circumstances, a U-shaped relationship exists between visual attractiveness and perceived performance but that this relationship is moderated by both brand information and access to processing capabilities. By understanding the boundary conditions and mechanisms involved in this process of performance-related trait inference, we can begin to outline implications for when and how to use a product's visual design as a competitive tool.

At the root of this model lies Helson's (1964) adaptation-level theory. Person perception research from social psychology has already demonstrated that individuals maintain adaptation levels of acceptance around cues such as physical attractiveness of others. Whether or not the person's attractiveness falls within a latitude of acceptance, people are either shown to assimilate information to a "what is beautiful is good" stereotype or to make a contrasting judgment. In the present study, this finding is extended to the domain of product design and consumers are similarly thought to have a latitude of acceptance around a product's visual attractiveness. In the case that processing capabilities are unconstrained, individuals first consider the extent to which the product being evaluated falls within an acceptable range of attractiveness. Depending on whether or not they deem the product to fall within this range, different beliefs are drawn upon.

In Study 1, we demonstrate that depending on the level of attractiveness- either within or beyond one's latitude of acceptance-individuals draw upon different belief structures. We show that in absence of other information, when a product's level of attractiveness if low or moderate, consumers draw upon a "what is beautiful is good" structure such that more attractive products are rated as being of higher quality than less attractive products. However, when a product's level of attractiveness exceeds a threshold, consumers draw upon a "too good to be true" belief structure such that highly attractive products are be rated as being of lower quality than moderately attractive products. But when consumers have access to external information, such as brand reputation of the manufacturer, they adjust their initial judgments to accommodate this information. In the high brand reputation condition, evaluations of products at all three levels of attractiveness are enhanced, resulting in suppression of the "too good to be true" belief. However, in the poor brand reputation condition the belief remains in tact.

While in Study 1 we show that individuals process visual information in a cognitive manner under conditions of unconstrained processing ability, the same is not true under conditions of low processing ability. In Study 2, when individuals are faced with limited processing capabilities they engage in perceptual processing of visual information based on an affect-transfer process. In absence of other information, regardless of whether or not a product falls within latitude of acceptance, consumers process visual information through a process of affect transfer such that more attractive products are preferred to less attractive products. Thus, perceived performance is thought to increase monotonically with increased attractiveness and brand information is not shown to interact with product attractiveness.

The findings of this research hold interesting implications for product designers and brand managers in helping assess when investment a product's visual design is beneficial and when this investment might backfire. Although the present paper makes progress toward outlining visual design and positioning guidelines for managers, there are still question that might be pursued by future researchers. For example, the model described in this paper accounts for the possibility that product category might moderate the impact of attractiveness upon perceptions of quality found in high processing capability conditions. Different product categories (e.g. primarily functional products versus primarily hedonic products) are thought to have different latitudes of acceptance around what is considered acceptable in terms of attractiveness and might have different belief structures associated with each level of attractiveness.

REFERENCES

Alba, J. W. (2007). "A Role for Aesthetics in Consumer Psychology." *Handbook of Consumer Psychology*.

Albright, L., D. A. Kenny, et al. (1988). "Consensus in personality judgments at zero acquaintance." *Journal of Personality and Social Psychology* 55(3): 387-395.

Ashmore, R. D. and F. K. Boca (1979). "Sex stereotypes and implicit personality theory: Toward a cognitive—Social psychological conceptualization." *Sex Roles* 5(2): 219-248.

Creusen, M. E. H. and J. P. L. Schoormans (2005). "The Different Roles of Product Appearance in Consumer Choice." *Journal of Product Innovation Management* 22(1): 63-81.

Dion, K., E. Berscheid, et al. (1972). "What is beautiful is good." *Journal of Personality and Social Psychology* 24(3): 285-90.

Eagly, A. H., R. D. Ashmore, et al. (1991). "What is beautiful is good, but..: A meta-analytic review of research on the physical attractiveness stereotype." *Psychological Bulletin* 110(1): 109-128.

Helson, H. (1964). *Adaptation-level theory: an experimental and systematic approach to behavior*, New York: Harper & Row.

Kahle, L. R. (1984). *Attitudes and Social Adaptation: A Person-Situation Interaction Approach*, Pergamon.

Nussbaum, B. (2000). Designs for the Future. *Business Week.* 28: 60.

Schmitt, B. and A. Simonson (1997). *Marketing aesthetics*, Free Press New York.

Do We Judge a Book by its Cover and a Product by its Package? How Affective Expectations are Contrasted and Assimilated into the Consumption Experience

Sharon Horsky, Bar Ilan University, Israel

Heather Honea, San Diego State University, USA

EXTENDED ABSTRACT

Marketing actions can serve to activate expectancies that impact consumption experiences and product efficacy. For instance, Shiv et. al. (2005) show that consumption of the exact same product differently impacts performance when the product is purchased at a discount versus at regular price. They confirm that the impact of consumer perception on performance is mediated by expectations.

When consumers do not have prior knowledge of a product's qualities, a product's visual aesthetic is a marketing action that serves to set consumers expectations. Attractive visual aesthetics generate favorable responses and impact product expectations (Postrel 2003). We propose that attractiveness generates *affective expectations* (beliefs about the pleasure or positivity associated with a consumption experience). In the case of hedonic products, where the benefit of the product is primarily determined by the affect experienced during consumption, affective expectations driven by product packaging may be contrasted to or assimilated into actual consumption beliefs and experiences.

An initial product survey validates the relationship between attractive aesthetics and product expectations. Then three experimental studies test propositions regarding the relationship between expectations set by packaging and consumer perceptions. The studies investigate the effect packaging aesthetics have on actual consumer beliefs and consumption evaluations and examine whether these effects carry through to purchase intentions. To create a context for contrast and assimilative effects, product quality and consumer affective expectations were varied across conditions.

Intuition might suggest that a more appealing packaging would increase consumers' product evaluations, purchase intentions, and beliefs. We show that this is not always the case. A contrast effect was found in the case of high quality product. The high quality product was evaluated more positively when it was paired with a package that was not particularly beautiful. This was due to surprise that was elicited from the incongruence between an individual's affective expectations generated by context and the actual product experience.

Study 1 was conducted to examine the relationship between hedonic product aesthetics and consumer expectations. Five hundred individuals were shown two inch pictures of 44 different hedonic product packages. Brand name was intentionally obscured but the product package was visible in terms of design and color. Participants rated the product on six semantic differential scales anchored by 1 and 7. The scales were Ugly-Pretty, Boring-Exciting, Unattractive-Attractive, Lame-Cool, Unsophisticated-Sophisticated, Unstylish-Stylish. Finally, participants rated their affective expectations of the product on a scale anchored by very low=1 and very high=5. Highly correlated semantic measures were combined. The Pretty and Attractive measures were combined to form a Beauty indicator (r= 0.862). Cool and Exciting were combined to form a Coolness indicator a (r=0.813). Sophisticated and Stylish were combined to form a Style indicator (r=0.851). Regressing these three indicators on expectation shows that they explain over 70% of the variance in participants' affective expectations for a product.

Having established the relationship between aesthetics and expectations we investigated the effects of aesthetics on the accep-tance of non-verifiable highly positive credence claims. Study 2 employed a 2x2 between-subjects experimental design with product package (high vs. low attractive) and product quality (high vs. low) as experimental factors was utilized. Packaging aesthetics interacted with product quality to influence belief in credence claims and purchase intentions. When the context for a low quality product is an attractive package, consumers are marginally more likely to accept credence claims. When the context for a high quality product is aesthetically low, consumers are marginally more likely to accept credence claims. Study 2 indicates that expectations are set based on packaging and product quality interacts with expectations. However, affective expectations from the packages were not perfectly contrasted or assimilated into consumer beliefs regarding credence claims. Perhaps credence claims, although positively valenced were not sufficiently affective in nature, therefore contrast or assimilation with affective expectations was imperfect.

We expect that hedonic product experiences are more affective in nature. This leads to specific predictions regarding the interaction between affective expectations and hedonic product experience.

Proposition A: All that Glitters is Gold Effect. Beautiful aesthetics, such as attractive packaging, increase initial positive response to a product. This positive response positively biases hedonic product experiences.

Proposition B: Frogs can be Princes Effect. Lack of aesthetics, such as plain packaging, does not increase initial positive response to a product. When hedonic product experience exceeds expectations generated by the low level product aesthetics, the resulting positive response biases hedonic product experiences.

Study 3 was conducted to determine the implications of packaging on perceptions of verifiable product attributes by examining actual product experience and purchase intentions. A 2x2 between-subjects experimental design with product package (high vs. low attractive) and product quality (high vs. low) as experimental factors was utilized. As predicted packaging aesthetics interacted with actual product quality to influence taste evaluations and purchase intentions. We find that a highly attractive package pattern positively biases taste evaluation in the low product quality case (assimilation)—providing evidence of the *All that Glitters is Gold Effect*. Purchase intentions appear to follow a similar pattern, with increased intention to purchase with low quality product when presented in the context of a highly attractive vs. low attractive package. The contrast bias was not significant with the high quality product in the low attractive package, though the means are directionally consistent with the *Frogs can be Princes Effect*.

Study 4 was conducted to further examine the unique impact low aesthetics and a high quality product to determine whether a contrast effect occurs. Participants' post-taste responses were measured to assess whether feeling surprise played a role in their perceptions and intentions. A between-subjects experimental design was employed, with product package (high vs. low attractive) and identical very high quality product in both packages. We find that if the packaging signal does not generate a positive response because of its low aesthetic appearance, then the individual is delighted when she experiences a high quality product. This surprise increases evaluation. Purchase intention follows a similar pattern. Apparently, when an individual kisses a frog that turns out to be a prince, her subsequent assessment is more positive than it would have been if she had expected to be kissing a prince initially. However, this *Frogs can be Princes Effect* appears to come into play only in the case of very high quality product. It seems that a product must be pretty "charming" to be contrasted to the low aesthetics of its package.

REFERENCES

Postrel, Virginia (2003), *Substance of Style,* New York, NY: HarperCollins Publisher.

Shiv, Baba , Ziv Carmon and Dan Ariely (2005), "Placebo Effects of Marketing Actions: Consumer May Get What They Pay For," *Journal of Marketing Research*, 42 (November), 383-393.

Bilingualism and the Emotional Intensity of Advertising Language

Stefano Puntoni, Erasmus University, The Netherlands
Bart de Langhe, Erasmus University, The Netherlands
Stijn van Osselaer, Erasmus University, The Netherlands

EXTENDED ABSTRACT

Regardless of their cultural heritage and native language, consumers around the world are routinely addressed by large numbers of marketing messages in a foreign language, mostly English. Calls for an increased focus on the consequences of globalization for consumers (e.g., Johar, Maheswaran, and Peracchio 2006) emphasize the need to improve current understanding of how the globalization of advertising language influences consumer response to marketing communications. In particular, no previous research has examined the emotional consequences of the use of a foreign language in commercial messages. This issue is important because generating emotional experiences around a brand is an important goal of brand communication and it is currently unclear what the emotional consequences of the globalization of advertising language are. Extending recent literature on the emotions of bilinguals (e.g., Pavlenko 2005), we propose a language-specific episodic trace theory of language emotionality to explain how the emotionality of marketing messages is influenced by the language used.

Following Hintzman's influential Minerva 2 model (Hintzman 1986, 1988), we argue that each experience is stored as an array of elements. At the time of retrieval, presenting one or more elements of such an experience activates memory traces of experiences that contain that or those elements. Activation of an experience makes therefore the other elements of that experience that were not in the probe accessible. Although Minerva 2 was not designed to deal with linguistic issues or emotions, a multiple-trace view may be applicable to emotional appraisals of advertising in one's first (L1) or second (L2) language. It seems possible that consumers' episodic memory traces include not only the direct, external perceptual elements of an experience, but also the emotions that were felt during an episode. In addition, it seems natural that the sights and sounds of words or series of words perceived during an episode would be stored as elements of the episodic trace as well. This would imply that if a word or series of words is encountered later, it functions as a probe for the multi-trace memory of experiences. Thus, advertising copy or slogans in L1 or L2 may function as memory probes which lead to the activation, and feeling, of emotions experienced before in same-language contexts. Assuming that emotional *echo content* is a positive function of the number of activated emotional traces (e.g., Hintzman 1986), this would imply that the perceived emotionality of marketing messages depends on the number of experiences in which the words of that message, in that language, have been encountered previously. In the context of the globalization of advertising language, it is reasonable to assume that the number of events experienced by consumers in concomitance with an L1 language context outnumbers that of events experienced in an L2 language context. L1 marketing communication should in general therefore trigger stronger emotional responses that L2 marketing communication. We assessed the language-specific trace theory of language emotionality in a number of studies.

In Study 1, Dutch-English-French trilinguals were addressed in English and rated a series of Dutch and French advertising slogans on emotionality and originality. Half of participants were L1 speakers of French and half were instead L1 speakers of Dutch.

We observed a two-way interaction between language and type of appraisal such that L1 slogans were rated as more emotional than L2 slogans, with no difference between L1 and L2 slogans in perceived originality. The two-way interaction, moreover, was not qualified by a three-way interaction with population: the emotional advantage of L1 was in fact exactly the same for Dutch and French native speakers.

In Study 2, nonnative speakers of English from a variety of countries rated the emotionality of single English words after having copied the word either in English or in their native language. Participants for whom the native language translation had been made more accessible rated the English words as more emotional. In this experimental paradigm all participants rated the same stimuli, ruling out a comprehension account for the effect of language on emotionality.

In Study 3, we provided direct evidence for the role of the context of language use for the effect of language on emotionality obtained in the previous studies. A set of L1/L2 word pairs was selected based on a pretest to differentiate between pairs that had been predominantly encountered in L1 versus L2 language contexts. Participants in the main study (Dutch native speakers who were fluent in English) then rated the emotionality of both L1 and L2 words from each pair. We observed a crossover interaction between language and language context. For concepts encountered predominantly in L1 language contexts we replicated the emotional advantage of L1 found in previous experiments but for concepts encountered predominantly in L2 language contexts we observed a reversal of this effect: in this case L2 words were rated as more emotional than L1 words.

In Study 4, we replicated the emotional advantage of L1 using ads featuring congruent visual information. Moreover, we manipulated the language of the rating scales. Participants reported more extreme ratings of emotional intensity when performing the task using L2 than L1 rating scales. This reversal of the effect of language across the two stimulus elements (ads and rating scales) is consistent with the stronger emotional intensity of L1 by showing that language shifts the perceived intensity of the anchoring points of semantic differentials. That is, the emotionality scale anchors are perceived as less extreme in L2, leading to more extreme ratings of stimuli on the L2 scale.

This article is the first to focus on the consequences of language for the perceived emotionality of marketing messages and, from a broader point of view, the first to adopt a psycholinguistic perspective on the emotional consequences of the process of globalization for consumers. Bilingualism is a growing area in consumer research (e.g., Luna and Peracchio 2001) and the article adds a new dimension to this body of literature.

REFERENCES

Hintzman, Douglas L. (1986), "'Schema Abstraction' in a Multiple-Trace Memory Model," *Psychological Review*, 93 (4), 411-428.

_____ (1988), "Judgments of Frequency and Recognition Memory in a Multiple-Trace Memory Model," *Psychological Review*, 95 (4), 528-551.

Johar, Gita V., Durairaj Maheswaran, and Laura A. Peracchio (2006), "MAPping the Frontiers: Theoretical Advances in Consumer Research on Memory, Affect, and Persuasion," *Journal of Consumer Research*, 33 (June), 139-149.

Luna, David and Laura A. Peracchio (2001), "Moderators of Language Effects in Advertising to Bilinguals: A Psycholinguistic Approach," *Journal of Consumer Research*, 28 (September), 284-294.

Pavlenko, Aneta (2005), *Emotions and Bilingualism*. Cambridge: Cambridge University Press.

The Role of Brand Personality and Consumer Attachment Style in Strengthening Brand Relationships

Vanitha Swaminathan, University of Pittsburgh, USA
Karen Stilley, University of Pittsburgh, USA
Rohini Ahluwalia, University of Minnesota, USA

EXTENDED ABSTRACT

Background. That brands have personalities or human characteristics is now well established in the literature; as is the idea that brand personality is a vehicle of consumer self-expression and can be instrumental in helping consumers express different aspects of their self (Aaker 1997). Humanizing a brand empowers it to play a more central role in the consumer's life: potentially enabling the consumer to project an aspect of their self which might be desirable for relationships they seek (Aaker 1997); or possibly even give them a sense of comfort at having found a brand that "fits" with their self-concept (Aaker 1999). In order to harness the potential of brand personality, it is important from both a managerial and a theoretical point, to understand the underlying mechanisms invoked under different circumstances, and identify moderators that provide more specific insights into which brand personality traits are going to matter to consumers. We adopt an attachment theory (Bowlby 1980) perspective to provide a richer understanding of the role of brand personality in influencing consequential branding outcomes such as brand attachment and purchase likelihood, especially under marketplace settings where consumers are not explicitly directed to pay attention to the brand's personality.

Predictions. Attachment theory has identified two dimensions of attachment style based on the individuals' view of self and view of others, i.e., anxiety and avoidance respectively, which are expected to influence the type of relationships they engage in and their potential for forming attachments in the interpersonal domain (Bartholemew and Horowitz 1991; Bartz and Lydon 2004). We propose that a consumer's attachment style (based on these two dimensions) will moderate the effect of brand personality on crucial outcomes such as brand attachment and purchase likelihood.

Method. Through a series of three experiments, our research demonstrates that consumers' attachment styles are likely to moderate the impact of brand personality on marketplace outcomes. We examine these hypotheses across three studies. The first study examines the extent to which consumers' attachment styles moderate the role of brand personality in predicting their existing brand attachments for favorite clothing brands. In Study 2 and 3, the key variables of attachment style and brand personality are manipulated (instead of measured), to provide a cleaner test of the hypotheses. Generalizability of the pattern of effects obtained with favorite brands in the first study is extended to the context of brand extensions (study 2) and new product introductions (study 3). The last two studies also attempt to provide process related insights (study 2) as well as identify boundary conditions for the effects obtained (study 3).

Results. Our research reveals that consumers who have an anxious attachment style are more likely to be influenced by a brand's personality than those who are less anxious about relationships. For the anxious types, when the brand is associated with a personality trait which the consumer considers important or relevant for maintaining relationships with others, brand attachment and purchase likelihood are enhanced. In this regard, our research reveals that high anxiety types who tend to avoid relationships are likely to be influenced by exciting brands; whereas high anxiety individuals who are low on relationship avoidance are attracted to sincere brands. In contrast, consumers who do not have an anxious attachment style, tend not to be influenced to the same extent by the brand's personality, demonstrating similar brand outcomes (attachment as well as purchase likelihood) for sincere and exciting brands. Importantly, this pattern of effects is replicated whether attachment style is measured or manipulated; across different product categories (clothing, shoes, and clocks); for well known favorite brands to new and unfamiliar brands; for outcomes varying from brand attachment to purchase likelihood. Further, these results appear to be more important in the context of publicly consumed goods rather than for privately consumed goods.

Conclusions. As such, our research points out to an interesting but counterintuitive finding: brand personality can be most useful for forging consumer-brand connections in a domain where past literature in the interpersonal relationship context suggests brand attachments are most unlikely (e.g., the high anxiety high avoidance consumers). Interestingly, brand personality might hold the key to forming relationships with and enhancing purchase likelihood of these consumers. Specifically, although high anxiety and high avoidance type of individuals (fearfuls) have been shown to demonstrate the lowest levels of attachment potential in past literature (e.g., Bartholomew and Horowitz 1991), the use of an exciting brand personality led them to exhibit brand attachment levels similar to low anxiety low avoidance (secure) individuals, associated with highest attachment potential in the interpersonal domain. Furthermore, it appears these relationships are formed with a view to projecting one's image as more desirable. Hence, this relationship potential is most likely for products which tend to be consumed publicly.

Our research sheds light on the processes underlying these effects. We contrast the mediating role of self-brand relevance and self-brand similarity. We find that self-brand relevance offers a better account of the processes by which individuals use brand personality in an instrumental way to building brand attachments.

Implications. At this point, it is important to note that several potential roles of brand personality have been discussed in the literature, ranging from a match with the consumer's self-concept to impression management via brand personality with the goal of developing positive relationships (Aaker 1999). Our research suggests that consumer attachment styles might be more likely to invoke the impression management type of mechanisms, serving as a tool to enhance one's attractiveness as a relationship partner.

By illuminating the important role of attachment styles, this research may serve to encourage scholars to re-think some of the fundamental notions of the universality of brand personality traits and their meaningfulness across groups of consumers differentiated based on attachment styles. This research contributes to the literature by demonstrating the important role of consumers' view of self and view of others, which, developed during infancy, influences how consumers seek brands with personality traits that are self-relevant or important. Brand personalities help consumers derive symbolic meaning from their relationships with brands. Sincere brand personality traits, for instance, are meaningful to consumers who seek relationships (less avoidant), but who have a highly anxious view of self. Exciting brands also symbolic meaning and are particularly meaningful to those anxious individuals who are focused on self-reliance.

REFERENCES

Aaker, Jennifer L. (1997), "Dimensions of Brand Personality," *Journal of Marketing Research*, 34 (3), 347-56.

Aaker, Jennifer L. (1999), "The Malleable Self: The Role of Self-Expression in Persuasion," *Journal of Marketing Research*, 36 (1), 45-57.

Bartholomew, Kim and Leonard M. Horowitz (1991), "Attachment styles among young adults: A test of a four-category model," *Journal of Personality and Social Psychology*, 61(2), 226-244.

Bartz, Jennifer A. and John E. Lydon (2004), "Close Relationships and the Working-Self Concept: Implicit and Explicit Effects of Priming Attachment on Agency and Communion," *Personality and Social Psychology Bulletin*, 30 (11), 1389-1401.

Bowlby, John (1980), *Attachment and Loss. Vol. 3*, New York: Basic Books.

The Impact of Employee Behavior on Brand Personality Impressions: The Moderating Effect of Pseudorelevant Information

Daniel Wentzel, University of St. Gallen, Switzerland
Sven Henkel, University of St. Gallen, Switzerland

EXTENDED ABSTRACT

Sales employees frequently disclose personal information to consumers in order to gain their trust and to improve the course of an interaction (Crosby, Evans, and Cowles 1990). A salesperson at an Apple store, for instance, may tell a customer who is looking to buy an iPod that she owns a particular model herself and uses it when she goes running on the weekends. The information that is disclosed on such occasions may be irrelevant for the final outcome of the interaction and for judging whether the salesperson has successfully performed her prescribed role. Information of this kind, however, may be indicative of the salesperson's general character, for which reason such pieces of rich, nondiagnostic information are referred to as "pseudorelevant" information (Hilton and Fein 1989). Even though the disclosure of pseudorelevant information should be a common occurrence in many sales interactions, there are no studies that have investigated how such information influences brand personality impressions. In this research, we propose that pseudorelevant information affects the extent to which consumers update their existing brand personality impressions after interacting with an employee whose behavior is consistent or inconsistent with these impressions.

To develop our predictions, we draw on studies that have been conducted in the area of stereotyping theory. The disclosure of pseudorelevant information during a sales interaction may determine how typical the employee is considered to be. This, in turn, can affect the extent to which the employee's behavior is generalized to the brand personality. When an employee does not disclose any pseudorelevant information, customers are likely to stereotype the employee and should regard him or her as a typical representative of the brand (Matta and Folkes 2005). When, however, pseudorelevant information has been disclosed, consumers may dissociate the employee from the brand and should consider the employee as a relatively unique, less typical member of the brand. This process is referred to as "fencing off" or subtyping (Kunda and Oleson 1995; Yzerbyt, Coull, and Rocher 1999). Stereotyping and subtyping processes should also determine to what extent an employee affects brand personality impressions. Because people produce less generalization from atypical than from typical group members (Rothbart and Lewis 1988), consumers' brand personality impressions should not be affected as strongly by the employee's behavior when they have received pseudorelevant information during the interaction. Two studies were conducted to test this prediction.

In the first study, participants read a scenario that depicted an interaction between a customer and an employee of a fictitious biking brand. In these scenarios, the employee's behavior was either consistent or inconsistent with the brand's personality. In addition, the amount of pseudorelevant information was varied through a conversation that took place between the customer and the employee. The results showed a significant interaction between the consistency of the employee's behavior and the disclosure of pseudorelevant information. When participants did not receive pseudorelevant information, their brand personality impressions were strongly influenced by the employee's behavior. That is, consistent behavior strengthened brand personality impressions, whereas inconsistent behavior weakened them. When participants received pseudorelevant information, however, they subtyped the employee. As a consequence, they transferred the employee's behavior to a lesser extent to the brand.

The second study extended these findings and showed that the impact of pseudorelevant information is moderated by accuracy motivation. More specifically, the second study manipulated the availability of pseudorelevant information and the degree to which participants were motivated to form an accurate impression of the employee. The analyses revealed a significant interaction between these two variables. When accuracy motivation was high, brand personality impressions were less strongly affected by the employee's behavior if participants had received pseudorelevant information. When accuracy motivation was low, however, brand personality impressions did not differ as a function of the information that had been disclosed. These results show that pseudorelevant information can block generalization because consumers are motivated to arrive at an accurate impression of the employee they are interacting with.

These results have implications for the literature on self-disclosure by showing that disclosing personal information can affect the extent to which consumers generalize an employee's behavior. This may entail positive as well as negative implications. On the one hand, the brand is not harmed as badly when the employee's behavior is inconsistent with the brand personality; on the other hand, the brand does not benefit as strongly when the behavior is consistent. Furthermore, our findings also contribute to research on the formation and updating of brand personality impressions (Aaker, Fournier, and Brasel 2004; Johar, Sengupta, and Aaker 2005). Earlier studies have suggested that personality traits come to be associated with a brand in a direct way by the company's employees. Our results indicate that the strength of this association depends on the information that consumers possess about an employee and their accuracy motivation. In fact, without knowing how the employee is perceived, it may be impossible to predict how brand personality impressions are affected by an employee's behavior.

REFERENCES

Aaker, Jennifer L., Susan Fournier, and Adam S. Brasel (2004), "When Good Brands Do Bad," *Journal of Consumer Research*, 31 (June), 1-16.

Crosby, Lawrence A., Kenneth R. Evans, and Deborah Cowles (1990), "Relationship Quality in Services Selling: An Interpersonal Influence Perspective," *Journal of Marketing*, 54 (July), 68-81.

Hilton, James L. and Steven Fein (1989), "The Role of Typical Diagnosticity in Stereotype-Based Judgments," *Journal of Personality and Social Psychology*, 57 (2), 201-11.

Johar, Gita Venkataramani, Jaideep Sengupta, and Jennifer L. Aaker (2005), "Two Roads to Updating Brand Personality Impressions: Trait Versus Evaluative Inferencing," *Journal of Marketing Research*, 42 (November), 458-69.

Kunda, Ziva and Kathryn C. Oleson (1995), "Maintaining Stereotypes in the Face of Disconfirmation: Constructing Grounds for Subtyping Deviants," *Journal of Personality and Social Psychology*, 68 (4), 565-79.

Matta, Shashi and Valerie S. Folkes (2005), "Inferences About the Brand from Counterstereotypical Service Providers," *Journal of Consumer Research*, 32 (September), 196-206.

Rothbart, Myron and Scott Lewis (1988), "Inferring Category Attributes from Exemplar Attributes: Geometric Shapes and Social Categories," *Journal of Personality and Social Psychology*, 55 (6), 861-72.

Yzerbyt, Vincent Y., Alastair Coull, and Steve J. Rocher (1999), "Fencing Off the Deviant: The Role of Cognitive Resources in the Maintenance of Stereotypes," *Journal of Personality and Social Psychology*, 77 (3), 449-62.

Happy Now or Overall? The Measurement of Local versus Global Well-Being

Stacy L. Wood, University of South Carolina, USA
Adam W. Craig, University of South Carolina, USA

EXTENDED ABSTRACT

The diversity of measures used in recent research illustrates that many researchers take different approaches to measuring happiness. While many of these approaches are logical given specific research questions, a lack of discussion about inherent measurement differences slows the progress we make in knowledge building because it keeps us from knowing how to compare results from disparate measures or, worse, leads us to make inappropriate comparisons between results. In this research, we assess the potential for measurement differences to arise from the respondent's own interpretation of what the researcher means when s/he asks "How happy are you?"

Here, we investigate two common interpretations of happiness that may be equally normatively appropriate for respondents, and yet, may be conceptually distinct (i.e., rely on inputs that do not perfectly overlap). These two interpretations originate in differences in temporal orientation–happiness that is perceived as an enduring or overarching assessment and happiness that is perceived as immediate and transitory pleasure Kahneman and Krueger (2007). We use the terms, *global* and *local,* to describe these two interpretations. Many cultures understand happiness as two related but distinct concepts—the temporary enjoyment of positive affect (local happiness) and a more static disposition suggestive of positive life choices and satisfaction (global happiness). Individuals may understand this difference as "Am I feeling happy right now?" versus "Am I happy overall?" Importantly, we propose that very similar response items may prompt either interpretation. In other words, people may understand the simple direction to "rate your happiness" as an injunction to report on their current short-term pleasure or the degree to which they have good lives. In this work, we investigate (1) the methodological and conceptual implications of these two interpretations, (2) how measurement vehicles may prompt one versus the other, (3) how the assessments may rely on different inputs and, (4) how the assessments may be differentially correlated with common well-being measures.

In this research, we present five studies that demonstrate consistent differences in the evaluation of happiness and provide process evidence that differences are due to one's temporally-oriented interpretation of happiness. This evidence offers behavioral researchers a better understanding of what existing (and future) findings from happiness and well-being studies may be validly compared.

Because the word "happiness" is used in common parlance to capture both global and local interpretations of happiness, we suggest that respondents are impacted by the nature of the item or the context in which the item is asked in determining whether they should respond in terms of their long-standing global well-being or their more changeable short-term enjoyment. In order to investigate this, we consider the influence of three context factors that may influence local/global interpretations: (1) the existence of local/global primes, (2) the temporal context of other items, and (3) the item language itself. Finally, we consider the process of temporal orientation through which these influences impact happiness ratings.

Our empirical data suggest that respondents use surprisingly subtle cues in happiness measures to determine whether they are being asked how happy they are now or how happy they are in general and that this distinction leads to consistent differences in reported happiness. Study 1 examines whether priming respondents with the concept of "local" versus "global" can influence their subsequent report of happiness. Respondents report lower happiness when primed with a local cue than those who are primed with a global cue. Study 2 is to replicate the priming effect found in study 1 and to additionally test the influence of item wording on reported happiness (Wierzbicka 2004). We observe lower reported happiness with the use of the word "pleased" versus the word "happy." Additionally, in replicating the main effect found in study 1, we observe lower reported happiness (with either wording) in the Local Prime condition. Study 3 tests the effect of survey context on local versus global interpretations of assessed happiness and finds that manipulating the type of survey questions that surround the item measuring happiness (e.g., local items such as "hungry" versus global items such as "stingy") prompts respondents to interpret happiness as local and to report lower happiness ratings than global contexts. Study 4 replicates the context effect (H3) found in study 3 and additionally examines process evidence (cognitive responses that capture inputs) that differences in responses may be due to differences in the respondents' local (immediate/situational) or global (enduring/static) inputs to the rating. Finally, Study 5 examines process evidence that differences in correlations to life satisfaction may be due to differences in the respondents' local or global interpretation. When participants responded to a cognitive response task after evaluating their happiness, those in the local context condition expressed more immediate reasons for their evaluation (e.g. "It's sunny today," or "I had a good breakfast") and those in the global context condition expressed more static reasons (e.g. "I have a good family," or "I like my job").

In conclusion, cues that signal a local (happy now) interpretation lead to lower ratings of happiness in lab settings than do global (happy overall) interpretations. Cues can consist of unintentional priming, context, or wording differences in the scale/item. Local interpretation leads respondents to consider more immediate short-term inputs (e.g., good day, not hungry) and global interpretation leads respondents to consider more long-term inputs (e.g., family, career) when assessing their happiness.

REFERENCES

Kahneman, Daniel and Alan B. Krueger (2006), "Developments in the Measurement of Subjective Well-Being," *Journal of Economic Perspectives*, 20 (1), 3.

Wierzbicka, Anna (2004), "'Happiness' in Cross-Linguistic and Cross-Cultural Perspective," *Daedalus*, 133 (Spring), 34-43.

Reducing the Spoiler Effect in Experiential Consumption

Alex S.L. Tsang, Hong Kong Baptist University, China
Dengfeng Yan, Hong Kong University of Science and Technology, China

EXTENDED ABSTRACT

A spoiler is a summary or description of a narrative product (e.g., comic book, movie, novel, TV drama), in which a dramatic "twist", such as the identity of the murderer in a detective story, is revealed. The spoiler effect denotes a phenomenon that a consumer's interest in consuming a particular narrative is reduced after exposure to a spoiler. We identify the psychological process underlying the spoiler effect, from an affective forecasting and focusing illusion perspective. Following the same logic, we further suggest a method for marketers to neutralize this effect.

Spoilers are a common phenomenon with narratives. When consumers consult external information sources, the source may intentionally or unintentionally leak information about the plot. Spoiler exposure creates a satiation effect (Redden, 2008) and an explanation effect (Wilson, Centerbar, Kermer, and Gilbert, 2005) that hinder favorable affective forecasting. As a result, intention to consume the narrative is reduced. In this research, we propose a psychological mechanism that underlies the spoiler effect and accounts for the satiation and explanation effects. We hypothesize that affective forecasting mediates the relationship between spoiler exposure and consumption intention of a narrative. Specifically, exposure to a spoiler produces an unfavorable forecasted affect, in turn reducing consumers' consumption intention (H1).

Study 1 was designed to test H1. Participants were provided with a scenario saying that a friend phoned the participant and revealed (spoiled version) or did not reveal (non-spoiled version) the identity of the murderer of a movie that the participant was planning to see; then, forecasted affects and narrative consumption intention were measured.

We adopted Baron and Kenny's (1986) three-step procedure to test the main and mediating effects, the first step shows that spoiler exposure was significantly related to movie-seeing intention in a negative way. The second step shows that spoiler exposure significantly affected excitement and surprise negatively. Step three shows that, when both spoiler exposure and the two forecasted affects were regressed on narrative-consumption intention, only surprise, but not excitement, was significant in explaining narrative-consumption intention. However, spoiler exposure was still significant in the model, but its β was significantly reduced. The results suggest only a partial mediation effect between spoiler exposure and narrative-seeing intention. H1 is partially supported. We suspect this outcome is caused by the usage of a "generic" scenario without explicitly providing the plot of the movie making it difficult for participants to forecast their affects. Thus, Study 2 reassesses the mediating effect by using a hypothetical movie synopsis.

Spoilers are commonly spread by WOM; however, marketers can still limit their negative impact. We argue that the spoiler effect is caused by a cognitive bias called focusing illusion, which denotes assigning a heavier weight to an attended attribute than to other unattended attributes in predicting the affect produced by a particular object (Kahneman, Krueger, Schkade, Schwarz, and Stone, 2006). A spoiler draws consumers' attention to a twist in a plot, thus they will rely heavily on the plot to forecast their affective responses for consuming the narrative. However, a leaked plot creates a satiation or explanation effect that reduces the forecasted enjoyment. Eventually, consumers' interest in consuming the narrative is reduced.

According to this proposed mechanism, a feasible way to debias focusing illusion is to move consumers' attention ways from the focal attribute. When other experience attributes (e.g., audio-visual effects) are made more salient at the time consumers forecast their affects, the plot's influence will be reduced. Hence, we hypothesize that spoilers do not significantly reduce consumers' narrative consumption intention if other experience attributes are made salient when they forecast their affect (H2).

Study 2 used a 2 (ad theme: plot focused / experience focused) x 2 (spoiler exposure: yes / no) between subjects factorial design. We designed an ad slogan emphasizing outstanding audiovisual performance instead of the unpredictable plot, so some other experiential attributes are made salient when consumers forecast their affects. They then read a movie excerpt, which contained or did not contain a spoiler. Eighty students and teachers participated in this study.

In order to test the debiasing mechanism; we split the sample according to which ad slogan the participants read. We then adopted Baron and Kenny's procedure to test the mediating effect. For the sample that was exposed to the experiential-attribute-focused slogan (n=38), the first step failed. Spoiler exposure does not produce a lower movie-seeing intention.

For the sample that was exposed to the plot-focused slogan (n=42), the first step shows that spoiler exposure significantly affects movie-seeing intention in a negative way. Step two was also successful. It shows that spoiler exposure significantly affects only two (happy and surprise) affects in a negative way. Surprise is consistently significant in both Study 1 and 2. If a participant was first exposed to a plot-focused slogan, spoiler exposure significantly reduced their forecasted happiness and forecasted surprise. Step three shows that, when both spoiler exposure and the two forecasted affects were regressed on movie-seeing intention, both happiness (at $p=.05$) and surprise (at $p=.10$) fulfill the mediating requirement by being significant in the model. At the same time, spoiler exposure becomes no longer significant after the mediator enters the model. The results suggest that forecasted affects can fully mediate the effect of spoiler exposure on the intention to purchase narratives. These results not only support H2 but also provide some evidence supporting H1.

In this paper, we introduce affective forecasting as a mediator and empirically test how it mediates spoiler exposure to reduce consumers' narrative consumption intention. We further postulate that focusing illusion biases affective forecasting and suggest a feasible way for marketers to defocus it. Our experimental results show that the negative impact of spoilers can be controlled. These findings are particularly valuable to practitioners. They provide guidance for promotional message formulation if narrative marketers do not want consumers' patronage interest to be hampered by spoilers.

REFERENCES

Baron, Reuben M. and David A. Kenny (1986), "The Moderator-Mediator Variable Distinction in Social Psychological Research: Conceptual, Strategic, and Statistical Considerations," *Journal of Personality and Social Psychology*, 51 (6), 1173-82.

Kahneman, Daniel, Alan B. Krueger, David Schkade, Nobert Schwarz, and Arthur A. Stone (2006), "Would You be Happier If You were Richer? A Focusing Illusion," *Science*, 312 (June), 1908-10.

Redden, Joseph P. (2008), "Reducing Satiation: The Role of Categorization Level," *Journal of Consumer Research*, 34 (5), 624-34.

Wilson, Timothy D., David B Centerbar, Deborah A. Kermer, and Daniel T. Gilbert (2005), "The Pleasure of Uncertainty: Prolonging Positive Moods in Ways People do Not Anticipate," *Journal of Personality and Social Psychology*, 88 (1), 5-21.

Geographic Differences in the Consumption of Hedonic Products: What the Weather Tells the Marketer!

Wenbin Sun, University of Mississippi, USA
Rahul Govind, University of Mississippi, USA
Nitika Garg, University of Mississippi, USA

EXTENDED ABSTRACT

Research has substantiated the association between weather and unrelated consumer behaviors. It has linked changes in states of weather to helping behavior (Cunningham 1979), consumer satisfaction (Mittal, Kamakura, and Govind 2004), consumer choice (Fergus 1999), retail sales (Starr-McCluer 2000), and stock returns (Hirshleifer and Shumway 2003) amongst others. In most of the studies in this stream, positive weather (e.g. presence of sunshine) has been linked to positive outcome (e.g. more helping behavior) and vice versa. The underlying assumption in all these studies examining the link between weather and consumption is that affect mediates this relationship. That is, weather manipulates affect which in turn influences behavior.

Recently, researchers have started focusing on the relation between weather and a specific type of consumer behavior–hedonic consumption. Weather has been found to affect aggregate consumption differences across countries for products such as alcohol, and coffee (Parker and Tavassoli 2000); purchase of lottery tickets (Bruyneel et al. 2005); and individual level consumption differences for variety of hedonic goods such as tobacco, food products (chocolate, cookies), and even choice of gift cards for stores varying in their degree of hedonicity (Govind, Garg, and Mittal 2008). In addition to demonstrating the relation between weather and hedonic consumption, Govind et al. (2008) also establish weather-induced affect as the driving force behind the weather-consumption relationship.

Given that hedonic consumption is vulnerable to contextual factors like advertising (Wansink and Ray 1996), packaging (Wansink 1996), and affect (Garg, Wansink, and Inman 2007); and that social marketing is concerned with increasing consumer and societal welfare by controlling (negative) hedonic consumption, it will be insightful to understand the role of weather, an exogenous factor, on consumption and the regional variations in the relationship. Thus, the current research will not only seek to replicate the weather-hedonic consumption association established by prior research but also, extend the literature by examining geographical variations in that relationship. Specifically, the current research will seek to answer questions such as, "will the impact of changes in amount of sunlight on hedonic consumption be the same in the east coast (which displays huge annual differences in temperature) as compared to the west coast (which displays less variance)?" This is important from the perspective of policy makers who spend millions of dollars in resources to manage and curb hedonic consumption.

The analysis utilizes secondary data from the entire continental United States on the consumption of two negative hedonic products, tobacco and alcohol consumption. Weather data consisted of twenty weather variables from The National Oceanic and Atmospheric Administration. In line with the prior literature, negative weather conditions are characterized by lower temperatures, reduced sunlight and increased precipitation. In addition to these factors, we include several unstudied factors such as danger due to hail, tornado and wind. We suspect that an increase in these weather risk factors will also increase hedonic consumption. In addition to the weather variables, we also include socio-economic and demographic factors since prior research has found these variables to have an effect on the consumption of products such as alcohol and tobacco.

We first conduct a factor analysis on the twenty weather variables to reduce the impact of multi-collinearity and to make the subsequent predictions more actionable. The resulting three factors are labeled as, (1) The Temperature Based Factor (2) The Weather-Risk Based Factor and (3) The Precipitation Based Factor. An Ordinary Least Squares (OLS) analysis was then conducted to establish the effect of weather (i.e. the three weather based factors) on hedonic consumption (alcohol and tobacco consumption) across the entire United States with each zip-code acting as a single data point. This analysis controlled for the effects of socio-economic and demographic variables such as income and age, which have been known to impact the consumption of the two hedonic goods. Following this, we explored regional patterns in the effect of weather on hedonic consumption by using Geographically Weighted Regression (GWR). This technique has some important advantages for our current research. For example, the assumption of OLS that the effect of weather on hedonic consumption is homogeneous across the country is not strictly reasonable. GWR addresses this problem by providing one set of coefficients for each zip code area, taking their special characteristics into consideration.

In addition to showing a significant association between weather factors and hedonic consumption, we find evidence of the space varying nature of the relationship across the US. Specifically, as the weather factors deteriorate, consumers become more likely to increase their consumption of tobacco and alcohol. Furthermore, in our analysis of regional patterns in the weather effects on consumption for these negative, hedonic products, we find that regions in the continental United States exhibit distinct spatial patterns in terms of their susceptibility to negative consumption with changes in weather. For example, the effect of changes in temperature on the consumption of alcohol is higher in the North-Eastern United States as compared to the Southern United States.

Although these regional patterns might differ based on the hedonic product being considered, it is clear that they vary significantly with shifts in weather conditions and that policy/ marketing initiatives designed to influence consumption of such products should adequately account for these patterns. Thus, stakeholders can utilize our findings to implement concrete policies based on the specific needs of the regions and consumers' propensity to succumb to inclement weather factors. Such focused effort can result in enhancing the effectiveness of these initiatives from both, the monetary and the social welfare aspects.

REFERENCES

Bruyneel, Sabrina, Siegfried Dewitte, Philip H. Franses, and Marnik G. Dekimpe (2005), "Why Consumers Buy Lottery Tickets When the Sun Goes Down on Them-The Depleting Nature of Weather-Induced Bad Moods," *Erim Report Series Research in Management*, 1-37.

Cunningham, Michael R. (1979), "Weather, Mood, and Helping Behavior: Quasi-experiments with the Sunshine Samaritan," *Journal of Personality and Social Psychology*, 37, 1947-56.

Fergus, James T. (1999), "Where, When, and by How Much Does Abnormal Weather Affect Housing Construction?" *Journal of Real Estate Finance and Economics*, 18 (1), 63-87.

Garg, Nitika, Brian Wansink, and Jeffrey J. Inman (2007), "The Influence of Incidental Affect on Consumers' Food Intake," *Journal of Marketing*, 71 (Jan), 194-206.

Govind, Rahul, Nitika Garg, and Vikas Mittal (2008), "Weather and Hedonic Consumption: What's Feeling Bad Got to Do With It!" working paper, University of Mississippi, University, MS 38677.

Hirshleifer, David and Tyler Shumway (2003), "Good day Sunshine: Stock Returns and the Weather," *Journal of Finance,* 58 (3), 1009–32.

Mittal, Vikas, Wagner A. Kamakura, and Rahul Govind (2004), "Geographic Patterns in Customer Service and Satisfaction: An Empirical Investigation," *Journal of Marketing*, 68 (July), 48-62.

Parker, Philip M. and Nader T. Tavassoli (2000), "Homeostasis and Consumer Behavior Across Cultures," *International Journal of Research in marketing*, 17 (Mar), 33-53.

Starr-McCluer, Martha (2000), "The Effects of Weather on Retail Sales," Board of Governors of the Federal Reserve System (US), *Finance and Economics Discussion Series 2000-08*, 1-25.

Wansink, Brian (1996), "Can Package Size Accelerate Usage Volume?" *Journal of Marketing*, 60 (July), 1-15.

Wansink, Brian and Michael L. Ray (1996), "Advertising Strategies to Increase Usage Frequency," *Journal of Marketing,* 60 (1), 31-46.

The Effects of Time on Customer Revenge and Avoidance: An Examination in Online Public Complaining Contexts

Yany Gregoire, Washington State University, USA
Thomas Tripp, Washington State University, USA
Renaud Legoux, HEC Montreal, Canada
Jeffrey Radighieri, Washington State University, USA

EXTENDED ABSTRACT

The potential for customers to get even with service firms after a service failure has grown exponentially with the advent of the Internet. As highlighted by Ward and Ostrom (2006), disgruntled customers can develop their own anti-corporation websites to denounce firms' misbehaviors. Based on a review of consumer advocacy websites (Yahoo! 2007), "homemade" anti-corporation websites represent only the tip of the iceberg of *online public complaining*, a phenomenon broadly defined as the act of using the Internet to publicly complain about a firm (cf. Singh 1988). A vast array of online third-party organizations now offers preformatted platforms that customers can use with even more convenience and at virtually no cost. As a general purpose, this study examines the phenomenon of public complaining made via online third-party organizations.

Online public complaining is intimately related to the notion of *customer revenge*, defined as the actions taken by a customer to cause harm to a firm for the damages it has caused (Bechwati and Morrin 2003). Given its managerial and financial implications (Luo 2006), research on customer revenge has recently gained in popularity (Bechwati and Morrin 2003 and 2007; Grégoire and Fisher 2006 and 2008).

Although progress has been made concerning our comprehension of customer revenge, a simple but important question still remains: How does customer revenge evolve over time? Does it grow stronger, or does it fade away? Managers should have a special interest in this question, because they need to know whether "online retaliators" will naturally reduce their vengeful activities over time, or persist in their efforts.

Our research here fills this gap by examining the effects of time on customer revenge. Moreover, we extend the revenge literature by incorporating another dimension reflecting a lack of forgiveness, *avoidance*. In this study, we suggest that customers fail to forgive as long as they stay motivated (a) to seek revenge against the firm, and (b) to avoid any form of interaction with the firm (cf., McCullough and colleagues 1998; 2007). Overall, we posit that time has differentiated effects on revenge versus avoidance.

Our hypotheses are tested with a longitudinal field study that was performed in collaboration with two established online third-party organizations over a two-month period. The study involves a series of four questionnaires that were administered at a regular interval of two weeks (cf., McCullough, Root and Bono 2007). Our sampling frame was composed of customers who made an online complaint at consumeraffairs.com (CA) or initiated a blog on rip-off_report.com (RR) in the 10 days preceding the first questionnaire. Initially, the sampling frames were composed of 1,434 and 952 individuals for CA and RR, respectively, for an overall sampling frame of 2,386. After the first wave, 431 participants completed the first survey, with 247 and 184 participants for RR and CA, respectively. For wave 1, the overall response rate was of 18.1%—17.2% and 19.3% for CA and RR, respectively. The number of respondents decreased by 131 between waves 1 and 2, by 85 between waves 2 and 3, and by 43 between waves 3 and 4. Overall, 172 respondents completed the four phases of the survey, with 111 and 61 respondents for CA and RR, respectively.

The central question of this research has both theoretical and managerial implications, and it can be formulated as follows: Do customers forgive firms over time? Our results suggest that customers have difficulties forgiving firms after a service failure that led to an online public complaining (see Figure 1). While customers lose their desire for revenge over time, which is perhaps satisfied after their online actions, their desire for avoidance *increases* over time, showing that they hold grudges. Overall, our results show little evidence that time would help the restoration of a relationship as it was before the service failure episode.

Despite an unforgiving tendency, the decrease of a desire for revenge over time constitutes encouraging news for managers. Let us remember that a desire for revenge is found to be associated with online public complaining for help-seeking in this research, and that this desire was found to be an important driver leading to harmful behaviors such as negative word-of-mouth, and vindictive complaining in previous research (Bonifield and Cole 2007). Compared to the results reported in the case of intimate relationships (McCullough, Bono, and Root 2007), the desire for revenge experienced by customers seems less sustainable. Overall, managers can find some comfort in these findings. The use of revenge is very demanding for customers in terms of time and emotional energy, and maintaining this response seems unproductive and unnecessarily costly. Note that these findings provide an explanation about the disappearance and lack of maintenance of many anti-corporation websites, after a given period of time (Ward and Ostrom 2006).

Although the consequences of a desire for avoidance are arguably less spectacular than those of revenge, they also come with costs that should not be underestimated by managers. In light of the influential work on lifetime customer value, the definite loss of a customer patronage can have non-negligible long-term financial repercussions (Luo 2007), especially in the case of strong-relationship customers. In addition, the service paradox literature has highlighted the importance of the recovery process through which a firm has the ability to create a renewed sense of loyalty (Maxham and Netemeyer 2002). Based on this paradox, customers' definite withdrawal from the recovery process may constitute the loss of a firm's last chance to restore a valuable relationship.

REFERENCES

Aggarwal, Pankaj (2004), "The Effects of Brand Relationship Norms on Consumer Attitudes and Behaviors," *Journal of Consumer Research*, 31 (June), 87-101.

Anderson, James C. and David W. Gerbing (1988), "Structural Equation Modeling: A Review and Recommended Two-Step Approach," *Psychological Bulletin*, 103 (May), 411-423.

Aquino, Karl, Thomas M. Tripp, and Robert J. Bies (2001), "How Employees Respond to Personal Offense: The Effects of Blame Attribution, Victim Status, and Offender Status on Revenge in the Workplace," *Journal of Applied Psychology*, 86 (February), 52-59.

_____, Steven L. Grover, Barry Goldman, and Robert Folger (2003), "When Push Doesn't Come to Shove: Interpersonal Forgiveness in Workplace Relationships," *Journal of Management Inquiry*, 12 (September), 209-219.

FIGURE 1
Changes in Revenge and Avoidance over Time (Observed Means)

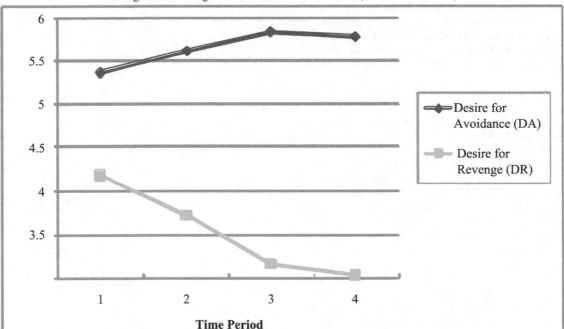

Ariely, Dan (2007), "HBR Case Study: The Customers' Revenge," *Harvard Business Review*, 85 (December), 31-42.

Bechwati, Nada N. and Maureen Morrin (2003), "Outraged Consumers: Getting Even at the Expense of Getting a Good Deal," *Journal of Consumer Psychology*, 13 (4), 440-453.

_____ and _____ (2007), "Understanding Voter Vengeance," *Journal of Consumer Psychology*, 17 (4), 277-291.

Bies, Robert J., and Thomas M.Tripp (1996), "Beyond Distrust: Getting Even and the Need for Revenge," In *Trust in Organizations*, ed. Roderick M. Kramer, & Tom R. Tyler, Newbury Park, CA: Sage Publications, 246-260.

Bitner, Mary Jo, Bernard H. Booms, and Mary S. Tetreault (1990), "The Service Encounter: Diagnosing Favorable/ Unfavorable Incidents," *Journal of Marketing*, 54 (January), 71-84.

Bliese, Paul D. and Robert E. Ployhart (2002), "Growth Modeling Using Random Coefficient Models: Model Building, Testing and Illustrations," *Organizational Research Methods*, 5 (October), 362-387.

Bolton, Ruth N. and Katherine N. Lemon (1999), "A Dynamic Model of Customers' Usage of Services: Usage as an Antecedent and Consequence of Satisfaction," *Journal of Marketing Research*, 36 (May), 171-186.

Bonifield, Carolyn and Catherine Cole (2007), "Affective Responses to Service Failure: Anger, Regret, and Retaliatory and Conciliatory Responses," *Marketing Letters*, 18 (January), 85-99.

De Wulf, Kristof, Gaby Oderkerken-Schröder and Dawn Iacobucci (2001), "Investment in Consumer Relationships: A Cross-Country and Cross-Industry Exploration," *Journal of Marketing*, 65 (October), 33-50.

Douglas, Scott C. and Mark J. Martinko (2001), "Exploring the Role of Individual Differences in the Prediction of Work-place Aggression," *Journal of Applied Psychology*, 86 (August), 547-560.

Finkel, Eli J., Caryl E. Rusbult, Madoka Kumashiro and Peggy A. Hannon. (2002), "Dealing with Betrayal in Close Relationships: Does Commitment Promote Forgiveness," *Journal of Personality and Social Psychology*, 82 (January), 956-974.

Folkes, Valerie S. (1984), "Consumer Reactions to Product Failures: An Attributional Approach," *Journal of Consumer Research*, 10 (March), 398-409.

Grégoire, Yany and Robert J. Fisher (2006), "The Effects of Relationship Quality on Customer Retaliation," *Marketing Letters*, 17 (January), 31-46.

_____ and _____ (in press), "Customer Betrayal and Retaliation: When your Best Customers Become your Worst Enemies," *Journal of the Academy of Marketing Science*, (Forthcoming).

Luo, Xueming (2007), "Consumer Negative Voice and Firm-Idiosyncratic Stock Returns," *Journal of Marketing*, 71 (July), 75-88.

Maxham, James G. III and Richard G. Netemeyer (2002), "A Longitudinal Study of Complaining Customers' Evaluation of Multiple Service Failures and Recovery Efforts," *Journal of Marketing*, 66 (October), 57-71.

McCullough, Michael E, K. Chris Rachal, Steven J. Sandage, Everett L. Worthington Jr., Susan Wade Brown, and Terry L. Hight (1998), "Interpersonal Forgiving in Close Relation-ship: II. Theoretical Elaboration and Measurement," *Journal of Personality and Social Psychology*, 75 (December), 1586-1603.

_____, C. Garth Bellah, Shelley Dean Kilpatrick, Judith L. Johnson (2001), "Vengefulness: Relationships with Forgiveness, Rumination, Well-Being, and the Big Five," *Personality and Social Psychology Bulletin*, 27 (May), 601-610.

_____, Giacomo Bono, and Lindsey M. Root (2007), "Rumination, Emotion, and Forgiveness: Three Longitudinal Studies," *Journal of Personality and Social Psychology*, 92 (March), 490-505.

Podsakoff, Philip M., Scott B. MacKenzie, Jeong-Yeon Lee, and Nathan P. Podsakoff (2003), "Common Method Biases in Behavioral Research: A Critical Review of the Literature and Recommended Remedies," *Journal of Applied Psychology*, 88 (October), 879-903.

Rindfleisch, Aric, Alan J. Malter, Shankar Ganesan, and Christine Moorman (in press), "Cross-Sectional versus Longitudinal Survey Research: Concepts, Findings, and Guidelines," *Journal of Marketing Research*, (Forthcoming).

Roehm, Michelle L. and Michael K. Brady (2007), "Consumer Responses to Performance Failures by High-Equity Brands," *Journal of Consumer Research*, 34 (December), 537-545.

Singh, Jagdip (1988), "Consumer Complaint Intentions and Behavior: Definitional and Taxonomical Issues," *Journal of Marketing*, 52 (January), 93-107.

Smith, Amy K., Ruth N. Bolton, and Janet Wagner (1999), "A Model of Customer Satisfaction with Service Encounters Involving Failure and Recovery," *Journal of Marketing Research*, 36 (August), 356-372.

Sydell, Laura (2007), "On the Internet, Is Everyone an Expert?," (accessed December 12, 2007), [available at http://www.npr.org/templates/story/story.php?storyId=15671312].

Tax, Stephen S., Stephen W. Brown and Murali Chandrashekaran (1998), "Customer Evaluations of Service Complaint Experiences: Implications for Relationship Marketing," *Journal of Marketing*, 62 (April), 60-76.

Wade, Susan H. (1989), "The Development of a Scale to Measure Forgiveness," Unpublished Doctoral Dissertation, Fuller Theological Seminar, Pasadena, California.

Ward, James C, and Amy L. Ostrom (2006), "Complaining to the Masses: The Role of Protest Framing in Customer-Created Complaint Web Sites," *Journal of Consumer Research*, 33 (December), 220-230.

Yahoo! (2007), "Consumer Advocacy and Information in the Yahoo! Directory," (accessed June 2, 2007) [available at http://dir.yahoo.com/Society_and_Culture/Issues_and_Causes].

The Persuasiveness of Stylistic Properties: The Moderating Role of Ideal-self vs. Ought-self

Jing Zhang, University of Wisconsin-Milwaukee, USA
Xiaojing Yang, University of Wisconsin-Milwaukee, USA
Laura Peracchio, University of Wisconsin-Milwaukee, USA

EXTENDED ABSTRACT

Stylistic properties refer to a variety of factors that impact the manner in which visual material is displayed (Peracchio and Meyers-Levy 2005). Studies have suggested that visual images often convey semantically meaningful concepts that impact consumer judgments via their stylistic properties (Messaris 1997). Take camera angle for example, when a product is depicted with a low, upward-looking camera angle, viewers tend to associate the product with potency and powerfulness. This interpretation was found to influence viewers' brand evaluations (Peracchio and Meyers-Levy 2005).

Despite a steady increase in the study of stylistic properties, little research has examined the effect of self-concept in determining the interpretation as well as the persuasion outcome of these stylistic properties. This research issue is important to address given that self-concept has been found to play intriguing roles in explaining various consumer behaviors, ranging from the persuasiveness of ad messages, to consumers' brand extension evaluations, and to memory and recall (e.g., Ng and Houston 2006). In this paper, we study a particular self-concept, ideal-self vs. ought-self, and examine whether and how it moderates the effect of camera angle on product attitudes.

Ideal-self refers to whom people want themselves to be and is closely related to people's hopes, wishes, and aspirations. Ought-self refers to whom people think they should be and is closely related to people's obligations, duties, and responsibilities. These two selves are associated with distinct motivations (promotion- vs. prevention– focused) and distinct self-regulatory systems (approach vs. prevention strategies) (Higgins 1998). And they have shown to affect the type of information (affective vs. substantive) consumers rely on to form judgment (Pham and Avnet 2004).

We propose that the persuasiveness of camera angle is moderated by the type of self (i.e., ideal vs. ought) that is activated at the exposure to ads. Specifically, when an upward-looking (low) angle is used, consumers whose ought-self is activated would form more favorable brand evaluations than consumers whose ideal-self is activated. This is because consumers with ought-self focus on avoiding loss to achieve their goals and tend to make conservative choices (Liberman et al. 1999), they are more likely to be bound by the hierarchy relationship and to yield to powerful figures. A product shot from a low, upward-looking angle is more likely to make those consumers feel positively about products. Conversely, when a downward-looking (high) angle is used to promote a brand, consumers whose ideal-self is activated would form more favorable brand evaluations than consumers whose ought-self is activated. This is because consumers with ideal-self are less likely to be bound by status-quo interpretations of the stylistic properties and tend to interpret a downward-looking angle favorably.

Study 1, a 2 (self manipulation: ideal-self vs. ought-self) x 2 (camera angle: downward-looking vs. upward-looking) between-subjects design, was conducted to test the prediction. A target ad for a cereal brand was used as a stimulus. The ad featured a large box of the cereal photographed from either one of these camera angles. Participants completed a series of seeming unrelated studies: 1) complete the exercise that is pertinent to manipulation of self (Pham and Avnet 2004); 2) complete the manipulation check items; and 3) review the ad, list their thoughts, and rate their product attitudes.

The manipulation of self was deemed satisfactory. A 2x2 ANOVA yielded a significant two-way Self x Camera Angle effect on product evaluations. Contrast analyses confirmed our expectations.

Study 2 was designed to examine the boundary conditions under which the Self x Camera Angle effect emerges. We argue that although the meaning of the visual stylistic properties is subtle, these properties could serve like central arguments by conveying diagnostic information. We therefore expect that the 2-way interaction effect will emerge only under high motivation of processing. To test this hypothesis, a 2 (self manipulation: ideal-self vs. ought-self) x 2 (camera angle: downward-looking vs. upward-looking) x 2 (processing motivation: high vs. low) between-subjects design was employed. Results confirmed our hypotheses.

To summarize, we find that when a high, downward-looking camera angle is utilized to photograph a product, consumers reported more favorable brand evaluations and thoughts when their ideal-self is temporarily accessible. Conversely, when a low, upward-looking camera angle is utilized, consumers reported more favorable brand evaluations and thoughts when their ought-self is temporarily accessible. In addition, these effects occurred under the high motivation of information processing. Taken together, these results contribute to the visual processing literature by showing the effect of self-concept on the interpretation of the meaning imparted by one stylistic property-camera angle. This project also contributes to the self-concept literature by revealing the power of self in yet another dimension of persuasion efforts-the visual aspect of persuasive messages.

REFERENCES

Higgins, E. Tory (1998), "Promotion and Prevention: Regulatory Focus as a Motivational Principle," in *Advances in Experimental Social Psychology*, Vol. 30, ed. Mark P. Zanna, San Diego, CA: Academic Press, 1–46.

Liberman, Nira, Lorraine Chen Idson, Christopher J. Camacho, and E. Tory Higgins (1999), "Promotion and Prevention Choices between Stability and Change," *Journal of Personality and Social Psychology*, Vol. 77 (December), 1135-45.

Messaris, Paul (1997), *Visual Persuasion: The Role of Images in Advertising*. Thousand Oaks, CA: Sage.

Ng, Sharon and Michael J. Houston (2006), "Exemplars or Beliefs? The Impact of Self-View on the Nature and Relative Influence of Brand Associations," *Journal of Consumer Research,* Vol. 32 (March), 519-29

Peracchio, Laura A. and Joan Meyers-Levy (2005), "Using Stylistic Properties of Ad Pictures to Communicate with Consumers." *Journal of Consumer Research* 32 (June): 29-40.

Pham, Michel Tuan and Tarmar Avnet (2004), "Ideals and Oughts and the Reliance on Affect versus Substance in Persuasion," *Journal of Consumer Research*, Vol. 30 (March), 503-18.

Promotion Framing Effects on Consumers' Perceptions of Customized Pricing

Fei Lee Weisstein, University of Illinois at Urbana-Champaign, USA
Kent B. Monroe, University of Illinois at Urbana-Champaign, USA

EXTENDED ABSTRACT

The Internet provides online retailers an opportunity to tailor product prices depending on consumers' individual characteristics. While modeling research suggests that there are positive benefits (Elmaghraby and Keskinocak 2003), behavioral research seems to discourage e-tailers to practice customized pricing since researchers have identified negative effects on consumers' perceived fairness, trust, and (re)purchase intentions (Garbarino and Lee 2003; Grewal, Hardesty, and Iyer 2004; Haws and Bearden 2006). The different conclusions from research raise a question: if it is practiced, can consumers' negative reactions be minimized? Recently, it was shown that price framing may reduce consumers' negative reactions (Lee and Monroe 2008). However, will price framing tactics influence consumers' perceptions similarly for high-priced versus low-priced products? Would perceived differences across product-price levels affect perceived price fairness and its outcomes? In this paper, we extend previous research by examining whether price framing can mitigate consumers' negative perceptions of customized pricing for both high-priced and low-priced products and further investigate the causal relationship of perceived fairness outcomes.

Research has shown that different price presentations affect consumers' evaluations of a deal offer (Krishna et al. 2002). That is, various promotions of the same magnitude framed differently may be perceived differently in terms of gains versus reduced losses (Diamond and Campbell 1989). Compared to a transaction with no framing, price promotions (e.g., discounts or gift rewards) may introduce a positive perception of differences. Therefore, consumers' negative perceptions of customized pricing could be reduced by making prices for apparently similar transactions less or not comparable. We predict that a price framing will induce higher consumers' perceived transaction dissimilarity. The more consumers perceive the transactions to be dissimilar; the lower will be their perceptions of price unfairness. Perceived price fairness may further positively influence perceived value, trust, and purchase satisfaction, and consequently have a positive impact on repurchase intentions. Pricing research suggests that consumers are often inaccurate when performing mental arithmetic calculations (Estelami 2003). Consumers may use simplifying heuristics rather than engage in more difficult mental arithmetic when integrating pieces of product information to form an overall judgment. We hypothesized that a discount framed in dollars (percentage) will be more effective for a high-priced (low-priced) product, and vice versa in reducing consumers' negative perceptions. Nevertheless, consumers perceive nonmonetary promotions differently than monetary promotions with the same nominal value. Consumers tend to segregate the benefits and perceive them as gaining something extra (Campbell and Diamond 1990). For example, a free gift with purchase promotions can lead to inferences about the value of the gift. Consumers tend to attach higher value to the same gift if it is given by a higher-priced brand name and vice versa (Raghubir, 2004). Thus, we predict that using free gift for a high-priced product may be effective in reducing consumers' negative perceptions of customized pricing since the free gift can enhance the transactional value of the purchase (Monroe 2003).

Studies 1 and 2 involved both discount framing (dollar off versus percentage off) and reward framing (free cash coupon versus free gift) for a high-priced desktop PC versus a low-priced movie DVD in a between-subjects factorial design. Participants first read a short scenario asking them to consider buying a HP desktop PC (or a movie DVD) on the Internet. The manipulation of price presentation format was introduced via a web page with the product image, name and model number, price, and product description. All participants were presented the same desktop PC (DVD) web page with the same product but with a different promotion presentation framing format. Participants were randomly assigned to either the control or one of the four framing conditions ($ off, % off, cash coupon, or a free gift). In the control group, participants were simply presented with the same product at the final price without any framing manipulations. The final computer (DVD) price for all participants was the same amount, $599.00 ($19.99). After all participants rated their willingness to buy, they were told that a friend had bought the same computer (DVD) from the same online store for a lower price, $499.00 ($16.99). Finally, participants evaluated the dependent measures of perceived fairness, perceived value, purchase satisfaction, perceived transaction dissimilarity, trust, and repurchase intentions. Open-ended thoughts data were collected to investigate participants' responses towards promotion framing, transaction dissimilarity compared to their friends, and overall purchase experiences.

The conceptual model of the underlying transaction dissimilarity mechanism was assessed using latent variable structural equation modeling in AMOS and showed a good fit. Our findings confirmed the proposition that the degree of transaction similarity is highly related to perceptions of price unfairness (Xia et al. 2004). Our findings further show that as perceived fairness increased, consumers perceived a higher value, purchase satisfaction, and trust. Consumers' repurchase intentions were mainly driven by trust (i.e., mediator of price fairness on repurchase intentions) in the high-priced product category while it was driven by both trust and perceived value in the low-priced product category. Contradictory to previous literature and our prediction, surprisingly, our results reveal that percentage off and free gift framing are more effective than dollar off and cash coupon framing in reducing consumers' negative perceptions of customized pricing not only for low-priced but also high-priced products. Both free gift and percentage off are in different units from the initial list price (monetary unit). The non-dollar promotion format also will produce a dissimilarity effect such that consumers, when comparing with other people's purchases, will perceive their own purchases differently. Additional comparisons between these two framings reveals that free gift framing in the high-priced product category and percentage off in the low-priced category yields the best results in enhancing consumers' perceptions. Overall, the findings suggest that promotion framing tactics influences consumers' reactions of customized pricing differently across different product-price levels. Consumers' perceived transaction dissimilarity is an important antecedent of perceived price fairness. We demonstrate that different promotion framing tactics can effectively mitigate consumers' negative perceptions of customized pricing.

REFERENCES

Adams, J. Stacey (1965), "Inequity in Social Exchange," in *Advances in Experimental Social Psychology*, Vol. 2, ed. L. Berkowitz, New York: Academic Press, 267-99.

Bagozzi, Richard P. and Youjae Yi (1988), "On the Evaluation of Structural Equation Models," *Journal of the Academy of Marketing Science*, 16 (1), 74-94.

Baker, Walter, Mike Marn, and Craig Zawada (2001), "Price Smarter on the Net.," *Harvard Business Review*, 79 (2), 122-27.

Bakos, Yannis (2001), "The Emerging Landscape for Retail E-Commerce," *Journal of Economic Perspectives*, 15 (1), 69-80.

Bolton, Lisa E., Luk Warlop, and Joseph W. Alba (2003), "Consumer Perceptions of Price (Un)Fairness," *Journal of Consumer Research*, 29 (4), 474-91.

Campbell, Leland and William D. Diamond (1990), "Framing and Sales Promotions: The Characteristics of a 'Good Deal'," *Journal of Consumer Marketing*, 7 (4), 25-31.

Chen, Haipeng (Allan) and Akshay R. Rao (2007), "When Two Plus Two Is Not Equal to Four: Errors in Processing Multiple Percentage Changes," *Journal of Consumer Research*, 34 (3), 327-40.

Chen, Shih-Fen S., Kent B. Monroe, and Yung-Chien Lou (1998), "The Effects of Framing Price Promotion Messages on Consumers' Perceptions and Purchase Intentions," *Journal of Retailing*, 74 (3), 353-72.

Cox, Jennifer Lyn (2001), "Can Differential Prices be Fair?" *Journal of Product & Brand Management*, 10 (5), 264-75.

Darke, Peter R. and Cindy M. Y. Chung (2005), "Effects of Pricing and Promotion on Consumer Perceptions: It Depends on How You Frame It," *Journal of Retailing*, 81 (1), 35-47.

Darke, Peter R. and Darren W. Dahl (2003), "Fairness and Discounts: The Subjective Value of a Bargain," *Journal of Consumer Psychology*, 13 (3), 328-38.

Diamond, William D. and Leland Campbell (1989), "The Framing of Sales Promotions: Effects on Reference Price Change," in *Advances in Consumer Research*, Vol. 16, ed. Thomas Srull, Provo, UT: Association for Consumer Research, 241-47.

Diamond, William D. and Abhijit Sanyal (1990), "The Effect of Framing on the Choice of Supermarket Coupons," *Advances in Consumer Research*, Vol.17, eds. Marvin Goldberg, Gerald Gorn, and Richard Pollay, Provo, UT: Association for Consumer Research, 488-93.

Elmaghraby, Wedad and Pinar Keskinocak (2003), "Dynamic Pricing in the Presence of Inventory Considerations: Research Overview, Current Practices, and Future Directions," *Management Science*, 49 (10), 1287-309.

Estelami, Hooman (2003), "The Effect of Price Presentation Tactics on Consumer Evaluation Effort of Multi-dimensional Prices," *Journal of Marketing Theory & Practice*, 11 (2), 1-15.

Garbarino, Ellen and Mark S. Johnson (1999), "The Different Roles of Satisfaction, Trust, and Commitment in Customer Relationships," *Journal of Marketing*, 63 (2), 70-87.

Garbarino, Ellen and Olivia F. Lee (2003), "Dynamic Pricing in Internet Retail: Effects on Consumer Trust," *Psychology & Marketing*, 20 (6), 495-513.

Gendall, Philip, Janet Hoek, Tracy Pope, and Karen Young (2006), "Message Framing Effects on Price Discounting," *Journal of Product & Brand Management*, 15 (7), 458-65.

Grewal, Dhruv, David M. Hardesty, and Gopalkrishnan R. Iyer (2004), "The Effects of Buyer Identification and Purchase Timing on Consumers' Perceptions of Trust, Price Fairness, and Repurchase Intentions," *Journal of Interactive Marketing*, 18 (4), 87-100.

Haws, Kelly L. and William O. Bearden (2006), "Dynamic Pricing and Consumer Fairness Perceptions," *Journal of Consumer Research*, 33 (3), 304-11.

Kahneman, Daniel, Jack L. Knetsch, and Richard Thaler (1986), "Fairness as a Constraint on Profit Seeking: Entitlements in the Market," *American Economic Review*, 76 (4), 728-41.

Kahneman, Daniel and Amos Tversky (1979), "Prospect Theory: An Analysis of Decision under Risk," *Econometrica*, 47 (2), 263-91.

Krishna, Aradhna, Richard Briesch, Donald R. Lehmann, and Hong Yuan (2002), "A Meta-analysis of the Impact of Price Presentation on Perceived Savings," *Journal of Retailing*, 78 (2), 101-18.

Kukar-Kinney, Monika, Lan Xia, and Kent B. Monroe (2007), "Consumers' Perceptions of the Fairness of Price-matching Refund Policies," *Journal of Retailing*, 83 (3), 325-37.

Kung, Mui, Kent B. Monroe, and Jennifer L. Cox (2002), "Pricing on the Internet," *Journal of Product & Brand Management*, 11 (4), 274-87.

Lee, Fei and Kent B. Monroe (2008), "Dynamic Pricing on the Internet: A Price Framing Approach," in *Advances in Consumer Research*, Vol. 35, eds. Angela Lee and Dilip Soman, Duluth, MN: Association for Consumer Research, 637-38.

Marn, Michael V. (2000), "Virtual Pricing," *McKinsey Quarterly* (4), 128-30.

Monroe, Kent B. (2003), *Pricing: Making Profitable Decisions*, Burr Ridge, IL: McGraw-Hill/Irwin.

Monroe, Kent B. and Joseph D. Chapman (1987), "Framing Effects on Buyers' Subjective Product Evaluations," in *Advances in Consumer Research*, Vol. 14, eds. Paul Anderson and Melanie Wallendorf, Provo, UT: Association for Consumer Research, 193-97.

Morwitz, Vicki G., Eric A. Greenleaf, and Eric J. Johnson (1998), "Divide and Prosper: Consumers' Reactions to Partitioned Prices," *Journal of Marketing Research*, 35 (4), 453-63.

Mussweiler, Thomas (2003), "'Everything is Relative': Comparison Processes in Social Judgement," *European Journal of Social Psychology*, 33 (6), 719-33.

Ordonez, Lisa D., Terry Connolly, and Richard Coughlan (2000), "Multiple Reference Points in Satisfaction and Fairness Assessment," *Journal of Behavioral Decision Making*, 13 (3), 329-44.

Payne, John W. (1982), "Contingent Decision Behavior," *Psychological Bulletin*, 92 (2), 382-402.

Raghubir, Priya (2004), "Free Gift with Purchase: Promoting or Discounting the Brand?" *Journal of Consumer Psychology*, 14 (1/2), 181-86.

Ramasastry, Anita (2005), "Web Sites Change Prices Based on Customers' Habits," http://www.cnn.com/2005/LAW/06/24/ramasastry.website.prices/.

Singh, Jagdip and Deepak Sirdeshmukh (2000), "Agency and Trust Mechanisms in Consumer Satisfaction and Loyalty Judgments," *Journal of the Academy of Marketing Science*, 28 (1), 150-67.

Sinha, Indrajit and Michael F. Smith (2000), "Consumers' Preferences of Promotional Framing of Price," *Psychology & Marketing*, 17 (3), 257-75.

Thaler, Richard (1985), "Mental Accounting and Consumer Choice," *Marketing Science*, 4 (3), 199-214.

Xia, Lan, Kent B. Monroe, and Jennifer L. Cox (2004), "The Price Is Unfair! A Conceptual Framework of Price Fairness Perceptions," *Journal of Marketing*, 68 (4), 1-15.

Yang, Zhilin and Robin T. Peterson (2004), "Customer Perceived Value, Satisfaction, and Loyalty: The Role of Switching Costs," *Psychology & Marketing*, 21 (10), 799-822.

Effects of a Scarcity Message on Product Judgments: Role of Cognitive Load and Mediating Processes

Junsang Yeo, Dongguk University, Korea
Jongwon Park, Korea University, Korea

EXTENDED ABSTRACT

The literature on the scarcity of objects has shown a generally positive effect of the scarcity in forming preferences and behaviors in diverse contexts (See Lynn 1991 for a review). Yet, the research on the effect of a scarcity message in marketing communication context (e.g., advertising) is relatively limited and provides mixed results. The present research intended to examine the effect of a scarcity message in a persuasive marketing communication and the processes that underlie the effect. While doing so, we also identified moderating conditions for the effect that have not previously been reported.

Consumers often hear a company announcing a plan for limited production of special products for a special occasion or encounter a retailer announcing the limited number of items remaining in stock. As such, consumers are frequently exposed to information about the scarcity of a product or service. A scarcity claim in a persuasive marketing context is likely to elicit positive thoughts about the product such as enhanced quality and exclusiveness. Yet, the claim can also provoke a second, negative thought, i.e., suspicion about marketers' manipulative intent (i.e., persuasive attempt). To this extent, the effect of a scarcity message is largely dependent on whether the second thought is actively generated.

Based on the research on dispositional attribution (Gilbert and Malone 1995; Trope and Gaunt 1999) and persuasion knowledge (e.g., Ahluwalia and Burnkrant 2004; Campbell and Kirmani 2000), we expect that generating the second thought (suspicion about the persuasive intent) and acting on it is relatively an effortful and controlled process, and thus requires considerable amount of cognitive resources. Consequently, it is hypothesized that a scarcity message in marketing communication can produce a positive impact on consumer evaluations only in a situation in which the cognitive resource is limited so that inference processes regarding the marketer's manipulative intent in using the message are unlikely to operate. When the cognitive resource is available, inferences about the manipulative intent are likely to occur, which in turn reduce or eliminate any positive consequence of the scarcity message.

These expectations were examined and confirmed in two experiments. In experiment 1, participants received a promotion pamphlet for a MP3 player that contained either a scarcity or a non-scarcity message. In addition, the cognitive resource was manipulated (high vs. low) by providing a cognitively distracting vs. non-distracting secondary task (i.e., memorizing an 8-digit vs. 2-digit number) at the time participants process the target message. A significant two-way interaction of cognitive resource and message type on evaluations indicated that the scarcity message, compared to the non-scarcity message, led to more favorable evaluations of the target product only when the cognitive resource was distracted. In addition, an analysis of participants' perceptions about persuasive attempts also yielded a significant 2-way interaction effect, indicating that indeed participants who received a scarcity message were more suspicious about the marketers' manipulative intent under no distraction conditions than under high distraction conditions, whereas the suspicion level in the latter conditions were comparable to the level in the non-scarcity message conditions.

Experiment 2 replicated findings from experiment 1 and in addition, examined the two alternative possibilities regarding the processes underlying the effect of the distraction task. The first, "discounting-inhibition" hypothesis posits that a distraction task inhibits discounting processes on target evaluations based on perceptions of the marketer's manipulative intent. The second, "activation-inhibition" hypothesis posits that the distraction task inhibits activation of persuasion knowledge per se from memory that is relevant to process the scarcity message. To examine these alternative possibilities, the persuasion knowledge was either primed or not before participants received the target information. Results showed that the effect of the cognitive distraction on the effectiveness of the scarcity message relative to the non-scarcity message was evidenced only when the persuasion knowledge was not primed. This supports the "activation-inhibition" hypothesis, suggesting that the effect of the distraction task was due to its influence on activation of persuasion knowledge rather than its influence on discounting process based on perceptions of the manipulative intent.

REFERENCES

Ahluwalia, Rohini and Robert E. Burnkrant (2004), "Answering Questions about Questions: A Persuasion Knowledge Perspective for Understanding the Effects of Rhetorical Questions," *Journal of Consumer Research*, 31(June), 26-42.

Amaldoss, Wilfred and Sanjay Jain (2005), "Pricing of Conspicuous Goods: A Competitive Analysis of Social Effects," *Journal of Marketing Research*, 42 (February), 30-42.

Baron, R. M., & Kenny, D. A. (1986), "The Moderator-Mediator Variable Distinction in Social Psychological Research: Conceptual, Strategic, and Statistical Considerations," *Journal of Personality and Social Psychology*, 51, 1173-1182.

Becker, Gary S. (1991), "A Note on Restaurant Pricing and Other Examples of Social Influences on Price," *Journal of Political Economy*, 99 (October), 1109-16.

Brock, T. C. (1968), "Implications of Commodity Theory for Value Change," In Greenwald, A. G., Brock, T. C. and Ostrom, T. M.(eds), in *Psychological Foundations of Attitudes*, New York: Academic.

Campbell, Margaret C. and Amna Kirmani (2000), "Consumers' Use of Persuasion Knowledge: The Effects of Accessibility and Cognitive Capacity on Perceptions of an Influence Agent," *Journal of Consumer Research*, 27(June), 69-83.

Cialdini, R. B. (2001), *Influence: Science and practice*, Boston, MA: Allyn and Bacon.

Fein, Steven (1996), "Effects of Suspicion on Attributional Thinking and the Correspondence Bias," *Journal of Personality and Social Psychology*, 70 (June), 1164-1184.

Fromkin, H. L.(1970), "Effects of Experimentally Aroused Feelings," *Journal of Personality and Social Psychology*, 16, 521-529.

Gilbert, Daniel T. and Patrick S. Malone (1995), "The Correspondence Bias," *Psychological Bulletin*, 117 (1), 21-38.

Gilbert, Daniel T., Brett W. Pelham, and Douglas S. Krull (1988), "On Cognitive Busyness: When Person Perceivers Meet Persons Perceived," *Journal of Personality and Social Psychology*, 54 (May), 733-740.

Inman, J. Jeffrey, Anil C. Peter, and Priya Raghubir (1997), "Framing the Deal: The Role of Restrictions in Accentuating Deal Value," *Journal of Consumer Research*, 24(June), 68-79.

Lynn, M. (1991), "Scarcity Effects on Value : A Quantitative Review of the   Commodity Theory Literature," *Psychology and Marketing*, 8, 67-78.

Stock, Axel and Subramanian Balachander (2005), "The Making of a "Hot Product": A Signaling Explanation of Marketers' Scarcity Strategy," *Management Science*, 51 (August), 1181-92.

Trope, Yaacov and Ruth Gaunt (1999), "A Dual-Process Model of Overconfident Attributional Inferences," in *Dual-Process Theories in Social Psychology*, New York: The Guilford Press, 161-178.

Williams, Patti, Gavan J. Fitzsimons, and Lauren G. Block (2004), "When Consumers Do Not Recognize "Benign" Intention Questions as Persuasion Attempts," *Journal of Consumer Research*, 31(3), 540-550.

The Effect of Creative Mindset on Consumer Information Processing

Xiaojing Yang, University of Wisconsin-Milwaukee, USA
Torsten Ringberg, University of Wisconsin-Milwaukee, USA
Huifang Mao, University of Central Florida, USA
Laura Peracchio, University of Wisconsin-Milwaukee, USA

EXTENDED ABSTRACT

Framing of persuasive messages becomes an important topic for researchers and managers alike in recent years (Lee and Aaker 2004; Wheeler, Petty and Bizer 2005). However, there are disagreements in the literature regarding the effectiveness of message framing. Many researchers (Edwards 1990; Lee and Aaker 2004; Wheeler, Petty and Bizer 2005) maintained that messages framed in a way that is consistent with consumers' natural mode of processing (as determined by their personality, processing motivation etc.) are more appealing ("matching effect" of persuasion). By contrast, some other researchers found the reverse to be true ("mismatching effect" of persuasion). That is, sometimes consumers are more susceptible to messages that are framed in a way that is inconsistent with their natural mode of processing (Aaker and Williams 1998; Millar and Millar 1990). We posit that consumers' mindset at the time of processing messages will determine the effectiveness of message framing. Specifically, we expect that a creativity mindset could reverse the commonly observed "matching effect" of persuasion.

Existing literature reveals that when there is a match between the framing of the message and consumers' personality schemata, consumers are likely to feel comfortable when processing incoming messages because these messages are consistent with how they naturally think about issues. This has been described as "processing fluency (Lee and Aaker 2004)" and "processing readiness (Thompson and Hamilton 2005)." This subjective experience of processing fluency could in turn influence subsequent evaluations. Thus, more positive evaluations are formed. By contrast, when the framing of the message is inconsistent with how they naturally process information, consumers are likely to feel frustrated and thus negative evaluations about the issue will result. Another explanation for this "matching effect" is elaboration-based. For instance, Wheeler, Petty and Bizer (2005) found that if the message framing is compatible with one's self-schemata, consumers will scrutinize the message more carefully.

We posit that this "matching effect" is likely to occur when consumers are in their "normal/natural" processing mode, without some sort of internal or external disruptions. Prior research (Sassenberg and Moskowitz 2005) has demonstrated that priming people with "thoughtfulness" mindset can trigger their common associations with the target issue. In these circumstances, consumers automatically relate the messages in a way that is consistent with how they "naturally" process information. Under this logic, when there is a mismatch between the two (i.e. message framing and how consumers naturally think), consumers will find the message more difficult to process and thus form less favorable evaluations. Thus, mismatching appeals would be ineffective.

We expect the reverse to be true when consumers are in a creativity mindset. By definition, being "creative" implies that consumers should stay away from common solutions to an issue, and avoid activation of typical associations related to the issue at hand. Once primed to think "creatively', we posit that this activated mindset will affect consumers' subsequent information processing activities —we expect that consumers will prefer something different and novel from how they naturally process information. Since mismatching appeals are framed in a way that is inconsistent with how consumers naturally think about the issue, consumers may be attracted to these novel and different appeals (Aaker and Williams 1998). Thus, we expect consumers should be more likely to elaborate on these "novel" messages, which ultimately affect their evaluations of the brand.

We examined this hypothesis across two studies in the context of mental construal (i.e., abstract vs. concrete thinking; see Trope and Liberman 2003). In both studies, we asked respondents to view an ad with different level of abstraction (abstract claim vs. concrete claim). We expect and found that when inducted with creativity mindset, abstract thinkers should find concrete (vs. abstract) ad claims more appealing, while concrete thinkers should be more susceptible to abstract(vs. concrete) ad claims, revealing a "mismatching" pattern. By contrast, when primed with thoughtfulness, abstract thinkers should find abstract (vs. concrete) ad claims more appealing, while concrete thinkers should be more susceptible to concrete (vs. abstract) ad claims, showing support for a "matching pattern."

Together, the results of study 1 and 2 indicate that consumers' mindset at the time of information processing is an important predictor of the "matching" or "mismatching" effect of persuasion. In line with conventional wisdom, when primed with thoughtfulness, consumers' common processing mode is reinforced and thus a "matching" effect of persuasion is observed. Specifically, respondents find messages that are consistent with their natural way of processing, as dictated by such factors as their personality, motivation or processing goals etc., more persuasive. By contrast, when we primed creativity, we found a "mismatching" effect of persuasion. That is, respondents are more susceptible to incoming messages that are inconsistent with their natural way of thinking.

REFERENCES

Aaker, L. Jennifer and Patti Williams (1998), "Empathy versus Pride: The Influence of Emotional Appeals across Cultures," *Journal of Consumer Research*, 25 (December), 242-61.

Edwards (1990), "The Interplay of Affect and Cognition in Attitude Formation and Change," *Journal of Personality and Social Psychology*, 59 (2), 202-16.

Lee, Angel Y. and Jennifer L. Aaker (2004), "Bringing the Frame Into Focus: The Influence Of Regulatory Fit on Processing Fluency and Persuasion," *Journal of Personality and Social Psychology*, 86 (2), 205-18.

Millar, Murray G. and Karen U. Millar (1990), "Attitude Change as a Function of Attitude Type and Argument Type," *Journal of Personality and Social Psychology*, 59 (2), 217-28.

Sassenberga, Kai and Gordon B. Moskowitz (2005), "Don't Stereotype, Think Different! Overcoming Automatic Stereotype Activation by Mindset Priming," *Journal of Experimental Social Psychology*, 41(5), 506-14.

Thompson, Debora Viana and Rebecca Hamilton (2006), "The Effects of Information Processing Mode on Consumers' Responses to Comparative Advertising," *Journal of Consumer Research*, 32 (4), 530-40.

Wheeler, S. Christian, Richard E. Petty and George Y. Bizer (2005), "Self-Schema Matching and Attitude Change: Situational and Dispositional Determinants of Message Elaboration," *Journal of Consumer Research*, 31 (March), 787-97.

Intention-Behavior Consistency: The Effect of Time Perspective

Muge Capar, Georgia Tech, USA
Koert van Ittersum, Georgia Tech, USA

EXTENDED ABSTRACT

Predicting future behavior is one of the central research topics in marketing and consumer research. Most of the theories developed to predict behavior, such as the theory of reasoned action (Fishbein and Ajzen 1975), the theory of planned behavior (Ajzen 1985, 1991), the model of interpersonal behavior (Triandis 1980), the theory of goal setting (Locke and Latham 1990), and the social-cognitive theory (Bandura 1977, 1998) propose that intention is the key predictor of behavior. Although intentions help predict behavior, there is often a substantial gap between people's intentions and their subsequent behavior–an intention-behavior inconsistency, meaning that people behave inconsistently with their intentions. To improve our understanding of the origin of this intention-behavior inconsistency, this research focuses on one of the key differences between intention and behavior: time. There is always a time interval between the formation or measurement of intentions and the performance of behavior. Despite the central role of time in the intention-behavior relationship, research that focuses on time-related aspects is scarce. Research has studied the effects of temporal distance and the characteristics of behavior (or the object of behavior) on people's decisions regarding future behaviors. In terms of intention-behavior relationship, in addition to the importance of temporal distance between intention and behavior, it is also important how the person approaches time. In order to fill this gap, we examine the effect of people's time perspective–a personality construct that reflects people's approach to past, present, and future–on the intention-behavior consistency. It is important to understand how this personality characteristic affects self-prediction of behavior in order to control for and correct errors in self-prediction so that more accurate and confident results can be obtained. Based on Zimbardo and Boyd's (1999) time perspective factors, we examine the effect of future, present-fatalistic, and present-hedonistic time perspectives on intention-behavior relationship in the concept of new product adoption. We hypothesize on the effect of these factors both on stated intentions, and intention-behavior consistency. We also hypothesize on the moderating role of attitude on these effects.

In order to test our hypotheses, we conducted an experiment with student subjects, in which we asked them their intention to pick up a stainless steel mug in a given time period in the near future, as well as measured their time perspective using Zimbardo Time Perspective Inventory. In the second part of the experiment we kept track of the participants that picked up or did not pick up the mug. To test the effects of these variables on stated intentions, we used logistic regression analysis with self reported behavioral intention as the dependent variable. Participants' attitudes towards the mug, the three time perspectives–present-hedonistic, future, and present-fatalistic, and the interactions between their attitude and the three time perspectives, were included as independent variables. To test the effects of the same variables on intention-behavior consistency, we again used logistic regression analysis with the intention-behavior consistency (0=inconsistent, 1=consistent)as the dependent variable. Those who followed through on their intentions (self-reported intention=yes; behavior is performed; self-reported intention=no; behavior is not performed) were classified as consistent, while those who did not follow through on their intentions (self-report intention=yes; behavior is not performed; self reported intention=no; behavior is performed) were classified as inconsis-

tent. Participants' attitudes, their time perspectives, and the interaction terms were included as independent variables.

We find that present-hedonism positively influences self-reported intentions, and this positive effect is strengthened by consumers' attitudes towards the mug. While we do not find a main effect for present-fatalism, we do find that the effect of present-fatalism on self-reported intentions is moderated by consumers' attitudes towards the mug. More specifically, consumers' attitudes towards the mug strengthen the negative influence of present-fatalism on self-reported intentions. We also find that people with high future time perspective are more conservative in stating their intentions and have a tendency to state lower intentions than individuals with a low future time perspective.

In line with their desire to achieve future goals, we find that more future-oriented individuals display a higher intention-behavior consistency. On the other hand, more present-oriented individuals tend to display a lower intention-behavior consistency. A strong orientation toward present pleasure, with little concern for future consequences, causes more present-hedonistic people to overstate their intentions, as a result of which they display a lower intention-behavior consistency. More present-fatalistic people display a lower intention-behavior consistency because of their hopeless attitude towards the future, which causes them to either overstate or understate their intentions. Furthermore, consumers' attitudes towards the mug moderate the effect of present-fatalism on the intention-behavior consistency–the more favorable consumers' attitudes, the weaker the relationship between present-fatalism and the intention-behavioral relationship.

On Believing Our Imagination: The Role of Mental Imagery in Belief Generation and Resilience

Massimiliano Ostinelli, McGill University, Canada
Ulf Böckenholt, McGill University, Canada

EXTENDED ABSTRACT

Theoretical evidence suggests the existence of a deliberate and an implicit route to believing. Deliberate beliefs are purposively held through a validating frame (e.g., explicit argumentation or source credibility), whereas implicit beliefs are derived from spontaneous and nonconscious inferences generated by perceptual-like experiences (Sperber, 1997). This distinction is akin to the one discussed by Gilbert and colleagues (e.g., Gilbert, Krull, & Malone, 1990) concerning the Cartesian approach—which suggests that people mentally represent ideas and then decide whether to accept them as true or false—and the Spinozan approach—which suggests that, once encoded, ideas are automatically endorsed as true and deliberation is needed to discard them.

Drawing on this literature, we propose that imagery-provoking messages (e.g., narrative, imagery instructions) induce both deliberate beliefs—due to the strength of the arguments and/or the credibility of the source—and implicit beliefs—due to the experience of mental images generated by the message—, whereas abstract messages (e.g., product ratings, abstract messages) induce only deliberate beliefs. For example, an abstract consumer review stating that "dialing with this cell phone is a tiring, error-filled process" might be believed only deliberately (e.g., I trust the reviewer, therefore I believe that the phone is bad), whereas an imagery-provoking one, such as "the buttons of this cell phone are too small so our fingers are always pushing the wrong button" can, in addition to deliberate beliefs, lead to the generation of implicit beliefs due to the experience of mental images (e.g., a person experiencing difficulty while dialing a phone number).

Moreover, we propose that beliefs derived by abstract messages, being held deliberately, should be relatively easy to discard. Once the credibility or the arguments of the message has been questioned, there is no reason to purposely maintain these beliefs. However, implicit beliefs generated by mental images should be less affected by deliberate attempts to discard the content of the message. That is, once generated, the mental images of a product will affect product evaluation even when the message has been discounted as unreliable.

The advantage of imagery-provoking messages, however, holds to the extent that consumers are able and motivated to generate mental images. Therefore, factors undermining an individual's willingness (or ability) to imagine might reduce the resilience of beliefs induced by imagery-provoking messages. One of these factors might be represented by consumers' expectations about the credibility of a message. Being suspicious about the trustworthiness of a message should reduce consumers' willingness to imagine product-related behaviors (e.g., why should I imagine something that is not true?). For this reason, the resilience of beliefs generated by imagery-provoking messages should be lower when discrediting cues (e.g. information about the credibility of the message) are provided before, rather than after, the encoding of the message.

Three studies were conducted to test our propositions. In Study 1, respondents judged imagery-provoking product claims as more believable than abstract ones, despite the fact that they were told that there was no "objective" reason to infer the believability of the product claims. Interestingly, almost 60% of the variability in claim believability was accounted for by the average imaginability rating of product claims. Study 2 examined how product evaluation was affected by mental imagery generated by a message that was afterwards declared either credible or non-credible. Results showed that source credibility had a stronger effect on product evaluation among participants reporting low mental imagery than among those reporting high mental imagery. This finding suggests that respondents who reported high mental imagery kept holding positive beliefs about the product despite knowing that the message was unreliable. In Study 3, participants evaluated a restaurant after being presented with two contradictory reviews presented either in an imagery-provoking (i.e., narrative) or an abstract manner (i.e., product ratings). Results showed that impressions formed by imagery product reviews were more resilient to subsequent challenges than those formed by abstract ones. Study 3 also suggested that the resilience of imagery-provoking messages was lower when the contradictory review was provided before, rather than after, the encoding of the message.

By suggesting that imagery-provoking messages induce beliefs that are more resilient than those generated by abstract ones, this work contributes to the literature on beliefs generation and correction (e.g., Gilbert & Ebert, 2002; Gilbert, Gill, & Wilson, 2002; Johar & Simmons, 2000; Schul & Burnstein, 1985; Schul & Mazursky, 1990). Our findings have significant implications for marketing practice given that people often imagine consumption-related behaviors (e.g., MacInnis & Price, 1987; Petrova & Cialdini, 2007; Shiv & Huber, 2000) to form product impressions that might need to be adjusted or even discounted. Our results apply not only to the case of mental images prompted by messages that are later found to be unreliable, but also to cases in which consumers need to integrate contradictory evidence presented either in an imagery-provoking or abstract format (e.g., imagery-provoking ads vs. consumer reports).

REFERENCES

Gilbert, D. T., & Ebert, J. E. J. (2002). Decisions and Revisions: The Affective Forecasting of Changeable Outcomes. *Journal of Personality and Social Psychology, 82*(4), 503-514.

Gilbert, D. T., Gill, M. J., & Wilson, T. D. (2002). The Future is Now: Temporal Correction in Affective Forecasting. *Organizational Behavior and Human Decision Processes 88*(1), 430-444.

Gilbert, D. T., Krull, D. S., & Malone, P. S. (1990). Unbelieving the Unbelievable: Some Problems in the Rejection of False Information. *Journal of Personality and Social Psychology, 59*(4), 601-613.

Johar, G. V., & Simmons, C. J. (2000). The Use of Concurrent Disclosures to Correct Invalid Inferences. *Journal of Consumer Research, 26*(4), 307-322.

MacInnis, D. J., & Price, L. L. (1987). The Role of Imagery in Information Processing: Review and Extensions. *Journal of Consumer Research, 13*(4), 473-491.

Petrova, P. K., & Cialdini, R. B. (2007). Evoking the Imagination as a Strategy of Influence. In *Handbook of Consumer Psychology* (pp. 505-523): Psychology Press.

Schul, Y., & Burnstein, E. (1985). When Discounting Fails: Conditions Under Which Individuals use Discredited Information in Making a Judgment. *Journal of Personality and Social Psychology, 49*(4), 894-903.

Schul, Y., & Mazursky, D. (1990). Conditions Facilitating Successful Discounting in Consumer Decision Making. *The Journal of Consumer Research, 16*(4), 442-451.

Shiv, B., & Huber, J. (2000). The Impact of Anticipating Satisfaction on Consumer Choice. *Journal of Consumer Research, 27*(2), 202-216.

Sperber, D. (1997). Intuitive and Reflective Beliefs. *Mind & Language, 12*(1), 67-83.

The Effects of Imagery, False Memory and Experience on Attitude Confidence

Priyali Rajagopal, Southern Methodist University, USA
Nicole Montgomery, College of William and Mary, USA

EXTENDED ABSTRACT

Two key variables that have been little considered in the marketing literature on imagery are the creation of false memories and attitude strength. A false memory may consist of a mistaken belief that a fictitious event occurred (e.g., being lost in a mall as a child) or a distortion of an event that actually did occur (e.g., meeting Bugs Bunny at Disneyland instead of Mickey Mouse). Recent research in psychology (e.g. Mazzoni and Memon 2003) has suggested that imagery can lead to the development of false memories. Thus, imagery can make respondents incorrectly believe that an event was actually experienced by them.

Based on this stream of research, we suggest that if false memories are implanted through imagery, these false memories may exhibit some effects that are similar to genuine product experience. Past research in marketing has demonstrated that product experience leads to stronger attitudes as compared to attitudes that are based on indirect product experience such as exposure to advertising (e.g., Regan and Fazio 1977). If imagery results in a mistaken belief that consumers have direct experience with a product (i.e., false memory), then it follows that imagery and experience may have equivalent effects on attitude strength. Therefore, we propose that attitudes based on imagery-evoking information will be stronger than attitudes based on information that is not imagery-evoking due to the creation of false product experience memories following exposure to a high-imagery advertising message.

Study 1

Design: 2 (image-provoking ability of the ten ads: high-imagery vs. low-imagery) x 10 (different products) mixed design, with imagery as the between-subjects factor and the different products as the within-subjects factor with 100 undergraduate students.

Procedure: Respondents were given a series of 10 print advertisements and given 45 seconds to view each ad. One week following the presentation of the ads, respondents were asked to complete an online survey containing the dependent measures.

Dependent measures

False memory. We used two different measures of false memory. The first measure was a product usage memory measure wherein, participants were provided with a list of fifty brands, amongst which were the ten target brands contained in the series of ads. Respondents were asked to select all of the brands that they believe they had used at least once. For the second measure, five brands (two target brands and three filler brands from the list) were each presented to respondents with a series of three statements ("I have purchased this product," "I have seen this product in local grocery stores," "I have heard about this product from friends or family members") and respondents were asked to select all statements that apply.

Attitude and attitude strength. Attitude was measured through the use of a four-item, seven-point scale (bad-good, negative-positive, unfavorable-favorable and undesirable-desirable). Attitude strength was measured using a three-item, seven-point scale ("how strongly do you hold the opinion about ___?", "how confident are you in your opinion of ___?" and "how certain are you in your opinion of ___?")

Results

There were no differences in self-reported involvement between any of the experimental conditions (all p-values>.1). There was no effect of imagery on attitudes towards the two target brands ($M_{High\ Imagery}$=5.21, $M_{Low\ Imagery}$=5.02, $F (1, 73)$=0.75, p>.1).

Attitude strength. There was a significant main effect of imagery on attitude strength towards the two target brands ($F (1, 73)$=6.36, p<.05). Respondents exposed to the high-imagery ads reported stronger attitudes (M=6.01) than respondents exposed to the low-imagery ads (M=5.06). Thus, H1 was supported.

Product Usage Memory. There was a significant main effect of imagery ($F (1, 73)$=5.26, p<.05) such that respondents that were exposed to the high-imagery ads selected more targets from the list on average (M=2.50) than respondents that were exposed to the series of low-imagery ads (M=1.69). Thus, H2 was supported.

Second memory measure. Respondents that read the high-imagery ads selected more false memory statements on average for each of the target brands (M=1.14) than respondents that read the low-imagery ads (M=0.61, ($F (1, 73)$=13.20, p<.05), supporting H2. There was not a significant difference between the two conditions in terms of the number of false memory statements selected for the filler brands (p >.05).

Mediation analysis. To test whether false memory mediated the effect of imagery on attitude strength, we conducted analyses in line with the procedure outlined in Baron and Kenny (1986). The following three relationships were established: (1): Imagery predicts attitude strength (β=.28, p<.05) (2): Imagery predicts false memory (β=.39, p<.05) and (3): When imagery and false memory are included as predictor variables, only false memory significantly predicts attitude strength (?=.25, p<.05) and imagery is reduced to non-significance (β=.19, p>.1). These results suggest that false memory fully mediates the effect of imagery on attitude strength.

Study 2

Design: 2 (direct product experience: yes vs. no) x 2 (imagery: high vs. low) between-subjects design with 113 undergraduate students.

Procedure: Respondents were exposed to the same set of 10 ads used in study 1 and were given 45 seconds to read each ad. Respondents in the no-experience condition then moved on to another study. Respondents in the experience conditions were informed that they would be given one of the advertised products to taste. The target product used in the study was Orville Redenbacher's Blue Corn popcorn. Respondents were given half of a cup of popcorn to taste. Since the target brand was a fictitious brand, we used ACTII popcorn for the taste experience. One week after the experiment, respondents were contacted by e-mail and instructed to complete a survey online

Dependent measures: We measured false memory, attitude and attitude strength for the Orville Redenbacher popcorn using the same measures as in study 1.

Results

False memory. Planned contrasts revealed that in the no-experience conditions, there was a significant effect of imagery on false memory such that respondents that read the high imagery ads selected a significantly higher mean number of statements in the false memory measure (M=.91) than respondents that read the low imagery ads (M=.46, t=1.97, p=.05). In the product experience conditions, as expected, there was no effect of imagery on false memory. There were no main or interactive effects of experience and imagery on the false memory for any of the filler brands and none of the planned contrasts were significant (all p-values>.1). Thus, as expected, the false memory creation was specific to the target brand alone.

The two experience conditions did not differ significantly on any of the dependent variables (all p's>.1) including attitude strength (supporting H3a), and hence we averaged the two experience conditions and conducted planned contrasts to test H3..

Attitude strength. In line with expectations, we found that the experience conditions elicited significantly higher attitude strength than the low imagery alone condition ($M_{Experience}$= 6.1, $M_{Low Imagery}$=4.41, t=3.59, p<.01), supporting H3d. The high imagery-no experience condition also elicited significantly higher attitude strength than the low imagery-no experience condition ($M_{High Imagery}$=5.40, $M_{Low Imagery}$=4.41, t=2.08, p<.05), supporting H3b. The experience and high imagery alone conditions were not significantly different (t=1.60, p>.1), supporting H3c.

Attitude. In line with expectations, we found that attitudes towards the target brand were significantly higher in the experience conditions (M=4.93) as compared to the high imagery-no experience (M=4.39, t=2.13, p<.05) and the low imagery-no experience conditions (M=4.31, t=2.22, p<.05). There were no differences between the high imagery and low imagery no experience conditions (p>.1).

Our research contributes to the literatures in imagery, product experience, and false memory. We extend the effects of imagery to include attitude strength, a variable that has not been previously considered in the imagery literature. Contrary to much of the previous research on product experience, we find that experience only results in stronger attitudes than an ad if the ad is pallid; an extremely vivid ad leads to equivalently strong attitudes as experience. Further, we find that the effect of imagery on attitude strength persists for as long as one week, suggesting that the effect is strong. In addition to contributing to research on imagery, we extend the false memory literature by considering the effects of false memory on attitudes and attitude strength.

REFERENCES

Mazzoni, Giuliana and Amina Memon (2003), "Imagination Can Create False Autobiographical Memories," *Psychological Science*, 14, 186-188.

Regan, Dennis T. and Russell Fazio (1977), "On the Consistency Between Attitudes and Behavior: Look to the Method of Attitude Formation," *Journal of Experimental Social Psychology*, 13, 28-45.

Mental Simulation and the Evaluation of New Products: The Affective and Cognitive Dimensions of Process- Versus Outcome-Focused Thoughts

Min Zhao, University of Toronto, Canada
Steve Hoeffler, Vanderbilt University, USA
Gal Zauberman, University of Pennsylvania, USA

EXTENDED ABSTRACT

Really new products (RNPs) allow consumers to do something they have not been able to do before. In this research we identify a key difference between RNPs and INPs regarding the natural mental representation that is formed when consumers consider the product: a focus on the process of using the product versus a focus on the end benefits provided by the product. More importantly, we proceed to address the question of how process- and outcome-focused visualization can be applied to INP and RNP to enhance evaluations. Further, we explore the efficacy of each type of mental simulation to enhance evaluation under each specific information processing mode (i.e. cognitive and affective) for RNPs.

Natural Mental Representations

According to Hoeffler (2003), consumers have less knowledge and greater performance uncertainty for RNPs than for INPs. Recent work (Wood and Lynch 2001) showed that high prior knowledge leads to learning complacency and lower motivation for information processing. This suggests consumers may not consider all aspects of INPs due to lower motivation, while they may have a higher motivation to learn different aspects of RNPs (i.e. both product benefits and the adoption and usage process). In addition, past research suggests that consumers focus more on the benefits for products with low complexity, but could consider both benefits and learning cost for products with high complexity (Mukherjee and Hoyer 2001). Thus we predict that:

H1: While consumers will focus more attention on the benefits than the process of using a product for INPs, they will focus equally on both aspects when evaluating RNPs.

Process- versus Outcome-Focused Mental Simulation

Research in psychology has identified two distinct types of mental simulation: process simulation that is focused on the process of reaching a goal versus outcome simulation that is focused on the desirable outcome of achieving the goal (Taylor et al. 1998). Multiple studies show that process simulation is more effective than outcome simulation in facilitating goal attainment (e.g., Taylor et al. 1998) or behavioral intentions (Escalas and Luce 2003, 2004). However, recent work in the context of preference over time (Zhao, Hoeffler and Zaubermam 2007) has demonstrated that each type of simulation is more effective when it augments the mental representation of an event that is naturally neglected. Based on consumers' natural focus of INP and RNP, and the complementary role of mental simulation in terms of activating the naturally less accessible considerations, we suggest that:

H2: While process simulation increases evaluations more than outcome simulation for INPs, the effect of process and outcome simulation will not differ for RNPs.

Impact on RNPs: Cognitive vs. Affective Processing Mode

To explore the potential effect of mental simulation on the evaluation of RNP, we reviewed the mental simulation literature and argue that the existing literature in mental simulation has either confounded process and outcome simulation with cognitive and affective components (i.e. process simulation with a cognitive focus vs. outcome simulation with an affective focus (Taylor et al. 1998)), or incorporated both cognitive and affective components into process and outcome simulation (Escalas and Luce 2003, 2004). Our approach here is to tease apart the cognitive and affective processing focus and investigate the unique effect of process and outcome simulation on the evaluation of RNPs under each type of processing. We predict that:

H3: When evaluating RNPs under a cognitive focused processing mode, outcome simulation leads to higher product evaluations than process simulation; whereas the reversal is true under an affective focused mode.

Experiments and Findings

In experiment 1, we asked participants to read a mock ad for an INP (ThinkPad) or a RNP (AudioPC) and indicate how much they thought about the process of using the product and how much they thought about the end benefits of using the product. The results showed that participants naturally made more thoughts about the end benefits than about the process of using the product for INP. However, they indicated similar amount of thoughts about both aspects for RNP. H1 was confirmed.

In experiment 2, we examined the role of classic process and outcome simulation (i.e. combined focus on both the cognitive and affective components) on the evaluation of new products. We asked participants to practice either a process-oriented (i.e. visualizing the steps of using the product) or outcome-oriented (i.e. visualizing the benefits of using the product) mental visualization task after they read the ad. The results showed that for INPs, process simulation indeed led to higher product evaluation because it activated the naturally ignored thoughts regarding the process of using the product. However, for RNPs which naturally evoked thoughts about both the product benefits and the process of using, the effect of process and outcome simulation on product evaluation did not differ. This supported H2.

In study 3, we tested the specific effect of process and outcome simulation on the evaluation of RNP by teasing apart the effect of cognitive vs. affective processing mode. Participants performed either a process-focused or outcome-focused visualization task that emphasized either the cognitive or affective components. The results indicated that under a cognitive processing mode, outcome simulation increased product evaluation more, whereas under an affective mode, process simulation was more effective than the opposite type of simulation. This provided support for H3. In addition, we found a partial mediating role of performance uncertainty on this pattern.

Conclusion

Our research centers on the role of mental representations in new product evaluation. Our findings provide better understanding to this important and complex question by showing the differential effects of process and outcome simulations, and by showing the role of affective and cognitive considerations in the different effectiveness of these two types of simulations. We further identified performance uncertainty as a mediator. We believe that our research provides some answers to the open questions about new product preference development, and well as open questions about the exact nature of different types of mental simulations and their effectiveness.

REFERENCES

Baron, Reuben M. and David A. Kenny (1986), "The Moderator-Mediator Variable Distinction in Social Psychological Research: Conceptual, Strategic, and Statistical Considerations," *Journal of Personality and Social Psychology*, 51 (6), 1173–82.

Burnkrant, Robert and Rao Unnava (1989), "Self-Referencing: A Strategy for Increasing Processing of Message Content," *Personality and Social Psychology Bulletin*, 15 (December), 628–38.

Burnkrant, Robert and Rao Unnava (1995), "Effect of Self-Referencing on Persuasion," *Journal of Consumer Research*, 22 (June), 17–26.

Castano, Raquel, Mita Sujan, Manish Kacker, and Harish Sujan (2006), "Temporal Distance and the Adoption of New Product: The Why and How of Adoptions," working paper, Tulane University.

Dahl, Darren W. and Steve Hoeffler (2004), "Visualizing the Self: Exploring the Potential Benefits and Drawbacks for New Product Evaluation," *Journal of Product Innovation Management*, 21, 259–67.

Debevec, Kathleen and Jean Romeo (1992), "Self-Referent Processing in Perceptions of Verbal and Visual Commercial Information," *Journal of Consumer Psychology*, 1 (1), 93–102.

Escalas, Jennifer Edson (2007), "Self-Referencing and Persuasion: Narrative Transportation versus Analytical Elaboration," *Journal of Consumer Research*, 33 (March), 421–29.

Escalas, Jennifer Edson and Mary Frances Luce (2004), "Understanding the Effects of Process-Focused Versus Outcome-Focused Thought in Response to Advertising," *Journal of Consumer Research*, 31 (September), 274–85.

Garbarino, Ellen and Julie Edell (1997), "Cognitive Effort, Affect, and Choice," *Journal of Consumer Research*, 24 (September), 147–58.

Green, Melanie and Timothy Brock (2000), "The Role of Transportation in the Persuasiveness of Public Narratives," *Journal of Personality and Social Psychology*, 79 (5), 701–21.

Hoeffler, Steve (2003), "Measuring Preferences for Really New Products," *Journal of Marketing Research*, 40 (November), 406–20.

Hsee, C. K. and Yuval Rottenstreich (2004), "Music, Pandas and Muggers: On the Affective Psychology of Value," *Journal of Experimental Psychology: General*, 133, 23–30.

Keren Gideon, and Lewis Charles (1979), "Partial Omega Squared for ANOVA Designs," *Educational and Psychological Measurement*, 39, 119–28.

Lehmann, Donald (1994), "Characteristics of Really New Products," paper presented at the *Marketing Science Institute Conference*, Boston, MA.

Metcalfe, J. and W. Mischel (1999), "Hot/Cool-System Analysis of Delay of Gratification: Dynamics of Willpower," *Psychological Review*, 106 (1), 3–19.

Moreau, C. Page, Arthur B. Markman, and Donald R. Lehmann (2001), "'What Is It?' Categorization Flexibility and Consumers' Responses to Really New Products," *Journal of Consumer Research*, 27 (March), 489–98.

Mukherjee, Ashesh and Wayne D. Hoyer (2001), "The Effect of Novel Attributes on Product Evaluation," *Journal of Consumer Research*, 28 (December), 462–72.

Pennington, N. and R. Hastie (1986), "Evidence Evaluation in Complex Decision Making," *Journal of Personality and Social Psychology*, 51, 242–58.

Sujan, Mita, James Bettman, and Hans Baumgartner (1993), "Influencing Consumer Judgments Using Autobiographical Memories: A Self-Referencing Perspective," *Journal of Marketing Research*, 30 (November), 422–36.

Taylor, Shelley E., Lien B. Pham, Inna D. Rivkin, and David A. Armor (1998), "Harnessing the Imagination: Mental Simulation, Self-Regulation and Coping," *American Psychologist*, 53 (April), 429–39.

Taylor, Shelley E. and Sherry K. Schneider (1989), "Coping and the Simulation of Events," *Social Cognition*, 7 (2), 174–94.

Trope, Yaacov and Nira Liberman (2003), "Temporal Construal," *Psychological Review*, 110 (3), 403–21.

Trope, Yaacov, Nira Liberman, and Cheryl Wakslak (in press), "Construal Levels and Psychological Distance: Effects on Representation, Prediction, Evaluation, and Behavior," *Journal of Consumer Psychology*.

Wood, Stacy and John Lynch (2001), "Prior Knowledge and Complacency in New Product Learning," *Journal of Consumer Research*, 29 (December), 416–26.

Zauberman, Gal, Kristin Diehl, and Dan Ariely (2006), "Hedonic and Informational Evaluations: Task Dependent Preferences for Sequences of Outcomes," *Journal of Behavioral Decision Making*, 19 (3), 191–211.

Zhao, Min, Steve Hoeffler, and Gal Zauberman (2007), "Mental Simulation and Preference Consistency over Time: The Role of Process- Versus Outcome-Focused Thoughts," *Journal of Marketing Research*, 44 (August).

Visual Inferences and Advertising Spending in Political Marketing

Michael Lewis, Washington University in St. Louis, USA
JoAndrea Hoegg, University of British Columbia, Canada

EXTENDED ABSTRACT

This paper explores how advertising spending and candidate appearance influence Congressional electoral outcomes. Our analyses reveal that campaign spending and visual inferences about candidate personality traits significantly predict vote share, but these factors have asymmetric effects across the major parties.

Introduction

Political campaign managers are increasingly utilizing marketing tools, and spending on political advertising is growing rapidly (Teinowitz 2004), yet political campaigns have received little attention within marketing. Our research considers the role of two marketing variables in political campaigns: product appearance, (i.e. the physical appearance of the candidate) and advertising spending strategies. In particular we explore how the role of party brand image and incumbency moderate the influence of these factors in political campaigns.

Background

Candidate Appearance and Impression Formation

Almost all products are subject to visual inferences that arise out of initial exposure when reactions can result in an established attitude before other information is considered. For political candidates, where visual contact with the candidate is often solely through short news clips or advertisements, personality inferences based on brief visual exposure may be critical. Research has demonstrated how personality inferences based on photographs of political candidates can influence elections (Todorov et al. 2005). Todorov et al. had study participants make relative personality judgments of U.S. Senate and Congressional candidates based solely on their photographs. Results indicated that the appearance of competence was highly predictive of electoral success.

The results of Todorov et al. (2005) are striking but may be incomplete. Because political parties function like brands in that they strive to develop distinct positions, such stereotypes likely differ across party. Thus, the visual qualities that mean success for a Republican may differ from those that mean success for a Democrat. We investigate this possibility.

Advertising Spending

We also consider the role of advertising spending. A consistent finding in prior research on campaign spending is that while challenger spending is found to influence vote shares, spending by incumbents usually has a statistically insignificant effect. The main explanation is that much like an early market entrant, incumbents start with advantages in awareness, which impacts the marginal effects of advertising investments. In contrast, challengers often start from a point of relative anonymity, so marginal spending has a greater effect. We examine this effect and also consider whether asymmetries exist across political party.

Finally we explore effects of advertising tone to see whether the effectiveness of negative advertising is altered as a function of incumbency and political party. As the later entrant into the market, challengers may gain relatively more by employing negative ads that highlight familiar deficiencies in their competitors because they enable alignable comparisons. On the other hand, negative advertising by incumbents that emphasizes the risk of switching to the challenger may be relatively more effective. Party affiliation may also have an effect. Given that political parties have estab-lished brand images and distinct positions, negative advertising may be differentially effective for Democratic versus Republican candidates.

Data

We obtained personality judgments based on candidate photographs for 112 congressional races from 2000 and 2002. Participants were presented with photographs of the two main candidates side by side, labeled "Candidate A" and "Candidate B" (picture position counterbalanced). Participants provided relative ratings on four personality trait questions (competence, intelligence, likeability, and trustworthiness), each on a seven-point scale from "Candidate A looks much more [intelligent]" to "Candidate B looks much more [intelligent]."

Advertising tone data was obtained from the University of Wisconsin's Political Science Department, which has compiled a database containing information on elections in the top 75 media markets in 2000 and the top 100 markets in 2002.[1] The database includes information on whether campaign ads were primarily positive or negative in tone, as well as estimated costs for each airing. We use the estimated costs and tone judgments to calculate the percentage of negative advertising used by each candidate. In addition, we use campaign fundraising and spending statistics from the Federal Election Commission.

Results

We first conduct an analysis of only the visual inference data for Democrats and Republicans. As predicted, the results suggest that the various visual assessments operate differently for the two parties. Republicans benefit from being perceived (visually) as more competent and trustworthy. Appearing more likeable or more intelligent has negative effects. The pattern is strikingly reversed for Democrats.

In the second stage of the analysis we examine the relationships between candidate spending, advertising tone and vote shares. Consistent with results in the political science literature, we find spending for challengers has a significant positive impact but for incumbents has a negligible effect. We also find that spending on negative advertising by Republican challengers is found to be significantly more effective than for Democratic challengers.

As a final step we use the personality inferences data and the spending data in a combined model. We find that spending levels and candidate appearance both significantly influence election results. Including the spending variables and the visual effects in a single model provides an opportunity to quantify the value of inferred personality traits. For example, a Republican incumbent gains the same benefit in vote share from a competence appearance

[1] The data were obtained from a project of the Wisconsin Advertising Project, under Professor Kenneth Goldstein and Joel Rivlin of the University of Wisconsin-Madison, and includes media tracking data from the Campaign Media Analysis Group in Washington, D.C. The Wisconsin Advertising Project was sponsored by a grant from The Pew Charitable Trusts. The opinions expressed in this article are those of the authors and do not necessarily reflect the views of the Wisconsin Advertising Project, Professor Goldstein, Joel Rivlin, or The Pew Charitable Trusts.

advantage of .1 as from shifting from a spending ratio (incumbent spending to total spending) of .5 to .56. If the Democratic challenger is spending the average of $450,000 this represents an incremental investment of approximately $115,000.

Discussion

Our research extends previous work in political marketing by examining how party brand image moderates the effectiveness of certain marketing variables in political campaigns. We show that visual inferences of candidate personalities have asymmetric effects on elections across the parties. We also extend research on the effectiveness of negative advertising by showing that effectiveness varies by party and incumbency. Future research is needed to understand the drivers of these asymmetries.

REFERENCES

Teinowitz, I. (2004). Election ad spending hits record 1.6 billion. *Advertising Age, Oct 25*, 75, 43.

Todorov, A., Mandisodza, A. N., Goren, A., & Hall, C., (2005). Inferences of competence from faces predict election outcomes. *Science*, 308, 1623-1626.

Mellowing Skeptical Consumers: An Examination of Sponsorship Linked Advertising

Sarah J. Kelly, University of Queensland, Australia
T. Bettina Cornwell, University of Michigan, USA
Leonard V. Coote, University of Queensland, Australia

EXTENDED ABSTRACT

The current research examines a communication form, namely sponsorship-linked advertising, having arisen since Friestad and Wright (1994) developed their persuasion knowledge framework. Sponsorship, defined as "…investing in causes and/or events to support overall corporate objectives and/or marketing objectives" (Cornwell 1995 p.15) has developed into a mainstream communications approach in the last two decades. Sponsorship-linked advertising has emerged as a way to leverage sponsorship relationships. It is also often misappropriated by event ambushers and thus has an interestingly complex relationship with the potential development of skepticism.

Cognitive psychology theory is used to propose a model of consumer response to sponsorship-linked advertising, in terms of underlying information processing dynamics. The theoretical model used is novel in that it incorporates skepticism and attributed advertiser motives as important resistance mechanisms to persuasion. The results obtained from experimental research support the existence of widespread consumer skepticism toward advertising generally, and a propensity for consumers to infer attributions on advertiser motive depending upon contextual cues both within and ancillary to ads. Moreover, differential processing of sponsorship-linked advertising is confirmed, such that sponsorship-linked advertising is associated with more favorable cognitive outcomes, including more positive thoughts, less ad skepticism and more favorable attributions. Results support existing conceptualizations of consumer skepticism which suggest that it may be transitory, depending upon contextual cues. This study contributes to sponsorship research by offering empirical evidence of favorable consumer response to sponsorship-linked advertising, suggesting that it is a viable leveraging tool. Moreover, consumer behavior research is advanced, with the study gaining insight into the complex relationship between persuasion attempts and skepticism. Interestingly, results imply that consumers may actually derive enjoyment, or at least feel less skepticism when viewing sponsorship linked ads as compared to non sponsorship linked ads.

REFERENCES

Cornwell, T. Bettina (1995), "Sponsorship-Linked Marketing Development," *Sport Marketing Quarterly,* 4 (4), 13-24.
Friestad, Marion and Peter W. Wright (1994), "The Persuasion Knowledge Model: How People Cope With Persuasion Attempts," *Journal of Consumer Research,* 21, 1-31.

Consumers' Response to Advocacy Advertising: A Process Model of Consumer Skepticism, Empathic Response, and Prosocial Behavior

Robert Madrigal, University of Oregon, USA
Johnny Chen, University of Oregon, USA
Monica LaBarge, University of Montana, USA
Namika Sagara, University of Oregon, USA

EXTENDED ABSTRACT

Advocacy ads are often produced by organizations wishing to promote a particular position on an issue. These ads typically feature a call to action such as asking consumers to write letters to public officials, donate money, protest, volunteer, or boycott a company's products. Advocacy ads are expected to be most effective when they create an emotional response in consumers that is premised on feelings of empathy for the affected parties. We build on Escalas and Stern (2003) by exploring in greater detail the process associated with empathic response. We contend that consumers' empathic emotional reactions will reflect a mixture of discrete emotions that directly predict related to a set of active coping behaviors aimed at attenuating the stressful situation. Implicit in the hypothesized model is the ability of empathy to mediate the influence of sympathy on each emotion. We also expect that each emotion will mediate the direct effect of empathy on active coping.

We propose a hierarchical model in which consumers' skepticism (ad credibility and inferences of manipulative intent) toward an advocacy ad influences their empathic response (i.e., sympathy and empathy) toward the affected parties featured in the ad which then, in turn, predicts specific empathic emotions (anger, hope, worry, and guilt). Both are considered antecedent to empathic response because if it is unlikely that viewers will have sympathetic feelings to an ad if they believe the ad is not credible and/or if they consider it to be manipulative (Cotte, Coulter, and Moore 2005).

Two studies examine an empathic hierarchy and subsequent coping responses. In study 1, blame (people vs. oil company) and self-blame (moderate vs. high) were manipulated to elicit empathic responses. Structural equation modeling was used to assess the fit of the proposed model to the data. The hierarchical model provided an excellent fit to the data (χ^2=38.82, df=34, p=.26; RMSEA=.022; SRMR=.04; CFI=.99). Two alternative models were examined. The first was identical to our final model except that the positions of empathy and sympathy were reversed. The model tests for the possibility that reactions to the ad affect feelings of empathy initially and that this then predicts sympathy which, in turn, influences the discrete emotions. The resulting model provided a very poor fit to the data (χ^2=147.61, df=34, p<.001; RMSEA=.12; SRMR=.093; CFI=.90). We also considered the sequence reported by Bagozzi and Moore (1994) having each discrete emotion (hope, worry, guilt, and anger) related directly to empathy, and empathy predicting active coping. This sequencing resulted in a poor fitting model (χ^2=69.45, df=24, p<.001; RMSEA=.095; SRMR=.11; CFI=.93).

The primary purpose of the study 2 was to replicate the findings in study 1 using a different set of stimuli. In study 2, appeal type (emotional vs. cognitive) and peer advocacy (single vs. group) were manipulated. First, the ad either made an emotional or cognitive appeal. People may be moved to action due to the effects of either appeal type, yet little is known about how these approaches are likely to influence consumers' empathic responses. Second, past research has shown that people are more likely to help a victim represented as a single person than a group (Kogut and Ritov 2005; Slovic 2007), but nothing is known about a single versus multiple endorsers of an issue. In addition, we examined two related concepts thought to influence empathic responses. First, respondent sex was included as a predictor in study 2 as prior research has assumed that women show greater empathy than men (Argo, Zhu, and Dahl 2008). Second, humanitarianism-egalitarianism (HE) was also considered as a predictor. HE is concerned with the "ideals of equality, social justice, the concern for others' well-being" (Katz and Hass 1988, 894) and is thought to contribute to people's coping behavior and feelings.

The overall structural configuration of the model in study 2 was consistent with study 1 except that two additional latent variables (HE and Gender) had been introduced and allowed to load across all endogenous variables. The resulting model provided excellent fit to the data (χ^2=581.40, df=205, p<.001; RMSEA=.038; SRMR=.069; CFI=.99) and also replicated our initial findings and lend support to our proposed model that describes the underlying relationship between consumer skepticism, feelings, and coping behaviors.

The current research expands our knowledge of the processes underlying consumers' empathic response to advertising and its consequences. We focused on advocacy advertising because of its reliance on connecting emotionally with consumers. Results indicate that respondents' skepticism toward an ad directly affects their empathic response which, in turn, gives rise to a set of discrete empathic emotions that each individually predict specific actions aimed at coping with the situation. Our results support the temporal sequence outlined by Escalas and Stern (2003). Consistent with their view, we found that a model specifying a direct effect from sympathy to empathy outperformed one in which those effects were reversed. Moreover, significant indirect effects of sympathy on each emotion through empathy were found. Our results also indicate that the influence of empathy on active coping is mediated by each of the empathic emotions. Finally, we also contribute to the research on empathy by providing an alternative to the variable sequencing reported by Bagozzi and Moore (1994). In contrast to their hypothesized ordering, we found that our model predicting an empathy→emotion→coping sequence provided a better fit to the data than their emotion→empathy→coping hierarchy.

REFERENCES

Argo, Jennifer J., Rui (Juliet) Zhu, and Darren W. Dahl, "Fact or Fiction: An Investigation of Empathy Differences in Response to Emotional Melodramatic Entertainment," *Journal of Consumer Research*, 34 (5), 614-23.

Bagozzi, Richard P. and David J. Moore (1994), "Public Service Advertisements: Emotions and Empathy Guide Prosocial Behavior," *Journal of Marketing*, 58 (1), 56-70.

Cotte, June, Robin A. Coulter, and Melissa Moore (2005), "Enhancing or Disrupting Guilt: The Role of Ad Credibility and Perceived Manipulative Intent," *Journal of Business Research*, 58 (3), 361-68.

Escalas, Jennifer E. and Barbara B. Stern (2003), "Sympathy and Empathy: Emotional Responses to Advertising Dramas," *Journal of Consumer Research*, 29 (4), 566-78.

Katz, Irwin and Glen R. Hass (1988), "Racial ambivalence and American value conflict: Correlational and priming studies of dual cognitive structures," *Journal of Personality and Social Psychology*, 55 (6), 893-905.

Kogut, Tehila and Ilana Ritov (2005), "The Identified Victim Effect: An Identified Group, Or Just a Single Individual?" *Journal of Behavioral Decision Making*, 18 (3), 157-67.

Slovic, Paul (2007), "If I Look at the Mass I Will Never Act: Psychic Numbing and Genocide," *Judgment and Decision Making*, 2 (2), 79-95.

Consumer Expectations and the Automatic Shifting of Standards in Brand Evaluations

Claudiu Dimofte, Georgetown University, USA
Johny Johansson, Georgetown University, USA

EXTENDED ABSTRACT

Biernat, Manis, and Nelson (1991) developed a schematic model of a "shifting standards effect" to explain the process by which prior, schema-based expectations can influence the word-based ratings elicited from respondents. Their SSE model proposes that recourse to commonly used stereotypes will change the meaning of subjective scales for respondents and thus shift their evaluative scores. This shift will not occur for objective scales. Biernat et al. (1991) empirically tested the model in the context of judgments about the financial success of several profiled men and women. When actual dollar figures for annual income were used as scale units, the resulting target ratings reflected the judges' more objective knowledge (i.e., factual beliefs) confirming the stereotype that males earn more than females. However, when word-based scales were used (anchored by *financially very unsuccessful* and *financially very successful*), judges differentially adjusted the meanings of the anchors for the two genders, rating the same profiled women as more successful than the same men. The subjective scales effectively reversed the well-known income stereotype (Biernat et al., 1991). Briefly put, we seem to relax our evaluative standards for stimuli associated with lower expectations, and in the process "cut them some slack."

In applying the SSE model to marketing research, we are testing whether marketing scales evaluating consumer response to brands might also exhibit the biases described by Biernat et al. (1991). This is an important issue, as at the core of consumer marketing lies the intent to differentiate the company or its brands from similar offerings in the marketplace on one or more evaluative dimensions. Applying the propositions of the Shifting Standards Model to the case of numerical and word-based brand ratings, we should be able to trace the shifting effect of brand expectations on consumer response.

Our starting point is the notion that when two brands evoke differing expectations of performance on some dimension, the observed differences in performance evaluations on that dimension may depend on the type of scale employed (i.e., numerical or word-based). Thus, product quality expectations for Japanese and U.S. electronics brands will likely favor the former, such that, compared to U.S. brands, Japanese brands are expected to be of higher quality. If the SSE model is correct, we should find instances when numerical judgments reveal this expectation, whereas more subjective, word-based judgments do not. Thus, under a scenario where consumers expect brand A to be superior to brand B, the following should occur:

H1: The use of subjective judgment standards (inherent to word-based measures) will automatically shift consumers' reported evaluations in accordance with prior brand expectations. Given the posited scenario, brand A will be judged as superior to brand B on a numerical scale, but this difference will be attenuated in word-based units.

The next hypothesis involves the precise explanatory account and proposed automatic nature of the hypothesized shift. We propose that the shifting standards effect derives from an internally generated, implicit anchor (i.e., the associated expectation). Further, when word-based scales are used to elicit the ratings, individuals engage in an unconscious corrective process that leads to attenuation of expectation-based differences. If true, this automatic component of the SSE could be captured by measures of implicit cognition. Formally put, using the same "A superior to B" scenario:

H2: Consumers will show weaker automatic associations with favorable attributes for brand B than for brand A. However, this difference will be less pronounced after responding to word-based rating scales than after responding to numerical rating scales.

Our results suggest that a common but unconscious consumer cognitive response to brand information may significantly impact the measured differentiation. Whereas more objective, numerical scores would indicate a sustainable differentiation between two brands along a particular dimension, more subjective, word-based responses may in fact show the very same brands to be virtually indistinguishable. This anomalous inconsistency was shown to originate in consumers' use of different evaluative standards for high and low expectations brands. In word-based judgments, evaluative standards are automatically more relaxed for the brand associated with lower expectations, allowing it to match its competitor's advantage. Study 1 established the effect in the context of expectations related to brand extension fit. Studies 2a and 2b uncovered the automatic nature of the shift by actually measuring the automatic adjustment of standards (i.e., comparative anchors) for word-based scales both directly and indirectly. Finally, study 3 eliminated the shifting effect by bringing this cognitive heuristic into individuals' awareness.

We also presented results that suggested a way to prevent consumers from making these automatic adjustments. By framing the word-based scales explicitly against respondents' expectations, we showed that it is possible to prevent the unconscious shift and to obtain the same ratings as for the numerical scales. In a sense, this manipulation and objective scales in general appear to induce what cognitive psychology terms a confirmation bias, whereas subjective scales avoid this bias and instead induce another–the SSE.

REFERENCE

Biernat, Monica, Melvin Manis, and Thomas E. Nelson (1991), "Stereotypes and Standards of Judgment," *Journal of Personality and Social Psychology*, 60 (4), 485-499.

Re-Examination of Maximization: Psychometric Assessment and Derivation of a Short Form of the Maximization Scale

Gergana Y. Nenkov, Boston College, USA
Maureen Morrin, Rutgers University, USA
Andrew Ward, Swarthmore College, USA
Barry Schwartz, Swarthmore College, USA
John Hulland, University of Pittsburgh, USA[1]

EXTENDED ABSTRACT

The purpose of this paper is to develop a revised and more psychometrically sound version of the Maximization Scale (Schwartz et al. 2002) that would enhance the use of the scale among behavioral researchers across several of the social science disciplines. The research presented in this paper is based on an analysis of both pre-existing datasets and new data. The pre-existing data consist of 12 pre-existing datasets, representing a total of over 5,800 respondents, were obtained from several authors, across several disciplines, in both the U.S. and overseas, who have used the Maximization Scale in their research. The new data were collected in three studies: (1) a questionnaire administered to academic researchers (n=8) regarding the content validity of the Maximization Scale; (2) a survey among a general population sample (n=40) regarding readability of the individual scale items; and (3) an experiment in the domain of financial decision making among a sample of adult participants (n=176) that tested both the new and original versions of the scale.

In this paper we conduct four sets of analyses. In *Analysis 1* we examine 10 pre-existing datasets containing the Maximization Scale in order to confirm the factor structure of the scale, assess its internal consistency and dimensional purity, and reduce the number of items. Based on these analyses we conclude that the some of the scale's psychometric properties are unsatisfactory. In *Analysis 2* we employ both pre-existing data (10 datasets) and new data (n=48) in order to develop revised versions of the Maximization Scale (9-item, 6-item, and 3-item versions). In the process of revising the Maximization Scale, we follow a set of rules and procedures consistent with past work (Richins 2004; Smith, McCarthy, and Anderson 2000; Stanton et al. 2002), which rely on internal, external, and judgmental criteria. Next, we evaluate the discriminant and nomological validity of the newly developed revised scales by relating them to existing constructs-anticipated regret (Schwartz et al. 2002), subjective happiness (Lyubomirsky and Lepper 1997), satisfaction with life (Diener et al. 1985), and optimism (Scheier, Carver, and Bridges 1994). In *Analysis 3* we cross-validate the three shorter versions of the scale employing 12 pre-existing datasets. We use both internal and external criteria in order to confirm their dimensionality, reliability and validity. Finally, in *Analysis 4* (n=176) we experimentally examine the revised scales' predictive validity and look into the relationship between consumers' maximizing tendencies, as measured by the revised Maximization scales, and their information processing and choices in an investment decision context. In this study we also measure several additional traits that are expected to be related to maximization to see whether maximization can predict consumers' decision-making beyond these other related variables. We measure regret, happiness, satisfaction with life, and optimism, mentioned above, as well as depression (Cole et al. 2004), perfectionism (Hewitt and Flett 1990), and need for cognition (Cacioppo and Petty 1982)

Based on results from our analyses of reliability, predictive, and nomological validity, and model fit, we conclude that the revised 6-item Maximization Scale exhibits superior psychometric properties as compared to the other versions of the scale we tested, namely, the original 13-item scale and the 9-item, and 3-item scales. The 6-item scale possesses good internal consistency and superior model fit as compared to the other two scale versions. Furthermore, it possesses good validity: its nomological net is similar to that of the original 13-item scale and its validity correlations, i.e. correlations with related traits, are more consistent with our predictions and past literature than those of both the 9-item scale and the original scale. The 6-item scale's predictive validity, as indicated by its capacity to distinguish between the decision-making processes of maximizers and satisficers in an investment decision making context, was also superior to that of the other two scale versions.

In this paper we also define and examine the three dimensions of maximization and conclude that the scale consists of three sub-dimensions–'high standards', 'alternative search', and 'decision difficulty', which converge on a higher-order latent construct. In our analysis we examine not only consumers' summed maximization scores, but also their scores on the three scale sub-dimensions. Our results suggest that the three dimensions of maximization might be differentially predictive of various consumer traits and behaviors. Therefore, we recommend that future researchers examine not only consumers' maximization scores but also their sub-dimension scores.

Past research has found a clear tendency for maximizers to report being significantly less happy, less satisfied with life and with their choices, and more depressed than satisficers (Iyengar, Wells, and Schwartz 2006; Schwartz et al. 2002). Our results build on these findings and suggest that the real problem with maximizing is not having high standards (as this dimension was not correlated with depression, satisfaction with life, or happiness), but rather, having high standards in a world of limitless alternatives, which demands extensive search and creates decision difficulty. It seems that the source of maximizers' psychological trouble is the need to search extensively and make difficult decisions, and not their tendency to set high standards for themselves.

The present research contributes to the existing literature on maximization in several important ways. First, we reduce the Maximization Scale length by more than half (from thirteen to six items), while improving its psychometric properties. There is growing interest in the maximization construct on behalf of researchers in areas such as social psychology, positive psychology,

[1]The authors gratefully acknowledge support for this research provided by a generous grant from the FINRA (formerly NASD) Investor Education Foundation (#2005-08). The authors would like to thank Tilottama Chowdhury, Samuel M.Y. Ho, Matt Wallaert, Rachael E. Wells, and the authors of the original Maximization scale—Barry Schwartz, Andrew Ward, John Monterosso, Sonja Lyubomirsky, Katherine White, and Darrin R. Lehman for generously providing their datasets for the analysis in this paper.

and consumer psychology. The shorter revised Maximization Scale proposed in this paper will provide these researchers with a measure of the construct that is brief, yet reliable and valid. Second, we show that the revised 6-item scale possesses very high predictive validity, since it was uniquely capable of differentiating between the information processing and decision making patterns of maximizers vs. satisficers in an investment decision-making situation, after controlling for several other related constructs. Third, we assess the Maximization Scale's dimensionality, and define and examine the three scale sub-dimensions. Our results suggest that the three dimensions are related to different traits, and researchers should examine people's scores on the three maximization sub-dimensions in addition to their summed maximization scores.

Having a shorter, yet more valid and reliable instrument with which to measure people's tendency to maximize should enhance research efforts examining how consumers' tendencies to maximize or satisfice during the choice process affect their decisions and choices and ultimately their happiness and well-being.

REFERENCES

Cacioppo, John T. and Richard E. Petty (1982), "The Need for Cognition," *Journal of Personality and Social Psychology*, 4 (1), 116-31.

Cole, Jason C., Adele S. Rabin, Tom L. Smith, Alan S. Kaufman (2004), "Development and Validation of a Rasch-Derived CES-D Short Form" *Psychological Assessment,* 16 (4), 360-72.

Diener, Ed, Robert A. Emmons, Randy J. Larsen, and Sharon Griffin (1985), "The Satisfaction with Life Scale," *Journal of Personality Assessment,* 49 (1), 71-75.

Hewitt, P. L. and G. L. Flett (1990), "Perfectionism and Depression: A Multidimensional Analysis," *Journal of Social Behavior and Personality,* 5, 423-438.

Iyengar, Sheena S., Rachael E. Wells, and Barry Schwartz (2006), "Doing Better but Feeling Worse: Looking for the 'Best' Job Undermines Satisfaction," *Psychological Science,* 17(2), 143-150

Lyubomirsky, Sonja and Heidi S. Lepper (1997), "A Measure of Subjective Happiness: Preliminary Reliability and Construct Validation," *Social Indicators Research*, 46, 137-55.

Richins, Marsha L. (2004), "The Material Values Scale: Measurement Properties and Development of a Short Form," *Journal of Consumer Research*, 31 (June), 209-219.

Scheier, Michael F., Charles S. Carver, and Michael W. Bridges (1994), "Distinguishing Optimism from Neuroticism (and Trait Anxiety, Self-Mastery, and Self-Esteem): A Reevaluation of the Life Orientation Test," *Journal of Personality and Social Psychology,* 67 (6), 1063-78.

Schwartz, Barry, Andrew Ward, John Monterosso, Sonja Lyubomirsky, Katherine White, and Darrin R. Lehman (2002), "Maximizing versus Satisficing: Happiness is a Matter of Choice," *Personality and Social Psychology,* 83 (5), 1178-97.

Smith, Gregory T., Denis M. McCarthy, and Kristen G. Anderson (2000), "On the Sins of Short-Form Development," *Psychological Assessment,* 12 (1), 102-111.

Stanton, Jeffrey M, Evan F. Sinar, William K. Balzer, and Patricia C. Smith (2002), "Issues and Strategies for Reducing the Length of Self-Report Scales," *Personnel Psychology*, 55, 167-194.

Deception at a Distance: How and When Does Temporal Distance Affect Persuasion Knowledge Activation?

Ryan Rahinel, University of Minnesota, USA
Norman O'Reilly, Laurentian University, Canada

EXTENDED ABSTRACT

Friestad and Wright (1994) theorize that consumers acquire persuasion knowledge over the lifespan. Such knowledge structure contains beliefs about the ways by which marketers and other persuasion agents attempt to persuade consumers and how consumers cope with these persuasion attempts. Researchers have theorized that when a consumer perceives a marketing agent to be appealing to psychological factors that the consumer believes to mediate persuasiveness (e.g., attention, emotion), the agent is perceived to be engaging in persuasive activities and the current (and, to some extent, future) encounters are evaluated by the consumer in this light (Friestad & Wright, 1994). At this point the consumer engages in one or more coping strategies to deal with the persuasion attempt (Kirmani & Campbell, 2004) and the consumers' persuasion knowledge is said to be activated. This entire process of persuasion knowledge activation has often been shown to result in decreased evaluations of the stimuli, product, brand, and even future messages by the brand (Main, Dahl, & Darke, 2007; Kirmani & Zhu, 2007; Wei, Fischer, & Main, 2006; Campbell & Kirmani, 2000). This research builds on previous work in persuasion knowledge by focusing on situations in which consumers are engaged in non-imminent (i.e., temporally distant) purchase decisions and where message cues vary in terms of the product feature mentioned in the persuasive message.

Conceptually, we draw on the work in Construal Level Theory (CLT) to arrive at our hypotheses. CLT argues that when events or objects are temporally distant, physically far, less like ourselves, or less probable, we tend to think about (and therefore describe) them in terms of their more abstract, stable, and general features (Trope, Liberman, & Wakslak, 2007). In other words, we form a high-level construal of the subject. Conversely, when events or objects are imminent, physically closer, more like ourselves, or more probable, CLT argues that we tend to think about and describe them in terms of their detailed, less stable, and peripheral features (Trope et al, 2007). That is, we engage in low-level construal. One implication of this is that we tend to focus on the primary features of a product when the purchase decision is temporally distant, but on the secondary features when the purchase decision is imminent (Trope & Liberman, 2000). Based on this, we arrived at three hypotheses. H1 suggests that a temporally distant purchase decision will lead to significantly higher persuasion knowledge activation and perceived ad deceptiveness than a temporally proximal purchase decision, but only when the product feature mentioned in the persuasive message cue is a primary feature. When the product feature mentioned in the persuasive message cue is a secondary feature, no differences will be present. H2a followed by suggesting that a temporally distant purchase decision will lead to significantly lower product and brand evaluations than a temporally proximal purchase decision, but only when the product feature mentioned in the persuasive message cue is a primary feature. When the product feature mentioned in the persuasive message cue is a secondary feature, no differences in product and brand evaluations will be present. Further, H2b suggests that the negative relationship between the temporal distance/product feature interaction effect and brand attitude will be mediated by persuasion knowledge activation.

We conducted a 2 (product feature mentioned: primary or secondary) X 2 (temporal distance: proximal vs. distant) experiment using 167 undergraduate students who were randomly assigned to treatments. The first page of the instrument package was a scenario in which subjects were told to imagine either that they would like to buy a digital camera *today* (temporally proximal) or *one year from now* (temporally distant), just before they leave to go on vacation to Europe. In both conditions, subjects were then asked to imagine browsing through a magazine *today*, and while doing this, encountering the advertisement on the following page of the package. The one-page print advertisement was for a new digital camera manufactured by a fictional brand named Eyelum. The second claim in the advertisement was highly deceptive in reporting either that the studies conducted by Eyelum found that the LCD screen used by the Eyelum e2000 was of higher quality than the LCD screen used by Canon (secondary feature condition) or studies conducted by Eyelum found that the lens used by the Eyelum e2000 is of higher quality than the lens used by Canon (primary feature condition).

Controlling for factors such as depth of processing and previous individual differences in importance of lenses vs. LCD screens, we find full support for H1 and H2a, and partial support for H2b. With regard to H1, there was a significant interaction effect on both persuasion knowledge thoughts (measured by coding thoughts of suspicion) (p<.04) and perceived ad deceptiveness (measured as three likert items: truthfulness, believability, and non-deceptiveness) (p<.05). Most importantly, while there were no differences between respondents in the secondary feature conditions, temporally distant subjects reported more persuasion knowledge thoughts and more perceived ad deceptiveness than temporally proximal subjects (Persuasion Knowledge Thoughts: p<.01; Perceived Ad Deceptiveness: p<.02). Consistent with H2a, we found no main effects but significant interaction effects on product quality (measured as five likert items: quality, reliability, performance, stylishness, and produces sharper pictures) and brand evaluations (measured as three likert items: likeable, appealing, favourable) (both ps<.02). Again, while there were no differences between the secondary feature treatments, we found differences between the primary feature treatments for both measures (both ps <.02). For H2b, we attempted two mediation analyses first using persuasion knowledge thoughts as the mediating variable and then using perceived ad deceptiveness as the mediating variable. Results showed that only perceived deceptiveness moderated the relationship between the temporal distance/product feature interaction and brand attitudes, providing evidence that the mediating role of persuasion knowledge operates via an automatic process.

REFERENCES

Aaker, J. L., & Lee, A. Y. (2001). "I" seek pleasures and "we" avoid pains: The role of self-regulatory goals in information processing and persuasion. *Journal of Consumer Research, 28*, 33-49.

Baron, R.M., & Kenny, D.A. (1986). The moderator-mediator distinction in social psychological research: Conceptual, strategic, and statistical considerations. *Journal of Personality and Social Psychology*

Campbell, M.C. (1995). When attention-getting advertising tactics elicit consumer inferences of manipulative intent: The importance of balancing benefits and investments. *Journal of Consumer Psychology*, 4(3), 225-254.

Campbell, M.C., & Kirmani, A. (2000). Consumers' use of persuasion knowledge: The effects of accessibility and cognitive capacity on perceptions of an influence agent. *Journal of Consumer Research*, 27(2), 69-83.

Darke, P.R., & Ritchie, R.J.B. (2007). The defensive consumer: Advertising deception, defensive processing, and mistrust. *Journal of Marketing Research*, 44(1), 114-127.

Friestad, M, & Wright, P. (1994). The Persuasion Knowledge Model: How people cope with persuasion attempts. *Journal of Consumer Research*, 21(1), 1-31.

Friestad, M., & Wright, P. (1995). Persuasion knowledge: Lay people's and researchers' beliefs about the psychology of advertising. *Journal of Consumer Research*, 22(1), 62-74.

Henderson, M. D., Fujita, K. F., Trope, Y., & Liberman, N. (2006). The effect of spatial distance on social judgment. *Journal of Personality and Social Psychology*, 91, 845–856.

Kirmani, A. & Zhu, R. (2007). Vigilant against manipulation: The effect of regulatory focus on the use of persuasion knowledge. *Journal of Marketing Research*, forthcoming.

Kirmani, A. & Campbell, M. (2004). Goal seeker and persuasion sentry: How consumer targets respond to interpersonal marketing persuasion. *Journal of Consumer Research*, 31(3), 573-582.

Liberman, N., Sagristano, M., & Trope, Y. (2002). The effect of temporal distance on level of construal. *Journal of Experimental Social Psychology*, 38, 523–535.

Liviatan, I., Trope, Y., & Liberman, N. (2006). Interpersonal similarity as a social distance dimension: A construal level approach to the mental representations and judgments of similar and dissimilar others' actions. Unpublished manuscript, New York University.

Main, K.J., Dahl, D.W., & Darke, P.R. (2007). Deliberative and automatic bases of suspicion: Empirical evidence of the sinister attribution error. *Journal of Consumer Psychology*, 17(1), 59-69.

Nussbaum, S., Trope, Y., & Liberman, N. (2003). Creeping dispositionism: The temporal dynamics of behavior prediction. *Journal of Personality and Social Psychology, 84*, 485-497.

Todorov, A., Goren, A., & Trope, Y. (2007). Probability as a psychological distance: Construal and Preferences. *Journal of Experimental Social Psychology*, 43, 473-482.

Trope, Y., Liberman, N., & Wakslak, C. (2007). Construal levels and psychological distance: Effects on representation, prediction, evaluation, and behavior. *Journal of Consumer Psychology*, 17(2), 83-95.

Trope, Y., & Liberman, N. (2000). Temporal construal and time-dependent changes in preference. *Journal of Personality and Social Psychology*, 79, 876-889.

Wei, M., Fischer, E. & Main, K.J. (2006). When does persuasion knowledge influence brand evaluations? In the *Proceedings for the Society of Consumer Psychology*, Miami, FL.

Physiological Arousal Mediates the Persuasive Impact of Positive Peripheral Cues in Threatening Communication

Zhenfeng Ma, University of Ontario Institute of Technology, Canada
Laurette Dubé, McGill University, Canada

EXTENDED ABSTRACT

Threat-related communication, such as health communication, is often processed in stressful contexts. For recipients under stress due to perceived threat, a desirable objective of health communication is to increase recipients' self-efficacy beliefs. We review a psychophysiological perspective of stress and the excitation transfer theory to propose how physiological arousal, above and beyond affect, can mediate the impact of positive peripheral cues (PPC) in threatening communication on recipients' self-efficacy beliefs.

Hypotheses

Research form various domains suggests that stress is a psychophysiological process that concurrently involves psychological (e.g. negative affect) and physiological responses (Ursin and Eriksen 2004; Ledoux 1995). Physiological responses include autonomic response such as increased skin conductance, and endocrine response such as increased salivary cortisol. Because the various psychological and physiological components of stress are mediated by relatively distinct neural pathways, they may each uniquely predict consumer behavior or attitude under stress.

Based on the framework of mediation analysis proposed by Kraemer et al. (2002), we propose that physiological arousal meet the essential criteria as the mediator of the persuasive impact of PPC. Specifically, physiological arousal can 1) occur during the communication exposure and be influenced by communication cues; 2) have a direct or interactive effect on the persuasive outcome. Research has shown that for individuals under stress, positive stimuli can alleviate psychological distress and physiological arousal (Fredrickson and Levenson 1998; Berk et al. 1989). For such individuals, PPC may function as safety signals which convey the presence of safety or the absence of threat, thereby leading to improved psychophysiological wellbeing. It can be expected that for recipients under stress due to perceived health threat, PPC in threatening communication can decrease physiological arousal and negative affect. However, such stress-buffering impact of PPC may be negligible for recipients in normal contexts, as the safety-signal value for these individuals will be minimal. We thus hypothesize:

> *H1*: Relative to threatening communication featuring no positive peripheral pictures, threatening communication featuring positive peripheral pictures reduces psychological distress and physiological arousal among recipients who have undergone prior stress due to perceived threat, but not among recipients in normal contexts.

We further posit that physiological arousal, in addition to affect, may have unique impact on persuasion. The excitation transfer theory (Zillmann 1971) argued that physiological arousal resulting from a prior nontrivial event decays relatively slowly and often remains operative after the individual has physically withdrawn from the stimulus. Because people generally do not distinguish between the portions of arousal that are due to prior stimuli and those caused by present stimulation, they may misattribute their residual arousal from prior episodes to an attitude object that is immediately present. In the context of health communication, when the communication is presented without PPC, recipients may misattribute their lingering arousal to their low self-efficacy beliefs ("I must feel bad because I lack confidence in the information."). On the contrary, when the communication is presented with PPC, the negative misattribution may be attenuated due to mitigated psychological distress and physiological arousal. It is even possible that the recipients may misattribute their improved psychophysiological wellbeing to their enhanced self-efficacy. Thus, for recipients who have undergone a prior threat, PPC in threatening communication may mitigate the negative impact of residual physiological arousal on self-efficacy beliefs, or may even transform arousal and distress from a negative impact into a positive influence on persuasion. Thus we hypothesize:

> *H2*: Positive peripheral pictures in threat-related communication mitigate or reverse the negative impact of psychological distress and physiological arousal on self-efficacy beliefs among recipients who have experienced prior stress.

Methods

We tested the research hypotheses through an experimental study of a 2 (stressful vs. non-stressful contexts) by 2 (cue-present vs. cue-absent communication) between-subject design. Eighty healthy women (mean age=58 ± 7.8) from the local community participated in this study. We first manipulated prior stress via a mental imagery task pertaining either to a high- or low-threat scenario, and then asked participants to browse a consumer health information website that either used PPC or did not use PPC. Physiological responses (skin conductance, heart rate variability and salivary cortisol) and affect during both the mental imagery and web-browsing tasks were recorded. Self-efficacy beliefs were measured after the web-browsing task as an index of persuasive outcome.

Results and Discussion

The stressful imagery task induced higher autonomic and endocrine responses, as well as high negative affect relative to the non-stressful task. Thus the stress manipulation was successful. A series of ANCOVAs showed that the PPC-present website decreased psychological distress and physiological arousal, but increased positive affect among participants who had undergone a prior threat, but not among those in the non-stressful condition. Thus H1 was supported.

Based on Kraemer colleagues' (2002) framework for mediation and moderation, our analysis showed that for participants who had gone through the stressful imagery task, PPC mitigated the negative impact of psychological distress and autonomic responses on self-efficacy beliefs. Further, for those participants, PPC turned physiological responses from a negative impact into a positive influence on self-efficacy beliefs. Further, the physiological pathway to persuasion was more evident in the stressful versus normal context. Overall, for participants who had undergone health threat, PPC enhanced persuasion by either mitigating or reversing the negative impact of psychological distress and physiological arousal on self-efficacy beliefs. Thus H2 was supported.

This study provided initial evidence that communication cues can interact with both affect and physiological arousal to determine the persuasive outcome. The physiological arousal revealed an important mechanism that can not be captured by self-reported affect. Future research can examine the impact of physiological processes on consumer behavior and decision making in a variety of different settings.

REFERENCES

Batra, Rajeev and Michael L. Ray (1986), "Affective Responses Mediating Acceptance of Advertising," *Journal of Consumer Research*, 13 (2), 234-249.

Berk, Lee S., Stanley A. Tan, William F. Fry, B.J. Napier, Jerry W. Lee, Richard W. Hubbard, John E. Lewis, and William C. Eby (1989), "Neuro-Endocrine and Stress Hormone Changes During Mirthful Laughter," *American Journal of Medical Science*, 298 (6), 390-396.

Cantor, Joanne R, Dolf Zillmann, and Jennings Bryant (1975), "Enhancement of Experienced Sexual Arousal in Response to Erotic Stimuli through Misattribution of Unrelated Residual Excitation," *Journal of Personality and Social Psychology*, 32(1), 69-75.

Curran, Shelley L., Michael A. Andrykowski, and Jamie L. Studts (1995), "Short Form of the Profile of Mood States (POMS-SF): Psychometric Information," *Psychological Assessment*, 7 (1), 80-83.

Damasio, Antonio (1994), *Descarte's Error*, New York: Penguin Books.

Edell, Julie A. and Marian Chapman Burke (1987), 'The Power of Feelings in Understanding Advertising Effects,' *Journal of Consumer Research*, 14 (3), 421-433.

Fredrickson, Barbara L., and Robert W. Levenson (1998), "Positive Emotions Speed Recovery from the Cardiovascular Sequelae of Negative Emotions," *Cognition and Emotion*, 12 (2), 191-220.

Kraemer, Helena Chmura, Christopher G. Fairburn and W. Stewart Agras (2002), "Mediators and Moderators of Treatment Effects in Randomized Clinical Trials," *Archives of General Psychiatry*, 59, 877-883.

LeDoux, Joseph E. (1989), "Cognitive-Emotional Interactions in the Brain," *Cognition and Emotion*, 3 (4), 267-289.

Lohr, Jeffery M., Bunmi O. Olatunji, and Craig N. Sawchuk (2007), "A Functional Analysis of Danger and Safety Signals in Anxiety Disorders," *Clinical Psychology Review*, 27 (1), 114-126.

Muller, Dominique, Charles M. Judd and Vincent Y. Yzerbyt (2005), "When Moderation Is Mediated and Mediation Is Moderated," *Journal of Personality and Social Psychology*, 89 (6), 852-863.

Schwarzer, Ralf and Britta Renner (2000), "Social-Cognitive Predictors of Health Behavior: Action Self-Efficacy And Coping Self-Efficacy," *Health Psychology*, 19(5), 487-495.

Shacham, Saya (1983), "A Shortened Version of the Profile of Mood States," *Journal of Personality Assessment*, 47 (3), 305-306.

Task Force of the European Society of Cardiology and the North American Society of Pacing and Electrophysiology (1996), "Heart Rate Variability: Standards of Measurement, Physiological Interpretation, and Clinical Use," *European Heart Journal*, 17, 354-381.

Ursin, Holger and Hege R. Eriksen (2004), "The Cognitive Activation Theory of Stress," *Psychoneuroendocrinology*, 29 (5), 567-592.

Zillmann, Dolf (1971), "Excitation Transfer in Communication-mediated Aggressive Behavior," *Journal of Experimental Social Psychology*, 7, 419-434.

Levels of Focus: The Impact of Optimism on Consumer Information Processing

Kai-Yu Wang, Brock University, Canada
Xiaojing Yang, University of Wisconsin-Milwaukee, USA
Laura Peracchio, University of Wisconsin-Milwaukee, USA

EXTENDED ABSTRACT

Substantial research has investigated individual differences in consumer information processing, such as gender (Meyers-Levy and Maheswaran 1991), involvement (Petty, Cacioppo, and Schumann 1983), and cultural orientation (Aaker and Maheswarn 1997). For example, males' information processing is more likely to be influenced by overall message themes or schemas whereas females' processing involves detailed elaboration of message content (Meyers-Levy and Maheswaran 1991). Few studies, if any, have examined the influence of optimism on consumer information processing in response to advertising.

For the past two decades, optimism has been investigated extensively in the areas of social, personality, and clinical psychology. Most of the previous research in psychology examined how optimists and pessimists process information and cope with a variety of situations that they face in their daily life, including chronic illness and major life transitions (Aspinwall, Richter, and Hoffman 2001). Optimism has gained increasing attention and been applied in consumer contexts. In the consumer finance area, previous research has examined how optimism influences consumers' financial behavior, such as consumers' investment in individual stocks, savings behavior, and economic decision-making, (Puri and Robinson 2007). Moreover, studies found that optimism is negatively related to maximization. That is, more optimistic consumers feel worse off as their options increase (Schwartz, Ward, Monterosso, and Lyubomirsky 2002). In marketing, research indicated that optimism has significant and unique influence on consumer shopping behavior (Kahle, Shoham, Rose, Smith, and Batra 2003). However, little has been known about how optimism impacts consumers processing ad information.

In addition to replicating the findings in the previous research that optimists and pessimists adopt different information processing styles in consumer contexts, the purpose of this research is to investigate the impact of optimism on brand attitudes in response to advertising. According to Craik and Lockhart's (1972) levels of processing theory, we propose that message relevance would determine the information processing styles that optimists/pessimists adopt. Moreover, the processes underlying the effects are examined.

Two experiments were designed to examine the moderating role of optimism on consumer information processing. The first experiment investigated the relationship between dispositional optimism and consumers' responses to advertising information, and further explored the effects that underlie this process. The second experiment provided a conceptual replication of experiment 1 by manipulating situational optimism and replicated the findings observed in experiment 1.

In experiment 1, two versions of ad message relevance (high and low) and two versions of ad format (comparative and noncomparative) were manipulated. We hypothesized that when the ad message is low in relevance and presented in a noncomparative format, optimists evaluate the advertised brand more favorably than pessimists. In contrast, when the ad message is low in relevance and presented in a comparative format, pessimists evaluate the advertised brand more favorably than optimists. We hypothesized a different pattern of when the ad message was highly relevant. In high relevant ad message conditions, pessimists were expected to evaluate the advertised brand more favorably than optimists when the ad format is noncomparative while optimists evaluated the advertised brand more favorably than pessimists when the ad format is comparative. The results were consistent with our predictions. Examination of thought measures provided additional support for the hypotheses.

Experiment 2 replicated findings in experiment 1. In addition, optimism was manipulated with two social situational scenarios instead of being measured as we did in experiment 1. Most of our predictions were supported. Examination of thought measures also provided additional support for the predictions.

Taken together, these two studies support most of our proposed theorizing about how optimism and message relevance affect consumers' brand attitudes in response to comparative advertising. This research suggests that optimists use global information processing whereas pessimists use local information processing when the ad message is low in relevance. Different processing modes were used when the ad message is highly relevant. When messages are highly relevant, optimists adopt rational information processing styles while pessimists adopt experiential information processing styles. This research demonstrated that optimists and pessimists have different levels of focus when processing irrelevant and relevant ad information. The results illustrate the underlying process of how optimists and pessimists process ad information.

From a managerial standpoint, this research has implications for advertising efforts. Specifically, when advertisers adopt comparative advertising, they should take the individual difference variable, optimism, into considerations. This research also enhances our understanding of how different processing styles of optimists and pessimists impact their brand attitudes in response to comparative advertising.

REFERENCES

Aaker, Jennifer L. and Durairaj Mahswaran (1997), "The effect of cultural orientation on persuasion," *Journal of Consumer Research*, 24 (December), 315-328.

Aspinwall, Lisa G, Linda Richter, and Richard R. Hoffman III (2001), "Understanding how optimism works: An examination of optimists' adaptive moderation of believe and behavior," In *Optimism & pessimism: Implications for theory, research, and practice*, ed. Edward C. Chang, Washington, DC: American Psychological Association, 217-238.

Craik, Fergus I. and Robert S. Lockhart (1972), "Levels of processing: A framework for memory research," *Journal of Verbal Learning and Verbal Behavior*, 11 (December), 671-684.

Kahle, Lynn R, Aviv Shoham, Greg Rose, Malcolm Smith, Rajeev Batra (2003), "Economic versus personal future-oriented attitudes as consumer shopping indicators," *Journal of Euro-Marketing*, 12 (3/4), 35.45.

Meyers-Lvey, Joan and Durairaj Maheswaran (1991), "Exploring differences in males' and females' processing strategies," *Journal of Consumer Research*, 18 (June), 63-70.

Petty, Richard E., John T. Cacioppo, and David Schumann (1983), "Central and peripheral routes to advertising effectiveness," *Journal of Consumer Research*, 10 (September), 135-46.

Puri, Manju and David T. Robinson (2007), "Optimism and economic choice," *Journal of Financial Economics*, 86 (1), 71-99.

Schwartz, Barry, Ward Andrew, John Monterosso, Sonia Lyubomirsky (2002), "Maximizing versus satisficing: Happiness is a matter of choice," *Journal of Personality and Social Psychology*, 83 (5), 1178-1185.

Relational versus Group Collectivism and Optimal Distinctiveness in a Consumption Context

Robert Kreuzbauer, University of Illinois at Urbana-Champaign, USA
Shengdong Lin, Sun Yat-Sen University, China
Chi-Yue Chiu, University of Illinois at Urbana-Champaign, USA

EXTENDED ABSTRACT

Across various research in cross-cultural consumer psychology as well as social psychology the probably most widely used framework to study differences how people feel, think and behave in different cultures is the individualism–collectivism distinction However, the individualism–collectivism distinction has recently been conceptually and methodologically criticized from various researchers (see Brewer & Chen, 2007) In order to reduce these shortcomings Brewer & Chen (2007) have introduce a new theoretical framework conceptualization of individual, relational and collective selves. They protect individualism as a reliable and useful construct for the study of cross-cultural differences of various aspects, however within collectivism they make a distinction between relational *(relational collectivism)*, and collective levels *(group collectivism)* of self-definition which embody two distinct forms of self-representation. Relational collectivism refers to aspects where the self is defined in terms of connections and role relationships to significant others whereas group collectivism occurs when the social self is defined as a depersonalized social category.

Although in every society people must be able to satisfy both individual and collective needs, that is, no culture, group or society is per se 'individualistic' or 'collectivistic'. This view is also consistent with optimal distinctiveness theory (ODT; Brewer, 1991) which asserts that individuals desire to attain an optimal balance of connectedness and distinctiveness *within* and *between* social groups and situations. The goal of this article is to demonstrate that consumers from Western cultures use different strategies to satisfy their need for connectedness or belongingness (i.e. the collective need) than consumer from East Asian cultures. The main prediction of ODT is that social identity is driven by two basic social needs, the need for assimilation or connectedness with a group and the need for distinctiveness, that is, perceiving oneself as a unique and independent individual. These two motives are in constant opposition with each other; when there is too much of one motive, the other must increase in order to counterbalance it and vice versa. Whereas distinctiveness or uniqueness is a common element that most companies try to achieve with their brand images and which has also been extensively researched since in consumer science, ODT so far has only received little attention. This is insofar surprising as several of the most successful commercials and brand provide a balanced image between both distinctiveness and belongingness. A well known example would be the Apple brand which on the one hand provides distinctiveness from Microsoft, but on the other hand creates a feeling of being connected to a group of highly creative and freaky consumers.

Extending these thoughts we believe that consumers from different cultures are also likely to choose different strategies to achieve optimal distinctiveness. Consistent with the framework of relational and group collectivism, it seems plausible that when activating the need for belongingness Westerners tend to satisfy this need through group collectivism whereas Easterners rather focus on relational collectivism.

To test this hypothesis, we conducted two experimental studies where subjects from one US and one Chinese university had to evaluate consumption scenarios that asked subjects to personalize products such as cell phones, laptops, back bags etc. Each scenario contained three choice options: With option one, subjects could personalize the respective product by putting a picture or symbol on the product that expresses their personality. Option two and three offered them to express their personality by putting a picture or symbol on the product that shows either their family or their university. The first study was designed to compare the responses between the different ethnic sample types (European Americans, Asian Americans and Chinese). In the second study we tested how the subjects' responses might differ when their need for distinctiveness or belongingness is manipulated through a deceived feedback procedure (one group was informed that their personal values would substantially differ from those of their colleagues (to activate need for belongingness), the other group was informed that their personal values were very similar to those of their colleagues (to activate distinctiveness need)).

Consistent with our hypotheses, we found that Chinese subjects preferred the relational over group collectivism choice option, that is, they would rather personalize their products with a picture or symbol from their family than from their university, whereas European American subjects showed the opposite preference. However, in both studies we could not find any significant differences between Asian Americans and other ethnic subject types and we did also not find any significant cross-cultural differences regarding the individualism choice option (i.e. whether they want to personalize the product with their own picture). Here further research is needed in order to get a better understanding of these findings. In study two, we again found evidence for the fact that Chinese show a clear preference towards the relational collectivism option. In addition to that, this study revealed that Chinese consumers change their choice behavior when their need for belongingness is activated. That is, when Chinese subjects have been brought into a situation of overly distinctiveness and therefore into an increased need for belongingness (in accordance with ODT) their preference shifts towards the relational choice option. This manipulation did not have any significant effect on their preference towards the group collectivism choice option (i.e. personalize the product with a University symbol).

The contribution of this article is twofold. First, it provides a first empirical proof of the recently suggested framework (Brewer & Chen, 2007) of relational and group collectivism in a consumption context. This shows that Westerners achieve collectivism rather through group collectivism whereas Easterners prefer to rely on relational collectivism. The second contribution is the extension of this approach towards optimal distinctiveness theory, that is, when their need for belongingness is activated, Easterners achieve an optimal level of distinctiveness through relational collectivism, whereas Westerners tend to be rather ambivalent between the two collectivism choice options. This research therefore contributes to a better understanding of the collectivism concept in cross-cultural consumption.

REFERENCES

Brewer MB, Chen YR (2007), Where (who) are collectives in collectivism? Toward conceptual clarification of individualism and collectivism. *Psychological Review,* 114/1, pp. 133-151

Brewer, MB (1991), The Social Self-On Being The Same And Different At The Same Time; *Personality And Social Psychology Bulletin,* 17, Issue 5, pp.475-482

"Accept a Gift or Reject it? That is Not A Simple Question": A Cross-Cultural Study of Gift Acceptance and the Mediating Role of Feelings of Appreciation and Indebtedness

Hao Shen, The Chinese University of Hong Kong, China
Fang Wan, University of Manitoba, Canada
Robert S. Wyer, Jr., Hong Kong University of Science & Technology, China

EXTENDED ABSTRACT

People often share a consumption experience with others. For example, they have dinner with friends at a restaurant or share a taxi ride. After doing so, one of the parties might offer to pay the bill. What factors determine whether the others accept the offer or insist on paying their share?

The present research investigated cultural differences in reactions to a gift or favor and, therefore, the likelihood that it is accepted or refused. In conceptualizing these differences, we assumed that people typically have both positive and negative reactions to a gift. That is, they normally have feelings of appreciation but also feel obligated to reciprocate. The likelihood of accepting a gift may depend on whether the feelings of appreciation for the gift outweigh the negative feelings of indebtedness that are likely to result from its acceptance. To this extent, cultural differences in the likelihood of accepting a gift may be the result of differences in the relative magnitude of these anticipated affective reactions. Asians, for example, are more inclined than North Americans to be concerned with the social norm of reciprocity (Hofstede 1980; Singelis 1994). Consequently, they may anticipate feeling more indebted if they receive a gift and less inclined to accept it.

Experiments 1 and 2 confirmed the existence of a cultural difference in the likelihood of accepting a gift in two different consumption situations. In Experiment 1, Hong Kong and Canadian participants imagined a scenario in which they shared at taxi with a friend and the friend offered to pay the fare. We found that Hong Kong participants were less willing to accept this offer than Canadians were. Experiment 2 replicated the results of the first experiment using a different scenario. In addition, we found that Asians were not only less likely than Canadians to accept a gift, but also expect others to be less willing to accept a gift from them.

Experiment 3 provided further evidence of this difference and confirmed our assumptions underlying it. In particular, Asians were more likely than North Americans to attribute the offer of a gift to ulterior motives and, as a result, were less appreciative. At the same time, Asians anticipated feeling relatively more indebted if they accepted the gift.

The first three experiments confirmed the general cultural difference between Asians' and North Americans' willingness to accept a gift and the feelings of appreciation and indebtedness that underlie this difference. However, the magnitude of these reactions can depend on a number of situational factors that influence perceptions of the gift-giver's motives. Experiment 4 investigated how cultural different in gift acceptance was moderated by the age of gift giver.

In experiment 4, Hong Kong and Canadian participants imagined being offered a gift from either a student who had just entered the university or a senior who was about to graduate. Upperclassmen were assumed to have higher social status in the eyes of Hong Kong participants than in the eyes of Canadians. We therefore expected that Hong Kong participants would report feeling less indebted if they received a gift from a senior than if they received a gift from a first year student, whereas this difference would be less evident among Canadian participants. To this extent, the effect of the gift-giver's age on acceptance of the gift should be greater among Hong Kong participants. The result of experiment 4 was consistent with this assumption.

Individuals who are concerned about being indebted are likely to keep track of the benefits they give and receive (Fong 2006). Thus, they feel disinclined to accept favors from a person that are greater than those they have given to the person in the past. (Cialdini 2001; Greenberg 1980). If this is so, and if Asians are more sensitive than North Americans to feelings of indebtedness, differences in the relative magnitude of the benefits they give and receive may have a relatively greater impact on their gift acceptance. Experiment 5 investigated this possibility by looking at actual gift acceptance behavior.

In experiment 5, the experiment was conducted at the student center of a Canadian university. The center was frequented by Chinese students from mainland China because it hosted courses in English as a second language. Students were randomly approached and asked to complete either a long (10-minute) or short (1-minute) survey. After doing so, participants were offered candy bars as a gift, being urged to take as many as they wished. We expected that Chinese participants would base the number of candies they selected on their perception of the benefit they had provided the experimenter (that is, the length of the questionnaire they had completed), and would avoid taking candy that would make them feel indebted. Thus, they were expected to take fewer candies if they had completed a short questionnaire than if they had completed a long one. In contrast, we expected North Americans to be less concerned about feeling indebted and that the amount of candy they took would be less dependent on the length of the questionnaire they had completed. These assumptions were confirmed by the data of experiment 5.

The studies we have reported provide one of the first demonstrations of a cultural difference in gift acceptance. Moreover, they provide insight into the reason why this difference occurs.

REFERENCES

Cialdini, Robert. B. (2001). *Influence: Science and Practice* (4th ed.). Needham Heights, MA: Allyn & Bacon.

Fong, Candy P. S. (2006), "The Impact of Favor-elicited Feelings on Reciprocity Behavior across Time," Unpublished doctoral dissertation, Hong Kong University of Science and Technology.

Greenberg, Martin S. (1980), "A Theory of Indebtedness," in *Social Exchange: Advances in Theory and Research*, Eds. Kenneth J. Gergen, Martin S. Greenberg, Richard H. Willis, NY: Plenum, 3-26

Hofstede, Geert (1980), *Culture's Consequences*, Newbury Park, CA: Sage.

Singelis, Theodore M. (1994), "The Measurement of Independent and Interdependent Self-Construals," *Personality and Social Psychology Bulletin*, 20 (October), 580–591.

Ptolemy vs. Copernicus: Self-Construal and Social Consumption

Sarah G. Moore, Duke University, USA
Gavan J. Fitzsimons, Duke University, USA

EXTENDED ABSTRACT

Copernicus was the first astronomer to suggest that the Sun, not the Earth, was the center of the universe. Despite initial controversy, his theory prevailed, displacing the Earth from its central location. On a non-cosmic level, the self-construal literature demonstrates that individuals differ in how they define themselves relative to others in their social universes. Interdependent individuals, whom we refer to as Copernican, define themselves in terms of relationships, such that their sense of self includes others in their social world (Markus and Kitayama 1991). Independent individuals, following Ptolemy, define themselves as autonomous, such that the center of an independent individual's universe is himself.

While past research has examined individual consumer decisions in great detail (Bettman, Luce, and Payne 1998), the study of social consumption contexts where consumers observe and respond to others' choices (Ariely and Levav 2000) or make choices for others (Botti, Iyengar, and Orfali 2008; Pöhlmann, Carranza, Hannover, and Iyengar 2007) has been relatively neglected, despite its ubiquity in everyday life. Little work has focused on how individuals respond to others' choices independent of their own, how individuals respond to making choices for others, or how well they perform this task. We investigate how individuals respond to others' choices and how they make choices for others, and propose that self-construal (Singelis 1994) is a fundamental moderator of how individuals react and behave in social consumption contexts.

Interdependent individuals are sensitive to others even when making self-choices and are comfortable having others choose for them (Pöhlmann et al. 2007), and thus should be sensitive to others' needs and preferences whether observing, predicting, or making choices on behalf of others. Conversely, independent individuals should display a Ptolemaic view of social consumption that leads to a self-focus and a concomitant neglect of others whether observing, predicting, or making choices for others. These two points of view lead to a paradox: while interdependents are well calibrated about what others would do and make better choices for others, they do so at an emotional cost. In social consumption, self-construal creates a double-edged sword that balances sensitivity for others with protecting the self. In four studies, we consider how self-construal influences observation, prediction, and choice in social consumption.

In Study 1, we examine how individuals respond to observing others' choice outcomes independent of their own. Using a restaurant scenario, we find that independent individuals respond more strongly to personal service failures (not getting what they ordered) than to the same service failure experienced by a friend, in terms of dissatisfaction and negative emotion. Interdependent individuals do not distinguish between self and other service failures, and respond equally negatively whether they or their friend had a poor choice outcome.

Study 2 considers how well independent versus interdependent individuals predict what others would do in different decision contexts. Consistent with Study 1, we find that independent individuals' predictions about others' actions are biased by their self-focus. Independents predict that their friends will ask their advice more often than they would ask a friend's advice; this is particularly pronounced in difficult choice situations. Interdependent individuals show no such bias. Similarly, independents, unlike interdependents, fail to recognize that others will respond as strongly as they will to a negative outcome, and underestimate others' emotional responses in addition to mispredicting their choices.

Studies 3 and 4 examine active choice on behalf of others. In Study 3, we evaluate how closely individuals adhere to their friend's preferences and investigate a moderator that impacts adherence. We find that independent individuals default to ignoring their friend's preferences and choose a friend's preferred option less often than interdependents. However, when their freedoms are threatened by a recommendation against their friend's favorite option, independents do choose this option—but do so in order to re-assert their freedom. Interdependents default to choosing a friend's favorite option, but move away from the choice upon receiving a recommendation against the friend's option because they are unwilling to inflict potentially negative outcomes on their friend. Corroborating these results, independents who receive no recommendation are quite happy, while individuals in the other conditions experience more negative emotion—independents because their freedom was threatened, interdependents because they feel responsible for choosing for others.

Finally, in Study 4, we allow individuals to decide whether they want to choose for others and investigate a moderator of willingness to choose. We use closeness as a proxy for self-construal: individuals who feel less (more) close to others should mirror independents (interdependents). Consistent with a Ptolemaic self-focus, non-close individuals are most likely to choose for others, and feel more satisfied and happier with their choices. However, when the stakes are high (when there are serious health consequences for making a choice), nobody is willing to choose for others. When the stakes are high enough, even independent individuals feel responsibility for choosing on behalf of others, close or distant.

In the context of social consumption, then, is it better to have a self-focused (Ptolemaic) or an other-focused (Copernican) point of view? While the Copernican point of view is probably best if one wishes to avoid being excommunicated by one's friends, it is the more emotionally difficult path to follow. Interdependent (Copernican) individuals are better calibrated about how others would make decisions, and make decisions that are closer to others' preferences. However, these other-focused individuals also respond more negatively if others come to grief in their choices, and suffer more negative emotional reactions when they choose for others.

REFERENCES

Ariely, Dan, and Jonathan Levav (2000), "Sequential Choice in Group Settings: Taking the Road Less Traveled and Less Enjoyed," *Journal of Consumer Research,* 27(3), 279-281.

Bettman, James R., Mary Frances Luce and John W. Payne (1998), "Constructive Consumer Choice Processes," *Journal of Consumer Research,* 25(3), 187-218.

Markus, Hazel R., and Shinobu Kitayama (1991), "Culture and the self: Implications for Cognition, Emotion, and Motivation," *Psychological Review,* 98, 224-253.

Singelis, Theodore M. (1994), "The Measurement of Independent and Interdependent Self-construals," *Personality and Social Psychology Bulletin,* 20, 580-591.

Pöhlmann, Claudia, Erica Carranza, Bettina Hannover, and
Sheena S. Iyengar (2007), "Repercussions of self-construal
for self-relevant and other-relevant choice," *Social
Cognition,* 25 (2), 284-305.

Botti, Simona, Sheena S. Iyengar, and Kristina Orfali (2008),
"Tragic Choices: Autonomy and Emotional Responses to
Life-Altering Decisions," working paper, Marketing
Department, London Business School, London UK, NW1
4SA.

'Fit for Charity':
The Moderating Role of Private Self-Focus in the Persuasiveness of Regulatory Fit

Marieke L. Fransen, University of Amsterdam, The Netherlands
Bob M. Fennis, Utrecht University, The Netherlands
Kathleen D. Vohs, University of Minnesota, USA
Ad Th. H. Pruyn, University of Twente, The Netherlands

EXTENDED ABSTRACT

In a world full of societal problems such as hunger, homelessness, illiteracy, and diseases, the need for charity support cannot be exaggerated. Many individuals already engage in volunteering and donate money to charity (Giving USA foundation 2007), but fundraisers have to keep up and continue advocating for more attention, effort, and donations to support their cause. Previous research on the determinants of charitable behavior has primarily focused on either demographic and individual characteristics of the volunteers and donators (e.g., Matsuba, Hart, Atkins 2007), or on the persuasive techniques that are used by charities to convince people to help (e.g., Cialdini and Goldstein 2004). However, what happens when these two components meet? Is a charity appeal more persuasive when its motives and values are framed in congruence with the (potential) volunteer's motivating strategies? The present research proposes that the interaction between either individual or situational differences in regulatory focus on the one hand (Higgins 1997) and the framing of a persuasive message on the other, can influence whether and to what extent people are willing to involve in charitable behavior. In addition, it is expected that these regulatory fit effects on charitable behavior are stronger for individuals with a high private self-focus because these individuals are especially affected by external information that is optionally relevant for the self (Hull et al. 2002). It is argued that private self-focus increases the activation of self-knowledge making it easier to process information that fits with this activated self-knowledge (i.e., regulatory focus).

Regulatory Focus Theory (Higgins 1997) states that there are two distinct mechanisms to regulate judgments and behavior, labeled promotion and prevention focus. When individuals are concerned with their ideal self, they adopt a promotion focus. This focus involves an eager strategy in the pursuit of hopes, wishes, and aspirations. On the other hand, when individuals are concerned with their ought self, they adopt a prevention focus which entails vigilant strategies to fulfill duties, obligations, and responsibilities. Individuals experience regulatory fit when they use goal pursuit strategies that match their (current) focus orientation, which in turn increases the perceived value of their behavior. Previous research on regulatory fit in the domain of advertising has demonstrated that individuals show more persuasion when an advertisement is framed in line with individuals' current orientation focus than when an advertisement mismatches with individuals' regulatory focus (e.g., Aaker and Lee 2006; Cesario, Grant, and Higgins 2004). In recent studies, the effects of regulatory fit on product evaluations and other types of outcome measures have been explained by the process of 'processing fluency': the experienced ease of processing or recalling information (e.g., Labroo and Lee 2006; Lee and Aaker 2004). These studies show that information that fits with one's regulatory focus is processed more easily than information that does not fit, and is therefore evaluated more positively. Extending on the processing fluency account for regulatory fit effects one could argue that regulatory fit effects are stronger for individuals with a high private self-focus. This is based on work by Hull and colleagues on the relation between private self-focus and information processing (Hull and Levy 1979; Hull et al. 2002). They propose

that a state of high private self-focus (i.e., attentiveness to one's inner state, personal history or any other aspect of oneself) primarily relates to the encoding of information in terms of its self-relevance. They argue that private self-focus has an effect on behavior by enhancing sensitivity and responsivity to aspects of the environment that are (potentially) relevant to the self. High private self-focus is proposed to facilitate processing of external information in self-relevant terms. More specifically, a state of high private self-focus enhances processing of self-relevant stimuli by activating knowledge about the self (Geller and Shaver 1976). We propose that especially information that already fits with stored self-knowledge (i.e., information that fits with current regulatory focus) will be easily related to the self by consumers high in private self-focus. This implies that charity appeals framed in promotion terms are easily perceived as self-relevant to consumers with a promotion focus, and charity appeals framed in prevention terms are easily perceived as self-relevant to consumers with a prevention focus. Hence, we expect that individuals high in private self-focus (as opposed to low in private self-focus) experience greater processing fluency when they accept information that fits with stored or activated self-knowledge. The misattribution of processing fluency is subsequently expected to positively influence attitudes and actual behavior.

In a series of three studies, in which participants were presented with charity information that either matched or mismatched their regulatory (promotion or prevention) focus, we tested our hypothesis that consumers engage in greater charity support when there is fit than when fit is absent. Moreover, we expected that the effects of regulatory fit are stronger for consumers with a high (as opposed to low) private self-focus. As predicted, the results demonstrated that consumers with a promotion focus donate more money to charity (studies 1a en 1b), and have a more positive attitude towards the charity (study 2) when the charity describes its goals in eager terms (aimed at attaining positive outcomes; promotion frame) than when vigilant terms (aimed at preventing negative outcomes; prevention frame) are used. The opposite was found for consumers with a prevention focus. Moreover, we found evidence for the moderating role of private self-focus. The three studies revealed that the aforementioned regulatory fit effects were stronger for individuals with a high (as opposed to low) private self-focus. Furthermore, the results demonstrated that processing fluency is the underlying mechanism accounting for the role of private self-focus (study 2).

Charities could take advantage of this knowledge by framing their message in congruence with receivers' (current) regulatory mechanism to make consumers experience fit. Moreover, this strategy would be especially fruitful when consumers are focused on their private selves because the present results show that particularly high private self-focused consumers donate more to charity when they experience fit. The focus on oneself may thus result in enhanced motivation to help others rather than -what might be intuitively expected- to merely serve the self. Hence, when advocating for charity it might be advantageous to remind consumers of themselves before asking to support another cause. In this way consumers can relate the charity information more easily to themselves, especially when this information is framed in congruence with consumers' individual regulation strategies.

REFERENCES

Aaker, Jennifer L., and Angela Y. Lee (2001), "'I' seek pleasures and 'we' avoid pains: The role of self-regulatory goals in information," *Journal of Consumer Research,* 28(1), 33-49.

Cesario, Joseph, Heidi Grant, and E. Tory Higgins (2004), "Regulatory Fit and Persuasion: Transfer From 'Feeling Right'," *Journal of Personality and Social Psychology*, 86 (3), 388-404.

Cialdini, Robert B. and Noah J. Goldstein (2004), "Social Influence: Compliance and Conformity," *Annual Review of Psychology*, 55, 591-621.

Higgins, E. Tory (1997), "Beyond pleasure and pain," *American Psychologist,* 52 (12), 1280-1300.

Geller, Vallerie and Philip Shaver (1976), "Cognitive consequences of self-awareness," *Journal of Experimental Social Psychology,* 12 (January), 99-108.

Giving USA Foundation (2007). www.givingusa.org

Hull, Jay. G. and Alan S. Levy (1979). "The organizational functions of the self: An alternative to the Duval and Wicklund model of self-awareness," *Journal of Personality and Social Psychology, 37*(5), 756-768.

Hull, Jay. G., Laurie B. Slone,Karen B. Meteyer, and Amanda R. Matthews (2002), "The nonconsciousness of self-consciousness," *Journal of Personality and Social Psychology,* 83(2), *406-24.*

Labroo, Aparna A. and Angela Y. Lee (2006), "Between Two Brands: A Goal Fluency Account of Brand Evaluation," *Journal of Marketing Research*, 43 (3), 374-85.

Lee, Angela Y. and Jennifer L. Aaker (2004), "Bringing the frame into focus: The influence of regulatory fit on processing fluency and persuasion," *Journal of Personality & Social Psychology,* 86 (2), 205-18.

Matsuba, M.K., Hart, D., & Atkins, R. (2007). "Psychological and social-structural influences on commitment to volunteering," *Journal of Research in Personality, 41*(4), 889-907.

The "I" of the Beholder: The Impacts of Gender Differences and Self-Referencing on Charity Advertising

Chun-Tuan Chang, National Sun Yat-sen University, Taiwan
Yu-Kang Lee, National Sun Yat-sen University, Taiwan

EXTENDED ABSTRACT

With decreasing governmental support for social services, requests for charitable donations have become more frequent over the past decade. How to maximize the responses among public contributors is an important arena in the marketing of non-profit organizations (NPOs) especially when the fund-raising competitions among NPOs are fierce. To date, research that has attempted to better elucidate the relationship between charity promotion and donation behavior has focused largely on cognitive mechanisms to increase compliance rates of donation solicitation. The researched mechanisms include foot-in-the-door techniques, visual aids, and request size. Less attention is directed toward examining how to frame charity messages effectively.

Charitable donations can be promoted through altruistic-value framed messages (e.g., "As a caring person, you are going to do something good to others in need") or egoistic-value framed ones (e.g., "As a successful person, you are going to do something good to protect your future") with the same goal (i.e., donation behavior promotion). Framing messages with these two main motives (altruistic and egoistic) for helping can be different between men and women. This article contributes to this evolving stream of research by applying framing concepts in promoting charitable campaigns to demonstrate that message framing might not be equally persuasive in all conditions, and could be moderated by two variables in social psychology: gender role and self-referencing. Gender roles can be an important determinant of reactions to charitable appeals that indicate donations either helps oneself (i.e., egoistic advantages) or someone else (i.e., altruistic benefits). How individuals process information by relating to the self-concept, is also relevant for charity advertising research. The current research tests the idea that responses to charitable appeals could be influenced by gender differences, and examines whether charitable information differently framed in a message would modify the effects of gender differences. How should advertisers frame a message for promoting a charitable donation? Should they frame the donation message as egoistic or altruistic appeals? Will self-referencing affect responses to egoistic versus altruistic appeals? Are the impacts of gender differences and self-referencing additive or multiplicative in influencing consumer attitudes toward donation promotion and inducing compliance with a request?

Influences of self-referencing in the relation between gender differences and charity framing appeal on advertising effectiveness were explored in a 2 (gender: female vs. male) X 2 (charity framing appeal: egoistic vs. altruistic) X 2 (self-referencing: low vs. high) factorial design. Self-referencing was manipulated through the nature of a NPO. The experiment was conducted through the Internet. Potential participants received an email invitation to participate in the study through a highlighted hyperlink to instantly access the designed website. Respondents were informed to evaluate a poster that would be launched for a forthcoming charitable campaign regarding the importance of making personal donations. They were then randomly exposed to one of the four treatment versions by viewing a designed poster. Finally, respondents continued to complete a questionnaire containing post-manipulation measures and manipulation checks, and clicked the "submit" button.

After successful manipulation checks, a series of analysis of variance were conducted to examine proposed hypotheses. The results support the general proposal that advertising effectiveness depends on complicated interrelationships among gender differences, charity framing appeal, and self-referencing. Specifically, the altruistic appeal results in more favorable intention than the egoistic appeal for the female audience, with the results reverses for the male counterparts. This lends qualified support to the phenomenon of *value congruity* (Brunel and Nelson, 2000; Supphellen and Nelson, 2001) in a charitable communication context. Contradictory to conventional wisdom (e.g., Block, 2005; Meyers-Levy and Peracchio, 1996; Shavitt and Brock, 1986, high self-referencing is not found to be always prevailing. The results further suggest that compared with women, men are more likely to be influenced by self-referencing. Self-referencing has a multiplicative impact on consumer attitudes toward donation promotion and behavioral intention when gender differences are considered.

Most importantly, we find that the interaction effect of gender differences and charity framing appeal can be attributed to and are moderated by different degrees of self-referencing. When the values delivered in the ad are accessible and easily activated by self-referencing techniques and match well with message claims, women are expected to resonate with altruistic claims that label them as caring because of socialization forces that encourage women to focus on others' welfare, and men are expected to resonate with egoistic claims that label themselves as successful because of the traditional male role. It appears that if the charity framing appeal fits the social role of audience member, it should motivate that person to behave in an appeal-consistent manner. As such, self-referencing can be an explicit form of conveying values in terms of gender differences if they match with the social nature of the audience member. The results reflect previous studies in that when activated values are self-relevant, assimilation effects may occur in line with gender expectations (Aaker and Williams, 1998; Nelson et al., 2006). However, our research challenges these views and shows that the effects of value congruity do not always have a positive impact. In fact, the opposite could occur in the absence of self-referencing. When self-referencing is low, the congruence between gender and charity framing appeal may cause a boomerang effect on advertising persuasion of charity message. This is true for both women and men encountering a donation solicitation by a NPO which is perceived as a charity providing low self-referencing needs. The altruistic appeal becomes more effective to men, but the egoistic appeal is more effective to women. It could be due to that people rely on the heuristic cue in information processing when self-referencing is low. The framing appeal depicting the opposite traditional gender social role could catch more attention in serving a heuristic cue.

This study provides important insights into social psychological influences of gender differences and self-referencing that occur when charitable donation messages are pitched to the public. How an individual being socially perceived, and how he/she perceives a NPO would determine the effectiveness of two major framing appeals. Different types of NPOs should employ appropriate framing appeals, depending on the audience member's gender. When individuals perceive a NPO as having a higher level of self-referencing, the effects of the *"I" of the beholder* (i.e., congruence between the gender and the message theme) may facilitate advertising persuasion. Conversely, when facing a NPO with a lower level of self-referencing, the *"I"* may be determined by how a charity message is framed (egoistic vs. altruistic). In short, incongruity between the gender and message theme lead to higher advertising effectiveness.

REFERENCES

Aaker, J. L., and Williams, P. (1998), "Empathy versus Pride: The Influence of Emotional Appeals across Cultures," *Journal of Consumer Research*, 25(4), 241-261.

Block, L. G. (2005), "Self-Referenced Fear and Guilt Appeals: The Moderating Role of Self-Construal," *Journal of Applied Social Psychology*, 35(11), 2290-2309.

Brunel, F. F., and Nelson, M. R. (2000), "Explaining Gendered Responses to "Help-Self" and "Help-Others" Charity Ad Appeals: The Mediating Role of World-Views," *Journal of Advertising*, 29(3), 15-28.

Meyers-Levy, J. (1989), "Gender Differences in Information Processing: A Selectivity Interpretation," in *Cognitive and Affective Responses to Advertising*, P. Cafferata and A. M. Tybout (eds.), Lexington, MA: Lexington Books.

Nelson, M. R., Brunel, F. F., Supphellen, M., and Manchanda, R. V. (2006), "Effects of Culture, Gender, and Moral Obligations on Responses to Charity Advertising Across Masculine and Feminine Cultures," *Journal of Consumer Psychology*, 16(1), 45-56.

Shavitt, S., and Brock, T. C. (1986), "Self-Relevant Responses in Commercial Persuasion: Field and Experimental Tests," in *Advertising and consumer psychology* (Vol.3, pp. 149-171), J. Olson and K. Sentis (eds.), New York: Praeger.

Supphellen, M., and Nelson, M. R. (2001), "Developing, Exploring, and Validating a Typology of Private Philanthropic Decision Making," *Journal of Economic Psychology*, 22(5), 573-603.

Social Value Orientation as a Moral Intuition: Decision-Making in the Dictator Game

Gert Cornelissen, Universitat Pompeu Fabra, Spain
Siegfried Dewitte, Katholieke Universiteit Leuven, Belgium
Luk Warlop, Katholieke Universiteit Leuven, Belgium

EXTENDED ABSTRACT

The types of consumer decisions studied by social marketers often have a social dilemma-type structure. They involve a conflict, either between pursuing the collective interest (e.g., avoiding environmental degradation by buying eco-friendly laundry detergent or by using public transport rather than one's own car) and one's personal interest (e.g., buying a cheaper non eco-friendly laundry detergent or the comfort and flexibility of taking one's own car), or between one's delayed self-interest (e.g., eating a healthy salad and a piece of fruit as a snack) and one's immediate self-interest (e.g., eating a pizza, and a chocolate mousse for desert). We studied the decision-making process in such situations in which self-interest conflicts with the collective interest. Based on the findings, we propose some public policy recommendations for the promotion of social desirable, or social responsible consumer behaviors.

In this context of social dilemmas, *social value orientation* (SVO) is a heavily studied concept (e.g., Van Lange et al., 1998; e.g., Mark Van Vugt et al., 1995). It categorizes people according to preferred patterns of outcomes between the self and others in interdependence situations. Commonly used categorizations distinguish people who are cooperators, individualists, or competitors. Cooperators (or pro-socials) prefer to maximize group outcomes and equality in outcomes. Individualists and competitors (or pro-selfs) prefer to maximize personal outcomes. Van Lange, De Bruin, Otten, and Joireman (1997b) argued that these tendencies develop during our lifetime through experiences with interdependence situations. The analogy with moral intuitions, which, according to Haidt (2001), are automatically activated moral judgments that develop through social and cultural interactions, made us expect that these social value orientations may be automatically activated preferences for pursuing the public interest versus pursing the self-interest.

This idea contrasts with the commonly held believe that pursuing the self-interest is an automatically activated goal (van den Bos et al., 2006), and that engaging in pro-social (consumer) behavior requires some kind of cognitive operation. We hypothesized that this would be true for pro-selfs, but not for pro-socials. On the other hand, we expected that if decisions would be based on a more elaborated thinking process, pursuing the self-interest would be a salient motive for all people. We attribute this to the fact that behaving selfishly has become a social norm in our society (Miller, 1999) and that private costs and benefits are more salient than public costs and benefits (Rothschild, 1979; Warlop et al., 2003) when thinking about outcome distributions.

A series of four studies, in which Dictator Games were played as a simulation for decision making in real life social dilemmas (like consumers' conflicts between pursuing collective or private interests), supported these hypotheses. In a Dictator Game two participants are paired. One of them receives an amount of money and is instructed to divide the money between himself and his partner. The size of a dictator's "donation" is a measure for cooperation level, or the degree to which one is motivated to pursue the collective interest. We showed that decisions to pursue the collective interest are the result of a two-step process. In an initial, automatic and intuitive step, participants anchored their donations according to their social value orientations. We elicited such intuitive decisions using a distraction manipulation, which existed of asking half of our participants to remember a 7-digit number. Pro-socials intuitively tended to support the collective interest to a larger degree than pro-selfs. In a second step, in which dictators think more elaborately about the decision at hand, both pro-socials and pro-selfs tended to benefit their immediate self-interest.

Additionally, we showed that the automatic effect of social value orientations is partly due to a differential perception of the closeness of one's relationship with the interaction partner. Pro-socials chronically feel "closer" to anonymous other people than pro-selfs. This is, at least partly, the reason for their intuitive tendency to value collective interests. Interestingly, we also showed it is possible to influence such perceptions and the resulting automatic decisions. By making people feel "closer" to their interaction partner, donation sizes increase if the decision is made automatically, but not when it is contemplated more elaborately.

The present results may offer new perspectives on the way social marketing strategies may reach their objectives of promoting behavior that benefits the collective interest (like consumer decisions supporting environmentally friendly products, fair trade or items produced in circumstances in which human rights are not violated) or individual's long-term self interest (e.g., eating healthy, abstaining from smoking or consuming illegal drugs). They suggest that techniques, which activate people's pro-environmental, ethical, or health values, while preventing them from contemplating extensively on a current decision, could be efficient tools to achieve these goals. Obviously, being able to activate such values implies that these values need to develop first, and in this respect traditional social marketing techniques based on argumentation and education are indispensible. Based on our results we propose, however, that the motivation to contemplate should be minimized on the moment actual decisions are made, since a thinking process tends to result in people pursuing their immediate self-interest.

REFERENCES

Haïdt, J. (2001). The emotional dog and its rational tail: A social intuitionist approach to moral judgment. *Psychological Review, 108*(4), 814-834.

Miller, D. T. (1999). The norm of self-interest. *American Psychologist, 54*(12), 1053-1060.

van den Bos, K., Peters, S. L., Bobocel, D. R., & Ybema, J. F. (2006). On preferences and doing the right thing: Satisfaction with advantageous inequity when cognitive processing is limited. *Journal of Experimental Social Psychology, 42*(3), 273-289.

Van Vugt, M., Meertens, R. M., & Van Lange, P. A. M. (1995). Car versus public transportation? The role of social value orientations in a real-life social dilemma. *Journal of Applied Social Psychology, 25*(3), 258-278.

Van Lange, P. A. M., De Bruin, E. M. N., Otten, W., & Joireman, J. A. (1997b). Development of prosocial, individualistic, and competitive orientations: Theory and preliminary evidence. *Journal of Personality and Social Psychology, 73*(4), 733-746.

Van Lange, P. A. M., Van Vugt, M., Meertens, R. M., & Ruiter, R. A. C. (1998). "A social dilemma analysis of commuting preferences: The roles of social value orientation and trust". *Journal of Applied Social Psychology, 28*(9), 796-820.

The Pervasive Effect of Aesthetics on Choice: Evidence from a Field Study

Jan R. Landwehr, University of St. Gallen, Switzerland
Aparna A. Labroo, University of Chicago, USA
Andreas Herrmann, University of St. Gallen, Switzerland

EXTENDED ABSTRACT

When it comes to purchasing expensive consumer durables, most people believe the choices they make result from thoughtful contemplation. For example, few people are likely to respond that they bought a car because the design was pleasing and familiar. However, a century of research on mere exposure effects suggests the intriguing possibility that visual design features and, in particular, the ease with which they are processed might play a powerful role in everyday decision processes. Research indicates that because important and personally relevant products are familiar and come to mind easily, people implicitly associate ease and familiarity with importance and personal relevance. As a consequence, archetypical designs, which are easier to process and more familiar, also seem more important, self-relevant, and likeable. These ease of processing effects are significantly stronger for visually complex than for simple designs because people might become aware of the ease of processing simple stimuli and correct their evaluations; if the design seems too familiar it might even feel boring.

While laboratory studies provide robust evidence of this phenomenon, its effect size in a high-involvement real world context with real financial implications (e.g., a car purchase) is unclear. The current investigation systematically examines this issue.

To investigate the impact of design features on sales in an important, real-life setting, we obtained six months (January 2007–June 2007) of officially recorded car sales data from the German Federal Transport Authority. Two objective design aspects were considered for each car: archetypicality and complexity. In accordance with the laboratory findings, we expected that archetypicality would increase sales of visually complex, but not of simple, cars. That is, complex cars would benefit from the ease of processing their design features and appeal most when they are archetypical, whereas for simple designs the ease of processing archetypical features would be non-informative.

Objective design archetypicality. A professional frontal photograph was taken of each car under standardized conditions controlling for stylistic aspects. Using morphing software from research done on human facial appeal, a morph was created. An archetype similarity score calculated by summing the Euclidian difference of each of 50 feature points of a car from the averaged position of the corresponding feature in the morphed (archetypical) car was created. A higher score indicated that a particular car was more archetypical and presumably easier to process.

Objective design complexity. Based on perception research which proposes that a computer algorithm for compression of an image file can measure picture complexity because it removes redundancies, ZIP algorithm was selected as an objective measure of design complexity.

Validating objective measures with subjective ratings. To confirm the two objective measures depict the proper constructs, 564 U.S. consumers rated the cars for typicality and complexity of design. As we expected, Euclidian (objective) archetype similarity significantly correlated with subjective archetype similarity ($r=0.46$, $p<0.02$) but not with subjective visual complexity ($r=-0.29$, $p>0.15$). Similarly, ZIP (objective) complexity significantly correlated with subjective complexity ratings ($r=0.56$, $p<0.01$) but not with subjective archetype similarity ($r=-0.35$, $p>0.09$). Furthermore, Euclidian

similarity and ZIP complexity were unrelated ($r=0.05$, $p>0.81$), suggesting that our measures capture conceptually distinct constructs and are suitable independent predictors. Only 15.1% of all of the images were recognized correctly, indicating the designs were difficult to identify and ratings unlikely to be biased by established associations. The results were not altered by removing ratings of images that were recognized.

Sales by objective archetypicality and complexity. To control for the correlative nature of our sales data, we included retail price, advertisement spending, technological sophistication, brand preferences, and time since market launch for each car in the analysis. Importantly, *none* of these controls was significantly correlated with either objective measure. The predicted pattern of results emerged: a positive effect of archetypicality ($\beta=0.35$, $p=0.049$), a positive effect of complexity ($\beta=0.28$, $p=0.031$), and an interaction between these two factors ($\beta=0.43$, $p=0.026$). With respect to the control variables, we observed substantial effects of retail price ($\beta=-0.29$, $p=0.023$) and brand preference ($\beta=0.62$, $p<0.001$), but the other three variables did not influence sales ($P \geq 0.30$). The model including design and control variables explained 87% of sales variance, and design factors alone explained 42% of sales variance. Because of this high level of explained variance, it is likely all important variables are included in the model. Additional analysis based on MM estimation which iteratively readjusts and reduces the weights of possible outliers to find the optimal solution with unbiased estimates yielded the same results.

Sales predictions with subjective measures. As additional evidence, we used the subjective ratings of archetypicality and complexity collected from U.S. consumers to predict German car sales. We observed a positive effect of increased archetypicality ($\beta=3.47$, $p=0.015$) and increased complexity ($\beta=3.60$, $p=0.01$) and the interaction term ($\beta=3.55$, $p=0.032$), thus replicating the effects observed with the objective scores. Including the five control variables did not alter the results, nor did *excluding* the 15.1% ratings of designs that were recognized; the three terms remained significant, with the model explaining 74% of sales variance.

General discussion. Our investigation provides evidence in a real market setting of the extent to which visual design features affect a purchase people presumably contemplate a great deal. The effect, observed on six months of car sales, is independent of retail price, technological sophistication, brand associations, advertising, time in the market, and replicates for both compact and executive cars. We observed it with subjective measures that controlled for brand recognition, suggesting it occurs outside conscious recognition, and with objective measures applying equal weight to the visual features of all cars.

Critics might suggest cars "rationally" best also have the best-liked designs. However, it is unclear why "rational" features correlate with "archetypicality" of "visually complex" cars, or how some manufacturers intuit the importance of such features for design of some but not all of their brands. Others might suggest two sets of consumers exist in the market, some who value design and others who value descriptive features, and design-valuing consumers somehow buy archetypical, visually complex cars. However, this implies that "rational" consumers are randomly and equally spread across remaining three conditions suggesting they are unable to distinguish a better car.

REFERENCES

Anand, Punam, Morris B. Holbrook, and Debra Stephens (1988), "The Formation of Affective Judgments-The Cognitive-Affective Model versus the Independence Hypothesis," *Journal of Consumer Research*, 15 (December), 386-91.

Baronchelli, Andrea, Emanuele Caglioti, and Vittorio Loreto (2005), "Measuring Complexity with Zippers," *European Journal of Physics*, 26 (September), 69-77.

Benson Philip J. and David I. Perrett (1993), "Extracting Prototypical Facial Images from Exemplars," *Perception*, 22 (March), 257-62.

Berlyne, Daniel E. (1966), "Curiosity and Exploration," *Science*, 153 (July), 25-33.

_____ (1974), *Studies in the New Experimental Aesthetics,* Washington, DC: Hemisphere.

Bornstein, Robert F. (1989), "Exposure and Affect: Overview and Meta-Analysis of Research, 1968-1987," *Psychological Bulletin*, 106 (September), 265-89.

Bornstein, Robert F. and Paul R. D'Agostino (1994), "The Attribution and Discounting of Perceptual Fluency: Preliminary Tests of a Perceptual Fluency/Attributional Model of the Mere Exposure Effect," *Social Cognition*, 12 (Summer), 103-28.

Bornstein, Robert F., Amy R. Kale, and Karen R. Cornell (1990), "Boredom as a Limiting Condition on the Mere Exposure Effect," *Journal of Personality and Social Psychology,* 58 (May), 791-800.

Deffenbacher, Kenneth A., Thomas Vetter, John Johanson, and Alice J. O'Toole (1998), "Facial Aging, Attractiveness, and Distinctiveness," *Perception*, 27 (October), 1233-43.

Donderi, Don C. (2006), "Visual Complexity: A Review," *Psychological Bulletin*, 132 (January), 73-97.

Lee, Angela Y. and Aparna A. Labroo (2004), "The Effect of Conceptual and Perceptual Fluency on Brand Evaluation," *Journal of Marketing Research*, 49 (May), 151-65.

Li, Ming and Paul Vitányi (1997), *An Introduction to Kolmogorov Complexity and Its Applications*, New York: Springer.

Mandler, George, Yoshio Nakamura, and Billie Jo Shebo Van Zandt (1987), "Nonspecific Effects of Exposure on Stimuli that cannot be Recognized," *Journal of Experimental Psychology: Learning, Memory and Cognition*, 13 (October), 646-8.

Perret, David I., Karen A. May, and Sin Yoshikawa (1994), "Facial Shape and Judgments of Female Attractiveness," *Nature*, 368 (March), 239-42.

Reber, Rolf, Piotr Winkielman, and Norbert Schwarz (1998), "Effects of Perceptual Fluency on Affective Judgments," *Psychological Science*, 9 (January), 45-8.

Schwarz, Norbert (2004), "Metacognitive Experiences in Consumer Judgment and Decision Making," *Journal of Consumer Psychology*, 14 (4), 332-48.

Sullivan, Susan A. and Leann L. Birch, "Pass the Sugar, Pass the Salt: Experience Dictates Preference," *Developmental Psychology*, **26** (July), 546-51.

Thorndike, Edward L. and Irving Lorge (1944), *The teacher's Word Book of 30,000 Words*, New York: Teachers College Press.

Winkielman, Piotr, Jamin Halberstadt, Tedra Fazendeiro, and Steve Catty (2006), "Prototypes are Attractive because they are Easy on the Mind," *Psychological Science*, 17 (9), 799-806.

Yohai, Victor, Werner A. Stahel, and Ruben H. Zamar (1991), "A Procedure for Robust Estimation and Inference in Linear Regression," in *Directions in Robust Statistics and Diagnostics Part II*, eds. Werner Stahel and Sanford Weisberg, New York: Springer, 365-74.

Zajonc, Robert B. (1968), "Attitudinal Effects of Mere Exposure," *Journal of Personality and Social Psychology Monographs*, 9 (2, Pt. 2), 1-27.

_____ (1980), "Feeling and Thinking: Preferences Need no Inferences," *American Psychologist*, 35(February), 151-75.

First Is Best: First Exposure Effects in Aesthetic Judgments

Mario Pandelaere, Ghent University, Belgium
Kobe Millet, Catholic University Leuven, Belgium
Bram Van den Bergh, Catholic University Leuven, Belgium

EXTENDED ABSTRACT

People differ from each other in their likes and dislikes. For example, a mother may disagree with her son's assessment that Madonna's version of *American Pie* is better than Don McLean's. Individual differences in number of exposures to the two versions of *American Pie* (e.g., the mother has been exposed more often to Don McLean and the son has heard Madonna more frequently) may explain the mother-son disagreement. Indeed, the more frequently people are exposed to a stimulus, the more they tend to like that stimulus (i.e., mere exposure, Zajonc 1968). Nevertheless, even when the mother and her son are equally familiar with the two versions of *American Pie*, we conjecture that the mother-son disagreement would persist if differences in order of exposure exist. More specifically, we hypothesize that a first encountered aesthetic stimulus tends to be preferred over related stimuli that are encountered later. The hypothesized *first exposure effect* differs from the mere exposure effect, because it refers to attitudinal effects of *first*, rather than *repeated*, exposure.

Bruine de Bruin and Keren (2003) argue that in sequential rating formats, items may be compared to earlier items. The analysis of Bruine de Bruin and Keren (2003) may apply only to situations where people process the different items analytically. In many situations, however, people may be less inclined to process analytically, but rather process stimuli in a less effortful, holistic fashion. We believe this may be the case in everyday consumption of aesthetic works. In those situations, we propose that a first encountered stimulus may be liked more than later encountered ones.

Our first real-life, correlational study (The music study) demonstrates that the appreciation of a song version not only depends on its familiarity (i.e., a mere exposure effect), but also on the order in which it has been encountered. In particular, a first encountered version of a song is appreciated more than a later encountered version. In a subsequent experiment (the song study), participants were exposed to different versions of the song *Boom Boom*. They preferred the version they heard first over the version they heard second. In the Landscape studies, participants were exposed to pictures of landscapes and the corresponding mirror-reversed pictures. Again, participants liked the picture they saw first more than the corresponding mirror-reversed picture they saw later. Moreover, the preference for the picture they saw first did not depend entirely on the correct identification of the picture they had seen first. Finally, in the Pollock study, participants were exposed to different orientations of abstract paintings. They appreciated the first orientation more than any subsequent orientation they were exposed to. This lower appreciation for subsequent orientations was not due to boredom.

Numerous studies suggest that earlier events and items are processed differently than later ones, either quantitatively (e.g., earlier items receive more attention) or qualitatively (e.g., earlier items bias the processing of later items). Although these studies demonstrate that the *cognitive* processing of first presented items may be different from later presented items, they do not imply *attitudinal* effects of first exposure. Nevertheless, across modalities (visual and auditory), across stimuli (music, abstract art and photographs) and across rating procedures (absolute evaluations and relative preferences), we demonstrated that a first encountered stimulus tends to be liked better than later encountered similar ones.

The type of processing may determine whether a first exposure effect is observed. In the contestant studies, jurors may be more inclined to think analytically about the contestants' performances. As such, features may be detected that allow comparison processes to focus on unique features. In the current studies, in contrast, the items probably were processed holistically, i.e. as a whole without trying to analyze the stimuli into features. Possibly, items appear more similar when people process stimuli holistically than when they process stimuli more analytically. Hence, any effect of type of processing on the first exposure effect may be mediated by perceived item similarity.

If the first exposure effect on aesthetic judgments is due to the type of processing, similar first exposure effects may be obtained for non-aesthetic products as well. As such, current findings may extend research on the pioneering advantage (i.e. preference for a brand that enters a market first over follower brands, Carpenter and Nakamoto, 1989) because several studies indicate a cognitive basis for the pioneering advantage (Kardes and Kalyanaram 1992). The present studies found higher evaluations for items that are encountered first than for items encountered later without the necessity of recognizing the first items as having encountered first. This suggests that higher evaluations of pioneering brands may even be obtained when a brand is not recognized as a pioneer.

The effect of exposure on attitudes is epitomized by the mere exposure effect: people develop a preference for initially neutral objects as they are *more* exposed to it. The current paper demonstrates that people's preferences are not only shaped by repeated exposure or by exposure duration (Bornstein 1989), but also by first exposure. Future studies need to address the mechanism involved in the current findings. For now, however, it appears that aesthetic judgments may reveal strong primacy effects.

REFERENCES

Bornstein, F. Robert. (1989), " Exposure and affect: Overview and meta-analysis of research, 1968-1987," *Psychological Bulletin,* 106 (September), 265-289.

Bruine de Bruin, Wändi and Gideon Keren (2003), "Order effects in sequentially judged options due to the direction of comparison," *Organizational Behavior and Human Decision Processes,* 92 (1-2), 91–101.

Carpenter, Gregory S. and Kent Nakamoto (1989), "Consumer preference formation and pioneering advantage," *Journal of Marketing Research*, 26 (August), 285-298.

Kardes, Frank R.,and Gurumurthy Kalyanaram, G. (1992), "Order-of-Entry Effects on Consumer Memory and Judgment: An Information Integration Perspective," *Journal of Marketing Research*, 29 (August), 343-357.

Zajonc, Robert (1968), "Attitudinal Effects of Mere Exposure," *Journal of Personality and Social Psychology Monographs*, 9 (No. 2, Part 2), 1–27.

Resolving Aesthetic Incongruity

Vanessa M. Patrick, University of Georgia, USA
Henrik Hagtvedt, University of Georgia, USA

EXTENDED ABSTRACT

The current research proposes a theoretical framework to explain the phenomenon of Aesthetic Incongruity Resolution (AIR). We empirically investigate the affective and behavioral consequences of the aesthetic incongruity that often arises in everyday consumption. With a set of four experiments, we investigate the consequences of a mismatch (aesthetic incongruity) between a product and the existing *consumption environment*. Consumers' existing possessions constitute their consumption environment, and what the specific consumption environment is thus depends on the new acquisition and the purpose it is meant to fulfill. For instance, the existing wardrobe may be the consumption environment for a new shirt, while the living room and all the furniture and decorations therein may be the consumption environment for a new rug. Thus, the consumption environment is defined as the set of pre-existing possessions amongst which the new acquisition will be introduced and utilized.

The current research demonstrates that aesthetic incongruity between an acquired product and its consumption environment may result in a consumer's decision to either return the product or to spend more on additional purchases. This decision is moderated by product appeal. Specifically, for a product high in aesthetic appeal, incongruity results in feelings of frustration due to the lack of fit, while for a product low in aesthetic appeal, incongruity results in regret for having made the purchase. We demonstrate that feelings of frustration motivate additional purchases to accommodate the product within one's consumption environment while feelings of regret are more likely to result in product returns.

In study 1, photographs of lamps were pretested to be high versus low in aesthetic appeal. Two photographs were selected and were rated equally in terms of incongruity with the picture of a room in which the lamp was to be placed. Participants were randomly assigned to one of two experimental conditions and asked to imagine that they had purchased the lamp (high vs. low appeal) for their living room (i.e., the room in the photograph), and they completed a questionnaire based on this scenario. Results revealed that participants in the high appeal condition experienced significantly more frustration than regret resulting from the incongruity, while those in the low appeal condition experienced significantly more regret than frustration. Further, the high appeal products were more likely to lead to additional purchases, while the low appeal products were more likely to be returned.

In study 2, participants read a scenario in which they purchased a shirt (high appeal vs. low appeal) that either fit well or not at all well with the rest of their wardrobe. Results revealed that when the product was high in appeal, participants were more frustrated by the lack of fit than they were regretful, but when the product was low in appeal, participants were more regretful than they were frustrated. For the high (low) appeal product, participants were more likely to make additional purchases (return the product) as a result of poor fit. Mediation analysis demonstrates that the difference score of frustration minus regret mediates the effect of appeal on the decision to buy more versus return the product. Interestingly, participants reported satisfaction with the high appeal product regardless of incongruity, indicating that the desire to accommodate the product itself resulted in the feelings of frustration and motivated the purchase of additional items in the low fit condition.

In study 3, participants read a scenario in which they bought curtains for decorative purposes (consummatory goal) or blinds to shade the room from the sun (instrumental goal), with high or low aesthetic appeal, that did not fit with the rest of the things in the bedroom. Results replicated the results from the previous studies, regardless of consumption goal. In other words, when the product was high (low) in appeal, participants were more frustrated (regretful) by the lack of fit than they were regretful (frustrated), and they were more likely to make additional purchases (return the product). Again, mediation analysis demonstrates that the difference score of frustration minus regret mediates the effect of aesthetic appeal on the decision to buy more versus return.

Study 4 was designed to illustrate a key managerial implication of the current research, namely that for high appeal products, the option to buy additional items to accommodate the product within the consumption environment (versus the option to return the product) results in greater satisfaction and more repeat purchases. Participants were told that a consumer had purchased a high (low) appeal rug that did not fit with the rest of the things in her living room. They then read a dialogue between the consumer and a sales clerk from the store in which the consumer explains her predicament. In one condition, the sales clerk gives the consumer the options of returning the rug to the store or mailing it back to the store, and in the other condition the sales clerk gives the consumer the options of returning the rug to the store or being shown additional items to purchase that would complement the rug and make it fit in the living room. Results revealed that in the high appeal condition, participants rated the sales clerk as friendlier and more competent, and they were more likely to buy again from the store in the future, when they were offered the option to buy more. However, this was not the case for the low appeal product.

Thus, this research does not only provide insights into the affective and behavioral responses to aesthetic incongruity between new purchases and the existing product environment. It also provides managerial guidance in terms of how to resolve instances of aesthetic incongruity, leading to increased customer satisfaction and future repeat purchases.

Unexpected Benefits of Being Less Rather Than More Similar: The Influence of Consumer Mindset and Brand Presence on Copycat Evaluation

Femke van Horen, Tilburg University, The Netherlands
Rik Pieters, Tilburg University, The Netherlands
Diederik A. Stapel, Tilburg University, The Netherlands

EXTENDED ABSTRACT

Suppose you are in a Wal-Mart supermarket and want to buy peanut butter. The Wal-Mart private label peanut butter is located next to the incumbent Skippy brand on the shelf. The Wal-Mart peanut butter has the same light-blue lid, an identical blue label with red lettering and the jar is of similar material and size. How would you evaluate the Wal-Mart peanut butter? Previous copycatting research would predict that the Wal-Mart private label is evaluated more positively the higher its similarity with the Skippy peanut butter is (Kapferer 1996; Loken, Ross and Hilke 1986; Warlop and Alba 2004). That is the general idea in the marketing literature is that increased similarity with the incumbent uniformly improves the evaluation of the copycat. We argue, instead, that in addition to similarity, copycat evaluation depends critically on the physical arrangement of the brands at the point-of-purchase and on the specific mindset that is activated in consumers while evaluating brands.

To date, remarkably little is known about how, in addition to the sheer degree of similarity, characteristics of the shopping situation, such as the physical arrangements in the supermarket and the consumers' mindset, influence the evaluation of copycats. Moreover, because the focus in theory and practice has traditionally been on highly similar, more blatant copycats (Zaichkowsky 2006), the effects of more subtle degrees of copycatting are largely unknown. That is, whereas blatant forms of copycatting are fairly straightforward to detect and taken to court, subtle forms of copycatting appear abound and are more difficult to detect, but—as we expect—may ironically benefit more from the incumbent's equity.

Social cognition theory (Sherif and Hovland 1961) and research in marketing (Herr 1989) has shown that contrast effects may occur when information about a product or brand is used as a comparison standard. Then, judgments about the brand will be displaced away from these comparison standards. Moreover, recent theories (Stapel and Suls 2004) suggest that the consumers' mindsets critically determine whether or not such comparison standards will be employed. Building on these ideas, the present research posits and shows that copycat evaluation is critically dependent on the i) consumer mindset (judge–consumer) and ii) brand presence (incumbent present–absent), as these prompt copycat-incumbent comparisons. Thus, when the Skippy peanut butter is in physical proximity when evaluating the Wal-Mart copycat, the latter might actually be evaluated less positively, as the incumbent brand is more likely to be used as a comparison standard, resulting in comparative contrast. In addition, when people are in a judgmental frame of mind (judge mindset) instead of an experiential frame of mind (consumer mindset) the Wal-Mart private label might be evaluated less positively as well. In a judge mindset, people are more inclined to critically appraise and gauge the copycat in terms of the acceptability of its trade dress tactics. In order to judge the copycat, a distinct representation of the incumbent brand will become accessible, which will be used as a comparison standard. This will result in a contrastive judgment, i.e., a devaluation of the copycat. We predict, however, that even when comparison is instigated, contrast will only occur for highly similar, but not for moderately similar copycats, because information needs to be similar and extreme, rather than moderate, for comparison to result in contrast (Stapel, Koomen and Van der Pligt, 1997). Empirical support for these predictions would imply that contrary to common belief, lower similarity, subtle copycats can be as damaging as or even more damaging than higher similarity, blatant copycats.

Three studies tested the hypothesis that evaluation of copycats is dependent on the degree of similarity, but also, and critically, on the consumer's mindset and brand presence. In these studies the degree of similarity between a supermarket private label and an incumbent brand was systematically varied. Study 1 tested the prediction that the evaluation of degrees of copycat similarity is affected by the activated mindset. In the context of the introduction of a new olive oil, participants were asked to imagine either that they were considering to buy (consumer mindset) or that they were determining the acceptability of (judge mindset) an olive oil with a particular brand name. Next, they evaluated 25 brand names that differed in degree of similarity to the incumbent brand (no, low, moderate, high and extreme). The results showed, in support of the hypothesis, that when a consumer mindset was activated, highly similar copycats were preferred over less similar copycats. However, when a judge mindset was activated, highly similar copycats were liked less. Study 2 tested, in addition to similarity and consumer mindset, the influence of brand presence on copycat evaluation. Six brand names from Study 1 were selected with low and high similarity to an incumbent brand. Again either a consumer or a judge mindset condition was activated. And for half of the participants within each condition the incumbent brand name was present on the screen while they were evaluating each of the six brand names. The results of Study 2 replicated the results of Study 1 when the incumbent brand name was not present. However, when the incumbent brand name was present the results completely reversed: participants in the consumer mindset liked highly similar copycats less. In fact, when the incumbent brand name was present, participants in a consumer mindset evaluated the high similarity copycat as negative, as did participants in the judge mindset. Study 3 tested whether degree of copycat similarity and evaluation are, as our theory would predict, curvilinearly instead of linearly related, when the incumbent brand is present. In this study, brand packages instead of brand names were used respectively with low, moderate or high degree of copycat-incumbent similarity. In support of our predictions, the moderate similarity copycat was evaluated more positively than the low and high similarity copycat, when the incumbent brand was present.

These results demonstrate that in addition to the degree of similarity, the evaluation of copycats is influenced by characteristics of the shopping situation, such as the physical arrangements in the supermarket and the consumers' mindsets, as these aspects are likely to instigate explicit comparisons between copycat and incumbent brand. We showed that under circumstances that are conducive to explicit comparisons, moderately similar copycats are in fact liked more than highly similar copycats. This reveals the unexpected benefits of being subtly similar for copycats, and the potential harm for the equity of incumbent brands that focus on combating the blatant copycats, whilst letting the subtle ones go by undetected.

REFERENCES

Herr, Paul M. (1989), "Priming Price: Prior Knowledge and Context Effects," *Journal of Consumer Research*, 16 (1), 67-75.

Kapferer, Jean-Noel (1995), "Brand Confusion: Empirical Study of a Legal Concept," *Psychology & Marketing*, 12 (6), 551-68.

Loken, Barbara, Ivan Ross and Ronald L. Hinkle (1986), "Consumer 'Confusion' of Origin and Brand Similarity Perceptions," *Journal of Public Policy & Marketing*, 5, p. 195-211

Sherif, Muzafer and Carl I. Hovland (1961), *Social Judgment: Assimilation and Contrast Effects in Communication and Attitude Change*, New Haven, Connecticut: Yale University Press.

Stapel, Diederik A., and Jerry Suls (2004), "Method Matters: Effects of Explicit Versus Implicit Social Comparisons on Activation, Behavior, and Self-Views," *Journal of Personality and Social Psychology*, 87, 860.

Stapel, Diederik A., Willem Koomen and Joop Van der Pligt (1997), "Categories of Category Accessibility: The Impact of Trait Concept Versus Exemplar Priming on Person Judgments," *Journal of Experimental Social Psychology*, 33 (1), 47-76.

Warlop, Luc, and Joseph W. Alba (2004), "Sincere Flattery: Trade-Dress Imitation and Consumer Choice," *Journal of Consumer Psychology*, 14, 21-27.

Zaichkowsky, Judith L. (2006), *The Psychology Behind Trademark Infringement and Counterfeiting*, New Jersey: Lawrence Erlbaum Associates, Inc.

Contrast or Assimilation As a Result of Upward Social Comparison with Idealized Images: The Role of Mode of Exposure and Priming

Fang Wan, University of Manitoba, Canada
Tamara Ansons, University of Manitoba, Canada
Jason Leboe, University of Manitoba, Canada
Dirk Smeesters, Erasmus University, The Netherlands

EXTENDED ABSTRACT

The popular use of highly attractive women in advertising has received some support from consumer research in terms its positive impacts on product evaluation, ad evaluation and purchase intention (Belch et al. 1987; Kang and Herr 2006). However, this line of research is increasingly challenged by the mounting research evidence that exposure to idealized images in advertising media elicits upward social comparison, resulting in negative mood (e.g., Stice and Shaw 1994), decreased body satisfaction (see review Groesz et al. 2002), decreased self-assessed attractiveness (e.g., Smeesters and Mandel 2006) and even increased problematic eating patterns (e.g., Harrison 2000) among young women. At the same time, other researchers have documented that idealized images of female models can enhance women's body satisfaction and self esteem (e.g., Myers and Biocca 1992; Mills et al. 2002; Henderson-King et al. 2001). Our understanding of the processes and boundary conditions of positive and negative effects of idealized images on women's self perceptions has an important marketing implication: if the idealized images in advertising are detrimental to women's body and self esteem, how can products and brands endorsed by idealized female images be successfully marketed at and received by female consumers (Bower 2001)? Therefore, consumer researchers need to re-scrutinize the impact of idealized images on young women and resolve previous research discrepancies.

The task of this research is to examine the boundary conditions of positive and negative impacts of idealized images on young women. Whereas most research attention has been devoted to the negative effects of idealized images on self evaluations among young women (see review, Groesz et al. 2002), we are interested in examining the mechanism and processes that gives rise to other observations that exposure to idealized images can enhance self perceptions (e.g., Henderson-King et al. 2001; Meyers and Biocca 1992). Employing the framework of social comparison theory, we propose that social comparison process can take place via either an implicit or an explicit route. An implicit social comparison, when taking place automatically, or outside viewers' awareness, can lower viewers' self-perception and body satisfaction and lead to a *contrast effect*. However, when taking place within the scope of viewers' attention and awareness, an *explicit social comparison* will allow viewers' to engage in conscious efforts to boost their own self-esteem through counter-argument. Such an explicit social comparison, therefore, will lead to more positive self-perceptions and enhanced body satisfaction, resulting in an *assimilation effect*. We tested these propositions with three experiments.

The first experiment explored the role of mode of exposure to idealized images in triggering differential social comparison processes. To induce either implicit or explicit social comparison, participants were asked to engage in one of two tasks while being exposed to idealized images. Participants in the implicit social comparison group were led to believe that they were participating in a study that examined peoples' natural intuition about the types of sunglasses that are most suitable for different face shapes. In contrast, participants in the explicit social comparison group were asked to rate the attractiveness of each of the women. In line with our predictions, participants in the implicit social comparison group reported lower evaluations of their weight related body traits compared to participants in the explicit social comparison group.

To further explore this finding, our goal of Experiment 2 was to examine whether participants' evaluations of their weight related body traits could be modified by inducing either a positive or negative interpretive frame. We expected that altering the interpretive frame would not influence the participants in the explicit social comparison group since they would be able to shield themselves from the impact of the interpretive frame by being consciously aware of, therefore combating the negative impact of threatening upward social comparison. In contrast, we expected that the participants in the implicit social comparison group would be influenced by the interpretive frame, leading to a contrast effect when the interpretive frame is positive, and an attenuated contrast effect when the interpretive frame is negative. In line with our expectations, we found that participants in the explicit social comparison group were unaffected by the interpretive frame. However, participants in the implicit social comparison group were affected by the interpretive frame: their self-perception was more negative when the content of the priming task biases them to interpret characteristics of the idealized females positively than when the priming task encourages a more negative interpretive frame. Thus, our results suggest that after explicit exposure to idealized female images, participants are able to insulate themselves from the negative impact of these idealized female images, whereas after implicit exposure participants are not able to shield themselves from negative impact of these female images, but are influenced by inducing either a positive or negative interpretive frame.

To account for the differences found for the participants in the explicit and implicit social comparison groups in Experiments 1 and 2 we speculated that participants in explicit social comparison are more aware of the upward social comparison process and tend to engage in counter-arguments to insulate themselves from the negative impact of exposure to a highly attractive comparison target. However, engaging in ego-protective strategies during the explicit social comparison process is cognitively demanding, therefore, such explicit social comparison processes requires more cognitive resources than social comparison processes that are implicit. To test this notion, our third experiment was conducted to mainly examine the role of the availability of cognitive resources in modulating the impact of exposure to idealized female images on participants' self-evaluations. Supporting our predictions, participants found the sunglasses task more cognitively demanding, which, consequently, meant that they had fewer cognitive resources available to engage in conscious strategies and counter-arguments that would help in protecting them from the negative consequences of exposure to idealized female images.

Altogether, these three experiments contribute to our understanding of the impact of social comparison processes on self evaluations. Surprisingly, our results indicate that participants were best equipped to deal with exposure to idealized images when this exposure was explicit. Thus, rather counterintuitively, we have found that women may be most susceptible to the negative consequences of exposure to idealized female images precisely when they are not focusing on their level of attractiveness.

REFERENCES

Banaji, Mahzarin R., Curtis Hardin and Alexander J. Rothman (1993), "Implicit Stereotyping in Person Judgment," *Journal of Personality and Social Psychology*, 65 (August), 272-81.

Bargh, John A. (1982), " Attention and Automaticity in the Processing of Self-Relevant information," *Journal of Personality and Social Psychology*, 43 (September), 425-436.

_____ (1990), "Auto-motives: Preconscious Determinants of Social Interaction," in E. Tory Higgins and R. M. Sorrentino (Eds.), *Handbook of Motivation and Cognition*, Vol.2, pp93-130. New York: Guilford Press.

_____ (1994), "The Four Horsemen of Automaticity: Awareness, Efficiency, Intention and Control in Social Cognition," in Robert S. Wyer Jr. and T. K. Srull (Eds.), *Handbook of Social Cognition*, pp1-40. Hillsdale, NJ: Erlbaum.

_____ (2002), "Losing Consciousness: Automatic Influences on Consumer Judgment, Behavior and Motivation," *Journal of Consumer Research*, 29 (September), 280-285.

Bargh, John A., Mark Chen and Lara Burrows (1996), "Automaticity of Social Behavior: Direct Effects of Trait Construct and Stereotype Activation on Action," *Journal of Personality and Social Psychology*, 71 (August), 230-44.

Bargh, John A. and Melissa J. Ferguson (2000), "Beyond Behaviorism: On the Automaticity of High Mental Processes," *Psychological Bulletin*, 126(6), 925-45.

Bargh, John A., Peter M. Gollwitzer, Annette Lee-Chai, Kimberly Barndollar and Roman Trotschel (2001), "The Automatic Will: Nonconscious Activation and Pursuit of Behavioral Goals," *Journal of Personality and Social Psychology*, 81, 1014-1027.

Bower, Amanda B. (2001), "Highly Attractive Models in Advertising and the Women who Loathe them: The Implications of Negative Affect for Spokesperson Effectiveness," *Journal of Advertising*, 30 (3), 51-63.

Bodenhausen, Galen V. and Neil C. Macrae (1998). Stereotype activation and inhibition. In Robet. S. Wyer, Jr. (Ed.), Stereotype activation and inhibition: Advances in social cognition (Vol. 11, pp. 1-52). Mahwah, NJ: Erlbaum.

Cattarin, Jill A., J. Kevin Thompson, Carmen Thomas, and Robyn Williams (2000), "Body Image, Mood, and Televised Images of Attractiveness: The Role of Social Comparison," *Journal of Social and Clinical Psychology*, 19(2), 220-239.

Chartrand, Tanya (2005), "The Role of Conscious Awareness in Consumer Behavior," *Journal of Consumer Psychology*, 15(3), 203-210.

Duke, Lisa (2002), "Get Real!: Cultural Relevance and Resistance to the Mediated Feminine Ideal," *Psychology and Marketing*, 19(2), 211-233.

Engeln-Maddox, Renee (2005), "Cognitive Responses to Idealized Media Images of Women: The Relationship of Social Comparison and Critical Processing to Body Image Disturbance in College Women," *Journal of Social and Clinical Psychology*, 24(8), 1114-1138.

Faludi, Susan (1991). *Backlash: The Undeclared War Against American Women*. New York: Crown.

Franzoi, Stephen L. and Stephanie A. Shields (1984), "The Body Esteem Scale: Multidimensional Structure and Sex Differences in a College Population," *Journal of Personality Assessment*, 48 (April), 173-78.

Fredrickson, Barbra L. and Tomi Ann Roberts, "Objectification Theory: Toward Understanding Women's Lived Experiences and Mental Health Risks," *Psychology of Women Quarterly*, 21 (June), 173-206.

Freedman, Rita J. (1986). *Beauty Bound*. Lexington, MA: D. C. Heath.

Freedman, Rita J. (1988). *Body Love: Learning to Like Our Looks and Ourselves*. New York: Harper & Row.

Garner, David M., Paul E. Garfinkel, Donna Schwartz and Michael Thompson (1980), "Cultural expectations of thinness in women,"*Psychological Reports, 47*, 483-491.

Garner, David M (1997), "The 1997 Body Image Survey Results," *Psychological Today, 30(1),33-84.*

Groesz, Lisa M., Michael P. Levine and Sarah K. Murnen (2002), "The Effect of Experimental Presentation of Thin Media Images on Body Satisfaction: A Meta-Analytic Review," *International Journal of Eating Disorder*, 31, 1-16.

Harrison, Kristen (2000), "The body electric: Thin-ideal media and eating disorders in adolescents," in *Journal of Communication, 51 (2)*, 119-143.

Henderson-King, Donna, Eaaron Henderson King and Lisa Hoffman (2001), "Media Images and Women's Self-Evaluations: Social Context and Importance of Attractiveness as Moderators," *Personality and Social Psychology Bulletin*, 27(11), 1407-1416.

Kang, Yong Soon and Paul M. Herr (2006), "Beauty and the Beholder: Toward an Integrative Model of Communication Source Effects," *Journal of Consumer Research*, 33 (June), 123-130.

Levine, Michael (1999). Media literacy in the prevention of disordered eating. Paper presented at the annual convention of the American Psychological Association, Boston.

Martin, Mary C. and James W. Gentry (1997), "Stuck in the Model Trap: The Effects of Beautiful Models in Ads on Female Pre-Adolescents and Adolescents," *Journal of Advertising*, 26(June), 19-33.

Meyers, Phillip & Frank A. Biocca (1992). The Elastic Body Image: The Effect of Television Advertising and Programming on Body Image Distortions in Young Women. *Journal of Communication, 42 (3), 108-133.*

Mills, Jennifer S., Janet Polivy, C. Peter Herman, and Marika Tiggemann (2002), "Effects of Exposure to Thin Media Images: Evidence of Self-Enhancement Among Restrained Eaters," *Personality and Social Psychology Bulletin*, 28(December), 1687-1699.

Richins, Marsha L. (1991), "Social Comparison and the Idealized Images of Advertising," *Journal of Consumer Research, 19* (June), 71-83.

Schwartz, Norbert (2004), "Metacognitive Experiences in Consumer Judgment and Decision Making," *Journal of Consumer Psychology*, 14, 332-348.

Smeesters, Dirk and Naomi Mandel (2006), "Positive and Negative Media Image Effects on the Self," *Journal of Consumer Research*, 32 (March), 576-82.

Sypeck, Mia F., James J. Gray, Sarah F. Etu, Anthony H. Ahrens, James E. Mosimann and Claire V. Wiseman (2006), "Cultural representations of thinness in women, redux: *Playboy* magazine's depiction of beauty from 1979 to 1999," *Body Image, 3(3)*, 229-235.

Stapel, Diederik A. and Willem Koomen (2001), "Lets not Forget the Past When We Go to the Future: On Our Knowledge of Knowledge Accessibility Effects," In G. Moskowitz (Eds.), *Cognitive Social Psychology* (pp.229-246). Mahwah, NJ: Erlbaum.

Stapel, Diederik A. and Jerry Suls (2004), "Method Matters: Effects of Deliberate versus Spontaneous Social Comparisons on Activation," *Journal of Personality and Social Psychology,* 87 (December), 860-75.

Stice, Eric and Heather E. Shaw (1994), "Adverse effects of the media portrayed thin-ideal on women and linkages to bulimic symptomatology," *Journal of Social and Clinical Psychology, 13 (3)*, 288-308.

Wolf, Naomi (1991). *The Beauty Myth: How Images of Beauty Are Used Against Women*. New York: William Morrow.

The Role of Social Comparison for Maximizers and Satisficers: Wanting the Best or Wanting to Be the Best

Kimberlee Weaver, Virginia Tech, USA
Norbert Schwarz, University of Michigan, USA
Keenan Cottone, University of Michigan, USA
Kimberly Daniloski, Virginia Tech, USA

EXTENDED ABSTRACT

The distinction between maximizing, attempting to examine every option before determining which choice is best, and satisficing, choosing the first option one comes across that meets a threshold of acceptability, was first posited by Herbert Simon in the 1950s. More recent work on the topic has led to the conceptualization of a maximization individual differences scale (Schwartz et al., 2002) as well as assessments of the impact of maximization behaviors on both objective and subjective outcomes (Schwartz et al., 2002; Iyengar, Wells, & Schwartz, 2006; Parker, Bruine de Bruin, & Fischhoff, 2007). The current paper seeks to further this literature by addressing a question that previous work has left open–the underlying motivation behind maximizing versus satisficing behavior.

Research on maximization behaviors has revealed that they tend to be highly correlated with a reliance on social comparison information (Parker, Bruine de Bruin, & Fischhoff, 2007). As Schwartz et al. (2002) point out, "whereas 'good enough' usually is judged in absolute terms, 'the best possible' may…require social comparison" (p. 1184). While social comparison can certainly be a useful, and even necessary, way to gain information about what choice is best, there is an alternate explanation for maximizers' reliance on it. Instead of seeking social comparison information in an effort to discover the best choice in an objective sense, it is possible that maximizers are seeking social comparison information to ensure they are the best in a relative sense. In other words, instead of being motivated to *find* the absolute best, maximizers may be motivated to *be* the best in a social rivalry. The current studies seek to parse apart these two motivational possibilities by explicitly pitting them against each other in a series of experiments.

Across three studies, maximizers and satisficers were given a series of two hypothetical versions of the world (an absolute choice and a positional choice) and were asked which one they would prefer (adapted from Solnick & Hemenway, 1998). For example:

- You make $60,000 per year and nearly all of your co-workers make $80,000 (absolute).
- You make $50,000 per year and nearly all of your co-workers make $30,000 (positional).

In the first option, subjects have a higher yearly income than in the second option (an absolute best), but they are making less than those around them. In the second option, though subjects have a lower income in an absolute sense, they are making more than those around them (a positional best). Results from Study 1 showed, across a wide range of scenarios, that maximizers are more willing than satisficers to sacrifice objective superiority in order to be the best relative to others.

Studies 2 and 3 presented respondents with absolute or positional choices while also manipulating the public visibility of the choice outcome. If maximizers place more weight on social comparison as a way to determine what *is* the best, then the social visibility of the outcome should be irrelevant and they should choose the same option in public as in private. In contrast, if maximizers place more weight on social comparison for positional standing, then they should be more likely to choose positionally when others will know about the decision outcome, but may instead choose to maximize objective quality when the outcome is private.

Confirming predictions, Study 2 showed a significant *Visibility X Maximization Score* interaction, $\chi^2(1)=4.66$, p<.05. Overall, maximizers were more likely to choose the positional option when the outcome of the choice was publicly visible than when it was private and known only to the decision maker, while satisficers' choices were unaffected by the visibility manipulation. Study 3 replicated this finding with products that were either naturally publicly visible (e.g., sunglass, car, cell phone) or naturally private (e.g., pajamas, ice maker, mattress).

The results from these three studies suggest that the motivations of maximizers are multi-faceted. While maximizers tend to make more positional choices than satisficers when their choices are publicly visible, this effect is not found when the outcome of the choice is private and known only to the decision maker. Future research should examine the individual factors of the maximization scale to ascertain whether there are "types" of maximizers who are more or less susceptible to the effects of public visibility. Overall, the current studies add complexity to the current literature on maximizing and decision making. Rather than focusing on the "best" option, three studies indicate that the motivation behind maximization behaviors can change across contexts. When social rivalry is salient, maximizers appear to be motivated to be the best in a relative sense. When social rivalry is not salient, maximizers appear to be motivated to choose the best an objective sense of the word.

REFERENCES

Iyengar, Sheena, Wells, Rebecca, & Schwartz, Barry (2006), "Doing better but feeling worse: Looking for the "best" job undermines satisfaction," *Psychological Science*, 17(2), 143-150.

Parker, Andrew, Bruine de Bruin, Wandi, Fischhoff, Baruch (2007), "Maximizers versus satisficers: Decision making styles, competence, and outcomes," *Judgment and Decision Making*, 2, 342-350.

Schwartz, Barry, Ward, Andrew, Monterosso, John, Lyubomirsky, Sonja, White, Katherine, & Lehman, Darrin (2002), "Maximizing versus satisficing: Happiness is a matter of choice," *Journal of Personality and Social Psychology*, 83(5), 1178-1197.

Simon, Herbert (1955), "A behavioral model of rational choice," *Quarterly Journal of Economics*, 59, 99-118.

Simon, Herbert (1956), "Rational choice and the structure of the environment," *Psychological Review*, 63, 129-138.

Simon, Herbert (1957), *Models of man, social and rational: Mathematical essays on rational human behavior*. New York: Wiley.

Solnick, Sara, & Hemenway, David (1998), "Is more always better?: A survey about positional concerns," *Journal of Economic Behavior and Organization*, 37(3), 373-83.

When Will People Tell You Something You Do Not Know?

Lei Huang, Dalhousie University, Canada
Sema Barlas, McGill University, Canada[1]

EXTENDED ABSTRACT

Word-of-mouth (WOM) is considered to be an important source of information for individual decisions based on a widely held assumption that other people can bring diverse perspectives to the individual's decision process (Heath and Gonzalez 1995). For any given decision problem, individuals may hold unique knowledge that may be acquired through personal experiences as well as common knowledge that may be obtained from mass media. According to Grecian norms of conversations (Grice 1975) and information theory (Shannon 1964), people should exchange unique information in order to maximize the informational content of available information for decisions. Also, at the deliberate level, people agree to these prescriptions and ascertain that it is the unique information that should be exchanged in interpersonal communications. However, extant empirical research demonstrated that "what people talk about" in actual conversations is not always what is the most informative for decisions. For instance, overwhelming evidence has been accumulated in the literature demonstrating that conversations are dominated by the information that members hold in common before discussions, the information that is consistent with members' pre-existing preferences (Stasser and Titus 1985, 1987), and the information that is extreme or negative. In addition, Huang and Barlas (2006) demonstrated that people exchange emotional and recreational information more often than cognitive and utilitarian information in WOM in order to establish social connections.

This paper investigates the exchange of unique information in WOM depending on the nature of this information (e.g., whether it is emotional or cognitive). Note that bias for emotional information in WOM reported by Huang and Barlas (2006) might be observed because emotional information (e.g., consumption experiences) is often uniquely held by participants. If this is the case, one would expect that the bias for emotional information should diminish when emotional information is commonly held by WOM participants. However, causal observation suggests that bias for emotional information is amplified when it is shared knowledge among individuals. For instance, most political conversations revolve around emotional topics (e.g., the gay marriage issue in the 2004 U.S. elections). Candidates' positions on issues that spur emotions among the voters are widely communicated by the mass media, and therefore, are likely to be common information among voters, whereas cognitive information (e.g., foreign aid) is likely to be the unique knowledge held by individual voters since it is often not publicized. Also, much literature suggests that people try to validate the messengers as well as the messages by talking about the commonly shared information (Stasser and Titus 1985) in order to validate that their partners are similar to them with respect to interests. Indeed, talking about common topics establishes social connections among participants in the same way sharing of emotional information. Thus, this paper aims to tease out the effects of information types (emotional versus cognitive) and the distribution of information among communicators (common versus unique) on the sampling of information for conversations and choices. We hypothesize that common information is exchanged more often than unique information in conversations; however, people demonstrate strong preference for common emotional information, but exchange unique information socially when it is emotional.

We used a political decision-making task where participants chose between two candidates for the Student President position after discussing candidates' profiles. Participants exchanged information with two other individuals before deciding to cast their vote. 120 participants (64 females) were recruited from undergraduate business courses as groups working on a class project together. Some groups were self-selected friends and others were formed by the course instructor choosing randomly among acquaintances. The 40 three-person groups were equally divided into two WOM conditions: common-cognitive-unique-emotional (briefed as common-cognitive) or common-emotional-unique-cognitive (briefed as common-emotional) condition. A control condition of 99 volunteered participants performed the same tasks as did the WOM participants except for exchanging information with others.

In the common-cognitive condition, the profile descriptions of electoral candidates included the same cognitive information across members, but emotional information was unique to the profile each member received. In contrast, identical emotional information was included in the profiles of all members in the common-emotional condition while each member received unique cognitive information. All participants were explicitly informed that their information was not complete before the discussion. All conversations were audio-taped for further content analysis.

Our results support the widely accepted conclusion in the literature that common information (mean=0.58) is exchanged more often than unique information (mean=0.42) in conversations. However, our results also suggest that unique emotional information (mean=0.61) that would facilitate interpersonal connections is, indeed, shared with others more often than common cognitive information (mean=0.39), but still less than common emotional information (mean=0.77). Thus one major contribution of this paper is the finding that emotional information enjoys a sampling advantage in WOM; this bias is inflated when emotional information is also commonly held by the members prior to conversations (e.g., as in online user groups). That is, the nature of the information plays a more significant role in conversations than the distribution of information among individuals. Additionally, these biases in information sampling lead to similar biases in the influence of information on decisions. There was a strong preference for the candidate who was favorable on the basis of common emotional information. By contrast, preference for the candidate who was favorable on the basis of cognitive information was not strong because participants exchanged the unique emotional information in conversations. The biases reported above were more pronounced when members in the group were similar with respect to the importance of emotional and cognitive attributes in their decisions. However, neither gender nor social ties (friends versus acquaintance) had significant impact.

Most existing research in the political marketing focuses on the impact of information valence on voting behavior. Differing from previous research, results from our study suggest that the nature of the information has considerable impact on conversations about candidates as well as on the votes and the size of this impact

---

[1]This article is based on the first author's dissertation research and is funded by a grant provided by the Social Sciences and Humanities Research Council of Canada. Authors are grateful for the comments of Joshua Klayman, Jackie Gnepp, Ashesh Mukherjee, Ulf Bockenholt, and Renaud Legoux on earlier versions of this article.

varies depending on the distribution of information among communicators. By focusing on the affective versus cognitive nature of information, our paper thus opens a new direction for future research to discover what other aspects of information determines the dynamics of voters' WOM behavior and their subsequent ballots. In conclusion, our findings suggest that WOM participants herd into commonly known emotional-options more often than individuals making the same choices privately. Also, it appears that, although cognitive information may inform one person, the emotional information engage many individuals.

REFERENCES

Grice, H. Paul (1975), "Logic and Conversation," in *Syntax and Semantics 3: Speech Acts*, Peter Cole and Jerry L. Morgan, eds. New York: Seminar Press.

Heath, Chip and Rich Gonzalez (1995), "Interaction with Others Increases Decision Confidence but not Decision Quality: Evidence against Information Collection Views of Interactive Decision Making," *Organizational Behavior and Human Decision Processes*, 61, 305-326.

Huang, Lei and Sema Barlas, "Sharing of Hedonic and Utilitarian Information in Word-of-Mouth Communications," in *APA 114th Annual Convention Program 2006* (Society for Consumer Psychology Annual Conference), New Orleans: American Psychological Association, p. 229.

Shannon, Claude E. (1964), *The Mathematical Theory of Communication*, Urbana University of Illinois Press.

Stasser, Garold and William Titus (1985), "Pooling of Unshared Information in Group Decision Making: Biased Information Sampling during Discussion," *Journal of Personality and Social Psychology*, 48 (6), 1467-1478.

_____ and _____ (1987), "Effects of Information Load and Percentage of Shared Information on the Dissemination of Unshared Information during Group Discussion," *Journal of Personality and Social Psychology*, 53 (1), 81–93.

What Do People Talk About in Word-of-Mouth Communications?

Sema Barlas, McGill University, Canada
Lei Huang, Dalhousie University, Canada[1]

EXTENDED ABSTRACT

Consumers perceive Word-of-Mouth information (WOM) as more credible than marketer-originated information (Bickart and Schindler 2001). Consequently, extant research focused on the antecedents and outcomes of WOM, and the question of what information consumers exchange with others (depending on "why", "about what", and "to whom" they are talking) has not received much research attention. It has been commonly assumed that people engage in WOM to improve quality of decisions, and thus, exchange diagnostic information to reduce their uncertainty with respect to offerings (Herr, Kardes and Kim 1991). Recent research indicates that people also engage in WOM to establish social connections (Sassenberg 2002). This paper aims to demonstrate that the social bonding goal increases the value of engaging marketing information in WOM. In our context, information is considered as socially engaging whenever it spurs shared emotions among communicators (e.g., funny or interesting information). More importantly, we also demonstrate that social-bonding efforts in WOM depend on "to whom" (e.g., friends vs. acquaintances) and "about what" people could talk (e.g., nature of marketing information).

According to our theoretical framework, people make trade-offs between different communication goals, depending on the characteristics of available topics and relationships among the communicators. Availability of highly engaging topics stimulates the social-bonding goal, and availability of relatively significant incentives resulting from attending to informative topics, facilitates the uncertainty reduction goal. Similarly, establishing social bonds via talking about engaging marketing information might be more prevalent among people with weak social-ties than among people with strong-social ties, especially when the given information is not about product benefits, and thus, does not trigger conversations about intimate consumption experiences (e.g., a funny joke in an advertisement). That is, impersonal marketing information might be a good conversation topic among strangers who lack other common topics. Lastly, we assume that goals influence selection of particular topics for conversations; therefore, observed bias for engaging information in social settings is an indication of the social bonding goal. More specifically, we predict that:

H1: Engaging information becomes significantly more valuable when it is consumed socially than when it is consumed individually.

H2: Acquaintances that are in need of social connections are more likely to promote the social bonding goal via engaging conversations about marketing information than other goals.

H3: The choice of engaging option increases over time during the WOM episode and conversations at early stages of a WOM episode exert disproportional influence on later choices.

[1]This article is based on the second author's dissertation research and is funded by a grant provided by the Social Sciences and Humanities Research Council of Canada. Authors are grateful for the comments of Joshua Klayman, Jackie Gnepp, Ashesh Mukherjee, Ulf Bockenholt, and Renaud Legoux on earlier versions of this article.

We applied an experimental paradigm in which participants were asked to choose between furniture and personal ads for proofreading to earn between $5 and $9, depending on the number of misspelled words they could identify over ten trials. Furniture and personal ads had, respectively, seven and three misspelled words. The task required participants to make a tradeoff between engaging conversations with others and their individual earning/savings as in consumer choice between discount ads and humorous ads. Furthermore, although participants were told in advance that furniture ads had more spelling mistakes and that personal ads were more interesting, they did not know the exact number of spelling errors; nor did they know how much more interesting personal ads were relative to furniture ads. Finally, there were two independent conditions in the study: subjects made their choices either privately or together with three other participants, in which case they could talk about the ads. All participants distributed 100 points between the spelling-error rate and the content to reflect the importance of these attributes in their choice of ads at the end of the study and indicated the number of people they were friends with in their group. All conversations were audio-taped for further content analysis.

Data support our predictions ($p<.05$). In general, engaging information became significantly more valuable when it was consumed socially than when it was consumed individually (H1) and the advantage of engaging information in social setting increased in conversations with weak ties (H2). More specifically, the importance of the content in making choices was significantly larger in the WOM condition than in the individual condition, suggesting that WOM participants intentionally shifted their goals in the direction of the social bonding goal. The intentional shift was larger for acquaintances than for friends. Also, WOM participants talked about the most relevant information for decisions, the spelling-error rate/money, only 23% of the time despite the fact that the importance of the spelling-error rate in making their choices was 42%. Note that the importance of money in the individual condition was 68%. That is, WOM groups deliberately switched their interest or preferences in favor of content, but they conversed about money even less than what would be expected given the intentional shifts in goals. In contrast to the conversations about money, intentional shifts determined the frequency of conversations about personal ads to a great extent; participants talked about personal advertisements 60% of the time and the importance of the content was 58% (32% for individuals); however, conversations systematically diverged from the intentional shifts in goals depending on the social ties. In particular, exclusively-acquaintance (mean=0.74) and exclusively-friend (mean=0.66) groups talked about the personal advertisements significantly more than the mixed groups (mean=0.56) did. Also, exclusively-friends groups talked about personal advertisements less than they intended to whereas exclusively-acquaintance groups talked about personal advertisements more than they intended to. Furthermore, WOM participants chose personal ads more than they intended to, compared with individuals. While the individual goal determined the initial choices, later choices were governed by the goal of the group and the nature of the conversations during the early stages of communications (H3).

Overall, our results suggest that WOM participants herd into engaging options disproportionately more with conversations over time in comparison to the individual decision-makers. Furthermore, acquaintances choose the engaging option more than friends especially at the beginning of the WOM episode. However, the influence of social ties on the herding behavior at later stages of WOM is absorbed by the group level intentional shifts in goals and conversations. Interestingly, biased sampling of information in conversations and its effect on choices diminishes in diverse groups.

REFERENCES

Bickart, Barbara and Robert M. Schindler (2001), "Internet Forums as Influential Sources of consumer Information," *Journal of Interactive Marketing*, 15 (3), 31-40.

Herr, Paul M., Frank R. Kardes, and John Kim (1991), "Effects of Word-of-Mouth and Product-Attribute Information on Persuasion: An Accessibility-Diagnosticity Perspective," *Journal of Consumer Research*, 17 (March), 454-62.

Sassenberg, Kai (2002), "Common Bond and Common Identity Groups on the Internet: Attachment and Normative Behavior in On-Topic and Off-Topic Chats," *Group Dynamics: Theory, Research, and Practice*, 6 (1), 27-37.

Too Much to Take In? The Role of Advertising Variables, Emotions and Visual Attention in Consumer Learning for Really New Products

Stephanie Feiereisen, Aston Business School, UK
Veronica Wong, Aston Business School, UK
Amanda J. Broderick, Coventry Business School, UK

EXTENDED ABSTRACT

"Learning is not attained by chance; it must be sought for with ardor and attended to with diligence" (Eugene S. Wilson)

RNPs create new product categories or at least significantly expand existing ones, and can lead to major shifts in market shares (Lehmann, 1994). For instance, Personal Digital Assistants (PDAs) qualified as RNPs at the time of launch. RNPs are a priority for most companies as, without the success of such novel products, market shares ultimately drop off (Hoeffler, 2003). The difficulty for consumers to comprehend the nature of a RNP using their existing cognitive knowledge structures can be a significant barrier to the success of the product, due to their highly innovative nature. Past research has shown that two learning processes may help consumers understand RNPs: analogical learning (Roehm and Sternthal, 2001) and mental simulation (Dahl and Hoeffler, 2004). However, existing studies have typically examined responses to advertising for RNPs conveyed using words. As decision-making research has shown that visualization tools can make product concepts more accessible (Lurie and Mason, 2007), we seek to add to the extant literature by determining whether advertising strategies rendered by pictorials may be more effective. We also argue that emotional influence is likely to be greatest during the early stages of product learning (Wood and Moreau, 2006). Therefore, acknowledging the role of emotions should contribute to a better understanding of consumer learning for RNPs. Furthermore, the use of an unbiased physiological measure of visual attention may decrease the uncertainty involved when investigating consumer learning processes by offering a 'window to the mind' (Pieters, Wedel and Zhang, 2007).

The present research extends the literature on consumer responses to RNPs by exploring a) advertising variables that can be manipulated to enhance consumer comprehension of the product (learning strategy and presentation format), b) the extent to which an emotion (i.e. discouragement) acts as a mediator between the advertising variables and product comprehension and c) the explanatory role of visual attention in learning processes for RNPs.

The knowledge transfer paradigm identifies an analogy as the comparison between a "base" and a "target" which share relations but lack common attributes (Gentner, 1989). Mental simulation is defined as the nonverbal representation of perceptual information and sensory experiences in memory (Baddeley, 1986). Analogies and mental simulation have been proved useful to deal with uncertain environments (Hoeffler, 2003) and therefore should help consumers learn about RNPs. However, the academic interest for analogies and mental simulations has largely been confined to the use of words. Research in visual syntax indicates that one of the main properties of visual communication is its lack of explicit means to identify how images relate to each other (Messaris, 1997). Two types of inferences may be drawn from a claim: strong and weak implicatures (Sperber and Wilson, 1986). Strong implicatures call for one interpretation which varies little across individuals whereas weak implicatures yield a wider range of inferences. Using analogies or mental simulations conveyed by images should trigger weak implicatures (Messaris, 1997), hence a risk that consumers lack guidance to merge the RNP with their existing usage patterns.

Contrarily, the explicitness of verbal syntax may help respondents to vicariously experience the consequences of product use (Walker and Olson, 1997). Thus, we posit that both mental simulation and analogical learning strategies are more likely to increase product comprehension when conveyed by words rather than by pictures.

Moreover, drawing on the E3 model of emotional influence (Wood and Moreau, 2006), we argue that the difficulties involved in learning about complex new products will trigger strong emotional responses such as discouragement, which in turn will affect product comprehension. We hypothesize that an increase in discouragement will mediate the effects of presentation format and learning strategy on product comprehension.

We also intend to demonstrate how visual attention can contribute to our understanding of the links between conceptual and perceptual analyses when learning for a RNP. We use the physiology of reading literature (Rayner, 1998), and the inverse inference model (Feng, 2003) with the aim to discriminate the state of higher-order cognitive processing from observed patterns of eye movements. We hypothesize that when the message is conveyed with words attention increments to the advertising message will reflect an increase in product comprehension, whereas when the message is conveyed with pictures an increase in attention will indicate confusion.

A total of eight hundred fifty three respondents participated in Study 1. The design was a 3 within-subjects (learning strategy: mental simulation vs. analogy vs. no analogy/ no mental simulation) x 2 between-subjects (presentation format: words vs. pictures) X 3 between-subjects (product: Digipen vs. Video glasses vs. Intelligent Oven). Each participant was thus exposed to three adverts. Study 1 provides us with two important results. First, as expected, both analogies and mental simulations enhance product comprehension to a greater extent when conveyed using words than using pictures. An analysis per product reveals that the video glasses are a notable exception, which suggests that the combination of mental simulation and pictures may actually facilitate comprehension for RNPs of a more hedonic nature. Second, discouragement partially mediates the effects of presentation format and learning strategy on product comprehension.

Study 2 measures individuals' visual attention to adverts for RNPs using an eye-tracking technique. The results suggest that when the message is conveyed using words, an increase in attention to the message reflects enhanced comprehension for the RNP. However, when the message is conveyed using pictures, an increase in attention reflects confusion towards the nature of the product. This study adds evidence to a growing body of literature which shows that eye movements reflect higher order cognitive processes (Pieters, Wedel and Zhang, 2007). Our research also demonstrates that the link between attention and comprehension is not always straightforward as an increase in attention may actually reflect confusion as opposed to comprehension.

REFERENCES

Baddeley, Alan D. (1986), *Working Memory*, New York: Oxford University Press.

Dahl, Darren W. and Steve Hoeffler (2004), "Visualizing the Self: Exploring the Potential Benefits and Drawbacks for New Product Evaluation", *Journal of Product Innovation Management*, 21 (4), 259-267.

Feng, Gary (2003), "From Eye Movement to Cognition: Toward a General Framework of Inference, Comment on Liechty et al., 2003", *Psychometrika*, 68 (4), 551-556.

Gentner, Dedre (1989), "The Mechanisms of Analogical Learning". In S. Vosniadou and A. Ortony (Eds.) *Similarity and analogical reasoning* (pp. 199-241), London: Cambridge University Press.

Hoeffler, Steve (2003), "Measuring Preferences for Really New Products", *Journal of Marketing Research*, 40 (4), 406-420.

Lehmann, Donald R. (1994), "Characteristics of "Really" New Products", paper presented at the Marketing Science Institute Conference, Boston.

Lurie, Nicholas H., and Charlotte H. Mason (2007), "Visual Representation: Implications for Decision Making", *Journal of Marketing*, 71 (1), 160-177.

Messaris, Paul (1997), *Visual Persuasion: The Role of Images in Advertising*, Sage Publications.

Pieters, Rik, Michel Wedel and Jie Zhang (2007), "Optimal Feature Advertising Design Under Competitive Clutter", *Management Science*, 53 (11), 1815-1828.

Rayner, Keith (1998), "Eye Movements in Reading and Information Processing: 20 years of research", Psychological Bulletin, *124 (3),* 372-422.

Roehm, Michelle L. and Brian Sternthal (2001), "The Moderating Effect of Knowledge and Resources on the Persuasive Impact of Analogies", *Journal of Consumer Research*, 28 (2), 257-272.

Sperber, Deirdre and Dan Wilson (1986), *Relevance: Communication and Cognition*, Oxford: Basil Blackwell.

Walker, Beth A. and Jerry C. Olson (1997), "The Activated Self in Consumer Behavior: A Cognitive Structure Perspective", *Research in Consumer Behavior*, 8, 135-171.

Wood, Stacey L. and C. Page Moreau (2006), "From Fear to Loathing? How Emotion Influences the Evaluation and Early Use of Innovations", *Journal of Marketing*, 70 (3), 44-57.

Enough is Enough! Or Is It? Factors that Impact Switching Intentions In Extended Service Transactions

Keith S. Coulter, Clark University, USA

EXTENDED ABSTRACT

Research has documented that customers leave corporations and service providers for a variety of reasons (Bolton 1998). Keveaney (1995) found that core service failures and service-encounter failures were the two most common "determinant incidents" that cause customers to terminate service relationships. In the case of extended service transactions (which typically occur over a period of hours, days, or even weeks), a critical determinant incident may continue over a prolonged period of time, or the service transaction may continue after the critical incident has occurred. Thus, even though a determinant incident has led the customer to decide to terminate the service relationship, the decision to terminate the relationship may later be revoked, depending upon the service provider's reaction(s) to the core service failure.

We posit that that a negative incident such as an extended service *delay* may be perceived as a core service failure that can culminate in service dissolution (Edvardsson and Roos 2001; Roos, Edvardsson, and Gustafsson 2004). Employee response to that service failure (i.e., service recovery efforts) may or may not serve to overturn the decision to terminate the service relationship (Hess, Ganesan, and Klein 2003). Because the extended service encounter is on-going, the customer/provider relationship may reach a point where even satisfactory recovery efforts may not be sufficient to prevent the customer from seeking dissolution. Thus we propose that (H1): As the length of the core service delay increases, satisfactory recovery efforts will be less likely to negate subsequent switching intentions.

In addition, because a core service failure (delay) that occurs early in an extended service transaction gives the firm and its employees more *opportunity* to respond, we expect that:

(H2): As the core service delay occurs later within an extended service transaction, satisfactory recovery efforts will be less likely to negate subsequent switching intentions.

Various factors may impact whether a specific service failure recovery attempt is likely to be judged as "satisfactory." These factors may be classified in terms of four recovery attributes-compensation, response speed, apology, and initiation (Smith, Bolton and Wagner 1999; Smith and Bolton 2002). Because in the case of extended service encounters the consumer is frequently unable to exit the transaction before its scheduled conclusion, and because customer-initiated complaints are likely to be less necessary due to the fact that front-line personnel have a greater period of time over which to recognize the service failure, we expect that (H3): response time and initiation will be less important than compensation or an apology in driving customer satisfaction.

Customers assume lower service provider inputs for controllable compared with uncontrollable failures, and they therefore expect greater recovery efforts by the service provider in order to restore equity to the exchange (Hess, Ganesan, and Klein 2003). In the case of extended service transactions, however, there may come a point where controllability of the situation becomes a moot point, and *no* amount of recovery effort is likely to lead to customer satisfaction. Thus we expect that: (H4) as the length of the core service delay increases, controllability will be less likely to have a positive impact on satisfactory recovery efforts.

Airline passengers (n= 451) who had experienced "significant" travel delays during the period from September 2006 to June 2007 filled out an on-line survey that provided retrospective accounts of their experience at different points in time. Customer satisfaction with the recovery effort as well as the four satisfaction antecedents were assessed with measures consistent with prior research (Bitner and Hubber 1994; Taylor 1994; Smith, Bolton, and Wagner 1999). Length of service delay was estimated for five different time periods: a) prior to arriving at the airport, b) prior to boarding the flight, c) after boarding the flight but prior to takeoff, d) in-flight prior to landing, and e) after landing but prior to gate arrival. The length of delay measure was formed by summing across categories; the time of delay variable was formed by selecting the category with the greatest number of minutes. Changes in switching intention were assessed by comparing intentions at the time period of greatest delay to those at the time of questionnaire item completion.

Of our total sample of 451 passengers, 91% (n= 410) expressed a greater intention to stay with their present service provider at time period two (M=5.12) than at time period one (M=2.63). Because the tendency to negate switching behavior was defined as a *positive* change in intentions, only those subjects who indicated this positive change (n=410) were included in further analyses. We first examined the impact of satisfactory recovery efforts on (negated) switching intentions utilizing OLS regression. The overall regression equation as well as the satisfaction independent variable was significant. We next examined the impact of the five independent variables on satisfaction. Again the overall regression equation (as well as all independent variables) was significant. The magnitude of the beta coefficients suggested that compensation and apology have a greater impact on satisfaction than response speed or initiation; thus H3 was supported.

We then employed hierarchical regression to examine our remaining hypotheses. The procedure involved constructing regression models that included main effect terms for all independent variables, as well as product terms representing each moderator effect. After calculating models containing only the main effects of the independent variables, each product term (i.e., moderator effect) was entered individually. The key test was whether the product term accounted for a significant amount of incremental variance, and whether the sign of the interaction terms was in the predicted (negative) direction. Results supported H1 and H2, but H4 was not supported. Overall, the two significant interaction terms accounted for nearly 9% incremental variance. We also replicated our H1-H2 results utilizing only that subset of subjects whose intentions changed by +5 or greater.

Overall, our results provide insights into those factors that impact the relationships between length of core service failure, time of core service failure, and satisfaction with service recovery efforts. These interrelationships are shown to impact customers' decisions to dissolve a service relationship.

REFERENCES

Bansai, H.S. and Shirley Taylor (1999), "The Service Provider Switching Model (SPSM)," *Journal of Services Research* 2(2), 200-218.

Berry, Leonard L. (1995), "Relationship Marketing of Services-Growing Interest, Emerging Perspectives," *Journal of the Academy of Marketing Science*, 23 (4), 236-245.

Bitner, M.J., Booms, B.H. and Tetreault, M.S. (1990), "The Service Encounter: Diagnosing Favorable and Unfavorable Incidents," *Journal of Marketing*, 54, 71-84.

Bitner, Mary Jo, and Hubbert, Amy. R. (1994), "Encounter Satisfaction Versus Overall Satisfaction Versus Quality: The Customer's Voice," in *Service Quality: New Directions in Theory and Practice*, Eds. Roland T. Rust and Richard Oliver, Thousand Oaks, CA: Sage, 72-94.

Bolton, R.N. (1998), "A Dynamic Model of the Duration of the Customer's Relationship with a Continuous Service Provider: The Role of Satisfaction," *Marketing Science*, 17, 45-65.

Boulding, William, Kalra, Ajay, Staelin, R., and Zeithaml, V.A. (1993), "A Dynamic Process Model of Service Quality: From Expectations to Behavioral Intentions," *Journal of Marketing Research*, 30, pp. 7-27.

Clark, Gary L., Peter Kaminski, and David Rink (1992) "Consumer Complaints: Advice on How Companies Should Respond Based on an Empirical Study," *Journal of Services Marketing*, 6 (1), 41-50.

Coulter, R.A. and Ligas, M. (2000), "The Long Good-bye: The Dissolution of Customer-Service Provider Relationships," *Psychology and Marketing*, 17 (8), 669-695.

Dube, Laurette and Michael S. Morgan (1998), "Capturing the Dynamics of In-process Consumption Emotions and Satisfaction in Extended Service Transactions," *International Journal of Research in Marketing*, 15 (4), 309-320.

Durrande-Moreau, A. (1999), "Waiting for Service: Ten Years of Empirical Research," *International Journal of Service Industry Management*, 10 (2), 171-189.

Edvardsson, Bo and Inger Roos (2001), "Critical incident techniques: Towards a framework for analysing the criticality of critical incidents," *International Journal of Service Industry Management* 12 (3), 251-268.

Gronroos, Christian (1988), "Service Quality: The Six Criteria of Good Perceived Service Quality," *Review of Business* 9 (Winter), 10-13.

Hess, Ronald L., Shankar Ganesan, and Noreen M. Klein (2003), "Service Failure and Recovery: The Impact of Relationship Factors on Customer Satisfaction," *Journal of the Academy of Marketing Science*, 31 (2), 127-145.

Keaveney, S.M. (1995), "Customer Switching Behavior in Service Industries: An Exploratory Study," *Journal of Marketing*, 59, 71-82.

Kelly, Scott, Douglas Hoffman, and Mark Davis (1993), "A Typology of Retail Failures and Recoveries," *Journal of Retailing* 69 (Winter), 429-452.

Oliver, R.L. and Swan, John E. (1989), "Consumer Perceptions of Interpersonal Equity and Satisfaction in Transactions: A Field Survey Approach," Journal of Marketing, 53 (April), 21-35.

Patterson, P.G., Johnson, L.W., and Spreng, R. (1997), "Modeling the determinants of Customer Satisfaction for Business-to-Business Professional Services," *Journal of the Academy of Marketing Science*, (Winter), 4-17.

Pruyn, A. and Smidts, A. (1998), "Effects of Waiting on the Satisfaction with the Service: Beyond Objective Time Measures," *International Journal of Research in Marketing*, 15 (4), 321-334.

Roos, I., and Strandvik, T. (1997), "Diagnosing the Termination of Customer Relationships," *Relationship Marketing Conference* (pp.617-631). Dublin: American Marketing Association.

Roos, I., Edvardsson, B. and Anders Gustafson (2004), "Customer Switching Patterns in Competitive and Non-Competitive Service Industries," *Journal of Service Research*, 6(3), 256-271.

Smith, Amy K. and Ruth N. Bolton (2002), "The Effect of Customers' Emotional Responses to Service Failures on Their Recovery Effort Evaluations and Satisfaction Judgments," *Journal of the Academy of Marketing Science*, 30 (5), 5-23.

Smith, Amy K., Ruth N. Bolton and Janet Wagner (1999), "A Model of Customer Satisfaction with Service Encounters Involving Failure and Recovery," *Journal of Marketing Research*," 36 (August), 356-372.

Taylor, Shirley (1994), "Waiting for Service: The Relationship between Delays and Evaluations of Service," *Journal of Marketing* 58 (2), 56-69.

Tax, Stephen, Stephen Brown, and Murali Chandrashekaran (1998), "Customer Evaluations of Service complaint Experiences: Implications for Relationship Marketing," *Journal of Marketing* 62 (April), 60-76.

Contact the Author for a complete list of references.

A Typology of Consumer Territorial Rudeness

Merlyn A. Griffiths, University of North Carolina-Greensboro, USA
Mary C. Gilly, University of California-Irvine, USA

EXTENDED ABSTRACT

Commercial and services settings are evolving in functional provisions for customers, serving as a place to conduct business, study, hangout, cyber connection, reading room, mental rejuvenation space, etc. The expectation is that consumers will linger and mingle and have a positive interactional experience. However, although the invitation to socialize with unknown others is encouraged by the myriad of offerings, layout, physical features and ambience, consumers often do not socialize. In fact, as a norm in the setting, social interaction seems frowned upon and may be even considered against proper etiquette in these settings (McGrath 2006). Instead of socializing, some consumers in these settings behave territorially over the space they occupy. Some consumers who have had territorial encounters with another customer within these linger and mingle places become morally outraged, as they perceive another's territorial actions as being rude. What is unclear is what aspects of territoriality do consumers perceive to be rude?

Researchers have empirically shown that consumer–to–consumer interaction frequently do occur in service environments with great frequency, and can impact evaluation of the overall experience, satisfaction, repatronage and loyalty (Bitner et al., 1990; McGrath and Otnes 1995). However the concept of territorial rudeness as a component of consumer-to-consumer interaction in service environments has been less explored. To categorize a person's behavior as rude is to make definitive judgments that the person's communicative actions are intentional displays of contempt and lack of respect (Tracy and Tracy 1998). Along this line rudeness can be considered as discourteous behavior, which is in opposition of normal, rational practice of social life; polite, face-attentive interaction (Goffman 1955). According to Thomas (1965) "rude behavior is the kind of behavior which hurts people's feelings and causes them offence…it must give offence or be intended to offend, or be generally judged offensive" (p. 403). Rudeness therefore can be defined as "insensitive or disrespectful behavior enacted by a person that displays a lack of regard for others" (Porath and Erez 2007, p. 1181). We employ qualitative methods to develop a typology of consumer territorial rudeness.

Understanding Territoriality

Territorial behavior is defined as "a self/other boundary-regulation mechanism that involves personalization of or marking of a place or object and communication that it is 'owned' by a person or group. Personalization and ownership are designed to regulate social interaction and to help satisfy various social and physical motives. Defense responses may sometimes occur when territorial boundaries are violated" (Altman 1975, p. 107). Thus, territoriality involves three distinct behavioral dimensions; marking, encroachment and defense.

Marking: Territorial markers serve as a mechanism to dissuade or delay others from invading space already spoken for (Shaffer and Sadowski 1975; Sommer and Becker 1969). Markers also serve preventative and regulatory functions (Altman 1975). They regulate the level of social interaction, and offer individuals or group the choice to not engage others or allow them into claimed space.

Encroachment: When these self-relevant spaces are invaded, the response is likely to be commensurate in intensity with the loss of control. Lyman and Scott (1967) distinguished three forms of territorial encroachment: *violation*, *invasion*, and *contamination*.

The term *intrusion* which refers to someone who uses and claims the space of another group or person was introduced by Goffman (1971) to encapsulate both violation and invasion.

Defense: The most common defensive behaviors are verbal responses like arguments and discussions. Other defensive behaviors can include gestures, facial expressions and body posture changes (Altman 1975). Knapp (1978) identified two types of territorial defenses: *prevention defenses* and *reaction defenses*.

Methods

Since the existing literature revealed little in terms of research on consumer territorial rudeness, qualitative methods of depth interviews and a territoriality thematic apperception test were chosen to allow for full exploration, clarification and development of the concept of territorial rudeness (see Strauss and Corbin 1998; Murstein 1963; Morgan 2002). Data were analyzed using the thematic analytic technique (Brun and Clark 2006; Boyatzis 1998).

Findings

We determined territorial rudeness is context, situational and individual characteristic dependent. With this in mind, we define *territorial rudeness* as territorial actions (including ignoring a person and language) and demeanor (including personality characteristics and attitude) that is interpreted by others in the setting as ill-mannered or discourteous to customers, the place or the owners. The results indicate that consumers perceive lingering, disregard for others in the usage of space, and intrusion to be rude.

REFERENCES

Altman, Irwin (1975), *The Environment and Social Behavior: Privacy, Personal Space, Territory, Crowding.* Monterey, CA: Wadsworth Publishing Company, Inc.

Bitner, Mary Jo (1990), "Evaluating Service Encounters: The Effects of Physical Surroundings and Employee Responses," *Journal of Marketing*, 54 (April), 69-82.

Boyatzis, Richard E. (1998), *Transforming Qualitative Information: Thematic Analysis and Code Development.* Thousand Oaks, CA: Sage Publications.

Braun, Virginia and Victoria Clarke (2006), "Using Thematic Analysis in Psychology," *Qualitative Research in Psychology*, 3, 77-101.

Goffman, Erving, (1955), "On Facework: An Analysis of Ritual Elements in Social Interaction," *Psychiatry,* 18, 213-31.

Goffman, Erving (1971), *Relations in Public.* New York: Basic Books.

Knapp, Mark L. (1978), *Nonverbal Communication in Human Interaction.* New York: Reinhart and Winston.

Lyman, Stanford M. and Marvin B. Scott (1967), "Territoriality: A Neglected Sociological Dimension," *Social Problems*, 15 (2), 236-49.

McGrath, Ben (2006), *"The Latte Class,"* in The New Yorker Vol. 1/9/06: http://www.newyorker.com/talk/content/articles/060109ta_talk_mcgrath.

McGrath, M.A., Otnes, Cele. (1995), "Unacquainted influencers: when strangers interact in the retail setting", *Journal of Business Research*, Vol. 32 No.3, pp.261-72.

Morgan, Wesley G. (2002), "Origin and History of the Earliest Thematic Apperception Test Pictures," *Journal of Personality Assessment*, 79 (3), 422-45.

Murstein, Bernard I. (1963), *Theory and Research in Projective Techniques (emphasizing the TAT).* New York, NY: John Wiley & Sons, Inc.

Porath, Christine. L. and Amir Erez (2007), "Does Rudeness Really Matter? The Effects of Rudeness on Task Performance and Helpfulness," *Academy of Management Journal,* 50 (5) 1181-1197.

Shaffer, David R. and Cyril Sadowski (1975), "This Table is Mine: Respect for Marked Barroom Tables as a Function of Gender of Spatial Marker and Desirability of Locale," *Sociometry,* 38 (3), 408-19.

Sommer, Robert and Franklin D. Becker (1969), "Territorial Defense and The Good Neighbor," *Journal of Personality and Social Psychology,* 11 (2), 85-92.

Strauss, Anselm and Juliet Corbin (1998), *Basics of Qualitative Research: Techniques and Procedures for Developing Grounded Theory.* Thousand Oaks, CA: Sage Publications Inc.

Thomas, Anne Lloyd (1965), "Facts and Rudeness," *Mind,* 74 (295), 399-410.

Tracy, Karen and Sarah J. Tracy (1998), "Rudeness at 911: Reconceptualizing Face and Face Attack," *Human Communication Research,* 25 (2), 225-51.

The Sprinter Effect: When Involvement and Self-Control Fail to Overcome Ego-Depletion

Danit Ein-Gar, Tel-Aviv University, Israel
Yael Steinhart, University of Haifa, Israel

EXTENDED ABSTRACT

Recent studies have explored the mechanisms that can help individuals overcome a depleted state. These studies pointed to several mechanisms such as increasing glucose levels in the blood, introducing humor, raising situational involvement, and personality dimensions such as chronic self-control. The current research focuses on exploring what happens when two of the above mechanisms interact together in depleting states. More specifically, we focus on the joint effect of situational involvement and chronic self-control on performance under depleted states. The literature has demonstrated the separate effects of each factor in dealing with ego-depletion. Thus, the separate effect of enhancing situational involvement helped overcome an ego-depleted state and similarly having high dispositional self-control decreased the likelihood of spending money even under depleted states.

However, little attention was given to what happens when the two take place simultaneously, as most often occurs in real life. The current research posits that although self-control and involvement separately may lead to the same pattern of behavior, when joined together they cause a turnover effect resulting in less controlled behavior under depleted states.

Individuals with high self-control and high involvement have a greater need to perform well in an ego-depleting task compared to individuals who have little involvement or low levels of self-control. Consequently, these high self-controlled and high involved consumers allocate extended resources in order to perform well in an ego-depleting task. When faced with a series of such tasks, however, this extended effort may leave them with fewer available resources for subsequent tasks. In other words, these extremely motivated consumers over exhaust their resources up to the point of no recovery. Therefore, when faced with the next self regulating task, even their high motivation will fail to help them perform well. In contrast, consumers who are less motivated are expected to invest fewer resources in a demanding task, so they suffer less from ego-depletion. As a result, when they encounter a subsequent task, they will be able to perform relatively well because they have not expended all their resources on the former demanding task.

Study 1 tested participants' performance in an ego-depleting task and then their performance in recognizing "jumbled-up" known brand-names. Under the depleting condition, high self-controlled, high involved participants performed well in the ego depletion task in comparison to less motivated participants. However, the same high self-controlled, high involved participants had fewer resources available for the following task, and therefore, performed worse in the brand recognizing task. That is, after being depleted, extremely motivated participants recognized fewer brand names compared to those with lower levels of motivation.

Study 2 was conducted in a grocery store with shoppers. Both involvement and ego-depletion were activated before participants entered the store, and the resulting effects on shoppers' impulsive buying behaviors were measured as they were leaving the store. As hypothesized, under a depleted state, involved shoppers with high self-control were more likely to engage in impulsive buying than other, less involved or less self-controlled shoppers.

It is, however, an over generalization to claim that very involved, very self-controlled consumers are always prone to reach the ego-depletion low-point-of- no-recovery and consequently act less rationally or perform poorly in subsequent tasks. Hence, we postulate that a state of mind metaphorically resembling a "marathon" runner's mindset will cause the opposite effect. When a runner is about to run a short sprint without being informed in advance that there will be a number of sprints, she may put all her efforts into the first sprint and then will be left with no available resources for the following ones. However, if the same runner was informed that she were running a marathon consisting of a number of runs one after the other, she would probably manage her efforts differently, reserving some strength for the last runs.

Accordingly, in the last study (Study 3) we wish to show that informing consumers about the number of tasks they are expected to perform and giving them a general description of the tasks, (without indicating anything about the need for self-control) will allow them to activate a resources conservation strategy and consequently to avoid the burnout. In this case, when highly involved, high self-controlled consumers know in advance that they are about to conduct multiple consumption tasks, they enter a "marathon" state of mind. They try not to expend all their efforts on the first task; they try not to exhaust themselves so that they ensure they have enough resources to perform well in later tasks as well.

In Study 3, we repeated the procedures used in Study 1 with two exceptions; First, participants were informed about the total number of tasks at the outset. Informing participants about the outline of the tasks was expected to make the difference between a "sprint" mindset and a "marathon" mindset. Second, after the depleting task, participants read a hypothetical consumption scenario and indicated their probability of buying impulsively different grocery products.

As expected, the results of this study altered the results of studies 1 and 2 and show that when planning ahead, the sprinter effect is diminished. In the ego-depleting condition, high involved participants with high self-control were less willing to buy impulsively grocery products than participants with lower motivation levels.

At What Stage of Process Does Depletion Hurt the Most?

Darlene Walsh, Concordia University, Canada
Antonia Mantonakis, Brock University, Canada

EXTENDED ABSTRACT

Researchers have offered many different theoretical models to better understand self-regulation. One such model is the ego-depletion model, whereby the self has a limited reserve of some resource, that is analogous to strength or energy, which is used whenever the self actively regulates, changes, or overrides responses. According to this model, when an individual engages in an initial task that requires self-regulation, they do not have the resources available to exert self-regulation on a subsequent, unrelated task also requiring self-regulation (e.g., Baumeister, Bratslavsky, Muraven and Tice 1998; Baumeister, Heatherton and Tice, 1994; Muraven and Baumeister, 2000; Baumeister, Sparks, Stillman and Vohs 2008).

Many researchers interested in self-regulation and consumer behaviour have examined various applications of this model, and have observed that depletion results in more passive, uncompromising, and affective consumer decision making (Baumeister et al. 2008). However, the goal of our research is to obtain a better understanding of the mechanism underlying the ego-depletion model. Specifically, we investigate whether there is a point within a self-regulation task that the effects of depletion are most detrimental. Our research question is, are the effects of depletion more evident at initial stages of a self-regulation task (i.e., when getting started on the task) or does depletion impede performance consistently throughout the entire self-regulation process? To answer this question, we designed and conducted two experiments described below.

In experiment 1, we created a self-regulation task that captures the process of learning a basic skill and assessed participants' ability to learn this task while they were depleted or not (Baumeister and Showers 1986). The self-regulation task required that the participants type out six-letter strings using only the index finger of their dominant hand. To assess the point that depletion influences performance, we recorded both the time it took participants to initiate a response (i.e., the time it took to type the first letter of the string) and the time it took participants to complete the response once it was initiated (i.e., the time it took to type the remaining letters of the string). We term these two components of the behavior response initiation and response completion, respectively. We manipulated depletion using self-presentation (see Baumeister and Showers 1986), such that participants in the depletion condition completed the task while the experimenter stood directly to the left of them, which induced self-attention, and as a result, self-presentation concerns (e.g., Baumeister and Steinhilber 1984). Participants in the no depletion condition were not watched.

We found that participants were slower to initiate the response on the self-regulation task when they were depleted than when they were not depleted. However, once depleted and non-depleted participants had initiated the task, they required the same amount of time for response completion. These results suggest that depletion influences an individuals' capacity to initiate the appropriate self-regulation response, but does not influence the self-regulation process once it has begun. Said differently, we found that depletion influences response initiation, but not response completion.

In experiment 2, we tested whether the detrimental influence of depletion caused primarily by a slowing of response initiation can be attenuated as participants learn the self-regulatory task. Assuming that performance can be described as either a controlled process, which is typically described as slow and effortful, or as an automatic process, which is usually described as fast and effortless, it is likely that controlled processes are dominant early in learning but give way to automatic processes later in learning (Shiffrin and Schneider 1977; Shiffrin and Schneider 1984). In other words, once a task is well-learned, the negative influences of depletion might have less of an impact on performance. Thus, the primary purpose of experiment 2 was to test whether the effect of depletion on response initiation dissipates as a task becomes well-learned. To do this, we used the same self-regulation task and depletion manipulation that we used in experiment 1, but extended the number of trials of learning, making the task relatively well-learned.

We replicated the results of experiment 1, showing that it is the initiation component of responding that is influenced by depletion, not the response completion component. In addition, we found that as experience in this self-regulation task grows (i.e., as the task becomes habitual) the effect of depletion on response initiation was reduced.

REFERENCES

Baumeister, Roy F., Bratslavsky, Ellen, Muraven, Mark, and Tice, Dianne M. (1998), "Ego depletion: Is the active self a limited resource," *Journal of Personality and Social Psychology,* 74, 1252-1265.

Baumeister, R.F., Heatherton, Todd F., and Tice, Dianne M. (1994). *Losing Control: How and Why People Fail at Self-Regulation.* CA: Academic Press.

Baumeister, Roy F. and Showers, Carolin J. (1986), "A review of paradoxical performance effects: Choking under pressure in sports and mental tests," *European Journal of Social Psychology,* 16, 361-383.

Baumeister, Roy F., Erin A. Sparks, Tyler F. Stillman, and Kathleen D. Vohs (2008), "Free will in consumer behaviour: Self-regulation, ego depletion, and choice," *Journal of Consumer Psychology,* 18(1), 4-13.

Baumeister, Roy F. and Steinhilber, Andrew (1984), "Paradoxical effects of supportive audiences on performance under pressure: The home filed disadvantage in sports championships," *Journal of Personality and Social Psychology,* 47 (1), 85-93.

Muraven, Mark, and Baumeister, Roy F. (2000), "Self-Regulation and Depletion of Limited Resources: Does Self-Control Resemble a Muscle?" *Psychological Bulletin,* March, 247-259.

Shiffrin, Richard M. and Schneider, Walter (1977), "Controlled and automatic human information processing: II. Perceptual learning, automatic attending and a general theory," *Psychological Review,* 84, 127-190.

Shiffrin, Richard M. and Schneider, W. (1984), "Automatic and controlled processes revisited," *Psychological Review, 91,* 269-276.

Forgetting Without Inhibition: A Resource Depletion Account of Retrieval-Induced Forgetting

Andrea Hughes, University of the Fraser Valley, Canada
Antonia Mantonakis, Brock University, Canada

EXTENDED ABSTRACT

The construct of inhibition has long been part of language, both in daily life as well as in scientific theorizing. From an experimental psychology perspective, the term inhibition has two primary functions: to explain basic neuronal behavior within the central nervous system, and to account for a variety of *deficits* in both cognitive and social phenomena (Aron 2007). It is the latter function that is the focus of this paper. The goal of the present research was to examine the utility of the concept of inhibition within the domain of memory and we use the retrieval induced forgetting paradigm–a paradigm which has been paramount in the development of the cognitive inhibition account–as a tool to demonstrate the limitations of the notion of inhibition as a psychological construct. In the case of the retrieval-induced forgetting effect, which is the observation that retrieval of some items in memory impairs other items in memory (Anderson, Bjork and Bjork 1994), we suggest a mechanism involving resource depletion (Muraven and Baumeister 2000; Vohs and Heatherton 2000).

The resource depletion mechanism takes into account both a person's capacity limitations (Baddeley 1996) and the strategies used to perform a memory task. According to the resource depletion view, the self has a limited reserve of a resource that is deployed whenever the self actively regulates, changes, or overrides a response (Baumeister and Heatherton 1996). Resource depletion is observed by some deficit in task performance; when participants must engage in some sort of self-regulatory task, performance on a subsequent task is inferior compared to a baseline for which no such regulatory task has been engaged in (Vohs and Heatherton 2000).

The resource depletion view does not suggest overarching deficits in motivation or ability, as depletion occurs only in tasks that require active control of the self. Depletion occurs when a person engages in more complex, but not simple, cognitive tasks, suggesting that, when depletion occurs, performance on subsequent, but also resource-laden, cognitive tasks declines (Schmeichel, Vohs and Baumeister 2003).

In light of the findings in the literature on self regulation, we questioned whether retrieval practice involves a form of self-regulation. That is, retrieval practice requires the individual to control responses on some task. Therefore, performance on the subsequent task (final recall) is inferior compared to a baseline for which no retrieval practice has taken place; failure to remember during final recall seems to not be due to inhibition, but rather, to the depletion of the resource needed to be successful during retrieval practice and again in the final recall test.

We first replicated the basic retrieval-induced forgetting effect (experiment 1) using the standard procedures which employ a 30 second recall opportunity. We posited that during the initial task–the retrieval practice session–one must actively practice some items from some categories, which depletes resources. In consequence, given that the final test requires the same set of resources as those required for the retrieval practice, and given that it is easier to report the practiced items; unpracticed items are not reported on the final test. We reasoned that allowing more time on the final test may provide an unconstrained context that allows report of all items. According to the resource depletion view, allowing participants more time to recall may provide a better context for which participants can use whatever is left over from their self-regulatory resources. Thus, experiment 2 was virtually identical in procedure to that of experiment 1 with the exception of the amount of time given to recall each category on the final test. We observed no retrieval-induced forgetting, providing evidence to support the hypothesis that the forgetting effect is, at least in part, determined by the demands of the recall task.

The aim of experiment 3 was to investigate resource depletion in an alternate way. We manipulated recall order on the final recall test. A resource depletion account would suggest that there should be greater decrements in recall for whatever is retrieved second, which is what we observed. An inhibition account would argue that "retrieval induced forgetting" should be observed regardless of output order.

A resource depletion account would predict that the self begins with a limited stock of any given resource, which is consumed when one engages in cognitive activity. This consumption results in decrements in performance on subsequent tasks that require the same resource. As long as the same resource is required in the second task as the first, decrements should be observed. An inhibition account instead makes specific predictions about when inhibition should occur at the taxonomic level. For example, there cannot be inhibition across categories: repeated practice in retrieving some members of a class should impair retrieval of other member of that class, not members of other classes (Anderson, et al 1994; Alba and Chattopadhyay 1986).

Based on this assumption, in experiment 4 we carried out a between-subjects manipulation which varied the number of categories used. Based on the findings of our previous experiments, we predicted that the amount of retrieval-induced forgetting will decrease as the number of categories decreases. Such a finding would further call into question the need for the mechanism of inhibition. That is, if the forgetting effect is attenuated by reducing the number of categories, there can not be a role for inhibition, as inhibition occurs within a particular category. However a finding that the forgetting effect is attenuated by reducing the number of categories would provide additional support of a resource depletion account. That is because, by reducing the number of categories, the resource required for retrieval practice is depleted to a lesser extent than with more categories. As such, reducing the number of categories should lead to a lower likelihood of performance decrements. Comparing the decrement in recall for the 8-category group to the same means of the 6-category group, there was a reliable decrease in retrieval induced forgetting for the 6-category group. This result provides compelling support for the resource depletion account of retrieval induced forgetting.

REFERENCES

Alba, Joseph W. and Amitava Chattopadhyay. (1986), "Salience Effects in Brand Recall," *Journal of Marketing Research,* 23 (November), 363-369.

Anderson, Michael. C., Robert A. Bjork, and Elizabeth L. Bjork. (1994), "Remembering can cause forgetting: Retrieval dynamics in long-term memory," *Journal of Experimental Psychology: Learning, Memory, and Cognition, 20,* 1063-1087.

Aron, Adam R. (2007), "The neural basis of inhibition in cognitive control," *The Neuroscientist, 13*, 214-228.

Baddeley, Alan D. (1996), "Exploring the central executive," Quarterly Journal of *Experimental Psychology: Human Experimental Psychology, 49*, 5-28.

Baumeister, Roy F., and Heatherton, Todd F. (1996), "Self-regulation failure: An overview," *Psychological Inquiry, 7,* 1-15.

Muraven, Mark, and Baumeister, Roy F. (2000), "Self-Regulation and Depletion of Limited Resources: Does Self-Control Resemble a Muscle?" *Psychological Bulletin*, March, 247-259.

Schmeichel, Brandon J., Kathleen D. Vohs, and Roy F. Baumeister. (2003), "Intellectual performance and ego depletion: Role of the self in logical reasoning and other information processing," *Journal of Personality and Social Psychology, 85*, 33-46.

Vohs, Kathleen D., and Todd, F. Heatherton. (2000), "Self-regulatory failure: A resource-depletion approach," *Psychological Science, 11*, 249-254.

"The Name Remains the Same for Fans"–Why Fans Oppose Naming Right Sponsorships

David M. Woisetschlaeger, University of Dortmund, Germany
Vanessa J. Haselhoff, University of Dortmund, Germany

EXTENDED ABSTRACT

The selling of a stadium's naming right is one very common type of sponsorship. For example, 14 out of 18 German soccer stadiums have sold their stadium's name in the last 15 years. Although financially highly profitable for a club, naming right sponsorships are not without risk. Clark, Cornwell, and Pruitt talk of "high controversy surrounding sponsorship deals" (Clark, Cornwell, and Pruitt 2002, p.17). Greenberg and Gray (1996) as well as Crompton and Howard (2003) refer to some examples of public opposition to stadiums' name selling. While the fit between sponsor and sponsee is empirically examined as a success factor of sponsorship (e.g. Simmons and Becker-Olsen 2006, Speed and Thompson 2000), little knowledge exists to guide the management of such companies that are in the particular situation of a low fit or even reactance of consumers. The present article contributes to the literature by examining the determinants and consequences of sponsorship fit using a qualitative and a quantitative study.

To gain a first idea of possible reactance motives of soccer fans, we followed an explorative approach by conducting in-depth interviews with 22 fans of Borussia Dortmund. The popular German soccer club sold the stadium's naming right to a local insurance company which was followed by negative reactions of its fans. To uncover the fans' deeper motives, the laddering-technique was applied (Gutman 1982, Reynolds and Gutman 1988). In summary, several aspects seem to influence the naming right-reactance. These include the fans' sense of tradition and their regional identification, their fan identity, and their attitude towards commercialization. Other aspects compromise the sponsor's regional identity as well as the perceived benefit of the sponsorship for the soccer club. A central factor was the perceived fit between the sponsor and the sponsee.

The second study aims to quantify the directions and strengths of effects that the attitudes identified in study 1 have on the evaluation of the sponsorship. More precisely, in accordance with findings from existing literature we propose that the perceived fit between sponsor and sponsee is crucial for the evaluation of the brand (club) image and intentions toward the brand (club), i.e. positive word-of-mouth. From a theoretical point of view, a miss-fit perceived by the consumer is equivalent to incongruence between sponsor and sponsee. Such incongruence causes psychological tensions in the consumer's mind and forces to reestablish congruence (Festinger 1957, Heider 1946 and 1958, Osgood and Tannenbaum 1955). Hence, a perceived miss-fit should be related to a more negative evaluation of the sponsor and the sponsee.

Due to the crucial role of fit for the success of the sponsor partnership, it is important to assess the effects of possible determinants of fit. The aspects derived from study 1 are used to develop theoretical explanations for possible effects on the perceived sponsor-sponsee fit. First, the degree to which fans identify themselves with the soccer club could be negatively related to the perceived fit. Consumers classify themselves and other consumers as being an in-group member or as being a member of the out-group (Carlson 2005). We propose that fans that identify themselves strongly with their soccer club are more likely to treat a sponsor as an intruder. Taking the same rationale, we propose that regional connectedness and tradition consciousness contribute to consciousness of kind and consequently increase the likelihood that the sponsor is not accepted as in-group member. Moreover, a negative attitude towards commercialization in general is likely to have a negative influence on sponsorship-fit. Finally, two positive aspects were mentioned in study 1 that could contribute to a positive perception of sponsor-sponsee fit: perceived benefits of the partnership and perceived regional identification of the sponsor.

To test the hypotheses, data was collected via an online survey. A total of 524 respondents participated, who are mostly male (93.2%), young (m=24 years), and highly involved fans showing a strong identification with their soccer club Borussia Dortmund. We measured attitude-related variables with multi-item scales. The dependent variables (brand image and word-of-mouth intention) are operationalized for the club (sponsee) and the sponsor. Three items are used to measure the brand/club image. Word-of-mouth intention is measured by four items adopted from existing literature again for the sponsor and the sponsee (e.g. Algesheimer, Dholakia, and Herrmann 2005). The evaluation of the sponsor-sponsee fit is included as a mediating construct (Simmons and Becker-Olsen 2006). As determinants of sponsor-sponsee fit, scales for attitude toward commercialization (Lee, Sandler, and Shani 1997), and fan identification (Algesheimer, Dholakia, and Herrmann 2005) were adopted from existing literature. Based on the findings of study 1, the fans' sense of tradition and their regional identification, and the sponsor's regional identification as well as the perceived benefit of the sponsorship for the soccer club were measured by multi-items scales developed by the authors.

Structural equation modeling was used to estimate the parameters of the structural model. Goodness-of-fit statistics indicate the overall acceptability of the structural model. The proposed positive relationship of fit and the dependent constructs brand (club) image, and brand (club) WOM intention is only valid for the sponsoring brand. The negative fit is attributed to the sponsor, while the sponsee's image remains unaffected. Furthermore, the perceived benefits for the club have the strongest positive impact on fit. The regional identification of the sponsor is another important positive determinant. The degree of regional connectedness and the attitude toward commercialization have a negative influence on fit. No significant influence is found for fan identification and tradition consciousness. A total of 63.6 % of the variance of fit is captured by the determinants above.

Results of the two studies demonstrate that negative effects of sponsorships are especially relevant for the sponsoring company since both brand image and WOM-intention are affected negatively. Some attitudes that affect the sponsor-sponsee fit like attitude toward commercialization and regional connectedness seem to be difficult to influence. The good news is that the strongest determinants of the sponsor-sponsee fit are at least potentially manageable by the sponsor: through communication of the benefits of the partnership, and by communicating the regional identification of the sponsor.

REFERENCES

Algesheimer, René, Utpal M. Dholakia and Andreas Herrmann (2005), "The Social Influence of Brand Community: Evidence from European Car Clubs," *Journal of Marketing*, 69 (3), 19-34.

Carlson, Bradley D. (2005), *Brand-based community: The role of identification in developing a sense of community among brand users,* Oklahoma, USA.

Clark, John M., T. Bettina Cornwell and Stephen W. Pruitt (2002), "Corporate Stadium Sponsorships, Signaling Theory, Agency Conflicts, and Shareholder Wealth," *Journal of Advertising Research*, 42 (6), 16-32.

Crompton, John L. and Dennis R. Howard (2003), "The American Experience with Facility Naming Rights: Opportunities for English Professional Football Teams," *Managing Leisure*, 8, 212–226.

Festinger, Leon (1957), *A Theory of Cognitive Dissonance*, Stanford: Stanford University Press.

Gutman, Jonathan (1982), "A Means-End Chain Model Based on Consumer Categorization Processes," *Journal of Marketing*, 46, 60-72.

Greenberg, Martin J. and James T. Gray (1996), *The Stadium Game*, Marquette University Law School, National Sports Law Institute.

Heider, Fritz (1946), "Attitudes and cognitive organization," *Journal of Psychology*, 21, 107-12.

Heider, Fritz (1958), "The Psychology of Interpersonal Relations," New York.

Lee, Myung-Soo, Dennis M. Sandler, and David Shani (1997), "Attitudinal Constructs Towards Sponsorship: Scale Development Using Three Global Sporting Events," *International Marketing Review*, 14 (3), 159-69.

Osgood, Charles E. and Percy H. Tannenbaum (1955), "The principle of congruity in the prediction of attitude change," *Psychological Review*, 62 (1), 42-55.

Reynolds, Thomas J. and Jonathan Gutman (1988), "Laddering Theory, Method, Analysis, and Interpretation," *Journal of Advertising Research*, 11-31.

Simmons, Carolyn J. and Karen L. Becker-Olsen (2006), "Achieving Marketing Objectives Through Social Sponsorships," *Journal of Marketing*, 70 (4), 154-69.

Speed, Richard and Peter Thompson (2000), "Determinants of Sports Sponsorship Response," *Journal of the Academy of Marketing Science*, 28 (2), 226-38.

Why Thematization?

A. Fuat Firat, The University of Texas-Pan American, USA
Ebru Ulusoy, The University of Texas-Pan American, USA

EXTENDED ABSTRACT

Thematization, a flourishing phenomenon, has attracted attention by scholars who observe contemporary culture. Many scholars observe thematization as a recent trend and make a distinction between themed spaces and the rest of the world. We argue that thematization is not a recent phenomenon and that the distinction made between environments considered themed and not themed is one of perspective, not present in the nature of the phenomenon. We investigate the reasons why a distinction is favored in popular culture and why interest in thematization has increased lately to propose an extension to explanations that concentrate on theming as a profitable business in contemporary culture. Our exploration of the history and conceptualization of thematization, indicates that the main force underlying the increased interest in thematization is cultural rather than economic.

Past conceptualization of thematization basically evolve around elements that constitute themed environments, such as social control, entertainment, fantasy, decentralization and privatization, and the spectacle (Gottdiener 1995, Ritzer 1999). In order to provide a direct definition without a prejudgment of its separation from the everyday, we define thematization as the patterning of space, activity or event to symbolize experiences and/or senses from a special or a specific past, present, or future place, activity or event as currently imagined.

Two themes are common to many of the theses regarding thematization (Gottdiener 2001; Sorkin 1992; Baudrillard 1996; Davis 1999; Beardsworth and Bryman 1999; Ritzer 1999): (1) thematization is driven by corporations and (2) contemporary consumers are accomplices in the theming of the world.

For corporations, competing for consumers who pay greater attention to the symbolic and the spectacle (Debord 1983), thematization is a sophisticated marketing technique (Gottdiener 2001) that serves economic interests by transforming the mundane to attractive, thus rendering it marketable. Humanistic values and enchanted forms in theme production are also means that help thematization serve the economic interests of corporations. Corporations institutionally create themes to imply social action and caring for the ecosystem.

Recent themed environments impact on all human senses by utilizing a multidimensional system of signs. They are, thus, are attractive to contemporary consumers who need multidimensionality in spaces and experiences (Featherstone 1990). Consumers who visit themed environments enjoy and appreciate them if they find experiences of meaning and substance (Fırat 2001), and as their needs for emotional, symbolic, and spiritual relief through encounters with public space, nature, democracy, and other cultures are fulfilled (Gottdiener 2001). Theming also provides securities sought in modernity, such as physical safety and hygiene (Beardsworth and Bryman 1999). Themed places introduce alternative visions of what people seek and become a new source of cultural capital (Hannigan 1998).

The most telling explanation for consumer interest in themed environments is the growth of a postmodern cultural sensibility where people develop a tacit understanding of the futility of making a distinction between the 'real' and the 'fantasy', everyday spaces and themed spaces. Thus, we find consumers ready to experience the thematic without reservations.

Consequently, the special interest in distinguishing certain spaces as themed and others as not themed tends to be an aberration of contemporary culture and a consequence of modernity that is maintained and reinforced by the emerging postmodern cultural sensibility where alternative modes of being and living are sought, and commitment to or the belief in the possibility of constructing one ideal order has waned. Recognizing this quest for difference and multiplicity, the corporations find production of 'themed' environments as a panacea a to their cultural bane, their guilt in having constructed a disenchanting modern order, as at the same time they profit from offering such environments to consumers. Furthermore, maintaining the illusory distinction of the 'themed' versus 'everyday', 'fantasy' versus the 'real', absolves them from being blamed as the culprit in humanity's disenchantment. In this absolution, they are aided by the members of the middle class who also tacitly recognize their complicity in having passively accepted and gone along with the lives that modern corporations created, at the same time they also seem aware of the illusory distinctions so maintained.

Representing the 'themed environment' as an economic strategy to develop market offerings, scholars have also inadvertently aided corporate interests. It is important, therefore, to deconstruct the current theses about thematization and provide insights that may further humanity's quest in building meaningful and substantive lives.

When reality is perceived as constructed and thematic, people afford greater power to reconstruct it as can be imagined. When reality is perceived as 'out there', people feel resigned to what they have inherited. As the illusory nature of the distinction between where people live everyday and where they go to have fun is articulated, the consciousness is gained that maintaining the distinction and organizing lives accordingly is not only limiting humanity's potentials to build more habitable worlds, but that it also perpetuates certain interests and a human condition that humanity can better do without.

REFERENCES

Baudrillard, Jean (1996), "Disneyworld Company," *CTheory.net*, www.ctheory.net/articles.aspx?id=158.

Beardsworth, Alan, Alan Bryman (1999), "Late Modernity and the Dynamics of Quasification: The Case of the Themed Restaurants," *The Editorial Board of the Sociological Review*, 228-257.

Davis, Susan G. (1999), *Spectacular nature, corporate culture, and the Sea World experience*, Berkeley, CA: University of California Press.

Debord, Guy (1983), *Society of the Spectacle*, Detroit, MI: Black and Red.

Featherstone, Mike (1990), "Perspectives on Consumer Culture," *Sociology*, 24, 1, 5-22.

Fırat, A. Fuat. (2001), "The Meanings and Messages of Las Vegas: The Present of our Future", *M@nagement*, 4(3), 101-120.

Gottdiener, Mark (1995), *Postmodern Semiotics: Material Culture and the Forms of Postmodern Life*, Oxford: Blackwell.

Gottdiener, Mark (2001), *The Theming of America, 2nd edition*, Cambridge, MA: Westview Press.

Hannigan, John (1998), *Fantasy City: Pleasure and Profit in the Postmodern Metropolis*, New York: Routledge.

Ritzer, George (1999), *Enchanting a Disenchanted World: Revolutionizing the Means of Consumption*, Thousand Oaks, California: Pine Forge Press.

Sorkin, Michael, ed. (1992), *Variations on a theme park: The new American City and the End of Public Space*. New York: Noonday.

Product Bundles and the Compositional Nature of Contextual Information

Dan Rice, University of Florida, USA
Alan Cooke, University of Florida, USA

EXTENDED ABSTRACT

With all of the attention that examinations of bundle evaluations have garnered in the literature, it is surprising that no research has investigated how consumers process contextual information when the context, target, or both are composed of bundles. The evaluation of individual product offers has been shown to be sensitive to dominance (Huber, Payne and Puto 1982), attribute tradeoffs (Simonson and Tversky 1992), tradeoff extremity (Simonson and Tversky 1992), attribute range and spacing (Cooke and Mellers 1998; Mellers and Cooke 1994; Parducci 1965), timing of product presentation (Wedell, Parducci and Geiselman 1987), and the extremity of the contextual products (Herr 1989), to name a few. Despite these results, little research has investigated how contextual information is processed when the target or contextual offers consist of product bundles. Here, contextual information is available not only in the distributions of each product category, but also in the joint distributions of attributes across different bundles containing these products. This compositional information may also serve as a context relative to which bundles are evaluated.

The primary goal of this research is to demonstrate that consumers are sensitive to how single contextual products are combined into bundles when evaluating target stimuli. To avoid confusion, we refer to this previously unexplored compositional contextual information as "bundle context," and the context created by single products as "single product context." After demonstrating the existence of bundle context effects, we further examine the process by which consumers account for the bundle context and explore moderators of the effects. We propose that the influence of bundle context is due to effortful comparisons between the bundle and the surrounding context, and the relative difficulty of these comparisons moderates the effects of the context. Three experiments provide evidence to support our hypotheses.

Our first experiment used a constant set of eight individual products that were pretested for attractiveness. The four moderately attractive products were combined into high and low attractiveness target bundles. Bundle context was manipulated by differentially combining the remaining four contextual products in different conditions. In the wide bundle contexts, the two most attractive products were bundled together in one contextual bundle and the two least attractive products were bundled together in the other. This created a wide range of overall attractiveness at the bundle level. In the narrow bundle context, the most attractive contextual item was paired with the least attractive contextual item and the second most attractive item with the second least attractive, forming a relatively narrow range of overall bundle attractiveness with the same individual products.

The results of experiment 1 show that bundle context influences the way consumers perceive contextual stimuli even when single product context is held constant. Target bundles appeared more similar in the wide context, where contextual bundles had widely disparate overall evaluations, than in the narrow context, where contextual bundles were more similar in overall evaluation. If consumers were only sensitive to single product context or were insensitive to context effects, the evaluations of the target bundles should have been constant across all conditions.

The results also revealed that bundle attractiveness was significantly less than the most attractive product it contained in all but the wide context, high context bundle comparison. This might be due to a ceiling effect of the two best products combined together in one bundle. This pattern of results is inconsistent with an additive model, even one allowing for extreme subadditivity. However, it is consistent with a number of alternative combination processes including both averaging and anchoring and adjustment processes.

A second experiment investigated whether the effects could be attributed to response language effects in the judgment process. The results of experiment 2 provide evidence that bundle choice reversals are possible and consumers are sensitive to the aggregate levels of attributes within the bundles of the contextual set even when the individual products in the set are held constant. From a theoretical standpoint, the choice reversal between target bundles is important because it shows that bundle context effects are a representational phenomenon that cannot be explained away by response language effects or single product context. That is, we obtain choice reversals between target bundles in a constant product set where the attribute levels only change at the bundle level. From a managerial perspective, the findings are important because they show that it is possible to create choice reversals between bundles simply by rearranging the products surrounding those bundles without adding new products to the set.

The third experiment investigates the process by which consumers account for the extra compositional information of how the individual products are paired in bundles (i.e. the bundle context). The results of experiment 3 indicate that bundle context effects are due to effortful contextual comparisons between bundles in the set. Participants found the bundle context information useful and tried to extract the information, but they were influenced more by the more attractive product in the bundle when under load.

Recognition analyses provide evidence that the attractiveness of the product influences recognition of the product. The analyses also show that the effect of attractiveness on recognition is greater under load. We interpret these results as an indication that the more attractive products were processed more deeply, creating better memory for those products (Craik and Lockhart 1972). This is consistent with consumers anchoring on the more attractive product and adjusting for the less attractive products in bundle evaluations (Yadav 1994).

REFERENCES

Adams, William J. and Janet L. Yellen (1976), "Commodity Bundling and the Burden of Monopoly," *Economic Journal*, 87 (September), 427-49.

Bettman, James R., Mary Frances Luce, and John W. Payne (1998), "Constructive Consumer Choice Processes," *Journal of Consumer Research*, 25 (December), 187-217.

Chaiken, Shelly and Yaacov Trope (1999), *Dual Process Theories in Social Psychology*. New York: Guilford Press.

Chakravarti, Dipankar and John G. Lynch, Jr. (1983), "A Framework for Exploring Context Effects On Consumer Judgment and Choice," in *Advances in Consumer Research*, 10, ed. Richard Bagozzi and Alice Tybout, Ann Arbor, MI: Association for Consumer Research, 289-97.

Cooke, Alan D. J. and Barbara A. Mellers (1998), "Multiattribute Judgment: Attribute Spacing Influences Single Attributes," *Journal of Experimental Psychology: Human Perception and Performance*, 24 (April), 496-504.

Cooke, Alan D. J., Claude Pecheux, and Elise Chandon (2005), "Subadditive Bundle Evaluations and the Value of Variety," working paper, Marketing Department, Warrington College of Business Administration, University of Florida, Gainesville, FL 32611.

Craik, Fergus I and Robert S. Lockhart (1972), "Levels of processing: A Framework for Memory Research," *Journal of Verbal Learning & Verbal Behavior,* 11(December) 671-684.

Gaeth, Gary J., Irwin P. Levin, Goutam Chakraborty, and Aron M. Levin (1990), "Consumer Evaluation of Multi-Product Bundles: An information Integration Analysis," *Marketing Letters*, 2 (January), 47-57.

Gilbert, Daniel T. (2002), "Inferential Correction," in *Heuristics and Biases: the Psychology of Intuitive Judgment*, ed. T. Gilovich, D. Griffin, and D. Kahneman, Cambridge, England: Cambridge University Press, 167-184.

Herr, Paul M. (1989), "Priming Price: Prior Knowledge and Context Effects," *Journal of Consumer Research*, 16 (June), 67-75.

Hicks, John R. and Roy G. D. Allen (1934a), "A Reconsideration of the Theory of Value. Part I," *Economica*, 1 (February), 52-76.

––––––– (1934b), "A Reconsideration of the Theory of Value. Part II. A Mathematical Theory of Individual Demand Functions," *Economica*, 1 (May), 196-219.

Hsee, Christopher K. (1998), "Less is better: When low-value options are valued more highly than high-value options," *Journal of Behavioral Decision Making*, 11 (June), 107-121.

Huber, Joel, John W. Payne and Christopher Puto (1982), "Adding Asymmetrically Dominated Alternatives: Violations of Regularity and the Similarity Hypothesis," *Journal of Consumer Research*, 9(June), 90-98.

Janiszewski, Chris and Donald R. Lichtenstein (1999), "A Range Theory Account of Price Perception," *Journal of Consumer Research*, 25(March), 353-68.

Kahneman, Daniel and Shane Frederick (2002) , "Inferential Correction," in *Heuristics and Biases: the Psychology of Intuitive Judgment*, ed. T. Gilovich, D. Griffin, and D. Kahneman, Cambridge, England: Cambridge University Press, 49-81.

Lancaster, Kelvin J. (1966), "A New Approach to Consumer Theory," *Journal of Political Economy*, 74 (2), 132-58.

Martin, Leonard L., John J. Seta, and Rick A. Crelia (1990), "Assimilation and contrast as a function of people's willingness and ability to expend effort in forming an impression," *Journal of Personality and Social Psychology*, 59 (July), 27-37.

Mellers, Barbara A. and Alan D. J. Cooke (1994), "Trade-Offs Depend on Attribute Range," *Journal of Experimental Psychology: Human Perception and Performance*, 20 (October), 1055-67.

Meyers-Levy, Joan and Brian Sternthal (1993), "A two-factor explanation of assimilation and contrast effects," *Journal of Marketing Research*, 30 (August), 359-368.

Meyers-Levy, Joan and Alice Tybout (1997), "Context effects at encoding and judgment in consumption settings: The role of cognitive resources," *Journal of Consumer Research*, 24 (June), 1-14.

Parducci, Allen (1965), "Category Judgment: A Range-Frequency Model," *Psychological Review*, 72 (November), 407-18.

Samuelson, Paul A. (1974), "Complementarity: An Essay on the 40th Anniversary of the Hicks-Allen Revolution in Demand Theory," *Journal of Economic Literature*, 12 (December), 1255-89.

Schneider, Walter and Richard M. Shiffrin (1977), "Controlled and Automatic Human Information Processing: I. Detection, Search, and Attention," *Psychological Review*, 84 (January), 1-66.

Simonson, Itamar, and Amos Tversky (1992), "Choice in Context: Tradeoff Contrast and Extremeness Aversion," *Journal of Marketing Research*, 29 (August), 281-95.

Wänke, Michaela, Herbert Bless, and Norbert Schwarz (1999a), "Assimilation and Contrast in Brand and Product Evaluations: Implications for Marketing," *Advances in Consumer Research,* 26 (1), 95-98.

––––––– (1999b), "Lobster, Wine, and Cigarettes: Ad Hoc Categorizations and the Emergence of Context Effects," *Marketing Bulletin,* 10 (May), 52-56.

Wedell, Douglas H., Allen Parducci, and R. Edward Geiselman (1987), "A Formal Analysis of Ratings of Physical Attractiveness: Successive Contrast and Simultaneous Assimilation," *Journal of Experimental Social Psychology*, 23 (May), 230-49.

Yadav, Majit S. (1994), "How Buyers Evaluate Product Bundles: A Model of Anchoring and Adjustment," *Journal of Consumer Research*, 21 (September), 342-53.

The Impact of Anticipated Follower Entry on Consumer Acceptance of Pioneer Brands

Zhenfeng Ma, University of Ontario Institute of Technology, Canada
Ying Jiang, University of Ontario Institute of Technology, Canada

EXTENDED ABSTRACT

Existing research on pioneering advantage has implicitly treated followers as a threat to the pioneers (Shankar, Carpenter and Krishnamurthi 1998; Golder and Tellis 1993). However, Carpenter and Nakamoto (1989) suggest that the market entry by late movers may actually increase consumers' preference for the leaders, especially when the late movers' products are not sufficiently differentiated (i.e. 'me-too' followers). In this study, we propose that the impact of the anticipated market entry by 'me-too' followers on the pioneer brands depend on the innovation newness and network externalities of the products. We show that the me-too followers' market entry announcements increased consumers' acceptance of the pioneer of really new products but not incrementally new products. We also demonstrate that for the pioneers of really new products, the positive impact of anticipated follower entry is more evident when the products exhibit high (versus low) indirect network externalities.

The Moderating Effect of Innovation Newness

Consumers usually perceive higher risks in buying really new products (RNPs) (Ram and Sheth 1989). Based on the research on category learning, we propose that the anticipated market entry by me-too followers may increase the conceptual clarity of the RNP category, thereby reducing consumers' uncertainty about the pioneer brand. Specifically, for a RNP category, me-too followers serve as category exemplars to increase the perceptual and conceptual salience of the RNP as a distinct product category. The increased conceptual clarity about the category can in turn reduce consumers' uncertainty and enhance consumers' acceptance of the pioneer. Moreover, the market entry by followers may be perceived as endorsement of the technologies used by the pioneer of a RNP, which increases consumers' confidence in the pioneer. In contrast, followers' entry may decrease consumers' acceptance of the pioneer of an incrementally new product (INP), because when the innovation newness of the product is low, the perceptual dominance of the pioneer is low, and it is easy for late comers to design products that deliver better performance than the pioneer brand. We thus hypothesize:

H1: Anticipated follower entry increases consumers' purchase intention toward the pioneer of a really new product, but decrease consumers' purchase intention toward the pioneer of an incrementally new product.

H2: The effect of anticipated follower entry on consumers' purchase intention toward the pioneer brand of a really new product is mediated by consumers' perceived risks.

The Moderating Effect of Indirect Network Externalities

Indirect network externalities (INE) exist when a customer's utility for a product increases as the number of complementary products increases (Srinavasan, Lilien and Rangaswamy 2004). Consumers often adopt a "wait-and-see" attitude toward pioneer brands with high INE, because they cannot obtain the full benefits of such products until there are sufficient complementary products. We posit that for the pioneer of a RNP with high INE, followers' market entry increases consumers' anticipated availability of the complementary products, thereby increasing the expected utility of the products. However, the impact of follower entry on the pioneer

of low-INE will be minimal, for the link between anticipated availability of complementary products and the perceived utility is weak for such products (Farrell and Saloner 1986), We thus hypothesize:

H3: Anticipated follower entry is more effective in increasing consumers' purchase intention toward the pioneer of really new products that exhibit high versus low indirect network externalities.

Study 1

Research hypotheses were examined by two experimental studies. The purpose of Study 1 is to examine the effect of anticipated follower entry on consumers' purchase intention towards the pioneer brand of a RNP versus an INP, and the underlying psychological mechanism of such an effect. One hundred and forty-five undergraduate students (94 males and 53 females) participated in this study. The study was a 2 x 2 design with anticipated follower entry (with- vs. without-follower) and innovation newness (RNP vs. INP) as the between-subjects conditions.

Anticipated follower entry and product type were manipulated by a purported news report about a new TV. In the RNP conditions, the product was described as a TV which can display vivid 3D images without the need for special glasses. In the INP conditions, the product was a LCD TV which outperforms existing models in several key attributes. In the with-follower entry conditions, the news report stated that the major competitors of the pioneer brand have announced plans to introduce their own LCD (3D) TVs based on technologies similar to those of the pioneer. In the without-follower entry conditions, the news report stated that the pioneer brand is the only LCD (or 3D) TV of its kind in the market and will remain as the sole player in the foreseeable future.

Consistent with H1, anticipated follower entry increased consumers' purchase intention toward the pioneer brand of a RNP, but had decreased consumers' purchase intention toward the pioneer of an INP. Consistent with H2, the effect of anticipated follower entry on purchase intention toward the pioneer brand of a RNP was mediated by perceived risk, especially by perceived financial risk.

Study 2

Study 2 tests the impact of anticipated follower entry and indirect network externalities on consumer acceptance of the pioneer brands. The study used a 2 (high vs. low INE) x 2 (with vs. without anticipated followers) between-subject design. Seventy-two undergraduate students (48 males and 24 females) participated in this study. INE and follower conditions were both manipulated by a news report about a 3D TV. In the low NE condition, the news report claimed that the TV either require (high INE) or did not require (low INE) any specially formatted TV programs or DVDs to show the 3D images. The anticipated follower condition was manipulated in the same way as in Study 1.

Consistent with H3, anticipated follower entry increased consumers' purchase intention toward the pioneer of high-INE products to a larger extent than toward the pioneer of a low-INE product.

Discussion

Previous research on pioneering advantage has focused on situations where the pioneer's best strategy is to create and defend a market position that minimizes competition. In this study we found that the positive impact of the me-too follower's entry on the pioneer is contingent on the innovation newness and network externalities of the product. Thus, marketing managers need to take into account these specific product characterizes when formulating competitive strategies.

REFERENCES

Ali, Abdul. (1994), "Pioneering versus Incremental Innovation: Review and Research Propositions," *Journal of Product Innovation Management*, 11, 46–61.

Carpenter, Gregory S. and Kent Nakamoto (1989), "Consumer Preference Formation and Pioneering Advantage," *Journal of Marketing Research*, 26(3), 285-298.

Farrell, Joseph and Garth Saloner (1986), "Installed Base and Compatibility: Innovation, Product Pre-announcement and Predication," *American Economic Review*, 76 (4), 940-55.

Golder, Peter N and Gerard J. Tellis (1993), "Pioneer Advantage: Marketing Logic or Marketing Legend?" *Journal of Marketing Research*, 30(May), 158-170.

Hauser, John, Gerard J. Tellis, and Abbie Griffin (2006), "Research on Innovation: A Review and Agenda for Marketing Science," *Marketing Science*, 25(November-December), 687-717.

Katz, M. and Carl Shapiro (1986), "Technology Adoption in the Presence of Network Externalities," *Journal of Political Economy*, 94 (August), 822-841.

Kirmani, Amna and Akshay R. Rao (2000), "No Pain, No Gain: A Critical Review of the Literature on Signaling Unobservable Product Quality," *Journal of Marketing*, 64(2), 66-79.

McDougal, Yancy B. (1995), "Decision Making under Risk: Risk Preference, Monetary Goals and Information Search," *Personality and Individual Differences*, 18 (6), 771-782.

Medin, D.L. and Schaffer, M.M. (1978), Context Theory of Classification Learning, *Psychological Review*, 85, 207-238.

Min, Sungwook, Manohar U. Kalwani, and William T. Robinson (2006), "Market Pioneer and Early Follower Survival Risks: A Contingency Analysis of Really New Versus Incrementally New Product-Markets," *Journal of Marketing*, 70(January), 15-33.

Nofosky, Robert M. (1986), "Attention, Similiarity, and the Identification-Categorization Relationship," *Journal of Experimental Psychology, General*, 115, 39-57.

_____ (1988), "Similarity, Frequency and Category Representations," *Journal of Personality and Social Psychology*, 14(1), 54-65.

Novemsky, Nathan, Ravi Dhar, Norbert Schwarz, and Itamar Simonson (2007), "Preference Fluency in Choice," *Journal of Marketing Research*, 44(August), 347-356.

Ram, Sundaresan and Jagdish N. Sheth (1989), "Consumer Resistance to Innovations: The Marketing Problem and Its Solutions," *Journal of Consumer Marketing*, 6(Spring), 5-14.

Shankar, Venkatesh, Gregory S. Carpenter and Lakshman Krishnamurthi (1998), "Late Mover Advantage: How Innovative Late Entrants Outsell Pioneers," *Journal of Marketing Research*, 35(1), 54-70.

Srinivasan, Lilien and Rangaswamy (2004), "First in, First out? The Effects of Network Externalities on Pioneer Survival," *Journal of Marketing*, 68 (January), 41-58.

Stone, R.N. and K. Gronhaug (1993). "Perceived Risk: Further Considerations for the Marketing Discipline," European Journal of Marketing, 27(3) 39–50.

Sungwook, Min, Manohar U. Kalwani and William T. Robinson (2006), Market Pioneer and Early Follower Survival Risks: A Contingency Analysis of Really New Versus Incrementally New Product-Markets, *Journal of Marketing*, 70, 15-33.

Urban, Glen L., Bruce D. Weinberg, and John R. Hauser (1996), "Premarket Forecasting of Really-New Products," *Journal of Marketing*, 60(January), 47-60.

Whalen, Paul J. (1998), "Fear, Vigilance and Ambiguity: Initial Neuroimaging Studies of the Human Amygdala," *Current Directions in Physiological Science*, 7(December), 177-188.

How to Overcome Customers' Adoption Barriers?

Sabine Kuester, University of Mannheim, Germany
Silke Hess, University of Mannheim, Germany

EXTENDED ABSTRACT

Customers' resistance to innovations turns out to be a significant managerial problem as it is a major cause of new product failure. Resistance refers to a negative outcome of new product evaluation and is evoked by several adoption barriers, which inhibit the intention to adopt the innovation. Prior research has focused on functional adoption barriers such as innovations' perceived risk or expected value and has identified marketing instruments to overcome these barriers (Bearden and Shimp 1982; Ziamou and Ratneshwar 2003). Other studies in a new product context point to the need to target customers' cognitive barriers that refer to the complexity associated with the evaluation of innovations and lead to an unfavorable judgment (Moreau, Lehmann, and Markman 2001; Ozanne Brucks, and Grewal 1992; Peracchio and Tybout 1996). Therefore, in this research, we identify marketing communication instruments that decrease perceived complexity of new products and reduce customers' difficulties in evaluating innovations. In doing so, we also account for innovation-specific and customer-specific factors that may moderate the effects of these instruments on customers' adoption barriers.

In our study, cognitive barriers signify situations when the innovation is difficult to evaluate and to categorize into existing schemas. In this regard, cognitive barriers refer to the complexity associated with innovations and are the potential cause of resistance. Communicating that the new product belongs to an existing category may help customers to better understand and evaluate the innovation. In line with prior studies, we propose that providing a categorization cue in the presentation of a new product will reduce perceived complexity and in turn decrease innovation resistance (Gregan-Paxton and Moreau 2003; Moreau, Markman, and Lehmann 2001).

Furthermore, it is expected that innovation-specific and customer-specific factors moderate the effect of a categorization cue on perceived complexity. Prior research shows that the degree of newness perceived by customers is a crucial factor in the evaluation of new products (Veryzer 1998). Besides fundamental differences between more radical or incremental new products, consumer behavior research of new product evaluation shows that the relationship of judgment making and newness of information is not linear (Meyers-Levy and Tybout 1989; Ozanne et al. 1992). Therefore, following Robertson's (1971) continuum model of innovations, characterizing innovations as continuous, dynamically continuous, and discontinuous, we propose a U-shaped moderating effect of product newness on the relationship between categorization cue and complexity.

Since the objective of this study is to analyze the emergence of adoption barriers within a new product evaluation process, we regard customers' involvement and need for cognition as relevant moderating variables. Involvement leads to more extensive processing of new information. Consequently, we expect that a categorization cue will be more effective in a high involvement situation. Similarly, we hypothesize that individuals' willingness to make a cognitive effort is a prerequisite for the effectiveness of a categorization cue. Hence, we propose that individuals showing high need for cognition will be more engaged in using a provided categorization cue for new product evaluation.

Furthermore, we assume that experts are more competent than novices in evaluating new products of a particular category, since experts possess more distinct category knowledge. Yet, empirical research provides an interaction effect between expertise and incongruity in such a way that experts and novices respond differently to a match or mismatch of new information (Sujan 1985). Therefore, we hypothesize a three-way-interaction between the impact of the categorization cue, expertise, and product radicalness.

In our experiment members of an online panel evaluated a continuous, a dynamically continuous, and a discontinuous product innovation. Overall, results support our hypotheses. Presenting new products with a categorization cue significantly decreases customers' perceived complexity and consequently innovation resistance. We also observed a significant interaction effect of categorization cue and product radicalness. As expected, this interaction effect was best described by an U-shaped curve. In this respect, the categorization cue is less effective for dynamically continuous new products as they are more incongruent to the induced category than incremental ones. To categorize dynamically continuous new products individuals need a larger amount of information, hence, the provided categorization cue is not sufficient and cannot resolve the discrepancy. In case of discontinuous innovations, individuals tend to analyze information more analytically and can use the categorization cue to reorganize cognitive structures. Besides, we found a moderating effect of customers' need for cognition and conclude that the effectiveness of a categorization cue requires the willingness to engage in cognitive processes. In line with our proposition, the impact of the categorization cue was larger in high involvement situations, although the interaction effect was not significant. Furthermore, the effect of the categorization cue on complexity was smaller for experts when evaluating an incremental new product. However, when evaluating a radical new product, this effect was larger for experts. We conclude that experts are more competent to categorize congruent information within their field of expertise.

We derive implications for innovation management and recommend managers to assist customers in evaluating and categorizing new products. Our research suggests that by providing a categorization cue innovation resistance can be prevented, and thus, new product failure avoided. Furthermore, when designing marketing communication instruments for new product launch, managers have to carefully consider the impact of innovation-specific and customer-related factors. In particular, our empirical results point to the need for customer-specific launch tactics such as a new product communication campaign that targets either experts or novices.

REFERENCES

Bearden, William O. and Terence A. Shimp (1982), "The Use of Extrinsic Cues to Facilitate Product Adoption," *Journal of Marketing Research*, 19 (May), 229-39.

Gregan-Paxton, Jennifer and C. Page Moreau (2003), "How Do Consumers Transfer Existing Knowledge? A Comparison of Analogy and Categorization Effects," *Journal of Consumer Psychology*, 13 (September), 422-30.

Meyers-Levy, Joan and Alice M. Tybout (1989), "Schema Congruity as a Basis for Product Evaluation," *Journal of Consumer Research*, 16 (June), 39-54.

Moreau, C. Page, Donald R. Lehmann, and Arthur B. Markman (2001), "Entrenched Knowledge Structures and Consumer Response to New Products," *Journal of Marketing Research*, 38 (February), 14-29.

_____, Arthur B. Markman, and Donald R. Lehmann (2001), ""What Is It?" Categorization Flexibility and Consumers' Responses to Really New Products," *Journal of Consumer Research,* 27 (March), 489-98.

Ozanne, Julie L., Merrie Brucks, and Dhruv Grewal (1992), "A Study of Information Search Behavior during the Categorization of New Products," *Journal of Consumer Research,* 18 (March), 452-63.

Peracchio, Laura A. and Alice M. Tybout (1996), "The Moderating Role of Prior Knowledge in Schema-Based Product Evaluation," *Journal of Consumer Research,* 23 (December), 177-92.

Robertson, Thomas S. (1971), *Innovative Behavior and Communication*, New York et al.: Holt, Rinehart & Winston.

Sujan, Mita (1985), "Consumer Knowledge: Effects on Evaluation Strategies Mediating Consumer Judgments," *Journal of Consumer Research*, 12 (June), 31-46.

Veryzer, Robert W. J. (1998), "Key Factors Affecting Customer Evaluation of Discontinuous New Products," *Journal of Product Innovation Management,* 15 (March), 136-50.

Ziamou, Paschalina and Srinivasan Ratneshwar (2003), "Innovations in Product Functionality: When and Why Are Explicit Comparisons Effective?," *Journal of Marketing*, 67 (Spring), 49-61.

Measuring Salesperson Orientation of Consumers

Jeffrey S. Larson, Brigham Young University, USA
Sterling A. Bone, Brigham Young University, USA

EXTENDED ABSTRACT

Research on customer-salesperson relationships and sales performance has been plentiful (Churchill et al. 1985; Franke and Park 2006). This research can be divided into two major categories: 1) research that focuses on the properties of specific customer-salesperson relationships and the effects of those properties, and 2) research on enduring salesperson characteristics and their consequents.

More recently, researchers have begun to focus on the role of the consumer in the salesperson-customer interaction (Kirmani and Campbell 2004). Much of this study has grown from the acknowledgement of the Persuasion Knowledge Model of consumer behavior (Friestad and Wright 1994). This recent consumer-focused literature parallels the first category of the salesperson-focused stream of literature—an assessment of situation-specific consumer behavior in the sales process. We develop the Salesperson Orientation of Consumers (SOC) Scale to aid researchers and practitioners alike in understanding the many enduring consumer characteristics that affect the consumer-salesperson interaction.

We define the Salesperson Orientation of Consumers (SOC) as the enduring disposition of a consumer to engage in particular salesperson-related thoughts and behaviors across a variety of marketplace encounters with salespeople. Previous research on consumer behavior regarding salespeople has focused on how this behavior changes as a result of the properties of a particular interaction. By developing the SOC scale, we hope to identify and measure the salesperson-related behaviors that are determined more by consumer traits than the interaction.

To develop the Salesperson Orientation of Consumers (SOC) scale, we followed the procedures for creating and validating scales developed by Churchill (1979). First, an initial set of items were drafted. The original list of potential scale items came from several sources. A literature review on consumer-salesperson interaction turned up a 13-item scale from Goff, Bellenger and Stojack (1994) which measured consumers' orientation toward automobile salespeople. We adapted their scale items to address general salesperson orientation, rather than car-salesperson-specific orientation.

A second source of preliminary scale items came from a two-stage brainstorming process. In the first stage, we hypothesized various factors that consumers could use to describe their feelings and orientations toward salespeople, including factors from the literature and some of our own hypothesis. After brainstorming these factors with ourselves and by informal consultation with various colleagues, we generated several items to measure each of these factors. We then removed redundant measures, which resulted in a pool of 35 items.

Scale Purification: Study 1

The 35-item scale was administered to three different samples. The data from all three studies were subjected to separate exploratory factor analyses with a varimax rotation. In all three studies, the results suggested a four-factor structure with similar loadings across the 35 items. Individual scale items that either 1) did not load strongly on any of the four dimensions or 2) did not load consistently across all three studies were dropped. This left the 18 items below. Items 1-5, 6-10, 11-15, and 16-18 loaded on factors 1, 2, 3, and 4, respectively.

1. When a salesperson is helping me, I usually take his/her advice.
2. I value the opinion of salespeople.
3. I feel more comfortable buying something when a salesperson has recommended it to me.
4. I want salespeople to help me make decisions.
5. I trust the information I get from salespeople.
6. I feel some obligation to please salespeople.
7. I sometimes wonder if a salesperson thinks better of me as a result of my buying something.
8. I sometimes wonder if a salesperson thinks ill of me when I don't purchase anything.
9. I am sometimes afraid that a salesperson will think I'm cheap if I don't buy something.
10. When I decline to buy something, I feel bad for the salesperson.
11. I avoid stores with a lot of salespeople.
12. When shopping, I would rather make the decision on my own before talking to any salespeople.
13. I wish salesclerks only answered questions instead of trying to convince you to buy something.
14. I feel more comfortable entering a store where I know salespeople will not approach me.
15. I wish I could forever avoid having to talk to a salesperson.
16. I am a person who is easily convinced by salespeople.
17. I could be talked into a purchase by a persuasive salesperson.
18. For reasons I don't fully understand, pushy salespeople are often successful in getting a sale from me.

Factor Structure: Study 2

To test the new 18-item scale, 532 undergraduates completed the scale in exchange for extra credit in a marketing course. The data were then submitted to the same factor analysis with varimax rotation as previously performed to check that the factor loadings concurred with the data collected from the 35-item scale. The resulting factor structure aligned precisely with the one predicted. The data were also subjected to a confirmatory factor analysis in Lisrel 8.8, which confirmed the four-factor structure on all measures.

Interpretation of Factors

Information Seeking. Previous research has made much of the function of salespeople as experts aiding consumers to make better decisions (Wernerfelt 1994). Of course, consumers are likely to differ in their beliefs about salesperson motivations. The first factor in the SOC scale captures the consumer tendency to seek and value the information provided by salespeople.

Self Presentation. Personal interaction with a salesperson is one type of social interaction. In social interactions with salespeople, consumers are likely to vary in their concern for the impression they give to the salesperson (Lennox and Wolfe 1984). The second factor of the SOC scale measures this concern.

Avoidance. Previous research has shown that consumer heterogeneity in tolerance for salesperson interaction can lead to a differentiated retail equilibrium (Chu, Gerstner and Hess 1995).

Advances in Consumer Research
Volume 36, © 2009

The existence of this third SOC subscale provides some empirical evidence in support of their model specification. Consumers vary in the extent to which they seek to avoid salesperson interaction.

Convinceability. Despite universal contempt for high pressure selling tactics, salespeople continue to use them. Asch's conformity experiments and Milgram's fake-shock experiments illustrate the powerful effect of social pressure (Asch 1952; Milgram 1974). It should come as no surprise then that salespeople can often use social pressure to extract sales from not-entirely-willing consumers. Of course, consumers vary in the extent to which such sales tactics work on them. This fourth and final SOC subscale measures the extent to which consumers are influenced by salespeople.

Predictive Validity: Study 4

In study 4, participants responded to a number of vignettes about marketplace behavior relating to salespeople. Due to space limitations, we cannot present the results here, but the full working paper is available from the authors.

REFERENCES

Asch, Solomon E. (1952), *Social Psychology,* New York: Prentice Hall.

Churchill, Gilbert A. (1979), "A Paradigm for Developing Better Measures of Marketing Constructs," *Journal of Marketing Research*, 16, 64-73.

Churchill, Gilbert A. Jr., Neil M. Ford, Steven M. Hartley and Orville C. Walker Jr. (1985), "The Determinants of Salesperson Performance: A Meta-Analysis," *Journal of Marketing Research*, 22(2), 103-118.

Franke, George R. and Jeong-Eun Park (2006), "Salesperson Adaptive Selling Behavior and Customer Orientation," *Journal of Marketing Research*, 43(4), 693-702.

Friestad, Marian and Peter Wright (1994), "Persuasion Knowledge Model: How People Cope with Persuasion Attempts," *Journal of Consumer Research*, 21(1), 1-31.

Goff, Brent G., Danny N. Bellenger and Carrie Stojack (1994), "Cues to Consumer Susceptibility to Salesperson Influence: Implications for Adaptive Retail Selling," *Journal of Personal Selling and Sales Management*, 2, 25-39.

Kirmani, Amna and Margaret C. Campbell (2004), "Goal Seeker and Persuasion Sentry: How Consumer Targets Respond to Interpersonal Marketing Persuasion," *Journal of Consumer Research*, 31(3), 573-582.

Lennox, Richard D., and Raymond N. Wolfe (1984), "Revision of the Self-Monitoring Scale," *Journal of Personality and Social Psychology*, 46, 1349-1364.

Milgram, Stanley (1974), *Obedience to Authority: An Experimental View*. New York, Harper & Row.

Wernerfelt, Berger (1994), "On the Function of Sales Assistance," *Marketing Science*, 13(1), 68-82.

Does the Patient Really Act Like a Supermarket Shopper?
A Semiotic Typology of Patients' Attitudes and Expectations towards the Health-Care System and the Consumption of Medicines

Isabelle Chalamon, Groupe ESC Dijon Bourgogne, France
Benoit Heilbrunn, ESCP EAP, France
Ines Chouk, IUT Cergy-Pontoise, France

EXTENDED ABSTRACT

What do patients expect of the health-care system? How can we explain the diversity of these expectations and how can we classify them? The purpose of this paper is to answer these questions by proposing a general typology of patients' attitudes and expectations towards the health-care system and medicines consumption.

In the health-care sector, the patient occupies a more and more central place. Increasingly active in health-care decision making (Shaffer and Sherrell 1995; Charles, Gafni, and Whelan 1999; Stevenson, Barry, Britten, Barber, and Bradley 2000), the patient is often treated as a "participant actor", as a "patient-expert" (Barbot 2002; Fox, Ward, and O'Rourke 1999), or as a "consumer" of medicine and health-care. He (or she)'s involved in his/her own diagnosis and treatment, (Herzlich and Pierret 1984) and is actively in search of information (Risker 1996; Wagner, Hu, and Hibbard 2001). The patient, as a final user of the health care system, is thus emerging as an increasingly pivotal research object.

The existing literature presents many typologies such as patients' preferences for various attributes of the doctor-patient relationship (Vick and Scott 1998), patients' participation in healthcare decision-making (Flynn, Smith, and Vanness 2006), patient's behaviours in health-care services (Shaffer and Sherrell 1995) and of patients' satisfaction (Singh 1990). Two main limits of these approaches can be identified. Firstly, these typologies focuse only on one dimension of the relationship between patients and the health-care system. A more global approach is required in order to really understand patients' preferences and expectations with respect to the health-care system and medicines consumption. Secondly, these typologies are based on "fixed" positions: each patient of the sample is "classified" in one cluster. But the points of view expressed are largely dependant on situational variables. We need to identify "virtual positions" and, based on theses positions, built situational "scenarios". In this context, our research objective is *to develop a general conceptual framework to understand and classify patients' expectations towards the health-care system and medicines consumption*. Furthermore, from a managerial point of view, there is no clear market "segmentation" of patients behaviours in this sector. Thus, the aim of our research, is to propose a relevant "segmentation tool" in the health-care context. It will provide professionals in this sector with a global vision of the final consumer's expectations. Based on this segmentation, improvements in service quality and patients' global satisfaction could be made. Indeed, the proposed classification will help doctors and institutional organizations to better understand patients' expectations and hence to meet their preferences more accurately. Moreover, based on this typology, pharmaceutical firms and actors in the field of health-care could provide a better positioning of their offers and develop more adapted communication strategies.

In order to develop a typology based on virtual positions, we carried out a semiotic analysis (Greimas 1983; Greimas and Courtès 1983) of patient's representations and expectations of the health-care system and medicines consumption, on the base of 38 semi-structured interviews. Four types of values expressed by patients were identified: the functional, the existential, the critical and the hedonistic values. The "functional" patient has a problem/solution logic and a functional approach towards health-care. On the other hand, the "existential patient" values health-care in a more global way: his definition of good health is more than just "not to be ill". This kind of patient trusts the system greatly and has a social approach to medicine: he feels that dialogue is a part of treatment and his choice may be influenced by peers or professional advice. The "critical patient" has a consumerist approach towards medicine. He is in a logic of comparison and budget-optimisation. Hedonistic valorisation is the negation of practical values. For this type of patient, health-care is a kind of "game" in which only the ludic dimension of the service is considered. Based on these values, a quantitative study was carried out in order to identify a typology of patients: data were collected on 200 patients. We identified four patient profiles: Hedonist, Functional, Optimizer, and Skeptic.

This study has two main contributions. First, this research underlines the interest of a structural semiotic approach to study the behaviour of health-care consumers. This approach provides an analytic tool to understand the variety of patients' attitudes and behaviours regarding health, health-care and medicines consumption. From a theoretical point of view, we can conclude that patients may be studied as consumers, and that medicine and health-care services are evaluated and valorised in the same way as other products or services. Second, this study provides a segmentation of patient behaviours. Based on patients' values, a typology of four patient profiles was proposed: hedonists, functionals, skeptics and optimizers. Based on the real-world heterogeneity of health-care consumers, our analysis should permit the development of a more targeted approach for each patient-type, and indeed a more global, uniform, yet accurately partitioned communication strategy. Depending on the cluster characteristics, different communication strategies should be adopted. For example, for skeptics, communication should be concentrated on the benevolence of the pharmacist/doctor. Optimizers, on the contrary, are more interested in cheaper products. Functionals are sensitive to the promptness of service, and hedonists to the benefits of the products on their welfare. Given the specificity of the context (France) and the size of our sample, additional research should be realized to determine the extent to which the results can be generalized.

REFERENCES

Barbot, Janine (2002), *Les Malades en Mouvement, la Médecine et la Science à l'Epreuve du Sida,* Paris, Balland.

Charles, Cathy, Amiram Gafni, and Tim Whelan (1999), "Decision-Making in the Physician-Patient Encounter: Revisiting the Shared Treatment Decision-Making Model", *Social Science and Medicine*, 49, 651-61.

Flynn, Kathryn E., Maureen A. Smith, and David Vanness (2006), "A Typology of Preferences for Participation in Healthcare Decision Making", *Social Science and Medicine,* 63, 1158-69.

Floch, Jean Marie (1988), "The Contribution of Structural Semiotics to the Design of a Hypermarket", *International Journal of Research in Marketing*, 4, 3, 233-53.

_____ (2001), *Semiotics, Marketing and Communication: Beneath the Signs, the Strategies*, Palgrave Macmillan.

Fox, Nicholas J., Katie J. Ward, and Alan J. O'Rourke (1999), "The 'expert patient': empowerment or medical dominance? The case of Weight loss, pharmaceutical drugs and the Internet", *Social Science and Medicine*, 60, 1299-309.

Greimas Algirdas J. (1983), Structural Semantics: An Attempt at a Method, Lincoln, University of Nebraska Press.

Greimas, Algirdas J. and Joseph Courtès (1983), *Semiotics and language: an Analytical Dictionary*, Indiana University Press.

Herzlich, Claudine and Janine Pierret (1984), *Malades d'Hier, Malades d'Aujourd'hui. De la Mort Collective au Devoir de Guérison,* Paris, Payot.

Risker, Christopher D. (1996), "The Health Belief Model and Consumer Information Searches: towards an integrated Model", *Health Marketing Quarterly*, 13, 3, 13-26.

Singh, Jagdip (1990), "A Multifacet Typology of Patient Satisfaction with Hospital Stay", *Journal of Health-care Marketing*, 10, 4, 8-20.

Shaffer, Teri R. and Daniel L. Sherrell (1995), "Exploring Patient Role Behaviors for Health-care Services: The Assertive, Activated and Passive Patient", *Health Marketing Quarterly*, 13, 1, 19-35.

Stevenson, Fiona A., Christine A. Barry, Nicky Britten, Nick Barber, and Colin P. Bradley (2000), "Doctor-patient communication about drugs: the evidence for shared decision making", *Social Science and Medicine*, 50, 829-40.

Vick, Sandra and Anthony Scott (1998), "Agency in Health-care. Examining Patients' Preferences for Attributes of the Doctor-Patient Relationship", *Journal of Health Economics*, 17, 587-605.

Wagner, Todd H., Teh- wei Hu, and Judith H. Hibbard (2001), "The Demand for Consumer Health Information" *Journal of Health Economics*, 20, 1059-75.

Zandbelt, Linda C., Ellen M. A. Smets, Frans J. Oort, and Hanneke C. J. M. De Haes (2005), "Coding Patient-Centred Behaviour in the Medical Encounter, *Social Science and Medicine*, 61, 661-71.

Intersectionality: Insights for Consumer Research

Ahir Gopaldas, York University, Canada
Ajnesh Prasad, York University, Canada
David Woodard, Ontario Ministry of the Attorney General, Canada

EXTENDED ABSTRACT

Intersectionality is a research paradigm that considers how multiple social systems (such as race, class, gender, education, marital status, sexuality, religion, nationality, immigration status, disability, etcetera) co-determine the experience of human life (Collins 1986, 1990; Crenshaw 1989, 1991). Over the past decade, numerous, diverse, and even conflicting definitions, methods, and applications of intersectionality have preoccupied social theorists and paradoxically popularized the paradigm across the social sciences (Davis 2008). In this article, we conduct a multidisciplinary review of literature on intersectionality to chart a brief history, distinguish it from prior perspectives, organize its various meanings, and delineate McCall's (2005) tri-partite classification of (*anticategorical*, *intracategorical*, and *intercategorical*) methodological approaches to intersectional research. Next, we consider the general intellectual utility of intersectionality across the social sciences and specific implications for important topics in three consumer research paradigms. We believe this line of inquiry is important for a number of reasons:

Proliferation. The intersectionality paradigm is gaining currency in theory, education, and practice. It has been hailed as the "most important contribution that women's studies has made so far" (McCall 2005: p.1771). Major social science journals now expect intersectional approaches, while race-, class-, and gender-only studies can be seen as "theoretically misguided, politically irrelevant, or simply fantastical" and are thus often rejected (Davis 2008: p.68). Intersectionality is now also taught in introductory undergraduate and graduate courses (Ritzer 2007). Collins' (1990) foundational text on intersectionality (*Black Feminist Thought*) has been discussed and applied widely across the social sciences (its citation count currently exceeds 3000), and in 2008, Collins became the 100th President of the *American Sociological Association*. Finally, though theory is several steps ahead of practice (Verloo 2006), legal awareness of intersectionality is slowly reformulating governance policies in domains such as affirmative action, human rights advocacy, and social work.

Conceptual confusion. Despite its "spectacular success," Davis (2008: p.67) notes that intersectionality remains a confusing concept because it suffers from "ambiguity" and "incompleteness" (p.76). Hence, in this article, we aim to clarify the meanings of intersectionality by contrasting intersectional and non-intersectional approaches to social research and disentangling the paradigm's ontological, axiological, epistemological, and methodological facets.

Methodological complexity. Acknowledging the intersectional nature of social systems challenges researchers to account for an incredible amount of phenomenological complexity. However, the task of intersectional research is itself also a complex endeavor requiring careful methodological considerations to make it comprehensible. McCall (2005) offers the most extensive review of methodological approaches to date. We build on her tripartite classification of approaches to develop a comparative framework that elaborates on the distinctive features of each approach.

Transferable utility. Thus far, intersectionality has been applied to a limited number of substantive topics. We argue that intersectionality can be applied to any systematic study of difference, among or within social systems, in economic, cognitive, social, or cultural processes, in quantitative or qualitative research.

Transformative Consumer Research (TCR). TCR (Mick 2006) is an emerging paradigm that emphasizes the public policy goal of achieving consumer welfare in an otherwise theoretical discipline of consumer research. To further bridge the transformative-theoretical divide, we discuss how intersectionality is particularly well suited to address the theoretical concern of consumer vulnerability, a top TCR priority.

Consumer Psychology. Diversity is an important but significantly overlooked domain of consumer psychology (Williams, Lee, and Henderson 2008). We suggest how future diversity research can be attuned to the intersectional nature of social categories without losing sight of consumer psychologists' current methodological competencies (i.e. experimental and quantitative methods).

Consumer Culture Theory (CCT). The CCT paradigm (Arnould and Thompson 2005) has already begun to tacitly appropriate intersectional ways of thinking, especially studies of the *sociohistoric patterning* of consumption. In this article, we discuss less apparent implications for studies on *identity interpellation*.

The meanings of intersectionality. A multidisciplinary review of the current literature on intersectionality generates a plethora of nuanced meanings. Intersectionality has been described as a social phenomenon, a theoretical perspective, a set of normative guidelines, and a set of methodological practices. To encompass this wide array of meanings, we describe intersectionality as a paradigm and attempt to disentangle its ontological, axiological, epistemological, and methodological facets. The foundational ontological proposition of the intersectionality paradigm is that identity categories (*American, European, Black, White, Poor, Working-class, Middle-class, Professional, Men, Women, Illiterate, Educated, Single, Married, Divorced*, etcetera) are integrated in subjects (e.g. *White Professional Men*) and collude to produce unique social experiences, which cannot be adequately accounted for by the sum of essences (e.g. *White-ness, Professional-ness, Masculinity*) or the interaction effects at the level of systems (e.g. race, class, gender). However, the intersectionality paradigm does *not* make a universal statement about the extent or manner in which systems of categories are integrated *but* contends that this question be left open to empirical investigation in context. The paradigm's purpose is to highlight the prospect of partial to extensive integration of systems and to prescribe concepts and methods to investigate the extent and manner of such integration. In addition, the intersectionality paradigm also posits that the nature of being for any social subject is always multi-categorical, sometimes multi-level, internally heterogeneous, dynamic, crosscutting, and context-specific. In axiological terms, the paradigm is a two-fold political project to (1) reveal the matrix of privilege/oppression and (2) amplify the lived experience of marginalized individuals. For example, McCall (2001) empirically demonstrates the intersectional roles of race, class, gender, and context in producing wage inequality. The remainder of this article uses McCall's (2005) tri-partite classification of (*anticategorical, intracategorical*, and *intercategorical*) intersectional approaches to social research to organize a discussion of methodology. While all methodological approaches share the paradigm's ontological and axiological facets, they diverge on epistemological counts. We hope our discussion highlights the theoretical potency of the intersectionality paradigm and draws more research attention to the dynamic interplay of social systems.

REFERENCES

Arnould, Eric J. and Craig J. Thompson (2005), "Consumer Culture Theory (CCT): Twenty Years of Research," *Journal of Consumer Research*, 31 (March), 868–82.

Collins, Patricia Hill (1986), "Learning From the Outsider Within: The Sociological Significance of Black Feminist Thought," *Social Problems*, 33 (6), S14-S32.

Collins, Patricia Hill (1990/1999), *Black Feminist Thought: Knowledge, Consciousness, and the Politics of Empowerment*. New York: Routledge.

Crenshaw, Kimberlé Williams (1989), "Demarginalizing the Intersection of Race and Sex: A Black Feminist Critique of Antidiscrimination Doctrine, Feminist Theory, and Anti-Racist Politics," *University of Chicago Legal Forum*, 139-67.

Crenshaw, Kimberlé Williams (1991), "Mapping the Margins: Intersectionality, Identity Politics, and Violence against Women of Color," *Stanford Law Review* 43 (6): 1241-79.

Davis, K. (2008), "Intersectionality as buzzword: A sociology of science perspective on what makes a feminist theory successful," *Feminist Theory*, 9 (1), 67.

McCall, Leslie (2001), *Complex Inequality: Gender, Class and Race in the New Economy*, New York: Routledge.

McCall, Leslie (2005), "The Complexity of Intersectionality," *Signs: Journal of Women in Culture and Society*, 30(3): 1771-800.

Mick, David Glen (2006), "Meaning and Mattering Through Transformative Consumer Research," in *Advances in Consumer Research*, Volume 33, Cornelia Pechmann and Linda L. Price (eds.).

Ritzer, G. (2007). *Contemporary Sociological Theory and Its Classical Roots: The Basics*. Boston: McGraw-Hill.

Verloo, M. (2006), "Multiple Inequalities, Intersectionality and the European Union," *European Journal of Women's Studies*, 13 (3), 211.

Williams, J., W.N. Lee, and G. Henderson (2008), "Diversity Issues in Consumer Psychology," in *Handbook of Consumer Psychology*, C. Haugtvedt, F. Kardes, and P. Herr (eds.), Mahwah, NJ: Erlbaum.

Sequencing Promotion and Prevention Features: The Moderating Role of Regulatory Focus

Subimal Chatterjee, Binghamton University, USA
Ashwin Vinod Malshe, Binghamton University, USA
Timothy B. Heath, Miami University, USA

EXTENDED ABSTRACT

Consider a recent advertisement for Crest Pro-Health toothpaste highlighting seven brand benefits: preventing cavities, preventing tartar, whitening teeth, freshening breath, preventing sensitivity, preventing gingivitis, and preventing plaque (http://www.crest.com/prohealth/). Since the brand lists more prevention features (i.e., information focusing on avoiding negative outcomes) than promotion features (i.e., information focusing on achieving positive outcomes; Aaker and Lee, 2001), it is likely to appeal more to prevention-focused consumers as opposed to promotion-focused consumers (Higgins 1997). However, the advertisement also uses a mixed sequence to present the information (alternating between prevention and promotion features) instead of blocking them (presenting all prevention features before all promotion features, or vice versa). We claim that a mixed sequence might appear less organized than a blocked sequence, a sense of disorganization that could increase the perception that the brand offers more variety (Kahn and Wansink 2004). Moreover, should the enhanced variety perception give the impression that the toothpaste is a change from the status-quo, the mixed sequence should appeal more to promotion-focused as opposed to prevention-focused consumers (Chernev 2004). This is because the desire for change fits better with the advancement goals of promotion-focused consumers than the security and safety goals of prevention-focused consumers.

In Study 1, sixty undergraduate students (26 females), from a large university in the northeast, read that the makers of a new brand of toothpaste, positioned on two promotion features (fresh breath and white teeth) and two prevention features (plaque buildup and tooth cavity), were investigating three different methods of ordering the features in their advertisements. The mixed sequence alternated between the promotion and prevention features. The two blocked sequences put the two promotion features either first, or last. We asked participants which sequence maximized the perception that the brand offers a variety of features. Thereafter, the participants completed the Regulatory Focus Questionnaire (RFQ; Higgins et al. 2001) that contained six promotion items (e.g., *I feel like I have been successful in making progress toward being successful in my life*) and five prevention items (e.g., *Not being careful enough has gotten me into trouble at times*; reverse scaled). Seventy percent of our participants (42/60) reported that the mixed sequence maximized feature variety ($z=3.10, p<.01$). We classified each participant as either promotion-focused (average promotion score-average prevention score>0) or prevention-focused (difference score<0; see Higgins et al. 2001) and examined the feature variety perceptions of the two groups. Seventy-one percent (21/41) of the promotion-focused participants thought that the mixed sequence offered more variety (than the two other blocked sequences), and 68% (13/19) of the prevention focused participants thought likewise.

In Study 2, we tested whether a mixed presentation of promotion and prevention features led to superior brand evaluation relative to a blocked presentation of the same features, and whether the favorable assessment was stronger among promotion as opposed to prevention-focused consumers. One-hundred-eighteen undergraduate students (77 females) participated in the study. We randomly assigned the participants into one of two regulatory focus conditions. Following the procedure outlined by Higgins and others (1994), we asked participants in the promotion-focused (prevention-focused) conditions to write a brief essay about their hopes and aspirations (duties and obligations), at present as well as five years from now. After participants had completed their essays, we directed them to a different task where they read that a toothpaste manufacturer was conducting a market survey to find out what consumers thought about the four different features of their brand. The selected features were identical to Study 1. To mimic a sequence, we presented the four features, one page at a time. The mixed sequences alternated between a promotion feature and a prevention feature or between a prevention feature and a promotion feature. The blocked sequences presented all the promotion features first or last. After reading about each feature, the participants evaluated the feature on two 7-point scales (very attractive/very unattractive, very important/very unimportant), and then turned the page to read about the next feature. After the participants had read and evaluated all four features, they evaluated the brand on a 100-point (Best/Worst) scale (see Escalas 2007, for a similar scale).

The attractiveness/importance ratings of the features were sufficiently correlated ($\alpha=0.75$) to merit creating a composite weight measure for the promotion and prevention features. We modeled brand evaluation as a function of all main and interaction effects of regulatory focus (prevention, promotion) sequence (mixed, blocked), prevention-feature weights, and promotion-feature weights. We controlled for gender (males, females), and the felt intensity of the prime (the number of words written by the participants in their essays) by treating these as covariates in the model. On the average, the brand received higher evaluation when the features were mixed ($M=89.19$) than blocked ($M=80.37$; $F(1, 98)=4.99$, $p<.05$). The sequence main effect was qualified by regulatory focus ($F(1,98)=5.33, p<.05$). Promotion-focused participants gave higher brand evaluation when the features were mixed ($M=90.93$) than blocked ($M=78.50$; $F(1,98)=7.99, p<.01$). The prevention-focused participants gave marginally higher brand evaluation when the features were mixed ($M=87.83$) than blocked ($M=82.39$), but the difference was not statistically significant.

Our results hold both theoretical and practical significance. From a theory perspective, to the best of our knowledge this is the first attempt to connect the concept of regulatory focus to information sequencing, and therefore adds to previous research on self-regulation in different contexts (Brockner et al. 2002, Chernev 2004, Liberman et al. 1999). From a managerial perspective, given that marketers often cannot customize their appeals to the promotion-focused and prevention-focused target segments (e.g., one Crest Pro-Health advertisement targeted to both promotion-focused and prevention-focused segments), it would make sense to include both promotion as well as prevention appeals in their communications. However, to get the maximum impact out of such mixed advertisements, our results show that marketers would need to use a mixed (alternating) feature sequence.

REFERENCE

Aaker, Jennifer L. and Angela Y. Lee (2001), "'I' Seek Pleasures and 'We' Avoid Pains: The Role of Self-Regulatory Goals in Information Processing and Persuasion," *Journal of Consumer Research*, 28 (1), 33-49.

Avnet, Tamar and E. Tory Higgins (2006), "How Regulatory Fit Affects Value in Consumer Choices and Opinions," *Journal of Marketing Research*, 43 (1), 1-10.

Brockner, Joel, Srikanth Paruchuri, Lorraine Chen Idson, and E. Tory Higgins (2002), "Regulatory Focus and the Probability Estimates of Conjunctive and Disjunctive Events," *Organizational Behavior and Human Decision Processes*, 87 (1), 5-24.

Cesario, Joseph, Heidi Grant, and E. Tory Higgins (2004), "Regulatory Fit and Persuasion: Transfer from 'Feeling Right,'" *Journal of Personality and Social Psychology*, 86 (3), 388–404.

Chernev, Alexander (2004), "Goal Orientation and Consumer Preference for the Status Quo," *Journal of Consumer Research*, 31 (3), 557-65.

Escalas, Jennifer E. (2007), "Self-Referencing and Persuasion: Narrative Transportation Versus Analytical Elaboration," *Journal of Consumer Research*, 33, 421-29.

Frederick, Shane, George Loewenstein, and Ted O'Donoghue (2002), "Time Discounting and Time Preference: A Critical Review," *Journal of Economic Literature*, 40 (2), 351-401.

Higgins, E. Tory (1997), "Beyond Pleasure and Pain," *American Psychologist*, 52 (12), 1280-300.

Higgins, E. Tory, Ronald S. Friedman, Robert E. Harlow, Lorraine Chen Idson, Ozlem N. Ayduk, and Amy Taylor (2001), "Achievement Orientations from Subjective Histories of Success: Promotion Pride Versus Prevention Pride," *European Journal of Social Psychology*, 31 (1), 3-23.

Higgins, E. Tory, Christopher J. Roney, Ellen Crowe, and Charles Hymes (1994), "Ideal Versus Ought Predilections for Approach and Avoidance: Distinct Self-Regulatory Systems," *Journal of Personality and Social Psychology*, 66 (2), 276-86.

Hoch, Stephen J., Eric T. Bradlow, and Brian Wansink (1999), "The Variety of an Assortment," *Marketing Science*, 18 (4), 527-46.

Idson, Lorraine Chen, Nira Liberman, and E. Tory Higgins (2000), "Distinguishing Gains from Nonlosses and Losses from Nongains: A Regulatory Focus Perspective on Hedonic Intensity," *Journal of Experimental Social Psychology*, 36 (3), 252-74.

Kahn, Barbara E. and Brian Wansink (2004), "The Influence of Assortment Structure on Perceived Variety and Consumption Quantities," *Journal of Consumer Research*, 30 (4), 519-33.

Lau-Gesk, Loraine (2005), "Understanding Consumer Evaluations of Mixed Affective Experiences," *Journal of Consumer Research*, 32 (1), 23-28.

Liberman, Nira, Lorraine Chen Idson, Christopher J. Camacho, and E. Tory Higgins (1999), "Promotion and Prevention Choices between Stability and Change," *Journal of Personality and Social Psychology*, 77 (6), 1135-45.

Loewenstein, George and Drazen Prelec (1992), "Anomalies in Intertemporal Choice: Evidence and an Interpretation," *The Quarterly Journal of Economics*, 107 (2), 573-97.

Pham, Michel Tuan, Joel B. Cohen, John W. Pracejus, and G. David Hughes (2001), "Affect Monitoring and the Primacy of Feelings in Judgment," *Journal of Consumer Research*, 28 (2), 167-88.

Rodin, Judith and Peter Salovey (1989), "Health Psychology," *Annual Review of Psychology*, 40 (1), 533-79.

Trijp, Hans C. M. Van, Wayne D. Hoyer, and Jeffrey J. Inman (1996), "Why Switch? Product Category: Level Explanations for True Variety-Seeking Behavior," *Journal of Marketing Research*, 33 (3), 281-92.

Wang, Jing and Angela Y. Lee (2006), "The Role of Regulatory Focus in Preference Construction," *Journal of Marketing Research*, 43, 28–38.

Williams, Patti and Jennifer L. Aaker (2002), "Can Mixed Emotions Peacefully Coexist?" *Journal of Consumer Research*, 28 (4), 636-49.

Consumer Response to Harmful Products with Cause-Related Marketing: Influences of Product-Cause Fit and Product Type

Chun-Tuan Chang, National Sun Yat-sen University, Taiwan

EXTENDED ABSTRACT

Partnering charitable causes with products has become a common practice for many marketing programs, referred to strategically cause-related marketing (CRM). CRM is one major philanthropic activity for a corporation to donate money to a charity each time a consumer makes a purchase. Sharing the business ethics and value of "paying back to society", CRM has become popularly adopted by industries or companies which have brought about many of environmental problems (e.g., water and air pollution, land degradation, and chemical contamination, and transport) because of the manufactured products or production process.

Recent studies have begun to examine potential factors that might affect CRM effectiveness and how consumers respond to CRM initiatives. One important variable that has been identified to determine the success of CRM is the *fit* between a product and a cause. Although researchers agree that selecting the "right" cause is a key to a successful CRM strategy, little is known in terms of what constitutes a good fit and how the fit nature can moderate the CRM effectiveness. In the present study, two high-fit natures are explored: *consistent fit* (i.e., a cause and a product have consistent images or similar values) and *complementary fit* (i.e., a selected cause is used to improve the harmful image through a compensation act). This issue especially draws our attention in the circumstances that consumers already have inherent negative evaluations toward a product when they perceive it as harmful. The other factor investigated previously is product type. Hedonic products are motivated by the desire for sensual pleasure and utilitarian ones are provoked by a basic need. CRM is more likely to be effective in promoting hedonic products than utilitarian ones because of guilt feeling accompanied with the purchase. However, contingent effects of product type with harmful nature remains unexplored.

Using the context of harmful products, this research extends the concept of product-cause fit by exploring how consumer perceptions of fit nature affect attitudes toward the sponsoring company and behavioral intention in purchase situations with different product types (i.e., utilitarian or hedonic), and consequently determine whether product-cause fit and its nature are necessary criteria to influence CRM effectiveness. Hypotheses were drawn from attribution theory including non-common effects and argumentation versus discounting principle (Kelley, 1967; Kelley, 1973; Kelley and Michela, 1980). An experiment in a 3 (product-cause fit: consistent fit vs. complementary fit vs. low fit) X 2 (product type: utilitarian vs. hedonic) between-subjects design is developed to test the relative CRM effectiveness of advertisement messages to promote products that consumers perceive as harmful. Products containing plastic (including packaging) are used as harmful products. In order to eliminate the effects of product-selection bias, two products with different price levels were chosen for each type (hedonic vs. utilitarian) based on a pre-test. Therefore, 12 experimental versions were produced. Prior to the experiment, the treatment booklets were randomized. Participants were randomly assigned to one of the 12 conditions above.

After successful manipulation checks, a series of analysis of variance were conducted to examine proposed hypotheses. The main effect of fit was first examined to replicate previous results. Participants preferred the product with a high-fit cause to that with a low-fit cause. The research supports the common assertion that

"fit" is important for successful CRM programs (Gupta and Pirsch, 2006; Hamlin and Wilson, 2004; Lafferty, 2007; Pracejus and Olsen, 2004; Trimble and Rifon, 2006). Participants tend to accept a product with a cause more easily when the cause is perceived as a high fit with the product image than as a low fit. Using the harmful product contexts, the experimental results are also analogous with recent works that the hedonic products bundled with a charity incentive are more effective than the utilitarian ones (Strahilevitz, 1999; Strahilevitz and Myer, 1998). More importantly, the present study raises concerns over the comprehensive understanding of "fit" and how it works. With a high-fit cause, the assessment of "fit nature" between a product and a cause may be an important consumer heuristic. Three observations are noteworthy.

First, when promoting a utilitarian product, the consistent fit between a product and a cause is more effective than the complementary fit. The results echo what previous research (e.g., Campbell and Kirmani, 2000; Szykman, 2004; Yoon et al., 2006) suggests that perceptions of a company's profit opportunities as obvious can lead to positive attitudes to the product bundled with a cause. Such perceptions of consistency could be the common node that would be activated in an individual's associative networks. *Second*, compared with the consistent fit, the complementary fit between a product and a cause is more effective when the charity incentive is associated with hedonic products. The purchase of hedonic products that have negative consequences on the environment may lead to dispositional blame. There is a motivation to alleviate the blame. Discovering that the manufacturer donates part of the profit from sales to an environment cause is consistent with this motivation and leads to increased behavioral intention to buy this product. With the purchase of utilitarian products that are environmentally harmful, the dispositional blame is diluted by the situational attribution that it is necessary to buy the product. Learning that part of the profit will go towards improving the environment is less consistent to consumers' goal. Behavioral intention to purchase thus becomes lower. *Third*, the influences of fit nature are stronger when the price of the harmful product is low. A possible reason could be that high price of the item may be associated with the downbeat impression that the company exploits the cause and that consumers would be better off making a direct contribution to the non-profit than purchasing products on CRM (Gupta and Pirsch, 2006). The effects of fit nature are thus reduced because of criticism of this exploitation.

This article has theoretical and practical contributions to CRM, consumer purchase decision-making, and societal marketing practice. It is important to go beyond simple demonstrations of the effects of fit, and to clarify *when* a cause-related promotion of a harmful product is likely to be observed, reversed, or eliminated because of fit nature. Investigating impacts of fit nature is an important marketing and public policy issue because both complementarity and consistency are commonly used as good-faith attempts to promote the charity incentive. However, they may not be equivalent with respect to their ability to enhance CRM effectiveness when different product types are considered. In practice, marketers hence stand to gain not only by choosing the appropriate fit strategy for their advertised products but also by taking the perceived product type of the offered bundles into consideration to optimize the effectiveness of cause-related campaigns.

REFERENCES

Campbell, M. C., and Kirmani, A. (2000), "Consumers' Use of Persuasion Knowledge: The Effects of Accessibility and Cognitive Capacity on Perceptions of an Influence Agent," *Journal of Consumer Research*, 27(2), 69-83.

Hamlin, R. P., and Wilson, T. (2004), "The Impact of Cause Branding on Consumer Reactions to Products: Does Product/ cause 'Fit' Really Matter?" *Journal of Marketing Management*, 20 (7-8), 663-681.

Kelley, H. H. (1967), "Attribution Theory in Social Psychology," in *Nebraska Symposium on Motivation*, Levine, D. (ed.), University of Nebraska Press, Lincoln, NB, 192-240.

Kelley, H. H. (1973), "The Process of Causal Attribution," *American Psychologist*, 28, 107-128.

Kelley, H. H. and Michela, J. L. (1980), "Attribution Theory and Research," *Annual Review of Psychology*, 31, 457-501.

Lafferty, B. A. (2007), "The Relevance of Fit in a Cause-Brand Alliance When Consumers Evaluate Corporate Credibility," *Journal of Business Research,* 60(5), 447-453.

Pracejus J. W., and Olsen G. D. (2004), "The Role of Brand/ Cause Fit in the Effectiveness of Cause-Related Marketing Campaigns," *Journal of Business Research*, 57(6), 635-540.

Strahilevitz, M. (1999), "The Effects of Product Type and Donation Magnitude on Willingness to Pay More for a Charity-Linked Brand," *Journal of Consumer Psychology*, 8(3), 215-241.

Strahilevitz, M., and Myers, J. G. (1998), "Donations to Charity as Purchase Incentives: How Well They Work May Depend on What You Are Trying to Sell," *Journal of Consumer Research*, 24(1), 434-446.

Szykman, L. R. (2004), "Who Are You and Why Are You Being Nice? Investigating the Industry Effect on Consumer Reaction to Corporate Societal Marketing Efforts," in Advances in Consumer Research, Vol. 31, Kahn, B. and M. F. Luce (eds.), 306-315.

Trimble, C. S., and Rifon, N. J. (2006), "Effects of Consumer Perceptions of Compatibility in Cause-Related Marketing Messages," *International Journal of Nonprofit and Voluntary Sector Marketing*, 11(1), 29-47.

Yoon, Y., Gurhan-Canli, Z., and Schwarz, N. (2006), "The Effects of Corporate Social Responsibility (CSR) Activities on Companies with Bad Reputations," *Journal of Consumer Psychology*, 16(4), 377-390.

The Category Label and Overall Similarity in Hybrid Products: Matches/Mismatches and Categorization Asymmetry in Consumer Preferences

Maria Saaksjarvi, Delft University of Technology, The Netherlands and HANKEN, Finland
Ewa Pulkkinen, HANKEN, Finland

EXTENDED ABSTRACT

Numerous studies show that consumers categorize a product based on its name, or based on its visual appearance to other products (i.e., its overall similarity) (e.g., Gregan-Paxton et al. 2005; Rips 1989). The relative dominance of the cues in categorization has been debated. A number of researchers claim superiority for the category label, stating that it is a more accurate cue for categorization, as a product's appearance does not necessarily reveal much of a product's purpose (Rips 1989; Yamauchi and Markman 2000). Others hold that overall similarity determines categorization to a much greater extent than the category label, as consumers are more susceptible to visual than verbal cues in categorizing new products (Gregan-Paxton et al. 2005; Rosch 1978). Although the category label and overall similarity have been widely studied, their conjoint effect is less known. Taking the approach of Yamauchi and Markman (2000) we define the category label and overall similarity on the level of mismatches and matches. The *category label* represents a product's category membership, whereas *overall similarity* refers to the degree of overlap a new product has to existing ones.

Our objective is to investigate the role of matches (and mismatches) of the category label and overall similarity in consumer preference for hybrid products. Hybrid products are products that combine two previously independent product categories into one product (Jain and Ziamou 1995). As compared to other products, they have multiple category labels, and overall similarity that links the product to multiple product categories. Considering that consumers categorize products in multiple ways, focusing on hybrid products allows us to examine how the way in which a product is categorized influences how consumers react to matches (mismatches) between overall similarity and the category label. By focusing on hybrid products, we extend on Yamauchi and Markman's study, which focused on a product with a single plausible category label with a single plausible category membership.

Studies that have addressed joint effects of *category labels and overall similarity* have received mixed results regarding their relative influences. Rips (1989) showed that similarity does not completely determine category membership, but neither does the category label alone. Rosch (1978) proposes that the effect of the category label is supportive to that of overall similarity, but cannot determine categorization by itself. Yamauchi and Markman (2000) propose that the conjoined influence of category labels and overall similarity primarily emerges from if they match or mismatch. In case of a mismatch, consumers follow the category label, presumably as it is more reliable and allows them to link the product to a taxonomic category.

The matches and mismatches in hybrid product can be linked to product categorization. Hybrid products can be interpreted using an asymmetrical or symmetrical categorization. If the categorization is *asymmetrical*, consumers use one of the product categories combined in the hybrid, reaching the interpretation that the product has one main category, and a single functionality (Costello and Keane 2000). In a *symmetrical* categorization, consumers use both of the product categories the hybrid product combines in classifying the product, thereby reaching the interpretation that the product has two main categories and two functionalities (Goldvarg and Glucksberg 1998; Wisniewski 1997).

In two studies, we examine the influence of matches/mismatches of consumer preference for hybrid products. Study 1 was an eye-tracking study conducted using 25 students. The results showed that consumers paid more attention to overall similarity than the category label, but that the importance of the category label increased in the mismatch condition. Study 1 also showed (tentatively) that consumers who engage in asymmetrical categorization were be positively (negatively) influenced by matches (mismatches) between overall similarity and the category label in assessing their preference for a hybrid product, whereas consumers who engage in symmetrical categorization are not likely to be influence by matches (mismatches) between overall similarity and the category label in assessing their preference for a hybrid product.

Study 2 was a questionnaire (paper and pencil study) with 75 consumers. In study 2, we replicated the hypothesis concerning the influence of categorization strategy (asymmetrical vs. symmetrical) and found support for the notion that consumers engaging in asymmetrical (vs. symmetrical) categorizations are susceptible to matches (mismatches). We also extended the applicability of the match/mismatch hypothesis to product characteristics, and showed that consumers are influenced by matches (mismatches) between the category label and overall similarity when assessing a product's net benefits and complexity. A match between the category label and overall similarity resulted in more benefits and less perceived complexity for a new hybrid product. Further, by comparing the match/mismatch hypothesis to the individual effects of the category label and overall similarity, we show that matches/mismatches account for a larger number of consumer responses to new products than the individual effects of the category label or overall similarity.

Taken together, the results provide support for the match/mismatch hypothesis in assessing the importance of the category label and overall similarity in consumer preferences.

REFERENCES

Barsalou, Lawrence W. (1985), "Ideals, Central Tendency, and Frequency of Instantiation as Determinants of Graded Structure in Categories," *Journal of Experimental Psychology: Learning, Memory, and Cognition*, 11, 629-649.

Chin, Wynne W. (1998b), "The Partial Least Squares Approach to Structural Equation Modeling," *Modern Methods for Business Research*, George A. Marcoulides, (ed.), Mahwah, New Jersey: Lawrence Erlbaum Associates, 295-336.

Costello, Fintan J. and Mark T. Keane (2000), "Efficient Creativity: Constraint-Guided Conceptual Combination," *Cognitive Science*, 24 (2), 299-349.

Estes, Zachary and Sam Glucksberg (2000), "Interactive Property Attribution in Concept Combination," *Memory and Cognition*, 28 (1), 28-34.

Goldvarg, Yevgeniya and Sam Glucksberg (1998), "Conceptual Combinations: The Role of Similarity," *Metaphor and Symbol*, 13 (4), 243-255.

Gregan-Paxton, Jennifer, Steve Hoeffler and Min Zhao (2005), "When Categorization Is Ambiguous: Factors That Facilitate the Use of a Multiple Category Inference Strategy," *Journal of Consumer Psychology*, 15 (2), 127–140.

Grice, H. Paul (1975), "Logic and conversation", in Peter Cole and Jerry L. Morgan, (eds.): *Syntax and Semantics*, 3, Speech Acts, New York, Academic Press, 41-58.

Jain, Kapil and Paschalina Ziamou (1995), "Hybrid Products: A Taxonomy and Propositions from a Categorization Perspective," in the Proceedings of the *COTIM*, Ruby Ray Dholakia and David R. Fortin (eds.), Newport, Rhode Island, 375-380.

Miller, Elizabeth G. and Barbara E. Kahn (2005), "Shades of Meaning: The Effect of Color and Flavor Names on Consumer Choice, " *Journal of Consumer Research*, 32 (1), 86-92.

Moore, Gary C. and Izak Benbasat (1991), "Development of an Instrument to Measure the Perceptions of Adopting an Information Technology Innovation," *Information Systems Research*, 2 (3), 173-191.

Moreau, C. Page, Donald R. Lehmann, and Arthur B. Markman (2001a), "Entrenched Knowledge Structures and Consumer Response to New Products," *Journal of Marketing Research*, 38 (1), 14-29.

Moreau, C. Page., Artur B. Markman and Donald R. Lehmann (2001b), "What Is It?' Categorization Flexibility and Consumers' Responses to Really New Products," *Journal of Consumer Research*, 27 (4), 489-98.

Ostlund, Lyman E. (1974), "Perceived Innovation Attributes as Predictors of Innovativeness," *Journal of Consumer Research*, 1, 23-9.

Rips, Lance J. (1989), "Similarity, Typicality, and Categorization," in Stella Vosniadou and Andrew Ortony (eds.), *Similarity and Analogical Reasoning*, Cambridge, England: Cambridge University Press, 21-59.

Roehm, Michelle L. and Brian Sternthal (2001), "The Moderating Effect of Knowledge and Resources on the Persuasive Impact of Analogies," *Journal of Consumer Research*, 28 (2), 257-272.

Rogers, Everett M. (1995). *Diffusion of Innovations*, 4th edition, New York: The Free Press.

Rosch, Eleanor. (1978), "Principles of Categorization," *Cognition and Categorization*, Rosch Eleanor and Barbara Lloyd (eds.), Erlbaum, Hillsdale NJ, 27-48.

Shafto, Patrick and John D. Coley (2003), "Development of Categorization and Reasoning in the Natural World: Novices to Experts, Naive Similarity to Ecological Knowledge," *Journal of Experimental Psychology: Learning, Memory, and Cognition*, 29 (4), 641-649.

Tversky, Amos (1977), "Features of similarity," *Psychological Review*, 84, 327-352.

Wisniewski, Edward J. and Bradley C. Love (1998), "Relations versus Properties in Conceptual Combination," *Journal of Memory and Language*, 38 (2), 177-202.

Wisniewski, Edward J. and Bradley C. Love (1997), "When Concepts Combine," *Psychonomic Bulletin and Review*, 4 (2), 167-183.

Wisniewski, Edward J. and Bradley C. Love (1996), "Construal and Similarity in Conceptual Combination," *Journal of Memory and Language*, 35 (3), 434-53.

Wood, Stacy L. and C. Page Moreau (2006), "From Fear to Loathing? How Emotion Influences the Evaluation and Early Use of Innovations," Journal of Marketing, 70 (July), 44-57

Yamauchi, Takashi and Arthur B. Markman (2000), "Inference Using Categories," *Journal of Experimental Psychology: Learning, Memory, and Cognition*, 26 (3), 776-795.

Yamauchi, Takashi and Arthur B. Markman (1998), "Category Learning by Inference and Classification," *Journal of Memory and Language*, 39, 124–148.

Examining Discourses of Gender and Consumption in the Media

Linda Tuncay, Loyola University Chicago, USA
Katherine Sredl, University of Illinois, USA
Marie-Agnès Parmentier, York University, Canada
Catherine Coleman, University of Illinois, USA

EXTENDED ABSTRACT

Gender identity is a fluid concept that has changed considerably over time, not only in its representation in media and its interpretation by consumers, but also in its conceptualization by researchers. Using hermeneutic analysis, a method used by prior consumer researchers, (e.g., Humphreys forthcoming; Coskuner 2006; Sherry 1995; Hirschman 1988), this paper explores gender and consumption discourses in popular media. Because gender is a relational and evolving construct, this study explores masculinity and femininity together to gain a holistic view of gender discourses in today's society. Specifically, the authors draw from two popular television shows, *Entourage* and *Sex and the City*, to illustrate how contemporary notions of femininity and masculinity are intertwined with consumption. The researchers found that the characters in both shows struggled with tensions between more traditional gender roles and the assumption of new, postmodern roles intimately associated with consumption (see, for example, Firat and Venkatesh 1995 for discussion on the assumption of postmodern roles). The nuances of these tensions are less frequently mentioned in popular media.

Three themes of masculinity emerged in *Entourage* that were both rooted in prior research as well as interwoven with more feminized notions of masculinity not extensively examined in previous inquiries. The first theme that emerged in the show was the Peter Pan ethos of childhood play and fun (Register 2001) and the Playboy lifestyle of self-indulgence and sexual conquests (Osgerby 2001). For the characters in *Entourage*, consumption is instrumental in enacting the masculine themes of the Peter Pan and Playboy lifestyles. At the same time, it is intertwined with traditionally feminized notions of gift giving and shopping. Second, the theme of buddydom, or the celebration of friendships with other men, was prevalent in *Entourage*. However, the characters' enactment of this relationship was more closely associated with a non-traditional family unit than with traditional notions of male bonding. While women are most often associated with communal goals, the portrayal of the *Entourage* "family" is reflective of broader shifts in the U.S. towards "non-traditional" households, including men living together beyond their college years (Lavigne 2004). Third, the consumption of "toys" has been demonstrated in prior research to be an important part of the enactment of masculinity (Fiske 1987) and is a central part of the male characters' lives in *Entourage*. But the quest for acquisition sometimes causes internal struggles for the characters when it conflicts with their desire to remain authentic. The motivation for authenticity has been demonstrated as a core theme of masculinity for Gen X men in prior research (Tuncay 2005). This struggle was particularly evident in the breadwinner, Vince, in a tension between his desire to take on "meaningful" acting parts in independent films and offers to act in commercialized, yet lucrative studio roles that would subsidize the characters' Hollywood consumption habits. Thus, in *Entourage*, several themes of masculinity emerged that resonated with prior research on gender and consumer behavior. However, the themes of this study were intertwined with conceptualizations of gender more traditionally associated with females, such as familial relationships, gift giving, shopping, and emphasis on physical appearance. While in the recent past, these behaviors have been associated with a segment of male consumers called "metrosexuals," such behaviors have now moved into the mainstream Thus, it is evident that new forms of masculinity are emerging, and are represented in popular media.

Three themes of gender fluidity and consumption also emerged in *Sex and the City*. While some of these themes have been discussed in prior research, the show demonstrates anxieties about balancing traditional and changing notions of femininity and masculinity. First, tensions between strict traditional gender roles and gender fluidity are prevalent. Negotiations over gender roles are demonstrated in the character Miranda, who struggles with her nonconformity to traditional gender roles when, for example, she prioritizes her career as a corporate lawyer, purchases a home and is faced with housekeeping. This tension is further demonstrated in the second theme that explores the costs of freedom and independence. *Sex and the City* displayed notable violations of traditional gender roles; in particular, the narratives of Samantha Jones portray striking examples of female sexual freedom. In asserting her independence and power through professional accomplishment, financial independence, sex without ties and home ownership, she is also forced to face her vulnerabilities. Third, the characters of *Sex and the City* struggle with the quest for authenticity, both in their consumption and in their identities. Much like in *Entourage*, the theme of authenticity builds through various storylines in which consumption actions are developed as metaphors for broader themes of life. For example, for the women of *Sex and the City*, the Playboy Mansion epitomizes notions of fantasy—sexual freedom and an idealized and luxurious lifestyle, especially for Samantha. However, their visit to the mansion ultimately signifies a lack of authenticity and fails to maintain the positive connotations of fantasy.

This research demonstrates that the characters of both shows actively explore masculine and feminine roles, though not without anxiety, as they move through new and fluid identities of gender that often are enacted through consumption. Tensions between traditional masculinity and alternative masculinities have been examined by past researchers (see, for example, Holt and Thompson 2004; Otnes and McGrath 2001). But in *Entourage*, the characters find ways to reestablish and reinforce their masculinities as they create new roles. In *Sex and the City*, several themes of gender found in prior research also emerged. While the notion of juggling and independence has been discussed in prior research (e.g., Thompson 1996) and despite acclaim in the popular press about ground-breaking portrayals of contemporary women, it is evident that the characters of *Sex and the City* still struggle to negotiate the gains of feminism with more traditional feminine ideals, much like how the characters of *Entourage* balance traditional gender roles with new masculine ideals. The authors find that these themes are reflective of ideological gains and shifts exemplified in feminist agenda and that, to a greater extent, they question what happens when these gains have been made.

REFERENCES

Coskuner, Gokcen (2006) "Grooming Masculinities: A Poststructuralist Analysis of Masculinity Discourses in Films," *Advances in Consumer Research*, 33, 63.

Firat, A. Fuat and Allandi Venkatesh (1995), "Liberatory Postmodernism and the Reenchantment of Consumption", *Journal of Consumer Research*, 22 (3), 239-267.

Hirschman, Elizabeth C. (1988) "The Ideology of Consumption: A Structural-Syntactical Analysis of 'Dallas' and 'Dynasty'," *Journal of Consumer Research*, 15 (3), 344-359.

Holt, Douglas and Craig Thompson (2004), "Man-of-action heroes: The pursuit of heroic masculinity in everyday consumption," *Journal of Consumer Research*, 31(2), 425-440.

Humphreys, Ashlee (Forthcoming), "Stacking the Deck: Gambling in Film and the Legitimization of Casino Gambling", *Explorations in Consumer Culture Theory*, Eds. Eileen Fischer and John Sherry, Routledge Press.

Lavigne, Paul (2004), "Roommates: It's a guy thing," *Dallas Morning News*, Accessed January 5, 2008, at www.baylor.edu/pr/bitn/news.php?action=story&story=34968

Osgerby, Bill (2001), *Playboys in Paradise*, New York, NY: Oxford International Publishers.

Otnes, Cele C. and Mary Ann McGrath (2001), "Perceptions and realities of male shopping behavior," *Journal of Retailing*, 77, 111-37.

Register, Woody (2001), "Everyday Peter Pans: Work, Manhood, and Consumption in Urban America, 1900-1930," in *Boys and Their Toys*, ed. Roger Horowitz, New York, NY: Routledge, 199-228.

Sherry, John F. (1995), "Bottomless Cup, Plug in Drug: A Telethnography of Coffee," *Visual Anthropology*, v.7 (4), 355-74.

Thompson, Craig J. (1996) "Caring Consumers: Gendered Consumption Meanings and the Juggling Lifestyle," *Journal of Consumer Research*, 22 (4), 388-408.

Tuncay, Linda (2005), "Men's Responses to Depictions of Ideal Masculinity in Advertising," *Advances in Consumer Research*, 2006, 33, 63.

Video Games, Processing Fluency and Choice: Exploring Product Placement in New Media

Haiming Hang, Lancaster University, UK
Susan Auty, Lancaster University, UK

EXTENDED ABSTRACT

Only recently has the increasing use of product placements in video games attracted academic attention. Video games, unlike TV or films, increase interactivity and sensory immersion, which may increase players' involvement with the placed product (Schneider and Cornwell, 2005). However, up to now no research has examined this advantage in detail, especially with regard to children who are believed to be more vulnerable to commercials (e.g. Auty and Lewis, 2004).

Furthermore, all previous research exploring product placement effectiveness was done without any consideration of contextual influences. But in reality consumers are not exposed to brands without contexts. For example, some consumers might indulge in video games (and be exposed to the brand) to demonstrate their game skills while others might only play the video game at their friends' request. Recently research has found that advertising effectiveness could be moderated by its context, an area that is worthy of further exploration (e.g. Malaviya, 2007).

In order to fill the above gaps, three experiments were done to explore the underlying mechanism of product placement in video games in affecting children's choice and to see whether its effectiveness would be moderated by one contextual factor—children's regulatory fit/nonfit when playing the game. By doing so, this study extends previous product placement research on several fronts: it is the first research to explore with children whether there is a unique advantage in encouraging interactive engagement with brands in video games; secondly it tries to demonstrate that a contextual factor such as children's regulatory fit/nonfit can moderate product placement effectiveness. Furthermore, while all previous research documented positive affect in participants after exposure to brands in the media, this research explores a possible boundary condition of this effect.

The main purpose of Study 1 was to explore the effect of product placement when brands were used as background in the game. The experimental design was a 2 (exposed to product placement vs. not exposed) x 2 (visual stimuli test vs. auditory stimuli test) between subjects factorial design. Children (n=131) were invited to either play a branded game (7 Up logo was used as background) or play a no-brand game for a similar length. The results show that product placement had a significant effect on children's choice, although the effect disappeared when the modality of presentation was changed from a visual display to a verbal offer. Therefore, it appears that when there was no interaction with the brand, perceptual but not conceptual fluency led to the effectiveness of product placement.

Study 2 was conducted to see if there is a unique advantage of placing brands in interactive media. Children (n=97) were randomly placed into four conditions: 1) control group playing an unbranded tennis game; 2) perceptual group playing a football game where the teams displayed the Nike logo on their shirts; 3) a conceptual group where children listened to a tape asking them to guess the team sponsor (Nike, Coke or Toshiba) and then played the unbranded tennis game; 4) a conceptual-perceptual group where children listened to the tape, "guessed" the sponsor and then played the same branded game as Group 2. Half of each group was asked to make a stimulus-based choice for the brands while the other half was asked to write down the brand names without the stimuli being provided (Lee, 2002). In order to keep conscious recall separate from unconscious fluency, children in both test modes were asked to exclude brands they had encountered in the game. The findings suggest that elaboration at the time of exposure led to conceptual priming. Prior exposure to the verbal stimulus of possible sponsors made children more likely to choose the brand in a written test (without cues) even though no child could recall being exposed to the brand. But there appeared to be no synergistic effects when children experienced both perceptual and conceptual fluency. It may be that perceptual fluency or conceptual fluency alone is sufficient to enhance the liking of a brand, and there are no additive effects on preference.

While previous research always reported a positive effect after exposure to product placement, Study 3 was done to see whether children's regulatory fit/nonfit when playing the game would moderate a placement's effectiveness. Children (n=100) were randomly allocated to the following four conditions: 1) a control group (playing a video game without any brand), 2) a test control group (playing a branded game only), 3) a regulatory fit group (playing a branded game while experiencing regulatory fit) and 4) a regulatory nonfit group (playing a branded game while experiencing regulatory nonfit). Children in both regulatory fit and nonfit conditions were asked to watch a TV ad about a cream preventing athlete's foot (a prevention focus) before playing the video game—FIFA 2002. Then when playing the video game, children who were allocated to the nonfit condition were told that the key strategy for playing the game was to score as many goals as possible (a promotion focus) while children who were allocated to the fit condition were told they needed to avoid letting the other team score (a prevention focus).

The results suggested that children in the regulatory fit condition were more likely to choose the brand in the game into their consideration set than children in the nonfit condition. Furthermore, children in the nonfit condition were also significantly less likely to choose the brand than children in the test control group (exposed to the brand only). Thus it appears that regulatory nonfit might block children from processing the stimulus even minimally.

In short, while previous research has attributed the effect of product placement to perceptual fluency, this study found that when the priming entailed a conceptual elaboration, such as being asked to choose a brand for players to wear—a common occurrence—children's subsequent choice of brand could be influenced even without perceptual fluency. However, its effect may be moderated by children's regulatory fit/nonfit when playing the game.

REFERENCES

Auty, Susan and Charlie Lewis (2004), "Exploring Children's Choice: The Reminder Effect of Product Placement," *Psychology & Marketing,* 21(9), 697-713.

Lee, Angela (2002), "Effects of Implicit Memory on Memory-Based Versus Stimulus-Based Brand Choice," *Journal of Marketing Research,* 39, 440-454.

Malaviya, Prashant (2007), "Amount and Type of Elaboration and Evaluation", *Journal of Consumer Research,* 34(June), 32-40.

Schneider, L-P and Cornwell, T. B. (2005) "Cashing In on Crashes via Brand Placement in Computer Games," *International Journal of Advertising,* 24(3), 321-343.

The Signaling Effects of Advertising and Distribution

Yaqin Shi, Hakuhodo, Japan
Akinori Ono, Keio University, Japan

EXTENDED ABSTRACT

Research Objective

The "signaling effect" stands as one of the most important topics in studies of consumer behavior. Previous research has focused primarily on price-quality associations in the consumers' cognitive processes (i.e., whether price has signaling effects on consumers' perceptions regarding the quality of a product). Some studies have confirmed the signaling effects of price, whereas others claim that there is only weak relationship between perceived price and quality. Advertising and distribution, in combination with price and quality, represent the key components of a marketing mix, known as the 4Ps: price, product, promotion, and place. However, little signaling research has dealt with advertising and distribution as signals, and no studies have examined associations among price, quality, advertising, and distribution. Here, we propose a causal model to examine the signaling effects of advertising and distribution on the perception of price and quality.

Proposed Model

Our proposed model includes the main hypotheses underlying previous signaling research, namely, that perceived price has direct and negative effects on purchase intention, as well as indirect and positive signaling effects on purchase intention via mediation by perceived quality. We expand this model by adding the construct of "subjective norm." This model is regarded as a variant of the Theory of Reasoned Action (TRA) insofar as it incorporates three determinants of purchase intention within the same general framework. Unlike the original TRA—and other purchase intention models proposed by signaling researchers—our model does not include attitude—and perceived value—because of evidence demonstrating direct links between belief and intention and also because of the difficulty in disentangling the direct effects of subjective norm on intention from the indirect effects as mediated by attitude. Finally, the signaling effects of perceived amounts of advertising and distribution on perceived price, quality, and subjective norm were introduced in this model.

The signaling effects of perceived amount of advertising on the perception of quality rest on the idea that honest sellers that provide high-quality products are more likely to expect repeat purchases compared to dishonest sellers that provide low-quality products. Moreover, heavy advertising may leads to inferences by consumers that these advertised products are more familiar to other consumers than unadvertised products, increasing the likelihood of the subjective norm. Consumers may also infer that well-advertised products are higher in price simply because the heavy advertising results in higher cost.

The presumed signaling effects of perceived amount of distribution on perceived quality rest on the idea that highly distributed products (i.e., products sold by many retailers and/or occupying more retail shelf space) are perceived as higher in quality because of some assumed link between product value and its prevalence. Moreover, consumers may infer that highly distributed products are popular and hold higher subjective norm. However, our model does not include the hypothesis that higher distribution causes the perception of higher prices because consumers have equally direct access to both price and distribution when they visit stores.

Methodology and Results

Our proposed model was tested empirically by distributing questionnaires to 263 university students. Consumer data of pertaining to a new released hard-disc-driven (HDD) portable music player/recorder (i.e., a competitor of iPod) were collected. For the structural equation modeling, we used multiple scales developed in previous signaling research.

Scaling and model estimation were conducted successfully, resulting in support for seven of nine hypotheses examined. It may have been that the hypothesis regarding the direct effect of perceived price on purchase intention was not supported because the respondents did not regard price as important when choosing high-tech HDD portable music players. The hypothesis regarding the signaling effect of perceived price on perceived quality and, therefore, indirect effect of perceived price on purchase intention, may have lacked support because the respondents may have preferred advertising and distribution to price as signals of quality.

Our results suggest that perceived amounts of both advertising and distribution might be stronger signals than perceived price. This finding is pertinent to the controversy concerning the weakness of the signaling effects of perceived price on perceived quality. Our results demonstrate that the signaling effects of the amount of advertising carry the greatest effect on the subjective norm, whereas those of price and distribution carry the greatest effects on perceived quality. We believe that these findings will fill an important void in the literature regarding the signaling effects in studies of consumer behavior.

FILM FESTIVAL

Summary

Russell Belk, York University, Canada
Marylouise Caldwell, University of Sydney, Australia

This was the seventh annual North American ACR Film Festival. Despite competition from the Latin American, European, and Asia-Pacific ACR Film Festivals that have also emerged in recent years, as well as at least three consumer research journals with special DVD issues, the quality and number of submissions just keep getting better. This year's submissions continue to represent a truly global interest in film, both in terms of topical focus and the geographic origin of the filmmakers. This is evident in this year's two prizes as well. The **Jurors' Award** went to Marta Rabikowska and Matthew Hawkins, University of East London, for their feature length film *Consumption, Belonging and Place*. The film shows how members of a multi-racial community located in South London negotiate their identities via a range of socially embedded consumption activities largely located in the local High Street. An earlier version of this film garnered a parallel prize at 2007 European ACR Conference. The prize carries a cash award from the Center for Consumer Culture (3C), Georgetown University, and the University of California, Irvine. The **People's Choice Award** went to Ebru Ulusoy and Handan Vicdan, University of Texas-Pan American, for their capsule-length entry: *Bodily Experiences of Second Life Consumers*. Their film provides preliminary evidence of how consumers experience their bodies as avatars in virtual worlds such as Second Life. Ebru Ulusoy has also become a repeat winner and this was her third film to win an ACR Award. Additional Film Festival submissions covered a variety of topics, including amongst others, the consummate loving relationships that some consumers have with their cars, the way Middle Eastern house design reflects Islamic gender power relations, the meaning of luxurious experiences to upper class Japanese consumers, and the methodological and representational challenges that researchers face when striving to produce academically sound films. For the time being these films are not available online. Those wishing to see or use one of the films are encouraged to contact the filmmakers.

PRESENTATIONS

"Can Buy Me Love"

John L. Lastovicka, Arizona State University, USA
Nancy J. Sirianni, Arizona State University, USA
Danny Kunz, Arizona State University, USA

The videography "Can Buy Me Love" portrays exhibitors of classic cars, muscle cars, and hotrods at public car shows in the Phoenix, Arizona metropolitan area. In contrast to Susan Fournier's work, these auto-enthusiasts reveal deeper and more intimate relationships with their possessions than previously reported in the consumer research literature. We show how these auto-enthusiast consumers have personified their automobiles as partners in–as what psychologist Robert Sternberg defines as–a consummate loving relationship. Consummate loving relationships exhibit three components, namely: passion, intimacy and commitment. Our videography contains a sampling of the behaviors, emotions and words of informants manifesting these three components with respect to their beloved cars.

"Can't Buy Me Love" also discusses the emotive benefits consumers receive from these relationships with their cars. We reveal that such relationships appear to fill an emotional void in their lives. Thus we conclude that the loving relationship that consumers have with their beloved possessions is asymmetric. Consumers invest their own time, energy, money and emotions into their possessions. In exchange, these beloved possessions help fill an emotional need for consumers. This is similar to what psychiatrists Donald Horton and Richard Wohl have characterized as the "para-relationships" that some television viewers have with media personalities.

The videography concludes by discussing what our insights offer marketers. First, we note that monogamy is not required in these loving relationships. Thus those who madly, truly, and deeply love one car have the opportunity to have more than one of these special cars in their garage. It was not uncommon for our informants to have more than one special car. Second, part of achieving intimacy with a loved possession means investing time, money, and effort into the loved possession. That means a host of complementary material possessions are often needed in support of the loved possession. We illustrate this point with the hundreds of dollars of potions, lotions and machines that informants can spend on keeping a dazzling mirror-like finish on the car's body. As the French philosopher Denis Diderot noted, consumers' possessions require other possessions. We believe this is especially true for consumers' most be-loved possessions.

"This Day is to be Special: The Role of Exaggerated Contrast in an Indian Wedding"

Ekant Veer, University of Bath, UK

The role of sacred and profane objects has been well founded in consumer research for some time. Belk, Wallendorf, & Sherry's (1989) seminal paper underlines the pervasiveness of the sacred within modern consumer culture. This research takes a reflexive look at one particular aspect of the sacred and profane relationship; that is, the way in which the sacred is kept separate and detached from the profane as a means of maintaining the importance and power associated with the sacred.

By drawing on a reflexive stance to this research the film presents the results of one interpretation of an Indian wedding. Reflexivity in this case, allows for the researcher to engage with the research site, but also accept his or her own biases and theoretical dispositions (Joy et. al 2006). The results presented show how audial and visual cues are exaggerated to illustrate the importance of sacred events in the lives of Hindu Indians. Although this research focuses specifically on a North Indian Hindu wedding the results from the research offer explanations for the exaggeration of audial and visual cues in other contexts.

This research uses the artistic concept of *negative space* as an analogy for how the sacred is contrasted with the profane. White space, Negative space or Silence all refer to the role that pauses or emptiness play in promoting the focus of a particular subject (Murray 2005).

For example, in music, without the silence between notes the notes themselves lose meaning (Zakia 1993). One may not consciously be aware of the negative space that encompasses a piece, but without it the nature of the artistic creation is often muddled and lost in the composition (Brittain & Beittel 1960). It is when the difference between the negative and positive space is overly exaggerated that one can more clearly see the positive, but also the role that the negative plays in framing the subject itself.

This research shows how the contrast between the positive, in this case a wedding, and the negative, the everyday lives of the participants, is exaggerated to more clearly understand and appreciate the positive or sacred as being differentiated from the profane and everyday. Although all five Aristotelian senses are exaggerated in an Indian wedding this movie only focuses on the exaggerated contrast of audial and visual cues.

The methodology employed in the research was that of a videoethnographic study. The chosen context was a typical North Indian Hindu wedding held in December 2006. The research followed the marriage participants throughout the many different Hindu wedding rituals as well as interviewing family members to understand the cultural meanings associated with the various aspects of the wedding. In total, 14 hours of video tape was recorded focusing on the wedding itself. However, to understand the everyday lives of the participants the researcher continued to follow the couple before and after the wedding as they lived their lives away from the sacredness of the ceremonies. A further 11 hours of video was taken of non-wedding context. The final dataset comprised primarily of observational data and interviews with various people living in Delhi.

From the research it was seen that colour was the most prominently exaggerated visual cue used to differentiate the wedding from the negative space of the participants' everyday lives. Gold, red, orange and silver all play a prominent role in the observed ceremonies, but are rarely seen in such brilliance and concentration in everyday Delhi life. Clothing is also used as a means of contrast with *turbans* and finest *saris* worn especially for the ceremonies, but are rarely worn at other times. The central focus of the main wedding ceremony is the *Hawan* or holy fire that grows in intensity as the ceremony progresses. The combination of rhythmic chanting and growing flames offer an almost hypnotic audial and visual contrast from the often mundane nature of city life.

Audial cues are clearly contrasted in a number of ways. For example, when the groom approaches the bride on the wedding day he is led by a large band playing traditional and auspicious instruments such as the *Shehnai*. The sounds experienced by participants are in stark contrast to the soundscape of traffic and white noise that typify modern Delhi life.

Based on the research it is possible to see a number of areas where audial and visual cues are overly exaggerated to promote the importance of the sacred and positive and differentiate it from the negative space that the profane offers. This effect is also seen in many other contexts beyond the Hindu wedding ceremony, such as the prominence of Washington monument over the relatively flat landscape of Washington D.C.; the use of stained glass in Christian architecture and even the importance of a singular finger set aside for wedding rings in western culture. When mixed with the profane the sacred loses its efficaciousness (Durkheim 1915 [1928]); however, by exaggerating the difference between the sacred and profane the sacredness of the Hindu wedding is more easily recognised as such.

References

Belk, Russell W., Wallendorf, Melanie, & Sherry Jr., John F. (1989), "The Sacred and Profane in Consumer Behaviour: Theodicy on the Odyssey," *Journal of Consumer Research,* **16**(June), 1-38.

Brittain, W. Lambert, & Beittel, Kenneth R. (1960), "Analyses of Levels of Creative Performances in the Visual Arts," *The Journal of Aesthetics and Art Criticism,* **19**(1), 83-90.

Durkheim, Emile (1915 [1928]), *Elementary Forms of Religious Life: A Study in Religious Sociology*, (J. W. Swain, Trans.), London: George Allen & Unwin Ltd.

Joy, Annamma, John F Sherry, Gabriele Troilo, and Jonathan Deschenes (2006), "Writing it Up, Writing it Down: Being Reflexive in Accounts of Consumer Behaviour," in *Handbook of Qualitative Research Methods in Marketing*, Russell W. Belk, Ed., Cheltenham: Edward Elgar Publishing, 345-360.

Murray, Joddy (2005) "White Space as Rhetorical Space: Usability and Image in Electronic Texts," in *Rhetorical Agendas: Political, Ethical, Spiritual*, P. Bizzell (Ed.), Lawrence Erlbaum Associates, 145-150,

Zakia, Richard D. (1993), "Photography and Visual Perception," *Journal of Aesthetic Education, 27*(4), 67-81.

"Behind Closed Doors: Gendered Home Spaces in a Gulf Arab State"

Russell Belk, York University, Canada
Rana Sobh, University of Qatar, Qatar

In the United States misunderstandings of Middle Eastern women are particularly strong. As Read (2003) observes, "Cultural stereotypes of Arab-American women tend to collapse religion and ethnicity into synonymous components of culture, portraying them as veiled Islamic traditionalists" (p. 208). These misunderstandings are fueled by prejudice and are, if anything, stronger when it comes to Arab women in the Middle East rather than emigrants to the United States. While Western xenophobia and prejudices toward the Middle East and Islam have grown stronger since the September 11th attacks on the Twin Trade Towers, there is a long history of vilifying Arabs in Hollywood films (Shaheen 2001). These stereotypes of Arab women over a century of Hollywood films include those of the closeted, subservient, and oppressed wife, the exotic, scantily clad, and sexually seductive harem maiden, the fat, unattractive beast of burden, the shapeless, ululating bundle of black, and the mindless fanatical terrorist. Never do we see normal Arab women at home with their families, in the office or workplace, or occupying professional positions as professors, engineers, or doctors. In other words, rather than portray a common humanity, Middle Eastern women are depicted in the Western media as objects, villains, threats, and victims.

By focusing on the home and gendered spaces and objects within it, our research presents a more accurate, normal, and human face for Qatari women. In so-doing, we hope to help create greater understanding as well as contribute to research streams concerning home, identity, culture, consumption, and gender. We sought to know what goes on behind the closed doors of the Middle Eastern household. As a crossroads of the Middle East, Qatar offers a unique opportunity to understand what is unique as well as what is common in Middle Eastern and Western values involving women, privacy, identity, and the home.

The consumption of spaces and places within our homes is expressive of culture. Using observation and ethnographic depth interviews with 30 middleclass Qatari families, we hoped to understand the meanings of home spaces and artifacts in their lives. We find that the home and its spaces and objects are encoded differently by men and women, particularly in terms of notions of privacy. Historically, the idea of personal versus shared spaces within homes is a relatively new one. Tuan (1982) shows that it is only within the last few hundred years that notions of privacy and of separate public and private spaces within the home have emerged. Notions of private space are also encoded architecturally and intimacy within the nuclear family is a concept that has grown as the presence of extended families sharing the same home has diminished. As Rybcynski (1986) points out, it was highly unusual for someone in the sixteenth century to have his or her own room and it was another century before people had rooms where they could retreat from the public view. In the process of privatization of areas of the home, individual family members began to think of areas of the home as being their territories (Altman 1975). Even when a particular area like the bathroom must be shared with other family members, it is common to temporarily claim private space for hygienic, purifying, and beautification rituals, on either a scheduled or first-come/first-served basis (Kira 1970). All of these distinctions are expanded in the Arabian Gulf. When these spaces are encroached upon by others, there is a sense of violation of privacy and person. There is therefore an inclination to formally or informally designate spaces and boundaries defining personal space, spaces for close kin, and spaces where gender-segregated friends, neighbors, and strangers can meet within the home.

The Middle Eastern sense of what is totally private is more absolute, due largely to the moral concerns of Islam. Within Arab Muslim homes, there is a sharper distinction between men's and women's spaces as well as transitional spaces in moving from one to another. Compared to the West there is also a sharper distinction in these homes between public and private space, often with high exterior perimeter walls and inward facing rooms. Furthermore, there is a sense of private space that a Muslim woman carries with her as she goes from home to marketplace. As Cooper (2001) found for women in Niger, creating and decorating a room of their own was extremely important to their identities as well as their sense of social and economic status. Although some (e.g, Nageeb 2004) have called this enclaving of space a "neo-harem," reducing rather than increasing women's sense of space and of control over their lives, our informants find it liberating. While there are also gendered areas within Western households, we find sharper and more formally drawn boundaries within the present study in Qatar. The basis for these differences are cultural and do not arise from prescriptions within Islam, although there is disagreement on this point (Campo 1991; Nageeb 2004).

If clothing can be thought of as a second skin for the individual, home and personal possessions may be seen as a third skin defining who we are by forming a part of our extended self (Belk 1988). Wallendorf and Arnould (1988) found that Americans' favorite objects were more likely to be linked to personal memories, while those from Muslim Niger were more likely to mention objects linked to social status. They also found gender differences, with men in Niger more likely to cite the Quran and women more likely to cite silver jewelry as well as objects given to them by others. On the other hand, we found less difference, with favorite possessions within the home likely to be sentimental objects, especially for women in out study. The present video focuses more on home spaces and provides a context for further on-going examination of favorite possessions.

"Urban Archetypal Hedonistas"

Marylouise Caldwell, University of Sydney, Australia
Paul Henry, University of Sydney, Australia

A meta-analytic review of research into a market orientation suggests that successfully implementing a marketing orientation associates with higher revenue and profits (Kirca, Jayachandran and O'Bearden 2005). Yet academic literature provides limited guidance as to how this goal is practically achieved (For an exception see Gebhardt, Carpenter and Sherry 2007). One observed barrier is an inability by firm personnel to readily empathize with target consumers and understand their values, consumption priorities and lifestyles. In this film, we present representations of female consumer archetypes found to resonate strongly with marketing practitioners operating in markets for food, fun, fashion and furniture in Sydney Australia. The representations are the result of academic research, consultation with market researchers and empirical testing of the film on consumers and marketing professionals.

"Bodily Experiences of Second Life Consumers"

Ebru Ulusoy, The University of Texas-Pan American, USA
Handan Vicdan, The University of Texas-Pan American, USA

This video studies the meanings of the body concept in virtual worlds to provide an alternative perspective to the embodiment/disembodiment debate. We explore whether the body is present in virtual worlds, and if it is, how this presence takes place.

The concept of body has long been an interest for consumer researchers. The main focus of this interest evolved around the corporeal body, 1) as a means of self-presentation and socialization (Thompson and Hirschman 1995), and 2) as a project that modern consumers work on (Featherstone, Hepworth and Turner 1991; Schouten 1991). Thus, modern consumers treated their bodies as not an 'end' but a 'means' of conveying a desirable image to others. Moreover, with the emergence of new communication technologies, the focus of the debate among social scientists has become the presence of the body. Some argued that these technologies have enabled people to break out of the finitude of their embodiment and engage in disembodiment (Balsamo 2000; Stone 2000; Turkle 1995; Ward 2001). Others contested the idea of the body becoming futile in virtual worlds, and advocated the essential role of embodiment in any human experience (Argyle and Shields 1996; Flichy 2007; Froy 2003; Hansen 2006; Mingers 2001). These perspectives in the literature have been briefly reviewed in the video.

The growing semiotic potential of the virtual worlds allows for visual representation of one's physical self through images such as avatars and photos, which brought another perspective to the embodiment/disembodiment debate. In this videography, we explore the symbolic and experiential construction of body through avatars, which can be defined as "graphic icons representing users through various forms" (Chung 2005, p.538), in a three-dimensional virtual world called Second Life (SL), where experiences are completely user created.

Experiencing the body in this symbolic realm brings us new inquires concerning the meanings attached to the avatars by their creators, how these avatars are constructed and reconstructed, and how and what consumers experience through these virtual bodies.

For the purpose of this videography, we interviewed three people (Skyler, Jesse, Fred) in physical everyday life settings, such as their offices or a computer lab at a university. These interviewees were logged in SL during the interviews, and were able to share their avatar (re)construction processes and bodily experiences with us visually. In addition, we interviewed five people (Raven, Esme, Spiff, Ginny, Cecil) online in their SL settings. First, we asked informants to talk about their initial involvement in SL and their feelings when they first found out about SL. Then, we asked them to describe what an avatar means to them and how having an avatar influences their SL experiences. Then we asked them to talk about the processes of avatar creation and recreation and what influences them in these processes. The informants talked about the number of avatars they created, the reasons behind creating several avatars, and how they created and modified their avatar(s). Lastly, we asked them to talk about the characteristics of the avatar(s) they created and whether there are any similarities or differences when they compare the characteristics of their avatar(s) and their first life selves. In sum, the questions mainly focused on the feelings and motives concerning their lives in SL, the processes of the (re)creation of virtual bodies/avatars, the motives behind these processes, and the experiences with these avatars in SL.

Concerning the concept of body in virtual worlds, our findings from the inquiry of involvement in SL, "avatar" meanings, avatar (re)construction and avatar experiences basically reveal that the body concept is perceived and experienced differently in many ways when compared to its perceptions and experience in first life. In virtual worlds, the body concept is more a reflection of contemporary consumers' desire to experiment with different identities, experiences, and modes of life independent and free of nature and any one particular way of being and living. Preoccupation with the body is an essential part of virtual lives. The (re)construction of symbolic corporeal selves reflects the transforming urge of a modern consumer from perceiving his/her body as less of a tool for communication with and impression to others to an experience itself, an end that s/he playfully engages in for its own sake. The body itself becomes the experience in SL, rather than solely being a communication or impression management medium as it is perceived in first life.

The video concludes that the presence of the body in virtual worlds becomes symbolic in nature and enables people to playfully engage in (re)constructing several bodily selves. Freed from the physical constraints, the body is experienced in the symbolic realm of the virtual worlds. Consumers reconcile their urge for physicality with the non-physicality of cyberspace in symbolic forms. We call this process as symembodiment and our explorations in SL reveal that body is present in virtual worlds, yet not with its physical constraints but with its symbolic meanings.

References

Balsamo, Anne (2000), "The Virtual Body in Cyberspace," In D. Bell and B. M. Kennedy (eds.), *The Cybercultures Reader,* London and New York: Routledge, 489-503.

Chung, Donghun (2005), "Something for Nothing: Understanding Purchasing Behaviors in Virtual Environments," *Cyberpsychology & Behavior,* 6, 538-554.

Featherstone, Mike, Mike Hepworth and Bryan S. Turner (1991), *The Body: Social Process and Cultural Theory,* London: Sage.

Schouten, John W. (1991), "Selves in Transition: Symbolic Consumption in Personal Rites of Passage and Identity Reconstruction," *Journal of Consumer Research,* 17, 412-425.

Stone, Allucquère R. (2000), "Will the Real Body Please Stand Up? Boundary Stories about Virtual Cultures," in D. Bell and B. M. Kennedy (eds.), *The Cybercultures Reader,* London and New York: Routledge, 504-528.

Thompson, Craig J. and Elizabeth Hirschman (1995), "Understanding the Socialized Boy: A Poststructuralist Analysis of Consumers' Self-Conceptions, Body Images and Self-Care Products," *Journal of Consumer Research,* 22(September), 139-153.

Turkle, Sherry (1995), *Life on the Screen: Identity in the Age of the Internet,* New York: Simon and Schuster.

"The Ties That Bind: Being Black, Buying, and Hope"
Linden Dalecki, Pittsburg State University, USA

Consumer culture involves a quest for meaning in life primarily through consumption. With our logo-laden clothing and shopping bags, we roam the shopping mall in search of an identity and in search of meaning in life.

—Russell Belk, 2006

Can individuals use consumer culture to transcend the internalized or habituated orientations that emanate from their socialization in class, gender, ethnicity, and other dimensions of social structuring?

—Arnould & Thompson, 2007

The Ties That Bind: Being Black, Buying, and Hope (2007), is an 8-minute consumer ethnography shot on miniDV that was commissioned by Burrell Advertising as part of the 2007 Proctor & Gamble Ethnic Marketing Conference. Burrell's main interest was to get a "30,000 foot view" of African American

consumption patterns and attitudes. It is expected that a dialogue will be generated around the following theme: to what extent do the videography typologies proposed by Kozinets and Belk (2007) in the *Handbook of Qualitative Research Methods in Marketing* result in different sorts of consumer information? For example, *The Ties That Bind* videography utilizes (1) videotaped interviews and (2) observational videography, as well as (6) impressionistic forms. Given that the short has participants from a range of socioeconomic backgrounds with a range of views regarding African American consumption and representations in marketing, it is also expected that discussion will be generated on the subject of various distinct consumer sub-segments within the African American community. In particular, given what appeared to be a common interest for highly-education African Americans in "marketing which targets healthy eating and healthy living"—something which this sub-segment felt was particularly lacking in contemporary marketing—a discussion of emerging trends and solutions could be invaluable.

Other interesting themes expressed by participants included the notion that marketers will all to often "whitewash black culture and try to sell it back to the black community" as well as the notion that blacks are still being represented in a manner that stereotypes them (i.e. offensive character depictions in fried chicken commercials, offense character depictions in stomach-medicine commercials, etc.), and the finally the idea that African Americans are sensitive to the difference between brands that "get them" and speak to them authentically, versus brands that are simply pandering.

Another relevant area touched on by the project is the notion of variations on "intergenerational brand loyalty"— on the one hand many professional African American participants mentioned wanting to distance themselves from brands to which their parents were loyal, but on the other many discuss "strange attachments" that are felt to particular products and/or brands. One of the more interesting examples was an executive woman whose mother was loyal to "regular Tide" and who wanted to distance herself from the brand, but then felt drawn to and eventually became loyal to a higher-end Tide line-extension.

"Binomial Structure in Luxury: Analyzing Overseas Trip Experiences of Japanese Well-to-dos"
Junko Kimura, Hosei University, Japan
Hiroshi Tanaka, Kato University, Japan

Introduction

What is luxury? What does luxury mean to consumers? This is the basic research question we would like to advance. So far we have been investigating the meaning of luxury, interviewing with people around the globe. Up until 2007, we interviewed mainly with ordinary people in New York and Tokyo, asking questions about their own properties which they think luxurious. Those properties were; plates of matrimonial gifts, collections of combs of her passed-away mother's, her father-in-law's curios, etc. We found that if the thing is to be her/his luxury, it has to have the following four characteristics: 1 Rarity, 2 Conspicuity, 3 Escape, and 4 Identity Reinforcement. This finding suggests that luxurious things mean not just gorgeous and deluxe appearances, but relevant and beneficial experiences to ordinary consumers. In the summer of 2007, we visited homes of Italian aristocrats in Florence, Italy. These aristocrats live in grand mansions which they inherited from their ancestors. We, however, found that for these ancestors the wealthy properties are not their luxury. Again, material abundance does not necessarily mean luxury.

This time our investigation turns from luxurious things to non-things, such as luxurious experiences. The reason is that during our interviews consumers frequently pointed out non-materialistic consumption are important part of their luxury. For example, one informant in New York told us bath a–la-Japanese at her home is her luxury. Bath tub itself is a thing but its use and experience is her luxury. For this purpose in mind, we picked up wealthy people's overseas trip as a typical example of non-materialistic luxurious consumption. Wealthy people frequently go overseas for traveling. For the Japanese rich people, overseas trip appears to be one of the few entertaining moments in life, as they are having busy city life and have strong needs to escape. They already own gorgeous houses and expensive branded fashions. Their abundant expenses go naturally to overseas trips. The question here is as follows: Why overseas trip is a luxury for wealthy consumers. What are they feeling while they are enjoying trips in foreign countries?

Methodology

This time we adopted a method what we call photo-confrontation narrative. We first asked informants to pick up ten photos which they feel of luxury during their overseas trip. Then we interviewed the informants in what way they felt luxury during the overseas trip. We tried to search deeper meanings of their luxury. The informants were Keiichi, Junko and Mr and Mrs Tadenuma. These three people all live in the most upscale districts in Tokyo area, such as Shoto at Shibuya.

Findings

Our utmost important finding is that luxurious experience of overseas trip arises from binomial concepts: two competing and contrastive concepts appeared simultaneously in their luxurious experience narratives.

Extra-ordinariness versus Ordinariness

Overseas trip is usually extraordinary experience for everyone. People visit foreign countries, walking down towns they never knew, eating exotic foods, and meeting people of different habits and cultures. Overseas trip is thought to be unusual experience. However, as we take a close look how people feel during overseas trip, "ordinary feelings" are strongly sought in overseas trips. These wealthy people are enjoying luxury assuming they live there. They enjoy themselves when the tourists act and behave as local people, eating local foods, walking local streets, looking at the scenery as if local people see the scenery.

Expectedness versus Unexpectedness

When we travel abroad, we usually make plans prior to visit, what to see, and what to eat. When we first visit Paris, many of us visit Eiffel tower. First time travelers expect to see what they have expected beforehand. However, unexpectedness is another thing they expect to experience. Expectedness and Unexpectedness is another dimension in rich people's overseas trip experiences.

Separateness versus Connectedness

In overseas trip, each moment is a precious experience. People meet new and curious things in each moment. In this regards, overseas trip is a moment-by-moment experience. However, if the trip has to be luxurious, the experience has to have factors related to past experiences and memory. Past experience and memory have an important meaning for overseas travelers. To repeat the past experience adds more luxury to the present oversea trip.

Non-wastefulness of time versus Wastefulness of time

Time devoted to overseas trip is a valuable resource for everybody. They do not want to waste time during trips in foreign countries. They try to fully utilize the time while staying in overseas. However, wealthy people feel luxuriousness when they waste time. Wasting time is a luxury while they are spending time efficiently doing overseas trips. Not useful time spending is another way to feel luxuriousness.

Conclusion

Why is overseas trip luxury for wealthy consumers? It was found that overseas trip has binomial meaning structure. Binomial means contrasting, competing concepts appear during their overseas trip experiences and creates luxurious feelings. As business implications, manufacturers and service providers of luxurious products tend to believe that they have to provide something gorgeous and deluxe looking. We would like to suggest that luxury is created not just from gorgeous appearing things, but luxury is created from internal meaning structures of consumers. All in all, luxury is produced not just from one pillar of this two pillar diagram but also from another side of the diagram.

"Everything You Always Wanted to Know About the Pre-Party* (*But Were Afraid To Ask)"

Christoffer Dymling, Stockholm University, Sweden
Jonas Olofsson, Stockholm University, Sweden
Eric Uggla, Stockholm University, Sweden
Jacob Ostberg, Stockholm University, Sweden

This videography focuses on a distinct social and cultural phenomenon in Sweden commonly known as the pre-party. This consumption phenomenon is familiar to virtually all Swedish youth from the age where people start familiarizing themselves with alcohol to the age where they have formed more or less stable relationships. There are some unique institutional characteristics that foster a milieu in which the pre-party is a necessary form for youth eager to engage in nightlife activities. First, the legal drinking age is 18 for drinking in a bar or at a restaurant and 20 if you wish to buy alcoholic beverages in the state-owned liquor store, Systembolaget. As most Swedish youngsters feel an urge to drink alcohol before the age of 18 they have to do so outside of bars or restaurants. A second institutional characteristic is the extremely high taxation on alcoholic beverages in Sweden; especially if you buy the beverages in a restaurant you have to pay more money than most youngsters can afford. Consequently the pre-party attendants save money by drinking cheap, often privately imported alcohol before going out. Previous studies on alcohol consumption has tended to emphasize the negative aspects of alcohol consumption and have, we would claim, disregarded potential positive aspects of social drinking (cf. Banister and Piacentini 2006). Reading previous studies on youth and drinking thus leaves one confused over the apparent popularity of this consumption activity; if drinking only leads to unwanted social encounters, is fueled by negative peer pressure, and has negative consequences for one's self and social identity, why is it such an enormously popular consumption activity?

To learn more about the consumption phenomena of the pre-party, ethnographic research methods, focus groups, and an Internet survey have been used to gather empirical material. This material has been analyzed using the framework of ritual consumption (Rook 1985; Wallendorf and Arnould 1991). The study thus illuminates and enhances the understanding of the symbolic aspects of the consumption culture phenomena. Findings suggest that the pre-party can be understood as a consumption ritual containing an artifact, an audience, performance roles, and script phases: the meet & greet, the synchronization, the intoxication, the critical phase, and the ending. The ritual becomes meaningful to its participants by providing security, community and a possibility to escape everyday life.

We have chosen to structure the videography as a fictional story rather than the conventional documentary style (Kozinets and Belk 2007). The reason is that we would like to push the boundaries of the video format and explore its potential for representing consumption phenomena in creative non-fiction style (Brown 2005; Sunderland 2007).

References

Banister, Emma N. and Piacentini, Maria G. (2006), "Getting Hammered?... Students Coping with Alcohol," *Journal of Consumer Behaviour*, 5 (March/April), 145-156.

Brown, Stephen (2005), "I Can Read You Like a Book! Novel Thoughts on Consumer Behavior," *Qualitative Market Research: An International Journal*, 16 (2), 219-237.

Kozinets, Robert V. and Belk, Russell W. (2007), "Camcorder society: quality videography in consumer and marketing research," in *Handbook of qualitative research methods in marketing*, ed. Russell W. Belk, Cheltenham, UK: Edward Elgar Publishing, 335-344.

Rook, Dennis W. (1985), "The Ritual Dimension of Consumer Behavior," *Journal of Consumer Research*, 12 (December), 251-264.

Sunderland, Patricia L. (2007), "Entering entertainment: creating consumer documentaries for corporate clients," in *Handbook of qualitative research methods in marketing*, ed. Russell W. Belk, Cheltenham, UK: Edward Elgar Publishing, 371-383.

Wallendorf, Melanie and Arnould, Eric J. (1991), ""We Gather Together": Consumption Rituals of Thanksgiving Day," *Journal of Consumer Research*, 18 (June), 13-31.

"Behind Closed Doors: Opportunity Identification Through Observational Research"

Cynthia Webster, Macquarie University, Australia
Richard Seymour, The University of Sydney, Australia
Kate Dallenbach, Victoria University, New Zealand

To thrive in today's competitive marketplace, businesses constantly need to search for opportunities to develop. Organisations frequently draw on consumers' experiences, creative thoughts and usage behaviours for inspiration. The rationale for using consumers for creative solutions is that different individuals have different experiences, abilities, beliefs and needs (Shane and Venkataraman 2000). Such differences lead to unique interpretations of existing functional capabilities, possible product transformations to develop new solutions and novel conjectures for applications in new product areas (Henderson and Cockburn 1994; Kirzner 1997; Zahra and Nielson 2002).

In his seminal work on innovation, von Hippel (1986, 1988, 2005) emphasises the importance of those outside the organisation, especially "lead users" in identifying opportunities for innovation. von Hippel argues that new product concepts generated through consumer discussions or within artificial environments, as in a laboratory or computer simulations, are limited as real usage situations typically are not encountered. Along with other consumer researchers, von Hippel (2001) advocates an observational approach to opportunity identification, focussing on the ways in which users in authentic, real world situations modify and interact with products and services (Griffin and Hauser 1993; Leonard-Barton 1995). With this in mind, the purpose of the short film "Behind Closed Doors" is to: 1) further our understanding of the ways in which consumers transform ordinary products to serve their everyday needs, and 2) broaden our appreciation of the role observational research and videography play in opportunity identification.

As videography is a precise way to vividly document the "lived realities of every day consumption" (Belk and Kozinets 2005, p.128), it is ideal for the purposes of opportunity identification. Within consumer research videographic methods are increasingly being used both to provide rich sources of data and as a dynamic format to present results. Not only does videography compliment other methods by providing stimuli for support and analysis, it extends research because the recordings can be viewed repeatedly and analysed from multiple perspectives, stimulating further insights and adding another layer to the research. Videography also is consistent with von Hippel's (1986, 1988, 2005) lead user approach to innovation in that recorded images of observed behaviour document the actual ways in which participants use objects within social environments. Observation of existent behaviours is important as studies show that what people say and what they do are two different things (Bernard, Killworth, Kronenfeld and Sailer 1984; Freeman and Webster 1994; Webster 1994). Moreover, some groups of individuals, such as children, do not have sophisticated verbal skills and as a result are unable to provide comprehensive explanations of their behaviours (Valkenburg and Buijzen 2005). Finally, the entrepreneurial research points out that people do not report innovative behaviours, in part, because they do not have full information and so do not realise what is unique (Shane 2000). Videography, therefore, is a valid technique to manage such difficulties.

In this film, results from trace analysis and usage behaviors are presented in five themes: "Fresh Ideas", "Storage", "Playing", "Repairs" and "Food Combinations". Results exemplify the distinctive ways in which mundane, household products are transformed through novel applications. In each category ordinary, everyday products are shown to have unusual applications. For example, in "Fresh Ideas" bull clips are used to preserve food items, yogurt is placed in the freezer, baking soda keeps the freezer and shoes smelling fresh and clothes are put on hangers before placing them on the clothesline. Under "Storage" the same type of plastic box is used to store shoes, videos and toys while metal stands are used in place of beside tables and bookcases. In "Playing" items such as stickers, yarn, bracelets and plastic string are used to decorate walls, windows, dresser drawers, musical instruments and toys. The social play of two children reveals multiple uses for a trampoline. Not only do the children jump, but they introduce soft toys to the jumping. Play is then extended with the toys to underneath the trampoline. Video boxes are used as blocks to build enclosures for a pretend zoo. With "Repairs" many items are not repaired, instead a quick fix occurs. Tape is used to hold the washing machine hose in place, Blu Tack keeps bathroom tiles on, ties fasten foam padding to the trampoline and frozen peas are used as an ice pack for a hurt arm. In "Food Combinations" the mother manually inserts corn into pasta tubes for her son, the young girl wraps a gelatine snake around a banana, she also modifies a biscuit into a form to be eaten with hommous. The social interaction between the two children is highlighted through the making of their ice-cream sundaes. They obviously are in a state of excitement showing off to one another adding unusual ingredients such as Milo (a chocolate milk powder) and various cake decorations while creating their masterpieces.

Understanding of innovation and innovative organisations is relatively limited (Salaman and Storey, 2002). Very low success rates of innovation suggest that 'successful' companies can expect around one third of their innovations will fail, yet it is not always clear why these new products fail (Cooper and Kleinschmidt, 1987; Poolton and Barclay, 1998). The challenge for practitioners and researchers alike is to develop methods that will lead to a 'pipeline' of potential project innovations that are consumer-driven, and 'understood' clearly within and across the innovating organisation. "Behind Closed Doors" highlights how naturalistic observations incorporated with videography are able to expose the creativity, problem solving, and variety seeking behaviors of one family. This research suggests alternative approaches for future research into opportunity identification, making use of observation and videography. Moreover, the current work emphasises that innovation and creativity require consideration of the relational rather than just self-seeking behaviours, needs or events.

References

Belk, Russell W. and Robert V. Kozinets (2005), "Videography in Marketing and Consumer Research," *Qualitative Market Research: An International Journal*, 8, 2, 128-141.

Bernard, H. Russell, Peter Killworth, David Kronenfeld and Lee Sailer (1984), "The Problem of Informant Accuracy: The Validity of Retrospective Data," *Annual Review of Anthropology*, 13, 495-517.

Cooper, Robert G. and Elko J. Kleinschmidt (1987), "New Products: What Separates Winners from Losers?" *Journal of Product Innovation Management*, 4, 169-184.

Freeman, Linton C. and Cynthia M. Webster (1994), "Interpersonal Proximity in Social and Cognitive Space," *Social Cognition*, 12, 223-247.

Griffin, Abbie and John R. Hauser (1993), "The Voice of the Customer," *Marketing Science*, 12, 1, 1–27.

Henderson, Rebecca and Iain Cockburn (1994), "Measuring Competence? Exploring Firm Effects in Pharmaceutical Research," *Strategic Management Journal*, 15 (winter), 63–84.

Kirzner, Israel M. (1997), "Entrepreneurial Discovery and the Competitive Market Process: An Austrian Approach," *Journal of Economic Literature*, 35, 1, 60-85.

Leonard-Barton, Dorothy (1995), *Wellsprings of Knowledge*. Boston, Harvard Business School Press.

Poolton, Jenny and Ian Barclay (1998), "New Product Development from Past Research to Future Applications," *Industrial Marketing Management*, 27, 197-212.

Salaman, Graeme and John Storey (2002), "Managers' Theories about the Process of Innovation," *The Journal of Management Studies*, 39(2), 147-165.

Shane, Scott (2000), "Prior Knowledge and the Discovery of Entrepreneurial Opportunities," *Organization Science*, 11(4), 448-469.

Shane, Scott and Sankaran Venkataraman (2000), "The Promise of Entrepreneurship as a Field of Research," *The Academy of Management Review*, 25, 1, 217-226.

Valkenburg, Patti M. and Moniek Buijzen (2005), "Parental Mediation of Undesired Advertising

Effects," *Journal of Broadcasting & Electronic Media*, 49, 2, 153-165.

von Hippel, Eric (1986), "Lead Users: A Source of Novel Product Concepts," *Management Science*, 32, 7, 791–805.

von Hippel, Eric (1988), *The Sources of Innovation*. New York, USA: Oxford University Press.

von Hippel, Eric (2001), "Perspective: User Toolkits for Innovation," *The Journal of Product Innovation Management*, 18, 247–25.

von Hippel, Eric (2005), *Democratizing Innovation*. Cambridge, USA, MIT Press.

Webster, Cynthia M. (1994), "Data Type: A Comparison of Cognitive and Observational Measures," *Journal of Quantitative Anthropology*, 4, 313-328.

Zahra, Shaker A. and Anders P. Nielson (2002), "Sources of Capabilities, Integration and Technology Commercialization," *Strategic Management Journal*, 23, 5, 377–98.

"Consumption, Belonging and Place"

Marta Rabikowska, University of East London, UK
Matthew Hawkins, University of East London, UK

A documentary, *Consumption, Belonging, and Place* is part of a bigger project on the relationships between consumption, ethnicity and material reality in which video ethnography was applied as a main method, accompanied by interactive methods of communicating with the receiving community, such as local screenings, exhibitions, and internet blogging. The role of the marketplace and the distributions of social and cultural meanings in creating the community has been investigated in this film within the time span of one year: 2006-2007 . The film was designed and executed to probe a methodological basis of research involving a voice of the researcher and her own experience in the community. In its current form the film represents the researcher's interpretation of the results from semi-structured interviews which were conducted among two groups of inhabitants of the community: the owners of businesses and the shoppers in the High Street. The street–the marketplace delineates spatio-material topography of the study but also serves as a symbolic representation of the socio-cultural practices of the local community. As in Nigel Thrift's theory of space in this research the street is "porous"- with no boundary to incoming memories, messages, or encounters, and with no stable landscape for communication (2002), though, as my ethnographic film shows, there will be plenty of attempts to make that space static and stable.

The film is an interpretative tool which shows that the street is made up of many kinds of stories and practices brought in to relation with one another through a continuous and largely involuntary process of encounters. The space of one street, however, emphasizes the 'materiality of thinking' (Carter 2004) which in this research is accepted as an epistemological foundation for consumption practices. Such practices are observed in relation to space and ethnicity which are themselves the products of interpretation of the consumption of the street and its facilities by different informants.

The film shows the researcher's own story of the place and other stories provided by the inhabitants of which none can become a dominant narrative. The intrepretivist approach is articulated through a subjective process of editing combined with self-referential images which reveal the process of film-making and the researcher's personal engagement (Cohen 1994). Both a textual and meta-textual level in the film is to accentuate the awareness of a tension between representation and everyday life practices, including the practice of research too.

To acknowledge the mutual exchange between those levels, the self-reflective visual 'footnotes' were utilized in the film which come from the reality of the researcher and the production-team. This approach recognizes the interconnectedness of objects, texts, images and technologies in people's lives which are the object of an ethnographic research. This is to state that, unlike in Collier's traditional approach, in this film ethnography is regarded as an aspect of research and an aspect of representation as well, while the whole project represents the narrative-based communication story constructed by the researcher (Clifford 1986).

The recorded interviews indicate that most of the stories told by the informants find their opposite versions in other informants. This differs mostly across different ethnic groups using the same street but also across generations and lifestyles. Nonetheless, in the process of editing, those stories acquire another form which depends only on a researcher who interprets them from her own point of view.

References

Burrawoy, M., Burton, A., Ferguson, A.A., & Fox, K.J. (1991) *Ethnography Unbound: Power and resistance in the modern metropolis*, Berkley: University of California Press.

Cohen, A. (1992) 'Self-conscious anthropology' in J.Okely and H.Callaway (eds), *Anthropology and Autobiography*, London: Routledge.

Collier, John. (1986). Visual Anthropology: Photography as a Research Method. In John Collier, Jr., and Malcolm Collier. Revised and Expanded Edition. Albuquerque: University of New Mexico Press.

Clifford, J. (1986) 'Introduction: partial truths' in J.Clifford and G.Marcus (eds), *Writing Culture: The Poetics and Politics of Ethnography*, Berkley: University of California Press.

Carter, P. (2004) *Material Thinking. The Theory and Practice of Creative Research*, Melbourne: University of Melbourne Press.

Thrift. N. and A.Amin (2002) *Cities*, Oxford: Polity.

Understanding and Improving Consumer Personal Finances

Chairs:
Lisa E. Bolton, The Pennsylvania State University, USA
Paul Bloom, Duke University, USA
Joel Cohen, University of Florida, USA

Participants:
David Glen Mick, University of Virginia, USA
Ron Paul Hill, Villanova University, USA
Kathleen D. Vohs, University of Minnesota, USA
Amar Cheema, Washington University, USA
John G. Lynch, Duke University, USA
Vanessa Perry, The George Washington University, USA
Gal Zauberman, University of Pennsylvania, USA
James Burroughs, University of Virginia, USA
Cynthia Cryder, Carnegie Mellon University, USA
Scott Rick, University of Pennsylvania, USA
Eldar Shafir, Princeton University, USA
Stephen Spiller, Duke University, USA

How do consumers make decisions about budgeting, spending, saving, investing, and borrowing? And what can be done to improve consumer personal finances? The recent sub-prime meltdown and related developments have focused attention on these important aspects of consumer behavior, yet research on consumer personal finances is scant. The objectives of this roundtable are 1) to encourage research on important issues related to consumer personal finances; 2) to bring together academic researchers and consumer organizations in order to identify issues of mutual interest; and 3) to improve consumer welfare through the development and dissemination of knowledge that improves personal financial decision-making among consumers. This roundtable will include participants from academia and industry, including the National Endowment for Financial Education and the Federal Reserve Bank, who are consumer advocates and sources of research funding.

ROUNDTABLE
Aesthetics and Consumption

Chairs:
Henrik Hagtvedt, University of Georgia, USA
Vanessa Patrick, University of Georgia, USA

Participants:
Wesley Hutchinson, University of Pennsylvania, USA
Joan Meyers-Levy, University of Minnesota, USA
JoAndrea Hoegg, University of British Columbia, Canada
Darren Dahl, University of British Columbia, Canada
Rajagopal Raghunathan, The University of Texas at Austin, USA
Rui Juliet Zhu, University of British Columbia, Canada
Rolf Reber, University of Bergen, Norway

C. Page Moreau, University of Colorado at Boulder, USA
Frederic Brunel, Boston University, USA
Annamma Jamy Joy, University of British Columbia, Canada
Jonathan Schroeder, University of Exeter, UK
Ravi Chitturi, Lehigh University, USA
Joseph Alba, University of Florida, USA
Michael Luchs, College of William & Mary, USA
Xiaoyan Deng, University of Pennsylvania, USA
Rishtee Kumar Batra, Boston University, USA

Aesthetics is increasingly becoming an important criterion by which consumers evaluate and differentiate between product offerings and make purchasing decisions. Recognizing this growing trend in the marketplace, a number of consumer researchers have begun focusing on this area of research. However, there exists no comprehensive, overarching, or integrative theoretical framework for aesthetics research in the consumption domain. Indeed, the concept of aesthetics is itself understood in diverse ways, and researchers variously equate it with, for instance, beauty, intrinsic interestingness, artistic appeal, pleasantness to the senses, or a combination of these and other concepts. It may therefore often be necessary for researchers in this area to specify how aesthetics is to be conceptualized in a given research project.

The topic of aesthetics tends to inspire interesting philosophical debate, as it also did during the roundtable, and different philosophical perspectives may help shape different research agendas. Notwithstanding these perspectives, it was noted that a general challenge for marketing scholars is to maintain a focus that is relevant for consumer behavior. Otherwise, aesthetics may become an esoteric topic for those of us with a special interest in the area, rather than the fertile and broadly influential area of research that it has the potential to be, based on the central role it plays in consumers' everyday evaluation and choice. Keeping this focus in mind, a number of issues brought up during the discussion are presented here in a brief, summary fashion.

Areas of Discussion
- Aspects of the aesthetic experience shaped both by universal influences stemming from our common evolutionary heritage and by individual differences stemming from culture and other sources.
- The aesthetic experience is often characterized as one that is enjoyed purely for its own sake, without regard to other, more practical considerations.
- Some argue that aesthetics is divorced from considerations of functionality, while others argue that the perception of a form-function relationship can help shape an aesthetic experience.
- Aesthetics as an all-consuming experience versus minor moments of pleasure.
- Emotions implicated in the experience of aesthetics.
- Is aesthetics a unique experience? If so, how?
- What is the relationship between aesthetics and hedonics?
- Aesthetic value. How does this translate to profit?
- Aesthetics as rich experience versus instant judgment, complexity versus fluency, cognition versus emotion. The race model: some aesthetic experiences may be instantaneous while others are elaborate and nuanced. What distinguishes these experiences?
- Aesthetics as a flow experience, leaving little cognitive capacity for reflection and analysis.
- Aesthetic schema, with innate and learned components.
- Aesthetics as a visual phenomenon, versus aesthetics incorporating all sensory perception. Perhaps the aesthetic schema is more fully developed for visual perception. This is also important for mass customization, where marketers must assume that consumers know what they like.

Contentious Areas

- Are concepts like the sublime relevant to consumer behavior research? Perhaps more mundane concepts tend to be more relevant for the majority of products, while the sublime can be relevant to other consumer experiences?
- According to Maslow, hedonic needs or higher order needs are taken care of only after functional needs have been met. Other evidence suggests that the need for aesthetics is present even when functional needs have not been adequately addressed.
- To which extent is aesthetics high culture or related with luxury, and to which extent is it more pervasive and found even in the most mundane consumption experiences?
- How immediately obvious should the managerial relevance be of research in aesthetics? What are, for instance, some issues related to trade dress, that is, the ownership by the firm of aesthetic presentation (look and feel)?
- Is there a good way to measure the aesthetic experience and to capture the rationale of the emotional choice?
- How does the work on aesthetics add to extant theory? We need to avoid conceptual replications. We need to establish different processes. Is aesthetics just another attribute?

One of the biggest challenges facing researchers in the domain of aesthetics is publishing in top journals. However, given the substantial and growing managerial importance of aesthetics, it seems reasonable that this area be given increasing attention in the marketing literature, as long as the theoretical contribution is also sufficient.

Perhaps interesting empirical effects without substantial theory should also be publishable on occasion, but this will not be sufficient to grow the topic of aesthetics as a viable and broadly influential area of research. Since research on aesthetics in marketing is still at a stage of infancy, it is likely to remain fragmented for some time to come. However, as the area matures over time a broader understanding of aesthetics is likely to emerge, as tends to be the natural progression for most areas of scientific inquiry. The current roundtable, where many researchers were not able to enter and partake in the discussion because the room was too full, clearly demonstrates that an increasing number of marketing scholars realize the importance of aesthetics as an area of research in marketing. Therefore, it seems realistic to hope that academic research in this area will eventually catch up with managerial practice and increase our general understanding of consumer behavior phenomena pertaining to aesthetics.

Building the Transformative Consumer Research Community: Opportunities and Obstacles for Rising Scholars

Chair:
Julie L. Ozanne, Virginia Polytechnic Institute and State University, USA

Participants:
Dipankar Chakravarti, University of Colorado at Boulder, USA
Ron Paul Hill, Villanova University, USA
David Glen Mick, University of Virginia, USA
Benet DeBerry-Spence, University of Illinois at Chicago, USA
David Crockett, University of South Carolina, USA
Krittinee Nuttavuthisit, Chulalongkorn University, Thailand
Amitava Chattopadhyay, INSEAD, Singapore
Simone Pettigrew, University of Western Australia, Australia
Peter Wright, University of Oregon, USA
Rohit Varman, Indian Institute of Management, India
Laurel Anderson, Arizona State University, USA
Stacey Menzel Baker, University of Wyoming, USA
Lisa Bolton, Pennsylvania State University, USA
Tonya Williams Bradford, University of Notre Dame, USA
June Cotte, University of Western Ontario, Canada
Susan Dobscha, Bentley College, USA
Cornelia Pechmann, University of California, Irvine, USA
Linda L. Price, University of Arizona, USA
Jose Antonio Rosa, University of Wyoming, USA
Namika Sagara, University of Oregon, USA
Sridhar Samu, Indian School of Business, India
Andrea Scott, Pepperdine University, USA
Sonya Grier, American University, USA
Humaira Mahi, San Francisco State University, USA
Dilip Soman, University of Toronto, Canada
Ashlee Humphreys, Northwestern University, USA
John Kozup, Villanova University, USA

Since David Mick's rousing 2005 presidential address calling for more transformative consumer research (TCR), we have seen a flurry of activity and increased institutional support. For example, a special issue on TCR will be published in the *Journal of Consumer Research* in the Fall of 2008, the first TCR conference was held at Dartmouth in 2007 (and a second one is being planned for 2009 at Villanova University), and a Handbook of Transformative Consumer Research is currently underway.

The primary people involved in building the TCR community, such as the members of the TCR task force and TCR Board, have been senior researchers who are well established in their careers. While resources in the form of research grants have been distributed to support the research of young scholars, junior scholars have not been directly involved in the formal deliberations that have shaped the direction of TCR. Moreover, given the diversity of issues spanned by TCR, some emerging scholars have voiced a desire and need to network within the larger community of researchers studying social problems. The long term success of any program of research, of course, depends on the ability to attract, foster, and develop a cadre of new researchers.

HLM: Hierarchical Linear Models

Chair:
Dawn Iacobucci, Vanderbilt University, USA

Participants:
Gerri Henderson, Northwestern University, USA
Adam Duhachek, Indiana University, USA
Jim Oakley, University of North Carolina, USA
Steve Hoeffler, Vanderbilt University, USA
Steve Posavac, Vanderbilt University, USA
Simona Botti, London Business School, UK
Katherine A. Burson, University of Michigan, USA
Pankaj Aggarwal, University of Toronto, Canada

HLM, or Hierarchical Linear Models, is a technique that Org Behavior scholars are finding very useful, and that marketing might also use in certain applications. The models integrate data that represent different (usually only two) levels of analyses. For example, individuals might state certain purchase preferences, and groups (households, buying centers, departments) might express others, and it would be naïve to model one part of the data without considering the other.

This workshop will provide an introduction to HLM models. We'll talk about why these techniques are an improvement over naïve methods to approaching the multi-level problem. We'll also talk briefly about how these models compare to other linear models.

Syntax will be provided, and attendees guided through, both stand-alone HLM software and SAS's means of analyzing HLM data.

Conducting Consumer Research in Emerging Markets: Challenges, Issues and New Directions

Chair:
Humaira Mahi, San Francisco State University, USA

Participants:
Laurel Anderson, Arizona State University, USA
Eric Arnould, University of Wyoming, USA
Russ Belk, York University, Canada
Dipankar Chakravarti, University of Colorado, Boulder, USA
Amitava Chattopadhyay, INSEAD, Singapore
Catherine Demangeot, Strathclyde University, UK
Rika Houston, California State University–Los Angeles, USA
Eric Li, York University, Canada
Tamara Masters, University of Utah, USA
Mary Ann McGrath, Loyola University, Chicago, USA
Alokparna Monga, University of South Carolina, USA
Anirban Mukhopadhyay, University of Michigan, USA
Aysegul Ozsomer, Koc University, Istanbul, Turkey
Raj Raghunathan, University of Texas at Austin, USA
Akshay Rao, University of Minnesota, USA
Bill Rhyne, University of California, Davis, USA
Umberto Rosin, Ca Foscari University of Venice, Italy
Baba Shiv, Stanford University, USA
Yiping Song, Fudan University, Shanghai, China
Mourad Touzani, ISG, University of Tunis, Tunisia
Linda Tuncay, Loyola University, Chicago, USA
Hester Van Herh, VU University, The Netherlands
Alladi Venkatesh, University of California, Irvine, USA

A roundtable was held at the 2007 ACR conference to discuss the issues and challenges with conducting consumer research in India and China. In our pre-conference discussions via an online group forum, and at the 2007 conference we identified and discussed some key issues and challenges and agreed upon the need to expand the discussion of the topic from India and China to include all transitional economies/emerging markets. This roundtable is thus a continuation and an expansion of the discussion started at the 2007 conference.

In order to facilitate pre-conference discussion, participants as well as forty researchers working on emerging markets that are a part of an online forum were asked to send in questions on topics relating to methodology, research and geographic area issues with conducting research in emerging markets. Since this roundtable is a part of an ongoing discussion started at ACR 2007 and to be continued at ACR–Asia Pacific, 2009, the discussion topics and questions identified were ones that could continue the discussion started last year. The discussion at this roundtable therefore centered on several key areas:

1. Capturing Cultural Nuances: Several respondents talked about the difficulty of capturing cultural and contextual nuances when conducting research in emerging markets. From practical issues such as finding good translators to finding a comfort level and understanding before starting research in these markets, participants discussed several complexities in emerging markets that require good research partners in these settings as well as a willingness on the part of the researcher to immerse themselves in the culture and understand the local context before collecting data. A participant from China talked about the diversity of the Chinese market and how consumer behavior changes from city to city within China based on the level of development in each city. This was echoed by researchers working in some other emerging markets such as India about tier I versus tier II or III cities and the urban-rural divide in most markets that makes generalization very difficult. A need and a platform to share these experiences among researchers working in these markets were felt to be useful.

2. Data Collection Issues: Several participants last year expressed a view that it is important for researchers to share our experiences with using various methodological tools in these markets. This year's discussion centered on using the right kind of research partners. Participants mentioned partnering with local universities as a way to get access to students and student assistants to help with data collection. Several participants shared issues with research partners and assistants not understanding exact research procedures and thus possibly affecting the quality of the data being collected. Again a need for a database to share experiences with other researchers who have worked in these markets before was agreed upon as being a very useful tool.

3. Theoretical issues: Last year we had discussed briefly the applicability of theories from developed markets being used in emerging ones. This year we extended this discussion by talking about the importance of recognizing context and its influence before

deciding on applying a particular theory in a new market. The idea that some theories are more amenable to cross-cultural application than others was discussed with the conclusion that researchers need to be very sensitive to the issue of context with theory translatability across cultures. Further, some participants discussed the need to clarify what their unit of analysis is when studying these markets. Is it the individual consumer or is it the market itself? Also, a researcher pointed out that the idea of multi-sited research with interpretive research which is typically not done by anthropologists is ideal for our field since there are topics within consumer research that lend themselves well to this type of work.

4. Geographic Area Uniqueness & Challenges: An important element of expanding the discussion from 2007 was to include work in geographical areas that do not have as much representation. For instance, what are some challenges with working in Latin America and Africa? A participant from Tunisia talked about the difficulty of connecting with researchers from other parts of the world. Since a majority of consumer research work is published in the United States and Europe, he talked about better accessibility to publishing outlets when working with these researchers. He talked about the need for more dialogue between researchers in other parts of the world and those based in the United States. Again, the usefulness of a database that would connect researchers working in various countries with each other was thought to be very useful.

5. Miscellaneous issues (Publishing Outlets, IRB issues, research contacts for local firms): Last year we talked about the difficulty sometimes of getting IRB approval due to various local level research collection methods not being agreeable to human subjects committees in several US universities. This time the discussion centered on finding solutions to these human subjects issues by talking to other researchers who had managed to clear this issue with their boards. Again the need for a dialogue among researchers was felt to be essential to find out about human subjects approval requirements in the countries where the research is being conducted as well as with getting approvals quickly in home countries. The other issue that researchers were interested in is was on how researchers might be able to contact local companies and managers in particular countries. Another issue discussed was the need to document and list some key publishing outlets for research on emerging markets. Given the changing nature of these markets, some topics may get outdated if these are under review for longer periods hence information on which outlets may be ideal was felt to be good information to share with other researchers.

6. Database: this year the main thread running through the discussions on the various topics listed above was the need to build a database and a community so that researchers could share their experiences on various aspects of conducting research in emerging markets. The database ideally would contain a list of research centers that fund research in emerging markets; a list of key contacts with firms/respondents in emerging markets; a list of potential journals to publish in and very key would be a list of researchers working in various emerging markets. Researchers' ability to post questions and receive responses from other researchers would add value given the need expressed by most researchers at the roundtable for a forum to discuss various issues. We currently have more than 50 ACR members that are a part of an existing online forum that was created last year. Ideas on where to site this database and how to structure it were discussed and these discussions will continue with participants to get consensus on the best way to structure this database/forum.

The next roundtable to continue this discussion will be held at ACR-Asia Pacific in India in January 2009. That discussion will involve a dialogue between researchers based in India working on consumer behavior issues and those based elsewhere that are interested in these issues.

In summary, the 2008 ACR-SF roundtable reinforced the idea that conducting consumer research in emerging markets is gaining tremendous interest among researchers as these markets expand rapidly. There are also various challenges to conducting research in these markets as discussed at this roundtable. Researchers working in these markets therefore strongly need a forum and a community to share their experiences on methodological tools and other issues to be able to be more efficient with conducting research in emerging markets.

ROUNDTABLE
Intro To Social Network Methods

Chair:
Dawn Iacobucci, Vanderbilt University, USA

Participants:
Gerri Henderson, Northwestern University, USA
Adam Duhachek, Indiana University, USA
Jim Oakley, University of North Carolina, USA
Steve Hoeffler, Vanderbilt University, USA
Steve Posavac, Vanderbilt University, USA
Simona Botti, London Business School, UK
Katherine A. Burson, University of Michigan, USA
Pankaj Aggarwal, University of Toronto, Canada

Networks are currently enjoying a great deal of popularity. Popular business press features regular articles speculating on how companies can make money off of the Facebook-and variant-like phenomena (cf., an entire special issue of Forbes last spring). Marketing has long acknowledged the importance of word-of-mouth, e.g., in diffusion models, and in recommendations for selections of service providers, yet only recently have they begun to embrace social network concepts. Further from acceptance still is the use of the social network analytical tools that might actually contribute to the understanding of network structures.

This workshop will provide an introduction to social network methods—the micro, actor-level indices, the meso, group-level methods, and the macro, network-level approaches. Attendees have probably heard of such concepts as centrality, and we'll see the many ways of computing it. Similarly, we'll look at techniques for identifying, cliques, structural equivalence, etc.

This overview will give attendees an appreciation of what social network methods are, e.g., as they read journal articles in which the techniques are used, or as they attend talks by their management colleagues. Perhaps some attendees will also be inspired to experiment with some social network aspect of their own research. To that end, we will also spend some time talking about how social network data are collected (not just modeled).

Consumer Neuroscience: Current State of Knowledge and Future Research Directions

Chairs:
James R. Bettman, Duke University, USA
Drazen Prelec, Massachusetts Institute of Technology, USA
Carolyn Yoon, University of Michigan, USA

Participants:
William Hedgcock, University of Iowa, USA
Mary Frances Luce, Duke University, USA
Hilke Plassmann, California Institute of Technology, USA and INSEAD, France
Baba Shiv, Stanford University, USA
Ale Smidts, Erasmus University, The Netherlands
Stacy Wood, University of South Carolina, USA
Akshay Rao, University of Minnesota, USA
Brian Knutson, Stanford University, USA
Adam Craig, University of South Carolina, USA
Vinod Venkatraman, Duke University, USA
Martin Reimann, Stanford University, USA
Scott Rick, University of Pennsylvania, USA

This roundtable session sought to discuss recent approaches in the field of consumer neuroscience that aim at understanding the neural systems supporting and affecting marketing-relevant behavior. The session brought together researchers currently using neuroscientific methods to investigate questions related to marketing in order to 1) assess the current state of knowledge and 2) discuss directions for future research. The session began with a discussion of the marketing-relevant questions that have been investigated within consumer neuroscience, as well as decision neuroscience and neuroeconomics. This was followed by a discussion to elicit ideas about research future directions.

Generating eReferrals Using Incentives and Bribes: A Field Experiment Testing Various Incentives for online Referrals

Jan Ahrens, Golden Gate University, USA

Michal Ann Strahilevitz, Golden Gate University, USA

Abstract

This research examines several methods for generating company-initiated electronic referrals (eReferrals). A field experiment was conducted with 45,000 participants using different online referral techniques. We manipulated the incentive magnitude for senders and receivers. Dependent measures included the number of eReferral emails sent, the number of eReferrals made and the number of eReferrals that led to sales. Our results show that incentives to both the receiver and the sender lead to higher eReferral rates. We also identified an interaction where relatively higher incentives for the sender of the eReferral were most effective when the receiver of the eReferral also was offered an incentive, albeit a lower incentive.

Introduction

The trend toward consumers generating their own marketing messages is increasingly taking the power of attracting customers out of the hands of the marketers. Traditional referrals can be described as one consumer's promotion of goods or services to another consumer. Electronic referrals (eReferrals) are those referrals that occur online. Firms are making great efforts to respond to this new technology-enabled phenomenon. This has led many firms to invest in encouraging customer acquisition via electronic referrals. eReferrals offer marketers a way to acquire new customers from current customers, at a potentially higher quality and lower cost than advertising.

The research used a large-scale field experiment measuring actual eReferral, registration and purchase behavior. Participants in the study were customers of Ebates and the individuals to whom they referred. Ebates is a website offering services and discounts to online shoppers who purchase through their portal.

When financial incentives to both senders and receivers are offered, equity theory suggests the two parties will be affected by what they each receive. Intuitively we may think that the person making a recommendation cares only about what incentive is offered to him or her, however, equity theory suggests otherwise. In general, equity theory can be described as the proposition that individuals seek equity in what they give and what they receive (Walster, Berscheid & Walster 1973). So the sender may believe that the receiver should also receive an incentive for efforts made. Equity exists when both parties receive the same incentive, such as $5 for the sender and $5 for the receiver.

Inequity may be present when the perceived inputs of one person are in opposition to what that person perceives are the inputs of another person (Adams 1963). Or, stated another way, inequity may be present when the incentive levels to the two parties are of different magnitudes. For example, assuming equal effort, if the sender gets $10 and the receiver gets $5, there is positive inequity for the sender. That said, assuming equal effort, if the sender gets $5 and the receiver gets $10, there is negative inequity for the sender.

Field Experiment Measuring Actual eReferral Rates Under Different Incentive Conditions

The field experiment was conducted with 45,000 participants who were customers of Ebates. Ebates offers a percentage of cash back on purchases to its customers who can shop at over 900 popular online stores. Participants were randomly selected from Ebates' base of customers who had purchased goods through Ebates within the past twelve months and had not opted-out of email communication from the company. The study was a two-factor between-subject experiment, where the size of the financial incentives offered to the senders and receivers of the eReferrals were manipulated. Specifically, the two independent variables were 1) *Incentive magnitudes to senders of the eReferrals* ($5, $10, $25, and $50), and 2) *Incentive magnitudes to receivers of the eReferrals* ($5, $10, $25, and $50). There were a total of eight conditions, representing the different incentive combinations (the first incentive level is for the sender, the second is for the receiver): $5/$5, $5/$10, $5/$25, $5/$50, $10/$5, $25/$5, $50/$5, $25/$25. Participants were randomly assigned to one of the eight conditions.

The eReferral initiation process began by Ebates contacting 45,000 current customers via a "prospecting email" with one of eight financial incentive offer combinations in exchange for referring others. These members then chose to make eReferral invitation attempts to friends, relatives, acquaintances or other persons. Receivers of these eReferrals then had the opportunity to register contact information with Ebates and thus become new Ebates members. As indicated in the invitations, for both parties to earn the financial incentive offered, the new member must have made a purchase within the offer expiration period of three weeks. Once this step occurred, the new member's status changed to that of a buyer, and the promised incentives were rewarded to both parties.

There were three dependent variables in the field experiment: 1) the number of eReferral invitation emails sent in attempts of creating an eReferral ("invitation emails"), 2) the number of new Ebates members acquired through the eReferral efforts ("new members"), and 3) the number of those new members that converted to become buyers ("new buyers"). Of the 45,000 "prospecting emails" sent from Ebates, 37,601 were actually delivered (i.e. "good" email addresses).

A unique URL was included in each email to enable tracking by condition. The URL was tied to each unique sender who then received the promised incentive when a receiver became both a member and a buyer by both registering and then purchasing through Ebates. A total of 2,226 "invitation emails" were sent from Ebates' Senders. There were 810 "new members" who registered and then subsequently 391 "new buyers" who purchased during the three-week offer expiration period.

Results

We hypothesized that in equal financial offer combination eReferral situations (e.g. the same amount for each party such as $5/$5), the higher the total financial incentive offer combination for senders and receivers combined, the more eReferral results would occur. All three dependent variables increased significantly between the group that received $5 for both parties ($5/$5) compared to the group that received $25 for both parties ($25/$25) as follows: 1) the rate of eReferral "invitation emails" sent out increased from 40.1 to 100.4 per thousand ($p < 0.0001$), 2) the rate of "new members" increased from 13.9 to 42.9 per thousand, ($p < 0.0001$), and 3) the rate of "new buyers" increased from 7.1 to 21.1 per thousand, ($p < 0.0001$).

In unequal financial offer combination eReferral situations (e.g. a different amount for each party such as $5/$10), we also hypothesized that the higher the total financial incentive offer combination for senders and receivers combined, the more eReferral results would occur. Groups in this analysis included $5/$10 and $10/$5 ($15 total), $5/$25 and $25/$5 ($30 total), $5/$50 and $50/$5 ($55 total). Significant increases of all three dependent variables occurred as each total incentive level increased ($p < 0.0001$). As an example, the rate of eReferral "invitation emails" sent increased from 47.2 per thousand in the $15 total group, to 59.5 in the $30 group, to 71.3 in the $55 group ($p < 0.0001$).

We also hypothesized that in cases with an unequal financial offer combination (e.g. $10/$5), those conditions with the sender receiving a higher financial offer than the receiver would yield higher eReferral rates than when the receiver's incentive is higher. Subjects with offer conditions of $5/$10, $5/$25 and $5/$50 were combined into a '*sender lower*' financial offer group, while subjects with offer conditions of $10/$5, $25/$5 and $50/$5 were combined into a '*sender higher*'. An ANOVA analysis was performed. The hypothesis was supported as eReferral results increased significantly from the "sender lower" to the "sender higher" groups. The rate of eReferral "invitation emails" sent increased from 48.1 to 68.8 per thousand ($p < 0.01$); the number of "new members" increased from 17.2 to 23.5 per thousand ($p < 0.05$); and the number of "new buyers" increased from 7.5 to 12.1 per thousand ($p < 0.05$).

When conditions within the unequal financial offer combination eReferral situations were isolated, those with the offer combinations of $50/$5 and $25/$5 showed significantly better measures in all three dependent variables than all three conditions in which the senders offer was lower ($5/$10, $5/$25 and $5/$50).

Conclusion

The results of this field experiment provide insight into consumer responsiveness to company-initiated eReferrals under different conditions. Not surprisingly, as the incentive to the referrer increased, so did the sender's eReferral effort and success in referring others. eReferrals rates also correlated positively to higher incentive levels for receivers of the eReferral. There were significant increases in eReferrals as the offer incentives increased both to senders and receivers. However, the effect of the size of the incentive to the sender was stronger than the effect of the size of the incentive to the receiver. When incentives to senders and receivers were unequal in size, eReferral results were higher when the sender's incentive was higher.

On a deeper level, the results suggest that mild positive inequity (i.e., inequity favoring the receiver of the offer) is tolerable, and in fact may motivate the highest level of effort (as measured by eReferral rates). Yet, too great a level of positive inequity may have a negative effect on motivation (as measured by eReferral rates). In short, the power of greed may only motivate consumers up to a point. At some maximum level of tolerance for positive inequity, our results suggest that consumers may be more motivated by offers that involve sharing rewards with others.

References

Adams, J.S. (1963). "Toward an understanding of inequity." *Journal of Abnormal and Social Psychology*, Vol. 67, Iss. 6, p. 422-436.

Walster, E., Berscheid, E., & Walster, G.W. (1973). "New directions in equity research." *Journal of Personality and Social Psychology*, Vol. 25, Iss. 2, p. 151-176.

Preferences for Food with Nutrition and Health Claims in a Close-to-Realistic Choice Context

Jessica Aschemann, University of Kassel, Germany

Ulrich Hamm, University of Kassel, Germany

Abstract

In 2007, the EU introduced a regulation on nutrition and health claims on food products in response to the increasing importance of claims. However, to what extent and how European consumers react to claims remains an open question. This study analyses purchase behaviour in a close-to-realistic laboratory choice test. The results show that foods with nutrition and health claims are generally preferred. Determinants of choice are perception of healthiness of the product, extent of information search and credibility of the claim. Participants' behaviour and statements indicate that the premise of designing a close-to-realistic choice context has been met.

Introduction

Health is an important motive for food choices and increasingly used as an argument in the communication strategies of food companies. In reaction to this trend, the EU commission developed the regulation (EC) No 1924/2006 on nutrition and health claims. Its aims are an EU-wide harmonisation in the handling of claims and consumers' protection from misguidance with regard to the "healthiness" of products. However, research on European consumers' reactions towards such claims on food is scarce so far, especially in a realistically designed decision context. This study, funded by the German Research Foundation, examines the influence that claims have on purchase decisions and the determinants of food choice in the presence of claims, using the choice-test method.

Methodology

A multi-measurement approach was developed combining a discrete choice-test in the laboratory with unobtrusive video-recording and a subsequent face-to-face-interview. The task was designed as realistically as possible, in reaction to the frequently expressed critique that previous studies on such claims might lack external validity (e.g. Keller et al. 1997; Garretson and Burton 2000; Van Trijp and van der Lans 2007), as well as consumer research (Liefeld 2000). We used three-dimensional, authentic products with brand names and inconspicuously added the claims with professionally designed adhesive stickers. The test persons were not forcefully exposed to the claims, were allowed a no-choice option (Dhar and Simonson 2003) and acted under budget constraints as well as increased relevance due to the non-hypothetical choice (Lusk and Schroeder 2004). Each of the 210 regular buyers of the products invited to the laboratory experiment was asked to imagine that they had strawberry-yoghurt, fruit-muesli and spaghetti on the shopping-list. They could choose one out of five alternatives each. The claims were present on two alternatives at a time (expected frequency of random choice of a product with claim therefore being 40%) and its appearance rotated between the brands in order to minimise the brand influence. Furthermore, the claim phrasing alternated between a nutrition claim, a health claim and a health risk reduction claim. We did not manipulate the products with further positive information in order to control for a mere-label-effect (Van Trijp and van der Lans 2007), because the authentic layout of the products already included other positive information (for example "with honey", "deliciously creamy", etc.).

Results

The sample size consisted of 630 cases, with the no-choice-option selected in 5% of all. 50.5% of the respondents were 45 years or older and 71.4% female. The proportion of choice for products with a claim was significantly different from the expected with 44.4% (n=599, χ^2=4.848*; with $p \leq .001$=***; $p \leq .05$=*). Hence, the subjects preferred the products with a claim, even though only 52.4% of the respondents stated that they had actually noticed the claim during the experiment and 38.7% said they had selected the habitually chosen brand. Additionally, the mean duration of information search for all three choice decisions was very short, 1.81 minutes only, and, on average, subjects touched 1.2 products per product category.

Binary logistic regression was applied for each of the three food categories in order to determine which of the independent variables contributed to the explanation of choice behaviour. Age, sex, credibility of the claim, knowing the nutrition-health-relationship and a positive attitude to functional food were insignificant influencing factors in all three models. Only perception of healthiness of the product with a claim had a significant and positive influence on choice for each food category. Choosing the habitual brand has a negative influence on choice of a product with a claim for pasta and yoghurt, scepticism towards texts on food packages has a positive influence for muesli but a negative for yoghurt and the fact that the claim is presented on the cheapest of the alternatives has a positive influence for pasta but a negative for yoghurt. Further variables are only significant for one of the food categories. All three models (yoghurt; muesli; pasta) are significant (Likelihood-Ratio Test: χ^2=76.511; df=11; p=.000; : χ^2=22.224; df=11; p=.023; χ^2=32.131; df=11; p=.001) but differently satisfying (Nagelkerke R^2=.464; .168; .218).

Conclusions

The study shows that products with claims are preferred. We conclude that the probability of preference for a product with a claim is higher when the person regards the product alternative as relatively healthy and does not choose the habitually chosen brand. Which are the determinants of choice as well as the direction of its influence depends very much on the food category and, related to that, the content of the claim. We deduce from the participants´ behaviour and statements that we might have been successful in meeting the premise of a realistically designed choice decision context. It can therefore be assumed that claims on food products increase the likelihood of purchase by consumers, even under the impact of the various influences at the point of sale.

References

Dhar, R. and I. Simonson (2003), "The effects of forced choice on choice," *Journal of Marketing Research*, 40 (2), 146–160.

Garretson, J. A. and S. Burton (2000). "Effects of nutrition facts panel values, nutrition claims, and health claims on consumer attitudes, perceptions of disease-related risks, and trust," *Journal of Public Policy & Marketing*, 19 (2), 213–227.

Keller, S. B.; Landry, M.; Olson, J.; Velliquette, A. M.; Burton, S. and J. C. Andrews (1997). "Thee of nutrition package claims, nutrition facts panels, and motivation to process nutrition information on consumer product evaluations," *Journal of Public Policy & Marketing*, 16 (2), 256–269.

Liefeld, J. P. (2002), "External (in)validity characteristics of consumer research reported in academic journals," *Canadian Journal of Marketing Research*, 20 (2), 84–94.

Lusk, J. L. and T. C. Schroeder (2004), "Are choice-experiments incentive compatible? A test with quality-differentiated beef steaks," *American Journal of Agricultural Economics*, 86 (2), 467–482.

Van Trijp, H. C. M. and I. A. van der Lans (2007), "Consumer perceptions of nutrition and health claims," *Appetite*, 48 (3), 305-324.

Should I Keep or Should I Give: The Effects of Mortality Salience on Disposing

A. Selin Atalay, HEC School of Management, Paris, France

Meltem Türe, Bilkent University, Turkey

Reminders of human mortality, mortality salience (MS) are inevitable in consumers' everyday lives. Terror Management Research (TMT; Greenberg et al.1997), explains how individuals deal with MS. TMT has shown that MS induces excessive spending and greed (Kasser and Sheldon 2000), preference for high status products and increased expression of materialistic values (Arndt et al. 2004, Mandel and Heine 1999). We extend this research by investigating how consumers dispose their possessions after acquiring new ones.

When mortality is salient, individuals try to establish a sense of control by reinforcing their belief in a cultural worldview (CWV), and enhancing their self-esteem (Pyszczynski et al. 2003). Self-esteem which mitigates the effects of MS, is enchanced by being a valuable member of a valuable culture (Arndt et al. 2002). A CWV also helps reduce anxiety by providing literal, and symbolic immortality (Pyszczynski et al.1998).

Disposing is an important consumption phenomenon. By disposing possessions, one can create, maintain or negotiate an identity (Belk 1988; Price et al. 2000), and can deal with aging and death (Marcoux 2001; Kates 2001; Price et al. 2000). As such, that it is important to understand how disposing shapes up under MS. The relationship between MS and disposition has not yet been investigated. Disposition of possessions may be both physical and psychological 'therapy' for consumers (Scwebke 2006) as it induces symbolic immortality, and presents a way to create a certain type of self. It helps an individual preserve a certain identity or construct and communicate a desired one (McAlexander 1991, Wallendorf and Young 1989).

From a TMT perspective we study how consumers dispose their possessions when mortality is salient. We hypothesize:

H1a: When mortality is salient individuals will dispose their possessions in ways that will help them create a sense of symbolic immortality.

H1b: When mortality is salient individuals will dispose their possessios in ways that will allow them to form a socially valued identity.

Study 1

Study 1, an experiment conducted with 41 undergraduates, tested how MS impacts disposing. MS was manipulated and its effect on disposing was measured.

Manipulation. In the MS condition, participants responded to two open-ended questions about death: 1) "Please briefly describe the emotions that the thought of your own death arouses in you."; 2) "Jot down, as specifically as you can, what you think will happen to you as you physically die and once you are physically dead." Participants in the control condition responded to a neutral topic: 1) "Please briefly describe the emotions that the thought of going to the dentist arouses in you."; 2) "Jot down, as specifically as you can, what you think will happen to you the next time you get a painful procedure done at the dentist's office." Standard distracter tasks followed to ensure that MS was present at a non-conscious level (Greenberg et al. 1990; Harmon-Jones et al. 1997).

Disposing. After the manipulation, participants reviewed a scenario which asked them to imagine that their family gave them an upgraded version of their existing camera. Participants were asked to indicate what they would do with their existing camera.

Results. In the MS condition, 68% indicated they would give their camera to someone else, while in the control condition 33% indicated they would give their camera to someone else. The remaining 34% of the participants in the MS condition indicated they would keep their old camera, while 67% of participants in the control condition indicated they would keep their old camera.

A binary logistic regression, with disposition typer as the dependent variable (choice of giving the old camera coded as 1) and MS as the independent variable, showed a significant effect of MS on disposition type (b=1.5, Wald χ^2=4.4, p<.05) indicating individuals in the MS condition preferred to give their old cameras to someone else more than those participants in the control condition.

In explaining their motivations, the MS participants reported that they would give their camera to someone else to prevent waste, achieve symbolic immortality and because giving is the *"right thing to do"*. Individuals in the MS condition who chose to keep their camera reported an emotional connection with the item. Participants in the control condition who chose to keep their cameras did so because they might need the item. They stated that they they might give it to someone they knew, which allows them to still have access to it.

To make sure that the effect of MS on disposition choice was not driven by a mood induced by MS, the Positive Affect Negative Affect Schedule (Watson, Clark and Tellegen 1998) was administered. The ANOVAs on positive and negative affect indicated no differences (p>.64 and p>.40, respectively) between the experimental groups.

Personality measures; Self-esteem (Rosenberg 1965), Desirability of Control (Burger and Cooper 1979), and Materialism (Richins 1989) indicated no differences between the groups (p>.32, p>.50 and p>.60, respectively).

Discussion. As predicted, MS caused individuals to dispose their item in ways that provide them a socialy accepted identity and symbolic immortality. MS induces a striving for symbolic immortality and self-esteem. Disposing literature suggests that giving away one's belongings can help one achieve a desired identity and symbolic immortality. Hence, giving away possessions help invididuals mitigate the effects of MS.

Future Studies

This work investigated the effects of the needs for self-esteem and symbolic immortality induced by MS on disposing. In the studies that follow it will be important to understand the effects of the other needs induced by MS on disposing namely; need for control and materialism.

General Discussion

MS is widely experienced, thus it is important to understand its effects on all phases of consumption. This research helps us understand how consumers evaluate their possessions and detach themselves from them under MS which in turn have implications for charitable donations, waste management, increasing recycling and sustainable consumption.

So, what will you do with your old item the next time you replace a possession?

References

Arndt, Jamie, Jeff Greenberg, Jeff Schimel, Tom Pyszczynski and Sheldon Solomon (2002), "To Belong or Not to Belong, That is the Question: Terror Management and Identification with Gender and Ethnicity," *Journal of Personality and Social Psychology*, 83(July), 26-43.

Arndt, Jamie, Jeff Greenberg, Tim Kasser, Kennon M. Sheldon (2004), "The Urge to Splurge: A Terror Management Account of Materialism and Consumer Behavior," *Journal of Consumer Psychology*, 14(3), 198-212.

Belk, Russell W. (1988), "Possessions and the Extended Self," *Journal of Consumer Research*, Vol. 15, 139-68.

Burger, Jerry M. and Harris M. Cooper (1979)The desirability of control, *Motivation and Emotion*, 3(4), 381-393.

Greenberg, Jeff, Sheldon Solomon, and Tom Pyszczynski (1997), "Terror Management Theory of Self-esteem and Cultural Worldviews: Empirical Assessments and Conceptual Refinements," In Mark P. Zanna (Ed.), *Advances in Experimental Social Psychology*, 29, 61-139, Orlando, FL: Academic Press.

Greenberg, Jeff, Tom Pyszczynski, Sheldon Solomon, Abram Rosenblatt, Mitchell Veeder, Shari Kirkland, and Deborah Lyon (1990), "Evidence for Terror Management Theory II: The Effects of Mortality Salience on Reactions to Those Who Threaten or Bolster the Cultural Worldview," *Journal of Personality and Social Psychology*, 58(February), 308-318.

Harmon-Jones, Eddie, Linda Simon, Jeff Greenberg, Tom Pyszczynski, Sheldon Solomon, and Holly McGregor (1997), "Terror Management Theory and Self-esteem: Evidence That Increased Self-esteem Reduces MS effects," *Journal of Personality and Social Psychology*, 72(January), 24-36.

Kasser, Tim and Sheldon Solomon (2000) Of Wealth and Death: Materialism, Mortality Salience and Consumption Behavior, Psychological Science, 11(4), 348-351.

Kates, Steven M. (2001) Disposition of Possessions Amoung Families of People Living with AIDS. *Psychology and Marketing*. Vol.18, 365-387

Mandel, Naomi and Steven J. Heine (1999), "Terror Management and Marketing: He Who Dies with the Most Toys Wins," *Advances in Consumer Research*, 26, 527-532.

Marcoux, Jean-Sebastien (2001). The 'Casser Maison' Ritual: Constructing the Self by Emptying the Home. *Journal of Material Culture*. Vol. 6, 213-235

McAlexander, J.H. (1991). Divorce, the Disposition of Relationships, and Everything. *Advances in Consumer Research*, vol.18, pp.43-48

Price, Linda, Eric Arnould, and Carolyn Curasi (2000), Older Consumers' Disposition of Valued Possessions, *Journal of Consumer Research*, Vol.27, 179-201

Pyszczynski, Tom, Jeff Greenberg, and Sheldon Solomon (1998), "A Terror Management Perspective on the Psychology of Control: Controlling the Uncontrollable," In Kofta, Weary and Sedek (Eds.), *Personal Control in Action*, 85-108, New York: Plenum Press.

Pyszczynski, Tom, Sheldon Solomon, and Jeff Greenberg (2003), *In the wake of 9/11: The Psychology of Terror*. Washington, DC: American Psychological Association.

Richins, Marsha (1989) in *American Marketing Association Educators Proceedings*, eds. Patrick Murphy et al., Chicago: The American Marketing Association.

Rosenberg, M. (1965). *Society and the adolescent self-image*. Princeton, NJ: Princeton University Press.

Schwebke, F. (2006). *Weg mit dem Ballast! Feel good!* Gräfe & Unzer

Wallendorf, M., & Young, M. M. (1989). Ashes to ashes, dust to dust: Conceptualizing consumer disposition of possessions. In T. Childers, R. Bagozzi, P.Peter, A. Firat, C. Kumcu, A. Sawyer, J. Frazier, M. Rothschild, &M. Strong (Eds.), Marketing Theory and Practice, AMA Winter Educators Conference (pp. 33–38). Chicago: American Marketing Association.

Watson, David, Lee A. Clark, and Auke Tellegen (1998), "Development and Validation of Brief Measures of Positive and Negative Affect: The PANAS Scales," *Journal of Personality and Social Psychology*, 54(June), 1063-1070.

Environmentally Friendly Consumption Preferences: Understanding the Impact of Consumption Routines

Tugba Orten, Izmir University of Economics, Turkey
Deniz Atik, Izmir University of Economics, Turkey

Since the 1970s, environmental issues have been increasingly studied by many marketing scholars. Especially in the early stage, majority of the studies attempted to identify environmentally concerned consumers (e.g., Murphy, Kangun, and Locander, 1978) under different names such as socially conscious consumers (e.g., Anderson and Cunningham, 1972; Brooker, 1976; Webster, 1975), voluntary simplifiers (e.g., Leonard-Barton, 1981; Shama, 1985), or green consumers (e.g., Diamantopoulus, Schlegelmilch, Sinkovics, and Bohlen, 2003). As it can be understood from these various denominations, these studies could not reach a common definition of who are the environmentally concerned consumers (Connolly, McDonagh, Polonsky, and Prothero, 2006). This may be because identifying who is a green consumer is not easy or not even possible. Consumers, regardless of the degree of their ecological consciousness, do not buy environmentally friendly products only on the basis of their ecological impacts (Henion, Gregory, and Clee, 1981). There may be many other reasons beyond the environmental aims motivating those purchasing decisions such as the health concerns of consumers for themselves or their families, economic constraints, quality issues, availability or pleasure (Connolly, McDonagh, Polonsky, and Prothero, 2006; Leonard-Barton, 1981).

Although after 1980s, the general focus of the studies has altered, investigating the underlying factors motivating proenvironmental behaviors like values, norms, beliefs, awareness, knowledge, concern and attitudes (e.g., Fransson and Garling, 1999; Garling, Fujii, Garling, and Jakobsson, 2003; Kim and Choi, 2005; Minton and Rose, 1997; Roberts and Bacon, 1997; Olander and Thogersen, 2006; Osterhus, 1997; Thogersen and Grunert-Beckmann, 1997), the results were again inconclusive in explaining why there is a weak relation between these predicators and the actual behaviors (Kilbourne and Beckmann, 1998). Moreover, studies underlined that there are different proenvironmental behaviors which are affected by different factors, and even at different levels under different structural conditions (Guagnano, Stern, and Dietz, 1995; Poortinga, Steg, and Vlek, 2004; Roberts and Bacon, 1997; Olander and Thogersen, 2006). For instance, Stern (2005) argued that personal variables (e.g., financial resources, literacy, social status, and behavior-specific knowledge and skills) are less likely to influence proenvironmental behavior when contextual factors (e.g., laws and regulations, financial incentives and penalties, and social pressure) are strong. The interrelationships of these personal and contextual variables might also vary depending on different types of environmentally significant behaviors such as green purchasing, recycling, or energy conservation behavior (Kim and Choi, 2005).

From a broader perspective, there are so many distinct green issues (Zimmer, Stafford, and Stafford, 1994) and for each one there are different types of proenvironmental behaviors that can be performed (Thogersen and Grunert-Beckmann, 1997). For example, if one concerns for waste management, buying biodegradable, recyclable or reusable products and separating waste are some of the alternative behaviors that can be followed. To put it in another way, in such a case, a consumer may buy beverages with refillable bottles but not separate his/her kitchen waste or may continue to buy hair sprays which contribute to another environmental deterioration, air pollution. In such situation, the critical questions are: are we going to define that person as an environmentally conscious consumer or not? Or, is it satisfying to place that person in a category and make predictions about his/her environmentally benign behaviors depending on that category?

Beyond this ambiguity and its inconclusive results in promoting environmentally friendly behavior, this study aims to understand: Which kinds of proenvironmental consumptions are preferred, and what are the reasons behind those preferences? In accordance with this desire to understand rather than explain, an unstructured interviewing method was chosen to have "a greater breadth of data, given its qualitative nature" (Fontana and Frey, 2000, p.652). Consequently, open-ended, in-depth interviews were conducted with twelve respondents, performing different levels of environmentally friendly consumption behaviors. This diversity in green consumption degrees also contributes to the discovery of dominant green consumption choices, and enables us to develop a better understanding of the common motivators behind consumers' choices.

Preliminary results show that consumers mostly tend to express their environmental concerns by their green buying behaviors rather than reducing their current consumption amounts. The data also reveals that there are some preeminent green purchasing preferences among respondents such as buying energy saving light bulbs. Even though some of the participants who proclaimed that they were aware of some other possible environmentally friendly consumption choices like buying paper-packs, they stated that high mark-ups, lack of less damaging alternatives or the limited availability of reaching those alternatives were the main reasons for not buying them. However, the in-depth look at their consumption preferences indicates that the most prominent difference between the preferred consumption choices and the ones not preferred was the frequency of buying. This interesting result stimulates further research on understanding the impact of consumption routines on environmentally friendly consumption preferences.

References

Anderson, Thomas. W. and Cunningham, William. H. (1972), "The Socially Conscious Consumer," *Journal of Marketing*, 36, 23-31.

Brooker, George (1976), "The Self-Actualizing Socially Conscious Consumers," *Journal of Consumer Research*, 3, 107-112.

Connolly, John; McDonagh, Pierre; Polonsky, Michael and Prothero, Andrea (2006), "Green Marketing and Green Consumers: Exploring the Myths," *Environmental Technology Management in Business Practices*, 251-268.

Diamantopoulos, Adamantios; Schlegelmilch, Bodo B.; Sinkovics, Rudolf R. and Bohlen, Greg (2003), "Can Socio-Demographics Still Play a Role in Profiling Green Consumers? A Review of the Evidence and an Empirical Investigation," *Journal of Business Research*, 56 (6), 465-480.

Fransson, Niklas and Garling, Tommy (1999), "Environmental Concern: Conceptual Definitions, Measurement Methods, and Research Findings," *Journal of Environmental Psychology*, 19, 369-382.

Fontana, Andrea and Frey, James H. (2000), "The Interview: From Structured Questions to Negotiated Text," In Denzin, Norman K. and Lincoln, Yvonna S. (eds.), *Handbook of Qualitative Research* (p.645-672), London: Sage.

Garling, Tommy; Fujii, Satoshi; Garling, Anita and Jakobsson, Cecilia (2003), "Moderating Effects of Social Value Orientation on Determinants of Proenvironmental Behavior Intention," *Journal of Environmental Psychology*, 23, 1-9.

Guagnano, Gregory A.; Stern, Paul C. and Dietz, Thomas (1995), "Influences on Attitude-Behavior Relationships: A Natural Experiment With Curbside Recycling," *Environment and Behavior*, 27 (5), 699-718.

Henion, Karl E.; Gregory, Russell and Clee, Mona A. (1981), "Trade-Offs In Attribute Levels Made By Ecologically Concerned and Unconcerned Consumers When Buying Detergents," *Advances in Consumer Research*, 624-629.

Kilbourne, William E. and Beckmann, Suzanne C. (1998), "Review and Critical Assessment of Research on Marketing and the Environment," *Journal of Marketing Management*, 14, 513-582.

Kim, Yeonshin and Choi, Sejung M. (2005), "Antecedents of Green Purchase Behavior: An Examination of Collectivism, Environmental Concern, and PCE," *Advances in Consumer Research*, 32, 592-599.

Leonard-Barton, Dorothy (1981), "Voluntary Simplicity Lifestyles and Energy Conservation," *Journal of Consumer Research*, 8, 243-252.

Minton, Ann P. and Rose, Randall L. (1997), "The Effects of Environmental Concern on Environmentally Friendly Consumer Behavior: An Exploratory Study," *Journal of Business Research*, 40, 37-48.

Murphy, Patrick E.; Kangun, Norman and Locander, William B. (1978), "Environmentally Concerned Consumers: Racial Variations," *Journal of Marketing*, 42 (4), 61-66.

Olander, Folke and Thogersen, John (2006), "The A-B-C of Recycling," *Advances in Consumer Research*, 7, 297-302.

Osterhus, Thomas L. (1997), "Pro-social Consumer Influence Strategies: When and How Do They Work," *Journal of Marketing*, 61, 16-29.

Poortinga, Wouter; Steg, Linda and Vlek, Charles (2004), "Values, Environmental Concern, and Environmental Behavior: A Study into Household Energy Use," *Environment and Behavior*, 36 (1), 70-93.

Roberts, James A. and Bacon, Donald R. (1997), "Exploring the Subtle Relationship between Environmental Concern and Ecologically Conscious Consumer Behavior," *Journal of Business Research*, 40, 79-89.

Shama, Auraham (1985), "The Voluntary Simplicity Consumer," *Journal of Consumer Marketing*, 2, 57-64.

Stern, Paul C. (2005), "Understanding Individuals' Environmentally Significant Behaviors," *ELR News and Analysis*, 35, 10785-10790.

Thogersen, John and Grunert-Beckmann, Suzanne C. (1997), "Values and Attitude Formation towards Emerging Attitude Objects: From Recycling To General, Waste Minimizing Behavior," *Advances in Consumer Research*, 24, 182-189.

Webster, Frederick E. (1975), "Determining the Characteristics of Socially Conscious Consumer," *Journal of Consumer Research*, 2, 188-196.

Zimmer, Mary R.; Stafford, Thomas F. and Stafford, Marla R. (1994), "Green Issues: Dimensions of Environmental Concern," *Journal of Business Research*, 30, 63-74.

From Saver Society to Consumer Society: The Case of the East European Consumer

Eleonora Axelova, York University, Canada

Russell Belk, York University, Canada

During the last nineteen years, the world has witnessed an important transition in Central and Eastern Europe, unprecedented in contemporary history–the move from a centrally planned to a market economy. In this short period of time, East European consumers have faced a new environment with changes in all spheres of their lives as well as an influx of new goods, services, media, and market institutions. The prior poor selection of products with shabby packaging, displayed in drab places with a lack of information was rapidly replaced by a wide choice of new products and brands from new countries-of-origin. These new goods came with attractive packaging, modern retailing, and clever and exciting advertising.

The East European consumer has now been amply exposed to marketing that is quite like that of the West. They have had enough time to become accustomed to the novelty of the market economy, but the communism of the past is not forgotten. Based on ethnographic participant observation and interviews in Bulgaria and Romania, we consider whether a market economy necessarily leads to a consumer society or whether some of the practices of earlier consumption patterns continue. At a macro level there is some evidence of nostalgia for communism seen in manifestations as diverse as the re-emgergence of East German rock music, the Trabi automobile, and Cultural Revolution restaurants (Berdahl 1999; Yang 2003). But we are interested in the more micro-level and perhaps deeper imprints of communism on the Eastern European consumer. Just as those raised in the Great Depression often evidenced cautious consumption and parsimony for many years after the Depression (Cohen 2003), it is possible that East Europeans may show similar traces of their prior ingenuity in surviving communism (Drakuli? 1991). Although there is some consumer research on East European consumers after Communism (e.g. Axelova 2004 and 2005; ; Belk 1997; Coulter, Price, and Feick 2003; Ettenson 1993; Feick, Coulter, and Price 1995; Ger, Belk, and Lascu 1993; Lofman 1993; Shama 1992; Shultz, Belk, and Ger 1994; Witkowski 1993), there is little that explores the persistence of old consumption habits, such as those we discovered in Bulgaria and label the "Saver Society."

What is the "Saver Society"?

The Bulgarian proverb "Prepare for winter and if summer comes say : 'Welcome!'" shows the cautious character of the Bulgarian people. At the heart of the Saver Society is a notion of "Saving," while the heart of Consumer Society lies consuming and spending. Saving was necessary under communism where credit did not exist. To buy a major appliance or an automobile, could take years of savings and patience. Thrift was necessary in daily life to allow any savings. Consumers were also frugal in using things. An old nylon stocking could become a fan belt, bottles for cooking oil or beer were returned to the store to be refilled. Vegetables, rabbits, and chickens were raised for food where possible. Sharing with relatives was another means of making do. Nothing went to waste. But besides thrift, there was also a cultural value placed on modesty. Another Bulgarian proverb says "Modesty makes the person beautiful, impertinence makes him ugly." When everyone was poor during the communist years it was also dangerous to stand out through even a small amount of conspicuous consumption. But savings patterns were no doubt easier in a time of scarcity and income parity when there were no stores full of attractive merchandise, glittering advertising, and nouveau riche consumers displaying alternative consumption models. So what has happened since 1989?

After defining the Saver Society and its characteristics, we describe how each characteristic has been transformed in light of the changes since communism. The initial conditions for the emergence of a Consumer Society in Eastern Europe now exist. These conditions include an attractive array of goods including Western brand names, media and tourists displaying the external world, plus feelings of deservingness (Belk, 1997) among local consumers, many of whom believe that after years of thrift and modesty, they have been earned the right to a better life.

Another change in Eastern Europe after 1989 has been new social stratification. Disparities that have arisen in income and class have provided new incentives for displaying wealth. Emphasis for many has shifted from hiding signs of wealth so as not to provoke others' envy, to openly displaying wealth and inviting envy.

Two extremes reactions toward Consumer Society in Eastern Europe have emerged. One is the case of the priviledged consumers with high incomes and more cosmopolitan lifestyles. They can travel abroad, buy expensive foreign brands, and acquire a knowledge of lifestyle trends elsewhere. They have easy access to the consumer credit and the Internet. These favoured consumers are already part of the Consumer Society.

The other extreme is the low income, often older, consumer. These consumers buy local brands and have difficulty obtaining credit. They do not belong to the Consumer Society. They, of necessity, remain part of the Saver Society. But between these two extremes we find others who remain a part of the Saver Society by choice. They continue to buy cheap, reuse what they can, display thrift and modesty in consumption, share with relatives, and avoid credit.

Conclusion and Discussion: The Broader Notion of the Saver Society.

Should we regard the group of voluntary members of the Saver Society in Bulgaria as a fossil of another time that will disappear with the next generation of children raised in a growing Cousumer Society? It is possible, but we don't think that this will be the case. There are lingering lessons of childhood and culture just as there are lingering lessons of communism. Besides the voluntary members of Saver Societies there are many poor within rich countries who are also more likely to be Savers. Hill and Stamey's (1990) work with American homeless, Stack's (1974) work with residents of an impoverished housing development, and Chin's (2001) work with poor black children all find instances of Saver Societies alongside Consumer Societies. We believe that our knowledge of both will be advanced by examining the coexistence of such vastly different consumption orientations.

Feedback Effects and Evaluation Process of Health-related Perceived Risk and Health Behavior: A Conceptual Model and an Empirical Test

Yi Zhang, University of Manchester, UK
Zheng Yin, University of Manchester, UK
Jikyeong Kang, University of Manchester, UK
David Baxter, National Health Service, UK

Abstract

Many theories have identified perceived risk as a predictor of behavior. However, contradicting findings from empirical studies have caused researchers to question the role of perceived risk.

This study aims to explore the internal mechanism behind the inconsistencies and to provide further insights. Based on an empirical study concerning the use of condoms, we propose a two-stage dynamic model, involving a process of "evaluation" of an initial action and a construct of "feedback effect" of perceived risk.

Our model will aid researchers and practitioners in social medicine and marketing in achieving a better understanding of health prevention behaviors.

Introduction

Perceived risk has been an interesting research topic for more than four decades. Bauer (1960) first coined the concept of perceived risk in the marketing area. Since then, numerous studies have been conducted to define, measure, and model perceived risk in the context of consumer behavior. Perceived risk has also been applied in various areas, including the food industry (Eiser, Miles, and Frewer 2002), e-commerce (Liebermann and Stashevsky 2002), banking (Gorton 2004), and health services (Kreuter and Strecher 1995). Many studies have illustrated the significant relationship between consumers' health behaviors and their perceived risk, and, indeed, the importance of perceived risk has been widely recognized.

Perceived Risk and Health Preventive Behavior

Perceived risk, as an important element of various health behavior models, has a strong relationship with health behavior or the intention of health behavior (Lindan et al. 1991). Many recent studies, however, state that perceived risk does not have a significant relationship with behavior and has little predictive power in health behavior models(Brewer et al. 2007; Leventhal, Kelly, and Leventhal 1999), such as the Health Belief Model, and the Theory of Reasoned Action. These contradicting findings have led several researchers to conduct meta-analyses in order to bring a more holistic picture of the importance of perceived risk and the relationship between health-related perceived risk and behavior (Brewer et al. 2007; Floyd 2000; e.g., Harrison, Mullen, and Green 1992). Those studies, however, failed to provide a clear explanation of inconsistent findings. Thus, the main purpose of this study is to provide a better understanding of the relationship between perceived risk and consumers' health-related behavior.

Brewer et al. (2004) attempt to explain the inconsistencies by proposing a reappraisal hypothesis, which provides a semi-dynamic structure explaining the inconsistencies. Their study clearly illustrates a relation between preventive health behavior and perceived risk using a longitudinal method. Nevertheless, Brewer et al.'s study did not observe the inconsistencies directly and failed to provide necessary background information of participants by assuming that all other factors are constant. More importantly, a vital "evaluation process" was not illustrated in their study, which explains the decision process during the formation of perceived risk and consistent health behavior.

In our study, health-related perceived risk and behavior are not considered in a static model, which naturally neglects the fact that either perceived risk or behavior can be changed or interrelated in a dynamic way with the progression of time. Instead, we propose a two-stage dynamic model to provide a possible explanation of the inconsistencies found in past studies. In addition, a new construct of "feedback effect" between perceived risk and behavior has been defined and explained.

Proposed Model

The model shown in Figure 1 illustrates the formation of consistent preventive behavior and the mechanism of feedback effect. We hypothesize that the contradicting findings from previous empirical studies are partially due to the fact that participants are at various stages

FIGURE 1
Proposed Model

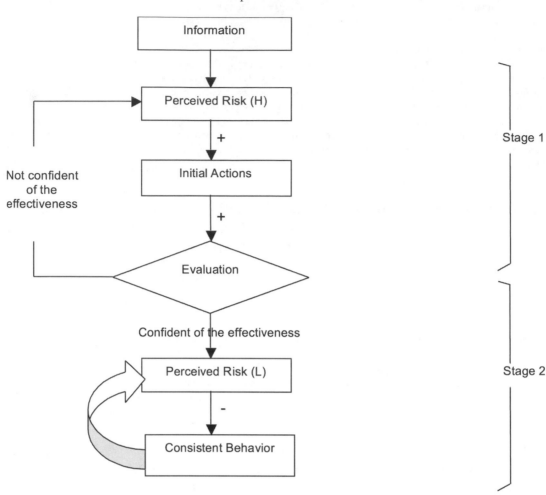

of perceived health risk. At the beginning stage, people obtain information from various sources which can improve the knowledge of a particular hazard or disease. They tend to have a high level of perceived risk after obtaining such information or having enough knowledge on a particular hazard. Based on previous behavioral models, a high level of perceived risk will lead people to engage in preventive behavior, which is then demonstrated in the second stage of the model. After an initial action, an evaluation process which determines the perceived effectiveness of the preventive behavior is carried out. When a person finds the preventive behavior cannot provide enough confidence, he/she stays at a high level of perceived risk. If a person believes that the preventive behavior can offer an effective protection against the particular risk, his/her perceived risk will be reduced and he/she will move to the 2nd stage which is stable.

In the 2nd stage, people have a low level of perceived risk and exhibit a consistent preventive behavior. Preventive behavior provides "feedbacks", which establish people's confidence and further reduce the perceived risk. On the other hand, a low level of perceived risk negatively related with a preventive behavior increases people's willingness to continue engaging in further preventive behaviors.

Study Design

In order to test the proposed model, we conducted a survey research based on a high-risk population in Manchester, UK. Participants were Female Commercial Sex Workers (FCSWs) who had a high risk of catching Sexually Transmitted Infections (STIs). We gained access to our participants by collaborating with a local organization, MASH (Manchester Action on Street Health) which provides sexual health services to FCSWs. Structured interviews were conducted to measure the perceived risks involved. The preventive behavior used in this study is a consistent use of condoms.

Data Collection

FCSWs' responses to the statement "I am at risk of being infected with HIV/AIDS" were recorded, and the reasons for their perceived risk status were also asked, using a four-point Liker-type scale. Higher scores represent a perception of greater risks. After participants evaluated their risks, they were asked to briefly explain the reasons. In addition, participants' knowledge of STIs, the years of working as FCSWs.

Results

Using the qualitative data, we observed that the perceived risk and the stages of FCSWs are significantly correlated ($\chi^2(1)$=107.76, p<.001). FCSWs' working-years also played an important role; the longer the participants had worked in the industry, the more likely they entered into the later stage in which they tend to use condoms consistently and with low perceived risks ($\chi^2(1)$=3.75, p<.05). Knowledge of STIs, the indicator of the information obtained by FCSWs, also affected which stage participants were at. When FCSWs obtained better knowledge on STIs, they were normally in stage 2 of the proposed model ($\chi^2(1)$=5.20, p<.05).

Summary and Contributions

Our study, which focuses on health-related perceived risk and behavior, filled a gap and explained the reasons why perceived risk has little predictive impact in many empirical studies. Feedback effects and the evaluation process, as proposed in our model, explain the interaction between perceived risk and health preventive behavior. Social marketers will benefit from our research whilst providing health preventive campaigns.

References

Bauer, R.A. (1960), "Consumer Behavior as Risk Taking," in *Dynamic Marketing for a Changing World, 43rd Conference of the American Marketing Association*, ed. R.S. Hancock, 389-98.

Brewer, N. T. Noel T., G. B. Gretchen B. Chapman, F. X. Frederick X. Gibbons, M. Meg Gerrard, K. D. Kevin D. McCaul, and N. D. Neil D. Weinstein (2007), "Meta-Analysis of the Relationship between Risk Perception and Health Behavior: The Example of Vaccination," *Health psychology*, 26 (2), 136-45.

Brewer, Noel T., Neil D. Weinstein, Cara L. Cuite, and James E. Herrington (2004), "Risk Perceptions and Their Relation to Risk Behavior," *Annals of Behavioral Medicine*, 27 (2), 125-30.

Eiser, J. R., S. Miles, and L. J. Frewer (2002), "Trust, Perceived Risk and Attitudes toward Food Technologies," *Journal of Applied Social Psychology*, 32 (11), 2423.

Floyd, D. L. (2000), "A Meta-Analysis of Research on Protection Motivation Theory," *Journal of Applied Social Psychology*, 30 (2), 407.

Gorton, G. (2004), "Banking Panics and Business Cycles*," *Oxford Economic Papers*, 40 (4), 751.

Harrison, Ja J. A., Pd P. D. Mullen, and Lw L. W. Green (1992), "A Meta-Analysis of Studies of the Health Belief Model with Adults," *Health Education Research*, 7 (1), 107-16.

Kreuter, Mw M. W. and Vj V. J. Strecher (1995), "Changing Inaccurate Perceptions of Health Risk: Results from a Randomized Trial," *Health psychology*, 14 (1), 56-63.

Leventhal, Howard, Kim Kelly, and Elaine A. Leventhal (1999), "Population Risk, Actual Risk, Perceived Risk, and Cancer Control: A Discussion," *J Natl Cancer Inst Monogr*, 1999 (25), 81-85.

Liebermann, Y. and S. Stashevsky (2002), "Perceived Risks as Barriers to Internet and E-Commerce Usage," *Qualitative market research*, 5 (4), 291.

Lindan, C. C., S. S. Allen, M. M. Carael, F. F. Nsengumuremyi, P. P. Van de Perre, A. A. Serufilira, J. J. Tice, D. D. Black, T. T. Coates, and S. S. Hulley (1991), "Knowledge, Attitudes, and Perceived Risk of Aids among Urban Rwandan Women: Relationship to Hiv Infection and Behavior Change," *AIDS*, 5 (8), 993-1002.

The Values and Lifestyles of Prior Mature Chinese Consumers

Lien-Ti Bei, National Chengchi University, Taiwan
Chih-Ping Wang, National Chengchi University, Taiwan
Hung-Miao Lin, Chinatrust Commercial Bank, Taiwan

Aging is a major issue in most developed and developing countries. The fact that the baby-boomer generation is approaching retirement age has attracted the attentions of governments in the areas of health care, social security, and retirement plan issues. In Italy, Germany, France, and North Europe, aging people occupy 15% of each nation's population. This enormous amount of consumers will also form a large senior market in ten years. Since they will have time after retirement and better health and financial conditions than the depression generation, the potential of this market cannot be ignored. Therefore, the consumption habits, values, and lifestyles of senior consumers have become an emergent issue for marketing researchers and practitioners (Gibler, Lumpkin, and Moschis, 1997; Moschins, Lee, and Mathur, 1997).

Gibler et al. (1997) referred to consumers aged 60 and above as "mature consumers." The present study follows this notion and refers to consumers who are approaching retirement as "prior mature consumers." The cohort of consumers, the 45 to 65 age group, is the ideal target for the study of the future senior market.

After closing its door for more than 50 years, China market has opened to the world and gained worldwide attention. Its prior mature population is around 150 million people. Therefore, this study targets on prior mature Chinese consumers. The purpose of this study is not only to explore the consumption habits, values, and lifestyles of consumers in this booming market but also to reveal the endurance and influences of traditional Chinese culture and Confucian values on consumer behavior when faced with the influences of western culture.

This cohort of Chinese consumers was educated with traditional Confucianism; they have experienced and admired the western modern life and materialism in their adulthood; and they gradually accept the concept of individualism. The conflicting value systems provide the best research targets to illustrate the durations and influences of various consumption values on purchase behaviors and patterns. Four metropolitan cities, Beijing, Shanghai, Guangzhou, and Taipei, were selected due to their economic and political representative status. In January and February 2006, 2075 respondents, 511 to 527 in each city, at the age of 45 to 65 were face-to-face surveyed via a demographic quota sampling procedure.

Other than demographic and consumption items, the questionnaire includes 133 Likert-type 6-point items on values and lifestyles. These items were designed for eight categories of values and concepts: concern about health, financial attitudes, gender issues, career and retirement plans, social relationships, attitude toward aging, consumption values, and other life perspectives. The result of factor analysis extracted 25 important factors. Under the control of age, gender, and work status, the 25 value and lifestyle factors of respondents among the four cities were compared by general linear models. The main findings are:

1) *Health concern and financial attitude*: In the industrial city Guangzhou, prior mature consumers care about their own health condition less and retain fewer traditional Chinese values, such as "limiting expenses within the income boundary and avoiding borrowing money." They are also more willing to invest through professional financial assistance than consumers in other cities.

2) *Consumption value*: In the most internationalized city, Shanghai, consumers prefer products endorsed by celebrities and enjoy the "taste of life" most.

3) *Career and retirement*: In a city where the economy is booming, such as Shanghai and Beijing, prior mature consumers worry about retirement less; while in a city with a slight recession, such as Taipei, prior mature consumers sense that "retiring means not having money" and tend to keep working after age 65.

4) *Social relationships*: Living in the political center, consumers in Beijing, unsurprisingly, care about all kinds of social issues most.

5) *Attitude toward aging*: prior mature consumers in Taipei are more accepting of aging. It can be explained by the traditional Confucian value of respecting the elderly that people in Taipei hold.

In general, family values, respect for seniors, and compliance with authority in traditional Confucianism are still obvious in the value systems of Chinese prior mature consumers. The results suggest these values are more enduring than others. On the other hand, traditional Chinese values regarding gender issues, conservative consumption rules, and desirable social behavior are influenced by western values more. Also, reflecting the economic prospects, in a city where consumers enjoy economic growth, future mature consumers tend to focus on enjoying the western-style life more and rapidly moving toward individualism. Our results suggest that marketers may emphasize the better and more enjoyable life provided by western imported brands; meanwhile, they should also emphasize how the product can contribute to the whole family or is acceptable to the society when targeting these prior mature consumers at present or in the future.

Reference

Gibler, Karen Martin, James R. Lumpkin, and George P. Moschis (1997), "Mature Consumer Awareness and Attitudes Toward Retirement Housing and Long-Term Care Alternatives." *The Journal of Consumer Affairs*, 31(1), 113-138

Moschis, George P., Euehum Lee, and Anil Mathur (1997), "Targeting the Mature Market: Opportunities and Challenges." *Journal of Consumer Marketing*, 14(4), 282-293

Intergenerational Study on the Effects of Attachment Style on Eating Behaviors

Aida Faber, McGill University, Canada
Laurette Dube, McGill University, Canada
Sophie Belanger, L'Oreal Canada, Canada

The family as a collective enterprise is central to consumer behavior, in particular in domains that pertain to lifestyle choice[1]. In today's world of plenty, individuals within families face many challenges and find it hard at times to maintain healthy diets and exercise patterns[2,3] as indicated by soaring obesity rates due to over-consumption and lack of exercise[4]. Yet, little research has attempted to combine the most recent theoretical developments in health and consumer psychology with others from family and parental processes. Such a combination would allow for a more sophisticated understanding of lifestyle decisions that may guide parents and children toward a better balance between health and the many other factors that drive choice and behavior. In this paper, we combine recent psychology research on self-regulation with that of attachment style to examine from an intergenerational perspective the effect of attachment styles on eating behavior in a large sample of child-parent dyads.

Research background

Attachment deals with regulatory functions and consequences of maintaining proximity to others[5]. According to attachment theory, children are born with a "repertoire of behaviors (attachment behaviors) aimed at seeking and maintaining proximity to supportive others (attachment figures)"[5]. In the face of threat or when inner resources are depleted, cognitive representations of attachment figures are automatically activated, thus increasing the person's confidence that there is protection available and facilitating self-regulation[5,6]. There are individual differences in attachment styles. When significant others are available in times of need, a sense of secure attachment is developed. On the other hand, when significant others are unavailable or unresponsive to one's needs, distress and a sense of insecurity are omnipresent.

Secure attachment styles are linked with effective coping skills, constructive ways of dealing with stress and conflict, and healthier interpersonal relationships[7,8]. On the other hand, insecure attachment styles are linked with eating disorders, trouble sleeping, and feeling of ineffectiveness and helplessness[7,9]. Interestingly, these differences in coping styles between securely and insecurely attached individuals can be linked to differences in self-regulation focuses that have recently received robust evidence in health and consumer psychology research. Self-regulation refers to the ability of setting and striving for goals in the face of ongoing challenges[2,10] and is widely applied to healthy lifestyles behaviors[2] because people seem to give in to temptation and not follow through with their long-term goals[11,12].

Hence, attachment security can be said to be associated with healthier lifestyles, i.e., engaging in health promotion behaviors and avoiding risky behaviors, and attachment insecurity with unhealthier lifestyles, i.e., engaging in risky behaviors and avoiding health promotion behaviors[7]. As a result, the objective of this paper is to study attachment styles and their link to food knowledge and consumption. Thus, in this study, we hypothesize that more secure attachment styles in parents and children will be linked with knowing more fruits and vegetables (F&V, hereafter) and having healthier diets. Because there are reliable gender differences in dealing with distress, with males coping in a non-rational manner by trying to distract themselves[13,14], we furthermore hypothesize that attachment security will have a beneficial role for them in that securely attached males will know more F&V and have better diets. Finally, the mediation effects of parental attachment on their children's food knowledge and consumption will be tested.

Method

Design and procedures

To test the above hypotheses, only the pre-intervention questionnaires of a web nutrition intervention aiming to increase children's F&V consumption were analyzed. In total 238 children (157 girls and 79 boys; M_{age}=10.15 years; M_{BMI}=21.42) and 210 parents (37 males and 183 females; M_{age}=41.05 years; M_{BMI}=25.48) completed the questionnaire. Although the 12-step parent/child web intervention took place at home, children between 8 and 12 years old were recruited from 28 French primary schools in a major Canadian city.

Measures

Attachment was measured using an adapted scale from Bowlby[15] from insecurely to securely attached (Crobach's alpha parents=.890, children=.855). F&V knowledge was assessed by asking participants whether or not they knew 31 fruits (fruit knowledge) and 39 vegetables (vegetable knowledge). F&V consumption was assessed by calculating the average fruit, vegetable and F&V intake of all the previously known F&Vs. High caloric food and snack (HCF and HCS, hereafter) consumption was calculated as the average number of times participants ate respectively eight specific HCFs, i.e., hot dogs, and six specific HCSs, i.e., cookies, during a day.

Results

For children, results showed that more securely attached children knew more fruits. There were also two significant interaction effects, in that vegetable and F&V knowledge was the same for girls regardless of their level of attachment whereas it was higher for more vs. less securely attached boys. Furthermore, there was an interaction effect for vegetable consumption in children, in that average vegetable consumption for girls remained the same regardless of their level of attachment whereas for boys, the more secure the attachment the higher the vegetable consumption. Attachment levels did not significantly predict fruit and fruit and vegetable consumption. Lastly, the more securely attached the children, the less HCF and HCS they consumed.

For parents, results showed that more securely attached parents, as measured in relation to their own parents, knew more vegetables and F&V. For fruits and vegetables separately, consumption was the same for women regardless of their attachment levels but was higher for more vs. less securely attached men. For F&V, HCF and HCS consumption, a more secure attachment was linked to higher F&V consumption and lower HCF and HCS consumption.

Mediation analyses showed that parents' attachment mediated the children's relationship between attachment and fruit, vegetable, and F&V knowledge, and HCS consumption but only partially mediated HCF consumption.

Conclusion and Discussion

In conclusion, this study shows that attachment, a variable closely linked with self-regulation focus, is an important predictor of healthy eating habits, not only for children but also for parents. Most importantly, through their own attachment styles, parents influence the role of their children's attachment in predicting healthy eating, which further confirms the pervasive influence of attachment in the every day consumption choices of two generations.

References

[1]Epp, A. M., & Price, L. L. (2008). Family identity: A framework of identity interplay in consumption practices. *Journal of Consumer Research, 35.* (Electronically published February 13, 2008)

[2] Ridder, D., de Witt, J. (2006). Self-regulation in Health Behavior: Concepts, Theories, and Central Issues. In: D. De Ridder & J. De Witt (Eds.), *Self-regulation in health behavior.* (pp. 1- 24). West Sussex: John Wiley & Son.

[3]Rothman, A. J., Baldwin, A., & Hertel, A. (2004). Self-regulation and behavior change: Disentangling behavioral initiation and behavioral maintenance. In K. Vohs and R. Baumeister (Eds.), *The handbook of self-regulation.* (pp. 130-148). New York: Guilford Press.

[4]Centers for Disease Control and Prevention (2005). The burden of obesity in the United States: A problem of massive proportions. *Chronic Disease Notes and Reports, 17,* 4-9.

[5]Mikulincer, M., Shaver, P. R., & Pereg, D. (2003). Attachment Theory and Affect Regulation: The Dynamics, Development, and Cognitive Consequences of Attachment-Related Strategies. *Motivation and Emotion, 27,* 77-102.

[6]Mikulincer, M., Gillath, O., & Shaver, P. R. (2002). Activation of the attachment system in adulthood: Threat-related primes increase the accessibility of mental representations of attachment figures. *Journal of Personality and Social Psychology, 83,* 881-895.

[7]Scharfe, E, & Eldredge, D. (2001). Associations between attachment representations and health behaviors in late adolescence. *Journal of Health Psychology, 6,* 295-307.

[8]Feeney, J. A., & Ryan, S. M. (1994). Attachment style and affect regulation: Relationships with health behavior and family experiences of illness. *Health Psychology, 13,* 334-345.

[9]Ward, A., Ramsay, R., & Treasure, J. (2000). Attachment research in eating disorders. *British Journal of Medical Psychology, 73,* 35–51.

[10]Mischel, W., Cantor, N., & Feldman, S. (1996). Principles of self-regulation: The nature of willpower and self-control. In E. T. Higgins & A. W. Kruglanski (Eds.), *Social psychology: Handbook of basic principles* (pp. 329–360). New York: Guilford.

[11]Muraven, M., & Baumeister, R. F. (2000). Self-regulation and depletion of limited resources: Does self-control resemble a muscle? *Psychological Bulletin, 126,* 247-259.

[12]Schmeichel, B. J., & Baumeister, R. F. (2004). Self-regulatory strength. In R. F. Baumeister & K. D. Vohs (Eds.), *Handbook of self-regulation* (pp. 84-98). New York: Guilford Press.

[13]Conway, M. A., Difazio, R., & Bonnevile J. (1991). Sex, sex roles, and response styles for negative affect. Selectivity in a free recall task. *Sex Roles, 25,* 687-700

[14]Conway, M., Giannopoulos, C., & Stiefenhofer, K. (1990). Response styles to sadness are related to sex and sex-role orientation. *Sex Roles, 22,* 579-587.

[15]Bowlby, J. (1973). *Attachment and loss: Vol 2. Separation: Anxiety and Anger.* New York: Basic Books.

The Role of Consumption in the Organization of Urban Space: The Case of Neo-Bohemia

Yesim Ozalp, York University, Canada

Russell W. Belk, York University, Canada

"Though locals will tell you that West Queen Street West extends all the way down to Gladstone Street, where the oh-so-hip Gladstone Hotel opened in late 2006, walking any farther than the intersection of Ossington and Queen Street West is an exercise in diminishing returns— with appliance stores more numerous than trendy cafes. This part of this street, it seems, is still waiting for its own renaissance." (New York Times, September 02, 2007)

Although Consumer Culture theoretics scholars have studied issues of class (Allen 2002; Henry 2005; Holt 1998), gender (Holt and Thompson 2004) and ethnicity (Crockett and Wallendorf 2004) in the socio-historic patterning of consumption (Arnould and Thompson 2005), urban life and urban space, where consumption is structured by and structures these socio-historic forces, have been left in the background (an exception is a study of gentrification by Ilkucan and Sandikci 2005). Consequently, our understanding of both low involvement everyday consumption choices and practices and high involvement consumption choices (e.g., buying a house) has been isolated from the dynamics of urban life and urban space, including the strategies used by actors in the consumption scene to create or to contest value and their struggles over symbolic and social spaces where value is created. This study follows a Bourdieudian tradition in order to understand acts of legitimization, performative consumption, value dynamics and cultural politics of consumption. We focus on conversion of capital and strategies and struggles in the field that enable and/or impede this conversion, different from other Bourdieudian studies in CCT which have focused on the concepts of capital (Bernthal, Crockett, and Rose 2005; Holt 1998) and habitus (Allen 2002; Henry 2005).

Within the limits of this research, we present a very specific type of neighborhood, often referred to as neo-bohemia. According to (Lloyd 2006), neo-bohemia is the current shelter of the post-modern creative class (Florida 2002), the *Bobos* (Brooks 2000) and the hipsters (Leland 2004). The most important aspect of both modern bohemia and post-modern neo-bohemia is the non-stable relationship between the mainstream, the market and the commercial on one hand and the alternative, creative and cultural on the other. Tensions in this non-stable relationship are constantly played out in urban life and urban space through both daily mundane consumption activities and momentous consumption choices such as buying a loft.

In order to understand the relations between consumption and the organization of neo-bohemian urban space, we selected the Queen Street West neighborhood in Toronto as our context. It was gentrified by the artists who moved out of an increasingly elite Yorkville neighborhood starting in the 1970s (Caulfield 1994) and now has the highest concentration of art galleries in Toronto. In addition to art galleries, the part declared as the Business Improvement Area (BIA) is occupied by new fashionable stores, restaurants and clubs, loft buildings and new commercial developments. Although the neo-bohemian trend has existed in the neighborhood, it has recently become "hot" after two companies announced and sold their loft developments in the area.

Our investigation of Queen Street West is an ongoing multi-method study. Our data include ethnographic observations conducted since early 2007. In addition, we have conducted interviews with neighborhood residents and art gallery owners. We have also collected two types of archival material: promotional material and media texts. Promotional material includes sales brochures and a bi-weekly publication promoting new condominium developments in Toronto. In addition to advertisements, the publication also has articles on condominium lifestyles, real estate trends, and decor. The media text, comprised of articles from Toronto newspapers and Canadian magazines, addresses not only the changes in the neighborhood, but also the lifestyle promoted by these new developments.

Our analysis addresses how consumption organizes and is organized by urban space, and our current findings involve themes of acts of legitimization, performative consumption, value dynamics and the cultural politics of consumption. Despite a backlash, the acts of legitimization provide a central strategy followed by the developers and which they seek to transfer to their customers. Developers depict the bohemian and hipster lifestyle as being among the "amenities" of their high-rise "lofts" in order to attract the "new urbanites" and invite them to be part of this "scene". One of these developments has even used the word bohemian in its name, although it has generated negative reactions among the Queen West art community. It also has staged community events such as fashion shows, which was only open to an exclusive crowd of designers and loft buyers. Another developer has purchased art products from local galleries with the intent of benefiting both galleries and their development. This created controversy among art galleries and some refused to sell. Central to all these acts is an attempt to convert economic capital into commodified and reified cultural capital, since position-taking and legitimacy in this field requires both forms of capital.

An important characteristic of these acts of legitimization involves performative consumption. The new buyers are asked to be part of this neo-bohemian lifestyle through their "consumption performances". This performative lifestyle, as our opening quote depicts, became central to the value dynamics in the neighborhood. Our interviewees suggest that recently opened shops in the neighborhood were mostly one-of-a-kind design stores and boutique shops selling non-mainstream clothing and decorating, replacing hardware stores and even some art galleries. Even the daily activity of having lunch has been affected by such value dynamics, and one of our informants maintains that she can longer find a good place to lunch within her budget.

This example brings us to our final theme, the cultural politics of consumption. We find mechanisms of both inclusion and exclusion in this urban space and show how consumption plays a key role in this. We also problematize the relationship between these new developments and the neighborhood, to show how the exclusionary mechanisms can also impede the capital conversion process, since it diminishes and alters available resources. Through these four themes we build an understanding of the mutual effects of changing neighborhood, consumption lifestyles, and public and private meanings of community.

References

Allen, Douglas E. (2002), "Toward a Theory of Consumer Choice as Sociohistorically Shaped Practical Experience: The Fits-Like-a-Glove (Flag) Framework," *Journal of Consumer Research*, 28 (4), 515-32.

Arnould, Eric J. and Craig J. Thompson (2005), "Consumer Culture Theory (CCT): Twenty Years of Research," *Journal of Consumer Research*, 31 (4), 868-82.

Bernthal, Matthew J., David Crockett, and Randall L. Rose (2005), "Credit Cards as Lifestyle Facilitators," *Journal of Consumer Research*, 32 (1), 130-45.

Brooks, David (2000), *Bobos in Paradise: The New Upper Class and How They Got There*, New York; London: Simon & Schuster.

Caulfield, Jon (1994), *City Form and Everyday Life: Toronto's Gentrification and Critical Social Practice*, Toronto: University of Toronto Press.

Crockett, David and Melanie Wallendorf (2004), "The Role of Normative Political Ideology in Consumer Behavior," *Journal of Consumer Research*, 31 (3), 511-28.

Emmrich, Stuart (2007), "Go West, Young Hipsters", *The New York Times, September 02, 2007* [Available from http://travel.nytimes.com/2007/09/02/travel/02DayOut.html, accessed September, 05, 2007]

Florida, Richard L. (2002), *The Rise of the Creative Class: And How It's Transforming Work, Leisure, Community and Everyday Life*, New York, NY: Basic Books.

Henry, Paul C. (2005), "Social Class, Market Situation, and Consumers' Metaphors of (Dis)Empowerment," *Journal of Consumer Research*, 31 (4), 766-78.

Holt, Douglas B. (1998), "Does Cultural Capital Structure American Consumption?," *Journal of Consumer Research*, 25 (1), 1-25.

Holt, Douglas B. and Craig J. Thompson (2004), "Man-of-Action Heroes: The Pursuit of Heroic Masculinity in Everyday Consumption," *Journal of Consumer Research*, 31 (2), 425-40.

Ilkucan, Altan and Ozlem Sandikci (2005), "Gentrification and Consumption: An Exploratory Study," *Advances in Consumer Research*, 32 (1), 474-79.

Leland, John (2004), *Hip: The History*, New York: Harper Collins.

Lloyd, Richard D. (2006), *Neo-Bohemia: Art and Commerce in the Postindustrial City*, New York: Routledge.

Empowered Consumers=Benevolent Consumers? The Effects of Priming Power on the Appeal of Socially Responsible Products

Swati Bhargava, New York University, USA
Amitav Chakravarti, New Ykrk University, USA

Cause related marketing or marketing of products that have social cause attached with them seems to be a good way to respond to consumer expectations of social initiatives and this has led to the popularity of corporate social responsibility (CSR) initiatives to influence consumers and differentiate product offerings. There is a general assumption that consumers will reward firms for their support of social programs and this has led many firms to adopt social causes (Levy, 1999). Till date research in cause-related marketing domain has looked at consumer's response to these endeavors based on the fit between cause and company (Barone et.al.,2007), consumer's perceptions of company's motivation (Dacin & Brown, 1997, Barone et.al., 2000), consumer attitudes toward such firms(Berger, Cunningham, and Kozinets,1996; Ross, Stutts, and Patterson 1990-91), and its products. However, the impact of power on consumer benevolence has largely gone unexamined.

Potentially, there are two very distinct, and opposing, possibilities associated with elevated power. On the one hand, "power" has been associated with corrupting people and exerting negative influence (Kipnis, 1972; Fiske,1992). On the other hand, power can also elicit social responsibility goals that increase the salience of others in decision-making (Chen et.al., 2001). The latter goals elicit behavior that enhances and reflects attentiveness and responsiveness to others' needs. We hypothesize that enhancing the salience of social responsibility goals for consumers by empowering them can enhance the relative importance of consumers in the process of buying socially responsible products. This should lead to increased purchase likelihood for products that support pro social endeavors. We introduce the construct of "power" as a variable that can influence the way message for a socially responsible product is perceived and processed. Support for why power would lead to socially responsible behavior is derived from Keltner et.al.(2003) theorizing on the effects of elevated power. The authors in this paper posit that elevated power activates the behavioral approach system (BAS), which regulates behavior associated with rewards (e.g., Carver & White, 1994; Sutton & Davidson, 2000). This is because increased power is correlated with increased resources, which in the consumption or consumer behavior context are the monetary resources available to spend on products. Powerful individuals are also aware of the abundance of social resources such as esteem and praise that are available in their environment. This has message framing implications for promotion of a cause-related product. Thus, such a message, by eliciting high power for prospective consumer can also elicit the realization of control of not only the ability to make a difference but also the realization of positive social rewards from the environment by enacting in a responsible way. This should enhance approach tendencies for socially responsible products. Across our studies we find evidence for positive influence of power on consumer responsiveness towards products that promote social causes.

In Study 1, we exposed participants to GAP (RED) advertisements. The computer based study presented the advertisement as a banner ad that is usually seen on various websites. The two conditions that participants were exposed to differed on power dimension. In one frame the tagline read "We Can Make a Difference. You can help" (original GAP commercial). This frame was meant to put the corporation i.e. GAP in position of power to make a difference in lives of people suffering from AIDS. The other frame was the consumer empowering frame where the tagline read, "You Can Make a Difference. We can help." (manipulated commercial). In each condition, participants reported the extent to which they felt powerful relative to the corporation. In addition they indicated their liking and purchase likelihood of the product in the two conditions. We expected the consumers to feel empowered in the condition where the tagline put the onus of helping needy on them and respond favorably towards the product. Our results were consistent with our hypothesis. However, there was no difference in the appeal of the tagline across two conditions.

In the second study we replicated the effect using a rather unknown European brand "Mobistar". This was done in order to take care of the potential confounding effect of liking and familiarity with the GAP brand. We get much robust effects in this study. The consumer empowering frame is certainly the preferred frame for consumers as they report feeling more power in this frame. This is evident in the significantly enhanced purchase likelihood in the consumer empowered frame. Further, we see the enhanced appeal of the tagline and enhanced overall opinion for the brand in the message that places consumers in the position of power. Participants also report liking the product better.

In sum we find that the construct of power can be used in consumption domain to influence evaluations of products that promote a social cause. This work shows that empowering message frames have the ability to influence consumer behavior in a way that it leads to win-win situation for all involved. The results presented here also have a number of important managerial implications. It provides marketers a unique opportunity to frame messages for cause-related marketing so as to garner maximum support for a cause. Typically, it is assumed that only those who are in position of power by virtue of their abundant resources such as financially sound individuals have the power to pursue social responsibility goals and make a difference in improving others' lives. This work shows by priming power, social responsibility goals can be evoked in any individual and their response for cause-related marketing can be much enhanced.

References

Barone, Michael J., Andrew T. Norman and Anthony D. Miyazaki (2007), "Consumer response to retailer use of cause-related marketing: Is more fit better?", *Journal of Retailing,* 83(4), 437-445.

_____, Anthony D. Miyazaki and Kimberly A. Taylor (2000), "The Influence of cause-related marketing on consumer choice: does one good turn deserve another?", *Journal of Academy of Marketing Science,* 28(2), 248-262.

Berger, Ida E. , Peggy H. Cunningham and Robert V. Kozinets (1996), "The processing of cause-related marketing claims: cues, biases, or motivators?" 1996 AMA Summer Educators Conference: Enhancing Knowledge Development in Marketing, Chicago: American Marketing Association.

Carver, C. S., & White, T. L. (1994). Behavioral inhibition, behavioral activation, and affective responses to impending reward and punishment: The BIS/BAS scales. *Journal of Personality and Social Psychology, 67,* 319–333.

Chen, Serena, Annette Y. Lee-Chai, and John A. Bargh (2001), "Relationship orientation as a moderator of the effects of social power", *Journal of Personality and Social Psychology,* 80(2), 173-187.

Dacin, Peter A. and Tom J. Brown (1997), "The Company and the Product: Corporate associations and consumer product responses." *Journal of Marketing* 61(January), 68-64.

Fiske, Alan. P. (1992), "The four elementary forms of sociality: framework for a unified theory of social relations", *Psychological Review,* 99, 689–723.

Keltner, Dacher, Deborah H. Gruenfeld and Cameron Anderson (2003), "Power, approach, and inhibition." *Psychological Review ,* 110(2), 265-284.

Kipnis, David (1972), "Does power corrupt?" *Journal of Personality and Social Psychology,* 24, 33-41.

Levy, Reynold (1999), *Give and Take.* Cambridge, MA, Harvard Business School Press.

Ross, John K. , Larry Peterson, and Mary Ann Stutts (1992). "Consumer perceptions of organozations that use cause-related marketing." *Journal of the Academy of Marketing Science,* 20(1): 93-97.

Sutton, S. K., & Davidson, R. J. (1997), "Prefrontal brain asymmetry: A biological substrate of the behavioral approach and inhibition systems" *Psychological Science, 8,* 204–210.

The Effects of Drug and Supplement Marketing on a Healthy Lifestyle

Amit Bhattacharjee, University of Pennsylvania, USA
Lisa Bolton, Pennsylvania State University, USA
Americus Reed II, University of Pennsylvania, USA

Obesity has been declared a public health epidemic in the United States, and food marketing has been implicated as one important factor in its pervasiveness (Seiders and Petty, 2004; Wadden, Brownell, and Foster, 2002). While high-fat eating remains attractive to many Americans, an assortment of weight management and fat-fighting products (both drugs and supplements) have proliferated. Indeed, in 2006, advertising expenditures ballooned to $4.8 billion for the pharmaceutical industry and $981 million in the supplement industry (Langreth and Herper, 2006; Brandweek, 2007). Though such fat-fighting remedies appeal to many consumers, recent research suggests that there may be unintended consequences that actually undermine consumers' intentions to engage in a healthy lifestyle. Hence marketing of such remedies may unwittingly exacerbate risky decision making and reduce, rather than improve, consumer welfare.

Bolton, Cohen, and Bloom (2006) found that problem status (or the relative attractiveness of the problem domain) moderates the effects of remedy marketing messages on consumers. Specifically, remedy messages undermine risk avoidance and increase risky behavioral intentions, particularly for those consumers most at risk. Though this boomerang effect exists across several domains, Bolton, Reed, Volpp, and Armstrong (2008) recently extended this work, identifying the psychological mechanisms that drive this phenomenon in the health domain. Their results indicate that drug marketing boomerangs and sabotages healthy lifestyle intentions in consumers via two mechanisms. First, drug marketing reduces consumer perceptions of health risk and lessens the perceived importance of complementary health-protective behaviors. Thus, consumers are less motivated to engage in these healthy behaviors. Second, drugs are associated with poor health, reducing consumers' perceptions of their own health and their self-efficacy, and thereby diminishing their perceived ability to engage in complementary behaviors (Bolton et al., 2008). Lacking both motivation and perceived ability to undertake health-supportive behaviors, consumers are unlikely to do so, leading to less healthy lifestyle intentions and a reduction in consumer welfare. Interestingly, this pattern does not hold for supplements: unlike drugs, supplements are not associated with poor health, and suggest by their very name that they are meant to be used as part of an overall health-protective regimen. Notably, Bolton et al's (2008) results also indicate that the drug marketing boomerang may be neutralized with a corrective intervention that addresses both motivation and ability to engage in health-protective behaviors in concert.

Building on prior research, we present a series of five studies conducted across samples of university students and field samples of adults from a daycare center and members of a fitness club. These studies seek to further investigate the boomerang phenomenon and its robustness in a substantive domain. We extend past research to address a problem of particular concern to society—the obesity epidemic— by focusing specifically on the effects of weight management drug marketing on healthy lifestyle behaviors in consumers. Results thus far can be summarized as follows: 1) Actual consumption of high-fat foods increases with mere exposure to weight management drug versus supplement remedy messages, particularly for those participants who are hungriest, and thus most attracted to the problem domain; 2) Healthy behavioral intentions decrease when participants imagine taking a weight management drug versus supplement, particularly for those participants who suffer from body image issues and have a problematic relationship with this domain of unhealthy behaviors; 3) As theorized, the boomerang effect of weight management drug marketing on healthy behavioral intentions is mediated by decreased motivation and a perceived decrease in ability to engage in health protective behaviors; 4) Evidence from two field samples of real consumers with a range of knowledge levels suggests that erroneous consumer beliefs about drugs and supplements underlie the boomerang effect of weight management drug marketing. While the boomerang is partially mitigated by more accurate knowledge, only the highest levels of knowledge (reflecting specialized training or expertise in drugs and supplements) are sufficient to eliminate it completely.

Overall, the present research builds on past research and contributes to the literature in several notable ways. First, past research has tended to investigate the boomerang phenomenon by examining behavioral intentions after imagined consumption of a remedy, and these results are replicated here in the domain of weight management. However, to our knowledge, the present research is the first to demonstrate the boomerang effect of drug marketing on actual behavior, and the first to demonstrate a boomerang arising from mere exposure to a drug marketing message. Second, the present research indicates that the boomerang effect can be influenced by both transient visceral factors (e.g., hunger) and relatively stable individual differences (e.g., body image) that alter the relative attractiveness of the problem domain. Taken together, these results provide evidence that while drug marketing can influence mindful, intended consumer behavior, it can also impact consumer behavior in relatively mindless eating contexts, highlighting the power and robustness of the boomerang phenomenon. Third, the present research provides evidence for the underlying role of consumer beliefs, suggesting that consumer activation of a drug-and-supplement-knowledge schema in response to weight management remedy marketing may account for the results in these contexts. Finally, the present research investigates the role of consumer knowledge underlying the boomerang phenomenon in field samples of real consumers. Only highly specialized training appears to mitigate the erroneous beliefs underlying the boomerang; otherwise, even well-educated consumers are susceptible, supporting the robustness of the phenomenon. In summary, the present research represents a call to action to develop efforts to mitigate the boomerang of drug remedy marketing for weight management, a domain crucial to the health and well-being of consumers.

References

Bolton, Lisa E., Joel B. Cohen, and Paul N. Bloom (2006), "Does Marketing Products as Remedies Create 'Get Out of Jail Free Cards'?" *Journal of Consumer Research*, 33 (1), 71-81.

Bolton, Lisa E., Americus Reed II, Kevin G. Volpp, and Katrina Armstrong (2008), "How Does Drug and Supplement Marketing Affect a Healthy Lifestyle?" *Journal of Consumer Research*, 34 (5), 713-726.

Brandweek (2007), "Gulping the Profit: The Unusual, Lucrative Life of the Supplement Business," April 2.

Langreth, Robert and Matthew Herper (2006), "Pill Pushers," *Forbes*, 177 (10), 94-102.

Seiders, Kathleen, and Ross D. Petty (2004), "Obesity and the Role of Food Marketing: A Policy Analysis of Issues and Remedies," *Journal of Public Policy and Marketing*, 23 (2), 153-169.

Wadden, Thomas A., Kelly D. Brownell, and Gary D. Foster (2002), "Obesity: Responding to the Global Epidemic," *Journal of Consulting and Clinical Psychology*, 70 (3), 510-525.

The Impact of Product Review Writing on Attitude Formation

Stephen Xihao He, Georgia Tech, USA
Samuel Bond, Georgia Tech, USA

Abstract

Putting emotional experiences into words has been shown to evoke various health and psychological consequences. Extending these ideas, our research examines the impact of writing on the evaluation of consumption objects. We argue and demonstrate that under certain conditions, consumers' ratings of a product are systematically biased when they are first given the chance to write a product review. In an experiment using short films, the bias was obtained for two different review manipulations which focused on distinct properties of the viewing experience. Importantly, most participants did not believe that their evaluations were affected by the review-writing process, and the effect was not moderated by lay theories about its existence.

Introduction

Consumers frequently rely on the opinions of others to make their purchase decisions. Although many recent studies have explored the influence of reviews on audiences' attitude toward a product, little existing research has considered how the process of writing a review might influence the attitude of the reviewer. Our work addresses two primary questions. First, does writing a review systematically impact the evaluation of a target product (and if so, in what direction)? Second, to what degree are consumers aware that this influence may occur?

Writing helps people to think and reason about their experiences. The highly structured nature of language and syntax often leads to a "search for meaning" and enhanced understanding of an experience or attitude object (Singer, 2004). Numerous studies have demonstrated positive health and social outcomes of writing about intense emotional episodes (Bootzin, 1997; Frattaroli, 2006; Slatcher & Pennebaker, 2006). On the other hand, verbalizing an episode may impair memory for details (Lane & Schooler, 2004), and deliberating about one's attitudes may alter those attitudes (Millar & Tesser, 1986) or impair decision quality (Wilson & Schooler, 1991).

Our framework relies on a set of attitude models involving the construal of targets and standards (Feldman & Lynch, 1988; Schwarz, 1999). These models assume that contextual influences make certain information temporarily accessible (Higgins, 1996), and that the influence of accessible information on judgment occurs through the formation of different mental representations. Typically, the inclusion (exclusion) of information in one's representation of a target results in assimilation (contrast) effects on their evaluations of the target.

Applying these ideas to the consumer review process, we suggest that the act of writing about a consumption experience makes certain details of the experience more salient and accessible. Importantly, we predict based on theories of memory and cognition that content of reviews is going to be biased by the overall valence of the experience. Consequently, because information retrieved and analyzed during the writing task will be deemed diagnostic, it will be included in one's mental representation of the experience, triggering assimilation effects. An implication of this proposal is that consumer "ratings" may depend on whether or not they are preceded by a review (e.g., ratings of a generally favorable product will be higher following a review.)

Hypothesis 1: Writing a product review prior to assigning a rating will systematically alter evaluations of the product.

Review instructions vary dramatically across different consumer forums (e.g., *Amazon.com* vs. *epinions.com*). Therefore, we consider two different types of review, *self-focused* and *target-focused* (described below). Self-relevant information is likely to be salient even without writing; however, target-focused reviews should make accessible facets of the experience that would otherwise go unnoticed, enhancing the influence of the writing task.

Hypothesis 2: The effect of review writing on evaluations will be stronger for reviews that are target-focused rather than self-focused.

Abundant research suggests that individuals are poor at introspecting into their mental processes (Nisbett & Wilson, 1977). Hence, if the review task does alter evaluations, it is unlikely that consumers will be aware of the existence (or direction) of the effect.

Hypothesis 3: Individuals will not be aware of the effect of reviews on their evaluations.

Design

The study was conducted in a university lab with 121 student participants. The target stimulus was a short movie clip (*George Lucas in Love*) that parodies the popular *Star Wars* franchise. After viewing the move clip on a computer, participants were given different instructions according to condition. Participants in the *target-focused review* group answered a series of questions focusing on attributes of the clip: e.g., "Please comment on the PLOT of the movie clip"; participants in the *self-focused review* group answered a series of questions focusing on their own feelings and responses: e.g., "Please comment on HOW YOU FELT as you were watching the movie clip." Participants in the *control group* wrote for five minutes about events of the previous day. Next, all participants rated the movie on four 7-point attitude scales and one ten-star "movie evaluation" scale. They were then asked whether they believed that their ratings were affected by the writing task, and (if so) in what direction. In addition, participants completed various demographic measures and follow-up questions (not discussed here).

Results and Conclusions

Participants were excluded from the analysis if they had seen the clip before, did not finish, or were not native English speakers, leaving a sample of 99 participants. A composite rating measure was formed by combining the standardized residuals of the four attitude questions and the ten-star scale. Univariate ANOVA on this measure revealed an overall effect of condition ($t=-2.29$, $p=.03$), indicating that review writing did in fact influence ratings. Ratings assigned by the control group ($M=-.280$) were significantly lower than those assigned by both the *target-focused* group ($M=.278$, $t=2.43$, $p=.02$) and the *self-focused* group ($M=.109$, $t=1.83$, $p=.07$), supporting Hypothesis 1. The difference in ratings of the two review groups was directionally consistent with Hypothesis 2 but not significant ($p>.4$).

Supporting Hypothesis 3, the data revealed a fundamental lack of awareness regarding the effect of review writing, The vast majority of participants in the review groups (44 out of 60) did not believe that writing affected their evaluations, yet the ratings of this subset were significantly higher than the control group ($F=5.18$, $p=.026$). Of the remaining 16 participants, most (11) suggested that the review process *negatively* influenced their evaluations; however, the ratings for these participants were also (directionally) higher than those of the control group. Overall, lay theories had no significant effect on ratings ($F=.06$, *ns*).

Further analysis revealed that the total number of words written was not significantly different across the treatment and control groups ($M=116.67$ vs. 130.13, *ns*), suggesting that it was not writing in itself that enhanced attitudes. Coding conducted by an independent assistant confirmed that both target-focused and self-focused reviews were generally positive in valence ($M=5.71$ and 5.34 on a 7-pt scale). Interestingly, the correlation between review valence and ratings was directionally lower for the target-focus group than the self-focus group ($r=.71$ vs. $.91$, *ns*).

Overall, these initial results support our contention that the act of writing a review can influence consumers' evaluations of the products they consume. In following up this research, we plan to explore the robustness of this effect to consumption experiences which differ in product category, valence, intensity, etc. Also, we plan to isolate the underlying mechanism by varying features of the review process. For example, our construal approach suggests that when review instructions are obviously nondiagnostic, consumers may discount the review from their mental representation, resulting in contrast effects.

References

Bootzin, R. R. (1997). Examing the Theory and Clinical Utility of Writing About Emotional Experiences. *Psychological Science, 8*(3), 167-169.

Feldman, J. M., & Lynch, J. G. (1988). Self-generated validity and other effects of measurement on belief, attitude, intention, and behavior. [Print]. *Journal of Applied Psychology, 73*(3), 421-435.

Frattaroli, J. (2006). Experimental Disclosure and Its Moderators: A Meta-Analysis. *Psychological Bulletin, 132*(6), 823-865.

Higgins, E. T. (Ed.). (1996). *Knowledge activation: Accessibility, applicability, and salience*. New York: Guilford Press.

Lane, S. M., & Schooler, J. W. (2004). Skimming the surface. Verbal overshadowing of analogical retrieval. *Psychological Science: A Journal Of The American Psychological Society / APS, 15*(11), 715-719.

Millar, M. G., & Tesser, A. (1986). Effects of affective and cognitive focus on the attitude-behavior relation. [Print]. *Journal of Personality and Social Psychology, 51*(2), 270-276.

Nisbett, R. E., & Wilson, T. D. (1977). Telling more than we can know: Verbal reports on mental processes. [Print]. *Psychological Review, 84*(3), 231-259.

Schwarz, N. (1999). Self-reports: How the questions shape the answers. *American Psychologist, 54*(2), 93-105.

Singer, J. A. (2004). Narrative identity and meaning making across the adult lifespan: An introduction. *Journal of Personality, 72*(3), 437-459.

Slatcher, R. B., & Pennebaker, J. W. (2006). *How Do I Love Thee? Let Me Count the Words-The Social Effects of Expressive Writing*. Paper presented at the Psychological Science.

Wilson, T. D., & Schooler, J. W. (1991). Thinking Too Much: Introspection Can Reduce the Quality of Preferences and Decisions. *Journal of Personality and Social Psychology, 60*(2), 181-192.

"My Fifty Pairs of Shoes are all Different!": Exploring and Explaining Exorbitant Buying

Mousumi Bose, Louisiana State University, USA
Alvin C. Burns, Louisiana State University, USA
Judith Anne Garretson Folse, Louisiana State University, USA

"I like shopping but I am not a compulsive buyer. When I find something I want, I sleep it through and when I think I still want it, I head to buy ... I still have 73 pairs of shoes."

Why do some of us have the fourteenth black shoe? Fifty pens? Thirty fishing rods? These questions have intrigued researchers studying buying behavior, and diverse explanations exist. While some motivations relate to compulsive buying (O'Guinn and Faber 1989), others involve impulsive buying (Rook 1987) and still others refer to conspicuous (Frank 2000) and status buying (O'Cass and McEwen 2004), excessive buying (Ridgway, Kukar-Kinney and Monroe 2006; Wu, Malhotra and van Ittersum 2006), collecting (Arnould, Zinkhan and Price 2004) and fixated buying (Schiffman and Kanuk 2007). However, there is a set of consumers who purchase recurrently, have an inventory far greater than that of a typical consumer and yet do not share the negative characteristics of the extreme buying mentioned earlier. This set of consumers is termed 'exorbitant buyers' and little research exists to understand them (ACR Exorbitant Buying Roundtable 2007).

Only three inquiries of exorbitant buying exist that relate to shopping and ownership experience, and motivations of product purchase and their subsequent non-consumption (Danziger 2002, Trocchia and Janda 2002, and Strack, Werth and Deutsch 2006). These studies have identified buyer characteristics and motivations in non-consumption, but have failed to acknowledge the underlying intent of buying a great many products in certain categories. This exploratory study seeks to define and describe exorbitant buying and to understand the underlying processes, motivations and factors affecting it. A second goal of this study is to analyze and explain exorbitant buying using concept mapping, based on social representations theory (concept map formed by sense-making of the participants about their inventory of products, Moscovici 1981).

Characterizing Exorbitant Buying

Exorbitant buying may be defined as an extensive acquisition of products to augment one's inventory of goods (of a certain category such as shoes, tools and others), for which logical justification, defensible in the mind of the buyer, exists. Central to the phenomenon are the fine-grained, thin-slicing 'needs' for which an ever-expanding list of products that necessitate buying in a bid to stay prepared for any eventuality ("I need black, open-toed shoes just in case I am invited to the party"). Individuals observe minute distinctions in their inventory of products such that they "see uniqueness in each of their products" that form the basis of rationalizing their purchases.

"People may look at them and say, they're all blue... I wouldn't say that any of them are exactly alike. They all have sort of a unique character in my mind, something different about them."

With a highly developed consumption vocabulary, these individuals are "picky" in their buying behavior; purchasing only items that fit their preference criteria. Detailed understanding of the nature of the phenomenon emerged from in-depth interviews conducted with students and non-student subjects; analysis of the former is presented here.

Methodology

Twenty exorbitant buyers were interviewed. During each interview, informants shared self-taken photographs of the products they buy exorbitantly for themselves. Questions related to the types of inventory that participants possessed, the reasons for such an inventory, and the process and outcomes of shopping (to understand inventory acquisition and consequences). Interviews were tape-recorded, transcribed and analyzed using an open coding process. A total of 38 themes emerged from these data. Next, *QDA Miner* was used to develop the concept map.

To elicit the structure of social representations, analysis of similarity (Flament 1986) was used with the assumption that the more themes are used together; the closer they are in the social representation. Inter-attribute similarity coefficients defined relationships among the themes; while a nearest neighbor algorithm identified the important relationships (Kruskal 1956). Next, core and periphery analysis of the social representation was conducted (Abric 2001). Core elements represent themes that constitute the essence of the representation. Coreness (Borgatti and Everett 1999), salience and sum similarity (Pawlowski, Kaganer and Carter 2007) were used to determine the core/peripheral concepts (map to be supplied at presentation).

Results: Dominant themes of Exorbitant Buying
- More articulated 'needs' per product category and average or more products per articulated need
  - o Owing to refined preferences with the ability to differentiate products based on minute, exacting differences (of looks, styles and purposes).
  - o Because of the perfectionist nature (pickiness in buying and consumption)
  - o Ever-expanding list of needs to be acquired.
  - o Look for variety in trends and styles to fit their needs.
- High level of self-control in shopping; with no purchases made if the products do not fit certain preference criteria.
- An extensive consumption vocabulary, with detailed knowledge about products in a particular product category.
- Products are consequential to 'staying prepared' and 'in control' in response to current or anticipated events.
- Switch brands; not brand loyal as products are bought to fulfill particular needs rather than be used for display.
- An 'insider-outsider' phenomenon in which the buyer (insider) rationalizes the purchase and may not consider the purchase excessive while the observer (outsider) deems it superfluous.
- Constant, deliberate and purposive search for a perfect purchase; short span of attention in terms of post-purchase consumption and a likelihood to "move on" to the next product; high attachment for the product rather than the process.
- No pronounced feelings of regret or guilt on the part of the buyer; low levels of financial stress as a result of buying unlike other extreme buying forms.

Conclusion

While commonly observed, exorbitant buying has had virtually no research attention. This study is the first attempt towards explaining consumer's rationalization of their inventory of products. The social representation approach helped identify that though shopping tends to be a positive emotional experience, the choice of items of the ever-increasing inventory tends to be based on analytic justification, defensible in the mind of the consumer.

References
Abric, J.C. (2001), "A Structural approach to Social Representations," in *Representations of the Social: Bridging Theoretical Traditions*, K. Deaux and G. Philogene (Eds.), Blackwell Publishers, Oxford, 42-47.

Borgatti, S. P. and M. G. Everett (1999), "Models of Core/Periphery Structures," *Social Networks*, Vol. 21, 375-395.

Burns, A. C., J. Folse and M. Bose (2007), "Defining and Exploring Exorbitant Buying Behavior," Roundtable in *Association for Consumer Research.*

Danziger, Pamela N. (2002), *Why People Buy Things They Don't Need*, PMP.

Flament, C. (1986), "L'Analyse de Similitude: Une Technique Pour les Recherches sur les Representations Sociales," in *L'Etude des Representations Sociales*, W. Doise (Ed.), Delachaux & Niestle, Paris, 139-156.

Frank, Robert (2000), *Luxury Fever: Money and Happiness in the era of excess*, Princeton University Press.

Kruskal, J. B. (1956), "On the Shortest Spanning Subtree of a Graph and the Traveling Sales Problem," in *Proceedings of the American Mathematical Society,* Vol. 7, 48-50.

Moscovici, S. (1981), "On Social Representations," in *Social Cognition: Perspectives on Everyday Understanding*, J. Forgas (Ed.), American Press, London, 181-209.

O'Cass, Aron and Hmily McEwen (2004), "Exploring Consumer Status and Conspicuous Consumption," *Journal of Consumer Behavior*, Vol. 4 (1), 25-39.

O'Guinn, Thomas C. and Ronald J. Faber (1989), "Compulsive buying: A Phenomenological Exploration, *Journal of Consumer Research*, Vol. 16 (September), 147-157.

Pawlowski Suzanne, Evgeny Kaganer and John Cater (2007), "Focusing the research agenda on burnout in IT: social representations of burnout in the profession," *European Journal of Information Systems* Vol. 16, 612–627.

Ridgway, Nancy M, Monika Kukar-Kinney and Kent B. Monroe (2006), "The Development and Validation of a Scale to Measure Excessive Buying," *Advances in Consumer Research*, Vol. 33, 132.

Rook, Dennis W. (1987), "The Buying Impulse, *Journal of Consumer Research*, Vol. 14 (September), 189-199.

Schiffman, L. and L. Kanuk (2007), *Consumer Behavior*, (Ed. 9), Prentice Hall, NY.

Strack, Fritz, Lioba Werth and Roland Deutsch (2006), "Reflective and Impulsive Determinants of Consumer Behavior," *Journal of Consumer Research*, Vol. 16 (3), 205–216.

Trocchia, Philip J. and Swinder Janda (2002), "An investigation of product purchase and subsequent non-consumption," *Journal of Consumer Marketing*, Vol. 19 (2), 188-204.

Wu, Lan, Naresh K. Malhotra and Koert van Ittersum (2006), "Excessive Buying: Conceptual Typology and Scale Development," *Advances in Consumer Research*, Vol. 33, 401-402.

Confused, Frustrated, and Angry: Consumer Responses to Promotional Messages in Online Service Transactions

S. Adam Brasel, Boston College, USA

Promotional nesting in online services, such as offering music downloads when purchasing concert tickets, is increasingly commonplace. In a goal-driven service transaction, consumers cannot simply avoid unwanted promotional messages as they are unsure of the promotional content's goal-relevance. An online study shows that nested promotions confuse and frustrate web novices, who are unsure if promotion participation is necessary to continue the central service transaction. Experts find nested promotions frustrating when they are on the same page as service content; promotions on separate (interstitial) pages elicit anger. While immediate compliance with promotions appears high, actual consumer follow-through expectations are very low.

Empty Pockets Full Stomachs: How Money Cues Induce People to Hoard Calories

Barbara Briers, HEC Paris, France
Sandra Laporte, HEC Paris, France

Abstract

Building on the security function of both money and food, we show in 5 studies that monetary cues can induce people to hoard calories as a means of securing their resources. In study 1 we test the main effect of money cues on food (caloric) preferences. In study 2 and 3 we illustrate the moderating effects of a resource manipulation (study 2) and individual differences in the security-worry meaning of money (study 3). Study 2 also reveals that calorie underestimation is mediating the effect of monetary stimuli on food preferences. Finally, in study 4, a general reward explanation is ruled out.

According to standard economics, money can be considered a conditioned reinforcer that gains its motivational property only because of its repetitive association with unconditioned reinforcers, such as food (e.g., Camerer, Loewenstein, and Prelec 2005). In psychological terminology, this tool theory about money (Lea and Webley 2006) corresponds to the security meaning of money (Rose and Orr 2007; Yamauchi and Templer 1982): money is considered to be instrumental; money is viewed as a means to obtain biologically relevant incentives. For most of humankind's history, however, food was the most relevant biological incentive (Diamond 1997), the ultimate form of resource security (Fieldhouse 1995). Building on the security function of both money and food, it seems reasonable then, to suggest that money as a conditioned reinforcer, is in particular 'conditioned' to food, and probably more to food than to other 'unrelated' rewards.

In behavioral studies there is a growing body of research supporting a close relationship between money and food. Nelson and Morrison (2005) found that men who feel either poor or hungry prefer heavier women than men who feel rich or satiated. This idea is consistent with the finding that in cultures with scarce resources, heavier women are preferred to slim women (e.g., Pettijohn and Jungeberg 2004; Symons 1979). Most relevant to the current research, however, are the findings of Briers et al. (2006). Briers and colleagues showed that cues signaling scarcity in one domain (e.g., food) motivated people to acquire or maintain resources in the other domain (e.g., money). In a similar vein, we propose that exposure to money cues motivates people to eat more, that is, to hoard caloric resources. We will argue that the effect of money cues on food consumption is driven by the need to secure one's resources.

We present five studies that tested this hypothesis. In *study 1a,* after inducing fantasies about winning the lottery (see Briers et al. 2006), participants had to rank 6 dishes according to their preference. After exposure to a high monetary cue, the most caloric dish 'hamburger & fries' was rated significantly better than after exposure to a low monetary cue. In *study 1b,* we incorporated caloric estimation as a subtle measure of people's desire for 'calories', since it has been proven that the more you value a good, the lower you estimate its availability (Dai, Wertenbroch, and Brendl 2008). After inducing fantasies about winning the lottery (Briers et al. 2006), participants exposed to high money cues estimated the caloric content of regular strawberry yoghurt (125 grams) significantly lower than participants exposed to low money cues. In *study 2,* it is shown that monetary satiation (e.g., Nelson & Morrison 2005) eliminates the effect of money primes on need for calories. In a 2 (money vs. fish screensavers; see Vohs, Mead, and Goode 2006) X 2 (monetary satiation vs. control) between subjects design, participants primed with money on average chose a larger brownie and again underestimated the caloric content, but only when they were not satiated with money. Additionally, study 2 revealed that calorie underestimation is mediating the effect of monetary stimuli on food preferences. In *study 3,* we showed more directly that people hoard calories (i.e., resources) as a means of protection or security from an uncertain future. For this, we relied on the moderating role of an individual difference in the meaning attached to money (Rose and Orr 2007). For people with a low tendency to worry about money, monetary satiation versus deprivation (e.g., Nelson & Morrison 2005), had no effect on the estimation of the fattening content of a brownie; For people with a high tendency to worry about money, monetary satiation compared to deprivation, significantly increased the estimation of the fattening content of a brownie (and thus decreased its value; Dai et al. 2008). Finally, in *study 4,* a general reward explanation is ruled out. We show (1) that monetary cues affect food related choices, but have no influence on non-food items, and (2) that participants' sensitivity for reward is not moderating this effect.

In sum, five studies show how monetary cues can induce an internal need to consume more (caloric) food. The emerging evidence that monetary rewards and food rewards share a brain region (e.g., Breiter et al. 2001; O'Doherty et al. 2002) raises the question of the extent to which this region is involved in the processing of all kinds of rewards (Montague and Berns 2002; Wilson and Daly 2004). In case of the latter, appetite for money should give rise to an even higher caloric need among individuals with a sensitive reward system, compared to people with an insensitive reward system. However, unlike other studies testing this idea of a general reward system (e.g., Van den Bergh, Dewitte, and Warlop 2008; Wadhwa, Shiv, and Nowlis 2008), in our studies no moderation with sensitivity for reward could be proven. Besides the alternative reward explanation, we also rule out an alternative mood explanation.

The demonstrated effect of different money manipulations on an internal need for calories may help explain why poor people are especially vulnerable to overeating and have ill health as a result. The prevalence of obesity has increased substantially since 1970 (Keith et al. 2006). In industrialized countries such as the United States (Drewnowsky and Specter 2004), as well as in developing countries (James 2004), obesity is usually associated with poverty. Although the Big Two (*reduced physical activity* and *specific food marketing practices*) might be (partly) responsible for the difference in obesity rates between the rich and the poor, so far, no attempts have been made to investigate whether poor people actually have a stronger need (at the individual level) to consume more (caloric) food than rich people. Perhaps in our material world, the attraction to money is so powerful that people who, relatively speaking, fail in their quest for (more) money, tend to substitute their lack of money by consuming more calories than is healthy.

References

Breiter, Hans C., Itzhak Aharon, Daniel Kahneman, Anders Dale, and Peter Shizgal (2001), "Functional Imaging of Neural Responses to Expectancy and Experience of Monetary Gains and Losses," *Neuron*, 30, 619–39.

Briers, Barbara, Mario Pandelaere, Siegfried Dewitte, and Luk Warlop (2006),"Hungry for Money: The Desire for Caloric Resources Increases the Desire for Financial Resources and Vice Versa," *Psychological Science*, 17, 939-43.

Camerer, Colin, George Loewenstein, and Drazen Prelec (2005), "Neuroeconomics: How Neuroscience Can Inform Economics," *Journal of Economic Literature*, 43 (1), 9-64.

Dai, Xianchi, Klaus Wertenbroch, and Miguel C. Brendl (2008), "The Value Heuristic in Judgments of Relative Frequency, " *Psychological Science*, 19, 18-19.

Diamond, Jared (1997), *"Guns, Germs, and Steel: The Fates of Human Societies,"* New York: W.W. Norton.

Drewnowski, Adam and SE Specter (2004), "Poverty and Obesity: The Role of Energy Density and Energy Costs, *American Journal of Clinical Nutrition*, 79, 6–16.

Fieldhouse, Paul (1995), *"Food and Nutrition,"* London: Chapman and Hall.

James, Philip T. (2004), "Obesity: The Worldwide Epidemic," *Clinics in Dermatology*, 22, 276–280.

Keith, S.W. et al. (2006), "Putative Contributors to the Secular Increase in Obesity: Exploring the Roads less Traveled," *International Journal of Obesity*, 30, 1585–94.

Lea, Stephen E.G. and Paul Webley (2006), "Money as Tool, Money as Drug: The Biological Psychology of a Strong Incentive," *Behavioral and Brain Sciences*, 29, 161–209.

Montague, P. Read and Gregory S. Berns (2002), "Neural Economics and the Biological Substrates of Valuation," *Neuron*, 36 (2), 265-84.

Nelson, Leif D. and Evan L. Morrison (2005), "The Symptoms of Resource Scarcity: Judgments of Food and Finances Influence Preferences for Potential Partners, *Psychological Science*, 16, 167–73.

O'Doherty, J.P., Deichmann, R., Critchley, H.D., & Dolan, R.J. (2002), "Neural Responses During Anticipation of a Primary Taste Reward," *Neuron*, 33, 815–826.

Pettijohn, Terry F. and Brian J. Jungeberg (2004), "Playboy Playmate Curves: Changes in Facial and Body Feature Preferences across Social and Economic Conditions," *Personality and Social Psychology Bulletin*, 30, 1186–97.

Rose, Gregory M. and Linda M. Orr (2007), "Symbolic Money Meanings: Refinements in Conceptualization and Measurement," *Psychology and Marketing*, 24(9), 743-61.

Symons, Donald (1979), *The Evolution of Human Sexuality*, New York: Oxford University Press.

Van den Bergh, Bram, Siegfried Dewitte, and Luk Warlop (2008), "Bikinis Instigate Generalized Impatience in Intertemporal Choice, *Journal of Consumer Research*, 35, 85-97.

Vohs, Kathleen D., Nicole L. Mead, Miranda R. Goode (2006), "The Psychological Consequences of Money, *Science*, 314, 1154-6.

Wadhwa, Monica, Baba Shiv, and Stephen M. Nowlis (2008), "A Bite to Whet the Reward Appetite: The Influence of Sampling on Reward-Seeking Behaviors," *Journal of Marketing Research*, 45 (4), 403-13.

Wilson, Margo and Martin Daly (2004), "Do Pretty Women Inspire Men to Discount the Future?" *Proceedings of the Royal Society London B (Suppl.)*, 271 (4), S177–79.

Yamauchi, Kent T. and Donald J. Templer (1982), "The Development of a Money Attitude Scale," *Journal of Personality Assessment*, 46(5), 522–28.

Explaining Obesity: An Inquiry into the Lives of the Obese

Jeff B. Murray, University of Arkansas, USA

Myla Bui, University of Arkansas, USA

Amy Stokes, University of Arkansas, USA

The United Nations' World Health Organization (WHO) has declared obesity to be the fourth major disease of the new century, alongside AIDS, cancer, and heart disease (2000). In 2003, Dr. Julie Gerberding, the director of The Centers for Disease Control and Prevention (CDC), argued that the health impact of obesity may be worse than the influenza epidemic of the early twentieth century or the black plague of the Middle Ages (Johnson 2005). For consumer researchers, the phenomenon has become a symbol of over-consumption and it is in this sense that it represents the dysfunctions of our consumer culture. This article reflects critically on the social construction of cultural discourses and therefore contributes to the critical tradition in consumer research (Murray and Ozanne 1991; Murray, Ozanne, and Shapiro 1994).

Conceptualization

The dominant paradigm in obesity research assumes that obesity is a serious preventable *disease* and is therefore part of the domain of epidemiology. By conceptualizing the topic in this way, researchers place the phenomenon in the context of the medical model. The organization of this paradigm is based on two guiding assumptions: the body as a machine metaphor and the energy imbalance thesis. Focusing on the environment completes the epidemiological triangle.

Although the medical model has taught us a lot about obesity as a risk factor, it has turned our attention away from the day-to-day experiences of obese consumers. Developing a more empathetic understanding of obesity shifts inquiry from medical discourses to social and cultural ones; this involves reclaiming the obesity topic from the study of physiology and developing it in terms of a body politics. The phrase "body politics" suggests a critical orientation directed to an institutionalized system of values and practices that discriminate against individuals that deviate from cultural standards. This article is directed by two research questions: How do obese consumers understand and conceptualize their corporeal experiences? How can an understanding of the experience of obese consumers be used with other perspectives in developing new explanations for obesity?

Our explanation for the rise in obesity rates involves three macro level perspectives: evolutionary, historical, and cultural. These are combined with the micro level perspective based on the hermeneutic analyses of our case studies. By beginning with the most macro (i.e., evolutionary) and ending with the micro (i.e., interpretive), we draw attention to the connections creating a *meso* level explanation. It is this meso level explanation that takes into account the consumer's day-to-day experience. Weight gain cannot be disentangled from the stories of consumers.

Method

Textual data were generated by means of existential-phenomenological interviews (Thompson, Locander, and Pollio 1989). The sample included nine females and five males. Nine of the 14 informants were married and their ages ranged from 25 to 62 with a mean age of 41. The BMI of all informants was over 30. Informants were from a variety of locations in the United States. Interviews were unstructured, focusing on narrative and context when discussing issues related to eating and weight.

Key Findings

Significant social and cultural events such as the Great Depression and World War II were found to have influenced many of our informants' attitudes toward diet and food. The *clean-your-plate* mentality is one of the consequences of this cultural socialization. In an era of abundance and fast food, this waste-not sensibility was patterned in the life stories of our informants as a contributing factor, passed down from previous generations, to their obesity.

Another key theme that emerges from the context of experience is the negative consequence of dramatic lifestyle changes. Divorce, physical injury, and the significant time constraints caused by attending school and working long hours were found to be common triggers of weight gain. Exhaustion, over-consumption, and eventual obesity, was the result of family circumstances, health issues, and scheduling conflicts that cannot be understood outside of a body politics.

The medical model, combined with media representations, fuels a fat prejudice and a cultural fat phobia, which makes it difficult to negotiate a fat identity. This phobia, combined with a struggle with weight, contributed to the poor self-esteem and anxiety experienced by our informants. Ironically, comfort food was the widespread coping mechanism used by many to regulate these negative emotions. Emotional eating was found to be a destructive spiral throughout our interviews: feeling anxiety over body image caused them to reach for comfort food to feel better, which led to weight gain and ultimately increased anxiety.

A large number of obese consumers see their bodies as both a subject and an object. The subject of the body involves the perception of the world through one's body. The objectified body is the body as perceived by the world; this is the socially constructed body. Many of the informants fragmented their bodies and described particular parts. It is the tension created by thinking that the world perceives a part of the body as inferior that makes it so difficult to negotiate a fat identity. The constant monitoring and regulation necessary to approximate the cultural ideal is challenging and requires cultural and economic capital; access to these resources is critical to having control over one's body project, yet is not accounted for when interpreting obesity using medical discourses.

By reintroducing, and working to combine experience with other historical and cultural perspectives, it is possible to construct an explanation for obesity that has additional implications beyond those provided by the medical model. Implications that respect personhood and take into account the importance of self-concept and self-esteem. As we continue to investigate this complexity, we need to include narrative and embrace a body politics. We need to construct explanations that are multilayered, bridging macro and micro perspectives, and we need to liberate consumers from repressive cultural discourses. This is the hope and vision of transformative consumer research. This article takes a small step toward this vision by bringing the voice of the obese to the conversation.

References

Bordo, Susan (1993), *Unbearable Weight: Feminism, Western Culture, and the Body*, Berkeley, CA: University of California Press.

Gawande, Atul (2005), "The Man Who Couldn't Stop Eating," in *Scoot Over Skinny*, ed. Donna Jarrell and Ira Sukrungruang, New York: Harcourt, 69-99.

Honeycutt, Karen (1999), "Fat World/Thin World: 'Fat Busters,' 'Equivocators,' 'Fat Boosters,' and the Social Construction of Obesity," in *Interpreting Weight*, ed. Jeffrey Sobal and Donna Maurer, Hawthorne, New York: Aldine De Gruyter, 165-82.

Johnson, Patrick (2005), "Obesity: Epidemic or Myth?" *Skeptical Inquirer*, September/October.

Murray, Jeff B. and Julie L. Ozanne (1991), "The Critical Imagination: Emancipatory Interests in Consumer Research," *Journal of Consumer Research*, 18 (September), 129-44.

Murray, Jeff B., Julie L. Ozanne, and Jon M. Shapiro (1994), "Revitalizing the Critical Imagination: Unleashing the Crouched Tiger," *Journal of Consumer Research*, 21 (December), 559-65.

Schroeder, Jonathan E. and Detlev Zwick (2004), "Mirrors of Masculinity: Representation and Identity in Advertising Images," *Consumption, Markets and Culture*, 7(1) (March), 21-52.

Thompson, Craig J., William B. Locander, and Howard R. Pollio (1989), "Putting Consumer Experience Back into Consumer Research: The Philosophy and Method of Existential-Phenomenology," *Journal of Consumer Research*, 16 (September), 133-47.

World Health Organization (2000), "Obesity: Preventing and Managing the Global Epidemic" (WHO Technical Report Series 894), Geneva: WHO.

Technology Addiction: An Exploratory Study of the Negative Impact of Technology on Consumer Welfare

Monica A. Hodis, Southern Illinois University, USA
Gordon C. Bruner II, Southern Illinois University, USA

Abstract

The purpose of this article is to bring the technology addiction (TA) discussion into the realm of consumer research and to sensitize researchers, policy makers and practitioners to the idea that TA poses a real threat to consumer welfare. The extant literature on consumer pathological use of various technologies is reviewed to support the necessity of adopting technology in general as a unit of analysis. Evidence from a qualitative study suggests that TA is a behavioral addiction and that the object of addiction is not the technology itself but rather the cumulative experience it affords.

Technology is one of the most important symbols of advancement and has been reshaping the fabric of society for generations. While normal use of technology will improve and enrich the consumer's life, overuse and abuse of technology can lead to addiction and have a long-lasting negative impact on consumer welfare. Yet, the adverse impact of technology on consumer welfare is a greatly under-researched area. The purpose of this article is to introduce technology addiction (TA) to consumer researchers as well as policy makers and practitioners so that it may begin to be viewed more seriously.

Consumer behaviorists with an interest in consumer welfare have only investigated deviant consumer behaviors such as compulsive buying, drug abuse, and eating disorders. TA and the adverse impact of technology on consumer welfare have remained largely untouched. However, mounting evidence suggests that TA is a serious problem and can no longer be ignored. Americans are starting to show serious signs of dependence to their cell phones (Licoppe and Heuritin 2001; Wikle 2001). College students spend increasing amounts of time playing online games, resulting in decreased academic performance, poorer interpersonal relationships, and increase in social anxiety (Chou, Condron, Bellan 2005; Lo, Wang, and Fang 2005). Neuroscientists have recently discovered evidence indicating that video games have an addictive potential not much different from drug or gambling addiction (Singer 2005).

Based on the extant knowledge, TA is defined here as *a compulsive, unnecessary use of technology that interferes with the individual's life, as well as his/her mental and/or physical well being. It is a psychological addiction to the cumulative experience one derives from one's involvement with the technology.* As a process addiction, TA dulls and distorts the addicts' reality allowing them to escape dealing with their true feelings and interfering with normal functioning and information processing (Schaef 1987). In their compulsive pursuit, tech addicts will neglect important aspects of their lives and will display symptoms of loneliness, depression, even isolation from friends and family. They will experience anxiety and withdrawal symptoms as well as craving when denied their habitual involvement with technology (Greenfield 1999).

Addiction is not as much a factor of the time spent or of the specific technology used, but of the activities performed and the purpose and outcome of the consumer's involvement with the technology. The use of technology for socio-affective regulation has a high chance of resulting in addiction, while using the same technology for information acquisition will most likely not result in addiction (Weiser 2001; Park 2005). Addiction is more likely to be severe when technology acts as a depressant to alleviate dissatisfaction by enabling individuals to escape from the negative aspects of their lives (Park 2005; Wan and Chiou 2006). On the other hand, the potential for addiction is also possible when technology is used as a stimulant, as a means of deriving excitement and entertainment.

A method of establishing whether TA is truly an addiction is to compare it against clinical criteria for other established addictions (Griffiths 1995). Qualitative evidence was gathered to determine if TA, as a behavioral addiction, exhibited the six core characteristics of addiction as identified by Griffiths (2000): salience, mood modification, tolerance, withdrawal, conflict and relapse. Focus group and in depth interviews with heavy users of technology were conducted in order to gain insights into the drivers of technology overuse and serve as a basis for a more extensive quantitative study. Previous research suggests that young, well educated individuals, college students in particular, are most likely to become addicted to technology (Kandell 1998; Hall and Parsons 2001). Given this, the participants in the focus group were college students attending a large, Midwestern U.S. university. The study used the interpretive research template recommended by Altheide and Johnson (1994).

The participants who exhibited the characteristics of addiction viewed technology as central to their lives. They often lost track of the increasing amount of time spent using it, indicating that a state of flow is one of the antecedents to addiction. Their compulsive use of technology was driven by the derived benefits, combined with a sense of necessity and duty to be "on call." One of the perceived benefits was the fact that it gives individuals a sense of control over their lives. Paradoxically, however, the large number of contact points often generated internal conflicts and made them feel like they were loosing control over areas of their lives. Other perceived benefits were indicative of mood management (boredom, relaxation, escape) as well as a need for entertainment and arousal, supporting both the depressant and stimulant models of addiction.

An important insight gained was that consumers do not use different technologies in isolation but interchangeably and in conjunction. The focus is to achieve the desired goal, to gain the desired benefit, and consumers will use the technology they find most contextually appropriate out of those available at that time. It was evident that a study of consumer addiction to individual technologies would present an incomplete picture of reality. In order to truly understand the dysfunctional consumption of technology, it is urged that technology products (in general) be the unit of analysis. The direct and indirect insights gained into the behavior of tech addicts clearly suggest that the object of addiction is not the technology itself, but rather the cumulative experience that it enables, as suggested by Peele (1985). The findings also indicate that a major part of learning how to cope with the disadvantages of technology is knowing that they exist. This suggests that there might be a need for educating the public about the addictive potential of technology and how to cope with it to minimize that eventuality.

Based on the insights gained, future research should test a model of technology use and addiction on a larger population. Since abstinence is not a realistic option for TA, a model that accounts for the factors and stages responsible for the onset of addiction is essential in understanding and combating the negative effects of dysfunctional technology use on consumer welfare.

References

Altheide, David L. and John M. Johnson (1994), *Criteria for Assessing Interpretive Validity in Qualitative Research*, in N. Denzin and Y. Lincoln (eds.) Handbook of Qualitative Research, Thousand Oaks: Sage, 485-499.

Chou, Chien, Linda Condron and John C. Belland (2005), "A Review of the Research on Internet Addiction, *Educational Psychological Review*," 17 (4), 363-388.

Griffiths, Mark (1995), "Technological Addictions," *Clinical Psychology Forum*, 76, 14-19.

Griffiths, Mark (2000), "Does Internet and Computer "Addiction" Exist? Some Case Study Evidence," *Cyberpsychology & Behavior*, 3 (2), 211-218.

Greenfield, David N. (1999), *Virtual Addiction: Help for Netheads, Cyberfreaks, and Those Who Love Them*, Oakland: New Harbinger Publications, Inc.

Hall, Alex S. and Jeffrey Parsons (2001), "Internet Addiction: College Student Case Study Using Best Practices in Cognitive Behavior Therapy," *Journal of Mental Health Counseling*, 23 (4), 312-327.

Kandell, Jonathan J. (1998), "Internet Addiction on Campus: The Vulnerability of College Students," *CyberPsychology & Behavior*, 1 (1), 11-17.

Licoppe, Christian and Jean P. Heuritin (2001), "Managing One's Availability to Telephone Communication through Mobile Phones: A French Case Study of Development Dynamics of Mobile Phone Use," *Personal and Ubiquitous Computing*, 5 (2), 99-108.

Lo, Shao-Kang, Chih-Chien Wang and Wenchang Fang (2005), "Physical Interpersonal Relationships and Social Anxiety among Online Game Players, *CyberPsychology & Behavior*, 8 (1), 15-20.

Park, Woong K. (2005), *Mobile Phone Addiction*, in Rich Ling and Per E. Pedersen (eds.), Mobile Communications. Re-negotiation of the Social Sphere, London: Springer, 253-272.

Peele, Stanton (1985), *The Meaning of Addiction. Compulsive Experience and Its Interpretation*, Lexington: Lexington Books.

Schaef, Anne W. (1987), *When Society Becomes an Addict,* San Francisco: Harper and Row.

Singer, Emily (2005), "Game Away the Day," *Technology Review: Emerging technologies and their impact*, November 15 2005. Available at http://www.technologyreview.com/Infotech/15884/?a=f (Accessed on July 25, 2008).

Wan, Chin-Sheng and Wen-Bin Chiou (2006), "Psychological Motives and Online Games Addiction: A Test of Flow Theory and Humanistic Need Theory for Taiwanese Adolescents," *Cyberpsychology & Behavior*, 9 (3), 317-324.

Weiser, Eric B. (2001), "The Functions of Internet Use and Their Social and Psychological Consequences," *Cyberpsychology & Behavior*, 4 (6), 723-743.

Wickle, Thomas A. (2001), "America's Cellular Telephone Obsession: New Geographies of Personal Communication," *The Journal of American Culture*, 24 (1-2), 123-128.

The Lived Experience of Consuming Violence

Hillary A. Leonard, University of Rhode Island, USA

Julianne Cabusas, University of Rhode Island, USA

Violence today is pervasive. The United States is currently in what might appear to be perpetual state of war. The threat of terrorism lurks behind many aspects of public life. Schools have become shooting grounds. In 2006 alone, more than 1.4 million violent crimes were reported to law enforcement agencies (Federal Bureau of Investigation, 2007). February 2008 marked the expansion of prison population of the United States to an all time high of one percent of the population (Liptak, 2008). All of this is part of what has been termed a culture of violence. As a consumer society, this culture of violence translates to consumption. We consume media accounts of the violence reported above. Eighty-nine percent of the top video games contain violent content and the majority of this violence is of a serious nature (Media Education Foundation, 2005). Music lyrics, particularly music consumed by teens and young adults are rife with violent messages. Roughly two thirds of Hollywood films are rated R (Media Education Foundation, 2005). Violent sports such as football, ultimate fight club and dog fighting enjoy widespread patronage. Despite the prevalence of the consumption of violence, marketing research has largely neglected the consumer side of consuming violence: why violence sells and what the consumption of violence means to consumers.

Violence and its consumption is not a new phenomenon. Violence has been explained as a fundamental feature of all societies (Denzin, 1984). Using violence for entertainment has a long tradition in many societies (Pinker, 2007)and (1973). Modern sensibilities have changed and despite its prevalence, much of the world today publicly condemns and tries to minimize many forms of violence (Pinker, 2007). Accordingly, much of the research on violent consumption considers the consequences and effects of consuming violence (Allen et.al 1995, Bushman 1998, Bushman and Philips 2001, Felson 1996 (Grier, 2001)).

Researchers have found that viewing violent media primes aggression (Hogben 1998, Smith and Donnerstein 1998), increases hostile feelings (Anderson 1997, Bushman 1995) and serves as an antecedent of aggressive behavior (Anderson and Bushman 2002). Research also indicates that media influences perceptions of the consequences of violent actions (Potter and Smith1999), and that certain personality traits are linked with favorable attitudes towards media violence (Bushman 1995, Aluja-Fabregat and Torrubia-Beltri1998). While there is relative agreement that the consumption of violence is correlated to aggressive behavior there is substantial debate regarding its causal effects and the role of additional factors (Grier, 2001). (For a review of research on this topic see the FTC's Report, Marketing Violent Entertainment to Children, Appendix A, 2000) (Federal Trade Commission, 2000).

While it has been found that people voluntarily expose themselves to, and often search out, images of violence (Zuckerman and Little, 1986), research into the attraction of consuming violence has been understudied. Research suggests that violent video games appeal to adolescent males as safe environment to experiment with controversial emotions (Jansz 2005). In the context of hockey, researchers found that presence of violence correlates positively with higher attendance rates (Jones, Ferguson and Stewart 1993). According to Zillman (1998), it is not necessarily the violence that accounts for the attractions of violent entertainment; it is what violence means to its audience that determines whether it will be appealing or not.

To uncover participants' feelings and meanings surrounding the consumption of violence this study uses the projective technique of collage creation. Projective techniques are useful for studying concepts that may be difficult to articulate or are uncomfortable topics of discussion (Rook, 1988; Zaltman, 1996). Because enjoying the consumption of violence may not be perceived as socially desirable, the projective approach is well suited for this study. Seventy-three participants recruited from an undergraduate consumer behavior course, each created a collage of what it means to consume violence and how it makes them feel. No materials were provided so that participants were free to use any material they chose in their collages. In addition to the collage created, all participants provided a short narrative explanation of their collage. Together, the collage and the narrative formed the text for analysis.

While this research is only at very early stage, preliminary analysis suggests that consumers feel conflicted by their consumption of violence. The consumption of violence is confrontational. The prevalence and appeal of consuming violence makes consumers feel trapped, and overrun, alone and powerless to resists the temptation of violence. They desire protection and escape. Yet it may be precisely these feelings of helplessness that lead consumers to feel empowered by violence. They describe their experience of consuming violence of one of human strength. And because they are consuming rather than enacting the violence, it is not a physical battle but a mental one. Living the experience of violent consumption results in feelings of triumph, against the violence consumed and ironically, against the societal pressures to consume it.

References

Anderson, C.A. (1997). Effects of violent movies and trait irritability on hostile feelings and aggressive thoughts. Aggressive Behavior, 23, 161–178.

Anderson, C.A., & Bushman, B.J. (2001). Effects of violent video games on aggressive behavior, aggressive cognition, aggressive affect, physiological arousal, and prosocial behavior: A meta-analytic review of the scientific literature. *Psychological Science*, 12, 353-359

Allen, M., Emmers, T., & Gebhardt, L. (1995). Exposure to pornography and acceptance of the rape myths. *Journal of Communication, 45,* 5–26.

Aluja-Fabregat, A. and Torrubia-Beltri, R. (1998) Viewing of mass media violence, perception of violence, personality and academic achievement. *Personality & Individual Differences,* Vol. 25 No. 5, pp. 973-89

Bandura, Albert. 1986.*Social foundations of thought and action: A social cognitive.* Englewood Cliffs, NJ: Prentice Hall. xiii, 617 pages. 013815614X.

Baumeister, R. F. (1997). *Evil. Inside human cruelty and violence.* New York: Freeman.

Berkowitz, L. (1999). "Evil Is More Than Banal: Situationism and the Concept of Evil." *Personality and Social Psychology Review* 3(3): 246-253.

Bushman, B. J. (1998). Effects of television violence on memory for commercial messages. *Journal of Experimental Psychology: Applied, 4,* 291–307.

Bushman, B. J., & Huesmann, L. R. (2001). Effects of televised violence on aggression. In D. G. Singer & J. L. Singer (Eds.), *Handbook of children and the media* (pp. 223–254). Newbury Park, CA: Sage.

Bushman, B. J., & Phillips, C. M. (2001). If the television program bleeds, memory for the advertisement recedes. *Current Directions in Psychological Science, 10,* 44-47

Cole, J. (1995). *The UCLA violence monitoring report.* Los Angeles: UCLA Cen

Denzin, Norman K., Toward a phenomenology of domestic, family violence. *The American Journal of Sociology* 90 (November 1984): 483-513.

Durant, Will. *The Story of Philosophy: The Lives and Opinions of the Greater Philosophers.* 1961. New York, New York, Washington Square Press.

Federal Bureau of Investigation, *Uniform Crime Report, Crime in the United States 2006.* September 2007.

Federal Trade Commission, *Marketing Violent Entertainment to Children: A Review of Self-Regulation and Industry Practices in the Motion Picture, Music Recording and Electronic Game Industries.* September 2000.

Felson, R. (1996). Mass media effects on violent behavior. *Annual Review of Sociology,* 22, 103-129.

Geertz, Clifford, *The Interpretation of Cultures,* Basic Books Inc., New York, New York. 1973.

Glaser, Barney and Anselm Strauss (1967), *The Discovery of Grounded Theory: Strategies for Qualitative Research,* Chicago: Aldine.

Grier, Sonya A., The Federal Trade Commission's report on the marketing of violent entertainment to youths: Developing policy-tuned research. *Journal of Public Policy and Marketing* 20 (Spring 2001): 123-132.

Hogben, M. (1998). Factors moderating the effect of televised aggression on viewer behavior. *Communication Research,* Vol. 25 No. 2, pp. 220-47.

Jansz, J. (2005). The emotional appeal of violent video games for adolescent males. *Communication Theory,* 15, 219-241.

Jones, J. C. H., D. G. Ferguson, et al. (1993). "Blood Sports and Cherry Pie: Some Economics of Violence in the National Hockey League." *American Journal of Economics and Sociology* 52(1): 63-78.

Krcmar, M. (1998). The contribution of family communication patterns to children's interpretations of television violence. *Journal of Broadcasting & Electronic Media,* Vol. 42 No. 2, pp. 250-64.

Liptak, Adam, *1 in 100 U.S. Adults Behind Bars, New Study Says.* February 28, 2008. The New York Times Company.

Media Education Foundation, *Media Violence: Facts and Statistics.* 2005.

Miles, M. B., & Huberman, A. M. (1994). Qualitative Data Analysis. Thousand Oaks: Sage.

Pinker, Steven, A History of Violence. *The New Republic* 236[12], 18-21. March 19, 2007. Washington D.C., The New Republic. 2007.

Potter, W. and Smith, S. (1999) Consistency of contextual cues about violence across narrative levels. *Journal of Communication,* Vol. 49 No. 4, pp. 121-33.

Smith S.L. & Donnerstein, E. (1998). Harmful effects of exposure to media violence: Learning of aggression, emotional desensitization, and fear. In R.G. Geen and E. Donnerstein, (Ed.), *Human aggression: Theories, research and implications for social policy* (pp. 168–202), Academic Press, San Diego, CA.

Staub, E. (1999). "The Roots of Evil: Social Conditions, Culture, Personality, and Basic Human Needs." *Personality and Social Psychology Review* 3(3): 179-192.

Thompson, C. (1997). Interpreting consumers: a hermeneutical framework for deriving marketing insights from texts of consumers' consumption stories. *Journal of Marketing Research,* 34, 438-455.

Thompson, C. J., Locander, W. B., & Pollio, H. R. (1989). Putting consumer experience back into consumer research: the philosophy and method of existential-phenomenology. *Journal of Consumer Research,* 16(2), 133-146.

Zillmann, D. (1998). "The psychology of the appeal of portrayals of violence." In J. H. Goldstein (Ed.), *Why we watch: The attractions of violent entertainment* (pp. 179-211). New York: Oxford University Press.

Zuckerman M, Little P. (1986) Personality and curiosity about morbid and sexual events. *Personality and Individual Differences,* 7, 49-56.

Restoring Hope and Enhancing Self-Regulation

Chiu-chi Angela Chang, Shippensburg University, USA

The purpose of this research is to understand the relationship between hope and self-regulation. Specifically, the research question is: how are individuals able to keep on regulating themselves in situations where they are losing hope or having low confidence about achieving their self-regulating goal? As an example, consider the situation where an individual sets a goal of losing weight and then devises a plan to achieve the goal by exercising regularly. However, a myriad of outside influences keeps the individual from exercising on regular basis. Consequently, this person becomes discouraged and starts to losing hope. Therefore, the inquiry is: how would this individual get back on track to adhere to the exercise plan again in order to reach the goal?

There are separate research lines in the marketing literature for the concepts of hope and self-regulation. MacInnis and de Mello (2005) define hope as "a positively valenced emotion evoked in response to an uncertain but possible goal-congruent outcome." These authors suggest that hope interacts with such consumer variables as involvement and expectations, to affect outcome variables, including brand attitudes and satisfaction. On the other hand, the concept of self-regulation is defined in Hong and Lee (2008) as "the exercise of control over oneself to bring the self in line with a desirable outcome or goal." The literature provides different theories to explain self-regulation, for example, self-regulatory resource availability (Vohs and Faber 2007), regulatory fit (Aaker and Lee 2006), and goal-directed behavioral intentions (Gollwitzer and Brandstatter 1997). The present research aims to synthesize these research areas and examine strategies to help consumers restore hope and enhance self-regulation.

MacInnis and de Mello (2005) indicate that "enhancement of hope may also increase a critical predictor of intentions to stop consumption: self-efficacy." This research focuses on the role of self-efficacy in the relationship between hope and self-regulation, and proposes that a promotion (versus prevention) regulatory focus can more effectively enhance perceived self-efficacy and thus self-regulation when hope is threatened. Formally,

Proposition 1: When confidence about what one hopes for is threatened, priming respondents with a promotion (vs. prevention) regulatory focus would enhance their perception of self-efficacy.

Proposition 2: Self-efficacy is positively related to self-regulation.

Proposition 3: Self-efficacy mediates the relationship between regulatory focus and self-regulation.

The rationales for the above propositions are as follows. When people have low confidence about achieving their hoped-for goals, they may be engaged in motivating reasoning about products touted as problem solutions in order to restore their hope (de Mello, MacInnis, and Stewart 2007). The present research further suggests that in the context of self-regulation, people may also be engaged in the (biased) appraisal of self-efficacy as a way to restore hope. Given that low confidence in the hoped-for goal is likely associated with low perceived self-efficacy, a relevant issue is to boost the perception of self-efficacy. This research proposes that because a promotion focus is oriented toward ease of taking actions or the consideration of self efficacy (Keller 2006) making a promotion (vs. prevention) focus salient will help enhance or sensitize an awareness of self-efficacy. In addition, the idea of regulatory fit indicates the significance of pairing a promotion (prevention) focus with eagerness (vigilance) strategies in enhancing motivation and self-regulation (Hong and Lee 2008). In the current context, restoring hope is in line with pursuing eagerness strategies. Thus, a regulatory fit may be obtained when a promotion focus is primed in the context of restoring hope. Moreover, perceived self-efficacy has been found to positively influence self-regulation intentions (Bolton, Reed, Volpp, and Armstrong 2008; Milne, Sheeran, and Orbell 2000), which provides support to Proposition 2. This research additionally suggests that the mechanism through which a regulatory focus impacts self-regulation is by affecting self-efficacy (Proposition 3). Note that, even if the sense of self-efficacy is mildly inflated or distorted (i.e., confidence in one's capabilities is overestimated), this bias is still deemed helpful in increasing the likelihood of accomplishing self-regulating goals (cf. Taylor and Brown 1994, p. 23).

In terms of methodology, in order to test the three propositions in this paper, it is recommended that a scenario similar to de Mello et al. (2007) be used, causing some respondents to lose hope in an endeavor (e.g., exercising). Then, respondents would be primed with a promotion (or a prevention) focus by writing about their hopes and aspirations (or duties and obligations), following the procedures in Freitas and Higgins (2002). Respondents would then rate themselves on self-efficacy using six semantic-differential scales (powerless-powerful, weak-strong, ineffectual-effectual, dependent-independent, reliant-self-reliant, undisciplined-disciplined) (Bolton et al. 2008). Finally, respondents' persistence in continuing their endeavor would be measured.

In conclusion, individuals are faced with self-regulation issues on a continual basis and are often overcome with failures. When consumers are losing confidence in achieving their hoped-for goals (i.e., when hope is threatened), the need to restore hope and enhance self-regulation is enormous. This research explicates the role of self-efficacy in connecting hope with self-regulation and explores the effect of priming a promotion or prevention regulatory focus in this context. It is the intention of this terse conceptual paper to stimulate a stream of research to benefit consumers' pursuits of self-regulating goals, particularly when hope is threatened.

References

Aaker, Jennifer L. and Angela Y. Lee (2006), "Understanding Regulatory Fit," *Journal of Marketing Research*, 43 (February), 15-9.

Bolton, Lisa E., Americus Reed II, Kevin G. Volpp, and Katrina Armstrong (2008), "How does Drug and Supplement Marketing Affects a Healthy Lifestyle?" *Journal of Consumer Research*, 34 (February), 713-26.

de Mello, Gustavo, Deborah J. MacInnis, and David W. Stewart (2007), "Threats to Hope: Effects on Reasoning about Product Information," *Journal of Consumer Research*, 34 (August), 153-61.

Frietas, Antonio L. and E. Tory Higgins (2002), "Enjoying Goal-Directed Actions: The Role of Regulatory Fit," *Psychological Science*, 13 (January), 1-6.

Gollwitzer, Peter M. and Veronika Brandstatter (1997), "Implementation Intentions and Effective Goal Pursuit," *Journal of Personality and Social Psychology*, 73 (July), 186-99.

Hong, Jiewen and Angela Y. Lee (2008), "Be Fit and Be Strong: Mastering Self-Regulation through Regulatory Fit," *Journal of Consumer Research*, 34 (February), 682-95.

Keller, Punam A. (2006), "Regulatory Focus and Efficacy of Health Messages," *Journal of Consumer Research*, 33 (June), 109-14.

MacInnis, Deborah J. and Gustavo de Mello (2005), "The Concept of Hope and Its Relevance to Product Evaluation and Choice," *Journal of Marketing*, 69 (1), 1-14.

Milne, Sarah, Paschal Sheeran, and Sheina Orbell (2000), "Prediction and Intervention in Health-Related Behavior: A Metaanalytic Review of Protection Motivation Theory," *Journal of Applied Social Psychology*, 30, 106–43

Taylor, Shelley E. and Jonathon D. Brown (1994), "Positive Illusions and Well-Being Revisited: Separating Fact from Fiction," *Psychological Bulletin*, 116 (1), 21-7.

Vohs, Kathleen D. and Ronald J. Faber (2007), "Spent Resources: Self-Regulatory Resource Availability Affects Impulse Buying," *Journal of Consumer Research*, 33 (March), 537-47.

When Electronic Recommendation Agents Backfire: Negative Effects on Choice Satisfaction, Attitudes, and Purchase Intentions

Joseph Lajos, INSEAD, France
Amitava Chattopadhyay, INSEAD, Singapore
Kishore Sengupta, INSEAD, France

Abstract

Many websites provide electronic recommendation agents that ask users questions about individual factors and their preferences for product attributes, and then rate and rank order the available products. Previous research has hailed these agents as rescuing consumers from choice overload. However, we report the results of an experiment in which use of an electronic recommendation agent negatively impacted participants' choice satisfaction, attitudes, and purchase intentions over a period of between one and two weeks. The data support our hypothesis that use of an electronic recommendation agent leads consumers to overweight utilitarian product attributes and underweight hedonic product attributes in choice.

Online nutrition retailers offer consumers an enormous selection of highly nutritious foods, drinks, and dietary supplements. For a novice health and fitness enthusiast, deciding which of these categories of products are likely to be helpful, and then choosing individual products within those particular categories, can be confusing, even when only a few options are available. For example, when selecting a nutrition bar, consumers may consider a diverse array of product attributes, including Calories, fat content, fiber content, glycemic index, protein to carbohydrate ratio, protein quality, and vitamin and mineral content, among others. Typically, the product that is best for a given consumer will depend on a variety of individual factors, such as age, eating patterns, exercise frequency and intensity, gender, and strength and weight goals, among others.

This example illustrates how the increasing selection of products and product features available in the marketplace, and especially online, has increased the complexity of many purchase decisions. Since consumers do not want more choices per se, but rather the more customized options that expanded choice can bring (Pine, Peppers, and Rogers 2005), it follows that the attractiveness of the expanded choice set offered by internet retailers depends on the ability of consumers to sort through it efficiently (Alba et al. 1997).

Product recommendation websites assist consumers in making complex purchase decisions in diverse product categories. These websites provide electronic recommendation agents that first ask users questions about individual factors and their preferences for product attributes, and then rate and rank order available products on the basis of their responses. The goals of these agents include improving decision quality and increasing satisfaction (West et al. 1999).

Although previous research has extensively examined the influence of electronic recommendation agent use on decision quality (e.g., Haubl and Trifts 2000), far less research has examined effects on satisfaction. Furthermore, those papers that have examined satisfaction have primarily focused on satisfaction with the choice process (e.g., Bechwati and Xia 2003), rather than on satisfaction with the choice itself. However, choice satisfaction is important to marketers, since it has been shown to influence attitudes and purchase intentions (Oliver 1980).

In this paper, we examine how use of an electronic recommendation agent for nutrition bars impacts consumers' choice satisfaction, attitudes, and purchase intentions over a period of one to two weeks, the time frame in which repurchase decisions for nutrition bars are typically made.

We conducted an experiment within the nutrition bar product category. The experimental design had two between-subjects conditions (recommendation agent vs. control). People recruited outside a behavioral laboratory near a large, urban university were assigned to one of the conditions and asked to examine descriptions of eight brands of nutrition bars and to select one of these brands to sample at home. At the conclusion of the in-lab portion of the experiment, participants received a package containing five sample bars of the brand that they had selected. One week after the experimental session, participants received an email that contained a link to an online follow-up survey that assessed their satisfaction with the brand that they selected, as well as their attitudes, purchase intentions, and other relevant variables.

Based on our hypothesis that use of an electronic recommendation agent leads consumers to overweight utilitarian product attributes and underweight hedonic product attributes, we predicted that participants in the agent condition would be more likely to choose one of the four utilitarian brands compared to participants in the control condition. Furthermore, we predicted that the total amount of time that participants spent examining the brands would not differ between the two conditions, as a lack of difference would indicate that participants in the agent condition did not just blindly follow the recommendations provided to them. However, we predicted that participants who ultimately selected a utilitarian brand would spend more time examining the brands than would participants who ultimately selected a hedonic brand, since utilitarian choices typically result from more intensive processing than do hedonic choices (Shiv and Fedorikhin 1999). The data supported all of these predictions.

Based on our hypothesis that use of an electronic recommendation agent reduces consumers' long-term choice satisfaction, we predicted that participants in the agent condition would like the bars less than would participants in the control condition. Furthermore, based on our hypothesis that use of an electronic recommendation agent leads consumers to overweight utilitarian product attributes and underweight hedonic product attributes in choice, we predicted that among participants in the agent condition, liking would be greater among those who chose a utilitarian brand than among those who chose a hedonic brand, whereas among participants in the control condition, liking would not differ between those who chose a utilitarian or hedonic brand. The data supported all of these predictions.

Finally, based on the hypothesis that use of an electronic recommendation agent negatively impacts consumers' attitudes, purchase intentions, and other relevant variables, we predicted that participants' ratings of the bars' taste, their likelihood of purchasing the chosen brand, and their likelihood of recommending the chosen brand to a friend would all be lower among participants in the agent condition than among those in the control condition. The data supported all of these predictions.

By showing that including a product in an electronic recommendation agent can have negative consequences, our results give a word of caution to managers. In particular, our results suggest that marketers who manage relatively utilitarian brands within product categories in which both relatively hedonic and relatively utilitarian brands are established should be especially cautious. Although agents might help increase short-term sales of such products by leading consumers to overweight utilitarian product attributes and underweight hedonic product attributes, this boost may come at the cost of long-run profitability.

References

Alba, Joseph, John Lynch, Barton Weitz, Chris Janiszewski, Richard Lutz, Alan Sawyer, and Stacy Wood (1997), "Interactive Home Shopping: Consumer, Retailer, and Manufacturer Incentives to Participate in Electronic Marketplaces," *Journal of Marketing*, 61 (July), 38-53.

Ansari, Asim, Skander Essegaier, and Rajeev Kohli (2000), "Internet Recommendation Systems," *Journal of Marketing Research*, 37 (August), 363-75.

Batra, Rajeev and Olli T. Ahtola (1991), "Measuring the Hedonic and Utilitarian Sources of Consumer Attitudes," *Marketing Letters*, 2 (2), 159-70.

Bechwati, Nada Nasr and Lan Xia (2003), "Do Computers Sweat? The Impact of Perceived Effort of Online Decision Aids on Consumers' Satisfaction with the Decision Process," *Journal of Consumer Psychology*, 13 (1&2), 139-48.

Bergkvist, Lars and John R. Rossiter (2007), "The Predictive Validity of Multiple-Item Versus Single-Item Measures of the Same Constructs," *Journal of Marketing Research*, 44 (May), 175-84.

Dhar, Ravi and Klaus Wertenbroch (2000), "Consumer Choice Between Hedonic and Utilitarian Goods," *Journal of Marketing Research*, 37 (February), 60-71.

Fitzsimons, Gavan J. and Donald R. Lehmann (2004), "Reactance to Recommendations: When Unsolicited Advice Yields Contrary Responses," *Marketing Science*, 23 (1), 82-94.

Gershoff, Andrew D., Susan M. Broniarczyk, and Patricia M. West (2001), "Recommendation or Evaluation? Task Sensitivity in Information Source Selection," *Journal of Consumer Research*, 28 (December), 418-38.

Glover, Steven M., Douglas F. Prawitt, and Brian C. Spilker (1997), "The Influence of Decision Aids on User Behavior: Implications for Knowledge Acquisition and Inappropriate Reliance," *Organizational Behavior and Human Decision Processes*, 72 (2), 232-55.

Goldberg, Lewis R. (1968), "Simple Models or Simple Processes? Some Research on Clinical Judgments," *American Psychologist*, 23, 483-96.

Haubl, Gerald, Benedict Dellaert, and Murat Usta (2007), "Ironic Effects of Personalized Product Recommendations on Subjective Consumer Decision Outcomes," presented at the *Marketing Science Conference*, June 28, Singapore.

Haubl, Gerald and Kyle B. Murray (2001), "Recommending or Persuading? The Impact of a Shopping Agent's Algorithm on User Behavior," in Michael P. Wellman and Yoav Shoham (eds.), *Proceedings of the 3rd ACM Conference on Electronic Commerce*, New York, NY: Association for Computing Machinery, 163-70.

_____ (2003), "Preference Construction and Persistence in Digital Marketplaces: The Role of Electronic Recommendation Agents," *Journal of Consumer Psychology*, 13 (1&2), 75-91.

Haubl, Gerald and Valerie Trifts (2000), "Consumer Decision Making in Online Shopping Environments: The Effects of Interactive Decision Aids," *Marketing Science*, 19 (1), 4-21.

Iyengar, Sheena S. and Mark R. Lepper (2000), "When Choice is Demotivating: Can One Desire Too Much of a Good Thing?," *Journal of Personality and Social Psychology*, 79 (6), 995-1006.

Jacoby, Jacob, Donald E. Speller, and Carol Kohn Berning (1974), "Brand Choice Behavior as a Function of Information Load: Replication and Extension," *Journal of Consumer Research*, 1 (June), 33-42.

Kmett, Carla M., Hal R. Arkes, and Steven K. Jones (1999), "The Influence of Decision Aids on High School Students' Satisfaction with Their College Choice Decision," *Personality and Social Psychology Bulletin*, 25 (10), 1293-1301.

Mandel, Naomi and Eric J. Johnson (2002), "When Web Pages Influence Choice: Effects of Visual Primes on Experts and Novices," *Journal of Consumer Research*, 29 (September), 235-45.

Mano, Haim and Richard L. Oliver (1993), "Assessing the Dimensionality and Structure of the Consumption Experience: Evaluation, Feeling, and Satisfaction," *Journal of Consumer Research*, 20 (December), 451-66.

Millar, Murray G. and Abraham Tesser (1986), "Effects of Affective and Cognitive Focus on the Attitude-Behavior Relation," *Journal of Personality and Social Psychology*, 51 (2), 270-6.

Oliver, Richard L. (1980), "A Cognitive Model of the Antecedents and Consequences of Satisfaction Decisions," *Journal of Marketing Research*, 17 (November), 460-9.

Payne, John W., James R. Bettman, and Eric J. Johnson (1993), *The Adaptive Decision Maker*, Cambridge, UK: Cambridge University Press.

Pine, B. Joseph II, Don Peppers, and Martha Rogers (1995), "Do You Want to Keep Your Customers Forever?" *Harvard Business Review*, 73 (March-April), 103-14.

Rossiter, John R. (2002), "The C-OAR-SE Procedure for Scale Development in Marketing," *International Journal of Research in Marketing*, 19 (December), 305-35.

Russo, J. Edward (1977), "The Value of Unit Price Information," *Journal of Marketing Research*, 14 (May), 193-201.

Rust, Roland T., Debora Viana Thompson, and Rebecca W. Hamilton (2006), "Defeating Feature Fatigue," *Harvard Business Review*, 84 (February), 98-107.

Schwartz, Barry (2000), "The Tyranny of Freedom," *American Psychologist*, 55 (1), 79-88.

Shiv, Baba and Alexander Fedorikhin (1999), "Heart and Mind in Conflict: The Interplay of Affect and Cognition in Consumer Decision Making," *Journal of Consumer Research*, 23 (December), 278-92.

Shugan, Steven M. (1980), "The Cost of Thinking," *Journal of Consumer Research*, 7 (September), 99-111.

Swaminathan, Vanitha (2003), "The Impact of Recommendation Agents on Consumer Evaluation and Choice: The Moderating Role of Category Risk, Product Complexity, and Consumer Knowledge," *Journal of Consumer Psychology*, 13 (1&2), 93-101.

Thompson, Debora Viana, Rebecca W. Hamilton, and Roland T. Rust (2005), "Feature Fatigue: When Product Capabilities Become Too Much of a Good Thing," *Journal of Marketing Research*, 42 (November), 431-42.

Todd, Peter and Izak Benbasat (1991), "An Experimental Investigation of the Impact of Computer Based Decision Aids on Decision Making Strategies," *Information Systems Research*, 2 (2), 87-115.

_____ (1992), "The Use of Information in Decision Making: An Experimental Investigation of the Impact of Computer-Based Decision Aids," *MIS Quarterly*, 16 (September), 373-93.

_____ (1999), "Evaluating the Impact of DSS, Cognitive Effort, and Incentives on Strategy Selection," *Information Systems Research*, 10 (4), 356-74.

West, Patricia M., Dan Ariely, Steve Bellman, Eric Bradlow, Joel Huber, Eric Johnson, Barbara Kahn, John Little, and David Schkade (1999), "Agents to the Rescue?" *Marketing Letters*, 10 (3), 285-300.

Widing, Robert E. II and W. Wayne Talarzyk (1993), "Electronic Information Systems for Consumers: An Evaluation of Computer-Assisted Formats in Multiple Decision Environments," *Journal of Marketing Research*, 30 (May), 125-41.

Wilson, Timothy D. and Dana S. Dunn (1985), "Effects of Introspection on Attitude-Behavior Consistency: Analyzing Reasons versus Focusing on Feelings," *Journal of Experimental Social Psychology*, 22, 249-63.

Wilson, Timothy D., Douglas J. Lisle, Jonathan W. Schooler, Sara D. Hodges, Kristen J. Klaaren, and Suzanne J. LaFleur (1993), "Introspecting About Reasons Can Reduce Post-Choice Satisfaction," *Personality and Social Psychology Bulletin*, 19 (3), 331-9.

Zajonc, Robert B. and Hazel Markus (1982), "Affective and Cognitive Factors in Preferences," *Journal of Consumer Research*, 9 (September), 123-31.

Zhang, Shi and Gavan J. Fitzsimons (1999), "Choice-Process Satisfaction: The Influence of Attribute Alignability and Option Limitation," *Organizational Behavior and Human Decision Processes*, 77 (3), 192-214.

Consumer Ethnic Identity: The Implications of Short Term Exposure to a Similar Culture

Helene Cherrier, Luiss University, Italy
Caroline Munoz, Fairleigh Dickinson University, USA
Natalie Wood, Saint Joseph's University, USA

The concept of ethnic identity is a popular yet perplexing subject among consumer researchers. Unlike the term race, the concept of ethnicity disregards generic heritage and focuses on one's sociocultural history. Broadly, consumer research considers two main aspects of ethnic identity. First, how can marketers use consumer ethnicity as a segmentation variable (Guilherme, Stanton, and Cheek 2003; Armstrong and Peretto Strata 2004). Second, how does cross-cultural experience impact cultural selves and ethnic identities (Askegaard, Arnould, and Kjeldgaard 2005). Within the second stream of research, acculturation theorists address the impact of cross-cultural adaptation, adjustment, integration, assimilation, and acculturation on cultural selves and ethnic identities (Penaloza 1994). For them, cultural identities are not fixed, but are deconstructed and reconstructed as consumers cross cultural boundaries. Ethnic identities are fluid identities that evolve through processes of acculturation.

Acculturation theorists provide undeniable insights concerning the development of consumer ethnic identities. However, most of their research assumes the idea of a dominant culture; a culture that contrasts with identifiable marginalized other cultures. For example, researchers on acculturation processes have considered dominant cultures such as the United States or the Danish culture and looked at marginalized ethnic groups such as the Mexicans (Penaloza 1994), the francophone Haitian and Haitian Creole (Oswald 1999) and Greenlandic immigrants (Askegaard et al. 2005). Focusing on conflicting or clashing cultures between a dominant and a dominated culture tends to simplify current multicultural environments and accelerated trans-cultural interactions. For example, in contexts such as London or Dubai, the distinction between a dominant and dominated culture blurs in the face of increasing multi-cultural incomers. Our research considers the acculturation process that individuals undergo when immigrating to a culture similar to that of their home country, leading us to ask the question:

RQ1: What impact, if any, does relocation to a similar culture exert on consumer ethnic identity?

In addition to focusing on clashing cultures, most studies on acculturation tend to consider cases of permanent or prolonged culture contact. In today's global arena, consumers can experience multiple and short term cross-cultural living arrangements. For example, individuals often travel abroad for work assignments and students are increasingly required to spend one semester abroad. This then raises the question:

RQ2: What, if any, impact does short term (maximum of six months) cultural contact exert on consumer ethnic identity?

This study considers consumer ethnic identity in the context of short-lived, cross-cultural experiences where home and host cultures are not distinctively dissimilar (i.e. comparable cultural and linguistic environment). We study the acculturation process of eight American exchange informants studying at a London university. The eight students selected for the study all originate from a strong trans-national consumer culture: the United States. The small sample size enabled us to acquire a deep understanding of the process through which each student experiences the modification, negotiation, or assimilation of ethnic identities. They all have been living in London for less than six months and intend to move back to their country of origin after one year abroad. One of the authors spent five months lecturing to the students. This enabled the author to observe the evolution of each American student in the host country. Beyond personal observations made by the instructor, a projective technique was used and analysed. The use of projective techniques enabled us to consider all aspects of consumer ethnic identities within the process of acculturation without influencing the informants (Lindzey 1961). Each student is asked to construct a collage that depicts "the life of a college student today." They are instructed to use any materials they desired and include any information that they deem relevant to the assignment. Furthermore, the respondents prepare a two to five page report which explains why they have included each image. They are also asked to explain the relative importance of their presented images. To further explore the potential cultural changes and how they are incorporated into their identities, the United States sample is benchmarked against ten students residing solely in the United States. For both analyses each researcher independently reviewed the collages and reports. Next, the independent analyses were shared and common themes were identified and agreed upon by all researchers.

Similarly to previous studies on long-term migrations, our findings support that consumer ethnic identities are fluid. After a six months exposure to a comparable consumer culture, our informants did not solely identify themselves with "American" symbols. They incorporated aspects of "trans-national consumer culture." At the same time, our study emphasizes that acculturation processes do not completely dissolve ethnic identities into "trans-national consumer culture," or a "global youth cultural segment" (Kjerldgaard and Askegaard 2006). On the contrary, the acculturation representing host and home global consumer cultures triggers its own resistance to global consumer culture.

The capacity of acculturation processes to simultaneously dissolve ethnic identities into global consumer culture and create its own resistance leads us to consider the concept of "symbolic ethnicities" rather than nation grounded ethnicities in consumer behavior studies. Symbolic ethnicities have little or no connection with actual ethnic communities (Alba 1990; Alba and Nee 2003). Through the acculturation process, consumer ethnic identities no longer represent countries of origin. Considering the concept of symbolic ethnic identity in consumer behavior research has important implications. First, the concept of symbolic ethnicity recognizes that the expansion of trans-cultural interactions generates similarities among consumers and at the same time evokes different associations according to the consumer's individual experience, both past and present. Second, the concept of symbolic ethnicity respects the multiplicity of singularities present in global consumer culture (Kjerldgaard and Askegaard 2006).

References

Alba, Richard D. (1990), *Ethnic Identity: the Transformation of White America*, New Haven, CT: Yale University Press.
Alba, Richard D. and Victor Nee (2003), *Remaking the American Mainstream: Assimilation and Contemporary Immigration*, Cambridge, MA: Harvard University Press.
Armstrong, Karen L. and Terese M. Peretto Strata (2004), "Market Analyses of Race and Sport Consumption," *Sport Marketing Quarterly,* 13(1), 7-16.
Askegaard, Soren, Eric Arnould, and Dannie Kjeldgaard (2005), "Postassimilationist Ethnic Consumer Research: Qualifications and Extensions, " *Journal of Consumer Research,* 32(1), 160-170.
Guilherme, Pires, John Stanton and Bruce Cheek (2003), "Identifying and Reaching an Ethnic Market: Methodological Issues," *Qualitative Market Research: An International Journal*, 6(4), 224-236.
Kjeldgaard, Dannie and Soren Askegaard (2006), "The Glocalization of Youth Culture: The Global Youth Segment and Structures of Common Differences," *Journal of Consumer Research,* 33(2), 231-247.
Lindzey, Gardner (1961), *Projective Techniques and Cross-Cultural Research*, New York: Appleton-Century-Crofts.
Oswald, Laura R. (1999), "Culture Swapping: Consumption and the Ethnogenesis of Middle-Class Haitian Immigrants," *Journal of Consumer Research*, 25 (4), 303-318.
Penaloza, Lisa (1994), "Atravesando Fronteras/Border crossings: A Critical Ethnographic Exploration of the Consumer Accultura-tion of Mexican Immigrants," *Journal of Consumer Research,* 21 (1), 32-54.

Black & White, or Only Shades of Gray? Exploring the Influence of Consumer Ambivalence on Female Contraceptive Choice and Usage

Piyush Sharma, The Hong Kong Polytechnic University, Hong Kong
Cindy M. Y. Chung, Nanyang Technological University, Singapore
M. Krishna Erramilli, Illinois Institute of Technology, USA
Bharadhwaj Sivakumaran, Indian Institute of Technology, India

Good healthcare and effective health education are major issues today for most governments and healthcare organizations. One of the biggest challenges for health education is to raise world-wide contraception prevalence rates in order to improve female health and welfare. To this end, sex-education in schools was expected to alleviate the problem of teenage pregnancies rampant in many developed countries on one hand and control the population growth in developing countries on the other (Erramilli et al. 2005). However, the results have been mixed so far.

Interestingly, the introduction of comprehensive sex education in American schools has coincided with an increase in teenage sex among girls from 29% in 1975 to 55% in 1990, increase in multiple partners from 14% in 1971 to 34% in 1988 and a 23% increase in teen pregnancies and deliveries from 1972 to 1990 (Hymowitz 2003). These problems have been attributed partly to the continued ambivalence about chastity, childbearing and working, with the American teens both liberated (sexually active) and yet not liberated enough (low contraceptive usage) at the same time (Gress-Wright 1993). In contrast, teenage pregnancy rates in Europe range from 0.4% in Netherlands to about 2% (90,000) in UK (Hollander 2004; Short 2004). In Asia, sex-education is largely information-based, focusing mainly on human reproduction and anatomy with little discussion about specific sexual practices (Smith et al. 2003).

Prior research shows that inconsistent contraceptive usage by females is an important direct cause of contraceptive failure leading to unwanted pregnancies and considerable physical and psychological discomfort (Fisher et al. 2005; Layte et al. 2007). Various factors are associated with the propensity to take contraceptive risks including an abortion history, dissatisfaction with current contraceptive method, low education, ambivalence towards getting pregnant, and a history of contraceptive risk taking (Snell and Wooldridge 2001). However, the issue of ambivalence towards different contraceptive methods has not been addressed adequately.

Recently there is an upsurge of interest in ambivalence in social psychology area (Nordgren et al. 2006). Ambivalence reflects the co-existence of positive and negative evaluations of an attitude object, and it is a different construct from 'indifference' or 'dissonance' (Nowlis et al. 2002). Prior research draws distinction between cognitive and affective ambivalence as well as psychological, social and cultural antecedents of ambivalence (Otnes et al. 1997). Empirical findings about the ability of ambivalent attitudes to predict behavior are mixed with some showing these attitudes as weaker and less predictive of behavior (Conner et al. 2003), and less resistant to persuasion (Armitage and Conner 2000). Others have found ambivalent attitudes to be more predictive of behavioral intentions (Jonas et al. 1997).

In this paper, we investigate the impact of ambivalence towards different contraceptive methods with female consumers in Singapore. We first review the extant literature in sex education, contraception, and ambivalence to develop a conceptual framework and several hypotheses about the influence of ambivalence on contraceptive usage behavior. Next we describe the findings from our qualitative study consisting of in-depth interviews with influencers such as doctors, nurses and male partners, and focus group discussion with female consumers, followed by a discussion of the results from a large scale survey-based study (N=1000).

Our results show that female consumers in general have ambivalent attitudes towards different contraceptive methods resulting in their inconsistent usage despite the risk of unwanted pregnancies. However, the influence of these ambivalent attitudes on the choice and usage of different contraceptive methods is moderated by the importance given to the opinion of different influencers. Specifically, female consumers have mixed attitude towards oral contraceptive pills because they are perceived to be highly effective but also potentially harmful in the long run because of their use of hormones. In contrast, withdrawal and rhythm are seen as less reliable but more natural contraceptive methods. Interestingly, condoms are the most popular contraceptive method because of their convenience but they are considered a hindrance to sexual pleasure.

Our results show that users of oral contraceptive pills continue to use them if they attached high importance to the opinions of their gynecologist. In contrast, females with mixed attitudes towards the relatively unsafe contraceptive methods such as withdrawal or rhythm methods continue to use these if they attach high importance to the opinion of their male partners. Finally, condoms seem to be most popular but their usage is still quite low because of the male partners' unwillingness to compromise on sexual pleasure. These findings provide valuable insights into the underlying reasons for inconsistent usage of contraceptives among females, which may have dire consequences for the physical and psychological health of female consumers. We discuss several implications of these findings for healthcare and consumer organizations. Finally, we discuss some limitations of our research and suggest some directions for future research.

References

Armitage, C. J. and M. Conner (2000), "Attitudinal Ambivalence: A test of three key hypotheses," *Personality and Social Psychology Bulletin*, 26, 1421–32.

Conner, Mark, Rachel Povey, Paul Sparks, Rhiannon James, and Richard Shepherd (2003), "Moderating role of attitudinal ambivalence within the theory of planned behaviour," *British Journal of Social Psychology*, 42, 75-94.

Erramilli, M. Krishna, Piyush Sharma, Cindy M. Y. Chung, and Bharadhwaj Sivakumaran (2005), "Health Literacy, Sex Education and Contraception: The Singapore Experience," *Studies in Communication Sciences*, 5 (2), 147-58.

Fisher, William A., Sukhbir S. Singh, Paul A. Shuper, Mark Carey, Felicia Otchet, Deborah MacLean-Brine, Diane Dal Bello, and Jennifer Gunter (2005), "Characteristics of women undergoing repeat induced abortion," *Canadian Medical Association Journal*, 172 (5), 637-41.

Gress-Wright, Jessica (1993), "The Contraceptive Paradox," *Public Interest*, 113 (Fall), 15-25.

Hymowitz, Kay S. (2003), "What to tell the kids about sex," *Public Interest*, 153 (Fall), 3-18.

Jonas, Klaus, Michael Diehl, and Philip Bromer (1997), "Effects of Attitudinal Ambivalence on Information Processing and Attitude-Intention Consistency," *Journal of Experimental Social Psychology*, 33 (2), 190-210.

Layte, Richard, Hannah McGee, Kay Rundle, and Collette Leigh (2007), "Does ambivalence about becoming pregnant explain social class differentials in use of contraception?," *European Journal of Public Health*, 17 (5), 477-82.

Nordgren, Loran F., Frenk van Harreveld, and Joop van der Pligt (2006), "Ambivalence, discomfort, and motivated information processing," *Journal of Experimental Social Psychology*, 42 (2), 252-58.

Nowlis, Stephen M., Barbara E. Kahn, and Ravi Dhar (2002), "Coping with ambivalence: The effect of removing a neutral opinion on consume," *Journal of Consumer Research*, 29 (3), 319-34.

Otnes, Cele, Tina M. Lowrey, and L. J. Shrum (1997), "Toward an understanding of consumer ambivalence," *Journal of Consumer Research*, 24 (1), 80-93.

Smith, Gary, Susan Kippax, Peter Aggleton, and Paul Tyrer (2003), "HIV/AIDS School-based Education in Selected Asia-Pacific Countries," *Sex Education*, 3 (1), 3-21.

Snell, W. E., Jr. and D. G. Wooldridge (2001), "Sexual awareness: Contraception, sexual behaviors, and sexual attitudes," *in New directions in the psychology of human sexuality: Research and theory*, Jr. W. E. Snell, Ed. Cape Girardeau, MO: Snell Publications.

A Role of Referring Website on Online Shopping Behavior

HoEun Chung, Purdue University, USA
JungKun Park, Purdue University, USA

Abstract

Despite several attempts have been made to understand online consumer behavior across from different situational settings, little is known of referring website's functionality on purchasing behavior. The purpose of the present study is two-folds. Firstly, the study defines different behavior patterns when consumers visit an online store through a referring website versus when consumers directly enter to an online store sans a referring website. Secondly, we investigated on the types of products (i.e. high-involvement product vs. low involvement product) purchased by access manner. Total number of 3,885 online consumers was used to conduct the study based on their detailed transaction activities.

As Internet penetrates everywhere, e-commerce has become a crucial axis in understanding contemporary consumer behavior. From rudimentary stage of e-commerce, researchers have been putting strenuous efforts to determine on deciding factors of online purchasing behavior from almost all the possible angels. However, not so much attention has been paid to how online consumer behaviors are affected contingent on the manners of access to online retail store.

The manners of online shoppers are largely divided into two venues; 1) access to an online store directly and 2) access to an online store by other website namely a referring website. In this paper, we examine different purchasing behavioral patterns when consumers access to an online retail store directly versus when they access to a site through a referring website. The present study is consisted of two parts. Firstly, we attempted to identify consumer behavioral patterns depending upon the access manner (i.e. direct access vs. indirect access via referring website). Secondly, we investigated on the types of products purchased by access manner.

The concept of referring website has been existed and perceived by consumers in e-commerce but not recognized yet. In its literal meaning, the word refer denotes "to direct or send for decision" (Merriam-Webster's Collegiate Dictionary, 1993). In this light, this present study defines a referring website as "a third-party website that directs consumer to an online retail store for a possible purchase decision." However, this is not to say on a narrow meaning of referring website taking a proactive role of recommendation by using recommending agents on a specific website but to include a broader indication of meaning of guiding consumers to another website by exposure of a brand or store name. If a consumer received some type of navigational cues by e-advertising means to be directed to an online retail store, it could be viewed that a website exerted a role of "referring".

Product information search phase has been identified as important in shopping context (Hodkinson et al. 2000; Haubl and Trifts, 2000). Janiszewski (1998) dichotomized consumer search patterns for shopping into two categories of goal-directed search and exploratory search. The characteristic of goal-directed search behavior is highlighted as having specific plans or specifications for purchase in mind. In contrast, exploratory search behavior is distinguished from goal-directed behavior in that it is undirected and stimulus-driven. Distinctive characteristics of each search type by various scholars can be recapitulated as follow; 1) Goal-directed search type consumers regard shopping as task-related work or problems to be solved ;their behavior patterns are geared to complete transaction fast, being efficient but deliberate at the same time. Simply put, utilitarian perspective is taken by this type of consumers. 2) Exploratory search type or experiential search type consumers have a tendency to immerse themselves in browsing behavior itself or navigating sites randomly without a planned purchasing goal. They are considered to be less focused on promptness of completing a shopping behavior. This type of behavior has often been linked with hedonic motives (Sherry, 1990).

Based on the dual characteristics of consumer search types mentioned in the above, the following hypotheses were developed:

H1: A consumer who enters online store directly not through a referring website will display goal-directed search type behavior spending 1) less time in total duration 2) more time per page 3) high-purchase intention.

H2: A consumer who enters online store through a referring website will display exploratory search type behavior spending 1) more time in total duration 2) less time per pages 3) low-purchase intention.

Petty and Cacioppo (1981) proposed a notable framework of Elaboration Likelihood Model (ELM) to explain persuasion process of consumers. The model postulates the cognition process is identified as two major routes: (1) Central route and (2) Peripheral route. Central route instigates consumer to elaborate on product allowing more thoughts on attributes and therefore more likely to lead altered product beliefs and brand attitude to purchase intention. In contrast, peripheral route provokes consumer to less cogitate on product with shallow thoughts and to pay attention on non-product information. Based on ELM, we assume that consumers with direct access manner would more cogitate and more likely to display purchase intention on high-involvement product. In contrast, consumers with indirect access manner are expected to be less influenced by the length of time spend at the site and less relevant of product involvement level when purchasing a product.

H3: Purchasing behavior of a consumer who enters online store directly not through a referring website will be associated with product involvement level.

H4: purchasing behavior of a consumer who enters online store through a referring website will be less likely to be associated with product involvement level.

Dataset were drawn from the ComScore 2004 Disaggregate data set. Our dataset is consists of 3,885 users who visited Amazon.com and made purchase on random items between July 1, 2004 to December, 2004. Product categories were grouped as in either high-involvement product or low-involvement product according to its price range and in reference to the FCB Grid (1986, Berger). Independent variables included total duration time, number of pages viewed, duration per page, connection speed, basket total, total price, and the ratio of total price to basket total. In the present study, the price ratio of total price divided by basket total was contrived to measure purchase intention. We define the price ratio that approximates to 1 as having higher purchase intention (ex. 0.1= low purchase intention; 0.9= high purchase intention).

Independent sample t-tests were used to determine if any significant differences existed in 1) total duration 2) duration per page 3) the price ratio between consumers who directly logged on to Amazon.com and who were mediated to the site through other referring websites. T-test was conducted to test hypothesis1 and hypothesis2. The logit regression was performed to test hypothesis3 and hypothesis4. The value of the each product category was compared to the criterion for the involvement level (i.e. high-involvement).

As expected, in measuring total duration and in number of pages viewed, consumers with direct access manner stayed during less amount of time than consumers with indirect access manner with significance level less than .001. The price ratio was higher in direct access manner group than indirect access manner group with significance level less than .05. This implies direct access manner group had greater purchase intention than indirect access group. Hypothesis 1 and hypothesis 2 were supported.

None of independent variables were significant in indirect access manner group in terms of product-involvement level from logit regression analysis. In direct access group, number of pages viewed, time spent per page, and the price ratio showed significance level less than .05 and total price less than .001. Among consumer with direct access manner to the site, as number of pages viewed by consumers decreased, it was more likely that high-involvement product was purchased. As time spent per page increased, it was more likely that high-involvement product was purchased. For both of total price and price ratio, it was more likely that high-involvement product was purchased as each dollar amount was increased. Hypothesis3 and hypothesis 4 were supported.

References

Berger, D. Theory into Practice: The FCB Grid. *European Journal.* 1986(Jan):35.

Haubl, G., and Trifts V. Consumer Decision Making in Online Shopping Environments: The Effects of Interactive Decision Aids. *Marketing Science 2000*;19(1) :4-21.

Hodkinson C, Kiel G. and McColl-Kennedy JR. Consumer Web Search Behaviour: Diagrammatic Illustration of Wayfinding on the Web.International *Journal of Human-Computer Studies* 2000;52:805-830.

Janiszewski C. The influence of display characteristics on visual exploratory search behavior. *Journal of Consumer Research.* 1998 ;25:290-301.

Petty RE ,Cacioppo JT, and David S. Central and Peripheral Routes to Advertising Effectiveness: The Moderating Role of Involvement. *Journal of Consumer Research* 1983;135-146 (September).

Sherry J F. A sociocultural analysis of a midwestern flea market. *Journal of Consumer Research* 1990; 17:13-30.

Using Brands to Communicate Self: How Effective Are We?

Renu Emile, Auckland University of Technology, New Zealand

Margaret Craig-Lees, Auckland University of Technology, New Zealand

Ken Hyde, Auckland University of Technology, New Zealand

The notion that tangible objects and modes of behaving communicate the role and status of individuals within a society has a long history (Gardner & Levy, 1955; Levy, 1959; Simmel, 1904, 1950, 1957; Veblen, 1899). A characteristic of contemporary societies is the centrality of the self and the wide acceptance that individuals use brands and/or products to create, maintain and communicate aspects of their self. The use of brands and/or products in this way has been extensively studied by consumer researchers. Aspects examined include: matching product and brand characteristics with the self; investigating the use of products and brands to reflect gender, role, status and prestige, reference group membership, ethnicity within and across cultural boundaries (Belk, 1988, 2004; Elliott, 1994; Elliott & Wattanasuwan, 1998; Goffman, 1951; Hogg, 1998; Holt, 1997; Lamont & Molnar, 2001; Cracken, 1988; Thompson & Haytko, 1997; Chaplin & Roedder-John, 2005).

The studies are primarily unidirectional, in that they report how the individual thinks the brand works to support aspects of their self. The question of whether the communication is actually effective, that is, does the sent or communicated message match with the read message, has had minimal attention. Advertising related research, while proposing a dialectical relationship between advertising and the consumer (Mick & Buhl, 1992; Sherry, 1987), also suggests that the construction of product and brand meaning ultimately builds up through interpersonal communication among consumers (Elliott & Wattanasuwan, 1998; Ritson & Elliott, 1999). Yet, advertising research continues to focus on the solitary subject at the expense of a more social orientation, neglecting the significance, use and interpretation of advertising messages in reciprocal social interactions. This observation can be applied to product and brand use. More specifically-are the messages that an individual wishes to send via the use of products and brands understood by intended audiences?

Grubb and Hupp (1968) found consumers of a specific brand to have self concepts similar to those of other consumers of the same brand. Grubb & Stern (1971) also found that users of a specific brand perceived that other users of the same brand would have similar self-concepts i.e., be the same type of people. Both studies were limited to the matching of perceptions of selected brands between two groups-consumers and their reference groups, rather than the matching of communicated messages by the self with messages received by audiences. Though these studies have examined shared perceptions, they are still unidirectional. Accepted wisdom is that consumers use brands and products to communicate aspects of the self. What is largely unknown is their degree of success. This study asks the question: *If young adults use brands to develop, maintain and communicate aspects of their self, what aspects of their self do they communicate and how successful are they?* To answer this question the study will address the following issues and tasks:

- Confirmation/disconfirmation of the premise that young adults use brands and products to construct and/or communicate aspects of their identity.
- Identifying the products and brands young adults use, the meanings constructed, and the ways in which they think the meanings associated with brands and products express aspects of their self-identity.
- Determining how the intended audiences interpret the identity that the brand and products are meant to communicate.

Identity development is a central facet of adolescence and self-brand connections begin in early adolescence (Moschis & Churchill, 1978; Chaplin & Roedder- John, 2005). GenY are highly brand conscious and are cognizant of the symbolic value of the brands they consume (Galician, 2004). They are also sophisticated consumers of entertainment media. Though parents do have an influence, superstar role models also wield significant influence and entertainment media is a key source of information about lifestyles and behaviours (Martin & Bush 2000; Lockwood & Kunda, 1997). This literature suggests that young adults will have developed use and interpretation skills-having developed shared meanings within their age cohorts.

The study intends to draw upon a loose collection of socially oriented perspectives of the self from within the marketing and consumer behaviour literature. In particular, it will draw upon Goffman's (1959) notion that the self is constantly engaged in performances, routinely playing specific roles within particular social interactions. The study will also take a consumer culture orientation that conceptualizes consumption as a mode of socio-cultural practice, and that which focuses not only on the economic, social and political dimensions of consumption, but also on the symbolic boundaries that structure personal and group identities (Arnould & Thompson, 2005). This study assumes a shared perception of reality, identifying with the Berger and Luckmann (1966) notion of social constructionism; that when people interact, they do so with the understanding that their respective perceptions of reality are related. A common thread in social constructionism is the force of language as a principal assumption and the need to identify shared constructions of meanings (Burr, 2003). The study draws upon phenomenological approaches to research design (Husserl, 1970; Schutz, 1962, 1964, 1967, 1970; Thompson, Locander & Pollio, 1989).

The study will employ the use of photography and semi-structured interviews and be conducted in two stages (Harper, 2000; Kjeldgaard, 2003, 2004; May, 2001; Noland, 2006, Quinney, 1995; Ziller, 1990). In the first stage, young adults (18-21) will be asked to photograph brands and products that they use to express self and asked to describe that self. In the second stage, collage boards of the photographs will be presented to other young adults and other age cohorts (not known to the first set of participants) who will be asked to describe the persona of the person in the pictures. Factors such as gender and actual physical appearance will be controlled for.

References

Arnould, Eric .J., & Thompson, Craig .J. (2005). Consumer culture theory (CCT): Twenty years of research. *Journal of Consumer Research, 31*, 868-883.

Berger, Paul., & Luckmann, T. (1966). *The social construction of reality: A treatise in the sociology of knowledge.* New York: Doubleday and Co.

Belk, Russell.W. (1988). Possessions and the extended self. *Journal of Consumer Research, 15*, 139-168.

Belk, Russell.W. (2004). Men and their machines. *Advances in Consumer Research, 31*, 273-278.

Burr,Vivian. (2003). *Social Constructionism.* London & New York: Routledge.

Chaplin, Lan. N and Roedder John, Deborah. (2005) The development of self- brand connections in children and adolescents *Journal of Consumer Research, 32*, 119-129.

Denzin, Norman .K., & Lincoln, Yvonne .S. (2000). The discipline and practice of qualitative research. In N.K. Denzin & Y.S. Yvonna Lincoln, (Eds.), *Handbook of qualitative research* (pp. 1-28). London: Sage.

Elliott, Richard. (1994). Exploring the symbolic meanings of brands. *British Journal of Management, 5*, Special Issue, S13-S19.

Elliott, Richard., & Wattanasuwan, K. (1998). Brands as symbolic resources for the construction of identity. *International Journal of Advertising, 17*(2), 131-144.

Gardner, Burleigh.B., & Levy, Sidney .J. (1955) The product and the brand. *Harvard Business Review, March-April*, 33-39.

Galician, Maurice .L (2004). Handbook of product placement in the mass media: New strategies in marketing theory, practice, trends, and ethics. Toronto: The Haworth Press.

Grubb, Edward.L., & Hupp, Greg. (1968). Perception of self, generalised stereotypes, and brand selection. *Journal of Marketing Research, 5*(1), 58-63.

Grubb, Edward .L., & Stern, Barbara.L. (1971). Self-concept and significant others. *Journal of Marketing Research, 8*(3), 382-385.

Goffman, Erving. (1951). Symbols of class status. *The British Journal of Sociology, 2*(4), 294-304.

Goffman, Erving . (1959). *The presentation of self in everyday life.* New York, N.Y.: Doubleday Press.

Harper, Douglas. (2000). Reimagining visual methods. In N.K. Denzin & Y.S. Yvonna Lincoln, (Eds.), *Handbook of qualitative research* (pp. 717-732). London: Sage.

Hogg, Margaret .K. (1998). Anti-constellations: Exploring the impact of negation on consumption. *Journal of Marketing Management, 14*(1-3), 133-158.

Holt, Douglas .B. (1997). Poststructuralist lifestyle analysis: Conceptualizing the social patterning of consumption in postmodernity. *Journal of Consumer Research, 23*(4), 326-350.

Husserl, Edward. (1970). *Logical investigation.* Atlantic Highlands, NJ; Humanities Press.

Kjeldgaard, Danni. (2003). Youth identities in the global cultural economy: Central and peripheral consumer culture in Denmark and Greenland. *European Journal of Cultural Studies.* 6 (3), 285-304.

Kjeldgaard, Danni . (2004). *Consumption and the global youth segment: Peripheral positions, central immersion.* Odense: University Press of Southern Denmark. Lannon, J., & Cooper, P. (1983). Humanistic Advertising: A holistic cultural perspective. *International Journal of Advertising, 2,* 195-213.

Lamont, Michelle., & Molnar, Virag (2001). How blacks use consumption to shape their collective identity. *Journal of Consumer Culture, 1*(1), 31-45.

Lockwood, Penlope., & Kunda, Zna. (1997). Superstars and me: Predicting the impact of role models on the self. *Journal of Personality and Social Psychology, 73*(1), 91-103

Levy, Sidney .J. (1959). Symbols for sale. *Harvard Business Review, 37,* 117-124.

Martin Craif .A., Bush Alan .J (2000) –Do role models influence teenagers; purchase intentions and behaviour?*; Journal of Consumer Marketing,* vol 17, no. 5, pp 441-453

May, Tim. (2001). *Social research: Issues, methods and process.* Buckingham & Philadelphia, PA: Open University Press.

McCracken, Grant. (1988). *Culture and consumption: New approaches to the symbolic character of consumer goods and activities.* Bloomington: Indiana University Press.

Mick, David.G., & Buhl, C. (1992). A meaning based model of advertising experiences. *Journal of Consumer Research, 19,* 317-338.

Moschis, G.P., & Churchill, Jr., G.A. (1978). Consumer socialization: A theoretical and empirical analysis. *Journal of Marketing Research, 15*(4), 599-609.

Noland, C.M. (2006). Auto-photography as a research practice: Identity and self-esteem research. *Journal of Research Practice, 2* (1), Article M1. Retrieved July 15, 2006, from http://jrp.icaap.org/content/v2.1/noland.html

Quinney, R. (1995). A sense sublime: Visual sociology as a fine art. *Visual Sociology, 10*(1-2), 61-84.

Ritson, Mark , & Elliott, Richard. (1999). The social uses of advertising: An ethnographic study of adolescent advertising audiences. *Journal of Consumer Research, 26*(3), pp. 260-277

Schutz, Alfred. (1962). *The problem of social reality.* The Hague: Martinus Nijhoff

Schutz, Alfred. (1964). *Studies in social theory.* The Hague: Martinus Nijhoff.

Schutz, Alfred. (1967). *The phenomenology of the social world.* Evanston, IL: Northwestern University Press.

Schutz, Alfred. (1970). *On phenomenology and social relations.* Chicago: University of Chicago Press.

Simmel, George. (1904). Fashion. *International Quarterly, 10.*

Simmel, George. (1950). The metropolis and mental life. In K. Wolff (Ed.) *The Sociology of Georg Simmel* (pp. 23-31). London: Collier Macmillan.

Simmel, George. (1957). Fashion. *The American Journal of Sociology, 62*(6), 541-558.

Thompson, Craig.J., Locander, W.B., & Pollio, H.R. (1989). Putting consumer experience back into consumer research: The philosophy and method of existential-phenomenology. *Journal of Consumer Research, 16,* 133–146.

Thompson, Craig J., & Haytko, D.L. (1997). Speaking of fashion: Consumers' uses of fashion discourses and the appropriation of countervailing cultural meanings. *Journal of Consumer Research, 24,* 15-41.

Thompson, Craig. J, & Tambyah, S.K. (1999). Trying to be cosmopolitan. *Journal of Consumer Research, 26,* 214-241.

Veblen, Theodore. (1934). *The theory of the leisure class: An economic study of institutions.* New York: The Modern Library.

Ziller, Robert. (1990). *Photographing the self: Methods for observing personal orientations.* Newbury Park, CA: Sage.

Consumer Animosity a Two-Way Street? A Story of Three Countries

Annie Peng Cui, West Virginia University, USA

Theresa A. Wajda, Slippery Rock University, USA

Micheal Y. Hu, Kent State University, USA

Much research has been done examining why consumers buy; less attention has been given to investigations of why consumers do not buy. Studies in consumer animosity, representing one of the latter streams, focus on what makes consumers shun products from certain countries in spite of high product quality. This study represents a first inquiry into the reciprocal nature of consumer animosity, as well as its impact on consumers' willingness to purchase foreign products in a cross-country setting (i.e., the U.S., China and Japan).

The objective of this study is twofold. First of all, this study examines whether the construct of consumer animosity is reciprocal in nature. Most of the studies that addressed the topic of animosity (e.g., Klein, Ettenson and Morris 1998, Klein 2002, Kalliny and Lemaster 2005, Hong and Kang 2006, Russell and Russell 2006, Shoham et al. 2005, Hinck 2004) studied consumer animosity as a one-directional construct in a single-country setting. The present study represents a first attempt to examine consumer animosity as a two-way street, namely, consumers' animosity attitude toward a foreign country should influence consumers from this foreign country and affect their purchase decisions as well. Studying consumer animosity in the U.S., China and Japan and its impact of on consumers' willingness to buy foreign products, this study contributes to the literature by examining the dynamics of consumer animosity in a cross-country setting.

Secondly, this study investigates the relationship between consumer animosity, product evaluation, consumer ethnocentrism and consumers' purchase intentions (i.e., willingness to buy). We want to extend the current literature on consumer animosity to examine if consumer animosity, product evaluation, consumer ethnocentrism and purchase intentions interact differently under different levels of animosity (e.g., high vs. low). Since consumers may hold different levels of animosity toward two different countries and toward the products from those countries, another major contribution of this research is to examine the impact of various levels of consumer animosity on purchase intentions.

We tested two hypotheses in study 1: 1) Chinese consumers have a higher level of animosity toward Japan than toward the U.S., and prefer American products over Japanese products; 2) even when consumer animosity is low, as long as it is present, it has a negative impact on purchase intentions. We adopted Klein, Ettenson and Morris's (1998) multi-item animosity scale and asked 175 Chinese participants to indicate their evaluations of products from the U.S. and Japan, their animosity toward the two countries, consumer ethnocentrism, and willingness to buy products from these two countries. We found that Chinese participants had a higher level of animosity toward Japan than toward the U.S. (Animosity$_{Japan=}$5.32, Animosity$_{U.S.=}$4.27, t=11.35 p=0.01, on scales of 1-7, 1 indicates low level of animosity and 7 indicates high level of animosity). Furthermore, though participants evaluated the American products and the Japanese products as equal in quality, they were more willing to purchase American products rather than Japanese products. Regression analysis revealed that even when consumer animosity was relatively low (in the case of the U.S.), as long as it was present, it had a negative impact on consumer's purchase intentions (U.S. coefficient=-0.17, p=0.01). Our hypotheses were confirmed by this initial investigation.

In our next studies, we will examine American consumers' animosity toward China and Japan, and Japanese consumers' animosity toward China and the U.S., as well as their perceptions of products from these countries. We hypothesize that although consumer animosity tends to be reciprocal (the sources of animosity such as war, culture, and politics should have impact on both sides), consumers from two countries may have different levels of animosity toward each other due to different perceptions of these animosity sources.

This research moves beyond the current animosity literature to investigate the reciprocal nature of the construct in a cross-country setting, different levels of consumer animosity and its impact on purchase intentions among Chinese, American and Japanese consumers. Preliminary findings in one of the three countries supported our hypotheses. We intend to conduct further studies in all three countries to achieve a better understanding of the construct of consumer animosity and its impact on consumers' willingness to purchase foreign products.

Brand Personality Profiles: A Pick-A-Winner Study of Two Methods

Annie Peng Cui, West Virginia University, USA
Robert Jewell, Kent State University, USA
Jie Xin, Shandong University, China

Brand personality, a multi-dimensional construct, provides a holistic view of a brand that goes beyond merely describing brand attributes (Keller 2003). A brand's personality is an aggregate representation of the benefits, usage, user and relative marketplace imagery associated with a particular brand. Examining what human personality characteristics consumers often endow a brand with will lead to a better understanding of the consumers' perception of the brand.

Aaker (1997, p. 347) defined brand personality as the "set of human characteristics associated with a brand." The purpose of Aaker's (1997) research was to assess and describe the aggregate structure of brand personality across brands and product categories. Aaker (1997) selected 37 brands from the EquiTrend study (1992) that were rated high on salience and represented different profiles of brand personality. Using a lexical approach similar to the Big Five model of human personality in psychology, the author developed a 42-item measurement scale from the original set of 114 traits and identified five dimensions of brand personality: excitement, sincerity, competence, sophistication and ruggedness.

Aaker's (1997) work inspired a stream of brand personality measurement studies. Some researchers attempted to measure brand personality using the five-factor model assuming each brand should have the same five-dimensional personality (e.g. Kim 2000; Best 2005). Rojas-Mendez, Erenchun-Podlech, and Silva-Olave (2004) applied Aaker's scale to the study of one specific brand, Ford. Kim (2000) and Best (2005) suggested that a brand's personality can be measured by the 15 facets of the five dimensions, instead of the full set of the 42-item scale.

Another group of researchers (Cui, Albanese, Jewell and Hu, 2007) adopted Q methodology to assess the brand personality of a single brand. They believe that Q methodology is uniquely suited for measuring the personality of a single brand because it allows researchers to measure a subjective construct in a holistic way without reducing the construct to factors (Cui, Albanese, Jewell and Hu, 2007). The instrumental basis of Q methodology is the Q-sort technique (Brown, 1996), a comparative ranking task in which participants rank order a set of statements (i.e., 42 brand personality traits), under certain instructions. Subjects are instructed to express their perceptions of a certain subject matter by rank ordering the provided statements into a continuum of categories, ranging from extremely characteristic to extremely uncharacteristic. Each category has a fixed number of statements. The number of statements required in the two extreme categories is the smallest, and the number gradually increases toward the middle of the categories; the distribution of the number of statements across categories resembles a normal distribution. Participants have to make comparisons among the statements before putting them into each category; therefore, the decision of assigning each statement to a particular category is made relative to the placement of the other statements. The subjective perspective of the brand's personality is constantly referred to by the sorter during the sorting process. The data then will be analyzed using Q-factor analysis to uncover groups of opinion about the subject matter.

The intention of the present study is to compare and contrast the two methodologies and to examine, based on consumers' evaluations, which method generates a more accurate and appropriate brand personality profile for consumer products. This research has two studies. In the first study, the authors will generate two separate personality profiles of the same brand using Q-methodology and the traditional survey method (e.g., Aaker 1997). A group of consumers will be presented with the two profiles (in words) and be asked to indicate which profile more accurately describes the brand's personality in their mind. This is followed by open-ended questions asking them to explain how they make their decisions and why they think a specific profile accurately depicts the brand's personality. Both the qualitative and quantitative data will be incorporated in the data analysis to draw the conclusion. Study 2 differs from study 1 in how the brand personality profiles are presented to the participants. Instead of using words to describe the two profiles, we will demonstrate the brand personality profiles by print ads. Accordingly, two print ads will be developed based on the two brand personality profiles. The ads will be pre-tested to ensure that they represent respective brand personality profiles. Another group of consumers will be presented with the two ads and be asked to answer the questions similar to those from study 1. The purpose of study 2 is 1) cross-validate the findings of study 1, and 2) illustrate the brand personality profiles in a more natural marketing setting (than description in words), namely, print advertising.

The literature of brand personality suggests two different profiling methods. The goal of this study is to identify which method generates a more accurate and appropriate brand personality profile of a single brand. The present study contributes to the literature as the first attempt to compare the two methods and demonstrate the pros and cons of each method using consumers' evaluations.

Service Value Chains to Support Knowledge-Based Personalized Recommendations

Sonja Wendel, Erasmus University Rotterdam, The Netherlands
Amber Ronteltap, Wageningen University, The Netherlands
Benedict G.C. Dellaert, Erasmus University Rotterdam, The Netherlands
Hans C.M. van Trijp, Wageningen University, The Netherlands

Sophisticated consumer and market information databases increasingly allow firms to provide consumers with personalized recommendations that can assist them in finding lower prices and better quality items in the marketplace (Xiao and Benbasat 2007). Most research pertaining to personalized recommendations to date has focused on the development of new methods to improve the quality of these product recommendations or analyzed how consumers make product choices when they use product recommendation systems (Ricci and Werthner 2006). Increasingly it is argued that it would be desirable if product recommendation systems were extended to also allow for more complex, knowledge-based recommendations in service domains such as health and personal finance (Felfernig et al. 2006). Such knowledge-based recommendations are likely to require the exchange of more complex, more fuzzy, and often more sensitive information between consumers and the supply chain (Punj and Moore 2007). Typically, also these recommendations would rely on a greater involvement of the consumer (in sharing detailed information), and of multiple partners in the service supply chain (to provide the necessary expertise to generate a recommendation) (Prahalad and Ramaswamy 2004). Thus, knowledge-based recommendations are expected to require a much more elaborate type of service value chain.

In the current study, we address the question how consumers evaluate such service value chains designed to create and deliver knowledge-based personalized recommendations. To do so, we conceptualize the underlying cost-benefit trade-offs that consumers make in evaluating knowledge-based personalized recommendation systems as being determined by a psychological contract in which consumers contribute personal information and effort in exchange for a more useful, tailored recommendation by the firm (Rousseau 1989, Zeithaml 1988). This overall structure provides the basis for two key contributions of our study.

First, since service value chains to support knowledge-based personalized recommendation systems require input from consumers at different stages of the value creation process our initial research objective is to investigate how consumers evaluate the fact that they need to actively participate in the recommendation generation process. We anticipate that service stages in which consumers maintain decision control and can choose the contributions they wish to make freely (e.g., in applying a recommendation in their own home) will be evaluated differently from stages in which consumers are more dependent on firms' input (e.g., when exchanging information with firms) (Namasivayam 2004). We expect that for stages in which little or no firm input is required, consumers will be overly optimistic about the quality, efficiency, and pleasure connected with their own contributions to the personalized recommendation systems (Metcalfe 1998; Pelletier et al. 2001). In particular, we expect that consumers' perceptions of usefulness, ease of use, and enjoyment are influenced less by variations in these stages than by variations in other stages, during which consumers are more dependent on firms. At the same time we expect that this level of optimism will not hold for the consumers' evaluations of the privacy safety of their personal information. The reason is that even in service stages in which consumers can freely determine their own actions they will still depend on firms to safely handle their personal information.

Second, we address the impact of service channel task context on the benefit trade-offs that determine consumers' willingness to use a service value chain with knowledge-based personalized recommendations. Previous research shows that benefit trade-offs may vary depending on the task context in which consumers are introduced to a product or service (Wendel and Dellaert 2005). We anticipate that the service channel through which a personalized recommendation is introduced plays crucial role as a key contextual factor in determining consumers' cost-benefit trade-offs. In particular, we investigate how consumers' cost-benefit trade-offs may shift when they are introduced to the service value chain out of their own interest, compared to when they use the system because of service channel requirements (Novak, Hoffman, and Duhachek 2003).

We test our proposed conceptualization and hypotheses in the area of nutrition recommendations. Recently a number of health organizations (commercial and non-commercial) have begun to implement personalized nutrition recommendations that rely on both detailed consumer input and on sophisticated firm expertise, and that offer a very promising tool to assist consumers in their decision making (Brug, Oenema, and Campbell 2003; Kreuter et al. 1999). Data collection involved 204 respondents from a large, ongoing consumer panel in the Netherlands who responded to hypothetical scenarios of different nutrition recommendation value systems. Our findings provide support for the proposed conceptual model and hypotheses. The results also provide managerial guidance to firms and public health policymakers wishing to promote the use of personalized health recommendations by consumers, as well as to consumers, who may find that they overestimate their own ability (or underestimate the effort involved) to implement the recommendations provided by personalized health recommendation systems.

References

Brug, Johannes, Anke Oenema, and Marci Campbell (2003), "Past, Present and Future of Computer-Tailored Nutrition Education," *American Journal of Clinical Nutrition*, 77 (4), 1028S-34S.

Alexander Felfernig, Gerhard Friedrich, Dietmar Jannach, and Markus Zanker (2006), "An Integrated Environment for the Development of Knowledge-Based Recommender Applications," *International Journal of Electronic Commerce*, 11(2), 11–34.

Kreuter, Matthew W., David Farell, Laura Olevitch, and Laura K. Brennan (1999), *Tailored Health Messages: Customizing Communication with Computer Technology*. Mahwah, NJ: Lawrence Erlbaum Associates.

Metcalfe, Janet (1998), "Cognitive Optimism: Self-Deception or Memory-Based Processing Heuristics?" *Personality and Social Psychology Review*, 2 (2), 100-10.

Namasivayam, Karthik (2004), "Action Control, Proxy Control, and Consumers' Evaluations of the Service Exchange," *Psychology & Marketing*, 21 (July), 463-80.

Novak, Thomas P., Donna L. Hoffman, and Adam Duhachek (2003), "The Influence of Goal-Directed and Experiential Activities on Online Flow Experiences," *Journal of Consumer Psychology*, 13 (1&2), 3-16

Pelletier, Luc G., Michelle S. Fortier, Robert J. Vallerand, and Nathalie M. Brière (2001) "Associations Among Perceived Autonomy Support, Forms of Self-Regulation, and Persistence: A Prospective Study," *Motivation and Emotion*, 25 (4), 279 -306.

Ricci, Francesco, and Hannes Werthner (2006), "Introduction to the Special Issue: Recommender Systems," *International Journal of Electronic Commerce*, 11(2), 5-7.

Rousseau, Denise M. (1989), "Psychological and Implied Contracts in Organizations," *Employee Responsibilities and Rights Journal*, 2 (2), 121-39.

Wendel, Sonja and Benedict G.C. Dellaert (2005), "Situation Variation in Consumers' Media Channel Consideration," *Journal of the Academy of Marketing Science*, 33 (4), 575-84.

Xiao, Bo, and I. Benbasat, (2007) "Consumer Decision Support Systems for E-Commerce: Design and Adoption of Product Recommendation Agents," *Management Information Systems Quarterly*, 31 (1), 317-209.

Zeithaml, Valarie A. (1988), "Consumer Perceptions of Price, Quality, and Value: A Means-End Model and Synthesis of Evidence," *Journal of Marketing*, 52 (July), 2-22.

Gender Differences in the Cognitive Organization of Spending Attitudes
Leslie D. Dinauer, University of Maryland University College, USA

This applied study, part of a larger ongoing project, examined Galileo cognitive maps of shopping concepts in men and women in order to inform the design of more effective debt counseling messages.

To study Galileo cognitive maps, a space containing attitude concepts that are relevant to the target population must be generated and analyzed. Several pilot studies were conducted to determine an appropriate set of shopping-related concepts to occupy such a space. Then, the final study employed Galileo spatial plot analysis and structural equation modeling to test the hypotheses about gender differences between the maps. The participants in this phase of the project were undergraduate students at a large eastern university.

Three hypotheses were tested:

H1: Men and women will possess different cognitive organizations of shopping-related concepts.
H2: When an individual receives a persuasive message directed toward a single concept, the force of that message will cause attitude change that will be reflected by motion in linked concepts.
H3: Gender will affect attitude change among linked concepts in a structure of shopping-related concepts.

So, the purpose of the study was two-fold: (1) to examine the effects of an inter-attitudinal structure upon attitude change for shopping-related concepts, and (2) to determine if gender affects such change. In order to induce attitude change, three persuasive messages differing only in their focal concept were employed. These focal concepts represented the categories of the first independent variable, Message target. The second independent variable was Gender. Finally, because there was a concern that some participants may have greater accessibility of the study's theorized concept relationships, Priming was added as a third independent variable.

The primary dependent variable of the study was attitude. Magnitude estimation was used to measure attitudes. Consistent with Galileo mapping theory, an attitude was represented by the distance between a concept and *things I like* whereas an analogous evaluative believe was represented by the distance between a concept and *good*. It was also necessary to create one new dependent variable that captured the movement of the concepts in the study that were not targeted by any message. The existence of non-targeted concepts allowed examination of the indirect effect of the target message on concepts merely associated with the target concept.

The Galileo computer program V56 calculated the adjusted geometric mean distances among the nine experimental concepts which resulted in 2 sets of distances, one for men and one for women. When the distances were plotted together, a multidimensional cognitive space resulted. The program then rotated each space to the same orientation and transformed it to a least-squares best fit so that the spaces would be similarly aligned and visual comparison could be made between them to detect the changes across experimental conditions. Additionally, structural equation modeling determined the causal relationships between the variables of interest.

The Galileo results showed that, overall, the women's cognitive space of shopping concepts was significantly smaller than the men's, which corresponds with a greater liking of the shopping concepts overall (recall that smaller distances=more liking, greater distances=less liking). This was further supported by the results of a 2 (Gender: male vs. female) x 2 (Priming: primed vs. unprimed) x 3 (Message Target: shopping vs. clothes vs. food) analysis of variance on attitude toward shopping which found, as expected, that women like the shopping concepts significantly more (M=4.55, SD=.06) than do men (M=4.79, SD=.09), F (1, *177*)=4.78, p<.05, η^2=.02.

Also, shopping is more central to the concept "needs" and the concept "wants" in the women's space. This might represent women's understanding of shopping as having equivalent roles in both necessary and unnecessary-but-desirable consumption. Women appear to closely relate shopping with a wider range of buying activities than do men. For example, the Galileo plot shows that women identify shopping and clothes as much more closely related than men (a *t*–test on the distance between shopping and clothes confirms this observation: t [205]=1.99, p<.05). It appears as if men consider shopping a not-so-good, disliked activity that, paradoxically, is most closely related to the acquisition of wants. For men, it appears, pain equals gain.

The structural equation models determined the causal relationships that existed between the variables of interest. These models suggested that women's attitudes about shopping seem to activate a chain reaction of evaluations toward clothes, then food, then needs, wants, gifts and luxuries. These results have tremendous implications for application in debt counseling and education: It's not enough, for example, for counselors to suggest, "Buy only what you need" when needs and wants are only marginally distinguishable.

The findings further suggest that (1) messages can be designed that attempt to influence attitudes toward and beliefs about shopping and debt indirectly, through related concepts, and (2) messages used for debt counseling might be much more effective if they employed gender-specific strategies that address men's and women's different understandings of shopping and related concepts. Even the act of determining an individual's specific shopping-related space and revealing the significant relationships to him or her (i.e., making the space accessible and salient) may increase the effectiveness of debt counseling by creating a new awareness of associations between attitudes that may previously have seemed irrelevant. This prediction will be tested in an upcoming study.

Under the Cover of Alcohol: The Impact of Alcohol Consumption and Preventive Media on Intentions to Engage in Deviant Behavior

Kivilcim Dogerlioglu-Demir, Washington State University, USA
Kristine Ehrich, Washington State University, USA
Darrel Muehling, Washington State University, USA

Previous research has established that alcohol impairs judgments and increases the likelihood of engaging in risky behaviors. It has been reported in the alcohol literature that alcohol consumption leads to increased rates of sexual assault and acquaintance rape (Champion, Foley, DuRant, Hensberry, Altman, Wolfson 2004).

As a part of social marketing efforts, the sponsors of warning ads use diverse message themes (such as fear appeals, social norm tactics and novel information) to attract attention and caution individuals against heavy drinking and its consequences (Kalsher, Clark and Wogalter 1993). Research on preventive media indicates mixed results: some studies suggest that when carefully designed, warning ads are influential (MacKinnon and Lapin 1998; Kalsher et al. 1993) while others posit that they are ineffective (Steele and Josephs 1990) and may even result in resistance to comply and/ or counterproductive (boomerang) effects (Synder and Blood 1992).

Most of these works, however, ignore the impact of an individual's subjective assessment of impairment ("perceived intoxication") and the motivation behind such an assessment on these risky actions. We investigate whether the link between alcohol consumption and intention to engage in deviant acts results solely from alcohol's pharmacological effects or from placebo effects as a consequence of the belief that alcohol has been consumed (Barthalow and Heinz 2006). Since individuals' perceived extent of impairment is "a viable decision making component" (Nicholson, Wang, Collins, Airhihenbuwa, Mahoney and Maney 1992), we believe that "perceived intoxication" may be a better predictor of intentions. We suggest that "perceived intoxication" is a variable that mediates the relationship between alcohol consumption and sexually aggressive tendencies. In addition, we argue that there is an individual difference variable (Alcohol Expectancy-AE) that may help explain the tendency of individuals to overestimate their intoxication levels (MacAndrew and Edgerton 1969; Brown, Goldman, Inn and Anderson1980). The beliefs that individuals hold about the effects of alcohol on their behavior, moods, and emotions are expected to moderate the relationship between alcohol consumption and perceived intoxication.

It has been suggested in the literature that a person's desire to experience a product's expected benefits increases the efficacy of placebo effects (Shiv, Ziv and Ariely 2005; Irmak and Fitzsimons 2005). In a similar vein, we suggest that AE is the main motivation behind one's self reported high intoxication levels. When people believe alcohol has the power to make them stronger, sexier, more confident and immune to dangers (high AE), they report their perceived intoxication levels much higher. We argue that this may even hold for individuals who are administered a placebo drink. "Perceived Intoxication" derived from the AE trait will act as a "cover" or permission to consider exhibiting an ordinarily forbidden behavior (such as sexual aggression). We also introduce an important individual difference variable, Rape Myth Acceptance (RMA), to explain individuals' tendencies to engage in sexually aggressive behaviors (Wells 2003) and violent acts (Burt 1980; Stephens and George 2004). More specifically, the tendency to support adversarial sexual beliefs, tolerate interpersonal violence and stereotype gender roles are expected to moderate the relationship between perceived intoxication and the likelihood to engage in sexual aggression. These myths act as "psychological neutralizers" that allow individuals to turn off social prohibitions (Burt 1980).

In our model, Alcohol Expectancy constitutes the motivational aspect behind higher reported intoxication levels whereas Rape Myth Acceptance determines one's likelihood to be acceptant of sexual aggression towards women. We provide a framework to examine the processes underlying deviant behaviors that arise as a result of alcohol consumption. We believe that it is meaningful to study the effectiveness of warning ads only after considering this broader framework.

In a pilot study, 52 heterosexual male undergraduate students of legal drinking age were recruited. Participants were screened via an online survey conducted a month before the actual experiment, where Alcohol Expectancy (adopted from Brown et al. 1980) and Rape Myth Acceptance (adopted from Burt 1980) measures were collected. The experiment was conducted in a design similar to a drinking occasion where participants consumed four drinks. They were then asked to rate perceived intoxication levels ("how intoxicated do you feel?" scale is from -9 to 9, with 0 meaning "at the legal limit"), attitude towards the ad and intention to engage in sexual aggression. It was a 3 (alcohol condition: alcohol; no alcohol; placebo) x 2 (ad condition: anti-sexual aggression ad; control -Pepsi ad) between subjects design. In the alcohol condition, participants were given drinks with high alcohol concentration (.80 g/kg ethanol), in the no alcohol condition, participants were to taste and spit out the alcohol and in the placebo condition, participants were made to believe that they were actually consuming alcohol by using a drink that tasted and smelled like alcohol (.04 g/kg ethanol). The blood alcohol levels of all participants were measured throughout the experimental session using a breathalyzer device.

Our results suggest that the alcohol manipulation worked. While individuals in both alcohol ($M= 2.8$ $SD=4.4$) and placebo ($M= -2.0$ $SD=3.3$) conditions reported higher levels of perceived intoxication ($p>.05$), the no alcohol group ($M= -6.8$ $SD=2.8$) indicated significantly lower perceived intoxication levels ($p<.05$). The results of a Sobel test ($p<.05$) indicated that perceived intoxication is a mediator between alcohol consumption and sexual aggression intentions, suggesting that individuals' perceived extent of impairment is a key factor in explaining deviant behaviors. Moreover, RMA had a significant main effect on sexually aggressive intentions ($p<.05$) indicating that one's tendency to support adversarial sexual beliefs has a strong impact on behavioral tendencies. However, we were not able to show a moderation effect between RMA and perceived intoxication. We also failed to show an interaction effect between AE and alcohol consumption. We were not able to demonstrate a significant interaction between ad condition and perceived intoxication. However, the signs of these variables were in the expected direction. We believe these non-significant findings may be primarily a power issue. A follow-up study with more participants is planned.

With this study, we hope to fill a gap in the social marketing and transformative consumer research literatures by providing a more inclusive conceptual framework on the relationship between the influence of alcohol and deviant behaviors. Our expectation is that alcohol has differing consequences on individuals that cannot be solely explained by pharmacological effects. The proposed framework may help explain the effect of warning ads on individuals' proclivity to engage in socially undesirable behaviors.

References available upon request

The Commodification of Marriage: "Mail-Order Brides" in the Electronic Age

Kivilcim Dogerlioglu-Demir, Washington State University, USA

Patriya Tansuhaj, Washington State University, USA

The film opens with kaleidoscopic shots of beautiful women posing for the camera. A man flips through the pages of a catalog resembling a catalog shopping for clothing. Looking at the booklet closely, one realizes that he is looking at the pictures of attractive women. Carefully examining these images, he is searching for a wife to take home. This is the opening scene of the 2003 documentary, *In the name of love,* directed by Shannon O'Rourke. The documentary tracks a number of women who are signed up with marriage agencies in Russia and rich American men searching for brides. O'Rourke examines commercialization of modern love and romance by looking at the lives of these women and the processes involved in this modern matchmaking business.

There are approximately 200 mail-order bride agencies in the United States, with an estimate by the U.S. Citizenship and Immigration Services to be 4,000 to 6,000 American men finding wives through those agencies each year (www.uscis.gov). This multi-million-dollar mail-order bride industry continues to thrive rapidly at a global scale and scope, with mixed reports on whether marriages via this international match making arrangement result in positive outcomes or in domestic violence. This international marketing practice has long been unregulated until recently when the International Marriage Broker Regulation Act was signed into law in 2006. Although this Act aims at protecting women from potential abuses, it in effect legitimizes the industry, and the volume of transactions continues to rise. A closer look at the law also indicates a sexist language in such a statement as, "The *seller* must obtain the man's record from the National Sex Offenders Public Registry database." (www.govtrack.us) We believe that it is worthwhile investigating this phenomenon from the perspective of morality of market exchange (Prasad 1999).

Advances in electronic commerce and internet technology accelerate speed, scope and scale of the mail order bride transactions on a global scale. Although these services represent a truly global consumption phenomenon, the mail order bride issue has not received sufficient attention from consumer researchers. This study aims at providing a better understanding of the nature of the mail-order bride service, causes of "commodification of love" and its consequences on gender relations, family and marriage formations. In an era where foreign brides are being marketed on the internet resulting in growing commodification of marriage, there is a high potential for violating personal identity of women in this process (Hughes 2000).

There are two dominant perspectives in studying consumption patterns as symbolic expressions in consumer research: Personality/values lifestyle analysis suggests that lifestyles are behavioral expressions of personality traits, and object signification research that posits that consumption objects (goods, services and events) represent social categories. Holt (1997) proposes the third, post-structuralist approach. He argues that this method is more appropriate for explaining consumption patterns in advanced capitalist societies. Meanings are realized in relation to peoples, times, places and objects. Moreover, meanings accumulate. They are not disconnected from history. They are "symbolic chains" that are constantly constructed. These meanings are multiple resources from which social actors select and combine. Hence, meaning of any object is dependent on which linkages are made. Consumption of marriage, for example, however individual, always works with the existing societal frameworks. Our research relies on Holt's perspective to offer a more comprehensive explanation of this complex phenomenon of commodification of marriage in the free market world.

The content analysis of currently active mail order bride websites includes virtual images, electronic presentations of brides, and other information on product and service offerings. Our initial review shows that most of the marketing activities concentrate on attracting American men to their one-stop shopping electronic bridal search service. Subservient and traditional women are typically portrayed as "products" offered as choices for men. They are described with such adjectives or phrases as, *untainted by Western feminism, family-oriented, innocent, pure,* and *loyal to the husband.*

We then develop a multi-stage model representing the international match-making process. Searching stage is characterized by clients viewing hundreds of mail-order bride agencies' websites and deciding the way he wants to connect with those potential brides. Clients can either choose to buy addresses or catalogs and magazines from agencies. Based on the photo and figure information (weight, height, or age), men get to know a bit about their future brides. In this process, women typically receive only very limited information about the man, mostly from what he chooses to tell her in the letters or emails. In the virtual contact stage, upon obtaining addresses, the client can start to write to women. The duration of pen-pal relationships lasts differently from client to client. In the rendezvous stage, mail-order bride agencies become travel and tour agencies. After a brief contact period, the client decides whether to take the next step of meeting prospective brides in person. In the bringing-home stage, it is often not the bride but rather the groom who makes the decision.

Following introduction of the above multi-stage framework, we plan to seek a theoretical explanation for commodification of women. We will conduct an interpretive study, via in-depth interviews and additional content analyses of websites, to account for consumption patterns evident in the mail-order bride industry. Visits with both women and men would allow us to hear their stories, stereotypes, expectations, emotions and satisfaction (or lack thereof). Coupled with our content analysis of mail order bride websites, we then will use themes and terms generated from the qualitative research to determine patterns of perceptions of and motives for mail order bride service participation from both the *seller* and the *consumer* perspectives. We expect to develop a theoretical model and related propositions for future empirical research on this global consumption phenomenon of social and human significance.

References

Holt, Douglas B. (1997), "Poststructuralist Lifestyle Analysis: Conceptualizing the Social Patterning of Consumption in Post-modernity," *Journal of Consumer Research*, 23 (March), 326–350.

Hughes, D.M. (2000), "The Internet and Sex Industries: Partners in Global Sexual Exploitation," *Technology and Society Magazine,* 19 (1), 35-42.

Prasad, Monica (1999), The Morality of Market Exchange: Love, Money, and Contractual Justice," *Sociological Perspectives,* 42 (2), 181-214.

(Full list of references is available upon request.)

An Investigation Into Individuals' Repeated Attempts at Behavior Change

Courtney Droms, Valdosta State University, USA

Recent research has shown that individuals make repeated attempts at behavior change prior to actually being successful. For example, typically individuals try to change their dieting behaviors on 4 to 5 occasions prior to actually being successful (Polivy and Herman 2002). Many of the dark side of consumer behavior areas identified by Mick (1996), such as smoking, drug use, shopping, and gambling, are behaviors that individuals try to change on a repeated basis. As consumer researchers, however, we do not have a clear understanding of how people interpret behavior change failures and persist in their efforts to change their behaviors after such failures.

In an effort to understand these behavior change attempts, this dissertation replicates and extends the Theory of Trying (Bagozzi and Warshaw 1990), to include feedback loops from the outcomes of behavior change attempts to attitudes towards trying to change again. The main objective of this research to address the question of how individuals interpret behavior change failure and persist post-failure. These feedback loops include several factors (i.e. attributions, self-esteem, and hope) to aid in understanding how an individual interprets behavior change outcomes and uses those interpretations as inputs into attitudes towards trying in the future.

Theoretical Model

The theoretical model is based on the model developed in the Theory of Trying (Bagozzi and Warshaw 1990). The theory of trying is employed in this context because it includes two variables that seem very relevant to repeated attempts at changing behaviors (i.e. the frequency and recency of prior attempts at changing behaviors). However, the model proposed by Bagozzi and Warshaw (1990) ends at trying to change behaviors. While the authors do suggest that the outcomes of these behavior change attempts feedback into attitudes, they do not explore the nature of the feedback. In order to explore the nature of the feedback from outcomes to attitudes, this paper employs three constructs–attributions for outcomes, self-esteem, and hope. Each of these factors will now be briefly discussed.

Attribution Theory. Weiner's (1974) theory of attributions posits that there are three dimensions to attributions–locus, stability, and controllability–that assist individuals in understanding the causes of their behaviors and behavioral outcomes. In the model, specific hypotheses, consistent with prior literature on attributions and the self-serving bias, have been developed that explicate how outcomes for success and failure are attributed along each dimension. These attributions also act as input to attitudes towards trying again and as such, hypotheses have been developed to examine several combinations of dimensions that will have the most impact on attitudes.

Self-Esteem. Self-esteem is defined as in individual's subjective appraisal of him or herself (Sedikides and Gregg 2003), which can be influenced by both goal achievement and goal failure (Crocker et al. 2003). As such, individuals in this study are expected to have lower levels of self-esteem post-failure rather than post-success at trying to change behaviors. Hypotheses were also developed and tested to capture the complexity of the interplay between self-esteem and attributions. Finally, an individual's self-esteem is also hypothesized to have a direct effect on that individual's attitudes towards trying to change in the future.

Hope. MacInnis and de Mello (2005) define hope as a positive emotion attached to a goal. There are three important dimensions to hope: goal congruency (i.e. the extent to which an environment is conducive to fulfilling a specific goal), certainty (i.e. the level of confidence an individual has in being able to achieve his or her goal), and importance of the goal. All three of these dimensions should be affected by the individual's success or failure at trying to change behaviors, such that failure at trying to change behaviors should lower an individual's level of hope. Hope is also hypothesized to affect the ways in which individuals understand and attribute the causes of their behavior change outcomes. Finally, individuals with high levels of hope should have a more positive outlook on the possibilities present in the future, which should enable them to have more positive attitudes towards changing in the future.

Methodology

An internet survey of 363 people who are currently trying to diet was completed. Modifying the procedure employed by Bagozzi and Warshaw (1990), data was collected in two stages, one month apart. Participants were asked to complete a series of measures in the first stage designed to capture their attitudes and intentions to try, the frequency and recency of prior attempts at trying to change behavior, and their current levels of self-esteem and hope. At stage two, one month later, individuals completed a second survey including measures of trying, the outcome of trying, and attitudes towards trying again in the future. Participants will also complete measures capturing their attributions for the outcome of their attempts at behavior change, as well as their updated levels of self-esteem and hope.

Discussion

Overall, this research will enlighten the discussion of how people repeatedly change their health behaviors. The theoretical model extends the Theory of Trying (Bagozzi and Warshaw 1990) by presenting a framework for understanding the various factors affected by the success or failure of a goal and how those factors then feedback into the attitude system. By incorporating concepts such as attributions, self-esteem, and hope into the feedback loops, we introduce several factors that are important in the interpretation of behavior change failure as well as the persistence towards the goal post-failure. There are important implications for both marketing and public policy as a result of this study. From a consumer behavior perspective, this model should shed some light on the effects of goal failure on an individual's attitudes and behaviors. From a public policy perspective, this study could suggest ways in which social marketing campaigns, policy recommendations, and health interventions should be designed.

References

Bagozzi, Richard P. and Paul R. Warshaw (1990), "Trying to Consume," *Journal of Consumer Research*, 17 (September), 127-140.
Crocker, Jennifer, Andrew Karpinski, Diane M. Quinn, and Sara K. Chase (2003), "When grades determine self-worth: Consequences of contingent self-worth for male and female engineering and psychology majors," *Journal of Personality and Social Psychology*, 85, 507-516.
MacInnis, Deborah J. and Gustavo E. de Mello (2005), "The Concept of Hope and Its Relevance to Product Evaluation and Choice," *Journal of Marketing*, 69 (January), 1-14.
Polivy, Janet, and C. Peter Herman (2002), "If at First You Don't Succeed: False Hopes of Self-Change," *American Psychologist*, 57(9), 677-689.
Sedikides, Constantine and Aiden P. Gregg (2003), "Portraits of the self," in M. A. Hogg & J. Cooper (Eds.), *Sage Handbook of Social Psychology*, London: Sage Publications, 110-138.
Weiner, Bernard (1974), *Achievement Motivation and Attribution Theory*, Morristown, NJ: General Learning Press.

The Role of "Interpretive Communities" in the Interpretation of "Open Text" Advertisements

Natalia Yannopoulou, University of Warwick, UK
Richard Elliott, University of Bath, UK

There has been a noticeable shift in print advertisements from functional to symbolic approaches as the use of rhetorical style in magazine advertisements has grown progressively more complex and elaborated over time (O'Donohoe, 2001). Thus the interpretation of brands and marketing communication has become extremely challenging, mainly due to the plethora of available cultural meanings and interpretive perspectives in combination with the instability of social categories (Firat and Venkatesh, 1995; Holt, 2002; Kates, 2002). The aim of this paper is to examine print advertising interpretation by different 'interpretive communities', in order to empirically explore how audiences interpret 'open' advertisements.

Multiple Readings

Empirical studies have not only established the existence of multiple readings of advertisements (Elliott, Eccles and Hodgson, 1993, Elliott and Ritson, 1995, Mick and Buhl, 1992), but they have also suggested that ambiguity and complex, non-anchored rhetorical figures may increase elaboration, because the consumer must figure out the advertisement's message (McQuarrie and Mick, 1999; Mothersbaugh, Huhman and Franke, 2002; Warlaumont, 1995). Increased elaboration in turn may increase the memorability of the advertisement (Kardes, 1998). In addition, consumers' pleasure in solving the puzzle of a rhetorical figure can lead to increased attention (McQuarrie and Mick, 1996) and a positive attitude towards the advertisement (McQuarrie and Mick, 1992; Peracchio and Meyers-Levy, 1994).

Open and Closed Texts

Advertising is consumed in a society composed of a variety of groups with different, often conflicting interests, requiring its texts to be what Eco (1979) calls open'. By this he means texts that do not attempt to close off alternative meanings and restrict their focus to one, easily attainable meaning.

This does not, however, imply that reading is completely idiosyncratic. In contrast, reader-response theorists believe that reading is based on collective conventions and that groups of readers can share certain reading strategies, allowing for the possibility of grouping similar readings and shared responses (Scott, 1994a).

Interpretive Communities

One way of achieving this, is through the concept of 'interpretive communities', which was introduced by Fish (1980) and proposes that it is "Interpretive communities…that produce meanings…Interpretive communities are made up of those who share interpretive strategies…" (p. 14). Regarding advertising, interpretive communities have been envisioned as a cultural formation with a shared social and historical context that results in similar interpretations (Elliott and Ritson, 1997; Schroder, 1994). As a result, the current study examines interpretive communities based on gender and social class.

Gender and Interpretation of Advertising

Gender differences in meaning interpretation of advertisements has been previously reported by Mick and Politi (1989), and Stern (1992) where males and females interpreted advertising visuals in noticeably different ways. Also Elliott (1995) found considerable differences in the way males and females responded to overt sexuality in advertising.

Social Class and Interpretive Codes

Consumers of different social classes code reality, language, products and advertisements in different ways (Durgee, 1986). Research by Bernstein (1973) on social relationships and linguistic patterns among middle and working class London school children, found two code types, restricted codes and elaborated codes.

Their implications for consumer behavior and advertising interpretation suggest that lower class consumers may perceive products based on their implied meanings and rely on context for their evaluation. They may prefer advertisements that use literal and concrete language and convey an image of a gratifying world in which products fit functionally into the drive for a stable and secure life. On the other hand, middle and upper class consumers may be more attuned to subtle differences of design and style and prefer appeals to more distant benefits, through the use of more symbolic and abstract language (Durgee, 1986).

Research Questions & Method

More specifically, this study will aim to answer the following:

- How do males and females interpret open advertisements?
- How do working and middle class audiences interpret open advertisements?

A reader-response approach was adopted since it emphasizes the meanings that consumers draw from advertisements (McQuarrie and Mick, 1999; Mick and Politi, 1989; Scott 1994). We conducted 40 in-depth interviews in the U.K. with working and middle class participants within the age range of eighteen to sixty years old. Ten advertisements were selected from magazines, based on their open versus closed approach to meaning and on the product categories whose target groups' correspond to the audience of the research. The concepts emerged were analyzed using the interpretive thematic analysis technique (Spiggle 1994).

Findings

Findings of the in-depth interviews indicate that people of different genders and from different social classes do interpret print advertisements in different ways. As a result and based on the different themes that emerged during the data analysis, we organised our initial findings in the following four propositions, where the first two propositions refer to the gender differences and the last two propositions refer to the social class observed differences.

Proposition I: Male participants approach the advertisement in a descriptive way.

When an advertisement was shown to a male participant, he would approach it by describing it as a picture, stating its figures and elements and by giving an interpretation based on the intended meaning by the advertiser. It can be therefore inferred that the primary concern for males is to state that they are smart enough to understand the advertisement and capable of reading between the lines.

Proposition II: Female participants approach the advertisement in an interpretive way.

On the other hand, when an advertisement was shown to a female participant, she would talk about the elements of the advertisement as they appealed to her and then try to reveal the advertiser's intended meaning. This observation leads us to think that females are willing to talk about and share personal emotions and past experiences more openly and more quickly than males. Consequently, it seems that females want to appear as free thinkers who no matter what, have something to say.

Proposition III: Working class participants approach advertisements in an implicit way.

Participants from the working class found advertisements that use simple adjectives and descriptors more appealing to them and more appropriate to convey a message that stressed the inherent quality of the featured product. Hence, they approached advertisements in a context dependent way and seemed to be more interested in the implicit fit of the product with their total lifestyle.

Proposition IV: Middle class participants approach advertisements in an explicit way.

In contrast, participants from the middle class approached advertisements in an explicit way. They enjoyed talking about implied meanings and how these could be seen in different contexts.

Thus this study provides insights into how people interpret advertisements and explores through the use of reader-response theory, the symbolic meanings that are drawn by them when consuming an advertisement. These findings present implications for designing marketing communications, with regards to the search and formation of different strategies concerning positioning and brand relationships, towards more flexible, multidimensional tactics and ambiguous messages, in order to be successfully communicated to multiple target groups conceptualized as 'interpretive communities'.

References

Bernstein, Basil B. (1973), *Class, Codes and Control*, London, Routledge & Kegan Paul.

Durgee, Jeffrey F. (1986), "How consumer sub-cultures code reality: A look at some code types", *Advances in Consumer Research*, 13 (1) 332-37.

Eco, Umberto (1979), *The Role of the Reader; Explorations in the Semiotics of Texts*, Bloomington and London, Indiana University Press.

Elliott, Richard, Eccles Susan, and Hodgson Michelle (1993), "Re-Coding Gender Representations: Women, Cleaning Products, and Advertising's New Man", *International Journal of Research in Marketing*, 10 (3) 311-24.

Elliott, Richard, and Ritson Mark (1995), "Practicing Existential Consumption: The Lived Meaning of Sexuality in Advertising" in *Advances in Consumer Research*, 22, (ed.) Kardes F. and Sujan, Provo, UT: Association of Consumer Research, 740-45.

_____ (1997), "Post-structuralism and the Dialectics of Advertising", Consumer Research: Postcards from the Edge, ed. Stephen Brown and Darach Turley, London, Routlrdge.

Elliott, Richard and Jones Abigail (1995), "Overt Sexuality in Advertising: A Discourse Analysis of Gender Responses", *Journal of Consumer Policy*, 18 (June), 187-217.

Firat, A. Fuat, and Venkatech Alladi (1995), "Liberatory Postmodernism and the Reenchantment of Consumption", *Journal of Consumer Research*, 22 (December), 239-67.

Fish, Stanley Eugene (1980), *Is There a Text in This Class? The Authority of Interpretive Communities*, Massachusetts, Harvard University Press.

Holt, Douglas (2002), "Why Do Brands Cause Trouble? A Dialectical Theory of Consumer Culture and Branding", *Journal of Consumer Research*, 29 (June), 70-90.

Kardes, Frank (1988), "Spontaneous Inference Processes in Advertising: The Effects of Conclusion Omission and Involvement on Persuasion", *Journal of Consumer Research*, 15 (September), 225-233.

Kates, Steven (2002), "Doing Brand and Subcultural Ethnographies: Developing the Interpretive Community Concept in Consumer Research", *Advances in Consumer Research*, 29 (1), 43-65.

McQuarrie, Edward, and Mick David Glen (1999), "Visual Rhetoric in Advertising: Text-Interpretive, Experimental, and Reader-Response Analyses", *Journal of Consumer Research*, 26 (June), 37-54.

_____ (1996), "Figures of Rhetoric in Advertising Language", *Journal of Consumer Research*, 22 (March), 424-38.

_____ (1992), "On Response: A Critical Pluralistic Inquiry into Advertising Rhetoric", *Journal of Consumer Research*, 19 (September), 180-97.

Mick, David Glel, and Buhl Claus (1992), "A Meaning Based Model of Advertising", *Journal of Consumer Research*, 19 (December), 317-38.

_____ and Politi Laura (1989), "Consumers' Interpretations of Advertising Imagery: A Visit to the Hell of Connotation", in *Interpretive Consumer Research*, (ed.) Hirschman E., Provo, UT, 85-96.

Mothersbaugh, David, Huhmann Bruce, and Franke George (2002), "Combinatory and Separative Effects of Rhetorical Figures on Consumers' Efforts and Focus in Ad Processing", *Journal of Consumer Research*, 28 (March), 589-602.

O'Donohoe, Stephanie (2001), "Living With Ambivalence: Attitudes to Advertising in Postmodern Times", *Marketing Theory*, 1, 91-108.

Peracchio, Laura, and Meyers-Levy Joan (1994), "How Ambiguous Cropped Objects in Ad Photos Affect Product Evaluations", *Journal of Consumer Research*, 21 (June), 190-204.

Phillips, Barbara (2000), "The Impact of Verbal Anchoring on Consumer Respose to Images Ads", *Journal of Advertising*, 29 (1), 15-24.

Schroder, Kim Christian (1994), "Audience semiotics, interpretive communities and the ethnographic turn in media research", *Media Culture & Society*, 16, 337-346.

Scott, Linda (1994), "Images in advertising: The Need for a Theory of Visual Rhetoric", *Journal of Consumer Research*, 21 (September), 252-73.

Spiggle, Susan (1994), "Analysis and Interpretation of Qualitative Data in Consumer Research", *Journal of Consumer Research*, 21 (December), pp. 491-503.

Stern, Barbara (1992), "Feminist Literary Theory and Advertising Research: A New "Reading" of the Text and the Consumer", *Journal of Current Issues and Research in Advertising*, 14 (1), 9-21.

Warlaumont, Hazel (1995), "Advertising Images: From Persuasion to Polysemy", *Journal of Current Issues and Research in Advertising*, 17 (1), 19-31.

Is Effective Product Placement in Movies?: A Cross-Cultural Study Between French and Spanish Consumers.

Jose Torrano, Technical University of Cartagena, Spain
Enrique Flores, Technical University of Cartagena, Spain

Abstract

Product placement (PP) has taken its place as a major promotional medium, especially these days when consumers have an increasing array of media choices and have the ability to switch in and out of various media as and when they chose too. Based on Dual Mediation Hypothesis Model (Mackenzie et al., 1986), we have analyses PP effectiveness within the international context, and we have compared the results obtained from samples of consumers (French and Spanish). This intercultural framework is justified for the increase of international operations of firms that sell their products and services to a higher number of markets, directed to consumers of different cultures and nationalities.

Conceptualization

Several recent studies have demonstrated that Product Placement (PP) as an advertising technique is more acceptable for viewers than conventional advertising and some of them have demonstrated its effectiveness as an advertising technique (McKecnie and Zou, 2003; Choi and Miracle, 2004). PP has been defined as "the paid inclusion of branded products or brand identifiers through audio and/or visual means, within mass media programming" (Karrh, 1998). The volume and sophistication of PP have grown impressively and rapidly, easily outpacing research efforts in the field (Tiwsakul et al, 2005).

The main contribution of this paper lies in show an effectiveness cross-cultural model in base on Dual Mediation Hypothesis Model DMH (Mackenzie et al, 1986) using French and Spanish consumers. We have chosen France and Spain because they are Western countries, both of them are Mediterranean and Hofstede (2001) indicates that this countries are very similar in his four dimensions (Power Distance Index, Individualism, Masculinity, and Uncertainty Avoidance Index).

The variables of the model: Thoughts about PP, .Attitudes towards PP, Thoughts about brand, Attitudes towards brand and Purchase Intention.

Choi and Miracle (2004) indicate that advertising effectiveness may be implemented by the attitude towards advertising, attitude towards brand and buyer's intention; a relationship which is widely supported by literature (Mackenzie and Lutz, 1989; Babins and Burns, 1997). Our model, in base on DMH, considers that thoughts generated about Product Placement influence directly on attitude towards PP (Yoon et al., 1995):

H1: Independently of the country, the attitude towards PP will be more positive for consumers with more thoughts about PP than for those consumers with a less thoughts about PP.

With respect to the attitude towards the brand Petty and Cacioppo (1986), with regard to PP, when consumer is exposed to PP, one of the first reactions to that exposure tends to be to demonstrate those feelings evoked.

H2: Independently of the country, the attitude towards the brand is more positive for individuals with more favourable attitude towards PP than for individuals with less favourable attitude towards PP.

As Petty and Cacioppo (1996) indicate, there are a direct relationship between those thoughts about the brand and the attitude towards brand.

H3: Independently of the country, the attitude towards the brand will be more positive for individuals with greater thoughts about the brand than for individuals with fewer thoughts about the brand.

As Makenzie et al. (1986) established, attitude towards advertising influence on thoughts about brand.

H4: Independently of the country, thoughts about the brand will be more positive when the attitude towards PPL is more positive than when the attitude towards the PPL is less positive.

According with (Mackenzie et al., 1986) effectiveness of advertising, finally, is determinate for relationship between attitude towards brand and purchase intention.

H5: Independently of the country, the purchase intention is greater for individuals with a more favourable attitude toward the brand than for individuals with a less favourable attitude.

Method

Subjects: 409 (205 French and 204Spanish undergraduate students).

Design: A 2x2 all between subjects full factorial experiment designs. The independent factors: frequency of watching movies (high, low), and frequency of using the product (high, low). Them a marketing jury determined the movie (actor/actress, brands and film were not Spanish or French). Four groups of these students (1.camera-on set, 2.camera-creative, 3.computer-on set, and 4.computer-creative) watched ten minutes of the film each one, in the university theatre. Those students filled the questionnaire with Karrh's (1998) Product Placement definition.

Major Findings

The results of the hypotheses:

H1: [F (1,405)=16.058; p<0.1], so it is supported. The results [F(1,405)= 1.469; p=0.226] also indicate that there are no differences between French and Spanish consumers.

H2: [F (1,405)=0.115; p= 0.735] make us reject this relationship and refuse this hypothesis. With respect to the possible differences between French and Spanish consumers, the analysis indicates that there are no significant differences [F(1,405)= 2.041; p= 0.154].

H3: [F (1,405)=4.683; p<0.1] indicate that this relationship is significant. Regarding the existence of possible differences between French and Spanish consumers we have indicates that there are significant differences [F (1,405)=40.573; p<0.1].

H4: [F(1,405)= 7.848; p<0.1], we accept hypothesis H4. The analysis indicates that there are no significant differences between French and Spanish consumers [F(1,405)= 0.152; p= 0.697].

H5: [F (1,405)=58.586; p< 0.1], it is a significant relationship, and there are significant differences between both groups of consumers [F(1,405)= 7.535; p< 0.1].

The results have demonstrated that we can conclude that we can use MDH model, made to advertising, to demonstrate the effectiveness of PP, but in our study, the relationships are as follow: thoughts about PP influences on attitude towards PP, attitude toward PP influences on thoughts about brand, thoughts about brand influences on attitude towards brand, and attitude towards brand influences on purchase intention.

With reference to cross-cultural aspect, the results show that there are not significant differences between French and Spanish consumers. These outcomes are very important for Marketers and firm that works in international markets. For our study Hoftede's model (2001) is a good predictor for cross-cultural studies.

References

Babins, L.A. and Burns, A.C. (1997), "Effects of Print Ad Pictures and Copy Containning Instructions to Imagine on Mental Imagery That Mediates Attitudes", *Journal of Advertising*, 26 (3), 33-44.

Choi and Miracle (2004), "The Effectiveness of Comparative Advertising in Korea and the United States", *Journal of Advertising, 33* (4).

Hofstede, G. (2001). *Culture's consequences (2nd ed.).* Beverly Hills, CA: Sage.

Karrh, J.A. (1998), "Brand Placement: A Review", *Journal of Current Issues and Research in Advertising*, 20 (2), 31-48.

McKechnie, S.B. and Zhou, J. (2003), "Product Placement In Movies: A Comparison Of Chinese And American Consumers´ Attitudes". *International Journal of Advertising*, 22, 349-374.

Mackenzie, S. B. and Lutz, R. J. (1989). "An Empirical Examination Of The Structural Antecedents Of Attitude Toward The Ad In An Advertising Pretesting Context", *Journal of Marketing, 53,* 48-65.

Mackenzie, S.B., Lutz, R.J. and Belch, G.E. (1986), *"The* Role Of Attitude Toward The Ad As A Mediator Of Advertising Effectiveness: A Test Of Competing Explanations", *Journal of Marketing Research 23, 130-143.*

Petty, R.E. and Cacioppo, J.T. (1986), "Communication and Persuasion. Central and Peripheral Routes to Advertising Effectiveness: The Moderating Role of Involvement", *Journal of Consumer Research, 10, 135-146.*

Petty, R. E. and Cacioppo, J. T.(1996), "Aderessing disturbing and disturbed consumer behaviour: is necessary to change the way we conduct behavioural science?", *Journal of Marketing Research. 33(1),1-9.*

Tiwsakul, Rungpaka; Hackley, Chris and Szmigin, Isabelle (2005), "Explicit, Non-Integrated Product Placement in British Television Progammes". *International Journal of Advertising*, 24 (Issue 1), 95-111.

Yoon, K.; Laczniak, R.N.; Muehing, D.D. and Reece, B.B. (1995), "A Revised Model Of Advertising Processing: Extending the Dual Mediation Hypothesis", *Journal of Current Issues and Research in Advertising*, 17 (2), 53-67.

Teenagers' Willingness to Share Personal Information with Marketers

Anu Sivaraman, University of Delaware, USA
Dan Freeman, University of Delaware, USA
Stewart Shapiro, University of Delaware, USA

Despite growing concerns, few empirical studies have examined how teenagers respond to marketers' information collection and use practices. The objective of this research is to understand how factors like materialistic values and dislike of marketing tactics may affect the extent to which teenagers are willing to share personal information with marketers. Consistent with study hypotheses, results from a representative sample of 709 U. S. teens indicate that the dislike of marketing tactics plays a moderating role in the positive relationship between materialism and willingness to share information. Self-esteem and susceptibility to peer influence also affect willingness to share personal information.

Why Do We Overbuy? Value from Engagement and the Shopping-consumption Discrepancy

Dilney Goncalves, INSEAD, France

The recent decades have witnessed an unprecedented increase in consumer discretionary income. The increased income allied with cheaper consumer goods shifted consumption from necessities to more hedonic products. With this trend, another phenomenon became more apparent and important: *overbuying*. Overbuying, or the act of purchasing an object and not consuming it, may have several causes. It may result from bad predictions about future and needs or from changes in taste. We propose another explanation, namely that engagement in the act of shopping temporarily increases the value of objects to shoppers.

We build on Higgins' theoretical framework on value from hedonic consequences and engagement. Higgins (2006) proposes that the value of an outcome depends not only on the hedonic consequences (pleasure or pain), but also on the strength of engagement in obtaining the outcome. According to this conceptualization, hedonic consequences contribute to value by determining the valence (positive or negative) and influencing its intensity. However, intensity is also determined by the strength of engagement. When people are strongly engaged in obtaining a certain outcome, its value becomes more extreme: negative outcomes become even more negative and positive outcomes become even more positive. To be engaged is "to be involved, occupied, and interested in something. Strong engagement is to concentrate on something, to be absorbed or engrossed with it." Differently from the valuation effect (Brendl, Markman, and Messner 2003), value from engagement is not caused by activation of goals. Instead, it comes from the way a goal is pursued and how the goal pursuit is experienced.

Four sources of engagement are described by Higgins: opposition to interfering forces, overcoming personal resistance, use of proper means, and regulatory fit. For the purposes of our study, the most relevant of these sources is opposition to interfering forces. The experience of motivational force increases with the presence of interfering forces as long as these forces are not strong enough as to make people abandon the goal altogether.

The contribution of this research is twofold: (1) we show that there is a discrepancy in value between shopping and consumption occasions and (2) we demonstrate that engagement increases WTP; Additionally we provide a novel way of manipulating engagement in an online shopping context. From a consumer welfare point-of-view, our research suggests that consumers should try to correct their estimates of enjoyment of a particular product, especially when the shopping environment is engaging. From a marketer's perspective our second experiment suggests a simple way of increasing engagement in online shopping, leading to greater valuation of products.

In the first experiment, we explored discrepancies in value between shopping and consumption. One hundred eleven participants were randomly assigned to one of four conditions. They were asked to report a recent purchase or to predict a future purchase. The design was a 2x2 between-subjects factorial. The first factor was reporting past experience or predicting a future experience. The second factor was focusing on the shopping occasion or the consumption occasion. The dependent variable was "when you think about the moment you bought (consumed) this product, how happy does it make you feel?"

An ANCOVA with days from actual (expected) purchase and price as covariates revealed only a significant effect of the time X focus interaction. Thinking about future consumption leads to greater happiness than thinking about past consumption (M_{future}=7.12; M_{past}=6.33; p=0.032). When thinking about shopping, subjects' happiness from past shopping did not differ significantly from future shopping (M_{past}=6.85; M_{future}=6.48; p=0.19). These results suggest that people make inaccurate predictions about consumption but relatively accurate predictions about shopping. Importantly, there seems to be a discrepancy between shopping and consumption: while shopping, people expect greater pleasure from products than they actually experience.

The second study was designed to test whether greater engagement leads to greater valuation of products and greater purchase likelihood. Participants were 158 members of the community of a large Brazilian university. They were recruited by email. As an incentive, they were entered in a lottery to win one MP3 player. The email contained a link to a webpage with the experiment. The first page introduced the research and the cover story that we were investigating how people evaluate and choose products online. Participants were randomly assigned to one of two conditions. They were asked to state their willingness to pay for three models of MP3 player and how much they liked each model. We also measured engagement using three items: how involved, how absorbed, and how focused on the task they were.

Engagement was manipulated by varying the effort in information search. Half the subjects (high-engagement) had to click on a link to access each product's attribute information whereas the other half (low-engagement) got all the attribute information with just one click. By making it more difficult to access product information, subjects in the high-engagement had to actively seek information. High-engagement subjects were required to click on each link at least once. On clicking, they saw a page with a picture and description of the MP3 player. The number of times subjects clicked on each link was recorded. In the low-engagement condition, subjects saw the same pictures of MP3 players, but all the features appeared on the same page in a table under the pictures. No action was required in this condition. The dependent variables were willingness-to-pay for and liking of each model.

Effort was found to increase engagement up to a certain point, after which more effort reduced engagement (inverted-U relationship). More importantly, we found that people who engage more in the process of product information search and comparison stated greater willingness-to-pay than do those who engage less in the process. This result supports our hypothesis that engaging in shopping increases value.

Although we have shown that engagement increases willingness-to-pay, a next study will be executed to examine whether this translates in greater purchase.

References

Ariely, Dan, George Loewenstein, and Drazen Prelec (2003), "'Coherent Arbitrariness': Stable Demand Curves Without Stable Preferences," *Quarterly Journal of Economics*, 118 (1), 73.

Brendl, C. Miguel, Arthur B. Markman, and Claude Messner (2003), "The Devaluation Effect: Activating a Need Devalues Unrelated Objects," *Journal of Consumer Research*, 29 (4), 463-73.

Carmon, Ziv and Dan Ariely (2000), "Focusing on the Foregone: How Value Can Appear So Different to Buyers and Sellers," *Journal of Consumer Research*, 27 (3), 360-70.

Cialdini, Robert B. (1993), *Influence: Science and practice* (3rd ed.). New York, NY, US: HarperCollins College Publishers.

Frederick, Shane and George Loewenstein (1999), "Hedonic adaptation," in *Well-being: The foundations of hedonic psychology.*, Daniel Kahneman and Ed Diener and Norbert Schwarz, Eds. New York, NY, US: Russell Sage Foundation.

Higgins, E. Tory (2006), "Value From Hedonic Experience and Engagement," *Psychological Review*, 113 (3), 439-60.

Kahneman, Daniel and Jack L. Knetsch (1991), "The Endowment Effect, Loss Aversion, and Status Quo Bias," *Journal of Economic Perspectives*, 5 (1), 193-206.

Kahneman, Daniel, Jack L. Knetsch, and Richard H. Thaler (1990), "Experimental tests of the endowment effect and the Coase theorem," *Journal of Political Economy*, 98 (6), 1352.

Kahneman, Daniel and Jackie Snell (1992), "Predicting a Changing Taste: Do People Know What They Will Like?," *Journal of Behavioral Decision Making*, 5 (3), 187-200.

Shin, Jiwoong and Dan Ariely (2004), "Keeping Doors Open: The Effect of Unavailability on Incentives to Keep Options Viable," *Management Science*, 50 (5), 575-86.

Thaler, Richard (1985), "Mental Accounting and Consumer Choice," *Marketing Science*, 4 (3), 199-214.

_____ (1980), "Toward a Positive Theory of Consumer Choice," in *Choices, Values, and Frames*, Daniel Kahneman and Amos Tversky, Eds. New York: Cambridge University Press.

Tversky, Amos and Daniel Kahneman (1973), "Availability: A heuristic for judging frequency and probability," *Cognitive Psychology*, 5 (2), 207-32.

Advice from a Caterpillar: Mainstreaming Hookah Consumption Into American Pop Culture

Merlyn A. Griffiths, University of North Carolina-Greensboro, USA
Tracy R. Harmon, Syracuse University, USA

Hookah smoking is a less known entity for consumer behavior researchers. Research on consumers' smoking behaviors have been vast in the marketing area, and has offered compelling evidence of the negative effects of smoking. The majority of these studies have focused primarily on cigarette consumption and the effects of advertising messages, antismoking messages and placement in media, as well as the addictive effects on adolescents, teenagers and young adults (see Pechmann and Reibling 2006; Pechmann and Reibling 2000; Pechmann and Shih 1999; Pechmann and Ratneshwar 1994; Pechmann et al. 2003). However, no studies to date have focused on American consumers' adoption or practice of hookah smoking. Just what is the appeal of this practice, and to what might we attribute its epidemic-like spread in mainstream culture. We investigate this phenomenon and identify factors relating to consumer attitudes, beliefs and attributed meanings that are contributing to the proliferation of hookah smoking.

Employing qualitative methods, our findings point to a significant disconnect for consumers in their perceptions. We have found nostalgic emotional disconnections, and disconnection of the risks and consequences involved in hookah consumption relative to cigarette and cigar smoking. Hookah consumption is viewed as a positive pleasurable experience that fosters group bonding.

References

Pechmann, C. and E.T. Reibling (2006), "Antismoking Advertisements for Youths: An Independent Evaluation of Health, Counter-Industry, and Industry Approaches," *American Journal of Public Health*, 96 (5), 906-13.

Pechmann, C., G. Z. Zhao, M. E. Goldberg, and E. T. Reibling (2003), "What To Convey In Antismoking Advertisements For Adolescents: The Use Of Protection Motivation Theory To Identify Effective Message Themes," *Journal of Marketing*, 67 (2), 1-18.

Pechmann, C. and E. T. Reibling (2000), "Anti-smoking Advertising Campaigns Targeting Youth: Case Studies From USA and Canada," *Tobacco Control*, 9 (Summer),18-31.

Pechmann, C. and C. Shih (1999), " Smoking Scenes in Movies and Antismoking Advertisements before Movies: Effects on Youth," *Journal of Marketing*, 63 (3), 1-13.

Pechmann, C. and S. Ratneshwar (1994), "The Effects of Antismoking and Cigarette Advertising on Young Adolescents Perceptions of Peers Who Smoke," *Journal of Consumer Research*, 21 (2), 236-51.

Who to Choose? Source Credibility and Attractiveness of Endorsers in the 2008 Presidential Primaries

Pamela Grimm, Kent State University, USA
Hyunjung Lee, Kent State University, USA
Neslihan Yilmaz, Kent State University, USA

Endorsements in politics are ubiquitous, especially in the run-up to a presidential election. Though both marketers and politicians try to influence consumer/voter behavior through endorsements, the endorsement process in politics is more complicated than in marketing for several reasons. First, in marketing the endorser is usually a celebrity or expert on the product category, is paid for his or her endorsement and, typically, an endorsement is not made unless a relationship (usually contractual) exists between the firm and the endorser.

In politics, celebrity endorsements seem less important that endorsements from sources such as other politicians. Endorsements in politics are not paid, there are no contractual relationships and some endorsements are rejected by the candidate because they are viewed as liabilities rather than assets. This rejection of an endorsement is a phenomenon seldom seen outside of the political arena.

It is especially clear in the 2008 Presidential Primary that endorsements matter. The campaigns make a point of sharing news about positive endorsements and several candidates have found themselves in the position of either having to reject or explain endorsements from sources viewed as negative by some voters. Yet, despite this obvious importance, there is only a limited understanding of the relative importance of different types of endorsers or the factors that drive the importance of an endorser.

This research provides insight into four broad categories of endorsers. These categories are: politicians, newspapers, organizations representing interest groups (ex: labor and religious groups) and celebrities. Evidence of the importance of most of these types of endorsements is found primarily in the Political Science literature, though the popular press has also been weighing in on this question as well. Political endorsements (Schulte 2008; Thomas 2008; Tumulty 2008), newspaper endorsements (Cooper,2007; Erikson 1976; Stengel 2008), interest group endorsements (Grossman & Helpman 1999; Maher 2008; McDermott 2006; Rapoport, Stone, & Abramowitz 1991), and celebrity endorsements (Celeb in chief 2007; Goodnight 2005; Jones & Carroll 2007; Payne, Hanlon, & Twomey III 2007; Weiskel 2005) have all been studied, though typically in isolation from other types of endorsements.

This paper examines and compares these different types of endorsers utilizing the Source Credibility and, in the case of celebrities, the Source Attractiveness models of endorser effects (Ohanian 1990). Application of these models in the context of political endorsements has not been done, though this application was suggested by Ohanian (1990). Using these models should provide greater insight into the mechanisms underlying endorsement effects in a political context.

Subjects in the research were undergraduate students from an Ohio public university who were given extra credit for participating in the research. The survey was administered online and was made available 36 hours before the March 2008 Primary in Ohio. The survey included items designed to gather information regarding party affiliation, primary candidate preferences, source credibility for each of the four categories of endorsers (politicians, newspapers, interest groups and celebrities) and attractiveness and importance of eight specific endorsers. Subjects rated two actual endorsers for each of the four categories of endorsers, for a total of eight endorsers. The eight specific endorsers rated by a subject depended on the subject's primary candidate preference. The items used for source credibility and attractiveness were those developed by Ohanian (1990). A single seven point item (with 1 as "not at all important" and 7 as "very important") was used to gauge the importance that a subject assigned to a given endorser.

Overall, 355 surveys were retained; 85 respondents were registered Republicans, 135 were Democrats and 40 were independent. The remaining subjects were not registered. The source credibility items were administered to all subjects, but the source attractiveness and importance items were only administered to those subjects who were registered to vote.

The ten items representing source credibility were averaged, as were the five items representing source attractiveness. The results demonstrate that, in general, consumers/voters evaluate the different endorsers in significantly different ways based on source credibility. Other politicians are viewed as most credible (mean=4.9 average on a seven point scale), followed by newspapers (4.3), interest groups (4.2) and celebrities (3.6) (p<.001).

The rank ordering produced by the Source Credibility items is mirrored in the importance ratings assigned to the specific celebrities in each category for each candidate. The average importance for politicians was 4.7; for newspapers 4.3; for interest groups 3.9 and for celebrities 2.9. Politicians are considered most credible and important and celebrities are considered least credible and important.

The Source Credibility scale can be further decomposed into two sub-factors: trustworthiness and expertise. A factor analysis of the scale items for each of the four categories of endorsers showed that the pattern of factor loadings followed the results of Ohanian except for celebrity endorsers. Means were computed on the two sub-factors for politicians, newspapers and interest groups. Results show significant differences between the three groups in terms of trustworthiness and expertise. Politicians are rated higher in terms of both expertise (5.42) and trustworthiness (4.39) than the other two groups, though the difference between politicians and interest groups, in terms of trustworthiness, is not significant. Newspapers are rated second in terms of expertise (4.49) but third, behind interest groups, in terms of trustworthiness (4.14). Interest groups are not significantly different from politicians in terms of trustworthiness (4.31) but are significantly lower than politicians and newspapers in terms of expertise (4.17).

Source attractiveness measures were collected for the two celebrities endorsing each of the four specific candidates. The average attractiveness measure was 4.11 across the eight celebrities included in the study. The relationship between attractiveness and the importance assigned the endorser was positive and significant (r=.406, p<.001).

This research demonstrates the value of utilizing the Source Credibility and Attractiveness framework in a political context. There are significant differences in how different types of endorsers are viewed in terms of credibility in general, and trustworthiness and expertise in particular. Further, credibility is mirrored in the importance assigned to endorsers by consumers. Celebrity attractiveness is also linked to the importance assigned to a celebrity's endorsement.

References

"Celeb in chief," (2007), *Time,* 170 (26), 25.

Cooper, Christopher (2007), "Odds are on obama to get iowa paper's endorsement," *Wall Street Journal-Eastern Edition,* 250 (141), A2.

Erikson, Robert S. (1976), "The influence of newspaper endorsements in presidential elections: The case of 1964," *American Journal of Political Science,* 20 (2), 207-33.

Goodnight, G. T. (2005), "The passion of the christ meets fahrenheit 9/11: A study in celebrity advocacy," *American Behavioral Scientist,* 49 (3), 410-35.

Grossman, Gene M., and Elhanan Helpman (1999), "Competing for endorsements," *The American Economic Review,* 89 (3), 501-24.

Jones, Jeffrey M., and Joseph Carroll (2007), "Most voters not moved by oprah's endorsement of obama: Majority say endorsements generally not an important factor in vote," *Gallup Poll Briefing, ,* 16-21.

Maher, Kris (2008), "Key union may back obama run," *Wall Street Journal-Eastern Edition,* 251 (7), A9.

McDermott, Monika L. (2006), "Not for members only: Group endorsements as electoral information cues," *Political Research Quarterly,* 59 (2), 249-57.

Ohanian, Roobina (1991), "The impact of celebrity spokespersons' perceived image on consumers' intention to purchase," *Journal of Advertising Research,* 31 (1), 46-54.

Payne, J. G., John P. Hanlon, and David P. Twomey III (2007), "Celebrity spectacle influence on young voters in the 2004 presidential campaign: What to expect in 2008," *American Behavioral Scientist,* 50 (9), 1239-46.

Rapoport, Ronald B., Walter J. Stone, and Alan I. Abramowitz (1991), "Do endorsements matter? group influence in the 1984 democratic caucuses," *The American Political Science Review,* 85 (1), 193-203.

Schulte, Bret (2008), "Endorsement envy. (cover story)," *U.S.News & World Report,* 144 (6), 41.

Stengel, Richard (2008), "Taking sides," *Time,* 171 (9), 6.

Thomas, Evan (2008), "Welcome to the family," *Newsweek,* 151 (6), 37.

Tumulty, Karen (2008), "Endorsement politics," *Time,* 171 (6), 50.

Weiskel, T. C. (2005), "From sidekick to sideshow-celebrity, entertainment, and the politics of distraction: Why americans are "sleepwalking toward the end of the earth," *American Behavioral Scientist,* 49 (3), 393-409.

Yes, The Poor Can Be Taught To Save-Evidence From a Survey of IDA Program Participants

Caezilia Loibl, The Ohio State University, USA
Beth Red Bird, The Ohio State University, USA
Michal Grinstein-Weiss, The University of North Carolina at Chapel Hill, USA
Min Zhan, University of Illinois at Urbana-Champaign, USA

Abstract

The question whether multi-year, intensive financial literacy programs aimed at helping those with low incomes and few assets actually work out in the long-run has not yet been answered. The current study is the first to scrutinize the outcome of participation in the Individual Development Account program in order to fill this void. The findings of a mail survey suggest that those who completed the program are more likely to accumulate assets, continue saving, and establish investment accounts, compared to those leaving the program prematurely. The influence of self-control and future orientation on savings behavior is discussed.

Conceptualization

Though saving is important to many low-income families, it can appear to be an impossible task in the context of a day-to-day effort to make ends meet. A number of psychological factors hamper regular savings. The lower the income, the higher tends to be the rate of time preference due to the many unfulfilled needs, which, in turn, leads to a lower willingness to delay gratification and to consider future consequences of current financial choices. Procrastination and naivety about this tendency contribute to people's belief that they will save tomorrow even if they are not saving today. Loss aversion suggests that people weigh the reduction of disposable income due to savings deposits more heavily than an equivalent future gain in consumption provided by the accumulated wealth.

The Individual Development Account (IDA) program has been designed with these factors in mind to help participants overcome the barriers to regular savings. IDAs are tax-protected, matched savings accounts designed to help those with low incomes and few assets to buy a home, capitalize a business, or fund higher education (Schreiner and Sherraden 2007). The current study is the first (to the best of the investigators' knowledge) to study the long-term outcomes of IDA program participation in order to answer the question whether those who complete the program continue to save and accumulate assets.

Method

A survey was mailed to all 465 former participants of an IDA program provider in the Midwest using best survey practices. A total of 164 usable questionnaires were returned (response rate: 43%); of those, 126 were returned by program graduates and 38 by program dropouts. A weighting correction was applied to the data to account for non-responses using normalized inverses of modeled response probabilities (Lohr 1999). The questionnaire inquired about six psychological (self-mastery; future orientation; self-control; economic strain; finances since IDA program; finances in a year), four program-related (graduation, months passed since IDA program, months in the program, asset.type), nine financial (own checking/ savings/ investment/ credit card/ fixed-payment/ mortgage account; household savings; credit card debt; decision authority), and nine basic demographic measures.

Major findings

Do IDA program graduates continue to save?

An OLS regression model was fit to the data using household savings as the dependent variable and the demographic, financial, program-specific, and psychological metrics as independent variables. Program graduation emerged as a highly significant predictor of household savings. Program graduation resulted in $341 higher household savings. Consistent with previous studies, we find future orientation to increase household savings.

Do future orientation and self-control develop during program participation?

To further assess the role of program graduation in individuals' future orientation, an OLS regression model was fit to the data using future orientation as dependent variable and the demographic, financial, program-specific, remaining psychological metrics, and the interaction terms with program graduation as independent variables. The results showed that a set of important savings predictors seemed unaffected by program graduation. We find the relationship between future orientation and self-control to be most important here. This observation may point toward the notion of a certain similarity in these psychological dispositions among those entering the IDA program, regardless of outcomes. While program graduation helped develop self-control, it did not affect future orientation, which emerged as a main effect in predicting household savings.

In conclusion, we propose that successful IDA program completion creates financial dispositions and behavior that provide long-term benefits. The program graduation variable itself provided a good predictor of household savings. The strict program structure and intensive financial training over several years time, we suggest, might succeed in building the willpower needed to achieve savings goals independently, long after leaving the care of the IDA program.

References

Lohr, Sharon L. 1999. *Sampling: Design and analysis.* Pacific Grove: Duxbury Press.

Schreiner, Mark, and Michael Sherraden. 2007. *Can the poor save? Saving and asset accumulation in Individual Development Accounts.* New Brunswick: Transaction.

Falling in Love with Brands: An Inductive Qualitative Exploration of Pathways to Emotional Attachment

Doug Grisaffe, University of Texas at Arlington, USA

Hieu Nguyen, California State University, Long Beach, USA

Introduction

Emotional attachment to brands (EAB) is a relatively new construct in the consumer behavior literature and little is known about the construct except a seminal scale development paper (Thomson, MacInnis and Park 2005–hereinafter referred to as TMP). The process through which EAB, as a basis of deep "brand relationships" (Park and MacInnis 2006), is developed remains far from well understood. The purpose of our paper is to explicate a set of *underlying psychological mechanisms* that consumers themselves cite as reasons for developing and exhibiting devoted EAB. Our paper contributes to the understanding of the EAB construct and expands the discoveries of TMP's work by presenting the pathways through which EAB is formed. We also address some issues that TMP point out as unanswered in their research.

Method

Given the relative infancy of this line of research, we intentionally designed our study to be inductive in nature. We asked 125 respondents to explain in their own words the reasons why they feel emotionally attached to brands that they listed. We then used a thematic content analytic approach to extract a set of data-reductive codes that capture and summarize the original responses. To interpret our findings, and to provide initial support for their validity, we bridge back to broader theoretical and empirical literature in consumer research. Eighteen frequently-mentioned themes emerged from our analysis which we grouped into four "pathways" reported below.

Findings

Pathway 1: Marketing Characteristics, Value, and Satisfaction

Oliver (1989) proposes a research approach that has been extensively used in the satisfaction literature: the comparison standards paradigm. The paradigm suggests that consumers hold certain product standards prior to consumption, observe product performance, compare the actual performance with their standards, form confirmation/disconfirmation perceptions, combine these perceptions with standard levels, and form satisfaction judgments with the product. Many respondents in our study cited satisfaction with the focal brand as the main driver for their EAB. This satisfaction is derived from perceived values including pricing (better prices), product (superior product quality and design), promotion (corporate image and advertising/market communication activities), and distribution (product/service availability, physical facilities). We propose that the first pathway to EAB is through customer satisfaction with superior product and service values as reflected in marketing characteristics.

Pathway 2: Utilitarian and Hedonic Benefits-What the Brand Does for Me

Fournier (1998) suggests that in close consumer-brand relationships, consumers come to identify and be involved with many of the brands they regularly consume. One important reason why people form lasting brand relationships is that such behavior helps create their personal identity and construct their own self concept (Ball and Tasaki 1992; Belk 1988). Work by Park, Jaworski, and MacInnis (1986) and Keller (1993) shows that there are three general dimensions of brand identities: functional, symbolic, and experiential. Brand functional attributes represent the utilitarian function or benefits of the product. Our data show that oftentimes consumers tried different brands but only one brand would provide the most satisfying solution to their problem, which formed the foundation of their EAB. These brands can aid consumers in fulfilling either a self-oriented goal (internally driven, e.g. having younger looking skin, softer hair, stronger teeth) or a social-oriented goal (supporting consumers' identity and social/professional roles, e.g. expressing self identity). Enhancing consumers' role in and out of the home is another attribute that these brands often possess.

Pathway 3: Consumer Socialization and Intergenerational Influence

Brands can also serve a social purpose by reflecting social ties to one's family, community, or cultural group (Muniz and O'Guinn 2001). Since the family is typically a consumer's most significant reference group, one way in which these social ties may be formed is via intergenerational transfer (Moschis 1985, 1987). In our surveys, many consumers revealed that they became emotionally attached to brands that they grew up with and their parents never used other brands. Many respondents also reported EAB with brands that their parents used as a way to "honor" the family tradition. The "family tradition" theme is not only limited to high-involvement, expensive branded goods, our respondents also reported their attachment to brands of fast-moving consumer goods such as soft drinks, laundry detergent, mayonnaise, and cookies.

Pathway 4: Sentimentality and Emotional Memories

Our fourth pathway to EAB involves an especially personal and meaningful pairing between a brand and some situation(s), experience(s), place(s), and/or person/people. For example, a woman might recall the "ritual" of visiting her grandfather as a child, sitting on the front porch of his house, and sharing Coca-cola and a Snickers candy bar. Now as an adult, she often has Coca-cola and a Snickers bar, and it reminds her of her grandfather, his house, and their front porch talks. With Pathway 4, specific brands become powerfully connected to sentimental and emotionally-imbued memories involving some meaningful place, situation, experience and/or person. It is as if repeatedly returning to the brands invokes a commemorative re-experiencing of some favorable or even longed-for past. It should be noted that inter-generational transfer doesn't require sentimental/emotional memory. Transfer alone could involve a user of Tide simply saying her grandmother used it, her mother used it, and so she uses it too. Likewise, Sentimental and Emotion memory does not require inter-generational dynamics. Someone might say he drank Taster's Choice coffee with his first long-term girlfriend in college while they stayed up nights to study. He reflects back fondly on those times to this day when he buys Taster's Choice. Thus Pathway 4 can correlate with Pathway 3, but not necessarily.

Conclusion

We expand the understanding of the EAB construct, initiated by TMP, by showing the pathways through which consumers form their EAB. We were also successful in having respondents report on brands with extreme levels of emotional attachment. While TMP's results suggest that brands to which consumers are emotionally attached tend to be high involvement and symbolically or hedonically related, out results show that EAB is also evidenced in low involvement and functionally related product categories. This finding could be more formally tested by controlling brands within different product categories (e.g. low vs. high involvement, utilitarian vs. hedonic). Future research should also examine the strength of each pathway, as well as the relation between EAB and market leadership.

References

Ball, A. Dwayne and Lori H. Tasaki, (1992), "The Role and Measurement of Attachment in Consumer Behavior," *Journal of Consumer Psychology*, 1(2), 155-132.

Belk, Russell W. (1988), "Possession and the Extended Self," *Journal of Consumer Research*, 15(2), 139-168.

Fournier, Susan (1998), "Consumer and Their Brands: Developing Relationship Theory in Consumer Research," *Journal of Consumer Research*, 24, 343-373.

Keller, Kevin Lane (1993), "Conceptualizing, Measuring, and Managing Customer-Based Brand Equity," Journal of Marketing, 57, 1-22.

Moschis, George P. (1985), "The Role of Family Communication in Consumer Socialization of Children and Adolescents," *Journal of Consumer Research,* 11(3), 898-913.

_____ (1987), *Consumer Socialization: A Life-Cycle Perspective*, Lexington, MA: Lexington Books.

Muniz Jr., Albert M. and Thomas C. O'Guinn (2001), "Brand Community," *Journal of Consumer Research*, 27(4), 412-432.

Oliver, Richard L. (1989), "Processing of the Satisfaction Response in Consumption: A Suggested Framework and Research Propositions," *Journal of Consumer Satisfaction, Dissatisfaction, and Complaining Behavior,* 2, 1-16.

Park, C. Whan and Deborah MacInnis (2006), "What's In and What's Out: Questions on the Boundaries of the Attitude Construct," *Journal of Consumer Research*, 33, 16-18.

_____, Jaworski, B. J., MacInnis, D. J. (1986), "Strategic Brand Concept/Image Management," *Journal of Marketing*, 50, 135-145.

Thomson, Matthew, Deborah MacInnis, and C.W. Park (2005), "The Ties that Bind: Measuring the Strength of Consumers' Emotional Attachments to Brands," *Journal of Consumer Psychology*, 15(1), 77-91.

What We Will Feel Depends on Who We Are: Cross-Cultural Differences in Affective Forecasting of "Ego-focused" Versus "Other-focused" Emotions

Vanessa Patrick, University of Georgia, USA
Henrik Hagtvedt, University of Georgia, USA

Abstract

In this research we aim to demonstrate that cross-cultural differences exist in the way individuals construct future events and consequently predict specific emotions. Five hundred and sixty-two participants from USA and India completed one of ten different versions of a questionnaire that varied 1) the positivity of the future experience, 2) whether the future experience was an individual vs. a group experience, and 3) familiarity with the future experience. Open-ended analysis is designed to reveal cross-cultural differences in the way future events are constructed. Quantitative assessment is designed to reveal differences in the forecasted emotions associated with these events.

There never was in the world two opinions alike, no more than two hairs or two grains; the most universal quality is diversity.
-Michel de Montaigne (1533-1592)

Recent research in consumer behavior has begun to examine the role of emotions in a cross-cultural context (Aaker and Maheshwaran 1997; Aaker and Williams 1998; Aaker and Lee 2001; Williams and Aaker 2002). However, the role of cross-cultural differences in the forecasting of emotions is an area that remains uninvestigated in the extant literature and forms the focus of the current research.

Affective Forecasting: Prediction of Future Affective States

A vast array of consumption activity is based on how consumers predict they are likely to feel at a future point in time. The choice and decision to consume is often based on a prediction of the emotional consequences of the consumption experience.

Affective forecasting (Gilbert et al. 1998) deals with a person's prediction of a future affective state. Recent research has demonstrated that making accurate affective forecasts is difficult and susceptible to a variety of errors and biases (Gilbert et al. 1998; Loewenstein and Schkade 2000) leading to affective misforecasting (Patrick, MacInnis, and Park 2007). Indeed, people exhibit what has been referred to as "impact" bias (Gilbert et al. 1998), where people tend to overestimate what the duration of their affective states will be, and "intensity" bias (Buehler and McFarland 2001), where people tend to overestimate the intensity with which they will experience a particular affective state.

In this research, we contribute to the extant research in two ways: 1) we investigate these biases in a cross-cultural context, and 2) we demonstrate these biases with specific emotions, namely ego-focused versus other-focused emotions.

Cross-cultural Differences in Affective Forecasting of Emotions

Extant research has demonstrated that the recognition and experience of many emotions appear to be cross-culturally robust. There has been support for the universality of basic emotions (Osgood, May, and Miron 1975), specific emotions like anger, surprise, fear, and empathy (Matsumoto 1989), and the recognition of these emotional states (Ekman 1984). However, significant cross-cultural differences do exist. Indeed, Triandis (1993) demonstrated that cross-cultural differences in emotions were a result of systematic cultural variations in the concerns of individuals, which in turn arose from differences in self-construal.

Based on this notion, cross-cultural research on emotions focused on "ego-focused" and "other-focused" emotions, and examined "the degree to which specific emotions systematically vary in the extent to which they follow from, and also foster or reinforce, an independent versus interdependent self" (Markus and Kitayama, 1991, p. 235). Thus, one would expect that in individualistic cultures (e.g., the United States, Western Europe, and Canada) the personal and subjective part of one's emotional experience is dominant, and "ego-focused" emotions like happiness, pride, frustration, and anger are more salient. On the other hand, in collectivist cultures (e.g., India, China, and Japan) the interpersonal and inter-subjective aspects of one's emotional experience is dominant, and "other-focused" emotions like empathy, guilt, and shame are more salient.

One might therefore posit that in predicting one's future emotional state (affective forecasting) people from different cultures would be likely to focus on different emotional/affective states, take into consideration different factors while making the affective forecast, and exhibit different errors or biases in their affective forecasts. The current thinking on the process of affective forecasting is that predictions of future affective states are made by conjuring up images of the future situation and predicting emotional reactions based on reactions to these images (Gilbert et al 2002).

Based on this we can expect that in individualist cultures the prediction of future affective states and subsequent decision to consume will be based solely on one's own personal tastes and preferences (happiness, pleasure, pride) while in collectivist cultures this prediction will also take into account the interpersonal and inter-subjective aspects of this decision (social approval, guilt, empathy).

Empirical Investigation and Data Analysis

This study employed a survey-based method designed to discern the categories of emotions that are forecasted and the nature of the thoughts associated with making the forecast for a variety of future events.

Five hundred and sixty-two participants (from India and USA) completed one of ten different versions of a questionnaire that asked individuals to forecast future experiences that varied 1) the positivity of the experience (e.g., restaurant vs. dentist visit), 2) whether the experience was an individual versus a group experience (e.g., a first job vs. a wedding), and 3) the familiarity of the experience (e.g., a vacation vs. winning the lottery). After constructing and describing the future experience, participants reported the extent to which they predicted a set of emotions would occur. Prediction of general positive and negative emotions, as well as ego-focused and other-focused emotions, was assessed. In addition, we measured individual differences in optimism, future orientation, and ability to consider future consequences. We expect that these variables in conjunction with the affective forecasts will help us discern cultural differences in individuals' ability to construct their future.

The analysis of both the quantitative and the qualitative aspects of the data are underway and will be completed by ACR 2008. The qualitative analysis has required the development of an extensive coding scheme to analyze the open-ended data. A brief summary of the preliminary quantitative results are outlined below:

- Participants in the individualist culture (USA) predicted more "ego-focused" versus "other-focused" emotions compared to participants in the collectivist culture (India)
- Participants in the individualist culture (USA) are more polarized in their affective forecasts (demonstrate a stronger impact bias) than participants in the collectivist culture (India). In other words, participants from individualist cultures predict more intense positive emotions for positive events and more intense negative emotions for negative events compared to collectivist cultures
- Participants in the individualist culture (USA) are more confident of their future feelings than participants in the collectivist culture (India)

Contributions of this research:

From a theoretical perspective, this research contributes to the extant literature by 1) demonstrating cross-cultural differences in the way future events are constructed, 2) introducing cross-cultural differences as an important variable that influences prediction of future affective states, and 3) demonstrating affective misforecasting biases for specific emotions, namely ego-focused versus other-focused emotions.

The Effects of Negative Feelings Caused by Forced Exposure to Banner Ads on Advertising Responses

Jung Ok Jeon, Pukyong National University, Korea
Hyun-Hee Park, Kyungpook National University, Korea
Jin-Hwa Lee, Pusan National University, Korea
Yoon-Ho Kim, Pukyong National University, Korea
Hee-Young Han, Pukyong National University, Korea

Most exposures to advertisements in traditional media occur at the same level of forced or intrusive exposure conditions. Unlike traditional media, the internet advertising makes it possible for the audience to be exposed to advertisements at many different levels of forced exposure. Moreover, as presentation techniques of the web rapidly advanced and sophisticated, the advertisers can generate different levels of advertising conditions. Despite such unique characteristics of the internet advertising, there are little research regarding the negative impact of different levels of forced exposure conditions on consumers' feelings, as well as on ad processing including avoidance behavior.

This study examines the possibility that the intensity level of forced exposure in banner ads may affect consumer's negative feelings, ad avoidance, and ad attitude. Especially this study sheds light on the moderating roles of negative feelings and ad avoidance. Based on literature review, it was hypothesized that: (H1) level of forced exposure and involvement would cause differences in relationships among negative feelings, ad avoidance, and ad attitude; (H2) negative feelings would be positively related to ad avoidance; and (H3) ad avoidance would be negatively related to ad attitude.

For the experiment, 2(forced level: no-skip 5" vs no-skip 10") x 2(involvement: high vs low) factorial designs were used. A total of 161 undergraduate students in Korea participated in the experiment. To represent different experimental conditions, two different types of banner presentation formats were created. For each condition, a pop-up window containing banner ad appeared when subjects opened the designated website. For the measure, negative feelings consisted of 3 dimensions: annoyance, irritation, and embarrassment. And, ad avoidance consisted of 2 dimensions: cognitive avoidance and physical avoidance.

It was found that the level of forced exposure showed significant differences in relationships among negative feelings, ad avoidance, and ad attitude. And, among negative feelings, feelings of annoyance significantly induced both of cognitive avoidance and physical avoidance, while irritation induced cognitive avoidance only. Also, both of ad avoidance dimensions negatively affected ad attitude. With the implications of these findings, extensive suggestions for future research are provided.

References

Aaker, Davis S. and Donald E. Bruzzone(1985), "Cause of Irritation in Advertising," *Journal of Marketing,* 49(2), 47-57.

_____, Douglad M. Stayman, and Michael R. Hagerty(1986), "Warmth in Advertising: Measurement, Impact, and Sequence Effects," *Journal of Consumer Research,* 12(March), 365-381.

Cho, Chang-Hoan, Jung-Gyo Lee, and Marye Tharp(2001), "Different Forced-Exposure Levels to Banner Advertisements," *Journal of Advertising Research, 41*(August), 45-56.

Cronin, John J. and Nancy E. Menelly(1992), "Discrimination vs. Avoidance: 'Zipping of Television Commercials," *Journal of Advertising,* 21(Summer), 1-7.

Edwards, Steven M., Hairong Li, and Joo-Hyun Lee(2002), "Forced Exposure and Psychological Reactance: Antecedents and Consequences of the Perceived Intrusiveness of Pop-Up Ads," *Journal of Advertising, 31(3),* 83-95.

Friestad, Marian and Peter Wright(1994), "The Persuasion Knowledge Model: How People Cope with Persuasion Attempts," *Journal of Consumer Research,* 21(June), 1-31.

Milward Brown Interactive(1999), *Evaluating the Effectiveness of the Superstitials,* Milward Brown Interactive, (October), [http://www.unicast.com/downloads/mbi.pdf].

Murry, John P., Jr, John L. Lastovicka, and Surendra N. Singh(1992), "Feeling and Liking Responses to Television Programs: An Examination of Two Explanations for Media Context Effects," *Journal of Consumer Research,* 18(March), 441-451.

Sherman, Lee and John Deighton(2001), "Banner Advertising: Measuring Effectiveness and Optimizing Placement," *Journal of Interactive Marketing, 15(2),* 60-64.

Consumers, Companies and Virtual Social Worlds: A Qualitative Analysis of Second Life

Andreas M. Kaplan, ESCP-EAP European School of Management, France
Michael Haenlein, ESCP-EAP European School of Management, France

When a company wishes to receive press coverage these days, a fairly safe bet is to announce corporate activities within the online application "Second Life". Second Life (SL) is a three-dimensional virtual social world that opened to the public in 2003 and in which users can interact with others in real time using personalized avatars. SL residents can explore their environment, meet and speak with each other and buy a wide variety of virtual products. The currency in SL is the Linden Dollar, which can either be obtained by exchanging US$ via the SL Exchange or by searching for a job for the avatar. More interestingly, Linden Dollars can also be re-exchanged into US$, making it possible to earn Real Life (RL) money by selling virtual products and services within SL.

SL is part of a group of Internet applications that can be subsumed under the term "virtual social worlds" and which can be considered as specific forms of virtual hyperrealities. Hyperrealities are one of the five conditions of postmodernism (e.g. Firat, Sherry, and Venkatesh 1994; Firat and Venkatesh 1993; Venkatesh, Sherry, and Firat 1993) and have previously been discussed in consumer research in the context of tourist attractions (e.g. Grayson and Martinec 2004) and media products (e.g. Rose and Wood 2005). We hypothesize that virtual social worlds offer unique benefits compared to traditional hyperrealities in the areas of marketing research and advertising. With respect to marketing research, we refer to Kozinets (2002) and his concept of netnography within online communities. Regarding advertising, we draw on previous literature showing that product placements in online games (e.g. Lee and Faber 2007; Nelson 2002) and virtual worlds (e.g. Schlosser 2003, 2006) positively impact brand attitudes and purchase intentions. However, despite these potential business benefits, few researchers have until now investigated consumer behavior within virtual social worlds.

Our analysis of SL is based on a series of 29 qualitative in-depth interviews with SL residents which we summarize in one integrated conceptual framework (e.g. Spiggle 1994). In the center of this framework is the SL resident, who appears in form of an avatar that can be considered as the virtual representation of an associated RL user. Similar to the RL user, who maintains a RL social network and RL exchange relationships with RL companies, the SL resident interacts as part of a SL social network and consumes products and services provided by SL stores. Such stores can either be set up and run by other SL residents (SL resident-owned stores) or be the virtual representations of RL companies within SL (SL flagship stores). This SL experience is connected to RL in two different ways: First, there is a potential connection between the SL resident and RL company if the latter uses Second Life for functions such as marketing research or the distribution of RL products (virtual commerce). Second, there can a connection between the RL user and the SL flagship store, for example if brand exposure within SL impacts RL purchase decisions similar to the effect of traditional or banner advertising.

Based on our conversations, we identify four key motivations for using SL: the search for diversion, the desire to build personal relationships, the need to learn and the wish to earn money. The first three motivations are similar to the gratifications sought from traditional mass media consumption (e.g. McQuail, Blumler, and Brown 1972), while the last one appears to be specific to SL. In line with previous findings in the context of personal webpages (Schau and Gilly 2003) there is a close resemblance between their RL personality and their SL avatar for some users, while for others there tends to be a substantial difference. The key social reference group for SL residents is their virtual friends within SL, while their RL friends are often unaware of their SL usage. Regarding purchase behavior, we observe impulse as well as planned purchases. This implies that at least for some part of their purchases SL users "plan ahead" before buying specific items, which closely mirrors behavior that can be observed in RL settings. SL users generally expect that the products available in SL flagship stores closely mirror the ones offered by the company in RL. This does not, however, imply that such products cannot be mildly adapted to the specific conditions of SL. Our interviews provided mixed support for ideas raised in the business press (e.g. Enright 2007) that companies could use their SL flagship stores to improve RL brand awareness, mainly because respondents stated to only rarely visit such stores. However, the idea of considering SL flagship stores as an extension of traditional e-Commerce activities and use them to distribute RL products generally seems to evoke positive reactions among SL users. Especially categories such as music, computers and books were named as prime examples for this form of distribution.

Overall, our analysis shows that users do not consider SL as a mere computer game, but as an extension of their RL. At some point (most likely with increasing usage intensity or consumption frequency), SL users seem to start engaging in activities that span beyond the single usage occasion so that the planning horizon that underlies SL usage goes beyond the actual time spent within the virtual social world. Regarding the business potential of this new medium, we find mixed support regarding SL's ability to influence RL brand attitudes and purchase intent. Simply setting up a flagship store within the virtual world is unlikely to be a promising advertising strategy. Instead, companies may need to supplement their virtual SL presence by regular events in order to maintain its attractiveness and attract a sufficient number of SL users. However, SL flagship stores could be used for the distribution of RL products and potentially help to overcome some of the drawbacks still associated with electronic mass customization (Kaplan and Haenlein 2006) and e-Commerce in certain product categories, such as the lack of physical product contact in the context of fashion items (Keeney 1999).

References

Enright, Allison (2007), "How the Second Half Lives," *Marketing news*, 41 (3), 12-14.
Firat, A. Fuat, John F. Jr. Sherry, and Alladi Venkatesh (1994), "Postmodernism, Marketing and the Consumer," *International journal of research in marketing*, 11 (4), 311-16.
Firat, A. Fuat and Alladi Venkatesh (1993), "Postmodernity: The Age of Marketing," *International journal of research in marketing*, 10 (3), 227-49.
Grayson, Kent and Radan Martinec (2004), "Consumer Perceptions of Iconicity and Indexicality and Their Influence on Assessments of Authentic Market Offerings," *Journal of consumer research*, 31 (2), 296-312.
Kaplan, Andreas M. and Michael Haenlein (2006), "Toward a Parsimonious Definition of Traditional and Electronic Mass Customization," *Journal of product innovation management*, 23 (2), 168-82.

Keeney, Ralph L. (1999), "The Value of Internet Commerce to the Customer," *Management science*, 45 (4), 533-42.

Kozinets, Robert V. (2002), "The Field Behind the Screen: Using Netnography for Marketing Research in Online Communities," *Journal of marketing research*, 39 (1), 61-72.

Lee, Mira and Ronald J. Faber (2007), "Effects of Product Placement in on-Line Games on Brand Memory," *Journal of advertising*, 36 (4), 75-90.

McQuail, Denis, Jay G. Blumler, and J. R. Brown (1972), "The Television Audience: A Revised Perspective," in *Sociology of Mass Communication*, ed. Denis McQuail, Harmondsworth: Pengium Books, 135-65.

Nelson, Michelle R. (2002), "Recall of Brand Placements in Computer/ Video Games," *Journal of advertising research*, 42 (2), 80-92.

Rose, Randall L. and Stacy L. Wood (2005), "Paradox and the Consumption of Authenticity through Reality Television," *Journal of consumer research*, 32 (2), 284-96.

Schau, Hope Jensen and Mary C. Gilly (2003), "We Are What We Post? Self-Presentation in Personal Web Space," *Journal of consumer research*, 30 (3), 385-404.

Schlosser, Ann E. (2003), "Experiencing Products in the Virtual World: The Role of Goal and Imagery in Influencing Attitudes Versus Purchase Intentions," *Journal of consumer research*, 30 (2), 184-98.

— (2006), "Learning through Virtual Product Experience: The Role of Imagery on True Versus False Memories," *Journal of consumer research*, 33 (3), 377-83.

Spiggle, Susan (1994), "Analysis and Interpretation of Qualitative Data in Consumer Research," *Journal of consumer research*, 21 (3), 491-503.

Venkatesh, Alladi, John F. Jr. Sherry, and A. Fuat Firat (1993), "Postmodernism and the Marketing Imaginary," *International journal of research in marketing*, 10 (3), 215-23.

Consumer Hope Scale: Development and Validation of Dispositional and Situational Measures

David Hardesty, University of Kentucky, USA
Blair Kidwell, University of Kentucky, USA
Jason Rowe, University of Kentucky, USA

Abstract

This research details the development and validation of measures to assess consumer hope. We develop both dispositional and situational measures to capture the three dimensions of hope; "to hope", "to have hope", and "to be hopeful." Results supported the scale's reliability and its discriminant and nomological validity. Our domain-specific dispositional consumer hope measure predicted consumer outcomes, such as subjective knowledge, better than domain-general alternatives. Furthermore, our context-specific situational consumer hope measure in the context of healthy food choice, predicted food-related outcomes such as impulsive eating, involvement toward food choices, and anticipated regret from making poor food choices, beyond alternatives.

Introduction

Recent work by MacInnis and colleagues (MacInnis and de Mello 2005; de Mello, MacInnis and Stewart 2007) has established the importance of hope in consumer research. Despite these contributions, an appropriate hope scale has yet to be developed and psychometrically assessed that can effectively distinguish hopeful from less hopeful consumers, and the important marketing outcomes that might result. Furthermore, researchers continue to pose questions for future research, such as, what is the role of hope in exchange relationships and how do consumers use hope to make decisions (de Mello, MacInnis and Stewart 2007). These questions have remained largely unanswered. Without the ability to recognize the hope of customers, and in turn, understand the ramifications of hopeful versus hopeless consumers, there remains a significant aspect of consumer behavior that is not only neglected and not well understood, but one that could provide meaningful prediction of important consumer outcomes.

In this research, we develop and validate two measures that assess related yet distinct aspects of consumer hope–dispositional and situational–that will allow researchers to extend our knowledge of consumer hope and further realize the important role hope plays in consumers achieving various outcomes such as purchase decisions, satisfaction, and subjective knowledge. With this knowledge of consumer hope, we may be better able to distinguish consumers who make the highest (and lowest) quality consumer decisions. In the next sections, we provide an overview of consumer hope, discuss dispositional and situational influences of hope, provide a three-dimension structure underlying consumer hope, and offer a rationale for how the consumer domain and the context of healthy eating provides specificity by which dispositional and situational hope measurement is needed.

Conceptualization

MacInnis and de Mello (2005) define hope as a positively valenced emotion evoked in response to an uncertain but possible goal-congruent outcome. Further, de Mello and MacInnis (2005) provide a three faceted conceptualization of the hope construct including "to hope", "to have hope", and "to be hopeful". The "to hope" facet is defined as "a positive emotion that varies as a function of the degree of yearning for a possible, goal-congruent, future outcome". The second facet, "to have hope", is viewed as "a positive emotion that arises when a goal-congruent future outcome is judged to be possible" while the final facet, "to be hopeful", is "a positive emotion that arises as a function of expectations regarding the likelihood of a possible future goal-congruent outcome".

We propose an overarching view of consumer hope in which it is divided into two basic categories–dispositional consumer hope (DCH) and situational consumer hope (SCH). We have developed two measures of consumer hope that tap into each of these levels of analysis. Dispositional consumer hope is a long-term, stable predisposition in individuals to view consumption experiences as either hopeful or hopeless. Our DCH scale is designed to be specific enough to capture the entire domain of consumer behavior, but more specific than domain-general measures of hope that capture less specificity of consumer outcomes.

Situational consumer hope is a relatively short-term affective reaction to a specific environmental stimulus. As opposed to DCH, which is longer lasting but more diffuse, SCH tends to have a clear cause or object and is more focused and intense. Our SCH scale, therefore, is designed to more precisely measure outcomes related to specific contexts, but less effectively assesses broader consumer outcomes.

Scaled Development Methodology

Taking into consideration the conceptualization of hope by MacInnis and de Mello (2005) and remaining consistent with the authors' theorizing, we treat the "to have hope" and "to be hopeful" dimensions as necessary elements for hope to exist. However, we focus our scale development on the "to hope" dimension as this is the dimension we believe is most relevant for consumer research. While we create measures for the "to have hope" and "to be hopeful" dimensions of consumer hope in order to ensure that hope exists, we focus most of our validation efforts on the "to hope" dimension.

We develop items tapping both dispositional and situational aspects of consumer hope. First, we use methodological procedures to generate and purify our initial pool of items. Next, we use data from study 1 to select items based on a battery of psychometric criteria. Then, study 2 data are subjected to confirmatory factor analysis to provide evidence regarding the unidimensionality, scale reliability, and discriminant validity of the dispositional and situational consumer hope measures. Data from both studies 1 and 2 are then analyzed to provide further evidence of discriminant validity and initial assessments of the nomological validity of the scales. Study 3 is currently underway to evaluate the predictive validity of the newly developed consumer hope scales and study 4 is planned for the purpose of providing evidence for construct validation of our two measures in a food choice context.

Major Findings

In study 1, evidence is provided that both dispositional and situational consumer hope discriminate from optimism, a global measure of state-based hope, a global measure of trait-based hope, and a global measure of hopelessness. In study 2, we first provide validation for the unidimensional structure of the consumer hope scales. We then show that the dispositional consumer hope measure predicts subjective knowledge and customer satisfaction better than an existing global hope scale and optimism and that the DCH scale is distinct from both the Herth Hope Scale (Herth 1991) and the Life Orientation Test (Scheier et al. 1994). Moreover, we show that the SCH measure using a healthy food context predicts involvement with food choices, anticipated regret from making bad food choices, and impulsive eating better than an existing global state-based measure and that the SCH scale is distinct from the Herth Hope Index (Herth 1992). The results of two additional studies are forthcoming. In study 3, the DCH and SCH measures will be assessed for predictive validity while in study 4; we aim to demonstrate the predictive ability of both scales in a consumer food choice context.

References

de Mello, Gustavo E. and Deborah J. MacInnis (2005), "Why and How Consumers Hope: Motivated Reasoning and the Market-place" in *Inside Consumption: Consumer Motives, Goals, and Desires*, ed. S. Ratneshwar and David Glen Mick, New York: Routledge, 44-66.

de Mello, Gustavo E., Deborah J. MacInnis, and David W. Stewart (2007), "Threats to Hope and Motivated Reasoning of Product Information," *Journal of Consumer Research*, 34 (August), 153-161.

Herth, Kaye (1991), "Development and Refinement of an Instrument to Measure Hope," *Journal of Scholarly Inquiry in Nursing*, 5 (1), 39-51.

Herth, Kaye (1992), "An Abbreviated Instrument to Measure Hope: Development and Psychometric Evaluation," *Journal of Advanced Nursing*, 17, 1251-1259.

MacInnis, Deborah J. and Gustavo E. de Mello (2005), "The Concept of Hope and Its Relevance to Product Evaluation and Choice," *Journal of Marketing*, 69 (January), 1-14.

Scheier, Michael F., Charles S. Carver, and Michael W. Bridges (1994), "Distinguishing Optimism from Neuroticism (and Trait Anxiety, Self-Mastery, and Self-Esteem): A Reevaluation of the Life Orientation Test," *Journal of Personality and Social Psychology*, 67 (6), 1063-1078.

Product Meaning and Consumer Creativity

Kelly Herd, University of Colorado, USA
Ethan Pew, University of Colorado, USA
Caleb Warren, University of Colorado, USA

Abstract

Product meanings are negotiated by a variety of social actors in a particular historical context. In this study we use a series of long interviews to explore product meanings actively created by consumers. We find that consumers create meaning through irony, through use innovation, and by adopting abandoned products. Consumers are motivated to create meaning because consumer-created meanings provide flexibility in constructing an identity, economic rewards, and intrinsic enjoyment. Leveraging creativity enables consumers to develop a space free from commoditized identities bartered in the marketplace.

Introduction

Consumer products are not merely commodities, but symbols consumers use to construct identities, strengthen relationships, and understand their social environment (Arnould and Thompson 2005; Hirschman and Holbrook 1982; Solomon 1983). Consumers interpret a product's meaning by associating the product with other cultural signs. These signs include its physical appearance, its intended purpose, the meanings established by manufacturers, and the personal identities and autobiographical memories linked to the product (Hirschman 1986; Hodder 2000; Mick 1986). To the extent that consumers can alter the signs associated with a product, they are able to create new product meanings.

Most product meanings are not created by individual consumers (McCracken 1986). More often meaning is shaped through a firm's branding efforts. For example, Wheaties is "The Breakfast of Champions," a meaning established through extensive athlete endorsements. Occasionally, however, consumers go beyond established interpretations to instill products with new meanings. For example, by converting Altoids tins into Buddhist shrines, HAM radios, or thumb pianos consumers cause the tins to become more than packaging for curiously strong mints.

There is growing interest in the role of consumer creativity as it relates to design (Moreau and Dahl 2005), product co-creation (Bendapudi and Leone 2003; Vargo and Lusch 2004) and innovation (Hirschman 1980). Yet limited research links creativity to the meaning creation process. Our study attempts to fill this gap by exploring the strategies and motivations that underlie consumer-created product meaning.

Method

The authors conducted depth interviews using a purposeful sample of six informants in the greater Denver area. Interviews followed methodological procedures outlined by McCracken (1988). Informants were asked a series of grand tour questions concerning their identity, sense of style, and methods of self-expression followed by more specific prompts.

We interpreted the interviews first by looking for emic meanings embedded in the text. We next searched for broader themes and categories emerging in the interviews, interpreting these in light of our pre-understanding shaped by the literature and our own experiences (Arnold and Fisher 1994).

Findings

Strategies

Our interviews revealed three partially overlapping strategies informants used to create product meaning: irony, use innovation, and adopting abandoned products.

Irony was achieved by using products with a dominant meaning in clever and unexpected ways. One informant described a bookcase built from bear traps welded to form supports for glass shelves. This one-of-a-kind piece contrasts sharp metal teeth with smooth glass playfully requiring the user to reach across powerful steel jaws to access books. Another informant described an outfit pairing a men's A-shirt, which she referred to as a "wife-beater," with a sequined shirt passed down from her grandmother. This combination created ironic tension by pairing the "wife-beater," a symbol of female submission in society generally associated with rural, working class men, with sparkle and flair, symbols more frequently tied to garishness and conspicuous fashion consumption.

Our informants relied on juxtaposed associations to create new meanings that abstract away from dominant interpretations. While the specific ironic meaning did not exist prior to the informants' creations, the formula of using tension to create meaning remains constant.

Informants also generated meaning by using products in ways not initially intended, a practice known as use innovation (Hirschman 1986). Given that a product's purpose largely determines its meaning, consumers create new meanings through new uses. Examples include a swim buoy used as a living room decoration and a lemon used as a cosmetic. A swim buoy means something very different when placed on a wall for aesthetic value than when placed on a ship deck for safety. Similarly, the interpretation of a lemon depends on its use.

A final way our informants created meaning was by adopting abandoned or cast-aside products. By adopting vintage clothing or obsolete electronics, and associating them with new people and new contexts, our informants created new meanings for these products.

Motivations

Informants reaped both intrinsic pleasure and economic benefits by creating product meanings. Informants described acts of meaning creation, such as turning a "scarf into a new window treatment," as an enjoyable way to spend free time. Informants who created meaning themselves avoided paying brand or fashion premiums and, in some cases, profited from reselling the fruit of their creation. One informant saved money by purchasing abandoned clothing at second-hand stores. Another profited directly by selling products infused with new meanings. Dan re-sold a generic $70 table purchased at Target for several hundred dollars after converting it to a custom made "Michael Jordan table" incorporating images from "his entire career."

Informants also created product meanings as a vehicle for controlling their identity. As product meanings are often leveraged in a quest to construct a self-image (Belk 1988), meaning creation affords consumers greater autonomy in shaping their identity. Creating novel product meanings enables consumers to construct a unique identity uncontaminated by meanings associated with undesirable, mainstream trends or commercialization. One informant sidestepped undesirable, dominant cultural meanings by purchasing obscure or second hand goods and by altering or combining products in ironic ways.

Discussion

This study hopes to illuminate an overlooked source of product meaning: consumer creativity. Through irony, use innovation, or by adopting abandoned products consumers can alter the signs, associations, and contexts of a product to establish new meanings. Given that identity is heavily shaped by possessions, meaning creation may be an essential step in developing a space free from the commoditized identities bartered in the marketplace (Firat and Venkatesh 1995; Kozinets 2002).

While this study represents an initial step towards understanding consumer-created meaning, many questions remain. To what extent do created meanings draw from existing, shared cultural understandings (Thompson et al. 1994)? Also, what types of consumers are most likely to create product meanings? Meaning creation may be especially prevalent amongst influential consumers (Gladwell 1997), consumers high in need for uniqueness (Tian et al. 2001), and consumers with above average cultural capital (Holt 1998). By continuing to pursue our study we hope to initiate an informative and enriching line of research furthering our understanding of consumer-created product meaning.

References

Arnold, Stephen J and Eileen Fisher (1994), "Hermeneutics and Consumer Research," *Journal of Consumer Research*, 21, 55-70.

Arnould, Eric J. and Craig J. Thompson (2005), "Consumer Culture Theory (CCT): Twenty Years of Research," *Journal of Consumer Research*, 31 (4), 484-505.

Belk, Russell W. (1988), "Possessions and the Extended Self," *Journal of Consumer Research*, 15, 139-68.

Bendapudi, Neeli and Robert P. Leone (2003), "Psychological Implications of Customer Participation in Co-Production," *Journal of Marketing*, 67 (1), 14-28.

Firat, W. Fuat and Alladi Venkatesh (1995), "Liberatory Postmodernism and the Reenchantment of Consumption," *Journal of Consumer Research*, 22 (3), 239-67.

Gladwell, Malcolm (1997), "The Coolhunt," The New Yorker, 11.

Hirschman, Elizabeth C. (1980), "Innovativeness, Novely Seeking, and Consumer Creativity," *Journal of Consumer Research*, 7 (3), 283-95.

_____ (1986), "The Creation of Product Symbolism," *Advances in Consumer Research*, 13 (1), 327-31.

Hirschman, Elizabeth C. and Morris B. Holbrook (1982), "Hedonic Consumption: Emerging Concepts, Methods, and Propositions," *Journal of Marketing*, 46 (3), 92-101.

Hodder, Ian (2000), "Interpreting Documents and Material Culture," in *The Sage Handbook of Qualitative Research*, Norman Denzin and Y. Lincoln, Eds. 3rd ed. Thousand Oaks, CA: Sage.

Holt, Douglas B. (1998), "Does Cultural Capital Structure American Consumption," *Journal of Consumer Research*, 25, 1-25.

Kozinets, Robert V. (2002), "Can Consumers Escape the Market? Emancipatory Illuminations fro Burning Man," *Journal of Consumer Research*, 29, 20-38.

McCracken, Grant (1986), "Culture and Consumption: A Theoretical Account of the Structure and Movement of the Cultural Meaning of Consumer Goods," *Journal of Consumer Research*, 13, 14.

_____ (1988), *The Long Inverview*. Thousand Oaks, CA: Sage Publications.

Mick, David Glen (1986), "Consumer Research and Semiotics: Exploring the Morphology of Signs, Symbols, and Significance," *Journal of Consumer Research*, 13, 196-212.

Moreau, C. Page and Darren W. Dahl (2005), "Designing the Solution: The Impact of Constraints on Consumers' Creativity," *Journal of Consumer Research*, 32 (1), 13-22.

Solomon, Michael R. (1983), "The Role of Products as Social Stimuli: A Symbolic Interactionism Perspective," *Journal of Consumer Research*, 10, 319-29.

Thompson, Craig J., Howard H Pollio, and William B Locander (1994), "The Spoken and the Unspoken: A Hermeneutic Approach to Understanding the Cultural Viewpoints That Underlie Consumers' Expressed Meanings," *Journal of Consumer Research*, 21, 432-52.

Tian, Kelly Tepper, William O. Bearden, and Gary L. Hunter (2001), "Consumers' Need for Uniqueness: Scale Development and Validation," *Journal of Consumer Research*, 28, 50-66.

Vargo, Stephan L. and Robert F. Lusch (2004), "Evolving to a Dominant Logic for Marketing," *Journal of Marketing*, 68, 1-17.

The Effects of Spoke-Avatars' Personalities on Source Expertise, Trustworthiness, and Attractiveness in the 3D Virtual Environment

Seung-A Jin, Boston College, USA
Yongjun Sung, The University of Texas at Austin, USA

Background

Second Life is the fastest growing virtual environment and has received considerable attention from researchers and practitioners in the fields of marketing and consumer behavior. To date, about 6.5 million people have entered *Second Life*, and the impact of this technology is beginning to be felt by society (Bainbridge 2007).

E-commerce already thrives in this digital world— approximately $1,199,460 was spent in one 24 hour period (*Second Life* 2007). One of the most distinguishing key features of *Second Life* is that users can navigate, interact, and view the world through their own customized avatar. Avatars are increasingly used as company representatives and persuasion agents on commercial Web sites and virtual environments (Holzwarth, Janiszewski, and Neumann 2006).

Theoretical Framework

The notion of inanimate objects, such as commercial brands, becoming associated with human characteristics has been given a considerable amount of attention in consumer research. This symbolic meaning that commercial brands acquire is often called *brand personality* (Aaker 1997). For example, a brand can be described by characteristics such as gender, age, social class, and lifestyle as well as classic human personality traits such as rugged (e.g., Harley Davidson), trendy (e.g., Apple), and sophisticated (e.g., Mercedes Benz).

This study aims to examine the relationship between symbolic consumption and consumer choice and to develop an understanding of what factors influence brand marketing and e-commerce in *Second Life*. This study empirically tests the role of brand personalities in persuasion and in the decision making process of the consumer. More importantly, the experiment was conducted in the avatar-based 3D virtual environment *Second Life*.

Although anthropomorphic qualities are most commonly associated with living creatures, consumers can also imbue non-human entities such as avatars with human personality traits. As sales representatives do in real life, avatars interact with consumers and make the online shopping experience more interpersonal (Holzwarth et al. 2006). Therefore, avatar-based 3D virtual environments are a promising marketing communications channel for brand management—not only online, but also in the real world— because marketers can effectively communicate personalities and images of their brands. Avatars are virtual sources or endorsers that can be used as company representatives. Thus, a company or brand's credibility can be created by any direct or indirect brand contact that the consumer experiences with avatars in virtual environments.

The purpose of the present study is to investigate the consequences of spokes-avatars' personalities on source credibility. More specifically, it conceptually links two streams of research (brand personality and source credibility) and examines the impact of two of Aaker's (1997) brand personality dimensions (Sincerity and Excitement) on three key constructs of source credibility: expertise, trustworthiness, and attractiveness. After reviewing prior research on brand personality and source credibility (e.g., Aaker 1997; Ohanian 1990), we predict that sincere spoke-avatars are more likely to be perceived as having source expertise (H1) and trustworthiness (H2) than exciting spoke-avatars, whereas exciting spoke-avatars are more likely to be perceived as having source attractiveness (H3) than sincere spoke-avatars. Towards the end, we conducted an experiment in the avatar-based 3D virtual environment *Second Life*.

Method

The present experiment is a two-group comparison design. Participants were 82 college students (43 females, 39 males) recruited from communication courses at a university in Massachusetts. We designed two different versions (featuring either an exciting or sincere spokes-avatar) of a 5-minute promotional script. We designed and manipulated the exciting avatar to appear young, trendy, unique, and contemporary. The avatar introduced itself by saying, "hi there! welcome to our store in second life!" and, then promoted the brand with an exciting tone consistent with the avatar's personality. On the contrary, we designed the sincere avatar to look honest, friendly, and wholesome. The avatar introduced itself by saying, "Hello. Welcome to our store in Second Life," and then promoted the brand with a sincere tone consistent with the avatar's personality. Subjects were told that they would be in a clothing store where they would interact with a sales-avatar, who would then tell them about online shopping inside *Second Life* and introduce a new line of clothes that the company had recently released. They were then asked to listen to the spokes-avatar's promotional dialogue and interact with it.

Results

To test the proposed hypotheses, a series of t-tests were conducted. Consistent with the predictions, the results indicated that subjects who interacted with sincere spoke-avatars showed higher scores for source expertise ($\alpha = .92$, $M_{expert} = 5.51$) and trustworthiness ($\alpha = .93$, $M_{trust} = 4.94$) than those who interacted with exciting spoke-avatars ($M_{expertise} = 4.79$, $t = 3.02$, $p < .01$; $M_{trust} = 4.24$, $t = 2.83$, $p < .01$), thereby supporting H1 and H2. Further, as predicted, the results suggest that subjects who interacted with exciting spoke-avatars showed higher scores for source attractiveness ($\alpha = .78$, $M_{attract} = 3.84$) than those who interacted with sincere spoke-avatars ($M_{attract} = 3.32$, $t = -2.01$, $p < .05$), thereby supporting H3.

Discussion

Despite the growing interest in the concept of brand personality, work in this area has been fairly limited and has made little progress in empirically supporting the importance of brand personality. Most of the research has focused on its structure and scales, but very limited research has empirically examined the consequences of brand personality. To fill the gap in the literature and expand application of brand personality to more diverse contexts (i.e., virtual environment and characters), this study investigated the predictive roles of spoke-avatars' personalities on key dimensions of source credibility. Our findings suggest that spoke-avatars' personalities can enhance source credibility in terms of expertise, trustworthiness, and attractiveness. The results showed that sincere avatars increased perceived source expertise and trustworthiness. Further, exciting avatars increased perceived source attractiveness.

From a managerial perspective, the findings of this study provide strategic insight into spoke-avatars and associated personality selection decisions. Avatars can serve as endorsers, sales agents, store assistants, and even as brands in virtual environments. Marketers can easily and effectively create, design, and manipulate spokes-avatars' personalities to convey personalities and images of products and companies, thereby increasing the persuasiveness of brand communications.

References

Aaker, Jennifer (1997), Dimensions of brand personality, *Journal of Marketing Research*, 34, 347-56.

Bainbridge, William Sims (2007), The scientific research potential of virtual worlds. *Science*, 317(5847), 472-76.

Holzwarth, Martin, Chris Janiszewski, and Marcus M. Neumann (2006), The influence of avatars on online consumer shopping behavior, *Journal of Marketing*, 70, 19-36.

Ohanian, Roobina (1990), Construction and validation of a scale to measure celebrity endorsers' perceived expertise, trustworthiness, and attractiveness, *Journal of Advertising*, 19, 39-52.

Second Life (2007), *Economic Statistics* Retrieved October 29, 2007, from http://secondlife.com/whatis/economy_stats.php

Are All Referrals Created Equal? The Impact of Social Connections on Consumer Discounts

Bryan R. Johnson, The Pennsylvania State University, USA
William T. Ross, Jr., The Pennsylvania State University, USA

Conceptualization

Throughout history, social relationships have played a critical role in facilitating communication and cooperation among individuals. Given their importance in social interactions, relationships possess the ability to shape various aspects of human behavior, including those related to consumption. Due to the important influence of these ties, many consumers incorporate relationships, either directly or indirectly, into purchasing products and services (Beaty et al. 1996; DiMaggio and Louch 1998). Accordingly, the purpose of this paper is to investigate the extent to which consumers receive benefits based on their structural relationships with firms, by identifying the economic impact of the different types of links (referrals) used to make purchases. More specifically, this paper examines how a referrer's connection to a firm (i.e., business relationship, personal relationship, customer relationship, etc.) impacts the size of the discount received by the consumer being referred. Interestingly, the basic question of whether or not consumers receive benefits based on structural relationships, including which connections have the greatest impact, has not been examined in the marketing literature. Nevertheless, given the extent to which consumers are socially connected to one another, and to firms, addressing this question is important if scholars are to understand the social dimension of consumer behavior.

To highlight the impact of social structure on discounts received by consumers, we draw upon social capital theory, which posits that individuals obtain benefits or returns as a result of their social relationships with others (Portes 1998; Lin 2001). In general, social capital theory focuses on the resources ingrained in an individual's social relationships and how these resources benefit the individual. These resources are considered social because they can only be accessed through direct and indirect ties with others. Common forms of social resources include advice, information, and ideas. Ultimately, to possess social capital, an individual must have relationships with others; it is only through social interactions that social capital can exist and provide benefits to individuals (Coleman 1988; Portes 1998; Lin 2001).

Scholars have explored the impact of social capital in a variety of settings within the social sciences (e.g., Lin and Huang 2005; Mouw 2003; Ream 2005; Seidel, Polzer, and Stewart 2000; Smoldt 1998). Although somewhat less prevalent, marketing scholars have also contributed to research in this area by highlighting the impact of social ties on consumption (Frenzen and Davis 1990; Brown and Reingen 1987; Reingen and Kernan 1986). To further contribute to theory in this developing research area, we highlight the economic consequences of using social ties to connect to firms. In the remainder of this paper, we evaluate the impact of a referrer's relationship to a firm on the consumer's discount, using a combination of qualitative and quantitative data. As the first of several studies, the main contribution of this research is that it demonstrates the economic impact of connecting to firms through various types of associations.

Method & Findings

The research site used for this case study, Car Concepts (a pseudonym), is a small automotive business located in the Western United States, specializing in basic to high-end products and services. This site is particularly appropriate for the current study because it is associated with an industry in which customers tend to rely heavily upon others to locate and connect to firms. Data for the study were drawn from the firm's archival records and from multiple interviews with the business owner between October and November 2007. These initial data include information for 35 consumers and the individuals who referred them to the firm. Additional data are currently being collected as part of an ongoing case study with the company.

To determine the impact of the referrer's relationship to the firm on the customers' discounts, we estimated an ordinal logit model with *customer discount* as the dependent variable and *referrer connection type* as the independent variable. We included *job size* and *customer type* as control variables. The results indicate that customers receive significantly smaller discounts when connecting through unknown individuals, through businesses, and through the firm's previous customers, than through those the owner deems to be friends. Stated differently, the odds of receiving larger discounts are much higher among those connecting through the owner's friends than through all other types of linkages to the firm. Amazingly, the average discount for those connecting through the owner's friends is $88, compared to $31, $12, and $7 for those connecting through previous customers, businesses, and unknown individuals, respectively. Clearly, our data strongly suggest that all referrals are not created equal.

Based on the overwhelming impact of friendship referrals, we conducted additional analyses among those customers connecting through friends of the owner. We created a cognitive friendship network, using the owner's perception of the relationships that existed among those he identified as friends. To construct this cognitive network, we asked the owner to identify whether or not each of the friends in his ego network were friends with one another, as done in previous research (Kilduff and Krackhardt 1994; Krackhardt 1990). We then used these responses to map the relationships among the owner's friends.

With this cognitive network in place, we used UCINET 6 to estimate the centrality of the owner's friends in the network. Then, we performed a median split to allocate these individuals to one of two categories: *central* or *non-central*. To test the impact of referrer centrality in the friendship network on the size of discounts received by customers, we estimated an ordinary least squares regression model with *customer discount* as the dependent variable, *referrer centrality* as the independent variable, and *job size* and *customer type* as control variables.

As expected, we find that customers receive significantly higher discounts when connecting through central friends than through non-central friends. After controlling for job size and customer type, the difference in the total discount received by customers who connect through a central versus a non-central referrer is approximately $107. Hence, while it is beneficial for consumers to connect to firms through friendship relationships, friends who are central in the friendship network tend to yield even greater benefits.

In summary, the main contribution of this research is that it demonstrates the economic impact of connecting to firms through various types of referral relationships. Our research not only confirms social capital theory's fundamental premise in the context of consumption, but it goes above and beyond the notion that individuals benefit from their social connections, by determining a dollar value associated with the different types of relationships employed in transactions with the focal firm. Although our findings emerge from a particular context, the theoretical implications of this study have broad applicability for consumer research.

References

Beaty, Sharon E., Morris Mayer, James E. Coleman, Kristy Ellis Reynolds, and Jungki Lee (1996), "Customer-Sales Associate Relationships," *Journal of Retailing*, 72 (3), 223-47.

Brown, Jacqueline Johnson and Peter H. Reingan (1987), "Social Ties and Word of Mouth Referral Behavior," *Journal of Consumer Research*, 14 (3), 350-362.

DiMaggio, Paul and Hugh Louch (1998), "Socially Embedded Consumer Transactions: For What Kinds of Purchases Do People Most Often Use Networks?" *American Sociological Review*, 63, 619-637.

Frenzen, Jonathan and Harry L. Davis (1990), "Purchasing Behavior In Embedded Markets," *Journal of Consumer Research*, 17 (1), 1-12.

Killduff, Martin and David Krackhardt (1994), "Bringing the Individual Back In: A Structural Analysis of the Internal Market for Reputation in Organizations," *Academy of Management Journal*, 37, 87-108.

Krackhardt, David (1990), "Assessing the Political Landscape: Structure, Cognition, and Power in Organizations," *Administrative Science Quarterly*, 35, 342-369.

Lin, Nan (2001), *Social Capital: A Theory of Social Structure and Action* (1 ed.). Cambridge: Cambridge University Press.

Lin, Shu-Chi and Yin-Mei Huang (2005), "The role of social capital in the relationship between human capital and career mobility: Moderator or mediator?" *Journal of Intellectual Capital*, 6 (2), 191-216.

Mouw, Ted (2003), "Social Capital and Finding a Job: Do Contacts Matter?" *American Sociological Review*, 68 (6), 868-98.

Portes, Alejandro (1998), "Social capital: Its origins and applications in modern sociology," *Annual Review of Sociology*, 24, 1-24.

Ream, Robert K. (2005), "Toward Understanding How Social Capital Mediates the Impact of Mobility on Mexican American Achievement," *Social Forces*, 84 (1), 201-24.

Reingen, Peter H. and Jerome B. Kernan (1986), Analysis of Referral Networks in Marketing: Methods and Illustration," *Journal of Marketing Research*, 23 (4), 370-378.

Seidel, Marc-David L., Jeffrey T. Polzer, and Katherine J. Stewart (2000), "Friends in high places: The effects of social networks on discrimination in salary negotiations," *Administrative Science Quarterly*, 45 (1), 1-24.

Smoldt, Robert K. (1998), "Turn word of mouth into a marketing advantage," *The Healthcare Forum Journal*, 41 (5), 47-49.

Understanding Why Temporally Myopic People Have More Credit Card Debt: Two Complementary Explanations

Jeremy Kees, Villanova University, USA
Jeff Joireman, Washington State University, USA
David Sprott, Washington State University, USA

Given the growing trend toward large credit card balances and confusion as to what types of information influence consumers' perceptions of credit card offers, it is important to examine predictors of credit card debt and how consumers process and utilize financial information on credit card offers. In the present paper, we focus on the role of one theoretically-relevant individual difference variable, the consideration of future consequences (CFC; Strathman et al. 1994). Individuals high in CFC are more likely to engage in a variety of personally-beneficial behaviors (for a review, see Joireman, Strathman, and Balliet 2006), and recent research has demonstrated that CFC can influence certain types of financial decisions (Joireman, Sprott, and Spangenberg 2005). While theory suggests a link between CFC and credit cards, no studies to date have not directly examined the relationship between CFC and actual credit card debt. We address this issue in the current research and also explore *why* CFC predicts credit card debt. In short, we focus on two possible explanations: first, CFC may predict compulsive buying which in turn predicts credit card debt; second, CFC may predict attraction to credit card offers, especially those promising immediate rewards (e.g., a $50 gift card after one's first purchase). In what follows, we briefly review work on CFC and fiscal responsibility, develop our hypotheses, and report two studies testing these hypotheses. We discuss the implications of our findings for both theory and practice.

Study 1

In Study 2, 84 participants completed the diagnostic screener for compulsive buying (DSCB; Faber and O'Guinn 1992), the CFC scale (Strathman et al. 1994), and reported their credit card debt. Originally, the CFC scale was reported to have a single underlying factor (Strathman et al. 1994). Recent research, however, suggests that the scale may contain two subscales, one comprised of the future-oriented items, which we will call CFC-Future, the other comprised of the immediate-oriented items, which we will call CFC-Immediate (Petrocelli 2003).

As expected, the CFC-Immediate subscale correlated significantly (and positively) with credit card debt. Findings also show that all of the CFC scales predicted compulsive buying, and compulsive buying was positively correlated with credit card debt. The pattern of results suggested that compulsive buying might mediate the relationship between CFC-Immediate and credit card debt. To test this mediation model, we conducted a two-step regression analysis predicting credit card debt. On Step 1, we entered CFC-Immediate. On Step 2, we entered compulsive buying. For mediation to hold, CFC-I should predict compulsive buying (which it does; $\beta=.50$, $p<.001$), CFC-I should predict credit card debt (which it does; $\beta=.24$, $p<.05$), compulsive buying should predict credit card debt (which it does;

?=.53, p<.001). Consistent with a full mediation model, the relationship between CFC-I and credit card debt became non-significant (?=-.04, p=.74) when compulsive buying was entered into the model (Baron & Kenny 1986). A Sobel (1982) test further confirmed that the reduction in the relationship between CFC-I and credit card debt was significant (z=3.63, p<.001). In summary, findings offer support for H2-H3 and partial support for H1.

Study 2

The goal of Study 2 was to evaluate whether those concerned with the immediate consequences of their actions would be more attracted to credit card offers that promised immediate rewards but implied long-term losses (i.e., through an extremely high interest rate). In Study 2, 145 participants participated in a 2 (temporal frame) X 2 (CFC) between-subjects experiment. The temporal frame of the offer was manipulated by altering the terms of the credit card offer; future orientation was a measured variable. For the temporal frame manipulation, participants were randomly assigned to one of two conditions. Participants assigned to the "short term gain / long term loss" framing condition or a "short term loss / long term gain" condition. We held constant the monetary benefits of the two credit card offers. After reading the credit card offer, participants indicated how likely they would be to apply for the credit card.

The analysis using the CFC-Immediate scale revealed a marginally significant main effect of condition $F(1, 142)$=2.88, p=.09, as well as a marginally significant interaction between CFC-Immediate and condition, $F(1, 142)$=2.77, p=.10. Follow-up analyses were run within each level of CFC-Immediate and within each temporal framing condition. Among those low in CFC-I, there was a significant preference for the credit card with the lower interest rate (STLoss-LTGain), $t(70)$=2.56, p=.02; in other words, they avoided the card with the short-term gain but a higher interest rate. However, among those high in CFC-I, there was no significant preference based on condition, $t(72)$<1; they liked each card equally. Within the STGain-LTLoss condition, those high in CFC-I were significantly more likely to apply for the card than those low in CFC-I, $t(70)$=2.26, p=.03. However, within the STLoss-LTGain condition, there was not a significant difference based on CFC-I, $t(72)$<1.

Brief Discussion

Findings from two studies provide insight into how consumer differences (i.e., CFC, compulsive buying) and types of information provided within credit card advertisements (e.g., fees, interest rates, and rewards) can influence consumers' financial decisions. Results across two studies were largely supportive that CFC can predict credit card debt (Study 1) and can impact evaluations of credit card offers (Study 2). Results are consistent with conceptualization of the CFC construct and prior CFC research in that some consumers tend to do a better job recognizing actions or behaviors that might jeopardize their long-term well-being. In addition to extending work on CFC, the present work also contributes to a better understanding of compulsive buying behavior.

The Effects of Implicit Color Preference and Implicit Racial Preference on Implicit Attitude towards the Ad

Ioannis Kareklas, University of Connecticut, USA
Robin Coulter, University of Connecticut, USA

Choosing an appropriate spokesperson is a critical decision for advertisers, given the mounting evidence in the persuasion literature which suggests different sources delivering the same message produce varied outcomes among recipients (Whittler and Spira 2002). Spokespersons who are perceived to be more credible, attractive, and similar to recipients are typically more persuasive (for a review, see Eagly and Chaiken 1993). In the context of ethnicity, extant research (using explicit measures) suggests that consumers respond more favorably (generate more positive advertisement and brand evaluations) to persuasive messages delivered by spokespersons of similar race (for a review, see Whittler 1991).

An important caveat regarding earlier work in this domain is that the bulk of this research has employed explicit (i.e., self-report) measures, which may suffer from response biases because the topic of race is socially sensitive, and explicit measures allow participants to consciously control their responses (Ashburn-Nardo, Knowles, and Monteith 2003; Brunel, Tietje, and Greenwald 2004). More recent work has employed implicit measures such as the Implicit Association Test (IAT; Greenwald, McGhee, and Schwartz 1998) to circumvent such response biases. Findings suggest that both Black and White participants exhibit an automatic "pro-White" preference when asked to sort Black versus White racial stimuli (Banaji, Greenwald, and Rosier 1997; Nosek, Banaji, and Greenwald 2002).

Additionally, research on the neural basis of social group processing has found that indirect measures of race evaluation correlate with functional magnetic resonance imaging (fMRI)-assessed activation of the amygdala (Phelps et al. 2000). Given that the amygdala is known to be involved in responding to threatening and to novel stimuli, and since research has shown that both Black and White participants demonstrate greater amygdala activity to unknown Black faces than to unknown White faces, Lieberman et al. (2005) posit that amygdala activity associated with race-related processing may be a manifestation of "culturally learned negative associations regarding African-American individuals." This explanation is consistent with System Justification Theory (SJT; Jost and Banaji 1994), which has previously been used to explain why Black participants exhibit a lack of ingroup preference in implicit racial evaluations (e.g., Brunel et al. 2004).

SJT posits that people are motivated to believe in a just world, and that a history of discrimination can lead even minorities to internalize negative attitudes toward their own groups as a means of justifying the status quo (Rudman, Feinberg, and Fairchild 2002). Jost and Banaji (1994) emphasize that such attitudes and the motive to sustain them are likely to be nonconscious, which explains why this phenomenon may not be picked up by self-report measures, but can be unearthed by implicit measures (Rudman, Feinberg, and Fairchild 2002).

Within the advertising context, Brunel et al. (2004) using the IAT found that White participants exhibited a significant implicit preference for ads that featured a White (vs. Black) spokesperson, but no significant explicit preference, whereas Black participants exhibited a significant explicit preference for Black spokespersons but no significant implicit preference between Black and White spokespersons. These findings underscore the importance of utilizing implicit measures to assess the effectiveness of advertisements that feature spokespersons that are of a similar (vs. different) race than the target audience.

Research suggests that another variable that may impact consumers' evaluations of African-American and White-American spokespersons is their implicit color preference for the color white as compared to the color black. Specifically, in the United States and many other countries, the cultural associations related to the color white are more positive, whereas the associations with the color black are more negative (Smith-McLallen et al. 2006). Williams, Tucker, and Dunham (1971) note that the color white has been used in religion, literature, and the mass media as a symbol of "goodness," while the color black has been used as a symbol of "badness." Similarly, Longshore (1979) observes that white is used to connote decency and purity, while black is used to connote evil and disgrace.

The purpose of this paper is to develop a theoretical model of the effects of implicit racial preference (IRP) and implicit color preference (ICP) on consumers' implicit attitude towards the ad (IAad). The aforementioned literature suggests that consumers' advertising evaluations are likely to be impacted by their implicit racial preference and their implicit color preference. Thus, we posit the following:

H1: Regardless of race, participants will exhibit an implicit racial preference for stimuli illustrating White-American (vs. African-American) faces.

H2: Regardless of race, participants will exhibit an implicit preference for advertisements featuring White-American (vs. African-American) spokespersons.

H3: Implicit racial preference will have a direct and positive effect on participants' implicit advertising evaluations, such that participants who implicitly prefer White-American (African-American) faces will also implicitly prefer ads that feature White-American (African-American) spokespersons.

H4: Regardless of race, participants will exhibit an implicit color preference for the color white as compared to the color black.

H5: Implicit color preference will have a direct and positive effect on participants' implicit racial preference, such that participants who implicitly prefer the color white (black) will also implicitly prefer White-American (African-American) faces.

H6: Implicit color preference will have a direct and positive effect on participants' implicit advertising evaluations, such that participants who implicitly prefer the color white (black) will also implicitly prefer White-American (African-American) spokespersons.

H7: Implicit racial preference will partially mediate the effect of implicit color preference on participants' implicit advertising evaluations, such that controlling for participants' implicit racial preference will reduce the effect of their implicit color preference on their implicit advertising evaluations.

We propose testing our hypotheses using three IAT procedures: an implicit color preference IAT, an implicit racial preference IAT, and an implicit attitude toward the ad IAT. Equal samples of Black and White participants will be recruited. As a consequence of our research, we will be able to provide insights about the respective individual and joint effects of implicit color preference and implicit racial preference on attitudes toward advertisements featuring White or Black spokespersons, as well as provide guidance related to the development of ads that feature Black or White spokespersons targeting Black or White consumers.

References

Ashburn-Nardo, Leslie, Megan L. Knowles, and Margo J. Monteith (2003), "Black Americans' Implicit Racial Associations and Their Implications for Intergroup Judgment," *Social Cognition*, 21 (1), 61-87.

Banaji, Mahzarin R., Anthony G. Greenwald, and M. Rosier (1997), "Implicit Esteem: When Collectives Shape Individuals," in *Self & Identity Preconference* Toronto.

Brunel, Frederic F., Brian C. Tietje, and Anthony G. Greenwald (2004), "Is the Implicit Association Test a Valid and Valuable Measure of Implicit Consumer Social Cognition?," *Journal of Consumer Psychology*, 14 (4), 385-404.

Eagly, Alice H. and Shelly Chaiken (1993), *The Psychology of Attitudes*, Fort Worth, TX Harcourt Brace Jovanovich College Publishers.

Greenwald, Anthony G., Debbie E. McGhee, and Jordan L. K. Schwartz (1998), "Measuring Individual Differences in Implicit Cognition: The Implicit Association Test," *Journal of Personality and Social Psychology*, 74 (6), 1464-80.

Jost, John T. and Mahzarin R. Banaji (1994), "The Role of Stereotyping in System-Justification and the Production of False Consciousness," *British Journal of Social Psychology*, 33 (1), 1-27.

Lieberman, Matthew D., Ahmad Hariri, Johanna M. Jarcho, Naomi I. Eisenberger, and Susan Y. Bookheimer (2005), "An Fmri Investigation of Race-Related Amygdala Activity in African-American and Caucasian-American Individuals," *Nature Neuroscience*, 8 (6), 720-22.

Longshore, Douglas (1979), "Color Connotations and Racial Attitudes," *Journal of Black Studies*, 10 (2), 183-97.

Nosek, Brian A., Mahzarin Banaji, and Anthony G. Greenwald (2002), "Harvesting Implicit Group Attitudes and Beliefs from a Demonstration Web Site," *Group Dynamics: Theory, Research, and Practice*, 6 (1), 101-15.

Phelps, Elizabeth A., Kevin J. O'Connor, William A. Cunningham, E. Sumie Funayama, J. Christopher Gatenby, John C. Gore, and Mahzarin R. Banaji (2000), "Performance on Indirect Measures of Race Evaluation Predicts Amygdala Activation," *Journal of Cognitive Neuroscience*, 12 (5), 729-38.

Rudman, Laurie A., Joshua Feinberg, and Kimberly Fairchild (2002), "Minority Members' Implicit Attitudes: Automatic Ingroup Bias as a Function of Group Status," *Social Cognition*, 20 (4), 294-320.

Smith-McLallen, Aaron, Blair T. Johnson, John F. Dovidio, and Adam R. Pearson (2006), "Black and White: The Role of Color Bias in Implicit Race Bias," *Social Cognition*, 24 (1), 46-73.

Whittler, Tommy E. (1991), "The Effects of Actors' Race in Commercial Advertising: Review and Extension," *Journal of Advertising*, 20 (1), 54-60.

Whittler, Tommy E. and Joan Scattone Spira (2002), "Model's Race: A Peripheral Cue in Advertising Messages?," *Journal of Consumer Psychology*, 12 (4), 291-301.

Williams, John E., Richard D. Tucker, and Frances Y. Dunham (1971), "Changes in the Connotations of Color Names among Negroes and Caucasians: 1963-1969," *Journal of Personality and Social Psychology*, 19 (2), 222-28.

Integral Affect and Attitude Strength in a Health Communications Context

Monica LaBarge, University of Montana, USA

An ongoing goal of practitioners and academics interested in health communications has been to improve their effectiveness (Keller and Lehmann, 2008). Research on the message effectiveness of health communications has largely focused on two major types of influences: 1) message characteristics such as positive versus negative framing, vividness, presentation of statistics, argument strength, and source effects; and 2) individual difference variables such as race, gender, need-for-cognition, regulatory focus, and involvement (Keller & Lehmann working paper). A variable that has been explored on a relatively limited basis in comparison to these other factors is the role of affect, and integral affect in particular, in influencing attitudes to health communications.

This is in spite of the contention by researchers that integral affect should be a relatively important influence in the context of health-related attitudes and decisions because of the very personal and potentially serious consequences associated with health behaviors (Slovic et al. 2005, Luce 2005). Research directed towards improving the effectiveness of health communications has explored the influence of affect in two primary ways. The majority of research on affect in this area has examined how antecedent mood states influence individuals' responses to health communications (Keller et al. 2003). A second stream of research has explored how the emotional presentation of information, such as the use of fear appeals or the vividness of the message (Keller 1999, Rothman and Salovey 1997), influence subsequent reactions to and perceptions of the message. With respect to information processing, Schwarz and Clore (1996) suggest that the role of affect can be framed in terms of two general streams: 1) an experiential approach that postulates an informational role of subjective experiences, including moods, emotions, bodily sensations, and cognitive experiences; and 2) a cognitive approach, which explores the impact of affective states on the content of thoughts rather than on the actual experience of thinking. Within the first stream, relatively little research has been directed towards improving our understanding of the hardwired, automatic (also called "somatic") processes that reflect affect. Within the somatic processes, the influence of affect includes not only emotion states stimulated by bodily processes, but also includes affect triggered by features of a stimulus that in turn activate schematic structures linked through conditioning to particular emotional responses (Pham 2004). The affect that is stimulated within an individual in response to an object or message can be termed integral affect. It is this internally-generated affect that is of interest in the current research.

The current research examines two research streams with respect to the role they each assign to integral affect in the processes of attitude formation. The first stream of research, based on the Elaboration Likelihood Model, has found that processing dominated by affect produces relatively weak attitudes compared to more cognitive processing. The second stream of research, based on the affect heuristic and two-systems theory, has determined that integral affective responses may be particularly important in situations where the decision to be made is extremely important and personally-relevant, or when the information presented is very complex and unfamiliar, as is frequently the case in the context of health-related choices (Slovic et al. 2005). Given these conflicting perspectives and a lack of empirical research that specifically investigates the strength of affectively-based attitudes, there appears to be a need for further exploration of how integral affective responses influence important persuasion-related variables such as attitude formation and attitude strength.

A series of laboratory experiments conducted with undergraduates at a major public university explored differences in affectively- and cognitively-based attitudes developed in response to health-related advertising. These differences were examined in measures of intention to engage in the advocated behavior; two measures of attitude strength (persistence and resistance), and three measures of attitude: overall attitude, and the affective and cognitive components of attitude.[1] Affectively-based attitudes were shown across studies to be stronger than cognitively-based attitudes for the measures of overall attitude and the cognitive component of attitude. The affective attitude component did not change significantly over time or in response to an attack, regardless of whether the attitude was initially formed based on affect or cognition. This suggests that the affective component of attitude is particularly stable when compared to overall attitudes and the cognitive component of attitude. In general, intentions to seek out information about or engage in the behavior advocated by the ad were more favorable for individuals in the affectively-based attitude condition. Together these results can be interpreted as supporting the contention of this research that affectively-based attitudes are more persistent over time and resistant to change and that intentions will be more favorable among individuals who hold affectively- than cognitively-based attitudes.

An additional methodological contribution of this research was to test a promising but relatively unproved experimental method for strengthening affectively-based attitudes (Peters and Slovic 2007). Elaboration tasks intended to strengthen the cognitive basis of an attitude, such as thought listings, have been well-validated (Petty et al. 1995), but few options have existed for similar strengthening of an affectively-based attitude. The goal of the silent feeling elaboration task employed in this study was to reduce disruption of affective processes underlying affectively-based attitudes, thus allowing for the maintenance of the affective basis of the attitude. Preliminary

---

[1]This separation of attitude into three components is consistent with Crites et al. (1994), Fabrigar and Petty (1999), Verplanken et al (1998), and Peters et al. (forthcoming), and the methodology used to measure and analyze these components was also consistent with these authors.

results show that the silent feeling task was successful in strengthening affectively-based attitudes, facilitating accurate comparison of the persistence of affectively- and cognitively-based attitudes.

Selected References

Crites, Stephen L., Leandre R. Fabrigar, and Richard E. Petty (1994), "Measuring the Affective and Cognitive Properties of Attitudes: Conceptual and Methodological Issues," *Personality and Social Psychology Bulletin*, 20 (6), 619-634.

Fabrigar, Leandre R. and Richard E. Petty (1999), "The Role of Affective and Cognitive Bases of Attitudes in Susceptibility to Affectively and Cognitively Based Persuasion," *Personality and Social Psychology Bulletin*, 25 (3), 363-81.

Keller, Punam Anand (1999), "Converting the Unconverted: The Effect of Inclination and Opportunity to Discount Health-Related Fear Appeals," Journal of Applied Psychology, 84 (3) 403-15.

Keller. Punam Anand and Donald R. Lehmann, (2008), "Designing Effective Health Communications: A Meta-Analysis," *Journal of Public Policy & Marketing*, 27 (2), 117-30.

Keller, Punam Anand, Isaac Lipkus and Barbara Rimer (2003), "Affect, Framing and Persuasion," *Journal of Marketing Research*, 40 (1), 54-65.

Luce, Mary Frances (2005), "Decision Making as Coping," *Health Psychology*, 24 (4), S23-28.

Peters, Ellen, Nathan Dieckmann, Daniel Vastfjall, C.K. Mertze, Paul Slovic, and Judith Hibbard (forthcoming), "Bringing Meaning to Numbers: The Functions of Affect in Choice," *Journal of Experimental Psychology: General*.

Peters, Ellen and Paul Slovic (2007), "Affective Asynchrony and the Measurement of the Affective Attitude Component," *Cognition & Emotion*, 21 (2), 300-329.

Petty, Richard E., Curtis P. Haugtvedt, and Stephen M. Smith (1995), "Elaboration as a Determinant of Attitude Strength: Creating Attitudes that are Persistent, Resistant and Predictive of Behavior," in *Attitude Strength: Antecedents and Consequences*, ed. Richard E. Petty and Jon A. Krosnick, Hillsdae, NJ: Lawrence Erlbaum Associates, 93-130.

Pham, Michel Tuam (2004), "The Logic of Feeling," *Journal of Consumer Psychology*, 14 (4), 360-69.

Rothman, Alexander J. and Peter Salovey (1997), "Shaping Perceptions to Motivate Healthy Behavior: The Role of Message Framing," *Psychological Bulletin*, 121 (1), 3-19.

Schwarz, Norbert, and Gerald L. Clore (1996), "Feelings and Phenomenal Experinces," in *Social Psychology: Handbook of Basic Principles*, ed. E. Tory Higgins and Arie W. Kruglanski, New York: Guilford Press, 433-65.

Verplanken, Bas, Godelieve Hofstee, and Heidi J. Janssen (1998), "Accessibility of Affective versus Cognitive Components of Attitude," *European Journal of Social Psychology*, 28 (1), 23-35.

Blurring the Boundaries between Real and Virtual: Consumption Experiences and the Self Concept in the Virtual World

Ereni Markos, University of Massachusetts, Amherst, USA
Lauren Labrecque, University of Massachusetts, Amherst, USA

Introduction

Millions of people currently have accounts in virtual worlds such as Second Life (SL). Members of these online communities customize avatars that can mimic real world activities such as shopping, socializing at a bar, going to the beach, driving a car, engaging in an intimate relationship as well as countless of other endeavors. In a commercial website, avatars enhance a shopping experience by serving as guides, conversation partners, and personal shopping assistants (Holzwarth, Janiszewski, & Neumann, 2006). In a virtual setting the key element is the user and as such users design virtual representations of themselves, to function and interact with other avatars in order to keep this world alive.

Virtual worlds are revolutionizing the online experience by extending the Web from a two dimensional platform to a three dimensional one. These platforms are growing in size and number at an exponential rate, creating an increased interest among businesses and the marketing community (Carr 2007; Kirkpatrick 2007; Stein 2006; Reena and Aili 2006). Interestingly, past research has shown that marketers see benefits in studying online communities as a tool in understanding consumption behavior (Kozinets 1999, 2002; Bromberg 1996; Muniz and O'Guinn 2001; Armstrong and Hagel 1996).

Our study focuses on one of the most rapidly growing virtual worlds, Second Life. The purpose of this paper is to better understand what drives virtual consumption and how these experiences play out in the virtual world and influence consumption in the real world. Further, drawing on the self concept theory we explore the implications in a virtual setting. We begin our investigation by conducting an exploratory study to learn more about SL and its residents. In our second study (ongoing), we create a survey instrument and collect data from residents in Second Life both inside and outside of the virtual world.

Methodology

In study 1 we explore SL by use of qualitative research methods. We employ a combination of structured and dialogic interviews coupled with participant observation to capture meaningful information. Research within virtual worlds is a relatively new area where 'there is no established precedent as to how to collect data' (Ward 1999). Research suggests that an efficient manner to gather data and conduct research in a virtual community is through using participant observations (Kozinets 2002; Reid 1995) and informal interviews (Turkle 1996).

In order to perform Study 1 we created two separate SL accounts (one for each author) and designed our unique avatars. Prior to interviewing, we spent time familiarizing ourselves with the landscape, etiquette, and functionality of SL. Throughout the research period, we established relationships with many residents, were invited into their SL homes and were introduced to their SL community and friends. Our exploration in SL spanned a one month period, consisting of daily visits and interviews. Research was performed throughout the day to accommodate SL's 24 hour global access. The overall approach was to enter SL, go to stores or locations where there were other avatars, engage in unstructured dialogs, record conversations and capture moments with photos. Our conversations were conducted through a text based instant messaging interface, however after our initial research VOIP was added as an option and will be used in subsequent studies. Photo elicitation served as another means of collecting data in our study. During conversations with residents we captured our interactions by using the photo feature enabled in the SL interface. Notably there is a built in option that enables this function, therefore most residents are aware of this and most were welcoming. Finally, we disclosed that we were conducting research and received verbal consent to use residents' comments.

Preliminary findings

Our initial findings suggest that in SL one can live out desires and seemingly unattainable dreams. Extant research shows that desires and fulfillment of fantasies serve as the impetus for many consumption activities (Belk, Ger, and Askergaard 2003). Virtual worlds are ripe with occasions to engage in behavior to fulfill these types of longings. For instance, we frequented an island where residents shared a love for Greece and her culture. This island mirrors a traditional Greek island with blue and white buildings, turquoise water, Greek music and activities particular to this culture. Even though we are thousands of miles away from Greece we felt as if we were on a sun-drenched island on the Mediterranean Sea. Regardless of the backdrop people can purchase villas, motorcycles, convertible cars, appliances, accessories, clothes and luxury services similar to the real world but at a minuscule price.

Exploring different facets of oneself is within reach and an exciting feature of virtual worlds (Turkle 1995). Applying Belk's (1988) concept of the extended self, virtual possessions can "symbolically extend the self", which he states "allows us to do things which we would otherwise be incapable" (Belk 1988 p.145). Whether it's an avatars form, a sports car, a villa, or an island, these possessions allow users to explore different facets of their identity. The ability to customize an avatar allows one to explore ethnicity, gender and other aspects of self. One resident elaborated on the freedom SL allows to explore gender and race. Even though he is a man in RL he tried out the role of woman. He also spoke about changing his racial identity and his ability to be more social on SL. Since SL is a computer mediated environment people are seemingly less inhibited and more inclined to experiment outside societal norms and possibilities.

Our findings show that people embrace the opportunity to explore their creativity and support the notion that in SL dreams become reality and consumption based daydreams that are otherwise unfeasible are attainable (Molesworth 2006). A user can experience what it feels like to fly, cross gender boundaries or even live out a non-human existence (many users create avatars that take on the form of an animal, alien or other creatures). Ultimately, anything is possible in a virtual world.

In our follow-up study (Study 2), which is still on-going, we conduct survey research of Second Life residents, using a participant panel. This second data collection will be used to gain a better understanding of how virtual worlds can be used to explore the self and how this ties into both virtual and real life consumption.

References

Armstrong, Arthur and John Hagel III (1996), "The Real Value of On-line Communities," *Harvard Business Review,* 74 (May/June), 134-141.

Belk, Russell W. (1988), "Possessions and the Extended Self," *Journal of Consumer Research,* 15 (September), 139-168.

Belk, Russell, Guliz Ger and Soren Askegaard (2003), "The Fire of Desire: A multisided Inquiry into Consumer Passion," *Journal of Consumer Research,* 30 (December), 326-351.

Bromberg, Heather (1996), "Are MUDs communities: identity, belonging and consciousness in virtual worlds," In R. Shields (Ed.), *Cultures of Internet.* London: Sage.

Carr, David F. (2007), "Is Business Open for Second Life?" *Baseline,* (70), 30-47.

Holzwarth, Martin, Chris Janiszewski and Marcus M. Neumann (2006), "The Influence of Avatars on Online Consumer Shopping Behavior," *Journal of Marketing,* 70 (4), 19-36.

Kirkpatrick, David (2007), "It's Not a Game," *Fortune,* 155(2), 56.

Kozinets, Robert V. (1999), "E-Tribalizing Marketing? The Startegic Implication of Virtual Communities of Consumption," *European Management Journal,* 17(3), 252-264.

Kozinets, Robert V. (2002), "The Field Behind the Screen: Using Netnography for Marketing Research in Online Communities," *Journal of Marketing Research,* 29(1), 61-72.

Molesworth, Mike (2006), "Real brands in imaginary worlds: investigating players' experiences of brand placement in digital games," *Journal of Consumer Behavior,* 5 (4), 355.

Muniz, Albert M., Jr. and Thomas O'Guinn C. (2001), "Brand Community," *Journal of Consumer Research,* 27 (March), 412-432.

Reena, Jana and Ailli McConnon (2006),"Second Life Lessons," *Businessweek,* (4011), 17.

Reid, Elizabeth (1995), "Virtual worlds: culture and imagination," In S. Jones (Ed.), *Cybersociety: Computer Mediated Communication and Community,* London: Sage.

Stein, Joel (2006), "My So-Called Second Life," *Time,* 168(26), 76.

The Economist (2006), Special Report: Living a Second Life-Virtual online worlds. *The Economist,* 380(8497), 98.

Turkle, Sherry (1996), *Life on Screen: Identity in the Age of the Internet,* London: Weidenfeld and Nicholson.

Ward, Katie (1999), "Cyber-ethnography and the emergence of the virtually new community," *Journal of Information Technology,* 14, 95-105.

Theoretical Foundation of Brand Personality for Postmodern Branding Dynamics: A Critical Review and Research Agenda

Eun-Jung Lee, Kent State University, USA

Abstract

This article attempts to contribute to a solid theoretical base for postmodern branding dynamics with a mediation of a popular market-oriented branding concept: *brand personality*. While re-illuminating market-oriented functions and common misconceptions about brand personality and discussing the limitation of its prevailing theoretical approach, a new and expansive conceptual ground has been suggested for brand personality upon *the theory of consumption symbolism*, a rising sub-stream in the consumer research literature, which speculates upon the meaning production and consumption in the postmodern marketplace. Based on its marketing-homegrown and interdisciplinary perspectives, some new research agendas have been suggested for the future academic approaches for deepening the academic understandings of the dynamics of brand personality and of the postmodern branding.

1. Conceptual Foundation

1.1 Brand personality in postmodern branding dynamics

Meanings of products play a critical role in contemporary consumers' choices. In the postmodern marketplace, commercial goods often perform as social identity markers, as well as carriers of functional qualities (McCracken, 1986). With a myriad of diverse meanings and symbols floating in the marketplace, consumers need heuristics for their decision-making regarding such non-utilitarian product— and brand—attributions. Marketers and managers need to make their branding activities compatible with their customers' interests (e.g., Solomon, 2003), and they require a systematic and organization-wide management for non-utilitarian facets of a brand. Brand personality has been devised and gradually elaborated upon to fulfill some of those needs in a more structured manner.

Brand personality, generally referring to the human characteristics associated with a brand (e.g., Aaker, 1997), is a branding concept that explains a facet of branding dynamics (e.g., Batra et al., 1993; Carr, 1996; Kapferer, 1998; Upshaw, 1995; Keller, 2001; 2003) which is about (some) non-utilitarian brand attributions (e.g., Keller, 1993). Brand personality is the core of postmodern branding dynamics, which fulfills a multi-faceted function in consumer-organization as well as within-organization communications (Davis, 2000; Aaker & Joachimsthaler, 2000; Silverstein & Fiske, 2005). Brand personality serves as an effective consumer-organization communication tool. It allows an organization to identify consumers' brand perceptions–even the hidden ones–by its projection techniques with (human) metaphor (Dent-Read & Szokolszky,1993; Zalthman, 1997). Marketers can then use consumers' perceptions to make their marketing strategies become more focused on consumers. It also provides a useful research method for consumer studies. On the other hand, brand personality serves as an organization-wide guide for brand meaning communication. It helps marketers communicate brand meaning which otherwise might not be easy to understand and/or share (among marketers). By adding robust, descriptive, and realistic explanations for core yet abstract brand identity, brand personality makes the brand meaning understandable and contemporary (Aaker & Joachimsthaler, 2000).

The most unique and useful brand personality function comes from a synergy of these two functions above. As a result, it helps marketers to actualize market-oriented and consumer-empowered brand management, which are the most critical in postmodern branding dynamics (Simonson, 2003; Wathieu et al., 2002).

1.2 Trait-based theoretical approach: Limitation

There have been great amounts of practitioners' efforts expended in identifying "what brand personality is" and "how it works." The prevailing research stream has been based on the trait-theory of psychology. Almost every brand personality study has adopted the trait theory (recently more focusing on the five factor theory) that was originally devised for human personality in psychology (e.g., Aaker, 1997; Carprara et al., 2001; Sung &Tinkham, 2005).

Having contributed to gaining fundamental understanding into brand personality and boosting academic interests in the subject, however, the trait-based brand personality approaches have been questioned for their incomplete explanation of the whole dynamics of brand personality (Sweeney & Brandon, 2006). For example, the trait-based approach has been examined for its critical limitation in explaining some core functions of brand personality, such as identifying brands with their symbolic attributions within the same product category (e.g., Romaniuk et al., 2003; Austin et al., 2003). As such, brand personality lacks a complete theoretical understanding about its unique functioning, and there has been a conceptual discrepancy between the theoretical and empirical developments of brand personality (Azoulay & Kapferer, 2003).

This limitation is caused partly by the intrinsic limitations of traits (e.g., Pervin, 2003; Braun-LaTour et al., 2007), but moreover, it is mainly due to some common misconceptions amongst academics. Previously, academics contended that brand and human personality share the same conceptual framework as well as scales-which is not true. Brand and human personalities are not analogous–brand personality is beyond the lexical scope of human personality (Sung & Tinkham, 2005). As a marketing-homegrown concept, brand personality demands a marketing-homegrown theory (Rook, 2006)-which the prevailing theories are not.

2. The theory of consumption symbolism: A market-oriented approach

2.1 Suggesting a new theoretical base: The theory of consumption symbolism

This article suggests a new and expansive theoretical base for brand personality-the theory of consumption symbolism, which is a marketing-homegrown research stream with an interdisciplinary academic basis. With all the diverse approaches and terms, scholars have consistently pursued the same goal-to identify and tabulate symbols beneath the surface of consumer goods (e.g., Arnould & Thompson, 2005; Belk, 1988; Hirschman & Holbrook, 1992; Holt, 1997; 2004; Kate, 2002; Mick, 1986). The theory of consumption symbolism refers to a rising research sub-stream in the marketing literature, which aims at identifying the mechanisms of meaning of consumption in the contemporary marketplace and its relation with consumer behavior. To address the market-oriented research topics, the theory of consumption symbolism has its roots in diverse basic disciplines such as philosophy, psychology, anthropology, economics, and sociology.

2.2 Application to brand personality studies

In-depth understanding of brand personality and its market-oriented mechanisms can be pursued within the theoretical base of the theory of consumption symbolism. This article presents two major new concepts that are required for the new brand personality studies to actualize market-oriented approaches. With the base of the theory, studies about brand personality can be expected to gain a market-oriented (i.e., context-oriented and consumer-oriented) perspective.

Context-oriented. According to the theory of consumption symbolism, the meaning of brand is established by consumers by being projected the everyday life stories of the consumers, which are inevitably contextual. The meanings of products should be understood and decoded based on "contextual" understandings that are essential in addressing consumption symbolism (Holt, 1997; Kates, 2002)–as should brand personality. However, the previous trait-based approaches considered brand personality with regard to customers' demands for "traits," which are inner-related and psychiatric characteristics of a human–therefore it is not apparently related to consumer behaviors in the marketplace. Therefore, the conceptual references of brand personality studies should be interdisciplinary, instead of single-disciplinary (e.g., psychology).

Consumer-oriented. Furthermore, studies about brand personality should maintain consumer-oriented perspectives. According to the theory, meaning of products should be understood from consumers' perspectives, not from others, since the meaning is generated and interpreted by consumers themselves. What has been largely missed in the trait-based approach is that, with few exceptions, they have tried to build a conceptual framework for brand personality by referring other concepts in other areas. Brand personality is not a concept that has adopted other concepts and theories (e.g., traits) from different disciplinary (e.g., psychology), but rather it is a concept that is developed by customers within a marketplace (e.g., Upshaw, 1995). The consumer-oriented approach can also be actualized with the experimental consumer research methods suggested by scholars in the theory of consumption symbolism, such as hermeneutics (e.g., Thompson, 1997) or narrative approach (e.g., Bruan-LaTour et al., 2007).

3. Discussion and Research agenda

3.1 A new conceptual framework with a multi-method approach

To start up new theoretical approaches for brand personality, brand personality needs a new conceptual framework from the new theoretical base. To be useful in the marketplace, the new conceptual framework should be able to explain the meaning and symbols that are projected to brands (with human metaphor) by the majority of consumers. Based on its common definitions (e.g., Aaker, 1997), the conceptual boundary of brand personality can literally have all the human characteristics that consumers associate with a brand–traits and personality are only part of them. To investigate this, it may require a fundamental literature review regarding a basic question: what the human characteristics are–and this can be narrowed down into actual structural components, based on consumers' perception about brand personality. This requires exploratory qualitative studies with a ground theory (e.g., Charmaz, 2006).

3.2 A systematic approach on non-utilitarian brand management

On many occasions, management skills regarding brand meaning have largely been left unidentified. Only a few celebrated gurus can figure them out on the basis of their intuitions and instincts. With the elaborated conceptual framework of brand personality, it is expected to reveal and explain some essential functions of brand personality (e.g., non-utilitarian differentiation points among brands) in a more structured manner which gives useful insight for practitioners as well as academicians.

Useful brand personality measurements can also be identified based on the framework, but it requires in-depth understandings about the social and cultural contexts surrounding the marketplace. Some structural components of brand personality would be highly contextual, and others (e.g., traits) not. Eventually, this also brings us to the idea of multi-level in the structural components of brand personality (e.g., those that are more stable and essential and others that are more contextual).

Moreover, practically useful brand personality measurements should be different according to diverse contexts, and it also derives to studies about cultural difference which can give useful inspiration for global marketing.

3.3 Decoding brand meanings with the mediation of brand personality

Finally, brand personality can be a mediator for understanding brand meanings and the dynamics of postmodern branding. There have been a great contribution for brand meaning with a provocative approaches (e.g., Aaker & Joachimsthaler, 2000), theoretical explanations about brand meaning and the non-utilitarian characteristics of brands are still in its infantry stage, and the developments have mostly been accomplished only in practical marketing circles. With a well-developed conceptual framework of brand personality, some aspects of the non-functional attributions of brands, or of the brand meaning, or the consumption symbolism, can be decoded.

References

Aaker, D. A. and Joachimsthaler, E. (2000), *Brand Leadership: The Next Level of the Brand Revolution*, New York, NY: Free Press.

Aaker, J. L. (1997), Dimensions of Brand Personality, *Journal of Marketing Research*, 34, 347-356.

Arnold E. J. and Thompson C. J. (2005), Consumer Culture Theory (CCT): Twenty Years of Research, *Journal of Consumer Research*, 31, 868-882.

Austin, J. R., Siguaw, J. A. and Mattila, A. S. (2003), A Re-Examination of the Generalizability of the Aaker Brand Personality Measurement Framework, *Journal of Strategic Marketing*, 11, 77-92.

Azoulay, A. and Kapferer, J.-N. (2003), Do brand personality scales really measure brand personality? *Brand Management*, 11, 143-155.

Batra, R., Lehmann, D. R. and Singh, D. (1993), The brand personality component of brand goodwill: some antecedents and consequences. In D. A. Aaker & A. L. Biel (Eds.), *Brand Equity and Advertising* (pp.83-97), Hillsdale, NJ: Lawrence Erlbaum Associates.

Belk, R. (1988), Possessions and the extended self, *Journal of Consumer Research*, 15 (2), 139-168.

Blackstone, M. (1995), The qualitative dimensions of brand equity, *Journal of Advertising Research*, 35, RC2- RC7.

Braun-LaTour, K. A., LaTour, M. S. and Zinkhan, G. M. (2007), Using Childhood Memories to Gain Insight into Brand Meaning, *Journal of Marketing*, 71 (April), 45-60.

Caprara, G. V., Barbaranelli, C. and Guido, G. (2001), Brand personality: How to make the metaphor fit? *Journal of Economic Psychology*, 22, 377-395.

Carr, S. D. (1996), The cult of brand personality, *Marketing News*, 30, 4-9.

Charmaz, K. (2006), *Constructing Grounded Theory: A Practical Guide Through Qualitative Analysis*, Thousand Oaks, CA: Sage Publications

Davis, S. M. (2000), *Brand asset management*, San Francisco: Jossey-Bass Inc.

Dent-Read, C. H. and Szokolszky, A. (1993), Where Do Metaphors Come From? *Metaphor and Symbolic Activity*, 8, 227-242.

Hirschman, E. C. and Holbrook, M. B. (1992), Postmodern Consumer Research, Newburg Park, CA: Sage Publication.

Holt, D. B. (2004), *How brands become icons*, Boston, MA: Harvard Business School Press.

Kapferer, J-N. (1998), *Strategic Brand Management* (2nd ed.), London and New York: Kogan Page.

Kates, S. M. (2002), The Protean Quality of Subcultural Consumption: An Ethnographic Account of Gay Consumers, *Journal of Consumer Research*, 29, 383-399.

Keller, K. L. (1993), Conceptualizing, measuring, and managing customer-based brand equity, *Journal of Marketing*, 57, 1-22.

Keller, K. L. (2001), Building customer-based brand equity, *Marketing Management*, 10, 14-19.

Keller, K. L. (2003), Brand Synthesis: The Multidimensionality of Brand Knowledge, *Journal of Consumer Research*, 29, 595-600.

Levy, S. J. (1981), Interpreting Consumer Mythology: A Structural Approach to Consumer Behavior, *Journal of Marketing*, 45, 49-61.

McCracken, G. (1986), Culture and Consumption: A Theoretical Account of the Structure and Movement of the Cultural Meaning of Consumer Goods, *Journal of Consumer Research*, 13, 71-84.

Mick, D. G. (1986), Consumer Research and Semiotics: Exploring the Morphology of Signs, Symbols, and Significance, *Journal of Consumer Research*, 13, 196-213.

Ogilvy, D. (1983), *Confession of an advertising man*, New York, NY: Dell.

Pervin, L. A. (2003), *The Science of Personality*, New York, NY: Oxford University Press.

Plummer, J. T. (1985), How Personality makes a difference, *Journal of Advertising Research*, 24, 27-31.

Romaniuk, J. and Ehrenberg A, (2003), Do Brands Lack Personality? Marketing Science Centre Research Report, 14, University of South Australia.

Rust, R. T. (2006), From the editor: The maturation of marketing as an academic discipline, *Journal of Marketing*, 70, 1-2.

Silverstein, M. J. and Fiske, N. (2005), *Trading up*, New York, NY: Penguin Group Portfolio.

Solomon, M. R. (2003), *Conquering consumerspace*, New York, NY: American Management Association.

Sung, Y. and Tinkham, S. F. (2005), Brand Personality Structures in the United States and Korea: Common and Culture-Specific Factors, *Journal of Consumer Psychology*, 15, 334-350.

Sweeney, J.C. and Brandon, C. (2006), Band personality: Exploring the potential to move from factor analytical to circumplex models, *Psychology and Marketing*, 23, 639-663.

Thompson, C. J. (1997), Interpreting Consumers: A Hermeneutical Framework for Driving Marketing Insights from the Texts of Consumers' Consumption Stories, *Journal of Marketing Research*, 34, 438-455.

Upshaw, L. B. (1995), *Building Brand Identity: A Strategy for Success in a Hostile Marketplace*, New York. NY: John Wiley & Sons.

Wathieu, L., Brenner, L., Carmon, Z., Chattopadhyay, A, Wertenbroch, K., Drolet, A., Gourville, J., Muthukrishnan, A. V., Novemsky, N., Ratner· R. K. and Wu. G. (2002), Consumer Control and Empowerment, *Marketing Letters*, 13, 297-305.

Zalthman, G. (1997), Rethinking Market Research: Putting People Back In, *Journal of Marketing Research*, 32, 424-437.

Endorser Influence on Product Judgment and Choice: A Comparative Study of Children and Their Parents

Aron M. Levin, Northern Kentucky University, USA
Irwin P. Levin, University of Iowa, USA

In this paper we will describe the next phase in our longitudinal study of the development of decision-making competence in children (National Science Foundation Grant No. SES07-21103). Whereas earlier phases focused on general decision-making style and riskiness of choice in games of chance, the current research focuses on an important class of real-world judgments and choices, namely the development of product preferences.

There is growing concern about how manufacturers of food products capitalize on the undue influence of favorite cartoon characters as "virtual persons" promoting unhealthy (e.g., sugar-laden) products. Specifically, we focus on the role of endorser influence as a peripheral cue affecting consumer judgments and decisions. Previous research on the general topic of endorser influence has been conducted within the context of Petty and Cacioppo's (1986) Elaboration Likelihood Model which distinguishes between central and peripheral routes to persuasion and considers "need for cognition" as a key individual difference variable. The bulk of this work has been done with adult consumers. We extend this work to children.

As in the earlier phases, the key to this research is developing tasks and measures suitable for both children and adults. In the present case, these developments required the following: 1) selecting both healthy and unhealthy food products used by children and adults; 2)

collecting normative data to identify favorite cartoon characters as "celebrity endorsers" for the target child group; 3) constructing a children's version of the Need for Cognition (NFC) scale; 4) using each child's parent as a "yoked control."

Research Design

A 2x2x2 factorial design was used to generate 8 unique stimuli (product descriptions) for each child and parent. The factors were whether or not the product's brand name was familiar, whether or not the product could be classified as "healthy," and whether or not the product description included a well-known endorser. Each participant received each of the 8 combinations, constructed such that no person received the same brand name or endorser more than once.

Hypotheses

Based on prior research with adults (Homer, & Kahle, 1990; Petty, Cacioppo, & Schumann, 1983), the following hypotheses (H) are provided for parents' data. In addition, a new research question (Q) will be addressed.

H1. Endorser effects should be greater for those scoring low on NFC than for those scoring high.
H2. Endorser effects should be less for known brand names than for unknown brand names.
Q1. How are endorser effects moderated by whether the product falls into the "healthy" or "unhealthy" category?

Based on prior research showing that children of the targeted age are less responsive to risk level in their decisions (Levin, et al., 2007) and that they strongly identify with their favorite cartoon characters (Chapman, et al., 2006), the following hypotheses and question deal with comparisons between children and adults:

H3. Children will weight endorser more and health benefits less than adults in their product ratings.
H4. As with adults, the endorser effect will be moderated by need for cognition and brand name familiarity.
Q2. Across child-parent pairs, will endorser effects be correlated such that parents who are most susceptible to endorser influence will have children who are similarly inclined?

Method

In the initial phase of the study of decision-making competence, 37 children age 5-7 and 43 children age 8-11, and their parents were administered a risky decision-making task especially designed to determine how riskiness of choice varies in response to contingencies that make risky choices advantageous or disadvantageous in the long run. For the new phase approximately 50 pairs of 7-8 year-old children and their accompanying parent are being recruited through the Child Research Participant Registry of a large midwestern university. Because some of these same children had participated in the initial phase, we will have background material on many of them.

Based on our pilot work, the following "endorsers" were selected for the children: Sponge Bob, Shrek, Scooby-Do, and The Incredibles. Their images were affixed to photos of the product package. Based on published norms of celebrity popularity, the following were selected as adult endorsers: Tiger Wood, Jay Leno, Katherine Heigl, and Adam Sandler. A photo of the endorser and a statement of endorsement appeared next to the photo of the product.

"Healthy" products were breakfast cereals and yogurts; unhealthy products were potato chips and sweet tarts. Within each product category the brand name was either well known or fictitious (ex. Yoplait vs. Emmi Yogurt). Each of the eight product depictions appeared as a separate laminated colored sheet. Participants are asked to rate each one on likeability, desirability and purchase intent. Standard Likert scales are used for adults; previously used frowning/smiling face scales are used for children.

Adult and child versions of the NFC scale are shown in the appendix. The adult version is the 18-item scale developed by Cacioppo, Petty, and Kao (1984). The child version retains 13 of these items in slightly modified form for each parent to rate her child.

Results and Discussion

The current results will add to our existing data which show that: 1) The decision-making style of young children age 5-7 closely adheres to that of their parents but diverges as they get older (8-11). 2) Younger children's choices are less affected by risk level than are older children's or adults'. 3) Children make riskier choices than their parents but their riskiness is moderated by dispositional traits such as "surgency".

We expect data collection and analysis for the new phase to be completed by the beginning of the summer. Among the more important results we are expecting are that children will be more susceptible to endorser effects than adults, that the effects in children will be less subject to the moderating influences of brand familiarity and healthiness, but that there will be a relationship between child and parent susceptibility. Such results will advance our understanding of children as consumers and will provide guidelines for identifying the profile of children especially susceptible to adverse advertising influences.

References

Cacioppo, J.T., Petty, R.E., & Kao, C.F. (1984). The efficient assessment of need for cognition. *Journal of Personality Assessment*, 48, 306-307.

Chapman, K., Nicholas, P., Banovic, D., & Supramanium, R. (2006). The extent and nature of food promotion directed to children in Australian supermarkets. *Health Promotion International*, 21, 331-339.

Homer, P.M., & Kahle, L.R. (1990). Source expertise, time of source identification, and involvement in persuasion: An elaborative processing perspective. *Journal of Advertising*, 19, 30-39.

Levin, I.P., Weller, J.A., Pederson, A.A., & Harshman, L.A. (2007). Age-related differences in adaptive decision making: Sensitivity to expected value in risky choice. *Judgment and Decision Making*, 2, 225-233.

APPENDIX

Need for Cognition Scale (Adults)

Write in the number that best fits your view:

1	2	3	4
completely true	mostly true	mostly false	completely false

_____1. I would prefer complex to simple problems.

_____2. I like to have the responsibility of handling a situation that requires a lot of thinking.

_____3. Thinking is not my idea of fun.

_____4. I would rather do something that requires little thought than something that is sure to challenge my thinking abilities.

_____5. I try to anticipate and avoid situations where there is likely chance I will have to think in depth about something.

_____6. I find satisfaction in deliberating hard and for long hours.

_____7. I only think as hard as I have to.

_____8. I prefer to think about small, daily projects to long-term ones.

_____9. I like tasks that require little thought once I've learned them.

_____10. The idea of relying on thought to make my way to the top appeals to me.

_____11. I really enjoy a task that involves coming up with new solutions to problems.

_____12. Learning new ways to think doesn't excite me very much.

_____13. I prefer my life to be filled with puzzles that I must solve.

_____14. The notion of thinking abstractly is appealing to me.

_____15. I would prefer a task that is intellectual, difficult, and important to one that is somewhat important but does not require much thought.

_____16. I feel relief rather than satisfaction after completing a task that required a lot of mental effort.

_____17. It's enough for me that something gets the job done; I don't care how or why it works.

_____18. I usually end up deliberating about issues even when they do not affect me personally.

Need for Cognition Scale (Parental report of their children)

Now we are going to ask you similar questions about your child. Please write in the number that best fits your view:

1	2	3	4
completely true	mostly true	mostly false	completely false

_____1. My child prefers complex to simple problems.

_____2. My child likes to have the responsibility of handling a situation that requires a lot of thinking.

_____3. Thinking is not my child's idea of fun.

_____4. My child would rather do something that requires little thought than something that is sure to challenge his or her thinking abilities.

_____5. My child tries to anticipate and avoid situations where there is likely chance that he or she will have to think in depth about something.

_____6. My child thinks only as hard as he or she has to.

_____7. My child prefers to think about small, daily projects to long-term ones.

_____8. My child likes tasks that require little thought once he or she has learned them.

_____9. My child really enjoys a task that involves coming up with new solutions to problems.

_____10. Learning new ways to think doesn't excite my child very much.

_____11. My child prefers his or her life to be filled with puzzles to solve.

_____12. My child feels relief rather than satisfaction after completing a task that required a lot of mental effort.

_____13. It's enough for my child that something gets the job done; he or she doesn't care how or why it works.

Petty, R.E., & Cacioppo, J.T. (1986). *The Elaboration Likelihood Model of Persuasion.* New York: Academic Press.

Petty, R.E., Cacioppo, J.T., & Schumann, D. (1983). Central and peripheral routes to advertising effectiveness: The moderating role of involvement. *Journal of Consumer Research*, 10, 135-146.

The Intersubjectivity of Family Consumption: Intra-family Consumer Identity and the Family Scape

Jeppe Trolle Linnet, University of Southern Denmark, Denmark

This paper is based on ongoing ethnographic fieldwork among four Danish middle-class families in Copenhagen. It is a phenomenological account of how consumption constitutes the intersubjectivity of family life, interpreting a detailed case of one family´s car ownership and purchase. This family used to drive a Volvo that long-term ownership had sacralized and decommodified (McCracken 1986; Belk, Wallendorf et al. 1989). The purchase of a new Ford marks a sea change in their constellation of individual identities, family identity and brand meanings. I use the phenomenological concept of intersubjectivity as a lens through which I analyze this process (Schutz 1970; Jackson 1996, 1998), and suggest two concepts for the analysis of family consumption: *Intra-family consumer identity* and *family scape*.

The paper contributes to uncovering the dynamics of consumer identity projects, and how the structures and normative views of society influence consumption (Arnould and Thompson 2005), as well as collective, long-term, narratively embedded forms of consumption rather than individual, isolated acts (Fournier 1998; Muniz Jr. and O'Guinn 2001).

I consider ways that the different family members exert individual agency as they negotiate their way towards a purchase decision balancing individual desires and collective needs. However, the paper is not focused on the modeling of collective decision-making and individual influences that has been a major preoccupation of family consumption research. Rather, the paper contributes to current research that aims to conceptualize the participatory roles of consumption objects and activities in fluid, multi-layered processes of family identity enactment (Epp and Price 2008), adding to this research a focus on intra-family negotiations and inter-family processes of identity construction through consumption.

I find the term *intersubjectivity of consumption* suggestive for describing the ongoing give and take of intra-family consumer relations, and how family consumption becomes meaningful in the context of a wider social network of families who evaluate each other's consumption practices and identities. To this end I present a detailed analysis of how family members both contest and resonate with each other's consumer desires and preferences. I emphasize that even in the "sacred" sphere of home and family life, access to which consumers often deny market messages (Coupland, Iacobucci et al. 2005), family members know each other *as consumers*. Each family member has a set of desires, preferences and values whereby other family members know him or her. I suggest the concept of *intra-family consumer identity:* An individual set of dispositions–changing over time–for certain practices of consumption, ownership and disposition that present our fellow family members with a window upon our needs, desires, values and fears, and thus a potential for collective or dyadic bonding and empathy, but also challenge them with potential transgressions and dominations of their lifeworld. In families as in wider consumer society, having desires is seen as a positive human trait, but can also as a potential disposition towards excess that collide with the surrounding social world (Belk, Ger et al. 2003). I outline a family-specific dynamic of mutual social knowledge about each other's everyday consumption patterns and desires, in which empathy and conflict coexist as intersubjective fundamentals of family consumption.

The concept of intra-family consumer identity allows for my observation that family members draw different meanings from the same consumption objects, but also that they are aware of the meanings perceived by their fellow family members. I argue that in order to conceptualize more fully family consumption, we must consider intra-familial diversity of interpretation, as well as conflicts. The temporal perspective is also important: in being less voluntary and fluid than brand communities, and involving long-term (even multi-generational; (Price, Arnould et al. 2000) interactions across a wide range of consumption categories, the dynamics of family consumption differ from other consumption communities.

The last aspect to this analysis is how family consumption connects to society and social networks. The normativities and classifications of wider society impinge on family consumption in several ways documented by this paper: The moralized opposition between consumer restraint and excess, or between thrift and "the treat" (Miller 1998), repeat themselves in a fractal-like manner at each level from *inter*-family social distinctions to the gendered interactions of *intra*-family consumer identities, and at the individual level in the ongoing moral self-reflexivity of the individual consumer. Intra- and inter-familial consumer identities thus mirror the discourses and ideologies of the marketplace (Kozinets 2008).

Another structuring force influencing family consumption, which has also been suggested by other family consumption researchers, is the "familial gaze" of families observing and critically evaluating each other lifestyle (Epp and Price 2008). My paper shows the existence of a heavily moralized model for how a family ought to consume, one which sanctifies authenticity and hard earned rewards (such as home cooking or physically demanding family trips to the Norwegian mountains) while denigrating convenience (take away food or package tours to Tenerife). And just like the gaze of "absent others" is internalized and present in how people organize their material home (Miller 2002), the intra-family consumer identities simultaneously face inward towards the family sphere, as they are actualized in interaction with other family members, and outward towards the symbolic, libidinous and moral structures of the consumer culture, which they both resist and draw upon.

I suggest the concept of the *family scape* to denote this complex of meanings that structure family consumption, while also being appropriated by the family in its ongoing construction of identity. This scape is a general cultural model, transmitted partly through marketing, of what a family is and is not, and what being a family means in consumption terms. In several variations, the concept of the scape has shown its potential for consumer research and social science in theorizing how overarching structural codes and commonalities shape and constrict local communities, groups and individuals, who are thereby also empowered with a means for communicating identity and exercising agency (Billig 1995; Wilk 1995; Kjeldgaard and Askegaard 2006)

References

Arnould, E. J. and C. J. Thompson (2005). "Consumer Culture Theory (CCT): Twenty Years of Research." *Journal of Consumer Research* 31(4): 868-882.

Belk, R. W., G. Ger, et al. (2003). "The Fire of Desire: A Multisited Inquiry into Consumer Passion." *Journal of Consumer Research* 30(3): 326-351.

Belk, R. W., M. Wallendorf, et al. (1989). "The Sacred and the Profane in Consumer Behavior: Theodicy on the Odyssey." *Journal of Consumer Research* 16(1): 1.

Billig, M. (1995). *Banal Nationalism*, Sage Publications Ltd.

Coupland, J. C., D. Iacobucci, et al. (2005). "Invisible Brands: An Ethnography of Households and the Brands in Their Kitchen Pantries." *Journal of Consumer Research* 32(1): 106-118.

Epp, A. M. and L. L. Price (2008). "Family Identity: A Framework of Identity Interplay in Consumption Practices." *Journal of Consumer Research* 35(1): 50-70.

Fournier, S. (1998). "Consumers and Their Brands: Developing Relationship Theory in Consumer Research." *Journal of Consumer Research* 24(4): 343-353.

Jackson, M. (1996). *Things As They Are: New Directions in Phenomenological Anthropology*, Indiana University Press.

Jackson, M. (1998). *Minima Ethnographica*, University of Chicago Press.

Kjeldgaard, D. and S. Askegaard (2006). "The Glocalization of Youth Culture: The Global Youth Segment as Structures of Common Difference." *Journal of Consumer Research* 33(2): 231-247.

Kozinets, R. V. (2008). "Technology/Ideology: How Ideological Fields Influence Consumers' Technology Narratives." *Journal of Consumer Research* 34(6): 865-881.

McCracken, G. (1986). "Culture and Consumption: A Theoretical Account of the Structure and Movement of the Cultural Meaning of Consumer Goods." *Journal of Consumer Research* 13(1): 71.

Miller, D. (1998). *A Theory of Shopping*, Cornell University Press.

Miller, D. (2002). *Home Possessions*, Berg.

Muniz Jr., A. M. and T. C. O'Guinn (2001). "Brand Community." *Journal of Consumer Research* 27(4): 412.

Price, L. L., E. J. Arnould, et al. (2000). "Older Consumers' Disposition of Special Possessions." *Journal of Consumer Research* 27(2): 179-201.

Schutz, A. (1970). *Alfred Schutz on Phenomenology and Social Relations. Edited and with an introduction by Helmut R. Wagner.* Chicago and London, The University of Chicago Press.

Wilk, R. R. (1995). Learning to be Local in Belize: Global Systems of Common Difference. *Worlds apart : modernity through the prism of the local.* D. Miller. London ; New York, Routledge: 110-133

The Role of Voice Design Features in Effective Self-Service Technologies

Jiayun Wu, The University of Arizona, USA
Sherry L. Lotz, The University of Arizona, USA

Abstract

This study aims to advance the understanding of effective self-service technologies (SSTs) in an ever increasing technology-mediated environment. The study hypothesizes a positive relationship between the voice design features (i.e., ease of voice) and customers' voice intention. This relationship is also mediated by customers' interface evaluation of SSTs. The study also evaluates how customers' likelihood of successful voice outcome moderates the relationship between customers' interface evaluation and voice intention. Hypotheses are proposed to be tested by using a computer-based online shopping experiment and a questionnaire given to college students.

Justification and Purpose

Self-service technologies (SSTs)–defined by Meuter, Ostrom, Roundtree, and Bitner (2000, p. 50) as "technological interfaces that enable customers to produce a service independent of direct service employee involvement" – are increasing in prevalence and becoming an important component of marketing (Zhu, Nakata and Sivakumar 2007). SSTs provide various services including monetary transactions, e.g., retail purchases; customer services such as hotel check out; and self-help, e.g., distance learning. These services benefit retail organizations and customers alike. Retailers are drawn to SSTs by their promise of greater cost efficiency, enhanced service quality, and their appeal to new customers when compared to in-person services (Parasuraman and Grewal 2000). Customer benefits include increased convenience, increased perceived control, money and time savings, and product/service customization (Robertson and Shaw 2005).

Given these benefits, customers in technology-mediated shopping environments value considerably the features of the technological interfaces, viz., the core components of SSTs (e.g., Alba et al. 1997; Zeithaml, Parasuraman and Malhotra 2002). Past research on SSTs and e-services provide some evidence for the positive impact of design features. For instance, Zhu, Nakata, and Sivakumar (2007) show how combined interface characteristics (i.e., comparative information and interactivity) and their interactions with individual traits influence SST effectiveness. However, researchers still know little about SST voice design features from the perspective of customers.

The purpose of this study is to address the existing literature's knowledge gap regarding the factors that may lead to greater SST effectiveness. More specifically, it investigates the relationships between SST voice design features, customers' interface evaluation of SSTs, and SST customers' voice intention. It also examines whether and how customers' perceived likelihood of successful voice outcome influences the relationship between customers' interface evaluation and voice intention.

Theoretical Framework and Hypotheses

As SSTs prevail and increase within marketing (Zhu, Nakata and Sivakumar 2007), researchers and practitioners recognize the need to understand the effectiveness of SSTs. This study focuses on one design element of the SST interface, viz., voice, which has received only limited systematic research regarding its relationship to SST effectiveness. Using SSTs, an organization can provide efficient and effective interface features to facilitate and encourage customer voice.

This study includes four constructs in its theoretical framework. These include SST voice design features (i.e., ease of voice), customers' interface evaluation of SSTs, customers' voice intention, and customers' perceived likelihood of successful voice outcome. The literature defines ease of voice as customers' perceptions of the effort or trouble required to lodge a complaint with the service organization (Robertson and Shaw 2005). This study defines customers' voice intention as the customers' aim or intention to direct complaints to the service organization through various means. Interface evaluation refers to the judgments or attitudes about an SST based on customers' experience with it (Zhu, Nakata and Sivakumar 2007). This study defines likelihood of successful voice outcome as the customer's perception of the level of positive outcome resulting from a service organization's efforts to remedy a service problem. The definition of likelihood of successful voice outcome is a modification of the definition for likelihood of success of the voice, which refers to customers' perceptions of the service organization's willingness to remedy service problems without "hassle" (Hirschman 1970). Two major reasons underlie this modification. First, Hirschman's definition does not account for various scenarios within a more complicated picture. For example, customers might perceive a service organization's willingness to remedy service problems as very high, but success-of-voice likelihood could be low (due to factors such as a service organization's incapacity to remedy service problems to the degree it desires). Second, the experience customers gain from directing complaints to a specific service organization in addition to customers' previous experience with other organizations and/or technologies, may significantly influence their perceived likelihood of successful voice outcome. For instance, research has demonstrated that previous non-store experience may help predict customers' intention to adopt interactive electronic formats (Eastlick 1996) and to also shop electronically (Shim and Drake 1990).

The study proposes the following four hypotheses:

H1: Customers' perceived ease of voice of SST voice design features will relate positively to customers' voice intention.

H2: Customers' perceived ease of voice of SST voice design features will relate positively to customers' interface evaluation.

H3: Customers' positive SST interface evaluation will relate positively to customers' voice intention.

H4: Customers' perceived likelihood of successful voice outcome will moderate the relationship between customers' interface evaluation of SST and their voice intention.

Methodology

This study will utilize a combined methodological approach consisting of focus-group interviews, a computer-based online shopping experiment, and self-administered questionnaires to evaluate voice design features in the SST environment. First, focus-group interviews, comprised of a sample of 15 college students, will identify: 1) a typical product that they have commonly purchased via a website, 2) typical SST voice design features that are considered to be easy, and 3) typical factors that may influence customers' perception of likelihood of successful voice outcome. Fifteen college students will complete the focus-group interviews in approximately 40 to 60 minutes on average. Next, this study will develop and test a computer-based experiment that simulates the self-service process that occurs with online shopping. The experiment will allow participants to respond to and evaluate the SST based on their actual interaction with the technology rather than through a hypothetical scenario. Interacting directly with the technology will enable participants to develop a sense of the level of ease of voice and the likelihood of successful voice outcome in the study's SST environment, and to thereby assess the technology in a more realistic and practical fashion. Prior to using the website for the final online shopping experiment, the website will be pre-tested using 15 college students from the same university to ensure that the website is both feasible and realistic. Fifteen students will complete the website pre-test in approximately 25 to 40 minutes on average.

Finally, participants will be asked to complete the questionnaire and to provide individual demographic information to be used in the data analysis phase of the study.

References

Alba, Joseph and John Lynch, et al. (1997), "Interactive Home Shopping: Consumer, Retailer, and Manufacturer Incentives to Participate in Electronic Marketplaces," *Journal of Marketing,* 61 (07), 38-53.

Eastlick, Mary Ann (1996), *Consumer Intention to Adopt Interactive Teleshopping,* Marketing Science Institute.

Hirschman, Albert O. (1970), *Exit, Voice, and Loyalty: Responses to Decline in Firms, Organization, and States,* Cambridge, Massachusetts: Harvard University Press.

Meuter, Matthew L., Amy L. Ostrom, Robert I. Roundtree and Mary Jo Bitner (2000), "Self-Service Technologies: Understanding Customer Satisfaction with Technology-Based Service Encounters," *Journal of Marketing,* 64 (Jul), 50-64.

Parasuraman, A. and Dhruy Grewal (2000), "The Impact of Technology on the Quality-Value-Loyalty Chain: A Research Agenda," *Academy of Marketing Science. Journal,* 28(1), 168-174.

Roberson, Nichola and Robin N. Shaw (2005), "Conceptualizing the Influence of the Self-Service Technology Context on Consumer Voice," *Services Marketing Quarterly,* 27(2) 33-50.

Shim, Soyeon and Mary Frances Drake (1990), "Consumer Intention to Utilize Electronic Shopping," *Journal of Direct Marketing,* 4 (3), 22-33.

Zeithaml, Valarie A., A Parasuraman and Arvind Malhotra (2002), "Service Quality Delivery through Web Sites: A Critical Review of Extant Knowledge," *Academy of Marketing Science. Journal,* 30(4), 362-375.

Zhu, Zhen, Cheryl Nakata, K. Sivakumar and Dhruv Grewal (2007), "Self-service Technology Effectiveness: The Roles of Design Features and Individual Traits. *Journal of the Academy of Marketing Science, 35 (4),* 492-506.

Is it Always Good to Feel in Control? Effects of Mortality Salience and Health Locus of Control on Health Behaviors

Adriana Samper, Duke University, USA
Mary Frances Luce, Duke University, USA
Devavrat Purohit, Duke University, USA

According to Terror Management Theory (TMT), individuals invest in their worldviews to assuage the fear aroused by a reminder of their mortality when death is made salient (Greenberg, Solomon & Pyszczynski, 1997; Shehryar & Hunt, 2005). These worldviews act as anxiety buffers by creating order and meaning, by providing standards of value, and by offering symbolic death transcendence to those who strive to meet these standards (Greenberg et al., 1997). Research has suggested that reminders of one's mortality increase the need to believe that others share one's worldview, leading to inflated estimates of consensus of one's opinions (Pyszczynski, Wicklund et al., 1996). Communications to consumers regarding health behavior often take place in settings where the threat of death may be salient (e.g., in a physician's office, as part of negatively emotion-laden appeals). Hence, we believe it is important to investigate the implications of TMT for consumer health behaviors.

Past research has examined the role of TMT on worldview and its influence on attitudes and behavior in a health context (e.g., Goldenberg, 2005; Shehryar and Hunt 2005). To date, however, research has yet to examine how the worldview of *perception of control over one's health* affects actions and thoughts surrounding disease risk and prevention, particularly in the context of a contagious disease. We utilize the construct of Health Locus of Control (Wallston, Wallston, Kaplan & Maides, 1976; Wallston & Wallston, 1981) to measure perceived control over health. On this scale, "health internals" believe that one's health is largely a result of his or her own behavior. At the other end of the dimension, health externals have generalized expectancies that the factors that determine their health are largely uncontrollable (i.e., external factors such as luck, fate, chance or powerful others). In this research, we add to the relatively small literature on worldview, perceptions of control and contagion to examine how mortality salience affects behaviors and perceptions of risk in a fatal and contagious disease context.

Previous research on Health Locus of Control (HLC) suggests that the feeling that one is in control of one's health leads to more adaptive health behaviors. A more internal HLC has been associated with certain preventive health behaviors (Norman, Bennett, Smith & Murphy, 1998), such as the ability to stop smoking (e.g., Kaplan & Cowles, 1978), and performance of exercise and dieting behaviors (Norman et al., 1998). In this research, we examine the effects of Health Locus of Control under mortality salience to see how health locus of control affects risk perceptions and behaviors. In particular, we examine how the drive to resolutely defend worldview will lead to inflated views of consensus of one's worldview under mortality salience. We suggest that under mortality salience, a more internal locus of control causes individuals to externalize their worldview of personal control over health onto others, leading to the notion that others are also at lower risk for disease. This in turn should lead to reduced unrealistic optimism (Weinstein, 1980) of not being infected with HIV as well as reduced future HIV prevention intentions. Hence, we hypothesize that the traditional relationship between HLC and health behavior will reverse in environments characterized by mortality salience.

In Study 1, participants were presented with the threat of HIV following a mortality salience (versus a dental pain) prime, and were asked to rate their own risk of being infected with HIV, the average other's risk of being infected with HIV, and their intentions to engage in future HIV-preventive behaviors. A moderated regression analysis on both unrealistic optimism (likelihood of having HIV–likelihood of the average other of having HIV) and prevention intentions (e.g., index of condom use, selectivity in sexual partners, etc.) revealed that a more internal health locus of control, while leading to greater unrealistic optimism and increased HIV prevention intentions at baseline (dental pain prime), becomes maladaptive and leads reduced unrealistic optimism and lower preventive intentions under mortality salience. We interpret these findings as reflecting a process whereby mortality salience leads to an increased perception of consensus of others' risks being similar to one's own, reducing the perceived population risk, and thus reducing overall HIV prevention intentions.

In order to test our proposed mechanism (i.e., that mortality salience causes individuals to externalize their worldview such that they see that others' estimates as their own), Study 2 manipulated the (self versus other) focus of the health message while again measuring health locus of control. Thus, this study directed participants to either take on a self-view, or an 'average other'-view (akin to the externalized worldview that we propose happens under mortality salience in Study 1) when reading the involving HIV information. In this sense, Study 2 allowed us to examine whether the mechanism of false consensus (encouraged by other focus) would cause more internal individuals to reduce their heightened unrealistic optimism of avoiding HIV infection and erode the preventive advantage of internals, as seen in Study 1. Again, a moderated regression analysis on unrealistic optimism and prevention intentions revealed that a more internal health locus of control, while leading to directionally greater unrealistic optimism and increased HIV prevention intentions with a self-focus, becomes maladaptive and leads reduced unrealistic optimism and lower preventive intentions with an other-focus.

This research has important implications for the communication of health messages, specifically those that convey death as a possible consequence. This type of message could potentially lead to increased risk-taking behaviors among those individuals who would normally engage in very protective, preventive behaviors, as evidenced by our initial study. Our research will help elucidate why certain health appeals may be more or less effective depending on the presence or absence mortality salience, and the degree of an individual's health locus of control.

References

Coan, Richard W. (1973), "Personality variables associated with cigarette smoking," *Journal of Personality and Social Psychology, 26,* 86-104.

Goldenberg, Jamie Lynn (2005), "The Body Stripped Down: An existential account of the threat posed by the physical body," *American Psychological Society, 14,* 224-228.

Greenberg, Jeff, Sheldon Solomon and Tom Pyszczynski (1997), "Terror management theory of self-esteem and social behavior: Empirical assessments and conceptual refinements." In M. P. Zanna (Ed.), Advances in experimental social psychology (Vol 29, pp. 61-139). New York: Academic Press.

Kaplan, Gordon D. and Ann Cowles (1978), "Health Locus of Control and Health Value in the Prediction of Smoking Reduction," *Health Education and Behavior, 6,* 129-137.

Norman, Paul, Paul Bennett, Christopher Smith and Simon Murphy (1998), "Health Locus of Control and Health Behavior," *Journal of Health Psychology, 3,* 171-180.

Pyszczynski, Tom, Robert A. Wicklund, Stefan Floresku, Holgar Koch, Gerardine Gauch, Sheldon Solomon and Jeff Greenberg (1996), "Exaggerated whistling in the dark: Consensus estimates in response to incidental reminders of mortality." *Psychological Science, 7,* 332-336.

Shehryar, Omar and David M. Hunt (2005), A Terror Management Perspective on the Persuasiveness of Fear Appeals," *Journal of Consumer Psychology, 15,* 275-287.

Wallston, Barbara S., Kenneth A. Wallston, Gordon D. Kaplan and Shirley A. Maides (1976), "A. Development and validation of the health locus of control [HLC] scale," *Journal of Consulting and Clinical Psychology, 44,* 580-585.

Wallston, Kenneth A. and Barbara S. Wallston (1981), "Health locus of control scales." In H. Lefcourt (Ed.) Research with the locus of control construct, Vol 1, pp. 189-243. New York: Academic Press.

Changing Behaviors toward Stigmatized Diseases

Linyun Yang, Duke University, USA

Mary Frances Luce, Duke University, USA

One of the major barriers to getting individuals with stigmatized diseases (i.e. STDs and psychiatric disorders) to seek treatment is the shame and distress caused by having to admit one has the disease. A large amount of research has documented the many consequences an individual must endure should he or she be associated with a stigmatized group. For example, Young et al. (2007) found that people not only view individuals suffering from STDs as being immoral in the sexual domain (e.g. being promiscuous, having premarital sex) but people also view these individuals as being immoral in nonsexual domains (e.g. lying, shoplifting). Being associated with a stigmatized group can be so debilitating that individuals are reluctant to seek treatment despite the obvious health and social benefits of doing so. For example, in the United States, approximately 60% of people with psychiatric disorders failed to receive any treatment within a one year period (Wang et al. 2005). This sample included both individuals with relatively minor disorders (e.g. adjustment disorders) and individuals with serious illnesses (e.g. schizophrenia), suggesting that even those who should have had the ability to seek help (i.e. those with minor disorders) decided not to do so.

Recent research from the stereotype literature suggests a method to directly address this stigma associated with the disease. The stereotypes associated with individuals suffering from stigmatized diseases often motivate others' negative expectations and prejudices (Corrigan 2004). Thus, one way to address stigma is by leveraging the finding that the way exemplars are categorized can change the evaluations (and hence the stereotypes) of groups they belong to (Bless et al. 2001; Kunda & Oleson 1995). More specifically, when positive exemplars are *included* in a group, the characteristics associated with the exemplar will be assimilated to the evaluations of the group. For example, when a favorable exemplar like Colin Powell is included in the group of Republicans, subsequent evaluations of the Republican Party become more positive (Stapel & Schwarz 1998). On the other hand, the *exclusion* of a favorable exemplar will lead to subsequently more negative evaluations of the group. This occurs because the exemplar is used as a standard of comparison, so the group as a whole appears worse off, leading to a contrast away from the positive attitudes toward the exemplar. Thus, we predict that inclusion of a positive exemplar will have beneficial effects for individuals with a negative stereotype regarding a particular patient group (e.g., the mentally ill).

We hypothesize that this is moderated by preexisting attitudes towards treatment. The degree to which negative stereotyping is a barrier to treatment, and hence the benefit of the inclusion mechanism, should be particularly strong for individuals who doubt the efficacy of mental health treatment. Specifically, inclusion of positive exemplars should be beneficial for individuals with preexisting negative attitudes toward treatment seeking. That is, inclusion of a positive exemplar should, by reducing negative group stereotypes, motivate these individuals to take steps towards treatment, even if these steps will involve (potentially prolonged) association with the stigmatized group. Conversely, when their views of those suffering from a stigmatized disease are altered, individuals with preexisting positive attitudes toward seeking treatment will likely react very differently. For individuals who are already highly inclined to seek treatment and readily believe in its effectiveness, making them view the group more positively (through inclusion) may *reduce* treatment seeking by undermining the perceived extremity or severity of the disease, in turn reducing motivation to use treatment to be rid of the disease and dissociate themselves from the stigmatized group.

In our experiment, we measure whether or not individuals express intentions to seek treatment if they experience symptoms of the mental disorder depression. Prior to participating in the formal experiment, participants completed the "Attitudes toward Seeking Professional Psychological Help Scale" (Mackenzie, Knox, Gekoski, & Macaulay 2004). During the formal experiment, participants read an article describing the symptoms of depression and were also introduced to a positive exemplar, Uma Thurman, who had suffered from depression in the past. Next, participants completed questions that lead them to either include or exclude Uma Thurman from the group of individuals suffering from depression (Bless & Wänke 2000). Following this task, participants read a scenario that described a situation in which they were experiencing symptoms of depression and then answered questions related to treatment seeking behavior. We find a 2-way interaction ($? = -0.51$, $p < .05$) between manipulated inclusion (versus exclusion) and measured attitudes where individuals with more negative attitudes toward mental health services are more likely to seek treatment when they *include* Uma Thurman compared to when they exclude her. However, individuals who have more positive attitudes toward mental health services display the opposite pattern where they are more likely to seek treatment when they *exclude* Uma Thurman. Follow up research manipulating (rather than measuring) underlying beliefs regarding treatment and disease is underway.

These results indicate that efforts to increase treatment seeking for stigmatized diseases must address both the stigma associated with individuals suffering from the disease and also people's preexisting attitudes toward seeking such services. This suggests that public service campaigns featuring celebrities with stigmatized diseases can be detrimental to some while beneficial to others, depending on each individual's preexisting attitudes toward mental health services and also how the celebrities are categorized. As we gain a better understanding of how stigma serves as a barrier to getting tested and seeking treatment for stigmatized diseases, we will be able to develop and implement effective strategies for combating this obstacle and encourage individuals with stigmatized diseases to request help to improve their health.

References

Bless, Herbert & Wänke, Michaela (2000). Can the same information be typical and atypical? How perceived typicality moderates assimilation and contrast in evaluative judgments. *Personality and Social Psychology Bulletin, 26,* 306-314.

Corrigan, Patrick W. (2004). How stigma interferes with mental health care. *American Psychologist, 59,* 614-625.

Day, Emer N., Edgren, Kara, & Eshlemn, Amy (2007). Measuring stigma toward mental illness: Development and application of the mental illness stigma scale. *Journal of Applied Social Psychology, 37,* 2191-2219.

Kunda, Ziva & Oleson, Kathryn C. (1995). Maintaining stereotypes in the face of disconfirmation: Constructing grounds for subtyping. *Journal of Personality and Social Psychology, 68,* 656-579.

Mackenzie, Corey S., Knox, V. Jane, Gekoski, William L., & MaCaulay, Helen L. (2004). An adaptation and extension of the attitudes toward seeking professional psychological help scale. *Journal of Applied Social Psychology, 34,* 2410-2435.

Stapel, Dierderick A. & Schwarz, Norbert (1998). The Republican who did not want to become President: An inclusion/exclusion analysis of Colin Powell's impact on evaluations of the Republican Party and Bob Dole. *Personality and Social Psychology Bulletin, 24,* 690-698.

Wang, Phillip S., Lane, Michael, Olgson, Mark, Pincus, Harold A., Wells, Kenneth B., & Kessler, Ronald C. (2005). Twelve-month use of mental health services in the United States. *Archives of General Psychiatry, 62,* 629-640.

Young, Sean, Nussbaum, David A., & Monin, Benoit (2007). Potential moral stigma and reactions to sexually transmitted diseases: Evidence for a disjunction fallacy. *Personality and Social Psychology Bulletin, 10,* 1-11.

Choosing Between American and Chinese Brands

Jingjing Ma, University of California, Los Angeles, USA
Shi (shir) Zhang, University of California, Los Angeles, USA

As the world's largest consumer market, China attracts many multinational corporations and foreign products and brands. The Chinese consumers' choices of these products and brands have changed in the past few years. For example, compared to Chinese products, American products used to have many competitive advantages, such as high quality and prestige. Due to recent surge of economic development and progress in technology and manufactory capabilities, more and more consumers in China begin to prefer domestic products to American products and in some situations they perceive Chinese products to be better choices than American products. Given that consumer choice decision making can be driven to a large extent by situational variables (e.g., psychological reactions to marketing activities), it is important, in terms of both consumer research theory and managerial significance, to investigate when and how Chinese consumers prefer products from American versus from their own country is important, and the role of brand plays in the decision making. This research aims to provide insights into Chinese consumers' psychology of decision making, relative to what we already know about Americans.

Theoretical background

Earlier research findings show that when choosing products such as clothes, cosmetics, and high-tech gadgets like cell phones and laptops, Chinese consumers usually prefer American brands, but when facing durable goods, TV sets, food etc, they prefer domestic brands. We note that those preferred American products are hedonic products, which seem to provide more utility on the dimension of experiential consumption, fun, pleasure, and excitement, whereas those preferred Chinese products are in general utilitarian products, primarily functional and instrumental.

Drawing from existing research, we suggest that the above observed behavior tendency in choice decision making can be moderated by decision contexts. For example, Bohm and Pfister (1996) show that asking participants to justify their choices can enhance their preferences for utilitarian products. Similarly, Bazerman, Tenbrunsel, and Wade-Benzoni (1998) find that making a choice can force consumers to choose what they should buy (vs. want to buy), so that they are more likely to buy utilitarian products. Furthermore, Dhar and Wertenbroch (2000) find that requiring subjects to list reasons for their choices can de-emphasize the hedonic focus relative to the utilitarian focus in subjects' product evaluations. Based on findings from this earlier research, we suggest that Chinese consumers should prefer utilitarian products more in with-justification condition than in without-justification condition, as providing reasons to justify decisions make consumers more likely focus on the utilitarian aspects of products and less likely on the hedonic dimension. Further, since Chinese consumers view western products to be more image driven, while Chinese products are pragmatic, Chinese consumers should prefer Chinese brands more in the justification condition than in the no justification condition, and versa vice for American brands.

Experiment and Result

One hundred and forty students were recruited from Peking University in Beijing, China. They were paid for their participation. Participants reported to an amphitheater and were assigned randomly to four conditions by receiving four kinds of questionnaires. The two independent variables are product category (hedonic and utilitarian) and justification (without-justification and with-justification). This constitutes a 2 (product category) *2(justification) between subjects design. The dependent variable is participants' choice between a Chinese brand product and an American brand product. In this experiment we find that in without-justification condition, Chinese consumers prefer American products regardless of hedonic or utilitarian; however, in with-justification condition, their preference varies across categories: in hedonic category, more participants prefer American products, but in utilitarian category, more participants prefer Chinese products.

Discussion

Much country of origin research points out that in developing countries consumers generally prefer products from developed countries to their own products. We find that this is not necessarily the case, depending on specific choice situations. In without-justification condition, Chinese consumers generally prefer American products regardless of product categories; but in with-justification condition, their preference varies across categories: they prefer American products in hedonic category but prefer Chinese products in utilitarian category. Although previous research finds that product types or levels of justification may influence consumers' preference, no research combines these two factors together to explore their interaction.

Some research finds that levels of justification may influence consumers' preference toward hedonic and utilitarian products. Specifically in without-justification condition consumers are likely to prefer hedonic products, but in with-justification their preference towards utilitarian products may increase. The focus of this previous research is on the influence of levels of justification on choice of products types (hedonic or utilitarian). In our research, we use the previous independent variable-levels of justification and dependent variable-product categories as two independent variables, and focus on their interaction effect on choice between American products and Chinese products. We find that not only does justification influence preference towards utilitarian versus hedonic products, it also changes the pattern of consumers' preference toward American versus Chinese products in hedonic and utilitarian categories.

References

Ahmed, Sadrudin A. and Alain d'Astous (2004), "Perceptions of Countries as Producers of Consumer Goods: A T-shirt Study in China," *Journal of Fashion Marketing and Management*, 8 (2), 187-200.

Bazerman, Max H., Ann E. Tenbrunsel, and Kimberly Wade-Benzoni (1998), "Negotiating with Yourself and Losing: Understanding and Managing Conflicting Internal Preferences," *Academy of Management Review*, 23, 225-41.

Bohm, Gisela and Hans-Rudiger Pfister (1996), "Instrumental or Emotional Evaluations: What Determines Preferences?" *Acta Psychologica*, 93 (1-3), 135-48.

CIA (2002), *World Fact Book*, CIA, Washington, DC, available at www.cia.gov

Cordell, Victor V. (1992), "Effects of Consumer Preferences for Foreign Sourced Products," *Journal of International Business Studies*, 23(2), 251-69.

Darling, John R. (1987), "A Longitudinal Analysis of the Competitive Profile of Products and Associated Marketing Practices of Selected European and Non-European Countries," *European Journal of Marketing*, 21(3), 17-29.

Darling, John R. and Van R. Wood (1990), "A Longitudinal Study Comparing Perceptions of U.S. and Japanese Consumer Products in a Third/Neutral Country: Finland 1975-1985," *Journal of International Business Studies*, 21(3), 427-50.

Dhar, Ravi and Klaus Wertenbroch (2000), "Consumer Choice Between Hedonic and Utilitarian Goods," *Journal of Marketing Research*, 37 (Feb), p60-71.

Dornoff, Ronald J., Clint B. Tankersley and Gregory P. White (1974), "Consumers' Perceptions of Imports," *Akron Business and Economic Review*, 5 (Summer), 26-29.

Festervand, Troy A., James R. Lumpkin and William J. Lundstrom (1985), "Consumers' Perceptions of Imports: An Update and Extension," *Akron Business and Economic Review*, 16 (Spring), 31-36.

Gaedeke, Ralph. (1973), "Consumer Attitudes Toward Products 'Made in' Developing Countries," *Journal of Retailing*, 49 (Summer), 13-24.

Hampton, Gerald M. (1977), "Perceived Risk in Buying Products Made Abroad by American Firms," *Baylor Business Studies*, 113(August), 53-64.

Hirschman, Elizabeth C. and Morris B. Holbrook (1982), "Hedonic Consumption: Emerging Concepts, Methods and Propositions," *Journal of Marketing*, 46 (Summer), 92-101.

Johansson, Johny K., Susan P. Douglas and Ikujiro Nonaka (1985), "Assessing the Impact of Country of Origin on Product Evaluations: A New Methodological Perspective," *Journal of Marketing Research*, 22 (November), 388-96.

Kaynak, Erdener and Orsay Kucukemiroglu (2001), "Country-of-Origin Evaluations: Hong Kong Consumers' Perception of Foreign Products after the Chinese Takeover of 1997", *International Journal of Advertising*, 20 (1), 117-138.

Kaynak, E., O. Kucukemiroglu, and A. S. Hyder (2000), "Consumers' Country-of-Origin (COO) Perceptions of Imported Products in a Homogeneous Less-Developed Country", *European Journal of Marketing*, 34 (9/10), 221-41. no such sitation

Krishnakumar, Parameswar (1974), "An Exploratory Study of the Influence of Country of Origin on the Product Images of Persons from Selected Countries," Ph.D. dissertation, The University of Florida.

Kwan, C. Y., K. W. Yeung, and K. F. Au (2003), "A Statistical Investigation of the Changing Apparel Retailing Environment in China," *Journal of Fashion Marketing and Management*, 7(1), 87-100.

Lee, E. (2002), "Dress to be Seen," *Asia Textile and Apparel Journal*, 13 (3), 78-9.

Lee, Moonkyu and Sevgin Eroglu (1995), "Product-Country Images: Impact and Role in International Marketing (Bood Rivew)," *Journal of International Marketing*, 3(2), 107-109. Abstract: Reviews the book "Product-Country Images: Impact and Role in International Marketing," edited by Nicolas Papadopoulos and Louise A. Heslop, International Business Press, Binghamton, New York, 1993, 477pp.; (AN 4453869)

Nagashima, Akira (1970), "A Comparison of Japanese and U.S. Attitudes toward Foreign Products," *Journal of Marketing*, 34 (January), 68-74.

Nagashima, Akira (1977), "A Comparative Product 'Made in' Image Survey among Japanese Businessmen," *Journal of Marketing*, 41 (July), 95-100.

Niffenegger, Phillip B., J. White and G. Marmet (1980), "How British Retail Managers View French and American Products," *European Journal of Marketing*, 14(8), 493-98.

Reierson, Curtis (1966), "Are Foreign Products Seen as National Stereotypes?" *Journal of Retailing*, 42 (Fall), 33-40.

Roth, Martin S. and Jean B. Romeo (1992), "Matching Product Category and Country Image Perceptions: A Framework for Managing Country-of-Origin Effects," *Journal of International Business Studies*, 23(3), 477-97.

Samiee, Saeed (1994), "Customer Evaluation of Products in a Global Market," *Journal of International Business Studies*, 25 (3), 579-604.

Schooler, Robert D. and Don H. Sunoo (1971), "Bias Phenomena Attendant to the Marketing of Foreign Goods in the U.S. ," *Journal of International Business Studies*, 2 (Spring), 71-80.

Strahilevitz, Michal and John G. Myers (1998), "Donations to Charity as Purchase Incentives: How Well They Work May Depend on What You Are Trying to Sell," *Journal of Consumer Research*, 24 (March), 434-46.

Tongberg, Richard C. (1972), "An Empirical Study of Relationships between Dogmatism and Consumer Attitudes towards Foreign Products," Ph.D. dissertation, Pennsylvania State University.

Wang, Chih-Kang (1983), "The Impact of Selected Environmental Forces upon Consumers' Willingness to Buy Foreign Product," *Journal of the Academy of Marketing Science*, 11 (Winter), 71-84.

Zhang, Li and Jingjing Ma (2006), "Xiao Fei Jing Yan, Wen Hua Yi Han Ji Fishbein Mo Xing" [Consumption Experience, Cultural Meaning and Fishbein Model], *Journal of Marketing Science*, 2(3) (in Chinese).

Understanding Shopping Stress Using Perceived Risk and Cognitive Appraisal Theory: A Synthesis, Elaboration and Application

Elaine MacNeil, Cape Breton University, Canada
Peter MacIntyre, Cape Breton University, Canada

It is important to identify not only shopping stressors but to understand why some events are perceived as stressful if we are to provide sound advice to retailers and consumers to reduce the stress associated with shopping. Unfortunately, stress has been a neglected area of enquiry in the field of consumer behaviour. Our research into shopping stress uncovered two concepts, previously studied independently, that shed light on this area: perceived risk and cognitive appraisal theory (CAT). The overlap between these conceptual schemes is striking and their synthesis provides a potentially powerful theoretical tool with which to study shopping stress. In providing this synthesis we propose two extensions that further our understanding of stress: the role of emotion and optimal challenge. Finally, we apply the conceptualization, emerging from a grounded theory approach, in an iterative fashion to the study of men who tell us they hate shopping. Consistent with this year's conference theme of Port of Call, we wish to reflect on where we have been and suggest a new direction for where we might go.

Raymond Bauer introduced the concept of perceived risk at the 43rd conference of the AMA in 1960, the same year in which Magda Arnold (1960) introduced the concept of appraisal into the stress literature. Over the years, the two research traditions have grown up quite independently, risk taking primarily studied in the field of marketing and CAT research primarily studied in the domain of psychology. Yet the conceptual overlap is astonishing. We propose that the integration of these concepts is useful to understanding stress, in particularly the *differences* among people not only in what shopping events they consider stressful but why these events are stressful.

In synthesizing the literature on these concepts we considered the following categories: definitions, processes, and consequences. According to Cox (1967) the amount of perceived risk involved in any behavioral act is assumed to be a function of (1) what is at stake and (2) the individual's subjective feeling of certainty that the consequences will be unfavorable (Cox 1967, p. 37). Similarly, in CAT Lazarus suggested that "we must consider our chances of mastering the transaction and having a positive outcome, what we have to do to attain the goal, and what price we must pay for success and failure" (Lazarus 1999, p. 71). Cognitive appraisal results in a subjective emotional experience that helps to orient a person to the relevance of an object or event. Both perceived risk and cognitive appraisal theories draw attention to how persons evaluate and cope with stressors. The definitions of perceived risk and cognitive appraisal both emphasize the subjectiveness of the experience and the interaction of person-specific and situational factors. Experiences such as risk and stress are not viewed as objective properties of situations, therefore reactions differ greatly person to person. Perceived risk and CAT also share similarities in terms of the way people define what is at stake, including the potential cost of wasted time (Roselius1971), physical wellbeing, financial resources, and threats to self-esteem (Jacoby and Kaplan 1972). Decision making is perhaps the key outcome in both theories. Coping with stress is a function of resources available, including spending more time or money and accessing knowledgeable others for support. Both theories also highlight goals as motivational supports. Cox (1967) proposed that "...whereas certainty and consequences determine the amount of perceived risk, the nature of the perceived risk should be a function of the nature of the buying goals involved" (Cox 1967 p.38). Similarly, stress occurs as a function of the strength of one's goal commitment and the degree to which the goal is endangered (Lazarus 1999). Sujan, Bettman and Verhallen (1999) identified the largest categories of stressors as choice-related stressors (e.g., having too many options) and in-store ambient stressors (e.g., music). However the question of why these factors were perceived as stressors in the first place largely was ignored.

In considering the convergence of these two theories, we note that at least two elaborations are required. First, a greater emphasis is needed on the importance of emotion in studying perceived risk. According to Taylor (1974) "risk is often perceived to be painful in that it may produce anxiety" (Taylor 1974, p.54), yet the role emotion plays in perceived risk has generally been ignored (Chaudhuri 1997). In the second area for elaboration, we recommend greater emphasis on the concept of optimal challenge, and with it potentially positive emotional reactions to risk. Within CAT, emotions associated with challenges include eagerness, excitement and exhilaration. Perceived risk in the consumer behaviour literature focuses almost exclusively on the negative consequence associated with uncertainty. We suggest that both the positive and negative outcomes should be considered in assessing perceived risk (Dholakia 1997). The perceived risk literature highlights the importance of uncertainty as a source of stress, but we believe that both certainty and uncertainty might have positive or negative consequences. For example, uncertainty might be perceived as a welcome challenge to the recreational shopper; product certainty might predispose a reluctant shopper to frustration if unanticipated delays occur.

We used classical grounded theory to inform this perspective. We interviewed 35 men who said they hate shopping. Emerging from this rich data was a complex relationship between stress, ability, and behaviour that we propose is mediated by the men's level of certainty. For example, in the context of gift shopping, certainty of a negative outcome affected expenditure of effort, one man said:

No matter what you buy it's the wrong size or it's the wrong style or it's I don't need that. What the hell do you get?" I just end up getting something. If she doesn't like it she will return it.

Uncertainty also affected risk taking, with anticipated time loss outweighing the potential benefits of shopping, as in this excerpt:

I won't go to a store looking for things that might be there. It's too chancy. There might be nothing there or a special I don want. I've just wasted half an hour.

A focus on positive and negative consequences associated with challenges and uncertainty has the potential to increase our understanding of the differences between enjoyable and stressful shopping situations. By integrating the literature on cognitive appraisal theory and perceived risk, and elaborating on the notion of the emotional processes accompanying challenges and uncertainties, future research can address not only the question of what shopping events are perceived stressful but why they are stressful for one shopper and enjoyable challenges for another.

References

Bagozzi, Richard, Mahesh Gopinath, and Prahanth U. Nyer (1999), "The Role of Emotions in Marketing," *Journal of the Academy of Marketing Sciences,* spring 1999, Vol. 27 (2), 184-206.

Bauer, Raymond (1960). "Consumer Behavior as Risk Taking" in Donald Cox's *Risk Taking and Information Handling*, 23-33, Harvard University, Boston.

Chaudhuri, Arjun (1997). "Consumption Emotion and Perceived Risk: A Macro analytic Approach," *Journal of Business Research*, 39, 81-92.

Cox, Donald F. (1967) ed. *Risk Taking and Information Handling in Consumer Behaviour,* Boston: Harvard University Press, 1967.

Dholakia, Utpal M. (1997). "An Investigation of the Relationship between Perceived Risk and Product Involvement," in *Advances in Consumer Research,* vol24. eds. Merrie Brucks and Deborah J. MacInnis, Provo, UT: Association for Consumer Research, 159-167.

Jacoby, Jacob and Leon B. Kaplan (1972) "The Components of Perceived Risk," in *Advances in Consumer Research*, ed. M.Venkatesan, Chicago: Association of Consumer Research, 382-393.

Lazarus, Richard. S. (1999), *Stress and Emotions: A New Synthesis.* New York, N.Y: Springer Publishing Company.

Luce, Mary Frances, James R. Bettman, and John W. Payne (2001), "An Integrated Model of Trade-off Difficulty and Consumer Choice," *Journal of Consumer Research*, 11-35.

Nyer, Prashanth U. (1997), "A Study of the Relationships between Cognitive Appraisals and Consumption Emotions," *Journal of the Academy of Marketing Sciences*, Vol. 25 (4) 296-304.

Roselius, Edward (1971), "Consumer Ranking of Risk Reduction Methods," *Journal of Marketing,* 35, 56-61.

Sujan, Mita., Harish Sujan, James Bettman and Theo Verhallen (1999), "Sources of Consumers Stress and their coping strategies", *European Advances in Consumer Research* (4), ed. Bernard Dubois, Tina M. Lowrey, L.J. Shrum, Marc Vanhuele, Provo, UT: Association for Consumer Research, 182-187.

Taylor, James W. (1974), The Role of Risk in Consumer Behavior, *Journal of Marketing (38)* (April),54-60.

Forming Brand Personality: Company-Based vs. Consumer-Based Sources

Natalia Maehle, Norwegian School of Economics and Business Administration, Norway
Chunyan Xie, Stord/Haugesund University College, Norway
Magne Supphellen , Norwegian School of Economics and Business Administration, Norway

In the modern consumer society we buy products not only for what they can do but also for what they symbolize. Brands encapsulate social meaning, and that allows us to use them to acquire or reinforce our identities (Johar and Sirgy 1991). Therefore, brand personality (brand's human-like characteristics) becomes one of the essential features that we consider while choosing a brand.

Not surprisingly, brand personality concept has got a lot of attention in marketing literature. However, the primary focus of previous studies has been either on understanding the effects of brand personality or on measurement issues related to the construct (Aaker 1997; Azoulay and Kapferer 2003; Govers and Schoormans 2005). Although it is also important to understand how consumers form their perceptions of brand personality, there has been little research in this direction (Batra, Lehmann, and Singh 1993). Moreover, the existing literature considers mostly company-based sources of brand personality such as company's employees, company's director, brand's endorsers (McCracken 1989), product-related attributes, product category associations, brand name, symbol or logo, advertising style, price, and distribution channel (Batra et al. 1993). Little, if any, attention has been paid to the possible consumer-based sources.

Nevertheless, consumer's voice is becoming more and more influential so that companies cannot just ignore it. Consumer based sources are important for forming brand personality both before and after consumer purchases the brands. Before the purchase take place, word-of-mouth effect will be significant in shaping consumers' understanding of the brand personality proposed by the company through the marketing mix. The formation of numerous discussion groups and brand online communities extend and strengthen the word-of-mouth effect from close others to a much larger group of people connected through a virtual network (McWilliam 2000). Compared to the company based sources, word-of-mouth will be treated as a more reliable information sources by consumers (Keller 2007). After the purchase and consumption, consumers' first hand experiences with the brands will be critical for them to reject or reinforce the proposed brand personality.

Brand personality encompasses five different dimensions: Sincerity, Excitement, Competence, Sophistication, and Ruggedness (Aaker 1997). We expect that consumer-based sources can be relevant for forming at least some of them.

Thus, the purpose of the current study is to find out which sources are relevant for forming different dimensions of brand personality. A set of sixty six semi-structured interviews was conducted to address these issues. Every respondent got questions about two different dimensions of brand personality. So, we got between twenty-five and twenty-seven answers for each dimension.

We started the interviews by explaining the concept of brand personality and the chosen brand personality dimensions in particular. Then we asked respondents to name a couple of brands that they think score high on a particular dimension. Respondents also explained their reasons why they thought so. Finally, respondents were asked to look on the list of possible sources of brand personality and choose five of them which they think are especially relevant for a particular personality dimension. Our final list included thirteen company-based and four consumer-based sources such as *company's employees, company's managing director, endorser, typical brand user, product attributes, product category, brand name, brand logo, advertising style, price, retail stores, country of origin, company's moral values, own experience when using the product, on-line consumer community, word-of-mouth, and own value system / own opinions.*

Both consumer-based sources and company-based sources were found to be important for forming brand personality. But they contributed differently in different dimensions. The results show that consumer-based sources such as own experience, word-of-mouth, and own value system play an important role for forming Sincerity and Competence dimensions. According to the respondents, "when you experience the brand by your own you can see if the brand is competent or not… you can check it…", "…It overshadows what I hear from others". However, "rumours [word-of-mouth] tell how good they [the brand] are" and "rumours influence what I believe".

On the other hand, company-based sources such as advertising style, brand name, product attributes, and typical brand user are dominant for forming Sophistication and Ruggedness dimensions. "It is all about the brand and its image", mentions one of the respondents. As for Excitement, it is formed by a blend of consumer- and company-based sources (e.g. advertising style, product attributes, word-of-mouth, own experience, and brand logo).

Thus, consumer-based sources are highly relevant for Sincerity and Competence but at the same time do not almost have any effect on Sophistication and Ruggedness. One of the reasons could be that consumers cannot accurately assess many of the brand's features related to Competence and Sincerity (e.g. product quality, product performance, product lifetime, value-for-money) before they purchase the brand. These features are the experience qualities which cannot be determined before consumers try the brand themselves (Nelson 1974). At the same time, Sincerity and Competence are vital features for every brand; they represent a kind of hygiene factors (Herzberg 1974) that any brand should have. Consumers being risk averse do not trust only company-based sources when they judge these dimensions; they need to get the confirmation from more credible sources such as their own experience or word-of-mouth (Keller 2007).

Sophistication and Ruggedness are of symbolic and intangible nature. They correspond to intersubjective quality emphasizing accepted cultural norms, often in the form of symbols and images (Pirsig 1999). These features are difficult to judge just from the direct contact with a product itself, and they are mostly based on the images and symbols which companies provide in their promotional campaigns. Excitement is related to both what you feel or think while experiencing a brand (subjective quality) and product characteristics like special technical features or exciting appearance (objective quality). Therefore, both company- and consumer-sources are relevant.

Thus, the current study indicates which sources tend to be more relevant for forming each brand personality dimension. Moreover, we have found out that consumer-based sources are extremely relevant for some dimensions, especially for Sincerity and Competence. However, further research is necessary to get a better understanding of how consumers form their brand personality judgments.

References

Aaker, Jennifer (1997), "Dimensions of Brand Personality", *Journal of Marketing Research*, 34 (3), 347-356.

Azoulay, Audrey and Jean-Noël Kapferer (2003), "Do Brand Personality Scales Really Measure Brand Personality?", *Journal of Brand Management*, 11 (2), 143-155.

Batra, Rajeev, Donald R. Lehmann, and Dipinder Singh (1993), "The Brand Personality Component of Brand Goodwill: Some Antecedents and Consequences" in *Brand Equity and Advertising*, ed. David A. Aaker and Alexander Biel, Hillsdale, NJ: Lawrence Erlbaum Associates, 83-96.

Govers, P.C.M. and J.P.L. Schoormans (2005), "Product Personality and Its Influence on Consumer Preference", *Journal of Consumer Marketing*, 22(4), 189-197.

Herzberg, Frederick (1974), "Motivation-Hygiene Profiles: Pinpointing What Ails The Organization", *Organizational Dynamics*, 3 (2), 18-29.

Johar, J.S. and M. Joseph Sirgy (1991), "Value-Expressive versus Utilitarian Advertising Appeals: When and Why to Use Which Appeal", *Journal of Advertising*, 20 (3), 23-33.

Keller, Ed (2007), "Unleashing the Power of Word of Mouth: Creating Brand Advocacy to Drive Growth", *Journal of Advertising Research*, 47 (4), 448-452.

McCracken, Grant (1989), "Who Is the Celebrity Endorser? Cultural Foundations of the Endorsement Process", *Journal of Consumer Research*, 16 (3), 310-321.

McWilliam, Gil (2000), "Building Stronger Brands through Online Communities", *Sloan Management Review*, 41 (3), 43-54.

Nelson (1974), "Advertising as Information", *Journal of Political Economy*, 83 (July-August), 729-54.

Pirsig, Robert M. (1999), *Zen and the Art of Motorcycle Maintenance: An Inquiry into Values*, New York: Quill.

Functional Regret: The Positive Effects of Regret on Learning from Negative Experiences

Noelle Nelson, University of Minnesota, USA

Selin Malkoc, Washington University, USA

Baba Shiv, Stanford University, USA

Popular wisdom encourages people to "Learn from experiences" while placing equal importance on not regretting anything. This implies that people can gain all the necessary information from their mistakes, without enduring any of the pain. Previous literature has focused mainly on the detrimental effects of regret. For example, Zeelenberg and Beattie (1997) found that participants who have lost money in a negotiation task perform badly (to the point of losing money) on a subsequent negotiation task.

Other related literature has shown that emotion, in general, can cause negative outcomes. Shiv, Loewenstein and Bechara (2005) showed that brain damaged patients who do not suffer negative emotional feedback after a financial loss end up making more money in the task. These patients were not swayed to a set of investments that had low-yield, but less risky, outcomes. In the current research, we take the evolutionary perspective that regret, as with any emotion, is functional. Therefore, we posit that regret (i.e., negative emotion) is a necessary condition for learning from negative experience.

Further, we make an important contribution by testing the effects of the emotional side of regret, while keeping cognitive feedback constant. Zeelenberg (1999) has noted that regret is made up of both cognitive and emotional components. To the best of our knowledge, no research has examined only the emotional component. Rather, comparisons have always been drawn between groups of people who have had negative cognitive feedback (experience regret) and groups of people who do not experience negative feedback. Our research draws conclusions on the effects of regret on learning from comparing people who feel more or less regret. Also, much research has shown the effects of anticipated regret, while we show that experienced regret can be beneficial.

The current research provides evidence that regret is helpful for learning from past mistakes. In addition, we show that this emotion-learning is domain dependent. That is, feeling regret does not result in a global state where people make better decisions. In fact, we posit that the negative emotion caused by regret will negatively affect decisions made outside the domain in which it was felt. However, subsequent decisions that are similar to the decisions that caused regret will benefit from regret. This results in our two hypotheses:

H1: For participants who experience regret to a greater degree, subsequent decisions that are similar to the regretted decisions will be better than for participants who experienced regret to a lesser degree.

H2: For participants who experience regret to a greater degree, subsequent decisions that are dissimilar to the regretted decisions will be worse than for participants who experienced regret to a lesser degree.

Our design results in two factors: felt-regret (high vs. low) and decision type (domain: similar vs. dissimilar). Regret was manipulated between subjects and decision type was measured within subjects. Undergraduates entered the lab and were seated in individual rooms. Past literature has shown that caffeine can heighten emotional arousal (see Sawyer, Julia and Turin 1982 for a review), so we manipulate the extent of felt-regret with caffeine. Participants were told that they'd be asked to drink and evaluate coffee. Half of the participants were given regular coffee (caffeinated) and half were given decaffeinated coffee.

Participants were then asked to evaluate pairs of products, and were given the chance to purchase the products with five endowed tokens. Three products (pencil, car decal and electronic game) were presented in increasing order of desirability (pre-tested), but participants believed the order was random and did not know when their last chance to "buy" a product would be. Therefore, most people purchased the second product (car decal) and were not able to buy the third product (electronic game). This resulted in our regret manipulation.

After the regret manipulation, participants were asked how much they would require to delay the arrival of a DVD they ordered by three or ten days. This delay measure measured impulsivity on a domain dissimilar decision (because shipping delays are quite different than decisions to buy small objects). Domain similar decisions were measured by taking willingness-to-pay measures on items similar to the regret manipulation items (e.g., keychain, game book, photo-frame). The key difference between the domain dissimilar (shipping delay) and domain similar (small objects) measures is that the shipping delay question is measuring impatience to receive an item, while the product measure is simply willingness-to-pay for an item.

Consistent with our conceptualization, we found in a repeated measures analysis that participants who had consumed caffeine (high felt-regret condition) were willing to pay less on similar items than participants who had decaf coffee (low felt-regret condition). This evidence is in line with hypothesis H1.

Consistent with hypothesis H2, participants who were in the high felt-regret condition did not perform as well when it came to decisions outside the learning domain as did the decaf participants. That is, when asked how much money they would need to delay the shipping of a DVD, participants who experienced greater regret required more money to delay the shipping by three or ten days.

Overall, we propose that regret is a necessary component for learning from mistakes and is, therefore, functional. We provide contributions to the literature by separating the effects of emotional regret from cognitive regret and by manipulating experienced regret (instead of anticipated). Further, regret learning is domain-specific and guides decision making in a directed way. Regret does not cause people to become more conservative with all decisions, but leads them to make better decisions after they have experienced regret in a certain domain.

References

Sawyer D.A., H.L. Julia and A.C. Turin (1982), "Caffeine and Human Behavior: Arousal, Anxiety, and Performance Effects," *Journal of Behavioral Medicine*, 5, 415-39.

Shiv, Baba, George Loewenstein and Antoine Bechara (2005), "The Dark side of Emotion in Decision-Making: When Individuals with Decreased Emotional Reactions Make More Advantageous Decisions," *Cognitive Brain Research,* 23 (1), 83-92.

Zeelenberg, Marcel (1999), "Anticipated Regret, Expected Feedback and Behavioral Decision-making," *Journal of Behavioral Decision Making*, 12, 93-106.

Zeelenberg, Marcel and Jane Beattie (1997), "Consequences of Regret Aversion:Additional Evidence for Effects of Feedback on Decision Making," *Organizational Behavior and Human Decision Processes*, 72, 63-78.

Factors Affecting Response Accuracy in Virtual Worlds

Francesco Massara, IULM University, Italy

Thomas P. Novak, University of California, Riverside, USA

Virtual worlds are emerging online environments that are beginning to be leveraged as a platform for consumer and marketing research (Bloomfield 2007; Hemp 2006; Menti 2007; Novak 2007, 2008). We compare the accuracy of responses obtained in virtual worlds with responses collected from traditional web-based research. We hypothesize that under certain conditions, data collected within a virtual world environment will generate more accurate responses than surveys administered through traditional Web browsers. We focus on low elaboration recognition tasks involving visual and text-based stimuli, and on how consumer motivational and characteristics of virtual worlds moderate accuracy on these tasks.

As highly visual environments, imagery plays an important role in information processing in virtual worlds. Because of their visual nature, virtual worlds induce imagery rather than discursive processing (MacInnis and Price 1987). For example, interacting with virtual objects has been found to facilitate mental imagery, which in turn has a positive impact on behavioral intentions (Schlosser 2003). A visual rather than text stimulus is congruent with the context of a virtual world, and this will predispose respondents toward imagery processing, resulting in a more accurate processing of images than text in virtual worlds. Thus:

H1: Response accuracy is greater for a visual (text) stimulus in surveys administered in virtual worlds (traditional Web browsers).

Three features differentiate virtual worlds from traditional two-dimensional Web environments: sensory experience, social networking, and virtual economy. First, human-computer interaction in virtual worlds is driven by a highly visual technology that engenders a more deeply immersive sensory experience than in the incorporeal, largely text-based *environment of the Web. Second, despite the fact that virtual worlds merely simulate the realism of physical places, the social interactions within them can be strikingly real (Grimmelmann 2004); Gorini et al. 2007; Bainbridge 2007; Chesney et al. 2007; Yee et al. 2007). Third, virtual worlds such as Second Life support internal economies with convertible currencies, intellectual property and free market exchange, resulting in increased realism and greater motivation to play (Ondrejka 2007).

These three features of virtual world relate to Yee's (2007) model of user motivations for playing in online games. Yee identifies three dominant dimensions: immersion (curiosity and escapism), social (behaving altruistically by helping others) and achievement (the desire to gain power and for the accumulation of wealth symbols and status).

Within virtual worlds, the level of user motivation along each of the three dimensions of immersion, social and achievement is expected to related to the user's response accuracy; we would further expect the relationship of user motivation to response accuracy to be stronger in virtual worlds than for studies fielded via traditional Web browsers. In addition, the salience of the three virtual world features of sensory experience, social networking and virtual economy would be expected to further moderate the relationship of motivation and response accuracy. Each of the three virtual world characteristics acts as moderators, each on a corresponding aspect of user motivation:

H2: The difference in the level of accuracy between consumers looking for high and low immersive sensory experience will be larger in virtual worlds compared to traditional Web-based research, and this difference will be further increased in the virtual world condition when sensory experience is more salient.

H3: The difference in the level of accuracy between consumers looking for high and low social networking opportunities will be larger in virtual worlds compared to traditional Web-based research, and this difference will be further increased in the virtual world condition when social networking is more salient.

H4: The difference in the level of accuracy between consumers looking for high and low achievement will be larger in virtual worlds compared to traditional Web-based research, and this difference will be further increased in the virtual world condition when the virtual economy is more salient.

These hypotheses will be tested in a series of four planned studies. Respondents will be randomly selected from a university panel of Second Life users, contacted via e-mail, and assigned to one of three survey context conditions: 1) In-world using survey fielded entirely in Second Life; 2) In-then-out-world (i.e., the respondent is sent into Second Life and their avatar remains in Second Life while the respondent is directed to a Web-based survey), and 3) Out-world using a Web-based survey.

In a first study, we compare response accuracy for visual vs. text stimuli in research studies administered in virtual worlds vs. via Web browsers. Dependent measures include objective statistics d' and ? from a signal detection task (SDT). The SDT will be a memory exercise featuring three sets of stimuli (picture, text, picture and text). Signal strength will be manipulated by varying the degree to which stimuli in a set differ from each other. Three consumer motivations for using virtual worlds–immersion, social, and achievement, are tested as moderators of response accuracy.

The parameter d' indicates the strength of the signal relative to noise, and larger values of d' indicate greater sensitivity of the respondent in recognizing previous information. The parameter ? captures whether the respondent's decision style in a memory task is liberal or conservative, meaning that the responder has a tendency to say "yes" or "no" (Tashchian, White and Pak 1988). Values of ? less than 1 indicate a liberal decision style with a greater tendency to say "yes," while values of ? greater than 1 indicate a conservative decision style with greater tendency to say "no." We expect that for image recall in a virtual world, d' will be higher and the response criterion will be stricter with ?>1, as compared to a traditional web setting.

In a series of three additional studies, we manipulate the salience of the there aforementioned characteristics of virtual worlds–sensory experience, social networking, and virtual economy–and test these as moderators along with median splits on the three consumer motivations for using virtual worlds.

This research will provide evidence of the relative accuracy of virtual worlds vs. traditional Web-based research for different marketing stimuli and consumer motivations. Response accuracy has important marketing applications ranging from advertising recall to accuracy in market research surveys. Our emphasis upon low-elaboration imagery processing has direct implications for advertising and consumer learning about product information in virtual worlds, and provides a methodological and theoretical foundation for extensions of this research to alternative modes of imagery instantiation and to higher-elaboration imagery and cognitive processing.

References

Bainbridge W.S. (2007), "The Scientific Research Potential of Virtual Worlds," *Science*, 317 (5837), 472–476.

Bloomfield, Robert (2007), "Worlds For Study: Invitation–Virtual Worlds for Studying Real-World Business, working paper, Johnson Graduate School of Management, Cornell University (http://ssrn.com/abstract=988984).

Chesney T., S. Chuah and R. Hoffmann (2007), "Virtual World Experimentation: An Exploratory Study," available at http://ssrn.com/abstract=1068225.

Gorini A., Gaggioli A. and G. Riva (2007), "Virtual Worlds, Real Healing," *Science*, 318 (5856), 1549.

Grimmelmann, J.T.L. (2004), "Virtual Worlds as Comparative Law," *New York Law School Law Review*, Vol. 49 (1), p. 147-184.

Hemp, Paul (2006), "Avatar-Based Marketing," *Harvard Business Review,* June, 48-57.

MacInnis D.J. and L.L. Price (1987), "The Role of Imagery in Information Processing: Review and Extensions," *Journal of Consumer Research*, 13(4), 437-491.

Menti, M. (2007), "Conducting Research in Second Life," *Quirks Marketing Research Review,* May, 44-48.

Novak T.P., (2007), "Consumer Behavior Research in Second Life: Issues and Approaches," *Association for Consumer Research Pre-Conference*, Memphis, TN, October 25 2007.

Novak, T.P. (2008), "eLab City: A Platform for Consumer Behavior Research in Virtual Worlds," *Marketing Science Institute Conference, Leveraging Online Media and Online Marketing,* Palm Springs, CA, February 6-8.

Ondrejka C.R. (2007), "Aviators, Moguls, Fashionistas and Barons: Economics and Ownership in Second Life," available at http://ssrn.com/abstract=614663.

Schlosser A. (2003), "Experiencing Products in the Virtual World: The Role of Goal and Imagery in Influencing Attitudes versus Purchase Intentions," *Journal of Consumer Research*, 30 (2), 184-198.

Tashchian A., J.D. White and S. Pak (1988), "Signal Detection Analysis and Advertising Recognition: An Introduction to Measurement and Interpretation Issues," *Journal of Marketing Research*, 25 (4), 397-404.

Yee N. (2007), "Motivations of Play in Online Games," *Journal of CyberPsychology and Behavior*, 9, 772-775.

Yee N., J.N. Bailenson, M. Urbanek, F. Chang, and D. Merget (2007), "The Unbearable Likeness of Being Digital: The Persistence of Nonverbal Social Norms in Online Virtual Environments," *Journal of CyberPsychology and Behavior*, 10 (1), 115-121.

Conscious Consumption and its Components: An Exploratory Study

Caroline Roux, McGill University, Canada

Jacques Nantel, HEC Montréal, Canada

Background

Socially responsible, environmentally friendly, or ethical consumption, as well as other terms that are often used in a conceptually similar manner, are frequently found in the marketing literature (Antil and Benett, 1979). Yet, there does not seem to be much consistency in the various terminologies and definitions that have been offered (Antil and Benett, 1979) about these components of "conscious" consumption.

For example, Roberts (1995) states that research in marketing often equates socially responsible and environmentally conscious consumer behavior. Leigh, Murphy and Enis (1988), on the other hand, believe that ecologically concerned consumers are a subset of the socially conscious category. Anderson, Henion, and Cox (1974), however, state that it would be unwise to interpret socially responsible and ecologically conscious consumers as constituting a single group. Furthermore, Webster (1975), as well as many other authors (e.g., Brooker, 1976; Antil and Bennett, 1979; Antil, 1984; Roberts, 1995; Roberts, 1996b), state that they were studying socially responsible consumers, but used dependent variables that concerned only the environment. Similarly, Carrigan and Attalla (2001) don't make a distinction between ethical and socially responsible consumers; while Copper-Martin and Holbrook (1993) state that the only significant stream of research on ethical consumer behavior has focused so far on environmental concerns. However, Shaw and Shiu (2003) mention that it is important to distinguish between "green" and "ethical" consumerism, because more wide-ranging ethical issues can add significantly to the complexity of consumer decisions, and ethical concerns are often ongoing and irresolvable.

Following Anderson, Henion and Cox's (1974) investigation more than 30 years ago, this study aims at better understanding the similarities and differences among the various types of "conscious" consumption. We focus on environmentally conscious, socially conscious and ethical consumption, because these domains received the most attention in the literature and also created the most confusion. Clearly, clarifying the main "conscious" consumption concepts is very important, because it will provide a foundation in understanding individual differences in consumption patterns that are becoming increasingly critical in the context of global warming.

Method

In order to study "conscious" consumption, a questionnaire was built from three major consumption scales. Socially responsible consumption was measured with the help of Roberts' (1995) SRCB scale (Socially Responsible Consumer Behavior), environmentally conscious consumption was assessed with Roberts' (1996a) ECCB scale (Environmentally Conscious Consumer Behavior), and ethical consumption was measured with Creyer and Ross' (1997) scale. These scales were selected because they appeared to be the most reliable ones available in the literature. They were pretested twice, mostly to test for their reliability and to reduce the number of items in each of them, in order to have a more parsimonious questionnaire. The final version of the questionnaire included 28 items taken from the three previous scales–eight from Roberts' (1995) scale, ten from Roberts' (1996a) scale and ten from Creyer and Ross' (1997) scale–which were randomized. It also included three items that measured participants' perceived level of identification with these three types of "conscious" consumption. The final version of the questionnaire was sent to the participants of a major Canadian Internet panel. All items were measured on a 5 point scale (with response categories ranging from totally disagree to totally agree).

Results

1338 questionnaires were returned (56,7% female, mean age=45), but many of them included missing data, which left us with 910 completed questionnaires for the environmentally conscious consumption scale, 949 for the socially responsible consumption scale, and 1200 for the ethical consumption scale. All scales provided satisfying results both at the exploratory (principal component analysis) as well as the confirmatory (structural equation modeling) level. The composition of two scales (Roberts, 1996a; Creyer and Ross, 1997) were however different from the original number of dimensions obtained by the authors. Indeed, three components were obtained for Roberts' (1996a) scale, instead of the two stated in his paper, and two for the Creyer and Ross (1997) scale, instead of the four stated in their article.

The factorial score of each scale was used to test for the correlation between each of them. All scales were highly correlated (SRCB-ECCB=0.588, SRCB-Ethical=0.544, and ECCB-Ethical=0.450; all $p<0.001$), which suggests that there is an overlap among these different concepts of "conscious" consumption. In addition, the scales factor score and the respective participants' perception measures were strongly related (SRCB=0.504, ECCB=0.556, and Ethical=0.555; all $p<0.001$).

Conclusion and Discussion

The results of this exploratory study suggest that the different concepts of "conscious" consumption overlap. We therefore investigated whether the different types of conscious consumption are nested or hierarchically ordered. Indeed, the percentages of participants' perceived level of identification to the different types of conscious consumption indicate that there are more participants who identify themselves as environmentally friendly (67.4%) than socially responsible (48.6%) or ethical (44.6%).[2] Further analyses partially supported this hierarchical relationship: People appear to become concerned about the environment first, possibly because it is concrete and easy to understand, and then become more conscious about their social responsibility (which involves broader issues like human and animal rights) and ethics (which takes into account the morality of our actions and is thus much more abstract). Although these results warrants further experimental investigations, it provides an avenue for reconciling the inconsistent use of these concepts in the literature. Equally important, a hierarchical view of "concern" or "consciousness" has important implications. Indeed, most field interventions aimed at raising consumers' "consciousness" seem to rely on more concrete actions first (e.g., making small behavioral changes), and then on more abstract actions (e.g., changing your mindset about consumption in general). Moreover, this conception of "conscious" consumption share defining characteristics with goal hierarchies and means-end chains, because the elements of their structure are organized hierarchically; with lower-level elements serving as means to achieve higher-level elements as ends (Pieters, Baumgartner, and Allen; 1995).

References

Anderson, Thomas W. Jr., Karl E. Henion and Eli P. Cox (1974). "Socially vs. Ecologically Responsible Consumers." In Ronald C. Curhan (Ed.), *1974 AMA Combined Proceedings: New Marketing for Social and Economic Progress and Marketing's Contributions to the Firm and to the Society* (Series No. 36, pp. 304-311). Chicago, IL : American Marketing Association.

Antil, John H. (1984). "Socially Responsible Consumers: Profile and Implications for Public Policy," *Journal of Macromarketing*, 4 (fall), 18-39.

---

[2] The percentages do not add up to 100 because participants could assign themselves to more than one type of conscious consumption.

Antil, John H. and Peter D. Bennett (1979). "Construction and Validation of a Scale to Measure Socially Responsible Consumption Behavior." In Karl E. Henion II and Thomas C. Kinnear (eds.), *The Conserver Society* (pp. 51-68), Chicago : American Marketing Association.

Brooker, George (1976). "The Self-Actualizing Socially Conscious Consumer," *Journal of Consumer Research*, 3 (2), 107-112.

Carrigan, Marylyn and Ahmad Attalla (2001). "The myth of the ethical consumer-do ethics matter in purchase behaviour?," *Journal of Consumer Marketing*, 18 (7), 560-577.

Copper-Martin, Elizabeth and Morris B. Holbrook (1993). "Ethical Consumption Experiences and Ethical Space [online]," *Advances in Consumer Research*, 20, 113-118.

Creyer, Elizabeth H. and William T. Ross Jr (1997). "The influence of firm behavior on purchase intention: do consumers really care about business ethics?," *Journal of Consumer Marketing*, 14 (6), 421-432.

Leigh, James H., Patrick E. Murphy and Ben M. Enis (1988). "A New Approach to Measuring Socially Responsible Consumption Tendencies," *Journal of Macromarketing*, 8 (spring), 5-20.

Pieters, Rik, Hans Baumgartner and Doug Allen (1995). "A means-end chain approach to consumer goal structures," *International Journal of Research in Marketing*, 12, 227-244.

Roberts, James A. (1995). "Profiling levels of socially responsible consumer behavior: A cluster analytic approach and its implications for marketing," *Journal of Marketing Theory and Practice*, 3 (4), 97-117.

Roberts, James A. (1996a). "Green Consumers in the 1990s: Profile and Implications for Advertising," *Journal of Business Research*, 36, 217-231.

Roberts, James A. (1996b). "Will the socially responsible consumer please step forward?," *Business Horizons*, 39 (1), 79-84.

Shaw, Deirdre and Edward Shiu (2003). "Ethics in consumer choice: A multivariate modelling approach," *European Journal of Marketing*, 37 (10), 1485-1518.

Webster, Frederick E. Jr (1975). "Determining the Characteristics of the Socially Conscious Consumer," *Journal of Consumer Research*, 2 (3), 188-196.

From Trash to Treasure: Freecycle.org as a Case of Generalized Reciprocity

Michelle R. Nelson, University of Illinois at Urbana-Champaign, USA
Mark A. Rademacher, University of Wisconsin–Madison, USA

FREE! Free software, songs, and stuff. The Internet provides a place to share technology, art and goods. Thus, Cyberspace may be fostering a new age of altruism that contrasts the egoism of commoditization (Belk 2007). Whereas sharing source code or Napster files offers a way to give without sacrificing ownership (Gielser 2006), giving tangible goods means letting go of the stuff-for good. Members of Freecycle.org do just that. Unlike traditional market systems or other second order (used) systems (e.g., craigslist), members give and receive goods absent monetary exchange. Thus, Freecycle serves as an apt forum to explore contemporary consumer gift systems and the phenomenon of reciprocity (Giesler 2006).

Reciprocity, a "set of rules and obligations that builds the complex pattern of give and take and helps establish moral standards of social solidarity" (Gouldner 1960, cf Gielser 2006), need not be tit-for-tat. Anthropological literature has revealed a continuum from *generalized reciprocity* (people give without expectation of anything in return) to *balanced reciprocity* (some expectation of repayment in a future exchange) to *negative reciprocity* (expectation of immediate repayment; Sahlins 1972).

We investigate Freecycle as an example of a traditional gift system with a focus on identifying how reciprocity is enacted and enforced. The multi-method approach included: (1) netnographic analysis of post content over a 1-month period; (2) an online survey (n=183) to elicit motivations for membership and to measure consumption attitudes and behaviors; and (3) depth interviews with nine members from a Freecycle group to gain a deeper understanding of Freecycle attitudes and behaviors. Analysis included both inductive and deductive as well as qualitative and quantitative approaches.

Findings

Gift Economy? Our analyses revealed distinct differences between Freecycle and traditional gift economies (e.g., Mauss 1925/1990). Traditional gift economies are defined by feelings of reciprocity (Malinowski 1953) that seem to represent a balanced or negative reciprocity. In this view, the "pure" gift does not exist (Mauss 1925/1990). Rather than being a "free and disinterested" social process, gift giving is inherently "constrained and self-interested." Gifts establish ties of reciprocity and interdependency among social actors and specific entities that provide benefits for both the gift giver and recipient (Hyde 1983; Malinowski 1953; Mauss 1925/1990). This traditional framework is altered, however, for Freecycle.org because of the predominance of a "generalized" reciprocity present within this community, as evidenced through the forum's structure, social rules, community and trust, articulated motivations and benefits of use.

Forum Structure. An average of 82 "offer and wanted" posts per day were observed in this community. Consequently, Freecyclers witness the flow of goods from one to another and see generalized reciprocity in action. These observations along with personal experience with Freecycle (the majority of our informants had experience in giving and receiving goods) may reinforce generalized reciprocity. Behavioral studies on humans (Berkowitz and Daniels 1964) and rats (Rutte and Taborsky 2007) suggest individuals may base cooperative behavior on prior experiences—irrespective of the identity of their partners. In other words, we can practice generalized reciprocity if we believe that others are doing so and we have experienced such acts of kindness in the past.

Rules and Social Norms. Although generalized reciprocity is typically witnessed in kinship groups or among villagers who know one another (Sahlins 1972), research in economics has found even with "constantly changing partners" (a.k.a strangers), elements of generalized reciprocity were witnessed when self-enforcing social norms encouraged such behaviors (e.g., Bó 2007; Kandori 1992). The Freecycle group offered rules to ensure reciprocity and social norms helped enforce it. Guidelines were offered for the number of "Wanted requests" an individual could post; the frequency of repeat requests; and the requirement of placing an Offer before a Wanted post. Further, Moderators promote reciprocity by monitoring Offers-to-Wanted ratios and sending notes to those who practice negative reciprocity.

Community and Trust. Research on kinship groups has observed that there is maximum trust and minimum social distance among people who engage in generalized reciprocity (Sahlins 1972). Despite critiques of Internet communities as "faceless and fleshless" (DeGraff, Wann, Naylor and Robin 2001, 61) and arguments suggesting reciprocity may diminish among larger communities (Hyde 1983), Freecyclers repeatedly referred to the group as community and felt connected to other members. The connection, however, mirrors relationships of "limited liability" (Muñiz and O'Guinn 2001); nothing more is expected from members other than to donate and request items, and to pick up those items on time. Still, members discussed a consciousness of kind ("atypical consumers") that manifested itself as a shared identity, which fostered trust (Muñiz and O'Guinn 2001).

Motivations & Benefits For Use. Although predicated on environmental activism, when asked why they use Freecycle, members repeatedly and passionately referred to receiving free stuff (egoism) and the "life" left in their goods and the possibility of sharing with others who needed them rather than environmental motives. This sort of generalized reciprocity is similar to that observed outside of kin groups–especially from those with wealth when they shared goods with those in need (Udehn 1996). Rather than leaving goods on the curb or donating to charity shops, Freecycle members wanted to know that someone would really benefit from their goods. Thus, the perceived need was an important part of this generalized reciprocity. Giving to those who demonstrated the most need in their 'stories' was a common practice. Thus, the deserving heuristic was applied, much like in dispositional strategies with family members (Price, Arnould, and Curasi 2000). Throughout the gift process, Freecyclers sacrifice monetary reward in favor of a feeling of helping others.

In sum, the existence of generalized reciprocity appears to operate in a contemporary online community. Different from traditional kin-based reciprocity, this forum allowed 'strangers' to freely give without expecting anything in return from the recipient. Rather, the group itself experiences reciprocity and perpetuates the gift exchange. Through this continuous exchange members appear to practice a new form of altruism while fulfilling the egoism of commoditization (Belk 2007). Freecycle is not a form of escape from the market (Kozinets 2002); the community remains firmly entrenched in the market (Arnould 2007).

References

Arnould, Eric J. (2007), "Should Consumer Citizens Escape the Market?" *The Annals of the American Academy of Political and Social Science, 611*, 96-111.

Belk, Russell W. (2007), "Why Not Share Rather Than Own?" *The Annals of the American Academy of Political and Social Science, 611*, 126-140.

Berkowitz Leonard and Louise R. Daniels (1964), "Affecting the Salience of the Social Responsibility Norm: Effects of Past Help on the Response to Dependency Relationships," *Journal of Abnormal Social Psychology, 68*, 275–281

Bó, Pedro Dal (2007), "Social Norms, Cooperation and Inequality," *Economic Theory, 30*, 1, 89-105.

DeGraff, John, David Wann, Thomas H. Naylor, and Vicki Robin (2001), *Affluenza: The all-consuming epidemic*, New York: Bennett-Korehler.

Giesler, Markus (2006), "Consumer Gift Systems," *Journal of Consumer Research*, 33(June), 283-290.

Hyde, Lewis (1983), *The Gift: Imagination and the Erotic Life of Property*, New York: Vintage Books.

Kandori, Michihiro (1992), "Social Norms and Community Enforcement," *Review of Economic Studies, 59*, 63–80.

Kozinets, Robert (2002), "Can Consumers Escape the Market? Emancipatory Illuminations from Burning Man," *Journal of Consumer Research, 29*(June), 20-38.

Malinowski, Bronislaw (1953), *Argonauts of the Western Pacific: An Account of the Native Enterprise and Adventure in the Archipelagoes of Melanesian New Guinea*, New York: E. P. Dutton & Co., Inc.

Mauss, Marcel (1925/1990), *The Gift: Forms and Functions of Exchange in Archaic Societies*, New York: Norton.

Muniz, Albert and Thomas C. O'Guinn (2001),"Brand Community," *Journal of Consumer Research* 27(March), 412-432.

Price, Linda L., Eric J. Arnould, and Carolyn F. Curasi (2000), "Older Consumers' Disposition of Special Possessions," *Journal of Consumer Research*, 27 (September), 179-201.

Rutte, Claudia and Michael Taborsky (2007), "Generalized Reciprocity in Rats," *PLoS Biology, 5*, 7. Available for download at http://biology.plosjournals.org/perlserv/?request=get-document&doi=10.1371/journal.pbio.0050196&ct=1. Accessed March 24, 2008.

Sachlins, Marshall (1972), *Stone Age Economies*, New York: Aldine Books.

Udehn, Lars (1996), *The Limits of Public Choice: A Sociological Critique of the Economic Theory of Politics*, London: Routledge.

Consumer Entrepreneurs: A Netnographic Study of Facebook's Next Top Model

Marie-Agnès Parmentier, York University, Canada

"Have you always thought that you would do a better job than the girls on ANTM and CNTM and have always wanted to enter the competition? Well now you can!!! Get ready for this competition! Inspired by America's and Canada's Next Top Model, we are going to have our own Facebook Model Search."
Silvia[3], *founder of the Facebook's Next Top Model Competition*

---

[3]Pseudonyms are used to preserve informants anonymity.

Consumer Culture Theory has an established tradition of examining consumers' creative appropriation of marketers' offerings (see Arnould and Thompson 2005). Concepts such as co-creation (Vargo and Lusch 2004), countervailing market responses (Thompson and Coskuner-Balli 2007), interagency (Kozinets et al. 2004), textual poaching (Jenkins 1992), and prosumption (Kozinets 2007) are part of that tradition.

Following the stream of research on audience participation in media culture (e.g., Jenkins 1992, 2006; Kozinets 2001; 2007) and the current interest in entrepreneurship in consumer tribes (Cova, Kozinets and Shankar 2007), this working paper focuses on fans who attempt to overcome the limited chances for participation in a particular institutional field. The project explores consumer entrepreneurship in the context of the grassroots Facebook competition for aspiring fashion models based on the reality TV hit *"America's Next Top Model."* One objective of the project is to refine our understanding of fans' producerly consumption activities and their relation to consumer entrepreneurship. A second objective is to examine the implications for marketers and other institutional members.

Background

On May 20th 2003, supermodel Tyra Banks launched the reality television series *America's Next Top Model* (ANTM). Now in its 10th cycle (season), ANTM has become a worldwide phenomenon broadcast in 90 countries (www.channelcanada.com/Article1140.html) with franchises in 40 including (www.tyrabanks.com) Australia, Britain, Canada, China, Germany, Israel, Norway, the Philippines, and Russia.

On ANTM, viewers are exposed to the transformation of everyday young women into potential top models as they compete for the chance at a modeling career. The show opens up a window– albeit a limited and potentially distorted one–on the modeling industry and allows viewers to learn about the norms and practices of the field via exclusive footage of high fashion photo shoots, runway shows, casting sessions, and advertising production.

Fashion modeling reality TV first appeared on North American screens only five years ago. Its emergence and popularity constitute a novel reality for the modeling field in that its production practices are increasingly being commodified (Sadrai-Orafai 2005). Fans' enthusiasm for the show paired with new affordable technologies and the possibilities of the Web 2.0. are resulting in producerly consumption activities ranging from fan fiction to wikimedia (cf. Kozinets 2007) to grassroots modeling competitions.

Method

Countless blogs (e.g., www.topmodelgossip.com), online discussion boards (e.g., www.fansofrealitytv/america-s-next-top-model-10/), and social networking groups (e.g., Addicted to America's Next Top Model) devoted to fans' interest in ANTM can be found on the Internet.

The focal site of investigation for this project is the Facebook's Next Top Model Competition (FNTM). This competition was launched in March 2007 by a fan of ANTM, an 18 year old high school student who created an outlet where aspiring models can compete for modeling exposure. In less than 5 days, the group grew from 100 members to 900. One year later, the FNTM competition, now in its third cycle, counts more than 3,000 members, making it the largest and most popular group of its kind on Facebook.

This paper is part of a larger netnographic (Kozinets 2002) project on the fandom of fashion modeling reality TV. I became interested in this grassroots competition while I was researching the different fan groups devoted to ANTM. My initial interest for this specific group was triggered by its professionalism. For instance, just like on television, contestants vie for "real" modeling prizes including photo shoots with professional photographers.

I made my entrée in June 2007. I contacted the founder and posted a comment to disclose my identity as a researcher. I since have been monitoring the activities of the group on a weekly basis. The data collected so far is comprised of a formal online interview and informal ongoing email exchanges with the founder, discussion threads, pictures, and posts. I plan on conducting additional interviews with members such as judges and contestants in order to reach theoretical saturation.

From the start, I have been engaged in an iterative process that is the hallmark of grounded theory (Strauss and Corbin 1998). My interpretation of the data is constructed through continuously moving between the literature and the individual postings, chunks of postings, entire discussion threads, interview data and the emergent understanding of the data set.

Preliminary Findings

Producerly consumption and consumer entrepreneurship

Not all fans actively engage in creative appropriation of the object of their fandom. Those who do, however, help co-create new meanings and products for other fans to appreciate. They add layers to the consumption experience of the original market offerings. In the FNTM group, fans who are aspiring models and those who are aspiring judges compete for a spot in the competition. The remaining members of the group can vote for their favourite contestants–an important difference from the television show-and share their critical evaluations of the different modeling performances.

On the one hand, consumer entrepreneurship surfaces on the part of the aspiring models who promote their potential and manage their trajectory in the competition. On the other hand, judges and lay-members alike participate in the management of an outlet for aspiring models to gain exposure, build photographic experience and win significant help to start a modeling career.

Implications for marketers and producers

These consumer entrepreneurs are reworking the traditional institutional arrangements of the field by expanding its modes of entry. They are also challenging–to some extent-the established legitimizing process typically experienced by fashion models.

Closer examination of the ripple effects of producerly consumption that results in consumer entrepreneurship should further our understanding of the co-creation paradigm.

References

Arnould, Eric and Craig Thompson (2005), Consumer Culture Theory (CCT): Twenty Years of Research, *Journal of Consumer Research*, 31 (4), 868-882.

Cova, Bernard, Robert V. Kozinets and Avi Shankar (2007) *Consumer Tribes*, Burlington, MA: Butterworth-Heinemann.

Jenkins, Henry (2006) *Convergence Culture: Where Old and New Media Collide*, New York: NYU Press.

_____ (1992) *Textual Poachers: Television Fans & Participatory Culture*, New York: Routledge.

Kozinets, Robert V. (2007) "Inno-Tribes: *Star Trek* as wikimedia," in eds. Bernard Cova, Robert V. Kozinets and Avi Shankar, *Consumer Tribes*, Burlington, MA: Butterworth-Heinemann, 194-209.

_____, John F. Sherry, Jr., Diana Storm, Adam Duhachek, Krittinee Nuttavuthisit and Benét DeBerry-Spence (2004), "Ludic Agency and Retail Spectacle," *Journal of Consumer Research*, 31 (3), 658-672.

Kozinets, Robert V. (2002) "The Field Behind the Screen: Using Netnography for Marketing Research in Online Communities," *Journal of Marketing Research*, 39 (1), 61-72.

_____ (2001) "Utopian Enterprise: Articulating the Meanings of *Star Trek's* Culture of Consumption," *Journal of Consumer Research*, 28 (1), 67-88.

Sadrai-Orafai, Stephanie (2005) "Evidentiary vs. Aesthetic Evaluations: Production & the Fashion Image on *America's Next Top Model*," American Anthropological Association Annual meeting, Washington DC, November 30-4.

Strauss, Anselm and Juliet Corbin (1998), *Basics of Qualitative Research: Techniques and Procedures for Developing Grounded Theory*. Thousand Oaks, CA: Sage.

Thompson, Craig J. and Gokcen Coskuner-Balli (2007) "Countervailing Market Responses to Corporate Co-optation and the Ideological Recruitment of Consumption Communities," *Journal of Consumer Research*, 34 (August), 135-152.

Vargo, Stephen L. and Robert F. Lusch. (2004) "Evolving to a New Dominant Logic for Marketing," *Journal of Marketing*, 68 (1), 1-17.

www.channelcanada.com/Article1140.html, last access: 11-22-2007.

www.tyrabanks.com, last access: 07-03-2007.

Culture, Self-Control, and Consumer Financial Behavior

Dante Pirouz, University of California, Irvine, USA

Some people are better at saving money for the future, paying their bills on time, sticking to their diets, and living up to their promises. One common trait for these people is the ability to regulate behavior. Maintaining self-control, defined as the ability to monitor one's behaviors and choose actions that minimize negative outcomes (Baumeister 2002), is important to living a healthier and happier life. Individuals who exhibit self-control are more likely to have higher grades in school, more wealth accumulation, higher self-esteem, lower reports of psychopathology, less binge eating, lower levels of alcohol abuse, lower levels of addictions of all kinds, better relationships and more secure interpersonal attachments (Tangney, Baumeister, and Boone 2004).

Is there a cultural aspect to self-control? Previous work has found that culture can have a profound impact on how people process information and make decisions (Aaker and Sengupta 2000; Nisbet 2003; Nisbett et al. 2001; Nisbett, Peng, and Ji 2000). There is also evidence that the ability of self-control may have developed in humans as a result of the benefits gained from belonging to a close-knit cultural community (Vohs and Baumeister 2004). Experiments have shown that when people are excluded from social groups, they tend to demonstrate a decreased ability to regulate their behavior.

A key dimension of cultural orientation is collectivism-individualism. Collective cultures tend to emphasize group cohesion and harmony while individualistic cultures emphasize individualism and uniqueness. On the level of the individual, this construct is operationalized as an independent versus interdependent construal (Mandel 2003; Markus and Kitayama 1991; Singelis 1994). People who tend to hold more independent views are more likely to see themselves as distinct from others and view autonomy, self-sufficiency and the individual as important. Those who hold an interdependent self view will see themselves as interconnected with others and view connectedness, social context and the group as important. The independent view is usually ascribed to Westerners for example Americans and the interdependent view is usually associated with Easterners for example Chinese. One study found that subjects who were primed with an interdependent self-construal were more likely to take on financial risk but less likely to take on social risk versus those primed with a independent self-construal (Mandel 2003). However, this research emphasized the mediating effect of social network without looking at the role of self-control.

It has been argued that cultures vary in terms of the value they place on self-control (Fox and Calkins 2003; Logue 1995). Cultures where group cohesion and interdependence are important would be more likely to value self-control from their group members. If self-control is indeed a skill that can be taught and improved with practice, whether the development of this skill is coveted within a cultural group will have important implications for control-related behaviors in its members.

On the other hand, ethnic groups in the U.S. vary greatly in their propensity for financial risk. For example, recent work found that investment portfolios of Hispanic Americans tended to favor near-term savings, liquid and low risk investments versus non-Hispanic Americans even when controlling for income (Plath and Stevenson 2005). This leads to lower investment value and slower wealth accumulation rates for Hispanic American households. African American consumers also differ significantly from other Americans in their financial decision making in terms of financial product preference, product research and investment asset portfolio composition (Plath and Stevenson 2000). Investment portfolios for African Americans tend to concentrate in more conservative investments such as real property and life insurance assets in contrast with most Caucasian Americans who tend to hold higher corporate debt and equity securities. Overall, a test of the effect of race and ethnicity on financial risk tolerance found that Caucasian Americans had the highest financial risk tolerance, followed by African Americans and Hispanic Americans (Yao, Gutter, and Hanna 2005). While in these studies Asian Americans were not included in the samples, these findings seem to indicate nonetheless that culture has an impact on consumers' financial risk decisions and product choices. This is contrary to the intuitive expectation that individuals with more self-control would tend to refrain from taking risks (Tangney et al. 2004; Weber, Blais, and Betz 2002). It may be that increased self-control allows individuals to feel confident taking on more financial risk. The seeming contradiction between self-control and risk-taking financial behavior among different ethnic groups offers an opportunity to investigate how culture impacts choices involving risk and whether these behaviors can explain the divergent financial choices that ethnic groups exhibit. These issues are the topic of this study.

While no study has yet been conducted on cultural variations in self-control, Kacen and Lee (2002) conducted a study on the opposite trait, impulsiveness, and found that collectivists have the same likelihood of the trait impulsiveness but show less overall impulse buying behavior. While the trait impulsiveness seems to be equally distributed regardless of culture, culture was an important determinant in the expression of that trait exhibited in impulse buying behavior. It may be that certain cultures and ethnic groups value self-control more than others and therefore tend to teach and reinforce this skill. That would mean that individuals in these cultures have more stamina when exercising their self-control "muscle."

Data were collected from 534 participants on their attitudes and behaviors when making financial choices. In addition, demographic (ethnicity, age, gender, etc.), investing and income information was collected. The survey was administered via an online questionnaire. These data were analyzed using partial least squares (PLS) to examine the latent and structural relationship between the variables. PLS was chosen as the method of analysis since it allows for complex measurement and theoretical models to be estimated simultaneously (Falk and Miller 1992; West and Graham 2004). Preliminary results of the analysis found that the participants who belong to collectivist ethnicities, such as Asian Americans, tended to have higher levels of self-control when making financial decisions. These participants also had lower levels of impulsive behavior versus ethnic groups with higher levels of individualism. This resulted in higher levels of savings behavior versus spending behavior and higher propensity for financial risk.

References

Aaker, Jennifer L. and Jaideep Sengupta (2000), "Additivity Versus Attenuation: The Role of Culture in the Resolution of Information Incongruity," *Journal of Consumer Psychology*, 9 (2), 67-82.

Baumeister, Roy F. (2002), "Yielding to Temptation: Self-Control Failure, Impulsive Purchasing, and Consumer Behavior," *Journal of Consumer Research*, 28 (4), 670.

Falk, R. Frank and Nancy B. Miller (1992), *A Primer for Soft Modeling*, Akron, OH: University of Akron.

Fox, Nathan A. and Susan A. Calkins (2003), "The Development of Self-Control of Emotion: Intrinsic and Extrinsic Influences," *Motivation and Emotion*, 27 (1), 7-26.

Kacen, Jacqueline J. and Julie Anne Lee (2002), "The Influence of Culture on Consumer Impulsive Buying Behavior," *Journal of Consumer Psychology*, 12 (2), 163-76.

Logue, A.W. (1995), *Self-Control: Waiting until Tomorrow for What Your Want Today*.

Mandel, Naomi (2003), "Shifting Selves and Decision Making: The Effects of Self-Construal Priming on Consumer Risk-Taking," *Journal of Consumer Research*, 30 (1), 30.

Markus, Hazel Rose and Shinobu Kitayama (1991), "Culture and the Self: Implications for Cognition, Emotion, and Motivation," *Psychological Review*, 98 (2), 224-53.

Nisbett, Richard E. (2003), *The Geography of Thought*, New York, NY: Free Press.

Nisbett, Richard E., Incheol Choi, Kaiping Peng, and Ara Norenzayan (2001), "Culture and Systems of Thought: Holistic Versus Analytic Cognition," *Psychological Review*, 108 (2), 291-301.

Nisbett, Richard E., Kaiping Peng, and Li-Jun Ji (2000), "Culture, Control, and Perception of Relationships in the Environment," *Journal of Personality & Social Psychology*, 78 (5), 943-55.

Plath, D. Anthony and Thomas H. Stevenson (2000), "Financial Services and the African-American Market: What Every Financial Planner Should Know," *Financial Services Review*, 94, 343-59.

_____ (2005), "Financial Services Consumption Behavior across Hispanic American Consumers," *Journal of Business Research*, 58 (8), 1089-99.

Singelis, T.M. (1994), "The Measurement of Independent and Interdependent Self-Construals," *Personality & Social Psychology Bulletin*, 20, 580-91.

Tangney, June P., Roy F. Baumeister, and Angie Luzio Boone (2004), "High Self-Control Predicts Good Adjustment, Less Pathology, Better Grades, and Interpersonal Success," *Journal of Personality*, 72 (2), 271-322.

Vohs, Kathleen D. and R. F. Baumeister (2004), "Ego Depletion, Self-Control, and Choice," in *Handbook of Experimental Existential Psychology*, ed. Jeff Greenberg, Sander L. Koole and Tom Pyszczynski, New York, NY: Guillford.

Weber, Elke U., Ann-Rene Blais, and Nancy E. Betz (2002), "A Domain-Specific Risk-Attitude Scale: Measuring Risk Perceptions and Risk Behaviors," *Journal of Behavioral Decision Making*, 15, 263-90.

West, Joel and John L. Graham (2004), "A Linguistic-Based Measure of Cultural Distance and Its Relationship to Managerial Values," *Management International Review*, 44 (3), 239-60.

Yao, Rui, Michael S. Gutter, and Sherman D. Hanna (2005), "The Financial Risk Tolerance of Blacks, Hispanics and Whites," *Association for Financial Counseling and Planning Education*, 16 (1), 51-62.

The Collecting Continuum: Incorporating Amateur Scientists and Scholarly Collecting Behaviors

Greta L. Polites, Bucknell University, USA

Natural history collections have seen a resurgence in popularity in recent years. Wealthy collectors from around the world successfully compete with museums to obtain rare specimens such as complete dinosaur skeletons. Tiny yet rare seashells can sell for thousands of dollars. Even ordinary collectors with limited funds can purchase fossils and archaeological treasures online. However, such collectors increasingly find themselves at odds with environmentalist sentiments and societal norms, manifested in calls for legislation to close collecting sites to non-scientists and preserve finds solely for the benefit of the general public. Thus developing an better understanding of the collecting behaviors of these individuals is important not only from a consumer behavior perspective (due to the large amounts of money exchanged), but also to society as a whole, so that responsible collecting behaviors can be encouraged while still allowing individuals to fulfill their innate need to "collect things."

Collecting has been defined as "the process of actively, selectively, and passionately acquiring and possessing things removed from ordinary use and perceived as part of a set of non-identical objects or experiences" (Belk, 1995, p.479). Collecting is differentiated from hoarding, accumulating, investment acquisitions, and ordinary consumption. It is viewed as a form of "materialistic luxury consumption," as the collected objects have been removed from their ordinary use or instrumental purpose (Belk, 1995). A "true" collection is believed to assume such importance to the collector that it will not be dispensed with unless absolutely necessary (Pearce, 1992).

Prior research has classified collectors based on either their *motivations for collecting* (see McIntosh and Schmeichel, 2004), *level of interest* (Wright and Ray, 1969), *types of objects collected* (Bryant, 1989), or overall *mode of collecting* (Danet and Katriel, 1989). While specific types of collections (e.g., stamp, book, teapot) have been investigated, researchers have tended to make generalized statements about all collectors, while pointing out that many exceptions occur. Most notably, prior literature has discussed in passing, but never clearly delineated, "scholarly" or "scientific" collecting. We argue that the motives, behaviors, and characteristics of "amateur scientist" collectors (i.e., advanced collectors in fields possessing professional counterparts, such as the natural sciences), like those of their counterparts, can differ substantially from those of the collecting population at large.

In particular, altruistic motives for collecting have been largely ignored or discounted. This results from the view that collecting to preserve items for future generations is simply a personal justification for extreme collecting behaviors, rather than a legitimate motivation (Belk, 1995). In other cases, such collecting has been associated with a personal need for purpose and destiny, and thus with a goal of achieving immortality (McIntosh and Schmeichel, 2004). However, fossil and artifact collectors have historically donated specimens to museums, provided curators with important scientific information on their finds, and assisted research efforts in numerous other ways, often without demanding any special recognition in return. Thus, is a denial of altruistic or selfless motives for collecting always appropriate where scientific collecting is concerned? Do amateur scientists truly donate only because the "pursuit is more important than the possession" (Belk et al., 1988)? Conversely, do institutional scholars always have altruistic motives for the collecting undertaken in their own jobs?

Using natural history collecting as a backdrop, and drawing from the author's own years of experience as an amateur paleontologist, we present a series of hypothesized differences between "typical" consumer collecting (as described in Belk, 1995) and "scientific" or "scholarly" collecting. We further propose a new taxonomy of collectors, grounded in theories of serious leisure (Stebbins, 1979) and the amateur/professional continuum (Leadbeater and Miller, 2004), and incorporating features of past classification schemes, that includes all types of collectors while more accurately representing "scientific" or "scholarly" collecting.

On one end of the continuum are dabblers, novices, and casual collectors. Three different branches may occur from here (representing commercial, "popular," and scientific collecting). In the realm of "popular" (e.g., stamp, coin) collecting, serious hobbyists may become "scholarly" hobbyists, but no true professional counterpart exists. In the realm of scientific collecting, devoted amateurs may become pro-ams, the latter of which have professional/scholarly counterparts.

This taxonomy focuses on differentiating collectors at each major stage on the continuum based on *form*, *scope*, *expertise*, *motivation*, and *roles*. Overall, the continuum represents a transition not just from *undisciplined* to *disciplined* collecting behaviors, but also from *individualism* to *collectivism*. As we move further along each branch of the continuum, collectors exhibit an increasingly research-oriented approach to collecting, a narrower collecting focus, more specialized knowledge, and "altruistic" behavior.

Two phases of data collection support the proposed taxonomy. The first phase involved textual analysis of archived content from a listserv that promotes modern seashell collecting. Coding and analysis of discussions on the purpose and value of shell collecting indicate tension between casual collectors (interested primarily in the beauty of shells, enjoyment of collecting activities, or building of social bonds), and more advanced collectors (who, while sharing some of these interests, work closely with professional scientists and are very concerned with limiting the harm, via destruction of habitats and entire species populations, caused by widespread shell collecting). The latter group intentionally restricts their collecting activities to prevent environmental damage.

The second phase consists of a series of in-depth (1-2 hour), semi-structured interviews with fossil collectors ranging from novices and amateur scientists to institutional scholars. Findings indicate that many collectors (including professionals) feel conflicted by the internal compulsion to increase/complete their collections while still acting "responsibly." Of particular interest are experiences and events that lead some collectors to move from one end of the continuum to the other over time. By determining what motivates a collector to work more closely with professionals, become more scholarly in their approach, and even relinquish valued specimens in their collection, we can inform research institutions on how to improve relations with amateur collectors and motivate them to collect in more "socially responsible" ways. Thus this study contributes not only to the collecting literature, but also informs the literature on individual motivation, particularly in regards to the practice of socially responsible behavior.

References

Allmon, Warren D. (1997), "Collections in Paleontology," in *Paleontology in the 21st Century Workshop; International Senckenberg Conference*, H. R. Lane, J. Lipps, F. F. Steininger, and W. Ziegler, Eds., Kleine Senckenberg-Reihe No. 25. W. Kramer, Frankfurt, 155-159.

_____ (2005), "The Importance of Museum Collections in Paleobiology," *Paleobiology*, 31, 1-5.

Andreoni, James (1990). "Impure Altruism and Donations to Public Goods: A Theory of Warm-Glow Giving," *The Economic Journal*, 100, 464-477.

Belk, Russell W., Melanie Wallendorf, John Sherry, Morris Holbrook, and Scott Roberts (1988), "Collectors and Collecting," *Advances in Consumer Research*, 15, 548-553.

Belk, Russell W. (1995), *Collecting in a Consumer Society*. New York, NY: Routledge.

Bryant, John (1989), "Stamp and Coin Collecting," in *Handbook of American Popular Culture*, 2nd ed., Vol. 3, Thomas Enge, Ed., New York, NY: Greenwood Press, 1329-1365.

Danet, Brenda and Tamar Katriel (1989), "No Two Alike: Play and Aesthetics in Collecting," *Play and Culture*, 2 (3), 253-277.

Ebeling, Ashlea (2000), "Dig It," *Forbes Magazine*, June 12, 2000, http://www.forbes.com/forbes/2000/0612/6514418a.html

Formanek, Ruth (1991), "Why They Collect: Collectors Reveal Their Motivations," in Rudmin, F.W. (ed.), To Have Possessions: A Handbook on Ownership and Property [Special Issue], *Journal of Social Behaviour and Personality*, 6 (6), 275-286.

Hughes, N. C., F. J. Collier, J. Kluessendorf, J. Lipps, W. L. Taylor, and R. D. White (2000), "Fossil Invertebrate and Microfossil Collections: Kinds, Uses, Users," in White, R. D. and W. D. Allmon, Eds., *Guidelines for the Management and Curation of Invertebrate Fossil Collections*, The Paleontological Society Special Publications, 10, 25-35.

Larson, Peter and Kristin Donnan (2004), *Rex Appeal: The Amazing Story of Sue, the Dinosaur that Changed Science, the Law, and My Life*. Montpelier, VT: Invisible Cities Press.

Leadbeater, C., and Miller, P. (2004), "The Pro-Am Revolution: How Enthusiasts are Changing Our Economy and Society," *Demos*, (November), 5-74.

Long, Mary M. and Leon G. Schiffman (1997), "Swatch Fever: An Allegory for Understanding the Paradox of Collecting," *Psychology and Marketing*, 14 (5), 494-509.

Martin, Paul (1999), *Popular Collecting and the Everyday Self: The Reinvention of Museums?*. London and New York: Leicester University Press.

McIntosh, William D. and Brandon Schmeichel (2004), "Collectors and Collecting: A Social Psychology Perspective," *Leisure Sciences*, 26 (1), 85-97.

Pearce, Susan M. (1993), *Museums, Objects, and Collections: A Cultural Study*. Washington, DC: Smithsonian Institution Press.

Pettitt, Charles (1991) "What Price Natural History Collections, or 'Why Do We Need All These Bloody Mice?'," *Museum Journal*, 91 (8), 25-28.

_____ (1994), "Using the Collections," in *Manual of Natural History Curatorship*, G. Stansfield, J. Mathias, and G. Reid, Eds., London: HMSO.

_____ (1997), "The Cultural Impact of Natural Science Collections," in *The Value and Valuation of Natural Science Collections: Proceedings of the International Conference, Manchester, 1995*, J. R. Nudds and C. W. Pettitt, Eds. London: The Geological Society, 94-103.

Polites, Greta L. (2005), "The Florida Paleontological Society: Bridging the Gap Between Amateur and Professional Paleontologists," University of Georgia, working paper.

Stebbins, Robert A. (1992). *Amateurs, Professionals, and Serious Leisure*. Montreal: McGill-Queen's University Press.

Tanselle, G. Thomas (1998). "A Rationale of Collecting," *Studies in Bibliography*, 51, 1-25.

Wright, Louis B. and Gordon N. Ray (1969), *The Private Collector and the Support of Scholarship (Papers Read at the Clark Library Seminar, April 5, 1969)*. Los Angeles, CA: William Andrews Clark Memorial Library, University of California.

Beyond Vanity: An Investigation into Romanian Women's Beauty Identities

Larisa Puslenghea, University of Illinois at Urbana-Champaign, USA
Michelle R. Nelson, University of Illinois at Urbana-Champaign, USA

Women's perceptions of beauty are important not only because they determine beauty practices that, in turn, translate into consumption patterns, but also because they shape women's lives. In Eastern Europe, the transition from socialism to capitalism, beyond its political, economic and social components, has also implied a change of lifestyles (Coulter, Price and Feick 2003). These new lifestyles offer the possibility to reinscribe the obsolete socialist notion of gender equality into a new capitalist notion that allows for female empowerment. This study departs from the approach of authors such as Coulter et al. who argue that the 1990s have been a period of radical shift in the way women relate to beauty. Quite on the contrary, this undertaking shows that Romanian women have used the proliferation of market options to evolve along the same conceptual lines as before the fall of communism, instead of going through a phase of serious disruption.

Conceptualization

The paper reviews the main positions represented in the 'nature' versus 'culture' debate (Bordo, 1993; Brush, 1998; Fraser, 2001; Hurd and Griffin, 2007). On the one side, nature is defined as the raw material awaiting to be amended and thus inferior to culture, whereas the opposing approach presents nature as the perfect blueprint and, therefore, superior to culture. However, 'nature' is usually presented as a discrete category, defying historical change, situated outside of culture and, thus, not subject to power relations. Paralleling this conceptualization is the discussion of the different approaches to a mind/body dualism focusing on the postmodern notion of 'natural' body as text, inseparable from its inscription. Such discussions are placed within the context of the broader debate on empowerment and cultural politics where the body is a "locus of social control" (Bordo, 1993, p. 33), acknowledging feminist works and Foucault's contribution. Particular attention is given to Foucault's notion of modern power and the way individual self-surveillance can be imposed with just one gaze, which plays in the normalization of the beauty industry. Finally, the recent theoretical contestation of the opposition between men and women is addressed in the light of postmodernism, insisting on women's agency even in processes that may be categorized as oppressive in previous conceptualizations.

Method

Fourteen semi-structured in-depth interviews were conducted with Romanian women ages 20 to 54 in 2007. Each interview was audio recorded and then transcribed and translated into English. The transcripts were then perused in an iterative process for emerging themes in a process of open coding and axial coding.

Major findings: Meanings of Beauty and Beauty Practices

These Romanian women relate repeatedly and in a decidedly nonlinear fashion to a multitude of beauty forms that could be subsumed under both 'cultural' and 'natural' models. In the constellation of perceptions with a cultural currency in Eastern Europe there appear to be competing hierarchies and complex dynamics among beauty types. For example, Cristina thinks that natural beauty is valued more than artificial appearance "with very flashy makeup", and Madalina feels this has to do with the implied deceitfulness since make up, through "tricks", makes even unattractive people look pretty. Beauty, for the women interviewed, is an intricate concept that simultaneously feeds into and emerges from almost all facets of life. Notably, beauty is a very mutable feature constantly being constituted, interpreted and contested through everyday interaction. For instance, Ana explains she appraises herself as beautiful or ugly based on how good she is at her job on a specific day or how well her romantic relationship is evolving at a given time.

For most respondents cosmetic use and the aura of artificiality that it brings about is acceptable only insofar as it covers up imperfections, that is only as long as it presents itself as an attempt of *mimesis* that reinforces the superiority and high social desirability of the 'natural' blueprint. Women are wary of the negative associations of cosmetic practices within their culture and therefore are much more willing to identify with practices termed "taking care of oneself" or "avoiding sloppiness" that somehow seem to feebly relate to traditional female roles such as nurturer or aesthetic arbitrator of the family.

Nevertheless, in this specific case, 'natural' beauty is not synonymous with the lack of any kind of cosmetic interaction (thus, not identified with nature as an ideal, untouched state), but it is a beauty that imitates the 'natural' look using makeup. In this case, 'naturalness' comes in degrees and hues and it is clearly culturally defined. Moreover, 'natural' beauty needs to be achieved and it requires significant efforts to maintain this 'natural' status. Here, the force of the belief in the superiority of nature is necessarily—yet paradoxically—complemented by an appeal to culture: with the supreme valuing of nature as a standard comes the realization of the fact that bodies are imperfect and need to be amended. Ironically, it is not the faith in the superiority of culture over nature, but the utopia of the natural body that makes these women resort to makeup in an attempt to emulate that ideal state.

The respondents in this study, regardless of age, seemed to agree that beauty is a specifically female characteristic and, thus, also a typically female responsibility. However, in the true spirit of postmodernism, it became apparent that there is no one linear discourse on beauty; instead there are a multitude of separate and often contradicting discourses (even stemming from the same woman!) that are being combined and recombined to construct meaning during the course of the conversation. Respondents did not rigorously adhere to one ideology, instead they switched between ideas belonging to such diverse intellectual sources as neo-Platonicism, feminism, postmodernism and so on. Moreover, in their use of these ideas they recombined them in original ways to create new and interesting meaning. For example, although the ascendancy of the natural ideal was predominant among interviewees, they saw makeup, and thus culture, as the way to attain—even if just fleetingly and illusorily—an impression of that ideal. So, for them, nature and culture are both oppositional and complementary terms.

References

Bordo, Susan (1993), *Unbearable Weight: Feminism, Western Culture, and the Body*. Berkeley, CA: University of California Press.

Brush, Pippa (1998), "Metaphores of inscription: Discipline, plasticity and the rhetoric of choice," *Feminist Review*, 58 (spring), 22-44.

Coulter, Robin A., Linda L. Price and Lawrence Feick (2003), "Rethinking the origins of involvement and brand commitment: insights from postsocialist Central Europe," *Journal of Consumer Research*, 30.2 (September), 151- 170.

Fraser, Suzanne (2001), "'Woman-Made Women': Mobilisations of nature in feminist accounts of cosmetic surgery," *Hecate*, 27.2 (October), 115-133.

Hurd Clarke, Laura and Meridith Griffin (2007), "The body natural and the body unnatural: Beauty work and aging," *Journal of Aging Studies*, 21. 3 (August), 187-201.

When Strangers Converse in Marketplace Environments: Effect of Service Provider-Related Versus Service Provider-Unrelated Conversations

Kaleel Rahman, American University in Dubai, UAE
Ulku Yuksel, University of Sydney, Australia

Customer-to-customer (C-to-C) interaction in service-oriented marketplace environments is an important aspect of consumer behavior (Harris and Baron, 2004). Hotels, airlines, hospitals, theatres, sporting events and trains are some examples of services where these interactions commonly occur. Understanding the C-to-C interactions is important for several reasons. Increased competition resulting in more choices to consumers has led to a situation where consumers seek compatibility of other customers in high contact services settings (Pratner and Martin, 1991) Increasing isolation of consumers due to divorce, lack of real social contacts and other similar reasons, consumers turn to marketplace environments to supplement interpersonal relationships (Martin and Pratner, 1989). In addition, service providers themselves expect their customer to share certain facilities like a queue, lounge and buffet.

Researchers have paid some attention to understand C-to-C interactions. For example, using market-oriented ethnography, Harris and Baron (2004) identified a stabilizing effect of conversations between strangers through *consumer anxiety reduction*, the *enactment of a partial employee role*, and the *supply of social interaction*. As McGrath and Otnes (1995) found in their taxonomy, roles performed by consumers in conversations with strangers include *help seeker, proactive helper, and reactive helper*. Using critical incidence techniques, Grove and Fisk (1997) categorized the percentage of different types of C-to-C interactions such as *verbal* (conversations), *waiting in line*, and *physical incidents* (other people's actions) and further categorized them into whether they are satisfying or dissatisfying incidents. Even though C-to-C interactions take different forms such as frowning at queue jumpers and smiling (Grove and Fisk, 1997), we limit our study to C-to-C conversations only.

Our research is an attempt at contributing to present literature by two dimensions. First, through a critical incidence technique, we divide C-to-C conversations into two types: *service provider-related* conversations and *service provider-unrelated* conversations. Second, we examine both positive and negative affective reaction to C-to-C conversations and their relationships with positive and negative word-of-mouth. We expect that affective reactions to service provider related conversations would be correlated to word-of-mouth behavior because the contents of these conversations are uniquely about the service provider. However, as we expect, affective reactions to service provider unrelated conversations would NOT be correlated to word-of-mouth behavior because the contents of these conversations involve customers' own interests but nothing about the service provider.

Data for this study was collected using the critical incidence technique (Gremler, 2004). Students enrolled in a senior undergraduate marketing course at a major university in an Eastern State in Australia participated in the study as part of their assignment requirement. In the beginning of their course, participants were informed about an assignment involving the importance of C-to-C conversations in services. They were asked to think about an incident in any services context where they had a conversation with another customer (but not with the service provider) whom they had never met before. The following week, in the beginning of the session, they were given a two-page response sheet. The original content of these two pages have diverse objectives and cover more issues than those relevant for the present paper. Bellow we describe only the relevant contents. On the first page respondents described the details of the incident.

The second part (page) of the task involved responding to the survey questions. For affective reaction, following from Holbrook and Batra (1987) we asked students *"What was your affective/emotional reaction to that interaction (your conversation with the other customer)? (Your reaction to the experience, not to how you would describe the experience)"*.

Having collected the response sheets, the open ended responses from the first pages were analyzed. Then, both authors sitting in tandem divided service provider related and unrelated responses. The first pile included those incidents involving a conversation that directly refers to the service provider. Following is an example of the first pile:

"My seat on a long flight to London was next to that of an extremely friendly Irish woman. She spent the whole trip comparing the service, quality of food, prices and various other aspects of the service company (airline). We discussed the lack of leg room and space for our handbags in our economy seating, the poor and very minimal attendance of the hostesses and our anger (particularly hers) at the lack of an explanation for circling the airport many times before proceeding to land and the lack of warning as we entered an area of bad turbulence".

The second pile included those incidents involving a conversation that does not directly refer to the service provider but refers to other types of conversations like weather, personal background, and life in general. Following is an example of the second pile:

"I recently went to the USA for a holiday and on the return leg my plane was delayed in Hawaii for what turned out to be one night. Whilst we were waiting in the terminal one of the other passengers chatted and lent me his mobile phone so that I could call my parents and advise of the delay as he has free calls anywhere in the world on weekends as part of his phone deal. This was definitely a memorable event for me as I appreciated the fact he is a very nice person to be chatting and also helpful"

This procedure resulted in 64 responses for service provider related interactions, 37 responses for service provider unrelated interactions and 23 responses being excluded from the study which could not be categorized into one of the two piles.

In terms of measures, first, we measured both positive (joy) and negative (anger) affective response to C-to-C conversations using scales developed by Richins (1997) in consumer research. For "joy" two items, *happy* and *pleased* were used on a five point scale with endpoints of *did not feel at all* and *felt strongly*. The two items were strongly correlated (r .89) and internally consistent (alpha .94) hence we used these two items to form a single item measure of joy. For "anger", two items, *angry* and *irritated,* were used on a five point scale with endpoints of did not feel at all and felt strongly. The two items were strongly correlated (r .90) and internally consistent (alpha .95) hence we used these two items to form a single item measure of Anger.

Second, we measured both positive and negative word-of-mouth behavior using items developed by Brown et. al. (2005). For both positive word-of-mouth (PWOM) and negative word-of-mouth (NWOM) we used two items each on a seven point scale with endpoints of *strongly disagree* and *strongly agree*. The two PWOM items were strongly correlated (r .93) and internally consistent (alpha .96) thus we used these two items to form a single item measure of PWOM (e.g., I spoke positively of the company to others). The two NWOM items were strongly correlated (r .82) and internally consistent (alpha .89) (e.g., I said negative things about the company to other people). Hence, we used these two items to form a single item measure of NWOM.

Noting the mean evaluations regarding service provided related versus unrelated conversations, results show that consumers react more joyfully (*m* 3.2) when they engage in service provider-unrelated conversations than when they converse about the service provider (*m* 2.6) but the level of anger between the two groups are almost the same (*m* 2.5 vs. 2.4). We attribute these findings to the nature of conversations themselves. For example, consumers who find opportunities to talk about something of their own interests are likely to be happier than when they talk about anything else. But negative aspects of these conversations do not have to be different depending whether a conversation is about their own interests or not.

PWOM (*m* 3.8 vs. 3.4) are higher among those who conversed something unrelated to the service provider. However, NWOM is higher among those who talked about the service provider (*m* 3.5 vs. 2.5). These results are surprising and may have strong implications for consumer behavior in services marketing. We turned to correlation analysis for an alternative perspective.

Correlationwise, in terms of service *provider related* conversations, Joy and PWOM (.655**) have significant positive relationships and Anger and NWOM (.627**) have significant positive relationships (supports proposition). As these results indicate, when consumers talk about the company and become happy, they go and tell good things about the company. Similarly, when they talk about the company and become angry, they go and tell bad things about the company.

Interestingly, in terms of service *provider unrelated* conversations, relationship between Joy and PWOM (.246) are not significant (supports proposition). Hence, when consumers talk about something of their own interests and become happy, they do not go and tell good things about the company. However, relationship between Anger and NWOM (.332*) is significant (rejects proposition). As this indicates, most interestingly, even when the conversations with strangers had nothing to do with the service provider, consumers tend to go and tell other people bad things about the service provider.

In sum, an effort previously not undertaken, we examine customer to customer conversations in services in terms of service provider related versus unrelated conversations. Then we examine positive and negative affective reactions to these conversations and their relationships with positive and negative word of mouth behavior. Contrary to our expectation, when the conversations with strangers had nothing to do with the service provider, consumers tend to go and tell other people bad things about the service provider. Implications of these findings, limitations and future research avenues are to be discussed in the completed paper.

References

Brown, T., Barry, T., Dacin, P., and Gunst, R. (2005) "Spreading the word: Investigating antecedents of consumer's positive word-of-mouth intentions and behaviors in a retailing context", *Journal of the Academy of Marketing Science*, 33 (2) pp. 123-138

Gremler, T. (2004) "The critical incident technique in service research", *Journal of Service Research*, 7 (August) pp. 65-89

Grove, S. J. and Fisk, R. P. (1997). "The Impact Of Other Customers On Service Experiences: A Critical Incident Examination Of "Getting Along"", *Journal of Retailing*, 73 (1), pp. 63-85.

Harris, K. and Baron, S. (2004). "Customer-to Customer Conversations in Service Settings", *Journal of Service Research*, (6) 3, pp. 287-303.

Holbrook, M. and Batra, R. (1987) "Assessing the role of emotions as mediators of consumer responses to advertising", *Journal of Consumer Research*, 14 (December), pp. 404-420

Martin, C. L. and Pranter, C. A. (1989) "Compatibility management: Customer-to-customer relationships in service environments", *Journal of Services Marketing*, 3, pp. 5-15

McGrath & Otnes, (1995). "Unacquainted influencers: When strangers, interact in the retail setting", *Journal of Business Research*, 32 93), pp. 261-272.

Pranter, C. A. and Martin, C. L. (1989) "Compatibility management role roles in service performers", *Journal of Services Marketing*, 5, pp. 43-53

Richins, M. (1997). "Measuring emotions in the consumption experience" *Journal of Consumer Research*, 24 (September), pp. 127-146

The Moderating Role of Social Networks in Loss Aversion: Testing How Consumption in Network Subcultures Can Strengthen Consumer-Brand Relationships

Renée Ann Richardson, Harvard Business School, USA

The literature on consumers' relationships with their brands emphasizes that, when people form relationships with brands that mirror their social relationships, the norms of social relationships are used as guiding principles in their interactions with brands. Recent experimental research has shown that the types of relationship norms present during an exchange can moderate the degree of loss aversion that consumers experience. Building on this research, I use an experimental approach to investigate the impact of social networks on loss aversion, and how purchase behavior embedded in a network setting (for example, group shopping or an at-home party), impacts the degree of loss aversion felt by a consumer. Results show that respondents in the socially embedded exchange condition have a higher degree of loss aversion, as demonstrated by the gap between their selling prices (willingness to accept) and buying prices (willingness to pay). With this research, I hope to build a stronger bridge between social network literature and decision making theory.

Automatic and Effortful Processes in Socially Desirable Responding: A Cross-Cultural View

Hila Riemer, Ben-Gurion University, Israel

Abstract

In this paper we develop a theory to account for differences in Socially Desirable Responding (SDR) across cultures. Specifically, we deal with differences in the mechanism through which individuals from different cultures engage in the form of SDR/Impression Management (IM) in attitude questions. Based on a distinct definition of attitude in Eastern cultures and on the notion that collectivists are practiced at correcting for situational factors, we argue that collectivists engage in IM through an automatic process. Individualists' IM, on the other hand, is more effortful. Implications and directions for future investigation are discussed.

Introduction

This paper deals with the process through which people from different cultures engage in socially desirable responding (SDR) for impression management (IM). Despite the existing knowledge about cultural differences in people's tendency for SDR (e.g., van Hemet, van de Vijver, Poortinga, and Georgas 2002), researchers are not clear about the underlying mechanism for SDR (Johnson and van de Vijver 2002). We argue that for those with an individualistic cultural background or context SDR takes place through a deliberate or effortful process, whereas for those with an collectivistic cultural background or context it is more spontaneous or automatic. Next we present the theoretical background and develop our propositions. Then we discuss implications and directions for future investigation.

Theoretical Background and Conceptual Development

Research suggests that collectivists are more likely to engage in SDR compared to individualists (e.g., Triandis et al. 2001; van Hemert et al 2002). The reasoning for this is that collectivists conform in order to maintain good relationships. In contrast, individualists value uniqueness and social independence, and thus are less likely to conform (Triandis 1995). Further, according to Lalwani, Shavitt, and Johnson (2006), individualists see their responses as means for self-enhancement, but collectivists see them as means for IM.

Focusing on responses to attitude questions in survey settings, we address cultural differences in the underlying mechanisms of SDR/IM. Research on attitude measurement suggests that there may be cultural differences in the attitude construct. According to cultural researchers, collectivists are more comfortable with contradictory propositions than Individualists (Aaker and Sengupta 2000, Wong, Rindfleisch, and Burroughs 2003). Further, research conducted in western societies proposes that attitude consists of different dimensions (cognitive, affective, and behavioral), and that these dimensions will often be, at least to some extent, consistent with one other. Inconsistancies will lead to weaker or less stable attitudes (Festinger 1957; Breckler 1984; Cacioppo, Petty, and Geen 1989; Chaiken and Yates 1985). However, given that collectivists are comfortable with contradictory propositions, it would be reasonable to expect that in the East there is less pressure to bring components of attitude toward internal consistency. Moreover, definitions of attitude imply an *enduring* disposition. However, if collectivists are comfortable with contradictions between the different components at a given time, then they might also feel comfortable with contradictions between the same component at different times.

If collectivists are indeed more prone to expressing different attitudes in different situations, then the case of SDR can be viewed as a special case for this tendency. We argue that collectivists are more likely to engage in SDR in response to attitude questions because they make situational corrections. Individualists are less likely to make those situational corrections and thus are less likely to engage in SDR. This notion of situational correction in response to attitude questions is equivalent to the situational correction in attribution, that it is more prevalent in collectivists (relative to individualists, who make more dispositional attributions in social judgment) (Morris and Peng 1994).

How do these situational corrections take place? The possibility that variations in expressed attitudes of collectivists are due to different characteristics of attitude (more complex, situational dependent, and less enduring relative to attitudes of individualists), implies that differences in expressed social attitudes will occur spontaneously without need for deliberate editing and processing. This idea is also in line with recent research by Knowles et al. (2001) that claims that collectivists' correction for situational factors in making attributions takes place automatically. These researchers maintain that because this correction has been practiced frequently in collectivists it has become "automatized", and thus does not require substantial cognitive resources.

Whereas with regard to collectivists it is possible to claim *automatic* situational correction, the case with individualists is different. Based on the Western view, an attitude refers to an enduring disposition. Thus, all else being equal, people's actual attitude (unless changed) should stay similar across situations. What can change, though, is the *expressed* attitude. Adjustments in the expressed attitude may take place when one wishes to engage in IM using SDR. To be able to make this adjustment, however, one should invest cognitive resources in order to edit one's response. This implies an effortful process (Gilbert, Pelham, and Krull 1998). Thus, we propose:

P1: When collectivists engage in SDR/IM in responding to attitude questions, they do it automatically without investing substantial cognitive resources.
P2: When individualists engage in SDR for IM in attitude questions, they do it through a more effortful process.

Discussion

This perspective has theoretical and practical implications. Theoretically it contributes to an understanding of the processes through which people respond to surveys, and particularly to sensitive survey questions. Further, this research contributes to the understanding of cultural differences in the construct of attitudes. The idea that there are differences in the construct of attitude across culture is new. Insight into this notion may open a new stream of research into the differences between cultures, not only in terms of cognitive processes but also in terms of understanding concepts such as attitudes and emotions.

Practically, this research contributes to understanding the conditions in which SDR is more likely to occur. Insights into the role of culture in SDR may improve our ability to assess the validity of cross-cultural comparisons based on survey data.

Future research is needed to provide empirical support for the propositions presented here and to assess cultural differences in response to other types of questions (e.g., knowledge and behavior rather then attitude).

References

Aaker, Jennifer and Jaideep Sengupta (2000), "Averaging versus Attenuation: The Role of Culture in the Resolution of Information Incongruity," *Journal of Consumer Psychology*, 9 (2), 67-82.

Breckler, Steven J. (1984), "Empirical Validation of Affect, Behavior, and Cognition as Distinct Components of Attitude," *Journal of Personality and Social Psychology*, 47 (Dec), 1191-1205.

Cacioppo, John T., Richard E. Petty, and Thomas R. Geen (1989), "Attitude Structure and Function: From the Tripartite to the Homeostasis Model of Attitudes," In Anthony R., Pratkanis, Steven J. Breckler, and Anthony G. Greenwald (Eds). *Attitude Structure and Function*. (pp. 275-309). The third Ohio State University volume on attitudes and persuasion. Hillsdale, NJ, England: Lawrence Erlbaum Associates, Inc.

Chaiken, Shelly and Suzanne Yates (1985), "Affective-Cognitive Consistency and Thought-Induced Attitude Polarization," *Journal of Personality and Social Psychology*, 49(Dec), 1470-1481

Festinger, L. (1957), *A Theory of Cognitive Dissonance*, Stanford, CA: Stanford University Press.

Gilbert, D. T., B. W. Pelham, and D. S. Krull, (1988), "On Cognitive Busyness: When Person Perceivers Meet Persons Perceived," *Journal of Personality and Social Psychology*, 54, 733-740.

Johnson, T. P. and F. J. R. van de Vijver, (2002), "Social Desirability in Cross-Cultural Research," In J. A. Harkness, F. J. R. van de Vijver, and P. P. Mohler (Eds.), *Cross-Cultural Survey Methods*, (pp. 193-202). Hoboken, NJ.Europe: Wiley.: Wiley Interscience.

Knowles, E. D., M. W. Morris, C. Chiu, and Y. Hong, (2001), "Culture and the Process of Person Perception: Evidence for Automaticity among East Asians in Correcting for Situational Influences on Behavior," *Personality and Social Psychology Bulletin*, 27(10), 1344-1356.

Lalwani, A. K., S. Shavitt, and T. Johnson, (2006), "What is the Relation between Cultural Orientation and Socially Desirable Responding?" *Journal of Personality and Social Psychology*, 90(1), 165-178.

Morris, M. W. and K. Peng, (1994), "Culture and Cause: American and Chinese Attributions of Social and Physical Events," *Journal and Personality and Social Psychology*, 67 (6), 949-971.

Triandis, H. C. (1995), *Individualism and Collectivism*, Boulder: Westview Press.

Triandis, H. C., P. Carnevale, M. Gelfand, C. Robert, S. A. Wasti, T. Probst, E. S. Kashima, T. Dragonas, D. Chan, X. P. Chen, U. Kim, C. de Dreu, E. van de Vliert, S. Iwao, K. I. Ohbuchi, and P. Schmitz (2001), "Culture and Deception in Business Negotiations: A Multilevel Analysis," *International Journal of Cross-cultural Management*, 1, 73-90.

van Hemert, D. A., F. J. van de Vijver, Y. H. Poortinga, and J. Georgas, (2002), "Structural and Functional Equivalence of the Eysenck Personality Questionnaire within and between Countries," *Personality and Individual Differences, 33*(8), 1229-1249.

Wong, N., A. Rindfleisch, and J. Burroughs, (2003), "Do Reverse-Worded Scales Confound Results in Cross-Cultural Research? The Case of the Materialism values Scale," *Journal of Consumer Research*, 30(1), 72-91.

Flow and Attitude Toward the Website on the Evaluation of Products Present by Means of Virtual Reality: A Conceptual Model

Eva Tomaseti, Polytechnic University of Cartagena, Spain
Salvador Ruiz, University of Murcia, Spain
Nina Reynolds, Bradford University, UK

Abstract

The website represents the future of a company's business communications on the Internet, since it allows supplying large amount of information as well as creating virtual experiences with the product. In this context, virtual reality constitutes a technology which provides users with realistic and interactive virtual environments. In this paper, based on five groups of models, we analyze the effect of virtual reality presentations, by means of interactivity and richness, on flow and attitude toward the website, and the subsequent effect of those variables on online product evaluation.

Introduction

The key characteristic for the assessment of virtual reality in terms of consumer's experience is the concept of telepresence defined as the sensation of being in an environment created by a communication medium (Steuer, 1992). On the basis of sensory stimuli transmitted by Virtual Reality, individuals feel the perceptual illusion of being present and highly involved in the environment created by the medium, whereas they are physically in another place (Kim and Biocca, 1997). Telepresence is determined by two factors: interactivity and richness (Suh and Lee, 2005; Coyle and Thorson, 2001; Klein, 2003; Steuer, 1992).

Likewise, literature has highlighted flow (Hoffman and Novak, 1998) and attitude toward the website (Fortin and Dholakia, 2005; Fiore and Jin, 2003; Taylor and Todd, 1995) as important antecedents of Internet behavior. On the basis of this approach, we propose a model of the effect of interactivity and richness on product evaluation, including flow and the attitude toward the website as mediating variables.

Proposed Model

The model tested draws from five areas. First, the effect of interactivity and richness on attitudes draws from the work of Fortin and Dholakia (2005). In this study, the authors analyze the effect of interactivity on attitude toward the brand, attitude toward the ad, and purchase intention. Second, attitude toward the Web has been considered by Technology Acceptance Model (TAM) (Karahanna et al., 2006; O'Cass and Fecench, 2003) as antecedent of technology acceptance. Third, an extension of TAM, the Web Acceptace Model (WAM) (Castañeda et al., 2007) substitutes attitude toward the Web by attitude toward the website as predictor of future re-visit intention. Fourth, latter research in the adoption of innovations theory has used the evaluation of products to predict adoption (Nabih et al., 1997; Parthasarathy et al., 1995; Rogers, 1995; Klonglan and Coward, 1970). Fifth, Hoffman and Novak's (1996) model takes into account the effect of telepresence on flow, and the effect of this outputs on behavioral variables.

In virtual reality literature, Sheridan (1992) uses the term interactivity to refer to the control of sensations and the ability to modify the environment, while Zeltner (1992) refers to the relationship between autonomy and interaction. Based on those dimensions, interactivity is then defined as the degree to which two or more communication parties can act on each other, the comunication medium, and the messages, as well as the degree to which such influences are synchronized (Liu and Shrum, 2002). Richness is defined as the form in which the environment presents the information to the senses (Steuer, 1992).

Although different studies have analysed how the use of virtual reality affects attitudes towards the website (Fiore et al., 2005; Martin et al., 2005; Schlosser, 2003), there is no agreement on the interaction effect of attitude towards the website, interactivity and richness on intentions (Fortin and Dholakia, 2005; Park et al., 2005; Hopkins et al., 2004). However, based on Coyle and Thorson's study, which tested that higher levels of interactivity and richness increase attitudes toward web sites, due to the fact that the virtual experience with the product is perceived as more similar to a direct experience, we proposed:

H1: Interactivity is positively related to attitude toward the website
H2: Richness is positively related to attitude toward the website

The flow state is defined as the holistic sensation that people feel when they act with total involvement (Csikszentmihalyi, 1977). Hoffman and Novak (1996) suggest that the success of online marketers depends on their ability to create opportunities for consumers to experience flow. They found a positive effect of interactivity and richness on telepresence and, consequently, of this variable on flow. The interactivity offered by virtual reality through a website favors communication, personalises the way the information and the product are presented, and increases enjoyment (Fiore and Jin, 2003). Similarly, the realistic experience provided by richness facilitates the occurrence of flow.

H3: Interactivity is positively related to flow
H4: Richness is positively related to flow

Marketing literature has also verified the positive relationship between attitude toward the ad and attitude toward the brand (Ko et al., 2005; Hopkins et al., 2004; MacKenzie et al., 1986). As such, we expect that attitude toward the website will influence attitude toward the product, yielding higher product evaluations. Therefore, an increase in attitude toward the website, as a result of increased interaction with the product and the possibility of obtaining detailed information (Ward and Lee, 1999), will positively impact product evaluation. As well, higher levels of flow imply a positive consumer experience (Finneran and Zhang, 2005) which will be manifested in a higher product evaluation.

H5: Attitude toward the website is positively related to product evaluation
H6: Flow is positively related to product evaluation

Finally, a higher level of flow is capable of conferring value to the online experience, which will positively influence attitudes toward the website (Finneran and Zhang, 2005; Mathwick and Rigdon, 2004).

H7: Flow is positively related to attitude toward the website

Method

The study was carried out with a sample of 177 university students. The experimental design was based on a website. The data collection process was completed online. We used a sport watch as the product as it belongs to a category frequently marketed on the Internet, and has been frequently used in virtual reality studies (Jiang and Benbasat, 2007; Daugherty et al., 2005; Jiang and Benbasat, 2005).

After visiting various websites, with a focus on well known brands of watches, we chose one representative commercial presentation which fulfilled the objectives of the study. The level of interactivity was manipulated through allowing subjects to obtain images of the product from different perspectives, as well as displaying information related to the product by using the mouse (Klein, 2003; Coyle and Thorson, 2001). In order to manipulate the variable richness, we followed the methodology used by Li et al. (2001) and Klein (2003). The product is presented in two sizes.

The initial page of the website presented the sport watch under one of four conditions (interactive/non interactive; high/low level of richness). Subsequently, participants evaluated the product (Mukherjee and Hoyer, 2001), the level of interactivity (Coyle and Thorson, 2001), their attitude toward the website (Martin, et al., 2005) and their flow state (Hoffman and Novak, 1996) during the visit to the website.

Results

We used confirmatory factor analysis (CFA) to test the discriminant validity of the measures. Results show that the model fit the data well. Then, we checked whether the correlations among the latent constructs were significantly less than one which provided evidence of discriminant validity. The internal consistency of the scales were tested using both the composite reliability (ρ_ε), and the average variance extracted (AVE). All values were significantly greater than 0.60, and 0.50, respectively, and demonstrate internal consistency.

In order to verify the hypotheses, we used structural equation modelling with the Robust Maximum Likelihood Method and the asymptotic variance-covariance matrix. The fit statistics for the full model ($\chi^2(96)=238.49$; p-value=0.0; CFI=0.98; SRMR=0.050; RMSEA=0.072; NNFI=0.98) were within the acceptable ranges (the chi-square is significant, p<0.05; SRMR and RMSEA ≤0.08; and NNFI and CFI ≥0.90), which indicated a good model fit.

Results showed that interactivity and richness have a strong direct effect on attitude toward the website (β=.74; p<0.01; β=.70; p<0.01), and flow (β=.98; p<0.01; β=.58; p<0.01), therefore confirming H1, H2, H3, and H4. Moreover, we found a positive impact of attitude toward the website (β=.37; p<0.01), and flow (β=.13; p<0.01) on product evaluation, supporting H5 and H6. Finally, we observed a direct effect of flow on attitude toward the website, as proposed in H7 (β=-.18; p<0.05).

One important criterion of a model's success is its performance compared with that of rival models (Bagozzi and Yi, 1988). Based on Luna et al's (2003) model, we developed a rival model which hypothesized the opposite relationship between attitude toward the website and flow.

We compared our proposed model with the rival model using the following criteria: overall fit, percentage of the models' statistically significant parameters, and explained variance of the endogenous constructs. The overall fit for the rival model was equal to that of proposed model. However, in the rival model, the effect of attitude toward the website on flow was not significant at 95%. Finally, the explained variances for all endogenous constructs were the same in the proposed and rival model. These findings provided more confidence to the proposed model.

References

Bagozzi, R.P., Yi, Y. (1988). On the Evaluation of Structural Equation Models. *Journal of the Academy of Marketing Science, 16* (1), 74-94.

Castañeda, J.A., Muñoz-Leiva, F., Luque, T. (2007). Web Acceptance Model (WAM): Moderating Effects of User Experience. *Information & Management, 44*, 384-396.

Csikszentmihalyi, M. (1977). Beyond Boredom and Aniety, San Francisco: Jossey-Bass.

Coyle, J.R., Thorson, E. (2001). The Effects of Progressive Levels of Interactivity and Vividness in Web Marketing Sites. *Journal of Advertising, 30* (3), 65-77.

Daugherty, T., Li, H., Biocca, F. (2005). Experiential Ecommerce: A Summary of Research Investigating the Impact of Virtual Experience on Consumer Learning. *Online Consumer Psychology: Understanding and Influencing Consumer Behavior in the Virtual World*, Haugtvedt, C., Machleit, K, & Yalch, R. (eds), Lawrence Erlbaum Associates.

Finneran, C.M., Zhang, P. (2005). Flow in Computer-Mediated Environments. *Communications of the Association for Information Systems, 15*, 82-101.

Fiore, A.M., Kim, J., Lee, H.H. (2005). Effect of Image Interactivity Technology on Consumer Responses Toward the Online Retailer. *Journal of Interactive Marketing, 19* (3), 38-53.

Fiore, A.M., Jin, H. (2003). Influence of Image Interactivity on Approach Responses toward an Online Retailer. *Internet Research: Electronic Networking Applications and Policy, 13* (1), 38-48.

Fortin, D.R., Dholakia, R,R, (2005). Interactivity and Vividness Effects on Social Presence and Involvement with a Web-Based Advertisement. *Journal of Business Research, 58*, 387-396.

Hoffman, D.L., Novak, T.P. (1996). Marketing in Hypermedia Computer-Mediated Environments: Conceptual Foundations. *Journal of Marketing, 60*, 50-68.

Hopkins, C.D., Raymond, M.A., Mitra, A, (2004). Consumer Responses to Perceived Telepresence in the Online Advertising Environment: The Moderating Role of Involvement. *Marketing Theory, 4* (1/2), 137-162.

Jiang, Z., Benbasat, I. (2007). The Effects of Presentation Formats and Task Complexity on Online Consumers' Product Understanding. *MIS Quarterly, 31* (3), 475-500.

Jiang, Z., Benbasat, I. (2005). Virtual Product Experience: Effects of Visual and Functional Control of Products on Perceived Diagnosticity and Flow in Electronic Shopping. *Journal of Management Information Systems, 21* (3), 111-147.

Karahanna, E., Agarwal, R., Angst, C.M. (2006). Reconceptualizing Compatibility Beliefs in Technology Acceptance Research. *Mis Quarterly, 30* (4), 781-804.

Kim, T., Biocca, F. (1997). Telepresence via Television: Two Dimensions of Telepresence May Have Different Connections to Memory and Persuasion. *Journal of Computer-Mediated Communication, 3* (2).

Klein, L.R. (2003). Creating Virtual Product Experiences: The Role of Telepresence. *Journal of Interactive Marketing, 17* (1), 41-55.

Klonglan, G.E., Coward, E, W. (1970). The Concept of the Symbolic Adoption: A suggested Interpretation. *Rural Sociology, 35*, 77-83.

Ko, H., Cho, C.H., Roberts, M.S. (2005). Internet Uses and Gratifications. *Journal of Advertising, 34* (2), 57-70.

Li, H., Daugherty, T., Biocca, F. (2001). Characteristics of Virtual Experience in Electronic Commerce: A Protocol Analysis. *Journal of Interactive Marketing, 15* (3), 13-30.

Liu, Y., Shrum, L.J. (2002). What is Interactivity and Is It Always Such a Good Thing? Implications of Definition, Person, and Situation for the Influence of Interactivity on Advertising Effectiveness. *Journal of Advertising, 31* (4), 53-64.

Luna, D., Peracchio, L.A., De Juan, M.D. (2003). Flor in Individual Web Sites: Model Estimatio and Cross-Cultural Validation. *Advances in Consumer Research, 30*, 280-281.

MacKenzie, S.B., Lutz, R.J., Belch, G. E. (1986). The Role of Attitude toward the Ad as a Mediator of Advertising Effectiveness: A Test of Competing Explanations. *Journal of Marketing Research, 13*, 130-143.

Martin, B., Sherrard, M.J., Wentzel, D. (2005). The Role of Sensation Seeking and Need for Cognition on Web-Site Evaluations: A Resource-Matching Perspective. *Psychology & Marketing, 22* (2), 109-126.

Mathwick, C., Rigdon, E. (2004). Play, Flow, and the Online Search Experience. *Journal of Consumer Research, 31*, 324-332.

Mukherjee, A., Hoyer, W.D. (2001). The Effect of Novel Attributes on Product Evaluation. *Journal of Marketing Research, 28*, 462-472.

Nabih, M.I., Bolem, J.G., Poiesz, T. (1997). Conceptual Issues in the Study of Innovation Adoption Behaviour. *Advances in Consumer Research, 24*,190-196.

O'Cass, A., Fenech, T. (2003). Web Retailing Adoption: Exploring the Nature of Internet Users' Web Retailing Behaviour. *Journal of Retailing and Consumer Services, 10*, 81-94.

Park, J.S., Lennon, J., Stoel, L. (2005). On-Line Product Presentation: Effects on Mood, Perceived Risk, and Purchase Intention. *Psychology & Marketing, 22* (9), 695-719.

Parthasarathy, M., Rittenburg, T.L., Ball, A.D. (1995). A Re-evaluation of the Product Innovation-Decision-Process: The Implications for Product Management. *Journal of Product & Brand Management, 4* (4), 35-47.

Rogers, E.M. (1995). Diffusion of Innovations. Fourth Edition, The Free Press, New York.

Schlosser, A.E. (2003). Experiencing Products in the Virtual World: The Role of Goal and Imagery in Influencing Attitudes versus Purchase Intentions. *Journal of Consumer Research, 30*, 184-198.

Sheridan, T.B. (1992). Musing on Telepresence and Virtual Presence. *Presence: Teleoperators and Virtual Environments, 1* (1), 120-126.

Steuer, J. (1992). Defining Virtual Reality: Dimensions Determining Telepresence. *Journal of Communication, 42 (4)*, 73-93.

Suh, K.S., Lee, Y.E. (2005). The Effects of Virtual Reality on Consumer Learning: An Empirical Investigation. *MIS Quarterly, 29*, 1-25.

Taylor, S., Todd, P. (1995). Assessing IT Usage: The Role of Prior Experience. *MIS Quarterly, 19* (4), 561-570.

Ward, M.R., Lee, M. J. (1999). Internet shopping, consumer search and product branding. *Journal of Product and Brand Management, 9(1)*, 20-25.

Zeltzer, D. (1992). Autonomy, Interaction, and Presence. *Presence: Teleoperators and Virtual Environments, 1* (1), 127-132.

The Evaluation of New Utilitarian and Symbolic Products: The Effect of Attribute Type and Product Knowledge

Eva Tomaseti, Polytechnic University of Cartagena, Spain
Salvador Ruiz, University of Murcia, Spain

Abstract

Companies introduce new products whose success depends on consumer's product evaluation. In this paper, we analyze the effect of the addition of three types of new attributes to a product (beneficial and image attributes and characteristics), with utilitarian or symbolic meaning, on its evaluation, and how this effect is moderated by product knowledge. Results show that the impact of attribute type and product knowledge depends on product meaning.

Introduction

The introduction of new attributes is one of the most common methods for developing new products. The impact of a new feature or attribute on product evaluation depends on the characteristics of the feature itself, the type of product to which the feature is added, the characteristics of the buying task, and other factors such as the marketing strategy or the competitive and social environment (Nowlis and Simonson, 1996). Besides the important stream of research which has already analized the impact of new attributes on new product evaluation (Mukherjee and Hoyer, 2001; Brown and Carpenter, 2000), little is known about the interaction effect of the different attributes added and the other factors. Focusing on the first two factors proposed by Nowlis and Simonson (1996), we propose that the impact of a new feature on new product evaluation must be analized considering not only the type of attribute and the type of product (in our case utilitarian or symbolic) as intrinsic elements to the product development, but also by individual factors, such as product knowledge.

The effect of the addition of new characteristics, beneficial attributes and image attributes on the evaluation of utilitarian and symbolic products

Although marketing literature has analized different attributes of products, Lefkoff-Hagius and Mason (1993) concluded that product attributes presented in marketing research (Hauser and Clausing, 1988; Hirschman, 1980) can be classified into three types: characteristics, beneficial attributes, and image attributes. These authors defined characteristics as those attributes related to physical properties, beneficial attributes as those related to the task or outcome referent, and image attributes as those wich possess symbolic meaning (Meenaghan, 1995), and are related with visual (Eckman and Wagner, 1994) and promotional aspects. More recent classifications, as those presented by Veryzer (1998) and Michaut et al. (2002) are somehow equivalent to that of Lefkoff-Hagius and Mason.

Literature disagrees concerning the importance of the three kinds of attributes on product evaluation. Some authors, as Meenaghan (1995), Eckman and Wagner (1994), and Michaut et al. (2002), concluded that consumers tend to show a higher preference for image attributes than for functional aspects of the product. However, Hirschman (1987) and Moreau et al. (2001) concede more significance to technological and performance aspects. This discrepancy can be explained by product meaning. One of the most accepted classifications distinguishes two kinds of products, functional or utilitarian and symbolics. It arises as a result of the existence of two individual necessities, functional ones, related to specific problems, and symbolic ones, that are the expression of self-image and social identification (Park et al., 1986). Then, functional products are those that possess some tangible characteristics that offer benefits to consumers (Fournier, 1991; Park et al., 1991; Bhat and Reddy, 1998; Kempf, 1999; Addis and Holbrook, 2002; Del Río et al., 2001), or have the ability to accomplish specific acts, based on properties such as their physical characteristics and features (Fournier 1991). Symbolic products are used to signify social position and/or self identity, not for functional benefits (Hirschman, 1981; Levy, 1959).

Literature related to the effect of different attributes on product evaluation observed a greater impact of brand name, compared to product benefits, on products with symbolic meaning (Del Río et al, 2001), while functional products tend to be evaluated on tangible features and cost, then secondarily on their intangible/image attributes (Sirgy and Johar, 1985). Furthermore, in their study centered in brand extensions, Park et al. (1991) found more favourable consumers' reaction when the new attribute is consistent with the brand concept. As such, consumers display a more positive reaction to functional than prestige extensions for functional brands, and to prestige than functional extensions for prestige brands. Therefore, applying this consistency to the combination of attribute types and product meanings as described above, we propose:

H1: Compared with the case where the new attribute is absent, the presence of a new characteristic or benefit in functional products increases the product evaluation more than the presence of a new image attribute.
H2: Compared with the case where the new attribute is absent, the presence of a new image attribute in symbolic products increases product evaluation more than the presence of a new characteristic or benefit.

Product knowledge and its effects on new product evaluation

Within the context of the adoption of innovations, marketing literature has highlighted the significant influence of knowledge on consumer's decisions (Saaksjarvi, 2003; Gatignon and Robertson, 1991; Alba and Hutchinson, 1987). Pre-existing knowledge of a product or service category determines the evaluation of new products connected with it (Saaksjarvi, 2003; De Bont and Schoormans, 1995). Product knowledge depends on the quantity of specific knowledge acquired by experience or training (Wood and Lynch, 2002). This influences the ability to understand and interpret information about products (Balabanis and Reynolds, 2001; MacInnis and Jaworski, 1989).

Based on Saaksjarvi's analogical learning theory, expert subjects value products upon new functions and intrinsic characteristics of the product (such as characteristics and benefits), while non experts based their evaluation on physical aspects (such as image attributes). Therefore, even when individuals value new products based on analogies (where there are no shared physical attributes), experts center their evaluation, mostly, on functional attributes, perceiving more utility (Irani, 2000), while non experts do it based on superficial or visible aspects of the product (Roehm and Sternthal, 2001; Roehm et al., 1999).

However, the degree of preference for functional attributes will be determined by product meaning. For utilitarian products, the understanding of new characteristics and new benefits will determine consumer decisions, but not for symbolic products, where those attributes lose importance in favour of image attributes. As such, for expert subjects, the difference of new utilitarian product evaluation obtained by the introduction of new characteristics and beneficial attributes will be higher than for non-experts. On the other hand, for symbolic products there will be no difference between experts and non-experts on product evaluation when new attributes are added, due to the fact that the image attribute (more valued for non-experts subjects) will be equally understandable for both experts and non-experts.

H3: The improvement on product evaluation based on the presence of a new characteristic or benefit in utilitarian products is higher for experts than for non-experts
H4: The improvement on product evaluation based on the presence of a new attribute (characteristic, benefit or image attribute) in symbolic products does not differ for experts and non-experts

Method

In order to choose a utilitarian and a symbolic product, a questionnaire was administered to forty students to evaluate different products (Allen and Ng, 2002; Allen and Ng, 1999). The product with the most utilitarian meaning was a personal computer and the one with the most symbolic meaning was a pair of casual sport shoes. To distinguish between characteristics, benefits and image attributes, a pretest was conducted with sixty students to classify a list of attributes related to PCs and casual sport shoes. In order to choose the new attributes, a new pretest was conducted to select the ones with the highest evaluation in the three categories and for both products.

To test the above hyphoteses, three hundred and fourteen students participated in the 2 x 2 x 3 experiment: high vs. low product knowledge; utilitarian and symbolic product; and the three attribute types, characteristics and benefits vs. image.

All participants received a questionnaire booklet. The first page presented the product (a PC or a pair of casual sport shoes), which provided eight attributes without brand name. The selection of attributes included was based on the analysis of real ads and interviews with some experts. Then, they were asked to evaluate the product on a six-item, seven-point scale anchored by "bad/good", "like/dislike", "not useful/useful", "desirable/undesirable", "high quality/low quality", "favourable/unfavourable" (Mukherjee and Hoyer, 2001). After completing this initial evaluation, they were asked to provide some information related to product meaning and product knowledge (Smith and Park, 1992). The last page showed a new product. Fifty-three students evaluated a new PC with a new characteristic (Intel Pentium V), fifty-one with a new beneficial attribute (SODIMM SDRAM DDR NP CL2.5 PC2100 of 512MB for Thinkpad) and forty-two a new design in PCs, presented with the slogan "Dimension 4600C, the PC for those who enjoy the future, nowadays" (Lefkoff-Hagius and Mason, 1993). Concerning the symbolic product, a total of forty-three students completed the questionnaire with the new pair of casual sport shoes with a new characteristic (Ultralite midsole), forty-four with the new beneficial attribute (CLIMAWARM) and forty-six with a new design in shoes presented with the slogan "Columbia 23, for those who want something different". All brand names were fictitious. Although real products did not have the combination of characteristics set in the questionnaire, all of the attributes were real and exist in the market. Therefore, the level of novelty of each new attribute was analized, and they obtained very similar values.

Results

We used ANOVA to test the hypotheses. Results show that the improvement on evaluation of utilitarian products based on the additional introduction of a new characteristic or a new beneficial attribute was higher than when a new image attribute was added (M_c=0.64 vs. M_b=0.54, p=0.82; M_c vs. M_i=0.12, p<0.05; M_b vs. M_i, p<0.05), providing support for hypothesis H1. For the symbolic product, the presence of the new image attribute was similarly valued to the added new characteristic or new beneficial attribute (M_c=0.36 vs. M_b=0.26, p=0.79; M_c vs. M_i=0.38, p=0.99; M_b vs. M_i, p=0.74). Therefore, hypothesis H2 was not supported.

In order to test hypotheses H3 and H4, the sample was divided into two levels of product knowledge. High product knowledge level was attributed to those individuals who scored higher than the median. The rest were classified as non-experts.

For the utilitarian product, evaluation improvements based on the addition of the new beneficial attribute was higher for experts than for non-experts (M_{expert}=0.73 vs. $M_{non\,expert}$=0.26; p<0.05), but there were no significant differences on evaluation improvements when the new characteristic (M_{expert}=0.58 vs. $M_{non\,expert}$=0.73; p=0.29) or the new image attribute were incorporated (M_{expert}=0.23 vs. $M_{non\,expert}$=0.03; p=0.56), which partially supported H3. For the symbolic product, evaluation improvements of expert and non-experts were similar when adding a new characteristic (M_{expert}=0.30 vs. $M_{non\,expert}$=0.43; p=0.61), a new beneficial attribute (M_{expert}=0.18 vs. $M_{non\,expert}$=0.35; p=0.34) and a new image attribute (M_{expert}=0.27 vs. $M_{non\,expert}$=0.45; p=0.47), which provided support for H4.

References

Addis, M., Holbrook, M.S. (2002). On the Conceptual Link Between Mass Customisation and Experiential Consumption: An Explosion of Subjectivity. *Journal of Consumer Behaviour, 1 (1)*, 50-66.

Alba, J.W., Hutchinson, J.W. (1987). Dimensions of Consumer Expertise. *Journal of Consumer Research, 13*, 411-454.

Allen, M.M., Ng, S.H. (1999). The Direct and Indirect Influences of Human Values on Product Ownership. *Journal of Economic Psychology, 20 (1)*, 5-39.

Allen, M.M., Ng, S.H., Wilson, M. (2002). A Functional Approach to Instrumental and Terminal Values and the Value-attitude-behaviour System of Consumer Choice. *European Journal of Marketing, 36 (1/2)*, 111-135.

Balabanis, G., Reynolds, N.L. (2001). Consumer Attitudes Towards Multi-Channel Retailers' Web Sited: The Role of Involvement, Brand Attitude, Internet Knowledge and Visit Duration. *Journal of Business Strategies, 18 (2)*, 105-131.

Bhat, S., Reddy, S.K. (1998). Symbolic and Functional Positioning of Brands. *Journal of Consumer Marketing, 15 (1)*, 32-43.

Brown, C.L., Carpenter, G.S. (2000). Why is the trivial important? A reasons-based account for the effects of trivial attributes on choice. *Journal of Consumer Research, 26*, 372-385.

De Bont, C.J.P.M., Schoormans, J.P.L. (1995). The Effects of Product Expertise on Consumer Evaluations of New-Product Concepts. *Journal of Economic Psychology, 16*, 599-615.

Del Río, A.B., Vázquez, R., Iglesias, V. (2001). The Role of the Brand Name in Obtaining Differential Advantages. *Journal of Product & Brand Management, 10 (7)*, 452-465.

Eckman, M., Warner, J. (1994). Judging the attractiveness of Product Design: The Effect of Visual Attributes and Consumer Characteristics. *Advances in Consumer Research, 21*, 560-564.

Fournier, S. (1991). Meaning-Based Framework for the Study of Consumer-Object Relations. *Advances in Consumer Research, 18*, 736-742.

Gatignon, H., Robertson, T.S. (1991). Innovative Decision Processes in Robertson, T.S. and Kassarjian, H.H. (eds.), *Handbook of Consumer Behaviour*, Prentice Hall, 316-348.

Hauser, J.R., Clausing, D. (1988). The House of Quality. *Harvard Business Review, 66*, 63-73.

Hirschman, E.C. (1980). Innovativeness, Novelty Seeking, and Consumer Creativity. *Journal of Consumer Research, 7*, 283-295.

Hirschman, E.C. (1981). Comprehending Symbolic Consumption: Three Theoretical Issues In Elizabeth C. Hirschman and Morris B. Holbrook (eds.), *Symbolic Consumer Behaviour*, Association for Consumer Research, Ann Arbor, MI.

Hirschman, E.C. (1987). Adoption of an Incredibly Complex Innovation: Propositions from a Humanistic Vantage Point. *Advances in Consumer Research, 14*, 57-60.

Irani, T. (2000). Prior Experience, Perceived Usefulness and the Web: Factors Influencing Adoption of Internet Communication Tools. Southern Association of Agricultural Scientists, Lexington, KY.

Kempf, D.S. (1999). Attitude Formation from Product Trial: Distinct Roles of Cognition and Affect for Hedonic and Functional Products. *Psychology & Marketing, 16 (1)*, 35-50.

Lefkoff-Hagius, R., Mason, C.H. (1993). Characteristics, Beneficial, and Image Attributes in Consumer Judgments of Similarity and Preference. *Journal of Consumer Research, 20*, 100-110.

Levy, S.J., (1959). Symbols for Sale. *Harvard Business Review, 37*, 117-124.

MacInnis, D.J., Jaworski, B.J. (1989). Information Processing from Advertisements: Toward an Integrative Framework. *Journal of Marketing, 53 (4)*, 1-24.

Meenaghan, T. (1995). The Role of Advertising in Brand Image Development. *Journal of Product & Brand Management, 4 (4)*, 23-34.

Michaut, A.M.K., Van Trijp, H.C.M., Steenkamp, J.B.E.M. (2002). Dimensions of Product Newness and their Differential Effect on Market Success. *Paper presented at 31st EMAC Conference*, May 28-31, Braga, Portugal.

Moreau, C.P., Lehmann, D.R., Markman, A.B. (2001). Entrenched Knowledge Structures and Consumer Response to New Products. *Journal of Marketing Research, 38*, 14-29.

Mukherjee, A. Hoyer, W.D. (2001). The Effect of Novel Attributes on Product Evaluation. *Journal of Marketing Research, 28*, 462-472.

Nowlis, S., Simonson I. (1996). The Effect of New Product Features on Brand Choice. *Journal of Marketing Research, 33*, 36-46.

Park, C.W., Jaworski, B.J., MacInnis, D.J. (1986). Strategic Brand Concept-Image Management. *Journal of Marketing, 50*, 135-145.

Park, C.W., Milderg S., Lawson R. (1991). Evaluation of Brand Extensions: The Role of Product Feature Similarity and Brand Concept Consistency. *Journal of Consumer Research, 18*, 185-193.

Roehm, M.L., Boone, D.S., Roehm H.A. Jr. (1999). Analogical Reasoning About New Product Introductions by Experts and Novices. *European Advances in Consumer Research, 4*, 161-165.

Roehm, M.L., Sternthal, B. (2001). The Moderating Effect of Knowledge and Resources on the Persuasive Impact of Analogies. *Journal of Consumer Research, 28*, 257-272.

Saaksjarvi, M. (2003). Consumer Adoption of Technological Innovations. *European Journal of Innovation Management, 6 (2)*, 90-100.

Sirgy, M.J., Johar, J.S. (1985). Measures of Product Value-Expressiveness and Utilitarianism: Initial Test of Reliability and Validity. *Proceedings of the Division of Consumer Psychology Convention*, Northridge, 99-103.

Smith, D.C., Park, C.W. (1992). The Effects of Brand Extensions on Market Share and Advertising Efficiency. *Journal of Marketing Research, 29*, 296-313.

Veryzer, R.W. (1998). Key Factors Affecting Customer Evaluations of Discontinuous New Product. *Journal of Product Innovation Management, 15*, 136-150.

Wood, S.L., Lynch, J.G. Jr. (2002). Prior Knowledge and Complacency in New Product Learning. *Journal of Consumer Research, 29*, 416-426.

The Influence of Evaluablility in Nutrition Tables on Consumers' Food Preferences

Vivianne Visschers, ETH Zurich, Switzerland

Michael Siegrist, ETH Zurich, Switzerland

Consumers seem to scarcely use nutrition tables printed on food products (Cowburn & Stockley, 2005). If they pay attention to these tables, they often seem to have difficulties in understanding the nutritional value of the products. Based on the evaluability principle, we suggest that people's nutritional value understanding may be facilitated when they can compare products.

The evaluability principle posits that when people evaluate a product on an attribute that does not have clear boundaries or references (e.g. the amount of fat in a product), the presence of similar information about another product can affect this evaluation (Hsee, 1996). The information about the other product then functions as a reference class. Thus, a nutrition table that includes nutrition information about other, perhaps similar products should influence consumers' perception of this product. Furthermore, consumers do not consider multiple attributes at the same time when choosing between food products but prefer to base their choice on one attribute of these products (Scheibehenne, Miesler, & Todd, 2007). This implies that consumers may benefit from summary information in nutrition tables when evaluating the nutritional value of a product.

Based on the evaluability heuristic and previous studies, we hypothesize that nutrition tables with information about a reference product, that is, in addition, summarized, are easier to understand and are more likely to affect consumers' evaluation of the products. So that the latter is more in agreement with the products' nutritional value.

We tested this in a between-subjects experiment. Six different nutrition tables were developed, which varied on summary information and on evaluability. The summary information was the nutrition density index (NDI) of the food product, which is based on the product's balance between the amount of nutrients and the amount of energy (cf. Drewnowski, 2005). This resulted in a value between 1 (low NDI) and 5 (high NDI). Evaluability was varied by presenting, along side the NDI score of the product at hand, either the average NDI score of the product category or the NDI score of a very healthy product, namely an orange. In sum, we tested six different nutrition tables, a standard nutrition table (*control*) and five tables that contained the standard table plus one of the following: the product's NDI score (*NDI score*), the percentage daily value of each nutrient (*%DV*), a positive, negative or neutral smiley for each nutrient (*smiley's*), a bar on which the product's NDI score and the average NDI of the product category were presented (*NDI plus product category*), or a bar on which the product's NDI score and the NDI score of an orange (*NDI plus orange*) were shown. These six tables were developed for two products: yogurt, which is a relatively healthy product, and chocolate, which is a relatively unhealthy product. Each respondent viewed one of these tables for one of the two products and was then asked to complete a questionnaire. This contained items about their liking of and intention to buy the product, its perceived healthiness, knowledge about the different nutrients, the evaluation of the nutrition table, which information in the nutrition table had drawn their attention, the importance of food for their health, and some demographics.

Overall, respondents perceived the yogurt as healthier than the chocolate. In addition, they rated the chocolate as more attractive and had greater intention to buy it than the yogurt. Respondents' knowledge of the two products seemed sufficient; they correctly indicated that the yogurt contained more sodium than the chocolate and that the chocolate contained more energy, fat, saturated fat, carbohydrates, sugar, and fibers than the yogurt.

The type of nutrition table influenced respondents' liking and intention to buy the chocolate. Respondents who had viewed the control table liked the chocolate more and had greater intention to buy it than the respondents who had seen the NDI score, %DV, smiley's, or NDI plus product category. This effect was not found for the yogurt. The chocolate's liking-buying score was higher in the control table condition than in the other nutrition table conditions, and higher compared to the yogurt's liking-buying rating. This may indicate that the tables that included reference information, summary information, or both changed people's perception of chocolate so that it became more in line with its nutritional value, which was actually relatively low.

A second study, in which we examined three nutrition tables for a healthy yogurt and an unhealthy yogurt, showed that the reference information changed people's healthiness perception of the unhealthy yogurt. The results of our two studies may imply two things. First, nutrition tables that provide reference information only seem to change people's perception of food products with low nutritional value, so that people like them less or consider them to be less healthy. Second, reference information only influences people's primary association with a product, and only when this association is not in line with the product's actual nutritional value. Consumers primarily associate chocolate with hedonic value and more with healthiness, reference information therefore changed these two perceptions of the two products.

In sum, this study suggests that the evaluability of nutrition table information can influence consumers' perception of a food product so that it corresponds to a greater degree with the product's nutritional value. An interesting suggestion for further research may be to study what kind of reference class induces this effect, thereby focusing on different food products.

References

Cowburn, G., & Stockley, L. (2005). Consumer understanding and use of nutrition labelling: A systematic review. *Public Health Nutrition, 8*, 21-28.

Drewnowski, A. (2005). Concept of a nutritious food: toward a nutrient density score. *American Journal of Clinical Nutrition, 82*, 721-732.

Hsee, C. K. (1996). The evaluability hypothesis: An explanation for preference reversals between joint and separate evaluations of alternatives. *Organizational Behavior and Human Decision Processes, 67*, 247-257.

Scheibehenne, B., Miesler, L., & Todd, P. M. (2007). Fast and frugal food choices: Uncovering individual decision heuristics. *Appetite, 49*, 578-589.

The IAT is Not Enough: The Added Value of Projective Techniques in Consumer Research

Hendrik Slabbinck, Ghent University, Belgium
Patrick Van Kenhove, Ghent University, Belgium

Introduction

Consumers do not only think and act rational. Also implicit or subconscious processes can influence their (consumer) behavior (e.g. Maison, Greenwald, and Bruin 2004). Consequently, in order to fully understand the consumer, both explicit and implicit attitudes have to be measured. Moreover, explicit attitudes can best be measured with direct measures and implicit attitudes with indirect measures (Greenwald and Banaji 1995).

One indirect measure that gets a fast growing support is the Implicit Association Test (IAT: Greenwald, McGhee, and Schwartz 1998). Apart from some exceptions (e.g. Blanton et al. 2006), the extensively tested psychometric properties of the IAT have mostly been approved (for an overview: see Nosek, Greenwald, and Banaji 2007). Whereas the IAT is frequently applied in research about stereotyping and prejudices, the interest by consumer researchers is also growing (e.g. Friese, Wanke, and Plessner 2006; Maison et al. 2004).

Another class of indirect measures are projective techniques. These research techniques appeared for the first time in consumer research in the 50's (Haire 1950). However, due to a lack of consensus on their psychometric qualities and subjective interpretation, these techniques disappeared virtually from attitude research. Yet, the interest in projective techniques seems to grow again (e.g. Boddy 2005; Vargas, von Hippel, and Petty 2004).

To conclude, two distinct indirect research techniques coexist, but, up to now, comparisons between both are very scarce (Sheldon et al. 2007). Hence, a clear need exists to compare the IAT with projective techniques. One important question that needs to be answered in this context is: "Are both techniques interchangeable, or do they measure distinct aspects of implicit attitudes?"

The relationship between the IAT and projective techniques

In the few studies in which the IAT was combined with a projective technique, the correlation between both is mostly non-significant or rather low. In the literature, we found correlations ranging from 0,11 (Vargas et al. 2004) to 0,28 (Meagher and Aidman 2002). Brunstein and Schmitt (2004) attribute this lack of correlation to method variance inherent to projective techniques, but Vargas et al. (2004) argue that low correlations can also indicate that projective techniques and the IAT asses different aspects of implicit attitudes. Next to Vargas et al. (2004) also Sheldon et al. (2007) showed that projective measures predict independently from the IAT a unique part of behavior. What is not clear yet is whether the IAT and projective techniques predict the same kind of behavior. According to McClelland et al. (1989), projective techniques outperform direct measures in the prediction of long term behavior and especially when behavior is triggered by activity incentives (e.g. long term job performance, ...), rather than social incentives. McClelland (1980) classifies this type of behavior as operant behavior. The IAT from its side, seems to outperform direct measures, especially if behavior is triggered by social incentives (e.g. prejudices, stereotyping, ...) (for an overview: Nosek et al. 2007). This kind of behavior can be classified as respondent behavior (McClelland 1980). Based on these findings, we hypothesized that projective techniques predict operant behavior whereas the IAT predicts respondent behavior.

Methodology

In order to operationalize this hypothesis, a exploratory study with 60 business students, was set up in which the personality dimension 'extraversion' was assessed by an IAT and a projective photoelicitation technique (selection of the most and least liked paintings out of a list 20 pre-tested paintings, followed by a semantic differential (based on the BFI: John, Donahue, and Kentle 1991)) measuring the extraversion of the paintings. The correlation between the liking of the painting and its extraversion rating can than be interpreted as a projective measure of the respondent's extraversion (procedure: see Liggett 1959).

Operant and respondent behavior were measured by nine five point likert items about impulsive buying behavior (IBB). IBB was chosen because a clear link exists between extraversion and IBB (Verplanken and Herabadi 2001). Respondent items comprised a stimulus element while operant items did not. An exemplar respondent item is "After having seen a TV commercial about sweets, I regularly indulge

FIGURE 1

Correlations between extraversion and impuslive buying behavior (n=60)

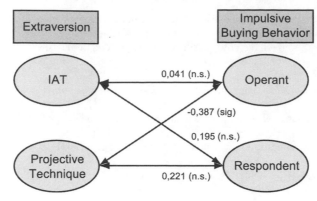

myself with some candy that I have in stock". An exemplar operant item is "When I come home from shopping, I am regularly surprised from all the unnecessary things that I bought". The items were factor analyzed and after deletion of three items, two factors could be maintained. The first factor clearly measured operant behavior and the second respondent behavior. The scores of each factor were summed which yielded into two reliable constructs (Operant: a=0,67; Respondent: a=0,75).

Results

As depicted in Figure 1, the results indicate that the projective measure indeed outperforms the IAT in predicting operant behavior. The projective, but not the IAT measure of extraversion correlated significantly with operant IBB ($r_{IAT-operant}$=0,041; p>0,05; $r_{projective-operant}$=-,387; p<0,01).

Concerning respondent behavior, we could not find any difference between both implicit measures of extraversion. The IAT nor the projective measure correlated with respondent IBB ($r_{IAT-respondent}$=0,192; p>0,05; $r_{projective-respondent}$=,221; p>0,05).

Discussion and follow up

In this first study, we found evidence that projective techniques and the IAT indeed predict different classes of behavior. However, it is not yet clear *why* they do so. A possible explanation could be that projective techniques are better in assessing personality traits than the IAT whereas (McClelland et al. 1989) the IAT will probably outperform projective techniques in the assessment of attitudes. (e.g. Nosek et al. 2007). This may also be a reason why in the current study, the IAT did not correlate with respondent IBB. Hence, to clarify the relation between implicit personality and attitudes, we will extend the current study in such a way that both, personality and attitudes are assessed separately by a projective technique and an IAT. We hypothesize firstly that personality assessed by a projective technique will outperform the IAT in predicting operant behavior. Next, we hypothesize that implicit attitudes measured by the IAT will outperform projective techniques in the assessment of respondent behavior.

References

Blanton, H., J. Jaccard, P. M. Gonzales, and C. Christe (2006), "Decoding the Implicit Association Test: Implications for Criterion Prediction," *Journal of Experimental Social Psychology*, 42 (2), 192-212.

Boddy, C. (2005), "Projective Techniques in Market Research: Valueless Subjectivity or Insightful Reality? A Look at the Evidence for the Usefulness, Reliability and Validity of Projective Techniques in Market Research," *International Journal of Market Research*, 47 (3), 239-54.

Brunstein, J. C. and C. H. Schmitt (2004), "Assessing Individual Differences in Achievement Motivation with the Implicit Association Test," *Journal of Research in Personality*, 38 (6), 536-55.

Friese, M., M. Wanke, and H. Plessner (2006), "Implicit Consumer Preferences and Their Influence on Product Choice," *Psychology & Marketing*, 23 (9), 727-40.

Greenwald, A. G., D. E. McGhee, and J. L. K. Schwartz (1998), "Measuring Individual Differences in Implicit Cognition: The Implicit Association Test," *Journal of Personality and Social Psychology*, 74 (6), 1464-80.

Greenwald, A.G. and M.R. Banaji (1995), "Implicit Social Cognition-Attitudes, Self-Esteem, and Stereotypes," *Psychological Review*, 102 (1), 4-27.

Haire, M. (1950), "Projective Techniques in Marketing Research," *The Journal of marketing*, 14 (5), 649.

John, O. P., E. M. Donahue, and R. L. Kentle (1991), *The Big Five Inventory-Versions 4a and 5*, Berkeley: University of California, Berkeley, Institute of Personality and Social Research.

Liggett, J. (1959), "The Paired Use of Projective Stimuli," *British Journal of Psychology*, 50 (3), 269-75.

Maison, D., A. G. Greenwald, and R. H. Bruin (2004), "Predictive Validity of the Implicit Association Test in Studies of Brands, Consumer Attitudes, and Behavior," *Journal of Consumer Psychology*, 14 (4), 405-15.

McClelland, D C (1980), "Motive Dispositions; the Merits of Operant and Respondent Measures," in *Review of Personality and Social Psychology*, ed. L Wheeler, Beverly Hills: Sage, v.

McClelland, D. C., R. Koestner, and J. Weinberger (1989), "How Do Self-Attributed and Implicit Motives Differ," *Psychological Review*, 96 (4), 690-702.

Meagher, BE and EV Aidman (2002), "The Effects of Implicit and Explicit Self-Esteem on Sensitivity to Unfavourable Performance Evaluation," *Australian Journal of Psychology*, 54, 44-44.

Nosek, B.A., A.G. Greenwald, and M.R. Banaji (2007), "The Implicit Association Test at Age 7: A Methodological and Conceptual Review," in *Automatic Processes in Social Thinking and Behavior*, ed. J. A. Bargh, Philadelphia, PA: Psychology Press, 265–92.

Sheldon, KM, LA King, L Houser-Marko, R Osbaldiston, and A Gunz (2007), "Comparing Iat and Tat Measures of Power Versus Intimacy Motivation," *European Journal of Personality*, 21 (3), 263-80.

Vargas, P. T., W. von Hippel, and R. E. Petty (2004), "Using Partially Structured Attitude Measures to Enhance the Attitude-Behavior Relationship," *Personality and Social Psychology Bulletin*, 30 (2), 197-211.

Verplanken, B and A Herabadi (2001), "Individual Differences in Impulse Buying Tendency: Feeling and No Thinking," *European Journal of Personality*, 15, S71-S83.

The Meaning of 'Product Placement': An Interpretive Exploration of Consumers' Experiences of Television Programme Product Placement in the United Kingdom and Thailand

Rungpaka Amy Tiwsakul, University of Surrey, UK

Chris Hackley, Royal Holloway, University of London, UK

Television programme product placement is increasing in significance from both a managerial and a consumer cultural perspective. Product placement refers in this research to the inclusion of or reference to branded products or services in scripts or plots in any form of non-advertising mediated entertainment for promotional purposes. In Thai there is no precise translation for product placement. It is known as 'implicit advertising' or 'kod-sa-na-faeng'. Television studios are seeking new revenue streams to offset the decline in conventional paid-for advertising revenues, while branding and advertising agencies are moving towards more 'experiential' marketing tools to access consumers 'under the radar'. Questions arise about the implications of this practice for international managerial practice and consumer experience, with attendant issues concerning ethics, public policy and regulation in a climate of increasing globalisation of brands. To date, with a small number of exceptions, research in the area has focussed largely on single-country studies measuring the attitudes of non-segmented audiences towards placements in movies.

Product placement has played an important role as a relatively new emerging tool of integrated marketing communications (IMC) for several decades. Brand marketing organisations have typically been content with seeing brand exposure in mediated entertainment as an add-on, but many are now putting resources into the technique. One of its perceived advantages over traditional advertising is the access it affords to consumers' daily experiences. Through placements in television soap operas, situation comedies, quiz shows, and other genres, brands can be featured as meaningful artefacts in narrative contexts which have a powerful resonance for consumers. This popular culture phenomenon blurs the boundaries between entertainment and promotion. The meanings of the media and promotions, as a result, are intertwined through the postmodern practice of intertextuality by which consumers engage in endless cross-referencing (Jansson, 2002; Gould and Gupta, 2006). In other words, consumers bring an intertextual network of meanings through which they interpret and react to the placements to the product placements and media that brands are embedded in.

Although some literature (e.g. Fazio and Zanna, 1978; Smith and Swinyard, 1988) suggests that "attitudes formed through lived experience are stronger, more accessible, held more confidently, and more predictive of behaviour than those derived from mediated experience through advertising" (Wattanasuwan, 2003, p.72), in postmodernity mediated experiences of, for example advertising, product placement and television programmes, may be as powerful as lived experiences in forming attitudes relevant to 'the symbolic project of the self' (ibid). Branded goods are consumed not only for their utility but also for their symbolic value (Elliott and Wattanasuwan, 1998). Media representations of brands in advertising and entertainment can be powerful in suggesting particular meanings in association with marketed products and brands. Effectively, products become commodity signs (Baudrillard, 1981).

Product placement in movies has been studied by academic researchers, usually from a neo-positivist perspective which measures the brand recall, attitudes of consumers, and purchase intention to the practice. There are some robust findings but more studies are needed which take into account several other dimensions. Firstly, television is potentially a more powerful channel than movies for reaching into consumers' lives because the consumer engagement with favourite soap operas or dramas or other genres of the television show is more intimate and more regular than visits to the movies. Secondly, this quality of engagement cannot easily be accessed through quantitative data gathering methods. Thirdly, the strategies and rationalisations behind product placement practices need to be understood to complete the overall picture, since consumer interpretations are only one half of the process. In particular, the managerial strategies are important not only in making assessments about the contribution of product placement to the marketing management of brands but also in making judgements about the attendant ethical and public policy implications. Furthermore, product placement seems to carry features consistent with the 'interpretive' or 'postmodern' turn in consumer and marketing research, especially with regard to the symbolic role brands may play as resources for the production of self and social identity. In this regard it is important to consider product placement from an interpretive consumer cultural perspective, a perspective not yet evident in the literature. Finally, much is made today of the globalisation of brands and the emergence of consumer communities separated by ethnicity, nationality and religion yet linked through brand allegiance. It is therefore useful to examine the cross-cultural context. Consumers under forty constitute a useful group in this research as they are typically fully engaged with media and brand culture and are known to use brands in their self-identification processes.

This study, then, uses qualitative data gathering methods to explore television programme product placement from the subjective perspective of young consumers in the UK and Thailand. This perspective is supplemented by a detailed account of managerial practices of product placement offered by leading agencies in the field. In-depth interviews with agency practitioners, and discussion groups and elicited auto-ethnographic passages with consumers were the main data-gathering methods. All data were fully translated and transcribed. Data were then subject to an interpretive thematic analysis which, drawing on elements of discourse analysis, focussed on the 'interpretive repertoires' which seemed to constitute the major themes drawn upon in articulating experiences of product placement.

The UK and Thailand were chosen because the UK is an advanced economy with a relatively immature television product placement industry while Thailand is a developing economy in which television product placement is a well-established practice. The intention of the study is not to compare the respective cultures as such, since culture is not a fixed entity which allows direct comparison, although it is important to consider product placement within its local media infrastructure and consumer culture. Rather, the intention is to juxtapose two contrasting contexts in order to add contrast and shade to the respective findings.

The findings offer a thematic interpretation of some 40,000 words of transcribed data with consumers and practitioners focusing on three main areas: 1) the managerial practices and strategies surrounding the use of television product placement as an aspect of marketing communications management 2) the ways in which consumers engage with, understand and interpret brand placements in television shows and 3) the ways in which these interpretations feed into ideas of self identity and consumer culture. The study concludes that product placement on television is a sophisticated managerial practice which constitutes a powerful discourse of brand consumption. Consumers are highly attuned to this discourse and draw on it reflexively in their expressions of self-concept.

References

Baudrillard, Jean (1981), *For a critique of the political economy of the sign*, St Louis MI: Telos Press.

Elliott, Richard, and Wattanasuwan, Kritsadarat (1998), Brands as symbolic resources for the construction of identity, *International Journal of Advertising*, Vol. 17, Iss. 2, p. 131-144.

Fazio, Russell, and Zanna, Mark P. (1978), On the predictive validity of attitudes: the role of direct experience and confidence, *Journal of Personality*, Vol. 46, Iss. p. 228-243.

Gould, Stephen J., and Gupta, Pola B. (2006), "Come on down" How consumers view game shows and the products placed in them, *Journal of Advertising*, Vol. 35, Iss. 1, p. 65-81.

Jansson, Andre (2002), The mediatisation of consumption: towards an analytical framework of image culture, *Journal of Consumer Culture*, Vol. 2, Iss. 1, p. 5-31.

Smith, Robert E., and Swinyard, William R. (1988), Cognitive response to advertising and trial: belief strength, belief confidence and product curiosity, *Journal of Advertising*, Vol. 17, Iss. 3, p. 3-14.

Wattanasuwan, Kritsadarat (2003), The young nouveau riche and luxury-brand consumption, *Journal of Commerce and Accountancy, Thammasat University, Thailand*, Vol. 97, Iss. January-March, p. 61-86.

Exploring Consumer Risk Across Multiple Domains

Gulnur Tumbat, San Francisco State University, USA

Extended Abstract

Consumer live in a world filled with risk which has become a big debate in the last decades in various areas such as destruction of nature and environment, pollution of air, water, and food, health problems, national security issues and politics, crime, and technology (Beck 1992, Giddens 1992, Furedi 2002). Within psychology and its manifestation in consumer research (e.g., brand preference, product choice), decision making and information processing under risk and uncertainty has been of considerable interest to both judgment and decision making literatures. So far consumer researchers have created a useful yet incomplete picture of consumer risk since consumers are largely viewed as responding individually to risks according to various "heuristics" or frames of perception that structure their judgment According to Paul Slovic (2000), one of the foremost theoreticians of the psychology of risk, "the perception and acceptance of risk have their roots in social and cultural factors" (p. 221). Similarly, Lopes (1997) argues that attempts to explain all of risky choice behavior in the narrow terms of purely perceptual, purely cognitive, or purely motivational mechanisms will necessarily miss much of what impels people toward or away from particular risks. Douglas and Wildawsky (1982), for instance, explain that risk is a constructed idea and that humans act less as individuals and more as social beings that have internalized social structures. Socio-cultural aspects of consumers risk perceptions and risk-taking behavior offer significant contributions to consumer risk studies along with economic and cognitive approaches to study risk. Yet, despite their widely acknowledged significance, particularly in the context of consumption, social and cultural contexts have been largely ignored in our field [see few notable exceptions. Thompson (2005)'s study on birth practices reveals how people's risk perceptions are culturally constructed. Celsi, Rose, Leigh (1993) investigated cultural motivations and dramatic worldview that effect people's risk taking behavior in the case of high-risk leisure activities].

These prior studies, focus on single and isolated risk discourses around issues such as product or brand choice, health, finances, and leisure, among some others. Various streams of literature, however, suggest that modern day consumers are faced with a vast array of multiple and competing demands that they try to deal with simultaneously. Building on Beck and Giddens, Furedi (2002) for instance argues that we now live in a culture of fear and discourses around risks of life produce what he calls a cautious individual. Consumers are embedded in social systems and in their day-to-day lives they encounter multiple foci on risk. Examples of various domains may include financial (e.g., investments, future considerations, debts to pay), environmental (e.g., pollution, global warming, depletion of natural resources), social/cultural (e.g., changing society, changing needs, relationships), terrorism (e.g., terrorist attacks, bombings, hijackings), crime/safety (e.g., security systems, gated communities), health (e.g., organic food, holistic approaches), and natural (e.g., natural disasters such as earthquakes and hurricanes) risks. However, with the existing research on risk, we are unable to address possible variance in assessing risks in cross-context. How do people perceive risks in different risk domains? How do they manage (tensions and) their perceptions across these domains? How consumers live/ cope with various (and sometimes countervailing) risk discourses (e.g., economic, political, technological, environmental, social) and what kind of role consumption plays in those experiences? How various risk discourses are activated and negotiated in everyday life? How are consumers' practices related to one discourse is mediated through other risk discourses? Do they balance their practices related with competing risk discourses? Or do they trade off one against another? Do the risk perceptions and resultant practices shift toward one risk domain to another? Consumer researchers need to answer these important questions and thus reveal embedded and complex quality of multiple risk discourses and their reflections on consumption practices.

To address this theoretical gap, a poststructuralist perspective would offer insights into how consumers experience multiple risk discourses and what role their consumption practices play. The methods used for data collection include multiple steps. First, a questionnaire was distributed to 50 graduate students as part of a graduate course. After giving some information to them about the project, questions asked were about the types of risk discourses they can identify, how they think they are related to consumption, and how they deal with them in their daily life, and how they think they effect their consumption in general. The purpose of this step was to gather a sense of potential areas to probe in the second step of the data collection process that is in-depth interviews. Preliminary analysis suggests several themes around these practices as prioritization (focusing one over the other depending on context), distraction (choosing to be distracted by other issues about their lives), ignorance, accommodation (trying to be careful), and some shift (in consumption practices).

This study hopes to add to the existing body of research around risk in consumer behavior field by studying risks as discourses in order to provide a deeper understanding about social, historical, cultural constructions of risk. Furthermore, it attempts to shift the focus from individual and isolated risk domains as they are tackled in previous research to a more broader perspective of multiple risk domains as experienced and lived by consumers on a daily basis. Sharing these ideas and preliminary findings at ACR would definitely provide much needed feedback and comments, and would also open up potential collaboration among other consumer risk researchers.

References

Beck, Ulrich (1992), *Risk Society: Towards a New Modernity*, London: Sage.

Celsi, Richard L., Randall L. Rose, and Thomas W. Leigh, (1993), "An Exploration of High-Risk Leisure Consumption through Skydiving," *Journal of Consumer Research*, 20 (June), 1-23.

Douglas, Mary and Aaron Wildavsky (1982), *Risk and Culture*, Berkeley, CA: University of California Press.

Foucault, Michel (1979), *Discipline and Punish*, trans. Alan Sheridan, NY: Vintage Books.

Furedi, Frank (2002), *Culture of Fear: Risk Taking and the Morality of Low Expectation*, London: Continuum.

Giddens, A. (1992), *Modernity and Self-Identity: Self and Society in the Late Modern Age*, Stanford, CA: Stanford University Press.

Slovic, Paul (2000), *The Perception of Risk*, London, UK: Earthscan.

Thompson, Craig J. (2005), "Consumers' Risk Perceptions in a Community of Reflexive Doubt," *Journal of Consumer Research*, 32 (September), 235-248.

Exploring the (Re)construction of The Body in Virtual Worlds: Consumption of Body as Experience

Handan Vicdan, The University of Texas-Pan American, USA
Ebru Ulusoy, The University of Texas-Pan American, USA

The main focus of interest on the body concept in consumer research evolved around the corporeal body. Body has been investigated as a project that modern consumers work on (Featherstone, Hepworth and Turner 1991; Schouten 1991), and as a means of self-presentation and socialization (Thompson and Hirschman 1995). Thus, modern consumers treated their bodies as not an 'end' but a 'means' of conveying a desirable image to others. Furthermore, with the emergence of new technologies, the presence of the body has been questioned. Some argued that these technologies have enabled people to break out of the finitude of their embodiment (Balsamo 2000; Turkle 1995). Others advocated the essential role of embodiment in any human experience (Argyle and Shields 1996; Froy 2003; Hansen 2006).

The growing semiotic potential of virtual worlds through multiplicity of symbols (Venkatesh 1999) allows for visual representation of one's physical self through avatars, which are "graphic icons representing users through various forms" (Chung 2005, p. 538). In this study, we explore the meanings attached to the avatars, and how and what consumers experience through these virtual bodies, in a 3-D virtual world called Second Life (SL).

We conducted netnographic research, which helped us understand the symbolic aspects of body, and develop alternative perspectives to the presence of the body in virtual worlds. Our preliminary data consist of our experiences as SL residents, and online/offline interviews with eight informants, all of which were in-depth and semistructured.

Findings derived from the meanings attributed to avatars reveal that preoccupation with the body is an essential part of virtual lives. The (re)construction of symbolic corporeal selves reflects the transforming urge of a modern consumer from perceiving his/her body as less of a tool for communication with and impression to others to an experience itself, an end that s/he playfully engages in for its own sake. The body itself becomes the experience in SL, rather than solely being a communication or impression management medium as it is perceived in first life (FL). Whereas FL is limited in the bodily creations; SL provides consumers the freedom to (re)construct their desired bodily creations and experiences.

Yet, the construction of body and the experiences lived through it in this symbolic realm are affected by consumers' FL selves and vice versa. In SL, consumers engage in experiences they can(not) immerse into in FL (e.g., flying, skydiving), and experiences they symbolically (e.g., death, suicide) and literally immerse into (e.g., having the sense of blood rush while the avatar is falling down). They gain the ability to engage in bodily experiences that they couldn't engage with their FL bodies because of physical or psychological constraints. Nevertheless, consumers build higher levels of empathy with their avatars, which strengthens the feeling aspect of experiences. Thus, SL experiences are not purely separated from those of FL and vice versa. FL selves are reflected on SL selves and vice versa during avatar (re)creation. In continuous (re)construction of bodily experiences, the paradoxes of *segregation* (e.g. SL gives the opportunity to do things one can't do in FL, and help mask FL appearances through avatars making socializing easier than FL) and *inseparableness* (incorporation of SL in FL or vice versa), and *possible* and *proper* are further intensified. SL consumers reflect their FL selves on SL selves and vice versa (e.g., keeping social distance in SL just like in FL; making avatars look like their FL selves and reflecting their SL selves on their FL selves, gaining skills through SL and reflecting that self-esteem gained in SL on FL experiences).

In SL, self-presentation is enhanced by immersion into SL experiences involving symbolic (re)construction and experience of several bodily selves. *Symembodiment*, a process in which consumers (re)construct and playfully engage in the symbolic creation and experiencing of their avatars, replaces the concept of disembodiment. Consumers reconcile their urge for physicality with the non-physicality of cyberspace in symbolic forms. They are devoid of bodily constraints, and are embedded in the scheme of symbolic forms (Venkatesh 1999). A person can become a mermaid and all of a sudden, grows a tail and experiences the transition into a leopard. A half-human cyborg changes his deep voice into a soft female voice while reading poems in SL. The body is experienced for the sake of itself rather than solely being used as a medium of self-presentation. "The boundaries delineated by cultural constructions of the body are both subverted and given free rein in virtual environments. With the body freed from the physical, it completely enters the realm of the symbol" (Reid-Steere 1996, p. 36). Hence, the continuous (re)construction of body through avatars becomes a symbolic experience, in which the body is present, not with its constraints but with its symbolic significance.

References

Argyle, Katie and Rob Shields (1996), "Is there a Body on the Net?" in *Cultures of Internet,* Shields, Ron, ed., London: Sage.

Balsamo, Anne (2000), "The Virtual Body in Cyberspace," In D. Bell and B. M. Kennedy (eds.), The Cybercultures Reader, NY: Routledge, 489-503.

Chung, Donghun (2005), "Something for Nothing: Understanding Purchasing Behaviors in Virtual Environments," *Cyberpsychology & Behavior,* 6, 538-554.

Featherstone, Mike, Mike Hepworth and Bryan S. Turner (1991), *The Body: Social Process and Cultural Theory,* London: Sage.

Froy, Francesca (2003), "Indeterminacy in Cyberspace," in Indeterminate Bodies, Segal, Naomi, Lib Taylor and Roger Cook, (eds.), NY: Palgrave Macmillan, 139-151.

Hansen, Mark B. N. (2006), *Bodies in Code: Interfaces with Digital Media,* NY: Routledge.

Reid-Steere, Elizabeth (1996), "Text-Based Virtual Realities: Identity and the Cyborg Body," in P. Ludlow (ed.), *High Noon on the Electronic Frontier: Conceptual Issues in Cyberspace,* MIT Press, 30-42.

Schouten, John W. (1991), "Selves in Transition: Symbolic Consumption in Personal Rites of Passage and Identity Reconstruction," *Journal of Consumer Research,* 17, 412-425.

Thompson, Craig J. and Elizabeth Hirschman (1995), "Understanding the Socialized Boy: A Poststructuralist Analysis of Consumers' Self-Conceptions, Body Images and Self-Care Products," *Journal of Consumer Research,* 22, 139-153.

Turkle, Sherry (1995), *Life on the Screen: Identity in the Age of the Internet,* NY: Simon and Schuster.

Venkatesh, Alladi (1999), "Postmodernism Perspectives for Macromarketing: An Inquiry into the Global Information and Sign Economy", *Journal of Macromarketing,* 19, 2, 153-169.

Reproducing and Subverting the Global Hierarchy: Revisiting Advertising in a Postcolonial Setting

Rohit Varman, Indian Institute of Management-Calcutta,, India

Both consumers and marketers draw upon extant sociocultural discourses to give meaning to the products they consume or sell (Belk 1988; Costa 1998; Thompson and Haytko 1997; Zukin and Maguire 2005). Advertising is an important tool employed by marketers to draw upon the culturally constituted world to establish symbolic equivalence with dominant sociocultural discourses (McCracken 1988; Sahlins 1976). Several studies in the past have drawn upon the post-colonial framework (Bhabha 1994; Breckenridge and Van der Veer 1993; Chakrabarty 1992; Guha 1998) and have highlighted the role of orientalism in advertising (Cayla and Koops-Elson 2006; Mazarella 2003; Rajagopal 2001). My research adds to this body of knowledge by offering an understanding of the manner by which advertising draws upon extant sociocultural discourses of 'self' and 'other' to give meaning to products.

In order to understand the socio-cultural codes embedded in Indian advertising, I conducted content analysis of print and television advertising. This helped me to understand the representations and discursive practices of some of the advertising firms. My data base comprised of around 500 advertisements, which were collected over a period of one year. In order to understand the process of creation of advertisements and deployment of extant sociocultural codes, I conducted indepth interviews with executives working in the Creative area in advertising firms. I conducted these interviews with 13 Creative Executives working in the domains of copywriting and art direction from three large advertising firms in India. My sampling was purposeful and involved interviews with junior and senior creative personnel from Indian and Multinational advertising firms. This also helped me to achieve triangulation that is necessary for the trustworthiness of data.

In uncovering the creative process through which 'auto-orientalism'(Mazarella 2003; Said 1978) is employed, I argue that extant theorization based on the post-colonial framework has overemphasized the 'orientalist' discourse and has failed to comprehend two other significant features embedded in Indian advertising texts. First, building on Foucault's (1978) conceptualization of representation and power, I show that a subversive discourse of 'occidentalism' is an important part of comprehending the relationship between advertising and otherness in India. In this discourse of 'occindentalism', the west is interpreted as profane, impure, and perfidious. My dialectical interpretation of self-orientalism and occidentalism helps in overcoming the passivity imparted to a post-colonial society. The reinforcement and subversion of the local-global/East-West hierarchy in Indian advertising contribute to a richer understanding of cultural processes in a post-colonial setting that have been elided in extant interpretation. Second, my research shows that Indian advertising cannot be sufficiently situated within the post-colonial framework. Here, I argue that the privilege imparted to the colonial encounter in the post-colonial framework ignores the cultural elements that have emerged from other possible historical processes (Ahmad 1992). In particular, I highlight the role of social class in Indian advertising that has emerged from the society's experience of capitalism. I show that the class hierarchy is reinforced through representations that emerge from advertisers who belong to the social and economic elite of the society. I draw upon Bourdieu's (1984) conceptualization of *habitus* to analyze the role of creative personnel in the production of these class-based representations. Finally, I apply a critical perspective to advertising and understand its functioning as part of the culture industry (Horkheimer and Adorno 1944/1998; Jhally 1987). I critique this ideological role and see it as a ramification of, and further catalyst to, hegemony, globalization, and the maintenance and exploitation of cultural difference and hierarchy.

References

Ahmad, Aijaz (1992), *In Theory: Classes, Nations, Literatures*, New Delhi: Oxford.

Belk, Russell W. (1988) "Possessions and the Extended Self," *Journal of Consumer Research*, 15 (September), 139-168.

Bhabha, Homi (1994), *The Location of Culture*, New York: Routledge.

Bourdieu, Pierre (1984), *Distinctions: A Social Critique of the Judgement of Taste*, London : Routeledge.

Breckenridge, Carol A. and Peter Van der Veer (1993), "Orientalism and Postcolonial Predicament," in *Orientalism and Postcolonial Predicament: Perspectives on South Asia*, ed. by Carol A. Breckenbridge and Peter van der Van, Calcutta: Oxford: 1-19.

Cayla, Julien and Mark Koops-Elson (2006), "Global Men and Local Roots: Representation and Hybridity in Indian Advertising, in *Gender and Consumer Behavior*, 8, Available on http://www.acrwebsite.org/volumes/gmcb_v08/ CP%20paper%2013%20Julien%20Cayla.pdf, Accessed on 02-01-2008.

Chakrabarty, Dipesh (1992), " Postcoliniality and the Artifice of History: Who Speaks for "Indian" Pasts?" *Representations*, 37 (Winter): 1-26.

Costa, Janeen (1998) "Paradisal Discourse: A Critical analysis of Marketing and Consuming Hawaii," *Consumption, Markets and Culture*, 14, 303-346

Foucault, Michel (1978), *The History of Sexuality: An Introduction Volume 1*, New York: Vintage Books.

Guha, Ranajit (1998), "On Some Aspects of the Historiography of Colonial India," in *Between Tradition and Modernity: India's Search of Identity*, edited by, Fred Dallmayr and G.N.. Devy, New Delhi: Sage, 279-300.

Holt, Douglas B. (2002) "Why Do Brands Cause Trouble? A Dialectical Theory of Consumer Culture and Branding," *Journal of Consumer Research*, 29 (June), 70-90.

Horkheimer, Max and Theodor Adorno. (1944/1998) *Dialectic of Enlightenment*, New York: Continuum.

Jhally, Sut (1987), *The Codes of Advertising: Fetishism and the Political Economy of Meaning in the Consumer Society*. New York: St. Martin's Press.

Mazarella,William (2003) *Shoveling Smoke: Advertising and Globalization in Contemporary India*, Durham, NC: Duke University Press.

Rajagopal, Arvind. (2001), *Politics After Television: Hindu Nationalism and the Reshaping of the Public in India*, Cambridge: University Press.

Sahlins, Marshall. (1976) *Culture and Practical Reason*, Chicago: University of Chicago Press.

Said, Edward W. (1978), *Orientalism*, New York: Random House.

Thompson, Craig and Diana L. Haytko (1997), "Speaking of Fashion: Consumers' Uses of Fashion Discourses and Appropriation of Countervailing Cultural Meanings," *Journal of Consumer Research*, 24 (June), 15-42.

Zukin, Sharon and Jennifer S. Maguire (2005), "Consumers and Consumption," *Annual Review of Sociology*, 30, 173-197.

The Consumer Who Knew Too Much: Online Movie Piracy By Young Adults

Iris Vermeir, University College Ghent & Ghent University, Belgium

Online movie piracy or the unauthorized, unpaid downloading of movies from the internet, is beginning to grow as internet connections become faster. Moreover, the anonymity of internet lowers the perception of illegality of unethical behavior, clearing the road for online unethical behavior (Freestone and Mitchell 2004). Research has demonstrated that consumers do not perceive the movie industry as a victim of movie piracy (especially because of the high prices charged at the box office) and hence, do not perceive the unethicalness of movie piracy (Freestone and Mitchell 2004). Consequently, all over the world, anti-movie piracy campaigns are developed to communicate that movie piracy is wrong. It is assumed that communicating the unethicalness of this illegal activity will decrease actual piracy behavior. However, ethical research shows that consumers engage in illegal behaviors, even though they perceive them as unethical (Sinha and Mandel 2008; Easly 2005). A lot of social psychological and consumer research has already shown that the link between attitudes or beliefs and behavior most often is not that straightforward and depends on several attitudinal, contextual, and personal variables that moderate this relation (for a meta-analysis see Glasman and Albarracin 2006; Kraus 1995).

The purpose of this study is to look at some of the variables that could explain why consumers engage in movie piracy behavior even though they find it unethical. More specifically, action related knowledge, price perception and perceived effort for the legal alternative were investigated.

Because stronger attitudes, lead to more consistent behaviors (e.g. Fabrigar et al. 2006), we can expect that higher perceptions of unethicalness will lead to less movie piracy. Obviously, limited knowledge of how to pirate a movie, will also lead to less movie piracy, even though movie piracy is perceived as an ethical alternative. Action related knowledge is a necessary condition for behavior (Frey et al. 2006). Fabrigar et al. (2006) already found that subjects who possess less relevant knowledge display less attitude-consistent behavior. The question remains however, if consumers who possess action related knowledge will engage in movie piracy despite unethical perceptions of movie piracy. Action related knowledge could explain why so many consumers engage in movie piracy, even though they know it is unethical.

Furthermore, we argue that consumers, who perceive the legal alternative as too expensive, will engage in movie piracy even though they consider this an unethical activity. High price perception decreases intentions to engage in an activity (Chiang and Dholakia 2003). Consequently, consumers could feel they are allowed to engage in an unethical activity because they have a good excuse: the legal alternative is too expensive. Consumers can diminish perceived guilt for inappropriate behavior by using neutralization techniques like condemning the condemners (e.g. the corporation deserves the mistreatment because he previously engaged in some form of misbehavior– i.e. charging too much) (Strutton et al. 1994).

Finally, high perceived effort for the legal alternative will lead to less consistent behavior. In other words, subjects who perceive movie piracy as unethical could engage in movie piracy if they perceive effort necessary for the legal alternative is too high. If a subject is not willing to spend time and energy for the legal alternative (e.g. going to the movie theatre), positive attitudes will not lead to behavior (Dik and Aarts, 2007).

In order to test our hypotheses, a total of 490 young adults between 18 and 22 years old completed an online questionnaire. Participants were asked six attitudinal questions on their attitude towards movie piracy on a 7-point Likert scale (α=.85). Furthermore, ethical perceptions of movie piracy were measured using 4 items (ethical, appropriate, permitted, proper) (α=.89) . Next, young adults indicate their action related knowledge (cfr. Roehm and Sternthal 2001), price perceptions and willingness to engage in effort for legal alternatives (cfr. Voss et al. 1998) on 7-point Likert scales. Finally, young adults were asked to indicate how much movie piracy they engage in (cfr. Cronin et al. 2000).

Significant main effects were found for ethical perception ($F_{(1,458)}$= 33,26, p<.01), knowledge ($F_{(1,458)}$= 510,301, p<.01), price perception ($F_{(1,458)}$= 2,87, p<.1) and willingness to engage in effort for a legal alternative ($F_{(1,458)}$= 10,58, p<.01). Young adults especially engaged in movie piracy when they perceive this activity as ethical, knew how to perform this behavior, and when price perception and perceived effort for legal alternatives was high. Significant interaction effects were found between ethical perception and knowledge ($F_{(1,458)}$= 8,33, p<.01) and ethical perception and price perception ($F_{(1,458)}$= 5,76, p<.05). Ethical perception determined behavior when behavioral knowledge was low: young adults, who did not really know how to pirate movies, engaged more in movie piracy when they perceived it as an ethical (versus unethical) activity. However, for knowledgeable young adults, ethical perception did not matter: they engaged in illegal movie piracy, regardless of their ethical perceptions. Furthermore, price perceptions of legal alternatives did not influence behavior differently for young adults who find movie piracy unethical. These 'ethical' young adults did not pirate movies a lot even if they perceived the legal alternatives as too expensive. On the contrary, 'unethical' consumers who find movie piracy ethical will engage more in movie piracy if they perceive legal alternatives as too expensive. We did not find an interaction effect between perceived effort and ethical perception. Young adults will engage more in movie piracy when they perceive the effort for the legal alternative as too high, regardless of their ethical perceptions. Possibly, perceived effort is rated relatively low in general (M=3,88, SD=1,09) to make young adults use this as an 'neutralization' to engage in unethical behavior.

Our results show that knowledge, price perception and willingness to perform effort influence movie piracy. Interestingly, it seems like young adults will engage in an illegal activity like movie piracy, despite their perceptions of unethicalness of movie piracy, if they know how to do it but not if they perceive legal alternatives as too expensive.

References

Chiang, Kuan-Pin and Ruby Roy Dholakia (2003),"Factors Driving Consumer to Shop Online: An Empirical Investigation", *Journal of Consumer Psychology*, 13(1&2), 177-183.

Cronin, Jr., J. Joseph, Michael K. Brady and Tomas M. Hult, (2000), "Assessing the Effects of Quality Value and Customer Satisfaction on Consumer Behavioral Intentions in Service Environments", *Journal of Retailing*, 79, 193-218.

Dik, Giel and Henk Aarts, (2007), "Behavioural cues to others' motivation and goal pursuits: The perception of effort facilitates goal inference and contagion", *Journal of Experimental Social Psychology*, 43(5), 727-737.

Easly, Robert F. (2005), "Ethical issues in the Music Industry Response to Innovation and Piracy", *Journal of Business Ethics*, 62, 163-168.

Fabrigar, Leandre R., Richard E. Petty, Steven E. Smith and Stephen L.Jr. Crites, (2006), "Understanding Knowledge Effects on Attitude-Behaviour Consistency: The Role of Relevance, Complexity, and Amount of Knowledge", J*ournal of Personality & Social Psychology*, 90(4), 556-577.

Freestone, Oliver and Vincent-Wayne Mitchell, (2004), "Generation Y Attitudes towards E-ethics and Internet-related Misbehaviours", *Journal of Business Ethics*, 54, 121-128.

Frey, Dieter, Heinz Mandl and Lutz Von Rosenstiel, (2006), "Knowledge and action", Ashland, OH, US: Hogrefe & Huber Publishers.

Glasman, Laura R. and Dolores Albarracín, (2006), "Forming Attitudes That Predict Future behaviour: A Meta-Analysis of the Attitude-Behaviour Relation", *Psychological Bulletin*, 132(5), 778-822.

Kraus, Stephen J., (1995), "Attitudes and the Prediction of Behaviour: A Meta-Analysis of the Empirical Literature", *Personality and Social Psychology Bulletin*, 21(1), 58-75.

Roehm, Michelle L. and Brian Sternthal, (2001), "The moderating effect of knowledge and resources on the persuasive impact of analogies", *Journal of Consumer Research*, 28, 257-272.

Sinha, Rajiv K. and Naomi Mandel (2008), "Preventing Digital Music Piracy: The Carrot or the Stick", *Journal of Marketing*, 27(January), 1-15.

Strutton, David, Scott. J. Vitell and Lou E. Pelton: (1994), "How Consumers May Justify Inappropriate behaviour in Market Settings: An Application on The Techniques of Neutralization", *Journal of Business Research* 30(3), 253-260.

Voss, Glenn B., A. Parasuraman and Dhruv Grewal, (1998), "The Roles of Price, Performance, and Expectations in determining Satisfaction in Service Exchanges", *Journal of Marketing*, 62, 46-61.

Team Purchase: Consumer Empowerment through Collective Actions

Jeff Wang, City University of Hong Kong, China
Xin Zhao, University of Hawaii, USA

Literature on consumer culture theory has illuminated the re-enchantment of consumption (Arnould and Thompson 2005; Firat and Venkatesh 1995). In contrast, the acquisition phase of purchasing is largely viewed as an individual decision-making process or an act framed by family traditions (Epp and Price 2008; Wallendorf and Arnould 1991). In this paper, we examine the phenomenon of team purchase as a collective act that is initiated and organized by groups of consumers in urban China (Areddy 2006). Through this ethnographic inquiry, we show how Chinese consumers have challenged the conventional market system and manipulated it to their own ends without necessarily aiming to escape the market as their counterparts in Western societies (see Kozinets 2002).

Team purchase is a consumer-organized collective activity gaining momentum just recently in urban China (Arredy 2006). It starts on the Internet, usually in chat rooms and discussion forums, where like-minded consumers devise plans to buy branded consumer products in large quantity at lower price. They then show up en masse at stores to demand discounts and more benefits. They usually defeat the merchants with their collective haggling. In addition to obtaining better pricing, they gain a sense of power and pride.

Team buyers unite to confront merchants. They defy the conventional retailer-buyer structure and demand concessions. By functioning as a team, they acquire negotiating power. The larger the team, the greater the discount they demand, knowing that sellers can make up their profits on larger volume. Instead of engaging in one-on-one negotiations, buyers collectively pressure the seller. The seller becomes an inferior in this face-to-face negotiation and often bends to consumers' demands. In other cases, consumers depend on the organizers—usually the Internet initiators—to reach deals with merchants. They save time and effort and rely on the savvy and pugnacity of other buyers to make deals for them. The team leaders are responsible for contacting the seller, negotiating the deals, and organizing other buyers to participate in the transaction. They may even take reasonability post-purchase if fellow buyers encounter problems with the products. In return, team leaders may receive a greater discount or a gift from the seller.

Team purchase is increasingly popular in China where multiple websites service consumers nationwide and numerous discussion forums facilitate discussions among interested people locally. With domestic market becoming increasingly complex, Chinese consumers have become more knowledgeable and self-protective than ever before. They have realized that individual effort is less effective than collective actions in the marketplace. Chinese consumers now apply the popular political ideology "solidarity is strength" and form groups to confront merchants. Collective acts are especially beneficial because consumer rights have yet to be effectively protected. When laws and regulations lack adequate enforcement, consumers use collective power to demand benefits and protection. The Internet serves as an important tool to organize people with similar concerns and interests. Consumers create alliances and act in unison against more dominant powers in the marketplace.

As an explorative study, we conducted depth-interviews with team buyers and merchants in four Chinese metropolises of Beijing, Shanghai, Guangzhou, and Shenzhen from June to August 2007. Our interviews started with grand tour questions that were followed by probing questions for meanings and experiences of team purchase (McCracken 1988). The interviews lasted from thirty minutes to one hour. They were conducted in Chinese and then transcribed and analyzed. We plan to participate in team purchases and collect more ethnographic data this summer. Through an iterative process (Arnould and Wallendorf 1994; Spiggle 1994), initial analysis has generated rich insights about the phenomenon. We have found that there exist distinctive differences between team purchase and other kinds of purchases such as Internet purchase, direct sale or wholesale. Participants employ a wide variety of strategies to ease transactions and reduce risks. Trust between buyers and merchants as well as between buyers and organizers emerges as an important issue. Organizer plays multiple roles as a negotiator, expert (or Prosumer, see Cova, Kozinets, and Shankar 2007), buyer, and a distributor. Interestingly, some buyers maintain their ties with team members by engaging in more team purchases and organizing activities afterward. For them, group purchases initiate consumption communities not necessarily based on brand (McAlexander, Schouten, and Koenig 2002; Muniz and O'Guinn 2001).

Although it has been recognized that consumers produce, acquire, and consume in form of communities (Belk and Costa 1998; Muniz and O'Guinn 2001; Schouten and McAlexander 1995) and that they protest against commercialization by engaging in consumer activism (Kozinets 2002; Kozinets and Handelman 2004), it is unclear how consumers collectively make purchase decisions and how they formulate a transient group to challenge the established orders in the marketplace. By studying team purchase, we explore the dynamics between consumers and merchants and examine how consumers collectively co-opt market offerings (Thompson and Coskuner-Balli 2007). We show the benefits, risks, rules and rituals of team purchase as compared to individual purchase. This research will also shed light on the discussions of strategies for consumer empowerment.

References

Areddy, James (2006), "Chinese Consumers Overwhelm Retailers with Team Tactics," *Wall Street Journal*, February 28.

Arnould, Eric J. and Craig J. Thompson (2005), "Consumer Culture Theory (CCT): Twenty Years of Research," *Journal of Consumer Research*, 31 (March), 868-82.

Arnould, Eric J. and Melanie Wallendorf (1994), "Market-Oriented Ethnography: Interpretation Building and Marketing Strategy Formulation," *Journal of Marketing Research*, 31 (November), 484-504.

Belk, Russell W. and Janeen Arnold Costa (1998), "The Mountain Man Myth: A Contemporary Consuming Fantasy," *Journal of Consumer Research*, 25 (December), 218-40.

Cova, Bernard, Robert V. Kozinets, and Avi Shankar Eds. (2007), *Consumer Tribes*. Oxford: Elsevier.

Epp, Amber M. and Linda L. Price (2008), "Family Identity: A Framework of Identity Interplay in Consumption Practices," *Journal of Consumer Research*, 35 (June), forthcoming.

Firat, A. Fuat and Alladi Venkatesh (1995), "Liberatory Postmodernism and the Reenchantment of Consumpiton," *Journal of Consumer Research*, 22 (3), 239-67.

Kozinets, Robert V. (2002), "Can Consumers Escape the Market? Emancipatory Illuminations from Burning Man," *Journal of Consumer Research*, 29 (June), 20-38.

Kozinets, Robert V. and Jay M. Handelman (2004), "Adversaries of Consumption: Consumer Movements, Activism, and Ideology," *Journal of Consumer Research*, 31 (December), 691-704.

McAlexander, James H., John W. Schouten, and Harold F. Koenig (2002), "Building Brand Community," *Journal of Marketing*, 66 (January), 38-54.

McCracken, Grant (1988), *The Long Interview*. Newbury Park: Sage Publications.

Muniz, Albert M. Jr. and Thomas C. O'Guinn (2001), "Brand Community," *Journal of Consumer Research*, 27 (March), 412-32.

Schouten, John W. and James H. McAlexander (1995), "Subcultures of Consumption: An Ethnography of the New Bikers," *Journal of Consumer Research*, 22 (June), 43-61.

Spiggle, Susan (1994), "Analysis and Interpretation of Qualitative Data in Consumer Research," *Journal of Consumer Research*, 21 (December), 491-503.

Thompson, Craig J. and Gokcen Coskuner-Balli (2007), "Countervailing Market Responses to Corporate Co-optation and the Ideological Recruitment of Consumption Communities," *Journal of Consumer Research*, 34 (August), 135-52.

Wallendorf, Melanie and Eric J. Arnould (1991), ""We Gather Together": Consumption Rituals of Thanksgiving Day," *Journal of Consumer Research*, 18 (June), 18-31.

The Impact of Source and Item Characteristics on Consumer Responses to Flattery in Retail Sales Transactions

Sutapa Aditya, York University, Canada
Kelley Main, University of Manitoba, Canada
Darren Dahl, University of British Columbia, Canada

Consumer behavior research over the last 25 years has significantly informed us about persuasive communications in the context of interpersonal interactions in the marketplace (Friestad & Wright 1994; Campbell & Kirmani 2000; Main, Dahl & Darke 2007). Flattery is a common method of interpersonal influence applied by agents in the marketplace. Although research on flattery in marketing has primarily focused on its negative influence (Main et al. 2007), studies conducted in other disciplines such as psychology and organizational behavior provide evidence of a positive influence of flattery (e.g., Cialdini, 2000; Watt, 1993; Wayne & Ferris 1990). The purpose of the present research was to search for similar positive evidence of flattery in the marketplace context and identify the boundary conditions of such an outcome.

We focus on two potential conditions under which flattery may have a positive influence on consumers. The first factor is the target item of flattery. To date, the literature has primarily looked at flattery on a store item that consumers try on (e.g. Campbell & Kirmani 2000). We are interested in learning if there is any difference in trustworthiness when the salesperson flatters the consumer on an item he/she wears to the store. Literature on mere ownership suggests that an object is evaluated more positively by individuals when it is owned by them vs. not (Beggan 1992) since possessions are considered as one's extended self (Belk 1988). Evaluation of one's own possessions is therefore linked to one's self perception and feeling of self enhancement (Beggan 1992). However, the literature has yet to explore the impact of a salesperson's flattery on a possession. It may be possible that when a consumer is flattered on an item she/he owns, it enhances his/her self-perceptions and creates a positive feeling towards the interaction experience as well as the flatterer.

The second factor proposed in the current study is the attractiveness of the source. Prior work demonstrated that messages from an attractive source are considered significantly more persuasive as compared to messages from an unattractive source (e.g. Baker & Churchill 1977) and can increase product evaluations of a contaminated product (Argo, Dahl & Morales 2008). In addition, attractiveness creates a halo effect, in which attractive people are considered to have many other socially desirable personality characteristics. Therefore, the source becomes more persuasive in the perceiver's eyes. We predict that flattery will lead to higher satisfaction with the interaction experience when the salesperson is attractive vs. unattractive. Moreover, this will be strengthened when a highly attractive salesperson compliments on an item owned by the consumer, as opposed to an item from the store.

A total of 50 participants (19 male and 31 female) from a large eastern university took part in a field study and received payment for their participation. A 2 (product: own vs. store) X 2 (attractiveness: high vs. average) between subjects experimental design was conducted. The product was a manipulated variable and attractiveness was a measured variable. The primary dependent measures included participant's satisfaction with the shopping experience, trust in the salesperson, and intentions to revisit the store. The cover story informed participants about a mystery shopping study on different stores on campus. The experimenter pretended to randomly choose a store from all stores on campus. In actuality, all respondents were sent to the same store and asked to try on a store item that appealed to them before returning to the experimenter to complete a questionnaire. The salesclerk in the store was a confederate who implemented the flattery manipulation either on the store or the own item.

Regression analysis revealed that the salesclerk's attractiveness had a significant main effect on participant's satisfaction with the shopping experience (b=0.215, t=3.559, p<0.05) and trustworthiness of the salesperson (b=0.19, t=3.052, p<0.01) which was qualified by a significant interaction of attractiveness and item on satisfaction (b =0.28, t=2.346, p<0.05) and salesperson trustworthiness (b=0.369, t=3.134, p<0.01). Simple slope analysis of the significant interaction effects revealed that when the clerk was less than average in attractiveness (1 standard deviation below the mean level of attractiveness), flattery on an item owned by the participant, as opposed to a store item, significantly reduced their satisfaction (b=-1.124, t=-2.44, p<0.05). However, when the salesclerk was above average in attractiveness, flattery did not lead to a significant difference in satisfaction level when the target of flattery was owned by the subject vs. a store item (b= 0.401, t=0.91, p >0.05). For trustworthiness, a less than average in attractiveness salesclerk was perceived as less trustworthy when flattery occurred on participants' own item (b =-1.004, t =-2.209, p<0.05). Participants reported significantly higher trustworthiness in the clerk who was above average in attractiveness when consumers were flattered on their own item as opposed to a store item (b=1.005, t=2.313, p<0.05). Findings also suggested a significant interaction effect of clerk attractiveness and item on participants' intention to revisit the store (b=0.742, t=4.19, p<0.001) that demonstrated the same pattern as the above findings (b=-2.331, t=-3.49, p<0.01; b=1.712, t=2.616, p<0.05).

In summary, this research supports our prediction that attractiveness of the source and the target item of flattery are two possible conditions that may result in a positive outcome of flattery. As predicted, flattery led to higher satisfaction, trustworthiness and intentions to revisit the store when the persuasive agent was highly attractive (vs. less attractive) and the target item is owned by the consumer (vs. a store item). Therefore, the present study contributes to the extant literature on persuasion knowledge by providing some of the first evidence of positive outcome of flattery in the marketplace context.

References

Argo, Jennifer J., Darren D. Dahl and Andrea Morales (2008), "Positive Consumer Contagion: Responses to Attractive Others in a Retail Context," forthcoming, *Journal of Marketing Research* .

Baker, Michael J and Gilbert Churchill Jr. (1977), "The Impact of Physically Attractive Models on Advertising Evaluations," *Journal of Marketing Research (JMR),* 14 (November), 538-555.

Beggan, James K. (1992), "On the Social Nature of Nonsocial Perception: The Mere Ownership Effect," *Journal of Personality and Social Psychology,* 62 (February), 229-237.

Belk, Russell (1988) "Possession and the Extended Self," *Journal of Consumer Research,* 15 (September), 139-168.

Campbell, Margaret C. and Amna Kirmani (2000), "Consumers' Use of Persuasion Knowledge: The Effects of Accessibility and Cognitive Capacity on Perceptions of an Influence Agent," *Journal of Consumer Research,* 27 (June), 69–83.

Cialdini, Robert B. (2000). *Influence: Science and Practice* (4th ed.). New York: Harper Collins.

Friestad, Marian and Peter Wright (1994), "The Persuasion Knowledge Model: How People Cope with Persuasion Attempts," *Journal of Consumer Research,* 21 (June), 1–31.

Main, Kelley J., Darren W. Dahl and Peter R. Darke (2007) "Deliberative and Automatic Bases of Suspicion: Empirical Evidence of the Sinister Attribution Error," *Journal of Consumer Psychology,* 17, 59-69.

Watt, J. D. (1993), "The Impact of the Frequency of Ingratiation on the Performance Evaluation of Bank Personnel," *The Journal of Psychology,* 127, 171–177.

Wayne, S. J., and G. R. Ferris (1990), Influence Tactics, Affect and Exchange Quality in Supervisor-Subordinate Interactions: A Laboratory Experiment and Field Study," *Journal of Applied Psychology,* 75, 487–499.

Exploring the Relationship between Brand Personality and Geographic Personality: Consumer Perceptions of Sport Teams and Cities

K. Damon Aiken, Eastern Washington University, USA

Richard M. Campbell, Sonoma State University, USA

While a good deal of previous research has investigated the strategic implications of branding and related consumer-processing intricacies, researchers have yet to test the effects of geographic associations within brand names. That is, researchers have not yet empirically examined the notion of a marketer leveraging the image of a geographic region in relation to a specific brand name–thereby creating and shaping unique brand associations in the minds of consumers.

The differential affects of geographic associations to brand names has been labeled "geographic equity" (Aiken, Koch, and Madrigal, 2000). The concept of geographic equity is thought to depend upon (1) geographic personality and related image associations of a region, as well as (2) geographic awareness and memory. In essence, geographic personality is much like human personality as cities, regions, countries–geographic locales in general–project observable and measurable personality traits. Geographic awareness and memory are important factors in eliciting cogent images in the minds of consumers. Kotler, Haider, and Rein (1993) utilize a notion of collective memory when they define place image as "the sum of beliefs, ideas, and impressions that people have of a place" (p. 141). Not only is this image a mental picture held in common by a group, but it is also used as a familiar way of communicating about a city.

Our central research question focuses on the relationship between brand personality (Aaker, 1997) and geographic personality. Do professional sports teams (*as brands*, held within the set of brands in a league) have brand personalities that take on some of the associative traits of the geographic locales in which they play? For example, are the NY Giants perceived as exciting partly because they are located in "the city that never sleeps?" Are the Steelers viewed as tough and hard-working because they play in the blue-collar, working-class town of Pittsburgh? Similarly, across leagues, are the Los Angeles Lakers thought of as glamorous and sophisticated because they are so relatable to the glitz of Hollywood? The answers to these questions would seem to have direct implications for corporate communication decisions for both sports marketing and tourism marketing.

The scope of our research question necessitated four versions of a four-part survey. Our desire was to test the brand personality characteristics of the ten most recent Super bowl teams (and cities). Data were collected from a total of 382 university students in five different locations (Indianapolis, Chicago, Seattle, Oakland, and Charlotte). This design allowed for the testing of "self-other congruence" (Funder and Colvin, 1997) with respect to those with direct city experience and those without such experience. Subjects in the test locations should take an insider's view with regards to their cities/teams. They were asked about their home cities/teams as well as two others (inclusive of those just mentioned as well as New York, Boston, Pittsburgh, Tampa Bay, and Philadelphia).

In general, fans do ascribe personality traits to both teams and cities. Moreover, measurements of the two constructs tend to correlate. Correlation coefficients ranged from .189 (the Ruggedness of Charlotte and the Ruggedness of the *Panthers*) to .623 (the competence of Pittsburgh and the competence of the *Steelers*). Interestingly, cities whose teams had recently participated in the playoffs were seen as more exciting (as were their teams). With regards to self-other congruence, perceptions between the insiders (with city experience) and the outsiders (without city experience) were quite different. In almost every case and across all five dimensions, city insiders consistently displayed lower ratings of the trait characteristics.

So, fans as consumers of sport likely tend to use geographic personality as a guide in formulating associative team/brand images. However, we should note that each of the five dimensions has a positive connotation. That is, people would probably like to think of their teams and their cities as sincere, exciting, competent, sophisticated, and rugged. Perhaps then, it should come as some surprise that city insiders relayed a downgraded view of their city's/team's personalities compared to outsiders. Alternatively, perhaps the insider's viewpoint is simply more realistic, while the outsider's viewpoint has been romanticized by various media. Regardless, we found no evidence of self-other congruence from this perspective.

In the future, given that personality evaluations seem to fluctuate according to win-loss records, it would be interesting to find out if fans go through a form of brand personality updating (Johar, Sengupta, and Aaker, 2005) from season to season. Perhaps, brand personality characteristics are not as resistant to change as widely believed, especially within the seasonal context of professional sports.

Finally, this research points to a number of other questions. In terms of the direction of the relationship for example, since the Chicago Bears are viewed as a tough, rugged, and mostly unsophisticated team, does this contribute to our views of the city of Chicago? Or, to the contrary, do we see Chicago as the birthplace of violent gangland behavior, the home of chilling lakeshore winds, and a place where only truly tough and rugged people could live; and consequently these opinions of the city shape our brand-image associations for the Bears? Moreover, how can we resolve brand image differences *within* the same city and *across* sports? Continuing with our Chicago example: Do the White Sox have a similar brand image as the Cubs? Or, looking across sports, do the Bears have a similar brand image as the Cubs? Thus, it appears that there are a great number of analytical intricacies yet to be explored.

References
Aaker, Jennifer (1997), "Dimensions of Brand Personality," *Journal of Marketing Research*, 34 (August), 347-356.
Aiken, Damon, Eric C. Koch, and Robert Madrigal (2000), "What's in a Name? Explorations in Geographic Equity and Geographic Personality," *American Marketing Association's Winter Educators' Conference*, Vol 11, 301-308.
Funder, David C. and C. Randall Colvin (1997), "Congruence of Others' and Self-Judgments of Personality," in *Handbook of Personality Psychology*, R. Hogan, J. Johnson, and S. Briggs, eds., San Diego: Academic Press, 617-647.
Kotler, Philip, Donald H. Haider, and Irving Rein (1993), *Marketing Places*, New York: The Free Press.
Johar, Gita Venkataramani, Jaideep Sengupta, and Jennifer Aaker (2005), "Two Roads to Updating Brand Personality Impressions: Trait Versus Evaluative Inferencing," *Journal of Marketing Research*, 42 (November), 458-469.

Appraisal Theory of Emotions and Advertising Rhetoric: A Model of Consumer Reactions

Pia A. Albinsson, New Mexico State University, USA

Theories in consumer psychology on emotions used in advertising research have predominantly concentrated on two dimensions: valence and arousal. Measures of valence and arousal are used, respectively, to evaluate the degree of positive and negative feelings towards an ad and a person's physiological level of excitement following exposure. The valence-arousal theory has been criticized for not measuring emotions that have distinct characteristics, but belong to the same valence (Lerner and Keltner 2000). For example, the difference between fear and anger or hope and happiness are hard to differentiate with the valence measures. In addition, these measures fail to specify whether emotions of the same valence differ in influencing consumer decision making and persuasion. Appraisal theory of emotion provides more emotional dimensions compared to the valence-arousal dichotomy and offers more detailed understanding of the antecedents and consequences of each emotion (Reisenzein and Hofmann 1993). Current research on emotion has found that emotions of the same valence differ in their antecedent appraisals (Smith and Ellsworth 1985; Roseman 2001). Appraisals also center on the individual consumers' assessment of his current situation with respect to well-being (Ruth, Brunel and Otnes 2002). In recent years, appraisal theories of emotions have been used by marketers to examine consumers' response to different health preventive advertising campaigns (Block and Keller 1998; Eppright, Tanner and Hunt 1994; Eppright et al. 2002; Tanner, Day and Crask 1989; Tanner, Hunt and Eppright 1991).

Another research stream that has shown to increase processing outcomes, such as persuasion, is advertising rhetoric. This relatively new area of research includes verbal and visual rhetorical works. Ads utilizing rhetorical works have been shown repeatedly to enhance ad processing and brand attitude goals (e.g., McQuarrie and Mick 2003; Mothersbaugh, Huhmann and Franke 2002; Tom and Eves 1999; Toncar and Munch 2001). Research on advertising rhetoric has, to date, been concerned with only cognitive aspects; the interface with emotional appeals or appraisal theory has not yet been explored. By studying both advertising rhetoric and the appraisals of emotional appeals, interaction effects can be explored to find the most efficient combination to induce systematic emotional influences on persuasion.

The purpose of this paper is to use existing knowledge of appraisal theory of emotion and combine this with recent research findings on advertising rhetoric to develop a more encompassing model of appraisal theory, namely the Emotional Appraisal and Reactions Model (EARM), which builds on appraisal theory (e.g., Lazarus 1968; Rogers 1975) and extends the ordered protection motivation model (Tanner et al. 1991) and the appraisal tendency framework (ATF) (Lerner, Han and Keltner 2007).

The EARM includes seven parts: (1) Information sources, (2) Relevance Appraisal and Ad Stimuli Appraisal, (3) Felt Emotion(s), (4) Secondary Appraisal, (5), Revised Felt Emotion(s), (6), Reaction(s), and (7) Personal and Social Norms and Values. The information sources in the EARM differ from previous coping models in that it includes positive and negative emotional appeals in addition to the more commonly examined fear appeal. It also includes advertising rhetoric (e.g., rhetorical works) in addition to ad characteristics, brand information and environmental benefits or threats. Since appraisal theory of emotion stresses that the individual consumer appraises each event based on his current situation, in regards to his well-being, several moderators are accounted for in the model. As in former appraisal models consumers go through an initial appraisal phase. The EARM divides this initial appraisal into two parts where the consumers appraise the information sources for overall relevancy and congruency of their desired state of well-being in addition to responses to the ad stimuli itself. The consumers, then in turn, appraise their own ability to handle the specific information based on their specific coping mechanisms. The last part of the model, reactions, includes both behavioral intentions and actual behavior in response to the ad stimuli.

The EARM is tested through an experiment which manipulates the presence and type of emotional appeal (i.e. hope, fear, and neutral) and verbal rhetorical works (i.e. trope, scheme, and nonfigurative) in a public service announcement (PSA) promoting a website endorsing a healthy lifestyle. Besides the emotional appeals and the verbal rhetorical works manipulated in the headlines and sub headlines all other elements of the target communication is held constant across conditions. In addition, several mediating and moderating variables were tested. Study 1 measured several dependent variables (depth of processing, memory and persuasion (behavioral intentions) while Study 2 measured only persuasion (actual behavior of visiting the advertised website) through a follow-up survey administered seven days later to the same participants as in Study 1. Results generally support the hypotheses that the dependent variables of depth of processing, memory and persuasion are increased when combining emotional appeals with advertising rhetoric in print advertising.

This research has useful implications for researchers, practitioners and consumers since it extends previous research streams in consumer research. The EARM contributes to researchers' understanding of how emotional appeals indirectly influence consumer reactions to ad stimuli, as well as assist practitioners in designing more effective ads and spending their limited ad budgets more efficiently. Future research needs to explore different combinations of advertising rhetoric and emotions to find the combination that is most effective in inducing desired preventive health behavior.

References

Block, Lauren G. and Punam Anand Keller (1998), "Beyond Protection Motivation: An Integrative Theory of Health Appeals," *Journal of Applied Social Psychology*, 28 (17), 1584-1608.

Eppright, David R., James B. Hunt, John F. Tanner, and George R. Franke (2002), "Fear, Coping, and Information: A Pilot Study on Motivating a Healthy Response," *Health Marketing Quarterly,* 20 (1), 51-72.

Eppright, David R., John F. Tanner and James B. Hunt (1994), "Knowledge and the Ordered Protection Motivation Model: Tools for Preventing AIDS," *Journal of Business Research,* 30, 13-24

Lazarus, Richard S. (1968), "Emotions and Adaptation: Conceptual and Empirical Relations," in Nebraska Symposium on Motivation, W.J. Arnold (Ed.), Lincoln, NE: University of Nebraska Press, 175-266.

Lerner, Jennifer S. and Dacher Keltner (2000), "Beyond Valence: Toward a Model of Emotion-Specific influences on Judgment and choice," *Cognition and Emotion,* 14 (4), 473-493.

Lerner, Jennifer S., Seunghee Han, Dacher Keltner (2007), "Feelings and Consumer Decision Making: Extending the Appraisal Tendency Framework," *Journal of Consumer Psychology,* 17 (3), 184-187

Mothersbaugh, David, L., Bruce A. Huhmann, and George R. Franke (2002) "Combinatory and Separative Effects of Rhetorical Figures on Consumers' Effort and Focus in Ad Processing," *Journal of Consumer Research*, 28 (4), 589-602.

McQuarrie, Edward, F. and David G. Mick (2003), "Visual and Verbal Rhetorical Figures under Directed Processing Versus Incidental Exposure to Advertising," *Journal of Consumer Research,* 29, (March), 579- 87.

Reisenzein, Rainer, and T. Hofmann (1993), "Discriminating Emotions from Appraisal-Relevant Situational Information: Baseline Data for Structural Models of Cognitive Appraisals," *Cognition and Emotion,* 7, 295-323.

Rogers, Ronald W. (1975), "A Protection Motivation Theory of Fear Appeals and Attitude Change," *Journal of Psychology,* 91, 93-114.

Roseman, Ira. J (2001), "A Model of Appraisal in the Emotion System: Integrating Theory, Research, and Applications," in Appraisal Processes in Emotion: Theory, Methods, Research, Klaus R. Scherer, Angela. Schorr, Tom Johnstone (Eds.), New York, NY: Oxford University Press, Inc., 68-120.

Ruth, Julie A., Frederic F. Brunel, and Cele C. Otnes (2002), "Linking Thoughts to Feelings: Investigating Cognitive Appraisals and Consumption Emotions in a Mixed-Emotions Context," *Journal of the Academy of Marketing Science,* 30 (1), 44-58.

Smith, Craig A and Phoebe C. Ellsworth (1985), "Patterns of Cognitive Appraisal in Emotions," Journal *of Personality and Social Psychology*, 48 (4), 813-838

Tanner, John F. Jr., James B. Hunt, and David R. Eppright (1991). "The Protection Motivation Model: A Normative Model of Fear Appeals," *Journal of Marketing*, 55, 36-45

Tanner, Jr. John F., Ellen Day, and Melvin R. Crask (1989), "Protection Motivation Theory: An Extension of Fear Appeals Theory in Communications," *Journal of Business Research*, 19, 267-76.

Tom, Gail and Anmarie Eves (1999), "The Use of Rhetorical Devices in Advertising," *Journal of Advertising Research*, 39 (4), 39-42.

Toncar, Mark and James Munch (2001), "Consumer Responses to Tropes in Print Advertising," *Journal of Advertising*, 30 (1), 55-65.

The Effect of Document Language Quality on Consumer Perceptions

Arancha Pedraz-Delhaes, Leger Marketing, Canada
Muhammad Aljukhadar, HEC Montreal, Canada
Sylvain Senecal, HEC Montreal, Canada

Abstract

The authors propose a model that describes how the quality of language in documents accompanying the product shapes consumer perceptions. Language quality impacts perceptions by determining document evaluation. Document evaluation fully mediated the relations between language quality and both product and organization evaluations, implying that documents accompanying the product are a vital extrinsic cue used by consumers to evaluate the product and the organization. For their part, product and organization evaluations formed consumer behavioral intentions. Findings also show comprehensibility to be affected by language quality, and support the notion that documents accompanying product are secondary products as document evaluation directly influenced intentions.

Empirical work on language quality is scant. As the majority of documents accompanying the product (hereafter, "documents" or "instruction guides") are initially written in English (TCEurope, 2005), and as studies of document quality have been mainly conducted by researchers in English-speaking milieus (where the quality of language in documents does not suffer from translation issues), little attention has been given to the role played by language quality. Simultaneously, literature delineates the importance of extrinsic cues in shaping consumer perceptions. In this work, we hypothesized that language quality will determine both document perceived quality and document evaluation or affection. We also hypothesized that documents accompanying the product are important extrinsic cues used by consumer to infer product quality. Similarly, based upon attribution theory, we postulated that document evaluation will shape consumer perceptions of the product's manufacturer and that product and organization evaluations will determine behavioral intentions.

The independent variable in our model and experiment was the language quality of the document, which is defined as the text's conformity to established linguistic conventions of the targeted audience. As the research was conducted in a French-speaking North American city, focus groups and the experiment were performed in French. Two focus groups indicated the soundness of the hypothetical relationships, showing consumers to exhibit low levels of tolerance to inferior language quality in documents and to express various negative responses ranging from deception to intentions of boycotting the manufacturer. In a following laboratory experiment that involved 116 participants drawn from a consumer panel, the independent variable was operationalized by three levels. Version A of the instruction guide had no errors, whereas version B had few spelling and grammatical errors, and version C had additional syntaxical and vocabulary errors. The versions were prepared based on real examples from existing guides. The task consisted in assembling a product (chest box) with one randomly assigned version. The manufacturer's identity was concealed from participants. Upon task performance, participants filled out a questionnaire which measured the dependent and potential influencing variables.

Document quality was measured using the document quality scale (Guillemette, 1990). We only included the items pertaining to six of the seven suggested dimensions (systematic arrangement, understandability, credibility, task relevance, demonstrativeness, and fitness). Where oblique rotation suggested the previous dimensions, factor analysis implied two dimensions. The first dimension (α=0.96) pertained to the majority of document quality dimensions and hence was used to reflect document quality in general. The second dimension (α=0.87) dealt mainly with document understandability and was thus used to examine whether language quality affected perceived comprehensibility.

Document evaluation (α=0.92) was measured using the five items of two scales reflecting the satisfaction toward a specific object (Eroglu and Machleit 1990, α reported=0.87; Spreng, MacKenzie, and Olshavsky 1996, α reported=0.94). Because product evaluation was considered by some researchers as cognitive (Smart, Madrigal, and Seawright, 1996) and by others as affective (Doll and Gholamzera, 1987; Eagly and Chaiken, 1993; Torkzadeh and Doll, 1993), we included both elements. Product evaluation was therefore measured using Peracchio and Meyers-Levy's scale (1994, α reported between 0.85 and 0.92) with the exception of one item removed and the addition of three of the four items proposed by Leclerc, Schmitt, and Dubé (1994, α reported>0.92). As expected, these items were found to result in one dimension (α=0.94).

Organization evaluation was measured using the only scale found to reflect the general attitude toward company (Goldsmith, Lafferty, and Newell, 2000, α reported=0.94, α obtained=0.97). Intentions were measured using the three items of intention to buy as in Patterson, Johnson, and Spreng (1997, α reported=0.97), the three items of positive recommendation intention of Price and Arnould (1999, α reported=0.95), and the three items of negative recommendation intention adapted from Blodgett, Hill, and Tax (1997, α reported=0.97). The previous items were adapted to each measure the product and organization intentions. One item was used to verify the manipulation.

ANOVA analysis revealed that language quality significantly affected document quality dimensions. The impact of language quality on document perceived comprehensibility was clear and significant for all language quality levels, leading us to conclude that even a few spelling and grammatical errors reduce comprehensibility. The presence of a marginal main effect of objective written language proficiency ($p=0.075$) implies that comprehensibility was affected more for individuals with better written language skills. The presence of a moderating role of gender ($p=0.057$) indicates that women enjoyed higher comprehensibility than men, although only for version A.

The impact of language quality on general document quality was apparent. Nevertheless, the presence of few grammatical and spelling errors (version B) marginally affect document general quality ($p=0.110$), while when there were more errors concerning the vocabulary and syntaxical elements (version C), the difference was pronounced and significant.

Language quality shapes perceptions of the product and organization by influencing document evaluation. The impact of language quality on document evaluation was important and significant for all levels, implying that document evaluation was determined by document language quality, regardless of personal or demographics factors. No main or moderating effects were found for educational level, objective written language proficiency, and importance accorded to language quality on the previous relationship. However, we found a main effect for age ($p=0.030$), implying that older consumers had higher document evaluation for all language quality levels and showed more tolerance to inferior language use. Interestingly, no significant correlation was found between educational level and objective written language skills.

Document evaluation fully mediated the relationships between language quality and both product and organization evaluations, implying that language quality impacts both product and organization evaluations through document evaluation. Product and product category knowledge were not found to influence the relationship between document evaluation and product evaluation, indicating the saliency of language quality on product perceptions. For their part, product evaluation shaped the intentions toward the product, and organization evaluation shaped the intentions toward the organization. Findings support the notion that documents accompanying the product are secondary products (Smart, Madrigal, and Seawright, 1996) as product evaluation partially mediated the relation between document evaluation and product intentions.

References

Blodgett, Jeffery, Donna J. Hill and Stephen Tax (1997), "The Effects of Distributive, Procedural and Interactional Justice on Postcomplaint Behavior," *Journal of Retailing*, 73(2), 185-210.

Doll, William and Gholamzera Torkzadeh (1987), "The Quality of User Documentation," *Information & Management*, 12(2), 73-78.

Eagly, Alice H. and Shelly Chaiken (1993), *The Psychology of Attitudes*. Belmont: Thomson Wadsworth.

Eroglu, Segin A. and Karen A. Machleit (1990), "An Empirical Study of Retail Crowding: Antecedents and Consequences," *Journal of Retailing*, 66(2), 201-21.

Goldsmith, Ronald E., Barbra A. Lafferty and Stephen J. Newell (2000), "The Impact of Corporate Credibility and Celebrity on Consumer Reaction to Advertisements and Brands," *Journal of Advertising*, 29(3), 30-54.

Guillemette, Ronald (1990), "What Readers Mean by 'Good Documentation'," *Information & Management*, 18(2) 69-77.

Leclerc, France, Bernd H. Schmitt and Laurette Dubé (1994), "Foreign Branding and Its Effects on Product Perceptions and Attitudes," *Journal of Marketing Research*, 31(2), 263-70.

Patterson, Paul G., Lester W. Johnson and Richard A. Spreng (1997), "Modeling the Determinants of Customer Satisfaction for Business-to-Business Professional Services," *Journal of the Academy of Marketing Science*, 25(1), 4-17.

Peracchio, Laura A. and Juan Meyers-Levy (1994), "How Ambiguous Cropped Objects in Ad Photos Can Affect Product Evaluations," *Journal of Consumer Research*, 21(1), 190-204.

Price, Linda L. and Eric J. Arnould (1999), "Commercial Friendships: Service Provider-Client Relationships in Context," *Journal of Marketing*, 63(4), 38-56.

Smart, Karl L., J. L. Madrigal and Kristie K. Seawright (1996), "The Effect of Documentation on Customer Perception of Product Quality," *IEEE Transactions on Professional Communication*, 39(3), 157-62.

Spreng, Richard A., Scott B. MacKenzie and Richard W. Olshavsky (1996), "A Reexamination of the Determinants of Consumer Satisfaction," *Journal of Marketing*, 60(3), 15-32.

TCEurope (2005), "Technical Documentation in the Enlarged EU: First Round-up on the Organisational, Technical and Economic Impacts," *Fifth Brussels Colloquium for User friendly Product Information*, March, 1-51.

Torkzadeh, Gholamzera and Doll William J. (1993), "The Place and Value of Documentation in End-User Computing," *Information & Management*, 24(3), 147-58.

I Really Want to Like It: Motivated Liking

Aner Tal, Duke University, USA
Dan Ariely, Duke University, USA

Motivations to like products can alter consumers' evaluations of and choices of products. Studies 1 and 2 demonstrate enhanced liking for music thought to indicate refinement and sophistication in people who like it. Study 3 demonstrates that these effects occur counter to people's expectations, ruling out belief-confirmation and social-desirability as explanations. Study 4 replicates the findings using choices that bear immediate consequences (listening to full songs) and a different motivation: believing oneself to have high emotional-intelligence. Further studies will explore additional motivations and product domains and investigate the process through which consumers learn to like products they are motivated to like.

Why do we like certain products rather than others? The traditional view in consumer choice theory has preferences develop based on processing of intrinsic product attributes (Simonson, in press; Bettman et al., 1998). However, liking can be based on reasons extrinsic to product attributes. You might, for instance, like something simply because of its "warm glow of familiarity" (Titchner, 1912), as demonstrated through extensive research on mere-exposure (Bornstein, 1989; Zajonc, 1968; 2000). You might like a product due to situational influences and cues (Berger & Fitzsimmons, in-press; Ferraro et al., in-press). Current physiological state, such as hunger or cold, might also influence liking (Cabanac, 1979). Prominently, expectations can also shape liking (Deliza & MacFie, 1996; Hirt, 1990; Lee et al., 2006; Ragunathan et al., 2006).

Motivational bases for evaluation are also prevalent. A broad literature regarding cognitive dissonance indicates that people can come to like items retroactively due to different motivations to justify their decisions and align them with attitudes (Cardozo, 1965; Cohen & Goldberg, 1970; Cummings & Venkatesan, 1976). Famously, Brehm (1955) showed that following choice people bias evaluations to favor their chosen alternative. Further, lack of a possibility to change one's choice may enhance liking (Gilbert and Ebert, 2002).

Some research outside the dissonance literature has also offered evidence for motivated liking. Berger & Heath (2007) showed effects of social group desirability on liking. Similarly, social motivations' influence on liking have been demonstrated by Escales and Bettman (2003; 2005), who showed the influence of identification groups on felt connection to brands. In psychology, merely expecting to interact with someone affected liking towards that person (Miller & Marks, 1982).

Dissonance primarily explores post-choice alterations of evaluation. The effects of motivations existing prior to choice and consumption have garnered less attention (though see Riis & McClure, in preparation). In this work, we explore whether motivation to like novel stimuli affected actual post-consumption liking and choice. Further, we seek to establish whether motivations can be artificially implanted by an external source, a possibility with potentially extensive marketing implications.

Study 1: Everybody Likes Opera

The first study aimed to examine whether thinking that liking for music shows one to be a more refined, sophisticated listener enhances liking for such music over alternatives associated with less sophistication.

Methods. Participants ($N=57$) listened to and evaluated two songs. The study was a 2 (song) X 2 (order) X 2 (motivation) within subjects design. The stimuli were international songs chosen following pretests that identified them as having moderate complexity and low familiarity.

After listening to each song, participants read reviews of the songs. Manipulations for motivation to like were embedded within the reviews, such that the songs were touted as either simple or complex, and indicating a person to be of either refinement and sophistication or of simple tastes. The wording was designed to avoid direct implications for enjoyability.

Dependent variables were self-reported enjoyment and desire for more information anchored by 1 (not at all) and 9 (very much) scales, and quality of song rated on a 9 point scale anchored by 1 (very low) and 9 (very high). Cronbach alpha for the three measures was .779, so the measures were averaged as a single DV.

Results. We ran ANOVA analysis controlling for song and order of manipulation, including song X condition interaction (non-significant). Participants reported enhanced impressions of the songs for which liking was ostensibly indicative of higher sophistication: $F(1, 106)=3.89$, $p=0.05$. LSmeans were 5.9 for low sophistication, and 6.6 for high sophistication.

Discussion. When liking for a song was described as indicating higher sophistication (due to its complexity), participants evaluated the song more highly than when it was described as indicating lower sophistication (due to its simplicity). The effects could potentially be explained by social desirability, as participants might indicate how participants *want to seem* rather than how they truly feel about the songs. Thus, in the next study we added a choice phase where participants could choose between CD collections of the two musical styles for a drawing. Given that such choices could have actual implications for the participants, the choice measure could reasonably be expected to be more indicative of participants' true liking for the songs.

Study 2: Effects on Choice

Method. The general methodology was similar to that of study 1. After completion of the first part of the study, participants ($N=59$) were asked to choose a compilation of one of the two musical styles for a drawing.

Results and discussion. As before, participants evaluated songs more highly when liking for them was presented as indicating greater sophistication: $F(1, 113)=4.82$, $p=0.03$, LSmeans 5.8 (low) vs. 6.4 (high). This enhanced evaluation seemed to reflect participants' genuine feelings about the songs, as it was reflected in CD choices that could have real consequences. Participants were more likely to choose the high-sophistication CD (70%) than the lower sophistication CD (30%): $F(1, 113)=20.84$, $p<.0001$. Again, note that both choice and evaluation occurred prior to choice, and so could not be explained by post-choice dissonance reduction.

Study 3: Belief Confirmation?

Arguably, being told that a more complicated song indicates greater sophistication would lead people to believe complex songs should and would be liked more, and subsequently lead to expectation fulfillment. The design of the studies reported above reduces the credibility of such an explanation. For one, information regarding the songs' complexity was presented either before or after each song was played (between-participants). If the process was one of expectation-fulfillment, information should have had greater effect if presented before songs. If anything, results indicate the opposite (information presented after each song yielded a greater effects).

We know, however, that beliefs can alter judgment retroactively, after consumption experiences (Braun, 1999). If this type of retroactive belief-confirmation occurred here, beliefs in a song's complexity indicating sophistication would lead people to expect they would like complex songs more than simple songs. If people do not think they would like such songs better, the process whereby the previous effects were obtained cannot, by definition, be one of simple belief-confirmation

To test this notion, we presented participants in the third study ($N=32$) with an account of the relation between liking for complex songs and sophistication similar to studies 1-2. However, instead of listening to the songs, participants just rated how much they expected to enjoy simple (condition 1) or complex (condition 2) songs. Participants assigned to the complex-song rating condition expected to enjoy songs less (3.73) than participants assigned to the low-complexity condition (4.58): $t(1, 50)=2.14$, $p=.04$. Thus, it appears that the process whereby consumers come to like that which they are motivated to like is not simply one of belief confirmation. Consumers' expectations for liking are in fact the reverse of their actual reported liking given a chance to listen to songs.

Study 4: The Bach Effect

Method. The current study employed a different motivation in order to generalize our results. Specifically, we told participants that liking for some music styles is diagnostic of emotional-intelligence. Under the guise of familiarizing them with the idea, participants heard three 30-second song samples in each of three styles. After listening to each sample, participants were told about its associated level of emotional-intelligence (high, low, or non-indicative). As an incentive-aligned dependent variable, participants (N=59) were asked to choose three songs to listen to. They could choose the full songs from which they'd heard clips, songs of the same styles, or unrelated control songs.

Results. Participants (N=45) chose more songs from styles presented as diagnostic of high emotional-intelligence (1.4) than from those presented as non-diagnostic (.77) or diagnostic of low emotional-intelligence (.84). The overall effect controlling for country and interaction (non-significant) was highly significant: $F(2, 126)$=8.29, p=.0004 contrast between low and medium to high.

Limitations and Further Studies

The studies reported here provided some evidence for the influence of different motivations on product evaluation and choice. Further studies will explore additional motivations and explore the process through which consumers learn to like what they want to like. Suggested mechanisms include differential encoding during consumption, post-choice editing of memories, and motivationally-biased construction of evaluation. Notably, motivations to like could be so powerful that they override the robust expectation fulfillment processes known in current research.

References

Berger, Jonah, and Grainne Fitzsimmons (in press), "Dogs on the Street and Pumas on Your Feet: How Cues in the Environment Influence Product Evaluation and Choice," *Journal of Marketing Research*.

_____ & Chip Heath (2007), "Where Consumers Diverge from Others: Identity-Signaling and Product Domains." *Journal of Consumer Research*, 34, 121-134.

Bornstein, R. F. (1989). Exposure and Affect: Overview and Meta-Analysis of Research, *Psychological Bulletin*, 106, 265–289.

Braun, Kathryn (1999), "Postexperience Advertising Effects on Consumer Memory," *Journal of Consumer Research*, 25 (4), 319-334.

Brehm, Jack (1955), "Post-decision Changes in the Desirability of Alternatives," *Journal of Abnormal and Social Psychology*, 52 (3), 384-389.

Cabanac, Michel (1979), "Sensory Pleasure," *Quarterly Review of Biology*, 54, 1-29.

Cardozo, (1965), "An Experimental Study of Customer Effort, Expectation, and Satisfaction," *Journal of Marketing Research*, 2 (3), 244-249.

Cohen, Joel, and Marvin Goldberg (1970), "The Dissonance Model in Post-Decision Product Evaluation," *Journal of Marketing Research*, 7, 315-321.

Cummings & Venkatesan (1976), "Cognitive Dissonance and Consumer Behavior: A Review of the Evidence," *Journal of Marketing Research*, 13 (3), 303-308.

Deliza, R., and H. J. H. MacFie (1996), "The Generation of Sensory Expectation by External Cues and its Effect on Sensory Perception and Hedonic Ratings: A Review," *Food Science*, 11, 103-128.

Escalas, Jennifer Edson and James R. Bettman (2003), "You Are What They Eat: The Influence of Reference Groups on Consumer Connections to Brands," *Journal of Consumer Psychology*, v. 13, n. 3, pp. 339-348.

_____ (2005), "Self-Construal, Reference Groups, and Brand Meaning, *Journal of Consumer Research*, 32 (3), 378-389.

Ferraro, Rosellina, Tanya L. Chartrand and Gavan J. Fitzsimons (in press), "The Effects of Incidental Brand Exposure on Consumption," to appear in *The Brand Experience: Handbook on Brand Management*, Ed. Bernd H. Schmitt, Elgar, MA.

Gilbert, Dan, & Ebert, Jane.E.J. (2002) Decisions and Revisions: The Affective Forecasting of Changeable Outcomes. *Journal of Personality and Social Psychology, 82, 503-514.*

Hirt, Edward R. (1990), "Do I See Only What I Expect? Evidence for an Expectancy-Guided Retrieval Model," *Journal of Personality and Social Psychology*, 58 (6), 937-951.

Lee, Leonard, and Dan Ariely (2006), "Try it, You'll Like it: The Influence of Expectation, Consumption, and Revelation on Preferences for Beer." *Psychological Science*. 17 (12), 1054–1058.

Miller, Norman, and Gary Marks, (1982), "Assumed Similarity Between Self and Other: Effect of Expectation of Future Interaction with That Other," *Social Psychology Quarterly*, 45 (2), 100-105.

Ragunathan, Rajagopal, Rebecca Walker Naylor, and Wayne D. Hoyer (2006), "The Unhealthy=Tasty Intuition and its Effects on Taste Inferences, Enjoyment, and Choice of Food Products," *Journal of Marketing*, 70 (4), 170-184.

Riis, J., & McClure, S. (In preparation), "Motivated Taste Change for Diet Coke."

Simonson, Itamar (in press), "Will I Like a Medium Pillow? Another Look at Constructed Preferences."

Titchner, E. B. (1912), "The Schema of Introspection," *American Journal of Psychology*, 23, 485-508.

Zajonc, R. B. (1968), "Attitudinal Effects of Mere Exposure," *Journal of Personality and Social Psychology Monographs*, 9 (2, pt. 2). Zajonc, 2000).

Zajonc, Robert B. (2000), "Feeling and Thinking: Closing the Debate Over the Independence of Affect," in Joseph E. Forgas (Ed.), *Feeling and Thinking: The Role of Affect in Social Cognition*, Cambridge University Press, Cambridge UK and New York, NY, USA

The Impact of Accent Stereotypes on Service Outcomes and Its Boundary Conditions

Ze Wang, University of Kansas, USA
Aaron Arndt, Old Dominion University, USA
Surendra Singh, University of Kansas, USA
Monica Biernat, University of Kansas, USA

"When we listened back to calls people had complained about often they were fine. Some people wanted the member of staff to fail because they were in India. I don't know why that should be, but when customers start voting with their feet, you have to respond."
—Adrian Web (Call Center Manager, BBC news, 2/14/2007)

The accent of service providers may positively or negatively bias customer perception of service quality—especially in service contexts where visual cues are absent (e.g., call centers). In this research, we explore the effects of accent stereotypes in a variety of call center situations. With two laboratory experiments, we demonstrate that even with identical service outcomes, customers' perception and interpretation of their service experience changed as a function of customer service employee accent (i.e., British, Indian and American). However, biases caused by accent stereotyping decrease when relevant objective information is available (i.e., the industrial norm).

Sociolinguistics literature (Lippi-Green 1994, Giles and Powesland 1975) suggests that accent is an important indicator of one's ethnicity, regional affiliation and social class. Even though accents may be subtle, individuals are still able to perceive and distinguish among different accents (Cargile 2000; Giles, Williams, Mackie and Rosselli 1995). People attribute positive traits to certain types of accents based on the prestige of the class or group that possess it (e.g., sophistication and politeness associated with British accent) (Ladegaard 1998). In contrast, people also discriminate against the speakers with foreign accents (e.g., African-American, Indian, and Mexican-American) which may "link to skin that isn't white, or signal a third-party homeland" (Lippi-Green, 1997, p.239). People's general tendency to evaluate individuals' performance more harshly than others upon accent has been a persistent finding in extant literature (Baugh 2000; Purkiss et al. 2000).

We extend these theories by examining accent stereotyping effect in the service context and testing its influence on customer satisfaction and customer evaluation of employee performance. Additionally, based on previous literature on stereotypical influence on causal attributions (Hewstone 1990; Jackson, Sullivan and Hodge1993), individuals tend to attribute stereotype-consistent behavior to internal stable causes and stereotype-inconsistent behavior to external unstable causes. We hypothesize that American customers are more likely to attribute favorable service to individual employee factors and attribute unfavorable service to external firm factors when an employee has an American or British accent. However, the attributions are reversed for employees with an Indian accent.

The impacts of accent stereotype on service outcomes depend on the informational context during the service. Research on stereotyping effect (Kunda and Thagard 1996) suggest that stereotyping is most likely to occur if customers do not have background information or other objective cues to make their judgment. Thus we hypothesize that the influence of employees' accent on customers' perception and evaluation of the service encounter should disappear, or at least decease, if customers are informed of industrial norms.

We conducted two empirical studies to test our hypotheses. The first study was designed to test the hypotheses that the accent stereotypes will bias customers' perception and evaluation of their service experience. Participants were asked to listen to taped phone calls between a customer and a bank employee from the perspective of the customer. Consistent with our hypotheses, we found that accent stereotypes influence both customer evaluation of employee performance and customer satisfaction. Even though service scenarios and conversation scripts were identical, customers rated the performance of employees with Indian accents much lower than the performance of employees with American and British accents. The influence of accent stereotyping on customer satisfaction was moderated by the service outcome. When the service outcome was favorable, the British accent was rated more positively than the American accent but, contrary to our hypothesis, the Indian accent was not rated more negatively than the American accent. However, when the service outcome was unfavorable, customer satisfaction in the Indian-accent condition was significantly lower than it was in American or British accent condition.

The second study examined the moderating effects of information availability. We tested whether accent stereotypical effects would decrease with the presence of other judgmental cues. In the high information condition, customers were informed of the industrial norms about the specific type of service; whereas in the low information condition, customers were not provided with any background information. As predicted, accent stereotypical effects on customer satisfaction were no longer significant after customers had more information to make judgment. However, the negative bias against the Indian accent was so strong that even when customers were informed of industrial norms, they still rated Indian-employee's performance as the lowest. Another noteworthy finding from this experiment was the difference in customer causal attribution across conditions. We measured customers' attributions by coding open-ended question responses. When employees from favorable outgroup (British) or ingroup (American) performed well, customers attributed this favorable outcome to their internal factors. When they provided poor service, customers attributed this unfavorable outcome to the external factors. The reverse is true when the employee was from an unfavorable outgroup (Indian).

In summary, we show across two studies that accent stereotypes bias customer evaluation and interpretation of service outcomes. Whereas they display a positive bias toward the British accent, customers show a strong negative bias against the Indian accent. They also make stereotype-consistent attributions about service outcomes. These stereotypical effects on service outcomes are partially reduced when customers are informed of other relevant information.

References

Baugh, John (2000), "Racial Identification by Speech," *American Speech*, 75(4), 362-364

Cargile, Aaron Castelan (2000), "Evaluations of Employment Suitability: Does Accent Always Matter?" *Journal of Employment Counseling*, 37 (3), 165-177.

Cowen, David A. (1986), "Developing a Process Model of Problem Recognition," *Academy of Management Review*, 11 (4): 763-776.

DeShields Jr., Oscar W and Gilberto de los Santos (2000), "Salesperson's Accent as a Globalization Issue," *Thunderbird International Business Review,* 42 (1), 29-46.

Giles, H. and P. F. Powesland (1975), *Speech styles and social evaluation.* Academic Press.

Giles, Howard, Angie Williams, Diane M. Mackie, and Francine Rosselli (1995), "Reactions to Anglo- and Hispanic-American-accented speakers: Affect, identity, persuasion, and the English-only controversy," *Language and Communication*, 15(2), 107-120.

Haslam, S. Alexander, Penelope J. Oakes, John C. Turner and Craig McGarty (1995), "Social Categorization and Group Homogeneity: Changes in the Perceived Applicability of Stereotype Content as a Function of Comparative Context and Trait Favourableness," *British Journal of Social Psychology*, 34 (2), 139-160.

Hennig-Thurau, Thorsten, Markus Groth, Michael Paul, and Dwayne D Gremler (2006), "Are All Smiles Created Equal? How Emotional Contagion and Emotional Labor Affect Service Relationships." *Journal of Marketing*, 70 (3), 58-73.

Hewstone, Miles (1990), "The 'Ultimate Attribution Error'?: A Review of the Literature on Intergroup Causal Attribution," *European Journal of Social Psychology*, 20 (4), 311-335.

Hilford, Andy, Murray Glanzer, Kisok Kim, and Lawrence T. DeCarlo (2002), "Regularities of Source Recognition: ROC analysis," *Journal of Experimental Psychology*, 131(4), 494-510.

Hosoda, Megumi, Eugene F. Stone-Romero, and Jennifer N. Walter (2007) "Listeners' Cognitive and Affective Reactions to English Speakers with Standard American English and Asian Accents," *Perceptual and Motor Skills*, 104 (1), 307-326.

Jackson, Linda, Linda Sullivan and Carole N. Hodge (1993), "Stereotype Effects on Attributions, Predictions, and Evaluations: No Two Social Judgments are Quite Alike," *Journal of Personality and Social Psychology*, 65(1), 69-84.

Kahneman, Daniel, Paul Slovic, and Amos Tversky (1982), *Judgment under Uncertainty: Heuristics and Biases*, New York: Cambridge University Press.

Ko, Sei Jin, Charles M. Judd, and Irene Blair (2006), "What the Voice Reveals: Within- and Between-Category Stereotyping on the Basis of Voice," *Personality and Social Psychology Bulletin*, 32(6), 806-819.

Kunda, Ziva and Thagard, Paul (1996), "Forming Impressions from Stereotypes, Traits, and Behaviors: A Parallel-Constraint-Satisfaction Theory," *Psychological Review*, 103(2), 284-308.

Ladegaard, Hans J. (1998), "National Stereotypes and Language Attitudes: The Perception of British, American and Australian language and Culture in Denmark," *Language and Communication*, 18 (4), 251-274.

Levi, Susannah and David B. Pisoni (2007), "Indexical and Linguistic Channels in Speech Perception: Some Effects of Voiceovers on Advertising Outcomes," in *Psycholinguistic Phenomena in Marketing Communications*, ed. Tina M. Lowrey, Mahwah, New Jersey: Lawrence Erlbaum Associates, 203-219.

Lippi-Green, Rosina L. (1997), *English with an Accent: Language, Ideology, and Discrimination in the United States*, London and New York: Routledge.

Locksley, Anne, Eugene Borgida, Nancy Brekke and Christine Hepburn (1980), "Sex Stereotypes and Social Judgment," *Journal of Personality and Social Psychology*, 39 (5), 821-831.

Matta, Shashi and Valerie S. Folkes (2005), "Inferences about the Brand from Counterstereotypical Service Providers," *Journal of Consumer Research*, 32 (2), 196-206.

Mount, Michael K. and Duane E. Thompson (1987), "Cognitive Categorization and Quality of Performance Ratings," *Journal of Applied Psychology*, 72 (2), 240-247.

Mullen, Brian, Brown, Rupert and Smith, Colleen (1992), "Ingroup Bias as a function of Salience, Relevance, and Status: An Integration," *European Journal of Social Psychology*, 22 (2), 1992, 103-122.

Oliver, Richard L. (1980), "A Cognitive Model of the Antecedents and Consequences of Satisfaction Decisions." *Journal of Marketing Research*, 17 (4), 460-469.

Parasuraman, A., Valarie A. Zeithaml, and Leonard L. Berry (1985), "A Conceptual Model of Service Quality and its Implications for Future Research." *Journal of Marketing*, 49 (4), 41-51.

Podberesky, Rosita, Robert H. Deluty and Stanley Feldstein (1990). "Evaluations of Spanish- and Oriental-accented English speakers." *Social Behavior and Personality*, 18 (1), 53-63.

Poster, Winifred R. (2007) "Who's on the line? Indian call center agents pose as Americans for U.S.-outsourced firms," *Industrial Relations*, 46 (2), 271-304.

Purkiss, Sharon L. Segrest , Pamela L. Perrewé, Treena L. Gillespie, Bronston T. Mayes and Gerald R. Ferris (2006), "Implicit Sources of Bias in Employment Interview Judgments and Decisions," *Organizational Behavior and Human Decision Processes*, 101 (2), 152-167.

Sandberg, Jared (2007), "'It Says Press Any Key; Where's the Any Key?': India's Call-Center Workers Get Pounded, Pampered," *Wall Street Journal (Eastern edition)*, Feb 20, B1.

Schneider, David J. (2004). *The Psychology of Stereotyping*, New York: Guilford Press.

Seta, J. J, Catherine E. Seta and Todd McElroy (2003), "Attributional Biases in the Service of Stereotype Maintenance: A Schema-Maintenance through Compensation Analysis," *Personality and Social Psychology Bulletin*, 29 (2), 151-163.

Solomon, Michael R. (1985), "A Role Theory Perspective on Dyadic Interactions: The Service Encounter." *Journal of Marketing*, 49 (1), 99-112.

Stockwell, Peter (2002), *Sociolinguistics: A Resource Book for Students*, Routledge, London and New York.

Tsalikis, John, Oscar W. DeShields Jr., and Michael S. LaTour (1991), "The Role of Accent on the Credibility and Effectiveness of the Salesperson," *The Journal of Personal Selling and Sales Management*, 11 (1), 31-42.

Yeung, Catherine W. M. and Dilip Soman (2007), "The duration heuristic," *Journal of Consumer Research*, 34 (3), 315-326.

How Does the Defensive Consumer Choose?

Laurence Ashworth, Queen's University, Canada
Andrew Wilson, York University, Canada
Peter Darke, York University, Canada

Abstract

The present study extends research on the defensive model of suspicion (Darke and Ritchie 2007) to the context of consumer choice. Prior research shows defensive suspicion induces negative product attitudes, but the implications for consumer choice have not yet been examined. We predict that defensive suspicion should lead to decisions that help minimize the chance of being tricked or misled. An experiment shows consumers who are experimentally induced into a suspicious mindset are more likely to defer their product choices when they have the opportunity, and more likely to choose an inexpensive versus premium alternative for forced choices.

Conceptualization

Historically, consumer choice research has focused on shifts in preferences related to the emphasis of various aspects of the choice task (e.g. Dhar and Sherman 1996; Dhar and Simonson 1992; Simonson and Tversky 1992). More recently, choice research has begun to focus on the goals of the consumer (Bettman, Luce, and Payne 2008). In this vein, the current research examines choice in the context of defensive goals evoked when consumers are actively suspicious about marketer tactics.

The current research adopted Darke and Ritchie's (2007) dual process model to predict the effects of suspicion on consumer choice. Their model distinguishes between specific and generalized suspicion, type of information processing (heuristic vs. systematic), and processing goals (accuracy vs. defense). Traditionally, trust has been regarded as a simple heuristic cue. Indications that a particular source is trustworthy lead to greater agreement without much thought about the argument's merits (e.g. Petty, Cacioppo, and Schumann 1983). Further, some forms of suspicion (e.g., ulterior motives) are known to increase systematic processing, leading to more careful thought and greater differentiation between strong and weak arguments (Priester and Petty 1995). This pattern is consistent with what Darke and Ritchie (2007) call accuracy-based suspicion, where initial distrust evokes the goal of forming a valid opinion, leading to greater objective processing, and attitudes reflective of the true merits of the arguments (see also Campbell and Kirmani 2000). However, they suggest that suspicion can also be more defensive in nature. Such defensive suspicion biases judgment in a way that helps protect the self-esteem or material interests of the consumer from perceived threats.

Darke and Ritchie (2007) support their defensive bias hypothesis in a series of experiments. A debriefing was used to inform subjects they had been deceived by an initial ad, followed by evaluations of a second advertisement for a different product presented under the guise of a separate study. The results indicated that advertising deception evoked defensive processing goals in the sense that consumers felt fooled or tricked. In order to avoid being misled again, consumers adopted more negative attitudes towards subsequently advertised products, even those advertised by unrelated second-parties. Process analyses showed that the initial deception led to generalized distrust towards advertisers—dubbed defensive stereotyping. Additional evidence argued against the alternative possibility that these effects were due to negative affect evoked by the deception manipulation. Importantly, there were a number of sources of evidence that these effects were produced through biased processing. For instance, advertising deception led to negative attitudes whether strong or weak arguments were included in the second ad, which is consistent with a defensive bias because accuracy-based processing should have produced greater differentiation between strong and weak arguments rather than uniformly negative responses. In addition, defensive stereotyping was observed only when consumers were the direct victims of the advertising deception (high ego-involvement), and not when they merely learned of it second-hand (low ego-involvement). Finally, consumers relied on their generalized suspicions to make attitude judgments even when highly diagnostic information was available that the second-party advertiser was trustworthy (Darke, Ashworth, and Ritchie 2008).

The above evidence suggests that advertiser deception evokes defensive goals that have the effect of negatively biasing subsequent product attitudes. However, it is not clear what implications such generalized suspicions have for consumer choices within a set. The study described here examines these implications. In general, we propose that consumer suspicion is likely to lead to more conservative choices. This can take the form of delaying choice when that option is available, in the same way that negative emotions (Luce 1998) or difficult decisions (Dhar 1997, Dhar and Nowlis 1999) can lead to delayed choice. When forced to choose, suspicious consumers are likely to avoid high priced options that purport to be of higher quality in favor of lower price (and quality) options because more modest product claims are less likely to evoke defensive concerns (Darke and Ritchie 2007).

Method

A sample of 229 adults (137 females), aged between 18 and 91 (mean 34.1) were randomly assigned to a 2 (suspicion: yes or no) x 2 (firms: same or different) between subjects design. Suspicion was manipulated by a procedure similar to Darke and Ritchie (2007) as described above. The effectiveness of this manipulation was confirmed through a check. Results showed that participants in the suspicion condition felt more fooled by the initial ad, relative to controls (Ms=5.32 versus 3.54, t(207)=13.66, p<.001; seven-point scales).

Following the suspicion manipulation, participants began what was ostensibly a separate study conducted by another researcher. Participants were presented with three choice tasks across different categories (binoculars, microwave ovens, and mp3 players). In each case, one option was presented as higher quality and price than its alternative. Subjects could choose either of the two options, or to delay their choice altogether. The second factor was manipulated by presenting the alternatives as being offered by a single retailer, or by two competing retailers. Note that these retailers were always fictitious and *were unrelated to the initial advertiser who had deceived participants*.

Major Findings

Participants in the suspicion condition were more likely to delay than were control participants ($F(1,224)=4.39$, $p=.037$). Delaying participants were asked to imagine circumstances in which a choice was necessary, and to choose between the two alternatives. In this case, suspicious participants were more likely to choose the inexpensive option compared to controls. Additional evidence showed that these effects occurred through generalized suspicion rather than any negative affect associated with the initial deception. Overall, this study provides initial support for the notion that suspicious consumers may defer choice when possible, and seek refuge in less expensive alternatives when a choice must be made.

Further experiments in this project will attempt to replicate these findings, while extending them by investigating boundary conditions. Stronger (weaker) effects are predicted under conditions of relatively subjective (objective) quality claims. When quality claims are attributed to an objective third party source (e.g. Consumer's Union), the effects of suspicion are hypothesized to be extinguished.

References

Bettman, J.R., Mary Frances Luce, and J.W. Payne (2008), "Consumer Decision Making: A Choice Goals Approach " in *Handbook of Consumer Psychology*, ed. C.P. Haugtvedt, P.M. Herr and F.R. Kardes, New York and London: Lawrence Erlbaum Associates, Taylor & Francis Group, 589-610.

Campbell, M. C. and A. Kirmani (2000), "Consumers' Use of Persuasion Knowledge: The Effects of Accessibility and Cognitive Capacity on Perceptions of an Influence Agent," *Journal of Consumer Research*, 27 (1), 69-83.

Darke, P. R., L.T.A. Ashworth, and R. J. B. Ritchie (2008), "Damage from Corrective Advertising: Causes and Cures," *Journal of Marketing*, in press.

Darke, P. R. and R. J. B. Ritchie (2007), "The Defensive Consumer: Advertising Deception, Defensive Processing, and Distrust," *Journal of Marketing Research*, 44 (1), 114-27.

Dhar, R. and S. J. Sherman (1996), "The Effect of Common and Unique Features in Consumer Choice," *Journal of Consumer Research*, 23 (3), 193-203.

Dhar, R. and I. Simonson (1992), "The Effect of the Focus of Comparison on Consumer Preferences," *Journal of Marketing Research*, 29 (4), 430-40.

Petty, R. E., J. T. Cacioppo, and D. Schumann (1983), "Central and Peripheral Routes to Advertising Effectiveness-the Moderating Role of Involvement," *Journal of Consumer Research*, 10 (2), 135-46.

Priester, J. R. and R. E. Petty (1995), "Source Attributions and Persuasion-Perceived Honesty as a Determinant of Message Scrutiny," *Personality and Social Psychology Bulletin*, 21 (6), 637-54.

Simonson, I. and A. Tversky (1992), "Choice in Context: Tradeoff Contrast and Extremeness Aversion," *Journal of Marketing Research*, 29 (3), 281-95.

How I Feel is More Important Than How You Feel: The Role of Process and Outcome Emotions on Object Evaluation

Sinem Atakan, University of Michigan, USA
Katherine A. Burson, University of Michigan, USA
Richard P. Bagozzi, University of Michigan, USA

All of the products we buy are produced either by other people or, in part, by us. Once we decide that we need a new product such as a coffee table, a sweater or a mug, we have the option to buy it or we can make it ourselves. The Home Depot, Build a Bear and other stores encourage consumers to become more involved in the production process. This research explores the effects of process-related and outcome-related emotions on object-self relationship and valuation of products. Specifically, three studies explore when and how making a product oneself will increase or decrease the final valuation of the object compared to a product constructed by someone else.

Common wisdom suggests that consumers will derive utility from participating in the construction of a product and perhaps be more satisfied with it than if they had simply purchased the product. However, imagine that the process of crafting a mug is quite unpleasant for the consumer (the clay feels clumpy and gross, etc.). This process is likely to color the consumer's final evaluation of the mug differently than if the process was pleasant (he loves the texture and smell of clay). Furthermore, the consumer is likely to have feelings about the final product that are unrelated to the process. For example, he may feel proud or ashamed of the outcome regardless of whether the process was pleasant or unpleasant. In either case, the object may be contaminated by the emotions and gain a symbolic meaning. As a result of the process and/or outcome emotions, consumers may identify with and become more attached to the object.

I propose that process and outcome emotions 1) contaminate the object by giving it a symbolic meaning, 2) symbolic meaning of the object affect identification with and attachment to the object, 3) alter valuation of the object. Previous research (Norton & Ariely, 2007) suggests that self involvement enhances the value of objects but does not explain the process or make any distinction between process and outcome emotions. Importantly, I predict that although both process and outcome emotions will affect evaluation, only process emotions will affect valuations of self made objects more than other made objects, despite the fact that the emotions themselves may not differ for self and the other person. When the outcome emotion is negative (positive), it does not matter whether it is self or another person who made the object. The consumer will be unhappy (happy) either way. However, when self is involved in the process, reactions to the object are likely to be stronger.

In the first two studies, all participants read a story describing the process of making a mug. The final outcome was held constant by showing the same mug picture in all conditions. Process emotions were manipulated by telling half of the participants that the process was pleasant and telling the other half that it was unpleasant. Producer in the story was either the participant himself or another participant in the experiment. As predicted, an ANOVA on object evaluation yielded a process emotion by producer interaction. Participants in the pleasant process condition evaluated the object more highly than the others. The effect of process on object evaluation was stronger if the participant imagined that he had made the object. This was not because participants could not imagine how another person would feel in the process. In fact, in both studies, they predicted no difference between their own process emotions and those of another person. Furthermore, study 2 reveals how the self-object relationship takes shape. Symbolic meaning of the object mediates the effect of the building process on identification as well as attachment. Process emotions contaminate the object and give it a symbolic meaning. People become attached to or identify with the object because of the object's symbolic meaning.

In a third study, I find evidence that outcome emotions affect evaluation of an object beyond the role of process emotions outlined above. Pride enhances evaluation of objects and shame diminishes the evaluation of the same object. Also, whether from the process or the outcome, positive emotions enhance symbolic meaning of objects and result in identification with as well as attachment to the object. Symbolic meaning of the object also mediates the effect of outcome emotions on attachment and identification. Unlike the first two studies, there was no interaction between producer and emotion on evaluation of the object, symbolic meaning of the object, or attachment. When emotions are related to the outcome (rather than the process), there is no distinction between self and other. Process emotions seem to be a stronger factor in shaping the self-object relationship than the outcome emotions.

My findings show that emotions that are evoked in the process as well as outcome emotions may enhance or diminish the value of objects by giving symbolic meanings to objects and therefore by shaping consumers identification with and attachment to the objects. If the outcome emotions are negative (positive), consumers are unhappy (happy) about the product regardless of who produced the object. On the other hand, process creates stronger response in object evaluation if self is involved. This research contributes to how self is extended to objects (Belk, 1988) and how consumers come to bond with the objects. The findings can help marketers to create additional value for consumers by understanding how the process and outcome emotions result in over or undervaluation of the objects.

References

Belk, Russell W. (1988), "Possessions and the Extended Self," *Journal of Consumer Research*, 15, Sept, 139-168
Norton, Michael and Dan Ariely (2007) "The IKEA Effect: How Labor Leads to Love", ACR Presentation, Oct 27

The Unexpected Impact of User Manual at the Pre-purchase Stage on Product Evaluation and Purchase Intention: An Exploratory Study

Benoit Aubert, Grenoble Ecole de Management / Customer Equity Institute, France
Olivier Trendel, Grenoble Ecole de Management / Customer Equity Institute, France
Daniel Ray, Grenoble Ecole de Management / Customer Equity Institute, France

Abstract

In order to better understand capability and usability of products, an increasing number of consumers read user manuals at the pre-purchase stage. The objective of this exploratory research is (i) to understand the impact of reading user manual at the pre-purchase stage on product evaluation and purchase intention and (ii) to investigate mediating and moderating effects. In an experiment, we found that user manual exposure may positively influence product evaluation and purchase intention, as long as the perceived pedagogical quality of the manual is high. User manual evoked usage vividness and perceived customer education are mediating this effect.

Research background

The rising number of products' features can overwhelm consumers with concerns on capability and usability of products (Thompson and al. 2005). Such complexity may lead consumers to face difficulties when evaluating an offer at the pre-purchase stage (Bell and Eisingerich 2007). Thus, consumers search more and more for product usage information at the pre-purchase stage such as product usage instructions (Higgins and Shanklin 1992). They can for instance easily download user manuals through companies' websites in order to get proper usage information.

It is thus reasonable to question the "return on investment" of letting consumers read user manuals at a pre-purchase stage. So far, literature on user manuals remains scarce and legitimately focuses on post-purchase issues (Celuch, Lust and Showers 1992; Wiese and al. 2004). The goal of this study is not to understand why some customers read user manual at the pre-purchase stage, but rather to explore the impact of such a behavior on product evaluation and purchase intention and also to propose a possible underlying mechanism. From a managerial point of view, this research provides companies with indications about the value of positioning user manuals as pre-purchase communication tools.

To analyze the effects of user manuals on product evaluation and buying intention, the role of perceived customer education and user manual evoked usage vividness has been investigated. Perceived customer education reflects the degree to which customers perceive having been educated on a product by a company and is an antecedent of skills improvement, usage and consumer satisfaction (Aubert 2007). User manual evoked usage vividness refers to the quality of product usage related mental imagery (Babin and Burns 1998; MacInnis and Price 1987).

From the existing literature we hypothesized that reading user manual before purchase improves perceived customer education and consequently product evaluation and buying intention (Honebein 1997). We also hypothesized that user manual evoked usage vividness mediates the link between user manual exposure and perceived customer education: the more a customer is able to clearly represent himself using the product mentally when reading a user manual, the more he should perceive having been well educated by the company (MacInnis and Price 1987).

Evidence of the impact of user manual at the pre-purchase stage

138 students from a major European business school participated in an experiment on the evaluation of a new digital multi-featured camera soon to be available on the local market. User manual (present, absent) was the only between subject factor that was manipulated. 68 students were provided with 4 original sources of information: one document on how to choose a digital camera, one copy of the web page for the camera, one document presenting the technical specification of the camera and a consumer report for this camera. The 70 other students were provided with the same 4 sources of information plus the original user manual for this camera. Students were asked to spend as much time as needed (up to 30 minutes) to study the different documents. They were informed that in a second part they would have to give their opinion on the camera.

We controlled that the average time spent reading the documents was greater in the user manual present condition than in the user manual absent condition (M=24.1 min. and 20.1 min., $p<.01$). We also controlled that product feature knowledge was the same for the 2 experimental groups (all p NS). As hypothesized, we found that students in the user manual present condition perceived being better educated to use the product by the company than students in the user manual absent condition (M=5.38 and 3.93, $p<.01$). We also found that product evaluation and purchase intention were greater in the user manual present condition ($p<.01$ and $p<.1$ respectively). In order to test the mediating role of perceived customer education we performed several regression analyses (Baron and Kenny 1986; Shrout and Bolger 2002) and found, as expected, that perceived customer education fully mediates the relationship between user manual exposure and product evaluation or purchase intention. In particular, the effect on user manual exposure on product evaluation or purchase intention disappears (p NS) when perceived customer education is entered in the model.

Understanding the underlying mechanism

In a second part we studied the specific impact, on perceived customer education, of 3 variables that qualify user manual exposure: exposure duration, level of attention and importance given to this source of information when evaluating the product. We found a significant relationship (marginally significant in the case of exposure duration) between these 3 variables and user manual evoked usage vividness (all $p<.01$ for attention and importance and $p<.1$ for exposure duration) and a significant relationship between user manual evoked usage vividness and perceived customer education ($p<.05$). Moreover, we found that user manual evoked usage vividness fully mediates the relationship between the 3 variables qualifying user manual exposure and perceived customer education.

Finally, as suggested by Hennig-Thurau and al. (2005), we tested the moderating effect of 2 variables: user manual perceived pedagogical quality (a key variable controllable by companies) and customer expertise with the product category, on the relationship between the 3 exposure variables and usage vividness. Following Jaccard, Wan and Turrisi (1990) procedure, we found that perceived pedagogical quality conditions the impact of the 3 exposure variables on user manual evoked usage vividness (all p for the interaction variables $<.05$) such as a poor level of pedagogical quality precludes the existence of the relationships. Interestingly, we found no moderating effect of customer expertise with digital cameras (all p for the interaction variables NS). Thus, companies do not have to take it into account.

Conclusion and further research

This research unveils that encouraging potential customers to read user manuals at the pre-purchase stage may positively influence product evaluation and purchase intention, as long as the perceived pedagogical quality of the manual is high. User manual evoked usage vividness and perceived customer education are key mediators between user manual exposure and behavioral antecedents. In further studies, we investigate the impact of other dimensions of user manual evoked imagery.

References

Aubert, Benoit (2008), "Toward a Better Understanding of the Effects of Customer Education on Usage Behaviour and Satisfaction", *Advances in Consumer Research,* Volume 35, eds. Angela Y. Lee and Dilip Soman, Duluth, MN : Association for Consumer Research.

Babin, Laurie A. and Alvin C. Burns (1998), "A Modified Scale for the Measurement of Communication Evoked Mental Imagery", *Psychology and marketing*, 15(3), 261–278.

Baron, Reuben M. and David A. Kenny (1986), "The Moderator-Mediator Variable Distinction in Social Psychological Research: Conceptual, Strategic, and Statistical Considerations", *Journal of Personality and Social Psychology*, 51(6), 1173-1182.

Bell, Simon J. and Andreas B. Eisingerich (2007), "The Paradox of Customer Education: Customer Expertise and Loyalty in the Financial Services Industry", *European Journal of Marketing*, 41, 466–486.

Celuch, Kevin G., John A. Lust, & Linda S. Showers (1992), "Product Owner Manuals: an Exploratory Study of Nonreaders versus Readers", *Journal of Applied Social Psychology*, 22(6), 492-507.

Hennig-Thurau, Thorsten, Peter C. Honebein and Benoit Aubert (2005), "Unlocking Product Value Through Customer Education," *American Marketing Association Winter Educators' Conference*, eds. Kathleen Seiders and Glenn B. Voss, San Antonio, TX: American Marketing Association.

Higgins, Susan H. and William L. Shanklin (1992), "Seeking Mass Market Acceptance for High-Technology Products", *Journal of Consumer Marketing*, 9(1), 5-14.

Honebein, Peter C. (1997), *Strategies for Effective Customer Education*, Chicago: NTC Books.

Jaccard, James, Robert Turrisi and Choi K. Wan (1990), "The Detection and Interpretation of Interaction Effects between Continuous Variables in Multiple Regression" *Multivariate Behavioral Research*, 25(4), 467-498.

MacInnis, Deborah J. and Linda L. Price (1987), "The Role of Imagery in Information Processing", *Journal of Consumer Research*, 13, (mach), 473-91.

Shrout, Patrick. E. and Niall Bolger (2002), "Mediation in Experimental and Nonexperimental Studies: New Procedures and Recommendations", *Psychological Methods*, 7(4), 422-445.

Thompson, Debora Viana, Rebecca W. Hamilton and Roland T. Rust (2005), "Feature Fatigue: When Product Capabilities Become Too Much of a Good Thing," *Journal of Marketing Research*, 42(4), 431-442.

Wiese, Bettina S., Jürgen Sauer and Bruno Rüttinger (2004), "Consumers' Use of Written Product Information", *Ergonomics*, 47 (11), 1180-1194.

Do Confident Consumers Search More? Examining The Relationship Between Multidimensional Self-confidence and External Information Search

Caezilia Loibl, The Ohio State University, USA
Soo Hyun Cho, The Ohio State University, USA
Florian Diekmann, The Ohio State University, USA
Marv Batte, The Ohio State University, USA

Conceptualization

The present study examines the implications of Bearden, Hardesty, and Rose's (2001) consumer self-confidence scale for external information search. While the consumer behavior literature has long suggested that consumer information search is influenced by their self-confidence, a rigorous analysis of the information search strategies of consumers with different levels of self-confidence is lacking. The present study aims to fill this void by employing the Bearden, Hardesty, and Rose scale to assess consumer self-confidence for the specific case of university extension provided consumer information. In particular, we examine the differences in information acquisition of high-confident and low-confident consumers and investigate which demographic variables influence consumer self-confidence measures in the context of information search.

Method

A total of 3,000 questionnaires were mailed to a random sample of Ohio residents in May and June 2007. An overall response rate of 32 percent was achieved, and a total of 787 responses were used for the analyses reported here. For this survey, we slightly revised the wording of the original consumer self-confidence scale to reflect the information search context and we excluded the market interface measure, which we deemed unrelated for the information search context. Our specific focus was on consumer information provided by a university extension program, including the following consumer interests: nutrition and health, youth and families, money matters, natural resources and environment, yard and garden, business and community, and farming and food production. The factor analysis described in Bearden, Hardesty, and Rose (Study 3), was repeated to confirm the validity of the revised scale.

K-means cluster analysis was used to identify consumer information strategies by analyzing the number of information sources respondents use to gather consumer information from a list of 29 information sources and the frequency of source use. The four-cluster solution proved the best solution: Cluster 1 (17% of the sample), representing consumers practicing a multi-source, high-information strategy; Cluster 2 (39%), representing consumers practicing an Internet-based moderate-information strategy; Cluster 3 (18%), representing consumers practicing a moderate-information strategy based on traditional, offline information sources; and Cluster 4 (26%), representing consumers practicing a low-information strategy.

Major findings

Relationship of self-confidence level and information search. The sample was split into high- and low-CSC consumers. Respondents whose scores on each of the five items assessing consumer self-confidence were above the midpoint (> 4) were classified as high-CSC consumers (N=105, 13.3%). A univariate general linear model was fit to the data using information cluster membership as the dependent variable. The CSC-level measure, demographic variables, and variables resulting from the interaction of the two were used as independent variables. We found that high-CSC consumers are significantly more likely to practice a high-information search strategy, even after controlling for the demographic variables and the interaction effects.

Predictors of consumer self-confidence level. Only a few studies have examined predictors of consumer self-confidence. Demographic influences had been found for age and gender. The literature is scarce despite Bearden, Hardesty, and Rose's call for examining demographic influences to identify variables that could serve as surrogates for consumer self-confidence measures. The present study extended previous analyses by examining the influence of nine demographic variables on consumer self-confidence measures. To test this proposition, several ordinary least squares regression models were fit to the data using the five consumer self-confidence measures as the dependent variables and demographic measures as independent variables. Our findings show that overall consumer self-confidence is primarily related to financial resources.

To conclude, Bearden, Hardesty, and Rose proposed a model of consumer self-confidence that distinguishes between six measures of self-confidence as related to consumer and marketplace phenomena. To date, this distinction has not been examined in the context of external information search. We have shown that consumer self-confidence measures act as significant predictors of information search activity, that high-CSC consumers are engaged in more search activity, and that consumer self-confidence scores are dependent on a limited number of demographic influences. These findings provide strong support for the view that consumer self-confidence improves the prediction of the search behavior of consumers.

Reference

Bearden, William O., David M. Hardesty, and Randall L. Rose. 2001. Consumer self-confidence: Refinements in conceptualization and measurement. *Journal of Consumer Research* June (1) (28):121-134.

A Research of the Effect of Gift Promotion and Its Spillover Effect

Chung-Hui Tseng, National Chengchi University, Taiwan
Yung-Chien Lou, National Chengchi University, Taiwan
Lien-Ti Bei, National Chengchi University, Taiwan

Gift promotion is taken as a common technique in most industry for a long time. However, the exact effect of gift promotion is nearly neglected by most managers as well as scholars, because it is believed that the higher the gift price is, the more successful gift promotion works. But, must it be true? In this study, the author questioned that the effect of gift promotion does not necessarily show a positive relationship with the gift price. In other words, if the gift price is much higher, even equal to the main product, consumer may think this is unreasonable, and then more possibly give a negative evaluation to the promotion deal. Thus, the purpose of this study was to deeply examine the effect of gift promotion.

In this study, gift promotion was defined as "buy A, get a free gift B"; that is, A and B were different products. Furthermore, promotion depth was taken as a main independent variable and defined as a percentage of gift price by main product price (eg. If an ad says: "Buy a Pair of Nike Running Shoes NT$2000, Get a Free Gift—a Casio Watch (Market Value NT$200)", the promotion depth is 10%; that is NT$200/NT$2000). By experiment design, promotion depth was manipulated as ten groups (10%, 20%,..., 100%), and brand images of main product and gift were chosen to be two moderators in this study.

Before main studies, a preliminary study was conducted in order to make sure the existence of turning-point of gift-promotion depth. Therefore, an one-factor experimental design (ten groups of gift-promotion depth) was conducted. The finding was that the turning-point of gift-promotion depth did exit. Following, an 10x2x2 between subject design was further held, and totally 975 valid questionnaires was gathered from two collages in Taipei city.

Three themes were arranged to further investigate effects of gift promotion. Inferences and discussions were based on literature of reference price and anchor-adjustment theory. In the first research theme, it is proposed that there is a turning point in promotion depth—50% of promotion depth, and the turning point was fluctuant in accordance with brand image. If the brand image was high, the turning point was 50%?however, if the brand image was low, the turning point was downward to 40% under low brand image of main product and downward to 20% under low brand image of gift. Based on these findings, promotion depth was divided into two categories—reasonable (depth before turning point) and exaggerated (depth after turning point) promotion depth—in order to do further investigations.

The second research theme focused on the effect of reasonable or exaggerated promotion depth and its interaction with brand image of main product and gift. Findings were (a) In the range of reasonable promotion depth, the deeper the promotion depth was, the higher the perceived value of product bundle was (eg. positive relationship). However, in the range of exaggerated promotion depth, negative relationship was exhibited. (b) The deeper the promotion depth was, the higher the price perception of gift was. In the range of reasonable promotion depth, as the depth increased, value-adding level of gift decreased. In the range of exaggerated promotion depth, as the depth increased, value-discounting level of gift increased. (c) The brand image of main product and gift did show significant moderating effect.

The third research theme was going to investigate whether the discounting perception toward gift would spill to other products with the same brand of the gift, or spill to the same product with other brand. In this study, we defined the phenomenon as a "spillover effect" of gift promotion. Findings were: (a) No matter in the range of reasonable or exaggerated promotion depth, gift promotion did cause discounting of perceived value toward other products with the same brand of the gift and to the same product with other brand. That is, spillover effect did exist. (b) As the promotion depth increased, the spillover effect would first go downward then upward. In other words, the relationship between promotion depth and spillover effect showed a type of U-shape. Findings of this study will enrich literature of promotion as well as offer practical suggestions to managers implementing strategies of gift promotions.

References

Aaker, D. A. (1991a), "Guarding the Power of Brand Name," *New York Times,* Dec., 313.

Aaker, D. A. (1991b), *Managing Brand Equity: Capitalizing on the Value of a Brand Name,* New York: The Free Press.

Aaker, D. A. (1996a), "Measuring Brand Equity across Products and Markets," *California Management Review,* 38(3), 102-120.

Aaker, D. A. (1996b), *Building Strong Brand,* New York: The Free Press.

Aaker, D. A. (1997), "Should You Take Your Brand to Where the Action Is?" *Harvard Business Review,* 75(5), 135-144.

Ahluwalia, R., H. R. Unnava, and R. E. Burnkrant (2001), "The Moderating Role of Commitment on the Spillover Effect of Marketing Communications," *Journal of Marketing Research,* 38(Nov.), 458-470.

Alba, J. W., S. M. Broniarczyk, T. A. Shimp, and J. E. Urbany (1994), "The Influences of Prior Beliefs, Frequency, Cues, and Magnitude Cues on Consumers' Perceptions of Comparative Price Data," *Journal of Consumer Research,* 21(Sep.), 219-235.

Alba, J. W., C. F. Mela, T. A. Shimp, and J. E. Urbany (1999), "The Effect of Discount Frequency and Depth on Consumer Price Judgment," *Journal of Consumer Research,* 26(Sep.), 99-114.

Alvarez, B. A. and R. V. Casielles (2005), "Consumer Evaluation of Sales Promotion: the Effect on Brand Choice," *European Journal of Marketing,* 39(Jan./Feb.), 54-70.

Anderson, J. R. (1983), "A Spreading Actication Theory of Memory," *Journal of Verbal Learning and Verbal Behavior,* 22(3), 261-295.

Anderson, E. T. and D. I. Simester (2004), "Long-run Effects of Promotion Depth on New versus Established Customers: Three Field Studies," *Marketing Science,* 23(1), 4-20.

Balachander, S. and S. Ghose (2003), "Reciprocal Spillover Effects: A Strategic Benefit of Brand Extentions," *Journal of Marketing,* 67(Jan.), 4-13.

Baron, R. M. and D. A. Kenny (1986), "The Moderator-Mediator Variable Distinction in Social Psychological Research: Conceptual , Strategic, and Statistical Considerations," *Journal of Personality and Social Psychology,* 51 (6), 1173-1182.

Baumgarth, C. (2004), "Evaluations of Co-Brands and Spillover Effects: Further Empirical Results," *Journal of Marketing Communications,* 10(June), 115-131.

Beckwith, N. E., H. H. Kassarjian, and D. R. Lehmann (1978), "Halo Effects in Marketing Research: Review and Prognosis," *Advance in Consumer Research,* 465-467.

Bell, D. R., G. Iyer, and V. Padmanabhan (2002), "Price Competition under Stockpiling and Flexible Consumptions," *Journal of Marketing Research,* 39(Aug.), 292-303.

Bertrand, K. (1998), "Premiums Prime the Market," *Advertising Age's Business Marketing,* 83(5), s6.

Biel, A. L. (1992), "How Brand Image Drives Brand Equity," *Journal of Advertising Research,* 32(6), RC6-12 (Special Section).

Biswas, A. and E. A. Blair (1991), "Contextual Effects of Reference Prices in Retail Advertisements," *Journal of Marketing,* 55(July), 1-12.

Biswas, A. (1992), "The Moderating Role of Brand Familiarity in Reference Price Perceptions," *Journal of Business Research,* 25(Nov.), 251-262.

Biwas, A., C. Pullig, B. C. Krishnan, and S. Burton (1999), "Consumer Evaluation of Reference Price Advertisements: Effects of Other Brands' Prices and Semantic Cues," *Journal of Public Policy and Marketing,* 18(Spring), 52-65.

Biswas, A. and S. Burton (1993), "Consumer Perceptions of Tensile Price Claims: An Assessment of Claim Types Across Different Discount Levels," *Journal of the Academy of Marketing Science,* 21(Summer), 217-230.

Blair, E. A. and E. L. Landon, Jr. (1981), "The Effects of Reference Price in Retail Advertising," *Journal of Marketing,* 45(Spr.), 61-69.

Blattberg, R. C. and A. Levin (1987), "Modeling the Effectiveness and Profitability of Trade Promotions," *Marketing Science,* 6, 124-146.

Block, R. A. and D. R. Harper (1991), "Overconfidence in Estimation: Testing the Anchoring and Adjustment Hypothesis," *Organizational Behavior and Human Decision Processes,* 49(Aug.), 188-207.

Broniarczyk, S. M. and J. W. Alba (1994a), "The Importance of the Brand in Brand Extension," *Journal of Marketing Research,* 31(May), 214-228.

Broniarczyk, S. M. and J. W. Alba (1994b), "The Role of Consumers' Intuition in Inference Making," *Journal of Consumer Research,* 21(Dec.), 393-407.

Carlson, B. W. (1990), "Anchoring and Adjustment in Judgment Under Risk," *Journal of Experimental Psychology,* 16(July), 665-676.

Chandon, P., B. Wansink, and G. Laurent (2000), "A Benefit Congruency Framework of Sales Promotion Effectiveness," *Journal of Marketing,* 64(Oct.), 65-81.

Collins, A. M. and E. F. Loftus (1975), "A Spreading Activation Theory of Semantic Processing," *Psychological Review,* 82(6), 407-428.

Cotton, B. C. and E. M. Babb (1978), "Consumer Response to Promotional Deals," *Journal of Marketing,* 42, 109-113.

Crites Jr., S. L., L. R. Fabrigar, and R. E. Petty (1994), "Measuring the Affective and Cognitive Properties of Attitudes: Conceptual and Methodological Issues," *Personality and Social Psychology Bulletin,* 20(6), 619-634.

Darke, P. R. and C. M. Chung (2005), "Effects of Pricing and Promotion on Consumer Perceptions: It Depends on How you Frame it," *Journal of Retailing,* 81(1), 35-47.

D'Astous, A. and I. Jacob (2002), "Understanding Consumer Reactions to Premium-Based Promotional Offers," *European Journal of Marketing,* 36(Nov./Dec.), 1270-1287.

D'Astous, A. and V. Landreville (2003), "An Experimental Investigation of Factors Affecting Consumers' Perceptions of Sales Promotions," *European Journal of Marketing,* 37(Nov./Dec.), 1746-1761.

D'Astous, A., R. Legoux, and F. Colbert (2005), "Consumer Perceptions of Promotional Offers in the Performing Arts: An Experimental Approach," *Canadian Journal of Administrative Science,* 21(3), 242-254.

Davis, H. L., S.J. Hoch, and E. K. Easton Ragsdale (1986), "An Anchoring and Adjustment Model of Spousal Predictions," *Journal of Consumer Research,* 13(June), 25-37.

Dawes, J. (2004), "Assessing the Impact of a Very Successful Price Promotion on Brand Category and Competitor Sales," *Journal of Product and Brand Management,* 13(5), 303-314.

Della Bitta, A. J., K. B. Monroe, and J. M. McGinnis (1981), "Consumer Perceptions of Comparative Price Advertisement," *Journal of Marketing Research,* 18(Nov.), 416-427.

DelVecchio, D., H. S. Krishnan, and D. C. Smith (2004), "Cents or Percent? Promotion Framing and Consumer Price Expectations," Working paper, University of Kentucky.

DelVecchio, D. (2005), "Deal-Prone Consumers' Response to Promotion: The Effects of Relative and Absolute Promotion Value," *Psychology and Marketing,* 22(5), 373-391.

DelVecchio, D., D. H. Henard, and T. H. Freling (2006), "The Effect of Sales Promotion on Post-Promotion Brand Preference: A Meta-Analysis," *Journal of Retailing,* 82(3), 203-213.

Desai, K. K. and K. L. Keller (2002), "The Effect of Ingrediant Branding on Strategies on Host Brand Extendibility," *Journal of Marketing,* 66(1), 73-93.

Dobni, D. and G. M. Zinkhan (1990), "In Search of Brand Image: A Foundation Analysis," *Advances in Consumer Research,* 17(1), 110-120.

Dobson, J. A. and B. Sternthal (1988), "Impact of Deals and Deal Retraction on Brand Switching," *Journal of Marketing Research,* 25 (Jan.), 72-81.

Dodds, W. B., K. B. Monroe, and D. Grewal (1991), "Effect of Price, Brand, Store Information on Buyers' Product Evaluation," *Journal of Marketing Research,* 28(Aug.), 307-319.

Einhorn, H. J. and R. M. Hogarth (1985), "Ambiguity and Uncertainty in Probabilistic Inference," *Psychological Review,* 92(Oct.), 456-461.

Friedlander, M. L. and S. J. Stockman (1983), "Anchoring and Publicity Effects in Clinical Judgment," *Jounal of Clinical Psychology,* 39(July), 637-643.

Gounaris, S. and V. Stathakopoulos (2004), "Antecedents and Consequences of Brand Loyalty: An Empirical Study," *Brand Management,* 11(4), 283-306.

Grewal, D., K. B. Monroe, and R. Krishnan (1998), "The Effects of Price-Comparison Advertising on Buyers' Perceptions of Acquisition Value, Transaction Value, and Behavioral Intentions," *Journal of Marketing,* 62 (Apr.), 46-59.

Grewal, D., R. Krishnan, J. Baker, and N. Borin (1998), "The Effects of Store Name, Brand Name and Price Discounts on Consumers' Evaluations and Purchase Intentions," *Journal of Retailing,* 73(3), 331-352.

Gupta, S. (1988), "Impact of Sales Promotion on When, What and How Much to Buy," *Journal of Marketing Research,* 25(Nov.), 342-355.

Gupta, S. and L. G. Cooper (1992), "The Discounting of Discounts and Promotion Thresholds," *Journal of Consumer Research,* 19(Dec.), 401-411.

Hardesty, D. M. and W. O. Bearden (2003), "Consumer evaluations of different promotion types and price presentations: the moderating role of promotional benefit level," *Journal of Retailing,* 79(1), 17-25.

Heilman, M. C., K. Nakamoto, and G. A. Rao (2002), "Pleasant Surprises: Consumer Response to Unexpected Instore Coupons," *Journal of Marketing Research,* 34, 242-252.

Helson, Harry (1964), *Adaptation-Level Theory: An Experimental And Systematic Approach To Behavior?* New York: Harper and Row

Herr, P. M., S. J. Sherman, and R. H. Fazio (1983), "On the Consequences of Priming: Assimilation and Contrast Effects," *Journal of Experimental Social Psychology,* 19, 323-340.

Herr, Paul M. (1989), "Priming Price: Prior Knowledge and Context Effects," *Journal of Consumer Research,* 16(June), 67-75.

Hogarth, R. M. and H. J. Einhorn (1989), "Order Effects in Belief Updating: The Belief Adjustment Model," Working Paper, Center for Decision Research, University of Chicago.

Hoyer, W. D. and S. P. Brown (1990), "Effects of Brand Awareness on Choice for a Common, Repeat-Purchase Product," *Journal of Consumer Research,* 17(2), 141-148.

Janiszewski, C. and S.M. J. Van Osselaer (2000), "A Connection Model of Brand Quality Associations," *Journal of Marketing Research,* 37(3), 331-350.

Johnson, E. J. and D. A. Schkade (1988), "Bias in Utility Assessments: Further Evidence and Explanations," *Management Sciences,* 35(April), 406-424.

Joyce, E. and G. C. Biddle (1981), "Anchoring and Adjustment in Probabilistic Inference in Auditing," *Journal of Accounting Research,* 19(Spring), 12-145.

Kalyanaram, G. and John D. C. Little (1994), "An Empirical Aanlysis of Latitude of Price Acceptance in Consumer Package Goods," *Journal of Consumer Research,* 21(Dec.), 408-418.

Keller, K. L. (1993), "Conceptualizing, Measuring, Managing Customer-Based Brand," *Journal of Marketing,* 57(1), 1-23.

Keller, K. L. and D. A. Aaker (1992), "The Effects of Sequential Introduction of Brand Extensions," *Journal of Marketing Research,* 29, 35-50.

Keller, K. L. (2001), "Building Customer-Based Brand Equity," *Marketing Management,* 10(2), 14-19.

Kotler, Philip (2003), *Marketing Management: Analysis, Planning, Implementation, and Control,* 11th ed., Englewood Cliff, NJ: Pretice-Hall, Inc.

Lichtenstein, D. R. and W. O. Bearden (1989), "Contextual Influences on Merchant-Supplied Reference Prices," *Journal of Consumer Research,* 16(June), 55-66.

Lichtenstein, D. R., R. G. Netemeyer, and S. Burton (1990), "Distinguishing Coupon Proneness form Value Consciousness: An Acquisition-Transaction Utility Theory Perspective," *Journal of Marketing,* 54, 54-67.

Liao, S. (2006), "The Effects of Nonmonetary Sales Promotions on Consumer Preferences: The Contigent Role of Product Category," *Journal of American Academy of Business,* 8 (2), 196-203.

Loken, B. and D. R. John (1993), "Diluting Brand Beliefs: When Do Brand Extensions Have a Negative Effect," *Journal of Marketing,* 57, 71-84.

Lola, L. L. (1982), "Toward a Procedural Theory of Judgment," Working Paper 17, Wisconsin Human Processing Program, Department of Psychology, University of Wisconsin, Madison.

Lola, L. L. (1985), "Averaging Rules and Adjustment Processes in Bayesian Inference," *Bulletin of the Psychonomic Society,* 23(6), 509-512.

Lola, L. L. (1987), "Procedural Debiasing," *Acta Psychologica,* 64(Feb.), 167-185.

Lola, L. L. and P. S. Ekberg (1980), "Test of an Ordering Hypothesis in Risky Decision Making," *Acta Psychologica,* 45(Aug.), 161-167.

Mano, H. (1990), "Anticipated Deadline Penalties: Effects on Goal Levels and Task Performance," in *Insights in Decision Making*, ed. R. M. Hogarth, Chicago: University of Chicago Press, 173-176.

Mitchell, V. W. and M. Greatorex (1993), "Risk Perception and Reduction in the Purchase of Consumer Services," *Service Industries Journal*, 13(4), 179-200.

Monroe, Kent B. (1990), *Pricing: Making Profitable Decisions*, 2nd Ed., McGraw-Hill Publishing Company.

Monroe, K. B. and S. M. Petroshius (1981), "Buyers' Perceptions of Price: An Update of the Evindence," in *Perspectives in Consumer Behavior*, eds. H. H. Kassarjian and T. S. Robertson, Glenview, IL: Scott Foresman, 43-55.

Morein, J. A. (1975), "Shift from Brand to Product Line Marketing," *Harvard Business Review*, 53(Sep.-Oct.), 56-64.

Northcraft, G. B. and M. A. Neale (1987), "Experts, Amateurs, and Real Estate: An Anchoring and Adjustment Perspective on Property Pricing Decisions," *Organizational Behivor and Human Decision Processes*, 39(Feb.), 84-97.

Njis, V. R., M. G. Dekimpe, Jan-Benedict Steenkamp (2001), "The Category-Demand Effect of Price Promotions," *Marketing Science*, 20(1), 1-22.

Palazon-Vidal, M. and E. Delgado-Ballester (2005), "Sales Promotions Effects on Consumer-Based Brand Equity," *International Journal of Market Research*, 47(2), 179-204.

Park, C. W., B. J. Jaworski, and D. J. MacInnis (1986), "Strategic Brand Concept-Image Management," *Journal of Marketing*, 50(Oct.), 135-145.

Park, C. W., S. Y. Jun, and A. D. Shocker (1996), "Composite Branding Alliances," *Journal of Marketing Research*, 33(4), 453-466.

Preton, R. H., F. Dwyer, and W. Rodelius (1978), "The Effectiveness of Bank Premiums," *Journal of Marketing*, 42(3), 96-101.

Raghubir, P. and K. P. Corfman (1999), "When Do Price Promotions Affect Brand Evaluations?" *Journal of Marketing Research*, 36(2), 211-222.

Raghubir, P. (2004), "Free Gift with Purchase: Promoting or Discounting the Brand," *Journal of Consumer Psychology*, 14(1&2), 181-186.

Raghubir, P., J. J. Inman, and H. Grande (2004), "The Three Face of Consumer Promotions," *California Management Review*, 46(4), 23-42.

Raghubir, P. (2005), "Framing a price bundle: the case of "buy/get" offers," *Journal of Product and Brand Management*, 14(2), 123-128.

Reibstein, D. J. and P. A. Traver (1982), "Factors Affecting Coupon Redemption Rates," *Journal of Marketing*, 46, 102-113.

Roehn, M. L. and A. M. Tybout (2006), "When Will a Brand Scandal Spill Over, and How Should Competitors Respond," *Journal of Marketing Research*, XLIII(Aug), 366-373.

Rossiter J. R. and L. Percy (1987), *Advertising and Promotion Management*, Singapore: McGraw-Hill.

Samu, S., H. S. Krishnan, and R. E. Smith (1999), "Using Advertising Alliance for New Product Introduction," *Journal of Marketing*, 63(1), 57-74.

Sherif, M. and C. I. Hovland (1961), *Social Judgment: Assimilaton and Contrast Effects in Communication and Attitude Change*, New Haven, CT: Yale University Press.

Shoemaker, R. W. and V. Tibrewala (1985), "Relating Coupon Redemption Rates to Past Purchasing of the Brand," *Journal of Advertising Research*, 25, 40-47.

Simonson, I., Z. Carmon, and S. O'Curry (1994), "Experimental Evidence on the Negative Effect of Product Features and Sales Promotions on Brand Choice," *Marketing Science*, 13(1), 23-40.

Simonin, B. L. and J. A. Ruth (1998), "Is a Company Known by the Company Its Keeps?" *Journal of Marketing Research*, 35(1), 30-42.

Swaminathan, V. and S. K. Reddy (2004), "Assessing the Spillover Effect of Ingredient Branded Strategies," (working paper).

Switzer, F. S. and J. A. Sniezek (1991), "Judgment Processes in Motivation: Anchoring and Adjustment Effects on Judgment and Behavior," *Organizational Behavior and Human Decision Processes*, 49(Aug.), 208-229.

Thaler, R. (1985), "Mental Accounting and Consumer Choice," *Marketing Science*, 4, (3), 199-214.

Thorndike, E. L. (1920), "A Constant Error in Psychological Ratings," *Journal of Applied Psychology*, 4, 25-29.

Till, B. D. and T. A. Shimp (1998), "Endorsers in Advertising: The Case of Negative Celebrity Information," *Journal of Advertising*, 27, 67-82.

Tversky, A. and D. Kahneman (1974), "Judgment under Uncertainty: Heuristics and Biases," *Science*, 185(Sep.), 1124-1131.

Urbany, J. E., W. O. Bearden, and D. C. Weilbaker (1988), "The Effect of Plausible and Exaggerated Reference Price on Consumer Perceptions and Price Search," *Journal of Consumer Research*, 15(June), 95-110.

Vaidyanathan, R. and P. Aggarwal (2000), "Stratigeic Brand Alliance," *Journal of Product and Brand Management*, 9(4), 214-226.

Washburn, J. H., B. D. Till, and R. Priluch (2000), "Co-Branding: Brand Equity and Trial Effect," *Journal of Consumer Marketing*, 17, 591-604

Wernerfelt, B. (1988), "Umbrella Branding as a Signal of New Product Quality: An Example of Signalling by Posting a Bond," *Rand Journal of Economics*, 19(Autumn), 458-466.

Wright, W. F. and U. Anderson (1989), "Effects of Situation Familarity and Financial Incentives on Use of the Anchoring and Adjustment Heuristic for Probability Assessment," *Organizaitonal Behavior and Human Decision Processes*, 44(Aug.), 68-82.

Yadav, M. S. (1994), "How Buyers Evaluate Product Bundles: A Model of Anchoring and Adjustment," *Journal of Consumer Research*, 21(Sep.), 342-353.

Zeithaml, V. A. (1985), "Consumer Perceptions of Price, Quality and Value: A Means-End Model and Synthesis of Evidence," *Journal of Marketing*, 52(July), 2-22.

What Really Matters When Differentiating: A Neuroscientific Approach

Martin Reimann, Stanford University, USA
Carolin Neuhaus, University of Bonn, Germany
Margit Enke, Technical University of Freiberg, Germany
Thomas Bender, Technical University of Freiberg, Germany
Bernd Weber, University of Bonn, Germany

Marketing managers' daily business is dedicated to fighting commoditization. That is, the process of trying to differentiate their firm's products in a marketplace where competitors offer essentially products with identical core attributes, e.g., in terms of quality. Prior research and managerial practice, however, lack insight about which aspects of differentiation resonate in acceptance and purchase among consumers. Moreover, consumers' affective and cognitive processes when deciding between a standard offering and a differentiated one are not yet well understood. Should the product packing be re-designed? Should marketing managers offer products at lower prices than the competition? Or, does a strong brand drive product success in a commoditized marketplace?

Methodology. To answer these questions, we digitally rendered pictures of 20 everyday products from sunscreen to table water along the line of three distinct variables: packaging design, brand, and price. For example, the well-known Evian spring water was shown in its original form (i.e., Evian brand, designed bottle, higher price) as well as in a rendered form with a different brand or a different bottle or at a lower price.

In a brain scanning session using functional magnetic resonance imaging (fMRI), 17 participants (gender: 9 male, 8 female; mean age: 24.9; occupation: students) bought or rejected original and rendered offerings. We chose fMRI because it has become one of the most prominent noninvasive methodologies for imaging brain activity in humans. Moreover, fMRI has made it possible to enhance our knowledge about how individuals process different stimuli. As such, fMRI allows for a direct measurement and localization of brain activations and offers several advantages over more traditional measurement approaches: (1) the ability to provide confirmatory evidence about the existence of an intrapersonal phenomenon; (2) the generation of a more fundamental conceptualization and understanding of underlying processes; and (3) the refinement of existing conceptualizations of various phenomena.

Results. Among other findings, our fMRI data suggest that design differentiated products activate areas related to reward anticipation to a significantly larger extend than non-differentiated and branded products. This suggests that marketing managers can trigger reward anticipation among consumers when offering products under a differentiated design.

In summary, we identified several relevant brain areas involved with three distinct differentiation strategies–packaging design differentiation, brand differentiation, and price differentiation. Utilizing fMRI, we were able to (1) provide confirmatory evidence about the existence of an intrapersonal phenomenon (i.e., reward anticipation relating to design differentiated products) and (2) generate a more fundamental conceptualization and understanding of these underlying processes.

References can be obtained from the first author upon request.

Brand Dilution Effects on Franchises

Noelle Nelson, University of Minnesota, USA
Barbara Loken, University of Minnesota, USA
Christine Bennett, University of Minnesota, USA

Prior literature on brand dilution has shown that when brands extend into new product domains, information about the extension that is inconsistent with the parent brand can affect the parent brand. However, most research on brand dilution has been performed in the context of product brand extensions. Product brand extensions are those in which the manufacturer is under the control of the parent brand and therefore, sanctioned by the parent brand manufacturer. Another context that may be potentially important for understanding brand dilution is the impact of a new retail opening with a franchised brand name.

Franchises are a good way for companies to expand quickly at relatively little cost. The franchisor charges a fee to the franchisee for the use of its brand, advertising, and other brand elements, while leaving varying amounts of control to the franchisee. A good example of a franchise is McDonalds. McDonald's franchisees benefit from McDonalds Corp. national advertising and brand strength, but are able to tailor some aspects of the store to the region or target market.

However, any McDonald's patron who has noticed the absence of his/her favorite item in a specific McDonald's can tell you that franchisees do not always deviate from the parent company in a positive way. This research examines cases in which parent brands have little control over some franchisee failures, but may, nonetheless, experience dilution effects. We examine the impact of consistent and inconsistent franchise openings through the use of brand partnerships. While research has examined the impact of co-branding (e.g. Siminon and Ruth 1998) in side-by-side retail contexts (Levin and Levin 2000) and in pairings of brands in retail displays (Buchanan, Simmons and Bickart 1999), researchers have not examined co-brands in franchise contexts in which the franchisee has some control over the use of co-brands.

In our research, we used a known company that was unlikely to yield ceiling or floor effects on loyalty: Bally's Fitness Centers. Bally's is a nation-wide chain of fitness centers that is operated on a franchise basis. Abundant past research has found that consistent extensions are better liked than inconsistent extensions. In the present study, we described Bally's as opening a new fitness center, and as part of the information received by participants, the new Bally's fitness center also housed a small restaurant.

Our consistent experimental condition was to combine Bally's with a small Panera (café/bistro). The inconsistent condition was Bally's with a small McDonald's restaurant. Because fast food sold through McDonald's is widely perceived to be unhealthy, it was expected to be perceived as quite inconsistent with the image of a fitness center. We also included a control condition, in which participants were not given information on a restaurant in the new Bally's.

Also, to rule out the argument that people simply do not know that Bally's is a franchise, and therefore apply negative information as if the parent company had control over the extension, we gave half of the participants information about Bally's as a franchise, and half no information. In particular, those who received franchise information were told that franchises are companies in which the franchisees can make decisions and changes to their specific store without interference from the parent company. The resulting experiment employed a three (extension type: inconsistent, consistent, control) by two (information about franchises vs. no information).

During the experiment, undergraduates completed a pencil and paper questionnaire about Bally's Fitness Centers. First, a description of the company Bally's was given, with franchise information either present or absent. Following the information about the parent company, information on the new Bally's (ostensibly opening in downtown Chicago) was given. Participants were told that the new Bally's would have a small Panera, McDonald's or were not given information about the new Bally's (control condition to obtain baseline views of Bally's).

Following the descriptions, participants were asked to rate both Bally's the parent company and the new downtown Chicago Bally's. Participants gave their impressions of whether Bally's (parent or extension) was roomy, high-end, and health-focused, as well as giving their overall evaluations.

Our results showed that though franchising should allow consumers to isolate negative feedback to the specific franchisee (i.e., the new Bally's store), information about the extension still leaks onto the parent company. Reminder information about Bally's as a franchise did not seem to help participants isolate the feedback to the specific store. Specifically, participants in the McDonald's condition rated both the parent Bally's and the new Bally's as being more crowded, less health-focused, less high-end, and overall more negative than the control condition.

However, it should be noted that the parent brand can also benefit from decisions made by the franchisee. That is, in the Panera condition, participants rated both the parent and new Bally's as being at least as good as the control condition (if not better) on the measures mentioned earlier.

Therefore, in the current research we replicate previous research that finds consistent extensions to be more favorably valued than inconsistent extensions. We extend these findings by showing that the parent brand (overall franchise in this case) can even benefit or be harmed by feedback from the extension when the extension is not under the parent's control.

In future research, we plan to examine whether high consumer familiarity with a brand will prevent negative spillover from extensions which are not controlled by the parent brand. Generally, we seek to find situations in which parent brands can be immune to these negative effects.

References

Levin, I.P. and A.M. Levin, "Modeling the Role of Brand Alliances in the Assimilation of Product Evaluations," *Journal of Consumer Psychology*, 9 (1), 43-52.

Buchanan L., C.J. Simmons and B.A. Bickart (1999), "Brand Equity Dilution: Retailer Display and Context Brand Effects," *Journal of Marketing Research*, 36 (3), 345-55.

Simonin, Bernard and Julie Ruth (1998), "Is a Company Known by the Company It Keeps? Assessing the Spillover Effects of Brand Alliances on Consumer Brand Attitudes," *Journal of Marketing Research*, 35 (February), 30–42.

Remembering Taste Experiences: Constructed Preferences from Suggestion

Amanda Wudarzewski, Brock University, Canada
Antonia Mantonakis, Brock University, Canada
Seema Clifasefi, University of Washington, USA
Daniel Bernstein, Kwantlen University College, Canada
Elizabeth F. Loftus, University of California, Irvine, USA

Abstract

It is well known in the literature on decision-making that utility can be derived from the anticipation of, the experience of, or the recollection of an event (Elster and Lowenstein 1992). We propose a fourth source of utility, utility derived from a false memory. We show that people can be influenced by false suggestion (for a consumption experience that did not occur), which can lead to a false memory, and result in a change in preference, which can be in either direction (i.e., preferences can increase or decrease). We propose a fluency hypothesis to account for our findings.

Memories are malleable, and current information can influence retrospective memory (Loftus and Palmer 1974). Utility can be derived from the anticipation of, the experience of, or the recollection of an event (Elster and Lowenstein 1992). We propose a fourth source: utility derived from false memory.

Post consumption feedback does not affect preferences (Lee, Frederick and Ariely 2006). Participants were assigned to one of three groups: where the ingredient was not disclosed; where participants received the "true" information *before* tasting the beer, or where they received the information *after* tasting the beer. Preferences towards the beer did not change in the *after* condition. However, "false" post-consumption feedback does affect preferences (Braun 1999). Participants tasted orange juice diluted with vinegar. After, an advertisement was presented claiming the juice was "great tasting". Participants used more positive words when describing their experiences with the juice, and the brand was more likely to be chosen.

Our investigation used these two somewhat contradictory findings as a motivator to our study. Our objective was to determine whether utility (either an increase or a decrease in preferences) can be derived from false memories. "Familiarity" is a possible mechanism that could play a role. Suggestion, which involves imagining having liked or disliked something, increases one's familiarity with an autobiographical experience. When a judgment is made on a subsequent occasion, this enhanced familiarity, or "fluency" could be misattributed to an autobiographical memory instead of to the suggestion (Bernstein et al. 2005b).The fluency hypothesis may account for why Lee et al. (2006) failed to observe a change in preference. Assuming that the post-consumption suggestion induced cognitions that were non-elaborative, participants may have not had the opportunity to experience "familiarity" that the beer tasted like vinegar.

We aim to first obtain increases and decreases in preferences within the same experiment, using the same critical item.. We chose an item that is relatively neutral for our sample of participants—white wine.

Hypotheses

H1: Participants who receive feedback that they loved (got sick from) wine will increase their confidence that such an experience occurred to them because of the cognitive elaboration that the experimental groups performed.

H2a: After feedback and elaboration, participants in the experimental groups will demonstrate an increase (decrease) in preference towards wine.

H2b: After feedback and elaboration, participants in the experimental groups will be more (less) likely to choose wine in a hypothetical situation.

H2c: After feedback and elaboration, participants in the experimental groups will show a higher (lower) willingness to pay (WTP) for wine.

Method

Participants

Ninety-three students from a large northeastern North American university participated.

Experimental Design

We used a 2 [valence (Love x Sick groups)] x 2 [suggestion (Suggestion x No Suggestion)] between-subjects design.

Procedure and Materials

We randomly assigned participants to the Love/Suggestion group, the Love/No Suggestion group, the Sick/Suggestion group, or the Sick/No Suggestion group. In an initial session, participants completed the Food History Inventory, which contained 24 events, including "loved (got sick from) drinking white wine" depending on what group they were assigned to. Participants also completed the Party Behavior Questionnaire, which asked participants to rate their likelihood of consuming food/drink items. Finally, participants completed the Food Preferences Questionnaire, where they rated food and drink items in terms of how much they enjoy eating/drinking each. Interspersed within these questionnaires were filler questionnaires to disguise the true nature of the experiment.

One week after session one, participants returned for a second session and half were given a false suggestion about their responses from session one. Participants were told their previous responses were entered into a computer, which generated a profile of their experiences with certain foods. The profiles were presented as if they had been individually tailored, although they contained the false suggestion. A portion of the profile was identical for all groups, but the critical event, "you loved (got sick from) drinking white wine," was embedded in the profile for the Suggestion groups. The No Suggestion (control) groups received filler items

Participants then completed an elaboration phase where they responded to questions about their profile. Participants were instructed to imagine the setting in which the experience might have taken place, where they may have been at the time and who they may have been with. The experimental groups answered these questions about the critical event.

Next, participants completed the Food History Inventory, Party Behavior Questionnaire, Food Preferences Questionnaire (to assess the change from session one), and the Food Costs Questionnaire where participants indicated their WTP for different food items (including "a bottle of white wine"). Finally, participants completed a Memory or Belief Questionnaire where they answered questions about their memory for the events mentioned in the profile, or to imagine what *might* have happened. Participants elaborated by providing as many details as possible.

Results and Discussion

Food History Inventory

The Love/Suggestion group (M=.92,SD=1.60) showed an increase in confidence that the event (loved drinking white wine) occurred, $t(12)$=2.07,p=.03. The Sick/Suggestion group (M=2.00,SD=2.57) also showed an increase in confidence that the event (got sick from drinking white wine) occurred, $t(13)$=2.91,p=.06.

Food Preferences Questionnaire

The Love/Suggestion group (M=1.00,SD=1.15) showed increased preference for wine, $t(12)$=3.12,p=.004. The Sick/Suggestion group (M=-.64,SD=.93) showed a decrease in preference for wine, $t(13)$=2.59,p=.011.

Party Behaviour Questionnaire

The Love/Suggestion group (M=62,SD=1.12) was more likely to indicate intent to consume wine, $t(12)$=1.98,p=.035. The Sick/Suggestion group (M=-.29,SD=.82) was more likely to avoid wine, $t(13)$=1.29, p=.10.

Food Costs Questionnaire

The Love/Suggestion group (M=\$13.92,SD=4.29) had a higher WTP for wine (M=\$10.53,SD=2.69), $t(28)$=2.65, p=.006. The Sick/Suggestion condition (M=\$13.71,SD=5.00) indicated a lower WTP for wine, (M=\$10.82,SD=4.51), $t(23)$=1.50,p=.073.

In summary, participants who received the suggestion had higher confidence that the critical event happened to them. We also found changes in preference based on the false suggestion. This is the first study to examine utility derived from false memory in terms of both increases and decreases in preference in the same experiment. We demonstrated that utility derived from false memory of an experience can form the basis of the subsequent recollection of (Food History Inventory), and the subsequent anticipation of (Party Behaviour Questionnaire), experience.

References

Bernstein, Daniel M., Cara Laney, Erin K. Morris, and Elizabeth F. Loftus (2005a), "False Beliefs about Fattening Foods can Have Healthy Consequences," *Proceedings of the National Academy of Sciences,* 102, 13724-13731.

_____ (2005b), "False Memories about Food can Lead to Food Avoidance," *Social Cognition,* 23(1), 11-34.

Braun, Kathryn A. (1999), "Post experience Advertising Effects on Consumer Memory," *Journal of Consumer Research,* 25 (March), 319-334.

Elster, Jon and George Lowenstein (1992), "Utility from Memory and Anticipation," in *Choice Over Time,* ed. George Lowenstein and Jon Elster, New York, NY, US: Russell Sage Foundation, 213-234.

Lee, Leonard, Shane Frederick, and Dan Ariely (2006), "Try It, You Will Like It: The influence of Expectation, Consumption, and Revelation on Preferences for Beer," *Psychological Science,* 17 (December), 1054-1058.

Loftus, F. Elizabeth, and John C. Palmer (1974), "Reconstruction of Automobile Destruction: An Example of the Interaction between Language and Memory," *Journal of Verbal Learning & Verbal Behavior,* 13 (October), 585-589.

Pezdek, Kathy, Iris Blandon-Gitlin, Shirley Lam, Rhiannon E. Hart, and Jonathan W. Schooler (2006), "Is knowing believing? The role of event plausibility and background knowledge in planting false beliefs about personal past," *Memory Cognition, 34*(8), 1628-1635.

Is It *Just* the Thought That Counts? Experimental Investigation into the Gift Giving Effort Effect

Risto Moisio, California State University, Long Beach, USA
Mariam Beruchashvili, California State University, Northridge, USA

Abstract

Even if consumer researchers have long contended that the effort put forth into a gift is vital, specific effects of gift-giving effort on one of its most important consequences–acts of reciprocity have not been examined. The purpose of this research is to investigate the phenomenon of perceived gift giving effort from the recipient's perspective. In this research, we empirically demonstrate what we describe as the gift giving effort effect, the idea that perceived gift giving effort sparks acts of reciprocation by the gift recipient in an array of everyday life situations.

If it is just the thought that counts, why have alongside the rows and rows of ready-made Hallmark greeting cards for any occasion a shelf with blank cards? Why offer consumers avenues to expand even more effort into gifts by providing countless gift selection workshops, online guides and tutorials, and even gift consulting services? If it is just the giving of a gift that counts, why do we see so many traces of consumers investing their emotional, psychic, and temporal efforts into the gift giving process? Why is the unifying theme of the effort in gift giving paradoxically important at the same time as the market parades more emphasis on gifts themselves? At least at the outset, it appears that a gift that reflects considerable amount of effort, not just the recognition of another person, is crucial to gift giving. The purpose of this research is to investigate the phenomenon of gift giving effort from the recipient's perspective. In this research, we empirically seek to examine what we describe as the gift giving effort effect. With this term we intend to capture the idea that perceived gift giving effort sparks one of the most fundamental processes in gift giving, acts of reciprocation by the gift recipient in an array of everyday life situations.

Our research builds on the extant literature in consumer behavior that has repeatedly recognized the pivotal role of gift giving effort in processes of gift giving (Sherry 1983). We build on the idea that the effort put forth into a gift is vital (e.g., Belk and Coon 1993; Sherry, McGrath, and Levy 1993). Gift giving effort is evidenced through multidimensional expansion of human energy, whether monetary or psychic in the form of gift giver's emotional investment that is highly valued by the recipient of the gift (Robben and Verhallen 1994). The effort expended in a gift in terms of money, time, and emotional effort is important, according to some researchers, because it signals to the recipient that the giver has made a selfless sacrifice, a characteristic of a perfect gift (Belk 1996; Belk and Coon 1993). Such sacrifice expressed through thought and effort invested in the gift by a marital partner makes a gift favorite to the gift recipient (Wolfinbarger 1990). Consumers also tend to perceive gifts that manifest effort as more successful (Wooten 2000). Others recognize how the adding of a hand-written message converts a generic birthday card into a personal gift to the recipient (Dodson and Belk 1996). In romantic relationships, a gift that reflects the expenditure of personal time and effort is perceived by the recipient as a symbol of love and of transference of the giver's self to the recipient (Belk and Coon 1993). Thus, while we learn from these studies that consumers associate emotional value with gifts imbued with effort, it remains unknown whether perceived gift giving effort impacts one of the most well-known consequences of gifts, reciprocation (e.g., Bodur and Ghromann 2005; Dorsch and Kelly 1994; Rynning 1989). The purpose of our research is to address this gap. We posit that the prevailing theory of gift giving grounded in reciprocity norm does not fully account for the gift giving effort effect.

In a series of experiments, we demonstrate that perceived gift giving effort affects the recipient in ways that cannot be explained by the prevailing theory of norm reciprocity. We examine a novel theoretical mechanism grounded in anthropological research by the seminal theorist of gift, Mauss (1954) who proposed that gifts represent vessels that contain and transmit the gift giver's spirit or *hau*. Across several studies, we investigate the gift giving effort effect. In studies 1a-1c, we demonstrate that perceived gift giving effort increases acts of reciprocity towards the gift giver in various everyday situations. We also seek to rule out alternative explanations of the gift giving effort effect. Specifically, our results show that neither gratitude, nor indebtedness, nor positive mood bias account for the gift giving effort effect. In study 2, we also examine gift giving effort effect in public (possibility of being evaluated by an audience) and private (no audience) situations. Consistent with social norm account, we find that gift giving effort increases reciprocation for high self-monitors in public but not in private situations. In private situations, social norm does not seem to account for our findings. In studies 3 and 4, we extend the underlying theoretical mechanism and the boundaries of the gift giving effort effect. We examine the role of reciprocation wariness and how it affects the gift giving effort effect. In study 3, we find that reciprocation wary participants are more likely to reciprocate in private as well as public situations. In study 4, we replicate and reverse the gift giving effort effect showing that gift giving effort may also backfire. Collectively, our findings speak to the importance of gift giving effort and particularly to the role of contagion in driving the gift giving effort effect. Our findings also show the boundaries of gift giving effort unaddressed in prior research on gifts more broadly.

References

Belk, Russell W. (1996), "The Perfect Gift," in *Gift Giving: A Research Anthology*, eds. Cele C. Otnes and Richard F. Beltramini. Bowling Green, OH: Bowling Green State University Popular Press, 59-84.

Belk, Russell W. and Gregory S. Coon (1993), "Gift Giving as Agapic Love: An Alternative to the Exchange Paradigm Based on Dating Experiences," *Journal of Consumer Research*, 20 (December), 393-417.

Bodur, H. Onur and Bianca Ghromann (2005), "Consumer Responses to Gift Receipt in Business-to-Business Consumer Contexts," *Psychology and Marketing*, 22 (May), 441-456.

Dodson, Kimberly J. and Russell W. Belk (1996), "The Birthday Card Minefield," in *Advances in Consumer Research*, Vol. 23, eds. Kim P. Corfman and John G. Lynch, Jr. Provo, UT: Association for Consumer Research, 14-20.

Dorsch, Michael J. and Stephen W. Kelly (1994), "An Investigation into the Intentions of Purchasing Executives to Reciprocate Vendor Gifts," *Journal of the Academy of Marketing Science*, 22 (4), 315-327.

Mauss, Marcel (1954), *The Gift: The Form and Reason for Exchange in Archaic Societies*, London: Cohen and West.

Robben, Henry S. J. and Theo M. M. Verhallen (1994), "Behavioral Costs as Determinants of Cost Perception and Preference Formation for Gifts to Receive and Gifts to Give," *Journal of Economic Psychology*, 15 (June), 333-350.

Rynning, M. (1989), "Reciprocity in a Gift-Giving Situation," *Journal of Social Psychology*, 129 (December), 769-778.

Sherry, John F., Jr. (1983), "Gift Giving in Anthropological Perspective," *Journal of Consumer Research*, 10 (September), 157-168.

Sherry, John F., Jr., Mary Ann McGrath, and Sidney Levy (1993), "The Dark Side of the Gift," *Journal of Business Research*, 28 (November), 225-244.

Wolfinbarger, Mary Finley (1990), "Motivations and Symbolism in Gift-Giving Behavior," in *Advances in Consumer Research*, Vol. 17, eds. Marvin E. Goldberg, Gerald Gorn, and Richard W. Pollay. Provo, UT: Association for Consumer Research, 699-706.

Wooten, David B. (2000), "Qualitative Steps toward an Expanded Model of Anxiety in Gift-Giving," *Journal of Consumer Research*, 27 (June), 84-95.

Consumer Alienation by Brands: Examining the Roles of Powerlessness and Relationship Type

Preeti Krishnan, University of Manitoba, Canada
Namita Bhatnagar, University of Manitoba, Canada
Rajesh Manchanda, University of Manitoba, Canada

The development of relationship theory in consumer research, with brands being considered as quasi-human relationship partners (Fournier 1998), has provided the foundation for examinations of consumer-brand relationships (e.g., Aaker, Fournier, and Brasel 2004; Aggarwal 2004, 2005; Muniz and O'Guinn 2001). The social relationship metaphor has been adopted in this domain and norms of *human* social ties have been found to govern consumption choices and behaviors (Fournier 1998; Aggarwal 2004). The negative fallouts of human ties many times include *felt alienation*—i.e., a sense of exclusion that is experienced by one of the relationship partners when the other induces a relationship stressor (i.e., a circumstance that is unfavorable or perceived as such; Panksepp 2005; Seeman 1959, 1975). Though studied extensively within sociological contexts (e.g., for women abandoned by their husbands; Arokach 2006), felt alienation remains unexamined within the domain of consumer-brand relationships. In this paper, we develop a process model of consumer alienation induced as a consequence of negative brand decisions, and propose that existing consumers can feel alienated by a brand, when their consumer-brand tie is subjected to a managerially-imposed relational stressor (e.g., closing of a convenient retail location, pulling of a product line from the shelf, or abandonment of a sub-brand; Fournier 1998; Muniz and Schau 2005).

We investigate how *powerlessness* (i.e., the perceived inability to amend an unfavorable situation or outcome, encompassing a sense of helplessness), considered by many scholars as an aspect of and antecedent to alienation (e.g., Ashforth 1989; Blauner 1964; Seeman 1959), influences consumer emotions, attitudes, and behavioral intentions under stressful situations, and specifically propose that a greater sense of alienation or exclusion will be experienced amongst those consumers that perceive themselves to be *powerless* (vis-à-vis *powerful*) in influencing brand decisions. This relationship is expected to be moderated by the relationship type that exists between brand and consumer, the treatment meted out by the brand during consumer efforts at decision reversal, outcomes of this effort, and perceived sincerity of any apologies proffered. Consumer-brand *relationship types* can vary on perceptual dimensions where they are seen as predominantly economic/transactional in nature (termed "exchange", as seen amongst business people) or based on social bonds (termed "communal", as seen amongst friends; Aggarwal 2004, 2005; Clark and Mills 1993). A change in perceived relationship type is expected once a stressor is introduced within a relationship—especially, one that transforms from communal to exchange amongst those consumers that feel powerless in influencing brand decisions.

Propositions of this research are tested within a series of laboratory experiments that use business undergraduate student samples. The service context of on-campus banking was used (found to be highly involving for the student sample, and used in prior research; Aggarwal 2004). Respondents were asked to imagine that they patronize the on-campus location of a hypothetical bank that then announces the intention to move far away off-campus (thus introducing a relational stressor). The first study examines the impact of variations in perceived powerlessness to change the bank's decision to relocate (control, powerless, versus powerful) and pre-existing relationship type (communal versus exchange) on attitudes toward the bank/employees/decision, felt alienation, emotions, behavioural intentions, and relationship transformation. The second study builds on the first by examining the additional impact of positive versus negative treatment by the bank while dealing with consumer efforts to reverse its relocation decision. Finally, study three examines the impact of perceived sincerity of apologies made by the bank upon reversal of its original stressful decision.

Results indicate that the mere presence of the stressor causes consumers to feel powerless to change the bank's decision and thus alienated by the brand. As the level of perceived power declines, consumers' sense of powerlessness, felt alienation, and intensity of negative emotions increase, making attitudes toward the bank/employees/decision and behavioral intentions unfavorable, and causing consumers to transform their relationship with the brand to be less social/friendly (communal) and more businesslike (exchange). Negative (positive) treatment of consumers by the bank is found to exacerbate (alleviate) the magnitude of perceived powerlessness, felt alienation, negative emotions, unfavorable attitudes and behavioral intentions. Attitude toward the decision (vis-à-vis bank/employees) is found to be most sensitive to perceptions of power, such that as perceived power declines, this attitude is least favourable—suggesting that consumers evaluate the stressor as a one-time negative event with the company and do not transfer negative emotions and cognitions generated from this event onto their more general attitudes towards the bank/employees. Felt alienation mediates the relationship between perceived powerlessness and consumer attitudes, which in turn mediate the impact of felt alienation on behavioural intentions.

This research has implications for both marketing theory and practice. From a theoretical standpoint, alienation and powerlessness find relevance and application within the domain of consumer-brand relationships, thereby, paving the way for interdisciplinary research. Our findings also support the stance of sociologists that consider powerlessness to be antecedent to alienation. Further, this research demonstrates that unlike human bonds, the perceived relationship dichotomy (communal and exchange) is not distinctive within consumer-brand ties, as the element of transaction/exchange is unavoidable here. From a managerial perspective, companies need to ensure that they avoid fostering feelings of powerlessness and perceptions of negative treatment amongst consumers while implementing unpopular brand decisions. Results found here also suggest that brands need not be overly anxious about overall equity dilution and consumer boycotts when a one-time negative decision has to be made.

Limitations and avenues for future research are also identified. Longitudinal data collection from real-life bank customers is planned to substantiate findings from student samples and to refine the process model. Future research is planned to evaluate the relevance of other aspects of alienation (delineated in sociology as—normlessness, meaninglessness, social isolation, and self-estrangement; Seeman 1959) to consumer-brand ties. Additional studies will also examine the impact of other relational stressors (e.g., breach of trust by company, presence of attractive alternatives) and contexts where relationship dichotomies are more distinct (e.g., high-risk investment banking, psychiatric counselling).

References

Aaker, Jennifer, Susan Fournier, and S. Adam Brasel (2004), "When Good Brands Do Bad," *Journal of Consumer Research*, 31 (1), 1-16.

Aggarwal, Pankaj (2004), "The Effects of Brand Relationship Norms on Consumer Attitudes and Behavior," *Journal of Consumer Research*, 31 (June), 87-101.

_____ and Sharmistha Law (2005), "Role of Relationship Norms in Processing Brand Information," *Journal of Consumer Research*, 32 (December), 453-64.

Arokach, Ami (2006), "Alienation and Domestic Abuse: How Abused Women Cope with Loneliness," *Social Indicators Research*, 78 (2), 327-40.

Ashforth, Blake E. (1989), "The Experience of Powerlessness in Organizations," *Organizational Behavior and Human Decision Processes*, 43 (2), 207-42.

Blauner, Robert (1964), *Alienation and Freedom: The Factory Worker and His Industry*, Chicago: University of Chicago Press.

Clark, Margaret S. and Judson Mills (1993), "The Difference Between Communal and Exchange Relationships: What It Is and What It Is Not," *Personality and Social Psychology Bulletin*, 19 (December), 684-91.

Fournier, Susan (1998), "Consumers and Their Brands: Developing Relationship Theory in Consumer Research," *Journal of Consumer Research*, 24 (March), 343-73.

Muniz, Albert M., Jr. and Thomas C. O'Guinn (2001), "Brand Community," *Journal of Consumer Research*, 27 (March), 412-32.

_____ and Hope J. Schau (2005), "Religiosity in the Abandoned Apple Newton Brand Community," *Journal of Consumer Research*, 31 (March), 737-47.

Panksepp, Jaak (2005), "Why Does Separation Distress Hurt? Comment on MacDonald and Leary," *Psychological Bulletin*, 131 (March), 224-30.

Seeman, Melvin (1959), "On the Meaning of Alienation," *American Sociological Review*, 24, 783-91.

_____ (1975), "Alienation Studies," *Annual Review of Sociology*, 1, 91-123.

Pulling-up or Pushing Down? Exploring Pro-leader and Anti-trailer Processing in Multi-option Consumer Choices

Simon J. Blanchard, Pennsylvania State University, USA
Margaret G. Meloy, Pennsylvania State University, USA
Kurt A. Carlson, Duke University, USA

Prior research has demonstrated that consumers distort new information to favor the option that is leading during a binary choice process (Carlson and Pearo 2004; Russo, Meloy and Medvec 1998). However, an unanswered question is whether and how consumers distort information in choices involving more than two options? Specifically, do decision makers evaluate new information to favor the leading option, to disfavor the trailing option(s), or do they do both? And what effect, if any, does the number of options in the consideration set have on how new information is evaluated? The current work seeks to address these questions.

Payne (1976) found that in multi-option settings, individuals quickly eliminate certain options from their consideration sets using limited information (see also Ordóñez, Benson, and Beach 1999). As such, the earliest focus in a choice process might be on eliminating options, perhaps by denigrating the trailing option(s). After the set is sufficiently reduced, processing to favor the leader may be the norm. As such, a primary objective of this work is to separate two types of processing: pro-leader and anti-trailer, and to determine if either or both dominate multi-option choice.

In *pro-leader* processing, respondents evaluate attribute information as overly favorable toward the option that is currently leading. Alternatively, *anti-trailer* processing involves the evaluation evaluate of new information as overly unfavorable toward the option that is trailing. The trailer is the option that was least preferred after seeing the previous piece of information. We test for both types of processing, as well as their onset, in an experimental study.

To examine the roles of pro-leader and anti-trailer processing in preferential choice, we traced not only how individuals processed new information, but we also tracked the relative strength of preference for each of the options throughout the choice process. Two decision contexts were used, restaurants and scholarship applicants. Restaurants represent a context in which individual preferences are more likely to drive the decision and the attributes used were more narrative. The scholarship scenario required that participants be more objective in their evaluations.

Participants and Design

The sample consisted of 244 students who received extra course credit for their research participation. Each was randomly assigned to one of twelve conditions. The manipulated factors were the number of available options (2, 4, or 6), the scenario (restaurants or scholarship applicants), and the order in which the attributes were presented (counter balanced forward or backward). Neither the scenario nor the information order had any impact on the results so they will not be discussed further.

Measures

Participants reviewed attribute information sequentially, where one page contained information for all of the options for that attribute. After reviewing the attribute information, participants gave two separate sets of responses. The first asked for an evaluation of each option using only the information on that page. Responses were captured on 9-point attractiveness scales (one for each option), where 1="very unattractive" and 9="very attractive". The second set of responses captured current cumulative preferences based on all the information seen to that point. This was accomplished with a race track image, on which participants placed the names of the options on the track for the portion of the choice process (i.e., race) that had been completed so far. Since the choice process was divided into six attributes, the race track was divided into six equal length segments. After each attribute was reviewed, participants put the name of the leading option at the front of the segment and the names of the other options somewhere further behind on the race track. The relative positions of the options were used to assess which option(s) were leading, trailing, or in between after each attribute.

By computing mean evaluations for each option on attribute t, conditional on whether the option was leading, trailing, or neither on attribute t-1, we can assess whether individuals engage in pro-leader, anti-trailer, or both types of processing. That is, pro-leader (anti-trailer) processing occurs when evaluations of the leading (trailing) option are significantly higher (lower) than when this same option is not leading (trailing).

Results

The evidence reveals that participants engaged in both pro-leader processing ($M=0.51$, $t(243)=7.87$, $p<.05$) and in anti-trailer processing ($M=0.42$, $t(243)=6.68$, $p<.01$). Moreover, analysis of variance revealed that both pro-leader processing and anti-trailer processing increased as the number of options present in the choice set increased (pro-leader: $F(2,232)=3.18$, $p<.05$; anti-trailer: $F(2, 232)=4.56$, $p<.05$). In other words, the greater the number of options being considered, the greater the tendency to support the leader and denigrate the trailer.

We used paired samples t-tests to assess the point at which (i.e., the serial position in the choice process where) each type of biased processing became significant. In the two-option case, the onset of pro-leader and anti-trailer processing were identical. In this case, biased processing occurred at the fourth attribute ($t(58)=2.64$, $p<.05$). In the four option case, pro-leader processing occurred earlier, on the third attribute (i.e., there was evidence of pro-leader processing on attribute three, four, five, and six, all $p<.05$), whereas anti-trailer processing did not appear until the fourth attribute (i.e., it existed for attributes four through six, all $p<.01$). In the six option case, pro-leader processing occurred even after just one attribute (all $p<.01$), while anti-trailer processing started with the third attribute (all $p<.05$).

Discussion

Participants engaged in both pro-leader and anti-trailer processing of new information, and the tendency to do so increased as the number of options increased. We did not find evidence to support the idea that consumers would use anti-trailer processing to eliminate options before using pro-leader processing to build support for an option to be selected. Rather, we found that both types of processing occur early in the choice process, and that the greater the number of options, the earlier they occur.

References

Carlson, Kurt A. and Lisa K. Pearo (2004), "Limiting predecisional distortion by prior valuation of attribute components," *Organizational Behavior and Human Decision Processes*, 94 (1), 48-59.

Payne, John W. (1976), "Task complexity and contingent processing in decision making: An information search and protocol analysis," *Organizational Behavior and Human Performance*, 16 (2), 366-87.

Russo, Edward J., Margaret G. Meloy, and Victoria H. Medvec (1998), "Predecisional distortion of product information," *Journal of Marketing Research*, 35 (4), 438-52.

The Effect of Social Trust on Consumers' Memory of Ads
Aiyin Wang, McGill University, Canada
Ulf Böckenholt, McGill University, Canada

Conceptualization

Social trust—opinions about whether one's fellow man can be trusted—have become important because of its observable consequences on economic exchanges (Warren 1999). A high level of social trust is commonly believed to encourage economic growth, because it reduces "transaction costs" resulting from social interactions. In contrast, a low level of social trust is argued to lead to economic barriers because of the lack of mutual confidence (Arrows 1972). In the marketing domain, marketing communication might be less effective to consumers with low levels of social trust because they tend to be more "defensive, watchful and vigilant" (Lewicki, McAllister and Bies 1998; p. 446). Consequently, they are more likely to scrutinize received information, and hence are less vulnerable to persuasive messages. However, as many advertisements receive little attention making them ineffective, close scrutiny by consumers can be valuable to the marketers. For instance, when the primary goal of the ad is to have consumers memorize some improved features of a new line of product, consumers with low level of social trust may look at the ad more carefully and therefore memorize better the features mentioned on the ad.

The extant literature suggests that people process information differently under different levels of trust (Schul and Mayo 2004; Priester and Petty 1995). Specifically, this research suggests that a low trust mind-set[4] motivates individuals to engage in more elaboration of the received messages than those with high trust mind-sets; even when the trust mind-set is unrelated to these messages. When information is processed at a deeper level by elaboration, recall and recognition of this information can also be enhanced as suggested by the "depth of processing model" (Craik and Jacoby 1976). Accordingly, consumers with mind-sets that are low in trust might be better at memorizing information in ads.

In this research, we are primarily concerned with high and low trust mind-sets induced by positive and negative generalized social trust (i.e. opinions about whether one's fellow man can be trusted) rather than ad-related trust. We expect that the activation of different levels of trust mind-sets will affect consumers' information processing style. That is, consumers with low trust mind-sets process ad information deeper than consumers with high trust mind-sets by securitizing the ads and possibly generating counter-arguments. We suggest that, this process will in turn improve the recall of ad information because of deeper information processing. Furthermore, we expect the effect of levels of trust mind-set on memory to be qualified by the type of messages provided in the ads (Darke and Ritchie 2007). Specifically, we expect that the effect of level of trust will be less pronounced when the type of message is about subjective claims as opposed to objective attributes.

Method

To test these hypotheses, we conducted a 2 (level of trust: high trust vs. low trust) x 2 (type of messages: objective attributes vs. subjective claims) mixed factorial design. One hundred and six university students were randomly assigned to either a high trust mind-set condition, or a low trust mind-set condition. All participants were asked to read a flyer which contained the manipulation of the high or low trust mind-set, and three experimental ads for three products. In the high trust mind-set condition, participants read a wallet dropping story from Reader's Digest (Mutz, 2005) with a trust-inducing content[5] prior to the presentation of the printed ads. In the low trust mind-set condition, participants read the same wallet dropping story but with a distrust-inducing content.[6] Involvement of the products was measured before the mind-set manipulation, and products with the highest and lowest involvement were selected for analyses. Each ad contains two types of information, objective attributes and subjective claims (e.g. "Ultra-Fiber fiber supplement is a source of natural fiber" vs. "Taking Ultra-Fiber fiber supplements, you will live healthier, better than ever!"). Need for cognition (Priester and Petty 1995) and general trust toward advertising (Darke and Richie 2007; Obermiller, Spangenberg and Maclachlan 2005) were measured as possible covariates for all the participants before presentation of the flyer. Subsequently, participants were asked to perform a recognition task regarding product attributes and claims made in the ads. Finally, purchase intentions were measured for all participants.

---

[4]Although there is debate on viewing trust and distrust as bipolar or two separate constructs, in the present research we assume that low trust refers to distrust and high trust refers to trust.

[5]In this condition, the story only reports about the people who try to return the wallet after finding it.

[6]In this condition, the story only reports about the people who kept the wallet after finding it.

Results

In order to dissociate memory accuracy from criterion shifts in the recognition of true and false statements, we conducted a signal detection theory (Green & Swets, 1966) analysis. Accuracy of memory (how well a person discriminates between correct and false statements) was estimated by the distance measure d. Results from a 2(level of trust) x 2(gender) x 2(product) x 2(types of message) ANOVA showed a significant two-way interaction of level of trust and message type (F (1, 102) =4.647, p-value=0.033). Specifically, when the message type is about objective attributes, participants with low trust mind-sets are higher in memory accuracy (d=1.12) than participants with high trust mind-sets (d=0.83; F (1, 104)=5.854, p =0.017); whereas when the message type is about objective claims, there is no difference between the two groups. There is also a main effect of message type (F (1, 105)=7.037, p=0.009), where objective attributes (d=0.97) are better memorized than subjective claims (d=0.79) for both groups in which participants have either high or low trust mind-sets. In summary, when the messages are objective attributes, participants with low trust mind-sets perform better in the recognition task than participants with high trust mind-sets. This result is consistent with the hypothesis that activation of a low trust mind-set triggers more careful processing of ad information and builds a stronger memory for participants with low- than high-trust mind-sets. However, when the messages are subjective claims, the level of trust did not have an effect on memory accuracy any longer, which supported the prediction that message type moderates the effect of level of trust. In addition, all participants memorized better the objective attributes than subjective claims. This result suggests that objective attributes may receive more attention than subjective claims, and that these attributes are scrutinized more by participants with low trust mind-sets than those with high trust mindsets. Subjective claims, on the other hand, may activate the negative stereotypes towards advertising in general (Darke and Ritchie 2007), and hence receive little attention from participants. Further analyses on possible covariates suggest that neither need for cognition nor general trust is correlated with the dependent variable d. The effect of level of trust on purchase intention is not significant for both products. This may due to the lack of a main effect of level of trust on memory accuracy. A significant difference in purchase intentions may be obtained in a future design in which stimuli ads contain only objective attributes as messages.

Contribution

Although much attention has been paid to the effect of low trust on information processing, little is known about its effect on memory. In addition, possible boundary conditions that qualify this effect have not been sufficiently discussed. The results of our research contribute to the theory of trust and distrust by suggesting that, when the ad information is about objective attributes, consumers with low trust mind-sets memorize ad information better; whereas when the ad information is about subjective claims, this effect weakens considerably. Second, research in consumer behavior has focused mostly on manipulating stimuli (ads)-relevant trust, and did not consider effect of social trust. The manipulation of different levels of social trust provides another dimension of trust that can influence consumers' information processing. Finally, our research offers also insights for practitioners by suggesting that low level of trust can enhance memory of certain type of ads information, whereby increase the effectiveness of marketing communication. From consumers' perspective, our research adds to their knowledge of persuasion by indicating that distrust does not always reduce the influences that ads impose on them.

References

Arrow , Kenneth (1972), "Gifts and Exchanges," *Philosophy and Public Affairs*, 1, 343-62.

Darke, Peter R. and Ritchie, Robin J. B. (2007), "The Defensive Consumer: Advertising Deception, Defensive Processing, and Distrust," *Journal of Marketing Research*, XLIV, 114-127.

Green, D.M., Swets J.A. (1966), *Signal Detection Theory and Psychophysics*, New York: Wiley.

Lewicki, Roy J., McAllister, Daniel J. and Bies, Robert J. (1998), "Trust and Distrust: New Relationships and Realities," *Academy of Management Review*, 23, 438-458.

Lockhart, R.D., Craik, F. I. M. and Jacoby, L. L. (1976), "Depth of Processing, Recognition and Recall: Some Aspects of a General Memory System," in *Recall and Recognition*, J. Brown, London: Wiley.

Mutz, Diana C. (2005), "Social Trust and E-commerce: Experimental Evidence for the Effects of Social Trust on Individuals' Economic Behavior," *Public Opinion Quarterly*, 69 (3), 393-416.

Obermiller, Carl, Spangenberg, Eric and MacLachlan, Douglas L. (2005), "Ad Skepticism: The Consequences of Disbelief," *Journal of Advertising*, 34 (3), 7-17.

Priester, Joseph R. and Petty, Richard E. (1995), "Source Attributions and Persuasion: Perceived Honesty as a Determinant of Message Scrutiny," *Personality and Social Psychology Bulletin*, 21, 637-654.

Schul, Yaacov, Mayo, Ruth and Burnstein, Eugene (2004), "Encoding Under Trust and Distrust: The Spontaneous Activation of Incongruent Cognitions," *Journal of Personality and Social Psychology*, 86 (5), 668-679.

Warren, Mark E (1999), "Introduction," in *Democracy and Trust*, ed. Mark E. Warren, Cambridge, UK: Cambridge University Press, 1-21.

The Impact of Perceptual Combination Effects on Asymmetry in Co-Branded Products

Lisanne Bouten, Delft University of Technology, The Netherlands
Effrosyni Petala, Delft University of Technology, The Netherlands
Amrita Kumar, Delft University of Technology, The Netherlands
Erik Jan Hultink, Delft University of Technology, The Netherlands

Abstract

Previous research has shown that perceptual (visual) and conceptual (textual) information can influence perceptions of (a)symmetry between two concepts that are part of a composite concept. We believe the same logic applies to co-branded products. One brand may be dominant over the other brand. An experiment with young women shows that perceptual cues influence perceptions of asymmetry (rather than conceptual cues). In addition, the perception of asymmetry mediates the effect of perceptual cues on product evaluation.

When two brands with different product portfolios develop a joint product, consumers perceive such a co-branded product as a composite concept. A composite concept is a combination of two categories referred to as a head and a modifier category (Wisniewski 1996, 1997). Park, Jun and Shocker (1996) studied the influence of combining conceptual cues on the consumers' perception of a co-branded product and found that respondents associated it more with the brand mentioned first (i.e., the header) than the brand mentioned last (i.e., the modifier). Thus, consumers perceive an asymmetry between the brands.

Besides the conceptual cues studied by Park et al. (1996), perceptual cues may also influence perceptions of asymmetry. Gregan-Paxton, Hoeffler, and Zhao (2005) examined how a single perceptual cue (i.e., a cell-phone or a PDA picture) and a single conceptual cue (i.e., a cell-phone or a PDA label) influenced the consumers' classification of a composite concept (e.g., combination of a PDA and a cell-phone). Their results showed that participants based their categorization on the perceptual cue rather than the conceptual cue.

Although these last results are relevant for the categorization literature, the before mentioned results do not necessarily apply to co-branded products. Gregan-Paxton et al. (2005) have not used any brands in their study, although a brand can form a relevant cue in itself (Boush and Loken 1991). In addition, the perceptual information of Gregan-Paxton et al. (2005) was similar to an existing product without any modification (e.g., it looked like a regular cell-phone). Co-branded products generally do not look exactly similar to an existing product of one brand, but are a modification of that product. This modification is achieved through the addition of design and/or brand elements of the other brand, creating a perceptual header-modifier relationship.

Here we compare the influence of combining perceptual cues to that of combining conceptual cues on perceptions of asymmetry between brands and on consumer evaluations of the co-branded product. For this purpose, we created an advertisement for a new co-branded moisturizing acne-control face-wash. This product combines the attributes of moisturizers (Nivea) and acne-control products (Clearasil) into a single product.

Method

The experiment used a two (combination of perceptual information more similar to Clearasil or Nivea) by two (combination of conceptual information more similar to Clearasil or Nivea) between subjects design. Based on this design we created four different advertisements. The relevant perceptual and conceptual cues were determined through a series of pre-tests. The combination of conceptual cues was similar to that used by Park et al. (1996)(e.g., "Clearasil acne-control face-wash with Nivea moisturizer"). A product designer created the perceptual cues: a thin white tube with blue graphics (more similar to Nivea), and a robust light- and dark blue tube with red graphics (more similar to Clearasil). The logo of the brand more similar to the perceptual information was visually superimposed over the logo of the other brand, imitating the conceptual header-modifier effect.

Our sample existed of 107 women between the age of 14 and 25 years ($M=17.9$), derived from the target population. Our dependent, perceptions of asymmetry between brands, was measured by three pre-tested items: "which brand does the product belong to more", "to which brand is the product more related", and, derived from Park et al. (1996), "which brand is more associated with the product" (7-point scale ranging from 'mostly Nivea' to 'mostly Clearasil', alpha>0.8). A two item 7-point scale measured product evaluation (Park et al. 1996). Finally, we controlled for familiarity, preference for one of the brands, relevance of 'moisturizing' and 'acne-control' for the target group, brand relevance during the purchase decision, and attitude toward the package.

Results

Perceptual information influences the perception of asymmetry between the brands ($F=78.63$, $p<.001$). The brand that is most similar to the perceptual information dominates. However, conceptual information has no influence on the perception of asymmetry ($F<1$, NS). Perceptual information also influences product evaluation ($F=6.61$, $p<.02$), with the perceptual information similar to Nivea more positively evaluated. Mediation analysis (Baron and Kenny 1986) shows that perception of asymmetry fully mediates the effect of perceptual information on product evaluation. Adding the control variables as covariates does not change these results.

Discussion

Gregan-Paxton et al. (2005) found that perceptual information influences categorization rather than conceptual information. However, they did not examine whether consumers perceive a possible asymmetry between the parts of a composite concept. We did, and we found that only perceptual information influences the perception of asymmetry in a co-branded product. Our findings also add to current co-branding literature, as this literature stream has only focused on the influence of conceptual information on evaluation (Park et al. 1996). We found that the consumers' perception of asymmetry mediates the effect of perceptual information on product evaluation. Thus, a co-branded product is differently evaluated when a particular brand is dominant through the product's visual appearance.

Previous categorization studies that investigated the simultaneous use of conceptual and perceptual information examined synthetic non-product stimuli (e.g., drawings with fictitious category labels)(Medin, Wattenmaker, and Hampson 1987; Yamauchi and Markman

2000). As a consequence of using synthetic stimuli, participants had to learn category membership during the experiment. Participants did this by combining both information sources offered. Thus, the independent influence of perceptual and conceptual information was difficult to assess. In contrast, we used familiar and discriminative conceptual and perceptual information, making the distinction between the influence of these cues on perceptions of asymmetry possible.

According to Gregan-Paxton et al. (2005) conceptual information becomes more important when perceptual information is less familiar. As we used both implicit and explicit perceptual and conceptual information it may be interesting to study the use of only implicit perceptual information (e.g., showing design elements of the brands without logos). It may be that when perceptual information is less explicit, consumers will rely more on conceptual information. Firms may thus be better able to influence the perception of asymmetry by adapting certain elements within the perceptual information, and thereby influencing product evaluation.

References

Baron, Reuben M. and David A. Kenny (1986), "The Moderator Mediator Variable Distinction in Social Psychological-Research-Conceptual, Strategic, and Statistical Considerations," *Journal of Personality and Social Psychology*, 51 (6), 1173-82.

Boush, David M. and Barbara Loken (1991), "A Process-Tracing Study of Brand Extension Evaluation," *Journal of Marketing Research, XXVIII*, 16-28.

Gregan-Paxton, Jennifer, Steve Hoeffler, and Min Zhao (2005), "When categorization is ambiguous: Factors that facilitate the use of a multiple category inference strategy," *Journal of Consumer Psychology*, 15 (2), 127-40.

Medin, Douglas L., William D. Wattenmaker, and Sarah E. Hampson (1987), "Family Resemblance, Conceptual Cohesiveness, and Category Construction," *Cognitive Psychology*, 19 (2), 242-79.

Park, C. Whan, Sung Youl Jun, and Allan D. Shocker (1996), "Composite branding alliances: an investigation of extension and feedback effects," *Journal of Marketing Research*, XXXIII, 453-66.

Wisniewski, Edward J. (1996), "Construal and similarity in conceptual combination," *Journal of Memory and Language*, 35 (3), 434-53.

— (1997), "When concepts combine," *Psychonomic Bulletin and Review*, 4 (2), 167-83.

Yamauchi, Takashi and Arthur B. Markman (2000), "Inference using categories," *Journal of Experimental Psychology-Learning Memory and Cognition*, 26 (3), 776-95.

Transfer of Value from Decision Interruption

Mathew S. Isaac, Northwestern University, USA
C. Miguel Brendl, Northwestern University, USA

Imagine a shopper whose cell phone rings while she is in the middle of choosing between two pairs of shoes at a department store. In consumption contexts like this one, purchase decisions are often temporarily delayed by unexpected and irrelevant interruptions. From a psychological standpoint, there is considerable evidence that decision interruption, and goal interruption more broadly, alters affect, attitudes, and choice. For example, Liu (2008) demonstrated that interruptions can impact the relative valuation of items in a choice set by shifting one's focus from feasibility to desirability of the potential options, thereby impacting choice itself. Our research contributes to the literature on goal interruption by providing the first empirical demonstration that the interruption and subsequent resumption of a decision task also affect the *value* placed on the chosen object.

Two opposing forces are activated when a decision, task, or goal is interrupted. On the one hand, an interruption generates negative feelings, such as annoyance and anxiety, and inhibits task performance since an impediment has been placed in front of an active goal (Bailey and Konstan 2006; Schiffman and Greist-Bousquet 1992; Schuh 1978). On the other hand, an interruption seems to be followed by a positive motivational force that increases recall (Zeigarnik 1927), resumption of the interrupted activity (Ovsiankina 1928), and valuation of the interrupted task (Cartwright 1942). It remains an open question as to when each of these forces is likely to dominate. Nelson, Meyvis, and Galak (working paper) recently found that participants watching an enjoyable television program evaluated the program more favorably when it was interrupted by commercials as compared to participants who viewed the program without interruption. The authors proposed a novel positive consequence of interruption, namely that it prevents hedonic adaptation to a pleasurable event.

Regardless of whether the net value of an interruption is positive or negative, we contend that individuals interrupted during a decision task routinely misattribute the value derived from task interruption to the decision object. There is considerable evidence that decision makers transfer the value created from using a specific decision-making process or strategy onto the outcome that they select. In explaining how value from a process can transfer to an object that is evaluated *after* goal pursuit has concluded, Higgins et al. (2003) proposed the concept of value confusion, claiming that "because people confuse the value experience [of the process or decision strategy] with the value experience of evaluating a subsequent object, they transfer the former to the latter." We argue here that, as a function of task involvement, interruption creates either net positive or net negative value for the decision task. This valuation subsequently spills over onto the chosen decision object.

Research by Wang and Calder (2006) on transportation (a highly analogous construct to involvement) supports our prediction that highly involved individuals will be more sensitive to the negative forces of decision interruption, whereas less involved individuals will be more sensitive to the positive forces of interruption. The authors found that participants who were highly transported by a narrative evaluated advertisements that did not intrude on their transportation experience (i.e. by appearing at the end of a magazine article) more positively than less transported participants. The pattern was reversed if the advertisements intruded on the transportation experience (i.e.

by appearing in the middle of the article). Evidently, participants who were highly transported by the narrative perceived an interruption to the transportation experience as a negative event that became associated with the advertisement. Of note is that Wang and Calder's research focused on evaluations of the interrupting event (the advertisement) rather than the task (the narrative) or a decision object, which may somewhat limit the applicability of their findings to the present research. Nevertheless, we reasonably hypothesize that involvement may moderate whether the positive forces or the negative forces associated with interruption will prevail.

In experiment 1, we attempted to show whether decision interruption would affect choice valuation, using task involvement as a potential moderator. Participants made a choice from a set of baby video monitors (if in the low involvement conditions) or a set of video iPods (if in the high involvement conditions). For half the subjects, this decision task was unexpectedly interrupted for 20 seconds. Stimuli were created such that one option in each choice set was objectively the most attractive and therefore chosen by nearly all participants across conditions. Four dependent variables related to the chosen object were captured after all participants had made a selection: Willingness to Pay (WTP), Satisfaction, Attitude, and Likelihood to Trade. On all four measures, highly involved participants who had been interrupted valued the chosen object (i.e., the selected iPod) less than participants who had not been interrupted. Conversely, participants in the low involvement conditions valued the chosen object (i.e., the selected baby monitor) more if they had been interrupted. A manipulation check confirmed that the experiment's involvement manipulation (the use of video iPods vs. baby monitors) was effective. We acknowledge that the involvement manipulation used in experiment 1 is subject to a host of alternate explanations since iPods and baby monitors differ along many dimensions, including familiarity and level of hedonism/utilitarianism. Nevertheless, our findings provide strong evidence that the effects of decision interruption transfer onto the chosen object, given the differences in valuation exhibited by interrupted and non-interrupted participants. The results also illustrate that interruption can cause spillover of *either* positive or negative affect onto the decision object, thereby raising the question as to when each type of affect will transfer, that is, which factors moderate the value transfer effect.

In subsequent experiments, we attempt to provide more rigorous support for task involvement as such a moderator by varying involvement at the level of the individual and keeping product information constant across participants. Assuming involvement moderates the value transfer effect, we intend to explore *why* increased involvement would cause individuals to be more influenced by the negative forces of decision interruption. Finally, we seek to implicate value confusion as the mechanism underlying the altered valuation of decision objects following an interruption.

References

Bailey, Brian P. and Joseph A. Konstan (2006), "On the need for attention-aware systems: Measuring effects of interruption on task performance, error rate, and affective state," *Computers in Human Behavior*, 22 (4), 685-708.

Cartwright, D. (1942), "The effect of interruption, completion, and failure upon the attractiveness of activities," *Journal of Experimental Psychology*, 31 (1), 1-16.

Higgins, E. Tory, Lorraine Chen Idson, Antonio L. Freitas, Scott Spiegel, and Daniel C. Molden (2003), "Transfer of Value From Fit," *Journal of Personality & Social Psychology*, 84 (6), 1140-53.

Liu, Wendy (2008), "Focusing on Desirability: The Effect of Decision Interruption and Suspension on Preferences" *Journal of Consumer Research*, 35, 640-52.

Nelson, Leif D., Tom Meyvis, and Jeff Galak (working paper), "Mispredicting Adaptation and the Consequences of Unwanted Disruptions: When Advertisements Make Television Programs More Enjoyable."

Ovsiankina, M. (1928), "The resumption of disrupted activities," *Psychologische Forschung*, 11, 302-79.

Schiffman, N. and S. Greist-Bousquet (1992), "The effect of task interruption and closure on perceived duration," *Bulletin of the Psychonomic Society*, 30 (1), 9-11.

Schuh, A.J. (1978), "Effects of an early interruption and note taking on listening accuracy and decision making in the interview," *Bulletin of the Psychonomic Society*, 12 (3), 242-44.

Wang, Jing and Bobby J. Calder (2006), "Media Transportation and Advertising," *Journal of Consumer Research*, 33, 151-62.

Zeigarnik, B. (1927), "On finished and unfinished tasks," in *A Source Book of Gestalt Psychology*, ed. W.D. Ellis, New York: Harcourt, Brace & World, 300-14.

The Appeal of Hidden Products

Aaron Brough, Northwestern University, USA

Can hiding a product from view increase its appeal? Normally, marketers aim to increase product visibility. However, this research suggests that products related to recently-fulfilled goals are evaluated more favorably when hidden than when visible, whereas the reverse is true for products relating to active goals. For example, a consumer who is not hungry may prefer food items in opaque packaging rather than transparent packaging, whereas a hungry consumer may exhibit the opposite preference.

Prior research has shown that objects relevant to active goals are evaluated more favorably than those relevant to recently fulfilled, inactive goals (Ferguson and Bargh 2004). The present research identifies an object's perceptual status as a moderator of this effect and suggests that occluding products relevant to fulfilled goals can boost their attractiveness, but occluding products relevant to active goals can decrease their attractiveness.

I propose a two-part explanation for this effect. First, given a limited capacity to attend to objects within the perceptual field, individuals may prefer not to clutter their surroundings with objects that could distract them from the pursuit of active goals. Thus, the adaptive practice of avoiding products related to already-fulfilled goals facilitates focusing on products relevant to active goals. Second, concealing a product from sight constitutes a form of avoidance. Therefore, obstructing one's view of an object related to a fulfilled goal reduces clutter in the visual field and helps satisfy the motivation to avoid potentially distracting objects. As this motive is satisfied, value is generated that can transfer to product evaluations. Across several studies, I attempt to demonstrate that compatibility between an individual's goal status and a product's perceptual status enhances product attractiveness.

A preliminary study examined how 58 participants differed in their evaluations of the U.S. Postal Service after reading a passage adapted from Horton and Rapp (2003) about a fictional character whose implied goal to walk to the mailbox was either fulfilled or unfulfilled. During the passage, the mailbox either remained visible or was hidden from the main character's view. When the character's goal was fulfilled, participants reported more favorable attitudes toward the U.S. Postal Service when the mailbox was hidden than when it was visible. However, this difference was not found among participants who read the version of the story in which the character's goal was unfulfilled. Because this study was not designed with the above hypothesis in mind, two additional studies were designed to more directly test the notion that products related to fulfilled goals are evaluated more favorably when hidden than when visible.

The first study compares evaluations of hidden products (opaque packaging) to visible products (transparent packaging) when participants have either an unfulfilled or a fulfilled goal to quench their thirst. Of 200 online participants, half were instructed to imagine that they were "extremely thirsty" and the other half were instructed to imagine that they were "not at all thirsty." All participants were then asked to choose between two plastic cups of water—one opaque and the other clear. Whereas the opaque cup was preferred by only 18% of participants in the thirsty condition, it was preferred by 27% of the participants in the not-thirsty condition. Thus, among participants whose goal to quench thirst was inactive, the water was more attractive when it was hidden from their sight by opaque packaging.

Because participants' choices may have been influenced by actual thirst levels, a second study was conducted in the laboratory in which thirst was manipulated. Furthermore, a behavioral measure rather than a self-reported measure was used as the primary dependent variable in the second study. Adopting a procedure similar to that used in Brendl et al. (2005), all participants consumed several salty pretzels upon arriving at the lab. Participants were then assigned to one of three conditions—very-thirsty, moderately-thirsty, or not-thirsty. Participants in the not-thirsty condition drank a full bottle of flavored water; those in the moderately-thirsty condition drank half of a bottle, and those in the very-thirsty condition did not drink anything. Participants who did not finish eating the pretzels or drinking the water were excluded from the analysis. Analysis of self-reported thirst confirmed that the thirst manipulation was successful.

Following the thirst manipulation and a filler task, participants learned about a new energy drink and were told that they would be permitted to sample it. On the desk of each participant were two cups—one opaque and one clear. Participants were instructed to bring one of the cups to the front of the room where they could pour as much or as little of the energy drink as they liked into their cup and drink it. The dependent measure of interest was the amount of beverage they consumed. As predicted, participants in the not-thirsty condition drank more when the beverage was poured into an opaque cup than when it was poured into a clear cup (M=53.8mL vs. 37.7mL). However, the reverse was true for moderately-thirsty participants; they consumed more of the beverage when it was easily visible in a clear cup than when it was partially occluded in an opaque cup (M=74.8mL vs. 50.0mL). Not surprisingly, the amount consumed by participants in the very-thirsty condition was higher than the other two conditions and did not differ by the cup into which it was poured (M=98.5mL (opaque) vs. 94.0mL (clear)).

Judging by consumption, the results of the second study suggest that participants whose thirst-quenching goal had already been fulfilled found the beverage more attractive in an opaque than in a transparent container, but that the opposite occurred for participants with an active goal to quench their thirst. A ceiling effect seems to exist in that once thirst levels reach a certain threshold, the container makes no difference in the attractiveness of the beverage.

Together, the evidence from these studies suggests that hiding a product from view can increase its appeal to consumers when that product is related to a recently fulfilled goal. By helping consumers avoid objects that might distract them from active goals, the act of visually concealing a product can actually enhance its attractiveness.

References

Brendl, C. Miguel, Amitava Chattopadhyay, Brett W. Pelham, and Mauricio Carvallo (2005), "Name letter branding: Valence transfers when product specific needs are active," *Journal of Consumer Research*. Vol 32(3) Dec 2005, 405-415.

Ferguson, Melissa J. and John A. Bargh (2004), "Liking Is for Doing: The Effects of Goal Pursuit on Automatic Evaluation," *Journal of Personality and Social Psychology*. Vol 87(5) Nov 2004, 557-572.

Horton, William S. and David N. Rapp (2003), "Out of sight, out of mind: Occlusion and the accessibility of information in narrative comprehension," *Psychonomic Bulletin & Review*. Vol 10(1) Mar 2003, 104-109.

The Interaction Effect of Mood and Price Level on Purchase Intention

Fengyan Cai, The Chinese University of Hong Kong, China
Felix Tang, The Chinese University of Hong Kong, China
Jian-Min Jia, The Chinese University of Hong Kong, China

Abstract

The present study examines the interaction of price level and mood on purchase intention. It integrates the mood congruency argument and mood regulation argument of affect influence by specifying how consumers' affective state influences their interpretation of price as a mood lifting, mood threatening, or neutral cue, which in turn guide their behavior. The experiment demonstrates that consumers in positive mood have higher intention to purchase a regular-priced product than consumers in negative mood, consistent with the mood congruency explanation. However, the reverse is true when the price of the product is high, as predicted by the mood regulation explanation.

Extant literature on impulsive and compulsive consumption demonstrated that people in positive or negative mood are more likely to buy than people in neutral mood (e.g., Faber and Christenson 1996). On the basis of the theory about mood congruency and mood regulation, the present study explores the interaction effect of price level and mood on consumers' purchase intention.

In terms of the impact of mood on behavior and judgment, there are two kinds of arguments. The mood congruency argument predicts that people in positive mood are more likely to believe the environment is benign and in turn more likely to do something (e.g., consumption), whereas negative mood is expected to lead to a less favorable evaluation of the environment, which inhibits actions (e.g., don't buy anything) (Bower 1981; Andrade 2005). The mood regulation argument states that people try to regulate their feelings to maximize their hedonic state (Isen 1987). It predicts people in positive mood will try to maintain and protect their positive mood, whereas people in negative mood are motivated to improve their mood. These motivations are contextual, stored in memory, and cannot be activated without situational cues (Vallerand 2004).

Price is an important marketplace cue for consumers (Gijsbrechts 1993). On one hand, it represents the amount of money consumers must give up to get the product (Volckner and Hofmann 2007). On the other hand, many consumers use price as a quality cue (Erickson and Johansson 1985). Thus, high price can be seen positively (good quality) and negatively (high cost). In the present study, we argue that whether consumers perceive high price as a good quality cue or as a high cost cue may depend on their incidental affective state. Specifically, since people in negative mood usually believe that shopping especially buying hedonic product will make them feel better (Faber 1992; Rook 1987), high price may be regarded as good quality and treated as a mood lifting cue; conversely, people usually avoid spending too much money on products they want to buy instead of products they should buy as such consumption may make them feel guilty later (Okada, 2005), in this respect, high price may be perceived as high cost and treated as a mood threatening cue. Interpreting the high price level as a signal of good quality product acts as a mood lifting cue; likewise, interpreting the high price level as high cost acts as a mood threatening cue. According to mood regulation argument mentioned above, people in positive mood have the motivation to protect their positive mood and people in negative mood try to improve their negative affective state, thus people in positive mood may be more sensitive to mood threatening cue (high cost), while people in negative mood are more likely to pay attention to the mood lifting cue (good quality). Therefore, we propose *H1a: For a high price product, people in negative mood are more likely to buy than those in positive mood.*

As utilitarian product with a regular price does not lift or threaten consumers' mood, both mood lifting cue and mood threatening cue are absent when a product's price is regular. Andrade(2005) demonstrated that people in positive mood are more likely to try a product than those in negative mood when mood lifting cue or mood threatening cue is absent. Based on mood congruent argument and Andrade's (2005) findings, we derived our *H1b: For a product with regular price, people in positive mood are more likely to buy than those in negative mood.*

Previously, we argue that people in positive mood perceive high price as a mood threatening cue while people in negative mood perceive high price as a mood lifting cue, so people in negative mood should perceive the quality of high-priced product better than those in negative mood do, which in turn influence consumers' purchase intention. Thus, we expect a mediation effect of perceived quality. That is, *H2: The interaction effect of mood and price on purchase intention is mediated by perceived quality.*

One hundred students participated a 2 (price level: high vs. regular) x 2 (mood: positive vs. negative) between-subject experiment for extra course credit. Mood manipulation method and experiment procedure were adopted from Zhang and Fishbach (2005). The stimulus was a ball pen, pretested and priced at RMB10 (approximately US$1.20) in the high price level condition and RMB3 (approximately US$0.40) in the regular price level condition. Perceived quality and purchase intention were the dependent variables. The manipulation of mood was successful ($F(1,98)=20.834$, $p<0.01$; $M_{positive}=5.76$, $M_{negative}=3.37$) and all scales were reliable, with Cronbach level above 0.70. The results of a two-way ANOVA showed that the interaction effect of mood and price level on purchase intention was significant ($F(1,96)=24.3$, $p<0.01$), the direction accorded with our expectation, and the simple main effects were also significant (Regular price condition: $M_{positive}=4.07$, $M_{negative}=3.11$; High price condition: $M_{positive}=2.91$, $M_{negative}=4.23$). Therefore, our H1a and H1b were supported. The results of hierarchical linear regression showed that the significant impact of the interaction term (Price*Mood) on purchase intention ($b=0.897$, $t=3.00$, $p<0.05$) became non-significant when perceived quality was added ($b=0.740$, $t=1.74$, $p>0.05$), supporting our H2.

This study contributes to the literature in two ways. Firstly, it extends existing literature about the impact of mood on behavior by demonstrating that it is consumers' perception of external cue instead of the cue per se that lead to different impact of mood on consumers' decision. Secondly, the evidence suggests that people in negative mood are more likely to buy expensive utilitarian product and people in positive mood tend to buy relatively cheap utilitarian product.

References

Andrade, E.B. (2005), "Behavioral Consequences of Affect: Combining Evaluative and Regulatory Mechanisms," *Journal of Consumer Research*, 32(December), 355-362.

Bower, G. H. (1981), "Mood and Memory," *American Psychologist*, 36(February), 129-148.

Erickson, G.M. and Johansson, J.K.(1985), "The Role of Price in Multi-attribute Product Evaluations," *Journal of Consumer Research*, 12(2), 195-199.

Faber, R.J. (1992), "Money Changes Everything: Compulsive Buying from a Biopsychosocial Perspective," *American Behavioral Scientist*, 35,809-819.

_____ and Christenson, G.A.(1996), "In the Mood to Buy: Differences in the Mood States Experienced by Compulsive Buyers and Other Consumers," *Psychology & Marketing,* 13(8), 803-819.

Forgas, J.P. (1995), "Mood and Judgment: The Affect Infusion Model (AIM)," *Psychological Bulletin*, 117(1), 39-66.

Gijsbrechts, E.(1993), "Prices and Pricing Research in Consumer Marketing: Some Recent Developments," *International Journal of Research in Marketing*, 10(2), 115-151.

Isen, A.M., Horn, N., and Rosenhan, D.L. (1973), "Effects of Success and Failure on Children's Generosity," *Journal of Personality and Social Psychology*, 27, 239-247.

Megill, J.L.(2003), "What Role Do the Emotions Play in Cognition?" *Consciousness & Emotion*, 41, 81-100.

Okada, E.M.(2005), "Justification Effects on Consumer Choice of Hedonic and Utilitarian Goods," *Journal of Marketing Research*, 42, 43-53.

Rook, J. (1973), "The Buying Impulse," *Journal of Consumer Research*, 14, 189-199.

Zhang, Y. and Fishbach, A. (2005), "The Role of Anticipated Emotions in the Endowment Effect," *Journal of Consumer Psychology*, 15, 4, 316-324.

Hear Is the Thing: The Influence of Sound-to-Writing Correspondence on Brand Name Processing

David Luna, City University of New York, USA
Marina Carnevale, City University of New York, USA
Dawn Lerman, Fordham University, USA

Abstract

Consumer research suggests that the sound of a brand name may influence consumer preferences. We explore how consumer auditorily process novel, non-word brand names and whether spelling the brand name correctly (e.g., when typing the name on a web browser) affects brand evaluations. Building on psycholinguistic research, we present the results of two empirical studies that investigate the underlying mechanisms of sound and sound-to-writing processing. Both phonetic and semantic associations to the auditorily presented brand name can lead to greater spelling accuracy.

A brand name may be a word or a non-word (i.e., a string of sounds that doesn't exist as a meaningful word, like Google). Consumer research has investigated some aspects of how brand sounds influence brand evaluations (e.g., phonetic symbolism; Lowrey and Shrum 2007; Yorkston and Menon 2004). However, little is known about how consumers process and later use sounds more generally. Moreover, the stimuli typically used to explore the effects of sound on evaluations have been visual, rather than auditory.

We present the results of two studies that explore how brand names are auditorily processed and how transcribing the auditory stimuli affects brand evaluations. Accurate spelling of a brand name presented auditorily (e.g., radio ads) is relevant because of the potential influence of correct spelling on the ability to find the brand (e.g., either online or at stores).

English is said to be a "deep" language, in which phonemes (i.e., sound representations) predominantly lack of a one-to-one relationship with graphemes (i.e., a letter or group of letters that represent a phoneme). The sound-to-writing correspondence of a word determines its level of consistency (Ziegler, Stone, and Jacobs 1997). For example, the phoneme /_@f/ corresponds to different graphemes, such as aff and alf. Therefore, the words staff and half have *inconsistent* sound-to-spelling mappings. Conversely, some phonemes (e.g., /_@g/) are represented by only one grapheme, so they have *consistent* mappings (ag), used in different words (e.g., tag, rag). This is an important distinction because it affects the process by which sound is transcribed.

There are two main routes to spelling (Coltheart 1981; Morton 1979). Through the direct route, that typically applies to frequently encountered words (Houghton and Zorzi 2003), individuals access the spelling of a word by retrieving semantic/phonological representations of the word stored in memory. When a non-word or an unfamiliar word is met, however, an indirect route occurs—that is, each of the phonemes is individually transcribed into its corresponding grapheme. Therefore, for novel non-word brand names, the consistency of a sound may facilitate their transcription by decreasing its ambiguity.

Non-word spelling might lead, however, to the use of both routes. For example, in cases of lexical priming (a word that sounds like the non-word is presented before the non-word), individuals can relate the non-word to one for which they already have a phonological representation, so the direct route could be used in addition to the indirect route (Cuetos 1993; Seymour and Dargie 1990).

In this research, we suggest that brand evaluations may be affected by the process of spelling the brand name. Successfully solving the spelling task may positively affect brand evaluations so the elaboration consumers engage into stimulates interest. This, however, should only happen for ambiguous (i.e., inconsistent) non-words.

Study 1

Method. Eighty-nine undergraduate business students participated in the study. We designed a 2 (consistency: consistent or inconsistent) x 2 (spelling prime: prime or no prime) between-subjects experiment. Each participant was exposed to eight audio clips, and, after each of them, had up to three trials to spell the brand name correctly. The sum of the number of trials left unused by each participant was utilized to assess one of the dependent variables: accuracy of spelling. Following the spelling task, the other dependent variable, brand evaluation, was measured through a seven-item scale.

Each audio clip provided the following information: product/service featured in the ad, last words in the website ad, and brand (website) name. We manipulated consistency of the brand names using the norms provided by Ziegler et al. (1997). The priming condition consisted of having the last word in the website ad prime (e.g., ..remove the t*ag*) or not prime (e.g., ..remove the paint) the intended spelling for the monosyllabic, non-word brand name that immediately followed (e.g., P*ag*.com).

Results. Results showed a significant interaction of priming and consistency on spelling accuracy (F(1, 88)=13.60, *p*<.001). For consistent brands, respondents were able to use the direct route to spelling regardless of priming condition. However, for inconsistent brands (which initially inhibit the direct route to spelling), priming had a positive effect on spelling accuracy (F(1, 85)=20.05, *p*<.001).

Interestingly, spelling accuracy influenced brand evaluations in the inconsistent condition (F(1, 49)=3.94, *p*<0.05), but not in the consistent condition (F(1, 38=.45, *p*=0.505). Therefore, only when the direct route to spelling was inhibited (inconsistent non-words), evaluations were enhanced by guessing the correct spelling.

Study 2

Study 2 examines how, when the direct route to spelling is inhibited, increased semantic elaboration can lead to greater spelling accuracy and higher evaluations. We expect that, for inconsistent brands, semantic elaboration will only enhance brand evaluations when the direct route is facilitated by priming.

Method. Seventy-five undergraduate students participated in the study. We designed a 2 (Semantic elaboration: elaboration or no elaboration) x 2 (spelling prime: prime or no prime) between-subjects experiment. Semantic elaboration was operationalized by changing the word used in the priming sentence to be congruent (e.g., fuel) or incongruent (e.g., staff) with the product category (e.g., cars). We used study 1's inconsistent brand names. The procedure and measures were the same as in study 1.

Results. Results showed that both elaboration and spelling prime had significant main effects on spelling accuracy (F (1, 74)=4.54, *p*<0.05 and F(1, 74)=18.45, *p*<.01, respectively). Those effects were qualified by a significant interaction of priming and elaboration on brand evaluations (F(1, 74)=5.75, *p*<0.05). As expected, when primed, participants in the elaboration condition had higher brand evaluations than those in the no-elaboration condition (F(1, 74)=4.10, *p*<.05). In the no-prime condition, however, there was no effect of elaboration on brand evaluations (F(1, 74)=1.816, *p*=.18). Finally, spelling accuracy proved to be a significant predictor of brand evaluations (F (1, 74)=5.99, *p*<0.05).

Conclusion

By exploring the underlying mechanisms of sound-to-writing processing, we develop a greater understanding of how consumers process brand names auditorily and how can these processes be facilitated and affect brand evaluations.

References

Coltheart, Max (1981), "Disorders of Reading and their implications for models of normal reading," *Visible language*, 15 (3), 245-86.

Cuetos, Fernando (1993), "Writing Processes in a Shallow Orthography," *Reading and Writing: An Interdisciplinary Quarterly*, 5, 17-28.

Houghton, George, and Marco Zorzi (2003), "Normal and Impaired Spelling in a Connectionist Dual-Route Architecture," *Cognitive Neuropsychology*, 20 (2), 115-62.

Lowrey, Tina M. and Larry J. Shrum (2007), "Phonetic Symbolism and Brand Name Preference," *Journal of Consumer Research*, 34 (October), 406-14.

McQuarrie, Edward F., and David G. Mick (1996), "Figures of Rhetoric in Advertising Language," *Journal of Consumer Research*, 22, (March), 424-37.

Morton, John (1979), "Word Recognition" in *Psycholinguistics 2: Structures and Processes,* ed. John Morton and John C. Marshall, Cambridge, MA: MIT, 107-156.

Seymour, Philip H.K., and Alison Dargie (1990), "Associative Priming and Orthographic Choice in Nonword Spelling," *The European Journal of Cognitive Psychology*, 2 (4), 395-480.

Yorkston, Eric Y. and Geeta Menon (2004), "A Sound Idea: Phonetic effects of Brand Names on Consumer Judgements," *Journal of Consumer Research*, 31 (June), 43-51.

Ziegler, Johannes, Gregory O. Stone, and Arthur M. Jacobs (1997), "What is the pronunciation for *-ough* and the spelling for /u/? A database for computing feedforward and feedback consistency in English," *Behavior Research Methods, Instruments & Computers,* 29 (4), 600-18.

The Influence of Service Employee Characteristics on Customer Choice and Post-Choice Satisfaction

Nancy J. Sirianni, Arizona State University. USA
Iana Castro-Nelson, Arizona State University. USA
Andrea C. Morales, Arizona State University. USA
Gavan J. Fitzsimons, Duke University. USA

Abstract

Interaction with a frontline employee is common in most retail and service encounters in which customers are looking to make product and service choices. During these customer-employee interactions, customers are exposed to service employees' personal characteristics, such as their displayed creativity, which can influence consumer behavior. The proposed research seeks to develop an understanding of how service employee characteristics influence customer choice and post-choice satisfaction.

Frontline employees are the store associates, sales floor personnel, and other service workers who personally interact with customers in retail and service encounters (Ellinger, Almadag, and Ellinger 2007). Past research notes the importance of these employees in their interactions with customers, as these workers can have a powerful impact on customers' perceptions of the brand and the firm, and on customers' overall satisfaction with the service encounter and the firm (Czepiel, Solomon, and Surprenant 1985; Zeithaml, Berry, and Parasuraman 1996; Zeithaml, Bitner, and Gremler 2006).

Each and every action by frontline employees can contribute to the total experience of customers (Pine and Gilmore 1999), including employee-demonstrated attitudes and behaviors, which can influence customers' perceptions of the service rendered (Bowen and Schneider 1985). In sum, the literature has demonstrated that customer-facing employees' actions play a pivotal role in shaping customers' experiences during the service encounter, but outside of studies of employee attractiveness (Reingen and Kernan 1993), little is known about how service employees' appearances can influence customer preferences and behavior during these interactions.

For example, does a person choosing to redecorate his or her house prefer a creative- or conservative-looking interior designer? Does having a creative-looking interior designer lead the person to make more creative choices and, if so, how high is the person's post-choice satisfaction? Our research seeks to address these questions.

Past work in psychology and marketing has provided compelling evidence that individuals can be primed to behave in certain ways. Priming studies are concerned with the temporary activation of an individual's representations and how these internal readinesses interact with environmental information to produce perceptions, evaluations, motivations and social behavior (Bargh 1997). Our proposed research seeks to extend priming theory by investigating how service employees' appearances can influence customers and their choices during service encounters and understanding how these choices are evaluated by customers.

Pre-tests-Method and Results

Three pre-tests were conducted to determine how respondents would evaluate customer-facing employees on five dimensions, some of which were derived from the services literature, including competence, internal personality factors, external personality factors, creativity and conservativeness. In pre-test I, respondents were asked to evaluate photographs of employees on the five dimensions mentioned above. In pre-test II, respondents were asked to evaluate job titles (for example, interior designer) on the same five dimensions. Based on the results of pre-tests I and II, photographs and job titles were chosen to be tested together. In pre-test III, participants were asked to evaluate the employee in the photograph based on the job title given. The conditions included photographs and job titles that were matched (creative photo and creative job title) and photographs and job titles that were mismatched (creative photo and conservative job title). Participants were also asked to indicate the likelihood that they would hire the employee in the photograph to perform the job title specified.

The results from the pre-tests indicate that customers evaluate service employees differently based on whether they look creative or conservative. Participants were more likely to hire the service employees in the conditions where the photograph and job title matched (creative photograph and creative job title or conservative photograph and conservative job title) than in the conditions where the photograph and job title did not match.

Study 1-Method and Preliminary Results

The goal of the pre-tests was to develop an understanding of how customers would evaluate service employees on five key dimensions (competence, internal personality factors, external personality factors, creativity, and conservativeness) and whether the employees' appearance (creative or conservative) would influence the customers' likelihood to hire that employee. Study I was designed to address the question: Do employee characteristics (for example displayed creativity) affect customer choice and, if so, how satisfied are customers with those choices?

Data were collected from a convenience sample of 271 students enrolled in an introductory Marketing course at a large southwestern university. Participants were randomly assigned to one of two conditions: creative or conservative. The study employed the use of a confederate who was either creatively dressed or conservatively dressed, based on the condition. The confederate provided participants with the cover story that she worked for a major office supply company that was seeking customer feedback on one of its products. Participants were told that they would be given a pen as a gift for their participation and that they could select the color of the pen. Participants were presented with both creative and conservative pen color choices and were asked to make an actual choice.

After completing a number of filler tasks, participants answered questions regarding their overall evaluations and quality of the pen, satisfaction and regret with their pen choice, evaluations of the service employee (confederate), their own need for uniqueness, and their own chronic creativity motivation.

To check that the confederate portrayed the desired characteristic, participants completed an evaluation of the confederate on the five dimensions discussed above. Participants in the creative condition rated the confederate as more creative and less conservative than participants in the conservative condition, who rated the confederate as less creative and more conservative. The differences in scores were statistically significant at the $p<.05$ level.

The initial analysis focused on the key dependent variable of pen choice. While there were no significant differences in pen choice between the creative and the conservative conditions, a large number of the participants (32 percent) chose a creative-colored pen in the creative conditions. Further analysis will be conducted for post-choice satisfaction and regret.

Discussion

Our initial findings shed light on the importance of service employee appearances, offering a fresh perspective that customers have preferences regarding the personal characteristics of the frontline employees with whom they interact and that these characteristics can potentially influence customer choice during customer-employee service encounters. Our future work in this area will extend this investigation to include post-choice satisfaction and regret to further understand how these choices are evaluated after they are made. The results of our study may have strong managerial implications, given that customers may not be as satisfied with their choices when these choices were influenced by the employees' characteristics, and their reduced satisfaction with the choice could influence their overall satisfaction with the experience and the firm.

References

Bargh, John A. (1997), "The Automaticity of Everyday Life," in *Advances in Social Cognition*, Vol. 10, ed. Robert S. Wyer, Jr., Mahwah, New Jersey: Earlbaum, 1-61.

Bowen, David E. and Benjamin Schneider (1985), "Boundary-Spanning Role Employees and the Service Encounter: Some Guidelines for Management and Research," in *The Service Encounter: Managing Employee/Customer Interaction in Service Businesses*, ed. John A. Czepiel, Michael R. Solomon and Carol F. Surprenant, Lexington, MA: D.C. Heath and Company, 127-47.

Czepiel, John A., Michael R. Solomon, and Carol F. Surprenant, eds. (1985), *The Service Encounter: Managing Employee/Customer Interaction in Service Businesses*, Lexington, Massachusetts: Lexington Books.

Ellinger, Alexander E., Ayse Banu Almadag, and Andrea D. Ellinger (2007), "An Examination of Organizations' Frontline Service Employee Development Practices," *Human Resource Development Quarterly*, 18 (3), 293-314.

Pine, B. Joseph and James H. Gilmore (1999), *The Experience Economy: Work is Theatre & Every Business a Stage*, Boston: Harvard Business School Press.

Reingen, Peter H. and Jerome B. Kernan (1993), "Social Perception and Interpersonal Influence: Some Consequences of the Physical Attractiveness Stereotype in a Personal Selling Setting," *Journal of Consumer Psychology*, 2 (1), 25-38.

Zeithaml, Valarie A., Leonard L. Berry, and A. Parasuraman (1996), "The Behavioral Consequences of Service Quality," *Journal of Marketing*, 60 (April), 31-46.

Zeithaml, Valarie A., Mary Jo Bitner, and Dwayne D. Gremler (2006), *Services Marketing*, Boston: McGraw-Hill Irwin.

The Consequences of Retailer vs. Media Communication About the Use of Intrusive Marketing Practices on Customer Attitudes, Satisfaction, Trust and Loyalty

Marco Lalos, University of Lausanne, Switzerland
Ghislaine Cestre, University of Lausanne, Switzerland

This study is encompassed in a broader research that investigates the boundaries of privacy and intrusiveness and differentiates their specific influence on consumer attitudes and customer-firm relationship constructs. Privacy has been extensively studied (Culnan, 1993; Dahl, Manchanda, & Argo, 2001; Hoffman & Novak, 1999; Phelps, Nowak, & Ferrell, 2000; White, 2004). Despite confusions between the two concepts by a number of authors, privacy can be defined as the perceived control over one's personal information and control over unsolicited presence of others (Goodwin, 1991), and intrusiveness as the interruption of a process (Li et al., 2002). Intrusiveness is considered to have deep implications on customer-firm relationships and in advertising (Aaker & Bruzzone, 1985; Edwards, Li, & Lee, 2002; Ha, 1996; Wang and Calder, 2006).

This study focuses on the impact that communication about the use of a data collection method, perceived to be intrusive, may have on consumers' attitudes, satisfaction, trust and loyalty. In this study, intrusiveness is contextualized in a retail environment, following the work of Larson, Bradlow and Fader (2005) and Klabjan (2005). The retail context provides flexibility to manipulate compensation, communication, and intrusiveness. Intrusiveness is operationalized in the form of a data collection method based on RFID[7] technology, earlier findings having revealed that RFID elicits high levels of perceived intrusiveness. Due to RFID's reported salient effect on consumers, it can be expected that individuals informed about the presence of such intrusive data collection method in the retailing environment, will report less favorable attitudes and satisfaction concerning their shopping experience, than if unaware of RFID's presence.

H1: Individuals' attitudes and satisfaction toward the retailer are less positive when information about the existence and purpose of an intrusive consumer data collection method is provided by the retailer, than when no information is provided

Building on the social exchange theory (Emerson 1981; White, 2004), it can be argued that intrusiveness effect can be outweighed (moderated) by an expected benefit, such as a compensation given to consumers. Individuals were shown to value compensations differently (Davis, Bagozzi and Warshaw, 1989), thus, different compensation types can be expected to arouse differently attitudes and satisfaction. Three types of compensations, economic, functional and hedonic, are defined in the literature (Gefen, Karahanna, and Straub, 2003; Moon and Kim, 2001). Younger individuals were shown to be more sensitive to economic rewards than more mature individuals, who may seek to experience diversity and service quality (Venkatesh et al. 2003). Economic compensation was thus retained in this study, based on a student sample, as it is expected to outweigh perceived intrusiveness, positively affecting attitudes and satisfaction.

H2: Individuals' attitudes and satisfaction toward the retailer are unaffected by information provided by the retailer about the existence and purpose of an intrusive consumer data collection method, when economic compensation is provided

---

[7]Radio Frequency Identification

Misleading communication can be perceived by consumers as deceiving (Darke & Ritchie, 2007). Hiding the purpose or existence of data collection practices will likely be perceived by consumers, upon awareness, as misleading, and may elicit feelings of irritation or betrayal, thus generating lower levels of trust and loyalty. Conversely, if the retailer openly communicates, consumer's levels of trust and loyalty may remain unchanged:

H3: Individuals' level of trust and loyalty remain unaffected when the retailer communicates openly about its data collection practices; it is negatively affected when the communication is made by a third party (media)

A scenario-based experiment was carried out among a group of 79 students, to test the hypotheses. Portrayed goods and store type were chosen to be familiar to respondents. To assess the effects of communication / no communication (H1), and of compensation (H2) on attitudes and satisfaction, respondents were placed in one of two scenarios: either the retailer informed them about the use of RFID (placed on shopping carts and product packagings), or there was no information provided. Three types of compensations (economic, functional or hedonic) were proposed by the retailer as means to arouse their attitude and satisfaction positively. To test retailer-induced vs. media-based communication on consumers' trust and loyalty (H3), respondents were placed in one of two scenarios: either the retailer informed them about the use of RFID, or they were later informed by the press about it. Loyalty and trust in the retailer were measured at different times with one hour interval. Validated Likert scales were used to measure every construct, reporting satisfactory Alphas. Manipulation checks were successful and intrusiveness was controlled: no RFID ($M=4.07$, $SD=1.47$) vs. RFID ($M=5.12$, SD=1.21, F $(1,40)=6.29$, $p=0.016$). ANOVAs and paired-sample t-tests were run to test the hypotheses.

H1 is supported. The averages of the three attitudes (under economic, functional and hedonic compensation) were calculated, lower attitudes toward the retailer under the retailer-communication scenario ($M=4.30$, $SD=1.42$) than under the no-communication scenario ($M=5.25$, $SD=1.17$, $F(1,40)=5.48$, $p=0.024$) were confirmed. Similarly, lower levels of satisfaction were confirmed under the retailer-communication scenario ($M=4.06$, $SD=1.23$), than under the no-communication scenario ($M=5.02$, $SD=1.13$, $F(1,40)=6.99$, $p=0.012$).

H2 is supported. No significant attitude change was reported between the no-communication scenario ($M=5.30$, $SD=1.49$) and the retailer-communication scenario ($M=4.66, SD=1.73, F(1,40)=1.632, p=$ n.s.). Also, no significant change in satisfaction occurred, despite the communication: no-communication ($M=5.15$, $SD=1.36$); retailer-communication ($M=4.50$, $SD=1.60$, $F(1,40)=1.955$, $p=$n.s.)

H3 is supported. Regarding trust: under the retailer-communication scenario, prior trust ($M=3.77$, $SD=1.32$) is not significantly higher than trust after stimulus ($M=3.66$, $SD=1.18$, $t(20)=0.51$, $p=$ n.s.). Under the media-communication scenario, prior trust ($M=4.03$, $SD=1.032$) is significantly higher than trust after stimulus ($M=3.27$. $SD=1.25$, $t(36)=4.40$, $p<0.001$). Regarding loyalty: under the retailer-communication scenario, prior loyalty ($M=4.43$, $SD=1.34$) is not significantly higher than loyalty after ($M=3.92$, $SD=1.48$, $t(20)=1.54$, $p=$ n.s.). Under the media-communication scenario, prior loyalty ($M=4.84$, $SD=1.33$) is significantly higher than loyalty after ($M=3.58$, $SD=1.70$, $t(36)=4.98$, $p<0.001$).

This research reveals the dilemma of choosing between disclosing truthfully the use of intrusive data collection methods knowing the impact on attitudes and satisfaction, and deciding not to communicate and bear the risk of a significant decrease in the levels of trust and loyalty should customers learn about the use of intrusive methods from a third party. These results encourage pursuing the research by manipulating new moderating variables over a heterogeneous population.

References

Aaker, David and Donald Bruzzone (1985), "Causes of Irritation in Advertising," *Journal of Marketing*, 49 (2), 47-57.

Culnan, Mary J. (1993), ""How did they get my name?": An Exploratory Investigation of Consumer Attitudes toward Secondary Information Use," *MIS Quarterly*, 17 (3), 341-363.

Dahl, Darren W., Rajesh V. Manchanda and Jennifer J. Argo (2001), "Embarrassment in Consumer Purchase: The Roles of Social Presence and Purchase Familiarity," *Journal of Consumer Research*, 28 (3), 473-481.

Darke, Peter R. and Robin J. B. Ritchie (2007), "The Defensive Consumer: Advertising Deception, Defensive Processing, and Distrust," *Journal of Marketing Research*, 44 (1), 114-127.

Davis, Fred D., Richard P. Bagozzi, and Paul R. Warshaw (1989), "User Acceptance of Computer Technology: A Comparison of two Models," *Management Science*, 35 (8), 982-1003.

Edwards, Steven M., Hairong Li and Joo-Hyun Lee (2002), "Forced Exposure and Psychological Reactance: Antecedents and Consequences of the Perceived Intrusiveness of Pop-Up Ads," *Journal of Advertising*, 31 (3), 84-95.

Emerson, Richard M. (1981), "*Social Exchange Theory*," In M. Rosenberg and R. H. Turner (Eds.), Social psychology: Sociological Perspectives (31-65). New York: Basic Books.

Gefen, David, Elena Karahanna, and Detmar W. Straub (2003), "Trust and TAM in Online Shopping: An Integrated Model," *MIS Quarterly*, 27 (1), 51-90.

Goodwin, Cathy (1991), "Privacy: Recognition of a Consumer Right", *Journal of Public Policy and Marketing*, 10 (1), 149-166.

Ha, Louisa (1996), "Advertising Clutter in Consumer Magazines: Dimensions and Effects," *Journal of Advertising Research*, 36 (4), 76-84.

Hoffman Donna L. and Thomas P. Novak (1999), "Building Consumer Trust Online," *Communications of the ACM*, 42 (4), 80-85.

Klabjan, Diego (2005), "In-Store One-to-One Marketing with RFID," in *Informs San Francisco-2005,*. San Francisco, USA.

Larson, Jeffrey S., Eric T. Bradlow and Peter S. Fader (2005), "An Exploratory Look at Supermarket Shopping Paths," *International Journal of Research in Marketing*, 22 (4), 395-414.

Li, Hairong, Steven M. Edwards and Joo-Hyun Lee (2002), "Measuring the Intrusiveness of Advertisements: Scale Development and Validation," *Journal of Advertising*, 31 (2), 37-47.

Moon, Ji-Won, and Young-Goul Kim (2001) "Extending the TAM for a World-Wide-Web context," *Information & Management*, 38 (2001), 217-230.

Phelps, Joseph, Glen Nowak and Elizabeth Ferrell (2000), "Privacy Concerns and Consumer Willingness to Provide Personal Information," *Journal of Public Policy and Marketing,* 19 (1), 27-41.

Venkatesh, Viswanath, Michael G. Morris, Gordon B. Davis, and Fred D. Davis (2003), "User Acceptance of Information Technology: Toward a Unified View," *MIS Quarterly,* 27 (3), 425-478.

Wang, Jing, and Bobby J. Calder (2006), "Media Transportation and Advertising," *Journal of Consumer Research,* 33 (3), 151-162.

White, Tiffany B. (2004), "Consumer Disclosure and Disclosure Avoidance: A Motivational Framework," *Journal of Consumer Psychology,* 14 (1&2), 41-51.

Is Seeing Believing? Consumer Responses to Opacity of Product Packaging

Sucharita Chandran, Boston University, USA
Rishtee Kumar Batra, Boston University, USA
Benjamin Lawrence, Boston University, USA

Product and packaging design has shown to influence consumer reactions and purchase behaviors (Bloch 1995; Holbrook and Anand 1992; Raghubir and Greenleaf 2006; Veryzer 1993, 1999). Research in visual aesthetics has focused on product shapes and dimensions (Krider, Raghubir, and Krishna 2001; Yang and Raghubir 2005) while one specific characteristic of packaging, its opacity or lack of transparency has received little attention (Dantas et al. 2004). This research addresses this important aspect of packaging design, transparency, which has been neglected in visual marketing research. Three studies investigate if and when transparency in packaging affects consumers' product attitudes and examines trust as a mediating factor.

Study One

Study one was an exploratory study aimed at understanding how packaging of familiar and unfamiliar brands affects consumers' perceived quality, trust, and willingness to pay. This study employed a 2(Brand: Familiar/Unfamiliar) X 2(Packaging: Clear/Opaque) between-subjects design in which 128 participants were asked to evaluate either an opaque package of mouthwash or a comparable clear package manufactured by either Landers (unfamiliar brand) or Listerine (familiar brand). Subjects were asked how much they would be willing to pay for the mouthwash and then to rate the perceived quality of the product. Next, participants were asked to describe what input they used when making their judgments of quality regarding the mouthwash. Finally, participants answered a series of four questions aimed at gauging their familiarity with the brand and attitude toward the brand. Neither novelty nor attractiveness of the packaging were found to be significant covariates in explaining any of the key dependent measures and were thus not used for further analysis.

With respect to perceived quality, a two-way ANOVA revealed a significant interaction effect between brand and packaging ($F(1,127)=3.85$, $p=.052$) such that for Lander's mouthwash, participants felt that the mouthwash was of better quality when packaged in a clear bottle than opaque bottle (mean 3.70 versus 3.47) but the opposite was true for Listerine (mean 5.38 versus 5.96). For willingness to pay, a two-way ANOVA also revealed a significant interaction effect between brand and packaging ($F(1,127)=5.41$, $p<.05$) such that for the unfamiliar brand of mouthwash (Lander's) participants were willing to pay significantly more for a clear bottle (mean=\$3.23) versus an opaque bottle (mean=\$2.73). Interestingly, however, when the brand of mouthwash was familiar (Listerine), there was no significant difference in participants willingness to pay for clear versus opaque bottles (mean=\$3.72 versus \$4.12). An analysis of participants' open-ended responses indicated that for unfamiliar brands, consumers were skeptical of the contents of bottle of mouthwash where as for a more familiar brand; there was not a sense of distrust due to packaging. Study two further examines the role of trust in the process of forming product attitudes based on packaging attributes.

Study Two

Study two examined the role of product type upon response to packaging design. In this 2(Product: Cough syrup/Toilet Cleaner) X 2(Packaging: Clear/Opaque), between-subjects study, 133 participants rated one of four possible product-packaging combinations along five performance-related dimensions. As in the past study, in order to rule out product attractiveness as an alternative explanation for the findings, two measures were utilized to gauge product attractiveness, but were not found to be significant.

With respect to perceived performance, a two-way ANOVA revealed a significant interaction effect between product and packaging ($F(1,132)=21.11$, $p=.000$), with all means being significantly different from one another. Participants evaluating the toilet bowl cleaner felt that a transparent package was of poorer quality than an opaque package (mean 1.74 versus 3.87) while for cough syrup, the opposite was true, they felt that a transparently packaged cough syrup was of better quality than an opaquely packaged cough syrup (mean 3.33 versus 2.77). A mediation analysis revealed that trust was a significant mediator in the inference of product quality from product packaging such that for combinations that were inconsistent with expectations (e.g. clear toilet bowl cleaner), participants' trust for the product was significantly lower than conditions in which packaging was consistent with expectations (e.g. opaque toilet bowl cleaner). Given that trust is a mediating mechanism that helps explain the results found in both study one and study two, the next study sought to reverse the effects of study two by enhancing trust in the inconsistent product packaging conditions.

Study Three

Study three was identical to study two in most dimensions. For this study, only the toilet cleaner product category was used, with the goal being to enhance trust in the transparently packaged toilet bowl cleaner and thus enhance ratings of product quality and performance. 89 subjects participated in a between-subjects study in which packaging (clear/opaque) was manipulated as well as the presence or absence of trust-enhancing information (eco-friendly claims made/no claims made). To increase the level of trust in the inconsistent toilet bowl cleaner package a claim was made that the packaging reflects an attempt to be environmentally friendly. The dependent measures taken in this study were identical to those in study two, however, additional measures of participants' eco-friendliness were taken to rule out environmental consciousness as a possible confound.

The results of study three support the claim that trust is a mediating mechanism in evaluating product packaging elements. We found a significant interaction between the presence of trust-enhancing eco-friendliness claims and packaging (F(1,88)=15.47, p=.014) such that when eco-friendliness claims were not made regarding the product packaging, participants preferred the opaque toilet bowl cleaner significantly to the transparent toilet bowl cleaner in terms of product quality (mean 3.48 versus 1.69) but when eco-friendliness claims were made, participants did not evaluate the product qualities as being different from one another (mean$_{opaque}$ 3.54 versus mean$_{clear}$ 3.45). Again, trust was found to be a significant mediator in this process. Though there seems to be clear preferences for product packaging across product categories, these preferences can be shifted when information is provided that will enhance the level of trust in non-traditional packaging.

In light of our significant findings related to packaging transparency and its influence on trust, willingness to pay, and perceived quality, product designers would be well served in contemplating which type of packaging in what contexts is appropriate. Going forward we would like to further investigate the process in which transparency influences attitudes toward products. For instance, when considering organic products the transparency of packaging may be a significant factor is relaying authenticity and perceptions of purity. While with other product categories transparency may negatively influence quality perceptions, for example when the package contains noxious chemicals such as bleach or when consumers prefer to avoid visual evidence of efficacy.

References

Bloch, Peter H. (1995), "Seeking the Ideal Form: Product Design and Consumer Response," *Journal of Marketing*, 59 (3), 16-29.

Dantas, Maria I. S., Valeria P. R. Minim, Rosires Deliza, and Rolf Puschmann (2004), "The Effect of Packaging on the Perception of Minimally Processed Products," *Journal of International Food & Agribusiness Marketing*, 16 (2), 71-83.

Holbrook, Morris B. and Punam Anand (1992), "The Effects of Situation, Sequence, and Features on Perceptual and Affective Responses to Product Designs. The Case of Aesthetic Consumption," *Empirical Studies of the Arts*, 10 (1), 19-31.

Krider, Robert E., Priya Raghubir, and Aradhna Krishna (2001), "Pizzas: P or Square? Psychophysical Biases in Area Comparisons," *Marketing Science*, 20 (4), 405-25.

Raghubir, Priya and Eric A. Greenleaf (2006), "Ratios in Proportion: What Should the Shape of the Package Be?" *Journal of Marketing*, 70, 95-107.

Veryzer, Robert W. (1993), "Aesthetic Response and the Influence of Design Principles on Product Preferences," *Advances in Consumer Research*, 20, 224-31.

_____ (1999), "A Nonconscious Processing Explanation of Consumer Response to Product Design," *Psychology and Marketing*, 16 (6), 497-522.

Yang, Sha and Priya Raghubir (2005), "Can Bottles Speak Volumes? The Effect of Package Shape on How Much to Buy," *Journal of Retailing*, 81 (4), 269-81.

The Perception of Family Brand Entitativity and Varieties of Family Brands

Joseph W. Chang, Vancouver Island University, Canada
Yung-Chien Lou, National Chengchi University, Taiwan

Conceptualization

Entitativity is defined as the degree to which a social aggregate is perceived as the degree of "being entitative" and "having the nature of an entity" (Campbell 1958, p. 17). Perceived entitativity has become the default concept of group perceptions for emerging research exploring the antecedents of perceived entitativity, as well as the organization, formation, function (or use), maintenance and revision of stereotypes (e.g. Fiske 1998). The antecedents of group perceptions, including interaction, importance, outcomes, goals, similarity, duration, size, and permeability (Lickel, Hamilton, Wieczorkowska, Lewis, Sherman and Uhles 2000), are suggestive cues for the perceptions of group coherence and entity, which lead to different routes of mental processes. Coherent groups are perceived as high entitative groups, whereas incoherent are perceived as low entitative groups. The perceived entitativity then affects the following psychological mechanisms of the formation of mental representation (stereotyping), trait attribution (or endowment) to group members, and subsequent group judgments (Crawford, Sherman, and Hamilton 2002). On-line (or integrated) processing is activated if the groups are perceived as high entitative groups, whereas memory-based (or retrospective) processing is elaborated if the groups are perceived as low entitative groups (McConnell, Sherman, and Hamilton 1997). As the cognitive processes underlying evaluations are common (Johar, Maheswaran, and Peracchio 2006; Loken 2006), it is expected that at least some influences on the perception of social groups apply also to the perception of family brands. The classification about social groups may be similar to the classification about family brands. Perceived entitativity may activate different cognitive processes and result in different evaluations about family brands. However, this concept has not yet been implemented to family brand evaluations. Therefore, this research examines the applicability of the eight entitativity measures in group perceptions on family brand evaluations.

Method

The eight measures of perceived entitativity are utilized to measure 40 prestigious family brands (e.g., Coca-Cola, Microsoft, IBM, etc.) selected from the Top 100 Global Brands of BusinessWeek (2006). Around 70 students (200 valid cases expected) participated in this study and received a reward of course credits for the participation. Participants are undergraduate business students at a university in North American. In order to ensure the quality of responses, voluntary participants were invited to a laboratory where the data were collected with one-on-one basis. To avoid systematic responding biases, participants were randomly assigned to one of the nine experimental groups with different orders of family brand names (three different orders) and measures (three different orders). In addition to a questionnaire of twelve pages, a 40-page booklet (one brand on a page) with color pictures of brand extension portfolios and brand logos of 40 popular family brands in consumer goods industries was provided for the evaluations. All the participants rated the 40 family brands on the extent to which each on qualified as a family brand (entitativity measure). Participants rated each family brand on a 9-point scale ranging from 1 (not a family brand at all) to 9 (very much a family brand) for the entitativity measure and then rated the same 40 family brands on the eight properties. In each case, after being given a definition of the property, participants rated the family brands on the 9-point scale. It took about 40 minutes to go through the rating process.

Results

Descriptive analyses were performed for the mean ratings of each family brand, which yielded a range of mean ratings from 4.41 to 7.56. This evidence indicates that participants did see substantial variation among the family brands. *Correlational analyses* were conducted to identify how the properties of these family brands were related to each other and to entitativity. The results indicated that seven properties, except permeability (as expected), were positively correlated with entitativity. Moreover, size was inter-correlated with five properties (duration, importance, interaction, and similarity); goals and importance were inter-correlated with four properties (duration, outcomes, importance, and similarity; duration, interaction, size, and goals); duration, outcomes, and similarity were inter-correlated with three properties; and permeability was inter-correlated with only two properties. Furthermore, *regression analyses* were performed to examine the relationship of these properties to entitativity. The results indicate that goals ($\alpha=.38$) and duration ($\alpha=.36$) were the most influential predictors of entitativity, followed by interaction ($\alpha=.22$), outcomes ($\alpha=.19$), importance ($\alpha=-.15$), size ($\alpha=.15$), permeability ($\alpha=.14$), and similarity ($\alpha=.06$). These eight properties were highly correlated with the entitativity measure ($R=.88$) and account for the large majority ($R^2=.77$) of the variance in entitativity ratings. In conclusion, these results indicated that several of these variables were strongly correlated with entitativity and accounted for a substantial portion of the variation in entitativity, which parallels the finding for social groups (Lickel et al. 2000). However, the pattern of inter-correlation acrossing properties for family brand evaluations is slightly different from the pattern for social groups which showed five properties (interaction, importance, goals, outcomes, and similarity) were highly inter-correlated. Finally, *k-means cluster analyses* were conducted specifying between three and six clusters to examine whether there were different types of family brands defined by unique patterns of property ratings, as well as whether these different types of family brands differed in entitativity. A 40 x 9 matrix in which each cell contained the average rating of a single family brand on a single property was created by averaging the 70 participants' ratings of each of the family brands for each of the nine properties. Clusters were then generated on the basis of the eight properties (entitativity exclusive). The five-cluster solution was found to be the most stable solution for the interpretation. Cluster 1 family brands (e.g., American Express) are small and have high levels of goals and similarity. Cluster 2 family brands (e.g., GE and Panasonic) are low in similarity, interaction, and outcomes, but of moderate duration and size. Cluster 3 family brands (e.g., Disney) are high in duration and size, but low in outcomes and similarity. Cluster 4 family brands (e.g., AVON) are relatively low in outcomes, size, importance, and interaction. Cluster 5 family brands (e.g., Toyota) are high in duration, goals, and similarity. Cluster 3 family brands are the highest in entitativity followed by Clusters 1, 2, 5, and 4. In conclusion, the results indicated that, as with social groups, properties of perceived entitativity are effective antecedents that may cluster family brands into groups, which subsequently elaborate different cognitive processes for family brand evaluations.

References

BusinessWeek, "The 100 Top Brands," *BusinessWeek Online*. Available from:<http://bwnt.businessweek.com/brand/2006/> [Accessed March 22, 2008].

Campbell, D. T. (1958), "Common Fate, Similarity, and Other Indices of the Status of Aggregates of Persons as Social Entities," *Behavioral Science*, Vol. 3, 14-25.

Crawford, M. T., S. J. Sherman, and D. L. Hamilton (2002), "Perceived Entitativity, Stereotype Formation, and the Interchangeability of Group Members," *Journal of Personality and Social Psychology*, 83 (5), 1076-1094.

Fiske, S. T. and S. L. Neuberg (1990), "A Continuum of Impression Formation, from Category-Based to Individuating Processes: Influences of Information and Motivation on Attention and Interpretation," in *Advances in Experimental Social Psychology*, Vol. 23, M. P. Zanna, ed. New York, NY: Academic Press, 1-74.

Johar, Gita Venkataramani, Durairaj Maheswaran, and Laura A. Peracchio (2006), "MAPping the Frontiers: Theoretical Advances in Consumer Research on Memory, Affect, and Persuasion," *Journal of Consumer Research*, 33 (June), 139-149.

Lickel, B., D. L. Hamilton, G. Wieczorkowska, A. C. Lewis, S. J. Sherman, and A. N. Uhles (2000), "Varieties of Groups and the Perception of Group Entitativity," *Journal of Personality and Social Psychology*, Vol. 78, 223-246.

Loken, Barbara (2006), "Consumer Psychology: Categorization, Inferences, Affect, and Persuasion," *Annual Review of Psychology*, Vol. 57 (January), 453-485.

McConnell, A. R., S. J. Sherman, and D. L. Hamilton (1997), "Target Entitativity: Implications for Information Processing about Individual and Group Targets," *Journal of Personality and Social Psychology*, Vol. 72, 750-762.

The Effects of Nine-ending Prices and the Need for Cognition in Price Cognition

Shih-Chieh Chuang, Chung Cheng University, Taiwan
Chaang-Yung Kung, Chao-yang University of Technology, Taiwan
Yin-Hui Cheng, National Penghu University, Taiwan
Shu-Li Yu, Chaoyang University of Technology, Taiwan

The use of nine-ending prices is popular among retailers. According to a previous report, 30% to 65% of all prices end in the digit nine, and evidence from an econometric analysis of UPC retail scanner data and surveys of retail price practices showed that consumers perceive nine-ending prices to be significantly lower than prices that are just one cent higher (Stiving and Winer, 1997; Schindler and Kirby, 1997; Thomas and Morwitz, 2005). This issue has attracted the interest of researchers since as early as 1936 (Ginzberg, 1936). More recently, Anderson and Simester (2003) suggested that the last digit of a price has a significant impact on receiving revenues, even though nine-ending prices change the price of products by just one cent.

Although monetary promotions such as nine-ending prices cause consumers to purchase more, some research has suggested that the effect of such prices depends on the amount of attention that consumers pay to the decision to purchase (Shindler and Warren, 1988; Zaichkowski, 1988). The amount of attention is likely to be affected by a variety of factors, including consumer involvement, motivation, and the opportunity to process price information. Another important variable that has largely been ignored in the literature is the need for cognition (NFC), which may be a crucial element that affects consumer perceptions of nine-ending prices. This research investigates the NFC as a facet of consumer personality that reflects a tendency to engage in and even enjoy evaluating prices, as it motivates comparative thought. It is proposed that consumers with a high and low NFC will exhibit different consumer behavior. The research divides consumers into two price cognition groups: high and low price cognition. Two subsequent experiments using these groups revealed that consumers with a low NFC tend to perceive nine-ending prices to be significantly cheaper than zero-ending prices.

Literature Review

Need For Cognition (NFC)

The need for cognition (NFC) is the tendency for people to engage in and enjoy thinking. Petty and Cacioppo (1986) demonstrated that the NFC is not related to the traditional conception of intelligence. Individuals with a high NFC are more likely to have a stronger intrinsic motivation to engage in cognition and to attempt to reduce any errors that they might have made. Being motivated by interest, enjoyment, or the challenge of work is termed intrinsic motivation. Individuals with a low NFC, in contrast, do not enjoy thinking.

Petty and Cacioppo (1986) indicated that the NFC is cognition to the extent that individuals engage in it on account of their intrinsic motivation. Based on this theory, numerous research associated with the NFC has verified that individuals with a high NFC possess stronger intrinsic motivation, and engage in cognition to reduce errors made when purchasing, whereas individuals with a low NFC do not enjoy the evaluation process. Park and Hastak (1994) found individuals with a low NFC to be reluctant when faced with cognitive endeavor and to prefer to avoid arduous discussions or deliberation; therefore, they tend to be easily influenced by others.

Given the foregoing ideas, we expect that the differences in consumer preferences for engaging in and enjoying relatively effortful cognitive processing of information, such as the NFC, are likely to influence the responses of consumers to nine-ending pricing tactics. In the sections that follow, we review the relevant literature and develop our hypotheses. We describe two experiments that we conducted to examine our predictions using the rightmost numerical digit (Study 1) and the leftmost numerical digit (Study 2) in a price.

Rightmost digit effect (nine-ending effects)

Previous studies have shown that consumers perceive a nine-ending price to be significantly lower than a price just one cent higher ($3.60 vs. $3.59). This pricing technique is termed "psychological pricing," apparently because of the belief that nine-ending prices act on the consumer via "special psychological effects" (Shindler and Kibarian, 1993; Bray and Harris, 2006).

Schindler and Kirby (1997) proposed two effects to explain this psychological effect. The first is the perceived-gain effect, which refers to the perception of consumers that nine-ending prices indicate that the retailer is giving a small amount back to the consumer. For example, a consumer might interpret a price such as $29 as involving a $1 discount from $30. The second reason is termed the underestimated price effect, which refers to the perception of consumers that a nine-ending price such as $29 is encoded as $20. Both the perceived-gain effect and the underestimated price effect make the product seem much cheaper to consumers than if it carried a zero-ending price, and trigger an enhanced buyer response (Gendall, Holdershaw, and Garland, 1997).

Brenner and Brenner (1982) explained that the perceived-gain and underestimated price effects are the result of a limited capacity on the part of consumers to make a cognitive effort to focus on directly accessible information. They held that consumers who are exposed to price information store only the more valuable parts of the message they receive, in this case the first digits of a number. For example, when the price is $299, the digit 2 is more significant information than the first 9, which in turn is more significant than the next 9. Consumers therefore recall that the price is $200, then that it is $290, but rarely that it is $299. This limit on cognitive capacity explains why consumers always perceive a nine-ending price to be a cheaper price than a zero-ending price. A study based on cognitive capacity by Shindler and Warren (1998) found that the effects of nine-ending prices depended on the amount of attention consumers paid to the decision to purchase. Consumers who were under greater time pressure paid less attention to each price and were therefore more likely to ignore the rightmost digits.

In accordance with the literature, we expect the NFC to moderate the perception of price for nine-ending prices. We expect individuals with a high NFC to pay more attention to information central to the purchase decision and to engage in more thought about the decision than individuals with a low NFC. Consumers with a high NFC are only influenced by actual price discounts, whereas consumers with a low NFC are affected by discount signals regardless of actual price discounts (Inman et al., 1990). Consumers with a high NFC are therefore less influenced by marketing or psychological tactics. When consumers with a high NFC are faced with a nine-ending price, they realize that it is only one cent lower than the zero-ending price, and no large discrepancy is created in their perception of price. Conversely, consumers with a low NFC are more likely to be affected by psychological tactics when faced with a nine-ending price, as they have a low motive to process price information and prefer to use heuristics by reading prices from left to right. This renders them liable to underestimate prices (Coulter, 2001).

Our hypothesis is therefore as follows:

H: Consumers with a low NFC will be more likely to perceive nine-ending prices to be lower than zero-ending prices than will consumers with a high NFC.

The data from the two experiments also provide cumulative evidence for the role played by the NFC in the nine-ending price effect. Consistent with our prediction, a high NFC reduces the magnitude of the nine-ending price effect. We demonstrate that consumers with a low NFC will be more likely to perceive nine-ending prices to be smaller than zero-ending prices than will individuals with a high NFC. We also found that the influence of the NFC on the price-ending effect is exerted not only on the rightmost digit (Study 1), but also on the leftmost digit (Study 2). This research contributes to the literature by offering empirical evidence that the NFC effect influences the nine-ending effect. A related question is whether it is important to use nine-ending prices. In response, we show that a nine-ending price is sometimes, but not always, perceived to be lower than a price that is one cent higher, and reveal that the perception is more likely to occur when consumers have a low NFC, as they are more likely to perceive no difference between nine-ending and zero-ending prices. There seems to be a domain invariant cognitive phenomenon underlying the popularity of nine-ending prices.

Reference

Anderson, E. T. & Simester, D. I. (2003). Effects of $9 price Endings on Retail Sales: Evidence from Field Experiments," *Quantitative Marketing and Economics,* 1(1), 93-110.

Bray, J.P. and Harris, C. (2006), "The Effect of 9-ending Prices on Retail Sales: A Quantitative UK Based Field Study," *Journal of Marketing Management*, 22, 601-617.

Brener, G. and Brenner, R. (1982), "Memory and Markets, or Why Are You Paying $2.99 for A Widget," *Journal of Business*, 55, 147-158.

Coulter, K. S. (2001), "Odd-ending Price Underestimation: An Experimental Examination of Left-to-right Processing Effects," *The Journal of Product and Brand Management*. 10(4/5), 276-292.

Gendall, P., Holdershaw, J. and Garland, J. (1997), "The Effect of Odd pricing on Eemand," *European Journal of Marketing*, 31, 799-813.

Inman, J. J., McAlister, L. & Hoyer, W. D. (1990), "Promotion Signal: Proxy for A Price Cut?" *Journal of consumer research*. 17(1), 74-81.

Park, J. W. and Hastak, M. (1994), "Memory-based Product Judgments: Effects of Involvement at Encoding and Retrieval," *Journal of Consumer Research*. 21, 534-547.

Petty, R. E. and Cacioppo, J. T. (1986), *Communication and Persuasion: Central and Peripheral Route to Attitude Change,* New York: Springer- Verlag.

Schindler, R. M. and Kirby, P. N. (1997), "Patterns of Rightmost Digits Used in Advertised Prices: Implications for Nine-ending Effects," *Journal of Consumer Research*, 24, 192-201.

Shindler R. M. & Warren, L.S. (1988), "Effect of Odd pricing on Choice of Items from A Menu," *Advances in Consumer Research*, 15, 348-353.

Shindler, R.M. and Kibarian, T.M. (1993), "Testing for Perceptual Underestimation of 9-ending Price," *Advances in Consumer Research*, 20, 580-585.

Stiving, M. & Winer, R. S. (1997), "An Empirical Analysis of Price Endings with Scanner Data," *Journal of Consumer Research*. 24, 57-67

Thomas, M. & Morwitz, V. (2005), "Penny Wise and Pound Foolish: The Left-digit Effect in Price Cognition," *Journal of Consumer Research*. 32, 54-64.

Zaichkowski, J.L. (1988), "Involvement and the Price Cue," *Advances in Consumer Research*, 15,323-327.

The Moderating Effect of Product Familiarity on the Endowment Effect

Ya-Chung Sun, Vanung University, Taiwan
Chien-Huang Lin, National Central University, Taiwan
Shih-Chieh Chuang, National Chung Cheng University, Taiwan
Yin-Hui Cheng, National Penghu University, Taiwan

In monetary-based trade, goods held by sellers are sold in exchange for monetary funds held by a buyer. Although the task of a seller is to sell its merchandise and the task of a buyer is to get the goods s/he needs, when doing so, the main goal of both seller and buyer is to maximize their gains (Goldman, Kraus, & Shehory 2004). But, how do consumers decide on the highest price they are willing to pay for a desired product? And, how do they decide on the lowest price they are willing to accept for a product they wish to sell?

The assessment of objective values refers to the fact that "people are required to estimate the least price they are willing to accept (WTA) when selling something and the ceiling price they are willing to pay (WTP) when buying something".

Most economists argue that the gap between WTA and WTP should converge for most commodities. However, experimental research has shown that the values of WTA and WTP might remarkably differ, even for the same object. This discrepancy in selling and buying price for the same object is rooted in the status of ownership and is termed "the endowment effect"(Kahneman et al. 1990).

Familiarity is defined as the number of product-related experiences that have been accumulated by the consumer (Abla and Hutchinson 1987). For example, familiarity with a product may lead to the use of prior product-related knowledge to direct the acquisition of information (e.g., information search; Brucks 1985) and the evaluation of information (e.g., to make compensatory trade-offs; Bettman and Park 1980).

Familiarity gives experienced consumers several advantages. It decreases the information search for existing alternatives (Bettman and Park 1980), provides a superior ability to encode new information (Jeffries et al. 1981), and allows the consumer to pay attention to relevant information and ignore irrelevant information (Johnson 1993).

Hence, this study explores whether consumer's product familiarity influences the endowment effect on the selling price and buying price. It is reasonable that the perceptions of value of both seller and buyer are influenced by product familiarity and therefore indirectly moderate the endowment effect.

Experiment 1

The purpose of this study is to test our hypotheses that ownership and the level of product familiarity interact and influence subjective valuation. The product familiarity of the participant was experimentally measured and its effect on endowment effect was observed.

The experiment was conducted by a factor-two level (ownership: owner vs. non-owner) between-subjects design. A total of 206 undergraduate students at the University of Vannung participated in this experiment as part of their course requirement marketing management class, and were randomly and equally assigned to one of two different experimental conditions.

These statistics strongly support our assumption that the endowment effect is larger when people have a lower level of product familiarity than people with higher level of product familiarity.

Experiment 2

Experiment 1 supports hypothesis one. However, the way we measured familiarity may not exclude the influence from other variables, such as prior knowledge or experience. To further demonstrate the endowment effect on product familiarity, experiment 2 manipulated the main variable to examine our hypotheses.

The objective of Experiment 2 aims to manipulate product familiarity rather than to measure product familiarity to test the robustness of the endowment effect.

The experiment was conducted by a 2 (ownership: owner versus non-owner) x 2 (product familiarity: high versus low) between-subjects design. A total of 204 undergraduate students at the University of Vannung participated in this experiment, and were randomly and equally assigned to one of four different experimental conditions.

As we expected, the analysis revealed a significant interaction between the endowment effect and product familiarity. The endowment effects are smaller when people have a higher level of product familiarity than for those who have a lower level of product familiarity.

Conclusion

All other things being equal, sellers tend to pursue a higher selling price for an owned object than they would be willing to pay as buyers (e.g. Kahneman, Knetsch, and Thaler 1990). However, as proven by the results of three experiments in this study, the level of product familiarity can affect the magnitude of the endowment effect. The endowment effects are smaller when people have a high level of product familiarity and the endowment effect is small when people have a low level of product familiarity. Hence, the level of product familiarity can be classified as a moderator in the endowment effect.

References

Alba, J.W., & Hutchinson, W. (1987), "Dimensions of Consumer Expertise," *Journal of Consumer Research*, 13, 411-453.

Bettman, James R., And C. Whan Park (1980b), "Effects of Prior Knowledge and Experience and Phase of the Choice Process on Consumer Decision Processes: A Protocol Analysis," *Journal of Consumer Research*, 7(December), 234-248.

Brucks, Merrie (1985), "The Effects of Product Class Knowledge on Information Search Behavior," *Journal of Consumer Research*, 12(June), 1-16

Goldman, Claudia V., Sarit Kraus, and Onn Shehory (2004), "On Experimental Equilibria Strategies for Selecting Sellers and Satisfying Buyers", *Decision Support Systems*, 38, 329-346.

Jeffries, Robin, Althea A. Turner, Peter G. Polson, and Michael E. Atwood (1981), "Processes Involved in Designing Software," in Cognitive Skills and Their Acquisition, ed. J. R. Anderson, Hillsdale, NJ: Lawrence Erlbaum.

Johnson, E. J., Hershey, J., Meszaros, J., & Kunreuther, H.(1993), "Framing, Probability Distortions, and Insurance Decision," *Journal of Risk and Uncertainty,* 7, 35-51.

Kahneman, Daniel, Jack L. Knetsch, and Richard H. Thaler (1990), "Experimental Tests of the Endowment Effect and the Coase Theorem," *Journal of Political Economy*, 98(December), 1325-1348.

Postconsumption Motivation–What Happens after a Need is Satisifed?

Robert Kreuzbauer, University of Illinois at Urbana-Champaign, USA
Chi-yue Chiu, University of Illinois at Urbana-Champaign, USA

This paper reports results from a new research direction called *Postconsumption Motivation* which tries to study motivational effects after basic social needs have been satisfied through consumption. Consumers purchase products or brands in order to satisfy certain needs, however, what are the motivational forces that drive consumers to act in a certain way after the brand is consumed? Is it even possibility to predict any kind of behavior after consumption? Based on the theory of optimal distinctiveness we demonstrate that consumers who consume a brand that allows them to satisfy their need for distinctiveness, have an increased desire for being connected to other people. This example is counterintuitive since (as existing theories in consumer behavior would predict) one would expect that when a consumer gets the feeling of being unique or distinctive by using a certain brand (e.g. wearing sunglasses from Gucci one feels distinctive from lower class people) this person should also continue to feel or act as a distinctive individual. However, as our studies showed, the opposite happens. Our theoretical concept is based on Brewer's theory of optimal distinctiveness (ODT, 1991) which asserts that individuals desire to attain an optimal balance of belongingness and distinctiveness *within* and *between* social groups and situations. These two motives are in constant opposition with each other; when there is too much of one motive, the other must increase in order to counterbalance it and vice versa. We tested this concept in 2x2x2 full-factoral between-subject experimental setting. In a first step consumers had to watch a 3 minutes slide presentation (that contained pictures from unique individuals combined with sentences and words that were associated with distinctiveness) that activated their need for distinctiveness. Then the experimental group (distinctiveness group) received a brief advertising message about a tea-bag brand which is associated with uniqueness (i.e. it helps the consumer to feel distinctive). In the control condition the participants received a message about the same tea-bag brand, but with a neutral content. Both groups had to rate the attractiveness of the advertising message (and returned the ratings to the experimenter) and then received one real tea-bag as a gift. That is, participants in both groups had an increased need for distinctiveness (through the slide presentation), then people in the experimental group learned that this brand is associated with distinctiveness and would therefore serve as a means to satisfy this particular need which finally happened after they received the tea-bag. After having rated how much this tea-bag would enable them to feel distinctive, participants were asked whether they would now prefer to work in a group or alone for the next task. We assumed that after their need for distinctiveness was satisfied through the tea-bag they would rather prefer to work in a group than alone since now–according to ODT-their need for belongingness would be activated. However, for the control group, this effect should be significantly weaker, since these participants never associated distinctiveness with the brand and would therefore not have successfully satisfied their need through the received tea-bag. The results confirmed our hypotheses. Participants in the experimental condition felt that the tea-bag would let them feel significantly more distinctive than participants in the control condition and also had a significantly higher preference towards working in a group (i.e. higher need for belongingness) than the control group. The experimental group also showed higher overall preference towards the tea-brand. In a second experiment we followed the same procedure than in study 1, however this time participants received a false tea-bag brand, that is, when the experimenter distributed the tea-bags he told the participants that his research assistant accidentally bought the wrong tea-bags, so he could only give them a different brand than the one in the advertising. The idea behind this procedure was that, in this experiment, both groups (1. group with distinctiveness message and 2. group with neutral message) were unable to satisfy their need for distinctiveness, as they haven't received the brand that was associated with distinctiveness. We therefore expected that both groups (compared to the experimental group from study 1) would also have a decreased feeling of distinctiveness for the tea-bag brand (since this was not associated with distinctiveness inside the ad) and consequently a decreased preference towards working in the group, since their need for belongingness wasn't activated accordingly due to the fact that distinctiveness wasn't sufficiently satisfied in the first task. Again our results were consistent with the hypotheses. In addition to that both studies also contained a memory recognition task where in the final part of the study participants were asked to recall adjectives which they read in the first rating of the advertising message. These results also confirmed the hypotheses. Participants who received the distinctiveness message and the correct tea-bag brand could remember significantly more adjectives than participants from the other three groups.

We believe that these results show important findings of a very new direction in consumer research where consumers motivational reactions are studied after a certain need has been satisfied. We assume that research in postconsumption motivation can help to better understand consumption as a continuing process that does not stop after a need has been satisfied. Our results are based on two strong experimental tests and also provide an explanation for the underlying theoretical framework of this process. In a further step we conduct studies that test the effect when consumers' need for belongingness is activated at the beginning and we will present these results together with those discussed above at the conference.

Reference

Brewer, MB (1991), The Social Self, *Personality and Social Psychology Bulletin*, 17(5), 475-482

The Role of Common Features in Decision Conflict Resolution

Anish Nagpal, The University of Melbourne, Australia
Adwait Khare, Quinnipiac University, USA
Tilottama Chowdhury, Quinnipiac University, USA
Ameet Pandit, The University of Melbourne, Australia

Abstract

During decision conflict resolution, features that are shared among alternatives are thought to cancel out and not play any role in choice because they are non-diagnostic; only the unique features help the consumer make a decision. In this research, we specifically examine how features that are shared among alternatives affect decision difficulty. Our results indicate that common attributes do matter; they do not simply cancel out. Further, how common attributes matter seems to depend on the type of decision conflict. Under approach-approach conflict, common attributes enhance the perceived advantage; thereby increasing the ease in decision-making. However, under avoidance-avoidance conflict, common attributes seem to enhance the perceived disadvantage, thereby increasing decision difficulty.

Introduction

Consider a consumer who faces a choice between two cars, car A and car B. Both the cars share a few bad features such as bad warranty, low horse-power, etc. However, each car has unique good features; car A has better fuel efficiency whereas car B is very safe. Such a decision creates an approach-approach conflict because the consumer is drawn towards both the alternatives. Alternatively, consumers face avoidance-avoidance conflict when they have to choose between two products that are equally unattractive. In the above example, consider both cars share a few good features such as good warranty, high horse-power, etc. However, each car has unique bad features; car A is not fuel efficient and car B is ranked low on safety. The literature argues that during such a conflict resolution process, the features that are shared among the alternatives cancel out and do not play a role in choice because they are non-diagnostic (Houston and Sherman 1995; Tversky 1972). The decision rests upon comparing only the unique features. Decisions that involve a comparison of only the good unique features (approach-approach conflict) are easier and take less time than those involving a comparison of only the bad features (avoidance-avoidance conflict).

In this research we question the assumption that common features cancel out and have no role to play in conflict resolution.

Decision Conflict and Decision Difficulty

Research shows that an approach-approach conflict takes less time and is easier to resolve than an avoidance-avoidance conflict. This has been verified in a number of experiments (Barker 1942; Chatterjee and Heath, 1995; Dhar and Nowlis 1999; Houston, Sherman, and Baker 1991; Hovland and Sears 1938; Sears and Hovland 1941; also see Anderson, 2003 for a review). The question of whether common features cancel out and play no role in the decision is an interesting one. Products often share a number of features with their competitor's products and it is logical to assume that the common features should cancel out and not affect the outcome. In fact, prospect theory (Kahneman and Tversky 1979) and the information restructuring framework (Coupey 1994) argue that the common features are cancelled out by consumers before they evaluate the relative attractiveness of the products. However, recent research has shown that common features can affect choice (Chernev, 1997, 2001). For example, using the confirmatory reasoning framework (Klayman 1995; Lord, Lepper, and Ross 1979; Russo, Medvec, and Meloy 1996; Russo, Meloy, and Medvec 1998), Chernev (2001) showed that that when consumers have already established preferences and the common features shared between the products are attractive, consumers make choices that confirm their prior preferences. However, when the attributes are equally important or consumers have no prior preferences, common features seem to have no impact on preferences. Even if that is the case, we believe that common features may impact other decision process characteristics such as decision difficulty.

Hypothesis Development

Consider the case of a consumer who is deciding between two cameras that have better features than a previously viewed camera, which is out of stock. This situation creates an approach-approach conflict (Chatterjee and Heath, 1995). Although consumers might face decision conflict, it is much easier to make a choice in such a situation because both the products are equally attractive (Chatterjee and Heath, 1995; Dhar and Nowlis 1999; Houston, Sherman, and Baker 1991). Once the consumer realizes that both the cameras are attractive and develops a liking towards one of the products, the other features of the camera, albeit shared with the other camera, should strengthen the already established preference for the camera and make the decision easier (Chernev 2001; Russo, Medvec, and Meloy 1996; Russo, Meloy, and Medvec 1998). Hence, as the number of common features increase, the decision to choose one of the two attractive cameras becomes more and more easy.

H1: In an approach-approach conflict, decision-making becomes easier as the number of common features shared between the products increases.

Now consider the case of a consumer who is deciding between two cameras that have worse features than a previously viewed camera, which is unfortunately out of stock. This situation creates an avoidance-avoidance conflict (Chatterjee and Heath, 1995), making the decision very difficult. It is reasonable to suggest that the consumer will process the other features of the cameras to help make the decision. However, if the other features are shared, it would add further to the frustration and disappointment of not being able to break the tie. Thus, we propose that when consumers face two unattractive products, the common features will make the decision even more difficult.

H2: In an avoidance-avoidance conflict, decision-making increases in difficulty as the number of common features shared between the products increases.

We now describe study 1 that tests the hypotheses stated above.

Study 1: Effect of Common Features on Decision Difficulty

Eighty-two undergraduate college students participated in study 1 in exchange for a chance to win a $50 gift certificate from the university bookshop. Participants were exposed to either approach-approach or avoidance-avoidance conflict using product descriptions that were adapted from Chatterjee and Heath (1996). Common features were manipulated at four levels, zero common features, one common feature, two common features, and three common features. The principal dependent variable was decision difficulty which was measured by asking the participants the following three questions, "How simple was the task to evaluate the cameras (reverse-coded)," "how difficult was the task to evaluate the cameras," and "how easy was the task to evaluate the cameras (reverse-coded)." All three questions were anchored at "Strongly Agree" and "Strongly Disagree." The mean of the three questions was calculated to give a single measure of decision difficulty (Cronbach-alpha=0.94).

Results

Conflict type significantly affected decision difficulty (α=-1.14, p<.05). This indicates that approach-approach conflict is more difficult to resolve than avoidance-avoidance conflict, which is a surprising result. The number of common attributes also significantly affected decision difficulty (α=-0.52, p<.05). More importantly, the interaction was also statistically significant (α=0.99, p<.05). We found that under approach-approach conflict, the number of common attributes significantly affected decision difficulty (α=-0.47, p<.05). The negative significant coefficient suggests that as the number of common attributes increases, decision difficulty decreases. Thus, H1 received support. Under avoidance-avoidance conflict, the number of common attributes also significantly affected decision difficulty (α=0.22, p<.05). The positive significant coefficient suggests that as the number of common attributes increases, decision difficulty increases. Thus, H2 received support. Results of both hypotheses' tests are unchanged when the importance ratings of all attributes, unique and common, are included in the model.

Discussion

Our results indicate that common attributes do matter; they do not simply cancel out leaving decision-making unaffected. Further, how common attributes matter seems to depend on the type of conflict in decision-making. When decision options are superior to an unavailable option (approach-approach conflict), common attributes enhance the perceived advantage even more and thereby increase the ease in decision-making. On the other hand, when decision options are inferior to an unavailable option (avoidance-avoidance conflict), common attributes seem to enhance the perceived disadvantage even more and thereby increase the discomfort in decision-making. Our findings indicate that assuming common attributes to be irrelevant can lead to incorrect conclusions about decision-making. Our results are promising and we intend to conduct further research to understand the role of attribute valence (both common and unique attributes can be positive vs. negative in valence) and consequences for the final decision (are some options more vs. less likely to get chosen).

References

Anderson, Christopher J. (2003), "The Psychology of Doing Nothing: Forms of Decision Avoidance Result from Reason and Emotion," *Psychological Bulletin,* 129 (1), 139-166.

Barker, Roger G. (1942), "An Experimental Study of the Resolution of Conflict by Children," in *Studies in Personality,* ed. McNemar Q. and M.A. Merrill, New York, NY, US: McGraw Hill, 13-34.

Chatterjee, Subimal and Timothy B. Heath (1996), "Conflict and Loss Aversion in Multiattribute Choice: The Effects of Trade-off Size and Reference Dependence on Decision Difficulty," *Organizational Behavior and Human Decision Processes,* 67 (June), 144-155.

Chernev, Alexander (1997), "The Effect of Common Features on Brand Choice: Moderating Role of Attribute Importance," *Journal of Consumer Research,* 23 (4), 304-311.

―――― (2001), "The Impact of Common Features on Consumer Preferences: A Case of Confirmatory Reasoning," *Journal of Consumer Research,* 27 (March), 475-488.

Coupey, Eloise (1994), "Restructuring: Constructive Processing of Information Displays in Consumer Choice," *Journal of Consumer Research,* 21 (June), 83-99.

Dhar, Ravi and Stephen M. Nowlis (1999), "The Effect of Time Pressure on Consumer Choice Deferral," *Journal of Consumer Research,* 25 (March), 369-84.

Houston, David A. and Steven J. Sherman (1995), "Cancellation and Focus: The Role of Shared and Unique Features in the Choice Process," *Journal of Experimental Psychology,* 31 (4), 357-378.

Houston, David A., Steven J. Sherman, and Sara M. Baker (1991), "Feature Matching, Unique Features, and the Dynamics of the Choice Process: Pre-decision Conflict and Post-decision Satisfaction," *Journal of Experimental Social Psychology,* 27 (5), 411-430.

Hovland, Carl I. and Robert R. Sears (1938), "Experiments on Motor Conflict: types of Conflict and Their Modes of Resolution," *Journal of Experimental Psychology,* 23, 477-493.

Kahneman, Daniel and Amos Tversky (1979), "Prospect Theory: An Analysis of Decision Under Risk," *Econometrica,* 47 (March), 263-291.

Klayman, Joshua (1995), "Varieties of Confirmation Bias," *Decision Making from the Perspective of Cognitive Psychology*, ed. J. R. Busemeyer, R. Hastie, and Douglas L. Medin, New York: Academic Press, 385–418 .

Lord, Charles G., Mark R. Lepper, and Lee Ross (1979), "Biased Assimilation and Attitude Polarization: The Effects of Prior Theories on Subsequently Considered Evidence," *Journal of Personality and Social Psychology*, 37 (November), 2098-2110.

Russo, J. Edward, Victoria Husted Medvec, and Margaret G. Meloy (1996), "The Distortion of Information during Decisions," *Organizational Behavior and Human Decision Processes*, 66 (April), 102-110.

Russo, J. Edward, Margaret G. Meloy, and Victoria Husted Medvec (1998), "Predecisional Distortion of Product Information," *Journal of Marketing Research*, 35 (November), 438-452.

Sears, Robert R. and Carl. I. Hovland (1941),"Experiments on Motor Conflict: Determination of Mode or Resolution by Comparative Strengths of Conflicting Responses," *Journal of Experimental Psychology*, 28, 280-286.

Tversky, Amos (1972), "Elimination by Aspects: A Theory of Choice," *Psychological Review*, 79 (July), 281-299.

The Inertia of Motion

Sunaina Chugani, The University of Texas at Austin, USA

Rajagopal Raghunathan, The University of Texas at Austin, USA

Ying Zhang, The University of Texas at Austin, USA

A mindset has been described as a highly accessible set of cognitive procedures that are activated upon use (Gollwitzer, Heckhausen, & Stellar, 1990; Gollwitzer & Bayer, 1999). Extant literature has confirmed that if a cognitive procedure gets activated in a certain situation, it is more likely to be activated for use in subsequent behavior to which it is applicable (Smith, Branscombe, & Bormann, 1988; Smith 1990, 1994; Gollwitzer & Bayer, 1999). Thus, we posit that Newton's first law–an object at rest (motion) stays at rest (motion) unless acted on by an outside force–has parallels in the human realm. Specifically, individuals in a state of psychological motion (e.g. who perceive that they have begun a task) will exhibit a greater propensity to maintain the motion state (e.g. by engaging in a subsequent task) than those in a state of rest. This "Inertia of Motion Hypothesis" predicts that an individual in a state of motion will (1) exhibit a greater propensity to engage in a subsequent task and, due to the greater readiness for motion, (2) exhibit a faster rate of progress through a given task. Two studies test these predictions.

In Study 1, participants were seated at separate computers and were asked to answer some simple demographic questions. Upon completion, half were told that they had completed the first section of the study (motion state condition), and the other half were told that the demographic questions were merely preliminary and that they had not yet started the study (rest state condition). Both groups were then informed that they would be required to wait for about five minutes until all participants were ready to proceed. In addition, participants were told that, if they wished, they could engage in an optional task while waiting by clicking on an icon at the bottom of the screen. The optional task consisted of word puzzles in which participants had to create as many words as possible from a string of letters presented to them. The amount of time it took for participants to click on the optional task icon served as a measure for their propensity to engage in a subsequent task. The rate at which participants generated the words in the task was taken as their rate of progress through the task. Results showed that those in the motion condition clicked on the icon for the optional task sooner (after M=61.48 seconds) than participants in the rest condition (after M=104.60 seconds), $t(117)=3.38$, $p<.01$. Further, those in the motion condition generated each word at a faster rate (M=12.08 seconds per word) than those in the rest condition (M=17.28 seconds per word), $t(113)=3.18$, $p<.01$. Thus, those in the motion condition exhibited a greater propensity to maintain their motion by choosing to engage in an optional task sooner than those in the rest condition, and, because of their greater readiness for further motion, proceeded through the optional task at a faster rate than those in the rest condition.

Study 2 was designed to provide triangulating evidence for the intertia of motion hypothesis by exploring the effect of taking away the experience of psychological motion. After the same state manipulation used in Study 1 (state: rest vs. motion), half of the participants simply proceeded to the next part of the study (no interrupt condition). The other half were interrupted by learning that they had to wait for "about two minutes" to make sure all participants were ready to proceed to the next part of the study (interrupt condition). For those in the motion condition, the period of disengagement imposed by the interruption was expected to take away their experience of psychological motion and thus mitigate their propensity to maintain that motion. For those in the rest condition, the interruption should simply extend their period of rest and was not expected to alter their state. Next, all participants then encountered an impression formation task; they were presented with one piece of information at a time about a target person and were instructed to stop requesting more information when they felt confident enough to form an impression of the target (adapted from Martin, Ward, & Achee, 1993). The average time spent on each piece of information was recorded as a measure of speed of progress through the task. Analysis of this data revealed an interaction between the state and interrupt variables, $F(3, 39)=3.73$, $p=.06$. As expected, without an interruption, individuals in motion spent significantly less time on average examining each piece of information (M=3.05 seconds per piece) than those at rest (M=4.34 seconds per piece), $F(1, 19)=3.55$, $p<.05$. This was a replication of the rate of progress findings from Study 1. In the interrupt condition, there was no significant difference between those in the motion condition (M=3.91 seconds per piece) and those in the rest condition (M=3.36 seconds per piece), $F(1,20)=0.43$, $p>.50$. So, taking away the experience of psychological motion mitigated the propensity of those in the motion condition to maintain their motion, causing them to behave no differently from those in the rest condition. A simple contrast illustrates the overall effect more clearly: the motion, no interrupt condition (the only condition in which participants experienced unmitigated motion) proceeded through the pieces of information at a faster rate (M=3.05 seconds) than those in the other three conditions combined (M=3.90 seconds per piece), $F(1,41)=3.92$, $p=.05$. So, these results triangulate the results from Study 1 by showing that taking away psychological motion results in a mitigation of the propensity to maintain motion.

These studies provide evidence that once an individual perceives himself to be "moving", the experience of psychological motion activates a motion state, resulting in a propensity to maintain motion. This exhibits itself behaviorally through (1) an increase in the propensity to engage in a subsequent task, and (2) a faster rate of progress through a given task. The relationship between psychological motion and the propensity to maintain that motion was reinforced by showing that when psychological motion is absent, so too is the propensity to maintain motion.

References

Gollwitzer, P.M. & Bayer, U. (1999). "Deliberative versus implemental mindsets in the control of action." In S. Chaiken & Y. Trope (Eds) *Dual-process theories in social psychology* (pp. 403-422). New York: Guilford Press.

Gollwitzer, P.M., Heckhausen, H., & Steller, B. (1990). "Deliberative and implemental mind-sets: Cognitive tuning toward congruous thoughts and information." *Journal of Personality and Social Psychology*, 59(6), 1119-1127.

Martin, L.L., Ward, D.W., & Achee, J.W. (1993). "Mood as input: People have to interpret the motivational implications of their moods." *Journal of Personality and Social Psychology*, 64(3), 317-326.

Smith, E. R. (1990). "Content and process specificity in the effects of prior experiences." In T.K. Srull & R.S. Wyer (Eds), *Advances in Social Cognition* (Vol. 3, pp. 1-59). Hillsdale, NJ: Erlbaum.

Smith, E. R. (1994). "Procedural knowledge and processing strategies in social cognition." In R.S. Wyer & T.K. Srull (Eds), *Handbook of Social Cognition* (Vol 1, pp. 101-51). Hillsdale, NJ: Erlbaum.

Smith, E.R., Branscombe, N.R., & Bormann, C. (1988). "Generality of the effects of practice on social judgment tasks." *Journal of Personality and Social Psychology*, 54(3), 385-395.

Self-Image Congruence Models Conceptualized as a Product Affirmation Process

Michael K. Coolsen, Shippensburg University, USA
Madoka Kumashiro, Goldsmiths University of London, UK

Marketing scholars understand and account for the process of self-image congruence models—we incorporate products/brands into our self-concepts (e.g., Onkvisit and Shaw, 1987, Prentice, 1987) and often desire those products that match and express to others our self-concept, personality traits, and core values (Dolich, 1969). However, does this desire extend to products that represent both the "good and bad" of who we are? Additionally, can such products affect one's emotions and actually help to change one's self-concept? While self-image congruence models suggest that we tend to seek brands that match our personality, the distinction between the expression of one's actual self (both the "good and bad" aspects of one's self-concept), one's enhanced self (self-concept aspects that others tend to favor) and one's ideal self (the aspects to which an individual aspires but not necessarily to which others aspire) in consumer behavior remains less clear. Solomon (2007) has suggested that the vast amount of consumer research has been mixed regarding the influence of the different types of self-concept traits on product evaluation, and Solomon seems less certain that self-image congruency models can explain preference for simple/functional products, such as a toaster or a day-planner. In an attempt to clarify the mixed evidence regarding self-image congruence models, we sought to apply a robust theory of close relationships, namely the Michelangelo Phenomenon (Drigotas, Rusbult, Wieselquist, and Whitton, 1999, Rusbult et al., 2005), to explain the evaluation of products that match our actual, enhanced, and ideal selves and the effects of these products on one's emotions and personality.

Drigotas and his colleagues developed a model of partner affirmation in close relationships (Drigotas, Rusbult, Wieselquist, and Whitton, 1999). These authors proposed that the process of behavioral confirmation (Darley and Fazio, 1980, Snyder, Tanke, and Berscheid, 1977) is likely to be quite powerful in that close partners exert strong/frequent impact on one another across diverse behavioral domains. Accordingly over time, each person is likely to exert considerable impact on the other's "self"—the other's traits, values, and behavioral tendencies. To the extent that the confirmation process aligns with each person's ideal self, each is likely to enjoy movement toward his or her ideal self, and the relationship will flourish. Affirmation describes the extent to which the partner's perception and behavior aligns with the individual's ideal self. Such affirmation is termed the "Michelangelo Phenomenon." Affirmation has been shown to yield enhanced personal and couple well-being (Campbell, Sedikides, and Bosson 1994; Drigotas et al. 1999).

The process of affirmation seems more intuitive in the context of a romantic relationship than in consumer behavior—indeed, one must be willing to accept that a consumer and a brand can have an interdependent relationship in which each exerts powerful effects on the other. Susan Fournier (1998) put out such a call to researchers to use close relationship theories in psychology to understand the relationship between consumer and brand, conceptualizing the brand as an animated partner to the consumer. At present, we make the argument that products can affirm the consumer's ideal self. Additionally, we offer the presumption that "product affirmation" exerts significantly more powerful effects on a consumer's emotions, personality, and product evaluations than products which verify or enhance one's self-concept (alternatively labeled as "product verification" and "product enhancement" respectively). Furthermore, if our assumption of product affirmation is reasonable, then any type of product which brings one closer to his/her ideal self, whether it is used for hedonic or utilitarian purposes, should yield significant affirmation effects.

We conducted three studies to empirically test the proposition of product affirmation. The first study (study 1) was a simple non-experimental (survey design) study to initially establish the association of product affirmation with changes in a consumer's emotions, personality, and product evaluations. Study 1 used a sample of alumni students of a moderately sized state-funded university in the northeastern United States, and results provided significant support for product affirmation effects. Using college student samples, the second and third studies used experimental manipulations to pit product affirmation effects on a consumer's emotions, personality, and product evaluations against product verification effects (study 2) and product enhancement effects (study 3). Study 2 asked participants to generate traits in their actual and ideal selves, whereas study 3 asked participants to generate traits in their enhanced and ideal selves. Both studies then prompted participants to think about and list a product for each of the two traits that would seem to show the participant as a person possessing each respective trait. Finally, after coming up with a product for each trait, participants were asked to rate their agreement on a series of Likert-type scales measuring the hedonic and utilitarian value of each respective product and the extent to which they would feel confident, lovable, attractive, excited, anxious, relaxed, disappointed, happy, and annoyed as a result of owning/using the product. Participants were also asked to rate their agreement on Likert-type scales measuring the extent that they liked each product associated with its respective trait.

Analyses employing mixed analysis of covariates (ANCOVA) designs (with product affirmation as the between-subjects factor and product verification (study 2)/product enhancement (study 3) as the within-subjects factors and using the product's hedonic and utilitarian scores as covariates) yielded strong and consistent support for product affirmation effects on a consumer's emotions, personality, and product evaluations and decidedly weaker and inconsistent product verification and product enhancement effects. That is, products aligned with the consumer's ideal self were evaluated more favorably and brought about more positive changes in the consumer's emotions and personality compared to products aligned with the consumer's non-ideal self. Alternatively, analyses did not exhibit parallel support for products aligned with the consumer's actual self (product verification) or products aligned with the consumer's enhanced self (product enhancement). Finally, these product affirmation effects operated above and beyond the product's hedonic or utilitarian value to the consumer. Such results seem to have profound implications for the revision of self-image congruence models in accounting for the apparently superior effect of product affirmation.

References

Campbell, Keith W., Constantine Sedikides and J. Bosson (1994), "Romantic Involvement, Self-Discrepancy, and Psychological Well-Being: A Preliminary Investigation," *Personal Relationships*, 1, 399-404.

Darley, John. M. and R. H. Fazio (1980), "Expectancy Confirmation Processes Arising in the Social Interaction Sequence," *American Psychologist*, 35, 867-881.

Dolich, I. J. (1969), "Congruence Relationship Between Self-Image and Product Brands," *Journal of Marketing Research*, 6, 80-84.

Drigotas, Stephen M., Caryl E. Rusbult, Jennifer Wieselquist and S. Whitton (1999), "Close Partner as Sculptor of the Ideal Self: Behavioral Affirmation and the Michelangelo Phenomenon," *Journal of Personality and Social Psychology*, 77, 293-323.

Fournier, Susan (1998), "Consumers and Their Brands: Developing Relationship Theory in Consumer Research," *Journal of Consumer Research*, 24, 343-373.

Onkvisit, S. and J. Shaw (1987), "Self-Concept and Image Congruence: Some Research and Managerial Implications," *Journal of Consumer Marketing*, 4, 13-24.

Prentice, D. A. (1987), "Psychological Correspondence of Possessions, Attitudes, and Values," *Journal of Personality and Social Psychology*, 53, 993-1002.

Rusbult, Caryl E., Madoka Kumashiro, Shevaun L. Stocker, Jeffrey L. Kirchner, Eli J. Finkel and Michael K. Coolsen (2005), "Self Processes in Interdependent Relationships: Partner Affirmation and the Michelangelo Phenomenon," *Interaction Studies: Social Behaviour and Communication in Biological and Artificial Systems*, 6, 375-391.

Solomon, Michael R. (2007), *Consumer Behavior (7th edition)*, Pearson.

Snyder, M., E. Tanke and Ellen Berscheid (1977), "Social Perception and Interpersonal Behavior: On the Self-Fulfilling Nature of Social Stereotypes," *Journal of Personality and Social Psychology*, 35, 656-666.

Taking Cues from Others: The Effect of Distinct Self-Views on the Persuasiveness of Extrinsic Brand Popularity Information

Yun Lee, University of Iowa, USA

Abstract

This research examines how the situational accessibility of distinct self-views influences the persuasiveness of extrinsic popularity information used in advertising. Two studies provide initial support for the hypothesis that the accessibility of different types of self-views affects how people interpret extrinsic brand popularity information used in advertising. Study 1 showed that the more individuals were accessible with interdependent self-views, they were more likely to favorably evaluate a brand presented with extrinsic popularity information in advertising. Study 2 showed that individuals with interdependent self-views were more likely to favorably evaluate a brand presented with extrinsic popularity information than individuals with independent self-views.

Conceptual Framework

Prior work has suggested that consumers use the relative brand popularity as a positive indicator of the brand's quality (Dean 1999; Huang and Chen 2006; Szymanski, Bharadwaj, and Varadarajan 1993). However, while brand popularity information has been frequently incorporated into advertising as a common practice for companies (Dean 1999), the effect of distinct self-views on the persuasiveness of extrinsic brand popularity information is yet to be clearly understood. Therefore, this research examines how the situational accessibility of distinct self-views influences the persuasiveness of extrinsic popularity information used in advertising. In this research, I propose that, due to different types of goals associated with distinct self-views, consumers with interdependent self-views are more likely to favorably evaluate a brand presented with extrinsic popularity information than consumers with independent self-views.

The distinction between the interdependent and independent self-views has been made through the different types of conflicted structure of goals (Singelis 1994; Triandis 1989). Individuals with interdependent self-views tend to be more sensitive to situations and social contexts and contingent upon the feelings, thoughts, and behavior of others (Kanagawa, Cross, and Markus 2001). The goals of individuals with dominant interdependent self-views are flexibility and variability to be connected with and belonged to others. Thus, those with interdependent self-views show greater relationship-relevant self-view tendencies enacting appropriate behaviors based on others' views, fostering harmony and fitting in with others. Since interconnectedness with and belongingness to others are the central focus of individuals with interdependent self-views (Kitayama et al. 1997), these individuals are more likely to hold a flexible and variant self-view to conform to situational and contextual norms (Kim and Markus 1999) and act in accordance with behaviors and decisions of others over their internal, personal attributes or characteristics (Markus and Kitayama 1991; Signelis 1994; Stapel and Koomen 2001).

In contrast, the goals of individuals with dominant independent self-views are uniqueness, individuality, autonomy, assertiveness, and independence distinctly separate from others (Aaker and Lee 2001). Thus, individuals with independent self-views tend to be more autonomous and invariant across situations and social contexts, and more focus on their own feelings and thoughts. Therefore, those with independent self-views show greater relationship-irrelevant self-view tendencies to accentuate self-related features and minimize the influence of others, resulting in emphasizing uniqueness, separateness, and distinctness of individuals (Baaren et al. 2003). Since expressions of one's unique, personal attributes are the main focus of individuals with independent self-views, these individuals are more likely to hold a bounded, stable and invariant self-view to pursue individualized internal characteristics and attributes that are clearly distinguished from others.

The preceding discussions suggest that the impact of extrinsic brand popularity information should vary based on relative accessibility of interdependent versus independent self-views, due to goal (in)compatibility between different types of self-views and extrinsic brand popularity information. Specifically, I predict that consumers with interdependent self-views should interpret extrinsic brand popularity information as values by which they can harmoniously fit in with others and maintain interconnections with and belongingness to others (Aaker and Lee 2001). In contrast, consumers with independent self-views should interpret a brand with extrinsic popularity information less favorably than consumers with interdependent self-views, because their goals characterized with being unique, distinct, separate, and different from others (Aaker and Lee 2001; Singelis 1994; Triandis 1989) are not compatible with values extrinsic brand popularity information represent. Therefore, I hypothesize that the more consumers are accessible with interdependent self-views, the more they will favorably evaluate a brand presented with extrinsic brand popularity information (study 1). I also hypothesize that individuals with interdependent self-views will be more likely to favorably evaluate a brand presented with extrinsic brand popularity information in advertising than individuals with independent self-views (study 2).

Study 1

To test H1, the extent of interdependent self-views was measured by instructing participants to write down short stories about similarities they have with family members or friends (Trafimow, Triandis, and Goto 1991). Then they were asked to indicate the degree to which they focused on others than selves (Lee, Aaker, and Gardner 2000) on a seven-point scale (1=not at all, 7=very much). Participants, were then asked to review the 2008 Tiburon GS print ad presented with extrinsic popularity information (i.e., the bestselling car! 89% of consumers who reviewed 2008 Tiburon GS selected this car) and indicate their favorability toward the brand on a seven-point scale (1=very unfavorable, 7=very favorable). As predicted, the results showed that the more participants were assessable with interdependent self-views, they were more likely to favorably evaluate a brand presented with extrinsic brand popularity information in advertising ($F(1, 96)=6.618, p=.012$).

Study 2

In study 2, interdependent versus independent self-views were manipulated. Participants were asked to think about how they are similar to (interdependent) or different from (independent) family members or friends and write down short stories about their thoughts (Trafimow, Triandis, and Goto 1991). The procedure to measure brand favorability was similar to study 1. The results showed marginally significant effect of different types of self-views on the persuasiveness of extrinsic brand popularity information. Participants with interdependent self-views were more likely to favorably evaluate a brand presented with extrinsic popularity information than participants with independent self-views ($M_{inter}= 5.12$ vs. $M_{indep}=4.75, t(98)=1.804, p=.074$).

Results and Discussion

These results are consistent with the previous findings showing that people tend to more focus on features, benefits, and values which are compatible with their goals of self-views (Aaker and Lee 2001; Gardner, Pickett, and Brewer 2000). Two studies reported here provide initial evidence that different types of self-views affect how consumers interpret extrinsic popularity information used in advertising. Distinct self-views encourage consumers to have different perspectives on goal pursuit (Aaker and Lee 2001; Lee, Aaker, and Gardner 2000) and then seek values and benefits which is consistent with their goals of self-views, which in turn affects their attitudes toward the brands shown in advertising.

References

Aaker, Jennifer L. and Angela Y. Lee (2001), " 'I' Seek Pleasures and 'We' Avoid Pains: The Role of Self-Regulatory Goals in Information Processing and Persuasion," *Journal of Consumer Research*, 28 (June), 33-49.

Barren, Rick B., William W. Maddux, Tanya L. Chartrand, Cris de Bouter, and Ad van Knippenberg (2003), "It Takes Mimic: Behavioral Consequences of Self-Construals," *Journal of Personality and Social Psychology*, 84(5), 1093-1102.

Dean, Dwane Hal (1999), "Brand Endorsement, Popularity, and Event Sponsorship as Advertising Cues Affecting Consumer Pre-Purchase Attitudes," *Journal of Advertising*, 28(3), 1-12.

Gardner, Wendi L., Cynthia L. Pickett, and Marilynn B. Brewer (2000), "Social Exclusion and Selective Memory: How the Need to Belong Affects Memory," *Personality and Social Psychology Bulletin*, 26 (April), 486-96.

Huang, Jen-Hung and Yi-Fen Chen (2006), "Herding in Online Product Choice," *Psychology and Marketing*, 23(5), 413-28.

Kanagawa, C., S.E. Cross, and Hazel Markus (2001), "Who am I: The Cultural Psychology of the Conceptual Self," *Personality and Social Psychology Bulletin*, 27, 90-103.

Kim, Heejung, and Hazel R. Markus (1999), "Deviance or Uniqueness, Harmony or Conformity? A Cultural Analysis," *Personality Processes and Individual Differences*, 77 (4), 785-800.

Kitayama, Shinobu., Hazel R. Markus, H. Matsumoto, and V. Norasakkunkit (1997), "Attitudes and Social Cognition: Individual and Collective Processes in the Construction of the Self: Self-Enhancement in the United States and Self-Criticism in Japan," *Journal of Personality and Social Psychology*, 72, 1245-67.

Lee, Angela Y., Jennifer L. Aaker, and Wendi L. Gardner (2000), "The Pleasures and Pains of Dstinct Self-Construals: The Role of Interdependence in Regulatory Focus," *Journal of Personality and Social Psychology*, 78 (June), 1122-34.

Markus, Hazel and Shinobu Kitayama (1991), "Culture and the Self: Implications for Cognition, Emotion, and Motivation," *Psychological Review*, 98 (April), 224-53.

Singelis, Theodore M. (1994), "The Measurement of Independent and Interdependent Self-Construals," *Personality and Social Psychology Bulletin*, 20 (5), 580-91.

Stapel, Diederik A. and Willem Koomen (2001), "I, We, and the Effects of Others on Me: How Self-Construal Level Moderates Social Comparison Effects," *Journal of Personality and Social Psychology*, 80 (5), 766-81.

Szymanski, David M., Sundar G Bharadwaj and P. Rajan Varadarajan (1993), "An Analysis of the Market Share-Profitability Relationship," *Journal of Marketing*, 57, 1-18.

Trafimow, David, Harry Triandis, and Sharon Goto (1991), "Some Tests of the Distinction between the Private Self and the Collective Self," *Journal of Personality and Social Psychology*, 60 (May), 649-55.

Triandis, Harry C. (1989), "The Self and Social Behavior in Differing Cultural Contexts," *Psychological Review*, 96 (3), 506-20.

Moderating Role of Member Identification on the Relationship Between Network Centrality and Opinion Leadership / Satisfaction

Seung Hwan (Mark) Lee, University of Western Ontario, Canada

June Cotte, University of Western Ontario, Canada

Opinion leaders are defined as individuals who influence the purchasing behavior of other consumers in a specific product domain (Flynn, Goldsmith, and Eastman 1996). Opinion leaders play a critical role in diffusing information across social systems (Chaney 2001). Burt (1999) posited that opinion leaders need to be socially connected inside a network, not isolated, to effectively spread information. However, we believe that the degree to which individuals become opinion leaders is not only tied to the extent which they are socially connected, but also the level in which they identify with their network.

Member identification is the degree to which one feels belongingness to an organization of which the person is a member (Bhattacharya, Rao, and Glynn 1995). When a person identifies with a club, he/she tends to define him/herself in terms of the club (Mael and Ashforth 1992). We believe that a person with high member identification (HMI) is likely to accrue greater benefits from being in a central position than a person with low member identification (LMI). As HMIs are passionate about their social club, they are likely to be recognized as the face of the club, thus having higher likelihood that they become strong influencers.

Furthermore, we test whether network centrality predicts satisfaction with the club, and whether member identification also acts as a moderator to this relationship.

H1: *Network centrality is positively related to opinion leadership.*
H2: *Network centrality is positively related to club satisfaction.*
H3: *The relationship between network centrality and opinion leadership is higher for HMI than LMI.*
H4: *The relationship between network centrality and club satisfaction is higher for HMI than LMI.*

Methodology

Participants & Procedure. In total, we collected data from 64 of 125 (response rate, 51.2%) students who were members of a university ethnic social club. To be a member of the club, one was required to purchase a membership at any point in the academic year. Network data were collected using the roster method (Wasserman and Faust 1997). In this method, we provided the students with an alphabetical listing of the names of all of the club members and asked to them to indicate their degree of friendship regarding each member.

Measures. We used the friendship matrix (64x64) into the network program UCINET (Borgatti, Everett, and Freeman 1999) to obtain differences in closeness centrality scores. Closeness centrality measures how many nodes on average it takes for an individual to reach everyone else in the network. Individual with high closeness centrality has the shortest path to all other nodes (Freeman 1979).

We obtained differences in centrality scores for the QAP regression analysis (non-parametric technique) to overcome the issues of non-independence of data points. Using ordinary least squares (OLS) is inappropriate as network data do not suffice the assumptions of independence of observation (e.g. Gibbons and Olk 2003). We interpret the outcomes of QAP analysis as having a higher (lower) closeness centrality score compared to others in the network.

For other measures, we used established scales from previous literatures. We assessed opinion leadership using a 6-item scale developed by Flynn et al. (1996). We assessed satisfaction using a 6-item scale developed by Baldwin, Bedell, and Johnson (1997). We measured member identification using a 6-item scale developed by Mael and Ashforth (1992). Lastly, we used gender as control in all of our analysis as studies have shown differences in gender effects in networks (e.g. Burt 1992)

Data Analysis. To test our hypothesized moderation of member identification, we used a median split (m=4.33) to divide the data into two groups. Data from high member identification (HMI, n=33) and from low member identification (LMI, n=31) were analyzed separately using QAP network regression analysis to test the relationship between closeness centrality and opinion leadership / club satisfaction. The use of two-group comparison using QAP is not uncommon (Borgatti and Cross 2003), and is used to identify possible moderators.

Results

All of our four hypotheses were supported by our data. Closeness centrality was positively related to opinion leadership ($\alpha=7.725$, $p<0.01$, $r^2=15.8\%$). Closeness centrality was also positively related to club satisfaction ($\alpha=6.83$, $p<0.01$, $r^2=11.8\%$). As for our test for moderation, we found full support for hypotheses 3 and 4. For the HMI group, closeness centrality was positive and significant in predicting opinion leadership ($\alpha=4.741$, $p<0.05$, $r^2=14.0\%$) and club satisfaction ($\alpha=6.639$, $p<0.01$, $r^2=18.1\%$). However, for the LMI group, the regression coefficient was not significant ($p>.05$, ns). The control variable gender was not significant.

Discussion

This study has few limitations. First, we acknowledge that the extent of the individuals' network reach beyond the social club which can influence the level of opinion leadership and satisfaction with the club. However, we feel that using the club network was appropriate as our dependent variables are likely to depend heavily on the network itself. Second, scholars have noted that response rate of under 50% would deem the network data to be unreliable and 70% to be desirable (Burt and Minor 1983; Scott 2000). Because we were only able to obtain 51.2% of the entire network, the network measure of closeness centrality is inevitably affected by the non-response. Thus, future research should devote to examining network with higher response rates.

The research can be extended in several ways. First, a longitudinal study would be appropriate to examine the development of friendship networks over time with respect to the variables mentioned in this study. In addition, this research can be enhanced by examining other structural dimensions (e.g. betweenness centrality, structural holes), and how it plays a role in predicting outcomes.

Albeit preliminary, this research provides contribution to the opinion leadership and the satisfaction literature. We find that in social clubs, member identification with the club plays an important role in identifying effective opinion leaders. Therefore, marketers should target those in central positions who identify strongly with their social club. Additionally, this research also shows that individual's who identify with their club garner higher satisfaction as a result of being in a central position.

References

Baldwin, Timoth T., Michael D. Bedell, and Jonathan L. Johnson (1997), "The Social Fabric of a Team-Based Mba Program: Network Effects on Student Satisfaction and Performance," *Academy of Management Journal*, 40 (December), 1369-97.

Bhattacharya, C. B., Hayagreeva Rao, and Mary A. Glynn (1995), "Understanding the Bond of Identification: An Investigation of Its Correlates among Art Museum Members," *Journal of Marketing*, 59 (October), 46-57.

Borgatti, Stephen P. and Rob Cross (2003), "A Relational View of Information Seeking and Learning in Social Networks," *Management Science*, 49 (April), 432-45.

Borgatti, Stephen P., Martin G. Everett, and Linton C. Freeman (2007), "Ucinet for Windows: Software for Social Network Analysis," Harvard, MA: Analytic Technologies.

Burt, Ronald S. (1992), *Structural Holes: The Social Structure of Competition*, Cambridge, MA: Harvard University Press.

_____ (1999), "The Social Capital of Opinion Leaders," *The ANNALS of the American Academy of Political and Social Science*, 566 (November), 37-54.

Burt, Ronald S. and M.J. Minor (1983), *Applied Network Analysis: A Methodological Introduction*, Beverly Hills, CA: Sage Publications.

Chaney, Isabella M. (2001), "Opinion Leaders as a Segment for Marketing Communications," *Planning*, 19 (5), 302-08.

Flynn, Leisa R., Ronald E. Goldsmith, and Jacqueline K. Eastman (1996), "Opinion Leaders and Opinion Seekers: Two New Measurement Scales," *Journal of the Academy of Marketing Science*, 24 (Spring), 137-47.

Freeman, Linton C. (1979), "Centrality in Social Networks: Conceptual Clarification," *Social Networks*, 1 (3), 215-39.

Gibbons, Deborah and Paul M. Olk (2003), "Individual and Structural Origins of Friendship and Social Position among Professionals," *Journal of Personality and Social Psychology*, 84 (February), 340-51.

Mael, Fred and Blake E. Ashforth (1992), "Alumni and Their Alma Mater: A Partial Test of the Reformulated Model of Organizational Identification," *Journal of Organizational Behavior*, 13 (March), 103-23.

Wasserman, Stanley and Katherine Faust (1994), *Social Network Analysis: Methods and Applications*, Cambridge, MA: Cambridge University Press.

An Investigation of College Students' Influence on Parents' Innovation Adoption

Jianping Liang, University of Western Ontario, Canada
June Cotte, University of Western Ontario, Canada

It has been twenty years since Gatignon and Robertson (1985) developed a model of the diffusion process. However, little research has been done in the context of a family's adoption of innovation, especially Gatignon and Robertson's unique focus on interpersonal communication transfer, one of the most important issues in diffusion research. Herein, we extended the intra-family influences on innovation literature with a study of college students' influences on their parents' innovation adoption.

Building on Cotte and Wood (2004), we suggested that influence within a family may be one important indicator of adoption probability. Prior family influence research has focused on intergenerational (parent to child) or intragenerational (sibling to sibling) influences in consumer socialization (Cotte and Wood 2004; Moore, Wilkie, and Lutz 2002). Intergenerational influence (IGI) research literature assumed that the direction of the influence on consumer behavior is from the older parent to the younger child (Moschis 1988). Comparatively little work has yet been explicitly done on upward intergenerational "influence", i.e., the "influence" of children on parents, and none explicitly has considered the role of adult offspring as innovation "influences" on their parents. In Brooks' (1957) seminal study, the difference between "influences" and "requests", especially within the family, was discussed. For example, if a mother is asked by her child to buy a brand of coffee, it is considered the child's "request". If a mother is told by her child that a brand of coffee is good, and she takes her child's words into consideration and is free to make the purchase, it is considered the child's "influence". Although the child's "request" was the focus in most of the previous research (see John 1999), the child's "influence" is the focus of this paper. "Influence" is defined as the power to affect somebody's actions, character or beliefs, especially by providing examples for them to follow and winning their admiration (p.611), while "request" is defined as an act of asking for a thing in this way (p.996, Crowther 1995).

Most of the previous research involving children in a family has investigated the "request" of adolescents under the age of 18 in the family (see John 1999). As children become adults, they are often considered being more mature, knowledgeable, and trustworthy by parents. Potentially they may become opinion leaders and "influence" parents, rather than merely "request" purchase. An opinion leader is considered to have the distinguishing characteristic of being sought by others for information and advice regarding the field in which s/he is a leader (Brooks 1957; Gatignon and Robertson 1985; Childers 1986; Rogers 2003). At the college stage, most young adult children live with people other than family members. However, many college students are not totally independent and still need various kinds of support from parents. The frequent communication and interaction possibly lead to a potential channel for the innovation diffusion process to occur.

Methodology. To the best of our knowledge, this is the first study to explore the influence of college students on their parents' innovation adoption. In order to investigate further on the mechanism of innovation diffusion from college students to parents, we conducted in-depth interviews with thirteen college students at a large North American university. Based on the in-depth interviews, we conducted a survey with 119 college students, as well as 51 of their parents. Data from both college students and their parents were cross-validated and used in the data analyses. Logistic regression was used to examine factors related to whether college students have told parents on innovation and whether parents have adopted the innovation told by their children in the last six month.

Major Findings. We found that college students' opinion leadership does not directly influence parents' innovation adoption. Rather, college students' opinion leadership influences parents' product category knowledge, which subsequently influences parents' innovation adoption.

We also found that the relationship between parents' product category knowledge and their innovation adoption is moderated by the innovativeness of the innovation such that the higher the parents' knowledge, the more likely their adoption, regardless of the innovativeness of the innovation, whereas when parents have lower knowledge, they are much more likely to adopt low innovative innovation than high innovative innovation.

According to the innovation diffusion literature, both homophily (i.e., the degree of similarity between pairs of individuals) and heterophily (i.e., the degree of dissimilarity) are important in determining the innovation diffusion (Rogers 2003). We only found the effects of homophily in social value, which indicated that the more similar the social value between college students and parents, the more likely that the college students tell parents about innovations and the more likely that their parents adopt the innovations.

Finally, Ekstrom, Tansuhaj and Foxman (1987) found that children's influence varies by family communication pattern and thus is stronger in families high in concept-orientation (i.e., children are encouraged to develop their own ideas and express their views more openly, see also McLeod and Chaffee 1972). We found that college students in more concept-oriented families are more likely to tell parents about innovations, but have no more influence on parents' innovation adoption than those in less concept-oriented families. On the other hand, emotional closeness between college students and parents does not influence whether college students tell parents about innovations, but influence parents' adoption, such that the higher the emotional closeness, the more likely the parents' adoption.

References

Brooks, Robert C. (1957), "'Word-of-Mouth' Advertising in Selling New Products," *Journal of Marketing*, 22, 154-161.

Childers, Terry L. (1986), "Assessment of the psychometric properties of an opinion leadership scale," *Journal of Marketing Research*, XXIII, 184-188.

Cotte, June and Stacy L. Wood (2004), "Families and Innovative Consumer Behavior: A Triadic Analysis of Sibling and Parental Influence," *Journal of Consumer Research*, 6, 78-86.

Crowther, Jonathan (1995), *Oxford Advanced Learner's Dictionary*, Oxford University Press.

Ekstrom, K.M., Patriya S. Tansuhaj, and Ellen R. Foxman (1987), "Children's Influence in Family Decisions and Consumer Socialization: A Reciprocal View," *Advances in Consumer Research*, 14, 283-287.

Gatignon, Hubert and Thomas S. Robertson (1985), "A Propositional Inventory for New Diffusion Research," *Journal of Consumer Research*, 3 (March), 849-867.

John, Deborah Roedder (1999), "Consumer Socialization of Children: A Retrospective Look at Twenty-Five Years of Research," *Journal of Consumer Research*, December, 183-213.

McLeod, J.M. and S.H. Chaffee (1972), "The Construction of Social Reality," in *The Social Influence Process*, J.T. Tiedeschi (Ed.), Chicago: Aldine-Atherton, 50-99.

Moore, Elizabeth S., W. L. Wilkie and R. J. Lutz (2002), "Passing the Torch: Intergenerational Influence as a Source of Brand Equity," *Journal of Marketing*, 66 (April), 17-37.

Moschis, George P. (1988), "Methodological Issues in Studying Intergenerational Influences on Consumer Behavior," in *Advances in Consumer Research*, Vol. 15, ed. M. J. Houston, Provo, UT: Association for Consumer Research, 569-573.

Rogers, Everett M. (2003), *Diffusion of Innovations* (5th ed.), New York: The Free Press.

The Effects of Phonetic Symbolism on Comparative Price Perceptions

Keith S. Coulter, Clark University, USA

Psycholinguistics is a specialized area within the field of cognitive psychology that is focused upon the development, production, comprehension, and usage of language. In general, psycho-linguistic features may influence both the memorability and perception of words through their ability to convey meaningfulness (Eysenck 1979). One attribute that has been shown to have an impact on the meaningfulness of a word is phonetic (or "sound") symbolism, which refers to the ability of particular phonemes (i.e., the fundamental building blocks of sound in a language) to convey information.

At the broadest level, researchers typically categorize phonemes in terms of vowels versus consonants. Vowels are then sub-categorized on a front versus back distinction (which refers to the position of the highest point of the tongue during pronunciation), whereas consonants are typically categorized as either fricatives (i.e., s, f, v, and z) or stops (i.e., p, k, t, b, g, d, and hard c). These front/back and fricative/stop distinctions are important because they have been consistently related to a variety of spatial dimensions. For example back-vowel sounds (e.g., "u" as in "dusk") and stop consonants are typically associated with perceptions of *large* size, whereas front vowel sounds (e.g., "e" as in "bee") and fricatives are typically associated with perceptions of *small* size (Sapir 1929; Newman 1933; Klink 2000; Yorkston and Menon 2004). The effect may be the evolutionary result of using resonant cavity and "formant dispersion" (i.e., the difference between resonance frequencies) as a cue to body size (Fitch 1994; 1997; Fitch and Hauser 2002).

Research in numerical cognition suggests that price-name phonemes may impact price perceptions due to the manner in which prices are processed and encoded. According to Dehaene's (1992) triple code model, numbers can be mentally represented and manipulated in three different forms: visual, auditory, and analog. The visual (Arabic) code represents numbers on a spatial visual medium on the basis of their written form in Arabic numerals (e.g., 72); the auditory verbal code is generated through a phonological representation in which each number is represented by a sequence of phonemes (e.g., "seventy" and "two"); the analogue magnitude code represents numbers as judgments of relative "size" arrayed in parallel-format along a left-to-right-oriented mental number line (Dehaene, Bossini, and Giraux 1993). Research has demonstrated that the verbal, visual, and analog representations are neurologically connected: paths link the different representations both within and across (i.e., through the corpus callosum) left and right hemispheres of the brain (Noel 2001).

Consistent with prior research in this area, we expect that *both* phonological and analog magnitude representations will be evoked when consumers are exposed to comparative price advertisements, and that the phonological representations may affect relative analog encoding (Monroe and Lee 1999; Roediger and McDermott 1993; Coulter and Coulter 2005; Coulter and Norberg 2007; Vanhuele, Laurent, and Dreze 2006; Vanhuele and Dreze 2002). More specifically, sale-price phonological codes that have been demonstrated to be associated with perceptions of "smallness" (i.e., fricatives and front vowels) should increase the likelihood that sale prices are perceived as small in comparison to regular prices, and that regular prices are perceived as large in comparison to sale prices, thereby increasing the magnitude of the perceived discount. Conversely, phonological codes typically associated with perceptions of "largeness" (i.e., back vowels and stops) should decrease the likelihood that sale prices are perceived as small in comparison to regular prices, thereby decreasing the magnitude of the perceived discount. We tested these assumptions in the context of three experiments.

Experiment 1 involved a between subjects (n= 150) design in which participants were exposed to comparative price advertisements. Regular prices in the target ads were identical, but the sale prices contained either fricative and front vowel (e.g., $7.66) or back vowel and stop (e.g., $7.22) price endings (cents digits). To ensure verbal encoding and consistent with previous studies in this area (cf. Vanhuele, Laurent, and Dreze 2006), participants were instructed to read silently to themselves any (sale) prices they encountered; they were further told to rehearse the prices internally to keep them in memory. To account for the effects of cross-condition differences in actual percentage discounts, we derived an adjusted perceived price discount measure (APD) by subtracting the actual from the perceived percentage discount, and then dividing by the actual percentage discount. ANOVA revealed that APD [$F(4,130)= 37.51, p<.001$], value assessments, and purchase intentions were significantly greater in the front vowel/fricative conditions than in the back vowel/stop conditions, even though actual discount was lower in the former case(s).

A limitation of our first Experiment was that the automatic and non-conscious nature of the numeric processing precluded our ability to administer a direct and definitive manipulation check. Thus, one could argue that extraneous factors associated with the specific sale price numbers (e.g., size, appearance, or "representativeness") might have impacted our results. Therefore, in Experiment 2 we utilized a task paradigm that employed *phonological suppression* to impede auditory price encoding (Dehaene 1992).

We hypothesized that verbal rehearsal of three different attribute-related phonological phrases during stimulus viewing would cause participants to suppress the phonological codes associated with price processing, while still encoding the appropriate analog magnitude representations (Lee and Kang 2002). Suppression of auditory codes associated with front vowel/fricative and back vowel/stop consonant sale prices should then assuage the relative distortion of analog magnitude representations associated with price discount encoding observed in Experiment 1. ANOVA results confirmed that supposition.

One might still argue, however, that findings were driven by *non*-phonetic characteristics of the chosen number combinations, and that these effects were suppressed when participants recited attribute-related information. Therefore in Experiment 3, we again examined the effects of phonetic suppression on price discount perceptions associated with two different regular/sale price combinations. However, we examined the proposed effects across English versus Chinese-speaking subjects. We utilized sale prices that may be characterized as front vowel/fricatives in one language, but back vowel/stops in another. ANOVA results revealed significant price phoneme x suppression x language effects, thus lending strong support to our hypotheses.

References

Ashcraft, Mark H. (1992), "Cognitive Arithmetic: A Review of Data and Theory," *Cognition*, 44 (1-2), special issue, 75-106.

Baddeley, Alan D. (1992), "Working Memory," *Science*, 255 (5054), 556-559.

Baddeley, Alan D. (2001), "Is Working Memory Still Working?" *American Psychologist*, 56 (November), 851-864.

Becker, Judith A. and Sylvia K. Fisher (1988), "Comparison of Associations to Vowel Speech Sounds by English and Spanish Speakers," *American Journal of Psychology*, 101 (1), 51-57.

Birch, D. and Erickson, M. (1958), "Phonetic Symbolism with Respect to Three Dimensions from the Semantic Differential," *Journal of General Psychology*, 58, 291-297.

Brysbaert, Marc, Wim Fias, and Marie-Pascale Noel (1998), "The Whorfian Hypothesis and Numerical Cognition: Is Twenty-four Processed in the Same Way as Four-and-Twenty," *Cognition*, 66 (1) April, 51-77.

Clark, John and Colin Yallop (1990), *An Introduction to Phonetics and Phonology*. London: Basil Blackwell.

Cortese, Michael J. (1998), "*Revisiging Serial Position Effects in Reading*," Journal of Memory and Language, 39, 652-665.

Coulter, Keith S. and Patricia A. Norberg, (2007) "The Impact of Physical Distance on Price Discount Perceptions," *AMA Summer 2007 Marketing Educators' Conference Proceedings*, Washington, D.C., August 3-5, 2007.

Dehaene, Stanislas (1992), "Varieties of Numerical Abilities," *Cognition*, 44 (1-2), special issue, 1-42.

Dehaene, Stanislas (1997), *The Number Sense*, Oxford: Oxford University Press.

Dehaene, Stanislas and Cohen, L. (1995), "Towards an Anatomical and Functional Model of Number Processing," *Mathematical Cognition*, 1 (1), 83-120.

Dehaene, Stanislas and Cohen, L. (1997), "Cerebral Pathways for Calculation: Double Dissociation Between Rote Verbal and Quantitative Knowledge of Arithmetic," *Cortex*, 33, 219-250.

Dehaene, S. Dupoux, E., and Mehler, J. (1990), "Is Numerical Comparison Digital? Analogical and Symbolic Effects in two-Digit Number Comparison," *Journal of Experimental Psychology: Human Perception and Performance*, 16, 626-641.

Dehaene, Stanislas, Bossini, S., and Giraux, P. (1993), "The Mental Representation of Parity and Number Magnitude," *Journal of Experimental Psychology: General*, 122, 371-396.

DeStefano, Diana and Jo-Anne leFevre (2004), "The role of working Memory in Mental Arithmetic," *European Journal of Cognitive Psychology*, 16 (3), 353-387.

Eysenck, M.W. (1979), "Depth, Evaluation, and Distinctiveness," in L.s. Cermak and F.I. M. Craig (Eds.), *Levels of Processing in Human Memory* (pp. 89-123). Hillsdale, NJ: Lawrence Erlbaum Associates.

Fitch, W. Tecumseh (1994), "Vocal Tract Length Perception and the Evolution of Language," Unpublished doctoral dissertation, Brown University.

Fitch, W. Tecumseh (1997), "Vocal Tract Length and Formant Frequency Dispersion Correlate with Body Size in Rhesus Macaques," *Journal of the Acoustical Society of America*, 102 (2), 1213-1222.

Fitch, W.T. and M.D. Hauser (2002), "Unpacking Honesty: Vertebrate Vocal Production and the Evolution of Acoustic Signals," in A. Simmons, R.R. Fay, and A.N. Popper (Eds.), *Springer Handbook of Auditory Research* (pp. 65-137), New York: Springer.

French, P.L. (1977), "Toward an Explanation of Phonetic Symbolism," *Word*, 28, 305-322.

Gallistel, C.R., and Gelman, R. (1992), "Preverbal and Verbal Counting and Computation," *Cognition* (44), 43-74.

Hinton, Leanne, Hohanna Nichols and John Ohala (1994), "*Introduction: Sound Symbolism Processes*," in Sound Symbolism, Hinton, Nichols, and Ohala (Eds.). Cambridge, England: Cambridge University Press.

Jesperson, O. (1922), *Language: Its Nature, Development, and Origin*. London: Allen and Unwin.

Johnson, R.C. 1967, "Magnitude Symbolism of English Words," *Journal of Verbal Learning and Verbal Behavior*," 6, 508-511.

Kim, Hyeong Min and David Luna (2007), "Do You Remember the Price of Your Shopping Basket? The Role of Linguistic Number Processing on Total Price Recall," Working Paper.

Klink, Richard R. (2000), "Creating brand Names with Meaning: The Use of Sound Symbolism," *Marketing Letters* 11 (1), 5-20.

Klink, Richard R. (2003), "Creating Meaningful Brands: The Relationship between Brand Name and Brand Mark," Marketing Letters, 14, 143-157.

Leahy, Thomas H. and Richard J. Harris (1996), *Learning and Cognition*, Englewood Cliffs, NJ: Prentice-Hall.

Lee, Kyoung-Min and So-Young Kang (2002) "Arithmetic Operation and Working Memory: Differential Suppression in Dual Tasks," *Cognition* (83), B63-B68.

Logie, Robert H., Kenneth J. Gillhooly, and Valerie Wynn (1994), "Counting on working Memory in Arithmetic Problem Solving," *Memory and Cognition*, 22(4), 395-410.

Lowrey, Tina M., L.J. Shrum and Tony M. Dubitsky (2003), "The Relation Between Brand-Name Linguistic Characteristics and Brand-Name Memory," *Journal of Advertising*, 32 (3), 7-17.

McCloskey, Michael, and Paul Macaruso (1995), "Representing and Using Numerical Information," *American Psychologist*, 50 (5) May, 351-363.

Morton, Eugene S. (1994), "*Sound Symbolism and Its Role in Non-Human Vertebrate Communication*," in Hinton, Nichols, and Ohala (Eds.), Sound Symbolism. Cambridge, England: Cambridge University Press.

Newman, S.S. (1933), "Further Experiments in Phonetic Symbolism," American Journal of Psychology, 45, 53-75.

Noel, Marie-Pascale (2001), "Numerical Cognition," in *Handbook of Cognitive Neuropsychology: What Deficits Reveal About the Human Mind*, Brenda Rapp, Ed., New York, NY: Psychology Press.

Ohala, John (1994), "*The Frequency Code Underlies the sound-Symbolic Use of Voice Pitch*," in Hinton, Nichols, and Ohala (Eds.), Sound Symbolism. Cambridge, England: Cambridge University Press.

Pinel, P., LeVlec, H.G., Van de Moortele, P.F., Naccache, L., LeBihan, D., and Dehaene, S. (1999), "Event-Related fMRI Analysis of the Cerebral Circuit for Number Comparison," *Neuroreport*, 10 (7), 1473-1479.

Pinker, S. (1994), *The Language Instinct*. New York: William Morrow.

Sapir, E. (1929), "A Study in Phonetic Symbolism," Journal of Experimental Psychology, 12, 225-239.

Shrum, L.J., and Tina M. Lowrey (2007), "Sounds Convey Meaning: The Implications of Phonetic Symbolism for Brand Name Construction," in *Psycholinguistic Phenomena in Marketing Communications*, Tina M. Lowrey and L.J. Shrum (Eds.), Lawrence Erlbaum Associates, 39-58.

Thomas, Manoj, and Vicki Morwitz (2005), "Penny Wise and Pound Foolish: The Left Digit Effect in Price Cognition," *Journal of Consumer Research*, 32 (June), 54-64.

Trbovich, Patricia L. and Jo-Anne LeFevre (2003), "Phonological and Visual Working Memory in Mental Addition," *Memory and Cognition*, 31(5), 738-745.

Ultan, R. (1978), "Size-Sound Symbolism," in J.H. Greenberg, C.A. Ferguson, and E.A. Moravcsik (Eds.), Universals of Human Language: Volume 2 Phonology (pp. 525-568). Stanford, CA: Stanford University Press.

Vanden Bergh, Bruce G., J. Collins, M. Schultz and K. Adler (1984), "Sound Advice on Brand Names," *Journalism Quarterly*, 61, 835-840.

Vanhuele, Marc, and Xavier Dreze (2002), "Measuring the Price Knowledge Shoppers Bring to the Store," *Journal of Marketing*, 66 (October), 72-85.

Vanhuele, Marc, Gilles Laurent, and Xavier Dreze (2006), Consumers' Immediate Memory for Prices, *Journal of Consumer Research*, 33 (2), 163-172.

Yorkston, Eric A. and Geeta Menon (2004), "A Sound Idea: Phonetic Effects of Brand Names on Consumer Judgments," *Journal of Consumer Research*, 31 (June), 43-51.

Does the Devil Really Wear Prada? Social Relations Analysis of Brand and Human Personalities

Maxim Polonsky, University of Connecticut, USA
Robin A. Coulter, University of Connecticut, USA

Nearly a half-century ago, Levy (1959) advanced the idea that brands are reflective symbols of the self. In the ensuing years, marketers and consumer researchers have focused on leveraging and understanding the many facets of brand symbolism. Aaker's seminal work (1997) linking brand personality characteristics to human personality characteristics is noteworthy, and has served as the bases for others' investigation of these associations (Caprara, Barbaranelli, and Guido; Johar, Sengupta, and Aaker 2005). This human-brand personality research is directly related to other work that has considered how consumers use brands to communicate something about their own identity (Belk 1988; Escalas and Bettman 2005; Kleine, Kleine and Kernan 1993), as well as to reinforce personality and attitudes toward themselves (Escalas and Bettman 2003; Fennis and Pruyn 2007; McCracken 1988).

Indeed companies expend great efforts to create brand images that are meaningful to consumers (Gobé 2007), and research on self-congruity theory (Sirgy 1982; Swann, Stein-Seroussi, and Giesler1992) argues that consumer brand purchasing behavior is determined by the interaction between perceptions of the product and the personality of the consumer; that is, consumers prefer brands with a symbolic function that is congruous with their self-identity. Thus, individuals often engage in selective exposure behaviors that maximize both, consistency and pleasure of self-expression. Fennis, Pruyn and Maasland (2005, 376) found a transfer effect from brand personality to consumer personality and concluded that "brands are capable to 'make us who we are.' Not only are brands chosen by consumers because they highlight some aspect of who we are or want to be, they also shape or highlight these aspects." Aaker (1999) documented that self-schematic traits lead to stronger brand preferences; that is, people prefer brands with which they share personality characteristics.

Another important theoretical aspect of the human-brand personality association is symbolic interactionism (Solomon 1983). Specifically, Solomon (1983, 320) focused on three perspectives: 1) a consumer's self-concept is based on perceptions of the responses of others, 2) a consumer's self-concept functions to direct behavior, and 3) a consumer's perception of the responses of others to some degree reflects those responses. Relatedly, research has demonstrated that consumers evaluate and compare their self-concept with the image of a stereotypic and generalized brand user (Sirgy 1982). Further, some have argued that individuals may have a preference for one brand over the other because they perceives themselves as similar to and identify with people who are generally perceived to use that brand. Further, numerous studies has supported this in-group brand association effect (Ericksen and Sirgy 1992; Heath and Scott 1998; Hong and Zinkhan 1995; Sirgy 1985).

Although there have been many contributions to the human-brand personality association within the past decade, research has not captured the duality of human-brand personality in a social context. The purpose of our research is to draw and build upon theoretical work on brand personality, self-congruity theory, symbolic interactionism, and interpersonal perception, as well as the social relations modeling work (Kenny 1994; Kenny and Albright 1987) to delve into the association of brand and human personality characteristics. We introduce the Social Relations Model (SRM) as a means to consider the social meaning and perception formation as dynamic processes, and where the self is both, a perceiver and a target of perception. The SRM model "permits simultaneous estimation of dispositional, situational, and interactional determinants of behavioral phenomena" by employing round-robin experimental design, and recognizes individuals to be both, a target and a perceiver (Malloy and Kenny 1986, 222). Specifically, the social relations modeling approach enables us assess dyadic data to address the questions such as: If a person is seen to be extraverted, is she also associated with extraverted brands? If a person sees herself to be extraverted and prefers extraverted brands, do others also see her as extraverted and preferring those brands? If a person sees herself using some particular brand, does she see others using the same brand? To further assess the SRM and its contributions related to understanding the human-brand associations, we conducted two studies.

The purpose of study 1 was to identify brands in the automobile and clothing categories that had a "consensus" personality. Study 1 involved two data collections. First, 70 undergraduates at a large northeastern university participated in an online study in which they rated 24 automobiles and 24 clothes brands (34 semantic differential items) to with regard to the Big Five personality characteristics–Agreeableness, Extraversion, Conscientiousness, Emotional Stability, and Openness (Goldberg 1990) and two additional traits, Sophistication and Ruggedness, identified by Aaker (1997). We identified automobile and clothing brands with a high Cronbach's alphas for the personality scale, high means, and low variances. In the second data collection, 40 MBA students were provided with a definition of the seven personality characteristics and asked via a free association task to name a brand that they associated with each personality characteristic. Based on these data collections, we identified to 22 brands, 11 each for automobiles (i.e., extroversion–Volkswagon; emotional stability–Volvo; ruggedness–Hummer) and clothing (i.e., extroversion–NIKE; emotional stability–Old Navy; ruggedness–Levis). Consistent with the SRM in study 2, we conducted a round-robin experiment, with 25 groups consisting of 3 or 4 members per group. The group participants (who were not previously acquainted with one another) were asked to interact with one another for ten minutes, so that each participant could have an initial understanding of the individual's personality characteristics. After the introduction period, each participant rated each group member on 25 semantic differential personality items. Next, the participants reported the likelihood (7-point Likert-scale) of brand use for their group members for each of the 22 brands (from study 1), and then reported their own likelihood of use. Finally, group participants were whether they perceived other group members as thinking they would use the brand. Our work contributes by extending the theoretical and empirical work related to human-brand associations, and our findings provide useful insights about the social meanings of brands.

References

Aaker, Jennifer (1997), "Dimensions of Brand Personality," *Journal of Marketing Research*, 34 (8), 347–56.

Belk, Russell W. (1988), "Possessions and the Extended Self," 15 (January), *Journal of Consumer Research*, 15 (2), 139-68.

Escalas, Jennifer Edson and James R. Bettman (2005), "Self-Construal, Reference Groups, and Brand Meaning," *Journal of Consumer Research*, 22 (December), 497-549

Escalas, Jennifer Edson and James R. Bettman (2003), "You are what they eat: The influence of reference groups on consumers' connections to brands," *Journal of Consumer Psychology*, 13 (3), 339-48.

Caprara, Gian Vittorio, Claudio Barbaranelli, and Gianluigi Guido (2001), "Brand Personality: How to Make the Metaphor Fit?" *Journal of Economic Psychology*, 22 (3), 377–95.

Ericksen, Mary K. and M. Joseph. Sirgy (1989), "Achievement Motivation and Clothing Behavior: A Self-Image Congruence Analysis," *Journal of Social Behavior and Personality*, 4 (4), 307–326.

Fennis Bob M. and Ad Th. H. Pruyn (2007), "You Are What You Wear: Brand Personality Influences on Consumer Impression Formation," *Journal of Business Research*, 60 (June), 634-639.

Fennis, Bob M., Ad Th.H Pruyn, and M. Maasland (2005), "Revisiting the Malleable Self: Brand Effects on Consumer Self-Perceptions of Personality Traits," in *Advances in Consumer Research*, Vol. 32, Geeta Menon and Akshay R. Rao, eds. Duluth, MN : Association for Consumer Research, Pages: 371-377.

Gobé, Marc (2001). *Emotional branding*. NY: Allworth Press.

Goldberg, Lewis R. (1990), "An Alternative 'Description of Personality': The Big-Five Factor Structure," Journal of Personality and Social Psychology, *59*, 1216–29.

Heath, Adam P. and Don Scott (1998), "The Self-Concept and Image Congruence Hypothesis: An Empirical Evaluation in the Motor Vehicle Market," *European Journal of Marketing*, 32 (11/12), 1110–23.

Hong, Wong J. and George M. Zinkhan (1995), "Self-Concept and Advertising Effectiveness: The Influence of Congruency, Conspicuousness, and Response Mode," *Psychology and Marketing*, 12 (1), 53–77.

Johar, Gita V., Jaideep Sengupta, and Jennifer Aaker (2005), "Two Roads to Updating Brand Personality Impressions: Trait versus Evaluative Inferencing," *Journal of Marketing Research,* (November), 458–69.

Kenny David A. (1994), *Interpersonal Perception: A Social Relations Analysis*. New York: Guilford.

Kenny, David A. and Linda Albright (1987), "Accuracy in Interpersonal Perception: A Social Relations Analysis," Psychological Bulletin*, 102,* 390–402.

Kleine, Robert E. III, Susan Schultz-Kleine, and Jerome B. Kernan (199), "Mundane Everyday Consumption and the Self: A Social Identity Perspective," *Journal of Consumer Psychology*, 2 (3) 209–35.

Levy, Sidney J. (1959), "Symbols for Sale," Harvard Business Review (July-August), 117–24.

Malloy Thomas E. and David A. Kenny (1986), "The Social Relations Model: An Integrative Method for Personality Research, *Journal of Personality*, 54 (1), 199–225.

McCracken, Grant (1988), *Culture and Consumption: New Approaches to the Symbolic Character of Consumer Goods and Activities*, Bloomington, IN: Indiana University Press.

Sirgy, M. Joseph (1982), "Self-Concept in Consumer Behavior: A Critical Review," *Journal of Consumer Research*, 9 (December), 287–300.

_____ (1985), "Using Self-Congruity and Ideal Congruity to Predict Purchase Motivation," *Journal of Business Research*, 13 (3), 195-206.

Solomon, Michael R. (1983), "The Role of Products as Social Stimuli: A Symbolic Interactionism Perspective," *The Journal of Consumer Research*, 10 (December), 319-29.

Swann, William B., Alan Stein-Seroussi, and Brian R. Giesler (1992), "Why People Self-Verify," *Journal of Personality and Social Psychology*, 62 (3), 392-401.

Brands: The Opiate of the Non-Religious Masses?

Ron Shachar, Tel Aviv University, Israel and Duke University, USA
Tülin Erdem, New York University, USA
Gavan J. Fitzsimons, Duke University, USA
Keisha M. Cutright, Duke University, USA

Brands have become a ubiquitous presence in today's world, affecting the everyday lives of consumers in many ways. Beyond providing general product benefits, brands maintain unique personalities (Aaker 1997) that consumers often capitalize on to express who they are to themselves and others in their lives (Aaker 1999). The personalities of brands also seem to enable their ascent to cult-like, or even religious, status in the lives of their consumers, supporting the notion that the sacred realm of religion and the secular world of consumption are often intertwined (e.g. Belk, Wallendorf and Sherry 1989). The popular press has even proclaimed brands as the "new religion" (Financial Times 2001).

While the potential relationship between religion and brands has generally been acknowledged, systematic research on the relationship between religiosity and the importance of brands in consumers' lives is noticeably lacking (but, see Rindfleisch, Burroughs & Wong's working paper for a recent exception). Thus, this research focuses on the relationship between religiosity and one indicator of the importance of brands in consumers' lives that we refer to as "brand reliance". We define brand reliance as the degree to which consumers prefer branded goods over goods without a well-known national brand (e.g., generics). Our objective is to establish that a relationship exists whereby individuals with different levels of religious commitment (religiosity) differ systematically in their brand reliance.

In our first study, we examine the relationship between religiosity and brand reliance at a macro level, using state level data. We find that higher religiosity, as measured by the number of congregations and self-reported church attendance, is associated with lower levels of brand reliance (as measured by two separate indexes reflecting the relative presence of brand focused vs. non-brand focused retailers). Further, we find that this result is strongest in high income states.

In our second study, we complete a micro-level analysis. We measure brand reliance by asking participants to make a series of choices among branded and generic products. We then relate the responses to individuals' reported church attendance. Consistent with the macro-level analysis results, we find that higher religiosity is associated with lower brand reliance, but only among high income individuals.

Given these two highly consistent studies, we aim to conduct additional research to allow us to better understand the factors underlying this relationship between religiosity and brand reliance. We speculate that religion and brands satisfy a common need, and it is this underlying need that links religiosity and brand reliance. For example, our findings may reflect differential strategies for maintaining a sense of belonging between religious and nonreligious individuals. For the religious, this need may be fulfilled through attendance at religious services. For the nonreligious, this need may be fulfilled by belonging to brand communities.

We also aim to better understand why we observe the link between brand reliance and religiosity largely for high income consumers. A number of plausible explanations are possible for this finding, but perhaps the most intuitive and parsimonious is that high income consumers have larger consideration sets. In other words, their income allows for the consideration of a much broader range of products than that of low income consumers. This leaves room for factors such as religiosity to influence their choices. Alternatively, low-income and high-income individuals may have qualitatively different consumption goals. Low-income individuals may use consumption as largely a means of survival. Conversely, high-income individuals may use consumption to serve higher-order goals (e.g. need for belonging, risk compensation) that can also be achieved through religion.

In addition to exploring the psychological explanations for the observed effects, future research might also explore the implications to firms. For example, retailers who are interested in promoting their store brands (versus the national brands) might consider using physical cues that remind shoppers of their religious beliefs in the store (e.g. dramatic cathedral ceilings at the entrance, religious-like music). Similarly, they might consider advertising their store brands through media that attract a greater percentage of religious consumers, or using spokespersons that are associated with strongly held religious beliefs. Conversely, retailers that focus on national brands or place lower strategic importance on their store brand lines should probably avoid such cues and outlets.

In terms of what implications our results may have for consumers, one could argue that our findings should not promote any changes in their behaviors if the status quo leads to the greatest consumer satisfaction. Thus, future research should determine whether or not the nonreligious are more satisfied after buying a brand, while the religious are more satisfied after buying a store brand.

In sum, this research has identified what we believe to be a very interesting empirical phenomenon, supported by two distinct methodological approaches. We believe this evidence will be of great interest to the consumer research community, and hope that it will spur research as to why there is a relationship between religiosity and brand reliance, as well as how an understanding of this relationship might best be applied.

References

Aaker, Jennifer (1997), "Dimensions of Brand Personality," *Journal of Marketing Research*, 34 (August), 347-56.

Aaker, Jennifer (1999), "The Malleable Self: The Role of Self-Expression in Persuasion," *Journal of Marketing Research,* 36 (February), 45-57.

Belk, Russell W., Melanie Wallendorf & John Sherry, Jr. (1989), "The Sacred and the Profane in Consumer Behavior: Theodicy on the Odyssey," *Journal of Consumer Research*, 16 (1), 1-39.

Financial Times (2001), (accessed July 14, 2007), [available at http://www.humphreys.co.uk.articles/e_commerce_3.htm].

Rindfleisch, Aric, James Burroughs, & Nancy Wong (working paper), "Religiosity and Brand Commitment".

In Death and in Love: Sacred Trade-offs in the Death Care and Wedding Industries

A. Peter McGraw, University of Colorado at Boulder, USA

Derick Davis, University of Colorado at Boulder, USA

Funerals and weddings represent two of the largest purchases consumers make. In the United States, the average funeral costs $6,500 (and can reach $10,000 with burial costs) and the average wedding costs more than $27,000 (AARP 2000; FTC.gov; Rheault 2007).

Funeral and wedding purchases pose unique challenges; consumers typically have little purchasing experience and make decisions under time pressure, while subject to the scrutiny of friends, family, and acquaintances. Furthermore, the respective industries have been subject to criticism for unscrupulous sales and marketing practices (e.g., Mitford 1998; Boden 2003; Mead 2007).

We examine a particular challenge facing consumers purchasing funerals or weddings. Consumers purchasing products and services in these domains are reluctant to engage in price-based trade-offs, which we contend puts them at risk of overspending. A growing literature examines how consumers are unwilling to engage in trade-offs between the secular (e.g., money) and the sacred (e.g., love and commitment; Baron and Spranca 1997; Belk, Wallendorf, and Sherry 1989; Fiske and Tetlock 1997; McGraw, Tetlock, and Kristel 2003). Such taboo trade-offs produce a variety of negative outcomes, including moral distress, moral contamination, decision avoidance, and decision refusal (Tetlock, et al. 2000; McGraw and Tetlock 2005; see also Luce, Bettman, and Payne 1997). We examine how price-based trade-off avoidance leads to non-compensatory decision strategies and spendthrifty decisions.

A funeral purchase implicitly requires a price be placed on a deceased loved one's memorial. A wedding purchase similarly requires a price be placed on a ceremony that represents a couple's love and commitment. We argue such purchases are seen as secular-sacred transactions and lead to price-based trade-off avoidance. Consumers do not want to undervalue sacredly held values by trading off price versus other attributes, such as product quality or quantity. Thus, consumers engage in non-compensatory choice strategies and chose premium options rather than balancing price against other attributes.

We present three studies that demonstrate consumers' greater willingness to pay for death care and wedding products compared to other routine purchase situations. We also show the effect is due, in part, to consumers' reluctance to engage in price-quality trade-offs.

Study 1 demonstrates that consumers are willing to pay more for products that are associated with funerals and weddings than no specific association, even when those products are judged to be of the same quality. Participants stated their willingness to pay (WTP) for four products (e.g., candles, thank you cards) that were randomly assigned for use in either a funeral, a wedding, or for "any reason" (control). Participants' WTP for products used as part of a funeral (*M*=$31.42) or memorial service (*M*=$35.21) were significantly higher than for the control (*M*=$18.23). Despite higher WTP values for funeral- and wedding-related products, judged quality of these products did not differ from control.

Study 2 used a matching versus choice procedure (Slovic 1991; see also Luce, Payne, and Bettman 1999) to examine consumer's unwillingness to make price-based trade-offs in funeral purchase decisions. Participants were randomly assigned to either a control or memorial dinner condition and were presented with two product options for use at the dinner. Respondents were asked to state the missing price (taboo trade-off) or quantity (routine trade-off) that would make them indifferent between low and high quality options. They were then asked to choose between the two matched options.

When faced with a price vs. quality trade-off, participants in the funeral condition chose the high-quality/price option more often than control (68% vs. 51%) and chose more of the same product when faced with a price vs. quantity trade-off (75% vs. 38%). But consistent with our hypothesis that non-price-based trade-offs are not taboo, quantity-quality trade-off choices did not differ between conditions (68% vs. 65% for the funeral and control condition, respectively).

Study 3 examined the effect of different techniques to reduce spendthrifty preferences for high-price high-quality goods with sacred associations. Participants were instructed to perform a price matching task between lower-quality/lower-priced thank you cards and a higher-quality option with no price listed (as in Study 2). The cards were to be sent to attendees of a wedding or funeral. Participants in the control condition were subsequently asked to make a choice between either option. The debiasing conditions were designed to encourage price-quality trade-offs by presenting either sacred or economic reasons to make price-based trade-offs. First, the difficult nature of price-based trade-offs in sacred domains was described, and the subsequent inclination of consumers to choose premium options was stated. Respondents in the economic debais condition were told that rational consumers recognize trade-offs are necessary in all situations including sacred events. Respondents in the sacred debias condition were told that no amount of money captures the importance of the situation, and therefore the meaning of the event should not be expressed through spending. In both conditions, participants were then encouraged, in light of this information, to treat the choice between the matched options as they would any run-of-the-mill purchasing decision.

Participants in the control condition chose the high-price, high-quality option 86% of the time, which is consistent with findings from Study 2. Those who read the economic debiasing statement chose the high-price, high-quality option 60% of the time, whereas participants who read the sacred debaising statement chose the high-price, high-quality option only 41% of the time, a significantly different proportion than the control.

The project has implications for when and how policy makers and consumer advocates should intervene on behalf of consumers. Specifically, we address how interventions that simply encourage rational economic behavior of consumers without removing the taboo nature of the exchange may not be as effective as interventions that take into account the value-signaling role money in the evaluation of sacred purchases.

References

AARP (2000). "The Deathcare Industry." Washington D.C.: AARP Public Policy Institute.

Baron, Jonathan, and Mark Spranca (1997), "Protected Values," *Organizational Behavior and Human Decision Processes,* 70(1), 1-16.

Belk, Russell W., Melanie Wallendorf, and John Sherry (1989). "The Sacred and the Profane in Consumer Behavior: Theodicy on the Odyssey." *Journal of Consumer Research,* 16 (June), 1-38.

Boden, Sharon (2003). *Consumerism, Romance and the Wedding Experience,* Hampshire: Palgrave MacMillian.

Fiske, Alan P., and Philip E. Tetlock (1997), "Taboo Trade-offs: Reactions to Transactions That Transgress the Spheres of Justice," *Political Psychology,* 18(2), 255-297.

FTC.gov (n.d.). "Funerals: A Consumer Guide." Retrieved March 23, 2008, from The Federal Trade Commission website: http://www.ftc.gov/bcp/conline/pubs/services/funeral.pdf

Luce, Mary F., James Bettman, and John Payne (1997). "Choice Processing in Emotionally Difficult Decisions." *Journal of Experimental Psychology: Learning, Memory, and Cognition.* 23, (2) 384-405.

Luce, Mary F., John W. Payne, and James R. Bettman (1999). "Emotional Trade-off Difficulty and Choice." *Journal of Marketing Research,* 36(May), 143-159.

Mitford, Jessica (1998), *The American way of Death Revisited,* New York: Alfred A. Knopf.

McGraw, A. Peter and Philip E. Tetlock (2005). "Taboo Trade-offs, Relational Framing and the Acceptability of Exchanges," *Journal of Consumer Psychology*, 15(January) 2-15.

McGraw, A. Peter, Philip E. Tetlock, and Orie V. Kristel (2003), "The Limits of Fungibility: Relational Schemata and the Value of Things," *Journal of Consumer Research,* 30(September), 219-229.

Mead, Rebecca (2007), *One Perfect Day: The Selling of the American Wedding,* New York: The Penguin Group.

Rheault, Magali (2007). "Americans Underestimate the Cost of Tying the Knot" Retrieved August 14, 2008 from the Gallup Poll website: http://www.gallup.com/poll/27844/ Americans-Underestimate-Cost-Tying-Knot.aspx

Slovic, Paul (1991). "The Construction of Preferences." *American Psychologist.* 50, 364-371.

Tetlock, Philip E., Orie V. Kristel, Beth Elson, Melanie Green, and Jennifer Lerner (2000), "The Psychology of the Unthinkable: Taboo Trade-offs, Forbidden Base Rates, and Heretical Counterfactuals," *Journal of Personality and Social Psychology,* 78 (May), 853-870.

The Impact of Semantic vs. Lexical Relations on the Strength of Inter-brand Linkages

Jing Lei, University of Ontario Institute of Technology, Canada
Niraj Dawar, University of Western Ontario, Canada

Research Background and Hypotheses

Brands are not cognitively independent in the way that consumers store them in memory. Rather, due to a variety of reasons, including common product category or common features, similar trade dress and design, similar or related advertising, complementary usage, and even proximate shelf location, consumers may establish associative linkages between brands to help them navigate the "brandscape" in which they consume. The strength of these linkages are said to be an important predictor of the magnitude of spillover effects in which external information (e.g. advertising or negative news) about a brand can change evaluations of related brands that are not directly implicated (Lei et al. 2008; Roehm and Tybout 2006). Therefore, it becomes important to understand what determines the strength of associative linkages between brands.

Prior research has primarily examined brand-related linkages based on semantic similarities such as common product features and shared product category (e.g., KitKat-Smarties). However, brands may also be linked through more superficial lexical similarities such as phonetically or orthographically similar brand names (e.g., Nescafé-Nestea). We propose that brand linkages based on these two types of relations (i.e. semantic vs. lexical) have different levels of strength, depending on the manner in which brand information was learned. Specifically, we propose that semantic linkages will be stronger when consumers learn interrelations between brands in a high task involvement condition, whereas lexical linkages will be stronger when consumers rely on heuristics to associate brands in a low task involvement condition. These propositions are explained in detail below.

Associative network theory (Collins and Loftus 1975) suggests that consumers organize information in networks that represent both semantic (e.g., Maid-Servant) and lexical (phonemic and orthographic similarities) relationships (e.g., Maid-Made) (see also Hennessey et al. 2005). These associations are encoded or learned through exposure to, and elaboration of information in the environment (Gardial and Biehal 1985). A critical aspect of the learning process is the level of task involvement (Petty and Cacioppo 1981). Task involvement determines the cognitive capacity allocated to the encoding and, therefore, the extent of elaboration that the information receives (Schmitt et al. 1993). In particular, high task involvement is characterized by a thoughtful, intentional learning process that allows elaboration of the stimulus information (Petty and Cacioppo 1986). In contrast, under low involvement, product/brand information may be learned incidentally with little cognitive effort or elaboration.

Therefore, when brand information is learned under high (vs. low) task involvement, consumers are more likely to rely on "deep" (vs. "surface") cues to establish links between new and existing brand information. "Deep" cues include abstract, underlying functional properties of a brand such as product and category similarity, and common or complementary usage, whereas "surface" cues refer to more concrete, sensory properties of the brand such as the linguistic characteristics of brand names, and the color of the product and its package (Zhang and Sood 2002). The elaboration of "deep" cues is facilitated by systematic processing but requires more cognitive effort, whereas "surface" cues are often used as heuristics, with little effort involved. We propose that linkages based on semantic relations will be stronger when consumers learn interrelations between brands in a high involvement condition. However, lexical linkages will be stronger when consumers rely on heuristics to associate brands in a low involvement condition.

Experiment and Results

To test the impact of semantic vs. lexical relations between brands, we developed a fictitious brand Nestello (a chocolate candy bar). Nestello is lexically linked with brands such as Nescafé but semantically linked with brands such as KitKat (we also developed seven other filler brands). Each fictitious brand was presented on a card describing information such as the product category, the company, and the brand name, and each card was printed in a different font and size. Eighty subjects were randomly assigned to a 2 (high vs. low task involvement) X 2 (lexical vs. semantic relation) between-subjects ANOVA design. Following established practice (Schmitt et al. 1993), we manipulated the level of task involvement by instructing subjects to focus on either the information presented or the font and size of the text information on each card. Strength of association between brands was measured using a computer-assisted response time sequential priming method (e.g., Bargh and Chartrand 2000; Herr et al. 1996).

The results showed a significant interaction term (F $(1, 72)$=25.38, $p<0.001$) between task involvement and type of relations between brands. Specifically, the Nestello-to-KitKat association (semantic relation) was significantly stronger in the high involvement condition than in the low involvement condition (5.95 vs. 5.05, $p<0.05$), whereas the Nestello-to-Nescafé association (lexical relation) was significantly stronger in the low involvement condition than in the high involvement condition (4.53 vs. 3.40, $p<0.05$). Thus our hypotheses were supported.

Implications

The above finding suggests that consumers rely on different types of cues (semantic vs. lexical) to establish brand associations in different learning environment. In other words, the strength of a linkage is influenced by not only the type of relations between brands, but also the cognitive process through which the linkage is initially established. Our finding also suggests that surface-level lexical attributes are important conduits through which brands can be associated in memory. It implies that lexical similarities can help firms position a new brand closely to an established brand for positive halo effects, irrespective of whether the new brand is in the same or a different product category. However, it also suggests that the scope of contamination imposed by a negative message may be larger than what is normally expected. For example, a brand that seems to be "unrelated" due to the absence of semantic similarities, may nevertheless be affected by the negative information about a related brand through lexical linkages. To further test this, we are conducting follow up studies to examine the impact of semantic vs. lexical brand linkages on spillover effects between brands. Overall, this research shows that the lexical attributes of a brand, which have not received much attention in previous research, can have significant influence on the cognitive structure of inter-brand linkages.

References

Bargh, John A. and Tanya L. Chartrand (2000), "Studying the Mind in the Middle: A Practical Guide to Priming and Automaticity Research". In H. Reis and C. Judd (Eds.), *Handbook of Research Methods in Social Psychology* (pp253-285). New York: Cambridge University Press.

Collins, Allan M. and Elizabeth F. Loftus (1975), "A Spreading-Activation Theory of Semantic Processing," *Psychological Bulletin*, 82 (6), 407-28.

Gardial, Sarah Fisher and Gabriel J. Biehal (1985), "Memory Accessibility and Task Involvement as Factors in Choice," *Association for Consumer Research*, Vol.12, 414-19.

Hennessey, Judith E., Theodore S. Bell, and Robert J. Kwortnik (2005), "Lexical Interference in Semantic Processing of Simple Words: Implications for Brand Names", *Psychology & Marketing*, Vol. 22 (January), 51-69.

Herr, Paul M., Peter H. Farquhar, and Russell H. Fazio (1996), "Impact of Dominance and Relatedness on Brand Extensions," *Journal of Consumer Psychology*, Vol. 5 (2), 135-59.

Lei, Jing Niraj Dawar, and Jos Lemmink (2008), "Negative Spillover in Brand Portfolios: Exploring the Antecedents of Asymmetric Effects", *Journal of Marketing*, forthcoming.

Petty Richard E. and John T. Cacioppo (1981), *Attitudes and Persuasion: Classic and Contemporary Approaches*, Dubuque, IA: Wm. C. Brown.

Petty Richard E. and John T. Cacioppo (1986), "The Elaboration Likelihood Model of Persuasion," *Advances of Experimental Social Psychology*, Vol.19, 123-205.

Roehm, Michelle and Alice M. Tybout (2006), "When Will a Brand Scandal Spillover and How Should Competitors Respond?" *Journal of Marketing Research*, Vol.43 (August), 366-73.

Schmitt, Bernd H., Nader T. Tavassoli, and Robert T. Millard (1993), "Memory for Print Ads: Understanding Relations among Brand Name, Copy, and Picture", *Journal of Consumer Psychology*, Vol. 2 (1), 55-81.

Zhang, Shi and Sanjay Sood (2002), "'Deep' and 'Surface' Cues: Brand Extension Evaluations by Children and Adults", *Journal of Consumer Research*, Vol. 29 (June), 129-41.

Hot Stimuli and Arousal: Implications for Temporal Orientation, Trial and Price

Brittany Duff, University of Minnesota, USA
Ron Faber, University of Minnesota, USA

Recently studies have empirically demonstrated the effects of 'hot' stimuli on temporal orientation and consumption impatience. Hot stimuli are appetitive, rewarding or hedonic stimuli (Berridge 2004) that activate an affective 'go' system, in contrast to the cool, cognitive system (Metcalfe and Mischel 1999). It has been shown that exposure to hot stimuli results in activation of the relevant neural systems which focuses the individual on smaller-sooner rewards, increases probability of making unplanned purchases and increases consumption impatience, even in domains unrelated to the stimuli (Li 2008; Van den Bergh, Dewitte and Warlop 2008).

Hot stimuli can be any sensory input including visual stimuli. Interestingly, visual-based studies select stimuli that vary primarily on arousal, yet arousal is not viewed as a causal mechanism. For example, the pictures Li (2008) chose from the International Affective Picture System (IAPS; Lang, Bradley and Cuthbert 2005) to represent hot versus cool stimuli had similar positive affective valence but differed on arousal (food vs. landscapes).

While, in these studies, appetitive activation has been found to focus attention on immediate rewards (and therefore devalue future rewards) differences in post-exposure arousal have not been found. This is surprising since the manipulations used, such as exposure to 'sexy images' of women, have previously been found to have effects through arousal (LaTour, Pitts and Snook-Luther 1990). Additionally, IAPS pictures are often used in research on motivated attention where arousal level is seen as representing the intensity of activation of the appetitive or aversive nature of the image (Lang, Bradley and Cuthbert 1998).

Past work has found that arousal at time of information processing can affect that processing (Sanbonmatsu and Kardes 1988). However, initial arousal was not assessed in the studies on appetitive stimuli. Initial arousal may impact the effect of the arousal level of the stimulus such that attentional focus to an immediately available reward is greatest when the stimulus matches the initial arousal level of the individual. Zajonc (1980) argued that hot system activation occurs at both the level of the stimulus and the individual, and, therefore, both should be measured. Therefore, examining initial activation or arousal states may be important for research on hot stimuli.

Method

To assess whether initial arousal may be affecting this process, an experiment similar to Li (2008) was conducted. Initially, 2 pictures with similar valence but differing in arousal were selected based on IAPS normative ratings. These images were of a deer drinking water (cool) and a team of skydivers jumping (hot). To further ensure the selected images met the desired criteria, a pre-test was conducted with 52 undergraduate students. As expected, the images were perceived as similar in valence [M_{deer}=6.37, $M_{skydive}$=6.84, t(51)=1.65, p>.1, n.s], but, were significantly different in arousal [M_{deer}=5.73, $M_{skydive}$=7.48, t(51)=6.76, p<.001].

These images were placed in constructed advertisements for either a hedonic or utilitarian product to see if product type would have an effect separate from the arousal level of the picture. A pre-test of products showed that a vacation/travel company and an insurance company differed significantly on perceptions of being hedonic [M_{travel}=8.0, $M_{insurance}$=4.5; t(17)=5.72, p<.001] as well as 'utilitarian' [M_{travel}=3.94, $M_{insurance}$=7.78; t(17)=-7.47, p<.001].

The primary study was conducted with 190 undergraduates. Subjects first filled out a questionnaire assessing their initial arousal on a 4-item scale along with other filler items. After completing the questionnaire, participants were exposed to one of the four ads (arousing picture/hedonic product; arousing picture/utilitarian product; non-arousing picture/hedonic product; non-arousing picture/utilitarian product). Participants then answered questions about the ad and then were asked to assess their happiness at winning a $100 prize today, in one month, six months and one year. This was followed by filler items as well as questions assessing post-exposure arousal level.

Results

A repeated-measures ANOVA for happiness at receiving $100 was run with time (today vs. one month, six months and one year in the future) as a within-subjects variable and picture arousal, product type and initial arousal as between-subjects variables. A median split was performed on initial arousal scores. The mean level of arousal for the low group was 2.93, while the high groups mean arousal was 5.45 [t (189)=-19.73, p<.001].

Ad-type (hedonic vs. utilitarian) with happiness at time of receiving $100 (F(1.62, 292=2.26, p>.1, n.s.), was not significant nor was ad –type and initial arousal, (F(1.62, 292)=.91, p>.3, n.s.). However, as predicted, there was a significant interaction with picture type (arousing vs. unarousing) and initial individual arousal level (high vs. low) affecting happiness at receiving money over time [F(1.62, 292)=6.91, p<.05]. This indicates that these pictures, similar to those chosen as 'hot' stimuli, do interact with initial arousal level in terms of the steepness of the discounting curve.

The means demonstrate opposite patterns for those with low and high initial arousal. For those low in initial arousal, discounting is steepest when exposed to the ad with the low arousal picture. For those high in initial arousal, the discounting curve is steepest when exposed to the ad with the high arousal picture. The results of discounting for the high arousal group (which showed more delay discounting when exposed to the high arousal picture) mirror those found in other studies (e.g. Li 2008). However, the fact that the low arousal group exhibited the opposite pattern is striking and points to the importance of assessing initial arousal and the role it may play in consumption impatience. Work in health communication has similarly pointed to the need to match arousal level of the message with the arousal level of the viewer for optimal effects (Stephenson and Southwell 2006).

As predicted, picture type (arousing/non-arousing) had a significant effect on arousal difference score: arousal at time 2 (post-exposure) minus arousal at time 1 (pre-picture exposure) [t(189)=-1.884, p<.05, one-tailed]. This arousal difference score, was higher for the arousing picture (skydivers) than the unarousing picture (deer) ($M_{deerdifference}$=.42, $M_{skydivediff}$=.19). In turn, this arousal difference score had significant effects on trial of the product [$M_{lowdiff}$=4.59 vs. $M_{highdiff}$=5.17; F(1,173)=3.99, p<.05] and price participants were willing to pay [$M_{lowdiff}$=$893.81 vs. $M_{highdiff}$=$1626.03; F(1,173)=3.9, p<.05].

References

Berridge, K. C. (2004), "Motivation Concepts in Behavioral Neuroscience," *Physiology & Behavior*, 81(2), 179-209.

Lang, P.J., M. M. Bradley and B.N. Cuthbert (1998), "Emotion and Motivation: Measuring Affective Perception," *Journal of Clinical Neurophysiology: Neuroscience of Emotion*, 15(5), 397-408.

Lang, P. J., *M. M. Bradley and B.N. Cuthbert* (2005), "International affective picture system (IAPS): Instruction manual and affective ratings," *Technical Report A-6, The Center for Research in Psychophysiology*, University of Florida.

Latour, M.S., R.E. Pitts and D.C. Snook-Luther (1990), "Female Nudity, Arousal and Ad Response: An Experimental Investigation," *Journal of Advertising*, 19(4), 51-62.

Li, X. (2008), "The Effects of Appetitive Stimuli on Out-of-Domain Consumption Impatience," *Journal of Consumer Research*, 34(5), 649-656.

Metcalfe, J. and W. Mischel (1999), "A Hot/Cool System Analysis of Delay of Gratification: Dynamics of Willpower," *Psychological Review*, 106(1), 3-19.

Sanbonmatsu, D.M. and F.R. Kardes (1988), "The Effects of Physiological Arousal on Information Processing and Persuasion," *Journal of Consumer Research*, 15, 379-385.

Stephenson, M.T. and B.J. Southwell (2006), "Sensation Seeking, the Activation Model, and Mass Media Health Campaigns: Current Findings and Future Directions for Cancer Communication," *Journal of Communication*, 56(1), s38-s56.

Van den Bergh, B., S. Dewitte and L. Warlop (2008), "Bikinis Instigate Generalized Impatience in Intertemporal Choice," *Journal of Consumer Research*, 35, 85-97.

Zajonc, R.B. (1980), "Feeling and Thinking: Preferences Need No Inferences," *American Psychologist*, 35(2), 151-175.

Mental Ownership as Important Imagery Content

Silvia Feuchtl, University of Vienna, Austria
Bernadette Kamleitner, Queen Mary, University of London, UK

Abstract

Previous research has shown that mental imagery influences consumer experiences. Most research on mental imagery has focused on imagery vividness. What people actually imagine has hardly been assessed. We propose mental ownership as a powerful imagery content. An online experiment supports this proposition. Path models show that mental ownership partially mediates the effect of imagery vividness on attachment and attitudes, which in turn influence behaviour. In particular, mental ownership strongly predicts attachment, which significantly increases intentions towards getting the mere-mentally owned product.

Phrases such as "Yes, I can see myself driving that car" indicate that mental imagery is present in consumers' everyday language, and it seems that consumers use their imagination to decide on what to buy. Indeed, marketing scholars and practitioners are well aware of the importance of mental imagery for consumer behaviour (e.g., MacInnis & Price, 1987; Phillips, 1996; Schroeder, 2005).

Several studies have shown that the more vivid and strong mental imagery, the more attitudes towards an ad or a product improve (e.g., Babin & Burns, 1998; Gregory, Cialdini, & Carpenter, 1982). Interestingly, whereas we know quite well that vividness matters, we know much less about what people actually imagine. This paper aims at contributing to our understanding of the importance of imagery content by proposing mental ownership as a particularly powerful imagery content

There are at least three criteria that a powerful and marketing-relevant imagery content needs to meet. Ownership meets them all: First, consumers must be able to experience or feel what they imagine. People are able to develop a "sense" of ownership (e.g., Heyman, Orhun, & Ariely, 2004; Pierce, Kostova, & Dirks, 2003), and experiences of psychological ownership are clearly not restricted to factual possessions (e.g., De Dreu & van Knippenberg, 2005; F. W. Rudmin, 1994).

Second, a powerful imagery content needs to be something that frequently preoccupies consumers and is hence able to come to one's mind spontaneously or "naturally". Ownership considerations and consequences clearly impact everyday life and differentiating between "mine" and "not mine" is a routine practice in most cultures.

Third and in order to be relevant for marketing, a powerful imagery content must be able to influence how consumers feel and behave towards an object. As indicated by several theoretical streams rooted in economics (endowment effect; e.g., Thaler, 1980) and psychology (mere-ownership effect and attachment; e.g., Beggan, 1992) ownership has the capacity to significantly influence how consumers feel about and behave towards an owned object.

To deal with the specific case of a sense of ownership in situations where there is no actual ownership we coin the term 'mental ownership'. Mental ownership is defined as a sense of ownership for a factually not owned product. The phrase 'a sense of ownership' denotes that mental ownership is more than merely imagining a situation of possession. It requires a shift in the person-product relation (or reference point), thus, that not getting a mentally owned product feels like a loss instead of a non-gain.

Our research model proposes that vivid mental imagery about an object can lead to mental ownership which, in turn, leads to the typical consequences of actual ownership: an increase in attachment and attitudes. Subsequently, attachment and attitudes are supposed to influence behavioural intentions and behaviours aiming at making the mere mentally owned object actually available to the imaginer.

To test the research model, 613 participants were presented with the information that either a new coffeemaker or a new car was being introduced to the market. Participants were then shown depictions of the same product in three different colours in an online experiment. To manipulate the degree of mental ownership, participants either had to actively choose a model in a particular colour (experimental group, EG), or they were simply informed that the product was available in three different colours (control group, CG). The rationale behind this manipulation was that the act of choosing can create an ownership like association between the chooser and the chosen object

(Gawronski, Bodenhausen, & Becker, 2007). After being informed of the different colour options participants were presented an ad for the (chosen) product. Subsequently, participants were asked to fill in a questionnaire assessing reactions to the ad (imagery vividness, mental ownership, attachment, attitudes, and behavioral intentions) and demographic characteristics. Overall, a 2 (choice EG vs. no-choice CG) x 2 (car vs. coffeemaker) experimental design was achieved.

The manipulation of mental ownership was successful and it was not due to an effect of the manipulation on mental imagery. To test the proposed research model we ran several path models in AMOS. First, we assessed a model without mere-mental ownership. In this model we restrained all paths leading to and from mental ownership to 0. None of the fit-indices reached the required levels. Second and to test the proposed mediating function of mere-mental ownership, we assessed a model with mere-mental ownership as a mediator, which led to satisfying levels of model fit. Overall there is support for the partial mediation proposed in the research model. Mere-mental ownership decreases the influence of imagery vividness on attachment and attitudes and it significantly predicts product attachment and attitudes. These main results hold for both products even when the paths are constrained across groups.

In addition and in contrast to most previous research we show that neither mental imagery nor mental ownership directly influence behaviour. In particular, attachment seems to predict behavioural intentions. This finding fits into a growing stream of research which indicates that attachments rather than attitudes are important indicators of behaviour (e.g., Park, MacInnis, & Priester, 2006; Thomson, MacInnis, & Park, 2005). Interestingly, the importance of attachment also underlines the importance of mere-mental ownership. Our results show that mere-mental ownership has considerably more impact on attachment than on attitudes. Hence, mental ownership seems to be indeed a powerful imagery content. Considering that people's imagery content can probably be influenced, mental ownership, like factual ownership, might prove to be of tremendous theoretical and practical importance in several contexts and disciplines.

Dinner Out with Independent Self-Construal Consumers: Wow, This is Bad Wine
Eugenia C. Wu, Duke University, USA
Sarah G. Moore, Duke University, USA
Gavan J. Fitzsimons, Duke University, USA

Imagine that you are asked to select a restaurant for dinner with a group of friends. Which restaurant do you choose? We usually know what to choose for ourselves, but what happens when there are others involved? More specifically, how do you choose when you must consider not just your own preferences but the predilections of those around you?

As consumers we are often required to choose collectively, on behalf of ourselves and others. We decide on behalf of others when we select the restaurant for a dinner outing, pick the toppings for a shared pizza or choose the movie for a group jaunt to the theater. Despite the frequency of such decisions, existing research has focused primarily on choices made for and by individual consumers (Bettman, Luce and Payne 1998). Decisions in a group context have been addressed mainly in research on family decision-making (Corfman and Lehmann 1987) and in the negotiations literature in terms of collective decisions made for and by the group (Oetzel 1998). In this research, we attempt to understand some of the factors which influence consumption choices on behalf of others.

We focus on self-construal and expertise, both factors which have a substantial impact on consumer behavior (West, Brown and Hoch 1996; Aaker and Schmidt 2001). Self-construal theory proposes that individuals differ fundamentally in how they construe the self; independents see themselves as unique and autonomous while interdependents define themselves in the context of their social relationships, roles and duties (Markus and Kitayama 1991). Research on expertise suggests that consumers may also differ in their levels of knowledge concerning particular consumption decisions (Alba and Hutchinson 1987). In two studies, we examine the influence of these factors on a common decision made on behalf of others: choice of wine for the table at a restaurant.

The wine choice situation requires individuals to balance their own preferences with those of the group—but unlike past research that investigates how individuals' self-choices are influenced by others' choices (Ariely and Levav 2000), we put individual and group preferences in conflict by asking individuals to make a choice for the entire group and not just themselves. We expect that independents will choose better (more expensive) wines of the type of wine they prefer (e.g., red versus white), sacrificing the group's welfare to maximize their own utility. Interdependents should make more balanced choices and choose bottles that are equally expensive; they may even self-sacrifice by choosing more expensive bottles of the type they prefer less.

We conducted the studies online, using a national sample of participants who self-identified as wine drinkers. Participants read that they went out to dinner with a group of friends, and that they had been elected to choose the wine for the evening–one bottle of red and one bottle of white–and that they were not to exceed a total budget of $110. Individuals then viewed a real wine list and selected one red and one white wine; we asked them to indicate the prices of the wines and to rate the quality of the two wines. We measured preferences for red and white wine by asking how often participants drank red versus white wine and measured self-construal (Singelis 1994). In Study 2, we also asked a number of wine-related questions to ascertain individuals' expertise.

As an initial illustration of our predicted effects, in Study 1, one strongly independent individual, a white-wine drinker, disregarded our instructions and selected two bottles of white wine, ignoring the group and satisfying his own preferences (he was excluded from our analysis). Our major dependent variables were the prices of the two bottles of wine individuals selected. We conducted a repeated measures analysis on the prices of red and white wine, using self-construal, wine preference, and expertise as independent variables. In both studies 1 and 2, we found similar results. First, we found an interaction between self-construal and wine preference. As predicted, independents' wine choices were influenced strongly by their preferences: the more they preferred red (white) wine, the more expensive a bottle of red (white) wine they chose. Interdependents chose more equally priced wines regardless of their preferences—in fact, they chose slightly more expensive bottles of the wine they did not prefer.

In Study 2, we measured expertise and found a three-way interaction between self-construal, wine preference, and expertise. While expertise did not influence the decisions of interdependents, independents' wine choices were influenced by their knowledge of wine.

Independent novices were the most self-interested, choosing red and white wines that were as expensive as possible, depending on their wine preferences. Independent experts also significantly increased the prices of red and white wines they chose according to their own preferences, but did so to a lesser degree than novices.

Importantly, these results are not driven by individuals' assumptions about others' preferences—independents who liked red wine did not choose more expensive red wines because they assumed everyone at the table would be drinking red wine, just like them. Most participants thought the break down of red versus white wine drinkers at the table would be about 50/50, and these predictions did not differ according to self-construal.

Our initial study suggests that independents sacrifice others' interests for their own and behave selfishly even when making decisions for a group. This initial study raises a number of interesting questions. What motivated independent experts in our study to make less biased choices for the group? What might encourage independent individuals to make better group choices? In a future study, we plan to manipulate group characteristics to answer some of these questions: for example, what if the group is comprised of wine experts vs. novices, or red vs. white wine drinkers? Manipulating these characteristics will uncover the dynamics that underlie individuals' choices on behalf of others.

In conclusion, when selecting someone to make a decision for other people, choose individuals with interdependent self-construals—or you might end up drinking house wine while they enjoy an award winning blend.

References

Aaker, Jennifer and Bernd Schmidt (2001), "Culture-Dependent Assimilation and Differentiation of the Self," *Journal of Cross-Cultural Psychology,* 32(5), 561-576.

Alba, Joseph W. and J. Wesley Hutchinson (1987), "Dimensions of Consumer Expertise," Journal of Consumer Research, 13(4), 411-454.

Ariely, Dan, and Jonathan Levav (2000), "Sequential Choice in Group Settings: Taking the Road Less Traveled and Less Enjoyed," *Journal of Consumer Research,* 27(3), 279-281.

Bettman, James R., Mary Frances Luce and John W. Payne (1998), "Constructive Consumer Choice Processes," *Journal of Consumer Research,* 25(3), 187-218.

Corfman, Kim P., and Donald R. Lehmann (1987), "Models of Cooperative Group Decision-Making and Relative Influence: An Experimental Investigation of Family Purchase Decisions," *Journal of Consumer Research,* 14(1), 1-13.

Markus, Hazel R., and Shinobu Kitayama (1991), "Culture and the self: Implications for Cognition, Emotion, and Motivation," *Psychological Review,* 98, 224-253.

Oetzel, John G. (1998), "Culturally Homogeneous and Heterogeneous Groups: Explaining Communication Processes Through Individualism-Collectivism and Self-Construal," *International Journal of Intercultural Relations,* 22(2), 135-161.

Singelis, Theodore M. (1994), "The Measurement of Independent and Interdependent Self-construals," *Personality and Social Psychology Bulletin,* 20, 580-591.

West, Patricia M., Christina L. Brown and Stephen J. Hoch (1996), "Consumption Vocabulary and Preference Formation," *Journal of Consumer Research,* 23(2), 120-135.

The Influence of Observed Body Movements on Consumer Behavior

Simon Ineichen, University of Basel, Switzerland
Arnd Florack, Zeppelin University, Germany
Oliver Genschow, University of Basel, Switzerland

An astonishing finding of research on embodied cognition is that motor behaviors and muscle contractions affect cognitive processes (Strack, Stepper, & Martin, 1988; Förster & Strack, 1996; Strack & Neumann, 2000; see for an overview Niedenthal, Barsalou, Winkielman, Krauth-Gruber, & Ric, 2005). In line with this research, recent studies found that body movements also have an impact on consumer judgments and behaviors (Förster, 2003; 2004). In these studies, participants rated products (Förster, 2003) or tasted a soft drink (Förster, 2004) and, at the same time, were asked to execute certain body movements. For instance, they were instructed to press their hand either up against the table from underneath, or down onto the table. Pressing one's hand up from underneath results in arm flexion, a movement that is related to grabbing something and pulling it towards oneself. It is argued that such movements are associated with approach-related behaviors and cognitive representations. In contrast, pressing one's hand down, results in arm extension, a defensive movement used to keep something at distance. It was found that arm flexion led to more positive judgments of a drink (Förster, 2003) and an increased drink intake (Förster, 2004).

In this study, we examined whether not only the execution, but already the observation of body movements affects consumer behavior. There is evidence that, observing other's actions, observing individuals seem to run an internal simulation of the observed behavior. This simulation occurs automatically (Gallese, 2001) and leads to neural activation in brain areas associated with the execution of the movements (Buccino et al., 2001). Also, there is indirect evidence for such a simulation to occur. Some mental disorders as well as orbito-frontal lesions lead to the symptom of echopraxia: the impulsive repetition of observed actions or heard sentences that occur with reflex-like immediacy (Lhermitte, Pillon, & Serdaru, 1986). We assumed that the observation of a body movement leads to a mental simulation of the movement and, thus, affect cognitive processes in the same way as the execution does.

However, we also assumed that individuals differ in the degree to which they are susceptible to the effects of observed body movements. Research on empathy has shown that people differ significantly in the degree to which they can feel the internal states of others

(Chlopan, McCain, Carbonell, & Hagen, 1985). Based on these findings, we assumed that for observers that are empathic with the observed person, observing the execution of motor actions should result in automatic cognitive responses similar to those elicited by actually carrying out those actions.

Method

Fifty-nine female undergraduate psychology students participated in the study for a small reward and partial course credit. Participants first completed a questionnaire for trait empathy (Leibetseder, Laireiter, Riepler, & Köller, 2001). Subsequently, they answered questions according to sports and recent consumption of food, drinks, and alcohol. Then, the experimenter provided participants with a glass of water and asked them to drink from it until they feel not thirsty any longer. Afterwards, the experimenter presented them a short video showing an athlete exercising with a bell bar. In the approach condition, the athlete was standing upright, pulling the weight from his waist to his chest, executing arm flexions against the weight. In the avoidance condition, he was lying on his back, pushing the weight up from his chest, doing arm extensions. Before the video started, participants obtained a glass with 300 ml of a drink which was said to be a new functional sports drink. The experimenter told participants that they should taste the drink and could drink as much as they wanted to do. After participants watched the video and tasted the drink, the experimenter thanked and debriefed the participants. The main dependent measure was the amount participants drank from the offered drink.

Results

We conducted a regression analysis with the amount participants drank as dependant variable and empathy as well as the dummy coded type of movement in the video as predictors. As expected, we found empathic observers to consume more of the drink while watching the approach related arm flexion movement than while observing the avoidance related arm extension movement. Observers low in empathy drank less when watching arm flexions than when watching arm extensions. The interaction term of empathy and type of movement had a significant effect on the amount participants drank from the offered drink. The main effects of empathy, and type of movement were not significant.

Discussion

Studies have shown that body movements and muscle contractions influence judgments and behaviors (e.g., Förster, 2003; 2004). Since the observation of other people's movements tends to elicit neural activations similar to those elicited by executed movements (Buccino et al., 2001), we assumed that also the observation of body movements affects consumer behavior. Our findings support this assumption for empathic observers. When observing arm flexion, a movement that is associated with grabbing and pulling something closer, high empathic observers drank more of an offered drink. When observing an arm flexion, a defensive movement that is involved in keeping distance and essentially incompatible with consumption, empathic observers drank less. Less empathic observers, in contrast, exhibited the inverse pattern.

Our findings extend recent research on embodied cognition showing that consumer behavior might be affected by processes related to motor areas in the brain. Previous research has shown the influence of own body movements. We showed that also the representation of body movements of others leads to similar effects. Further research should examine whether body movements, for instance in TV advertising spots, may have long time effects on the product evaluations or whether observing body movements has only immediate effects on evaluations and behavior.

References

Buccino, G., Binkofski, F., Fink, G. R., Fadiga, L., Fogassi, L., Gallese, V., Seitz, R. J., Zilles, K., Rizzolatti, G., & Freund, H.-J. (2001). Action observation activates premotor and parietal areas in a somatotopic manner: an fMRI study. *European Journal of Neuroscience, 13*, 400–404.

Chlopan, B., McCain, J., Carbonell, J., & Hagen, R. (1985). Empathy: Review of available measures. *Journal of Personality and Social Psychology, 48*, 635-653,

Förster, J. (2003). The influence of approach and avoidance motor actions on food intake. *European Journal of Social Psychology, 33*, 339-350.

Förster, J. (2004). How body feedback influences consumers' evaluation of products. *Journal of Consumer Psychology, 14*, 416-426.

Förster, J., & Strack, F. (1997). Motor actions in retrieval of valenced information: A motor congruence effect. *Perceptual and Motor Skills, 85*, 1419-1427.

Gallese, V. (2001). The "shared manifold" hypothesis: from mirror neurons to empathy. *Journal of Consciousness Studies, 8*, 33-50.

Leibetseder, M., Laireiter, A.-R., Riepler, A., Köller, T. (2001) E-Skala: Fragebogen zur Erfassung von Empathie–Beschreibung und psychometrische Eigenschaften [E-scale: Questionnare for the assessment of empathy–description and psychometric properties. Zeitschrift für Differentielle und Diagnostische Psychologie, 22, 70-85.

Lhermitte, F., Pillon, B., & Serdaru, M. (1986). Human autonomy and the frontal lobes. Part I: Imitation and utilization behavior: a neuropsychological study of 75 patients. *Annals of Neurology, 19*, 326-334.

Niedenthal, P. M., Barsalou, L. W., Winkielman, P., Krauth-Gruber, S., & Ric, F. (2005). Embodiment in attitudes, social perception, and emotion. *Personality and Social Psychology Review, 9*, 184-211.

Strack, F., & Neumann, R. (2000). Furrowing the brow may undermine perceived fame: The role of facial feedback in judgments of celebrity. *Personality and Social Psychology Bulletin, 26*, 762-768.

Strack, F., Stepper, S., & Martin, L. L. (1988). Inhibiting and facilitating conditions of the human smile: A nonobtrusive test of the facial feedback hypothesis. *Journal of Personality and Social Psychology, 54*, 778-777.

Determinants of Customer Dependence and its Effects on Customer Trust in Interpersonal based Buyer-Seller Relationships

Kareem Abdul Waheed, Institute of Management Technology, Dubai, UAE
Sanjay S. Gaur, Auckland University of Technology, New Zealand

Abstract

Traditionally, customer dependence is viewed as a structural constraint in relationship outcomes. The effect of customer dependence on power, control and opportunistic behavior in buyer-seller relationship context is well researched. This paper views customer dependence as a positive relationship construct, identifies the determinants of customer dependence and explains the effects of customer dependence on customer satisfaction and customer trust. The paper is based on an empirical study carried out in farmer-chemical fertilizer retailer relationship-a commonly found interpersonal based buyer-seller relationship in India.

Conceptualization

Many customers in developing country like India build and maintain personal relationships directly with the small-scale retailers. Customer dependence, satisfaction, trust and loyalty on retailer play an important role for building and maintaining such relationships (Anderson and Narus, 1990; Morgan and Hunt, 1994; Andaleeb, 1995). There is considerable research in retailing that focuses on customer's satisfaction, trust and loyalty (e.g. Westbrook, 1981; Macintosh and Lockshin, 1997; Reynolds and Beaty, 1999). Customer dependence has been studied in marketing channels and industrial buying literature (e.g. Andaleeb, 1995; 1996; Lusch and Brown, 1996; Gassenheimer, *et al.,* 1996; Gassenheimer, *et al.,* 1998; Joshi and Arnold, 1998) and not well in retailing. Retailing involves interpersonal based buyer-seller relationships. To the best of our knowledge in the field, no study has researched customer dependence in the interpersonal based buyer-seller relationships. In this paper, we have proposed a model on determinants of customer dependence and its effects on customer trust in interpersonal based buyer-seller relationships context.

We identified product familiarity and market uncertainty as two determinants of customer dependence. First, if the customers' knowledge is limited in understanding their own requirements and how well the supplier's product could be used, they have to depend on their supplier to supply the products in accordance with their requirements. Second, if there is perceived uncertainty about availability of alternative supplies and suppliers, it would act as an exit barrier for the relationship with one supplier and would lead to a dependence based relationship.

Further, we examined the effects of customer dependence on trust. We proposed two types of positive effects on trust-one direct effect and the other indirect effect via satisfaction. A widely prevailing argument suggests a hypothesis-increased levels of perceived customer dependence on the supplier has a negative impact on customer trust, which was however not empirically supported (Monczka *et al.,* 2002; Handfield and Bechtel 2002). An interpersonal trust development perspective of Lewicki and Bunker (1996) is adopted in this paper to support the hypothesis–customer dependence on supplier leads to customer trust. Lewicki and Bunker (1996) posit three stages of trust development in interpersonal relationships in professional context: calculus-based trust, knowledge-based trust and identification-based trust. We equate customer dependence to calculus-based trust and hence it further leads to enhancement of trust. We contend, even when the buyers are in dependent position, the extent and quality of experience gained during the interactions could lead to positive effects on trust. Similarly, majority of the studies that focus on TCA (transactional cost analysis) approach suggest direct or indirect negative causal relationship between dependence and satisfaction (Gassenheimer, *et al.,* 1998; Andaleeb, 1996). By applying Lewicki and Bunker model, we contend, customer dependence also leads to satisfaction. Many studies empirically proved the positive relationship between satisfaction and trust (Batt and Rexha 1999; Kennedy *et al.* 2001).

Last, we proposed a negative moderating role of satisfaction on the relationship between customer dependence and trust to reemphasize that satisfaction acts as a major contributor in developing trust rather than dependence.

Method

A survey was carried out to empirically validate the model in farmer-chemical fertilizer retailer relationship, which is an example of a typical interpersonal based buyer-seller relationship in Indian context. Madurai, Pudukottai and Trichy districts of Tamil Nadu state were selected for the study. One taluk having higher fertilizer consumption from each of the above districts was selected. A taluk is the major revenue, administrative and planning unit in the district. The total sample size for this study was 300 farmers. The questionnaire was first translated to Tamil and then was translated back to English with the help of English and Tamil language translators independently (Brislin, 1980; McGorry, 2000). The earlier version of the English questionnaire was compared to the back-translated questionnaire and inconsistencies were removed after consultation with the translators (Brislin, 1980; McGorry, 2000). All the variables included in the study were measured using the scales available in the literature [product familiarity-Oliver and Bearden (1985); market uncertainty-Batt (2000); customer dependence-Batt (2000); customer satisfaction-Kennedy *et al.* (2001); customer trust-Holden (1990)].

All the measures were subjected to convergent validity and discriminant validity test using AMOS. Hypotheses testing were carried out specifically for determinants of customer dependence and its direct effect on trust by Confirmatory Factor Analysis using AMOS. The indirect effect of customer dependence on trust via satisfaction and the moderation effect of satisfaction hypotheses were tested by multiple regression analysis using SPSS.

Major Findings

There are well-documented researches suggesting the importance of customer dependence for long-term buyer-seller relationships. But limited researches in marketing domain have looked at the phenomenon of customer dependence in the market place. Our study conceptualized and empirically tested the determinants of customer dependence and its effects on customer trust. The customer perception of market uncertainty was empirically proven as an important determinant for the customer dependence. Perceived product familiarity was also found to reduce customer dependence on the seller.

Our main contention of the study that analyzes the effect of customer dependence on customer trust was well supported. Basically, this result emphasized the applicability of interpersonal trust development perspective in interpersonal based buyer-seller relationships. We view the development of calculus-based trust as a process that leads to the customer dependence. The possible subsequent interactions between the buyer and seller add to the knowledge of each other and positive experiences, which could possibly lead to information symmetry between them. Information symmetric situation between the buyer and seller evolves when the customer has identification-based trust on the seller. Identification-based trust between the buyer and seller leads to joint goals, cooperative behavior, collective decision-making and collective efforts. Hence, this result negates the exaggerated negative consequences of customer dependence in buyer-seller relationships.

Our other contention of the study, the customer dependence has positive impact on customer satisfaction, did not get empirical support. We suggest this research question for further probe. Finally, our last hypothesis is related to the negative moderating effect of customer satisfaction on the positive relationship between customer dependence and customer trust was also supported. This result again emphasizes the importance of customer satisfaction in creating customer trust when compared to other variables.

References

Andaleeb, Syed Saad (1995) "Dependence Relations and the Moderating Role of Trust: Implications for Behavioral Intentions in Marketing Channels," *International Journal of Research in Marketing*, 12 (2), 157-72

_____ (1996), "An Experimental Investigation of Satisfaction and Commitment in Marketing Channels: The Role of Trust and Dependence," *Journal of Retailing*, 72 (1), 77-93.

Anderson, James, C. & James, A. Narus (1990), "A Model of Distributor Firm and Manufacturer Firm Working Partnerships," *Journal of Marketing*, 54 (January), 42-58.

Batt, Peter J. (2000), "Modeling Buyer-Seller Relationships in Agribusiness in South East Asia", Paper No: 17. in *Proceedings of 16th Annual IMP Conference*, 7-9 September, Bath, University of Bath-University of Birmingham.

_____ and Nexhmi Rexha (1999), "Building Trust in Agribusiness Supply Chains: A Conceptual Model of Buyer-Seller Relationships in the Seed Potato Industry in Asia," *Journal of International Food and Agribusiness Marketing*, 11 (1), 1-17.

Brislin, Richard W. (1980), "Translation and Content Analysis of Oral and Written Materials," in *Hand Book of Cross-cultural Psychology*, Volume-2, Triandis, Harry C. and Berry, John W. eds. Boston: Allyn & Bacon, Inc. 389-444.

Gassenheimer, Jule B., J. Charlene Davis, and Robert Dahlstrom (1998), "The Effects of Incongruency: Is Dependent What We Want To Be?", *Journal of Retailing*, 74 (Summer), 247-271.

Gassenheimer, Jule B., Jay U. Sterling, and Robert A. Robicheaux (1996), "Long-term Channel Member Relationships." *International Journal of Physical Distribution & Logistics*, 26(5), 94-116.

Handfield, Robert.B., and Christian, Bechtel. (2002), "The Role of Trust and Relationship Structure in Improving Supply Chain Responsiveness", *Industrial Marketing Management*, 31, 367– 382.

Holden, R. K. (1990), "An Exploratory Study of Trust in Buyer-Seller Relationships," A Dissertation, Ann Arbor, MI: University Microfilms International.

Joshi, A.W. and Arnold, S.J. (1998), "How Relational Norms Affect Compliance in Industrial Buying", *Journal of Business Research*, 41(2), 106-14.

Kennedy, Mary S., Linda K. Ferrel, Debbie T. LeClair, D.T. (2001), "Consumers' Trust of Salesperson and Manufacturer: An Empirical Study," *Journal of Business Research*, 51 (1), 73-86.

Lewicki, Roy and Bunker, Benedict (1996), "Developing and Maintaining Trust in Work Relationships," in *Trust in organizations: frontiers of theory and research*. Tom Tyler and Roderick Kramer, eds., Thousand Oaks, California: Sage. 114-139.

Lusch, Robert. F. and Brown, James R. (1996), Interdependency, Contracting, and Relational Behavior in Marketing Channels", *Journal of Marketing*, Vol. 60, October, pp. 19-38.

Macintosh, Gerrard. and Lockshin, Lawrence.S. (1997), "Retail Relationships and Store Loyalty: A Multi-level Perspective", *International Journal of Research in Marketing*, 14(5), 487-497.

McGorry, Susan Y. (2000), "Measurement in a Cross-Cultural Environment: Survey Translation Issues," *Qualitative Market Research: An International Journal*, 3 (2), 74-81.

Monczka, Robert M., Thomas J. Callahan and Ernest L Nichols (1995), "Predictors of Relationships among Firms Predictors of Relationships among Buying and Supplying Firms", *International Journal of Physical Distribution & Logistics Management*, 25 (10), 45-59.

Morgan, Robert M. and Shelby D. Hunt (1994), "The Commitment-Trust Theory of Relationship Marketing," *Journal of Marketing*, 58 (3), 20-38.

Oliver, Richard L. and William O. Bearden (1985), "Crossover Effect in the Theory of Reasoned Action: A Moderating Influence Attempt," *Journal of Consumer Research*, 12 (December) 324-340.

Reynolds, Kristy. E. and Sharon E. Beatty (1999), "Customer Benefits and Customer Consequences of Customer-Salesperson Relationships in Retailing," *Journal of Retailing*, 75 (1), 11-32.

Westbrook, Robert. A. (1981), "Sources of Customer Satisfaction with Retail Outlets," *Journal of Retailing*, 57(Fall), 68-85.

The Effects of Intimacy on Consumer-Brand Relationships

Katharina Guese, University of Lausanne, Switzerland
Karine Gautschi Haelg, University of Lausanne, Switzerland

Interest in consumer-brand relationships (CBR) has emerged among scientists over the last decade (e.g., Fournier 1998). Nevertheless, no study investigated the effects of intimate CBR within an experiment. Subsequently, we examine the effects of intimacy and anthropomorphization on consumer brand perception. Moreover, this paper investigates whether a consumer feels more intimate with an anthropomorphized brand .

In the marketing literature, the assumption predominates that consumers attribute human characteristics to brands (e.g., Aaker 1997). For instance, given that brands are received as a gift or that they are utilized by a close friend or a family member, people are encouraged to humanize them (Rajagopal 2006). Anthropomorphization can be defined as viewing human characteristics in non human forms or events (Guthrie, 1993). Extending this line of thought, Fournier (1998) suggests that brands, like humans, serve as a legitimate relationship partner. One of the characteristics of human relationships (Miller and Lefcourt 1982) as well as of CBR (Fournier 1994; Fournier 1998) is intimacy. Intimacy can be described as "feelings of closeness, connectedness, and bondedness in loving relationships" (Sternberg 1986, p. 119). According to researchers in the field of interpersonal relationships, intimacy is an essential component of relationships among adults (Gaia 2002). In marketing research, Fournier (1994; 1998) assesses that intimacy is characterized by a detailed knowledge of the brand and a special brand meaning for the customer.

Following the perspective that life is given to a brand in the consumer's mind (Aggarwal 2004; Ouwersloot and Tudorica 2001), we can assume that customers tend to build relationships with brands as with human beings. This in turn leads to the proposition that consumers tend to elaborate relationships with brands. The first overall prediction is that individuals who established an intimate relationship with a brand feel more trust towards this brand and a higher level of brand partner quality than if they do not sense this intimacy. Secondly, it is assumed that people tend to feel more trust towards the brand and a higher level of brand partner quality if it is perceived as having human characteristics.

To analyze these hypotheses, we conducted a scenario-based 2 (intimate/ non intimate) x 2 (anthropomorphized/ non anthropomorphized) ANCOVA with a final number of 63 participants. A ficticious fashion brand served as stimulus. The wording of the non intimate condition was mainly copied from an existing marketing text utilized by a famous brand. As defined by Hook et al. (2003), the brand description of the intimate condition included the components of intimacy: elements of love and affection, personal validation, self-disclosure and trust. The manipulation check was performed on the basis of a 9-item intimacy scale (Cronbach's Alpha=.926) by Nysveen and his colleagues (2001), which was modified from Fournier (1994). While the non anthropomorphized scenario was written in an impersonal style, in the anthropomorphized scenario, the brand expressed itself as a person. A single item represented the brand's anthropomorphization. As regards the dependent variables, the partner quality scale by Fournier (1994) was first utilized to measure to what extent the respondent perceives the brand as a good partner. Five items reflected this variable (Cronbach's Alpha=.926). Secondly, participants completed the 10-item scale by Hess (1995) to indicate their trust level towards the brand (Cronbach's Alpha=.761). Respondents fashion involvement served as covariate (Tigert et al. (1976); Cronbach's Alpha=.769).

The main purpose of the experiment reported here was to examine the effects of intimacy and anthropomorphization on brand trust and brand partner quality. First, we successfully manipulated intimacy in the case where the brand was not anthropomorphized by the use of brand descriptions. Participants who received the intimate and non anthropomorphized text presented higher levels of intimacy than participants in the non intimate and non anthropomorphized condition $F(1,27)=8.89$, $p<.01$. In terms of our first hypothesis, we found that the use of intimate components in creating a CBR results in significantly higher levels of trust; $F(1,27)=5.05$, $p<.05$ and partner quality; $F(1,27)=6.36$, $p<.05$, compared to the use of traditional non intimate cues. Therefore, we propose that intimacy increases brand trust and brand partner quality. Analyses to test the second hypothesis, could not be completed because the manipulation did not present the expected results.

The first contribution of this work consists in its being the first study to successfully manipulate the perceived intimacy of a customer in the course of an experiment and, subsequently, to assess its effects on brand trust and brand partner quality. Therefore, the research question suggesting that marketers can establish an intimate relationship with a brand is affirmed. This result is even more significant, as intimacy is known to increase over time (Shimp and Madden 1988) and as it has never been manipulated in an experiment to analyze the CBR. Secondly, this work provides further insight into the performance aspects of brand management because the study proposes and empirically supports the idea that intimacy plays a pivotal role in a CBR. Additionally, this enlarged understanding of intimate relationships is crucial for marketers as it lays emphasis on the necessity to elaborate intimate feelings in CBRs because they represent a competitive advantage compared to competitor brands.

Notwithstanding these contributions, there are some limitations which suggest interesting opportunities for future research. First, the limited number of observations per experimental condition lowers the generalizability of the results. Furthermore, the external validity is limited due to the overrepresentation of women in the sample. Future research may replicate our study by using a larger counterbalanced sample. Secondly, given that a well-established multidimensional measurement of brand anthropomorphization does not exist in the literature, our unidimensional measurement limits the internal validity of the results. It is possible that the absence of a main effect on anthropomorphization stems from this lack of internal validity and that a replication of the study using a multidimensional scale could increase this validity. Therefore, future research should elaborate an appropriate scale and may replicate our study.

References

Aaker, Jennifer L. (1997), "Dimensions of Brand Personality," *Journal of Marketing Research*, 34 (3), 347-56.
Aggarwal, Pankaj (2004), "The Effects of Brand Relationship Norms in Consumer Attitudes and Behavior," *Journal of Consumer Research*, 31 (1), 87-101.

Fournier, Susan (1994), *Consumer-Brand Relationship Framework for Strategic Brand Management*, Ph.D. dissertation, University of Florida.

_____ (1998), "Consumers and Their Brands: Developing Relationship Theory in Consumer Research," *Journal of Consumer Research*, 24 (4), 343-73.

Gaia, Celeste A. (2002), "Understanding Emotional Intimacy: A review of conceptualization, assessment and the role of gender." *International Social Science Review;* 77(3/4), 151-171.

Guthrie, Stewart (1993), *Faces in the Clouds: A New Theory of Religion*, New York: Oxford University Press.

Hess, J. (1995), "Construction and Assessment of a Scale to Measure Consumer Trust" Chapter in Barbara B. Stern and George M. Zinkhan (Eds.), *AMA Educator's Proceedings*, 6, 20-26. Chicago: American Marketing Association.

Hook, Misty K.; Lawrence H. Gerstein; Lacy Detterich and Betty Gridley (2003), "How close are we? Measuring Intimacy and Examining Gender Differences" *Journal of Counseling & Development*, 81(4), 462-472.

Miller, Rickey S. and Herbert M. Lefcourt (1982), "The Assessment of Social Intimacy" *Journal of Personality Assessment,* 46 (5), 514-18.

Nysveen, Herbjorn, Per E. Pedersen and Helge Thorbjornsen (2001), "Merkerelasjoner via Internett: en sammenligning av statisk nettsted, nettsted med kundefellesskap og personalisert nettsted som applikasjoner for å bygge merkerelasjoner via Internett", *SNF-rapport, 12/01, 6220*, Bergen.

Ouwersloot, Hans and Anamaria Tudorica (2001), "Brand Personality Creation through Advertising," *MAXX Working Paper Series,* 2001-01. Maastricht.

Rajagopal (2006), "Insights from research. Brand excellence: measuring the impact of advertising and brand personality on buying decisions" *Measuring Business Excellence*, 10 (3), 56-65.

Shimp, Terence A. and Thomas J. Madden (1988), "Consumer-Object Relations: A Conceptual Framework Based Analogously on Stemberg's Triangular Theory of Love," *Advances in Consumer Research,* 15 (1), 163-68.

Sternberg, Robert J. (1986), "A Triangular Theory of Love" *Psychological Review*, 93 (2), 119-135.

Tigert, Douglas J., Lawrence J. Ring, and Charles W. King (1976), "Fashion Involvement and Buying Behavior: A Methodological Study," *Advances in Consumer Research*, 3 (1), 46-52.

A Meta-Analytic Review of Fear Appeals: A Terror Management Perspective

David M. Hunt, University of Wyoming, USA
Stephanie Geiger-Oneto, University of Wyoming, USA
Omar Shehryar, Montana State University, USA

Fear appeals–persuasive messages designed to scare people into complying with a message by threatening negative consequences of non-compliance (Witte 1992)–are used in a broad range of social marketing contexts including drinking and driving, smoking cessation and prevention, domestic violence, food safety, and HIV/AIDS prevention. Scholarly interest in fear-based communications has been maintained for over fifty years. Three theories, drive theory (Janis & Feschbach, 1953), protection motivation theory (PMT; Rogers, 1983), and the parallel response theory (PRT; Tanner, Hunt, & Eppright, 1991) have guided much of the extant research on the efficacy of fear appeals. This body of research has demonstrated weak, but reliable effects of fear upon attitudes, intentions, and behaviors (Boster and Mongeau 1984; Mongeau 1998; Witte 2000). Relatively weak associations between fear and outcome variables has led to calls for research to identify plausible moderators between fear and persuasive outcomes (Witte 2000).

Across all three major theoretical approaches to fear appeal research, the dominant paradigm asserts that differences in the level of fear lead to differences in the persuasiveness of a message (Keller and Block 1996; Rogers 1985; Witte 1994). However, this approach overlooks the potential influence of the qualitative nature of the threatened consequence. Fear appeal messages vary not only in terms of the level of fear, but also in terms of the qualitative nature of the threatened consequence. For instance some consequences pose social threats, some pose threats of injury, and some pose threats of death. Terror Management Theory (TMT) (Greenberg, Pyszczynski, & Solomon 1986) suggests that messages threatening death produce responses to fear appeal messages that differ from responses to social threats or to threats of injury (Shehryar and Hunt 2005). Specifically, TMT suggests that fear appeals that make mortality salient may result in rejection of messages inconsistent with the cultural worldviews of message recipients. This suggests that extant theoretical approaches grounded in the level-of-fear paradigm under-predict the conditions under which fear-based messages will be rejected.

Terror Management Theory posits that even subtle reminders of mortality increase the need to defend and strengthen one's cultural worldview. Treatments considered equally noxious, such as threatening someone with serious injury, intense pain, or social embarrassment do not evoke mortality salience and do not lead to a defense of cultural worldviews (Greenberg, Pyszczynski, Solomon, Simon, & Breus, 1994). The distinction between responses to the fear of death versus responses to other noxious consequences has important implications for fear appeal research. Specifically, when individuals highly committed to a worldview are exposed to a death-threat-based message that conflicts with that worldview, they will reject the message's recommendation.

We hypothesize that when messages conflict with recipients' cultural worldviews, the qualitative nature of the threatened consequence will moderate the relationship between commitment to that worldview and persuasiveness of the message such that:

Hypothesis1: When messages conflict with the cultural worldview of recipients, fear appeals that threaten death as a consequence will be negatively related to message acceptance and positively related to message rejection.

To test this hypothesis, we employ meta-analytic techniques to synthesize the findings of extant fear appeal research. Drawing on Terror Management Theory (Greenburg, et al., 1986), we distinguish between studies that used death as a threatened consequence from studies that did not. Studies included in the analysis are coded for the nature of threatened consequence and the degree to which the recommended message conflicts with the cultural worldview of the sample. To assess the moderating influence of nature of threat, effect sizes across a 2x2 experimental design (mortality salient vs. mortality non-salient threat) and (consistent cultural worldview vs. inconsistent cultural worldview) will be compared.

The purpose of this meta-analysis is not to settle any dispute among competing theoretical approaches. Instead, we offer a complimentary theoretical perspective to supplement extant understanding of fear appeal efficacy. Specifically, exploring the efficacy of fear appeals from the perspective of TMT contributes to fear appeal research in at least two ways. First, the categories of death and non-death-related consequences are discrete. Comparatively, there are no broadly accepted standards for what constitutes a high fear appeal, a moderate fear appeal, or a low fear appeal (Keller 1999). Fear communications differentiated by the qualitative nature of the threatened consequence avoids the debate over the constitution of fear levels. Second, this meta-analysis extends the theoretical domain of fear appeal research by offering TMT as an additional framework from which to examine the efficacy of fear-based communications. The TMT perspective allows future inquiry to examine the nature of fear as a factor moderating fear appeal outcomes thereby extending current research beyond the one-dimensional level of fear paradigm.

References

Arndt, J., Goldenberg, J. L., Greenberg, J., Pyszczynski, T., & Solomon, S. (2000), "Death can be hazardous to your health: Adaptive and ironic consequences of defenses against the terror of death," In *Psychodynamic Perspectives on Sickness and Health*, P. R. Duberstein & J. M. Masling (Eds.), Washington, DC: American Psychological Association, 201-257.

Greenberg, J., Pyszczynski, T. & Solomon, S. (1986), "The causes and consequences of a need for self-esteem: A terror management theory," In *Public Self and Private Self*, R. F. Baumeister (Ed.), NY: Springer, 189-212.

Janis, I. L. & Feshbach, S. (1953), "Effects of fear-arousing communications," *Journal of Abnormal and Social Psychology*, 48 (1), 78-92.

Keller, P. A. (1999), "Converting the unconverted: The effect of inclination and opportunity to discount health-related fear appeals," *Journal of Applied Psychology*, 84 (June), 403-415.

Rippetoe, P. A. & Rogers, R. W. (1987), "Effects of components of protection-motivation theory on adaptive and maladaptive coping with a health threat," *Journal of Personality & Social Psychology*, 52 (March), 596-604.

Rogers, R. W. (1983), "Cognitive and physiological processes in fear appeals and attitude change: A revised theory of protection motivation, "In *Social Psycho-physiology*, J. T. Cacioppo & R. E. Petty (Eds.), New York: Guilford Press.

Shehryar, Omar and David Hunt (2005), "A terror management perspective on fear appeals," *Journal of Consumer Psychology*, 15 (4), 275-287.

Tanner, J. F., Hunt, J. G., & Eppright, D. R. (1991), "The protection motivation model: A normative model of fear appeals," *Journal of Marketing*, 55 (July), 36-45.

Witte, K. (1994), "Fear control and danger control: A test of the extended parallel process model (EPPM), *Communication Monographs*, 61 (June), 113-134.

Why 'Fast Food' Triggers 'McDonald's' and 'Burgerking' Triggers 'Fast Food': Antecedents of Brand Typicality and the Relationship Between Category and Brand

Jia Liu, Monash University, Australia
Els Gijsbrechts, Tilburg University, The Netherlands
Dirk Smeesters, Erasmus University, The Netherlands

Very typical brands are assumed to be categorized faster upon a brand cue (brand-to-category direction) and to be recalled faster upon a category cue (category-to-brand direction) than less typical brands. We, however, propose that brand typicality effects are asymmetric in the brand-to-category and category-to-brand direction. We examine to what extent two different antecedents of brand typicality drive this asymmetry, namely family resemblance (FR) and frequency of instantiation (FOI). Three studies examine the relationship between FR and FOI, and their impact on the link between brand and category, in a context of real brands. The findings reveal that FR is more important in determining how fast a brand is categorized given a brand cue, whereas FOI is more influential in determining the speed of brand recall in the presence of a category name.

The Portion-Size Effect: How Increasing the Number of Portion-Size Options Can Increase the Volume of Food Consumption

Jing Lei, University of Ontario Institute of Technology, Canada
Tripat Gill, University of Ontario Institute of Technology, Canada

Research Background and Hypotheses

Among the many contributing factors to obesity, the steadily increasing portion-sizes of food over the past 30 years (also know as "super-sizing") are among the most criticized (e.g., Cutler et al. 2003; Wansink 2004). The increase in portion-sizes is said to have affected both the consumption norms (i.e., how much is appropriate to eat?) and the consumption monitoring accuracy (i.e., how much has been eaten?), and has ultimately led to increasing food intake (Chandon and Wansink 2007; Wansink and Ittersum 2007). While these two factors may explain why consumers overeat in a given portion size, it is not clear what causes them to choose a portion size (e.g., large) that is larger than their physiological need (e.g., medium) in the first place. In the current research, we propose that consumers' choice for portion-sizes is influenced by the number of portion-size options available in the environment. Specifically, it is proposed that merely adding larger portion-size options (e.g., adding an "Extra Large" option to the set of "Small, Medium and Large") can increase the volume of food consumed. In other words, over-consumption can occur not only by increasing the portion-size of existing options but also by adding new (and larger) portion-size options. We propose that this effect occurs as a result of 1) the change in consumption norms for the appropriate portion-size, and 2) the reduction in the consumption guilt associated with consuming larger portion-sizes. These two mechanisms are explained in detail below.

Wansink and colleagues (e.g., Kahn and Wansink 2004) suggest that people tend to rely on consumption norms to decide how much is appropriate to eat. These norms can be influenced by external cues that are present in the environment. The number of available portion-size options can be one such cue. For example, if the number of larger portion-size options (e.g., large, extra large drink; double, triple hamburger) increases, people may assume that there is a reason that these larger options are offered and use this information to guide their choices (Schwartz 1996). Specifically, the increasing presence of larger size options may signal that it is appropriate or socially acceptable to order a larger portion-size. As a result, the choice for larger portion-sizes may increase and accordingly the average consumption volume of food would increase.

Secondly, while the current super-sized environment may lead consumers to believe that "more is better" (Wansink 2004), the current environment of "calorie-consciousness" also leads consumers to regulate how much they consume (Cutler et al. 2003). The latter self-regulation may make consumers feel guilty to choose the "large" option from the set of "small/medium/large" (S/M/L) options. However, if another "extra-large" (XL) option is added to this set, consumers may feel less guilty to choose the "large" option from the set of S/M/L/XL options. The reduced feeling of guilt may consequently increase the choices for larger sizes as the number of portion-size options increases.

Experiments and Results

Two experimental studies were conducted to test the effect of increasing portion-size options on consumption volume. The studies used hypothetical scenarios where subjects were told to imagine that they were in a restaurant and decided to order either a beverage or a fast food meal from different sets of portion-size options. Experiment 1 (n=64) employed a 2 (3 vs. 4 portion-size options) * 1 (vanilla milkshake) between-subjects design, in which participants had to choose from either 3 options (small/medium/large) or 4 options (small/medium/large/extra large) of vanilla milkshake. We also asked the participants to estimate the amount of calories contained in each portion-size after they made the choice. We found that in the 4 (vs. 3) option condition, more people chose the "Large" option (33.3% vs. 13.4%, z=1.69, p=0.05) and fewer people chose the "Small" option (26.2% vs. 45.5%, z= -1.56, p=0.06). The proportion of people choosing "Medium" was not significantly changed (35.7% vs. 40.9%, z=-0.41, p=0.34). We also found that the average number of calories consumed was significantly increased when participants were given 4 (vs. 3) portion-size options (629 vs. 523 calories, t=2.49, p=0.02). Furthermore, we found that participants significantly underestimated the number of calories contained in each portion-size (p<0.001 for all conditions).

Experiment 2 was conducted to investigate if the above results can be replicated in a fast food meal scenario and whether providing calorie information would influence participants' portion-size choices. Experiment 2 (n=187) employed a 2 (3 vs. 4 portion-size options) * 2 (calorie information provided vs. not provided) between-subjects design using a fast food meal scenario (chicken salad). We found that more people chose the "Large" option in the 4 (vs. 3) option condition when no calorie information was provided (45.7% vs. 20%, z=2.69, p<0.001), whereas this change was not significant when calorie information was provided (38.8% vs. 31.0%, z=0.78, p=0.22). We also found that fewer people chose the "Small" option in the 4 (vs. 3) option condition regardless of whether calorie information was provided or not (8.2% vs. 21.4%, z= -1.80, p=0.04; 6.5% vs. 18.0%, z= -1.70, p=0.04). Furthermore, the results show that the average number of calories consumed was significantly increased when participants were given 4 (vs. 3) portion-size options (393 vs. 333, t=4.42, p<0.001).

Implications

The above results confirm our prediction that the choice for larger portion-sizes increases as the number of portion-size options increases. This finding violates the principle of regularity based on the normative probability choice model (e.g., Tversky 1972); specifically that the probability of choosing a particular option (e.g., "large") cannot be increased when the number of offered options increases. More importantly, our finding indicates that the mere increase in the number of portion-size options offered can lead to over-consumption. The two proposed underlying reasons that lead to this effect, namely the changes in consumption norms and consumption guilt, are to be tested in subsequent studies. Overall, this research aims to provide insights into the impact of a specific type of environmental factor (i.e. number of portion-size options) on food consumption and suggest implications for managers / public-policy makers to address the issue of over-consumption.

References

Chandon, Pierre and Brian Wansink (2007), "Is Obesity Caused by Calorie Underestimation? A Psychophysical Model of Meal Size Estimation", *Journal of Marketing Research*, Vol. 44 (February), 84-99.

Cutler, David M., Edward L. Glaeser, and Jesse M. Shapiro (2003), "Why Have Americans Become So Obese?" *Journal of Economic Perspectives*, Vol. 17 (summer), 93-118.

Kahn, Barbara E. and Brian Wansink (2004), "The Influence of Assortment Structure on Perceived Variety and Consumption Quantities", *Journal of Consumer Research*, Vol. 30 (March), 519-33.

Schwarz, Norbert (1996), *Cognition and Communication: Judgmental Biases, Research Methods and the Logic of Conversation*, Mahwah, NJ: Erlbaum.

Tversky, Amos (1972), "Elimination by Aspects: A Theory of Choice," *Psychological Review*, Vol. 79 (4), 281-99.

Wansink, Brian (2004), "Environmental Factors That Increase the Food Intake and Consumption Volume of Unknowing Consumers", *Annual Review of Nutrition*, Vol. 24, 455-79.

Wansink, Brian and Koert Van Ittersum (2007), "Portion Size Me: Downsizing Our Consumption Norms", *Journal of the American Dietetic Association*, Vol. 107 (July), 1103-6.

A Taxonomy of Price Behaviour

Björn Ivens, University of Lausanne, Switzerland
Brigitte Müller, University of Lausanne, Switzerland
Katharina Guese, University of Lausanne, Switzerland

Abstract

Many of the classical retail chains attempt to counter discounters' aggressive expansion strategy by introducing low-priced private label product assortments. In this paper, we analyze the relationship between consumers' price behavior and their reactions toward the classical retailers' low price products. Based on survey data we first develop a taxonomy of customers' price behavior. This taxonomy is built from several dimensions of consumers' price behavior. We then analyze if the price behavior cluster consumers' belong to has an impact on their response to classical retailers' low-price products. The paper closes with a discussion of the results and directions for future research.

Over the past years, the international expansion of hard-discounters such as Aldi or Lidl has led to a shift in the European retail landscape. The relative market share of this type of retail format has constantly grown (Denstadli et al. 2005; Business Insights 2006). Traditional retail chains have long had difficulties finding an appropriate strategic reply. The most important move for many retailers has consisted in introducing an assortment of low-priced products which are sold at prices comparable to those of the hard-discounters products. For example, in Switzerland two major players dominate the retail market, i.e. Coop and Migros. Together they hold approximately 72% of the national retail market and traditionally both have been selling their products at average to upper price points (Von Ungern-Sternberg and Jametti 2007). When German hard-discounters Aldi and Lidl have entered the Swiss market, both Swiss retail chains have established discount price product ranges. The strategic function of these new product assortments in both cases is to retain price sensitive customers and prevent them from switching to the new competitors. An important question in this context is whether these products attract all types of customers or whether specific customer groups are more likely to buy them. The purpose of this paper is to provide elements to answer this question.

Consumer's price behaviour

In a broad stream of research, different constructs describing customers' price behavior have been conceptualized (e.g. Lichtenstein et al. 1990; Vanhuele and Drèze 2002) and their impact on purchasing decisions has been demonstrated (e.g. Ailawadi et al. 2001; Estelami and Lehmann 2001).

Lichtenstein et al. (1993) distinguish several constructs describing different aspects of customers' price behavior. Four constructs reflect the negative role of price: (1) Price consciousness; (2) Value consciousness; (3) Sale proneness; (4) Price mavenism. Two constructs reflect the positive role: (5) Price-quality scheme; (6) Prestige sensitivity.

The extent to which a consumer is price conscious or a price maven varies between individuals. These concepts describe the personality of each consumer. While scholars have analyzed the relationship between various aspects of consumers' price behavior and outcome variables, little is known about the extent to which typical patterns of price behavior exist. From a managerial vantage point, however, the existence of price behavior clusters or segments would be of high relevance. To the best of our knowledge, the constructs described above have not yet been used in order to segment customers.

Research methodology and results

A total number of 471 questionnaires were collected from consumers. The structure of respondents corresponds to the one in the relevant regional population with regard to gender and age. The scales included in the questionnaire are mostly drawn based upon the ones developed by Lichtenstein et al. (1993): Value consciousness (4 items, $\alpha=.692$), Price consciousness (3 items, $\alpha=.869$), Sale proneness (3 items, $\alpha=.703$), Price mavenism (4 items, $\alpha=.780$), Price quality scheme (3 items, $\alpha=.746$) and Prestige sensitivity (3 items, $\alpha=.729$).

In our analysis, we proceeded in two steps. First, we used cluster analysis in order to uncover a potential segment structure in consumers' price behavior. Analysis of variance shows that the three identified clusters differ significantly along five of the six active cluster variables. Only for prestige sensitivity we observe no significant differences. Analysis of discriminance shows that the probability that objects in the data base are correctly allocated to the clusters is 92.5%:

Cluster 1 (value-oriented shoppers) is characterized by high value and low price consciousness. Sale proneness is also lower as for the other two clusters. Consumers see themselves as price mavens and score the highest on price-quality scheme.

Cluster 2 (price-oriented shoppers) is composed of consumers who show low value but high price consciousness as well as relatively high sale proneness. On price mavenism and prestige sensitivity they have average scores.

Cluster 3 (sale-driven shoppers) is composed of sale prone consumers who score low on both price and value consciousness, on price mavenism and on price quality scheme.

The second step aims at identifying the buyers of discount-price products. Using analysis of variance, we also analyzed whether significant differences exist in the three groups' response to low price product assortments at classical retailers. We included three independent variables in the analysis, i.e. consumer attitude towards discount-priced products, consumer attitude towards that specific retail brand and consumers frequency of buying the specific retail brand. For all three independent variables there are significant differences ($p<0.05$) between the three shopper clusters. Value-oriented and price-oriented shoppers buy more frequently low price products than those driven by sales. A similar pattern is observed concerning cluster 3. Sale-driven consumers have the least favorable attitude toward discount-priced assortments and the specific assortment brand and also buy less frequently the brand. On the contrary, we can observe that value and price-oriented consumers evaluate these types of products more favorably and buy them more frequently.

Implications and future research

By elaborating this taxonomy, we shed light on the link between key constructs in behavioral pricing and consumer response to discount concepts. For managerial practice, our results imply that the managers of retail brands should adapt the positioning of their discount-price brand(s). In particular, strategies need to be designed to communicate precisely with the price segment who responds positively to the discount-priced brands as compared to the segment of sale prone shoppers which is mainly focusing upon price promotions for national brands.

Future research is undertaken in order to focus not only focus upon respondents' reactions toward the classical retailers' discount-priced assortments but also compare consumers' attitudes towards the discount retailers (Aldi and Lidl) with attitudes toward discount-priced assortments. This would allow identifying potential motivational gaps in buying one or the other offering.

References

Ailawadi, Kusum L., Scott A. Neslin and Karen Gedenk (2001). "Pursuing the value-conscious consumer: Store brands versus national brand promotions," *Journal of Marketing*, 65(1): 71-89.

Business Insights (2006). *Brand Success in Discounters: Strategies for Driving Sales Growth and New Customer Acquisition*, London : Business Insights.

Denstadli, Jon M., Rune Lines and Kjell Gr?nhaug (2005). "First mover advantages in the retail grocery industry," *European Journal of Marketing*, 39 (7/8): 872-884.

Estelami, Hooman and Donald R. Lehmann (2001). "The impact of research design on consumer price recall accuracy: An integrative review," *Journal of the Academy of Marketing Science*, 29 (1): 36-49.

Jin, Brenda and Byoungho Sternquist (2003). "The influence of retail environment on price perceptions: An exploratory study of US and Korean students," *Service Industries Journal*, 20 (6): 643-660.

Lichtenstein, Donald R., Richard G. Netemeyer and Scot Burton (1990). "Distinguishing coupon proneness from value consciousness: An acquisition-transaction utility theory perspective," *Journal of Marketing*, 54 (July): 54-67.

Lichtenstein, Donald R., N. M. Ridgway, and Richard G. Netemeyer (1993). "Price perceptions and consumer shopping behaviour: A field study," *Journal of Marketing Research*, 30 (May): 234-245.

Vanhuele, Marc and Xavier Drèze (2002). "Measuring the Price Knowledge Customers Bring to the Store, *Journal of Marketing*, 66: 72-85.

Von Ungern-Sternberg, Thomas and Mario Jametti. (2007). "Die Übernahme von Denner durch Migros verstösst gegen das Kartellgesetz," Economic working paper series 07-02, Department of Econometrics and Economy, University of Lausanne.

Effects of Personal Values on Brand Equity

Eda Gurel Atay, University of Oregon, USA

Brand equity, "marketing effects uniquely attributable to the brand" (Keller 1993, p. 1), has been studied by several researchers (Aaker and Keller 1990; Sivakumar and Raj 1997). Many of these studies found that high equity brands benefit from more loyal and satisfied customers, higher purchase intentions, and more frequent use of the product/service. Because brand equity has so many important implications, it is essential to understand how to build brand equity (Keller 1993; Kirca, Jayachandran, and Bearden 2005). One way to build brand equity is to position a brand accordingly. Positioning is a fundamental part of a company's marketing strategy since it describes the distinctive place of each brand in the target consumers' minds and provides clear bases to compare different brands in a product category (Kotler, 2003; Prince, 1990). In a way, the result of successful positioning is the successful creation of brand equity. And, since consumers decide with their purchases which brands have more equity than others, it is important to consider them when establishing a brand's position. One of the most important characteristics of people, hence consumers, is their personal values. Accordingly, the aim of this paper is to examine effects of brand positioning based on personal values on brand equity.

Values are described as the most important construct by many researchers (Rokeach 1973; Kahle 1996) in social science. They are central to people's lives (Kahle and Timmer 1983), are enduring and difficult to change (Rokeach 1973), and guide behaviors and judgments across specific situations (Rokeach 1973; Kahle and Timmer 1983) including consumer behaviors. Indeed, research on consumer means-end chains (Gutman, 1982; Reynolds, 1985) consistently finds that the core reason consumers choose products is value fulfillment. These findings suggest that values can have a strong impact on brand equity. Specifically, in this paper, it is hypothesized that customers form more favorable attitudes toward a brand if its position in their minds is consistent with their values (Jayawardhena 2004). Favorably formed attitudes, in turn, contribute to paying more attention to the brand (Roskos-Ewoldsen and Fazio 1992). Finally, paying more attention to a brand contributes to higher brand equity (Dhar and Simonson 1992) in terms of purchase intentions, positive word-of-mouth intentions, and actual buying behaviors.

To test these hypotheses, an online study was conducted with 226 university students. After completing List of Values (cf. Kahle 1996), participants were directed to a web site where they could have an online shopping experience. This web site gave information on three brands from a single product category. Two of the brands were aimed to represent different value dimensions characterized by Homer and Kahle (1988): external values (i.e., sense of belonging, being well-respected, and warm relationships with others) or internal values (i.e., self-fulfillment, self-respect, and sense of accomplishment). The other brand did not highlight any specific value. To stress external values, the message included phrases like "new member of your family, taking care of others, loved ones, and being appreciated". To stress internal values, in contrast, phrases like "reward yourself, just for you, and what you want" were used. Each participant was presented with these three messages in a random order. After examining the brands by reading product descriptions, participants completed measures of attitude toward each brand (bad/good, negative/positive, unfavorable/favorable, something I dislike/something I like, not at all attractive/attractive, and undesirable/desirable). Then, participants were asked to buy one product from several product categories. There were eight brands in each product category and participants had 10 seconds to examine these eight brands and decide which one they would buy (of course, without paying money). Three of the brands were the same as in the first part of the study. The time a participant spent in examining each brand was recorded as a measure of attention. After participants chose one brand from each category to buy, they completed purchase intention and word-of-mouth intention questions for these three brands. Moreover, participants' choices were used to measure their actual buying behaviors.

Regression analyses indicated that as the score on the composite index of external values increased, attitudes toward the brand that stressed external values became more favorable (α=.142, t=2.145, p<.033). However, the relationship between the composite index of internal values and attitudes toward the brand reflecting internal values was significant only at .087 level. In other words, attitudes were predicted significantly by external values but not by internal values. In contrast, attention paid to brands that reflected internal values was significantly influenced by attitudes toward those brands (α=.157, t=2.374, p<.018) while attention paid to brands stressing external values was not affected by the attitudes toward those brands. Similarly, spending more time in examining the brands reflecting internal values resulted in significantly higher purchase intentions for those brands (α=.187, t=2. 857, p<.005) but not for other brands. Attention had also a significant positive impact on word-of-mouth intentions for brands stressing internal values (α=.191, t=2. 866, p<.005). However, the relationship between attention and purchase intention for brands reflecting external values was significant only at .066 level (β=.123, t=1.847, p<.066) and the results were not significant for word-of-mouth intentions. Finally, to look at the relationship between attention and buying behavior, attention was recoded as "less attention" and "more attention" by using median-split. The analyses revealed that while only four participants who paid less attention to the brands reflecting internal values chose those brands to buy, 25 participants who paid more attention to those brands chose them to buy (χ^2 (1, N=226)=17.445, p<.001). Likewise, only 15 participants who paid less attention to the brands reflecting external values chose those brands to buy while 31 participants who paid more attention to the brands reflecting external values chose them to buy (χ^2 (1, N=226)=7.543, p<.006).

The present research shows that even a single message based on personal values is capable of increasing brand equity through attitudes and attention. That is, positioning messages highlighting some personal values affect attitudes positively. Attitudes, on the other hand, affect brand equity through attention. However, most of the results were confirmed for brands associated with internal values. One reason for this might be the characteristics of the sample. University students were employed to run this study and it is highly possible that these participants endorsed internal values more than external values.

Overall, even though the conceptual model was partially supported by the data, it provides some insights into the importance of values in creating brand equity. Indeed, it is expected that brand equity studies will be more meaningful if personal values are taken into consideration.

References

Aaker, D. A. & Keller, K. L. (1990), "Consumer Evaluations of Brand Extensions," *Journal of Marketing*, 54 (1), 27-41.
Dhar, R. & Simonson, L. (1992), "The Effect of the Focus of Comparison on Consumer Preferences," *Journal of Marketing Research*, 29, November, 430-440.
Gutman, J. (1982), "A Means-End Chain Model Based on Consumer Categorization Processes," *Journal of Marketing*, 46, 60-72.
Homer, P. M. & Kahle, L. R. (1988), "Structural Equation Test of the Value-Attitude-Behavior Hierarchy," *Journal of Personality and Social Psychology*, 54 (4), 638-646.
Jayawardhena, C. (2004), "Personal Values' Influence on E-Shopping Attitude and Behavior," *Internet Research*, 14 (2), 127-138.

Kahle, L. R. (1996), "Social Values and Consumer Behavior: Research from the List of Values," in The Psychology of Values: The Ontario Symposium Volume 8, ed. Clive Seligman, James M. Olson, and Mark P. Zanna, Mahwah, NJ: Lawrence Erlbaum Associates, 135-152.

Kahle, L. R., & Timmer, S. G. (1983), "A Theory and a Method for Studying Values," in Social Values and Social Change, ed. Lynn R. Kahle, New York: Praeger Publishers, 43-72.

Keller, K. L. (1993), "Conceptualizing, Measuring, and Managing Customer-Based Brand Equity," Journal of Marketing, 57, 1-22.

Kirca, Ahmet H., Satish Jayachandran, and William O. Bearden (2005), "Market Orientation: A Meta-Analytic Review and Assessment of Its Antecedents and Impact on Performance," Journal of Marketing, 69 (2), 24-41.

Kotler, P. (2003), A Framework for Marketing Management. New Jersey: Pearson Education, Inc.

Prince, M. (1990), "How Consistent is the Information in Positioning Studies," Journal of Advertising Research, 30 (3), 25-30.

Reynolds, T. J. (1985), "Implications for Value Research: A Macro vs. Micro Perspective," Psychology & Marketing, 2(4), 297-305.

Rokeach, M. (1973), The Nature of Human Values. In J. W. Berry, M. H. Segall, & Ç. Ka?ıtçıba?ı (Eds.), Handbook of Cross-Cultural Psychology (2th ed., Vol.3, pp.79–118). Boston: Allyn and Bacon.

Roskos-Ewoldsen, D. R. & Fazio, R. H. (1992), "On the Orienting Value of Attitudes: Attitude Accessibility as a Determinant of an Object's Attraction of Visual Attention," Journal of Personality and Social Psychology, 63 (2), 198-21.

Sivakumar, K. & Raj, S. P. (1997), "Quality Tier Competition: How Price Change Influences Brand Choice and Category Choice," Journal of Marketing, 61, July, 71-84.

Comparative Knowledge and Consumer Choice

Liat Hadar, University of California at Los Angeles, USA
Sanjay Sood, University of California at Los Angeles, USA

Abstract

We examined whether manipulating consumers' subjective knowledge would alter their preferences. In two studies we manipulated participants' feeling of relative knowledge or ignorance by presenting a reference group which was more or less knowledgeable or by presenting a loosely related question that varied in difficulty. Participants' choices were affected by their perceived relative knowledge. We found that participants who felt relatively knowledgeable were less susceptible to judgmental biases and reported that they were more likely to join retirement saving plan they knew little about.

Previous research on risky choice has shown that when people are primed to believe that they are comparatively ignorant they become more risk averse; when they are primed to believe that they are comparatively knowledgeable they become more risk seeking (Fox & Tversky, 1995; Fox & Weber, 2002).

The current paper examines whether non-risky consumer choice can be altered by manipulating consumers' feeling of knowledge. Such findings may have very valuable consequences to domains in which consumers make suboptimal decisions such as employees' tendency not to sign up for retirement saving plans. By designing plan information that would make consumers feel more or less knowledgeable about retirement saving, we might be able to help more consumers by encouraging them to save for retirement. We conducted two studies that provide preliminary evidence for the role of subjective knowledge in consumer choice.

In Study 1 we examined the effect on comparative knowledge on the conjunction fallacy, the mistaken belief that the conjoint events (A?B) are more likely than their constituents (A or B) when instances of the conjunctions are easier to recall (Tversky & Kahneman, 1983). 196 students were asked to imagine that they are offered four new medication packets, similar in number of pills and costs. These medications treated different symptoms: sore throat, weakness, fever, or fever particularly caused by sore throat. Participants were asked which medication they would be more likely to buy if they were to buy one of them. Participants in the "relative knowledge" condition were told that "The pharmaceutical company is presenting this choice to random people in downtown xx as well as to UCLA undergraduate students"; participants in the "relative ignorance" condition were told that "The pharmaceutical company is presenting this choice to Medical students and doctors at the university as well as to UCLA undergraduate students". This information was given to the participants after the four medications had been presented and before they made their choice. We hypothesized that participants would feel relatively knowledgeable compared to random people in downtown, but relatively ignorant relative to Medical students and doctors.

Following the conjunction fallacy, we expected that, overall, more participants would choose the medication that treats fever caused by sore throat than the medication that treats fever only. Moreover, we expected participants in the "relative knowledge" condition to be more confident in their knowledge about medications compared to participants in the "relative ignorance" condition, and thus be more careful in their choice of medication and less susceptible to the conjunction fallacy.

The results supported our hypotheses: the proportion of participants who chose the "fever by sore throat" treatment (i.e., the conjunction) was lower than the proportion of participants who chose the "fever" treatment (i.e., the constituent event) in the "relative knowledge" condition (33.96% versus 66.04%, p=.001 one-tailed). No differences were found in the "relative ignorance" condition (46% versus 54%, p=.2142 one-tailed). In other words, making people feel that they are more knowledgeable made them less susceptible to the disjunction fallacy.

Study 2 examined the role of subjective knowledge in saving choices. Participants were provided information about retirement saving plans and were told that they would subsequently be asked to estimate on a 7-point Likert scale the likelihood that they would join such retirement plan in the future, when they have steady jobs. Participants were further informed that before they estimate the chances of joining the retirement plan, they would be asked a question that would allow the researchers to estimate their general knowledge about financial markets. Half of the participants were given a difficult question and half were given an easy question. We hypothesized that those who received the easy question would feel knowledgeable about financial markets and thus more comfortable announcing that they are likely to join a retirement plan they know only little about; in contrast, participants who received the difficult question would feel less knowledgeable about financial markets and thus less comfortable announcing that they are likely to join a plan they know only little about.

An analysis of the results revealed that participants who received the easy question indicated that they were more likely to join a retirement saving plan in the future than participants who received the difficult question, although both received the same amount of information about retirement saving (5.5 versus 5, on average, p<.05).

The results of the two studies provide preliminary support to the notion that subjective knowledge may impact judgment and consumer choice, and that consumer choice may be altered by manipulating subjective knowledge.

References

Fox Craig R. and Amos Tversky (1995), "Ambiguity Aversion and Comparative Ignorance." *Quarterly Journal of Economics*, 110, 585-603.

Fox Craig R. and Martin Weber (2002), "Ambiguity Aversion, Comparative Ignorance, and Decision Context." *Organizational Behavior and Human Decision Processes*, 88, 476–498.

Tversky, Amos and Daniel Kahneman (1983), "Extensional Versus Intuitive Reasoning: The Conjunction Fallacy in Probability Judgment." *Psychological Review*, 90(4), 293-315.

Choosing How Many Options to Choose From: Does it Depend on Affective Priming?

Sebastian Hafenbrädl, University of Lausanne, Switzerland

Ulrich Hoffrage, University of Lausanne, Switzerland

Chris M. White, University of Lausanne, Switzerland

When making purchase decisions, how many options do people wish to have available? Does this number depend on people's affect towards the product? To address this, we combined two research areas, the "tyranny of too much choice" and "affective decision making".

Tyranny of too much choice

Larger choice sets offer advantages: As compared to smaller choice sets, they are likely to contain better options (assuming options are randomly sampled from the population), leading to better decision outcomes. On the other hand, larger choice sets also have disadvantages: More options require more computation, both for screening and comparing the options, leading to a more effortful and time consuming decision process. This trade-off between outcome-satisfaction and process-satisfaction is therefore integral to understanding how people determine the number of options they wish to have available, which we refer to as their desired-set-size (DSS).

Reutskaja and Hogarth (2009) measured satisfaction with a choice made from a set of gift boxes whose size ranged from 5 to 30 options. They observed an inverse U-shaped relationship between satisfaction and the size of the choice set. This suggests that initially the benefits of having a larger choice set are greater than the costs, causing satisfaction to increase. However, as the size of the choice set continues to increase, the additional costs exceed the additional benefits, causing satisfaction to decrease.

Despite recent interest in the tyranny of too much choice, the size of the choice set has nearly always been determined by the experimenter (e.g., Iyengar & Lepper, 2000; White et al., submitted). In real life, however, people can usually determine the size of their choice set themselves by visiting as many stores as they wish and stop considering more options at any time. Much could be learned by asking participants to determine the size of the choice set themselves, but as far as we are aware, this has only been done in studies reported by Salgado (2005) and Chernev (2006).

Affective decision making

The above cost-benefit analysis ignores affect and emotions even though they play a role in choice situations. It is not only options themselves that evoke affect, rather, what happens prior to a judgment or decision can also cause options to be evaluated in an affective manner. Hsee and Rottenstreich (2004) found that people's Willingness-to-pay (WTP) for items depended on whether a person is computationally primed (achieved with a questionnaire containing items that required them to perform computations) or affectively primed (achieved with a questionnaire containing items that required them to examine and report their feelings).

Predictions

Similar to Hsee and Rottenstreich (2004), we predicted that people who were computationally-primed would exhibit a constant sensitivity to an increase in the number of items. In contrast, we predicted that people who were affectively-primed would appear to be insensitive to the number of items.

Procedure. First, the 160 participants were told that they could choose 5 (or 10, manipulated between subjects) postcards of their university's campus. Second, they completed either the affective or computational-priming questionnaire (adapted from Hsee and Rottenstreich 2004). Third, they determined their WTP and their DSS from which they could choose their 5 (or 10) cards. The minimum set size was either 5 postcards (or 10, according to the condition); the maximum was 100 postcards. Fourth, these three steps were repeated with Christmas present tags (order counterbalanced) and with different priming questions. Participants were given the opportunity to take home their chosen items.

Results and Discussion

The calculation-primed participants were willing to pay significantly more for 10 cards than for 5. In contrast, the affectively-primed participants were largely insensitive to the number of items they would choose. This predicted pattern was only significant for some of the dependent variables and was affected by whether outliers were removed from the data. In the full dataset, the interaction was significant when considering all dependent variables together (with a MANOVA), but when each dependent variable was analyzed separately (with separate ANOVAs) it was only statistically significant for the DSS that was stated a second time at the end of the experiment, although there was also a tendency towards this interaction for the DSS that was stated initially. In the trimmed dataset, the interaction was significant when considering all dependent variables together, but when each dependent variable was analyzed separately, it was only statistically significant for the DSS that was stated a second time and marginally significant for WTP.

After the experiment, several participants said that they did not perceive watching the pictures as an investment of time, that is, a cost they had to pay in order to select some good ones, but that they had intrinsically enjoyed seeing them. This could explain the added noise in the measures elicited before people actually watched the pictures.

There was no correlation between the two measures of costs, hypothetical financial costs (WTP) and expected temporal and cognitive costs that will subsequently be realized (DSS). This was surprising because these variables showed similar patterns of mean data. This suggests that, contrary to the well-known expression "time is money", people do not naturally treat the two concepts as being equal. Investigating the mental relationship between these two concepts could therefore be a fruitful area for further research.

We also measured participants' satisfaction with the choosing process and the chosen items. Reutskaja and Hogarth (2009) found satisfaction to be an inverse U-shaped function of the manipulated choice set size. In contrast, we found that there was no linear or nonlinear relationship between DSS and the two reported satisfaction measures. The fact that participants determined the size of the choice set themselves provides two plausible explanations for the lack of a relationship. First, people may have been able to determine the set size that would yield the maximum overall satisfaction for them. Second, people may have become committed to their stated DSS and therefore did not want to report regretting having too many or too few options, as that would imply that they had previously made an imperfect judgment.

References

Chernev, A. (2006). Decision focus and consumer choice among assortments. *Journal of Consumer Research, 33,* 50-59.

Hsee, C. K. & Rottenstreich, Y. (2004). Music, pandas and muggers: On the affective psychology of value. *Journal of Experimental Psychology, 133,* 23–30.

Iyengar, S. S. & Lepper, M. R. (2000). When choice is demotivating: Can one desire too much of a good thing? *Journal of Personality and Social Psychology, 79,* 995-1006.

Reutskaja, E. & Hogarth, R. M. (2009). Satisfaction in choice as a function of the number of alternatives: When 'goods satiate'. *Psychology & Marketing,* 26, 197-202.

Salgado, M. (2005). Choosing to have less choice. Unpublished manuscript, Northwestern University, USA. *http://ageconsearch.umn.edu/bitstream/123456789/24078/1/wp060037.pdf*

White, C. M., Reisen, N., & Hoffrage, U. (submitted). Choice deferral arising from absolute evaluation or relative comparison. Manuscript submitted for publication.

Multiple Motives, Multiple Selves: What Motivates Consumption

Tracy R. Harmon, Syracuse University, USA
Anand Kumar, University of South Florida, USA
David Ortinau, University of South Florida, USA

One of the least contested claims in marketing is that individuals are motivated to enhance their self-esteem and establish consistency in their self-concept when engaging in symbolic consumption (Levy 1959; Grub and Grathwohl 1967; Levy 1986). However, less attention has been directed towards additional identity motives guiding self-brand interactions. Recently, in the social psychology literature, motives beyond self-esteem and self-consistency were found to aid in identity construction namely: efficacy, meaning, distinctiveness, and belonging (Vignoles, Regalia, Manzi, Golledge, and Scabini 2006). These alternative motives can provide a richer understanding of how and why individuals are motivated to engage in self-brand interactions.

When brand associations are used to construct one's identity or to communicate one's self to others, a self-brand connection is formed (Escalas and Bettman 2000; 2005). Self brand connections measure the degree to which individuals have incorporated brands into their self-concept (Escalas and Bettman 2003; 2005). Presumably, self-brand connections will be enhanced as brands are chosen to achieve specific identity goals. This is due to identity commitment, which is associated with expectations of behavior relevant to identity goals (Foote 1951). Identity commitment serves as a boundary criterion in determining how motivations from social influence will be handled. To illustrate, a person committed to the identity of "soccer mom" will interpret marketing stimuli differently than one committed to a "corporate executive" identity.

An individual is likely to support and be more committed to preserving a particular identity when it is more central (Settles 2004). As stated earlier, centrality is influenced by multiple identity motives, which are related to a specific identity within the individual. Therefore a highly central identity should lead to stronger self-brand connections as various motives are satisfied. The key determinant of this proposed relationship is brand associations congruent with the self-image. Therefore the following hypothesis is offered:

A brand that is very popular and used by many different types of people (e.g., a BMW) may have different meanings to consumers based on the different identities that are presented through brand usage. It is expected brand symbolism will moderate the formation of self-brand connections due to the brands ability to communicate something about the individual. It is hypothesized that in cases when centrality is low, brand symbolism will be the primary source of self-brand connections. Thus it is expected that brand symbolism will moderate the effects of identity centrality on self-brand connections.

Methodology

Using a methodology developed by Vignoles et al. (2002), participants freely generated a list of identities then rated them for its centrality on automobile purchases (dependent variable) and for its association with motivations of self-esteem, distinctiveness, continuity, self-efficacy, belonging, meaning, recognition, consistency, and security (independent variables). The main analysis was designed to evaluate the unique contributions of each motive rating to predictions to identity centrality.

Results

Overall, the results indicate individuals do in fact assign varying levels of importance to their identities in a consumption environment. The findings suggest centrality is a viable construct for understanding how individuals manage multiple identities in consumption decisions. Participants rated as more central, those identities that provided a sense of self-esteem and that gained them recognition with regard to their automobile. Together, these motives seem to suggest individuals are motivated more so by internal self aspects (self-esteem) compared to other's acknowledgement of them (recognition). This finding is quite interesting because it these motives are not consistent with Grub and Grathwohl's Model of Consuming Behavior (1967) and Sirgy's (1982) Product-Image Congruity Theory. Ideally, the more participants rated an identity as satisfying feelings of self-esteem or self-consistency, the more they should have considered it as central to their decisions. However, when considered with the other eight motives, the effects of these two motives were attenuated and failed to be strong predictors of identity centrality. Brand symbolism as a moderator between identity centrality and self-brand connection was evidenced from the findings. Brands that were perceived as more symbolic resulted in higher self-brand connections when the identity was central to the automobile category. When combined with the psychological importance, an identity that is congruent with brand associations, but is also congruent with the typical user and/or brand personality, stronger connections to the brand are likely. This interactive effect between brand symbolism and identity centrality is worth exploring further.

References

Bagozzi, Richard P., M. Bergami and Robert L. Leone (2003), "Hierarchical Representation of Motives in Goal-Setting," *Journal of Applied Psychology*, 88 (4) 915-943.

Grubb, Edward and Harrison L. Grathwohl (1967), Consumer Self-Concept, Symbolism and Market Behavior: A Theoretical Approach," *Journal of Marketing*, 31 (October), 22-27.

Levy, Sidney J. (1959), "Symbols for Sale," *Harvard Business Review*, 37 (July-August), 117- 24.

Levy, Sidney J. (1986), "Meanings in Advertising Stimuli," in J. Olson and K. Sentis (Eds.), *Advertising and Consumer Psychology* (214–226), Westport, CT: Praeger.

Markus, Hazel and Ziva Kunda (1986), "Stability and Malleability of the Self-Concept," *Journal of Personality and Social Psychology*, 51, 858-866.

Settles, Isis H. (2004), "When Multiple Identities Interfere: The Role of Identity Centrality," *Personality and Social Psychology Bulletin*, 30 (4), 487-500.

Stets, Jan E. and Peter J. Burke, (2000), "Identity Theory and Social Identity Theory," *Social Psychology Quarterly*, 63, 224–237.

Stryker, Sheldon and Richard T. Serpe (1994), "Identity Salience and Psychological Centrality: Equivalent, Overlapping, or Complementary Concepts?," *Social Psychology Quarterly*, 57, 16–35.

Thoits, Peggy A. (1986), "Multiple Identities: Examining Gender And Marital Status Differences In Distress," *American Sociological Review*, 51, 259-272.

Vignoles, Vivian L., Xenia Chryssochoou and Glynis M. Breakwell (2002), "Sources of Distinctiveness: Position, Difference and Separateness in the Identities of Anglican Parish Priests," *European Journal of Social Psychology*, 32(6), 761-780.

Vignoles, Vivian L., Camillo Regalia, Claudia Manzi, Jen Golledge and Eugenia Scabini (2006), "Beyond Self-Esteem: Influence of Multiple Motives on Identity Construction," *Journal of Personality and Social Psychology*, 90(2), 308-333.

When the Ingroup Fails to Indicate Brand Meaning: Exploring the Role of Identity Centrality in Self-brand Connections

Tracy R. Harmon, Syracuse University, USA
Anand Kumar, University of South Florida, USA
David Ortinau, University of South Florida, USA

Self-brand connections are defined as the degree to which a consumer has incorporated the brand into their self-concept (Escalas and Bettman 2003, 2005). Escalas and Bettman (2005) found that brand associations consistent with an ingroup led to stronger self-brand connections compared to brand associations inconsistent with an ingroup. This is because brands become more meaningful the more closely they are linked to an individual's identity. But what happens to this relationship if another identity other than the ingroup identity is associated with the brand? Or how are self-brand connections influenced if the reference group is associated with multiple brands? This study seeks to address the former question by examining the nature of multiple identities in the formation of self-brand connections.

Markus and Kunda (1986) put forth the term "malleable" (or working) self-concept to refer to an individual's various self-conceptions (e.g. ideal self, perceived self, social self) which function to provide an interpretative and evaluative context for the overall view of the self (Markus and Wurf 1987). To date the consideration of multiple selves has been omitted from research linking reference group influence to self-brand connections (Escalas and Bettman 2005; Chaplin and Roedder-John 2005). This omission leads to questions surrounding the differential attitudes and cognitions within the perceived reference group. This is supported by literature in social psychology which suggests individuals assign a level of significance to their identities which directly impacts group driven attitudes, behaviors, and cognitions (Vignoles, Regalia, Manzi, Golledge, and Scabini 2006; Settles 2004; Stryker and Serpe 1994). It is argued that because individuals possess multiple identities, an individual's self-brand connection should be reflective of the identity that is most central to the brand. In simpler terms, if the brand is associated with a particular ingroup, then the ingroup identity should carry the most psychological importance in interactions with the brand.

Identity centrality, defined as the psychological importance one places on a given identity (Settles 2004) can aid in explaining how individuals negotiate multiple identities exacerbating one and buffering others. Identity centrality requires conscious awareness and is usually measured by asking individuals to rank different identities according to their importance (Rane and McBride 2000). Self-brand connections are likely to be enhanced when an ingroup identity is central to the brand compared to when it is not. This research shows that the differential self-brand connections within the ingroup are due to the lack of value expressive influence by other reference group members when centrality is taken into consideration.

Methodology

The procedure was a replication of that used by Escalas and Bettman (2005). Changes dealt with the order of measures and the incorporation of the identity centrality measure.

Results

The consideration of identity centrality in this study was based on the expectation that ingroup members will form differential self-brand connections for the brand image match condition. Extending these findings, identity centrality positively moderated self-brand connections for the ingroup. This result is significant in that it reveals the significance of centrality in examining self-brand interactions. It is not enough to say that an identity is salient to a particular brand. As evidenced in the results, identity centrality leads to stronger self-brand connections in the brand image does match condition. This difference among ingroup members indicates there is varying levels of importance within the group. From a marketer's stand point this could mean the difference in message effectiveness. Salience may be sufficient enough to encourage an individual to attend to a particular message. But is it enough to create an emotional bond? Is it enough to get the consumer to buy the product? It is argued that centrality is true a catalyst for self-brand connections.

The moderating influences of identity centrality on outgroup brand associations was insignificant. It difficult to hypothesize the directional influence of identity centrality in outgroup effects due to various meanings associated with outgroups. Identity importance can be hypothesized to influence the outgroup but it will vary depending on the desired degree of divergence from the outgroup. For instance, an individual may declare an outgroup but may desire to eventually become one its members (e.g. fraternities and sororities). Or perhaps an individual may have some level of similarity with the outgroup. These scenarios make it difficult to predict how identity centrality will influence self-brand connections.

Brand associations not matching the image of the outgroup were lower for individuals with an independent self-construal compared to interdependent self-construal. This finding was consistent with Escalas and Bettman's (2005) results. They reasoned that outgroup brand associations will have the greatest effect on participants with independent self construals due to their strong differentiation needs. This was evidenced in this study as well.

Identity centrality moderated the influence of self-construal such that the degree of self-brand connections for independent versus interdependent self-construal was reversed. Interdependents formed lower self-brand connections than independents. Interdependents were thought to shift their focus from outgroup differentiation to ingroup differentiation, leading to lower self-brand connections. By doing this they are attempting to show ingroup favoritism and seeking distinctiveness from the outgroup. Lower self-brand connections for individuals with interdependent self-construals is more in line with the self-construal research which views interdependents are more collectivist in nature (Singelis 1994).The contrast in findings due to identity centrality may be worth investigating the continued use of the self-construal to examine individual differences in self-brand connections.

Overall, the pattern of results supports the general idea proposed in this essay: individuals use brands to create or communicate their self-concept partly in an effort to meet certain identity goals (e.g. self-verification, self-enhancement) and do it more so when a particular identity is central.

References

Chaplin, Lan Nguyen and Deborah Roedder John (2005), "The Emergence of Self-Brand Connections in Children and Adolescents," *Journal of Consumer Research*, 32 (June), 119-125.

Escalas, Jennifer E. and James R. Bettman (2003), "You Are What They Eat: The Influence of Reference Groups on Consumer Connections to Brands," *Journal of Consumer Psychology*, 13 (3), 339-48.

Escalas, Jennifer E. and James R. Bettman (2005), "Self-Construal, Reference Groups, and Brand Meaning," *Journal of Consumer Research*, 32 (December), 378-389.

Markus, Hazel and Ziva Kunda (1986), "Stability and Malleability of the Self-Concept," *Journal of Personality and Social Psychology*, 51, 858-866.

Markus, Hazel and Wurf, E. (1987), "The Dynamic Self Concept: A Social Psychological Perspective," *Annual Review of Psychology*, 38, 299-333.

Rane, T.R., and McBride, Brent A. (2000), "Identity Theory As a Guide to Understanding Fathers' Involvement With Their Children," *Journal of Family Issues*, 21, 347-366.

Settles, Isis H. (2004), "When Multiple Identities Interfere: The Role of Identity Centrality," *Personality and Social Psychology Bulletin*, 30 (4), 487-500.

Stryker, Sheldon and Richard T. Serpe (1994), "Identity Salience and Psychological Centrality: Equivalent, Overlapping, or Complementary Concepts?," *Social Psychology Quarterly*, 57, 16–35.

Vignoles, Vivian L., Camillo Regalia, Claudia Manzi, Jen Golledge and Eugenia Scabini (2006), "Beyond Self-Esteem: Influence of Multiple Motives on Identity Construction," *Journal of Personality and Social Psychology*, 90(2), 308-333.

Brand Origin or Product Origin? The Effects of Country of Origin Fit on Brand Evaluation

Sangwon Lee, University of Central Florida, USA

Zachary Johnson, University of Central Florida, USA

Xin He, University of Central Florida, USA

In previous research streams on the topic, the term country of origin has been defined as either brand origin or product origin (country of manufacture); brand origin referring to the home country of the brand, and product origin referring to where the product was actually made. Regardless of the definition used for country of origin in a particular paper, the research outcome has consistently shown that consumers make inferences about product quality based on either definition of country of origin. Alternatively, this research argues that country of origin evaluations are comprised of three components: 1) brand origin 2) product origin, and 3) fit between brand origin and product origin.

The term "country of origin fit" refers to whether or not the brand origin is the same as the product origin; if the brand origin and product origin are the same country, this congruence leads to a fit. No fit refers to the situation when the brand origin is one country and the product origin is another country. To this concept of country of origin fit, previous research has been silent.

The current research offers a theory-based empirical examination of country of origin fit. The purpose of the present study is to examine whether processing fluency enhanced by fit will affect brand evaluation. The product origin is often different from brand origin due to several management reasons, but the exact influence on brand evaluation was not clear. This research suggests that the effects of fit between brand origin and product origin can be explained by processing fluency.

The findings of this research extend the country of origin research streams. First, this research extends the previous research by expanding the country of origin evaluation to three components: 1) brand origin 2) product origin, and 3) fit. Second, several studies examined country of origin effects on product quality evaluations from the management perspective (Paterson and Jolibert 1995; Maheswaran 1994). However, little theory-based research has examined consumer perceptions that influence country of origin evaluations (Gurhan-Canli and Maheswaran 2000). This research extends the extant research by introducing information fluency theory from the consumer's perspective. Third, the findings of this research extend processing fluency research. Theoretically, previous researches have examined processing fluency within the single category of product or word. This research extends the literature by adding another stimulus for processing fluency such as fit between two different levels of brand and product. Fourth, this research extends the previous country of origin research by introducing fit which will strengthen the country of origin effects on brand evaluation.

To examine how fit influences brand evaluation, two streams of research will be discussed. First, stereotype literature is examined to show the relationship between fit and information processing fluency. Second, processing fluency literature is reviewed to show the relationship between information processing fluency and brand evaluation (Lee and Aaker 2004). Stereotype literature suggests that if the information is more consistent with stereotypes, people can more easily process information because consistent information is expected and is therefore conceptually more fluent (Bodenhausen and Lichtenstein 1987; Lee and Aaker 2004; Macrae et al. 1994; Sherman et al. 1998). In our context, if the brand origin is the same as the product origin, people can more readily process information because product information is consistent with consumer stereotypes (brand information) and will be more fluent. Processing fluency literature has shown that processing fluency can lead to enhanced affective judgments (Lee and Aaker 2004). According to this view, when people are presented with a brand that is easy to process, the positive experience of fluent processing leads to more positive evaluation of the brand. Similarly, in the context of this research, the processing fluency enhanced by the country of origin fit may lead to more positive attitude toward the brand.

Hypothesis 1 suggests that the fit of the country of the brand origin and the product origin will lead to more positive attitude toward the brand than no fit. To test this hypothesis, 170 undergraduate business students from a major southeastern university participated in the between subject experiment that is designed to test whether the country of origin fit will affect brand evaluations. To control the quality inferences from the brand name and country, mock brand and country names were created for the stimuli (e.g. GLOBAL brand and Country J, K). The stimuli also specified that both countries are known for producing the same quality product. Study 1 supports the notion that the fit of the country of brand origin and product origin has an impact on attitude toward the brand. There was a statistically significant difference at the p<.05 level in attitude toward the brand scores for two different fit conditions (F (1,168)=4.50, p<.05). Thus, the fit leads to more positive attitude toward the brand than no fit.

Based on the result of study 1, study 2 will be designed to further explore the moderating effect of the quality of brand origin on the relationship between fit and attitude toward the brand. Previous research shows that country of origin is likely to affect interpretation of information about specific product attributes especially when country of origin is conveyed before the attribute descriptions (Hong and Wyer 1990). In the context of this research, we propose that processing fluency enhanced by the country of origin fit will strengthen the country of origin effects on brand evaluation. Thus, depending on initial quality of brand origin, the attitude toward the brand will be either more positive or more negative.

For the second study, 2 brand origin (high quality, low quality) x 2 country of origin (fit, no fit) between subjects experiment will be designed to create one of four possible experimental conditions: (1) High-quality brand origin with the same product origin, (2) High-quality brand origin with the different product origin that produces equally high-quality products, (3) Low-quality brand origin with the same product origin and (4) Low-quality brand origin with the different product origin that produces equally low-quality products.

References

Allen, Chris T. and Chris A. Janiszewski (1989), "Assessing the Role of Contingency Awareness in Attitudinal Conditioning with Implications for Advertising Research," *Journal of Marketing Research*, 26 (February), 30-43

Bodenhausen, G. V., & Lichtenstein, M. (1987), "Social Stereotypes and Information-Processing Strategies: The Impact of Task Complexity." *Journal of Personality and Social Psychology*, 52, 871-880

Gurhan-Canli, Zeynep and Durairaj Maheswaran (2000), "Determinants of Country of Origin Evaluations," *Journal of Consumer Research*, 27 (June), 96-108

Holbrook, Morris B. (1986), "Aims, Concepts, and Methods for the Representation of Individual Differences in Esthetic Responses to Design Features," *Journal of Consumer Research*, 13 (December), 337-347

Hong, Sung-Tai and Robert S. Wyer (1990), "Determinants of Product Evaluation: Effects of the Time Interval between Knowledge of a Product's Country of Origin and Information about Its Specific Attributes," *Journal of Consumer Research*, 17 (December), 277-288

Jacoby, L.L., & Dallas, M. (1981), "On the Relationship between Autobiographical Memory and Perceptual Learning," *Journal of Experimental Psychology*, 110, 306-340

Lee, Angela Y. (2001), "The Mere Exposure Effect: An Uncertainty Reduction Explanation Revisited" *Personality and Social Psychology Bulletin*, 27, 1255-1266

Lee, Angela Y. and Aparna A. Labroo (2004), "The Effect of Conceptual and Perceptual Fluency on Brand Evaluation," *Journal of Marketing Research*, May, 151-165

Lee, Angela Y. and Jennifer L. Aaker (2004), "Bringing the Fame into Focus: The Influence of Regulatory Fit on Processing Fluency and Persuasion." *Journal of Personality and Social Psychology*, 86, 205-218

Macrae,C.N., Milne, A.B., & Bodenhausen, G. V. (1994), "Stereotype as Energy Saving Devices: A Peek inside the Cognitive Tool Box," *Journal of Personality and Social Psychology*, 66, 37-47

Maheswaran, Durairaj (1994), "Country of Origin as a Stereotype," *Journal of Consumer Research*, 21, 354-365

Peterson, Robert A. and Alain Jolibert (1995), "A Meta Analysis of Country of Origin Effects," *Journal of International Business Studies*, 26, 883-900

Putrevu, Sanyay and Kenneth R. Lord (1994), "Comparative and Noncomparative Advertising: Attitudinal Effects under Cognitive Affective Involvement Conditions," *Journal of Advertising* (June), 77-90

Reber, R., Winkielman P., & Schwarz N. (1998), "Effects of Perceptual Fluency on Affective Judgments," *Psychological Science*, 9, 45-48

Seamon, J.G., Williams, P.C., Crowley, M.J. Kim,I.J., Langer, S.A., Orne,P.J. and Wishengrad D.L. (1995), "The Mere Exposure Effect is based on Implicit Memory: Effects of Stimulus Type, Encoding Conditions, and Number of Exposures on Recognition and Affect Judgments," *Journal of Experimental Psychology*, 21, 711-721

Sherman, J.W., Lee, A.Y., Bessenoff, G.R., & Frost, L.A. (1998), "Stereotype Efficiency Considered: Encoding Flexibility under Cognitive Load" *Journal of Personality and Social Psychology*, 75, 589-606

Why Humor Breaks Resistance to Influence: Implicit Effects of Distraction and Positive Affect

Madelijn Strick, Radboud University Nijmegen, The Netherlands
Rick B. van Baaren, Radboud University Nijmegen, USA
Rob W. Holland, Radboud University Nijmegen, USA
Ad van Knippenberg, Radboud University Nijmegen, USA

Humor in advertising has been identified as a peripheral cue that can enhance the effectiveness of advertisements without conveying any information about the quality or function of the brand. Furthermore, it has often been suggested that humor has the unique quality to overcome resistance to persuasion (e.g. Sternthal and Craig 1973; Nabi, Moyer-Guse, and Byrne 2007). How does humor do this?

To approach this topic it is very useful to have a clear definition of humor. Researchers have decomposed the experience of humor into two phases: (1) a cognitive phase needed for incongruency-resolution, which poses cognitive demands, and (2) an affective phase, in which positive emotions are experienced (Deckers and Devine 1981; Suls 1972; Watson, Matthews, and Allman 2007). Given the relation between cognitive distraction and yielding to persuasive messages (e.g. Festinger and Maccoby 1964; Keating and Brock 1976) and the general beneficial effects of positive affect on advertising effectiveness (e.g., Stuart, Shimp, and Engle 1987), both the cognitive and the affective phase may be responsible for breaking resistance. We present three experiments that disentangle these two components of humor and examine their influence on product memory, attitudes, behavior and resistance to influence.

Nowadays, implicit associative processes play an important role in shaping our views of products and brands. Therefore, in the present research we used an evaluative conditioning paradigm to unobtrusively associate products with humor (see De Houwer, Thomas, and Baeyens 2001 for a review). To rule out confounding mood effects, humor was manipulated within subjects.

In Experiment 1, novel energy drink brands were unobtrusively associated with either humorous or control (i.e. non-humorous) cartoons. In line with the conceptualization of humor as a distracter, humor impaired the recognition of associated products. Yet, an evaluative priming task (Fazio 2001) showed that the automatic evaluations of these products were enhanced due to association with unrelated humor. These memory and implicit liking effects were not correlated. Finally, these enhanced evaluations mediated the relation between association with humor and overt product choice. These findings indicate that humor dissociates product memory from implicit product liking and choice.

In Experiment 2, novel energy drink brands were consistently paired with humorous (i.e. cognitively demanding and positive) sentences, whereas other products were paired with sentences that were either (1) equally demanding but neutral (2) equally positive but undemanding (3) undemanding and neutral. Afterwards, product recognition and explicit product liking were assessed. Furthermore, behavioral consequences were assessed by giving participants the opportunity to spend discount coupons on the beverages. The results showed that cognitively demanding sentences reduced product recognition, whereas the positivity of the sentences had no effect on product recognition. These findings suggest that the cognitive demands of humor, not the positive affect it evokes, underlie the distraction effect. Furthermore, positive sentences enhanced attitudes and behavioral preferences towards products, irrespective of cognitive demands. Overall, these findings indicate that the dissociating effect of humor on product memory and liking are unique to humor. Other positive cues also enhanced product liking, but they did not distract attention.

In Experiment 3, attitudes toward novel peppermint brands were conditioned using the same experimental conditions and stimulus material as Experiment 2. For half of the participants, the conditioning phase was preceded by a written instruction that provoked resistance to influence. In this resistance condition, it was explained to participants that the experiment was conducted in collaboration with an untrustworthy advertising agency that would use the research results to spam them with E-mail and SMS text messages. Participants in the control condition read a neutral control instruction instead. Next, all participants were exposed to the same conditioning procedure. Afterwards, brand recognition and implicit brand liking (using the evaluative priming task) were employed. The memory and liking effects of Experiment 1 and 2 were replicated. In addition, the results of the implicit attitude measure indicated that humorous information enhanced implicit brand attitudes in both the resistance and control condition. Other (i.e. less-distracting) positive cues, however, only enhanced implicit brand attitudes in the control condition. Furthermore, we found a significant positive correlation between distraction (i.e. brand recognition impairment) and implicit product liking in the resistance condition. These results indicate that humor overcomes resistance due to its quality to distract attention from products, not by evoking positive affect.

These three experiments show a robust pattern of results that extend our knowledge of implicit effects of humor in advertising in several ways. First, as far as we know, we are the first to show conditioning effects of humor on implicit attitudes, which in turn predict overt product choice. Interestingly, association of a product with unrelated humor enhances its attractiveness in a way that is dissociated from the accessibility of the product in memory. This finding suggests that humor can affect responses to brands even if consumers do not explicitly infer and/or memorize them. Furthermore, unlike previous research, we directly compared humor with other positive, non-humorous, emotions and show that the distraction effect is unique to humor. These findings fit very well with theories of humor processing that focus on incongruency-resolution (Deckers and Devine 1981; Suls 1972; Watson, et al. 2007).

Finally, we have found clear evidence that humor overcomes resistance to influence by distracting attention. Participants that were motivated to offer resistance were able to discount the influence of positive cues when these cues were undistracting. They were unable, however, to resist the positive influence of humor. The positive correlation between distraction and implicit brand attitudes indicates that the distraction of humor is responsible for this effect. The conceptualization of humor as both a distracter and a motivator of liking and approach behavior has interesting implications for various research domains in consumer psychology that involve self-regulation.

References

De Houwer, Jan, Sarah Thomas, and Frank Baeyens (2001), "Associative learning of likes and dislikes: A review of 25 years of research on human evaluative conditioning," *Psychological Bulletin,* 127 (November), 853-69.

Deckers, Lambert and John Devine (1981), "Humor by violating an existing expectancy," *Journal of Psychology, 108,* 107-10.

Fazio, Russell H. (2001), "On the automatic activation of associated evaluations: An overview," Cognition and Emotion, 15, 115-41.

Festinger, Leon and Nathan Maccoby (1964), "On resistance to persuasive communications," *Journal of Abnormal and Social Psychology,* 68, 359-66.

Keating, John P. and Timothy Brock (1976), "Acceptance of persuasion and the inhibition of counterargumentation under various distraction tasks," *Journal of Experimental Social Psychology,* 10, 301-09.

Nabi, Robin L., Emily Moyer-Gusé, and Sahara Byrne (2007), "All joking aside: A serious investigation into the persuasive effect of funny social issue messages," *Communications Monographs*, 74(1), 29-54.

Sternthal, Brian and C. Samuel Craig (1973), "Humor in advertising," *Journal of Marketing,* 37 (October), 12–8.

Stuart, Elnora W., Terence A. Shimp, and Randall W. Engle (1987), "Classical Conditioning of Consumer Attitudes: Four Experiments in an Advertising Context," *Journal of Consumer Research,* 14 (December), 334-49.

Suls, Jerry M. (1972). "A two-stage model for the appreciation of jokes and cartoons: An information-processing analyses" in *The psychology of humor*, Jeffrey H. Goldstein & Paul E. McGhee (Eds.), New York: Academic Press, 81-100.

Watson, Karli K., Benjamin J. Matthews, and John M. Allman (2007). "Brain activation during sight gags and language-dependent humor," *Cerebral Cortex, 17,* 314-24.

Existential Anxiety and Essentialism Explain Negative Reactions Toward Brand Extensions

Pelin Kesebir, University of Illinois at Urbana-Champaign, USA

Ying-yi Hong, University of Illinois at Urbana-Champaign, USA

Terror Management Theory posits that the knowledge of one's mortality, combined with a biologically rooted desire for self-preservation, is apt to create paralyzing existential terror. As revealed by a variety of studies, individuals seem to hold on to their cultural worldviews in an attempt to manage this terror (Greenberg et al. 1990). Cultures, as shared symbolic conceptions of reality, not only give meaning and order to existence, but also provide a venue for expanding and perpetuating oneself in a larger beyond. Individuals thus seek solace in the knowledge that whereas they might be mere mortals, the cultural worldviews they subscribe to are imperishable and ever-lasting.

Brands, to the extent they represent cultural values, may carry a similar death-anxiety mollifying function. Highly revered brands that represent the culture's core values and are perceived to be "timeless" are also commonly referred as iconic brands. If such brands function as a buffer against death anxiety, it stands to reason that brand extensions may be perceived as contamination of these icons and thus lead to increased death anxiety and engender negative responses.

One individual difference variable that might influence the degree of negative reactions toward brand extensions is essentialism. Essentialism is the tendency to believe that there are stable and unchangeable underlying essences to entities. Previous research on essentialism has examined essentialism toward social categories, such as race, sexual orientation and ethnic groups, and found that essentialist beliefs are associated with stereotyping and prejudice (Haslam et al. 2006). For example, people who believe that there are important, inherent, and stable differences between heterosexuals and homosexuals are more likely to endorse stereotypes about homosexuals.

People who generally endorse essentialistic beliefs may also exhibit essentialism toward brands—a tendency to believe that there are stable and unchangeable underlying essences to brands. Such people might be bothered by brand extensions, since brand extensions by definition damage the "essence" of the original brand and "contaminate" it. We hypothesized that a high degree of essentialism might engender negative reactions toward brand extensions, particularly when the brand in questions is representative of cultural values and the individual has chronically high or experimentally increased death anxiety.

Study 1 aimed to show that when reminded of their mortality, highly essentialistic participants would disapprove more of a brand extension scenario involving a highly iconic brand. Participants first completed a 21-item measure of Essentialism, and then were randomly assigned into a mortality salience or control condition. In the mortality salience condition participants were asked to answer two open-ended questions about their mortality, whereas in the control condition they answered two similar questions about dental pain. After this manipulation, all participants read a scenario about Coca Cola Peppermint—"a beverage that is quite similar to regular Coke, however has a distinct peppermint aftertaste." Following this, participants responded to three questions about Coca Cola Peppermint on a seven-point Likert scale. These questions were: (a) "How good do you think Coca Cola Peppermint is going to taste," (b) "How much do you approve of Coca Cola's efforts to come up with new tastes," and (c) "How much do you agree or disagree with the following statement: Products such as Coca Cola Peppermint dilute the image of Coca Cola, and weaken the brand."

Participants' responses to these questions were separately submitted to univariate general linear model analyses, which revealed, as expected, a significant Mortality prime x Essentialism interaction, for all three different questions: Participants in the mortality salience condition were more likely to think that Coca Cola Peppermint would taste bad, to the extent that they were high in essentialism. Similarly, participants reminded of their mortality disapproved more of Coca Cola's efforts to come up with new tastes, and believed that products such as Coca Cola Peppermint diluted the image of Coca Cola and hurt the brand—again to the extent that they were essentialistic. Importantly, in our analyses we controlled for the need for cognitive closure (Kruglanski and Webster 1996), which allows us to conclude that the observed effect of essentialism is unique and different from a general potential effect of closed-mindedness.

Study 2 replicated and extended Study 1 by demonstrating that high death accessibility combined with high essentialism leads to more negative reactions toward brand essentialism, and the magnitude of this effect is influenced by how much the brands in question represent cultural values. Participants first completed an implicit measure of death-thought accessibility. The measure was designed as a word-completion task and included word fragments that can be completed in either death-related or unrelated ways (e.g., G R A _ E can be completed as "grave" or "grape"). After this measure of death accessibility, participants rated on a seven-point scale how much they believed certain brands/cultural icons (e.g., Crest, Tom Hanks) represented American values. This was followed by brand extension scenarios involving the brands participants were just asked about. These scenarios were: (a) Crest coming up with a lip moisturizer, (b) Lipton introducing "Lipton Soup," (c) Tom Hanks recording a rock album, and (d) Some producers filming a sequel to the movie Casablanca. After each scenario, participants answered the same questions about their reaction toward these extensions as in Study 1.

Our results revealed a significant Death Accessibility x Essentialism interaction as a predictor of negative reactions toward brand extensions, across four different scenarios. Furthermore, we found a Death Accessibility x Essentialism x Value representativeness interaction, which confirmed our hypothesis that a combination of high death anxiety and essentialism leads to particularly antagonistic responses toward brand extensions when the brands are highly representative of cultural values.

These two studies, taken together, suggest that a brand extension can be interpreted as threatening and perceived negatively, if the brand is highly representative of the culture's values, and if the consumer is high in essentialism and death-thought accessibility. It seems that individuals embrace iconic brands as instances of their cultural worldview, and the desire to hold on to them, in their "pure form", is more pronounced for people who are experiencing a combination of high essentialism and death anxiety.

References

Greenberg, Jeff, Tom Pyszczynski, Sheldon Solomon, Abram Rosenblatt, Mitchell Veeder, Shari Kirkland, and Deborah Lyon (1990), "Evidence for Terror Management Theory II: The Effects of Mortality Salience on Reactions to Those who Threaten or Bolster the Cultural Worldview," *Journal of Personality and Social Psychology*, 58 (February), 308–318.

Haslam, Nick, Brock Bastian, Paul Bain, and Yoshihisa Kashima (2006), "Psychological Essentialism, Implicit Theories, and Intergroup Relations," *Group Processes Intergroup Relations*, 9 (January), 63–76

Kruglanski, Arie W., Donna M. Webster (1996), "Motivated Closing of the Mind: 'Seizing' and 'Freezing'," *Psychological Review*, 103 (April), 263–283.

The Role of Affect, Music and Self-awareness in Consumer Information Processing

Iris W. Hung, National University of Singapore, Singapore
Robert S. Wyer, Jr., Hong Kong University of Science and Technology, China

Although consumers' evaluations of a product are obviously based in part on the favorableness of their attributes, at least two other factors can come into play. First, consumers may base their evaluations of a product on their positive or negative affective reactions to it. Second, they might imagine using the product in a particular situation and base their judgments on the desirability of doing so. Both effects depend on people's use of their subjective reactions as a basis for judgment. A contingency in the effects, therefore, may be the extent to which individuals are likely to consult these reactions for use as a basis for judgment rather than relying on more objective criteria. The present research examined this possibility.

Theoretical Background

Affect as information. People's tendency to use the affect they are experiencing and attribute to an object as a basis for judging this object is well established (Schwarz & Clore 1996). In the product domain, however, there are two qualifications. First, people are only likely to base their judgments of a product on their feelings if the product is normally based on hedonic criteria rather than utilitarian considerations (Pham 1998; Yeung & Wyer 2004, 2005). Second, the affect consumers are experiencing may influence their judgments only if these feelings are salient to them at the time and, therefore are a prominent source of information.

Contextual influences on product judgments. Consumers who are called upon to evaluate a product may often imagine themselves using the product in a particular situation and base their judgments on the feeling they anticipate to result from doing so. To this extent, their evaluation may depend in part on the particular situation they happen to consider, and this, in turn, may be influenced by features of the situational context in which the evaluation is made. For example, people who are asked to evaluate products while listening to music may imagine themselves using the products in a situation similar to that in which this music is often encountered, and may base their judgments on their feelings about doing so.

Effects of self-awareness. Note that people's use of the affective reactions as an informational basis for judgments, and the thoughts and feelings that result from imagining the use of the product in a given situational context, both require consultation of their subjective emotional or cognitive responses. To this extent, it may depend on their general sensitivity to these responses. This sensitivity may be influenced by their self-awareness, or the attention they pay to themselves as an object (Duval & Wicklund 1973). According to Scheier and Carver (1977), increasing people's consciousness of their internal feelings should increase their use of their feelings as a basis for judgment. In the present context, this could have two effects. First, if products spontaneously elicit positive or negative affect, self-awareness may increase the tendency to use this affect as a basis for evaluating these products. Second, self-awareness may increase the tendency to imagine oneself using the product in a particular situation and to base evaluations of the product on the desirability of doing so. Thus, if listening to music activates thoughts and feelings about a situation in which this type of music is normally played, self-awareness might increase evaluations of products that are typically used in this situation. Evaluations of products that are *not* typically used in that particular situation, however, should not be influenced by people's self-awareness. Two experiments investigated these possibilities.

Method

In experiment 1, participants were asked to evaluate a series of products under conditions in which their self-awareness was experimentally manipulated by placing participants in front of a mirror (for evidence of the effectiveness of this procedure, see Duval and Wicklund 1972). Participants were randomly assigned to six conditions of a 2 (high vs. low self-awareness) x 3 (music type: social vs. relaxing vs. none) design. The products they judged varied systematically in terms of the criteria used to evaluate them (hedonic vs. utilitarian) and the context in which they were used (social vs. non-social).

In the music conditions, participants were told that the purpose of the study was to investigate how students do two things at the same time. They were listening to either the social or non-social relaxing music while reading a simple passage. After listening to the music for 3 minutes, they were asked to perform an ostensibly unrelated product evaluation task while the music was playing. On this pretense, they evaluated 14 products that pretested to vary in terms of the criteria normally used to judge them (hedonic vs. utilitarian) and the situational context in which they were typically used (social vs. nonsocial). After making these evaluations, participants reported their reactions to the music. In the no-music conditions, participants evaluated the products without the music playing.

Experimental design and procedures in experiment 2 were identical to those in experiment 1 except that participants evaluated a list of products that were typically used either in a social, or in a non-social relaxing environment.

Results

The results of both experiments confirmed our predictions. Participants reported being more likely to report imagining themselves using the products when they participated in front of a mirror (high self-awareness conditions). Furthermore, participants in both studies evaluated hedonic products more favorably in the presence of a mirror than in its absence, whereas their judgments of utilitarian products were unaffected. When social music was played, self-awareness increased evaluations of product that were normally used in a social environment, and when relaxing music was played, it increased evaluations of products that were normally used in a relaxing environment.

In combination, the results provided insight into the conditions in which consumers are likely to use their affective reactions as a basis for product evaluations, the impact of situational context on these evaluations, and the different ways that self-awareness can exert an influence on consumer judgments.

References

Duval, Shelley T. and Robert A. Wicklund (1972) *A Theory of Objective Self Awareness*. Oxford, England: Academic Press.

Pham, Michel T. (1998). "Representativeness, Relevance, and the Use of Feelings in Decision Making", *Journal of Consumer Research*, 25(September), 167-88.

Scheier, Michael F. and Charles S. Carver (1977) "Self-focused Attention and the Experience of Emotion: Attraction, Repulsion, Elation, and Depression." *Journal of Personality and Social Psychology*. 35(9), 625-36

Schwarz, Norbert and Gerald L. Clore (1996) "Feelings and Phenomenal Experiences." in Social Psychology:Handbook of Basic Principles, *ed. Higgins, Edward Tory and Kruglanski, Arie W., New York, Guilford Press. 433-65*.

Yeung, Catherine W. M. and Robert S. Wyer, Jr. (2004) "Affect, Appraisal, and Consumer Judgment", *Journal of Consumer Research*. 31(2), 412-24.

_____ and _____ (2005) "Does Loving a Brand Mean Loving Its Products? The Role of Brand-Elicited Affect in Brand Extension Evaluations". *Journal of Marketing Research*. 42(4), 495-506.

The Effect of Option Number in Directional Comparison

Yu-chen Hung, National University of Singapore, Singapore

Catherine Yeung, National University of Singapore, Singapore

Research shows that when consumers compare between two options based on their specific attributes, they pay more attention to one of the options (the "focal" option) than the other one (Dhar and Simonson 1992). They map attributes of the focal option onto the attributes of the non-focal option, and weight the unique attributes of the focal option more heavily than those of the non-focal option. Hence, they prefer the focal option more (less) when the unique attributes are favorable (unfavorable)(Houston, Sherman and Baker 1989). This is referred as the "direction-of-comparison" effect. The direction of comparison effect has only been demonstrated in experiments in which two alternatives were considered, and has not been generalized to a more realistic, multiple-option comparison settings (Sanbonmatsu, Kardes and Gibson 1991, Mantel and Kardes 1999, Houston and Sherman 1995, Houston, Sherman and Baker 1991). The purpose of our study is to investigate the direction of comparison effect in multiple-option comparison.

Past research has shown that the direction-of-comparison effect requires one to store the specific attributes of the available options in memory, such that they can later serve as a basis for an attribute-based comparison(Mantel and Kardes 1999). When specific attributes are not available in memory, no feature matching occurs between the focal option and the non-focal option, so the focal option is not preferred more (or less). When the number of alternatives increases, it becomes harder to store attribute information in memory. Feature matching among options is also less likely. If so, the direction-of-comparison effect should disappear as the option number increases. We, however, showed that this was not the case in 3 lab experiments and 1 field study. In experiment 1, we required participants to compare 2, 3, and 4 alternatives, respectively, and showed that the direction-of-comparison effect not only sustained, but became more and more apparent as the number of option increased from 2 to 4. We demonstrated the focal option was more likely to be chosen when the comparisons were among attractive attributes, while the focal option was more likely to be rejected when the comparisons were among unattractive attributes. Besides, participants' willingness to pay increased (decreased) when comparison was among attractive (unattractive) attributes, as option number went from 2 to 4. We showed that the direction-of-comparison effect was augmented, rather than attenuated, in multiple-option comparison. The augmentation reflected in choice and willingness to pay.

The augmented direction-of-comparison effect in multiple-option settings has two implications. First, the focal option benefits from comparison among attractive alternatives. Second, the focal option disadvantages when comparison is among unattractive alternatives. We refer to the former as beneficial effect, and the later as disadvantage effect. If the augmentation show in study 1 is robust, we expect that the beneficial effect helps focal option, even when the focal option is objectively the weakest options among all alternatives. On the other hand, the disadvantage effect harms the focal option, even when it is the strongest among all options. For example, consider a house with designer furniture versus a house with good location. Although designer furniture is attractive, it is not as important as good location. A house with designer furniture is referred as weak option in this example. When the house with designer furniture becomes the focal option, it is not necessarily appealing because people compare it with the other house in good location. But as the number of option increases, the direction-of-comparison effect predicts that the house with designer furniture, which is the weak focal option, enjoys the beneficial effect and would be well chosen. We conducted experiment 2 to test the prediction that the beneficiary effect promotes a focal option, to the extent that it can help a weak alternative. We selected a number of house attributes from pretests and composed the focal option with the weaker attributes. In experiment 2, our participants were required to compare either 2, 3 or 4 houses and indicated which house they would like to visit most. In supportive of this prediction, we demonstrated that the focal option was mostly chosen among all alternatives, despite that it was the weak option.

The second implication from the augmented direction-of-comparison effect is the disadvantage effect. The disadvantage effect transpires when people compare across unattractive attribute. We reason that the disadvantage effect hurts the focal option, even when it is the relatively stronger alternative. We tested the disadvantage effect in study 3. Similarly, we had pretests and composed the focal option with minor negative attributes (e.g. poor pool maintenance in a condominium), whereas the other options had major negative attributes (e.g. the rooms are too small). The participants compared either 2, 3 or 4 options and indicated which condominium they would like to visit. Consistent with our prediction, the focal option lost its choice share significantly as the number of option increased, despite that it was the strongest among all alternatives.

We offer an explanation for the augmented direction-of-comparison effect. The direction-of-comparison effect happens because of the differential attention received by the focal option to the non-focal option. As the number of option increases, people still pay more attention to the focal option, and the non-focal options share the rest of attention. Therefore, the differential attention paid to the focal option relative to the each non-focal option increases. As a result, the direction-of-comparison effect enlarges when people have more options to choose from. The differential attention contributes to the beneficiary effect shown in experiment 2 and the disadvantage effect shown in experiment 3. To test this explanation and replicate findings from previous experiments, we conducted a field study. In this study, the participants compared attractive hampers by sequentially reading the hampers in a booklet. The results showed that people took the last hamper as the focal option, and the choice share of the weak hamper increased significantly when it was presented last. On the other hand, the participants who flipped the booklet back and forth paid no differential attention. Hence, there was no beneficiary effect for the weak hamper when it was presented at last.

References

Dhar, Ravi & Itamar Simonson (1992), "The Effect of the Focus of Comparison on Consumer Preferences," *Journal of Marketing Research,* 29, 430-440.

Houston, David A. & Steve J. Sherman (1995), "Cancellation and Focus: The Role of Shared and Unique Features in the Choice Process." *Journal of Experimental Social Psychology,* 31, 357-378.

Houston, David A., Steve J. Sherman & Sara M. Baker (1989), "The influence of unique features and direction of comparison of preferences," *Journal of Experimental Social Psychology,* 25, 121-141.

———— (1991) "Feature matching, unique features, and the dynamics of the choice process: Predecision conflict and postdecision satisfaction, "*Journal of Experimental Social Psychology,* 27, 411-430.

Mantel, Susan Powell & Frank. R. Kardes (1999)," The Role of Direction of Comparison, Attribute-Based Processing, and Attitude-Based Processing in Consumer Preference," *The Journal of Consumer Research,* 25, 335-352.

Sanbonmatsu, David M., Frank R. Kardes & Bryan D. Gibson (1991), "The role of attribute knowledge and overall evaluations in comparative judgment," *Organizational Behavior and Human Decision Processes,* 48, 131-146.

Perceived Quality, Packaging and Self-Image Congruence: An Application in the Cosmetics Market

Ahmad Jamal, Cardiff University, UK
Mohammed Sajid Khan, American University of Sharjah, UAE
Matoula Stamatia Tsesmetzi, Cardiff University, UK

The study aims to explore the impact of perceived quality, perceptions of packaging and self-image congruence on customer satisfaction, loyalty and word of mouth intentions. The study specifically focuses on make-up cosmetics, and in particular cosmetics choices made by women, for which no previous research exists. The market analyst, Key Note (2007), highlights a number of important trends in the market including the dominance of global brands enjoying strong brand awareness and loyalty levels with a need to strike a balance between persuading consumers to try new products and retaining brand loyalty to existing favourites. Also, the main users tend to be the younger people (mainly females) showing a heightened sense of pride in the way they look. Also, most customers recognize the potential of cosmetic products in making a positive contribution towards their self images. Moreover, usage of premium cosmetics, particularly those bearing the name of international fashion houses, leads to the development of feel good factor supported by high prices and exclusivity offered by the brands (Key Note, 2007). Despite the significance of perceived quality, packaging and self-concept, no previous research has investigated their effects on important performance measures such as satisfaction, loyalty and word of mouth within this crucial market. The paper aims to fill these gaps in the literature.

Following Zeithaml (1988), we consider perceived quality (PQ) to be a consumer's judgment about a product/brand' overall excellence or superiority (Zeithaml, 1988). PQ is an important subjective attribute (e.g., Grapentine, 1995) and an information cue (Lee and Lou, 1996; Monroe and Dodds, 1988). As perceptions of quality go up, consumers can better recognise the differentiation and superiority of the brand through their long term personal experiences with the brand (Llusar; 2001; Yoo et al., 2000). Such perceptions help develop strong, favourable and unique brand associations in consumer minds (Keller, 2001). Prior research has reported PQ to be an important antecedent of satisfaction (e.g., Cronin and Taylor, 1992). Moreover, Oliver (1999) argues that consumer perceptions of product quality and/or product superiority can generate a strong sense of brand-directed preference leading to the development of loyalty. Hence, we expect direct links from PQ to satisfaction, loyalty and word of mouth intentions.

The cosmetic industry is highly competitive and product innovation is the key to success as the product life cycle tends to be short (Kumar et al., 2006; Underwood, 1999, 2003). The emphasis is on creating differentiation at the point of sale through packaging (Doyle 2004). Bottles are designed that are softer to the touch, have sleeker and sexier shapes, are easier to hold and less likely to break. Moreover, products have to offer added value with dual functionality and special visual effects to stand out and get attention from the consumer (Doyle, 2004). To achieve this effect, the industry relies on consumers' perceptions of beauty and the recent developments in new technology have allowed firms to create a wide scheme of colours and packs (Kumar et al., 2006; Silayoi and Speece, 2007, Underwood et al., 2001). We argue that positive evaluations of packaging can help in meeting customer expectations and hence influence satisfaction judgements, loyalty levels and word of mouth intentions.

A review of literature suggests that consumers can express themselves by choosing brands whose personalities are perceived to be congruent with their own personalities (Aaker, 1999; Sirgy 1997). Moreover, during the consumption process, a product-user image interacts with the consumers' self concept generating a subjective experience referred to as self-image congruence (Sirgy, et al. 1997). A number of studies have established the effects of self-image congruence on attitudes, brand preference, purchase intentions, customer satisfaction and word of mouth intentions (Ericksen, 1996; Sirgy et al., 1997, 1991; reference to authors' prior published work). While the effects of self-image congruence have been tested for different product categories (e.g., automobiles, mobile phones, athletic shoes, jewellery), these have never been tested within the cosmetics market. We expect self image congruence to be related to satisfaction, loyalty and word of mouth intentions. Moreover, as per prior research, we also expect direct links from satisfaction to loyalty (e.g., Oliva et al. 1992; Selnes 1993 and from loyalty to word of mouth (Dick and Basu 1994).

Data was obtained from female cosmetic users in a leading metropolitan city in the UK using self-administered questionnaire, which contained measures adopted from previous research. After the pilot testing, 300 questionnaires were distributed among users of cosmetics make-up brands who expressed their willingness to participate using a mall intercept procedure. The procedure resulted in 193 usable questionnaires. This was followed by exploratory factor analysis, Pearson correlation tests and quantification of scale reliabilities via alpha scores. Three multiple regressions were computed. The first one revealed high and significant beta weights for PQ (β=0.383, p<0.000, t value=6.374), packaging (β=0.296, p<0.000, t value =4.6702) and low but significant beat for self-congruence (β =0.166, p<0.042, t value=2.046) with the independent variables accounting for about 47% of the variance in satisfaction scores (adjusted R square=0.465, F statistic56.714). Second equation revealed high and significant beta weights for satisfaction (β=0.554, p<0.000, t value=6.176), packaging (β=0.235, p<0.008, t value =4.6702) and low but significant beta for self-congruence (β =0.149, p<0.014, t value=2.478) with the independent variables accounting for about 48% of the variance in loyalty scores (adjusted R square=0.481, F statistic 45.408). However, the PQ to loyalty link was neither high nor significant. Results for final equation revealed high and significant beta weights for satisfaction (β=0.432, p<0.000, t value=6.506) and PQ (β=0.291, p<0.000, t value=4.530) and low and significant beta weights for loyalty (β=0.165, p<0.001, t value=3.363) and packaging (β=0.187, p<0.002, t value =3.082) with the independent variables accounting for about 88% of the variance in word of mouth scores (adjusted R square=0.684, F statistic84.062). Hence, all except quality to loyalty and self-image to word of mouth links were supported. Given that no prior research has investigated the effects perceived quality, packaging perceptions, self-image congruence on satisfaction, loyalty and word of mouth intentions, we believe our study will go some way in helping brand managers developing a better understanding of consumer behavior within the rapidly growing and multibillion pounds cosmetic and personal care industry (Chandler 1995; Wurdinger 1996).

References

Aaker, J.L, 1999, "The malleable self: the role of self-expression in persuasion", *Journal of Marketing Research*, 36, 1, 45-57.

Chandler, S. (1995), "Au nature? Au contraire", Business Week, (May 22), 50.

Cronin, J. J. Jr., and Taylor, S. A. (1992), "Measuring Service Quality: A Reexamination and Extension", *Journal of Marketing*, 56(3), pp. 55-68.

Ericksen, M.K, 1996, "Using self-congruity and ideal congruity to predict purchase intention: a European perspective", *Journal of Euro-Marketing*, 6, 1, 41-56.

Grapentine, T. (1995), "Dimensions of An Attribute," *Marketing Research*, Summer, Vol. 7, Issue 3, pp.18-27.

Keller, K. L. (2001), "Building customer-based brand equity" *Marketing Management*, 10 (2), pp. 14-20.

Key Note (2007), Cosmetics & Fragrances, *Market Report Plus 2007*, 20th edition, March.

Kumar, S., Massie, C., and Dumonceaux, M. D., (2006), "Comparative innovative business strategies of major players in cosmetic industry", *Industrial Management + Data Systems*, Vol. 106, No. 3, pp. 285-306.

Lee, M. and Lou, Y-C. (1996), "Consumer Reliance on Intrinsic and Extrinsic Cues in Product Evaluations: A Conjoint Approach," *Journal of Applied Business Research*, Vol.12, Issue 1, pp.21-29

Llusar, J.C.B., Zornoza, C.C. and Tena, A.B.E. (2001), "Measuring the relationship between firm perceived quality and customer satisfaction and its influence on purchase intentions", *Total Quality Management*, 12, pp. 719–734.

Monroe, K. B. and Dodds, W.B. (1988), "A Research Program for Establishing the Validity of the Price-Quality Relationship", *Journal of the Academy of Marketing Science*, 16 (Spring), pp.151-68.

Oliva, T. A., Oliver, L. R., and MacMillan, C. I. (1992), "A catastrophe model for developing service satisfaction strategies", *Journal of Marketing*, Vol. 56 (July), pp. 83-95.

Oliver, R. L. (1999), "Whence consumer loyalty?", *Journal of Marketing*, Vol. 63 (Special Issue), pp.33-44.

Oliver, R. L. (1997), *Satisfaction: A Behavioral Perspective on the Consumer*, McGraw-Hill, New York.

Oliver, R. L. (1993), "Cognitive, affective, and attribute bases of the satisfaction response", *Journal of Consumer Research*, Vol. 20, No. 3, pp. 418-430.

Oliver, R. L. (1980), "Cognitive model of the antecedents and consequences of satisfaction decisions", *Journal of Marketing Research*, Vol. 17 (November), pp. 460-469.

Selnes, F. (1993), "An examination of the effect of product performance on brand reputation, satisfaction and loyalty" *European Journal of Marketing,* 27(9), pp. 19-35.

Silayoi, P. and Speece, M. (2007), "The importance of packaging attributes: a conjoint analysis approach" *European Journal of Marketing* Vol. 41 No. 11/12, pp. 1495-1517.

Sirgy, J. M. (1982), "Self-concept in consumer behavior: a critical review", *Journal of Consumer Research*, Vol. 9, No. 3, pp. 287-300.

Sirgy, J. M., Johar, J. S., Samli A. C. and Claiborne C. B. (1991), "Self-congruence versus functional predictors of consumer behavior", *Journal of the Academy of Marketing Science*, 19 (4), pp. 363-375.

Sirgy, Joseph M., Grewal Dhruv., Mangleburg, F. Tamara., Park Jae-ok., Chon, Kye-Sung., Claiborne, C. B., Johar, J. S. and Berkman Harold (1997), "Assessing the Predictive Validity of Two Methods of Measuring Self-Image Congruence," *Journal of the Academy of Marketing Science*, 25(3), 229-241.

Underwood, R. (1999), "Construction of brand identity through packaging: A qualitative inquiry" American Marketing Association. Conference Proceedings: 1999 AMA Winter Educators' Conference: Marketing Theory, 10, pp.147.

Underwood, R., Klein, N.M. and Burke, R.R. (2001), "Packaging communication: attentional effects of product imagery" *Journal of Product & Brand Management*, Vol. 10(7), 403-22.

Underwood, R. and Klein, N.M. (2002), "Packaging as brand communication: effects of product pictures on consumer responses to the package and brand", *Journal of Marketing Theory and Practice*, Vol. 10 No. 4, pp. 58-69.

Underwood, R. (2003), "The communicative power of product packaging: creating brand identity via lived and mediated experience", *Journal of Marketing Theory and Practice*, Winter, pp. 62-76.

Wansink, B. (1996), "Can package size accelerate usage volume?", *Journal of Marketing*, Vol. 60, No. 3, pp. 1-14.

Wurdinger, V. (1996), "Hair Care Report", *Drug & Cosmetic Industry*, 158 (4), pp. 24-3

Yoo, B., Donthu N. and Lee S. (2000), "An examination of selected marketing mix elements and brand equity", *Journal of the Academy of Marketing Science*, 28 (2), pp. 195-211.

Zeithaml, V. A. (1988), "Consumer perceptions of price, quality, and value: a means-end model and synthesis of evidence", *Journal of Marketing*, 52 (July), pp. 2-22.

Payment Frequency Discount vs. Payment Amount Discount: The Framing Effect on Preference Reversal

Ji Hoon Jhang, University of Colorado, USA
Jungkeun Kim, University of Minnesota, USA

Theoretical Background

Across many product categories, widespread are multiple payments plans with which consumers pay certain amounts of money by schedule. By allowing consumers to choose the plan that serves them best, companies are attracting more consumers. Despite the topic's importance and pervasiveness, empirical studies on the effects of different payment plan framings are scarce.

In addition, multiple payment plans are often accompanied with price discounts. These price discounts are one of the most common promotional tools used by marketers to attract consumers (Monroe 2003). In this situation, we can think of several ways to frame a price discount. For example, imagine that the suggested price of a product is $160. Consumers are required to pay 4 payments of $40. The store can provide the $40 price discount and can quote $120 as the final selling price with multiple payments. Specifically, price discount can be either: 1) a payment *frequency discount*-which reduces the payment frequency from 4 to 3, holding the amount of each payment constant; or 2) a payment *amount discount*-which reduces each payment amount from $40 to $30 without changing the payment frequency. In addition, we can generate several framing methods to express the price discount as below[8] (Figure 1).

Mainly drawing on prospect theory (Kahneman and Tversky 1979; Tversky & Kahneman 1991) and mental accounting (Thaler 1985), we investigate consumers' preferences between the payment frequency discount and the amount discount across different framing conditions. Therefore, the purpose of this research is to explore: 1) how framings influence consumers' preferences between the payment frequency discount and the amount discount, yielding a preference reversal; and 2) under what conditions the effect of framings is attenuated.

Preference Reversal between Gain Framing and Loss Framing

Researchers have shown that people have different preferences for multiple gains and losses (Linville and Fischer 1991; Thaler 1985). Put differently, people prefer segregated gains and integrated losses. On the basis of this theory, we can predict preference reversal. Specifically, in our loss framing condition, based on $\{U_{FD}[(-\$40) + (-\$40) + (-\$40)] > U_{AD}[(-\$30) + (-\$30) + (-\$30) + (-\$30)]\}$, we can expect that people prefer the payment frequency discount to the payment amount discount. On the other hand, in our gain framing condition, based on $\{U_{FD}(\$40) < U_{AD}(\$10+\$10+\$10+\$10)\}$, we can expect the opposite pattern:

H1a: People will prefer the payment frequency discount to the payment amount discount in loss framing condition.
H1b: People will prefer the payment amount discount to the payment amount frequency in gain framing condition.
H1c: There will be a preference reversal across loss framing and gain framing conditions.

Study 1

Drawing on the notion that people prefer segregated gains and integrated losses, we investigated consumers' preferences for two discount plans (the payment frequency discount vs. the payment amount discount) with different framings (loss framing vs. gain framing). Sixty-two participants (average age=21.7, 59.7% female) were offered two discount plans, along with one of two framings, as shown in Table 1. The participants were then asked to rate their likelihood of choosing one plan over the other with a 10-point scale (i.e., (-5)-frequency discount preferred; (5)–amount discount preferred).[9] Responses were recoded such that "1" represents a preference for the payment frequency discount and "10" represents a preference for the payment amount discount. Therefore, a value of "5.5" indicates no preference between the two discount plans.

The ANOVA revealed a main effect of the framings ($F_{1,60}$=9.45, p =.003), indicating the preference reversal between two framing conditions. Specifically, the participants preferred the frequency discount to the amount discount in the loss framing condition (mean=4.21, t^{10}=2.22, p=.035), but showed an opposite preference in the gain framing condition (mean=6.70, t =2.14, p=.045). Furthermore, we analyzed the inferred choice. Sixty-one percent of the participants in the loss framing condition chose the frequency discount plan, whereas, in the gain framing condition, only 32.3% chose the frequency discount plan (Chi-Square=5.25, p=.022). In sum, the results support Hypothesis 1.

This result shows that consumers prefer paying less frequently to paying lower amounts of money each time when they regard the payment plans as losses, while they show the opposite pattern if they consider the payment plans as gains.

Preference Reversal between Double Loss Framing I and II Conditions

In the double loss framing I condition, we expect that people will show no preference between the two discount plans because the "frequency discount" and the "amount discount" are both losses for consumers. In contrast, in the double loss framing II condition, we expect that people will prefer the frequency discount to the amount discount because people are expected to be more sensitive to changes in the frequency than in the amount.[11]

H2a: People will show no preference between the two discount plans in the double loss framing I condition.
H2b: People will prefer the payment frequency discount to the payment amount discount in the double loss framing II condition.
H2c: There will be a preference reversal across the double loss framing I and II conditions.

Study 2

The purpose of Study 2 is to examine the preference reversal in the double loss framing I and II conditions. Except for the double loss framing conditions, the other experimental procedures were identical to those of Study 1. Sixty-two participants (average age=21.8, 41.9% female) were randomly assigned one of two experimental conditions.

The ANOVA revealed a main effect of framings ($F_{1,60}$=5.03, p =.029), indicating a preference reversal between the two framing conditions. Specifically, the participants preferred the frequency discount to the amount discount in the double loss framing II condition (mean=4.13, t =2.56, p=.016), but showed no difference in the double loss framing I condition (mean=5.50, t <1). Therefore, the result supports Hypothesis 2.

---

[8] We named the first category above "loss framing" because it merely shows the payment amounts, which are definitely perceived as losses to consumers whereas we named the second category "gain framing" because it focuses on price discounts, which are definitely gains to consumers. We also named the remaining two categories "double loss framing" because they contain the payment frequency and payment amount, which are double losses to consumers.

[9] We measured choice and relative preference with one scale.

[10] All *t* statistics hereafter refer to comparing the mean with the neutral point (i.e., "5.5").

[11] We assume that people calculate the payment frequency and payment amount along with the same scale. In addition, we also assume diminishing sensitivity (Tversky and Kahneman 1991).

FIGURE 1

Framing	Payment Frequency Discount	Payment Amount Discount
Loss framing:	$40, $40, $40	$30, $30, $30, $30
Gain framing:	~~$40, $40, $40, $40~~ $40, $40, $40	~~$40, $40, $40, $40~~ $30, $30, $30, $30
Double loss framing I:	3 payments of $40 each	4 payments of $30 each
Double loss framing II:	~~4 payments of $40 each~~ 3 payments of $40 each	~~4 payments of $40 each~~ 4 payments of $30 each

Disappearing Preference Reversal under the Provision of Reasons

Previous studies have demonstrated that people show different preferences when asked to provide reasons or not (Shafir, Simonson, & Tversky 1993; Simonson 1989). In our discount condition, we expect that people prefer the payment frequency discount when they are asked to provide reasons for their preferences because the reason(s) regarding the payment frequency discount is (are) easier to generate than the reason(s) regarding the payment amount discount.[12]

> *H3: People will prefer the payment frequency discount to the payment amount discount when they are asked to provide reasons for their preferences.*

Study 3

Study 3 explored the boundary condition in which the effects of previous studies are attenuated. The experimental design was a 4 (Framings: loss vs. gain vs. double loss I vs. double loss II) between-subject design. All experimental materials were the same as those in Studies 1 and 2. The only difference was that all participants were asked to provide reasons for their preferences. We expected that the frequency discount would be preferred in all four framing conditions, insofar as it is much easier for the participants to provide reasons for fewer payments. One-hundred-sixty-five participants (average age=20.7, 58.2% female) were randomly assigned one of four experimental conditions.

As anticipated, there were no differences across the experimental conditions ($(F_{3,161}=2.53, p > .05)$. Specifically, the frequency discount was preferred to the amount discount in most framing conditions (means=3.59, 3.77, & 4.40, all $p's < .05$) except in the double loss framing II condition (mean=5.14, t <1). The reasons provided by the participants also confirmed Hypothesis 3; most participants mentioned fewer payments as reasons.

General Discussion

This study examined the preference reversal between the payment frequency discount and the payment amount discount across four different framings. Three experiments demonstrated that consumers' relative preference for the frequency vs. the amount discount is systematically changed by different framings. In addition, this research showed that this preference reversal disappeared when people were asked to provide reasons for their preference. This research demonstrates the tenets of mental accounting (i.e. the segregation of gains and the integration of losses) and finds interesting results regarding the relative importance of the frequency vs. the amount discount in consumers' preferences. In sum, this study can contribute to an understanding of the role of the framing effect on price discounts.

References

Kahneman, Daniel and Amos Tversky (1979), "Prospect Theory: An Analysis of Decision under Risk," *Econometrica*, 47(March), 263-92.

Linville, Patricia W. and Gregory W. Fischer (1991), "Preferences for Separating or Combining Events," *Journal of Personality and Social Psychology*, 60(January), 5-23.

Monroe, Kent B. (2003), *Pricing: Making Profitable Decisions*, 3d ed. Burr Ridge, IL: McGraw-Hill/Irwin.

Shafir, Eldar, Itamar Simonson and Amos Tversky (1993), "Reason-Based Choice," *Cognition*, 49(October-November), 11-36.

Simonson, Itamar (1989), "Choice Based on Reasons: The Case of Attraction and Compromise Effects," *Journal of Consumer Research*, 16(September), 158-174.

Thaler, Richard (1985), "Mental Accounting and Consumer Choice," *Marketing Science*, 4(Summer), 199-214.

Tversky, Amos and Daniel Kahneman (1991), "Loss Aversion in Riskless Choice: A Reference-Dependent Model," *The Quarterly Journal of Economics*, 106(November), 1036-61.

---

[12]Currently, we are preparing an empirical study supporting this assumption.

Attribute Order Effects on Consumer Judgment: The Role of Ideal Point Availability and Attribute Importance

Ying Jiang, University of Ontario Institute of Technology, Canada
Jing Lei, University of Ontario Institute of Technology, Canada

The primacy effect in a decision context refers to the fact that information appearing early in the sequence has a stronger effect on judgment than does subsequent information (e.g., Kardes and Herr 1990). One explanation to this effect is that individuals bias their interpretation of the subsequent information to cohere with the disposition evoked by the initial information (also known as the "information-distortion" effect). For example, Bond et al. (2007) found that consumers tend to form an initial disposition (e.g., like or dislike) toward a product based on a positive or negative attribute, and this disposition subsequently biases their evaluations of other attributes. This finding suggests that presenting positive (negative) attribute information early in the sequence increases (decrease) consumers' favorability toward the product.

An underlying assumption of the above finding is that consumers' initial disposition toward a product is installed by valenced attribute information. However, in many occasions product information is presented neutrally or is perceived to be neutral. Hence, an interesting question is whether neutral information can also evoke an evaluative disposition that subsequently influences the interpretation of other attributes. Further, the two attributes used to install the initial disposition in Bond et al.'s (2007) study are both important attributes (e.g., functionality and price of a PAD). Thus, it is yet to know whether the disposition evoked by a trivial attribute can bias the evaluation of subsequent important attributes. In this research we propose that the impact of a target neutral attribute on the evaluation of other attributes depends on whether consumers have readily available preferences (or ideal points) for attributes and the relative importance of the target attribute. These propositions are explained in detail below.

When approaching a decision problem, some consumers have well articulated preferences for product attributes whereas others do not (Chernev 2003). For example, consumer A wants an MP3 player with a memory of at least 8GB, a battery that can last for at least 24 hours of audio play, and a price within the range of 200 dollars; whereas consumer B does not have specific requirements although acknowledging the importance of these attributes. Previous research suggests that the availability of ideal points influences consumers' decision process (Chernev 2003). In particular, consumers with readily available preferences evaluate product alternatives in search of attributes that match and confirm these preferences. Therefore, when a target attribute, although presented neutrally, matches (does not match) a consumer's ideal point for the attribute, it may lead to a positive (negative) predisposition that can influence the evaluation of subsequent attributes. However, this predisposition is only likely to have a strong effect on other attributes when the target attribute is perceived to be more important than or at least equally important as the subsequent attributes. In contrast, when consumers do not have specific requirements for attributes, the neutral target attribute is less likely to cause a strong evaluative disposition that can bias the interpretation of subsequent attributes. Therefore, we propose that:

H1: When a target neutral attribute is perceived to be more important than or at least equally important as other attributes presented later in the sequence, the neutral attribute will have a stronger distortion effect on other attributes for consumers with (vs. without) ideal points for attributes.

When the target neutral attribute is less important than the attributes presented later, consumers are likely to form a weak disposition toward the product regardless of the availability of ideal points. For consumers with readily available ideal points, a weak disposition may not bias their evaluation of other attributes because they will use the ideal points as a benchmark to judge these attributes and form strong evaluative opinions. However, for consumers without readily available ideal points, a weak preliminary disposition may still influence their evaluations of other attributes presented later as they do not have specific criteria to judge these attributes. Therefore, we propose that:

H2: When a target neutral attribute is perceived to be less important than other attributes presented later in the sequence, the neutral attribute will have a stronger distortion effect on other attributes for consumers without (vs. with) ideal points for attributes.

To test the above hypotheses, we conducted an experimental study using undergraduate students from a North American university. The study employed a 2(ideal point availability: available vs. not available) x 2(target attribute importance: important vs. less important) between-subject design. Participants were first given a decision scenario in which they needed to purchase an MP3 player as a gift for their friend. In the scenario, the ideal point availability and the relative importance of the target attribute were manipulated. Based on the established procedure of Bond et al. (2007), we used the *stepwise evolution of preference* (SEP) method to measure if the target attribute presented early in the sequence would 1) bias the evaluation of the subsequent attributes; 2) influence consumers' purchase decision of the product; and 3) influence consumers' confidence about their decisions. Furthermore, follow up studies have been designed to replicate the expected findings from the current experiment by using different products and decision scenarios.

Our research expects to contribute to the literature of information distortion in product judgment in several ways. First, previous research shows that consumers' preliminary disposition toward a product can be evoked by valanced attribute information (Bond et al. 2007) or product comparison (Carlson, Meloy, and Russo 2006). However, we suggest such predispositions can also be installed by neutral attribute information. This extends the existing theory by generalizing the information-distortion effect to different judgment tasks. Second, prior research has primarily examined the information-distortion effect as a main effect. Little is known about the moderating factors that could lead to a more nuanced set of effects. This research aims to take our understanding about the information-distortion effect beyond the simple main effects by demonstrating key interactions and contingences in the contexts of product judgment.

References

Bond, Samuel D., Kurt A. Calson, Margaret G. Meloy, J. Edward Russo, and Robin J. Tanner (2007), "Information Distortion in the Evaluation of a Single Option," *Organizational Behavior and Human Decision Processes*, 102, 240-254.

Carlson, Kurt A., Margaret G. Meloy, and J. Edward Russo (2006), "Leader-Driven Primacy: Using Attribute Order to Affect Consumer Choice," *Journal of Consumer Research*, 32(March), 513-518.

Chernev, Alexander (2003), "When More Is Less and Less Is More: The Role of Ideal Point Availability and Assortment in Choice," *Journal of Consumer Research*, 30(September), 170-.

Kardes, Frank K. and Paul M. Herr (1990), "Order Effects in Consumer Judgment, Choice, and Memory: the Role of Initial Processing Goals," *Advances in Consumer Research*, 17, 541-546.

Does Feedback Always Facilitate Learning?: Degree of Preference Development and Degree of Feedback Complexity

Jaewoo Joo, University of Toronto, Canada

A long tradition of research based on the MCPL paradigm suggests that when feedback is provided, people learn functional relationships between cues and outcomes (Brehmer and Brehmer 1988; Hammond 1955). It has been found that feedback not only facilitates learning of the relationship between attributes and product quality (Meyer 1987) and between attributes and others' preferences (West 1996) but also stabilizes preferences by providing a framework to correctly identify the relationship between attributes and self preferences (West, Brown and Hoch 1996).

As classic papers emphasized feedback as a learning facilitator, it has been extensively discussed what influences the impact of feedback on task outcomes (Hutchinson and Alba 1991). The moderators that have been found include learner variables such as goal or motivation, situation variables such as memory load or time pressure, cue characteristics such as salience or valence, and finally feedback type such as cognitive feedback. Further, at least two previous research projects revealed that outcome feedback, when an error on a particular task is large, can lead to negative task performance because people keep changing their original strategies and learning does not occur (Arkes et al. 1986; Hogarth et al. 1991).

As it is found that outcome feedback does not always facilitate learning, some researchers pay attention to a different type of feedback: cognitive feedback (Balzer, Doherty, and O'Connor 1989; Doherty and Balzer 1988; Todd and Hammond 1965). Compared with outcome feedback that provides information only about a true model, cognitive feedback provides information about relations: relations among cues, subject's judgment, and criterion variable in environment. This approach is mapped on to Lens model suggested by Hammond et al. 1975).

The present research aims to demonstrate that even cognitive feedback does not always lead to an improved task outcome. More broadly speaking, our objective is to investigate when cognitive feedback hinders or does not hinder people from improving outcomes. In the present research, we consider learning as stabilizing self preferences (West, Brown and Hoch 1996) and consider feedback as cognitive feedback: providing information about a functional relationship between attributes and pre-feedback preferences.

Here, we aim to demonstrate that the extent to which preferences are stabilized differs depending on one variable about learners and one variable about feedback quality: how much a pre-feedback preference is developed and how complicated a feedback is. The former variable, *the degree of preference development*, refers to how much pre-feedback preferences can be explained by available cues (attributes). For instance, some people are aware of several wine-related attributes that determine their preferences. In this case, their wine preferences are highly developed. Whereas, others evaluate wines without knowing much about what makes them prefer or choose, suggesting that their wine preferences are poorly developed. The proportion of pre-feedback preferences predicted by attributes will determine preference consistency. The latter variable, *the degree of feedback complexity*, refers to the amount of relationship-relevant information contained by feedback. For instance, suppose that a type of grape, a winery, and a production year can fully determine pre-feedback preferences. Simple feedback provides information about only one key factor and how it affects preferences (e.g., "you like wine produced later"), whereas complex feedback provides information about how all three attributes affects preferences (e.g., "you like the wine produced later, the wine created at a certain region of France, and the wine made by Shiraz....). In other words, the number of attribute about which feedback provides information determines feedback complexity.

We have two testable hypotheses: feedback stabilizes the preferences of (1) those who developed a low degree of pre-feedback preferences more greatly than the preferences of those who developed a high degree of pre-feedback preferences and (2) when the degree of complexity is lower than higher. The former hypothesis (1) is suggested by an idea that people who do not develop their own preferences (i.e., novices) have more rooms to learn their own preferences than those who already develop preferences (i.e., experts). The latter hypothesis (2) is consistent with the effect of information overload on decision making, suggesting that overwhelming information confuses people and prevent from learning (Lurie 2004). Interestingly, the second hypothesis that the fewer attributes will benefit preference stabilization suggests a discrepancy with a finding in West, Brown and Hoch (1996).

We conducted a 2 (degree of preference development: low vs. high) x 2 (degree of feedback complexity: low vs. high) between-subjects design study by using 30 carefully designed chair pictures which consist of 5 binary attributes. Participants rated their preferences about 15 chairs, received one feedback, and then rated preferences about another 15 chairs. People whose R^2 about the first 15 preferences were lower than 0.6 are categorized as a lowly developed pre-feedback preference group and others belong to a highly developed pre-feedback preference group. Half the participants received simple feedback which provides directional relationship about only one strongest attribute, whereas the other half received complex feedback which tells directional relationships about all five attributes.

FIGURE 1
RESEARCH FRAMEWORK

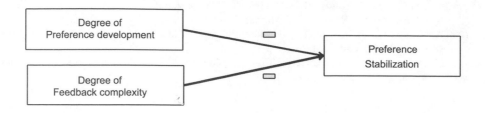

FIGURE 2
R-SQUARE OF PREFERENCES BEFORE AND AFTER FEEDBACK IS PROVIDED

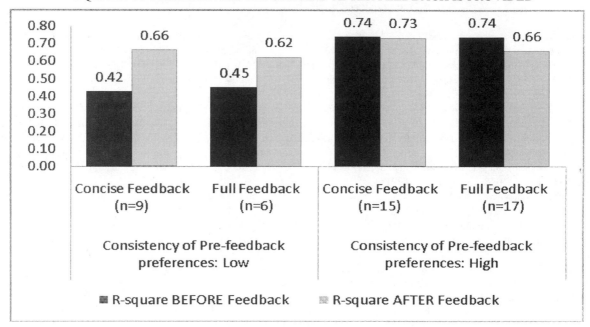

Results suggest hypothesis 1 but not hypothesis 2. The R^2 about the preferences increases when pre-feedback preferences are lowly developed, whereas it decreases when pre-feedback preferences are highly developed (0.21 vs. -0.4, $F=17.71$, $p<.01$), supporting the former hypothesis. As for the latter hypothesis, although the effect is not significant, data provide a directional support by demonstrating that simple feedback more strongly stabilizes preferences than complex feedback (0.12 vs. 0.05, $F=1.38$, $p>.2$). We hope to increase the number of observations to increase statistical significance. It is worth nothing that neither those who lowly develop pre-feedback preferences (+0.09) nor those who highly develop pre-feedback preferences (-0.02) fail to increase their R^2 after feedback was provided.

Probably, the most interesting findings come from those who highly develop pre-feedback preferences and receive complex feedback. Their preferences become significantly destabilized after feedback is provided (-0.08, $t=-1.67$, $p=.10$), implying that feedback does not simply benefit but harms those who already developed their own preferences.

Accept or Reject?: How Task Valence Interacts With Product Information Processing To Alter Purchase Decisions

Uma Karmarkar, Stanford University, USA
Brian Knutson, Stanford University, USA
Baba Shiv, Stanford University, USA

Though behavioral research on decision-making has described in rich detail the ways that framing can affect the nature of a decision, we still do not fully understand the emotional and cognitive processes by which this takes place. Previous studies have investigated decisions framed as either choosing a desirable option, or rejecting an insufficiently appealing one, and have found results suggesting that the type of decision increases the salience of positive (choose) or negative (reject) information (e.g. Shafir 1993, Ganzach and Schul, 1995.) However, in these experiments the decisions are between two or more items and always lead to one option emerging as a winner. Thus the decision task changes the nature of the comparison or tradeoff between options as opposed to the evaluation of each one.

Recent work has illuminated the importance of positive and negative affect when evaluating individual products in a shopping context. Knutson et al. (2007) used functional magnetic resonance imaging (fMRI) to show that presentation of a product activated brain areas that respond to reward anticipation such as the nucleus accumbens. Price information appeared to activate the insula, a separate brain region. Thus this work supported the notion of distinct gain and loss neural centers whose balance contributed to the final decision whether or not to purchase the product. Focal analyses in these areas revealed that activation in these regions enabled prediction of the decision based on the comparative strengths of the localized signals. These results appear to reflect a "translation" of the overall complex cognitive and affective response to a balance of distinct affective evaluations.

Using a combination of fMRI and behavioral experiments, we look to build on this work by examining whether task information that emphasizes processing related to gain and loss can also change the desirability of an individual item in a shopping type context. In our design, participants made an accept or reject decision about purchasing a single item after being presented dichotomous information related to that item's perceived reward value versus the potential negative impact of its price. This design was based off the task used in the Knutson et al. (2007) work, and the list of products were selected to be highly desirable to the participant pool of young adults. Each person made forty do (do not) accept decisions and forty do (do not) reject decisions; thus eighty separate products were presented in total. The order of accept versus reject choice tasks and the decision type for any individual product were counterbalanced across participants. Participants received an endowment at the beginning of the experiment and their decisions had real monetary consequences. One accept trial and one reject trial were chosen randomly at the end of the experiment and if a participant had chosen to buy the product on those trials, they were required to pay back part of the endowment to receive it.

In our first experiments, for each trial, participants viewed a discounted price, and were then shown the associated product. Findings indicated that people chose to buy approximately the same total number of items in both the accept and reject conditions. Moreover, decision reaction times in trials where the participant chose to buy the item were longer than those in no-buy trials, possibly indicating more conflict or difficulty in the decision to make a purchase. However, there was no difference between reaction times in the accept and reject tasks for buy choices or in reaction times for no-buy choices. Average preference and willingness-to-pay ratings, reported on seven-point scales, were also not significantly different between accept and reject framed decisions.

For a second set of participants, the salience or impact of the price was minimized by presenting a photo of the product first, and then listing its price afterwards. Results showed that under these conditions, significantly *more* products were purchased under reject than accept decisions. Again, there was a main effect of slower reaction times on any trials (accept- or reject-type) in which an item was bought. However, across both buy and no-buy choices, reaction times for reject decisions were significantly slower than accept ones, indicating that it was more difficult to reject purchase of an item when the salience of price was decreased. Interestingly, average preference for the purchased items was higher in the accept condition than in the reject condition though willingness to pay ratings were the same across decision types.

These behavioral findings imply that minimizing price, an easily processed feature that can be used as a decision heuristic, makes the nature of evaluation in a reject decision more complex. Additional experiments involving fMRI will complement this work and examine activation of specific brain areas such as the anterior cingular cortex, shown to be involved in conflict during decision making. We predict greater anterior cingulate activation in tasks where the information most congruent with the choice type is minimized in the decision process. This methodology can also allow us to investigate the question of whether accept and reject decisions preferentially activate positive or negative emotional neural circuitry respectively.

References

Knutson, B., Scott Rick, G. Elliott Wimmer, Drazen Prelec, and George Lowenstein. (2007) "Neural Predictors of Purchases", *Neuron*, 53, 147-156.

Ganzach, Yoav and Schul, Yaacov. (1995) "The Influence of Quantity of Information and Goal Framing on Decision", *Acta Psychologica*, 89, 23-36.

Shafir, Eldar. (1993) "Choosing Versus Rejecting: Why some options are both better and worse than others," *Memory and Cognition*, 21, 546-556.

Moderate Copy Complexity Enhances the Persuasiveness of Direct Marketing

Tina M. Lowrey , University of Texas at San Antonio, USA
Youngseon Kim, University of Texas at San Antonio, USA

Copywriters increase readability by eliminating complicated words and reducing sentence length, hoping that more individuals will read the piece, resulting in increased response rates. Whether this yields the desired results has not been fully addressed. In exploratory research, we obtained samples from two direct mail houses that had conducted split-copy tests on simple vs. complex versions of their direct marketing. In all cases, simplification involved shortening the copy, so the effects of complexity were confounded with length. Research on complexity in advertising has been done on magazine copy—much briefer than the average direct marketing piece. Moderate complexity seems to enhance memory and persuasiveness, but no research has been conducted on longer texts such as direct marketing. We present two laboratory experiments that isolated complexity from length as the independent variables that could impact order intentions, and a third experiment which tested whether the medium carrying the message also influences persuasiveness.

Experiment 1

In Experiment 1, we expected that:

H1: Moderate complexity offers will be associated with greater intention to order than simple offers.
H2: Those higher in involvement will be associated with greater intention to order than those low in involvement.
H3: Order intentions will be greatest for those high in involvement exposed to moderately complex versions.

Method

Participants and Procedure. Eighty-five college students participated in for course credit, ran in groups of 12 seated at cubicles in a laboratory. Participants were asked to read at their own pace the material on the desk in front of them, which was the direct marketing offer. When finished reading, participants were instructed to raise their hands to receive the next phase. The researcher collected the offer and provided the participants with the measurement booklet, which they were instructed to complete at their own pace. Upon completion, the participants were free to leave the laboratory.

Stimuli. The direct marketing pieces for a collectible were written after extensive pre-testing. The four versions created were: short/simple; short/moderate; long/simple; long/moderate. Simple versions had high school level Fog indices of 10.75 (long) and 11.45 (short), whereas the moderate versions had college level Fog indices of 14.60 (long) and 13.70 (short). The short versions had 600-650 words, and the long versions had 850-900 words.

Dependent Variables. Intention to order was measured on a nine-point scale with a higher number indicating a greater intention to order, and a thought-listing task was included.

Results and Discussion

H1, H2 and H3 were supported. Those who received the moderate versions had higher intentions to order (Mean=2.98) than those who received the simple versions (Mean=2.05; $F(1, 83)=3.99, p<.05$). Those who reported high levels of involvement had greater order intentions (2.96 vs. 2.04; $F(1, 83)=3.78; p<.05$) than those at low levels of involvement.

High involvement participants who received the moderate offer had higher order intentions than all other participants ($F(1, 81)=9.24; p <.005$), and had a marginally higher mean number of positive thoughts (1.91 vs. 1.43; $F(1, 51)=3.53; p=.07$)

In Experiment 1, the expected results were obtained but the order intensions were quite low on a nine-point scale. Experiment 2 was designed to provide an offer that might be of more overall interest to all participants. The same hypotheses were tested.

Experiment 2

Method

Participants and Procedure. One hundred three college students participated for course credit, with an identical procedure to that of Experiment 1.

Stimuli. The offer was re-written for a different collectible selected after additional pre-testing.

Dependent Variables. An intention to order scale and a thought-listing task were included.

Results and Discussion

Complexity exerted a main effect on order intentions (5.00 vs. 3.77; $F(1, 101)=6.23; p<.05$). Involvement exerted a main effect, with high involvement participants having higher order intentions (5.57 vs. 3.36; $F(1, 101)=23.48; p<.001$). Involvement did not moderate the impact of complexity on order intentions, as in Experiment 1, but t-tests showed partial support for the relation.

Experiment 3

Experiment 3 involved a 3 (simple vs. moderate vs. complex copy) X 2 (short vs. long) X 2 (print vs. broadcast) manipulation of direct marketing for the same item used in Experiment 2. The addition of a radio commercial was intended to test the hypothesis that the persuasiveness of copy in radio commercials will decrease as the complexity of copy gets beyond moderate complexity. However, the persuasiveness of copy in the print offer is not expected to decrease as the copy gets more complex.

Method

Participants and Procedure. Two hundred forty-one college students participated for credit in 16 sessions run in the same laboratory. However, a computer-mediated experiment was utilized. Each of the participants was randomly assigned to a cubicle with a computer monitor, which showed a randomly pre-selected condition. The participants in the print conditions read the direct marketing offer on the screen at their own pace and then responded to the questionnaire. The participants in the radio conditions listened to the commercial on headsets and then responded to the questionnaire.

Stimuli. Six print versions of direct marketing offers and six radio commercials were prepared, with an addition of an even more complex version (over 15 for both short and long versions).

Dependent Variables. Intention to order was measured on a five-point scale and a thought listing task was included.

Results and Discussion

There was no main effect for complexity but there was one for involvement, such that those who reported high levels of involvement had greater order intentions (2.91 vs. 2.16; $F(1, 239)=21.69$; $p=.000$) than those at low levels of involvement. The interaction between length and medium on intentions was also significant ($F(1, 182)=4.338$; $p =.039$).

The effect of length on counterarguments, with long versions having more counterarguments than short versions, was significant ($F(1, 227)=3.92$; $p =.049$). The effect of medium on support arguments, with print versions having more support arguments than radio versions was marginally significant ($p=.091$).

Reference

Gunning, Robert (1968), *The Technique of Clear Writing*, New York: McGraw Hill.

The Influence of Progress Presentation Format on Repurchase Intention in Loyalty Programs
Jessica Y. Y. Kwong, The Chinese University of Hong Kong, China
Susanna Y. N. Wong, The Chinese University of Hong Kong, China

Studies on loyalty programs have identified important antecedents that facilitate consumers' decision to join a loyalty program (Kivetz 2003), choice of a particular kind of program (Kivetz and Simonson 2002), and program evaluation (Yi and Jeon 2003). However, getting consumers to join a loyalty program is only half the battle. A loyalty program is effective in building customer loyalty only if the program encourages its members to persist and do repurchases.

Progress, defined as the percentage of goal completion, plays a critical role in people's motivation to persist toward a goal. As described by goal gradient principles (Hull 1932), people become more motivated as their progress towards a goal increases. Similarly, consumers have higher intention to repurchase as they get nearer to the end of a loyalty program. A few studies have thus far shown that repurchase intention increases when actual progress increases (Garland and Conlon 1998; Kivetz et al. 2006) and when progress is artificially advanced (Nunes and Dreze 2006). The present research adds to this line of works by showing that the same actual progress could result in different repurchase intentions when the progress information is presented using different formats.

Specifically, we argue that progress information presented by figure displays (e.g., a status triangle) can be more effective in enhancing customers' repurchase intention as compared to the same information expressed in numbers (e.g., 874 points out of 1,900 points). This is because figure displays can induce a greater perceived progress as compared to numerical display when designed appropriately. When expressed in figure displays, progress is indicated by the percentage of shaded area. Because area estimation is often biased by the salient dimension of a figure (Krider, Raghubir, and Krishna 2001), estimation of progress should be biased accordingly.

To illustrate the bias in progress estimation, consider a case where progress is presented using a status triangle. A progress of 46% would be represented by shading 46% of the triangle (shading starts from the top of the triangle). Because people estimate the area of a triangle mainly on the basis of its height, the ratio between the area of the shaded triangle and that of the full triangle (which indicates the progress) will be driven by the ratio of the heights of the two. This will always lead to an overestimation of the percentage of the shaded area and hence the perceived progress. This should in turn enhance program members' intention to persist and repurchase.

We further argue that the above prediction on the greater influence from figure displays will uphold even when the two display formats are used simultaneously. A simultaneous presentation not only provides a more direct test for the unique influence of one format over the other but it also allows us to explore the underlying mechanism for their relative dominance. We propose that figure displays dominate over numerical displays because estimation of progress via the former path is easier.

It is cognitively less demanding to estimate progress in figure displays because consumers substitute the area calculations with a direction comparison of the relative size of the salient dimension only. This turns a numerical computation process into a relatively simple perceptual task. Thus, we may expect that the relative dominance of figure displays should be particularly pronounced when the numerical computation of progress is non-trivial. In other words, figure dominance should be attenuated when the numerical computation of progress is facilitated.

Two scenario experiments with undergraduates as participants were designed to assess our notions. Experiment 1 assessed how perceived progress and repurchase intentions in a loyalty program differed with the use of figure displays versus numerical displays. Participants reported significantly higher perceived progress and intention to repurchase ($ps<.05$) when the progress information was supplemented by a figure display (i.e., a status triangle in which 46% of the area was shaded) than when the same progress information was presented in numbers alone (i.e., you accumulated 874 points out of 1,900 points). This supports the idea that repurchase intention could be enhanced by presenting the same progress in figure displays as compared to numerical displays.

Experiment 2 further tested if the relative influence of figure versus numerical displays is attenuated when the computation of numerical information is easy. A 2 (presentation format: figure displays vs. no figure displays) x 2 (ease of computation: easy vs. difficult) factorial design was employed. In the easy condition, the participants accumulated 460 loyalty points out of 1,000 points, whereas in the difficult condition, the participants accumulated 874 out of 1,900 points. Thus across all the conditions, the participants had completed 46% of the loyalty program but they differed in the ease in calculating the progress (percentage). The interaction between presentation format and ease of computation was significant on both perceived progress and intention to repurchase ($p<.05$). The presence of figure displays significantly increased the perceived progress and intention to repurchase only when the numerical computation is difficult ($ps<.05$), but not when the computation is easy (NS). The results were consistent with our notion that the influences of the two display formats stem from the ease in processing the two modes of information. The advantages of using figure displays to encourage repurchase are compromised when the computation of the actual progress is inherently easy.

In sum, we demonstrated that the formats in which progress information is presented play a substantial role in encouraging loyalty program members to persist and repurchase. The findings also suggest that the effects of presentation formats depend on the ease in processing the two different modes of information.

References

Garland, Howard and Donald E. Conlon (1998), "Too Close to Quit: The Role of Project Completion in Maintaining Commitment," *Journal of Applied Social Psychology*, 28 (22), 2025-2048.

Hull, Clark L. (1932), "The Goal-Gradient Hypothesis and Maze Learning," *Psychological Review*, 39 (January), 25-43.

Kivetz, Ran (2003), "The Effects of Effort and Intrinsic Motivation on Risky Choice," *Marketing Science*, 22 (Fall 2003), 477-502.

Kivetz, Ran and Itamar Simonson (2002), "Earning the Right to Indulge: Effort as a Determinant of Customer Preferences Toward Frequency Program Rewards," *Journal of Marketing Research*, 39 (May), 155-170.

Kivetz, Ran, Oleg Urminsky, and Yuhuang Zheng (2006), "The Goal-Gradient Hypothesis Resurrected: Purchase Acceleration, Illusionary Goal Progress, and Customer Retention," *Journal of Marketing Research*, 43 (February), 39-58.

Krider, Robert E., Priya Raghubir, and Aradhna Krishna (2001), "Pizzas: Pi or Square? Psychophysical Biases in Area Comparisons," *Marketing Science*, 20 (Fall 2001), 405-425.

Nunes, Joseph C. and Xavier Dreze (2006), "The Endowed Progress Effect: How Artificial Advancement Increase Effort," *Journal of Consumer Research*, 32 (March), 504-512.

Yi, Youjae and Hoseong Jeon (2003), "Effects of Loyalty Programs on Value Perception, Program Loyalty, and Brand Loyalty," *Journal of the Academy of Marketing Science*, 31 (3), 229-240.

Consumer Entry Decision in Promotional Games Based on Chance: Do the Perceived Odds of Winning Matter?

Sandra Laporte, HEC Paris, France

Promotional games represent significant investments for marketers: $1.83 billion were spent in 2006 in this kind of sales promotion (Promo Magazine, 2007). Their goals may be to make a product or service known, to collect information for direct marketing purposes or to build brand image. To achieve this, firms often wish to maximize the number of participants. This is particularly true for promotional games relying on a chance mechanism to designate winners (lotteries, sweepstakes, instant win games, etc.), which potentially address a greater number of entrants than skill-based contests. However, so far, consumer research has offered few guidelines on the impact of design characteristics on participation likelihood for promotional games based on chance (Ward and Hill, 1991).

One of these characteristics which directly impacts the cost of the promotion for the firm is the number of prizes, i.e. the number of winners. This piece of information is considered to contribute significantly to the game attractiveness and is made as salient as possible in the associated advertisement (Feinman, Blashek and McCabe, 1987). But are consumers actually sensitive to the number of prizes when making their entry decision? This number is an incomplete indication of the probability to win (i.e. the numerator), since typically no indication is given on the number of participants (i.e. the denominator). Thus, the consumer is placed in a decision under uncertainty, in which the ambiguity on the probability to win stems from the limited availability of probability cues. Following research on scope neglect and magnitude insensitivity (e.g. Frederick and Fischoff, 1998, Kahneman, Ritov and Schkade, 2000, Hsee and Rottenstreich, 2004), our hypothesis is that in most cases, people estimation of their probability to win, and then their participation likelihood, is not an increasing function of the number of prizes. We contend it is due to the lack of *evaluability* of this variable, i.e. the "impossibility to evaluate the desirability of one level when it is presented in isolation" (Hsee, 1996; Hsee et al., 2005): a consumer may not be able to judge if a game offering 10 prizes is associated with a *good* or *bad* probability to win.

Three scenario-based pilot studies investigate the impact on consumer entry likelihood of different kinds of probability cues embedded in advertisements for promotional games based on chance. By probability cue, we refer to the elements in the game design contributing to the probability to win but insufficient to estimate it precisely, like the number of prizes (study 1a: 1 vs. 10 week-end trips to win), the geographical scope of the game (study 1b: 100 winners in Paris vs. 100 in France) or the frequency of drawings (Study 1c: A winner every day vs. every week vs. every month). We only find an impact of the magnitude of the probability cue on participation likelihood in the temporal frequency format: In study 1c, respondents (N=165) declare on a 9-point scale to play more often when the winning instants are happening every day than every month (m_{day}=3.790, m_{month}=1,374, p<0.05). Thus, the evaluability of the probability cue seems greater when it takes the form of the temporal frequency of drawing compared to the number of prizes or the geographical scope of the game.

In Study 2, we test if the insensitivity to the geographical scope of the game is due to the incapacity to estimate the number of participants it represents. People have to give their likelihood to choose between a Gaumont or an UGC movie theater to watch a movie on a Saturday night: the UGC is 10-minute further but is randomly drawing 100 spectators among its multiplexes[13] who each win 10 free tickets. In a full factorial design, we manipulated the geographical scope of the sweepstake (low scope: all spectators in Paris vs. high scope: all spectators in France) and the amount of information (no information vs. the average number of UGC screens and spectators on a

---

[13]In most countries, the entry in a promotional game must not require any monetary consideration in order not to be regarded by the legal interdiction against commercial lotteries (Feinman, 1987).

Saturday night in Paris/France). The probability cue has no impact on respondents estimated probability to win (N=107, m_{Paris}=.389, m_{France}=.586, p=.357[14]), while the amount of information has a main negative effect (m_{noinfo}=1.020, $m_{nbspectators}$=-0.045, p<.001). More interestingly, the interaction between the information amount and the geographical scope is not significant (p=.531), meaning that people do not become more sensitive to the scope when they know its value with precision. It does not reduce the difficulty to figure out if the geographical scope covered by the game is a positive or a negative signal for their probability to win.

Study 3 tests how visualizing the number of prizes makes consumers more sensitive to this probability cue by helping them realizing if, taken into isolation, a given number is large or small. Two between-subject factors are manipulated orthogonally in the ad for a sweepstake: the number of prizes (2 vs. 12 iPods), which is given in digits and the number of pictures showing the prizes (1 picture vs. as many pictures as iPods to win, i.e. 2 or 12 pictures). When only one picture shows the prize category, people estimated probability is not sensitive to the number of prizes, thus replicating study 1a (N=108, m_{2iPods}=0.104, $m_{12iPods}$=0.109, p=0.984), while when there are as many pictures as prizes at stake, respondents estimations become magnitude sensitive (m_{2iPods}= -0.76, $m_{12iPods}$=0.532, p=0.02).

We are currently looking for other means to increase the sensitivity of estimated probability to win to the number of prizes, while gaining more insights about the underlying mechanism. Moreover, this research tackles consumer decision making under an original kind of uncertainty, which is an intermediate case between the absence of any probability cue (i.e. choice under ignorance, e.g. Hogarth and Kunreuther, 1995) and vaguely (or imprecisely) defined probabilities through numerical ranges, verbal expressions or graphical representations (e.g. Kuhn, 1997, Hönekopp, 2003). Here, uncertainty is contextualized in the case where people are only provided with one of the elements necessary to come up with probability estimation, either the numerator part (number of prizes, drawing frequency) or the denominator part (geographical scope).

References

Promo Magazine, 2007 Industry Trends Report http://promomagazine.com/lp/research/2007_Ind_Trnd_Rpt/

Feinman, Jeffrey P., Robert D. Blashek and Richard J. McCabe (1987), *Sweepstakes, Prize Promotios, games and Contests*, McGraw-Hill Education.

Frederick, Shane, & Baruch Fischhoff (1998), « Scope (in)sensitivity in elicited valuations », *Risk, Decision, and Policy*, 3, 109 – 123.

Hogarth, Robin M. and Howard Kunreuther (1995), «Decision Making under Ignorance : Arguing with Yourself », *Journal of Risk and Uncertainty*, 10, 15-36.

Hönekopp, Johannes (2003), « Precision of Probability information and Prominence of Outcomes: A Description and Evaluation of Decision under Uncertainty », *Organizational Behaviors and Human Decision Processes*, 90, 124-138.

Hsee, Christopher K. (1996), « The evaluability hypothesis: An explanation for preference reversals between joint and separate evaluations of alternatives » *Organizational Behavior and Human Decision Processes*, 67, 247–257.

Hsee, Christopher K. and Yuval Rottenstreich (2004), "Music, Pandas and Muggers: On the affective psychology of value", *Journal of Experimental Psychology: General*, 133 (1), 23-30.

Hsee, Christopher K., Yuval Rottenstreich and Zhixing Xiao (2005), "When is more better? On the relationship between magnitude and subjective value", *Current directions in Psychological Science*, 14 (5), 234-237.

Kahneman, Daniel, Ilana Ritov, and David Schkade (2000), « Economic preferences or attitude expressions? An analysis of dollar responses to public issues », In Daniel Kahneman and Amos Tversky (Eds.), Choices, values, and frames (pp. 642– 672). New York: Cambridge University Press.

Kuhn, Kristine, M. (1997), « Communicating Uncertainty: Framing Effects on Responses to Vague Probabilities », *Organizational Decisions and Human Decision Processes*, 71 (1), 55-83.

Ward, James C. and Ronald P. Hill (1991), "Designing effective promotional games: Opportunities and problems", *Journal of Advertising*, 20 (3), 69-81.

The Interpersonal Hot Hand Fallacy: Endorsement of Promotional Games by Previous Winners

Sandra Laporte, HEC Paris, France

Extensive research has already emphasized the specific role of similarity with others on beliefs, judgments (e.g. Feick and Higie 1992; Suls et al. 2000) and behaviors (Burger et al. 2004; Shang et al. 2008) in contexts characterized by incomplete information. This research deals with a new effect of interpersonal similarity: we contend that similarity can affect judgment under uncertainty in the context of promotional games based on chance or state lotteries. This kind of entry decision is characterized by uncertainty since the advertisements designed to recruit the participants do not communicate the probability to win. Thus to answer the question "How likely am I to win this drawing?", we show that people rely on their similarity with the previous winners and believe they have more chances to win the random drawing when they are similar to the previous winner than when they are dissimilar.

A common advertising practice used by brands or national lotteries is consistent with this assumption: it consists in featuring winners of previous drawings, with pictures and few personal details (e.g. first name, age, place of living, occupation), in order to foster the participation in the next drawing (Roger 2005). We confirmed this hypothesis in lab: we manipulated the similarity between subjects and

[14]Analyses were realized on estimated probability to win after the transformation recommended by Tukey (1977, p397). We add 0.5 to the probabilities and then take the Napierian logarithm of the sum.

featured previous winners through age. In the similar condition, the advertisement for the sweepstake showed the picture of a couple of previous winners with about the same age as the respondents, while in the dissimilar condition featured previous winners were older. Age similarity had a significant effect on how much time respondents were willing to spend to enter the sweepstake[15] measured by a 7-point scale (N=113, $m_{sameage}$=3.115 vs. m_{older}=2.03, t=1.799, p<0.05 (one-tailed)).

We contend that similarity with previous winners enhances the entry likelihood through the estimated probability to win. In line with the Attribute Substitution Model (Kahneman and Frederick 2002), consumers may substitute their similarity with previous winners (heuristic attribute) for probability to win the next drawing (target attribute). The three conditions to apply this model are indeed satisfied: First, the probability to win the lottery is not directly available. Secondly, similarity judgment is a natural assessment in social judgment and represents a good candidate as a heuristic attribute: social perception theories have shown that people tend to automatically rely on salient attributes such as gender, age, ethnicity or national origin to categorize people as similar or dissimilar (Brewer and Harasty Feinstein 1999; Fiske et al. 1999; Mussweiler 2003). Thirdly, consumers are likely to rely on heuristics to estimate their probability to win a promotional game based on chance because time and not money is required to participate (Monga and Saini, 2008) and the entry decision is likely to be low-involving. Hence, our main hypothesis is that people may estimate their probability to win as higher when previous winners are similar to them. This pattern of results extends the well-established Hot Hand Fallacy (Gilovich, Vallone and Tversky 1985) from the intrapersonal to the interpersonal domain: People treat similar or dissimilar previous winners as the two possible outcomes of a binary random process. The hot hand is interpersonal because the two consecutive winners are not the same person but are similar. In line with research showing that gamblers tend to believe that luck is an individual attribute responsible for winning (Wagenaar and Keren, 1988; Rogers and Webley, 2001), luck benefits here to a category of persons.

Studies 1a&b tested the Interpersonal Hot Hand Fallacy when interpersonal similarity was manipulated through gender (1a) and educational background (1b). Respondents estimated their probability to win the impending drawing to be greater when the last two winners had the same gender as them (N=50, $m_{samegender}$ =0.872[16] vs. $m_{differentgender}$ =0.286, t=1.817, p (one-tailed)<0.05) or when they were pursuing the same kind of academic studies as them ($m_{samestudies}$=1.077 vs. $m_{differentstudies}$ =0.252; t=2.643 ; p<0.05).

Study 2 replicated the influence of similarity with previous winners on the estimated odds of winning by manipulating similarity through age: the photograph and the associated legend presented either a 70-year old couple (dissimilar condition) or a 29 year-old couple (i.e. the average age of respondents, similar condition). Respondents thought they had higher chances to win the next drawing when they were similar to the previous winners ($m_{sameage}$=0.354[16]) than dissimilar (m_{older}=-0.140, t=2.109, p<0.05), and this difference could not be attributed to the Availability Heuristic. The estimated probability of winning mediated the impact of similarity on participation likelihood (Baron and Kenny 1986, MacKinnon 2007).

Study 3 investigated the impact of the number of similar/dissimilar previous winners featured, as the number of observed previous outcomes has been shown to be a moderator of the Hot Hand Fallacy (Ayton and Fisher, 2002; Johnson, Tellis and Macinnis, 2005). When one single previous winner was featured, the Interpersonal Hot Hand occurred as in previous studies: people estimated they had a higher chance to win the next drawing when the previous winner had the same gender as them than when the previous winner had a different gender (N=43 ; $m_{same\ gender}$= 0.124 vs. $m_{different\ gender}$= -0.870 ; t=2.095 ; p<0.5). When three previous winners were featured, gender similarity had no effect (N=51 ; $m_{same\ gender}$= -0.907 vs. $m_{different\ gender}$= -0.970 ; t=0.135 ; p>0.5). Moreover, the alternative explanation related to the activation persuasion knowledge was ruled out.

The main contribution of this research is to show a new kind of hot hand fallacy caused by a similarity judgment. It also extends the existing literature dealing with the influence of similarity and identity congruency. While unrealistic optimism can bias the evaluation of anonymous, random-picked in-group member on social traits (Klar and Giladi 1997), here we show that the observation of what happened to an anonymous in-group member can also influence the likelihood judgement of an event occurring to oneself.

References

Ayton, Peter and Illan Fischer (2004), "The Hot Hand Fallacy and the Gambler's Fallacy: two faces of subjective randomness?", *Memory and Cognition*, 32 (8), 1369-1378.

Baron, Reuben M. and David A. Kenny (1986), "The moderator-mediator variable distinction in social psychological research: Conceptual, strategic, and statistical considerations", *Journal of Personality and Social Psychology*, 51 (6), 1173-1182.

Brewer, Marilynn B., and Harasty Feinstein, Amy S. (1999), "Dual processes in the cognitive representation of persons and social categories," in *Dual-process theories in social psychology*, Edited by S. Chaiken, and Y. Trope. New York: Guilford Press.

Burger, Jerry M., Nicole Messian, Shebani Patel, Alicia del Prado, and Carmen Anderson (2004), "What a Coincidence! The Effects of Incidental Similarity on Compliance," *Personality and Social Psychology Bulletin*, 30 (1), 35-43.

Feick, Lawrence F. and Robin A. Higie (1992), "The effects of preference heterogeneity and source characteristics on ad processing and judgments about endorsers," *Journal of Advertising*, 21 (2), 9-24.

Festinger, Leon (1954), « A Theory of Social Comparison Processes », *Human Relations*, (7), 117-140.

Fiske, Susan T., Monica Lin, and Steven L. Neuberg (1999), "The continuum model: Ten years later," in *Dual-process theories in social psychology*, Edited by S. Chaiken, and Y. Trope. New York: The Guilford Press, 231-54.

Gilovich, Thomas, Robert Vallone and Amos Tversky (1985), "The hot hand in basketball: on the misperception of random sequences", *Cognitive Psychology*, 17, 295-314.

Johnson, Joseph, Gerard J. Tellis and Deborah J. Macinnis, (2005), "Losers, Winners, and Biased Trades", *Journal of Consumer Research*, 32 (september), 324-329.

---

[15] We use this dependent measure to be consistent with the interdiction in many countries to ask for a consideration to enter a game based on chance. Thus, the cost of participating is related to time and effort spent.

[16] Analyses were realized on estimated probability to win after the transformation recommended by Tukey (1977, p.397). We added 0.5 to the probabilities and then took the Napierian logarithm of the sum.

Kahneman, Daniel and Shane Frederick (2002), "Representativeness revisited: Attribute substitution in intuitive judgment". pp. 49-81 in Thomas Gilovich, Dale Griffin, and Daniel Kahneman [eds]. *Heuristics & Biases: The Psychology of Intuitive Judgment.* New York. Cambridge University Press.

Klar, Yechiel, and Eilath E. Giladi (1997), "No one in my group can be below the group's average: A robust positivity bias in favor of anonymous peers." *Journal of Personality and Social Psychology,* 73, 885-901.

MacKinnon, David P., Amanda J. Fairchild, and Matthew S. Fritz (2007), "Mediation analysis," *Annual Review of Psychology,* 58 (1), 593-614.

Monga, Ashwani and Ritesh Saini (2008), "How I decide depends on what I spend: Use of Heuristics is greater for Time than for Money", *Journal of Consumer Research,* 34 (6), 914-922.

Mussweiler, Thomas (2003), "Comparison processes in social judgment: Mechanisms and consequences," *Psychological Review,* 110 (3), 472-89.

Roger, Patrick (2005), *Lotomania : Approche scientifique du jeu et du comportement des joueurs*, Village Mondial: Paris.

Rogers, Paul and Paul Webley (2001), "It could be us! Cognitive and Social Psychological factors in UK National Lottery Play", *Applied Psychology: An International Review,* 50 (1), 181-199.

Shang, Jen, Americus I. Reed, and Rachel Croson (2008), "Identity congruency effects on donations," *Journal of Marketing Research,* 45 (3), 351-61.

Suls, Jerry, René Martin, and Ladd Wheeler (2000), "Three kinds of opinion comparison: The triadic model," *Personality and Social Psychology Review,* 4 (3), 219-37.

Tukey, John W. (1977), *Exploratory Data Analysis*, Addison-Wesley Publishing Company, Inc.

Wagenaar, Willem A. & Gideon B. Keren (1988), « Chance and Luck are not the same », *Journal of Behavioral Decision Making,* 1, 65-75.

The Effects of Expertise on the Processing of Alignable Versus Nonalignable Features

Myungwoo Nam, INSEAD, Singapore

Jing (Alice) Wang, University of Iowa, USA

Angela Y. Lee, Northwestern University, USA

What makes a product different than other competing products? To come up with a brand positioning, marketers need to identify a point of difference that makes its product different from other competing brands. For example, Sharp argues that its LCD panels have superior response times compared to other brands, making its TVs better equipped to show fast-action programs such as sporting events. On the other hand, Sony's Playstation 3 emphasizes that it is the only new generation console that is capable of playing Blu-ray discs and differentiate itself from Microsoft's XBOX 360 which cannot play high definition video format without an add-on HD DVD drive. All of these positioning strategies strive to win over consumers by communicating product information that differentiates their brand from the competitors. They differ, however, in the type of differentiating feature they promote. The first positioning strategy focuses on attribute values that are different along the same dimension. We refer to this strategy as emphasizing alignable differences. On the other hand, the latter strategy emphasizes the feature that is unique to a particular brand. We refer to this type of strategy as differentiating on nonalignable differences.

An important question to marketers is which of these two strategies is more effective in differentiating its brand compared to other competing options. Prevailing findings in the literature suggest that alignable differences influence consumer decisions more than nonalignable differences because alignable differences are easier to compare than nonalignable differences (Gentner and Markman 1993; Zhang and Markman 1998).

The current study investigates a condition under which nonalignable differences are used as a basis of product evaluation that differentiates alternative options. Specifically, consumer expertise is identified as a moderating variable that influences processing of alignable versus nonalignable options.

The relative importance of alignable differences in product comparison and choice can be explained by the diagnosticities of types of attributes as well as ease of processing of alignable features relative to nonalignable features (Feldman and Lynch 1988; Zhang and Markman 1998). Specifically, alignable differences can be directly compared across different options and allow unambiguous comparisons (Slovic and MacPhillamy 1974). The ease of comparison between two alignable features makes them diagnostic in product evaluation. For example, even a novice consumer who has little knowledge about digital cameras can use number of pixels as an indicator of picture quality in choosing camera. On the other hand, consumers will have difficulties in comparing two brands on nonalignable differences. One of the reasons is that it is difficult for consumers to determine how good nonalignable attributes are without making direct comparisons with other brands. When judging the expected utility of a nonalignable attribute value, consumers need to have sufficient knowledge to interpret the expected benefit of attribute level, and make a comparison between it and the relevant standard from memory. Given the difficulty of interpreting expected benefit of the nonalignable attribute, novice consumers would resort to cognitively less demanding task of comparing alignable attributes.

The current study focuses on the effects of expertise on processing of alignable versus nonalignable features. Experts' familiarity with the product category reduces cognitive effort and frees up cognitive resources (Alba and Hutchinson 1987). In addition, experts are better able to infer associated benefits from attributes than novices (Maheswaran and Sternthal 1990).

This analysis suggests that despite the majority of studies that found dominance of alignable differences over nonalignable differences in product judgment, consumer expertise may moderate this effect. When consumers have substantial knowledge about the product category, it is likely that they would focus more on nonalignable features rather than alignable features. Specifically, we hypothesize that more knowledgeable consumers are better able to infer the benefits of nonalignable features, and that this ability would make them to pay more attention to nonalignable features and use them as a basis for their judgments.

Three studies were conducted to test this hypothesis. Study 1 investigated relative attention that participants place on alignable versus nonalignable differences. It was expected that experts would pay more attention to nonalignable differences than novices because their abilities to process and compare nonalignable differences is greater than those of novices. The study had a one factor (expertise: high vs. low) between-subject design. MP3 player category was chosen as a focal product category. The results showed that there was a main effect of expertise. The analysis revealed that the percentage of experts who chose alignable difference (8.7%) was much smaller than experts who chose nonalignable differences (91.3%) as the most distinguishing feature. On the other hand, 37.5% of novices chose alignable difference and 62.5% of them chose nonalignable difference as the most distinguishing feature (χ^2 (45)=5.44, $p<.02$).

Study 2 investigated how experts and novices search for alignable versus nonalignable product information. The study had a 2 (alignable vs. nonalignable) x 2 (experts vs. novices) mixed design. One hundred twenty seven undergraduate participants were asked to evaluate two brands of tennis racquet after reviewing product information on the computer. The results showed a main effect of alignability, such that participants reviewed more alignable features than nonalignable features ($M=5.01$ vs. 3.88; $F(1, 125)=62.66$, $p<.001$). Subsequent planned contrasts showed that novices reviewed more alignable features than experts ($M=5.16$ vs. 4.86; $t(125)=2.05$, $p<.05$), whereas experts reviewed more nonalignable features than novices ($M=4.03$ vs. 3.73; $t(125)=1.96$, $p<.05$). The results of study 2 showed that experts focused more on nonalignable features than alignable features. On the other hand, novices paid more attention to alignable features than nonalignable features.

Study 3 used brand evaluations as a dependent measure to test the effects of expertise on processing of alignable versus nonalignable features. A 2 (experts vs. novices) x 2 (superior alignable vs. superior nonalignable) design was used. Similar to study 1, MP3 player category was used. The results indicated that the interaction between these factors was significant. Follow up contrasts revealed that experts evaluated the target brand more favorably in superior nonalignable condition ($M=5.81$) than those in superior alignable condition ($M=4.98$, $F(1, 96)=10.80$, $p<.001$). The result is consistent with our expectation that experts focus on nonalignable attributes and are able to infer benefits from these attributes. On the other hand, novices evaluated the target brand less favorably in superior nonalignable condition ($M=5.35$) than those in superior alignable condition ($M=3.81$, $F(1, 96)=5.75$, $p<.05$), replicating previous studies that showed consumers' initial focus on alignable features (Zhang and Markman 1998).

References

Alba, Joseph W. and J. Wesley Hutchinson (1987), "Dimensions of Consumer Expertise," *Journal of Consumer Research*, 13 (March), 411-454.

Feldman, Jack M. and John G. Lynch Jr. (1988), "Self-Generated Validity and Other Effects of Measurement on Belief, Attitudes, Intention, and Behavior," *Journal of Applied Psychology*, 73 (August), 421-435.

Gentner, Dedre and Arthur B. Markman (1994), "Structural Alignment in Comparison: No Difference without Similarity," *Psychological Science*, 5(3), 152-158.

Maheswaran, Durairaj and Brian Sternthal (1990), "The Effects of Knowledge, Motivation, and Type of Message on Ad Processing and Product Judgments," *Journal of Consumer Research*, 17 (June), 66-73.

Slovic, Paul and Douglas MacPhillamy (1974), "Dimensional Commensurability and Cue Utilization In Comparative Judgment," *Organizational Behavior and Human Performance*, 11(2), 172-194.

Zhang, Shi and Arthur B. Markman (1998), "Overcoming the Early Entrant Advantage: The Role of Alignable and Nonalignable Differences," *Journal of Marketing Research*, 35, 413-426.

Best-Laid Plans…: Understanding the Processes Underlying the Planning Fallacy

Jaehoon Lee, University of Texas at San Antonio, USA
L. J. Shrum, University of Texas at San Antonio, USA
Jongwon Park, Korea University, Republic of Korea

Abstract

The planning fallacy refers to the systematic tendency to hold a confident belief that one's own task will proceed as planned. Research has provided evidence of the tendency to underestimate the completion time for future tasks. The purpose of this research is to extend the previous research to a consumer behavior context and examine possible underlying processes. Our findings suggest that people underestimate their shopping completion times but overestimate their shopping duration times. Our findings also indicate that people with a high interpersonal locus of control tend to underestimate the shopping times more so than those with a low interpersonal locus of control.

Conceptual Background

Most people have probably had the experience of planning to complete a paper within a few days but taking a week to complete it because they underestimated the time to complete the paper. This is referred to as the *planning fallacy*, which is the systematic tendency for people to underestimate how long a task will take to complete, even though they are often aware that certain types of tasks invariably take longer to complete. A number of studies (Buehler and Griffin 2003; Buehler, Griffin, and Ross 1994; Byram 1997; Newby-Clark et al. 2000) have demonstrated that this tendency is surprisingly robust and has been shown to persist regardless of whether people are asked to consider various possibilities (e.g., future, pessimistic, or optimistic scenarios, need for accuracy, task decomposition). However, despite this robustness, surprisingly little is known about the underlying processes (but see Kruger and Evans 2004). The purpose of the current research is to address that issue. As a first step, we begin by investigating possible individual differences variables that may moderate the effect.

One individual difference variable we expected to moderate the planning fallacy effect is locus of control. Locus of control refers to the degree to which people believe that outcomes of their actions are under their own control (internal locus of control) or outside their own control (external locus of control(Paulhus 1983). Paulhus specified three primary spheres of control: *personal efficacy* that is associated with personal achievement, *interpersonal control* that is associated with other people and groups, and *sociopolitical control* that is associated with social and political events. Within each of these dimensions, people with an internal locus of control believe they have control over their actions and outcomes, whereas people with an external locus of control believe they have little control. If one explanation for the planning fallacy effect is that people tend to underestimate the external forces that can upset their plans for task completion and overestimate their ability to control those external forces, then we would expect internals (relative to externals) to exhibit more of a planning fallacy effect and thus underestimate the time it would take to complete a given task.

A second individual difference variable we investigated was regulatory focus (Higgins 1987). Regulatory focus is a theory of self-regulation that proposes two types of foci: a promotion focus (primarily concerned with maximizing gains) and a prevention focus (primarily concerned with minimizing losses). Promotion-focused people are oriented towards fulfilling their hopes and aspirations, whereas prevention-focused strive to avoid negative outcomes and failures. If one explanation for the planning fallacy effect is that people look at shorter completion times as more "successful" than longer completion times, then promotion-focused people should show a larger planning fallacy effect than prevention focused people.

In sum, we expect a planning fallacy main effect, but we expect this effect to be qualified by two separate interactions with locus of control and regulatory focus.

Method

About three weeks before Valentine's Day, students (n=133) who had a significant other, were planning on buying a Valentine's Day gift, and had not completed the gift purchase yet were randomly assigned to one of three experimental conditions: a best-case scenario (assume that "things will go as well as they possibly can"), worst-case scenario (assume that "things will go as poorly as they possibly can"), and a no-scenario condition. In the best- and worst-case conditions, participants were instructed to make predictions based on the scenarios (i.e., told that if the scenario they described is what actually happens to them, when will they complete their Valentine's Day shopping (completion time) and how long will it actually take them to do the shopping (duration)). Next, participants were asked to make final predictions on their actual completion time and shopping duration (ignoring their scenarios). Participants in the no-scenario condition made final predictions only. Next, participants completed the locus of control (Paulhus 1983) and regulatory focus measures (Higgins et al. 2001). A few days after Valentine's Day, participants were contacted and asked when they had completed their shopping (actual completion times) and how long it took them (actual duration times).

Results

We tested for an overall planning fallacy effect by examining the differences between the predicted and actual completion time and shopping duration as a function of scenario condition. People underestimated their shopping completion times regardless of their scenario condition (ps<.001). The planning fallacy effect is indicated in the no-scenario condition in which participants' predicted completion times averaged 12.4 days but their actual completion times averaged 15.6 days, or about a 25% underestimation. In spite of this general underestimation of completion time, however, participants *overestimated* how long it would take them to actually conduct the shopping (duration), again regardless of condition (ps<.02). In addition, the degree of the overestimates of shopping duration was greater in the best-case scenario than in the worst-case scenario (p<.05).

We next investigated the effects of the individual difference variables on the planning fallacy effect. The magnitude of the planning fallacy did not differ as a function of any of the individual difference variables. However, in terms of estimating the duration of shopping time, those with low interpersonal control overestimated their shopping duration time (M=67.9 min.) to a greater degree than those with high interpersonal control (M=38.6 min.). However, due to high variability, this difference was not significant (p=0.14). In addition, interpersonal control moderated the planning fallacy effect in the best-case condition, with those high in interpersonal control underestimating to a greater degree than those low in interpersonal control (M=2.67 days vs. -.21 days, with a negative number indicating overestimation, p<.10). We also found that people with high sociopolitical control overestimated shopping duration to a greater degree (M=81.05 min.) than those with low sociopolitical control (M=42.06 min., p<.05) and that people with high prevention focus overestimated shopping duration to a greater degree (M=62.1 min.) than those with a low prevention focus (M=32.65 min., p<.10).

In conclusion, in this experiment we replicated previous research on the planning fallacy effect, and did so within a consumer behavior context. We also provided preliminary evidence of some possible underlying mechanisms. Future research will be aimed at better understanding the individual differences results and developing methods for manipulating the underlying processes.

References

Buehler, Roger and Dale Griffin (2003), "Planning, Personality, and Prediction: The Role of Future Focus in Optimistic Time Predictions," *Organizational Behavior and Human Decision Processes*, 92, 80-90.

Buehler, Roger, Dale Griffin, and Michael Ross (1994), "Exploring the "Planning Fallacy": Why People Underestimate Their Task Completion Times," *Journal of Personality and Social Psychology*, 67 (3), 366-81.

Byram, Stephanie J. (1997), "Cognitive and Motivational Factors Influencing Time Prediction," *Journal of Experimental Psychology: Applied*, 3 (3), 216-39.

Higgins, E. Tory (1987), "Self-Discrepancy: A Theory Relating Self and Affect," *Psychological Review*, 94 (3), 319-40.

Kruger, Justin and Matt Evans (2004), "If You Don't Want to Be Late, Enumerate: Unpacking Reduces the Planning Fallacy," *Journal of Experimental Social Psychology*, 40, 586-98.

Newby-Clark, Ian R., Michael Ross, Roger Buehler, Derek J. Koehler, and Dale Griffin (2000), "People Focus on Optimistic Scenarios and Disregard Pessimistic Scenarios While Predicting Task Completion Times," *Journal of Experimental Psychology: Applied*, 6 (3), 171-82.

Paulhus, Delroy (1983), "Sphere-Specific Measures of Perceived Control," *Journal of Personality and Social Psychology*, 44 (6), 1253-65.

Preserve Self or Impress Others: Mortality Proximity and Guilt Advertising
Sooyeon Nikki Lee-Wingate, Fairfield University, USA

Since the initial discussions by Ghingold (1981), the construct of consumer guilt has received some attention in the consumer behavior literature (e.g., Lascu 1991), mostly related to hedonic or luxury consumption (Kivetz and Simonson 2002). To further enrich understanding of the guilt construct, the current research investigates conditions under which advertising utilizing guilt appeals can be more effective.

Guilt appeals stress how you should (or should not) do something in order to avoid violating moral standards, as such transgressions will produce unwanted guilt. I classify guilt appeals into two categories, based on the focal users of the market offering and the direction of intended guilt manipulation. Interestingly, these two types attempt to manipulate the amount of guilt people anticipate in two opposite directions. The first category, *guilt-lessening appeals*, focuses on indulgences for purchasers themselves (e.g., spa treatment, expensive jewelry, etc.) to lessen guilt most consumers feel about self-indulgent consumption. These argue: "It's about time you *should* do something for yourself. You are worth it." The second category, *guilt-magnifying appeals*, intends other people than the purchaser as the focal users (e.g., children's education, birthday gifts, insurance, wills, etc.) and attempt to magnify the level of guilt most consumers feel about having to uphold socially desirable behaviors involving their loved ones. These ask "Are you doing what you *should* be doing for your loved ones?" In this research, the compliance to these two types of guilt appeals is the primary dependent variable.

The extant literature suggests a list of mediators of the process within which advertising appeals influence guilt perceptions and purchase intentions of consumers: self-esteem (Ghingold 1981; Lascu 1991), locus of control (Rotter 1966; Ghingold 1981; Lascu 1991), susceptibility to guilt (Kivetz and Simonson 2002), motivation to comply (Carlsmith and Gross 1969), and self-competence (Deci 1975; Lascu 1991), to name a few. However, few moderators have been studied. Specifically, under which conditions can guilt appeals be more effective, regardless of individual-level mediators? Moreover, do these moderators operate in unique processes?

The key moderator in this research is drawn from mortality salience, a well-studied construct in the Terror Management Theory (TMT; see Greenberg, Solomon, and Pyszczynski 1997). I draw on the two different motivations underlying TMT: self-preservation and impression management. Mortality salience has been shown to increase likelihood of behaviors that *a)* preserve own material interests, under self-preservation motivation, and *b)* are socially desirable, under impression motivation (Maheswaran and Agrawal 2004). Consistent with the self-preservation motivation of defending own material interests and increasing self-worth, mortality facilitates purchase of high-status objects (Mandel and Heine 1999), for which guilt-lessening appeals are usually employed. Similarly, materialism helped buffer consumers from mortality (Arndt, Solomon, Kasser, and Sheldon 2004). In these contexts, mortality salience appears to foster the motivation where a boost of self-worth becomes compulsory–which may simultaneously favor compliance to guilt-lessening appeals. At the same time, mortality salience has also been linked to impression motivation that promotes socially desirable behaviors (Jonas, Schimel, Greenberg and Pyszczynski 2002). Socially desirable behaviors usually involve other people, who often are the foci of guilt-magnifying appeals. In this line of reasoning, I hypothesize that preservation motivation will increase compliance to guilt-lessening appeals that promote self-indulgent consumption, whereas impression management will increase compliance to guilt-magnifying appeals that recommend socially desirable consumption.

It is important to distinguish these two distinct mechanisms of motivation (Maheswaran and Agrawal 2004). I hypothesize a new variable of mortality proximity to do exactly that. It is interesting that TMT literature does not differentiate the focal death person in terms of proximity to the perceivers (proximal vs. distal). If a consumer feels a specific type of death is proximal to him or herself, then it will not only generate stronger effects of death-thought accessibility, but also create and strengthen specific motivation regarding self-preservation (versus social impression management) for subsequent behaviors. For example, if a college-aged student views news about how some college students commit suicides, then the resulting death-thought accessibility will be more focused on self-preservation motivation (perhaps resulting in the purchase of a luxury item for oneself) than viewing a story about rising occurrences of deaths caused by breast cancer in middle-aged women, which may perhaps be more focused on impression management motivation regarding their mothers (perhaps resulting in buying a luxury gift for mother's day).

Thus the hypotheses to be tested in this research are as follows:

H1: Proximal mortality will increase compliance to guilt-lessening appeals via inducing motivation of self-preservation.

H2: Distal mortality will increase compliance to guilt-magnifying appeals via inducing motivation to enhance socially desirable impressions.

The results of this research will theoretically aid the understanding of how consumer guilt construct operates in the advertising context, considering mortality proximity as a moderator. In addition, results will contribute to the progress of literature on mortality by suggesting a moderator that determines which process is evoked under mortality salience. Practical recommendations of this research inform advertisers using guilt appeals to choose a context that primes the appropriate sort of mortality proximity. For example, TV shows such as ER, House, Law and Order, or CSI mentioning particular sicknesses, murders, or accidental deaths that may proximally affect a particular segment more so than others can be considered to maximize favorable receptivity of guilt appeals.

References

Arndt, Jamie, Sheldon Solomon, Tim Kasser, and Kennon M. Sheldon (2004), "The Urge to Splurge: A Terror Management Account of Materialism and Consumer Behavior," *Journal of Consumer Psychology*, 14 (3), 198-212.

Carlsmith, J. Merrill and Alan E. Gross (1969), "Some Effects of Guilt on Compliance," *Journal of Personality and Social Psychology*, 11 (3), 232-239.

Deci, Edward (1975), *Intrinsic Motivation*, New York: Plenum Press.

Ghingold, Morry. (1981). "Guilt Arousing Communications: An Unexplored Variable," in Kent Monroe (ed.), *Advances in Consumer Research*, 8, 442-8. Ann Arbor: Association for Consumer Research.

Greenberg, Jeff, Sheldon Solomon, and Tom Pyszczynski (1997), "Terror Management Theory of Self-esteem and Social Behavior: Empirical Assessments and Conceptual Refinements," in M. P. Zanna (ed.), *Advances in Experimental Social Psychology*, New York: Academic, 61-139.

Jonas, Eva, Jeff Schimel, Jeff Greenberg, and Tom Pyszczynski (2002), "The Scrooge Effect: Evidence that Mortality Salience Increases Prosocial Attitudes and Behavior," *Personality and Social Psychology Bulletin*, 28(10), 1342-1353.

Kivetz, Ran and Itamar Simonson. (2002a). "Self Control for the Righteous: Toward a Theory of Pre-commitment to Indulgence," *Journal of Consumer Research*, 29 (September), 199-217.

Lascu, Dana-Nicoleta. (1991). "Consumer Guilt: Examining the Potential of a New Marketing Construct," in Rebecca Holman and Michael Solomon (eds.), *Advances in Consumer Research*, 18, 290-93. Provo: Association for Consumer Research.

Maheswaran, Durairaj and Nidhi Agrawal, (2004), "Motivational and Cultural Variations in Mortality Salience Effects: Contemplations on Terror Management Theory and Consumer Behavior," *Journal of Consumer Psychology*, 14 (3), 213-218.

Mandel, Naomi and Steven J. Heine (1999), "Terror Management and Marketing: He Who Dies with the Most Toys Wins," *Advances in Consumer Research*, 26, 527-532.

Rotter, Julian B. (1966), "General Expectancies for Internal Versus External Control of Reinforcement," *Psychological Monographs*, 609, 1-28.

Mood Awareness and Brand Extension

Kang-Ning Xia, Yuan Ze University, Taiwan
Yu-Tse Lin, Fu Jen Catholic University, Taiwan

This study primary explored the effects of mood on brand extension. Previous research indicated that mood did influence consumers' acceptance of brand extension (Kahn, 1995; Menon and Kahn, 1995). For example, consumers with positive mood may adopt more diverse brand extensions than consumers with negative mood (Barone, Miniard, and Romeo, 2000). In other words, the happy ones can accept the larger difference between extension brand and parent brand than the sad ones. In spite of rich evidence that show the influence of mood on brand extension, there was little research discussing the mechanism behind the influence process.

Furthermore, previous research about the relationship of mood and brand extension neglected the issue of the mode of brand extension. When firms execute brand extensions, there are at least two types of extension policy (Park, Mileberg, and Lowson, 1991); the first is to focus on the similarity of brand concepts or brand image, for example, Rolex watches extended to its bracelets series. The other is to emphasize on the similarity of product characteristics, such as Timex watches extended to its timekeepers. Therefore, the objective of this study is to discuss if mood has the same influence on these two types of brand extension and the mechanism behind the influence process.

Actually, mood influences consumers' attitudes in a quite complicated way, and the purpose of this study is to probe that in various mood awareness (conscious and unconscious) and mood level (good mood and bad mood), the consumers' acceptance and preference to brand extension may be different. There are two mood awareness condition should be discussed: motivational mood and backdrop mood (Luomala and Laaksonen, 2000). As to the motivational mood, people experience mood in a conscious way and can aware of the source of mood; this kind of mood may involve cognition process. As to the backdrop mood, people are just in good or bad mood without being aware of it.

Mood awareness is the critical factor that influences whether mood influence attitude directly or via cognition components (Xia, 2007). When consumers are under backdrop mood and doesn't aware the source of mood, the mood can reflect to the attitude directly. It means good mood lead to more acceptance of brand extension, while bad mood lead less preference to the brand extension.

On the contrary, when the consumers are under motivational mood and can aware the sources of moods, the mood effect is indirect and involved cognition elements. It means in motivational mood, good mood leads to the heuristic thinking approach, and consumers will care more about the heuristic cues (Monroe, 2003; Suri and Monroe, 2003), for example, the brand image. On the contrary, bad mood leads to the systematic thinking style (Bless, Bohner, Schwarz, and Strack, 1990; Bless, Mackie, and Schwarz, 1992; Mackie and Worth, 1989; Sinclair, Mark, and Clore, 1994; Worth and Mackie, 1987), and the consumers will pay more attention to the attributes that related to the product itself (Xia, 2007).

When applying the above discussion to brand extension, it is suggested that in backdrop mood (unconscious situation), mood influences brand extension attitude directly; It leads to the hypothesis 1:

H1: When consumers in happy mood and can't aware of it (backdrop mood), their preference and recall to brand extension will be higher than the bad mood one.

On the other hand, in motivational mood (conscious) situation, mood will influence consumers' attitude via biasing information process. Good mood leads to pay attention to heuristic cues, for example, the brand image. Therefore, when facing brand extension, consumers prefer the brand concept similarity extension to the product characteristic similarity extension. It leads to the hypothesis 2:

H2: When consumer in a happy mood and can aware of it (motivational mood), their preference and recall to brand concept similarity extension will be higher than to product characteristic similarity extension.

On the contrary, bad mood leads to the systematic thinking style, and the consumers will pay more attention to the attributes that related to the product itself. Hence, bad mood consumers incline to accept the product characteristic similarity extension more. It leads to hypothesis 3:

H3: When consumer in a sad mood and can aware of it (motivational mood), their preference and recall to brand concept similarity extension will be lower than to product characteristic similarity extension.

A 2 (mood level: good vs. bad)*2 (mood awareness: motivational vs. backdrop)*2 (brand extension type: product similarity vs. brand concept similarity) experiment was designed to examined the hypotheses, and there were 160 respondents random assigned in one of the above conditions.

The result of this study can be discussed in two parts. First, in the backdrop mood (unconscious) situation, it is hypothesized mood influences attitude directly. The results supported H1, and show that good mood leads to higher acceptance to brand extension, while bad mood leads to lower preference to brand extension. In the backdrop mood, there is no difference between the acceptances of two modes of brand extension.

In motivational mood, it is hypothesized good mood leads to focus on brand image. The results also supported H2 and indicated that consumers prefer the brand concept similarity extension to the product characteristic similarity extension. Moreover, H3 was also supported by the results that indicated bad mood consumers prefer product characteristic similarity extension more, and relative to product characteristic similarity extension, they don't like brand concept similarity extension.

Reference

Barone, M. J., Miniard, P. W., & Romeo, J. B. (2000). The influence of positive mood on brand extension evaluations. *Journal of Consumer Research*, 26 (3), 386-400.

Bless, H., Clore, G. L., Schwarz, N., Golisano, V., Rabe, C., & Wölk, M. (1996). Mood and the use of scripts: Does happy mood really lead to mindlessness? *Journal of Personality and Social Psychology*, 71, 665-679.

Bless, H., Mackie, D. M., & Schwarz, N. (1992). Mood effects on attitude judgments: Independent effects of mood before and after message elaboration. *Journal of Personality and Social Psychology*, 63, 585-595.

Kahn, B. E. (1995). Consumer variety-seeking among goods and services: An integrative review. *Journal of Retailing and Consumer Services*, 2, 139-148.

Luomala, H., & Laaksonen, M. (2000). Contribution from mood research. *Psychology & Marketing*, 17 (3), 195-233.

Mackie, D. M., & Worth, L. T. (1989). Processing deficits and the mediation of positive affect in persuasion. *Journal of Personality and Social Psychology*, 57, 27-40.

Menon, S., & Kahn, B. E. (1995). The impact of context on variety seeking in product choices. *Journal of Consumer Research*, 22, 275-295.

Monroe, K. B. (2003). *Pricing: Making profitable decisions*. IL: McGraw-Hill/Irwin.

Park, W., Mileberg, S., & R Lowson, R. (1991). Evaluation of brand extensions: The role of product feature similarity and brand concept consistency. *Journal of Consumer Research,* 18 (2), 185-193.

Sinclair, R. C., Mark, M. M., & Clore, G. L. (1994). Mood-related persuasion depends on (mis)attributions. *Social Cognition*, 12, 309-326.

Suri, R., & Monroe, K. B. (2003). The effects of time constraints on consumers' judgments of prices and products. *Journal of Consumer Research*, 30, 92-104.

Xia, K. (2007). *The Effects of Consumers' Moods on Advertising Cognition and Product Attitude*. The PhD Dissertation of Department of Business Administration, National Chengchi University.

Action-Driven Evolution of General and Enduring Preference Hierarchies

Ab Litt, Stanford University, USA

Abstract

How can 'mere' actions and choices, independent of their expected or actual outcomes, shape preferences and choice rationales themselves? A difficulty-varying-α model is constructed to investigate the effects on preferences of making cross-domain product choices in attribute trade-off conflicts. Employing principles of persistence and generality, the model inspires a set of hypotheses regarding the evolution of stable and generalized attribute importance hierarchies, as well as preference amplification and switching behaviors.

Supporting simulation results are described, which form the basis for behavioral experiments in development to test model predictions. Implications for taste acquisition, "lifestyle marketing", and personality are also currently under study.

Conceptualization

The emphasis in much of behavioral decision research is on the processes by which preferences lead to actions, such as choices and judgments. The present work examines the less studied reverse of this relationship: how actions and choices, independent of expected or actual outcomes, affect preferences and choice rationales themselves. A difficulty-varying-α model is constructed to investigate the effects on preferences of making cross-domain product choices in attribute trade-off conflicts (ATCs). The model and accompanying simulations inspire a set of hypotheses concerning the generality of the action-to-preference effects in terms of cross-context evaluation attributes. For instance, if I choose comfy clogs over durable boots, might I become more likely to choose a power-drill with a soft-grip handle than one with a lifetime warranty? Through this generality, the model provides a precise explanatory framework for within-domain findings of Hoeffler and Ariely (1999), and also allows for extended behavioral predictions that both cut across domains and explore more complicated phenomena in action-driven preference evolution. It embodies two basic principles by which actions shape preferences:

1) Persistence: The effects of an individual's actions can influence how the individual continues to act, e.g., in subsequent choices, and so on. That is, preference attribute weights don't simply *shift* following an action, but are able to systematically *evolve* over time and a series of actions.
2) Generality: Re-valuations occur via attribute re-weighting, and so actions can have effects beyond any specific options at hand, on any process or decision which taps those same attributes.

Simulations of multiple ATC decisions are useful for testing and exploring these principles, because they allow for the exact control (or randomization) of initial weights, choice difficulty, ATC presentation order, and interactions thereof. The simulations also inspire behavioral paradigms currently being designed to test various model predictions.

Model and Primary Hypothesis

Choice options are represented as fixed vectors of attribute values, which identify the specific attributes defined as choice-relevant for that option, and the nature of the information available on that attribute (divergence from zero). For instance, products A=[.9, .2, __, __] and B=[.1, .8, __, -.7] might both be defined on durability and price, but eco-friendliness might only be of relevance to product B. A weight vector, w, captures the importance and valence of all the attributes to an overall valuation, V, of an option. This is naturally defined as the dot product of these vectors:

$$V(\text{option X}; w) = <X, w>$$

In an ATC between two options, X and Y, the choice policy is defined to be the selection of the option with higher overall valuation, $V(X; w)$ or $V(Y; w)$. After a choice has been made, attribute weight updating occurs in response to the motivation to resolve dissonance aroused by having to make the ATC choice. Components of w are increased for attributes on which the chosen option, X, is strong and decreased for those on which the X is weak, and vice versa for the rejected option, Y. Given the manner in which w, X, and Y are defined as vectors, this translates into the update rule

$$w \blacklozenge \leftarrow w + \alpha \cdot X - \alpha \cdot Y \text{ (for choosing X, rejecting Y)}$$

The degree to which w is updated in this way on any single choice is determined by the value of α. Here, a variable-alpha approach can be utilized to produce psychologically realistic results. The notion of a variable a (i.e., systematic epoch-to-epoch differences in how much weight is given to new information) is a powerful general principle in machine learning, and seems relevant to other domains of psychology as well. For instance, in learning behaviors, it seems plausible that people use high alphas in early-stage learning (since they have little expertise, and a high alpha allows quick learning of basic and general facets), and then move to reduced alpha values when they have proceeded to later, fine-tuning stages (since low alphas allow behaviors that have already been learned to stay robust against deviations encountered in the exploration of limiting and extreme cases).

Here, it seems natural that a be correlated with the *difficulty* of the decision, since more difficult decisions arouse more dissonance, and greater efforts for dissonance reduction. A clear formulation of ATC difficulty is the degree to which options have close value equivalence, and also exhibit a high degree of trade-off between different attributes. The first aspect is akin to the absolute valuation *difference* between two options. The second corresponds directly to the *orthogonality* of the two option vectors, which is simply the closeness of their dot product to zero. Thus, ATC difficulty for a choice between A and B is defined as follows:

$$\text{difficulty} \propto 1/(<A, B> \cdot |V(A) - V(B)|)$$

This difficulty determination is fed into a sigmoid clamp to define $0 < \alpha < 1$ for a given ATC, giving α approaching 1 with increasing decision difficulty:

$$a = 1/(1 + e^{<A, B> \cdot |V(A) - V(B)|})$$

A key consequence of this variable-α policy and the persistence and generality principles is that, as repeated choices are made in ATCs between different options, the spreading out of attributes caused by a higher a in the early stages will make later choices *easier*, since attribute preferences have been "pulled apart" from each other by choices in earlier ATCs with high between-attribute trade-offs.

This will reduce a for these later choices, and hence the relative change to the weight vector. Thus, even with randomized or zeroed initial weights, and randomized ATC presentation of randomly defined options, a *stabilizing dominance structure* for the attribute weights should eventually arise.

H1: Repeated ATC choices will evolve a stabilized attribute importance weight hierarchy.

Additional behaviors predicted by this model reflect the outcomes of such choice-driven evolution of attribute hierarchies. First, if the evolution process spreads out weights in a manner consistent with how those attributes favored an earlier choice, it can make an individual more satisfied with that earlier choice:

H2: Repeated ATC choices can result in preference amplifications on re-evaluation.

Conversely, if the evolution process spreads out weights in a manner *inconsistent* with how those attributes favored an earlier choice, it can make an individual less satisfied with the earlier choice, and indeed reverse preference directionality:

H3: Repeated ATC choices can result in preference switches/(de-)acquisitions on re-evaluation.

Findings and Future Directions

Support for H1-H3 is provided by a series of six simulation experiments, each using 25 products randomly defined either within-domain (i.e., on all of the same attributes) or sharing definitions for only a sub-set of general attributes. For H1, simulations using five-attribute products beginning with random initial weights evolved dispersed and stable dominance hierarchies within 10 binary ATC iterations (H_a: $\sigma_{init} < \sigma_{final}$; $F(4, 4) = 56.7453$, $p < 0.001$). Similar dominance evolution for *only* shared attributes evolved when ATC choices were simulated for products across different domains. For H2 and H3, valuation computations using initial versus evolved weights showed that, even if the weight evolution process occurred over different product domains, initial preferences could be amplified in some cases ($\approx 44\%$ of pairs, max(|increase|)=187%) and switched in others ($\approx 15\%$ of pairs, max(|reversal|)=213%), depending on the degree to which the sequence of ATC decisions conforms to either the preconditions of H2 or H3.

The low iteration requirements for these simulations suggest practical behavioral tests. Currently under design are repeated cross-domain ATC tasks measuring effects on confidence, WTP, difficulty judgments, distortion, switching propensity, and direct measurement of attribute weights using conjoint analysis techniques. Broader implications of H2-H3 for taste acquisition, "lifestyle marketing", and personality stability are also under study.

Reference

Hoeffler, Steve and Dan Ariely (1999), "Constructing Stable Preferences: A Look into Dimensions of Experience and their Impact on Preference Stability," *Journal of Consumer Psychology*, 8 (2), 113-139.

Consumers Commit the Planning Fallacy for Time but not for Money
Stephen A. Spiller, Duke University, USA
John G. Lynch, Jr., Duke University, USA

The planning fallacy is defined as: "The tendency to hold a confident belief that one's own project will proceed as planned, even while knowing that the vast majority of similar projects have run late" (p. 366, Buehler, Griffin, & Ross, 1994). Because individuals plan for money as well as time, discussions of the planning fallacy often conflate underestimating time costs with underestimating money costs. Kahneman and Tversky (1979), Buehler and colleagues (1994), and others use both cost overruns and schedule overruns as motivating examples of the fallacy, but most subsequent research examines the fallacy only as it pertains to time (though see Ulkumen, Thomas, & Morwitz, 2008, for work on duration-based budgets rather than project-based budgets). We consider the extent to which consumers underestimate time and money expenditures and find that the planning fallacy for money is absent or considerably reduced relative to the planning fallacy for time.

The planning fallacy is usually attributed to using singular data about the plan under consideration to the neglect of distributional data regarding other similar plans (Kahneman & Tversky, 1979; see Buehler, Griffin, & Ross, 2002, for a review), but there is nothing inherently different about using singular vs. distributional data for time or money. Recent research has considered the extent to which time is perceived more flexibly than money (e.g., Okada & Hoch, 2004; Zauberman & Lynch, 2005). To the extent that predictions of money expenditures are either less biased (due to less flexible perceptions) or more binding (due to greater ability or willingness to constrain costs) than predictions for time expenditures, the planning fallacy will be more pronounced for time than for money. Kruger and Evans's (2005) study 1 provides preliminary suggestive evidence by showing that participants who listed everyone on their holiday shopping list (compared to those who did not) estimated that their holiday shopping would require 40% more days, 96% more hours, but only 9% more money. We test the cross-resource difference in the planning fallacy directly using self-reported susceptibility to the planning fallacy and measures of actual and predicted expenditures.

Studies 1a and 1b

In studies 1a and 1b, we measure consumers' beliefs about their own time and money expenditure predictions. In study 1a, 1113 online panelists reported the severity and frequency with which they committed the planning fallacy for time spent on "major projects" or money spent on "major purchases". Participants reported a greater planning fallacy for time than for money as assessed by both severity ($t(1111)=5.13$, $p<.0001$; $M_{Time}=8.417$, $M_{Money}=7.723$ on 13-point scales) and frequency ($t(1111)=7.50$, $p<.0001$, $M_{Time}=2.939$, $M_{Money}=2.284$ on 6-point scales). In study 1b, 1551 online panelists reported the severity and frequency with which they committed the planning fallacy for time or money on "major shopping trips". We replicated the effect for frequency ($t(1549)=3.476$, $p=.0005$; $M_{Time}=2.442$, $M_{Money}=2.199$ on 6-point scales) but not severity ($t(1549)<1$, $p=.3771$; $M_{Time}=4.224$, $M_{Money}=4.171$ on 7-point scales).

Study 2

If consumers commit the planning fallacy for time but not for money, forming more time plans will be associated with having less time than expected, whereas forming more money plans will not be associated with having less money than expected. One hundred five participants reported their propensity to form time or money plans for the short- and long-runs and how much they agreed with the statement "I often find I have less [time / money] at the end of the [day / month] than I expect"; resource was varied between subjects, time span was varied within subjects. Individuals with high propensities to form time plans report having less time than expected ($r_{short-run}=.398$, $p=.003$; $r_{long-run}=.399$, $p=.003$), but individuals with high propensities to form money plans do not report having less money than expected ($r_{short-run}=-.046$, $p>.5$; $r_{long-run}=-.217$, $p>.1$). These cross-resource differences are significant (p's$<.02$).

Study 3

In study 3, we measure actual cross-resource differences in the planning fallacy using predicted and actual time and money expenditures. Ninety-three undergraduate participants completed up to ten online surveys. In survey 1, they described four plans they recently formed (short- and long-run plans for time and money), and how much time or money they expected to spend on each. Every other day for 16 days, participants reported in surveys 2-9 whether they completed each of their short-run plans and, if so, how much time or money they spent on it. Seven to eight weeks later, participants reported in survey 10 the same measures for their long-run plans. Plans that did not have an identified goal or endpoint (e.g., "I plan to stay caught up in my studies daily" has no completion date) were excluded from our analyses. We used log(actual expenditures / expected expenditures) as our dependent variable to allow cross-resource comparisons in the same metric. For uncompleted time plans, we took participants' last report of *not* completing their plan as a conservative proxy for their actual completion time.

Thirty-six participants had useable plans of all four types. A 2 (time, money) x 2 (short-run, long-run) repeated measures ANOVA indicated a main effect of resource ($F(1,35)=18.57$, $p<.0001$); neither the effect of horizon nor the interaction approached significance (p's$>.4$). Participants underestimated their time expenditures ($M_{Log(Actual/Expected)}=.522$, indicating 41% underestimation) and overestimated their money expenditures ($M_{Log(Actual/Expected)}=-.173$, indicating 18% overestimation). A similar analysis using only participants who completed all four plans ($N=21$) showed similar results (Time: $M_{Log(Actual/Expected)}=.175$, indicating 16% underestimation; Money: $M_{Log(Actual/Expected)}=-.189$, indicating 21% overestimation; $F(1,20)=3.32$, $p=.0832$).

Discussion

In three studies, we demonstrated that consumers commit the planning fallacy for time but not for money, that they acknowledge this difference, and that individuals who form more time plans have less time than expected whereas individuals who form more money plans do not have less money than expected. We have not yet explored boundary conditions or tested the process behind these differences. One explanation we are currently examining is that because it may be easier to constrain money expenditures than time expenditures, money expenditure predictions are just as optimistic as time expenditure predictions but are self-correcting because actual money expenditures are constrained to meet the optimistic predictions whereas actual time expenditures are not.

References

Buehler, Roger, Dale Griffin, and Michael Ross (1994), "Exploring the 'Planning Fallacy': Why People Underestimate Their Task Completion Times," *Journal of Personality and Social Psychology*, 67 (September), 366-81.

_____ (2002), "Inside the Planning Fallacy: The Causes and Consequences of Optimistic Time Predictions," in *Heuristics and Biases: The Psychology of Intuitive Judgment*, ed. Thomas Gilovich, Dale Griffin, Daniel Kahneman, New York, NY: Cambridge University Press, 250-70.

Kahneman, Daniel, and Amos Tversky (1979), "Intuitive Prediction: Biases and Corrective Procedures," *TIMS Studies in Management Science*, 12, 313-327.

Kruger, Justin, and Matt Evans (2004), "If You Don't Want to be Late, Enumerate: Unpacking Reduces the Planning Fallacy," *Journal of Experimental Social Psychology*, 40, 586-98.

Okada, Erica Mina, and Stephen J. Hoch (2004), "Spending Time Versus Spending Money," *Journal of Consumer Research*, 31 (September), 313-23.

Ulkumen, Gulden, Manoj Thomas, and Vicki G. Morwitz (2008), "Will I Spend More in 12 Months or a Year? The Effect of Ease of Estimation and Confidence on Budget Estimates," *Journal of Consumer Research*, 35 (August), 245-56.

Zauberman, Gal, and John G. Lynch, Jr. (2005), "Resource Slack and Propensity to Discount Delayed Investments of Time Versus Money," *Journal of Experimental Psychology: General*, 134 (1), 23-37.

Principles of Geometric Accounting. Is Bigger Always Better When It's Free?

Igor Makienko, University of Nevada, Reno, USA

While planning sales promotion campaigns retailers often face a dilemma what to offer as a free gift. Monetary value or cost of a gift is probably the main factor in such a situation. However, gifts of the same monetary value may be very different in their sizes and this factor may affect consumers' deal perceptions.

According to Taylor et al. (1979) visual stimuli that are more salient but not necessary more important may have disproportionate effect on consumer's judgments.

To our knowledge nobody investigated the effect of the actual size of a free gift on deal perceptions and purchase intentions. Literature review reveals few studies that are only reminiscent of our topic. For example, Wansink (1996) reports that larger packages encourage consumption. Package shapes that attract more attention are perceived to contain greater volume of a product (Folkes and Matta, 2004).

In our research we investigate how the price of a promoted product (high vs. low) and the size of a free gift (smaller than vs. bigger than the promoted product) affect consumers' deal evaluations and purchase intentions.

Conceptual Background

We suggest that when the value of a free gift is ambiguous consumers may infer it based on its size and the price of a promoted product.

Krider et al. (2001) propose that initial comparison between two figures is based on a single, most salient at a time of evaluation dimension. Though in sales promotion context consumers do not choose between the two items it is still a joint outcome context (Nunes and Park, 2003) and size dimension may be very salient especially if a gift is bigger than a promoted product.

To estimate the value of a gift, consumers may use some heuristic relating the monetary value of a gift to its size. Based on one of the main assumptions of normative economics-that more is preferred to less we suggest that size-value relation is likely to be positive. However, another factor–price of a promoted product may reverse this relationship.

Low and Lichtenstein (1993) investigated double promotions–when consumers are offered a price discount (Was… Now…) and a free gift–and found that when stated reference price was high, respondents evaluated deals with expensive gifts more favorably than those with cheap gifts. The reverse was true when the stated reference price was low. The authors conclude that higher reference prices 'absorbed' both the discount and high monetary value of a free gift while low reference prices resulted in a 'too-good-to-be-true' situation and negative consumers' attributions that adversely affected deal perceptions. When consumers feel that retailer is giving too much they may question the quality of a product or a gift or both (Friestad and Wright, 1994). Retailer's credibility is likely to be low as well.

In a similar vein Raghubir (2004) suggests that consumers make inferences about the value of a free gift based on the price of a promoted product and expected discount rate in the industry. The author shows that well-established brands may be adversely affected when they are offered as free gifts with low-priced products.

Extending this logic to our context we expect an interaction between the size of a gift and the price of a promoted product. When the price of a promoted product is high, offering bigger size gifts is likely to improve deal perceptions. On the other hand, with low-priced products bigger size gifts will hurt deal perceptions and retailer's credibility.

Methodology

In our study we chose a backpack as a promoted product and a plush toy dog as a free gift and employed a 2 ($60/high vs. $30/low promoted product price) x 2 (gift size smaller than vs. gift size bigger than that of a promoted product) between-subjects full-factorial design.

Results and Major Findings

Manipulation checks showed that price levels and sizes were perceived as intended. Respondents were not significantly different in their perceptions of believability of presented sales promotion and quality of a backpack.

Dependent variables were measured with well-established scales and all scales were reliable (αs ranged from 0.809 to 0.945).

To analyze the data we used one-way ANOVA where condition served as an independent variable. Results for attitude toward the deal ($F(3,114)=5.692$, $p=0.001$), perceived value ($F(3,114)=5.395$, $p=0.002$), purchase intentions ($F(3,114)=3.072$, $p=0.031$) and retailer's credibility ($F(3,114)=3.87$, $p=0.011$) were significant.

Post-hoc tests showed that when a $60 backpack was offered with a smaller dog, respondents had significantly lower deal perceptions and perception of retailer's credibility than in any other condition. This result may be related to a noticeable discrepancy between a $60 price that respondents were exposed to and their estimates of a fair price for a backpack ($31.42) in high price condition. While a bigger size gift was able to justify high deal price, a smaller size gift could not do this job. Enhanced deal perception was due to respondents' higher quality evaluations of a bigger size gift ($p=0.005$).

In a low price condition counter to our hypothesis bigger size gifts did not hurt respondents' deal perceptions and retailer's credibility. Probably $30 price was not low enough to make respondents generate negative attributions about the quality of the dog and influence their deal perceptions. Indeed, perceived quality of the dog in low price conditions did not vary significantly with the change in its size.

Overall our study supports the notion that the size of a free gift may affect deal perceptions. Bigger size gifts with ambiguous monetary values are likely to enhance perception of a deal when they are offered with high-priced products. On the other hand, when price of a promoted product is low bigger size gifts may not help in enhancing deal perceptions.

References

Folkes, Valerie and Shashi Matta (2004), "The Effect of Package Shape on Consumers' Judgments of Product Volume: Attention as a Mental Contaminant," *Journal of Consumer Research*, 31 (2), 390-401.

Friestad, Marian and Peter Wright (1994), "The Persuasion Knowledge Model: How People Cope with Persuasion Attempts," *Journal of Consumer Research*, 21 (1), 1-31.

Krider, Robert E, Priya Raghubir and Aradhna Krishna (2001), "Pizzas: π or Square? Psychophysical Biases in Area Comparisons," *Marketing Science*, 20 (4), 405-26.

Low, George S. and Donald R. Lichtenstein (1993), "The Effect of Double Deals on Consumer Attitudes," *Journal of Retailing*, 69 (4), 453-66.

Nunes, Joseph and Whan C. Park (2003), "Incommensurate Resources: Not Just More of the Same," *Journal of Marketing Research*, 40 (1), 26-38.

Raghubir, Priya (2004), "Free Gift with Purchase: Promoting or Discounting the Brand?" *Journal of Consumer Psychology*, 14 (1/2), 181-6.

Taylor, Shelley E. and Susan T. Fiske (1978), "Salience, Attention and Attribution: Top of the Head Phenomena," in *Advances in Experimental Social Psychology*, Vol. 11, ed. L. Berkowitz, New York: Academic Press, 249-288.

Wansink, Brian (1996), "Can package size accelerate usage volume?" *Journal of Marketing*, 60 (3), 1-15.

Accuracy and Affiliative Motivations in Socially Influenced Decision Making

Ted Matherly, University of Maryland, USA

People are often asked to make decisions based solely on socially acquired information–that is, their observations of the choices of others. Social influence has generally concluded that the general desire to make accurate decisions (Chaiken, Giner-Sorolla and Chen 1996) will lead individuals to conform to the choice of a large number of people, because consensus creates a perception of accuracy (Martin and Hewstone 2001). Recent research by Berger and Heath (2007) demonstrated that this generalized conformity may be moderated by the degree to which a product category is able to serve as a signal of group identity. Given the biasing effects of multiple motivations suggested by social judgment theory (Kruglanski and Sleeth-Keppler 2007), we believe the presence of an affiliative goal, where individuals make choices to express their connections to other people, provides a compelling explanation for observed differences in behavior based on the size of the group of people who have made a particular choice.

We propose that, in a socially influenced choice scenario where an individual can observe groups of differing sizes choosing among options, which are otherwise the same, the individual's varying motivations will influence their choices in a specific way. When no other motivations are active, choices will be consistent with classic theories of social influence (Sherif 1936), such that option selected by the largest group of people will be instrumental to their fundamental accuracy goal. However, when individuals possess an affiliative motivation, it will interact with their accuracy motivation to lead them to seek a means of achieving both goals simultaneously (Kruglanski, et al. 2002). Because options preferred by smaller groups are presumed to be stronger signals of identity (Berger and Heath 2007), the presence of an affiliative motivation will bias their perceptions of what their most accurate choice is, such that they will perceive the option preferred by the smallest group as the most likely means of achieving both goals (Kruglanski and Ajzen 1983).

In a preliminary study, we manipulated participant's affiliative motivation through an article describing a recent victory by their university's football team and answering a series of elaboration questions designed to elicit recollections of the game and the participants' affective reactions to the outcome. In a subsequent, presumably unrelated study, they were asked to make the "best" choice between three brands of a product: one preferred by a majority of a national sample and a small minority of their university's students, another preferred by a small minority of a national sample and a majority of their university's students, and a third choice preferred by larger minorities of both the national and university samples. The modal choice of those participants whose affiliative motivations were not activated by the elaboration task (based on a median split) was that chosen by the majority of the national sample, thereby satisfying an accuracy motivation. On the other hand, those whose affiliative motivations were more likely to select the option preferred by the minority of the national sample and the majority of their fellow university students. These results suggest that the presence of an affiliative motivation may alter perceptions of the "best" choice in a socially influence decision making scenario.

Our program of studies will begin with a more exacting test of the proposed relationships. Participants will first be asked to list several small campus groups that they feel they are a part of. Next, we will activate a general affiliative motivation (as opposed to the university-specific affiliative motivation of the preliminary study) through a lexical decision task combined with subliminal priming of words either associated with the concept of affiliation or of neutral words. Participants will then be presented with a series of supposed product usage data sets; wherein a majority of one of the campus groups they have listed earlier will use the product. In one condition, a minority of the students' full campus will be users, while, in the other, a majority of the campus will be users. Participants will rate their purchase likelihoods and satisfaction with their choices. Thus, our study will use a 2 (prime: affiliative, neutral) between- x 2 (campus user group size: small, large) within- subjects design. We anticipate an interaction of these two factors, such that those in the affiliative prime condition would be more likely to purchase when the campus user group is small vs. large, while we expect the opposite pattern in the neutral prime condition, where accuracy concerns would encourage purchase when a larger number of people have also purchased.

While our findings would provide evidence to suggest a motivational account for varying social influence outcomes, they are somewhat limited due to the artificial nature of the study itself. As a more realistic test of our hypotheses, our second study is designed to replicate a real-world choice situation. Fifteen participants will first complete the same lexical decision priming task from our first study. Next, a networked computerized choice system will present a choice among several brands of products, along with information about how many of the other participants in the lab have chosen each brand. Immediately after, three confederates will register the same choice, creating a small group within the session. Participants will then make their choices at their own pace. We anticipate that those participants with in the affiliative prime condition will be more likely to make their choices earlier, compared to those in the neutral prime condition. They will be more likely to choose with the confederates early on, but as more people choose and the adopting group becomes larger, this likelihood will decrease. On the other hand, those in the neutral prime condition will be more likely to choose with the largest group who has made the same choice.

Our results will provide a convincing demonstration of the role of motivation in guiding the interpretation of social influence information. These findings present useful extensions into other areas of marketing research, including the diffusion of innovations, hot products, as well as the role of individual and decision-level situational factors in influencing decision making.

References

Berger, Jonah and Chip Heath (2007), "Where Consumers Diverge from Others: Identity Signaling and Product Domains," *Journal of Consumer Research*, 34 (August), 121-34.

Chaiken, Shelly, Roger Giner-Sorolla, and Serena Chen (1996), "Beyond Accuracy: Defense and Impression Motives in Heuristic and Systematic Information Processing," in *The Psychology of Action: Linking Cognition and Motivation to Behavior*, ed. Peter M. Gollwitzer and John A. Bargh, New York: Guilford, 553-78.

Kruglanski, Arie W. and David Sleeth-Keppler (2008), "The Principles of Social Judgment." In *Social Psychology: Handbook of Basic Principles*, ed. Arie W. Kruglanski and E. Tory Higgins, New York: Guilford, 116-37.

Kruglanski, Arie W. and Icek Azjen (1983), "Bias and Error in Human Judgment," *European Journal of Social Psychology*, 13 (1), 1-44.

Kruglanski, Arie W., James Y. Shah, Aylet Fishbach, Ron Friedman, Woo Young Chun, and David Sleeth-Keppler (2002), "A Theory of Goal Systems," in *Advances in Experimental Social Psychology*, ed. Mark P. Zanna, 34, 331-376, New York: Academic Press.

Martin, Robin and Martin Hewstone (2001), "Conformity and Independence in Groups: Majorities and Minorities," in *Blackwell Handbook of Social Psychology*, ed. Michael A. Hogg and R. Scott Tindale, 209-34.

Sherif, Muzafer (1936), *The Psychology of Social Norms,* New York: Harper.

Narrative Transportation for Product Evaluation: Can Consumers Make the Difference?

Ellis A. van den Hende, Delft University of Technology, The Netherlands
Brent McFerran, University of British Columbia, Canada

Abstract

Narrative transportation (i.e., immersion into a story) has shown positive results in both psychology and marketing studies. In our product evaluation research with narrative scenarios, increased transportation experienced by the consumer (i.e., the reader) helps to surrogately experience the product and helps to list more benefits. Our results indicate that for some products transportation will increase evaluation, but for others it does not. Transportation, as opposed to what previous literature suggests, provides diverse consumer evaluations.

Visual imagery has shown to facilitate consumers' evaluation of a product (e.g., Hoeffler 2003). One way to facilitate imagination is by using narratives. When reading a narrative, people get lost in the story and experience what the main character experiences. This process is called narrative transportation (Green and Brock 2000). The narrative experience allows readers to have a vivid image of what they read, they feel what the character is feeling, and thus forget the world around them. Solely positive effects of transportation have been reported so far; we aim to extend these findings by showing that transportation can also result in diverse and negative evaluations.

Various studies show that transportation changes the beliefs of the reader. For example, Green and Brock (2000) found that after reading a murder story, increased narrative transportation resulted in a change of beliefs of real world statements (e.g., penalties for murder). Transportation also resulted in more positive evaluations of advertisements (e.g., Escalas 2007). Extending previous research, we will provide deeper understanding of the effects of narrative transportation for product evaluation research with consumers.

We propose that transportation increases differences in product evaluations and predictions of product success. Transported readers should not evaluate all products equally. These readers recognize differences in attractiveness of products. When using product scenarios (i.e., narratives in which a main character is using a product) to evaluate the potential success of products in a new market, increased transportation on the part of the reader facilitates surrogately experiencing the new product. The more the reader gets transported, the more experience is gained and the more benefits are perceived. Perceiving the benefits allows for consideration of these benefits. People who were less transported have not experienced the benefits and will give a lower evaluation. We expect that differences in evaluations and success predictions will be present between people who were transported to a greater extent versus people who were transported to a lesser extent, but this will depend on the valence of the focal product. Transportation facilitates picking up the differences in valence of products. Thus, consumers who are more transported into a scenario about a product that is new to the market will not evaluate all products equally. Thus, we predict an interaction, rather than a main effect, where transportation heightens evaluations for products with high potential market success more than those with a lower likelihood, rather than boosting evaluations for all products.

Products were selected with various levels of success in other markets than the market of the participant population. Pretesting with experts from industry confirmed two food products distinct in level of predicted success on the target market. A scenario was written in which a main character was either eating a special microwaveable ice cream (pretested as a less attractive product for the target market) or drinking a special fruit juice (pretested as a more attractive product for the target market). Both storylines were identical, except for the focal product. Numbers of product features and benefits were balanced. Transportation was manipulated directly (increased vs decreased) through instructions (see Green and Brock 2000), and the two scenarios were used (ice cream vs fruit juice) in a between subjects design (n=107). Levels of transportation (adapted from the Green and Brock 2000 scale), success prediction and product evaluation were measured.

The manipulation check on transportation was successful (F=9.301, p<.01). Results showed a main effect for transportation on the number of benefits listed by the participants (F=4.805, p<.05). Results also showed a significant interaction between the focal product and transportation on product evaluation (F=3.809, p=.05) as well on success prediction (F=9.186, p<.01). Comparing contrasts indicated that the product success predictions and product evaluations differed significantly between increased and decreased transported participants in the fruit juice condition (fruit juice: increased transportation>decreased transportation; product evaluation t=2.296, p<.05, success prediction t=3.558, p<.01), but not in the ice cream condition (product evaluation, t=-.525, NS, success prediction, t=-.822, NS). Thus, higher levels of transportation on the side of the reader into a scenario did not result in more positive evaluations and success predictions for both products. For the fruit juice, higher levels of transportation resulted more positive product evaluation and success prediction. However, for the ice cream the product evaluations and success predictions were equal for higher and lower levels of transportation on the side of the reader.

This study used a positive and negative product (as pretested). Apparently, either our scenario or our transportation manipulation was not strong enough to reverse the effect of transportation for the ice cream that was pretested as a product with more negative valence. In a next study we will manipulate the valence of the ice cream in the scenario directly (positive vs negative). We will combine this variable with transportation instructions (increased vs decreased) in a between subjects design. We expect to find that transportation increases the perceived negative impression of the ice cream that was showing up in the first study.

Discussion

With our studies we provide insight in the process of transportation for product evaluations. Our results indicate that for some products transportation will increase evaluation, but for others it does not. Transportation, as opposed to what previous literature suggests, provides diverse evaluations of competing products. In a follow up study we would like to show the mechanism of benefit processing. It could be that with the help of narrative transportation consumers can behave like experts and predict market success successfully through the use of narratives or scenarios.

References

Escalas, Jeniffer Edson (2007), "Self-Referencing and Persuasion: Narrative Transportation Versus Analytical Elaboration," *Journal of Consumer Research*, 33 (March), 421-29.
Green, Melanie C. and Timothy C. Brock (2000), "The Role of Transportation in the Persuasiveness of Public Narratives," *Journal of Personality and Social Psychology*, 79 (November), 701-21.
Hoeffler, Steve (2003), "Measuring Preferences for Really New Products," *Journal of Marketing Research*, 40 (November), 406-20.

Blue or Red? Exploring the Effect of Color on Cognitive Task Performances

Ravi P. Mehta, University of British Columbia, Canada
Rui (Juliet) Zhu, University of British Columbia, Canada[17]

Color is a basic aspect of human perception and has intrigued many researchers to study its impact on cognition and behavior. For example, color has been shown to affect test performance (Soldat et al.1997) and well being of hospital patients (Verhoeven et al. 2006). Research in marketing has shown that cool colors (e.g., blue) are often associated with more favourable product evaluations, higher purchase intentions, and a stronger inclination to shop (Babin et al. 2003).

While the above findings are intriguing, they often lack rigorous theoretical understanding of why those effects occur. In addition, inconsistent results have been reported in the color literature. For example, conflicting results have been found as to whether warm versus cool colors enhance cognitive task performance. While some researchers have found that cool color (e.g., blue) led to better performance than warm color (e.g., red; Elliot et al. 2007; Soldat et al. 1997), others have observed the opposite (e.g., Hatta et al. 2002; Kwallek and Lewis 1990).

This paper intends to reconcile the above discrepancy and advance theoretical understanding of how and why color affects human cognition. We suggest that different colors can activate alternative types of regulatory focus, and consequently affect performances on different types of cognitive tasks. People also develop shared associations with colors (Elliot et al. 2007). While red is often associated with dangers and mistakes (Elliot et al. 2007), blue is frequently associated with openness and freedom (e.g., sky and ocean; Kaya and Epps 2004). Such color-induced associations have the potential to activate alternative types of regulatory focus. Regulatory focus theory suggests that people can achieve their goals in two different ways, either with a promotion or a prevention regulatory focus (Higgins 1987). Individuals who adopt a promotion focus perceive their goals as hopes and aspiration, and *eagerly* approach matches to their goals. In contrast, those who adopt a prevention focus perceive their goals as duties and obligations, and *vigilantly* avoid mismatches to their goals. We propose that red, due to its associations to danger and failures, is likely to activate a prevention focus because it cautions people to guard against such negative outcomes. Blue, however, is expected to activate a promotion focus, due to its associations to openness and freedom and thus its focus on achieving positive outcomes. Further, empirical studies involving regulatory focus theory have revealed that while a promotion focus increases performance speed and creativity, a prevention focus enhances performance accuracy (Friedman and Forster 2001; Forster et al. 2003). Following this line of research, we hypothesize that red, if activating a prevention focus, should enhance performance on detail-oriented cognitive tasks, whereas blue, if activating a promotion focus, should lead to better performance on creative tasks. A series of experiments provide systematic support to our theorizing.

[17]The authors would like to thank Joan Meyers-Levy for her very helpful comments on an earlier version of the paper. Financial support from the Social Sciences and Humanities Research Council of Canada is gratefully acknowledged.

All studies were run on computers and color was manipulated via background screen color. The first study employed two tasks to test the basic hypothesis that red/blue can induce primarily a prevention/promotion focus. First task involved indicating a preference for a prevention or a promotion focused brand from the same product category (Zhou and Pham 2004). The second task asked participants to solve a set of anagrams containing prevention, promotion or control target words. Results supported our hypothesis that red (blue) activates primarily a prevention (promotion) focus. Individuals in the red (blue) condition showed higher preference for brands featuring prevention (promotion) benefits and took significantly less time to solve prevention (promotion) focused anagram words. An auxiliary study demonstrated that our color manipulation did not affect mood.

Study 2 examined whether red (blue), due to activated prevention (promotion) focus, can enhance performance on detail-oriented (creative) cognitive tasks. A detailed-oriented task (a memory task) and a creative task (generating creative uses of a brick) were employed. As anticipated, better performance (i.e., accuracy) was observed in the red versus blue or control condition for the memory task, while those in the blue condition produced more creative responses in the creative task.

Study 3 replicated study 2 results using a different set of tasks, namely a proofreading task (detail-oriented) and a Remote Associates Test (creative task; Mednick 1962). More importantly, it offered insights on the underlying mechanism. We found that red can activate a prevention focus and thus enhance performance on a task requiring attention to detail, whereas blue can activate a promotion focus and therefore enhance performance on the creative task.

In the final study, we tested an important marketing implication from our theorizing. If red leads to prevention focus, it should enhance persuasion when paired with an ad that features images that are unambiguously related to the target product (e.g., specific product details). This is so because such clearly unambiguous, product-related images ensure these prevention-focused individuals that everything is in order and the ad involves no ambiguity. In contrast, blue, due to its activation of promotion focus, should enhance persuasion when paired with an ad that features images that are remotely related to each other and to the product. As such a setup provides opportunities for these promotion-focused individuals to engage in creative processing. An ad featuring either unambiguously or remotely related images was adopted from Zhu and Meyers-Levy (2007). As expected, those in the red condition were more persuaded when the ad featured unambiguously related images than remotely related ones, whereas the opposite was true for those in the blue condition.

In sum, findings from this paper contribute to our knowledge in two ways. First, it reconciles a conflicting set of results observed in the color literature (i.e., whether red or blue enhances cognitive performance?). We demonstrate that while red leads to a prevention focus and thus better performance on detail-oriented tasks, blue leads to a promotion focus and thus better performance on creative tasks. Second, findings from this research offer important marketing insights. While prior research has demonstrated that blue generally leads to more favorable consumer responses, our theory and data suggest conditions where red can enhance persuasion.

References

Babin, Barry J., David M. Hardesty and Tracy A. Suter (2003), "Color And Shopping Intentions: The Intervening Effect Of Price Fairness And Perceived Affect," *Journal of Business Research*, 56, 541– 551.

Elliot, Andrew J., Markus A. Maier, Arlen C. Moller, Ron Friedman and Jorg Meinhardt (2007), "Color and Psychological Functioning: The Effect of Red on Performance Attainment," *Journal of Experimental Psychology: General*, 136(1), 154–168.

Forster, Jens, Tory E. Higgins, and Amy Taylor Bianco (2003), "Speed/accuracy decisions in task performance: Built-in trade-off or separate strategic concerns? ," *Organizational Behavior and Human Decision Processes*, 90, 148-164.

Friedman, Ronald S., and Jens Forster (2001), "The Effects of Promotion and Prevention Cues on Creativity," *Journal of Personality and Social Psychology*, 81 (6), 1001-1013.

Hatta, Takeshi, Hirotaka Yoshida, Ayako Kawakami, Masahiko Okamoto (2002), "Color Of Computer Display Frame In Work Performance, Mood, And Physiological Response," *Perceptual Motor Skills*, 94, 39-46.

Higgins, E. Tory (1987), "Self-Discrepancy: A Theory Relating Self and Affect," *Psychological Review*, 94 (July), 319–40.

Kaya, Naz and Helen H. Epps (2004), "Relationship Between Color And Emotion: A Study of College Students," *College Student Journal*, 38 (3), 396-405.

Kwallek, Nancy and Carol M. Lewis (1990), "Effects of environmental colour on males and females: A red or white or green office," Applied Ergonomics, December, 275-278.

Mednick, Sarnoff A. (1962), "The Associative Basis Of The Creative Process," *Psychological Review*, 69 (3), 220-232.

Soldat Alexander S., Robert C. Sinclair and Melvin M. Mark (1997), "Color as an Environmental Processing Cue: External Affective Cues Can Directly Affect Processing Strategy without Affecting Mood," *Social Cognition*, 15(1), 55-71.

Verhoeven, Joost W. M., Marcel E. Pieterse and Ad Th. H. Pruyn (2006), "Effects of Interior Color on Healthcare Consumers: A 360 degree Photo Simulation Experiment," *Advances in Consumer Research*, 33, 292-293.

Zhou, Rongrong and Michel T. Pham (2004), "Promotion and Prevention across Mental Accounts: When Financial Products Dictate Consumers' Investment Goals," *Journal of Consumer Research*, 31 (June), 125-135.

Zhu, Rui (Juliet) and Joan Meyers-Levy (2007), "Exploring the Cognitive Mechanism that Underlies Regulatory Focus Effects," *Journal of Consumer Research*, 34 (June), 89-96.

Unconscious Information Processing Reduces Information Overload and Increase Product Satisfaction

Claude Messner, University of Basel, Switzerland

Michaela Waenke, University of Basel, Switzerland

Abstract

Consumers are less satisfied with a product chosen from an extended assortment than one from a limited assortment (Iyengar & Lepper, 2000). Presumably, information overload is responsible for decreased satisfaction. Decreasing information overload during the decision process should therefore increase satisfaction. One possibility to increase processing capacity is unconscious information processing (Dijksterhuis et al. 2006). We demonstrate that a spontaneous selection from an extended assortment leads to an information overload as well as extensive conscious information processing. However, unconscious information processing is one way to enjoy the advantages of an extended assortment without an information overload.

When given the choice between a limited and an extended assortment, consumers tend to prefer the extended assortment. Indeed large assortment sizes have some advantages: consumers experience more fun (Iyengar & Lepper, 2000) and the probability that the consumer's needs will be satisfied increases with the assortment size (McAlister & Pessemier, 1982; Kahn, 1995). Nevertheless, surprisingly, consumers are less satisfied with a product chosen from an extended assortment than one from a limited assortment (Iyengar & Lepper, 2000). Presumably, information overload is responsible for decreased satisfaction. Decreasing information overload during the decision process in a large assortment should therefore increase satisfaction relative to a small assortment size.

One possibility to increase processing capacity is unconscious information processing (Dijksterhuis, Bos, Nordgren & van Baaren, 2006). Unconscious information processing is an unconscious rumination, which starts automatically as soon as a consumer is consciously thinking about something other than the target product. Compared with conscious information processing, the capacity of the unconscious is less limited (Dijksterhuis & Nordgren, 2006). Previous research has shown that after complex decisions, consumers are more satisfied with their decision when they processed information unconsciously than consciously (Dijksterhuis, 2004; Dijksterhuis & von Olden 2006; Dijksterhuis et al., 2006). Based on these assumptions we expect that unconscious information processing could be one solution for consumers to benefit from an extended choice by reducing the negative effects of information overload. We predict that the negative effect on satisfaction when choosing from a large assortment compared to a small assortment diminishes when consumers base their choice on unconscious information processing.

Method

We conducted a study in which the participants chose a praline in a 3 (selection mode) x 2 (assortment size) between-subject design. A third of the participants saw the assortment once and were asked to write down their thoughts on the pralines before they chose one praline (conscious condition), a third chose one praline spontaneously (spontaneous condition) and a third saw the assortment once and solved anagrams for five minutes before they selected a praline (unconscious condition). Half of the participants selected one praline from a limited assortment (6) and the other half from an extended assortment (24). After the selection, the participants evaluated the taste and hedonic experience of the praline as well as the pleasure and satisfaction with their choice on a seven-point scale. Because of the high intercorrelation, we report the mean of the four variables (Cronbach α=.78).

Results

The results are in line with our predictions. As expected, the interaction between selection mode and assortment size is significant, $F(2, 174)$=7.41, p=.0008. Participants in the conscious condition evaluated the praline from an extended assortment less positively (M=5.26, SD=1.12) than from a limited choice (M=5.81, SD=0.74), t (58)=2.24, p=.03, replicating previous findings. Similarly, the participants in the spontaneous condition evaluated the taste of the praline from an extended choice less positively (M=5.33, SD=0.81) than from a limited choice (M=5.84, SD=0.99), t (58)=2.17, p=.03. However, the participants in the unconscious condition evaluated the taste of the praline from an extended choice more positively (M=6.04, SD=0.54) than from a limited choice (M=5.50, SD=0.96), t (58)=2.71, p=.009.

Conclusion

The aim of this study was to investigate conditions in which the consumer could profit from an extended choice. Elaborating choices from an extended assortment quickly reaches the limits of conscious information processing. However, unconscious information processing is one way to enjoy the advantages of an extended assortment without an information overload. Retailers may be well advised to provide distraction from choosing when increasing the range of options.

References

Dijksterhuis, Ap. (2004). Think different: the merits of unconscious thought in preference development and decision making. *Journal of Personality and Social Psychology, 87*(5), 586-598.

Dijksterhuis, Ap., Bos, Maarten. W., Nordgren, Loran. F., & van Baaren, Rick. B. (2006). On Making the Right Choice: The Deliberation-Without-Attention Effect. *Sience*, 311, 1005-1007

Dijksterhuis, Ap., & Nordgren, Loran F. (2006). A theory of unconscious thought. *Perspectives on Psychological Science, 1*(2), 95-109.

Dijksterhuis, Ap., & van Olden, Zeger. (2006). On the benefits of thinking unconsciously: Unconscious thought can increase post-choice satisfaction. *Journal of Experimental Social Psychology, 42*(5), 627-631.

Iyengar, Sheena S., & Lepper, Mark. R. (2000). When choice is demotivating: Can one desire too much of a good thing. *Journal of Personality and Social Psychology, 79*(6), 995-1006.

Kahn, Barbara. E. (1995). Consumer variety-seeking among goods and services An integrative review. *Journal of Retailing and Consumer Services, 2*(3), 139-148.

McAlister, Leigh., & Pessemier, Edgar. (1982). Variety Seeking Behavior: An Interdisciplinary Review. *Journal of Consumer Research, 9*(3), 311.

Matching Product Newness to Consumer Exploratory Buying Behavior: Strategies for Effective New Product Launch

Anne Michaut, HEC Paris, France

The topic of new product acceptance has figured prominently in the marketing literature. Understanding and predicting accurately new product acceptance has become a key success factor on today's markets. As a consequence, innovation features as a key challenge in business research today. A plethora of studies have focused on consumer response to innovation (Hauser, Griffin and Tellis 2006). Yet, only few studies investigated the relationship between new products' and consumers' characteristics. Moreover, the cross-cultural dimension has become increasingly vital to companies in terms of new product diffusion (e.g. Tellis et al. 2003; Golder and Tellis 2004). This paper proposes to match elements of product newness to the existing two-dimensional conceptualization of exploratory buying behavior (see Baumgartner and Steenkamp 1996). It also intends to integrate cultural variations by testing the hypotheses in a cross-national context, using 5 countries in Europe (UK, Germany, France, Italy and Spain).

In terms of consumers' personality characteristics, researchers quickly recognized the applicability of exploratory behaviors to important areas of consumer behavior. Activities such as innovative behavior in product purchase, variety seeking, brand switching, recreational shopping, and information search are manifestations of exploratory tendencies in the consumer buying process (Baumgartner and Steenkamp 1996). Yet, Baumgartner and Steenkamp (1996) proposed that a two-factor conceptualization of exploratory consumer buying behavior might be more useful than the initial seven facets. Following this observation, they developed the Exploratory Buying Behavior Tendency (EBBT) scale, with two forms of exploratory buying behavior: Exploratory Acquisition of Products (EAP) and Exploratory Information Seeking (EIS) based on the distinction between *sensory* and *cognitive* stimulation seeking.

In terms of new product characteristics, past studies have shown that perceived product newness can have a major impact on the product's diffusion and adoption (Gatignon & Robertson 1991; Rogers 1976). Yet, more recently, Calantone and colleagues (2006) concluded that product innovativeness *per se* has no direct effect on new product profitability and meta-analyses results (Szymanski, Kroff and Troy 2007; Montoya-Weiss and Calantone 1994; Henard and Szymanski 2001) revealed that newness and performance are positively related but that the average bivariate effect remains small to moderate in size. In terms of marketing research, it appears relevant to study the effect of variables associated to product newness rather than the effect of newness in itself. Following this observation, recent research has focused on more specific product characteristics associated to product newness: e.g. complexity (Mukherjee and Hoyer 2001), uncertainty related to really new products (Hoeffler 2003), and familiarity with the product category (Dahl and Hoeffler 2004). We propose to follow Berlyne's theory of collative variables, stating that newness is accompanied by other properties, closely related, but sufficiently distinct from newness itself to produce their own influence on the direction of stimulus selection or the strength of any stimulus selection process (Berlyne, 1960, 1966). We argue product newness can create *sensory* or *cognitive* stimulation depending on its accompanying variables. Namely, we propose that variables such as change or surprise produce *sensory* stimulation (further labeled sensory newness). In contrast, variables such as complexity or puzzlingness produce *cognitive* stimulation (further labeled cognitive newness).

What are the likely effects of the product newness on liking? And more importantly, what are the likely interactions between product newness, consumer exploratory behavior and cultural characteristics? Drawing a parallel between the consumer exploratory buying behavior (EAP and EIS) and the product profile (sensory and cognitive newness); we expect congruency between the product profile and the consumer profile to yield higher product liking than incongruency between the two. More specifically, we expect (1) consumers with high (low) EAP to show higher (lower) liking for sensory new products as sensory newness should satisfy *sensory* stimulation seeking. Similarly, we expect (2) consumers with high (low) EIS to show higher (lower) liking for cognitive new products as cognitive newness should satisfy *cognitive* stimulation seeking. At the cultural level, individualism and uncertainty avoidance have been related to consumer innovativeness. We expect (3) consumers in countries with high (low) individualism to show higher (lower) liking for sensory new products as they are 'different' from existing ones; and (4) consumers in countries with high (low) uncertainty avoidance to show lower (higher) liking for cognitive new products as they comprise more uncertainty.

The results from a large study conducted in 5 European countries (i.e. UK, Germany, France, Italy and Spain) with 150 to 180 respondents per country evaluating 36 new products each (in the detergent category) partially supported our predictions. The analysis was conducted using a three-level hierarchical linear model with product characteristics (Level 1), personality characteristics (Level 2) and cultural characteristics (Level 3). Multigroup confirmatory factor analysis (Steenkamp and Baumgartner 1998; Byrne 1998) was previously performed to address the issue of measurement invariance across countries.

Specifically, in terms of main effects, we find a positive effect of consumer exploratory behavior on new product liking (EAP and EIS), a positive effect of sensory newness and negative effect of cognitive newness on new product liking. Moreover, we find that the negative effect of product cognitive newness on liking increases as EIS increases and that the positive effect of sensory newness decreases as EAP increases. This suggests that *in*congruity between the personality and product profile yields higher product liking. In terms of cultural characteristics, we find that the negative effect of product cognitive newness on liking is reinforced as uncertainty avoidance increases and that the positive effect of sensory newness on liking is emphasized as individualism increases. Hence we find that congruity between the culture and product profile yields higher product liking In conclusion, our results show that personality and cultural characteristics are not a negligible source of variation in new product evaluation and new product liking in particular. Product characteristics should not be dissociated from personality and cultural characteristics when evaluating new product liking.

As always, our research has several limitations that present opportunities for future work. The present study is based on a reduced number of product and personality characteristics. Further research should examine the influence of more extent product and personality characteristics.

References

Baumgartner, H. and J.-B. E. M. Steenkamp (1996). Exploratory consumer buying behavior: Conceptualization and measurement. *International Journal of Research in Marketing*, 13: 121.

Berlyne, D. C. (1960). *Conflict, arousal and curiosity* McGraw-Hill, New-York.

Berlyne, D. E. (1966). Curiosity and exploration, *Science* 153: 25-33.

Byrne, Barbara M. (1998). *Structural Equation Modeling* with Lisrel, Prelis and Simplis: Basic concepts, application and programming. Lawrence Erlbaum Associates, Inc., NJ. p. 412.

Calantone, R.J., Chan, K.; Cui, A. S. (2006). Decomposing Product Innovativeness and Its Effects on New Product Success. *Journal of Product Innovation Management*, 23 (5), p408-421.

Dahl, D.W. and Hoeffler, S. (2004). Visualizing the Self: Exploring the Potential Benefits and Drawbacks for New Product Evaluation. *Journal of Product Innovation Management*, 21 (4), p259-267.

Gatignon, H. and T. Robertson (1991). Innovative decision processes, in: *Handbook of consumer behavior*. K. e. Robertson, Englewood Cliffs, NJ: Prentice Hall: 316-48.

Golder, P. N. and G. J. Tellis (2004). Growing, Growing, Gone: Cascades, Diffusion, and Turning Points in the Product Life Cycle. *Marketing Science*, 23(2): 207-218.

Hauser, J., Tellis, G.J., Griffin, A. (2006). A Review and Agenda for Marketing Science. *Marketing Science*, 25 (6), p687-717.

Henard, D.H. and Szymanski, D.M. (2001). Why some products are more successful than others, Journal of Marketing Research 38 (August): 362-375.

Hoeffler, S. (2003). Measuring preferences for really new products. *Journal of Marketing Research*, 40(4), 406-420.

Montoya-Weiss, Mitzi M.; Calantone, R. (1994). Determinants of New Product Performance: A Review and Meta-Analysis. *Journal of Product Innovation Management*, 11 (5), p397-417.

Mukherjee, Ashesh and Hoyer, Wayne D. (2001). The Effect of Novel Attributes on Product Evaluation. *Journal of Consumer Research*, 28 (3): p462-472.

Rogers, E. (1976). New product adoption and diffusion. *Journal of Consumer Research*, 2, 290-301.

Steenkamp, J.-B. E. M., Baumgartner, Hans (1998). Assessing measurement invariance in cross-national consumer research. *Journal of Consumer Research*, 25: 78.

Szymanski, D. M., Kroff, M. W. and Troy, L. C. (2007). Innovativeness and new product success: insights from the cumulative evidence. *Journal of the Academy of Marketing Science*, 35 (1), p35-52.

Tellis, G. J., S. Stremersch, et al. (2003). The International Takeoff of New Products: The Role of Economics, Culture, and Country Innovativeness. *Marketing Science*, 22(2): 188-208.

Understand the Role of Hybrid-level Country of Origin in Consumers' Product Evaluations.

Yupin Patara, Rutgers University, USA

Kent B. Monroe, University of Illinois at Urbana-Champaign and University of Richmond, USA

The Country of Origin Labeling Act 2002 will become effective in 2009. There has been concerned by consumers as to the relative quality of products led to questions as to the meaning of a "Made in ..." label especially from more than one origin. Using Cue Consistency Theory as a theoretical foundation, how multiple extrinsic cues such as brand, price and certification cobrand interact with a hybrid-level of the country of origin to influence consumers' perceptions of quality is studied. The findings explain the role of a hybrid-level of the country of origin in consumers' product evaluations.

This research investigates a series of studies to examine the influence of the pattern of cues, namely cues consistency such as *brand, price, certification cobrand and a hybrid-level of the country of origin* upon the manner in which these cues are used in product evaluations. The situation to be studied is when several extrinsic cues are provided how consumers form their perceptions of product quality, value and willingness to buy.

The research questions are:—(1) How do consumers evaluate "Made in ..." label as a hybrid-level of country of origin? (2) How do consumers utilize a hybrid-level of country of origin information along with *brand, price and certification cobrand* when evaluating products' quality?

Conceptualization

When consumers are uncertain about the quality of products, they may use extrinsic cues to judge the quality claims made by the sellers (Monroe 2003). A product's *brand name* is a cue for customers representing images that they have formed about the brand and may be used as an indicator of quality (Rao and Monroe 1989). Brucks, Zeithaml and Naylor (2000) find that when price is paired with a consistent brand cue, the quality evaluation is enhanced. Chao (1989) finds the same enhancement when pairing price with positive country of origin brand.

According to cue consistency theory (Slovic 1966; Maheswaran and Chaiken 1991; Miyazaki, Grewal, and Goodstein 2000) when a set of cues is consistent each cue will reinforce a subsequent judgment. If a brand name is capable of signaling quality, then the presence of country of origin as an additional signal to endorse and signal the primary brand's product quality may enhance quality perceptions.

It is because they provide enhancing impact and are likely to be used jointly in overall evaluations. Similarly, *country of origin* cues can also influence consumers' quality perceptions and their confidence in the quality of the product. People form an initial concept of a product on the basis of its country of origin and this concept once formed can influence how information about the product's specific attributes is interpreted (Hong and Wyer 1990).

Inconsistent cues may signal contradictory information. Moreover, evaluations with inconsistent cues may depend upon some consistent subset of the inconsistent cues. Consumers may focus on the negative cue and anchor their perceptions of quality based more on the negative cues (Ahluwalia 2002; Campbell and Goodstein 2001).

Hypotheses

H1: There will be an interaction effect of price and *a hybrid-level of the country of origin* on consumers' perceptions of product quality, such that the effect of either cue will be stronger when paired with a consistent (i.e., High *price*/ Strong *hybrid-level of the country of origin*) versus inconsistent cue.

H2: There will be an interaction effect of brand and country of ingredient origin on consumers' perceptions of product quality, such that the effect of either cue will be stronger when paired with a consistent (i.e., Familiar *Brand*/ Strong *hybrid-level of the country of origin*) versus inconsistent cue.

For a High Price Level of a Product

H3a: When the brand is highly familiar cobranded with a reputable certification agency, an increase in proportion of *hybrid-level of the country of origin* from a strong country of origin will result in an increase in the perception of quality.

H3b: When the brand is highly familiar cobranded with a reputable certification agency, an increase in proportion of *hybrid-level of the country of origin* from a strong country of origin will result in an increase in the perception of quality.

H3c: When the brand is highly familiar cobranded with a reputable certification agency, an increase in proportion of *hybrid-level of the country of origin* from a strong country of origin will result in an increase in the perception of quality.

Findings

Study 1. The hypothesized effect from H1 reveals a significant price x ingredient origin information interaction on perceived quality ($F_{(170)}=6.95$, $p<.001$). We found no mean differences for the inconsistent conditions relative to price and ingredient origin pairing ($F <1$, NSP). The effect of either cue will be stronger when paired with a consistent (i.e., High *price*/ Strong *hybrid-level of the country of origin*) versus inconsistent cue.

Study 2. The hypothesized effect from H2 reveals a significant brand x ingredient origin information interaction on perceived quality ($F_{(162)}=5.51$, $p<.01$, see figure 5). We found no mean differences for the inconsistent conditions relative to brand and ingredient origin pairing ($F <1$, NSP). The effect of either cue will be stronger when paired with a consistent (i.e., Familiar brand/ Strong *hybrid-level of the country of origin*) versus inconsistent cue.

Study 3. The hypothesized effect from H3 reveals that when the brand is highly familiar cobranded with a reputable certification agency, an increase in proportion of *hybrid-level of the country of origin* from a strong country of origin will result in an increase in the perception of quality ($t_{(150)}=3.83$, $p<0.001$), increase in the perception of value ($t_{(150)}=4.73$, $p<0.001$), and willingness to buy ($t_{(150)}=1.88$, $p<0.05$).

Discussion

Study 1 and 2 provide strong support for the cues consistency hypotheses. The target cue is a stronger predictor of perceived quality when paired with a consistent. Study 3 provide support for the proportion of the *hybrid-level of the country of origin* hypotheses that when the brand is highly familiar cobranded with a reputable certification agency, an increase in proportion of *hybrid-level of the country of origin* from a strong country of origin will result in an increase in the perception of quality, value and willingness to buy.

References

Carey, John (2007), "Not Made in China," *Business Week*, July, 41-43.

Hong, Sung-Tai and Robert S. Wyer (1990), "Determinants of Product Evaluation: Effects of the Time Interval between Knowledge of a Product's Country-of-origin and Information about Its Specific Attributes," *Journal of Consumer Research*, 17 (December), 277-88.

Hong, Sung-Tai and Dong Kyoon Kang (2006), "Country-of-Origin Influences on Product Evaluations: The Impact of Animosity and Perceptions of Industriousness Brutality on Judgments of Typical and Atypical Products," *Journal of Consumer Psychology*, 16 (3), 232-39.

Miyazaki, Anthony D., Dhruv Grewal and Ronald C. Goodstein (2005), "The Effect of Multiple Extrinsic Cues on Quality Perceptions: A Matter of Consistency," *Journal of Consumer Research*, 32 (March), 146-53.

Monroe, Kent B. (2003), *Pricing: Making Profitable Decisions*, 3rd ed., Boston, MA: McGraw-Hill/Irwin.

Rao, Akshay R. and Kent B. Monroe (1989), "The Effect of Price, Brand Name, and Store Name on Consumers' Perceptions of Quality," *Journal of Marketing Research*, 26 (August), 351-57.

Slovic, Paul (1966), "Cue-Consistency and Cue-Utilization in Judgment," *The American Journal of Psychology*, 79 (3), 427-34.

Urbany, Joel E., Ajit Kaicker, and Melinda Smith-de Borrero (1996), "Transaction Utility Effects When Quality is Uncertain," *Journal of the Academy of Marketing Science*, 25 (1), 45-55.

Verlegh Peeter W.J. and Steenkamp Jan-Benedict E.M. (1999), "A Review and Meta-Analysis of Country-of-Origin Research," *Journal of Economic Psychology*, 20, 521-46.

Does Time Fly When You're Counting Down? The Effect of Counting Direction on Subjective Time Judgment

Edith Shalev, New York University, USA
Vicki G. Morwitz, New York University, USA

Web users watching video clips of commercials, news items, or music online can tell how much time has elapsed from the beginning of the video and the total duration of the video clip by looking at a digital counter usually located at the bottom of the pop-up media player. Are these video segments more entertaining when the timer counts the elapsed time downward or upward? Suppose your gym instructor asks you to do 25 sit-ups. Does time seem to pass by more quickly and are you more willing to do additional sets of sit-ups if you count down from 25 to 1 or up from 1 to 25?

This research examines the impact of counting events upward *vs.* downward on the perceived duration of the interval containing the events as well as on consequences associated with the duration of the interval. We propose that the end of a counting down sequence (7, 6, 5, 4, 3, 2, 1) evokes more favorable feelings than the end of a counting up sequence (for example 19, 20, 21, 22, 23, 24, 25) because it draws the counter's attention to the prospect of goal attainment at an earlier stage (assuming that adults do not consider the mere act of counting itself to be enjoyable or engaging, we suspect they hold an implicit goal of completion towards most tasks that involve counting). Past research suggests that an earlier perception of proximity to the goal results in greater positive emotions than a later one (Carver and Scheier 1990, Kivetz et al 2006, Nunes and Dreze 2006). Additionally, it has been shown that individuals tend to misattribute the favorability associated with the end of an experience to the overall favorability of that experience (Fredrickson and Kahneman, 1993). As a result, we hypothesize that individuals will interpret a counting down experience as more favorable and shorter than a counting up experience. Since individuals high in need for cognition (NFC) have been shown to devote more attention to their own thinking and meta-cognitive experiences (Petty et al, 2007), we expect the effect of counting up *vs.* down will be larger for individuals high in NFC.

In study 1 we asked participants to imagine doing twenty five sit-ups. Half were asked to count their sit-ups from 1 to 25 (upward) and half were asked to count from 25 to 1 (downward). Counting downward resulted in estimation of shorter exercise duration and in perception of faster completion pace compared to counting upward. Conversely, downward counters held more favorable attitudes towards the counting task and were more willing to continue counting sit-ups than upward counters.

In study 2 we asked participants to count twenty five geometrical shapes. We manipulated two factors between participants: counting direction–upward or downward and counting range–half counted between 1 and 25 and half counted between 26 and 50. We hypothesized that counting downward will be perceived as shorter and as more enjoyable than counting upward only for the 1-25 range where the final countdown sequence is indicative of the distance to one's completion goal (5, 4, 3, 2, 1), but not for the 26-50 range (where the countdown ends with 29, 28, 27, 26, 25). The results were consistent with our hypotheses. Downward counters estimated the duration of the counting task to be shorter than upward counters in the 1 to 25 ranges but not in the 26 to 50 ranges. This study also rules out task complexity as an alternative account for the downward counting effect. Regardless of the range counted, participants indicated that downward counting is more difficult than upward counting (yet the downward counting effect was not obtained in the 26 to 50 range).

In Study 3 participants were asked to estimate the duration of a waiting interval in which they counted either from 1 to 60 or from 60 to 1. They were asked to imagine waiting on the phone for a service representative. We manipulated the counting direction between participants and measured NFC. Consistent with our hypotheses, the counting direction effect was found only for individuals high in NFC.

In Study 4 we manipulated two factors between conditions: counting direction–upward vs. downward–and primed goal–completion vs. accomplishment. We also measured NC. Following the priming manipulation, we used the same procedure as in the sit-up study. The results replicated the NFC moderation obtained in study 3: only participants who were high in NFC demonstrated the downward counting effect on time perception. Furthermore, only for those high in NFC was the counting direction effect moderated by the primed goal. Specifically, participants who were primed with a completion goal perceived time to be shorter following downward counting. On the other hand, those who were primed with an accomplishment goal perceived time to be shorter following upward counting.

In sum we find across studies that counting down experiences are perceived as shorter and as more favorable than counting up experiences. Our results support the hypothesis that this effect depends on the implicit goal one holds towards the counting task. These findings have important managerial implications because they suggest that consumers may find the same experience more enjoyable and effective when the events or time units associated with it are counted downward. To mention just a few examples where this effect can be applied: managers of call centers, directors of fitness DVDs and designers of online video segments can improve the appeal and effectiveness of their products with hardly any effort.

References

Carver, C.S., Scheier, M.F. (1990). Origins and functions of positive and negative effect. A control-process view. *Psychological Review*, 97, 19-35.

Fredrickson, B. L., & Kahneman, D. (1993). Duration neglect in retrospective evaluations of affective episodes. *Journal of Personality and Social Psychology*, 65, 45-55.

Kivetz, Ran, Oleg Urminsky, and Yuhuang Zheng (2006), "The Goal-Gradient Hypothesis Resurrected: Purchase Acceleration, Illusionary Goal Progress, and Customer Retention," *Journal of Marketing Research*, 43 (1), February, 39-58.

Nunes, J. C., Dreze, X. (2006). The Endowed Progress Effect: How Artificial Advancement Increases Effort. *Journal of Consumer Research*, 32, 504-512.

Petty, R. E., Briñol, P., Tormala, Z. L., & Wegener, D. T. (2007) The role of meta-cognition in social judgment. In E. T. Higgins & A. Kruglanski (Eds), *Social psychology: A handbook of basic principles (2nd ed.)*. New York: Guilford Press.

The Influence of Consumer Mood State on Mental Imagery Processing of Advertisement and Brand Evaluation

Jun R. Myers, California State Polytechnic University, USA
Sela Sar, Iowa State University, USA

Advertising appeals that encourage imagined consumption imagery are well known to be effective marketing communication tools to enhance brand attitudes and behavioral intentions. However, our understanding of the effectiveness of using mental imagery of consumption is still far from clear. This research focuses on exploring the influence of consumers' mood state on the generation of consumption mental imagery and product and brand evaluations.

Mental imagery processing is defined as a process by which sensory information is represented in working memory during encoding, processing and retrieving of information (McInnis and Price, 1987). According to this definition, imagery processing is a processing mode, not a knowledge structure (e.g., specific schemas or scripts). The instantiation of a schema or script generates imagery. In consumer research, the *availability-valence hypothesis* directly addresses the persuasion effects of message evoked imagery on judgment and evaluation (Kisielius and Sternthal, 1986). It suggests that sensory imagery information is more available than semantic information at the time of judgment, and more likely to activate existing information structures. Therefore, effects of imagery processing on learning, evaluation and judgment are stronger than the processing of non-vivid, pallid or abstract information (Anderson and Bower, 1980; Kisielius and Sternthal, 1984, 1986; Tversky and Kahneman, 1974). Furthermore, the availability-valence hypothesis postulates that whether vivid information enhances, undermine or has no effect on persuasion depends on the relative valence (or "favorability") of the information in relation to the message advocacy. When the valence of thoughts in working memory is positive toward message advocacy, it will enhance persuasion. (Kisielius and Sternthal, 1986).

Recently in psychology, the influence of mood state on information processing has drawn a lot of attention. It has been shown that mood state can significantly influence how people process incoming and self-generated information (e.g., Forgas, 1995; Schwarz, 1990). However, little research has investigated the influence of mood state on consumers' use of mental imagery in processing marketing communication messages. Two theoretical frameworks suggest great potential to predict how different consumer mood states can affect the way consumers use mental imagery in processing brand information and forming brand evaluations.

The "cognitive capacity view" (Mackie & Worth, 1989) contends that positive affective state renders people less able to process incoming information because happy affect activates many positive thoughts in memory, and these thoughts occupy people's attentional capacity. In contrast, negative affect is less likely to generate thoughts to the extent that could take up much cognitive capacity. This view is consistent with the findings in current consumer behavior literature involving the use of positive consumption imagery in advertisement to induce greater extent of mental imagery processing, and reduce cognitive scrutiny and counter-arguments of message claims (Escalas, 2004). From this view, positive mood provides more resources for consumers to engage in imagery generation, and thus facilitates the generation of mental images regarding positive consumption experience, and reduces consumers' critical scrutiny and analytical examination of the message argument.

The "hedonic contingency view" suggests that people in a negative mood state are motivated to process information. They think that such processing can have hedonic value to their mood state (Wegener and Petty, 1994). This view renders support for the use of positive consumption imagery: when consumers are in a negative mood state (versus positive mood state), they are more likely to be motivated to engage themselves in the hedonically pleasant experience of imagining the future consumption. The motivation to change negative mood should be higher than the motivation to keep the positive mood state. Based on the hedonic contingency view, it would be expected that the ease of imagery generation in response to imagery appeals in the ad message will depend on the hedonic consistency of the mood state in regard to the valence of the imagery. When consumers are in negative mood, there is a heightened hedonic value to engage in positive consumption imagery processing. When consumers are in positive mood, such hedonic value to engage in positive consumption imagery processing should be diminished.

The two theoretical frameworks suggest different predictions in regard to the generation of consumption mental imagery and brand evaluations. The "cognitive capacity view" suggests that positive mood state (versus negative mood state) will provide more resources for the generation of mental imagery of consumption by reducing the resource allocated on message scrutiny. The "hedonic contingency view" predicts that negative mood state provides heightened motivation to the use of mental imagery of future consumption. This research aims to test these two seemingly competing views.

An experiment involving 254 subjects was conducted to test the influence of mood state on consumers' use of mental imagery to process advertising information. The experiment was a 3 (mood state: negative vs. neutral vs. positive) x 2 (imagery appeal: present vs. absent) between subject factorial design. Results support that mood state influences the extent of mental imagery processing and brand evaluations. Specifically, the more positive consumer's mood state is, the more extensive mental imagery is used in the processing of advertisement, and the more positively consumers evaluate the advertised brand. Results also suggest that the extent of imagery processing mediates the influence of mood state on brand evaluation. In short, results indicate that processing resources seem to play an important role in determining the impact of consumers' mood state on mental imagery processing and brand evaluation.

References

Anderson, John and Gordon Bower (1980), *Human Associative Memory*, Hillsdale, NJ: Lawrence Erlbaum.

Escalas, J. E. (2004), "Imagine Yourself in the Product: Mental Simulation, Narrative Transportation, and Persuasion," *Journal of Advertising*, 33 (2), 37-48.

Forgas, P. J. (1995), "Mood and Judgment: The affect Infusion Model (AIM)," *Psychological Bulletin*, 116, 39-66.

Kisielius, Jolita and Brian Sternthal (1984), "Detecting and Explaining Vividness Effect in Attitudinal Judgments," *Journal of Marketing Research*, 21, 54-64.

Kisielius, Jolita and Brian Sternthal (1986), "Examining the Vividness Controversy: An Availability-Valence Interpretation," *Journal of Consumer Research*, 12 (March), 418-431.

Mackie, D. M. and L. T. Worth (1989), "Processing Deficits and the Mediation of Positive Affect in Persuasion," *Journal of Personality and Social Psychology*, 57, 27-40.

MacInnis, Deborah J. and Linda L. Price (1987), "The Role of Imagery in Information Processing: Review and Extensions," *Journal of Consumer Research*, Vol. 13 (March), 437-491.

Schwarz, N. (1990), "Feelings as Information: Information and Motivation Functions of Affective States," in R. M. Sorrentino and E. T. Higgins (Eds.), *Handbook of Motivation and Cognition: Foundations of Social Behavior* (pp. 527-561), New York: Guilford.

Taylor, Shelly E. and Sherry K. Schneider (1989), "Coping and the Simulation of Events," *Social Cognition*, 7(2), 174-194.

Wegener, Duane T., Richard E. Petty (1995), "Positive Mood Can Increase or Decrease Message Scrutiny: The Hedonic Contingency View of Mood and Message Processing," *Journal of Personality and Social Psychology*, Vol. 69, No. 1, 5-15.

Seeing Ourselves in Others: Consumer Compliance with Recommendations Made by Ambiguous Agents

David A. Norton, University of South Carolina, USA
Rebecca W. Naylor, University of South Carolina, USA

Abstract

This research investigates how compliance with a recommendation made by another consumer is affected by the amount of information provided about the reviewer and the perceived similarity of the reviewer. In Study 1 we demonstrate that, given no information about a reviewer (i.e., the reviewer's characteristics are ambiguous), consumers project their own characteristics onto the reviewer, resulting in compliance likelihoods that are similar to compliance with a recommendation made by a reviewer presented as similar (vs. dissimilar) to the target consumer. In Study 2 we demonstrate that the false consensus effect is responsible for these results.

Consumers seeking recommendations on products and services have typically obtained this information from two primary sources, professional agents who are paid to make such recommendations (e.g., movie critics, interior decorators) (Solomon 1986; West 1996) or friends and family members who provide this information through word-of-mouth communication (Brown and Reingen 1987). However, Internet technology now offers consumers a new source for product information: consumer-to-consumer recommendations in which no personal information is provided about the reviewer (e.g., online user reviews that are posted with no identifying information about the reviewer other than a user name).

The primary research question we seek to address is: how do consumers respond to recommendations made by an ambiguous reviewer (whom we define as a reviewer about whom no personal information is available)? Previous research on agent recommendations suggests that giving consumers more information about a product recommender will increase compliance with the recommendation if that recommender is demographically similar to the consumer (Feick and Higie 1992). Gershoff and Johar (2006) demonstrate, for example, that consumers overestimate an agent's knowledge based on over-reliance on similarity cues in a close relationship. Hence, past research suggests that reviewer ambiguity would *decrease* compliance with reviewer recommendations since consumers will be unsure whether the reviewer is similar (which would increase compliance) or dissimilar (which would decrease compliance) to themselves. However, Norton, Frost, and Ariely (2007) argue that ambiguity can be beneficial in some contexts (e.g., potential dating partners are liked more when people have less information about them because more information increases the likelihood of discovering dissimilarity between oneself and a potential partner).

We propose that, when provided with no identifying information about a reviewer, consumers project their own characteristics onto that reviewer in a manner consistent with the false consensus effect (in which consumers tend to overestimate the prevalence of their own attitudes in the general population; Ross, Greene, and House 1977), such that consumers respond as positively to recommendations made by ambiguous reviewers as they do to recommendations by reviewers that they know are similar to themselves. Essentially, we propose that when information about reviewers' tastes is left ambiguous, participants assume these reviewers share their own tastes and attitudes.

To test our hypotheses, in Study 1 each participant read a restaurant review ostensibly written by another consumer and then indicated their intentions to visit the restaurant they read about. The review was designed to be slightly positive in order to make the restaurant attractive but to avoid ceiling effects. The text of the review was held constant across all conditions, and amount and type of reviewer information was manipulated such that participants saw either (1) no information about the reviewer (ambiguous reviewer condition), (2) information about a reviewer who was similar to the average student at their university (similar reviewer condition), or (3) information about a reviewer who was different from the average student at their university (dissimilar reviewer condition). In the similar and dissimilar reviewer conditions, the participants saw nine units of demographic information (e.g., age, gender, university attended, etc.) that were either similar or dissimilar to themselves (gender) or to the average student at their university (age, university attended). After reading the review, participants rated, on a scale of one ("not at all likely") to nine ("extremely likely"), how likely they would be to try the restaurant. Participants also rated how similar they thought the reviewer was to themselves in terms of similarity in restaurant taste.

In order to analyze the results of Study 1, we used orthogonal contrast codes comparing (1) the similar reviewer condition to the ambiguous reviewer condition and (2) the ambiguous and similar reviewer conditions to the dissimilar reviewer condition. We found, as predicted, that participants in the similar reviewer (M=5.99) condition showed no difference in likelihood of trying the recommended restaurant compared to participants in the ambiguous reviewer condition (M=6.00), $F(1, 216)$=0.00, p>.95. However, compliance with the recommendation was significantly lower for the dissimilar reviewer condition (M=5.37) compared to the similar and ambiguous reviewer conditions, $F(1, 216)$=11.01, p<.01. In order to demonstrate that the differences we find in restaurant trial are indeed caused by differing perceptions of similarity, we compared participants' ratings of similarity in the similar versus ambiguous reviewer conditions. As expected, participants perceived the reviewer in the ambiguous condition to be equally similar to themselves (M=5.42) compared to the reviewer in the similar reviewer condition (M=5.59), supporting our false consensus explanation. Further, the difference in perceived similarity between the dissimilar reviewer condition (M=4.46) and the other two conditions mediated the relationship between the dissimilar versus similar and ambiguous reviewer conditions and likelihood of trying the restaurant, z=3.93, p<.01.

The goal of Study 2 was to provide additional evidence that these results are driven by the false consensus effect. We hypothesize that alerting participants to the potential bias of the effect (i.e., warning participants about the tendency to see oneself in ambiguous others) decreases compliance with an ambiguous reviewer's recommendation. Hence, Study 2 used the same restaurant review context and three-level (ambiguous reviewer vs. similar reviewer vs. dissimilar reviewer) variable and added a two-level warning variable (such that participants were either warned about the false consensus effect or not warned).

The results of Study 2 support our predictions; we found a significant interaction between the warning variable and the similar reviewer versus ambiguous reviewer contrast, $F(1, 286)$=2.90, p<.01. With no warning about the false consensus effect, the results of Study 1 were replicated such that there was no difference in compliance with the recommendation between the similar and ambiguous reviewer information condition (M=6.17 for both conditions). However, when participants received a warning about the potential impact of the false consensus effect, they were significantly less likely to try the restaurant in the ambiguous reviewer condition (M=5.18) than in the similar reviewer (M=6.35) condition, thus providing additional evidence that the false consensus effect drives our results.

References

Brown, Jacqueline Johnson and Peter H. Reingen (1987), "Social Ties and Word-of-Mouth Referral Behavior," *Journal of Consumer Research*, 14 (December), 350–362.

Feick, Lawrence and Robin A. Higie (1992), "The Effects of Preference Heterogeneity and Source Characteristics on Ad Processing and Judgments about Endorsers." *Journal of Advertising*, 21 (Summer), 9-24.

Gershoff, Andrew D. and Gita Venkataramani Johar (2006), "Do You Know Me? Consumer Calibration of Friends' Knowledge," *Journal of Consumer Research*, 32 (March), 496-503.

Norton, Michael I., Jeana H. Frost, and Dan Ariely, "Less Is More: The Lure of Ambiguity, or Why Familiarity Breeds Contempt." *Journal of Personality and Social Psychology*, Vol 92(1), Jan 2007. pp. 97-105.

Ross, Lee, David Greene, and Pamela House (1977), "The False Consensus Effect: An Egocentric Bias in Social Perception and Attribution Processes," *Journal of Experimental Social Psychology*, 13 (May), 279–301.

Solomon, Michael R. (1986), "The Missing Link: Surrogate Consumers in the Marketing Chain," *Journal of Marketing*, 50 (October), 208–218.

West, Patricia M. (1996), "Predicting Preferences: An Examination of Agent Learning," *Journal of Consumer Research*, 23 (June), 68–80.

Corporate Syntheses: Consumers' Role in Mergers and Acquisitions

Eleni-Zoi Papavasileiou, Boston University, USA

Mergers and Acquisitions (M&As) have been a major trend over the past three decades; companies internationalize and strengthen their presence by acquiring profitable targets. In 2005, the total value of M&As worldwide was $2.7 trillion, an increase of 38% compared to that of the previous year (Ettenson 2006). Thus, very few topics have gained as much attention in media and business research as M&As (Bouwman, Fuller, and Nain 2003). However, even though the total value and number of M&As continue to increase, a recent Mc Kinsey report (1997) notes that only one in five deals manages to create shareholder value.

Conceptualization

Research in various disciplines such as finance and strategy has investigated M&As. Existing research examines post-acquisition financial performance and points to a poor conclusion: "acquisitions do not create superior post acquisition performance for acquiring firms" (King et al. 2004).

One of the failures of the finance-based view of M&As is that managers pay little attention to the way they should present the M&A to consumers. Ettenson and Knowles (2007) notice that prior to an M&A deal, managers try to identify only the "hard" assets- property, equipment, patent, and drilling rights, but very rarely discuss the "relational" assets- corporate reputation, consumers' goodwill, and brands. Basu (2002) wonders *"who's thinking about customers and critically-the brands? At the moment no one"*. However, the success of an M&A also depends on how external stakeholders and more specifically consumers perceive the M&A. They could either like it and support it, or dislike it and abandon their support towards the company after the M&A. Therefore, researchers and practitioners call for moving from "deal breaker-factors that prevent a deal from closing" to "deal maker-factors that enhance the chances of success after the merger" (Ettenson and Knowles 2007).

This paper suggests two main antecedents for consumers' attitudes and behavioral intentions after the M&A: 1) consumers' perceptions of the degree to which the two corporate images match, 2) naming of the company.

Corporate Image Matching

Broniarczyk and Alba (1994) extend the brand extension literature suggesting that in their brand extension evaluation, consumers consider the *psychological similarity* between the two brands (perceived similarity between the associations of the two brands). Broniarczyk and Alba (1994) and Park et al. (1991) suggest that the effect of consumers' perceived "fit" between the two brands dominates the effects of brand affect and category similarity. Similarly, this paper suggests that in their M&A evaluation, consumers consider the degree to which the two corporate images match.

Corporate Name

Cohen and Murphy (1984) investigate the attribute formation when two concepts come together to form a composite concept. The two authors report a minimum rule for the attribute formation of a composite concept: "*if something is not a 'good' A, it cannot be a 'good' AB*". In the M&A case two companies come together to form a new company. Following Cohen's and Murphy's (1984) minimum rule, when the matching between the two corporate images is low, the use of a combined name (i.e. after the FedEx UPS merge, both companies will operate under the FedEx UPS name) may be confusing and harm consumers' attitudes.

Cohen and Murphy (1984) and Hampton (1987) report a maximum rule; when a constituent of a composite concept is salient on a particular attribute, then this attribute will also be salient in the composite concept. Applied in the M&A context, when the two corporate images match, both companies' images will be stronger in the event that both companies start to operate under a combined name.

Tversky and Kahneman (1981) suggest that consumers are "less willing to accept a surcharge than to forego a discount." In other words, the two authors suggested that losses (negative events) loom larger than gains (positive events). In the M&As context, the low matching pair of companies could be perceived as a negative event (loss) and the high matching pair of companies as a positive event (gain). This paper suggests that consumers are more likely to support the separate naming strategy in the low matching case- loss case (each company continues to operate under its own name) than the combined naming strategy in the high matching case- gain case (both companies start to operate under a combined name).

Methodology

We used a 2 (high/ low matching) x 4 (4 naming strategies) within-subjects experimental design, with 107 college students participating. The experiment was conducted in two phases. First, we asked participants to provide the associations that came to their minds upon the presentation of one pair of companies. We used two pairs of companies: Starbuck's-Dunkin Donuts and FedEx-UPS. Each participant was randomly assigned to one pair. Participants were also asked to rate the degree of matching between the two corporate images. Afterwards, participants were informed that the two companies merged and were asked to express their attitudes and behavioral intentions toward each one of the four naming strategies: Strategy 1: both companies start to operate under a combined name (i.e. FedEx UPS), Strategy 2: both companies start to operate under the name of the first company (i.e. FedEx), Strategy 3: both companies start to operate under the name of the second company (i.e. UPS), Strategy 4: each company continues to operate under its own name (i.e. FedEx, UPS). At the end, potential covariate measures were collected.

Results

The data were analyzed in a regression framework. The dependent variables were the differences between consumers' attitudes and behavioral intentions vis-à-vis the four alternative naming strategies (for example: consumers' attitudes vis-à-vis Strategy 1- consumers' attitudes vis-à-vis Strategy 2, consumers' behavioral intention vis-à-vis Strategy 1- consumers' behavioral intention vis-à-vis Strategy 2). The independent variable was the degree to which the two corporate images match (High/ Low).[17] The results provided broad support for our conceptualization.

Consistent with our predictions, consumers preferred naming strategy 1 (combined naming) in the high matching case and naming strategy 4 (separate naming) in the low matching case ($\beta_{str.1-str.4}=-.477$, $p_{str.1-str.4}=.000$). Consumers also preferred naming strategy 1 (combined naming) in the high matching case and naming strategies 2 and 3 (names of the 1st and 2nd company) in the low matching case ($\beta_{str.1-str.2}=-.348$, $p_{str.1-str.2}=.000$, $\beta_{str.1-str.3}=-.228$, $p_{str.1-str.3}=.025$). Finally, consumers preferred naming strategies 2,3 in the high matching case and naming strategy 4 in the low matching case ($\beta_{str.2-str.4}=-.246$, $p_{str.2-str.4}=.014$, $\beta_{str.3-str.4}=-.295$, $p_{str.3-str.4}=.004$). Matching had an expected analogous effect on consumers' purchase intentions. Consumers are more likely to purchase when naming strategy 1 is used in the high matching case and naming strategy 4 is used in the low matching case ($\beta_{str.1-str.4}=-.319$, $p_{str.1-str.4}=.003$, $\beta_{str.1-str.2}=-.145$, $p_{str.1-str.2}=.112$, $\beta_{str.2-str.4}=-.234$, $p_{str.2-str.4}=.021$, $\beta_{str.3-str.4}=-.280$, $p_{str.3-str.4}=.002$).

As expected, consumers were more likely to support the separate naming strategy in the low matching case than the combined naming strategy in the high matching case. More specifically, in the low matching case, 69% of consumers chose naming strategy 4 (separate naming) as the most appropriate, whereas 27% of consumers chose naming strategy 1 (combined naming) as the most appropriate in the high matching case (if y is our dependent variable and x our independent variable, $y=-1.877x+0.509$, for $x=0$ -high matching-, $y_0=0.509$ and for $x=1$ –low matching-, $y_1=-1.368$, $|y_1|$ is significantly higher than $|y_0|$).

Implications

Both researchers (Basu 2006; Ettenson and Knowles 2007) and practitioners (Knowles and Ettenson 2007) begin to acknowledge that marketing could play a beneficial role when companies negotiate an M&A. More specifically, this paper proposes two key factors that influence consumers' reactions to M&As: degree to which the two corporate images match and naming strategy. Apart from the financial analysis that managers should do when considering an M&A, they may also need to think of more marketing-oriented assets such as consumers, corporate images and rebranding. This paper suggests that the matching between the two corporate images as well

---

[18]All regression coefficients are standardized. Coding for the matching between the two corporate images is 0 (1)=high (low) matching.

as the naming strategy (combined vs. separate) affect consumers' perceptions of M&As. Choosing the less favorable naming strategy may harm both consumers' attitudes and purchase intentions. Thus, managers should first understand how consumers think of the two corporate images, and choose the naming strategy accordingly.

References

Basu, Kunal (2002), "Merging Brands: Designing the Post M&A Portfolio," *Ivey Business Journal*, 67 (2), 1.

_____ (2006), "Merging Brands after Mergers," *California Management Review*, 48 (4), 28-40.

Bouwman, Christa H. S., Kathleen Fuller, and Amrita S. Nain (2003), "Stock Market Valuation and Mergers," *MIT Sloan Management Review*, 45 (1), 9-11.

Broniarczyk, Susan M. and Joseph W. Alba (1994), "The Importance of the Brand in Brand Extension," *Journal of Marketing Research*, 31 (2), 214.

Cohen, Benjamin and Gregory L. Murphy (1984), "Models of Concepts," *Cognitive Science: A Multidisciplinary Journal*, 8 (1), 27-58.

Ettenson, Richard and Jonathan Knowles (2006), "Merging the Brands and Branding the Merger," *MIT Sloan Management Review*, 47 (4), 10.

Hampton, James A. (1987), "Inheritance of Attributes in Natural Concept Conjunctions," *Memory & Cognition*, 15 (1), 55-71.

King, David R., Dan R. Dalton, Catherine M. Daily, and Jeffrey G. Covin (2004), "Meta-Analyses of Post-Acquisition Performance: Indications of Unidentified Moderators," *Strategic Management Journal*, 25 (2), 187-200.

Knowles, Jonathan and Richard Ettenson (2007), "Reconcilable Differences," *Harvard Business Review*, 85 (6), 24-26.

Park, C. Whan, Sandra Milberg, and Robert Lawson (1991), "Evaluation of Brand Extensions: The Role of Product Feature Similarity and Brand Concept Consistency," *Journal of Consumer Research*, 18 (2), 185-93.

Tversky, Amos and Daniel Kahneman (1981), "The Framing of Decisions and the Psychology of Choice," *Science*, 211 (4481), 453-458.

The Role of Regret under Task Difficulty: A Boomerang Effect

Kirsten Passyn, Salisbury University, USA

Mita Sujan, Tulane University, USA

Previous research has documented the advantages of high self-accountability emotions, such as guilt and regret, over low self-accountability emotions, such as fear, in motivating self-protection behaviors, such as wearing sunscreen or eating high fiber foods (Passyn and Sujan, 2005). In accord with functional theories of emotion (Frijda 1986, Lazarus 1981), this research supports the idea that high self-accountability emotions motivate and drive self-protection behaviors. However, these findings are limited to simple domains where perceptions of self-efficacy are high.

Thus, previous research has only shown the ability of emotions to impact behaviors that participants feel capable of engaging in. This raises the questions as to the impact of high-self accountability emotions in more complex and demanding domains, for example, resisting peer pressure. When you heighten task difficulty, creating more uncertainty of ones ability to perform the task, Protection Motivation Theory (PMT) would predict a decline in self protection behavior (Rogers 1983). Thus, when a person feels incapable of performing the task they are less likely to do so.

The purpose of this research is to examine the impact of high self-accountability emotions under conditions of high task difficulty. We tested our hypotheses in the context of condom usage. Outwardly, most people perceive condoms usage as an efficacious behavior, they are readily available and easy to use. However, actual rates of condom usage are low because in the heat of the moment the task of actually stopping, finding, and using a condom is difficult (Bradford and Beck 1991). In a pretest we assessed participants' perceptions of condom usage difficulty and self-efficacy. Participants were either exposed to an in the moment message describing the difficulty of actually stopping and asking to use a condom or not exposed to any message. As predicted the results indicated when simply asked about condom usage participants report low task difficulty (M=2.8) and strong levels of self-efficacy, (M=3.78). However, when they were exposed to the manipulation perceptions of task difficulty increased significantly (M=4.2) and self-efficacy dropped significantly (M=2.73)*. In conclusion, our pretest demonstrates that while college students believe that condom usage is easy, reminding them of the urgency of the moment significantly increases perceptions of the real difficulty of using condoms.

Our study was a 2(task difficulty: present vs. absent) X 2(emotion: fear vs. regret) design. Task difficulty was manipulated using the manipulation described above. Emotions were manipulated using either a fear/low self-accountability message or a regret/high self-accountability message that discussed the threat of Chlamydia. Both messages concluded with a tagline to use condoms. Manipulation checks confirmed that participants in the fear (regret) conditions felt significantly more fear (regret) than participants in the other conditions. Additionally, the self-efficacy manipulation did not impact the intensity of the felt emotions, so there was no difference among the fear(regret) conditions. Furthermore, the task difficulty measure indicated significantly higher perceptions of task difficulty when participants were exposed to the "in the moment" message. Thus the manipulations were effective.

In support of previous emotion research the regret conditions combined resulted in significantly stronger behavioral intentions than the fear conditions combined (M=7.5 vs. 4.8, respectively). Among the fear conditions, as predicted by PMT, task difficulty significant decreased perceptions of self-efficacy (M=3.7 vs. 2.7) and intentions to use condoms (M=5.5 vs. 4.1). However, and in conflict with PMT, among the regret conditions there is a boomerang effect; increasing task difficulty significantly increases perceptions of self-efficacy (M=3.7 vs. 4.3) and boosts behavioral intentions (M=6.9 vs. 8.1). Thus in the process of motivating difficult behaviors regret actually erases self-efficacy doubts.

The pattern of results cannot be attributed to emotional intensity. Thus the boomerang effect did not result from increased emotional intensity but instead increased motivation through personal responsibility. That is regret, when the task is difficulty forces individuals to be more determined enhancing perceptions of personal responsibility (M=7.4 vs. 8.4) and therefore self-efficacy and behavioral intentions.

In conclusion, as predicted by PMT for traditional fear appeals increasing task difficulty result in minimal self protection behavior. As predicted by emotion research regret results in strong self-protection behaviors. Importantly however, perceptions of self-responsibility override even perceptions of task difficulty, resulting in a boomerang effect and enhanced self-efficacy and behavioral intentions. This research illustrates the power of regret to promote self-protective behaviors even when the behaviors are difficult.

* For space reasons the term significant is only used when p<.05.

Self-Relevant Brand Alliances: When Do Consumers (Not) Fit?

Nicole Verrochi, University of Pennsylvania, USA
Americus Reed II, University of Pennsylvania, USA

Abstract

Successful brand alliances possess high fit between brands forming the alliance. However, many brand alliances contain elements relevant to consumers' identities. Two studies demonstrate that regardless of fit between the parent brands, if one brand is low in fit with the consumer's identity, the brand alliance is perceived poorly. Thus, current conceptualizations of brand alliances need to be broadened to include consumers and their identities. By considering the target market's conception of each brand, and how each is self relevant to the target, it is possible to build a more comprehensive and accurate representation of successful brand alliances.

During the mega-merger boom of the late 1980s and early 1990s, joint branding flourished in the marketplace. Consumers are now accustomed to seeing ingredient branding (NutraSweet in Diet Coke), co-branding (Frito-Lay chips with KC Masterpiece barbeque sauce), and other forms of branding alliances. Despite this abundance, empirical research on how consumers perceive these co-brands is still in its infancy, and what determines a successful brand alliance remains unclear.

The purpose of the current research is to demonstrate the need for a wider view when considering the role of fit in brand alliances. Specifically, we suggest that there are three connections that need to be high in fit for a brand alliance to have the highest probability of success (positive attitudes, purchase intention, choice). These three connections are the link between the two brands, which is commonly examined in brand alliance research, and the two links between each parent brand and the consumer. By including the consumer in our conceptualization of fit, researchers on brand alliances will better understand the mechanisms driving attitude transfer and, ultimately, choice.

Research on effective brand alliances has grown out of the brand extension literature. In this way, many similar factors reappear—specifically the question of fit: do these two brands fit? Because the most prevalent comparison in brand alliances is one brand with another, fit is often conceptualized as complementary product attributes, functions or uses (Park, Jun and Shocker 1996; Samu, Krishnan and Smith 1999). Complementarity can be defined as the requirement of one product for the use or operation of the second product (Samu et al. 1999). And, as with brand extensions, the degree of complementarity is related to the ability of activation to spread from one product to the other. The point of difference is that with brand alliances researchers examine the transfer of attitude from two branded products to a new concept.

In the attitude literature, there is an associated stream of literature regarding consumers' social identity-based attitudes (e.g., Reed 2004). Brands that are strongly connected to a consumer's identity allow people to express themselves, and have been shown to be more resistant to counterpersuasion tactics than less identity-relevant brands (Bolton and Reed 2004). These papers suggest that incorporating the fit (conceptualized as identity relevance) between each of the two parent brands and the consumer will enhance our understanding of successful brand alliances.

This paper incorporates the theoretical approaches of both the brand extension and social identity-based attitude literatures to test whether higher fit between a consumer and the two parent brands may enhance attitudes toward the brand alliance. A set of two experiments test the hypothesis that low fit between consumer and either parent brand will result in lower attitudes toward the brand alliance. Fit is manipulated through priming participants with either high-fit or low-fit identities, or by manipulating the brands involved in the brand alliance effort. All other aspects of the stimuli are the same between conditions. Participants were exposed to an advertisement, and then subsequently asked for evaluations of the alliance.

Study 1A primed three different identities that consumers can possess: athlete, student and fashionista. After increasing the salience of one identity, participants were asked to evaluate a current brand alliance, Nike+ iPod, indicating their perceptions if inter-brand fit and attitude toward the alliance. Systematic differences were found across the three identities, such that those participants viewing the advertisement through the lens of their stylish identity expressed more positive attitudes and perceived greater fit than the participants with athlete or student identity primed (attitude: F(2, 63)=4.972, p<.01; fit: F(2, 63)=6.136, p<.01). While this data demonstrates that a salient identity can influence consumers' attitudes, it remained unclear whether this was due to the stylish identity or to the hypothesized match between perceptions of the shoe (its relative fashion versus functionality) and the relative identity.

Study 1B sought to demonstrate that it is the match between the values of the salient identity (functionality for runners versus fashion for stylish identities) and perceptions of the product that drive the change in perceived fit and attitude. To this end, a more specific identity (runner) was primed in order to focus on the functionality of the shoe, and different sneaker brands were used to manipulate the perceived deliverables of the product. Specifically, we hypothesized that runners would perceive higher fit and possess a more positive attitude toward brand alliances containing shoe brands perceived as highly functional (Mizuno, New Balance) versus highly stylish brands (Nike, Adidas). The converse would be true for the participants with fashionista identity activated. The interaction of shoe brand and identity was, as hypothesized, significant for both attitude (F(1, 130)=4.797, *p*<.05) and perceptions of brand alliance fit (F(1, 130)=8.943, *p*<.005). These results implicate the need for a match between the consumer identity and the product perceptions in order for a brand alliance to be evaluated positively.

To our knowledge, there has been no effort to include consumer self-conceptions in models of brand alliance success. This set of studies represents a first attempt to consider how different consumer identities can impact both perceptions of brand alliance fit and attitude toward the alliance. Drawing from the social identity-based attitude literature, we extend the concept of complementarity, or brand alliance fit, to include the consumer. Moving from a dyadic to triadic level of analysis allows consumer researchers to have a deeper understanding of the products that consumers are likely to see as "acceptable" in brand alliances. The experiments presented here provide reliable evidence for the importance of including this consumer-focused fit into evaluations of brand alliance structure, suggesting that successful efforts require not only high inter-brand fit, but also a strong brand-consumer connection. Taken together, these studies provide support for the value in taking the consumer into account when defining brand alliance fit, as different identities will emphasize diverse brand values—not all of which are complementary.

References

Bolton, Lisa E. and Americus Reed, II (2004), "Sticky Priors: The Perseverance of Identity Effects on Judgment," *Journal of Marketing Research*, 41 (4), 397-410.

Park, C. Whan, Sung Youl Jun and Allan D. Shocker (1996), "Composite Branding Alliances: An Investigation of Extension and Feedback Effects," *Journal of Marketing Research*, 33 (4), 453-466.

Reed, Americus, II (2004), "Activating the Self-Importance of Consumer Selves: Exploring Identity Salience Effects on Judgments," *Journal of Consumer Research*, 31 (September), 286-295.

Samu, Sridhar, H. Shanker Krishnan and Robert E. Smith (1999), "Using Advertising Alliances for New Product Introduction: Interactions Between Product Complementarity and Promotional Strategies," *Journal of Marketing*, 63 (1), 57-74.

Looking for Great Discounts–How Store Coupons Shape Attention, Product Memory, and Store Impressions

Charles Y. Z. Zhang, University of Michigan, USA
Norbert Schwarz, University of Michigan, USA

Coupons are a widely used tool of sales promotion and numerous studies examined their impact on consumer behavior (see Raghubir, Inman and Grande, 2004, for a review). While most of the available research focused on product or brand coupons, retailers may use generic coupons to attract customers to their stores. Such coupons take a variety of forms, typically as conditional dollar-off coupon ($X off any purchase above $Y), unconditional dollar-off coupon ($X off any purchase), or percentage-off coupon (Z% off any purchase). On theoretical grounds, it is likely that store coupons influence what customers attend to once they are in the store. The present research addresses this possibility. We predict, and find, that such coupons induce consumers to focus on products in a price range close to the minimum purchase requirements of the coupon, as indicated by biases in consumers' memory for the goods offered.

Rationale

Several lines of research suggest that consumers who receive a dollar-off coupon may attempt to make a purchase in the price range of the coupon's minimum purchase requirement. First, the perceived value of a given discount increases with the percentage saving it provides. For example, Tversky and Kahneman (1981) observed that consumers are more willing to drive 20 minutes for $5 off a $15 product than for $5 off a $125 product. Similarly, Krishna et al. (2002) found in a meta-analysis of 20 coupon studies that consumers' think they saved more money when a given face value results in a high rather than low percentage discount. Second, specifically for unconditional coupon holders, purchasing a product at or just above the coupon's face value amounts to receiving the product for "free", which is particularly attractive (Ariely, 2008). Hence, consumers with and without a dollar-off coupon may pay differential attention to items at different price levels. This differential attention, in turn, may affect their later recall of the items offered as well as their impression of the store. This prediction is consistent with psychological research that shows that attention and memory are a function of goals and motivation (e.g., Anderson and Pichert, 1978; Klinger, 1977).

Studies

Method. We built an online office supply store using a real online shopping platform. The store had about 20 items, priced $5-$30, with product descriptions, pictures, and price information copied from the website of a major office supplies store. The lower priced items (below $10) where stationary and paper products, whereas the higher priced items (above $20) were computer accessories.

Study 1. Fifty-four business undergraduates browsed the store and did vs. did not receive a coupon that offered "$5 off any purchase." Participants were encouraged to make a hypothetical purchase decision during browsing, but were not required to do so. Next, participants completed an unrelated experiment as a filler task. Subsequently they estimated the average price of all items offered in the store, and evaluated how much variety the store offers in the lower and higher priced product categories (paper products vs. computer accessories).

As predicted, participants who received a $5-off coupon purchased items that had a lower price than participants who received no coupon, estimated that the average price of all items offered in the store is lower, and provided more favorable ratings of the variety that the store offers in the paper products category

Study 2. Following the same procedures, participants received either a "$5-off-any-purchase" or a "$5-off-a-$20-purchase" coupon. Going beyond Study 1, participants' click-stream data were captured as a measure of what they attended to and a memory task with free recall of all items offered was added.

Compared to the $5-off-$20 group, the $5-off group clicked on more low-price and fewer high-price items, confirming that the type of coupon influences product search. Moreover, they also recalled more low-price items and fewer high-price items.

Conclusions

Our findings highlight an unintended side-effect of dollar-value coupons. Consumers perceive the identical coupon as more valuable when it provides a high (e.g., $5 off $10) rather than low (e.g., $5 off $50) percentage discount (Krishna et al., 2000). To maximize the benefit of a given coupon they attempt to find products that are priced close to the purchase requirement of the coupon, thus maximizing the percentage discount. As a result, consumers who receive a low requirement coupon pay more attention to low-priced products than consumers who do not, biasing their memories and impressions of the store. While the specific effects will depend on the specific coupon type, our findings provide first evidence that coupons channel consumers' attention with downstream effects on store impressions. Unfortunately, these impressions may be more important in the long run than any short-term sales increase.

References

Anderson, R.C. & Pichert, J.W. (1978). "Recall of previously unrecallable information following a shift in perspective" *Journal of Verbal Learning and Verbal Behavior*, 1978, 17, 1-12.

Ariely, D. (2008). *Predictably irrational*, New York: Harper Collins.

Klinger, E. (1977), *Meaning and void: Inner experience and the incentives in people's lives*, Minneapolis: University of Minnesota Press

Krishna, Aradhna, Richard Briesch, Donald R. Lehmann, and Hong Yuan (2002) "A Meta-Analysis of the Impact of Price Presentation on Perceived Savings", *Journal of Retailing*, 78, Summer, 101-18.

Raghubir, Priya, J. Jeffrey Inman, and Hans Grande (2004), "The Three Faces of Price Promotions: Economic, Informative and Affective," *California Management Review*, 46 (4), Summer, 1-19.

Tversky, Amos and Daniel Kahneman (1981), "The Framing of Decisions and the Psychology of Choice," *Science*, 211, 453-58.

The Effect of Temporal Framing on Product Choice

Andrea Heintz Tangari, University of Arkansas, USA
Ronn J. Smith, University of Arkansas, USA

This research focuses on the temporal framing of a cost savings message for an energy efficient product, a compact fluorescent light (CFL) bulb. In two experiments, we examine the effects of three different temporal frames of cost savings (one month, one year, and lifetime). We investigate how the framing impacts product choice, purchase intentions, attitudes, and perceptions of savings. Additionally, we look to see if consumers' temporal orientation (a predisposition toward future outcomes versus present outcomes) will moderate the effect of the temporal framing of savings.

Conceptual Background

Research on the level of construal in decision making has led to formulation of Construal Level Theory (CLT), which demonstrates how people's perceptions of proximal events are construed in lower-level, concrete terms; whereas distal events are construed in higher-level, abstract terms (e.g. Liberman and Trope 1998). CLT can affect choice and preference such that a product that is favored in the near future, due to framing of specific concrete attributes, might not be favored in the distant future based on those same attributes. CLT also posits that the value associated with distant future situations is increased over delay while the value associated with near future situations is discounted over delay.

A person's temporal orientation also has the possibility to play a role in how a person construes different events. Some have suggested that temporal orientation–a predisposition to focus one's attention on the past, present, or future–influences subsequent behavior and attitudes (e.g. Lasane and Jones 1999; Strathman, et al. 1994).

Study 1

The first study examines how the temporal framing of savings of a CFL bulb influences purchase intentions, attitudes, and perceptions of savings. We predict that consumers will have higher evaluations regarding the CFL bulb in the temporally proximal savings frames compared to the more abstract and temporally distal lifetime savings frame.

A total of 78 undergraduate research participants completed the survey. The sample was 68% male with a mean age of 21. Subjects received a sheet that showed a picture of a 60-watt equivalent CFL bulb in its packaging. The label on the CFL package differed across the three temporal framing conditions and indicated the average amount of savings in one month, one year, and lifetime one could expect from changing one bulb and all bulbs in their home to this CFL bulb.

Results: To analyze our prediction we ran the three temporal framing of savings conditions on the dependent variables purchase intentions, CFL attitude, and perception of savings. The temporal framing of savings did significantly influence perceptions of savings ($F=10.83$, $p<.001$) and purchase intentions ($F=3.16$, $p<.05$). Perceptions of savings and purchase intentions were significantly higher in the proximal one month and one year frames than the temporally distant lifetime frame ($p<.05$). The temporal framing of savings did not significantly influence attitude toward the CFL bulb ($F=2.43$, $p=.09$) although the means were in the expected directions such that attitude decreased as the temporal distance of the savings frame increased.

Study 2

In study 2 we tested if a consumer's temporal orientation moderated the effect of the temporal framing of savings. We predict that given the distal lifetime frame, future-oriented consumers will not discount savings, will have higher attitudes and will choose CFL bulbs over incandescent bulbs compared to present-oriented consumers. A total of 69 undergraduate research participants completed the survey. The sample was 47% male with a mean age of 21. Temporal framing of savings was manipulated, while temporal orientation was a measured variable. The temporal framing of savings was similar to the first study and had three temporal framing conditions. To measure temporal orientation the Temporal Orientation Scale (Lasane and Jones 1999) was used to determine if subjects were present or future-oriented.

Results: To analyze our predictions we ran 3 (temporal framing of savings: one month vs. one year vs. lifetime) x 2 (temporal orientation: present vs. future) MANOVA on the dependent variables of CFL attitude, and perceived CFL savings. Given the dichotomous light bulb choice variable, we ran logistic regression to test the interaction.

The logistic regression results indicate that the interaction between the temporal framing of savings and temporal orientation was significant for product choice ($\chi^2=14.70$, $p<.01$). In the lifetime condition, future-oriented subjects are much more likely to buy CFL bulbs (100%) compared to present-oriented subjects (33%; $\chi^2=9.59$, $p<.005$).

The interaction was significant for perception of savings ($F=3.66$, $p<.05$). Future-oriented subjects ($M=5.91$) had higher perceptions of savings given the lifetime condition compared to present-oriented subjects ($M=4.50$, $p<.05$). For attitude, the interaction was not significant ($p>.10$).

Discussion

In two experiments we assessed the effects of temporal framing on purchase intentions, product choice, attitude, and perception of savings. In the first study we found that in general, participants had lower purchase intentions and somewhat lower attitudes given the most distal lifetime frame compared to the proximal frames. It also appears that consumers discount the savings from a CFL bulb as temporal distance increases. In the second study we found that given the lifetime frame, present-oriented consumers were *less* likely to choose the CFL bulb over the incandescent and also viewed the savings from a CFL bulb as much lower compared to future-oriented consumers. These results seem to indicate that present-oriented consumers discount savings at a greater rate than future-oriented consumers.

This research is especially important given the recent focus on energy efficiency. Thus, this research also provides managerial implications. It appears that more consumers can be reached using proximal compared to distal frames of savings. Finding the most effective way to communicate the savings and efficiency of a product that will help consumers choose the better product is not only important to the manufacturers and marketers, but will be better for society in general.

References

Lasane, Terell P. and James M. Jones (1999), "Temporal Orientation and Academic Goal-Setting: The Mediating Properties of a Motivational Self," *Journal of Social Behavior & Personality*, 14 (1), 31-44.

Liberman, Nira and Yaacov Trope (1998), "The Role of Feasibility and Desirability Considerations in Near and Distant Future Decisions: A Test of Temporal Construal Theory," *Journal of Personality and Social Psychology*, 75 (1), 5-18.

Strathman, Alan J., Faith Gleicher, David S. Boninger, and C. Scott Edwards (1994), "The Consideration of Future Consequences: Weighing Immediate and Distant Outcomes of Behavior," *Journal of Personality and Social Psychology*, 66 (4), 742-752.

Impact of CSR Communication Strategies on Attitude Change after a Crisis

Virginie Solelhac, Pompeu Fabra University, Spain

Recent studies have shown that consumers demand more information about companies' corporate social responsibility (CSR). However, communicating only positively about CSR, guaranteeing the absence of any unethical process along the whole supply chain, may result in greater deterioration in consumers' attitude in the event of an ethical crisis. Building from the literature on schema discrepancy and attribution theory, we analyze the effect of several communication strategies on attitudes and attitude change after a crisis. Evidence is found that using a two-sided communication message is the strategy that minimizes the impact of a crisis on attitudes towards the company.

A Painful Choice: Embodied Influences on Choice Perception

Aner Tal, Duke University, USA

Elements of consumers' overall situation might infuse judgments of choice difficulty and product dimensions. Contrary to prior research, such choice-extrinsic influences on judgment may not be susceptible to discounting through attribution. Further, choice-extrinsic effects on judgment might be somewhat specific in that physical difficulty affects judgments relating to a feeling of discomfort, but not ones tangential to it, such as choice satisfaction. I demonstrate that the physical discomfort caused by a hand-press leads to judgments of greater choice difficulty as well as lower ratings of manufacturer ethics, but not to lower choice satisfaction (studies 1-2). If explicitly asked to exclude the hand-press difficulty from judgment, consumers can discount the physical pain from judgments of difficulty, but not from judgments of the ethicality of manufacturing conditions (study 2), demonstrating that attribution-discounting is limited.

Making choices is effortful and depleting (Johnson & Payne, 1985; Iyengar & Lepper, 2000). Choosing one option often involves giving up others, which consumers are reluctant to do (Anderson, 2003; Gilbert and Ebert, 2002; Shin & Ariely, 2004).

But what determines how painful choices are, both in terms of the effort involved and in terms of post-choice feelings such as regret? Aspects of the choice set itself are obvious candidates. The more options there are, for instance, the harder the choice (Iyenger et al., 2006; Schwartz, 2004). Similarly, the greater the quantity of information, the harder it is to analyze (Johnson & Payne, 1985; Bockenholt et al., 1991). The extent of differences among options (Iglesias-Parro et al., 2002) and emotionality of the product domain (Luce, 1998) also make choice harder.

Elements external to the choice itself that are not directly relevant to the choice itself can also affect the pain of choosing. Mood, for instance, might alter the manner in which people approach choice and experience its painfulness (Tice et al., 2001). Affect in general might transfer from an unrelated source in the environment to an object of judgment. Extensive research in psychology has documented instances where affect generated by elements unrelated to an object infuses judgment (Forgas, 1995; Mayer et al., 1992). People tend to attribute their feelings to objects, and thus, when focused on an object of evaluation, believe affect emanates from the object (Higgins, 1998). More generally, people see their feelings as indicative of the adaptiveness of their environment, so that judgments might become negatively infused given negative feelings due to ambiguity as to the source of the low adaptiveness indicated by negative feelings (Fridja, 1999; Barret and Salovey, 2002).

Generally, it's believed that affect should only influence unrelated judgments if the source of affect is unknown. When people are aware of the true source of their feelings, they realize that the feelings are unrelated to the object of judgment, and can discount them (Schwartz & Clore, 1983). Thus, people will only use affect in judgment if they believe it to be relevant (Clore, 1992; Yeung & Wyer, 2004) and cannot attribute it to judgment-external elements (Reber et al., 2004; Schwarz & Clore, 2003). If affect is attributed to external sources, people will discount it and avoid its influence on judgment (Higgins et al., 2003; Darke et al., 2006).

However, one might question the pervasiveness of people's ability to discount irrelevant sources of affect given correct attribution. After all, if people are bad at identifying the source of sensations as irrelevant to begin with, why should they be able to correctly parse out extraneous feelings out once those are pointed out (Winkielman, 1997)? Further, people may be able to discount extraneous effects in some instances, but not in others. In other words, some feelings might more easily infuse some judgments (e.g., physical difficulty and mental difficulty). Similarly, people might have an easier time discounting certain affective sources (e.g., physical difficulty) from specific, analogous evaluations (e.g., mental difficulty), while being unable to discount these affective sources from less obviously related evaluations (e.g., ethics).

Study 1 focuses on decision effort. I posit that physical difficulty might be a generalized feeling that is not discounted even if its source is apparent and obviously extraneous to the decision. The negative emotion aroused by choice effort can in turn influence evaluation of the option chosen (Gabriano & Edell, 1997). However, if the infusion of irrelevant feelings is specific to judgments that are alignable with the feeling, satisfaction might not be influenced by physical difficulty.

Study 1: Hard Pressed

Methods. Participants (N=109) were asked to hold a hand-press while choosing among four digital cameras. Each option was represented by a name and a picture, along with a description along 11 product attributes. We manipulated difficulty by altering the pressure level on the hand-press, and by requiring participants in the difficult condition to press the device to its limit. In contrast, participants in the easy condition used the device on its easiest setting and were asked to press it on a level that's comfortable for them. All participants held the hand-presses pressed until making their choice.

At the end of the choice participants were asked to report how effortful the choice was and how pleased they were with their choice. They were then asked to report to what extent they followed instructions, as well as felt pressure and pain (manipulation checks that indicated increased pain and pressure on the higher difficulty level).

Results and discussion. Participants who reported not using the hand-press as instructed (n=10) were dropped from analysis. Participants in the "difficult" condition reported greater choice effort (5.43) than participants in the "easy" condition (4.57): $F(1, 96)$=4.49, p=.04. There was no effect on how pleased participants were with their choice (p>.4).

It appears, then, that difficulty of pressing the hand-press seeped into judgment of choice effort, but not into product evaluation. The differential effects on perceived effort and evaluation might indicate a difference in the manner of arriving at those judgments. It might be that difficulty affects difficulty judgments, but not option evaluation and satisfaction. Thus, it might be that the *influence of choice-extrinsic elements on judgment is restricted to judgments on dimensions similar to that of the choice-extrinsic element.*

Study 2: Good and Hard

Judgment of ethics should also be influenced by physical discomfort, since moral judgments are related to feelings of emotional discomfort (Haidt, 2003). However, the link of ethics to discomfort is less clear than the link of (physical) discomfort) to (mental) discomfort. Accordingly, I predicted that: A) There would be a significant effect of hand-press difficulty on judgment of ethical manufacturing conditions. B) Given explicit instructions to discount hand-press difficulty from evaluation, participants would no longer display the effect on choice difficulty, but would continue to display the effect on ethics judgment.

Methods. Participants (N=23) faced the exact same scenario as in study 1. However, all participants were instructed to note that the questions are about the choice rather than about the hand-press task. In addition, a measure of judged ethicality of manufacturing conditions was added.

Results and discussion. Given instructions to discount the hand-press task from their judgment, participants in the hard hand-press condition did not rate choice difficulty as being higher than those in the easy hand-press condition (p>.5). However, despite instructions to discount the hand-press task from judgment, participants in the hard condition still judged manufacturing conditions as being less ethical

(4.7) than participants in the easy condition (6): F(1, 22)=4.82, p=.04. A further study will attempt to reverse the order of judgment to determine whether the lack of discounting in ethics judgment was due to the nature of the judgment or simply due to the fact that physical difficulty had already been discounted from the choice difficulty judgment. Even if the latter is true, the findings would be interesting in the context of attribution and discounting of irrelevant inputs, since they would indicate that once people have discounted an irrelevant input from one judgment, they would not discount it from further judgments even if it does affect those latter judgments.

General Discussion

Irrelevant inputs to judgment might be more limited in their "contaminative" effects than generally believed. Accordingly, it appears that physical difficulty due to an unrelated task external to the choice process affects judgments of choice difficulty and manufacturer ethics, but not judgments of choice satisfaction. Irrelevant feelings might affect judgment only on dimensions that are allignable with the specific feeling. Directly relatable (mental difficulty) as well as less directly relatable (ethics) judgments can be affected. However, when the relation of the irrelevant input is less obvious than the relation of physical to mental difficulty, people might not be able to discount the irrelevant input even given explicit instructions to do so. Thus, people's capacity to discount an irrelevant input from judgment might be more limited than generally believed.

References

Anderson, Christopher J. (2003), "The Psychology of Doing Nothing: Forms of Decision Avoidance Result From Reason and Emotion," *Psychological Bulletin*, 129, 139-167.

Meyer, John D., Lisa Feldman Barrett, and Peter Salovey (2002), The Wisdom in Feeling: Psychological Processes in Emotional Intelligence, Guilfod: New York.

Bockenholt, Ulf, Albert Dietrich, Michael Aschenbrenner, and Franz Schmalhofer (1991), "The Effects of Attractiveness, Dominance, and Attribute Differences on Information Acquisition in Multiattribute Binary Choice," *Organizational Behavior and Human Decision Processes*, 49(2), 258-281.

Clore, Gerald L. (1992), "Cognitive phenomenology: Feelings and the construction of judgment," in Eds., Martin, Leonard L., and Abraham Tesser, The Construction of Social Judgments, Lawrence Erlbaum: New York.

Darke, P.R., Chattopadhyay, A., & Ashworth, L.T.B. (2006). The Importance and Functional Significance of Affective Cues in Choice. *Journal of Consumer Research, 33 (3)*, 322-328.

Forgas, Joseph P. (1995), "Mood and judgment: The affect infusion model (AIM)," *Psychological Bulletin*, 117 (1), 39-66.

Frijda, Nico, (1999), "Emotions and Hedonic Experience," in Eds. Kahenman, Daniel, Ed Diener, and Norbert Schwartz, Well-Being: The Foundations of Hedonic Psychology, Russel-Sage: New York.

Gabriano, Ellen C., and Julie A. Edell (1997), "Cognitive Effort, Affect, and Choice," in *Journal of Consumer Research*, 24 (2), 147-158.

Gilbert, Dan, & Ebert, Jane.E.J. (2002), "Decisions and Revisions: The Affective Forecasting of Changeable Outcomes," *Journal of Personality and Social Psychology, 82, 503-514.*

Haidt, Jonathan (2003), "The Moral Emotions," In Eds. R. J. Davidson, K. R. Scherer, & H. H. Goldsmith Handbook of Affective Sciences, Oxford: Oxford University Press.

Higgins, E. Tory (1998), "The Aboutness Principle: A Pervasive Influence on Human Inference," *Social Cognition*, 16 (1), 173-198.

Higgins, E. Tory, Lorraine Chen Idson, Antonio L. Freitas, Scott, Spiegel, and Daniel C. Molden (2003), "Transfer of Value from Fit," *Journal of Personality and Social Psychology*, 84 (6), 1140-1153.

Iglesias-Parro, S., E. I. De La Fuenta, and A. R. Ortega (2002), "The Effect of Context Variables on Cognitive Effort in Multiattribute Binary Choice," *Theory and Decision*, 52 (2), 101-125.

Iyengar, Sheena S., and Mark R. Lepper (2000), "When choice is demotivating: Can one desire too much of a good thing?" *Journal of Personality and Social Psychology*, 79 (6), 995-1006.

Iyenger, Sheena S., Rachael E. Wells, and Barry Schwartz (2006), "Doing Better But Feeling Worse: Looking for the "Best" Job Undermines Satisfaction," *Psychological Science*, 17 (2), 143-150.

Johnson, Eric J., and John W. Payne (1985), "Effort and Accuracy in Choice," *Management Science*, 31 (4), 395-414.

Luce, Mary Frances (1998), "Choosing to Avoid: Coping with Negatively Emotion-Laden Consumer Decisions," *Journal of Consumer Research*, 24 (4), 409-433.

Mayer John D., Yvonne N. Gaschke, Debra L. Braverman, and Temperance W. Evans (1992), "Mood-Congruent Judgment is a General Effect," *Journal of Personality and Social Psychology*, 63 (1), 119-132.

Schwartz, Barry (2004), The Paradox of Choice: Why More is Less, Eco: New York.

Schwarz, Norbert (2004), "Meta-Cognitive Experiences in Consumer Judgment and Decision Making," *Journal of Consumer Psychology*, 14 (4), 332-348.

Schwarz, Norbert, and Gerald Clore (1983), "Mood, Misattribution, and Judgments of Well-Being: Informative and Directive Functions of Affective States," *Journal of Personality and Social Psychology*, 45 (3), 513-523.

Schwarz, Norbert, and Gerald Clore (2003), "Mood as Information: 20 Years Later," *Psychological Inquiry*, 14 (3, 4), 296-303.

Shin, Jiwoong and Dan Ariely (2004), "Keeping Doors Open: The Effect of Unavailability on Incentives to Keep Options Viable," *Management Science*, 50 (5), 575-586.

Reber, Rolf, Norbert Schwartz, and Piotr Winkielman (2004), "Processing Fluency and Aesthetic Pleasure: Is Beauty in the Perceiver's Processing Experience?" *Personality and Social Psychology Review*, 8 (4), 363-382.

Tice, Dianne M., Ellen Bratslavsky, and Roy F. Baumeister (2001), "Emotional Distress Regulation Takes Precedence Over Impulse Control: If You Feel Bad, Do It!" *Journal of Personality and Social Psychology*, 80 (1), 53-67.

Winkielman, Piotr, Robert B. Zajonc, and Norbert Schwartz (1997), "Subliminal Affective Priming Resists Attributional Interventions," *Cognition and Emotion*, 11 (4), 433-465.

Yeung, Catherine, and Robert S. Wyer, Jr. (2004), "Affect, Appraisal, and Consumer Judgment," *Journal of Consumer Behavior*, 31 (2), 412-424.

Author Index